The Practical Works *of*
RICHARD BAXTER

The Practical Works *of*
RICHARD BAXTER
Selected Treatises

HENDRICKSON PUBLISHERS

Engraved by William Holl

SELECT TREATISES

FROM

THE PRACTICAL WORKS

OF

RICHARD BAXTER:

INCLUDING

THE SAINTS' EVERLASTING REST,

THE DIVINE LIFE,

TREATISE ON CONVERSION, CALL TO THE UNCONVERTED,
DIRECTIONS TO A SOUND CONVERSION, MISCHIEF OF
SELF-IGNORANCE, DYING THOUGHTS, &c.

WITH

PREFATORY REMARKS AND MEMOIR OF THE AUTHOR.

The Practical Works of Richard Baxter: Selected Treatises
Richard Baxter

Hendrickson Publishers Marketing, LLC
P. O. Box 3473
Peabody, Massachusetts 01961-3473

ISBN 978-1-59856-571-3

Printed in the United States of America

First Printing — October 2010

ADVERTISEMENT.

THE PRACTICAL WORKS of RICHARD BAXTER have gained for their author a high place among writers on practical religion. They are characterized by genuine and fervent piety, earnestness, and unction; and they press home the truths of Scripture upon the conscience of the sinner in a manner so clear, searching, and convincing, that none can rise from their perusal without feeling roused from spiritual carelessness or torpor, comforted under distress, or strengthened and encouraged in the path of duty. A well-known puritan writer remarks of them: "His books on practical divinity have been effectual for more numerous conversions of sinners to God than any printed in our time; and while the church remains on earth, will be of continual efficacy to recover lost souls. There is a vigorous pulse in them that keeps the reader awake and attentive."

These writings, however, are so voluminous, and consequently so expensive, that the great mass of readers could neither spare the time required for their entire perusal, nor the sum needful for their purchase. To obviate this difficulty, editions of many of his treatises separately, have from time to time been published, and by this means several of BAXTER'S writings have obtained a very extensive circulation among all classes of the community.

In the present selection, the Publishers have endeavoured to embody those treatises that have been found most useful, and have been most approved by the Christian public, along with several others of an equally valuable nature, but not so generally known. In particular, this selection includes the SAINTS' EVERLASTING REST, the first book that Baxter wrote, and the second which he published; and had he never written another, it alone would have endeared his memory for ever to all who cherish the sublime hopes of the gospel; the DIVINE LIFE, an admirable experimental treatise written with great sweetness—soft, tender, and full of simplicity, and abounding with passages of great beauty, illustrative not only of the fine genius, but the intense ardour of Baxter's spirit and feelings; the TREATISE ON CONVERSION; CALL TO THE UNCONVERTED; NOW OR NEVER; DIRECTIONS TO A SOUND CONVERSION; DIRECTIONS TO WEAK CHRISTIANS FOR THEIR ESTABLISHMENT, GROWTH, AND PERSEVERANCE; CHARACTER OF A CONFIRMED CHRISTIAN, ALSO OF A WEAK AND OF A SEEMING CHRISTIAN—books that must ever rank among the highest of the writings of Baxter; THE MISCHIEF OF SELF-IGNORANCE, a work clear, concise, and simple beyond several of his other pieces, while it is second to none of them in persuasive eloquence and impressive fervour, clothing thoughts that are not familiar in very perspicuous language, and adapting itself with uncommon felicity to the inexperienced and the undisciplined; and DYING THOUGHTS, written for his own use in the latter times of his corporal pains and weakness, abounding in admirable sentiments, expressed in appropriate and beautiful language, worthy of a believer in the near prospect of eternity. The works on conversion treat of the most important subject which can occupy the attention of mankind in its degenerate state, and discuss it with a power rarely equalled in human writings. While BAXTER's talents were adequate to any subject to which they might be directed, the conversion of men was the grand object to which he devoted them, in the fullest extent in which they could be exercised.

The whole of the treatises have undergone a careful revision, and the Latin quotations with which some of them abound, being often obstructive to the general reader, have either been omitted or translated into English. Short prefatory remarks accompany each book, and a Memoir of Baxter precedes the whole. That these improvements may lead to an extended perusal of these invaluable writings, is the earnest wish of the projectors of this Edition.

CONTENTS.

THE DIVINE LIFE, in Three Treatises. The first, Of the Knowledge of God; the second, Of Walking with God; the third, Of Conversing with God in Solitude.

PART I. THE KNOWLEDGE OF GOD.

"And this is life eternal, that they might know thee the only true God, and Jesus Christ whom thou hast sent" (John xvii. 3).

THE MISCHIEFS OF SELF-IGNORANCE,
AND THE BENEFITS OF SELF-ACQUAINT-
ANCE, opened in divers Sermons at St. Dunstan's
West, and published in answer to the accusations
of some and the desires of others.

"For if a man think himself to be something
when he is nothing, he deceiveth himself; but let
every man prove his own work, and then shall he
have rejoicing in himself alone, and not in another.
For every man shall bear his own burden" (Gal.
vi. 3–5).

DYING THOUGHTS on Phil. i. 23.

A

MEMOIR

RICHARD BAXTER.

RICHARD BAXTER's 'devotional and practical works' have long and deservedly occupied a very elevated station among the standard works of British theology. 'The tooth of time,' the progress of events, and the modern 'march of mind,' have neither rendered them antiquated, nor thrown them materially into the shade. They possess the seeds of sanctified genius, and the imperishable principles of spiritual grandeur, and permanent moral worth. After upwards of a century and a half, the works of the author continue 'to praise him in the gates.' They form the best biographical monument of their author's unparalleled industry and well-earned fame. The call for works of this kind by the reading and religious public, is, in our apprehension, 'a token for good.' It indicates an improved and improving *taste* among the pious portion of our population, for the solid, substantial, staple nourishment, of the ancient puritanic and non-conformist school. While they could descend to feed the 'babes in Christ with the unmixed milk of the word,' they could also cover the gospel board with 'strong meat,' suited 'to men of full age, even those who, by reason of use, had their senses exercised to discern both good and evil.'

In the age and country in which we live, there is a numerous class of readers who love to luxuriate in the antiquarian lore of 'the olden times,' especially when it is presented to the imagination in the plastic drapery of novels, poetry, plays, and 'border tales,' which record the costumes, the customs, the habits, and modes of thought and expression, and the valorous deeds of our great-grandfathers on 'the flood and the field.' These are run upon, like paintings of the Flemish and Italian schools. They are many of them *fancy* pictures of men and manners; and, perhaps, owe more than two-thirds of their interest to the ingenuity of the literary artist. It is well that there is another, and pretty numerous class of readers, who prefer dealing in the facts and principles of antiquity, and who can appreciate sound sense and sterling piety under a plain puritanic garb; who can recognise the advocate of civil and religious liberty, and the unflinching friend of grace, and truth, and gospel holiness, under the antiquated costume of an old non-conformist. Sacred principles are immortal; 'they live and abide for ever.' In the bosoms of this latter class of men, piety and patriotism maintained a fervent heat, and diffused a cheering and salutary radiance in dark and troublous times. They were the 'Elijahs' and 'Elishas' of their age—they were men of faith and prayer—they were England's glory and strength—though, during the turmoil, they were sometimes treated 'as the filth of the world, and as the offscouring of all things.' They planted, and watered, and watched, and trained the tree of civil freedom and religious liberty, under the shade of which we can now securely sit, and 'eat the fat, and drink the sweet, and send portions' to our more distant and destitute brethren of mankind, 'for whom nothing is prepared.'

Baxter's Call to the Unconverted has obtained a range of circulation, and a degree of popularity, little inferior to the Pilgrim's Progress, or Paradise Lost. It has come into thousands and tens of thousands of the cottages of our British peasantry. With many the author's name has become familiar as household words. His Reformed Pastor has found its way into the libraries and hands of hundreds, or thousands, of ministers. Its pungent pathetic appeals to the consciences of the torpid, the languid, and the lukewarm, have been productive of the most salutary effects, first upon the pastors, and then upon the people. Baxter's Saints' Rest has long and deservedly been a favourite with decided Christians of all denominations. His Dying Thoughts, though, perhaps, less known, have gilded the gloom of many a sick chamber, and cheered and charmed the desponding spirits of many a dying penitent, and taught him to repose his hopes upon the riches of revealed mercy. Many other treatises of Baxter's devotional and practical works, though less known than the above, are not less valuable, and calculated, by the Divine blessing, to prove highly beneficial to various classes of readers. The present edition of his Devotional and Practical Works, which this brief biographical sketch is intended to precede, will place the best productions of the author's prolific pen before the reader in a pleasing and portable form, in a style of typographical execution, agreeable, if not alluring to the eye, and at such a moderate cost as to place them within the reach of those who relish such massy and pathetic productions of 'the olden times.' They will amply reward the serious and inquisitive reader.

An author whose writings we have frequently perused with ardour and interest, with pleasure and profit—who has informed our judgment—corrected our errors—dispelled our darkness, and dissolved our doubts—who has warmed our hearts, invigorated our hopes, and taught us how to live with credit and comfort, and die in peace and safety—it is natural for us to wish to know something of his private character, his public life, his labours, and his latter end. We wish to have some personal intimacy with the man, and to see the Christian in his every day attire. Baxter, who was copious as the Nile on almost every subject which he treated, has left ample materials in his 'Life and Times,' which exhibit a full-length portrait of 'the man and his communications.' The 'Reliquæ Baxterianæ,' or his autobiography of 'The most remarkable Passages of his Life and Times,' though prolix, has all the charms, and some of the defects, of this species of writing. Silvester and Calamy, his early biographers, have adjusted and wrought up these materials to great advantage. The abridgment by the one, and the original by the other, contain a mine of matter, though some parts of it are rather tedious, and of minor importance. The patient, laborious student, and the black-letter men of antiquarian taste, who form only a minority of the reading republic, may love such a repast in the antiquated style. Something was still required to be done, to compress and modernise the work—to lop off extraneous and redundant matter—to separate the alloy, and preserve every particle of the solid gold—and present the interesting life and eventful times of Richard Baxter to the public, in a more readable dress and attractive form. This has been executed with much sound judgment and critical skill, by Baxter's last biographer, the late Rev. William Orme of Camberwell, and author of the Life of John Owen, D. D., &c. It is a work of singular and superior excellence. For more than half a century, Baxter occupied an ample and elevated space in the public eye. He lived in critical and stormy times. He stood high in an age pre-eminently distinguished by great and good men, of intellectual power and high character. His biographer had drunk deeply into the spirit of the nonconformist age. He was familiar with the facts, and details, and contested principles of that eventful period of our civil and ecclesiastical story. He could appreciate the work, and delineate the character, of such a man as Baxter; and by his candour and critical sagacity, exhibit 'the lights and shades' in his character, and the excellencies and defects of his elaborate writings. He has done so with great propriety, force, and feeling, and has presented us with a likeness, as large as life, of the intellectual and moral character of Richard Baxter. All we can contemplate here is a miniature sketch in profile. Our chief difficulties are selection and compression.

Among the great and good men whom Divine providence raised up, and qualified to counteract the encroachments of arbitrary power, and to give a salutary impulse and a safe direction to the public mind in Great Britain, through a considerable portion of the seventeenth century, the name of Richard Baxter ranks not among the least. He was born on the 12th of November, 1615, at Rowtan, near High Ercal, in Shropshire. His father was also named Richard Baxter. He was a sober, respectable, and rather religiously disposed man, who had a small freehold estate at Eaton-Constantine, about five miles from Shrewsbury. His mother's name was Adeney, and a native of the same county. The early part of his infancy was spent under the roof of his maternal grandfather. While yet in childhood, his father conceived that he saw some buds of early piety, and fondly hoped that young Richard was 'sanctified from the birth.'

The state of religion and morals at that period in the country and neighbourhood, was extremely low; nor was he more favourably situated with respect to his schoolmasters. They were neither distinguished for learning nor morals. The genius and industry of the youth, however, surmounted these untoward circumstances. The father's small estate did not afford sufficient resources for enabling him to send his son to the university; but he placed him for a time under private tutors, who were alleged to have performed their duty to their pupil very imperfectly. Young Baxter's thirst for information, his native ardour of mind, and untiring application, however, conquered most of the difficulties which he encountered. Though Baxter never enjoyed the mental discipline of an academical life, nor realized the literary and varied advantages of a university course, yet he happily escaped many of the snares and temptations incident to such a situation, at a very critical period of life; and by the pure dint of invincible application, and the elastic spring of his opening genius, he acquired more varied and substantial knowledge of men and things—of books and systems—of principles and character, than thousands who have, for ten or fifteen years, breathed the air of academic groves. At a very opportune period of his early life, he had access to an excellent library, which proved of incalculable service to him. At the request of Lord Newport he went to Wrexeter, where he taught in a free school for six months.

In 1633, before Baxter had completed his teens, he was persuaded, by a Mr Wickstead, to wave the studies in which he was then engaged, and try his fortune at court. He accordingly went to Whitehall. He carried with him recommendations to Sir Henry Herbert, master of the revels, by whom he was cordially received. Our author was then only eighteen, a period of life when the fascinations and blandishments of a court are very apt to exert a powerful influence over the youthful imagination. To what pitch of political power his extraordinary talents and constitutional ardour might have raised him, as a senator or statesman, we know not; but it soon became apparent that the Lord designed him for purer and nobler employment. The dissolute character of the court of Charles I., in which the Book of Sports had been concocted, where interludes and plays were more relished than serious piety, and puritanism was as much disliked and shunned as the plague—presented a tainted moral atmosphere very uncongenial to Baxter's then existing state of mind. A single month sufficed him of a court life. It was not his proper element; and he left Whitehall with disgust. Like Moses, he 'chose rather to suffer affliction with the people of God, than to enjoy' the honours and emoluments of a court, and 'the pleasures of sin for a season.' 'He had respect to the recompence of reward,' 'and endured as seeing Him who is invisible.' Though Baxter's religious character had been at that period but partially developed, and his religious principles were by no means matured, yet some of the books which he had read with interest and profit, such as Burney's Resolution, Sibb's Bruised Reed, Perkins on Repentance, on Living and Dying Well, &c., had been the means, under the Divine blessing, of generating in his mind the principle of vital piety.

An incipient desire for 'the work of the ministry' had early taken possession of Baxter's mind. It is frequently a feeling consequent upon conversion to God. It is often secretly cherished long before it is openly avowed, or the ulterior steps towards its attainment are distinctly defined to the mind of the subject. This predilection, and the severe affliction of his mother, will partly account for his rapid removal from court. He resumed his studies with increased intensity. His mother died, under deep distress, in May following, 1634. His own health was also greatly shaken. The Lord was training him for future usefulness in the furnace; and ingenuously as he confessed, and deeply as he deplored, the defects of his early education—his want of a regular academical training—and the honours and advantages of a course at the university, as apparently interposing insurmountable obstructions to his most sanguine wishes; yet all the while his heavenly Father was proving, and tempering, and training him in the furnace, ultimately to make him 'a workman who needs not to be ashamed, rightly dividing the word of God,' and that 'he might be able to comfort others, who are in any trouble, with the same consolations wherewith he had been comforted of God.' What he lacked, or lost in the acquisition of languages, literature, and mathematical science, he gained in experimental piety, close communion with God, and the acquisition of those spiritual attainments which so pre-eminently fitted him for the efficient discharge of the pastoral functions, and for doing 'the work of an evangelist.'

When Baxter arrived at the age of twenty-one, his health and strength were very much wasted. He apprehended that he could not survive above a year or two; and though deeply sensible of his deficiencies, yet seeing numbers perishing around him for lack of knowledge—feeling the frailty of his frame—a fervent desire to be useful to souls—and conceiving that he possessed some portion of the powers of persuasion, he took orders in the Church of England from the bishop of Worcester. His family connections, and personal predilections, were then all in favour of the church. He had then read but little, and studied less, of the subject of church government and discipline, or of the nonconformist controversy.

He received a license to teach a school at Dudley, where he also, for a short season, preached the gospel with much acceptance, and some success. It was while here that he became acquainted with some nonconformists. His first impressions of them were, that they were splenetic, and that their strictures were too severe against the bishops; yet he averred, that 'he found them to be both godly and honest men.' They furnished him with several writings upon their own side of the question, and amongst others, with Ames' Suit Against Ceremonies, which he read with care, comparing it with Dr Burges's Rejoynder. The former work shook his faith in the divine right of modern Episcopacy, and several of its ceremonies, and made him feel, that he had acted either ignorantly, or rashly, in taking orders before he had maturely weighed what his oaths and subscription implied. His active mind ultimately took a wider range of reading upon both sides. This rather increased than diminished his scruples with respect to some parts of the church service. After labouring for nine months in Dudley, he removed to Bridgenorth, and became assistant to Mr William Madstone, an aged minister, who treated him with much respect and cordiality. He performed those parts of the church service himself, of the scriptural authority of which Baxter's conscience had begun to entertain serious scruples. At first a considerable excitement was produced by his ministrations in his new sphere of labour, and some portion of fruit appeared. Though then in the ardour of youth, his soul burning with zeal, and his heart melting with compassion for perishing sinners—though his aim was simple, and his eye single, yet the excitement subsided, and he was made to feel that his 'sufficiency' and his success alike, were 'of the Lord.'

About this time arbitrary power and ecclesiastical tyranny were making rapid inroads upon the civil liberties of the subjects, and recklessly invaded the sacred rights of conscience. What in our ecclesiastical annals is called the et cætera oath, came to be imposed about this period. It had been devised as a kind of test, and enacted as a clap-trap. Such crooked carnal policy generally overshoots the mark —it defeats the very object which it seeks to secure. Many men of principle, who 'feared an oath,' and could afford to 'keep a conscience,' were justly stumbled and startled at such an imposition, which was little short of the Romish claim to infallibility. This famous, or rather, infamous oath, induced Baxter and many more to study the authority of English Episcopacy, and the arrogant claims of the hierarchy, more carefully than ever. The clause at which his conscience revolted runs in these terms:—'Nor will I ever give my consent to alter the government of the church by archbishops, bishops, deans, and archdeacons, &c., as it stands now established, and as by right it ought to stand.' Expulsion from the altars of the church was the stern penalty of not swallowing this oath. If a church rule her sons with a rod of iron, and seek to bind them to her interests, as slaves, in chains of brass, she is not to wonder at the alleged *weakness* of the men who demur at her mandates; but she ought to blush at her own wickedness in seeking to rivet human fetters upon Christ's free men. In some instances they might have silently submitted to parts of the principle in detail; but deliberately to swear to it by compulsion and penalty, changed the complexion of the case.

An interesting era in the life of Baxter now occurred. In the year 1640 he received an invitation by the bailiff and principal inhabitants of Kidderminster, to come and preach the gospel among them. He embraced it. His salary was £60 per annum. He who holds the key of David set before him an open door. The vicar and his two curates had been accused by them as incompetent for the functions of the offices which they nominally, but inefficiently filled. Probably under the dread of formal inquiry, and the scrutiny of parliamentary *triers*, the vicar consented to grant the above allowance to an acceptable preacher. As he was a man who neither had capacity nor inclination to preach—seldom gave them a sermon but once a quarter—and was a noted frequenter of ale-houses—and as the curates he employed were of the same stamp, it is very likely, in the then existing state of the country, they would feel perfectly willing to keep the peace with one of such devotedness of heart to his proper work, and energy and decision of character, as Richard Baxter.

The moral change produced by the labours of Baxter formerly, and latterly at Kidderminster, was, perhaps, without a parallel in Great Britain. It presented a noble field for unfolding the sleepless energies and the indefatigable labours of 'the man of God.' It seemed a spot selected by heaven for a spiritual experiment. By the Divine blessing it succeeded to an astonishing extent. By his labours and prayers, his 'teaching and preaching publicly, and from house to house,' the moral 'wilderness and solitary place were made glad.' This once dreary and cheerless desert assumed the fragrance of Carmel, and the fertility of Lebanon. He early felt a predilection to the people and the place. It was just such a field as suited Baxter's genius and taste; though, with the exception of a very small remnant of pious persons, who were ready to enter into his sentiments, sympathies, and plans, the minds and morals of the overwhelming majority of the people were very few removes from a state of pure heathenism; but bad as they were, they were in a more hopeful state than those among whom he had laboured, and recently left, at Bridgenorth. They had sunk into the arms of carnal security, and into a system of selfishness, under a sound and awakening ministry. To the great body of Baxter's new charge, the gospel was quite a new thing. They had not previously heard it, nor were they hardened in the guilt of having rejected it. The few praying people who were there, had longed for it, and prepared the way for it. 'When the poor and the needy seek water, and there is none, and their tongue faileth for thirst, I the Lord will hear, I, the God of Israel, will not forsake them: I will open rivers in high places, and fountains in the midst of the valleys: I will make the wilderness a pool of water, and the dry land springs of water. . . . That they may see, and know, and consider, and understand together, that the hand of the Lord has done this, and the Holy One of Israel has created it.' It was here that Baxter, in a pre-eminent degree, 'did the work of an evangelist;' it was here that he displayed the unexampled diligence of the Christian pastor; it was here that 'he fed the church of God' with the kindness of a father, and the tenderness of a mother, 'which he had purchased with his own blood;' it was here that he received many for his 'joy and crown;' it was chiefly in this favoured spot that he immortalized his own name, and has given all but permanent celebrity to the place, having identified it, in the associations of the reading and religious public, with the Northampton of America.

Baxter had scarcely got the fallow-ground fully broken up at Kidderminster, after two years' active labour, when the civil war broke out. The tide of party feeling ran very high. The country became divided between the King and the Long Parliament. The cavaliers, or royalists, as they styled themselves, rallied round the standard of the King; and the friends of liberty and serious piety generally sided with the Parliament. Baxter ranked among the latter. His residence at Kidderminster was interrupted by the civil war. Persons who dared to leave the beaten track, or deviate from the forms of the Established Church, were suspected by the royalists, and treated by the rabble, as enemies to the King, and hostile to the church. Mr Baxter became a marked man by the king's troops. Without the restraints of military discipline, having little pay and no principle, they were allowed to pillage and plunder the puritans, as fair game, with perfect impunity. Having suffered in his person, his family, and property, in the most rude and barbarous manner, he was induced, for a time, to retire from his favourite field of labour.

In order to avoid such annoyances, he was persuaded to retire to Coventry, where he might remain with safety. That place had been garrisoned by Parliament; and there he found thirty other ministers, who, for similar reasons, had sought refuge under the wing of the garrison 'from the face of the spoilers.' He remained there for two years, as 'in strong hold,' and preached once every Lord's day to the garrison, and once to the inhabitants of the town. However unfavourable a season of civil commotion is for the preaching and patient hearing of the tidings of pardon and peace among men embroiled in a civil contest, yet, in other respects, there seems to be an imperious call for 'the still small voice of mercy' during the solemn pauses between contending parties, and the relentless ravages of the sword. In this new and strictly militant sphere of labour, Baxter did not forget the apostolic charge: 'Preach the word; be constant in season and out of season; reprove, rebuke, exhort with all long-suffering and doctrine.' After the decisive action of Naseby, and the favourable aspect of affairs to the Parliamentary men, Baxter accepted the appointment of chaplain to Whalley's regiment of dragoons. The extravagant notions which obtained at that time in the army upon subjects of religion and politics, required a man of sound judgment, to check party feeling, repress enthusiasm, and lay before the opening and inquisitive minds of these patriotic men, the sacred and substantial principles of Divine revelation. This Baxter laboured to perform, without fear or flattery, with some considerable degree of success. After following the camp for some time, he left the army early in the year 1657. A profuse bleeding at the nose, and several alarming symptoms, compelled him to retire to the house of Sir Thomas Rouse, in which he continued for some time in a very precarious state of health. On his recovery, he returned again to Kidderminster—he resumed his labours among the people of his choice—and remained their faithful, affectionate, and successful pastor, during the lapse of fourteen additional years. During the sixteen years of his energetic and devoted ministrations in this favoured spot—while the country was convulsed with a civil war—while he was the subject of no ordinary share of personal afflictions, and incessant bodily infirmities—while he had an ample share of the trials incident to a life of fearless, active benevolence in 'the kingdom and patience of Jesus Christ'—yet he was honoured, under God, to effect an astonishing spiritual change in the minds and morals of the people. The wide moral wastes were brought under a process of successful cultivation—'Zion's wilderness was made like Eden, and her desert like the garden of the Lord; joy and gladness were found therein, thanksgiving, and the voice of melody.' The bright visions of ancient prophecy were palpably realized: 'Instead of the thorn there came up the fir tree; and instead of the briar there sprang forth the myrtle tree; and it became to the Lord for a name, and an everlasting sign that should not be cut off.'

It was during the time Baxter was at Coventry that the celebrated Westminster Assembly of Divines was convened by order of Parliament. Though not himself a member of that body, he had paid particular attention to their proceedings; he was well acquainted with the principles, characters, talents, and various parties who composed it; and in his Life and Times, has given a pretty full and candid account of their deliberations and chief transactions. Had he been a member, he would in all probability have been a leading man among the Presbyterian party, or those who wished to introduce a species of modified Episcopacy. In doctrinal sentiments, he substantially accorded with the pious of all parties; but upon the constitution, discipline, and government of the church, it is questionable if he would have agreed entirely with any one of them. He decidedly disliked the Erastianism of some of the high church party; he disapproved of the intolerant spirit of some of the Presbyterians; and though he eulogised the piety and talents of the leading men among the Independents, who formed but a fractional part of the Assembly, yet he blamed them for bigotry—ranked them and the Baptists among the minor sectaries—thought them too strict and exclusive in their discipline and membership—would allow the civil magistrate no power in the church—and conceived that they carried the principles of religious liberty and the inviolable right of conscience to an unreasonable extent. He has, however, given a more impartial account of the character and proceedings of the Westminster Assembly, than has been given either by Lord Clarendon, Baillie, or Milton.

Baxter's details of this celebrated convocation

forms an important chapter in his Life and Times, and throws a considerable portion of light upon the state of parties during an eventful crisis of our ecclesiastical annals. Marking their discussions and decisions, as an attentive and impartial observer, stationed on an elevated neck of neutral territory, he has expressed his opinions of the men, and the matters of discussion, with candour and freedom; and although it would be quite incompatible with the restricted limits of this brief sketch, in which our author was a spectator rather than an actor, to enter into those lengthened details, yet we presume a few sentences by such a writer as our author, upon the principles, spirit, and character of the parties who composed this far-famed Assembly, will be gratifying to the reader. For more ample details, we would refer him to the Life and Times, or Orme's Life of Baxter.

Respecting the High Church party, he thought that 'they made too light of the power of the ministry, church, and excommunication—that they made church communion more common to the impenitent than Christ would have it—that they made the church too like the world, by breaking down the hedge of spiritual discipline, and laying it almost common with the wilderness; and that they misunderstood and injured their brethren, affirming that they claimed, as from God, a coercive power over the bodies and consciences of men. . . . I utterly disliked their extirpation of the true discipline of Christ, not only as they omitted or corrupted it, but as their principles and church state had made it impracticable. They thus altered the nature of churches, and the ancient nature of bishops and presbyters. They set up secular courts—vexed honest Christians—countenanced ungodly teachers—opposed faithful ministers—and promoted the increase of ignorance and profaneness.' *

As to the Presbyterians, he says:—' I saw, too, that in England, the persons who were called Presbyterians were eminent for learning, sobriety, and piety; and the pastors so called were those who went through the work of the ministry in diligent and serious preaching to the people, and edifying men's souls, and keeping up religion in the land. ... But I disliked their order of lay elders, who had no ordination, or power to preach and administer sacraments; for though I grant that lay elders, as the chief of the people, were often employed to express the people's conduct, and preserve their liberties, yet these were no church officers at all, nor had any charge of private oversight of the flocks. I disliked, also, the course of some of the more rigid of them, who drew near to the way of prelacy by grasping at a kind of secular power, not using it themselves, but binding the magistrate to confiscate or imprison men, merely because they were excommunicated, and so corrupting the true discipline of the church, and turning the communion of the saints into the communion of the multitude, who must keep in the church against their wills, for fear of being undone in the world; whereas a man whose conscience cannot feel a just excommunication, unless it be backed with confiscation or imprisonment, is no fitter to be a mem-

* Life, part ii. pp. 139, 140. Orme's Life, chap. iv. pp 72, 73.

ber of a Christian church, than a corpse is to be a member of a corporation. I disliked, also, some of the Presbyterians, that they were not tender enough to dissenting brethren; but too much against liberty, as others were too much for it; and thought by votes and numbers to do that which love and reason should have done.' Baxter's candour here is the more manifest, as his connections and opinions were, at that period, more identified with the Presbyterians than any of the other parties. His enlightened views of the distinction between civil and ecclesiastical power, and the absurdity of coercion in matters of conscience, are also strongly and distinctly expressed, though in some other parts of his writings these things are not so happily expressed. Though he was the friend of liberty, yet he seemed at times to be afraid of too much of it.

Baxter was less friendly to the Independents than to some other of the sects then prevalent. As some of the most powerful minds which figured on the political arena during the commonwealth, were considered, either from religious or political predilections, to lean to this minor party, he very possibly was suspicious of their moderation, if, as a party, they came into power. Many of them, also, were prepared to go further than Baxter in curing acknowledged corruptions, pruning away human inventions from the worship of God, and carrying forward the principles of reformation. He had possibly some jealousy, that some, in their dislike to ecclesiastical tyranny, and others, in their zeal for a purer and better order of things, might run either too fast or too far, and injure the peace of the church, and the tranquillity of the commonwealth; yet the opinions he expresses of this minor section of the Assembly is alike honourable to the candour of the writer, and the character of the man. He says, 'Most of the Independents were zealous, and very many learned, discreet, and godly men, fit to be very serviceable in the church. In the search of scripture and antiquity, I found that in the beginning a governed church, and a stated worshipping church, were all one, and not two several things; and that though there might be other bye meetings in places like our chapels, or private houses, for such as age or persecution hindered to come to the solemn meetings, yet churches there were, no bigger, in respect of number, than our parishes now. These were societies of Christians, united in personal communion, and not only for communion by meetings of officers and delegates in synods, as many churches in associations; but I saw if once we go beyond the bounds of personal, as the end of particular churches, in the definition, we may make a church of a nation, or of ten nations, or what we please, which will have none of the nature and ends of the primitive particular churches. I saw also a commendable care of serious holiness and discipline in most of the Independent churches; and I found that some Episcopal men, as bishop Usher himself, did hold, that every bishop was independent as to synods; and that synods were not proper governors of particular bishops, but only for their concord.'

He however adds: 'But in the Independent way I disliked many things. They made too light of or-

dination. They also had their office of lay eldership. They were commonly stricter about the qualification of church membership than scripture, reason, or the practice of the universal church would allow, not taking a man's bare profession as credible, and as sufficient evidence of his title to church communion, unless either by a holy life, or the particular narration of the passages of a work of grace, he satisfied the pastors and all the church that he was truly holy; whereas, every man's profession is the valid reason of the thing professed in his heart, unless it be disproved by him who questions it, by proving him guilty of heresies, or impiety, or sins inconsistent with it.'

There are several other things alleged of the Independents, against which Baxter expressed his disapprobation, some of which might or might not be correct. Their principles were unpopular—they were much in the minority—they were deemed *ultras* in religion—some misapprehended, and others misrepresented, their sentiments—a good deal of his information had been obtained by hearsay—and Baxter, with all his candour and straightforward honesty, was sometimes credulous and rash in his conclusions. Both in spirit and sentiment he approached nearer to this despised sect than he was himself aware of. The above is only a brief specimen of the general outline which Baxter has drawn of the celebrated Assembly at Westminster. Of its general fairness no party have much cause of complaint. His impression of the men who composed it was certainly favourable. For solid learning, fervent piety, zeal for the interests of religion, and concern for the good of their country, there has seldom, if ever, been such an Assembly of great and good men. There were portions of alloy among all parties; but with all these deductions, there was a vast preponderance of excellence. It was a period of great excitement. The best men in the nation felt that much was at stake. Their civil privileges, and religious liberties, had been but recently torn from the fangs of kingcraft and ecclesiastical tyranny—a determined appeal had been made to the sword—the elements of society were put in a state of fusion—the social, civil, and ecclesiastical systems underwent an ordeal—the errors and misrule of centuries had to be cleared away—the science of government was but imperfectly learned—but piety and patriotism guided their footsteps in the midst of the paths of judgment, amid sects and schisms, which intimidated the weak, and alarmed the selfish.

Much more was expected from the sessions of the Assembly than it was in their power, or that of any other, to achieve. The idol of uniformity was 'cast down, but not destroyed.' A portion of 'the old leaven' still lurked in the minds of some of these good men. It is very little that large Assemblies have been able to accomplish in composing religious differences; and when they have called in the civil sword to enforce their decisions, they have done infinitely more mischief than ever they did good—originated more controversies than ever they have composed—made more hypocrites by terror, than cordial believers by love—and given birth to more sects and schisms than they have found it politic to extirpate, or possible to convert.

During the *interregnum*, or period of the commonwealth, the minds of many good men were divided upon the propriety of past proceedings to the late king, and the present principles of government, as well as upon religious subjects and matters of ecclesiastical regimen. Baxter had no more friendly feelings to what he deemed usurpation on the part of the Protector, than to the despotism and reckless stretches of arbitrary power in his predecessor, as if a legitimate king had 'a divine right' to oppress his subjects, and 'establish iniquity by law.' He signed, or entered 'the submission' to Cromwell and the Parliament; but his predilections were in favour of monarchy. He had little personal attachment to Cromwell, and no great partiality for several measures of his government, though, like many others, he found the most exceptionable of these preferable to the state of things subsequent to the Restoration. He does not appear to have had much confidence in the Protector; nor does the Protector appear to have reposed much confidence in him. Through the influence of Lord Broghill and the Earl of Warwick, he was once brought to preach before him. He chose for his text 1 Cor. i. 10, and expatiated upon the divisions and distractions of the church, showing how mischievous it was for politicians to maintain such divisions for their own ends, that they might fish in troubled waters. Sometime afterwards Cromwell had a long private interview with him, during which he gave expression to some sentiments which could not be palatable to Oliver. It was a part of his policy to gain and attach influential and talented men by patience and moderation, and probably passed over what was unpalatable to himself in forbearance and dignified silence. At all events, Baxter does not appear to have been a favourite or confidential person at the Protector's court. Whatever was objectionable in the Lord Protector's private character or public administration, it must be allowed that he had a difficult part to act. The agitated jarring materials of which the commonwealth was composed, required a master mind 'to ride in the whirlwind and rule the storm.' His discrimination, decision, and the liberal policy which he in general pursued, reflect honour upon his memory, after the heat of party feeling had subsided. This, Baxter was candid enough to confess. The commonwealth men who had lived under the first Charles, and during the administration of the second Charles, were furnished with ample materials for painful contrast between what preceded, and what succeeded, the portion of civil liberty and religious freedom enjoyed by all parties under the alleged fanaticism and republican usurpation of Oliver Cromwell.

The Restoration banished Baxter from his beloved flock at Kidderminster for ever; but the happy effects of his labours lingered there for more than a century. The Restoration issued in the expulsion of the faithful pastor, and the restoration of the old vicar. Gladly would he have remained among them as his curate; but this, bishop Morley would by no means tolerate, nor allow him, under the wing of the church of England, to labour in any part of his diocese. When he requested liberty to labour in a village that had no endowment, Morley replied,

'They are better to be without any, than have you to preach to them.' It is not to be wondered at that such rude cavalier treatment should have for ever severed him from the church of England; and although he neither lusted after her honours nor emoluments—for he afterwards refused from Lord Chancellor Clarendon the bishopric of Hereford—yet he lingered for a season after her altars, and was an occasional conformist. The two following years of his life he spent chiefly in London. He was looked upon as a friend to monarchy, and was chosen to preach before the Parliament in April 1660, which was the day preceding that on which they voted the king's return. By his years, his intelligence, his standing, and weight of character, he gave an impulse to the returning tide of loyalty to the banished prince of the house of Stuart. He soon afterwards preached a thanksgiving sermon at St Paul's, for General Monk's success. After the Restoration he became one of the king's chaplains in ordinary, and preached before him once. But Baxter was not a courtly man. He had too much conscience and principle to get far into the confidence of such a king, or ever to become popular in a profane court. He, however, was appointed one of the commissioners at the Savoy, took part in the conferences, and drew up the reformed liturgy. He was exceedingly anxious for a comprehension between the church of England and the nonconformists. He laboured late and early for it. He used all his influence and arguments with the most unyielding of each party, and with the king himself; but it proved labour in vain. They were heterogeneous materials—they could not be amalgamated. Baxter's motives were pure, his intentions were upright; but the ardour of his zeal surpassed the soundness of his judgment, in imagining that such discordant elements could cordially coalesce. Some of his nonconforming brethren, much inferior to him in talent, saw the impracticability of such a scheme. The king himself never honestly wished, nor intended it. Sheldon, and several of the bishops, were equally hostile to any alteration in the liturgy, or any concessions to the nonconformists. The whole ended very like a farce; and the king seemed determined to dragoon his subjects into conformity to the church, or compel them to leave the kingdom. The first fruits of the Restoration were bitter disappointment and grief; the full harvest filled up the drama with the Act of Uniformity, which, like the prophet's roll, was 'filled with lamentation, mourning, and woe.'

All Baxter's attempts towards a comprehension having proved abortive, being precluded from labouring near his former flock, and having no stated charge, he preached occasionally in and about London. In order to obtain this liberty, he procured a license from bishop Sheldon, for which he had to subscribe a promise 'not to preach any thing against the doctrine and ceremonies of the church.' He occasionally assisted Dr Bates at St Dunstan's, and preached sometimes at Blackfriar's. His principles, character, and deserved celebrity, both as a preacher and writer, might have been deemed a sufficient passport for him into any pulpit in Great Britain; but Baxter, now in the maturity of his intellectual and moral vigour, after more than sixteen years' faithful service, and unexampled success in winning souls to Christ, and in feeding and ruling the Lord's flock, must be restrained as a suspected heretic newly landed from Rome or Spain, and gagged by pledges to a bishop, as if he were a fierce fiery novice who plotted the overthrow of church and state! Could any thing be more preposterous? Great guilt must fall somewhere, for either restraining or interdicting such a man from preaching the gospel freely, when thousands were 'perishing for lack of knowledge.' He preached a farewell sermon at Blackfriar's in May, 1662. He afterwards retired to Acton in Middlesex, where he usually went to the church one part of the Lord's day, and spent the remainder of it with his family, and any of his poor neighbours who chose to come unto him. The vexations and annoyances to which he was subjected during the rigid reign of terror, subsequent to the passing and enforcing the Act of Uniformity, were neither few nor small. Like most of his brethren, he drank deeply into the bitter cup of persecution. By mulcts, fines, successive imprisonments, spoliation, and loss of goods, he suffered much in body, in mind, and in substance. One of his imprisonments lasted upwards of two years. Yet all these he bore with the equanimity and meekness of a Christian. Even then his active mind was meditating on executing something for the glory of God, the good of the church, or the benefit of his species.

The Act of Uniformity, which was passed in May, 1662, took effect on Bartholomew's day, the 24th August following. It naturally awakened painful associations in the minds of many of the best men who ministered at the Episcopal altars. It reminded them of the French massacre which occurred on the same day, when upwards of forty thousand Protestants perished by the hands of the Roman Catholics. That barbarous and sanguinary act formed an arbitrary and gloomy sequel in England to its prototype of Catholic cruelty and French fury. If the one resembled the reckless havoc of Robespierre, the other, equally intolerant in its character, under forms of an unrighteous law, was calculated 'to wear out the saints of the Most High.' This atrocious deed, chiefly concocted by Hyde and Sheldon, and passed by the British Parliament, led to the ejection of two thousand of the most conscientious ministers of the Church of England, and entailed countless calamities and intolerable grievances upon thousands of the most useful and inoffensive subjects that ever trod the British soil. Of these, Baxter, while he survived, had an ample share. He seldom preached in public but he was surrounded with spies. Rarely could he commend the principles of the common salvation to the consciences of his auditors, or condemn the common vices of fallen humanity, without being taxed with sedition, heresy, and schism. Little relaxation was to be expected, and less was realised, while such a libertine as Charles II. and his infatuated brother, and successor, swayed the British sceptre. It was the revolution of 1688 that brought them effectual relief.

An event of considerable importance occurred about this time in the history of Baxter. He married a Miss Charlton, a pious young lady of his native county, not much more than a month after the Act of Uniformity came into operation. It occasioned a considerable deal of speculation for a time, as did that of Luther the German reformer. This arose chiefly from two circumstances. While engaged in his pastoral labours at Kidderminster, his whole soul was absorbed in his work, and he, perhaps, seldom thought of such an act. He considered the marriage relation as lawful and 'honourable,' though in his own case he for a long time deemed it inexpedient. His remarks upon ministers who saw and acted differently from him, were too free. This afforded some ground for retaliation when he married himself, at the age of forty-seven, a young lady only in her twenty-third year. The disparity of years between Baxter and the object of his choice, furnished some materials for idle speculation and private gossip. He says himself, 'that the news of it rung about every where, partly as a wonder, and partly as a crime; and that the king's marriage was scarcely more talked of than his.' Subsequent to the death of Miss Charlton's father, she and her mother came to reside in Kidderminster before Baxter left it. Her mother seems to have been a pious woman. 'She was a blessing among many of the poor weavers in Kidderminster, and preferred their society above all the vanities of the world.' The preaching of Baxter appears to have been blessed to Miss Charlton when about eighteen years of age. She was one of the many fruits of his efficient ministry. She had cause to love him as her spiritual father, counsellor, and friend. They seem to have enjoyed a larger portion of connubial comfort than is common where there is such a disparity in years between the husband and the wife, and when her family and fortune had raised her a grade above her husband in society. Decided piety was the basis and bond of their union. It kindled and kept alive between them reciprocal affection. Her deep-toned devotion, sound discretion, talents, and industry for family management, her services too, and well-timed sympathies with her husband in his various chequered fortunes, proved her to be a fit companion in life to Richard Baxter. She was an eminent blessing to him in his advanced years. 'They lived together as heirs of the grace of life, and their prayers were not hindered' by internal discord. Like 'Zacharias and Elisabeth,' they were both righteous before God, walking in all the commandments and ordinances of the Lord blameless,' as far as the temper of those turbulent times would admit. More than once they were called, for the sake of a good conscience, to 'take joyfully the spoiling of their goods, knowing in themselves that they had in heaven a better and more enduring substance.' It does not appear that they had any family. His 'Breviate of the Life of Mrs Baxter' is highly creditable to the piety and domestic character of both. This small volume, which forms a concise outline of the religious character of Mrs Baxter and her mother Mrs Charlton, is not the least valuable of the author's minor productions, and affords an admirable specimen of the stamina and strength of female piety among the nonconformists of old England. In every respect she was a suitable 'help meet for him' during nineteen of the most trying and eventful years of his life. She soothed his sorrows—tenderly sympathized with his bodily sufferings—softened some of the asperities of his natural temper—supplemented and balanced some of his minor defects—shaded his infirmities—afforded him every facility to pursue his proper labour—and displayed a moral courage in taking up the cross, and cheerfulness in bearing it, every way worthy of the wife of Richard Baxter. She frequently followed him to jail, and contributed to render his cell a little Bethel, where they frequently had more Christian visitors than in the calm current of every-day life. He says himself, ' My poor wife made nothing of prisons, distrainings, reproaches, and such crosses; but her burden was most inward, from her own tenderness, and next from those whom she over loved.'

Baxter drank deeply into the cup of calamity from the period of the Restoration, till the Revolution afforded him enlargement ' at the eleventh hour.' Through nineteen years of that dark, dreary, perilous period, Mrs Baxter's domestic services and society were an incalculable blessing to him. He, with hundreds more of faithful devoted ministers of Christ, could for a length of time only preach publicly by stealth. Their peaceful and useful labours were viewed by the jealous eye of the church as schism, and by the jaundiced eye of the state as sedition. The Act of Uniformity was soon followed by the Oxford, or Five Mile Act, the principle of which was more fitted for the meridian of Rome or of Spain in the palmy days of the inquisition, or for the abject slaves of an oriental despot, than to the souls and circumstances of free born Englishmen in the middle of the seventeenth century, who had previously tasted some of the sweets of civil and religious liberty under the Commonwealth. The oath ran in the following terms : ' I, A. B., do swear, that it is not lawful, upon any pretence whatsoever, to take up arms against the king; and that I do abhor that traitorous position of taking arms by his authority, against his person, or against those who are commissioned by him in pursuance of such commission; and that I will not at any time endeavour any alteration of the government, either in church or state.'

These sanguinary enactments were designed to silence every faithful minister of Christ without the pale of the Church of England, and were calculated to grieve every humane and honest-minded man within it. Sheldon, the archbishop of Canterbury, Seth, the bishop of Salisbury, and chancellor Hyde, the accredited directors and keepers of the king's conscience, obtained the credit of framing and carrying through Parliament those despotic principles which were long a deep disgrace to the statute book of Great Britain. Many, or most of the nonconformist flocks 'fainted' for the lack of wholesome pastures; the waters of the sanctuary had been poisoned, and agitated from the bottom by the breath of intolerance; and the poor people, hungering and thirsting for the bread and the water of life, were 'scattered abroad as sheep that had no shepherd.' Spoliation and distraint spread in every corner of the country where the people possessed a vestige of principle, and had faith and fortitude to keep a good conscience. To be compelled, right or wrong, to worship at the Episcopal altars, when Ichabod was legibly inscribed upon thousands of her pulpits—to swear eternal and unalterable allegiance to her semi-popish service-book—swallow in silence, like the slaves of the Grand Turk, the doctrine of ' passive obedience and non-resistance'—and pledge themselves, with the solemnity of an oath, never to endeavour any alteration in the then existing condition of the church and state—such oaths, promises, and pledges, they justly considered as a distinct assumption of the popish principle of infallibility, and on their part as a dereliction of the great principle of Christian liberty, an invasion on the unalienable rights of conscience, and an abject abandonment of their civil duties to their country and posterity as Englishmen. It is not to be wondered that there were then many thousands in Britain who would not bow the knee to this image of Baal, nor, to escape the gloom of a dungeon, worship this ' golden image' which the king, the intolerant part of the prelates, and a servile Parliament, had been pleased to set up. Baxter was a person of much too tender a conscience to take such an oath. He consulted some of his legal friends upon its implications—submitted some queries as to its bearing, to which he received lengthened replies; but to his mind they proved unsatisfactory. He drew up certain strictures upon ' the Act,' with a distinct avowal of loyalty to the king, subjection to government where their enactments did not interfere with obedience to Christ, and special reasons for not taking the oath. These he showed to some of his friends, whom he considered better versed in legal matters than himself. They dissuaded him from giving publicity to them, as they would, in all probability, only make bad worse; and that the only remedy which he and his brethren like-minded had, was to bear all with silence and patience.

While these intolerant and arbitrary principles were carried into effect with relentless rigour, Divine Providence saw meet to visit the metropolis and some parts of the country with severe judgments. The plague raged in London and its vicinity in the most fearful and appalling manner. It commenced at Acton, where Baxter resided, in the end of July, 1665, and continued till the month of March following. Being absent from his family for a time, on his return he found the churchyard in the neighbourhood of his dwelling ' ploughed like a field with graves,' and many of his neighbours numbered with the dead; but by the protection of a kind providence, he found his own family safe, and his habitation uninfected. He made ' the Lord his refuge, and the Most High his habitation,' therefore ' no evil befel him,' nor did the plague, in an infected atmosphere, ' come near his dwelling.' The court, and a large portion of the conforming clergy, fled, and left their suffering fellow-citizens and flocks to the ravages of ' the pestilence that walketh in darkness, and the destruction that wasted at noon-day.' ' Their own shepherds pitied them not.' The moral heroism, however, displayed by not a few of the silenced ministers on that mournful and perilous occasion, reflects immortal honour upon their memories. The names of Vincent, Chester, Janeway, Turner, and many others, were conspicuous in those labours of love. While the judgments of Heaven were consuming the people by hundreds and thousands, these intrepid men fearlessly 'stood between the living and the dead,' and 'preached the unsearchable riches of Christ,' that there was still 'balm in Gilead, and a Physician there' capable, in the prospect and the agonies of death, of 'healing the hurt of the daughter of the people.' 'He sent his word and healed them, and delivered them from their destructions.' 'O that men would praise the Lord for his goodness, for his wonderful works to the children of men!' Baxter and his generous partner in life had too much Christian principle in their hearts, and too much of the milk of human kindness in their bosoms, to shun the post of danger and duty in the day of peril, and remain as idle spectators of such heart-rending scenes of human woe. It has been calculated that upwards of 100,000 of the population, on that occasion, fell victims to that dreadful scourge. But when the Lord's hand is lifted up, many of the most guilty are the most blind and obdurate, and 'will not see; but they shall see, and be ashamed for their envy at the people; yea, the fire of thine enemies shall devour them.'

The plague had not long subsided till 'the great fire' broke out in London, on the 2d September, 1666, the ravages of which, for three days and three nights, within and without the walls of the city, spread universal consternation among the people, and entailed untold calamities upon thousands of homeless, houseless inhabitants. Our author, in his Life and Times, gives copious and minute details of these unexampled scenes of devastation and consequent wretchedness. 'Thus,' he says, 'was the best, and one of the fairest, cities of the world turned into ashes and ruins in three days' space, with many scores of churches, and the wealth and necessaries of the inhabitants. It was a sight which might have given any man a lively sense of the vanity of the world, and of all its wealth and glory, and of the future conflagration, to see the flames mount upward towards heaven, and proceed so furiously without restraint—to see the streets filled with people, so astonished, that many had scarcely sense left them to lament their own calamity—to see the fields filled with heaps of goods, costly furniture, and household stuff, while sumptuous buildings, warehouses, and furnished shops, and libraries, &c., were all on flames, and none durst come near to secure any thing—to see the king and nobles ride about the streets, beholding all these desolations, and none could afford them relief—to see the air, so far as it could be beheld, so filled with the smoke, that the sun shined through it with a colour like blood; yea, even when it was setting in the west, it so appeared to them that dwelt on the west side of the city. But the dolefulest sight of all was afterwards to see what a ruinous confused place the city was, by chimneys and steeples standing, only standing, in the midst of cellars and heaps of rubbish, so that it was hard to know where the streets had been, and dangerous, for a long time, to pass through the ruins because of the vaults and fire in them. No man that seeth not such

a thing, can have a right apprehension of the dreadfulness of it.' *

These sweeping judgments, and disastrous dispensations, were, to some extent, over-ruled for good. By pestilence and fire the Lord pleaded the cause of his oppressed people, and, under the pressure of public calamity, for a short time set before the silenced ministers 'an open door.' The most of the parish churches were burned to ashes, or reduced to a pile of rubbish. The 'hireling' part of the clergy 'fled, because they were hirelings, and cared not for the flock,' and for a season simply suspended their hostility. The nonconformist ministers now resolved more than ever to preach to the houseless, homeless multitudes 'who had escaped' the ravages of the flames 'with the skin of their teeth,' till they were imprisoned. Their bowels yearned over the multitudes who fainted and were scattered abroad as sheep having no shepherd. Several of them, whose names are familiar to the annals of nonconformity, opened their houses, fitted up rooms, some of them erected plain temporary chapels, and booths, &c., to accommodate the people, who, stripped of their all, many of them were anxious to hear the gospel, and seemed disposed to seek indemnification in 'the unsearchable riches of Christ.' The people 'had none other to hear, save in a few churches, that could hold no considerable part of them; so that to forbid them to hear the nonconformists, was all one as to forbid them all public worship—to forbid them to seek heaven when they had lost almost all that they had on earth—to take from them their spiritual comforts after all their outward comforts were gone. They thought this a species of cruelty so barbarous, as to be unbeseeming any man who would not own himself to be a devil.' Baxter further adds: 'But all this little moved the ruling prelates, saving that shame restrained them from imprisoning the preachers so hotly and forwardly as before. The Independents also set up their meetings more openly than formerly. Mr Griffiths, Mr Brooks, Mr Caryl, Mr Barker, Dr Owen, Mr Philip Nye, and Dr Goodwin, who were their leaders, came to the city; so that many of the citizens went to those meetings called private, more than went to the public parish churches.' This was only a brief breathing time to those excellent men who had been restrained by gagging statutes, and intolerant enactments, from speaking to the people. The pressure of these public judgments was no sooner alleviated, than the king returned to his guilty pleasures, and the exercise of arbitrary power, which formed his native element, and the High Churchmen to their intolerance and cruelty. 'Though you should bray a fool in a mortar, with a pestle, among wheat, yet will he not be wise, nor will his folly depart from him.' The degree of connivance shown to the nonconformists and their meetings about that period, arose out of casual circumstances, not from any alteration of the laws, or respect to their property, their persons, or their principles. The attempts at a comprehension, and their failure, discovered the spirit by which the dominant party were actuated; and 'the Act of Indemnity' seemed more designed for the benefit of the

* Life, part i. pp. 98—100.

Roman Catholics than to afford relief to the noncon-formists. It was a bungling piece of patchwork to amend a vicious system of sanguinary legislation; and the awkward attempts at a comprehension ended in smoke.

While Baxter resided at Acton, he became acquainted with Sir Matthew Hale, who was lord chief baron of the exchequer. He was a person of preeminent piety, a judge of incorruptible integrity, an honour and a pattern to the legal profession, in a corrupt age, when the streams of public justice were often poisoned at the fountain head. Though men very dissimilar in their natural temperament and habits of study, yet they were kindred spirits on all the cardinal verities of the common salvation. They had a mutual predilection for metaphysical discussion; but the congenial sympathies of their minds found their sweetest solace and fervent friendship in the fundamental principles of the glorious gospel of the blessed God. Their mutual Christian friendship was maintained inviolate for life, and, we doubt not, was a blessing to both. Baxter says: 'The conferences which I had frequently with him, mostly about the immortality of the soul, and other philosophical and foundation points, were so edifying, that his very questions and objections did help me to more light than other men's solutions. . . . When the people crowded in and out of my house to hear, he openly showed me great respect, before them, at the door, and never spoke a word against it, as was no small encouragement for the people to go in; though the other sort muttered, that a judge should so far countenance that which they took to be against the law!'

After Baxter was released from prison, he seems to have resided for more than a year at Tatteredge, near Barnet. Here he was separated from part of his family. By the smallness of the apartments, smoke, and cold, the place was exceedingly uncomfortable; and if it was not the means of inducing some of his bodily complaints, certainly tended very much to aggravate them. Such, however, were the ardour and energy of his mind, his untiring and invincible perseverance at the pen and the page, when precluded from the labours of the pulpit, that during the five following years, from 1665 till 1670, he produced some of the most elaborate and valuable of his practical works. Within the same period, also, he had frequent and long discussions with Dr Owen, upon terms of agreement among Christians of all parties. On all the fundamental doctrines of the gospel, these two great men were essentially one. The character of their minds was widely different. On the constitution, union, and government of a gospel church, there was a considerable disparity in their respective sentiments. Perhaps the Doctor had studied these subjects more minutely than Baxter. He seems to have been more clear and correct, but much less ardent and sanguine than Baxter, as to the practicability of a cordial union among the different parties that then divided the professing world. Baxter looked more to rules, and details, and mutual concessions. Owen seems to have distrusted and suspected the efficacy of these, and looked more to identity of principle, and unity of spirit, and affection, as the most essential elements of church union,

and the amalgamation of different parties. 'The one expected to unite all hearts by attacking all understandings; the other trusted more to the gradual operation of Christian feeling, by which alone he believed that extended unity would finally be effected. The issue has proved, that in this case Owen had made the wiser calculation.' *

The Act against conventicles was again renewed in 1670, and enforced against the nonconformists with unmitigated rigour. Baxter alleged, that some of the new clauses, added to the old Act, had a reference to his own case. The most peaceful, loyal, and respectable among them, were not spared. Their meetings in London were infested with spies, and disturbed with bands of armed men. The partial liberty which the silenced ministers took to resume their labours among the remnant who had escaped the ravages of the recent pestilence, and the devastations of the fire, were now looked upon with an evil eye by the court and the High Church party, and they seemed resolved to put them down. Sheldon was as zealous in this business as any Spanish inquisitor could have been, to proscribe and punish heretics against 'the holy mother church.' He addressed the bishops of his province, urging them to promote, by every means in their power, 'so blessed a work as the preventing and suppressing of conventicles,' which the King and the Parliament, 'out of their pious care for the welfare of the church and kingdom,' had endeavoured to accomplish.

It was about this period that the Earl of Lauderdale sent for Baxter, and wished to engage him to accompany him on an expedition to make some alterations, and settle the state of ecclesiastical affairs in Scotland. By the king's permission, he professed to consult Baxter, and to induce his compliance, was authorised to offer him a bishopric, or professorship in one of our Scottish colleges. But Baxter, though he thought more favourably of this old Covenanter, and professed Presbyterian, than he really deserved, in a sensible, impressive, manly letter, respectfully, but decidedly, declined the proffered honour. He who had previously refused a bishopric in England, was not likely to be tempted to accept of one in Scotland, where the circumstances of temptation to enter into the arbitrary measures of the court, and to sacrifice principle at the shrine of courtly honour and ecclesiastical interest, were equally objectionable as in his native soil. Baxter was not a person of such flexible principles, nor of such an accommodating conscience, as to concur with his lordship in sanctioning these sanguinary enactments, and in carrying into effect those desperate measures of dragooning the Scottish Presbyterians into all the paraphernalia of Episcopal polity. Both Charles and his lordship had mistaken their man. It would have been an unnatural and uncomfortable yoke to each of the parties. The aged veteran, therefore, wisely declined the honours and emoluments of ecclesiastical preferment in Scotland, as he had already disposed of a similar offer in England. Such facts speak volumes of the high value which Baxter, and other of his contemporaries of kindred principles, set upon the

* See Orme's Life, vol. i. p. 284.

birth-right of civil freedom and religious liberty. In the letter addressed to his lordship he says:

'I would request that I might be allowed to live quietly to follow my private studies, and might once again have the use of my books, which I have not seen these ten years. I pay for a room for their standing in at Kidderminster, where they are eaten by worms and rats, having no sufficient security for my quiet abode in any place to encourage me to send for them. I would also ask that I might have the liberty, which every beggar has, to travel from town to town, I mean but to London, to oversee the press when any thing of mine is licensed for it. If I be sent to Newgate for preaching Christ's gospel (for I dare not sacrilegiously renounce my calling, to which I am consecrated *per sacramentum ordinis*), I would request the favour of a better prison, where I may but walk and write. These I would take as very great favours, and acknowledge your lordship as my benefactor if you procure them; for I will not so much injure you as to desire, or my reason as to expect, any greater matters, no, not the benefit of the law.' It is rare indeed that a bishopric is offered to a man in such circumstances, and much rarer to find a man possessed of so much principle as to refuse it, and to prefer the unrestrained liberty of 'a beggar, to travel from town to town,' as his own or his Master's business require him—the solitude of a cell to pursue his studies in peace, and the privilege of a prison yard for relaxation—to the splendid equipage and luxuries of a bishop's palace. Let none imagine that this arose from a weak enthusiastic mind, or that it was the obstinate whim of an ascetic, whose soul had been seared with misanthropy against his species, and who was incapable of relishing the sweets of social liberty, and the comforts of civilized life. Such a choice, and such a request, are indeed puzzling and perplexing to a time-serving and worldly-minded professor; but the subject is perfectly intelligible to a Christian who wishes 'to live in all good conscience toward God,' and 'to have this as his joy and rejoicing, even the testimony of his conscience, that in simplicity and godly sincerity, not by fleshly wisdom, but by the grace of God, he should have his conversation in the world.' He found himself in company with some of the Lord's holy prophets, many 'of whom the world was not worthy.' 'Moreover, Jeremiah said unto king Zedekiah, What have I offended against thee, or against thy servants, or against this people, that ye have put me in prison? Where are now your prophets who prophesied unto you, saying, The king of Babylon shall not come against you, nor against this land? Therefore hear now, I pray thee, O my lord the king, let my supplication, I pray thee, be accepted before thee, that thou cause me not to return to the house of Jonathan the scribe, lest I die there. Then Zedekiah the king commanded that they should commit Jeremiah to the court of the prison, and that they should give him daily a piece of bread out of the baker's street, until all the bread in the city was spent. Thus Jeremiah remained in the court of the prison.' In Baxter's future imprisonments it is questionable if lord Lauderdale ever did any thing to soften the rigours of his bondage; or if Charles

showed the same leniency to him that the weak and indecisive Jewish prince showed to the Lord's prophet.

In 1671, Baxter lost the greater part of his fortune by the shutting up of the king's exchequer, amounting to upwards of a thousand pounds. He had intended it for a benevolent purpose, and not to soothe and support himself in his declining years. He says: 'All the money and estate that I had in the world, of my own, was there, except £10 per annum which I enjoyed for 11 or 12 years. Indeed it was not my own, which I mention to counsel those that would do good, to do it speedily, and "with all their might."' I had got, in all my life, the sum of £1000. Having no child, I devoted almost all of it to a charitable use—a free school. I used my best and ablest friends, for seven years, with all the skill and industry I could, to help me to purchase a house, or land to lay it out on, that it might be accordingly settled.' This was an infamous transaction. It produced distress and ruin among many. Baxter never recovered a shilling of it. His chief regret, however, was, that it deprived him of carrying his benevolent intentions into effect; and he records the fact for the instruction and direction of posterity, that they should become their own executors, lay out their substance, for the glory of God and the good of man, with their own hands, and enjoy the gratification of seeing its happy effects in their lifetime. There is often much misappropriation and embezzlement in posthumous charities.

An event of considerable importance occurred in the spring of 1672. The king issued a declaration, dispensing with the penal statutes in operation against the nonconformists. This document declares, 'That his Majesty, by virtue of his supreme power in matters ecclesiastical, suspends all penal laws thereabout; and that he will grant a convenient number of public meeting-places to men of all sorts who conform not, provided the persons are approved by him, and that they only meet in places sanctioned by him, with open doors, and do not preach seditiously, nor against the Church of England.' The Earl of Shaftesbury got the credit of advising this measure; but neither he nor his master deserved the credit which they claimed for having issued it, from any relentings for the injuries previously inflicted upon the nonconformists. Their design was to afford relief to the Roman Catholics. It was rather a kind of clap-trap for the silenced ministers, and several of them refused to avail themselves of the privilege which this morally just, but politically illegal, measure afforded them. Had the laws been founded in substantial justice, the king had no legal right to dispense with the execution of them. This 'dispensing power,' and suspicious act of grace, were not from sympathy with the principal sufferers; but to favour a party whose principles were more in unison with the secret sympathies of the king's heart. When a public plunderer scours the country, and pillages the population of their all, he may affect great generosity in giving back a tithe to a few of his favourites, when justice would have demanded restitution of the whole, and doomed the plunderer to the gallows. Nor need there be any demur among the plundered people as to the lawfulness of taking back the tithe as an instalment, while they insist upon the restitution of the whole as their lawful and unalienable property. Some good men of all parties were disposed to avail themselves of the indulgence occasioned by the king's dispensing power to promote the interests of religion.

After recovery from a dangerous fit of sickness, Baxter had resolved to seek a license from the king to preach the gospel on the indulgence principle; but wished it simply as a nonconformist, and not under the title either of an Independent or Presbyterian. It appears that Sir Thomas Player, chamberlain of London, had procured one for him without any knowledge or effort of his own. And he says: ' The 19th of November was the first day, after ten years' silence, that I preached in a tolerated public assembly, though not yet tolerated in any consecrated church, but only against law in my own house.' About the same time he was chosen one of six ministers as a lecturer at Pinner's Hall; but his service there was not of long continuance.

As the times seemed, for a short season, to become more favourable, Baxter was induced to erect or procure a place for meeting in Oxendon street. He had scarcely opened it, when an attempt was made to surprise and apprehend him, and commit him to the county jail on the Oxford Act; and though he, through an accidental absence, escaped, yet the person who officiated for him was apprehended, and committed to the Gatehouse for three months. Having been kept out of his new meeting house for a whole year, he took another in Swallow street. There also he was prevented from preaching to the people, as a guard had been set for several sabbaths together to prevent him from occupying it. Little do many dissenting churches and congregations, on these and similar sites, now think, while peacefully worshipping God ' under their vine and fig tree,' on those memorable spots, what hardships and incessant annoyances those fathers and founders of the nonconformist interest endured in wresting the privileges which they now enjoy from the iron grasp of civil tyranny and religious intolerance. ' The indulgence' and ' the king's license,' arising out of his ' dispensing power,' which promised much, yielded little substantial benefit to the ejected ministers. But a man like Baxter, of an ardent mind, and whose heart is in his Master's work, if he fail in one plan of operations, his inventive resources will lead to the adoption of another, in which he will succeed. In the month of January, 1672-3, he commenced a week-day lecture at Mr Turner's church in New Street, near Fetter Lane, where he preached the gospel freely, as he says, ' with great convenience and God's encouraging blessing.' On the Lord's day, however, he had no stated congregation to preach to, but occasionally gave his services to those who required them.

Like the great apostle of the Gentiles, Baxter felt that ' necessity was laid upon him to preach the gospel.' Even in his advanced years, and frequently labouring under a load of bodily infirmities, his bowels yearned for the spiritual necessities of his countrymen. While the snows of advanced age shaded his temples, in the midst of a thousand vexatious and harassing circumstances, his ardent soul glowed with seraphic ardour for opportunities to preach to the people ' the unsearchable riches of Christ.' By the precipitancy and crooked policy of his persecutors, several of their attempts to ensnare, imprison, and pillage him, failed. This, instead of mollifying, only exasperated them. In 1682, he suffered more severely than ever for his nonconformity. One day he was suddenly surprised in his house by a band of constables and officers, who apprehended him by a warrant to seize his person for coming within five miles of a corporate town, producing, at the same time, no less than five more warrants to distrain for £195, for five sermons which he had preached. He had just risen from bed, in great weakness from a severe paroxysm of pain, and was following the officers to jail, when met by Dr Thomas Cox, a medical gentleman, who ordered him back to his bed, while he went immediately to five of the justices, and deponed upon oath that Mr Baxter could not be lodged in jail but at the peril of his life. Upon this a delay was obtained till they should consult with the king, who graciously permitted the postponement of his incarceration, that he might be suffered to die at home. Meanwhile they executed their warrants on the books and effects in his house, the former of which were not his own, and they sold even the bed upon which this venerable minister of the Lord Jesus lay sick. ' The tender mercies of the wicked are cruel.' Baxter, however, had many pious firm friends, who could not be uninterested spectators of such a scene. They promptly advanced the money at which the articles seized in his house were appraised, in consequence of which they were retained. He afterwards reimbursed them. This iniquitous process, under covert of law, was originated and carried on without any previous notice or summons being sent him, or without his being acquainted who his accusers had been, and who were to be his judges. What a mockery of law, and insult upon the first principles of common justice! ' Shall the throne of iniquity have fellowship with the moral Governor of the universe, which frameth mischief by a law? They gather themselves together against the soul of the righteous, and condemn the innocent blood.' But Baxter could add, in the language of scripture, ' The Lord is my defence, and my God is the rock of my refuge.'

The king, now drawing near the end of his life and reign, was sunk in the sensuality of his court, and callous to the sufferings of thousands of the best of his subjects. The fires of intolerance burned with redoubled fury. Prosecutions were multiplied to an unexampled extent. Under the guise of an unrighteous and execrable law, like the statutes of Draco, tinged with blood, one class of subjects were sanctioned to live on pillage, and prey upon another. The one was pampered to live as beasts of prey; and the other was doomed to suffer all manner of indignities as beasts of burden. Many of the cormorants of the canon and civil law were insatiable. Their scent in hunting out alleged heresy was keen as that of a Roman inquisitor; and with all the *sang froid* of Turks, they could relentlessly ride rough shod over many valuable men, ' of whom the world was not worthy. Let us listen for a moment to the aged veteran himself. He says: 'But when they had taken and sold all, and I had borrowed some bedding and necessaries of the buyer, I was never the quieter, for they threatened to come upon me again, and take all, as mine, whosesoever it was, which they found in my possession, so that I had no remedy but utterly to forsake my house, and goods, and all, and take lodgings at a distance in a stranger's house; but having a long lease of my own house, which binds me to pay a greater rent than now it is worth, wherever I go I must pay that rent.' He 'took joyfully the spoiling of his goods, knowing in himself that he had in heaven a better and enduring substance.' He had been long separated from the greater part of his books. The few that he had borrowed from friends for consultation and reference, while composing some of his most valuable treatises, were seized and sold, regardless of either remonstrance or redress. This threw him entirely upon his bible, and the inexhaustible resources of heaven. Neither his faith nor his philosophy failed him under these privations. He consoled himself that he was near the end of that life and labour where no books are needed; and he says: 'I the more easily let all go.' 'Naked came I into the world, and naked must I go out; but I never wanted less that man can give, than when men had taken all away.' 'My old friends and strangers were so liberal, that I was fain to restrain their bounty.'

Although the House of Commons had passed certain resolutions in order to mitigate some of the more rigorous statutes against the nonconformists; and although 'the king's dispensing power' held out a promise of some amelioration, yet neither the one nor the other afforded the aggrieved any essential relief. By spies, officers, and interested informers, and not a few judges, they were continually harassed in various parts of the country. Orders were issued from the king and the council board to suppress all conventicles, and in the hands of these administrators, they were not allowed to lie as a dead letter. They had quietly to bear the brunt of 'Jedburgh justice,' 'Irish evidence,' and 'Lynch law;' and although Baxter was a man formed of 'sterner stuff' than to flinch from the cross in any case in which the dictates of his conscience, and the principles of Divine revelation, were implicated, yet he was by no means the most forward to offend in infringing upon those intolerant statutes, which had ejected and silenced more than two thousand of the most conscientious and able ministers in England, and so seriously circumscribed the liberties of her best subjects. He was loyal to the constitution of his country, and was by no means a red-hot radical reformer. On matters of church polity, though not a latitudinarian, he was moderate almost to a fault. He was in a sickly emaciated state, deeply afflicted with stone, and now well stricken in years, yet he was a marked man. None of these things could screen him from the jealousy of High Church feeling, and the vengeance of the court. In 1683-4, the Rev. Thomas Mayot, a beneficed clergyman of the Church of England, died, and left a bequest of £600 in favour of sixty-four ejected ministers, and appointed Baxter as the sole executor, 'not because they were nonconformists, but on account of their piety and poverty.' This fact plainly shows, that that generous and compassionate conformist considered Baxter as 'a faithful steward' to administer his bounty to these worthy but deeply injured men. Indeed, he had a large share of the confidence of pious men of all parties. The bequest, however, was for a time intercepted. The king's attorney sued for it in chancery, and the lord keeper North gave it all to the king. Shortly after the Revolution, the commissioners of the Great Seal restored it to Baxter, to be appropriated to the proper persons, agreeably to the Will of the testator. The sleepless eye of Divine Providence frequently marks the dark deeds of human rapacity with determined disapprobation, and restores to the injured poor the portion designed for them.

During a great part of 1683, Baxter made little appearance in public; but he was unremitting in his application in private. His active mind was incessantly engaged with some of his numerous and various treatises, either upon practical or controversial theology. His pregnant mind was constantly teeming with something of a beneficial character for his species—either some pamphlet to answer an opponent on the spur of the moment, or some more elaborate production for the instruction and profit of future generations. His facility at composition was extraordinary. In that, he scarcely has had a superior, and in few ages an equal. Even to a green old age, in the midst of nameless bodily infirmities, it seems to have been wrought into a habit. Activity seemed necessary to his very being. He has thrown a vast amount of soul into his works. They bear the impress of a powerful energetic mind.

From repeated molestations by the public powers, Baxter's health was greatly broken down in 1684. While he lay in a state of languishing and pain, the justices of the sessions sent warrants to apprehend him. At that time there were about a thousand more whose names were upon the catalogue, all to be bound over to their good behaviour. He expected at least six months' imprisonment for not taking the Oxford oath, and for venturing to reside in London. He refused to open his chamber door to the officers. Their warrant did not authorise them to break it open. But the six officers were bent upon their object. They stationed themselves at his study door all night, and kept him from bed and food, and closely maintained the siege till he surrendered. They conveyed him, while scarcely able to stand upon his own feet, to the sessions, and bound him over to good behaviour under a bond of four hundred pounds. He simply wished to know his crime and accusers; but they gave him evasive answers, that it was for no substantive fault, but for the security of the government in evil times, and that they had a list of suspected persons who were to be treated in a similar manner. He told them that he would rather that they would at once send him to jail, than leave him at large involuntarily to implicate others, for if but five persons came in when he was praying, it would be construed into a breach of good behaviour, and subject them all to fine and imprisonment. His judges replied: 'That if they came unexpectedly, and on other business, and not to a set meeting, nor yet if we did nothing contrary to law and the practice of the church.' He rejoined, ' Our innocency is not now any security to us. If but two beggar women did but stand in the street, and swear that I spake contrary to the law, though they heard me not, my bonds and my liberty were at their will.' Nor was this a mere imaginary case—he accordingly adds: ' For I myself, lying in my bed, heard Mr J. R. preach in a chapel on the other side of my chamber, and yet one Sibil Dash, and Elizabeth Coppel, two miserable poor women, who made a trade of it, swore to the justices that it was another that preached; and they had thus sworn against very many worthy persons in Hackney and elsewhere, on which their goods were seized for great mulcts or fines. To all this I had no answer, but that I must give bond, when they knew that I was not likely to break the behaviour, unless by lying in bed in pain.

Towards the latter years of Baxter's eventful life, both the political and ecclesiastical horizon were invested with a dark and dense gloom. The king's court was little better than a common brothel. The monarch himself, though he wore a diadem, was a cold blooded tyrant to the liberties of his country, and the happiness of his subjects, the sworn foe of serious piety and moral restraint, a Papist in heart, under a Protestant mask, a profane wit, and a licentious rake. He had brought the religion and liberties of the country to the verge of ruin. In February 1684-5, Charles II. closed his arbitrary and inglorious reign, and was called to appear at the tribunal of the Almighty, who ' cuts off the spirit of princes, and is terrible to the kings of the earth;' ' who brings the princes to nothing; he maketh the judges of the earth as vanity.' Those who wear the crown, and the coronet, and the mitre, and those who occupy the judgment-seat, who ' are clothed in purple and fine linen, and fare sumptuously every day,' would do well to remember, that when their immortal spirits pass the boundaries of time to take their just award from the Judge of the quick and the dead, impartial posterity will stamp their verdict of their principles and deeds upon monuments durable as marble. ' The seed of evil-doers shall never be renowned.' ' Is this man Coniah a despised broken idol ? Is he a vessel wherein is no pleasure ? Wherefore are they cast out, he and his seed, and are cast into a land that they know not ?' Even these despotic and dark deeds which distress the human family, and rend the frame-work of society, present a multitude of monitory lessons to posterity. ' O earth, earth, earth, hear the word of the Lord! Thus saith the Lord, Write ye this man childless, a man that shall not prosper in his days, for no man of his seed shall prosper sitting upon the throne of David, and ruling any more in Judah.'

Happily for Great Britain, at that period of trouble and darkness, of dimness and anguish, which covered the land when James II. ascended the throne, with avowedly Popish principles, and high notions of princely prerogatives, there was a pious praying remnant in the country. They had much reason to fear, that

* Orme's Life of Baxter, vol. i. pp. 331-2.

if Charles had ' chastised them with whips,' for keeping conventicles, James, his successor, ' would scourge them with scorpions.' They had too good reason to complain with the church of old, ' Therefore is judgment far from us, neither doth justice overtake us; we wait for light, but behold obscurity; for brightness, but we walk in darkness. . . . We roar all like bears, and mourn sore like doves; we look for judgment, but there is none; for salvation, but it is far from us. . . . Judgment is turned away backward, and justice standeth far off; truth is fallen in the street, and equity cannot enter; yea, truth faileth, and he that departeth from evil maketh himself a prey; and the Lord saw it, and it displeased him that there was no judgment.'

Sometime before the demise of Charles, he had raised the famous, or rather infamous, Jefferies to the dignity of the bench. As might be expected, Baxter soon fell into his hands. There was an understanding between Charles and James, prior to the death of the former, and which the latter did not conceal when Duke of York, that Baxter was marked out for jail. When bound over, under a high penalty, to his good behaviour, the intention was to keep hold of him till matter of accusation was found against him. Judge Jefferies was a fit person to go any length with such a detestable deed. If any person in England could out-Herod Herod, this was the man. Profane in his principles, coarse in his character, a bully in his manners, sanguinary in his dispositions, capable of packing and brow-beating a jury, insulting the prisoner's counsel, and delivering decisions that would have disgraced a Spanish inquisitor, he did not scruple to disgrace the ermine, outrage the first principles of common justice, and expose the law to the contempt of every intelligent and well constituted mind. Of all Baxter's previous prosecutions, this conclusion of the drama certainly exceeded, as a dishonour to the British bench, an abandonment of all gravity, decency, and decorum, and a mere mockery of all law and justice. The pretext for the prosecution was, a supposed reference, in Baxter's Commentary on the New Testament, to the bishops of the Church of England; which was stigmatised as a scandalous and seditious book against the government, the bishops, and the church. The author was accordingly apprehended, and committed to the King's-Bench prison, by a warrant from Lord Chief Justice Jefferies, in the depth of winter, 1685. He applied for a *Habeas Corpus*, obtained it, and subsequently retired to the country till the approaching session in May following. At his advanced stage of life, and by the incessant pain to which he was subject, it was conceived that he could not bear the confinement of a prison. He, however, appeared at the appointed time in Westminster Hall, to wait his trial. On the 14th of May he pleaded not guilty. Being much indisposed on the 18th, it was moved that he might have further time given him before his trial came on. This reasonable request, by his counsel, was rudely and peremptorily denied by Jefferies.

It does not appear that Baxter wrote any detailed account of this singular trial himself. No regular report appears to have been made of it in ' the State

'Trials,' except what has been copied from Calamy's abridgement of Baxter's Life. His biographers, however, have collected and recorded the principal facts of the case. In the Biographia Britannica, vol. ii. p. 15, and in Middleton's Biographia Evangelica, vol. iv. pp. 26, 27, pretty copious notes are given of this memorable trial, toward the close of our author's life. To these, and especially Mr Orme's Life of Baxter, we must refer the reader for more ample details. All in all, the accounts are of a sickening and disgusting character, and a burlesque upon the administration of public justice. All we can attempt in this sketch is a brief specimen or two, of the coarse invective and foul ribbaldry of Baxter's judge, the Lord Chief Justice of England, during the trial, which will sufficiently justify the character we have given of the man in the preceding paragraph. On Baxter's counsel moving in court that his trial might be put back for a short time, owing to his severe indisposition, the Lord Chief Justice in wrath replied, 'I will not give him a minute's more time to save his life. We have had to do with other sorts of persons, but now we have a saint to deal with, and I know how to deal with saints as well as sinners. Yonder (says he) stands Oates in the pillory, in New Palace garden, and he says he suffers for the truth, and so does Baxter; but if Baxter did but stand on the other side of the pillory with him, I would say that two of the greatest rogues and rascals in the kingdom stood there.'

On the 30th May, 1685, he was brought up to his trial before the Lord Chief Justice Jefferies, at Guildhall. Sir Henry Ashurst, who would ' not forsake his own and his father's friend,' stood by him all the while. 'Mr Baxter came first into the court, with all the marks of serenity and composure, waited for the coming of the Lord Chief Justice, who appeared quickly after, with great indignation in his face. He no sooner sat down, than a short cause was called and tried; after which the clerk began to read the title of another cause. ' You blockhead (says Jefferies) the next cause is between the king and Richard Baxter;' upon which Mr Baxter's cause was called. The passages mentioned in the information was his Paraphrase on Matt. v. 19; Mark ix. 39; xii. 38—40; Luke x. 2; John xi. 57; Acts xv. 12. These passages were picked out by Sir Roger L'Estrange, and some of his fraternity; and a certain noted clergyman, who shall be nameless, put into the hands of his enemies some accusations out of Rom. xiii. &c., as against the king, to touch his life; but no use was made of them. The great charge was, that in these several passages he reflected on the prelates of the Church of England, and so was guilty of sedition, &c. The king's counsel opened the information at large, with its aggravations. Mr Wallop, Mr Williams, Mr Rotheram, Mr Attwood, and Mr Phipps, were Mr Baxter's counsel.

Let another brief specimen of this infamous process suffice. 'Mr Baxter beginning to speak again, Jefferies exclaimed, 'Richard, Richard! dost thou think we will hear thee poison this court, &c. Richard, thou art an old fellow, an old knave. Thou hast written books enough to load a cart, every one as full of sedition as an egg is full of meat. Hadst thou been whipped out of thy writing trade forty years ago, it had been happy. Thou pretendest to be a preacher of the gospel of peace, and thou hast one foot in the grave. 'Tis time for thee to begin to think what account thou intendest to give; but leave thee to thyself, and I see thou wilt go on as thou hast begun ; but, by the grace of God, I will look after thee. I know thou hast a mighty party, and I see a great many of the brotherhood in corners waiting to see what will become of their mighty don, and a doctor of the party clerking too (Dr Bates) at your elbow ; but, by the grace of Almighty God, I will crush you all.' When Jefferies had summed up the alleged evidence in a violent tirade of profanity and low abuse, that would have disgraced a Turkish tribunal, Baxter said, ' Does your lordship think that any jury will pretend to pass a verdict upon me upon such a trial ?' Jefferies replied, ' I'll warrant you, Mr Baxter; don't trouble yourself about that.' The jury accordingly brought him in guilty ! On the 29th June he had judgment given against him. He was fined five hundred merks, condemned to lie in prison till it was paid, and bound to his good behaviour for seven years. Jefferies had proposed that he should be whipped through the city; but his brethren would not agree to it. In his fine and imprisonment they acquiesced. In 1686, the king, at the mediation of Lord Powes, granted him a pardon ; and on the 24th of November, he was discharged out of the King's Bench. Securities, however, were required for his good behaviour; but it was entered on his bail-piece, by direction of the king, that his remaining in London, contrary to the Oxford Act, should not be taken as a breach of the peace.'*

This farce of a trial was calculated to fix the stain of indelible infamy upon the bench of British justice, and to bring all the principles of civil law into universal contempt. What man's property, liberty, or life, could be safe in the hands of such a judge, or proof against the verdict of a packed jury, brow-beat into an iniquitous decision by ' an unjust judge, who neither feared God nor regarded man ?' At the close of the second edition of the Paraphrase, upon which this prosecution was founded, Baxter inserts the following note: ' Reader, it is like you have heard how I was, for this book, by the instigation of Sir Roger L'Estrange and some of the clergy, imprisoned nearly two years by Sir George Jefferies, Sir Francis Wilkins, and the rest of the judges of the King's Bench, after their preparatory restraints and attendance, under the most reproachful words, as if I had been the most odious person living, and not suffered at all to speak for myself. Had not the king taken off my fine, I had continued in prison till death. Because many desire to know what all this was for, I have written the eight accusations, which, (after the clergy search of my book) were brought in as seditious. I have altered never a word accused, that ye may know the worst. What I said of the murderers of Christ, and of the hypocrite Pharisees and their sins, the judge said I meant of the Church of England, though I have written for it,

* See Middleton's Lives, vol. iv. pp. 26—30.; and Biographia Britannica.

and still communicate with it.' Having given the passages of scripture, &c., he adds: ' These were all, by one that knoweth his own name, put into their hands, with some accusations out of Rom. xiii. (supposed by Dr Sherlock) as against my life; but their discretion forbade them to use them, or name them.' It was well that Baxter was enabled to maintain a portion of ' the meekness and gentleness of Christ,' under this vexatious and iniquitous trial; but subsequent generations have had no difficulty to see, that his persecutors, accusers, and judges, were men actuated by a similar spirit, and influenced by kindred principles, with those men who accused Paul ' as a pestilent fellow, a mover of sedition among all the Jews throughout the world, and a ringleader of the sect of the Nazarenes; who also has gone about to profane the temple, whom we took, and would have judged according to our law.' It is long since the British public have formed their opinion, and passed their verdict, upon his principal judge and his master, as influenced by prejudices and passions, not far dissimilar to those who ' gnashed upon Stephen with their teeth,' and who doomed the Prince of peace to the accursed tree, as ' an enemy to Cæsar, and a mover of sedition throughout all Jewry.' ' If they have called the Master of the house Beelzebub, how much more they of the household?'

The last two years of Baxter's imprisonment yielded him more tranquillity and composure to pursue his studies, and complete some of his works, than he had enjoyed since the Restoration; and although his physical strength was greatly exhausted, his frame much attenuated, his infirmities daily multiplying, and the shadows of the evening were stretching out upon him; and although he had not now Mrs Baxter to nurse and cheer him, and convert the solitude of a cell, and the gloom of a prison, into a palace or a paradise, yet he enjoyed solid confidence in God; he found ' consolation in Christ, comfort of love, fellowship of the Spirit, bowels of mercies,' joy in the Holy Ghost, and the hallowed hope of eternal life. While ' tribulation for Christ abounded, consolation by Christ much more abounded.' A large portion of the pious in London and its vicinity, some in, and many of different denominations out of, the Establishment, sincerely sympathised with him, visited him in prison, and did not fail ' to minister to him in his bonds.' Among these was the celebrated Matthew Henry, the well known commentator, when quite a young man. He communicated, in a letter to his father, dated 17th November, 1685, an outline of his interview with this ' aged disciple,' and ' now also a prisoner of Jesus Christ.' As young Henry had come up from the country, it might have been supposed that a thousand objects would have seized his fancy, and engaged his inquiries before Richard Baxter, an aged emaciated man, shut up in prison, under the odium of heresy against the polity of the church, and sedition against the state. But like another Onesiphorus, when he came to London ' he sought out' Baxter ' very diligently, and found him.' We have no doubt but ' he refreshed him, and was not ashamed of his chain;' and it is obvious from Henry's letter to his father Philip, that he found himself well repaid in the solemn, seasonable, and affectionate coun-

sels tendered to him by the aged veteran to that young soldier of Jesus Christ, who was then preparing for the field to carry on the conflict. Henry says: ' I found him in pretty comfortable circumstances, though a prisoner in a private house near the prison, attended by his own man and maid. . . . He is in as good health as one can expect, and methinks looks better, and speaks heartier, than when I saw him last. The token you sent he would by no means be persuaded to accept, and was almost angry when I pressed it from one ousted as well as himself. He said he did not use to receive; and I understand since his need is not great. He gave us some good counsel to prepare for trials, and said, the best preparation for them was, a life of faith, and a constant course of self-denial.' This is a noble and lovely spectacle. It is like ' a well of living water' in an African wilderness, or an *oasis* in the midst of a Lybian desert. Mr Williams, Henry's biographer, says of it, ' It is one of those lovely pictures of days which are past, which, if rightly viewed, may produce lasting and beneficial effects, emotions of sacred sorrow for the iniquity of persecution, and animating praise that the demon in these happy days of tranquillity is restrained, though not destroyed.' *

* Hard as often was Baxter's lot, and roughly as he was sometimes handled ' for conscience sake,' of which the preceding sketches furnish only a few specimens; and though, from his commanding talents, and wide range of influence, he was often black-balled as a wicked man, yet he was by no means the greatest sufferer among the ejected ministers, and poor persecuted nonconformists. He was sometimes under softer skies than some of his brethren. He was certainly a man of moderation. Some of his brethren thought him so to a fault. He contended with men of extreme opinions on both sides. He sometimes enjoyed the sunny side of the hill, when some others more bitterly felt the blast. This arose from the character of his mind, but not from a desertion of his principles, nor a dastardly dread of the cross. We may present to the reader a bird's-eye view, by a modern writer, of the nameless sufferings and sanguinary persecutions to which the nonconformists were subjected, in both quarters of the United Kingdom, under the second Charles.

' Charles II., on his restoration, renewed all the persecutions of his bloody race. He pursued the Scottish Covenanters to the mountains and morasses with fire and sword, enacting all the horrors of racks, thumb-screws, and the iron boot, as may be seen vividly detailed in Sir Walter Scott's Tales of a Grandfather, and Old Mortality. Neale, says the writer of the preface to Mr De Laune's Plea for Nonconformists, states: " That De Laune was one of near eight thousand who had perished in prison in the reign of Charles II.; and that merely for dissenting from the church in some points, for which they are able to bring good reason." As for the severe penalties inflicted on them for seditious and riotous assemblies, designed only for the worship of God, he adds: " That they suffered in their trades and estates, within the compass of five years, at least two millions of money!" Another writer adds, that Mr Jeremy White had carefully collected a list of the dissenting sufferers, and of their sufferings, and had the names of sixty thousand persons who had suffered on a religious account, between the restoration of Charles II. and the revolution of king William, five thousand of whom died in prison. It is certain, that besides those who suffered in their own country, great numbers retired to the plantations and different parts of America. Many transported themselves and their effects to Holland, and filled the English churches of Amsterdam and the Hague, &c. If we admit the dissenting families of the several denominations in England to be one hundred and fifty thousand, and that each family suffered no more than the loss of three or four pounds per annum, from the Act of Uniformity, the whole will amount to twelve or fourteen millions, a prodigious sum for those times. But these are only conjectures. The damage done to the trade and the property of the nation was undoubtedly immense; and the wounds that were made in the estates of private families were deep and

When Baxter obtained his full enlargement from the rules of the King's Bench, where young Henry had visited him, which he did in February, 1687, he removed to his house in the Charterhouse Yard. For about four years and a half he continued to assist Mr Silvester, until bodily debility rendered it requisite for him to confine himself to his room. He preached gratuitously for him while his ability admitted, on the mornings of the Lord's day, and every alternate Thursday morning. Preaching was Baxter's proper element. He loved his Master, his work, and the souls of men, and 'he was willing to spend, and be spent, though the more abundantly he loved, the less he was loved.' Like a star of the first magnitude, in the right hand of Him who walks in the midst of the seven golden candlesticks, his life, his light, and his lustre, remained undiminished almost to the latest stages of his mortal career. 'In old age, when others fade, he was fat and full of sap, and always flourishing, to show (to succeeding generations) that the Lord is a rock, and there is no unrighteousness with him.' And when unable to travel to the place of worship, and officiate in public, he, as on former occasions, when interdicted by 'the powers that be,' opened 'his own hired house, and received all that came in to him, preaching the kingdom of God, and the things which concern the Lord Jesus, with all confidence, no man forbidding him.'

In the latter part of James II.'s reign, Baxter took little or no part in public affairs. It was an evil time; it was wise to say little. They could 'make a man an offender for a word, and lay a snare for him who reproved in the gate, and turn aside the just for a thing of nought.' Matters were rapidly ripening, and rushing on to a crisis. The Stuart dynasty was upon the eve of being broken up, which, for three successive reigns, had thrown the nation into fits of fever and ague, by their king-craft, the golden image of uniformity, which they had set up for universal worship, and their monkish and inquisitorial maxims of church polity. They had set every man's hand against his brother, and made the flower of the nation writhe upon the rack, and bleed at every pore. But as the deepest darkness sometimes precedes the approaching dawn, so it was in this case. Baxter had long and fruitlessly laboured to reconcile jarring parties, and amalgamate materials which had no common principle of affinity, no doubt with the best intentions; but he lived long enough to see, that 'that which is crooked cannot be made straight; and that which is wanting cannot be numbered.' It is likely at last he tried what prayer to God could do, when persuasion with men had failed. 'At eventime it was light.' He lived to see the last of the Stuarts desert the British throne, and to witness the morn-

ing star of a bloodless revolution dawn through a dark horizon, and promise a brighter and better day to the interests of civil freedom and religious liberty, under the mild lustre of which he might for a short time walk, and, like 'a shock of corn fully ripe,' be gathered to glory, and descend to the grave in a good old age in peace. It was so. There can be no doubt but Baxter's soul rejoiced in this happy change, though his bodily weakness precluded him from making any conspicuous appearance in those singular, merciful, and memorable events. He had no doubt been taught since the Restoration, in tones solemn as thunder, and in characters glaring as the lurid lightning, 'not to trust in princes nor men's sons, in whom there is no stay,' &c. After the snows of threescore years and ten had blanched his locks, he should have learned many mortifying lessons to little purpose, if he had not learned to 'cease from man, whose breath is in his nostrils, for wherein is he to be accounted of?' Yet it was a solace to the soul of this venerable servant of Christ, after weathering the storms of a long, dark, dreary night, to see a prince ascend the British throne, who, though he had breathed republican air, had sucked the breasts of freedom, was a thorough paced Protestant, enlightened advocate of civil liberty, and the fast friend of religious freedom to all the loyal subjects of the civil state. When 'Jacob saw the waggons' which his son had sent, 'his spirit revived;' 'he said, It is enough, Joseph is yet alive; I will go down, and see him before I die.'

We come at last to witness this venerable man in his sick chamber, and upon his death-bed. We see him close his career like the summer setting sun; the glare of his beams are softened; but his disc large, calm, and clear, he descends, in silent majesty, under the horizon. To such a man as Richard Baxter, who, for more than half a century, had walked with God, lived a life of faith upon the Lord Jesus, whose 'affections' were so uniformly and incessantly 'set on things that are above;' who was almost a daily, but patient, martyr to the stone; whose shattered frame kept him constantly hovering upon the confines of the eternal world; whose unearthly life, and unparalleled labours, demonstrated, in ten thousand different ways, 'whose he was, and whom he served,'—the gleanings of the sick chamber, and the records of the death-bed, can add little to the ample blaze of such accumulated evidence. 'He feared the Lord from his youth,' if he was not, as his father supposed, 'sanctified from the womb.' Baxter was emphatically 'a living epistle of Christ, known and read of all men.' 'His works praise him in the gates.' His gigantic labours attest him to have been a man of astonishing calibre of mind. His Devotional and Practical Works attest the worth of his character, and have immortalised his name. They form a monument to his memory more durable than the pyramids of Egypt. His Christian friends, Silvester, Calamy, Dr Bates, Mather of New England, &c. &c., who witnessed the closing scene of the venerable saint, have culled and collected a few flowers of his 'last sayings,' to strew around his tomb; but it is unnecessary, in this brief sketch, to give them in detail. His last days and dying hours were in har-

---

large, many of whom, to my knowledge, wear the scars of them to this day.

'The nature of the Christian religion is essentially free, and the voice of Christ proclaims to men, "the truth shall make you free." The spirit of Christianity shrinks from the touch of the iron and blood-stained hand of political rule. It is so boundless in its aspirations, and expansive in its energies, that it must stand on the broad champaign of civil and intellectual liberty, ere it can stretch its wings effectively for that flight which is destined to encompass the earth, and end only in eternity.'—*Neale and Hewitt.*

mony and proper keeping with his life. His end was calm and comfortable, without raptures. When asked, on the eve of dissolution, how he did, he distinctly replied, ' Almost well.' He expired on Tuesday morning, 8th December, 1691, aged seventy-six years. ' Mark the perfect man, and behold the upright, for the latter end of that man is peace.' ' They enter into peace, they rest in their beds, each one walking in his uprightness.'

Few pious men ever more steadily and conscientiously gave all diligence to make their calling and election sure, than did Richard Baxter. At a very early period of his mortal career, he ' thus judged, that if one died for all, then were all dead; and that he died for all, that they who live should not henceforth live unto themselves, but to him who died for them, and rose again.' Nothing could surpass his undivided and unwavering consecration of heart, of head, of hand, of time, and talents of a high order; of powers, and person, and property, to the glory of God, the benefit of the church of Christ, and the best interests of his species, than were put and kept in constant requisition by this singularly devoted man. Like Howard and Clarkson, he had *one* great object to occupy a life time, and it completely absorbed him. His great practical maxim seems to have been, ' Whether we live, we live unto the Lord; or whether we die, we die unto the Lord; living or dying, we are the Lord's.' ' Write, Blessed are the dead who died in the Lord; yea, saith the Spirit, for they do rest from their labours, and their works follow them.' ' Here are the patience and faith of the saints; here are they who keep the commandments of God, and the faith of the Lord Jesus.'

As might be expected, ' many devout men carried' the remains of Baxter ' to his burial, and made great lamentation over him.' He was buried in Christ Church, where the ashes of his wife and mother-in-law had been mouldering. His funeral was numerously attended by persons of different ranks, especially of ministers, conformists as well as nonconformists. All were eager to testify their respect to the memory of a man who had as strong a head, and as sound a heart, as any man of the age in which he lived; and of whom it might have been said, with as much truth as was said by a Scotch Earl of the intrepid Knox, ' Here lies one who never feared the face of man.'

In order to maintain continuity in the preceding imperfect outline of Baxter's eventful life, and to present the narrative and the facts with some degree of coherence to the mind of the reader, we have followed the fortunes of our author over an extended tract, from his birth to his burial, through a lapse of ' threescore years and ten,' of one of the most important epochs of British history. Still our sketch, though it has already exceeded the limits we originally prescribed for ourselves, is very imperfect. We have been necessitated to pass over many important and memorable transactions in his life. His character must be taken in all its length, and breadth, and depth, and lofty moral bearing, to fit us for forming an accurate estimate of the vigour of his mind, the acuteness of his reasoning powers, the depth of his

piety, the warmth of his heart, the strength of his sensibilities, the wide range of his mental and moral resources, the fire and force of his genius, and the weight and worth of his moral character. The reader who enters into the spirit of his devotional and practical works, which succeed this sketch, will naturally inquire what were the cardinal elements that entered into the composition of that master mind, that fitted him for grappling with all the wiles of satan, and the subtleties of error; that fitted him for laying bare the moral anatomy of the heart; that qualified him to make the thunders of Sinai burst upon the uncircumcised ear, and the terrors of Tophet to alarm the slumbering conscience; and that equally fitted him for pouring the balm of mercy into the broken heart, and the oil of gladness into the lacerated spirit ? The secret lay in his *pre-eminent personal piety.* Although we have already exceeded our intended limits, yet there are still a few points in the character of Baxter upon which we beg leave briefly to touch.

The face, the figure, and the form of a writer who has interested and profited us, are minor points, which more or less awaken the curiosity of the most of readers; ' the soul,' however, ' is the measure of the man.' Both Baxter and his biographers have reserved a few fragments to gratify this feeling among those who feel interested in his mental productions. The great Architect of the human frame and ' face divine,' sometimes lodges a soul of superior power and opulence in a casement of the firmest texture, and the most elegant and masterly mould. Many instances will occur to the reader. Baxter's constitution was originally sound. Though early, deeply, and long afflicted, he was a personable man. He was tall of stature, spare of flesh, had a considerable share of bone and muscle; had rather an agreeable intelligent countenance, and a clear, piercing, melting eye. Toward the latter part of his life, he stooped forward. In early life he was the subject of numerous and complicated bodily complaints. He was successively in the hands of no fewer than thirty-six gentlemen of the healing art. He was long the victim of medical treatment and experiment. Doctors differed on the character of his case; and after he had taken drugs without number, and all prescriptions failed, he discontinued all these attempts, except in taking advice for some particular symptom. He was literally diseased from head to foot; his stomach flatulent and acidulous; violent rheumatic headachs; profuse bleedings at the nose; his blood so thin and acrid, that it oozed out from the points of his fingers, and kept them often raw and bloody; his legs swelled and dropsical, &c. His physicians called it hypochondria, he himself considered it *primatura senectus*—premature old age; so that at twenty he had the symptoms, in addition to disease, of fourscore. Seldom has there been an instance in which the quenchless energy and ardour of the soul has more illustriously triumphed over the countless and complicated infirmities of the body, and constrained its enfeebled organs to yield an amount of service to her superior dictates, that astonishes and confounds succeeding generations. It is doubtless ' the Lord's doings,' and it may well be ' wondrous in our eyes.' Baxter had a soul of fire, and it would have required a frame of flint to sustain its pressure, and execute its multifarious and stupendous functions. He had some reason, like Paul, to 'glory even in his infirmities, that the power of Christ might rest upon him.'

As to the character of his mind, it was eminently acute, discriminating, and capacious. In the early part of his career he had dipped pretty deeply into the dialectics of the old school. He loved at times to indulge his metaphysical predilections. If these studies tended to sharpen and polish his powers, and improve his love of order and arrangement in his controversial and theological discussions, they were the chief advantages which he derived from them. In most other respects they are more a blemish than a beauty in his writings, and are felt a burden, rather than a benefit, to nine-tenths of his readers. It is certain that the most arid pages of his voluminous writings are those in which he indulges in his metaphysical disquisitions; and the most rich and racy are those far more numerous pages in which he seems to forget his metaphysical and logical distinctions, and opens all the fountains of pious feeling, and the rich stores of theological lore with which his mind was replenished, and carries his reader captive at pleasure. It is then that his mind is in its proper element. It moves with the majesty of a vessel richly laden, under a spring tide, a fair gale, all her canvass spread, and the port in full view. His sentiments then came warm from the heart, and readily find their way to it. The elements of his intellect were simplicity, transparency, and downright honesty. Richard Baxter was a straight-forward honest man, in 'the spirit of his mind.' His mind loved order, and generally aimed at it. The plan, the division, the parts and proportions of several of his treatises and sermons, are by no means sufficiently simple, clear, and accurate. This usually arose from the multiplicity and pressure of his labours. He seldom had leisure deliberately to form a plan, calmly to correct its defects, and deliberately to fill it up. Baxter possessed an active, vigorous, and fertile mind. He seems to have had an inexhaustible spring of ideas. His mind went from the centre to the whole circumferences of revealed religion. No section of the vast field was left unexplored. He was a student con amore. Theology, in all its departments, was his native element. His accumulations were vast and varied. He was more 'a ready scribe' in the principles and laws of the kingdom of Christ and of God, than a profound and elegant scholar. He had as much exquisite pleasure in the communication, as he had delight in the acquisition, of divine knowledge. He was 'like a giant refreshed with wine,' while wielding the weapons of inspired truth, and his soul exulted in its anticipated success, as 'a strong man who runs a race.' The weapons of the Christian warfare he could and did use with great dexterity and effect.

The extent and variety of Baxter's talents were of a very high order. He lived in an age of great men. The character of the times in which they lived, put them all in requisition. No man of tolerable talent, of decided piety and patriotism, could,

without dishonour to himself, and disgrace to his country, skulk into the shade. It may be styled the Augustan age of Great Britain. Some of the noblest characters for piety, integrity, talent, and moral courage, that grace the annals of our country, were Baxter's contemporaries. Though he was chiefly a companion of those who feared the Lord, and 'his delight' was principally with 'the saints and the excellent of the earth,' yet he was often in the society of men of the first order of intellect, talent, and rank in society. Had the bar, the senate, or the court, been the object of his taste, his talents were of such an order as might have raised him to distinction in either. Had mere science, literature, and scholarship, been the objects of his ambition, even at 'the eleventh hour,' under all his early disadvantages, his talents might have clothed him with the honours of either of the universities, and planted him in some of the principal chairs. 'Seest thou a man diligent in his business, he shall stand before kings, he shall not stand before mean men.' Had Baxter lived at an early age, he would have ranked among 'the fathers.' While the Nonconformists called 'no man father' or 'master upon earth,' yet Baxter's mind and talents were of such an order, as to call forth the affectionate respect of such men as Drs Owen, Bates, Howe, Manton, Goodwin, and others among the Nonconformists, and some of the most distinguished men for piety and talent in the Church of England. His intimacy with, and moral influence among, some of the most pious and talented laymen, such as Sir Matthew Hale and Sir Robert Boyle, both within and without the church; and his correspondence with several of the pious and *literati* of Europe, all go to show, that Baxter was no ordinary man, both as to piety, talent, and moral influence.

But Baxter's genius early obtained a sacred and sublimated character. It was wisely and well directed to the glory of its great Author who conferred it; to the honour of the Saviour who had lived, and laboured, and died for the redemption of a lost world; it was consecrated to the elucidation and publication of 'the unsearchable riches of Christ;' to the conversion and sanctification of perishing souls; and to the establishment and enlargement of the spiritual kingdom of God in the world. His genius did not run in a new, but it ran in a noble channel. It is a cause so sacred, a subject so sublime, and a work so arduous and stupendous, as to be worthy of the best energies of an archangel. His choice was 'to prophesy over the dry bones.' He carried the vestal fire of his genius into the pulpit. He studied, he prayed, and he preached, like an angel who had lighted from a distant orb. His searching sermons, his solemn tones, and pointed appeals to the heart, were sanctioned by heaven, and kindled conviction and concern into the most callous consciences. His inventive mind plied every scriptural measure to make evangelical truth to bear with effect upon the people of his charge. He in good earnest 'did the work of an evangelist.' 'He taught' the mass of the people 'publicly, and from house to house,' 'preaching repentance toward God, and faith toward our Lord Jesus Christ.' Kidderminster, which had long been a moral desert, by the divine blessing soon became as the garden of the Lord, and assumed the fragrance of Carmel, and the fertility of Lebanon.

The celebrated and eloquent Dr Bates, in his funeral sermon on Baxter, gives an admirable epitome of his talents, genius, and character. He knew his friend to the core; and in his fine chaste classic style, he has given the lineaments from the life, with the hand of a master, who had dipped his pencil in the variegated and harmonious hues of the rainbow. He says. ' In his sermons there was a rare union of arguments and motives to convince the mind and gain the heart. All the fountains of reason and persuasion were open to his discerning eye. There was no resisting the force of his discourses, without denying reason and divine revelation. He had a marvellous felicity and copiousness in speaking. There was a noble negligence in his style, for his great mind could not stoop to the affected eloquence of words. He despised flashy oratory; but his expressions were clear and powerful—so convincing the understanding—so entering into the soul—so engaging the affections, that those were deaf as adders who were not charmed by such a charmer. He was animated with the Holy Spirit, and breathed celestial fire to inspire heart and life into dead sinners, and to melt the obdurate in their frozen tombs.' And in the dedication of the same sermon to Sir Henry Ashurst, Baxter's steady and long-tried friend, who 'had not left off his kindness to the living and the dead,' Dr Bates goes on to say:

' I cannot omit the mentioning, that Mr Boyle and Mr Baxter, those incomparable persons in their several studies, and dear friends, died within a short space of one another. Mr Boyle was engaged in the contemplation of the design and architecture of the visible world, and made rare discoveries in the system of nature, not for curiosity and barren speculation, but to admire and adore the perfections of the Deity, in the variety, order, beauty, and marvellous artifice of the creatures that compose this great universe. Mr Baxter was conversant in the invisible world. His mind was constantly applied to understand the harmonious agreement of the Divine attributes in the economy of our salvation, and to restore men to the image and favour of God. They are now admitted into the enlightened and purified society above, where the immense volumes of the divine wisdom are laid open, and by one glance of the eye they discover more perfectly the glorious and wonderful works of God in heaven and earth, than the most diligent inquirers can do here in a thousand years' study, though they had the sagacity of Solomon. By the light of glory they see the face of God, and are satisfied with his likeness for ever.' *

As a preacher, Baxter has been styled ' the English Demosthenes.' His pulpit powers were of a very high order. If he was not uniformly happy in his divisions, logically clear and correct in his arrangement; if his style was sometimes rugged, his particulars multiplied to an undue extent without a palpable distinction, and some of his discourses had less of the pruning knife, and the polish of a classical diction, than could have been desired; yet few sermons, in either earlier or later times, have been more fitted, all in

* Middleton's Lives, vol. iv. pp. 47, 48.

all, to answer the great ends of preaching—the conviction and conversion of sinners, the nourishment, stability, and practical godliness of the saints. His reasoning is generally clear—his arguments conclusive, though sometimes redundant—his style terse and nervous—his remonstrances rousing—his warnings solemn as thunder—his reproofs piercing and vivid as lightning—and his appeals to the heart so tender and melting, that it could not be easy for the most obdurate to withstand them. His addresses are free as the vital air, and clear as the light of heaven. Nature, art, and eloquence, laid all their varied stores at his feet, for immediate use, when ' beseeching sinners to be reconciled to God.' His mind was never fettered nor cramped with ' the modern question,' whether it was the duty of sinners, of every grade, without delay ' to repent and believe the gospel.' His success was answerable to his efforts. If he did not study preaching as a science, as some have done, his love to the Saviour, the labour, and the souls of men, had enwrought it into the very texture of his soul as an art. It was not more his duty than it was his delight, ' to warn every man, and teach every man, in all wisdom, that he might present every man perfect in Christ Jesus.'

It is as a writer, however, that the vitality, the vigour, the variety, and versatility of Baxter's genius chiefly appear. Very few writers, in any age, have traversed the fields of theology to a wider extent. No corner of the vast continent seems to have escaped his eagle eye—no crevice is left unexplored. There were few authors of any note, foreign or domestic, who had written on theological subjects, with whom he did not seem to have a familiar acquaintance. He could, and did, quote them without parade. It was the order of the day, for the authors of the seventeenth century to overload their margins and columns with copious quotations from the Greek and Latin fathers, and from continental divines. Baxter, as a matter of course, went into the custom. It is now wisely discontinued. He was a man who read the bible, prayed to the Father of lights, and thought for himself; and the best parts of his varied and voluminous productions, are those that seem to have sprung from his own spontaneous contemplations of the inspired volume, irrespective of any previous writer, any suspected sentiments, or jarring system. When he ceased to think of the thorns and thickets of controversy—got out of the smoke and dust of polemics—wrestled in secret prayer with God —and took large and deep draughts from the fountain of Israel—he pours out such a rich flood of vital and varied thought, that, like the Jordan in harvest, he overflows his banks, and sweeps thought and feeling of his readers into the powerful current.

Baxter's active and vigorous mind delighted to expatiate over the whole encyclopedia of religion, natural and revealed; and his inquisitive soul, with a wing that never wavered, loved to trace it out in all its reasons and ramifications. He was master of himself and his subject. He seemed equally at home with the histories, the facts, the principles, the precepts, the promises, the consolations, and the evidences of divine revelation. With the different de partments of doctrinal, vital, experimental, and practical theology, he was quite familiar. From 'the first principles of the doctrine of Christ,' through all the intermediate stages of divine truth, to the profundity of the divine decrees, which set bounds to created intellect, his sleepless, ceaseless inquiries were directed. What was minute, and what was magnificent in the system of sacred truth, shared their proportion in his attention. At one time we find him 'a teacher of babes, and an instructor of the foolish;' at another, breaking the bread of life in crumbs to the humble rural rustic, in his Poor Man's Book; framing catechisms to the poor peasant; and unfolding the principles of personal and domestic piety to the English farmer. At another time you find him contending with the most cultivated minds of the sceptical class and infidel school; again, detecting and exposing the sophistry of the Jesuits, and laying bare the arbitrary principles and abominations of Popery. At one time we find him composing Compassionate Counsels to Young Men; and at another, contending with Stillingfleet, the archbishop of Canterbury, or writing his Humble Advice to the Members of Parliament. At one time writing his Call to the Unconverted; and at another Directing Justices in corporations to discharge their duty to God; at one time persuading the ignorant sinner to become 'a saint,' or submit to the shameful alternative of living and dying 'a brute;' and at another, writing his Reformed Pastor, and remonstrating with the slothful and inert of his own profession with a searching solemnity, that thrills through the secret recesses of the heart. Prose, in all its doctrinal and didactic forms, was his main *forte;* but sacred poetry was sometimes resorted to as a kind of relaxation, and to feed and fan the flame of personal and domestic devotion.

The magnitude and variety of Baxter's works, as a writer, fill us with astonishment. Had he been a recluse, or a mere book-worm, all his life, the extent of his mental productions would have been less wonderful; but he was a man of public spirit, of catholic feeling, and of active habits. It is astonishing how he could husband time for such herculean labours of the pen and the press. The late Mr Orme, his last biographer, has given the titles, dates, and list of no less than one hundred and sixty-eight distinct treatises and sermons, from the folio and thick quarto, to his single sermons and minor pieces. Mr Orme says: 'The age in which he lived was an age of voluminous authorship; and Baxter was, beyond comparison, the most voluminous of all his contemporaries. Those who have been acquainted only with what are called his practical or spiritual writings, form no correct estimate of the extent of his works. These form twenty-two vols. octavo in the present edition; and yet they are but a small portion of what he wrote. The number of his books has been variously estimated. As some of the volumes which he published contained several distinct treatises, they have sometimes been counted as one, and sometimes reckoned four or five. The best way of forming a correct opinion of Baxter's labours from the press, is by comparing them with some of his brethren who wrote a good deal. The works of bishop Hall amount

to ten volumes octavo; Lightfoot's extend to thirteen; Jeremy Taylor's to fifteen; Dr Goodwin's would make about twenty; Dr Owen's extend to twenty-eight; Richard Baxter's, if printed in a uniform edition, could not be comprised in less than sixty volumes, making more than from thirty to forty thousand closely printed octavo pages!'

His biographer continues: 'On this mass of writing he was employed from 1649, when his first work appeared, till near the time of his death, in 1691, a period of forty-four years. Had he been chiefly engaged in writing, this space was amply sufficient to have enabled him to produce all his works with ease. But it must be recollected, that writing was but a small part of his occupation. His labours as a minister, and his engagements in the public business of his times, formed his chief employment for many years, so that he speaks of writing but as a recreation from more severe duties. Nor is this all, his state of health must be taken into consideration in every estimate of his work. A man more diseased, or who had more to contend with in the frame of his body, probably never existed in the same circumstances. He was a constant martyr to sickness and pain, so that how he found it practicable to write with the composure that he generally did, is one of the greatest mysteries in his history. The energy of his mind was superior to any discouragement; for though it often felt the burden and clog of the flesh, it never gave way to its desire of ease, or succumbed under the pressure of its infirmities. He furnishes an illustrious instance of what may be done by principle, energy, and perseverance, in the most untoward and discouraging circumstances.'* Numerous and various as have been the productions of the prolific pen of 'the author of Waverley,' with a firm constitution, flexible materials among his hands to take the form of his fancy, like melted wax; enjoying perfect freedom from the harpies of persecution; in the sunshine of his study, or the tranquillity of his mansion; with every facility which books and leisure could afford; if mere quantity alone—not to speak of the very different character and qualities of the themes which occupied these authors' time and talents—I suspect that the mental opulence and manual operations of our afflicted and emaciated Nonconformist, will leave the celebrated novelist, poet, and baronet, far in the rear.

That Baxter would have written better had he written less, is highly probable. Had he taken more time to form the plan of some of his treatises—had he taken more pains to mature and assort his ample materials—given a more simple and lucid form to some of his discussions—had he dropped some extraneous digressions, pruned some exuberances, and polished some parts of his style, it would have unquestionably added much to the value of some of his incomparable productions. It is also highly probable, if not absolutely certain, that had Baxter's mind been less distracted with polemical discussions—had he allowed many of the vagaries and crudities then broached—and some of the violent attacks against himself to pass unnoticed and unanswered, and, like the ephemera and weeds of summer, to die a natural

* Orme's Life of Baxter, pp. 785-6.

death—and had he restricted the operations of his mind, and the labours of his pen, more to the doctrinal, devotional, and practical parts of theology, which were so congenial to the high-toned spirituality of his mind, it would have added materially to their worth. A deep sense of duty, and an impression of the dangerous and deleterious influence of error, with the urgency of the case, and the temper of the times, however, all conspired to urge him to write on those multifarious topics. It was, perhaps, one of the weaknesses of this great and good man, that, as a kind of inquisitor general, he considered himself bound to expose, counteract, and condemn, all that he considered erroneous. His controversial talents were of a superior order. His brethren knew it, and sometimes urged him to engage in it. On these subjects he at times used too much acerbity of expression. He was apt to overdo the thing, and overlay his opponent with arguments. Many of his controversial pieces were of a local and ephemeral character. But none was ever more severe in sifting and searching out his own defects and faults than he was himself; and few have ever been so candid in confessing them, and conscientious in correcting them. He says himself:—

'Concerning almost all my writings, I must confess that my own judgment is, that fewer, well studied and polished, would have been better; but the reader who can safely censure the books, is not fit to censure the author, unless he had been upon the place, and acquainted with all the occasions and circumstances. Indeed, for the Saints' Rest, I had four months vacancy to write it, in the midst of continual languishing and medicine; but for the rest, I wrote them in the crowd of all my other employments, which would allow me no great leisure for polishing, and exactness, and ornament; so that I scarce ever wrote one sheet twice over, nor stayed to make any blots or interlinings, but was fain to let it go as it was first conceived; and when my own desire was rather to stay upon one thing long, than run over many, some sudden occasion or other extorted almost all my writings from me; and the apprehensions of present usefulness, or necessity, prevailed against all other motives; so that the divines that were at hand with me, still put me on, and approved of what I did, because they were moved by present necessities as well as I. But those who were far off, and felt not those nearer motives, did rather wish that I had taken the other way, and published a few elaborate writings; and I am ready myself to be of their mind, when I forget the case that I then stood in, and have lost the sense of former motives.' This is a noble instance of Baxter's searching self-discernment and ingenuous candour, in giving an impartial verdict upon his own mental offspring, to which the most of authors are blind and partial to a proverb. In the document from which the above extract is taken, there is much to the same effect. Indeed, no modern critic, sitting in his self-imaginary chair, hearing evidence, examining witnesses, sifting discrepancies, and seeking facts, and passing judgment, could go through the process with more impartiality and severity than Baxter has done with the productions of his own pen.

But Baxter, with all these occasional slips, minor defects, metaphysical obscurities, casual exuberances, and inadvertent digressions, I love thee still! There is no lack of rich gold ore in the mine, though found amidst a few rough incrustations. The man who has patience to ponder your pages, and eyes to behold spiritual excellence, may dig diamonds from the veins which you have opened in the inexhaustible mine of divine revelation. Your defects are only like spots upon the disk of the sun. You have furnished your table with ample variety of wholesome well dressed provisions; if they are not set with all the finery of French cookery, they have all the substantial qualities that are befitting an English table. All that your guests require is a healthful appetite, to feel themselves at home, and happy in your society.

There is a cloud of witnesses who bear concurrent and unequivocal testimony to the high character and useful tendency of Baxter's writings, especially his devotional and practical works. They were extensively read, and highly appreciated, by many of his contemporaries. It was a reading as well as a writing age. Dr Barrow (who was no mean judge) said, 'His practical writings were never mended, and his controversial ones seldom confuted.' The Hon. Robert Boyle declared, that 'He was the fittest man of the age for a casuist, because he feared no man's displeasure, nor hoped for any man's preferment.' Bishop Wilkins remarked of him, 'that he had cultivated every subject he had handled; that if he had lived in the primitive times, he would have been one of the fathers of the Church; and that it was enough for one age to produce such a man as Mr Baxter.' Archbishop Usher entertained the highest opinion of his abilities; and it was by his persuasion he was induced to write his treatises upon Conversion. Dr Manton thought 'he came nearer to the apostolical writings than any man of the age.' Dr Bates says, 'that his books, for their number and variety of matter, make a library. They contain a treasure of controversial, casuistical, and practical divinity. His books of practical divinity have been effectual for more numerous conversions of sinners to God, than any printed in our time; and while the church remains on earth, will be of continual efficacy to recover lost souls. There is a vigorous pulse in them that keeps the reader awake and attentive.' Addison says, 'I once met with a page of Mr Baxter. Upon the perusal of it, I conceived so good an idea of the author's piety, that I bought the whole book.' The celebrated Dr Johnson has quoted Baxter more than once in his Rambler. When asked by Boswell, 'what works of Richard Baxter he should read?' the doctor, in his sage epigrammatic style, replied, 'Read any of them, for they are all good.' Job Orton, who laboured some time in Kidderminster, and after many years had rolled by, had opportunity of witnessing the remote effects of his successful labours, entertained the highest opinion of Baxter's piety, talents, and character. Dr Doddridge styled him 'the English Demosthenes,' and called Baxter 'his particular favourite;' and adds, 'It is impossible to tell how much I am charmed with the devotion, good sense, and pathos, which is every where to be found in him. I cannot forbear looking upon him as one of the greatest orators, both with regard to copiousness, acuteness, and energy, that our nation has produced,' &c. &c. I shall only add the testimony of the late William Wilberforce, who comes down to our own times, and whose fine taste and sterling piety fully qualified him to mark the beauties, and appreciate the excellencies, of Baxter, as an author, with whose writings he was long familiar. In writing of him he says: ' With his controversial pieces I am little acquainted; but his practical writings, in four massy folios, are a treasury of Christian wisdom. It would be a most valuable service to mankind to revise them, and perhaps to abridge them, to render them more suited to the taste of modern readers.'

In reference to the above suggestion of the deceased Christian statesman, the writer of this article takes leave to say, that it is extremely difficult to abridge such an author as Baxter, or materially to alter the arrangement of his treatises, without the spirit of the work evaporating; and the freshness, the fervour, the feeling, and the unction, stamped upon the original work, being dissipated, and a naked, nerveless skeleton, under a misnomer, being put into the reader's hands. The publishers of the present edition of Baxter's Practical Works, therefore, have wisely determined not to present the public with an abridgment. They have resolved minutely and rigidly to revise, and select, and arrange the treatises in consecutive order; but in absolute good faith to give Richard Baxter, in his own native cut and costume, to the public, with only the antiquated dust decently brushed from his venerable vestments. The reader will *bona fide* find himself conversing with 'the mighty dead.'

This sketch has already far exceeded our intended limits, yet a tenth has not been told of what is really interesting in the fertile and eventful life and times of Richard Baxter. With the utmost cordiality we refer the inquisitive reader to Orme's Life of Baxter, to which we have already frequently referred with unqualified praise, and to which we have been not a little indebted in drawing up the preceding sketch. Much remains yet to be said and seen of Baxter's deep-

toned piety, which has given such an imitable charm to the productions of his pen—his unflinching fidelity and inviolable integrity, which neither men nor money, friends nor foes, frowns nor flatteries, could shake— his mortification to all the blandishments and fascinations of time, of ' the lust of the flesh, the lust of the eye, and the pride of life,' and singular self-denial—his gravity and Christian cheerfulness, so beautifully blended and happily balanced in his character. We might multiply paragraphs and pages in writing of his quenchless ardour—his incessant diligence— his herculean labours—his child-like simplicity—his love of peace—and his fruitless and ill-judged attempts to effect union among materials that had no common principle of affinity—the painful position in which he sometimes placed himself between High Churchmen and decided Nonconformists—his want of sound judgment in some matters, even while 'his failings leaned to virtue's side.' Much might be mentioned of his active benevolence, which embraced the necessities of the soul as well as those of the body— his zeal for ameliorating the miseries of fallen humanity—some of his embryo schemes for circulating the scriptures at home, and for sending the gospel to some of the accessible parts of the heathen world, partly anticipating, by more than a century, some of those excellent institutions of modern times, which have been an honour to our native country, and a blessing to the heathen world. In one word, though he was not a perfect nor a faultless man, yet, with all his faults and infirmities, he was a very extraordinary person. He possessed much largeness of soul. The sensibilities of his heart were warm. He was a man of faith and prayer. He lived near to God, and walked with him. This was the secret of his support, the spring of his untiring activity, and the source of his success. What he was, he was by the grace of God, and to him belongs all the glory. ' The righteous shall be held in everlasting remembrance.' ' The record' of Richard Baxter ' is on high;' and ' his works will praise him in the gates' while sound searching theology is valued in the church of Christ, and respected within the boundaries of the British Isles.

THE

SAINTS' EVERLASTING REST;

OR

A TREATISE

OF

THE BLESSED STATE OF THE SAINTS IN THEIR ENJOYMENT OF GOD.

INTRODUCTORY REMARKS.

The Saints' Everlasting Rest, though the second book which Baxter published, was the first he wrote; and had he never written another, it alone would have endeared his memory for ever, to all who cherish the sublime hopes of the gospel. "It was written by the author for his own use during the time of his languishing, when God took him off from all public employment;" and furnishes an admirable illustration of the richness and vigour of his mind, as well as of the great sources of its consolation. "While I was in health," he says, "I had not the least thought of writing books, or of serving God in any more public way than preaching, but when I was weakened with great bleeding, and left solitary in my chamber at Sir John Cook's in Derbyshire, without any acquaintance but my servant about me, and was sentenced to death by the physicians, I began to contemplate more seriously on the everlasting rest, which I apprehended myself to be just on the borders of. That my thoughts might not too much scatter in my meditation, I began to write something on that subject, intending but the quantity of a sermon or two; but being continued long in weakness, where I had no books and no better employment, I followed it on, till it was enlarged to the bulk in which it is published. The first three weeks I spent on it was at Mr. Nowel's house, at Kirkby Mallory, in Leicestershire; a quarter of a year more, at the seasons which so great weakness would allow, I bestowed on it at Sir Thomas Rous's, in Worcestershire; and I finished it shortly after at Kidderminster."

Thus, in less than six months, and those months of pain and sickness, he produced a quarto volume of more than eight hundred pages, rich in Chris-tian sentiment, wonderfully correct and pointed in style, and fertile in most beautiful illustrations. "The marginal citations," he tells us, "I put in after I came home to my books, but almost all the book itself was written when I had no book but a Bible and a Concordance; and I found that the transcript of the heart hath the greatest force on the hearts of others."

The success and approbation which this work experienced were very great. The first edition was published in 1649, the ninth edition appeared in 1662, and it passed through several other editions in quarto in the course of the few following years.

The Saints' Rest is divided into four parts. Of these the first and the last were all that the author originally designed; the one containing the explanation of the nature of the rest, the other "a directory for getting and keeping the heart in heaven by heavenly meditation." The last, indeed, he tells us, was the main thing intended in the writing of the book, and to which all the rest is subservient. The second part treats of the certainty of the future rest, where he enters much further than is necessary in such a book into the evidences of revelation, mixed up with discussions and stories about apparitions, witches, and compacts with the devil, which are blemishes on the fair face of this beautiful production. The third is on the use which ought to be made of the doctrine and prospect of the everlasting rest, the first four chapters of it being intended for secure and sensual sinners who might happen to read the book, and the three last for Christians, to direct and comfort them in the time of affliction, and to stir them up to seek the salvation of their brethren.

The very title of this book operates like a charm on the mind of a Christian, and leads him to associate with it the most delightful ideas. EVERLASTING REST presents to the wearied, harassed, suffering spirit, a prospect full of glory and repose. As the cessation of labour, the termination of suffering, and the end of all evil, in connection with the eternal enjoyment of God, it is the sum of Christian blessedness, comprehending in it all that is calculated to reconcile to the trials of life, and to sustain under its labours and sorrows. It is a rest which consists not in indisposition or incapacity for action, or in the indulgence of indolence and sloth, but which implies activity without weariness, and exertion without fatigue; the constant employment of our best faculties on the worthiest objects and employments securing that felicity which is to be found only in doing the will of God, without involving exhaustion of spirits or diminution of strength. What more can man desire to render him supremely happy?

To such a person as Baxter, a martyr to disease and pain, possessed of a spirit characterized by restless activity, which was constantly repressed and counteracted by a body ill adapted to be the instrument of its boundless desires; but who, notwithstanding this counteraction, continually struggled to do the work of God, the hope of rest must have been exquisitely delightful. Surrounded as he was at the same time with all that grieved his spirit and resisted his efforts, it is not wonderful that he fled to the promise of rest as his refuge and his anchor. While he did this, however, he did not surrender himself to the mere contemplation of the joy set before him; it roused and excited him to still greater exertions, or induced that patience *with joyfulness* of which the apostle speaks, and which is the peculiar effect of the Christian hope.

It is sweet to look forward to the restitution of all things—to think of a world where God is entirely glorified, and entirely loved, and entirely obeyed, where sin and sorrow are no more, where severed friends shall meet never again to part, where the body shall not weigh down the spirit, but shall be its fit medium of communication with all the glorious inhabitants and scenery of heaven, where no discordant tones or jarring feelings shall interrupt or mar the harmony of that universal song which shall burst from every heart and every tongue, to Him who sitteth upon the throne and to the Lamb. And it is not only

sweet but most profitable to meditate on these prospects. It is a most healthful exercise. It brings the soul into contact with that society to which it properly belongs, and for which it was created.

The world think that these heavenly musings must unqualify the mind for present exertion, but this is a mistake arising from an ignorance of the nature of heaven. The happiness of heaven is the perfection of those principles which lead to the discharge of duty, and therefore the contemplation of it must increase our sense of the importance of duty. That happiness is not entirely a future thing, but rather the completion of a present process, in which every duty bears an important part. The character and the happiness of heaven, like the light and heat of the sunbeams, are so connected that it is impossible to separate them, and the natural and instinctive desire of the one is thus necessarily linked to the desire of the other. Full of peace as the prospect of heaven is, there is no indolent relinquishment of duty connected with the contemplation of it, for heaven is full of action. Its repose is like the repose of nature—the repose of planets in their orbits; it is a rest from all controversy with God, from all opposition to his will. His servants serve Him. Farewell, vain world! no rest hast thou to offer which can compare with this. The night is far spent; soon will *that* day dawn, and the shadows flee away.

The Saints' Rest has been one of the most useful of Baxter's works—the most useful to Christians, for whom it was chiefly intended. The late Mr. Fawcett, of Kidderminster, published an excellent abridgment of it in 1758. It makes no alteration on the sense or even language of the author, but diminishes the bulk of the work by omitting many digressions, controversial discussions, together with the prefaces, dedications, and other things of a temporary and local nature. From that time the circulation of the original work has been greatly diminished; but I have no doubt the design of the author has been fully accomplished, as a much greater circulation has been given to his sentiments in a moderate 12mo than could have been obtained for the bulky 4to.

The foregoing account of this Treatise is extracted from Orme's *Life of Baxter*, and, we may add, that Fawcett's abridgment, as most suitable for general use, is that here presented to the reader.

THE

SAINTS' EVERLASTING REST.

"There remaineth therefore a Rest to the people of God."

HEBREWS IV. 9.

CHAPTER I.

THE INTRODUCTION TO THE WORK, WITH SOME AC-
COUNT OF THE NATURE OF THE SAINTS' REST.

Sect. 1. The important design of the Apostle in the text, to which
the Author earnestly bespeaks the attention of the Reader. 2.
The Saints' Rest defined, with a general plan of the Work. 3.
What this rest pre-supposes. 4. The Author's humble sense of
his inability fully to show what this rest contains. 5. It contains,
(1.) A ceasing from means of grace; 6. (2.) A perfect freedom
from all evils; 7. (3.) The highest degree of the saints' personal
perfection, both in body and soul; 8. (4.) The nearest enjoyment of God the Chief Good; 9—14. (5.) A sweet and constant
action of all the powers of soul and body in this enjoyment of God;
as, for instance, bodily senses, memory, love joy, together with a mutual love and joy. 15. The Author's humble
reflection on the deficiency of this account.

1. It was not only our interest in God, and
actual enjoyment of him, which was lost in Adam's
fall, but all spiritual knowledge of him, and true
disposition towards such a felicity. When the
Son of God comes with recovering grace, and
discoveries of a spiritual and eternal happiness
and glory, he finds not faith in man to believe it.
As the poor man, that would not believe any one
had such a sum as a hundred pounds, it was so
far above what himself possessed: so men will
hardly now believe there is such a happiness as
once they had, much less as Christ hath now
procured. When God would give the Israelites
his sabbaths of rest, in a land of rest, he had
more ado to make them believe it, than to overcome their enemies, and procure it for them.
And when they had it, only as a small intimation
and earnest of an incomparably more glorious
rest through Christ, they yet believe no more
than they possess, but say, with the glutton at
the feast, Sure there is no other heaven but this!
Or, if they expect more by the Messiah, it is only
the increase of their earthly felicity. The apostle bestows most of this epistle against this distemper, and clearly and largely proves, that the
end of all ceremonies and shadows, is to direct
them to Jesus Christ the substance; and that the
rest of sabbaths, and Canaan, should teach them
to look for a farther rest, which indeed is their
happiness. My text is his conclusion, after
divers arguments; a conclusion, which contains
the ground of all the believer's comfort, the end
of all his duty and sufferings, the life and sum of
all gospel promises and Christian privileges.
What more welcome to men, under personal
afflictions, tiring duties, successions of sufferings,
than rest? It is not our comfort only, but our
stability. Our liveliness in all duties, our enduring tribulation, our honouring of God, the
vigour of our love, thankfulness, and all our
graces; yea, the very being of our religion and
Christianity, depend on the believing serious
thoughts of our rest. And now, reader, whatever thou art, young or old, rich or poor, I entreat thee, and charge thee, in the name of thy
Lord, who will shortly call thee to a reckoning,
and judge thee to thy everlasting unchangeable
state, that thou give not these things the reading
only, and so dismiss them with a bare approbation; but that thou set upon this work, and take
God in Christ for thy only rest, and fix thy heart
upon him above all. May the living God, who
is the portion and rest of his saints, make these
our carnal minds so spiritual, and our earthly
hearts so heavenly, that loving him, and delighting in him, may be the work of our lives; and
that neither I that write, nor you that read this
book, may ever be turned from this path of life;
lest a promise being left us of entering into his
rest, we should come short of it, through our own
unbelief or negligence!

2. The Saints' Rest is the most happy state of a Christian; or it is the perfect endless enjoyment of God by the perfected saints, according to the measure of their capacity, to which their souls arrive at death, and both soul and body most fully after the resurrection and final judgment. According to this definition of the Saints' Rest, a larger account of its nature will be given in this Chapter; of its preparatives, Chap. II.; its excellencies, Chap. III.; and Chap. IV. the persons for whom it is designed. Farther to illustrate the subject, some description will be given, Chap. V. of their misery who lose this rest; and Chap. VI. who also lose the enjoyments of time, and suffer the torments of hell. Next will be showed, Chap. VII. the necessity of diligently seeking this rest; Chap. VIII. how our title to it may be discerned; Chap. IX. that they who discern their title to it should help those that cannot; and Chap. X. that this rest is not to be expected on earth. It will then be proper to consider, Chap. XI. the importance of a heavenly life upon earth; Chap. XII. how to live a heavenly life upon earth; Chap. XIII. the nature of heavenly contemplation, with the time, place, and temper fittest for it; Chap. XIV. what use heavenly contemplation makes of consideration, affections, soliloquy, and prayer; and likewise, Chap. XV. how heavenly contemplation may be assisted by sensible objects, and guarded against a treacherous heart. Heavenly contemplation will be exemplified, Chap. XVI. and the whole work concluded.

3. There are some things necessarily pre-supposed in the nature of this rest; as, for instance —that mortal men are the persons seeking it. For angels and glorified spirits have it already, and the devils and damned are past hope. That they choose God only for their end and happiness. He that takes any thing else for his happiness, is out of the way the first step.—That they are distant from this end. This is the woful case of all mankind since the fall. When Christ comes with regenerating grace, he finds no man sitting still, but all posting to eternal ruin, and making haste towards hell; till, by conviction, he first brings them to a stand, and then, by conversion, turns their hearts and lives sincerely to himself. —This end, and its excellency, is supposed to be known, and seriously intended. An unknown good moves not to desire or endeavour. And not only a distance from this rest, but the true knowledge of this distance, is also supposed. They that never yet knew they were without God, and in the way to hell, did never yet know the way to heaven. Can a man find he hath lost his God, and his soul, and not cry, I am undone? The reason why so few obtain this rest, is, they will not be convinced, that they are, in point of title, distant from it; and, in point of practice, contrary to it. Who ever sought for that, which he knew not he had lost? "They that be whole need not a physician, but they that be sick."— The influence of a superior moving cause is also supposed; else we shall all stand still, and not move toward our rest. If God move us not, we cannot move. It is a most necessary part of our Christian wisdom, to keep our subordination to God, and dependence on him. "We are not sufficient of ourselves to think any thing as of ourselves, but our sufficiency is of God." "Without me," says Christ, "ye can do nothing."—It is next supposed, that they who seek this rest, have an inward principle of spiritual life. God does not move men like stones, but he endows them with life, not to enable them to move without him, but in subordination to himself the first mover.—And farther, this rest supposes such an actual tendency of soul towards it, as is regular and constant, earnest and laborious. He that hides his talent shall receive the wages of a slothful servant. Christ is the door, the only way to this rest. "But strait is the gate, and narrow is the way," and we must strive, if we will enter, for "many will seek to enter in, and shall not be able;" which implies, that "the kingdom of heaven suffereth violence." Nor will it bring us to the end of the saints, if we begin in the spirit, and end in the flesh. He only "that endureth to the end shall be saved." And never did a soul obtain rest with God, whose desire was not set upon him above all things else in the world. "Where your treasure is, there will your heart be also." The remainder of our old nature will much weaken and interrupt these desires, but never overcome them. And considering the opposition to our desires, from the contrary principles in our nature, and from the weakness of our graces, together with our continued distance from the end, our tendency to that end must be laborious, and with all our might.—All these things are pre-supposed, in order to a Christian's obtaining an interest in heavenly rest.

4. Now we have ascended these steps into the outward court, may we look within the vail? May we show what this rest contains, as well as what it pre-supposes? Alas, how little know I of that glory! The glimpse which Paul had, contained what could not, or must not, be uttered. Had he spoken the things of heaven in the language of heaven, and none understood that language, what the better? The Lord reveal to me

what I may reveal to you! The Lord open some light, and show both you and me our inheritance! Not as to Balaam only, whose eyes were opened to see the goodliness of Jacob's tents, and Israel's tabernacles, where he had no portion, and from whence must come his own destruction! Not as to Moses, who had only a discovery, instead of possession, and saw the land which he never entered! But as the pearl was revealed to the merchant in the gospel, who rested not till he had sold all he had, and bought it! And as heaven was opened to the blessed Stephen, which he was shortly to enter, and the glory showed him which should be his own possession!—The things contained in heavenly rest are such as these;—a ceasing from means of grace;—a perfect freedom from all evils;—the highest degree of the saints' personal perfection, both of body and soul;—the nearest enjoyment of God the chief good;—and a sweet and constant action of all the powers of body and soul in this enjoyment of God.

5. (1.) One thing contained in heavenly rest is, the ceasing from means of grace. When we have obtained the haven, we have done sailing. When the workman receives his wages, it is implied he has done his work. When we are at our journey's end, we have done with the way. ' Whether prophecies, they shall fail; whether tongues, they shall cease; whether knowledge, it also," so far as it had the nature of means, "shall vanish away." There shall be no more prayer, because no more necessity, but the full enjoyment of what we prayed for: neither shall we need to fast and weep, and watch any more, being out of the reach of sin and temptations. Preaching is done; the ministry of man ceaseth; sacraments become useless; the labourers are called in, because the harvest is gathered, the tares burned, and the work finished; the unregenerate past hope, and the saints past fear, for ever.

6. (2.) There is in heavenly rest a perfect freedom from all evils. All the evils that accompanied us through our course, and which necessarily follow our absence from the chief good; besides our freedom from those eternal flames, and restless miseries, which the neglecters of Christ and grace must remedilessly endure; a woful inheritance, which, both by birth, and actual merit, was due to us, as well as to them. In heaven there is nothing that defileth or is unclean. All that remains without. And doubtless there is not such a thing as grief and sorrow known there: nor is there such a thing as a pale face, a languid body, feeble joints, unable infancy, decrepit age, peccant humours, painful or pining sickness, griping fears, consuming cares, nor whatsoever deserves the name of evil. We did weep and lament when the world did rejoice; but our sorrow is turned into joy, and our joy shall no man take from us.

7. (3.) Another ingredient of this rest is, the highest degree of the saints' personal perfection, both of body and soul. Were the glory ever so great, and themselves not made capable of it, by a personal perfection suitable thereto, it would be little to them. " Eye hath not seen, nor ear heard, neither have entered into the heart of man, the things which God hath prepared for them that love him." For the eye of flesh is not capable of seeing them, nor this ear of hearing them, nor this heart of understanding them: but there the eye, and ear, and heart are made capable; else how do they enjoy them? The more perfect the sight is, the more delightful the beautiful object. The more perfect the appetite, the sweeter the food. The more musical the ear, the more pleasant the melody. The more perfect the soul, the more joyous those joys, and the more glorious to us is that glory.

8. (4.) The principal part of this rest, is our nearest enjoyment of God the chief good. And here, reader, wonder not if I be at a loss; and if my apprehensions receive but little of that which is in my expressions. If it did not appear, to the beloved disciple, what we shall be, but only in general, " that when Christ shall appear, we shall be like him," no wonder if I know little. When I know so little of God, I cannot much know what it is to enjoy him. If I know so little of spirits, how little of the Father of spirits, or the state of my own soul, when advanced to the enjoyment of him? I stand and look upon a heap of ants, and see them all with one view; they know not me, my being, nature, or thoughts, though I am their fellow-creature: how little then must we know of the great Creator, though he with one view clearly beholds us all? A glimpse the saints behold, as in a glass; which makes us capable of some poor, dark apprehensions of what we shall behold in glory. If I could tell a worldling what the holiness and spiritual joys of the saints on earth are, he cannot know; for grace cannot be clearly known without grace: how much less could he conceive it, should I tell him of this glory? But to the saints I may be somewhat more encouraged to speak; for grace gives them a dark knowledge and slight taste of glory. If men and angels should study to speak the blessedness of that state in one word, what could they say beyond

this, that it is the nearest enjoyment of God? O the full joys offered to a believer in that one sentence of Christ, 'Father, I will that those whom thou hast given me be with me where I am, that they may behold my glory which thou hast given me!' Every word is full of life and joy. If the queen of Sheba had cause to say of Solomon's glory, 'Happy are thy men, happy are these thy servants, who stand continually before thee, and hear thy wisdom;' then sure they that stand continually before God, and see his glory, and the glory of the Lamb, are more than happy. To them will Christ give to eat of the tree of life, and to eat of the hidden manna : yea, he will make them pillars in the temple of God, and they shall go no more out; and he will write upon them the name of his God, and the name of the city of his God, which is New Jerusalem, which cometh down out of heaven from his God, and he will write upon them his new name ; yea, more, if more may be, he will grant them to sit with him on his throne. 'These are they who came out of great tribulation, and have washed their robes, and made them white in the blood of the Lamb: therefore are they before the throne of God, and serve him day and night in his temple, and he that sitteth on the throne shall dwell among them. The Lamb which is in the midst of the throne shall feed them, and shall lead them unto living fountains of water; and God shall wipe away all tears from their eyes.' O blind, deceived world! Can you show us such a glory? This is the city of our God, where the tabernacle of God is with men, and he will dwell with them and they shall be his people, and God himself shall be with them, and be their God. The glory of God shall lighten it, and the Lamb is the light thereof. And there shall be no more curse ; but the throne of God and of the Lamb shall be in it; and his servants shall serve him, and they shall see his face, and his name shall be in their foreheads. These sayings are faithful and true, and the things which must shortly be done. And now we say, as Mephibosheth, 'Let the world take all, for as much as our Lord will come in peace.' Rejoice, therefore, in the Lord, O ye righteous, and say, with his servant David, 'The Lord is the portion of mine inheritance : the lines are fallen unto me in pleasant places ; yea, I have a goodly heritage. I have set the Lord always before me : because he is at my right hand, I shall not be moved. Therefore my heart is glad, and my glory rejoiceth ; my flesh also shall rest in hope. For thou wilt not leave my soul in hell, neither wilt thou suffer thine Holy One to see corruption. Thou wilt show me the path of life ; in thy pre-

sence is fulness of joy ; at thy right hand there are pleasures for evermore.' What presumption would it have been, once to have thought or spoken of such a thing, if God had not spoken it before us? I durst not have thought of the saints' preferment in this life, as Scripture sets it forth, had it not been the express truth of God. How indecent to talk of being sons of God—speaking to him—having fellowship with him—dwelling in him, and he in us, if this had not been God's own language ; how much less durst we have once thought of shining forth as the sun—of being joint heirs with Christ—of judging the world— of sitting on Christ's throne—of being one in him and the Father, if we had not all this from the mouth, and under the hand of God? But hath he said, and shall he not do it ? Hath he spoken, and shall he not make it good ? Yes, as the Lord God is true, thus shall it be done to the man whom Christ delighteth to honour. Be of good cheer, Christian, the time is near, when God and thou shalt be near, and as near as thou canst well desire. Thou shalt dwell in his family. Is that enough ? 'It is better to be a door-keeper in the house of God, than to dwell in the tents of wickedness.' Thou shalt ever stand before him, about his throne, in the room with him, in his presence-chamber. Wouldst thou yet be nearer? Thou shalt be his child, and he thy Father ; thou shalt be an heir of his kingdom ; yea, more, the spouse of his Son. And what more canst thou desire? Thou shalt be a member of the body of his Son ; he shall be thy Head ; thou shalt be one with him, who is one with the Father, as he himself hath desired for thee of his Father, 'that they all may be one, as thou, Father, art in me, and I in thee, that they also may be one in us ; and the glory which thou gavest me, I have given them, that they may be one, even as we are one ; I in them and thou in me, that they may be made perfect in one, and that the world may know that thou hast sent me, and hast loved them as thou hast loved me.'

9. (5.) We must add, that this rest contains a sweet and constant action of all the powers of the soul and body in this enjoyment of God. It is not the rest of a stone, which ceaseth from all motion when it attains the centre. This body shall be so changed, that it shall no more be flesh and blood, which cannot inherit the kingdom of God ; but a spiritual body. We saw not that body that shall be, but God giveth it a body as it hath pleased him, and to every seed his own body. If grace makes a Christian differ so much from what he was, as to say, I am not the man I was ; how much more will glory make us differ?

As much as a body spiritual, above the sun in glory, exceeds these frail, noisome, diseased lumps of flesh, so far shall our senses exceed those we now possess. Doubtless as God advanceth our senses, and enlargeth our capacity, so will he advance the happiness of those senses, and fill up with himself all that capacity. Certainly the body should not be raised up and continued, if it should not share in the glory. As it hath shared in the obedience and sufferings, so shall it also in the blessedness. As Christ bought the whole man, so shall the whole partake of the everlasting benefits of the purchase. O blessed employment of a glorified body! to stand before the throne of God and the Lamb, and to sound forth for ever, ' Thou art worthy, O Lord, to receive glory, and honour, and power. Worthy is the Lamb that was slain, to receive power, and riches, and wisdom, and strength, and honour, and glory, and blessing; for thou hast redeemed us to God by thy blood, out of every kindred, and tongue, and people, and nation; and hast made us unto our God kings and priests. Alleluia; salvation, and glory, and honour, and power, unto the Lord our God. Alleluia, for the Lord God omnipotent reigneth.' O Christians! this is the blessed rest; a rest as it were, without rest : for 'they rest not day and night, saying, Holy, holy, holy Lord God Almighty, who was, and is, and is to come.' And if the body shall be thus employed, O, how shall the soul be taken up! As its powers and capacities are greatest, so its actions are strongest, and its enjoyments sweetest. As the bodily senses have their proper actions, whereby they receive and enjoy their objects, so does the soul in its own actions enjoy its own objects, by knowing, remembering, loving, and delightful joying. This is the soul's enjoyment. By these eyes it sees and by these arms it embraces.

10. Knowledge of itself is very desirable. As far as the rational soul exceeds the sensitive, so far the delights of a philosopher, in discovering the secrets of nature, and knowing the mystery of sciences, exceed the delights of the glutton, the drunkard, the unclean, and of all voluptuous sensualists whatsoever. So excellent is all truth. What, then, is their delight who know the God of truth? How noble a faculty of the soul is the understanding? It can compass the earth : it can measure the sun, moon, stars, and heaven; it can foreknow each eclipse to a minute, many years before. But this is the top of all its excellency, that it can know God, who is infinite, who made all these, a little here, and more, much more hereafter. O the wisdom and goodness of our blessed Lord! He hath created the understanding with a natural bias and inclination to truth as its object; and to the prime truth, as its prime object. Christian, when, after long gazing heavenward, thou hast got a glimpse of Christ, dost thou not sometimes seem to have been with Paul in the third heaven, whether in the body, or out, and to have seen what is unutterable? Art thou not, with Peter, ready to say, ' Master, it is good to be here !' ' O that I might dwell in this mount! O that I might ever see what I now see!' Didst thou never look so long upon the Sun of Righteousness, till thine eyes were dazzled with his astonishing glory? And did not the splendour of it make all things below seem black and dark to thee? Especially in the day of suffering for Christ, when he usually appears most manifestly to his people, didst thou never see one walking in the midst of the fiery furnace with thee, like the Son of God? Believe me, Christians, yea, believe God, you that have known most of God in Christ here, it is as nothing to what you shall know; it scarce, in comparison of that, deserves to be called knowledge. For as these bodies, so that knowledge must cease, that a more perfect may succeed. Knowledge shall vanish away. 'For we know in part. But when that which is perfect is come, then that which is in part shall be done away. When I was a child, I spake as a child, I understood as a child, I thought as a child; but when I became a man, I put away childish things. For now we see through a glass, darkly, but then face to face; now I know in part, but then shall I know even as also I am known.' Marvel not, therefore, Christian, how it can be life eternal, to know God, and Jesus Christ. To enjoy God and Christ, is eternal life; and the soul's enjoying is in knowing. They that savour only of earth, and consult with flesh, think it a poor happiness to know God. But 'we know that we are of God, and the whole world lieth in wickedness: and we know that the Son of God is come, and hath given us an understanding, that we may know him that is true; and we are in him that is true, even in his Son Jesus Christ. This is the true God, and eternal life.'

11. The memory will not be idle, or useless, in this blessed work. From that height the saint can look behind him, and before him. And to compare past with present things, must needs raise in the blessed soul an inconceivable esteem and sense of its condition. To stand on that mount, whence we can see the wilderness and Canaan, both at once; to stand in heaven, and look back on earth, and weigh them together in

the balance of a comparing sense and judgment, how must it needs transport the soul, and make it cry out, 'Is this the purchase that cost so dear as the blood of Christ? No wonder. O blessed price! and thrice blessed love, that invented, and condescended! Is this the end of believing? Is this the end of the Spirit's workings? Have the gales of grace blown me into such a harbour? Is it hither that Christ hath allured my soul? O blessed way, and thrice blessed end! Is this the glory which the Scriptures spoke of, and ministers preached of, so much? I see the gospel is indeed good tidings, even tidings of peace and good things, tidings of great joy to all nations. Is my mourning, my fasting, my sad humblings, my heavy walking, come to this? Is my praying, watching, fearing to offend, come to this? Are all my afflictions, Satan's temptations, the world's scorns and jeers, come to this? O vile nature, that resisted so much, and so long, such a blessing! Unworthy soul, is this the place thou camest so unwillingly to? Was duty wearisome? Was the world too good to lose? Didst thou stick at leaving all, denying all, and suffering any thing, for this? Wast thou loath to die, to come to this? O false heart, thou hadst almost betrayed me to eternal flames, and lost me this glory! Art thou not now ashamed, my soul, that ever thou didst question that love which brought thee hither? that thou wast jealous of the faithfulness of thy Lord? that thou suspectedst his love, when thou shouldst only have suspected thyself? that ever thou didst quench a motion of his Spirit? and that thou shouldst misinterpret those providences, and repine at those ways, which have such an end? Now thou art sufficiently convinced, that thy blessed Redeemer was saving thee, as well when he crossed thy desires, as when he granted them; when he broke thy heart, as when he bound it up. No thanks to thee, unworthy self, for this received crown; but to Jehovah, and the Lamb, be glory for ever.'

12. But, O! the full, the near, the sweet enjoyment, is that of love. 'God is love; and he that dwelleth in love, dwelleth in God, and God in him.' Now the poor soul complains, 'O that I could love Christ more!' Then, thou canst not choose but love him. Now thou knowest little of his amiableness, and therefore lovest little; then, thine eyes will affect thy heart and the continual viewing of that perfect beauty will keep thee in continual transports of love. Christians, doth it not now stir up your love, to remember all the experiences of his love? Doth not kindness melt you, and the sunshine of divine goodness warm your frozen hearts? What will it do then, when you shall live in love, and have all in him, who is all? Surely love is both work and wages. What a high favour, that God will give us leave to love him! That he will be embraced by those, who have embraced lust and sin before him! But more than this, he returned love for love; nay, a thousand times more. Christian, thou wilt then be brim-full of love; yet, love as much as thou canst, thou shalt be ten thousand times more beloved. Were the arms of the Son of God open upon the cross, and an open passage made to his heart by the spear, and will not his arms and heart be open to thee in glory? Did he begin to love before thou lovedst, and will not he continue now? Did he love thee, an enemy? Thee, a sinner? Thee, who even loathedst thyself? and own thee, when thou didst disclaim thyself? And will he not now immeasurably love thee, a son? Thee, a perfect saint? Thee, who returnedst some love for love? He that in love wept over the old Jerusalem when near to its ruin, with what love will he rejoice over the new Jerusalem in her glory? Christian, believe this, and think on it —thou shalt be eternally embraced in the arms of that love, which was from everlasting and will extend to everlasting; of that love which brought the Son of God's love from heaven to earth, from earth to the cross, from the cross to the grave, from the grave to glory; that love which was weary, hungry, tempted, scorned, scourged, buffeted, spit upon, crucified, pierced; which did fast, pray, teach, heal, weep, sweat, bleed, die;— that love will eternally embrace thee. When perfect created love, and most perfect uncreated love, meet together, it will not be like Joseph and his brethren, who lay upon one another's necks weeping; it will be loving and rejoicing, not loving and sorrowing. Yet it will make Satan's court ring with the news, that Joseph's brethren are come, that the saints are arrived safe at the bosom of Christ, out of the reach of hell for ever. Nor is there any such love as David's and Jonathan's, breathing out its last into sad lamentations for a forced separation. Know this, believer, to thy everlasting comfort, if those arms have once embraced thee, neither sin, nor hell, can get thee thence for ever. Thou hadst not to deal with an inconstant creature, but with him 'with whom is no variableness, nor shadow of turning.' His love to thee will not be as thine on earth to him, seldom, and cold, up and down. He that would not cease nor abate his love, for all thine enmity, unkind neglects, and churlish resistances, can he cease to love thee,

when he hath made thee truly lovely? He that keepeth thee so constant in thy love to him, that thou canst challenge tribulation, distress, persecution, famine, nakedness, peril, or sword, to separate thy love from Christ, how much more will himself be constant? Indeed thou mayest be ' persuaded, that neither death, nor life, nor angels, nor principalities, nor powers, nor things present, nor things to come, nor height, nor depth, nor any other creature, shall be able to separate us from the love of God which is in Christ Jesus our Lord.' And now are we not left in the apostle's admiration, ' What shall we say to these things?' Infinite love must needs be a mystery to a finite capacity. No wonder angels desire to look into this mystery. And if it be the study of saints here, to know the breadth, and length, and depth, and height, ' of the love of Christ, which passeth knowledge;' the saints' everlasting rest must consist in the enjoyment of God by love.

13. Nor hath joy the least share in this fruition. It is that, which all the former lead to, and conclude in ; even the inconceivable complacency which the blessed feel in their seeing, knowing, loving, and being beloved of God. This is the white stone which no man knoweth, saving he that receiveth it. Surely this is the joy which a stranger doth not intermeddle with. All Christ's ways of mercy tend to, and end in, the saint's joys. He wept, sorrowed, suffered, that they might rejoice : he sendeth the Spirit to be their Comforter ; he multiplies promises ; he discovers their future happiness, that their joy may be full. He opens to them the fountain of living waters, that they may thirst no more, and that it may spring up in them to everlasting life. He chastens them, that he may give them rest. He makes it their duty to rejoice in him alway, and again commands them to rejoice. He never brings them into so low a condition wherein he does not leave them more cause of joy than sorrow. And hath the Lord such a care of our comfort here? O what will that joy be, where the soul, being perfectly prepared for joy, and joy prepared by Christ for the soul, it shall be our work, our business, eternally to rejoice! It seems the saints' joy shall be greater than the damned's torment : for their torment is the torment of creatures, prepared for the devil and his angels ; but our joy is the joy of our Lord. The same glory which the Father gave the Son, the Son hath given them, to sit with him in his throne, even as he is set down with his Father in his throne. Thou, poor soul, who prayest for joy, waitest for joy, complainest for want of joy,

longest for joy : thou then shalt have full joy, as much as thou canst hold, and more than ever thou thoughtest on, or thy heart desired. In the mean time, walk carefully, watch constantly, and then let God measure out to thee thy times and degrees of joy. It may be he keeps them until thou hast more need. Thou hadst better lose thy comfort than thy safety. If thou shouldst die full of fears and sorrows, it will be but a moment, and they are all gone, and concluded in joy inconceivable. As the joy of the hypocrite, so the fears of the upright are but for a moment. ' God's anger endureth but a moment ; in his favour is life ; weeping may endure for a night, but joy cometh in the morning.' O blessed morning! Poor, humble, drooping soul, how would it fill thee with joy now, if a voice from heaven should tell thee of the love of God, the pardon of thy sins, and assure thee of thy part in these joys! What then will thy joy be, when thy actual possession shall convince thee of thy title, and thou shalt be in heaven, before thou art well aware?

14. And it is not *thy* joy only ; it is a mutual joy, as well as a mutual love. Is there joy in heaven at thy conversion, and will there be none at thy glorification? Will not the angels welcome thee thither, and congratulate thy safe arrival?—Yea, it is the joy of Jesus Christ ; for now he hath the end of his undertaking, labour, suffering, dying, when we have our joys ; when he is glorified in his saints, and admired in all them that believe ; when he sees of the travail of his soul, and is satisfied. This is Christ's harvest, when he shall reap the fruit of his labours ; and it will not repent him concerning his sufferings, but he will rejoice over his purchased inheritance, and his people will rejoice in him.—Yea, the Father himself puts on joy too, in our joy. As we grieve his Spirit, and weary him with our iniquities, so he is rejoiced in our good. O how quickly does he now spy a returning prodigal, even afar off! How does he run and meet him! And with what compassion does he fall on his neck, and kiss him, and put on him the best robe, and a ring on his hand, and shoes on his feet, and kills the fatted calf to eat and be merry. This is indeed a happy meeting ; but nothing to the embracing and joy of that last and great meeting. Yea, more ; as God doth mutually love and joy, so he makes this His rest, as it is our rest. What an eternal sabbatism, when the work of redemption, sanctification, preservation, glorification, is all finished, and perfected for ever! ' The Lord thy God in the midst of thee is mighty ; he will save, he will

2

rejoice over thee with joy, he will rest in his love, he will joy over thee with singing.' Well may we then rejoice in our God with joy, and rest in our love, and joy in him with singing.

15. Alas! my fearful heart scarce dares proceed. Methinks I hear the Almighty's voice saying to me, ' Who is this that darkeneth counsel by words without knowledge?' But pardon thy servant, O Lord, I have not pried into unrevealed things. I bewail that my apprehensions are so dull, my thoughts so mean, my affections so stupid, and my expressions so low, and unbeseeming such a glory. I have only heard by the hearing of the ear; O, let thy servant see thee and possess these joys; and then shall I have more suitable conceptions, and shall give thee fuller glory; I shall abhor my present self, and disclaim and renounce all these imperfections— ' I have uttered that I understood not, things too wonderful for me, which I know not.' Yet ' I believed, and therefore have I spoken.' What, Lord, canst thou expect from dust but levity? or from corruption but defilement? Though the weakness and irreverence be the fruit of my own corruption, yet the fire is from thine altar, and the work of thy commanding. I looked not into thy ark, nor put forth my hand unto it, without thee. Wash away these stains also in the blood of the Lamb. Imperfect or none, must be thy service here. O take thy Son's excuse—' The spirit is willing, but the flesh is weak.'

CHAPTER II.

THE GREAT PREPARATIVES TO THE SAINTS' REST.

Sect. 1. The happiness of Christians in having a way open into paradise. There are four things which principally prepare the way to enter into it; 2, 3. particularly, (1.) The glorious appearing of Christ; 4. (2.) The general resurrection; 5—8. (3.) The last judgment; 9, 10, and, (4.) The saints' coronation; 11. Transition to the subject of the next chapter.

1. The passage of paradise is not now so blocked up, as when the law and curse reigned. Wherefore finding, beloved Christians, a new and living way consecrated for us, through the vail, that is to say, the flesh of Christ, by which we may, with boldness, enter into the holiest, I shall draw near with fuller assurance. And finding the flaming sword removed, shall look again into the paradise of our God. And because I know that this is no forbidden fruit, and withal that it is good for food, and pleasant to the spiritual eyes, and a tree to be desired to make one truly wise and happy, I shall, through the assistance of the Spirit, take and eat thereof myself, and give to you according to my power, that you may

eat. The porch of this temple is exceeding glorious, and the gate of it is called Beautiful. Here are four things, as the four corners of this porch. Here is the most glorious coming and appearance of the Son of God;—that great work of Jesus Christ in raising our bodies from the dust, and uniting them again to the soul;—the public and solemn process at their judgment, where they shall first themselves be acquitted and justified, and then with Christ judge the world;—together with their solemn coronation, and receiving the kingdom.

2. (1.) The most glorious coming and appearance of the Son of God may well be reckoned in his people's glory. For their sake he came into the world, suffered, died, rose, ascended, and for their sake it is that he will return. To this end will Christ come again, to receive his people unto himself, that where he is, there they may be also. The bridegroom's departure was not upon divorce. He did not leave us with a purpose to return no more. He hath left pledges enough to assure us to the contrary. We have his word, his many promises, his sacraments, which show forth his death till he come; and his Spirit, to direct, sanctify, and comfort, till he return. We have frequent tokens of love from him, to show us he forgets not his promise, nor us. We daily behold the forerunners of his coming, foretold by himself. We see the fig-tree putteth forth leaves, and therefore know that summer is nigh. Though the riotous world say, ' My Lord delayeth his coming;' yet let the saints lift up their heads, for their redemption draweth nigh. Alas, fellow Christians, what should we do if our Lord should not return? What a case are we here left in? What! leave us in the midst of wolves, and among lions, a generation of vipers, and here forget us? Did he buy us so dear, and then leave us sinning suffering, groaning, dying daily, and will he come no more to us? It cannot be. This is like our unkind dealing with Christ, who, when we feel ourselves warm in the world, care not for coming to him; but this is not like Christ's dealing with us. He that would come to suffer, will surely come to triumph. He that would come to purchase, will surely come to possess. Where else, were all our hopes? What were become of our faith, our prayers, our tears, and our waiting? What were all the patience of the saints worth to them? Were we not left of all men the most miserable? Christians, hath Christ made us forsake all the world, and be forsaken of all the world? to hate all and be hated of all? and all this for him that we might have him, instead of all? And will he, think you, after all this, for-

get us, and forsake us himself? Far be such a thought from our hearts! But why staid he not with his people while he was here? Why? Was not the work on earth done? Must he not take possession of glory in our behalf? Must he not intercede with the Father, plead his sufferings, be filled with the Spirit, to send forth, receive authority, and subdue his enemies? Our abode here is short. If he had staid on earth, what would it have been to enjoy him for a few days, and then die? He hath more in heaven to dwell among; even the spirits of many generations. He will have us live by faith, and not by sight.

3. O fellow-Christians, what a day will that be, when we, who have been kept prisoners by sin, by sinners, by the grave, shall be fetched out by the Lord himself! It will not be such a coming as his first was, in poverty and contempt, to be spit upon, and buffeted, and crucified again. He will not come, O careless world! to be slighted and neglected by you any more. Yet that coming wanted not its glory. If the heavenly host, for the celebration of his nativity, must praise God, with what shoutings will angels and saints at that day proclaim glory to God, peace and good-will towards men! If a star must lead men from remote parts of the world to come to worship a child in a manger, how will the glory of his next appearing constrain all the world to acknowledge his sovereignty! If, riding on an ass, he enter Jerusalem with hosannas, with what peace and glory will he come toward the New Jerusalem! If, when he was in the form of a servant, they cried out, 'What manner of man is this, that even the winds and the sea obey him?' what will they say, when they shall see him coming in his glory, and the heavens and the earth obey him! 'Then shall all the tribes of the earth mourn.' To think and speak of that day with horror, doth well beseem the impenitent sinner, but ill the believing saint. Shall the wicked behold him, and cry, 'Yonder is he whose blood we neglected, whose grace we resisted, whose council we refused, whose government we cast off?' And shall not the saints with inconceivable gladness, cry, 'Yonder is he whose blood redeemed us, whose Spirit cleansed us, whose law did govern us, in whom we trusted, and he hath not deceived our trust; for whom we long waited, and now we see we have not waited in vain! O cursed corruption! that would have had us turn to the world, and present things, and say, Why should we wait for the Lord any longer? Now we see, Blessed are all they that wait for him. And now, Christians, should we not put up that petition heartily, ' Thy kingdom come?' The

Spirit and the bride say, Come : and let him that heareth,' and readeth, 'say, Come.' Our Lord himself says, 'Surely I come quickly, Amen: even so, come, Lord Jesus.'

4. (2) Another thing that leads to paradise is, that great work of Jesus Christ, in raising our bodies from the dust, and uniting them again unto the soul. A wonderful effect of infinite power and love! Yea, wonderful indeed, says unbelief, if it be true. What! shall all these scattered bones and dust become a man?—Let me with reverence plead for God, for that power whereby I hope to arise. What beareth the massy body of the earth? What limits the vast ocean of the waters? Whence is that constant ebbing and flowing of the tides? How many times bigger than all the earth is the sun, that glorious body of light? Is it not as easy to raise the dead, as to make heaven and earth, and all of nothing?—Look not on the dead bones, and dust, and difficulty, but at the promise. Contentedly commit these carcasses to a prison that shall not long contain them. Let us lie down in peace, and take our rest; it will not be an everlasting night, nor endless sleep. If unclothing be the thing thou fearest, it is that thou mayest have better clothing. If to be turned out of doors be the thing thou fearest, remember, that ' when the earthly house of this tabernacle is dissolved, thou hast a building of God, an house not made with hands, eternal in the heavens.' Lay down cheerfully this lump of corruption; thou shalt undoubtedly receive it again in incorruption. Lay down freely this terrestial, this natural body; thou shalt receive it again a celestial, a spiritual body. Though thou lay it down with great dishonour, thou shalt receive it in glory. Though thou art separated from it through weakness, it shall be raised again in mighty power—'In a moment, in the twinkling of an eye, at the last trump; (for the trumpet shall sound;) and the dead shall be raised incorruptible, and we shall be changed.' ' The dead in Christ shall rise first. Then they who are alive and remain, shall be caught up together with them in the clouds, to meet the Lord in the air.' Triumph now, O Christian, in these promises; thou shalt shortly triumph in their performance. This is the day which the Lord will make, we shall rejoice and be glad in it. The grave, that could not keep our Lord, cannot keep us. He arose for us, and by the same power will cause us to arise. For if we believe that Jesus died, and rose again, even so them also who sleep in Jesus, will God bring with him. Let us never look at the grave, but let us see the

resurrection beyond it. ' Yea, let us be steadfast, immoveable, always abounding in the work
of the Lord, for as much as we know our labour
is not in vain in the Lord.'

5. (3.) Part of this prologue to the saints' rest,
is the public and solemn process at their judgment, where they shall first themselves be acquitted and justified, and then with Christ judge
the world. Young and old, of all estates and
nations, that ever were, from the creation to that
day, must here come, and receive their doom.
O terrible! O joyful day! Terrible to those that
have forgot the coming of their Lord! Joyful
to the saints, whose waiting and hope was to see
this day! Then shall the world behold the goodness and severity of God: on them who perish,
severity; but to his chosen, goodness. Every
one must give an account of his stewardship.
Every talent of time, health, wit, mercies, afflictions, means, warnings, must be reckoned for.
The sins of youth, those which they had forgotten, and their secret sins, shall all be laid open
before angels and men. They shall see the Lord
Jesus, whom they neglected, whose word they
disobeyed, whose ministers they abused, whose
servants they hated, now sitting to judge them.
Their own consciences shall cry out against them,
and call to their remembrance all their misdoings. . Which way will the wretched sinner look?
Who can conceive the terrible thoughts of his
heart? Now the world cannot help him; his old
companions cannot; the saints neither can nor
will. Only the Lord Jesus can; but, there is
the misery, he will not. Time was, sinner, when
Christ would, and you would not; now, fain
would you, and he will not. All in vain, to cry
to the mountains and rocks, ' Fall on us, and
hide us from the face of Him that sitteth upon
the throne;' for thou hast the Lord of mountains
and rocks for thine enemy, whose voice they
will obey, and not thine. I charge thee, therefore before God, and the Lord Jesus Christ, who
shall judge the quick and the dead at his appearing, and his kingdom, that thou set thyself seriously to ponder on these things.

6. But why tremblest thou, O humble gracious
soul? He that would not lose one Noah in a
common deluge, nor overlook one Lot in Sodom:
nay, that could do nothing till he went forth; will
he forget thee at that day? The Lord knoweth how to deliver the godly out of temptations,
and to reserve the unjust unto the day of judgment to be punished. He knoweth how to make
the same day the greatest terror to his foes, and
yet the greatest joy to his people. ' There is
no condemnation to them that are in Christ

Jesus, who walk not after the flesh, but after the
Spirit.' ' Who shall lay any thing to the charge
of God's elect?' Shall the law? The law of
the spirit of life in Christ Jesus, hath made them
free from the law of sin and death. Or shall
conscience? ' The Spirit itself beareth witness
with their spirit, that they are the children of
God.' ' It is God that justifieth, who is he that
condemneth?' If our judge condemn us not,
who shall? He that said to the adulterous woman, ' Hath no man condemned thee? Neither
do I;' will say to us, more faithfully than Peter
to him, ' Though all men deny thee, or condemn
thee, I will not.' Having confessed me before
men, thee ' will I also confess before my Father
who is in heaven.'

7. What inexpressible joy, that our dear
Lord, who loveth our souls, and whom our
souls love, shall be our Judge! Will a man
fear to be judged by his dearest friend? Or
a wife by her own husband? Christian, did
Christ come down and suffer, and weep, and
bleed and die for thee, and will he now condemn
thee? Was he judged, condemned, and executed in thy stead, and now will he condemn thee
himself? Hath he done most of the work already,
in redeeming, regenerating, sanctifying, and
preserving thee, and will he now undo all again?
Well, then, let the terror of that day be ever so
great, surely our Lord can mean no ill to us in
all. Let it make the devils tremble, and the
wicked tremble; but it shall make us leap for
joy. It must needs affect us deeply with the
sense of our mercy and happiness, to see the
most of the world tremble with terror, while we
triumph with joy; to hear them doomed to everlasting flames, when we are proclaimed heirs of
the kingdom; to see our neighbours that lived in
the same towns, came to the same congregation,
dwelt in the same houses, and were esteemed
more honourable in the world than ourselves,
now, by the Searcher of hearts, eternally separated. This, with the great magnificence and
dreadfulness of the day, the apostle pathetically
expresses: ' It is a righteous thing with God, to
recompense tribulation to them that trouble you;
and to you who are troubled, rest with us, when
the Lord Jesus shall be revealed from heaven,
with his mighty angels, in flaming fire, taking
vengeance on them that know not God, and that
obey not the gospel of our Lord Jesus Christ;
who shall be punished with everlasting destruction from the presence of the Lord, and from the
glory of his power; when he shall come to be
glorified in his saints, and to be admired in all
them that believe in that day.'

8. Yet more, we shall be so far from the dread of that judgment, that ourselves shall become the judges. Christ will take his people, as it were into commission with himself, and they shall sit and approve his righteous judgment. 'Do you not know that the saints will judge the world?' Nay, 'know ye not that we shall judge angels?' Were it not for the word of Christ that speaks it, this advancement would seem incredible, and the language arrogant. 'Even Enoch, the seventh from Adam, prophesied this saying, Behold the Lord cometh with ten thousands of his saints, to execute judgment upon all, and to convince all that are ungodly among them, of all their ungodly deeds which they have ungodly committed, and of all their hard speeches which ungodly sinners have spoken against him.' Thus shall the saints be honoured, and the upright shall have dominion in the morning. O that the careless world 'were wise, that they understood this, that they would consider their latter end!' That they would be now of the same mind as they will be, when they shall see the heavens pass away with a great noise, and the elements melt with fervent heat, and the earth also, and the works that are therein, burnt up,—when all shall be in fire about their ears, and all earthly glory consumed! For the heavens and the earth, which are now, are reserved unto fire against the day of judgment, and perdition of ungodly men. 'Seeing then that all these things shall be dissolved, what manner of persons ought ye to be in all holy conversation and godliness, looking for and hasting unto the coming of God, wherein the heavens, being on fire, shall be dissolved, and the elements shall melt with fervent heat.'

9. (4.) The last preparative to the saints' rest is their solemn coronation, and receiving the kingdom. For, as Christ, their Head, is anointed both King and Priest, so, under him, are his people made unto God both kings and priests, to reign, and to offer praises for ever. The crown of righteousness, which was laid up for them, shall by the Lord, the righteous Judge, be given them at that day. They have been faithful unto death, and therefore he will give them a crown of life. And according to the improvement of their talents here, so shall their rule and dignity be enlarged. They are not dignified with empty titles, but real dominion. Christ will grant them to sit with him on his throne: and will give them power over the nations, even as he received of his Father; and

he 'will give them the morning-star.' The Lord himself will give them possession with these applauding expressions; 'Well done, good and faithful servant, thou hast been faithful over a few things, I will make thee ruler over many things; enter thou into the joy of thy Lord.

10. And with this solemn and blessed proclamation shall he enthrone them: 'Come, ye blessed of my Father, inherit the kingdom prepared for you from the foundation of the world.' Every word is full of life and joy. 'Come'—this is the holding forth of the golden sceptre, to warrant our approach unto this glory. Come now as near as you will; fear not the Bethshemite's judgment; for the enmity is utterly abolished. This is not such a 'Come' as we were wont to hear, 'Come, take up your cross, and follow me.' Though that was sweet, yet this much more. 'Ye blessed'—Blessed indeed, when that mouth shall so pronounce us! For though the world hath accounted us accursed, and we have been ready to account ourselves so; yet certainly those that he blesseth, are blessed; and those whom he curseth, only are cursed, and his blessing cannot be reversed. 'Of my Father'—Blessed in the Father's love, as well as the Son's, for they are one. The Father hath testified his love in their election, donation to Christ, sending of Christ, and accepting his ransom, as the Son has also testified his. 'Inherit'—No longer bondmen, nor servants only, nor children under age, who differ not in possession, but only in title, from servants; but now we are heirs of the kingdom, and joint heirs with Christ. 'The kingdom'—No less than the kingdom! Indeed, to be King of kings, and Lord of lords, is our Lord's own proper title; but to be kings, and reign with him, is ours. The enjoyment of this kingdom is as the light of the sun; each have the whole, and the rest never the less. 'Prepared for you'—God is the Alpha, as well as the Omega of our blessedness. Eternal love hath laid the foundation. He prepared the kingdom for us, and then prepared us for the kingdom. This is the preparation of his counsel and decree; for the execution whereof Christ was yet to make a further preparation. 'For you'—Not for believers only in general, who, without individual persons, are nobody; but for you personally. 'From the foundation of the world'—Not only from the promise after Adam's fall, but from eternity.

11. Thus we have seen the Christian safely landed in paradise, and conveyed honourably to his rest. Now let us a little further, in the next

chapter, view those mansions, consider their privileges, and see whether there be any glory like unto this glory.

CHAPTER III.

THE EXCELLENCIES OF THE SAINTS' REST.

Sect. 1. The excellencies of the Saints' Rest are enumerated. 2. (1.) It is the purchased possession. 3, 4. (2.) A free gift. 5. (3.) Peculiar to saints. 6. (4.) An association with saints and angels. 7. (5.) It derives its joys immediately from God himself. 8. (6.) It will be seasonable. 9. (7.) Suitable. 10—12. (8.) Perfect without sin and suffering. 13. (9.) And everlasting. 14. The chapter concludes with a serious address to the reader.

1. Let us draw a little nearer, and see what further excellencies this rest affordeth. The Lord hide us in the clefts of the rock, and cover us with the hands of indulgent grace while we approach to take this view! This rest is excellent for being—a purchased possession,—a free gift,—peculiar to saints, an association with saints and angels,—yet deriving its joys immediately from God:—and because it will be a seasonable—suitable—perfect—and eternal rest.

2. (1.) It is a most singular honour of the saints' rest, to be called 'the purchased possession.' That is, the fruit of the blood of the Son of God; yea, the chief fruit, the end, and perfection of all the fruits and efficacy of that blood. Greater love than this there is not, to lay down the life of the lover. And to have this our Redeemer ever before our eyes, and the liveliest sense and freshest remembrance of that dying, bleeding love still upon our souls! How will it fill our souls with perpetual joy, to think, that in the streams of this blood we have swam through the violence of the world, the snares of Satan, the seducements of flesh, the curse of the law, the wrath of an offended God, the accusations of a guilty conscience, and the vexing doubts and fears of an unbelieving heart, and are arrived safe at the presence of God! Now, he cries to us, Is it 'nothing to you, all ye that pass by? behold, and see if there be any sorrow like unto my sorrow!' and we scarce regard the mournful voice, nor scarce turn aside to view the wounds. But then our perfected souls will feel, and flame in love for love. With what astonishing apprehensions will redeemed saints everlastingly behold their blessed Redeemer! the purchaser, and the price, together with the possession! Neither will the view of his wounds of love, renew our wounds of sorrow. He, whose first words after his resurrection were

to a great sinner, 'Woman, why weepest thou?' knows how to raise love and joy, without any cloud of sorrow, or storm of tears. If any thing we enjoy was purchased with the life of our dearest friend, how highly should we value it? If a dying friend deliver us but a token of his love, how carefully do we preserve it! and still remember him when we behold it, as if his own name were written on it! And will not then the death and blood of our Lord everlastingly sweeten our possessed glory? As we write down the price our goods cost us; so, on our righteousness and glory, write down the price, the precious blood of Christ. His sufferings were to satisfy the justice that required blood, and to bear what was due to sinners, and so to restore them to the life they lost, and the happiness they fell from. The work of Christ's redemption so well pleased the Father, that he gave him power to advance his chosen, and gave them the glory which was given to himself, and all this 'according to his good pleasure, and the counsel of his own will.'

3. (2.) Another pearl in the saints' diadem is, that it is a free gift. These two, purchased and free, are the chains of gold which make up the wreaths for the tops of the pillars in the temple of God. It was dear to Christ, but free to us. When Christ was to buy, silver and gold were nothing worth; prayers and tears could not suffice, nor any thing below his blood; but our buying is receiving; we have it freely, without money, and without price. A thankful acceptance of a free acquittance, is no paying of the debt. Here is all free: if the Father freely give the Son, and the Son freely pay the debt; and if God freely accepts that way of payment, when he might have required it of the principal; and if both Father and Son freely offer us the purchased life on our cordial acceptance, and if they freely send the Spirit to enable us to accept; what is here then that is not free? O the everlasting admiration that must needs surprise the saints to think of this freeness! 'What did the Lord see in me, that he should judge me meet for such a state? That I, who was but a poor, diseased, despised wretch, should be clad in the brightness of this glory! That I, a creeping worm, should be advanced to this high dignity! That I, who was but lately groaning, weeping, dying, should now be as full of joy as my heart can hold! yea, should be taken from the grave, where I was rotting, and from the dust and darkness, where I seemed forgotten, and be here set before his throne! That I should be taken, with Mordecai, from captivity, and be set next unto the king;

and, with Daniel, from the den, to be made ruler of princes and provinces! Who can fathom unmeasurable love?' If worthiness were our condition for admittance, we might sit down and weep with St John, 'Because no man was found worthy. But the Lion of the tribe of Judah is worthy, and hath prevailed;' and by that title we must hold the inheritance. We shall offer there the offering that David refused, even praise for that which cost us nothing. Here our commission runs, 'Freely ye have received, freely give;' but Christ has dearly bought, yet freely gives.

4. If it were only for nothing, and without our merit, the wonder were great; but it is moreover against our merit, and against our long endeavouring our own ruin. What an astonishing thought it will be, to think of the unmeasurable difference between our deservings and receivings! Between the state we should have been in, and the state we are in! To look down upon hell, and see the vast difference that grace hath made between us and them! To see the inheritance there, which we were born to, so different from that which we are adopted to! What pangs of love will it cause within us to think, 'Yonder was the place that sin would have brought me to, but this is it that Christ hath brought me to! Yonder death was the wages of my sin, but this eternal life is the gift of God, through Jesus Christ my Lord! Who made me to differ? Had I not now been in those flames, if I had had my own way, and been let alone to my own will? Should I not have lingered in Sodom, till the flames had seized on me, if God had not in mercy brought me out?' Doubtless this will be our everlasting admiration, that so rich a crown should fit the head of so vile a sinner! That such high advancement, and such long unfruitfulness and unkindness, can be the state of the same person! And that such vile rebellions can conclude in such most precious joys! But, no thanks to us, nor to any of our duties and labours, much less to our neglects and laziness: we know to whom the praise is due, and must be given for ever. Indeed to this very end it was, that Infinite Wisdom cast the whole design of man's salvation into this mould of purchase and freeness, that the love and joy of man might be perfected, and the honour of grace most highly advanced; that the thought of merit might neither cloud the one nor obstruct the other; and that on these two hinges the gate of heaven might turn. So, then, let DESERVED be written on the door of hell, but on the door of heaven and life, THE FREE GIFT.

5. (3.) This rest is peculiar to saints, belongs to no other of all the sons of men. If all Egypt had been light, the Israelites would not have had the less; but to enjoy that light alone, while their neighbours lived in thick darkness, must make them more sensible of their privilege. Distinguishing mercy affects more than any mercy. If Pharaoh had passed as safely as Israel, the Red Sea would have been less remembered. If the rest of the world had not been drowned, and the rest of Sodom and Gomorrah not burned, the saving of Noah had been no wonder, nor Lot's deliverance so much talked of. When one is enlightened, and another left in darkness; one reformed, and another by his lust enslaved; it makes the saints cry out, 'Lord, how is it that thou wilt manifest thyself unto us and not unto the world?' When the prophet is sent to one widow only of all that were in Israel, and to cleanse one Naaman of all the lepers, the mercy is more observable. That will surely be a day of passionate sense on both sides, when there shall be two in one bed, and two in the field, the one taken and the other left. The saints shall look down upon the burning lake, and in the sense of their own happiness, and in the approbation of God's just proceedings, they shall rejoice and sing, 'Thou art righteous, O Lord, who wast, art, and shalt be, because thou hast judged thus.'

6. (4.) But though this rest be proper to the saints, yet it is common to all the saints; for it is an association of blessed spirits, both saints and angels; a corporation of perfected saints, whereof Christ is the head; the communion of saints completed. As we have been together in the labour, duty, danger, and distress: so shall we be in the great recompense and deliverance. As we have been scorned and despised, so shall we be owned and honoured together. We, who have gone through the day of sadness, shall enjoy together that day of gladness. Those, who have been with us in persecution and prison, shall be with us also in that palace of consolation. How oft have our groans made, as it were, one sound? our tears one stream? and our desires one prayer? But now all our praises shall make up one melody; all our churches, one church; and all ourselves, one body: for we shall all be one in Christ; even as he and the Father are one. It is true, we must be careful, not to look for that in the saints, which is alone in Christ. But if the forethought of sitting down with Abraham, and Isaac, and Jacob, in the kingdom of heaven, may be our lawful joy; how much more the real sight and actual possession? It cannot choose but be comfortable to think of that day, when we

shall join with Moses in his song, with David in his psalms of praise, and with all the redeemed in the song of the Lamb for ever; when we shall see Enoch walking with God; Noah enjoying the end of his singularity; Joseph of his integrity; Job of his patience; Hezekiah of his uprightness; and all the saints the end of their faith. Not only our old acquaintance, but all the saints, of all ages, whose faces in the flesh we never saw, we shall there both know and comfortably enjoy. Yea, angels as well as saints, will be our blessed acquaintance. Those who now are willingly our ministering spirits, will willingly then be our companions in joy. They, who had such joy in heaven for our conversion, will gladly rejoice with us in our glorification. Then we shall truly say, as David, 'I am a companion of all them that fear thee;' when 'we are come unto mount Zion, and unto the city of the living God, the heavenly Jerusalem, and to an innumerable company of angels: to the general assembly, and church of the first-born, who are written in heaven, and to God the Judge of all, and to spirits of just men made perfect, and to Jesus the Mediator of the new covenant.' It is a singular excellence of heavenly rest, that 'we are fellow-citizens with the saints, and of the household of God.'

7. (5.) As another property of our rest, we shall derive its joys immediately from God. Now we have nothing at all immediately, but at the second or third hand, or how many, who knows? From the earth, from man, from sun and moon, from the ·ministration of angels, and from the Spirit, and Christ. Though in the hand of angels, the streams savour not of the imperfection of sinners, yet it does of the imperfection of creatures; and as it comes from man, it savours of both. How quick and piercing is the word in itself! Yet many times it never enters, being managed by a feeble arm. What weight and worth is there in every passage of the blessed gospel! Enough, one would think, to enter and pierce the dullest soul, and wholly possess its thoughts and affections; and yet how oft does it fall as water upon a stone! The things of God, which we handle, are divine; but our manner of handling is human. There is little we touch, but we leave the print of our fingers behind. If God speak the word himself, it will be a piercing, melting word indeed. The Christian now knows by experience, that his most immediate joys are his sweetest joys; which have least of man, and are most directly from the Spirit; Christians, who are much in secret prayer and contemplation, are men of greatest life and joy, because they have all more immediately from God himself. Not that we should cast off hearing, reading, and conference, or neglect any ordinance of God; but to live above them, while we use them, is the way of a Christian. There is joy in these remote receivings; but the fulness of joy is in God's immediate presence. We shall then have light without a candle, and perpetual day without the sun; for 'the city has no need of the sun, neither of the moon, to shine in it; for the glory of God lightens it, and the Lamb is the light thereof: there shall be no night there, and they need no candle, neither light of the sun; and they shall reign for ever and ever.' We shall then have enlightened understandings without Scripture, and be governed without a written law; for the Lord will perfect his law in our hearts, and we shall be all perfectly taught of God. We shall have joy, which we drew not from the promises, nor fetched home by faith or hope. We shall have communion without sacraments, without this fruit of the vine, when Christ shall drink it new with us in his Father's kingdom, and refresh us with the comforting wine of immediate enjoyment. To have necessities, but no supply, is the case of them in hell. To have necessity supplied by means of the creatures, is the case of us on earth. To have necessity supplied immediately from God, is the case of the saints in heaven. To have no necessity at all, is the prerogative of God himself.

8. (6.) A farther excellence of this rest is, that it will be seasonable. He that expects the fruit of his vineyard at the season, and makes his people 'like a tree planted by the rivers of water, that bringeth forth his fruit in his season,' will also give them the crown in his season. He that will have a word of joy spoken in season, to him that is weary, will surely cause the time of joy to appear in the fittest season. They who are not weary in well-doing, shall, if they faint not, reap in due season. If God giveth rain even to his enemies, both the former and the latter in his season, and reserveth the appointed weeks of harvest, and covenants that there shall be day and night in their season; then surely the glorious harvest of the saints shall not miss its season. Doubtless he that would not stay a day longer than his promise, but brought Israel out of Egypt on the self-same day, when the four hundred and thirty years were expired; neither will he fail of one day or hour of the fittest season for his people's glory. When we have had in this world a long night of darkness, will not the day-breaking and the rising of the Sun of Righteousness, be then seasonable? When we have passed a long

and tedious journey, through no small dangers, is not home then seasonable? When we have had a long and perilous war, and received many a wound, would not a peace with victory be seasonable? Men live in a continual weariness; especially the saints, who are most weary of that which the world cannot feel: some weary of a blind mind; some of a hard heart; some of their daily doubts and fears; some of the want of spiritual joys; and some of the sense of God's wrath. And when a poor Christian hath desired and prayed, and waited for deliverance many years, is it not then seasonable? We grudge that we do not find a Canaan in the wilderness, or the songs of Zion in a strange land; that we have not a harbour in the main ocean, nor our rest in the heat of the day, nor heaven before we leave the earth; and would not all this be very unseasonable?

9. (7.) As this rest will be seasonable, so it will be suitable. The new nature of the saints doth suit their spirits to this rest. Indeed their holiness is nothing else but a spark taken from this element, and by the Spirit of Christ kindled in their hearts; the flame whereof, mindful of its own divine original, ever tends to the place from whence it comes. Temporal crowns and kingdoms could not make a rest for saints. As they were not redeemed with so low a price, neither are they endued with so low a nature. As God will have from them a spiritual worship, suited to his own spiritual being, he will provide them a spiritual rest, suitable to their spiritual nature. The knowledge of God and his Christ, a delightful complacency in that mutual love, an everlasting rejoicing in the enjoyment of our God, with a perpetual singing of his high praises: this is a heaven for a saint. Then we shall live in our own element. We are now as the fish in a vessel of water, only so much as will keep them alive; but what is that to the ocean? We have a little air let into us, to afford us breathing; but what is that to the sweet and fresh gales upon Mount Sion? We have a beam of the sun to lighten our darkness, and a warm ray to keep us from freezing; but then we shall live in its light, and be revived by its heat for ever.—As the natures of saints are, such are their desires; and it is the desires of our renewed nature which this rest is suited to. Whilst our desires remain corrupted and misguided, it is a far greater mercy to deny them, yea, to destroy them, than to satisfy them; but those which are spiritual are of his own planting, and he will surely water them, and give the increase. He quickened our hunger and thirst for righteousness, that he might make us happy in a

full satisfaction. Christian, this is a rest after thy own heart; it contains all thy heart can wish; that which thou longest, prayest, labourest for, there thou shalt find it all. Thou hadst rather have God in Christ, than all the world: there thou shalt have him. What wouldest thou not give for assurance of his love? There thou shalt have assurance without suspicion. Desire what thou canst, and ask what thou wilt, as a Christian, and it shall be given thee, not only to half of the kingdom, but to the enjoyment both of kingdom and King. This is a life of desire and prayer, but that is a life of satisfaction and enjoyment.—This rest is very suitable to the saints' necessities also, as well as to their natures and desires. It contains whatsoever they truly wanted; not supplying them with gross created comforts, which like Saul's armour on David, are more burden than benefit. It was Christ and perfect holiness which they most needed, and with these shall they be supplied.

10. (8.) Still more, this rest will be absolutely perfect. We shall then have joy without sorrow, and rest without weariness. There is no mixture of corruption with our graces, nor of suffering with our comfort. There are none of those waves in that harbour, which now so toss us up and down. To-day we are well, to-morrow sick; to-day in esteem, to-morrow in disgrace; to-day we have friends, to-morrow none; nay, we have wine and vinegar in the same cup. If revelation raise us to the third heaven, the messenger of Satan must presently buffet us, and the thorn in the flesh fetch us down. But there is none of this inconstancy in heaven. If perfect love casteth out fear, then perfect joy must needs cast out sorrow, and perfect happiness exclude all the relics of misery. We shall there rest from all the evil of sin, and of suffering. 11. Heaven excludes nothing more directly than sin, whether of nature or of conversation. 'There shall in nowise enter any thing that defileth, neither whatsoever worketh abomination or maketh a lie.' What need Christ at all to have died, if heaven could have contained imperfect souls? 'For this purpose the Son of God was manifested, that he might destroy the works of the devil.' His blood and Spirit have not done all this, to leave us after all defiled. 'What communion hath light with darkness? and what concord hath Christ with Belial?' Christian, if thou be once in heaven, thou shalt sin no more. Is not this glad news to thee, who hast prayed, and watched against it so long? I know, if it were offered to thy choice, thou wouldst rather choose to be freed from sin, than have all the world. Thou shalt have thy de-

3

sire.—That hard heart, those vile thoughts, which accompanied thee to every duty, shall now be left behind for ever.—Thy understanding shall never more be troubled with darkness. All dark Scriptures shall be made plain; all seeming contradictions reconciled. The poorest Christian is presently there a more perfect divine than any here. O that happy day, when error shall vanish for ever! When our understanding shall be filled with God himself, whose light will leave no darkness in us! His face shall be the Scripture, where we shall read the truth. Many a godly man hath here, in his mistaken zeal, been a means to deceive and pervert his brethren, and when he sees his own error, cannot again tell how to undeceive them. But there we shall conspire in one truth, as being one in him who is the truth.—We shall also rest from all the sin of our will, affection, and conversation. We shall no more retain this rebelling principle, which is still drawing us from God: no more be oppressed with the power of our corruptions, nor vexed with their presence: no pride, passion, slothfulness, insensibility, shall enter with us; no strangeness to God, and the things of God; no coldness of affections, nor imperfection in our love; no uneven walking, nor grieving of the Spirit; no scandalous action, nor unholy conversation: we shall rest from all these for ever. Then shall our will correspond to the divine will, as face answers face in a glass, and from which, as our law and rule, we shall never swerve. 'For he that is entered into his rest, he also hath ceased from his own works, as God did from his.'

12. Our sufferings were but the consequences of our sinning, and in heaven they both shall cease together. We shall rest from all our doubts of God's love. It shall no more be said, that 'Doubts are like the thistle, a bad weed, but growing in good ground.' They shall now be weeded out, and trouble the gracious soul no more. We shall hear that kind of language no more, 'What shall I do to know my state? How shall I know that God is my Father? that my heart is upright? that my conversion is true? that faith is sincere? I am afraid my sins are unpardoned; that all I do is hypocrisy; that God will reject me; that he does not hear my prayers.' All this is there turned into praise. We shall rest from all sense of God's displeasure. Hell shall not be mixed with heaven. At times the gracious soul remembered God, and was troubled; complained, and was overwhelmed, and refused to be comforted; divine wrath lay hard upon him, and God afflicted him with all

his waves. But that blessed day shall convince us, that though God hid his face from us for a moment, yet with everlasting kindness will he have mercy on us. We shall rest from all the temptations of Satan. What a grief is it to a Christian, though he yield not to the temptation, yet to be solicited to deny his Lord! What a torment, to have such horrid motions made to his soul! such blasphemous ideas presented to his imagination! Sometimes cruel thoughts of God, undervaluing thoughts of Christ, unbelieving thoughts of Scripture, or injurious thoughts of Providence! To be tempted sometimes to turn to present things, to play with the baits of sin, and venture on the delights of flesh, and sometimes to atheism itself! Especially, when we know the treachery of our own hearts, ready, as tinder, to take fire, as soon as one of those sparks shall fall upon them! Satan hath power here to tempt us in the wilderness, but he entereth not the holy city: he may set us on a pinnacle of the temple in the earthly Jerusalem, but the new Jerusalem he may not approach; he may take us up into an exceeding high mountain, but the Mount Sion he cannot ascend; and if he could, all the kingdoms of the world, and the glory of them, would be a despised bait to a soul possessed of the kingdom of our Lord. No, it is in vain for Satan to offer a temptation more. All our temptations from the world and the flesh shall also cease. O the hourly dangers that we here walk in! Every sense and member is a snare; every creature, every mercy, and every duty is a snare to us. We can scarce open our eyes, but we are in danger of envying those above us, or despising those below us; of coveting the honours and riches of some, or beholding the rags and beggary of others with pride and unmercifulness. If we see beauty, it is a bait to lust; if deformity, to loathing and disdain. How soon do slanderous reports, vain jests, wanton speeches, creep into the heart! How constant and strong a watch does our appetite require! Have we comeliness and beauty? What fuel for pride! Are we deformed? What an occasion of repining! Have we strength of reason, and gifts of learning? O how prone to be puffed up, hunt after applause, and despise our brethren! Are we unlearned? How apt then to despise what we have not! Are we in places of authority? How strong is the temptation to abuse our trust, make our will our law, and cut out all the enjoyments of others by the rules and model of our own interest and policy! Are we inferiors? How prone to grudge at other's preeminence, and bring their actions to the bar of our judgment! Are we rich, and not too much exalted? Are we poor, and not discontented? Are we not lazy in our duties, or make a Christ of them? Not that God hath made all these things our snares; but through our own corruption they become so to us. Ourselves are the greatest snare to ourselves. This is our comfort, our rest will free us from all these. As Satan hath no entrance there, so neither any thing to serve his malice: but all things there shall join with us in the high praises of their great Deliverer. As we rest from the temptations, we shall likewise from the abuses and persecutions of the world. The prayers of the souls under the altar will then be answered, and God will avenge their blood on them that dwell on the earth. This is the time for crowning with thorns; that for crowning with glory. Now, 'all that live godly in Christ Jesus, shall suffer persecution;' then they that suffered with him, shall be glorified with him. Now, we must be hated of all men for Christ's name's sake. Then, Christ will be admired in his saints that were thus hated. We are here made a spectacle unto the world, and to angels, and to men; as the filth of the world, and the offscouring of all things; men separate us from their company, and reproach us, and cast out our names as evil: but we shall then be as much gazed at for our glory, and they will be shut out of the church of the saints, and separated from us, whether they will or not. We can scarce pray in our families, or sing praises to God, but our voice is a vexation to them: how must it torment them then, to see us praising and rejoicing, while they are howling and lamenting! You, brethren, who can now attempt no work of God, without losing the love of the world, consider, you shall have none in heaven but will further your work, and join heart and voice with you in your everlasting joy and praise. Till then, possess ye your souls in patience. Bind all reproaches as a crown to your heads. Esteem them greater riches than the world's treasures. 'It is a righteous thing with God, to recompense tribulation to them that trouble you; and to you, who are troubled, rest with Christ.' We shall then rest from all our sad divisions, and unchristian quarrels with one another. How lovingly do thousands live together in heaven, who lived at variance upon earth! There is no contention, because none of this pride, ignorance, or other corruption. There is no plotting to strengthen our party, nor deep designing against our brethren. If there be sorrow or shame in heaven, we shall then be both sorry and ashamed, to remember all this carriage

on earth; as Joseph's brethren were to behold him, when they remembered their former unkind usage. Is it not enough that all the world is against us, but we must also be against one another? O happy days of persecution, which drove us together in love, whom the sunshine of liberty and prosperity crumbles into dust by our contentions! O happy day of the saint's rest in glory, when, as there is one God, one Christ, one Spirit, so we shall have one heart, one church, one employment for ever! We shall then rest from our participation of our brethren's sufferings. The church on earth is a mere hospital. Some groaning under a dark understanding, some under an insensible heart, some languishing under unfruitful weakness, and some bleeding for miscarriages and wilfulness, some crying out of their poverty, some groaning under pains and infirmities, and some bewailing a whole catalogue of calamities. But a far greater grief it is, to see our dearest and most intimate friends turned aside from the truth of Christ, continuing their neglect of Christ and their souls, and nothing will awaken them out of their security: to look on an ungodly father or mother, brother or sister, wife or husband, child or friend, and think how certainly they shall be in hell for ever, if they die in their present unregenerate state: to think of the gospel departing, the glory taken from our Israel, poor souls left willingly dark and destitute, and blowing out the light that should guide them to salvation! Our day of rest will free us from all this, and the days of mourning shall be ended: then thy people, O Lord, shall be all righteous; they shall inherit the land for ever, the branch of thy planting, the work of thy hands, that thou mayest be glorified. Then we shall rest from all our own personal sufferings. This may seem a small thing to those that live in ease and prosperity; but to the daily afflicted soul it makes the thoughts of heaven delightful. O the dying life we now live! as full of sufferings as of days and hours! Our Redeemer leaves this measure of misery upon us, to make us know for what we are beholden, to mind us of what we should else forget, to be serviceable to his wise and gracious designs, and advantageous to our full and final recovery. Grief enters at every sense, seizes every part and power of flesh and spirit. What noble part is there, that suffereth its pain or ruin alone? But sin and flesh, dust and pain, will all be left behind together. O the blessed tranquillity of that region, where there is nothing but sweet, continued peace! O healthful place, where none are sick! O fortunate land, where all are kings! O holy assembly, where all are priests! How free a state, where none are servants, but to their supreme Monarch! The poor man shall no more be tired with his labours: no more hunger or thirst, cold or nakedness; no pinching frosts or scorching heats. Our faces shall no more be pale or sad; no more breaches in friendship, nor parting of friends asunder; no more trouble accompanying our relations, nor voice or lamentation heard in our dwellings: 'God shall wipe away all tears from our eyes.' O my soul, bear with the infirmities of thine earthly tabernacle; it will be thus but a little while; the sound of thy Redeemer's feet is even at the door. We shall also rest from all the toils of duties. The conscientious magistrate, parent, and minister, cries out, 'O the burden that lieth upon me!' Every relation, state, age, hath variety of duties; so that every conscientious Christian cries out, 'O the burden! O my weakness that makes it burdensome!' But our remaining rest will ease us of the burdens. Once more we shall rest from all these troublesome afflictions which necessarily accompany our absence from God. The trouble that is mixed in our desires and hopes, our longings and waitings, shall then cease. We shall no more look into our cabinet, and miss our treasure; into our hearts, and miss our Christ; no more seek him from ordinance to ordinance; but all be concluded in a most blessed and full enjoyment.

13. (9.) The last jewel of our crown is, that it will be an everlasting rest. Without this, all were comparatively nothing. The very thought of leaving it, would imbitter all our joys. It would be a hell in heaven, to think of once losing heaven: as it would be a kind of heaven to the damned, had they but hopes of once escaping. Mortality is the disgrace of all sublunary delights. How it spoils our pleasure, to see it dying in our hands! But, O blessed eternity! where our lives are perplexed with no such thoughts, nor our joys interrupted with any such fears! where 'we shall be pillars in the temple of God, and go no more out.' While we were servants, we held by lease, and that but for the term of a transitory life; 'but the son abideth in the house for ever.' 'O my soul, let go thy dreams of present pleasures, and loose thy hold of earth and flesh. Study frequently, study thoroughly, this one word—ETERNITY. What! Live and never die! Rejoice, and ever rejoice!' O happy souls in hell, should you but escape after millions of ages! O miserable saints in heaven, should you be dispossessed, after the age of a million of worlds! This word, everlasting,

contains the perfection of their torment, and our glory. O that the sinner would study this word! methinks it would startle him out of his dead sleep. O that the gracious soul would study it, methinks it would revive him in his deepest agony! 'And must I, Lord, thus live for ever? Then will I also love for ever. Must my joys be immortal; and shall not my thanks be also immortal? Surely, if I shall never lose my glory, I will never cease thy praises. If thou wilt both perfect and perpetuate me and my glory; as I shall be thine, and not my own; so shall my glory be thy glory. And as thy glory was thy ultimate end in my glory; so shall it also be my end, when thou hast crowned me with that glory which hath no end. 'Unto the King eternal, immortal, invisible, the only wise God, be honour and glory, for ever and ever.''

14. Thus I have endeavoured to show you a glimpse of approaching glory. But how short are my expressions of its excellency! Reader, if thou be an humble sincere believer, and waitest with longing and labouring for this rest, thou wilt shortly see, and feel the truth of all this. Thou wilt then have so high an apprehension of this blessed state, as will make thee pity the ignorance and distance of mortals, and will tell thee, all that is here said falls short of the whole truth a thousand-fold. In the mean time, let this much kindle thy desires, and quicken thy endeavours. Up, and be doing; run, and strive, and fight, and hold on; for thou hast a certain, glorious prize before thee. God will not mock thee; do not mock thyself, nor betray thy soul by delaying, and all is thine own. What kind of men, dost thou think, would Christians be in their lives and duties, if they had still this glory fresh in their thoughts? What frame would their spirits be in, if their thoughts of heaven were lively and believing? Would their hearts be so heavy? their countenances be so sad? or would they have need to take up their comforts from below? Would they be so loath to suffer; so afraid to die: or would they not think every day a year till they enjoy it? May the Lord heal our carnal hearts, lest we enter not into this rest, because of unbelief!

CHAPTER IV.

THE CHARACTER OF THE PERSONS FOR WHOM THIS REST IS DESIGNED.

Sect. 1. It is wonderful that such rest should be designed for mortals. 2. The people of God, who shall enjoy this rest, are, (1.) Chosen from eternity. 3. (2.) Given to Christ. 4. (3.) Born again. 5—8 (4.) Deeply convinced of the evil of sin, their misery by sin, the vanity of the creature, and the all-sufficiency of Christ. 9. (5.) Their will is proportionably changed. 10. (6.) They engage in covenant with Christ. 11. and, (7.) They persevere in their engagements. 12. The reader invited to examine himself by the characteristics of God's people. 13. Further testimony from Scripture that this rest shall be enjoyed by the people of God. 14. Also that none but they shall enjoy it. 15, 16. And that it remains for them, and is not to be enjoyed till they come to another world. 17. The chapter concludes with showing, that their souls shall enjoy this rest while separated from their bodies.

1. While I was in the mount, describing the excellencies of the saints' rest, I felt it was good being there, and therefore tarried the longer; and was there not an extreme disproportion between my conceptions and the subject, much longer had I been. Can a prospect of that happy land be tedious? Having read of such a high and unspeakable glory, a stranger would wonder for what rare creatures this mighty preparation should be made, and expect some illustrious sun should break forth. But, behold! only a shell-full of dust, animated with an invisible rational soul, and that rectified with as unseen a restoring power of grace; and this is the creature that must possess such glory. You would think it must needs be some deserving piece, or one that brings a valuable price: but, behold! one that hath nothing; and can deserve nothing; yea, that deserves the contrary, and would, if he might, proceed in that deserving: but being apprehended by love, he is brought to him that is All: and most affectionately receiving him, and resting on him, he doth, in and through him, receive all this. More particularly, the persons for whom this rest is designed, are—chosen of God from eternity—given to Christ, as their Redeemer—born again—deeply convinced of the evil and misery of a sinful state, the vanity of the creature, and the all-sufficiency of Christ—their will is renewed—they engage themselves to Christ in covenant—and they persevere in their engagements to the end.

2. (1.) The persons for whom this rest is designed, whom the text calls 'the people of God,' are 'chosen of God before the foundation of the world, that they should be holy and without blame before him in love.' That they are but a small part of mankind is too apparent in Scripture and experience. They are the little flock to whom 'it is their Father's good pleasure to give the kingdom.' Fewer they are than the

world imagines: yet not so few as some drooping spirits think, who are suspicious that God is unwilling to be their God, when they know themselves willing to be his people.

3. (2.) These persons are given of God to his Son, to be by him redeemed from their lost state and advanced to this glory. God hath given all things to his Son. 'God hath given him power over all flesh, that he should give eternal life to as many as the Father hath given him.' The Father hath given him all who repent and believe. The difference is clearly expressed by the apostle—'he hath put all things under his feet, and gave him to be the head over all things to the church.' And though Christ is, in some sense, a ransom for all, yet not in that special manner, as for his people.

4. (3.) One great qualification of these persons is, that they are born again. To be the people of God without regeneration, is as impossible as to be the children of men without generation. Seeing we are born God's enemies, we must be new-born his sons, or else remain enemies still. The greatest reformation of life that can be attained to without this new life wrought in the soul, may procure our further delusion, but never our salvation.

5. (4.) This new life in the people of God discovers itself by conviction, or a deep sense of divine things. As for instance: they are convinced of the evil of sin. The sinner is made to know and feel, that the sin, which was his delight, is a more loathsome thing than a toad or serpent, and a greater evil than plague or famine; being a breach of the righteous law of the most high God, dishonourable to him, and destructive to the sinner. Now the sinner no more hears the reproof of sin, as words of course; but the mention of his sin speaks to his very heart, and yet he is contented you should show him the worst. He was wont to marvel, what made men keep up such a stir against sin; what harm it was for a man to take a little forbidden pleasure; he saw no such heinousness in it, that Christ must needs die for it, and a Christless world be eternally tormented in hell. Now the case is altered: God hath opened his eyes to see the inexpressible vileness of sin.

6. They are convinced of their own misery by reason of sin. They who before read the threats of God's law, as men do the story of foreign wars, now find it their own story, and perceive they read their own doom, as if they found their own names written in the curse, or heard the law say, as Nathan, 'Thou art the man.' The wrath of God seemed to him before but as a storm to a

man in a dry house, or as the pains of the sick to the healthful stander-by : but now he finds the disease is his own, and feels himself a condemned man; that he is dead and damned in point of law, and that nothing was wanting but mere execution to make him absolutely and irrecoverably miserable. This is a work of the Spirit, wrought in some measure in all the regenerate. How should he come to Christ for pardon, that did not first find himself guilty, and condemned? or for life, that never found himself spiritually dead? 'The whole need not a physician, but they that are sick.' The discovery of the remedy, as soon as the misery, must needs prevent a great part of the trouble. And perhaps the joyful apprehensions of mercy may make the sense of misery sooner forgotten.

7. They are also convinced of the creature's vanity and insufficiency. Every man is naturally an idolater. Our hearts turned from God in our first fall; and, ever since, the creature hath been our god. This is the grand sin of nature. Every unregenerate man ascribes to the creature divine prerogatives, and allows it the highest room in his soul; or, if he is convinced of misery, he flies to it as his saviour. Indeed, God and his Christ shall be called Lord and Saviour; but the real expectation is from the creature, and the work of God is laid upon it. Pleasure, profit, and honour, are the natural man's trinity; and his carnal self is these in unity. It was our first sin to aspire to be as gods; and it is the greatest sin that is propagated in our nature from generation to generation. When God should guide us, we guide ourselves; when he should be our sovereign, we rule ourselves: the laws which he gave us we find fault with, and would correct; and, if we had the making of them, we would have made them otherwise: when he should take care of us, (and must, or we perish,) we will take care for ourselves; when we should depend on him in daily receivings, we had rather have our portion in our own hands: when we should submit to his providence, we usually quarrel at it, and think we could make a better disposal than God hath made. When we should study and love, trust and honour God, we study and love, trust and honour our carnal selves. Instead of God, we would have all men's eyes and dependence on us, and all men's thanks returned to us, and would gladly be the only men on earth extolled and admired by all. Thus we are naturally our own idols. But down falls this Dagon, when God does once renew the soul. It is the chief design of that great work to bring the heart back to God himself. He convinceth the sinner,

that the creature can neither be his god to make him happy, nor his Christ, to recover him from his misery, and restore him to God, who is his happiness. God does this, not only by his word, but by providence also. This is the reason, why affliction so frequently concurs in the work of conversion. Arguments which speak to the quick, will force a hearing, when the most powerful words are slighted. If a sinner made his credit his god, and God shall cast him into the lowest disgrace, or bring him, who idolized his riches, into a condition wherein they cannot help him; or cause them to take wing, and fly away; what a help is here to this work of conviction! If a man made pleasure his god, whatsoever a roving eye, a curious ear, a greedy appetite, or a lustful heart could desire, and God should take these from him, or turn them into gall or wormwood, what a help is here to conviction! When God shall cast a man into languishing sickness and inflict wounds on his heart, and stir up against him his own conscience, and then, as it were, say to him, 'Try if your credit, riches, or pleasure can help you. Can they heal your wounded conscience? Can they now support your tottering tabernacle? Can they keep your departing soul in your body? or save you from mine everlasting wrath? or redeem your soul from eternal flames? Cry aloud to them, and see now whether these will be to you instead of God and Christ.' O how this works now with the sinner! Sense acknowledges the truth, and even the flesh is convinced of the creature's vanity, and our very deceiver is undeceived.

8. The people of God are likewise convinced of the absolute necessity, the full sufficiency, and perfect excellency of Jesus Christ: as a man in famine is convinced of the necessity of food; or a man that had heard or read his sentence of condemnation, of the absolute necessity of pardon; or a man that lies in prison for debt, is convinced of his need of a surety to discharge it. Now, the sinner feels an unsupportable burden upon him, and sees there is none but Christ can take it off; he perceives the law proclaims him a rebel, and none but Christ can make his peace: he is as a man pursued by a lion, that must perish if he finds not a present sanctuary: he is now brought to this dilemma; either he must have Christ to justify him, or be eternally condemned; have Christ to save him, or burn in hell for ever; have Christ to bring him to God, or be shut out of his presence everlastingly. And no wonder if he cry out as the martyr, 'None but Christ! none but Christ!' Not gold, but bread, will satisfy the hungry; nor any thing

but pardon will comfort the condemned. 'All things are counted but dung now, that he may win Christ; and what was gain, he counts loss for Christ.' As the sinner sees his misery, and the inability of himself, and all things to relieve him, so he perceives there is no saving mercy out of Christ. He sees, though the creature cannot, and himself cannot, yet Christ can. Though the fig-leaves of our own unrighteous righteousness are too short to cover our nakedness, yet the righteousness of Christ is large enough: ours is disproportionate to the justice of the law, but Christ's extends to every tittle. If he intercede, there is no denial: such is the dignity of his person, and the value of his merits, that the Father grants all he desires. Before, the sinner knew Christ's excellency, as a blind man knows the light of the sun; but now, as one that beholds its glory.

9. (5.) After this deep conviction, the will discovers also its change. As for instance—The sin, which the understanding pronounces evil, the will turns from with abhorrence. Not that the sensitive appetite is changed, or any way made to abhor its object: but when it would prevail against reason, and carry us to sin against God, instead of Scripture being the rule, and reason the master, and sense the servant; this disorder and evil the will abhors.—The misery also which sin hath procured, is not only discerned, but bewailed. It is impossible that the soul should now look, either on its trespass against God, or yet on its own self-procured calamity, without some contrition. He that truly discerns that he hath killed Christ, and killed himself, will surely, in some measure, be pricked to the heart. If he cannot weep he can heartily groan; and his heart feels what his understanding sees. The creature is renounced as vanity, and turned out of the heart with disdain. Not that it is undervalued, or the use of it disclaimed; but its idolatrous abuse, and its unjust usurpation. Can Christ be the way, where the creature is the end? Can we seek to Christ to reconcile us to God, while in our hearts we prefer the creature before him? In the soul of every unregenerate man, the creature is both God and Christ. As turning from the creature to God and not by Christ, is no true turning; so believing in Christ, while the creature hath our hearts, is no true believing. Our aversion from sin, renouncing our idols, and our right receiving Christ, is all but one work, which God ever perfects where he begins. At the same time, the will cleaves to God the Father, and to Christ. Having been convinced that nothing else can be his happiness,

the sinner now finds it is in God. Convinced, also, that Christ alone is able and willing to make peace for him, he most affectionately accepts of Christ for Saviour and Lord. Paul's preaching was 'repentance toward God, and faith toward our Lord Jesus Christ.' And life eternal consists, first in 'knowing the only true God, and then Jesus Christ, whom he hath sent.' To take the Lord for our God, is the natural part of the covenant: the supernatural part is, to take Christ for our Redeemer. The former is first necessary, and implied in the latter. To accept Christ without affection and love, is not justifying faith. Nor does love follow as a fruit, but immediately concurs; for faith is the receiving of Christ with the whole soul. 'He that loveth father and mother more than Christ, is not worthy of him,' nor is justified by him. Faith accepts him for Saviour and Lord: for in both relations will he be received, or not at all. Faith not only acknowledges his sufferings, and accepts of pardon and glory, but acknowledges his sovereignty, and submits to his government and way of salvation.

10. (6.) As an essential part of the character of God's people, they now enter into a cordial covenant with Christ. The sinner was never strictly, nor comfortably, in covenant with Christ till now. He is sure by the free offers, that Christ consents; and now he cordially consents himself; and so the agreement is fully made.— With this covenant Christ delivers up himself in all comfortable relations to the sinner; and the sinner delivers up himself to be saved, and ruled by Christ. Now the soul resolutely concludes, 'I have been blindly led by flesh and lust, by the world and the devil, too long, almost to my utter destruction; I will now be wholly at the disposal of my Lord, who hath bought me with his blood, and will bring me to his glory.'

11. (7.) I add, that the people of God persevere in this covenant to the end. Though the believer may be tempted, yet he never disclaims his Lord, renounces his allegiance, nor repents of his covenant; nor can he properly be said to break that covenant, while that faith continues which is the condition of it. Indeed, those that have verbally covenanted, and not cordially, may 'tread under foot the blood of the covenant, as an unholy thing, wherewith they were sanctified,' by separation from those without the church; but the elect cannot be so deceived. Though this perseverance be certain to true believers, yet it is made a condition of their salvation; yea, of their continued life and fruitfulness, and of the continuance of their justification,

though not of their first justification itself. But eternally blessed be that hand of love, which hath drawn the free promise, and subscribed and sealed to that which ascertains us, both of the grace which is the condition, and the kingdom which on that condition is offered!

12. Such are the essentials of this people of God: not a full portraiture of them in all their excellencies, nor all the notes whereby they may be discerned. I beseech thee, reader, as thou hast the hope of a Christian, or the reason of a man, judge thyself, as one that must shortly be judged by a righteous God, and faithfully answer these questions. I will not inqure whether thou remember the time or the order of these workings of the Spirit: there may be much uncertainty and mistake in that. If thou art sure they are wrought in thee, the matter is not so great, though thou know not when or how thou camest by them. But carefully examine and inquire, Hast thou been thoroughly convinced of a prevailing depravation through thy whole soul? and a prevailing wickedness through thy whole life? and how vile sin is? and that, by the covenant thou hast transgressed, the least sin deserves eternal death? Dost thou consent to the law, that it is true and righteous, and perceive thyself sentenced to this death by it? Hast thou seen the utter insufficiency of every creature, either to be itself thy happiness, or the means of removing this thy misery? Hast thou been convinced, that thy happiness is only in God, as the end; and in Christ, as the way to him; and that thou must be brought to God through Christ, or perish eternally? Hast thou seen an absolute necessity of thy enjoying Christ, and the full sufficiency in him, to do for thee whatsoever thy case requires? Hast thou discovered the excellency of this pearl, to be worth thy 'selling all to buy it?' Have thy convictions been like those of a man that thirsts; and not merely a change in opinion, produced by reading or education? Have both thy sin and misery been the abhorrence and burden of thy soul? If thou couldst not weep, yet couldst thou heartily groan under the insupportable weight of both? Hast thou renounced all thy own righteousness? Hast thou turned thy idols out of thy heart, so that the creature hath no more the sovereignty, but is now a servant to God and Christ? Dost thou accept of Christ as thy only Saviour, and expect thy justification, recovery, and glory, from him alone? Are his laws the most powerful commanders of thy life and soul? Do they ordinarily prevail against the commands of the flesh, and against the greatest interest of thy credit, profit, pleasure or life? Has Christ the highest room in thy heart and affections, so that, though thou canst not love him as thou wouldst, yet nothing else is loved so much? Hast thou to this end made a hearty covenant with him, and delivered up thyself to him? Is it thy utmost care and watchful endeavour that thou mayest be found faithful in this covenant; and though thou fall into sin, yet wouldst thou not renounce thy bargain, nor change thy Lord, nor give up thyself to any other government for all the world?—If this be truly the case, thou art one of the people of God in my text; and as sure as the promise of God is true, this blessed rest remains for thee. Only see thou 'abide in Christ,' and 'endure to the end;' for 'if any man draw back, his soul shall have no pleasure in him.' But if no such work be found within thee; whatever thy deceived heart may think, or how strong soever thy false hopes may be; thou wilt find to thy cost, except thorough conversion prevent it, that the rest of the saints belongs not to thee. 'O that thou wert wise, that thou wouldst understand this, that thou wouldst consider thy latter end!' That yet while thy soul is in thy body, and 'a price in thy hand,' and opportunity and hope before thee, thine ears may be open, and thy heart yield to the persuasions of God, that so thou mightest rest among his people, and enjoy ' the inheritance of the saints in light !'

13. That this rest shall be enjoyed by the people of God, is a truth which the Scripture, if its testimony be further needed, clearly asserts in a variety of ways: as, for instance, that they are ' fore-ordained to it, and it for them.—God is not ashamed to be called their God, for he hath prepared for them a city.' They are styled 'vessels of mercy, afore prepared unto glory. In Christ they have obtained an inheritance, being predestinated according to the purpose of him who worketh all things after the council of of his own will.' And 'whom he did predestinate, them he also glorified.' Who can bereave his people of that rest which is designed for them by God's eternal purpose?—Scripture tells us, they are redeemed to this rest. ' By the blood of Jesus we have boldness to enter into the holiest;' whether that entrance means by faith and prayer here, or by full possession hereafter. Therefore the saints in heaven sing a new song unto him who has 'redeemed them to God by his blood, out of every kindred, and tongue, and people, and nation, and made them kings and priests unto God.' Either Christ, then, must lose his blood and sufferings, and never ' see of the travail of his soul, or else ' there remaineth a rest

to the people of God.' In Scripture this rest is promised to them. As the firmament with stars, so are the sacred pages, bespangled with these divine engagements. Christ says 'Fear not, little flock, for it is your Father's good pleasure to give you the kingdom.' 'I appoint unto you a kingdom, as my Father hath appointed unto me; that ye may eat and drink at my table in my kingdom.' All the means of grace, the operations of the Spirit upon the soul, and gracious actings of the saints, every command to repent and believe, to fast and pray, to knock and seek; to strive and labour, to run and fight, prove that there remains a rest for the people of God. The Spirit would never kindle in us such strong desires after heaven, such love to Jesus Christ, if we should not receive what we desire and love. He that 'guides our feet into the way of peace,' will undoubtedly bring us to the end of peace. How nearly are the means and end conjoined! 'The kingdom of heaven suffereth violence, and the violent take it by force.' They that 'follow Christ in the regeneration shall sit upon thrones of glory.' Scripture assures us, that the saints have the 'beginnings, foretastes, earnests, and seals,' of this rest here. 'The kingdom of God is within them.' 'Though they have not seen Christ, yet loving him, and believing in him, they rejoice with joy unspeakable and full of glory; receiving the end of their faith, even the salvation of their souls.' They 'rejoice in hope of the glory of God.' And does God 'seal them with that Holy Spirit of promise, which is the earnest of their inheritance,' and will he deny the full possession? The Scripture also mentions, by name, those who have entered into this rest,—as Enoch, Abraham, Lazarus, the thief that was crucified with Christ, &c. And if there be a rest for these, sure there is a rest for all believers. But it is vain to heap up Scripture proofs, seeing it is the very end of Scripture to be a guide to lead us to this blessed state, and to be the charter and grant by which we hold all our title to it.

14. Scripture not only proves that this rest remains for the people of God, but also that it remains for none but them; so that the rest of the world shall have no part in it. 'Without holiness no man shall see the Lord. Except a man be born again, he cannot see the kingdom of God. He that believeth not the Son shall not see life, but the wrath of God abideth on him. No whoremonger, nor unclean person, nor covetous man, who is an idolater, hath any inheritance in the kingdom of Christ and of God. The wicked shall be turned into hell, and all the nations that forget God. They all shall be damned, who believe not the truth, but have pleasure in unrighteousness. The Lord Jesus shall come, in flaming fire, taking vengeance on them that know not God, and that obey not the gospel of our Lord Jesus Christ; who shall be punished with everlasting destruction from the presence of the Lord, and from the glory of his power.' Had the ungodly returned before their life was expired, and been heartily willing to accept of Christ for their Saviour and their King, and to be saved by him in his way, and upon his most reasonable terms, they might have been saved. God freely offered them life, and they would not accept it. The pleasures of the flesh seemed more desirable to them than the glory of the saints. Satan offered them the one, and God offered them the other; and they had free liberty to choose which they would, and they chose 'the pleasures of sin for a season,' before the everlasting rest with Christ. And is it not a righteous thing that they should be denied that which they would not accept? When God pressed them so earnestly, and persuaded them so importunately, to come in, and yet they would not, where should they be but among the dogs without? Though man be so wicked, that he will not yield till the mighty power of grace prevail with him, yet still we may truly say, that he may be saved, if he will, on God's terms. His inability being moral, and lying in wilful wickedness, is no more excuse to him, than it is to an adulterer that he cannot love his own wife, or to a malicious person that he cannot but hate his own brother: is he not so much the worse, and deserving of so much the sorer punishment? Sinners shall lay all the blame on their own wills in hell for ever. Hell is a rational torment by conscience, according to the nature of the rational subject. If sinners could but then say, It was wrong of God, and not of us, it would quiet their consciences, and ease their torments, and make hell to them to be no hell. But to remember their wilfulness, will feed the fire, and cause the worm of conscience never to die.

15. It is the will of God, that this rest should yet remain for his people, and not be enjoyed till they come to another world. Who should dispose of the creatures, but he that made them? You may as well ask, Why have we not spring and harvest without winter? or, Why is the earth below and the heavens above? as, Why have we not rest on earth? All things must come to their perfection by degrees. The strongest man must first be a child. The greatest scholar must first begin with the alphabet. The tallest oak was once an acorn. This life is our infancy; and

would we be perfect in the womb, or born at full stature? If our rest was here, most of God's providences must be useless. Should God lose the glory of his church's miraculous deliverances, and the fall of his enemies, that men may have their happiness here? If we were all happy, innocent, and perfect, what use was there for the glorious works of our sanctification, justification, and future salvation?—If we wanted nothing, we should not depend on God so closely, nor call upon him so earnestly. How little should he hear from us, if we had what we would have! God would never have had such songs of praise from Moses at the Red Sea and in the wilderness, from Deborah and Hannah, from David and Hezekiah, if they had been the choosers of their condition. Have not thy own highest praises to God, reader, been occasioned by thy dangers or miseries? The greatest glory and praise God has through the world, is for redemption, reconciliation, and salvation by Christ; and was not man's misery the occasion of that?— And where God loses the opportunity of exercising his mercies, man must needs lose the happiness of enjoying them. Where God loses his praise, man will certainly lose his comforts. O the sweet comforts the saints have had in return to their prayers! How should we know what a tender-hearted Father we have, if we had not, as the prodigal, been denied the husks of earthly pleasure and profit? We should never have felt Christ's tender heart, if we had not felt ourselves weary and heavy laden, hungry and thirsty, poor and contrite. It is a delight to a soldier, or traveller, to look back on his escapes when they are over; and for a saint in heaven to look back on his sins and sorrows upon earth, his fears and tears, his enemies and dangers, his wants and calamities, must make his joy more joyful. Therefore the blessed, in praising the Lamb, mention his 'redeeming them out of every nation, and kindred, and tongue;' and so, out of their misery, and wants, and sins, 'and making them kings and priests to God.' But if they had had nothing but content and rest on earth, what room would there have been for these rejoicings hereafter?

16. Besides, we are not capable of rest upon earth.—Can a soul that is so weak in grace, so prone to sin, so nearly joined to such a neighbour as this flesh, have full content and rest in such a case? What is soul-rest but our freedom from sin, and imperfection, and enemies? And can the soul have rest that is pestered with all these, and that continually? Why do Christians so often cry out, in the language of Paul. 'O

wretched man that I am! who shall deliver me?' What makes them 'press towards the mark, and run that they may obtain, and strive to enter in,' if they are capable of rest in their present condition?—And our bodies are incapable as well as our souls. They are not now those sunlike bodies which they shall be, when this corruptible hath put on incorruption, and this mortal hath put on immortality. They are our prisons and our burdens; so full of infirmities and defects, that we are fain to spend most of our time in repairing them, and supplying their continual wants. Is it possible that an immortal soul should have rest in such a distempered noisome habitation. Surely these sickly, weary, loathsome bodies, must be refined, before they can be capable of enjoying rest. The objects we here enjoy are insufficient to afford us rest. Alas! what is there in all the world to give us rest? They that have most of it, have the greatest burden. They that set most by it, and rejoice most in it, do all cry out at last of its vanity and vexation. Men promise themselves a heaven upon earth: but when they come to enjoy it, it flies from them. He that has any regard to the works of the Lord, may easily see, that the very end of them is to take down our idols, to make us weary of the world, and seek our rest in him. Where does he cross us most, but where we promise ourselves most content? If you have a child you dote upon, it becomes your sorrow. If you have a friend you trust in, and judge unchangeable, he becomes your scourge. Is this a place or state of rest? And as the objects we here enjoy are insufficient for our rest, so God, who is sufficient, is here little enjoyed. It is not here that he hath prepared the presence-chamber of his glory. He hath drawn the curtain between us and him. We are far from him as creatures, and farther as frail mortals, and farthest as sinners. We hear now and then a word of comfort from him, and receive his love-tokens to keep up our hearts and hopes; but this is not our full enjoyment. And can any soul, that hath made God his portion, as every one hath that shall be saved by him, find rest in so vast a distance from him, and so seldom and small enjoyment of him? Nor are we now capable of rest, as there is a worthiness must go before it. Christ will give the crown to none but the worthy. And are we fit for the crown, before we have overcome? or for the prize, before we have run the race? or to receive our penny, before we have wrought in the vineyard? or to be rulers of ten cities, before we have improved our ten talents? or to enter into the joy of our Lord, before we have well done, as good and faithful servants? God will not alter the course of justice, to give you rest before you have laboured, nor the crown of glory till you have overcome. There is reason enough why our rest should remain till the life to come. Take heed, then, Christian reader, how thou darest to contrive and care for a rest on earth; or to murmur at God for thy trouble, and toil, and wants in the flesh. Doth thy poverty weary thee? Thy sickness, thy bitter enemies, and unkind friends? It should be so here. Do the abominations of the times, the sins of professors, the hardening of the wicked, all weary thee? It must be so while thou art absent from thy rest. Do thy sins, and thy naughty distempered heart weary thee? Be thus wearied more and more. But under all this weariness, art thou willing to go to God thy rest, and to have thy warfare accomplished, and thy race and labour ended? If not, complain more of thy own heart, and get it more weary, till rest seem more desirable.

17. I have but one thing more to add, for the close of this chapter,—that the souls of believers do enjoy inconceivable blessedness and glory, even while they remain separated from their bodies. What can be more plain than those words of Paul—'we are always confident, knowing that whilst we are at home,' or rather, sojourning, 'in the body, we are absent from the Lord; for we walk by faith, not by sight. We are confident, I say, and willing rather to be absent from the body, and to be present with the Lord.'—Or those, 'I am in a strait betwixt two, having a desire to depart, and to be with Christ, which is far better.'—If Paul had not expected to enjoy Christ till the resurrection, why should he be in a strait, or desire to depart? Nay, should he not have been loath to depart upon the very same grounds? For while he was in the flesh, he enjoyed something of Christ.—Plain enough is that of Christ to the thief, 'To-day shalt thou be with me in paradise.'—In the parable of Dives and Lazarus, it seems unlikely Christ would so evidently intimate and suppose the soul's happiness or misery presently after death, if there were no such matter. Our Lord's argument for the resurrection supposes that, 'God, being not the God of the dead, but of the living,' therefore Abraham, Isaac, and Jacob, were then living in soul.—If the 'blessedness of the dead that die in the Lord,' were only in resting in the grave, then a beast or a stone were as blessed; nay, it were evidently a curse, and not a blessing. For was not life a great mercy? Was it not a greater mercy to serve God, and to

do good; to enjoy all the comforts of life, the fellowship of saints, the comfort of ordinances, and much of Christ in all, than to lie rotting in the grave? Therefore some further blessedness is there promised.—How else is it said, 'We are come to the spirits of just men made perfect.' Sure, at the resurrection, the body will be made perfect, as well as the spirit. Does not Scripture tell us, that Enoch and Elias are taken up already? And shall we think they possess that glory alone?—Did not Peter, James and John see Moses also with Christ on the mount? yet the Scripture saith, Moses died. And is it likely that Christ deluded their senses, in showing them Moses, if he should not partake of that glory till the resurrection?—And is not that of Stephen as plain as we can desire? 'Lord Jesus, receive my spirit.' Surely, if the Lord receive it, it is neither asleep, nor dead, nor annihilated: but it is where he is, and beholds his glory.— That of the wise man is of the same import: 'The spirit shall return unto God who gave it.' Why are we said to have eternal life; and that to 'know God is life eternal;' and that a believer 'on the Son hath everlasting life?' Or how is 'the kingdom of God within us?' If there be as great an interruption of our life, as till the resurrection, this is no eternal life, nor everlasting kingdom.—The cities of Sodom and Gomorrah are spoken of as 'suffering the vengeance of eternal fire.' And if the wicked already suffer eternal fire, then, no doubt, but the godly enjoy eternal blessedness.—When John saw his glorious revelations, he is said to be 'in the Spirit,' and to be 'carried away in the Spirit.' And when Paul was caught up to the third heaven, he knew not 'whether in the body or out of the body.' This implies, that spirits are capable of these glorious things, without the help of their bodies.—Is not so much implied, when John says, 'I saw under the altar the souls of them that were slain for the word of God?' When Christ says, 'Fear not them who kill the body but are not able to kill the soul,' does it not plainly imply, that when wicked men have killed our bodies, that is, have separated the souls from them, yet the souls are still alive? The soul of Christ was alive when his body was dead, and therefore so shall be ours too. This appears by his words to the thief, 'To-day shalt thou be with me in paradise;' and also by his voice on the cross, 'Father, into thy hands I commend my spirit.' If the spirits of those that were disobedient in the days of Noah, were in prison, that is, in a living and suffering state; then certainly, the separate spirits of the just are in an opposite condition of happiness. Therefore, faithful souls will no sooner leave their prisons of flesh, but angels shall be their convoy; Christ, with all the perfected spirits of the just, will be their companions: heaven will be their residence, and God their happiness. When such die, they may boldly and believingly say, as Stephen, 'Lord Jesus, receive my spirit;' and commend it, as Christ did, into a Father's hands.

CHAPTER V.

THE GREAT MISERY OF THOSE WHO LOSE THE SAINTS' REST.

Sect. 1. The reader, if unregenerate, urged to consider what the loss of heaven will be. 2. (I.) The loss of heaven particularly includes, 3. (1.) The personal perfection of the saints; 4. (2.) God himself; 5. (3.) All delightful affections towards God; 6. (4.) The blessed society of angels and glorified spirits. 7. (II.) The aggravations of the loss of heaven: 8. (1.) The understanding of the ungodly will then be cleared; 9. (2.) also enlarged; 10. (3.) Their consciences will make a true and close application. 11. (4.) Their affections will be more lively; 12—18. (5.) Their memories will be large and strong. 19. Conclusion of the chapter.

1. If thou reader, art a stranger to Christ, and to the holy nature and life of his people, who art before described, and shalt live and die in this condition, let me tell thee, thou shalt never partake of the joys of heaven, nor have the least taste of the saints' eternal rest. I may say, as Ehud to Eglon, ' I have a message to thee from God;' that, as the word of God is true, thou shalt never see the face of God with comfort. This sentence I am commanded to pass upon thee; take it as thou wilt, and escape it if thou canst. I know thy humble and hearty subjection to Christ would procure thy escape; he would then acknowledge thee for one of his people, and give thee a portion in the inheritance of his chosen. If this might be the happy success of my message, I should be so far from repining, like Jonah, that the threatenings of God are not executed upon thee, that I should bless the day that ever God made me so happy a messenger. But if thou end thy days in thy unregenerate state, as sure as the heavens are over thy head, and the earth under thy feet, thou shalt be shut out of the rest of the saints, and receive thy portion in everlasting fire. I expect thou wilt turn upon me, and say, When did God show you the Book of Life, or tell you who they are that shall be saved, and who shut out? I answer, I do not name thee, nor any other; I only conclude it of the unregenerate in general, and of thee, if thou be such a one. Nor do I go about to determine who shall repent, and who shall not: much less, that thou shalt never repent. I had

rather show thee what hopes thou hast before thee, if thou wilt not sit still, and lose them. I would far rather persuade thee to hearken in time, before the door be shut against thee, than tell thee there is no hope of thy repenting and returning. But if the foregoing description of the people of God does not agree with the state of thy soul, is it then a hard question, whether thou shalt ever be saved? Need I ascend up into heaven to know, that ' without holiness no man shall see the Lord;' or, that only ' the pure in heart shall see God;' or, that ' except a man be born again, he cannot enter into the kingdom of God?' Need I go up to heaven, to inquire that of Christ, which he came down to earth to tell us; and sent his Spirit in his apostles to tell us; and which he and they have left upon record to all the world? And though I know not the secrets of thy heart, and therefore cannot tell thee by name, whether it be thy state or not; yet, if thou art but willing and diligent, thou mayest know thyself, whether thou art an heir of heaven or not. It is the main thing I desire, that if thou art yet miserable, thou mayest discern and escape it. But how canst thou escape, if thou neglect Christ and salvation? It is as impossible as for the devils themselves to be saved: nay, God has more plainly and frequently spoken it in Scripture of such sinners as thou art, than he has of the devils. Methinks a sight of thy case would strike thee with amazement and horror. When Belshazzar ' saw the fingers of a man's hand that wrote upon the wall, his countenance was changed and his thoughts troubled him, so that the joints of his loins were loosed, and his knees smote one against another.' What trembling then should seize on thee, who hast the hand of God himself against thee, not in a sentence or two, but in the very scope of the Scriptures, threatening the loss of an everlasting kingdom! Because I would fain have thee lay it to heart, I will show thee—the nature of thy loss of heaven,—together with its aggravations.

2. (I.) In their loss of heaven, the ungodly lose—the saints' personal perfection,—God himself,—all delightful affections towards God,—and the blessed society of angels and saints.

3. (1.) The glorious personal perfection which the saints enjoy in heaven, is the great loss of the ungodly. They lose that shining lustre of the body, surpassing the brightness of the sun at noonday. Though the bodies of the wicked will be raised more spiritual than they were upon earth, yet that will only make them capable of the more exquisite torments. They would be

glad then, if every member were a dead member, that it might not feel the punishment inflicted on it; and if the whole body were a rotten carcass, or might lie down again in the dust. Much more do they want that moral perfection which the blessed partake of; those holy dispositions of mind ; that cheerful readiness to do the will of God ; that perfect rectitude of all their actions ; instead of these, they have that perverseness of will, that loathing of good, that love to evil, that violence of passion, which they had on earth. It is true, their understandings will be much cleared by the ceasing of former temptation, and experiencing the falsehood of former delusions; but they have the same dispositions still, and fain would they commit the same sins, if they could : they want but opportunity There will be a greater difference between these wretches, and the glorified Christians, than there is betwixt a toad and the sun in the firmament. The rich man's purple and fine linen, and sumptuous fare, did not so exalt him above Lazarus while at his gate full of sores.

4. (2.) They shall have no comfortable relation to God, nor communion with him. ' As they did not like to retain God in their knowledge,' but said unto him, ' Depart from us, for we desire not the knowledge of thy ways ;' so God will abhor to retain them in his household. He will never admit them to the inheritance of his saints, nor endure them to stand in his presence, but ' will profess unto them, I never knew you ; depart from me ye that work iniquity.' They are ready now to lay as confident claim to Christ and heaven, as if they were sincere believing saints. The swearer, the drunkard, the whoremonger, the worldling, can say, Is not God our Father as well as yours ? But when Christ separates his followers from his foes, and his faithful friends from his deceived flatterers, where then will be their presumptuous claim ? Then they shall find that God is not their Father, because they would not be his people. As they would not consent that God by his Spirit should dwell in them, so the tabernacle of wickedness shall have no fellowship with him, nor the wicked inhabit the city of God. Only they that walked with God here, shall live and be happy with him in heaven. Little does the world know what a loss that soul hath who loses God. What a dungeon would the earth be, if it had lost the sun! What a loathsome carrion the body, if it had lost the soul! Yet all these are nothing to the loss of God. As the enjoyment of God is the heaven of the saints, so the loss of God is the hell of the ungodly ; and as the enjoying of God is the enjoying of all, so the loss of God is the loss of all.

5. (3.) They also lose all delightful affections towards God. That transporting knowledge ; those delightful views of his glorious face ; the inconceivable pleasure of loving him : the apprehensions of his infinite love to us ; the constant joys of his saints, and the rivers of consolation with which he satisfies them—Is it nothing to lose all this ? The employment of a king in ruling a kingdom, does not so far exceed that of the vilest slave, as this heavenly employment exceeds that of an earthly king. God suits men's employments to their natures. Your hearts, sinners, were never set upon God in your lives, never warmed with his love, never longed after the enjoyment of him ; you had no delight in speaking or hearing of him ; you had rather have continued on earth, if you had known how, than to be interested in the glorious praises of God. Is it meet, then, that you should be members of the celestial choir ?

6. (4.) They shall be deprived of the blessed society of angels and glorified saints. Instead of being companions of those happy spirits, and numbered with those triumphant kings, they must be members of the corporation of hell, where they shall have companions of a far different nature and quality. Scorning and abusing the saints, hating them, and rejoicing in their calamities, was not the way to obtain their blessedness. Now you are shut out of that company from which you first shut out yourselves ; and are separated from them, with whom you would not be joined. You could not endure them in your houses, nor towns, nor scarce in the kingdom. You took them, as Ahab did Elijah, for the 'troublers of the land,' and, as the apostles said, for 'men that turned the world upside down.' If any thing fell out amiss, you thought all was owing to them. When they were dead or banished, you were glad they were gone, and thought the country well rid of them. They molested you by faithfully reproving your sins. Their holy conversation troubled your consciences, to see them so far excel you. It was a vexation to you to hear them pray, or sing praises in their families. And is it any wonder if you be separated from them hereafter ? The day is near, when they will trouble you no more. Betwixt them and you will be a great gulf fixed. Even in this life, while the saints were mocked, destitute, afflicted, tormented, and while they had their personal imperfections ; yet, in the judgment of the Holy Ghost, they were such ' of whom the world was not

worth. Much more unworthy will the world be of their fellowship in glory.

7. (II.) I know many will be ready to think, they could spare these things in this world well enough, and why may they not be without them in the world to come ? Therefore, to show them that this loss of heaven will then be most tormenting, let them now consider—their understandings will be cleared to know their loss, and have more enlarged apprehensions concerning it—their consciences will make a closer application of it to themselves—their affections will no longer be stupified, nor their memories be treacherous.

8. (1.) The understanding of the ungodly will then be cleared, to know the worth of that which they have lost. Now they lament not their loss of God, because they never knew his excellence ; nor the loss of that holy employment and society, for they were never sensible what they were worth. A man that has lost a jewel, and took it but for a common stone, is never troubled at his loss ; but when he comes to know what he lost, then he laments it. Though the understanding of the damned will not be sanctified, yet they will be cleared from a multitude of errors. They now think that their honours, estates, pleasures, health, and life, are better worth their labour, than the things of another world ; but when these things have left them in misery, when they experience the things which before they did but read and hear of, they will be of another mind. They would not believe that water would drown, till they were in the sea ; nor the fire burn, till they were cast into it ; but when they feel, they will easily believe. All that error of mind which made them set light by God, and abhor his worship, and vilify his people, will then be confuted and removed by experience. Their knowledge shall be increased, that their sorrows may be increased. Poor souls ! they would be comparatively happy, if their understandings were wholly taken from them, if they had no more knowledge than idiots, or brute beasts ; or if they knew no more in hell, than they did upon earth, their loss would less trouble them. How happy would they then think themselves, if they did not know there is such a place as heaven ! Now, when their knowledge would help to prevent their misery, they will not know, or will not read or study that they may know ; therefore, when their knowledge will but feed their consuming fire, they shall know whether they will or not. They are now in a dead sleep, and dream they are the happiest men in the world ; but when death awakes them, how will their judgments be changed in a moment!

and they that would not see, shall then see and be ashamed.

9. (2.) As their understanding will be cleared, so it will be more enlarged, and made more capacious to conceive the worth of that glory which they have lost. The strength of their apprehensions, as well as the truth of them, will then be increased. What deep apprehensions of the wrath of God, the madness of sinning, the misery of sinners, have those souls that now endure this misery, in comparison with those on earth, that do but hear of it. What sensibility of the worth of life has the condemned man that is going to be executed, compared with what he was wont to have in the time of his prosperity ! Much more will the actual loss of eternal blessedness make the damned exceedingly apprehensive of the greatness of their loss : and as a large vessel will hold more water than a shell, so will their more enlarged understandings contain more matter to feed their torment, than their shallow capacity can now do.

10. (3.) Their consciences also will make a truer and closer application of this doctrine to themselves, which will exceedingly tend to increase their torment. It will then be no hard matter to them to say, ' This is my loss ! and this is my everlasting remediless misery !' The want of this self-application is the main cause why they are so little troubled now. They are hardly brought to believe that there is such a state of misery ; but more hardly to believe that it is like to be their own. This makes so many sermons lost to them, and all threatenings and warnings in vain. Let a minister of Christ show them their misery ever so plainly and faithfully, they will not be persuaded they are so miserable. Let him tell them of the glory they must lose, and the sufferings they must feel, and they think he means not them, but some notorious sinners. It is one of the hardest things in the world, to bring a wicked man to know that he is wicked, or to make him see himself in a state of wrath and condemnation. Though they may easily find, by their strangeness to the new-birth, and their enmity to holiness, that they never were partakers of them ; yet they as verily expect to see God, and be saved, as if they were the most sanctified persons in the world. How seldom do men cry out, after the plainest discovery of their state, I am the man ! or acknowledge, that if they die in their present condition, they are undone for ever ! But when they suddenly find themselves in the land of darkness, feel themselves in scorching flames, and see they are shut out of the presence of God for ever,

then the application of God's anger to themselves will be the easiest matter in the world : they will then roar out these forced confessions, ' O my misery ! O my folly ! O my inconceivable, irrecoverable loss !'

11. (4.) Then will their affections likewise be more lively, and no longer stupified. A hard heart now makes heaven and hell seem but trifles. We have showed them everlasting glory and misery, and they are as men asleep; our words are as stones cast against a wall, which fly back in our faces. We talk of terrible things, but it is to dead men ; we search the wounds, but they never feel us : we speak to rocks rather than to men ; the earth will as soon tremble as they. But when these dead souls are revived, what passionate sensibility ! what working affections ! what pangs of horror ! what depth of sorrow will there then be ! How violently will they fly in their own faces ? How will they rage against their former madness ! The lamentations of the most affectionate wife for the loss of her husband, or of the tenderest mother for the loss of her children, will be nothing to theirs for the loss of heaven. O the self-accusing and self-tormenting fury of those forlorn creatures ! How will they even tear their own hearts, and be God's executioners upon themselves ! As themselves were the only meritorious cause of their sufferings, so themselves will be the chief executioners. Even Satan, as he was not so great a cause of their sinning as themselves, he will not be so great an instrument of their torment. How happy would they think themselves then, if they were turned into rocks, or any thing that had neither passion nor sense ! How happy, if they could then feel, as lightly as they were wont to hear! if they could sleep out the time of execution, as they did the time of the sermons that warned them of it ! But their stupidity is gone ; it will not be.

12. (5.) Their memories will, moreover, be as large and as strong as their understandings and affections. Could they but lose the use of their memory, their loss of heaven being forgot, would little trouble them. Though they would account annihilation a singular mercy, they cannot lay aside any part of their being. ' Understanding, conscience, affections, memory, must all live to torment them, which should have helped to their happiness. As by these they should have fed upon the love of God, and drawn forth perpetually the joys of his presence, so by these must they feed upon his wrath, and draw forth continually the pains of his absence. Now they have no leisure to consider, nor any room in their memories for the things of another life ; but

then they shall have nothing else to do : their memories shall have no other employment. God would have had the doctrine of their eternal state ' written on the posts of their doors, on their hands and hearts :' he would have had them mind it, 'and mention it when they lay down and rose up, when they sat in their houses, and when they walked by the way ;' and seeing they rejected this counsel of the Lord, therefore it shall be written always before them in the place of their thraldom. that. which way soever they look, they may still behold it. It will torment them to think of the greatness of the glory they have lost. If it had been what they could have spared, or a loss to be repaired with any thing else, it had been a smaller matter. If it had been health, or wealth, or friends, or life, it had been nothing. But, O ! to lose that exceeding eternal weight of glory !—It will also torment them to think of the possibility they once had of obtaining it. Then they will remember, ' Time was, when I was as fair for the kingdom as others. I was set upon the stage of the world : if I had played my part wisely and faithfully, I might now have had possession of the inheritance. I, who am now tormented with these damned fiends, might have been among yonder blessed saints. The Lord did set before me life and death ; and having chosen death, I deserve to suffer it. The prize was held out before me; if I had run well. I might have obtained it ; if I had striven, I might have had the victory ; if I had fought valiantly, I had been crowned.'—It will yet more torment them to remember, that their obtaining the crown was not only possible, but very probable. It will wound them to think, 'I had once the gales of the Spirit ready to have assisted me. I was proposing to be another man, to have cleaved to Christ, and forsake the world. I was almost resolved to have been wholly for God. I was once even turning from my base seducing lusts. I had cast off my old companions, and was associating with the godly—yet I turned back, lost my hold, and broke my promises. I was almost persuaded to be a real Christian, yet I conquered those persuasions. What workings were in my heart, when a faithful minister pressed home the truth ! O how fair was I once for heaven ! I almost had it, and yet I have lost it. Had I followed on to seek the Lord, I had now been blessed among the saints.'

13. It will exceedingly torment them to remember their lost opportunities. ' How many weeks, and months. and years, did I lose, which if I had improved, I might now have been happy. Wretch that I was ! could I find no time to study

the work, for which I had all my time? no time among all my labours, to labour for eternity? Had I time to eat, and drink, and sleep, and none to save my soul? Had I time for mirth and vain discourse, and none for prayer? Could I take time to secure the world, and none to try my title to heaven? O precious time! I had once enough, and now I must have no more. I had once so much, I knew not what to do with it; and now it is gone, and cannot be recalled. O that I had but one of those years to live over again? How speedily would I repent! How earnestly would I pray! How diligently would I hear! How closely would I examine my state! How strictly would I live! But it is now too late, alas! too late!'

14. It will add to their calamity to remember how oft they were persuaded to return. ' Fain would the minister have had me escape these torments. With what love and compassion did he beseech me! and yet I did but make a jest of it. How often did he convince me! and yet I stifled all these convictions. How did he open to me my very heart! and yet I was loathe to know the worst of myself. O how glad would he have been, if he could have seen me cordially turn to Christ! My godly friends admonished me: they told me what would become of my wilfulness and negligence at last; but I neither believed nor regarded them. How long did God himself condescend to entreat me! How did the Spirit strive with my heart, as if he was loathe to take denial! How did Christ stand knocking, one Sabbath after another, and crying to me, ' Open, sinner, open thy heart to thy Saviour, and I will come in, and sup with thee, and thou with me, ' Why dost thou delay? How long shall thy vain thoughts lodge within thee? Wilt thou not be pardoned, and sanctified, and made happy? When shall it once be?'—O how the recollection of such divine pleadings will passionately transport the damned with self-indignation! ' Must I tire out the patience of Christ? Must I make the God of heaven follow me in vain, till I had wearied him with crying to me, Repent! return! O how justly is that patience now turned into fury, which falls upon me with irresistible violence! When the Lord cried to me, Wilt thou not be made clean? when shall it once be? my heart, or at least my practice, answered, Never. And now when I cry, How long shall it be till I am freed from this torment? how justly do I receive the same answer, Never, never!'

15. It will also be most cutting to remember on what easy terms they might have escaped their misery. This work was not to remove moun-

tains, nor conquer kingdoms, nor fulfil the law to the smallest tittle, nor satisfy justice for all their transgressions. The yoke was easy, and the burden light, which Christ would have laid upon them. It was but to repent, and cordially accept him for their Saviour; to renounce all other happiness, and take the Lord for their supreme good; to renounce the world and the flesh, and submit to his meek and gracious government; and to forsake the ways of their own devising, and walk in his holy delightful way. ' Ah,' thinks the poor tormented wretch, ' how justly do I suffer all this, who would not be at so small pains to avoid it! Where was my understanding, when I neglected that gracious offer; when I called the Lord a hard master, and thought his pleasant service a bondage, and the service of the devil and the flesh the only freedom? Was I not a thousand times worse than mad, when I censured the holy way of God as needless preciseness; when I thought the laws of Christ too strict, and all too much that I did for the life to come? What would all sufferings for Christ and well-doing have been, compared with these sufferings that I must undergo for ever? Would not the heaven, which I have lost, have recompensed all my losses? And should not all my sufferings have been there forgotten? What if Christ had bid me to do some great matter; whether to live in continual fears and sorrows, or to suffer death a hundred times over: should I not have done it? How much more, when he only said, ' Believe and be saved. Seek my face, and thy soul shall live. Take up thy cross, and follow me, and I will give thee everlasting life.' O gracious offer! O easy terms! O cursed wretch, that would not be persuaded to accept them !'

16. This also will be a most tormenting consideration, to remember what they sold their eternal welfare for. When they compare the value of the pleasures of sin, with the value of 'the recompense of reward,' how will the vast disproportion astonish them! To think of the low delights of the flesh, or the applauding breath of mortals, or the possessing heaps of gold, and then to think of everlasting glory. ' This is all I had for my soul, my God, my hopes of blessedness!' It cannot possibly be expressed how these thoughts will tear his very heart. Then will he exclaim against his folly—' O miserable wretch! Did I set my soul to sale for so base a price? Did I part with my God for a little dirt and dross; and sell my Saviour, as Judas, for a little silver? I had but a dream of delight, for my hopes of heaven; and now I am awakened, it is all vanished. My morsels are now turned to

gall, and my cups to wormwood. When they were past my taste, the pleasures perished. And is this all that I have had for the inestimable treasure? What a mad exchange did I make! What if I had gained all the world, and lost my soul? But, alas! how small a part of the world was it for which I gave up my part in glory!' O that sinners would think of this, when they are swimming in the delights of the flesh, and studying how to be rich and honourable in the world! When they are desperately venturing upon known transgression, and sinning against the checks of conscience!

17. It will add yet more to their torment, when they consider that they most wilfully procured their own destruction. Had they been forced to sin, it would much abate the rage of their consciences; or if they were punished for another man's transgressions; or any other had been the chief author of their ruin. But to think it was the choice of their own will, and that none in the world could have forced them to sin against their wills; this will be a cutting thought. ' Had I not enemies enough in the world, (thinks this miserable creature,) but I must be an enemy to myself? God would never give the devil, nor the world, so much power over me, as to force me to commit the least transgression. They could but entice; it was myself that yielded and did the evil. And must I lay hands upon my own soul, and imbrue my hands in my own blood? Never had I so great an enemy as myself. Never did God offer any good to my soul, but I resisted him. He hath heaped mercy upon me, and renewed one deliverance after another to draw my heart to him; yea, he hath greatly chastised me, and made me groan under the fruit of my disobedience; and though I promised largely in my affliction, yet never was I heartily willing to serve him.' Thus will it gnaw the hearts of these sinners, to remember that they were the cause of their own undoing, and that they wilfully and obstinately persisted in their rebellion, and were mere volunteers in the service of the devil.

18. The wound in their consciences will be yet deeper, when they shall not only remember it was their own doing, but that they were at so much cost and pains for their own damnation. What great undertakings did they engage in to effect their ruin; to resist the Spirit of God; to overcome the power of mercies, judgments, and even the word of God; to subdue the power of reason, and silence conscience. All this they undertook and performed. Though they walked in continual danger of the wrath of God, and knew he could lay them in the dust, and cast them into hell in a moment; yet would they run upon all this. O the labour it costs sinners to be damned! Sobriety, with health and ease, they might have had at a cheaper rate; yet they will rather have gluttony and drunkenness, with poverty, shame, and sickness. Contentment they might have, with ease and delight: yet they will rather have covetousness and ambition, though it costs them cares and fears, labour of body, and distraction of mind. Though their anger be self-torment, and revenge, and envy consume their spirits; though uncleanness destroy their bodies, estates, and good names; yet will they do and suffer all this, rather than suffer their souls to be saved. With what rage will they lament their folly, and say, ' Was damnation worth all my cost and pains? Might I not have been damned on free cost, but I must purchase it so dearly? I thought I could have been saved without so much ado, and could I not have been destroyed without so much ado? Must I so laboriously work out my own damnation, when God commanded me to work out my own salvation? If I had done as much for heaven, as I did for hell, I had surely had it. I cried out of the tedious ways of godliness, and the painful course of self-denial; and yet I could be at a great deal more pains for Satan and for death. Had I loved Christ as strongly as I did my pleasures, and profits, and honours, and thought on him as often, and sought him as painfully, O how happy had I now been! But justly do I suffer the flames of hell, for buying them so dear, rather than have heaven, when it was purchased to my hands!'

19. O that God would persuade thee, reader, to take up these thoughts now, for preventing the inconceivable calamity of taking them up in hell as thy own tormentor! Say not that they are only imaginary. Read what Dives thought, being in torments. As the joys of heaven are chiefly enjoyed by the rational soul in its rational actings, so must the pains of hell be suffered. As they will be men still, so will they feel and act as men.

———

CHAPTER VI.

THE MISERY OF THOSE, WHO, BESIDES LOSING THE
SAINTS' REST, LOSE THE ENJOYMENTS OF TIME, AND
SUFFER THE TORMENTS OF HELL.

Sect. 1. The connection of this with the preceding chapter. 2. (I.)
The enjoyments of time which the damned lose: 3. (1.) Their
presumptuous belief of their interest in God and Christ; 4. (2.)
All their hopes; 5. (3.) All their peace of conscience; 6. (4.) All
their carnal mirth; 7. (5.) All their sensual delights. 8. (II.) The
torments of the damned are exceeding great: 9. (1.) The principal author of them is God himself: 10. (2.) The place or state of
torment; 11. (3.) These torments are the effects of divine vengeance; 12. (4.) God will take pleasure in executing them; 13.
(5.) Satan and sinners themselves will be God's executioners; 14.
(6.) These torments will be universal; 15. (7.) Without any mitigation; 16. (8.) And eternal. 17. The obstinate sinner convinced
of his folly in venturing on these torments; 18. And entreated to
fly for safety to Christ.

1. As godliness hath a promise of the life that
now is, and of that which is to come; and if we
' seek first the kingdom of God and his righteousness,' then all meaner ' things shall be added
unto us ;' so also are the ungodly threatened with
the loss both of spiritual and temporal blessings ;
and because they sought not first God's kingdom
and righteousness, therefore shall they lose both
it and that which they did seek, and there ' shall
be taken from them that little which they have.'
If they could but have kept their present enjoyments, they would not have much cared for the
loss of heaven. If they had lost and forsaken all
for Christ, they would have found all again in
him ; for he would have been all in all to them.
But now they have forsook Christ for other things,
they shall lose Christ, and that also for which
they forsook him; even the enjoyments of time,
besides suffering the torments of hell.

2. (I.) Among the enjoyments of time, they
shall particularly lose—their presumptuous belief of their interest in the favour of God, and
the merits of Christ—all their hopes—all their
false peace of conscience—all their carnal mirth
—and all their sensual delights.

3. (1.) They shall lose their presumptuous belief of their interest in the favour of God, and
the merits of Christ. This false belief now supports their spirits, and defends them from the
terrors that would otherwise seize upon them.
But what will ease their trouble, when they can
believe no longer, nor rejoice any longer ? If a
man be near to the greatest mischief, and yet
strongly conceit that he is in safety, he may be
as cheerful as if all were well. If there were no
more to make a man happy, but to believe that
he is so, or shall be so, happiness would be far
more common than it is like to be. As true faith
is the leading grace in the regenerate, so is false
faith the leading vice in the unregenerate. Why
do such multitudes sit still, when they might

have pardon, but that they verily think they are
pardoned already ? If you could ask thousands
in hell, what madness brought them thither ? they
would most of them answer, ' We made sure of
being saved, till we found ourselves damned.
We would have been more earnest seekers of
regeneration, and the power of godliness, but we
verily thought we were Christians before. We
have flattered ourselves into these torments, and
now there is no remedy.' Reader, I must in
faithfulness tell thee, that the confident belief of
their good state, which the careless, unholy, unhumbled multitude so commonly boast of, will
prove in the end but a soul-damning delusion.
There is none of this believing in hell. It was
Satan's stratagem, that being blindfold they might
follow him the more boldly : but then he will uncover their eyes, and they shall see where they
are.

4. (2.) They shall lose also all their hopes. In
this life, though they were threatened with the
wrath of God, yet their hope of escaping it bore
up their hearts. We can now scarce speak with
the vilest drunkard, or swearer, or scoffer, but
he hopes to be saved for all this. O happy world,
if salvation were as common as this hope ! Nay,
so strong are men's hopes, that they will dispute
the cause with Christ himself at judgment, and
plead their ' having eat and drank in his presence,
and prophesied in his name, and in his name cast
out devils ;' they will stiffly deny that ever they
neglected Christ in hunger, nakedness, or in prison, till he confutes them with the sentence of
their condemnation. O the sad state of those
men, when they must bid farewell to all their
hopes ! ' When a wicked man dieth, his expectation shall perish ; and the hope of unjust men
perisheth. The eyes of the wicked shall fail,
and they shall not escape, and their hope shall
be as the giving up of the ghost.' The giving up
the ghost, is a fit, but terrible resemblance of a
wicked man giving up his hopes. As the soul
departeth not from the body without the greatest
pain ; so doth the hope of the wicked depart. The
soul departs from the body suddenly, in a moment,
which hath there delightfully continued so many
years : just so doth the hope of the wicked depart. The soul will never more return to live
with the body in this world ; and the hope of the
wicked takes an everlasting farewell of his soul.
A miracle of resurrection shall again unite soul
and body, but there shall be no such miraculous
resurrection of the damned's hope. Methinks,
it is the most pitiable sight this world affords, to
see such an ungodly person dying, and to think
of his soul and his hopes departing together

With what a sad change he appears in another world! Then if a man could but ask that hopeless soul, 'Are you as confident of salvation as you were wont to be?' what a sad answer would be returned! O that careless sinners would be awakened to think of this in time! Reader, rest not till thou canst give a reason of all thy hopes, grounded upon Scripture-promises—that they purify thy heart; that they quicken thy endeavours in godliness; that the more thou hopest, the less thou sinnest, and the more exact is thy obedience. If thy hopes be such as these, go on in the strength of the Lord, hold fast thy hope, and never shall it make thee ashamed. But if thou hast not one sound evidence of a work of grace on thy soul, cast away thy hopes. Despair of ever being saved, except thou be born again; or of seeing God, without holiness; or of having part in Christ, except thou love him above father, mother, or thy own life. This kind of despair is one of the first steps to heaven. If a man be quite out of his way, what must be the first means to bring him in again? He must despair of ever coming to his journey's end in the way that he is in. If his home be eastward, and he is going westward, as long as he hopes he is right, he will go on; and as long as he goes on hoping, he goes farther amiss. When he despairs of coming home, except he turn back, then he will return, and then he may hope. Just so it is, sinner, with thy soul: thou art born out of the way to heaven, and hast proceeded many a year; thou goest on, and hopest to be saved, because thou art not so bad as many others. Except thou throwest away these hopes, and see that thou hast all this while been quite out of the way to heaven, thou wilt never return and be saved. There is nothing in the world more likely to keep thy soul out of heaven, than thy false hopes of being saved, while thou art out of the way to salvation. See, then, how it will aggravate the misery of the damned, that, with the loss of heaven, they shall lose all that hope of it which now supports them.

5. (3.) They will lose all that false peace of conscience, which makes their present life so easy. Who would think, that sees how quietly the multitude of the ungodly live, that they must very shortly lie down in everlasting flames? They are as free from the fears of hell as an obedient believer; and for the most part have less disquiet of mind than those who shall be saved. Happy men, if this peace would prove lasting! 'When they shall say, peace and safety; then sudden destruction cometh upon them, as travail upon a woman with child; and they shall not escape.' O cruel peace, which ends in such a war! The soul of every man by nature is Satan's garrison: all is at peace in such a man till Christ comes, and gives it terrible alarms of judgment and hell, batters it with the ordnance of his threats and terrors, forces it to yield to his mere mercy and take him for the Governor —then doth he cast out Satan, 'overcome him, take from him all his armour wherein he trusted, and divideth his spoils,' and then doth he establish a firm and lasting peace. If, therefore, thou art yet in that first peace, never think it will endure. Can thy soul have lasting peace, in enmity with Christ? Can he have peace, against whom God proclaims war? I wish thee no greater good, than that God break in upon thy careless heart, and shake thee out of thy false peace, and make thee lie down at the feet of Christ, and say, 'Lord, what wouldst thou have me to do?' and so receive from him a better and surer peace, which will never be quite broken, but be the beginning of thy everlasting peace, and not perish in thy perishing, as the groundless peace of the world will do.

6. (4.) They shall lose all their carnal mirth. They will themselves say of their 'laughter, it is mad; and of their mirth, what doeth it?' It was but 'as the crackling of thorns under a pot.' It made a blaze for a while, but it was presently gone, and returned no more. The talk of death and judgment was irksome to them, because it damped their mirth. They could not endure to think of their sin and danger, because these thoughts sunk their spirits. They knew not what it was to weep for sin, or to humble themselves under the mighty hand of God. They could laugh away sorrow, and sing away cares, and drive away those melancholy thoughts. To meditate, and pray, they fancied would be enough to make them miserable, or run mad. Poor souls! what a misery will that life be, where you shall have nothing but sorrow; intense, heart-piercing, multiplied sorrow; when you shall neither have the joys of saints, nor your own former joys! Do you think there is one merry heart in hell; or one joyful countenance, or jesting tongue? You now cry, 'A little mirth is worth a great deal of sorrow:' but surely, a little godly sorrow, which would have ended in eternal joy, had been worth much more than all your foolish mirth; for the end of such mirth is sorrow.

7. (5.) They shall also lose all their sensual delights. That which they esteemed their chief good, their heaven, their god, must they lose, as well as God himself. What a fall will the proud,

ambitious man, have from the top of his honours! As his dust and bones will not be known from the dust and bones of the poorest beggar; so, neither will his soul be honoured or favoured more than theirs. What a number of the great, noble, and learned, will be shut out from the presence of Christ! They shall not find their magnificent buildings, soft beds, and easy couches. They shall not view their curious gardens, their pleasant meadows, and plenteous harvests. Their tables will not be so furnished, nor attended. The rich man is there no more 'clothed in purple and fine linen, nor fareth sumptuously every day.' There is no expecting the admiration of beholders. They shall spend their time in sadness, and not in sports and pastimes. What an alteration will they then find! The heat of their lust will be then abated. How will it even cut them to the heart, to look each other in the face! What an interview will there be, cursing the day that ever they saw another! O that sinners would now remember, and say, 'Will these delights accompany us into the other world? Will not the remembrance of them be then our torment? Shall we then take this partnership in vice for true friendship? Why should we sell such lasting, incomprehensible joys, for a taste of seeming pleasure? Come, as we have sinned together, let us pray together, that God would pardon us; and let us help one another towards heaven, instead of helping to deceive and destroy each other.' O that men knew but what they desire, when they would so fain have all things suited to the desires of the flesh! It is but to desire their temptations to be increased, and their snares strengthened.

8. (II.) As the loss of the saints' rest will be aggravated by losing the enjoyments of time, it will be much more so by suffering the torments of hell. The exceeding greatness of such torments may appear by considering—the principal author of them, who is God himself—the place or state of torment—that these torments are the fruits of divine vengeance—that the Almighty takes pleasure in them—that Satan and sinners themselves shall be God's executioners —that these torments shall be universal—without mitigation —and without end.

9. (1.) The principal author of hell-torments is God himself. As it was no less than God whom the sinners had offended, so it is no less than God who will punish them for their offences. He hath prepared those torments for his enemies. His continued anger will still be devouring them. His breath of indignation will kindle the flames. His wrath will be an intole-

rable burden to their souls. If it were but a creature they had to do with, they might better bear it. Woe to him that falls under the strokes of the Almighty! 'It is a fearful thing to fall into the hands of the living God.' It were nothing in comparison to this, if all the world were against them, or if the strength of all creatures were united in one to inflict their penalty. They had now rather venture to displease God, than displease a landlord, a customer, a master, a friend, a neighbour, or their own flesh; but then they will wish a thousand times in vain, that they had been hated of all the world, rather than have lost the favour of God. What a consuming fire is his wrath! If it be kindled here but a little, how do we wither like the grass! How soon doth our strength decay, and turn to weakness, and our beauty to deformity! The flames do not so easily run through the dry stubble, as the wrath of God will consume these wretches. They that could not bear a prison, or a gibbet, or a fire, for Christ, nor scarce a few scoffs, how will they now bear the devouring flames of divine wrath?

10. (2.) The place or state of torment is purposely ordained to glorify the justice of God. When God would glorify his power, he made the worlds. The comely order of all his creatures, declareth his wisdom. His providence is shown in sustaining all things. When a spark of his wrath kindles upon the earth, the whole world, except only eight persons, are drowned; Sodom, Gomorrah, Admah, and Zeboim, are burnt with fire from heaven; the sea shuts her mouth upon some, the earth opens and swallows up others; the pestilence destroys by thousands. What a standing witness of the wrath of God, is the present deplorable state of the Jews! Yet the glorifying the mercy and justice of God is intended most eminently for the life to come. As God will then glorify his mercy in a way that is now beyond the comprehension of the saints that must enjoy it; so also will he manifest his justice to be indeed the justice of God. The everlasting flames of hell will not be thought too hot for the rebellious; and, when they have there burned through millions of ages, he will not repent him of the evil which has befallen them. Woe to the soul that is thus set up as a butt for the wrath of the Almighty to shoot at! and as a bush that must burn in the flames of his jealousy, and never be consumed!

11. (3.) The torments of the damned must be extreme, because they are the effect of divine vengeance. Wrath is terrible, but revenge is implacable. When the great God shall say, 'My rebellious creatures shall now pay for all the

abuse of my patience. Remember how I waited your leisure in vain, how I stooped to persuade and entreat you. Did you think I would always be so slighted?' Then will he be revenged for every abused mercy, and for all their neglects of Christ and grace. O that men would foresee this, and please God better in preventing their woe!

12. (4.) Consider also, that though God had rather men would accept of Christ and mercy, yet, when they persist in rebellion, he will take pleasure in their execution. He tells us, 'fury is not in me:' yet he adds, 'who would set the briers and thorns against me in battle; I would go through them, I would burn them together.' Wretched creatures! when he that made them will not have mercy upon them, and he that formed them will show them no favour. As the Lord rejoiced over them to do them good; so the Lord will rejoice over them to destroy them, and to bring them to nought. Woe to the souls whom God rejoiceth to punish! 'He will laugh at their calamity, he will mock when their fear cometh: when their fear cometh as desolation, and their destruction cometh as a whirlwind; when distress and anguish cometh upon them.' Terrible thing, when none in heaven or earth can help them but God, and he shall rejoice in their calamity! Though Scripture speaks of God's laughing and mocking, not literally, but after the manner of men; yet it is such an act of God, in tormenting the sinner, which cannot otherwise be more fitly expressed.

13. (5.) Consider that Satan and themselves shall be God's executioners. He that was here so successful in drawing them from Christ, will then be the instrument of their punishment, for yielding to his temptations. That is the reward he will give them for all their service; for their rejecting the commands of God, forsaking Christ, and neglecting their souls at his persuasion. If they had served Christ as faithfully as they did Satan, he would have given them a better reward. It is also most just, that they should be their own tormentors, that they may see their whole destruction is of themselves; and then, whom can they complain of but themselves?

14. (6.) Consider also that their torment will be universal. As all parts have joined in sin, so must they all partake in the torment. The soul, as it was the chief in sinning, shall be the chief in suffering; and as it is of a more excellent nature than the body, so will its torments far exceed bodily torments: and as its joys far surpass all sensual pleasures, so the pains of the soul exceed corporeal pains.—It is not only a soul, but a sinful soul, that must suffer. Fire will not burn, except the fuel be combustible; but if the wood be dry, how fiercely will it burn? The guilt of their sins will be to the damned souls like tinder to gunpowder, to make the flames of hell take hold upon them with fury. — The body must also bear its part. That body, which was so carefully looked to, so tenderly cherished, so curiously dressed, what must it now endure! How are its haughty looks now taken down! How little will those flames regard its comeliness and beauty! Those eyes, which were wont to be delighted with curious sights, must then see nothing but what shall terrify them; an angry God above them, with those saints whom they scorned, enjoying the glory which they have lost; and about them will be only devils and damned souls. How will they look back, and say, 'Are all our feasts, and games, and revels come to this?' Those ears which were accustomed to music and songs, shall hear the shrieks and cries of their damned companions: children crying out against their parents, that gave them encouragement and example in evil; husbands and wives, masters and servants, ministers and people, magistrates and subjects, charging their misery upon one another, for discouraging in duty, conniving at sin, and being silent, when they should have plainly foretold the danger. Thus will soul and body be companions in woe.

15. (7.) Far greater will these torments be, because without mitigation. In this life, when told of hell, or if conscience troubled their peace, they had comforters at hand; their carnal friends, their business, their company, their mirth. They could drink, play, or sleep away their sorrows. But now all these remedies are vanished. Their hard presumptuous unbelieving heart was a wall to defend them against trouble of mind. Satan was himself their comforter, as he was to our first mother: 'Hath God said, ye shall not eat? Ye shall not surely die. Doth God tell you that you shall lie in hell? It is no such matter: God is more merciful. Or if there be a hell, what need you fear it? Are not you Christians? Was not the blood of Christ shed for you?' Thus, as the Spirit of Christ is the comforter of the saints, so Satan is the comforter of the wicked. Never was a thief more careful lest he should awake the people, when he is robbing the house, than Satan is not to awaken a sinner. But when the sinner is dead, then Satan hath done flattering and comforting. Which way, then, will the forlorn sinner look for comfort? They that drew him into the

snare, and promised him safety, now forsake him, and are forsaken themselves, his comforts are gone, and the righteous God, whose forewarnings he made light of, will now make good his word against him to the least tittle.

16. (8.) But the greatest aggravation of these torments will be their eternity. When a thousand millions of ages are past, they are as fresh to begin as the first day. If there were any hope of an end, it would ease the damned to foresee it; but *for ever* is an intolerable thought. They were never weary of sinning, nor will God be weary of punishing. They never heartily repented of sin, nor will God repent of their suffering. They broke the laws of the eternal God, and therefore shall suffer eternal punishment. They knew it was an everlasting kingdom which they refused, and what wonder if they are everlastingly shut out of it. Their immortal souls were guilty of the trespass, and therefore must immortally suffer the pains. What happy men would they think themselves, if they might have lain still in their graves, or might but there lie down again! How will they call and cry, ' O death! whither art thou now gone? Now come and cut off this doleful life. O that these pains would break my heart, and end my being! O that I might once at last die! O that I had never had a being!' These groans will the thoughts of eternity wring from their hearts. They were wont to think sermons and prayers long; how long then will they think these endless torments. What difference is there betwixt the length of their pleasures and their pains! The one continued but a moment, the other endureth through all eternity. Sinner, remember how time is almost gone. Thou art standing at the door of eternity; and death is waiting to open the door, and put thee in. Go, sleep out a few more nights, and stir about a few more days on earth, and then thy nights and days shall end: thy thoughts, and cares, and pleasures, shall all be devoured by eternity; thou must enter upon the state which shall never be changed. As the joys of heaven are beyond our conception, so are the pains of hell. Everlasting torment is inconceivable torment.

17. But methinks I see the obstinate sinner desperately resolving, ' If I must be damned, there is no remedy. Rather than I will live as the Scripture requires, I will put it to the venture; I shall escape as well as the rest of my neighbours, and we will even bear it as well as we can.' Alas! poor creature, let me beg this of thee, before thou dost so flatly resolve, that thou wouldst lend me thy attention to a few questions, and weigh

them with the reason of a man. Who art thou, that thou shouldst bear the wrath of God? Art thou a god or a man? What is thy strength? Is it not as the strength of wax, or stubble, to resist the fire; or as chaff to the wind; or as dust before the fierce whirlwind? If thy strength were as iron, and thy bones as brass; if thy foundation were as the earth, and thy power as the heavens, yet shouldst thou perish at the breath of his indignation. How much more, when thou art but a piece of breathing clay, kept a few days from being eaten with worms, by the mere support and favour of him whom thou art thus resisting!—Why dost thou tremble at the signs of almighty power and wrath? at claps of thunder, or flashes of lightning; or that unseen power which rends in pieces the mighty oaks, and tears down the strongest buildings; or at the plague, when it rageth around thee? If thou hadst seen the plagues of Egypt, or the earth swallow up Dathan and Abiram; or Elijah bring fire from heaven to destroy the captains and their companies, would not any of these sights have daunted thy spirit? How then canst thou bear the plagues of hell?—Why art thou dismayed with such small sufferings as befal thee here? A toothache; a fit of the gout, or stone; the loss of a limb, or falling into beggary and disgrace? And yet all these laid together will be one day accounted a happy state, in comparison of that which is suffered in hell.—Why does the approach of death so much affright thee? O how cold it strikes to thy heart! And would no, the grave be accounted a paradise, compared with that place of torment which thou slightest? —Is it an intolerable thing to burn part of thy body, by holding it in the fire? What then will it be to suffer ten thousand times more for ever in hell?—Why does the thought or mention of hell occasion any disquiet in thy spirit? And canst thou endure the torments themselves?— Why doth the rich man complain to Abraham of his torments in hell? Or thy dying companions lose their courage, and change their haughty language?—Why cannot these make as light of hell as thyself?—Didst thou never see or speak with a man under despair? How uncomfortable was his talk! How burdensome his life! Nothing he possessed did him good: he had no sweetness in meat or drink; the sight of friends troubled him; he was weary of life, and fearful of death. If the misery of the damned can be endured, why cannot a man more easily endure these foretastes of hell? What if thou shouldst see the devil appear to thee in some terrible shape? Would not thy heart fail thee, and thy hair stand on an end? And how wilt thou endure to live for ever, where thou shalt have no other company but devils, and the damned, and shalt not only see them, but be tormented with them and by them? Let me once more ask, if the wrath of God be so light, why did the Son of God himself make so great a matter of it? It made him 'sweat as it were, great drops of blood falling down to the ground.' The Lord of life cried, ' My soul is exceeding sorrowful, even unto death ;' and on the cross, 'My God, my God, why hast thou forsaken me?' Surely if any one could have borne these sufferings easily, it would have been Jesus Christ. He had another measure of strength to bear it than thou hast. Woe to thee, sinner, for thy mad security ! Dost thou think to find that tolerable to thee, which was so heavy to Christ? Nay, the the Son of God is cast into a bitter agony, and bloody sweat, only under the curse of the law; and yet thou, feeble, foolish creature, makest nothing to bear also the curse of the gospel, which requires a much sorer punishment. The good Lord bring thee to thy right mind by repentance, lest thou buy thy wit at too dear a rate !

18. And now, reader, I demand thy resolution, what use wilt thou make of all this? Shall it be lost to thee? or wilt thou consider it in good earnest? Thou hast cast away many a warning of God, wilt thou do so by this also? Take heed: God will not always stand warning and threatening. The hand of revenge is lifted up, the blow is coming, and woe to him on whom it lighteth! Dost thou throw away the book, and say, it speaks of nothing but hell and damnation? Thus thou usest also to complain of the preacher. But wouldst thou not have us tell thee of these things ? Should we be guilty of the blood of thy soul, by keeping silent that which God hath charged us to make known? Wouldst thou perish in ease and silence, and have us to perish with thee, rather than displease thee, by speaking the truth? If thou wilt be guilty of such inhuman cruelty, God forbid we should be guilty of such sottish folly. This kind of preaching or writing, is the ready way to be hated ; and the desire of applause is so natural, that few delight in such a displeasing way. But consider, are these things true, or are they not? If they were not true, I would heartily join with thee against any that fright people without a cause. But if these threatenings be the word of God, what a wretch art thou, that wilt not hear it, and consider it! If thou art one of the people of God, this doctrine will be a comfort to thee, and not a terror. If thou art yet unre-

generate, methinks thou shouldst be as fearful to hear of heaven as of hell, except the bare name of heaven or salvation be sufficient. Preaching heaven and mercy to thee, is entreating thee to seek them, and not reject them; and preaching hell is but to persuade thee to avoid it. If thou wert quite past hope of escaping it, then it were in vain to tell thee of hell; but as long as thou art alive, there is hope of thy recovery, and, therefore, all means must be used to awake thee from thy lethargy. Alas! what heart can now possibly conceive, or what tongue express, the pains of those souls, that are under the wrath of God ! Then, sinners, you will be crying to Jesus Christ, ' O mercy ! O pity, pity on a poor soul!'. Why, I do now, in the name of the Lord Jesus, cry to thee, ' O have mercy, have pity, man, upon thy own soul !' Shall God pity thee, who will not be entreated to pity thyself? If thy horse see but a pit before him, thou can scarcely force him in ; and wilt thou so obstinately cast thyself into hell when the danger is foretold thee ? ' Who can stand before the indignation of the Lord ? and who can abide the fierceness of his anger?' Methinks thou shouldst need no more words, but presently cast away thy soul-damning sins, and wholly deliver up thyself to Christ. Resolve on it immediately, and let it be done, that I may see thy face in the rest among the saints. May the Lord persuade thy heart to strike this covenant without any longer delay ! But if thou be hardened unto death, and there be no remedy, yet say not another day, but that thou wast faithfully warned, and hadst a friend, that would fain have prevented thy damnation.

CHAPTER VII.

THE NECESSITY OF DILIGENTLY SEEKING THE SAINTS' REST.

Sect. 1. The saints' rest surprisingly neglected ; particularly, 2. By the worldly-minded ; 3. The profane multitude ; 4. Formal professors ; 5—8. And by the godly themselves, whether magistrates, ministers, or people. 9. The author mourns the neglect, and excites the reader to diligence, by considering, 10. The ends we aim at, the works we have to do, the shortness and uncertainty of our time, and the diligence of our enemies ; 11. Our talents, mercies, relations to God, and our afflictions. 12. What assistances we have, what principles we profess, and our certainty never to do enough. 13. That every grace tends to diligence, and to trifle is lost labour ; that much time is misspent, and that our recompense and labour will be proportionable. 14. That striving is the divine appointment, all men do or will approve it, the best Christians at death lament their want of it, heaven is often lost for want of it, but never obtained without it. 15. God, Christ, and the Holy Spirit are in earnest: God is so in hearing and answering prayer : ministers in their instructions and exhortations : all the creatures in serving us ; sinners in serving the devil, as we were once, and now are, in worldly things, and in heaven and hell are all in earnest. 16. The chapter concludes with proposing some awakening questions to the ungodly, and, 17. also to the godly.

1. If there be so certain and glorious a rest for the saints, why is there no more industrious seek-

ing after it? One would think, if a man did but once hear of such unspeakable glory to be obtained, and believed what he heard to be true, he should be transported with the vehemency of his desire after it, and should almost forget to eat and drink, and should care for nothing else, and speak of and inquire after nothing else, but how to get this treasure. And yet people who hear of it daily, and profess to believe it as a fundamental article of their faith, do as little mind it, or labour for it, as if they had never heard of any such thing, or did not believe one word they hear. This reproof is more particularly applicable to the worldly-minded; the profane multitude; the formal professors, and even to the godly themselves.

2. The worldly-minded are so taken up in seeking the things below, that they have neither heart nor time to seek this rest. O foolish sinners, who hath bewitched you? The world bewitches men into brute beasts, and draws them some degrees beyond madness. See what riding and running, what scrambling and catching for a thing of nought, while eternal rest lies neglected! What contriving and caring to get a step higher in the world than their brethren, while they neglect the kingly dignity of the saints! What insatiable pursuit of fleshly pleasures, while they look on the praises of God, the joy of angels, as a tiresome burden! What unwearied diligence in raising their posterity, enlarging their possessions, (perhaps for a poor living from hand to mouth) while judgment is drawing near; but, how it shall go with them then, never puts them to one hour's consideration! What rising early, and sitting up late, and labouring from year to year, to maintain themselves and children in credit till they die; but, what shall follow after, they never think on! Yet these men cry, 'May we not be saved without so much ado?' How early do they rouse up their servants to their labour; but how seldom do they call them to prayer, or reading the scriptures! What hath this world done for its lovers and friends, that it is so eagerly followed, and painfully sought after, while Christ and heaven stand by, and few regard them? or what will the world do for them for the time to come? The common entrance into it, is through anguish and sorrow. The passage through it, is with continual care and labour. The passage out of it, is the sharpest of all. O unreasonable, bewitched men! Will mirth and pleasure stick close to you? Will gold and worldly glory prove fast friends to you in the time of your greatest need? Will they hear your cries in the day of your ca-

lamity? At the hour of your death, will they either answer or relieve you? Will they go along with you to the other world, and bribe the judge, and bring you off clear, or purchase you a place among the blessed? Why, then, did the rich man want a drop of water to cool his tongue? Or, are the sweet morsels of present delight and honour of more worth than eternal rest? And will they recompense the loss of that enduring treasure? Can there be the least hope of any of these? Ah, vile, deceitful world! how oft have we heard thy most faithful servants at last complaining—' O the world hath deceived me, and undone me! It flattered me in my prosperity, but now it turns me off in my necessity. If I had as faithfully served Christ, as I have served it, he would not have left me thus comfortless and hopeless.' Thus they complain; and yet succeeding sinners will take no warning.

3. As for the profane multitude, they will not be persuaded to be at so much pains for salvation, as to perform the common outward duties of religion. If they have the gospel preached in the town where they dwell, it may be they will give the hearing to it one part of the day, and stay at home the other; or if the master come to the congregation, yet part of his family must stay at home. If they want the plain and powerful preaching of the gospel, how few are there in a whole town, who will travel a mile or two to hear abroad; though they will go many miles to the market for provision for their bodies! They know the scripture is the law of God, by which they must be acquitted or condemned in judgment; and that 'the man is blessed who delights in the law of the Lord, and in his law doth meditate day and night;' yet will they not be at pains to read a chapter once a day. If they carry a bible to church, and neglect it all the week, this is the most use they make of it. Though they are commanded to pray without ceasing, and to pray always; yet they will neither pray constantly in their families, nor in secret. Though Daniel would rather be cast to the lions, than forbear praying three times a day in his house, where his enemies might hear him; yet these men will rather venture to be an eternal prey to Satan, the roaring lion, than thus seek their own safety. Or their cold and heartless prayers invite God to a denial: for among men it is taken for granted, that he who asks but slightly and seldom, cares not much for what he asks. They judge themselves unworthy of heaven, who think it is not worth their more constant and earnest requests. If every door was marked, where families do not, morning and

evening, earnestly seek the Lord in prayer, that his wrath might be poured out upon such prayer-less families, our towns would be as places over-thrown by the plague, the people being dead within, and the mark of judgment without. I fear where one house would escape, ten would be marked out for death; and then they might teach their doors to pray, 'Lord, have mercy upon us,' because the people would not pray themselves. But especially, if we could see what men do in their secret chambers, how few would you find in a whole town that spend one quarter of an hour, morning and night, in ear-nest supplication to God for their souls! O how little do these men set by eternal rest! Thus do they slothfully neglect all endeavours for their own welfare, except some public duty in the con-gregation, which custom or credit engages them to. Persuade them to read good books, learn the grounds of religion in their catechism, and sanctify the Lord's-day in prayer, and medita-tion, and hearing the word, and forbearing all worldly thoughts and speeches; and what a te-dious life do they take this to be! As if they thought heaven were not worth doing so much for.

4. Another sort are formal professors, who will be brought to an outward duty, but to the inward work of religion they will never be per-suaded. They will preach, or hear, or read, or talk of heaven, or pray in their families, and take part with the persons or causes that are good, and desire to be esteemed among the godly; but you can never bring them to the more spiritual duties—as, to be constant and fervent in secret prayer and meditation; conscientious in self-ex-amination; heavenly-minded; to watch over their hearts, words, and ways; to mortify the flesh, and not make provision to fulfill its lusts; to love, and heartily forgive an enemy, and pre-fer their brethren before themselves; to lay all they have, or do, at the feet of Christ, and prize his service and favour before all; to prepare to die, and willingly leave all to go to Christ. Hy-pocrites will never be persuaded to any of these. If any hypocrite entertains the gospel with joy, it is only in the surface of his soul; he never gives the seed any depth of earth: it changes his opinion but never melts and new-moulds his heart, nor sets up Christ there in full power and authority. As his religion lies most in opinion, so does his chief business and conversation. He is usually an ignorant, bold, conceited dealer in controversies, rather than an humble embracer of known truth, with love and obedience. By his slighting the judgments and persons of others,

and seldom talking with seriousness and humili-ty of the great things of Christ, he shows his re-ligion dwells in the brain, and not in his heart. The wind of temptation carries him away as a feather, because his heart is not established with Christ and grace. He never, in private conver-sation, humbly bewails his soul's imperfections, or tenderly acknowledges his unkindness to Christ; but gathers his greatest comforts from his being of such a judgment or party. The like may be said of the worldly hypocrite, who chokes the gospel with the thorns of worldly cares and desires. He is convinced that he must be religious, or he cannot be saved; and therefore he reads, and hears, and prays, and forsakes his former company and courses; but he resolves to keep his hold of present things. His judgment may say, God is the chief good; but his heart and affections never said so. The world hath more of his affections than God, and therefore it is his god. Though he does not run after opinions and novelties, like the former, yet he will be of that opinion which will best serve his worldly advantage. And as one whose spirits are enfeebled by some pestilential disease; so this man's spirits being possessed by the plague of a worldly disposition, how feeble is he in se-cret prayer! how superficial in examination and meditation! how poor in heart-watchings! how nothing at all in loving and walking with God, rejoicing in him, or desiring him!—So that both these, and many other sorts of hypocrites, though they will go with you in the easy outside of re-ligion, yet will never be at the pains of inward and spiritual duties.

5. And even the godly themselves are too lazy seekers of their everlasting rest. Alas! what a disproportion is there between our light and heat! our profession and prosecution! Who makes that haste as if it were for heaven? How still we stand! How idly we work! How we talk, and jest, and trifle away our time! How de-ceitfully we perform the work of God! How we hear, as if we heard not; and pray, as if we prayed not; and examine, and meditate, and re-prove sin, as if we did it not; and enjoy Christ, as if we enjoyed him not; as if we had learned to use the things of heaven, as the apostle teacheth us to use the things of the world! What a fro-zen stupidity has benumbed us! we are dying, and we know it, and yet we stir not; we are at the door of eternal happiness, or misery, and yet we perceive it not; death knocks, and we hear it not; God and Christ call and cry to us, 'To-day, if ye will hear my voice, harden not your hearts; work while it is day, for the night cometh when

none can work. Now ply your business, labour for your lives, lay out all your strength and time; now or never;' and yet we stir no more than if if we were half asleep. What haste do death and judgment make! how fast do they come on! they are almost at us, and yet what little haste we make! Lord, what a senseless, earthly, hellish thing is a hard heart! Where is the man that is in earnest a Christian? Methinks men every where make but a trifle of their eternal state. They look after it but a little by the by; they do not make it the business of their lives. If I were not sick myself of the same disease, with what tears should I mix this ink; with what groans should I express these complaints! and with what heart-grief should I mourn over this universal deadness!

6. Do magistrates among us seriously perform their work? Are they zealous for God? Do they build up his house? Are they tender of his honour? Do they second the word? and fly in the face of sin and sinners, as the, disturbers of our peace, and the only cause of all our miseries? Do they improve all their power, wealth, and honour, and all their influence, for the greatest advantage to the kingdom of Christ, as men that must shortly give an account of their stewardship?

7. How thin are those ministers that are serious in their work! Nay, how mightily do the very best fail in this? Do we cry out of men's disobedience to the gospel in the demonstration of the Spirit, and deal with sin as the destroying fire in our towns, and by force pull men out of it? Do we persuade people, as those should, that know the terrors of the Lord? Do we press Christ, regeneration, and faith, and holiness, believing that, without these, men can never have life? Do our bowels yearn over the ignorant, careless, and obstinate multitude? When we look them in the face, do our hearts melt over them, lest we should never see their faces in rest? Do we, as Paul, tell them, weeping, of their fleshly and earthly disposition? 'And teach them publicly, and from house to house, at all seasons, and with many tears?' And do we entreat them, as for their soul's salvation? Or rather, do we not study to gain the approbation of critical hearers; as if a minister's business were of no more weight but to tell a smooth tale for an hour, and look no more after the people till the next sermon? Does not carnal prudence control our fervour, and make our discourses lifeless, on subjects the most piercing? How gently do we handle those sins, which will so cruelly handle our people's souls! In a word,

our want of seriousness about the things of heaven, charms the souls of men into formality, and brings them to this customary careless hearing, which undoes them. May the Lord pardon the great sin of the ministry in this thing; and, in particular, my own!

8. And are the people more serious than magistrates or ministers? How can it be expected! Reader, look but to thyself, and resolve the question. Ask conscience, and suffer it to tell thee truly. Hast thou set thy eternal rest before thine eyes, as the great business thou hast to do in this world? Hast thou watched and laboured, with all thy might, 'that no man take thy crown?' Hast thou made haste, lest thou shouldst come too late, and die before thy work be done? Hast thou pressed on through crowds of opposition, 'towards the mark, for the prize of the high calling of God in Christ Jesus,' still 'reaching forth unto those things which are before?' Can conscience witness your secret cries, and groans, and tears? Can your family witness, that you taught them the fear of the Lord, and warned them not to go to that place of torment? Can your minister witness, that he has heard you cry out 'What shall I do to be saved?' and that you have followed him with complaints against your corruptions, and with earnest inquiries after the Lord? Can your neighbours about you witness, that you reprove the ungodly, and take pains to save the souls of your brethren? Let all these witnesses judge this day between God and you, whether you are in earnest about eternal rest. You can tell by his work, whether your servant has loitered, though you did not see him; so you may by looking at your own work. Is your love to Christ, your faith, your zeal, and other graces, strong or weak? What are your joys? What is your assurance? Is all in order with you? Are you ready to die, if this should be the day? Do the souls, among whom you have conversed, bless you? Judge by this, and it will quickly appear whether you have been labourers or loiterers.

9. O blessed rest, how unworthily art thou neglected! O glorious kingdom, how art thou undervalued! Little know the careless sons of men, what a state they set so lightly by. If they once knew it, they would surely be of another mind. I hope thou, reader, art sensible what a desperate thing it is to trifle about eternal rest; and how deeply thou hast been guilty of this thyself. And I hope also, thou wilt not now suffer this conviction to die. Should the physician tell thee, 'If you will observe but one thing, I doubt not to cure your disease;' wouldst thou

not observe it? So I tell thee, if thou wilt observe but this one thing for thy soul, I make no doubt of thy salvation—shake off thy sloth, and put to all thy strength, and be a Christian indeed: I know not then what can hinder thy happiness. As far as thou art gone from God, seek him with all thy heart, and no doubt thou shalt find him. As unkind as thou hast been to Jesus Christ, seek him heartily, obey him unreservedly, and thy salvation is as sure as if thou hadst it already. But full as Christ's satisfaction is, free as the promise is, large as the mercy of God is, if thou only talk of these, when thou shouldst eagerly entertain them, thou wilt be never the better for them; and if thou loiter, when thou shouldst labour, thou wilt lose the crown. Fall to work, then, speedily and seriously, and bless God that thou hast yet time to do it. And to show that I urge thee not without cause, I will here add a variety of animating considerations. Rouse up thy spirit, and, as Moses said to Israel, 'Set thy heart unto all the words which I testify unto thee this day; for it is not a vain thing, because it is your life.' May the Lord open thy heart, and fasten his counsel effectually upon thee!

10. Consider how reasonable it is, that our diligence should be answerable to the ends we aim at, to the work we have to do, to the shortness and uncertainty of our time, and to the contrary diligence of our enemies. The ends of a Christian's desires and endeavours are so great, that no human understanding on earth can comprehend them. What is so excellent, so important, or so necessary, as the glorifying of God, the salvation of our own and other men's souls, by escaping the torments of hell, and possessing the glory of heaven? And can a man be too much affected with things of such moment? Can he desire them too earnestly, or love them too strongly, or labour for them too diligently? Do not we know, that if our prayers prevail not, and our labour succeeds not, we are undone for ever? —The work of a Christian here is very great and various. The soul must be renewed; corruptions must be mortified; custom, temptations, and worldly interests, must be conquered; flesh must be subdued; life, friends, and credit must be slighted; conscience on good grounds be quieted; and assurance of pardon and salvation attained. Though God must give us these without our merit, yet he will not give them without our earnest seeking and labour. Besides, there is much knowledge to be got, many ordinances to be used, and duties to be performed: every age, year, and day; every place we come

to; every person we deal with; every change of our condition, still require the renewing of our labour: wives, children, servants, neighbours, friends, enemies, all of them call for duty from us. Judge, then, whether men that have so much business lying upon their hands, should not exert themselves; and whether it be their wisdom either to delay or loiter. Time passeth on. Yet a few days, and we shall be here no more. Many diseases are ready to assault us. We that are now preaching, and hearing, and talking, and walking, must very shortly be carried, and laid in the dust, and there left to the worms in darkness and corruption: we are almost there already; we know not whether we shall have another sermon, or sabbath, or hour. How active should they be who know they have so short a space for so great a work! And we have enemies that are always plotting and labouring for our destruction. How diligent is Satan in all kind of temptations! Therefore, 'be sober, be vigilant; because your adversary the devil, as a roaring lion, walketh about, seeking whom he may devour: whom resist, steadfast in the faith.' How diligent are all the ministers of Satan! False teachers, scoffers, persecutors, and our inbred corruptions, the most busy and diligent of all! Will a feeble resistance serve our turn! Should not we be more active for our own preservation, than our enemies are for our ruin?

11. It should excite us to diligence, when we consider our talents, and our mercies, our relation to God, and the afflictions he lays upon us. The talents which we have received are many and great. What people breathing on earth have had plainer instructions, or more forcible persuasions, or more constant admonitions, in season and out of season? Sermons, till we have been weary of them; and sabbaths, till we have profaned them; excellent books, in such plenty that we know not which to read. What people have had God so near them? or have seen so much of Christ crucified before their eyes? or have had heaven and hell so open unto them? What speed should such a people make for heaven? How should they fly that are thus winged? And how swiftly should they sail that have wind and tide to help them! A small measure of grace beseems not such a people, nor will an ordinary diligence in the work of God excuse them. All our lives have been filled with mercies. God hath mercifully poured out upon us the riches of sea and land, of heaven and earth. We are fed and clothed with mercy. We have mercies within and without. To num-

ber them, is to count the stars or the sands of the sea-shore. If there be any difference betwixt hell and earth, yea, or heaven and earth, then certainly we have received mercy. If the blood of the Son of God be mercy, then we are engaged to God by mercy. Shall God think nothing too much, nor too good for us; and shall we think all too much that we do for him? When I compare my slow and unprofitable life, with the frequent and wonderful mercies received, it shames me, it silences me, and leaves me inexcusable. Besides our talents and mercies, our relations to God are most endearing. Are we his children, and do we not owe him our most tender affections, and dutiful obedience? Are we 'the spouse of Christ,' and should we not obey and love him? 'If he be a Father, where is his honour? and if he be a Master, where is his fear? We call him Master, and Lord, and we say well.' But if our industry be not answerable to our relations, we condemn ourselves in saying we are his children or his servants. How will the hard labour, and daily toil, which servants undergo to please their masters, judge and condemn those who will not labour so hard for their Great Master? Surely there is no master like him; nor can any servants expect such fruit of their labours as his servants. And if we wander out of God's way, or loiter in it, how is every creature ready to be his rod, to reduce us, or put us on! Our sweetest mercies will become our sorrows. Rather than want a rod, the Lord will make us a scourge to ourselves: our diseased bodies shall make us groan; our perplexed minds shall make us restless; our conscience shall be as a scorpion in our bosom. And is it not easier to endure the labour than the spur? Had we rather be still afflicted, than be up and doing? And though they that do most, meet also with afflictions; yet surely according to their peace of conscience, and faithfulness to Christ, the bitterness of their cup is abated.

12. To quicken our diligence in our work, we should also consider, what assistances we have, what principles we profess, and our certainty that we can never do too much.—For our assistance in the service of God, all the world are our servants. The sun, moon, and stars, attend us with their light and influence. The earth, with all its furniture of plants and flowers, fruits, birds, and beasts; the sea, with its inhabitants; the air, the wind, the frost and snow, the heat and fire, the clouds and rain, all wait upon us while we do our work Yea, the angels are all our ministering spirits. Nay more, the

patience of God doth wait upon us; the Lord Jesus Christ waiteth, in the offers of his blood; the Holy Spirit waiteth, by striving with our backward hearts; besides the ministers of the gospel, who study and wait, preach and wait, pray and wait, upon careless sinners. And is it not an intolerable crime for us to trifle, while angels and men, yea, the Lord himself, stand by, and look on, and, as it were, hold us the candle while we do nothing? I beseech you, Christians, whenever you are praying, or reproving transgressors, or upon any duty, remember what assistances you have for your work, and then judge how you ought to perform it. The principles we profess, are, that God is the chief good; that all our happiness consists in his love, and therefore it should be valued and sought above all things; that he is our only Lord, and therefore chiefly to be served; that we must love him with all our heart, and soul, and strength; that our great business in the world is to glorify God, and obtain salvation. Are these doctrines seen in our practice? or, rather, do not our works deny what our words confess?—But however our assistances and principles excite us to our work, we are sure we can never do too much. Could we do all, 'we are unprofitable servants;' much more when we are sure to fail in all. No man can obey, or serve God too much. Though all superstition, or service of our own devising, may be called a 'being righteous overmuch;' yet, as long as we keep to the rule of the word, we can never be righteous too much. The world is mad with malice, when they think, that faithful diligence in the service of Christ is foolish singularity. The time is near when they will easily confess that God could not be loved, or served too much, and that no man can be too busy to save his soul. We may easily do too much for the world, but we cannot for God.

13. Let us further consider, that it is the nature of every grace to promote diligence, that trifling in the way to heaven is lost labour, that much precious time is already mispent, and that in proportion to our labours will be our recompense.—See the nature and tendency of every grace. If you loved God, you would think nothing too much that you could possibly do to serve him, and please him still more. Love is quick and impatient, active and observant. If you love Christ, you would keep his commandments, nor accuse them of too much strictness. If you had faith, it would quicken and encourage you—if you had the hope of glory, it would, as the spring in the watch, set all the wheels of

your souls a-going—if you had the fear of God, it would rouse you out of your slothfulness—if you had zeal, it would inflame, and eat you up. In what degree soever thou art sanctified, in the same degree thou wilt be serious and laborious in the work of God. But they that trifle, lose their labour. Many who, like Agrippa, are but almost Christians, will find in the end, they shall be but almost saved. If two be running in a race, he that runs slowest loses both prize and labour. A man that is lifting a weight, if he put not sufficient strength to it, had as good put none at all. How many duties have Christians lost, for want of doing them thoroughly? 'Many will seek to enter in, and shall not be able,' who if they had striven, might have been able. Therefore, put to a little more diligence and strength, that all you have done already be not in vain. Besides, is not much precious time already lost? With some of us childhood and youth are gone; with some their middle age also; and the time before us is very uncertain. What time have we slept, talked, and played away, or spent in worldly thoughts and cares! How little of our work is done! The time we have lost cannot be recalled; should we not then redeem and improve the little which remains? If a traveller sleep, or trifle most of the day, he must travel so much faster in the evening, or fall short of his journey's end. Doubt not but the recompense will be according to your labour. The seed which is buried and dead, will bring forth a plentiful harvest. Whatever you do, or suffer, everlasting rest will pay for all. There is no repenting of labours or sufferings in heaven. There is not one says, 'Would I had spared my pains, and prayed less, or been less strict, and done as the rest of my neighbours.' On the contrary, it will be their joy to look back upon their labours and tribulations, and to consider how the mighty power of God brought them through all. We may all say, as Paul, 'I reckon that the sufferings' and labours 'of this present time, are not worthy to be compared with the glory which shall be revealed in us.' We labour but for a moment, but we shall rest for ever. Who would not put forth all his strength for one hour, when for that hour's work he may be a prince while he lives? 'God is not unrighteous, to forget our work and labour of love.' Will not 'all our tears be wiped away,' and all the sorrows of our duties be then forgotten?

14. Nor does it less deserve to be considered, that striving is the divinely appointed way of salvation, that all men either do or will approve it, that the best Christians at death lament their

negligence, and that heaven itself is often lost for want of striving, but is never had on easier terms. The sovereign wisdom of God has made striving necessary to salvation. Who knows the way to heaven better than the God of heaven? When men tell us we are too strict, whom do they accuse, God or us? If it were a fault, it would lie in him that commands, and not in us who obey. These are the men that ask us, Whether we are wiser than all the world besides? and yet they will pretend to be wiser than God. How can they reconcile their language with the laws of God? 'The kingdom of heaven suffereth violence, and the violent take it by force. Strive to enter in at the strait gate; for many will seek to enter in, and shall not be able. Whatsoever thy hand findeth to do, do it with thy might: for there is no work, nor device, nor knowledge, nor wisdom in the grave, whither thou goest. Work out your own salvation with fear and trembling. Give diligence to make your calling and election sure. If the righteous scarcely be saved, where shall the ungodly and the sinner appear?' Let them bring all the seeming reasons they can, against the holy violence of the saints; this sufficeth me to confute them all, that God is of another mind, and he hath commanded me to do much more than I do; and though I could see no other reason for it, his will is reason enough. Who should make laws for us, but he that made us? And who should point out the way to heaven, but he that must bring us thither? And who should fix the terms of salvation, but he that bestows the gift of salvation? So that, let the world, the flesh, or the devil, speak against a holy laborious life, this is my answer—God hath commanded it. Nay, there never was, nor ever will be, a man, but will approve such a life, and will one day justify the diligence of the saints. And who would not go that way, which every man shall finally applaud? True, it is now a way everywhere spoken against. But let me tell you, most that speak against it, in their judgments approve of it; and those that are now against it, will shortly be of another mind. If they come to heaven, their mind must be changed before they come there. If they go to hell, their judgment will then be altered, whether they will or not. Remember this, you that love the opinion and way of the multitude; why then will you not be of the opinion that all will be of? Why will you be of a judgment, which you are sure all of you shortly to change? O that you were but as wise in this, as those in hell! Even the best of Christians, when they come to die. exceedingly lament their negligence. They then wish, ' O that I had been a thousand times more holy, more heavenly, more laborious for my soul! The world accuses me for doing too much, but my own conscience accuses me for doing too little. It is far easier bearing the scoffs of the world, than the lashes of conscience. I had rather be reproached by the devil for seeking salvation, than reproved of God for neglecting it.' How do their failings thus wound and disquiet them, who have been the wonders of the world for their heavenly conversation! It is for want of more diligence, that heaven itself is often lost. When they that have. ' heard the word, and anon with joy received it, and have done many things, and heard,' the ministers of Christ gladly, shall yet perish; should not this rouse us out of our security? How far hath many a man followed Christ, and yet forsook him, when all worldly interests and hopes were to be renounced! God hath resolved, that heaven shall not be had on easier terms. Rest must always follow labour. ' Without holiness, no man shall see the Lord.' Seriousness is the very thing wherein consists our sincerity. If thou art not serious, thou art not a Christian. It is not only a high degree in Christianity, but the very life and essence of it. As fencers upon a stage differ from soldiers fighting for their lives, so hypocrites differ from serious Christians. If men could be saved without this serious diligence, they would never regard it; all the excellencies of God's ways would never entice them. But when God hath resolved, that, without serious diligence here, you shall not rest hereafter, is it not wisdom to exert ourselves to the utmost?

15. But to persuade thee, if possible, Reader, to be serious in thy endeavours for heaven, let me add more considerations. As for instance, consider,—God is in earnest with you; and why should you not be so with him? In his commands, his threatenings, his promises, he means as he speaks. In his judgments he is serious. Was he not so, when he drowned the world? when he consumed Sodom and Gomorrah? and when he scattered the Jews? Is it time, then, to trifle with God? Jesus Christ was serious in purchasing our redemption. In teaching, he neglected his meat and drink: in prayer, he continued all night: in doing good, his friends thought him beside himself: in suffering, he fasted forty days, was tempted, betrayed, spit upon, buffeted, crowned with thorns, sweat drops of blood, was crucified, pierced, died. There was no jesting in all this. And should we not be serious in seeking our own salvation?—The Holy

Spirit is serious in soliciting us to be happy. His motions are frequent, pressing, and importunate. He striveth with us. He is grieved when we resist him. And should we not be serious, then, in obeying and yielding to his motions?—God is serious in hearing our prayers, and bestowing his mercies. He is afflicted with us. He regardeth every groan and sigh, and puts every tear into his bottle. The next time thou art in trouble, thou wilt beg for a serious regard of thy prayers. And shall we expect real mercies, when we are slight and superficial in the work of God? The ministers of Christ are serious in exhorting and instructing you. They beg of God, and of you; and long more for the salvation of your souls, than for any worldly good. If they kill themselves with their labour, or suffer martyrdom for preaching the gospel, they think their lives are well bestowed, so that they prevail for the saving of your souls. And shall other men be so painful and careful for your salvation, and you be so careless and negligent of your own?—How diligent and serious are all the creatures in serving you! What haste makes the sun to compass the world! The fountains are always flowing for thy use; the rivers still running; spring and harvest keep their times. How hard does thy ox labour for thee from day to day! How speedily does thy horse travel with thee! And shalt thou only be negligent? Shall all these be so serious in serving thee, and thou so careless in thy service to God?—The servants of the world and the devil are serious and diligent: they work as if they could never do enough: they make haste, as if afraid of coming to hell too late: they bear down ministers, sermons, and all before them. And shall they be more diligent for damnation, than thou for salvation? Hast thou not a better master, sweeter employment, greater encouragements, and a better reward?—Time was when thou wast serious thyself in serving Satan and the flesh, if it be not so yet. How eagerly didst thou follow thy sports, thy evil company, and sinful delights! And wilt thou not now be as earnest and violent for God? You are to this day in earnest about the things of this life. If you are sick, or in pain, what serious complaints do you utter! If you are poor, how hard do you labour for a livelihood! And is not the business of your salvation of far greater moment? There is no jesting in heaven or hell. The saints have a real happiness, and the damned a real misery. There are no remiss or sleepy praises in heaven, nor such lamentations in hell. All these are in earnest. When thou, Reader, shalt come to death and judgment, O what deep, heart-piercing thoughts wilt thou have of eternity! Methinks I foresee thee already astonished to think how thou couldst possibly make so light of these things. Methinks I even hear thee crying out thy stupidity and madness.

16. And now, Reader, having laid down these undeniable arguments, I do, in the name of God, demand thy resolution—wilt thou yield obedience, or not? I am confident thy conscience is convinced of thy duty. Darest thou now go on in thy common, careless course, against the plain evidence of reason, and commands of God, and against the light of thy own conscience? Darest thou live as loosely, sin as boldly, and pray as seldom as before? Darest thou profane the sabbath, slight the service of God, and think of thine everlasting state, as carelessly as before? Or dost thou not rather resolve to gird up the loins of thy mind, and set thyself wholly to the work of thy salvation, and break through the opposições, and slight the scoffs and persecutions of the world, and 'lay aside every weight, and the sin which doth so easily beset thee, and run with patience the race that is set before thee?' I hope these are thy full resolutions. Yet, because I fear the obstinacy of the heart of man, and because I am solicitous thy soul might live, I once more entreat thy attention to the following questions; and I command thee from God, that thou stifle not thy conscience, nor resist conviction; but answer them faithfully, and obey accordingly. If, by being diligent in godliness, you could grow rich, get honour or preferment in the world, be recovered from sickness, or live for ever in prosperity on earth; what lives would you lead, and what pains would you take in the service of God? And is not the saints' rest a more excellent happiness than all this? If it were felony to break the sabbath, neglect secret or family worship, or be loose in your lives, what manner of persons would you then be? And is not eternal death more terrible than temporal? If God usually punished with some present judgment every act of sin, as he did the lie of Ananias and Sapphira, what kind of lives would you lead? And is not eternal wrath far more terrible?—If one of your acquaintance should come from the dead, and tell you that he suffered the torments of hell for those sins you are guilty of; what manner of persons would you afterwards be? How much more should the warnings of God affright you?—If you knew that this were the last day you had to live in the world, how would you spend it? And you know not but it may be your last, and are sure your last is near.—If

you had seen the general dissolution of the world, and all the pomp and glory of it consumed to ashes, what would such a sight persuade thee to do? Such a sight you shall certainly see.—If you had seen the judgment-seat, and the books opened, and the wicked stand trembling on the left hand of the Judge, and the godly rejoicing on the right hand, and their different sentences pronounced; what persons would you have been after such a sight? This sight you shall one day surely see. If you had seen hell open, and all the damned there in their ceaseless torments; also heaven opened, as Stephen did, and all the saints there triumphing in glory; what a life would you lead after such sights? These you will see before it be long.—If you had lain in hell but one year, or one day, or hour, and there felt the torments you now hear of; how seriously would you then speak of hell, and pray against it! And will you not take God's word for the truth of this, except you feel it?—Or if you had possessed the glory of heaven but one year, what pains would you take rather than be deprived of such incomparable glory?—Thus I have said enough, if not to stir up the sinner to a serious working out his salvation, yet at least to silence him, and leave him inexcusable at the judgment of God. Only as we do by our friends when they are dead, and our words and actions can do them no good, yet to testify our affection for them we weep and mourn; so will I also do for these unhappy souls. It makes my heart tremble, to think how they will stand before the Lord, confounded and speechless: when he shall say, 'Was the world, or Satan, a better friend to you than I? Or had they done more for you than I had done? Try now whether they will save you, or recompence you for the loss of heaven, or be as good to you as I would have been.' What will the wretched sinner answer to any of this? But though man will not hear, we may hope in speaking to God. 'O thou that didst weep and groan in spirit over a dead Lazarus, pity these dead and senseless souls, till they are able to weep and groan in pity to themselves! As thou hast bid thy servants speak, so speak now thyself: they will hear thy voice speaking to their hearts, who will not hear mine speaking to their ears. Lord, thou hast long knocked at these hearts in vain; now break the doors, and enter in!'

17. Yet to show the godly why they, above all men, should be laborious for heaven, I desire to ask them, what manner of persons should those be whom God hath chosen to be vessels of mercy? Who have felt the smart of their

negligence in their new birth, in their troubles of conscience, in their doubts and fears, and in other sharp afflictions? Who have often confessed their sins of negligence to God in prayer? Who have bound themselves to God by so many covenants? What manner of persons should they be, who are near to God, as the children of his family; who have tasted such sweetness in diligent obedience; who are many of them so uncertain what shall everlastingly become of their souls? What manner of persons should they be in holiness, whose sanctification is so imperfect; whose lives and duties are so important to the saving or destroying a multitude of souls; and on whom the glory of the great God so much depends?—Since these things are so, I charge thee, Christian, in thy Master's name, to consider, and resolve the question, 'What manner of persons ought we to be in all holy conversation and godliness?' And let thy life answer the question as well as thy tongue.

CHAPTER VIII.

HOW TO DISCERN OUR TITLE TO THE SAINTS' REST.

Sect. 1. The folly of men in not inquiring after a title to the saints' rest; 2. and their cause for terror, as long as they are destitute of a title. 3. Self-examination is urged upon them; 4. (1.) From the possibility of arriving at a certainty; 5—9. (2.) From the hinderances which will be thrown in our way by Satan, sinners, our own hearts, and many other causes; 10. (3.) From considering how easy, common, and dangerous it is to be mistaken; that trying will not be so painful as the neglect; that God will soon try us, and that to try ourselves will be profitable; 11. And therefore the reader is entreated no longer to delay the trial. 12. Then, (4.) Directions are given how to try; 13. (5.) Marks for trial are added, particularly, 14. Do we make God our chief good? 15. Do we heartily accept of Christ for our Lord and Saviour? 16, 17. The chapter concludes with illustrating the great importance of these two marks.

1. Is there such a glorious rest so near at hand? And shall none enjoy it but the people of God? What mean most of the world, then, to live so contentedly without assurance of their interests in this rest, and neglect the trying of their title to it? When the Lord has so fully opened the blessedness of that kingdom which none but obedient believers shall possess; and so fully expressed those torments, which the rest of the world must eternally suffer; methinks they that believe this to be certainly true, should never be at any quiet in themselves, till they were fully assured of their being heirs of the kingdom. Lord, what a strange madness is this, that men, who know they must presently enter upon unchangeable joy or pain, should yet live as uncertain what shall be their doom, as if they had never heard of any such state; yea, and live as quietly and merrily in this uncertainty, as if all were made sure, and there were no danger!

Are these men alive or dead? Are they awake or asleep? What do they think on? Where are their hearts? If they have but a weighty suit at law, how careful are they to know whether it will go for or against them? If they were to be tried for their lives at an earthly bar, how careful would they be to know whether they should be saved or condemned, especially if their care might surely save them! If they be dangerously sick, they will inquire of the physician, What think you, Sir, shall I escape or not? But in the business of their salvation, they are content to be uncertain. If you ask most men 'a reason of the hope that is in them,' they will say, 'Because God is merciful, and Christ died for sinners,' and the like general reasons, which any man in the world may give as well as they: but put them to prove their interest in Christ, and in the saving mercy of God, and they can say nothing to the purpose. If God or man should say to them, What case is thy soul in, man? Is it regenerate, sanctified, and pardoned, or not? He would say, as Cain of Abel, 'I know not; am I my soul's keeper? I hope well, I trust God with my soul; I shall speed as well as other men do: I thank God, I never made any doubt of my salvation.' Thou hast cause to doubt, because thou never didst doubt; and yet more, because thou hast been so careless in thy confidence. What do thy expressions discover, but a wilful neglect of thy own salvation? As a shipmaster that should let his vessel alone, and say, 'I will venture it among the rocks, and waves, and winds; I will trust God with it; it will speed as well as other vessels.' What horrible abuse of God is this, to pretend to trust God, to cloak their own wilful negligence! If thou didst really trust God, thou wouldst also be ruled by him, and trust him in his own appointed way. He requires thee to give 'diligence to make thy calling and election sure,' and so trust him. He hath marked thee out a way in scripture, by which thou art charged to search and try thyself, and mayest arrive at certainty. Were he not a foolish traveller, that would hold on his way, when he does not know whether he be right or wrong; and say, 'I hope I am right; I will go on, and trust in God?' Art thou not guilty of this folly in thy travels to eternity? not considering, that a little serious inquiry, whether thy way be right, might save thee a great deal of labour, which thou bestowest in vain, and must undo again, or else thou wilt miss of salvation, and undo thyself.

2. How canst thou think or speak of the great God without terror, as long as thou art uncer-

tain whether he be thy Father, or thy enemy, and knowest not but all his perfections may be employed against thee? Or of Jesus Christ, when thou knowest not whether his blood hath purged thy soul; whether he will condemn or acquit thee in judgment; or whether he be the foundation of thy happiness, or a stone of stumbling to break thee, and grind thee to powder? How canst thou open the bible, and read a chapter, but it should terrify thee? Methinks every leaf should be to thee as Belshazzar's writing on the wall, except only that which draws thee to try and reform. If thou readest the promises, thou knowest not whether they shall be fulfilled to thee. If thou readest the threatenings, for any thing thou knowest, thou readest thy own sentence. No wonder thou art an enemy to plain preaching, and say of the minister, as Ahab of the prophet, ' I hate him; for he doth not prophesy good concerning me, but evil.' How canst thou without terror join in prayer? When thou receivest the sacrament, thou knowest not whether it be thy bane or bliss. What comfort canst thou find in thy friends, and honours, and houses, and lands, till thou knowest thou hast the love of God with them, and shalt have rest with him when thou leavest them? Offer a prisoner, before he knows his sentence, either music, or clothes, or preferment; what are they to him till he knows he shall escape with his life? for if he knows he must die the next day, it will be a small comfort to die rich or honourable. Methinks it should be so with thee, till thou knowest thy eternal state. When thou liest down to take thy rest, methinks the uncertainty of thy salvation should keep thee waking, or amaze thee in thy dreams, and trouble thy sleep. Doth it not grieve thee to see the people of God so comfortable in their way to glory, when thou hast no good hope of ever enjoying it thyself? How canst thou think of thy dying hour? Thou knowest it is near, and there is no avoiding it, nor any medicine found out that can prevent it. If thou shouldst die this day, (and who 'knows what a day may bring forth?') thou art not certain whether thou shalt go to heaven or hell. And canst thou be merry, till thou art got out of this dangerous state? What shift dost thou make to preserve thy heart from horror, when thou rememberest the great judgment day, and everlasting flames? When thou hearest of it, dost thou not tremble, as Felix? If the 'keepers shook, and became as dead men, when they saw the angel come and roll back the stone from Christ's sepulchre,' how canst thou think of living in hell with devils, till thou hast some well-grounded assurance that thou shalt escape it? Thy bed is very soft, or thy heart is very hard, if thou canst sleep soundly in this uncertain case.

3. If this general uncertainty of the world about their salvation were remediless, then must it be borne as other unavoidable miseries. But, alas! the common cause is wilful negligence. Men will not be persuaded to use the remedy. The great means to conquer this uncertainty is self-examination, or the serious and diligent trying of a man's heart and state by the rule of scripture. Either men understand not the nature and use of this duty, or else they will not be at the pains to try. Go through a congregation of a thousand men, and how few of them shall you meet with, that ever bestowed one hour in all their lives in a close examination of their title to heaven! Ask thy own conscience, Reader, when was the time, and where was the place, that ever thou solemnly tookest thy heart to task, as in the sight of God, and didst examine it by scripture, whether it be renewed or not? Whether it be holy or not? whether it be set most on God or the creatures, on heaven or earth? When didst thou follow on this examination till thou hadst discovered thy condition, and passed sentence on thyself accordingly? But because this is a work of so high importance, and so commonly neglected, I will therefore show—that it is possible, by trying, to come to a certainty; what hinders men from trying and knowing their state; then offer motives to examine—and directions,—together with some marks out of scripture, by which you may try, and certainly know, whether you are the people of God or not.

4. (1.) Scripture shows, that the certainty of salvation may be attained, and ought to be laboured for, when it tells us so frequently, that the saints before us have known their justification and future salvation: when it declares, that 'whosoever believeth in Christ, shall not perish, but have everlasting life:' which it would be in vain to declare, if we cannot know ourselves to be believers or not; when it makes such a wide difference between the children of God, and the children of the devil: when it bids us ' give diligence to make our calling and election sure;' and earnestly urges us to examine, prove, know our ownselves, whether we be in the faith, and whether Jesus Christ be in us, except we be reprobates: also when its precepts require us to rejoice always, to call God our Father, to live in his praises, to love Christ's appearing, to wish that he may come quickly, and to comfort ourselves with the mention of it. But who can do

any of these heartily, that is not in some measure sure that he is the child of God.

5. (2.) Among the many hinderances which keep men from self-examination, we cannot doubt but Satan will do his part. If all the power he hath, or all the means and instruments he can employ, can do it, he will be sure, above all duties, to keep you from this. He is loth the godly should have the joy, assurance, and advantage against corruption, which the faithful performance of self-examination would procure them. As for the ungodly, he knows if they should once earnestly examine, they would find out his deceits, and their own danger, and so be very likely to escape him. How could he get so many millions to hell willingly, if they knew they were going thither? And how could they avoid knowing it, if they did but thoroughly try : having such a clear light and sure rule in the scripture to discover it? If the snare be not hid, the bird will escape it. Satan knows how to angle for souls better than to show them the hook and line, or fright them away with a noise, or with his own appearance. Therefore he labours to keep them from a searching ministry ; or to keep the minister from helping them to search, or to take off the edge of the word, that it may not pierce and divide ; or to turn away their thoughts : or to possess them with prejudice. Satan knows when the minister has provided a searching sermon, fitted to the state and necessity of a hearer ; and, therefore, he will keep them away that day, if it be possible ; or cast him into a sleep ; or steal away the word by the cares and talk of the world ; or some way prevent its operation.

6. Another great hinderance to self-examination, arises from wicked men. Their examples ; their merry company and discourse ; their continually insisting on worldly concerns ; their raillery and scoffs at godly persons ; also their persuasions, allurements, and threats, are each of them exceedingly great temptations to security. God doth scarcely ever open the eyes of a poor sinner, to see that his way is wrong, but presently there is a multitude of Satan's apostles ready to deceive and settle him again in the quiet possession of his former master. 'What!' say they, 'do you make a doubt of your salvation, who have lived so well, and done nobody any harm? God is merciful ; and if such as you shall not be saved, God help a great many! What do you think of all your forefathers? And what will become of all your friends and neighbours that live as you do? Will they all be damned? Come, come, if you hearken to these preachers, they will drive you out of your wits. Are not all men sinners? And did not Christ die to save sinners? Never trouble your head with these thoughts, and you shall do well.' O how many thousands have such charms kept asleep in deceit and security, till death and hell have awakened them! The Lord calls to the sinner and tells him, ' The gate is strait, the way is narrow, and few find it : try and examine, give diligence to make sure.' The world cries, ' Never doubt, never trouble yourselves with these thoughts.' In this strait, sinner, consider, it is Christ, and not your forefathers, or neighbours, or friends, that must judge you at last ; and if Christ condemn you, these cannot save you : therefore common reason may tell you, that it is not from the words of ignorant men, but from the word of God you must fetch your hopes of salvation. When Ahab would inquire among the multitude of flattering prophets, it was his death. They can flatter men into the snare, but they cannot tell how to bring them out. ' Let no man deceive you with vain words : for because of these things cometh the wrath of God upon the children of disobedience. Be not ye therefore partakers with them.'

7. But the greatest hinderances are in men's own hearts.—Some are so ignorant, that they know not what self-examination is, nor what a minister means when he persuadeth them to try themselves : or they know not that there is any necessity for it, but think every man is bound to believe that his sins are pardoned, whether it be true or false, and that it is a great fault to make any question of it ; or they do not think that assurance can be attained ; or that there is any great difference between one man and another, but that we are all Christians, and therefore need not trouble ourselves any further ; or at least they know not wherein the difference lies. They have as gross an idea of regeneration as Nicodemus had.—Some will not believe that God will ever make such a difference betwixt men in the life to come, and therefore will not search themselves, whether they differ here. —Some are so stupified, say what we can to them, that they lay it not to heart, but give us the hearing, and there is the end.—Some are so possessed with self-love and pride, that they will not so much as suspect they are in danger : like a proud tradesman, who scorns the prudent advice of casting up his books ; as fond parents will not believe or hear any evil of their children. —Some are so guilty, that they dare not try, and yet they dare venture on a more dreadful trial.—Some are so in love with sin, and so dis-

like the way of God, that they dare not try their ways, lest they be forced from the course they love, to that which they lothe.—Some are so resolved never to change their present state, that they neglect examination as a useless thing. Before they will seek a new way, when they have lived so long, and gone so far, they will put their eternal state to the venture, come of it what will. Many men are so busy in the world, that they cannot set themselves to the trying their title to heaven. Others are so clogged with slothfulness of spirit, that they will not be at the pains of an hour's examination of their own hearts.—But the most common and dangerous impediment is that false faith and hope, commonly called presumption, which bears up the hearts of the greatest part of the world, and so keeps them .from suspecting their danger.

8. And if a man should break through all these hinderances, and set upon the duty of self-examination, yet assurance is not presently attained. Too many deceive themselves in their inquiries after it, through one or other of the following causes. There is such confusion and darkness in the soul of man, especially of an unregenerated man, that he can scarcely tell what he doth, or what is in him.—As in a house where nothing is in its proper place, it will be difficult to find what is wanted ; so it is in the heart where all things are in disorder.—Most men accustom themselves to be strangers at home, and too little observe the temper and motions of their own hearts.—Many are resolved what to judge before they try ; like a bribed judge, who examines as if he would judge uprightly, when he is previously resolved which way the cause shall go.—Men are partial in their own cause ; ready to think their great sins small, and their small sins none ; their gifts of nature to be the work of grace, and to say, ' all these have I kept from my youth ; I am rich, and increased in goods, and have need of nothing.'—Most men search but by the halves. If it will not easily and quickly be done, they are discouraged and leave off. They try themselves by false marks and rules ; not knowing wherein the truth of Christianity doth consist ; some looking beyond, and some short of the scripture-standard. And frequently they miscarry in this work by attempting it in their own strength : as some expect the Spirit should do it without them, so others attempt it themselves, without seeking or expecting the help of the Spirit. Both these will certainly miscarry in their assurance.

9. Some other hinderances keep even true Christians from comfortable certainty. As for instance : the weakness of grace. Small things are hardly discerned. Most Christians content themselves with a small measure of grace, and do not follow on to spiritual strength and manhood. The chief remedy for such would be to follow on their duty, till their grace be increased. Wait upon God, in the use of his prescribed means, and he will undoubtedly bless you with increase. O that Christians would bestow most of that time to getting more grace, which they bestow in anxious doubtings whether they have any or none ; and lay out those serious affections in praying for more grace, which they bestow in fruitless complaints ! I beseech thee, Christian, take this advice as from God ; and then, when thou believest strongly, and lovest fervently, thou canst no more doubt of thy faith and love, than a man that is very hot can doubt of his warmth, or a man that is strong and lusty, can doubt of his being alive. Christians hinder their own comfort by looking more at signs, which tell them what they are, than at precepts, which tell them what they should do : as if their present case must needs be their everlasting case ; and if they be now unpardoned, there were no remedy. Were he not mad, that would lie weeping because he is not pardoned, when his prince stands by all the while offering him a pardon, and persuading him to accept of it ? Justifying faith, Christian, is not thy persuasion of God's special love to thee, but thy accepting Christ to make thee lovely. It is far better to accept Christ as offered, than spend so much time in doubting whether we have Christ or not.— Another cause of distress to Christians is, their mistaking assurance for the joy that sometimes accompanies it.—As if a child should take himself for a son no longer than while he sees the smiles of his father's face, or hears the comfortable expressions of his mouth ; and as if the father ceased to be a father, whenever he ceased those smiles and speeches.—The trouble of souls is also increased by their not knowing the ordinary way of God's conveying comfort. They think they have nothing to do but to wait when God will bestow it. But they must know, that the matter of their comfort is in the promises, and thence they must fetch it as often as they expect it, by daily and diligently meditating upon the promises ; and in this way they may expect the Spirit will communicate comfort to their souls. The joy of the promises, and the joy of the Holy Ghost, are one ; add to this, their expecting a greater measure of assurance than God usually bestows. As long as they have any doubting, they think they have no assurance. They consider not

that there are many degrees of certainty. While they are here, they shall ' know but in part.'—Add also, their deriving their comfort at first from insufficient grounds. This may be the case of a gracious soul, who hath better grounds, but doth not see them. As an infant hath life before he knoweth it, and many misapprehensions of himself and other things, yet it will not follow that he hath no life. So when Christians find a flaw in their first comforts, they are not to judge it a flaw in their safety. Many continue under doubting, through the exceeding weakness of their natural parts. Many honest hearts have weak heads, and know not how to perform the work of self-trial. They will acknowledge the premises, and yet deny the apparent conclusion. If God do not some other way supply the defect of their reason, I see not how they should have clear and settled peace. One great and too common cause of distress is, the secret maintaining some known sin. This abates the degree of our graces, and so makes them more undiscernible. It obscureth that which it destroyeth not; for it beareth such sway that grace is not in action; nor seems to stir, nor is scarce heard speak for the noise of this corruption. It puts out or dimmeth the eye of the soul, and stupifies it, that it can neither see nor feel its own condition. But especially it provokes God to withdraw himself, his comforts, and the assistance of his Spirit, without which we may search long enough before we have assurance. God hath made a separation between sin and peace. As long as thou dost cherish thy pride, thy love of the world, the desires of the flesh, or any unchristian practice, thou expectest comfort in vain. If a man setteth up his idols in his heart, and putteth the stumbling-block of his iniquity before his face, and cometh to a minister, or to God, to inquire for comfort, instead of comforting him, God ' will answer him that cometh, according to the multitude of his idols.'—Another very great and common cause of the want of comfort is, when grace is not kept in constant and lively exercise. The way of painful duty is the way of fullest comfort. Peace and comfort are Christ's great encouragements to faithfulness and obedience; and, therefore, though our obedience does not merit them, yet they usually rise and fall with our diligence in duty. As prayer must have faith and fervency to procure it success, besides the blood and intercession of Christ, so must all other parts of our obedience. If thou grow seldom, and customary, and cold in duty, especially in thy secret prayers to God, and yet findest no abatement in thy joys, I cannot but

fear thy joys are either carnal or diabolical. Besides, grace is never apparent and sensible to the soul, but while it is in action; therefore, want of action must cause want of assurance. And the action of the soul upon such excellent objects, naturally bringeth consolation with it. The very act of loving God in Christ is inexpressibly sweet. The soul that is best furnished with grace, when it is not in action, is like a lute well stringed and tuned, which, while it lieth still, maketh no more music than a common piece of wood; but when it is handled by a skilful musician, the melody is delightful. Some degree of comfort follows every good action, as heat accompanies fire, and as beams and influence issue from the sun. A man that is cold, should labour till heat be excited; so he that wants assurance, must not stand still, but exercise his graces, till his doubts vanish. The want of consolation in the soul is also very commonly owing to bodily melancholy. It is no more wonder for a conscientious man, under melancholy, to doubt, and fear, and despair, than for a sick man to groan, or a child to cry when it is chastised. Without the physician in this case, the labours of the divine are usually in vain. You may silence, but you cannot comfort them. You may make them confess they have some grace, and yet cannot bring them to the comfortable conclusion. All the good thoughts of their state which you can possibly help them to, are seldom above a day or two old. They cry out of sin, and the wrath of God, when the chief cause is in their bodily distemper.

10. (3.) As for motives to persuade to the duty of self-examination, I entreat you to consider the following:—To be deceived about your title to heaven is very easy. Many are now in hell, that never suspected any falsehood in their hearts, that excelled in worldly wisdom, that lived in the clear light of the gospel, and even preached against the negligence of others. To be mistaken in this great point is also very common. It is the case of most in the world. In the old world, and in Sodom, we find none that were in any fear of judgment. Almost all men among us verily looked to be saved; yet Christ tells us, 'there be few that find the strait gate, and narrow way which leadeth unto life.' And if such multitudes are deceived, should we not search the more diligently, lest we should be deceived as well as they?—Nothing is more dangerous than to be thus mistaken. If the godly judge their state worse than it is, the consequences of this mistake will be sorrowful; but the mischief flowing from the mistake of the ungodly is un-

speakable. It will exceedingly confirm them in the service of Satan. It will render ineffectual the means that should do them good. It will keep a man from compassionating his own soul. It is a case of the greatest moment, where everlasting salvation or damnation is to be determined: and if you mistake till death, you are undone for ever. Seeing then the danger is so great, what wise man would not follow the search of his heart both day and night, till he were assured of his safety? Consider how small the labour of this duty is in comparison of that sorrow which followeth its neglect. You can endure to toil and sweat from year to year, to prevent poverty, and why not spend a little time in self-examination, to prevent eternal misery? By neglecting this duty, you can scarce do Satan a greater pleasure, nor yourselves a greater injury. It is the grand design of the devil, in all his temptations, to deceive you, and keep you ignorant of your danger, till you feel the everlasting flames; and will you join with him to deceive yourself? If you do this for him, you do the greatest part of his work. And hath he deserved so well of you, that you should assist him in such a design as your damnation? The time is nigh when God will search you. If it be but in this life by affliction, it will make you wish that you had tried and judged yourselves, that you might have escaped the judgment of God. It was a terrible voice to Adam, 'where art thou? Hast thou eaten of the tree?' And to Cain, 'where is thy brother?' Men 'consider not in their hearts that I,' saith the Lord, 're-member all their wickedness: now their own doings have beset them about; they are before my face.' Consider also what would be the sweet effects of this self-examination. If thou be upright and godly, it will lead thee straight towards assurance of God's love; if thou be not, though it will trouble thee at the present, yet it will tend to thy happiness, and at length lead thee to the assurance of that happiness. Is it not a desirable thing to know what shall befal us hereafter? especially what shall befal our souls? and what place and state we must be in for ever? And as the very knowledge itself is desirable, how much greater will the comfort be of that certainty of salvation? What sweet thoughts wilt thou have of God! All that greatness and justice, which is the terror of others, will be thy joy. How sweet may be thy thoughts of Christ, and the blood he hath shed, and the benefits he hath procured! How welcome will the word of God be to thee, and how beautiful the very feet of those that bring it! How sweet will be the

promises when thou art sure they are thine own! The very threatenings will occasion thy comfort, to remember that thou hast escaped them. What boldness and comfort mayest thou then have in prayer, when thou canst say, 'Our Father,' in full assurance! It will make the Lord's supper a refreshing feast to thy soul. It will multiply the sweetness of every common mercy. How comfortably mayest thou then undergo all afflictions! How will it sweeten thy forethoughts of death and judgment, of heaven and hell! How lively will it make thee in the work of the Lord, and how profitable to all around thee? What vigour will it infuse into all thy graces and affections, kindle thy repentance, inflame thy love, quicken thy desires, and confirm thy faith, be a fountain of continual rejoicing, overflow thy heart with thankfulness, raise thee high in the delightful work of praise, help thee to be heavenly-minded, and render thee persevering in all! All these sweet effects of assurance would make thy life a heaven upon earth.

11. Though I am certain these motives have weight of reason in them, yet I am jealous, Reader, lest you lay aside the book, as if you had done, and never set yourself to the practice of the duty. The case in hand is of the greatest moment, whether thou shalt everlastingly live in heaven or hell. I here request thee, in behalf of thy soul; nay, I charge thee, in the name of the Lord, that thou defer no longer, but take thy heart to task in good earnest, and think with thyself, 'Is it so easy, so common, and so dangerous to be mistaken? Are there so many wrong ways? Is the heart so deceitful? Why, then, do I not search into every corner, till I know my state? Must I so shortly undergo the trial at the bar of Christ? And do I not presently try myself? What a case were I in, if I should then miscarry? May I know by a little diligent inquiry now; and do I stick at the labour?' But perhaps thou wilt say, 'I know not how to do it.' In that I am now to give thee directions; but alas! it will be in vain, if thou art not resolved to practise them. Wilt thou, therefore, before thou goest any further, here promise before the Lord, to set thyself upon the speedy performance of the duty, according to the directions I shall lay down from the word of God. I demand nothing unreasonable or impossible. It is but to bestow a few hours, to know what shall become of thee for ever. If a neighbour, or a friend, desire but an hour's time of thee in conversation, or business, or any thing in which thou mayest be of service, surely thou wouldst not deny it; how much less shouldst thou deny this

to thyself in so great an affair! I pray thee to take from me this request, as if, in the name of Christ, I presented it to thee on my knees; and I will betake me on my knees to Christ again, to beg that he will persuade thy heart to the duty.

12. (4.) The directions how to examine thyself are such as these :—Empty thy mind of all other cares and thoughts, that they may not distract or divide thy mind. This work will be enough at once, without joining others with it. Then fall down before God in hearty prayer, desiring the assistance of his Spirit, to discover to thee the plain truth of thy condition, and to enlighten thee in the whole progress of this work. Make choice of the most convenient time and place. Let the place be the most private ; and the time, when you have nothing to interrupt you; and, if possible, let it be the present time. Have in readiness, either in memory, or writing, some scriptures, containing the descriptions of the saints, and the gospel terms of salvation ; and convince thyself thoroughly of their infallible truth. Proceed then to put the question to thyself. Let it not be, whether there be any good in thee at all ? nor, whether thou hast such or such a degree and measure of grace ? but whether such or such a saving grace be in thee in sincerity or not ? If thy heart draw back from the work, force it on. Lay thy command upon it. Let reason interpose, and use its authority. Yea, lay the command of God upon it, and charge it to obey, upon the pain of his displeasure. Let conscience also do its office, till thy heart be excited to the work.—Nor let thy heart trifle away the time, when it should be diligently at the work. Do as the Psalmist —'My spirit made diligent search.' He that can prevail with his own heart, shall also prevail with God.— If, after all thy pains, thou art not resolved, then seek out for help. Go to one that is godly, experienced, able, and faithful, and tell him thy case, and desire his best advice. Use the judgment of such a one, as that of a physician for thy body : though this can afford thee no full certainty, yet it may be a great help to stay and direct thee. But do not make it a pretence to put off thy own self-examination. Only use it as one of the last remedies, when thy own endeavours will not serve. When thou hast discovered thy true state, pass sentence on thyself accordingly; either that thou art a true Christian, or that thou art not. Pass not this sentence rashly, nor with self-flattery, nor with melancholy terrors ; but deliberately, truly, and according to thy conscience, convinced by scripture and reason. Labour to get thy heart affected with its condition, according to the sentence passed on it. If graceless, think of thy misery : if renewed and sanctified, think what a blessed state the Lord hath brought thee into. Pursue these thoughts till they have left their impression on thy heart. Write this sentence at least in thy memory—' At such a time, upon thorough examination, I found my state to be thus, or thus.' Such a record will be very useful to thee hereafter. Trust not to this one discovery, so as to try no more ; nor let it hinder thee in the daily search of thy ways: neither be discouraged, if the trial must be often repeated. Especially take heed, if unregenerated, not to conclude of thy future state by the present. Do not say, ' Because I am ungodly, I shall die so ; because I am a hypocrite, I shall continue so.' Do not despair. Nothing but thy unwillingness can keep thee from Christ, though thou hast hitherto abused him, and dissembled with him.

13. (5.) Now let me add some marks by which you may try your title to the saints' rest. I will only mention these two,—taking God for thy chief good—and heartily accepting Christ for thy only Saviour and Lord.

14. Every soul that hath a title to this rest, doth place his chief happiness in God. This rest consisteth in the full and glorious enjoyment of God. He that maketh not God his chief good and ultimate end, is in heart a pagan and a vile idolater. Let me ask, then, dost thou truly account it thy chief happiness to enjoy the Lord in glory, or dost thou not ? Canst thou say, ' The Lord is my portion ? Whom have I in heaven but thee? and there is none upon earth that I desire besides thee.' If thou be an heir of rest, it is thus with thee. Though the flesh will be pleading for its own delights, and the world will be creeping into thine affections ; yet in thy ordinary, settled, prevailing judgment and affections, thou preferrest God before all things in the world.—Thou makest him the very end of thy desires and endeavours. The very reason why thou hearest and prayest, and desirest to live on earth, is chiefly this, That thou mayest seek the Lord, and make sure of thy rest. Though thou dost not seek it so zealously as thou shouldst ; yet it has the chief of thy desires and endeavours, so that nothing else is desired or preferred before it. Thou wilt think no labour or suffering too great to obtain it. And though the flesh may sometimes shrink, yet thou art resolved and contented to go through all. Thy esteem for it will also be so high, and thy affection to it so great, that thou wouldst not exchange thy title to it, and hopes of it, for any

worldly good whatsoever. If God should set before thee an eternity of earthly pleasures on the one hand, and the saints' rest on the other, and bid thee take thy choice ; thou wouldst refuse the world, and choose this rest. But if thou art yet unsanctified, then thou dost in thy heart prefer thy worldly happiness before God ; and though thy tongue may say, ' that God is thy chief good,' yet thy heart doth not so esteem him. For the world is the chief end of thy desires and endeavours. Thy very heart is set upon it. Thy greatest care and labour is to maintain thy credit, or fleshly delights. But the life to come hath little of thy care or labour. Thou didst never perceive so much excellency in that unseen glory of another world, as to draw thy heart after it, and set thee a labouring heartily for it. The little pains thou bestowest that way, is but in the second place. God hath but the world's leavings ; only that time and labour which thou canst spare from the world, or those few, cold, and careless thoughts which follow thy constant, earnest, and delightful thoughts of earthly things. Neither wouldst thou do any thing at all for heaven, if thou knewest how to keep the world. But lest thou shouldst be turned into hell, when thou canst keep the world no longer, therefore thou wilt do something. For the same reason, thou thinkest the way of God too strict, and wilt not be persuaded to the constant labour of walking according to the gospel rule ; and when it comes to the trial, that thou must forsake Christ, or thy worldly happiness, then thou wilt venture heaven rather than earth, and so wilfully deny thy obedience to God. And certainly if God would but give thee leave to live in health and wealth for ever on earth, thou wouldst think it a better state than rest. Let them seek for heaven that would, thou wouldst think this thy chief happiness. This is thy case, if thou art yet an unregenerate person, and hast no title to the saints' rest.

15. And as thou takest God for thy chief good, so thou dost heartily accept of Christ for thy only Saviour and Lord, to bring thee to this rest. The former mark was the sum of the first and great command of the law, ' thou shalt love the Lord thy God with all thy heart.' The second mark, is the sum of the command of the gospel, ' believe in the Lord Jesus Christ, and thou shalt be saved.' And the performance of these two, is the whole of godliness and Christianity. This mark is but the definition of faith. Dost thou heartily consent that Christ alone shall be thy Saviour ? and no further trust to thy duties and works, than as means appointed in subordination to him ? and looking at them as not in the least measure able to satisfy the curse of the law, or as a legal righteousness, or any part of it ; but consent to trust thy salvation on the redemption made by Christ ? Art thou also content to take him for thy only Lord and King, to govern and guide thee by his laws and Spirit ; and to obey him, even when he commands the hardest duties, and those which most cross the desires of the flesh ? Is it thy sorrow when thou breakest thy resolution herein ? and thy joy when thou keepest closest in obedience to him ? Wouldst thou not change thy Lord and Master for all the world ? Thus is it with every true Christian. But if thou be a hypocrite, it is far otherwise. Thou mayest call Christ thy Lord and thy Saviour ; but thou never foundest thyself so lost without him, as to drive thee to seek him and trust him, and lay thy salvation on him alone. At least, thou didst never heartily consent that he should govern thee as thy Lord, nor resign up thy soul and life to be ruled by him, nor take his word for the law of thy thoughts and actions. It is likely thou art content to be saved from hell by Christ when thou diest ; but in the mean time he shall command thee no further than will stand with thy credit, or pleasure, or other worldly ends. And if he would give thee leave, thou hadst far rather live after the world and flesh, than after the word and Spirit. And though thou mayest now and then have a motion or purpose to the contrary ; yet this that I have mentioned is the ordinary desire and choice of thy heart. Thou art therefore no true believer in Christ ; for though thou confess him in words, yet in works thou dost deny him, ' being abominable, and disobedient, and unto every good work reprobate.' This is the case of those that shall be shut out of the saints' rest.

16. Observe, it is the consent of your hearts, or wills, which I especially lay down to be inquired after. I do not ask, whether thou be assured of salvation, nor whether thou canst believe that thy sins are pardoned, and that thou art beloved of God in Christ ? These are no parts of justifying faith, but excellent fruits of it, and they that receive them, are comforted by them ; but, perhaps, thou mayest never receive them while thou livest, and yet be a true heir of rest. Do not say then, ' I cannot believe that my sins are pardoned, or that I am in God's favour ; and therefore I am no true believer.' This is a most mistaken conclusion.— The question is, Whether thou dost heartily accept of Christ, that thou mayest be pardoned, reconciled to God, and so saved ? Dost thou consent

that he shall be thy Lord, who hath bought thee, and that he shall bring thee to heaven in his own way? This is justifying, saving faith, and the mark by which thou must try thyself. Yet still observe, that all this consent must be hearty and real, not feigned or with reservations. It is not saying, as that dissembling son, 'I go, Sir; and went not.' If any have more of the government of thee than Christ, thou art not his disciple. I am sure these two marks are such as every Christian hath, and none but sincere Christians. O that the Lord would now persuade thee to the close performance of this self-trial! that thou mayest not tremble with horror of soul, when the Judge of all the world shall try thee; but be so able to prove thy title to rest, that the prospect and approach of death and judgment may raise thy spirits, and fill thee with joy.

17. On the whole, as ever Christians would have comforts that will not deceive them, let them make it the great labour of their lives to grow in grace, to strengthen and advance the interest of Christ in their souls, and to weaken and subdue the interest of the flesh. Deceive not yourselves with a persuasion, that Christ hath done all, and left you nothing to do. To overcome the world, the flesh, and the devil; and in order to that, to stand always armed upon our watch, and valiantly and patiently to fight it out, is of great importance to our assurance and salvation. Indeed it is so great a part of our baptismal vow, that he who performeth it not, is no more than a nominal Christian. Not to every one that presumptuously believeth, but 'to him that overcometh, will Christ give to eat of the hidden manna, and will give him a white stone, and in the stone a new name written, which no man knoweth, saving he that receiveth it; he shall eat of the tree of life, which is in the midst of the paradise of God, and shall not be hurt of the second death. Christ will confess his name before his Father, and before his angels, and make him a pillar in the temple of God, and he shall go no more out; and will write upon him the name of his God, and the name of the city of his God, which is new Jerusalem, which cometh down out of heaven from his God, and will write upon him his new name.' Yea, 'He will grant to him to sit with him on his throne, even as he also overcame, and is set down with his Father on his throne. He that hath an ear, let him hear what the Spirit saith unto the churches.'

CHAPTER IX.

THE DUTY OF THE PEOPLE OF GOD TO EXCITE OTHERS TO SEEK THE REST.

Sect. 1. The Author laments that Christians do so little to help others to obtain the saints' rest: 2. (I.) Shows the nature of this duty; particularly, 3. (1) In having our hearts affected with the misery of our brethren's souls; 4—6. (2.) In taking all opportunities to instruct them in the way of salvation; 7. (3.) In promoting their profit by public ordinances; 8 (II.) Assigns various reasons why this duty is so much neglected; 9. And answers some objections against it: 10—13 Then. (III.) Urges to the discharge of it, by several considerations. 14. Addressed to such as have knowledge, learning, and utterance; 15. Those that are acquainted with sinners; 16. Physicians that attend dying men; 17. Persons of wealth and power; 18. Ministers; 19 And those that are intrusted with the care of children or servants 20. The chapter concludes with an earnest request to Christian parents to be faithful to their trust.

1. Hath God set before us such a glorious prize as the saints' rest, and made us capable of such inconceivable happiness? Why, then, do not all the children of this kingdom exert themselves more to help others to the enjoyment of it? Alas, how little are poor souls about us beholden to most of us! We see the glory of the kingdom, and they do not: we see the misery of those that are out of it, and they do not: we see some wandering quite out of the way, and know, if they hold on, they can never come there; and they themselves discern it not. And yet we will not seriously show them their danger and error, and help to bring them into the way, that they may live. Alas, how few Christians are there to be found, that set themselves with all their might to save souls! No thanks to us, if heaven be not empty, and if the souls of our brethren perish not for ever. Considering how important this duty is, to the glory of God, and the happiness of men, I will show—how it is to be performed—why it is so much neglected—and then offer some considerations to persuade to it.

2. (I.) The duty of exciting and helping others to discern their title to the saints' rest, doth not mean that every man should turn a public preacher, or that any should go beyond the bounds of their particular callings: much less does it consist in promoting a party spirit; and, least of all, in speaking against men's faults behind their backs, and be silent before their faces. This duty is of another nature, and consists of the following things—in having our hearts affected with the misery of our brethren's souls—in taking all opportunities to instruct them in the way of salvation—and in promoting their profit by public ordinances.

3. (1.) Our hearts must be affected with the misery of our brethren's souls. We must be compassionate towards them, and yearn after

their recovery and salvation. If we earnestly longed after their conversion, and our hearts were solicitous to do them good, it would set us on work, and God would usually bless it.

4. (2.) We must take every opportunity that we possibly can, to instruct them how to attain salvation. If the person be ignorant, labour to make him understand the chief happiness of man; how far he was once possessed of it; the covenant God then made with him; how he broke it; what penalty he incurred; and what misery he brought himself into: teach him his need of a Redeemer; how Christ did mercifully interpose, and bear the penalty; what the new covenant is: how men are drawn to Christ; and what are the riches and privileges which believers have in him. If he is not moved by these things, then show him the excellency of the glory he neglects; the extremity and eternity of the torments of the damned: the justice of enduring them for wilfully refusing grace; the certainty, nearness, and terrors of death and judgment; the vanity of all things below; the sinfulness of sin; the preciousness of Christ; the necessity of regeneration, faith, and holiness, and the true nature of them. If, after all, you find him entertaining false hopes, then urge him to examine his state; show him the necessity of doing so; help him in it; nor leave him till you have convinced him of his misery and remedy. Show him how vain and destructive it is to join Christ and his duties, to compose his justifying righteousness. Yet be sure to draw him to the use of all means: such as hearing and reading the word, calling upon God, and associating with the godly: persuade him to forsake sin, avoid all temptations to sin, especially evil companions, and to wait patiently on God in the use of means, as the way in which God will be found.

5. But because the manner of performing this work is of great moment, observe therefore these rules.—Enter upon it with right intentions. Aim at the glory of God in the person's salvation. Do it not to get a name, or esteem to thyself, or to bring men to depend upon thee, or to get thee followers; but in obedience to Christ, in imitation of him, and tender love to men's souls. Do not as those, who labour to reform their children or servants from such things as are against their own profit or humour, but never seek to save their souls in the way which God hath appointed. Do it speedily. As you would not have them delay their return, do not you delay to seek their return. While you are purposing to teach and help him, the man goes deeper in debt; wrath is heaping up; sin taking root; custom fastens him; temptations to sin multiply; conscience grows seared; the heart hardened; the devil rules; Christ is shut out; the Spirit is resisted; God is daily dishonoured; his law violated; he is without a servant, and that service from him which He should have; time runs on; death and judgment are at the door; and what if the man die, and drop into hell, while you are purposing to prevent it? If, in the case of his bodily distress, you must not say to him, ' Go, and come again, and to-morrow I will give, when thou hast it by thee;' how much less may you delay the succour of his soul? That physician is no better than a murderer, who negligently delayeth till his patient be dead or past cure. Lay by excuses, then, and all lesser business, and ' exhort one another daily, while it is called To-day; lest any be hardened through the deceitfulness of sin.' Let your exhortation proceed from compassion and love. To jeer and scoff, to rail and vilify, is not a likely way to reform men, or convert them to God.—Go to poor sinners with tears in your eyes, that they may see you believe them to be miserable, and that you unfeignedly pity their case. Deal with them with earnest humble entreaties. Let them perceive it is the desire of your hearts to do them good; that you have no other end but their everlasting happiness; and that it is your sense of their danger, and your love to their souls, that forceth you to speak; even because you know the terrors of the Lord, and for fear you should see them in eternal torments. Say to them, ' Friend, you know I seek no advantage of my own: the method to please you, and keep your friendship, were to soothe you in your way, or let you alone; but love will not suffer me to see you perish, and be silent. I seek nothing at your hands, but that which is necessary to your own happiness. It is yourself that will have the gain and comfort, if you come to Christ.' If we were thus to go to every ignorant and wicked neighbour, what blessed fruit should we quickly see!—Do it with all possible plainness and faithfulness. Do not make their sins less than they are, nor encourage them in a false hope. If you see the case dangerous, speak plainly—' Neighbour, I am afraid God hath not yet renewed your soul: I doubt you are not yet recovered from the power of Satan to God; I doubt you have not chosen Christ above all, nor unfeignedly taken him for your sovereign Lord. If you had, surely you durst not so easily disobey him, nor neglect his worship in your family, and in public; you could not so eagerly follow the world, and talk of nothing but the things of

the world. If you were in Christ, you would be a new creature : old things would be passed away, and all things would become new. You would have new thoughts, new talk, new company, new endeavours, and a new conversation. Certainly, without these you can never be saved ; you may think otherwise, and hope otherwise, as long as you will, but your hopes will all deceive you, and perish with you.' Thus must you deal faithfully with men, if ever you intend to do them good. It is not in curing men's souls, as in curing their bodies, where they must not know their danger, lest it hinder the cure. They are here agents in their own cure ; and if they know not their misery, they will never bewail it, nor know their need of a Saviour. Do it also seriously, zealously, and effectually. Labour to make men know that heaven and hell are not matters to be played with, or passed over with a few careless thoughts.—' It is most certain, that one of these days thou shalt be in everlasting joy or torment; and doth it not awaken thee ? Are there so few that find the way of life ? So many that go the way of death ? Is it so hard to escape ? so easy to miscarry ? and yet do you sit still and trifle ? What do you mean ? The world is passing away : its pleasures, honours, and profits, are fading and leaving you : eternity is a little before you ; God is just and jealous : his threatenings are true : the great day will be terrible : time runs on : your life is uncertain : you are far behindhand : your case is dangerous : if you die to morrow, how unready are you ! With what terror will your souls go out of your bodies ! And do you yet loiter ! Consider, God is all this while waiting your leisure ; his patience bears : his long-suffering forbears : his mercy entreats you ; Christ offereth you his blood and merits : the Spirit is persuading : conscience is accusing : Satan waits to have you. This is your time, now or never. Had you rather burn in hell, than repent on earth ? have devils your tormentors, than Christ your governor ? Will you renounce your part in God and glory, rather than renounce your sins ? O friends, what do you think of these things ? God hath made you men ; do not renounce your reason where you should chiefly use it.' Alas ! it is not a few dull words, between jest and earnest, between sleep and awake, that will rouse a dead-hearted sinner. If a house be on fire, you will not make a cold oration on the nature and danger of fire, but will run and cry, Fire, fire ! To tell a man of his sins as softly as Eli did his sons ; or to reprove him as gently as Jehoshaphat did Ahab, ' Let not the king say so ;' usually doth as much

harm as good. Lothness to displease men, makes us undo them.

6. Yet, lest you run into extremes, I advise you to do it with prudence and discretion.— Choose the fittest season. Deal not with men when they are in a passion, or where they will take it for a disgrace. When the earth is soft, the plough will enter. Take a man when he is under affliction, or newly impressed under a sermon. Christian faithfulness requires us, not only to do good when it falls in our way, but to watch for opportunities. Suit yourselves also to the quality and temper of the person. You must deal with the ingenious more by argument than persuasion. There is need of both to the ignorant. The affections of the convinced should be chiefly excited. The obstinate must be sharply reproved. The timorous must be dealt with tenderly. Love and plainness, and seriousness, take with all ; but words of terror some can scarce bear. Use also the aptest expressions. Unseeming language makes the hearers lothe the food they should live by ; especially if they be men of curious ears, and carnal hearts.—Let all your reproofs and exhortations be backed with the authority of God. Let sinners be convinced that you speak not of your own head. Turn them to the very chapter and verse where their sin is condemned, and their duty commanded. The voice of man is contemptible, but the voice of God is awful and terrible. They may reject your words, that dare not reject the words of the Almighty.—Be frequent with men in this duty of exhortation. If we are always to pray, and not to faint, because God will have us importunate with himself ; the same course, no doubt, will be most prevailing with men. Therefore, we are commanded ' to exhort one another daily ;' and, 'with long-suffering.' The fire is not always brought out of the flint at one stroke ; nor men's affections kindled at the first exhortation. And if they were, yet if they be not followed, they will soon grow cold again. Follow sinners with your loving and earnest entreaties, and give them no rest in their sin. This is true charity, the way to save men's souls, and will afford you comfort upon review.—Strive to bring all your exhortations to an issue. If we speak the most convincing words, and all our care is over with our speech, we shall seldom prosper in our labours : but God usually blesses their labours, whose very heart is set upon the conversion of their hearers, and who are therefore inquiring after the success of their work. If you reprove a sin, cease not till the sinner promises you to leave it, and avoid the occasion of it. If you

are exhorting to a duty, urge for a promise to set upon it presently. If you would draw men to Christ, leave not till you have made them confess the misery of their present unregenerated state, and the necessity of Christ, and of a change, and have promised you to fall close to the use of means. O that all Christians would take this course with all their neighbours that are enslaved to sin, and strangers to Christ!—Once more, be sure your example exhort as well as your words. Let them see you constant in all the duties you persuade them to. Let them see in your lives that superiority to the world which your lips recommend. Let them see, by your constant labours for heaven, that you indeed believe what you would have them believe. A holy and heavenly life is a continual pain to the consciences of sinners around you, and continually solicits them to change their course.

7. (3.) Besides the duty of private admonition, you must endeavour to help men to profit by the public ordinances. In order to that—endeavour to procure for them faithful ministers, where they are wanting. 'How shall they hear without a preacher?' Improve your interest and diligence to this end, till you prevail. Extend your purses to the utmost. How many souls may be saved by the ministry you have procured! It is a higher and nobler charity than relieving their bodies. What abundance of good might great men do, if they would support, in academical education, such youth as they have first carefully chosen for their integrity and piety, till they should be fit for the ministry! And when a faithful ministry is obtained, help poor souls to receive the fruit of it. Draw them constantly to attend it. Remind them often what they have heard; and, if it be possible, let them hear it repeated in their families, or elsewhere. Promote their frequent meeting together, besides publicly in the congregation; not as a separate church, but as a part of the church, more diligent than the rest in redeeming time, and helping the souls of each other heaven-ward. Labour also to keep the ordinances and ministry in esteem. No man will be much wrought on by that which he despiseth. An apostle says, 'We beseech you, brethren, to know them who labour among you, and are over you in the Lord, and admonish you; and to esteem them very highly in love for their work's sake.'

8. (II.) Let us now a little inquire, what may be the causes of the gross neglect of this duty; that the hinderances being discovered, may the more easily be overcome.—One hinderance is, men's own sin and guilt. They have not themselves been ravished with heavenly delights; how then should they draw others so earnestly to seek them? They have not felt their own lost condition, nor their need of Christ, nor the renewing work of the Spirit; how then can they discover these to others? They are guilty of the sins they should reprove, and this makes them ashamed to reprove.—Another is, a secret infidelity prevailing in men's hearts. Did we verily believe, that all the unregenerated and unholy should be eternally tormented, how could we hold our tongues, or avoid bursting into tears, when we look them in the face, especially when they are our near and dear friends? Thus doth secret unbelief consume the vigour of each grace and duty. O Christians, if you did verily believe that your ungodly neighbours, wife, husband, or child, should certainly lie for ever in hell, except they be thoroughly changed before death shall snatch them away, would not this make you address them day and night till they were persuaded? Were it not for this cursed unbelief, our own and our neighbours' souls would gain more by us than they do.—These attempts are also much hindered by our want of charity and compassion for men's souls. We look on miserable souls, and pass by, as the priest and levite by the wounded man. What though the sinner, wounded by sin, and captivated by Satan, do not desire thy help himself; yet his misery cries aloud. If God had not heard the cry of our miseries, before he heard the cry of our prayers, and be moved by his own pity before he was moved by our importunity, we might long have continued the slaves of satan. You will pray to God for them to open their eyes, and turn their hearts; and why not endeavour their conversion, if you desire it? And if you do not desire it, why do you ask it? Why do you not pray them to consider and return, as well as pray to God to convert and turn them? If you should see your neighbour fallen into a pit, and should pray to God to help him out, but neither put forth your hand to help him, nor once direct him to help himself, would not any man censure you for your cruelty and hypocrisy? It is as true of the soul as of the body. If any man 'seeth his brother have need, and shutteth up his bowels of compassion from him, how dwelleth the love of God in him?' Or what love hath he to his brother's soul?—We are also hindered by a base, man-pleasing disposition. We are so desirous to keep in credit and favour with men, that it makes us most unconscionably neglect our own duty. He is a foolish and unfaithful physician that will let a sick man die for

fear of troubling him. If our friends are distracted, we please them in nothing that tends to their hurt. And yet, when they are beside themselves in point of salvation, and. in their madness, posting on to damnation, we will not stop them, for fear of displeasing them. How can we be Christians, that 'love the praise of men more than the praise of God?' For, if we 'seek to please men, we shall not be the servants of Christ.'—It is common to be hindered by sinful bashfulness. When we should shame men out of their sins, we are ourselves ashamed of our duties. May not these sinners condemn us, when they blush not to swear, be drunk, or neglect the worship of God; and we blush to tell them of it, and persuade them from it? Bashfulness is unseemly, in cases of necessity. It is not a work to be ashamed of, to obey God in persuading men from their sins to Christ. Reader, hath not thy conscience told thee of thy duty many a time, and put thee on to speak to poor sinners; and yet thou hast been ashamed to open thy mouth, and so let them alone to sink or swim? O read and tremble, 'Whosoever shall be ashamed of me, and of my words, in this adulterous and sinful generation, of him also shall the Son of man be ashamed, when he comes in the glory of his Father, with his holy angels.' An idle and impatient spirit hinders us. It is an ungrateful work, and sometimes makes men our enemies. Besides, it seldom succeeds at the first, except it be followed on. You must be long teaching the ignorant, and persuading the obstinate. We consider not what patience God used towards us when we were in our sins. Woe to us if God had been as impatient with us as we are with others!—Another hinderance is, self-seeking. 'All seek their own, not the things which are Jesus Christ's' and their brethren's. With many, pride is a great impediment. If it were to speak to a great man, and it would not displease him, they would do it; but to go among the poor, and take pains with them in their cottages, where is the person that will do it? Many will rejoice in being instrumental to convert a gentleman, and they have good reason; but overlook the multitude, as if the souls of all were not alike to God. Alas, these men little consider how low Christ stooped to us! Few rich, and noble, and wise, are called. It is the poor that receive the glad tidings of the gospel.—And with some, their ignorance of the duty hindereth them from performing it. Either they know it not to be a duty, or, at least, not to be their duty. If this be thy case, Reader, I am in hope thou art now acquainted with thy duty, and will set upon it.

9. Do not object to this duty, that you are unable to manage an exhortation: but either set those on the work who are more able, or faithfully and humbly use the small ability you have, and tell them, as a weak man may do, what God says in his word.—Decline not the duty, because it is your superior who needs advice and exhortation. Order must be dispensed with, in cases of necessity. Though it be a husband, a parent, a minister, you must teach him in such a case. If parents are in want, children must relieve them. If a husband be sick, the wife must fill up his place in family affairs. If the rich are reduced to beggary, they must receive charity. If the physician be sick, somebody must look to him. So the meanest servant must admonish his master, and the child his parent, and the wife her husband, and the people their minister; so that it be done when there is real need, and with all possible humility, modesty, and meekness.—Do not say, 'This will make us all preachers;' for every good Christian is a teacher, and has a charge of his neighbour's soul. Every man is a physician, when a regular physician cannot be had, and when the hurt is so small that any man may relieve it; and in the same cases every man must be a teacher!—Do not despair of success. Cannot God give it? And must it not be by means? Do not plead, it will only be casting pearls before swine. When you are in danger to be torn in pieces, Christ would have you forbear; but what is that to you that are in no such danger? As long as they will hear, you have encouragement to speak, and may not cast them off as contemptible swine.—Say not it is a friend on whom I much depend, and by telling him his sin and misery, I may lose his love, and be undone.' Is his love more to be valued than his safety? or thy own benefit by him, than the salvation of his soul? or wilt thou connive at his damnation, because he is thy friend? Is that thy best requital of his friendship? Hadst thou rather he should burn in hell for ever, than thou shouldst lose his favour, or the maintenance thou hast from him.

10. (III.) But that all who fear God may be excited to do their utmost to help others to this blessed rest, let me entreat you to consider the following motives. As, for instance, not only nature, but especially grace, disposes the soul to be communicative of good. Therefore, to neglect this work is a sin both against nature and grace. Would you not think him unnatural that would suffer his children or neighbours to starve in the streets, while he has provision at hand? And is not he more unnatural, that will let them

eternally perish, and not open his mouth to save them? An unmerciful, cruel man, is a monster to be abhorred of all. If God had bid you give them all your estates, or lay down your lives to save them, you would surely have refused, when you will not bestow a little breath to save them. Is not the soul of a husband, or wife, or child, or neighbour, worth a few words? Cruelty to men's bodies is a most damnable sin; but to their souls much more, as the soul is of greater worth than the body, and eternity than time. Little know you what many a soul may now be feeling in hell, who died in their sins, for want of your faithful admonition.—Consider what Christ did towards the saving of souls. He thought them worth his blood; and shall we not think them worth our breath? Will you not do a little where Christ hath done so much?—Consider what fit objects of pity ungodly people are. They are dead in trespasses and sins, have not hearts to feel their miseries, nor to pity themselves. If others do not pity them, they will have no pity; for it is the nature of their disease to make them pitiless to themselves, yea, their own most cruel destroyers.—Consider it was once thy own case. It was God's argument to the Israelites, to be kind to strangers, because themselves had been 'strangers in the land of Egypt.' So should you pity them that are strangers to Christ, and to the hopes and comforts of the saints, because you were once strangers to them yourselves. Consider your relation to them. It is thy neighbour, thy brother, whom thou art bound to love as thyself: 'He that loveth not his brother whom he seeth daily, doth not love God whom he never saw.' And doth he love his brother that will see him go to hell, and never hinder him?

11. Consider what a load of guilt this neglect lays upon thy own soul. Thou art guilty of the murder and damnation of all those souls whom thou dost thus neglect; and of every sin they now commit, and of all the dishonour done to God thereby; and of all those judgments which their sins bring upon the town or country where they live.—Consider what it will be to look upon your poor friends in eternal flames, and to think that your neglect was a great cause of it. If you should there perish with them, it would be no small aggravation of your torment. If you be in heaven, it would surely be a sad thought, were it possible that any sorrow could dwell there, to hear a multitude of poor souls cry out for ever, 'O, if you would but have told me plainly of my sin and danger, and set it home, I might have escaped all this torment, and been now in rest!' What a sad voice will this be!—

Consider what a joy it will be in heaven, to meet those there whom you have been the means to bring thither. To see their faces, and join with them for ever in the praises of God, whom you were the happy instruments of bringing to the knowledge and obedience of Jesus Christ?—Consider how many souls you may have drawn into the way of damnation, or hardened in it. We have had, in the days of our ignorance, our companions in sin, whom we incited, or encouraged. And doth it not become us to do as much to save men, as we have done to destroy them?—Consider how diligent are all the enemies of these poor souls to draw them to hell. The devil is tempting them day and night: their inward lusts are still working for their ruin: the flesh is still pleading for its delights: their old companions are increasing their dislike of holiness. And if nobody be diligent in helping them to heaven, what is like to become of them?

12. Consider how deep the neglect of this duty will wound, when conscience is awakened. When a man comes to die, conscience will ask him, 'What good hast thou done in thy lifetime? The saving of souls is the greatest good work; what hast thou done towards it? How many hast thou dealt faithfully with?' I have often observed that the consciences of dying men very much wounded them for this omission. For my own part, when I have been near death, my conscience hath accused me more for this than for any sin. It would bring every ignorant profane neighbour to my remembrance, to whom I never made known their danger. It would tell me, 'Thou shouldst have gone to them in private, and told them plainly of their desperate danger, though it had been when thou shouldst have eaten or slept, if thou hadst no other time.' Conscience would remind me how, at such or such a time, I was in company with the ignorant, or was riding by the way with a wilful sinner, and had a fit opportunity to have dealt with him, but did not; or at least did it to little purpose. The Lord grant I may better obey conscience while I have time, that it may have less to accuse me of at death!—Consider what a seasonable time you now have for this work. There are times in which it is not safe to speak; it may cost you your liberties, or your lives. Besides, your neighbours will shortly die, and so will you. Speak to them, therefore, while you may.—Consider, though this is a work of the greatest charity, yet every one of you may perform it; the poorest as well as the rich. Every one hath a tongue to speak to a sinner.—Once more, consider the happy consequences of this work, where it is faithfully done.

You may be instrumental in saving souls, for which Christ came down and died, and in which the angels of God rejoice. Such souls will bless you here and hereafter. God will have much glory by it. The church will be multiplied and edified by it. Your own souls will enjoy more improvement and vigour in a divine life, more peace of conscience, more rejoicing in spirit. Of all the personal mercies that I ever received, next to the love of God in Christ to my own soul, I must most joyfully bless him for the plentiful success of my endeavours upon others. O what fruits then might I have seen if I had been more faithful! I know we need be very jealous of our deceitful hearts in this point, lest our rejoicing should come from our pride. Naturally we would have the praise of every good work ascribed to ourselves: yet to imitate our Father in goodness and mercy, and to rejoice in the degree of them we attain to, is the duty of every child of God. I therefore tell you my own experience, to persuade you, that if you did but know what a joyful thing it is, you would follow it night and day through the greatest discouragements.

13. Up, then, every man that hath a tongue, and is a servant of Christ, and do something of your Master's work. Why hath he given you a tongue, but to speak in his service? And how can you serve him more eminently, than in saving souls? He that will pronounce you blessed at the last day, and invite you to 'the kingdom prepared for you,' because you 'fed him, and clothed him, and visited him,' in his poor members, will surely pronounce you blessed for so great a work as bringing souls to his kingdom. He that saith, 'the poor you have always with you,' hath left the ungodly always with you, that you might still have matter to exercise your charity upon. If you have the hearts of Christians or of men, let them yearn towards your ignorant, ungodly neighbour. Say as the lepers of Samaria, 'We do not well; this day is a day of good tidings, and we hold our peace.' Hath God had so much mercy on you, and will you have no mercy on your poor neighbours? But as this duty belongs to all Christians, so especially to some, according as God hath called them to it, or qualified them for it. To them, therefore, I will more particularly address the exhortation.

14. God especially expects this duty at your hands to whom he hath given more learning and knowledge, and endued with better utterance, than your neighbours. The strong are made to help the weak; and those that see must direct the blind. God looketh for this faithful improvement of your parts and gifts, which, if you neglect, it were better you had never received them; for they will but aggravate your condemnation, and be as useless to your own salvation as they were to others.

15. All those that are particularly acquainted with some ungodly men, and that have particular interest in them, God looks for this duty at your hands. Christ himself did eat and drink with publicans and sinners; but it was only to be their physician, and not their companion. Who knows but God gave you interest in them to this end, that you might be the means of their recovery? They that will not regard the words of a stranger, may regard a brother, or sister, or husband, or wife, or near friend; besides that, the bond of friendship engages you to more kindness and compassion than ordinary.

16. Physicians that are much about dying men should, in a special manner, make conscience of this duty. It is their peculiar advantage, that they are at hand; that they are with men in sickness and dangers, when the ear is more open, and the heart less stubborn than in time of health: and that men look upon their physician as a person in whose hands is their life; or, at least, who may do much to save them; and, therefore, they will the more regard his advice. You that are of this honourable profession, do not think this a work beside your calling, as if it belonged to none but ministers; except you think it beside your calling to be compassionate, or to be Christians. O help, therefore, to fit your patients for heaven? And whether you see they are for life or death, teach them both how to live and die, and give them some physic for their souls, as you do for their bodies. Blessed be God, that very many of the chief physicians of this age have, by their eminent piety, vindicated their profession from the common imputation of atheism and profaneness.

17. Men of wealth and authority, and that have many dependants, have excellent advantages for this duty. O what a world of good might lords and gentlemen do, if they had but hearts to improve their influence over others? Have you not all your honour and riches from God? Doth not Christ say, 'Unto whomsoever much is given, of him much shall be required?' If you speak to your dependants for God and their souls, you may be regarded, when even a minister shall be despised. As you value the honour of God, your own comfort, and the salvation of souls, improve your influence over your tenants and neighbours; visit their houses; see

whether they worship God in their families; and take all opportunities to press them to their duty. Despise them not. Remember God is no respecter of persons. Let men see that you excel others in piety, compassion, and diligence in God's work, as you do in the riches and honours of the world. I confess you will by this means be singular, but then you will be singular in glory; for few of the 'mighty and noble are called.'

18. As for the ministers of the gospel, it is the very work of their calling, to help others to heaven.—Be sure to make it the main end of your studies and preaching. He is the able, skilful minister, that is best skilled in the art of instructing, convincing, persuading, and consequently of winning souls: and that is the best sermon that is best in these. When you seek not God, but yourselves, God will make you the most contemptible of men. It is true of your reputation, what Christ says of your life, 'He that loveth it shall lose it.' Let the vigour of your persuasions show, that you are sensible on how weighty a business you are sent. Preach with that seriousness and fervour, as men that believe their own doctrine, and that know their hearers must be prevailed with, or be damned. —Think not that all your work is in your studies and pulpit. You are shepherds, and must know every sheep, and what is their disease, and mark their strayings, and help to cure them, and fetch them home. Learn of Paul, not only to 'teach your people publicly, but from house to house.' Inquire how they grow in knowledge and holiness, and on what grounds they build their hopes of salvation, and whether they walk uprightly, and perform the duties of their several relations. See whether they worship God in their families, and teach them how to do it. Be familiar with them, that you may maintain your interest in them, and improve it all for God. Know of them how they profit by public teaching. If any too little 'savour the things of the Spirit,' let them be pitied, but not neglected. If any walk disorderly, recover them with diligence and patience. If they be ignorant, it may be your fault as much as theirs. Be not asleep while the wolf is waking.—Deal not slightly with any. Some will not tell their people plainly of their sins, because they are great men; and some, because they are godly; as if none but the poor and the wicked should be dealt plainly with. Yet labour to be skilful and discreet, that the manner may answer to the excellency of the matter. Every reasonable soul hath both judgment and affection; and every rational, spiritual sermon. must have

both. Study and pray, and pray and study, till you are become 'workmen that need not be ashamed, rightly dividing the word of truth;' that your people may not be ashamed, nor weary in hearing you.—Let your conversation be teaching, as well as your doctrine. Be as forward in a holy and heavenly life, as you are in pressing others to it. Let your discourse be edifying and spiritual. Suffer any thing, rather than that the gospel and men's souls should suffer. Let men see that you use not the ministry only for a trade to live by; but that your hearts are set upon the welfare of souls. Whatsoever meekness, humility, condescension, or self-denial you teach them from the gospel, teach it them also by your undissembled example. Study and strive after unity and peace. If ever you would promote the kingdom of Christ, and your people's salvation, do it in a way of peace and love. It is as hard a thing to maintain in your people a sound understanding, a tender conscience, a lively, gracious, heavenly frame of spirit, and an upright life, amidst contention, as to keep your candle lighted in the greatest storms. 'Blessed is that servant, whom his Lord, when he cometh, shall find so doing.'

19. All you whom God hath intrusted with the care of children and servants, I would also persuade to this great work of helping others to the heavenly rest.—Consider what plain and pressing commands of God require this at your hands: 'These words thou shalt teach diligently unto thy children, and shalt talk of them when thou sittest in thine house, and when thou walkest by the way, and when thou liest down, and when thou risest up.'—'Train up a child in the way he should go; and when he is old he will not depart from it.'—'Bring up your children in the nurture and admonition of the Lord.' Joshua resolved, that 'he and his house would serve the Lord.' And God himself says of Abraham, 'I know him, that he will command his children, and his household after him, and they shall keep the way of the Lord.'—Consider it is a duty you owe your children in point of justice. From you they received the defilement and misery of their natures; and, therefore, you owe them all possible help for their recovery.—Consider, how near your children are to you. They are parts of yourselves. If they prosper when you are dead, you take it as if you lived and prospered in them; and should you not be of the same mind for their everlasting rest? Otherwise you will be witnesses against your own souls. Your care, and pains, and cost for their bodies, will condemn you for your neglect of their

precious souls. Yea, all the brute creatures may condemn you. Which of them is not tender of their young?—Consider, God hath made your children your charge, and your servants too. Every one will confess they are the minister's charge. And have not you a greater charge of your own families, than any minister can have of them? Doubtless at your hands God will require the blood of their souls. It is the greatest charge you were ever intrusted with, and woe to you, if you suffer them to be ignorant or wicked for want of your instruction or correction. Consider, what work there is for you in their dispositions and lives. There is not one sin, but thousands. They have hereditary diseases, bred in their natures. The things you must teach them are contrary to the interests and desires of the flesh. May the Lord make you sensible what a work and charge lieth upon you!—Consider what sorrows you prepare for yourselves by the neglect of your children. If they prove thorns in your eyes, they are of your own planting. If you should repent and be saved, is it nothing to think of their damnation, and yourselves the occasion of it? But if you die in your sins, how will they cry out against you in hell: 'All this was wrong of you; you should have taught us better, and did not; you should have restrained us from sin, and corrected us, but did not.' What an addition will such outcries be to your misery. On the other side, think what a comfort you may have, if you be faithful in this duty. If you should not succeed you have freed your own souls, and have peace in your own consciences. If you do, the comfort is inexpressible, in their love and obedience, their supplying your wants, and delighting you in all your remaining path to glory. Yea, all your family may fare the better for one pious child or servant. But the greatest joy will be, when you shall say, 'Lord, here am I, and the children thou hast given me;' and shall joyfully live with them for ever.—Consider, how much the welfare of church and state depends on this duty. Good laws will not reform us, if reformation begin not at home. This is the cause of all our miseries in church and state, even the want of a holy education of children. I also entreat parents to consider, what excellent advantages they have for saving their children. They are with you while they are tender and flexible. You have a twig to bend, not an oak. None in the world have such interest in their affections as you have. You have also the greatest authority over them. Their whole dependence is upon you for a maintenance. You best know their temper and in-

clinations. And you are ever with them, and can never want opportunities: especially you, mothers, remember this, who are more with your children while young, than their fathers. What pains are you at for their bodies! What do you suffer to bring them into the world! And will you not be at as much pains for the saving of their souls! Your affections are tender; and will it not move you to think of their perishing for ever? I beseech you, for the sake of the children of your bowels teach them, admonish them, watch over them, and give them no rest, till you have brought them to Christ.

20. I shall conclude with this earnest request to all Christian parents that read these lines—That they would have compassion on the souls of their poor children, and be faithful to the great trust that God hath put on them. If you cannot do what you would for them, yet do what you can. Both church and state, city and country, groan under the neglect of this weighty duty. Your children know not God, nor his laws, but take his name in vain, and slight his worship, and you neither instruct them nor correct them; and therefore God corrects both them and you. You are so tender of them, that God is the less tender of both them and you. Wonder not if God make you smart for your children's sins; for you are guilty of all they commit, by your neglect of your duty to reform them. Will you resolve, therefore, to set upon this duty, and neglect it no longer? Remember Eli. Your children are like Moses in the bulrushes, ready to perish if they have not help. As ever you would not be charged before God as murderers of their souls, nor have them cry out against you in everlasting fire, see that you teach them how to escape it, and bring them up in holiness and the fear of God. I charge every one of you, upon your allegiance to God, as you will very shortly answer the contrary at your peril, that you will neither refuse nor neglect this most necessary duty. If you are not willing to do it, now you know it to be so great a duty, you are rebels, and no true subjects of Jesus Christ. If you are willing, but know not how, I will add a few words of direction to help you. Lead them, by your own example, to prayer, reading, and other religious duties. Inform their understandings. Store their memories. Rectify their wills. Quicken their affections. Keep tender their consciences. Restrain their tongues, and teach them gracious speech. Reform and watch over their outward conversation. To these ends, get them bibles and pious books, and see that they read them. Examine them often what they learn; especially

spend the Lord's day in this work, and suffer
them not to spend it in sports or idleness. Show
them the meaning of what they read or learn.
Keep them out of evil company, and acquaint
them with the godly. And fail not to make
them learn their catechism. Especially show
them the necessity, excellency, and pleasure of
serving God; and labour to fix all upon their
hearts.

CHAPTER X.

THE SAINTS' REST IS NOT TO BE EXPECTED ON EARTH

Sect. 1. In order to show the sin and folly of expecting rest here. 2.
(I.) The reasonableness of present afflictions is considered: 3. (1.)
That they are the way to rest; 4. (2.) Keep us from mistaking our
rest; 5. (3.) From losing our way to it; 6. (4.) Quicken our pace
towards it; 7. (5.) Chiefly incommode our flesh; 8, 9. and (6.)
Under them the sweetest foretastes of rest are often enjoyed. 10.
(II.) How unreasonable to rest in present enjoyments; 11. (1)
That it is idolatry: 12. (2) That it contradicts God's end in giving
them; 13. (3.) Is the way to have them refused, withdrawn, or
imbittered; 14. (4.) That to be suffered to take up our rest here is
the greatest curse; 15. (5) That it is seeking rest where it is not;
16. (6.) That the creatures, without God, would aggravate our
misery; 17. (7.) And all this is confirmed by experience. 18. The
author laments that this is nevertheless a most common sin. 19—
23. (III.) How unreasonable our unwillingness to die, and possess
the saints' rest, is largely considered. 24. The author apologizes
for saying so much on this last head.

1. We are not yet come to our resting place.
Doth it remain? How great then is our sin
and folly to seek and expect it here! Where
shall we find the Christian that deserves not this
reproof? We would all have continual prosperity, because it is easy and pleasing to the
flesh; but we consider not the unreasonableness
of such desires. And when we enjoy convenient
houses, goods, lands, and revenues; or the necessary means God hath appointed for our spiritual good; we seek rest in these enjoyments.
Whether we are in an afflicted or prosperous
state, it is apparent, we exceedingly make the
creature our rest. Do we not desire creature enjoyments more violently, when we want them,
than we desire God himself? Do we not delight
more in the possession of them, than in the enjoyment of God? And if we lose them, doth it
not trouble us more than our loss of God? Is it
not enough, that they are refreshing helps in
our way to heaven, but they must also be made
our heaven itself? Christian Reader, I would
as willingly make thee sensible of this sin, as of
any sin in the world, if I could tell how to do it;
for the Lord's greatest quarrel with us is in this
point. In order to this, I most earnestly beseech
thee to consider—the reasonableness of present
afflictions—and the unreasonableness of resting

in present enjoyments;—as also of our unwillingness to die, that we may possess eternal rest.

2. (I.) To show the reasonableness of present
afflictions, consider—they are the way to rest—
they keep us from mistaking our rest, and from
losing our way to it—they quicken our pace towards it—they chiefly incommode our flesh;—
and under them God's people have often the
sweetest foretastes of their rest.

3. (1.) Consider, that labour and trouble are
the common way to rest, both in the course of
nature and grace. Can there possibly be rest
without weariness? Do you not travail and
toil first, and rest after? The day for labour is
first, and then follows the night for rest. Why
should we desire the course of grace to be perverted, any more than the course of nature? It
is an established decree, 'that we must through
much tribulation enter into the kingdom of God.'
And that, 'if we suffer, we shall also reign with
Christ.' And what are we, that God's statutes
should be reversed for our pleasures?

4. (2.) Afflictions are exceedingly useful to us,
to keep us from mistaking our rest. A Christian's
motion towards heaven is voluntary, and not constrained. Those means, therefore, are most profitable which help his understanding and will.
The most dangerous mistake of our souls is, to
take the creature for God, and earth for heaven.
What warm, affectionate, eager thoughts have
we of the world, till afflictions cool and moderate them? Afflictions speak convincingly, and
will be heard when preachers cannot. Many a
poor Christian is sometimes bending his thoughts
to wealth, or flesh-pleasing, or applause, and so
loses his relish of Christ, and the joy above;
till God break in upon his riches, or children,
or conscience, or health, and break down his
mountain which he thought so strong. And then,
when he lies in Manasseh's fetters, or is fastened
to his bed with pining sickness, the world is nothing, and heaven is something. If our dear Lord
did not put these thorns under our head, we
should sleep out our lives, and lose our glory.

5. (3.) Afflictions are also God's most effectual
means to keep us from losing our way to our
rest. Without this hedge of thorns on the right
hand and left, we should hardly keep the way
to heaven. If there be but one gap open, how
ready are we to find it, and turn out at it!
When we grow wanton, or worldly, or proud,
how doth sickness, or other affliction, reduce us!
Every Christian, as well as Luther, may call
affliction one of the best schoolmasters; and with
David may say, 'Before I was afflicted I went
astray; but now have I kept thy word.' Many

9

thousand recovered sinners may cry, ' O healthful sickness ! O comfortable sorrows ! O gainful losses ! O enriching poverty ! O blessed day that ever I was afflicted !' Not only the ' green pastures, and still waters, but the rod and staff, they comfort us.'—Though the word and Spirit do the main work, yet suffering so unbolts the door of the heart, that the word hath easier entrance.

6. (4.) Afflictions likewise serve to quicken our pace in the way to our rest. It were well, if mere love would prevail with us, and that we were rather drawn to heaven, than driven. But seeing our hearts are so bad that mercy will not do it ; it is better to be put on with the sharpest scourge, than loiter, like the foolish virgins, till the door is shut. O what a difference is there betwixt our prayers in health and in sickness ! betwixt our repentings in prosperity and adversity ! Alas, if we did not sometimes feel the spur, what a slow pace would most of us hold toward heaven ! Since our vile natures require it, why should we be unwilling that God should do us good by sharp means ? Judge, Christian, whether thou dost not go more watchfully and speedily in the way to heaven, in thy sufferings, than in thy more pleasing and prosperous state.

7. (5.) Consider further, it is but the flesh that is chiefly troubled and grieved by afflictions. In most of our sufferings the soul is free, unless we ourselves wilfully afflict it. ' Why then, O my soul, dost thou side with this flesh, and complain, as it complains ? It should be thy work to keep it under, and bring it into subjection ; and if God do it for thee, shouldst thou be discontented ? Hath not the pleasing of it been the cause of almost all thy spiritual sorrows ? Why then may not the displeasing of it further thy joy ? Must not Paul and Silas sing, because their feet are in the stocks ? Their spirits were not imprisoned. Ah, unworthy soul ! is this thy thanks to God for preferring thee so far before thy body ? When it is rotting in the grave, thou shalt be a companion of the perfected spirits of the just. In the meantime, hast thou not consolation which the flesh knows not of ? Murmur not then at God's dealings with thy body ; if it were for want of love to thee, he would not have dealt so by all his saints. Never expect thy flesh should truly expound the meaning of the rod. It will call love, hatred ; and say, God is destroying, when he is saving. It is the suffering party, and therefore not fit to be the judge. Could we once believe God, and judge of his dealings by his word, and by their usefulness to our souls, and reference to our rest, and could

we stop our ears against all the clamours of the flesh, then we should have a truer judgment of our afflictions.

8. (6.) Once more consider, God seldom gives his people so sweet a foretaste of their future rest, as in their deep afflictions. He keeps his most precious cordials for the time of our greatest faintings and dangers. He gives them, when he knows they are needed, and will be valued ; and when he is sure to be thanked for them, and his people rejoiced by them. Especially, when our sufferings are more directly for his cause, then he seldom fails to sweeten the bitter cup. The martyrs have passed the highest joys. When did Christ preach such comforts to his disciples, as when their hearts were sorrowful at his departure ? When did he appear among them, and say, ' peace be unto you,' but when they were shut up for fear of the Jews ? When did Stephen see heaven opened, but when he was giving up his life for the testimony of Jesus ? Is not that our best state, wherein we have most of God ? Why else do we desire to come to heaven ? If we look for a heaven of fleshly delights, we shall find ourselves mistaken. Conclude then, that affliction is not so bad a state for a saint in his way to rest. Are we wiser than God ? Doth he not know what is good for us as well as we ? or is he not as careful of our good, as we are of our own ? Woe to us, if he were not much more so ; and if he did not love us better than we love either him or ourselves !

9. Say not, ' I could bear any other affliction but this.' If God had afflicted thee where thou canst bear it, thy idol would neither have been discovered nor removed. Neither say, ' if God would deliver me out of it, I could be content to bear it.' Is it nothing that he hath promised it shall work for thy good ? Is it not enough that thou art sure to be delivered at death ? Nor let it be said, ' if my affliction did not disable me from my duty, I could bear it.' It doth not disable thee for that duty which tends to thy own personal benefit, but is the greatest quickening help thou canst expect. As for thy duty to others, it is not thy duty when God disables thee. Perhaps thou wilt say, ' the godly are my afflicters ; if it were ungodly men, I could easily bear it.' Whoever is the instrument, the affliction is from God, and the deserving cause thyself ; and is it not better to look more to God than thyself ? Dost thou not know that the best men are still sinful in part ? Do not plead, ' If I had but that consolation, which you say God reserves for suffering times, I should suffer more contentedly ; but I do not perceive any

such thing.' The more you suffer for righteousness' sake, the more of this blessing you may expect; and the more you suffer for your own evil doing, the longer it will be before that sweetness comes. Are not the comforts you desire, neglected or resisted? Have your afflictions wrought kindly with you, and fitted you for comfort? It is not suffering that prepares you for comfort, but the success and fruit of suffering upon your hearts.

10. (II.) To show the unreasonableness of resting in present enjoyments, consider—it is idolizing them—it contradicts God's end in giving them—it is the way to have them refused, withdrawn, or imbittered—to be suffered to take up our rest here, is the greatest curse—it is seeking rest where it is not to be found—the creatures, without God, would aggravate our misery—and to confirm all this, we may consult our own and others' experience.

11. (1.) It is gross idolatry to make any creature, or means, our rest. To be the rest of the soul, is God's own prerogative. As it is apparent idolatry to place our rest in riches, or honours; so it is but a more refined idolatry to take up our rest in excellent means of grace. How ill must our dear Lord take it, when we give him cause to complain, as he did of our fellow-idolaters, ' My people have been lost sheep, they have forgotten their resting place ?' ' My people can find rest in any thing rather than in me. They can delight in one another, but not in me. They can rejoice in my creatures and ordinances, but not in me. Yea, in their very labours and duties they seek for rest, but not in me. They had rather be any where, than be with me. Are these their gods? Have these redeemed them? Will these be better to them than I have been, or than I would be ?' If yourselves have a wife, a husband, a son, that had rather be any where than in your company, and be never so merry as when furthest from you, would you not take it ill? So must our God needs do.

12. (2.) You contradict the end of God in giving these enjoyments. He gave them to help thee to him, and dost thou take up with them in his stead? He gave them to be refreshments in thy journey, and wouldst thou dwell in thy inn, and go no further? It may be said of all our comforts and ordinances, as is said of the Israelites, ' The ark of the covenant of the Lord went before them, to search out a resting place for them.' So do all God's mercies here. They are not that rest; as John professed he was not the Christ; but they are voices crying in the wilderness, to bid us prepare; 'for the kingdom of God,' our true rest, 'is at hand.' Therefore to rest here, were to turn all mercies contrary to their own ends, and to our own advantages, and to destroy ourselves with that which should help us.

13. (3.) It is the way to cause God, either to deny the mercies we ask, or to take from us those we enjoy, or at least imbitter them to us. God is no where so jealous as here. If you had a servant whom your wife loved better than yourself, would you not take it ill of such a wife, and rid your house of such a servant? So, if the Lord see you begin to settle in the world and say, ' here I will rest;' no wonder if he soon in his jealousy unsettle you. If he love you, no wonder if he take that from you with which he sees you are destroying yourselves. It hath long been my observation of many, that when they have attempted great works, and have just finished them; or have aimed at great things in the world, and have just obtained them; or have lived in much trouble, and have just overcome it: and began to look on their condition with content, and rest in it—they are then usually near to death or ruin. When a man is once at this language, ' Soul, take thy ease:' the next news usually is, ' thou fool, this night,' or this month, or this year, ' thy soul shall be required, and then whose shall these things be ?' What house is there, where this fool dwells not? Let you and I consider, whether it be not our own case. Many a servant of God hath been destroyed from the earth, by being overvalued and overloved. I am persuaded, our discontents and murmurings are not so provoking to God, nor so destructive to the sinner, as our too sweet enjoying, and resting in, a pleasant state. If God hath crossed you in wife, children, goods, friends, either by taking them away, or the comfort of them; try whether this be not the cause : for wheresoever your desires stop, and you say, ' now I am well;' that condition you make your god, and engage the jealousy of God against it. Whether you be friends to God or enemies, you can never expect that God should suffer you quietly to enjoy your idols.

14. (4.) Should God suffer you to take up your rest here, it is one of the greatest curses that could befall you. It were better never to have a day of ease in the world; for then weariness might make you seek after true rest. But if you are suffered to sit down and rest here, a restless wretch you will be through all eternity. To ' have their portion in this life,' is the lot of the most miserable perishing sinners. Doth

it become Christians, then, to expect so much here? Our rest is our heaven; and where we take our rest, there we make our heaven. And wouldst thou have but such a heaven as this?

15. (5.) It is seeking rest where it is not to be found. Your labour will be lost; and if you proceed, your soul's eternal rest too. Our rest is only in the full obtaining of our ultimate end. But that is not to be expected in this life; neither is rest therefore to be expected here. Is God to be enjoyed in the best church here, as he is in heaven? How little of God the saints enjoy under the best means, let their own complainings testify. Poor comforters are the best ordinances, without God. Should a traveller take up his rest in the way? No; because his home is his journey's end. When you have all that creatures and means can afford, have you that you believed, prayed, suffered for? I think you dare not say so. We are like little children strayed from home, and God is now fetching us home, and we are ready to turn into any house, stay and play with every thing in our way, and sit down on every green bank, and much ado there is to get us home. We are also in the midst of our labours and dangers; and is there any resting here? What painful work doth lie upon our hands? Look to our brethren, to our souls, and to God; and what a deal of work, in respect to each of these, doth lie before us! And can we rest in the midst of all our labours? Indeed we may rest on earth, as the ark is said to have 'rested in the midst of Jordan,' a short and small rest. Or as Abraham desired the 'angels to turn in and rest themselves' in his tent, where they would have been loth to have taken up their dwelling. Should Israel have fixed their rest in the wilderness, among serpents, and enemies, and weariness, and famine? Should Noah have made the ark his home, and have been loth to come forth when the waters were assuaged? Should the mariner choose his dwelling on the sea, and settle his rest in the midst of rocks, and sands, and raging tempests? Should a soldier rest in the thickest of his enemies? And are not Christians such travellers, such mariners, such soldiers? Have you not fears within, and troubles without? Are we not in continual dangers? We cannot eat, drink, sleep, labour, pray, hear, converse, but in the midst of snares; and shall we sit down and rest here? O Christian, follow thy work, look to thy dangers, hold on to the end, win the field. and come off the ground, before thou thinkest of a settled rest. Whenever thou talkest of a rest on earth, it is like Peter on the mount, 'thou knowest not what thou sayest.' If, instead of telling the converted thief, 'This day shalt thou be with me in paradise,' Christ had said he should rest there upon the cross; would he not have taken it for a derision? Methinks it would be ill resting in the midst of sickness and pains, persecutions and distresses. But if nothing else will convince us, yet sure the remainders of sin, which do so easily beset us, should quickly satisfy a believer, that here is not his rest. I say, therefore, to every one that thinketh of rest on earth, 'Arise ye, and depart; for this is not your rest, because it is polluted.' These things cannot in their nature be a true Christian's rest. They are too poor to make us rich; too low, to raise us to happiness; too empty, to fill our souls; and of too short a continuance, to be our eternal content. If prosperity and whatsoever we here desire, be too base to make gods of, they are too base to be our rest.—The soul's rest must be sufficient to afford it perpetual satisfaction. But the content which creatures afford, waxes old, and abates after a short enjoyment. If God should rain down angels' food, we should soon lothe the manna. If novelty support not, our delights on earth grow dull. All creatures are to us as the flowers to the bee; there is but little honey on any one, and therefore there must be a superficial taste; and so to the next.—The more the creature is known, the less it satisfieth. Those only are taken with it, who see no further than its outward beauty, without discerning its inward vanity. When we thoroughly know the condition of other men, and have discovered the evil as well as the good, and the defects as well as the perfection, we then cease our admiration.

16. (6.) To have creatures and means without God is an aggravation of our misery. If God should say, 'Take my creatures, my word, my servants, my ordinances, but not myself;' would you take this for happiness? If you had the word of God, and not 'the Word,' which is God; or the bread of the Lord, and not the Lord, which 'is the true bread;' or would cry with the Jews, 'The temple of the Lord,' and had not the Lord of the temple; this were a poor happiness. Was Capernaum the more happy, or the more miserable, for seeing the mighty works which they had seen, and hearing the words of Christ which they did hear? Surely that which aggravates our sin, and misery, cannot be our rest.

17. (7.) To confirm all this, let us consult our own and others' experience.— Millions have made trial, but did any ever find a sufficient rest for his soul on earth? Delights I deny not but

they have found, but rest and satisfaction they never found. And shall we think to find that which never man could find before us? Ahab's kingdom is nothing to him, without Naboth's vineyard; and did that satisfy him when he obtained it? Were you, like Noah's dove, to look through the earth for a resting-place, you would return confessing, that you could find none. Go, ask honour, Is there rest here? You may as well rest on the top of tempestuous mountains, or in Etna's flames. Ask riches, Is there rest here? Even such as is in a bed of thorns. If you inquire for rest of worldly pleasure, it is such as the fish hath in swallowing the bait: when the pleasure is sweetest, death is nearest. Go to learning, and even to divine ordinances, and inquire whether there your souls may rest? You might indeed receive from these an olive branch of hope, as they are means to your rest, and have relation to eternity; but in regard of any satisfaction in themselves, you would remain as restless as ever. How well might all these answer us, as Jacob did Rachel, 'Am I in God's stead,' that you came to me for soul-rest? Not all the states of men in the world; neither court nor country, towns nor cities, shops nor fields, treasures, libraries, solitude, society, studies, nor pulpits, can afford any such thing as this rest. If you could inquire of the dead of all generations, or of the living through all dominions, they would all tell you, 'Here is no rest.' Or if other men's experience move you not, take a view of your own. Can you remember the state that did fully satisfy you; or if you could, will it prove lasting? I believe we may all say of our earthly rest, as Paul of our hope, ' if it were in this life only, we are of all men the most miserable.'

18. If then either scripture or reason, or the experience of ourselves, and all the world, will satisfy us, we may see there is no resting here. And yet how guilty are the generality of us of this sin! How many halts and stops do we make, before we will make the Lord our rest. How must God even drive us, and fire us out of every condition, lest we should sit down and rest there! If he gives us prosperity, riches, or honour, we do in our hearts dance before them, as the Israelites before their calf, and say, ' these are thy gods ;' and conclude, ' it is good to be here.' If he imbitter all these to us, how restless are we till our condition be sweetened, that we may sit down again, and rest where we were! If he proceed in the cure, and take the creature quite away, then how do we labour, and cry, and pray, that God would restore it, that we may make it our rest again! And while we are de-

prived of our former idol, yet rather than come to God, we delight ourselves in the hope of recovering it, and make that very hope our rest; or search about from creature to creature, to find out something to supply the room; yea, if we can find no supply, yet we will rather settle in this misery, and make a rest of a wretched being, than leave all and come to God. O the cursed averseness of our souls from God! If any place in hell were tolerable, the soul would rather take up its rest there, than come to God. Yea, when he is bringing us over to him, and hath convinced us of the worth of his ways and service, the last deceit of all is here, we will rather settle upon those ways that lead to him, and those ordinances that speak of him, and those gifts which flow from him, than we will come entirely over to himself. Christian, marvel not that I speak so much of resting in these; beware lest it prove thy own case. I suppose thou art so far convinced of the vanity of riches, honour, and pleasure, that thou canst more easily disclaim these; and it is well if it be so; but the means of grace thou lookest on with less suspicion, and thinkest thou canst not delight in them too much, especially seeing most of the world despise them, or delight in them too little. I know they must be loved and valued; and he that delights in any worldly thing more than in them, is not a Christian. But when we are content with ordinances without God, and had rather be at a sermon than in heaven, and a member of the church here than of the perfect church above, this is a sad mistake. So far let thy soul take comfort in ordinances, as God doth accompany them; remembering, this is not heaven, but the first fruits. 'While we are present in the body, we are absent from the Lord;' and while we are absent from him, we are absent from our rest. If God were as willing to be absent from us as we from him, and as loth to be our rest as we to rest in him, we should be left to an eternal restless separation. In a word, as you are sensible of the sinfulness of your earthly discontents, so be you also of your irregular satisfaction, and pray God to pardon them much more. And above all the plagues on this side hell, see that you watch and pray against settling any where short of heaven, or reposing your souls on any thing below God.

19. (III.) The next thing to be considered, is, our unreasonable unwillingness to die, that we may possess the saints' rest. We linger, like Lot in Sodom, till ' the Lord being merciful unto us,' doth pluck us away against our will. I confess that death of itself is not desirable; but the soul's

rest with God is, to which death is the common passage. Because we are apt to make light of this sin, let me set before you its nature and remedy, in a variety of considerations. As for instance—it has in it much infidelity. If we did but verily believe, that the promise of this glory is the word of God, and that God doth truly mean as he speaks, and is fully resolved to make it good; if we did verily believe, that there is indeed such blessedness prepared for believers : surely we should be as impatient of living, as we are now fearful of dying, and should think every day a year till our last day should come. Is it possible that we can truly believe, that death will remove us from misery to such glory, and yet be loth to die ? If the doubts of our own interest in that glory make us fear, yet a true belief of the certainty and excellency of this rest, would make us restless till our title to it be cleared. Though there is much faith and Christianity in our mouths, yet there is much infidelity and paganism in our hearts, which is the chief cause that we are so loth to die.—It is also much owing to the coldness of our love. If we love our friend, we love his company; his presence is comfortable, his absence is painful : when he comes to us, we entertain him with gladness ; when he dies, we mourn, and usually overmourn. To be separated from a faithful friend, is like the rending a member from our body. And would not our desires after God be such, if we really loved him ? Nay, should it not be much more than such, as he is above all friends most lovely ? May the Lord teach us to look closely to our hearts, and take heed of self-deceit in this point ! Whatever we pretend, if we love either father, mother, husband, wife, child, friend, wealth, or life itself more than Christ, we are yet none of his sincere disciples. When it comes to the trial, the question will not be, Who hath preached most, or heard most, or talked most ? but, Who hath loved most ? Christ will not take sermons, prayers, fastings ; no, nor the ' giving our goods,' nor the ' burning our bodies,' instead of love. And do we love him, and yet care not how long we are from him ? Was it such a joy to Jacob to see the face of Joseph in Egypt ; and shall we be contented without the sight of Christ in glory, and yet say we love him ? I dare not conclude, that we have no love at all, when we are so loth to die ; but I dare say, were our love more, we should die more willingly. If this holy flame were thoroughly kindled in our breasts, we should cry out with David, ' As the hart panteth after the water-brooks, so panteth my soul after thee, O God.

My soul thirsteth for God, for the living God : when shall I come and appear before God ?'—By our unwillingness to die, it appears we are little weary of sin. Did we take sin for the greatest evil, we should not be willing to have its company so long. ' O foolish, sinful heart ! Hast thou been so long a cage of all unclean lusts, a fountain incessantly streaming forth the bitter waters of transgression, and art thou not yet weary ? Wretched soul ! hast thou been so long wounded in all thy faculties, so grievously languishing in all thy performances, so fruitful a soil of all iniquities, and art thou not yet more weary ? Wouldst thou still lie under thy imperfections ? Hath thy sin proved so profitable a commodity, so necessary a companion, such a delightful employment, that thou dost so much dread the parting day ? May not God justly grant thee thy wishes, and seal thee a lease of thy desired distance from him, and nail thy ears to these doors of misery, and exclude thee eternally from his glory ?'—It shows that we are insensible of the vanity of the creature, when we are so loth to hear or think of a removal. ' Ah, foolish, wretched soul ! doth every prisoner groan for freedom : and every slave desire his jubilee ; and every sick man long for health ; and every hungry man for food ; and dost thou alone abhor deliverance ? Doth the sailor wish to see land ? Doth the husbandman desire the harvest, and the labourer to receive his pay ? Doth the traveller long to be at home, and the racer to win the prize, and the soldier to win the field ?—and art thou loth to see thy labours finished, and to receive the end of thy faith and sufferings ? Have thy griefs been only dreams ? If they were, yet methinks thou shouldst not be afraid of waking. Or is it not rather the world's delights that are all mere dreams and shadows ? Or is the world become of late more kind ? We may at our peril reconcile ourselves to the world, but it will never reconcile itself to us. O unworthy soul ! who hadst rather dwell in this land of darkness, and wander in this barren wilderness, than be at rest with Jesus Christ ! who hadst rather stay among the wolves, and daily suffer the scorpion's stings, than praise the Lord with the host of heaven !'

20. This unwillingness to die, doth actually impeach us of high treason against the Lord. Is it not choosing of earth before him, and taking of present things for our happiness, and, consequently, making them our very god ? If we did indeed make God our end, our rest, our portion, our treasure, how is it possible but we should desire to enjoy him ?—It moreover discovers

some dissimulation. Would you have any believe you, when you call the Lord your only hope, and speak of Christ as all in all, and of the joy that is in his presence, and yet would endure the hardest life, rather than die, and enter into his presence? What self-contradiction is this, to talk so hardly of the world, and the flesh, to groan and complain of sin and suffering, and yet fear no day more than that, which we expect should bring our final freedom! What hypocrisy is this, to profess to strive and fight for heaven, which we are loth to come to! and spend one hour after another in prayer, for that which we would not have! Hereby we wrong the Lord and his promises, and disgrace his ways in the eyes of the world. As if we could persuade them to question, whether God be true to his word or not? whether there be any such glory as the Scripture mentions? When they see those so loth to leave their hold of present things, who have professed to live by faith, and have boasted of their hopes in another world, and spoken disgracefully of all things below, in comparison of things above, how doth this confirm the world in their unbelief and sensuality? ' Sure,' say they, ' if these professors did expect so much glory, and make so light of the world as they seem, they would not themselves be so loth to change.' O how are we ever able to repair the wrong which we do to God and souls by this scandal! And what an honour to God, what a strengthening to believers, what a conviction to unbelievers would it be, if Christians in this did answer their profession, and cheerfully welcome the news of rest!—It also evidently shows, that we have spent much time to little purpose. Have we not had all our lifetime to prepare to die? So many years to make ready for one hour, and are we so unready and unwilling yet! What have we done? Why have we lived? Had we any greater matters to mind? Would we have wished for more frequent warnings? How often hath death entered the habitations of our neighbours! How often hath it knocked at our own doors! How many distempers have vexed our bodies, that we have been forced to receive the sentence of death! And are we unready and unwilling after all this? O careless, dead-hearted sinners! unworthy neglectors of God's warnings! faithless betrayers of our own souls

21. Consider, not to die, is never to be happy. To escape death, is to miss of blessedness; except God should translate us, as Enoch and Elijah; which he never did before or since. ' If in this life only we have hope in Christ, we are of all men most miserable.' If you would not die, and go to heaven, what would you have more than an epicure or a beast? Why do we pray, and fast, and mourn? Why do we suffer the contempt of the world? Why are we Christians, and not pagans and infidels, if we do not desire a life to come? Wouldst thou lose thy faith and labour, Christian? all thy duties and sufferings, all the end of thy life, and all the blood of Christ, and be contented with the portion of a worldling or a brute? Rather say, as one did on his deathbed, when he was asked whether he was willing to die or not, ' Let him be loth to die, who is loth to be with Christ.' Is God willing by death to glorify us, and we are unwilling to die, that we may be glorified? Methinks, if a prince were willing to make you his heir, you would scarce be unwilling to accept it: the refusing such a kindness would discover ingratitude and unworthiness. As God hath resolved against them, who make excuses when they should come to Christ, ' none of those men, who were bidden, shall taste of my supper;' so it is just with him to resolve against us, who frame excuses when we should come to glory.— The Lord Jesus Christ was willing to come from heaven to earth for us, and shall we be unwilling to remove from earth to heaven for ourselves and him? He might have said, ' What is it to me, if these sinners suffer? If they value their flesh above their spirit, and their lusts above my Father's love; if they will sell their souls for nought, who is it fit should be the loser? Should I, whom they have wronged? Must they wilfully transgress my law, and I undergo their deserved pain? Must I come down from heaven to earth, and clothe myself with human flesh, be spit upon and scorned by man, and fast, and weep, and sweat, and suffer, and bleed, and die a cursed death; and all this for wretched worms, who would rather hazard their souls, than forbear one forbidden morsel? Do they cast away themselves so slightly, and must I redeem them so dearly?' Thus we see Christ had reason enough to have made him unwilling; and yet did he voluntarily condescend. But we have no reason against our coming to him; except we will reason against our hopes, and plead for a perpetuity of our own calamities. Christ came down to fetch us up; and would we have him lose his blood and labour, and go again without us? Hath he bought our rest at so dear a rate? Is our inheritance ' purchased with his blood?' And are we, after all this, loth to enter? Ah, Sirs, it was Christ, and not we, that had cause to be loth. May the Lord forgive, and heal this foolish ingratitude!

22. Do we not combine with our most cruel foes in their most malicious designs, while we are loth to die, and go to heaven? What is the devil's daily business? Is it not to keep our souls from God? And shall we be content with this? Is it not the one-half of hell which we wish to ourselves, while we desire to be absent from heaven? What sport is this to Satan, that his desires and thine, Christian, should so concur? that when he sees he cannot get thee to hell, he can so long keep thee out of heaven, and make thee the earnest petitioner for it thyself! O gratify not the devil so much to thy own injury! Do not our daily fears of death make our lives a continual torment? Those lives which might be full of joy, in the daily contemplations of the life to come, and the sweet delightful thoughts of bliss; how do we fill them up with causeless terrors! Thus we consume our own comforts, and prey upon our truest pleasures. When we might lie down, and rise up, and walk abroad, with our hearts full of the joys of God, we continually fill them with perplexing fears. For he that fears dying, must be always fearing; because he hath always reason to expect it. And how can that man's life be comfortable, who lives in continual fear of losing his comforts?—Are not these fears of death self-created sufferings? As if God had not inflicted enough upon us, but we must inflict more upon ourselves. Is not death bitter enough to the flesh of itself, but we must double and treble its bitterness? The sufferings laid upon us by God, do all lead to happy issues: the progress is, from tribulation to patience, from thence to experience, and so to hope, and at last to glory. But the sufferings we make for ourselves, are circular and endless, from sin to suffering, from suffering to sin, and so to suffering again; and not only so, but they multiply in their course; every sin is greater than the former, and so every suffering also: so that except we think God hath made us to be our own tormentors, we have small reason to nourish our fears of death.—And are they not useless, unprofitable fears? As all our care 'cannot make one hair white or black, nor add one cubit to our stature;' so neither can our fear prevent our sufferings, nor delay our death one hour: willing, or unwilling, we must away. Many a man's fears have hastened his end, but no man's ever did avert it. It is true, a cautious fear concerning the danger after death, hath profited many, and is very useful to the preventing of that danger; but for a member of Christ, and an heir of heaven, to be afraid of entering his own inheritance, is a sinful, useless fear.—And

do not our fears of dying ensnare our souls, and add strength to many temptations? What made Peter deny his Lord? What makes apostates in suffering times forsake the truth? Why doth the green blade of unrooted faith wither before the heat of persecution? Fear of imprisonment and poverty may do much, but fear of death will do much more. So much fear as we have of death, so much cowardice we usually have in the cause of God: beside the multitude of unbelieving contrivances, and discontents at the wise disposals of God, and hard thoughts of most of his providences, which this sin doth make us guilty of.

23. Let us further consider, what a competent time most of us have had. Why should not a man, that would die at all, be as willing at thirty or forty, if God see fit, as at seventy or eighty? Length of time doth not conquer corruption; it never withers nor decays through age. Except we receive an addition of grace, as well as time, we naturally grow worse. 'O my soul! depart in peace. As thou wouldst not desire an unlimited state in wealth and honour, so desire it not in point of time. If thou wast sensible how little thou deservest an hour of that patience which thou hast enjoyed, thou wouldst think thou hadst had a large part. Is it not divine wisdom that sets the bounds? God will honour himself by various persons, and several ages, and not by one person or age. Seeing thou hast acted thy own part, and finished thy appointed course, come down contentedly, that others may succeed, who must have their turns as well as thyself. Much time hath much duty. Beg therefore for grace to improve it better; but be content with thy share of time. Thou hast also had a competency of the comforts of life. God might have made thy life a burden, till thou hadst been as weary of possessing it, as thou art now afraid of losing it. He might have suffered thee to have consumed thy days in ignorance, without the true knowledge of Christ: but he hath opened thy eyes in the morning of thy days, and acquainted thee betimes with the business of thy life. Hath thy heavenly Father caused thy lot to fall in Europe, not in Asia, Africa, or America; in England, not in Spain or Italy? Hath he filled up all thy life with mercies, and dost thou now think thy share too small? What a multitude of hours of consolation, of delightful Sabbaths, of pleasant studies, of precious companions, of wonderful deliverances, of excellent opportunities, of fruitful labours, of joyful tidings, of sweet experiences, of astonishing providences, hath thy life partaken

of! Hath thy life been so sweet, that thou art loth to leave it? Is this thy thanks to him who is thus drawing thee to his own sweetness? O foolish soul, would thou wast as covetous after eternity, as thou art for a fading, perishing life! and after the presence of God in glory, as thou art for continuance on earth! Then thou wouldst cry, 'Why is his chariot so long in coming? Why tarry the wheels of his chariot? How long, Lord? how long?'—What if God should let thee live many years, but deny thee the mercies which thou hast hitherto enjoyed? Might he not give thee life, as he gave the murmuring Israelites quails? He might give thee life, till thou wert weary of living, and as glad to be rid of it as Judas, or Ahithophel; and make thee *like* many miserable creatures in the world, who can hardly forbear laying violent hands on themselves. Be not therefore so importunate for life, which may prove a judgment, instead of a blessing. How many of the precious servants of God, of all ages and places, have gone before thee! Thou art not to enter an untrodden path, nor appointed first to break the ice. Except Enoch and Elijah, which of the saints have escaped death? And art thou better than they? There are many millions of saints dead, more than now remain on earth. What a number of thine own bosom-friends, and companions in duty, are now gone, and why shouldst thou be so loth to follow? Nay, hath not Jesus Christ himself gone this way? Hath he not sanctified the grave to us, and perfumed the dust with his own body, and art thou loth to follow him too? Rather say as Thomas, 'let us also go, that we may die with him.'

24. If what hath been said, will not persuade, scripture and reason hath little force. And I have said the more on this subject, finding it so needful to myself and others; finding among so many Christians, who could do and suffer much for Christ, so few that can willingly die; and of many, who have somewhat subdued other corruptions, so few have got the conquest of this. I persuade not the ungodly, from fearing death. It is a wonder that they fear it no more, and spend not their days in continual horror.

———

CHAPTER XI.

THE IMPORTANCE OF LEADING A HEAVENLY LIFE UPON EARTH.

Sect. 1. The reasonableness of delighting in the thoughts of the saints' rest. 2. Christians exhorted to it, by considering, 3. (1.) It will evidence their sincere piety; 4. (2.) It is the highest excellence of the Christian temper; 5. (3.) It leads to the most comfortable life; 6—9. (4.) It will be the best preservative from temptations to sin; 10. (5.) It will invigorate their graces and duties; 11. (6.) It will be their best cordial in all afflictions; 12 (7.) It will render them most profitable to others; 13 (8.) It will honour God. 14. (9.) Without it, we disobey the commands, and lose the most gracious and delightful discoveries of the word of God. 15. (10.) It is the more reasonable to have our hearts with God, as his is so much on us; 16 17, and (11.) In heaven, where we have so much interest and relation; 18 (12.) Besides, there is nothing but heaven worth setting our hearts upon. 19. Transition to the subject of the next chapter.

1. Is there such a rest remaining for us? Why then are our thoughts no more upon it? Why are not our hearts continually there? Why dwell we not there in constant contemplation? What is the cause of this neglect? Are we reasonable in this, or are we not? Hath the eternal God provided us such a glory, and promised to take us up to dwell with himself, and is not this worth thinking on? Should not the strongest desires of our hearts be after it? Do we believe this, and yet forget and neglect it? If God will not give us leave to approach this light, what mean all his earnest invitations? Why doth he so condemn our earthly-mindedness, and command us to set our affections on things above? Ah, vile hearts! if God were against it, we were likelier to be for it; but when he commands our hearts to heaven, then they will not stir one inch: like our predecessors, the sinful Israelites; when God would have them march for Canaan, then they mutiny, and will not stir; but when God bids them not go, then they will be presently marching. If God say, 'love not the world, nor the things of the world,' we dote upon it. How freely, how frequently can we think of our pleasures, our friends, our labours, our flesh and its lusts; yea, our wrongs and miseries, our fears and sufferings! But where is the Christian whose heart is on his rest? What is the matter? Are we so full of joy, that we need no more? Or is there nothing in heaven for our joyous thoughts? Or rather, are not our hearts carnal and stupid? Let us humble these sensual hearts that have in them no more of Christ and glory. If this world was the only subject of our discourse, all would count us ungodly; why then may we not call our hearts ungodly, that have so little delight in Christ and heaven?

2. But I am speaking only to those whose

portion is in heaven, whose hopes are there, and who have forsaken all to enjoy this glory; and shall I be discouraged from persuading such to be heavenly-minded? Fellow-Christians, if you will not hear and obey, who will? Well may we be discouraged to exhort the blind, ungodly world, and may say, as Moses did, 'Behold the children of Israel have not hearkened unto me, how then shall Pharaoh hear me?' I require thee, Reader, as ever thou hopest for a part in this glory, that thou presently take thy heart to task, chide it for its wilful strangeness to God, turn thy thoughts from the pursuit of vanity, bend thy soul to study eternity, busy it about the life to come, habituate thyself to such contemplations, and let not those thoughts be seldom and cursory, but bathe thy soul in heaven's delights; and if thy backward soul begin to flag, and thy thoughts to scatter, call them back, hold them to their work, bear not with their laziness, nor connive at one neglect. And when thou hast, in obedience to God, tried this work, got acquainted with it, and kept a guard on thy thoughts, till they are accustomed to obey, thou wilt then find thyself in the suburbs of heaven, and that there is, indeed, a sweetness in the work and way of God, and that the life of Christianity is a life of joy. Thou wilt meet with those abundant consolations which thou hast prayed, panted, and groaned after, and which so few Christians do ever here obtain, because they know not this way to them, or else make not conscience of walking in it. Say not, 'We are unable to set our own hearts on heaven; this must be the work of God only.' Though God be the chief disposer of your hearts, yet next under him you have the greatest command of them yourselves. Though without Christ you can do nothing, yet under him you may do much, and must, or else it will be undone, and yourselves undone through your neglect. Christians, if your souls were healthful and vigorous, they would perceive incomparably more delight and sweetness in the believing, joyful thoughts of your future blessedness, than the soundest stomach finds in its food, or the strongest senses in the enjoyment of their objects; so little painful would this work be to you. But because I know, while we have flesh about us, and any remains of that 'carnal mind, which is enmity to God,' and to this noble work, that all motives are little enough, I will here lay down some considerations; which, if you will deliberately weigh, with an impartial judgment, I doubt not but they will prove effectual with your hearts, and make you resolve on this excellent duty. More particularly consider

—it will evidence your sincere piety— it is the highest excellence of the Christian temper—it is the way to live most comfortably—it will be the best preservative from temptations to sin—it will enliven your graces and duties—it will be your best cordial in all afflictions—it will render you most profitable to others—it will honour God. Without it you will disobey the commands, and lose the most gracious and delightful discoveries of the word of God: it is also the more reasonable to have your hearts with God, as his is so much on you—and in heaven, where you have so much interest and relation: besides, there is nothing but heaven worth setting your hearts upon.

3. (1.) Consider, a heart set upon heaven will be one of the most unquestionable evidences of your sincerity, and a clear discovery of a true work of saving grace upon your souls. You are often asking, 'How shall we know that we are truly sanctified?' Here you have a sign infallible from the mouth of Jesus Christ himself— 'where your treasure is, there will your hearts be also.' God is the saints' treasure and happiness; heaven is the place where they must fully enjoy him. A heart, therefore, set upon heaven, is no more but a heart set upon God; and, surely, a heart set upon God through Christ, is the truest evidence of saving grace. When learning will be no proof of grace; when knowledge, duties, gifts, will fail; when arguments from thy tongue or hand may be confuted; yet then will this, from the bent of thy heart, prove thee sincere. Take a poor Christian, of a weak understanding, a feeble memory, a stammering tongue; yet his heart is set on God, he hath chosen him for his portion, his thoughts are on eternity, his desires are there; he cries out, 'O that I were there!' He takes that day for a time of imprisonment, in which he hath not had one refreshing view of eternity. I had rather die in this man's condition, than in the case of him who hath the most eminent gifts, and is most admired for his performances, while his heart is not thus taken up with God. The man that Christ will find out at the last day, and condemn for want of a wedding garment, will be one that wants this frame of heart. The question will not then be, How much have you known, or professed, or talked? but, How much have you loved, and where was your heart? Christians, as you would have a proof of your title to glory, labour to get your hearts above. If sin and Satan keep not your affections from thence, they will never be able to keep away your persons.

4. (2.) A heart in heaven, is the highest excel-

lence of your Christian temper. As there is a common excellence, by which Christians differ from the world; so there is this peculiar dignity of spirit, by which the more excellent differ from the rest. As the noblest of creatures, so the noblest of Christians are they whose faces are set most direct for heaven. Such a heavenly saint, who hath been wrapt up to God in his contemplations, and is newly come down from the views of Christ, what discoveries will he make of those superior regions! how high and sacred is his discourse! Enough to convince an understanding hearer, that he hath seen the Lord, and that no man could speak such words, except he had been with God. This, this is the noble Christian. The most famous mountains and trees are those that reach nearest to heaven; and he is the choicest Christian, whose heart is most frequently and most delightfully there. If a man have lived near the king, or hath seen the sultan of Persia, or the great Turk, he will be thought a step higher than his neighbours. What then shall we judge of him that daily travels as far as heaven, and there hath seen the King of kings, hath frequent admittance into the divine presence and feasteth his soul upon the tree of life? For my part, I value this man before the noblest, the richest, the most learned, in the world.

5. (3.) A heavenly mind is the nearest and truest way to a life of comfort. The countries far north are cold and frozen, because they are distant from the sun. What makes such frozen, uncomfortable Christians, but their living so far from heaven? And what makes others so warm in comforts, but their living higher, and having nearer access to God? When the sun in the spring draws nearer to our part of the earth, how do all things congratulate its approach! The earth looks green, the trees shoot forth, the plants revive, the birds sing, and all things smile upon us. If we would but try this life with God, and keep these hearts above, what a spring of joy would be within us! How should we forget our winter sorrows! How early should we rise to sing the praise of our great Creator! O Christians, get above. Those that have been there, have found it warmer; and I doubt not but thou hast some time tried it thyself. When have you largest comforts? Is it not when thou hast conversed with God, and talked with the inhabitants of the higher world, and viewed their mansions, and filled thy soul with the forethoughts of glory? If thou knowest by experience what this practice is, I dare say thou knowest what spiritual joy is. If, as David professes, 'the light of God's countenance more gladdens

the heart than corn and wine;' then, surely, they that draw nearest, and most behold it, must be fullest of these joys. Whom should we blame then, that we are so void of consolation, but our own negligent hearts? God hath provided us a crown of glory, and promised to set it shortly on our heads, and we will not so much as think of it. He bids us behold and rejoice, and we will not so much as look at it; and yet we complain for want of comfort. It is by believing, that we are 'filled with joy and peace,' and no longer than we continue believing. It is in hope the saints rejoice, and no longer than they continue hoping. God's Spirit worketh our comforts, by setting our own spirits on work upon the promises, and raising our thoughts to the place of our comforts. As you would delight a covetous man by showing him gold; so God delights his people by leading them, as it were, into heaven, and showing them himself, and their rest with him. He does not cast in our joys while we are idle, or taken up with other things. He gives the fruits of the earth while we plough, and sow, and weed, and water, and dung, and dress, and with patience expect his blessing; so doth he give the joys of the soul. I entreat thee, Reader, in the name of the Lord, and as thou valuest the life of constant joy, and that good conscience which is a continual feast, to set upon this work seriously, and learn the art of heavenly-mindedness, and thou shalt find the increase a hundred fold, and the benefit abundantly exceed thy labour. But this is the misery of man's nature: though every man naturally hates sorrow, and loves the most merry and joyful life, yet few love the way to joy, or will endure the pains by which it is obtained; they will take the next that comes to hand, and content themselves with earthly pleasures, rather than they will ascend to heaven to seek it; and yet when all is done, they must have it there, or be without it.

6. (4.) A heart in heaven will be a most excellent preservative against temptations to sin. It will keep the heart well employed. When we are idle, we tempt the devil to tempt us; as careless persons make thieves. A heart in heaven can reply to the tempter, as Nehemiah did, 'I am doing a great work, so that I cannot come.' It hath no leisure to be lustful or wanton, ambitious or worldly. If you were but busy in your lawful callings, you would not be so ready to hearken to temptations; much less if you were also busy above with God. Would a judge be persuaded to rise from the bench, when he is sitting upon life and death, to go and play with children in

the streets? No more will a Christian, when he is taking a survey of his eternal rest, give ear to the alluring charms of Satan. The children of that kingdom should never have time for trifles, especially when they are employed in the affairs of the kingdom; and this employment is one of the saints' chief preservatives from temptations.

7. A heavenly mind is the freest from sin, because it hath truer and livelier apprehensions of spiritual things. He hath so deep an insight into the evil of sin, the vanity of the creature, the brutishness of fleshly, sensual delights, that temptations have little power over him. ' In vain the net is spread,' says Solomon, ' in the sight of any bird.' And usually in vain doth Satan lay his snares to entrap the soul that plainly sees them. Earth is the place for his temptations, and the ordinary bait; and how shall these ensnare the Christian, who hath left the earth, and walks with God? Is converse with wise and learned men the way to make one wise? Much more is converse with God. If travellers return home with wisdom and experience, how much more he that travels to heaven? If our bodies are suited to the air and climate we most live in; his understanding must be fuller of light, who lives with the Father of lights. The men of the world that dwell below, and know no other conversation but earthly, no wonder if their understanding be darkened, and Satan ' takes them captive at his will.' How can worms and moles see, whose dwelling is always in the earth? While this dust is in their eyes, no wonder they mistake gain for godliness, sin for grace, the world for God, their own wills for the law of Christ, and, in the issue, hell for heaven. But when a Christian withdraws himself from his worldly thoughts, and begins to converse with God in heaven, methinks he is, as Nebuchadnezzar, taken from the beasts of the field to the throne, and ' his reason returneth unto him.' When he hath had a glimpse of eternity, and looks down on the world again, how doth he charge with folly his neglects of Christ, his fleshly pleasures, his earthly cares! How doth he say to his laughter, It is mad; and to his vain mirth, What doth it? How doth he verily think there is no man in bedlam so truly mad as wilful sinners, and unworthy slighters of Christ and glory! This makes a dying man usually wiser than others, because he looks on eternity as near, and hath more heart-piercing thoughts of it than he ever had in health and prosperity. Then many of the most bitter enemies of the saints have their eyes opened, and like Balaam, cry out, ' O

that I might die the death of the righteous, and that my last end might be like his!' Yet let the same men recover, and lose their apprehensions of the life to come, and how quickly do they lose their understandings with it! Tell a dying sinner of the riches, honours, or pleasures of the world, and would he not answer, ' What is all this to me, who must presently appear before God, and give an account of all my life?' Christian, if the apprehended nearness of eternity will work such strange effects upon the ungodly, and make them so much wiser than before; O what rare effects would it produce in thee, if thou couldst always dwell in the views of God, and in lively thoughts of thy everlasting state! Surely a believer, if he improve his faith, may ordinarily have more quickening apprehensions of the life to come, in the time of his health, than an unbeliever hath at the hour of his death.

8. A heavenly mind is also fortified against temptations, because the affections are thoroughly prepossessed with the high delights of another world. He that loves most, and not he that only knows most, will most easily resist the emotions of sin. The will doth as sweetly relish goodness, as the understanding doth truth; and here lies much of a Christian's strength. When thou hast had a fresh, delightful taste of heaven, thou wilt not be so easily persuaded from it. You cannot persuade a child to part with his sweetmeats, while the taste is in his mouth. O that you would be much on feeding on the hidden manna, and frequently tasting the delights of heaven! How would this confirm thy resolutions, and make thee despise the fooleries of the world, and scorn to be cheated with such childish toys. If the devil had set upon Peter in the mount of transfiguration, when he saw Moses and Elias talking with Christ, would he so easily have been drawn to deny his Lord? What! with all that glory in his eye? No. So, if he should set upon a believing soul, when it is taken up in the mount with Christ, what would such a soul say? ' Get thee behind me, Satan; wouldst thou persuade me hence, with trifling pleasures, and steal my heart from this my rest? Wouldst thou have me sell these joys for nothing? Is any honour or delight like this? or can that be profit, for which I must lose this?' But Satan stays till we are come down, and the taste of heaven is out of our mouths, and the glory we saw is even forgotten, and then he easily deceives our hearts. Though the Israelites below, eat, and drink, and rise up to play before their idol, Moses in the mount will not do so. O if we could keep the taste of our

souls continually delighted with the sweetness above, with what disdain should we spit out the baits of sin !

9. Besides, whilst the heart is set on heaven, a man is under God's protection. If Satan then assault us, God is more engaged for our defence, and will doubtless stand by us, and say, ' My grace is sufficient for thee.' When a man is in the way of God's blessing, he is in the less danger of sin's enticing. Amidst thy temptations, Christian Reader, use much this powerful remedy— keep close with God by a heavenly mind ; follow your business above with Christ, and you will find this a surer help than any other. ' The way of life is above to the wise, that he may depart from hell beneath.' Remember that ' Noah was a just man, and perfect in his generation ;' for he ' walked with God :' and that God said to Abraham, ' Walk before me, and be thou perfect.'

10. (5.) The diligent keeping your hearts in heaven, will maintain the vigour of all your graces, and put life into all your duties. The heavenly Christian is the lively Christian. It is our strangeness to heaven that makes us so dull. How will the soldier hazard his life, and the mariner pass through storms and waves, and no difficulty keep them back, when they think of an uncertain perishing treasure ! What life then would it put into a Christian's endeavours, if he would frequently think of his everlasting treasure ! We run so slowly, and strive so lazily, because we so little mind the prize. Observe but the man who is much in heaven, and you shall see he is not like other Christians ; there is something of what he hath seen above, appeareth in all his duty and conversation. If a preacher, how heavenly are his sermons ! If a private Christian, what heavenly converse, prayers, and deportment ! Set upon this employment, and others will see the face of your conversation shine, and say, Surely he hath been ' with God on the mount.' But if you lie complaining of deadness and dulness, that you cannot love Christ, nor rejoice in his love ; that you have no life in prayer, nor any other duty, and yet neglect this quickening employment ; you are the cause of your own complaints. Is not thy life hid with Christ in God ? Where must thou go, but to Christ for it ? And where is that but to heaven, where Christ is ? ' Thou wilt not come to Christ, that thou mayest have life.' If thou wouldst have light and heat, why art thou no more in the sunshine ? For want of this recourse to heaven, thy soul is as a lamp not lighted, and thy duties as a sacrifice without fire. Fetch one coal daily from this altar, and see if thy offering will not

burn. Light thy lamp at this flame, and feed it daily with oil from hence, and see if it will not gloriously shine. Keep close to this reviving fire, and see if thy affections will not be warm. In thy want of love to God, lift up thy eye of faith to heaven, behold his beauty, contemplate his excellencies, and see whether his amiableness and perfect goodness will not ravish thy heart. As exercise gives appetite, strength, and vigour to the body ; so these heavenly exercises will quickly cause the increase of grace and spiritual life. Besides, it is not false or strange fire, which you fetch from heaven for your sacrifices. The zeal which is kindled by your meditations on heaven, is most likely to be a heavenly zeal. Some men's fervency is only drawn from their books, some from the sharpness of affliction, some from the mouth of a moving minister, and some from the attention of an auditory ; but he that knows this way to heaven, and derives it daily from the true fountain, shall have his soul revived with the water of life, and enjoy that quickening which is peculiar to the saints. ' By this faith thou mayest offer Abel's sacrifice, more excellent than' that of common men, and 'by it obtain witness that thou art righteous, God testifying of thy gifts,' that they are sincere. When others are ready, like Baal's priests, to cut themselves, because their sacrifice will not burn ; thou mayest breathe the spirit of Elijah, and in the chariot of contemplation soar aloft, till thy soul and sacrifice gloriously flame, though the flesh and the world should cast upon them all the water of their opposing enmity. Say not, how can mortals ascend to heaven ? Faith has wings, and meditation is its chariot. Faith is a burning-glass to thy sacrifice, and meditation sets it to the face of the sun : only take it not away too soon, but hold it there awhile, and thy soul will feel the happy effect. Reader, art thou not thinking, when thou seest a lively Christian, and hearest his lively fervent prayers, and edifying discourse, ' O now happy a man is this ! O that my soul were in this blessed condition !' Why, I here advise thee from God, set thy soul conscientiously to this work, wash thee frequently in this Jordan, and thy leprous dead soul will revive, 'and thou shalt know that there is a God in Israel,' and that thou mayest live a vigorous and joyful life, if thou dost not wilfully neglect thy own mercies.

11. (6.) The frequent believing views of glory are the most precious cordials in all afflictions. These cordials, by cheering our spirits, render our sufferings far more easy, enable us to bear them with patience and joy, and so strengthen

our resolutions, that we forsake not Christ for fear of trouble. If the way be ever so rough, can it be tedious if it lead to heaven? O sweet sickness, reproaches, imprisonments, or death, accompanied with these tastes of our future rest! This keeps the sufferings from the soul, so that it can only touch the flesh. Had it not been for that little (alas! too little) taste which I had of rest, my sufferings would have been grievous, and death more terrible. I may say, 'I had fainted, unless I had believed to see the goodness of the Lord in the land of the living.' Unless this promised rest had been my delight, I should then have perished in mine affliction. ' One thing have I desired of the Lord, that will I seek after ; that I may dwell in the house of the Lord all the days of my life, to behold the beauty of the Lord, and to inquire in his temple. For in the time of trouble he shall hide me in his pavilion : in the secret of his tabernacle shall he hide me ; he shall set me upon a rock. And now shall mine head be lifted up above mine enemies round about me : therefore will I offer in his tabernacle sacrifices of joy ; I will sing, yea, I will sing praises unto the Lord.' All sufferings are nothing to us, so far as we have these supporting joys. When persecution and fear hath shut the doors, Christ can come in, and stand in the midst, and say to his disciples, ' Peace be unto you.' Paul and Silas can be in heaven, even when they are thrust into the inner prison, their bodies scourged with 'many stripes, and their feet fast in the stocks.' The martyrs find more rest in their flames, than their persecutors in their pomp and tyranny ; because they foresee the flames they escape, and the rest which their fiery chariot is conveying them to. If the Son of God will walk with us, we are safe in the midst of those flames, which shall devour them that cast us in. ' Abraham went out of his country, not knowing whither he went ; because he looked for a city which hath foundations, whose builder and maker is God. Moses esteemed the reproach of Christ greater riches than the treasures in Egypt ; because he had respect unto the recompence of reward. He forsook Egypt, not fearing the wrath of the king ; because he endured, as seeing him who is invisible. Others were tortured, not accepting deliverance; that they might obtain a better resurrection. Even Jesus, the author and finisher of our faith, for the joy that was set before him, endured the cross, despising the shame, and is set down at the right hand of God.' This is the noble advantage of faith ; it can look on the means and end together. This is the great reason of our impatience, and censuring of God, because we gaze on the evil itself, but fix not our thoughts on what is beyond it. They that saw Christ only on the cross, or in the grave, do shake their heads, and think him lost ; but God saw him dying, buried, rising, glorified, and all this at one view. Faith will in this imitate God, so far as it hath the glass of a promise to help it. We see God burying us under ground, but we foresee not the spring, when we shall all revive. Could we but clearly see heaven, as the end of all God's dealings with us, surely none of his dealings could be grievous. If God would once raise us to this life, we should find, that though heaven and sin are at a great distance ; yet heaven and a prison, or banishment, heaven and the belly of a whale, or a den of lions, heaven and consuming sickness, or invading death, are at no such distance. But as ' Abraham saw Christ's day and rejoiced ;' so we, in our most forlorn state, might see that day. when Christ shall give us rest, and therein rejoice. I beseech thee, Christian, for the honour of the gospel, and for thy soul's comfort, be not to learn this heavenly art, when in thy greatest extremity thou hast most need to use it. He that, with Stephen, ' sees the glory of God, and Jesus standing on the right hand of God,' will comfortably bear the shower of stones. ' The joy of the Lord is our strength,' and that joy must be fetched from the place of our joy ; and if we walk without our strength, how long are we like to endure?

12. (7.) He that hath his conversation in heaven, is the profitable Christian to all about him. When a man is in a strange country, how glad is he of the company of one of his own nation ! How delightful is it to talk of their own country, their acquaintance, and affairs at home ! With what pleasure did Joseph talk with his brethren, and inquire after his father, and his brother Benjamin ! Is it not so to a Christian, to talk with his brethren. that have been above, and inquire after his Father, and Christ his Lord ? When a worldly man will talk of nothing but the world, and a politician of state affairs, and a mere scholar of human learning, and a common professor of his duties ; the heavenly man will be speaking of heaven, and the strange glory his faith hath seen, and our speedy and blessed meeting there. O how refreshing and useful are his expressions ! How his words pierce and melt the heart, and transform the hearers into other men ! How doth his doctrine drop as the rain, and his speech distil as the dew, as the small rain upon the tender herb, and as the showers upon the grass,

while his lips publish tne name of the Lord, and ascribe greatness unto his God! Is not his sweet discourse of heaven like the ' box of precious ointment,' which, being ' poured upon the head of Christ, filled the house with the odour ?' All that are near may be refreshed by it. Happy the people that have a heavenly minister! Happy the children and servants that have a heavenly father or master! Happy the man that hath a heavenly companion, who will watch over thy ways, strengthen thee when thou art weak, cheer thee when thou art drooping, and comfort thee with the comfort wherewith he himself hath been so often comforted of God! This is he that will always be blowing at the spark of thy spiritual life, and drawing thy soul to God, and will say to thee, as the Samaritan woman, ' Come, and see one that hath told me all that ever I did ;' one that hath loved our souls to the death. ' Is not this the Christ ?' Is not the ' knowledge of God and him eternal life ?' Is it not the glory of the saints to see his glory ? Come to this man's house, and sit at his table, and he will feast thy soul with the dainties of heaven ; travel with him by the way, and he will direct and quicken thee in thy journey to heaven ; trade with him in the world, and he will counsel thee to buy the pearl of great price. If thou wrong him, he can pardon thee, remembering that Christ hath pardoned his greater offences. If thou be angry, he is meek, considering the meekness of his heavenly pattern ; or if he fall out with you, he is soon reconciled, when he recollects that in heaven you must be everlasting friends. This is the Christian of the right stamp, and all about him are better for him. How unprofitable is the society of all other sorts of Christians, in comparison with this! If a man should come from heaven, how would men long to hear what reports he would make of the other world, and what he had seen, and what the blessed there enjoy! Would they not think this man the best companion, and his discourses the most profitable ? Why then do you value the company of saints no more, and inquire no more of them, and relish their discourse no better ? For every saint shall go to heaven in person, and is frequently there in spirit, and hath often viewed it in the glass of the gospel. For my part, I had rather have the company of a heavenly-minded Christian, than of the most learned disputants or princely commanders.

13. (8.) No man so highly honoureth God, as he whose conversation is in heaven. Is not a parent disgraced, when his children feed on husks, are clothed in rags, and keep company with none

but rogues and beggars ? Is it not so to our heavenly Father, when we, who call ourselves his children, feed on earth, and the garb of our souls is like that of the naked world ; and our hearts familiarly converse with, and ' cleave to the dust,' rather than stand continually in our Father's presence ? Surely we live below the children of the King, not according to the height of our hopes, nor the provision of our Father's house, and the great preparations made for his saints. It is well we have a Father of tender bowels, who will own his children in rags. If he did not first challenge his interest in us, neither ourselves nor others could know us to be his people. But when a Christian can live above, and rejoice his soul with the things that are unseen, how is God honoured by such a one! The Lord will testify for him, This man believes me, and takes me at my word ; he rejoiceth in my promise, before he hath possession ; he can be thankful for what his bodily eyes never saw ; his rejoicing is not in the flesh ; his heart is with me ; he loves my presence ; and he shall surely enjoy it in my kingdom for ever. ' Blessed are they that have not seen, and yet have believed. Them that honour me, I will honour.' How did God esteem himself honoured by Caleb and Joshua, when they went into the promised land, and brought back to their brethren a taste of the fruits, and spake well of the good land, and encouraged the people! What a promise and recompense did they receive!

14. (9.) A soul that doth not set its affections on things above, disobeys the commands, and loses the most gracious and delightful discoveries of the word of God. The same God that hath commanded thee to believe, and to be a Christian, hath commanded thee to ' seek those things which are above, where Christ sitteth on the right hand of God, and to set your affections on things above, not on things on the earth.' The same God that hath forbidden thee to murder, steal, or commit adultery, hath forbidden thee the neglect of this great duty ; and darest thou wilfully disobey him ? Why not make conscience of one, as well as the other ? He hath made it thy duty, as well as the means of thy comfort, that a double bond may engage thee not to forsake thy own mercies. Besides, what are all the most glorious descriptions of heaven, all those discoveries of our future blessedness, and precious promises of our rest, but lost to thee? Are not these the stars in the firmament of scripture, and the golden lines in that book of God ? Methinks thou shouldst not part with one of these promises, no, not for a world. As heaven is the perfection of

all our mercies, so the promises of it in the gospel are the very soul of the gospel. Is a comfortable word from the mouth of God of such worth, that all the comforts in the world are nothing to it? And dost thou neglect and overlook so many of them? Why should God reveal so much of his counsel, and tell us beforehand of the joys we shall possess, but to make us know it for our joy? If it had not been to fill us with the delights of our foreknown blessedness, he might have kept his purpose to himself, and never have let us know it till we came to enjoy it. Yea, when we had got possession of our rest, he might still have concealed its eternity from us, and then the fears of losing it would have diminished the sweetness of our joys. But it hath pleased our Father to open his counsel, and let us know the very intent of his heart, that our joy might be full, and that we might live as the heirs of such a kingdom. And shall we now overlook all? Shall we live in earthly cares and sorrows, and rejoice no more in these discoveries, than if the Lord had never wrote them? If thy prince had but sealed thee a patent of some lordship, how oft wouldst thou cast thy eyes upon it, and make it thy delightful study, till thou shouldst come to possess the dignity itself! And hath God sealed thee a patent of heaven, and dost thou let it lie by thee, as if thou hadst forgot it? O that our hearts were as high as our hopes, and our hopes as high as these infallible promises!

15. (10.) It is but just that our hearts should be on God, when the heart of God is so much on us. If the Lord of glory can stoop so low, as to set his heart on sinful dust, methinks we should easily be persuaded to set our hearts on Christ and glory, and ascend to him, in our daily affections, who so much condescends to us. Christian, dost thou not perceive that the heart of God is set upon thee, and that he is still minding thee with tender love, even when thou forgettest both thyself and him? Is he not following thee with daily mercies, moving upon thy soul, providing for thy body, preserving both? Doth he not bear thee continually in the arms of love, and promise that ' all shall work together for thy good,' and suit all his dealings to thy greatest advantage, and give his angels charge over thee? And canst thou be taken up with the joys below, and forget thy Lord, who forgets not thee? Unkind ingratitude! When he speaks of his own kindness for us, hear what he says—' Zion said, The Lord hath forsaken me, and my Lord hath forgotten me. Can a woman forget her sucking child, that she should

not have compassion on the son of her womb? Yea, she may forget, yet will I not forget thee. Behold, I have graven thee upon the palms of my hands; thy walls are continually before me.' But when he speaks of our regards to him, the case is otherwise. ' Can a maid forget her ornaments, or a bride her attire? yet my people have forgotten me days without number.' As if he should say, ' You will not rise one morning but you will remember to cover your nakedness, nor forget your vanity of dress; and are these of more worth than your God; of more importance than your eternal life? And yet you can forget these day after day.' Give not God cause thus to expostulate with us. Rather let our souls get up to God, and visit him every morning, and our hearts be towards him every moment.

16. (11.) Should not our interest in heaven, and our relation to it, continually keep our hearts upon it? There our Father keeps his court. We call him, ' Our Father, who art in heaven.' Unworthy children! that can be so taken up in their play, as to be mindless of such a Father. There also is Christ, our head, our husband, our life; and shall we not look towards him and send to him as oft as we can, till we come to see him face to face? Since ' the heavens must receive him until the times of restitution of all things;' let them also receive our hearts with him. There also is New Jerusalem, ' which is the mother of us all.' And there are multitudes of our elder brethren. There are our friends and old acquaintance, whose society in the flesh we so much delighted in, and whose departure hence we so much lamented, and is this no attractive to thy thoughts. If they were within thy reach on earth, thou wouldst go and visit them, and why not oftener visit them in spirit, and rejoice beforehand to think of meeting them there? ' Socrates rejoiced that he should die, because he believed he should see Homer, Hesiod, and other eminent persons. How much more do I rejoice, said a pious old minister, who am sure to see Christ my Saviour, the eternal Son of God, in his assumed flesh; besides so many wise, holy, and renowned patriarchs, prophets, apostles,' &c. A believer should look to heaven, and contemplate the blessed state of the saints, and think with himself, ' Though I am not yet so happy as to be with you, yet this is my daily comfort, you are my brethren and fellow-members in Christ, and therefore your joys are my joys, and your glory, by this near relation, is my glory; especially while I believe in the same Christ, and hold fast the same faith and obedience, by which you were thus digni-

fied, and rejoice in spirit with you, and congratulate your happiness in my daily meditations.'

17. Moreover, our house and home is above. ' For we know that if our earthly house of this tabernacle were dissolved, we have a building of God, an house not made with hands, eternal in the heavens.' Why do we then look no oftener towards it, and 'groan earnestly, desiring to be clothed upon with our house which is from heaven?' If our home were far meaner, sure we should remember it, because it is our home. If you were but banished into a strange land, how frequently would your thoughts be at home. And why is it not thus with us in respect of heaven? Is not that more truly and properly our home, where we must take up our everlasting abode, than this, which we are every hour expecting to be separated from, and to see no more? We are strangers, and that is our country. We are heirs, and that is our inheritance; even ' an inheritance incorruptible, undefiled, and that fadeth not away, reserved in heaven for us.' We are here in continual distress and want, and there lies our substance; even 'a better and an enduring substance.' Yea, the very hope of our souls is there; all our hope of relief from our distresses; all our hope of happiness, when here we are miserable: all this 'hope is laid up for us in heaven.' Why, beloved Christians, have we so much interest, and so few thoughts there? So near relation, and so little affection? Doth it become us to be delighted in the company of strangers, so as to forget our Father, and our Lord? or to be so well pleased with those that hate and grieve us, as to forget our best and dearest friends; or to be so fond of borrowed trifles, as to forget our own possession and treasure; or to be so much impressed with fears and wants, as to forget our eternal joy and rest? God usually pleads his property in us; and thence concludes he will do us good, even because we are his own people, whom he hath chosen out of all the world. Why then do we not plead our interest in him, and so raise our hearts above; even because he is our own God, and because the place is our own possession? Men commonly overlove and overvalue their own things, and mind them too much. O that we could mind our own inheritance, and value it half as much as it deserves!

18. (12.) Once more consider, there is nothing but heaven worth setting our hearts upon. If God have them not, who shall? If thou mind not thy rest, what wilt thou mind? Hast thou found out some other God? or something that will serve thee instead of rest? Hast thou found

on earth an eternal happiness? Where is it? What is it made of? Who was the man that found it out? Who was he that last enjoyed it? Where dwelt he? What was his name? Or art thou the first that ever discovered heaven on earth? Ah, wretch! trust not to thy discoveries, boast not of thy gain till experience bid thee boast. Disquiet not thyself in looking for that which is not on earth; lest thou learn thy experience with the loss of thy soul, which thou mightest have learned on easier terms; even by the warnings of God in his word, and the loss of thousands of souls before thee. If Satan should ' take thee up to the mountain of temptation, and show thee all the kingdoms of the world, and the glory of them;' he could show thee nothing that is worthy thy thoughts, much less to be preferred before thy rest. Indeed, so far as duty and necessity require it, we must be content to mind the things below; but who is he that contains himself within the compass of those limits? And yet if we ever so diligently contract our cares and thoughts, we shall find the least to be bitter and burdensome. Christians, see the emptiness of all these things, and the preciousness of the things above. If thy thoughts should, like the laborious bee, go over the world from flower to flower, from creature to creature, they would bring no honey or sweetness home, save what they gathered from their relations to eternity. Though every truth of God is precious, and ought to be defended; yet even all our study of truth should be still in reference to our rest; for the observation is too true, 'that the lovers of controversies in religion have never been warmed with one spark of the love of God.' And, as for minding the ' affairs of church and state;' so far as they illustrate the providence of God, and tend to the settling of the gospel, and the government of Christ; and, consequently, to the saving our own souls, and those of our posterity, they are well worth our diligent observation; but these are only their relations to eternity. Even all our dealings in the world, our buying and selling, our eating and drinking, our building and marrying, our peace and war, so far as they relate not to the life to come, but tend only to the pleasing of the flesh, are not worthy the frequent thoughts of a Christian. And now doth not thy conscience say, that there is nothing but heaven and the way to it, that is worth thy minding.

19. Now, Reader, are these considerations weighty, or not? Have I proved it thy duty to keep thy heart on things above, or have I not? If thou say, ' not,' I am confident thou contra-

11

dictest thy own conscience. If thou acknowledge thyself convinced of the duty, that very tongue of thine shall condemn thee, and that confession be pleaded against thee, if thou wilfully neglect such a confessed duty. Be thoroughly willing, and the work is more than half done. I have now a few plain directions to give you for your help in this great work; but, alas! it is in vain to mention them, except you be willing to put them into practice. However, I will propose them to thee, and may the Lord persuade thy heart to the work!

CHAPTER XII.

DIRECTIONS HOW TO LEAD A HEAVENLY LIFE UPON EARTH.

Sect. 1. (I.) Hinderances to a heavenly life must be avoided; such as, 2. (I.) Living in any known sin; 3. (2.) An earthly mind; 4. (3.) Ungodly companions; 5. (4.) A notional religion; 6. (5.) A haughty spirit; 7. (6.) A slothful spirit: 8. (7.) Resting in preparatives for a heavenly life, without the thing itself. 9. (II.) The duties which will promote a heavenly life are these: 10. (1.) Be convinced that heaven is the only treasure and happiness; 11, 12. (2.) Labour to know your interest in it; 13. (3.) and how near it is: 14. (4.) Frequently and seriously talk of it; 15. (5.) Endeavour in every duty to raise your affections nearer to it; 16. (6.) To the same purpose improve every object and event; 17, 18. (7.) Be much in the angelical work of praise: 19. (8.) Possess your souls with believing thoughts of the infinite love of God: 20. (9.) Carefully observe and cherish the motions of the Spirit of God: 21. (10.) Nor even neglect the due care of your bodily health.

1. (I.) As thou valuest the comforts of a heavenly conversation, I must here charge thee from God, to avoid carefully some dangerous hinderances; and then faithfully and diligently to practise such duties as will especially assist thee in attaining to a heavenly life. And, (1.) The hinderances to be avoided with all possible care, are—living in any known sin—an earthly mind—the company of the ungodly—notional religion—a proud and lofty spirit—a slothful spirit—and resting in mere preparations for this heavenly life, without any acquaintance with the thing itself.

2. (1.) Living in any known sin, is a grand impediment to a heavenly conversation. What havoc will this make in thy soul! O the joys that this hath destroyed! The ruin it hath made amongst men's graces! The soul-strengthening duties it hath hindered! Christian Reader, art thou one that hast used violence with thy conscience! Art thou a wilful neglecter of known duties, either public, private, or secret? Art thou a slave to thine appetite, or to any other commanding sense? Art thou a proud seeker of thine own esteem? Art thou a peevish and passionate person, ready to take fire at every word, or look, or supposed slight? Art thou a deceiver of others in thy dealings, or one that

will be rich, right or wrong? If this be thy case, I dare say, heaven and thy soul are very great strangers. These beams in thine eyes will not suffer thee to look to heaven; they will be a cloud between thee and thy God. When thou dost but attempt to study eternity, and gather comforts from the life to come, thy sin will presently look thee in the face, and say, ' These things belong not to thee. How shouldst thou take comfort from heaven, who takest so much pleasure in the lusts of the flesh?' How will this damp thy joys, and make the thoughts of that day and state become thy trouble, and not thy delight! Every wilful sin will be to thy comforts, as water to the fire; when thou thinkest to quicken them, this will quench them. It will utterly indispose and disable thee, that thou canst no more ascend in divine meditation, than a bird can fly when its wings are clipped. Sin cuts the very sinews of this heavenly life. O man! what a life dost thou lose! What daily delights dost thou sell for a vile lust! If heaven and hell can meet together, and God become a lover of sin, then mayest thou live in thy sin, and in the tastes of glory; and have a conversation in heaven, though thou cherish thy corruption. And take heed, lest it banish thee from heaven, as it does thy heart. And though thou be not guilty, and knowest no reigning sin in thy soul, think what a sad thing it would be, if ever this should prove thy case. Watch, therefore: especially resolve to keep from the occasions of sin, and out of the way of temptations. What need have we daily to pray, ' Lead us not into temptation, but deliver us from evil!'

3. (2.) An earthly mind is another hinderance carefully to be avoided. God and mammon, earth and heaven, cannot both have the delight of thy heart. When the heavenly believer is blessing himself in his God, and rejoicing in hope of the glory to come; perhaps thou art blessing thyself in thy worldly prosperity, and rejoicing in hope of thy thriving here. When he is comforting his soul in the views of Christ, of angels, and saints, whom he shall live with for ever; then thou art comforting thyself with thy wealth, in looking over thy bills and bonds, thy goods, thy cattle, or thy buildings, and in thinking of the favour of the great, of the pleasure of a plentiful estate, of larger provision for thy children after thee, of the advancement of thy family, or the increase of thy dependents. If Christ pronounced him a fool, that said, ' Soul, take thy ease, thou hast enough laid up for many years;' how much more so art thou, who knowingly speakest in thy heart the same words! Tell

me, what difference between this fool's expressions and thy affections? Remember, thou hast to do with the Searcher of hearts. Certainly, so much as thou delightest, and takest up thy rest on earth, so much of thy delight in God is abated. Thine earthly mind may consist with thy outward profession and common duties; but it cannot consist with this heavenly duty. Thou thyself knowest how seldom and cold, how cursory and reserved thy thoughts have been of the joys above, ever since thou didst trade so eagerly for the world. O the cursed madness of many that seem to be religious! They thrust themselves into a multitude of employments, till they are so loaded with labours, and clogged with cares, that their souls are as unfit to converse with God, as a man to walk with a mountain on his back; and as unapt to soar in meditation, as their bodies to leap above the sun! And when they have lost that heaven upon earth, which they might have had, they take up with a few rotten arguments to prove it lawful; though, indeed, they cannot. I advise thee, Christian, who hast tasted the pleasures of a heavenly life, as ever thou wouldst taste of them any more, avoid this devouring gulf of an earthly mind. If once thou come to this, that thou wilt be rich, thou 'fallest into temptation, and a snare, and into many foolish and hurtful lusts.' Keep these things loose about thee, like thy upper garments, that thou mayest lay them by whenever there is need; but let God and glory be next thy heart. Ever remember, 'that the friendship of the world is enmity with God. Whosoever therefore will be a friend of the world, is the enemy of God.'—' Love not the world, neither the things that are in the world. If any man love the world, the love of the Father is not in him.' This is plain dealing, and happy he that faithfully receives it.

4. (3.) Beware of the company of the ungodly. Not that I would dissuade thee from necessary converse, or from doing them any office of love; especially, not from endeavouring the good of their souls, as long as thou hast any opportunity or hope: nor would I have thee to conclude them to be dogs and swine, in order to evade the duty of reproof; nor even to judge them such at all, as long as there is any hope for the better: much less can I approve of their practice, who conclude men dogs or swine, before ever they faithfully and lovingly admonish them; or perhaps, before they have known them, or spoken with them. But it is the unnecessary society of ungodly men, and too much familiarity with unprofitable companions, that I dissuade you from. Not only the openly profane, the swearer, the drunkard, and the enemies of godliness, will prove hurtful companions to us, though these indeed are chiefly to be avoided; but too frequent society with persons merely civil and moral, whose conversation is empty and unedifying, may much divert our thoughts from heaven. Our backwardness is such, that we need the most constant and powerful helps. A stone, or a clod, is as fit to rise and fly in the air, as our hearts are naturally to move toward heaven. You need not hinder the rocks from flying up to the sky; it is sufficient that you do not help them: and surely if our spirits have not great assistance, they may easily be kept from soaring upward, though they should never meet with the least impediment. O think of this in the choice of your company! When your spirits are so disposed for heaven, that you need no help to lift them up; but, as flames, you are always mounting, and carrying with you all that is in your way; then, indeed, you may be less careful of your company; but till then, as you love the delights of a heavenly life, be careful herein. What will it advantage thee in a divine life to hear how the market goes, or what the weather is, or is like to be, or what news is stirring? This is the discourse of earthly men. What will it conduce to the raising thy heart God-ward to hear that this is an able minister, or that an eminent Christian, or this an excellent sermon, or that an excellent book, or to hear some difficult, but unimportant controversy? Yet this, for the most part, is the sweetest discourse thou art like to have from a formal, speculative, dead-hearted professor. Nay, if thou hadst newly been warming thy heart in the contemplation of the blessed joys above, would not this discourse benumb thy affections, and quickly freeze thy heart again? I appeal to the judgment of any man that hath tried it, and maketh observations on the frame of his spirit. Men cannot well talk of one thing, and mind another, especially things of such different natures. You, young men, who are most liable to this temptation, think seriously of what I say: can you have your hearts in heaven among your roaring companions in an alehouse or tavern? or, when you work in your shops with those whose common language is oaths, 'filthiness, or foolish talking, or jesting?' Nay, let me tell you, if you choose such company when you might have better, and find most delight in such, you are so far from a heavenly conversation, that as yet you have no title to heaven at all, and in that state shall never come there. If your treasure was there, your heart could not be on things so distant. In a word, our company will be a

part of our happiness in heaven, and it is a singular part of our furtherance to it, or hinderance from it.

5. (4.) Avoid frequent disputes about lesser truths, and a religion that lies only in opinions. They are usually least acquainted with a heavenly life, who are violent disputers about the circumstantials of religion. He whose religion is all in his opinions, will be most frequently and zealously speaking his opinions; and he whose religion lies in the knowledge and love of God and Christ, will be most delightfully speaking of that happy time when he shall enjoy them. He is a rare and precious Christian, who is skilful to improve well-known truths. Therefore let me advise you who aspire after a heavenly life, not to spend too much of your thoughts, your time, your zeal, or your speech, upon disputes that less concern your souls; but while hypocrites are feeding on husks or shells, do you feed on the joys above. I wish you were able to defend every truth of God, and, to this end, would read and study; but still I would have the chief truths to be chiefly studied, and none to cast out your thoughts of eternity. The least controverted points are usually most weighty, and of most necessary, frequent use to our souls. Therefore, study well such scripture precepts as these : 'him that is weak in the faith receive ye, but not to doubtful disputations. Foolish and unlearned questions avoid; knowing that they do gender strifes. And the servant of the Lord must not strive. Avoid foolish questions, and genealogies, and contentions, and strivings about the law; for they are unprofitable and vain. If any man teach otherwise, and consent not to wholesome words, even the words of our Lord Jesus Christ, and to the doctrine which is according to godliness ; he is proud, knowing nothing, but doting about questions and strifes of words, whereof cometh envy, strife, railings, evil surmisings, perverse disputings of men of corrupt minds, and destitute of the truth, supposing that gain is godliness : from such withdraw thyself.'

6. (5.) Take heed of a proud and lofty spirit. There is such an antipathy between this sin and God, that thou wilt never get thy heart near him, nor get him near thy heart, as long as this prevaileth in it. If it cast the angels out of heaven, it must needs keep thy heart from heaven. If it cast our first parents out of paradise, and separated between the Lord and us, and brought his curse on all the creatures here below, it will certainly keep our hearts from paradise, and increase the cursed separation from our God. Intercourse with God will keep men low, and that lowliness will promote their intercourse. When a man is used to be much with God, and taken up in the study of his glorious attributes, he abhors himself in dust and ashes ; and that self-abhorrence is his best preparative to obtain admittance to God again. Therefore, after a soul-humbling day, or in times of trouble, when the soul is lowest, it useth to have freest access to God, and savour most of the life above. The delight of God is in ' him that is poor, and of a contrite spirit, and trembleth at his word ;' and the delight of such a soul is in God ; and where there is mutual delight, there will be freest admittance, heartiest welcome, and most frequent converse. But God is so far from dwelling in the soul that is proud, that he will not admit it to any near access : ' The proud he knoweth afar off.'—' God resisteth the proud, and giveth grace to the humble.' A proud mind is high in conceit, self-esteem, and carnal aspiring ; a humble mind is high, indeed, in God's esteem, and in holy aspiring. These two sorts of high-mindedness are most of all opposite to each other, as we see most wars are between princes and princes, and not between a prince and a ploughman. Well then, art thou a man of worth in thy own eyes ? Art thou delighted when thou hearest of thy esteem with men, and much dejected when thou hearest that they slight thee ? Dost thou love those best that honour thee, and think meanly of them that do not, though they be otherwise men of godliness and honesty ? Must thou have thy humours fulfilled, and thy judgment be a rule, and thy word a law to all about thee ? Are thy passions kindled, if thy word or will be crossed ? Art thou ready to judge humility to be sordid baseness, and knowest not how to submit to humble confession, when thou hast sinned against God, or injured thy brother ? Art thou one that lookest strange at the godly poor, and art almost ashamed to be their companion ? Canst thou not serve God in a low place as well as a high ? Are thy boastings restrained more by prudence or artifice than humility ? Dost thou desire to have all men's eyes upon thee, and to hear them say, ' This is he ?' Art thou unacquainted with the deceitfulness and wickedness of thy heart ? Art thou more ready to defend thy innocence, than accuse thyself or confess thy fault ? Canst thou hardly bear a close reproof, or digest plain dealing ? If these symptoms be undeniably in thy heart, thou art a proud person. There is too much of hell abiding in thee, to have any acquaintance with heaven ; thy soul is too like the devil, to have any familiarity with God. A proud man makes

himself his god, and sets up himself as his idol; how then can his affections be set on God? How can he possibly have his heart in heaven? Invention and memory may possibly furnish his tongue with humble and heavenly expressions, but in his spirit there is no more of heaven than there is of humility. I speak the more of it, because it is the most common and dangerous sin in morality, and most promotes the great sin of infidelity. O Christian! if thou wouldst live continually in the presence of thy Lord, lie in the dust, and he will thence take thee up. 'Learn of him to be meek and lowly, and thou shalt find rest unto thy soul.' Otherwise thy soul will be 'like the troubled sea, when it cannot rest, whose waters cast up mire and dirt;' and instead of these sweet delights in God, thy pride will fill thee with perpetual disquiet. As he that humbles himself as a little child, shall hereafter be greatest in the kingdom of heaven; so shall he now be greatest in the foretastes of that kingdom. God 'dwells with a contrite and humble spirit, to revive the spirit of the humble, and to revive the heart of the contrite ones.' Therefore, 'humble yourselves in the sight of the Lord, and he shall lift you up.' And when others are cast down, 'then thou shalt say, there is lifting up; and he shall save the humble person.'

7. (6.) A slothful spirit is another impediment to this heavenly life. And I verily think, there is nothing hinders it more than this in men of a good understanding. If it were only the exercise of the body, the moving of the lips, the bending of the knee, men would as commonly step to heaven, as they go to visit a friend. But to separate our thoughts and affections from the world, to draw forth all our graces, and increase each in its proper object, and hold them to it till the work prospers in our hands; this, this is the difficulty. Reader, heaven is above thee, and dost thou think to travel this steep ascent without labour and resolution? Canst thou get that earthly heart to heaven, and bring that backward mind to God, while thou liest still, and takest thine ease? If lying down at the foot of the hill, and looking toward the top, and wishing we were there, would serve the turn, then we should have daily travellers for heaven. But 'the kingdom of heaven suffereth violence, and the violent take it by force.' There must be violence used to get these first-fruits, as well as to get the full possession. Dost thou not feel it so, though I should not tell thee? Will thy heart get upwards, except thou drive it? Thou knowest that heaven is all thy hope, that nothing below can yield thee rest; that a heart, seldom

thinking of heaven, can fetch but little comfort thence; and yet dost thou not lose thy opportunities, and lie below, when thou shouldst walk above, and live with God? Dost thou not commend the sweetness of a heavenly life, and judge those the best Christians that use it, and yet never try it thyself? As the sluggard that stretches himself on his bed, and cries, O that this were working! so dost thou talk, and trifle, and live at thy ease, and say, O that I could get my heart to heaven! How many read books, and hear sermons, expecting to hear of some easier way, or to meet with a shorter course to comfort, than they are ever like to find in scripture. Or they ask for directions for a heavenly life, and if the hearing them will serve, they will be heavenly Christians; but if we show them their work, and tell them they cannot have these delights on easier terms, then they leave us, as the young man left Christ, sorrowful. If thou art convinced, Reader, that this work is necessary to thy comfort, set upon it resolutely: if thy heart draw back, force it on with the command of reason; if thy reason begin to dispute, produce the command of God, and urge thy own necessity, with the other considerations suggested in the former chapter. Let not such an incomparable treasure lie before thee, with thy hand in thy bosom; nor thy life be a continual vexation, when it might be a continual feast, only because thou wilt not exert thyself. Sit not still with a disconsolate spirit, while comforts grow before thine eyes, like a man in the midst of a garden of flowers, that will not rise to get them, and partake of their sweetness. This I know, Christ is the fountain; but the well is deep, and thou must get forth this water before thou canst be refreshed with it. I know, so far as you are spiritual, you need not all this striving and violence; but in part you are carnal, and as long as it is so, there is need of labour. It was a custom of the Parthians, not to give their children any meat in the morning, before they saw the sweat on their faces with some labour. And you shall find this to be God's usual course, not to give his children the tastes of his delights till they begin to sweat in seeking after them. Judge, therefore, whether a heavenly life, or thy carnal ease, be better; and, as a wise man, make thy choice accordingly. Yea, let me add for thy encouragement, thou needest not employ thy thoughts more than thou now dost; it is only to fix them upon better and more pleasant objects. Employ but as many serious thoughts every day upon the excellent glory of the life to come, as thou now dost upon worldly affairs, yea, on vanities and impertinencies, and thy heart will soon be at heaven. On the whole, it is ' the field of the slothful, that is all grown over with thorns and nettles; and the desire of the slothful killeth his joy, for nis hands refuse to labour; and it is the slothful man that saith, ' There is a lion in the way, a lion is in the streets.'—' As the door turneth upon his hinges, so doth the slothful upon his bed. The slothful hideth his hand in his bosom; it grieveth him to bring it again to his mouth,' though it be to feed himself with the food of life. What is this but throwing away our consolations, and, consequently, the precious blood that bought them? For ' he that is slothful in his work, is brother to him that is a great waster.' Apply this to thy spiritual work. and study well the meaning of it.

8. (7.) Contentment with the mere preparatives to this heavenly life, while we are utter strangers to the life itself, is also a dangerous and secret hinderance. When we take up with the mere study of heavenly things, and the notions of them, or the talking with one another about them; as if this were enough to make us heavenly. None are in more danger of this snare, than those that are employed in leading the devotions of others, especially preachers of the gospel. O how easily may such be deceived! While they do nothing so much as read and study of heaven; preach, and pray, and talk of heaven; is not this the heavenly life? Alas! all this is but mere preparation: this is but collecting the materials, not erecting the building itself: it is but gathering the manna for others, and not eating and digesting it ourselves. As he that sits at home may draw exact maps of countries, and yet never see them, nor travel toward them, so may you describe to others the joys of heaven, and yet never come near it in your own hearts. A blind man, by learning, may dispute of light and colours; so may you set forth to others that heavenly light, which never enlightened your own souls, and bring that fire from the hearts of your people, which never warmed your own hearts. What heavenly passages had Balaam in his prophecies, yet how little of it in his spirit! Nay, we are under a more subtle temptation, than any other men, to draw us from this heavenly life. Studying and preaching of heaven more resembles a heavenly life, than thinking and talking of the world does; and the resemblance is apt to deceive us. This is to die the most miserable death, even to famish ourselves, because we have bread on our tables; and to die for thirst, while we draw water for others, thinking it enough that we have daily to do with it, though we never drink for the refreshment of our own souls.

9. (II.) Having thus showed thee what hinderances will resist thee in the work, I expect that thou wilt resolve against them, consider them seriously, and avoid them faithfully, or else thy labour will be in vain. I must also tell thee, that I here expect thy promise, as thou valuest the delights of these foretastes of heaven, to make conscience of performing the following duties; the reading of which, without their constant practice, will not bring heaven unto thy heart. Particularly, be convinced that heaven is the only treasure and happiness;—labour to know that it is thy own,—and how near it is;— frequently and seriously talk of it;—endeavour to raise thy affections nearer to it in every duty; —to the same purpose improve every object and event;—be much in the angelical work of praise; —possess thy soul with believing thoughts of the infinite love of God; carefully observe and cherish the motions of the Spirit of God;—nor even neglect the due care of thy bodily health.

10. (1.) Be convinced that heaven is the only treasure and happiness, and labour to know what a treasure and happiness it is. If thou do not believe it to be the chief good, thou wilt never set thy heart upon it; and this conviction must sink into thy affections; for if it be only a notion it will have little efficacy. If Eve once supposes she sees more worth in the forbidden fruit, than in the love and enjoyment of God, no wonder if it have more of her heart than God. If your judgment once prefer the delights of the flesh before the delights of the presence of God, it is impossible your heart should be in heaven. As it is ignorance of the emptiness of things below, that makes men so overvalue them; so it is ignorance of the high delights above, which is the cause that men so little mind them. If you see a purse of gold, and believe it to be but counters, it will not entice your affections to it. It is not the real excellence of a thing itself, but its known excellence, that excites desire. If an ignorant man see a book, containing the secrets of arts or sciences, he values it no more than a common piece, because he knows not what is in it; but he that knows it, highly values it, and can even forbear his meat, drink, and sleep, to read it. As the Jews killed the Messiah, while they waited for him, because they did not know him; so the world cries out for rest, and busily seeks for delight and happiness, because they know it not; for did they thoroughly know what it is, they could not so slight the everlasting treasure.

11. (2.) Labour also to know that heaven is thy own happiness. We may confess heaven to be the best condition, though we despair of enjoying it; and we may desire and seek it, if we see the attainment but probable; but we can never delightfully rejoice in it, till we are in some measure persuaded of our title to it. What comfort is it to a man that is naked, to see the rich attire of others? What delight is it for a man that hath not a house to put his head in, to see the sumptuous buildings of others? Would not all this rather increase his anguish, and make him more sensible of his own misery? So, for a man to know the excellencies of heaven, and not know whether ever he shall enjoy them, may raise desire, and urge pursuit, but he will have little joy. Who will set his heart on another man's possessions? If your houses, your goods, your cattle, your children, were not your own, you would less mind them, and less delight in them. O Christian! rest not, therefore, till you can call this rest your own: bring thy heart to the bar of trial: set the qualifications of the saints on one side, and of thy soul on the other, and then judge how near they resemble. Thou hast the same word to judge thyself by now, as thou must be judged by at the great day. Mistake not the scripture's description of a saint, that thou neither acquit nor condemn thyself upon mistakes. For as groundless hopes tend to confusion, and are the greatest cause of most men's damnation; so groundless doubts tend to, and are the great cause of, the saint's perplexity and distress. Therefore, lay thy foundation for trial safely, and proceed in the work deliberately and resolutely, nor give over till thou canst say, either thou hast, or hast not yet, a title to this rest. O! if men did truly know, that God is their own Father, and Christ their own Redeemer and Head, and that those are their own everlasting habitations, and that there they must abide and be happy for ever; how could they choose but be transported with the forethoughts thereof! If a Christian could but look upon sun, moon, and stars, and reckon all his own in Christ, and say, ' These are the blessings that my Lord hath procured me, and things incomparably greater than these;' what holy raptures would his spirit feel!

12. The more do they sin against their own comforts, as well as against the grace of the gospel, who plead for their unbelief, and cherish distrustful thoughts of God, and injurious thoughts of their Redeemer; who represent the covenant as if it were of works, and not of grace: and Christ as an enemy, rather than a Saviour; as if he were willing they should die in their unbelief, when he hath invited them so often and so affectionately, and suffered the agonies that they should suffer. Wretches that we are! to be keeping up jealousies of our Lord, when we should be rejoicing in his love. As if any man could choose Christ, before Christ hath chosen him, or any man were more willing to be happy, than Christ is to make him happy. Away with these injurious, if not blasphemous thoughts! If ever thou hast harboured such thoughts in thy breast, cast them from thee, and take heed how thou ever entertainest them more. God hath written the names of his people in heaven, as you use to write your names or marks on your goods; and shall we be attempting to raze them out, and to write our names on the doors of hell? But blessed be God, whose foundation standeth sure; and who ' keepeth us by his power through faith unto salvation!'

13. (3.) Labour to apprehend how near thy rest is. What we think near at hand, we are more sensible of than that which we behold at a distance. When judgments or mercies are afar off, we talk of them with little concern; but when they draw close to us, we tremble at, or rejoice in them. This makes men think on heaven so insensibly, because they conceit it at too great a distance; they look on it as twenty, thirty, or forty years off. How much better were it to receive ' the sentence of death in ourselves,' and to look on eternity as near at hand! While I am writing, and thinking of it, it hasteth near, and I am even entering into it before I am aware. While thou art reading this, whoever thou art, time posteth on, and thy life will be gone ' as a tale that is told.' If you verily believed you should die to morrow, how seriously would you think of heaven to-night! When Samuel had told Saul, ' To-morrow shalt thou be with me;' this struck him to the heart. And if Christ should say to a believing soul, ' To-morrow shalt thou be with me;' this would bring him in spirit to heaven beforehand. Do but suppose that you are still entering into heaven, and it will greatly help you more seriously to mind it.

14. (4.) Let thy eternal rest be the subject of thy frequent serious discourse; especially with those that can speak from their hearts, and are seasoned themselves with a heavenly nature. It is great pity Christians should ever meet together, without some talk of their meeting in heaven, or of the way to it, before they part. It is pity so much time is spent in vain conversation, and useless disputes, and not a serious word of heaven among them. Methinks we should meet together on purpose to warm our spirits

with discoursing of our rest. To hear a Christian set forth that blessed, glorious state, with life and power, from the promises of the gospel, methinks should make us say, 'Did not our hearts burn within us, while he opened to us the scriptures?' If a Felix will tremble when he hears his judgment powerfully represented, why should not the believer be revived, when he hears his eternal rest described? Wicked men can be delighted in talking together of their wickedness; and should not Christians then be delighted in talking of Christ; and the heirs of heaven in talking of their inheritance? This may make our hearts revive, as it did Jacob's, to hear the message that called him to Goshen, and to see the chariots that should bring him to Joseph. O that we were furnished with skill and resolution, to turn the stream of men's common discourse to these more sublime and precious things! and, when men begin to talk of things unprofitable, that we could tell how to put in a word for heaven, and say, as Peter of his bodily food, Not so, for I have never eaten any thing that is common or unclean.' O the good that we might both do and receive by this course! Had it not been to deter us from unprofitable conversation, Christ would not have talked of our giving an account of every idle word in the day of judgment. Say then, as the Psalmist, when you are in company, ' Let my tongue cleave to the roof of my mouth, if I prefer not Jerusalem above my chief joy.' Then you shall find it true, that a ' wholesome tongue is a tree of life.'

15. (5.) Endeavour, in every duty, to raise thy affections nearer to heaven. God's end in the institution of his ordinances was, that they should be as so many steps to advance us to our rest, and by which, in subordination to Christ, we might daily ascend in our affections. Let this be thy end in using them, and doubtless they will not be unsuccessful. How have you been rejoiced by a few lines from a friend, when you could not see him face to face! And may we not have intercourse with God in his ordinances, though our persons be yet so far remote? May not our spirits rejoice in reading those lines, which contain our legacy and charter for heaven? With what gladness and triumph may we read the expressions of divine love, and hear of our celestial country, though we have not yet the happiness to behold it! Men that are separated by sea and land, can by letters carry on great and gainful trades; and may not a Christian, in the wise improvement of duties, drive on this happy trade for rest? Come then, renounce formality, custom, and applause, and kneel down in secret or public prayer, with hope to get thy heart nearer to God, before thou risest up. When thou openest thy Bible, or other book, hope to meet with some passage of divine truth, and such blessing of the Spirit with it, as will give thee a fuller taste of heaven. When thou art going to the house of God, say, ' I hope to meet with somewhat from God to raise my affections, before I return; I hope the Spirit will give me the meeting, and sweeten my heart with those celestial delights; I hope Christ will appear to me in that way, and shine about me with light from heaven; let me hear his instructing and reviving voice, and cause the scales to fall from my eyes, that I may see more of that glory than I ever yet saw. I hope, before I return, my Lord will bring my heart within the view of rest, and set it before his Father's presence, that I may return as the shepherds from the heavenly vision, " glorifying and praising God, for all the things I have heard and seen." When the Indians first saw that the English could converse together by letters, they thought there was some spirit enclosed in them. So would by-standers admire when Christians have communion with God in duties—what there is in those scriptures, in that sermon, in that prayer, that fills their hearts so full of joy, and so transports them above themselves. Certainly God would not fail us in our duties, if we did not fail ourselves. Remember, therefore, always to pray for your minister, that God would put some divine message into his mouth, which may leave a heavenly relish upon your spirit.

16. (6.) Improve every object and every event, to mind thy soul of its approaching rest. As all providences and creatures are means to our rest, so they point us to that as their end. God's sweetest dealings with us at the present, would not be half so sweet as they are, if they did not intimate some further sweetness. Thou takest but the bare earnest, and overlookest the main sum, when thou receivest thy mercies, and forgettest thy crown. O that Christians were skilful in this art! You can open your Bibles; learn to open the volumes of creation and providence, to read there also of God and glory. Thus we might have a fuller taste of Christ and heaven in every common meal, than most men have in a sacrament. If thou prosper in the world, let it make thee more sensible of thy perpetual prosperity. If thou art weary with labour, let it make the thoughts of thy eternal rest more sweet. If things go cross, let thy desires be more earnest to have sorrows and sufferings for ever cease. Is thy body refreshed with food or

sleep? remember the inconceivable refreshment with Christ. Dost thou hear any good news? remember what glad tidings it will be, to hear the trump of God, and the applauding sentence of Christ. Art thou delighted with the society of the saints? remember what the perfect society in heaven will be. Is God communicating himself to thy spirit? remember the time of thy highest advancement, when both thy communion and joy shall be full. Dost thou hear the raging noise of the wicked, and the confusions of the world? think of the blessed harmony in heaven. Dost thou hear the tempest of war? remember the day, when thou shalt be in perfect peace, under the wings of the Prince of peace for ever. Thus, every condition, and creature, affords us advantages for a heavenly life, if we had but hearts to improve them.

17. (7.) Be much in the angelical work of praise. The more heavenly the employment, the more it will make the Spirit heavenly. Praising God is the work of angels and saints in heaven, and will be our own everlasting work; and if we were more in it now, we should be liker to what we shall be then. As desire, faith, and hope, are of shorter continuance than love and joy; so also preaching, prayer, and sacraments, and all means for expressing and confirming our faith and hope, shall cease, when our triumphant expressions of love and joy shall abide for ever. The liveliest emblem of heaven that I know upon earth is, when the people of God, in the deep sense of his excellency and bounty, from hearts abounding with love and joy, join together both in heart and voice, in the cheerful and melodious singing of his praises. These delights, like the testimony of the Spirit, witness themselves to be of God, and bring the evidence of their heavenly parentage along with them.

18. Little do we know how we wrong ourselves by shutting out of our prayers the praises of God, or allowing them so narrow a room as we usually do, while we are copious enough in our confessions and petitions. Reader, I entreat thee, remember this, let praises have a larger room in thy duties; keep matter ready at hand to feed thy praise, as well as matter for confession and petition. To this end, study the excellencies and goodness of the Lord, as frequently as thy own wants and unworthiness; the mercies thou hast received, and those which are promised, as often as the sins thou hast committed. 'Praise is comely for the upright. Whoso offereth praise, glorifieth God. Praise ye the Lord, for the Lord is good; sing praises unto his name, for it is pleasant. Let us offer the sacrifice of praise to God continually, that is, the fruit of our lips, giving thanks to his name.' Had not David a most heavenly spirit, who was so much in this heavenly work? Doth it not sometimes raise our hearts, when we only read the song of Moses, and the psalms of David? How much more would it raise and refresh us, to be skilful and frequent in the work ourselves! O the madness of youth, that lay out their vigour of body and mind upon vain delights and fleshly lusts, which is so unfit for the noblest work of man! And O the sinful folly of many of the saints, who drench their spirits in continual sadness, and waste their days in complaints and groans, and so make themselves, both in body and mind, unfit for this sweet and heavenly work! Instead of joining with the people of God in his praises, they are questioning their worthiness, and studying their miseries, and so rob God of his glory, and themselves of their consolation. But the greatest destroyer of our comfort in this duty, is our taking up with the tune and melody, and suffering the heart to be idle, which ought to perform the principal part of the work, and use the melody to revive and exhilarate itself.

19. (8.) Ever keep thy soul possessed with believing thoughts of the infinite love of God. Love is the attractive of love. Few so vile, but will love those that love them. No doubt it is the death of our heavenly life to have hard thoughts of God, to conceive of him as one that would rather condemn than save us. This is to put the blessed God into the similitude of Satan. When our ignorance and unbelief have drawn the most deformed picture of God in our imaginations, then we complain that we cannot love him, nor delight in him. This is the case of many thousand Christians. Alas, that we should thus blaspheme God, and blast our own joys! Scripture assures us, that 'God is love; that fury is not in him; that he hath no pleasure in the death of the wicked, but that the wicked turn from his way and live.' Much more hath he testified his love to his chosen, and his full resolution effectually to save them. O that we could always think of God as we do of a friend; as of one that unfeignedly loves us, even more than we do ourselves; whose very heart is set upon us to do us good, and hath therefore provided for us an everlasting dwelling with himself! it would not then be so hard to have our hearts ever with him! Where we love most heartily, we shall think most sweetly and most freely. I fear most Christians think higher of the love of a hearty friend, than of the love of God; and what wonder then if they love their friends bet-

ter than God, and trust them more confidently than God, and had rather live with them than with God.

20. (9.) Carefully observe and cherish the motions of the Spirit of God. If ever thy soul get above this earth, and get acquainted with this heavenly life, the Spirit of God must be to thee as the chariot to Elijah ; yea, the very living principle by which thou must move and ascend. O then, grieve not thy guide, quench not thy life, knock not off thy chariot wheels! You little think how much the life of all your graces, and the happiness of your souls, depend upon your ready and cordial obedience to the Spirit. When the Spirit urges thee to secret prayer, or forbids thee thy known transgressions; or points out to thee the way in which thou shouldst go ; and thou wilt not regard, no wonder if heaven and thy soul be strange. If thou wilt not follow the Spirit, while it would draw thee to Christ and thy duty ; how should it lead thee to heaven, and bring thy heart into the presence of God ? What supernatural help, what bold access, shall the soul find in its approaches to the Almighty, that constantly obeys the Spirit ? And how backward, how dull, how ashamed, will he be in these addresses, who hath often broken away from the Spirit that would have guided him ? Christian Reader, dost thou not feel sometimes a strong impression to retire from the world, and draw near to God ? Do not disobey, but take the offer, and hoist up thy sails while this blessed gale may be had. The more of the Spirit we resist, the deeper will it wound ; and the more we obey, the speedier will be our pace.

21. (10.) I advise thee, as a further help to this heavenly life, not to neglect the due care of thy bodily health. Thy body is a useful servant, if thou give it its due, and no more than its due ; but it is a most devouring tyrant, if thou suffer it to have what it unreasonably desires; and it is as a blunted knife, if thou unjustly deny it what is necessary to its support. When we consider, how frequently men offend in both extremes, and how few use their bodies aright, we cannot wonder if they be much hindered in their converse with heaven. Most men are slaves to their appetites, and can scarcely deny any thing to the flesh, and are therefore willingly carried by it to their sports, or profits, or vain companions, when they should raise their minds to God and heaven. As you love your souls, ' make not provisions for the flesh, to fulfil the lusts thereof;' but remember, ' to be carnally minded, is death ; because the carnal mind is

enmity against God, for it is not subject to the law of God, neither indeed can be. So then they that are in the flesh cannot please God. Therefore, brethren, we are debtors, not to the flesh, to live after the flesh. For if ye live after the flesh, ye shall die; but if ye through the Spirit do mortify the deeds of the body, ye shall live.' There are a few, who much hinder their heavenly joy, by denying the body its necessaries, and so making it unable to serve them: if such wronged their flesh only, it would be no great matter ; but they wrong their souls also ; as he that spoils the house, injures the inhabitants. When the body is sick, and the spirits languish, how heavily do we move in the thoughts and joys of heaven !

CHAPTER XIII.

THE NATURE OF HEAVENLY CONTEMPLATION, WITH THE TIME, PLACE, AND TEMPER, FITTEST FOR IT.

Sect. 1. The duty of heavenly contemplation is recommended to the Reader, 2. and defined. 3—6. (I.) The definition is illustrated. 7. (II.) The time fittest for it is represented, as, 8. (1.) stated ; 9—12. (2.) frequent ; 13. and (3.) seasonable every day, particularly every Lord's day, 14—17. but more especially, when our hearts are warmed with a sense of divine things ; or when we are afflicted or tempted ; or when we are near death : 18. (III.) The fittest place for it, is the most retired : 19. (IV.) And the temper fittest for it, is, 20. (1.) when our minds are most clear of the world, 21. (2.) and most solemn and serious.

1. Once more I entreat thee, Reader, as thou makest conscience of a revealed duty, and darest not wilfully resist the Spirit; as thou valuest the high delights of a saint, and the soul-ravishing exercise of heavenly contemplation ; that thou diligently study, and speedily and faithfully practise, the following directions. If, by this means, thou dost not find an increase of all thy graces, and dost not grow beyond the stature of common Christians, and art not made more serviceable in thy place, and more precious in the eyes of all discerning persons ; if thy soul enjoy not more communion with God, and thy life be not fuller of comfort, and hast it not readier by thee at a dying hour : then cast away these directions, and exclaim against me for ever as a deceiver.

2. The duty which I press upon thee so earnestly, and in the practice of which I am now to direct thee, is, ' The set and solemn acting of all the powers of thy soul in meditation upon thy everlasting rest.' More fully to explain the nature of this duty, I will here illustrate a little the description itself—then point out the fittest time, place, and temper of mind, for it.

3. (I.) It is not improper to illustrate a little the manner in which we have described this duty

of meditation, or the considering and contemplating of spiritual things. It is confessed to be a duty by all, but practically denied by most. Many that make conscience of other duties, easily neglect this. They are troubled, if they omit a sermon, a fast, or a prayer, in public or private; yet were never troubled that they have omitted meditation, perhaps all their lifetime to this very day; though it be that duty by which all other duties are improved, and by which the soul digesteth truths for its nourishment and comfort. It was God's command to Joshua, ' This book of the law shall not depart out of thy mouth, but thou shalt meditate therein day and night, that thou mayest observe to do according to all that is written therein.' As digestion turns food into chyle and blood, for vigorous health; so meditation turns the truths received and remembered into warm affection, firm resolution, and holy conversation.

4. This meditation is the acting of all the powers of the soul. It is the work of the living, and not of the dead. It is a work, of all others the most spiritual and sublime, and therefore not to be well performed by a heart that is merely carnal and earthly. They must necessarily have some relation to heaven, before they can familiarly converse there. I suppose them to be such as have a title to rest, when I persuade them to rejoice in the meditations of rest. And supposing thee to be a Christian, I am now exhorting thee to be an active Christian. And it is the work of the soul I am setting thee to, for bodily exercise doth here profit but little. And it must have all the powers of the soul to distinguish it from the common meditation of students; for the understanding is not the whole soul; and therefore cannot do the whole work. As in the body, the stomach must turn the food into chyle, and prepare for the liver, the liver and spleen turn it into blood, and prepare for the heart and brain; so in the soul, the understanding must take in truths, and prepare them for the will, and that for the affections. Christ and heaven have various excellencies, and therefore God hath formed the soul with different powers for apprehending those excellencies. What the better had we been for odoriferous flowers, if we had no smell? or what good would language or music have done us, if we could not hear? or what pleasure should we have found in meats and drinks, without the sense of taste? So, what good could all the glory of heaven have done us, or what pleasure should we have had in the perfection of God himself, if we had been without the affections of love and joy? And what strength or sweetness canst

thou possibly receive by thy meditations on eternity, while thou dost not exercise those affections of the soul, by which thou must be sensible of this sweetness and strength? It is the mistake of Christians to think that meditation is only the work of the understanding and memory; when every school-boy can do this, or persons that hate the things which they think on. So that you see there is more to be done than barely to remember and think on heaven: as some labours not only stir a hand, or a foot, but exercise the whole body; so doth meditation exercise the whole soul. As the affections of sinners are set on the world, are turned to idols, and fallen from God, as well as their understanding; so must their affections be reduced to God, as well as the understanding; and as their whole soul was filled with sin before, so the whole must be filled with God now. See David's description of the blessed man, ' His delight is in the law of the Lord, and in his law doth he meditate day and night.'

5. This meditation is set and solemn. As there is solemn prayer, when we set ourselves wholly to that duty; and ejaculatory prayer, when, in the midst of other business we send up some short request to God: so also there is solemn meditation, when we apply ourselves wholly to that work; and transient meditation, when, in the midst of other business, we have some good thoughts of God in our minds. And, as solemn prayer is either set, in a constant course of duty, or occasional, at an extraordinary season; so also is meditation. Now, though I would persuade you to that meditation which is mixed with your common labours, and also that which special occasions direct you to; yet I would have you likewise make it a constant standing duty, as you do by hearing, praying, and reading the scriptures; and no more intermix other matters with it, than you would with prayer, or other stated solemnities.

6. This meditation is upon thy everlasting rest. I would not have you cast off your other meditations; but surely as heaven hath the pre-eminence in perfection, it should have it also in our meditation. That which will make us most happy when we possess it, will make us most joyful when we meditate upon it. Other meditations are as numerous as there are lines in the scripture, or creatures in the universe, or particular providences in the government of the world. But this is a walk to Mount Zion; from the kingdoms of this world to the kingdom of saints; from earth to heaven; from time to eternity; it is walking upon sun, moon, and stars, in the garden and paradise of God. It

may seem far off; but spirits are quick; whether in the body, or out of the body, their motion is swift. You need not fear, like the men of the world, lest these thoughts should make you mad. It is heaven, and not hell, that I persuade you to walk in. It is joy, and not sorrow, that I persuade you to exercise. I urge you to look on no deformed objects, but only upon the ravishing glory of saints, and the unspeakable excellencies of the God of glory, and the beams that stream from the face of his Son. Will it distract a man to think of his only happiness? Will it distract the miserable to think of mercy, or the prisoner to foresee deliverance, or the poor to think of approaching riches and honour? Methinks it should rather make a man mad, to think of living in a world of woe, and abiding in poverty and sickness, among the rage of wicked men, than to think of living with Christ in bliss. 'But wisdom is justified of all her children.' Knowledge hath no enemy but the ignorant. This heavenly course was never spoken against by any but those that never knew it, or never used it. I fear more the neglect of men that approve it, than the opposition or arguments of any against it.

7. (II.) As to the fittest time for this heavenly contemplation, let me only advise, that it be—stated—frequent—and seasonable.

8. (1.) Give it a stated time. If thou suit thy time to the advantage of the work, without placing any religion in the time itself, thou hast no need to fear superstition. Stated time is a hedge to duty, and defends it against many temptations to omission. Some have not their time at command, and therefore cannot see their hours; and many are so poor, that the necessities of their families deny them this freedom: such persons should be watchful to redeem time as much as they can, and take their vacant opportunities as they fall, and especially join meditation and prayer, as much as they can, with the labours of their callings. Yet those that have more time to spare from their worldly necessities, and are masters of their time, I still advise to keep this duty to a stated time. And indeed, if every work of the day had its appointed time, we should be better skilled, both in redeeming time, and in performing duty.

9. (2.) Let it be frequent, as well as stated. How often it should be, I cannot determine, because men's circumstances differ. But, in general, scripture requires it to be frequent, when it mentions meditating day and night. For those, therefore, who can conveniently omit other business, I advise, that it be once a day at least. Frequency in heavenly contemplation is particularly important.

10. Frequent society breeds familiarity, and familiarity increases love and delight, and makes us bold in our addresses. The chief end of this duty is, to have acquaintance and fellowship with God; and, therefore, if thou come but seldom to it, thou wilt keep thyself a stranger still; for seldom conversing with God will breed a strangeness between thy soul and him. When a man feels his need of God, and must seek his help in a time of necessity, then it is great encouragement to go to a God we know and are acquainted with. 'O!' saith the heavenly Christian, 'I know both whither I go, and to whom. I have gone this way many a time before now. It is the same God that I daily converse with, and the way has been my daily walk. God knows me well enough, and I have some knowledge of him.' On the other side, what a horror and discouragement will it be to the soul, when it is forced to fly to God in straits, to think, 'Alas! I know not whither to go. I never went the way before. I have no acquaintance at the court of heaven. My soul knows not that God that I must speak to, and I fear he will not know my soul.' But especially when we come to die, and must immediately appear before this God, and expect to enter into his eternal rest, then the difference will plainly appear; then what a joy will it be to think, 'I am going to the place that I daily conversed in; to the place from whence I tasted such frequent delights; to that God whom I have met in my meditation so often. My heart hath been at heaven before now, and hath often tasted its reviving sweetness; and if my eyes were so enlightened, and my spirits so refreshed, when I had but a taste, what will it be when I shall feed on it freely?' On the contrary, what a terror will it be to think, 'I must die, and go I know not whither; from a place where I am acquainted, to a place where I have no familiarity or knowledge!' It is inexpressible horror to a dying man, to have strange thoughts of God and heaven. I am persuaded the neglect of this duty so commonly makes death, even to godly men, unwelcome and uncomfortable. Therefore I persuade to frequency in this duty. And as it will prevent strangeness between thee and God, so also,

11. It will prevent unskilfulness in the duty itself. How awkwardly do men set their hands to a work they are seldom employed in! Whereas, frequency will habituate thy heart to the work, and make it more easy and delightful.

The hill which made thee pant and blow at first going up, thou mayest easily run up, when thou art once accustomed to it.

12. Thou wilt also prevent the loss of that heat and life thou hast obtained. If thou eat but once in two or three days, thou wilt lose thy strength as fast as it comes. If in holy meditation thou get near to Christ, and warm thy heart with the fire of love, and then come but seldom, thy former coldness will soon return; especially as the work is so spiritual, and against the bent of depraved nature. It is true, the intermixing of other duties, especially secret prayer, may do much to the keeping thy heart above; but meditation is the life of most other duties, and the view of heaven is the life of meditation.

13. (3.) Choose also the most seasonable time. All things are beautiful and excellent in their season. Unseasonableness may lose the fruit of thy labour, may raise difficulties in the work, and may turn a duty to a sin. The same hour may be seasonable to one, and unseasonable to another. Servants and labourers must take that season which their business can best afford; either while at work, or in travelling, or when they lie awake in the night. Such as can choose what time of the day they will, should observe when they find their spirits most active and fit for contemplation, and fix upon that as the stated time. I have always found that the fittest time for myself is the evening, from sunsetting to the twilight. I the rather mention this, because it was the experience of a better and wiser man; for it is expressly said, ' Isaac went out to meditate in the field at the eventide.' The Lord's day is exceeding seasonable for this exercise. When should we more seasonably contemplate our rest, than on that day of rest which typifies it to us? It being a day appropriated to spiritual duties, methinks we should never exclude this duty, which is so eminently spiritual. I verily think this is the chief work of a Christian sabbath, and most agreeable to the design of its positive institution. What fitter time to converse with our Lord, than on the Lord's day? What fitter day to ascend to heaven, than that on which he arose from earth, and fully triumphed over death and hell? The fittest temper for a true Christian, is, like John, to ' be in the Spirit on the Lord's day.' And what can bring us to this joy in the Spirit, but the spiritual beholding of our approaching glory? Take notice of this, you that spend the Lord's day only in public worship; your allowing no time to private duty, and therefore neglecting this spiritual duty of meditation, is very hurtful to your souls. You

also that have time on the Lord's day for idleness and vain discourse, were you but acquainted with this duty of contemplation, you would need no other pastime; you would think the longest day short enough, and be sorry that the night had shortened your pleasure. Christians, let heaven have more share in your sabbaths, where you must shortly keep your everlasting sabbath. Use your sabbaths as steps to glory, till you have passed them all, and are there arrived. Especially you that are poor, and cannot take time in the week as you desire, see that you well improve this day: as your bodies rest from their labours, let your spirits seek after rest from God.

14. Besides the constant seasonableness of every day, and particularly every Lord's day, there are also more peculiar seasons for heavenly contemplation. As for instance:

15. When God hath more abundantly warmed thy spirit with fire from above, then thou mayest soar with greater freedom. A little labour will set thy heart a-going at such a time as this; whereas, at another time, thou mayest take pains to little purpose. Observe the gales of the Spirit, and how the Spirit of Christ doth move thy spirit. ' Without Christ, we can do nothing;' and therefore let us be doing while he is doing; and be sure not to be out of the way, nor asleep, when he comes. When the Spirit finds thy heart, like Peter in prison, and in irons, and smites thee, and says, ' Arise up quickly, and follow me,' be sure thou then arise, and follow, and thou shalt find thy chains fall off, and all doors will open, and thou wilt be at heaven before thou art aware.

16. Another peculiar season for this duty is, when thou art in a suffering, distressed, or tempted state. When should we take our cordials, but in time of fainting? When is it more seasonable to walk to heaven, than when we know not in what corner of earth to live with comfort? Or when should our thoughts converse more above, than when they have nothing but grief below? Where should Noah's dove be but in the ark, when the waters cover all the earth, and she cannot find rest for the sole of her foot? What should we think on, but our Father's house, when we have not even the husks of the world to feed upon? Surely God sends thy afflictions to this very purpose. Happy art thou, poor man, if thou make this use of thy poverty; and thou that art sick, if thou so improve thy sickness! It is seasonable to go to the promised land, when our burdens are increased in Egypt, and our straits in the wilderness.

Reader, if thou knewest what a cordial to thy griefs the serious views of glory are, thou wouldst less fear these harmless troubles, and more use that preserving, reviving remedy. 'In the multitude of my troubled thoughts within me,' saith David, 'thy comforts delight my soul.' 'I reckon,' saith Paul, 'that the sufferings of this present time are not worthy to be compared with the glory which shall be revealed in us.'—'For which cause we faint not, but though our outward man perish, yet the inward man is renewed day by day. For our light affliction, which is but for a moment, worketh for us a far more exceeding and eternal weight of glory, while we look not at the things which are seen, but at the things which are not seen; for the things which are seen are temporal; but the things which are not seen are eternal.'

17. And another season peculiarly fit for this heavenly duty is, when the messengers of God summon us to die. When should we more frequently sweeten our souls with the believing thoughts of another life, than when we find that this is almost ended? No men have greater need of supporting joys, than dying men; and those joys must be fetched from our eternal joy. As heavenly delights are sweetest, when nothing earthly is joined with them; so the delights of dying Christians are oftentimes the sweetest they ever had. What a prophetic blessing had dying Isaac and Jacob, for their sons! With what a heavenly song, and divine benediction, did Moses conclude his life! What heavenly advice and prayer had the disciples from their Lord, when he was about to leave them! When Paul was ready to be offered up, what heavenly exhortation and advice did he give the Philippians, Timothy, and the elders of Ephesus! How near to heaven was John in Patmos, but a little before his translation thither! It is the general temper of the saints to be then most heavenly when they are nearest heaven. If it be thy case, Reader, to perceive thy dying time draw on, O where should thy heart now be, but with Christ? Methinks thou shouldst even behold him standing by thee, and shouldst bespeak him as thy father, thy husband, thy physician, thy friend. Methinks thou shouldst, as it were, see the angels about thee waiting to perform their last office to thy soul; even those angels which disdained not to carry into Abraham's bosom the soul of Lazarus, nor will think much to conduct thee thither. Look upon thy pain and sickness as Jacob did on Joseph's chariots, and let thy spirit revive within thee, and say, 'It is enough, Christ is yet alive; because he liveth, I shall live also.' Dost

thou need the choicest cordials? Here are choicer than the world can afford; here are all the joys of heaven, even the vision of God, and Christ, and whatsoever the blessed here possess. These dainties are offered thee by the hand of Christ; he hath written the receipt in the promises of the gospel; he hath prepared the ingredients in heaven; only put forth the hand of faith, and feed upon them, and rejoice and live. The Lord saith to thee, as to Elijah, 'Arise and eat, because the journey is too great for thee.' Though it be not long, yet the way is miry: therefore obey his voice, arise and eat, and in the strength of that meat thou mayest go to the mount of God; and, like Moses, die in the mount whither thou goest up: and say, as Simeon, 'Lord, now lettest thou thy servant depart in peace; for my eye of faith hath seen thy salvation.'

18. (III.) Concerning the fittest place for heavenly contemplation, it is sufficient to say, that the most convenient is some private retirement. Our spirits need every help, and to be freed from every hinderance in the work. If, in private prayer, Christ directs us to 'enter into our closet, and shut the door, that our Father may see us in secret,' so should we do this in meditation. How often did Christ himself retire to some mountain, or wilderness, or other solitary place? I give not this advice for occasional meditation, but for that which is set and solemn. Therefore withdraw thyself from all society, even that of godly men, that thou mayst awhile enjoy the society of thy Lord. If a student cannot study in a crowd, who exerciseth only his invention and memory; much less shouldst thou be in a crowd, who art to exercise all the powers of thy soul, and upon an object so far above nature. We are fled so far from superstitious solitude, that we have even cast off the solitude of contemplative devotion. We seldom read of God's appearing by himself, or by his angels, to any of his prophets or saints, in a crowd; but frequently when they were alone. But observe for thyself what place best agrees with thy spirit; within doors or without. Isaac's example, in going out to meditate in the field, will, I am persuaded, best suit with most. Our Lord so much used a solitary garden, that even Judas, when he came to betray him, knew where to find him: and though he took his disciples thither with him, yet he was withdrawn from them for more secret devotions; and though his meditation be not directly named, but only his praying, yet it is very clearly implied; for his soul is first made sorrowful with the bitter medi-

tations on his sufferings and death, and then he poureth it out in prayer. So that Christ had his accustomed place, and consequently accustomed duty; and so must we; he hath a place that is solitary, whither he retireth himself, even from his own disciples, and so must we: his meditations go further than his thoughts, they affect and pierce his heart and soul, and so must ours. Only there is a wide difference in the object: Christ meditates on the sufferings that our sins had deserved, so that the wrath of his Father passed through all his soul; but we are to meditate on the glory he hath purchased, that the love of the Father, and the joy of the Spirit, may enter at our thoughts, and revive our affections, and overflow our souls.

19. (IV.) I am next to advise thee concerning the preparations of thy heart for this heavenly contemplation. The success of the work much depends on the frame of thy heart. When man's heart had nothing in it to grieve the Spirit, it was then the delightful habitation of his Maker. God did not quit his residence there, till man expelled him by unworthy provocations. There was no shyness or reserve till the heart grew sinful, and too lothesome a dungeon for God to delight in. And was this soul reduced to its former innocency, God would quickly return to his former habitation; yea, so far as it is renewed and repaired by the Spirit, and purged from its lusts, and beautified with his image, the Lord will yet acknowledge it as his own; Christ will manifest himself unto it, and the Spirit will take it for his temple and residence. So far as the heart is qualified for conversing with God, so far it usually enjoys him. Therefore, ' with all diligence keep thy heart, for out of it are the issues of life.' More particularly,

20. (1.) Get thy heart as clear from the world as thou canst. Wholly lay by the thoughts of thy business, troubles, enjoyments, and every thing that may take up any room in thy soul. Get it as empty as thou possibly canst, that it may be the more capable of being filled with God. If thou couldst perform some outward duty with a piece of thy heart, while the other is absent, yet this duty, above all, I am sure thou canst not. When thou shalt go into the mount of contemplation, thou wilt be like the covetous man at the heap of gold, who, when he might take as much as he could, lamented that he was able to carry no more: so thou wilt find so much of God and glory as thy narrow heart is able to contain, and almost nothing to hinder thy full possession, but the incapacity of thy own spirit. Then thou wilt think, ' O that

this understanding, and these affections, could contain more! It is more my unfitness than any thing else, that even this place is not my heaven. God is in this place, and I know it not. This mount is full of chariots of fire; but mine eyes are shut, and I cannot see them. O the words of love Christ hath to speak, and wonders of love he hath to show, but I cannot bear them yet! Heaven is ready for me, but my heart is unready for heaven.' Therefore, Reader, seeing thy enjoyment of God in this contemplation much depends on the capacity and disposition of thy heart, seek him here, if ever, with all thy soul. Thrust not Christ into the stable and the manger, as if thou hadst better guests for the chief rooms. Say to all thy worldly business and thoughts, as Christ to his disciples, ' Sit ye here, while I go and pray yonder.' Or as Abraham to his servants, when he went to offer Isaac, ' Abide ye here, and I will go yonder and worship, and come again to you.' Even as the priests thrust king Uzziah out of the temple, where he presumed to burn incense, when they saw the leprosy upon him; so do thou thrust those thoughts from the temple of thy heart, which have the badge of God's prohibition upon them.

21. (2.) Be sure to set upon this work with the greatest solemnity of heart and mind. There is no trifling in holy things. ' God will be sanctified in them that come nigh him.' These spiritual, excellent, soul-raising duties, are, if well used, most profitable; but, when used unfaithfully, most dangerous. Labour, therefore, to have the deepest apprehensions of the presence of God, and his incomprehensible greatness. If queen Esther must not draw near ' till the king hold out the sceptre;' think, then, with what reverence thou shouldst approach him who made the worlds with the word of his mouth, who upholds the earth as in the palm of his hand, who keeps the sun, moon, and stars in their courses, and who sets bounds to the raging sea. Thou art going to converse with him, before whom the earth will quake, and devils do tremble, and at whose bar thou and all the world must shortly stand, and be finally judged. O think! ' I shall then have lively apprehensions of his majesty. My drowsy spirits will then be awakened, and my irreverence be laid aside; and why should I not now be roused with the sense of his greatness, and the dread of his name possess my soul?' Labour also to apprehend the greatness of the work which thou attemptest, and to be deeply sensible both of its importance and excellency. If thou wast pleading for thy life at the bar of

an earthly judge, thou wouldst be serious, and yet that would be a trifle to this. If thou wast engaged in such a work as David against Goliath, on which the welfare of a kingdom depended; in itself considered, it were nothing to this. Suppose thou wast going to such a wrestling as Jacob's, or to see the sight which the three disciples saw in the mount, how seriously, how reverently wouldst thou both approach and behold! If but an angel from heaven should appoint to meet thee, at the same time and place of thy contemplations; with what dread wouldst thou be filled! Consider, then, with what a spirit thou shouldst meet the Lord, and with what seriousness and awe thou shouldst daily converse with him. Consider also the blessed issue of the work: if it succeed, it will be thy admission into the presence of God, and the beginning of thy eternal glory on earth; a means to make thee live above the rate of other men, and fix thee in the next room to the angels themselves, that thou mayest both live and die joyfully. The prize being so great, thy preparations should be answerable. There is none on earth live such a life of joy and blessedness, as those that are acquainted with this heavenly conversation. The joys of all other men are but like a child's play, a fool's laughter, or a sick man's dream of health. He that trades for heaven is the only gainer, and he that neglects it is the only loser. How seriously, therefore, should this work be done!

CHAPTER XIV.

WHAT USE HEAVENLY CONTEMPLATION MAKES OF CONSIDERATION, AFFECTIONS, SOLILOQUY, AND PRAYER.

Sect. 1. The reader is invited to engage in heavenly contemplation; 2. and to that end is, (I.) Directed in the use of consideration; 3—8. the great influence of which over the heart is represented in several instances; 9. Then, (II.) it is shown how heavenly contemplation is promoted by the affections; particularly, 10—12. (1.) by love, 13 (2.) desire, 14. (3.) hope, 15. (4.) courage, or boldness, 16.—18. and (5.) joy. 19. A caution is added concerning this exercise of the affections. 20—22. (III.) The chapter concludes with some account of the usefulness of soliloquy and prayer, in heavenly contemplation.

1. Having set thy heart in tune, we now come to the music itself. Having got an appetite, now approach to the feast, and delight thy soul as with marrow and fatness. Come, for all things are now ready. Heaven and Christ, and the exceeding weight of glory are before you. Do not make light of this invitation, nor begin to make excuses; whatever thou art, rich or poor, though in alms-houses or hospitals, though in highways and hedges, my commission is, if possible, to compel you to come in: and blessed is he that shall eat bread in the kingdom of God! The manna lieth about your tents; walk out, gather it up, take it home, and feed upon it. In order to this I am only to direct you—how to use your consideration—and affections—your soliloquy, and prayer.

2. (I.) Consideration is the great instrument by which this heavenly work is carried on. This must be voluntary, and not forced. Some men consider unwillingly; so God will make the wicked consider their sins, when he shall ' set them in order before their eyes;' so shall the damned consider of the excellency of Christ, whom they once despised, and of the eternal joys which they have foolishly lost. Great is the power which consideration hath for moving the affections, and impressing things on the heart; as will appear by the following particulars.

3. (1.) Consideration, as it were, opens the door between the head and the heart. The understanding having received truths, lays them up in the memory, and consideration conveys them from thence to the affections. What excellency would there be in much learning and knowledge, if the obstructions between the head and heart were but opened, and the affections did but correspond to the understanding! He is usually the best scholar, whose apprehension is quick, clear, and tenacious; but he is usually the best Christian, whose apprehension is the deepest and most affectionate, and who has the readiest passages, not so much from the ear to the brain, as from that to the heart. And though the Spirit be the principal cause; yet, on our part, this passage must be opened by consideration.

4. (2.) Consideration presents to the affections those things which are most important. The most delightful object does not entertain, where it is not seen, nor the most joyful news affect him that does not hear it; but consideration presents to our view those things which were absent, and brings them to the eye and ear of the soul. Are not Christ and glory affecting objects? Would they not work wonders upon the soul, if they were but clearly discovered, and our apprehensions of them were in some measure answerable to their worth? It is consideration that presents them to us: this is the Christian's perspective, by which he can see from earth to heaven.

5. (3.) Consideration also presents the most important things in the most affecting way. Consideration reasons the case with a man's own heart. When a believer would reason his heart to heavenly contemplation, how many arguments offer themselves from God and Christ, from

each of the divine perfections, from our former and present state, from promises, from present sufferings and enjoyments, from hell and heaven. Every thing offers itself to promote our joy, and consideration is the hand to draw them all out; it adds one reason to another, till the scales turn: this it does when persuading to joy, till it hath silenced all our distrust and sorrows, and your cause for rejoicing lies plain before you. If another's reasoning is powerful with us, though we are not certain whether he intends to inform or deceive us, how much more should our own reasoning prevail with us, when we are so well acquainted with our own intentions? Nay, how much more should God's reasoning work upon us, which we are sure cannot deceive, or be deceived? Now, consideration is but the reading over, and repeating God's reasons to our hearts. As the prodigal had many and strong reasons to plead with himself, why he should return to his Father's house, so have we to plead with our affections, to persuade them to our Father's everlasting mansion.

6. (4.) Consideration exalts reason to its just authority. It helps to deliver it from its captivity to the senses, and sets it again on the throne of the soul. When reason is silent, it is usually subject; for when it is asleep, the senses domineer. But consideration awakens our reason, till, like Samson, it rouses up itself, and breaks the bonds of sensuality, and bears down the delusions of the flesh. What strength can the lion exert while asleep? What is a king, when dethroned, more than another man? Spiritual reason, excited by meditation, and not fancy or fleshly sense, must judge of heavenly joys. Consideration exalts the objects of faith, and comparatively disgraces the objects of sense. The most inconsiderate men are most sensual. It is too easy and common to sin against knowledge, but against sober, strong, persevering consideration, men seldom offend.

7. (5.) Consideration makes reason strong and active. Before, it was a standing water, but now as a stream, which violently bears down all before it. Before, it was as the stones in the brook, but now, like that out of David's sling, which smites the Goliath of our unbelief in the forehead. As wicked men continue wicked, because they bring not reason into act and exercise; so godly men are uncomfortable, because they let their reason and faith lie asleep, and do not stir them up to action by this work of meditation. What fears, sorrows, and joys will our very dreams excite! How much more, then, would serious meditation affect us?

8. (6.) Consideration can continue and persevere in this rational employment. Meditation holds reason and faith to their work, and blows the fire till it thoroughly burns. To run a few steps will not get a man heat, but walking an hour may: and though a sudden occasional thought of heaven will not raise our affections to any spiritual heat, yet meditation can continue our thoughts till our hearts grow warm. Thus you see the powerful tendency of consideration to produce this great elevation of the soul in heavenly contemplation.

9. (II.) Let us next see how this heavenly work is promoted by the particular exercise of the affections.—It is by consideration, that we first have recourse to the memory, and from thence take those heavenly doctrines which we intend to make the subject of our meditation; such as promises of eternal life, descriptions of the saints' glory, the resurrection, &c. &c. We then present them to our judgment, that it may deliberately view them over, and take an exact survey, and determine uprightly concerning the perfection of our celestial happiness, against all the dictates of flesh and sense, and so as to magnify the Lord in our hearts, till we are filled with a holy admiration.—But the principal thing is to exercise, not merely our judgment, but our faith in the truth of our everlasting rest; by which I mean, both the truth of the promises, and of our own personal interest in them, and title to them. If we did really and firmly believe, that there is such a glory, and that within a few days our eyes shall behold it, O what passions would it raise within us! What astonishing apprehensions of that life would it produce! What love, what longing would it excite within us! O how it would actuate every affection! How it would transport us with joy, upon the least assurance of our title! Never expect to have love and joy move, when faith stands still, which must lead the way. Therefore, daily exercise faith, and set before it the freeness of the promise, God's urging all to accept it, Christ's gracious disposition, all the evidences of the love of Christ, his faithfulness to his engagements, and the evidences of his love in ourselves; lay all these together, and think, whether they do not testify the good-will of the Lord concerning our salvation, and may not properly be pleaded against our unbelief.—Thus, when the judgment hath determined, and faith hath apprehended the truth of our happiness, then may our meditation proceed to raise our affections, and, particularly,—love—desire—hope—courage, or boldness—and joy.

10. (1.) Love is the first affection to be excited in heavenly contemplation : the object of it is goodness. Here, Christian, is the soul-reviving part of thy work. Go to thy memory, thy judgment, and thy faith, and from them produce the excellencies of thy rest ; present these to thy affection of love, and thou wilt find thyself as it were in another world. Speak out, and love can hear. Do but reveal these things, and love can see. It is the brutish love of the world that is blind : divine love is exceeding quick-sighted. Let thy faith take hold of thy heart, and show it the sumptuous buildings of thy eternal habitation, and the glorious ornaments of thy Father's house, even the mansions Christ is preparing, and the honours of his kingdom ; let thy faith lead thy heart into the presence of God, and as near as thou possibly canst, and say to it, 'Behold the Ancient of Days, the Lord Jehovah, whose name is, I AM : this is he who made all the worlds with his word, who upholds the earth, who rules the nations, who disposes of all events, who subdues his foes, who controls the swelling waves of the sea, who governs the winds, and causes the sun to run its race, and the stars to know their courses. This is he who loved thee from everlasting, formed thee in the womb, gave thee this soul, brought thee forth, showed thee the light, and ranked thee with the chief of his earthly creatures ; who endued thee with thy understanding, and beautified thee with his gifts ; who maintains thy life and all its comforts, and distinguishes thee from the most miserable and vilest of men. O here is an object worthy thy love ! Here shouldst thou even pour out thy soul in love ! Here it is impossible for thee to love too much ! This is the Lord who hath blessed thee with his benefits, spread thy table in the sight of thine enemies, and made thy cup overflow ? This is he whom angels and saints praise, and the heavenly host for ever magnify !' Thus do thou expatiate on the praises of God, and open his excellencies to thine heart, till the holy fire of love begins to kindle in thy breast.

11. If thou feelest thy love not yet burn, lead thy heart farther, and show it the Son of the living God, whose name is, 'Wonderful, Counsellor, the mighty God, the everlasting Father, the Prince of Peace :' show it the King of saints on the throne of his glory, 'the First and the Last ; who is, and was, and is to come ; who liveth, and was dead, and behold he lives for evermore ; who hath made thy peace by the blood of his cross,' and hath prepared thee with himself a habitation of peace : his office is the great Peace-maker ; his kingdom is the kingdom of peace : his gospel is the tidings of peace ; his voice to thee now is the voice of peace ! Draw near and behold him. Dost thou not hear his voice ? He that bade Thomas come near, and see the print of the nails, and put his finger into his wounds, he it is that calls to thee, 'Come near and view the Lord thy Saviour, and be not faithless, but believing ; peace be unto thee, fear not, it is I.' Look well upon him. Dost thou not know him ? It is he that brought thee up from the pit of hell, reversed the sentence of thy damnation, bore the curse which thou shouldst have borne, restored thee to the blessing thou hadst forfeited, and purchased the advancement which thou must inherit for ever. And dost thou not yet know him ? His hands were pierced, his head, his side, his heart were pierced, that by these marks thou mightest always know him. Dost thou not remember when he found thee lying in thy blood, and took pity on thee, and dressed thy wounds, and brought thee home, and said unto thee, Live. Hast thou forgotten since he wounded himself to cure thy wounds, and let out his own blood to stop thy bleeding ? If thou knowest him not by the face, the voice, the hands, thou mayest know him by that heart ; that soul-pitying heart is his ; it can be none but his : love and compassion are its certain signatures : this is he who chose thy life before his own ; who pleads his blood before his Father, and makes continual intercession for thee ? If he had not suffered, what hadst thou suffered ? There was but a step between thee and hell, when he stepped in and bore the stroke. And is not here fuel enough for thy love to feed on ? Doth not thy throbbing heart stop here to ease itself, and, like Joseph, ' seek for a place to weep in ?' or do not the tears of thy love bedew these lines ? Go on, then, for the field of love is large ; it will be thy eternal work to behold and love ; nor needest thou want work for thy present meditation.

12. How often hath thy Lord found thee, like Hagar, sitting and weeping, and giving up thy soul for lost, and he opened to thee a well of consolation, and also opened thine eyes to see it ! How often, in the posture of Elijah, desiring to die out of thy misery, and he hath spread thee a table of unexpected relief, and sent thee on his work refreshed and encouraged ! How often, in the case of the prophet's servants, crying out, ' Alas ! what shall we do, for a host doth encamp us ;' and he hath ' opened thine eyes to see more for thee than against thee !' How often, like Jonah, peevish, and weary of thy life, and

he hath mildly said, ' dost thou well to be angry' with me, or murmur against me? How often hath he set thee on watching and praying, repenting and believing, 'and when he hath returned, hath found thee asleep,' and yet he hath covered thy neglect with a mantle of love, and gently pleaded for thee, that ' the spirit is willing, but the flesh is weak?' Can thy heart be cold, when thou thinkest of this? Can it contain, when thou rememberest those boundless compassions? Thus, Reader, hold forth the goodness of Christ to thy heart; plead thus with thy frozen soul, till, with David, thou canst say, ' My heart was hot within me; while I was musing, the fire burned.' If this will not rouse up thy love, thou hast all Christ's personal excellencies to add; all his particular mercies to thyself, all his sweet and near relations to thee, and the happiness of thy everlasting abode with him. Only follow them close to thy heart. Deal with it, as Christ did with Peter, when he thrice asked him, 'Lovest thou me?' till he was grieved, and answers, ' Lord thou knowest that I love thee.' So grieve and shame thy heart out of its stupidity, till thou canst truly say, ' I know, and my Lord knows, that I love him.

13. (2.) The next affection to be excited in heavenly contemplation, is desire. The object of it is goodness considered as absent, or not yet attained. If love be hot, desire will not be cold. Think with thyself, ' What have I seen? O the incomprehensible glory! O the transcendent beauty! O blessed souls that now enjoy it! who see a thousand times more clearly what I have seen at a distance, and through dark interposing clouds! What a difference between my state and theirs! I am sighing, and they are singing: I am offending, and they are pleasing God. I am a spectacle of pity, like a Job or a Lazarus, but they are perfect, and without blemish. I am here entangled in the love of the world, while they are swallowed up in the love of God. They have none of my cares and fears: they weep not in secret; they languish not in sorrows: these "tears are wiped away from their eyes." O happy, a thousand times happy souls! Alas, that I must dwell in sinful flesh, when my brethren and companions dwell with God! How far out of sight and reach of their high enjoyment do I here live! What poor feeble thoughts have I of God! What cold affections towards him! How little have I of that life, that love, that joy, in which they continually live! How soon doth that little depart, and leave me in thicker darkness! Now and then a spark falls upon my heart, and while I gaze

upon it, it dies, or rather my cold heart quenches it. But they have their light in his light, and drink continually at the spring of joys. Here we are vexing each other with quarrels, when they are of one heart and voice, and daily sound forth the hallelujahs of heaven with perfect harmony. O what a feast hath my faith beheld, and what a famine is yet in my spirit! O blessed souls! I may not, I dare not, envy your happiness; I rather rejoice in my brother's prosperity, and am glad to think of the day when I shall be admitted into your fellowship. I wish not to displace you, but to be so happy as to be with you. Why must I stay, and weep, and wait? My Lord is gone; he hath left this earth, and is entered into his glory; my brethren are gone; my friends are there; my home, my hope, my all, is there. When I am so far distant from my God, wonder not what aileth me, if I now complain: an ignorant Micah will do so for his idol, and shall not my soul do so for the living God? Had I no hope of enjoyment, I would go hide myself in the deserts, and lie and howl in some obscure wilderness, and spend my days in fruitless wishes; but since it is the land of my promised rest, and the state I must myself be advanced to, and my soul draws near, and is almost at it, I will love and long, I will look and desire, I will be breathing, " How long, Lord! how long wilt thou suffer this soul to pant and groan, and not open to him who waits, and longs to be with thee!"' Thus, Christian Reader, let thy thoughts aspire, till thy soul longs, as David, ' O that one would give me to drink of the wells of salvation!' And till thou canst say as he did, ' I have longed for thy salvation, O Lord;' and as the mother and brethren of Christ, when they could not come at him, because of the multitude, sent to him, saying, 'Thy mother and brethren stand without, desiring to see thee;' so let thy message to him be, and he will own thee; for he hath said, ' They that hear my word, and do it, are my mother and my brethren.'

14. (3.) Another affection to be exercised in heavenly contemplation, is hope. This helps to support the soul under sufferings, animates it to the greatest difficulties, gives it firmness in the most shaking trials, enlivens it in duties, and is the very spring that sets all the wheels a-going. Who would believe or strive for heaven, if it were not for the hope that he hath to obtain it? Who would pray, but for the hope to prevail with God? If your hope dies, your duties die, your endeavours die, your joys die, and your souls die. And if your hope be not in exercise, but asleep, it is next to dead. Therefore, Christian Reader, when

thou art winding up thy affections to heaven, forget not to give one lift to thy hope. Think thus, and reason thus with thy own heart : ' Why should I not confidently and comfortably hope, when my soul is in the hands of so compassionate a Saviour, and when the kingdom is at the disposal of so bountiful a God ? Did he ever discover the least backwardness to my good, or inclination to my ruin ? Hath he not sworn, that he delights not in the death of him that dieth, but rather that he should repent and live ? Have not all his dealings witnessed the same ? Did he not mind me of my danger, when I never feared it, because he would have me escape it ? Did he not mind me of my happiness, when I had no thoughts of it, because he would have me enjoy it ? How often hath he drawn me to himself, and his Christ, when I have drawn backward ! How hath his Spirit incessantly solicited my heart ! And would he have done all this, if he had been willing that I should perish ? Should I not hope, if an honest man had promised me something in his power ? And shall I not hope, when I have the covenant and oath of God ? It is true, the glory is out of sight; we have not beheld the mansions of the saints ; but is not the promise of God more certain than our sight ? We must not be saved by sight, but " by hope ; and hope that is seen is not hope ; for what a man seeth, why doth he yet hope for ? But if we hope for that we see not, then do we with patience wait for it." I have been ashamed of my hope in an arm of flesh, but hope in the promise of God maketh not ashamed. In my greatest sufferings, I will say, " The Lord is my portion ; therefore will I hope in him. The Lord is good unto them that wait for him, to the soul that seeketh him. It is good that a man should both hope and quietly wait for the salvation of the Lord. For the Lord will not cast off for ever. But though he cause grief, yet will he have compassion, according to the multitude of his mercies." Though I languish and die, yet will I hope; for " the righteous hath hope in his death." Though I must lie down in dust and darkness, yet there " my flesh shall rest in hope." And when my flesh hath nothing to rejoice in, yet will I " hold fast the rejoicing of the hope firm unto the end ;" for the hope of the righteous shall be gladness. Indeed, If I was myself to satisfy divine justice, then there had been no hope : but Christ hath brought in a better hope, " by the which we draw nigh unto God." Or, if I had to do with a feeble creature, there were small hope ; for, how could he raise this body from the dust, and lift me above the sun ? But what is this to the Almighty power, which made the heavens and the earth out of nothing ? Cannot that power which raised Christ from the dead, raise me ? and that which hath glorified the Head, glorify also the members ? Doubtless, by the blood of his covenant, God will send forth his prisoners out of the pit wherein is no water ; therefore will I " turn to the strong-hold, as a prisoner of hope." '

15. (4.) Courage or boldness is another affection to be exercised in heavenly contemplation. It leadeth to resolution and concludeth in action. When you have raised your love, desire, and hope, go on, and think thus with yourself—' Will God indeed dwell with men ? And is there such a glory within the reach of hope ? Why then do I not lay hold upon it ? Where is the cheerful vigour of my spirit ? Why do I not gird up the loins of my mind ? Why do not I set upon my enemies on every side, and valiantly break through all resistance ? What should stop me, or intimidate me ? Is God with me, or against me in the work ? Will Christ stand by me, or will he not ? If God and Christ be for me, who can be against me ? In the work of sin, almost all things are ready to help us, and only God and his servants are against us, yet how ill doth that work prosper in our hands ! But in my course to heaven, almost all things are against me, but God is for me ; and therefore how happily doth the work succeed ! Do I set upon this work in my own strength, or rather in the strength of Christ my Lord ? And " cannot I do all things through him that strengthens me ?" Was he ever foiled by an enemy ? He hath indeed been assaulted ; but was he ever conquered ? Why then doth my flesh urge me with the difficulties of the work ? Is any thing too hard for Omnipotence ? May not Peter boldly walk on the sea, if Christ give the word of command ? If he begin to sink, is it from the weakness of Christ, or the smallness of his faith ? Do I not well deserve to be turned into hell, if mortal threats can drive me thither ? Do I not well deserve to be shut out of heaven, if I will be frightened from thence with the reproach of tongues ? What if it were father, or mother, or husband, or wife, or the nearest friend I have in the world, if they may be called friends that would draw me to damnation, should I not forsake all that would keep me from Christ ? Will their friendship countervail the enmity of God, or be any comfort to my condemned soul ? Shall I be yielding to the desires of men, and only harden myself against the Lord ? Let them beseech me upon their knees, I will scorn to stop

my course to behold them; I will shut my ears to their cries : let them flatter or frown ; let them draw out tongues and swords against me ; I am resolved in the strength of Christ to break through, and look upon them as dust. If they would entice me with preferment, even with the kingdoms of the world, I will no more regard them than the dung of the earth. O blessed rest! O glorious state! Who would sell thee for dreams and shadows? Who would be enticed or affrighted from thee? Who would not strive, and fight, and watch, and run, and that with violence, even to the last breath, in order to obtain thee? Surely none but those that know thee not, and believe not thy glory.'

16. (5.) The last affection to be exercised in heavenly contemplation, is joy. Love, desire, hope, and courage, all tend to raise our joy. This is so desirable to every man by nature, and so essentially necessary to constitute our happiness, that I hope I need not say much to persuade you to any thing that would make your life delightful. Supposing you therefore already convinced that the pleasures of the flesh are brutish and perishing, and that your solid and lasting joy must be from heaven, instead of persuading, I shall proceed in directing. Reader, if thou hast managed well the former work, thou art got within sight of thy rest—thou believest the truth of it—thou art convinced of its excellency—thou art fallen in love with it—thou longest after it—thou hopest for it—and thou art resolved to venture courageously for obtaining it. But is there any work for joy in this? We delight in the good we possess; it is present good that is the object of joy; and thou wilt say, ' Alas, I am yet without it !' But think a little further with thyself. Is it nothing to have a deed of gift from God? Are his infallible promises no ground of joy? Is it nothing to live in daily expectations of entering into the kingdom? Is not my assurance of being hereafter glorified, a sufficient ground for inexpressible joy? Is it not a delight to the heir of a kingdom to think of what he must soon possess, though at present he little differ from a servant? Have we not both command and example, for ' rejoicing in hope of the glory of God ?'

17. Here then, Reader, take thy heart once more, and carry it to the top of the highest mount ; show it the kingdom of Christ, and the glory of it ; and say to it, ' All this will thy Lord give thee who hast believed in him, and been a worshipper of him. "It is the Father's good pleasure to give thee this kingdom." Seest thou this astonishing glory which is above thee ? All

this is thy own inheritance. This crown is thine, these pleasures are thine ; this company, this beautiful place, are all thine ; because thou art Christ's, and Christ is thine : when thou wast united to him, thou hadst all these with him.' Thus take thy heart into the land of promise ; show it the pleasant hills and fruitful valleys ; show it the clusters of grapes which thou hast gathered, to convince it that it is a blessed land, flowing with better than milk and honey. Enter the gates of the holy city, walk through the streets of the New Jerusalem, ' walk about Sion, and go round about her : tell the towers thereof: mark well her bulwarks ; consider her palaces ; that thou mayest tell it to thy soul.' Hath it not the glory of God, and is not her light like unto a stone most precious, even like a jasper stone, clear as crystal ? See the ' twelve foundations of her walls, and in them the names of the twelve apostles of the Lamb. And the building of the walls of it are of jasper ; and the city is pure gold, like unto clear glass ; and the foundations are garnished with all manner of precious stones. And the twelve gates are twelve pearls, every several gate is of one pearl, and the street of the city is pure gold, as it were transparent glass. There is no temple in it ; for the Lord God Almighty, and the Lamb, are the temple of it. It hath no need of the sun, neither of the moon in it, for the glory of God doth lighten it, and the Lamb is the light thereof ; and the nations of them which are saved shall walk in the light of it. These sayings are faithful and true ; and the Lord God of the holy prophets sent his angels,' and his own Son, ' to show unto his servants the things which must shortly be done.' Say now to all this, ' This is thy rest, O my soul ! And this must be the place of thy everlasting habitation. Let all the sons of Sion rejoice ; let the daughters of Jerusalem be glad ; for great is the Lord, and greatly to be praised in the city of our God, in the mountain of his holiness. Beautiful for situation, the joy of the whole earth, is Mount Sion. God is known in her palaces for a refuge.'

18. Yet proceed on. The soul that loves, ascends frequently, and runs familiarly through the streets of the heavenly Jerusalem, visiting the patriarchs and prophets, saluting the apostles, and admiring the armies of martyrs ; so do thou lead on thy heart as from street to street ; bring it into the palace of the great King ; lead it, as it were, from chamber to chamber. Say to it, ' Here must I lodge : here must I live ; here must I praise ; here must I love, and be beloved. I must shortly be one of this heavenly choir, and

be better skilled in the music. Among this blessed company must I take up my place; my voice must join to make up the melody. My tears will then be wiped away; my groans be turned to another tune; my cottage of clay be changed to this palace; my prison rags to these splendid robes; and my sordid flesh shall be put off, and such a sun-like spiritual body be put on; 'for the former things are here passed away.' 'Glorious things are spoken of thee, O city of God!' When I look upon this glorious place, what a dunghill and dungeon methinks is earth! O what difference betwixt a man feeble, pained, groaning, dying, rotting in the grave, and one of these triumphant shining saints! Here shall I drink of the river of pleasures, the streams whereof make glad the city of God. Must Israel, under the bondage of the law, serve the Lord 'with joyfulness, and with gladness of heart, for the abundance of all things?' Surely I shall serve him with joyfulness and gladness of heart, for the abundance of glory. Did perse-cuted saints 'take joyfully the spoiling of their goods;' and shall not I take joyfully such a full reparation of all my losses? Was it a celebrated 'day wherein the Jews rested from their ene-mies,' because it 'was turned unto them from sorrow to joy, and from mourning into a good day?' What a day then will that be to my soul, whose rest and change will be inconceivably greater! 'When the wise men saw the star' that led to Christ, 'they rejoiced with exceeding great joy;' but I shall shortly see him, who is himself 'the bright and morning Star.' If the disciples 'departed from the sepulchre with great joy,' when they had but heard that their Lord 'was risen from the dead;' what will be my joy, when I shall see him reigning in glory, and my-self raised to a blessed communion with him! Then shall I indeed have 'beauty for ashes, the oil of joy for mourning, and the garment of praise for the spirit of heaviness,' and Sion shall be made 'an eternal excellency, a joy of many generations.' Why then do I not arise from the dust, and cease my complaints? Why do I not trample on vain delights, and feed on the fore-seen delights of glory? Why is not my life a continual joy, and the savour of heaven perpetu-ally upon my spirit?

19. Let me here observe, that there is no necessity to exercise these affections, either ex-actly in this order, or all at one time. Some-times one of thy affections may need more ex-citing, or may be more lively than the rest; or if thy time be short, one may be exercised one day, and another upon the next; all which must

be left to thy prudence to determine. Thou hast also an opportunity, if inclined, to make use of it, to exercise opposite and more mixed affec-tions; such as—hatred of sin, which would de-prive thy soul of these immortal joys—godly fear, lest thou shouldst abuse thy mercy—godly shame and grief, for having abused it—unfeigned repentance—self-indignation—jealousy over thy heart—and pity for those who are in danger of losing these immortal joys.

20. (III.) We are also to take notice, how heavenly contemplation is promoted by soliloquy and prayer. Though consideration be the chief instrument in this work, yet, by itself, it is not so likely to affect the heart. In this respect, contemplation is like preaching, where the mere explaining of truths and duties is seldom attended with such success, as the lively application of them to the conscience; and especially when a divine blessing is earnestly sought for to accom-pany such application.

21. (1.) By soliloquy, or a pleading the case with thyself, thou must in thy meditation quicken thy own heart. Enter into a serious debate with it. Plead with it in the most moving and affect-ing language, and urge it with the most power-ful and weighty arguments. It is what holy men of God have practised in all ages. Thus David, 'Why art thou cast down, O my soul? and why art thou disquieted within me? Hope thou in God; for I shall yet praise him, who is the health of my countenance, and my God.' And again, 'Bless the Lord, O my soul! and all that is within me, bless his holy name! Bless the Lord, O my soul! and forget not all his bene-fits!' This soliloquy is to be made use of accor-ding to the several affections of the soul, and according to its several necessities. It is a preaching to one's self: for as every good master or father of a family is a good preacher to his own family; so every good Christian is a good preacher to his own soul. Therefore the very same method which a minister should use in his preaching to others, every Christian should endeavour after in speaking to himself. Ob-serve the matter and manner of the most heart-affecting minister; let him be as a pattern for your imitation; and the same way that he takes with the hearts of his people, do thou also take with thy own heart. Do this in thy heavenly contemplation; explain to thyself the things on which thou dost meditate; confirm thy faith in them by scripture; and then apply them to thyself, according to their nature, and thy own necessity. There is no need to object against this, from a sense of thy own inability. Doth

not God command thee to ' teach the scriptures diligently unto thy children, and talk of them when thou sittest in thine house, and when thou walkest by the way, and when thou liest down, and when thou risest up?' And if thou must have some ability to teach thy children, much more to teach thyself; and if thou canst talk of divine things to others, why not also to thy own heart?

22. (2.) Heavenly contemplation is also promoted by speaking to God in prayer, as well as by speaking to ourselves in soliloquy. Ejaculatory prayer may very properly be intermixed with meditation, as a part of the duty. How often do we find David, in the same psalm, sometimes pleading with his soul, and sometimes with God! The apostle bids us ' speak to ourselves in psalms, and hymns, and spiritual songs;' and no doubt we may also speak to God in them. This keeps the soul sensible of the divine presence, and tends greatly to quicken and raise it. As God is the highest object of our thoughts, so our viewing of him, speaking to him, and pleading with him, more elevates the soul, and excites the affections, than any other part of meditation. Though we remain unaffected, while we plead the case with ourselves: yet when we turn our speech to God, it may strike us with awe; and the holiness and majesty of him whom we speak to, may cause both the matter and words to pierce thee deeper. When we read, that ' Isaac went out to meditate in the field,' the margin says, ' to pray;' for the Hebrew word signifies both. Thus in our meditations, to intermix soliloquy and prayer; sometimes speaking to our own hearts, and sometimes to God, is, I apprehend, the highest step we can advance to in this heavenly work. Nor should we imagine it will be as well to take up with prayer alone, and lay aside meditation; for they are distinct duties, and must both of them be performed. We need the one as well as the other, and therefore shall wrong ourselves by neglecting either. Besides, the mixture of them, like music, will be more engaging; as the one serves to put life into the other. And our speaking to ourselves in meditation, should go before our speaking to God in prayer. For want of attending to this due order, men speak to God with far less reverence and affection than they would speak to an angel, if he should appear to them; or to a judge, if they were speaking for their lives. Speaking to the God of heaven in prayer, is a weightier duty than most are aware of.

CHAPTER XV.

HEAVENLY CONTEMPLATION ASSISTED BY SENSIBLE OBJECTS, AND GUARDED AGAINST A TREACHEROUS HEART.

Sect. 1. As it is difficult to maintain a lively impression of heavenly things, therefore, 2. (I.) Heavenly contemplation may be assisted by sensible objects; 3. (1.) If we draw strong suppositions from sense; and, 4—11. (2.) If we compare the objects of sense with the objects of faith, several instances of which are produced. 12. (II.) Heavenly contemplation may also be guarded against a treacherous heart, by considering, 13, 14. (1.) The great backwardness of the heart to this duty; 15. (2.) Its trifling in it; 16. 3.) Its wandering from it; and 17. (4.) Its too abruptly putting an end to it.

1. The most difficult part of heavenly contemplation is to maintain a lively sense of heavenly things upon our hearts. It is easier, merely to think of heaven a whole day, than to be lively and affectionate in those thoughts a quarter of an hour. Faith is imperfect, for we are renewed but in part; and goes against a world of resistance; and, being supernatural, is prone to decline and languish, unless it be continually excited. Sense is strong, according to the strength of the flesh; and being natural, continues while nature continues. The objects of faith are far off: but those of sense are nigh. We must go as far as heaven for our joys. To rejoice in what we never saw, nor ever knew the man that did see, and this upon a mere promise, in the Bible, is not so easy as to rejoice in what we see and possess. It must therefore be a point of spiritual prudence, to call in sense to the assistance of faith. It will be a good work, if we can make friends of these usual enemies, and make them instruments for raising us to God, which are so often the means of drawing us from him. Why hath God given us either our senses, or their common objects, if they might not be serviceable to his praise? Why doth the Holy Spirit describe the glory of the New Jerusalem, in expressions that are even grateful to the flesh? Is it that we might think heaven to be made of gold and pearl? or that saints and angels eat and drink? No: but to help us to conceive of them as we are able, and to use these borrowed phrases as a glass, in which we must see the things themselves imperfectly represented, till we come to an immediate and perfect sight.—And besides showing how heavenly contemplation may be assisted by sensible objects,—this chapter will also show how it may be preserved from a wandering heart.

2. (I.) In order that heavenly contemplation may be assisted by sensible objects, let me only advise to draw strong suppositions from sense, —and to compare the objects of sense with the objects of faith.

3. (1.) For the helping of thy affections in heavenly contemplation, draw as strong suppositions as possible from thy senses. Think on the joys above, as boldly as scripture hath expressed them. Bring down thy conceptions to the reach of sense. Both love and joy are promoted by familiar acquaintance. When we attempt to think of God and glory, without the scripture manner of representing them, we are lost, and have nothing to fix our thoughts upon; we set them so far from us, that our thoughts are strange, and we are ready to say, ' What is above us, is nothing to us.' To conceive of God and glory, only as above our conception, will beget but little love; or as above our love, will produce little joy. Therefore put Christ no farther from you than he hath put himself, lest the divine nature be again inaccessible. Think of Christ as in our own glorified nature. Think of glorified saints, as men made perfect. Suppose thyself a companion with John, in his survey of the New Jerusalem, and viewing the thrones, the majesty, the heavenly hosts, the shining splendour, which he saw. Suppose thyself his fellow-traveller into the celestial kingdom, and that thou hadst seen all the saints in their white robes, with palms in their hands; and that thou hadst heard those ' songs of Moses and of the Lamb.' If thou hadst really seen and heard these things, in what a rapture wouldst thou have been? And the more seriously thou puttest this supposition to thyself, the more will thy meditation elevate thy heart. Do not, like the papists, draw them in pictures; but get the liveliest picture of them in thy mind that thou possibly canst, by contemplating the Scripture account of them, till thou canst say, ' Methinks I see a glimpse of glory! Methinks I hear the shouts of joy and praise, and even stand by Abraham and David, Peter, and Paul, and other triumphant souls! Methinks I even see the Son of God appearing in the clouds, and the world standing at his bar to receive their doom; and hear him say, " Come ye blessed of my Father;" and see them go rejoicing into the joy of their Lord! My very dreams of these things have sometimes greatly affected me, and should not these just suppositions much more affect me? What if I had seen, with Paul, those "unutterable things?" Or, with Stephen, had seen " heaven opened, and Christ sitting at the right hand of God?" Surely that one sight was worth his storm of stones. What if I had seen, as Micaiah did, " the Lord sitting upon his throne, and all the host of heaven standing on his right hand, and on his left?" Such things did these men of God see; and I shall shortly see far more than ever they saw, till they were loosed from the flesh, as I must be. Thus you see how it excites our affections in this heavenly work, if we make strong and familiar suppositions from our bodily senses, concerning the state of blessedness, as the spirit hath in condescending language expressed it.

4. (2.) The other way in which our senses may promote this heavenly work, is, by comparing the objects of sense with the objects of faith. As for instance: you may strongly argue with your hearts from the corrupt delights of sensual men, to the joys above. Think with yourselves, ' Is it such a delight to a sinner to do wickedly? and will it not be delightful indeed to live with God? Hath the drunkard such delights in his cups, that the fears of damnation will not make him forsake them? Will the whoremonger rather part with his credit, estate, and salvation, than with his brutish delights? If the way to hell can afford such pleasure, what then are the pleasures of the saints in heaven! If the covetous man hath so much pleasure in his wealth, and the ambitious man in places of power and titles of honour; what then have the saints in everlasting treasures, and in heavenly honours, where we shall be set above principalities and powers, and be made the glorious spouse of Christ? How delightfully will the voluptuous follow their recreations from morning to night, or sit at their cards and dice nights and days together! O the delight we shall have when we come to our rest, in beholding the face of the living God, and in singing forth the praises unto him and the Lamb!' —Compare also the delights above, with the lawful and moderate delights of sense. Think with thyself, ' How sweet is food to my taste when I am hungry, especially if it be, as Isaac said, "such as I love," which my temperance and appetite incline to! What delight then must my soul have in feeding upon " Christ, the living bread," and in " eating with him at his table in his kingdom!" Was a mess of pottage so sweet to Esau in his hunger, that he would buy it at so dear a rate as his birthright? How highly then should I value this never-perishing food! How pleasant is drink in the extremity of thirst, scarcely to be expressed; enough to make the strength of Samson revive! O how delightful will it be to my soul to drink of that " fountain of living water, which whoso drinketh it shall thirst no more!" How delightful are grateful odours to the smell; or music to the ear; or beautiful sights to the eye! What fragrance then hath the precious ointment which is

poured on the head of our glorified Saviour, and which must be poured on the head of all his saints, and will fill all heaven with its odour! How delightful is the music of the heavenly host! How pleasing will be those real beauties above! How glorious the building not made with hands, the house that God himself dwells in, the walks and prospects in the city of God, and the celestial paradise!'

5. Compare also the delights above, with those we find in natural knowledge. These are far beyond the delights of sense; but how much further are the delights of heaven! Think then, 'Can an Archimedes be so taken up with his mathematical invention, that the threats of death cannot disengage him, but he will die in the midst of his contemplations? Should not I be much more taken up with the delights of glory, and die with these contemplations fresh upon my soul; especially when my death will perfect my delights, while those of Archimedes die with him? What exquisite pleasure it is to dive into the secrets of nature, and find out the mysteries of arts and sciences; especially if we make a new discovery in any one of them! What high delights are there then in the knowledge of God and Christ! If the face of human learning be so beautiful, as to make sensual pleasures appear base and brutish; how beautiful then is the face of God! When we meet with some choice book, how could we read it day and night, almost forgetful of meat, drink, or sleep! What delights are there then at God's right hand, where we shall know in a moment all that is to be known!' —Compare also the delights above with the delights of morality, and of the natural affections. What delight had many sober heathens in the rules and practice of moral duties, so that they took him alone for an honest man, who did well through the love of virtue, and not merely for fear of punishment; yea, so much valued was this moral virtue, that they thought man's chief happiness consisted in it. Think then, 'What excellency will there be in our heavenly perfection, and in that uncreated perfection of God which we shall behold! What sweetness is here in the exercise of natural love, whether to children, parents, yoke-fellows, or intimate friends! Does David say of Jonathan, "Thy love to me was wonderful, passing the love of women?" Did the soul of Jonathan cleave to David? Had Christ himself one disciple whom he especially loved, and who was wont to lean on his breast? If then the delights of close and cordial friendship be so great, what delight shall we have in the friendship of the most High, and in our mu-

tual intimacy with Jesus Christ, and in the dearest love of the saints! Surely this will be a stricter friendship, and these more lovely and desirable friends, than ever the sun beheld; and both our affections to our Father and Saviour, and especially theirs to us, will be such as we never knew here. If one angel could destroy a host, the affections of spirits must also be proportionably stronger, so that we shall then love a thousand times more ardently than we can now. As all the attributes and works of God are incomprehensible, so is this of love: he will love us infinitely beyond our most perfect love to him. What then will there be in this mutual love!'

6. Compare also the excellencies of heaven, with those glorious works of creation which our eyes now behold. What wisdom, power, and goodness, are manifested therein! How does the majesty of the Creator shine in this fabric of the world! 'His works are great, sought out of all them that have pleasure therein.' What divine skill in forming the bodies of men or beasts! What excellency in every plant! What beauty in flowers! What variety and usefulness in herbs, plants, fruits, and minerals! What wonders are contained in the earth and its inhabitants; the ocean of waters, with its motions and dimensions; and the constant succession of spring and autumn, of summer and winter! Think then, 'if these things, which are but servants to sinful men, are so full of mysterious worth, what is that place where God himself dwells, and which is prepared for just men made perfect with Christ! What glory is there in the least of yonder stars! What a vast resplendent body is yonder moon, and every planet! What an inconceivable glory hath the sun! But all this is nothing to the glory of heaven. Yonder sun must there be laid aside as useless. Yonder is but darkness to the lustre of my Father's house. I shall myself be as glorious as that sun. This whole earth is but my Father's footstool. This thunder is nothing to his dreadful voice. These winds are nothing to the breath of his mouth. If the "sending rain, and making the sun to rise on the just and on the unjust," be so wonderful, how much more wonderful and glorious will that sun be, which must shine on none but saints and angels!'—Compare also the enjoyments above, with the wonders of providence in the church and world. Would it not be an astonishing sight, to see the sea stand as a wall on the right hand and on the left, and the dry land appear in the midst, and the people of Israel pass safely through, and Pharaoh and his host

drowned? or to have seen the ten plagues of Egypt? or the rock gushing forth streams? or manna and quails rained from heaven? or the earth opening and swallowing up the wicked? But we shall see far greater things than these; not only sights more wonderful, but more delightful: there shall be no blood nor wrath intermingled; nor shall we cry out, as the men of Bethshemesh, 'Who is able to stand before this holy Lord God?' How astonishing, to see the sun stand still in the firmament; or the dial of Ahaz go back ten degrees! But we shall see when there shall be no sun; or rather shall behold for ever a sun of infinitely greater brightness. What a life should we live, if we could have drought or rain at our prayers; or have fire from heaven to destroy our enemies, as Elijah had; or raise the dead, as Elisha; or miraculously cure diseases, and speak all languages, as the apostles! Alas, these are nothing to the wonders we shall see and possess with God; and all of them wonders of goodness and love! We shall ourselves be the subjects of more wonderful mercies than any of these. Jonah was raised but from a three days' burial in the belly of a fish; but we shall be raised from many years' rottenness and dust; and that dust exalted to the glory of the sun; and that glory perpetuated through eternity. Surely, if we observe but common providences; as, the motions of the sun; the tides of the sea; the standing of the earth; the watering it with rain, as a garden; the keeping in order a wicked confused world; with many others, they are all admirable. But what are these to the Sion of God, the vision of the divine Majesty, and the order of the heavenly host?—Add to these, those particular providences which thou hast thyself enjoyed and recorded through thy life, and compare them with the mercies thou shalt have above. Look over the mercies of thy youth and riper age, of thy prosperity and adversity, of thy several places and relations; are they not excellent and innumerable, rich and engaging? How sweet was it to thee, when God resolved thy doubts; scattered thy fears; prevented the inconveniencies into which thy own counsel would have cast thee; eased thy pains; healed thy sickness; and raised thee up as from death and the grave! Think then, 'Are all these so sweet and precious, that without them my life would have been a perpetual misery? Hath his providence on earth lifted me so high, and his gentleness made me so great! How sweet then will his glorious presence be! How high will his eternal love exalt me! And how great shall I be made in

communion with his greatness! If my pilgrimage and warfare have such mercies, what shall I find in my home, and in my triumph! If God communicates so much to me while I remain a sinner, what will he bestow when I am a perfected saint! If I have had so much at such a distance from him, what shall I have in his immediate presence, where I shall ever stand before his throne!'

7. Compare the joys above with the comforts thou hast here received in ordinances. Hath not the bible been to thee as an open fountain, flowing with comforts day and night? What suitable promises have come into thy mind; so that, with David, thou mayest say, 'Unless thy law had been my delight, I should then have perished in mine affliction!' Think then, 'If his word be so full of consolations, what overflowing springs shall we find in God himself! If his letters are so comfortable, what will the glories of his presence be! If the promise is so sweet, what will the performance be! If the testament of our Lord, and our charter for the kingdom, be so comfortable, what will be our possession of the kingdom itself!'—Think farther, 'What delights have I also found in the word preached! When I have sat under a heavenly, heart-searching teacher, how hath my heart been warmed! Methinks I have felt myself almost in heaven. How often have I gone to the congregation troubled in spirit, and returned joyful! How often have I gone doubting, and God hath sent me home persuaded of his love in Christ! What cordials have I met with to animate me in every conflict! If but the face of Moses shine so gloriously, what glory is there in the face of God! If the feet of them that publish peace, that bring good tidings of salvation, be beautiful; how beautiful is the face of the Prince of peace! If this treasure be so precious in earthen vessels; what is that treasure laid up in heaven! Blessed are the eyes that see what is seen there, and the ears that hear the things that are heard there. There shall I hear Elijah, Isaiah, Jeremiah, John, Peter, Paul: not preaching to gainsayers, in imprisonment, persecution, and reproach; but triumphing in the praises of him that hath raised them to honour and glory.'—Think also, 'What joy is it to have access and acceptance in prayer; that I may always go to God, and open my case and unbosom my soul to him, as to my most faithful friend! But it will be a more unspeakable joy, when I shall receive all blessings without asking, and all my necessities and miseries will be removed, and when God himself will be the portion and inheritance of my soul.'—As for

the Lord's supper, ' What a privilege is it to be admitted to sit at his table, to have his covenant sealed to me there! But all the life and comfort there, is to assure me of the comforts hereafter. O the difference between the last supper of Christ on earth, and the marriage supper of the Lamb at the great day! Then his room will be the glorious heavens; his attendants, all the hosts of angels and saints; no Judas, no unfurnished guest, comes there; but the humble believers must sit down by him, and their feast will be their mutual loving and rejoicing.'—Concerning the communion of saints, think with thyself, ' What a pleasure is it to live with intelligent and heavenly Christians! David says of such, "they were all his delight." O what a delightful society then shall I have above! Had I but seen Job on the dunghill, what a mirror of patience! and what will it be to see him in glory? How delightful to have heard Paul and Silas singing in the stocks! how much more to hear them sing praises in heaven! What melody did David make on his harp! but how much more melodious to hear that sweet singer in the heavenly choir! What would I have given for an hour's free converse with Paul, when he was just come down from the third heaven! But I must shortly see those things myself, and possess what I see.' —Once more, think of praising God in concert with his saints: ' What if I had been in the place of those shepherds, who saw, and heard the heavenly host singing, " Glory to God in the highest, and on earth peace, good will towards men !" But I shall see and hear more glorious things. How blessed should I have thought myself, had I heard Christ in his thanksgivings to his Father! how much more, when I shall hear him pronounce me blessed! If there was such joy at bringing back the ark, or at rebuilding the temple; what will there be in the New Jerusalem! If the earth rent, when the people rejoiced at Solomon's coronation; what a joyful shout will there be at the appearing of the King of the church! If, " when the foundations of the earth were laid, the morning stars sang together, and all the sons of God shouted for joy; what a joyful song will there be, when the world of glory is both founded and finished, when the top-stone is laid, and when " the holy city is adorned as the bride, the Lamb's wife !" '

8. Compare the joys thou shalt have in heaven, with what the saints have found in the way to it, and in the foretastes of it. When did God ever reveal the least of himself to any of his saints, but the joy of their hearts was answerable to the revelation? In what an ecstacy was Peter on the mount of transfiguration! ' Master,' says he, ' it is good for us to be here; let us make three tabernacles; one for thee, and one for Moses, and one for Elias.' As if he had said, ' O let us not go down again to yonder persecuting rabble; let us not return to our mean and suffering state. Is it not better to stay here, now we are here? Is not here better company, and sweeter pleasure?' How was Paul lifted up with what he saw! How did the face of Moses shine, when he had been talking with God! These were all extraordinary foretastes; but little to the full beatific vision. How often have we read and heard of dying saints, who have been as full of joy as their hearts could hold; and when their bodies have felt the extremity of sickness and pain, have had so much of heaven in their spirits, that their joy hath far exceeded their sorrows! If a spark of this fire be so glorious, even amidst the sea of adversity; what then is glory itself! O the joy that the martyrs have felt in the flames! They were flesh and blood, as well as we; it must therefore be some excellent thing that filled their spirits with joy, while their bodies were burning. Think, Reader, in thy meditations, ' Sure it must be some wonderful foretaste of glory that made the flames of fire easy, and the king of terrors welcome. What then is glory itself? What a blessed rest, when the thoughts of it made Paul desire to depart, and be with Christ; and makes the saints never think themselves well, till they are dead! Shall Saunders embrace the stake, and cry, Welcome cross! and shall not I more delightfully embrace my blessedness, and cry, Welcome, crown? Shall Bradford kiss the faggot, and shall not I kiss the Saviour? Shall another poor martyr rejoice to have her foot in the same hole of the stocks in which Mr Philpot's had been before her? and shall not I rejoice, that my soul shall live in the same place of glory, where Christ and his apostles are gone before me? Shall fire and faggot, prisons and banishment, cruel mockings and scourgings, be more welcome to others than Christ and glory to me? God forbid !'

9. Compare the glory of the heavenly kingdom, with the glory of the church on earth, and of Christ in his state of humiliation. If Christ's suffering in the room of sinners had such excellency, what is Christ at his Father's right hand! If the church under her sins and enemies have so much beauty, what will she have at the marriage of the Lamb! How wonderful was the son of God in the form of a servant! When he is born, a new star must appear, and conduct the strangers to worship him in a manger! heavenly

hosts with their songs must celebrate his nativity ; while a child, he must dispute with doctors ; when he enters upon his office, he turns water into wine ; feeds thousands with a few loaves and fishes ; cleanses the lepers, heals the sick, restores the lame, gives sight to the blind, and raises the dead. How wonderful then is his celestial glory ! If there be such cutting down of boughs, and spreading of garments, and crying Hosanna, for one that comes into Jerusalem, riding on an ass ; what will there be when he comes with his angels in his glory ! If they that heard him preach the gospel of the kingdom, confess, ' Never man spake like this man ;' they then that behold his majesty in his kingdom, will say, ' There was never glory like this glory.' If, when his enemies came to apprehend him, they fell to the ground ; if, when he is dying, the earth quakes, the vail of the temple is rent, the sun is eclipsed, the dead bodies of the saints arise, and the standers by acknowledge, ' Verily this was the Son of God ;' O what a day will it be, when the dead must all arise, and stand before him ! when he will once more shake, not the earth only, but the heavens also ! when this sun shall be taken out of the firmament, and be everlastingly darkened with his glory ! and when every tongue shall confess him to be Lord and King ! If, when he rose again, death and the grave lost their power ; if angels must roll away the stone, terrify the keepers till they are as dead men, and send the tidings to his disciples ; if he ascend to heaven in their sight ; what power, dominion, and glory, is he now possessed of, and which we must for ever possess with him ! When he is gone, can a few poor fishermen and tentmakers cure the lame, blind, and sick, open prisons, destroy the disobedient, raise the dead, and astonish their adversaries ? what a world will that be, where every one can do greater works than these ! If the preaching of the gospel be accompanied with such power as to discover the secrets of the heart, humble the proud sinner, and make the most obdurate tremble : if it can make men burn their books, sell their lands, bring in the price, and lay it down at the preacher's feet ; if it can convert thousands, and turn the world upside down ; if its doctrine from the prisoner at the bar, can make the judge on the bench tremble ; if Christ and his saints have this power and honour in the day of their abasement, and in the time appointed for their suffering and disgrace ; what then will they have in their absolute dominion, and full advancement in their kingdom of glory !

10. Compare the glorious change thou shalt have at last, with the gracious change which the Spirit hath here wrought on thy heart. There is not the smallest sincere grace in thee, but is of greater worth than the riches of the Indies : not a hearty desire and groan after Christ, but is more to be valued than the kingdoms of the world. A renewed nature is the very image of God ; Christ dwelling in us ; and the Spirit of God abiding in us : it is a beam from the face of God ; the seed of God remaining in us : the only inherent beauty of the rational soul : it ennobles man above all nobility : fits him to understand his Maker's pleasure, do his will, and receive his glory. If this grain of mustard-seed be so precious, what is the 'tree of life in the midst of the paradise of God !' If a spark of life, which will but strive against corruptions, and flame out a few desires and groans, be of so much worth ; how glorious then is the fountain of this life ! If we are said to be like God, when we are pressed down with a body of sin ; sure we shall be much more like God, when we have no such thing as sin within us. Is the desire after, and love of heaven, so excellent ; what then is the thing itself ? Is our joy in foreseeing and believing so sweet ; what will be the joy of full possession ? How glad is a Christian when he feels his heart begin to melt, and be dissolved with the thoughts of sinful unkindness ! Even this sorrow yields him joy. O what then will it be, when we shall know, and love, and rejoice, and praise in the highest perfection ! Think with thyself, ' What a change was it, to be taken from that state wherein I was born, and in which I was rivetted by custom, when thousands of sins lay upon my score, and if I had so died, I had been damned for ever ! What an astonishing change, to be justified from all these enormous crimes, and freed from all these fearful plagues, and made an heir of heaven ! How often, when I have thought of my regeneration, have I cried out, O blessed day ! and blessed be the Lord that ever I saw it ! How then shall I cry out in heaven, O blessed eternity ! and blessed be the Lord that brought me to it ! Did the angels of God rejoice to see my conversion ? Surely they will congratulate my felicity in my salvation.—Grace is but a spark raked up in the ashes, covered with flesh from the sight of the world, and sometimes covered with corruption from my own sight ; but my everlasting glory will not be so clouded, nor my light be under a bushel, but upon a hill, even upon mount Sion the mount of God.

11. Once more, compare the joys which thou shalt have above, with those foretastes of it

which the Spirit hath given thee here. Hath not God sometimes revealed himself extraordinarily to thy soul, and let a drop of glory fall upon it? Hast thou not been ready to say, 'O that it might be thus with thy soul continually!' Didst thou never cry out with the martyr, after thy long and mournful expectations, 'He is come! He is come!' Didst thou never, under a lively sermon of heaven, or in thy retired contemplations on that blessed state, perceive thy drooping spirits revive, and thy dejected heart lift up thy head, and the light of heaven dawn on thy soul? Think with thyself, 'What is this earnest to the full inheritance! Alas! all this light that so amazeth and rejoiceth me, is but a candle lighted from heaven, to lead me thither through this world of darkness! If some godly men have been overwhelmed with joy, till they have cried out, "Hold, Lord, stay thy hand; I can bear no more!" what then will be my joys in heaven, when my soul shall be so capable of seeing and enjoying God, that though the light be ten thousand times greater than the sun, yet my eyes shall be able for ever to behold it!' Or if thou hast not yet felt these sweet foretastes, (for every believer hath not felt them,) then make use of such delights as thou hast felt, in order the better to discern what thou shalt hereafter feel.

12. (II.) I am now to show how heavenly contemplation may be preserved from a wandering heart. Our chief work is here to discover the danger, and that will direct to the fittest remedy. The heart will prove the greatest hinderance in this heavenly employment; either—by backwardness to it—or, by trifling in it—or, by frequent excursions to other objects—or, by abruptly ending the work before it is well begun. As you value the comfort of this work, these dangerous evils must be faithfully resisted.

13. (1.) Thou wilt find thy heart as backward to this, I think, as to any work in the world. O what excuses will it make! What evasions will it find out! What delays and demurs, when it is ever so much convinced! Either it will question whether it be a duty or not; or, if it be so to others, whether to thyself. It will tell thee, 'This is a work for ministers that have nothing else to study; or for persons that have more leisure than thou hast.' If thou be a minister, it will tell thee, 'This is the duty of the people; it is enough for thee to meditate for their instruction, and let them meditate on what they have heard.' As if it was thy duty only to cook their meat, and serve it up, and they alone must eat it, digest it, and live upon it. If all this will

not do, thy heart will tell thee of other business, or set thee upon some other duty; for it had rather go to any duty than this. Perhaps it will tell thee, 'Other duties are greater, and therefore this must give place to them, because thou hast no time for both. Public business is more important; to study and preach for the saving of souls, must be preferred before these private contemplations.' As if thou hadst not time to care for thy own salvation, for looking after that of others. Or thy charity to others were so great, that it obliges thee to neglect thy own eternal welfare. Or as if there were any better way to fit us to be useful to others, than making this proof of our doctrine ourselves. Certainly heaven is the best fire to light our candle at, and the best book for a preacher to study; and if we would be persuaded to study that more, the church would be provided with more heavenly lights; and when our studies are divine, and our spirits divine, our preaching will also be divine, and we may be called divines indeed. Or if thy heart have nothing to say against the work, it will trifle away the time in delays, and promise this day, and the next, but still keep off from the business. Or it will give thee a flat denial, and oppose its own unwillingness to thy reason. All this I speak of the heart, so far as it is still carnal; for I know, so far as it is spiritual, it will judge this the sweetest work in the world.

14. What is now to be done? Wilt thou do it if I tell thee? Wouldst thou not say, in a like case, 'What should I do with a servant that will not work? or with a horse that will not travel? Shall I keep them to look at?' Then faithfully deal thus with thy heart; persuade it to the work, take no denial, chide it for its backwardness, use violence with it. Hast thou no command of thy own thoughts? Is not the subject of thy meditations a matter of choice, especially under this conduct of thy judgment? Surely God gave thee, with thy new nature, some power to govern thy thoughts. Art thou again become a slave to thy depraved nature? Resume thy authority. Call in the Spirit of Christ to thine assistance, who is never backward to so good a work, nor will deny his help in so just a cause. Say to him, 'Lord, thou gavest my reason the command of my thoughts and affections: the authority I have received over them is from thee; and now, behold, they refuse to obey thine authority. Thou commandest me to set them to the work of heavenly meditation, but they rebel and stubbornly refuse the duty. Wilt thou not assist me to exercise that authority which thou hast given me? O send

down thy Spirit, that I may enforce thy commands, and effectually compel them to obey thy will ?' Thus thou shalt see thy heart will submit, its resistance be overcome, and its backwardness be turned into cheerful compliance.

15. (2.) Thy heart will also be likely to betray thee by trifling, when it should be effectually meditating. Perhaps, when thou hast an hour for meditation, the time will be spent before thy heart will be serious. This doing of duty, as if we did it not, ruins as many as the omission of it. Here let thine eye be always upon thy heart. Look not so much to the time it spends in the duty, as to the quantity and quality of the work that is done. You can tell by his work, whether a servant hath been diligent. Ask yourself, ' What affections have yet been exercised ? How much am I yet got nearer to heaven ?' Think not, since thy heart is so trifling, it is better to let it alone : for by this means, thou wilt certainly banish all spiritual obedience ; because the best hearts, being but sanctified in part, will resist, so far as they are carnal. But rather consider well the corruption of thy nature ; and that its sinful indispositions will not supersede the commands of God ; nor one sin excuse for another ; and that God has appointed means to excite our affections. This self-reasoning, self-considering duty of heavenly meditation, is the most singular means, both to excite and increase love. Therefore stay not from the duty, till thou feelest thy love constrain thee, any more than thou wouldst stay from the fire, till thou feelest thyself warm ; but engage in the work till love is excited, and then love will constrain thee to further duty.

16. (3.) Thy heart will also be making excursions from thy heavenly meditation to other objects. It will be turning aside, like a careless servant, to talk with every one that passeth by. When there should be nothing in thy mind but heaven, it will be thinking of thy calling, or thy affections, or of every bird, or tree, or place thou seest. The cure is here the same as before ; use watchfulness and violence. Say to thy heart, ' What ! did I come thither to think of my worldly business, of persons, places, news, or vanity, or of any thing but heaven, be it ever so good ? Canst thou not watch one hour ? Wouldst thou leave this world and dwell for ever with Christ in heaven, and not leave it one hour to dwell with Christ in meditation ? Is this thy love to thy friend ? Dost thou love Christ, and the place of thy eternal blessed abode, no more than this!' If the ravening fowls of wandering thoughts devour the meditations intended for heaven they devour the life and joy of thy thoughts ; therefore drive them away from thy. sacrifice, and strictly keep thy heart to the work.

17. (4.) Abruptly ending thy meditation before it is well begun, is another way in which thy heart will deceive thee. Thou mayest easily perceive this in other duties. In secret prayer, is not thy heart urging thee to cut it short, and frequently making a motion to have done ? So in heavenly contemplation, thy heart will be weary of the work, and will stop thy heavenly walk before thou art well warm. But charge it in the name of God to stay, and not do so great a work by halves. Say to it, ' Foolish heart ! if thou beg awhile, and goest away before thou hast thy alms, is not thy begging a lost labour ? If thou stoppest before the end of thy journey, is not thy travel lost ? Thou camest hither in hope to have a sight of the glory which thou must inherit ; and wilt thou stop when thou art almost at the top of the hill, and turn back before thou hast taken thy survey ? Thou camest hither in hope to speak with God, and wilt thou go before thou hast seen him ? Thou camest to bathe thyself in the streams of consolation, and to that end didst unclothe thyself of thy earthly thoughts, and wilt thou only touch the bank and return ? Thou camest to spy out the land of promise ; go not back without one cluster of grapes to show thy brethren, for their encouragement. Let them see that thou hast tasted of the wine, by the gladness of thy heart ; and that thou hast been anointed with the oil, by the cheerfulness of thy countenance ; and hast fed of the milk and honey, by the mildness of thy disposition, and the sweetness of thy conversation. This heavenly fire would melt thy frozen heart, and refine and spiritualize it ; but it must have time to operate.' Thus pursue the work till something be done, till thy graces be in exercise, thy affections raised, and thy soul refreshed with the delights above ; or if thou canst not attain these ends at once, be the more earnest at another time. ' Blessed is that servant, whom his Lord, when he cometh, shall find so doing.'

CHAPTER XVI.

HEAVENLY CONTEMPLATION EXEMPLIFIED, AND
THE WHOLE WORK CONCLUDED.

Sect. 1. The Reader's attention excited to the following example of meditation. 2. The excellencies of heavenly rest; 3. Its nearness; 4. dreadful to sinners, 5. and joyful to saints; 6. its dear purchase, 7 its difference from earth. 8. The heart pleaded with. 9. Unbelief banished. 10. A careless world pitied. 11—13. Heavenly rest the object of love, 14—21. and joy. 22. The heart's backwardness to heavenly joy lamented. 23—27. Heavenly rest the object of desire. 28 Such meditations as this urged upon the reader: 29. The mischief of neglecting it; 30. The happiness of pursuing it. 31. The Author's concluding Prayer for the success of his work.

1. And now, Reader, according to the above directions, make conscience of daily exercising thy graces in meditation, as well as prayer. Retire into some secret place, at a time the most convenient to thyself, and, laying aside all worldly thoughts, with all possible seriousness and reverence look up toward heaven, remember there is thine everlasting rest, study its excellency and reality, and rise from sense to faith, by comparing heavenly with earthly joys: then mix ejaculations with thy soliloquies; till having pleaded the case reverently with God, and seriously with thy own heart, thou hast pleaded thyself from a clod to a flame; from a forgetful sinner, and a lover of the world, to an ardent lover of God; from a fearful coward to a resolved Christian; from an unfruitful sadness to a joyful life: in a word, till thou hast pleaded thy heart from earth to heaven, from conversing below to walking with God, and till thou canst lay thy heart to rest, as in the bosom of Christ, by some such meditation of thy everlasting rest as is here added for thy assistance.

2. 'Rest! How sweet the sound! It is melody to my ears! It lies as a reviving cordial at my heart, and from thence sends forth lively spirits, which beat through all the pulses of my soul! Rest—not as the stone that rests on the earth, nor as this flesh shall rest in the grave, nor such a rest as the carnal world desires. O blessed rest! when we " rest not day and night, saying, Holy, holy, holy, Lord God Almighty !" When we shall rest from sin, but not from worship: from suffering and sorrow, but not from joy ! O blessed day! When I shall rest with God ! When I shall rest in the bosom of my Lord! When I shall rest in knowing, loving, rejoicing, and praising! When my perfect soul and body shall together perfectly enjoy the most perfect God ! When God, who is love itself, shall perfectly love me, and rest in his love to me, as I shall rest in my love to him; and rejoice over me with joy, and joy over me with singing, as I shall rejoice in him '

3. 'How near is that most blessed, joyful day! It comes apace. " He that shall come, will come, and will not tarry." Though my Lord seems to delay his coming, yet a little while and he will be here. What is a few hundred years, when they are over? How surely will his sign appear ! How suddenly will he seize upon the careless world, even as the lightning cometh out of the east, and shineth unto the west! He who is gone hence shall so come. Methinks I hear his trumpet sound ! Methinks I see him coming in clouds, with his attending angels, in majesty and glory !

4. 'O secure sinners ! What now will you do ? Where will you hide yourselves ? What shall cover you ? Mountains are gone ; the heavens and the earth, which were, are passed away ; the devouring fire hath consumed all, except yourselves, who must be the fuel for ever. O that you could consume as soon as the earth ; and melt away as did the heavens ! Ah, these wishes are now but vain ! The Lamb himself would have been your friend ; he would have loved you, and ruled you, and now have saved you ; but you would not then, and now it is too late. Never cry, " Lord, Lord ;" too late, too late, man. Why dost thou look about ? Can any save thee ? Whither dost thou run ? Can any hide thee ? O wretch, that hast brought thyself to this !

5. 'Now, blessed saints, that have believed and obeyed. This is the end of faith and patience. This is it for which you prayed and waited. Do you now repent your sufferings and sorrows, your self-denying and holy walking ? Are your tears of repentance now bitter or sweet? See how the Judge smiles upon you ; there is love in his looks ; the titles of Redeemer, Husband, Head, are written in his amiable shining face. Hark, he calls you ! he bids you stand here on his right hand : fear not, for there he sets his sheep. O joyful sentence ! " Come, ye blessed of my Father, inherit the kingdom prepared for you from the foundation of the world." He takes you by the hand, the door is open, the kingdom is his, and therefore yours ; there is your place before his throne ; the Father receives you as the spouse of his Son, and bids you welcome to the crown of glory. Ever so unworthy, you must be crowned. This was the project of free redeeming grace, the purpose of eternal love. O blessed grace ! O blessed love ! Oh how love and joy will rise ! But I cannot express it, I cannot conceive it.

6. 'This is that joy which was procured by sorrow, that crown which was procured by the

cross. My Lord wept, that now my tears might be wiped away ; he bled, that I might now rejoice; he was forsaken, that I might not now be forsook ; he then died, that I might now live. O free mercy, that can exalt so vile a wretch ! Free to me, though dear to Christ ! Free grace, that hath chosen me, when thousands were forsaken! When my companions in sin must burn in hell, I must here rejoice in rest ! Here must I live with all these saints ! O comfortable meeting of my old acquaintance, with whom I prayed, and wept, and suffered, and spoke often of this day and place ! I see the grave could not detain you ; the same love hath redeemed and saved you also.

7. 'This is not like our cottages of clay, our prisons, our earthly dwellings. This voice of joy is not like our old complaints, our impatient groans and sighs ; nor this melodious praise like the scoffs and revilings, or the oaths and curses, which we heard on earth. This body is not like that we had, nor this soul like the soul we had, nor this life like the life we lived. We have changed our place and state, our clothes and thoughts, our looks, language, and company. Before, a saint was weak and despised ; so proud and peevish, we could often scarce discern his graces : but now how glorious a thing is a saint! Where is now their body of sin, which wearied themselves and those about them ? Where are now our different judgments, reproachful names, divided spirits, exasperated passions, strange looks, uncharitable censures? Now we are all of one judgment, of one name, of one heart, house, and glory. O sweet reconciliation ! Happy union ! Now the gospel shall no more be dishonoured through our folly. No more, my soul, shalt thou lament the sufferings of the saints, or the church's ruins, nor mourn thy suffering friends, nor weep over their dying beds, or their graves. Thou shalt never suffer thy old temptations from Satan, the world, or thy own flesh. Thy pains and sickness are all cured ; thy body shall no more burden thee with weakness and weariness ; thy aching head and heart, thy hunger and thirst, thy sleep and labour, are all gone. O what a mighty change is this! From the dunghill to the throne ! from persecuting sinners to praising saints ! From a vile body, to this which " shines as the brightness of the firmament !" From a sense of God's displeasure, to the perfect enjoyment of him in love ! From all my doubts and fears, to this possession which puts me out of doubt ! From all my fearful thoughts of death, to this joyful life ! Blessed change! Farewell sin and sor-

row for ever : farewell my rocky, proud, unbelieving heart ; my worldly, sensual, carnal heart : and welcome now my most holy, heavenly nature. Farewell repentance, faith, and hope ; and welcome love, and joy, and praise. I shall now have my harvest, without ploughing or sowing ; my joy without a preacher, or a promise ; even all from the face of God himself. Whatever mixture is in the streams, there is nothing but pure joy in the fountain. Here shall I be encircled with eternity, and ever live, and ever, ever praise the Lord. My face will not wrinkle, nor my hair be gray ; " for this corruptible shall have put on incorruption, and this mortal, immortality, and death shall be swallowed up in victory. O death, where is now thy sting ? O grave, where is thy victory ?" The date of my lease will no more expire, nor shall I trouble myself with thoughts of death, nor lose my joys through fear of losing them. When millions of ages are passed, my glory is but beginning ; and when millions more are passed, it is no nearer ending. Every day is all noon, every month is harvest, every year is a jubilee, every age is full manhood, and all this is one eternity. O blessed eternity ! The glory of my glory ! the perfection of my perfection !

8. ' Ah, drowsy, earthly heart ! How coldly dost thou think of this reviving day ! Hadst thou rather sit down in dirt, than walk in the palace of God ? Art thou now remembering thy worldly business, or thinking of thy lusts, earthly delights, and merry company ? Is it better to be here, than above with God ? Is the company better ? Are the pleasures greater ? Come away ; make no excuse nor delay ; God commands, and I command thee ; gird up thy loins ; ascend the mount ; look about thee with faith and seriousness. Look not back upon the way of the wilderness, except it be to compare the kingdom with that howling desert, more sensibly to perceive the wide difference. Yonder is thy Father's glory ; yonder, O my soul, must thou remove, when thou departest from this body ; and when the power of thy Lord hath raised it again, and joined thee to it, yonder must thou live with God for ever. There is the glorious New Jerusalem, the gates of pearl, the foundation of pearl, the streets and pavements of transparent gold. That sun, which lighteth all this world, will be useless there ; even thyself shall be as bright as yonder shining sun : God will be the sun, and Christ the light, and in his light shalt thou have light.

9. ' O my soul ! dost thou " stagger at the promise of God through unbelief ?" I much sus-

pect thee. Didst thou believe indeed, thou wouldst be more affected with it? Is it not under the hand, and seal, and oath of God? Can God lie? Can he that is truth itself be false? What need hath God to flatter or deceive thee? Why should he promise thee more than he will perform? Dare not to charge the wise, almighty, faithful God, with this. How many of the promises have been performed to thee in thy conversion! Would God so powerfully concur with a feigned word? O wretched heart of unbelief! Hath God made thee a promise of rest, and wilt thou come short of it? Thine eyes, thine ears, and all thy senses, may prove delusions, sooner than a promise of God can delude thee. Thou mayest be surer of that which is written in the word, than if thou see it with thine eyes, or feel it with thine hands. Art thou sure thou art alive, or that this is earth thou standest on, or that thine eyes see the sun? As sure is all this glory to the saints; as sure shall I be higher than yonder stars, and live for ever in the holy city, and joyfully sound forth the praises of my Redeemer; if I be not shut out by this "evil heart of unbelief," causing me to "depart from the living God."

10. 'And is this rest so sweet and so sure? Then what means the careless world? Know they what they neglect? Did they ever hear of it, or are they yet asleep, or are they dead? Do they certainly know that the crown is before them, while they thus sit still, or follow trifles? Undoubtedly they are beside themselves, to mind so much their provision by the way, when they are hasting so fast to another world, and their eternal happiness lies at stake. Were there left one spark of reason, they would never sell their rest for toil, nor their glory for worldly vanities, nor venture heaven for sinful pleasure. Poor men! O that you would once consider what you hazard, and then you would scorn these tempting baits! Blessed for ever be that love which hath rescued me from this bewitching darkness!

11. 'Draw yet nearer, O my soul! with thy most fervent love. Here is matter for it to work upon, something worth thy loving. O see what beauty presents itself! Is not all the beauty in the world united here? Is not all other beauty but deformity? Dost thou now need to be persuaded to love? Here is a feast for thine eyes, and all the powers of thy soul: dost thou need entreaties to feed upon it? Canst thou love a little shining earth, a walking piece of clay? And canst thou not love that God, that Christ, that glory, which is so truly and unmeasurably lovely? Thou canst love thy friend, because he

loves thee; and is the love of a friend like the love of Christ? Their weeping or bleeding for thee, does not ease thee, nor stay the course of thy tears or blood; but the tears and blood that fell from thy Lord have a sovereign healing virtue.—O my soul! if love deserves, and should beget love, what incomprehensible love is here before thee! Pour out all the store of thy affections here, and all is too little. O that it were more! O that it were many thousand times more! Let him be first served, that served thee first. Let him have thy first-born, and strength of thy soul, who parted with strength, and life, and love for thee.—O my soul! dost thou love for excellency? Yonder is the region of light; this is a land of darkness. Yonder twinkling stars, that shining moon, and radiant sun, are all our lanterns hung out of thy Father's house, to light thee while thou walkest in this dark world. But how little dost thou know the glory and blessedness that is within!—Dost thou love for suitableness? What person more suitable than Christ? His Godhead and humanity, his fullness and freeness, his willingness and constancy, all proclaim him thy most suitable friend. What state more suitable to thy misery, than mercy? Or to thy sin and pollution, than honour and perfection? What place more suitable to thee than heaven? Does this world agree with thy desires? Hast thou not had a sufficient trial of it, or dost thou love for interest and near relation? Where hast thou better interest than in heaven, or nearer relation than there?

12. 'Dost thou love for acquaintance and familiarity? Though thine eyes have never seen thy Lord, yet thou hast heard his voice, received his benefits, and lived in his bosom. He taught thee to know thyself and him; he opened thee that first window through which thou sawest into heaven. Hast thou forgotten since thy heart was careless, and he awakened it; hard, and he softened it; stubborn, and he made it yield; at peace, and he troubled it; whole, and he broke it; and broken till he healed it again? Hast thou forgotten the times when he found thee in tears; when he heard thy secret sighs and groans, and left all to come and comfort thee? when he took thee, as it were, in his arms, and asked thee, "Poor soul, what ails thee? Dost thou weep, when I have wept so much? Be of good cheer, thy wounds are saving, and not deadly; it is I have made them, who mean thee no hurt: though I let out thy blood, I will not let out thy life." I remember his voice. How gently did he take me up! How carefully did he dress my wounds! Methinks I hear him still saying

to me, " Poor sinner, though thou hast dealt un-kindly with me, and cast me off; yet I will not do so by thee. Though thou hast set light by me, and all my mercies, yet they and myself are all thine. What wouldst thou have that I can give thee? And what dost thou want that I cannot give thee? If any thing I have will give thee pleasure, thou shalt have it. Wouldst thou have pardon? I freely forgive thee all the debt. Wouldst thou have grace and peace? Thou shalt have them both. Wouldst thou have my-self? Behold I am thine, thy Friend, thy Lord, thy Brother, Husband, and Head. Wouldst thou have the Father? I will bring thee to him, and thou shalt have him, in and by me." These were my Lord's reviving words. After all, when I was doubtful of his love, methinks I yet re-member his overcoming arguments: " Have I done so much, sinner, to testify my love, and yet dost thou doubt? Have I offered thee my-self and love so long, and yet dost thou question my willingness to be thine? At what dearer rate should I tell thee that I love thee? Wilt thou not believe my bitter passion proceeded from love? Have I made myself in the gospel a lion to thine enemies, and a lamb to thee, and dost thou overlook my lamb-like nature? Had I been willing to let thee perish, what need have I done and suffered so much? What need I follow thee with such patience and importunity? Why dost thou tell me of thy wants; have I not enough for me and thee? Or of thy unworthi-ness; for if thou wast thyself worthy, what shouldst thou do with my worthiness? Did I ever invite, or save the worthy and the righteous; or is there any such upon earth? Hast thou nothing; art thou lost and miserable, helpless and forlorn? Dost thou believe I am an all-sufficient Saviour, and wouldst thou have me? Lo, I am thine, take me; if thou art willing, I am; and neither sin, nor Satan, shall break the match." These, O these, were the blessed words which his Spirit from his gospel spoke unto me, till he made me cast myself at his feet, and cry out, " My Saviour and my Lord, thou hast broken, thou hast revived my heart; thou hast overcome, thou hast won my heart; take it, it is thine; if such a heart can please thee, take it; if it cannot, make it such as thou wouldst have it." Thus, O my soul, mayest thou remember the sweet familiarity thou hast had with Christ; therefore, if acquaintance will cause affection, let out thy heart unto him. It is he that hath stood by the bed of sickness, hath eased thy pains, refreshed thy weariness, and removed thy fears. He hath been always ready, when thou hast earnestly sought him; hath met thee in public and private ; hath been found of thee in the congregation, in thy house, in thy closet, in the field, in thy waking nights, in thy deepest dangers.

13. ' If bounty and compassion be an attrac-tive of love, how unmeasurably then am I bound to love him! All the mercies that have filled up my life, all the places that ever I abode in, all the societies and persons I have been conver-sant with, all my employments and relations, every condition I have been in, and every change I have passed through, all tell me, that the foun-tain is overflowing goodness. Lord, what a sum of love am I indebted to thee! And how does my debt continually increase! How should I love again for so much love? But shall I dare to think of requiting thee, or of recompensing all thy love with mine? Will my mite requite thee for thy golden mines; my seldom wishes, for thy constant bounty ; mine which is nothing, or not mine, for thine which is infinite, and thine own? Shall I dare to contend in love with thee; or set my borrowed languid spark against the Sun of love? Can I love as high, as deep, as broad, as long as love itself? as much as he that made me, and that made me love, and gave me all that little which I have? As I cannot match thee in the works of power, nor make, nor pre-serve, nor rule the worlds ; no more can I match thee in love. No, Lord, I yield; I am overcome. O blessed conquest! Go on victoriously, and still prevail, and triumph in thy love. The cap-tive of love shall proclaim thy victory ; when thou leadest me in triumph from earth to heaven, from death to life, from the tribunal to the throne; myself, and all that see it, shall acknow-ledge thou hast prevailed, and all shall say "Be-hold how he loved him!" Yet let me love, in subjection to thy love; as thy redeemed captive, though not thy peer. Shall I not love at all, because I cannot reach thy measure? O that I could feelingly say, " I love thee, even as I love my friend, and myself!" Though I cannot say, as the apostle, ' Thou knowest that I love thee;" yet I can say, " Lord, thou knowest that I would love thee!" I am angry with my heart, that it doth not love thee; I chide it, yet it doth not mend; I reason with it, and would fain persuade it, yet I do not perceive it stir; I rub and chafe it in the use of ordinances, and yet I feel it not warm within me. Unworthy soul! Is not thine eye now upon the only lovely object? Art thou not now beholding the ravishing glory of the saints? And dost thou not love? Art thou not a rational soul, and should not reason tell thee,

that earth is a dungeon to the celestial glory? Art thou not thyself a spirit, and shouldst thou not love God, "who is a spirit, and the Father of spirits?" Why dost thou love so much thy perishing clay, and love no more the heavenly glory? Shalt thou love when thou comest there; when the Lord shall take thy carcass from the grave, and make thee shine as the sun in glory for ever and ever; shalt thou then love, or shalt thou not? Is not the place a meeting of lovers? Is not the life a state of love? Is it not the great marriage day of the Lamb? Is not the employment there the work of love, where the souls with Christ take their fill? O then, my soul, begin it here! Be sick with love now, that thou mayest be well with love there. Keep thyself now in the love of God; and let neither life, nor death, nor any thing separate thee from it; and thou shalt be kept in the fullness of love for ever, and nothing shall imbitter or abate thy pleasure; for the Lord hath prepared a city of love, a place for communicating love to his chosen, "and they that love his name shall dwell therein."

14. 'Awake then, O my drowsy soul! To sleep under the light of grace is unreasonable, much more in the approach of the light of glory. Come forth, my dull congealed spirit, thy Lord bids thee "rejoice, and again rejoice." Thou hast lain long enough in thy prison of flesh, where Satan hath been thy jailor; cares have been thy irons, fears thy scourges, and thy food the bread and water of affliction; where sorrows have been thy lodging, and thy sins and foes have made thy bed, and an unbelieving heart hath been the gates and bars that have kept thee in; the Angel of the covenant now calls thee, and bids thee arise, and follow him. Up, O my soul! and cheerfully obey, and thy bolts and bars shall all fly open; follow the Lamb whithersoever he goeth. Shouldst thou fear to follow such a guide? Can the sun lead thee to a state of darkness? Will he lead thee to death, who died to save thee from it? Follow him, and he will show thee the paradise of God; he will give thee a sight of the New Jerusalem, and a taste of the tree of life. Come forth, my drooping soul, and lay aside thy winter dress; let it be seen by thy garments of joy and praise, that the spring is come; and as thou now seest thy comforts green, thou shalt shortly see them "white and ripe for harvest," and then thou shalt be called to reap, and gather, and take possession. Should I suspend and delay my joys till then? Should not the joys of the spring go before the joys of harvest? Is title nothing before pos-session? Is the heir in no better a state than a slave? My Lord hath taught me to rejoice in hope of his glory, and how to see it through the bars of a prison, for when persecuted for righteousness' sake, he commands me to "rejoice and be exceeding glad," because my reward in heaven is great. I know he would have my joys exceed my sorrows, and as much as he delights in "the humble and contrite," he yet more delights in the soul that "delights in him." Hath my Lord spread me a table in this wilderness, and furnished it with the promises of everlasting glory, and set before me angels' food? Doth he frequently and importunately invite me to sit down, and feed, and spare not? Hath he, to that end, furnished me with reason, and faith, and a joyful disposition, and is it possible that he should be unwilling to have me rejoice? Is not his command, to "delight thyself in the Lord;" and his promise, to "give thee the desires of thine heart?" Art thou not charged to "rejoice evermore;" yea, to "sing aloud, and shout for joy!" Why should I then be discouraged? My God is willing, if I were but willing. He is delighted with my delights. He would have it my constant frame, and daily business, to be near him in my believing meditations, and to live in the sweetest thoughts of his goodness. O blessed employment, fit for the sons of God! But thy feast, my Lord, is nothing to me without an appetite. Thou hast set the dainties of heaven before me; but, alas, I am blind, and cannot see them! I am sick, and cannot relish them! I am so benumbed, that I cannot put forth a hand to take them. I therefore humbly beg this grace, that as thou hast opened heaven to me in thy word, so thou wouldst open mine eyes to see it, and my heart to delight in it; else heaven will be no heaven to me. O thou Spirit of life, breathe upon thy graces in me; take me by the hand, and lift me from the earth, that I may see what glory thou hast prepared for them that love thee!

15. 'Away then, ye soul-tormenting cares and fears, ye heart-vexing sorrows! At least forbear a little while: stand by; stay here below till I go up and see my rest. The way is strange to me, but not to Christ. There was the eternal abode of his glorious deity; and thither hath he also brought his glorified flesh. It was his work to purchase it; it is his to prepare it, and to prepare me for it, and bring me to it. The eternal God of truth hath given me his promise, his seal and oath, that, believing in Christ, I shall not perish, but have everlasting life. Thither shall my soul be speedily removed, and my body very shortly

follow. And can my tongue say, that I shall shortly and surely live with God ; and yet my heart not leap within me ? Can I say it with faith and not with joy ? Ah faith, how sensibly do I now perceive thy weakness ! But though unbelief darken my light, and dull my life, and suppress my joys, it shall not be able to conquer and destroy me ; though it envy all my comforts, yet some in spite of it I shall even here receive ; and if that did not hinder, what abundance might I have ! The light of heaven would shine into my heart ; and I might be almost as familiar there, as I am on earth. Come away then, my soul ; stop thine ears to the ignorant language of infidelity ; thou art able to answer all its arguments; or if thou art not, yet tread them under thy feet. Come away: stand not looking on that grave, nor turning those bones, nor reading thy lesson now in the dust ; those lines will soon be wiped out. But lift up thy head, and look to heaven, and see thy name written in golden letters " in the book of life of the Lamb that was slain." What if an angel should tell thee, that there is a mansion in heaven prepared for thee, that it shall certainly be thine for ever ; would not such a message make thee glad ? And dost thou make light of the infallible word of promise, which was delivered by the Spirit, and even by the Son himself ? Suppose thou hadst seen a fiery chariot come for thee, and fetch thee up to heaven, like Elijah ; would not this rejoice thee ? But thy Lord assures thee, that the soul of Lazarus hath a convoy of angels to carry it into Abraham's bosom. Shall a drunkard be so merry among his cups, or the glutton in his delicious fare, and shall not I rejoice who must shortly be in heaven ? Can meat and drink delight me when I hunger and thirst ? Can I find pleasure in walks and gardens, and convenient dwellings ? Can beautiful objects delight mine eyes ; or grateful odours my smell ; or melody my ears ? And shall not the forethought of celestial bliss delight me ? Methinks among my books I could employ myself in sweet content, and bid the world farewell, and pity the rich and great that know not this happiness ; what then will my happiness in heaven be, where my knowledge will be perfect ! If the Queen of Sheba came from the utmost parts of the earth to hear the wisdom of Solomon, and see his glory ; how cheerfully should I pass from earth to heaven, to see the glory of the eternal Majesty, and attain the height of wisdom, compared with which, the most learned on earth are but fools and idiots ! What if God had made me commander of the earth ; what if I could remove mountains, heal diseases with a word or a touch, or cast out devils, should I not rejoice in such privileges and honours as these, and shall I not much more rejoice that my name is written in heaven ? I cannot here enjoy my parents, or my near and beloved friends, without some delight : especially when I did freely let out my affection to my friend, how sweet was that exercise of my love ! O what will it then be to live in the perpetual love of God ! " For brethren to dwell together in unity here, how good and how pleasant it is !" To see a family live in love, husband and wife, parents, children, and servants, doing all in love to one another ; to see a town live together in love, without any envyings, brawlings, or contentions, lawsuits, factions, or divisions, but every man loving his neighbour as himself, thinking they can never do too much for one another, but striving to go beyond each other in love ; how happy, how delightful a sight is this ! O then, what a blessed society will the family of heaven be, and those peaceful inhabitants of the New Jerusalem, where there is no division, nor differing judgments, no disaffection nor strangeness, no deceitful friendship, no, not one unkind expression, not an angry look or thought ; but all are one in Christ, who is one with the Father, and all live in the love of him, who is love itself ! The soul is not more where it lives, than where it loves. How near then will my soul be united to God, when I shall so heartily, strongly, and incessantly love him ! Ah, wretched unbelieving heart, that can think of such a day, and work, and life as this, with such low and feeble joys ! But my future enjoyments will be more lively.

16. ' How delightful is it to me to behold and study these inferior works of creation ! What a beautiful fabric do we here dwell in ; the floor so dressed with herbs, and flowers, and trees, and watered with springs and rivers; the roof so widely expanded, so admirably adorned ! What wonders do sun, moon, and stars, seas, and winds contain ! And hath God prepared such a house for corruptible flesh, for a soul imprisoned : and doth he bestow so many millions of wonders upon his enemies ? O what a dwelling must that be, which he prepares for his dearly beloved children ; and how will the glory of the New Jerusalem exceed all the present glory of the creatures ! Arise, then, O my soul, in thy contemplation; and let thy thoughts of that glory as far exceed in sweetness thy thoughts of the excellencies below ! Fear not to go out of this body, and this world, when thou must make so happy a change ; but say, as one did when he

was dying, " I am glad, and even leap for joy, that the time is come in which that mighty Jehovah, whose majesty in my search of nature I have admired, whose goodness I have adored, whom by faith I have desired and panted after, will now show himself to me face to face."

17. ' How wonderful also are the works of Providence ! How delightful to see the great God interest himself in the safety and advancement of a few humble, praying, but despised persons ; and to review those special mercies with which my own life hath been adorned and sweetened ! How often have my prayers been heard, my tears regarded, my troubled soul relieved ! How often hath my Lord bid me be of good cheer ! What a support are these experiences, these clear testimonies of my Father's love to my fearful unbelieving heart ! O then, what a blessed day will that be, when I shall have all mercy, perfection of mercy, and fully enjoy the Lord of mercy ; when I shall stand on the shore, and look back on the raging seas I have safely passed ; when I shall review my pains and sorrows, my fears and tears, and possess the glory which was the end of all ! If one drop of lively faith was mixed with these considerations, what a heaven-ravishing heart should I carry within me ! Fain would " I believe ; Lord, help my unbelief !"

18. ' How sweet, O my soul, have ordinances been to thee ! What delight hast thou had in prayer, and thanksgiving, under heavenly sermons, and in the society of saints, and to see " the Lord adding to the church such as should be saved !" How then can my heart conceive the joy which I shall have, to see the perfected church in heaven, and to be admitted into the celestial temple, and with the heavenly host praise the Lord for ever ! If the word of God was sweeter to Job than his necessary food, and to David than honey and the honeycomb, and was the joy and rejoicing of Jeremiah's heart ; how blessed a day will that be, when we shall fully enjoy the Lord of this word, and shall no more need these written precepts and promises, nor read any book but the face of the glorious God ! If they that heard Christ speak on earth, were astonished at his wisdom and answers, and wondered at the gracious words that proceeded out of his mouth ; how shall I then be affected to behold him in his majesty !

19. ' Can the prospect of this glory make others welcome the cross, and even refuse deliverance ; and cannot it make thee cheerful under lesser sufferings ? Can it sweeten the flames of martyrdom; and not sweeten thy life, or thy sickness, or thy natural death ? Is it not the same heaven which they and I must live in ? Is not their God, their Christ, their crown, and mine, the same ? And shall I look upon it with an eye so dim, a heart so dull, a countenance so dejected. Some small foretastes of it have I myself had : and how much more delightful have they been, than any earthly things ever were : and what then will the full enjoyment be !

20. ' What a beauty is there here in the imperfect graces of the Spirit ! Alas ! how small are these to what we shall enjoy in our perfect state ! What a happy life should I here live, could I but love God as much as I would ; could I be all love, and always loving ! O my soul, what wouldst thou give for such a life ? Had I such apprehensions of God, such knowledge of his word as I desire ; could I fully trust him in all my straits ; could I be as lively as I would in every duty ; could I make God my constant desire and delight ; I would not envy the world their honours or pleasures. What a blessed state, O my soul ! wilt thou shortly be in, when thou shalt have far more of these than thou canst now desire, and shalt exercise thy perfected graces in the immediate vision of God, and not in the dark, and at a distance, as now.

21. ' Is the sinning, afflicted, persecuted church of Christ, so much more excellent than any particular gracious soul ? What then will the church be, when it is fully gathered and glorified ; when it is ascended from the valley of tears to mount Sion ; when it shall sin and suffer no more ! The glory of the Old Jerusalem will be darkness and deformity to the glory of the New. What cause shall we have then to shout for joy, when we shall see how glorious the heavenly temple is, and remember the meanness of the church on earth !

22. ' But, alas ! what a loss am I at in the midst of my contemplations ! I thought my heart had all the while attended, but I see it hath not. What life is there in empty thoughts and words, without affections ? Neither God, nor I, find pleasure in them. Where hast thou been, unworthy heart, while I was opening to thee the everlasting treasures ? Art thou not ashamed to complain so much of an uncomfortable life, and to murmur at God for filling thee with sorrows, when he in vain offers thee the delights of angels ? Hadst thou now but followed me close, it would have made thee revive and leap for joy, and forget thy pains and sorrows. Did I think my heart had been so backward to rejoice !

23. 'Lord, thou hast reserved my perfect joys for heaven; therefore, help me to desire till I may possess, and let me long when I cannot, as I would, rejoice. O my soul, thou knowest, to thy sorrow, that thou art not yet at thy rest. When shall I arrive at that safe and quiet harbour where there are none of these storms, waves, and dangers; when I shall never more have a weary restless night or day? Then my life will not be such a mixture of hope and fear, of joy and sorrow; nor shall flesh and spirit be combating within me; nor faith and unbelief, humility and pride, maintain a continual conflict. O when shall I be past these soul-tormenting fears, and cares, and griefs? When shall I be out of this soul-contradicting, ensnaring, deceitful flesh; this corruptible body, this vain, vexatious world? Alas! that I must stand and see the church and cause of Christ tossed about in contention, and made subservient to private interests, or deluded fancies! There is none of this disorder in the heavenly Jerusalem: there I shall find a harmonious concert of perfected spirits, obeying and praising their everlasting King. O how much better to be a door-keeper there, than the commander of this tumultuous world! Why am I no more weary of this weariness? Why do I so forget my resting-place? Up then, O my soul, in thy most raised and fervent desires! Stay not till this flesh can desire with thee; expect not that sense should apprehend thy blessed object, and tell thee when and what to desire. Doth not the dullness of thy desires after rest, accuse thee of most detestable ingratitude and folly? Must thy Lord procure thee a rest at so dear a rate, and dost thou no more value it? Must he go before to prepare so glorious a mansion for such a wretch, and art thou loth to go and possess it! Shall the Lord of glory be desirous of thy company, and thou not desirous of his? Must earth become a very hell to thee, before thou art willing to be with God? Behold the most lovely creature, or the most desirable state, and tell me where wouldst thou be, if not with God? Poverty is a burden; riches a snare; sickness unpleasing; health unsafe; the frowning world bruises thy heel; the smiling world stings thee to the heart: so much as the world is loved and delighted in, it hurts and endangers the lover; and if it may not be loved, why should it be desired? If thou art applauded, it proves the most contagious breath; if thou art vilified, or unkindly used, methinks this should not entice thy love. If thy successful labours, and thy godly friends, seem better to thee than a life with God, it is time for God to take them from thee.

If thy studies have been sweet, have they not also been bitter? And, at best, what are they to the everlasting views of the God of truth? Thy friends here have been thy delight; and have they not also been thy vexation and grief? They are gracious; and are they not also sinful? They are kind; and are they not soon displeased? They are humble; but, alas! how proud also! Their graces are sweet, and their gifts helpful; but are not their corruptions bitter, and their imperfections hurtful? And art thou so loth to go from them to thy God?

24. 'O my soul, look above this world of sorrows! Hast thou so long felt the smarting rod of affliction, and no better understood its meaning? Is not every stroke to drive thee hence? Is not its voice like that to Elijah, "What dost thou here?" Dost thou forget thy Lord's prediction, "In the world ye shall have tribulation; in me ye may have peace?" Ah, my dear Lord, I feel thy meaning; it is written in my flesh, engraved in my bones. My heart thou aimest at; thy rod drives, thy silken cord of love draws; and all to bring it to thyself. Lord, can such a heart be worth thy having; make it worthy, and then it is thine: take it to thyself, and then take me. This clod hath life to stir, but not to rise. As the feeble child to the tender mother, it looketh up to thee, and stretcheth out the hands, and fain would have thee take it up. Though I cannot say, "my soul longeth after thee;" yet I can say, I long for such a longing heart. "The spirit is willing, the flesh is weak." My spirit cries, "let thy kingdom come," or let me come to thy kingdom; but the flesh is afraid thou shouldst hear my prayer, and take me at my word. O blessed be thy grace, which makes use of my corruptions to kill themselves; for I fear my fears, and sorrow for my sorrows, and long for greater longs; and thus the painful means of attaining my desires increase my weariness, and that makes me groan to be at rest.

25. 'Indeed, Lord, my soul itself is in a strait, and what to choose I know not; but thou knowest what to give. "To depart and to be with thee, is far better;" but "to abide in the flesh seems needful." Thou knowest I am not weary of thy work, but of sorrow and sin: I am willing to stay while thou wilt employ me, and despatch the work thou hast put into my hands; but, I beseech thee, stay no longer when this is done; and while I must be here, let me be still amending and ascending; make me still better, and take me at the best. I dare not be so impatient, as to importune thee to cut off my time, and snatch me hence unready; because

I know my everlasting state so much depends on the improvement of this life. Nor would I stay when my work is done; and remain here sinning, while my brethren are triumphing. Thy footsteps bruise this worm, while those stars shine in the firmament of glory. Yet I am thy child as well as they; Christ is my Head as well as theirs: why is there then so great a distance! But I acknowledge the equity of thy ways: though we are all children, yet I am the prodigal, and therefore more fit in this remote country to feed on husks, while they are always with thee, and possess thy glory. They were once themselves in my condition, and I will shortly be in theirs. They were of the lowest form, before they came to the highest; they suffered, before they reigned; they came out of great tribulation, who are now before thy throne; and shall not I be content to come to the crown as they did; and to drink of their cup, before I sit with them in the kingdom? Lord, I am content to stay thy time, and go thy way, so thou wilt exalt me also in thy season, and take me into thy barn, when thou seest me ripe. In the mean time I may desire, though I am not to repine; I may believe and wish, though not make any sinful haste; I am willing to wait for thee, but not to loose thee; and when thou seest me too contented with thine absence, then quicken my languid desires, and blow up the dying spark of love; and leave me not till I am able unfeignedly to cry out, "As the hart panteth after the water-brooks, so panteth my soul after thee, O God. My soul thirsteth for God, for the living God; when shall I come and appear before God? My conversation is in heaven, from whence I look for a Saviour. My affections are set on things above, where Christ sitteth, and my life is hid. I walk by faith, and not by sight; willing rather to be absent from the body, and present with the Lord."

26. 'What interest hath this empty world in me; and what is there in it that may seem so lovely as to entice my desires from my God, or make me loth to come away? Methinks, when I look upon it with a deliberate eye, it is a howling wilderness, and too many of its inhabitants are untamed monsters. I can view all its beauty as deformity; and drown all its pleasures in a few penitent tears; or the wind of a sigh will scatter them away. O let not this flesh so seduce my soul, as to make me prefer this weary life before the joys that are about thy throne! And though death itself be unwelcome to nature, yet let thy grace make thy glory appear to me so desirable, that the king of terrors may be the messenger of my joy. Let not my soul be ejected by violence, and dispossessed of its habitation against its will; but draw it to thyself by the secret power of thy love, as the sunshine in the spring draws forth the creatures from their winter cells; meet it half way, and entice it to thee, as the loadstone doth the iron, and as the greater flame attracts the less! Dispel, therefore, the clouds that hide thy love from me; or remove the scales that hinder mine eyes from beholding thee; for the beams that stream from thy face, and the foretastes of thy great salvation, and nothing else can make a soul unfeignedly say, "Now let thy servant depart in peace!" But it is not thy ordinary discoveries that will here suffice: as the work is greater, so must thy help be. O turn these fears into strong desires, and this lothness to die into longings after thee! While I must be absent from thee, let my soul as heartily groan, as my body doth under its want of health! If I have any more time to spend on earth, let me live as without the world in thee, as I have sometimes lived as without thee in the world. While I have a thought to think, let me not forget thee; or a tongue to move, let me mention thee with delight; or a breath to breathe, let it be after thee, and for thee; or a knee to bend, let it daily bow at thy footstool; and when by sickness thou confinest me, do thou "make my bed, number my pains, and put all my tears into thy bottle!"

27. 'As my flesh desired what my spirit abhorred, so now let my spirit desire that day which my flesh abhorreth; that my friends may not with so much sorrow wait for the departure of my soul, as my soul with joy shall wait for its own departure! Then "let me die the death of the righteous, and let my last end be like his;" even a removal to that glory which shall never end! Then let thy convoy of angels bring my departing soul among the perfected spirits of the just, and let me follow my dear friends that have died in Christ before me; and while my sorrowing friends are weeping over my grave, let my spirit be reposed with thee in rest: and while my corpse shall lie rotting in the dark, let my soul be in 'the inheritance of the saints in light." O thou that numberest the very hairs of my head, number all the days that my body lies in the dust; and thou that "writest all my members in thy book," keep an account of my scattered bones! O my Saviour, hasten the time of thy return: send forth thy angels, and let that dreadful, joyful trumpet sound! Delay not, lest the living give up their hopes;

delay not, lest earth should grow like hell, and thy church, by division, be all crumbled to dust; delay not, lest thy enemies get advantage of thy flock, and lest pride, hypocrisy, sensuality, and unbelief prevail against thy little remnant, and share among them thy whole inheritance, and when thou comest thou find not faith on the earth; delay not, lest the grave should boast of victory, and having learned rebellion of its guest, should refuse to deliver thee up thy due! O hasten that great resurrection-day, when thy command shall go forth, and none shall disobey; when "the sea and the earth shall yield up their hostages, and all that sleep in the grave shall awake, and the dead in Christ shall rise first;" when the seed which thou sowest corruptible, shall come forth incorruptible; and graves that received rottenness and dust, shall return thee glorious stars and suns! Therefore dare I lay down my carcass in the dust, intrusting it, not to a grave, but to thee; and therefore my flesh shall rest in hope, till thou shalt raise it to the possession of everlasting rest. "Return, O Lord; how long? O let thy kingdom come!" Thy desolate bride saith, Come! for thy Spirit within her saith, Come; and teacheth her thus to "pray with groanings which cannot be uttered;" yea, the whole creation saith, Come, waiting to be delivered from the bondage of corruption into the glorious liberty of the children of God. Thou thyself hast said, "Surely I come quickly." Amen. Even so, come, Lord Jesus!'

CONCLUSION.

28. Thus, Reader, I have given thee my best advice for maintaining a heavenly conversation. If thou canst not thus meditate methodically and fully, yet do it as thou canst; only be sure to do it seriously and frequently. Be acquainted with this heavenly work, and thou wilt, in some degree, be acquainted with God; thy joys will be spiritual, prevalent, and lasting, according to the nature of their blessed object; thou wilt have comfort in life and death. When thou hast neither wealth, nor health, nor the pleasures of this world, yet wilt thou have comfort. Without the presence, or help of any friend, without a minister, without a book, when all means are denied thee, or taken from thee, yet mayest thou have vigorous, real comfort. Thy graces will be mighty, active, and victorious; and the daily joy, which is thus fetched from heaven, will be thy strength. Thou wilt be as one that stands on the top of an exceeding high mountain; he looks down on the world as if it were quite below him; fields and woods, cities and towns, seem to him but little spots. Thus despicably wilt thou look on all things here below. The greatest princes will seem but as grasshoppers; the busy, contentious, covetous world, but as a heap of ants. Men's threatenings will be no terror to thee; nor the honours of this world any strong enticement; temptations will be more harmless, as having lost their strength; and afflictions less grievous, as having lost their sting; and every mercy will be better known and relished. It is now, under God, in thy own choice, whether thou wilt live this blessed life or not; and whether all this pains I have taken for thee shall prosper or be lost. If it be lost through thy laziness, thou thyself wilt prove the greatest loser. O man! what hast thou to mind but God and heaven? Art thou not almost out of this world already? Dost thou not look every day, when one disease or other will let out thy soul? Does not the grave wait to be thine house; and worms to feed upon thy face and heart? What if thy pulse must beat a few strokes more? What if thou hast a little longer to breathe, before thou breathest out thy last; a few more nights to sleep, before thou sleepest in the dust? Alas! what will this be, when it is gone? And is it not almost gone already? Very shortly thou wilt see thy glass run out, and say to thyself, 'My life is done! My time is gone! It is past recalling! There is nothing now but heaven or hell before me!' Where then should thy heart be now, but in heaven? Didst thou know what a dreadful thing it is, to have a doubt of heaven when a man is dying, it would rouse thee up. And what else but doubt can that man then do that never seriously thought of heaven before?

29. Some there be that say, 'It is not worth so much time and trouble, to think of the greatness of the joys above; so that we can make sure they are ours, we know they are great.' But as these men obey not the command of God, which requires them to have their 'conversation in heaven, and to set their affections on things above;' so they wilfully make their own lives miserable, by refusing the delights which God hath set before them. And if this were all, it were a small matter; but see what abundance of other mischiefs follow the neglect of these heavenly delights. This neglect will damp, if not destroy their love to God,—will make it unpleasant to them to think or speak of God, or engage in his service,—it tends to pervert their judgments concerning the ways and ordinances of God,—it makes them sensual and

voluptuous,—it leaves them under the power of every affliction and temptation, and is a preparative to total apostacy,—it will also make them fearful and unwilling to die. For who would go to a God or a place he hath no delight in? Who would leave his pleasure here, if he had not better to go to? Had I only proposed a course of melancholy, and fear, and sorrow, you might reasonably have objected. But you must have heavenly delights, or none that are lasting. God is willing you should daily walk with him, and fetch in consolations from the everlasting fountain: if you are unwilling, even bear the loss; and, when you are dying, seek for comfort where you can get it, and see whether fleshly delights will remain with you; then conscience will remember, in spite of you, that you was once persuaded to a way for more excellent pleasures,—pleasures that would have followed you through death, and have lasted to eternity

30. As for you, whose hearts God hath weaned from all things here below, I hope you will value this heavenly life, and take one walk every day in the New Jerusalem. God is your love and your desire; you would fain be more acquainted with your Saviour; and I know it is your grief, that your hearts are not nearer to him, and that they do not more feelingly love him, and delight in him. O try this life of meditation on your heavenly rest! Here is the mount, on which the fluctuating ark of your souls may rest. Let the world see, by your heavenly lives, that religion is something more than opinions and disputes, or a talk of outward duties. If ever a Christian is like himself, and answerable to his principles and profession, it is when he is most serious and lively in this duty. As Moses, before he died, went up into mount Nebo, to take a survey of the land of Canaan; so the Christian ascends the mount of contemplation, and by faith surveys his rest. He looks upon the glorious mansions, and says 'Glorious things are' deservedly 'spoken of thee, thou city of God!' He hears, as it were, the melody of the heavenly choir, and says, 'Happy is the people that are in such a case; yea, happy is that people, whose God is the Lord!' He looks upon the glorified inhabitants, and says, 'Happy art thou, O Israel; who is like unto thee, O people, saved by the Lord, the shield of thy help, and who is the sword of thine excellency!' When he looks upon the Lord himself, who is their glory, he is ready, with the rest, to 'fall down and worship him that liveth for ever and ever and say,

Holy, holy, holy, Lord God Almighty, who was, and is, and is to come! Thou art worthy, O Lord, to receive glory and honour, and power!' When he looks on the glorified Saviour, he is ready to say, Amen, to that new song, 'Blessing, and honour, and glory, and power, be unto him that sitteth upon the throne, and unto the Lamb, for ever and ever. For thou wast slain, and hast redeemed us to God by thy blood, out of every kindred, and tongue, and people, and nation; and hast made us, unto our God, kings and priests!' When he looks back on the wilderness of this world, he blesses the believing, patient, despised saints; he pities the ignorant, obstinate, miserable world; and for himself, he says, as Peter, 'It is good to be here; or as Asaph, 'It is good for me to draw near to God; for lo, they that are far from thee shall perish.' Thus, as Daniel, in his captivity, daily opened his window towards Jerusalem, though far out of sight, when he went to God in his devotions; so may the believing soul, in this captivity of the flesh, look towards 'Jerusalem, which is above.' And as Paul was to the Colossians, so may the believer be with the glorified spirits, though absent in the flesh, yet with them in the spirit, joying and beholding their heavenly order. And as the lark sweetly sings while she soars on high, but is suddenly silenced when she falls to the earth; so is the frame of the soul most delightful and divine, while it keeps in the views of God by contemplation. Alas! we make there too short a stay; fall down again, and lay by our music!

31. But, 'O thou, the merciful Father of spirits, the attractive of love, and ocean of delights, draw up these drossy hearts unto thyself, and keep them there till they are spiritualized and refined; and second thy servant's weak endeavours, and persuade those that read these lines to the practice of this delightful, heavenly work! O suffer not the soul of thy most unworthy servant to be a stranger to those joys which he describes to others; but keep me, while I remain on earth, in daily breathings after thee, and in a believing, affectionate walking with thee! And when thou comest, let me be found so doing; not serving my flesh, nor asleep with my lamp unfurnished; but waiting and longing for my Lord's return! Let those who shall read these heavenly directions. nor merely read the fruit of my studies, but the breathing of my active hope and love: that, if my heart were open to their view, they might there read the same most deeply

engraven with a beam from the face of the Son of God; and not find vanity, or lust, or pride within, when the words of life appear without; that so these lines may not witness against me; but, proceeding from the heart of the writer, may be effectual, through thy grace upon the heart of the reader, and so be the savour of life to both! Amen.'

'Glory be to God in the highest; on earth peace; good-will towards men.'

THE EXIT.

From POETICAL FRAGMENTS, *by Richard Baxter, a little volume inestimable for its piety.*

MY soul, go boldly forth,
Forsake this sinful earth;
What hath it been to thee
   But pain and sorrow;
And think'st thou it will be
   Better to-morrow?

Why art thou for delay?
Thou cam'st not here to stay:
What tak'st thou for thy part
   But heavenly pleasure;
Where then should be thy heart
   But where's thy treasure?

Thy God, thy head's above;
There is the world of love,
Mansions there purchased are,
   By Christ's own merit,
For these He doth prepare
   Thee by his Spirit.

Jerusalem above,
Glorious in light and love,
Is mother of us all;
   Who shall enjoy them?
The wicked hell-ward fall;
   Sin will destroy them.

O blessed company,
Where all in harmony
Jehovah's praises sing,
   Still without ceasing;
And all obey their King
   With perfect pleasing.

What joy must there needs be,
Where all God's glory see;
Feeling God's vital love,
   Which still is burning;
And flaming Godward move,
   Full love returning.

Hath mercy made life sweet:
And is it kind and meet
Thus to draw back from God
   Who doth protect thee?
Look then for his sharp rod
   Next to correct thee.

Lord Jesus, take my spirit:
I trust thy love and merit:
Take home this wandering sheep,
   For thou hast sought it:
This soul in safety keep,
   For thou hast bought it.

THE DIVINE LIFE,

IN

THREE TREATISES.

FIRST.

THE KNOWLEDGE OF GOD, AND THE IMPRESSION WHICH IT MUST MAKE UPON THE HEART, AND ITS NECESSARY EFFECTS UPON OUR LIVES.

SECOND.

THE DESCRIPTION, REASONS, AND REWARD OF THE BELIEVER'S WALKING WITH GOD.

THIRD.

THE CHRISTIAN'S CONVERSE WITH GOD; OR THE INSUFFICIENCY AND UNCERTAINTY OF HUMAN FRIENDSHIP, AND THE IMPROVEMENT OF SOLITUDE IN CONVERSE WITH GOD; WITH SOME OF THE AUTHOR'S BREATHINGS AFTER HIM.

PREFATORY REMARKS.

THE work on the DIVINE LIFE was first published in 1664. The occasion of it, Baxter informs us, was this: "The Countess of Balcarras, before going into Scotland after her abode in England, being deeply sensible of the loss of the company of those friends which she left behind her, desired me to preach the last sermon which she was to hear from me, on these words of Christ: 'Behold the hour cometh, yea, is now come, that ye shall be scattered every man to his own, and shall leave me alone; and yet I am not alone, because the Father is with me.' At her request I preached on this text, and being afterwards desired by her to give it her in writing, and the publication being her design, I prefixed the two other treatises, to make it more considerable, and published them together. The treatise is upon the most excellent subject, but not elaborate at all; being but popular sermons preached in the midst of diverting businesses, accusations, and malicious clamours.

"When I offered it to the press, I was fain to leave out the quantity of one sermon in the end of the second treatise (that God took Enoch), wherein I showed what a mercy it is to one that walked with God to be taken to him from this world; because it is a dark, wicked, malicious, implacable, treacherous, deceitful world, &c. All which the bishop's chaplain must have expunged, because men would think it was all spoken of them. And so the world hath got a protection against the force of our baptismal vow."

This admirable treatise may be placed either under the head of the experimental or the devotional works of our author. It is divided into three parts—The Knowledge of God; Walking with God; and Converse with God in solitude. This division obviously embraces all the great points of Christian practice and experience. Without the knowledge of God, man can have no objective religion. He is the glorious object of love, veneration, and hope; the source of all pure and spiritual enjoyment; and the spring of all right conduct. He who knows God aright will, at the same time, walk with God, or in the course of obedience to him; and with this course will be invariably connected that spiritual fellowship with him which is at once the enjoyment of religion, and the best proof of its reality.

None of the works of Baxter is written with greater sweetness than this. The manner of it is in good keeping with the subject; soft, tender, and full of spirituality. He lays open to the reader, as it were, the very recesses of his own heart; and describes his own character and procedure in delineating the essential features of the Christian character and profession. In himself were combined, in an extraordinary degree, the contemplative and the active in religion. In the former he delighted no less than in the latter. To him the gospel of Christ was a continual feast. It presented to him a boundless and exhaustless subject; combining all that was holy, excellent, and sublime; all that was most worthy in itself, with everything calculated to inspire the love of goodness, and promote the most joyful compliance with the divine will. In meditation he found relief from the severity of bodily pain, from the anguish of disappointment, and the sorrow of unmerited suffering; from the pains and griefs occasioned by his own sins, or the sins of others. While all around was darkness and tempest, here he found repose to his spirit, and a quiet refuge. When languid, it recruited his strength; when discouraged, it reinvigorated his hope; when exposed to perils, or called to the discharge of arduous duties, it gave fresh energy and animation to his soul. God as revealed in the economy of redemption, was the grand centre of all the principles, feelings, and exercises of Baxter. It was to him at once an attractive as well as a repelling power; drawing him to holiness and happiness, and repelling everything that was mean and unworthy from his character, as well as what was more directly evil.

To the extraordinary degree in which the mind of Baxter was imbued with the spiritual knowledge of God, arising from the intimacy of his communion with him, arose no small portion of that energy of character for which he was so distinguished. The proper value of the contemplative life in him was thus strikingly illustrated. In many men contemplation operates as a principle of seclusion: it renders society disagreeable; the bustle and business of it intolerable. They can be happy only in retirement, and in abstraction from the duties of social obligation. Such persons become a kind of spiritual epicures: who can enjoy only what is exquisite, and adapted to the most delicate palate. The common food of Christianity is unsuited to them. Their religion assumes all the character of a refined, spiritual selfism; concerned only about one thing, and that thing comfort: it partakes not of the active principles or sympathies of apostolic Christianity.

In others, activity is too much separated from meditation. The leaves and the fruit are cultivated without due attention to the root of the tree. Enjoyment is found only or chiefly in the crowd, or on the stage of public life. Effect is studied rather than principle; and all is supposed to be well if others are but persuaded that it is so. There is little that is permanent and influential in this class of persons. What is thus produced is easily blasted and overthrown. There is a want of sufficient breadth and depth in the foundation, for the superstructure which they endeavour to rear, and hence it often tumbles into ruin. Professed concern for the good of others, when connected with indifference to our own, cannot be sincere in its nature or lasting in its duration. Baxter is a happy illustration of the two great constituent principles of the Christian character now adverted to, and which constitute the subject of the work under consideration.

The chief fault, says Mr. Orme, that presents itself to me in this work is, the extent to which he dwells on the natural attributes of God, such as his eternity, simplicity, omnipotence, &c., as comprehended in that knowledge which is eternal life. Not that I would exclude these things; but he has dwelt upon them in undue proportion, and to the exclusion of more extended views of the moral attributes of God, which constitute the grand subject of revelation, and the great objects of Christian faith and enjoyment. In the natural perfections of God, however, Baxter was furnished with delightful subjects for the exercise of his metaphysical powers. The uses of God's "simple and uncompounded essence of his incorporeality and invisibility," were quite to his taste; though likely to be regarded by the reader as more ingenious than profitable. He has also some disquisitions about sin, as whether "God decrees not, or wills not, *ut evenit peccatum;* and whether he wills *de eventu,* that sin shall not come to pass when it doth?" in which little light is thrown on these mysterious questions.

These, however, are but trifling blemishes in this valuable work, which abounds with passages of great beauty, illustrative not only of the fine genius, but the intense ardour of Baxter's spirit and feelings.

THE DIVINE LIFE.

PART I.

OF THE KNOWLEDGE OF GOD.

" And this is life eternal, that they might know thee, the only true God, and Jesus Christ whom thou hast sent."—JOHN xvii. 3.

INTRODUCTORY REMARKS.

GOD is the principal efficient, the supreme directive, and the ultimate final cause of man : for of him, and through him, and to him, are all things, and to him shall be glory for ever. The new life or nature in the saints, is his image. The principle of it is called the divine nature. The exercise of that principle, including the principle itself, is called the life of God, from which the Gentiles are said to be alienated by their ignorance. Therefore it is called holiness, which is a separation to God from common use : and ' God's dwelling in us,' and ' ours in him,' of whom we are said to be ' born and regenerated,' and our perfection in glory, is our living with God, and enjoying him for ever. Godliness then is the comprehensive name of all true religion. Jesus Christ himself came but to restore corrupted man to the love, obedience, and fruition of his Creator, and at last will give up the kingdom to his Father, that God may be all and in all : and the Son himself shall be subject to this end. The end of Christ's sacrifice and intercession is to reconcile God and man : the end of his doctrine is to teach us to know God : the end of his government is to reduce us to the perfect obedience of our Maker. It is therefore the greatest duty of a Christian to know God as revealed by his Son ; and it is such a duty about our ultimate end as is also our greatest mercy and felicity. Therefore doth the Lord Jesus here in the text describe that life eternal which he was to give to those whom the Father had given him, to consist in ' knowing the only true God, and Jesus Christ whom he had sent.' My purpose is in this treatise to speak only of the first part of the text, ' the knowledge of God,' and first I shall very briefly explain the text.

' This,' that is, this which I am describing.

' Life ;' life is taken sometimes for the soul's abode in the body, which is the natural life of man ; or the soul's continuation in its separated state, which is the natural life of the soul : and sometimes for the perfections of natural life : and that either its natural perfection, that is, it health and vivacity ; or its moral perfection or rectitude ; and that is either in the cause, and so God is our life, Christ is our life, the Holy Spirit is our life : or in itself, and so holiness is our life in the principle, seed or habit. Sometimes life is taken for the work, employment and exercise of life ; and so a holy conversation is our moral, spiritual, or holy life. Sometimes it is taken for the felicity of the living : and so it contains all the former in their highest perfection, that is, both natural life and moral, spiritual life, and the holy exercise thereof, together with the full attainment and fruition of God in glory, the end of all.

'Eternal,' that is, simply eternal, objectively, as to God the principal object : and eternal, subjectively, that is, everlasting.

' This is life eternal,' not natural life in itself considered, as the devils and wicked men shall have it ; but, 1. It is the same moral, spiritual life, which shall have no end, but to endure to eternity : it is a living to God in love ; but only initial, and very imperfect here, in comparison of what it will be in heaven. 2. It is the eternal felicity, 1. Seminally; for grace is as it were the seed of glory; 2. As it is the necessary way or means of attaining it; and that preparation which infallibly procures it. The perfect holiness of the saints in heaven, will be one part of their perfect happiness: and this holiness imperfect they have here in this life. It is the same God that we know and love, here and there; and with a knowledge and love that is of the same nature seminally. This imperfect holiness hath the promise of perfect holiness and happiness in the full fruition of God hereafter. So it is the seed and prognostic of life eternal.

'To know.' Not to know God here and hereafter in the same manner or degree; but to know him here as in a glass, and hereafter in his glory, as face to face. To know him by an affective practical knowledge: there is no text of scripture of which the rule is more clearly true and necessary than of this, that words of knowledge imply affection. It is the closure of the whole soul with God, which is here called the knowing of God, because it is not meet to name every particular act of the soul; when ever this duty is mentioned, it is all denominated from knowledge, as the first act, which infers all the rest. 1. Knowledge of God in the habit is spiritual life, as a principle. 2. Knowledge of God in the exercise, is spiritual life, as an employment. 3. The knowledge of God in perfection, with its effects, is life eternal, as it signifies full felicity. What it contains I shall further show anon.

'Thee.' That is, the Father, called by some divines the fountain, or foundation of the trinity: and often used in the same sense as the word 'God,' to signify the pure deity.

'The only.' He that believes that there is more gods than one, believes not in any. For though he may give many the name, yet the description of the true God can agree to none of them. He is not God indeed, if he be not one only.

This doth not at all exclude Jesus Christ, as the second person in trinity: but only distinguishes the pure deity, or the only true God, as such, from Jesus Christ, as mediator between God and man.

'True.' There are many that falsely and metaphorically are called gods: if we think of God but as one of these, it is not to know him, but deny him.

'God.' The word God doth not only signify the divine perfections in himself, but also his

relation to the creatures. To be a God to us, is to be one to whom we must ascribe all that we are or have; and one whom we must love, obey, and honour, with all the powers of soul and body: and one on whom we totally depend, and from whom we expect our judgment and reward, in whom alone we can be perfectly blessed.

'And Jesus Christ.' That is, as mediator, in his natures, (God and man) and in his office and grace.

'Whom thou hast sent.' That is, whom thy love and wisdom designed and commissioned to this undertaking and performance.

The knowledge of the Holy Ghost seems here left out, as if it were no part of life eternal: but 1. At that time the Holy Ghost in that eminent sort, as sent by the Father and Son on the apostles, after the resurrection and the ascension of Christ, was not yet so manifested as afterwards, and therefore not so necessarily to be distinctly known and believed in as after: the having of the Spirit being of more necessity than the distinct knowledge of him. Certain it is that the disciples were at first very dark in this article of faith: and scripture more fully reveals the necessity to salvation of believing in the Father and Son, than in the Holy Ghost distinctly; yet telling us, that 'if any man have not the Spirit of Christ, the same is none of his.' 2. But presently after, when the Spirit was to be sent, the necessity of believing in him is expressed; especially in the apostles' commission to baptize all nations, that were made disciples, in the name of the Father, Son, and Holy Ghost.

CHAP. I

The knowledge of the only true God, and of Jesus Christ the mediator, is the life of grace, and the necessary way to the life of glory.

As James distinguishes between such a dead faith as devils and wicked men had, and such a living and working faith as was proper to the justified; so must we here of the knowledge of God. Many 'profess that they know God, but in works they deny him, being abominable and disobedient, and to every good work reprobate.' There is a 'form of knowledge,' which the unbelievers had, and a 'knowledge which puffeth up,' and is void of love, which hypocrites have. But no man, spiritually, knows the things of God, but by the Spirit; and they that rightly 'know his name will put their trust in him.' Thus he gives the regenerated a 'heart to know him,' and the new creature 'is renewed in knowledge.' Vengeance shall be 'poured out on them that know not God.'

This saving knowledge of God, which is eternal life, contains and implies in it all these acts. 1. The understanding's apprehension of God according to the necessary articles of faith. 2. A belief of the truth of these articles : that God is, and is such as he is therein described. 3. A high estimation of God accordingly. 4. A volition, complacency, or love to him as God, the chief good. 5. A desiring after him. 6. A choosing him, with the rejection of all competitors. 7. A consent that he be our God, and a giving up ourselves to him as his people. 8. An intending him as our ultimate end in the use of means, in the course of our conversations. 9. A seeking him in the choice and use of means. 10. An obeying him as our sovereign governor. 11. An honouring and praising him as God. 12. And an enjoying him and delighting in him, in some small foretaste here, as he is seen by faith ; but perfectly hereafter, as beheld in glory. The effective practical knowing of God, which is life eternal, contains or implies all these parts.

Every Christian that hath any of this knowledge, desires more : it is his great desire to know more of God, and to know him with a more affecting, powerful knowledge. He that grows in grace, accordingly grows in this knowledge of God and of Jesus Christ. The vigour and alacrity of our souls live in it : the rectitude of our actions, and the holiness of them, flow from it : God is the excellency of our hearts and lives : our advancement and our joy are here only to be found. All other knowledge is so far desirable, as it conduces to the knowledge of God, or to the several duties which that knowledge requires. All knowledge of words or things, of causes and effects, of any creatures, actions, customs, laws, or whatsoever may be known, is so far valuable as it is useful ; and so far useful as it is holy, subserving the knowledge of God in Christ. What the sun is to all men's eyes, that God is to their souls, and more : it is to know him, that we have understandings given us : and our understandings enjoy him but so far as they know him ; as the eye enjoys the light of the sun, by seeing it. The ignorance of God is the blindness and part of the atheism of the soul, and infers the rest. They that know him not, desire not heartily to know him ; nor can they love him, trust him, fear him, serve him, or call upon him, whom they do not know. 'How shall they call upon him in whom they have not believed ?' The heart of the ungodly saith to God, 'depart from us ; for we desire not the knowledge of thy ways : what is the almighty, that we should serve

him ? And what profit shall we have if we pray unto him ?' All wickedness hath admission into that heart or land, where the knowledge of God is not the watch to keep it out : Abraham inferred that the men of Gerar would kill him for his wife, when he saw that 'the fear of God was not in that place.' It was 'God's controversy with Israel, because there was no truth, nor mercy, nor knowledge of God in the land ; but by swearing, lying, killing, and stealing, they brake out, and blood touched blood. They are called by God 'a foolish people, sottish children, of no understanding, that knew not God; though they were wise to do evil.' He will 'pour out his fury upon the heathen that know him not, and the families that call not on his name.' As the day differs from the night, by the light of the sun, so the church differs from the world, by the knowledge of God in Jesus Christ. 'In Judah is God known; his name is great in Israel: in Salem also is his tabernacle, and his dwelling place in Zion.' The love, unity and peace which shall succeed persecution and malice in the blessed times, shall be 'because the earth shall be full of the knowledge of the Lord, as the waters cover the sea.' Hypocrites shall know him superficially and ineffectually : and his holy ones shall know him so as to love him, fear him, trust him, and obey him ; with a knowledge effectual upon heart and life : and he will continue his loving kindness to them that know him.

He is the best Christian that hath the fullest impression made upon his soul, by the knowledge of God in all his attributes. Thus it is our life eternal to know God in Christ. It is to reveal the Father that the Son was sent ; and it is to reveal the Father and the Son, that the Holy Spirit is sent ; God is the light, the life, and felicity of the soul. The work of its salvation is but the restoring it to him, and putting it in possession of him. The beginning of this is regeneration and reconciliation ; the perfection of it is glorification, beatific vision, and fruition. The mind that hath least of God, is the darkest and most deluded mind : and the mind that hath most of him, is the most lucid, pure, and serene. How is God in the mind, but as the light and other visible objects are in the eye, as pleasant melody is in the ear, and as delightful meats and drinks are in the taste, but that God makes a more deep and durable impress on the soul, and such as is suitable to its spiritual, immaterial nature.

As your seal is to make a full impression on the wax of the whole figure that is upon itself, so hath God been pleased, in divers seals, to engrave his image, and these must make their impress upon us. 1. There is the seal of the creation: for the world hath much of the image of God: it is engraven also on the seal of providential disposals (though there we are incapable of reading it yet, so fully as in the rest). 2. It is engraven on the seal of the holy scriptures. 3. And on the person of Jesus Christ, who is the purest, clearest image of the Father, as also on the holy example of his life. 4. By the means of all these applied to the soul, in our sober consideration, by the working of the Holy Ghost, the image of God is made upon us.

Here note, 1. That all the revealed image of God must be made on the soul, and not a part only: and all is wrought where any is truly wrought. 2. That to the completeness of his image on us, it is necessary that each part of God's description be orderly made, and orderly make the impress on us, and that each part keep its proper place: for it is a monster that hath feet where the head should be, or the backside forward, or where there is any gross misplacing of the parts. 3. Note also, that all the three forementioned seals contain all God's image on them; but yet not all alike; but the first part is more clearly engraven upon the first of them, the second part upon the second of them, and the third part most clearly on the third and last.

To open this more plainly to you; unity in trinity, and trinity in unity, is the sum of our holy faith. In the deity there is revealed to us one God in three persons, the Father, Son, and Holy Ghost; the essence is but one; the subsistences are three. As we must conceive and speak of the divine nature according to its image, while we see it but in a glass; so we must say, that in this blessed deity in the unity of essence, there is a trinity of essential properties and attributes, that is, power, wisdom and goodness, life, light and love; the measure of which is to have no measure, but to be infinite. Therefore this being is eternal, and not measured by time, being without beginning or end: he is immense, as being not measured by place, but contains all places, and is contained in none. He is perfect, as not measured by parts or by degrees, but quite above degrees and parts. This infiniteness of his being communicates itself, or consists, in the infiniteness of his essential properties. His power is omnipotence, that is, infinite power; his knowledge or wisdom is omniscience, that is, infinite wisdom: his goodness is felicity itself, or infinite goodness.

The first seal on which he engraved this his image, was the creation. that is. 1. The whole world in general. 2. The intellectual nature, or man in special.

In the being of the creation and every particular creature, his infinite being is revealed; so wretched a fool is the atheist, that by denying God, he denies all things! Could he prove that there is no God, I would quickly prove that there is no world, no man, no creature: if he know that he is himself, or that the world or any creature is, he may know that God is: for God is the original being: and all being that is not eternal, must have some original: and that which hath no original is God, being eternal, infinite, and without cause.

The power of God is revealed in the being and powers of the creation. His wisdom is revealed in their nature, order, offices, effects, &c.; his goodness, in the creature's goodness, its beauty, usefulness, and accomplishments. But though all his image thus appear upon the creation, yet is it his omnipotence that principally there appears. The beholding and considering of the wonderful greatness, activity and excellence of the sun, the moon, the stars, the fire. and other creatures, doth first and chiefly possess us with apprehensions of the infinite greatness or power of the Creator.

In the holy word or laws of God, which is the second glass, or seal (more clear and legible to us than the former) there appears also all his image, his power in the narratives, predictions, &c. his wisdom in the prophecies, precepts, and in all: his goodness in the promises and institutions in a special manner. But yet it is his second property, his wisdom, that most eminently appears on this second seal, and is seen in the glass of the holy law. The discovery of such mysteries; the revelation of so many truths; the suitableness of all the instituted means; and the admirable fitness of all the holy contrivances of God, and all his precepts, promises and threatenings, for the government of mankind, and carrying him on for the attainment of his end, in a way agreeable to his nature; these show that wisdom that is most eminently here revealed, though power and goodness be revealed with it; so in the face of Jesus Christ, who is the third and most perfect seal and glass, there is the image of the power, wisdom and goodness of the Godhead: but yet it is the love or goodness of the Father that is most eminently revealed in the Son: his power appeared in the incarnation, the conquests over Satan and the world, the miracles, the resurrection and the ascension of Christ. His wisdom appears in the admirable mystery of redemption, and in all the parts of the office, works, and laws of Christ, and in the means appointed in subordination to him; but love and goodness shine most clearly and amiably through the whole; it being the very end of Christ in this blessed work, to reveal God to man in the riches of his love, as giving us the greatest mercies, by the most precious means, in the meetest season and manner for our good; reconciling us to himself, and treating us as children, with fatherly compassions, bringing us nearer him, and opening to us the everlasting treasure, having brought life and immortality to light in the gospel.

God being thus revealed to man from without, in the three glasses or seals of the Creation, Law, and Son himself, he is also revealed to us in ourselves, man being, as it were, a little world.

In the nature of man is revealed as in a seal or glass, the nature of the blessed God, in some measure. In unity of essence, we have a trinity of faculties of soul, even the vegetative, sensitive and rational, as our bodies have both parts and spirits, natural, vital and animal; the rational power in unity, hath also its trinity of faculties, even power for execution, understanding for direction, and will for command: the measure of power is naturally sufficient to its use and end; the understanding is a faculty to reason, discern, and discourse: the will hath that freedom which beseems an undetermined, self-determining creature here in the way.

Besides this physical image of God that is inseparable from our nature, we have also his law written in our hearts, and are ourselves objectively part of the law of nature; that is, the signifiers of the will of God. Had we not by sin obliterated somewhat of this image, it would have showed itself more clearly, and we should have been more capable of understanding it.

And when we are regenerated and renewed by the grace and Spirit of Christ, and planted into him, as living members of his body, we have then the third impression upon our souls, and are made like our Head in wisdom, holiness, and in effectual strength.

Considered as creatures endued with power, understanding and will, we have the impress of all the foresaid attributes of God: but eminently of his power

Considered as we were at first possessed with the light and law of works or nature, (of which we yet retain some part) so we have the impress of all these attributes of God; but most eminently of his wisdom.

Considered as regenerated by the Spirit, and planted into Christ, so we have the impress of all his said attributes; but most eminently of his love and goodness, shining in the moral accomplishments or graces of the soul.

Man being thus made at first the natural image of God, (with much of the image of his love) the Lord did presently, by necessary result and voluntary consent, stand related to us in such variety of relations, as answer the foresaid properties and attributes. These relations of God to us, are next to be known as flowing from his attributes and works.

As we have our derived being from God, who is the primitive, eternal being; so from our being given by creation, God is related to us as our maker; from this relation of a creator in unity, there arises a trinity of relations: this trinity is in that unity, and that unity in this trinity.

God having made us of nothing, is necessarily related to us as our Lord; by a Lord, we mean strictly a proprietary or owner, as you are the owner of your goods, or any thing that is your own. He is related to us as our ruler, our governor or king. This arises from our nature, made to be ruled in order to our end, being rational, voluntary agents; and also from the dominion and blessed nature of God, who only hath right to the government of the world, and only is fit and capable of ruling it. He is related also to us as our benefactor or Father; freely and of his bounty giving us all the good that we receive.

His first relation in this trinity, answers his first property in the trinity: he is our almighty Creator, and therefore is our owner, or our Lord.

The second of these relations answers the second property of God. He is most wise, and made an impress of his wisdom on the rational creature, and therefore is our governor.

The third relation answers the third property of God. As he is most good, so he is our benefactor; 'thou art good, and dost good.' Man's nature and disposition is known by his works, though he be a free agent; for 'the tree is known by its fruit;' and so God's nature is known by his works (as far as it is fit for us here to know) though he be a free agent.

In each of these relations, God hath other special attributes, which are denominated from his relations, or his following works.

As he is our Lord or owner, his proper attribute is to be absolute, having so full a title to us, that he may do with us what he chooses.

17

As he is our ruler, his proper attribute is to be our sovereign or supreme; there being none above him, or co-ordinate with him, nor any power of government but what is derived from him.

As he is our benefactor, it is his prerogative to be our chief, or all; the Alpha and Omega; the fountain, or first efficient cause of all that we receive or hope for; and the end or ultimate final cause that can make us happy by fruition, and that we must still intend.

As these are the attributes of God in these his great relations, so in respect to the works of these relations, he hath other subordinate attributes. As he is our owner, it is his work to dispose of us; and his proper attribute to be most free. As he is our ruler, it is his work to govern us; which is first, by making laws for us, and then by teaching and persuading us to keep them, and lastly by executing them, which is by judging, rewarding, and punishing. In respect to all these, his principal attribute is to be just or righteous; in which is comprehended his truth or faithfulness, his holiness, his mercy, and his divine power. As his attributes appear in the assertions of his word, he is true, his veracity being nothing but his power, wisdom, and goodness, expressing themselves in his word or revelations. For he that is able to do what he will, and so wise as to know all things, and so good as to will nothing but what is good, cannot possibly lie; for every lie is either for want of power, or knowledge, or goodness; he that is most able and knowing, need not deceive by lying; and he that is most good, will not do it on any account. As his first properties appear in the word of promise, he is called faithful, which is his truth in making good a word of grace. As he commands holy duties, and condemns sin as the most detestable thing, by a pure, righteous law, so he is called holy; and also as the fountain of this law, and the grace that sanctifies his people. As he fulfils his promises, and rewards and defends men according to his word, so he is called merciful and gracious, as a governor, (where his mercy is considered as limited or ordained by his laws.) As he fulfils his threatenings, he is called angry, wrathful, terrible, dreadful, holy, jealous, &c. But he is just in all.

As these are his attributes as our sovereign ruler; so as our benefactor, his special attribute is to be gracious, or bountiful, or benign; or to be loving, and inclined to do good. These are the attributes of God resulting from his nature as appearing in his image in the creation, laws, and the person of his Son; and resulting from his relations and the works of those relations; even as he is our creator in unity; and our Lord or owner, our ruler and benefactor in trinity.

Were it not my purpose to confine myself to this short discovery of the nature, attributes, and works of God, but to run deeper into the rest of the body of divinity, I should come down to the fall and the work of redemption, and show you in the gospel and all the ordinances, &c. the footsteps of this method of trinity in unity, which I have here begun; but that were to digress.

Besides what is said, we might name to you many attributes of God, that are commonly called negative, and do but distinguish him from the imperfect creature, by setting him infinitely above us in his perfections. Man hath a body; but God is not a body, but a spirit; man is mutable, but God immutable; man is mortal, but God immortal, &c. Now as I have showed you these properties, relations, and attributes of God, so I must next tell you that we also stand in answerable counter-relations to him; and must have the qualities, and do the works that answer those relations.

As God is our almighty Creator, so we are his creatures, impotent and insufficient for ourselves. We owe him therefore all that a creature that hath but our receivings, can owe his Maker. In this relation is contained a trinity of relations. We are his own, as he is our Lord. We are his subjects, as he is our ruler. We are his children, as he is our Father; or his obliged beneficiaries, as he is our benefactor. Now having opened to your observation the image of God, and the extrinsic seals, I have ripened the discourse so far, that I may the more fitly show you how the impression of this image of God is to be made upon the soul of the believer.

Chap. II.

OF THE KNOWLEDGE OF GOD'S BEING.

'He that cometh to God, must believe that God is, and that he is a rewarder of them that diligently seek him.' The first thing to be imprinted on the soul is, that there is a God: that he is a real, most transcendent being. As sure as the sun that shines hath a being, and the earth that bears us hath a being, so sure hath God that made them a being infinitely more excellent than theirs. As sure as the streams come from the fountain, and as sure as earth and stones, and beasts, and men did never make themselves, nor uphold themselves, or continue the course of nature in themselves and others, nor govern the world, so sure is there an infinite, eternal being that doth this. Every atheist who is not mad, must confess that there is an eternal being, that had no beginning or cause; the question is only, which this is? Which ever it is, it is this that is the true God. What now would the atheist have it to be? Certainly it is that Being that hath being itself from none, that is the first cause of all other beings: and if it causes them, it must necessarily be every way more excellent than they, and contain all the good that it hath caused; for none can give that which he hath not to give; nor make that which is better than itself; that being that hath made so glorious a creature as the sun, must needs itself be much more glorious. It could not have put strength and power into the creatures, if it had not itself more strength and power. It could not have put wisdom and goodness into the creature, if it had not more wisdom and goodness than all they. Whatever it is therefore that hath more power, wisdom and goodness than all the world besides, that is it which we call God. That cause that hath communicated to all things else, the being, power, and all perfections which they have, is the God whom we acknowledge and adore. If atheists will ascribe all this to atoms, and think that the motes made the sun; or if others will think that the sun is God, because it participates of so much of his excellency, let them be mad a while, till judgment shall convince them. So clear beyond all question to my soul, is the being of the Godhead, that the devil hath much lost the rest of his subtle temptations, when he hath foolishly and maliciously adjoined this, to draw me to question the being of my God, which is more than to question whether there be a sun in the firmament.

But what is the impress that the being of God must make upon the soul?

I answer, from hence, the holy soul discerns that the beginning and the end of his religion, the substance of his hope, is the being of beings, and not a shadow; and that his faith is not a fancy. The object is as it were the matter of the act. If our faith, hope, love, and fear, be exercised in a delusory work, God is to the atheist but an empty name; he feels no life or being in him; and accordingly he offers him a shadow of devotion, and a nominal service. But to the holy soul there is nothing that hath life and being but God, and that which receives a being from him, and leads to him. This real object puts a reality into all the devotions of a holy soul. They look upon the vanities of the world as nothing; therefore they look on worldly men as on idle dreamers that are doing nothing.

This puts a seriousness and life into the faith and holy affections of the believer. 'He knows whom he trusteth.' He knows whom he loveth, and in whom he hopeth. Atheists, and ungodly men, practically judge of God as the true believer judges of the world. The atheist takes the pleasures of the world to be the only substance; and God to be but as a shadow, a notion, or a dream. The godly take the world to be as nothing, and know it is but a fancy and dream, and shadow of pleasures, honour, profit, and felicity, that men talk of, and seek so eagerly below; but that God is the substantial object and portion of the soul. If you put into the mouth of a hungry man, a little froth, or breath, or air, and bid him eat it, and feed upon it, he will tell you, he finds no substance in it; so judges the graceless soul of God, and so judges the gracious soul of the creature, as separated from God.

Let this be the impression on thy soul, from the consideration of God's transcendent being; O look upon thyself and all things as not being without him; and as nothing in comparison of him! Therefore let thy love to them be as nothing, and thy desires after them, and care for them, as nothing; but let the being of thy love, desire, and endeavours, be let out upon the transcendent being. The creature hath its kind of being; but if it would be to us instead of God, it will be as nothing. The air hath its being, but we cannot dwell in it, nor rest upon it to support us as the earth doth. The water hath its being, but it will not bear us, if we would walk upon it. The name of the great Jehovah is, 'I am.' Try any creature in thy need, and it will say, as Jacob to Rachel, 'Am I in God's stead, that hath withheld thy desire from thee?' Send to it, and it will say as John Baptist, who confessed 'I am not the Christ.' Let none of all the affections of thy soul have so much life and being in them, as those that are exercised upon God. Worms and motes are not regarded in comparison of mountains; a drop is not regarded in comparison of the ocean. Let the being of God take up thy soul, and draw off thy observation from deluding vanities, as if there were no such things before thee. When thou rememberest that there is a God, kings and nobles, riches and honours, and all the world, should be forgotten in comparison of him; and thou shouldst live as if there were no such things, if God appear not to thee in them. See them as if thou didst not see them, as thou seest a candle before the sun; or a pile of grass, or particle of dust, in comparison with the earth. Hear them as if thou didst not hear them; as thou hearest the leaves of the shaken tree, at the same time with a clap of thunder. As greatest things obscure the least, so let the being of the infinite God so take up all the powers of thy soul, as if there were nothing else but he, when any thing would draw thee from him. O if the being of this God were seen by thee, thy seducing friend would scarcely be seen, thy tempting baits would scarcely be seen, thy riches and honours would be forgotten ; all things would be as nothing to thee in comparison of him.

Chap. III.

As the being of God should make this impression on thee, so the attributes that speak the perfection of that being must each one have their work ; as his unity or indivisibility, his immensity and eternity.

The thought of God's Unity should contract and unite thy straggling affections, and call them home from multifarious vanity. It should possess thy mind with deep apprehensions of the excellency of holy unity in the soul and in the church ; and of the evil of division, and misery of distracting multiplicity. 'The Lord our God is one God.' Perfection hath unity and simplicity. We fell into divisions and miserable distraction when we departed from God unto the creatures, for the creatures are many, and of contrary qualities, dispositions, and affections ; and the heart that is set on such an object, must needs be a divided heart ; and the heart that is divided among so many and contrary or discordant objects, must needs be a distracted heart. The confusions of the world confound the heart that is set upon the world. He that makes the world his god, hath so many gods, and so discordant, that he will never please them all ; and all of them together will never fully content and please him. And who would have a God that can neither please us, nor be pleased ? He that makes himself his god, hath a compounded god (and now corrupted) of multifarious, and now of contrary desires, as hard to please as any without us. There is no rest or happiness but in unity ; and therefore none in ourselves or any other creature ; but in God, the only centre of the soul. The further from the centre, the further from unity. It is only in God that differing minds can be well united. Therefore is the world so divided, because it is departed so far from God. Therefore have we so many minds and ways, and such diversity of opinions, and contrariety of affections, because men forsake the centre of unity. There is no uniting in any worldly, carnal, self-devised principles, or prac-

tices. When holiness brings these distracted, scattered souls to God, in him they will be one. While they cavil at holiness, and cry up unity, they show themselves distracted men. For holiness is the only way to unity, because it is the agreement of the soul with God. All countries, and persons cannot meet in any one interest or creature, but each hath a several interest of his own ; but they might all meet in God. If the pope were God and had his perfections, he would be fit for all the church to centre in ; but being man, and yet pretending to this prerogative of God, he is the grand divider and distracter of the church. The proverb is too true ; 'so many men, so many minds,' because that every man will be a god to himself, having a self-mind and self-will, and all men will not yield to be one in God. God is the common interest of the saints ; and thereof all that are truly saints, are truly united in him. If all the visible church, and all the world, would heartily make him their common interest, we should quickly have a common unity and peace, and the temple of double-faced Janus would be shut up. They that sincerely have one God, have also one Lord and Saviour, one faith, one spirit, one baptism ; (or holy covenant with God) even because they have 'one God and Father of all, who is above all, and through all, and in them all.' Therefore they must 'keep the unity of the Spirit in the bond of peace,' though yet they have different degrees of gifts, and therefore differences in opinion about abundance of inferior things. The further we go from the trunk or stock, the more numerous and small we shall find the branches. They are one in God, that are divided in many doubtful controversies. The weakest therefore in the faith must be received into this union and communion of the church ; but not to doubtful disputations. As the ancient baptism contained no more than our engagement to God, the Father, Son, and Holy Ghost, so the ancient profession of saving faith was of the same extent. God is sufficient for the church to unite in. A union in other articles of faith is so far necessary to the unity of the church, as it is necessary to prove our faith and unity in God, and the sincerity of this ancient, simple belief in God the Father, Son, and Spirit.

The unity of God is the attribute to be first handled and imprinted on the mind, even next unto his essence ; 'The Lord our God is one Lord.' The unity of the church is its excellency and attribute, that is first and most to be esteemed and preserved next unto its essence. If it be not a church, it cannot be one church ; and if we be not saints, we cannot be united saints. If we be not members, we cannot make one body. But when once we have the essence of saints and of a church, we must next be solicitous for its unity ; nothing below an essential point of faith will allow us to depart from the catholic unity, love, and peace that is due to saints; and because such essentials are never wanting in the catholic church, or any true member of it, therefore we are never allowed to divide from the catholic church, or any true and visible member. It is first necessary that the church be a church, that is, a people separated from the world to Christ ; and that the Christian be a Christian in covenant with the Lord. But the next point of necessity is, that the church be one and Christians be one. He that for the sake of lower points, how true soever, will break this holy bond of unity, shall find at last, to his shame and sorrow, that he understood not the excellency or necessity of unity. The prayer of Christ for the perfection of his saints is, ' that they all may be one, as thou Father art in me, and I in thee, that they also may be one in us : that the world may believe that thou hast sent me : and the glory which thou gavest me I have given them, that they may be one, even as we are one : I in them, and thou in me, that they may be made perfect in one, that the world may know that thou hast sent me, and hast loved them as thou hast loved me.' Here it appears that the unity of the church or saints is necessary to convince the world of the truth of Christianity, and of the love of God to his people, and necessary to the glory and perfection of the saints. The nearer any churches or members are to the divine perfections, and the more strictly conformable to the mind of God, the more they are one, and replenished with catholic love to all saints, and desirous of unity and communion with them. It is a most lamentable delusion of some Christians that think their ascending to higher degrees of holiness, doth partly consist in their withdrawing from the catholic church, or from the communion of most of the saints on earth, upon the account of some smaller differing opinions ; and they think that they should become more loose, and leave their strictness, if they should hold a catholic communion, and leave their state of separation and division ! Is there any strictness amiable or desirable, except a strict conformity to God ? Surely a strict way of sin and wickedness is not desirable to a saint. And is not God one, and his church one, and hath he not commanded all his servants to be one : and is not love the new and great commandment, by which they must be known to all

men to be his disciples ? Which then is the stricter servant of the Lord ? He that loveth much, or he that loveth little? He that loveth all Christians, or he that loveth but a few, with the special love ? He that loveth a Christian as a Christian ; or he that loveth him but as one of his party or opinion ? He that is one in the catholic body ; or he that disowns communion with the far greatest part of the body ? Will you say that Christ was loose and the pharisees strict; because Christ eat and drank with publicans and sinners, and the pharisees condemned him for it ? It was Christ that was stricter in holiness than they ; for he abounded more in love and good works ; but they were stricter than he in a proud, self-conceited moroseness and separation. Certainly he that is highest in love, is highest in grace, and not he that confines his love to few. Was it not the weak Christian that was the stricter in point of meats, drinks and days ? But the stronger that were censured by them, did more strictly keep the commandment of God.

Christian reader, let the unity of God have this effect upon thy soul, 1. To draw thee from the distracting multitude of creatures, and make thee long to be all in God. That thy soul may be still working toward him, till thou find nothing but God alone within thee. In the multitude of thy thoughts within thee, let his comforts delight thy soul. The multitude distracts thee ; retire into unity, that thy soul may be composed, quieted, and delighted. 2. Let it make thee long for the unity of saints, and endeavour it to the utmost of thy power, that the church in unity may be more like the Head. 3. Let it cause thee to admire the happiness of the saints, who are freed from the bondage of the distracting creature, and have but one to love, fear, trust, serve, seek, and know ; ' one thing is needful,' which should be chosen, but it is many that we are troubled about.

CHAP. IV.

The Immensity of God, which is the next attribute to be considered, must have this effect upon thy soul : 1. The infinite God that is every where, comprehending all places and things, and comprehended by none, must raise admiring, reverent thoughts in the soul of the believer. We wonder at the magnitude of the sun and the heavens, and of the whole creation ; but when we begin to think what is beyond the heavens, and all created being, we are perplexed. Why it is God that is in all, above all, beyond all, and beneath all, and where there is no place, because no creature, there is God : and if thy thoughts should imagine millions of millions of miles beyond all place and measure, all is but God ; and go as far as thou canst in thy thoughts, and thou canst not go beyond him. Reverently admire the immensity of God. The world and all the creatures in it, are not to God so much as a sand or atom is to all the world. The point of a needle is more to all the world, than the world to God. For between that which is finite and that which is infinite, there is no comparison. ' Who hath measured the waters in the hollow of his hand ? and meted out heaven with the span, and comprehended the dust of the earth in a measure, and weighed the mountains in scales, and the hills in a balance ? Behold the nations are as a drop of a bucket, and are counted as the small dust of the balance : behold he taketh up the isles as a very little thing. All nations before him are as nothing : and they are counted to him less than nothing, and vanity.'

2. From this greatness and immensity of God also, thy soul must reverently stay all its busy, bold inquiries, and know that God is to us and to every creature incomprehensible. If thou couldst fathom or measure him, and know his greatness by a comprehensive knowledge, he were not God. A creature can comprehend nothing but a creature. You may know God, but not comprehend him ; as your foot treads on the earth, but doth not cover all the earth. The sea is not the sea, if you can hold it in a spoon. Thou canst not comprehend the sun which thou seest, and by which thou seest all things else, nor the sea, or earth, no, nor a worm or pile of grass : thy understanding knows not all that God hath put into any the least of these ; thou art a stranger to thyself, and to somewhat in every part of thyself, both body and soul. And thinkest thou to comprehend God, that perfectly comprehendest nothing ? Stop then thy over-bold inquiries, and remember that thou art a shallow, finite worm, and God is infinite. First reach to comprehend the heaven and earth and whole creation, before thou think of comprehending him, to whom the world is nothing, or vanity; or so small a dust, or drop, or point. Saith Elihu, ' At this my heart trembleth, and is moved out of its place : hear attentively the noise of his voice. God thundereth marvellously with his voice ; great things doth he which we cannot comprehend.' How then should we comprehend himself ? When God pleads his cause with Job himself, what doth he but convince him of his infinitude and absoluteness, even from the greatness of his works, which are beyond our reach,

and yet are as nothing to himself : should he take the busy inquirer in hand, but as he did begin with Job. ' Who is this that darkeneth counsel with words without knowledge ? Gird up thy loins like a man, for I will demand of thee, and answer thou me,' &c. Alas ! how soon would he nonplus and confound us, and make us say as Job, ' Behold I am vile ! What shall I answer thee ? I will lay my hand upon my mouth : once have I spoken, but I will not answer ; yea, twice, but I will proceed no further.' Indeed there is mentioned in Eph. iii. 11. the saints' comprehending the dimensions of the love of Christ, but as the next verse saith, ' it passeth knowledge;' so comprehending there, signifies no more but a knowing according to our measure; an attainment of what we are capable to attain ; nay, nor all that either, but such a prevalent knowledge of the love of Christ as is common to all the saints; as there is nothing more visible than the sun, and yet no visible being less comprehended by the sight ; so is there nothing more intelligible than God (for he is all in all things,) and yet nothing so incomprehensible to the mind that knows him. It satisfies me not to be ignorant of God, or to know so little as I know, or to be short of the measure that I am capable of ; but it satisfies me to be incapable of comprehending him ; or else I must be unsatisfied because I am not God. O the presumptuous arrogancy of those men, if I may call them men, that dare prate about the infinite God such things as never were revealed to them, in his works or word ! Who dare pretend to measure him by their shallow understandings, and question, if not deny and censure, that of God which they cannot reach ; and sooner suspect the word that reveals him, than their shallow understandings, that should better conceive of him. Saith Elihu, ' Behold God is great, and we know him not, neither can the number of his years be searched out.' Though the knowledge of him be our life eternal, yet we know him not by any full and adequate conception. We know an infinite God, and therefore with an excellent knowledge objectively considered, but with a poor degree and kind of knowledge next to none, as to the act ; and it is a thousand thousand fold more that we know not of him, than that we know : for indeed there is no comparison to be here made.

3. The immensity of God, as it proves him incomprehensible, so it contains his omnipresence ; and therefore should continually affect us, as men that believe that God stands by them. As we would compose our thoughts, minds, and passions, if we saw, were it possible, the Lord stand over

us, so should we now labour to compose them. As we would restrain and use our tongues, and order our behaviour, if we saw his majesty, so should we do now, when we know that he is with us. An eye servant will work hard in his master's presence, whatever he doth behind his back. Bestir thee then, Christian, for God stands by; ' in him we live, and move, and have our being.' Loiter not till thou canst truly say that God is gone, or absent from thee; sin not by wilfulness or negligence, till thou canst say thou art behind his back. Alas, that we should have no more awakened, serious souls, and no more fervent, lively prayers, and no more serious, holy speech, and no more careful, heavenly lives, when we stand before the living God, and do all in his sight, and speak all in his hearing? O why should sense so much affect us, and faith and knowledge work no more? We can be awed with the presence of a man, and would not do before a prince what most men do before the Lord. Yea, other things affect us when we see them not; and shall not God? But of this more afterwards.

4. The immensity of God assures us much of his all-sufficiency. He that is every where, is easily able to hear all prayers, to help us in all straits, to supply all wants, to punish all sins. A blasphemous conceit of God as finite, and as absent from us, is one of the causes of our distrust. He that distrusts an absent friend, as thinking he may forget him, or neglect him, will trust him when he is with him; cannot he hear thee, pity thee, and help thee, that is still with thee? O what an awe is this to the careless! What a support to faith; what a quickener to duty; what a comfort to the afflicted, troubled soul! God is in thy poor cottage, Christian, and well acquainted with thy wants: God is at thy bedside when thou art sick, and nearer thee than the nearest of thy friends. What would thou do in want or pain if God stood by? Wouldst thou not pray and trust him if thou sawest him? So do though thou see him not, for he is surely there.

5. The immensity and infinite greatness of God assure us of his particular providence. Some blasphemous infidels imagine that he hath only a general providence, and hath left all to some inferior powers, and meddles not with particular things himself: they think that as he hath left it to the sun to illuminate the world, so hath he left all other inferior things and events to nature or inferior causes; and that he doth not himself regard, observe, reward, or punish the thoughts, words, and ways of men. And all

this is, because they consider not the immensity or infinite greatness of the Lord. It is true, that God hath framed the nature of all things, and delights to maintain and use the frame of second causes which he hath made; and will not easily and ordinarily work against or without this order of causes: but it is as true and certain, both that sometimes he makes use of miracles, and that in the very course of natural causes he is able to exercise a particular providence, as well as without them, by himself alone. The creature doth nothing but by him. All things move as he first moves them, in their natural agency. His wisdom guides, his will intends and commands; his power moves and disposes all. The sun would not shine, if he were not the light of it; and he is no less himself the light of the world, than if he did illuminate it without a sun. God is never the further off, because the creatures are near us; or never the less in the effect, because he uses a second cause, than if there were no second cause at all. What influence second causes have upon the souls of men, he hath for the most part kept unknown to us; but that himself disposes of us and all things after the counsel of his own will, is beyond all question. Can he that is most mean with thy thougths, be regardless of them? Can he be regardless of thy words and ways that is with thee, and sees and hears all? If thou believe not that he is as verily with thee as thou art there thyself, thou art then an atheist. If thou believe him not to be infinite, thou believest him not to be God. It is not God that can be absent, limited or finite. If thou be not such a senseless atheist but knowest that God is everywhere, how is it possible thou shouldst doubt of his care or observance, or particular providence about every thing?

No child is so foolish that will think his father cares not what he saith or doth, when he stands before him. Wouldst thou doubt of God's particular providence, whether he regard thy heart, talk and practice, if thou didst see him with thee? Surely it is scarcely possible. Why then dost thou question it when thou knowest that he is with thee?' If thou be an atheist and knowest not, look about thee on the world, and bethink thee whether stones, trees, and earth, whether beasts, or birds, or men, make themselves; if they do, thou hadst better uphold thyself, and be not sick, and do not die. If thou madest thyself, thou canst surely preserve thyself; but if any thing else made thee and all these lower things, either it was somewhat greater or less than they; either it was somewhat better or worse than they. If less, or worse, how could it make them greater or better than itself? Can any thing give that which it hath not? If it must needs be greater and better than the creatures, then as it must be wiser than they, and more holy, gracious, and just than they, so must it be more comprehensive than all they. Whoever made this earth, is certainly greater than the earth, or else he should give it more than he had to give. If he be greater, he must be present: if thou shouldst be so vain as to account any other higher thing the maker of this world, that is not God, thou must ascribe also a sufficiency to that maker, to exercise a particular providence, and moreover be put to consider who did make that maker. Nothing therefore is more certain, even to reason itself, than that the maker of the world must be greater than the world, therefore present with all the world; and therefore must observe and regard all the world. When thou canst find out a thought, or word, or deed that was not done in the presence of God, or any creature that is not in his presence, then believe and spare not that he sees or regards it not; yea, and that it has no being. O blind atheists! you see the sun before your eyes, which enlightens all the upper part of the earth at once; even millions of millions see all by its light; and yet do you doubt whether God beholds, regards, and provides for all at once.

Tell me, if God had never a creature to look to in all the world but thee, wouldst thou believe that he would regard thy heart, words, and ways or not? If he would, why not now, as well as then? Is he not as sufficient for thee, and as really present with thee, as if he had no other creature else? If all men in the world were dead save one, would the sun any more illuminate that one than now it doth? Mayest thou not see as well by the light of it now, as if it had never another to enlighten? And dost thou see a creature do so much, and wilt thou not believe as much of the creator? If thou think us worms too low for God so exactly to observe, thou mayest as well think that we are too low for him to create, or preserve; and then who made us and preserves us? Doth not the sun enlighten the smallest bird, and crawling insect, as well as the greatest prince on earth? Doth it withhold its light from any creature that can see, and say, I will not shine on things so base? And wilt thou more restrain the infinite God that is the maker, light, and life of all? It is he that filleth all in all, the heaven of heavens cannot contain him, and is he absent from thee? 'He doth beset thee before and behind, and layeth his hand upon thee; whither wilt thou go

from his Spirit, or whither wilt thou fly from his presence? If thou ascend up into heaven, he is there; if thou make thy bed in hell, thou wilt feel him there; if thou take the wings of the morning, and dwell in the uttermost parts of the sea, even there shalt thou find him to be to thee as thou art.' Thou mayest think, with sinful Adam and Eve, to hide thyself from the presence of the Lord: but thou wilt quickly find that he observes thee; and 'be sure thy sin will find thee out.' Thou mayest with Cain be turned out of the gracious presence of God, and cast out of his church and mercy; and with the damned thou mayest be turned out of the presence of his blessedness and glory: but thou shalt never be out of his essential presence, nor so escape the presence of his justice. It is the presence of his grace where the upright are promised here to dwell, and out of which they fear lest they be cast. 'Cast me not away from thy presence, and take not thy Holy Spirit from me.' It is the presence where is fulness of joy, which they aspire after, but there is also a presence that the earth shall tremble at, and that the wicked shall perish at; so that a particular providence must be remembered by them that believe and remember the immensity of God.

Chap. V.

The eternity of God is the next attribute to be known which also must have its work upon the soul. And, 1. This also shows us that God is incomprehensible; for man cannot comprehend eternity. When we go about to think of that which hath no beginning nor end, it is to our mind as a place a thousand miles off is to our eye; even beyond our reach; we cannot say there is no such place, yea, we know there is; but we cannot see it: so we know there is an eternal being; but our knowledge of his eternity is not intuitive, or comprehensive. Eternity therefore is the object of our faith, reverence, and admiration, but forbids our busy bold inquiries. O the arrogancy of those ignorantly learned, and foolishly wise disputing men, that have so long perplexed, if not torn in pieces, the church, about the priority and posteriority of the knowledge and decrees of God, when they confess them all to be eternal! As if they knew not that terms of priority and posteriority have not that significancy in or about eternity, as they have with us.

2. The eternity of God must draw the soul from transitory to eternal things. It is an everlasting blessedness, even the eternal God, that our souls are made for; the brutes are made for a mortal happiness; the immortal soul can-

not be fully content with any thing that will have an end. As a capacity of this endless blessedness distinguishes man from the beasts that perish ; so the disposition to it distinguishes saints from the ungodly, and the fruition of it distinguishes the glorified from the damned. Alas, what a silly thing were man if he were capable of nothing but these transitory things! What were our lives worth, and what were our time worth, and what were all our mercies worth, or what were all the world worth to us, or what were we worth ourselves? I would not under-value the works of God : but truly if man had no other life to live but this, I should esteem him a very contemptible creature. If you say that there is some excellency in the brutes, I answer, True ; but their usefulness is their chief excellency ; and what is their use but to be a glass in which we may see the Lord, and to be serviceable to man in his passage to eternity? They are not capable of knowing, or loving, or enjoying God themselves : but they are useful to man, who is capable of this ; and so they have an everlasting end and this is their excellency. Therefore the atheist that denies an everlasting life to man, brings himself into a far baser state then the brutes are in. For the brutes have an everlasting end, in promoting the happiness of man : but if man have no everlasting end himself, there is no other whose everlasting happiness he can promote. The unbeliever therefore debases his own soul and the whole creation : and faith and holiness advance the soul and all things with it, that are useful to our advancement. The true believer honours his horse, his dog, his food and raiment, the earth he treads on, and every creature, incomparably more than the infidel doth honour his own or any other's soul, or than he honours the greatest prince on earth. For the believer uses all things, even the vilest, in reference to eternity ; but the infidel uses his life and soul but to a transitory end ; and takes the greatest prince on earth to be but for a transitory use. As eternity is invaluable in comparison of time, so the use and excellency that a believer doth ascribe to a piece of bread, or the basest creature, in the sanctified improvement of it, is ten thousand times, even unspeakably, above the use and excellency that an unbeliever ascribes to his soul or to his prince. He that stamps the image of a dog or a toad upon gold, instead of the image of the prince, and would have ten thousand pounds worth go but for a farthing, doth not by a thousand degrees so much debase the gold, as the infidel debases his soul and all things. Infidelity is guilty of the destruction of all souls, and the destruction of all mercies, and the destruction of all divine revelations, of all graces, of all ordinances, and means, and of the destruction of the whole creation that was made for man : for he that destroys the end, destroys all the means : but the infidel destroys and denies the end of every one of these, and holiness only doth give them up, and use them to their ends.

1. He is guilty of the destruction of all souls : for as much as in him lies they are destroyed, while they are all made useless to the end for which they were created. If there be no other life and happiness everlasting, what are souls good for? What is the reasonable creature good for? Is it to be happy here? In what? Here is no happiness? Is it in eating, drinking, and sleeping? Why, these are to strengthen us for our service which tends to our end, and therefore cannot be themselves our end. Is it not better to be without either meat, or drink, or sleep, in point of happiness, so be it we also were without the need of them, than to need them and have them for our need, especially with the care and trouble which they cost us? I had an hundred times rather, for my part, if it were lawful to desire it, never have meat, or drink, or sleep, and be without the need of them, as I had rather be without a sore, than to have a plaster that will ease it, and be every day at the pains to dress it. Brutes have some advantage in these above men, in that they have not the care, fear, and sorrow of mind as we have, in the getting or keeping what they have or need. If you go downward, and say that men are made to govern brutes, then what are brutes made for, unless to manure the earth ; and so the basest shall be the end of the noblest, and God may be as wisely said to be for man, because he is to govern him. Truly if there were no everlasting life, but man were a mere terrestrial animal, I had rather never have been born, or should wish I had never been a man : I knew not what to do with myself, nor how to employ the faculties of my soul or body, but they would all seem to me as useless things. What should I do with my reason, if I had no higher an end than beasts? What should I do with a mind that knows there is a God, and another world, and that is capable of desiring him, seeking and enjoying him, if it must be frustrated of all? What should I do with a heart that is capable of the love of God, and delighting in his love, if I have no God to love and delight in, when this life is ended? Why have I a heart that so desires him, in fuller vision and fruition, if I be capable of no such thing? What then

13

should I do with my time and life? Verily I know, not, if I were fully of this sad opinion, whether I should turn brute in my life agreeably to my judgment, or whether I should make an end of my life to be eased of a useless burden; but confident I am I should not know what to do with myself; I should be like a cashiered soldier, or like one turned out of his service, that knew not where to have work and wages: and if you found me standing all day idle, I must give you the reason, because no man hath hired me. What do those wretches do with their lives, that think they have no God to serve and seek, or future happiness to attain? As men use to say of naughty ministers, so may I say of all mankind, according to the doctrine of the infidels, 'a naughty priest is good for nothing,' and it is true of him as such, for as Christ himself saith, 'Ye are the salt of the earth: but if the salt have lost its savour, wherewith shall it be salted? It is thenceforth good for nothing, but to be cast out, and to be trodden under foot of men: ye are the light of the world: men do not light a candle to put it under a bushel.' So I say of the reasonable creature: the grass is useful for the beasts: the beasts are serviceable unto man: a swine that cannot serve you living, is useful being dead. But if there were no God to seek and serve, and no life but this for us to hope for, for ought I know man were good for nothing: what were light good for, if there were no eyes? or eyes, if there were no light to see by? What is a watch good for, but to tell the hour of the day? All the curious parts and workmanship of it is worth no more than the metal is worth, if it be not useful to its proper end. And what reason, will, and affections in man are good for, I know not, if not to seek, to please, and to enjoy the Lord. Take off this poise, and all the wheels of my soul must stand still, or else do worse.

2. The infidel and ungodly man that looks not after an eternal end, destroys all the mercies of God, and makes them as no mercies at all: creation and our being, is a mercy; but it is in order to our eternal end. Redemption by Christ is an unspeakable mercy; but it is denied by the infidel, and rejected by the ungodly: what is Christ worth, and all his mediation, if there be no life for man but this? Peace and liberty, health and life, friends and neighbours, food and raiment, are all mercies to us, as a ship and sails are to the mariner, or a fair way, or horse, or inn, to a traveller: but if by denying our eternal end, you make our voyage or our journey vain, these mercies then are little worth: no more than a ship on the land, or a plough in the sea, or a

horse to him that hath no use for him. O what an ungrateful wretch is that, who will deny all the mercies of God to himself, and to all others! For once deny the use and the eternal end, and you deny the mercy.

3. He that believes not, or seeks not after an eternal end, destroys all the doctrine, law and government of God: for all is but to lead us to this end. All the holy scriptures, the precepts of Christ, and his holy example, the covenant of grace, the gifts and miracles of the Holy Ghost, the light and law of nature itself, are all to bring us to our eternal end: therefore he that denies that end, doth cancel them all, and cast them by as useless things.

4. He denies all the graces of the Spirit: for what use is there for faith, if the object of it be a falsehood? What use for hope, if there be no life to be hoped for? What use for holy desires and love, if God be not to be enjoyed? Grace is but the delusion and deformity of the soul, if the infidel and ungodly be in the right.

5. They destroy also all the means of our salvation, if they deny salvation, which is the end. To what purpose should men study, or read, or hear, or pray, or use either sacraments or any other means, for an end that is not to be had? To what end should men obey or suffer, for any such end that is not attainable?

6. Yea, they let loose the soul to sin, and take off all effectual restraint. If there be no eternal end, and no reward or punishment but here, what can effectually hinder the men of this opinion from stealing, whoredom, or any villany, when it may be done with secresy? What should hinder the revengeful man from poisoning or secretly murdering his enemy, or setting his house on fire in the night? If I know a man or woman who believes that there is no life to come, I take it for granted they are revengeful, thieves, deceivers, fornicators, or any thing that is bad, if they have but temptation, and secret opportunity For what hath he to seek but the pleasing of his flesh, that thinks he hath no God to seek or please, or no future reward or punishment to expect? He that confesses himself an infidel to me, confesses himself to be in all things else as bad as ever he can or dare Honesty is renounced by that man or woman that profess themselves to be atheists or infidels: methinks, in congruity with their profession, they should take it for a wrong to be called or reputed honest! If you tell me that heathens had a kind of honesty; I must tell you again, that most heathens believed the immortality of the soul, and that kind of seeming honesty which they had was only in those of

them that thus expected a life to come. But those that believe not another life where man is to have his punishment and reward, have nothing like to honesty in them, but live like greedy, ravenous beasts, where they are from under the laws and government of them that look for another life. The cannibals that eat men's flesh, and some such savages as they, are the nations that expect no life but this. It is believed so commonly by all the civil infidels and Turks, as shows it to be a principle that nature reveals.

7. Yea, the whole creation that is within the sight of man, is destroyed opinionatively by the infidels that look for no immortal life: for all things were made to further our salvation: the heavens to declare the glory of God, and the firmament to show his handy work, and all creatures to be our glass in which we must behold the Lord, and our book in which we must read and learn his nature and his will. The sun is to light us, and maintain our life, and the life of other lower creatures, while we prepare for immortality: the earth is to bear us, and to bear fruit for us; and the trees and plants and every creature to accommodate and serve us, while we serve the Lord and pass on to eternity. Therefore the atheist that denies us our eternity, denies the usefulness of all the world; what were all the creatures here good for, if there were no men? The earth would be a wilderness, and the beasts would for the most part perish, for want of sustenance, and all would be like a forsaken cottage that no man dwells in, and doth no good; and if man be not the heir of immortality, they can do him no good. All creatures are but our provision in the way to this eternity: therefore if there were no eternity, what should we do with them? And who will travel to a place that is not, or a city that is no where but in his imagination, besides a madman? It is evident therefore, that as all the tools in a workman's shop are made useless to him if he be forbidden to use his trade, and all the books in my library are useless, if I may not read them to get knowledge; so all creatures under heaven are made useless and destroyed doctrinally by the atheist, that thinks there is no eternal life for which they should be used. I must seriously profess if I believed this (being in other things of the mind I am) I knew not what to do with any thing. What should I do with my books, but to learn the way to this eternity? What should I do with my money, if there be no treasure to be laid up in heaven, or friends to be made with the mammon abused commonly to unrighteousness? What should I do with my

tongue, my hands, my time, my life my self, or any thing, if there were no eternity? I think I should dig my grave, and lay me down in it, to die and perish, to escape the sorrows of a longer life that must be my companions.

Remember then, Christians, and still remember it, that eternity is the matter of your faith and hope. Eternity is your portion and felicity; eternity is the end of all your desires, labours, and distresses. Eternity is your religion, and the life of all your holy motions; and as without the capacity of it, you would be but beasts, so without the love and desire of it, and title to it, you would be but wicked miserable men. Set not your hearts on transitory things, while you stand near unto eternity. How can you have room for so many thoughts on fading things, when you have an eternity to think on? What light can you see in the candles or glow-worms of this world, in the sunshine of eternity? O remember, when you are tempted to please your eyes, your taste, and sensual desires, that these are not eternal pleasures. Remember, when you are tempted for wealth or honour to wrong your souls, that these are not the eternal riches; houses and lands are not eternal: meats and drinks are not eternal: sports and pastimes, and jocund, sinful company, are not eternal. Alas, how short, how soon they vanish into nothing! But it is God and our dear Redeemer that are eternal. The flower of beauty withers with age, or by the nipping blast of a short disease; the honours of the world are but a dream; your graves will bury all its glory. Down comes the prince, the lord, the gallant, and suddenly takes his lodgings in the dust. The corpse that was pampered and adorned yesterday, is corruption to-day. The body that was bowed to, attended, and applauded but the other day, is now interred in the vault of darkness, with worms and moles. To-day it is corruption and a most lothesome thing, that lately was dreaming of an earthly happiness. One day he is striving for riches and pre-eminences, or glorying and rejoicing in them, that the next day may be snatched away to hell. O fix not your minds on fading things, that perish in the using, and by their vanishing mock you that set your hearts upon them. You will not fix your eye and mind upon every bird that flies by you, as you will on the houses that you must dwell in: nor will you mind every passenger, as you will do your friends that still live with you. And shall transitory vanity be minded by you above eternity?

3. It is eternity that must direct you in your estimate of all things. It is this that shows

you the excellency of man above the beasts: it is this that tells you the worth of grace, and the weight of sin, the preciousness of holy ordinances and helps, and the evil of hinderances and temptations : the wisdom of the choice and diligence of the saints, and the folly of the choice, and negligent, sinful lives of the ungodly ; the worth of God's favour, and the vanity of man's ; and the difference between the godly and the unsanctified world, in point of happiness.

Were not grace the egg, the seed, the earnest of an eternal glory, it were not so glorious a thing. But O how precious are all those thoughts, desires, delights and breathings of the soul, that bring us on to a sweet eternity ! Even those sorrows, groans, and tears are precious that lead to an eternal joy ! Who would not willingly obey the holy motions of the Holy Spirit, that is but preparing us for eternity ! This is it that makes a bible, a sermon, a holy book, to be of greater value than lands and lordships. It is eternity that makes the illuminated soul so fearful of sinning, so diligent in holy duties, so cheerful and resolved in suffering, because he believes it is all for an eternity. A Christian in the holy assemblies, and in his reading, learning, prayer, conference, is laying up for everlasting, when the worldling in the market, in the field or shop, is making provision for a few days or hours : thou gloriest in thy riches and pre-eminence now, but how long wilt thou do so ? To-day that house, that land is thine ; but canst thou say, it shall be thine to-morrow ? Thou canst not: but the believer can truly say, My God, my Christ, is mine to-day, and will be mine to all eternity ! O death ! thou canst take my friends from me, and my worldly riches from me, and my time, strength, and life from me ; but take my God, my Christ, my heaven, my portion from me, if thou canst ! My sin is all thy sting and strength ! But where is thy sting when sin is gone ; and where is thy strength when Christ hath conquered thee ? Is it a great matter that thou deprivest me of my sinful, weak, and troublous friends, when against thy will thou bringest me to my perfect blessed friends, with whom I must abide for ever ! Thou dost indeed bereave me of these riches ; but it is that I may possess the invaluable, eternal riches! Thou endest my time, that I may have eternity! Thou castest me down that I may be exalted ! Thou takest away my strength of life, that I may enter into life eternal ! And is this the worst that death can do ? And shall I be afraid of this ? I willingly lay by my clothes at night, that I may take my rest, and I am not loth to put off the old when I must put

on the new. The bird that is hatched is not grieved because he must leave the broken shell ; nor is it the grief of man or beast that he hath left the womb. Death doth but open the womb of time and let us into eternity, and is the second birth-day of the soul. Regeneration brings us into the kingdom of grace ; and death into the kingdom of glory.

Blessed are they that have their part in the new birth of grace and the first resurrection from the death of sin ; for to such the natural death will be gain ; and they shall have their part in the second resurrection, and on them the everlasting death shall have no power. It is eternity that tells you what you should mind, and be, and do, and that turns the scales in all things where it is concerned. Can you sleep in sin so near eternity ! Can you play and laugh before you are prepared for eternity ! Can you think him wise that sells his eternal joy for the ease, the mirth, the pleasure of a moment ; and trifles away the time in which he must win or lose eternity ? If these men be wise, there are no fools, nor any but wise men in bedlam. Dare thy tongue report, or thy heart imagine, that any holy work is needless, or a heavenly life too much ado, or any suffering too dear, that is for an eternity ! O happy souls that win eternity with the loss of all the world ! O bless that Christ, that Spirit, that light, that word, that messenger of God, that drew thy heart to choose eternity before all transitory things ! That was the day when thou began to be wise, and indeed to show thyself a man ! Thy wealth, thy honour, thy pleasure will be thine when the sensual world hath nothing to show, but sin and hell, of all they laboured for. Their pleasures, honours, and all die, when they die ; but thine will then begin their perfection ! The hopes of the ungodly are like an addle egg that when it is broken sends forth nothing but an odious smell, when another sends forth the living bird. O all you worldlings, rich and poor, you dream, play, and trifle, because you labour not for eternity ! Even worldly princes, and nobles of the earth, your glory is but a squib, a flash, a nothing, in comparison of the eternal glory which you lose ; you are doing nothing when you are striving for the world ; you are trifling and befooling your immortal souls while you are grasping a shadow, the uncertain riches : it is the believer whom you despise, that seeks for something, that loses not his labour, that shows himself a man of reason, who is caring, studying, labouring, praying, watching, and suffering for eternity.

Why is a day in the courts of God so much

better than a thousand in the tents or palaces of wickedness, but because it is the exchange where we have news of heaven, and trade for an eternity? And why is it better to be a door-keeper in the house of God, than to flourish in the prosperity of sinners, but because God's house is the porch or entrance to an eternity of delights; and the lowest room among the saints affords us a better prospect into heaven, than the highest state of worldly dignity? The ungodly are near to cutting down when they flourish in their greatest glory. Stay but a little, and he that flourisheth will be withered and cast into the fire, and the righteous shall see it when he is cut off, and shall seek him, but he is not to be found, for the enemies of God, and all that are far from him shall perish, their desire shall perish, their hope shall perish, their way shall perish, and themselves, and all that they sought, loved, and delighted in, shall perish, even the visible heavens and earth, which they abused, shall be consumed with fire. 'Seeing then that all these things shall be dissolved, what manner of persons ought we to be in all holy conversation and godliness, looking towards and waiting for the coming and appearance of our Lord!' Shall any man be accounted wise, that is not wise for eternal happiness? Shall any man be counted happy that must be most miserable to eternity? Christian, I charge thee to hold on, and look to thy soul, thy words, thy ways, for it is for eternity. O play not, loiter not, do nothing by the halves in the way to eternity! Let the careless world do what they will; they despise, and know not what they despise; they neglect, and know not what they neglect; but thou that seekest, labourest, and waitest, knowest what thou seekest, labourest, and waitest for. They sin and know not what they do. They know not what they are treasuring up for an eternity. But thou knowest why thou hatest and avoidest sin.

Sinners, be awakened by the call of God; do you know where you are, and what you do? You are every man of you stepping into eternity? Will you sin away, will you loiter away, will you sell for nothing, an eternal glory? Is thy sinful lust, gain, mirth, gluttony, and excess of drink, a price to set upon eternity? If heaven be no more worth to thee, art thou not as bad as Judas, who for thirty pieces of silver would sell his Lord? O eternity, eternity! what hearts have they that can so forget thee, neglect thee, and disesteem thee, when they stand so near thee! O sleepy souls; do you never use to rub your eyes, and look before you towards eternity? And doth it not amaze you to see whither it is that you

are going? Merrily you run down the hill; but where is the bottom? If you look but down from the top of a steeple, it may occasion an amazing fear; what then should it cause in you to look down into hell, which is your eternity? No good can possibly be small that is eternal; and no hurt or pain can be called little, that is eternal: an eternal tooth-ache, or an eternal gout, or stone, or fever, were a misery unspeakable; but O what are these to an eternal loss of heaven, and to an eternal sense of the burning wrath of God Almighty! To be out of heaven a day, and in hell that day, is a misery now unknown to sinners: but if it were as many thousand years as the earth hath sands, it were a greater misery; but to be there for ever, doth make the misery past all hope and all conceiving. O methinks the very name of eternity, should frighten the drunkard out of the ale-house, and the sleepy sinner out of his security, and the lustful, sportful, voluptuous sinner out of his sensual delights! Methinks the very name of eternity should call off the worldling to seek betimes a more enduring treasure, and should take down the gallant's pride, and bring men to look after other matters than the most do look after. Methinks to hear the name of eternity should with men of any faith and reason, even blast all the beauty, sully the glory, sadden the delights, weaken the temptations of the world, and make all its pleasure, pomp and splendour, to be to our apprehensions as a smoke, a shadow, as the dust that we tread upon. Methinks to hear the name of eternity, should lay so odious a reproach on sin, and so nakedly open the folly, shame, and misery of the ungodly, and so lively show the need and worth of faith and holiness, that men should be soon resolved in their choice, and soon be at the end of an ungodly course, and need no more words to make them the resolved servants of the Lord, before to-morrow. O methinks, that a thought of eternity should, with a believer, answer all temptations, and put life into all his prayers and endeavours.

If we were ever so cold, or dull, or sleepy one would think a serious thought of eternity should warm us, quicken us, and awake us! O Christians, shall we hear carelessly, or speak carelessly of eternity; shall we pray coldly, or labour negligently for eternity? O what an ocean of joy will eternity be unto the sanctified. It hath neither banks nor bottom. O what a gulf of misery and woe will eternity be to the ungodly! Wonderful, that on their dying beds they quake not with the horror, and that they cry not out with greatest lamentation, to think what a bottomless gulf of misery their departing souls must be cast into! To be for ever, ever, ever under the most heavy wrath of God. This is the appointed wages of ungodliness; this is the end of wicked ways; this is it that sinners chose, because they would not live to God; this they preferred or ventured on, before a holy, heavenly life; and this is it that believers are labouring to escape in all their holy care and diligence. It is an infinite value that is put upon the blood of Christ, the promises of God, the ordinances and means of grace, and grace itself, and the poorest duties of the poorest saints, because they are for an infinite, eternal glory. No mercy is small that tastes of heaven, as all doth or should do to the believer. No action is low that aims at heaven. O how lively should the resolutions and courage of those men be, that are travelling, fighting, and watching for eternity! How full should be their comforts, that are drawn from the foresight of infinite eternal comforts; as all things will presently be swallowed up in eternity, so methinks the present apprehension of eternity should now swallow up all things else in the soul.

Object. But, saith the unbeliever, if God have made man for eternity, it is a wonder that there are no more lively impressions of so infinite a thing upon the souls of all; our sense of it is so small, that it makes me doubt whether we are made for it.

Answ. Consider, 1. That benumbness, sleep, and death, is the very state of an unholy soul. Hast thou cast thyself into a sleepy, senseless disease, and wilt thou argue thence against eternity? This is as if the blind should conclude that there is no sun, or that the eye of man was not made to see it, because he hath no sight himself: or as if you should think that man hath not any life or feeling, because your palsied limbs do not feel: or that the stomach was not made for meat, because the stomachs of the sick abhor it.

2. And for believers, you may see by their lives that they have some apprehensions of eternity: why else do they differ from you, and deny themselves, and displease the world and the flesh itself? Why do they set their hearts above, if they have not lively thoughts of an eternity?

2. But if you ask me, why their apprehensions are not a thousand times more lively about so infinite a thing; I answer, their apprehensions must be suitable to their state. Our state here is a state of imperfection; and so will our apprehensions be; but a perfect state will have perfect apprehensions. It is no proof that the infant in the womb is not made to come into this world, and see the sun, and converse with men, because he hath no apprehensions of it. Our state here is a conjunction of the soul to a frail, distempered body: and so near a conjunction, that the actions of the soul must have great dependence on the body; therefore our apprehensions are limited by its frailty; and the soul can go no higher than the capacity of the body will allow. Our apprehensions now are fitted to our use and benefit; we are now believers, and must live by faith: and therefore must not be beholders, and live by sense. If eternity were open to men's natural sight, or we had here as clear and lively apprehensions of it, as those have that are there, then it were no thanks, no praise to us to be believers, or to obey and live as saints; then God should not govern man, as man, here in the way by a law, but as a beast by sense, or as the glorified that have possession. Where there are perfect apprehensions of God and glory, there will be also perfect love, joy, and praise, and consequently perfect happiness; and this were to make earth and heaven, the way and the end, to be all one. Perfect apprehensions are kept for a perfect state of happiness. But here it is well if we have such apprehensions as are fitted to the use of travellers and soldiers, as will carry us on, and prevail against the difficulties of our course. Moreover, the body, the brain, which the soul in apprehending now makes use of, cannot bear such apprehensions as are suitable to the thousandth part of the greatness of the object, without distraction. The smallest eye may see the sun, but the greatest cannot endure to gaze upon its glory; much less if it were at the nearest approach. It is a mercy of mercies to give us such apprehensions of eternity, as are meet for passengers to bring us thither; and it is part of our mercy that those apprehensions are not so great as to distract and overwhelm us.

4. The eternity of God must teach the soul contentment and patience under all labours, changes, sufferings and dangers that are here below. Believing soul, draw near; look seriously on eternity, and try whether it will not make such impressions as these upon thee. Art thou weary of labours, either of the mind or body? Is not eternity long enough for thy rest? Canst thou not afford to work out the day light of this life, when thou must rest with Christ to all eternity? Canst thou not run with patience so short a race, when thou lookest to so long a rest? Canst thou not watch one hour with Christ, who must reign with him to all eternity? Dost thou begin to shrink at sufferings for Christ,

when thou must be in glory with him for ever? How short is the suffering? How long is the reward? Dost thou begin to think hardly of the dealing of the Lord, because his people are here afflicted, and made the scorn and byeword of the world? Why, is not eternity long enough for God to show his love and bounty to his people in? Is not the day at hand, when Lazarus and the rich worldling both must hear, 'But now he is comforted, and thou art tormented.' Did not that *now*, come time enough which was the entrance of eternity? 'Even Jesus, the author and perfecter of our faith, for the joy that was set before him, endured the cross, despising the shame, and is set down at the right hand of the throne of God. Consider him that endured such contradiction of sinners against himself, lest ye be wearied and faint in your minds.'

Dost thou grudge at the prosperity of the wicked, and prevalency of the church's enemies? Look then unto eternity, and bethink thee whether that be not long enough, for the saints to reign, and the wicked to be tormented. Wouldst thou have them in hell before their time? Dost thou begin to doubt of the coming of Christ, or the truth of his promises, because he doth so long delay? O what is a thousand years to eternity? Is there not yet time enough before thee, for Christ to make good all the promises in? Were not those disciples sharply but justly rebuked as, 'fools and slow of heart to believe,' that when their Lord had been but two days dead, were unbelievingly saying, 'we hoped this had been he that should have redeemed Israel.' O remember, Christian, in all thy darkness and ignorance of the difficult passages of scripture, or of providence, that the things that are chained to eternity, cannot be perfectly understood by him that stands in an inch of time: but when eternity comes, thou shalt understand them. Remember when things seemed crooked in this world, and the best are lowest, and the worst are highest, that eternity is long enough to set all straight. Remember when sinners triumph, that eternity is long enough for their complaints. In thy poverty, pain, and longest afflictions, remember that eternity is long enough for thy relief. If thy sorrow be long, and thy comforts short, remember that eternity is long enough for thy joys. Cannot we be content to take up short in this life, when we believe eternity? Dost thou stagger at the length or strength of thy temptations: and art thou ready to draw back and venture upon sin? Why what temptation can there be, that should not be lighter than a feather, if eternity be put against it in the scales? In a word, if there be any man that escapes the foolish seductions of this world, and uses it as not abusing it, and hath all his worldly accommodations as if he had none, it is he that fixes his eye upon eternity, and sees that the fashion of these lower things doth pass away. No man can be ignorant of the necessity and worth of a holy life, who discerns that the eternal God is the end of it. The right apprehensions of God's eternity, supposing him our end, which is further to be manifested in its place, is a most powerful antidote against all sin, and a most powerful composer of a distempered mind, and a most powerful means to keep up all the powers of the soul in a resolute, vigorous, cheerful motion to the eternal God, for whom and by whom it was created.

CHAP. VI.

The next attribute of God that is to make its impress on us, is, that he is a Spirit. In this one are these three especially comprehended: 1. That he is simple, and not material or compounded, as bodies are: 2. That he is invisible, and not to be seen as bodies are: 3. That he is immortal and incorruptible, and not subject to death or change, as bodies are.

1. As simplicity signifies unity, in opposition to multiplicity, we have spoken of it before. As it is opposite to all materiality, mixture or composition, we are now to speak of it. The believing thoughts of God's immateriality and simplicity, should have these three effects upon the soul. 1. It should do much to win the heart to God, and cause it to close with him as its felicity: because as he hath no matter or mixture, so he hath nothing but pure and perfect goodness, and therefore there is nothing in him to discourage the soul. The creatures have evil in them with their good, and by contrary qualities hurt us, when they help us, and displease us when they please us: but in God there is nothing but infinite goodness. Should not the soul adhere to him, where it is sure to find nothing but simple, pure, and unmixed good? The creatures are all liable to some exceptions: in one thing they help us, but in another they hinder us; in one thing they are suitable to us, and in another thing unsuitable; but God is liable to no exceptions. This will for ever confound the ungodly that give not up themselves unto him: they did even for a thing of nought forsake that God that was purely and simply good, and against whom they had no exceptions. Had there been any thing in God to discourage the soul, or which his most malicious enemy could blame, the ungodly soul

had some excuse. But this will stop all the mouths of the condemned, that they had nothing to say against the Lord and yet they had no mind to him, no hearts for him, in comparison of the vain, vexatious creatures.

2. The simplicity of God should make us know the imperfection and vanity of all the creatures that are compounded things; and so should help to alienate us from them. Our friends have in them perhaps much holiness, but mixed with much sin. They may have much knowledge; but mixed with much ignorance. Their humility is mixed with pride; their meekness with some passions, their love with selfishness, and a small matter will cause them to distaste us: they may be much for God; but withal they may do much against him. They help the church; but through their weakness they may lamentably detract or wrong it: they are able to help us but in part; and willing but in part; and they have usually interests of their own, that are inconsistent with ours. We have no quality, but hath some alloy. Our houses, our families, our neighbours, our callings, our cattle, our land, our countries, churches, ministers, magistrates, laws and judgments, yea, even health, plenty, and peace itself, all have their mixtures of bitterness or danger, and those the most dangerous commonly that have least bitterness. But in God there is none of all this mixture, but pure uncompounded good. ' He is light, and with him is no darkness.' Indeed there is somewhat in God that an ungodly man distastes, and that seems in the state that he is in to be against him, and hurtful to him: as is his justice, holiness, truth, &c. But justice is not evil, because it doth condemn a thief or murderer: meat is not bad, because the sick distaste it. It is the cross position of the sinful soul, or his enmity to the Lord, that makes the Lord to use him as an enemy. Let him but become a subject fit for sweeter dealing from God, and he is sure to find it. Leave then the compounded, self-contradicting creature, and adhere to the pure, simple Deity.

3. God's simplicity must draw the soul to a holy simplicity, that it may be like to God. We that serve a pure simple God, must do it with simple pure affections, and not with hypocrisy, or a double heart. His interest in us should be maintained with a holy jealousy, that no other interest mix itself therewith. The soul should attain to a holy simplicity by closing with the simple infinite God, and suffering nothing to be a sharer with him in our superlative affections. All creatures must keep their places in our hearts, and that is only in a due subordination and sub-serviency to the Lord: but nothing should take up the least of that estimation, those affections, or endeavours that are his own peculiar. God will not accept of half a heart: a double-minded, double-hearted, double-faced, or double-tongued person, is contrary to the holy simplicity of a saint. As we would not bow the knee to any gods but one, so neither should we bow the heart or life to them. We should know what is God's prerogative, and that we should keep entirely for him. A subordinate esteem, love, and desire the creature may have, as it reveals God to us, or leads to him, or helps us in his work: but it should not have the least of his part in our esteem, love, or desire. This is the chastity, the purity, the integrity of the soul. It is the mixture, impurity, corruption and confusion of our souls, when any thing is taken in with God. See therefore, Christian, that in thy heart thou have no God but one, and that he have all thy heart, soul, and strength, as far as thou canst attain it. Because there will be still in imperfect souls, some sinful mixture of the creature's interest with God's, let it be the work of thy life to be watching against it, casting it out, and cleansing thy heart of it, as thou wouldst do with thy food if it fell into the dust. For whatever is added to God in thy affections, doth make no better an increase there, than the adding of earth unto thy gold, or of impurity unto thy meat, or of corrupted humours and sickness to thy body. Mixture will make no better work.

It may be thy rejoicing, if thou have ' the testimony of a good conscience, that in simplicity and godly sincerity, and not in fleshly wisdom, but by the grace of God, thou hast had thy conversation in the world.' It is the state of hypocrisy when one God is openly professed and worshipped and yet the creature lies deepest and nearest to the heart.

2. The invisibility of God also must have its due effects upon us.

1. It must warn us, that we picture not God to our eye-sight, or in our fancies in any bodily shape. Saith the prophet, ' To whom will you liken God? or what likeness will ye compare unto him?' So, 'no man hath seen God at any time; the only begotten Son, which is in the bosom of his Father, he hath declared him; and therefore we must conceive of him but as he is declared, ' Not that any man hath seen the Father, save he which is of God, he hath seen the Father.' If you ask me, how then you should conceive of God, if not in any bodily shape? I answer, get all these attributes, and relations of God to make their proper impress upon thy soul, as now I am

teaching you, and then you will have the true conceiving of God : this question therefore is to be answered at the end of this discourse, when you have seen all the attributes of God together, and heard what impression they must make upon you.

2. This must teach us, to think most highly of the things that are invisible, and more meanly of these visible things. Let it be the property of a beast, and not of a man, to know nothing but what he seeth or hath seen : let it be the mark of the brutish infidels, and not of Christians, to doubt of the invisible things, because they are invisible ; or to think that things visible are more excellent or sure. As the senses are more ignoble than the intellect, a beast having as perfect senses as a man, and yet no reasonable understanding, so the objects of sense must proportionably be below the objects of the understanding, as such. The grossest and most palpable objects are the basest. It is the subtle part that is called the spirits ; which being drawn out of plants or other vegetables, is most powerful and excellent, and valued, when the earthly dregs are cast away as little worth. It is that subtle part in our blood that is called the spirits, that hath more of the virtue of life, and doth more of the works than the feculent, gross and earthly part. The air and wind have as true a being as the earth, and a more excellent nature, though it be more gross and they invisible. The body is not so excellent as the invisible soul. Invisible things are as real as visible, and as suitable to our more noble invisible part, as visible things to our fleshly, baser part.

3. The invisibility of God must teach us to live a life of faith, and to get above a sensual life : and it must teach us to value the faith of the saints, as knowing its excellency and necessity. Invisible objects have the most perfectly excellent reality ; and therefore faith hath the pre-eminence above sense. Natural reason can live upon things not seen, if they have been seen, or can be known by natural evidence. Subjects obey a prince that they see not : and fear a punishment which they see not : and the nature of man is afraid of the devils, though we see them not. But faith lives upon such invisible things, as mortal eye did never see, nor natural, ordinary evidence demonstrate, but are revealed only by the word of God : though about many of its invisible objects, faith hath the consent of reason for its encouragement. Value not sight and sense too much. Think not all to be mere uncertainties and notions that are not the objects of sense. We should not have heard that God

is a spirit, if corporeal substances had not a baser kind of being than spirits : intelligence is a more noble operation than sense. If there be any thing properly called sense in heaven, it will be as far below the pure intellectual intuition of the Lord, as the glorified body will be below the glorified soul. But what that difference will be, we cannot now understand. Fix not your minds on sensible things. Remember that your God, your home, your portion are unseen : and therefore live in hearty affections to them, and serious prosecution of them, as if you saw them. Pray, as if you saw God, heaven, and hell. Hear, as if you saw him that sends his messenger to speak to you. Resist all the temptations to lust, sensuality, and every sin, as you would do if you saw God stand by. Love him, fear him, trust him, and serve him, as you would do if you beheld him. 'Faith is the evidence of things not seen.' Believing must be to you instead of seeing ; and make you as serious about things unseen, as sensual men are about things sensible. In every thing that you see, remember it is he that is unseen that appears in them. He enlightens you by the sun ; he warms you by the fire ; he bears you by the earth. See him in all these by the eye of faith.

3. The immortality, incorruptibility and immutability of God, must

1. Teach the soul to rise up from these mortal, corruptible, mutable things, and to fix upon that God who is the immortal, incorruptible portion of his saints.

2. It must comfort and encourage all believers in the consideration of their felicity ; and support them under the failings of all mortal corruptible things. Our parents, children, and friends are mortal : they are ours to-day, and dead to-morrow : they are our delight to-day, and our sorrow or horror to-morrow : but our God is immortal. Our houses may be burned ; our goods may be consumed or stolen ; our clothes will be worn out ; our treasure here may be corrupted. But our God is unchangeable, the same for ever. Our laws and customs may be changed ; our governors and privileges changed ; our company, employments, and habitation changed : but our God is never changed. Our estates may change from riches to poverty : and our names that were honoured, may incur disgrace. Our health may quickly turn to sickness, and our ease to pain : but still our God is unchangeable for ever. Our friends are inconstant and may turn our enemies : our peace may be changed into war ; and our liberty into slavery : but our God doth never change. Time will

change customs, families, and all things here: but it changes not our God. The creatures are all but earthen metal, and quickly dash in pieces: our comforts are changeable; ourselves are changeable and mortal: but so is not our God.

3. And it should teach us to draw as near to God as we are capable by unchangeable fixed resolutions, and constancy of endeavours; and to be still the same as we are at the best.

4. It should move us also to be more desirous of passing into the state of immortality, to long for our unchangeable habitation, and our immortal, incorruptible bodies, and to possess the kingdom that cannot be moved, and let not the mutability of things below much trouble us, while our rock, our portion, is immovable. God waxes not old: heaven doth not decay by duration: the glory of the blessed shall not wither, nor their sun set upon them, nor their day have any night; nor any mutations or commotions disturb their quiet possessions. O love and long for immortality and incorruption!

CHAP. VII.

Having spoken of the effects of the attributes of God's essence as such, we must next speak of the effects of his three great attributes which some call subsistential, that is, his omnipotency, understanding and will; or his infinite power, wisdom and goodness: by which it hath been the way of the schoolmen and other divines to denominate the three persons, not without some countenance from scripture phrase. The Father they call the infinite power of the Godhead; and the Son, the wisdom and word of God, and of the Father: and the Holy Ghost, the love and goodness of God, of the Father and Son. But, that these attributes of power, understanding and will, or power, wisdom and goodness, are of the same importance with the terms of personality, Father, Son, and Holy Ghost, we presume not to affirm. It suffices us, 1. That God hath assumed these attributes to himself in scripture. 2. And that man who bears the natural image of God, hath power, understanding and will; and as he bears the holy, moral image of God, he hath a power to execute that which is good, and wisdom to direct, and goodness of will to determine for the execution: and so while God is seen of us in this glass of man, we must conceive of him after the image that in man appears to us, and speak of him in the language of man, as he doth of himself.

The almightiness of God ought to make these impressions on our souls. It ought to possess the soul with very awful and reverent thoughts of God; and fill us continually with his holy fear. Infinite greatness and power, must have no common, careless thoughts, lest we blaspheme him in our minds, and be guilty of contempt. The dread of the heavenly majesty should be still upon us; and we must be in his fear all the day long, not under that slavish fear that is void of love, as men fear an enemy, or hurtful creature, or that which is evil: for we have not such a Spirit from the Lord, nor stand in a relation of enmity and bondage to him: but reverence is necessary; and from thence a fear of sinning and displeasing so great a God. 'The fear of the Lord is the beginning of wisdom.—By it men depart from evil. The fear of God, the want of which is sin, is often put for the whole new man, or all the work of grace within us, even the principle of new life: and it is often put for the whole work of religion, or service of God; therefore the godly are usually denominated such as fear God; the godly are ' devoted to the fear of God.' It is our 'sanctifying the Lord in our hearts, that he be our fear and dread.' If we fear him not, we take him not for our master. Evangelical grace excludes not this fear; 'though we receive a kingdom that cannot be moved,' yet must our acceptable service of God be with reverence and godly fear. With fear and trembling we must work out our salvation. In fear we must 'pass the time of sojourning here.' In it we must converse together; yea, 'holiness is to be perfected in the fear of God,' and that ' because we have the promises.' The most prosperous churches walk in this fear, it is a necessary means of preventing destruction, and of attaining salvation when we have the promises. 'God puts this fear in the hearts of those that shall not depart from him.' See therefore that the greatness of the Almighty God possess thy soul continually with his fear.

God's almightiness should also possess us with holy admiration of him, and cause us in heart and voice to magnify him. O what a power is that which made the world of nothing; which upholds the earth without any foundation but his will; which placed and maintains all things in their order in heaven and earth; which causes so great and glorious a creature as the sun, that is so much bigger than all the earth, to move so many thousand miles in a few moments, and constantly to keep its time and course! That gives its instinct to every brute, and causes every part of nature to do its office! By his power it is that every motion of the creature is performed, and that order is kept in the kingdoms of the world. 'He made the heaven and the earth by his great power, and stretched out arm, and nothing is too hard for him : the great, the mighty God, the Lord of hosts, is his name ; great in counsel, and mighty in work.—The great, the mighty, the terrible God.—To him therefore that alone doth great wonders, we must give the greatest praise.—O how great are his works, and his thoughts are very deep.—Great is our Lord and of great power.—Therefore in Zion must he be great.—And his great and terrible name must be praised.'

3. In the church where he is known, must his name be great; thus, ' For we know that the Lord is great, and our God is above all gods.' His saints delight to praise his greatness : ' Bless the Lord, O my soul! O Lord my God, thou art very great! Thou art clothed with honour and majesty, who coverest thyself with light as with a garment, who stretchest out the heavens like a curtain, who layeth the beams of his chambers in the waters, who maketh the clouds his chariot, who walketh upon the wings of the wind, who maketh his angels spirits, his ministers a flame of fire,' &c. From almightiness all things have their being, and therefore must honour the Almighty. ' Alpha and Omega, the beginning and the ending, saith the Lord, which is, and which was, and which is to come, the Almighty.' They that magnify the Lord with the song of Moses and of the Lamb, say, ' great and marvellous are thy works, O Lord God Almighty ; just and true are thy ways, thou King of saints.'

The almightiness of God must imprint upon our souls a strong and stedfast confidence in him, according to the tenor of his covenant and promises. Nothing more certain than that impotency and insufficiency will never cause him to fail us, or to break his word. O what an encouragement is it to the saints, that they are built on such an impregnable rock, and that omnipotency is engaged for them! O what a shame is this to our unbelief, that ever we should distrust omnipotency!

If God be almighty, remember in thy greatest wants, that there is no want but he can easily and abundantly supply. Remember in thy greatest suffering, pains, or dangers, that no pain is so great which he cannot mitigate and remove, and no danger so great from which he is not able to deliver thee. The servants of Christ dare venture on the flames, because they trust upon the Almighty. In confidence of omnipotency, they dare stand against the threatenings of the greatest upon earth. ' We are not careful,' said those three believers to the king, ' to answer thee in this matter : if it be so, our God whom we serve is able to deliver us.' He that is afraid to stand upon a slender bow, or upon the unstable waters, is not afraid to stand upon the earth ; and he that is afraid of robbers when he is alone, is bolder in a conquering army ; what will man trust, if he distrust omnipotency ? Where can we be safe, if not in the love, the covenant, the hands of the Almighty God ? When storms and winds had frighted the disciples, lest they should be drowned when Christ was in the ship, their sin was aggravated by the presence of their powerful Lord, whose mighty works they had often seen. ' Why fear ye, saith he, O ye of little faith ?' Cannot he rebuke the winds and waves ; and will not all obey the rebukes of the Almighty ? When thou hast a want that God cannot supply, or a sickness that he cannot cure, or a danger that he cannot prevent, then be thou fearful, distrust him, and spare not. Remember also in thy lowest state, and in the church's greatest sufferings or dangers, that the Almighty is able to raise up his church or thee even in a moment.

If you say, that it is true God can do it, but we know not whether he will; I answer, 1. I shall show you in due place, how far he hath revealed his will for such deliverances. In sum, we have his promise, that all things shall work together for our good, and what would we have more? would you have that which is evil for you ? 2. At present, see that omnipotency do establish thy confidence so far as it is concerned in the cause. Be sure that no work is too hard for the Almighty : do not so much as in the thoughts of thy heart, make question of his power, and say with those unbelievers, ' Can God furnish a table in the wilderness? Can he give bread also? Can he provide flesh ?' If really thou distrust not the power of God, believe then the most difficult or improbable things, as well as the easiest and most probable, if God reveal or promise them. The resurrection seems improbable to impotent man ; but God hath promised it : and nothing is difficult to omnipotency. The calling of the Jews ; the ruin of the Turk ; the downfall of the pope ; the unity of Christians, all seem to us unlikely things : but all things to God are not only possible, but easy. He is at no more labour to make a world, than to make a straw, or make a fly. ' Whatsoever pleased the Lord, that did he in heaven and earth, in the sea and in the depths.' Dost thou think it improbable that ever all thy sins should be conquered ; and that ever thy soul should live with Christ among the holy saints and angels; and that ever thy body, that must first be dust, should shine as the stars in the firmament of God? Why doth it seem to thee improbable? Is it not as easy to God as to cause the earth to stand on nothing, and the sun to run its daily course? If God had promised you to live a day longer, or any small and common things, thou couldst then believe him; and is it not as easy to him to advance thee to everlasting glory, as to cause thee to live another hour, or to keep a hair of thy head from perishing? Sin is too strong for thee to overcome, but not for God. Death is too strong for thee to conquer; but not for Christ. Heaven is too high for thee to reach by thy own strength; but he that is there, and prepared it for thee, can take thee thither.

Trust God or trust nothing: he that cannot trust in him shall despair for ever; for all other confidence will deceive him. They that know his name will put their trust in him; for the Lord hath not forsaken them that seek him. ' All those that trust in him shall rejoice, and ever shout for joy, because he defendeth them.— Blessed is the man that maketh the Lord his trust, and respecteth not the proud, nor such as turn aside to lies. Whoso putteth his trust in the Lord shall be safe.' O what hath almightiness done in the world; what for the church; what for thee; and yet wilt thou distrust him? ' O how great is the goodness that he hath laid up for them that fear him; which he hath wrought for them that trust in him before the souls of men?—The Lord redeemeth the souls of his servants, and none of them that trust in him shall be desolate.' Are thy straits too great; thy work too hard? ' Commit thy way unto the Lord: trust also in him, and he shall bring it to pass.' In thy lowest state look up to the Almighty, and say, ' what time I am afraid, I will trust in thee: in God have I put my trust; I will not fear what man can do unto me.—The Lord is my rock, and my fortress, and my deliverer: my God and my strength; in whom I will put my trust; my buckler, and the horn of my salvation, and my high tower.—He is a buckler to all that trust in him. Some trust in chariots, and some in horses; but we will remember the name of the Lord our God.' Trust not in the creature, that is, in vanity and infirmity. There is not almightiness in man, or any creature. ' It is better therefore to trust in the Lord, than to put confidence in man: it is better to trust in the Lord, than to put confidence in princes. What a working passage is that, ' Thus saith the Lord, cursed be the man that trusteth in man, and maketh flesh his arm, and whose heart departeth

from the Lord! For he shall be like the heath in the deserts, and shall not see when good cometh. Blessed is the man that trusteth in the Lord, whose hope the Lord is; for he shall be as a tree planted by the waters, and that spreadeth out her roots by the river, and shall not see when heat cometh.'

Trust also in God, as one that is assured that no enemy is too strong for the Almighty. Alas, what is an army of dust to omnipotency? If the Lord but arise, ' his enemies will be scattered, and they that hate him will flee before him; as smoke is driven away, and as wax melteth before the fire, the wicked shall perish at the presence of the Lord.' While the Lord of Hosts is for us, we need not fear if hosts come against us; at worst they can but kill our bodies; and greater is he that is in us, than he that is in the world. O what a match have the miserable enemies of the church; what a work do they undertake; what a desperate attempt do they enterprize; to strive against heaven, and overcome omnipotency?

Trust in the Lord, as one that believes that no means or instruments are too small or weak for almightiness successfully to use. No matter who the instrument be, how mean, weak, and despicable, if it be but an almighty hand that uses it. A few poor fishermen and despised people, shall pull down Satan's kingdom in the world, and conquer the greatest, and bring in the nations to the faith, if omnipotency be with them.

The almightiness of God must fill our hearts with courage and resolution in his cause, and make us go on with greater alacrity in his work. Though we must be doves and lambs for innocency and meekness; yet must we be soldiers for valour and stability. Shall we flag or shrink, that have omnipotency on our side? Whoever scorns thee, or hates, or threatens, and imprisons thee, is not the almighty enough to set against them all, for thy encouragement?

The almightiness of God must be the comfort of all that have interest in him. O, did the blind world but see him that is omnipotent, or know the strength that is engaged for the weakest saint, they would soon see which is the strongest side, and which to cleave to, for their security. O blessed people, that have the Almighty on their side, and engaged with them against their enemies, and to do their works, and answer their desires! How can any of them perish, when the almighty is engaged for their salvation? ' The Father is greater than all, and none shall take them out of his hands.' How glad would men be in the beginning of a war, to know which side will prove the stronger, that they may join with that? Can the side that God is on be conquered? If you are wise, observe what cause is his, and let that be yours. 'It is hard to kick against the pricks:' woe to those souls that the Almighty is against, and that dash themselves on the rock that they should build on.

Chap. VIII.

The next attribute that must work upon us, is the infinite wisdom, or omniscience of God. His understanding is infinite. The impressions that this should make upon our souls are these:

1. Delight in wisdom, that you may in your places be like to God. The new man is renewed in knowledge after the image of him that created him. If God be infinitely wise, those then are the most excellent that are the wisest. Ignorance is the soul's blindness, and the privation of the image of God on the understanding. 'Wisdom excelleth folly, as far as light excelleth darkness.' To desire, as Adam did, any of that knowledge that God hath reserved to himself, or is unnecessary for us, is not indeed to be wise in our desires: unnecessary knowledge is but a trouble. But to know the Lord, and his revealed will, and the way of life, is the light and glory of our minds. He that hath lost his eye-sight, hath lost his principal natural delight, and is as one out of the world while he is in it. The ignorant souls that are void of the heavenly illumination, must needs be void of the delights of grace, and though they live in the visible church, where the beauty of holiness is the excellency of the saints, yet they do not see this beauty; but are like the infidels that are out of the church, while they are in it. The blind are in continual danger; they know not where they set their feet. They know not when to be confident, nor when to fear; sometimes they are afraid where there is no cause, because there may be cause for aught they know; and sometimes they are fearless at the very brink of death, and little think of the evil that they are near. Why do our poor deluded people so boldly live in an unconverted state, but because they know not where they are? Why do they so carelessly lie down and rise in an unsanctified condition, unpardoned, unready for death and judgment, and under the condemnation of the law, but because they know not the misery or danger in which they stand? Why do they go on so carelessly and wilfully in sin, despise the counsel of their teachers and of the Lord, and take a holy life as needless, but because they know not what they do? Men could not go so quietly or merrily to hell, with their

eyes open, as they do when they are shut by ignorance.

Whence is it, that such multitudes are still ungodly, under all the teachings and warnings of the Lord? but because 'They have their understandings darkened, being alienated from the life of God, by the ignorance that is in them, because of the blindness of their heart; and therefore many being past feeling, have given them over to lasciviousness, to work all uncleanness with greediness.' Sin is the fruit of folly, and the greatest folly: they are 'fools that make a jest of it.' It is for want of wisdom that they die. The ignorant are prisoners to the prince of darkness. 'Knowledge is despised by none but fools.' The conquest of so many subtile enemies, the performance of so many spiritual duties, which we must go through, if we will be saved, are works too hard for fools to do. The saving of a man's soul, is a work that requires the greatest wisdom. Therefore the illumination of the mind is God's first work in the conversion of a sinner. If infinite wisdom communicate to you but the smallest beam of heavenly light, it will change your minds, and make you other men than before, and set you on another course; wisdom will be your guide, and keep you in safe paths; it will cause you to refuse the evil, and to choose the good: it will show you true happiness, and the way to obtain it: it will cause you to foresee the evil, and escape it, when fools go on and are destroyed. Wisdom will teach you to know the season, to redeem your time, and walk exactly, when folly will leave you to too late repentance. There is not a soul in hell but was brought thither by sinful folly; nor is there a soul in heaven (of them at age) but by heavenly wisdom was conducted thither. In worldly matters the wicked may seem wisest; and many a saint may be very ignorant: but when you see the end, you will all confess that those were the wise men, that had wisdom to repel temptations, to refuse the enticing baits of sin, and to make sure of everlasting joys.

O therefore apply your hearts to wisdom! go to Christ for it, who is the wisdom of God, and is appointed by him to be our wisdom. He will teach it you, who is the best master in the world, so you will but keep in his school, that is, his church, and will humbly learn as little children, and apply yourselves submissively to his Spirit, word and ministers: 'Ask wisdom of God, that giveth liberally, and upbraideth not' with former ignorance. Think not any pains in holy means too much to get it. 'If thou wilt receive the words of God, and hide his commandments with thee, and incline thy heart to wisdom, and apply it to understanding ; yea, if thou criest after knowledge, and liftest up thy voice for understanding ; if thou seekest her as silver, and searchest for her as for hid treasures, then shalt thou understand the fear of the Lord, and find the knowledge of God ; for the Lord giveth wisdom; out of his mouth is knowledge and understanding;' and fear not being a loser by thy cost or labour. For 'happy is the man that findeth wisdom, and the man that getteth understanding : for the merchandise of it is better than silver, and the gain thereof than of fine gold: she is more precious than rubies, and all the things thou canst desire, are not to be compared to her; her ways are ways of pleasantness, and all her paths are peace.'

2. The infinite wisdom of God, must resolve you to take him for your principal teacher, counsellor and director, in all your undertakings. Who would go and seek the advice of a fool, when he may have infallible wisdom to direct him ? In a work of so great difficulty and concern, a work that hell, and earth, and flesh oppose ; a work that our everlasting state depends on ; I think it behoves us to take the best advice that we can get. And who knows the will of God, like God ? or who knows the certain means of salvation, like him that is the author and giver of salvation? Would you know whether it be best to live a mortified, holy life ? Who shall be your counsellor? If you advise with the flesh, you know that it would be pleased. If you advise with the world or wicked men, you know, that they would be imitated, and judge as they are ; and are not likely to be wise for you, that are so foolish for themselves, as to part with heaven for a merry dream. If you advise with the devil, you know he would be obeyed, and have company in his misery. You can advise with none but God, but such as are your enemies ; and will you ask an enemy, a deadly enemy, what course you should take to make you happy? Will you ask the devil how you may be saved; or will you ask the blind, ungodly world, what course you should take to please the Lord ? Or will you ask the flesh, by what means you may subdue it, and become spiritual ? If you take advice of scripture, of the Spirit, of a holy well-informed minister, or Christian, or of a renewed, well-informed conscience, I take this for your advising with the Lord ; but besides these that are his mouth, you can ask advice of none but enemies. But if they were ever so much your friends, and wanted wisdom, they could but ignorantly seduce you. Do you think that any of them

all, is as wise as God? It is the constant course of a worldly man to advise with the world, and of carnal men to advise with the flesh ; and therefore it is that they are hurried to perdition The flesh is brutish, and will lead you to a brutish life ; and if you live after it, undoubtedly you shall die ; and if you sow to it, you shall but reap corruption. If you are tempted to lust, will you ask the flesh that tempts you, whether you should yield ? If the cup of excess be offered to you, or flesh-pleasing feasts prepared for you, will you ask the flesh whether you should take them, or refuse them ? You may easily know what counsel it will give you. The counsel of God, and of our flesh, are contrary ; and therefore the lives of the carnal and spiritual man are contrary. Will you venture on the advice of a brutish appetite, and refuse the counsel of the all-knowing God ? Such as is your guide, and counsellor, such will be your end.

Never man miscarried by obeying God ; and never man sped well by obeying the flesh : God leads no man to perdition, and the flesh leads no man to his salvation. God's motions are all for our eternal good, though they seem to be for our temporal hurt : the motions of the flesh are for our eternal hurt, though at present they seem to be for our corporal benefit. If at any time you be at a loss, and your carnal friends, or your ease, or pleasure advises you one way, and the word of God and his faithful ministers advise you another way, use but your reason well, and consider whether God or those that contradict him be the wiser, and accordingly suit your practice. Alas ! man, thy friend is ignorant, and knows not what is good for himself. Thy flesh is ignorant, and knows not what is good for thy soul ! But God knows all things. Your flesh and friends feel what pleases them at present, and judge accordingly : but what will be hereafter they understand not, or consider not : but God knows as well what will be, as what is : he counsels you as one that knows how your actions will appear at last, and what it is that will save you, or undo you, to all eternity. If you be but sick, it is two to one but the counsel of your physician and of your appetite will differ. If you obey your physician before your appetite, for your health or life, should you not obey God before it, for your salvation ? Do you think in your consciences, that any that persuade you to a careless, worldly, fleshly life, are as wise as God that persuades you to the contrary ? You dare not say so with your tongues : and yet the most dare say to their lives. O how justly do the ungodly perish, that deliberately choose a brutish appetite, a malignant world, and a malicious devil, as a wiser or fitter conductor than the Lord! But 'blessed is the man that walketh not in the counsel of the ungodly, but his delight is in the law of the Lord.' Woe to the ungodly, that reject and set at nought the counsel of the Lord, and will have none of it! that wait not for his counsel, 'that rebel against the words of God, and contemn the counsel of the most High.' Woe to them 'that take counsel against the Lord and his Christ, that they may break asunder his bonds, and cast away his obligations.' Woe to them that are 'given up to the lusts of their own hearts, and to walk in their own counsels;' for 'by their own counsels shall they fall.' But had they hearkened to the Lord, and walked in his way, with the fulness of his blessings would he have satisfied them. Resolve therefore, whatever the flesh or the world say, that 'the testimonies of God shall be your counsellors,' and 'bless the Lord that giveth thee counsel.' For his counsel is infallible; having guided thee by his counsel, he will bring thee to his glory.

3. The infinite wisdom of God, must resolve the soul to rest in his determinations. We are most certain that God is not deceived. Though all men seem liars to you, let God be true: for it is impossible for him to lie. If our reason be to seek, so is not God. When we are saying with Nicodemus, How can these things be? God knows how: and it is enough for us to know that they are so. If infinite wisdom say the word, believe it, though all the world contradict it. Though proud unbelievers say, that the words of God are improbable, let them know that God is not at a loss when men's dark understandings are at a loss: the sun is not taken out of the firmament, whenever a man closes or loses his eyes. What! will those cavillers puzzle the Almighty; will they pose omniscience? Doth it follow that the course of the planets, the heavens, and all the creatures are out of order, if these silly moles understand not the order of them? No more will it follow that any word of God is false, or any rule of God is crooked, because they see not its truth and rectitude. Shall dust and ashes judge the Lord? who hath been his counsellor, and with whom hath he advised for the making, redeeming, or governing of the world? There is no rest to an inquisitive soul, but in the infinite wisdom of the Lord. Find once that it is his word, and inquire no further. It is madness to demand a further proof. As all goodness is comprised in his will and love; so all truth is comprised in his wisdom and revela-

tions. There are no arguments but what are lower and subordinate to this. Therefore if thy reason be at a loss, as to the cause or manner, yet hast thou the greatest reason to believe that all is just and true that proceeds from the wisdom of the Lord. If flesh and blood, and all the world gainsay it, yet rest in the word of God.

4. The next effect that God's omniscience should have upon our minds, is to take all the sayings of men as folly, that are against the Lord. Let them be high or low, learned or unlearned, if they contradict the God of infinite wisdom, take it but as the words of a distracted man. Did you ever meet with any man of them, that durst say he was wiser than God himself? Herod, who was eaten to death with vermin, was applauded by the flattering crowd, but with this acclamation, 'It is the voice of a god, and not of a man.' Will you say of any man that he is wiser than God? If you dare not say so, how dare you hear them and believe them against the word of God? How dare you be drawn from a holy life, from a self-denying duty, or from the truth of God, by the words of a man, yea, perhaps of a fool, who speaks against the word of God! 'To the law, and to the testimony; if they speak not according to these, it is because there is no light in them.'

5. The infinite wisdom of God, should establish our confidence concerning the fulfilling of all his word. He will not fail for want of knowledge: when he spoke that prophecy, that promise, or that threatening, he perfectly knew all things that would come to pass, to all eternity. He knew therefore what he said when he gave out his word, and therefore will fulfil it. 'Heaven and earth may pass away, but one jot or tittle of his word shall not pass away till all be accomplished.'

6. From the infinite wisdom of God, the church must be encouraged in its greatest straits, and against all the cunning and subtilty of their enemies. Are we ever in such straits, that God knows not how to bring us out? When we see no way for our deliverance, doth it follow that he sees none? If cunning serpents are too subtle for us, do we think that they can deceive the Lord? What had become of us long ago, if God had not known whatever is plotted in Rome, or Spain, or hell against us? If he knows not of all the consultations of the conclave, and of all the contrivances of jesuits and friars; and of all the jugglings of the masked emissaries. If God had not known of Vaux and his powder mine, it might have blown up all our hopes. But while

we know that God is in their councils, hearing every word they say, and knowing every secret of their hearts, and every mischief which they enterprise, let us do our duty, and rest in the wisdom of our great protector, who will prove all his adversaries to have played the fool: for as sure as his omnipotency shall be glorified by overcoming all opposing powers, so sure shall his infinite wisdom be glorified, by conquering and befooling the wisdom that is against him.

7. If God be infinite in knowledge, it must resolve us all to live accordingly. O remember, whatever thou thinkest, that God is acquainted with all thy thoughts. Wilt thou feed on lustful, covetous, malicious, or unbelieving thoughts, in the eye of God? Remember in thy prayers and every duty, that he knows the very frame of all thy affections, and the manner as well as the matter of thy services. Wilt thou be cold and careless in the sight of God? O remember in thy most secret sins, and thy works of darkness, that nothing is unknown to God; and that before him thou art in the open light. Fearest thou not the face of the Almighty. Wilt thou do that when he knows it, that thou wouldest not do if man did know? He knows whether thou deceive thy neighbour, or deal uprightly: defraud not therefore, for the Lord is the avenger. Do nothing that thou wouldest not have God to know. For certainly he knows all things. Shall he not see, that made and illuminates the eye? And shall he not hear, that made both tongue and ears? Shall he not know that gives us understanding, and by whom we know?

Let this be thy comfort in thy secret duties. He that knows thy heart, will not overlook the desires of thy heart, though thou hadst not words as thou desirest to express them. He that knows thy uprightness, will justify thee, if all the world condemn thee. He that sees thee in thy secret alms, or prayers, or tears, will openly reward thee. Let this also comfort thee under all the slanders of malicious or misinformed men. He that must be thy judge and theirs, is acquainted with the truth; who will certainly ' bring forth thy righteousness as the light, and thy judgment as the noon-day.' O how many souls are justified with the omniscient God, that are condemned by the malignant world! How many blots will be wiped off before the world at the day of judgment, that here did lie upon the names of faithful, upright men! O how many hypocrites shall be then disclosed; what a cutting thought should it be to the dissembler, that his secret falsehood is known to God; and when he hath the reputation that he fought with men, he

hath his reward! For it is a more sad reward that God will give him.

Chap. IX.

The next of God's attributes that must make its impress on the soul, is his infinite goodness. The denomination of goodness, as all other of his attributes, is suited to the capacity or affections of the soul of man. That which is truly amiable is called good. Not as if there were no goodness, but what is a means to man's felicity, as some most foolishly have affirmed: for our end and felicity itself, and God as he is perfect and excellent in himself, is more amiable than all means.

In three respects therefore it is that God is called good, or amiable to man. 1. In that he is infinitely excellent and perfect in himself. For the love of friendship is a higher love than that of desire. The most perfect sort of love is that which wholly carries the lover from himself to the perfect object of his love. The soul delights to contemplate excellency, when excellency itself, and not the delight, is the ultimate end of that desire and contemplation. 2. God is called good, as he is the pattern and fountain of all moral good. As he makes us righteous, holy laws, commanding moral good, and forbidding and condemning evil. And thus his goodness is his holiness and righteousness, his faithfulness and truth. 3. God is called good, as he is the fountain of all the creature's happiness, and as he is bountiful and gracious, and ready to do good, and as he is the felicitating end and object of the soul.

This infinite goodness must have these effects upon us. 1. It must possess us with a superlative love to God. This blessed attribute is it that makes us saints indeed, and makes that impression on us, which is as the heart of the new creature. It is goodness that produces love. Love is that grace that closes with God as our happiness and end, and is the felicitating enjoying grace. Without it we are but as sounding brass, or tinkling cymbals, whatever our gifts and parts may be. Love is the very excellency of the soul, as it closes with the infinite excellency of God. It is the very felicity of the soul, as it enjoys him that is our felicity. Most certainly the prevailing love of God, is the surest evidence of true sanctification. He that hath most love, hath most grace; and is the best and strongest Christian; and he that hath least love, is the worst or weakest. Knowledge and faith are but to work our hearts to love; and when love is perfect, they have done their work. Teaching and distant revelations will not be for ever; and therefore such knowledge and faith as we have now, will not be for ever. But God will be for ever amiable to us, and therefore love will endure for ever. The goodness of God is called love, and as 'God is love, so he that dwelleth in love doth dwell in God, and God in him.' The knowledge of divine goodness makes us good, because it makes us love him that is good. It is love that acts most purely for God. Fear is selfish, and hath somewhat of aversion. Though there be no evil in God for us to fear, yet is there such good in him that will bring the evil of punishment upon the evil; and this they fear. But love resigns the soul to God, and that in the most acceptable manner. Make it therefore your daily work to possess your souls with the love of God. Love him once, and all that he saith and doth will be more acceptable to you; and all that you say or do in love, will be more acceptable unto him. Love him and you will be loth to offend him; you will be desirous to please him; you will be satisfied in his love. Love him and you may be sure that he loves you. 'Love is the fulfilling of his law.' That you may love him, this must be your work, to believe and contemplate his goodness. Consider daily of the infinite goodness or amiableness of his nature, and of his excellency appearing in his works, and of the perfect holiness of his laws. But especially see him in the face of Christ, and behold his love in the design of our redemption, in the person of the Redeemer, in the promises of grace, and in all the benefits of redemption. Yea, look by faith to heaven itself, and think how you must for ever live in the perfect blessed love of infinite enjoyed goodness. As it is the knowledge and sight of gold, beauty, or any other earthly vanity, that kindles the love of them in the minds of men; so is it the knowledge and serious contemplation of the goodness of God that must make us love him, if ever we will love him.

2. The goodness of God must also encourage the soul to trust him. For infinite good will not deceive us. Nor can we fear any hurt from him, but what we wilfully bring upon ourselves. If I knew but which were the best and most loving man in the world, I could trust him above all men; and I should not fear any injury from him. How many friends have I that I dare trust with my estate and life, because I know that they have love and goodness in their low degree! Shall I not trust the blessed God, that is love itself, and infinitely good? whatever he will be in justice to the ungodly, I am sure he delights

not in the death of sinners, but rather that they turn and live; and that he will not cast off the soul that loves him, and would wish to be fully conformed to his will. It cannot be that he should spurn at them who are humbled at his feet, and long, pray, seek, and mourn after nothing more than his grace and love. Think not of God as if he had less of love and goodness, than the creature has: If you have high and confident thoughts of the goodness and fidelity of any man on earth, and dare quietly trust him with your life and all; see that you have much higher thoughts of God, and trust him with greater confidence, lest you set him below the silly creature in the attributes of his goodness, which his glory and your happiness require you to know.

3. The infinite goodness of God must call off our hearts from the inordinate love of all created good whatever. Who would stoop so low as earth, that may converse with God? Who would feed on such poor delights, that hath tasted the graciousness of the Lord? Nothing more sure than that the love of God doth not reign in that soul where the love of the world, or of fleshly lust, or pleasure, reigns. Had worldlings, or sensual, or ambitious men, but truly known the goodness of the Lord, they could never have so fallen in love with those deceitful vanities. If we could but open their eyes to see the loveliness of their Redeemer, they would soon be weaned from other lovers. Would you conquer the love of riches, honour, or any thing else that corrupts your affections? O try this sure and powerful way! Draw nigh to God, and take the fullest view thou canst; in thy most serious meditation of his infinite goodness, and all things else will be vile in thy esteem, and thy heart will soon contemn them and forget them, and thou wilt never dote upon them more.

4. The infinite goodness of God should increase repentance, and win the soul to a more resolute, cheerful service of the Lord. O what a heart is that which can offend, and wilfully offend, so good a God! This is the odiousness of sin, that it is an abuse of an infinite good. This is the most heinous, damning aggravation of it, that infinite goodness could not prevail with wretched souls against the empty flattering world: but that they suffered a dream and shadow, to weigh down infinite goodness in their esteem. And is it possible for worse than this to be found in man? He that had rather the sun were out of the firmament, then a hair were taken off his head, were unworthy to see the light of the sun. And surely he that will turn

away from God himself, to enjoy the pleasures of his flesh, is unworthy to enjoy the Lord. It is bad enough that Augustine, in one of his epistles, says of worldly men, that 'they had rather there were two stars fewer in the firmament, than one cow fewer in their pastures, or one tree fewer in their woods or grounds.' But it is ten thousand times a greater evil that every wicked man is guilty of, who will rather forsake the living God, and lose his part in infinite goodness, than he will let go his filthy and unprofitable sins. O sinners, as you love your souls, 'despise not the riches of the goodness, forbearance, and long-suffering of the Lord; but know that his goodness should lead you to repentance. Would you spit at the sun? Would you revile the stars? Would you curse the holy angels? If not, O do not ten thousand-fold worse, by your wilful sinning against the infinite goodness itself.

But for you Christians that have seen the amiableness of the Lord, and tasted of his perfect goodness, let this be enough to melt your hearts, that ever you have wilfully sinned against him: O what a good did you contemn in the days of your unregeneracy, and in the hour of your sin! Be not so ungrateful and disingenuous as to do so again. Remember whenever any temptation comes, that it would entice you from the infinite good: ask the tempter, man or devil, whether he hath more than an infinite good to offer you: and whether he can out-bid the Lord for your affection?

And now for the time that is before you, how cheerfully should you address yourselves unto his service; and how delightfully should you follow it on from day to day! What manner of persons should the servants of this God be, that are called to nothing but what is good! How good a master; how good a work; and how good company, encouragements, and helps; and how good an end! All is good, because it is the infinite good that we serve and seek: and shall we be loitering, unprofitable servants!

5. Moreover, this infinite goodness should be the matter of our daily praises. He that cannot cheerfully magnify this attribute of God, so suitable to the nature of the will, is surely a stranger to the praises of the Lord. The goodness of God should be a daily feast to a gracious soul, and should continually feed our cheerful praises, as the spring or cistern fills the pipes. I know no sweeter work on earth, nay, I am sure there is no sweeter, than for faithful sanctified souls, rejoicing to magnify the goodness of the Lord, and join together in his cheerful praises. O Christians, if you would taste the joys of saints,

and live like the redeemed of the Lord indeed, be much in the exercise of this heavenly work, and with holy David, make it your employment, and say, 'O how great is thy goodness which thou hast laid up for them that fear thee.—The earth is full of the goodness of the Lord;' what then are the heavens? 'Thy congregation hath dwelt therein: thou, O Lord, hast prepared thy goodness for the poor.— O that men would praise the Lord for his goodness, and for his wonderful works to the children of men! For he satisfieth the longing soul, and filleth the hungry soul with goodness.—The goodness of God endureth continually.—Truly God is good to Israel, even to such as are of a clean heart.—O taste and see that the Lord is good, blessed is the man that trusteth in him.—The Lord is good, his mercy is everlasting, his truth endureth from generation to generation.—The Lord is good to all, and his tender mercies are over all his works.—O praise the Lord, for the Lord is good; sing praises to his name, for it is pleasant.' Call him as David, 'my goodness, and my fortress, my high tower, my deliverer, my shield, and he in whom I trust.—Let men therefore speak of the glorious honour of his majesty and of his wondrous works: let them abundantly utter the memory of his great goodness, and sing of his righteousness.' If there be a thought that is truly sweet to the soul, it is the thought of the infinite goodness of the Lord. If there be a pleasant word for man to speak, it is the mention of the infinite goodness of the Lord! And if there be a pleasant hour for man on earth to spend, and a delightful work for man to do, it is to meditate on, and with the saints to praise the infinite goodness of the Lord. What was the glory that God showed unto Moses, and the taste of heaven that he gave him upon earth, but this, 'I will make all my goodness pass before thee, and I will proclaim the name of the Lord before thee; and I will be gracious on whom I will be gracious, and will show mercy on whom I will show mercy.' And his proclaimed name was, 'the Lord, the Lord God, merciful and gracious, long-suffering, and abundant in goodness and truth.' These were the holy praises that Solomon did consecrate the temple with, 'Arise, O Lord God, into thy resting place, thou and the ark of thy strength: let thy priests, O Lord God, be clothed with salvation, and let thy saints rejoice in goodness.' O Christians, if you would have joy indeed, let this be your employment! Draw near to God, and have no low undervaluing thoughts of his infinite goodness; for 'how great is his goodness, and how great is his beauty?'

Why is it that divine consolations are so strange to us, but because divine goodness is so lightly thought upon ? As those that think little of God at all, have little of God upon their hearts; so they that think but little of his goodness in particular, have little love, or joy, or praise.

6. Moreover, the goodness of God must possess us with desire to be conformed to his goodness, in our measure. The holy perfection of his will, must make us desire to have our wills conformed to the will of God; we are not called to imitate him in his works of power, nor so much in the paths of his omniscience, as we are in his goodness, which as manifested in his work and word, is the pattern and standard of moral goodness in the sons of men. The impress of his goodness within us, is the chief part of his image on us; and the fruits of it in our lives is their holiness and virtue. As he is good and doth good, so must it be our greatest care to be as good, and do as much good as possibly we can. Any thing within us that is sinful and contrary to the goodness of God, should be to our souls as poison to our bodies, which nature is excited to strive against with all its strength, and can have no safety or rest till it be cast out; and for doing good, it must be the very study and trade of our lives. As worldlings study and labour for the world, and the pleasing of their flesh: so must the Christian study and labour to improve his master's talents to his use, and to do as much good as he is able, and to please the Lord. ' The desire of the righteous (as such) is only good. —To depart from evil and do good,' is the care of the just. ' We must please our neighbours for good to their edification.—While we have time we must do good to all men, as we are able ; but especially to them of the household of faith.' Not only to them that do good to us, but to our enemies. This is it that we must not forget; and which by ministers we must be put in mind of; which all that love life and would inherit the blessing, must devote themselves to. In this we must be like our heavenly Father, and approve ourselves his children.

7. From the perfect infinite goodness of God, we must learn to judge of good and evil, in all the creatures. To this must all be reduced as the standard, and by this must they be tried. It is a most wretched absurdity of sensual men, to try the will, word, or ways of God, by themselves, and by their own interests or wills; and to judge all to be evil in God that is against them. And yet, alas, how common is this case ! Every man is naturally loth to be miserable: suffering he abhors; and therefore that which causes his suffering he calls evil. So when he hath deserved it himself by his sin, he thinks that the law is evil for threatening it, and that God himself is evil for inflicting it; so that infinite goodness must be tried and judged by the vicious creature, and the rule and standard must be reduced to the crooked line of human actions or dispositions; and if God will please the worldling, the sensualist, the proud, the negligent, who should please him, then he shall be good, and he shall be God ; if not, say these judges, he shall be evil, and unmerciful, and no God. They will not believe that he is good that punishes them. Thus if the thief or murderer had the choice of kings and judges, you may know what persons he would choose; no one should be a judge, or accounted a good man, that would condemn and hang him.

But I beseech you consider, what is fit to be the rule and standard, if not perfection of goodness itself. Do you think that the will of ignorant, fleshly, sinful man, is more fit to be the rule of goodness, than the will of God ? We are sure that God is not deceived, and sure that there is no iniquity with him; but we know that all men are liable to deceit, and have private interests, and corrupted minds and wills that have some vicious inclination. O what blasphemy is in the heart of that man, that will sooner condemn the holy will and law of God, than his own will, or the wills of any men, be they ever so seemingly wise or great ! The will of God is revealed in his laws, concerning the necessity of a holy life; and the will of foolish, wicked men is by their scornful speeches and sinful lives revealed to be against it. Which of these do you follow ; which is it that prescribes you the better course ? The will of God that is infinitely good, or the will of man that is miserably evil ? If you know any better than God, follow him before God. But if none be greater and more powerful than he, if none be wiser or of more knowledge, it is as sure that none is better. Much less are those ignorant, wicked men, that despise the scripture and a holy life, and would persuade you that they can tell you of a better way. Let me speak it to the terror of the ungodly soul, who by the deceits or scorn of any sort of men is drawn away from Christ and holiness ; it shall stand on record against thee until the day of judgment, and it shall stick continually as a dagger in thy heart, that thou didst prefer the reason and the will of man, yea, perhaps of a drunkard, or a worldling, before the word or will of God: and though thy tongue durst not speak it, thy life did speak it, that thou thoughtest the word and will of man to be better than the word and will of God: yea more, that thou tookest the way of the devil to be better than God's ways, who is infinitely good: for surely thou choosest that which thou takest to be best for thee. Therefore if that man deserve condemnation, that sets up a man, a horse, or an image, and saith, This is a greater and wiser than God, and therefore this shall be my god, then dost thou deserve the same condemnation that settest up the words or will of man, even of wicked men, and sayest by thy practice, These are better than God, and his word, or will, and therefore I will choose or follow them. For God is full as jealous of the honour of his goodness, as of his power or wisdom.

Well, Christians, let flesh and blood say what it will, and let all the world say what they will, judge that best that is most agreeable to the will of God; for good and evil must be measured by this will. That event is best which he determines of, and that action is best which he commands. All is naught, and will prove so in the end, that is against this will of God, what policy or good soever may be pretended for it.

8. If the will of God be infinitely good, we must all labour both to understand it and perform it. Many say, 'Who will show us any good?' Would you not know what is best, that you may choose and seek it? As the inordinate desire of knowing natural good and evil did cause our misery, so the holy rectified desires of knowing spiritual good, must recover us: search the scriptures then, and study and inquire; for it more concerns you to know the will of God, than to know the will of your princes or benefactors, or know of any treasures of the world: the riches of grace are given to us, by God's 'making known the mystery of his will, according to his good pleasure which he purposed in himself.' Our desire to know the good will of God, must be that we may do it. For this must we pray, ' That we may be filled with the knowledge of his will, in all wisdom and spiritual understanding, that we may walk worthy of the Lord, unto all pleasing, being fruitful in every good work, that we may ' be made perfect in every good work to do his will, and have that wrought in us which is pleasing in his sight;' that we may not only ' know his will and approve the things that are excellent,' but may ' prepare ourselves to do according to his will,' lest we be punished the more. See that the will of no man be preferred before God's will; seek not your own wills, nor set them up against the Lord's: if Christ, whose will was pure and holy,

profess that he sought not his own will, but his Father's, and that he ' came not to do his own will, but his that sent him ;' should it not be our resolution, whose wills are so misguided and corrupt?

9. If God's will be infinitely good, we must rest in his will. When his ways are dark, or grievous to our flesh: when his word seems difficult; when we know not what he is doing with us, remember it is the will that is infinitely good, that is disposing of us. Only let us see that we stand not cross to the greater good of his church and honour; and then we may be sure that he will not be against our good. We that can rest in the will of a dear and faithful friend, should much more rest in the will of God: do your duty, and be not unwise, but understanding what the will of the Lord is for you to do, and then distract not your minds with distrustful fears about his will that is infinitely good, but say, The will of the Lord be done.

10. The infinite goodness of God should draw out our hearts to desire communion with him, and to long after the blessed fruition of him in the life to come. O how glad should we be to tread his courts! to draw near him in his holy worship, to meditate on him, and secretly open our hearts before him, and to converse with those gracious souls that love to be speaking honourably of his name! What will draw the heart of man, if goodness and infinite goodness will not? When the drunkard saith in the alehouse, It is good to be here, and the covetous man among his gains, and the sensual man among his recreations and merry companions, It is good to be here; the Christian that can get nigh to God, or have any prospect of his love in his ordinances, concludes that of all places upon earth, ' it is good to be here,' and that ' a day in his courts is better than a thousand.' But O, to depart and be with Christ, is far better.' With infinite goodness we shall find no evil, no emptiness, or defect; when we perfectly enjoy the perfect good, what more can be added, but for ever to enjoy it? O! therefore, think on this, Christians, when death is dreadful to you, and you would willingly stay here, as being afraid to come before the Lord, or loth to leave the things which you here possess, shall goodness itself be distrusted by you, or seem no more desirable to you? Are you afraid of goodness? even of your Father, of your happiness itself? Are you better here than you shall be with God? Are your houses, lands, friends, pleasures, or any thing better than infinite goodness? O meditate on this blessed attribute of God, till you distaste the world, till you

are angry with your withdrawing, murmuring flesh : till you are ashamed of your unwillingness to be with God, and till you can calmly look in the face of death, and contentedly hear the message that is posting towards you, that you must presently come away to God. Your natural birth-day brought you into a better place than the womb ; and your gracious birth-day brought you into a far better state than your former sinful, miserable captivity ; and will not your glorious birth-day put you into a better habitation than this world ? O know, choose, seek, and live to the infinite good, and then it may be your greatest joy when you are called to him.

Chap. X.

Having spoken of these three great attributes of God, I must needs speak of those three great relations of God to man, and of those three works in which they are founded, which have flowed from these attributes.

This one God in three persons, hath created man and all things, which before were not ; hath redeemed man when he was lost by sin ; and sanctifies those that shall be saved by redemption. Though the external works of the trinity are undivided, yet not indistinct, as to the order of working, and a special interest that each person hath in each of these works. The Father, Son, and Holy Ghost did create the world ; and they also did redeem us, and sanctify us ; but so as that creation is in a special sort ascribed to the Father, redemption to the Son, and sanctification to the Holy Spirit ; not only because of the order of operation, agreeably to the order of subsisting ; for then the Father would be as properly said to be incarnate, or to die for us, or mediate, as the Son to create us—which is not to be said—for he created the world by his Word, or Son, and Spirit, and he redeemed it by his Son, and sanctifies it by his Spirit. But scripture assures us that the Son alone was incarnate for us, and died and rose again, and not the Father or the Spirit ; and so that the human nature is peculiarly united to the second person in glory ; and so that each person hath a peculiar interest in these several works, the reason of which is much above our reach.

The first of these relations of God to man, which we are to consider of, is, that he is our Creator ; it is he that giveth being to us and all things ; and that gives us all our faculties or powers. Under this, for brevity, we shall speak of him also as he is our preserver ; because preservation is but a kind of continued creation, or a continuance of the beings which God hath caused. God then is the first efficient cause of all the creatures, from the greatest to the least. And easily did he make them, for he spake but the word, and they were created : they are the products of his power, wisdom and goodness. He commanded and they were created. He still produces all things that in the course of nature are brought forth. ' Thou sendest forth thy Spirit ; they are created ; thou renewest the face of the earth.' From hence these following impressions must be made upon the considering soul.

1. If all things be from God as the creator and preserver, then we must be deeply possessed with this truth, that all things are for God as their ultimate end. For he that is the beginning and first cause of all things, must needs be the end of all. His will produced them, and the pleasure of his will is the end for which he did produce them. ' I have created him for my glory. —The Lord hath made all things for himself, yea, even the wicked for the day of evil.' I think the Chaldee paraphrase, the Syriac and Arabic, give us the true meaning of this, who concordantly translate it, ' the wicked is kept for the day of evil ;' as Job hath it, ' the wicked is reserved to the day of destruction : they shall be brought forth to the day of wrath.—To reserve the unjust to the day of judgment to be punished.' God made not the wicked as wicked, or to be wicked ; but he that gave them their being and continues it, will not be a loser by his creation or preservation, but will have the glory of his justice by them in the day of wrath or evil, for which he keeps them, and till which he bears with them, because they would not obediently give him he glory of his holiness and mercy. So it is said of Christ, ' for by him were all things created that are in heaven and that are in earth, visible and invisible ; all things were created by him and for him.' If they are by him, they must needs be for him.—So ' thou art worthy, O Lord, to receive glory, honour, and power ; for thou hast created all things, and for thy pleasure they are and were created.' This pleasure of God's will is the end of all things ; and therefore it is certain that he will see that all things shall accomplish that end, and his will shall be pleased We have all in few words ; ' for of him, and through him, and to him are all things ; to whom be glory for ever, Amen.' Of him, as the first efficient that gives them their beings : and through him, as the preserver, disposer and conductor of them to their end : and to him, as the ultimate end.

If you say, but how is the pleasure of God's will attained from the wicked that break his laws, and displease his will?

I answer: understand but how his will is crossed or accomplished, pleased or displeased, and you will see, that his will is always done and pleased, even by them that displease him in violating his will. For God's will hath two sorts of objects or products, which must be still distinguished: 1. He wills what shall be due from us to him, and from him to us. 2. He wills entities and events, or what shall actually be, or come to pass. Strictly both these acts of God's will, perform the things willed, and so are not without their proper effect. God, as the cause and disposer of all things, attains his will concerning events: all things shall come to pass which he absolutely wills shall come to pass. He is not frustrated of his will herein, being neither unwise, nor impotent, nor unhappy. 'Whatsoever pleased the Lord, that did he in heaven and in earth, in the sea and in the depths.—Our God is in heaven, he hath done whatsoever he pleased.' As God as our governor, doth by his laws oblige man to his duty, his will hath its effect: a command doth but make the thing commanded to be our duty, and our duty it is: and so this act of the will of God is not in vain. Thus far he hath his will. By his promises he makes the reward to be due to all, on condition they perform the duty on which he hath suspended it, and to be actually due to those only that perform the condition: and all this is accomplished. Heaven is conditionally offered to all, and actually given to the faithful only. So that what God wills to be due as a lawgiver, is accordingly due; and what he actually wills shall come to pass, verily shall come to pass according to his will.

But perhaps you will say, he doth not will that all men shall eventually obey his laws, but only that it shall be their duty.

I answer, our speeches of God being borrowed from man, who is one of the glasses in which he is here seen by us; especially the manhood of Jesus Christ. We must accordingly conceive and say, acknowledging still the improprieties and imperfections of our conceptions and expressions, that as man doth simply and most properly will the event of some things, which he absolutely desires should come to pass, and doth not simply will some other things, but only *in tantum* ; he so far wills them, that he wills and resolves to do such and such things as have a tendency thereto, and to go no farther, and do no more for the attaining of them, though he

could ; so God doth simply and properly will some things, that is, the things which he decrees shall come to pass: but we must after our manner conceive and say, that there are other things which he wills but only so far as to make it man's duty to perform it, and persuade him to the doing of that duty, and give him such a measure of help, as leaves him without any just excuse, if he do it not ; and so far he wills the salvation of such, as to promise or offer it them on such terms : and no further doth he will the obedience or salvation which never comes to pass, but leaves it here to the will of man. For if he simply willed that every duty should be eventually done, it would be done ; and if he simply willed that all men should be actually saved, they would be saved. And that he simply wills their duty or obligation, and likewise so far, doth will the event of their obedience and salvation, as this comes to, as aforesaid, is certain, and in this we are all agreed ; and I am not so well skilled in dividing, as to understand where the real difference lies between the parties that here most contend : but about the bare name I know they differ, some thinking that this last is not to be named an act of God's will, or a willing of man's obedience or salvation, and some thinking that it is so to be named : who doubtless are in the right ; nor is there room for controversies, while we confess the impropriety of this and all our speeches of God, as speaking after the manner of men ; and while scripture, that must teach us how to speak of God, doth frequently so speak before us.

2. God being the maker and first cause of all things, that is, of all substantial beings, commonly creatures, we must conclude that sin is no such being, because it is most certain that he is not the Creator or the cause of it. Scripture assures us, and all Christians are agreed, that God is not the cause or author of sin. How odious then should that be to us, that is so bad as not to come from God? If God disclaim it, let us disclaim it. Let us abhor that it should come from us, seeing God abhors that it should come from him. Own not that which hath nothing of God upon it.

If you say, that it is an accident though not a substance, and therefore it must needs come from God, because even accidents have their being.

I answer, that among the most subtle disputers it is granted, that it hath no created being, or no being that is caused by God ; of this they are agreed. It is granted by all Christians that sin hath no other kind of being, but what the will of man can cause. And if that be so, the philosophical trifling controversy whether it be only a privation, or a relation, or *modus entis*, which the will thus causes, must be handled as philosophical, and valued but as it deserves: for this is all the controversy that here remains. If the form be relative, and the foundation be but a mere privation, the disconformity being founded in a defect, then the case is soon resolved, as to the rest. He that errs, understands amiss: that he understands is of God: that he errs, that is, is defective, and so false in his understanding, is of himself: that he wills when he chooses sin, is of God the universal cause: but that he wills a forbidden object, rather than the contrary, and fails in his understanding and his will, this is not of God, but of himself. If others say that the very foundation of that disconformity which is the form of sin, is sometimes an act, they must also say that it is not an act as such, but this act comparatively considered, or as circumstantiated, or as exercised on the forbidden object rather than another, or a volition instead of a nolition, and choosing that which should be refused, or a refusing that which should be chosen: and whether this be a privation, or a mode, is a philosophical controversy; and in philosophy, and not in theology, is the difficulty; divines being agreed as aforesaid, that whatever you name it, being, or privation, or mode, it is but such as must be resolved ultimately into the will of man as its original, or first cause, supposing God to be the Creator and conserver of that free power that is able to choose or to refuse, and as an universal cause to concur with the agent to the act as such. But philosophers indeed are at a loss, and are desirous to tell us of privations, modes, relations, denominations, *entia rationis*, and I know not what, that they say are neither beings nor nothing, but between both they know not what! The nature of things, in the utmost extremities of the branches, being spun with so fine a thread, that the understanding is not subtle enough to discern them. And shall this disturb us in divinity, or be imputed to it?

If you say, that the will of God is the cause of all things, and therefore of sin.

I answer, if you call sin nothing, as a shadow, darkness, death, &c. are nothing, for all that we abhor them, then you answer yourselves; if you call it something, we are all agreed, that it is but such a something as man can cause without God's first causing it: it suffices that God do the part of a Creator in giving man the free power of choosing or refusing; and the part of a preserver, in maintaining that power, and as an universal cause concurring to all acts *in genere*, as the sun doth shine on the dunghill and the flowers: and that he also do the part of a just governor in prohibiting, dissuading, and threatening sinners.

Object. But how can sin eventually be, if God decree it not, seeing all events are from his will?

I answer, 1. We are agreed that he causes it not. 2. That he doth not so much as will the event of sin as sin. 3. That he willingly permits what is by him permitted. 4. And that sin is such a thing as may be brought forth by a bare permission, if there be no positive decree for the event. As a negative in the effects, requires not a positive cause, so neither a positive will for its production. There are millions of millions of worlds, and individual creatures, and species possible, that shall never be: and it is audaciousness to assert, that there must be millions of millions of positive decrees, that such worlds or creatures shall not be. 5. Nor is it any dishonour to God, if he have not a positive decree or will about every negation, as that all the men in the world shall not be called by a thousand possible names rather than their own, &c.

These things being all certain, I add, 1. Let them dispute that dare, that yet indeed God doth positively will the events of all privations or negations of acts. 2. But when men are once habitually wicked, and bent to evil, it is just with him, if he permit them to follow their own lusts, and if he leaves before them such mercies as he foreknows they will wilfully make occasions of their sin; and if he resolve to make use of the sin which he knows they will commit, for his church's good, and for his glory.

Object. But doth not God will that sin eventually shall not be?

Answ. Even as I before said, he wills that obedience eventually shall be. If sin come to pass, it is certain that God did not simply will that it should not come to pass: for then he must be conquered and unhappy by every sin: but he wills simply that it shall be the duty of man to avoid it; and he may be said to disallow the event so far as that he will forbid it, threaten, and dissuade the sinner, and give him the helps, that shall leave him inexcusable if he sin, and so leave it to his will. Thus far he may be said to will that sin eventually shall not be; but not simply.

Though these things are not obvious to vulgar capacities, yet they are such, as the subject in

hand, viz. God's first causation and creation, together with the weight of them, and the contentions of the world about them, have made needful.

3. If God be the Creator and the cause of
all, then we must remember that all his works
are good : and therefore nothing must be hated
by us that he hath made, considered in his native
goodness. God hates sin, and so must we : for
that he made it not, and he hates all the workers of iniquity as such, and so must we ; but we
must love all of God that is in them, and love
them for it. There is somewhat good and amiable in every creature ; yea all of it, that is of
God. Though some insects are odious to us,
because they are hurtful, and seem deformed in
themselves, yet are they good in themselves, and
not deformed as parts of the universe, but good
unto the common end. The wants in the wheels
of your watch are as useful to the motion as the
solid parts. The night is part of the useful order
of the creation, as well as the day. The vacant
interspace in your writing, is needful as well as
the words : every letter should not be a vowel, nor
every character a capital ; every member should
not be a heart, or head, or eye : nor should every
one in a commonwealth be a king, or lord : so
in the creation the parts that seem base, are useful in their places, and good unto their ends.
Let us not therefore vilify or detest the works
of God, but study the excellencies of them, and
see, admire, and love them as they are of God.
It is one of the hardest practical points before
us, to know how to estimate all the creatures,
and to use them without running into one extreme. At the same time to love the world, and
not to love it ; to honour it, and despise it ; to
exalt it, and to tread it under our feet ; to mind
it, use it with delight, and yet to be weaned from
it as those that mind it not. And yet a great
part of our Christian duty lies in the doing of
this difficult work. As the world is the devil's
bait, and the flesher's idol, set up against God,
and would entice us from him, or hinder us in
his service, and either be our carnal end and
happiness, or a means thereto, so we must make
it the care of our hearts to hate it, despise it,
neglect it, and tread it under foot ; and the labour
of our lives to conquer it.

But the same creatures must be admired,
studied, loved, honoured, delighted in, and daily
used, as they are the excellent work of the almighty God, and reveal to us his attributes or
will, being the glass in which we must see him
while we are in the flesh ; and as they lead us to
God, and strengthen, furnish or help us in his

service. But to love them for God, and not for
themselves, O how hard is it ! To keep pure
affections towards them, and a spiritual delight
in them, that shall not degenerate into a carnal
delight, is a task for the holiest saint on earth,
to labour in with all his care and power, as long
as he here liveth. Yet this must be done ; and
the soul that hath obtained true self-denial, and
is dead to the world, devoted and alive to God,
is able in some good measure to perform it. To
love the world for itself, and make the creature
our chief delight, and live to it as our end, and
idol, this is the common damning course. To
cast away our possessions, and put our talents
into our fellow-servants' hands, and to withdraw
ourselves as it were out of the world into solitude, as monks or hermits do, this is too like the
hiding of our talents, and a dangerous course of
unfaithfulness and unprofitableness, unless in
some extraordinary case ; and is at best the too
easy way of cowards that will be soldiers only
out of the army, or where there is but little danger of the enemy : but to keep our stations, and
take honours, and riches as our master's talents,
as a burden that we must honour him by bearing,
and the instruments by which we must laboriously do him service ; and to see and love him
in every creature, and study him in it, and sanctify it to his use ; and to see that our lust get
no advantage by it, and feed not on it ; but that
we tame our bodies, and have all that we have
for God, and not for our flesh ; this is the hard,
but the excellent, most acceptable course of
living in this world.

And it is not only other creatures, but ourselves also, that we must thus admire, love, and
use for God, while we abase ourselves, as to ourselves, and deny ourselves, and use not ourselves
for ourselves, but as we stand in due subordination to him. Abase yourselves as sinful, and
abhor that which is your own, and not the Lord's;
but vilify not your nature in itself, nor any thing
in you that is the work of God. Pretend not
humility for the dishonouring of your maker.
Reason and natural freedom of the will, are
God's work, and not yours, and therefore must
be honoured, and not scorned and reviled ; but
the blindness and error of your reason, and the
bad inclinations and actions of your free-wills,
these are your own, and therefore vilify them,
hate them, and spare not. And when you lament the smallness of your graces, deny them
not ; and slight not, but magnify the preciousness of that little that you have, while you mourn
for the imperfection. And when men offend
you, or prove your enemies, forget not to value

and love that of God that yet is in them. All is good that is of God.

4. If all things be of God, as the creator and conserver, we must hence remember on whom it is that ourselves and all things else depend. 'In him we live, move, and have our being.—He upholds all things by the word of his power,' the earth stands upon his will and word. The nations are in his hands, so are the lives of our friends and enemies, and so are ourselves. Therefore our eye must be upon him; our care must be to please him; and our trust and quietness must be in him; and blessed is he that maketh sure of an interest in his special love.

5. Hence also we must observe the vanity of all creature-confidence, and our hearts must be withdrawn from resting in any means or instruments. They are nothing to us, and can do nothing for us, but what they have or do from him that made and preserves us.

6. And lastly, hence also we may see the patience and goodness of the Lord, that as he refused not to make those men that he foreknew would live ungodlily, so he denies not to uphold their being, even while they sin against him. All the while that they are abusing his creatures, they are sustained by him, and have those creatures from him. From him the drunkard hath his drink, and the glutton his meat, and the voluptuous youth their abused health and strength; and all men have from him the powers or faculties of soul and body by which they sin. And shall any be so ungrateful as to say therefore that God doth cause their sin? It is true, he can easily stop thy breath while thou art swearing, lying, and speaking against the service of God that made thee: and wouldst thou have him do so? He can easily take away the meat, drink, riches, health, and life which thou abusest; and wouldst thou have him do it? He can easily keep thee from sinning any more on earth, by cutting off thy life, and sending thee to pay for what thou hast done: and art thou content with this? Must he be taken to be a partaker in thy sin, because he doth not strike thee dead, or lame, or speechless, or disable thee from sinning? Provoke him not by thy blasphemies, lest he clear himself in a way that thou desirest not. But O wonder at his patience, that holds thee in his hand, and keeps thee from falling into the grave and hell, while thou art sinning against him! While a curse or oath is in thy mouth, he could let thee fall into utter misery. How often hast thou provoked him to take thee in thy lust, in thy rage, or in thy neglect of God, and give

thee thy desert! Would any of you support your enemy, as God doth you.

Chap. XI.

As we must know God as our Creator. so also as our Redeemer; of which I shall say but little now, because I have mentioned it more fully in the Directions for Sound Conversion. It is 'life eternal to know the Father, and Jesus Christ whom he has sent.' The Father redeems us by the Son, whom he sent, whose sacrifice he accepted, and in whom he is well pleased; and this must have these effects upon our souls.

1. We must be hence convinced, that we are not now in a state of innocency, nor to be saved as innocents, or on the terms of the law of our creation: but salvation is now by a Redeemer: and therefore consists in our recovery and restoration. The objects of it are only lapsed, sinful, miserable men. Name the creature if you can, since Adam, that stood before God here in the flesh, in a state of personal, perfect innocency, except the immaculate Lamb of God. If God, as Creator, should now save any, without respect to a redemption, it must be on the terms of the law of creation: upon which it is certain that no man hath or shall be saved; that is, upon perfect, personal, persevering obedience. You cannot exempt infants themselves from sin and misery, without exempting them from Christ the Redeemer, and the remedy. 'There is none righteous (in himself without a Redeemer) no not one.—They are all gone out of the way.—That every mouth may be stopped, and all the world may become guilty before God.' And if all the world be guilty, none are innocent: 'therefore by the deeds of the law there shall no flesh be justified in his sight.—For all have sinned, and come short of the glory of God; being justified freely by his grace, through the redemption that is in Jesus Christ.—All we like sheep have gone astray, we have turned every one to his own way, and the Lord hath laid on him the iniquity of us all.—Through the offence of one, many are dead.—And the judgment was by one to condemnation.—By the offence of one, death reigned by one.—By the offence of one, judgment came on all men to condemnation.—By one man's disobedience many were made sinners.—We were shapen in iniquity, and in sin did our mother conceive us.—We were by nature the children of wrath, and dead in trespasses and sins.—In Adam all die.—We thus judge, that if one died for all, then were all dead—Christ is the Saviour of the body.—Christ loved the church, and gave himself for it, that he might

sanctify and cleanse it with the washing of water, by the word, that he might present it to himself a glorious church.' If infants have no sin and misery, then they are none of the body, the church, which Christ loved and gave himself for, that he might cleanse it. But what further proof need we when we have the common experience of all the world? Would every man that is born of a woman, without exception, so early manifest sin in the life, if there were no corrupt disposition at the heart? And should all mankind without exception, taste of the punishment of sin, if they had no participation of the guilt? Death is the wages of sin; and 'by sin death entered into the world, and it passeth upon all men, for that all have sinned.' Infants have sickness, torments, and death, which are the fruits of sin. And were they not presented to Christ as a Saviour, when he took them in his arms and blessed them, and said, ' of such is the kingdom of God?' Certainly, none that never were guilty, or miserable, are capable of a place in the kingdom of the Mediator. For to what end should he mediate for them; or how can he redeem them, that need not a redemption? or how should he reconcile them to God, that never were at enmity with him? Or how can he wash them that never were unclean? Or how can he be a physician to them that never were sick; ' when the whole have no need of the physician.' He ' came to seek and to save that which was lost, and to save his people from their sins.' They are none of his saved people therefore, that had no sin. He came to ' redeem those that were under the law.' But it is most certain, that infants were under the law, as well as the adult: and they were a part of his people Israel, whom he visited and redeemed. If ever they be admitted into glory, they must praise him that redeemed them by his blood.

God doth first justify those whom he glorifies, and they ' must be born again, that will enter into his kingdom.' There is no regeneration or renovation but from sin, nor any justification but from sin, and from what we could not be justified from by the law of Moses, nor any justification but what contains remission of sin; and where there is no sin, there is none to be remitted. Nor is there any justification but what is through the redemption that is in Christ Jesus, and his propitiation.—' He is made of God redemption to us.' And the redemption that we have by him ' is remission of sins by his blood. —By his own blood entered he once into the holy place, having obtained eternal redemption for us:' the eternal inheritance is received ' by

means of death for the redemption of transgressions.' So that all scripture speaks this truth aloud to us, that there is now no salvation promised but to the church, the justified, the regenerated, the redeemed; and that none can be capable of these but sinners, and such as are lost and miserable in themselves. Till our necessity be understood, redemption cannot be well understood. They that believe that Christ died not only for this or that man in particular, but for the world, methinks, should believe that the world are sinners, and need his death. He is called ' the Saviour of the world,' and ' the Saviour of all men, especially of believers.—We have seen and do testify that the Father sent the Son to be the Saviour of the world. And from what doth he save them? ' From their sins,' and ' from the wrath to come.'—' For this is a faithful saying, and worthy of all acceptation, that Christ Jesus came into the world to save sinners.' Infants then are sinners, or none of those that he came to save. Christ hath made no man righteous by his obedience, but such as Adam made sinners by his disobedience; ' For as by one man's disobedience, many were made sinners, so by the obedience of one, many shall be made righteous.' Infants are not made righteous by Christ, if they were not sinners: and sinners they cannot be by any but original sin. ' God commended his love to us, in that while we were yet sinners Christ died for us: much more being now justified by his blood, we shall be saved from wrath through him: when we were enemies, we were reconciled to God by the death of his Son,' so that it is sinners that Christ died for, and sinners that are justified by his blood, and sinners that are reconciled to God. Infants therefore are sinners, or they are none of the redeemed, justified or reconciled. And when Jesus Christ, by the grace of God, did taste death for every man, infants are surely included. ' There is one mediator between God and man, the man Christ Jesus, who gave himself a ransom for all.' Therefore all had sin and misery, and needed that ransom. ' He is the propitiation for our sins, and not for ours only, but also for the sins of the whole world.' And is it not plain then that the whole world are sinners?

I speak all this for the evincing of original sin only, because that only is denied by such as yet pretend to Christianity; for actual sin is commonly confessed, and shows itself. And truly so doth original sin, in our proneness to actual: and in the earliness and commonness of such evil inclinations; and in the remnants of it, which the sanctified feel, though they are such as were sanctified ever so early, before actual sin had time to breed those evil habits, which therefore certainly were born with us.

If the image of God, consisting in true holiness, be not natural, or born in every infant in the world, then original sin must needs be born with them: for that sin is either only or chiefly the privation of that image or holiness. He that will say that this image is not requisite to infants, and so that the absence of it is a mere negation, doth make them brutes, and not of the race of man, whom God created after his image and leaves them incapable of heaven or hell, or any other life than beasts have. He that thinks so of infants to-day, may think so of himself to-morrow. He that will affirm that this image or holiness is born with every infant into the world, so wilfully contradicts common evidence, which appears in the contrary effects, that he is not worthy to be further talked with.

One thing more I will propound yet to the contrary-minded; can they say that any infants are saved or not? If not, either they perish as brutes, which is a brutish opinion, or they live in misery; and then, they had sin that did deserve it; yea, if they think that any of them perish in the wrath to come, it must be for sin. If they think that any of them are saved, it is either by covenant, or without: there is some promise for it, or there is none. If none, then no man can say that any of them are saved. For who hath known the mind of the Lord without his revelation? It is arrogancy to tell the world of the saving of any whom God did no way reveal that he will save. But if they plead a revelation or promise, it is either the covenant of nature or of grace; a promise contained in nature, law or gospel. The former cannot be affirmed, not only because the dissenters themselves deny any such covenant to have been in nature, or any way made to Adam, but because there is no such covenant or promise in nature to be found, for the salvation of all infants; and if not for all, then for none: and because it is contrary to abundance of plain passages in the scriptures, that assure us there is but one covenant of salvation now in force: and that ' all the world shall become guilty before God, and every mouth be stopped,' and that ' by the deeds of the law no flesh shall be justified in his sight,' and ' if righteousness come by the law, then Christ is dead in vain.—For as many as are of the works of the law, are under the curse.—And that no man is justified by the law in the sight of God, is evident; for the just shall live by faith;

and the law is not of faith; but the man that doth them shall live in them.' Certainly the law of nature requires not less than Moses' law to a man's justification, if not more. And ' if there had been a law given which could have given life, verily righteousness should have been by the law.—But the scripture hath concluded all under sin, that the promise by faith of Jesus Christ might be given to them that believe.'

By the fulness of this evidence, it is easy to see, that infants and all mankind are sinners, and therefore have need of the Redeemer.

2. To know God as our Redeemer, contains the knowledge of the great ends of our redemption, and of the manifestation of God to man thereby. Having treated of these on a former occasion, I shall now say but this in brief. It is beyond dispute, that God could have made man capable of glory, and kept him from falling by confirming grace, and, without a Redeemer, settled him in felicity as he did the angels. He that foresaw man's fall, and necessity of a Saviour, could easily have prevented that sin and necessity: but he would not; he did not: but chose rather to permit it, and save man by the way of a Redeemer. In which his infinite wisdom is exceedingly manifested. And in Christ, who is the power and wisdom of God, among others these excellent effects are declared to us, which the way of redemption attains, above what the saving us on the terms of nature would have attained.

1. God is now wonderfully admired and magnified in the person of the Redeemer. Angels themselves desire to pry into this mystery, as the frame of nature is set to us to see God in, where we daily as in a glass behold him and admire him; so the person of the Redeemer, and work of incarnation and redemption, is set to the angels for their contemplation and admiration, as well as to us: ' to the intent that now unto the principalities and powers in heavenly places, might be known, by the church, the manifold wisdom of God.' In the glorious perfection and dignity of the Redeemer, will God be for ever glorified; for his greatest works do most honour him: and as the sun doth now to us more honour him than a star, so the glorified person of the Redeemer, doth more honour God than man or angels. ' He is gone into heaven, and is on the right hand of God; angels, authorities, and powers, being made subject to him.—Being raised from the dead, God hath set him at his own right hand in heavenly places, far above all principalities, powers, might, dominion, and every name that is named, not only in this

world, but also in that which is to come; and hath put all things under his feet, and gave him to be the head over all things to the church, which is his body, the fulness of him that filleth all in all.—Who being the brightness of his glory, and the express image of his person, and upholding all things by the word of his power, when he had by himself purged our sins, sat down on the right hand of the Majesty on high, being made so much better than the angels, as he hath by inheritance obtained a more excellent name than they.'

Here a very great truth appears, which very many overlook, that the exaltation of the person of the Redeemer, and the glory that God will have in him, is a higher and more principal part of God's intent in the sending of him to be incarnate and redeem us, than the glorifying of man, and of God by us. Christ will be more glorious than men or angels, and therefore will more glorify God; and God will eternally take more complacency in him than in men or angels: and therefore, though in several respects he is for us, and the means of our felicity, and we are for him, and the means of his glory, as the head is for the body, and the body for the head, yet we are more for Christ as a means to his glory, than he for us: I mean he is the more excellent principal end. ' For to this end Christ both died, rose and revived, that he might be Lord both of the dead and living;—who being in the form of God, thought it not robbery to be equal with God; but made himself of no reputation, and took upon him the form of a servant, and was made in the likeness of men: and being found in fashion as a man, he humbled himself, and became obedient unto death, even the death of the cross: wherefore God also hath highly exalted him, and given him a name, which is above every name; that at the name of Jesus every knee shall bow, both of things in heaven and things in earth, and under the earth, and that every tongue should confess that Jesus Christ is Lord, to the glory of God the Father.—And I beheld, and I heard the voice of many angels round about the throne, and the beasts, and the elders, and the number of them was ten thousand times ten thousand, and thousands of thousands: saying with a loud voice, Worthy is the Lamb that was slain, to receive power, and riches, and wisdom, and strength, and honour, and glory, and blessing: and every creature which is in heaven, and in earth, and under the earth, and such as are in the sea, and all that are in them, heard I saying, Blessing, honour, glory and power be unto him that sitteth on the throne, and unto the Lamb for ever and ever.—The city had no need of the sun, neither of the moon to shine in it; for the glory of God doth lighten it, and the Lamb is the light thereof. —The throne of God and of the Lamb shall be in it, and his servants shall serve him; and they shall see his face, and his name shall be in their foreheads.' These and many other scriptures show us, that God will be for ever glorified in the person of the Redeemer, more than in either men or angels; and consequently that it was the principal part of his intention in the design of man's redemption.

In the way of redemption man will be saved with greater humiliation and self-denial than he should have been in the way of creation. If we had been saved in a way of innocency, we should have had more to ascribe to ourselves. It is meet that all creatures be humbled and abased and nothing in themselves, before the Lord.

3. By the way of redemption, sin will be the more dishonoured, and holiness more advanced, than if sin had never been known in the world. Contraries illustrate one another. Health would not be so much valued, if there were no sickness: nor life, if there were no death: nor day, if there were no night: nor knowledge, if there were no ignorance: nor good, if man had not known evil. The holiness of God would never have appeared in execution of vindictive justice against sin, if there had never been any sin; and therefore he hath permitted it, and will recover us from it, when he could have prevented our falling into it.

4. By this way also, holiness and recovering grace shall be more triumphant against the devil and all its enemies: by the many conquests that Christ will make over Satan, the world and the flesh, and death, there will very much of God be seen to us, that innocency would not thus have manifested.

5. Redemption brings God nearer unto man: the mystery of incarnation gives us wonderful advantages to have more familiar thoughts of God, and to see him in a clearer glass, than ever we should else have seen him in on earth, and to have ' access with boldness to the throne of grace.' The pure Deity is at so vast a distance from us, while we are here in flesh, that if it had not appeared in the flesh unto us, we should have been at a greater loss. But now ' without controversy great is the mystery of godliness; God was manifested in the flesh, justified in the Spirit, seen of angels, preached to the Gentiles, believed on in the world, and received up into glory.'

6. In the way of redemption, man is brought to more earnest and frequent addresses unto God, and dependence on him : necessity drives him : and he hath use for more of God, or for God in more of the ways of his mercy, than else he would have had.

7. Principally in this way of saving miserable man by a Redeemer, there is opportunity for the more abundant exercise of God's mercy, and consequently for the more glorious discovery of his love and goodness to the sons of men, than if they had fallen into no such necessities. Misery prepares men for the sense of mercy. In the Redeemer there is so wonderful a discovery of love and mercy, as is the astonishment of men and angels. 'Behold what manner of love the Father hath bestowed upon us, that we should be called the sons of God !'—' God, who is rich in mercy, for his great love wherewith he loved us, even when we were dead in sins, hath quickened us together with Christ, (by grace ye are saved) and hath raised us up together, and made us sit together in heavenly places in Christ Jesus ; that in the ages to come he might show the exceeding riches of his grace, in his kindness towards us by Christ Jesus ; for by grace ye are saved through faith, and that not of yourselves, it is the gift of God : not of works, lest any man should boast.'—'For we ourselves were sometimes foolish, disobedient, deceived, serving divers lusts and pleasures, &c. But after that the kindness and love of God our Saviour toward man appeared, not by works of righteousness which we have done, but according to his mercy he saved us, by the washing of regeneration and renewing of the Holy Ghost.' Never was there such a discovery of God as he is love, in a way of mercy to man on earth, as in the Redeemer, and his benefits.

8. In the way of redemption the soul of man is formed to the most sweet and excellent temper, and his obedience cast into the happiest mould. The glorious demonstration of love, doth animate us with love to God ; and the shedding abroad of his love in our hearts by the Spirit of the Redeemer, doth draw out our hearts in love to him again: and the sense of his wonderful love and mercy fills us with thankfulness : so that love is hereby made the nature of the new man ; and thankfulness is the life of all our obedience : for all flows from these principles, and expresses them : so that love is the compendium of all holiness in one word ; and thankfulness of all evangelical obedience. And it is a more sweet and excellent state of life, to be the spouse of Christ, and his members, and serve God as friends and children, with love and thankfulness, than to serve him merely as the most loyal subjects, or with an obedience that hath less of love.

9. In the way of redemption, holiness is more admirably exemplified in Christ, than it was, or would have been in Adam. Adam would never have declared it in that eminency of love to others, submission to God, contempt of the world, self-denial, and conquest of Satan, as Christ hath done.

10. In the way of redemption, there is a double obligation laid upon man for every duty. To the obligations of creation, all the obligations of redemption and the new creation are superadded : and this threefold cord should not so easily be broken. Here are moral means more powerfully to hold the soul to God.

11. In this way there is a clearer discovery of the everlasting state of man, and life and immortality are more fully brought to light by the gospel, than, for ought we find in scripture, they were to innocent man himself. 'No man hath seen God at any time : the only begotten Son that is in the bosom of the Father, he hath declared him.'—' For no man hath ascended up into heaven, but he that came down from heaven, even the Son of man, which is in heaven.'

12. Man will be advanced to the judging of the ungodly and of the conquered angels : even by the good will of the Father, and a participation in the honour of Christ our head, and by a participation in his victories, and by our own victories in his strength, by the right of conquest, we shall judge with Christ, both devils and men, that were enemies to him, and our salvation : and there is more in that promise than we yet well understand ; ' he that overcometh, and keepeth my words unto the end, to him will I give power over the nations, and he shall rule them with a rod of iron ; as the vessels of a potter shall they be broken to shivers, even as I received of my Father.'

13. That which Augustine so much insists on, I think is also plain in scripture, that the salvation of the elect is better secured in the hands of Christ, than his own or any of his posterities was in the hands of Adam. We know that Adam lost that which was committed to him : but ' we know whom we have believed, and are persuaded, that he is able to keep that which we commit to him, against that day.' Force not these scriptures against our own consolation, and the glory of our Redeemer, and then judge, ' as thou hast given him power over all flesh, that he should give eternal life to as many as thou hast

given him.'—' All that the Father giveth me, shall
come to me ; and him that cometh to me, I will
in no wise cast out.'—' And this is the Father's
will which hath sent me, that of all which he
hath given me I should lose nothing, but should
raise it up again at the last day.'—' But ye believe
not, because ye are not of my sheep, as I said
unto you : my sheep hear my voice, and I know
them, and they follow me, and I give unto them
eternal life, and they shall never perish, and none
shall take them out of my hands : my Father
which gave them me is greater than all, and no
man is able to pluck them out of my Father's
hands.'—' Blessed be the God and Father of our
Lord Jesus Christ, who hath blessed us with all
spiritual blessings in heavenly places in Christ,
according as he hath chosen us in him before the
foundation of the world, that we should be holy
and without blame before him in love : having
predestinated us to the adoption of children by
Jesus Christ to himself, according to the good
pleasure of his will, to the praise of the glory of
his grace, wherein he hath made us accepted in
the Beloved.'—'Being predestinated according to
the purpose of him that worketh all things after
the counsel of his own will.'

If faith, and repentance, and the right disposition of the will itself, be his resolved gift
to his elect, and not things left merely to our
uncertain wills, then the case is past all question. ' In meekness instructing those that oppose
themselves, if God peradventure will give them repentance to the acknowledging of the truth, and
that they may recover themselves out of the snare
of the devil.'—' By grace ye are saved through
faith, and that not of yourselves, it is the gift of
God.'—' The fruit of the Spirit is love, faith.'—
' To you it is given on the behalf of Christ, not only
to believe.'—' As many as were ordained to eternal
life believed.'—' And I will give them an heart to
know me, that I am the Lord, and they shall be
my people, and I will be their God ; for they
shall return unto me with their whole heart.'—
' And I will give them one heart, and I will put
a new Spirit within you ; and I will take the
stony heart out of their flesh, and will give them
an heart of flesh, that they may walk in my statutes, and keep my ordinances and do them, and
they shall be my people, and I will be their God.'
—' A new heart also will I give you, and a new
spirit will I put within you, and I will take
away the stony heart out of your flesh, and give
you an heart of flesh, and I will put my Spirit
within you, and cause you to walk in my statutes.'
See also in Hebrews, where this is called the *new
and better covenant.* ' I will put my laws in their
minds, and write them in their hearts.'—' And I
will give them one heart and one way, that they
may fear me for ever.'—' And I will make an everlasting covenant with them, and I will not turn
away from them to do them good, but I will put
my fear in their hearts that they shall not depart
from me.'—' Who makes thee to differ ? and what
hast thou that thou didst not receive ?' Much
more may be produced, from which it is evident
that Christ is the author and finisher of our faith :
and that the certainty of the salvation of his
elect, doth lie more on his undertaking and resolution infallibly to accomplish their salvation,
than upon our wisdom, or the stability of our
mutable free-wills : and that thus we are better in
the hands of the second Adam, than we were in
the hands of the first.

14. To conclude ; vindictive justice will be
doubly honoured upon them that are final reject-
ers of this grace. Though conscience would have
had matter enough to work upon for the torment
of the sinner, and the justifying of God, upon the
mere violation of the law of nature or works, yet
nothing to what it now will have on them that
are the despisers of this great salvation. ' For of
how much sorer punishment, suppose ye, shall he
be thought worthy, that hath trodden under foot
the Son of God ?' When it is wilful impenitency,
against most excellent means and mercies, that
is to be charged upon sinners, and when they
perish because they would not be saved, justice
will be most fully glorified before all, and in the
conscience of the sinner himself. All this considered, you may see that, besides what reasons
of the counsel of God are unknown to us, there
is abundant reason open to our sight, from the
great advantages of this way, why God would
rather save us by a Redeemer, than in a way of
innocency, as our mere Creator.

But, for the answering of all objections against
this, I must now desire you to observe these
two things following. 1. That we here suppose man a terrestrial inhabitant clothed with
flesh : otherwise it is confessed that if he were
perfect in heaven, where he had the beatific
vision to confirm him, many of these forementioned advantages to him would be none.
2. And it is supposed that God will work on
man by moral means ; and where he never so infallibly produces the good of man, he doth it in
a way agreeable to his nature and present state ;
and his work of grace is wise, magnifying the
contrivance and conduct of his wisdom, as well
as his power : otherwise indeed God might
have done all without these or any other means.

3. The knowledge of God in Christ as our

Redeemer, must imprint upon the soul those holy affections, which the design and nature of our redemption bespeak, and answer these forementioned ends.

As, 1. It must keep, the soul in a sense of the odiousness of sin, that must have such a remedy to pardon and destroy it.

2. It must raise us to most high and honourable thoughts of our Redeemer, the Captain of our salvation, that bringeth back lost sinners unto God: and we must study to advance the glory of our Lord, whom the Father hath advanced and set over all.

3. It must drive us out of ourselves, and bring us to be nothing in our own eyes, and cause us to have humble, penitent, self-condemning thoughts, as men that have been our own undoers, and deserved so ill of God and man.

4. It must drive us to a full and constant dependence on Christ our Redeemer, and on the Father by him: as our life is now in the Son as its root and fountain, so in him must be our faith and confidence, and to him we must daily have recourse, and seek to him, and to the Father in his name, for all that we need, for daily pardon, strength, protection, provision and consolation.

5. It must cause us the more to admire the holiness of God, which is so admirably declared in our redemption; and still be sensible how he hates sin and loves purity.

6. It must invite and encourage us to draw near to God, who hath condescended to come so near to us; and as sons we must cry ' Abba, Father,' and though with reverence, yet with holy confidence, must set ourselves continually before him.

7. It must cause us to make it our daily employment to study the riches of the love of God, and his abundant mercy manifested in Christ; so that above all themes in the world, we should most diligently and delightfully peruse the Son of God incarnate, and in him behold the power, wisdom, and goodness of the Father: and with Paul we should desire ' to know nothing but Christ crucified;' and ' all things should be counted but loss and dung for the excellency of the knowledge of Christ Jesus our Lord.'—' That we may be able to comprehend with all saints, what is the breadth, and length, and depth, and heighth, and to know the love of Christ, which passeth knowledge, that we may be filled with all the fulness of God.'

8. Above all, if we know God as our Redeemer, we must live in the power of holy love and gratitude. His manifested love must prevail with us so far, that unfeigned love to him may be the predominant affection of our souls. And being free from the spirit of bondage and slavish fear, we must make love and thankfulness the sum of our religion : and think not any thing will prove us Christians, without prevailing love to Christ, nor that any duty is accepted that proceedeth not from it.

9. Redemption must teach us to apply ourselves to the holy laws and example of our Redeemer for the forming and ordering of our hearts and lives.

10. And it must quicken us to love the Lord with a redoubled vigour, and to obey with double resolution and diligence, because we are under a double obligation. What should a people so redeemed esteem too much or too dear for God ?

11. Redemption must make us a more heavenly people, as being redeemed to the incorruptible inheritance in heaven : ' the blessed God and Father of our Lord Jesus Christ, according to his abundant mercy, hath begotten us again unto a lively hope, by the resurrection of Jesus Christ from the dead, to an inheritance incorruptible, undefiled, and that fadeth not away, reserved in heaven for us, who are kept by the power of God through faith unto salvation.'

12. Lastly, Redemption must cause us to walk the more carefully, and with a greater care to avoid all sin, and to avoid the threatened wrath of God, because sin against such unspeakable mercy is unspeakably great : and condemnation by a Redeemer for despising his grace, will be a double condemnation.

CHAP. XII.

The third relation in which God is to be known by us, is, as he is our sanctifier and comforter, which is specially ascribed to the Holy Ghost. And doubtless as the dispensation of the Holy Ghost is the perfecting dispensation, without which creation and redemption would not attain their ends ; and as the sin against the Holy Ghost, is the great and dangerous sin ; so our belief in the Holy Ghost, and knowledge of God as our sanctifier by the Spirit, is not the least or lowest act of our faith or knowledge. It implies or contains these things following.

1. We must hence take notice of the certainty of our common original sin. The necessity of sanctification proves the corruption, as the neces sity of a Redeemer proves the guilt : it is not one but all that are baptized, that must be baptized into the name of the Son and Holy Ghost, as well as of the Father : which is an entering

into covenant with the Son as our Redeemer, and with the Holy Ghost as our Sanctifier. So that infants themselves must be sanctified, or be none of the church of Christ, which consists of baptized and sanctified persons. 'Except a man be born again, even of the Spirit, as well as water, he cannot enter into the kingdom of heaven.'— 'For that which is born of the flesh is flesh, and that which is born of the Spirit is spirit,' and therefore the fleshly birth producing not a spiritual creature, will not save without the spiritual birth; the words are most plain; not only against them that deny original sin, but against them that misunderstanding the nature of redemption, think that all infants are merely, by the price paid, put into a state of salvation, and have the pardon of their original sin in common, attending their natural birth. But these men should consider, 1. That this text and constant experience tell us that the new birth doth not thus commonly to all accompany the natural birth: and yet without the new birth none can be saved, nor without holiness any see God. 2. That pardon of sin is no man's, upon the bare suffering of Jesus Christ; but must be theirs by some covenant or promise conveying to them a right to the benefits of his suffering. And therefore no man can be said to be pardoned or saved, without great arrogancy in the affirmer, that hath not from God a promise of such mercy. But no man can show any promise that gives remission of original sin to all infants. Produce it, or presume not to affirm it, lest you fall under the heavy doom of those that add to his holy word. The promise is to the faithful and their seed. The rest are not the children of the promise, but are under the curse of the violated law; which indeed is dispensable; and therefore we cannot say that God will pardon none of them; but withal, we cannot say that he will, unless he had told us so. All the world stand in need of a sanctifier: and therefore most certainly, even since Christ's death, they are naturally corrupted.

2. And as our belief in the Holy Ghost, as sanctifier, engages us to acknowledge our original sin and misery, so doth it engage us to magnify his renewing work of grace, and be convinced of the necessity of it, and to confess the insufficiency of corrupted nature to its own renovation. As no man must dishonour the work of our Creator; and therefore our faculties of reason and natural free-will are not to be denied or reproached: so must we be as careful that we dishonour not the works of our Redeemer or Sanctifier; and therefore the viciousness of these faculties, and the thraldom of our wills to their

own disinclinations, and to concupiscence, must be confessed; and the need of grace to work the cure. It is not ingenuous for us, when God made it so admirable a part of his work in the world, to redeem us, and save us from our sin and misery, that we should hide or deny our diseases, and make ourselves believe that we have but little need of the physician, and so that the cure is no great matter, and consequently deserves no great praise. I know the church is troubled by men of dark, yet self-conceited minds, that in these points are running all into extremes. One side denying the gracious method, and the other the omnipotent way of God in our recovery. One plainly casting our sin and misery principally on God; and the other as plainly robbing the Redeemer and Holy Spirit of the honour of our recovery. But it is the latter that my subject leads me now to speak of. I beseech you, take heed of any conceit that would draw you to extenuate the honour of our sanctifier. Dare you contend against the Holy Ghost for the integrity of your natures, or the honour of your cure? Surely he that hath felt the power of this renewing grace, and found how little of it was from himself, nay, how much he was an enemy to it, will be less inclined to extenuate the praise of grace than inexperienced men will be. Because the case is very weighty, give me leave, by way of question, to propound these considerations to you.

Quest. 1. Why is it, think you, that all must be baptized into the name of the Son and Holy Ghost, as well as of the Father? Doth it not imply that all have need of a sanctifier, and must be engaged to that end in covenant with the sanctifier? I suppose you know that it is not to a bare profession of our belief of the trinity of persons, that we are baptized. It is the covenant entrance into our happy relation to God the Father, Son, and Holy Ghost, that is then celebrated. And therefore as infants and all must be thus engaged to the sanctifier; so all must acknowledge their necessity of this mercy, and the excellency of it. It is essential to our Christianity, that we value it, desire it, and receive it. Therefore an error inconsistent with it proves us indeed no Christians.

Quest. 2. Why is it, think you, that the Holy Ghost and this renewing work, are so much magnified in the scripture? Is not the glory of it answerable to those high expressions; undoubtedly it is. I have already told you elsewhere of the eulogies of this work. It is that by which Christ dwells in them, and they are made a habitation of God by the Spirit. They are made by it 'the temples of the Holy Ghost.' It is the divine power, which is no other than omnipotency, that 'giveth us all things pertaining unto life and godliness.' Think not, I beseech you, any lower of this work than is consistent with these expressions. It is 'the opening of the blind eyes of our understanding, and turning us from darkness to light, and from the power of Satan unto God, and bringing us into his marvellous light.' It is an inward teaching of us by God, an effectual teaching and anointing, and 'a writing the laws in our hearts, and putting them in our inward parts.' I purposely forbear any exposition of these texts, lest I seem to distort them ; and because I would only lay the naked word of God before your own impartial considerations. It is God's work by the Spirit, and not our own, as ours, that is here so much magnified. And can all this signify no more but a common, bare proposal of truth and good to the intellect and will; even such as ignorant and wicked men have ? Doth God do as much to illuminate, teach, and sanctify them, that never are illuminated, or taught, and sanctified, as them that are? This work of the Holy Ghost is called 'a quickening,' or making men that were dead, 'alive;' it is called a 'new begetting or new birth,' without which none can enter into heaven ; a 'renewing us,' and making us 'new men,' and 'new creatures,' so far as that old things are past away, and all become new ; it is 'a new creating us after the image of God;' it makes 'us holy as God is holy ;' yea, it makes us 'partakers of the divine nature.' It gives us 'repentance to the acknowledging of the truth, that we may recover ourselves out of the snare of the devil, who were taken captive by him at his will.' It gives us that 'love by which God dwelleth in us, and we in God.' We are 'redeemed by Christ from all iniquity, and therefore it is that he gave himself for us, to purify to himself a peculiar people zealous of good works.' It is an 'abundant shedding of the Holy Ghost' on us for our renovation, and by it a 'shedding the love of God abroad in our hearts.' It is this Holy Spirit, given to believers, by which they pray, and by which they 'mortify the flesh.' By this Spirit we live, walk, and rejoice. Our joy, peace, and hope is through the power of the Holy Ghost. It gives us a spiritual mind, and takes away the carnal mind that is enmity against God, and neither is nor can be subject to his law. By this Spirit that is given to us, we must know that we are God's children. 'For if any man have not the Spirit of Christ, the same is none of his.' All holy graces are the fruits of the Spirit. It would be too long to

number the several excellent effects of the sanctifying work of the Spirit upon the soul, and to recite the eulogies of it in the scripture. Surely it is no low or needless thing which all these expressions intend.

Quest. 3. If you think it a most heinous sin to vilify the Creator and his work, and the Redeemer and his work, why should not you think so of the vilifying of the Sanctifier and his work, when God hath so magnified it, and will be glorified in it; and when it is the applying, perfecting work, that makes the purchased benefits of redemption to be ours, and forms our Father's image on us.

Quest. 4. Do we not doctrinally commit too much of that sin, if we undervalue the Spirit's sanctifying work, as a common thing, which the ungodly world manifest in practice, when they speak and live in a contempt or low esteem of grace ? And which is more injurious to God—for a profane person to jest at the Spirit's work, or for a Christian, or minister, deliberately to extenuate it ; especially when the preaching of grace is a minister's chief work, surely we should much fear partaking in so great a sin?

Quest. 5. Why is it that the scripture speaks so much to take men off from boasting or ascribing any thing to themselves ? 'That every mouth may be stopped;' and why doth not the law of works exclude boasting but only the law of faith ? Surely the actions of nature, except so far as it is corrupt, are as truly of God, as the acts of grace. And yet God will not take it well to deny him the glory of redemption, or sanctification, and tell him that we paid it him in another kind, and ascribed all to him as the author of our free-will by natural production. For as nature shall honour the Creator, so grace shall also honour the Redeemer and Sanctifier. God designs the humbling of the sinner, and teaching him to deny himself, and to honour God in such a way as may stand with self-abasement, leaving it to God to honour those by way of reward, that honour him in way of duty, and deny their own honour.

Quest. 6. Why is the blaspheming, and sinning against the Holy Ghost made so heinous and dangerous a sin, if the works of the Holy Ghost were not most excellent, and such as God will be most honoured by ?

Quest. 7. Is it not great ingratitude for the soul that hath been illuminated, converted, renewed, quickened, and saved by the Holy Ghost, to extenuate the mercy, and ascribe it most to his natural will ? O what a change was it that sanctification made ; what a blessed birth-day was that to our souls, when we entered here upon life eternal! And is this the thanks we give the Lord for so great a mercy?

Quest. 8. What mean those texts, if they confute not this unthankful opinion? 'It is God that worketh in you to will and to do of his good pleasure.'—' God hath raised us up together, and made us sit together in heavenly places in Christ Jesus, that in the ages to come he might show the exceeding riches of his grace, in his kindness towards us through Christ Jesus: for by grace ye are saved through faith, and that not of yourselves; it is the gift of God; not of works, lest any man should boast; for we are his workmanship created to good works in Christ Jesus.'—' Ye have not chosen me, but I have chosen you, and ordained you that you should go and bring forth fruit, and that your fruit should remain.'—' Herein is love : not that we loved God, but that he loved us.'—' For who maketh thee to differ; and what hast thou that thou didst not receive?' —No man can come unto me, except the Father which hath sent me draw him.'—' The natural man receiveth not the things of the Spirit of God, for they are foolishness unto him, neither can he know them, because they are spiritually discerned.'—' That which is born of the flesh is flesh, and that which is born of the Spirit is spirit,' that is plainly, the fleshly birth produces but flesh and not Spirit; if any man will have the Spirit, and so be saved, it must be by a spiritual birth by the Holy Ghost. ' The Lord opened Lydia's heart that she attended to the things that were spoken of Paul,' &c. Was the conversion of Paul, a murdering persecutor, his own work rather than the Lord's, when the means and manner were such as we read of? ' The God of our fathers hath chosen thee, that thou shouldst know his will, and see that Just One, and hear the voice of his mouth.' He was chosen to the means and to faith, and not only in faith unto salvation. When Christ called his disciples to come and follow him, was there no prevailing inward power that made them leave all and follow him? Was it not the power of the Holy Ghost that converted three thousand Jews at a sermon, of them that by wicked hands had crucified and slain the Lord Jesus? When the preaching and miracles of Christ converted so few, his brethren, and they that ' saw his miracles believed not on him ;' but when the Holy Ghost was given after his ascension, in that plenty which answered the gospel and promise, his words were fulfilled, ' And I, if I be lifted up from the earth, will draw all men unto me.' I pass by abundance more of such evidence.

Quest. 9. Doth it not tend to bring sin into credit, which holiness is contrary to, and to bring the love of God into discredit, and to hinder men's conversion, and keep them from a holy life, when holiness is taken for so low and natural or common a thing?

Quest. 10. And consequently, doth it not tend to the vilifying of the attribute of holiness in God, when the image and effect of it is so extenuated?

Quest. 11. And doth it not tend to the contempt of heaven itself, whose state of felicity consists much in perfect holiness? If sanctification be but some common motion, which Cain and Judas had, as well as Paul, surely it is less divine and more inconsiderable than we thought.

Quest. 12. Doth it not speak a very dangerous suspicion of a soul that never felt the special work of grace, that can make light of it, and ascribe it most to his own will? Would not sound humiliation do more than arguments to cure this great mistake? I never yet came near a thoroughly humbled soul, but I found them too low and vile in their own eyes to have such undervaluing thoughts of grace, or to think it best for them to leave all the efficacy of grace to their own wills. A broken heart abhors such thoughts.

Quest. 13. Dare any wise and sober man desire such a thing of God, or dare you say that you will expect no other grace, but what shall leave it to yourselves to make it effectual or frustrate it? I think he is no friend to his soul that would take up with this.

Quest. 14. Do not the constant prayers of all that have but a show of godliness, contradict the doctrine which I am contradicting? Do you not beg of God to melt, soften, and bow your hearts, and to make them more holy, and fill them with light, faith, and love, and hold you close to God and duty? In a word, do you not daily pray for effectual grace, that shall infallibly procure your desired ends? I scarcely ever heard a prayer from a sober man but was orthodox in such points, though their speeches would be heterodox.

Quest. 15. Do you not know that there is an enmity in every unrenewed heart against sanctification, till God remove it? Are we not greater enemies to ourselves, and greater resisters of the Holy Ghost, and of our own conversion, sanctification, and salvation, than all the world besides is? Woe to him that feels not this by himself. And is it likely, that we that are enemies to holiness, should do more to our own sanctification, than the Holy Ghost? Woe to us, if he conquer not our enmity.

Quest. 16. Is it probable that so great a work as the destroying of our dearest sins, the setting our hearts and all our hopes on an invisible glory, delighting in the Lord, and forsaking all for him, &c. should come rather from the choice of a will that loves those sins, and hates that holy, heavenly life, than from the Spirit of Christ? surely this is much above us.

Quest. 17. Whence is it that so often one man that hath been a notorious sinner is converted by a sermon, when a more civil man, of better nature and life, is never changed, though he have that and ten times more persuasions?

Quest. 18. Doth not experience tell impartial observers, that those who highly esteem the sanctifying work of the Holy Ghost, are ordinarily of more holy, heavenly lives, than they that use to ascribe the distinguishing work to their free wills? In my observation it is so.

Quest. 19. Should not every gracious, humble soul, be more inclined to magnify God than himself; and to give him the glory, than to give it to ourselves, especially in a case where scripture and experience tell us that we are more unlikely than God to deserve the praise? Our destruction is of ourselves, but in him is our help. When we see an effect and know it, and the causes that are in question, it is easy to conjecture, from the quality, which is the true cause. If I see a serpent brought forth, I will sooner think that it was generated by a serpent than a dove. If I see sin in the world, I shall easily believe it is the spawn of this corrupted will, that is so prone to it. But if I find a divine nature in me, or see a holy, heavenly life in any, I must needs think that this is likelier to be the work of the blessed God, than of such a naughty heart as man's, that hath already been a self-destroyer.

Quest. 20. What motive hath any man to exalt himself and sin against the Holy Ghost by such an extenuation of his saving grace? It is a causeless, fruitless sin. The only reason that ever I could hear for it, was lest the doctrine of differencing grace should make God a respecter of persons, or the author of sin, of which there is no reason of a suspicion. We all agree that no man perishes, or is denied grace, but such as deserve it: and when all deserve it, it is no more respect of persons in God to sanctify some only of those ill deservers, than it is that he makes not all men kings, nor every dog a man, nor every star a sun, or every man an angel. To clear all objections concerning this, would be but to digress.

3. Lastly, Our knowledge of the Holy Ghost must raise us to an high estimation of his works, a ready reception of his graces, and cheerful obedience to his motions. He sanctified our Head, who had no sin, by preventing sin in his conception, and he anointed him to his office, and came upon him at his baptism: he sanctified and anointed the prophets and apostles to their offices, and by them indited the holy scripture. He illuminates, converts, sanctifies, and guides all that are to be heirs of life. This is his work. Honour that part of it that is done on Christ, on the prophets, apostles, and the scriptures; and value and seek after that which belongs to yourselves. Think not to be holy without the sanctifier, nor to do any thing well without the Spirit of Jesus Christ, who is Christ's internal, invisible agent here on earth. O that men knew how much of their welfare depends on a faithful obeying of the Holy Ghost!

CHAP. XIII.

The next part of our knowledge of God is to know him in those great consequent relations, to which he is entitled by creation and redemption, viz. as he is our absolute Lord, or Owner, our most righteous Governor, and our most bountiful or gracious Father, or Benefactor.

1. God, both as our Creator and Redeemer, hath an absolute dominion of the world; that is, he is our Owner or Proprietor, and we are his own; for we take not the term, lordship or dominion, here in the looser sense as it signifies a ruler, but in the stricter sense, as it signifies an owner. Of this relation I have already spoken in a sermon of Christ's dominion: and therefore shall say the less in this place.

The knowledge of God's dominion or propriety must comprehend, 1. The certain truth of this his right. 2. The fulness of it. 3. The effects that it must have on us.

I. The truth of it is beyond dispute, even among infidels, that know there is a God. He that made us of his own materials, or of nothing, must needs be the owner of us; and so must he that bought us from destruction. 'Behold all souls are mine.'—'To this end Christ both died, rose, and revived, that he might be Lord both of the dead and living.'—'All things that the Father hath are mine.' The Father then hath this propriety by creation, and the Son by redemption: and the Father also by communication with the Son in redemption; and the Son by communication with the Father in creation.

II. And it must be the most absolute plenary dominion, because the very being of all the creatures is from God, and therefore no one can be co-ordinate with him, or his rival, nor any thing limit his interest in us.

III. And the effects that this must have upon us, are these following.

1. Hence we must conclude, and reverently and willingly confess, that further than he voluntary doth oblige himself to us, it is impossible that God should be our debtor; and consequently that upon terms of commutative justice we should merit any thing of God. For what can we render to him but his own; and how should he, properly and antecedently, be indebted to and for his own?

2. And we must conclude, that antecedently to his laws and promise, it is impossible that God can do us any wrong, or any thing that he can do, can be guilty of injustice: for justice gives to all their own: and therefore it gives nothing to us from God but what he voluntarily gives us himself, which therefore is first a gift of bounty, and but secondarily a due in justice.

3. And therefore we must hence learn, that God may do with his own as he will. Therefore we must take heed that we repine not at any of his decrees or providences, or any passages concerning them in his word. Much may we above us, because our blindness cannot reach the reasons of his ways; but nothing is unreasonable or evil; for all proceeds from infinite wisdom and goodness, as well as from omnipotency; as no man must feign any thing of God, and say, this is his decree, or word, or providence; and therefore it is good, when there is no such thing revealed to us; so when we find that it is indeed revealed, our reason must presently submit, and undoubtedly conclude it reasonable and good. Yet is there no cause from hence to fear, lest God should condemn the innocent, or break his promises, and deny us the reward; nor is there any hope to wicked men that he should violate his peremptory threatenings, or, as they call it in their selfish language, be better than his word: because though God have an absolute propriety, and therefore in regard of his interest or power, may do what he will, yet he is essentially also most wise and good, and accordingly hath fitted all things to their use, and taken upon him the relation of our government, and as it were obliged himself by his laws and covenants, and declared himself to be most just; and showed us hereby that he will do nothing contrary to these. As there is no contradiction, but most perfect unity, in God's omnipotency, wisdom, and goodness; his dominion or propriety, his kingdom and paternity;

so shall there be no contradiction, but a perfect concord of all these in the exercise. He therefore that, as our king or governor, hath undertaken to advance the godly, and destroy the wicked, will not, by the exercise of his absolute dominion, deny himself, nor be unfaithful to his people, or to his rules of government.

If you ask me, in what cases then this dominion is exercised? I answer, 1. In laying the foundations of laws and right. 2. In the disposal of the unreasonable creatures. 3. In abundance of things about his rational creatures, wherein, as rector, he is not engaged, nor hath in his laws declared his will; as about the various constitutions and complexions of men, their ranks and dignities in the world, their riches, or poverty, their health, or sickness, their gifts and parts, both natural and acquired; the first giving of the gospel, and of special grace, to such as had forfeited them, and had no promise of them: the degrees of outward means and mercies; the degrees of inward grace, more than what is promised, &c.

From hence also we must learn, not to repine at the providences of God about his church, which are strange to us, and past our reach, and seem to make against its welfare. Remember that as he may do with his own as he will, so we have no reason to think that he will be lavish or disregardful of his own. The church is not ours, but God's: and therefore he is fitter then we to be trusted with it.

And so in our own distresses by affliction; when flesh repineth, let us remember, that we are his own, and he may do with us as he pleases. If we be poor, despised, sick and miserable in the world, let us remember, that as it is no injury to the beasts that they are not men, or to the worms that they are not beasts, or to the plants that they have not sense, or to the stars that they are not suns, so it is no wrong to the subjects that they are not princes, or to the poor that they are not rich, or to the sick that they are not healthful. May not God do with his own, as he will; shall a beggar grudge that you give not all that he desires, when you are not bound to give him any thing?

4. Yea, hence we must learn to be the more thankful for all our mercies, because they proceed from the absolute Lord, who was not obliged to us. He might have made us idiots, or madmen; he might have made us beasts or insects, without any injury to us; and the mercies which are consequently from his promise, are antecedently from his propriety and dominion: for he might have put us into other capacities, and

have chosen not to have made those promises. And his promises bind us not to be less thankful but more. As his mercies are not the less mercies but the greater, for being promised ; because we have now the comfort and use of them in the promise, before we have them.

5. Hence also we must learn, that there can be no simple, absolute propriety in any creature. No creature gave all the being and well being to another that it hath, and this originally as of its own. We being not our own but God's, cannot have any thing that is absolutely our own. Human propriety is but derived, limited, and respective. Our goods, and lands, and lives are ours ; that is, they are ours to use for God, as the instruments of a workman to do his work : but not ours to use as we think meet. They are so ours, as that men may not take them from us, but God may take them from us at his pleasure. And therefore think not you may mis-spend a penny if you were ever so rich, because it is your own ; but know, that you must mis-spend nothing, because it is not your own but God's.

6. Principally, we must hence learn to deny ourselves, as being not our own, and having nothing in the world that is our own, in respect to God, the absolute owner. And therefore above all the sins of your souls, still watch against this selfishness ; lest you should grow to look at your time, your strength, your wealth, your interests, as your own, and forget that you are mere stewards ; and say as the ungodly, ' our lips are our own : who is Lord over us ?' O take heed that you use not your strength, or interest, or any thing for yourselves : no not so much as your food and raiment, that is, for yourselves ultimately, or not in subordination to the Lord. For self as subject unto God, or as closed with him in the bond of love, is no longer self in enmity and opposition, nor that which we are forbidden to seek or serve.

7. And this knowledge of the dominion of God, must prevail with us effectually to resign ourselves absolutely to him. Our consent doth give him no title to us, but it is necessary to our welfare that we confess his title. All men, even the wicked, are his own ; but that is against their wills : but the godly are willingly his own, and disclaim all interest in themselves but what is duly subordinate to his : the name of God is put upon them, as you put your names on your goods or sheep. ' I sware unto thee, and entered into a covenant with thee, saith the Lord, and thou becamest mine.'—' And they shall be mine, saith the Lord, in that day when I make up my jewels.' To be entirely his by covenant, is pro-

per to a saint : for sanctification hath these parts : one is the habitual devotion of the soul to God, and the other is the actual dedication, and a third is the relation of the person as thus dedicated, and the fourth is the actual using of ourselves for God. These four are the parts of sanctification ; so that all is but our giving up ourselves to God. But to be his in right, is common to the devils and most ungodly. The hearts of the sanctified do resolvedly and delightfully say, ' my beloved is mine, and I am his, and I am my beloved's and my beloved is mine.' See then that you keep not any thing back, but resign up yourselves entirely to God, as those that know they are wholly his.

8. And with ourselves we must resign up all to God that we have. For if we are not our own but his, then our children, our wealth, our senses, our time, our abilities and all that we have are his. All is not to be used one way for God : not all to the poor, nor all to the commonwealth, nor all to the direct promoting of his worship : but all must be his, and used for him, in one way or other, and in those ways which he requires. Possess not any thing merely for yourselves.

9. Especially see to it in the use and improvement, that you use yourselves, and all that you have for God. Let this be your intention, trade, and study. See that you be always at his work ; that if a man come in upon you any hour of the day, and ask you what you are a doing, and whose work it is that you are upon, you may truly be able to say, the Lord's. If you be asked, who you are now speaking for, or spending your time for, or for whom you expend your wealth ? You may truly say of every hour, and every penny, and every word, ' it is for the Lord.' Even that which you give your children or friends, and that which you receive for your support or comfort, may all be principally and ultimately for God : ' ye are not your own ; for ye are bought with a price : therefore glorify God in your body, and in your spirit, which are God's.'—' Christ died for all, that they which live, should not henceforth live unto themselves, but to him that died for them, and rose again.'

10. This must be a stay to the souls of true believers, and cause them with comfort to trust themselves and all their affairs in the hands of God. When we have first made it our care to give to God the things that are God's, and heartily consecrated ourselves and all that we have to him, as his own ; we have no reason to doubt of his acceptance, nor of his care, protection and merciful disposal of us. This is a wonderful comfort to poor Christians, to think that they

have such an owner. Whoever is against you, Christians, be sure of it God will look to you, as his own. And if you but promise another that you will be as careful of his child, his horse, his goods, as if they were your own, he will think you say as much as can be expected. If you be poor, or sick, or desolate, you may be sure that yet God will look to you as his own. And why should you think that he will be careless of his own? Ground your prayers and confidence on this, as David doth: ' I am thine, save me.' And in all our labours, and the affairs of our lives, when our consciences can say that we live to God, and study to do all we can for him, and to improve all our time, parts, and other talents, to his use, it may very much quiet us in all his disposals of us. If he keep us in the lowest case, if we be his, we must rest in his wisdom, that knows best how to use his own. If he take our friends from us, he takes but his own. If he deny his saving grace to our ungodly children, a heavy judgment of which we must be sensible, yet when we have devoted them to God, and done our own part, we must be silent, as Aaron was, when his sons were destroyed, and confess that ' the potter hath power over his own clay, to make of the same lump a vessel to honour, and another to dishonour. All his disposals shall work to that end which is the most universal perfect good, and most denominates all the means. But those that are his own by consent and covenant, may be sure that all shall work to their own good. Let us die with Christ, and be buried to the world, and know no Lord or owner but our great Creator and Redeemer, except in a limited sense, and then we may boldly argue with him to the quiet of our souls from this relation, ' I am thine, help me.'—' Stir up thyself, and awake to my judgment, even to my cause, my Lord and my God,' when faith and love have first said as Thomas, ' My Lord and my God.'

Chap. XIV.

The next relation to be spoken of, is God's sovereignty: both by creation and redemption he hath the right of governing us as our sovereign king, and we are obliged to be his willing subjects, and as such to obey his holy laws. He is the Lord or owner of all the world; even of brutes as properly as of man: but he is the sovereign king or governor only of the reasonable creature; because no others are capable of that proper moral government which now we speak of. Vulgarly indeed his physical motions and dispositions are called his rule or government:

and so God is said to govern brutes and inanimate creatures: but that is but a metaphorical expression: as an artificer metaphorically governs his clock, or engine, or a shepherd his sheep. But we now speak of proper moral government. God having made man a rational and free agent, having an immortal soul, and capable of everlasting happiness, his very nature and the end of his creation required, that he should be conducted to that end and happiness by means agreeable to his nature; that is, by the revelation of the reward before he sees it, that he may seek it and be fitted for it: and by prescribed duties that are necessary to obtain it, and to his living here according to his nature: and by threatened penalties to quicken him to his duty: so that he is naturally a creature to be governed, both as sociable, and as one to be conducted to his end. He therefore that created him having alone both sufficiency and right, doth by this very creation become his governor. His government hath two parts (the world being thus constituted the kingdom of God.) The first is by legislation, or making laws, and officers for execution. The second is by the procuring the execution of these laws; to which end he doth exhort and persuade the subjects to obedience, and judge them according to their works, and execute his judgment.

His first law was to Adam, the law of nature, obliging him to adhere to his Creator, and to love him, trust him, fear him, honour him, and obey him with all his might, in order to the pleasing of his Creator, and the attainment of everlasting life: to which was added a positive law, against the eating of the tree of knowledge: and death was the penalty due to the sinner: this law was quickly broken by man; and God delayed not his judgment, but sentenced the tempter, the woman and the man; though not according to their merits; but graciously providing a Redeemer, he presently stopped the execution of the far greatest part of the penalty, the Son of God undertaking, as our surety, to become a sacrifice and ransom for us. Hereupon the covenant of grace was made, and the law of grace enacted with mankind; but more obscurely in the beginning; being cleared up by degrees in the several promises to the fathers, types of the law, and the prophecies of the prophets of several ages, the law being interposed because of transgression: in the fulness of time the Messiah was incarnate, and the first promises concerning him fulfilled, and after his holy life, preaching, and conquest of the tempter and the world, he gave himself a ransom for us, and conquering death he rose again, ascended into heaven, being possessed in his manhood of the fulness of his power, and all things being delivered into his hands; so that he was made the general administrator and Lord of all. And thus he more clearly revealing his covenant of grace, and bringing life and immortality to light, commissioned his ministers to preach this gospel to all the world. And thus the primitive sovereign is God, and the sovereign by derivation is Jesus, the mediator, in his manhood united to the second person in the Godhead; and the laws that we are governed by, are the law of nature, with the superadded covenant of grace; the subordinate officers are angels, magistrates, and pastors of the church (having works distinct); the society itself is called the church and kingdom of God; the reward is everlasting glory, with the mercies of this life in order to it: and the punishment is everlasting misery, with the preparatory judgments, especially on the soul, which are here inflicted. Subjection is due upon our first being; and is consented to, or vowed in baptism, and is to be manifested in holy obedience to the death. This is the sovereignty and government of God. Now let us see how God, as our sovereign, must be known.

1. The princes, and all the rulers of the world, must understand their place and duty: they are first God's subjects, and then his officers, and can have no power but from God, nor hold any but in dependence on him, and subordination to him. Their power extends no further than the heavenly Sovereign hath signified his pleasure, and by commission to them, or command to us, conferred it on them. As they have no strength, or natural power, but from the omnipotent God, so can they have no authority, or governing power or right, but from the absolute king of all the world. They can less pretend to a right of governing not derived from God, than a justice or constable may to such power, not derived from the earthly sovereigns.

Princes and states also must hence understand their end and work. God who is the beginning, must be the end also of their government: their laws must be but by-laws, subservient to his laws, to further men's obedience to them. The common good, which is their lower nearer end, must be measured by his interest in the nations, and men's relations unto him. The common possession of his favour, blessing and protection is the greatest common good. His interest in us, and ours in him, must therefore be principally maintained.

2. The knowledge of God as our sovereign King, must bring the whole man into subjection to him. Our understandings must be subject to his doctrine, and resigned to him, as teachable and tractable: when we know what is his law and will, we must rest in it, though we know not the reasons of it. We take not on us to be competent judges of all the reasons of the laws of men, but must obey them without disputing the reasons (with the limitations after to be mentioned.) How much more must we submit to the wisdom of the infallible law-giver, that cannot deceive, or be deceived. Our wills also must be fully subject to his will, revealed by his precepts. We must desire no more to move us, or to stop us, but to know what God would have us do. As the first wheels in a watch or other engine, moves all the rest, so the will of God must move all our wills, and rule our lives. We must take heed above all things in the world, lest our wills (which are the lower wheels) should have any such defects, distempers, reserves, any carnal bias, interest, or inclination, that makes them unfit to receive the law of God, or be ruled by his will. We must imitate our Lord, and learn of the prophet David, 'I delight to do thy will, O God.' With cheerful readiness to obey, we must stand waiting for the word of his command; and say 'teach me to do thy will, for thou art my God,' and as Samuel, 'Speak, Lord, for thy servant heareth.' When a man's selfish, carnal will is mortified, and his will lies submissive before the Lord, and wholly applies itself to his will, and it is enough to a man to move him in the greatest matters, to know that it is the will of God, this is a state of true subjection. Thus must we be in subjection to the Father of spirits, submitting even to his sharpest dispensations, for all the church is subject unto Christ, and this is essential to our holy covenant and Christianity itself. When God is taken to be our God, and we give up ourselves to be his people; when Christ is taken to be our Saviour, and we give up ourselves to him as his members, and redeemed ones, it essentially contains our taking him for our chief governor, and giving up ourselves to him as his subjects. Take heed of that wisdom that would supersede the wisdom of God, and be your guide itself, without depending on his wisdom. This is the foolish, damning wisdom of the world. Take heed of that concupiscence or will that would be your ruler, and overturn the will of God. For this is the grand rebel, and greatest enemy of God and us.

3. And subjection must produce obedience; subjection is the consent of the will to be sub-

jects, and to obey : obedience is the actual performance of commanded duties. Subjection is the root of obedience, and virtually contains it : obedience is the fruit of subjection, and supposes it. If God be your master, show it by his fear, or service : it is not calling Christ our king, but obeying him before all, that will prove us subjects. ' Not every one that saith unto me, Lord, Lord, shall enter into the kingdom of heaven : but he that doeth the will of my Father which is in heaven.'—' I beseech you therefore, brethren, by the mercies of God, that you present your bodies a living sacrifice, holy, acceptable to God, your reasonable service : and be not conformed to this world, but be ye transformed,' or turned into other men, ' by the renewing of your mind, that you may prove what is that good, that acceptable and perfect will of God.'—' And this is the will of God, even your sanctification '— ' Forasmuch then as Christ hath suffered for us in the flesh, arm yourselves likewise with the same mind : for he that hath suffered in the flesh, hath ceased from sin : that he no longer should live the rest of his time in the flesh, to the lusts of men, but to the will of God.' Yea, we should ' stand perfect and complete in all the will of God,' and by the power of the word of God ' every thought should be brought in obedience unto Christ.' Our obedience should be public and exemplary, ' for so is the will of God, that with well-doing we put to silence the ignorance of foolish men.'—' Obedience is better than sacrifice.' Whatever you do, therefore, keep close to the law of God.

4. To this end we must labour to know the law, and be acquainted with God's will. The book of nature must be studied : the holy scriptures must be searched, and meditated in both day and night. Princes must have this book continually in their hands. Rich and poor must learn it, that they may obey it.

5. Our subjection to God obliges us to a subjection to the officers that he sets over us. If any man say to judges, justices, and constables, ' I will obey the king, but you are not kings, therefore I will not obey you,' he shall suffer as disobeying the king in his officers. Contempt of magistrates and ministers, reflects on God.

6. Yea, hence we must practically understand in what respect to obey our governors : not merely as the officers of men : not only as chosen by the people ; but as the officers of God, that from him have their authority. The atheistical politicians that derive authority no higher than the sword, or the people's choice, or natural strength,

teach men to obey their governors, but as a little dog submits unto a mastiff, or so far as their convenience persuades them, but not for conscience in obedience to God. They teach men to look to no higher end than common preservation and liberties, and not to expect protection or reward from the absolute sovereign. In a word, they entice all princes and people into damnable rebellion against the Lord ; as much as if they should entice all constables and justices to hold their places without dependence on the prince. But God teaches us that ' there is no power but of God : the powers that be, are ordained of God : whosoever therefore resisteth the power, resisteth the ordinance of God ; and they that resist, shall receive to themselves damnation : for he is the minister of God to us for good ; even the minister of God, an avenger to execute wrath upon him that doeth evil.'—' Wherefore we must needs be subject, not only for wrath, but also for conscience' sake.'—' For they are God's ministers continually attending upon this very thing ; and for this cause we must pay them tribute.'—' Submit yourselves to every ordinance of man for the Lord's sake, for so is the will of God.'— Judge righteously between every man and his brother, ye shall not respect persons in judgment, but shall hear the small as well as the great; you shall not be afraid of the face of man : for the judgment is God's.'—' And he said to the judges, take heed what ye do ; for you judge not for man, but for the Lord, who is with you in the judgment ; wherefore let the fear of the Lord be upon you.' But our atheistical politicians would teach rulers that they are none of the ministers of God, and that they judge for man only, and not for him. The nature of all true obedience is such as Paul describes in children and servants, that takes its rise and motives from the Lord : ' Children, obey your parents in the Lord, for this is right.'—' Servants, be obedient to them that are your masters, according to the flesh, with fear and trembling, in singleness of your heart, as unto Christ : not with eyeservice, as men-pleasers, but as the servants of Christ, doing the will of God from the heart ; with good-will, doing service as to the Lord and not to men.'

7. Hence also you must learn, that God's authority is the highest authority, and there is indeed no such thing in the world as true authority that is against him, or not subordinate unto him. Therefore if men command us to disobey God, by neglecting that which is a duty, or by sinning against him, their commands are from a disobedient will of their own, but from no au-

thority : and it is better in such cases to obey God than man. So many prophets, apostles, and other martyrs, would not have been sacrificed by the fury of persecutors, if they had thought it just to obey them before God. God never gave any man authority against him, nor to nullify his laws. The acts of a justice or constable against the king, or beyond their power, are private or rebellious acts, and not authoritative. So are the laws of men that are against God. Yet note well, that though we must rather disobey men, than God, yet we may not forcibly resist, when we may not obey them. And in some cases (as if a king would ravish a woman, or the like) when it is lawful to resist his deed, it is not lawful to resist his state, and disturb the government of the commonwealth. Obey men cheerfully when God forbids it not : but see that God be your absolute sovereign, whose laws can be dispensed with by none.

If parents or masters command you to break the laws of God, obey them not. Despise them not, but humbly deprecate their displeasure, and obey them in all other things ; but in the unlawful thing, obey them not: no, not if they were the greatest princes upon earth. But say as the three witnesses of God, ' we are not careful to answer thee in this matter : if it be so, our God whom we serve is able to deliver us from the burning fiery furnace, and he will deliver us out of thy hands, O king : but if not, be it known unto thee, O king, that we will not serve thy gods, nor worship the golden image which thou hast set up.'

What I have said of magistrates, in the two last cases, I mean of pastors in the church. They must be obeyed in and for the Lord ; but not against the Lord. Saith Paul of the churches of Macedonia, ' they gave their ownselves to the Lord, and unto us, by the will of God.'—' He that heareth you heareth me, and he that despiseth you despiseth me.' And yet the leaven of the pharisees must be avoided : and an angel from heaven be held as accursed, if he should preach another gospel. And I would not have flatterers to set either princes or pastors above the angels of heaven. Though yet in other respects we may be still obliged, as I said before, to hear and to obey them.

8. The knowledge of God's sovereignty, must teach us to fear his righteous threatenings, and reverence his justice, and prepare ourselves to be judged by him. He rules by his laws, and so by threatenings and promises, which he will make good. It is not a painted fire that he threatens. Judgment is a part of government.

Laws are but shadows if there be no execution. ' O worship the Lord in the beauty of holiness ; fear before him all the earth.'—' Say among the heathen, that the Lord reigneth.' As his promises, so his peremptory threatenings shall be fulfilled. He will not revoke his stablished laws for fear of hurting wilful sinners, who will not fear his judgments till they feel them. ' Let all the earth fear the Lord, let all the inhabitants of the world stand in awe of him : for he spake, and it was done ; he commanded, and it stood fast.' Mark also the present judgments of the Lord, and rush not on his indignation. For ' the Lord is known by the judgments which he executeth : the wicked is oft snared in the work of his own hands.' Though ' the wicked contemn God, and say in his heart, thou wilt not require it,' yet they shall find that ' he beholdeth mischief to requite it with his hand, and that he is the helper of the fatherless and poor that commit themselves unto him.'—' The Lord's throne is in heaven: his eyes behold, his eyelids try, the children of men : the Lord trieth the righteous ; but the wicked, and him that loveth violence, his soul hateth.'

9. The sovereignty of God is a comfort to his loyal subjects. They may be sure that he will protect them, and make good his word. ' Behold he cometh, and his reward is with him. The righteous judge at his appearing will give the crown of righteousness to all them that love his appearing.'—' O let the nations be glad and sing for joy, for thou shalt judge the people righteously, and govern the nations upon earth.' —' Let the heavens rejoice, and the earth be glad, before the Lord ; for he cometh, for he cometh to judge the world with righteousness, and the people with his truth.'

10. Lastly, the knowledge of God as our sovereign king, must cause us to desire and pray for and promote the glory of his kingdom, and the obedience of his subjects in the world : that his name may be hallowed, by the coming of his kingdom, and the doing of his will on earth as it is in heaven, must be the matter of our daily requests to God. It must be the grief of every subject of the Lord, to think of the heathen and infidel parts of the world ; and to see the rebellion of the profane among us ; and that the laws of God are unknown or despised by the most of men. Alas ! how very many are ruled by their lusts, self-conceit, corrupted wills, and the customs of the world, or the will of men ! but how few are ruled by the laws of God ! O how should it grieve an honest heart, to see God's kingdom hindered by infidelity, and weakened,

divided, and disturbed by popery, and heresy, and dishonoured by scandal and impiety, as it is! And to see the multitude, and the violence and industry of corrupters, dividers and destroyers : and the fewness, the coldness, and remissness of the builders, the healers and restorers! All you that are loyal subjects to your Lord, lament these ways of rebellion and disobedience, and the diminutions and distempers of the subjects of his kingdom, and the unfaithfulness and negligence of his ministers : and bend your cares, desires, and prayers, to the promoting of God's kingdom in you, and in the world, and befriend not any thing that hinders its prosperity.

Chap. XV.

The third of these relations, and the next point in the knowledge of God, to be spoken of, is, that he is ' our most loving father, or bountiful benefactor.' As he is good, so he, doth good. As he is the chief good, so he bestows the greatest benefits : and therefore is thence, by a necessary result, our most bountiful benefactor. The term 'Father' comprehends in it all his three great relations to us. 1. A father gives being to his children, and therefore hath some propriety in them ; and God is the first cause of our whole being, and therefore we are his own. 2. A father is the governor of his children : and God is our chief governor. 3. A father tenderly loves his children that are child-like, loving and obedient to him ; and seeks their felicity : and so doth God love, and will make happy, his loving and obedient children, who have not only their being from him as their Maker, but their new being, or holy nature, from him as their sanctifier. This last being the end and perfection of the rest, doth communicate its nature to the rest, as the means. And so, 1. The new nature that God thus gives us in our regeneration, is not from his common love, but is an act of special grace, proceeding from his special, fatherly love. 2. The government that he exercises over them, as his regenerated children, is not a common government, such as is that of the mere law of nature, or of works ; but it is a special government by a law of grace, a justifying, saving law, or covenant ; together with an internal illuminating, quickening, guiding spirit, with church-state, officers, and ordinances, all suited to this way of grace : even as his dominion or propriety by redemption, and our sanctification and resignation, is not a common propriety, but a gracious relation to us as our own father, who hath the endeared relation to him of being his own children. All is from love, and in a way of love, and for the exercise and demonstration of love : so that when I call God ' our benefactor,' I precisely distinguish this last part of his relation to us from the rest : but when I call him ' a Father,' I mean the same thing, or relation which a benefactor signifies ; but with fuller aspect on the foregoing relations, and joining of them as they are perfected all in this.

Here I shall briefly name the benefits on which this relation of God is founded. 1. Even in creating us, he acted as a benefactor, giving us the fundamental good of being, and the excellency of manhood. 2. By setting us in a well furnished world, and putting all things under our feet, and giving us the use of creatures. 3. By entering into the relation of a governor to us, and consequently engaging himself to terms of justice in his dealing with us, and to protect us, and reward us, if we did obey ; and making us capable of an everlasting happiness as our end, and appointing us sufficient means thereto. These benefits denominated God the great benefactor or father unto man, in the state of his creation.

But then, moreover, he is a common benefactor also. 4. By so loving the world, as to give his only begotten Son, to be their Redeemer ; a sufficient sacrifice for sin. 5. By giving out his promise or covenant of grace, and making a proclamation of pardon, reconciliation, and eternal life, to all that will accept it in and with Christ, to gospel ends. 6. By sending forth the messengers of this grace, commanding them to preach to every creature the gospel, or word of reconciliation committed to them, and to beseech men, in Christ's stead, as his ambassadors, as if God himself did intreat by them, to be reconciled to God. 7. By affording some common mercies without, and motions of his Spirit within, to second these invitations. But though by this much God hath a title to their dearest love, yet they have no title to his highest benefits, nor are in the nearest relation of children or beneficiaries to him.

But, 8. When he begets us again to a lively hope, by his incorruptible seed, and gives us both to will and to do, and when the Father effectually draws us to the Son, renews us according to his image, takes away our old and stony hearts from us, gives us new and tender hearts, and gives us to know him, and love him as a father ; then is he our Father in the dearest and most comfortable sense, and we are his children, that have interest in his dearest love. 9. Therefore we have his Spirit, and pardon, justification, and reconciliation with him. 10 Also we have special communion with him in prayer, praises, sacraments, and all holy ordinances and conversation. 11. We and our services are pleasing to him, and so we are in the light of his countenance, and under a special promise of his protection and provision, and that all things shall work together for our good. 12. And we have the promise of perfection in everlasting glory.

Now as you see how God is our benefactor or most gracious and loving Father, let us next see what this must work on us.

1. Goodness and bounty should shame men from their sin, and lead them to repentance. Love is not to be abused and requited with unkindness and provocation. He that can turn grace into wantonness, and do evil because grace hath abounded, or that it may abound, shall be forced to confess that his damnation is just. He that will not hate his sin, when he sees such exceeding benefits stand by, and hears mercy, and wonderful mercy, plead against it, and upbraid the sinner with ingratitude, is like to die a double death, and shall have no more sacrifice for sin.

2. The fatherly love and benefits of God call for our best returns of love. The benefits of creation oblige all to love him with all their heart, and soul, and might: much more the benefits of redemption, and especially, as applied by sanctifying grace, to them that shall be heirs of life, it obliges them by multiplied strongest obligations: the worst are obliged to as much love of God as the best; for none can be obliged to more than to love him with all their heart, &c. but they are not as much obliged to that love: we have new and special obligations; and therefore must return a hearty love, or we are doubly guilty. Mercies are love's messengers, sent from heaven to win up our hearts to love again, and entice us thither. All mercies therefore should be used to this end. That mercy that doth not increase, or excite and help our love, is abused and lost, as seed that is buried when it is sowed, and never more appears. Earthly mercies point to heaven, and tell us whence they come, and for what. Like the flowers of the spring, they tell us of the reviving approaches of the sun: but like foolish children, because they are near us, we love the flowers better than the sun; forgetting that the winter is drawing on. But spiritual mercies are as the sun-shine that more immediately depends on, and flows from, the sun itself. And he that will not see, and value, the

sun by its light, will never see it! These beams come down to invite our minds and hearts to God; and if we shut the windows, or play till night, and they return without us, we shall be left to utter darkness.

The mercies of God must imprint upon our minds the fullest and deepest conceptions of him, as the most perfect, suitable, lovely object to the soul of man; when all our good is originally in him, and all flows from him, that hath the goodness of a means, and finally himself is all; not to love God then, is not to love goodness itself; and there is nothing but good that is suited to our love. Night and day therefore should the believer be drawing and deriving from God, by the views and tastes of his precious mercies, a sweetness of nature, and increase of holy love to God, as the bee sucks honey from the flowers. We should not now and then for a recreation light upon a flower, and meditate on some mercy of the Lord; but make this our work from day to day, and keep continually upon our souls, the lively tastes, and deep impressions of the infinite goodness and amiableness of God. When we love God most, we are at the best, and most pleasing to God; and our lives are sweetest to ourselves: and when we steep our minds in the believing thoughts of the abundant fatherly mercies of the Lord, we shall most abundantly love him. Every mercy is a suitor to us from God. The scope of them all is this, 'My son, give me thy heart.' Love him that thus loves thee. Love him, or you reject him. O wonderful love! that God will regard the love of man! that he will enter into a covenant of love; that he will be related to us in a relation of love; that he will deal with us on terms of love; that he will give us leave to love him, who are so base, and have so loved earth and sin! yea, and that he will be so earnest a suitor for our love, as if he needed it, when it is only we that need! But the paths of love are mysterious and incomprehensible.

3. As God is in special a benefactor and father to us, we must be the readiest and most diligent in obedience to him. Child-like duty is the most willing and unwearied kind of duty. Where love is the principle, we shall not be eye-servants, but delight to do the will of God, and wish, O that I could please him more! It is a singular delight to a gracious soul to be upon any acceptable duty; and the more he can do good, and please the Lord, the more he is pleased. As fatherly love and benefits are the fullest and the surest, so will filial duty be. The heart is no fit soil for mercies, if they grow not up to

holy fruits. The more you love, the more cheerfully will you obey.

4. From hence we must learn, both how God is man's end, and what are the chief means that lead us to him.

1. God is not the end of reason, nakedly considered, but he is the end which love inclines us to, and which by love is attained, and by love enjoyed: the understanding of which would resolve many great perplexing difficulties that step into our way in theological studies. I will name no more now, but only that it teaches us, how both God and our own felicity in the fruition of him, may be said to be our ultimate end, without any contradiction, yet so that it be eminently and chiefly God. For it is a union, such as our natures are capable of, that is desired, in which the soul doth long to be swallowed up in God; understand but what a filial or friendly love is, and you may understand what a regular intention is, and how God must be the Christian's end.

2. Withal it shows us, that the most direct and excellent means of our felicity, and to our end, are those that are most suited to the work of love. Others are means more remotely, and necessary in their places; but these directly. Therefore the promises and narratives of the love and mercy of the Lord, are the most direct and powerful part of the gospel, conducing to our end: and the threatenings the remoter means. Therefore as grace was advanced in the world, the promissory part of God's covenant or law, grew more illustrious, and the gospel consisted so much of promises, that it is called 'glad tidings of great joy.' Therefore the most full demonstration of God's goodness and loveliness to our hearers, is the most excellent part of all our preaching, though it is not all. And therefore the meditation of redemption is more powerful than the bare meditation of creation, because it is redemption that most eminently reveals love. Therefore Christ is the principal means of life, because he is the principal messenger and demonstration of the Father's love, and by the wonders of love which he reveals and exhibits in his wondrous grace, he wins the soul to the love of God. For God will have external objective means, and internal effective means concur, because he will work on man agreeably to the nature of man. Though there was never given out such prevalent invincible measures of the Spirit, as Christ hath given for the renewing of those that he will save, yet shall not that Spirit do it without as excellent objective means. Though Christ, and the riches of his grace

revealed in the gospel, be the most wonderful objective means; yet shall not these do it without the internal effective means. But when love doth shine to us so resplendently without us, in the face of the glorious Sun of love, and is also set into us by the Spirit's illumination, that sheds abroad this love in our hearts, then will the holy fire burn, which comes from heaven, and leads to heaven, and will never rest till it have reached its centre, and brought us to the face and arms of God.

5. From the fatherly relation and love of God, we must learn to trust him, and rest our souls in his securing love. Shall we distrust a Father; an omnipotent father! Therefore is this relation prefixed to the petitions of the Lord's prayer, and we begin with ' our Father which art in heaven,' that when we remember his love, and our interest in him, and his all-sufficiency, we may be encouraged to trust him, and make our addresses to him. If a Father, and such a Father, smite me, I will submit, and kiss the rod: for I know it is the healing fruit of love. If a Father, and such a Father, afflict me, wound me, deal strangely with me, and grieve my flesh, let me not murmur or distrust him; for he well understands what he doth; and nothing that shall hurt me finally can come from omnipotent paternal love. If a Father, and such a Father, kill me, yet let me trust in him, and let not my soul repine at his proceedings, nor tremble at the separating stroke of death. A beast knows not when we strive with him, what we intend, whether to cure, or to kill him: but a child need not fear a killing blow, nor a loving soul a damning death, from such a Father. If he be a Father, where is his love and trust?

6. If God be our Father, and so wonderful a benefactor to us, then thanks and praise must be our most constant work, and must be studied above all the rest of duty, and most diligently performed. If the tongue of man, which is called his glory, be made for any thing, and good for any thing, it is to give the Lord his glory, in the thankful acknowledgment of his love and mercies, and the daily cheerful praises of his name. Let this then be the Christian's work.

7. The children of such a Father should live a contented, cheerful life. Diligence becomes them, but not contrivances for worldly greatness, nor cares for that which their Father hath promised them to care for. Humility and reverence beseems them, but not dejection and despondency of mind, and a still complaining, fearful, troubled, disconsolate soul. If the children of such a Father shall not be bold, confident, and cheerful, let

joy and confidence then be banished from the earth, and be renounced by all the sons of men.

Chap. XVI.

There are yet several subordinate attributes of God, that being comprised in the fore-mentioned, may be passed over with the briefer touch. The next that I shall speak of is, his freedom. God is free in more senses than one: but for brevity, I shall speak of all together.

1. God hath a natural freedom of will, being determined to will by nothing without him, nor liable to any necessity, but what is consistent with perfect blessedness and liberty. His own being, blessedness, and perfections, are not the objects of his election; and therefore not of that which we call free-will: but all his works without, as creation, providence, redemption, &c. are the effects of his free will: not but that his will concerning all these, hath a necessity of existence: for God did from eternity will the creation, and all that is done in time; and therefore from eternity that will existing, had a necessity of existence: but yet it was free, because it proceeds not necessarily from the very nature of God. God was God before he made the world, or redeemed it, or did the things that are daily done. Therefore one part of the schoolmen maintain, not only that there is contingency from God, but that there could be no contingency in the creature, if it had not its original in God: the liberty of God being the fountain of contingency.

2. There is also an eminency both of dominion and sovereignty in God, according to which he may be called free. His absoluteness of propriety frees him from the restraint of any obligation, but what flows from his own free will, from disposing of his own as he pleases. And his absolute sovereignty frees him from the obligation of his own laws, as laws, though he will still be true to his promises and predictions. Let man therefore take heed how he questions his Maker, or censures his laws, or works, or ways.

Chap. XVII.

Another attribute of God is his justice. With submission, I conceive that this is not to be said to be from eternity, any otherwise than all God's relations are, as Creator, Redeemer, &c. because there is no time with God. For though the blessed nature denominated *just* is from eternity, yet not the formality or denomination of justice. For justice is an attribute of God, as he is go-

vernor only: and he was not governor, till he had creatures to govern: and he could not be a just governor when he was no governor. The denomination did not arise till the creation had laid the foundation. Many questions may be resolved hence, which I will not trouble you to recite.

Justice in God is the perfection of his nature, as it gives every one his due, or governs the world in the most perfect order for the ends of government. Because he is just, he will reward the righteous, and distinguish between the godly and the wicked: for that governor that uses all alike, is not just. The crown of righteousness is given by him as a righteous judge.

1. The justice of God is substantially (in men we call it an inclination) in his nature, and so it is eternal.

2. It is founded formally in his relation of governor.

3. It is expressively, first, in his laws: for as a just governor he made them suited to the subjects, objects, and ends.

4. It is expressively, secondly, in his judgments and executions; which is when they are according to his law; or in the cases of penalty where he may dispense at least according to the state of the subject, and fitted to the ends of government.

(1.) The justice of God is the consolation of the just: he will justify them whom his gospel justifies, because he is just. The justice of God in many places of scripture, is taken for his fidelity in vindicating his people, and his judging for them, and procuring them the happy fruits of his government, and so is taken in a consolatory sense. 'Justice and judgment are the habitation of thy throne; mercy and truth shall go before thy face.'—'It is a righteous thing with God to recompence tribulation to them that trouble us, and rest to the troubled.'

(2.) The justice of God is the terror of the ungodly. As he would not make unrighteous laws, for the pleasure of unrighteous men, so neither will he pass unrighteous judgment. But look what a man sows, that shall he also reap. All his peremptory threatenings shall be made good, and his wrath poured out for ever upon impenitent souls, because he is the righteous God.

Chap. XVIII.

Another of God's attributes is his holiness. He is called holy. 1. As he is transcendently above and separated from all the creatures, in comparison of whom the heavens are not clean; and from whom all things stand at an infinite distance. 2. As the perfection of his nature is the fountain of all moral good; first, in the holiness of his law, the rule of holiness; second, in the holiness of the soul, and, third, in his holy judgments. And consequently as this perfect nature is contrary to all the moral pollution of the creature, lothing iniquity, forbidding and condemning it. That perfect goodness of the will of God, from whence flow holy laws, and motions, and the holiness of the soul of man, is it that scripture means usually by God's holiness; rather than the foresaid distance from the creatures. Therefore his holiness is usually given as the reason of his laws and judgments, and of his enmity to sin : and our holiness is called his image (who imitate not his transcendency) and we are commanded to be holy as he is holy. The nature of the image will best tell us what holiness is in God. Holiness in us is called the divine nature, and therefore is radically a right inclination and disposition of the soul; which hath its rise from transcendent holiness in God, even as our wisdom from his transcendent wisdom, and our being from his being. Holiness therefore being indeed the same with the transcendently moral goodness of God, which I have spoken of before, I shall say but little of it now. Thus must the holiness of God be known.

1. It must cause us to have a most high and honourable esteem of holiness in the creature, because it is the image of the holiness of God. Three sorts of creatures have a derivative holiness : the first is the law; which is the mere signification of the wise and holy will of God concerning man's duty, with rewards and penalties, for the holy governing of the world! This is the nearest image of God, engraven upon that seal which must be the instrument of imprinting it in our souls. Now the holiness of the word is not the mere product of the will of God, considered as a will; but of the will of God considered as holy, that is, as the infinite, transcendent, moral goodness in the architype or original. For all events that proceed from God, are the products of his will, which is holy, but not as holy, as the creating, preserving, disposing of every fly, or fish in the sea, or worm in the earth, &c. There is somewhat therefore in the nature of God, which is the perfection of his will, and is called holiness, which the holiness of the law flows from and expresses.

This holy word is the immortal seed that begets holiness in the soul, which is the second subject of derived holiness; and this our holiness is a conformity of the soul to the law, as the product of the holy will of God, and not a mere

conformity to his predictions, and decreeing will as such. It is a separation to God, but not every separation : Pharaoh was set apart to be the passive monument of the honour of God's name : and Cyrus was his servant to restore his people, and yet not thus holy : but it is a separation from common and unclean uses; and a purgation from polluting vice, and a renovation by reception of the image of God's holiness, whose nature is to incline the soul to God, and devote it wholly to him; both in justice, because we are his own, and in love, because he is most holy and perfectly good.

The third subject of holiness is those creatures that are but separated to holy uses, and these have but a relative holiness; as the temple, the holy utensils, the Bible as to the materials, the minister as an officer, the people as visible members, &c.

All these must be reverenced and honoured by us, according to the proportion of their holiness. Our principal reverence must be to the holy word of God : for holiness is more perfect there than in our souls. The holiness of the word, which is it that the ungodly hate or quarrel at, is the glory of it in the eyes of holy men. We may much discern a holy and an unholy soul, by their loving or not loving a holy law; especially as it is a rule to themselves. A distaste of the holiness of scripture, and of the holiness of the writings of divines, and of the holiness of their preaching, or conference, discovers an unholy soul. A love to holy doctrine shows that there is somewhat suitable to it in the soul that loves it. It is the eulogy of the scriptures, the promises, the covenant, the prophets and apostles, that they are all holy. The holiness of the scripture doth make it as suitable and savoury to a holy soul, as light is suitable to the eye-sight, and sweetness to the taste : and therefore it is to them as the honey comb. But to the unholy it is a mystery, and as foolishness, and that which is contrary to their disposition, and they have an enmity to it : which makes a wonderful difference in their judging of the evidences of scripture verity, and much facilitates the work of faith in one sort, and strengthens unbelief in the other. Holy doctrine is the glass that shows us the holy face of God himself, and therefore must needs be most excellent to his saints.

2. And we must honour and love also the holiness of the saints : for they also bear the image of the Lord. Their holy affections, prayers, discourses, and conversations must be beautiful in our eyes: and we must take heed of those

temptations, that either from personal injuries received from any, or from their blots or imperfections, or from their meanness in the world, or from the contempt, reproach, and slanders of the ungodly, would draw us to think dishonourably of their holiness. He that honours the holy God, will honour his image in his holy people. ' In his eyes a vile person will be contemned, but he will honour them that fear the Lord.'—' The saints on earth are the excellent in his eyes, and his delight is in them.' The breathings of divine love in the holy prayers, praises and speeches of the saints, and their reverend and holy mention of his name, are things that a holy soul doth sweetly relish, and take pleasure in, as we would do to hear an angel speak of the holy things of the invisible glory.

3. Relative holiness itself, though the lowest, must be honoured by us. Holy offices and persons in them must be reverenced for their relative holiness. Holy ordinances, which also participate of the holiness of the law, must be reverently used. Due reverence must be given even to that which is lawfully by men devoted to a holy use, as are temples, and utensils of worship, and the maintenance dedicated to the service of God. That which is holy, must not be devoured, nor used as we do things common and unclean.

2. God's holiness must make us holy : we must fall in love with it, and wholly conform ourselves unto it. Every part of sanctifying grace must be entertained, cherished, excited, and used by us. Sin must be lothsome to us, because it is contrary to the holiness of God. No vile insect should seem to us so ugly. A dead carcass is an unpleasant sight, because it shows us a privation of natural life : but an unholy soul is incomparably a more lothsome, ghastly sight, because it shows us the privation of the life of holiness. No man can well know the odiousness of sin, and the misery and lothsomeness of the unholy soul, that knows not the holiness of God. ' Speak unto all the congregation of Israel, and say unto them, Ye shall be holy: for I the Lord your God am holy.'—' Sanctify yourselves therefore, and be ye holy, for I am the Lord your God.'—' As he that hath called us is holy, so must we be holy in all manner of conversation.'—' It is an holy calling wherewith we are called.' We are sanctified to be ' a peculiar people to Christ.'—' That denying ungodliness and worldly lusts, we should live soberly, righteously and godly in this present world.' We are made 'an holy priesthood, to offer up spiritual sacrifice, acceptable to God, by Jesus Christ.' We must

therefore ' present our bodies a living sacrifice, holy, acceptable to God, our reasonable service, for we are ' chosen in Christ before the foundation of the world, that we should be holy, and without blame,' and are redeemed and sanctified by Christ, ' that we may be presented glorious, holy, and without blemish.' See therefore that you ' follow holiness, without which no man shall see the Lord.' For ' blessed are the pure in heart, for they shall see him.'

3. The holiness of God must be to us a standing, unanswerable argument to shun all temptations that would draw us to be unholy, and to confound all the words of wicked men that are spoken against holiness. Remember but that God is holy, and if thou like that which is spoken against God, thou art his enemy. Think on the prophecy of Enoch, ' Behold the Lord cometh with ten thousand of his saints, to execute judgment upon all, and to convince all that are ungodly among them, of all their ungodly deeds, which they have ungodly committed, and of all their hard speeches, which ungodly sinners have spoken against him.'—' God will not hold him guiltless that taketh his holy name in vain ;' much less that blasphemeth holiness, which is the perfection of his blessed nature.

4. The holiness of God must possess us with a sense of our uncleanness, and further our humiliation. When Isaiah heard the seraphim cry, ' Holy, holy, holy, is the Lord of hosts, the whole earth is full of his glory,' he said, ' Woe is me, for I am undone ; because I am a man of unclean lips, and I dwell in the midst of a people of unclean lips ; for mine eyes have seen the King, the Lord of Hosts.'

5. The holiness of God must cause us to walk continually in his fear, and to take heed of all the affections of our souls, and even of the manner of our behaviour, when we come near to him in his holy worship. What suffered the Bethshemites for irreverent looking into the holy ark, and Uzzah but for touching it ? And what a dreadful example is that of the two sons of Aaron, that were slain by a devouring fire from the Lord, for offering strange fire which he commanded not. And Aaron was awed into silence by this account from God : ' I will be sanctified in them that come nigh me, and before all the people I will be glorified. Take heed lest irreverence, or deadness, or customary, heartless wordy services, should be brought before a holy God. Take heed of hypocritical, carnal worship. The holy God will not be mocked with compliments and shows.

CHAP. XIX.

The next attribute of God to be spoken of, is his veracity, truth and faithfulness. This is the result of his perfect wisdom, goodness, and omnipotency: for because he is most wise and powerful, he cannot be necessitated to lie: and because he is most good, he will not lie. Though God speaks by none but a created voice, and signifies his will to us by men, that in themselves considered are defectible; yet what he makes his voice, shall speak truth; and what he chooses to signify his will, shall truly signify it. He therefore condemns lying in man, because it is contrary to his own veracity. For if any should say that God is under no law, and therefore is not bound to speak truth, or not deceive a prophet or apostle by his inspirations; I answer, that he hates lying as contrary to his perfect nature, and is himself against it, and cannot possibly be guilty of it, because of his own perfection; and not because he is under a law. Lying comes from some imperfection, either of knowledge, power, or goodness, which can none of them befal the Lord. The goodness of the creature is a goodness of conformity to a binding law; and the goodness of the law is a goodness of conformity to, and expressive of the good will of God. But the goodness of God is a perfection of essence, the primitive goodness, which is the fountain, standard, and end of all other good; and not a goodness of conformity to another.

This attribute of God is of very great use to his servants. 1. From hence we must be resolved for duty, and for a holy, heavenly life: because the commands of God are serious, and his promises and threatenings true. If God were not true, that tells us of these great eternal things, then might we excuse ourselves from godliness, and justify the worldling in his sensual way: there is nothing of common sense and reason that can be said against a holy life, by a man that denies not the truth of God, or of his word. And to deny God's truth, is most unreasonable of all. I beseech you when you read and hear of the wonderful weighty matters of the scripture, of an endless life, and the way thereto; bethink you, if these things be true, ' what manner of persons you should be, in all holy conversation and godliness!' If the word be true, that tells us of death, judgment, heaven and hell, is it time for us to sin, to trifle, and live unready?

2. The truth of God is the terror of his enemies. O happy men, if their unbelief could make void the threatenings of God, and doubting of them would make them false! and if their misery were as easily remedied as denied; and ended as easily as now forgotten! or forgotten hereafter as easily as now! But true and righteous is the Lord, and from the beginning his word is true, not a word shall fall to the ground, nor a jot or tittle pass unfulfilled.

3. The truth of God is the ground of faith, and the stay of our souls, and the rock of all our confidence and comfort: a Christian did not differ from another man unless in being somewhat more deluded, if God were not true. But this is the foundation of all our hopes, and the life of our religion, and all that we are as Christians proceeds from this. Faith is animated by God's veracity, and from thence all other graces flow, or are excited in us. O Christians, what a treasure is before your eyes, when you open the blessed book of God! What life should it put into your confidence and comforts, to think that all these words are true! All those descriptions of the everlasting kingdom, and all those exceeding precious promises of this life, and that which is to come, and all the expressions of that exceeding love of God unto his servants, all these are ' the true sayings of God.' A faithful witness will not lie, much less will the faithful God. Eternal life is promised by God that cannot lie ' Wherein God willing more abundantly to show unto the heirs of promise, the immutability of his counsel, confirmed it by an oath; that by two immutable things, in which it was impossible for God to lie, we might have a strong consolation, who have fled for refuge to lay hold upon the hope set before us.' Let faith therefore live upon the truth of God, and let us be strengthened, and rejoice therein.

4. Abhor all doctrines which deny the truth and faithfulness of God, for they destroy the ground of Christian faith, of all divine faith, and all religion. The veracity of God is the formal object of all divine faith: we believe God, because he cannot lie: if he can lie, and do lie, he is not credible. But you will say, Is there any that hold such odious doctrines? Answ. I like not the charging of persons with the consequences of their opinions which they discern not, but disclaim: God will not charge them with such consequences, who do their best to know the truth, and why should we? All men have some errors, whose consequences contradict some articles of faith. It is not the persons that I persuade you to dislike, but the doctrine. The doctrine is never the less to be abhorred, because a wise or good man may hold that which doth infer it.

I shall now instance only in the Dominicans'

predetermination. They that hold that it is necessary to the being of every circumstantiated act natural and free, that God be the principal, immediate, physical, efficient, predeterminating cause of it, hold that he so causes all the false speeches and writings, as well as other sins, that ever were spoken or written in the world: not only as they are acts in general, but as these words in particular; so that he so predetermined the tongues of Ananias and Sapphira to say those very words which they said, rather than others: Now seeing it is apparent, (1.) That God hath not a voice, but speaks to us by a created voice, even by prophets and apostles, and that the scripture was written by men : (2.) And that God's veracity, which is the formal object of our faith, consists in his not using lying instruments, nor sending a lying messenger to us: (3.) That no way of inspiration can make God to be any more the cause of the words or writings of an apostle, than his immediate, physical, efficient, specifying predetermination doth; for it can do no more than irresistibly as the first cause, physically to actuate the agent to this thought, will, word, or deed, considered with all its circumstances. It follows that we have no certainty when God actuates an apostle or prophet to speak true, and when to speak falsely; and that no words or writing are of certain truth upon any account of God's inspiration or promotion, because God not only can, but doth cause all the untruths that are spoken or written in the world: therefore no faith in God's revelations hath any sure foundation, nor any formal object at all: and so all religion is dashed out at a stroke. To say that God causes not the falsity of the word, nor the word as false, but the word which is false, might well be the justification of them that affirm God to be but the universal cause of the word or act in general, as a word or act; and that the specification is only from the sinner. But in them that say he is the particular cause of this word comparatively, rather than another, it is but a contradiction: 1st. For there is no other cause of the falsity, which is a mere relation, but that which causes the rule, and the word or writing, which is false, and so lays the foundation. 2d. It overthrows all certainty of faith, if God speak to us by his instruments, those words that are false: the agent being false as well as the thing, leaves us no ground of certainty. The Dominicans therefore have but one task in which their hope is placed, to excuse their opinion from plainly obliterating all divine belief and religion, and that is to prove that there is so great a difference between inspiration,

and their physical predetermination, that God cannot by inspiration premove to an untruth, though by physical predetermination he may: this is their task, which I see not the least possibility that ever they should perform : if God premove, and predeterminate every will, tongue, and pen, to every lie that is spoken or written, more potently and irresistibly than I move my pen in writing, it is past my power to understand what more he can do by inspiration, to interest him in the creature's act: or at least how the difference can be so great as that one of the ways he can predetermine all men to their falsities, and none the other way. But of this I have written a large disputation; yet think it not needless, even in a practical treatise, to say thus much here.

5. The truth of God must teach us to hate every motion to unbelief in ourselves and others: it is a heinous sin to give God the lie, though he speak to us but by his messengers: every honest man, so far as he is honest, is to be believed: and is God less true? A graceless gallant will challenge you the field for the dishonour, if you give him the lie. If you deny God's veracity, you do not only equal him with the worst of men, but with the devil, who was a liar from the beginning. Yea, you may make him incapable of being the governor of the world, or suppose him to govern it by deceits and lies. Abhor therefore the first motions of unbelief. It makes men somewhat worse than devils; for the devils know that God cannot lie, and therefore they believe and tremble. Unbelief of the truth of the word of God, is the curse of the soul; the enemy and bane of all grace and religion, so far as it prevails. Let it be the principal care and labour of your souls, to settle the foundation of your faith aright, and to discern the evidence of divine authority in the holy scriptures, and to extirpate the remnants of infidelity in your hearts.

6. Let the truth and faithfulness of God engage you to be true and faithful to him, and to each other. You have promised him to be his servants ; be faithful in your promises : you are in covenant with him: break not your covenant. Many a particular promise of reformation you have made to God: prove not false to him that is true to you.

Be as good as your word to all men that you have to do with. Abhor a lie, as the offspring of the devil, who is the father of it: remember you serve a God of truth : and that it is the rectitude and glory of his servants to be conformable to him. They say the Turks are of-

fended at Christianity, because of the lies and
falsehoods of Christians. But surely they were but
nominal Christians, and no true Christians, that
ever they found such : and it is a pity that Christianity should be judged of through the world,
by the lives of them that never were Christians
but from the teeth outward, and the skin that
was washed in baptism. They that will lie to
God, and covenant to be his holy servants, when
they hate his holy service, will lie to man, when
their self-interest requires it. When they seem
to repent, and honour him with their tongues;
' they flatter him with their mouth, and lie to him
with their tongues ; for their heart is not right
with him, neither are they stedfast in his covenant.' God saith, ' ye shall not steal, nor deal
falsely, nor lie one to another.'—' A righteous
man hateth lying.'—' The lying tongue is but for
a mòment ;' for God hates it, and it is an ' abomination to him.'—' The lovers and makers of
lies are shut out of the kingdom of Christ.'

But above all, false teachers that preach and
prophesy lies, and deceive the rulers and people
of the earth, are abominable to God. When Ahab
was to be destroyed, a lying spirit in the mouth
of his prophets deceived them. And 'if a ruler
hearken to lies, all his servants are wicked.'

7. Above all, false witness and perjury should
be most odious to the servants of the God of
truth. ' A false witness shall not be unpunished,
and he that speaketh lies shall perish.'—' When
thou vowest a vow to God, defer not to pay it,'
saith David.—' Thy vows are upon me, O God,'
and ' unto thee shall the vow be performed.'
Perjury is a sin that seldom escapes vengeance,
even in this life. The instances of Saul the
first, and Zedekiah the last of the kings of Judah,
before the desolation, are both very terrible.
Saul's posterity must be hanged, to stay the famine that came upon the people for his breaking
a vow that was made by Joshua, and not by
him, though he did it in zeal for Israel. Zedekiah's case you may see, in 2 Chron. xxvi. Ezek.
xvii. He that swears, appeals to God as the
searcher of hearts, and avenger of perjury. The
perjured person chooses the vengeance of God.
He is unfit, till he repent, to be a member of
any civil society. For he dissolves the bond of
all societies. He cannot well be supposed to
make conscience of any sin or villany in the
world, against God, his country, his king, his
friend or neighbour, that makes no conscience
of an oath. It is not easy to name a greater
wickedness out of hell, than to approve of perjury by laws or doctrine. And whether the
church of Rome do so or not, I only desire them
to consider that have read the third canon of
the council at Lateran under Pope Innocent the
Third, where an approved general council decrees, that the Pope discharges vassals from their
allegiance or fidelity to those temporal lords that
exterminate not heretics (as they call them) out
of their dominions. What shall restrain men
from killing kings, or any villany, if once the
bond of oaths be nullified ? But scripture saith,
' keep the king's commandment, and that in regard of the oath of God.' No man defends perjury by name : but to say that men that swear
to do that which God commands, or forbids not,
are not bound to keep that oath ; or that the
Pope may absolve men, or disoblige them that
swore fidelity to temporal lords, when once the
Pope hath excommunicated them, seems to me
of the same importance.

CHAP. XX.

The next attribute to be spoken of, is, his mercifulness, and his long suffering patience, which
we may set together. This is implied in his
goodness, and the relation of a Father before
expressed. Mercy is God's goodness inclining
him to prevent or remove his creatures' misery.
It is not only the miserable that are the objects of it, but also those that may be miserable ;
it being as truly mercy to keep us out of it foreseen, as to deliver us out of it when we were in
it. Hence it is, that ' he takes not pleasure in the
death of the wicked, but rather that he may turn
and live.' And hence it is that he afflicts not willingly, nor grieves the children of men. Not that
his mercy engages him to do all that he can do
for the salvation of every sinner, or absolutely
to prevent or heal his misery ; but it is his attribute, chiefly considered as governor of the rational creature ; and so his mercy is so great to
all, that he will destroy none but for their wilful
sin, and shut none among us out of heaven, but
those that were guilty of contemning it. God
doth not prevent the sinner with his judgment,
but with his grace he often doth. He never
punishes before we are sinners, nor ever decreed
so to do, as all will grant. He punishes none,
where his foregoing commands and warnings
have had their due effect for the prevention :
and therefore because the precept is the first
part of his law, and the threatening is but subservient to that, and the first intent of a governor
is to procure obedience, and punishing is but upon
supposition that he misses of the first; therefore is God said not to afflict willingly ; because
he doth it not, for so the distinction is found,
not as a law-giver, and ruler by those laws con-

sidered before the violation; but only as a judge of the law-breakers. But yet God's mercy is no security to the abusers of his mercy; but rather will sink them into deeper misery, as the aggravation of their sin: as God afflicts not willingly, and yet we feel that he afflicteth: so if he do not condemn you willingly, you shall find, if you are impenitent, that yet he will condemn you.

If you say, God can be forced to do nothing against his will: I answer you, that it is not simply against his will; for then it should never come to pass: but it is against the principal act of his will, which flows from him as a lawgiver, or ruler by laws, in which respect it may be said that he had rather that the wicked turn and live: but yet if they will not turn, they shall not live. A merciful judge had rather the thief had saved his life by forbearing to steal; but yet he had not rather that thieves go unpunished than he should condemn them.

But you will say, if God had rather men did not sin, why doth he not hinder it? I answer, 1. He had not absolutely and simply rather; that is, so far as to do all that he can to prevent it, nor all that without which he foreknows it will not be prevented: but he doth much against sin as a law-giver, and nothing for it; he causes us not, but persuades us from it; and therefore, as a ruler, he may be said to have rather that men did not sin, or rather that they would turn and live.

1. The mercy of God, therefore should lead sinners to repentance, and shame them from their sin, and lead them up to God in love.

2. Mercy should encourage sinners to repent, as well as engage them to it: for we have to do with a merciful God, that hath not shut up any among us in despair, nor forbid them to come in, but continues to invite when we have often refused, and will undoubtedly pardon and welcome all that return.

3. Mercy being specially the portion of the saints, must keep them in thankfulness, love and comfort: and all mercies must be improved for their proper ends: when a merciful God is pleased to fill up his servant's lives with such great and various mercies as he doth, it should breed a continual sweetness upon their hearts, and cause them to study the most grateful retribution. He should breathe forth nothing but thankfulness, obedience and praise, who breathes nothing but mercies from God. As the food that men live upon, will be seen in their temperature, health and strength; so they that live continually upon mercies, should be wholly turned into love and thankfulness: it should become as it were their

nature, temperature and constitution. How unspeakable is the love of God, that provides so sweet a life for his servants, even in their warfare and pilgrimage in this world; that mercy must be as it were the air that they breathe in, the food which they must live upon; and the remembrance, improvement, and thankful mention of it, must be the business and employment of their lives! With what sweet affections, meditations, and expressions should we live, if we lived but according to the rate of those mercies upon which we live! Love and joy, thanks and praise, would be our very lives. What sweet thoughts would mercy breed and feed in our minds when we are alone; what sweet apprehensions of the love of God, and life eternal, should we have in prayer, reading, sacraments, and other holy ordinances! Sickness and health, poverty and wealth, death as well as life would be comfortable to us: for all is full of mercy to the vessels of mercy. O Christians, what a shame is it that God is so much wronged, and ourselves so much defrauded of our peace and joy, by passing over such abundance of great invaluable mercies, without tasting their sweetness, or well considering what we receive! Had we David's heart, what songs of praise would mercy teach us to indite! How affectionately should we recount the mercies of our youth and riper age; of every place and state that we have lived in, to the honour of our gracious Lord, and the encouragement of those that know not how good and merciful he is!

But withal, see that you contemn not, or abuse not mercy: use it well; for it is mercy that you must trust to in the hour of your distresses. O do not trample upon mercy now, lest you be confounded when you should cry for mercy in your extremity.

4. The mercifulness of God, must cause his servants to imitate him in a love of mercy: 'be merciful, for your heavenly Father is merciful.'— 'Blessed are the merciful, for they shall obtain mercy.' Be merciful in your censures: be merciful in your retributions: you are none of God's children, if you love not your enemies, pray not for them that curse you, and do not good to them that hate and persecute you, according to your power. If you forgive not men their trespasses, but take your brother by the throat, neither will your heavenly Father forgive you your trespasses. Mark, that even while he is called 'your heavenly Father,' yet he will not forgive, if you forgive not. Unmerciful men are too unlike to God, to claim any interest in his saving mercy, in the hour of their extreme misery. Men

of cruelty, blood, and violence he abhors : and usually they do not live out half their days ; but they that bite and devour one another, are devoured one of another. The last judgment will pass much according to men's works of mercy to the members of Christ. ' He shall have judgment without mercy, that hath showed no mercy : and mercy rejoiceth against judgment.'—' Pure religion, and undefiled, before God and the Father, is this, to visit the fatherless and widows in their affliction, and to keep himself unspotted in the world.'—' He that having this world's goods, seeth his brother in need, and shutteth up the bowels of his compassion from him, how dwelleth the love of God in him ?' But above all cruelty, there is none more devilish than cruelty to souls. And in those that undertake the place of pastors, cruelty to men's souls is a far greater sin than in any others. To starve those that they undertake to feed ; and to seduce those whom they undertake to guide, and be wolves to those whose shepherds they pretend to be, and to prefer their worldly honours and ease, before the souls of many thousands ; to be so cruel to souls, when Christ hath been so merciful to them, as to come down on earth to seek and save them, and to give his life a ransom for them ; this will one day be so heavy a charge, that the man that must stand as guilty under it, will a thousand times wish, that a ' millstone had been hanged about his neck, and he had been cast into the bottom of the sea,' before he had betrayed or murdered souls, or offended one of the little ones of Christ. Be merciful to men's souls and bodies, as ever you would find mercy with a merciful God in the hour of your necessity and distress.

Chap. XXI.

The last of God's attributes which I shall now mention, is, his dreadfulness or terribleness, to those that are the objects of his wrath. This is the result of his other attributes, especially of his holiness, and governing justice, and truth in his comminations. ' He is a great and dreadful God.'—' A mighty God and terrible.'—' A great and terrible God.'—' With God is terrible majesty.'—' The Lord most high is terrible.'

1. His children therefore must be kept in a holy awe ; . God is never to be approached or mentioned, but with the greatest reverence. We must ' sanctify the Lord of Hosts himself, and he must be our fear and dread.' Even they that receive the unmovable kingdom, must have grace in their hearts to serve him acceptably, with reverence and godly fear, because our God

is a consuming fire. When we come to worship in the holy assemblies, we should think, as Jacob, ' How dreadful is this place This is none other but the house of God, and this is the gate of heaven.' Especially when God seems to frown upon the soul, his servants must humble themselves before him, and deprecate his wrath, as Jeremiah did ; ' Be not a terror to me.' It ill becomes the best of men, to make light of the frowns and threatenings of God. Also when he deals with us in judgment, and we feel the smart of his chastisements, though we must remember that he is a Father, yet withal we must consider that he shows himself an offended Father : therefore true and deep humiliation hath ever been the course of afflicted saints, to turn away the wrath of a terrible God.

2. But above all, what cause have the ungodly to tremble at the dreadfulness of that God, who is engaged in justice, (except they be converted) to treat them for ever as his unpardoned enemies. As there is no felicity like the favour of God ; and no joy comparable to his children's joys ; so is there no misery like the sense of his displeasure, nor any terrors to be compared to those, which his wrath inflicts without end on the ungodly. O wretched sinner ! what hast thou done to make God thine enemy ? what could hire thee to offend him by thy wilful sin ? and to do that which thou knewest he forbids and condemned in his word ? What madness caused thee to make a mock at sin and hell, and to play with the vengeance of the Almighty ; what gain did hire thee to cast thy soul into the danger of damnation ? Canst thou save by the match, if thou win the world and lose thy soul ? Didst thou not know who it was thou hadst to do with ; it had been better for thee that all the world had been offended with thee, even men and angels, great and small, than the most dreadful God ? Didst thou not believe him, when he told thee how he was resolved to judge and punish the ungodly? what caused thee to venture upon the consuming fire ? Didst thou not know that as he is merciful, so he is jealous, holy, just and terrible ? In the name of God, I require and intreat thee, fly to his mercy in Jesus Christ ; and hearken speedily to his grace, and turn at his reproof and warning ; to-day, while it is called to-day, harden not thy heart, but hear his voice, lest he resolve in his wrath that thou shalt never enter into his rest ; there is no enduring, there is no overcoming, there is no contending with an angry, dreadful, holy God : repent therefore and turn to him, and obey the voice of mercy that thy soul may live.

3. The dreadfulness of God, doth tell both good and bad, the great necessity of a Mediator. What an unspeakable mercy is it that God hath given us his Son ; and that by Jesus Christ we may come with boldness and confidence into the presence of the dreadful God, that else would have been to us a greater terror than all the world, yea, than Satan himself. The more we are apprehensive of our distance from God, and of his terrible majesty, and his more terrible justice against such sinners as we have been, the more we shall understand the mystery of redemption, and highly value the mediation of Christ.

4. Lastly, let the dreadfulness of God, prevail with every believing soul, to pity the ungodly that pity not themselves. O pray for them, O warn them, exhort them, intreat them, as men that know the terror of the Lord. If they knew, as well as you do, what sin is, and what it is to be children of wrath, and what it is to be unpardoned, unjustified, and unsanctified, they would pity themselves, and cry for mercy, mercy, mercy, from day to-day, till they were recovered into a state of life, and turned from the power of Satan unto God. Alas, they know not what it is to die, and to see the world to come, and to appear before a dreadful God : they know not what it is to be in hell-fire ; nor what it is to be glorified in heaven : they never saw or tried these things, and they want the faith by which they must be foreseen by those that are yet short of nearer knowledge : you therefore that have faith to foreknow these things, and are enlightened by the Spirit of God. O pity and warn, and help the miserable ! Tell them how much easier it is to escape hell, than to endure it : and how much easier a holy life on earth is, than the endless wrath of the most dreadful God. Tell them that unbelief, presumption, and security, are the certain means to bring them their misery, but will do nothing to keep it off ; though they may keep off the present knowledge and sense of it, which would have driven them to seek a cure. Tell them that death and judgment are at hand, and that when they laugh, or sport, or scorn, and jest at the displeasure of the dreadful God, it is posting toward them, and will be upon them before they are aware ; and when they slumber, their damnation slumbers not : but while unbelieving sinners say, Peace, peace, sudden destruction will come upon them, as unexpected travail on a woman with child, and they shall not escape. O tell them how dreadful a thing it is, for a soul that is unregenerated and unsanctified, to go from that body which it pampered, and sold its salvation to please, and to appear at the tribunal of God: and how dreadful it is for such a soul to fall into the hands of the living God. At least save your own souls, by the faithful discharge of so great a duty ; and if they will take no warning, let them at last remember, when it is too late, that they were told in time what they should see and feel at last, and what their latter end would prove ; and that God and man did warn them in compassion, though they perish because they would have no compassion or mercy upon themselves. Thus let the terribleness of God provoke you, to do your duty with speed and zeal, for the converting and saving of miserable souls.

Thus I have briefly set before you the glass in which you may see the Lord, and told you how he must be known : and how he must be conceived of in our apprehensions ; and how the knowledge of God must be improved, and what impressions it must make upon the heart, and what effect it must have upon our lives : blessed, and for ever blessed, are those souls, that have the true and lively image of this God, and all these his attributes imprinted on them, as to the creature they are communicable. O that the ' veil were taken from our hearts, that we all with open face, beholding as in a glass the glory of the Lord, may be changed into the same image, from glory to glory, as by the Spirit of the Lord,' and may increase and live in the knowledge of the true and only God, and of Jesus Christ, which is eternal life. Amen.

PART II.

OF WALKING WITH GOD.

" And Enoch walked with God, and he was not ; for God took him."—GEN. v. 24.

CHAP. I.

THE TEXT EXPOUNDED, AND THE DUTY DEFINED.

BEING to speak of our converse with God in solitude, I think it will not be unsuitable, nor unserviceable to the ends of that discourse, if I here premise a short description of the general duty of practical godliness, as it is called in scripture, ' a walking with God.' It is here commended to us in the example of holy Enoch, whose excellency is recorded in this signal character, that, ' he walked with God :' and his special reward expressed in the words following, ' and he was not, for God took him.' I shall speak most of his character, and then somewhat of his reward.

The Samaritan and vulgar Latin versions strictly translate the Hebrew as we read it: but the interpretation of the Septuagint, the Syriac, the Chaldee and the Arabic, are rather good expositions (all set together) of the meaning of the word, than strict translations. The Septuagint and Syriac read it, 'Enoch pleased God.' The Chaldee hath, 'Enoch walked in the fear of God.' The Arabic, 'he walked in obedience to God.' Indeed to walk in the fear and obedience of God, and thereby to please him, is the principal thing in our walking with God. The same character is given of Noah in Gen. vi. 19. and the extraordinary reward annexed: he and his family were saved in the deluge. And the holy life which God commanded Abraham is called, a walking before God: 'Walk before me, and be thou perfect.' In the New Testament the Christian conversation is ordinarily called by the name of 'walking.' Sometimes a 'walking in Christ:' sometimes a 'walking in the Spirit, in which we live,' and a 'walking after the Spirit;' sometimes a 'walking in the light, as God is in the light.' Those that 'abide in Christ must so walk even as he hath walked.' These phrases set together tell us, what it is to walk with God. But I think it not unprofitable somewhat more particularly to show you what this walking with God contains.

As atheism is the sum of wickedness, so all true religiousness is called by the name of godliness or holiness, which is nothing else but our devotedness to God, living to him, and our relation to him as thus devoted in heart and life. Practical atheism is a living as without God in the world. Godliness is contrary to practical atheism, and is a living as with and to God in the world and in the church, and is here called a walking with God. It contains in it these particulars.

1. To walk with God includes the practical acknowledgment, that is made by the will as well as the understanding, of the grand attributes of God, and his relations to man; that he is infinite in his being, that is, immense and eternal; as also in his power, wisdom and goodness: that he is the Creator, Redeemer and Sanctifier: that he is our absolute Lord, or owner, our most righteous governor, and most bountiful benefactor, or Father: that of him, and through him, and to him, are all things: that in him we live, and move, and have our being: that he is the fountain, or first cause, from which all proper being, truth and goodness in the creature is but

a derived stream. To have the soul unfeignedly resign itself to him as his own; and subject itself to him as our governor, walking in the awe of his sovereign power; sensible of the strong obligation of his laws, which reason, justice and necessity all command us to obey. To live as in full dependence on him; to have the first and greatest respect unto him: a more observant respect to him than to our rulers: a more obedient respect to him than to our masters: a more dependent, tender, and honourable respect to him than to parents, or our nearest friends. Thus 'he that comes to God,' as God, and so as to be accepted of him, 'must believe that he is,' and (what he is in his relations to man, especially that as our governor and benefactor) that 'he is the rewarder of them that diligently seek him.' The impress of a Deity in his essential and relative attributes must be upon the heart of him that walks with God. Yea, the being of God must be much more remarkable to him, than the being of all creatures; and his presence more regarded, than the presence of the creature: and all things must be to us in comparison of God, as a candle is in comparison of the sun: his greatness and transcendent excellencies must so overpower them all, as to make them less observed and regarded, by his taking up our chief observation and regard.

2. Our walking with God includes our reconciliation to him, and that we are not in our natural state of enmity, but made his children and friends in Christ. Can two walk together unless they be agreed? Enmity is against unity, disaffection causes aversion, and flying from each other: yea, the fears of a guilty child may make him fly from his father's presence, till there be a particular reconciliation, besides the general state of reconciliation. A provoking, faulty child doth dwell with God his Father, though under the continual terror of his frowns: but to walk with him, in the full sense, is more than to be related to him, and to dwell with him: in a large sense indeed all God's children may be said to walk with him, as it signifies only a conversation, ordered in godliness, sincerity and simplicity. But in this sublimer sense, as it signifies a lively exercise of faith, love, and heavenly-mindedness, and a course of complacent contemplation, and holy converse with God, so it is proper only to some of the sounder and more vigilant, industrious believers. And hereto it is necessary, not only that we be justified and reconciled to God from our state of enmity, but also that we be pardoned, justified, and reconciled from our particular falls, which are more than the ordinary

infirmities of believers. Also it is necessary that we have grateful, friendly thoughts of God: that we have so much sense of his excellency, goodness, and kindness to ourselves, as may give us a complacency in conversing with him, and may make the thoughts and mention of him to be desirable and pleasing to us. Walking with God doth import, though not the full assurance of his special love and grace to us; yet such an apprehension of his love and goodness, as may draw the heart to think of him with desire, if not with delight. A lothness to draw near him, to think of him, or to mention him, a weariness of his special service, are contrary to this special walking with God.

3. Our walking with God, doth include our esteeming and intending him as the ultimate end and felicity of our souls. He is not to be sought, or loved, or conversed with, as a means to any greater good, (for there is no greater) nor as inferior, or merely equal unto any; his goodness must be the most powerful attractive of our love: his favour must be valued as our happiness; and the pleasing of him must be our most industrious employment. To walk with him, is to live in the warming, reviving sunshine of his goodness, and to feel a delighting, satisfying virtue in his love and gracious presence. To live as those that are not their own, and that have their lives, faculties, provisions, and helps for their master's service: as a horse or dog is of so much worth, as he is of use to him that owns him; and that is the best that is the most serviceable to his master: yet with this very great difference, that man being a more noble and capacious creature, is admitted not only into a state of service, but of sonship, friendship, and communion with God; and is allowed and appointed to share more in the pleasure and fruits of his services, and to put in his own felicity and delight into his end; not only because self-love is natural and necessary to the creature, but also because he is under the promise of a reward; and because he is a lover, and not only a servant, and his work is principally a work of love, and therefore his end is the end of a lover, which is mutual complacency in the exercises of love.

He that seeks not first the kingdom and righteousness of God, and refers not other things to him, but seeks first the creature, and God only for it, doth but deny God in his heart, and basely subject him to the works of his own hands, and doth not walk with God, but vilify and reject him. If you live not to God, even to obey, please, and honour him, you do not walk with him; but walk contrary to him, by living to his enemies, the flesh, the world, and the devil, and therefore God will walk contrary to you. You were both created and redeemed, though for your own felicity, yet principally for the glory and pleasure of your Creator and Redeemer; and for no felicity of your own but what consists in pleasing him, glorifying him, and enjoying him; 'whether therefore we eat, or drink, or whatever we do, it should all be done to the glory of God.' He that regardeth a day, or regardeth it not; he that eateth, or that eateth not, must do it to the Lord. Though a good intention will not sanctify a forbidden action, yet sins of ignorance and mere frailty are borne and pardoned of God, when it is his glory and service that is sincerely intended, though there be a mistake in the choice of means: 'none of us liveth to himself, and no man dieth to himself: for whether we live, we live unto the Lord; and whether we die, we die unto the Lord: whether we live therefore, or die, we are the Lord's: for to this end Christ both died, rose, and revived, that he might be Lord both of the dead and living.' Our walking with God, is a serious labouring, 'that whether present or absent, we may be accepted of him.' To this the love of our Redeemer must constrain us: 'for he died for all, that they which live, should not henceforth live unto themselves, but unto him that died for them, and rose again. Religion therefore is called the seeking of God, because the soul doth press after him, and labour to enjoy him, as the runner seeks to reach the prize; or as a suitor seeks the love and fruition of the person beloved. All the particular acts of religion are oft denominated from this intention of the end, and following after it, and are all called a seeking the Lord.

Conversion is called a seeking the Lord. 'Seek ye the Lord, while he may be found.'— 'The children of Israel shall return and seek the Lord their God.'—'They do not return to the Lord their God, nor seek him.' Men that are called to conversion, are called to seek God. 'Break up your fallow ground, for it is time to seek the Lord, till he come and rain righteousness upon you.' The converted children of 'Israel and Judah shall go weeping together to seek the Lord their God.' The wicked are described to be men that do not seek the Lord. The holy covenant was to seek the Lord: if therefore you would walk with God, let him be the mark, the prize, the treasure, the happiness, the heaven itself, which you aim at, and sincerely seek. 'Now set your heart and your souls to seek the Lord your God.'—'Glory ye in his holy name: let the heart of them rejoice that seek the Lord: seek the Lord and his strength, seek his face for evermore.' As the life of a covetous man is a seeking of riches, and the life of an ambitious man is a seeking of worldly honour and applause, so the life of a man that lives to God, is a seeking him ; to please him, honour him, and enjoy him ; and so much of this as he attains, so much doth he attain of satisfaction and content. If you live to God, and seek him as your end and all, the want of any thing will be tolerable to you, which is but consistent with the fruition of his love. If he be pleased, man's displeasure may be borne : the loss of all things, if Christ be won, will not undo us. Man's condemnation of us signifies but little, if God the absolute judge do justify us. He walks not with God, that lives not to him, as his only happiness and end.

4. Moreover our walking with God includes our subjection to his authority, and our taking his wisdom and will to be our guide, and his laws in nature and scripture for our rule ; you must not walk with him as his equals, but as his subjects : nor give him the honour of an ordinary superior, but of the universal king : in our doubts he must resolve us ; and in our straits we must ask counsel of the Lord : ' Lord, what wouldest thou have me to do,' is one of the first words of a penitent soul. When sensual worldlings do first ask the flesh, or those that can do it hurt or good, what they would have them be or do ; none of Christ's true subjects, do call any man father or master on earth, but in subordination to their highest Lord. The authority of God doth awe them, and govern them more than the fear of the greatest upon earth. Indeed they know no power but God's, and that which he committeth unto man. Therefore they can obey no man against God, whatever it cost them : but under God they are most readily and faithfully subject to their governors, not merely as to men that have power to hurt them if they disobey ; but as to the officers of the Lord, whose authority they discern and reverence in them : but when they have to do with the enemies of Christ, who usurp a power which he never gave them, against his kingdom and the souls of men, they think it easy to resolve the question, whether it be better to obey God or man ? As the commands of a rebellious constable, or other fellow-subject, are of no authority against the king's commands : so the commands of all the men on earth, are of so small authority with them against the laws of God, that they fully approve of the resolute answer of those witnesses in Dan. iii., ' We are not careful to answer thee in this matter : if it be so, our God whom we serve is able

to deliver us,' &c. ' But if not, be it known unto thee, O king, that we will not serve thy gods, nor worship the golden image which thou hast set up.' Worldlings are ruled by their fleshly interest, wisdom, and self-will, and by the will of man so far as it doth comport with these : by these you may handle them and lead them up and down the world : by these doth satan hold them in captivity. But believers feel themselves in subjection to a higher Lord, and better law, which they faithfully, though imperfectly observe : therefore our walking with God is called a walking in his law, a walking in his statutes, and keeping and doing his commands,—walking in his paths. It is our following the Lamb, which way soever he goeth : to be given up to our own hearts' lusts, and to walk in our counsels, is contrary to this holy walk with God, and is the course of those that are departed from him : and 'they that are far from him shall perish ; he destroyeth those that go a whoring from him : but it is good for us to draw near to God.'

5. Our walking with God doth imply that as we are ruled by his will, so we fear no punishment like his threatened displeasure : and that the threats of death from mortal men, will not prevail with us so much as his ' threats of hell.' If God say, I will condemn thee to everlasting punishment if thou wilt not keep my laws. If men say, we will condemn thee to imprisonment or death, if thou keep them, the believer fears God more than man : the law of the king doth condemn Daniel to the lion's den, if he forbear not to pray for a certain time. But he fears God more, that will deny those that deny him, and forsake those that forsake him : therefore the forementioned witnesses ventured on the fiery furnace, because God threatened a more dreadful fire. Therefore a true believer dare not live, when an unbeliever dare not die : he dare not save his life from God, lest he lose it ; but loseth it that he may save it. But unbelievers that walk not with God, but after the flesh, do most fear them that they observe most powerful in the world, and will be more moved with the penalty of some worldly loss or suffering, than with God's most dreadful threats of hell : for that which they see not, is to them as nothing, while they want that faith by which it is foreknown, and must be escaped.

6. Moreover he that walks with God, doth from God expect his full reward. He ceases not his holy course, though no man observe him, or none commend him or approve him ; though all about him hate him and condemn him ; though he be so far from gaining by it with men that it

cost him all that he hath or hoped for in the world : for he knows that godliness is of itself great gain, and that it hath the promise of this life, and that to come, and none can make God's promise void : he knows that his 'Father which seeth in secret will reward him openly,' and that he shall have a treasure in heaven who parts with all on earth for Christ. He hath such respect to this promised recompense of reward, that for it he can suffer with the people of God, and account the very reproach of Christ a greater treasure than court or country can afford him in a way of sin. He accounts them blessed that are persecuted for righteousness' sake, because the kingdom of heaven is theirs. He judges it a cause of exceeding joy, to be reviled and persecuted, and to have all manner of evil falsely spoken of us for the sake of Christ, because our reward in heaven is great. For he verily believes, that as sure as these transitory pleasures will have an end, and forsake those miserable souls that were deluded by them, so certainly is there a life of endless joys, to be possessed in heaven with God and all the holy ones ; and this he will trust to, as that which will fully repair his losses, and repay his cost, and not deceive him : let others trust to what they will, it is this that he is resolved to trust to, and venture all to make it sure, when he is sure that all is nothing which he ventures, and that by the adventure he can never be a loser, nor ever save by choosing that which itself must perish. Thus he that truly walks with God expects his reward from God, and with God, and thence is encouraged in all his duty, and thence is emboldened in all his conflicts, and thence is upheld and comforted in his sufferings: when man is the rewarder, as well as the chief ruler, of the hypocrite, then earthly things are the poise and motives to his earthly mind.

7. Our walking with God imports that as we expect our reward from him, so also that we take his promise for our security for that reward. Believing his word and trusting his fidelity to the quieting and emboldening of the soul, is part of our holy walking with him. A promise of God is greater satisfaction and encouragement to a true believer, than all the visible things on earth : a promise of God can do more, and prevail further with an upright soul, than all the sensible objects in the world. He will do more, and go further upon such a promise, than he will for all that man can give him. Peruse the life of Christ's apostles, and see what a promise of Christ can do ; how it made them forsake all earthly pleasures, possessions and hopes, and part with friends, houses, and country, and travel up and

down the world, in dangers, sufferings, and unwearied labours, despised and abused by great and small : and all this to preach the gospel of the kingdom, which they had never seen, and to attain that everlasting happiness, and help others to attain it, for which they had nothing but the promise of their Lord. See what a promise well believed in will make a Christian do and suffer. Believers did those noble acts, and the martyrs underwent those torments, which are mentioned, Heb. xi. because 'they judged him faithful that had promised.' They considered not difficulties, and defect of means, and improbabilities as to second causes, nor 'staggered at the promise of God through unbelief ; but being strong in faith, gave glory to God ; being fully persuaded, that what he had promised he was also able to perform,' as it is said of Abraham.

8. To walk with God, is to live as in his presence, and that with desire and delight. When we believe and apprehend that wherever we are, we are before the Lord, who seeth our hearts and all our ways ; who knoweth every thought we think, and every word we speak, and every secret thing which we do : as verily to believe that God is here present and observes all, as we do that we ourselves are here : to compose our minds, our thoughts, our affections to that holy reverence and seriousness as beseems man before his Maker : to order our words with that care and gravity as beseems those that speak in the hearing of the Lord. That no man's presence do seem more considerable to us than his presence : as we are not moved at the presence of a fly, or worm, or dog, when persons of honour and reverence are present, so should we not comparatively be moved at the presence of man, how great, or rich, or terrible soever, when we know that God himself is present, to whom the greatest of the sons of men, are more inconsiderable than a fly or worm is unto them. As the presence of the king makes ordinary standers by to be unobserved, and the discourses of the learned make us disregard the babblings of children ; so the presence of God should make the greatest to be scarce observed or regarded in comparison of him : God, who is still with us, should so much take up our regard, that all others in his presence should be but as a candle in the presence of the sun.

Therefore it is that a believer composes himself to that behaviour which he knows God doth most expect, and beseems those that stand before him : when others accommodate themselves to the persons that are present, observing them, pleasing them, and showing them respect, while they take no notice of God at all, as if they believed not that he is there. Hence it is that the men of God were wont to speak, though reverently, yet familiarly of God, as children of their Father with whom they dwell, as being indeed fellow-citizens with the saints, who are his household: Abraham calls him, 'the Lord before whom I walk;' and Jacob, 'God before whom my fathers Abraham and Isaac walked;' and David resolves, 'I will walk before the Lord in the land of the living.' Yea, God himself is pleased to use the terms of gracious condescending familiarity with them. Christ dwelleth in them by faith, his Spirit dwelleth in them as his house and temple, yea, the Father himself is said to dwell in them, and they in him. 'He that keepeth his commandments dwelleth in him, and he in him.' —'If we love one another, God dwelleth in us.' —'Hereby we know that we dwell in him, and he in us, because he hath given us of his Spirit.' —'Whoever shall confess that Jesus is the Son of God, God dwelleth in him, and he in God.'— 'God is love, and he that dwelleth in love, dwelleth in God, and God in him.' Yea, God is said to walk in them, as they are said to walk with him: 'for ye are the temple of the living God; as God hath said, I will dwell in them, and walk in them, and I will be their God, and they shall be my people.'

Our walking with God then is not only a sense of that common presence which he must needs afford to all; but it is also a believing apprehension of his gracious presence, as our God and reconciled Father, with whom we dwell, being brought near unto him by Christ; and who dwells in us by his Spirit.

9. To walk with God, includes not only our believing in his presence, but also that we see him in his creatures, and his daily providence, that we look not on creatures as independent or separated from God; but see them as the glass, and God as the represented face; and see them as the letters and words, and God as the sense of all the creatures that are the first book which he appointed man to read. We must behold his glory declared by the heavens, and see him shining in the sun; and see his power in the fabric of the world, and his wisdom in the admirable order of the whole: we must taste the sweetness of his love in the sweetness of our food and in the comforts of our friends, and all our accommodations; we must see, and love his image in his holy ones; and we must hear his voice in the ministry of his messengers. Thus every creature must become a preacher to us, and we must see the name of God upon it: thus all things will be

sanctified to us, while 'Holiness to the Lord' is written upon all. Though we must not therefore make idols of the creatures, because God appears to us in them, yet must we hear the message which they bring us, and reverence in them the name of the Creator which they bear. By this way of conversing with them, they will not ensnare us, or deceive, or poison us, as they do the carnal unbelieving world: but as the fish brought money to Peter to pay his tribute, so every creature would bring us a greater, even a spiritual gain. When we behold it, we should say with pleasant admiration, 'This is the work of God, and it is wonderful in our eyes.' This is the true divine philosophy, which seeks, and finds, and contemplates, and admires the great Creator in his works: when that which sticks in the creature itself, whatever discovery it seem to make, is but a childish unprofitable trifling: like learning to shape all the letters aright, without learning to know their signification and sense. It is God appearing in the creatures, that is the life, beauty, use, and excellence of all the creatures; without him they are but useless, vain, insignificant things.

10. Our walking with God contains our willing and sincere attendance on him in the use of those duties in which he hath appointed us to expect his grace. He is everywhere in his essential presence, but he is not everywhere alike to be found in the communications of his grace. The assemblies of his saints that worship him in holy communion, are places where he is more likely to be found, than in an ale-house or a play-house. You are more likely to have holy converse with him among the holy, that will speak of holy things to your edification, than among the senseless ignorant sensualists, and the scornful enemies of holiness, that are the servants of the devil, whom he uses in his daily work for the deceiving and perdition of the world. Therefore the conversation of the wicked doth grieve and vex a righteous soul, as it is said the Sodomites did by Lot, because all their conversation is ungodly, far from God, not savouring of any true knowledge of him or love to him, but is against him by enmity and provocation. If God himself do dwell and walk in all his holy ones, then they that dwell and walk with them, have the best opportunity to dwell and walk with God. To converse with those in whom God dwelleth, is to converse with him in his image, and to attend him at his dwelling: and wilfully to run among the wicked, is to run far away from God. 'In his temple doth every man speak of his glory, when among his enemies every man speaks to

the dishonour of him in his word and ways. He is otherwise present with those that are congregated in his name and for his worship, than he is with those that are assembled for wickedness or vanity, or live as mere animals 'without God in the world.' And we must draw as near him as we can, if we would be such as walk with God.

We must not be strange to him in our thoughts, but make him the object of our most serious meditations: it is said of the wicked that they are 'far from God;' and that 'God is not in all their thoughts.' The thoughts are the mind's employment. It dwells on that which it frequently thinks of. It is a walk of the mind, and not of the body which we are treating of. To mind the world, and fleshly things, is contrary to this walk with God: we are far from him, when our thoughts are, ordinarily, far from him. I know that it is lawful and meet to think of the business of our callings, so far as is necessary to the prudent successful management of them; that it is not requisite that our thoughts be always actually upon God: but he that doth manage his calling in holiness doth all in obedience to God's commands, and sees that his work be the work of God, and he intends all to the glory of God, or the pleasing of his blessed will: and he oft renews these actual intentions; and oft interposes thoughts of the presence, or power, or love, or interest of him whom he is serving: he often lifts up his soul in some holy desire or ejaculatory request to God: he oft takes occasion from what he sees, or hears, or is doing, for some more spiritual meditation or discourse: so that still it is God that his mind is principally employed on or for, even in his ordinary work, while he lives as a christian.

It is not enough to think of God, but we must think of him as God, with such respect, reverence, love, trust, and submission (in our measure) as is due from the creature to his Creator. For as some kind of speaking of him is but a taking his name in vain: so some kind of thinking of him is but a dishonouring of him, by contemptuous or false unworthy thoughts. Most of our walking with God consists in such affectionate apprehensions of him as are suitable to his blessed attributes and relations. All the day long our thoughts should be working either on God, or for God: either upon some work of obedience which he hath imposed on us, and in which we desire to please and honour him, or else directly upon himself. Our hearts must be taken up in contemplating and admiring him, in magnifying his name, his word and works; and

in pleasant contented thoughts of his benignity and of his glory, and the glory which he confers on his saints. He that is unskilful or unable to manage his own thoughts with some activity, seriousness, and order, will be a stranger to much of the holy converse which believers have with God. They that have given up the government of their thoughts, and turned them loose to go which way fancy pleases, and present sensitive objects do invite them, and to run up and down the world as masterless unruly vagrants, can hardly expect to keep them in any constant attendance upon God, or readiness for any sacred work. The sudden thoughts which they have of God, will be rude and stupid, savouring more of profane contempt, than of holiness, when they should be reverend, serious, affectionate and practical, and such as conduce to a holy composure of their hearts and lives.

As we must walk with God, 1. In our communion with his servants. 2. In our affectionate meditations; so also 3. In all the ordinances which he hath appointed for our edification and his worship.

1. The reading of the word of God, and the explication and application of it in good books, is a means to possess the mind with sound, orderly, and working apprehensions of God, and of his holy truths: so that in such reading our understandings are oft illuminated with a heavenly light, and our hearts are touched with a special delightful relish of that truth; and they are secretly attracted and engaged unto God and all the powers of our souls are excited and animated to a holy obedient life.

2. The same word preached with a lively voice, with clearness and affection, hath a greater advantage for the same illumination and excitation of the soul. When a minister of Christ that is truly a divine, being filled with the knowledge and love of God, shall copiously and affectionately open to his hearers, the excellencies which he hath seen, and the happiness which he hath foreseen and tasted of himself, it frequently, through the co-operation of the Spirit of Christ, doth wrap up the hearers' hearts to God, and bring them into a more lively knowledge of him, actuating their graces, and enflaming their hearts with a heavenly love, and such desires as God hath promised to satisfy. Christ doth not only send his ministers furnished with authority from him, but also furnished with his Spirit, to speak of spiritual things in a spiritual manner; so that in both respects he might say, 'he that heareth you, heareth me:' and also by the same Spirit doth open and excite the hearts of the

hearers: so that it is God himself that a serious Christian is principally employed with, in the hearing of his heavenly, transforming word: therefore he is affected with reverence and holy fear, with some taste of heavenly delight, with obedient subjection and resignation of himself to God. The word of God is powerful, not only in pulling down all high exalting thoughts, that rise up against God, but also in lifting up depressed souls, that are unable to rise unto heavenly knowledge, or communion with God. If some Christians could but always find as much of God upon their hearts at other times, as they find sometimes under a spiritual powerful ministry, they would not so complain that they seem forsaken, and strangers to all communion with God, as many of them do. While God, by his messengers and Spirit, is speaking, and man is hearing him; while God is treating with man about his reconciliation and everlasting happiness, and man is seriously attending to the treaty and motions of his Lord, surely this is a very considerable part of our walking and converse with God.

3. Also in the sacrament of the body and blood of Christ, we are called to a familiar converse with God: he there appears to us by a wonderful condescension in the representing, communicating signs of the flesh and blood of his Son, in which he hath most conspicuously revealed his love and goodness to believers: there Christ himself with his covenant-gifts, are all delivered to us by these signs of his own institution. No where is God so near to man as in Jesus Christ: and no where is Christ so familiarly represented to us, as in this holy sacrament. Here we are called to sit with him at his table, as his invited welcome guests; to commemorate his sacrifice, to feed upon his very flesh and blood; that is, with our mouths upon his representative flesh and blood, and with our applying faith upon his real flesh and blood, by such a feeding as belongs to faith. The marriage covenant betwixt God incarnate, and his espoused ones, is there publicly sealed, celebrated, and solemnized. There we are entertained by God as friends, and not as servants only, and that at the most precious costly feast. If ever a believer may on earth expect his kindest entertainment, and near access, and a humble intimacy with his Lord, it is in the participation of this feast, which is called, 'the communion,' because it is appointed as well for our special communion with Christ as with one another. It is here that we have the fullest intimation, expression, and communication of the wondrous love of God; and therefore it is here that we have the loudest call, and best assistance to make a large return of love: and where there is the most of this love between God and man, there is most communion, and most of heaven, that can be had on earth.

But it much concerns the members of Christ, that they deprive not themselves of this communion with God in this holy sacrament through their miscarriage; which is too frequently done by one of these extremes, either by rushing upon holy things with a presumptuous careless common frame of heart, as if they knew not that they go to feast with Christ, and discerned not his body: or else by an excess of fear, drawing back, and questioning the good will of God, and thinking diminutively of his love and mercy: by this means satan deprives many of the comfortable part of their communion with God, both in this sacrament, and in other ways of grace; and makes them avoid him as an enemy, and be loth to come into his special presence; and even to be afraid to think of him, to pray to him, or to have any holy converse with him: when the just belief and observation of his love would stablish them, and revive their souls with joy, and give them experience of the sweet delights which are opened to them in the gospel, and which believers find in the love of God, and the foretaste of the everlasting pleasures.

4. In holy, faithful, fervent, prayer, a christian hath very much of his converse with God. For prayer is our approach to God, and calling to mind his presence and his attributes, and exercising all his graces in a holy motion towards him, and an exciting all the powers of our souls to seek him, attend him, and reverently to worship him: it is our treating with him about the most important businesses in all the world: a begging of the greatest mercies, and a deprecating his most grievous judgments; and all this with the nearest familiarity that man in flesh can have with God. In prayer, the Spirit of God is working up our hearts unto him, with desires expressed in sighs and groans: it is a work of God as well as of man: he blows the fire, though it be our hearts that burn and boil. In prayer we lay hold on Jesus Christ, and plead his merits and intercession with the Father: he takes us as it were by the hand, leads us unto God, hides our sins, procures our acceptance, and presents us amiable to his Father, having justified and sanctified us, and cleansed us from those pollutions, which rendered us lothsome and abominable. To speak to God in serious prayer, is a work so high, and of so great moment, that it calls off our minds from all things else, and gives no creature room

or leave to look into the soul, or once to be observed: the mind is so taken up with God, and employed with him, that creatures are forgotten, and we take no notice of them, unless when through the diversions of the flesh, our prayers are interrupted and corrupted, and so far degenerated, and are no prayer; so far, I say, as we thus turn away from God. So that the soul that is most and best at prayer, is most and best at walking with God, and hath most communion with him in the Spirit: to withdraw from prayer, is to withdraw from God: to be unwilling to pray, is to be unwilling to draw near to God; meditation or contemplation is a duty in which God is much enjoyed: but prayer hath meditation in it, and much more.

All that is upon the mind in meditation, is upon the mind in prayer, and that with great advantage, as being presented before God, and pleaded with him, and so animated by the apprehensions of his observing presence, and actuated by the desires and pleadings of the soul. When we are commanded to pray, it includes a command to repent, to believe, to fear the Lord, and desire his grace. For faith and repentance, fear, and desire, are altogether in action in a serious prayer: and, as it were, naturally each one takes his place, and there is a holy order in the acting of these graces in a Christian's prayers, and a harmony which he doth seldom himself observe. He that in meditation knows not how to be regular and methodical, when he is studiously contriving and endeavouring it; yet in prayer before he is aware, hath repentance, faith, fear, and desire, and every grace falling in its proper place and order, and contributing its part to the performance of the work. The new nature of a Christian is more immediately and vigorously operative in prayer, than in many other duties: therefore every infant in the family of God can pray, with groaning desires, and ordered graces, if not with well ordered words: when Paul began to live to Christ, he began aright to pray: ' behold he prayeth,' saith God to Ananias. ' Because they are sons, God sends the Spirit of his Son into the hearts of his elect, even the Spirit of adoption, by which they cry, Abba, Father,' as children naturally cry to their parents for relief. Nature is more regular in its works than art or human contrivance is. Necessity teaches many a beggar to pray better for relief to men, than many learned men, who feel not their necessities, can pray to God. The Spirit of God is a better methodist than we are. And though I know that we are bound to use our utmost care and skill for the orderly actuating of each holy affection

in our prayers, and not pretend the sufficiency of the Spirit for the patronage of our negligence or sloth; for the Spirit makes use of our understandings for the actuating of our wills and affections; yet withal it cannot be denied, but that it was upon a special reason that the Spirit that is promised to believers is called a spirit of grace and supplication. That it is given us to help our infirmities, even the infirmities of our understanding, when ' we know not what to pray for as we ought;' and that the Spirit itself is said to ' make intercession for us, with groanings which cannot be uttered.' It is not the spirit without that is here meant: such intercession is no where ascribed to that. How then is the prayer of the spirit within us distinguished from our prayer? Not as different effects of different causes: as different prayers by these different parties. But as the same prayer proceeding from different causes, having a special force, (for quality and degree,) as from one cause, (the spirit,) which it hath not from the other cause, (from ourselves,) except as received from the spirit.

The spirit is a new nature, or fixed inclination, in the saints: for their very self-love and will to good, is sanctified in them, which works so readily, though voluntarily, as that it is in a sort by the way of nature, though not excluding reason and will; and not as the motion of the brutish appetite. That God is their felicity, and the only help and comfort of their souls, and so the principal good to be desired by them, is become to them a truth so certain, and beyond all doubt, that their understandings are convinced, that to love good, and to love God, are words that have almost the same signification; and therefore here is no room for deliberation and choice, where there is nothing but unquestionable good. A Christian, so far as he is such, cannot choose but desire the favour and fruition of God in immortality, even as he cannot choose, because he is a man, but desire his own felicity in general: and as he cannot, as a man, but be unwilling of destruction, and cannot but fear apparent misery, and that which brings it; so, as a Christian, he cannot choose but be unwilling of damnation, and of the wrath of God, and of sin as sin, and fear the apparent danger of his soul, so that his new nature will presently cast his fear, repentance, and desires into their proper course and order, and set them on work on their several objects, about the main unquestionable things, however they may err, or need more deliberation about things doubtful: the new creature is not as a lifeless engine, as a clock, or watch, or ship, where every part must be set in order by the art and hand of man, and so kept and used : but it is like to the frame of our own nature, even like man who is a living engine, when every part is set in its place and order by the Creator, and hath in itself a living and harmonious principle, which disposes it to action, and to regular action, and is so to be kept in order and daily exercise, by ourselves, as yet to be principally ordered and actuated by the Spirit, which is the principal cause.

By all which you may understand how the Holy Ghost is in us a Spirit of supplication, and helps our infirmities, teaches us to pray, and intercedes in us ; and also that prayer is to the new man so natural a motion of the soul towards God, that much of our walking with God is exercised in this holy duty : and that it is to the new life as breathing to our natural life ; and therefore no wonder that we are commanded to pray continually, as we must breathe continually, or as nature which needs a daily supply of food for nourishment, hath a daily appetite to the food which it needs, so hath the spiritual nature to its necessary food, and nothing but sickness doth take it off.

Thus I have showed you how our walking with God contains a holy use of his appointed means.

11. To walk with God includes our dependence on him for our mercies, and taking them as from his hand. To live as upon his love and bounty ; as children with their father, that can look for nothing but from him. As the eye of a servant is upon his master's face and hand, so must our eye be on the Lord, for the gracious supply of all our wants. If men give us any thing, we take them but as the messengers of God, by whom he sends it to us : we will not be unthankful unto men ; but we thank them but for bringing us our Father's gifts. Indeed man is so much more than a mere messenger, as that his own charity also is exercised in the gift. A mere messenger is to do no more but obediently to deliver what is sent us, and he need not exercise any charity of his own ; and we owe him thanks only for his fidelity and labour, but only to his master for the gift : but God will so far honour man, as that he shall be called also to use his charity, and distribute his master's gifts with some self-denial ; and we owe him thanks, as under God he partakes in the charity of the gift; and as one child owes thanks to another who both in obedience to the Father, and love to his brother, doth give some part of that which his Father had given him before. But still it is from our Father's bounty, as the principal cause

that all proceeds. Thus Jacob speaks of God : ' God before whom my fathers, Abraham and Isaac did walk, the God which fed me all my life long unto this day, the angel which redeemed me from all evil, bless the lads,' &c. When he had mentioned his father Abraham and Isaac's walking with God, he describes his own by his dependence upon God, and receiving from him, acknowledging him the God that had fed him, and delivered him all his life. Carnal men that live by sense, depend upon inferior sensible causes ; and though they are taught to pray to God, and thank him with their tongues, it is indeed their own contrivances and industry, or their visible benefactors, which their hearts depend upon and thank. It were a shame to them to be so plain as Pharaoh, and to say, ' Who is the Lord ?' or to speak as openly as Nebuchadnezzar, and say, ' Is not this great Babylon that I have built, by the might of my power,' &c. Yet the same atheism and self-idolizing is in their hearts, though it be more modestly and cunningly expressed. Hence it is that they that walk with God, have all their gifts sanctified to them, and have in all a divine and spiritual sweetness, which those that take them but as from creatures never feel or understand.

12. Lastly, it is contained in our walking with God, that the greatest business of our lives be with him, and for him. It is not a walk for complement or recreation only, that is here meant; but it is a life of nearness, converse, and employment, as a servant or child that dwells with his master or father in the house. God should be always so regarded, that man should stand by as nothing, and be scarcely observed in comparison of him. We should begin the day with God, and entertain him in the first and sweetest of our thoughts : we should walk abroad and do our work as in his sight : we must resolve to do no work but his, no, not in our trades and ordinary callings : we must be able to say, It is the work which my master set me to do, and I do it to obey and please his will. At night we must take an account of ourselves, and spread open that account before him, desiring his acceptance of what was well, and his pardon for what we did amiss, that we may thus be ready for our last account. In a word, though men be our fellow-labourers and companions, yet the principal business of our care and diligence, must be our Master's service in the world. Therefore we must look about us, and discern the opportunities of serving him, and of the best improvement of his talents ; and must make it our daily study and business, to do him the greatest ser-

vice in the world. Therefore we must look about us, and discern the opportunities of serving him, and of the best improvement of his talents; and must make it our daily study and business to do him the greatest service we are able, whatever it may cost us through the malice of the enemies, being sure our labour shall not be in vain, and that we cannot serve him at too dear a rate. It is not as idle companions, but as servants, as soldiers, as those that put forth all their strength, to do his work and reach the crown, that we are called to walk with God. All this is done, though not in the same degree by all, yet according to the measure of their holiness by every one that lives by faith.

Having told you what it is to walk with God, as to the matter of it, I shall more briefly tell you as to the manner: the nature of God, of man, and of the work, will tell it you.

1. That our walk with God must be with the greatest reverence: were we ever so much assured of his special love to us, and ever so full of faith and joy, our reverence must be never the less for this. Though love cast out that guilty fear which discourages the sinner from hoping and seeking for the mercy which would save him, and which disposes him to hate and fly from God, yet doth it not cast out that reverence of God, which we owe him as his creatures, so infinitely below him as we are. It cannot be that God should be known and remembered as God, without some admiring and awful apprehensions of him. Infinitude, omnipotency, and inaccessible majesty and glory, must needs affect the soul that knows them, with reverence and self-abasement. Though we receive a kingdom that cannot be moved; yet if we will serve God acceptably, we must serve him with reverence and godly fear, as knowing that as he is our God, so he is also a consuming fire. We must so worship him as those that remember that we are worms and guilty sinners, and that he is most high and holy, and will be 'sanctified in them that come nigh him, and before all the people he will be glorified.' Irreverence shows a kind of atheistical contempt of God, or else a sleepiness and inconsiderateness of the soul. The sense of the goodness and love of God, must consist with the sense of his holiness and omnipotency. It is presumption, pride, or stupidity, which excludes reverence; which faith doth cause, and not oppose.

2. Our walking with God must be a work of humble boldness and familiarity. The reverence of his holiness and greatness, must not overcome or exclude the sense of his goodness and compassion, nor the full assurance of faith and hope.

Though by sin we are enemies and strangers to God, and stand afar off, yet in Christ we are reconciled to him, and brought near. ' For he is our peace, who hath taken down the partition, and abolished the enmity, and reconciled Jew and Gentile unto God.'—'And through him we have all an access to the Father by one spirit.'— ' We are now no more strangers and foreigners, but fellow-citizens of the saints, and of the household of God.'—' In him we have boldness and access with confidence by the belief of him.' Though of ourselves we are unworthy to be called his children, and may well stand afar off with the publican, and not dare to lift up our faces towards heaven, but smite our breasts, and say, ' O Lord, be merciful to me a sinner.'—' Yet have we boldness to enter into the holiest, by the blood of Jesus, by a new and living way which he consecrated for us, through the veil, that is to say, his flesh: and having an High-Priest over the house of God, we may draw near with a true heart, in full assurance of faith.' Therefore whensoever we are afraid at the sight of sin and justice, let us remember that ' we have a great High-Priest that is passed unto the heavens, even Jesus the Son of God: therefore let us come boldly to the throne of grace. that we may obtain mercy, and find grace to help in time of need.' He that allows us to walk with him, doth allow us such humble familiarity as · beseems those that walk together with him.

3. Our walking with God must be a work of holy pleasure and delight. We may unwillingly be dragged into the presence of an enemy, and serve as drudges upon mere necessity or fear. But walking together is the loving and delightful converse of friends. When we take sweet counsel of the Lord, and set him always at our right hand, and are glad to hear from him, glad to speak to him, and glad to withdraw our thoughts from all the things and persons in the world, that we may solace ourselves in the contemplations of his excellency, and the admirations of his love and glory, this is indeed to walk with God. You converse with him as with a stranger, an enemy, or your destroyer, and not as with God, while you had rather be far from him, and only tremble in his presence, and are glad when you have done and are got away, but have no delight or pleasure in him. If we can take delight in our walking with a friend, a friend that is truly loving and constant, a friend that is learned, wise and holy; if their wise and heavenly discourse be better to us, than our recreations, meat, or drinks, or clothes; what delight then should we find in our secret converse with the

most high, most wise and gracious God! How glad should we be to find him willing and ready to entertain us? How glad should we be that we may employ our thoughts on so high and excellent an object? What cause have we to say, ' my meditation of him shall be sweet, and I will be glad in the Lord.'—' In the multitude of my thoughts within me,' (my sorrowful, troublesome, weary thoughts) ' thy comforts do delight my soul.' Let others take pleasure in childish vanity or sensuality, but say thou as David, ' I have rejoiced in the ways of thy commandments, as much as in all riches : I will meditate in thy precepts and have respect unto thy ways : I will delight myself in thy statutes, and will not forget thy word.'—' I will delight myself in thy commandments which I have loved.'—' Let scorners delight in scorning, and fools hate knowledge, but make me to go in the path of thy commandments, for therein do I delight.' If thou wouldst experimentally know the safety and glory of a holy life, ' delight thyself in the Lord, and he shall give thee the desire of thine heart.' Especially when we draw near him in his solemn worship, and when we separate ourselves on his holy days from all our common worldly thoughts, to be conversant, as in heaven, with the blessed God; then may we with the holy apostles be ' in the Spirit on the Lord's day.'—' And if we turn away our foot from the sabbath, from doing our pleasure on that holy day, and call the sabbath a delight, the holy of the Lord, honourable, and shall honour him, not doing our own ways, nor finding our own pleasure, nor speaking our own words, then shall we delight ourselves in the Lord,' and understand how great a privilege it is to have the liberty of those holy days and duties for our sweet and heavenly converse with God.

4. Our walking with God must be a matter of industry and diligence : it is not an occasional idle converse, but a life of obedience, and employment, that this phrase importeth. The sluggish idle wishes of the hypocrite, whose hands refuse to labour, are not this walking with God : nor the sacrifice of fools, who are hasty to utter the overflowings of their foolish hearts before the Lord, while they keep not their foot, nor hearken to the law, nor consider they do evil. ' He that cometh to God (and will walk with him) must believe that he is, and that he is the rewarder of them that diligently seek him. God is with you while you are with him; but if you forsake him, he will forsake you.'—' Up and be doing, and the Lord will be with you.' If you would meet with God in the way of mercy, ' take

diligent heed to do the commandment and law, to love the Lord your God, and to walk in all his ways, and to cleave unto him, and to serve him with all your heart, and with all your soul.'

5. Our walking with God is a matter of some constancy : it signifies our course of life, and not some accidental action on the by ; a man may walk with a stranger for a visit, or in compliment, or upon some unusual occasion : but this walk with God, is the act of those that dwell with him in his family, and do his work. It is not only to step and speak with him, or cry to him for mercy in some great extremity, or to go to church for company or custom, or think or talk of him sometimes heartlessly on the by, as a man will talk of news, or matters that are done in a foreign land, or of persons that we have little to do with : but it is to be always with him, ' to seek first his kingdom and righteousness.'—' Not to labour (comparatively) for the food that perisheth, but for that which endureth to everlasting life.'—' To delight in the law of the Lord, and meditate on it day and night.' That ' his words be in our hearts, and that we teach them diligently to our children, and talk of them sitting in the house, and walking by the way, lying down, and rising up.' That ' we pray continually and in all things give thanks.' But ' will the hypocrite delight himself in the Almighty, or will he always call upon God ?'—' His goodness is as the morning cloud, and as the early dew it goeth away.'

So much of the description of this walking with God.

CHAP. II.

THE PRACTICAL INFLUENCE OF THE DOCTRINE UPON MAN'S HEART AND LIFE.

We are next to consider how far this doctrine doth concern ourselves, and what use we have to make of it upon our hearts and lives.

First, It acquainteth us with the abundance of atheism that is in the world, even among those that profess the knowledge of God. It is atheism not only to say there is no God, but to say so in the heart, while the heart is no more affected towards him, observant of him, or confident in him, or submissive to him, than if indeed there were no God: when there is nothing of God upon the heart, no love, no fear, no trust, no subjection ; this is heart-atheism. When men that have some kind of 'knowledge of God, yet glorify him not as God, nor are thankful to him, but become vain in their imaginations, and their foolish hearts are darkened; these men are heart-atheists; and 'professing themselves wise, they become fools, and are given up to vile affections: and as they do not like to retain God in their knowledge (however they may discourse of him, so) God oft giveth them over to a reprobate mind, to do those things that are not convenient, being filled with all unrighteousness, fornication, wickedness, covetousness, maliciousness, envy, murder, debate, deceit, malignity.' Many such atheists go up and down under the self-deceiving name of Christians: being indeed unbelieving and defiled, so void of purity that they deride it, and 'nothing is pure to them; but even their mind and conscience is defiled: they profess that they know God, but they deny him in their works, being abominable and disobedient, and to every good work reprobate.' What are they but atheists, when 'God is not in all their thoughts,' unless it be in their impious or blaspheming thoughts, or in their light, contemptuous thoughts! To take God for God indeed, and for our God, essentially includes the taking him to be the most powerful, wise and good, the most just and holy, the creator, preserver, and governor of the world, whom we and all men are obliged absolutely to obey and fear, to love and desire, whose will is our beginning, rule and end: he that taketh not God for such as here described, taketh him not for God, and therefore is indeed an atheist: what name soever he assumeth to himself, this is the name that God will call him by; even a 'fool that hath said in his heart there is no God: while they are corrupt and do abominably, they understand not, and seek not after God; they are all gone aside, and are altogether become filthy, there is none of them that doth good; they are workers of iniquity, they have no knowledge, and eat up the people of God as bread, and call not upon the Lord.' 'Ungodliness' is but the English for atheism. The atheist or ungodly in opinion, is he that thinks that there is no God, or that he is one that we need not love and serve, and that is but the same, viz. to be no God.

The atheist or ungodly in heart, or will, is he that consents not that God shall be his God, to be loved, feared and obeyed before all. The atheist in life, or outward practice, is he that lives as without God in the world; that seeks him not as his chief good, and obeys him not as his highest absolute Lord; so that indeed atheism is the sum of all iniquity, as godliness is the sum of all religion and moral good. If you see by the description which I have given you, what it is to be godly, and to walk with God, and what it is to be an atheist or ungodly, you may easily see that godliness is more rare, and atheism more common, than many that themselves are atheists will believe. It is not that which a man calls his God, that is taken by him for his God indeed. It is not the tongue, but the heart, that is the man. Pilate called Christ the king of the Jews, when he crucified him. The Jews called God their Father, when Christ tells them they 'were of their father the devil,' and proveth it, because whatever they said, 'they would do his lusts.' The same Jews pretended to honour the name of the Messiah, and expect him, while they killed him. The question is not what men call themselves, but what they are: not whether you say you take God for your God, but whether you do so indeed: not whether you profess yourselves to be atheists, but whether you are atheists indeed or not. If you are not, look over what I have here said, and ask your consciences: Do you walk with God, and who is it you submit yourselves willingly to be disposed of by? To whom are you most subject, and whose commands have the most effectual authority with you? Who is the chief governor of your hearts and lives, and whom is it that you principally desire to please? Whom do you most fear, and whose displeasure do you principally avoid? From whom is it that you expect your greatest reward, and in whom, and with whom, do you place and expect your happiness? Whose work is it that you do, as the greatest business of your lives? Is it the goodness of God in himself, and unto you, that draws up your hearts to him in love? Is he the ultimate end of your intentions, design, and the industry of your lives? Do you trust upon his word as your security for your everlasting hopes and happiness? Do you study and observe him in his works? Do you really live as in his presence? Do you delight in his word, and meditate on it? Do you love the communion of saints, and to be most frequent and familiar with them that are most frequent and familiar with Christ? Do you savour more the particular affectionate discourse about his nature, will and kingdom, than the frothy talk of empty wits, or the common discourse of carnal worldlings? Do you love to be employed in thanking him for his mercies, and in praising him, and declaring the glory of his attributes and works? Is your dependence on him as your great benefactor, and do you receive your mercies as his gifts.

If thus your principal observation be of God, your chief desire be after God, your chief confidence in God, and your chief business in the world be with God, and for God, and your chief joy be in the favour of God, (when you can apprehend it) and in the prosperity of his church, and your hopes of glory: and if your chief grief and trouble be your sinful distance from him, your backwardness and disability in his love and service, the fear of his displeasure, and the injuries done to his gospel and honour in the world; then I must needs say, you are savingly delivered from your atheism and ungodliness; you do not only talk of God, but walk with God; you are then acquainted with that spiritual life and work, which the sensual world is unacquainted with, and with those invisible, everlasting excellencies, which if worldlings knew, they would change their minds, choice, and pleasures: you are then acquainted with that rational, manly, saint-like life, which ungodly men are strangers to; and you are in the way of that well-grounded hope and peace to which all the pleasures and crowns on earth, if compared, are but chaff and misery. But if ye were never yet brought to walk with God, do not think you have a sound belief in God, nor that you acknowledge him sincerely, nor that you are saved from heart-atheism; nor is it piety in the opinion and the tongue, that will save him that is an atheist, or ungodly in heart and life. Divinity is practical science: knowing is not the ultimate or perfective act of man: but a means to holy love, joy and service. Nor is it clear and solid knowledge, if it do not somewhat affect the heart, and engage and actuate the life, according to the nature and use of the thing known. The soundness of knowledge and belief, is not best discerned in the intellectual acts themselves, but in their powerful, free and pleasant efficacy, upon our choice and practice. By these therefore you must judge, whether you are godly or atheistical. The question is not what your tongues say of God, nor what ceremonious observances you allow him, but what your hearts and your endeavours say of him, and whether you glorify him as God, when you say you know him: otherwise you will find that 'the wrath of God is revealed from heaven against all ungodliness and unrighteousness of men, who hold the truth in righteousness.'

Now alas, what matter of lamentation is here before us! To see how seriously men converse with one another; and how God is overlooked or neglected by the most! How men live together, as if there were more that is considerable in these particles of animated dust, than in the Lord Almighty, and in all his graces, service and rewards! To see how God is cast aside, and his interest made to give place to the inter-est-of the flesh, and his services must stay till men have done their service to their lusts, or to worldly men, that can do them hurt, or show them favour! And his will must not be done, when it crosses the will of sinful man! How little do all the commands, promises, and threatenings of God signify with these atheistical men, in comparison of their lusts, or the laws of men, or any thing that concerns their temporal prosperity. O how is the world revolted from their Maker! How have they lost the knowledge of themselves, and forgotten their natures, capacities and obligations, and what it is to be indeed a man. O hearken, sinners, to the call of your Redeemer! Return, O seduced, wandering souls, and know at last your resting place! Why is not God in all your thoughts? Or why is he thought on with so much remissness, unwillingness, and contempt, and with so little pleasure, seriousness or regard? Do you understand yourselves in this? Do you deal worthily with God, or wisely for yourselves? Do you take more pleasure, with the prodigal, to feed swine, and to feed with them, than to dwell at home with your heavenly Father; and to walk before him, and serve him in the world? Did you but know how dangerous a way you have been in, and how unreasonably you have dealt, to forsake God in your hearts, and follow that which cannot profit you, what haste would you make to leave the crowd, come home to God, and try a more noble and gainful conversation? If reasons may have room and leave to work upon you, I will set a few before you more distinctly, to call you off from your barren, inordinate creature-converse, to a believing, serious converse with God.

1. The higher and more excellent the object is, especially when it is also of most concern to ourselves, the more excellent is the converse. Therefore as nothing dare compare itself with God, so no employment may be compared with this of holy walking with him. How vile a contempt is it of the Almighty, and of our celestial joys, for the heart to neglect them, and turn away, and dwell upon vanity and trouble, and let these highest pleasures go! Is not God and glory worthy of thy thoughts, and all thy service?

2. What are those things that take thee up? Are they better than God, or fitter to supply thy wants? If thou think and trust in them accordingly, ere long thou shalt know better what they are, and have enough of thy cursed choice and confidence. Tell those that stand by thee at the parting hour, whether thou didst choose

aright and make a gaining or a saving match. O poor sinners! have you not yet warning enough to satisfy you that all things below are vanity and vexation, and that all your hope of happiness is above! Will not the testimony of God satisfy you? Will not the experience of the world for so many thousand years together satisfy you? Will not the ill success of the damned satisfy you? Will nothing but your own experience convince you? If so, consider well the experience you have already made, and seasonably retire, and try no further, and trust not so dangerous a deceiver to the last, lest you buy your knowledge at a dearer rate than you will now believe.

3. You have daily more to do with God, than with all the world, whether you will or not: therefore seeing you cannot avoid him if you would, prefer that voluntary obedient converse which hath a reward, before that necessitated converse which hath none. You are always in his hands: he made you for his service; and he will dispose of you and all that you have, according to his will. It shall not go with you as yourselves would have it, nor as your friends would have it, nor as princes and great ones of the world would have it; unless as their wills comply with God's; but as God would have it, who will infallibly accomplish all his will. If a 'sparrow fall not to the ground without him, and all the hairs of our heads are numbered,' then certainly he over-ruleth all your interests and affairs, and they are absolutely at his disposal. To whom then in reason should you so much apply yourselves as unto him? If you will not take notice of him, he will take notice of you: he will remember you, whether you remember him or not; but it may be with so strict and severe a remembrance, as may make you wish he did quite forget you. You are always in his presence; and can you then forget him, and hold no voluntary converse with him, when you stand before him? If it be but mean inferior persons that we dwell with, and are still in company with, we mind them more, and speak more to them, than we do to greater persons that we seldom see. But in God there is both greatness and nearness to invite you. Should not all the worms on earth stand by, while the glorious God doth call you to him, and offer you the honour and happiness of his converse? Shall the Lord of heaven and earth stand by, and be shut out, while you are chatting or trifling with his creatures? Nay, shall he be neglected that is always with you? You cannot remove yourselves a moment from his sight; and therefore you should not shut your eyes, and turn away your face, and refuse to observe him, who is still observing you.

Moreover, your dependence both for soul and body, is all on him: you can have nothing desirable but by his gift. He feeds, he clothes, he maintains you, he gives you life and breath, and all things: yet can you overlook him, or forget him; do not all his mercies require your acknowledgment? A dog will follow him that feeds him: his eye will be upon his master: and shall we live upon God, and yet forget and disregard him? We are taught a better use of his mercies by the holy prophet David, 'O bless our God, ye people, and make the voice of his praise to be heard: which holdeth our soul in life, and suffereth not our feet to be moved!'

Nay, it is not yourselves alone, but all the world that depends on God. It is his power that supports them, and his will that disposes of them, and his bounty that provides for them: and therefore he must be the observation and admiration of the world: it is less unreasonable to take no notice of the earth that bears us and yields us fruit, and of the sun that yields us heat and light, than to disregard the Lord that is more to us than sun, and earth and all things. 'The eyes of all things wait on him; and he giveth them their meat in due season: he openeth his hand and satisfieth the desire of every living thing.'—'The Lord is good to all, and his tender mercies are over all his works: all his works therefore shall praise him, and his saints shall bless him: they shall speak of the glory of his kingdom, and talk of his power.'

Moreover, God is so abundantly and wonderfully represented to us in all his works, as will leave us under the guilt of most unexcusable contempt, if we overlook him, and live as without him in the world. 'The heavens declare the glory of God, and the firmament showeth his handy-work: day unto day uttereth speech, and night unto night showeth knowledge.' Thus 'that which may be known of God is manifest; for the invisible things of him from the creation of the world, are clearly seen, being understood by the things that are made, even his eternal power and godhead: so that the ungodly are without excuse.' Cannot you see that which all the world reveals; nor hear that which all the world proclaims? 'O sing ye forth the honour of his name: make his praise glorious! Say to the Lord, How terrible art thou in thy works! Through the greatness of thy power shall thine enemies submit themselves unto thee: all the earth shall worship thee, and shall sing unto thee : they shall sing unto thy name : come and see the works of God : he is terrible in his doings towards the children of men.' Can we pass him by, that is every where present, and by every creature represented to us ? Can we forget him, when all the world are our remembrancers ? Can we stop our ears against the voice of heaven and earth ? Can we be ignorant of him, when the whole creation is our teacher ? Can we overlook that holy, glorious name, which is written so legibly upon all things that ever our eyes beheld, that nothing but blindness, sleepiness or distraction, could possibly keep us from discerning it! I have many a time wondered, that, as the eye is so dazzled with the beholding of the greatest light, that it can scarcely perceive the shining of a lesser, so the glorious transcendent majesty of the Lord, doth not even overwhelm our understandings, and so transport and take us up, as that we can scarcely observe or remember any thing else. For naturally the greatest objects of our sense, are apt to make us at that time insensible of the smaller : and our exceeding great business, is apt to make us utterly neglect and forget those that are exceeding small : O what trifles are the best and greatest of the creatures, in comparison of God! What toys and trifles are all our other businesses in the world in comparison of the business which we have with him! But I have been stopped in these admirations by considering that the wise Creator hath fitted and ordered all his creatures according to the use which he designs them to : therefore as the eye must be receptive only of so much light as is proportioned to its use and pleasure, and must be so distant from the sun, that its light may rather guide, than blind us, and its heat may rather quicken, than consume us ; so God hath made our understandings capable of no other knowledge of him here, than what is suited to the work of holiness: while we have flesh, and fleshly works to do, and lawful necessary business in the world, in which God's own commands employ us, our souls, in this lanthorn of the body, must see him through so thick a glass, as shall so far allay our apprehension, as not to distract us, and take us off the works which he enjoins us. God and our souls shall be at such a distance, as that the proportionable light of his countenance may conduct us, and not overwhelm us : and his love may be so revealed, as to quicken our desires, and draw us on to a better state, but not so as to make us utterly impatient of this world and utterly weary of our lives, or to swallow us up, or possess us of our most desired happiness, before we arrive at the state of

happiness. While the soul is in the body, it maketh so much use of the body in all its operations, that our wise and merciful Creator and governor doth respect the body as well as the soul, in his ordering, disposing, and representing of the objects of those operations : so that when I consider that certainly all men would be distracted, if their apprehensions of God were any whit answerable to the greatness of his majesty and glory (the brain being not able to bear such high operations of the soul, nor the greatness of the passions which would necessarily follow) it much reconciles my wondering mind to the wise and gracious providence of God, even in setting innocent nature itself at such a distance from his glory, allowing us the presence of such grace as is necessary to bring us up to glory. Though it reconciles me not to that doleful distance which is introduced by sin, and which is furthered by satan, the world, and the flesh, and which our Redeemer by his Spirit and intercession must heal.

It further reconciles me to this disposal and will of the blessed God, and this necessary natural distance and darkness of our mind, when I consider, that if God, heaven, and hell, were as near and open to our apprehensions, as the things are which we see and feel, this life would not be what God intended it to be, a life of trial and preparation to another, a work, a race, a pilgrimage, a warfare ; what trial would there be of any man's faith or love, or obedience, or constancy, or self-denial? If we saw God stand by, or apprehended him as if we saw him (in degree) it would be no more praiseworthy or rewardable for a man to abhor all temptations to worldliness, ambition, gluttony, drunkenness, lust, cruelty, &c. than it is for a man to be kept from sleeping that is pierced with thorns, or for a man to forbear to drink a cup of melted gold which he knows will burn out his bowels, or to forbear to burn his flesh in fire. It were no great commendation to his chastity, that would forbear his filthiness, if he saw or had the fullest apprehensions of God ; when he will forbear it in the presence of a mortal man: it were no great commendation to the intemperate and voluptuous, to have no mind of sensual delights, if they had but such a knowledge of God as were equal to sight. It were no thanks to the persecutor to forbear his cruelty against the servants of the Lord, if he ' saw Christ coming with his glorious angels, to take vengeance on them that know not God, and obey not the gospel, and to be admired in his saints, and glorified in them that now believe.' I deny not but this happily necessitated holiness is best in itself, and therefore will be our state in heaven; but what is there of trial in it? Or how can it be suitable to the state of man, that must have good and evil set before him, and life and death left to his choice; and that must conquer if he will be crowned, and approve his fidelity to his Creator against competitors, and must live a rewardable life before he have the reward?

But though in this life we may neither hope for, nor desire, such overwhelming sensible apprehensions of God, as the rest of our faculties cannot answer, nor our bodies bear; yet that our apprehensions of him should be so base, small, dull, and unconstant as to be borne down by the noise of worldly business, or by the presence of any creature, or by the tempting baits of sensuality, this is the more odious, by how much God is more great and glorious than the creature, and even because the use of the creature itself is but to reveal the glory of the Lord. To have such slight and stupid thoughts of him, as will not carry us on in uprightness of obedience, nor keep us in his fear, nor draw out our hearts in sincere desires to please him, and enjoy him, and as will not raise us to a contempt of the pleasures, profits, and honours of this world, this is to be despisers of the Lord, and to live as in a sleep, and to be dead to God, and alive only to the world, and flesh. It is no unjust dishonour or injury to the creature, to be accounted as nothing in comparison of God, that it may be able to do nothing against him and his interest; but to make such a nothing of the most glorious God, by our contemptuous forgetfulness or neglect, as that our apprehensions of him cannot prevail against the sordid pleasures of the flesh, and against the richest baits of sin, and all the wrath or allurements of man, this is but to make a God of dust, and nothing, and (in heart and practice) to make God worse than dust and ashes. It is a wonder that man's understanding can become so sottish, as thus to wink the sun itself into a constant darkness, and to take God as nothing, or as no God, who is so abundantly revealed to them in astonishing transcendent greatness and excellency, by all the creatures in the world, and with whom we have continually so much to do. O sinful man! into how great a depth of ignorance, stupidity and misery art thou fallen!

But because we may see by the lives of the ungodly, that they little think that they have so much to do with God, though I have spoken of this to the godly in the other part of this treatise, I shall somewhat more particularly acquaint those that have most need to be informed of it, what business it is that they have with God.

1. It is not a business that may be done, or left undone, like your business with men: but it is such as must be done, or you are undone for ever. Nothing is absolutely necessary but this: nothing in all the world doth so much concern you. You may at far cheaper rates forbear to eat, or drink, or clothe yourselves, or live, than forbear the dispatch of this necessary work.

2. Your business with God, and for God in the world, is that which you have all your powers and endowments for; it is that which you were born into the world for, and that which you have understanding and free-will for, and that which you have your thoughts, memories and affections for, and that which you have eyes, ears, and tongues, and all your corporal parts and abilities for; and that which you have your time for; and your preservation, protection and provisions: it is that which you have all your teaching for; which Christ himself came for into the world; which the scriptures are written for; which ministers are sent for, which all order and government in church and state is principally appointed for: in a word, it is that for which you have your lives, and all things, and without which all were as nothing, and will be to you worse than nothing, if they do not further your work with God: you will wish you had never seen them if they befriend you not in this.

3. Your business with God, and for him, is such as you must be continually doing: as is incumbent on you every hour, for you have every hour given you for this end. You may dispatch this man to-day, and another to-morrow, and have no more to do with them again for a long time: but you have always incessantly important works to do with God. For your common work should be all his work; and all should be done with principal respect to him.

But I shall yet more particularly tell the ungodly what business it is that they have with God, which it seems, by their careless negligent lives, they are not aware of.

1. You must be either saved or damned by him; either glorified with him, or punished by him to everlasting: and it is now that the matter must be determined, which of the two conditions you must be in: you must now obtain your title to heaven, if ever you will come thither: you must now procure deliverance from hell-fire, if ever you will escape it. Now it is that all that must be done, upon which the scales must turn for your salvation or damnation: you know this

work is principally to be done between you and God, who alone can save you or destroy you: and yet do you forget him, and live as if you had no business with him, when you have your salvation to obtain from him, and your damnation to prevent ? Have you such business as this with any other ?

2. You have a strict and righteous judgment to undergo in order to this salvation or damnation. You must stand before the holy majesty, and be judged by the governor of the world: you must be there accused, and found guilty or not guilty ; and judged as fulfillers, or as breakers of the holy covenant of grace : you must be set on the right hand or on the left : you must answer for all the time that you here spent, and for all the means and mercies which you here received, and for that you have done, whether it were good or evil : and it is now in this life that all your preparation must be made, and all that must be done, upon which your justification or condemnation will then depend. It is between God and you that all this business must be done : and yet can you live as negligently towards him, as if you had no business with him ?

3. You have a death to die, a change to make, which must be made but once ; which will be the entrance upon endless joy or pain : do you think this needeth not your most timely and diligent preparation : you must struggle with pains, and faint with weakness, and feel death taking down your earthen tabernacle : you must then have a life that is ending to review, and all that you have done laid open to your more impartial judgment ; you must then see time as at an end, and the last sand running, and your candle ready to go out, and leave the snuff ; you must then look back upon all that you have had from the world, as ending ; and upon all that you have done as that which cannot be undone again, that you may do it better ; and you must have a more serious look into eternity, when you are stepping thither, than you can now conceive of : and doth all this need no preparation ? It is with God that all that business must be now transacted, that must make your death to be comfortable or safe. If now you will only converse with men, and know no business that you have with God, you shall find at last to your exceeding terror, that you are in his hands, and passing to his bar, and that it is God that then you have to do with, when your business with all the world is at an end : he will then have something to do with you, if you will now find nothing to do with him.

4. In order to all this you have reconciliation to receive from God, and the pardon of all your sins to be obtained. For woe to you if then you are found under the guilt of any sin. Look back upon your lives, and remember how you have lived in the word, and what you have been doing : how you have spent your time, in youth, and in your riper age ; and how many sinful thoughts, words, and deeds you have been guilty of ; how often you have sinfully pleased your appetites, gratified your flesh, and yielded to temptations, abused mercy, and lost your time ; how often you have neglected your duty, and betrayed your souls : how long you have lived in forgetfulness of God and your salvation ; minding only the things of the flesh and of the world : how often you have sinned ignorantly and against knowledge, through carelessness and through rashness, through negligence and through presumption, in passion, and upon deliberation ; against convictions, purposes and promises : how often you have sinned against the precepts of piety to God, and of justice and charity to men. Think how your sins are multiplied and aggravated, more in number than the hours of your lives : aggravated by a world of mercies ; by the clearest teachings, and the loudest calls, and sharpest reproofs, and seasonable warnings, and by the long and urgent importunities of grace. Think of all these, and then consider whether you have nothing now to do with God, whether it be not a business to be followed with all possible speed and diligence, to procure the pardon of all these sins : you have no such business as these to transact with men : you may have business with them which your estates depend upon, or which touch your credit, or lives ; but you have no business with men, unless in subordination to God, which your salvation doth depend upon : your eternal happiness is not in their hands : they may kill your bodies, if God permit them, but not your souls. You need not solicit them to pardon your sins against God : it is a small matter how you are judged of by man : you have one that judgeth you, even the Lord. No man can forgive sin, but God only. O then how early, how earnestly should you cry to him for mercy ! Pardon must be obtained now or never : there is no justification for that man at the day of judgment, who is not forgiven and justified now. ' Blessed then is the man whose iniquity is forgiven, whose sin is covered, and to whom it is not imputed by the Lord.' Woe to that man that ever he was born, who is then found without the pardon of his sins ! Think of this as the case deserves, and then think if

you can, that your daily business with God is small.

5. Moreover, you have peace of conscience to obtain; and that depends upon your peace with God. Conscience will be your accuser, condemner, and tormentor, if you make it not your friend, by making God your friend. Consider what conscience hath to say against you, and how certainly it will speak home, when you would be loth to hear it: and bethink you how to answer all its accusations, and what will be necessary to make it a messenger of peace; and then think your business with God to be but small, if you are able. It is no easy matter to get assurance that God is reconciled to you, and that he hath forgiven all your sins.

6. In order to all this, you must be united to Jesus Christ, and be made his members, that you may have part in him, and that he may wash you by his blood, and that he may answer for you to his Father; woe to you if he be not your righteousness, and if you have not him to plead your cause, and take upon him your final justification! None else can save you from the wrath of God: and he is the Saviour only of his body, he hath died for you without your consent, and he hath made general proclamation of pardon and salvation, before you consented to it: but he will not be united to you, nor actually forgive, justify and save you, without your own consent: therefore, that the Father may draw you to the Son, and may give you Christ, and life in him, when all your hope depends on it, you may see that you have more to do with God, than your senseless hearts have hitherto understood.

7. That you may have a saving interest in Jesus Christ, you must have sound repentance for all your former life of wickedness, and a lively, effectual faith in Christ: neither sin nor Christ must be made light of. Repentance must tell you to the very heart, that you have done foolishly in sinning, and that ' it is an evil and a bitter thing that you forsook the Lord, and that his fear was not in you: and thus your wickedness shall correct you and reprove you.' Faith must tell you that Christ is ' more necessary to you than food or life, and that there is no other name given under heaven by which you can be saved,' and it is not so easy nor so common a thing to repent and believe, as ignorant presumptuous sinners imagine. It is a greater matter to have a truly humbled, contrite heart, and to lothe yourselves for all your sins, and to lothe those sins, and resolvedly give up yourselves to Christ and to his Spirit for a holy life, than

heartlessly and hypocritically to say, I am sorry or I repent, without any true contrition or renovation. It is a greater to betake yourselves to Jesus Christ as your only hope, to save you both from sin and from damnation, than barely through custom, and the benefit of education, to say, I do believe in Christ. I tell you it is so great a work to bring you to sound Repentance and Faith, that it must be done by the power of God himself, they are the gifts of God, you must have his Spirit to illuminate you, and show you the odiousness of sin, the intolerableness of the wrath of God, the necessity and sufficiency, the power and willingness of Christ; and to overcome all your prejudice, and save you from false opinions and deceits: and to repulse the temptations of Satan, the world and the flesh, which will all rise up against you. All this must be done to bring you home to Jesus Christ, or else you will have no part in him, his righteousness and grace: and can you think that you have not most important business with God, who must do all this upon you, or else you are undone for ever!

8. Moreover you must have all the corruptions of your natures healed, and your sins subdued, and your hearts made new by sanctifying grace, and the image of God implanted in you, and your lives made holy and sincerely conformable to the will of God. All this must be done, or you cannot be acceptable to God, nor ever will be saved: though your carnal interests rise against it; though your old corrupted natures be against it; though your custom, pleasure, and worldly gain and honour be against it; though all your carnal friends and superiors be against it; though the devil will do all that he can against it, yet all this must be done or you are lost for ever: all this must be done by the Spirit of God; for it is his work to make you new and holy: can you think then that the business is not great which you have with God; when you have tried how hard every part of this work is, to be begun and carried on, you will find you have more to do with God, than with all the world.

9. Moreover, in order to this, it is necessary that you read, hear and understand the gospel, which must be the means of bringing you to God by Christ: this must be the instrument of God, by which he will bring you to repent and believe, and by which he will renew your natures, and imprint his image on you, and bring you to love him, and obey his will. The word of God must be your counsellor, and your delight, and you must set your heart to it, and meditate in it day and night. Knowledge must be the means

to reclaim your perverse, misguided wills, and to reform your careless, crooked lives, and to bring you out of the kingdom of darkness, into the state of life and light. Such knowledge cannot be expected without a diligent attending unto Christ, the teacher of your souls, and a due consideration of the truth. By that time you have learned what is needful to be learned for a true conversion, a sound repentance, a saving faith, and a holy life, you will find that you have far greater business with God than with all the world.

10. Moreover, for the attaining of all this mercy, you have many a prayer to put up to God: you must daily pray for the forgiveness of your sins, and deliverance from temptations, and even for your daily bread, or necessary provisions for the work which you have to do: you must daily pray for the supplies of grace which you want, and for the gradual mortification of the flesh, and for help in all the duties which you must perform; and for strength against all spiritual enemies which will assault you; and preservation from the manifest evils which attend you: these prayers must be put up with unwearied constancy, fervency and faith. Keep up this course of fervent prayer, and beg for Christ, grace, pardon, and salvation in any measure as they deserve, and according to thy own necessity, and then tell me whether thy business with God be small, and to be put off as lightly as it is by the ungodly.

11. Moreover, you are made for the glory of your Creator, and must apply yourselves wholly to glorify him in the world: you must make his service the trade and business of your lives, and not put him off with something on the by: you are good for nothing else but to serve him; as a knife is made to cut, as your clothes are made to cover you, your meat to feed you, and your horse to labour for you; so you are made, redeemed, and maintained for this, to love and please your great Creator: and can you think that it is but little business that you have with him, when he is the end and master of your lives, and all you are or have is for him?

12. For the due performance of his service, you have all his talents to employ. To this end it is that he hath entrusted you with reason, health, and strength, with time, parts, interest, and wealth, and all his mercies, and all his ordinances and means of grace; and to this end must you use them, or you lose them: you must give him an account of all at last, whether you have improved them all to your Master's use. Can

you look within you, without you, about you, and see how much you are trusted with, and must be accountable to him for, and yet not see how great your business is with God?

13. Moreover, you have all the graces which you shall receive to exercise; and every grace doth carry you to God, and is exercised upon him, or for him: it is God that you must study, know, love, desire, and trust and hope in, and obey: it is God that you must seek after, and delight in, so far as you enjoy him: it is his absence or displeasure that must be your fear and sorrow: therefore the soul is said to be sanctified when it is renewed, because it is both disposed and devoted unto God. Therefore grace is called holiness, because it all disposes, carries the soul to God, and uses it upon and for him. Can you think your business with God is small, when you must live upon him, and all the powers of your soul must be addicted to him, and be in serious motion towards him; when he must be much more to you than the air which you breathe in, or the earth you live upon, or than the sun that gives you light and heat; yea, than the soul is to your bodies?

14. Lastly, you have abundance of temptations and impediments to watch and strive against, which would hinder you in the doing of all this work, and a corrupt and treacherous heart to watch and keep in order, which will be looking back, and shrinking from the service. Lay all this together, and then consider whether you have not more and greater business with God, than with all the creatures in the world.

If this be so, is there any cloak for that man's sin, who is all day taken up with creatures, and thinks of God as seldom and carelessly as if he had no business with him? Yet alas, if you take a survey of high and low, of court, city, and country, you shall find that this is the case of no small number, yea, of many that observe it not to be their case; it is the case of the profane that pray in jest, swear, curse, and rail in earnest. It is the case of the malignant enemies of holiness, that hate them at the heart who are most acquainted with this converse with God, and count it but hypocrisy, pride or fancy, and would not suffer them to live upon the earth, who are most sincerely conversant in heaven. It is the case of pharisees and hypocrites, who take up with ceremonious observances, as 'touch not, taste not, handle not,' and such like traditions of their forefathers, instead of a spiritual rational service, and a holy, serious walking with the Lord. It is the case of all ambitious men, and covetous worldlings, who make more ado to climb up a little higher than their brethren, to hold the reins, have their wills, and be admired and adored in the world, or to get a large estate for themselves and their posterity, than to please their Maker, or to save their souls. It is the case of every sensual epicure, whose belly is his God, and serves his fancy, lust, and appetite before the Lord. It is the case of every unsanctified man, that seeks first the prosperity of his flesh, before the kingdom and righteousness of God, and is most careful and laborious to lay up a treasure on earth, and laboureth more (with greater estimation, resolution, and delight) for the meat that perisheth, than for that which endureth to everlasting life. All these (who are too great a part of the world, and too great a part of professed Christians) are taken up with creature converse ; and yet think to escape the deluge of God's displeasure, because the Enochs and Noahs are so few who walk with God ; and they think God will not destroy so many : thus they think to be saved by their multitude, and to hide themselves in the crowd from God : they will go the wide and common path, and be of the mind that most are of: they will not be convinced till most men are convinced : that is, till their wisdom come too late, and cost them dearer than its worth. When all men are convinced that God should have been preferred before the world, and served before their fleshly lusts, as they will certainly and sadly be, then they will be convinced with the rest. When all men understand that life was given them to have done the work which eternal life depends on, then they will understand it with the rest. When all men shall discern between the righteous and the wicked ; between those that serve God, and that serve him not, then they will discern it with the rest : they will know what their business was in the world, and how much they had to do with God, when all men know it.

But O how much better for them had it been to have known it in time, while knowledge might have done them better service, than to make them feel the greatness of their sin and folly, and the hopes which once they had of happiness, and to help the sting of desperation continually to prick them at the heart : they would not be of so little a flock as that to which it was the good pleasure of God to give the kingdom. If you demand a reason of all this, their reason was in their sensual pleasures : they had fleshly appetites and lusts, and thereby could relish fleshly pleasures ; but spiritual life and appetite they had none, and therefore relished not spiritual things : had Christ, holiness, and heaven been

as suitable to their appetites, as the sweetness of their meat, drink, and lusts, and as suitable to their fancy as their worldly dignities and greatness were, they would then have made a better choice. They would have walked with God, if drunkenness, gluttony, pride, wantonness, covetousness and idleness, had been the way in which they might have walked with him. If these had been godliness, how godly would they have been ? How certainly would they have come to heaven, if this had been the way ? To be idle, proud, fleshly, and worldly, is that which they love ; and to be humble, holy, heavenly, and mortified, is that which they hate, and cannot away with : their love and hatred proceed from their corrupt natures ; and these are instead of reason to them. Their strong apprehensions of a present suitableness in fleshly pleasures to their appetites, and of a present unsuitableness of a holy life, keep out all effectual apprehensions of the excellencies of God, and of spiritual, heavenly delights, which cross them in the pleasures which they most desire.

But yet (their appetites corrupting their understandings as well as their wills) they will not be mad without some reason, nor reject their Maker and their happiness without some reason, nor neglect that holy work which they were made for, without some reason : let us hear then what it is.

CHAP. III.

OBJECTIONS STATED AND ANSWERED.

Object. 1. They say, ' It is true that God hath much to do with us, and for us : but it follows not that we have so much to do with him, or for him, as you would have us to believe : for he is necessarily good, and necessarily doth good; and therefore will do so, whether we think of him or not: the sun will not give over shining on me, though I never think on it, or never pray to it, or give it thanks. Nor doth God need any service that we can do him, no more than the sun doth : nor is he pleased any more in the praise of men, or in their works.'

Answ. 1. It is most certain that God is good as necessarily as he is God: but it is not true, that he must necessarily do good to you, or other individual persons, nor that he necessarily doth the good he doth them. As he is not necessitated to make toads and serpents as happy as men, or men as angels ; so he is not necessitated to save the devils or damned souls, for he will not save them. He was under no greater a necessity to save you, than them. He was not necessitated to give you a being: he could have passed you by, and caused others to have possessed your room. As it was God's freewill, and not any necessity, that millions more are never born that were in possibility of it: for all that is possible doth not come to pass. So, that you and millions more were born, was not of necessity but of the same free-will. And as God did not make you of necessity but of free-will: so he doth not necessarily but freely justify, or sanctify, or save. If he did it by necessity of nature, he would do it to all as well as some ; seeing all have a natural capacity of grace as well as those that receive it: God is able to sanctify and save more, yea, all, if it were his will: and it is not for want of power or goodness that he doth not. Millions of beings are possible which are not future. God doth not all the good which he is able, but communicates so much to his several creatures as to his wisdom seems meet. If the damned would be so presumptuous as to argue, that because God is able yet to sanctify, and save them, therefore he must do it of necessity of nature, it would not be long before they should thus dispute themselves out of their torments. God will not ask leave of sinners to be God: their denying him to be good, that is, to be God, because he complies not with their conceits and wills, doth but prove them to be fools and bad themselves.

Indeed some sciolists pretending to learning, while they are ignorant of most obvious principles of natural knowledge, have taught poor sinners to cheat their souls with such dreams as these. They have made themselves believe that goodness in God is nothing else but his benignity, or disposition to do good. As if the creature were the ultimate end, and all God's goodness but a means thereto: so God were the Alpha or first efficient, and yet the creature the Omega or last end : and all the goodness in God were to be estimated and denominated by its respect to the felicity of man : and so the creature hath the best part of the deity. Such notions evidently show us, that lapsed man is predominantly selfish, and is become his own idol, and is lost in himself, while he hath lost himself by his loss of God: when we see how powerful his self-interest is, both with his intellect and will: even men of great ingenuity, till sanctification hath restored them to God, and taught them better to know him and themselves, are ready to measure all good or evil by their own interests ; when yet common reason would have told them, if they had not perverted it by pride

and partial studies, that short of God even among the creatures, there are many things to be preferred before themselves and their own felicity : he is irrationally enslaved by self-love, that cannot see that the happiness of the world, or of his country, or of multitudes, is more to be desired than his happiness alone. That he ought rather to choose to be annihilated, or to be miserable, if it were made a matter of his deliberation and choice, than to have the sun taken out of the firmament, or the world, or his country to be annihilated or miserable. God is infinitely above the creature.

Object. But it may be said, that he needeth nothing to make him happy, having no defect of happiness.

Answ. And what of that? Must it needs therefore follow that he made not all things for himself, but for the creature finally ? He is perfectly happy in himself, and his will is himself : this will was fulfilled when the world was not made, for it was his will that it should not be made till it was made, and it is fulfilled when it is made, and fulfilled by all that comes to pass : and as the absolute simple goodness and perfection of God's essence is the greatest good, the eternal, immutable good ; so the fulfilling of his will is the ultimate end of all obedience : he hath expressed himself to take pleasure in his works, and in the holiness, obedience and happiness of his chosen: though pleasure be not the same thing in God as it is in a man, no more than will or understanding is, yet it is not nothing which God expresses by such terms, but something which we have no fitter expression for : this pleasing of the will of God being the end of all, even of our felicity, is better than our felicity itself.

They that will maintain that God, who is naturally and necessarily good, hath no other goodness but his benignity, or aptness to do good to his creatures, must needs also maintain that (God being for the creature, and not the creature for God) the creature is better than God, as being the ultimate end of God himself, and the highest use of all his goodness, being but for the felicity of the creature: as also that God doth all the good that he is able : and that all men shall be saved, and all devils, and every worm and insect be equal to the highest angel, or else that God is not able to do it. That he did thus make happy all his creatures from eternity, for natural necessary agents work always if they be not forcibly hindered ; and that there never was such a thing as pain or misery, in man or brute, or else that God was not able to prevent it. But abundance of such consequences must needs follow from the denying of the highest good, which is God himself, and confessing none but his efficient goodness. But some will be offended with me for being so serious in confuting such an irrational, atheistical conceit, who know not how far it prevails with an atheistical generation.

Be it known to you, careless sinners, that though the sun will shine on you whether you think on it or not, or love it, or thank it or not; and the fire will warm you whether you think on it, and love it or not; yet God will not justify or save you, whether you love him or think on him or not: God doth not operate unwisely in your salvation; but governs you wisely, as rational creatures are to be governed; and therefore will give you happiness as a reward; and therefore will not deal alike with those that love him, and that love him not; that seek him, and that seek him not; with the labourers and the loiterers, the faithful and the slothful servant. Would you have us believe that you know better than God himself what pleases himself, or on what terms he will give his benefits, and save men's souls? or do you know his nature better than he knows it, that you dare presume to say, because he needs not our love or duty, therefore they are not pleasing to him? Then what hath God to do in governing the world, if he be pleased and displeased with nothing that men do, or with good and evil actions equally? Though you cannot hurt him, you shall find that he will hurt you, if you disobey him: though you cannot make him happy by your holiness, you shall find that he will not make you happy without it.

If he did work as necessarily as the sun doth shine, according to your similitude; yet, 1. Even the shining of the sun doth not illuminate the blind nor doth it make the seeds of thorns and nettles to bring forth vines or roses, nor the gendering of frogs to bring forth men; but it actuates all things according to the several natures of their powers. Therefore how can you expect that an unbelieving and unholy soul, should enjoy felicity in God, when in that state they are incapable of it? 2. If the sun do necessarily illuminate any one, he must necessarily be illuminated; and if it necessarily warm or quicken any thing, it must be necessarily warmed and quickened; else you would assert contradictions. So if God did necessarily save you, and make you happy, you would necessarily be saved and made happy. That contains essentially your holiness, your loving, desiring and seeking after

God; to be saved or happy without enjoying God by love, or to love him and not desire him, seek him or obey him, are as great contradictions as to be illuminated without light, or quickened without life. What way soever it be that God conveys his sanctifying Spirit, I am sure that 'if any man have not the Spirit of Christ, the same is none of his,' and that 'without holiness none shall see God,' and that if you will have the kingdom of God, you must seek it first, preferring it before all earthly things. Then if all the question that remains undecided be, Whether God do you wrong or not in damning you, or whether God be good because he will not save you when he can, I shall leave you to him to receive satisfaction, who will easily silence and confound your impudence, and justify his works and laws. Prepare your accusations against him, if you will needs insist upon them, and try whether he or you shall prevail: but remember that thou art a worm, and he is God, and that he will be the only judge when all is done; and ignorance and impiety, that prate against him to their own confusion, in the day of his patience, shall not then usurp the throne.

Object. 2. But how can God be fit for mortals to converse with, when they see him not, and are infinitely below him?

Answ. I hope you will not say that you have nothing to do at home, with your own souls: yet you never saw your souls. It is the soul, the reason and the will of men that you daily converse with here in the world, more than their bodies, and yet you never saw their souls, their reason or their wills. If you have no higher light to discern by than your eye-sight, you are not men but beasts. If you are men, you have reason; and if you are Christians, you have faith, by which you know things that you never saw. You have more dependence on the things that are unseen, than on those which you see, and have much more to do with them.

Though God be infinitely above us, yet he condescends to communicate to us according to our capacities: as the sun is far from us, and yet doth not disdain to enlighten, warm, and quicken a worm or fly here below. If any be yet so much an atheist as to think that religious converse with God is but a fancy, let him well answer me these few questions.

Quest. 1. Doth not the continued being and well-being of the creatures, tell us that there is a God on whom, for being and well-being, they depend, and from whom they are, and have whatsoever they are and whatsoever they have? And therefore that passively all the creatures have more respect to him by far, than to one another.

Quest. 2. Seeing God communicates to every creature according to their several capacities; is it not meet then that he deal with man as man, even as a creature rational, capable to know, love, and obey his great Creator, and to be happy in the knowledge, love and fruition of him? That man hath such natural faculties, and capacities, is not to be denied by a man that knows what it is to be a man: that God hath not given him these in vain, will be easily believed by any that indeed believe that he is God.

Quest. 3. Is there any thing else that is finally worthy of the highest actions of our souls? or that is fully adequate to them, and fit to be our happiness? If not, then we are left either to certain infelicity, contrary to the tendency of our natures, or else we must seek our felicity in God.

Quest. 4. Is there any thing more certain than that by the title of creation, our Maker hath a full and absolute right to all that he hath made: and consequently to all our love and obedience, our time and powers? For whom should they all be used but for him from whom we have obtained them?

Quest. 5. Can any thing be more sure, than that God is the righteous governor of the world, and that he governs man as a rational creature, by laws and judgment? Can we live under his absolute sovereignty, under his many righteous laws, under his promise of salvation to the justified, and under his threatenings of damnation to the unjustified, and yet not have more to do with God than with all the world? If indeed you think that God doth not love and reward the holy and obedient, and punish the ungodly and disobedient, then either you take him not to be governor of the world, or, which is worse, you take him to be an unrighteous governor: then you must by the same reason say, that magistrates and parents should do so too, and love and reward the obedient and disobedient alike: but if any man's disobedience were exercised to your hurt, by slandering, or beating, or robbing you, I dare say you would not then commend so indifferent and unjust a governor.

Quest. 6. If it be not needless for man to labour for food and raiment, and necessary provision for his body, how can it be needless for him to labour for the happiness of his soul? If God will not give us our daily bread while we never think of it, or seek it, why should we expect that he will give us heaven though we never think on it, value it, or seek it?

Quest. 7. Is it not a contradiction to be happy in the fruition of God, and yet not to mind him, desire him, or seek him? How is it that the soul can reach its object, but by estimation, desire and seeking after it: how should it enjoy it but by loving it, and taking pleasure in it?

Quest. 8. While you seem but to wrangle against the duty of believers, do you not plead against the comfort and happiness of believers? For surely the employment of the soul on God, and for him, is the health and pleasure of the soul; to call away the soul from such employment, is to imprison it in the dungeon of this world, and to forbid us to smell the sweetest flowers, and confine us to a sink or dunghill, and to forbid us to taste of the food of angels, or of men, and to offer us vinegar and gall, or turn us over to feed with swine. He that pleads that there is no such thing as real holiness and communion with God, doth plead in effect that there is no true felicity or delight for any of the sons of men: and how welcome should ungodly atheists be unto mankind, that would for ever exclude them all from happiness, and make them believe they are all made to be remedilessly miserable?

Here take notice of the madness of the unthankful world, that hates and persecutes the preachers of the gospel, who bring them the glad tidings of pardon, hope, and life eternal, of solid happiness, and durable delight; and yet they are not offended at these atheists and ungodly cavillers, that would take them off from all that is truly good and pleasant, and make them believe that nature hath made them capable of no higher things than beasts, and hath enthralled them in remediless infelicity.

Quest. 9. Do you not see by experience that there are a people in the world whose hearts are upon God, and the life to come; and that make it their chief care and business to seek him and to serve him? How then can you say that there is no such thing, or that we are not capable of it, when it is the case of so many before your eyes? If you say that it is but their fancy or self-deceit: I answer, that really their hearts are set upon God, and the everlasting world, and that it is their chief care and business to attain it; this is a thing that they feel, and that you may see in the bent and labour of their lives; and therefore you cannot call that a fancy, of which you have so full experience; but whether the motives that have invited them, and engaged them to such a choice and course, be fancies and deceits or not, let God be judge, and let the awakened consciences of worldlings themselves be judge, when they have seen the end, and tried whether it be earth or heaven that is the shadow, and whether it be God or their unbelieving hearts that was deceived.

Quest. 10. Have you any hopes of living with God for ever, or not? If you have not, no wonder if you live as beasts, when you have no higher expectations than beasts: when we are so blind as to give up all our hopes, we will also give up all our care and holy diligence, and think we have nothing to do with heaven. But if you have any such hopes, can you think that any thing is fitter for the chief of your thoughts and cares, than the God and kingdom, which you hope for ever to enjoy? Or is there any thing that can be more suitable, or should be more delightful to your thoughts, than to employ them about your highest hopes, upon your endless happiness and joy, and should not that be now the most noble and pleasant employment for your minds, which is nearest to that which you hope to be exercised in for ever? Undoubtedly he that hath true and serious thoughts of heaven, will highly value that life on earth which is likest to the life in heaven: and he that hates or is most averse to that which is nearest to the work of heaven, does boast in vain of his hopes of heaven.

By this time you may see (if you love not to be blind) that man's chief business in the world is with his God, and that our thoughts, and all our powers, are made to be employed upon him, or for him; and that this is no such needless work as atheists make themselves believe.

Remember that it is the description of the desperately wicked, that 'God is not in all his thoughts.' And if yet you understand it not, I will a little further show you the evil of such atheistical unhallowed thoughts.

1. There is nothing but darkness in all thy thoughts, if God be not in them. Thou knowest nothing, if thou knowest not him; and thou usest not thy knowledge, if thou use it not on him. To know the creature as without God, is to know nothing: no more than to know all the letters in the book, and not to know their signification or sense. All things in the world are but insignificant cyphers, and of no other sense or use, if you separate them from God, who is their sense and end. If you leave out God in all your studies, you do but dream and doat, and not understand what you seem to understand. Though you were taken for the most learned men in the world, and were able to discourse of all the sciences, and your thoughts had no lower employment daily than the most sublime speculations which the nature of all the creatures doth

afford, it is all but folly and impertinent dotage, if it reach not unto God.

2. Yea, your thoughts are erroneous and false, which is more than barely ignorant, if God be not in them. You have false thoughts of the world, of your houses and lands, friends, and pleasures, and whatsoever is the daily employment of your minds. You take them to be something, when they are nothing; you are covetous of the empty purse, and know not that you cast away the treasure: you are thirsty after the empty cup, when you wilfully cast away the drink. You hungrily seek to feed upon a painted feast: you murder the creature by separating it from God who is its life, and then you are enamoured on the carcass; and spend your days and thoughts in its cold embraces. Your thoughts are straggling abroad the world, and following impertinencies, if God be not in them. You are like men that walk up and down in their sleep, or like those that have lost themselves in the dark, who weary themselves in going they know not whither, and have no end nor certain way.

3. If God be not in all your thoughts, they are all in vain. They are like the drone that gathereth no honey: they fly abroad and return home empty: they bring home no matter of honour to God, or profit or comfort to yourselves: they are employed to no more purpose than in your dreams: only they are more capable of sin: like the distracted thoughts of one that doteth in a fever, they are all but nonsense, whatever you employ them on, while you leave out God, who is the sense of all.

4. If God be not in all your thoughts, they are nothing but confusion: there can be no just unity in them, because they forsake him who is the only centre, and are scattered abroad upon incoherent creatures. There can be no true unity but in God: the further we go from him, the further we run into divisions and confusions. There can be no just method in them, because he is left out that is the beginning and the end. They are not like a well-ordered army, where every one is moved by the will of one commander, and all know their colours and their ranks, and unanimously agree to do their work: but like a swarm of flies, that buzz about they know not whither, nor why, nor for what. There is no true government in your thoughts, if God be not in them; they are masterless and vagrants, and have no true order, if they be not ordered by him, and to him, if he be not their first and last.

5. If God be not in all your thoughts, there is no life in them: they are but like the motion of

a bubble, or a feather in the air: they are impotent as to the resisting of any evil, and as to the doing of any saving good: they have no strength in them, because they are laid out upon objects that have no strength: they have no quickening, renewing, reforming, encouraging, resolving, confirming power in them, because there is no such power in the things on which they are employed: whereas the thoughts of God and everlasting life, can do wonders upon the soul: they can raise up men above this world, and teach them to despise the worldling's idol, and look upon all the pleasures of the flesh as upon animal delight in wallowing in the mire. They can renew the soul, and cast out the most powerful beloved sin, and bring all our powers into the obedience of God, and that with pleasure and delight: they can employ us with the angels, in a heavenly conversation, and show us the glory of the world above, and advance us above the life of the greatest princes upon earth: but the thoughts of earthly fleshly things have power indeed to delude men, mislead them, and hurry them about in a vertiginous motion; but no power to support us, or subdue concupiscence, or heal our folly, or save us from temptations, to lead us back from our errors, or help us to be useful in the world, or to attain felicity at last. There is no life, nor power, nor efficacy in our thoughts, if God be not in them.

6. There is no stability or fixedness in your thoughts if God be not in them. They are like a boat upon the ocean, tossed up and down with winds and waves: the mutable uncertain creatures can yield no rest or settlement to your minds. You are 'troubled about many things;' and the more you think on them, and have to do with them, the more are you troubled: but you forget the one thing necessary, and fly from the eternal Rock, on which you must build, if ever you will be established. While the creature is in your thought instead of God, you will be one day deluded with its unwholesome pleasure, and the next day feel it pierce you at the heart: one day it will seem your happiness, and the next you will wish you had never known it: that which seems the only comfort of your lives this year, may the next year make you weary of your lives. One day your are impatiently desiring and seeking it, as if you could not live without it: and the next day, or ere long, you are impatiently desiring to be rid of it: you are now taking in your pleasant morsels, and drinking down your delicious draughts, and jovially sporting it with your inconsiderate companions: but how quickly will you be repenting of all this, and complaining of

your folly, and vexing yourselves, that you took not warning, and made not a wiser choice in time? The creature was never made to be our end, or rest, or happiness: and therefore you are but like a man in a wilderness or maze, that may go up and down, but knows not whither, and finds no end, till you come home to God, who only is your proper end, and make him the Lord, and life, and pleasure of your thoughts.

7. As there is no present fixedness in your thoughts, so the business and pleasure of them will be of very short continuance, if God be not the chief in all. Who would choose to employ his thoughts on such things as he is sure they must soon forget, and never more have any business with to all eternity? You shall think of those houses, lands, friends, and pleasures but a little while, unless it be with repenting tormenting thoughts, in the place of misery: you will have no delight to think of any thing, which is now most precious to your flesh, when once the flesh itself decays, and is no more capable of delight; 'his breath goeth forth, he returneth to his earth; in that very day his thoughts perish.'

Call in your thoughts then from these transitory things, that have no consistency or continuance, and turn them unto him with whom they may find everlasting employment and delight: remember not the enticing baits of sensuality and pride, but 'remember now thy Creator in the days of thy youth, while the evil days come not, nor the years draw nigh when thou shalt say, I have no pleasure in them.'

8. Thy thoughts are but sordid, dishonourable and low, if God be not the object of them. They reach no higher than the habitation of beasts; nor do they attain to any sweeter employment than to meditate on the felicity of a brute: thou choosest with the fly to feed on corruption, when thou mightest have free access to God himself, and mightest be entertained in the court of heaven, and welcomed thither by the holy angels: thou wallowest in the mire with the swine, or diggest thyself a house in the earth, as worms and moles do, when thy thoughts might be soaring up to God, and might be taken up with high and holy and everlasting things. What if your thoughts were employed for preferment, wealth, and honour in the world? Alas! what silly things are these, in comparison of what your souls are capable of; you will say so yourselves when you see how they will end, and disappoint your expectations. Imprison not your minds in this infernal cell, when the superior regions are open to their access: confine them not to this

narrow vessel of the body, whose tossings and dangers on these boisterous seas will make them restless, and disquiet them with tumultuous passions, when they may safely land in paradise, and there converse with Christ. God made you men, and if you reject not his grace, will make you saints: make not yourselves like beasts. God gave you souls that can step in a moment from earth to heaven, and there foretaste the endless joys : do not you stick then fast in clay, and fetter them with worldly cares, or intoxicate them with fleshly pleasures, nor employ them in the worse than childish toys of ambitious, sensual, worldly men : your thoughts have manna, angels' food, provided them by God: if you will lothe this and refuse it, and choose with the serpent to feed on the dust, or upon the filth of sin, God shall be judge and your consciences one day shall be more faithful witnesses, whether you have dealt like wise men or like fools ; like friends or enemies to yourselves ; and whether you have not chosen baseness, and denied yourselves the advancement which was offered you.

9. If God be not the chief in your thoughts, they are no better than dishonest and unjust. You are guilty of denying him his own. He made not your minds for lust and pleasure, but for himself: you expect that your cattle, your goods, your servants, be employed for yourselves, because they are your own. But God may call your minds his own by a much fuller title : for you hold all but derivatively and dependently from him : what will you call it but injustice and dishonesty, if your wife, or children, or servants, or goods, be more at the use and service of others, than of you ? If any can show a better title to your thoughts than God doth, let him have them ; but if not, deny him not his own. O stray not so much from home ; for you will be no where else so well there : Desire not to follow strangers, you know not whither, nor for what ; you have a master of your own, that will be better to you than all the strangers in the world. Bow not down to creatures, that are but images of the true and solid good : commit not idolatry or adultery with them in your thoughts ; remember still that God stands by : bethink you how he will take it at your hands ; and how it will be judged of at last, when he pleads his right, his kindness, and solicitations for you; and you have so little to say for any pretence of right or merit in the creature. Why are not men ashamed of the greatest dishonesty against God, when all that have any humility left them, do take adultery, theft, and other dishonesty against creatures, for a shame ? The time will come when

God and his interest shall be better understood, when this dishonesty against him, will be the matter of the most confounding shame, that ever did or could befall men. Prevent this by the juster exercise of your thoughts, and keeping them pure and chaste to God.

10. If God be not in your thoughts there will be no matter in them of solid comfort or contentment. Trouble and deceit will be all their work : when they have fled about the earth, and taken a taste of every flower, they will come home loaded with nothing better than vanity and vexation. Such thoughts may excite the laughter of a fool, and cause that mirth that is called madness. But they will never conduce to settled peace, and durable content : therefore they are always repented of themselves, and are troublesome to our review, as being the shame of the sinner, which he would be cleared of, or disown. Though you may approach the creature with passionate fondness, and the most delightful promises and hopes, be sure of it, you will come off at last with grief and disappointment, if not with the loathing of that which you choose for your delight. Your thoughts are in a wilderness among thorns and briars, when God is not in them as their guide and end : they are lost and torn among the creatures ; but rest and satisfaction they will find none. It may be at the present it is more pleasant to you to think of recreation, or business, or worldly wealth, than to think of God : but the pleasure of these thoughts is as delusory, and short-lived, as are the things themselves on which you think. How long will you think with pleasure on such fading transitory things ? The pleasure cannot be great at the present, which reaches but the flesh and fancy, and which the possessed knows will be but short. Nay you will shortly find by sad experience, that of all the creatures under heaven there will none be so bitter to your thoughts, as those in which you now find greatest carnal sweetness. O how bitter will the thought of idolized honour, and abused wealth and greatness be, to a dying or a damned Dives ! The thoughts of that ale-house or play-house where thou hadst thy greatest pleasure, will trouble thee more than the thoughts of all the houses in the town besides : the thoughts of that one woman with whom thou didst commit thy pleasant sin, will wound and vex thee more than the thoughts of all the women in the town besides. The thoughts of that beloved sport which thou couldst not be weaned from, will be more troublesome to thee than the thoughts of a thousand other things in which thou hadst no inor-

dinate delight. For the end of sinful mirth is sorrow.

When Solomon had tried to please himself to the full, in mirth, in buildings, vineyards, woods, waters, in servants, and possessions, silver and gold, cattle and singers, and instruments of music of all sorts, in greatness, and all that the eye or appetite or heart desired; he finds when he awaked from this pleasant dream, that he had all this while been taken up with vanity and vexation, in so much that he saith on the review: ' therefore I hated life, because the work that is wrought under the sun is grievous to me, for all is vanity and vexation of spirit; yea, I hated all my labour which I had taken under the sun.' You may toil out and tire yourselves among these briars in this barren wilderness; but if ever you would feel any solid ground of quietness and rest, it must be by coming off from vanity, and seeking your felicity in God, and living sincerely for him and upon him, as the worldling doth upon the world. His pardoning mercy must begin your peace, forgiving you your former thoughts; and his healing, quickening mercy, must increase it, by teaching you better to employ your thoughts, and drawing up your hearts unto himself; and his glorifying mercy must perfect it, by giving you the full intuition and fruition of himself in heaven, and employing you in his perfect love and praise, not leaving any room for creatures, nor suffering a thought to be employed on vanity for ever.

Chap. IV.

EXPOSTULATION WITH OBJECTORS.

By this time I hope you may see reason to call yourselves to a strict account, what converse you have been taken up with in the world, and upon what you have exercised your thoughts: surely you must needs be conscious, that the thoughts which have been denied God, have brought you home but little satisfaction, and have not answered the ends of your creation, redemption or preservation; and that they are now much fitter matter for your penitential tears, than your comfort, in the review! I do not think you dare own, and stand to those thoughts which have been spent for fleshly pleasures, or in unnecessary worldly cares, or that were wasted in impertinent vagaries upon any thing, or nothing, when you should have been seeking God! I do not think you have now any great pleasure, in the review of those thoughts, which once were taken up with pleasure, when

your most pleasant thoughts should have been of God. Dare you approve of your rejecting your Creator, and the great concern of your soul, out of your thoughts, and wasting them upon things unprofitable and vain? Did not God and heaven deserve more of your serious thoughts than any thing else that ever they were employed on? Have you laid them out on any thing that more concerned you? Or on any thing more excellent, more honourable, more durable, or that could claim precedency upon any just account? Did you not shut heaven itself out of your thoughts, when you shut out God? Is it not just that God and heaven should shut out you? If heaven be not the principal matter of your thoughts, it is plain that you do not principally love it: if so, judge you whether those that love it not are fit to be made possessors of it.

O poor distracted, senseless world! Is not God great enough to command and take up your chief thoughts? Is not heaven enough to find them work, and afford them satisfaction and delight? And yet is the dotage of the world enough? Is your honour, wealth, fleshly delights and sports enough? God will shortly make you know whether this were wise and equal dealing! Is God so low, so little, so undeserving, to be so often and easily forgotten, and so hardly and so slightly remembered? I tell you, ere long he will make you think of him to your sorrow, whether you will or no, if grace do not now set open your hearts, and procure him better entertainment.

But perhaps you will think that you walk with God, because you think of him sometimes ineffectually and as on the by. But is he esteemed as your God, if he have not the command, and if he have not the precedency of his creatures? Can you dream that indeed you walk with God, when your hearts were never grieved for offending him, nor ever much solicitous how to be reconciled to him, nor much inquisitive whether your state or way be pleasing or displeasing to him? When all the business of an unspeakable importance, which you have to do with God, before you pass to judgment, is forgotten and undone, as if you knew not of any such work that you had to do; when you make no serious preparation for death, when you call not upon God in secret, or in your families, unless with a little heartless lip labour; and when you love not the spirituality of his worship, but only delude your souls with the mockery of hypocritical outside compliment Do you walk with God while you are plotting for preferment, and gaping after worldly greatness, while you are gratifying all the desires of your flesh, and making provision for the future satisfaction of its lusts? Are you walking with God when you are hating him in his holiness, his justice, his word and ways, and hating all that seriously love and seek him; when you are doing your worst to dispatch the work of your damnation, and put your salvation past all hope, and draw as many to hell with you as you can? If this be a walking with God, you may take further comfort that you shall also dwell with God, according to the sense of such a walk: you shall dwell with him as a devouring fire, and as just, whom you thus walked with in the contempt of his mercies, and the provocation of his justice.

I tell you, if you walked with God indeed, his authority would rule you, his greatness would much take up your minds, and leave less room for little things: you would trust his promises, fear his threatenings, be awed by his presence, and the idols of your hearts would fall before him: he would over-power your lusts, and call you off from your ambitious and covetous designs, and obscure all the creature's glory. Believing, serious effectual thoughts of God, are very much different from the common, doubtful, dreaming, ineffectual thoughts of the ungodly world.

Object. But perhaps some will say, ' This seems to be the work of preachers, and not of every Christian, to be always meditating of God: poor people must think of other matters: they have their business to do, and their families to provide for: ignorant people are weak-headed, and are not able either to manage or endure a contemplative life: so much thinking of God will make them melancholy and mad, as experience tells us it hath done by many: therefore this is no exercise for them.'

To this I answer: Every Christian hath a God to serve, and a soul to save, and a Christ to believe in and obey, and an endless happiness to secure and enjoy, as well as preachers: pastors must study to instruct their flock, and to save themselves, and those that hear them: the people must study to understand and receive the mercy offered them, and to make their own calling and election sure. It is not said of pastors only, but of every blessed man, that ' his delight is in the law of the Lord, and therein doth he meditate day and night.' The due meditation of the soul upon God, is so far from taking you off from your necessary business in the world, that it is the only way to your orderly and successful management of it. It is not a distracting

thoughtfulness that I persuade you to, or which is included in a Christian's walk with God: but it is a directing, quickening, exalting, comforting course of meditation: many a hundred have grown melancholy and mad with discontented thoughts of the world; it doth not follow therefore that no man must think of the world at all, for fear of being mad or melancholy; but only that they should think of it more regularly, and correct the error of their thoughts and passions: So is it about God and heavenly things: our thoughts are to be well ordered, and the error of them cured, and not the use of them forborn. Atheism and impiety, and forgetting God, are unhappy means to prevent melancholy; there are wiser means, for avoiding madness, than by renouncing all our reason, and living by sense like the beasts that perish, and forgetting that we have an everlasting life to live.

But yet because I am sensible that some here mistake on the other hand, and I would not lead you into any extreme, I shall fully remove the scruple contained in this objection, by showing you, in the following propositions, in what sense and how far your thoughts must be taken up with God, supposing what was said in the beginning, where I described to you the duty of walking with God.

Prop. 1. When we tell you that your thoughts must be on God, it is not a course of idle musing, or mere thinking, that we call you to, but it is a necessary practical thinking of that which you have to do, and of him that you must love, obey and enjoy. You will not forget your parents, or husband, or wife, or friend; and yet you will not spend your time in sitting still and thinking of them, with a musing, unprofitable thoughtfulness: but you will have such thoughts of them, and so many as are necessary to the ends, even to the love and service which you owe them, and to the delight that your hearts should have in the fruition of them. You cannot love, or obey, or take pleasure in those that you will not think of; you will follow your trades, or your master's service but unhappily, if you will not think on them. Thinking is not the work that we must take up with: it is but a subservient instrumental duty, to promote some greater, higher duty: therefore we must think of God, that we may love him, do his service, trust him, fear and hope in him, and make him our delight. All this is it that we call you to, when we are persuading you to think on God.

2. An hypocrite, or a wicked enemy of God, may think of him speculatively, and perhaps be more frequent in such thoughts than many prac-

tical believers. A learned man may study about God, as he doth about other matters, names, and notions ; and propositions and decisions concerning God, may be a principal part of his learning. A preacher may study about God, and the matters of God, as a physician or a lawyer does about the matters of their own profession, either for the pleasure which knowledge, as knowledge, brings to human nature, or for the credit of being esteemed wise and learned, or because their gain and maintenance comes in this way. They that fill many volumes with controversies concerning God, and fill the church with contentions and troubles by them, and their own heart with malice and uncharitableness against those that are not of their opinions, have many a thought of God, which yet will do nothing to the saving of their souls, no more than they do to the sanctifying of them. Such learned men may think more orthodoxly and methodically concerning God, than many an honest serious Christian, who yet thinks of him more effectually and savingly : even as they can discourse more orderly and copiously of God, when yet they have no saving knowledge of him.

3. All men must not bestow so much time in meditation as some must do : it is the calling of ministers to study so as to furnish their minds with all those truths concerning God which are needful to the edification of the church ; and so to meditate on these things as to give themselves wholly to them. It is both the work of their common and their special calling : the study necessary to Christians as such, belongs as well to others as to them : but other men have another special or particular calling, which also they must think of, so far as the nature and ends of their daily labours require. It is a hurtful error to imagine that men must either lay by their callings to meditate on God, or that they must do them negligently, or to be taken up in the midst of their employments with such studies of God as ministers are, that are separated to that work.

4. No man is bound to be continually taken up with actual, distinct thoughts of God : for in duty we have many other things to think on, which must have their time : and as we have callings to follow, and must eat our bread in the sweat of our brows, so we must manage them with prudence: 'a good man will guide his affairs with discretion.' It is both necessary as duty, and necessary as a means to the preservation of our very faculties, that both body and mind have their times of employment about our lawful business in the world : the understandings of many cannot bear it, to be always employed on the greatest and most serious things; like lute strings they will break, if they be raised too high, and be not let down and relaxed, when the lesson is finished. To think of nothing else but God, is to break the law of God, to confound the mind, and to disable it to think aright of God, or any thing. As he that bids us pray continually, did not mean that we should do nothing else, or that actual prayer should have no interruptions, but that habitual desires should on all meet occasions be actuated and expressed ; so he that would be chief in all their thoughts, did never mean that we should have no thoughts of any thing else, or that our serious meditation on him should be continual without interruption : but that the final intending of God, and our dependence on him should be so constant as to be the spring or mover of the rest of the thoughts and actions of our lives.

5. A habitual intending of God as our end, depending on his support, and subjection to his government, will carry on the soul in a sincere and constant course of godliness, though the actual, most observed thoughts of the soul be fewer in number about God, than about the means that lead unto him, and the occurrences in our way : the soul of man is very active and comprehensive, and can think of several things at once : when it is once clear and resolved in any case, it can act according to that knowledge and resolution, without any present sensible thought ; nay, while its actual most observed thoughts are upon something else. A musician that hath a habitual skill, can keep time and tune while he is thinking of some other matter : a weaver can cast his shuttle right, and work truly, while he is thinking or talking of other things. A man can eat and drink with discretion, while he talks of other things. Some men can dictate to two or three scribes at once, upon divers subjects : a traveller can keep on his way, though he seldom think distinctly of his journey's end, but be thinking or discoursing most of the way upon other matters : for before he undertook his journey, he thought both of the end and way, and resolved then which way to go, and that he would go through all both fair and foul, and not turn back till he saw the place : and this habitual understanding and resolution may be secretly and unobservedly active, so as to keep a man from erring, and from turning back, though at the same time the traveller's most sensible thoughts and his discourse may be upon something else. When a man is once resolved of his end, and hath laid his design, he is past deli-

berating of that, and therefore hath less use of his thoughts about it: but it is readier to lay them out upon the means, which may be still uncertain, or may require his frequent deliberation. We have usually more thoughts and speeches by the way, about our company, or our horses, or inns, or other accommodations, or the fairness, or foulness of the way, or other such occurrences, than we have about the place we are going to; and yet this secret intention of our end will bring us thither. So when a soul hath cast up his accounts,—hath renounced a worldly and sensual felicity,—hath fixed his hopes and resolution upon heaven,—is resolved to cast himself upon Christ, and take God for his only portion, this secret, habitual resolution will do much to keep him constant in the way, though his thoughts and talk be frequently on other things : yea, when we are thinking of the creature, and feel no actual thoughts of God, it is yet God more than the creature that we think of: for we did beforehand look on the creature as God's work, representing him unto the world, and as his talents, which we must employ for him, and as every creature is related to him: this estimation of the creature is still habitually, and in some secret, less perceived act, most prevalent in the soul. Though I am not always sensibly thinking of the king, when I use his coin, or obey his laws, &c. yet it is only as his coin still that I use it and as his laws that I obey them. Weak habits cannot do their work without great carefulness of thoughts ; but perfect habits will act a man with little thoughtfulness, as coming near the natural way of operation. Indeed the imperfection of our habitual godliness doth make our serious thoughts, vigilance, and industry, to be the more necessary to us.

6. There are some thoughts of God that are necessary to the very being of a holy state ; as that God be so much in our thoughts, as to be preferred before all things else, and principally beloved and obeyed ; and to be the end of our lives, and the bias of our wills : and there are some thoughts of God that are necessary only to the acting and increase of grace.

7. So great is the weakness of our habits, so many and great are the temptations to be overcome, so many difficulties are in our way, and the occasions so various for the exercise of each grace, that it behoves a Christian to exercise as much thoughtfulness about his end and work, as hath any tendency to promote his work, and to attain his end : but such a thoughtfulness as hinders us in our work, by stopping, or distracting,

or diverting us, is no way pleasing unto God. So excellent is our end, that we can never encourage and delight the mind too much in the fore thoughts of it. So sluggish are our hearts, and so loose and unconstant are our apprehensions and resolutions, that we have need to be most frequently quickening them, lifting at them, and renewing our desires, and suppressing the contrary desires, by the serious thoughts of God and immortality. Our thoughts are the excitements that must kindle the flames of love, desire, hope, and zeal : our thoughts are the spur that must urge on a sluggish tired heart. So far as they conduce to any such works and ends as these, they are desirable and good. But what master loves to see his servant sit down and think, when he should be at work ? Or to use his thoughts only to grieve and vex himself for his faults, but not to mend them ; to sit down lamenting that he is so bad and unprofitable a servant, when he should be up and doing his master's business as well as he is able ? Such thoughts as hinder us from duty, or discourage or unfit us for it, are real sins, however they may go under a better name.

8. The godly themselves are very much wanting in the holiness of their thoughts, and the liveliness of their affections. Sense leads away the thoughts too easily after these present sensible things ; while faith being infirm, the thoughts of God and heaven are much retarded by their invisibility. Many a gracious soul crieth out, O that I could think as easily and as affectionately and as unweariedly about the Lord, and the life to come, as I can do about my friends, my health, my habitation, my business, and other concerns of this life ! But, alas ! such thoughts of God and heaven have far more enemies and resistance, than the thoughts of earthly matters have.

9. It is not distracting, vexatious thoughts of God that the holy scriptures call us to : but it is to such thoughts as tend to the healing, peace, and felicity of the soul ; and therefore it is not a melancholy, but a joyful life. If God be better than the world, it must needs be better to think of him. If he be more beloved than any friend, the thoughts of him should be sweeter to us. If he be the everlasting hope and happiness of the soul, it should be a foretaste of happiness to find him nearest to our hearts. The nature and use of holy thoughts, and of all religion, is but to exalt, sanctify, and delight the soul, and bring it up to everlasting rest : and is this the way to melancholy or madness ? Or is it not more likely to make men melancholy, to think of nothing but

a vain, deceitful and vexatious world, that hath much to disquiet us, but nothing to satisfy us, and can give the soul no hopes of any durable delight ?

10. Yet as God is not equally related unto all, so is he not the same to all men's thoughts. If a wicked enemy of God and godliness, be forced and frightened into some thoughts of God, you cannot expect that they should be as sweet and comfortable thoughts as those of his most obedient children are. While a man is under the guilt and power of his reigning sin, and under the wrath and curse of God, unpardoned, unjustified, a child of the devil, it is not this man's duty to think of God, as if he were fully reconciled to him, and took pleasure in him, as in his own. Nor is it any wonder if such a man think of God with fear, and think of his sin with grief and shame. Nor is it any wonder the justified themselves think of God with fear and grief, when they have provoked him by some sinful and unkind behaviour, or are cast into doubts of their sincerity and interest in Christ, and when he hides his face, or assaults them with his terrors. To doubt whether a man shall live for ever in heaven or hell, may rationally trouble the thoughts of the wisest man in the world ; and it were but sottishness not to be troubled at it. David himself could say, 'in the day of my trouble I sought the Lord : my sore ran in the night and ceased not : my soul refused to be comforted : I remembered God and was troubled : I complained and my Spirit was overwhelmed : thou holdest mine eyes waking : I am so troubled that I cannot speak : will the Lord cast off for ever ?'

Yet all the sorrowful thoughts of God, which are the duty either of the godly or the wicked, are but the necessary preparatives of their joy. It is not to melancholy, distraction or despair, that God calls any, even the worst : but it is that ' the wicked' would ' seek the Lord while he may be found, and call upon him while he is near ; that he would forsake his way, and the unrighteous man his thoughts ; and return unto the Lord, and he will have mercy upon him, and to our God, for he will abundantly pardon.' Despair is sin ; and the thoughts that tend to it are sinful thoughts, even in the wicked. If worldly crosses, or the sense of danger to the soul, had cast any into melancholy, or overwhelmed them with fears, you can name nothing in the world that in reason should be so powerful a remedy to recover them as the thoughts of God, his goodness, mercy, and readiness to receive and pardon those that turn unto him ; his covenant,

promises, and grace through Christ, and the everlasting happiness which all may have that will accept and seek it in the time of grace, and prefer it before the deceitful, transitory pleasures of the world. If the thoughts of God, and of the heavenly, everlasting joys will not comfort the soul, and cure a sad despairing mind, I know not what can rationally do it. Though yet it is true, that a presumptuous sinner must needs be in a trembling state, till he find himself at peace with God : and mistaken Christians, that are cast into causeless doubts and fears by the malice of Satan, are unlikely to walk comfortably with God, till they are resolved and recovered from their mistakes and fears.

Chap. V.

ON THE PROPER DIRECTION OF THE THOUGHTS.

Object. But it may be the objector will be ready to think, that ' if it be indeed our duty to walk with God, yet thoughts are no considerable part of it : what more uncertain or mutable than our thoughts ? It is deeds and not thoughts that God regards : to do no harm to any, but to do good to all, this is indeed to walk with God. You set a man upon a troublesome and impossible work while you set him upon so strict a guard, and so much exercise of his thoughts : what cares the Almighty for my thoughts ?'

Answ. 1. If God know better than you, and is to be believed, then thoughts are not so inconsiderable as you suppose. Doth he not say, that ' the thoughts of the wicked are an abomination to the Lord ?' It is the work of the gospel, by its power, to ' pull down strong holds, casting down imaginations, and every high thing that exalteth itself against the knowledge of God, and bringing in to captivity every thought to the obedience of Christ.' The unrighteous man's forsaking his thoughts, is part of his necessary conversion. It was the description of the deplorable state of the old world that 'God saw that the wickedness of man was great in the earth, and that every imagination of the thoughts of his heart was only evil continually ; and it repented the Lord that he had made man on the earth, and it grieved him at his heart.' Judge by this, whether thoughts be so little regarded by God, as you imagine. David saith of himself, ' I hate vain thoughts.' Solomon saith ' the thoughts of the righteous are right.' Paul saith that ' charity thinketh not evil.'

2. Thoughts are the issue of a rational soul. If its operations be contemptible, its essence is

contemptible: if its essence be noble, its operations are considerable. If the soul be more excellent than the body, its operations must be more excellent. To neglect our thoughts and not employ them upon God, and for God, is to vilify our noblest faculties, and deny God, who is a spirit, that spiritual service which he requires.

3. Our thoughts are commonly our most cordial, voluntary acts, and show the temper and inclination of the heart: and therefore are regardable to God that searches the heart, and calls first for the service of the heart.

4. Our thoughts are radical and instrumental acts: such as they are, such are the actions of our lives. Christ tells us that out of the heart proceed evil thoughts, murders, adulteries, fornications, thefts, false witness, blasphemies, which defile the man.

5. Our thoughts are under a law, as well as words and deeds; 'the thought of foolishness is sin:' and Christ extends the law even to the thoughts and desires of the heart. And under the law it is said, 'beware that there be not a thought in thy wicked heart,' &c., namely, of unmercifulness towards thy brother.

6. Thoughts can reach much higher than sense, and may be employed upon the most excellent and invisible objects; and therefore are fit instruments to elevate the soul that would converse with God. Though God be infinitely above us, our thoughts may be exercised on him; our persons never were in heaven, and yet our conversation must be in heaven. How is that but by our thoughts? Though we see not Christ, yet by the exercise of believing thoughts on him, 'we love him, and rejoice with joy unspeakable and full of glory.' Though God be invisible, yet our 'meditations of him may be sweet, and we may delight in the Lord.' Say not that all this is but fanciful and delusory, as long as thoughts of things unseen are fitter to actuate and elevate the love, desires and delights of the soul, and to move and guide us in a regular and holy life, than the sense of lesser present good. The thoughts are not vain or delusory, unless the object of them be false, vain, and delusory. Where the object is great, sure, and excellent, the thoughts of such things are excellent operations of the soul. If the thoughts of vain glory, wealth and pleasure, can delight the ambitious, covetous and sensual; no wonder if the thoughts of God and life eternal afford us solid high delights.

7. The thoughts are not so liable to be counterfeit and hypocritical as are the words and outward deeds. Therefore they show more what the man is, and what is in his heart. For as Solomon saith, 'as he thinketh in his heart, so is he.'

8. Our thoughts may exercise the highest graces of God in man; and also show those graces, as being their effects. How is our faith, love, desire, trust, joy, and hope to be exercised, but by our thoughts? If grace were not necessary and excellent, it would not be wrought by the Spirit of God, called the divine nature, and the image of God. If grace be excellent, the use and exercise of it is excellent: therefore our thoughts by which it is exercised must needs have their excellency too.

9. Our thoughts must be the instruments of our improving all holy truth in scripture, and all the mercies which we receive, and all the afflictions which we undergo. What good will reading a chapter in the Bible do to any one that never thinks on it? Our delight in the law of God must engage us to 'meditate in it day and night.' What good shall he get by hearing a sermon that exercises not his thoughts for the receiving and digesting it? Our considering what is said, is the way in which we may expect that 'God should give us understanding in all things.' What the better will he be for any of the merciful providences of God, who never bethinks him whence they come, or what is the use and end that they are given for? What good will he get by any afflictions, that never bethinks him who it is that chastises him, and for what, and how he must get them removed, and sanctified to his good? A man is but like one of the pillars in the church, or like the corpse which he treads on, or at best but like the dog that follows him thither for company, if he use not his thoughts about the work which he hath in hand, and cannot say, 'we have thought of thy lovingkindness, O God, in the midst of thy temple.' He that bids you hear, doth also bid you 'take heed how you hear.' You are commanded to 'lay up the word in your heart and soul, and to set your hearts to all the words which are testified among you: for it is not a vain thing for you, because it is your life.'

10. Our thoughts are so considerable a part of God's service, that they are often put for the whole. 'A book of remembrance was written for them that feared the Lord, and that thought upon his name.' Our believing and loving God, trusting in him, and desiring him and his grace, are the principal parts of his service, which are exercised immediately by our thoughts: in praise and prayer it is this inward part that is the soul

and life of all. He is a foolish hypocrite that thinks to be heard for his much speaking.

On the contrary the thoughts are named as the sum of all iniquity. ' Their thoughts are thoughts of iniquity.'—' I have spread out my hands all the day long unto a rebellious people, which walketh in a way that was not good, after their own thoughts.'—' O Jerusalem, wash thy heart from wickedness, that thou mayest be saved: how long shall thy vain thoughts lodge within thee.'—' The fool hath said in his heart, There is no God.'

11. A man's thoughts are the appointed orderly way for the conversion of a sinner, and the preventing of his sin and misery. David saith, ' I thought on mine ways, and turned my feet unto thy testimonies.' The prodigal came to himself, and returned to his father, by the success of his own consideration. ' Thus saith the Lord of hosts, consider your ways,' is a voice that every sinner should hear. ' It is he that considereth and doth not according to his father's sins, that shall not die.' Therefore it is God's desire, ' O that they were wise and understood this, and that they would consider their latter end.' It is either men's inconsiderateness, or the error of their thoughts, that is the cause of all their wickedness : ' my people doth not consider.' Paul ' verily thought, that he ought to do many things against the name of Jesus.' Many ' deceive themselves by thinking themselves something when they are nothing.'—' They think it strange that we run not with them to excess of riot:' therefore they speak evil of us. Disobedient formalists consider not that they do evil when they think they are offering acceptable sacrifices to God. The very murder of God's holy ones hath proceeded from these erroneous thoughts ; ' they that kill you shall think they do God service.' All the ambition, covetousness, injustice, and cruelty following thereupon, which troubles the world, and ruins men's souls, is from their erroneous thoughts, overvaluing these deceitful things. ' Their inward thought is that their houses shall continue for ever, and their dwelling places to all generations.' The presumptuous and impenitent are surprised by destruction, for want of thinking of it to prevent it : ' in such an hour as you think not, the Son of man cometh.'

12. Lastly, The thoughts are the most constant actions of a man, and therefore most of the man is in them. We are not always reading, or hearing, or praying, or working : but we are always thinking. Therefore it doth especially concern us to see that this constant breath of the soul be sweet, and that this constant stream be pure

and run in the right channel. Well therefore did David make this his request, ' Search me, O God, and know my heart : try me, and know my thoughts : and see if there be any wicked way in me, and lead me in the way everlasting.' I say therefore to those that insist on this irrational objection, that these very thoughts of theirs, concerning the inconsiderableness of thoughts, are so foolish and ungodly, that when they understand the evil even of these, they will know that thoughts were more to be regarded. ' If therefore thou hast done foolishly in lifting up thyself, or if thou hast thought evil, lay thy hand upon thy mouth.'

Though, after all this, I still confess that it is so exceeding hard a matter to keep the thoughts in holy exercise and order, that even the best daily and hourly sin, in the omissions, the disorder or vanity of their thoughts ; yet for all that, we must needs conclude that the inclination and design of our thoughts must be principally for God, and that the thoughts are principal instruments of the soul, in acting in his service, and moving it towards him, and in all this holy work of our walking with God : therefore to imagine that thoughts are inconsiderable and of little use, is to unman us, and unchristen us. The labour of the mind is necessary for the attaining of the felicity of the mind : as the labour of the body is necessary for the things that belong unto the body. As bodily idleness brings unto beggary, when the diligent hand makes rich : so the idleness of the soul doth impoverish the soul, when the laborious Christian lives plentifully and comfortably, through the blessing of God upon his industry and labour. You cannot expect that God should appear to you in a bodily shape, that you may have immediate converse with him in the body. It is in the Spirit that thou must converse with God who is a Spirit. The mind sees him by faith, who is invisible to the bodily eyes. Nay, if you will have a true and saving knowledge of God, you must not liken him to any thing that is visible, nor have any corporal conceivings of him : earthly things may be the glass in which we may behold him, while we are here in the flesh. But our conceivings of him must be spiritual, and minds that are immersed in flesh and earth, are unmeet to hold communion with him : the natural man knows him not, and ' the carnal mind is enmity to him, and they that are in the flesh cannot please him.' It is the pure, abstracted, elevated soul, that understands by experience what it is to walk with God.

Chap. VI.

OBLIGATIONS AND ADVANTAGES OF WALKING WITH GOD.

Having in the foregoing uses, reproved the atheism and contempt of God which ungodly men are continually guilty of, and endeavoured to convince them of the necessity and desirableness of walking with God, and in particular of improving our thoughts for holy converse with him, and answered the objections of the impious and atheistical; I shall next endeavour to cure the remnants of this disease, in those that are sincerely holy, who live too strangely to God their Father in the world. In the performance of this, I shall first show you what are the benefits of this holy life, which should make it appear desirable and delightful; and then I shall show you why believers should addict themselves to it as doubly obliged, and that their neglect of it is a sin attended with special aggravations. This is the remainder of my task.

To walk with God in a holy and heavenly conversation, is the employment most suitable to human nature; not to its corrupt disposition, nor to the carnal interest and appetite; but to nature as nature, to man as man: it is the very work that he was made for: the faculties and frame of the soul and body were composed for it by the wise Creator: they are restored for it by the gracious Redeemer. Though in corrupted nature where sensuality is predominant, there is an estrangement from God, and an enmity and hatred of him, so that the wicked are more averse to all serious, holy converse with him in prayer, contemplation, and a heavenly life, than they are to a worldly, sinful life; yet all this is but the disease of nature, corrupting its appetite, and turning it against that proper food which is most suitable to its sound desires, and necessary to its health and happiness. Though sinful habits are become as it were a second nature to the ungodly, so depraving their judgments and desires that they verily think the business and pleasures of the flesh are most suitable to them; yet these are as contrary to nature as nature, that is, to the primitive tendencies of all our faculties, and the proper use to which they were fitted by our Creator, and to that true felicity which is the end of all our parts and powers, even as madness is contrary to the rational nature, though it were hereditary.

Sect. 1. What can be more agreeable to the nature of man, than to be rational and wise, and to live in the purest exercise of reason? Certainly there is nothing more rational than that we should live to God, and gladly accept of all that communion with him of which our natures on earth are capable. Nothing can be more reasonable than for the reasonable soul to be entirely addicted to him that did create it, that doth preserve it, and by whom it doth subsist and act. Nothing is more reasonable than that the absolute Lord of nature be honoured, and served wholly by his own: nothing is more reasonable than that the reasonable creature live in the truest dependence upon, and subordination to the highest reason; and that derived, imperfect wisdom, be subservient to, and guided by the primitive, perfect wisdom: it is most reasonable that the children depend upon the father, and the foolish be ruled by the most wise, and that the subjects be governed by the universal king, that they honour him and obey him, and that the indigent apply themselves to him that is all-sufficient, and is most able and ready to supply their wants; and that the impotent rest upon him that is omnipotent.

2. Nothing can be more reasonable than that the reasonable nature should intend its end, and seek after its true and chief felicity: that it should love good as good, and therefore prefer the chief good before that which is transitory and insufficient. Reason commands the reasonable creature to avoid its own delusion and destruction, and to rest upon him that can continually support us, and not upon the creature, that will deceive us and undo us: to prefer the highest and noblest converse before that which is inferior, unprofitable and base, and that we rejoice more in the highest, purest, and most durable delights, than in those that are sordid and of short continuance. Who knows not that God is the chief good, and true felicity of man, the everlasting rock, the durable delight, and to be preferred before his creatures? Who might not find, that would use his reason, that all things below are vanity and vexation?

3. Nothing can be more rational and agreeable to man's nature, than that the superior faculties should govern the inferior, that the brutish part be subject to the rational; and that the ends and objects of this higher faculty be preferred before the objects of the lower: that the objects of sense be made subservient to the objects of reason. If this be not natural and rational, then it is natural to man to be no man, but a beast, and reasonable to be unreasonable. Now it is evident that a holy living unto God, is but the improvement of true reason, and its employment

for and upon its noblest object, and its ultimate end : and that a sensual life is the exercise of the inferior brutish faculties, in predominancy above and before the rational : therefore to question whether God or the Creator should be first sought, loved, principally desired, delighted in, and served, is but to question whether we should live like men or like beasts, and whether dogs or wise men be fitter companions for us ? Whether the rider or the horse should have the rule ? Whether the rational or sensitive powers be superior and proper to the nature of a man ?

Object. But there is a middle state of life, betwixt the sensual and the divine or holy life, which sober philosophers did live, and this is the most natural life, and most properly so called.

Answ. I deny this ; there is no middle state of life, if you denominate the several states of life, from the several ends, or the several powers. I grant that the very sensitive powers in man, especially the imagination, is much advanced by the conjunction of reason, above that of a brute : I grant that the delights of the imagination may be preferred before the immediate pleasure of the senses : and I grant that some little distant knowledge of God, things divine, and hopes of attaining them, may affect an unsanctified man with an answerable pleasure. But all this is nothing to prove that there is a third sort of end, or of powers, and so a third or middle state of life, specially distinct from the sensitive and the holy life. Besides, the vegetative man hath no other life or faculties, than the sensitive and the rational : therefore one of these must be in predominancy or rule. Therefore he can have no middle sort or end ; and therefore no middle state of life, that can be said to be agreeable to his nature. Those that seek and take up their chief felicity in riches and plenty, and provisions for the flesh, though not in present pleasing of the sense, live but the life of sensuality. A fox or dog takes pleasure when he hath eaten his belly full, to hide and lay up the rest : and so doth the bee to fill the hive, and make provision for the winter. The proud that delight in honour and applause, and making others subject to their lusts, live but the life of sensuality : a dog, a horse, and other brutes, have something of the same. They that are grave through melancholy, or because they can reach no great matter in the world, and because their old or duller spirits are not much pleased with juvenile delights, and so live retiredly, and seek no higher pleasure or felicity, but only sit down with the weeping or the laughing philosopher, lamenting or deriding the vanity of the world, do yet live no

other than a sensual life : as an old dog that hath no pleasure in hunting or playfulness, as he had when he was a whelp. Only he is less deluded, and less vain, than other sensualists that find more pleasure in their course.

Object. All the doubt is concerning those that place their felicity in knowledge, and those that delight in moral virtues, or that delight in studying of God, though they are no Christians.

Answ. The point is weighty, and hath often unhappily fallen into injudicious hands. I shall endeavour to resolve it as truly, clearly and impartially as I can. It is a great error against the nature of man, to say, that knowledge, as such, is fit to be any man's chief and ultimate end. It may be that act which is next the enjoying act of the will, which is it that indeed is next the end, objectively considered : but it is not that act which we call the last end. This is plain, (1.) Because the object of the understanding, which is truth, is not formally the nearest object or matter of full felicity or delight : it is goodness that is the nearest object. (2.) Therefore the office of the intellect is but introductive and subservient to the office of the will, to apprehend the verity of good, and present it to the will to be prosecuted, or embraced, or delighted in. There are many truths that are ungrateful and vexatious, and which men would wish to be no truths : there is a knowledge which is troublesome, useless, undesirable and tormenting, which even a wise man would willingly avoid, if he knew how. Morality is but preparatively in the intellect : and therefore intellectual acts, as such, are not morally good, or evil, but only participatively, as subject to the will. Therefore knowledge, as such, being not a moral good, can be no other than such a natural good only so far as it tends to some welfare or happiness, or pleasure of the possessor or some other : and this welfare or pleasure is either that which is suited to the sensitive powers, or to the rational, which is to be found in the love of God alone.

I add therefore, that even those men that seem to take up their felicity in common knowledge, indeed do but make their knowledge subservient to something else which they take for their felicity. For knowledge of evil may torment them. It is only to know something which they take to be good, that is their delight. It is the complacency or love of that good at the heart, which sets them on work, and causes the delight of knowing. If you will say that common knowledge, as knowledge, doth immediately delight, yet will it be found but such a pleasing of the imagination as an ape hath in spying marvels, which if it have no end that is higher, is still but a sensitive delight; but if it be referred to a higher delight in God, it doth participate of the nature of it. Delight in general is the common end of men and brutes: but in their nature they are distinguished as sensual or rational.

If you suppose a philosopher to be delighted in studying mathematics, or any of the works of God, either he hath herein an end, or no end beyond the knowledge of the creature: either he terminates his desires and delights in the creature, or else uses it as a means to raise him to the Creator. If he study and delight in the creature ultimately, this is indeed the act of a rational creature, and an act of reason, as to the faculty it proceeds from, and so is a rational contrivance for sensual ends and pleasures: but it is but the error of reason, and is no more agreeable to the rational nature, than the deceit of the senses is to the sensitive. Nor is it finally to be numbered with the operations soliciting human nature, any more than an erroneous dream of pleasure, or than that man is to be numbered with the lovers of learning, who takes pleasure in the binding, leaves, or letters of the book, while he understands nothing of the sense. But if this philosopher seek to know the Creator in and by the creatures, and take delight in the Maker's power, wisdom and goodness, which appears in them, then this is truly a rational delight, in itself considered, and beseeming a man. If he reach so far in it, as to make God his highest desire and delight, overpowering the desires and delights of sensuality, he shall be happy, as being led by the Son unto the Father: but if he make but some little approaches towards it, and drown all such desires in the sensual desires and delights, he is then but an unhappy sensualist, and lives brutishly in the tenor of his life, though in some acts in part he operate rationally as a man.

The like I may say of them that are said to place their delight in moral virtues. Indeed nothing is properly a moral good, or virtue, but that which is exercised upon God as our end, or upon the creature as a means to this end. To study and know mere notions of God, or what is to be held and said of him in discourse, is not to study to know God, no more than to love the language and phrase of holy writing, is to love God. To study God, as one that is less desirable than our sensual delights, is but to blaspheme him. To study, seek and serve him as one that can promote or hinder our sensual felicity, is but to abuse him as a means to your sensuality. For the virtues of temperance, justice or charity, they are but analogically to be found in any ungodly person. Materially they may have them in an eminent degree; but not as they are informed by the end which moralizes them. Jezebel's fast was not formally a virtue, but an odious way of hypocrisy to oppress the innocent: he that doth works of justice and mercy, to evil ends only, as for applause, or to deceive, &c. and not from the true principles of justice and mercy, doth not thereby exercise moral virtue, but hypocrisy and other vice. He that doth works of justice and mercy, out of mere natural compassion to others, and desire of their good, without respect to God, as obliging, or rewarding, or desiring it, doth perform such a natural good work, as a lamb or a gentle beast doth to his fellows, which hath not the true form of moral virtue, but the matter only. He that in such works hath some little respect to God, but more to his carnal interest among men, doth that which on the by participates of moral good, or is such, being to be denominated from the part predominant. He that doth works of justice or charity principally to please God, and in true obedience to his will, and a desire to be conformed thereto, doth that which is formally a moral good, and holy, though there may be abhorred mixtures of worse respects.

So that there are but two states of life here: one of those that walk after the flesh, and the other of those that walk after the Spirit: however the flesh have several materials and ways of pleasure: even the rational actings have a carnal end, are carnal finally and morally, though they are acts of reason; for they are but the errors of reason, and defectiveness of true rationality; and being but the acts of erroneous reason as captivated by the flesh, and subservient to the carnal interest, they are themselves to be denominated carnal: so even the reasonable soul as biassed by sensuality, and captivated thereto, is included in the name of flesh in scripture.

How much moral good is in that course of piety or obedience to God, which proceeds only from the fear of God's judgments, without any love to him, I shall not now discuss, because I have too far digressed already.

All that I have last said, is to show you the reasonableness of living unto God, as being indeed the proper and just employment of the superior faculties of the soul, and the government of the lower faculties. For if any other, called moralists, seem to subject the sensual life to the rational, either they do but seem to do so; the sensual interest being indeed predominant, and their rational operations subjected thereto:

or at the best, it is but some poor and erroneous employment of the rational faculties which they exercise, or some weak approaches towards that high and holy life, which is indeed the life which the rational nature was created for, and which is the right improvement of it.

4. Moreover, nothing is more beseeming the nature of man, than to aspire after the highest and noblest improvement of itself; and to live the most excellent life that it is capable of. For every nature tends to its own perfection. But it is most evident, that to walk with God in holiness, is a thing that human nature is capable of; and that is the highest life that we are capable of on earth: therefore it is the life most suitable to our natures.

5. What can be more rational and beseeming a created nature, than to live to those ends which our Creator intended in the very forming of our natures? It is his ends that are principally to be served. But the very composure of our faculties plainly proves, that his end was that we should be fitted for his service: he gave us no powers or capacity in vain: and therefore to serve him and walk with him, is most suitable to our natures.

Object. That is natural which is first, and born with us: but our enmity to holiness is first, and not our holiness.

Answ. It may be called natural indeed, because it is first, and born with us: in that respect we confess that sin, and not holiness, is natural to us. But holiness is called natural to us, in a higher respect, because it was the primitive natural constitution of man, was before sin, is the perfection or health of nature, the right employment and improvement of it, and tends to its happiness. A hereditary leprosy may be called natural, as it is first, and before health, in that person: but health and soundness is natural, as being the well being of nature, when the leprosy is unnatural, as being but its disease, and tending to its destruction.

Object. But nature in its first constitution was not holy, but innocent only, and it was by a superadded gift of grace that it became holy, as some schoolmen think: and as others think, Adam had no holiness till his restoration.

Answ. These are popish improved fancies, and contrary to nature and the word of God.

1. They are no where written, nor have any evidence in nature, and therefore are the groundless dreams of men.

2. The work of our recovery to God is called in scripture a redemption, renovation, restoration, which imply that nature was once in that holy estate before the fall. It is expressly said, that the new man which we put on, is renewed in knowledge after the image of him that created him. After God's image Adam was created.

3. If it belong to the soundness and integrity of nature to be holy, that is, disposed and addicted to live to God, then it is rash and foolish, for men out of their own imagination, to feign, that God first made nature defective, and then mended it by superadded grace. But if it belong not to the soundness and integrity of human nature to be holy, then why did God give him grace to make him so? Nay then, it would follow, that when God sanctified Adam, or any since, he made him specifically another thing, another creature, of another nature, and did not only cure the diseases of his nature.

4. It is yet apparent in the very nature of man's faculties, that their very usefulness and tendency is to live to God, and to enjoy him: that God should make a nature apt for such a use, and give it no disposedness to its proper use, is an unnatural conceit. We see to this day that it is but an unreasonable abuse of reason, when it is not used holily for God; and it is a disease of nature to be otherwise disposed. Therefore primitive nature had such a holy inclination.

5. The contrary opinion tends to infidelity, and to brutify human nature. For if no man can believe that he must be holy, live to God, and enjoy him hereafter in heaven, but he that also believes that primitive nature was never disposed or qualified for such a life; and that God must first make a man another creature of another nature, and consequently not a man, this is not only so improbable, but so contrary to scripture and reason, that few considerate persons would believe it. As if we must believe that God would turn brutes into men. God heals, elevates, and perfects nature, but he doth not specifically change it, at least in this life.

Object. But let it be granted that he gives no man specifically another nature, yet he may give him such higher gifts as may be like another nature.

Answ. No doubt he may and doth give him such gifts as actuate and perfect nature: but some disposition to our ultimate end is essential to our nature; and therefore to assign man another ultimate end, and to give a disposition to it, of which he had no seed, or part, or principle before, is to make him another creature. I confess that in lapsed man, the holy disposition is so far dead, as that the change makes a man a new creature in a moral sense, as he is a new man that changes his mind and manners: but still nature hath its aptitude, as rational, to be employed for its Maker; so that he is not a new creature in a natural sense.

An actual or habitual willingness to his holy employment, a promptitude to it, and a due understanding of it, is the new creature, morally so called, which is given in our regeneration: but the natural aptitude that is in our faculties as rational, to this holy life, is essential to us as men, or as rational; even to have the natural power which must yet have further help or moral life to actuate it. Adam had both these: the one he retained, or else he had not continued a man; the other he lost, or else he had not had need of renovation.

If Adam's nature had not been disposed to God, as to his end and sovereign, then the law of nature, to adhere to God, and obey and serve him, was not written in his heart: then it would not have been his duty to adhere to God, and to obey and serve him: which is so false, that even in lapsed, unrenewed nature, there is left so much aptitude hereto, as will prove him to be still under the obligations of this law of nature, even actually to adhere to God, and to obey him, which a dead man, a madman, or an infant, is not immediately.

By all this you see, that though the blindness and disease of reason is contrary to faith and holiness, yet reason itself is so much for it, as that faith itself is but the act of elevated, well informed reason; and supernatural revelation is but the means to inform our reason, about things which have not a natural evidence, discernible by us. Sanctification, actively taken, is but the healing of our reason and rational appetite: and holiness is but the health or soundness of them. The error of reason must be renounced by believers, but not the use of reason: the sufficiency of reason and natural light, without supernatural light and help, we must all deny: but to set reason, as reason, in opposition to faith or holiness, or divine revelation, is as gross a piece of foolery, as to set the visive faculty in opposition to the light of the sun, or to its objects. It is the unreasonableness of sinners that is to be cured by illuminating grace. 'They are wise to do evil, but to do good they have no knowledge.' Their reason is wounded, depraved and corrupted about the matters of God: they have reason to serve the flesh, but not to master it. God doth renew men by giving them wisdom, and bringing them to a sound mind: as logic helps reason in discourse and arguing, so

theology informs reason about the matters of God and our salvation: and the Spirit of God makes his doctrine and revelation effectual. Make nature sound and reason clear, and then we will consent that all men be persuaded to live according to their nature and their reason. But if a madman will rave and tear himself and others, and say, This is according to my nature or my reason: it is fitter that chains and whips cure that nature and reason, than that he be allowed to live according to his madness. If a drunkard or whoremonger will say, My nature and reason incline me to please my appetite and lust: it is fit that the brutish nature be corrected, and the beast which rides and rules the man be taken down; and when indeed his nature is the nature of man, and fitted to the use and ends it was made for, then let him live according to it and spare not. If a malicious man will abuse or kill his neighbours, and say, This is according to my nature, let that nature be used as the nature of wolves and foxes, and other noxious creatures are. But let human nature be cured of its blindness, carnality and corruption, and then it will need no external testimony to convince it, that no employment is so natural and suitable to man, as to walk with God, in love and confidence, reverent worship, and cheerful obedience to his will. A worldly, fleshly, sensual life, will then appear to be below the rational nature of a man, as it is below us to go to grass with horses, or to live as mere companions of brutes. It will then appear to be as natural for us to love and live to our Creator and Redeemer, and to walk with God, as for a child to love his parents, and to live with them and serve them. When I say that this is natural, I mean not that it is necessary by natural necessity, or that grace doth operate as their rational motion is so called. There is a brutish or inanimate nature, and there is a rational, voluntary nature: grace works not according to the way of inanimate nature, in free agents. I may well say, that whatever is rational, is natural to a rational creature as such, so far as he discerns it. Yea, and habits, though they affect not necessarily, but freely in a rational nature, yet they incline necessarily, as by the order of nature. They contain in their being a natural aptitude and propensity to action.

Object. But thus you confound nature and grace, natural and supernatural operations, while you make grace natural.

Answ. No such thing: though walking with God be called natural, as it is most agreeable to nature so far as it is found, and is the felicity and best employment of the rational nature as such: Yet, 1. Diseased nature doth abhor it, as a diseased stomach the most pleasant and most wholesome food, as I said before. 2. This disease of nature cannot be cured without divine, supernatural grace. So that as to the efficient cause, our holiness is supernatural. But it is unsound doctrine of those that affirm that Adam in his pure natural state of innocency, had no natural holiness, or aptitude and promptitude to walk with God in order to everlasting happiness; but say that all this was either wanting to him, and was a state specifically distinct, which he fell short of by his sin, or that it was given him by superadded grace, and was not in his entire nature.

Yet we deny not but, as to degrees, Adam's nature was to grow up to more perfection: that his natural holiness contained not a sufficient, immediate aptitude and promptitude to every duty, which might afterwards be required of him: but this was to be obtained in the exercise of that holiness which he had: even as a vine or other fruit tree, though it be natural to it to bear its proper fruit, yet hath it not an immediate sufficient aptitude hereto, whilst it is but appearing out of the seed, before it be grown up to maturity. Or as it is natural to a man to discourse and reason; but yet his nature in infancy, or untaught and unexercised, hath not a sufficient immediate aptitude and promptitude hereunto. Or as grace inclines a renewed soul to every holy truth and duty: yet such a soul in its infancy of grace, hath not a sufficient immediate aptitude or promptitude to the receiving of every holy truth, or the doing of every holy duty; but must grow up to it by degrees. But the addition of these degrees is no specific alteration of the nature of man, or of that grace which was before received.

Having been so long upon this first consideration (that walking with God is most agreeable to human nature), I shall be more brief in the rest that follow.

Sect. II. To walk with God, and live to him, is incomparably the highest and noblest life. To converse with men only, is to converse with worms: whether they be princes or poor men, they differ but as the larger from the lesser. If they be wise and good, their converse may be profitable and delightful, because they have a beam of excellency from the face of God. O how unspeakable is the distance between his wisdom and goodness, and theirs! But if they be foolish, ungodly and dishonest, how lothsome is their conversation! What impure breath is in their profane and filthy language! In their lies and slanders of the just! In their sneers and scorns of those that walk with God! which expose at once their folly and misery to the pity of all that are truly understanding. When they are gravely speaking evil of the things which they understand not, or with a fleering confidence deriding merrily the holy commands and ways of God, they are much more lamentably expressing their infatuation than any that are kept in chains in bedlam: though indeed, with the most, they escape the reputation which they deserve, because they are attended with persons of their own proportion of wisdom, that always reverence a silk coat, and judge them wise that wear gold lace, and have the greatest satisfaction of their wills and lusts, and are able to do most mischief in the world: because good men have learned to honour the worst of their superiors, and not to call them as they are. But God is bold to call them as they are, and give them in his word such names and characters by which they might come to know themselves. Is it not a higher, nobler life to walk with God, than to converse in bedlam or with intoxicated sensualists, that live in a constant delirium?

Yea, worse than so: ungodly men are children of the devil, so called by Jesus Christ himself, because they have much of the nature of the devil, and the 'lusts of their father they will do;' yea, they are taken captive by him at his will. They are the servants of sin, and do the drudgery that so vile a master sets them on. Certainly as the spirits of the just are so like to angels, that Christ saith we shall be as they, and equal to them; so the wicked are nearer kin to devils than they themselves will easily believe. They are as like him as children to their father: he is a liar, and so are they: he is a hater of God, of godliness, and of godly men, and so are they: he is a murderer, and would devour the holy seed; and such are they. He envies the progress of the gospel, the prosperity of the church, and the increase of holiness, and so do they. He hath a special malice against the most powerful and successful preachers of the word of God, and against the most zealous and eminent saints; and so have they. He cares not by what lies and fictions he disgraces them, nor how cruelly he uses them; no more do they, (or some of them at least:) he cherisheth licentiousness, sensuality and impiety: and so do they. If they seem better in their adversity and restraint, yet try them but with prosperity and power, and you shall see quickly how like they are to devils. Shall we delight more to converse with brutes and incarnate devils, than with God. Is it not a more high and excellent conversation to walk with God, and live to him, than to be companions of such degenerate men, that have almost forfeited the reputation of humanity? Alas, they are companions so deluded and ignorant, and yet so wilful; so miserable, and yet so confident and secure, that they are, to a believing eye, the most lamentable sight that the whole world can show us out of hell. How sad a life must it then needs be, to converse with such, were it not for the hope that we have of furthering their recovery and salvation?

But to walk with God is a word so high, that I should have feared the guilt of arrogance in using it, if I had not found it in the holy scriptures. It is a word that imports so high and holy a frame of soul, and expresses such high and holy actions, that the naming of it strikes my heart with reverence, as if I had heard the voice to Moses, 'put off thy shoes from off thy feet, for the place whereon thou standest is holy ground.' Methinks he that shall say to me, Come see a man that walks with God, doth call me to see one that is next unto an angel, or glorified soul! It is a far more reverend object in mine eye, than ten thousand lords or princes, considered only in their fleshly glory. It is a wiser action for people to run and crowd together, to see a man that walks with God, than to see the pompous train of princes, their entertainments, or their triumph. O happy man, that walks with God, though neglected and contemned by all about him! What blessed sights doth he daily see! What ravishing tidings, what pleasant melody doth he daily hear, unless it be in his swoons or sickness! what delectable food doth he daily taste! He sees by faith the God, the glory, which the blessed spirits see at hand by nearest intuition: he sees that in a glass and darkly, which they behold with open face: he sees the glorious majesty of his Creator, the eternal King, the cause of causes, the composer, upholder, preserver, and governor of all worlds: he beholds the wonderful methods of his providence: what he cannot reach to see, he admires, and waits for the time when that also shall be open to his view! He sees by faith the world of spirits, the hosts that attend the throne of God; their perfect righteousness, their full devotedness to God: their ardent love, their flaming zeal, their ready and cheerful obedience, their dignity and shining glory, in which the lowest of thém exceeds that which the disciples saw on Moses and Elias when they appeared on the holy mount, and talked with Christ. They hear by faith the heavenly concert, the high and harmonious songs of praise, the joyful triumphs of crowned saints, the sweet commemorations of the things that were done and suffered on earth, with the praises of him that redeemed them by his blood, and made them kings and priests to God: herein he hath sometimes a sweet foretaste of the everlasting pleasures, which though it be but little, as Jonathan's honey on the end of his rod, or as the clusters of grapes which were brought from Canaan into the wilderness, yet are they more excellent than all the delights of sinners. In the beholding of this celestial glory, some beams penetrate his breast, and so irradiate his longing soul, that he is changed thereby into the same image, from glory to glory; the spirit of glory and of God doth rest upon him. O what an excellent holy frame doth this converse with God possess his soul of! How reverently doth he think of him! What life is there in every name and attribute of God which he hears or thinks on! The mention of his power, his wisdom, his goodness, his love, his holiness, his truth, how powerful and how pleasant are they to him! when to those that know him but by the hearing of the ear, all these are but like common names and notions; and even to the weaker sort of Christians, whose walking with God is more uneven and low, interrupted by their sins, doubts, and fears, this life and glory of a Christian course is less perceived.

The sweet appropriating and applying works of faith, by which the soul can own his God, and finds itself owned by him, are exercised most easily and happily in these near approaches unto God. Our doubts are cherished by our darkness, and that is much caused by our distance: the nearer the soul approaches to God, the more distinctly it hears the voice of mercy, the sweet reconciling invitations of love; and the more clearly it discerns that goodness and amiableness in God which makes it easier to us to believe that he loves us, or is ready to embrace us; and banishes all those false and horrid apprehensions of him, which before were our discouragement, and made him seem to us more terrible than amiable. As the ministers and faithful servants of Christ, are ordinarily so misrepresented by the malignant devil, to those that knew them not, that they are ready to think them some silly fools, or false-hearted hypocrites, and to shun them as strange persons; but when they come to thorough acquaintance with them by a nearer and familiar converse, they see how much they were mistaken, and wronged by their prejudice and belief of slanderers' reports: even so a weak believer, who is under troubles, in the apprehension of his sin and danger, is apt to hearken to the enemy of God, that would show him nothing but his wrath, and represent God as an enemy to him: in this case it is exceedingly hard for a poor sinner to believe that God is reconciled to him, or loves him, or intends him good, but he is ready to dread and shun him as an enemy, or as he would fly from a wild beast or murderer, or from fire or water, that would destroy him: and all these injurious thoughts of God are cherished by strangeness and disaffection. But as the soul doth fall into an understanding and serious converse with God, and having been often with him, doth find him more merciful than he was by Satan represented to him, his experience reconciles his mind to God, and makes it much easier to him to believe that God is reconciled unto him, when he hath found much better entertainment with God than he expected, and hath observed his benignity, and the treasures of his bounty laid up in Christ, and by him distributed to believers, and hath found him ready to hear and help, and found him the only full and suitable felicitating good; this banishes his former horrid thoughts, and makes him ashamed that ever he should think so suspiciously, injuriously, and dishonourably of his dearest God and Father.

Yet I must confess that there are many upright, troubled souls, who are much in reading, prayer, and meditation, that still find it hard to be persuaded of the love of God, and that have much more disquietude and fear since they set themselves to think of God, than they had before: but yet for all this, we may well conclude, that to walk with God is the way to consolation, and tends to acquaint us with his love. As for those troubled souls, whose experience is objected against, some of them are such as are yet but in their return to God, from a life of former sin and misery, and are yet but like the needle in the compass that is shaken, in a trembling motion towards their rest, and not in any settled apprehensions of it. Some of them by the straying of their imaginations too high, and putting themselves upon more than their heads can bear, and by the violence of fears, or other passions, make themselves incapable of those sweet consolations which else they might find in their converse with God; as a lute, when the strings are broken with straining, is incapable of making any melody. All of them have false apprehensions of God, and therefore trouble themselves by their own mistakes. If some per-

plex themselves by their error, doth it follow that therefore the truth is not comfortable? Is not a Father's presence consolatory, because some children are afraid of their fathers, who know them not because of some disguise? Some of God's children walk so unevenly and carelessly before him, that their sins provoke him to hide his face, and to seem to reject them and disown them, and so to trouble them that he may bring them home: but shall the comforts of our Father's love and family be judged of by the fears or smart of those whom he is scourging for their disobedience, or their trial? Seek God with understanding, as knowing his essential properties, and what he will be to them that sincerely and diligently seek him; and then you will quickly have experience that nothing so much tends to quiet, and settle a doubting, troubled, unstable soul, as faithfully to walk with God.

But the soul that estranges itself from God, may indeed for a time have the quietness of security; but so far, it will be strange to the assurance of his love, and to true consolation. Expect not that God should follow you with his comforts in your sinfulness and negligence, and cast them into your hearts whilst you neither seek nor mind them: or that he will give you the fruit of his ways in your own ways. Will he be your joy when you forget him; will he delight your souls with his goodness and amiableness, while you are taken up with other matters, and think not of him? Can you expect to find the comforts of his family among his enemies out of doors? The experience of all the world can tell you, that prodigals, while they are straggling from their Father's house, do never taste the comfort of his embraces. The strangers meddle not with his children's joys: they grow not in the way of ambition, covetousness, vain-glory, or sensuality; but in the way of holy obedience, and of believing contemplations of the divine, everlasting objects of delight. 'For lo, they that are far from him shall perish: he destroys them that go awhoring from him: but it is good for us to draw nigh to God.'

Sect. III. Walking with God, is the only course that can prove and make men truly wise. It proves them wise that make so wise and good a choice, and are disposed and skilled in any measure for so high a work. Practical wisdom is the solid, useful, profitable, wisdom: practical wisdom is seen in our choice of good, and refusal of evil, as its most immediate and excellent effect. No choosing or refusing doth show the wisdom or folly of man so much as that which is about the greatest matters, and which everlasting life or death depend on. He is not thought so wise among men that can write a volume about the orthography or etymology of a word, or that can guess what wood the Trojan horse was made of, as he that can bring home gold and pearls, or he that can obtain and manage governments, or he that can cure mortal maladies: for as in lading we distinguish between bulk and value, and take not that for the best commodity which is of greatest quantity or weight, but that which is most precious and of greatest use: so there is a bulky knowledge extended far, to a multitude of words and things, which are all of no great use or value; and therefore the knowledge of them is such as they: there is a precious sort of knowledge, which fixes upon the most precious things; which being of greatest use and value, do accordingly prove the knowledge such. Nothing will prove a man simply and properly wise, but that which will prove or make him happy. He is wise indeed, that is wise to his own and others' good: and that is indeed his good, which saves his soul, and makes him for ever blessed. Though we may admire the cunning of those that can make the most curious engines, or by deceiving others, advance themselves, or that can subtilly dispute the most curious niceties, or criticize upon the words of several languages: yet I will never call them wise that are all that while the devil's slaves, the enemies of God, the refusers of grace, and are making haste to endless misery. I think there is not one of those in hell who were once the subtle men on earth, that now take themselves to have been truly wise, or glory much in the remembrance of such wisdom.

As the choice proves men wise, so the practice of this holy walking with God doth make them much wiser than they were. As there must be some work of the Spirit to draw men to believe in Christ, and yet the Spirit is promised and given, in a special sort or measure, to them that believe; so must there be some special wisdom to make men choose to walk with God; but much more is given to them in this holy course. As Solomon was wiser than most of the world, before he asked wisdom of God, or else he would not have made so wise a choice, and preferred wisdom before the riches and honours of the world; and yet it was a more notable degree of wisdom that was afterwards given him in answer to his prayer; so it is in this case.

There are many undeniable evidences to prove, that walking with God doth do more to make men truly wise, than all other learning or policy in the world.

1. He that walks with God, doth begin aright and settles upon a sure foundation: we use to say, that a work is half finished that is well begun: he hath engaged himself to the best and wisest teacher: he is a disciple to him that knows all things. He hath taken in infallible principles, and taken them in their proper place and order: he hath learned those truths which will every one become a teacher to him, and help him to that which is yet unlearned. Whereas many that thought they were doctors in Israel, if ever they will be wise and happy, must become fools, that is, such as they have esteemed fools, if ever they will be wise, and must be called back with Nicodemus to learn Christ's cross, and to be taught that 'that which is born of the flesh is but flesh,' and 'that which is born of the Spirit is Spirit:' and that therefore they 'must be born again,' not only of water, but also of the Spirit, if ever they 'will enter into the kingdom of heaven.' O miserable beginning! and miserable progress! when men that never soundly learned the mysteries of regeneration, faith, love, self-denial, and mortification, proceed to study names and words, and to turn over a multitude of books, to fill their minds with airy notions, and their common places with such sayings as may be provision and furniture for their pride and ostentation, and ornament to their style and language; and know not yet what they must do to be saved, and indeed know nothing as they ought to know! As every science hath its principles, which are supposed in all the consequent verities; so hath religion, as doctrinal and practical, those truths which must be first received, before any other can be received as it ought; and those things which must be first done, before any other can be done, so as to attain their ends. These truths and duties are principally about God himself, and are known and done effectually by those, and only those, that walk with God, or are devoted to him. It is a lamentable thing to see men immersed in serious studies, even till they grow aged, and to hear them seriously disputing and discoursing about the controversies or difficulties in theology, or inferior sciences, before ever they had any saving knowledge of God, or of the work of the Holy Ghost in the converting and sanctifying of the soul, or how to escape everlasting misery!

2. He that walks with God hath fixed upon a right end, and is renewing his estimation and intention of it, and daily prosecuting it: this is the first and greatest part of practical wisdom. When a man once knows his end aright, he may better judge of the aptitude and seasonableness

of all the means. When we know once that heaven contains the only felicity of man, it will direct us to heavenly thoughts, and to such spiritual means as are fitted to that end: if we have the right mark in our eye, we are more likely to level at it, than if we mistake our mark. He is the wise man, and only he, who hath steadily fixed his eye upon that blessedness which he was created and redeemed for, and makes straight towards it, and bends the powers of soul and body, by faithful, constant diligence, to obtain it. He who hath rightly and resolvedly determined of his end, hath virtually resolved a thousand controversies that others are unsatisfied and erroneous in; he that is resolved that his end is to please and glorify God, and to enjoy him for ever, is easily resolved whether a holy life, or a sensual and worldly, be the way: whether the way is to be godly, or to make a mock at godliness: whether covetousness and riches, ambition and preferment, voluptuousness and fleshly pleasures, be the means to attain his end: whether it will be attained rather by the studying of the word of God, and meditating on it day and night, and by holy conference, fervent prayer, and an obedient life; or by negligence, or worldliness, or drunkenness, or gluttony, or cards and dice, or beastly filthiness, or injustice and deceit. Know once, but whither it is that we are going, and it is easy to know whether the saint or the swaggerer, be in the way.

But a man that mistakes his end, is out of his way at the first step; and the further he goes, the further he is from true felicity; and the more he errs, and the further he hath to go back again, if ever he return. Every thing that a man doth in the world, which is not for the right end, the heavenly felicity, is an act of foolishness and error, how splendid soever the matter or the name may make it appear to ignorant men. Every word that an ungodly person speaks, being not for a right end, is in him but sin and folly, however materially it may be an excellent and useful truth. While a miserable soul hath his back upon God, and his face upon the world, every step he goes is an act of folly, as tending unto his further misery. It can be no act of wisdom, which tends to a man's damnation. When such a person begins to inquire and bethink him where he is, and whither he is going, and whither he should go, and to think of turning back to God, then, and never till then, he is beginning to come to himself, and to be wise. Till God and glory be the end that he aims at, and seriously bends his study, heart, and life to seek, though a man were searching into the mysteries of nature, though he were studying or discussing the notions of theology, though he were admired for his learning and wisdom by the world, and cried up as the oracle of the earth, he is all the while but playing the fool, and going a cleanlier way to hell than the grosser sinners of the world! For is he wise that knows not whether heaven or earth be better? Whether God or his flesh should be obeyed? Whether everlasting joys, or the transitory pleasures of sin, should be preferred? Or that seems to be convinced of the truth in these and such like cases, and yet hath not the wisdom to make his choice, and bend his life according to his conviction? He cannot be wise that practically mistakes his end.

3. He that walks with God knows those things with a deep, effectual, heart-changing knowledge, which other men know but superficially, by halves, and as in a dream. True wisdom consists in the intensiveness of the knowledge subjectively, as much as in the extensiveness of it objectively. To see a few things in a narrow room perspicuously and clearly, doth show a better eye-sight than in the open air to see many things obscurely, so as scarcely to discern any of them aright: like him that saw men walk like trees. The clearness and depth of knowledge, which makes it effectual to its proper use, is the greatness and excellency of it: therefore it is that unlearned men, who love and fear the Lord, may well be said to be incomparably more wise and knowing men than the most learned that are ungodly. As he hath more riches who hath a little gold or jewels, than he who hath many load of stones: so he who hath a deep effectual knowledge of God the Father, and the Redeemer, and of the life to come, is wiser and more knowing than he who hath only a notional knowledge of the same things, and of a thousand more. A wicked man hath so much knowledge, as teaches him to speak the same words of God, Christ, and heaven, which a true believer speaks; but not so much as to work in him the same affections and choice, nor so much as to cause him to do the same work. As it is a far more excellent kind of knowledge, which a man hath of any country by travel and habitation there, than that which comes but by reading or report, or which a man hath of meat, of fruits, of wines, by eating and drinking, than that which another hath by hearsay; so is the inward heart-affecting knowledge of a true believer, more excellent than the flashy notions of the ungodly. Truth, simply as truth, is not the highest and most excellent object of the mind: but good, as

good, must be apprehended by the understanding, and commended to the will, which entertains it with complacency, adheres to it with choice and resolution, prosecutes it with desire and endeavour, and enjoys it with delight. Though it be the understanding which apprehends it, yet it is the heart or will that relishes it, and tastes the greatest sweetness in it, working upon it with some mixture of internal sense, which hath made some ascribe a knowledge of good, as such, unto the will. It is the will's intention that causes the understanding to be denominated practical: therefore I may well say, that it is wisdom indeed when it reaches to the heart. No man knows the truth of God so well as he that most firmly believes him: no man knows the goodness of God so well as he that loves him most: no man knows his power and mercy so well as he that doth most confidently trust him: no man knows his justice and judgment so well as he that fears him: no man knows or believes the glory of heaven so well as he that most esteems, desires, and seeks it, and hath the most heavenly heart and conversation: no man believes in Jesus Christ so well, as he that gives up himself unto him, with the greatest love and thankfulness, trust, and obedience. As James saith 'show me thy faith by thy works,' so say I, Let me know the measure and value of my knowledge by my heart and life. That is wisdom indeed, which conforms a man to God, and saves his soul: this only will be owned as wisdom to eternity, when dreaming notions will prove but folly.

4. He that walks with God hath an infallible rule, and takes the right course to have the best acquaintance with it, and skill to use it. The doctrine that informs him is divine; it is from heaven, and not of men: therefore if God be wiser than man, he is able to make his disciples wisest; and teaching will more certainly and powerfully illuminate. Many among men have pretended to infallibility, that never could justify their pretensions, but have confuted them by their own mistakes and crimes: but none can deny the infallibility of God. He never yet was deceived, or did deceive; he errs not, nor teaches error: Nicodemus knew Christ was to be believed, when he knew that he was a teacher come from God. Christ knew that the Jews themselves durst not deny the truths of John's doctrine, if he could but convince them that it was 'from heaven, and not of men.' 'It is impossible for God to lie:' it is the devil that was a liar from the beginning, and is yet the father of lies. No wonder if they believe lies that follow

such a teacher. Those that follow the flesh and the world, do follow the devil: they that will believe what their fleshly interests and lusts persuade them to believe, do believe what the devil persuades them to believe; for he persuades them by these, and for these. What marvel then, if there be found men in the world, that can believe that holiness is hypocrisy, or a needless thing;—that those are the worst men that are most careful to please God;—that the world is more worthy of their care and labour, than their salvation is;—that the pleasures of sin for a season are more desirable, than the everlasting happiness of the saints; that cards, dice, mirth, lust, wealth, and honour, are matters more delectable than prayer, and meditating on the word of God, and loving him, and obeying him, and waiting in the hope of life eternal; that gluttons, and drunkards, and whoremongers, and covetous persons, may enter into the kingdom of God, &c. What wonder, if a thousand such lies are believed by the disciples of the father of lies! What wonder, if there are so many haters of God in the world, as to fill the earth with persecutions and cruelties, or make a scorn of that which God most highly values; and all this under pretence of order, or unity, or justice, or something that is good, and therefore fit to palliate their sin! Is there any thing so false, or foul, or wicked, that Satan will not teach his followers? Is he grown modest, or moderate, or holy, or just? Is he reconciled to Christ, to scripture, to godliness, or to the godly? Or is his kingdom of darkness at an end? And hath he lost the earth? Or are men therefore none of the servants of the devil, because they were baptized, as Simon Magus was, and call and think themselves the servants of Christ? As if still it were not the art by which he gets and keeps disciples, to suffer them to wear the livery of Christ, and to use his name, that he may thus keep possession of them in peace, who else would be frighted from him, and fly to Christ!

He will give them leave to study arts and sciences, and to understand things excellent of inferior use, so be it they will be deceived by him in the matters of God and their salvation. He can allow them to be learned lawyers, excellent physicians, philosophers, politicians, to be skilful artists, so be it they will follow him in sin to their ruin, and will overlook the truth that should set them free. Yea he will permit them where there is no remedy, to study the holy scriptures, if he may but be the expounder and applier of it: yea, he will permit them notionally to understand it, if they will not learn by it to be converted, to be holy, and to be saved: he can suffer them to be eminent divines, so they will not be serious Christians. Thus is the world by the grand deceiver hurried in darkness to perdition, being taken captive by him at his will. But the sanctified are all illuminated by the Holy Ghost, by whom their eyes are so effectually opened, that they 'are turned from darkness unto light, and from the power of Satan unto God.'—' The Father of glory hath given them the Spirit of wisdom and revelation, in the knowledge of Christ, that the eyes of their understanding being enlightened, they may know what is the hope of his calling, and what the riches of the glory of his inheritance in the saints.' Certainly that illumination of the Holy Ghost, which is so often mentioned in scripture as given to all true believers, is not a fancy, nor an insignificant name: if it signifies any thing, it signifies somewhat that is much above the teaching of man. All that walk with God are taught of God. Can man teach like God? God hath access unto the heart, and there he doth transcribe his laws, and put them into our inward parts. They that walk with him have not only his word to read, but his Spirit to help them to understand it: and being with him in his family, yea, he dwells in them, and they in him; he is ready at hand to resolve their doubts: when he gave them his fear, he gave them the beginning of wisdom. He causes them to incline their ear to wisdom, and to apply their hearts unto it, and makes them to know it in the hidden parts.

It is his law that they have determined to make their rule; they live as under his authority: they are more observant of his will and government, than of any laws or government of man. As they obey man in and for the Lord, so they do it in subordination to him, and therefore not against him and his laws, which being the standard of justice, and the rule of rulers, and of subjects both, they are in the safest way of unerring wisdom, who walk with God according to that rule, and refuse to turn aside, though commanded by man, or enticed by Satan, the world, or the flesh.

5. He that walks with God is the most considerate person, and therefore hath great advantage to be wise. The frequent and serious thoughts of God, awaken all the powers of the soul, so that drowsiness doth not hinder the understanding, and so occasion its deceit: there is scarcely a more common and powerful cause of men's folly, delusion, and perdition, in all the world, than that sleepiness and stupidity which hinders reason from the vigorous performance of its office: in this senseless case, though a man both know and consider of the same truths, which in their nature are most powerful to cleanse and govern and save his soul, yet sluggishness doth enervate them: he knows them as if he knew them not, and considers them as if he never thought of them: they work little more upon him, than if he believed them not, or had never heard of them: even as a dream of the greatest matters moves not the sleeper from his pillow: in this senseless state the devil can do almost any thing with a sinner: he can make him sin against his knowledge: when conscience hath frightened him into some kind of penitence, and made him cry out, I have sinned and done foolishly, and caused him to promise to do so no more; yet doth the devil prevail with him to go on and to break his promises, as if he had never been convinced of his sins, or confessed them, or seen any reason or necessity to amend: he doth but imprison the truth in unrighteousness, and bury it in a senseless heart: whereas if you could but awaken all the powers of his soul, to give this same truth its due entertainment, and take it deeper into his heart, it would make him even scorn the baits of sin, and see that the ungodly are beside themselves, and make him presently resolve and set upon a holy life. Hence it is, that sickness which causes men to receive the sentence of death, doth usually make men bewail their former sinful lives, and marvel that they could be before so sottish as to resist such known and weighty truths: and it makes them purpose and promise reformation, and wish themselves in the case of those that they were wont before to deride and scorn: because now the truth is more deeply received and digested, by their awakened souls, and appears in its proper evidence and strength. There is no man but must acknowledge, that the same truth doth at one time command his soul, which at another time seems of little force: it is a wonder to observe how differently the same consideration works with a man when he is awakened, and when he is in a secure, stupid state.

Now this is his advantage that walks with God: he is much more frequently than others awakened to a serious apprehension of the things which he understands: the thoughts of the presence of the most holy God, will not suffer him to be secure and senseless as others are, or as he is himself, when he turns aside from this heavenly conversation. He hath in God such exceeding transcendent excellencies, such greatness, such goodness, continually to behold, that it keeps his soul in a much more serious, lively frame, than any other means could keep it in: so that whenever any truth or duty is presented to him, all his faculties are awake and ready to observe and improve it. A sermon, or a good book, or godly conference, or a mercy, when a man hath been with God in prayer and contemplation, will relish better with him, and sink much deeper, than at another time. Nay, one serious thought of God himself, will do more to make a man truly and solidly wise, than all the reading and learning in the world, which shuts him out.

6. Walking with God doth fix the mind, and keep it from diversions and vagaries, and consequently much helpeth to make men wise. A struggling mind is empty and unfurnished. He that hath no dwelling, for the most part hath no wealth. Wandering is the beggar's life. Men do but bewilder and lose themselves, and not grow wise, whose thoughts are ranging in the corners of the earth, and are like masterless dogs, that run up and down according to their fancy, and may go any whither, but have business no where. · The creature will not fix the soul: but God is the centre of all our thoughts: in him only they may unite, fix, and rest. He is the only loadstone that can effectually attract and hold it stedfast to himself. Therefore he that walks with God is the most constant and unmovable of men: let prosperity or adversity come ; let the world be turned upside down, and the mountains be hurled into the sea, yet he changes not : let men allure or threat, let them scorn or rage, let laws, customs, government, and interest change, he is still the same. For he knows that God is still the same, and that his word changes not. Let that be death one year, which was the way to reputation another, and let the giddy world turn about as the seasons of the year, this changes not his mind and life, though in things lawful he is of a yielding temper: for he knows that the interest of his soul doth not change with the humours or interests of men : he still fears sinning, for he knows that judgment is still drawing on, in all changes and seasons whatsoever : he is still set upon the pleasing of the most holy God, whoever be uppermost among men ; as knowing that the God whom he serves is able to deliver him from man, but man is not able to deliver him from God. He still goes on in the holy path, as knowing that heaven is as sure and as desirable as ever it was. ' Surely he shall not be moved for ever : the righteous shall be in everlasting remembrance : he shall not be afraid of evil tidings : his heart is fixed, trusting in the Lord : his heart is established, he shall not be afraid.'

7. He that walks with God, hath the great master-truths upon his heart which are the standard of the rest, and the stock, as it were, out of which they spring. The great truths about God, grace, and glory, have a greater power than many hundred truths of an inferior nature. Moreover, such a one is sure that he shall be wise in the greatest and most necessary points. He is guilty of no ignorance or error that shall keep him out of heaven, or hinder his acceptance with his God. If he be wise enough to please God and to be saved, he is wise indeed, as before was hinted.

8. Walking with God doth take off the vizor of deluding things, and keeps us out of the reach and power of those objects and arguments which are the instruments of deceit. When a man hath been believingly and seriously with God, how easily can he see through the sophistry of the tempting world ! How easily can he practically confute the reasonings of the flesh ! and discern the dotage of the seeming subtleties of wicked men, that will needs think they have reason for that which is displeasing to their Maker, and tends to the damning of their souls ! So far as a man is conversant with God, so far he is sensible that all things are nothing, which can be offered as a price to hire him to sin: that the name of preferment, honour, and wealth, or of disgrace, imprisonment, and death, are words almost of no signification, as to the tempter's ends, to draw the soul from God and duty. It is men that know not God, and know not what it is to walk with him, that think these words so big and powerful, to whom wealth and honour do signify more than God and heaven ; and poverty, disgrace and death, do signify more than God's displeasure and everlasting punishment in hell. As it is easy to cheat a man that is far from the light, so is it easy to deceive the most learned man that is far from God.

9. Walking with God, doth greatly help us against the deceitful and erroneous disposition of our own hearts. The will hath a very great power upon the understanding : therefore ungodly, fleshly men will very hardly receive any truth which crosses the carnal interest or disposition: and will hardly let go any error that feeds them: because their corrupted wills are a bias to their understandings, and make them desperately partial in all their reading and hearing, and hypocritical in their prayers and inquiries after truth. Interest and corruption lock up their hearts from their own observation. Whereas a man that walks with God, who is jealous, holy, and just, and a searcher of the heart.

is driven from hypocrisy, and forced to behave himself as in the open light, and to do all as in the sight of all the world, as knowing that the sight of God is of far greater concern and regard. The partiality, corruption and bias of the heart, are detected and shamed by the presence of God. Therefore to walk with God is to walk in the light, and as children of the light, and not in darkness. He that doth ' truth cometh to the light, that his deeds might be manifest, that they are wrought in God : when every one that doth evil hateth the light, neither comes to the light, lest his deeds should be reproved : this is their condemnation, that light is come into the world, and men love the darkness rather than the light, because their deeds are evil.' It tends therefore exceedingly to make men wise, to walk with God, because it is a ' walking in the light,' and in such a presence as most powerfully prevails against that hypocrisy, deceitfulness and partiality of the heart, which is the common cause of destructive error.

10. Lastly, they that walk with God are entitled by many promises, to the guidance and direction of his Spirit. Blessed are those that have such a guide : at once a light in the world without them, and a light immediately from God within them : for so far as he is received and works in them, he will lead them into truth, and save them from deceit and folly, and having ' guided them by his counsel, will afterward take them unto glory.' Whereas the ungodly are led by the flesh, and often 'given up to their own hearts' lusts, to walk in their own counsel,' till at last ' the fools do say in their hearts, There is no God, and they become corrupt and abominable, eating up the people of the Lord as bread, and call not on his name.'—' Deceiving and being deceived ; sensual, having not the Spirit, who shall receive the reward of their unrighteousness, as accounting it pleasure to riot in the day time.'

SECT. IV. Another benefit of walking with God, is, that it makes men good, as well as wise : it is the most excellent means for the advancement of man's soul to the highest degree of holiness attainable in this life. If conversing with good men doth powerfully tend to make men good; conversing with God must needs be more effectual ; which may appear in these particulars.

1. The apprehensions of the presence and attributes of God, do most effectually check the stirrings of corruption, and rebuke all the vicious inclinations and motions of the soul : even the most secret sin of the heart, is rebuked by his presence,

as well as the most open transgression of the life : for the thoughts of the heart are open to his view. All that is done before God, is done as in the open light : nothing of it can be hid : no sin can have the encouragement of secrecy to embolden it. It is all committed in the presence of the universal king and lawgiver of the world, who hath forbidden it : it is done before him that most abhors it, and will never be reconciled to it. It is done before him that is the judge of the world, and will shortly pass the sentence on us according to what we have done in the body. It stands up in his presence who is of infinite majesty and perfection, and therefore most to be reverenced and honoured ; therefore if the presence of a wise, grave, and venerable person, will restrain men from sin, the presence of God, apprehended seriously, will do it much more. It is committed before him that is our dearest friend, tender father, and chief benefactor : therefore ingenuity, gratitude and love, will all rise up against it in those that walk with God. There is that in God, before the eyes of those that walk with him, which is most contrary to sin, and most powerful against it, of any thing in the world. Every one will confess, that if men's eyes were opened to see the Lord in glory standing over them, it would be the most powerful means to restrain them from transgressing : the drunkard would not then venture upon his cups : the fornicator would have a cooling for his lusts : the swearer would be afraid to take his Maker's name in vain : the profane would scarce presume to scorn or persecute a holy life. He that walks with God, though he see him not corporally, yet sees him by faith, and lives as in his presence ; and therefore must needs be restrained from sin, as having the means which is next to the sight of God. If pride should begin to stir in one that walks with God, O what a powerful remedy is at hand ! How effectually would the presence of the great and holy God rebuke it ; and constrain us to say, ' I have heard of thee by the hearing of the ear ; but now mine eye seeth thee ; wherefore I abhor myself, and repent in dust and ashes.' If worldly love, or carnal lust, should stir in such a one, how powerfully would the terrors of the Lord repress it ; and his majesty rebuke it ; and his love and goodness overcome it ? If worldly cares or murmuring discontents begin to trouble such a one, how effectually will the goodness, the all-sufficiency and the faithfulness of God allay them, and quiet and satisfy the soul, and cause it to be offended at its own offence, and to chide itself for its repinings and distrust ? If passion arise and begin to discompose us; how powerfully will the presence of God rebuke it? and the reverence of his majesty, and the sense of his authority and pardoning grace will assuage it, and shame us into silent quietness; who dare let out his passions upon man, in the presence of his Maker, that apprehends his presence? The same I might say of all other sins.

2. The presence and attributes of God apprehended by those that walk with him, is the potent remedy against temptations. Who will once turn an eye to the gold and glory of the world, that is offered him to allure to sin, if he see God stand by; who would be tempted to lust or any sinful pleasure, if he observe the presence of the Lord? Satan can never come in so ill a time with his temptations, and have so little hope to speed, as when the soul is contemplating the attributes of God, or taken up in prayer with him, or any way apprehensive of his presence. The soul that faithfully walks with God, hath enough at hand in him to answer all temptations. The further any man is from God, and the less he knows him, the more temptations can do upon him.

3. The presence of God, affords the most powerful motives unto good, to those that walk with him. There is no grace in man, but is from God, and may find in God its proper object or incentive. As God is God, above the creature transcendently and infinitely in all perfections, so all the motives to goodness which are drawn from him, are transcendently above all that may be brought from any creature. He that lives always by the fire, or in the sun-shine, is likeliest to be warm. He that is most with God, will be most like to God in holiness. Frequent and serious converse with him, doth most deeply imprint his communicable attributes on the heart, and make there the clearest impression of his image. Believers have learned by their own experience, that one hour's serious prayer, or meditation, in which they can get nigh to God in the spirit, doth more advance their grace, than any help that the creature can afford them.

4. Moreover, those that walk with God, have not only a powerful, but an universal incentive for the actuating and increasing of every grace. Knowledge, faith, fear, love, trust, hope, obedience, and zeal, and all have in God their proper objects and incentives: one creature may be useful to us in one thing, and another in another thing; but God is the most effectual mover of all his graces: and that in a holy harmony and order. Indeed he hath no greater motive to draw us to love him, fear him, trust

him, and obey him, than himself. It is life eternal to know him in his Son, and that is, not only because it entitles to life eternal, but also because it is the beginning and incentive of that life of holiness which will be eternal.

5. Moreover, those that walk with God, have a constant as well as a powerful and universal incentive to exercise and increase their graces. Other helps may be out of the way: their preachers may be silenced or removed: their friends may be scattered or taken from them: their books may be forbidden, or not at hand: but God is always ready and willing: they have leave at all times to come to him, and be welcome. Whenever they are willing they may go to him by prayer or contemplation, and find all in him which they can desire. If they want not hearts, they shall find no want of any thing in God. At what time soever fear would torment them, they may draw near and put their trust in him. He will be a sure and speedy refuge for them, a very present help in trouble. Whenever coldness or lukewarmness would extinguish the work of grace, they may go to him, and find those streams of flaming love flow from him, those strong attractives, those wonderful mercies, those terrible judgments, of which, while they are musing, the fire may again wax hot within them.

6. Lastly, by way of encouraging reward, God uses to give abundantly of his grace, to those that walk most faithfully with him: he will show most love to those that most love him: he will be nearest to them that most desirously draw nigh to him; while he forsakes those that forsake him, and turns away from those that turn away from him. ' The hand of our God is for good upon all them that seek him: but his power and his wrath is against all them that forsake him.'

Thus it is apparent in all these evidences, that walking with God is not only a discovery of the goodness that men have, but the only way to increase their grace, and make them better. O what a sweet humility, seriousness, and spirituality appears in the conference, or conversation, or both, of those that newly come from a believing close converse with God; when they that come from men and books, may have but a common mind or life! Those that come from the business and pleasure of the world and flesh, and from the company of foolish, riotous gallants, may come defiled, as the swine out of the mire.

SECT. V. Lastly, to walk with God, is the best preparation for times of suffering, and for the day of death. As we must be judged according to what we have done in the body: so the nearer we find ourselves to judgment, the more we shall be constrained to judge ourselves according to what we have done, and shall the more perceive the effect upon our souls.

That this is so excellent a preparative for sufferings and death, will appear by the consideration of these particulars.

1. They that walk with God are safest from all destructive sufferings; and shall have none but what are sanctified to their good. They are near to God, where destruction comes not: as the chicken under the wings of the hen: they walk with him that will not lead them to perdition: that will not neglect them, nor sell them for nought, nor expose them to the will of men and devils, though he may suffer them to be tried for their good. No one can take them out of his hands. Be near to him, and you are safe: the destroyer cannot draw you thence. He can draw you, when the time is come, from the side of your merriest companions, and dearest friends; from the presence of the greatest princes; from the strongest tower, or most sumptuous palace, or from your heaps of riches, in your securest health: but he cannot take you from the arms of Christ, nor from under the wings of your Creator's love. 'For there is no God like him, in heaven above, or on the earth beneath, who keeps covenant and mercy with his servants, that walk before him with all their heart.' However we are used in our Father's presence, we are sure it shall be for good in the latter end: for he wants neither power nor love to deliver us, if he saw deliverance to be best.

2. Walking with God is the surest way to obtain a certainty of his special love, and of our salvation: what an excellent preparative for sufferings or death such assurance is, I need not tell any considerate believer. How easy may it be to us to suffer poverty, disgrace or wrongs, or the pains of sickness or death, when once we are certain that we shall not suffer the pains of hell! How cheerfully may we go out of this troublesome world, and leave the greatest prosperity behind us, when we are sure to live in heaven for ever! Even an infidel will say, that he could suffer or die, if he could but be certain to be glorified in heaven when he is dead.

3. Walking with God doth mortify the flesh, and all the affections and lusts thereof: the soul that is taken up with higher matters, and daily sees things more excellent, becomes as dead to the things below: thus it weans us from all that in the world which seems most desirable to carnal men. When the flesh is mortified, and the

world is nothing to us, or but as a dead and lothesome body, what is there left to be very troublesome in any suffering from the world, or to make us loth by death to leave it? It is men that know not God, that overvalue the profits and honours of the world; and men that never felt the comforts of communion with God, that set too much by the pleasures of the flesh: and it is men that set too much by these, that make so great a matter of suffering. It is he that basely overvalues wealth, that whines and repines when he comes to poverty: it is he that sets too much by his honour, and being befooled by his pride, doth greatly esteem the thoughts or applauding words of men, that swells against those that disesteem him, and breaks his heart when he falls into disgrace. He that is cheated of his wits by the pomp and splendour of a high and prosperous estate, doth think he is undone when he is brought low. But it is not so with him that walks with God: for being taken up with far higher things, he knows the vanity of these: as he sees not in them any thing that is worthy of his strong desires, so neither any thing that is worthy of much lamentation when they are gone. He never thought that a shadow, or feather, or a blast of wind, could make him happy: and he cannot think that the loss of these can make him miserable. He that is taken up with God, hath a higher interest and business, and finds not himself so much concerned in the storms or calms, that are here below, as others are, who know no better, and never minded higher things.

4. Walking with God doth much overcome the fear of man: the fear of him that can destroy both soul and body in hell fire, will extinguish the fear of them that can but kill the body. The threats or frowns of a worm are inconsiderable to him that daily walks with the great and dreadful God, and hath his power and word for his security. As 'Moses esteemed the reproach of Christ greater riches than the treasures of Egypt, because he had respect to the recompense of reward; so he feared not the wrath of the king, for he endured as seeing him that is invisible.'

5. Walking with God doth much prepare for sufferings and death, in that it promotes quietness in the conscience: so that when all is at peace within, it will be easy to suffer any thing from without. Though there is no proper merit in our works to comfort us, yet it is an unspeakable consolation to a slandered persecuted man to be able to say, 'These evil sayings are spoken falsely of me, for the sake of Christ: and I suffer not as an evil doer, but as a Christian.

It is matter of very great peace to a man that is hasting unto death, to be able to say as Hezekiah, 'remember now, O Lord, how I have walked before thee in truth, and with a perfect heart, and have done that which is good in thy sight :' and as Paul, 'I have fought a good fight, I have finished my course, I have kept the faith: henceforth there is laid up for me a crown of righteousness.'—'For our rejoicing is this, the testimony of our conscience, that in simplicity and godly sincerity, not with fleshly wisdom, but by the grace of God, we have had our conversation in the world.' Such a testimony of conscience is a precious cordial to a suffering or a dying man : the time we have spent in a holy and heavenly conversation, will be exceedingly sweet in the last review, when time spent in sinful vanity, idleness, and in worldly and fleshly designs, will be grievous and tormenting. The day is coming, and is even at hand, when those that are now the most hardened infidels, or obstinate presumptuous sinners, or scornful malicious enemies of holiness, would wish and wish a thousand times, that they had spent that life in a serious, obedient walking with God, which they spent in seeking worldly wealth, and laying up a treasure on earth, and feeding the inordinate desires of their flesh. I tell you, it is walking with God, that is the only way to have a sound and quiet conscience : he that is healing and settling his conscience upon the love of God and the grace of Christ, in the time of prosperity, is making the wisest preparation for adversity : the preparation thus made so long before, perhaps twenty, or forty, or threescore years or more, is as truly useful and comfortable at a dying hour, as that part which is made immediately before. I know that besides this general preparation, there should be also a particular special preparation for sufferings and death ; but yet this general part is the chief and most necessary part. A man that hath walked in his life-time with God, shall certainly be saved, though death surprise him unexpectedly, without any more particular preparation : but a particular preparation without either such a life, or such a heart as would cause it if he had recovered, is no sufficient preparation at all, and will not serve to any man's salvation. Alas ! what a pitiful provision doth that man make for death and for salvation, who neglects his soul, despises the commands of God, and disregards the promises of eternal life, till he is ready to die, and then cries out, 'I repent, I am sorry for my sin, I would I had lived better,' and this only from the constraint of fear, without any such love to God and holiness which would make him

walk with God if he should recover ! What if the priest absolve this man from all his sins ? Doth God therefore absolve him ? Or shall he thus be saved ? No, it is certain that all the sacraments and absolutions in the world will never serve to save such a soul, without that grace which must make it new and truly holy.

Nay, if you have not walked with God in the Spirit, but walked after the flesh, though your repentance should be sound and true at the last, it will yet very hardly serve to comfort you, though it may serve to your salvation : because you will very hardly get any assurance that it is sincere. It is dangerous lest it should prove but the effect of fear, which will not save, when it comes not till death fright you to it.

6. Moreover, to walk with God is an excellent preparation for sufferings and death, because it tends to acquaint the soul with God, and to embolden it both to go to him in prayer, and to trust on him, and expect salvation from him. He that walks with God is so much used to holy prayer, that he is a man of prayer, and is skilled in it, and hath tried what prayer can do with God : so that in the hour of his extremity, he is not to seek, either for a God to pray to, or a mediator to intercede for him, or a spirit of adoption to enable him as a child to fly for help to his reconciled Father. Having not only been frequently with God, but frequently entertained and accepted by him, and had his prayers heard and granted, it is a great encouragement to an afflicted soul in the hour of distress, to go to such a God for help. And it is a dreadful thing when a soul is ready to go out of the world, to have no comfortable knowledge of God, or skill to pray to him, or encouragement to expect acceptance with him : to think that he must presently appear before a God whom he never knew, nor heartily loved, being never acquainted with that communion with him, in the way of grace, which is the way to communion in glory, O what a terrible thought is this ! But how comfortable is it when the soul can say, 'I know whom I have believed ? The God that afflicts me is he that loves me, and hath manifested his love to me by his daily attractive, assisting and accepting grace ! I am going by death to see him intuitively, whom I have often seen by the eye of faith, and to live with him in heaven, with whom I lived here on earth ; from whom, and through whom, and to whom was my life ! I go not to an enemy, nor an utter stranger, but to that God who was the spring, the ruler, the guide, the strength, and the comfort of my life. He hath heard me so often, that I cannot

think he will now reject me : he hath so often comforted my soul, that I will not believe he will now thrust me into hell : he hath mercifully received me so often, that I cannot believe he will now refuse me : those that come to him in the way of grace, I have found he will in no wise cast out. As strangeness to God doth fill the soul with distrusting fears, so walking with him breeds that humble confidence which is a wonderful comfort in the hour of distress, and a happy preparation to sufferings and death.'

7. Lastly, to walk with God, doth increase the love of God in the soul, which is the heavenly tincture, and inclines it to look upward, and being weary of a sinful flesh and world, to desire to be perfected with God. How happy a preparation for death is this, when it is but the passage to that God with whom we desire to be, and to that place where we would dwell for ever! To love the state and place that we are going to, being made connatural and suitable thereto, will much overcome the fears of death. But for a soul that is acquainted with nothing but this life, and savours nothing but earth and flesh, and hath no co-naturality with the things above, for such a soul to be surprised with the tidings of death, alas, how dreadful must it be!

Thus I have showed you the benefits that come by walking with God, which if you love yourselves with a rational love, methinks should resolve every impartial, considerate reader, to give up himself without delay, to so desirable a course of life! Or, if he have begun it, to follow it more cheerfully and faithfully than he had done.

CHAP. VII.

DUTY OF WALKING WITH GOD, AND THE DANGER OF NEGLECTING IT.

I am next to show you that believers have special obligations to this holy course of life, and therefore are doubly faulty, if they neglect it : though indeed, to neglect it totally, or in the main drift of their lives, is a thing inconsistent with a living faith.

Consider, 1. If you are true Christians, your relations engage you to walk with God : is he not your reconciled Father, and you his children in a special sense? Whom should children dwell with, but with their Father? You were glad when he received you into his covenant that he would enter into so near a relation to you, as he expresses, 'I will receive you, and will be a father to you, and ye shall be my sons

and daughters, saith the Lord almighty.' Do you draw back, as if you repented of your covenant ; and were not only weary of the duty, but of the privileges and benefits of your relation? You may have access to God, when others are shut out : your prayers may be heard, when the prayers of the wicked are abominable : you may be welcome when the worldlings, ambitious, and carnal are despised : he that dwells in the highest heaven, is willing to look to you with respect, and dwell with you, when he beholds the proud afar off. Yet will you not come that may be welcome? Doth he put such a difference between you and others, as to feed you as children at his table, while others are called dogs, and are without the doors, and have but your crumbs, and yet will you be so foolish and unthankful, as to run out of your Father's presence, and choose to be without, among the dogs? How came your Father's presence to be so grievous to you; and the privileges of his family to seem so vile? Is it not some unchildlike carriage ; the guilt of some disobedience or contempt that hath first caused this? Or have you fallen again in love with fleshly pleasures, and some vanity of the world? Or have you had enough of God and godliness, till you begin to grow weary of him? If so, you never truly knew him. However it be, if you grow as indifferent to God, do not wonder if shortly you find him set as light by you : believe it, the day is not far off, in which the fatherly relation of God, and the privileges of children, will be more esteemed by you : when all things else forsake you in your last distress, you will be loth that God should then forsake you, or seem as a stranger to hide his face : then you will cry out, as the afflicted church, 'look down from heaven, and behold from the habitation of thy holiness and of thy glory : where is thy zeal and thy strength; the sounding of thy bowels, and of thy mercies towards me ; are they restrained? Doubtless thou art our Father : though Abraham be ignorant of us, and Israel acknowledge us not, thou, O Lord, art our Father, our Redeemer ; thy name is from everlasting.'

Nothing but God, and his fatherly relation, will then support you : attend him therefore, and with reverent, obedient cheerfulness and delight, converse with him as with your dearest father. For since the beginning of the world, men have not known by sensible evidence, either of the ear or the eye, besides God himself, what he hath prepared for him that waits for him Though he be ' wroth with us because we have sinned, yet doth he meet him that rejoices and works righteousness, that remembers him in his ways.' Say not, I have played abroad so long that I dare not now go home: I have sinned so greatly, that I dare not speak to him, or look him in the face. Come yet but with a penitent, returning heart, and thou mayest be accepted through the Prince of peace: prodigals find better entertainment than they did expect, when once they do but resolve for home. If he allow us to begin with ' our Father which art in heaven,' we may boldly proceed to ask 'forgiveness of our trespasses,' and whatever else is truly good for us. But, alas, as our iniquities seduce us away from God, so the guilt of them affrights some from returning to him, and the love of them corrupts the hearts of others, and makes them too indifferent as to their communion with him; so that too many of his children live as if they did not know their Father, or had forgotten him: we may say, ' but we are all as an unclean thing, and all our righteousnesses are as filthy rags, and we all do fade as a leaf, and our iniquities like the wind have taken us away: and there is none that calls upon thy name, that stirs up himself to take hold of thee; for thou hast hid thy face from us, and hast consumed us because of our iniquities; but now, O Lord, thou art our Father; we are the clay, and thou our potter, and we are all the work of thy hand. Be not wroth very sore, O Lord, neither remember iniquity for ever: behold, see we beseech thee, we are all thy people.' O do not provoke your Father to disown you, or to withdraw his help, or 'hide his face, or to send the rod to call you home! for if you do, you will wish you had known the privileges of his presence, and had kept nearer to him! Be not so unnatural, so unthankful, so unkind, as to be weary of your Father's presence, and such a Father too, and to take more delight in any other.

Moreover, you are related to God in Christ as a wife unto a husband, as to covenant union, and nearness and dearness of affection, and as to his tender care of you for your good: is it seemly, is it wisely or gratefully done of you, to desire rather the company of others, and delight in creatures more than him? How affectionately doth thy Maker call himself the husband of his people? Can thy heart commit adultery, and forsake him: ' my covenant they brake, though I was an husband to them, saith the Lord.' O put not God to exercise his jealousy. It is one of his terrible attributes, to be a jealous God. Can he be otherwise to thee, when thou lovest not his converse or company, and carest not how long thou art from him in the world? Woe to

thee if he once say as in Hos. ii. 2. 'she is not my wife, neither am I her husband.'

Nay, more than this, if you are Christians, you are ' members of the body of Christ.' Therefore how can you withdraw yourselves from him, and not feel the pain and torment of so sore a wound or dislocation? You cannot live without a constant dependence on him, and communication from him, ' I am the true vine, and my father is the husbandman: abide in me, and I in you. I am the vine, ye are the branches: he that abides in me, and I in him, the same brings forth much fruit: for without me ye can do nothing. If ye abide in me, and my words abide in you, ye shall ask what ye will, and it shall be done unto you.'

So near are you to Christ, that he delights to acquaint you with his secrets: O how many mysteries doth he reveal to those that walk with him, which carnal strangers never know! Mysteries of wisdom! Mysteries of love and saving grace! Mysteries of scripture, and mysteries of providence! Mysteries felt by inward experience, and mysteries revealed, foreseen by faith! Not only the strangers that pass by the doors, but even the common servants of the family, are unacquainted with the secret operations of the Spirit, and entertainments of grace, and joy in believing, which those that walk with God either do or may possess. Therefore Christ calls you friends, as being more than servants. ' Ye are my friends, if ye do whatsoever I command you. Henceforth I call you not servants; for the servant knows not what his Lord doth: but I have called you friends; for all things that I have heard of my Father, I have made known unto you.' It is true for all this, that every true Christian hath reason to complain of his darkness and distance from God. Alas, they know so little of him, and of the mysteries of his love and kingdom, that sometimes they are apt to think that they are indeed but utter strangers to him: but this is, because there is infinitely more still unknown to them than they know. What! can the silly shallow creature comprehend his infinite Creator? Or shall we know all that is to be known in heaven, before we enjoy all that is to be enjoyed in heaven? It is no more wonder to hear a believer pant and mourn after a fuller knowledge of God, and nearer access to him, than to seek after heaven, where this will be his happiness. But yet, though his knowledge of God be small, compared with his ignorance, that little knowledge of God which he hath attained, is more mysterious, sublime and excellent, than all the learning of the greatest unsanctified scholars in the world. Walk with him according to the nearness of your relations to him, and you shall have this excellent knowledge of his mysteries, which no books or teachers alone can give. You shall be effectually touched at the heart with the truths which others do ineffectually hear: you shall be powerfully moved, when they are but ineffectually exhorted. When they only hear the voice without them, you shall hear the voice within you, and as it were behind you, saying, This is the way, walk in it. O that you could duly value such a friend, to watch over you, and for you, and dwell in you, and tell you faithfully of every danger, and of every duty, and teach you to know good and evil, and what to choose, and what to refuse; how closely and delightfully would you converse with such a blessed friend, if you rightly valued him.

2. Moreover, you that are the servants of God, have by your covenant and profession, renounced and forsaken all things else, as they stand in any opposition to him, or competition with him, and have resigned yourselves wholly unto him alone: therefore with him must you converse, and be employed, unless you will forsake your covenant. You knew first that it was your interest to forsake the world and turn to God: you knew the world would not be instead of God to you, either in life, or at death: upon this knowledge it was that you changed your master, changed your minds, and changed your way, your work, your hopes: do you dream now that you were mistaken? Do you begin to think that the world is fitter to be your God or happiness? If not, you must still confess that both your interest and your covenant oblige you to turn your hearts and minds from the things which you have renounced, and to walk with him that you have taken for your God, and to obey him whom you have taken for your king and judge, and to keep close to him with purest love, whom you have taken for your everlasting portion. Mark what you are minding all the day, while you are neglecting God: is it not something that you have renounced? Did you not renounce it upon sufficient cause? Was it not a work of your most serious deliberation; and of as great wisdom, as any that ever you performed; if it were, turn not back in your hearts again from God unto the renounced creature. You have had many a lightning from heaven in to your understandings, to bring you to see the difference between them: you have had many a teaching, and many a warning, and many a striving of the Spirit, before you were prevailed with to renounce the world, the flesh and the devil, and to give up yourself entirely and absolutely so God. Nay, did it not cost you the smart of some afflictions, before you would be made so wise? Did it not cost you many a gripe of conscience, and many a terrible thought of hell, and of the wrath of God, before you would be heartily engaged to him, in his covenant? Will you now live as strangely and neglectfully towards him, as if those days were quite forgotten; and as if you had never felt such things; and as if you had never been so convinced or resolved? O Christians, take heed of forgetting your former case! your former thoughts, your former convictions, complaints, and covenants! God did not work all that upon your hearts to be forgotten: he intended not only your present change, but your after remembrance of it, for your close adhering to him while you live; and for your quickening and constant perseverance to the end. The forgetting of their former miseries, and the workings of God upon their hearts in their conversion, is a great cause of mutability and revolting, and of unspeakable hurt to many a soul.

Nay, may you not remember also what sorrow you had in the day of your repentance, for your forsaking and neglecting God so long? Will you grow again negligent of him? Was it then so heinous a sin in your eyes; and is it now grown less? Could you then aggravate it so many ways, and now do you justify or extenuate it? Were you then ready to sink under the burden of it; and were so hardly persuaded that it would be forgiven you: and now do you make so small a matter of it? Did you then so much wonder at your folly, that could so long let out your thoughts and affections upon the creature, while you neglected God and heaven; and do you begin to look that way again? Do you now grow familiar with a life so like to that which was once your state of death; and bear that easily that once was the breaking of your heart? O Christians, turn not away from that God again, who once brought you home, with so much smart and so much grace; with such love and fatherly severity! Methinks when you remember how you were once awakened, you should not easily fall asleep again. When you remember the thoughts which then were in your hearts, and the tears that were in your eyes, and the earnest prayers which you then put up, that God would receive, and take you for his own, you should not now forget him, and live as if you could live without him. Remember that so far as you withdraw your hearts from God, and let them follow inferior things, so far you contradict his works upon your hearts; so far you violate your covenant with him, or sin against it; so far you are revolters, and go against the principal part of your professed religion: yea, so far you are ungodly, as you thus withdraw your hearts from God. Cleave to him, and prosecute your covenant, if you will have the saving benefits of his love and covenant.

3. Moreover, the servants of God are doubly obliged to walk with him, because they have had that experience of the goodness, the safety and the sweetness of it, which strangers have not. Do you not remember how glad you were, when you first believed that he pardoned and accepted you? How much you rejoiced in his love and entertainments? How much better you found your Father's house, than ever you had found your sinful state? How much sweeter his service was, than you did before believe? It is likely you can remember something like that which is described in the words of Luke: 'And he arose, and came to his father: but when he was yet a great way off, his father saw him, and had compassion, and ran and fell on his neck and kissed him: and the son said unto him, Father, I have sinned against heaven, and in thy sight, and am no more worthy to be called thy son: but the father said to his servants, bring forth the best robe and put it on him, and put a ring on his hand, and shoes on his feet, and bring hither the fatted calf, and kill it, and let us eat and be merry: for this my son was dead, and is alive again, he was lost, and is found.' What would you have thought or said of this prodigal, if after all this, he should have been weary of his father's house and company, and have taken more pleasure in his former company? Would you not have said, he was a forgetful and unthankful man, and worthy never more to be received? I do not speak to you now as to apostates, that are turned ungodly, and have quite forsaken God and holiness: but I beseech you consider, what it is, after such experiences and obligations as these, so much as to abate your love, and grow remiss, unmindful, and indifferent, as if you were weary of God, and were inclined to neglect him, and look again to the world for your hope, satisfaction, and delight? As you love your souls, and as you would avoid the sorrows which are greater than any that ever you felt, take heed of slighting the love that hath done such wonders for you, and of dealing so unthankfully with the everlasting God, and of turning thus away from him that hath received you! Remember whilst you live, the love of your espousals: was God so good to you at the first, and holiness so desirable? and is it not so still?

I am sure that your own experience will bear witness, that since that time, in all your lives, it never was so well with you as when you walked most faithfully with God. If you have received any falls and hurts, it hath been when you have strayed from him: if ever you had safety, peace, or joy, it hath been when you have been nearest to him: your wounds, grief, and death, have been the fruit of your own ways, and of your forsaking him: your recovery, health, and life have been the fruit of his ways, and of your adhering to him: many a time you have confessed this, and have said, It is good for me to draw near to God. He hath helped you when none else could help you: and comforted you when none else could comfort you. How far are you above the worldling's happiness, when you are nigh to God? One lively thought of his greatness, and excellency, and of his love to you in Jesus Christ, will make the name of wealth, honour, favour, preferment, and sensual pleasure, to seem to you as words of no signification: how indifferent will you be, as to your prosperity in the world, when you feel what it is to walk with God? If you are lively experimental Christians, you have found this to be true: have you not found that it is the very health, ease, and proper employment of your souls to walk with God, and keep close to him? that all goes well with you while you can do thus, however the world doth esteem or use you? that when you grow strange or disobedient to God, and forgetful of his goodness, his presence, and his authority, you are like the stomach that is sick, and like a bone that is out of joint, that can have no ease till it be healed, and restored to its proper place? No meats or drinks, no company nor recreation, no wealth or greatness will serve to make a sick man well, or ease the dislocated bones. Nothing will serve a faithful holy soul but God; this is the cause of the sorrow of his heart, of the secret groans and complainings of his life, because in this life of distance and imperfection, he finds himself so far from God; and when he hath done all that he can, he is still so dark, and strange, and cold in his affections! When persecution drives him from the ordinances and public worship, or when sin hath set him at a greater distance from his God, he bemoans his soul, as David in his banishment from the tabernacle, 'as the heart panteth after the water-brooks, so panteth my soul after thee, O God: my soul thirsteth for God, for the living God: when shall I come and appear before God? My tears have been my meat day and night, while they continually say unto me.

Where is thy God?' It is no wonder if with his greatest joy, he be yet clouded with these sorrows, because he yet wants more of God than he enjoys : his enjoying graces—love and joy—are yet imperfect. But when he hath attained his nearest approach to God, he will have fulness of delight in fulness of fruition.

O Christians! Do I need to tell you, that after all the trials you have made in the world, you have never found any state of life, that was worthy your desires, nor that gave you any true contentment, but only this living upon God? If you have not found such comfort here as others have done, yet at least you have seen it afar off, within your reach : as men that in the Indies, in the discovery of plantations, expect gold mines, when they find those golden sands that promise it. You have found a life which is certainly desirable, and leads to joy in the midst of sorrow : it is no small joy to have a certain promise and prospect of everlasting joy. It is therefore more excusable in those that never tasted any better than the pleasures of the flesh, to neglect this sweeter heavenly life, than it is in you, that have been convinced by your own experience, that there is no life to be compared with it.

4. Your walking with God is the necessary prosecution of your choice and hopes of life eternal. It is your necessary preparation to your enjoying him in heaven. Have you fixed on those hopes with so great reason and deliberation, and will you now draw back and be slack in the prosecution of them? Have you gone so far in the way to heaven, and do you now begin to look behind you, as if you were about to change your mind? Paul sets you a better example : ' yea, doubtless, I count all things but loss for the excellency of the knowledge of Christ Jesus my Lord ; for whom I have suffered the loss of all things, and do count them but dung, that I may win Christ, and be found in him, if by any means I might attain to the resurrection of the dead : not as though I had already attained, either were already perfect : but I follow after, if that I may apprehend that for which also I am apprehended of Christ Jesus : brethren, I count not myself to have apprehended, but this one thing I do, forgetting those things which are behind, and reaching forth unto those things which are before, I press toward the mark for the prize of the high calling of God in Christ Jesus.' He compares himself to a runner in a race, that till he apprehend the prize or mark, doth still make forward with all his might, and will not so much as mind or look at any thing behind him, that would turn him back, or stop him in his course. The world and the flesh are the things behind us : we turned our backs upon them at our conversion, when we turned to God : it is these that would now call back our thoughts, and corrupt our affections, when we should run on, and reach forward to the heavenly prize : it is God and heaven, and the remaining duties of a holy life, that are the things before us! And shall we now look back ; what, we that are running and striving for a crown of endless glory ! we, that if we lose it, do lose our souls and hopes for ever! we that have loitered in the morning of our lives, and lost so much precious time as we have done ; we, that have gone so far in our way, and held out through so many difficulties and assaults ; shall we now grow weary of walking with God, and begin to look to the things behind us? Did he not tell us at the first, that father and mother, house, lands, life, and all things must be forsaken for Christ, if we will be his disciples? These are the things behind us, which we turned our back on when we consented to the covenant : and are they now grown better ; or is God grown worse, that we turn our hearts from him to them ; when we first begun our Christian race, it was upon supposition that it was for that immortal crown, which all the world is not to be compared to.

Have we not still the same consideration before us, to move us to hold on till we attain it? Hold on, Christians, it is for heaven : is there not enough in that word to drive back all the cares and pleasures, that importune your minds to forget your God? Is there not enough in that word to quicken you up in your greatest dullness ; and to call you home, when you are wandering from God : and to make you again fall out with all that would reduce you, or divert you, and call it vanity and vexation of spirit? Methinks the fore-thought of that life and work which you hope to have with God for ever, should make you earnestly desire to have as much of the life on earth, as is here to be attained! If it will be your heaven and happiness then, it must needs be desirable now. It is not beseeming a man that saith he is seeking for perfect communion with God in heaven, and that above all things,—as every Christian doth—to live in a daily neglect or forgetfulness of God on earth. Delightfully to draw near him, and exercise all our faculties upon him, or for him sometime in prayer and contemplation on himself, and always in works of obedience to him ; this is the life that beseems those that profess to seek eternal life. O therefore let us make it our daily work, to keep our God and glory in our eye, and to spur on our dull affections, and in the diligent attendance and following the Captain of our salvation, to prosecute our expected end.

5. Lastly, consider that God doth purposely provide you hard entertainment in the world, and causes every creature to deny you the pleasure and satisfaction which you desire, that so you may have none to walk with but himself, with any heart-settling comfort and content. If you see not enough in him to allure you to himself, you shall feel enough in the world to drive you to him : if his love and goodness will not serve you alone to make him your pleasure, and hold you to him in the best, and most excellent, way of love, at least the storms and troubles that are abroad shall show you the necessity of keeping close to God ; and the love of yourselves shall help you to do that which was not done by the attraction of his love alone. If you will put him to it, to send out his command to every creature to cross and vex you, and disappoint all expectations from it, that so he may force you to remember your Father and your home, deny not then but it is because of yourselves that you were not saved in an easier way. Would you wish God to make that condition pleasant to you, which he sees you take too much pleasure in already, or seek and desire it, at least ; when as it is the pleasantness of the creature that is your danger, and which detains your thoughts and affections from himself? If you could but learn to walk with him, and to take up your pleasure in his love appearing to you in his creatures, and to make their sweetness the means to your apprehension of the sweetness of his favour, and of the everlasting joys, then you might say the creature doth you good ; and then it is likely you might be permitted to possess and use it for such pleasure. The jealous God will watch your hearts, though you watch them not ; and he will make you know that he sees which way they run out from him, and what creature it is that is minded and delighted in, while he is neglected, as if he were unsuitable, and scarcely desirable. You must never look that he should long permit you those prohibited delights, or let you alone in those idolatrous inclinations : if he love you, he will cure that carnal love, and recover your love to himself that hath deserved it. If he intended not your salvation, he may let you go, and try again whether the creature will prove better to you than himself : but you cannot think that he will thus let go his children that must live with him for ever. Have you not perceived that this is the design and meaning of his afflicting and disappointing providences ; even to leave you no comfortable entertainment or converse but with himself, and with his servants, and with those means that lead you to himself. If you begin to desire to lodge abroad in strange habitations, he will uncover those houses, and will not leave you a room that is dry to put your head in ; or he will throw open the doors, and leave all open to the lust of ravenous beasts and robbers. He will have thy heart, and he will have thy company, because thou art his child, and because he loves thee. He will allow thee neither thy carnal delights nor hopes.

If he perceive thee either taking that pleasure in thy prosperity, which thou shouldst take in him alone, or hoping at least that the world may hereafter prove more amiable and delightful to thee ; the more he loves thee, the more his providence shall conspire with his grace, to change thy mind by depriving thee of thy unwholesome, dangerous delights, and of all thy hopes of such hereafter. Use the world as a traveller, for the ends to which it was ordained, to the service of God, and the furtherance of thy salvation, and then thou shalt find that God will furnish thee with all that is necessary to these necessary ends : but if the world must have your love and care, and must be your chief business and delight, and your excuse for not attending upon God, murmur not, nor marvel not, if he dispose of it and you accordingly. If you are yet too healthful to think with seriousness of your eternal state : if you are too rich to part with all for Christ, or openly to own his cause : if you are too much esteemed in the world to own a scorned, slandered religion : if you are so busy for earth that you cannot have time to think of heaven ; if you have so much delight in house or land, or in your employments, or recreations, or friends, that God and godliness can have little or none of your delight : marvel not then if God shake your health, or waste your riches, or turn your honour into contempt, and suffer men to slander and reproach you, and spit in your face, and make you of no reputation : marvel not if he turn you out of all, or turn all to your grief and trouble, and make the world a desert to you, and the inhabitants as wolves and bears. The great lesson that Christ hath undertaken to teach you, is the difference betwixt the Creator and the creature, and the difference betwixt heaven and earth. The great work that Christ hath undertaken to do upon you, is to recover your hearts from the world to God : this lesson he will teach you, and this work he will do upon you, whatever it cost you : for it must be done.

Yet is not the world unjust enough, or cruel, or vexatious enough to you, to teach you to come home, and take up your rest in God? It may then prove more cruel, and more vexatious to you, till you have better learned this necessary lesson. Yet is not your condition empty enough of carnal, delusory pleasures, to wean you from the world, and make you look to surer things? Yet are you keeping up your worldly hopes, that the world will again prove better to you, and that you shall have happy days hereafter? It seems you are not yet brought low enough: you must yet take another chastisement, and perhaps a sharper than you took before: you must have more blood letting, till your delirium cease, and your feverish thirst after creature-comforts abate. It is sad that we should be so foolish and unkind as to stay from God, as long as any preferments, or pleasures, or profits in the world, will entertain us: but seeing it is so, let us be thankful both to that grace and that providence which cures us. If you perceive it not better to dwell with God, than with a flattering prospering world, he will try whether you can think it better to dwell with God, than with a malicious, cruel, persecuting world: and whether it be better to have your hearts in heaven, than in poverty, prison, banishment or reproach. If you find it not better to converse with God, than with those that honour you, please you, or prefer you; he will try whether you can think it better to converse with him, than with those that hate, revile, and persecute you. Are these the wise and wholesome methods of our great Physician? Shall we not rather be ruled by him than by our brutish appetites; and think better of his counsels, than of the blind concupiscence of the flesh? Let this be the issue of all our sufferings, and all the cruelties and injuries of the world, to drive us home to converse with God, and to turn our desires, labours, and expectations to the true felicity that never will forsake us; and then, the will of the Lord be done! Let him choose his means, if this may be the end: let us kiss the rod, and not revile it, if this may be the fruit of his corrections. Who will not pray that God would deny us those enjoyments which keep us from seeking our happiness in him; and that he would deny us all those hurtful pleasures which hinder us from pleasing him, or from making him and his ways our chief pleasure? That he would permit us no such creature-converse, as hinders our converse with him? It is best living there (be it in prison or at liberty) where we may live best to God. Come home, O suffering Christian, to thy God!

take up thy rest and rest in him; be satisfied with him as thy portion; and remember where it is that he is to be fully and perpetually enjoyed; and then it is good for thee that thou wast afflicted; for all thy sufferings have their end.

This last consideration will be further prosecuted in the following part: and the directions for walking with God, which I should here give you, I have reserved for a peculiar treatise, entitled, A Christian Directory.

PART III.

OF CONVERSING WITH GOD IN SOLITUDE.

"*Behold the hour cometh, yea, is come, that ye shall be scattered every man to his own, and shall leave me alone: and yet I am not alone, because the Father is with me.*"—JOHN xvi. 32.

I. THE DEFINITION OF THE TEXT.

HAVING treated of our conformity to Christ in sufferings, in general, I since came distinctly to treat of his particular sufferings in which we must be conformed to him: and having gone over many of those particulars, I am this day to handle the instance of Christ's being forsaken by his friends and followers.

He thought meet to foretell them how they should manifest their infirmity and unsteadfastness in this temporary forsaking of him, that so he might more fully convince them, that he knew what was in man, and that he knew future contingencies, or things to come, which seem most dependent on the will of man, and that he voluntarily submitted to his deserted state, and expected no support from creatures, but that man should then do least for Christ, when Christ was doing most for man: that man, by an unthankful forsaking Christ, should then manifest his forsaken state, when Christ was to make atonement for his reconciliation to God, and was preparing the most costly remedy for his recovery. He foretold them of the fruit which their infirmity would produce, to humble them that were apt to think too highly of themselves for the late free confession they had made of Christ, when they had newly said, 'Now we are sure that thou knowest all things: by this we are sure that thou comest forth from God.'

He answers them, 'Do ye now believe? Behold the hour cometh,' &c. Not that Christ would not have his servants know his graces in them, but he would also have them know the corruption that is latent, and the infirmity consistent with their grace. We are very apt to judge of all that is in us, and of all that we shall do hereafter, by what we feel at the present upon our hearts. As when we feel the stirring of some corruption, we are apt to think that there is nothing else, and hardly perceive the contrary grace, and are apt to think it will never be better with us: so when we feel the exercise of faith, desire, or love, we are apt to overlook the contrary corruptions, and to think that we shall never feel more. But Christ would keep us both humble and vigilant, by acquainting us with the mutability and inconstancy of our minds. When it goes well with us, we forget that the time is coming when it may go worse. As Christ said to his disciples here in the case of believing, we may say to ourselves in that and other cases: do we now believe? It is well: but the time may be coming in which we may be brought to shake with the stirrings of our remaining unbelief, and shrewdly tempted to question the truth of Christianity itself, and of the holy scriptures, and of the life to come. Do we now rejoice in the persuasions of the love of God? The time may be coming when we may think ourselves forsaken and undone, and think he will esteem and use us as his enemies. Do we now pray with fervour, and pour out our souls to God? It is well: but the time may be coming when we shall seem to be as dumb and prayerless, and say, we cannot pray, or else we find no audience and acceptance of our prayers. Christ knows that in us which we little know by ourselves; and therefore may foreknow that we will commit such sins, or fall into such dangers, as we little fear.

What Christ here prophesies to them, did afterwards all come to pass. As soon as ever danger and trouble did appear, they began to flag, and to show how ill they could adhere unto him, or suffer with him, without his special corroborating grace: in the garden when he was sweating blood in prayer, they were sleeping; though the spirit was willing, the flesh was weak: they could not ' watch with him one hour.' When he was apprehended, they shifted each man for himself. ' Then all his disciples forsook him and fled'. And as this is said to be that the scriptures might be fulfilled, so it might be said to be, that this prediction of Christ himself might be fulfilled. Not that scripture prophecies did cause the sin by which they were fulfilled; nor that God caused the sin, to fulfil his own predictions, but that God cannot be deceived who foretold in scrip-

tures long before, that thus it would come to pass: when it is said that ' thus it must be, that the scripture may be fulfilled,' the meaning is not, that, thus God will make it be, or, thus he causes men to do that he may fulfil the scriptures: it is not a necessity of the thing itself, as caused by the prediction or decree; but a necessity of the truth of this conclusion in arguing; such a thing will be, because God hath decreed, foreknown, or foretold it: or whatever God foretells, must necessarily come to pass; that is, will certainly come to pass: but this God hath foretold: therefore this will come to pass.

II. THE APPLICATION OF THE PRINCIPLE.

Here are three observable points in the text, that are worthy our distinct consideration, though for brevity's sake I shall handle them together.

1. That Christ was forsaken by his own disciples and left alone.

2. When the disciples left Christ, they were scattered every one to his own. They returned to their old habitations, and old acquaintance, and old employment, as if their hopes and hearts had been almost broken, and they had lost all their labour in following Christ so long: yet the root of faith and love that still remained, caused them to inquire further of the end, and to come together in secret to confer about these matters.

3. When Christ was forsaken of his disciples and left alone, yet was he not forsaken of his Father, nor left so alone as to be separated from him or his love.

We are now to consider of this not only as a part of Christ's humiliation, but also as a point in which we must expect to be conformed to him. It may possibly seem strange to us that Christ would suffer all his disciples to forsake him in his extremity; and I doubt it will seem strange to us, when in our extremity, and our suffering for Christ, (and perhaps for them,) we shall find ourselves forsaken by those that we most highly valued, and had the greatest familiarity with. But there are many reasons of this permissive providence open to our observation.

(1.) No wonder, if when Christ was suffering for sin, he would even then permit the power and odiousness of sin to break forth, that it might be known he suffered not in vain. No wonder, if he permitted his followers to desert him, and show the latent unbelief, and selfishness, and unthankfulness that remained in them, that so they might know that the death of Christ was as necessary for them as for others; and the universality of the disease might show the need that the remedy should be universal. It is none of Christ's intent to make his servants to seem better than they are, to themselves or others, or to honour himself by the hiding of their faults, but to magnify his pardoning and healing grace, by the means or occasion of the sins which he pardons and heals.

(2.) Hereby he will bring his followers to the fuller knowledge of themselves, and show them that which all their days should keep them humble, and watchful, and save them from presumption and trusting in themselves: when we have made any full confession of Christ, or done him any considerable service, we are apt to say with the disciples, ' Behold we have forsaken all and followed thee ; what shall we have ?' As if they had rather been givers to Christ, than receivers from him ; and had highly merited at his hands: but when Peter forswears him, and the rest shift for themselves, and when they come to themselves, after such cowardly and ungrateful dealings ; then they will better understand their weakness, and know on whom they must depend.

(3.) Hereby also they shall better understand what they would have been, if God had left them to themselves, that so they may be thankful for grace received, and may not boast themselves against the miserable world, as if they had made themselves to differ, and had not received all that grace by which they excel the common sort : when our falls have hurt us and shamed us, we shall know to whom we must be beholden to support us.

(4.) Christ would permit his disciples thus far to forsake him, because he would have no support from man, in his sufferings for man : this was part of his voluntary humiliation, to be deprived of all earthly comforts, and to bear affliction even from those few, that but lately were his faithful servants : that men, dealing like men, and sinners, while he was doing like God, and as a Saviour, no man might challenge to himself the honour of contributing to the redemption of the world, so much as by encouraging the Redeemer.

(5.) Christ did permit the faith and courage of his disciples thus far to fail, that their witness to him might be of the greater credit and authority, when his actual resurrection, and the communication of the Spirit, should compel them to believe : when all their doubts were dissipated, they that had doubted themselves, and yet were constrained to believe, would be received as the most impartial witnesses by the doubting world.

(6.) Lastly, by the desertion and dissipation of his disciples, Christ would teach us whenever we are called to follow him in suffering, what to expect from the best of men : even to know that of themselves they are unfaithful, and may fail us : and therefore not to look for too much assistance or encouragement from them. Paul lived in a time when Christians were more self-denying and stedfast than they are now, and Paul was one that might better expect to be faithfully accompanied in his sufferings for Christ, than any of us : and yet he saith, ' at my first answer no man stood with me, but all men forsook me :' and prays, that it be not laid to their charge. Thus you have seen some reasons why Christ consented to be left of all, and permitted his disciples to desert him in his sufferings.

Yet note here, that it is but a partial, temporary forsaking that Christ permits ; and not a total or final forsaking or apostasy. Though he will let them see that they are yet men, he will not leave them to be but as other men : nor will he quite cast them off, or suffer them to perish.

Nor is it all alike that thus forsake him ; Peter doth not do as Judas : the sincere may manifest their infirmity ; but the hypocrites will manifest their hypocrisy.

Accordingly in our sufferings our familiars that were false-hearted, as being worldlings and carnal at the heart, may perhaps betray us, and set against us, or forsake the cause of Christ, and follow the way of gain and honour : when our tempted shrinking friends, that yet may have some sincerity, may perhaps look strange at us, and seem not to know us, and may hide their heads, and show their fears ; and perhaps also begin to study some self-deceiving arguments and distinctions, and to stretch their consciences, and venture on some sin, because they are afraid to venture on affliction ; till Christ shall cast a gracious, rebuking, quickening aspect on them, and shame them for their sinful shame, and fear them for their sinful fears, and inflame their love to him by the motions of his love to them, and destroy the love that turned them from him : and then the same men that dishonourably failed Christ and us, and began to shrink, will turn back and reassume their arms, and by patient suffering overcome and win the crown, as we have done before them.

I. *Christians are subject to the desertion of friends.*

Christians, expect to be conformed to your Lord in this part of his humiliation also. Are your friends yet fast and friendly to you ? For all that, expect that many of them, at least, should prove less friendly : and promise not yourselves an unchanged constancy in them.

Are they yet useful to you? Expect the time when they cannot help you. Are they your comforters and delight, and is their company much of your solace upon earth? Be ready for the time when they may become your sharpest scourges, and most heart-piercing griefs, or at least when you shall say, We have no pleasure in them. Have any of them, or all, already failed you? What wonder? Are they not men, and sinners? To whom were they ever so constant as not to fail them? Rebuke yourselves for your unwarrantable expectations from them: learn hereafter to know what man is, and expect that friends should use you as follows.

1. Some of them that you thought sincere, shall prove perhaps unfaithful and dissemblers, and upon fallings out, or matters of self-interest, may seek your ruin. Are you better than David, that had an Ahitophel: or than Paul, that had a Demas: or than Christ, that had a Judas? Some will forsake God: what wonder then if they may forsake you? 'Because iniquity shall abound, the love of many shall wax cold.' Where pride, vain-glory, sensuality, and worldliness are unmortified at the heart, there is no trustiness in such persons: for their wealth, or honour, or fleshly interest, they will part with God and their salvation; much more with their best deserving friends. Why may not you, as well as Job, have occasion to complain, 'he hath put my brethren far from me, and my acquaintance are verily estranged from me: my kinsfolk have failed, and my familiar friends have forgotten me: they that dwell in my house, and my maidens, count me for a stranger: I am an alien in their sight: I called my servant, and he gave me no answer: I entreated him with my mouth: my breath is strange to my wife; though I entreated for the children's sake of my own body: yea, young children despised me: I arose, and they spake against me: all my inward friends abhorred me; and they whom I loved are turned against me.' Why may not you, as well as David, be put to say, 'yea, mine own familiar friend in whom I trusted, which did eat of my bread, hath lifted up his heel against me.' Those that have been most acquainted with the secrets of your soul, and privy to your very thoughts, may be the persons that shall betray you, or grow strange to you. Those that you have most obliged by benefits, may prove your greatest enemies. You may find some of your friends like birds of prey, that hover about you for what they can get, and when they have catched it, fly away. If you have given them all that you have, they will forsake you, and perhaps reproach you, because you have no more to give them. They are your friends more for what they yet expect from you, than for what they have already received. If you cannot still be helpful to them, or feed their covetous desires, or supply their wants, you are to them but as one that they had never known. Many a faithful minister of Christ hath studied, preached, prayed, and wept for their people's souls, and after all have been taken for their enemies, and used as such: yea even because they have done so much for them. Like the patient, that being cured of a mortal sickness, sued his physician at law for making him sick with the physic. But it is indeed our uncured patients only that are offended with us. Paul was accounted an enemy to the Galatians, because he told them the truth. Ungrateful truth makes the most faithful preachers most ungrateful. It must seem no wonder to a preacher of the gospel, when he hath entreated, prayed, and wept night and day for miserable souls, and laid his hands as it were under their feet, in hopes of their conversion and salvation, to find them after all, his bitter enemies, and seeking his destruction, that could have laid down his life for their salvation. Jeremiah seemed too impatient under this affliction, when he said, 'give heed to me, O Lord, and hearken to the voice of them that contend with me: shall evil be recompensed for good? Remember that I stood before thee to speak good for them, and to turn away thy wrath from them: therefore deliver up their children to the famine, and pour out their blood by the force of the sword.'

Thus may ingratitude afflict you, and kindness be requited with unkindness, and the greatest benefits be forgotten, and requited with the greatest wrongs: your old familiars may be your foes: and you may be put to say as Jeremiah: 'for I heard the defaming of many: fear on every side: report, say they, and we will report it: all my familiars watched for my halting, saying, Peradventure he will be enticed, and we shall prevail against him, and we shall take our revenge on him.' Thus must the servants of Christ be used, in conformity to their suffering Head.

2. Some that are sincere, and whose hearts are with you, may yet be drawn by temptation to disown you: when malice is slandering you, timorous friendship may perhaps be silent, and afraid to justify you, or take your part: when a Peter in such imbecility and fear can disown and deny his suffering Lord, what wonder if faint-hearted friends disown you, or me, that may give them too much occasion or pretence? Why

may not you and I be put to say as David did, 'my lovers and my friends stand aloof from my sore, and my kinsmen stand afar of: they that seek after my life lay snares for me: and they that seek my hurt speak mischievous things, and imagine deceits all the day long!' They that in fearfulness will fail their Maker and Redeemer, and hazard their salvation, may by a smaller temptation be drawn to fail such friends as we.

3. Moreover, a hundred things may occasion fallings out, even amongst unfeigned friends: passions may cause inconvenient actions or expressions, and these may cause passions in their friends ; and these may grow so high till friends seem to one another to be like enemies: Paul and Barnabas may grow so hot, as to fall out to a parting. How easily can Satan set fire on the tinder which he finds in the best and gentlest natures, if God permit him? No friends so near and dear, that passionate weaknesses may not either alienate or make a grief to one another. How apt are we to take unkindnesses at one another, and to be suspicious of our friends, or offended with them? How apt to give occasion of such offence? How apt are we to censure one another, and to misinterpret the words and actions of our friends? How apt to give occasion of such mistakes and cutting censures? The more kindness we have found in, or expected from our friends, the more their real or supposed injuries will affect us. We are apt to say, 'had it been a stranger, I could have borne it: but to be used thus by my bosom or familiar friend, goes near my heart.' Indeed the unkindnesses of friends is no small affliction ; the suffering going usually as near the heart, as the person that caused it was near it : especially when our own weakness causes us to forget the frailty and infirmities of man, and with what allowances and expectations we must choose and use our friends ; and when we forget the love that remains in the midst of passions.

4. Also cross-interests and unsuitableness may exceedingly interrupt the fastest friendship. Friendship is very much founded in suitableness, and maintained by it : and among mortals, there is no perfect suitableness to be found ; but much unsuitableness still remains. That which pleaseth one, is displeasing to another: one likes this place, and the other that : one likes this habit, and the other that : one is for mirth, and the other for sadness : one for talk, and the other for silence : one for a public, and the other for a private life. Their personality having self-love as inseparable, will unavoidably cause

a contrariety of interests. The creature is insufficient for us : if one have it, perhaps the other must want it : like a covering too narrow for the bed. Sometimes our reputations seem to stand cross, so that one man's is diminished by another's : then how apt is envy to create a grudge, and raise unfriendly jealousies and distastes ? Sometimes the ease of one is the annoyance of the other : then mine and thine, which are contrary to the communion of friendship, may divide, alienate, and make two of those that seemed one. The instances of Abraham and Lot, upon the difference among their servants, of Isaac and Ishmael, of Jacob and Esau, of Laban and Jacob, of Leah and Rachel, of Joseph and his brethren, of Saul and David, and of Ziba, Mephibosheth and David, with many others, tell us this. It is rare to meet with a Jonathan, that will endearedly love that man to the death, who is appointed to deprive him of a kingdom. If one can but say, I suffer by him, or I am a loser by him, it seems enough to excuse unfriendly thoughts and actions. When you can gratify the desires of all covetous, ambitious, self-seeking persons in the world, or else cure their diseases, and possess their minds with perfect charity, then all the world will be your friends.

5. Cross opinions also are like to alienate many of your friends. This age hath over and over again given the world as full and sad demonstrations of the power of cross opinions to alienate friends, and make divisions, as most ages of the world have ever had. If your friend be proud, it is wonderful how he will slight you, and withdraw his love, if you be not of his mind. If he be zealous, he is easily tempted to think it a part of his duty to God to disown you if you differ from him, as taking you for one that disowns the truth of God, and therefore one that God himself disowns ; or at least to grow cold in his affection toward you, and to decline from you as he that thinks you do from God. As agreement in opinions doth strangely reconcile affections ; so disagreement doth secretly and strangely alienate them ; even before you are well aware, your friend hath lost possession of your hearts, because of an unavoidable diversity of apprehensions : when all your friends have the same intellectual complexion and temperature, and measure of understanding with yourselves, then you may have hope to escape the ruptures which unlikeness and differences of apprehensions might else cause.

6. Moreover, some of your friends may so far overgrow you in wisdom, wealth, honour, or

worth in their own conceits, that they may begin to take you to be unsuitable for them, and unmeet for their further special friendship. Alas, poor man, they will pity thee that thou art no wiser, and that thou hast no greater light to change thy mind as fast as they, or that thou art so weak and ignorant as not to see what seems to them so clear a truth ; or that thou art so simple to cast away thyself by crossing them that might prefer thee, or to fall under the displeasure of those that have power to raise or ruin thee : but if thou be so simple, thou mayest be the object of their lamentations, but art no familiar friend for them. They think it fittest to close and converse with those of their own rank and stature, and not with such children, that may prove their trouble and dishonour.

7. Some of your friends will think that by a more thorough acquaintance with you, they have found out more of your infirmities or faults ; and therefore have found that you are less amiable and valuable than at first they judged you : they will think that by distance, unacquaintedness, and an overhasty love and judgment, they were mistaken in you ; and that now they see reason to repent of the love which they think was guilty of some errors and excess: when they come nearer you, and have had more trial of you, they will think they are fitter to judge of you than before : indeed, our defects are so many, and all our infirmities so great, that the more men know us, the more they may see in us that deserves pity or reproof ; and as pictures, we appear less beautiful at the nearest view : though this will not warrant the withdrawing of that love which is due to friends, and to virtue, even in the imperfect : nor will excuse that alienation, and decay of friendship that is caused by the pride of such as overlook perhaps much greater failings and weaknesses in themselves, which need forgiveness.

8. Perhaps some of your friends will grow weary of their friendship, having that infirmity of human nature, not to be much pleased with one thing long. Their love is a flower that quickly withers : it is a short-lived thing that soon grows old. It must be novelty that must feed their love and their delight.

9. Perhaps they may have got some better friends in their apprehensions, they may have so much interest as to take them up, and leave no room for ancient friends. It may be, they have met with those that are more suitable, or can be more useful to them : that have more learning, or wit, or wealth, or power than you have, and therefore seem more worthy of their friendship.

10. Some of them may think when you are in a low and suffering state, and in danger of worse, that it is part of their duty of self-preservation to be strange to you, though in heart they wish you well. They will think they are not bound to hazard themselves upon the displeasure of superiors, to own or befriend you, or any other : though they must not desert Christ, they think they may desert a man for their own preservation.

To avoid both extremes in such a case, men must both study to understand which way is most serviceable to Christ, and to his church, and withal, to be able to deny themselves, and also must study to understand what Christ means in his final sentence, ' Inasmuch as you did it (or did it not) to one of the least of these my brethren, you did it (or did it not) to me.' As if it were to visit the contagious, we must neither cast away our lives to do no good, or for that which in value holds no proportion with them ; nor yet must we deny to run any hazard when it is indeed our duty : so is it in our visiting those that suffer for the cause of Christ: only here the owning them being the confessing of him, we need more seldom to fear being too forward.

11. Some of your friends may cover their unfaithfulness with the pretence of some fault that you have been guilty of, some error that you hold, or some unhandsome or culpable act that you have done, or some duty that you have left undone or failed in. For they think there is not a better shelter for unfaithfulness, than to pretend for it the name and cause of God, and so to make a duty of their sin. Who would not justify them, if they can but prove that God requires them, and religion obliges them, to forsake you for your faults ? There are few crimes in the world that by some are not fathered on God, that most hates them, as thinking no name can so much honour them. False friends therefore use this means as well as other hypocrites: and though God is love, and condemns nothing more than uncharitableness and malice, yet these are commonly by false-hearted hypocrites called by some pious, virtuous names, and God himself is entitled to them : so that few worldlings, ambitious persons or time-servers, but will confidently pretend religion for all their falsehood to their friends, or bloody cruelty to the servants of Christ who comply not with their carnal interest.

12. Perhaps some of your friends may really mistake your case, and think that you suffer as evil-doers, and instead of comforting you, may be your sharpest censurers : this is one of the most notable things set out to our observation

in the book of Job : it was not the smallest part of his affliction, that when the hand of God was heavy upon him, and then if ever was the time for his friends to have been his comforters, and friends indeed ; on the contrary they became his scourge, and by unjust accusations, and misinterpretations of the providence of God, did greatly add to his affliction! When God had taken away his children, wealth, and health, his friends would take away the reputation and comfort of his integrity; and under pretence of bringing him to repentance, did charge him with that which he was never guilty of : they wounded his good name, and would have wounded his conscience, and deprived him of his inward peace: censorious, false, accusing friends, cut deeper than malicious, slandering enemies : it is no wonder, if strangers or enemies misjudge and misreport our actions : but when your bosom friends, that should most intimately know you, and be the chief witnesses of your innocence against all others, shall in their jealousy or envy, or peevishness, or falling out, be your chief reproachers and unjust accusers, as it makes it seem more credible to others, so it will come nearest to yourselves. Yet this is a thing that must be expected ; yea, even your most self-denying acts of obedience to God, may be so misunderstood by godly men, and real friends, as by them to be taken for your great miscarriage, and turned to your rebuke: as David's dancing before the ark was by his wife ; which yet did but make him resolve to be yet more vile.

If you be cast into poverty, or disgrace, or prison, or banishment, for your necessary obedience to Christ, perhaps your friend or wife may become your accuser for this your greatest service, and say, This is your own doing : your rashness, or indiscretion, or self-conceitedness, or wilfulness hath brought it upon you : what need had you to say such words, or to do this or that? Why could not you have yielded in so small a matter ? Perhaps your costliest and most excellent obedience shall by your nearest friends be called the fruits of pride, or humour, or passion, or some corrupt affection, or at least of folly or inconsiderateness. When flesh and blood hath long been striving in you against your duty, and saying, Do not cast away thyself: O serve not God at so dear a rate : God doth not require thee to undo thyself: why shouldst thou not avoid so great inconveniences ? When with much ado you have conquered all your carnal reasonings, and denied yourselves and your carnal interests, you must expect, even from some religious friends, to be accused for these very actions, and perhaps their accusations may fasten such a blot upon your names, as shall never be washed out till the day of judgment. By difference of interests, or apprehensions, and by unacquaintedness with your hearts and actions, the righteousness of the righteous may be thus taken from him, and friends may do the work of enemies, yea, of satan himself, the accuser of the brethren ; and may prove as thorns in your bed, and gravel in your shoes, yea, in your eyes, and wrong you much more than open adversaries could have done. How it is likely to go with that man's reputation, you may easily judge, whose friends are like Job's and his enemies like David's, that lay snares before him, and diligently watch for matter of reproach : yet this may befall the best of men.

13. You may be permitted by God to fall into some real crime, and then your friends may possibly think it is their duty to disown you, so far as you have wronged God : when you provoke God to frown upon you, he may cause your friends to frown upon you : if you will fall out with him, and grow strange to him, no marvel if your truest friends fall out with you, and grow strange to you. They love you for your godliness, and for the sake of Christ ; and therefore must abate their love, if you abate your godliness : and must, for the sake of Christ, be displeased with you for your sins. If in such a case of real guilt, you should be displeased at their displeasure, and should expect that your friend should befriend your sin, or carry himself towards you in your guilt, as if you were innocent, you will but show that you understand not the nature of true friendship, nor the use of a true friend : and are yet yourselves too friendly to your sins.

14. Moreover, those few friends that are truest to you, may be utterly unable to relieve you in your distress, or to give you ease, or do you any good. The case may be such that they can but pity you, lament your sorrows, and weep over you: you may see in them that man is not as God, whose friendship can accomplish all the good that he desires to his friends. The wisest and greatest and best of men are miserable comforters, and ineffectual helps : you may be sick, pained, grieved, and distressed, notwithstanding any thing that they can do for you : nay, perhaps in their ignorance, they may increase your misery, while they desire your relief; and by striving indirectly to help and ease you, may tie the knot faster and make you worse. They may provoke those more against you that oppress you, while they think they speak that

which should tend to make you free: they may think to ease your troubled minds by such words as shall increase the trouble: or to deliver you as Peter would have delivered Christ, and saved his Saviour, first by carnal counsel, ' Be it far from thee, Lord; this shall not be unto thee.' Then by carnal unjust force, by drawing his sword against the officers; love and good meaning will not prevent the mischiefs of ignorance and mistake. Many thousand sick people are killed by their friends that attend them, with an earnest desire of their life: while they ignorantly give them that which is contrary to their disease, and will not be the less pernicious for the good meaning of the giver. Who have more tender affections than mothers to their children? Yet a great part of the calamity of the world of sickness, and the misery of man's life, proceeds from the ignorant and erroneous indulgence of mothers to their children, who, to please them, let them eat and drink what they will, and use them to excess and gluttony in their childhood, till nature be abused, mastered, and clogged with those superfluities and crudities which are the cause of most of the following diseases of their lives.

I might here also remind you how your friends may themselves be overcome with a temptation, and then become the more dangerous tempters of you, by how much the greater their interest is in your affections. If they be infected with error, they are the likeliest persons to ensnare you: if they be tainted with covetousness or pride, there is none so likely to draw you to the same sin: so your friends may be in effect your most deadly enemies, deceivers and destroyers.

15. If you have friends that are never so firm and constant, they may prove not only unable to relieve you, but even additions to your grief. If they are afflicted in the participation of your sufferings, as your troubles are become theirs, so their trouble for you will become yours, and so the stock of your sorrow will be increased. They are mortals, and liable to distress as well as you. Therefore they are like to bear their share in several sorts of sufferings: so friendship will make their sufferings to be yours: their sicknesses and pains, their fears and griefs, their wants and dangers, will all be yours. The more they are your hearty friends, the more they will be yours. So you will have as many additions to the proper burden of your griefs, as you have suffering friends: when you but hear that they are dead, you say as Thomas, ' let us also go that we may die with him.' Having many such friends you will almost always have

one or other of them in distress; and so be seldom free from sorrow; besides all that which is properly your own.

16. Lastly, If you have a friend that is both true and useful, yet you may be sure he must stay with you but a little while. ' The godly men will cease, and the faithful fail from among the children of men; while men of lying flattering lips, and double hearts, survive, and the wicked walk on every side, while the vilest men are exalted;' while swarms of false malicious men, are left round about you, perhaps God will take away your dearest friends: if among a multitude of unfaithful ones, you have but one that is your friend indeed, perhaps God will take away that one. He may be separated from you into another country; or taken away to God by death. Not that God doth grudge you the mercy of a faithful friend, but that he would be your all, and would not have you hurt yourselves with too much affection to any creature, and for other reasons to be named.

To be forsaken of your friends, is not all your affliction: but to be so forsaken is a great aggravation of it.

(1.) For they use to forsake us in our greatest sufferings and straits, when we have the greatest need of them.

(2.) They fail us most at a dying hour, when all other worldly comfort fails: as we must leave our houses, lands and wealth, so must we for the present leave our friends: as all the rest are feeble comforters, when we have once received our citation to appear before the Lord, so also are our friends but silly comforters: they can weep over us, but they cannot with all their care delay the separating stroke of death one day or hour.

Only by their prayers, and holy advice, reminding us of everlasting things, and provoking us in the work of preparation, they may prove to us friends indeed. Therefore we must value a holy, heavenly, faithful friend, as one of the greatest treasures upon earth. While we take notice how as men they may forsake us, we must not deny but that as saints they are precious, and of singular use to us; and Christ uses by them to communicate his mercies; and if any creatures in the world may be blessings to us, it is holy persons, that have most of God in their hearts and lives.

(3.) It is an aggravation of the cross, that they often fail us when we are most faithful in our duty, and stumble most upon the most excellent acts of our obedience.

(4.) Those are the persons that oft-times fail

us, of whom we have deserved best, and from whom we might have expected most.

Review the experiences of the choicest servants that Christ hath had in the world, and you shall find enough to confirm you of the vanity of man, and the instability of the dearest friends. How highly was Athanasius esteemed? and yet at last deserted and banished by the famous Constantine himself! How excellent a man was Gregory Nazianzen, and highly valued in the church? and yet by reproach and discouragements driven away from his church at Constantinople whither he was chosen, and envied by the bishops round about him. How worthy a man was the eloquent Chrysostom, and highly valued in the church? and yet how bitterly was he prosecuted by Hierom and Epiphanius; and banished, and died in a second banishment, by the provocation of factious, contentious bishops, and an empress impatient of his plain reproofs? What person more generally esteemed and honoured for learning, piety, and peaceableness, than Melanchthon? and yet by the contentions of Illyricus and his party, he was made weary of his life. As highly as Calvin was deservedly valued at Geneva, yet once in a popular lunacy and displeasure, they drove him out of their city, and in contempt of him some called their dogs by the name of Calvin; though after they were glad to intreat him to return. How much our Grindal and Abbot were esteemed, it appears by their advancement to the archbishopric of Canterbury: and yet who knows not that their eminent piety sufficed not to keep them from dejecting frowns! If you say, that it is no wonder if with princes through interest, and with people through levity, it be thus; I might heap up instances of the like unsteadiness of particular friends: but all history, and the experiences of the most, so much abound with them, that I think it needless. Which of us must not say, with David, that all men are liars, that is, deceitful and unfaithful, either through weakness or insufficiency; that either will forsake us, or cannot help us in the time of need?

Was Christ forsaken in his extremity by his own disciples, to teach us what to expect, or bear? Think it not strange then to be conformed to your Lord, in this, as well as in other parts of his humiliation. Expect that men should prove deceitful; not that you should entertain censorious suspicions of your particular friends: but remember in general that man is frail, and the best too selfish and uncertain; and that it is no wonder if those should prove your greatest

grief, from whom you had the highest expectations. Are you better than Job, or David, or Christ? and are your friends more firm and unchangeable than theirs.

Consider, 1. That creatures must be set at a sufficient distance from their Creator. All-sufficiency, immutability, and insoluble fidelity, are proper to Jehovah. As it is no wonder for the sun to set, or be eclipsed, as glorious a body as it is, so it is no wonder for a friend, a pious friend, to fail us, for a time, in the hour of our distress. There are some that will not: but there is none but may, if God should leave them to their weakness. Man is not your rock: he hath no stability but what is derived, dependent, uncertain, and defective. Learn therefore to rest on God alone, and lean not too hard or confidently upon any mortal man.

2. God will have the common infirmity of man to be known, that so the weakest may not be utterly discouraged, nor take their weakness to be gracelessness, whilst they see that the strongest also have their infirmities, though not so great as theirs. If any of God's servants live in constant holiness and fidelity, without any shakings or stumbling in their way, it would tempt some self-accusing troubled souls, to think that they were altogether graceless, because they are so far short of others. But when we read of Peter's denying his master in so horrid a manner, with swearing and cursing, that he knew not the man, and of his dissimulation and not walking uprightly, and of David's unfriendly and unrighteous dealing with Mephibosheth, the seed of Jonathan: and of his most vile and treacherous dealing with Uriah, a faithful and deserving subject; it may both abate our wonder and offence at the unfaithfulness of our friends, and teach us to compassionate their frailty, when they desert us; and also somewhat abate our immoderate dejection and trouble, when we have failed toward God or man ourselves.

3. Moreover, consider, how the odiousness of that sin, which is the root and cause of such unfaithfulness, is greatly manifested by the failing of our friends. God will have the odiousness of the remnants of our self-love and carnal-mindedness, and cowardice appear: we should not discern it in the seed and root, if we did not see and taste it in the fruits. Seeing without tasting will not sufficiently convince us: a crab looks as beautiful as an apple; but when you taste it, you better know the difference. When you must yourselves be unkindly used by your friends, and forsaken by them in your distress, and you have tasted the fruits of the remnants of their

worldliness, selfishness and carnal fears, you will better know the odiousness of these vices, which thus break forth against all obligations to God and you, and notwithstanding the light, the conscience, and perhaps the grace, that resists them.

4. Are you not prone to over-value and over-love your friends? If so, is not this the proper remedy for your disease. In the loving of God, we are in no danger of excess; and therefore have no need of any thing to quench it. In the loving of the godly, purely upon the account of Christ, and in loving saints as saints, we are not apt to go too far. But yet our understandings may mistake, and we may think that saints have more of sanctity than indeed they have; and we are exceedingly apt to mix a selfish, common love, with that which is spiritual and holy; and at the same time, when we love a Christian as a Christian, we are apt not only to love him, as we ought, but to over-love him because he is our friend, and loves us. Those Christians who have no special love to us, we are apt to undervalue, and neglect and love them below their holiness and worth: but those that we think entirely love us, we love above their proper worth, as they stand in the esteem of God: not but that we may love those that love us, and add this love to that which is purely for the sake of Christ; but we should not let our own interest prevail and over-turn the interest of Christ, nor love any so much for loving us, as for loving Christ: and if we do so, no wonder if God shall use such remedies as he sees meet, to abate our excess of selfish love.

O how highly are we apt to think of all that good which is found in those who most highly value us, and most dearly love us; when perhaps in itself it is but some ordinary good, or ordinary degree of goodness which is in them! Their love to us irresistibly procures our love to them: and when we love them, it is wonderful to observe how easily we are brought to think well of almost all they do, and highly to value their judgments, graces, parts and work: when greater excellencies in another perhaps are scarcely observed, or regarded but as a common thing. Therefore the destruction or want of love is apparent in the vilifying thoughts and speeches, that most men have of one another; and in the low esteem of the judgments, and performances, and lives of other men: much more in their contempt, reproaches and cruel persecutions. Now though God will have us increase in our love of Christ in his members, and in our pure love of Christians, as such, and in our common charity

to all, yea, and in our just fidelity to our friend; yet would he have us suspect and moderate our selfish and excessive love, and inordinate, partial esteem of one above another, when it is but for ourselves, and on our own account. Therefore as he will make us know, that we ourselves are no such excellent persons, as that it should make another so laudable, or advance his worth, because he loves us; so he will make us know, that our friends, whom we over-value, are but like other men: if we exalt them too highly in our esteem, it is a sign that God must cast them down; and as their love to us, was it that made us so exalt them: so their unkindness or unfaithfulness to us, is the fittest means to bring them lower in our estimation and affection. God is very jealous of our hearts, as to our over-valuing and over-loving any of his creatures: what we give inordinately and excessively to them, is some way or other taken from him, and given them to his injury, and therefore to his offence. Though I know that to be void of natural, friendly, or social affections, is an odious extreme on the other side; yet God will rebuke us if we are guilty of excess. It is the greater and more inexcusable fault to over-love the creature because our love to God is so cold, and so hardly kindled and kept alive! He cannot take it well to see us dote upon dust and frailty like ourselves, at the same time when all his wondrous kindness, and attractive goodness, cause but such a faint and languid love to him, which we ourselves can scarcely feel. If therefore he cure us by permitting our friends to show us truly what they are, and how little they deserve such excessive love, when God hath so little, it is no more wonder, than it is that he is tender of his glory, and merciful to his servants' souls.

5. By the failing and unfaithfulness of our friends, the wonderful patience of God will be observed and honoured as it is showed both to them and us. When they forsake us in our distress, especially when we suffer for the cause of Christ, it is God that they injure more than us: and therefore if he bear with them, and forgive their weakness upon repentance, why should not we do so, that are much less injured? The world's perfidiousness should make us think, how great and wonderful is the patience of God, that bears with, and bears up so vile, ungrateful, treacherous men that abuse him to whom they are infinitely obliged? And it should make us consider, when men deal treacherously with us, how great is that mercy that hath borne with, and pardoned greater wrongs, which I myself have done to God, than these can be which men have

done to me! It was the remembrance of David's sin, that had provoked God to raise up his own son against him, of whom he had been too fond, which made him so easily bear the curses and reproach of Shimei. It will make us bear abuse from others, to remember how ill we have dealt with God, and how ill we have deserved at his hands ourselves.

6. I have observed another reason of God's permitting the failing of our friends. It is, that the love of our friends may not hinder us when we are called to suffer or die. When we over-love them, it tears our very hearts to leave them: and therefore it is a strong temptation to draw us from our duty, and to be unfaithful to the cause of Christ, lest we should be taken from our too dear friends, or lest our suffering cause their too much grief. It is so hard a thing to die with willingness and peace, that it must needs be a mercy to be saved from the impediments which make us backward : and the excessive love of friends and relations, is not the least of these impediments : O how loth is many a one to die, when they think of parting with wife, or hus-band, or children, or dear and faithful friends! Now, I have often observed, that a little before their death or sickness, it is ordinary with God to permit some unkindness between such too dear friends to arise, by which he moderated and a-bated their affections, and made them a great deal more willing to die. Then we are ready to say, it is time for me to leave the world, when not only the rest of the world, but my dearest friends have first forsaken me! This helps us to remember our dearest everlasting Friend, and to be grieved at the heart that we have been no truer ourselves to him, who would not have for-saken us in our extremity. Sometimes it makes us even weary of the world, and to say as Elias, 'Lord, take away my life,' when we must say, I thought I had one friend left, and behold even he forsakes me in my distress. As the love of friends entangles our affections to this world, so to be weaned, by their unkindnesses, from our friends, is a great help to loosen us from the world, and proves often a very great mercy to a soul that is ready to depart.

As the friends that love us most, and have most interest in our esteem and love, may do more than others, in tempting us to be unfaithful to our Lord, to entertain any error, to commit any sin, or to flinch in suffering ; so when God hath permitted them to forsake us, and to lose their too great interest in us, we are fortified against all such temptations from them. I have known where a former intimate friend hath

grown strange, and broken former friendship, and quickly after turned to such dangerous ways and errors, as convinced the other of the merci-fulness of God, in weakening his temptation by his friend's desertion ; who might else have drawn him along with him into sin. I have often ob-served, that when the husbands have turned from religion to infidelity, or to some dangerous heresy, that God hath permitted them to hate and abuse their wives so inhumanly, as that it preserved the poor women from the temptation of following them in their apostacy or sin; when as some other women with whom their husbands have dealt more kindly, have been drawn away with them into pernicious paths.

Therefore still I must say, we were undone if we had the disposing of our own conditions. It would be long before we should have been will-ing ourselves to be thus unkindly dealt with by our friends : and yet God hath made it to many a soul, a notable means of preserving them from being undone forever. Yea, the unfaithfulness of all our friends, and the malice and cruelty of all our enemies, doth us not usually so much harm, as the love and temptation of some one deluded erring friend, whom we are ready to follow into the gulf.

7 Lastly, consider that it is not desirable or suitable to our state, to have too much of our comfort by any creature : not only because it is most pure and sweet, which is most immediately from God : but because also we are very prone to over-love the creature; and if it should but seem to be very agreeable to us, by serving our necessities or desires, it would seem the more amiable, and therefore be the stronger snare : the work of mortification doth much consist in the annihilation or deadness of all the creatures, as to any power to draw away our hearts from God, or to entangle us and detain us from our duty. The more excellent and lovely the creature ap-pears to us, the less it is dead to us, or we to it ; and the more will it be able to hinder or ensnare us.

When you have well considered all these things, I suppose you will admire the wisdom of God in leaving you under this kind of trial, and weaning you from every creature, and teaching you by his providence, as well as by his word, to 'cease from man, whose breath is in his nos-trils ; for wherein is he to be accounted of?' and you will see that it is no great wonder that cor-rupted souls, that live in other sins, should be guilty of this unfaithfulness to their friends: and that he that dare unthankfully trample upon the unspeakable kindness of the Lord, should deal unkindly with the best of men. You make no great wonder at other kind of sins, when you see the world continually commit them; why then should you make a greater or a stranger matter of this, than of the rest? Are you better than God? Must unfaithfulness to you be made more heinous, than that unfaithfulness to him, which yet you daily see and slight? The least wrong to God is a thousand fold more than the greatest that can be done to you, as such. Have you done that for your nearest friend, which God hath done for him, and you, and all men? Their obligations to you are nothing in comparison of their great and manifold obligations to God.

You know that you have more wronged God yourselves, than any man ever wronged you: if yet for all that, he bear with you, have you not great reason to bear with others?

Yea, you have not been innocent towards men yourselves: did you never wrong or fail another? Or rather, are you not apter to see and aggravate the wrong that others do to you, than that which you have done to others? May you not call to mind your own neglects, and say as Adonibezeck, 'threescore and ten kings having their thumbs and their great toes cut off, gathered their meat under my table: as I have done, so God hath requited me.' Many a one have I failed or wronged, and no wonder if others fail and wrong me.

Nay, you have been much more unfaithful and injurious to yourselves, than ever any other hath been to you. No friend was so near you, as yourselves: none had such a charge of you: none had such helps and advantages to do you good or hurt: yet all the enemies you have in the world, even in earth or hell, have not wronged and hurt you half so much as you have done yourselves. O, methinks the man or woman that knows themselves, and knows what it is to repent; that ever saw the greatness of their own sin and folly, should have no great mind or leisure to aggravate the failing of their friends, or the injuries of their enemies, considering what they have proved to themselves. Have I forfeited my own salvation, and deserved everlasting wrath, and sold my Saviour and my soul for so base a thing as sinful pleasure, and shall I ever make a wonder of it, that another man doth me some temporal hurt? Was any friend so near to me as myself; or more obliged to me? O sinful soul, let thy own, rather than thy friend's deceit, treachery, and neglects, be the matter of thy displeasure, wonder, and complaints!

Let thy conformity herein to Jesus Christ, be thy holy ambition and delight: not as it is thy suffering, nor as it is caused by men's sin: but as it is thy conformity and fellowship in the sufferings of thy Lord, and caused by his love.

I have already showed you that sufferers for Christ, are in the highest form among his disciples. The order of his followers usually is this: 1. At our entrance, and in the lowest form, we are exercised with the fears of hell, and God's displeasure, and in the works of repentance for the sin that we have done. 2. In the second form, we come to think more seriously of the remedy, and to inquire what we shall do to be saved, and to understand better what Christ hath done and suffered, and what he is and will be to us: and to value him, his love, and grace: here we are much inquiring how we may know our own sincerity, and our interest in Christ, and are labouring for some assurance, and looking after signs of grace. 3. In the next form or order we are searching after further knowledge, and labouring better to understand the mysteries of religion, and to get above the rudiments and first principles: and here if we escape turning bare opinionists or heretics, by the snare of controversy or curiosity, it is well. 4. In the next form we set ourselves to the fuller improvement of all our further degrees of knowledge; and to digest it all, and turn it into stronger faith, love, hope, and greater humility, patience, self-denial, mortification, and contempt of earthly vanities, and hatred of sin: and to walk more watchfully and holily, and to be more in holy duty. 5. In the next form we grow to be more public-spirited: to set our hearts on the church's welfare, and long more for the progress of the gospel, and for the good of others; and to do all the good in the world that we are able, for men's souls or bodies, but especially to long and lay out ourselves for the conversion and salvation of ignorant, secure, unconverted souls. The counterfeit of this is, an eager desire to proselyte others to our opinions, or that religion which we have chosen, by the direction of flesh and blood, or which is not of God, nor according unto godliness, but doth subserve our carnal ends. 6. In the next form we grow to study more the pure and wonderful love of God in Christ, and to relish and admire that love, and to be taken up with the goodness and tender mercies of the Lord, and to be kindling the flames of holy love to him that hath thus loved us; and to keep our souls in the exercise of that love: and withal to live in joy, thanks, and praise to him that hath redeemed us and loved us. Also by faith to

converse in heaven, and to live in holy contemplation, beholding the glory of the Father and
the Redeemer in the glass which is fitted to our
present use, till we come to see him face to face.
Those that are the highest in this form, do so
walk with God, and burn in love, and are so
much above inferior vanities, and are so conversant by faith in heaven, that their hearts even
dwell there, and there they long to be for ever.
7. In the highest form in the school of Christ,
we are exercising this confirmed faith and love,
in sufferings, especially for Christ : in following
him with our cross, and being conformed to him,
and glorifying God in the fullest exercise, and
discovery of his graces in us, and in an actual
trampling upon all that stands up against him,
for our hearts : in bearing the fullest witness to
his truth and cause, by constant enduring, though
to the death.

Not but that the weakest that are sincere,
must suffer for Christ if he call them to it: martyrdom itself is not peculiar to the strong believers: whoever forsakes not all that he hath for
Christ, cannot be his disciple. But to suffer with
that faith and love fore-mentioned, and in that
manner, is proper to the strong : usually God
doth not try and exercise his young and weak
ones with the trials of the strong ; nor set his
infants on so hard a service, nor put them in the
front or hottest of the battle, as he doth the ripe
confirmed Christians. The sufferings of their
inward doubts and fears doth take up such : it is
the strong that ordinarily are called to sufferings
for Christ, at least in any high degree ; I have
digressed thus far to make it plain to you, that
our conformity to Christ, and fellowship with
him in his sufferings, in any notable degree, is
the lot of his best confirmed servants, and the
highest form in his school among his disciples :
therefore not to be inordinately feared or abhorred, not to be the matter of impatience, but
of holy joy ; and in such infirmities we may
glory. If it be so of sufferings in the general,
for Christ, then is it so of this particular sort of
suffering, even to be forsaken of all our best and
nearest, dearest friends, when we come to be
most abused by the enemies.

For my own part, I must confess that as I am
much wanting in other parts of my conformity
to Christ, so I take myself to be yet much short,
of what I expect he should advance me to, as
long as my friends no more forsake me. It is
not long since I found myself in a low, if not a
doubting case, because I had so few enemies,
and so little sufferings for the cause of Christ,
though I had much of other sorts ; now that

doubt is removed by the multitude of furies which
God hath let loose against me. But yet, methinks, while my friends themselves are so friendly to me, I am much short of what I think I must
at last attain to.

II. *The cause of this desertion selfishness.*

But let us look further into the text, and see
what is the cause of forsaking Christ in the disciples : and what it is that they betake themselves
to, when they leave him.

' Ye shall be scattered every man to his own.'

Self-denial was not perfect in them, selfishness
therefore in this hour of temptation did prevail.
They had before forsaken all to follow Christ ;
they had left their parents, their families, their
estates, their trades, to be his disciples : but
though they believed him to be the Christ, yet
they dreamed of a visible kingdom, and did all
this with too carnal expectations of being great
men on earth, when Christ should begin his
reign. Therefore when they saw his apprehension
and ignominious suffering, and thought how they
were frustrate of their hopes, they seem to repent
that they had followed him, though not by apostacy and an habitual or plenary change of mind,
yet by a sudden passionate frightful apprehension, which vanished when grace performed its
part. They now began to think that they had
lives of their own to save, and families of their
own to mind, and business of their own to do:
they had before forsaken their private interests
and affairs, and gathered themselves to Jesus
Christ, and lived in communion with him, and
one another. But now they return to their trades
and callings, and ' are scattered every man to his
own.'

Selfishness is the great enemy of all societies,
of all fidelity and friendship : there is no trusting that person in whoever it is predominant. The
remnants of it, where it doth not reign, do make
men walk unevenly and unsteadfastly towards
God and men. They will certainly deny both
God and their friends, in a time of trial, who
are not unable to deny themselves : or rather he
never was a real friend to any, that is predominantly selfish. They have always some interest
of their own, which their friend must needs contradict, or is insufficient to satisfy. Their houses,
their lands, their monies, their children, their
honour, or something which they call their own,
will be frequently the matter of contention ; and
are so near them, that they can for the sake of
these, cast off the nearest friend. Contract no
special friendship with a selfish man : nor put
any confidence in him, whatever friendship he
may profess. He is so confined to himself, that

he hath no true love to spare for others: if he seem to love a friend, it is not as a friend, but as a servant, or at best as a benefactor: he loves you for himself, as he loves his money, or horse, or house, because you may be serviceable to him: or as a horse or dog doth love his keeper, for feeding him: therefore when your provender is gone, his love is gone: when you have done feeding him, he hath done loving you: when you have no more for him, he hath no more for you.

Object. But, some will say, it is not the falseness of my friend that I lament, but the separation, or the loss of one that was most faithful: I have found the deceitfulness of ordinary friends; and therefore the more highly prize those few that are sincere. I had but one true friend among abundance of self-seekers: and that one is dead, or taken from me, and I am left as in a wilderness, having no mortal man that I can trust, or take much comfort in.

Answ. Is this your case? I pray you answer these few questions, and suffer the truth to have its proper work upon your mind.

Quest. 1. Who was it that deprived you of your friend; was it not God? Did not he that gave him you, take him from you? Was it not his Lord and owner that called him home? Can God do any thing amiss? Will you not give him leave to do as he lists with his own? Dare you think that there was wanting either wisdom or goodness, justice or mercy, in God's disposal of your friend? Or will you ever have rest, if you cannot have rest in the will of God?

2. How know you what sin your friend might have fallen into, if he had lived as long as you would have him? You will say, that God could have preserved him from sin: it is true; but God preserves wisely, by means, as well as powerfully: sometimes he sees that the temptations to that person are like to be so strong, and his corruption like to get such advantage, that no means is so fit as death itself, for his preservation. If God had permitted your friend by temptation to have fallen into some scandalous sin, or course of evil, or into errors or false ways, would it not have been much worse than death to him and you? God might have suffered your friend that was so faithful, to have been sifted and shaken, as Peter was, and to have denied his Lord; and to have seemed in your own eyes, as odious, as he before seemed amiable.

3. How know you what unkindness to yourself, your dearest friend might have been guilty of? Alas, there is greater frailty and inconstancy in man, than you are aware of. There are sadder roots of corruption unmortified, that may spring up into bitter fruits, than most of us ever discover in ourselves. Many a mother hath her heart broken by the unnatural conduct of such a child, or the unkindness of such a husband, as if they had died before, would have been lamented by her, with great impatience and excess. How confident soever you may be of the future fidelity of your friend, you little know what trials might have discovered. Many a one hath failed God and man, that once were as confident of themselves, as ever you were of your friend. Which of us see not reason to be distrustful of ourselves? Can we know another better than ourselves: or promise more concerning him.

4. How know you what great calamity might have befallen your friend, if he had lived as long as you desired? When the righteous seem to men to perish, and merciful men are taken away, it is from the evil to come that they are taken. How many of my friends have I lamented as if they had died unseasonably, concerning whom some following providence quickly showed me, that it would have been a grievous misery to them to have lived longer! Little know you what calamities were imminent on his person, his family, kindred, neighbours, country, that would have broke his heart: what if a friend of yours had died immediately before some calamitous subversion of a kingdom, some ruins of the church, &c. and if ignorantly, he had done that which brought these things to pass, can you imagine how lamentably sad his life would have been to him, to have seen the church, the gospel, and his country, in so sad a case; especially if it had been caused by him? Many that have unawares done that which hath ruined a particular friend, have lived in so much grief and trouble, as made them consent that death should both revenge the injured on them, and conclude their misery. What then would it have been to have seen the public good subverted, and the faithful overwhelmed in misery, and the gospel hindered, and holy worship changed for deceit and vanity; and for conscience to have been daily saying, I had a hand in all this misery: I kindled the fire that hath burned up all!

What comfort can you think such friends, if they had survived, would have found on earth? Unless it were a comfort to hear the complaints of the afflicted, to see and hear such odious sins as sometimes vexed righteous Lot to see and hear; or to hear of the scandals of one friend, and the apostacy of another, and the sinful compliances and declinings ot a third; and to be under temptations, reproaches and afflictions themselves? Is it a matter to be so much lamented, that God hath prevented their greater miseries and woe?

5. What was the world to your friends while they did enjoy it? Or what is it now, or like to be hereafter to yourselves? was it so good and kind to them, as that you should lament their separation from it? was it not to them a place of toil and trouble, of envy and vexation, of enmity and poison, of successive cares, and fears, and griefs, and, worst of all, a place of sin? Did they groan under the burthen of a sinful nature, a distempered, tempted, troubled heart, of languishings and weakness of every grace; of the rebukes of God, the wounds of conscience, and the malice of a wicked world? And would you have them under these again; or is their deliverance become your grief? Did you not often join in prayer with them, for deliverance from malice, calamities, troubles, imperfections, temptations and sin? and now those prayers are answered in their deliverance: and do you now grieve at that, which then you prayed for!

Doth the world use yourselves so well and kindly, as that you should be sorry that your friends partake not of the feast? Are you not groaning from day to day yourselves? and are you grieved that your friends are taken from your griefs? you are not pleased with your own condition: when you look into your hearts, you are displeased and complain: when you look into your lives, you are displeased and complain: when you look into your families, into your neighbourhoods, unto your friends, unto the church, unto the kingdom, unto the world, you are displeased and complain: and are you also displeased that your friends are not under the same displeasure and complaints as you? Is the world a place of rest or trouble to you? And would you have your friends to be as far from rest as you?

If you have some ease and peace at present, you little know what storms are near! you may see the days, you may hear the tidings, you may feel the griefs and pains, which may make you call for death yourselves, and make you say, that a life on earth is no felicity, and make you confess that they are blessed that are dead in the Lord, as resting from their labours, and being past these troubles, griefs and fears. Many a poor troubled soul is in so great distress, as that they take away their own lives to have some taste of hell: and yet, at the same time, are grieving because their friends are taken from

them, who would have been grieved for their griefs, and for aught they know might have fallen into as sad a state as they themselves are now lamenting.

6. Do you think it is for the hurt or the good of your friend, that he is removed hence? It cannot be for his hurt, unless he be in hell. At least, it is uncertain whether to live would have been for his good, by an increase of grace, and so for greater glory. If he be in hell, he was no fit person for you to take much pleasure in upon earth: he might be indeed a fit object for your compassion, but not for your complacency. Surely you are not undone for want of such company as God will not endure in his sight, and you must be separated from for ever. But if they be in heaven, you are scarcely their friend if you would wish them thence. Friendship hath as great respect to the good of our friends as of ourselves. Do you pretend to friendship, and yet lament the removal of your friend to his greatest happiness! Do you set more by your own enjoying his company, than by his enjoying God in perfect blessedness: this shows a very culpable defect either in faith or friendship; and therefore beseems not Christians and friends. If love teaches us to mourn with them that mourn, and to rejoice with them that rejoice; can it be an act of rational love to mourn for them that are possessed of the highest everlasting joys?

7. God will not honour himself by one only, but by many: he knows best when his work is done: when our friends have finished all God intended them for, when he put them into the world, is it not time for them to be gone, and for others to take their places, and finish their work also in their time? God will have a succession of his servants in the world. Would you not come down, and give place to him that is to follow you, when your part is acted, and his is to begin? If David had not died, there had been no Solomon, no Jehosaphat, no Hezekiah, no Josiah, to succeed him and honour God in the same throne. You may as wisely grudge that one day only takes not up all the week, and that the clock strikes not the same hour still, but proceeds from one to two, from two to three, &c., as to murmur that one man only continues not, to do the work of his place, excluding his successors.

8. You must not have all your mercies by one messenger or hand: God will not have you confine your love to one only of his servants: and therefore he will not make one only useful to you: but when one hath delivered his message and done his part, perhaps God will send you

other mercies by another hand: and it belongs to him to choose the messenger, who gives the gift. If you will childishly dote upon the first messenger, and say you will have all the rest of your mercies by his hand, or you will have no more, your frowardness more deserves correction than compassion: and if you be kept fasting till you can thankfully take your food, from any hand that your Father sends it by, it is a correction very suitable to your sin.

9. Do you so highly value your friends for God, or for them, or for yourselves, in the final consideration? If it was for God, what reason of trouble have you, that God hath disposed of them, according to his wisdom and unerring will? Should you not then be more pleased that God has, and employs them in his highest service, than displeased that you want them?

But if you value, and love them for themselves, they are now more lovely when they are more perfect; and they are now more fit for your content and joy, than they could be in their sin and sorrows.

But if you valued and loved them but for yourselves only, it is just with God to take them from you, to teach you to value men to proper ends, and upon better considerations: and both to prefer God before yourselves, and better to understand the nature of true friendship, and better to know that your own felicity is not in the hands of any creature, but of God alone.

10. Did you improve your friends while you had them? or did you only love them, while you made but little use of them for your souls? If you used them not, it was just with God, for all your love, to take them from you. They were given you as your candle, not only to love it, but to work by the light of it: and as your garments, not only to love them, but to wear them; and as your meat, not only to love it, but to feed upon it. Did you receive their counsel, and hearken to their reproofs, and pray with them and confer with them upon those holy truths that tended to elevate your minds to God, and to inflame your breasts with sacred love? If not, be it now known to you, that God gave you not such helps and mercies only to talk of, or look upon and love, but also to improve for the benefit of our souls.

11. Do you not seem to forget where you are yourselves, and where you must shortly and for ever live? Where would you have your friends, but where you must be yourselves? Do you mourn that they are taken hence? why, if they had staid here a thousand years, how little of that time should you have had their company;

when you are almost leaving the world yourselves, would you not send your treasure before you to the place where you must abide? How quickly will you pass from hence to God, where you shall find your friends that you lamented as if they had been lost, and there shall dwell with them for ever? O foolish mourners! would you not have your friends at home? at their home and your home, with their Father and your Father, their God and your God! Shall you not there enjoy them long enough; can you so much miss them for one day, that must live with them to all eternity; and is not eternity long enough to enjoy your friends in?

Object. But I do not know whether ever I shall there have any distinct knowledge of them, or love to them, and whether God shall not there be so far all in all, as that we shall need no comfort from the creature.

Answ. There is no reason for either of these doubts: for, 1st. You cannot justly think that the knowledge of the glorified shall be more confused or imperfect than the knowledge of natural men on earth. We shall know much more, but not so much less. Heaven exceeds earth in knowledge, as much as it does in joy. 2d. The angels in heaven have now a distinct, particular knowledge of the least believers, rejoicing particularly in their conversion, and being called by Christ himself 'their angels.' Therefore when we shall be 'equal to the angels,' we shall certainly know our nearest friends that there dwell with us, and are employed in the same attendance. 3d. Abraham knew the rich man in hell, and the rich man knew Abraham and Lazarus: therefore we shall have as distinct a knowledge. 4th. The two disciples knew Moses and Elias in the mount, whom they had never seen before: though it is possible Christ told them who they were, yet there is no such thing expressed: and therefore it is as probable that they knew them by the communication of their irradiating glory: much more shall we be then illuminated to a clearer knowledge. 5th. It is said expressly, that our 'present knowledge shall be done away' only in regard of its imperfection; and not of itself, which shall be perfected: 'when that which is perfect is come, then that which is in part shall be done away.' As we put away childish thoughts and speeches, when we become men: the change will be from 'seeing in a glass' to 'seeing face to face,' and from 'knowing in part' to 'knowing even as we are known.'

2. That we shall both know, and love, and rejoice in creatures, even in heaven, notwithstanding that God is all in all, appears further

thus: 1st. Christ in his glorified humanity is a creature: and yet there is no doubt but all his members will there know and love him in his glorified humanity, without any derogation from the glory of his deity. 2d. The body of Christ will continue its union, and every member will be so nearly related, even in heaven, that they cannot choose but know and love each other. Shall we be ignorant of the members of our body: and not be concerned in their felicity with whom we are so nearly one? 3d. The state and felicity of the church hereafter, is frequently described in scripture, as consisting in society. It is a kingdom, the city of God, the heavenly Jerusalem: and it is mentioned as part of our happiness to be of that society. 4th. The saints are called kings themselves: and it is said that they shall judge the world, and the angels. Judging in scripture is frequently put for governing, therefore, whether there will be another world of mortals which they shall govern, as angels now govern men; or whether the misery of damned men and angels will partly consist in as base a subjection to the glorified saints, as dogs now have to men, or wicked reprobates on earth to angels; or whether in respect of both those together, the saints shall then be kings, and rule and judge; or whether it be only the participation of the glory of Christ, that is called a kingdom, I will not here determine; but it is most clear that they will have a distinct particular knowledge of the world, which they themselves must judge; and some concernment in that work. 5th. It is put into the description of the happiness of the saints, that they shall come from the east, and from the west, and shall sit down with Abraham, Isaac and Jacob, in the kingdom of God. Therefore they shall know them, and take some comfort in their presence. 6th. Love, even to the saints, as well as unto God, is one of the graces which shall endure for ever. It is exercised upon an immortal object (the image and children of the most high) and therefore must be one of the immortal graces. For grace, in the nature of it, dies not: and therefore if the object cease not, how should the grace cease, unless you will call its perfecting a ceasing?

It is a state too high for such as we, and I think for any mere creature, to live so immediately and only upon God, as to have no use for any fellow creature, nor no comfort in them. God can make use of glorified creatures, in such subserviency and subordination to himself, as shall be no diminution to his all-sufficiency and honour, nor to our glory and felicity. We must take heed of fancying such a heaven itself, as is above the capacity of a creature; as some very wise divines think they have done, that tell us we shall immediately see God's essence, his glory being that which is provided for our intuition and felicity, and is distinct from his essence; being not every where, as his essence is. As those do that tell us because that God will be all in all, therefore we shall there have none of our comfort by any creature. Though flesh and blood shall not enter into that kingdom, but our bodies will then be spiritual bodies; yet will they be really the same as now, and distinct from our souls; and therefore must have a felicity suitable to a body glorified: if the soul did immediately see God's essence, yet as no reason can conclude that it can see nothing else, or that it can see even created good, and not love it, so the body however must have objects and felicity fit for a body.

Object. But it is said, if we knew Christ after the flesh, henceforth know we him no more.

Answ. No doubt but all the carnality in principles, matter, manner and ends of our knowledge, will then cease, as its imperfection: but that a carnal knowledge be turned into a spiritual, is no more a diminution to it, than it is to the glory of our bodies, to be made like the stars in the firmament of our Father.

Object. But then I shall have no more comfort in my present friends than in any other.

Answ. First, If you had none in them, it is no diminution to our happiness, if indeed we should have all in God immediately and alone. Second, But if you have as much in others that you never knew before, that will not diminish any of your comfort in your ancient friends. Third, But it is most probable to us, that as there is a two-fold object for our love in the glorified saints; one is their holiness, and the other is the relation which they stood in between God and us, being made his instruments for our conversion and salvation, so that we shall love saints in heaven in both respects: in the first respect, which is the chief, we shall love those most that have most of God, and the greatest glory, though such as we never knew on earth. In the second respect we shall love those most, that were employed by God for our greatest good.

That we shall not there lay by so much respect to ourselves, as to forget or disregard our benefactors, is manifest. 1. In that we shall for ever remember Christ, love him, and praise him, as one that formerly redeemed us, and 'washed us in his blood, and hath made us kings and priests to God:' therefore we may also in just subordination to Christ, remember them with love and thankfulness, that were his instruments for the collation of these benefits. 2. This kind of self-love, to be sensible of good and evil, to ourselves, is none of the sinful or imperfect selfishness to be renounced or laid by, but part of our very natures, and as inseparable from us as we are from ourselves.

Much more, were it not digressive, might be said on this subject: but I shall only add, that as God doth draw us to every holy duty by showing us the excellency of that duty; and as perpetuity is not the smallest excellency, so he hath purposely mentioned that love endureth for ever, when he hath described the love of one another, as a principal motive to kindle and increase this love. Therefore those that think they shall have no personal knowledge of one another, nor personal love to one another,—for we cannot love personally, if we know not personally,—take a most effectual course to destroy in their souls all holy special love to saints, by casting away that principal or very great motive given them by the Holy Ghost. I am not able to love much where I foreknow that I shall not love long. I cannot love a comely inn, so well as a nearer dwelling of my own, because I must be gone to-morrow. Therefore must I love my Bible better than my law-books, or physic books, &c. because it leads to eternity. Therefore I must love holiness in myself and others, better than meat and drink, wealth and honour, beauty and pleasure, because it must be loved for ever, when the love of these must needs be transitory, as they are transitory. I must profess, from the very experience of my soul, that it is the belief that I shall love my friends in heaven, that principally kindles my love to them on earth. If I thought I should never know them after death, and consequently never love them more when this life is ended, I should, in reason, number them with temporal things, and love them comparatively but a little: even as I love other transitory things, allowing for the excellency in the nature of grace. But now I converse with some delight with my godly friends, as believing I shall converse with them for ever, and take comfort in the very dead and absent, as believing we shall shortly meet in heaven: I love them, I hope, with a love that is of a heavenly nature, while I love them as the heirs of heaven, with a love which I expect shall there be perfected, and more fully and for ever exercised.

12. The last reason that I give you, to move you to bear the loss or absence of your friends, is, that it gives you the loudest call to retire from all the world, and to converse with God himself, and to long for heaven, where you shall be separated from your friends no more. Your forsaken state will somewhat assist you to that solitary converse with God, which it calls you to: but this brings us up to the third part of the text.

III. *How the loss is supplemented.*

'Yet I am not alone, because the Father is with me.'

Doct. When all forsake us, and leave us (as to them) alone, we are far from being simply alone; because God is with us.

He is not without company that is with the king, though twenty others have turned him off. He is not without light that hath the shining sun, though all his candles be put out. If God be our God, he is our all, and is enough for us: if he be our all, we shall not much find the want of creatures while he is with us.

For, 1. He is with us who is every where, and therefore is never from us: and knows all the ways and projects of our enemies; being with them in wrath, as he is with us in mercy.

2. He is with us who is almighty, sufficient to preserve us, conquerable by none; and therefore while he is with us, we need not fear what man can do unto us: for they can do nothing but what he will: no danger, no sickness, no trouble or want, can be so great as to make it any difficulty to God to deliver us, when and how he pleases.

3. He is with us who is infinitely wise, and therefore we need not fear the subtilty of enemies; nor shall any of his undertaken works for his church or us miscarry for want of foresight, or through any oversight. We shall be preserved even from our own folly, as well as from our enemies' subtilty: for it is not our own wisdom that our greatest concerns do principally rest upon, nor that our safety and peace are chiefly secured by; but it is the wisdom of our great Preserver. He knows what to do with us, and what paths to lead us in, and what is best for us in all conditions. And he hath promised to teach us, and will be our sure, infallible guide.

4. He is with us who is infinitely good, and therefore is only fit to be a continual delight and satisfaction to our souls; that hath nothing in him to disaffect us, or discourage us: whom we may love without fear of over-loving; and need not set any bounds to our love, the object of it being infinite.

5. He is with us who is most nearly related to us, and most dearly loves us; and therefore will never be wanting to us in any thing that is

fit for us to have. This is he that is with us, when all have left us, and as to man we are alone ; and therefore we may well say that we are not alone. Of this I shall say more in the application.

Quest. But how is he with us? Answ. 1. He is with us not only in his essential presence, as he is every where, but by his gracious Fatherly presence : we are in his family, attending on him : even as the eye of a servant is to the hand of his master : we are always with him, and, as he phrases it himself in the parable, 'all that he hath is ours,' that is, all that is fit to be communicated to us, and all the provisions of his bounty for his children. When we awake, we should be still with him : when we go abroad, we should be always as before him : our life and works should be a walking with God.

2. He is always with us sufficiently to do us good ; though we have none else that cares for us, yet will he never cast us out of his care, but bids us cast our care on him, as promising that he will care for us. Though we have none else to provide for us, he is always with us, and our Father knows what we want, and will make the best provision for us. Though we have none else to defend us against the power of our enemies, he is always with us to be our sure defence : he is the rock to which we fly, and upon which we are surely built. He gathers us to himself as the hen gathers her chickens under her wings. And surely while love is thus protecting us, we may well say that the Father himself is with us. Though in all our wants we have no other to supply us, yet he is still with us to perform his promise, that no good thing shall be wanting to them that fear him. Though we may have none else to strengthen and help us, and support us in our weakness, yet he is always with us, whose grace is sufficient for us, to manifest his strength in weakness. Though we have no other to teach us, and to resolve our doubts, yet he is with us that is our chief master, and hath taken us to be his disciples, and will be our light and guide, and will lead us into the truth. Though we have none else to be our comforter, in our agony, darkness or distress ; but all forsake us, or are taken from us, and we are exposed as Hagar with Ishmael in a wilderness, yet still the Father of all consolations is with us; his Spirit, who is the Comforter, is in us : and he that so often speaks the words of comfort to us in his gospel, and says, 'be of good cheer; let not your hearts be troubled, neither be afraid,' &c., will speak them, in the season and measure which is fittest for us, unto our hearts.

Though all friends turn enemies, and would destroy us, or turn false accusers, as Job's friends, in their ignorance or passion ; though all of them should add affliction to our affliction, yet is our Redeemer and justifier still with us, and will lay his restraining hand upon our enemies, and say to their proudest fury, 'hitherto, and no further shalt thou go.' He is angry with Job's accusing friends, notwithstanding their friendship and good meaning, and though they seemed to plead for God and godliness against Job's sin. Who shall be against us while God is for us? or who shall condemn us when it is he that justifies us? Though we be put to say as David, ' I looked on my right hand, and beheld, but there was no man that would know me : refuge failed me ; no man cared for my soul ;' yet we may say with him, ' I cried unto thee. O Lord ; I said, Thou art my refuge and my portion in the land of the living : bring my soul out of prison, that I may praise thy name : the righteous shall compass me about : for thou shalt deal bountifully with me. I poured out my complaint before him; I showed before him my trouble : when my spirit was overwhelmed within me, then thou knewest my path : in the way wherein I walked have they privily laid a snare for me.' Thus ' God is our refuge and strength ; a very present help in trouble : therefore should we not fear though the earth were removed, and though the mountains were carried into the midst of the sea ; though the waters thereof roar and be troubled,' &c. Though as David saith, ' mine enemies speak evil of me : when shall he die, and his name perish ? And if he come to see me, he speaketh vanity : his heart gathereth iniquity to itself ; when he goeth abroad he telleth it : all that hate me whisper together against me : against me do they devise my hurt : an evil disease, say they, cleaveth fast unto him ; and now that he lieth, he shall rise up no more : yea, my own familiar friend, in whom I trusted, that did eat of my bread, hath lift up his heel against me.' Yet we may add as he, 'and as for me, thou upholdest me in mine integrity, and settest me before thy face for ever.' Though as Psal. xxxv. 7. &c. ' Without cause they have hid for me their net in a pit, which without cause they have digged for my soul : 11. and false witnesses did rise up, they laid to my charge things that I knew not : they rewarded me evil for good : 15, 16. In my adversity they rejoiced, and gathered themselves together ; the abjects gathered themselves together against me, and I knew it not ; they did tear and ceased not ; with hypocritical mockers in feasts, they gnashed upon me with their teeth : 20. For they speak not peace, but they devise deceitful matters against them that are quiet in the land.' Yet, verse 9. ' My soul shall be joyful in the Lord ; it shall rejoice in his salvation : 10. All my bones shall say, Lord, who is like unto thee, who deliverest the poor from him that is too strong for him, yea, the poor and the needy from him that spoileth him.' Though friends be far off, 'the Lord is nigh to them that are of a broken heart, and saveth such as be of a contrite spirit : many are the afflictions of the righteous, but the Lord delivereth him out of them all.'—'The Lord redeemeth the soul of his servants ; and none of them that trust in him shall be desolate.' Therefore, ' I will be glad and rejoice in his mercy, for he hath considered my trouble, and hath known,' and owned, 'my soul in adversity : and hath not shut me in the hand of the enemy. When my life was spent with grief, and my years with sighing, my strength failed because of mine iniquity, and my bones were consumed ; I was a reproach among all mine enemies, but especially among my neighbours, and a fear to mine acquaintance ; they that did see me without, fled from me : I was forgotten, and as a dead man out of mind ; I was like a broken vessel : I heard the slander of many : fear was on every side, while they took counsel together against me, they devised to take away my life : but I trusted in thee, O Lord : I said, thou art my God : my times are in thy hand : deliver me from the hands of mine enemies, and from them that persecute me : make thy face to shine upon thy servant : save me for thy mercies' sake. O how great is thy goodness which thou hast laid up for them that fear thee, which thou hast wrought for them that trust in thee before the sons of man ! Thou shalt hide them in the secret of thy presence from the pride of man : thou shalt keep them secretly in a pavilion from the strife of tongues.' Thus God is with us when men are far from us, or against us ; his people find, by happy experience, that they are not alone. Because he is nigh them, evil shall not come nigh them unless as it works for their good. He is their ' hiding place to preserve them from trouble : the great water-floods shall not come nigh them : he will compass them about with songs of deliverance.'

3. As God is with us thus relatively and efficiently, so also objectively, for our holy converse. Wherever our friends are, God is still at hand to be the most profitable, honourable, and delightful object of our thoughts. There is enough in him to take up all the faculties of my soul. He that is but in a well-furnished library, may find great and excellent employment for his thoughts many years together: and so may he that lives in the open world, and hath all the visible works of God to meditate upon : but all this were nothing if God were not the sense of books and creatures, and the matter of all these noble studies : he that is alone, and hath only God himself to study, hath the matter and sense of all the books and creatures in the world, to employ his thoughts upon. He never needs to want matter for his meditation, that hath God to meditate on. He need not want matter of discourse, whether mental or vocal, that hath God to talk of, though he have not the name of any other friend to mention. All our affections may have in him the highest and most pleasant work. The soul of man cannot have a more sweet and excellent work than to love him : he wants neither work nor pleasure, that in his solitude is taken up in the believing contemplations of eternal love, and of all his blessed attributes and works. O then what happy and delightful converse may a believer have with God alone ! He is always present, and always at leisure to be spoken with ; and always willing of our access and audience : he hath no interest opposed to our felicity, which should move him to reject us, as worldly great ones often have. He never misunderstands us, nor charges that upon us which we were never guilty of : if we converse with men, their mistakes, interests, passions, and insufficiencies, makes the trouble so great, and the benefit so small, that many have become thereby weary of the world, or of human society, and have spent the rest of their days alone in desert places. Indeed the more of God that appears in men, the more is their converse excellent and delightful : and theirs is the best that have most of God : but there is so much of vanity, and self, and flesh, and sin in the most, or all of us, as very much darkens our light, damps the pleasure, and blasts the fruit of our societies and converse. O how often have I been solaced in God, when I found nothing but deceit and darkness in the world ! How often hath he comforted me, when it was past the power of man ! How often hath he relieved and delivered me, when all the help of man was vain ! It hath been my stay and rest, to look to him, when the creature hath been a broken staff, and deceitful friends have been but as a broken tooth, or a foot that is out of joint, as Solomon speaks of confidence in an unfaithful man in the time of trouble. Verily, as the world were but an horrid dungeon without the sun, so it were a howling wilderness, a place of no considerable employment or delight, were it not that in it we may live to God and do him

service, and sometimes be refreshed with the light of his countenance, and the communications of his love. But of this more afterwards.

IV. *The advantages of solitude.*

We see our example and our encouragements. Let us now, as followers of Christ, endeavour to imitate him in this, and to live upon God when men forsake us, and to know that while God is with us, we are not alone, nor indeed forsaken while he forsakes us not.

I shall, 1. Show you here, negatively, what you must not do. 2. Affirmatively, what you must do, for the performance of your duty in this imitation of Christ.

1. You must not make this your pretence for the undervaluing your useful friends, nor for your unthankfulness for so great a benefit as a godly friend: nor for the neglect of your duty in improving the company and help of your friends: two is better than one: the communion of saints, and help of those that are wise and faithful, is a mercy highly to be esteemed. The undervaluing of it is at least a sign of a declining soul.

2. You must not hence fetch any pretence to slight your friends, and disoblige them, or neglect any duty that you owe them, or any means therein necessary to the continuation of their friendship.

3. You must not causelessly withdraw from human society into solitude. A weariness of converse with men is often joined with a weariness of our duty: a retiring voluntarily into solitude, when God doth not call or drive us thither, is often but a retiring from the place and work which God hath appointed us: consequently a retiring rather from God, than to God. Like some idle servants that think they should not work so hard, because it is but worldly business, and think their masters deal not religiously by them, unless they let them neglect their labour, that they may spend more time in serving God: as if it were not serving God to be faithful in their master's service.

I deny not but very holy persons have lived in a state of retirement from human converse: in such cases as these, it may become a duty: 1. In case of such persecution as at present leaves us no opportunity of serving or honouring God so much in any other place or state. 2. In case that natural infirmity, or disability, or any other accident, shall make one less serviceable to God and his church in society, than he is in solitude. 3. In case he hath committed a sin so heinous, and of indelible scandal and reproach, as that it is not fit for the servants of Christ any more

to receive him into their local communion, though he repent: for as to local communion, I think such a case may be. 4. In case a man, through custom and ill company, be so captivated to some fleshly lust, as that he is not able to bear the temptations that are found in human converse: but falls by them into frequent heinous sinning: in this case the right hand or eye is rather to be parted with, than their salvation Though a mere restraint by distance of temptations and opportunities of sinning, will not prove a man sanctified, nor save the soul that loves the sin, and fain would live in it: yet, 1. Grace may sometimes appear in the strength and self-denial which is exercised in the very avoiding of temptations, when yet perhaps the person hath not strength enough to have stood against the temptations if they had not been avoided. 2. The distance of temptations, and opportunity of serious and frequent consideration, may be a means to help them to sincerity that want it. 5. In case a man by age or sickness find himself so near to death, as that he hath now a more special call to look after his present actual preparation, than to endeavour any more the good of others; and find withal, that solitude will help him in his preparations, his society being such as would but hinder him. In these five cases, I suppose it lawful to retire from human converse into solitude.

But when there is no such necessity or call, it usually proceeds from one of these vicious distempers: 1. From cowardice and fear of suffering, when the soldiers of Christ do hide their heads, instead of confessing him before men. 2. From a laziness of mind and weariness of duty: when slothful and unprofitable servants hide their talents, pretending their fear of the austerity of their Lord. It is easier to run away from our work than to do it: and to go out of the reach of ignorance, malice, contradiction and ungodliness, than to encounter them, and conquer them by truth and holy lives. So many persons as we converse with, so many are there to whom we owe some duty: this is not so easy as it is to over-run our work, and to hide ourselves in some wilderness or cell, whilst others are fighting the battles of the Lord. 3. Or it may proceed from mere impatience: when men cannot bear the frown, scorns, and violence of the ungodly, they fly from sufferings, which by patience they should overcome. 4. Or it may come from humour and mutability of mind, and discontent with one's condition: many retire from human converse to please a discontented passionate mind; or expecting to find that in privacy, which in public they could not find, nor is any where to be found on earth. 5. Some do it in melancholy, merely to please a sick imagination, which is vexed in company, and a little eases itself in living as the possessed man among the tombs. 6. Sometimes it proceeds from self-ignorance, and an unhumbled state of soul: when men think much better of themselves than others, they think they can more comfortably converse with themselves than with others: whereas if they well understood that they are the worst or greatest enemies, or troubles to themselves, they would more fear their own company than other men's: they would then consider what proud, fleshly, worldly, selfish, and disordered hearts they are likely to carry with them into their solitude, and there to be annoyed with from day to day: that the nearest enemy is the worst, and the nearest trouble is the greatest.

These vices or infirmities carry many into solitude; and if they live where popish vanity may seduce them, they will perhaps imagine, that they are serving God, and entering into perfection, when they are but sinfully obeying their corruptions: and that they are advanced above others in degrees of grace, while they are pleasing a diseased fancy, and entering into a dangerous course of sin. No doubt but the duties of a public life are more in number, and greater in weight, and of more excellent consequence and tendency, even to the most public good, and greatest honour of God, than the duties of privacy or retirement. A good man is a common good. 'And,' saith Seneca, 'if every one have not some share or interest in them, how are they common?' Let me add these few considerations, to show you the evil of voluntary, unnecessary solitude.

1. You less contribute to the honour of your Redeemer, and less promote his kingdom in the world, and less subserve his death and office, while you do good but to few, and live but almost to yourselves.

2. You live in the poorest exercise of the grace of charity; and therefore in a low, undesirable condition.

3. You will want the communion of saints, and benefit of public ordinances, for I account not a college life a solitary life. You will want the help of the charity, graces and gifts of others, by which you might be benefited.

4. It will be a life of smaller comfort, as it is a life of smaller benefit to others. They that do but little good according to their ability, must expect but little comfort. They have usually most peace and comfort to themselves that are

the most profitable to others. 'No man can live well, that looketh but to himself: thou must live to another, if thou wilt live to thyself.'

O the delight that there is in doing good to many! None knows it that hath not tried it: not upon any account of merit; but as it pleases God, and as goodness itself is amiable and sweet; and as we receive by communicating; and as we are under promise; and as charity makes all the good that is done to another to be to us as our own!

5. We are dark, and partial, and heedless of ourselves, and hardly brought or kept in acquaintance with our hearts; and therefore have the more need of the eye of others: even an enemy's eye may be useful, though malicious; and may do us good, while he intends us evil. Saith Bernard, 'The evil that none seeth, none reproveth: and where the reprover is not feared, the tempter comes more boldly, and the sin is committed the more licentiously.' It is hard to know the spots in our own faces, when we have no glass or beholder to acquaint us with them. Saith Chrysostom, 'Solitude is the cover of all vices.' In company this cover is laid aside, and vice being more naked, is more ashamed. It is beholders that cause shame; which solitude is not acquainted with: and it is a piece of impenitency not to be ashamed of sin.

6. We are for the most part so weak and sickly, that we are unable to subsist without the help of others. 'Unwise men, or infants, or such like men, must not be left to themselves.' God hath left some impotency, insufficiency and necessity upon all that should keep men sociable, and make them acknowledge their need of others, and be thankful for assistance from them, and be ready to do good to others, as we would have others to do to us. He that feels not the need of others, is so unhumbled as to have the greater need of them.

7. Pride will have great advantage in private, and repentance great disadvantage, while our sins seem to be all dead, because there is not a temptation to draw them out, or an observer to reprove them. 'Many a man seems to himself patient and humble, while he keeps out of company; who would return to his own nature, if the commotion of any occasion did but provoke him.' It is hard to know what sin or grace is in us, if we have not such trials as are not to be found in solitude.

8. Flying from the observation and judgment of others, is a kind of self-accusation; as if we confessed ourselves so bad as that we cannot stand the trial of the light. Seneca says, 'A good

conscience will call in the crowd (or witnesses, not caring who seeth :) a bad conscience is anxious and solicitous even in solitude : if they be things honest which thou dost, let all men know : if they be dishonest, what good doth it thee that no man else knows it, when thou knowest it thyself? O miserable man, if thou despise this witness!' Something is suspected to be amiss with those that are always in their chambers, and are never seen. Tell not men that you cannot bear the light; it is he that doth evil that hates the light, lest his deeds should be reproved.

9. Solitude is too like death to be desirable: he lives that doth good, and he is dead that is useless. 'He lives that is profitable to many: he lives that is observed or perceived : but they that lie hid and drowsy, anticipate their death.' It is the most culpable death, and therefore the worst to have life, and not to use it.

10. A life of holy communion is likest unto heaven, where none shall be solitary, but all, as members of the heavenly Jerusalem, shall in harmony love and praise their Maker.

These reasons seem sufficient to me to satisfy you that no man should choose solitude without a special necessity or call : nor yet should it be taken for a life of greater perfection, than a faithful serving of God in public, and doing good to more.

I shall now come to the affirmative, and tell you for all this, that 'if God call us into solitude, or men forsake us, we may rejoice in this, that we are not alone, but the Father is with us.' Fear not such solitude, but be ready to improve it, if you be cast upon it. If God be your God, reconciled to you in Christ, and his Spirit be in you, you are provided for solitude, and need not fear if all the world should cast you off. If you be banished, imprisoned, or left alone, it is but a relaxation from your greatest labours; which though you may not cast off yourselves, you may lawfully be sensible of your ease, if God take off your burden. It is but a cessation from your sharpest conflicts, and removal from a multitude of great temptations. Though you may not cowardly retreat or shift yourselves from the sight and danger, yet if God will dispense with you, and let you live in greater peace and safety, you have no cause to murmur at his dealing. A fruit-tree that grows by the highway side, doth seldom keep his fruit to ripeness, while so many passengers have each his stone to cast at it. Seneca could say, ' I never bring home well from a crowd the manners which I took out with me : something is disordered of that which I had set in order : something of that which I

had banished doth return : the conversation of many, I find an enemy to me.' O how many vain and foolish words corrupt the minds of those that converse with an ungodly world, when your ears and minds who live in solitude, are free from such temptations ! You live not in so corrupt an air as they : you hear not the filthy speeches, which fight against modesty and chastity, and are the incitements of lust: you hear not the discontented, complaining words of the impatient; nor the passionate, provoking words of the offended ; nor the wrangling, quarrelsome words of the contentious: nor the censorious, or slanderous, or reproachful words of the malicious, who think it their interest to have their brethren supposed to be bad, and to have others hate them, because they themselves hate them ; and who are as zealous to quench the charity of others, when it is destroyed in themselves, as holy persons are zealous to provoke others to love, which dwells and rules in themselves. In your solitude with God, you shall not hear the lies and malicious revilings of the ungodly against the generation of the just: nor the subtle, cheating words of heretics, who being themselves deceived, would deceive others of their faith, and corrupt their lives. You shall not there be distracted with the noise and clamours of contending uncharitable professors of religion, endeavouring to make odious first the opinions, and then the persons of one another ; one saying here is the church, and another, there is the church : one saying, this is the true church-government, and another saying, nay, but that is it : one saying, God will be worshipped thus, another, not so, but thus, or thus. You shall not there be drawn to side with one against another, nor to join with any faction, or be guilty of divisions : you shall not be troubled with the oaths and blasphemies of the wicked, nor with the imprudent miscarriages of the weak ; with the persecutions of enemies, or the falling out of friends : you shall not see the cruelty of proud oppressors, that set up lies by armed violence, and care not what they say, or do, nor how much other men are injured and suffer, so that themselves may tyrannize, and their wills and words may rule the world, when they do so unhappily rule themselves. In your solitude with God, you shall not see the prosperity of the wicked, to move you to envy ; nor the adversity of the just, to be your grief; you shall see no worldly pomp and splendour to befool you, nor adorned beauty to entice you, nor wasting calamities to afflict you ; you shall not hear the laughter of fools, nor the sick man's groans, nor the wronged man's complaints, nor the poor man's murmurings, nor the proud man's boastings, nor the angry man's abusive ragings.

As you lose the help of your gracious friends, so you are freed from the fruits of their peevishness and passions; of their differing opinions, ways, and tempers; of their inequality, unsuitableness and contrariety of minds or interests; of their levity and unconstancy, and the powerful temptations of their friendship, to draw you to the errors or other sins which they are tainted with themselves. In a word, you are there half delivered from the vanity and the vexation of the world; and were it not that you are yet undelivered from yourselves, and that you take distempered corrupted hearts with you, O what a felicity would your solitude be! But alas, we cannot over-run our own diseases, we must carry with us the remnants of our corrupted nature; our deadness and dulness, our selfishness and earthly minds, our impatience and discontents; and worst of all, our lamentable weakness of faith, love, and heavenly-mindedness, and our strangeness to God, and backwardness to the matters of eternal life. O that I could escape these, though I were in the hands of the most cruel enemies! O that such a heart could be left behind; how gladly would I over-run both house, land, honour, and all sensual delights, that I might over-run it! O where is the place where there is none of this darkness, nor disaffection, nor distance, nor estrangedness from God! O that I knew it! O that I could find it! O that I might there dwell, though I should never more see the face of mortals; nor ever hear a human voice, nor ever taste of the delights of flesh! Alas, foolish soul, such a place there is, that hath all this, and more than this: but it is not in a wilderness, but in paradise, not here on earth, but above with Christ; and yet am I so loth to die? yet am I no more desirous of the blessed day, when I shall be unclothed of flesh and sin? O death, what an enemy art thou even to my soul! by affrighting me from the presence of my Lord, and hindering my desires and willingness to be gone; thou wrongest me much more than by laying my flesh to rot in darkness. Fain would I know God. and fain would I more love him and enjoy him. But O this hurtful love of life! O this unreasonable fear of dying, detains my desires from pressing on to the happy place where all this may be had! O wretched man that I am, who shall deliver me from this body of death! this carnal, unbelieving heart, that sometimes can think more delightfully of a wilderness than of heaven; that can go seek after God in desert solitude, among the birds, and beasts, and trees,

and yet is so backward to be loosed from the flesh that I may find him and enjoy him in the world of glory! Can I expect that heaven should come down to earth; and that the Lord of glory should remove his court, and either leave the retinue of his celestial courtiers, or bring them all down into this drossy world of flesh and sin, and this to satisfy my fleshly, foolish mind! Or can I expect the translation of Enoch, or the chariot of Elias? Is it not enough that my Lord hath conquered death, and sanctified the passage, and prepared the place of my perpetual abode?

Well, for all this, though a wilderness is not heaven, it shall be sweet and welcome for the sake of heaven, if thence I may but have a clearer prospect of it: and if by retiring from the crowd and noise of folly, I may but be more composed and better disposed to converse above, and to use my faith, alas, my too weak, languid faith, until the beatific vision and fruition come. If there may be but more of God, or readier access to him, or more heart-quickening flames of love, or more heart-comforting intimations of his favour, in a wilderness than in a city, in a prison than in a palace, let that wilderness be my city, and let that prison be my palace, while I must abide on earth. If in solitude I may have Enoch's walk with God, I shall in due season have such a translation as shall bring me to the same felicity which he enjoys; and in the mean time, as well as after, it is no disadvantage, if by mortal eyes I be seen no more. If the chariot of contemplation will in solitude raise me to more believing, affectionate converse with heaven, than I could expect in tumults and temptations, it shall reconcile me unto solitude, and make it my paradise on earth, till angels, instead of the chariot of Elias, shall convey me to the presence of my glorified Head, in the celestial paradise.

Object. But it is grievous to one that hath been used to much company. to be alone.

Answ. Company may so use you, that it may be more grievous to you not to be alone. The society of wasps and serpents may be spared; and bees themselves have such stings as make some that have felt them think they bought the honey dear.

But can you say you are alone while you are with God? is his presence nothing to you? doth it not signify more than the company of all men in the world? Saith Hierom, 'A wise man cannot be alone: for he hath with him the good men that are or have been. And if there be a want of men, he speaks with God.' He should rather have said, there can be no want of man when

we may speak with God : and were it not that
God is here revealed to us as in a glass, and
that we converse with God in man, we should
think human converse little worth.

Object. O but solitude is disconsolate to a
sociable mind.

Answ. But the most desirable soicety is no
solitude. Saith Hierom, ' Doth the infinite vast-
ness of the wilderness terrify thee ; but do thou
ascend in mind and walk in paradise : as often as
thou ascendest thither in thought and mind, so
often thou shalt not be in the wilderness.' If God
be nothing to thee, thou art not a Christian but
an atheist. If God be God to thee, he is all in
all to thee ; and then should not his presence be
instead of all ? O that I might get one step
nearer unto God, though I receded many from
all the world ! O that I could find that place
on earth, where a soul may have nearest access
unto him, and fullest knowledge and enjoyment
of him, though I never more saw the face of
friends ! I should cheerfully say with my blessed
Saviour, ' I am not alone, for the Father is
with me.' And should say so for these reasons
following :

1. If God be with me, the Maker, Ruler, and
Disposer of all is with me : so that all things are
virtually with me in him. I have that in gold
and jewels which I seem to want in silver, lead
and dross. I can want no friend, if God vouchsafe to be my friend ; and I can enjoy no benefit
by all my friends, if God be my enemy : I need
not fear the greatest enemies, if God be reconciled to me. I shall not miss the light of the
candle, if I have this blessed sun. The creature
is nothing but what it is from God and in God :
it is worth nothing, or good for nothing, but
what it is worth in order unto God, as it declares
him, and helps the soul to know him, serve him,
or draw nearer to him : as it is idolatry in the
unhappy worldling, to thirst after the creature
with the neglect of God, and so to make the
world his God ; so doth it savour of the same
heinous sin to lament our loss of creatures more
than the displeasure of God. If God be my
enemy, or I am fallen under his indignation, I
have then so much greater matters to lament
than the loss, or absence, or frowns of man, as
should almost make me forget that there is such
a thing as man to be regarded. But if God be
my Father and my friend in Christ, I have then
so much to think of with delight, and to recreate and content my soul, as will proclaim it most
incongruous and absurd to lament inordinately
the absence of a worm, while I have his love and
presence who is all in all. If God cannot con-

tent me, and be not enough for me, how is he
then my God ; or how shall he be my heaven
and everlasting happiness.

2. If God be with me, he is with me to whom
I am absolutely devoted. I am wholly his, and
have acknowledged his interest in me, and long
ago disclaimed all usurpers, and repented of
alienations, and unreservedly resigned myself to
him : where should I dwell but with him that is
my owner, and with whom I have made the
most solemn covenant that ever I made ? I never
gave myself to any other, but in subordination
to him, and with a stipulation for his highest inviolable right. Where should my goods be but
in my own house ; with whom should a servant
dwell but with his master ; and a wife but with
her husband ; and children but with their Father ?
I am more nearly related to my God, and to my
Saviour, than I am to any of my relations in this
world. I owe more to him than to all the
world : I have renounced all the world, as they
stand in competition or comparison with him :
and can I want their company then, while I am
with him ? How shall I hate father and mother,
wife, children, brother and sister for his sake,
if I cannot spare them, or be without them to en.
joy him ? To hate them is but to use them as
men do hated things, that is, to cast them away
with contempt, as they would alienate me from
Christ, and to cleave to him, and be satisfied in
him alone. I am now married to Christ, and
therefore must cheerfully leave father and mother,
and my native place, and all to cleave to him :
with whom should I now delight to dwell, but
with him who hath taken me into so near relation, to be, as it were, one flesh with him ! O my
dear Lord, hide not thou thy face from an unkind, an unworthy sinner ! let me but dwell with
thee and see thy face, and feel the gracious embraces of thy love, and then let me be cast off
by all the world, if thou seest it meet for me ;
or let all other friends be where they will, so that
my soul may be with thee ; I have agreed for
thy sake to forsake all, even the dearest that
shall stand against thee, and I resolve by thy
grace to stand to this agreement.

3. If God be with me, I am not alone, for he
is with me that loves me best. The love of all
the friends on earth is nothing to his love. O
how plainly hath he declared that he loves me,
in the strange condescension, the sufferings,
death, and intercession of his Son ? What love
hath he declared in the communications of his
Spirit, and the operations of his grace, and the
near relations into which he brought me ? What
love hath he declared in the course of his pro-

vidences; in many and wonderful preservations and deliverances; in the conduct of his wisdom, and in a life of mercies! What love appears in his precious promises, and the glorious provisions he hath made for me with himself to all eternity! O my Lord, I am ashamed that thy love is so much lost; that it hath no better return from an unkind, unthankful heart; that I am no more delighted in thee, and swallowed up in the contemplation of thy love; I can contentedly let go the society and converse of all others, for the converse of some one bosom friend, that is dearer to me than they all, as Jonathan to David: can I not much more be satisfied in thee alone, and let go all, if I may continue with thee? My very dog will gladly forsake all the town, and all persons in the world, to follow me alone! Have I not yet found so much love and goodness in thee, my dear and blessed God, as to be willing to converse alone with thee? All men delight most in the company of those that love them best: they choose not to converse with the multitude when they look for solace and content, but with their dearest friends: should any be so near to me as God? O were not thy love unworthily neglected by an unthankful heart, I should never be so unsatisfied in thee, but should take up, or seek my comforts in thee: I should then say, 'whom have I in heaven but thee, and there is none on earth that I desire besides thee.' Though not only my friends, but my flesh and heart themselves should fail me, it is thou that wilt still be the strength of my heart, and my portion for ever: it is good therefore for me to draw near to thee, how far soever I am from man: O let me there dwell where thou wilt not be strange, for thy loving kindness is better than life: instead of the multitude of my turmoiling thoughts, let me be taken up in the believing views of thy reconciled face, and in the glad attendance of thy grace: or at least in the multitude of my thoughts within me, let thy celestial comforts delight my soul. Let me dwell as in thy family; and when I awake, let me be still with thee! Let me go no where, but be still following thee: let me do nothing but thy work, nor serve any other, but when I may truly call it a serving thee: let me hear nothing but thy voice and let me know thy voice by whatever instrument thou shalt speak; let me never see any thing but thyself, and the glass that represents thee, and the books in which I may read thy name: let me never play with the outside, and gaze on words and letters as insignificant, and not observe thy name, which is the sense. Whether it be in company or in solitude, let me be

continually with thee, and do thou vouchsafe to hold me by my right hand: and ' guide me by thy counsel, and afterwards receive me unto thy glory.'

4. If God be with me I am not alone; for I shall be with him whose love is of greater benefit to me than the love of all my friends in the world. Their love may perhaps be some little comfort, as it flows from his: but it is his love by which, and upon which I live. It is his love that gives me life, time, health, food, and preservation; that gives me books, and gives me understanding: that gives me provision. and saves me from turning it to pernicious fleshliness and excess; that gives me even my friends themselves, and saves me from that abuse which might make them to me worse than enemies. The sun, the earth, the air is not so useful or needful to me as his love. The love of all my friends cannot make me well when I am sick: it cannot forgive the smallest of my sins; nor yet assure me of God's forgiveness: it cannot heal the maladies of my soul, nor give a solid lasting peace to the conscience which is troubled: if all my friends stand about me when I am dying, they cannot take away the fears of death, nor secure my passage to everlasting life: death will be death still, and danger will be danger, when all my friends have done their best. But my almighty friend is all-sufficient: he can prevent my sickness, or rebuke and cure it, or make it so good to me, that I shall thank him for it: he can blot out my transgressions, and forgive all my sin; and justify me when the world and my conscience do condemn me: he can teach me to believe, to repent, to pray, to hope, to suffer, and to overcome: he can quiet my soul in the midst of trouble, and give me a well-grounded, everlasting peace, and a joy that no man can take from me. He can deliver me from all the corruptions and distempers of my froward heart; and ease me and secure me in the troublesome war which is daily waged in my breast. He can make it as easy a thing to die, as to lie down and take my rest when I am weary, or to undress me at night and go to bed. He can teach death to lay by its terrible aspect, and speak with a mild and comfortable voice, and to me the most joyful tidings that ever came unto my ears; and to preach to me the last and sweetest sermon, even the same that our Saviour preached on the cross. ' Verily I say unto thee, To-day shalt thou be with Christ in paradise.'

Is this the difference between the love of man and of God? Yet do I lament the loss of man! Yet am I so backward to converse with God, and to be satisfied in his love alone! Ah my God, how justly mayest thou withhold that love which I thus undervalue; and refuse that converse which I have first refused? and turn me over to man, to silly, sinful man, whose converse I so much desire, till I have learned by dear experience the difference between man and God, and between an earthly and a heavenly friend! Alas, have I not tried it often enough, to have known it better before this day? Have I not often enough found what man is in a time of trial? Have I not been told it over and over, and told it to the quick, by deceitful friends, by self-seeking friends, by mutable, erroneous, deceived, scandalous, backsliding friends, by proud and self-conceited friends; by passionate, quarrelsome, vexatious friends; by self-grieving, troubled friends, that have but brought me all their calamities and griefs to be additions to my own; by tempting friends, that have drawn me to sin more effectually than enemies; by tender, faithful, but unable friends, that have but brought fire from my calamities and sorrows, to kindle their own, not equally sharing, but each one taking all my trouble entirely to himself: that have been willing, but insufficient to relieve me; and therefore the greater was their love, the greater was their own, and consequently mine affliction: that would have been with me, but could not; that would willingly have eased my pain, and strengthened my languishing body, but could not; that would gladly have removed all my troubles, and comforted my downcast mind, but could not. O how often have I found that human friendship is a sweet desired addition to our woe; a beloved calamity, and an affliction which nature will not be without, not because it loves evil, nor because it is wholly deceived in its choice, for there is good in friendship, and delight in holy love, but because the good which is here accompanied with so much evil, is the beginning of a more high and durable friendship, and points us up to the blessed, delightful society and converse which in the heavenly Jerusalem we shall have with Christ.

But O how much better have I found the friendship of the all-sufficient God! His love hath not only pitied me, but relieved me: he hath not only been as it were afflicted with me in my afflictions, but he hath delivered me seasonably and powerfully, and sweetly hath he delivered me: and when he had once told me that my afflictions were his own, I had no reason to doubt of a deliverance. My burdened mind hath been eased by his love, which was but more burdened by the fruitless love of all my friends.

Often have I come to man for help, ease, and comfort, and gone away as from an empty cistern, that had no water to cool my thirst; but God hath been a present help: could I but get near him, I was sure of light, how great soever was my former darkness; could I but get near him, I was sure of warming, quickening life, how dead soever I had been before: but all my misery was, that I could not get near him! My darkened estranged guilty soul, could not get quieting and satisfying acquaintance: my insensible heart lay dead on earth, and would not stir, or quickly fell down again, if by any celestial force it began to be drawn up, and move a little towards him: my carnal mind was entangled in diverting vanities: and thus I have been kept from communion with my God. Kept! not by force of human tyranny; not by bars or bolts, or distance of place, or by the lowness of my condition: nor by any misrepresentations or reproach of man; but, alas, by myself, by the darkness, deadness, sluggishness, earthliness, fleshliness, and passions of a naughty heart. These have been my bars, bolts, and jailors; these are they that have kept me from my God: had it not been for these, I might have got nearer to him; I might have walked with him, and dwelt with him; yea, dwelt in him, and he in me: and then I should not have missed any friends, nor felt mine enemies. Is it my sinful distance from my God that hath been my loss, my wilderness, my woe; and is it a nearer admittance to the presence of his love that must be my recovery and my joy, if ever I attain to joy? O then, my soul, lay hold on Christ the reconciler, and in him and by him draw near to God, and cease from man, whose breath is in his nostrils. Love God in his saints, and delightfully converse with Christ in them, while thou hast opportunity. But remember thou livest not upon them, or on their love, but upon God; and therefore desire their company but for his: and if thou hast his, be content if thou hast not theirs. He wants not man; that enjoys God. Gather up all the love, thoughts, and desires which have been scattered and lost upon the creatures, and set them all on God himself, and press into his presence, and converse with him, and thou shalt find the mistake of thy present discontents, and sweet experience shall tell thee thou hast made a happy change.

5. If God be with me, I am not alone, because he is with me with whom my greatest business lies: and what company should I desire, but theirs with whom I have my daily, necessary work to do? I have more to do with

God, than with all the world : yea, more and greater business with him in one day, than with all the world in all my life. I have business with man about houses, lands, or food, or raiment, or labour, or journeying, or recreations, about society and public peace : but what are these to my business with God ? Indeed with holy men, I have holy business ; but that is but as they are messengers from God, and come to me on his business, and so they must be dearly welcome. But even then my business is much more with God than with them ; with him that sent them, than with the messengers. Indeed my business with God is so great, that if I had not a mediator to encourage and assist me, to do my work and procure me acceptance, the thoughts of it would overwhelm my soul.

O therefore my soul, let man stand by : it is the eternal God that I have to do with ; and with whom I am to transact in this little time the business of my endless life. I have to deal with God through Christ, for the pardon of my sins, of all my great and grievous sins ; and wo to me, if I speed not, that ever I was born : I have some hopes of pardon, but intermixed with many perplexing fears : I have evidences much blotted, and not easily understood : I want assurance that he is indeed my Father and reconciled to me, and will receive me to himself when the world forsakes me : I have many languishing graces to be strengthened ; and alas, what obstinate, vexatious corruptions to be cured ! Can I look into my heart, into such an unbelieving, dead and earthly heart, into such a proud, peevish and disordered heart, into such a trembling, perplexed, self-accusing heart, and yet not understand how great my business is with God ? Can I peruse my sins, or feel my wants, and sink under my weaknesses, and yet not discern how great my business is with God ? Can I look back upon all the time that I have lost, and all the grace that I unthankfully resisted, and all the mercies that I trod under foot, or fooled away, or can I look before me and see how near my time is to an end, and yet not understand how great my business is with God ? Can I think of the malice and diligence of satan, the number, power and subtilty of mine enemies, the many snares and dangers that are still before me, the strength and number of temptations, and my ignorance, unwatchfulness and weakness to resist, and yet not know that my greatest business is with God ? Can I feel my afflictions and lament them, and think my burden greater than I can bear, and find that man cannot relieve me : can I go mourning in the heaviness of my soul, and water my bed with tears, and fill the air with my groans and lamentations, or feel my soul overwhelmed within me, so that my words are intercepted, and I am readier to break than speak, and yet not perceive that my greatest business is with God ? Can I think of dying ; can I draw near to judgment ; can I think of everlasting joys in heaven; and of everlasting pains in hell, and yet not feel that my greatest business is with God ?

O then, my soul, the case is easily resolved with whom it is that thou must most desirously and seriously converse. Where should thou be but where thy business is, and so great business ? Alas, what have I to do with man ? What can it do but make my head ache, to hear a deal of senseless chat, about preferments, lands, and dignities; about the words and thoughts of men, and a thousand toys that are utterly impertinent to my great employments, and signify nothing but that the dreaming world is not awake ? What pleasure is it to see the bustles of a bedlam world ? What a stir they make to prove or make themselves unhappy ? How long and of how little weight, are the learned discourses about syllables and words, names and notions, mood and figure, yea, or about the highest planets, when all are not referred unto God ? Were it not that some converse with men doth further my converse with God ; and that God did transact much of his business by his messengers and servants, it were no matter whether ever I more saw the face of man : were it not that my Master hath placed me in society, and appointed me much of my work for others, and with others, and much of his mercy is conveyed by others, man might stand by, and solitude were better than the best society, and God alone should take me up. O nothing is so much my misery and shame, as that I am no more willing, nor better skilled in the management of my great, important business ! That my work is with God, and my heart is no more with him! O what might I do in holy meditation, or prayer, one hour, if I were as ready for prayer, and as good at prayer, as one that has had so long opportunity and so great necessity to converse with God, should be ! A prayerless heart, a heart that flies away from God, is most inexcusable in such a one as I, that have so much important business with him : it is work that must be done ; and if well done, will never be repented of: I use not to return from the presence of God, when indeed I have drawn near him, as I do from the company of empty men, repenting that I have lost my time, and trembling that my mind is discomposed or depressed by the vanity and earthly savour of their discourse : I often repent that I have prayed to him so coldly, and conversed with him so negligently, and served him so remissly : but I never repent of the time, the care, the affections or the diligence employed in his holy work. Many a time I have repented that ever I spent so much time with man, and wished I had never seen the faces of some that are eminent in the world, whose favour and converse others are ambitious of : but it is my grief and shame that so small a part of all my life hath been spent with God ; and that fervent prayer and heavenly contemplations, have been so seldom and so short. O that I had lived more with God, though I had been less with the dearest of my friends ! How much more sweet then would my life have been ! How much more blameless, regular and pure ! How much more fruitful, and answerable to my obligations and professions ! How much more comfortable to my review ! How many falls, hurts, wounds, griefs, and groans might I have escaped ! O how much more pleasing is it now to my remembrance, to think of the hours in which I have lain at the feet of God, though it were in tears and groans, than to think of the time which I have spent in any common converse with the greatest, or the most learned, or the dearest of my acquaintance.

As my greatest business is with God, so my daily business is also with him : he purposely leaves me under wants, and suffers necessities daily to return, and enemies to assault me, and affliction to surprise me, that I may be daily driven to him : he loves to hear from me : he would have me be no stranger with him : I have business with him every hour, I need not want employment for all the faculties of my soul, if I know what it is to converse in heaven. Even prayer, and every holy thought of God, hath an object so great and excellent, as should wholly take me up. Nothing must be thought or spoken lightly about the Lord. His name must not be taken in vain : nothing that is common beseems his worshippers. He will be sanctified of all that shall draw near him : he must be loved with all the heart and might. His servants need not be wearied for want of employment, nor through the lightness or unprofitableness of their employment : if I had cities to build, or kingdoms to govern, I might better complain for want of employment, for the faculties of my soul, than I can when I am to converse in heaven. In other studies the delight abates when I have reached my desire, and know all that I can know : but in God there is infinitely more

to be known, when I know the most. I am never satiated with the easiness of knowing, nor are my desires abated by any uneasiness or unworthiness in the object : but I am drawn to it by its highest excellencies, and drawn on to desire more and more by the infinitude of the light which I have not yet beheld, and the infinitude of the good which yet I have not enjoyed. If I be idle, or seem to want employment, when I am to contemplate all the attributes, relations, mercies, works, and revealed perfections of the Lord, it is surely for want of eyes to see, or a heart inclined to my business : if God be not enough to employ my soul, then all the persons and things on earth are not enough.

When I have infinite goodness to delight in, where my soul may freely let out itself, and never need to fear excess of love, how sweet should this employment be ? As knowledge, so love is never stinted here, by the narrowness of the object : we can never love him in any proportion either to his goodness and amiableness in himself, or to his love to us. What need have I then of any other company or business, when I have infinite goodness to delight in, and to love, further than they subserve this greatest work ?

Come home then, O my soul, to God ; converse in heaven : turn away thine eyes from beholding vanity : let not thy affections kindle upon straw or briars, that go out when they have made a flash or noise, and leave thee to thy cold and darkness : but come and dwell upon celestial beauties, and make it thy daily and most diligent work, to kindle thy affections on the infinite, everlasting good ; and then they will never be extinguished or decay for want of fuel ; but the further they go, and the longer they burn, the greater will be the flame. Though thou find it hard while love is but a spark to make it burn, and complain that thy cold and backward heart is hardly warmed with the love of God, yet when the whole pile hath taken fire, and the flame ascends, fire will breed fire, love will cause love ; and all the malice of hell itself shall never be able to suppress or quench it unto all eternity.

6. It is a great encouragement to my converse with God, that no misunderstanding, no malice of enemies, no former sin or present frailty, no, nor the infinite distance of the most holy God, can hinder my access to him, or turn away his ear or love, or interrupt my leave and liberty of converse. If I converse with the poor, their wants afflict me, being greater than I can supply ; their complaints and expectations, which I

cannot satisfy, are my trouble. If I would converse with great ones, it is not easy to get access: and less easy to have their favour, unless I would purchase it at too dear a rate : how strangely and contemptuously do they look at their inferiors ! Great friends must be made for a word or smile : if you be not quickly gone, they are weary of you ; if you seek any thing of them, or would put them to any cost or trouble, you are as welcome to them as so many noisome creatures. They please them best that drive you away. With how much labour and difficulty must you climb, if you will see the top of one of these mountains ? When you are there, you are but in a place of barrenness ; and have nothing to satisfy you for your pains, but a larger prospect and dizzy view of the lower grounds which are not your own: it is seldom that these great ones are to be spoken with : perhaps their speech is but a denial to your request, if not some snappish and contemptuous rejection, that makes you glad when you are got far enough from them, and makes you better love the accessible, calm, and fruitful plains.

But O how much greater encouragements hath my soul to converse with God ! Company never hinders him from hearkening to my suit : he is infinite and omnipotent, and is sufficient for every individual soul, as if he had no other to look after in the world: when he is taken up with the attendance and praises of his heavenly host, he is as free and ready to attend and answer the groans and prayers of a contrite soul, as if he had no nobler creatures, and no higher service to regard. I am often unready, but God is never unready : I am unready to pray, but he is not unready to hear : I am unready to come to God, to walk with him, and to solace my soul with him ; but he is never unready to entertain me. Many a time my conscience would have driven me away, when he hath called me to him, and rebuked my accusing, fearful conscience. Many a time I have called myself a prodigal, a companion of fools, a miserable, hard-hearted sinner, unworthy to be called his son, when he hath called me child, and chid me for my questioning his love. He hath readily forgiven the sins which I thought would have made my soul the fuel of hell : he hath entertained me with joy, with music and a feast, when I better deserved to have been among the dogs without his doors. He hath embraced me in his sustaining, consolatory arms, when he might have spurned my guilty soul to hell, and said, 'depart from me, thou worker of iniquity, I know thee not.' O little did I think that he could ever have forgotten the vanity and villany of my youth ; yea, so easily have forgotten my most aggravated sins. When I had sinned against light ; when I had resisted conscience ; when I had frequently and wilfully injured love, I thought he would never have forgotten it : but the greatness of his love and mercy, and the blood and intercession of his Son, hath cancelled all.

O how many mercies have I tasted since I thought I had sinned away all mercies ! How patiently hath he borne with me, since I thought he would never have put up more ! Yet besides my sins and the withdrawings of my own heart, there hath been nothing to interrupt our converse. Though he be God, and I a worm, yet that would not have kept me out : though he be in heaven, yet he is near to succour me on earth, in all that I call upon him for : though he have the praise of angels, he disdains not my tears and groans : though he have the perfect love of perfect souls, he knows the little spark in my breast, and despises not my weak and languid love : though I injure and dishonour him by loving him no more, though I often forget him, and have been out of the way when he hath come or called me, though I have disobediently turned away mine ears, and unkindly refused the entertainments of his love, and unfaithfully dealt with those whose company he forbade me, he hath not divorced me, nor turned me out of doors. O wonderful ; that heaven will be familiar with earth : and God with man ; the highest with a worm : and the most holy with an unconstant sinner ! Man refuses me, when God will entertain me : man, that is no wiser nor better than myself. Those that I never wronged, or deserved ill of, reject me with reproach : God, whom I have unspeakably injured, doth invite me, and intreat me, and condescends to me, as if he were beholden to me to be saved : men, that I have deserved well of, do abhor me : God, that I have deserved ill of, doth accept me. The best of them are briars, and a thorny hedge, and he is love, rest, and joy : yet I can be more welcome to him, though I have offended him, than I can to them whom I have obliged : I have freer leave to cast myself into my Father's arms, than to tumble into those briars, or wallow in the mire. I upbraid myself with my sins, but he doth not upbraid me with them. I condemn myself for them, but he condemns me not : he forgives me sooner than I can forgive myself : I have peace with him, before I can have peace of conscience.

O therefore, my soul, draw near to him that is so willing of thy company ! That frowns thee not away, unless it be when thou hast fallen into the dust, that thou mayest wash thee from thy filthiness, and be fitter for his converse. Draw near to him that will not wrong thee, by believing misreports of enemies, or laying to thy charge the things thou knewest not : but will forgive the wrongs thou hast done to him, and justify thee from the sins that conscience lays to thy charge. Come to him who, by his word and Spirit, his ministers and mercies, calls thee to come ; and hath promised that those that come to him, he will in no wise shut out. O walk with him that will bear thee up, and lead thee as by the right hand, and carry his infants when they cannot go ! O speak to him that teaches thee to speak, and understands and accepts thy stammering, and helps thine infirmities, when thou knowest not what to pray for as thou oughtest ; and gives thee groans when thou hast not words, and knows the meaning of his Spirit in thy groans : that cannot be contained in the heaven of heavens, and yet hath respect to the contrite soul, who trembles at his word, and fears his displeasure : that pities the tears, and despises not the sighing of a broken heart, nor the desires of the sorrowful. O walk with him that is never weary of the converse of the upright soul ! that is never angry with thee but for flying from him, or for drawing back, or being too strange, and refusing the kindness and felicity of his presence. The day is coming when the proudest of the sons of men would be glad of a kind look from him that thou hast leave to walk with : even they that would not look on thee, and they that injured and abused thee, and they that inferiors could have no access to, O how glad would they be then of a smile, or a word of hope and mercy from their Father ! Draw near then to him, on whom the whole creation depends ; whose favour at last the proudest and the worst would purchase with the loudest cries, when all their pomp and pleasure is gone, and can purchase nothing. O walk with him that is love itself, and think him not unwilling or unlovely ; and let not the deceiver, by hideous misrepresentations, drive thee from him : when thou hast felt a while the storms abroad, methinks thou shouldst say, How good, how safe, how sweet is it to draw near to God !

7. With whom should I so desirously converse, as with him whom I must live with for ever? If I take pleasure in my house, or land, or country, my walks, my books, or friends themselves, as clothed with flesh, I must possess this pleasure but a little while : henceforth know we no man after the flesh : had we known Christ after the flesh, we must know him so no more for ever. Though his glorified spiritual body we shall know. Do you converse with father or mother ; with wives or children : with pastors and teachers ? Though you may converse with these as glorified saints, when you come to Christ, yet in these relations that they stand in to you now, you shall converse with them but a little while : ' For the time is short : it remaineth that both they that have wives, be as though they had none ; and they that weep, as though they wept not ; and they that rejoice, as though they rejoiced not ; and those that buy, as though they possessed not ; and that use this world, as not abusing it,' or as though they used it not : ' for the fashion of this world passeth away.'

Why then should I so much regard a converse of so short continuance ? Why should I be so familiar in my inn, and so much in love with that familiarity, as to grieve when I must but think of leaving it, or talk of going home, and look forward to the place where I must dwell for ever ? Shall I be fond of the company of a passenger that I travel with, yea, perhaps one that doth but meet me in the way, and goes to a contrary place, and shall I not take more pleasure to remember home ? I will not be so uncivil as to deny those I meet a short salute, or to be friendly with my fellow-travellers : but remember, O my soul, that thou dost not dwell, but travel here, and that it is thy Father's house where thou must abide for ever : yea, and he is nearer thee than man (though invisible) even in thy way. O see him then that is invisible : hearken to him when he speaks : obey his voice ; observe his way, speak to him boldly, though humbly and reverently, as his child, about the great concerns of thy state ; tell him what it is that aileth thee ; and seeing all thy smart is the fruit of thy own sin, confess thy folly and unkindness, crave his forgiveness, and remember him what his Son hath suffered, and for what. Treat with him about thy future course : desire his grace, and give up thyself to his conduct and his care : weep over in his ears the history of thy misdoings and unthankful course : tell it him with penitential tears and groans : but tell him also the advantage that he hath for the honouring of his grace, if it may now abound where sin abounds : tell him that thou art most offended with thyself, for that which he is most offended with : that thou art angry with thy disobedient, unthankful heart : that thou art even weary of that heart that loves him no more ; and that it shall never please thee, till it love him better, and be more desirous to please him : tell him of thy enemies, and crave the protection of his love, tell him of thy frailties, infirmities, and passions, and crave not only his tender forbearance, but his help : tell him that without him thou canst do nothing ; and crave the grace that is sufficient for thee, that through him that strengthens thee thou mayest do all things : when thou fallest, despair not, but crave his helping hand to raise thee.

Speak to him especially of the everlasting things, and thank him for his promises, and for thy hopes : for what thou shalt be, and have, and do among his holy ones for ever. Express thy joy in the promise of those joys ; that thou must see his glory, love him, and praise him better than thou canst now desire ! Begin those praises, and as thou walkest with him, take pleasure in the mention of his perfections ; be thankful to him and speak good of his name : solace thyself in remembering what a God, what a defence and portion, all believers have : and in considering whither he is now conducting thee, and what he will do with thee, and what use he will make of thee for ever : speak with rejoicing of the glory of his works, and the righteousness of his judgments, and the holiness and evenness of his ways : sing forth his praises with a joyful heart, and pleasant and triumphing voice ; and frown away all slavish fears, all importunate, malicious suggestions and doubts, all peevish, hurtful griefs, that would mar or interrupt the melody ; and would untune or unstring a raised, well composed soul. Thy Father loves thy very moans and tears : but how much more doth he love thy thanks and praise ? Or if indeed it be a winter time, a stormy day with thee, and he seem to chide or hide his face because thou hast offended him, let the cloud that is gathered by thy folly come down in tears and tell him, thou hast sinned against heaven and before him, and art no more worthy to be called his son ; but yet fly not from him, but beg his pardon and the privilege of a servant. Thou wilt find embraces when thou fearest condemnation, and find that he is merciful and ready to forgive : only return, and keep closer for the time to come. If the breach through thy neglect be gone so far, as that thou seemest to have lost thy God, and to be cast off, and left forsaken ; despair not yet : for he doth but hide his face till thou repent : he doth not forsake thee, but only tell thee what it is to walk so carelessly as if thou wouldst forsake him : thou art faster and surer in his love and covenant than thou canst believe or apprehend. Thy Lord was as dear as ever to his Father, when he cried out, ' my God, why hast thou forsaken me ? But yet neglect him not, and be not regardless of his withdrawings and of thy loss : lift up thy

voice and cry but ' Father ;' in despite of unbelief, cry out ' my Father, my Saviour, my God,' and thou shalt hear him answer thee at last, ' my child.' Cry out, ' O why dost thou hide thy face, and why hast thou forsaken me ; O what shall I do here without thee ; O leave me not, lose me not in this howling wilderness ; let me not be a prey to any ravenous beast ; to my sin, to satan, to my foes and thine ?' Lift up thy voice and weep, and tell him, they are the tears and lamentations of his child : O beg of him, that thy wanderings and childish folly may not be taken as acts of enmity, or at least that they may be pardoned ; and though he correct thee, that he will return and not forsake thee, but still take thee and use thee as his child, or if thou hast not words to pour out before him, at least smite upon thy breast, and though thou be ashamed or afraid to look up towards heaven, look down and say, ' O Lord, be merciful to me a sinner,' and he will take it for an acceptable suit, that tends to thy pardon and justification, and will number such a sentence with the prayers which he cannot deny. Or if thou cry and canst not hear of him, and hast long called out upon thy Father's name, and hearest not his voice and hast no return, inquire after him of those thou meetest : ask for him of them that know him, and are acquainted with his way. Make thy moan unto the watchmen, and ask them where thou mayest find thy Lord. At last he will appear to thee, and find thee first, that thou mayest find him, and show thee where it was that thou didst lose him, by losing thyself and turning from him ; seek him and thou shalt find him : wait and he will appear in kindness : for he never fails or forsakes those that wait upon him.

This kind of converse, O my soul, thou hast to prosecute with thy God. Thou hast also the concerns of all his servants ; his afflicted ones, to tell him of : tell him also of the concerns of his kingdom, the fury of his enemies, the dishonour they cast upon his name, the matters of his gospel, cause, and interest in the world : but still let his righteous judgment be remembered, and all be terminated in the glorious everlasting kingdom.

Is it not much better thus to converse with him that I must be with for ever, about the place, and the company, work, and concerns of my perpetual abode, than to be taken up with strangers in my way, and detained by their impertinencies.

I have found myself so long in these meditations that I will but name the rest and tell you what I had farther to have treated on, and leave the enlargement to your own meditations.

8. I have no reason to be weary of converse with God, seeing it is that for which all human converse is regardable. Converse with man is only so far desirable as it tends to our converse with God : and therefore the end must be preferred before the means.

9. It is the office of Christ, and the work of the Holy Ghost, and the use of all the means of grace, and of all creatures, mercies, and afflictions, to reduce our straying souls to God, that we may converse with him, and enjoy him.

10. Converse with God is most suitable to those that are so near to death; it best prepares for it : it most resembles the work that we are next to do. We had rather, when death comes, be found conversing with God than with man : it is God that a dying man hath principally to do with : it is his judgment that he is going to, and his mercy that he hath to trust upon ; therefore it concerns us to draw near him now, and be no strangers to him, lest strangeness then should be our terror.

11. How wonderful a condescension is it that God should be willing to converse with me! with such a worm and sinful wretch : therefore how inexcusable is my crime, if I refuse his company, and so great a mercy !

12. Lastly, heaven itself is but our converse with God and his glorified ones, though in a more perfect manner than we can here perceive. Therefore our holy converse with him here is the state that most resembles heaven, and that prepares for it, and all the heaven that is on earth.

V. *Directions to improve solitude.*

It remains now that I briefly tell you what you should do to attain and manage this converse with God, in the improvement of your solitude. For directions in general for walking with God, I reserve for another place. At present let these few suffice.

Direct. 1. If you would comfortably converse with God, make sure that you are reconciled to him in Christ, and that he is indeed your friend and Father. ' Can two walk together except they be agreed ?' Can you take pleasure in dwelling with the consuming fire ; or conversing with the most dreadful enemy ? Yet this I must add, that every doubting or self-accusing soul may not find a pretence to fly from God. (1.) That God ceases not to be a father whenever a fearful soul is drawn to question or deny it. (2.) That in the universal love and grace of God to miserable sinners, and in the universal act of conditional pardon and oblivion, and in the offers of grace, and the readiness of God to receive the penitent, there is glad tidings, that should exceed-

ingly rejoice a sinner ; and there is sufficient encouragement to draw the most guilty miserable sinner to seek to God, and sue for mercy. But yet the sweetest converse is for children, and for those that have some assurance that they are children.

But perhaps you will say, that this is not easily attained: how shall we know that he is our friend ?

In brief, I answer, If you are unfeignedly friends to God, it is because he first loved you. Prefer him before all other friends, and all the wealth and vanity of the world ; provoke him not by wilfulness or neglect : use him as your best friend, and abuse him not by disobedience or ingratitude ; own him before all, at the dearest rates, whenever you are called to it : desire his presence : lament his absence : love him from the bottom of your heart : think not hardly of him : suspect him not, misunderstand him not, hearken not to his enemies ; receive not any false reports against him : take him to be really better for you, than all the world. Do these, and doubt not but you are friends with God, and God with you : in a word, be but heartily willing to be friends to God, and that God should be your chief friend, and you may be sure that it is so indeed, and that you are and have what you desire. And then how delightfully may you converse with God.

Direct. 2. Wholly depend on the mediation of Christ, the great Reconciler: without him there is no coming near to God : but in his Beloved you shall be accepted. Whatever fear of his displeasure shall surprise you, fly presently for safety unto Christ : whatever guilt shall look you in the face, commit yourself and cause to Christ, and desire him to answer for you : when the doors of mercy seem to be shut against you, fly to him that bears the keys, and can at any time open to you and let you in: desire him to answer for you to God, to your own consciences, and against all accusers : by him alone you may boldly and comfortably converse with God ; but God will not know you out of him.

Direct. 3. Take heed of bringing a particular guilt into the presence of God, if you would have sweet communion with him : Christ himself never reconciled God to sin ; and the sinner and sin are so nearly related that notwithstanding the death of Christ, you shall feel that iniquity dwells not with God, but he hates the workers of it, and the foolish shall not stand in his sight ; and that if you will presume to sin because you are his children, ' be sure your sin will find you out.' O what fears, what shame, what self-abhorrence, and self-revenge will guilt raise in a penitent soul, when it comes into the light of the presence of the Lord! It will unavoidably abate your boldness and your comforts: when you should be sweetly delighting in his pleased face and promised glory, you will be befooling yourselves for your former sin, and ready even to tear your flesh, to think that ever you should do as you have done, and use him as you would not have used a common friend, and cast yourselves upon his wrath. But an innocent soul, or pacified conscience, walks with God in quietness and delight, without those frowns and fears which are a taste of hell to others.

Direct. 4. If you would comfortably converse with God, be sure that you bring not idols in your hearts: take heed of inordinate affection to any creature. Let all things else be nothing to you, that you may have none to take up your thoughts but God. Let your minds be further separate from them than your bodies: bring not into solitude or contemplation a proud, or lustful, or covetous mind: it much more concerns thee, what heart thou bringest, than what place thou art in, or what work thou art upon. A mind that is drowned in ambition, sensuality, or passion, will scarcely find God any sooner in a wilderness than in a crowd, unless he be there returning from those sins to God, wherever he sees him, God will not own and be familiar with so foul a soul. Seneca could say, ' What good doth the silence of all the country do thee, if thou have the noise of raging affections within?' And Gregory says, ' He that in body is far enough from the tumult of human conversation, is not in solitude, if he busy himself with earthly cogitations and desires: and he is not in the city, that is not troubled with the tumult of the worldly cares and fears, though he be pressed with the popular crowds.' Bring not thy house, land, credit, or carnal friend along with thee in thine heart, if thou desire and expect to walk in heaven, and to converse with God.

Direct. 5. Live still by faith: let faith lay heaven and earth as it were together: look not at God as if he were far off: set him always as before you, even as at your right hand. Be still with him when you awake. In the morning thank him for your rest; and deliver up yourself to his conduct and service for that day. Go forth as with him, and to do his work: do every action with the command of God, and the promise of heaven, before your eyes, and upon your hearts: live as those that have incomparably more to do with God and heaven, than with all this world; that you may say with David, as afore cited, ' Whom have I in heaven but thee?

and there is none on earth that I desire besides thee.' And with Paul, ' To me to live is Christ, and to die is gain.' You must shut up the eye of sense, save as subordinate to faith, and live by faith upon a God, a Christ, and a world that is unseen, if you would know by experience what it is to be above the brutish life of sensualists, and to converse with God. O Christian, if thou hast rightly learned this blessed life, what a high and noble soul-conversation wouldst thou have! How easily wouldst thou spare, and how little wouldst thou miss the favour of the greatest, the presence of any worldly comfort; city or solitude would be much alike to thee, saving that the place and state would be best to thee, where thou hast the greatest help and freedom to converse with God. Thou wouldst say of human society as Seneca, ' One is instead of all the people to me, and the people as one: one is enough for me, and none is enough.' Thus being taken up with God, thou mightest live in prison as at liberty, and in a wilderness as in a city, and in a place of banishment as in thy native land: ' for the earth is the Lord's, and the fulness thereof;' and every where thou mayest find him, and converse with him, and lift up pure hands unto him: in every place thou art within the sight of home, and heaven is in thine eye, and thou art conversing with that God, in whose converse the highest angels place their highest felicity and delight.

How little cause then have all the church's enemies to triumph, that can never shut up a true believer from the presence of his God; nor banish him into such a place where he cannot have his conversation in heaven? The stones that were cast at holy Stephen, could not hinder him from seeing the heavens opened, and Christ sitting at the right hand of God. A Patmos allowed holy John communion with Christ, being there in the Spirit on the Lord's day. Christ never so speedily and comfortably owns his servants, as when the world disowns them, and abuses them for his sake, and hurls them up and down as the scorn and off-scouring of all. He quickly found the blind man that he had cured, when once the Jews had cast him out. Persecutors do but promote the blessedness and exceeding joy of sufferers for Christ.

How little reason then have Christians to shun such sufferings, by unlawful means, which turn to their so great advantage; and to give so dear as the hazard of their souls by wilful sin to escape the honour, and safety, and glory of martyrdom?

Indeed we judge not, we love not, we live not, as sanctified ones must do, if we judge not that the truest liberty, and love it not as the best condition, in which we may converse with God. O how much harder is it to walk with God, in a court, in the midst of sensual delights, than in a prison or wilderness where we have none to interrupt us, and nothing else to take us up? It is our prepossessed minds, our earthly hearts, our carnal affections and concupiscence, and the pleasures of a prosperous state, that are the prisons and jailors of our souls. Were it not for these, how free should we be, though our bodies were confined to the straitest room? He is at liberty that can walk in heaven, and have access to God, and make use of all the creatures in the world, to the promoting of this his heavenly conversation. He is the prisoner whose soul is chained to flesh and earth, and confined to his lands and houses, and feeds on the dust of worldly riches, or wallows in the dung and filth of gluttony, drunkenness, and lust: that are far from God, and desire not to be near him; but say to him, Depart from us, we would not have the knowledge of thy ways: that love their prison and chains so well, that they would not be set free, but hate those with the most cruel hatred that endeavour their deliverance. Those are the poor prisoners of Satan that have not liberty to believe, nor love God, nor converse in heaven, nor seriously to mind or seek the things that are high and honourable; that have not liberty to meditate or pray, or seriously to speak of holy things, nor to love and converse with those that do so: that are tied so hard to the drudgery of sin, that they have not liberty one month, or week, or day, to leave it, and walk with God so much as for a recreation: but he that lives in the family of God, and is employed in attending him, and doth converse with Christ, and the host of holy ones above, in reason should not much complain of his want of friends, or company, or accommodations, nor yet be too impatient of any corporal confinement.

Lastly, be sure then most narrowly to watch your hearts, that nothing have entertainment there which is against your liberty of converse with God. Fill not those hearts with worldly cares, which are made, and new made, to be the dwelling-place of God. Desire not the company which would diminish your heavenly acquaintance and correspondence. Be not unfriendly, nor conceited of a self-sufficiency; but yet beware lest under the honest ingenuous title of a friend, a special, prudent, faithful friend, you should entertain an idol, or an enemy to your love of God, or a co-rival or competitor with your highest friend: for if you do, it is not the specious title of a friend that will save you from the thorns and briars of disquietude, and from greater troubles than ever you found from open enemies.

O blessed be that high and everlasting friend, who is every way suited to the upright souls! To their minds, their memories, their delight, their love, &c. by surest truth, by fullest goodness, by clearest light, by nearest love, by firmest constancy, &c. O why hath my drowsy and dark-sighted soul been so seldom with him; why hath it so often. so strangely, and so unthankfully passed by, and not observed him, nor hearkened to his kindest calls! O what is all this trash and trouble that hath filled my memory, and employed my mind, and cheated and corrupted my affections, while my dearest Lord hath been days and nights so unworthily forgotten, so contemptuously neglected and disregarded, and loved as if I loved him not! O that these drowsy and those waking nights, those loitered, lost, and empty hours had been spent in the humblest converse with him, which have been dreamed and doted away upon—now I know not what! O my God, how much wiser and happier had I been, had I rather chosen to mourn with thee, than to rejoice and sport with any other! O that I had rather wept with thee, than laughed with the creature? For the time to come let that be my friend, that most befriends my dark, dull, and backward soul, in its progress, and heavenly conversation: Or if there be none such upon the earth, let me here take no one for my friend! O blot out every name from my corrupted heart, which hinders the deeper engraving of thy name! Ah, Lord, what a stone, what a blind, ungrateful thing, is a heart not touched with celestial love; yet shall I not run to thee. when I have none else that will know me; shall I not draw near thee, when all fly from me? When daily experience cries out so loud, 'None but Christ: God or nothing.' Ah, foolish heart, that hast not thought of it? Where is that place, that cave or desert, where I might soonest find thee, and fullest enjoy thee; is it in the wilderness that thou walkest, or in the crowd, in the closet, or in the church? Where is it that I might soonest meet with God? But alas, I now perceive, that I have a heart to find, before I am like to find my Lord; O loveless, lifeless, stony heart; that is dead to him that gave it life; and to none but him? Could I not love, or think, or feel at all, methinks I were less dead than now? Less dead, if dead, than now I am alive? I had almost said, Lord, let me never love more till I can love thee? Nor think more on any thing till I can more willingly think of thee? But I must suppress that wish: for life will act: the mercies and motions of nature are necessary to those of grace. Therefore in the life of nature, and in the glimmerings of thy light, I will wait for more of the celestial life! My God, thou hast my consent! It is here attested under my hand: separate me from what and whom thou wilt, so I may but be nearer thee! Let me love thee more, and feel more of thy love, and then let me love or be beloved of the world, as little as thou wilt.

I thought self-love had been a more predominant thing: but now I find that repentance hath its anger, its hatred and its revenge: I am truly angry with my heart that hath so often and foolishly offended thee; methinks I hate that heart that is so cold and backward in thy love, and almost grudge it a dwelling in my breast. Alas, when love should be the life of prayer, the life of holy meditation, the life of sermons and of a holy conference, and my soul in these should long to meet thee, and delight to mention thee, I stray, Lord, I know not whither: or I sit still and wish, but do not rise and run, and follow thee; yea, I do not what I seem to do. All is dead, all is dead, for want of love; I often cry, O where is that place where the quickening beams of heaven are warmest, that my frozen soul might seek it out! But whither can I go, to city, or to solitude, alas, I find it is not place that makes the difference. I know that Christ is perfectly replenished with life and light, and love divine: I hear him as our head and treasure proclaimed and offered to us in the gospel! This is thy record, that he that hath the Son, hath life! O why then is my barren soul so empty? I thought I had long ago consented to thy offer; and then according to thy covenant, both head and life in him are mine? Yet must I still be dark and dead?

Ah, dearest Lord, I say not that I have too long waited; but if I continue thus to wait, wilt thou never find the time of love; and come and own thy dying worm? Wilt thou never dissipate these clouds, and shine upon this dead and darkened soul? Hath my night no day? Thrust me not from thee, O my God; for that is a hell, to be thrust from God. But surely the cause is all at home, could I find it out, or rather could I cure it; it is surely my face that is turned from God, when I say, his face is turned from me. But if my life must here be out of sight, and hidden in the root, with Christ in God, and if all the rest be reserved for that better world, and I must here have but

these small beginnings, O make me more to love and long for the blessed day of thine appearing, and not to fear the time of my deliverance, or unbelievingly to linger in this Sodom, as one that had rather stay with sin, than come to thee; Though sin hath made me backward to the fight, let it not make me backward to receive the crown: though it hath made me a loiterer in thy work, let it not make me backward to receive the wages which thy love will give to our pardoned, poor, accepted service. Though I have too often drawn back, when I should have come unto thee, and walked with thee in thy ways of grace, yet heal that unbelief and disaffection, which would make me to draw back, when thou callest me to possess thy glory? Though the sickness and lameness of my soul have hindered me in my journey, yet let their painfulness help me in my desire to be delivered from them and to be at home, where, without the interposing nights of thy displeasure, I shall fully feel thy fullest love, and walk with thy glorified ones in the light of thy glory, triumphing in thy praise for evermore. Amen.

But now I have given you these few directions for the improvement of your solitude, for converse with God, lest I should occasion the hurt of those that are unfit for the lesson I have given. I must conclude with this caution, which I have formerly also published, that it is not melancholy or weak-headed persons, who are not able to bear such exercises, for whom I have written these directions. Those that are not able to be much in serious, solitary thoughtfulness, without confusions, distracting suggestions, and hurrying, vexatious thoughts, must set themselves for the most part to those duties which are to be done in company by the help of others; and must be very little in solitary duties: for to them whose natural faculties are so diseased or weak, it is no duty, as being no means to do them the desired good; but while they strive to do that which they are naturally unable to endure, they will but confound, distract themselves, and make themselves unable for those other duties which yet they are not utterly unfit for. To such persons, instead of ordered, well digested meditations and much time spent in secret thoughtfulness, it must suffice that they be brief in secret prayer, and take up with such occasional abrupt meditations as they are capable of; and that they be the more in reading, hearing, conference, praying and praising God with others: until their melancholy distempers are so far overcome, as that by the direction of their spiritual guides, they may judge themselves fit for this improvement of their solitude.

FORSAKING ALL FOR CHRIST.

From BAXTER'S POETICAL FRAGMENTS, *the poem entitled " The Resolution," in which the author counts the cost of following Christ through good report and evil report.*

MUST I be driven from my books?
From house, and goods, and dearest friends?
One of thy sweet and gracious looks,
For more than this will make amends.
The world's thy book: there I can read,
Thy power, wisdom, and thy love;
And thence ascend by faith, and feed
Upon the better things above.

I'll read thy works of providence!
Thy spirit, conscience, and thy rod
Can teach without book all the sense
To know the world, myself, and God.
Few books may serve when thou wilt teach;
Many have stolen my precious time!
I'll leave my books to hear thee preach;
Churchwork is best when thou dost chime.

As for my house, it was my tent
While there I waited on thy flock:
That work is done; that time is spent:
There neither was my home nor stock.
Would I in all my journey have
Still the same inn and furniture?
Or ease and pleasant dwellings crave,
Forgetting what thy saints endure?

My Lord had taught me how to want
A place wherein to put my head:
While he is mine I'll be content
To beg or lack my daily bread.
Heaven is my roof, earth is my floor;
Thy love can keep me dry and warm:
Christ and thy bounty are my store;
Thy angels guard me from all harm.

As for my friends, they are not lost:
The several vessels of thy fleet
Though parted now, by tempests tost,
Shall safely in the haven meet.
Still we are centred all in thee;
Members tho' distant of one head;
In the same family we be,
By the same faith and Spirit led.

Before thy throne we daily meet,
As joint petitioners to thee:
In spirit we each other greet,
And shall again each other see.
The heavenly hosts, world without end,
Shall be my company above;
And thou my best and surest friend,
Who shall divide me from thy love?

Must I forsake the soil and air,
Where first I drew my vital breath?
That way may be as near and fair;
Thence I may come to thee by death.
All countries are my Father's lands;
Thy Son, thy love doth shine on all;
We may in all lift up pure hands,
And with acceptance on thee call.

What if in prison I must dwell,
May I not there converse with thee?
Save me from sin, thy wrath, and hell,
Call me thy child; and I am free.
No walls or bars can keep Thee out;
None can confine a holy soul;
The streets of heaven it walks about;
None can its liberty control.

Must I feel sicknesses and smart,
And spend my days and nights in pain?
Yet if thy love refresh my heart,
I need not overmuch complain.
This flesh hath drawn my soul to sin;
If it must smart, thy will be done;
O fill me with thy joys within,
And then I'll let it grieve alone!

I know my flesh must turn to dust,
My parted soul must come to thee,
And undergo thy judgment just,
And in the endless world must be.
In this there's most of fear and joy,
Because there's most of sin and grace;
Sin will this mortal frame destroy,
But Christ will bring me to thy face.

Shall I draw back and fear the end
Of all my sorrows, tears, and pain?
To which my life and labours tend,
Without which all had been in vain?
Can I for ever be content
Without true happiness and rest?
Is earth become so excellent
That I should take it for my best?

Or can I think of finding here
That which my soul so long had sought?
Should I refuse those joys through fear,
Which bounteous love so dearly bought?
All that doth taste of heaven is good;
When heavenly light doth me inform,
When heavenly life stirs in my blood,
When heavenly love my heart doth warm.

How many guiltless creatures die,
To be a feast or food to me,
Who love their lives as well as I;
And hath not God more right to me?
Must I be privileged alone?
Or no man die until he please?
And God deposed from his throne,
And human generation cease?

Though all the reasons I can see,
Why I should willingly submit,
And comfortably come to thee;
My God, thou must accomplish it.
The love which fill'd up all my days,
Will not forsake me to the end;
This broken body thou wilt raise,
My spirit I to thee commend.

A

TREATISE OF CONVERSION,

PREACHED AND NOW PUBLISHED FOR THE USE OF THOSE THAT ARE STRANGERS TO
A TRUE CONVERSION, ESPECIALLY THE GROSSLY IGNORANT AND UNGODLY.

PREFATORY REMARKS.

This treatise and the six that follow it in this volume, belong to a class of books which must ever rank high, perhaps I should say highest, among the works of Baxter. As they treat of the most important subject which can occupy the attention of mankind in its degenerate state; so they discuss that subject with a power which is probably unequalled in human writings. While Baxter's talents were adequate to any subject to which they might be directed, the conversion of men was the grand object to which he devoted them, in the fullest extent in which they could be exercised. Other things he might resort to as recreation, or submit to as duty; this employment constituted his sacred delight. His whole soul was here eminently at home; he revels and luxuriates in it, exulting in the privilege of calling sinners to repentance, and thus promoting the glory of his Lord and Master.

In this department of writing, I am not aware that he had properly any predecessor in the English language. Among the works both of the episcopal and puritan divines, many excellent discourses on most branches of Christian faith and duty had previously appeared. The Puritans excelled especially in the expository and didactic departments of instruction; while many Conformists produced very able treatises on the several branches of theological and moral truth. But by no one nor all of them was produced such a mass of pungent and powerful addresses to the consciences of ignorant, ungodly, and thoughtless men, as by Baxter. Conversion in all its important aspects, and unutterably important claims, had not before been discussed, at least in our language; nor had any man previously employed so boundless a range of topics, in conjunction with such an energetic and awakening style of addressing sinners.

To excel in this mode of preaching, requires talents and properties of no ordinary kind. There must be a combination of scriptural knowledge and ardent piety, with a correctness of thinking, as well as a fervency of imagination and manner, which are rarely found in one individual. Incorrect notions of the boundless grace and mercy of the gospel, led some of Baxter's predecessors in the awakening style of preaching, to deal out the unmitigated thunders of the law. These, however, will roll in the ears of sinners in vain, unless mellowed with the meek and persuasive allurements of the gospel. Baxter knew how to connect them, so as to alarm and convince, without driving to despair. Taylor could describe the loathsomeness and guilt of the sinner, and the certainty as well as awfulness of his danger, with an exhaustless and withering power of illustration. He could inculcate penance and mortification with great force of argument. But his manner partook more of monkish severity—of the gloom and austerity of the cloister—than of the faithfulness and tenderness of Jesus and his apostles. Baxter's severity never partakes of the nature of misanthropy. He never seems to take pleasure in wounding. He employs the knife with an unsparing hand; but that hand always appears to be guided by a tender sympathizing heart. He denounces sin in language of tremendous energy, and exposes its hideous nature by the light of the flames of hell itself, but it is to urge the sinner to flee from the wrath to come, and to lay hold on the hope set before him. He never appears as the minister of divine vengeance come to execute wrath, and to make men miserable before the time; but as an angel of mercy, brandishing a flaming sword to drive men to the tree of life.

In the writings of Owen and Howe, and the preachers of the same school, doctrinal discussion, and elaborate argument in support and illustration of gospel truths, are more prominent than their addresses to sinners. This, perhaps, may be accounted for, by the different circumstances of the people whom they addressed. Their congregations consisted chiefly of a select company of believers, or of those who made a credible profession of the gospel. Hence their discourses were chiefly employed in instructing and building up. Baxter's hearers in Kidderminster, where most of his works of this class were 'produced, were of a different description; a large mass of ignorant, wicked persons, chiefly in the lower walks of life. When he entered on his labours among them, there was scarcely a vestige of religion in the place. He studied the best methods of gaining their attention, and of rousing them to repentance and reformation. How admirably he succeeded is evident, both from the discourses which he produced, and the effects which resulted from them. The character of his early preaching remained, as is generally the case, to the last. The Christian minister who has this kind of work to do (and what Christian minister has it not to do more or less?) would therefore do well to study this portion of Baxter's writings.

To excel in this kind of preaching, he was eminently qualified. He possessed an untiring capability of application; an uncommon degree of acuteness and nicety of discernment; a profound knowledge of the depths of iniquity belonging to the human heart; a fearless fidelity in the discharge of his duty; a constant sense of the divine presence on his mind, along with an impression, which seems never to have left him, that death was just at hand.

> "He preach'd, as never sure to preach again,
> And as a dying man to dying men!"[1]

He was gifted with exhaustless powers of expression, and an exuberance of imagination which supplied unfailing stores of language and illustration. He had also a soft, flexible, melodious voice; a tenderness, pathos, and solemnity of manner, which clothed all he said with dignity and love.

With such qualifications, presenting themselves even on the very surface of those discourses by which his popularity is still maintained, it is not surprising that, like some distinguished men in other professions, he carried those labours in which he had no prototype to a perfection which has never been excelled. It might be easy to produce specimens, both from Baxter's time and since, of greater profundity of thought, and greater originality of conception; of more refinement of language—though his language is often peculiarly happy; of more accuracy of argument and statement; of detached passages more tremendous or more touching, than any occurring in Baxter's writings on Conversion: but we have nothing that will admit of comparison with them as a whole—nothing so pointed, so awful, and yet so full of tenderness and compassion.

It is to this preaching we must chiefly look as the means of those amazing effects which, under divine influence, were produced at Kidderminster, while Baxter laboured there. We have no account of any remarkable outpouring of the Spirit—of anything corresponding with what is now called a revival —during the period of Baxter's residence in that town. But the effects produced by his ministry are

perfectly intelligible to all who look at the means employed, and attend to the promised blessing of God in connection with them. Baxter was a man of faith and prayer; he was also a man of unwearied labour. He preached in season, and out of season. He was an instrument fit for the work, and diligently employed all the means which God had put in his power. While he did so, he found, what every faithful labourer will also find, that he did not labour for nought, or spend his strength in vain.

These general observations will supersede the necessity of repeating the same things, on noticing the other publications relative to Conversion, which follow this, and to which we shall prefix special prefatory remarks.

The first work of this class is a "Treatise of Conversion; preached and now published for the use of those that are strangers to a true conversion, especially the grossly ignorant and ungodly." 1657, 4to. "It was the substance," he says, "of some plain sermons on conversion, which Mr. Baldwin, who lived in my house, and learned the short-hand character in which I wrote my pulpit notes, had transcribed. Though I had no leisure for this or other writings, to take much care of the style, or to add any ornaments or citations of authors, I thought it might better pass as it was than not at all; and that if the author missed the applause of the learned, the book might yet be profitable to the ignorant, as it proved, through the great mercy of God."

He dedicates the volume, in a most affectionate and faithful manner, to the inhabitants of the borough and foreign of Kidderminster. A few sentences of this address deserve to be quoted, as they explain the nature of the work, and illustrate the spirit of the man.

"As it was the unfeigned love of your souls that hath hitherto moved me much to print what I have done, that you might have the help of those truths which God hath acquainted me with, when I am dead and gone, so is it the same affection that hath persuaded me here to send you this familiar discourse. It is the same that you heard preached: and the reasons that moved me to preach it do move me now to publish it; that if any of you have forgot it, it may be brought to your remembrance; or if it worked not upon you in the hearing, yet in the deliberate perusal it may work. I bless the Lord that there are so many among you that know, by experience, the nature of conversion, which is the cause of my abundant affection towards you, above any other people that I know. But I see that there is no place or people on earth that will answer our desires, or free us from those troubles that constantly attend our earthly state. I have exceeding cause to rejoice in very many of you; but in many, also, I have cause of sorrow. Long have I travailed (as Paul speaks, Gal. iv. 19), as in birth, till Christ be formed in you. For this have I studied, and prayed, and preached; for this have I dealt with you in private exhortation; for this have I sent you all such books as I conceived suitable to your needs, and yet, to the grief of my soul, I must speak it, the lives of many of you declare that this great work is yet undone. I believe God, and therefore I know that you must every soul of you be converted, or condemned to everlasting punishment. And, knowing this, I have told it you over and over again. I have showed you the proof and reasons of it, and the certain misery of an unconverted state; I have earnestly besought you and begged of you to return, and if I had tears at command I should have mixed all these exhortations with my tears; and if I had but time and strength (as I have not), I should have made bold to have come once more to you, and sit with you in your houses, and intreated you on the behalf of your souls, even twenty times for once that I have intreated you. The God that sent me to you knows that my soul is grieved for your blindness, and stubbornness, and wickedness, and misery, more than for all the losses and crosses in the world; and that my heart's desire and prayer for you to God, is that you may yet be converted and saved."

A man who speaks in this earnest and affectionate tone cannot fail to be heard. The people must have been impressed with his sincerity; his love gained their confidence; and his plain and striking appeals thus found access to their consciences and hearts.

The treatise itself is founded on Matt. xviii. 3, "Except ye be converted, and become as little children, ye shall not enter into the kingdom of heaven." In a series of chapters he explains the nature of conversion; proves that none but those who are converted can be saved; illustrates the misery of the unconverted, and the benefits of conversion; and discusses at length twenty hinderances to conversion.

It is easy to conceive of a more logical arrangement than what is here described and followed. Exceptions might also be taken to some of Baxter's definitions and distinctions, though they do not affect anything of importance. There will also be perceived an occasional redundancy and repetition in some of his thoughts; for which there is always an apology in preaching: yet it is altogether a very admirable treatise. He thus beautifully apologizes for the plainness and earnestness of his manner:

"The commonness and the greatness of men's necessity, commanded me to do anything that I could for their relief, and to bring forth some water to cast upon this fire, though I had not at hand a silver vessel to carry it in, nor thought it the most fit. The plainest words are the most profitable oratory in the weightiest matters. Fineness is for ornament, and delicacy for delight; but they answer not necessity, though sometimes they may modestly attend that which answers it. Yea, when they are conjunct, it is hard for the necessitous hearer or reader to observe the matter of ornament and delicacy, and not to be carried from the matter of necessity; and to hear or read a neat, concise, sententious discourse, and not to be hurt by it; for it usually hindereth the due operation of the matter, keeps it from the heart, stops it in the fancy, and makes it seem as light as the style. We use not to stand upon compliment, when we run to quench a common fire, nor to call men out to it by an eloquent speech. If we see a man fall into fire or water, we stand not upon mannerliness in plucking him out, but lay hands upon him as we can without delay."

Common as preaching is among us, the style best adapted to the pulpit, and to the great subjects which are there discussed, is, I fear, very imperfectly understood. In some instances the language of the preacher is correct, chaste, classical; but the discussion is flat, cold, and unimpressive. The truth is neither concealed nor misrepresented: but there is an entire absence of "thoughts that breathe and words that burn." In other cases the pulpit is degraded by vulgarity and oddity or every kind of low buffoonery. This is done for the avowed purpose of gaining attention and rendering truth familiar. Such persons would seem to forget that it is practicable to be plain without becoming low, to strike and secure attention without becoming harlequins and buffoons. Who ever heard of men being converted by apes and mountebanks? In a third class, finery and ornament are mistaken for eloquence; and the gospel is supposed to be preached with power, when it is little better than buried under the rubbish of words and masses of gorgeous or tawdry figures.

All these and many other vices which accompany preaching, arise from preachers being occupied with something else than their subject, and the eternal good of their audience. If the mind is but sufficiently impressed with these, there will be no disposition to cultivate either the ludicrous or the fine, the lofty or the low, in setting forth the words of eternal life. Simplicity with earnestness is the only style of speaking which becomes the ministry of the gospel. The one will enable the preacher to convey truth to the understanding, the other will give him the command of the heart. Impressed himself, he will impress others; and what he himself clearly understands, he will make intelligible to his audience. These were the things which Baxter studied; and they constituted the power and charm of his eloquence. Thousands hung upon his lips when he preached; not to be dazzled or amused, but to be convinced of their danger or led to the remedy. His popularity arose chiefly from his impassioned earnestness and solemnity. His hearers had no opportunity to be thinking of the man, or of anything about him; while he spoke, their thoughts were fixed on themselves or on Christ; and when they left him, they were compelled to think and to speak, not of Richard Baxter, but of the awful or delightful subject which he had brought before them.—Orme's *Life and Writings of Baxter.*

A

TREATISE OF CONVERSION,

TO THE READER.

You have here presented to you a common subject, handled in a plain style, not only without those subtilties and citations which might suit it to the palates of learned men, but also without that conciseness, sententiousness, and quickness, which might make it acceptable to the ingenious and acute. If you wonder why I should trouble the world with such an ordinary dull discourse, as I owe you an account of it, so I shall faithfully give it you. Besides, my defect of leisure and acuteness to satisfy the expectations of these sharper wits, I did here purposely avoid that little which I could have done. I was to preach not only to a popular auditory, but to the most ignorant, sottish part of that auditory ; for it is they that are principally concerned in the matter. And knowing that the whole nation abounds with such, I was easily persuaded to permit the press to offer it to their view, and even as it was preached, without alteration. For the subject, I know it is the most needful that can be offered them. The reason why they must be condemned is, because they are not converted ; and were they but truly converted they would escape. To convert a sinner from the error of his way, is to save a ' soul from death, and to cover a multitude of sins ;' to convert them, is to pull them out of the fire, it is to recover them out of the snare of the devil, who are taken captive by him at his will ; conversion is the most blessed work, and the day of conversion the most blessed day that this world is acquainted with. It takes a slave from Satan and a hand from his service ; it addeth a subject, a son, a member to the Lord Jesus : it rescueth a soul from everlasting torments, and maketh him an heir of everlasting joys. And for such a work, we can never do too much. And alas, the most are little sensible of the nature or necessity of this change : many that say they believe in God as their creator and in Christ as their redeemer, declare that they are deluded by their deceitful hearts, in that they believe not in the Holy Ghost as their sanctifier : for they know not what sanctification is, nor ever look much after it in themselves. The commonness and the greatness of men's necessity, commanded me to do any thing that I could for their relief, and to bring forth some water to cast upon this fire, though I had not at hand a silver vessel to carry it in, nor thought it the most fit. The plainest words are the most profitable oratory in the weightiest matters. Fineness is for ornament, and delicacy for delight ; but they answer not necessity, though sometimes they may modestly attend that which answers it. Yea, when they are conjunct, it is hard for the necessitous hearer or reader to observe the matter of ornament and delicacy, and not to be carried from the matter of necessity ; and to hear or read a neat, concise, sententious discourse, and not to be hurt by it ; for it usually hindereth the due operation of the matter, keeps it from the heart, stops it in the fancy, and makes it seem as light as the style. We do not to stand upon compliment or precedency, when we run to quench a common fire, nor to call men out of it, by an eloquent speech. If we see a man fall into fire or water, we stand not upon the manner in plucking him out, but lay hands on him as we can without delay. I shall never forget the relish of my soul, when God first warmed my heart with these matters, and when I had newly entered into a seriousness in religion : when I read such a book as Bishop Andrew's sermons, or heard such kind of preaching, I felt no life in it : methought they did but play with holy things. Yea, when I read such as Bishop Hall, or Henshaw's Meditations, or other such essays, resolves, and witty things, I tasted little sweetness in them; though now I can find much. But it was the plain and pressing downright preacher, that only seemed to me to be in good earnest, and to make somewhat of it, and to speak with life, light, and weight : it was such kind of writings that were wonderfully pleasant and savoury to my soul. I am apt to think that it is thus now with my hearers; and that I should measure them by what I was, and not by what I am. Yet I must confess, that though I can better digest exactness and brevity, than I could so long ago, yet I as much value seriousness and plainness; and I feel in myself, in reading or hearing, a despising of that wittiness as proud foolery, which savoureth of levity, and tendeth to evaporate weighty truths, to turn them all into very fancies, and keep them from the heart. As a stage-player, or moricedancer differs from a soldier or a king, so do these preachers from the true and faithful ministers of Christ: and as they deal liker to players than preachers in the pulpit, so usually their hearers do rather come to play with a sermon, than to attend a message from the God of heaven about the life or death of their souls.

Indeed, the more I have to do with the ignorant sort of people, the more I find that we cannot possibly speak too plainly to them. If we do not speak in their own plain dialect, they understand us not. Nay, if we do so, yet if we compose those very words into a handsomeness of sentence, or if we speak any thing briefly, they feel not what we say : nay, I find, if we do not purposely draw out the matter into such a length of words, and use some repetition of it that they may hear it inculcated on them again, we do but over-run their understandings, and they presently lose us. That very style and way, that is apt to be a little offensive to the exact, and that is tedious and loathsome to the curious ear, whose religion is most in air and fancy, must be it that must do good upon the ignorant, and is usually most savoury and acceptable to them. Upon such considerations, I purposely chose so plain a style in the handling of this subject: for I preached and wrote it, not for the judicious, but for the special use of the more ignorant sort. And indeed, I am very sensible that herein I have not reached the thing that I desired ; and yet have not spoken half so plainly as I should : especially, that there wanteth that life and piercing quickness, which may concur with plainness, and a subject of such necessity doth require. The true causes of this were, the dulness and badness of my own heart, and a continual decay of the quickness of my spirits, through the increase of various distempers, together with that exceeding scarcity of leisure, which weakness and oppressing business have caused. But if God will give help and leisure, I shall seek a little to amend it, in something more which on the same subject I have begun.

One other reason that moved me to consent to this publication, is the scarcity of books that are written purposely on this subject. Though, on the by and by parts, I know that nothing is more common in English, yet on this subject purposely and alone I remember scarce any besides Mr Whateley's New Birth (and some sermons on repentance) and indeed I have long persuaded all that I had opportunity to persuade, to buy that book of Mr Whateley's, and to give them abroad among the ignorant, ungodly people. And if I had seen any such fruit of my persuasions as I desired, I think I should never have published this. But when I could not prevail with the one sort to buy them, nor with the other sort to give them, I resolved to print somewhat on so necessary a point, were it never so meanly done, if it were but that I might have some books to give myself to some that need, and also that the newness and other advantages might entice this book into the hands of some, that are never like to read those which heretofore I have commended to them.

One thing more I observe is likely to be offensive in this writing, and that is, that the same things do here and there fall in, which formerly have been spoken. I confess my memory oft lets slip the passages that I have before written, and in that forgetfulness I write them again ; but I make no great matter of it. The writings of the same things is safe to the reader, and why then should it be grievous to me? Not because it is displeasing to the curious, till I set more by their applause, and take the approbation of men for my reward. I like to hear a man dwell much on the same essentials of Christianity. For we have but one God, one Christ, and one faith to preach ; and I will not preach another gospel to please men with variety, as if our Saviour and our gospel were grown stale. This speaking the same things is a sign that a man hath considered what he speaks, and that he hath made it his own, and utters not that which accidentally falls in. And it is a sign that he is still of the same belief, doth not change, and that he loves the truth, which he so much dwells upon ; that he looketh more at the feeding of men's souls, and strengthening their graces, than at the feeding of their itching fancies, and multiplying their opinions. For it is the essentials and common truths, as I have often said, that we daily live upon as our bread and drink. And we have incomparably more work before us, to know these better, and use them better, than to know more. The sea will afford us more water after we have taken out a thousand tuns, than an hundred of those wells and pits from whence we never yet brought any. I speak not against the need of clothing the same truths with a grateful variety in representing it to the world, nor against a necessary compliance with the diseases of some itching novelists in order to the cure ; but only give you an account of this publication, by him that had rather be charged with the greatest rudeness of style, than with the guilt of neglecting what he might have done for the saving of one soul.

RICHARD BAXTER.

CHAPTER I.

" *Verily I say unto you, except ye be converted, and become as little children, ye shall not enter into the kingdom of heaven.*"—MATTH. xviii. 3.

INTRODUCTION.

Though the gospel doth not presuppose grace in men, but brings it to them, yet doth it suppose them to be men, and therefore endued with natural principles : and though there is not enough in nature to convert men, yet doth grace find some advantage in nature for its reception, and somewhat which it may improve for a further good : otherwise we might as well plead with beasts as men. Supernatural light supposes natural : the doctrine of faith supposes reason ; and he that would draw you to be everlastingly happy, doth suppose you so much to love yourselves as to be willing to be happy, and loth to be absolutely miserable. I come not therefore to persuade any of you to these things, which are supposed : we are not sent to entreat men to be men, or reasonable creatures, or to love themselves, or to be willing to be happy : I will not be beholden to any of you for this, for you cannot do otherwise : but we are sent to tell you where your happiness lies, and where not, and to advise you to exercise your reason aright, and to know the way to happiness, and take that course by which it may be obtained.

I must confess to you, that ever since I knew what it was to be a minister of the gospel,—what labour it must cost,—how cold a reward is to be expected from our hearers, and what a troublesome errand we come upon, in the judgment of the most, I never could think any thing below the pleasing of God, and the saving of the souls of our people and ourselves, to be a motive sufficient to draw a man to this employment ? Nor do I think it meet to come once into the pulpit, with any lower ultimate ends than these : he that is a minister for lower ends than these, in heart and deed, is no minister of Christ ; but as he seeks himself, so will he serve himself, and must reward himself as he can ; and no wonder if he be unfaithful in all his course. And he that preacheth one sermon for lower ultimate ends than these, will seek himself and not Christ, and so be unfaithful in that sermon : and if such study smooth words and fine sentences, which tend more to please than to save men's souls, it is no wonder. Considering these things when I had purposed this day's work in this place, I remembered in whose name I must speak, and on whose errand I must go, and therefore that from him I must receive my message ; and I remembered also to whom I was to speak, even to men that must be everlastingly happy or miserable ; and that are now in the way, and have that to do in a little time, which this their everlasting state doth depend upon. I remembered also, that Christ hath assured me, that of the many that are called, few are chosen, and that most men perish, for all the mercy that is in God, for all that Christ hath done and suffered, and for all the grace that is offered them in the gospel : and I considered the reason, even because they will not receive this grace, nor entertain Christ and the mercy of God, as it is offered to them. I therefore resolved to preach to you, as one that hath but one sermon to preach to you, and knows not whether ever he shall speak to you more, and therefore to choose no lower subject than that which your life or death depends upon ; and accordingly, to handle it as far as I am able with that plainness a matter of such concern should be handled with. If my business were to be thought a learned man, or to procure your applause, or to please your ears, I should then have prepared some pleasing matter, tried to have adorned it with some flourishes of wit, and presented it to you in mixture of languages, which you do not understand, and with such pretty jingles and gaudy allusions as carnal fancies are used to be tickled with ; but knowing that this is not the way to please God, but to please the devil, nor to save myself, or those that hear me, but to hinder the salvation of us both, I soon resolved not only to avoid the study of such unprofitable, carnal ostentation, but even to study to avoid it: for I should be loth to please Satan any way by doing his work, but doubly loth to please him in preaching the gospel, and to be serving him in the choicest service of my Lord.

If the Lord but bless the word that I shall speak to the conversion of any souls here present, I have the ends I come for ; and shall believe that I have cause to bless his name that sent me hither to-day ; and in hope of this success, which I have begged of the Lord, I shall cheerfully address myself to the work.

THE TEXT EXPLAINED, AND THE SUBJECT STATED.

The occasion of these words of Christ was the carnal thoughts of his disciples concerning the state of his kingdom, as if it had been of earthly pomp and glory, like the great monarchs of the world ; and also their carnal, aspiring desires and contrivances to get the highest place in his kingdom : they found these conceits among the Jews, and nature easily entertained and cherished them, which is so dark and so disaffected to higher things. Christ thought it not yet seasonable to give them the full discovery of his kingdom, it being reserved for the Holy Ghost, who was miraculously to possess them, and teach them all things in Christ's bodily absence, that the world might see that his doctrine was not of his devising, but from above : yet he presently falls upon that sin which these inquiries discovered in them; and before he fully tells them the nature of his kingdom, he plainly tells them what they must be if they will have a part in that kingdom. It may seem a great doubt, whether the disciples were at this time unconverted, that Christ tells them of the necessity of a conversion, or whether it be but a particular conversion from some particular sins that he here speaks of; as there is a general conversion or repentance necessary to the unregenerated, and a particular conversion or repentance necessary

to the godly upon their particular falls. To this I answer, 1. Judas was undoubtedly unconverted, and so did continue. 2. The apostles were then ignorant of many truths which afterwards became of absolute necessity to salvation; as Christ's death, resurrection, ascension, the nature of his kingdom, &c. Yet I dare not say that they were not in a state of salvation when they were thus ignorant of them, because they were not then fundamentals, or of absolute necessity, as afterwards they were : yet Christ might well tell them that these truths must be believed hereafter, and they could not have that eminent measure of faith which was proper to his more illuminated church after his ascension, without believing them. Yea, if they had not believed them when they were made fundamentals of absolute necessity to be believed, they had ceased to be true disciples of Christ. And whether there be not some noble effects of this gospel doctrine upon the heart, which are also proper to the church after Christ's ascension, as well as these articles of belief were proper to them, and so that this text may speak of both, I leave to further consideration. 3. Many think that it is but a particular conversion and repentance that is here spoken of; that is, from this sin of ambition which the disciples did now manifest : but then they observe not that it will hence be concluded, that a true disciple may by a particular sin be in such a state, that if he should die in it, he should not be saved. But others that are learned and godly think that no hard conclusion, as long as God will not suffer them to die in it. 4. I purposely forbear to trouble you with the names of expositors, but I make no doubt but they are in the right, that suppose that Christ doth here reprehend their ambition, by describing the contrary temper of his true followers, showing them the absolute necessity of conversion, without any determination whether they were or were not converted at present. He tells them that except they be converted, humble persons, they cannot be saved, but doth not determine that now they are otherwise. Indeed it doth not seem likely that the disciples of Christ, had not then that conversion and humility of mind that was of absolute necessity to salvation. These words may well be used to converted men, to show them the necessity of that conversion which they have. As if a Christian begin to grow covetous, you may say, except you be a man converted from earthly-mindedness to heavenliness, you cannot enter into the kingdom of heaven ; which doth not deny him to be already converted. Though as to our present purpose the matter is not great which of these be taken for the sense, because they all afford us that doctrine that we shall gather : for if there be no salvation without a particular conversion from a particular sin, much less without a conversion from a state of sin. But the plain sense of the text I doubt not is this ; as if he should say, 'You strive for pre-eminency and worldly greatness in my kingdom, why, I tell you my kingdom is a kingdom of babes, it contains none but the humble that are small in their own eyes, and look not after great matters in this world ; and though nature be proud, yet except you be now or hereafter converted, and become as little children, you shall not enter into the kingdom of heaven.' By the kingdom of heaven is here meant, both the estate of true grace and also of glory. Not as if conversion were a preparation to their entering into this kingdom as begun on earth, but it is their very entrance itself, and so the beginning of it. The doctrine we shall hence handle shall be given you in no other but the words of the text, lest I seem to force them.

Doct. It is a most certain truth, proclaimed by Jesus Christ, that except men be converted and become as little children, they cannot enter into the kingdom of heaven.

The order which we shall observe in handling this, is,

I. To show you what this kingdom of heaven is.

II. What is it to be converted, and particularly what to become as little children.

III. Confirm the doctrine from other Scriptures.

IV. I shall give you the reasons why no man can enter the kingdom of heaven that is not converted.

V. We shall make use of all, and therein show you the hinderances of conversion, the marks of it, the motives to it, and the directions for attaining it; as the Lord shall enable me.

I. The kingdom of heaven is taken in Scripture both for *the state of grace and glory*. As all men are by nature in the kingdom of Satan here, by a willing obeying of him, and hereafter to be tormented by him; so all the converted are by grace in the kingdom of Christ, by a willing submission and obedience here, and hereafter to be glorified by him for ever: this is all one kingdom, because there is the same king and the same subjects ; yet they are diversified in this, that one is the way or means to the other, and that the laws and duties which belong to us in the way, are not all the same as those that shall continue at the end. It is called the king-

dom of heaven, both because the king is from above, and not a mere man, as earthly kings are ; and reigns in heaven invisibly, and not as earthly monarchs whom you may see: and because it is heaven to which all grace, means and duties tend, and it is heaven where is the end, the full felicity, and the most glorious part of the kingdom ; the guide and sanctifier of the church also is from heaven, even the Holy Ghost: the law is from heaven by the inspiration of the Spirit, the hearts of the subjects are heavenly, and their lives must be heavenly : it is here in the seed, it will be hereafter in the full tree. The difference between the egg and the bird, the acorn and the oak, is not nearly so great as the difference between the kingdom of grace and of glory. And yet a man that had never seen or known the production of such creatures would little believe, if you should show him an acorn, that that would come to be an oak. And it is no marvel if a carnal heart will not believe that the weak, despised graces of the saints, tend to such an inconceivable glory. When a poor Christian that is dead to this world lies praying and panting after God, looking and longing after glory, little doth the unbelieving world think what a blessed harbour it is, to which by these gales he is moving and hastening ; they now see him praying, and shall then see him possessing and praising : they now see his labour and suffering, but they will not believe his blessedness and perfection, till they see it to their own sorrow who have lost it.

SECTION I.

HOW CONVERSION, REPENTANCE, REGENERATION, VOCATION AND SANCTIFICATION AGREE OR DIFFER.

Before I proceed to open the nature of conversion, I shall say somewhat more of the word: and I shall show you the difference between conversion, repentance, regeneration, sanctification, and calling.

1. All these five words are used in Scripture to express the same work upon the soul: only they have some respective and other smaller differences, which I shall now manifest to you. And the first word vocation or calling is taken often for God's act of calling when it hath no success, and this is called ineffectual calling: so it is used, 'Because I called and ye refused, I have stretched forth my hands and no man regarded ; but ye have set at nought all my counsel, and would none of my reproof.—I called, but ye answered not.' And

many other places: sometimes it is taken for the act of God when it is successful; as 1 Thess. ii. 12. and many more places. 2. This success itself is termed our calling in a passive sense: and it is two-fold. First, *Common;* when men are brought but to outward profession and common gifts; and so the word is used often. Second, *Special;* when men are savingly converted to Christ; the former is common effectual calling, the latter is special effectual calling: and this last is the same with conversion: only these two differences are observable. (1.) As to the name, it is metaphorically taken from the outward call of the gospel, and so applied to the effect on the soul. (2.) It hath usually in scripture a principal respect to the first effect on the soul, even the act of faith itself above all other graces, and following obedience: yet not excluding the latter, but sometimes plainly comprehending them. So that some divines conceive that vocation is a work different from sanctification, because they conceive that it is only the Spirit's causing the first act of faith in the soul, and by that act a habit is effected, and therewith the seed of all graces, which they call the work of sanctification. And indeed the word vocation hath special respect to the gospel-call, to the act of believing in Christ, and the proper effect of that call, even our actual belief. But sometimes also it comprehendeth the whole Christian relation and state.

2. Repentance is the same thing as special effectual calling; so we take not calling in the most narrow sense of all, for the bare act of faith; only this difference there is. First, The word repentance especially denotes our motion from that sinful state from which we turn, and which we repent of: yet including essentially also the state to which we turn. Whereas the word vocation principally expresses the state to which we are called. Second, Also the word repentance principally respects our turning to God from whom we fell: but the word vocation doth as much or more respect our coming to Christ the Mediator as the way to the Father. There is a two-fold repentance, (1.) One is our turning from a state of sin and misery, such as the unconverted are in, and this is it that we mean now, as the same with conversion from the same state. (2.) There is also a particular repentance, which is a turning from a particular sin, and this must be daily renewed while we live. Repentance signifies and contains two things. The first is a hearty sorrow that ever we sinned; the second is a change of the mind from that sin to God. Indeed the former is but part of the latter: the changed mind is changed in this part, and manifests its change in a special manner, by remorse for former sins: though all remorse is not from such a change.

3. The word regeneration also signifies the same thing with conversion, but with this small difference. 1st. The term is metaphorical, taken from our natural generation; because there is so great a change, that a man is as it were another man. 2d. The word is, in scripture sense, I think more comprehensive than conversion, repentance or vocation; for it signifies not only the newness of our qualities, but also of our relations, even our whole new state. This is not ordinarily acknowledged, but if we view the places where the word is used, it will prove so. For as Paul describing the thing though he use not the word, saith, 'he that is in Christ is a new creature, old things are passed away, behold all things are become new.' Where relations must needs be a part of that all as the context will show. So it is called the laver or washing of regeneration; and is distinguished from the renewing of the Holy Ghost; at least as the general, comprehending that as a part. (1.) Most expositors think that the word hath reference to baptism, and expresseth its effects. And no doubt baptism is for remission of sins, and therefore the laver of regeneration is for remission of sins. (2.) The very text maintains plainly that grace by which we are saved: by free grace and that is our free justification as well as free sanctification. And our divines commonly cite that text against the papists upon that account, as pleading for free justification. 'Not by works of righteousness which we have done, but according to his mercy he saved us, by the washing of regeneration, and the renewing of the Holy Ghost.' Is not saving from the guilt of sin a part of our salvation? what reason to restrain saving here to sanctification only? Doubtless if there were reason to restrain the word regeneration to either, it would be to justification only: because the giving of the Holy Ghost is next mentioned by itself, but justification is not mentioned at all; if regeneration comprehends it not. And it is certain, that the apostle intends not only to tell us, that we are freely sanctified without works, but also that we are freely justified by grace without works. So it is said, 'except a man be born of water and of the Spirit, he cannot enter into the kingdom of God.' Where he at least, hath some respect to baptism, as most suppose, and baptism is for the remission of sins: to be born of water therefore must needs include remission of sin. And this regeneration maketh a man a new crea-

ture, and as Paul saith, in the 'new creature all things are become new,' and not the qualities only. But essentially, regeneration is the same with conversion.

4. The word sanctification also signifies the same thing generally, as conversion doth, only with the small differences following. Sanctification is more comprehensive, for it signifies our whole state of dedication or devotedness to God, which comprehends in it these four things. (1.) The change of a man's qualities, whereby he is made fit for the service of God, having his heart bent towards him, and set upon him. (2.) The actual dedication or devoting of a man's self to God by faith and a holy covenant; especially in baptism, by solemn vow or engagement. (3.) The relation of a person so dedicated or devoted to God, as he is one set apart to him for holy uses, and it is from this relation especially that the word sanctification is used. (4.) The holiness of life that follows hereupon, in the actual living to God, to whom we are devoted. Sanctification comprehends all this, and so comprehends in it vocation, and somewhat more.

But then perhaps it may be found, that sanctification is sometimes, if not often used in scripture for holiness of the life alone, as presupposing all the rest. Indeed there are more words than one, which we translate sanctification, which yet are not all of one sense. As δικαίοσις, δικαίωμα, and δικαιοσύνη, *righteousness*, differ: so doth ἀγιασμός, ἀγιότης and ἀγιωσύνη, *holiness*, differ: but I shall purposely forbear to trouble you with such matters. So that having opened before to you the word *conversion*, and now these four, vocation, repentance, regeneration and sanctification, you may see how far they are the same, or differ. The like may be said of the word changing, renewing, or making new, and the like, which all signify the same work of God upon the soul.

Those therefore that inquire whether vocation, regeneration, repentance, sanctification, &c. are the same thing, or different; and which of them goeth first, &c. must first be resolved of the sense of the term before they proceed to the matter: for most of these words are used in several senses, and that ambiguity must first be removed.

SECTION II.

NECESSITY OF CONVERSION.

I am next to show you what it is to be converted and become as little children: which can-

not be so well done till I have first given some brief description of the state of a man unconverted: to which end you must know, that God made man perfect, and gave him a perfect law to keep, which commanded perfect obedience upon pain of everlasting death: by the temptation of Satan, man broke this law, cast himself out of the favour of God, made himself the slave of Satan, and the child of death; this he did by a wilful adhering to the creature, and departing from God, so that the nature of man was thus become corrupt; and such as the first man Adam was, such must his posterity needs be, for who can bring a clean thing out of an unclean? And how can Adam convey to his posterity that image of God, which he had lost himself, or that right to the favour of God, and further happiness? So that we are all born with corrupted natures, inclined to earth and earthly things; strange and averse to heaven and heavenly things; prone to evil and backward to good; estranged from God, and making our carnal selves our God. Pride, self-love, covetousness, voluptuousness, unbelief, ignorance, error, hypocrisy, ungodliness, strife, contention, cruelty and all wickedness have their roots at once in us, and if temptation serve, we shall bring forth the fruit.

This being the state of every man by nature, by practice and custom in sinning, men become worse, and the longer they delay before they are converted, the worse usually do they grow, and the further do they go from God, and from their happiness. By all which methinks you may easily see, both what conversion is, and why there is such a necessity of it.

The word conversion is sometimes taken actively, for that act or work that converts us; and sometime passively, for that change which is thereby wrought; as man is the subject or patient, so is he also an agent in the actual turning of his own soul; so that God and man are both agents in this work. The word here in my text is active, and makes it the act of man, except 'ye convert yourselves:' but we translate it, 'be converted:' because the word is used reciprocally, as some speak in scripture: in a word, God, as the most laudable principal cause, doth cause man's will to turn itself. So that conversion actively taken, as it is the work of the Holy Ghost, is a work of the Spirit of Christ, by the doctrine of Christ, by which he effectually changes men's minds, heart, and life from the creature to God in Christ: conversion, as it is our work, is the work of man, wherein by the effectual grace of the Holy Ghost, he turns his mind, neart, and life from the creature to God in Christ. And conversion as taken passively, is the sincere change of a man's mind, heart and life from the creature to God in Christ, which is wrought by the Holy Ghost, through the doctrine of Christ, and by himself thus moved by the Holy Ghost. Here you may see, (1.) Who is the cause of this conversion, and what are the means. (2.) What is the change wrought. (3.) On whom. (4.) From what, and to what. First, The most laudable, principal cause is the Holy Ghost, who is the sanctifier of the elect. Second, The instrumental cause is the doctrine of Christ either read, or heard, or some way known; and brought by the Spirit to men's understandings and consideration. Third, Man himself is the subject of the Spirit's operation, and the proper agent of these holy actions of believing, repenting, &c. which the Holy Ghost doth cause him to perform. It is not the Holy Ghost that believes, but he causes man to believe. Fourth, That which we are turned from, is as to the object, the creature, which sinful man doth adhere to above God; and as to the act it is sin, that is, he ceases this vicious adhering to the creature. Fifth, That which man turns to, is God, in and by Christ the mediator. God hath again the heart of a sinner, when he is converted, and God will be his happiness; his reformation, recovery, reward and felicity consist in this.

The parts of this conversion are these three. 1. It is a change of the mind. 2. Of the heart. 3. Of the life.

SECTION III.

IN WHAT CONVERSION CONSISTS.

1. Conversion changes the mind. First, From ignorance. Second, From inconsiderateness. Third, From unbelief. Fourth, From error.

1. Every unconverted man is ignorant of the saving truths of the gospel, either by a total ignorance of the thing, or by an insufficient, superficial, ineffectual apprehension of it: the most of the world do not know what man is by nature and actual sin; how hateful sin and sinners are to God; how it deserves his everlasting wrath, and makes it our portion: how Christ hath satisfied and redeemed us from this misery, on what terms, and in what order he offers to man that pardon and life which he hath purchased: how he will judge them that believe,

repent and obey him at last to everlasting glory, and the rest to everlasting misery. Many poor souls are utterly ignorant of these very principles of the Christian religion, in the midst of gospel-light, and under all our most diligent instructions, and of those that have some knowledge of them, many know them but superficially and ineffectually.

Now the first thing that the Spirit of God doth either in or to the work of conversion, is, to open men's eyes to understand these mysteries: so that, the man that was wont to hear them as a strange thing, as if we spoke Greek or Hebrew to him, is now like a man that is brought out of a dungeon into the open light; or that hath his eye-sight recovered, and doth not only know these things, but knows them with a somewhat clear and affecting knowledge: and is much taken with the light, rejoices in it, and marvels at his former ignorance. I shall prove all this to you by scripture, in 1 Cor. ii. 14. the apostle tells us, 'the natural man receiveth not the things of the Spirit of God, for they are foolishness to him, neither can he know them, because they are spiritually discerned.' In 2 Cor. iv. 3. the apostle saith, 'If our gospel be hid, it is hid to them that are lost, in whom the god of this world hath blinded the minds of them which believe not, lest the light of the glorious gospel of Christ, who is the image of God, should shine unto them. And then the cure you may see in Acts xxvi. 18. 'I send thee to open their eyes, and turn them from darkness to light, and from the power of Satan unto God.' Many poor people think that utter ignorance may stand with grace, and that they may be saved without knowledge because they are not book-learned; but you hear God tells you otherwise. Many have much speculative knowledge that have no grace, but no man can have grace without solid knowledge: for who can hate sin till he knows it, and the evil of it? And who can love God till he knows him to be lovely? And who can do the duty that he understands not, or go the way to heaven that he is ignorant of? So that this is the first part of the change of the mind, from ignorance to knowledge.

2. The second part of the change of the mind, is from careless inconsiderateness to sober consideration; and this is a great help to all that followeth. The main reason why we cannot bring men out of love with this vain world, nor to yield to the call of God, seek after Christ, and their everlasting salvation, is, because we cannot bring them to consideration: men are heady and rash, and drown their own reason with wilfulness, or

passion, or worldly business, and will not give reason leave to work. Their vicious wills command their understandings to other objects, and will not let them dwell long enough on those that should do them good. All wicked men are inconsiderate men, and therefore inconsiderate, because wicked; and therefore wicked, because inconsiderate. If they hear of the greatest truths in the congregation, they go home and talk of other matters, and all runs out, and they are never the better: we cannot get them to go alone one hour, and seriously consider of what they heard. Ignorance doth much to men's perdition, but inconsiderateness much more. O if that little which our common people know, were but frequently and earnestly considered of, it would not suffer them to be such as they are! Well! but when the Spirit of God comes effectually to convert the soul, he makes them consider: he awakens the sleepy soul, and shows them that the matter so nearly concerns them, that if they love themselves, it is time to consider of it: he sets these truths still before their eyes, which formerly they cast behind their backs; he holds their thoughts upon them so, that they must needs consider them. They had heard perhaps an hundred times before of sin, Christ, and the necessity of conversion, of judgment, heaven, and hell, but they never thoroughly considered it till now. O this is a great part of the renewing work of the Spirit, to fix a man's thoughts upon the truths of God till they work, and to bring a man's reason to do its office! I will show you this but in two or three texts of scripture. In Acts xvii. 11. it is said that the Jews of Berea had more ingenuity than the rest, for 'they searched the scriptures daily, whether those things were so, therefore many of them believed:' when they came home they did not turn their thoughts presently to other matters and think no more of what they had heard, but they took their Bibles, considered and examined the sermons which they had heard, that they might be resolved whether it were so, indeed or not; that if it were so, they might obey it accordingly; and therefore they believed. In Psal. cxix. 59, 60. David saith, 'I thought of my ways, and turned my feet unto thy testimonies; I made haste and delayed not to keep thy commands:' when he thought on his ways he turned without delay: and God complains of the disobedient Israelites in Isa. i. 2, 3. that he had ' nourished and brought up children, and they rebelled against him;' and what was the cause? why, 'the ox knoweth his owner, and the ass his master's crib, but Israel doth not know; my people doth not

consider.' So that you may see the second part of the conversion of the mind is from inconsiderateness to consideration.

3. The third part of the change of the mind, is from unbelief to true believing: a customary belief upon the bare credit of their forefathers, and the common consent of the country they dwell in, most among us may have of the gospel; but this faith is like the ground of it and will not serve to establish and renew the soul. Men are not soundly persuaded of the infallible truth of all the word of God till converting grace doth bring them to believe it: they think it may be true, and it may be false for ought they know, they cannot tell: and therefore it is that when we come to those particulars that displease them, they will not believe them. When they do confess in general that the scripture is true, yet when we tell them particularly of those passages that speak of the necessity of conversion, the difficulty of salvation, the fewness of the saved, and the multitude that shall perish, with many the like truths, they will plainly show that they do not believe them. A word of such matters of heaven and hell, if it were well believed, would doubtless prevail against sensual allurements, and make them see that they have something else than this deceitful world to look after. Certainly all unconverted sinners are at best but such half-believers as in scripture are called rightly unbelievers. But when the Spirit by the word doth illuminate their understanding, they see then that all this is most certainly true: that the talk of sin, misery, Christ, grace, glory, and of everlasting torments to the impenitent, are no dreams nor doubtful suppositions. God tells them then to the very heart, that these are matters not to be questioned, but presently and seriously to be regarded: for God will prove true when all men prove liars: heaven and earth shall pass away, but a jot or tittle of his word shall not pass away till all be fulfilled.

Whatever unbelievers think of it now, nothing is more certain than that all men on earth shall shortly find themselves in heaven or hell. Now the soul perceives that this is true, as the God of heaven is true, and that it is madness to question the truth of his word, who is truth itself, and to think that word will shake or fail which bears up heaven and earth and is the best security that is possible to be had; and that he should deceive them who never deceived any; and doth so much to save them from being deceived by Satan, and their own deceitful hearts. Before conversion you might have heard by his cold prayers, and carnal conference, and seen by his careless, sinful life, that he did not heartily believe the word of God; but now you may hear and see by him that he doth believe it. If you tell a man that a bear, murderer, or a thief is following after him, if you see him not stir any faster, nor mend his pace, you will say surely he doth not believe it: but if you see him run as for his life, it is a sign that he believes it: when once a man is truly converted, you may see by his affection, diligence, and self denial, that he owns and believes the word of God indeed: if you over-heard him in his prayers, his tears, or at least his hearty groans will tell you that he believes: if he talk with you of his former life, his sobs and sighs, and his deep self-accusings will tell you that he believes it: his careful endeavours for the saving his soul, his earnest inquiries what he shall do to be saved, will tell you that he believes: the change of his company, his talk, his life, his casting away those sins with hatred which were his delight, and taking up that holy life with delight which before he had no heart to; all this will show that he is now a true believer. Because Noah believed, he was moved with fear, and prepared the ark: he that had seen him at work might perceive that he believed: he would never else have so laboured to escape the danger.

4. The fourth point wherein the change of the understanding doth consist, is in the healing of men's errors, and turning them from those false conceits which they had about God, his ways, and the matters of salvation. While they were unconverted, Satan had taught them, the world had taught them, and the flesh had taught them many things against God and their own safety: were they persuaded that either there was no heaven and hell, or that God would save them though they did not much look after it themselves. They thought sin was better than holiness, that it was a more desirable life to please the flesh, to be honourable, to eat, drink, and be merry, than to live in the thoughts of another world, deny the flesh that pleasure it desires, and to spend so much time in reading, hearing, praying and meditating. They thought this was a tedious, unnecessary life, and that all this was more ado than needs; that the wisest way was to follow their business in the world, take their pleasure while they might have it, and only come to church, forbear some heinous sins, and then believe that God will be merciful to them, and they shall do well enough without all this stir; that they may take what they can get of the pleasures of the world, and when they have done, if there be any heaven, they may have it with a

short repentance when they can keep the world no longer.

Many more such errors as these are in the minds of unconverted sinners, through the seducements of the deceiver: indeed they live a life of error. Some heretics err in one particular, and some in another, but wicked men err in the very drift of their lives. But when God converts, he changes all these opinions. The man is then of another mind. He that thought sin so pleasant, would now gladly purge it out; he that desired so to glut himself with the world and sinful delights, would now be rid of them: like a foolish person that will needs take poison, because it is sweet, and will not believe him that tells him it is deadly; but when he feels it begin to gripe him in the bowels, and to burn him at the heart, then he cries out, O now I believe you that it is poison: O give me a vomit that I may cast it up quickly, or else I die: then, if you see him retching and straining himself to get it up again, groaning, and crying out, O my heart, it burns me, it tears me; O that I could get it up; you may see then that the man's opinion is changed.

Sinners, believe it, if ever God will save you, it will be thus with you. You thought there was no great harm in taking now and then a cup with good fellows, in neglecting God and your souls, while you provide for your bodies, in dropping a curse or a small oath in the heat of your passion; you could ask, what harm is it to spend the Lord's day in idleness, or vain-talking, or recreations, when you had a God, and a soul, and an everlasting state to look after, which should have been the business of that day: perhaps you let down now and then some sharper poison of covetousness, malice, fornication, &c. O but if ever God convert you, all this must up again; you will groan and strain at it by the vomit of repentance, and cry out, O that I had never known it: O that I had never seen the faces of such ungodly companions: O that I could get up the very roots of this sin, I would never return to it again.

You that now think it so grievous a life to be godly, and that there needs not so much ado for your salvation; if ever God convert you, he will make you see, that it is both necessary and delightful: you will then say, What, shall I sit still when my everlasting salvation is at stake? I have but a little time to make sure of escaping eternal misery; I must very shortly be in heaven or hell; and now is the time that must turn the scales, for then I must be judged according to my works; and is this a time to loiter in; or is this a matter to be forgotten or made light of?

O sinners, if God open your eyes, you will marvel, I tell you, you will a thousand times marvel, that ever you should be so sottish, and in a manner besides yourselves, as to follow your business in the vain world, eat and drink, and sleep so quietly, while you knew not what should become of you for ever. You will cry out of yourselves, O where was my wit, that I should make so light of that which was my only business; and that I should sleep out that short time of my life which was given me on purpose to work out my salvation in; and that I should forget that judgment that I was told again and again was at the door?

Sinners, if God do once truly convert your souls, you will see, that if wife, children, friend, estate, life require your labour and care, your salvation requires an hundred times more. You will then say, What, can I make too much haste to heaven, or be at too much care or pains to make sure of it? Can any labour be too much to obtain such a glory, or to escape the flames of everlasting misery? If I lose the world and my life, I may be a saver and a gainer in the life eternal; but if I lose that life, how shall I be a saver; or which way shall I hope for a reparation of my loss? And what good will it then do me that I had pleasure, or credit, or riches in the world? Is it worth the labour of all my life to gather in this earth, and to live in more plenty of worldly vanity than other men a little while, till I drop into my grave? And is it not worth ten thousand times more care and pains to make sure that I live among the angels, and see the face of God in endless glory? O Lord, where is that man's senses that thinks he can pay too dear for heaven, and yet that all the stir of his life is not too dear a price for earth? To get him a pleasant passage to his grave, when he might have as much pleasure upon other terms? Where is that man's reason that will be at all this trouble for nothing, and yet will cry out to God, or to his minister, what need all this ado to be saved? Ask a gasping man on his death-bed, whether this labour had not been better laid out for heaven? And whether heaven or earth will pay a man better for his care and pains? What! Doth the Lord himself cry out to sinners, 'Lay not up to yourselves a treasure on earth, where rust and moth doth corrupt, but lay up for yourselves a treasure in heaven.—Seek first the kingdom of God, and his righteousness.—Labour not for the food which perisheth, but for that which endureth to everlasting life.' And shall men that call themselves Christians say, that this is more ado than needs? Thus sinners, will your minds be changed, if ever you be converted: you will then be quite of another mind concerning the world, God, the wicked, and the godly, than now you are. I tell you, God will unteach you again all these false opinions about these matters, which the devil, the world, and the flesh have been so long teaching you. It is his work to unteach you first, and then to teach you better things: this will be so. You that now say you will never believe but a man may be saved without so much ado; you will never believe that none shall be saved but those that are thus changed; you will never believe that God makes so great a matter of sin as preachers talk of: if God will convert and save you, he will make you believe it. Even the most confident of these conceits will be changed. Be not too peremptory, sinner, God can yet show thee so much mercy as to change thy mind: he hath changed as self-conceited men's minds as thine, and hath shaken as confident opinions as these. Paul thought himself as wise as you, before his conversion, and tells us, 'I verily thought myself that I ought to do many things contrary to the name of Jesus:' but when God had struck him down, and amazed him with his glory, and then illuminated him with his saving light, he crieth out, 'Lord, what wouldst thou have me to do?' And this with trembling and astonishment. He telleth you what he thought then of his former courses: 'we ourselves were sometimes foolish, disobedient, serving divers lusts and pleasures;' but how was he healed? 'But after that the kindness and love of God our Saviour towards man appeared, not by works of righteousness which we have done, but according to his mercy he saved us by the washing of regeneration and renewing of the Holy Ghost.' You say you will never be of another mind; ay, but God can make you of another mind: his light cannot be overcome by your darkness, if he mean you so much mercy as to shine in upon your souls. This is the fourth part of the change of men's understandings from error to saving truth in the matters of salvation.

SECTION IV.

CONVERSION—A CHANGE OF HEART AND PRINCIPLE.

2. The second part of the work of conversion is upon the heart or will, to which this change of the mind or understanding is preparative: and in this change of the heart, there are these several parts observable. (1.) The will is brought to like what it disliked, and to dislike what it liked before. (2.) It is brought to choose what it

refused; and to consent to that which it would not consent to. (3.) It is brought to resolve, where it was either resolved on the contrary; or unresolved. (4.) The several affections are changed, of love and hatred; desire and aversion; delight and sorrow; hope and despair; courage and fear; and anger with content and discontent. In al these respects the converted is changed, which we must therefore speak of in their order.

1. The first change that God maketh on the heart or will in the work of conversion, after the preparatory works, which we now pass over, is in the complacency or displacency of it: he causeth that to savour or relish as sweet to the will, which before was as bitter: the soul receiveth a new inclination; it liketh that which before it disliked, not only by a mere approbation, but by a willing agreement of the heart therewith. So that, these two things, a new inclination, and a new complacency, do go to make up this first part of the work. Before conversion the very bent of man's mind is toward the things below, and his heart is against the things of God: he relisheth the things below as sweet: and it pleaseth him to possess them, or to think of possessing them, but he hath no pleasure in God, nor in thinking or hearing of the life to come: all things please or displease a man, according as they agree or disagree to his inclination; and as they seem to him either suitable or unsuitable. Things do not please or displease according to their own goodness or badness, but according to the qualification of him that apprehendeth or entertaineth them. 'To the hungry soul every bitter thing is sweet, but the full soul loatheth the honey-comb.' But when a man is sick, there is scarce a greater torment than to eat or drink, when the stomach goeth against it. O how they loath it, and cannot get it down! They had rather cast the daintiest fare into the channel, than take it into their stomachs; so it is with the sick, unrenewed soul: he hath no pleasure in God, nor any holy things: it goeth against his heart to think of them, or seriously to speak or hear much of them. He marvelleth how other men can find so much delight in reading, hearing, praying, and the like; for his part he is weary to bear it, though for fashion, or fear of God's wrath, he comes to church, or sayeth over a few words of hypocritical, heartless prayer, yet he usually makes no long matter of it, but he longeth till it be done, and he is glad when it is over; therefore the scripture calleth such enemies to God, and haters of him; for their hearts are not with him, though with their tongues they may draw near him.

I know it is a very common thing with almost all men to profess that God hath more of their hearts than their pleasures, profits, or any thing else: but sin hath blinded them so, that they know not themselves: otherwise it would be a very easy matter for them to perceive that their very hearts are turned away from God. Many poor sinners are even willing to cheat their souls with a lie, when they might know that their hearts have no delight in God: but that the very thoughts of him and of his word, and service, and everlasting life, are rather grievous to them; and as the Psalmist saith, 'God is not in all their thoughts.—The Lord knoweth their thoughts, that they are vain.' Well, this is then the first change that God by his renewing grace doth make upon the heart—he turneth it to himself, he giveth it a new inclination and bias: he first openeth men's eyes to see God's excellency and the excellency of those glorious things which he hath promised; and thereby draweth their hearts unto them. It is a great and difficult matter to set the heart of man upon heaven, but God can do it, and doth it in this great change. I know the best are still earthly in part, too much in the dark, and too backward to the things of God, and God hath not nearly that room in their hearts which he deserves, and which they could wish he had. Yet a wonderful change is made on them: they that had no savour of God and glory before, do now savour nothing else so much; they can truly say, as David, though perhaps not so feelingly as he, 'Whom have I in heaven but thee, and there is none on earth that I can desire besides thee?' He that scarce thought of God before, now his mind runs upon him, now his thoughts are, whether God be reconciled to him, or not: and how God approveth of him, and his ways: were he sure of his favour he would think himself happy; could he but know him, and enjoy him more, he had the very desire of his heart. It is his greatest trouble that he is no nearer him, and no more fit to please and honour him; and God hath no more room in his heart. Unfeignedly he grudgeth at the remnants of sin, that they should so weary and grieve the Spirit of God, and hinder his more sensible enjoyment of his love; it grieveth him that any of that room in his heart should be taken up by fleshly and worldly vanities, which he knoweth doth of right belong to Christ. It is his care to give him yet better entertainment, and to get out those remnants of sin and vanity, that God at last may have it all to himself. It is his daily business to mortify sin, and dress up his disordered heart for Christ; and glad he is when he

38

can but find any signs of his presence, and feeleth any stirring of his grace ; and when he can but move towards him more swiftly by a stronger love ; this is the true condition and temper of a converted soul ; all other men do but talk of God, but it is only these that give him their heart.

Sirs, I would fain make this as plain as I can to you, and I would fain have you try as we go along, whether this change has been made in your own hearts, or not. You know that there is something or other that every man is most pleased in, and his mind is most towards ; and this complacency and bent of the mind is the very spring of almost all his conversation : but if he have no pleasure in it, nor mind to it, he will neglect it, whatsoever you can say or do. Here is the true root of the difference between the hearts of the carnal and of the spiritual : before a man is converted, his mind is not towards God, but upon other things : but afterwards nothing is so near and dear to him. Mark the discovery of both these states, Rom. viii. 5—9. 'For they that are after the flesh do mind the things of the flesh, but they that are after the Spirit, the things of the Spirit. For to be carnally minded is death, but to be spiritually minded is life and peace. Because the carnal mind is enmity against God, for it is not subject to the law of God, neither indeed can be ; so then, they that are in the flesh cannot please God. But ye are not in the flesh but in the Spirit, if so be that the Spirit of God dwell in you. Now if any man have not the Spirit of Christ, he is none of his.' Here you see in the very words of the Holy Ghost a plain description of these two different conditions of men ; till a man be converted, his mind is more on his fleshly pleasure, or credit in the world, than in God or the happiness of the world to come. Whatsoever he may say or pretend to the love of God, yet God knoweth that his mind is another way : but when converting grace comes, it taketh off the old bias, and setteth on a new one ; and now the man that was carnally minded is become spiritually minded. Sinners, if you would but enter into your own hearts, and ask them what it is that seemeth best to you in all the world ; what is it that most pleaseth you ; what you would have if you might have your choice ; by this you might know the bent of your mind ; and so know whether you are indeed converted, or not. You think it may be, that you may have worldly and fleshly minds, and yet have grace too : and that you may set your hearts most upon your fleshly and worldly pleasures, and yet be the children of God ; but deceive not yourselves, it cannot be : believe me, it cannot be. O that those men did think of this, that drown their hearts in the cares of this life ; or wilfully run on in gluttony, drunkenness, or other fleshly delights. If ever you escape the torments you have deserved, if ever you will see the face of God in peace, those hearts must be turned quite another way ; those delights must grow bitter to you : you must be ashamed of your present pleasure. Your souls must abhor them in comparison of Christ, and even abhor yourselves for all your abominations. And cast them all away as dross and dung, and account all as loss for the winning of Christ, which now you think your greatest gain, Phil. iii. 8, 9.

O sinners, how low will all these things be then in your hearts ? When you look upon all the glory of this world, it will be no more lovely than a dead carcass in your eyes : for you will be crucified to the world, and the world to you. If a man would then offer you all the kingdoms and glory of the earth, it would be but as a trifle to you, it would be disapproved in your thoughts if it tended to deprive you of everlasting glory. Many infirmities may stand with grace, but a carnal or worldly mind in a prevailing sense cannot. 'Love not the world nor the things of the world, for if any man love the world, the love of the Father is not in him.' I know there are few men so foolish and ungodly, but will say with their tongues, that God is better than the creature, and heaven than earth, and would give it as their judgment under their hand, and confirm it with an oath, that they do not dissemble. Yea, but the question is of the inclination and complacency of their hearts : which do these men love best, and which do they mind as the most suitable good ; never tell me, that their estimation of God is sincere, unless it affect the heart with an answerable complacency and inclination to him. They may apprehend it as truth that God is the chief good, but they do not truly, that is, thoroughly apprehend it.

But when converting grace comes, it doth this work. I know, when the best Christians have reached to the greatest knowledge of God, and sense of his love, which in this life they may expect, they will still be looking higher after more. And the apprehension of that which they yet come short of, will much darken the apprehension of their present attainment : infiniteness will quite over-match both our apprehensions and our affections : but though we are ready to call our present glimpse and taste of God a very nothing, when we compare our knowledge of him with our ignorance, and our enjoyments with our wants; yet when we compare these small things with all the pleasures or profits of this world, we see that we have chosen the better part. Alas, the poor converted soul hath quickly a taste of the vanity of this world in the very first heart-breaking and humbling that he was brought into; when his sin is set in order before him, and the voice of the law doth make his heart to tremble, and an angry God doth look him into terrors, what then can all the world do for his relief? How sensibly then doth he say, silly comforters! O what should I do if I had no better hopes? O what contemptuous thoughts and speeches then hath he of all these things that he once so much valued! He thinketh he can scarce find words that are base enough for them. If he could find worse than Paul's losses, dross, and dung, he would do it. O that men would now, in the day of their prosperity, bethink themselves of this, which all shall know at last. It is a most doleful sight to any man of wisdom and compassion, to see men that have wounded and loaded consciences, to run up and down, after pleasure and profit, as if these would heal them which have made their wounds: men that are even undone for want of healing, and are within a step of hell, and will certainly and very speedily be there, if Christ, by saving, renewing grace do not recover them, do quite forget the nature of their distress, and the thing they want, and mind the toys of worldly things as if they would save them. What, is sin still sweet to you, when it hath made such work against your souls? Is this world still so lovely in your eyes, when it hath enticed you already to the very brink of hell? O poor, bewitched souls, that will dote upon that which you confess deceiveth you! That will dig your own graves with such excessive pains, and purchase a room in everlasting torments at so dear a rate? Well, if ever God will have mercy on your souls, he will show you another kind of pleasure and felicity; he will acquaint you with, that which shall be worth your labour, he will bring those sick, distempered souls to another relish than now they have: he will make you abandon these guilty pleasures, and thirst for the living water that shall spring up in you to everlasting life. Instead of your over-eager seeking the food that perisheth, he will make you hunger after the bread of life. What the unsanctified man doth most love, we may see by experience; we see what he seeks after, partly by his life; and you will see out of scripture yet

more fully which way the heart of the sanctified is inclined. ' The love of God is shed abroad in your hearts by the Holy Ghost.' They are confident that ' nothing can separate them from this love, neither height, nor breadth,' &c. They can sometimes appeal to Christ himself with Peter, ' Lord, thou knowest that I love thee.—O how I love thy law!' said David, ' it is my meditation day and night, yea, I love them exceedingly, above gold; above their appointed or necessary food,' saith Job. ' Thy word was the joy, and rejoicing of my heart,' saith Jeremiah. So vehement was Paul against those men that could not love the Lord of love, that he pronounceth them accursed with the greatest curse. ' Thy law,' saith David, ' is within my heart.— How amiable are thy tabernacles, O Lord ; my soul longeth, yea, even fainteth for the courts of the Lord ; my heart and my flesh crieth out for the living God; blessed are they that dwell in thy house ; blessed is the man whose strength is in thee, in whose hearts are the ways of them. My soul breaketh for the longing it hath to thy judgments at all times.—Thou art my God, early will I seek thee, my soul thirsteth for thee, my flesh longeth for thee, to see thy power and thy glory, as I have seen thee in the sanctuary, because thy loving kindness is better than life, my lips shall praise thee: thus will I bless thee while I live, I will lift up my heart in thy name. My soul shall be satisfied as with marrow and fatness, and my mouth shall praise thee with joyful lips, when I remember thee upon my bed, and meditate on thee in the night season.'

2. The second part of the change of the heart is in its intents or objects of pursuit. Conversion setteth a man upon right ends: all the work of a man's life lieth in intending certain ends, and using certain means to obtain them: and all the work of Christianity lieth in intending right ends, and in using right means to obtain them. The chief part of man's corruption in his depraved natural state, doth consist in this, that he intendeth wrong ends: that is a man's end which he accounteth his felicity, his treasure, his chief good, and which he useth all things else to obtain. Whatsoever you think the best thing in the world for you, and had rather have it than any thing else ; and whatsoever you principally seek after in your life, and think yourself most happy if you could obtain it, and think yourself most miserable if you miss of it, and therefore had rather lose all than that, and make it your main business to be sure that you may enjoy it, that, and nothing else but that, is your end. In general, every man's happiness

is his end, and this nature itself, as nature doth so far adhere to, and intend that no man can do otherwise, and there is no indication of man's not intending this. However generals are nothing, but as they are found in particular things: when it comes to the particular object of fruition: and what it is wherein men's happiness doth consist, there it is that the depraved nature doth most culpably err: for every carnal man doth apprehend it the best condition for him to enjoy his carnal pleasure, profit, and vain glory in this world; or if he look for a life to come, he would have it consist of such kind of pleasures as he here enjoyed in this life; and therefore his very heart is most set upon these sensual, worldly things: he hath a nature so suitable to them, that he savoureth these as the sweetest delights, and things fittest for him: and therefore his very business, and daily care and work in the world, is to get, or increase, to keep or enjoy and draw out the sweetness of these sensual things. So that an earthly man hath an earthly mind and earthly ends, as Christ said to Nicodemus, that which is born of the earth is earthly: and a fleshly man hath a fleshly mind and fleshly ends, as I before showed, from Rom. viii. 7. They cannot see in the love of God, or the enjoyment of him, so certain, so suitable a good for them, as may be their felicity, and better to them than these earthly things. Either they doubt whether the happiness, which they see not be true, or a mere delusion; or else they think that it is too far off, and a place too strange to them to be their felicity: they think that God and man are at too great a distance to be so mutually loved, and that he is so strange to us, as to be an unsuitable object for our highest love. Nay, because of his holiness, justice, and the other blessed perfections of his nature, and because he will judge the ungodly world unto perdition, therefore their hearts are even against him, and they that call him their God, have a secret enmity to him: so that before conversion, it is the sinful, miserable state of all men, that God is not their end; he hath not their hearts: it is not he that they most seek after in their lives, nor in whom their souls apprehend the chiefest delight and felicity to consist: but it is in the fleshly pleasures, or profits, or honour of this world; it is some creature and not God that hath men's hearts, their care, and earnest diligence.

Hence it is, that they are said to have their portion in this life, and are there called the men of the world: they are such as lay up a treasure on earth; they think none can show them any greater good, and apprehend not the joy of the light of God's countenance; they seek only 'what they shall eat or drink, or wherewith they shall be clothed,' for this is the custom of the nations of the world. They make light of Christ, and the kingdom that he promiseth, in comparison of their farms, their oxen, their worldly wealth and pleasure; 'they lay up treasures for themselves here, but are not rich towards God;' if they have abundance, they cheer their souls, as having enough for many years, and so resolve to 'eat, drink, and be merry;' if they are called by a trial to part with all for Christ, and the hope of everlasting glory, 'they go away sorrowful, because of their riches,' or the dearness of that which they are called to forsake. In a word, they are such as a compassionate man should mention with tears; they are enemies to the cross of Christ, though not always to his name; 'their end is destruction, their god is their belly, their glory is in their shame, they mind earthly things;' they 'make provision for the flesh to fulfil the lusts thereof;' they have their 'good things in this life, when the godly have their evil things, and therefore when others are comforted, they shall be tormented.' All these scriptures declare to you what are the ends of unconverted men, and where are their hearts: 'for where their treasure is, there will their hearts be.'

But when the Spirit comes with converting grace, the very ends and intents of a man are changed; as he findeth the greatest excellency in God and the things of the life to come, so hath he there laid up his treasure and fixed his hopes: he hath reckoned what the world is worth, and how much it can afford him, how long it will last him, what it will do for him in the greatest need; and upon certain knowledge of its vanity and insufficiency he hath resolved that this cannot make him happy. If ever you be converted, you will know all this to be true by experience that I say: that it is the work of converting grace to make a man consider whether all that he can hope for in this world will make him indeed a happy man, and upon consideration he findeth it will not serve his turn. God bringeth it now close to his thoughts and affections, so that the mere splendour, alluring taste, and false appearances of worldly things, cannot deceive him as formerly they did; but he understandeth now the utmost they can do for him; he considereth how that they do but flatter him into the grave and hell, and leave him when he is in the depth of his distress: before he was as the prodigal, that thought it hard keeping to live in his father's house, but abroad and among his companions and pleasures he would go; but when he comes to himself, he finds that he must come home again, or perish with hunger: the poor soul then layeth these things to heart: alas, thinks he, I may be merry a few days more if I hold on in this company and course; but will this life last for ever? I may be somebody in the world for a while, if I can be rich or honourable; but how long can I keep it when I have got it? I may please my mind among my friends and worldly businesses, my corn and cattle, my pleasures and prosperity; but what shall I do shortly when these things are gone? I may think now that I can live without the favour of God, but can I do so when I have nothing else to live on? Alas! is that fit to be instead of God and heaven to me, that will not keep me out of the grave, nor keep my strongest or most beautiful parts from mouldering in the dust; no, nor keep my soul from everlasting torments? O, what shall I do if I have not a better portion than this? Wo to me, that ever I was born, if I be not better provided for before I die.

Thus doth God take off the soul in conversion from its former ends, and makes it say, 'Lord, these will not serve my turn; O, put me not off with such things as these.' When the soul is thus loosened from its former delight, and seeth that it must be something else that must be his happiness; then doth the Spirit by the word of God reveal to him the certainty and the fulness of that glory that is to be had by Christ in the everlasting love and fruition of God: and then he sees, that though it be not here to be had, yet it is to be had hereafter; and that man was made to higher things than he hath hitherto minded. Now he begins to bethink himself in good earnest that heaven may be had, and that for him as well as others; the impossibility is taken away by Christ, and the door is set open; the glory is unconceivable, and if he can but once get it, he is made happy for ever. These thoughts now work in the heart of the man that never had such lively working thoughts of it before. So that now he feeleth his heart burn within him, when he hath once found where his happiness is to be had; presently, the Spirit having touched his heart with an effectual inclination thereto, he is bent upon it, and sets his heart and face to seek it: and now this is his business; comparatively he hath nothing else to do: now it must be God or none, heaven or nothing, that will serve his turn: now if God should offer him, I will give thee mirth and riches for a thousand years without interruption, I will give thee the good word of all about thee, I will make thee the greatest man on earth, and thou shalt

have the world at will; but not my love and grace in Christ, nor the hope of everlasting glory: this would be the saddest news that ever came to his soul. It is not now the same thing that would please him as before: tell not him now of profit and pleasure; it is everlasting pleasure that he must have: he hath another journey to go, another home to regard, another kind of trade to drive on in the world than before he had. Now 'he looketh for a city, that hath foundations, whose builder and maker is God;' and therefore doth take himself but as a stranger on earth, and one that sojourneth in a foreign country. Now the best of worldly things will no longer satisfy them, but they 'desire a better country, that is, an heavenly: wherefore God is not ashamed to be called their God, for he hath prepared for them a city.' Now they are soundly persuaded that 'there is a God, and that he is the rewarder of them that diligently seek him,' and that this reward is beyond the grave, and therefore they have 'respect to the recompence of reward,' and are content to submit to the sufferings of this life, that so they may obtain a better resurrection. He now is to this world as a dead man in comparison; 'crucified to the world, and the world to him.—And his life is hid with Christ in God; and when Christ, who is his life, shall appear, then shall he appear also with him in glory.'

Beloved hearers, you may easily conceive that it is a very great change that causes a man to have other ends than ever he had before; that entirely turns the very bent of his heart and life, and makes him have a quite contrary business in the world than before he had: that sets a man's face another way, so that he who before went one way, doth now go the contrary. Alas! it is not the restraint of a wicked work or two, or the outward civilizing of your lives, that is true conversion. It is such a change as I am now describing to you, that turns you quite another way. If you are true Christians that hear me, you know it, or may know it to be thus with yourselves. For certainly, you have had experience of this in your souls. It were no impossible thing for you now, if you were but willing to know certainly, whether you be converted, or not. One would think that a man's end might be discerned above all things: cannot you know what you love best? And what you would willingly have? And what you cannot be content without? And what you aim at in the course of your lives? And what you place your hopes and happiness in, which you will have, though you part with all to get it? And what it is that beareth down all things else in your hearts and lives? Why something or other doth this, whatsoever it be, and this is your end. And one would think that this which so much takes one up, and so much sways, and is the business of his life, might be well discerned. Sirs, deal truly between God and your souls: what hath your hearts? What game do you follow? What do you mind above all? I ask not whether you set not a foot now and then out of the way: but which way are you travelling? For earth or for heaven? O that you would but be faithful to your souls in this trial! I have often told you, and will tell you yet again, and desire you to remember it as long as you live, that this is the true difference between every converted soul, and all hypocrites and carnal men in the world: that to the true Christian indeed, God and everlasting glory is his main end, religion is his business, and all worldly things come as they occur, and therefore he can have them, or be without them; whereas with all hypocrites and carnal men, the pleasing of their flesh in this world is their chief end, and therefore worldliness, voluptuousness or ambition is their business, and the matters of God and religion come as may happen, and therefore they can taste of them, or they can be without them. I would you would keep this one mark by you while you live: by which you may judge yourselves without deceit, and so the true Christian need not deny his sincerity, nor the hypocrite imagine that he is what he is not; but might certainly know that he is yet in the flesh. And thus I have shown you what is the second part of the work of conversion on the will or heart, even the change of a man's ends and intentions.

SECTION V.

CONVERSION ISSUES IN, AND IS MANIFESTED BY, A CHANGE OF LIFE.

3. The third part of the work of conversion on the will, is this, the same Spirit in the word, which changes a man's ends, doth also change him as to the choice of means, and causes him to choose what before he refused, and to consent to that which before he did reject. Heaven is not obtained in every way, but in God's own way, and if a man should never so much intend God as his end, and yet not seek him in the means of his appointment (though I think there is none that doth so, or that ever these indeed are separ-

ated, yet I say, if such a thing were) it would not save him. It is not enough to know where we must be happy, but we must also know how to come thither. There is but one right way to salvation in the main, and he that will be saved, must be sure to embrace it.

1. There are two sorts of means or ways to salvation, not contrary but one subordinate to the other, but one is the chief and principal way, that is, Jesus Christ and the Holy Ghost: the other is the subservient way, and that is the means that Christ hath appointed under himself. When man was lost, there was no remedy for him in heaven or earth, but the ever-living Son of God to come down from heaven, take our nature, perfectly obey the law, and suffer for our disobedience; this he did in compassion to mankind: he was born of a virgin, without man, and without sin, by the power of the Holy Ghost. He lived on earth without sin also, and proved his Godhead and doctrine by his works; he raised the dead, healed the lame, the blind, the sick, and at last offered himself on the cross a sacrifice for our sins, in suffering that which we must else have suffered; and being buried, he rose again the third day, and after forty days in the sight of his disciples, ascended into heaven, where he is now in our nature interceding for us and preparing us a place. Before he departed from earth, he ordained this law, and sent his disciples to preach it to all the world—that all they that would renounce their own works, and trust their souls upon his redemption and ransom, forsake the world, the flesh, and the devil, take him for their only Lord and Saviour, and so return to God himself, shall receive the pardon of all their sins, and be made the heirs of everlasting glory. He hath promised also to send his sanctifying Spirit to dwell and work in those that believe; thus you see what is the principal means of salvation: it is the Lord Jesus Christ, who having suffered for us, is offered to us in the gospel, to be our head and husband, our Saviour and our Lord.

Two things are here of absolute necessity to our salvation; the one is, to believe unfeignedly that Christ is the Messiah and Redeemer of the world: and the second is, to accept him as he is offered to us in the gospel: now the heart of an unconverted sinner is against both these. (1.) It doth not soundly believe the truth of Christ's incarnation, resurrection and ascension, but only by a common, customary, superficial belief: but of this I spoke before. (2.) He doth not welcome Christ to his soul, as he is offered to him: partly because men are unhumbled and feel not the need of Christ: for 'the whole needs not the physician, but they that are sick',—and partly, because that Christ would reclaim them from the way that they take pleasure in: and would bring them into a way, that is, against their hearts; and many other causes there are. So that, even where Christ seems to be much honoured, and men will bow, and do the greatest reverence to his name, and profess themselves his faithful servants, and that they trust their salvation on him alone; yet for all this they do not savingly or sincerely believe in him. They have learned to speak well of Christ, and they are willing to be forgiven by him; but they never laid hold on him, as a drowning man would do on that which might save him: nor did they ever feel at their hearts what a glorious work of mercy he hath wrought in their redemption; or how much he hath done for them, and how much he hath engaged their souls unto himself. They never had any of the saints' admiration at the height, breadth, length and depth, nor have they been taken up with this astonishing project of love, as men thus redeemed at such a rate must be: nor would they ever consent that Christ should rule over them, mortify their lusts, and bring them back from the flesh to God: and therefore they are unbelievers, even while they profess the faith of Christ. But when converting grace comes, as it raises the soul's estimation of Christ, as I have said before, so doth it open the heart to his entertainment. O what glad news is it to desolate, self-condemned souls to hear that the Son of God hath bought them with his blood! It is life to them to hear the glad tidings of their redemption. It is the very work of the Spirit in conversion, to bring the soul into this admiration of redemption; and to show it the riches of grace in Christ, and the mystery of this blessed work, when his eyes are opened to see how God designed here the magnifying of his love: and how glorious God is in his mercy in the work of redemption, even as glorious as in his power in the work of creation. And when his wounded soul hath well understood how Christ hath made him a balm of his blood, this makes him have other thoughts of Christ and redemption than before he had. O how much sweeter to him are the hearing, reading, and thinking of this Christ, than before they were! He that before did shut the door, and let Christ knock, and knock again, and could so often churlishly resist him, O how the case is now altered with him!

Now Christ is to him as cordial-waters to a man in a swoon; as a hand to a drowning man:

as drink to a man in a burning fever; as a pardon to a man condemned to die: the name of Christ doth even revive him, when withal he can but have some hope that he is his. O could you now assure him that Christ is willing to pass over all his unkind resistance, and to be friends with him, and wash his soul in his blood, how glad a man would he be! When sin stares him in the face, O then for a Christ to make his peace! When conscience is up in arms against him, now how doth Christ befriend him, to step in and bear the stroke! He saith not as Pharoah, 'who is the Lord that I should serve him?' Nor as they in Job, 'depart from us, we desire not the knowledge of thy ways:' nor as the common rebels of the world, 'we will not have this man to reign over us:' but as Laban to Abraham's servants, 'come in, thou blessed of the Lord; wherefore standest thou without? for the house and room is prepared for thee.' Too long have I made my soul a sink, a dungeon, when it might and should have been thy dwelling, and the temple of thy Holy Spirit. Come in, Lord, and let sin possess thy room no longer; hath here been room for the world, and room for fleshly lusts and pleasures, and is there no room for thee? Let thy graces dwell, where sin hath dwelt; here is room for them all: or if there be not room, O cast out sin, and make thee room; thou that madest all things ready for me, before thou callest me by the voice of the gospel, make all within me ready for thyself, and cast out him that is stronger than I, and hath held my heart so long in a peaceable captivity. Only thy presence now will do me good: I die if thou revive me not: I am devoured by the jaws of the devouring lion, if thou do not rescue me. I am tormented by my own conscience, and nothing but thine applied blood can mollify it: I am accused and condemned by the law, which I have broken, and what shall I say, or do, if thou come not in, and plead not thy blood, and answer for me? I have many thousand sins that will be brought in against me; and how shall I come off, but by the virtue of thy sacrifice? Hell is ready to devour me everlastingly, if thou do not save me: save me, save me, Lord, or I perish! I am a lost, undone man if thou do not save me! The devils that have deceived me, do but stay to torment me if thou do not save me. A just and angry God will be to me everlastingly a consuming fire, if his indignation be not quenched by thy blood and intercession. There is no other name under heaven by which I can be saved. No, no, it must be Christ alone, it must be Christ or none, Christ or I am lost.

Now doth the poor soul look upon Christ as on the fire or air, that he cannot live without; he sees an absolute necessity of him for the main, and an absolute necessity for every particular. Every sin that he remembereth, telleth him that he hath need of Christ. Every corruption that he feeleth stirring within him, telleth him of the absolute need of Christ. Every temptation that assaulteth him, telleth him of the need of Christ. He never falleth into any known sin again (which alas, is too often) but it maketh him see the need of Christ. He findeth he could not live a day or an hour safely without him; he cannot wash one spot, nor master one corruption without him: when he goes to God in prayer for his soul, he then findeth the need of Christ; he dare not draw near if Christ take him not by the hand: he knows there is no admittance in any other name. He durst not look God in the face, nor name him, nor worship him, nor hope for any mercy from him, but through Christ. In a word, without Christ, he dares neither live nor die. You see then where another part of conversion lieth in this true belief in the Lord Jesus Christ. You may know and say all this of Christ before conversion; but you never rightly apprehend it nor feel it till then.

And as the merit, so the Spirit of Christ is here comprehended; for I join both together for brevity. It is by his Spirit that Christ takes down the strong contradiction of the flesh, and bringeth all in subjection to himself; as light prevails against darkness, strength against weakness, and life against death, so doth the Spirit prevail for Christ in the souls of the elect. Before conversion, there is nothing but grieving and striving against, and quenching the Spirit, and using it like an enemy. But now how glad is the soul of his presence! How loth to grieve him! How fearful of quenching it! And if by some unkindness the Spirit seem to be withdrawn, what mourning doth he make! And how sadly doth he cry out as David did, 'restore to me the joy of thy salvation, and uphold me by thy free Spirit.' And if he feel the Spirit as it were departing from him, he calls aloud with David, 'cast me not away from thy presence, and take not thy holy Spirit from me.' As a living man is loth to die, and knoweth that when his spirit is gone from his body, it will return to corruption, and therefore will use all possible means to keep the soul and body from parting, even so the true believer knows, that if the Spirit of God were gone from his soul, the soul were dead or worse than dead, and therefore it is his daily care to keep the Spirit and his soul from parting. He appre-

hendeth it now to be a blessed privilege indeed, to have the Spirit of Jesus still within him, to be his temple, and by him to be preserved from temptation, excited to duties, animated in them, and sanctified to the service of him that did redeem him.

And now, I must needs say to those of you that are unconverted, that all these matters are strange to you; you hear me, but you have felt no such things as these within yourselves. O what a difference is there between this living faith in Christ, and the name of faith, and the image of Christianity, which you boast of and presume upon! what a difference is there between these warm, heart-reviving feelings in Christ, and your cold belief and dull profession! It is one thing for Christ to dwell in the heart by faith, and another thing for him to have the custom of the country, and the law of the land on his side, to make way for him. It is one thing for a man that is well, to honour a physician, and another thing for a sick man to seek after him, beg his help, take him for his physician, and willingly take down any thing that he gives him. I pray you mark what I say, because it is the most common delusion of unconverted men amongst us, that they verily think that they truly believe in Christ already: and there is a common belief that will never save them, and that they take up with, and look not after the saving faith: I cannot better open the difference to ordinary capacities, than by the aforesaid comparison. You know a man in health may truly believe that such a man is an able physician, and he may speak well of him, and honour him: now suppose a man were deadly sick of a consumption, and did not know it; if this man honour the physician as much as any other healthful man, will this cure him, or save his life? No, but the patient that prays him to come to him, and will trust his life in his hands, and will take the bitterest medicine that he gives him, and will forbear any hurtful meat or drink, be it never so pleasant to him, this is he that is like to be healed by him. Christ is known among us to be the able physician of souls: we all confess and praise his skill, and know that he can save us. We all hear of the freeness of his cure, that he takes nothing, but doth it as soon for the poorest beggar, as the greatest prince; but knowing all this, and speaking well of him, will cure no man: no, but you must go to him believingly, and beg his help, and take him for your physician, and trust your souls upon his blood and Spirit, and apply his means, and take the bitterest cup that he shall reach you, and forsake the morsels of fleshly pleasure that have been sweet to you heretofore. Do not say this is to be justified by works; for this is no other kind of works than what standeth in a necessary subserviency to Christ, even the work of grace itself. This is but the work that Christ calls thee to. ' This is the work of God, that ye believe in him whom the Father hath sent:' this is but coming to Christ that ye may have life, and taking his yoke and burden on you, that you may find rest to your souls. When the poor people followed him on earth from place to place, and hearkened to his words and took up his cross that they might be his disciples, and be justified and saved by him, he did not tell them, this is sinful working for justification. To conclude, if ever you be converted, thus must you follow Christ, and thus must you yield to the Spirit which you now resist.

Thus I have showed you how the converted soul doth accept of Christ and the Spirit, on the terms and to the ends that are mentioned in the gospel. Christ Jesus is accepted as the Redeemer of their souls, that hath satisfied justice by being a ransom for their sins, and hath merited everlasting glory for them; and as the Lord that by the title of his redemption must rule them as their head, that must provide for them and supply all their wants; and as the fountain and treasure of all that grace that must save them; the Holy Ghost is entertained as he that must sanctify and guide them in the way to life everlasting, having already sealed the truth of the doctrine.

SECTION VI.

CONVERSION, AS CONNECTED WITH A SYSTEM OF DIVINELY APPOINTED MEANS.

We are next to consider how the work of conversion doth turn the heart or will of man to these means that stand in a subordination to Christ: and indeed a natural man is disaffected not only to Christ, but to all his ordinances: he that minds not the end nor the chief means, cannot heartily mind the subordinate means.

1. One means that God hath appointed to salvation is confession of sin, with a broken heart for the sin confessed. A man unconverted doth neither see any such evil in sin as to drive him to this confession, nor to break his heart in godly sorrow; nor will his heart be brought to consent to the faithful performance of that. A heart unhumbled and unchanged doth think it but a piece of childish folly to weep and mourn

for sin, and lament it before the world: they are too stout to stoop to a disgraceful acknowledgment: they scorn to be so base as to make an open confession of their sins, or to lament their misery! They feel no such burden upon their consciences as should drive them into such repentance to seek to God for ease; and if they confess to God in secret, it is without a broken heart: they will not endure so much pain as to feel their own condition, and have their sores so faithfully searched as is necessary to a cure. This afflicting of the soul, their souls abhor.

But when converting grace hath changed their hearts, O how the case is altered with them! Then godly sorrow is even as it were natural to them; and they that could not endure it, do now even cherish and indulge it. It is a voluntary sorrow; they mourn and would mourn like him that cried out, 'labour not to comfort me,' that is, till God will comfort me. As a sore that is not ripe will not break nor run, and that which is not suppurative is oft uncurable; but when it is brought to suppuration and ripeness, then it will even break of itself, and run without any more ado: so is it with the impenitent soul and the penitent; till repentance comes, the soul is not ripe. Ministers are every day applying to it all the mollifying, dissolving remedies they can devise to bring it to suppuration, but all will not do; their hearts will not break, not a tear of unfeigned repentance will come forth; they hide their sin, and scorn to make a penitent confession. But O, when grace hath done the work, and softened the heart, and ripened the sore, then it will come out of its own accord. I would not have you take this upon my bare word, but see whether the scripture say not so before me. They were once a stubborn generation of sinners that the apostles had there to deal with, that durst have their hands in the blood of Christ himself; but when they were once converted, ' they were pricked at the heart, and said to Peter and the rest of the apostles, Men and brethren, what shall we do?' This did imply a confession of their sin; thus, ' We confess ourselves guilty, and we find our souls in a miserable case under the wrath and curse of God: O give us your advice what we shall do.' These were three thousand people at once that were brought to this conviction and confession. See how freely all comes out when the heart is once pricked by the word and Spirit! The like you know was the case of Saul at his conversion, as stout a hearted sinner before as another; but when God overpowered him by converting grace, then he calls out with trembling and astonishment, 'Lord, what wilt thou have me to do?' And when he relateth his own life and manner of conversion, how freely doth he confess his former persecution! And again, in Acts xxvi. 10, 11. confessing that he was a 'persecutor, yea, and punished Christians in the synagogue, and compelled them to blaspheme; yea, was mad, yea, exceedingly mad against them.' The like doth he confess in Tit. iii. 3. and Acts xvi. The apostles met with a stout-hearted jailor that put them in the inner prison, and their feet fast in the stocks; but when an earthquake opened the doors and set them free, and a heartquake brought him in and laid him at their feet, and grace took the opportunity to do its work; then he crieth out with trembling, 'Sirs, what must I do to be saved?' David tells you his own experience, 'I acknowledged my sins unto thee, and mine iniquity have I not hid: I said I will confess my transgression to the Lord, and thou forgavest the iniquity of my sin: for this shall every one that is godly pray to thee in a time when thou mayest be found.' After his grievous fall, the fifty-first Psalm will show you his confession. So 'many confessed and showed their deeds, and brought their books and burned them before all men.' These were such as were reputed wise and learned before; but when grace had changed them, they openly confess that all was folly. Many more such examples we have, and precepts where God requireth it. And indeed pardon itself is offered on these terms: 'If we confess, he is faithful and just to forgive.—He that covereth his sins shall not prosper; but whoso confesseth and forsaketh them shall have mercy.—Confess your faults one to another, and pray one for another.'

Indeed in the primitive times no man was baptized that did not confess his sins openly, and renounce them; even John himself caused the Jews to confess their sins before he would baptize them. So in Jeremiah, 'return thou backsliding Israel, saith the Lord, and I will not cause mine anger to fall upon you; for I am merciful, saith the Lord: and I will not keep mine anger for ever; only confess thine iniquity that thou hast transgressed against the Lord. Turn, O back-sliding children, saith the Lord, for I am married to you.' You see here that conversion hath ever confession accompanying it. He that turns must and will confess, as the repenting church, 'we acknowledge, O Lord, our wickedness, and the iniquity of our fathers; for we have sinned against thee: do not abhor us for thy name's sake.' And in Hosea it was the Lord's threatenings against them, 'I will go, and return unto my place, till they acknowledge

their offence, and seek my face: in their afflictions they will seek me early.' So that it is most evident that conversion opens the heart and mouth to confess, even to God or man, or both, according as the case requires: not but that a Judas will do it at last in horror, and cry out, 'I have sinned in betraying the innocent blood:' but this is forced by horror, and not by a gracious change. Many a thief will confess his sin at the gallows, that is not converted; but when conversion comes, the very mind being changed, is set against the sin, and therefore they long to cast it up. Hiding tends to keeping, confession tends to parting with sin: therefore he that is penitent doth not hide it, so far as he hath any call to confess it. O my people, that the Lord would bring this to the hearts of some of you that most need it: one may hear by your speeches that conversion is far from your hearts. How many among us are there that have little cause to justify themselves, and yet we cannot bring them to any confession, but what is general and common with all, that we are sinners! But for any hateful and disgraceful sin, they excuse it and hide it; and have nothing but good almost to say of themselves: you shall not hear one sad complaint almost that they will make against themselves.

If you have a froward wife, you will complain of that; if disobedient children, if careless or stubborn servants, you will complain of them. If you have unkind friends or neighbours, you will complain of them; but of yourselves, where you have greatest reason to complain, we can scarce hear a word. If any do you wrong, you are still harping upon it and making the worse of it; but for all the wrong that you have done to God and your own souls, you can lightly pass it over, and make little of it: and who heareth you half so oft complain of yourselves as others? What say you? Is it not thus with many among us? You know not how sad a mark this is. I tell you, if ever converting grace come to your hearts, it will make you pour out complaints against yourselves; it will make you cry with David, 'I have done foolishly,' and with Paul, 'I was foolish, disobedient, I was mad, yea, exceeding mad,' and, 'O wretched man that I am! who shall deliver me?' Mark the unconverted man in his talk, and you shall hear him, if not as the pharisee, saying, 'I am not like other men;' yet at least saying nothing against himself, but distracting from the good names of others, and making the devil more servants than indeed he hath, and God fewer, by their rash censures: they have the hypocrite's eye that was not made to see itself, that is good for little but to spy motes in others' eyes! But the beam in their own they cannot see: the infirmities of those that fear God they can talk of; but a graceless heart and a worldly, fleshly life of their own doth little trouble them. But when converting grace comes, you may hear by their very talk that the case is changed; they have no body then to talk against so much as themselves: their censures against themselves seem the most uncharitable; their talk is most of the sins of their own hearts and lives: and blame them not, for these are nearest them and most concern them: the mote in their own eye doth most grieve them, and till they have wiped out that, they have less mind to look into the eyes of others. In a word, whosoever is justified of God, and freed from condemnation, is a judger and condemner of himself; but they that lie under the condemnation of God, are commonly self-justifiers.

SECTION VII.

CONVERSION ACCOMPANIED WITH EARNEST PRAYER.

2. Another means that converting grace doth turn the heart to, is earnest *prayer* to God. A man unconverted is a stranger to true prayer; either he doth nothing in his duty, or that which is next to nothing: commonly they will not be brought so much as to the outside and form of the duty; but if they be, that is all; till some affliction or conviction come and awaken them to a little more for a time: but they never fall to this work to purpose, till saving grace do truly change them: a carnal heart feeleth no such need of God or mercy, as to drive him to beg for it from day to day: he feels himself well enough, and therefore saith with them in Job, 'What is the Almighty that we should serve him; and what profit should we have if we pray unto him?' They scarce think it worth their labour. It may be for fear of perishing with the ungodly, and from some general conviction of conscience, they may use some formal, cold expressions, or perhaps take up the outside of this duty: but it is not prayer without the desires of the soul which carry out a man to seek for mercy and relief from God: unconverted men are either dumb to this holy duty, or their hearts are dumb while their tongues are speaking: either they have nothing to say to God; or nothing but some words that they get by rote, and utter without the feeling of their souls; or else they have little else but words. Their consciences witness, and God himself is a witness, that they do not in secret beg earnestly for his mercy; they do not heartily call to him for pardoning grace and sanctifying grace: with their families they do not earnestly beg of God the same mercy, as a people that desire that he should dwell among them. For where there is no true feeling of sin and misery and desire after grace, there can be no hearty prayer to God: what need you any further mark of a graceless soul, than that they are prayerless.

But converting grace doth open the heart, and let in the Holy Ghost, which is a 'Spirit of supplication,' and 'this Spirit doth help their infirmities;' and whereas of themselves 'they know not what to pray for as they ought, he maketh request for them with groans that are unutterable.' As the new born infant, or any living creature, will quickly show whether it be alive, by making towards the parent for its nourishment: so will the new born Christian. It is not unlikely that the apostle referreth to this—'We have received the Spirit of adoption, whereby we cry, Abba, Father.' As the child doth first learn to cry Mamma, so doth the Christian first learn to make utterance to God as a Father, and by prayer to seek to him for relief; and for certain, as the Spirit of Christ is a Spirit of prayer, so if any man have not this Spirit, he is none of his. The evidence that God gives Ananias of Saul's conversion, was this, 'behold, he prayeth.' It was the proof of Cornelius' grace, that he prayed to God always, and the angel takes the time of his prayer to appear to him; and Peter, that must be sent unto him, is found at prayer. The new converted disciples 'continued in prayer.' It is no small part of a Christian's life to 'continue instant in prayer,' and watch in the same. It were easy to prove this by multitudes of scripture texts: he that hath not this breath of prayer, is either a dead man, or in a dangerous swoon. As the poor child, when any thing hurts or affrights it, runs to the mother or father for help; so doth the poor Christian to Christ. He may go to ministers, and go to other Christians, (as Cornelius to Peter, because Christ sends him, and so under Christ) but it is Christ to whom he goes directly, and whom he is most with. He hath a very praying Spirit within him, contrary to that dumb spirit that possesses the ungodly: so that he must needs go to God when any thing aileth him, and he will not be held back. His soul would be disconsolate, and as David in the wilderness, if he were kept from God. He would be overwhelmed with troubles if he might not go to ease his mind with God: some ease he may get from ministers and friends, but O, if he had not more from God, his case were very sad. He is in prayer as Jeremiah was in preaching—' The word was a consuming fire shut up in his bones, he was weary of forbearing and could not stay :' so are his sins and his necessities like a consuming fire shut up in his heart, he is weary with forbearing, he cannot hold them, to God he must go, as David, while he held ' his tongue, his sorrow was stirred, his heart was hot within him, the fire burned till he spake to God:' and ' while I kept silence my bones waxed old.'

You may better keep the converted Christians from food, raiment, home, or friends, than keep them from God: they had rather be without a shop to work in, a house to dwell in, a bed to lie in, than a place to pray in. But the best is, that God hath sanctified every place to him, and commanded him every where to lift up pure hands. His Lord and Saviour hath left him his example, who was sometimes in a wilderness, sometimes in a garden, and sometimes in other solitary places, purposely for prayer, and so accustomed to one that Judas knew of it. He that was perfect would show us his dependence on the infinite Godhead, by giving us an example of constancy in this duty : so that we find him even all night in prayer to God. And all his disciples do learn this lesson of him, and imitate him in their measure, in this holy work. If we ask for other examples, we may find Cornelius and Daniel at it in their families, Peter at it in the house top. Paul and Silas at midnight are at it in the inner prison in the stocks. From every place can the prayers of the godly have access to heaven. For God is every where present, and therefore though the places of public assemblies be in a special sort the house of prayer, yet doth he not confine his prayer to that house. The very soul of a Christian is habituated to prayer, and therefore he doth it as it were continually. And in every thing he maketh known his wants by it to God. So that he is seldom so deeply asleep in any lapse through security but that more or less he breathes this breath of grace in holy prayer. If he want *wisdom*, he asketh it of God, for he knoweth that he giveth liberally, and upbraideth not. If he want the *Spirit* itself in a further measure, he goes to God, who hath promised to give it to them that ask it. If he want *forgiveness of sin, deliverance from any evil or temptation*, it is the matter of his daily prayer, yea, is as his very daily bread, his health and life, and all the comforts of it: for

he knows that all things are sanctified by the word and prayer. If he be afflicted, he prays; and if in sickness, he desires the elders of the church to pray with him ; for he knows that the effectual fervent prayer of the righteous availeth much.

If the servants of Christ be in troubles, prayers without ceasing are the means of their relief. Even besides secret prayer, and church prayers upon any such occasion of their own and others, if a few Christians can get together to prayer, it is pleasanter to them than to the drunkard or voluptuous when they can get together for sports or wickedness. When Peter was in prison, many were got together in a house to prayer, when he came and knocked at the door, after the angel had set him free. In a word, the true convert begins his new life in prayer ; he continues it in prayer habitual or actual; sometimes by the secret motions of the heart, and sometimes by the expression also of his mouth, and he ends it, as to this world, most commonly in prayers—as the Lord Jesus himself, as his blessed martyr Stephen did, committing their spirits to God at the closing of their eyes ; and the saints do commonly follow them in that course : so by the help of these blessed gales we are carried through the waves and troubles of this world, and by this we land at the last in glory. Never think therefore to find a prayerless convert, no more than to find a breathless living man. O the poor Christian feels that he cannot live without prayer, because he cannot live without God. He cannot be without it one day: he cannot be at home or abroad without it; he cannot travel or return home without it; he cannot labour without it in the shop or in the field ; but when he wants a place to bow his knee in, he hath yet an opportunity to bow his soul : and if company or business shut his mouth, yet it must be business indeed that quite taketh off his heart ; for his eye is on God, as the eye of the servant on the hand of his master. Why may I not say, as the eye of our dogs, when they wait on us at our tables, is towards us for every bit they have : so the eye and dependence of the Christian for soul and for body, is upon God: and many a secret ejaculation doth he send up, and many a groan doth pass his heart, that those that even stand by him are unacquainted with. As a beggar is known by his needy begging tone, so is the Christian known by his begging of God. The poor useth entreaties, or speaketh supplication ; you may know them by it ; they make a trade of it ; they live by begging ; they will have no denial: such a one is the Christian, that even lives by begging as his very trade : as one that must always pray, and not be weary or wax faint. So that this is the second means that converting grace doth turn men's hearts to.

SECTION VIII.

CONVERSION ATTENDED WITH THE SERIOUS AND ATTENTIVE PERUSAL OF THE WORD OF GOD.

3. The third means subordinate to Christ and the Spirit, which converting grace doth turn the heart to, is, the *word* of God, whether heard, or read, or preached, or any way fitly made known. The word is the very seed that doth beget him to this life, the immortal seed of God, which always must remain in him. Of this incorruptible seed is he new born, and therefore it cannot be, but he must love it, and desire it. The scripture to a carnal man is as a common book : many things in it seem to be unlikely, and many things even next to foolishness, because he hath not the Spirit to discern them. To all the ungodly it is as a sealed book ; though some of them know the grammatical and logical sense, none of them taste the spiritual sweetness, nor partake of the life that it begets in the soul. Therefore we find so many of the learned papists making a jest of scripture, even while they confess it to be the word of God. Some of them daring to accuse the matter, and some the style, and many the words and manner of expression, as if it were obscure, or unfit, or insufficient to its proper use : a carnal man can easily spare it ; a chapter in the Bible to him is but as a common story. Many of them can delight to read a romance, or a book of fables and fictions, composed of vapid imaginings and meaningless expressions, or any such like wicked devices of men's brains that are made to rob God of men's hearts, and to rob themselves of their time and wit, than to read over the sacred story, and the holy precepts of Christ, and the spiritual doctrine of faith and salvation. We may see the difference between men's dispositions towards God's word in the papists and poor protestants, in the time and place of persecution. The protestants would make much of one leaf of the Bible; they would get together to hear a chapter read, as to a feast, when they knew their lives were endangered by it. The papists used all their power to suppress it, to hinder the promulgation of it, and keep the people from the knowledge of it, and burned them at a stake for the using of it. Their inquisition in Spain and Italy inquire after it, as if it were some book of treason or witchcraft ; while the poor Christians whose hearts are touched with it, do hide it and keep it, as the chief jewel in the world. Luther would not take a world for one leaf of the Bible, his adversaries would have been glad if they could have banished it out of the world.

In the primitive church the heathen persecutors did first seek after the Christian Bibles and other good books, that they might burn them. And if the ministers would deliver them all the books, sometime they would spare their lives; but the poor Christians would be torn in pieces and suffer any kind of death before they would deliver them one of those books to be burned. And if any through fear had yielded to deliver them, they were ever after looked upon by the other Christians as if they were apostates and deniers of Christ, and were commonly called by the name of traitors, and the very posterity of such was in disgrace after them. Insomuch that the schism of the Donatists sprung from an excessive zeal on this occasion : because a bishop was but ordained by one that had been a son of a traitor of the Bible, they separated from him, and from all the church that held communion with him, for his sake. So that you may see what thoughts the servants of Christ have ever had of the Holy Scriptures, and how contrary to these are the men of the world.

And we cannot blame them, for they know that it was by this word that God did first quicken them; by this he convinced them of sin and misery ; by this he revealed to them Christ and glory : in this is contained the covenant of grace, the charter for salvation, and that title to all the mercies of this life and that which is to come : here are the laws of heaven by which they must live, and by which they must all be judged: here are those promises which first revived their distressed souls ; the first cordials that refreshed their fainting spirits, the first news of pardon and glad tidings of salvation that ever they had, was from hence. They know it is a book inspired from heaven by the Spirit of God, containing the discovery of the will of God, and the highest mysteries, which flesh and blood cannot reveal; and that they are matters also of everlasting consequence, to which all the matters in this world are as nothing, and not worthy the naming or once remembering: and do you blame a poor Christian for being in love with this blessed book ? Especially when he knows these things not by mere hearsay only, but by many a sweet experience in his soul; many a sweet draught hath he here drunk in his extremity;

and many a feast hath his soul here had, if he be a Christian of long standing and experience. But however, this was the means of his conversion, and the very instrument of the Spirit for raising him from the dead; and as the Christian is so in love with the book of God, so is he with the doctrine of it, wherever he finds it. Any other book that is written to explain and apply this, is savoury to him; especially the public preaching of this word, which is most eminently the standing ordinance of God for man's conversion and edification.

The same sermons that would have made him sleep, or made his head ache, before his conversion, do now awaken him, and make his heart ache for his former folly; and yet he loves them, though they trouble and grieve him, for he loves that kind of trouble and grief which they beget. O how sweet is that word to his soul, which heretofore he was wont to lothe or quarrel at! he could live with David in the temple even day and night; other men can scarcely be drawn to it, but for custom or by respect, but it would be a death to him to be kept away; if there were a famine in the land of the word of God, he would wander from sea to sea before he would be without it; it is as natural, according to this new nature, for a true convert to seek after the word of God, as for the infant to seek to the breast; as new born babes, they desire the sincere milk of the word, that they may live and grow thereby: they receive with meekness the engrafted word; τὸν λόγον ἔμφυτον, *the word which is innaturalized* to them, and connatural with them, for it is it that is able to save their souls, able to do its own part thereto. Never did you know that Christian who could live without this word, any more than a man can live without meat. I told you the language of Job, David, and Jeremiah, before. O how certainly do the careless neglecters and despisers of this word discover that yet they are unconverted souls, that taste no sweetness in it; that will rather make it a matter of derision, when they see people read and hear so diligently, and talk so much of the word of God. But in the Bible the Christian hath grounded his hopes; here hath he built and bottomed his soul; and here will he live and die. This then is another part of the work of conversion—it turns men's hearts to the word of God, and makes them value it as their necessary food.

SECTION IX.

CONVERSION INDUCES THE SUBJECT TO SEEK THE COMMUNION OF THE SAINTS.

4. The fourth means of salvation to which conversion turns the heart of a man is, the *communion of the saints.* Before conversion, the nature, and sometimes the very name of a saint is lothesome to them, though God hath told us that without holiness none shall see him, and that all his people are called and sanctified, and none but they shall be glorified; yet how commonly do we hear men make a mock at the very name of saints: these are the saints, say they; these are the holy brethren. When the blood of Christ is shed to sanctify men; when the Spirit of grace is sent from heaven to sanctify men, and hath made it his office; when all that God doth by his word and ordinances is to sanctify men; when all true Christians are sanctified men, or saints; and the church itself is a company of saints; and when sanctification is nothing else but our devotedness to God that made and redeemed us,—yet dare these impious wretches open their mouths against sanctity, coming near to the scorning of God himself, and to reproaching the word and the will of God! Yea, and to some kind of blasphemy of the Holy Ghost. It is natural to a wicked man to hate a saint; an enmity is put between them; and the first two men that were born into the world manifested that enmity, for Cain killed his brother Abel; because his own works were evil, and his brother's righteous. Christ himself tells his disciples, ' that because they are not of the world, but he hath chosen them out of the world, therefore the world hates them; but if they were of the world, the world would love its own,' yea, on this very account it first hated Christ himself, and therefore no wonder if the communion of the saints be abhorred, or not delighted in by the ungodly, even while they make it an article of their creed. But when once their soul is truly converted, there is a likeness to God and his saints put upon them; and a natural love to them implanted in their hearts, and thereupon a strong inclination to have communion with them in the worship of God, and the way to heaven; as many drops of water will gather into one; or many streams will run into one river; or many small flames, if you bring them near, will make all into one; and every thing is inclined as it were to incorporate with its like, so is it with the truly sanctified soul: the same means will not serve their turns, if they have it not in communion. The multitude of them that believed were of one heart, and of one

soul, and they distributed to one another, as every one had need ; and charity made that common which law had made proper ; they continued stedfast in the apostles' doctrine and fellowship, and breaking of bread and prayer; and they that believed were together, and had all things common, that is, by charity, as I said before, and they continued daily with one accord in the temple, breaking bread from house to house.

Certainly, there is in all the children of God such a love to their brethren, that they love their company, especially in the holy worship of him that redeemed them. False hearted Christians, that have but the name, may have the hearts of heathens, and do as they did, who were unacquainted with Christian love, but so will not the true. Hence it is, that the Christians in all ages have so valued the Lord's supper, which hath been still called the communion of the church, or of saints; because there they all join together to feed upon one Christ, and taste of the supper of the Lord, as the fellow-heirs of his glory: and as many corns make one loaf of bread, so are they, as the apostle speaks, ' one bread and one body: for the bread which they break, it is the communion of the body of Christ, and the cup which they drink, is the communion of his blood.' And hence it is, that it hath ever been so heavy a punishment in the eyes of all Christians to be excommunicated, and shut out of the fellowship of the church: (though there are also other reasons greater than this) so that the poor Christians, if they had fallen into any sin that deserved excommunication, would have stood with tears at the church-doors, month after month, entreating the prayers of the church that they might be pardoned, and be fit to be taken in again ; and this even when Christianity was so persecuted, that it was matter of danger to a man's life to be a Christian, so precious then was the communion of saints: every Lord's day did they administer the Lord's supper, that they might be frequent in that part of communion : and therefore they highly esteemed the Lord's days, because they were the days of the church's holy communion. Do not marvel then, if any true converted soul have a closing, uniting, combining disposition ; and if they love to be together in the holy worship and service of God ; and if they are glad when they can get together in the public meeting-place, or any other convenient place, to join together, and help each other in the work that is common to all. I know there may be some upright souls who live among such as hinder them from that com-

munion which they would have ; but their hearts are towards it, and they will have it if they can : I know also that the heathens, papists, and all enemies of the church, have still defamed the communion of Christians, and such as join to seek the Lord ; and if any evil fall out among them, they would lay it all on their meeting and communion : but yet this malice of the devil could never break the assembly and communion of the saints.

I know also, that many heretics are much addicted to secret combination, and to unite together in their way ; but that is natural for men to love their like in evil ; but it is not so natural to delight in good : other men's communion in evil doth not disgrace, but commend our communion in the fear of God. Satan hath his legions that can agree in one man ; but they are not such as the legions that attended upon Christ. What, must Christ have no school or army, because Satan hath one? Must we disperse, because the wicked always associate? There are means sufficient left us to discern the communion of the church of Christ from all ungodly and heretical combinations whatsoever. Though there be some stings in the church of Christ among the bees, yet there is more honey. The meetings of heretics are like the nests of wasps, they are all sting and no honey. Saith Tertullian, Wasps have combs too and heretics make churches; the combs of the bees and of the wasps may be very similar to look upon ; but the honey is not like, nor the sting the same : it is not to feed on the doctrine of Christ and live to him, that heretics combine, but it is to divide the church, to show their error and pride, and to sting and despise others. So that their meetings are nothing like the meeting of the church in many regards. I beseech you now, beloved hearers, try how your hearts are affected to the matter in hand. If you are true converts, your very hearts are among the saints : it doth you good especially to join with them in public, and especially in the two duties of praising God, and receiving the sacraments, which are the most proper to the church. And also it will do you good to have communion with them in private. In prayer, in conference, in any holy work, you are where you would be when you are thus employed : you do not imitate the hypocritical world, saying, ' I believe the communion of saints ;' and at the same time either hate and scorn, or at least neglect, and set light by the communion of saints.

It is not to every wicked man that the promise is made, ' Where two or three are met together in Christ's name, there is he in the midst of them.'

And it is not for nothing that the saints delight in this communion. For as here is most of God's blessing, and most help from one another, so when they are nearest to one another, they are all nearest to Christ : and their communion is a foretaste of their communion in glory : for their happiness lieth in their being one with Christ and among themselves, and Christ died on purpose to 'gather into one the children of God that are scattered throughout the world.' And it is God's 'design in the work of redemption to gather together in one, all things in Christ. As he therefore 'gives his prophets, apostles, ministers to the church, for the perfection of the saints, and edifying of the body, till it be all come in the unity of the faith to a perfect man, that we may grow up in him, who is the head in all things, from whom the body, fitly joined together, and compacted by that which every joint supplieth, according to the effectual working in the measure of every part, maketh increase of the body, to the edifying of itself in love,' so also at the day of judgment shall the 'angels gather the elect together from the four winds,' and they shall be one in Christ for ever. Great reason therefore have the saints to look out after more of that which their perfection doth so much consist in. Other men may have some delight in the company and assembly of Christians for by-respect; but to love the communion of the saints, as such, and delight in them, as the body of Christ implied in his praises, this is the proper disposition of a saint. And this is another thing that conversion doth turn their hearts unto.

SECTION X.

CONVERSION PRODUCES DECISION OF MIND, AND DECISION OF SUBJECTS.

4. Having spoken of the third part of the conversion of the heart, which consisteth in the right choice of the means of salvation ; I proceed to the fourth, which consists in the *thorough resolving of the yet wavering and unsettled soul.* I make not this a part in itself different from all that are before mentioned, but the very life and perfection of them, especially of the two last. Some kind of willingness, and unsound consent there may be in the half converted; and many times it is long after the beginning of this change before it reach to a sound resolution ; but it is never a saving work of special grace indeed, and proper to the saints, till then. Men may have many convictions, and be brought to engage

themselves in covenant to God, and yet for want of this true resolution, their hearts may not be right with God, nor they be stedfast in his covenant. We are suitors for Christ to a backward and obstinate generation of men ; we are long persuading them before they will yield, and when they seem to yield, they are long in the beginning, deliberating and wavering before they will resolve. Sometimes God turneth the heart more suddenly at a sermon : but ordinarily, for ought I can find, men stick long under conviction and half purposes, before they are thus converted : when they see that all is not well with them, and that they are not in a safe condition to appear before God at judgment, in that they have not taken the right course that Christian wisdom required them to take, they feel then within them many persuadings of the Spirit of God, and their conscience reasoning the case with them, and saying, ' this life will not serve thy turn long, if death find thee in this condition, thou art an undone man : away then with thy negligence, idle company and courses, and set thyself to seek after Christ before it be too late ;' and under these persuasions the mind is sometimes purposed to do it : but these purposes are either for the time to come, that hereafter they will be new men ; or else they are but half purposes, that reach not to a resolution : and therefore if at present they make some kind of change, it is but by halves : and they usually turn back again : this is the case of the best men ordinarily before conversion.

But when conversion comes, it turns over the mind unfeignedly to God ; it brings the soul beyond its former waverings ; it shows men that there is no other remedy, the thing is of necessity, and that all is but vanity that can be said against it, and no good reason can be given to take any wise man off from the work of repentance and a heavenly life, and therefore he is resolved that this shall be his way. He hath considered and found for certain that there is no true felicity but in the favour of God, and that his love and promised glory is everlasting, and all things else are vain and transitory ; and therefore he is resolved that God should be his portion, and nothing but God ; heaven shall be the end of his desire and labour, and nothing but heaven : he hath also considered that there is no pardon of sin but by the blood of Christ, and no hope of salvation, but by cleaving to him, and yielding to his renewing Spirit, and therefore he is now resolved that Christ shall have his heart, and his Spirit shall do its work, and that the word of God hereafter shall be his rule : he is now determined to know nothing but Christ crucified. Before he was like a man that was weighing somewhat in the scales, and the other end was the heavier, or the scales stood as it were even : but now the Holy Ghost hath brought in those arguments, and set them home on the conscience, with that life that hath turned the scales. Before he was like a man that had lost his way, and standeth still, considering whether he shall turn back or not, or whether he shall go this way or that ; but now he is resolved, and he stands no longer considering, but turns without any more ado ; and this resolution is not rash or ungrounded, but having considered what can be said for God and for the world ; for sin and for repentance, and considering what he may meet with in the way to heaven, he resolves whatsoever it cost him, repent he will, return he will, for saved he must be : though he meet with hard dealing from the world, there is no remedy, he will go through it : though he may suffer much in the flesh, yet that shall not take him off : though he know he must leave his former pleasure, and wicked company, and live that life that the flesh doth abhor, yet all this shall not take him off.

O what a pleading and reasoning there is commonly between the flesh and the Spirit before the heart will be thus resolved. As it was with Caracciolus the marquess of Vicum, when his conscience bid him leave his land and friends and all for Christ, to forsake popery, and betake himself to these countries, where he might enjoy the gospel ; his house and lands then came in his eyes ; what, must I leave all these for mere conscience, and live I know not how ? His wife hangs upon him, his children with tears do cry after him, O father, leave us not : and many a sob and sigh it costs his heart before he could resolve to get away. And as it was with many of the martyrs when they were to die for Christ and for his truth : wife, children, and friends follow them to the fire, crying out, O turn, turn, and do not undo yourselves and us : so that they had almost as much ado to overcome that temptation, as to bear the flames. So is it with a sinner in the work of conversion ; when he looks to Christ and everlasting glory, and considers withal that these cannot be obtained without the loss of earthly, sinful pleasure ; and when he thinks of his old merry company and course, his ease and fleshly pleasure that he must leave ; when he thinks of the strangeness of the way that he must now turn to, and how unacquainted he is with it, and how many bitter scorns, and worse, he is like to meet with ; and how much care and pains it must cost him to be saved ; this keeps him sometimes at a stand, and also breeds in him many troublesome thoughts, so that he scarce knows which way to turn him, or what to do : if he repent and return to God, he must deny his flesh, and forsake all this world, and for ought he knows, have scarce any more of that kind of pleasure that he lived upon before, and if he do not do this, he must forsake God, and all hope of everlasting glory, and give up himself to eternal misery. This seems a very sad strait to one at the first ; because he yet hath had no experience of the joy of the Holy Ghost, and the higher comforts of a Christian life, nor of the help which God will afford him in his way : and therefore we cannot marvel if many a poor soul do here stick in the birth, and if it be long before they resolve for God ; while others turn back and perish for ever, since grace and only grace can resolve them. When Christ opens their eyes effectually and to the purpose, he lets them see, that between heaven and earth, God and the world, grace and sin, there is no comparison. They see then, this is not a matter to doubt of, or to stick at : God must be pleased, but there is no necessity that the world or the flesh be pleased.

God's favour must be had, but we may live without the favour of the world ; death and judgment must be provided for, but it is needless to provide for the desires of the flesh ; an hundred considerations comes in upon his soul, which make him say, Away with all these worldly vanities, and welcome Christ and a holy life. Now he casts off that great weight that hangs on him, and ' that sin that did so easily beset him, that he may run with patience the race that is before him, looking to Jesus the Author and Finisher of his faith, who for the joy that was set before him, endured the cross, despised the shame, and is set down at the right of the throne of God.' In a word, he is now thoroughly convinced that one thing is necessary, and therefore he hath chosen the better part, which shall not be taken from him. You are never truly converted till you have this resolution of the soul ; whatever good purposes you may make for the time to come, if you be not resolved presently to return ; I say, presently without delay, you are not yet truly converted to Christ, though you may verily think that the life of faith and holiness is the best life, and may have some mind to it, and purpose one of these days to return ; nay, though you may have some present purposes that are cold and faint, and come not up to the height of resolution ; and though you make some half trial hereafter, and change some of your company and your courses, all this is well, but it will not serve the turn without this resolution. Many a man that is lost for ever, hath had many a good wish and purpose, and made some assay to mend his life, and made some half reformation, and yet, being not resolved for Christ, they have perished. The principal part of the work of saving grace in the soul doth lie in this resolution. O that the wavering, the loitering, and the delaying soul would lay this well to heart. O that they understood this who are convinced that they must return and be new men, and yet cannot be brought to present resolution, but linger in their sins as being loth to come away; as Lot did in Sodom, till God, being merciful to him, caused the angel to carry him out. Well, this is the next work of converting grace. If ever you be converted, you will be resolved for Christ.

SECTION XI.

CONVERSION INTIMATELY CONNECTED WITH A CHANGE IN THE AFFECTIONS OF THE HEART AND DISPOSITIONS OF THE MIND.

5. The fifth part of the work of conversion in the heart, consists in the *change that is made upon the affections.* Though these are not so evident and certain always to try a man's state by—and therefore I would have Christians try especially by the former—yet it is certain that conversion changes these also; and because they are many, and I have been long in the description of this work already, I will the more briefly run them over.

1. The first of the affections that appear in this change, are love and hatred. Before conversion the heart loves not spiritual things and ways—there is an opposition to them, and enmity against them. It loves not inward holiness, nor a holy life; it loves not the people that are holy; nay, it loves not God himself, as he is just and holy; yea, it hath an inward lothing of him, and of his image and way; though yet it be so deceitful as perhaps not to know thus much by itself. But on the contrary, it loves fleshly pleasure, earthly profit, vain glory, ease, and the honour of the world; for it only savours of these kind of things. But conversion turns a man's love and hatred, and makes him love the holy God, and those holy people and ways that he could not heartily love before, and it makes him lothe those sins, that he before loved. That this is so in all that are converted, is evident from many texts of scripture. 'He that loveth father or mother,' &c. 'His delight is in the law of the Lord, and in his law doth he meditate day and night.—In his eyes a vile person is contemned, but he honoureth them that fear the Lord.—By this we may know that we are passed from death to life, because we love the brethren; he that loveth not his brother abideth in death.' They hated the light before, because it was against their deeds, but now they love it, and come to it. The very evil actions that they do, they now hate, yea, they hate even the garments spotted of the flesh, and all that bears the mark of a fleshly, sensual course. If you then be truly converted, this change will be upon your affections.

2. The second part of affections that show themselves in this change, are desire and aversion. These are so near akin to love and hatred, that I need to say the less of them. The unconverted man's desires are after the fleshly pleasures which he loves; of these they think they can never have enough, but cry as the horse-leech, Give, give. When do you hear the covetous man say he hath enough? Or the ambitious man say, I would be no higher? Or the sensual man say, my appetite and lust are now satisfied, I would have no more? Their very life is a thirsting after provision for the flesh and the fulfilling its desires; and sometimes God gives them much of what they desire, for a time, but it is in judgment, and a curse to them through their sin. But as for God and Christ, the Spirit, and holiness, to these they have no appetite, but naturally lothe them, and at the best have but cold and heartless wishes after them. Hence it is, that they refuse so many motions for their own good: move them to spiritual things, and there is somewhat within them that is against the motion, so that they will not hear us, or be persuaded by us. O, how backward is an unconverted soul to spiritual good! They will go no further than they are drawn, and they will not be drawn to give up themselves to it. Hence it is, that our ministerial labours are so much lost. We persuade sick men to their meat, that have no appetites for it: nay, whose stomachs rise against it and lothe it. It goeth against their carnal natures, against their former customs, against their ease, profit, and pleasure, and therefore it will not go down with them; they cannot away with it. We heave a stone that will stir no further than main force doth move it. O had they but desire after Christ and grace, as they

have after worldly, fleshly vanity: how happy might they be!

But when converting grace comes, it changes their desire. God calls to them then effectually by his word and Spirit. 'Ho, every one that thirsteth, come and drink of the water of life freely.' As if he should say, ' What mean you to desire that which will do so little good, and to lay out your labour for that which will not profit you, or save you? Come to me, and take the grace that I freely offer you, and follow my direction, and I will give you that which is worthy your desire.' When God hath once effectually touched the heart with converting grace, it leaves a secret thirsting after him in the soul. As when he called Peter and the other apostles, and said unto them, Follow me, they presently left all and followed him: then they cry out with David, ' My soul thirsteth after thee as the thirsty land.' The desire of their soul is to his name, and to the remembrance of him ; now they see that excellency in God's word, ways, and graces, that all things that may be desired are not to be compared to it ; ' they are more to be desired than gold, yea, than fine gold ;' before they desired many things, and nothing would satisfy them : now give them but one thing and they will be satisfied to the full. Before their desires were only after vanity ; but now, so far as they are renewed, they are only after good ; and that God that gave them these desires, will fulfil them. He that caused them to hunger and thirst after righteousness, will satisfy them ; and he that turned their minds from this world, and gave them to desire after a better country, will give them that promised land which they desire.

3. The next affections whose change is discovered in the work of conversion, are, their delight and sorrow : this is the next pair. An unconverted man doth naturally find no pleasure in God or spiritual things ; for a fool hath no delight in understanding,' it is fleshly lust and pleasure that they desire ; and the pleasure of sin for a season, for which they part with the highest delight; ' they live in pleasures on earth, and fat themselves as for a day of slaughter.' They account it pleasure to riot in the day light of the gospel, in that day which is given for other kinds of work; they not only do evil, but have pleasure in them that do it ; these 'fools hate knowledge, and scorners delight in scorning.' And if they have any delight in better things through a common work of grace, it is but a superficial, fading delight, ' a rejoicing in the light for a season, but no sound, well-grounded delight.' But when converting grace comes, it gives a man those new delights which he knew not of before. Then the things that he before saw not, nor well believed, the things which he distasted and lothed are his delight : God himself is his delight ; the doing of his will is their delight ; his law, his word, his statutes, are their delight ; on the Lord's day they delight in him ; in the multitude of troubling, perplexing thoughts, his comforts delight their souls ; their delight is in the saints on earth, and those that excel in virtue. It is their meat and drink to draw nigh to God : it doth them good at the heart, when they can but be enlarged towards him, and have more light and life than before they had. These are the new delights of a converted soul : ' He doth not part with all delight at his conversion ; he doth but change a brutish and sensual delight for such as are fit for a man and a Christian. The wicked think they shall never have a merry day again, if they should be thus changed ; but he meets with more truly comfortable days, than ever he did before ; nay, he never knew what true comfort was till now. I know every poor Christian hath not that measure of these delights as some have : some are clouded with darkness and infirmities, and live much more sadly than others do, but yet the delight which they have in these things, is more than in the things which they before delighted in : it glads them when they can but see a beam of heavenly light from the face of God: they have so much as shows the change that is made upon the soul.

The like we may say also of the sorrow of the converted. It is not the same that it was before. Before it went nearer their hearts to lose any pleasure or commodity in the world, or to be wronged, or suffer any disgrace from men, or to suffer any want in their estates, or any pain in their bodies, than it did to lie under the wrath of God, and live as without him, and his favour in the world: they were truly such as Satan falsely reported Job to be; had you but touched them in their estates or bodies, they would have quickly showed you what was next their hearts : but all the misery of their soul was no great trouble to them. A man would marvel, that knows what a miserable state that of sinful nature is, that so many thousands in the world can be void of God's image, strangers to the Spirit, and know no more of Christ but the very name, and yet be no more troubled at it : that they can bear such a weight of unpardoned sin as they do every day, and feel it no more : that they can live under the curse of God's righteous law, and remain in daily danger of damnation, so that if they should die before conversion, they are lost for ever, and yet be no more troubled at it : but alas, they are blind and see not the case that they are in ; they are dead and stupid, and therefore feel it not. It is the nature of their miserable condition to make them so; they are more troubled for a worldly trifle, than for all these things of everlasting consequence. But it is far otherwise with the converted soul; one doubt of the love of God is more grievous to them, than to doubt of their worldly happiness ; the remnant of their mortified sins is heavier on their soul, than the mountain of unmortified sin was to them before ; they send out more groans and cries to God, because of their daily failings and infirmities, than they did before for all their iniquity ; the utter gracelessness of their hearts was then not so grievous to them as the weakness of their graces now. He never before knew what it was to have the least spiritual communion with God, and yet he bore it lightly ; now the want of it one day and in one duty is more grievous to him. What need we prove this to you, when every gracious soul doth feel it, and the world about them may see it, that their sorrows are of another nature than they were before ? Were they wont to lie in tears for sin, and mourn for God's absence as now they do ? Before they were sorrowful, that they might not come to heaven without such a course as would impoverish them in the world. But now they are sorrowful that they can shake off the world and sin no better and get ground of the corruptions no faster than they do. Perhaps you will say, if conversion bring so much sorrow with it, is it not better to be without it ? Answ. No, for it is a willing sorrow, a necessary, healing sorrow, 'that worketh repentance to salvation, not to be repented of, and not the sorrow of the world that causeth death.' See the blessed effects of it at large, 2 Cor. vii. 9, 10. It is a sorrow mixed with greater joy ; for we are as sorrowful, yet always rejoicing. It is a very short sorrow that will quickly be forgotten ; for God hath promised himself to wipe away all tears from our eyes. It is a sorrow of God's own giving, and therefore it cannot choose but be good, for God giveth not evil; it is a sorrow preparing for everlasting joy ; and he that hath called us to it, hath foretold us that we 'shall be sorrowful, but our sorrow shall be turned into joy, which none shall take from us: we shall weep and lament, and the world shall rejoice ;' but mark the end, who it is that will be sorrowful or joyful then : 'mark the upright man and behold the just, for the end of that man is peace.' What wise man will refuse so short a sorrow for so long

a joy ? Who that is well in his wits, will choose rather to die of his sore, than to indure the smart of the lances to open it ? Nay, there is an ingenuity in a converted soul, which makes it, in a kind of holy revenge, even to be willing to taste somewhat of the smart of his own folly : he sees that it was himself that caused it, that brought all this upon himself, and the desert of a thousand times more, and therefore he even chooses in some measure to afflict his soul, and doth not thrust away sorrow from him, as before he was wont to do.

4. The next pair of affections that show their change, are hope and despair. Before conversion, the soul of sinners is either borne up on false ungrounded hopes, which is the common case, or else they drop into desperation. The hopes of an unconverted man are foolish and contrary to the word of God, and do but show the delusion of his soul, and tend to his destruction. They are like the hopes of a man that thinketh he is travelling to London, when he is in the way to York, and yet goes on, and hopes he shall come to London for all that, as well as they that go the right way. So do these men commonly hope to come to heaven, while they go in the way to hell,—though God have told them, and passed his word on it, that he who goes in these ways shall not see peace, and hath assured the world that there is no peace to the wicked. Yet still they will hope to find peace in evil ways ; these deceiving hopes are the common cause of the damnation of the world ; as the scripture frequently acquainteth us. But when converting grace comes, O what work it makes on the soul in this particular ! How it battereth down all the false hopes of sinners ; and maketh them see that they were all this while deceived ! O it maketh the poor soul even undone in its own apprehension, and shows then that all his hopes were vain in which he formerly trusted. Then he cries out, I had hoped to come to heaven without conversion, but now I see it will not be : I had hoped I was well enough before ; and that God would have mercy on me in that condition without any more ado, but now I see I did but deceive myself. I had hoped that I had a saving part in Christ, though I loved the world and followed my sins, but now I see it is not so. I had hoped I might have been saved if I had died in that condition, but now I see that I had certainly been damned.

Now the soul is brought to a kind of despair ; not an absolute despair that God will have no mercy on him ; no, he never escaped that till now ; but a conditional despair, that ever he should come to heaven without conversion: he despairs of ever being saved in the old condition that he was in. Then comes in another kind of hope than ever he knew before. Then the Spirit of grace doth bring him to hope upon grounds that will not deceive him. Now he hath a well-grounded hope that quickens and comforts him. Before he had a dull and dead hope to escape damnation; but now he hath 'a living hope' of seeing the face of God for ever.' He hath now that hope toward God by which we are saved, even the hope of the resurrection of the dead, and the hope of things not seen. Now he hath a hope which is built on the scripture, and bred by experience, and which will not make him ashamed. Before, as he was without God, so was he without hope; but now he hath that hope which is an anchor of the soul, a hope that he can give a reason of; a hope that purifies him, even the hope of eternal life, which none have but those that are heirs by faith, and are brought to it by this regeneration. And for this blessed hope at the glorious appearing of the great God our Saviour, doth his faith and patience expect and wait: so that now he hath some reason for his hopes, for he hath the promise of the faithful God to support them. The least hope that a poor troubled soul hath after conversion in the midst of all his fears and doubts, is of more value than all the most confident boastings of the unconverted: for there can be no hope of being saved out of the way that God hath appointed to salvation: and the bolder men are, and the more they hope and boast in a wrong way, the blinder they show themselves, and the more is their misery: but the godly are safe in an objective hope, even when they want much of the subjective. There is hope, yea, and assurance in itself, when they know it not, and they are safe in that which they do not perceive.

5. The next pair of affections that manifest their conversion, is courage and fear; an unconverted man is bold in sin, but fears not much the wrath of God, and the sorest evil that he threatens in his word. But when he should encounter with any of the enemies of his salvation, there he hath no courage. It is a marvel to see the strange distemper of a graceless soul. These poor wretches are so valiant in their wickedness, that they dare sin when the converted dare not; they dare break the Lord's day, dare drink, revel, take their pleasure, neglect their souls, and slight God and all his mercy: they dare run upon his sorest wrath, and upon hell itself. Tell them of these things, and you cannot much daunt them. It is their mad valour

that they dare damn their own souls: like a distracted man, that dares leap into water and drown himself, or a blind man that dares run into a coal pit, because he knows not what he doth. Such a kind of valour have unconverted men, when as in the way of their duty, they are the most notorious cowards in the world. They dare not venture upon a little suffering to prevent eternal sufferings; or upon the frowns of men, or the danger of being undone in their worldly estates, though it be for a hope of everlasting glory: nay, they dare not venture upon a very scorn; but when they have some mind to turn and set upon duty, a wicked man can mock them out of all: are not these valiant men indeed, that dare not look the feeblest enemy of their souls in the face, and yet dare venture on the flames of hell? This is the common case of the unconverted.

But when grace hath made this change, then they are very differently affected: then they are the most fearful men in the world, of God and his displeasure, and the most courageous against all the opposition of the world. Alas! they find then that it is madness, not valour, to be fearless of the wrath of God: there is no standing before his indignation, and no dealing with the Almighty, if he be set against us. Therefore doth the poor soul throw down all weapons of opposition, and lay himself at the feet of God, as Saul, and say, 'Lord, what wouldst thou have me to do?' Therefore we find converts use to come in trembling to Christ, and scripture tells us, 'the fear of God is the beginning of wisdom.' Now he dare not for his life do that which before he did. He durst have let fall an oath or a curse in his passion before; but now he dares not: he durst have secretly deceived others, and have committed secret filthiness; because no body saw him, he was out of fear; but now he dares not; for he fears him that is greater than all. He durst have neglected duty, and have been indifferent for all company, and taken his fleshly pleasures, but now he dare not: for his life he dare not. O thinks he, what if I should die in the act of that sin? What if God should deny me repentance and forgiveness? Where were I then? He durst before lie in a state of death, but now he dares not live quietly, till he have laboured after assurance of his salvation; that he may know it shall go well with him when he must be here no more. Now if he be tempted to know sin, this is his answer, I dare not do it, because I fear God. Other rulers oppressed the people, and so did not he; because he feared God. It is the description of the ungodly, that 'there is no fear of God before his eyes;' and the description of a wicked place, 'there is no fear of God in this place;' and the description of the godly, that 'they fear God.' By this 'fear of the Lord it is that men depart from evil;' this tends to life; in this is strong consolation. So that it is the work of conversion to bring the presumptuous hardened sinner to this fear of the Lord: none do so much fear God as they.

But then for the threats of men, for worldly troubles, crosses, losses, or any such thing that may stand in the way to heaven, how little do they fear them all! Here where the wicked are most cowardly, the converted soul is most courageous. Alas! he knows the difference between the creature and the Creator: and therefore when he hath once got God on his side, he sees he is safe, and the danger is most over. Then, O what light thoughts hath he of man, or of all that he can do! 'In God have I put my trust,' saith David, 'I will not fear what flesh can do unto me.' What is flesh to be compared with God? Can flesh resist him and cross his pleasure, and overcome him? 'The Lord is on my side, I will not fear what man can do unto me; God is our refuge and strength, a very present help in trouble; therefore will we not fear though the earth be removed, and though the mountains be carried into the midst of the sea, though the waters thereof roar.' He knoweth what encouragement God hath given him, 'Fear not, for I am with thee.—Fear ye not the reproach of man, neither be afraid of their revilings; for the moth shall eat them up like a garment, and the worm shall eat them like wool: but my righteousness shall be for ever, and my salvation from generation to generation.' These words of God are the instruments of that change that is made on the converted soul, and therefore will make an impression like themselves. When God doth change men, he makes them soldiers under the banner of Christ, and sets them in fight against principalities and powers, even against a world of wicked enemies; and therefore he will certainly give them courage. This courage is an essential part of our change, and without some measure of it we cannot be Christians. He that will come to heaven must forsake all, tread down all, and despise all in comparison of Christ, that he may not be a forsaker and a despiser of Christ: therefore we find the apostle, in the name of himself and his fellow-soldiers, courageously triumphing over death, and the grave, and every enemy, 'O death, where is thy sting? O grave, where is thy victory?—The sufferings of this life are not worthy to be compared to the glory that shall be revealed in us; what shall we say then to these things? If God be for us, who can be against us? It is God that justifieth, who shall condemn? What shall separate us from the love of God?' Read these triumphant words at leisure: it is certain that a true believer hath more valour than to be turned out of the way to heaven, by any assault that a creature can make upon him.

6. The next passion that shows the change, is anger. This is a single passion, and hath no contrary. Before conversion men are angry with those that trouble them in their sins. If you would but teach the ignorant, or persuade the obstinate, or cross them in the way of their beloved sins, O, how angry will they be! as if you were their enemy, and did them some deadly hurt: you cannot speak to them so tenderly in a reproof, but they will think you do it to disgrace them, or in ill will to them, or at least that you make them worse than they are, and they think you make more ado than needs; as Amaziah did by the prophet. They would stop his mouth if they could, who would stop their course of sinning. You shall not see one of many of them that have so much ingenuity as to take a close reproof in good part; no, not from a minister, whose calling doth specially bind him to it. Hence is the common indignation that we meet with from poor blinded wretches, when we do but our duty: nay, when we do not half, nor the tenth part of our duty, in persuading them to a greater care of their salvation, they are offended with us, as if we did too much. O what a difference is there between their judgment, and the judgment of God, and our own conscience! And what a strait a poor minister, or private Christian, must needs be in between both! I confess to you all here, to my shame, that I remember no one sin in the world, that my conscience doth so much accuse and judge me for, as for doing so little for the saving of men's souls, and dealing no more fervently and earnestly with them for their conversion, or reformation: and yet every body is not pleased with that little which I do.

I confess to you, that when I am alone, and think of the case of poor, ignorant, worldly, earthly, unconverted sinners, that live not to God, nor set their hearts on the life to come; my conscience tells me, that I should go to as many of them as I can, and tell them plainly and roundly what will become of them if they do not turn; and to beseech them with all the earnestness that I can, to come unto Christ, and change their course, and make no delay. And though I have many excuses come in from other business, and from disability and want of time, yet none of them all do satisfy my own conscience. When I consider what heaven and hell are, which will one of them be the end of every man's life; my conscience tells me, that I should follow them with all possible earnestness night and day, and take no denial of them till they return to God. But if a man should do thus, how would it be taken? Some of them would think of him as Christ's natural kindred did of him, when they were about to lay hands on him, and thought that he was beside himself; some would think him a precise fellow, that thought nobody should be saved but a few that make more stir than needs; and most would be angry with a man, as if he did them wrong, when he doth but seek to save them with fear, pulling them or keeping them out of the fire of sin. Christ himself is an offence to the ungodly world, and therefore no wonder if we offend them: they will even bear a secret grudge in their minds at those men that trouble them in their sins; and anger resteth in the bosom of these fools. If you should suddenly come in upon a thief or an adulterer with a light, who thought to have hidden his sin in the dark, he would be offended at it; and so are most wicked men with us.

But when converting grace hath changed the heart, the case is quite contrary: then he will thank you for that which before he was angry at; he loves no man so well as him that hath sought to save his soul. O those reproofs and exhortations that God did bless to his conversion will stick by him for ever: he will bless God that ever he saw your face, and remember those words that helped to save him, as long as he lives: he will take it for a greater benefit than if you had given him all your wealth. A special extraordinary love to those that were made the means of their conversion will stick for ever in their minds; the very words that you speak to them will be so remembered, that they would not for a world but they had heard these words. O, what a change is here suddenly wrought! he that was wont to say, 'look to yourselves, you shall not answer for me,' and be angry with them that troubled him in the way to hell; now loves their very names, and the remembrance of their kindness is pleasant to him; even like a poor distracted man, who abuses the physician, and calls them all to naught that would cure him, as if they came to kill him; but when he is come to himself again, then he will give them hearty thanks. Somewhat like it is in a beast: if he have

a thorn in his foot, he will strive against you, and not let you pull it out; and if you cast him down to force him to it, he lies as if you were about to kill him: but when it is out, and he perceives the ease, he will perceive you did not mean him any harm. So it is with a sinner before his conversion: he is angry with those that would do him good; but when once God hath turned his heart, he is quite of another mind: then he saith, 'let the righteous smite me, it shall be a kindness; and let him reprove me, it shall be an excellent oil, which shall not break my head,' and he takes open rebuke better than secret love; and the wounds of a friend to be better than the kisses of an enemy. I know by sad experience, that too much heart-rising against reproof doth remain in many that I hope are converted, but that is from their unconverted part; and if it were predominant, it would prove them unconverted men; for so far as they are gracious, thus it will be.

Yea, not only so; but when a man is converted, his anger is turned against himself: he was never so angry with others for reproving him, as he is now for sinning against God, and doing so much wrong to his own soul. Certainly there is in every converted soul a great indignation against themselves for their sin: they fall out with themselves, think ill of themselves, speak ill of themselves; yea, and could find in their hearts to be in part revenged upon themselves: you may see as much said by Paul in 2 Cor. vii. 11. where, among other effects of godly sorrow, he names indignation and revenge. A true repenting sinner could even find in his heart to execute some punishment upon himself: O, how he calls himself almost all that is naught! O, thinks he, what a fool, what a wretch, what a beast was I, to love the filth of sin better than the favour of God and the hopes of everlasting glory! What a madman was I, to be angry with those that would have kept me from damnation! Where was my wit and reason, when I so long forgot the work that I was born for, and made so light of the Lord that bought me, and thought so little of the place that I must live in for ever? I do not speak this of mine own head; I have heard many, and many a one, through God's great mercy, after conversion, calling themselves worse than all this amounts to; and expressing greater anger against themselves than the wicked now express against those that would convert them: and you read, that even the saints in scripture did the like; and that not by a secret confession, but left it on record to all generations. David calls himself an ignorant fool, and as a beast. He

cries out, when his heart smote him by true repentance, 'I have sinned greatly, I have done foolishly.' Paul himself saith, that he was even mad,
and exceedingly mad against the Christians before
his conversion, and of himself and the rest he
confesses 'ourselves were sometimes foolish, disobedient, deceived, serving divers lusts and pleasures, living in malice and envy, hateful, and
hating one another.' So that you see converted
men are very angry with themselves for their
sinful lives ; you hear how they call themselves.

If they used such language against another
man, you would think it were railing; to call
them fools and madmen, and all to naught : but
alas ! they know by sad experience what they
say, and yet by glad experience that it is now
better with them. Hence it is that they can more
easily bear the hard words of another, when they
are forced to say as bad by themselves. Therefore is every converted sinner a man that lothes
himself for his iniquity. Yea, they could find
in their hearts, as I said, to be partly revenged
on themselves. For though they must not destroy their own bodies, because they are not their
own, but Christ's, nor must not in any way hurt
them, so far as to make them the less serviceable unto God ; yet in any other case, they can
find in their heart to punish this flesh, and to
make it smart, that hath led them to so much
evil. Therefore they are the more easily brought
to fasting, and denying the flesh its desires, though
they put it to trouble and pain ; for as this doth
tend to master it, and subdue it for the time to
come, so a vindicative self-mortification for the
time past, voluntarily undertaken, is but a lawful
fruit of repentance, so that it do in no wise disable us from the service of God. Hence it is,
that a thorough convert doth more easily forbear
a carnal pleasure, than an hypocrite or half convert will do. For when they are pleading the
lawfulness of their pleasure, and saying, what
harm is it, and why may I not do this or that ;
he is willing to avoid it, though it should be but
indifferent, as long as there is any great danger of
sin in it. For what cares he if the flesh do smart
for it, if that be the worst, seeing it is the flesh
that he is fallen out with, and hath done so much
wrong to God and him. So that you see what a
change conversion makes on a man's anger a
well as other passions.

7. The last change we shall mention on the
affections that is made by converting grace, is
in regard of a man's content and discontent.
Before conversion a man is discontented if he had
not the desires of his flesh: he hath no rest in
his mind if he be poor or afflicted, and see not

some hope of coming out of it : but for the love
of God, and the life of grace, and the joys of
the godly, he can be well enough content without these. If he had but what he would have
in the world, take you the rest, for he thinks he
can live well enough without them. When Cain's
sacrifice was not accepted, as his brother's, he
was discontented at his brother, and consequently
at God himself. 'He was very wroth, and his
countenance fell.' Because his brother was preferred before him, and was judged righteous
when he was judged unrighteous : but he could
be content without true righteousness itself
though he could not be content without the estimation of it : so can all ungodly men be content
well enough to be ungodly, but not to be called
ungodly ; the name troubles them, when the thing
is so far from troubling them, that they will not
be persuaded by any means to leave it. In a
word, it is the things of this world that wicked
men do seek contentment in, though they find it
not : but as for spiritual and heavenly things,
they can be better content in the case that they
are now in ; without them, than with them.

But conversion turns the heart also in this
respect. For when a man is once truly changed,
he can be contented with any state, if he have
but the favour of God, and the life of his grace,
and communion with him, and without this he
can be content with nothing. Nothing but Christ
will serve his turn : if God will give him more
besides, he will take it and be thankful ; but without Christ he takes all things to be as nothing ;
what if he had lands and lordships, honour and
dignity, what will this do for him without God
in Christ ? And blame him not, for he hath felt
such a disease, that these things could not heal,
when Christ and Christ alone could do it : and
therefore Christ he must have whatsoever else
he go without. A little of the world will serve
with Christ, but nothing in the world will serve
without him. As a wicked man is troubled and
restless, because he hath not that which he would
have, when every thing is not according to his
mind, if friends, if estates, if his house, or his
body, or any thing be out of order, he is in discontent, because it is here that he seeks contentment, and therefore is troubled when he misses
it : so is it with a believer in respect of Christ
If God hide his face, if the Spirit seem to withdraw, if Christ seem strange to him, if doubts of
salvation come in upon his soul, he is as a bone
out of joint, pained and troubled, and nothing
will quiet him till he be set in joint again. Like
a child, that will be quieted with nothing but
that which he cries for : if you offer him any

thing else, he throws it away, for that is not it which he cries for. So is it with this poor Christian if you tell him of riches, or honour, or pleasure, and not of Christ, grace, and glory, you do but trouble him, for these are not the things that he looks after. There is but one thing in the world that can give him content; let him have that, and he hath enough. Did he but know that God is reconciled to him, that he is united to Christ, that the Spirit is in him, and that he is in the safe way to the kingdom of glory, then if he have but food and raiment, he can therewith be content, yea, or if he were without them, if God so dispose of it: for he hath learned, by the teaching of converting grace, to abound and to want, and in whatsoever state he is, therewith to be content, and therefore his conversation is without covetousness, and he is content with such things as he hath, because God hath promised him that he will never leave him nor forsake him. So this is another fruit of conversion about men's content or discontent.

SECTION XII.

GENUINE CONVERSION DISTINGUISHED BY A TEACHABLE SPIRIT.

Having said thus much of the change of the affections, I might proceed to show you what those particular reigning sins are that this work doth cast out of the heart, and what particular graces it there setteth up, and so go over all the chief sins and graces. But because this would hold me longer than I intend to stand upon this subject, and because these are comprehended in the change already mentioned, I shall pass these over; only that part which my text doth particularly express, I take it to be my duty particularly to handle.

'Except you become as little children.' You see here, that Christ places much of the work of conversion in the making of us to become as little children. I shall here therefore stay a while to tell you, first, what is not meant by this: and second, what is meant by it. 1. Christ doth not by this intend that little children are altogether innocent, and that there is nothing in them that is hateful to God: for certainly, they have all original sin; for who can bring a clean thing out of an unclean; or how can the parents beget holy children, that are unholy themselves; or righteous children, that are themselves unrighte-

ous? I mean without sin, when they are not themselves without sin. And therefore it is not by nature that children are righteous, or come to heaven. But it is by grace, through the blood of Christ that washes them, and covenant mercy that forgives them, and baptism that seals this unto them, and they are capable also of the Spirit, to sanctify them. If there were not a willing nature in infants disposing them to evil, before they do it, as there is a stinging venomous nature in a serpent before he stings, or in a wasp even in the comb; how should it come to pass that children should be so forward to evil as soon as they can commit it? Why are they not as forward to good? If children be not by nature, through original sin, even hateful to God, what need have they of the blood of Christ to wash them and cleanse them from it; or of the water of baptism to seal this cleansing? Doubtless, there is not an infant in the world but would be for ever damned, if Christ's blood did not procure their pardon and reconciliation with God. It is not therefore in absolute innocency that Christ here means that we must become as little children, before we can enter into the kingdom.

2. Nor yet is it in point of safety from the wrath of God; as if every child, or any by nature, were free from all danger of everlasting perdition: by grace many are, but by nature none at all. From the hour of their birth many may be sanctified; but it is the covenant of grace, and the grace of the covenant, that sanctifies them, and not the parent or nature.

The two things therefore that Christ intends in the words of my text, are these. 1. That as children are but newly entered into the world, beginning their lives, and all things are new to them, so he that will be saved must by conversion, as it were, begin the world anew. I pray you mark it, for Christ hath not given you this doctrine and example for nothing. Therefore it is that we find so often in the scripture mention made of laying by, or destroying, or putting off the old man. In Rom. vi. 6. 'Our old man is crucified with him, that the body of sin might be destroyed, that henceforth we should not serve sin.' He that hath truly learned Christ, 'hath put off concerning the former conversation the old man, which is corrupt according to the deceitful lusts, and are renewed in the spirit of their mind, and put on the new man, which after God is created in righteousness and true holiness.—Mortify therefore your members which are upon the earth, fornication, uncleanness, inordinate affection, evil concupiscence and covetousness, which is idolatry; for which things' sake, the wrath of God cometh on the children of disobedience: in the which ye also walked sometimes, when ye lived in them. But now ye also put off all these: anger, wrath, malice, blasphemy, filthy communication out of your mouth. Lie not one to another, seeing ye have put off the old man with his deeds: and have put on the new man, which is renewed in knowledge, after the image of him that created him.' Upon consideration of which great change, they are said also to be 'dead, and risen again, and their life now hidden with Christ in God.' You see then that here is an old man to be put off, and destroyed, and a new man to be put on; that is, there must be such a change of the qualities of the soul, and the practice of the life, that a man must not in his affection and conversation be the same man that he was before. For though he be the same in substance and person and the natural faculties of his soul, yet not the same in disposition and practice.

In regard of his old corrupt disposition and conversation he is called the old man, and in regard of his new disposition and conversation he is called the new man. As a man that hath been an ill husband, and run out of all, and having nothing left, is cast into prison, and when he lies there, he remembers his folly, and at last a friend comes and pays his debts, sets him up again, and gives him a stock to trade with; we say of this man, he begins the world anew. So when a poor sinner is in prison, under the wrath of God for his sin, and Christ comes in his gospel and tells him, 'I have paid thy debt, and now I will set thee free, and give thee the help of my Spirit and means; only see thou be faithful to me, and make better use of my mercy for the time to come.' Now this converted sinner is to begin the world as it were anew. As a man that hath fallen into a fever, that hath consumed all his flesh to the very bones, when he is cured, his natural parts make him new blood and flesh again: so when Christ hath cured the diseased soul, the old flesh is as it were consumed, and we are made anew. As a man that hath missed his way at the first setting out, and gone the contrary way all day, and at last comes to know that he was all this while out of his way, he is then to begin his journey anew. So is it with the converted man: when the illumination of the Spirit by the word, doth acquaint him, that he hath all this while been out of the way to heaven, he turns again and says, 'I am now to begin my life again.' The building that he hath been setting up all this while, is blown down by the breath of God's displeasure, or consumed by the fire of his curse. And therefore he must begin again, and build all anew from the very ground: not an earthly building like the old, but a spiritual house for himself, that may be fit for his holy spirit to dwell in. And may attain at last to the building not made with hands, eternal in the heaven.

I beseech you, beloved hearers, mark this as we go, and see whether this be so with your own souls. I must tell every carnal, worldly sinner of you all in the name of God, that your old condition is a miserable condition, and will not serve the turn for heaven: if ever you will be saved, you must become as little children, and even begin the world anew. A new heart you must have, a new life you must lead; a new course you must take, and a new end you must aim at and intend. But of this I must speak more afterwards, under the further proof and application.

2. Another thing that Christ here principally intends in the text, is, that we must become as little children, in regard of humility and all our designs and contrivances in the world. Though this be not the whole that he intends, yet this is the very reason for which he mentions the whole work of conversion, as necessary to salvation; and therefore he particularly gives instance in this part: though children have the seed of all these in their natures, yet are they not acquainted with the acts of all, even when they begin to be acquainted with some. Children will very early show their frowardness and disobedience, and sensuality, and some pride, but not by aspiring after great things in the world, and seeking after dominions, dignities and honours. They are in no care for enlarging possessions, for heaping up riches, for buying lands and lordships; they envy not the princes and lords of the world, but are as well contented with their lower matters, as kings and emperors are with their crowns; if they have meat and drink, clothes, and play, they are pleased: you never hear them murmur that they are not preferred to this office or that, in church or state: they do not contrive how to undermine others; nor to get above them in worldly dignities; nor to blast the name of others, that they may magnify their own. They disdain not those of the lowest rank; but the children of a lord will play familiarly, if they be not dissuaded by others, with the children of beggars: in a word, though they have pride, and show it in lower things, yet do they not look after the great matter of the world, as ambitious and covetous persons do. And this is the thing that Christ intends to his disciples, and to all Chris-

tians, that if ever they will enter into the kingdom of heaven, they must lay by their pride, vain-glory, and covetousness, and become as little children to all these honours and riches of the world. So that it is plain, that Christ makes humility an essential part of the work of conversion, and altogether inseparable from the heirs of his kingdom.

As pride is thought to be the first sin of the devil, and was certainly the first or one of the first that tainted the nature of man, when he would needs be as God, knowing good and evil; so is it not the last or least of the works of Christ on the soul in its recovery, to take down this pride, humble us, and make us little in our own eyes. Satan drew us to aspire after a kind of godhead, and to be more than men : and Christ brings us to be as little children, and almost less than men. Satan drew us to be like him in pride, and Christ draweth us by doctrine and example, to be like to him in meekness and lowliness : Satan would lift us up, that he might cast us down, and our fall might be the greater, by how much we attempted to mount the higher : and Christ casts us down, that he may lift us up, and that our glory may be the greater, by how much we are made the baser by humility. Satan did but unsettle us by taking us off our rock and foundation, when he pretended to exalt us : and Christ doth settle us again, by laying us low : and by teaching us meekness he causes us to find that rest to our souls, which in pride and vain-glory could not be found. Satan by sin did make us low and vile in God's eye, and high and excellent in his own : and Christ, by converting grace, doth make us low and vile in our own eyes, and high and excellent in God's. By corrupted nature, men are still inclined to rise higher and lift up themselves, but by grace he is disposed to think meanly of himself, and to set light by the honours and greatness of this world. And why is this, think you ; is it because grace debases men's spirits ? No, but because it raises and ennobles them. The converted soul doth slight the glory and greatness of the world, not on the same reasons as children do ; i. e. because they know it not, or because it is above them ; but because he is now acquainted with far greater things, and because that all on earth is below them. It is not because he would fain have greater matters, and cannot get them, but because he hath got a sight of such things in the world to come, in comparison of which these things are as nothing, and therefore to be disesteemed, and even trodden under foot. He slights not crowns and kingdoms, as things above him, but as things

below him. The very humility of the saints hath a high design : when they lie in the dust, in self-abhorrence and self-condemnation, they are aspiring thence as high as heaven : their humble confession, tears, and groans, have a tendency to that glory which is above the sun. As a child that casts his ball to the ground, that it may rebound the higher ; or as a man that means to make the highest building, will dig deepest to lay the foundation : in the depth of their debasement they are seeking to be as the angels of God. It is heaven that they mean in every duty, in every prayer, in every lamentation they make for their infirmities, yea, in all they do in the world, it is nothing lower than heaven that they intend.

Perhaps you will by this time turn your opinion of them, as much as the barbarians did of Paul, and as before you thought them too base, now you will say, that grace doth make them proud ; but it is no such matter. Pride is the undue estimation of a man's self, and a desire of undue estimation from others : and it provokes a man to seek after an unnecessary greatness in the world, which tendeth to lay him as low as hell. But these high desires and attempts, and expectations of the saints are accompanied with a deep sense of their own unworthiness. They confess beforehand that they are worthy of nothing, when they live in hope of all things : they acknowledge that hell is their desert, when they aspire after heaven. And when they come thither, they will confess it was not from their merit, but will for everlasting glorify that grace that did bestow it. They lean in all their endeavours upon Christ, and never think to rise so high by any strength, that is properly their own. They will readily confess, that they have nothing but what they received, and that it was God, and not themselves, that made them to differ : and therefore they dare not glory as if they received it not. When they have most, they most honour the giver : and when they do best, they magnify him that quickened and strengthened them : and say, ' not to us, O Lord, not to us, but to thy name give the glory.' The more they have, the better they know whence they had it. And as their light increases, so doth it lead them further from themselves, and show them their natural darkness, and the glory of that sun from whence all flows. It is not impossible for a low spirit to have high designs ; and for a man to lie in deep self-accusations, with strongest hope of an angelical glory. A man may look toward heaven that lies flat on the earth, so that his back be towards it, and not his face. It is no pride to desire that which God made for us : nor to seek after any greatness that he hath promised, offered, and commanded us to seek for.

The sin of pride lies not in the elevation, and aspiring after things so great ; but in the injustice and error of it, and in the falseness of the estimation : unless when it comes to desire to be even as God. It is not pride, but spiritual wisdom, to desire to be like to God in holiness, and to bear his image, for that is our perfection. It is not pride to be unsatisfied with all the greatness and glory of this world ; and restlessly to seek after a heavenly kingdom, and to hope to be like the Son in glory, and to be equal with the angels of God. For God hath made us for this, and set it before us, as the prize we run for, and given us an infallible promise of it in his word : God would not have us base, when he forbids us to be proud. His service dignifies us, if any thing be a dignity. He would not have us to be such earth-worms, so poor, so miserable, so blind, so naked, as to take up with the trifles of the world : but would have us live like men that have souls, which are immortal. Pride is the ruin of the soul, which consumes the substance, and is a mortal disease. He loves not our barrenness, nor is he against our substantial growth and nourishment, because he would cure us of this distemper that would kill us. So that, when God takes you down, it is that he may lift you up ; and he makes you lesser, that he may make you greater. And if you should yet imagine that humiliation is an unlikely way to exaltation, the Spirit of God and the life of grace hath taught the true convert the contrary by experience : he knows it is God's ordinary way to bring life out of death, light out of darkness, all things out of nothing, and to be glorified by weak things. He knows that Christ went by the cross unto the crown, and was nearest his glory when he was lowest in his humiliation ; and so must he. For he that will be conformed to him in his glory, must be conformed to him in his sufferings. We must suffer with him, that we may reign with him. The prison, the stocks, scourging, and scorns, were the preparation for the throne, that Paul and many another must undergo. The lark that soars highest, and sings as it were in the face of the sun, was bred under a clod, as low as any other bird.

Beloved hearers, I beseech you hear not these things as matters that concern you not, but as the true description of the heirs of heaven. Thus must it be with you if you will be saved. While you are unconverted, O what stoutness and stub-bornness is in the heart? How willingly would men be somebody in the world ! How ill do you take it to be lightly esteemed ! You would think it a gallant thing, if you could but be greatest, and have all things done as you would have them, and all men depending upon you, and you to be beholding to none ; to have men's knees bow to you, your word to be the law, and all men give you the pre-eminency ; to have your name to be great and famous, and to be honoured by all. What an excellent life were this in the eye of a carnal man : but converting grace will bring you down, if God in mercy please to give it you. It will make you call yourselves less than the least of all his mercies, ' a worm and no man—a wretched man.' It will make you think yourselves unworthy to live ; unworthy to come among the saints ; unworthy to mention the name of God, or taste of his favour ; and this not feignedly, but from your very hearts. It will make you marvel that God should do so much for such a wretch as you ; and that he had not damned you long ago. It will make confession of sin even natural to you, and make you lay your mouth in the dust. You will say worse of yourselves to God and man, than most others will say of you, and you will the more easily bear all slightings, reproaches and unworthy usings from the world, because you know how ill you deserve of God, as having used him and his grace so ill. Instead of sneering at those that observe you not, and honour you not, you will think yourselves unworthy to be observed, and think the dishonour less than your due. Instead of sneering that any should go before you, or be preferred above you, you will be ready to stoop to the feet of the meanest, for their good. You will esteem others, as far as reason will bear it, better than yourselves : and in honour prefer others before yourselves. Instead of lording it over your brethren, you will think it your greatness to be the servants of all.

It may be you will say, this is a strange person whom I now describe, and if there be no true converts but such as these, God help us all ; for they are but few. I answer, this is the description that I find in the word ; and be they few or many, these, and these only, are the disciples that Christ will own. ' For thus saith the Lord, the high and lofty One that inhabiteth eternity, whose name is holy, I dwell in the high and holy place, with him also that is of an humble and contrite spirit, to revive the spirits of the humble, and to revive the heart of the contrite ones.—To this man will I look, even to him that is poor, and of a contrite spirit, and trembleth at my word.—

Blessed are the poor in spirit, for theirs is the kingdom of heaven; blessed are they that mourn, for they shall be comforted; blessed are the meek, for they shall inherit the earth.' Read the text that Christ preached. 'Mind not high things, but condescend to men of low estate.' And Job, 'He shall save the humble person.—He that humbleth himself shall be exalted, and he that exalteth himself shall be brought low.—God resisteth the proud, but giveth grace to the humble.' I shall not trouble you to recite one half of the passages that speak in this strain, and assure us that there is no true grace and Christianity without true humility. I confess there are several degrees of it in the sanctified, according to the several degrees of their sanctification, but it is predominant in them all.

O that the ambitious great ones of the world would lay this to heart! O, that even all the leaders of Christ's flock, the preachers of humility, would lay this to heart! Then we should not have had the church so torn in pieces, by contending after precedency and pre-eminency: who should be lords, bishops, and above the rest, especially after such a check from Christ, as this and several other texts contain. When his disciples strove who should be the greatest, this is Christ's decision of the controversy: not by telling them that Rome shall be the ruler of all other churches, and the other four patriarchs shall be next to it; and the bishop of the metropolis or greatest cities shall rule those of the lesser cities, and these shall rule those that dwell in a village: no, Christ takes another course to decide the controversy, by setting before them a child, by telling them that 'the kings of the Gentiles exercise lordship over them, and they that exercise authority are called benefactors: but ye shall not be so; but he that is greatest among you, let him be as the younger, and he that is chief, as he that doth serve.' One would think that the very thoughts of Christ washing his disciples' feet, and saying to them that thus they should do to one another, should shame proud ambition from among the preachers of such a gospel. O that our stubborn people also would remember this, who are too good to obey the word of the Lord; and too stout to be admonished, or come for instruction to their ministers: yea, or patiently to bear a reproof! All these persons, and many more may call themselves Christians as long as they will, but Christ that knows his sheep will not own them. Believe it, it is as possible to be a true Christian without true humility, as for a house to be without a foundation.

I have showed now what it is to become as little children, so far as is beyond controversy. But there is somewhat more that might be worth our inquiry, whether they were not baptized and purified children, as such, that Christ here intends; in whom even the root of pride is mortified? But this I will not presume to meddle with, because on this subject I would deliver you nothing but what among the godly is commonly agreed on. But this I may well say in general, that this text in part, and others more fully tell us, that Christ did not look upon infants as at so great a distance from him, as some modern sects seem to do.

SECTION XIII.

CONVERSION PRODUCTIVE OF PRACTICAL FRUIT IN THE LIFE.

Having done with the work of conversion on the judgment and on the heart; the next thing to be done, is to show you the change that it makes on men's lives: for this must be looked after as well as the former. The same God that rules the heart, doth rule the life; and he that requires the cleansing of the heart, doth require also the cleansing of the hands. The soul commands the body, and the heart will dispose of the course of the life; if therefore the heart be changed, the life must needs be changed too: the root is for the fruit; and the life within is much to enable us to action without. When God gives us the root and life of grace and holiness, it is that we may bring forth the fruit, and do the works of grace and holiness. He makes not the new creature for nothing, or to be idle, much less to go on in serving the devil: but he makes him for a new work, even to serve the living God, 'for we are his workmanship, created to good works, which God hath ordained that we should walk therein.' The excellency of his peculiar people, is 'to be zealous of good works.' A good heart and a good life are inseparable; but the life may further out-go the heart, than the heart can out-go the life: for there may be a reformed life that is in many respects good, while the heart is bad; but the life is never worse than the heart: for there can be no evil of sin in this life, but what the heart is the proper cause of: 'For out of the heart come murders, adulteries, theft, false witnessing, blasphemy, and such like sins, which defile the man.' It is therefore a vain boast of those men that take on them to be converted, when they live as they did before: neither God nor any wise man will believe them, though they may thus deceive themselves. Seeing then, there must be a new life, with a new heart, or no salvation: let us a little particularly inquire wherein that *newness of life doth consist.*

The first and principal change of the life, consists in the covenant which the converted soul doth make with Christ. As this is principally in the heart, and so contains faith and holy resolution, we have spoken of it before: but now I mention it as expressed with the tongue; 'for as with the heart we believe to righteousness; so with the mouth is confession made to salvation.' A resolved heart will have a resolved tongue; it will carry a man to express his resolution, as there is convenient opportunity, both to God and man; this covenant might be verbally entered before in the face of the congregation, in our baptism by our parents, who are authorized by God in scripture and nature to enter their children into it, for their good; but if the heart did never truly own that covenant, when you come to the use of reason, you cannot expect to be saved by it. Your own covenant with Christ, when you come to age, is then as necessary to your salvation, as your covenant by your parent in baptism was before, to put you into that right which infants have by virtue of the promise; this covenant is the very bond and foundation of all the following obedience of your lives, when God hath opened the eyes of a sinner to see his great necessity of Christ, and the glory and felicity that he hath procured, and withal to see the universality and freeness of the promise: and that God doth call to him to consent to his terms, and accept the mercy freely offered. Converting grace doth move the heart to acceptance, and the tongue and life to make expression of it. There might be half covenant, and false hypocritical promises before, which, for want of sincerity, were soon broken, and come to naught: but conversion enters us into a true, firm and durable covenant. When the poor sinner doth once understand that it is not owing to God if he be shut out; and that Christ hath put in no bar of exception against him more than any other in the promise of pardon and salvation; and when he understands that God doth but stay for his consent, and that all the hinderance is at his own will, and he understands thoroughly what reason he hath to be willing, and how little there is to be said against it; then he doth set up his resolution, and give up himself in covenant unto God.

It may be before he misunderstood the cove-

nant, and thought that Christ was unwilling to show mercy to such a one that had done him so much wrong, and he doubted whether God would bid him welcome, if he should come home; but when he is better informed, he manifesteth his consent. God saith to him in the gospel, Sinner, wilt thou be mine? And he answereth, Yea, Lord, with all my heart; and glad that thou wilt accept of such a wretch as I. God saith to him in his gospel and by his ministers, 'Sinner, thou hast undone thyself, and art under my wrath and curse, I have redeemed thee by the blood of my dear Son; he hath bought thee and will save thee, if thou wilt be his: what sayest thou? Wilt thou heartily give up thyself to him to be saved? Shall he be thy Saviour and thy Lord?' And the sinner answereth: ' Yea, Lord, with all my heart; nothing more welcome to me than Christ. It is Christ that my wounded soul doth want. It is he, and only he that can save me: I will be his, and take him to be mine, and gladly make with him an everlasting covenant.' Before, though Christ were offered a thousand times, the stupid sinner laid it not to heart, and would not come to him that he might have life. But when he is drawn by the Father, and secretly illuminated and converted by his grace, then is he heartily glad of the match; he takes this as the day of marriage between Christ and him. Christ gives up himself to the sinner, and the sinner gives up himself to Christ. I know that the mere covenant of the lips alone will prove no man to be heartily converted: but this, in connexion with that of the heart, will prove it. Have you been brought to this, beloved hearers? To do that by yourselves at age, which you did by your parents in baptism? Have you gladly taken Christ, as he is offered to you? And have you delivered up yourselves to him? I tell you, converting grace will bring you into covenant: this covenant is the very sum of all your change: all is contained in this one word—the making a union between Christ and you. Yea, and it will even make you on every fit opportunity to manifest this to others; to glory in your Saviour, be willing openly to confess him before the world, and let it know that you are in covenant with him.

And I must tell you in a word, that if this covenant be sincere, it will have these qualifications following. First, It will be done in some competent measure of understanding and judgment: you will know what Christ is, what he hath done, what need you have of him, how he is offered, and upon what terms he is to be received and made yours. For there can be no true covenant, when you are utterly ignorant of the very substance of the covenant. Second, If it be a true covenant, it must be entire, you must take all that is offered you, and not only a part: you must yield to the terms of the covenant, and give up yourselves wholly to Christ again. It is not to take Christ to some uses, and not to others, as to justify and save you from hell, and not to sanctify or save you from sin. Third, You must do it resolvedly and habitually, from a rooted habit and resolution of the very heart; and not from a sudden fear, or flash of conviction under a moving sermon, and as many will do in sickness and extremity, and then forget all, or grow cold again, and return to their vomit, when the fit is over: like those, ' when he slew them, then they sought him, and they returned and enquired early after God, and they remembered that God was their rock, and the high God their redeemer: nevertheless, they did flatter him with their mouth, and lied unto him with their tongues, for their heart was not right with him, neither were they stedfast in his covenant.—They kept not the covenant of God, and refused to walk in his law.' Fourth, If you covenant sincerely, it must be for a present return, and not only for the time that is to come. It must be from that day forward, without any more delay. It is not a true covenant, which excepteth but a day. Fifth, If you truly covenant* with Christ, you will do it unreservedly: yea, and resolve against all reservation. You will not secretly make exceptions, and say in your hearts, I will be the servant of Christ, if he would use me as I would have him, and deal easily with my flesh, and not destroy my worldly interest; I will follow him as far as the way is fair, and no further; no, but you will unreservedly give up yourselves to his disposal and say, I am sure I cannot have Christ and life upon terms too hard. I am sure that however he deal with me, I can have no better master, nor can I take a better course; and if he do as hardly by me as ever he did by any of his servants, I know I shall be no loser by him, nor ever have cause to repent of the bargain. And therefore I am resolved I will give up myself to him. He is wise, just, and merciful, let him do with me as he will.

* Personal covenanting was a subject very much insisted upon by some of the old divines of the puritanical and non-conformist school. Some of them carried it to an unscriptural extent—calculated to foster a self-righteous spirit, and exhibit the scheme of salvation as a species of bargain-making between man and his Maker. In scripture, when man is spoken of as entering into covenant with God, it simply means his cordially believing the principles, and embracing the promises of God's everlasting and well-ordered covenant—or ' taking hold of his covenant.' In Old Testament style, it was equivalent to a sinner ' repenting, and believing the Gospel.'—*Editor.*

This is the principal effect of true conversion, to bring the soul thus to be reconciled to God in Christ.

2. And in the same covenant, as the converted soul doth close with Christ, so doth it renounce all other competitors. Before he served another master, but now he understands it must be so no more. There is no serving God and mammon, the Spirit and the flesh: Christ and Satan are as irreconcileable as light and darkness. It is the purpose of Christ to bring men from the captivity of Satan, and of sin; he lets the sinner know, that there is no hopes of joining these together: either the devil or Christ must be forsaken; either sin or mercy must be renounced. The word, Spirit, and ministers say to him, 'thou seest, sinner, how the case standeth; God is resolved, he will not change: never think of any other way; either let sin go, or let heaven go; take which thou wilt, and leave which thou wilt; but never think of keeping both.' Hereupon the sinner lets go his sins, and renounces the world, the flesh, the devil; and engages himself that Christ alone shall be his saviour and his Lord, and God alone his chief good: he will take the promised glory for his portion; and this is the other part of the covenant. At this one blow, the root of every sin is destroyed: but principally that which is the centre and sum of all the rest, and that is, self love and self seeking. Every unconverted sinner lives to himself, and is addicted principally to his carnal interest, and the main work that Christ hath to do upon the soul is, to take down this carnal self; this is the great enemy that he bends his force against. The subduing of this is his chief victory; this is the great idol of every unregenerated man, that must be taken down, or there is no salvation.

The very nature of conversion is, a turning from carnal self to God by Christ. This therefore is to be inquired after by all that would find this change upon themselves. And I beseech you, brethren, be very careful in this particular: for as this part of the work is of absolute necessity, so the interest of carnal self is very strong and deep rooted, and exceedingly much befriended by our nature: so that here is the main difficulty of all your work. O, it is no easy matter for a man unfeignedly to deny himself; it is a subtile enemy that will keep much secret life and strength, when it seems to be overcome. And though you may think in an affliction, or time of humiliation, that self is brought very low; yet when prosperity comes again, or when its interest lies at stake, and you are called, either to costly duties, or sufferings, you will then see better what strength your carnal self yet retains. Many a man hath gone far, and done much, and shamefully fallen away at the last, because they were never brought thoroughly to self-denial. It is the remaining interest of carnal self that leads some to fleshly lusts, some to proud, ambitious ways, and some to drown themselves in the cares of this world, and so prove wretched hypocrites at the last. I do therefore as earnestly advise every soul of you to all possible care in this point, as I would do to any thing in the world: whatever you do, be jealous of this sin. Fight neither against small nor great, but against this enemy, carnal self: and do not too easily believe that it is overcome: conquer this and conquer all. This is the life and soul of all sins. The very use and end of all sin is flesh-pleasing. As he that hath right ends, hath done more than half his work for his salvation: so he that keeps up his fleshly ends is still a servant of the flesh, whatever he may do that seems to be for God. He that hath got the victory of this self, hath broken the heart of every sin. And in this fall of carnal self, there are three great master sins go down,—pride, covetousness, and voluptuousness. He that before was set upon the exalting of himself, is now set upon the glorifying of God. He that lived to the world, and was a drudge for earth, is now employed for higher things; and he that must have his sports, pleasures, and fleshly ease, hath now learned to use his body as a servant, and no longer to suffer it to be the ruler of his soul. But of these I have spoken elsewhere. So that I will say no more of them now: only this, that the destroying of these three sins,—pride, covetousness, and voluptuousness, and in them carnal self, is one half of the work of true conversion as the other half is the setting up of God, and the turning of the soul by Christ to him; and an unreserved dedication and resignation of ourselves to him.

When the sinner is thus engaged in covenant to God, the next thing that he doth, is *actually to forsake that sin* which he hath renounced, and make good the covenant that even now he made. For it is not a false, dissembling promise that converted sinners make to God. There is no hold to take of another man's word: before conversion, all promises come from so low a principle that they quickly vanish, and the heart of such a man is as changeable as the moon. But when they are converted, you shall see that they are men of their word, did mean as they said, and were in good earnest with

God, and that they are indeed fallen out with sin: they do not now think to put off the righteous God with words, and keep that sin which in their covenant they did renounce; no, they know that that would but bring greater wrath upon them, and cause God to deal with them as perjured covenant-breakers, besides all the rest of their sins; and therefore the same grace that caused them to promise, causes them to perform. O, what a sudden change doth appear in the lives of such as these, when God hath thoroughly done his work! I know the work on the heart is the greatest work, but that is not seen so much by men, and therefore not so much admired. But the life is seen by others, and therefore it is a wonder in the eyes of the world, many times, to see the change of a converted sinner; when they see, that he that lived in fleshly pleasures doth now despise them, and hath no such mind of his former sports and delights! They marvel what aileth the man that he is so changed, when they hear him that was wont to curse and swear, and deride those that feared God, to lament now his wickednesses, to reprove others that do as he was wont to do, and warn them to take heed of going that way; people will marvel what hath befallen the man that hath made this alteration. They do not see what he hath seen, nor know the workings of the Spirit of God upon his soul; they know not how God hath been hammering his hard heart, melting it, and forming it to this; they were not witnesses of the strivings and conflict in his spirit, which was between Christ and the flesh: and therefore when they see not the cause within, the change without will seem the stranger to them.

Indeed it is a kind of miracle to see the effects of the power of Christ, and how suddenly oftentimes the change is made, that would never have been made by any other means. Take a man that hath only some light convictions, and a half repentance, and how long is he in making a half reformation. If he were wont to swear or curse, or frequent ale-houses and vain company, he cannot suddenly leave it, but sometimes he restrains it a little, as if he were reformed, and sometimes he falls to it again, because he is not truly changed. But when he is converted indeed, you shall see him ordinarily leave all these sins even on a sudden. He that was wont to swear or curse, you shall never hear him do it again: he will flee from the places that before he delighted in: he is moved by a more effectual principle, and therefore will not stand trifling in the business. Grace makes a man know, that sin, Satan, and the flesh are his deadly enemies, that seek the everlasting damnation of his soul, and therefore it is the less marvel if he use them as enemies. If friends have weapons in their hands, they will but play with them, but deadly enemies will seek the blood of one another. There is difference between fencing and fighting for life. Though a man that knows nothing of their meaning, might think a fencer is fighting in good earnest, seeing he seems to make as great a stir as if it were so indeed: yet the issue will show you that it is otherwise, because you see that there is no blood shed, nor men killed. So is it with an hypocrite in his seeming reformation; when he makes the greatest stir against his sin in confessing, and prayer, and other means, yet he will not resolvedly cast it away, but he secretly uses it as his friend, while he openly abuses it as his enemy; and he puts it into his bosom, while he calls it all to naught. He will not be brought unfeignedly to renounce it, give it a bill of divorce, and cast it out as a man doth his vomit, with resolution never to take it in more: O how sweetly doth he cherish it in his thoughts in secret, when he frowns upon it with the severest countenance! How easily is he drawn to it again and again, when he takes on him to repent of it and abhor it! But it is quite contrary with a man that is converted. Though the remnants of sin will remain in him while he lives, yet as to the reign of it he presently casts it off, and bids defiance to it: he fights against it in good earnest, as knowing that either he or it must die; he casts it up as a loathsome vomit, which he will not take into his stomach again; you shall quickly see, by the course of his life, that his heart is changed. Before true conversion comes, what a stir have we with wretched sinners to leave a base lust,—to forsake their drunkenness, or covetousness, or uncleanness; to leave their swearing and base speaking, and yet we cannot prevail with them; sometimes they will, and then again they will not; sometimes a flash of conviction flies in their faces, and they are a little affrighted, and then they will presently repent and mend; but when the fit is over, you shall see that it is not a change of his disposition or nature, it was but a little falling out with their sin, which leaves them faster friends when they are reconciled: but conversion makes an unreconcileable enmity. Away go former sinful customs and courses; away go covetous practices, wicked speeches, proud fashions, and evil courses; as Sarah thrust out Hagar and Ishmael out of her house, and would receive them no more. If you have deadly enemies in your house, you will thrust out them and all that they have. If a man should sit in a dark room among venomous reptiles, and think verily that there were no such matter, but he were in his bedchamber; you might persuade him long enough to come away, and tell him of the danger; but he will not stir, but laugh at you, because he does not believe you. But if you come into the room with a light, and he see them crawling all about him and making at him, then you need not another word to bid him begone; he is quickly up, and leaves them with abhorrence.

We tell unconverted sinners of the hatefulness of sin, the danger that they are in, and pray them to leave it, but they believe us not, and do but laugh at it; but when the Spirit of God brings in the light, and they see all this with their own eyes, that it is even worse than ever we made it; then away go their sins without any more ado. We entreat a fellow mortal to come away, telling him that sin hath a sting, and a deadly sting, and assure him, from the word of God, that it will be bitterness in the latter end, and he makes no great matter of our words, but can hear us, as if we came in the pulpit to tell him a tale, and not to save his soul from hell: and therefore he can go on in his old way for all this, and take his cups, or follow the world and his fleshly lusts, and give the preacher leave to talk. But when converting grace comes, it makes them taste the bitterness of sin, and then they quickly abandon it. It makes them feel the sting and smart, and then they cry to God for help, and wish they had never known it, and run away from it with detestation. Grace brings in that light from God, which shows them that which they did not see before. How that all this while they have had a multitude of serpents in their bosom, and they have been playing even at the brink of hell: and when they see this with their own eyes, it is time for them to take another course.

If you doubt of all this I say, whether conversion does make a man thus cast away his sin, while the hypocrite stands dallying with it, and cannot leave it, look into the example of all true converts. Or if that do not satisfy you, look into the infallible word of God. How eagerly was Saul going on in his persecution, till the light from heaven stopped his course, and the voice and grace of Christ changed his mind! But do you read if ever Paul persecuted any more? Or doth he delay and take time to consider of the matter before he would leave his former sin? No, but he presently forbears, and betakes himself to another course. When he confessed the former sinful course of himself and others, he tells you now how the matter is mended. And no marvel, for the man that lives in his former sinful way, can never be saved, whatever change of the heart he may pretend. 'Know ye not that the unrighteous shall not inherit the kingdom of God? Be not deceived, neither fornicators, nor idolators, nor adulterers, nor effeminate, nor abusers of themselves with mankind, nor thieves, nor covetous, nor drunkards, nor revellers, nor extortioners shall inherit the kingdom of God. And such were some of you; but ye are washed, but ye are sanctified, but ye are justified in the name of the Lord Jesus, and by the Spirit of our God.' Now you see that conversion makes an effectual change of the life : ye were such, but now it is not so, ye are washed, ye are sanctified by the Spirit of God. When God mentions the conversion of these people, he says concerning their former sins: 'thou shalt cast them away as a menstruous cloth, thou shalt say to it, Get thee hence.' With what detestation will a converted sinner say to his former sin, Get thee hence! It is by thee that I have suffered, and had like to have been undone for ever. It is by thee that I have so much wronged God, and therefore away with thee, get thee hence. So also Isaiah, 'Turn ye unto him, from whom the children of Israel have deeply revolted ; for in that day every man shall cast away his idols of silver, and his idols of gold, which your own hands have made you for a sin.' And the description of conversion runs thus: 'Cast away from you all your transgressions, whereby ye have transgressed against me, and make you a new heart, and a new spirit ; for why will you die, O ye house of Israel?' And in Ezekiel, God commands them, 'cast ye away every man the abomination of his eyes;' and also, 'they rebelled, and did not cast away every man the abomination of his eyes.—Let us therefore cast off the works of darkness, and let us put on the armour of light; let us walk honestly, as in the day, not in rioting and drunkenness, not in chambering and wantonness, not in strife and envying.—Wash. ye, make ye clean, put away the evil of your doings from before mine eyes ; cease to do evil, learn to do well.—Seek the Lord while he may be found, call upon him while he is near, let the wicked forsake his ways, and the unrighteous man his thoughts, and let him return again to the Lord, and he will have mercy upon him, and to our God for he will abundantly pardon.—Amend your ways and your doings, and obey the voice of the Lord your God, and he will repent him of the evil.' An hundred more such passages might be cited ;

wherein it is most evident that there is no true conversion of the heart, if the sin of the life be not also cast away.

If any will here desire to be curious, and to know how much conquest the least degree of grace doth make, and how much actual sins may stand with sincerity of grace ; or if any will imagine, that because there is yet actual sin in the converted, that therefore there is no discernable difference between their reformation and other men's ; I answer them as follows: First, A strong degree of grace is easily known by him that hath it, by the thorough reformation both of heart and life. Second, The weakest degree of grace is not ordinarily known, and therefore you cannot expect that I should make it known. For he that hath so little grace as to sin as much as will stand with true grace, shall scarce ever know that he hath any true grace at all in that condition : he is not fit for such a condition, nor would it do him good till he were fitter for it. Third, There is no change of the life that will discover sincerity certainly to others, nor to themselves considered alone, without the change of the heart ; but there is a wickedness of the life that will prove a wickedness of the heart, even unto others, much more to men themselves, who may know both immediately. Fourth, By this one mark you may know whether the sins of your lives, be they great or small, are certain proofs of an unconverted, graceless heart or not. In every truly converted man, the chief bent of his heart and life is against sin, and his chief desire and endeavour is to destroy it ; but in others it is not so. Whatsoever kind of sinning therefore will not stand with such a bent of heart and life, with such a desire and endeavour, will prove that man to be graceless or unconverted that doth commit it. Now how far a man's sin is with, or against the predominant bent of his own heart and life, he may discern himself by diligent observation.

I have hitherto spoken only of sins of commission, which are cast away when the soul is changed : the next part of the reformation of the life is in point of *duty*. A converted soul hath presently another *work to do*. As he hath set his heart upon another end, and looks after another portion and inheritance, so has he other means to use, which are suitable to the nature of the end which is to be obtained. A heavenly felicity is not gotten by earthly means. Learning to do well, therefore, is ever joined with ceasing to do evil. Seeking the Lord while he may be found, and calling on him while he is near, is joined with forsaking wicked ways He that is turned from the power of Satan, is turned to God. Before conversion the wretched sinner had no pleasure in God, and therefore no pleasure in his service ; and therefore was seldom, cold, and careless in it, and gave God nothing but the dregs of the world, the flesh, and what they could spare, and put him off with some formal, superficial, cheap kind of service that would cost them but little. But when converting grace hath made a change, as God is their delight, so is his work and worship. They see a world of work before them which they made no conscience of before: as I told you of Paul in Acts ix. 11. he falls a praying as soon as he is converted, and from praying he proceeds to the preaching of that gospel which he persecuted before. It made the people wonder to see him who had been persecuting all that called upon the name of Jesus, but a little before, to preach for them a little after. The scripture saith all that heard him were amazed, and said, ' Is not this he that destroyed them which called on this name in Jerusalem, and came hither to that intent, to bring them bound to the chief priests?' So is it to this day. When a poor sinner that was wont to mock at a holy life, and never was used to call upon God, or at least but heartlessly and with the lips ; that made no conscience of praying in his family, or instructing them, or holy spending the Lord's day, shall now be as diligent in these as any. When the Bible is in his hand, or other good books, that had rather before have had a pack of cards, or dice, or worldly business ; when a man that was wont to set light by these things, is now set upon them, and cannot live without them : this makes the world about him amazed and say, is not this he that scorned sermons, who now follows after sermons ? Is not this he that was against these things as much as any, that now is set so much upon them ? I know a man that is unconverted may be much in the use of means, but here is the difference: to a converted man the obedience of God is his chief work and business, to which all other things are made to stoop : but to the unconverted, the work of the flesh and world is the chief, and the service of God must stoop to that. If any of you dream that you are converted, and yet will not be brought to the works of obedience, both in holiness to God and righteousness to men, you do but wilfully deceive yourselves. Do you think a man can love God above all, as every true Christian does, and not seek him above all ; or that a man can have a heavenly heart, and not have a heavenly life ? It cannot be. If you had rather sit at home, when you should be attending upon God in the public assembly, or enjoying private helps for your souls, or are cumbered about many things, when you should be looking after the one thing necessary; it is a sign that you have not chosen the better part. Whenever the heart is changed to God, the main bent of the life will presently consist in the seeking of God.

A new heart will have a *new tongue.* The fruit of it will appear in the scope of a man's discourse: ' for out of the abundance of the heart the mouth speaketh.' I know a man may force his words, and therefore I still say to you that these proofs from the outward actions are stronger for the negative than the affirmative. An evil tongue will prove an evil heart, but to prove a man sincere there must be both heart and tongue. But certain it is, that though words may be counterfeit, yet true conversion doth always change the speech, and make the tongue also serviceable to those higher ends which the heart is newly set upon. He that before had no mind to speak of any thing but earthly and fleshly matters, he is now inquiring after other matters. The first words that we read of the converted Jews, of the converted jailer, and of Paul, when he was converted, were, ' what God would have them do that they might be saved.' Before, the very discourse of sin, grace, Christ, and the life to come, were a trouble to them, but now it is otherwise. They know they have their tongues for no greater use, nor can they better employ them, than in seeking direction for their everlasting happiness. Now if you mark them in the company that they come into, if they have any fit opportunity, they are lamenting their former sinful life, or warning others to avoid the way that they were led into, or telling men of the evil of sin, and the need of Christ and grace, or asking help of those that can help them : how to search their hearts ; how to overcome the remnant of their sins ; and how to carry on the work of God, that they may be ready for death and judgment, and get safe to heaven. You that are carnal, wonder that men speak so much of these things, and you are weary to hear them, but you know not the change that is made upon their hearts. Can you blame a man to talk of his everlasting condition, and of that which is of greater moment than all the matters of the world ? Can you blame a man to talk most of that which he minds most, and which his very heart is set upon ?

If his tongue be of heaven, while his heart is on earth, then he is an hypocrite : but would you not have a man's tongue to follow his heart when his heart is right? Yet some men are so perverse, and so against the things of God, that they are ready to say, why cannot they keep their faith or religion to themselves? Cannot they be religious in secret, without talking of it so much to others? As if the heart only were made for God, and the tongue for the world, the flesh or the devil. As if a man should talk of nothing but the childish toys and trifles of the world, for fear of seeming an hypocrite, or for fear of troubling these squeamish souls. Shall the Holy Ghost make such a change on the heart of a sinner, and shall not the tongue partake of it, or express it? Can Christ and his Spirit dwell in the heart, and the tongue conceal so blessed an inhabitant? Can a man have a taste of heaven upon his heart, and the kingdom of God begun within him, and yet not express his life or joy? Or is it meet for him that has found the way to heaven, to hold his tongue, and let others quietly post to hell? Should a man that hath narrowly escaped damnation himself be silent, when he sees others go in the same way that he had like to have perished in? Who will not call to another to take heed, that hath escaped a quicksand himself; or set up a bush, that those that follow may see the danger? Is it not a strange conceit of these men, that would have the converted so cruel to all that are yet unconverted; so unthankful to God that hath mercifully delivered them; so senseless of matters of the greatest weight, and so serviceable to Satan, the great deceiver, as to say nothing of such unspeakable things as these? What! have the love of God shed abroad in their hearts, and say nothing of it! Have the pardon of sin in the blood of Christ, and say nothing of it! What! see many souls in danger of damnation, and say nothing, but let them perish! It cannot be; it must not be: it is a most unreasonable thing to desire it.

Our tongue is our glory, it is the principal instrument of manifesting our mind, by which man differs from all other inferior creatures: and should we not use it for God and the greatest things? What sottish people are these to think their worldly matters fit for their discourse, and the matters of everlasting life unfit? To think it no harm to jest, talk foolishly, tell idle tales, and such a man they take for a pleasant companion, and never find fault with him. But for the things that may honour God, or tend to men's salvation, or to destroy sin and cross the devil, here we must be silent, and keep our religion to ourselves. Did ever these foolish persons believe Jesus Christ, 'that by their words they shall be justified, and by their words they shall be condemned?' Did they ever believe, or regard the words of the Holy Ghost, 'but forni-

cation, uncleanness, or lasciviousness, let it not be once named among you, as becometh saints; nor filthiness, nor foolish talking, nor jestings, which are not convenient, but rather giving of thanks?—Let no corrupt communication proceed out of your mouth, but that which is good to the use of edifying, that it may minister grace to the hearers, and grieve not the Holy Spirit of God.—Let the word of Christ dwell in you richly in all wisdom, teaching and admonishing one another.—Exhort one another daily while it is called to-day, lest any of you be hardened through the deceitfulness of sin.—If any man speak, let him speak as the oracle of God, that God in all things may be glorified.' Abundance of such passages are in scripture, which may tell you what to think of the folly of such carnal men; and may assure you that a converted, heavenly heart, will always have a new and heavenly tongue.

A changed heart will induce a person to seek a *change of company*, if it may be had. There is somewhat in nature that disposes all men to delight in that company which is most suitable to their disposition. While their hearts are carnal, they love the company of such: a man that is of their mind and way, and will break a jest, and be merry with them, or talk with them about their worldly matters, is the best companion for them; for the company of mortified and heavenly men, they have no pleasure in it. They mar their mirth with putting in words about the evil of sin, death and judgment, and everlasting things: they trouble them, and therefore they have no mind to their company. But when converting grace hath changed them, their minds in this are changed also. O, how unsavoury then is it to them to sit or walk in the company of such that have never a word of God, or that may help them in the matters that their hearts are set upon! Their merry talk, and fine discourse, is to him but as the crackling of thorns in the fire. It troubles him, and moves him to compassionate such empty souls that have no God, no Christ, no heaven to talk of, but mere unprofitable trifles; but the company of those is sweet to him that will discourse about the matters of his salvation—that will tell him how he may get more grace, and lay more open to him the mysteries of the gospel, and speak of the riches of God's love in Christ, or tell him of the dangers that are yet before him, or the duties that he must perform. These matters are now savoury to him, for these he knows do indeed concern him, and are worth the talking of.

When a man is in a strange country a thousand miles off, it doth him good to meet with his own countrymen, and talk with them about his friends, and family, his estate, and inheritance, and the home to which he must return. One hour of this discourse is sweeter to him than a hundred with the strangers of the country, about matters that are little to him: so is it here. A Christian that knows he is a stranger in this world, and that his God, his salvation, his home, his inheritance are all in the world to come, had rather far discourse with a heavenly-minded man about his Father and everlasting works and blessedness, than with worldly men about this world. Who loves not the company of his dearest friends and brethren more than of strangers or enemies? We know those that fear God are like to be our companions for ever, and therefore we would have them our companions here. You may see by scripture that it is thus with true Christians. ' In his eyes a vile person is contemned, but he honoureth them that fear God.—They take sweet counsel together, and walk to the house of God in company.—They that feared the Lord, spake often one to another.—I am a companion,' saith David, ' of all them that fear thee, and of them that keep thy precepts.' And it is one of the Hebrews' commendations, that they became companions of them that suffered for Christ. And on the contrary side, it was alleged to be one of Job's iniquities to go in company with the workers of iniquity, for men are supposed to be such as their company is: and we are commanded with such, no, not to eat, and to ' have no company with them, that they may be ashamed.' And Solomon saith, a 'companion of fools shall be destroyed.'

Another part of the change of the life, is this : true conversion makes a man *compassionate to those that are unconverted, and very desirous of their conversion*, and therefore sets men upon such endeavours as they can use to bring it to pass, yea, it makes men zealous of good works, and very careful and studious to do what good they can. It is the disposition of wicked men to draw others with them into wickedness, and to make others as bad as themselves : ' they not only do that which is evil, but have pleasure in them that do it.' They would have others as loose as they, and as careless of their own souls as they, and to make as light a matter of sin as they do. The drunkard would have companions, and the gamester would have them : every one that hates and derides a godly life, would have all others do so too. Men are loth to go to hell alone, but like men that are running violently

down a hill, they draw one another with them. It somewhat comforts them to see most of the world as bad as themselves, because they think then God will not condemn so many : as if the number of sinners did extenuate the wrong : and those unconverted men that are not so bad as to wish others as bad as themselves, yet have little zeal for men's recovery : for how can they love other men better than themselves ?

But when conversion hath given a man a sight and sense of the evil of sin, it makes him pity all that are misled, and earnestly desire their conversion and recovery. O, how much would the gracious soul have others to see the folly of sin, as he hath seen it! How desirous is he to have them see their need of Christ, that glory above, that felicity which lies in the favour of God, as he hath seen them ! It doth him good to have companions in good: he hath no mind to be happy alone. The number of partakers he knows will not at all diminish his joys. If he could tell how, he would have all the world to be as happy as himself, the more the better. And therefore he prays heartily for the conversion of other men : he pleads with them, and persuades them, and gladly he would have their eyes to be opened, and their hearts to be softened and turned to God. He remembers that their case was once his own, and how foolish and froward he was, even as they now are ! He remembers how miserable he then was, though he knew it not, and would not for all the world be in the same case again ; and therefore he cannot choose but pity those that he hath left behind him ; and long for their deliverance.

Truly, sinners, it is from hence that men fearing God do trouble you so much in your sins, and make such a stir with you about matters of your souls ; and tell you of your danger, and persuade you to turn and take another course : it is because they are loth to see you perish if they could help it. You would have them let you alone, but they are loth to let you alone, in such a case and way as that. If some that are running to drown themselves, or do any mischief to themselves, should bid you let them alone, and meddle with yourselves, and take no care for them, you would not let them alone for all that, but would hinder them if you could from making away with themselves. So if you are angry with men that would keep you out of hell, and bid them let you alone, and take no care for you, because you shall answer for yourselves, this will not satisfy them to stand still, and see you run into damnation, if they knew how to help it. Alas ! it is not because they love to be meddling with other people's matters, or take pleasure in reproving and controlling other men: if it were not for your sakes and the glory of God, it is more easy for us to let you alone. We have work enough of our own to do, and dangers enough of our own to prevent. It is small pleasure to any man that is well in his wits to meddle needlessly with other men's matters, and to contradict wilful sinners ; when he knows how little thanks he is like to have for it. What, do you think we long to have men hate us and fly in our faces ? Is it a pleasure to us to vex men, and make them our enemies ? No ! alas, it is so great a displeasure, that it becomes a strong temptation to us to be unfaithful or negligent in our duty. Many a minister is so loth to get the ill will of his people, that he lets them alone in their sins, or only tells them of it in public, or at the most but in an easy, ineffectual way, and so falls in danger of perishing with them for company. Nothing makes more negligent, unreasonable ministers (next the unfaithfulness of their own hearts) than people's hating their instructions and reproofs, and impatiently bearing the means that should recover them. Carnal ministers will not cast themselves upon the people's displeasure, but rather let them alone and venture them. They that dare venture their own souls to escape the ill will of men, will venture other men's too : and so it is also with private Christians.

The reason why so few will be brought to deal plainly and faithfully for the saving of others, is, because it is commonly so ill taken. Alas, sinners ! what ease, what profit, what good is it, think you, to other men to trouble you in your sins, if it were not for your good, and for the command and glory of God ? But what man who is not a tiger, or hath not a heart of stone within him, can see men within a little of damnation and let them alone ? Who can be so cruel as to hold his tongue, while he sees men in the high-way to hell ? If we were yet in our unbelief, and did not believe that the word of God is true, or that unconverted men shall certainly perish, then we might well be silent, for who would go to make men sad with melancholy fancies or fearful dreams that have no truth in them ? But O, do not blame a man that hath been in the same condition himself, and is mercifully delivered by converting grace, if he look back to those he hath left behind, and tell them of their danger ! Do not blame a man that hath his eyes opened by faith, and sees hell-fire a little before you, if he should call to you, call again, and call with tears, and greatest earnestness, to entreat you to stop and go no further. I dare say,

if you did see what he sees, you would be of the same mind, and would be as loth to go on in an unconverted condition as any one would be to suffer you. When the eyes of sinners are shut that they see not their own condition, nor what a storm is rising in heaven against them, they are content and quiet at the gates of hell ! But when either grace or torments have opened their eyes, the case will be quite changed with them. Well, this is certain, that whenever God converts the soul, he makes men very desirous of other men's conversion, and very compassionate to them that are yet in darkness and in bondage by their sins. Not only Paul and the preachers of the gospel say, ' necessity is laid upon me, and woe unto me if I preach not the gospel ;' but every Christian in his place doth find a necessity upon him to endeavour the good of others ; and he finds an earnest desire to it, and a delight in that which God hath made so necessary. And it is not in this matter of conversion only, but in all other things also, that a true Christian hath a special inclination to do good.

As he that is evil, delights to do evil ; so he that is good, delights to do good : though he be not perfectly good, for so is none till he come to heaven : much less primitively and of himself good, for so there is none good but God, yet hath he a derived and imperfect goodness, and in that measure as he is good, he must needs be inclined to do good ; for every thing will work according to its nature. It is a death to wicked men to do that which is a godly man's delight. A man or beast cannot fly in the air, but a bird can do it as easily as we can walk on the earth. A good man is never in his own element, but when he is doing some good ; his mind runs on it. He studies how he may effect it ; and he is not content to do good unless he do much good. He knows what Christ hath said : ' herein is my Father glorified, that ye bring forth much fruit,' he finds by experience that which others will not believe, that doing good is either a receiving of good, or inseparably conjunct with it. The more a man gives to the poor or to other good uses, with right intents, the more he receives. Whatever others receive by his endeavours, he is sure that he shall not lose his labour, or cost, as to himself. He that giveth to the poor, lendeth to the Lord. A carnal man is ever selfish, and draws all to him, as if there were no one but himself that he cared for : but a gracious man is in his place and measure like God, a communicative good. As God is good and doth good, so is he. That which a man's nature inclines him to, he cannot forget. A good man forgets not in the main to do good, for he knows that with such sacrifice God is well pleased. Mark this, all you that profess more zeal for God than others; believe it, true conversion will appear in good works. The true servants of Christ do as much exceed the world in a contempt of earthly things, and in compassion to the miserable, and in readiness and bounty, according to their ability, to those that want, as they do exceed them in praying or other duties. Other men part with the world as their treasure, and almost as their blood, but the heavenly Christian parts with it as his superfluity, or at least as that which he can spare. Faith teaches men to do good ; and good works are part of the riches of a saint. Doing good is so excellent and necessary a thing, that even an enemy must be made partaker of it. And want of thankfulness or requital from men, is no excuse to them who neglect it; even some works of piety may be forborne for doing good to others.

CHAPTER II.

THE INDISPENSIBLE NECESSITY OF CONVERSION TO SALVATION.

I have spoken of the work of conversion, as it contains the change of the judgment, and of the heart, and of the life, and so have finished the third particular promised, which was to shew you what conversion is, and wherein it doth consist. By what is said, you may easily see that it is a great change that is made on the soul and in the life, by this renewing grace of Christ. Methinks now all those men that know, or may know, that never such a work was wrought upon their hearts, should see that it is time to look about them, and to lay to heart the sad conclusion which Christ hath here delivered in my text. What! have all the people of this congregation found all this change upon judgment, heart and life, as I have here spoken of ? O that it were so well. What a joy were that to us, to angels, to Christ himself! And what everlasting joy would that be to themselves! But alas! their conversations and careless lives tell us, that with too many of them it is far otherwise. And what keeps such guilty souls in peace ? Can so many men hear such a text as this: that except they be converted they cannot be saved, and yet not look about them, nor be awakened from their security ? Yet it is too evident, by sad experience, that they who read this and know, or might know, that they are not converted, are yet as careless as if they could endure damnation well enough. But what is the matter, and how comes this to pass ? Doubtless, because they do not thoroughly believe the truth of what is said. I shall therefore come now to the next thing promised—briefly to show you, from the word of God the certain truth of what we have in hand, that you may see it is a matter past all doubt and question.

SECTION I.

THE LORD JESUS DECLARES IT NECESSARY IN ORDER TO A MAN ENTERING THE KINGDOM OF GOD AS A CONVERT.

First, What need you any more than the very words of the text ? Do you need further proof, where you have the words of Christ himself ? But you shall see yet more. He tells Nicodemus, that 'except a man be regenerated and born again, he cannot enter into the kingdom of heaven :' that is, as a child is as it were a new creature that lately received life, which had none before, and newly enters into the world; so must every man that will be saved, as it were receive a new spiritual life, and enter into the world of grace, even into the church of God, and begin his life as it were again. ' If any man be in Christ, he is a new creature, old things are passed away, behold, all things are become new! See here both the necessity and the nature of this change. It is not one or two, but *every* man who is in Christ that is thus converted. And he that is not in Christ, is not a Christian, and he that is not a Christian cannot be saved. Every true Christian, then, is a new creature, not in substance, but in quality and in life; 'old things are past away, behold, all things are become new !' What are all these things but those that I have before expressed to you ? A truly converted man hath not the same ends and intentions that he had before: he hath a new hope and happiness, new love, new desires, new sorrow, new delight, new resolution, and a new conversation : all is become new. He enters into a new covenant with Christ, and so he hath a new master, a new head, husband and Lord: and is now a member of a new society, and entered into a new kingdom and family. He hath a new work to do, he hath new company to converse with, he hath new thoughts in his heart, and speaks a new language. He leads his life by a new law : and thus all things are become new. Even relations are here included, as well as physical qualifications, for he hath a new Father, a new inheritance, and so of the rest. It must needs be a great change indeed, where all things are become new. If it were but one or two of these, it would make a great alteration; much more when it is in all. So are they likened ' to new born babes, who must therefore desire the sincere milk of the word, that they may live and grow by it.—For in Christ Jesus neither circumcision availeth any thing, nor uncircumcision, but a new creature.—The world must be crucified to us, and we to the world, that we may live anew to God.'

I told you before, that in conversion we 'put off the old man, which according to the deceitful lusts, is corrupt, and are renewed in the spirit of our mind, and put on the new man, which after God is created in righteousness and true holiness.' And that 'according to his mercy he saved us by the washing of regeneration, and the renewing of the Holy Ghost, which he sheddeth on us, through Jesus Christ our Saviour, that being justified by his grace, we might be made heirs according to the hope of eternal life. So we put on the new man which is renewed in knowledge after the image of him that created us.' He commands them to make them a new heart and a new spirit. And what he commands to all, he declares himself resolved to give to his elect. ' A new heart also will I give you, and a new spirit will I put into you, and I will take away the stony heart out of your flesh, and I will give you an heart of flesh; and I will put my Spirit within you, and cause you to walk in my statutes, and ye shall keep my judgments and do them.' So in the same prophet, 'I will give them one heart, and I will put a new spirit within them; and I will take the stony heart out of their flesh, and will give them an heart of flesh; that they may walk in my statutes, and keep my ordinances, and do them, and they shall be my people, and I will be their God.' And as they are new creatures, so they have a new commandment or law to live by; and a new promise or covenant for their inheritance. They have a new name, that no man knows but he that hath it, or at least they shall have. They have new employments, even serving God 'in newness of life, that as they were planted together in the likeness of Christ's death, they should be also in the likeness of his resurrection. Knowing this, that their old man is crucified with him, that the body of sin might be destroyed, that henceforth they should not serve sin. For he that is dead is justified or freed from sin.' And thus they 'serve God in newness of spirit.' And so the whole church is one new man in Christ. A new lump that is purged from the old leaven, must all particular churches of Christians be. But lest any doubt should be left, I will reduce the rest to some particular arguments.

1. It is the very office of Jesus Christ, which he came into the world to perform, to bring back ungodly sinners unto God. And shall we think that Christ came on a needless errand? Believe it, as his suffering was necessary for our ransom, so was his doctrine and Spirit as necessary for our conversion, and we can no more be saved without the one than without the other. Think with yourselves whether it be a likely thing that God should send his Son on earth by a miracle, surpassing all miracles, and this on purpose to call home straying, sinful souls, if they might be saved without conversion? If it had been possible for men to be happy without holiness, and to escape misery without escaping sin, what need Christ have come to sanctify them? The Lord Jesus is the great physician of souls, and he comes not to heal any petty diseases, that might as well have been healed without him: but he comes to cure a mortal plague, that no one else could have cured but himself. It was never the mind of Christ to come down from heaven to suffer for our sins, that we might be saved in them without a change. Never did it enter into his holy thoughts to bring men to glory in their sins; but to destroy their sins that would keep them out of glory. He never meant to bring you and your disease to heaven together; but to heal your disease, that else would be your ruin. What! shall we think that Christ came to impute a righteousness to the impenitent and unconverted; to make God believe that they are just in him, who are not in him at all; and to make men seem to be what they are not? Why, this were to feign the blessed Son of God to be the patron of iniquity, and to die for the upholding of sin; and not for the destroying of it. What greater blasphemy against Christ can there be, than to imagine that he befriends sin, which he doth so hate, or that he takes part with Satan, and strengthens his kingdom, when it was his very business in the world to destroy Satan and his works? What! must Christ come and so miraculously condescend to do and suffer what he did, and all to heal diseased souls, and kill that sin that else would kill them, and after all this shall he be made the patron of it?

Take this home with thee to thy heart, unconverted sinner, whoever thou art: if men could have been saved without conversion, Christ would never have done so much to convert them as he hath done. You comfort yourselves in Christ, while you live in wilful sinning, and you think that though you be not renewed, yet you shall be pardoned and saved by his blood shed. Why, I tell you from the word of God, you may extract much terror from the thoughts of Christ; but hope of salvation without conversion he will afford you none. You may rather think with yourselves, that if the changing of a sinner had not been a work of great necessity, Christ would never have come down to do it. I know that we have free pardon of sin by his blood, or else we had no hope: but the converted alone partake of that pardon; as Mark says, 'Lest at any time they be converted, and their sin should be forgiven them.' So also Paul, 'Repent ye therefore, that your sins may be blotted out.' If you had but that one chapter, (Luke xv.) to tell you in what manner Christ doth save men, you might easily see, it is not by bringing them to heaven in their ungodliness. He likens himself to one that having lost a sheep in the wilderness, goes and seeks after it, till he find it: and when he hath found it, doth he leave it? No, but lays it on his shoulders, and brings it home rejoicing; or like one that sweeps the house to find a piece of silver that was lost; or like the father that gladly receives the returning prodigal. But without returning, there had been no receiving him, nor no rejoicing over him.

But doth not Christ tell us of some that needed no repentance? Yes, true, why is that? Because they had truly repented before. They needed no conversion, or such conversion as the new converts have, which consists in a change, from a state of sin to God: but only a proceeding in obedience, and particular repentance for their particular slips. But if they had not been converted before, they would have needed such a conversion or repentance. For so the prophet Isaiah saith, 'all we like sheep have gone astray, and have turned every one to his own way:' and in like manner Peter saith 'ye were as sheep going astray, but are returned to the Shepherd and Bishop of your souls.' Or if there be any that were sanctified in their infancy, as no doubt there are, so that their actual going astray was prevented; yet as they went astray in Adam and their parents, so had they a straying disposition in their corrupted natures, which needs a turn, as well as the sins, which appear in the life. And thus it appears that Christ came of purpose to convert men, and not to pardon any soul without conversion. 'The Son of man is come to seek and to save that which was lost.—Who gave

himself for us,' not to pardon us, and to save without converting us, but 'to redeem us from all iniquity, and purify to himself a peculiar people, zealous of good works.' So that hence you may see the absolute necessity of conversion to salvation.

2. It is the very aim of the gospel, and principal design of the whole word of God, to convert men from sin to God, and build them up when they are once converted. And do you think that God would have made it the scope of his word, if it had not been necessary? If a man could be saved without conversion, what need God to inspire prophets and apostles to deliver his word to the world, and to seal it with the miraculous gifts of the Holy Ghost, and all to convert men and build up the converted? Would God make all this stir with us as he doth in the bible, for a needless thing? Alas, if he did not know that your disease will kill you except it be cured, he would never have prepared so many remedies against it. This is the very use and glory of the law of God. 'The law of God is perfect, converting the soul.' What else doth scripture call sinners to, but to repent and turn to God by Christ. 'As I live, saith the Lord, I have no pleasure in the death of the wicked, but that the wicked turn from his way and live; turn ye, turn ye from your evil ways; for why will ye die, O house of Israel?—But if the wicked shall turn from all his sins that he hath committed, and keep all my statutes, and do that which is lawful and right, he shall surely live; he shall not die.—Have I any pleasure at all that the wicked should die, saith the Lord God, and not that he should return from his ways and live?—Repent and turn yourselves from all your transgressions, so iniquity shall not be your ruin. Cast away from you all your transgressions, whereby you have transgressed, and make you a new heart, and a new spirit; for why will ye die, O house of Israel? For I have no pleasure in the death of him that dieth, saith the Lord God, wherefore turn yourselves and live ye.—Turn ye at my reproofs, and I will pour out my Spirit to you.—Turn ye to me with all your hearts, with fasting, weeping, and mourning; rend your hearts and not your garments, and turn to the Lord your God.' An hundred such passages might be brought, in which it is apparent, that the turning of sinners to God, is the main scope of the holy scriptures.

3. It is as certain, that to convert men to God by the faith of Jesus Christ, is the very business that the ministers of the gospel are appointed to. And is it likely that God would send

us to trouble the world with a needless work ?
For my part, if I did not know that repentance
and conversion are absolutely necessary to the
glory of God's grace and saving of the sinner, I
should be loth to trouble myself and others so
much about such matters as I do. Who could
find in his heart to study, preach, weary himself, vex the world, call men to such unwelcome duties, preach to them such unpleasant
truths, set them upon works that are so hard
to flesh and blood, and put them upon so many
sufferings in the world, if all this were for
a needless thing? John Baptist began to preach
repentance; Christ followed him, in preaching the same doctrine, and tells them, except
they repent, they shall all perish. The apostles
follow him in preaching the same repentance,
as that without which there is no salvation.
They tell us, ' God commandeth all men
every where to repent.' Paul's business was,
to 'shew all men that they must repent and
turn to God, and do works meet for repentance.'
And 'to open men's eyes, and turn them from
darkness to light, and the power of Satan to
God, that they may receive remission of sins,
and an inheritance among the sanctified by faith
in Christ.' As Christ himself came to call sinners to repentance. So doth he send his ministers on the same errand ; and after all his suffering, he will give men pardon on no other
terms : but repentance and remission of sins
must be preached in his name among all nations.
Mark the way of gospel preaching and salvation,
' The God of our fathers raised up Jesus, whom
ye slew and hanged on a tree, him hath God exalted with his right hand, to be a prince and a
Saviour, to give repentance to Israel, and forgiveness of sins ; repentance in order before forgiveness : when men turn from sin, God turns
from his punishing wrath ; but not before. ' God
hath granted to the gentiles repentance unto life.'
The sum of Paul's doctrine was, ' Repentance
toward God, and faith toward our Lord Jesus
Christ.' For this do God's ministers 'instruct
in meekness them that oppose themselves, if God
peradventure will give them repentance to the
acknowledging of the truth, that they may recover themselves out of the snare of the devil,
who are taken captive by him at his will.' It is
said, that ' God is not willing that any should
perish, but that all should come to repentance,'
which plainly implies ; that if they come not to
repentance, they must perish for all that. Therefore repentance is one of the fundamentals;
and preaching repentance is laying the foundation : and he that is grown incurable, and re-

mediless by apostacy, is said to be one that cannot be renewed by repentance ; which supposes
that there can be no other way of renewing : and
a desperate man is one that finds no place for repentance ; and that in the godly, all the fruits of
holiness are made the fruits of repentance.

4. The very providence of God in mercy and
affliction, are purposely to bring sinners to repentance: and therefore certainly, repentance is
necessary to salvation, ' Despisest thou the riches
of his goodness, and forbearance and long suffering, not knowing that the goodness of God
leadeth thee to repentance ? But after thy hardness and impenitent heart, treasurest up to thyself wrath against the day of wrath, and revelation of the righteous judgment of God.' If conversion were not necessary to salvation, God
would not make so much ado by affliction and
mercy to bring us to it.

5. God makes it the duty even of every man
in his place, to do all that he can for the conversion of others: and this he would never do,
if there were another way to salvation, ' They
that turn many to righteousness shall shine as
the stars for ever and ever.—If any of you do
err from the truth, and one convert him, let him
know,' that he that converteth a sinner from the
error of his ways, shall save a soul from death,
and cover a multitude of sins.' And David promises, if God would pardon and restore him,
that he will teach transgressors his way, that sinners may be converted to him. So that, lay all
this now together, and judge whether it be likely
that God would have set all the world on work
for the conversion of sinners, if there had been
any other way to save them. Should Christ
himself have come upon this errand ? Should
the word of God be written to this end ? Should
all the prophets, apostles and ministers of the
gospel be sent on this message ? Should all
mercies, and all afflictions be directed to this
use? Should it be made the duty of every
Christian to endeavour it? If men could be
saved without conversion, by any other way ;
doubtless the case is plain, it should not be.

I beseech you therefore, let this be received
by you as an unquestionable truth: make no
halt or doubt in the business; shift it not off
with foolish cavils ; but ground it even in the
bottom of your hearts, that without true conversion, there is no hope of salvation.

You have as good proof of it as you can desire of any truth in the world. Yea, besides all
that I have said, it is a thing that in general is
confessed by heathens, and discerned even by
the light of nature. They that will not believe

in Christ, will confess the necessity of repent- ance and reformation, which yet cannot be wrought without faith in Christ. Though I know there is a great deal more necessary to this work, yet I should think I had done something to-day, if you would but all go home resolved without all doubt of the truth of my text: and would never more think that there is any other way to salvation, besides conver- sion. For certainly, if you were once well re- solved, that you must every man of you be con- verted, or condemned, you would look a little better about you than most do. At least this would destroy your false hopes and presump- tion, and make you see what is yet to be done, and would much help to prepare you for a further work. And that none of you may say another day, that you never heard or knew the truth, I do here solemnly proclaim it to you all in the name of Christ, that there is no hope of salvation without true conversion. And I have fully proved it to you from the word of God. So that, if ever a man or woman that is here before the Lord this day, shall yet dare to live in an unconverted state, you are left without a cloak for your sin: you shall not be able to tell the Lord at judg- ment, that you never heard or knew so much. If he ask any of you at that day, how it came to pass that you turned not to God, nor sought after converting grace, and how you could ever think to look God in the face without conversion: you shall not be able to say 'we lived under a minister that never told us of it; we thought we might have done well enough without it, and some particular repentance might have served the turn.' The truth hath shone this day in your eyes: you have heard what Christ saith, and what his apostles say, and what is the drift of all the scripture. If yet you will believe that a man may be saved without conversion, it is your wil- ful obstinacy and unbelief that makes you think it: you must wink hard, and draw the curtains of carnal security about your ears: if in the midst of this day-light you will sleep as in the night of former darkness.

SECTION II.

ALL BY NATURE NEED CONVERSION.

But it may be asked are there not many in the world that need no conversion, even from their infancy? Doth not God regenerate men by baptism, or at least before: which baptism seal- eth, or at least by Christian education in their infancy? And what need have these of after- conversion? To this I shall answer briefly, but plainly, in these propositions following, namely, No doubt but God doth pardon original sin to multitudes of infants by the blood of Christ, through the covenant of grace, which is made to the faithful, and to their seed. And being thus pardoned, they may be truly said to be new creatures, or regenerate relatively: holy educa- tion of parents may be a means through God's blessing, of actually converting those that were before but partially changed, yea, and of those that were not. And if parents did their duty first in a believing dedication of their children to God by baptism, and then in a careful bring- ing them up in his fear: it is most certain, that this would be the most ordinary age and sea- son of regeneration and sanctification to life. For God would not be wanting to his own ordinances used in faith by his own people. He did not appoint them in vain; neither hath he given them a precept without a promise. If any one did re- ceive the seed of true grace in their infancy, it will certainly appear in a holy life even from their infancy upwards. And therefore there is the same work done in the hearts of such as were converted in infancy, and after were brought up in the fear of God, as I have before described to you in the truly converted. If any man did but live one year, month or week of his childhood after he had the use of reason, in a state utterly graceless, that man hath no reason to take the least comfort now to himself, upon any conceit that he was regenerated in his infancy. If he have from his childhood unfeignedly loved God above all, and been heavenly minded, if he has hated sin, and delighted in all holiness, feared God and repented of all known sin, laboured to sub- due it, and had the rest of the marks of grace in his heart, then he may be sure that he was sanctified betime. But if any man have lived to the world or the flesh but one month, since his infant state, never minding the life to come, nor loving the holy ways of God, nor hating ini- quity, he may be sure that he must have another conversion, than any he had in his infancy, or it will not serve his turn for heaven. An infant- conversion may serve for an infant state of sal- vation: but he that hath after that, lived to sin, must have an actual conversion, as he was actu- ally a sinner. And if he had grace in infancy, he must have the same working of it toward God and heaven, which in the work of conver- sion I described before. So that I do not call you to judge of your state by the time or manner of your change, so much as by the matter or thing itself: Find all that work upon your judgments, heart and life, which I have before laid down, and be sure it is there, and then whensoever you come by it, you are happy. But if it be not now there, it is a silly delusion, to glory in the conceits of an infant-baptismal change. Yet I doubt not but there is many a true Christian, who hath received this grace so early, that they have the greater cause to be for ever thankful for it to God.

So much for the confirmation of the point: that certainly this work of conversion is necessary to all that will be saved. One time or other the image of God must be imprinted on the heart, and in those that age expressed in the life.

SECTION III.

REASONS WHICH RENDER CONVERSION REQUISITE.

I am next, according to the method propounded, to give you the reasons of it. Why a man cannot enter into the kingdom of heaven except he be converted. The case is so clear, that we may easily see reason for it, if we be willing to see.

1. If there were no other reason apparent to us but the word of God, one would think it might satisfy such as we. Heaven is his own, and he may give it to whom he will, and he hath told us in his word that he will give it to no other, and should not that suffice us? May not he do with his own as he listeth? It is his hand that must set on the crown; and may not he set it on what head he please? We are sure of these two things. First, that God hath full power to dispose of it, and therefore can do no wrong to others by denying it. Second, that he is infinitely wise, good, and just, and therefore it must needs be the wisest and best way that he takes, though such sinners as we, could not see the wisdom, the goodness, or the justice of it. Do you grudge at this doctrine, that none shall be saved but those that are converted? Why, then you grudge at God. And do you think indeed that he knows not what he doeth? Are you wiser than he? Or are you more righteous than he? What! Must the God of heaven come down to you to learn wisdom, justice, or mercy? Will you question him at the bar of judgment, and ask him why he doth so? Will you charge him with injustice, or unmercifulness? And say, Lord, why art thou so unmerciful as to condemn all the unconverted? O poor fools! for so I dare call you, that dare so far presume. How easily will God answer you, and justify his wisdom, his justice, and his mercy? It is a fine world, when the Creator must be judged at the bar of a silly creature!

I tell you my religion, and my resolution. I believe all that God saith to be true, though the matter were never so much beyond my reach: and of this I am so confident, that I will venture my soul upon it. I have looked up and down to see if there be any better or more sure grounds for a wise man to venture his happiness upon, and I can find no better: nay, I am sure there is no better. If any man have found any better, let him take it, and make his boast of the gain when he hath it. For my part, I will take God's word, and I will trust my soul and hopes on this, and I will look for satisfaction of all my doubts and scruples, when I come to possess the promised felicity. And I am sure I can lose nothing, or no great matter by this resolution. For sure I am, that all other happiness is a shadow and delusion; and all other foundations are sandy, and will deceive. If God tell me in his word, that no man shall be saved except he be converted; I will take his word, and let them look well to their standing that refuse it. I will set this word of God against all the reasons in the world that you can bring. Well, you say it is a hard saying, that so few should be saved: will you say you cannot believe that God will deal so hardly? Against all these vain cavils I set the word of God. God hath said it, and will he not do it!

2. Well, but if we must needs go further to reasoning the case with you, and God's word will not satisfy you, I will proceed to show you some nearer reasons from the nature of the thing. And the first of these reasons shall be from the nature of God's government, and the state of men in this present life. We are set here as in the way to a further end: God never intended that this should be our home, nor that we should have the victory without a combat, nor the crown without the victory. God never meant that we should have the wages of his glory, how free soever, without a faithful performing of our work: at least the work of unfeigned repentance and conversion: would you have God reward men for serving the devil? Or to say at the last day, 'Come, sinner, thou hast lived to the devil all thy life, and set thy heart on the world, and abused or despised me and my grace, enter now into the promised glory.' Why, sinners, if self-love did not blind you, and make fools of you;

you could tell that this were a sentence unfit for the most wise and righteous God. What! must he reward the devil's servants? Shall not the Judge of all the world do righteously? And what is righteousness, but to give every man his due? And is not punishment naturally due to the disobedient? Especially when they have refused, or lightly valued a pardon? The case is plain. A wise and righteous governor, let him be never so merciful, must make a difference between the righteous and the wicked: and therefore God will so do. 'A righteous judge must pass sentence according to the law. Tell me! would you think well of that governor, that should let men rob you, beat you, or violently take possession of your house or land and never punish him? And will you think that God will suffer infinitely greater injury at your hands? Would you like such a law, that shall bid all men steal, kill, and spare not, for the judge will not be so cruel as to hang or punish them? I think you would say, this were but a foolish and unmerciful judge, that pretends thus to be merciful: do not then for shame impute this folly and unrighteousness to God.

If he should not have made righteous laws, which threaten punishment to sin, for the restraining of it; how should the world be governed? And if he should make laws, and never execute them, how should he be wise and righteous? He is not so weak as to be put to govern the world by mere deceit. It belongs to a righteous governor, to see that it go well with the good, and ill with the bad. And I think if God should deal so well with the worst as with the best, your own reason would be ready to question it. Why, what can he do more to the best, than to save them in his glory? for what more are they capable of? And should he do this also to the worst? Surely, if he must shut them out of glory, they must needs be in misery. For if there were no more, but to look towards the happiness which they so lost, and see Lazarus in Abraham's bosom, and the righteous whom they derided, possessing that glory which they valued not, it must needs fill their minds with anguish and vexation; and their own consciences would torment them for ever. Well! you see then some reason why the unconverted should not enter into the kingdom of heaven.

3. But further consider this. The holy nature of God will not permit the unclean, and unholy soul in his presence. 'There shall in no wise enter into it any thing that defileth, or whatsoever worketh abomination.—Thou art of purer eyes than to behold evil, and canst not look on iniquity.—For thou art not a God that hath pleasure in wickedness, neither shall evil dwell with thee. The foolish shall not stand in thy sight, thou hatest all the workers of iniquity: the righteous Lord loveth righteousness, but the wicked his soul hateth.—Therefore the ungodly shall not stand in judgment, nor sinners in the congregation of the righteous.—For God shall judge the world in righteousness; and minister judgment to the people in uprightness.—And he is known by the judgment which he executes, when the wicked is snared in the work of his own hand: so that the wicked shall be turned into hell, and all the nations that forget God.' What reason would you have more? There is a contradiction between the nature of God and the unconverted. 'What fellowship hath righteousness with unrighteousness, and what communion hath light with darkness?' Therefore it is that God also puts an enmity between the seed of the woman, and of the serpent. And calls his converted people to come out from the impenitent, unbelieving world; not by a schismatical, but by a godly separation. 'For what concord hath Christ with Belial? Or what part hath he that believeth with an infidel? And what agreement hath the temple of God with idols? For ye are the temple of the living God, as God hath said, I will dwell in them, and walk in them, and I will be their God, and they shall be my people. Wherefore come out from among them, and be ye separate, saith the Lord; and touch not the unclean thing, and he will receive you, and be a Father to you.' If God himself could endure communion with the unholy, then he would allow his people to endure it. But because they are his, and must be like him, therefore must they withdraw from such.

Sinners, I pray you judge as you would be judged of. Would you have communion yourselves with that which is against your nature? Why the holy nature of God is infinitely more against unholy sinners, as such, than your nature is against the most venomous creature: and therefore he cannot admit the unconverted into his kingdom. Therefore it is, that he will redeem and sanctify them, and cleanse them from their sin, that they may be presented spotless and unblameable to him by Christ, before they shall come to glory. Believe it, sinners, light and darkness, holiness and unholiness, God and sin, are utterly unreconcilable. If ever God and you must live together in glory, you must become holy as he is holy, that you may be such as he can dwell withal, and delight in: either he must turn unholy like you, or you must turn holy like him.

And which do you think is the more likely to be done? Can you expect that the Sun of righteousness should turn dark to comply with your darkness? Or that the immutable God should lay by his excellency, to suit himself with your vileness? Why, this were for God to cease to be God: for to be an unholy God, is to be an evil God, and this is to be no God. For to be God, is to be the chief good: see then what a fair issue the carnal reasonings, and confident hopes of wicked men have. They hope to be saved without conversion and holiness: and the issue is this—they hope that God will cease to be God, lest they should be damned, and shut out of his kingdom. Do not say I make worse of your reasoning than it is. The case is plain, it is no better.

I appeal to thy own conscience, whether the mind of man can be capable of greater madness. O, what a befooling thing is sin! Is it not more reasonable that thou shouldst cease to be ungodly, than that God should cease his blessed nature? There is some possibility yet that thou mayest cease to be a wilful, impenitent sinner: but there is no possibility that God should cease to be God. Wo to thee, if thou cast thy soul upon such hopes. Should God cease his goodness and blessed perfection, all the world would be confounded, or turn to nothing. Turn therefore, for be sure of it, he will not turn to thee. He hath commanded his servants that they come not one jot nearer the wicked; 'Let them return to thee, but return not thou to them.' And will he then do that which he forbids his servants? Many a sinner hath thought that God is like himself, even of his mind, and thought as lightly of sin as they. But they never found it so in the end: he did by wonderful, incomprehensible condescension become man to save sinners, but he will never become a sinner to save sinners; nor unholy to save the unholy. He took our flesh, and he took our curse, and in that sense became sin for us, who knew no sin: but he will never take to him sin itself. He is yet reconcilable to sinners, but he will never be reconciled to sin. Yet, if thou wilt turn to him, thou mayest be welcome; but never look he should turn like thee.

4. Do you not yet see reason enough why no unconverted sinner should be saved? Why come along with me, and I will show you yet more. God offered them salvation in this life, for the very taking. I may well say upon easy and reasonable terms, when it was no more but accept it, and have it; and they would not. It was propounded to their choice, and they refused it. They might have had Christ, and

pardon, holiness, and happiness, if they would, and they would not: and would you have God to save them whether they will or not? He set life and death before them, and bids them choose life, that they might live. He set before them blessing and cursing, and denounced to them that they should certainly perish if their hearts turned away, and they would not hear. He called heaven and earth to record against them; he sent his Son, his apostles, his ministers to them to entreat them, and in his name to beseech them to turn to him, and to be reconciled. He charged us to be 'instant with them in season, and out of season;' and 'to reprove, rebuke, exhort with all long-suffering and doctrine:' as suitors that would take no denial. He bids us even 'compel them to come in;' and yet they would not come, we could not prevail. Some would make excuses from one thing, and some from another: some had their farms, and some their trades, and some their wives, and all their sins to regard; they could not have leisure and inclination to be converted and fear God: some set light by us and our message: and some did openly oppose it, contradicting the truth and cavilling at it, as if they were wiser than to be converted and saved; as if they had more reason than to come in to God that called them, and accept of his salvation; and therefore even scorned the holy word and way of God that should have saved them. To our heart's grief we must witness it against the faces of thousands of our poor hearers, that this was the true case, and thus things were carried on between God and them: Christ called out to them when he was on earth, even with tears, and bids us do the like with tears now in his stead. 'O that thou hadst known at least in this thy day, the things that belong to thy peace!' but they would not, till they were hid from their eyes, and it was too late. 'How often would I have gathered thee, as an hen gathereth her chickens under her wings, and ye would not.'

Sinners, I beseech you, let not sin befool you, to make you fly in the face of God, instead of returning to him at his call. Can you think that God is unjust or unmerciful that would have given you heaven, and you would not accept of it? If he deny you that in eternity which you would not accept of in time, can you blame him or yourselves? I know what some hearts will be ready to imagine. You will say, 'I was willing to be saved, and therefore this is nothing to me.' But were you willing to take salvation as it was offered? If not, you may as well say plainly, you will have none of it: for you shall have none of it upon any other terms. You would have had mercy by halves and not in whole. You would have picked out that part of salvation which pleased you, and left the rest. God would have saved you from the guilt and power of sin, from hell, and from unholiness, and you would have but one of these, without the other: or would have been saved from hell and all other punishments, but you would not be sanctified and brought near to God, and taken off from this world, and set your hearts on the world to come: and you knew, or might know, that God would not halve and part his salvation: you shall have all, or you shall have none. If you will keep sin, you shall keep the curse with it: if you will keep the serpent, you shall have the sting and venom with it. If you will not take Christ for your Master, as well as your Saviour, and be ruled by him, when his yoke is so easy and his burden so light, never look to find rest to your souls, if you will not be converted, you may as well speak out, and say plainly you will not be saved: for it is all one. He that says he will not eat and drink, may as well say he will not live: and he that will not take physic, may as well say he will not be cured.

If Christ, grace and glory, had never been offered to you, nor you had any means to have brought you to the knowledge of him, then you had had some excuse. As Christ says, 'if I had not come and spoken to them, they had not had sin, but now they have no cloak for their sin.' If we had not in Christ's name entreated you to return, and offered you salvation, you had some excuse. But now, what can you reasonably say? I dare challenge the reason of all the world to answer this one reason, by which God will prove, that the unconverted should be condemned. It is reason that he that would not have heaven upon such reasonable terms as Christ did tender it him, should for ever be shut out. What will you say to this, when God shall question thee, and say, 'what sayest thou, sinner, did not I freely offer thee my grace and salvation?' Do you believe you shall have the face at the day of judgment to tell Christ he is unmerciful if he damn you, when he shall tell you that he would often have gathered you to him, as a hen gathereth her chickens under her wings, and ye would not? Will not that one word stop thy mouth for ever? What, dost thou complain of man? Is it for want of mercy? Why, what more tender mercy wouldst thou have had? 'I would have gathered thee as a hen,' &c. Sinners, I witness to you this day, that God, angels, and men shall judge of you, that if you be thrust into hell, it is because you would not be saved. And it is not because God was cruel to you, but because you were cruel and unmerciful to yourselves. I tell you this will prove true at the last.

5. Finally, if all these reasons do not satisfy you, I will show you more, and such as methinks should satisfy any man on earth, that the unconverted cannot be saved. Even because it is an impossible thing. It is a flat contradiction. Why, conversion is part of salvation here, and the perfection of it is an higher part hereafter. Why, sin is the soul's sickness, wounds, and death; and grace and holiness are its health and life: and were not that a fool, who expects you should make him well, and not remove his sickness and cure his wounds, and never heal or close them; or make a dead man alive, and yet let him be dead still? Why, it is as great a contradiction and impossibility for a man to be saved and not converted. What is it that we must be saved from, but sin and hell? and there is no saving from hell but by saving from sin. 'He shall save his people from their sins.' Do you know what the salvation is that God hath promised us in glory? Why, it is this: that we shall be perfectly freed from all sin, and have the image of his holiness perfected on our souls: that we shall be perfectly in love with God, perfectly beloved of him, live in the sight of his majesty, fill ourselves with the view of his pleased face, and breathe out his praise with the heavenly host for ever. Doth such a heaven as this is please you; or doth it not? If it do not, you must have none; for there is no other, except you will call a pot-house, or other sensual pleasures, your heaven. But if you will have this heaven which God doth offer you, you may easily see that it cannot be had without conversion. Can you be saved from sin, and yet keep it? Can you be perfected in holiness, and yet be unholy? Can you live in the everlasting love of God, and have no true love to him at all? Can you delight in him, and yet have no delight in him, but be weary of him, and delight in your worldly vanities more? Well, sinners, I think I need to say no more. The contradiction is so evident, that you may as well say, 'I will be saved, and I will not,' as to say, 'I will be saved, but not converted.'

But perhaps some vain caviller will say, It is true we cannot be glorified without conversion and holiness, but God might have given us that in another world, though he change us not here. But you do not know that this life is the appointed time of working, running, and fight-

ing for the crown? The life to come is the time
of reward, and of your receiving the prize that
here you run for: would you have God help you
in your race, when you are past it, and your time
is gone? Or, contrary to wisdom and governing
justice, to confound the way and the end; this
life, and that to come? You may with far more
wisdom expect that when you have loitered till
the sun be set, God shall call it back again, at
your desire, that you may have day-light to work
by. He gave thee time, and gave thee warning to
use it while thou hadst it; and told thee this
was the accepted time, 'this was the day of salvation;' and to trifle out this time, and then to
think that God should give thee both grace and
glory in that life where he hath resolved only to
perfect grace in glory, and crown those that have
overcome on earth,—this is such folly in so great
a business, as I desire no friend of mine may be
guilty of.

But it is our ignorance of God that makes us
unholy, you say, and therefore when death hath
opened our eyes, as we shall know him better
so we shall the more love him according to that
knowledge; and so we shall be sanctified: and
God cannot but love those that love him, and
therefore they will be saved.

Still it is not all knowledge of God that will
cause a love to him. If you know him as excellent, and yet as your enemy, and one that
stands resolved perpetually to punish you for
your sin, this will provoke no love to him, but
hatred. The dignity and worth of an enemy
may be some matter of admiration to us, and of
reverence, but not of such love as may tend to
fruition. It is inseparable from your natures to
love yourselves; and therefore you will love
that which you think is for your good, and hate
that which you think is against you, and tends
to your destruction. You will then find that
your damnation was part of God's righteous
government of the world: that the whole work
of government was one inseparable frame, begun
by legislation, and finished by judgment and
execution: and that God will no more break
the frame of government, than he will the frame
of nature, nor so much: for that he may do
when he pleases, though he will do it rarely, but
this his own perfection is against. So that when
you see God as it were obliged for ever to destroy you, you cannot close in love with him, as
your friend or chief good, as those do that enjoy him in the promised glory,

CHAPTER III.

CONFIRMATION AND PRACTICAL APPLICATION OF
THE DOCTRINE OF CONVERSION, AS PREVIOUSLY
STATED.

SECTION I.

THERE IS A KINGDOM TO BE ENTERED INTO
AND OBTAINED.

Having thus cleared the way, by showing you
the meaning and the truth of the point in hand,
I shall next come to the application of it to ourselves. And first, by way of inference, you see
from hence that there is a kingdom of heaven
to be obtained. It were in vain to talk who shall
come thither, and who shall not, if there were no
such thing to be had. Doubt not, Christian, thou
hast the word of the God of heaven for it.
Challenge the tempter, if he would draw thee
to doubting, to prove that ever the God of this
word deceived any. If he would tempt thee to
question, whether it be his word or not: show
him upon it his image and superscription, with
the seal of his manifold, uncontrolled miracles.
And ask him what better evidence mortals can
expect, unless they would have God, who cannot
be seen, to walk among them, and speak to every
particular man. O, that thou wouldst be true to
God and thyself, and then thou shalt find God
will be true to thee. As sure as there is an earth
for thee to tread on, and as sure as there is a sun
whose light thou seest, so sure is there an heavenly, everlasting glory, for every converted,
persevering soul. There can be no better ground
of assurance than the word of God. I know
that man, while he is in this flesh, is strange to
things beyond his sense, and hath a natural desire to have his senses themselves to be the inlets of his knowledge; and therefore he is apt
to think that either he is uncertain of all that he
sees not, (unless he hath seen the like that may
help him to understand it;) or else that his knowledge of it is as no knowledge: but this is a
weakness unworthy of a man.

What if you had never seen any large and populous city, and should hear the glory of it described by others; would you think it uncertain that
there is such a place because you have not seen
it? Nay further, you have not seen your souls:
do you think it therefore uncertain whether you
have a soul or not? A man that is born blind
did never see the sun, and yet he will not doubt
whether there be a sun, when all the world
about tells him so: and shall not the word of
God be taken as soon as the word of a man?

You never saw God himself, and yet it is the grossest error in the world to think that there is no God, when we see every hour the works that he hath made, and which we know, could none of them make themselves: you see that which assures you of the things that are unseen. You see the word of God: you see his works and daily providences; you see a divine testimony, the sufficient ground of your belief. Noah did not see the flood, when he laboured so many years in making the ark. But though the unbelieving world might deride him in the beginning, at last the flood came and did convince them. ' By faith Noah being warned of God, of things not seen as yet, moved with fear, prepared an ark, to the saving of his house, by the which he condemned the world, and became heir of the righteousness, which is by faith.' If the devil could once make you stagger at the truth of the promise, and make you doubt whether there be a heaven and a hell, because you see them not; he might then delude you with the vanities which you do see. But when you believe it upon God's word as verily as if you saw it, then you will be likely to be Christians indeed. Therefore the apostle brings such proof of the doctrine of the resurrection, and when he hath done, he builds this exhortation upon it—' Wherefore, my beloved brethren, be stedfast, unmoveable, always abounding in the work of the Lord, for as much as you know your labour is not in vain in the Lord.'

SECTION II.

THE IMPORTANCE OF EXAMINING WHETHER WE ARE THE SUBJECTS OF CONVERSION.

Having gone thus far with you, and showed you that there is a kingdom of heaven; and that certainly none but the converted shall enter it: my next business is, to come nearer your hearts, and to inquire of, and beseech you to inquire of yourselves, whether you are the converted heirs of this kingdom, or not? You hear from the mouth of Christ himself how the case stands. He that spoke this will be your judge, and according to this word it is that he will judge you. Believe you not this? I hope you do believe it. Methinks now I should need to say no more to reasonable men, to warn them presently to enter into their own consciences, and try, and try again whether they are converted. But because that this is so necessary a work, I will tell you some of those reasons that should move you presently

to set upon this trial: and show you how desirable it is to be well resolved in this point. For I know that the devil will be such an enemy to it, and the heart so backward to it, that all we can say is likely to be too little to bring the most of men but to a faithful examination of their own souls.

1. The first reason that moves me to intreat you to try yourselves, is the weight of the business in hand. A wise man may put a small thing to a venture, but he will not venture all his estate, or liberty, or life, if he can help it. How much less should a wise man venture his soul? Great things and eternal things should be made as sure of as we can. For a man to be in endless happiness, or misery, is a matter that should not have one cold, or dull and careless thought: Much less should it be ordinarily, or wholly made light of. I profess to you, brethren, I wonder how you can so little regard the assurance of your conversion and salvation, as most of the world doth! As if hell were grown sufferable, or heaven grown of smaller value, and the glory of it did begin to fade. For, a man that is no heathen, but believes that a departing soul goes somewhere, either to heaven or hell, methinks he should be willing to know whither it should go before it is gone. For, when it is once gone, it is past recalling. Methinks, as long as you are in much doubting of your salvation, this one thought should often be running in your mind,— What if I should not be converted or saved; what a case were I then continually to be in? Your hearts, it is likely, cherish hopes that you are converted, and all shall be well enough with you when you die: But what if it should prove otherwise? Methinks this one thought should even amaze you, while you are in that estate,— For all my hopes, what if I should perish? O what wise man would put his everlasting salvation or damnation to the venture, if he could possibly get it out of doubt! Therefore I beseech you, for the Lord's sake, get alone again and again, and put this question to your own consciences, ' How can I tell that I am truly converted?' And if you are ready to say, I hope it is so, when you have nothing for these hopes, but because you would have it so: call to your consciences for the proof of what they say: and do not take your own bare words. It is proof that must carry it, and not merely saying that you are converted. Ask therefore conscience, how canst thou prove it? What canst thou show that will evidence a conversion, more than unsanctified persons may show? And I pray you, see that you be not put off too easily,

and take not every gloss for evidence : but in a matter of such consequence, see that you deal faithfully, and go to the very quick: alas, almost all the comfort of your lives lies upon it : even your everlasting salvation lies upon it, which is much more.

2. Another reason which makes me the more earnestly desire that you would try whether you are a true convert, or not, is, because all men by nature are children of wrath and need conversion, and the greatest part of the world live and die in their natural state, and never come to be truly converted. Seeing, therefore, that it is a thing that every one must have that will be saved, and yet most men go without it, and therefore are damned, should it not waken you to examine whether you are of the number of those that are converted, yea or nay ? If it were a needless thing that might be spared without your undoing; or if it were a thing that every body has, or that almost all, or most have, you might be the more secure ; but it is not so. What need we more proof than God's express word ? 'The gate is strait, and the way narrow, and few there be that find it.' And common experience seconds this word of God. Do you see that most men are converted, and such as I before described to you ? O that it were so. But we shall speak more of this toward the end. Will any man that hath not lost his senses, now stand cavilling and quarrelling that so few should be saved, instead of making sure of his own salvation ? The reason that there is so few, is because they will not be saved upon God's terms. And if you will take their course, and quarrel with the gracious word and ways of God, instead of submitting to them, you will speed as they, and be carried down the stream for company. But those that care for their souls, will take warning by other men's miscarriages, and be awakened to make sure.

3. Another reason that should move you to examine whether you be indeed converted or not, is because the want of this is one of the greatest causes why so few come to be converted, and to be saved. Nothing doth more keep a man from turning back again, when he hath lost his way, than when he doth not know that he has lost it: and how can he know, that wanders in the night, and will not inquire and ask the way, or that is so wilful and self-conceited, that he will not believe any man that tells him he hath lost his way. As long as he is of this mind, he will never turn again. So it is with most of the careless world : they are going into the way of worldliness or vain glory, and live to

the flesh, which is quite contrary to the way to heaven, and yet they will not once seriously ask a minister, or ask any one that can inform them, whether that be the way or not ? Or whether they shall ever come to heaven in that way ? But they press on after their fleshly business, as if they had no tongue in their heads ; or as if it were not worth the asking, to know, whether they are in the way to heaven or hell. Surely, if men will not so much as inquire or consider with themselves, and examine their way by the word of God, to see whether they are right or wrong, they are never like to be saved. If you that never had this great cure done upon your souls did but know so much, you would not rest sure till it were done. You could not lie down quietly, nor rise quietly : you could not eat or drink, or sleep quietly. Tell me, either a man or woman of you, could you be quiet if you were sure that you were yet unconverted, and in a state, that if death should find you in, you must be damned? If you knew this by yourselves, how could you choose but get presently to God on your knees in secret, and cry out, Help, Lord, or I am everlastingly undone. O forgive me, and change my heart and life, or else I am a lost man and woman for ever. How could you choose, if you knew yourselves unconverted, but follow God with your prayers day and night till he had changed your hearts. You could not sit at home, but you would go to the ministers, and to experienced Christians, and ask them for some help, and advice for your salvation. But when men think all is well with them, who can expect that they should put themselves to so much trouble ; or seek much to God or man for cure, or make any great matter of the greatest misery ? I do not fear any one thing more to make me lose all this labour, and leave many of you after all this, unconverted, than this conceit that you are already converted, when you are not. This is it that is most like to hinder our work, and to undo your souls. And therefore, for the Lord's sake, deny me not this one request, to take a little pains to try whether you are converted. 'For if any man think he is something, when he is nothing, he deceiveth himself.'

4. Another reason that should make you never rest till you know that you are converted, is, because of the many and great benefits that the true knowledge of this one thing would afford you. For the truly converted, holding on to death, shall certainly be saved. If you had but this assurance once, you might live quietly, and abound with comforts! You might lie down,

and nothing make you afraid: you might rejoice in the mercies of the Lord, as the tokens of his love ; and bear his rod with greater peace, as being the chastisement of a Father. Had you but this assurance once, you might hear and read the word with comfort : and when you come to the promises, say, ' these are mine:' you might secretly and publicly pray with comfort, and have access with boldness to the throne of grace : you might run to God when any thing ails you, and call him your Father in confidence of his acceptance : you might gladly feast with the saints in the holy communion of the church : you might cheerfully sing God's praises, and glory in the thoughts of his great salvation. And when you are dying, you might look to heaven as your home, and long to be dissolved and to be with Christ, and might joyfully let go your departing souls, and say as Christ, ' Father, into thy hand I commend my spirit.' What a blessed life is this, when a man can look upon every thing with comfort ! If he look on the godly, he can say, they are my brethren ; if on the wicked, he can say, I am delivered from their sad estate. If he look on any of the mercies which he possesses, he can say, they are the fruits of the blood of Christ, and the tokens of his Father's love. If on his poverty, or want, he can say, my greater wants are supplied, and these prepare for the ever-during riches. If he look on the law, he can say, it hath nothing against him, because he hath pardon through him that hath borne the curse. If on the gospel, he can rejoice in it as the glad tidings of his salvation : if he look on the threatenings, he can say, it reacheth not to a pardoned sinner ; if on the promise, he can say, it is my charter for heaven. If he look upward to heaven, he can say, it is my own inheritance, thither I am going, and there I shall shortly be. If he look downward, toward the place of torments, he can say, from thence did grace deliver me. If there were any terror to a man's soul, it would be in sin, Satan, death, and hell, but none of these are matter of terror to him. Not sin, for it is pardoned, mortified in part, and will be perfectly so ere long : not Satan, for he is conquered and cast out of his possession ; not death, for it hath lost its sting, and is become the passage into everlasting life : not hell, for it will be our perpetual joy to see that we are delivered from such everlasting torments. In a word, because he can say, God is my Father, Christ is my Saviour and my head, the Holy Ghost is my sanctifier.' Therefore he can say, ' all is mine, as I am Christ's, and Christ is God's.' O my hearers, what

would you give ; nay, what would you not give, to be presently put into such a condition ? Had you not rather than all the world now, that you were sure that you are converted, and in this state of life ? Surely, if you are well in your wits, you had. Who would care what becomes of the world, if he were once sure of heaven ; or what becomes of his corruptible flesh, if he were sure it should go well with his soul ; and that flesh itself should rise again to glory. O what a terrible thing it is, for a soul to go out of the body, and not know whither ! And how much more to depart under the curse of God,—from the damnation of the law to the condemnation of the judge. But how blessed is it, to remove from the state of a frail and sinful man, to live with Christ,—to be equal with the angels.

What say you now, beloved hearers ? Is there not weight enough in these reasons to persuade you to try whether you are converted or not? Dare you say there is not? If you dare not, you are witnesses yourselves that you are convinced. You see it is your duty: or see it is necessary for your own good. Your labour will be small in comparison of the profit : the loss will be nothing ; the advantage gained may be unspeakable. Shall I then, as your minister, beseech you presently to fall to this work ? As a messenger of Christ shall I entreat it of you ? As a friend to your souls shall I entreat it of you ? It is for yourselves : it is no unreasonable matter you see, that I ask of you. Conscience shall witness one day to the face of refusers, that it was not unreasonable. My hearers, I pray you, for the Lord's sake, and for your souls' sake, do not deny it me. I profess, in the presence of the Lord, I had rather you would grant me this small request, than give me all you have in the world : even that you would but make it your business to try, and thoroughly try, whether you are yet converted, or not ? But then, let me entreat you to do it seriously, and make somewhat of it, and leave not till you have done your best to be resolved whether it be so with you or not ? You do not need to ask me what causes me to be so earnest with you for such a thing. You have heard by the foregoing reasons what causes me. You may see here in my text what causes me. When Christ himself saith, ' except you be converted, and become as little children, ye cannot enter into the kingdom of heaven.' This is the thing then that I entreat you to do : that you would betake yourselves, at your next opportunity, without delay into some private place, and there bethink yourselves what you have heard: or at least what is said here in my text: and say thus with yourselves, 'I see there is no hope of salvation without conversion; my heart must be turned from the world, the flesh, and sin, to God by Christ, or else I cannot enter into heaven: I know I shall shortly leave this life: doth it not concern me then to see by times that I be converted? Was ever such a change as this wrought in my heart, or not? There is no dissembling with God, he will not be mocked. What sayest thou conscience? Have I ever had such a change, or not? Thus follow on the inquiry, and leave it not till you can say, whether you have been converted, or not; or at least till you have some more light into the business than you had before: and if you cannot do it at one time, as it is likely you cannot fully, go do it again and again: think on it as you lie in bed: think on it when you are alone, and say to yourselves, seeing I must be converted, or condemned, is it not time for me to know whether it be so with me, or not?'

And if you cannot get the case well resolved, let me entreat one thing more, which I have often entreated of you,—that you would come to one of us that are your teachers, or go to some judicious, able Christian, and ask advice to help you in the trial: for in so great a business it is dangerous to be mistaken. I do not speak all this to those Christians that have lived long in the fear of God, and have doubts raised in their minds by the temptations of the enemy, or by their own great care of the matter of their salvation, and have asked help of ministers, taken pains, and done what lies in them to be resolved, and yet find some doubts remaining. It is not these to whom I now speak. Though I would not grudge my labour to these whensoever I can have time for it, to do them any good I could, yet I would rather advise them to acknowledge the light of grace that shines in their eyes, and not forget their own experiences, nor make light of the abundance of that mercy which hath translated them from darkness into the kingdom of Christ, and feed upon that glory which is propounded to their faith. But I speak to those that either never did yet set to the work of examination; or never followed it till they discerned their miserable state; or at least not till they got out of it, but are still clinging to the world and flesh: and also to those young, unsettled Christians that be not yet well resolved for a change; or at least those that never yet had the advice of any minister, or judicious person, for the right settling of their spiritual estate: for all these, but especially for those that never

set upon examination before, I would entreat them, if they find themselves in the dark, and cannot well manage it themselves, nor can find whether they are converted or not, that they would come to us and seek advice. I pray you, my hearers, do not think that we are either so stubborn, or so careless of your souls, as to despise you, or to think it much to take this pains with you. The poorest beggar shall be welcome to us, that will come to us on this errand. Indeed, ministers are set in every church, as the physician is in the town, for all that are in distress, to resort to for advice, that their diseases may not prove their death. It is not only to preach to you that we are made ministers, but especially to give advice and direction for their salvation to all that have special need, and come to us. Indeed for small matters you should no more trouble a minister, than you should trouble a physician for a cut finger, because you have others enough at hand to give you advice: if all the people of England would use their ministers to this kind of employment, it would be happier for their souls, and happy for the nation, and would make men know better the nature and need of the office of the ministry.

We do not desire you to come to us as the popish priests make all their people do, to confess every secret sin that they have committed in the Lent, before they receive the sacrament at Easter: but when you hear out the word of God, that no man can be saved except he be converted, and you set yourselves to try whether you are converted or not, and cannot find it out: here your salvation lies much on the business, and therefore common reason tells you that you should take the best advice you can, and that presently, without delay. And so you may be much better resolved, and your minds more quieted, and you may go upon surer grounds for your salvation than perhaps you would otherwise do. There is never an honest minister in England, but would be willing to forbear his meat, or sleep, as far as nature would bear, to help his people in such straits as these: when they come to us and tell us, 'I have taken some pains to try whether I am converted truly, or not, and I am not able to discern: I know it is your office to help me, I pray you help to resolve my doubt, for I am resolved I will not venture my soul so carelessly as I have done till now.' You do not know what good you might get, if you would but take this course to be resolved: for God will bless his own ordinances. I pray you therefore let no carelessness or bashfulness hinder you; for matters of salvation are not such things that you should either be careless or ashamed of : however say not but we offered you our help.

But perhaps you will ask me, when I am examining my conscience, how shall you know whether I am converted or not; by what marks may it be discerned? To this I answer; I have so often given you divers marks already in the sermons I have preached, and the books that I have written for your use, that I am loth to do the same thing over again. But for this time it may suffice, if you will but remember that description of the work of conversion which I gave you before. For in that are all the marks that are necessary.

When you are examining your own hearts, inquire then: 1. Whether you ever found that change upon your mind that I before mentioned. Are you soundly persuaded of the truth of the word of God and the life to come, and do you know and believe how vile a thing sin is? And what need you have of Christ, and what he hath done for you, and offers to do? And do you esteem the love of God, and the hopes of salvation, above all things in this world, and account of all but as dung, that you may win Christ: are you fully persuaded of the riches of free grace and of the necessity of a holy life, how much soever you may have slighted them heretofore?

2. And have your hearts been so far changed hereupon, as that you have laid up your treasure and hopes in the life to come, and that is it that you take for your felicity: so that you can truly say, that the main bent and drift of your life is, not for the pleasure or profits of the world, but how to please God and be happy for ever? Though you may step out of the way by human infirmity, yet this is the bent and scope of your life : this is your chief care, and this hath your most serious thoughts and business. Can you truly say you use the world for God and for heaven, and do not serve God for the world ; that you take all these outward things but as necessaries in your journey, and look at heaven as your home and happiness ; that God hath the highest room in your hearts, and the world and flesh stand under him ; that you do not prefer these things before him ; that you are resolved, whatsoever it cost you, to adhere to God, though you lose the world, and resolved not to cleave to it, when it forfeits to you the favour of God ; that God shall be first served, and the world shall have his refuse ; and not the world first served, and God have its dregs? Have you tasted of the infinite love which he hath manifested for your salvation in the blood of his Son, and admired that free grace that hath thus purchased your redemption? Have you fled to Christ, as the only refuge of a guilty soul, from the curse of the law, and the wrath of God, renouncing all conceits of any merit, or legal righteousness of your own, taking Christ and his merits for your righteousness? Do you find that you hate the former sins that you loved, and take pleasure in those holy ways that you had no pleasure in before, and are you resolved thus to hold on to the death?

3. Is all this to be seen in your life? Have you in good earnest changed your former courses, and resolved to turn to them no more? Have you left your old ungodly company further than your calling, or necessity, or charity requires you to be with them? And have you betaken yourselves into the company of those that fear God, and take pleasure in their holy communion, and in their help and company in the way to heaven? Especially, do you avoid those great transgressions, by which you were carried away in your ignorance? And are you willing to destroy the remnants of your sin, whatsoever it cost you, and not to spare, or cherish, or befriend it? So that there is no known sin that you wilfully live in, nor no known duty that you wilfully cast off; but you would gladly be what God would have you be, and your greatest sorrow is that you can be no better. And if you fall by any temptation, you rise again with shame and grief, and free confession, and renew your resolution by the grace of God, to take better heed for the time to come.

This is the sum of the work of conversion, and this is the state of a gracious soul. I have left out several particulars, lest I should be too tedious, because you may see them together before you ; but the rest are implied in these.

When you go then to examine your hearts, set these few questions before you, and put them to your hearts, or else peruse those marks that I have given you in my Saints' Rest. You do not need to be at a loss for marks to try yourselves by, books will help you, or ministers will help you, or friends will help you. But all the difficulty is in two things. First, To get your heart to the work. Second, To be able to know your own hearts. For they are so dark and deceitful, that without a special light and diligence, you may easily be mistaken in yourselves.

Well, brethren, I again renew my request to you, that seeing you must be converted, or condemned, will you set yourselves to try whether you are converted, or not? I hope you be not willing to be deceived; and I hope you do not think that salvation is not worth this much labour. I should hope that I might request as much as this from you. If it were for myself, or a friend, how much more when it is for your salvation. Tell me, therefore, will you do this much at my request, at Christ's request, yea, and at his command; or will you not? Will you bestow now and then a secret hour about it, and follow it on till you get resolution, and know whether you are converted, or not? Truly, neighbours, I do not speak these words to you carelessly, or customarily, as matters that I shall never look after when I am out of the pulpit; or as if I cared not whether you ever more minded them, or not. But it is the matter of practice that I regard: whether you will do the thing that I am desiring of you. I am loth you should spend another day in a state of condemnation, and not know it. I am loth you should spend another day in negligent uncertainty of your everlasting state. If you are converted, I would fain have you know it; if I could procure it, I would have you surely to go to heaven when you die, before you pass another week, or before you go this night to bed. And if you are not yet converted, I would fain have you know it, that you may lay to heart your condition, and without any more delay, may make out for the grace of Christ that must recover you. I pray you, do not think that it is utter despair that I am driving you to. If you should upon trial find that you are unconverted, you need not despair, and say, 'there is no hope:' no, but you must know that there is mercy before you. Christ hath prepared it for you, and offers it to you, and is willing you should have part in it if you be willing. Only you must consent to be changed now at last, and resolve to go no further in the old way. It is conversion, and not desperation, that God requires. And I hope a man may seek after his error to amend it, rather than to despair of the amendment. What if upon examination you should perceive that till this hour you have been in a state of death; it doth not follow that you must live and die so; but that you must make haste to get out of it, which you will hardly ever do, till you find that you are in it. It were a foolish traveller that will say, I will not ask the way, lest I find that I have missed it, and then I have no hope of getting home: but rather he should ask the way, that if he have missed it, he may know it, and get in the right way before it be night. And because it is my present business, rather to convince the unconverted for their recovery, than the converted for their comfort, I shall here tell you for the negative, who they be that are yet unconverted, and must be changed, if ever they will be saved.

SECTION III.

EVIDENCES OF A PERSON IN AN UNCONVERTED STATE.

1. That man or woman who never yet perceived and felt that sin is a great and detestable evil, deserving the wrath of God, and that never felt what need they stand in of the pardon of sin, by the blood of the Lord Jesus; nor was ever humbled in the apprehension of his unworthy dealing with God, but can bear his sin as a tolerable burthen, is yet unconverted; and without conversion cannot be saved.

2. That man or woman who was never driven to Christ for deliverance, nor beaten out of the conceits of merit or sufficiency in himself: nor brought to admire the glorious design of God in the great work of redemption; nor savoured the sweetness of the glad tidings of salvation, which are brought to distressed sinners in the gospel, so that his heart was never warmed with the sense of the Redeemer's love and blood, but hears and reads the gospel as a common story: or as if it were not he that was thus redeemed; is yet unconverted, whatsoever he may seem.

3. That person who hath not his heart and hopes in heaven, and looks not at that as his only happiness, and doth not make it the business of his life to attain it; but sets his heart more upon the things of this life, is certainly unconverted, whatever he may pretend.

4. That person who is not weary of all known sin, and hates it not, and would not be rid of it with all his heart, and is not willing to be at the labour or cost of duty, in the use of those means which God hath required for the obtaining of a conquest: but will venture his soul upon a careless life, rather than be brought to diligent godliness, and takes up godliness in part upon mere necessity, having rather let it alone if he durst; and takes it for a grievous thing to be hindered from his sin: that person is not as yet converted, but must have a further change before he can be brought into a state of life.

5. That person who doth not set himself to the duties of holiness, to God, righteousness, and mercy toward man; who hath not the Spirit of Christ within him, and the image of God upon him; who doth not express it in his worship and

obedience, and is not loving, compassionate and merciful to others, nor humble and low in his own eyes, nor delights in doing good, nor is willing to do as he would be done by; I say that person is not yet truly converted, whatsoever appearance of conversion he may have; but must yet be otherwise converted, or be condemned.

6. That man or woman who hath any thing in this world that is so dear to them that they cannot spare it and part with it for Christ, and obedience to his command, but will rather venture their souls upon his threatenings, and will only take up so much of religion as may stand with their worldly prosperity, of seeming felicity, and are not resolved, by strength of grace, rather to let go all than Christ. I say, that person is yet unconverted, and must have a further change or be condemned.

Now the Lord have mercy on poor sinners; what a world of them are yet in the state of death! How little do they believe it, or lay it to heart! I wonder what men think of such words in scripture when they meet with them. Surely they cannot choose but consider that they concern them as well as others: and if no man can be saved without conversion, they must needs know they cannot. What then do these men think of themselves? Do they think that they are converted, or that they are not? If they think they are not, then surely they durst not rest till they are. For I do not think they are willing to be damned. It must needs be, therefore, that they think they are converted, when they are not; and that is the thing that deceives and quiets them in their misery. But it is worth inquiry to find out what it is that so deceives men, that the grossest worldling, or the vilest sensualist, are yet persuaded that they are converted, gracious men: and I find among others these three things are the cause. First, They do not know what conversion is, but take that to be true conversion, which is no such thing. Second, They do not know themselves, but take themselves to have what they have not; and do what they do not, and be what they are not. And Third, They are resolved to believe what they would have to be true, be it ever so false; and therefore will rather think they are well already, than they will be at the trouble to know that it is otherwise, and to use the means for a thorough discovery.

_____

SECTION IV.

THE GRIEF WHICH UNCONVERTED SOULS OCCASION TO GODLY MINISTERS.

By the foregoing inquiry, we have certainly found, that conversion is too strange a thing in the world, and that the greatest part of the world, yea, of those that are called by the preaching of the gospel, are yet unconverted. The consideration of this must needs be a grief to the heart of every faithful minister, that knows the misery of an unconverted man and foresees his latter end. It will be a grief to any honest physician, if he have a whole hospital of sick persons under cure, to see that the most of their diseases are mortal, and to find but few recovered by the greatest skill and care that he can use: how much more must the everlasting danger of men's souls be grievous to those that are appointed to watch over them? Would the Lord but cause you to know your own misery, as we know it, and to compassionate yourselves as we must compassionate you, we should have the more hope of your recovery. Will you now join with us in lamenting your own condition, and lay to heart what a case it is to be unconverted? Truly, humanity, and much more Christianity, doth bind us to think on your condition with lamentation. Should we see an enemy, should we see an animal in torment, and have no compassion? How much less so many men and women that are so near us, and so dear to us in the flesh. Alas, that there is such a glory, and most men will miss of it. That there is such a fire prepared for the devil and his angels, and the most will run themselves wilfully into it! Why, faith makes absent things as if they were present. That which will be so one of these days, I look on it as if it were even so already. O! methinks I see the thousands of the unconverted, departing from the face of an angry judge, who hath newly shut them up under his final sentence, ' depart ye cursed into everlasting fire.'

If you ask me, why I tell you of such sad things? Truly, brethren, it is because they are much more sad to suffer than to hear of; and because you are yet alive in a possibility of preventing them. If you marvel that I should believe such things, when no man sees them; it is because I am a Christian. And if you believe them not as well as I, you would do well to say so plainly, and do not dissemble any longer, and presume to be Christians, when you are not: and to believe God's word, when you do not. I profess to you, I should take it but for a paltry profession, to ride up and down to preach the gospel, and trouble the minds of men in vain, and get the ill will of most of our neighbours, and tire and spend ourselves in this work, if it were not certainly true, which we must tell them: and if the gospel were a fable or human device. If the word of God were not true, ministers have the most unworthy employment upon earth. But if it be true, as nothing is more certain, O Lord, what hard hearts then have we, that we are no more affected with your condition! And what hearts have you, that are no more affected with your own! The Lord knows, if I were not confident that this word is true, that tells us of the danger of all that are unconverted, I would not have been here to-day; nay, I would shut up my books, and take another employment in hand, and never preach more. But shall a man that knows the unconverted will be condemned, forbear to tell them of the misery that is near them? Then were our case more sinful than yours, for you know it not, and therefore love not to hear of it. I believe it, and know it, and yet should I silence it? I know it is unpleasant doctrine, but it is necessary: and it is most true: God never yet did prove a liar: if he were not true, he were not God. You will believe yourselves the things that you see not, upon common experience; and why should not I believe that which I see not, upon a better ground? You do not see the sun at midnight, and yet you believe that it will rise the next morning; because it usually does so. You see no flowers or fruits on the earth in winter, and yet you believe that you shall see them the next year, because they usually come in their seasons. You are now all alive, and see not your graves digged, nor your friends about you, there laying you, and leaving you in darkness to the worms; and yet you know that such a day will come, though now you see it not: as truly do I know that there is endless wo to every sinner that dies unconverted. I see not the flames, nor do I hear the cries of damned souls, but yet I know that there they are, while we sit here, and there they will be to all eternity. It is likely the man in Luke xvi. was a man of quality, that had so bountiful a table, and was clothed so gorgeously every day. Alas, his poor brethren, it is likely, did little think what was become of his soul when they had laid his body in the earth. If a preacher should have told them, he was afraid he was in hell, do you think they would not have been ready to fly in his face, or account him intolerably self-conceited, or precise: and yet the Lord Jesus brings us news that he was

in hell-torment, wishing that one might be sent from the dead, to warn those his poor brethren that he had left behind him on the earth. No doubt, he knew that they were all of the same mind as he was, when he was alive: and as fleshly, worldly, and careless of their salvation, and therefore were in the highway to the same condemnation; or else, if he had known them to be godly, heavenly-minded men, he would never have thought them in such danger, as it seems he did. But we read not that they had any such fears of themselves as he had. If one had come to them from the dead, and told them that their late worshipful brother was in hell for his sin, and knowing them to be all in the way to the same misery, had sent to them to beseech them presently to be converted, lest they also come to that place of torment: what welcome, do you think, would such a messenger have had? I know not well what fear of a dead man appearing to them might have done; but I partly imagine what entertainment a minister should have had, that had said the like. Verily, hearers, the case of careless sinners is never the safer because they see not, and fear not the danger. A man in a consumption or dropsy is not the further from death, though he be never so confident that he shall not die. If a thief at the gallows have a conceit that he shall escape, that will not save his life. What if you should have an hundred men that you had known on earth sent to you from the dead one after another, and all of them should tell you this one sentence in my text, that there is none who enter into heaven but converted souls; would you not begin to look about you, and say to yourselves, am I converted, or not? What a case am I in then, that am yet in the flesh? It may be if one appeared to you in your chamber in the night, and told you this news, it would only affright you a little, and you would forget it. Perhaps, if two or three only should appear to you, and tell you it, you might forget it again; but if twenty should tell it you, methinks it should awaken you. Assuredly, the words of the Lord are of more weight, than the words of a thousand dead men are. 'If you will not believe him, neither will you be persuaded though one rise from the dead.'

Seeing these things are so, I do not blame ministers, if they be plain and earnest with you, though some may think them precise, and beside themselves. Paul was put to make this answer, 'for whether we be beside ourselves, it is to God; or whether we be sober, it is for your cause.' Truly, we are like a physician, that sees a foolish man swallowing arsenic, or mercury, and tells him 'O, what are you doing? It is deadly poison, you must presently take a vomit, or it will kill you. But because it is sweet, the man derides the physician, and bids him look to himself,' hoping he shall do as well as he, till he feel the griping and burning at his heart, and then he will believe it. O, the gripes of a damned man's conscience, when he reflects on the day of grace which he lost on earth! We tell you not of this to drive you to despair, but to persuade you to repentance, and cast away your sins before you are past hope. Do not think we wrong you, by foretelling you what will come of it, if you die unconverted. If there were any wrong in it, it must be laid on God that can do no wrong. If he have not bid us tell you of them, then take us for your enemies and spare not: call us liars, if we show you not his word for it. But alas, when God hath revealed your danger, must we hide it? And that when he hath foretold us, that if we told you not of it, your blood shall be required at our hands. Read that text well, and tell me then, whether you would have us such cruel enemies, I had almost said, such devils to you and to ourselves, as to hide a matter of such unconceivable moment from your eyes? What good would it do you to be thus flattered into hell? What good would it do you to have us to be damned with you, for being unfaithful for the preventing of your damnation? Who will laugh at this but Satan, the great enemy both of us and you? Alas, you may easily think with yourselves that it is no pleasure to a minister to tell you so sad a story of your misery. But if a Balaam must say, 'if Balak would give me the house full of gold and silver, I cannot go beyond the word of the Lord, to do less or more;' must not Christ's ministers be as faithful? I say again, if this gospel were not true, I would be a scavenger rather than a preacher; and I would join in a petition to have all ministers banished from the land: but seeing it is otherwise, I appeal to your consciences who it is that wrongs you: whether it belongs to Christ and his ministers to tell you of your danger, or yourselves to make light of it, and to refuse the cure?

CHAPTER IV.

THE GUILT AND DANGER OF THE UNCONVERTED.

Thus much I have spoken to you, to make you willing to hear and know the truth of your

condition; my next desire is, that you will lay it well to heart. You will never make out aright for the remedy, till you feel your misery. Alas, what abundance of people are there in the world that never were converted, and yet live as carelessly as if all were well with them! Come among twenty that are as merry as the best, and ask them one by one, whether they are converted, or not? Some will tell you they hope so, they cannot tell; and some will deride you, and most of them perhaps know not what conversion is, nor ever much minded any such thing: and yet these very men do read, or hear the word of God, that tells them so plainly that 'except they be converted, they shall not enter into the kingdom of heaven.' What do you think of such words, when you hear them, or read them? Are you never touched at the heart with them, and doth conscience never make you cry out, Alas then, what will become of me? Well, because I would have you sensible of your condition, lest you should rest in it to your undoing, I will tell you a little further what it is in some particulars: and may the Lord awaken you to lay them to heart!

SECTION I.

THE UNCONVERTED ARE THE CHILDREN OF THE WICKED ONE.

1. As long as you are unconverted, you are no true children of God nor members of Jesus Christ; and therefore you have no part in that fatherly, special love, but stand still before his eyes as enemies. For your hearts are not toward him, but toward the things below, as you know, or might know if you would. The world is divided into two sorts—the children of God and the children of the devil: the converted, and they only, are the children of God. All the unconverted are the children of the devil, as Christ himself has called some of them. It is said of them all, and long ago they were called the seed of the serpent. It is by faith in Christ Jesus that we are made the sons of God; but the unconverted have not true faith. When you go to God in prayer, if you cannot call him your Father, what comfort can you expect? If you look up for a blessing on your labours, and for supply of your wants, if it be not to a Father's hand that you look, how cold will the comfort of them be! Why, it is conversion that turns the heart to God, and if he have not your hearts, you are

not his children, and therefore none of the un-converted are his children. You are 'all by nature the children of wrath,' and therefore not the children of God. And by regeneration you are new-born children of God; and it is conversion that is this regeneration. You may call him Father as long as you will, but he will never call you children till you are converted. You may think you have as good right in him as another, but he will never own you till you are converted. You may call him Lord, Lord, even to the last, but he will tell you he knows you not. It is not nature, but renewing grace, that puts upon you his image, and puts within you his Spirit and holy nature, and if you have not that image, that Spirit, that holy nature, whatsoever you may think yourselves, he will never take you for his children. All the children of God are somewhat like him: 'they are holy as he is holy.' And it is conversion that makes men in their places, and measure, like to God. It is plain therefore, that the unconverted are none of his children; and then how can they expect his fatherly love, or his fatherly care of them in the time of their necessity? The goodness of God is the foundation of all the creature's hopes, but if you will keep out of the way of his goodness, and yet expect the benefit of it, you are likely to be deceived. For an enemy or a stranger cannot look for the portion of a child.

And as you are no children of God, so you are no members of Christ without conversion; for we are adopted only in Christ; and therefore children of God, because members of Christ, who is his natural Son. It is conversion that makes us members of Christ. I suppose you will confess, that if you were not Christians, you were miserable: and if you be not converted, you are not true Christians. You may have the name, but you have not the nature. You may keep a room among those that profess themselves Christians: but God that knows the heart will ask you, 'friend, how camest thou in hither, not having on a wedding garment?' And then you will be speechless. That man who has no part in Christ, how sad and miserable a condition is he in! It was the terrible description of the case of Simon Magus, 'thou hast no part nor lot in this matter; thou art yet in the gall of bitterness and the bond of iniquity.' And the proof was, 'because his heart was not right in the sight of God.' He was baptized, and had a kind of belief, but yet he was not converted, and therefore had no part in Christ. All the hopes and life of the world is laid up in Jesus Christ. He therefore that hath no part in him, hath no hope,

no life, no ground of peace, or comfort. Without a Saviour, how dare you draw near to God in prayer? How dare you think of death or judgment? What a sad appearance are you. there likely to make? O! wo, and ten thousand woes to that man, that must stand at the bar of God without a part in the blood of Christ, and must answer there without that advocate: nay, he will be judge himself, and will justify none but those that are his members. You will surely confess yourselves, that, if you have no part in Christ, you are in a most miserable case.

Why, brethren, the case is as plain in scripture as the high way, that if you are yet unconverted, you are no true Christians, and have no part in Christ, as to any saving interest. You are by nature in another stock, and it is converting grace that must cut you out, and plant you into Christ, the living vine. This is the very nature of true conversion: therefore must men be humbled, mortified, and broken off from themselves and all creatures, that they may be removed and planted into Jesus Christ; and may abide in him, and he in them, and that in him they may bring forth fruit: for out of him you are nothing, and can do nothing. And whatsoever you may profess, you are but withered branches, and must be gathered up, and cast away, and burnt in the fire. To be a man, and not to be born, is much the same as to be a true Christian, and not to be new born: for as our conception and birth is the passage into the life and world of nature, so our conversion or new birth is the passage into the life of grace. We that know not your hearts, do call you all Christians that seem to be so: but if we certainly knew who they be that are yet unconverted, we should tell these men to their faces they are no Christians. Their souls are not yet washed with the blood of Christ, nor are they sanctified by his Spirit, and therefore having not his Spirit, they are none of his. O therefore in the name of God look about you, and you that have lived so long unconverted, remember you have lived so long without a part in Christ. And therefore lament that you have taken on you to be Christians so long, when it is not so, and now be such as you have seemed to be. The union between Christ and true Christians is internal, in the heart: mere words and ceremonies unite not men to Christ.

SECTION II.

THE UNCONVERTED ARE VOID OF THE SOLID HOPE OF SALVATION.

2. Consider further, I beseech you : there is no hope of the salvation of any unconverted man, that so lives and dies. This is true, whether you like it, or not. If you are offended at this saying, you are offended with the saying of Christ that redeemed his people. And it were better for you to be offended with your sins, than with Christ that condemns them. If you say, it is a hard saying, I am sure it is a true saying, for God cannot lie. I gave you the proofs of it before at large : if you forget them, remember my text, and you need no more. What hypocrites then are those wretches, that say they will not believe it, and yet for all that, will take on them to be Christians, and to believe the word of God. You read here that Christ proclaims, ' verily, except ye be converted ye shall not enter into the kingdom of heaven.' And when you read it, yet you say, you will not believe it. And yet you will say, that you are Christians and believe Christ. What contradictions are these ? What, wilt thou worship a God, whom thou takest to be a liar ? This cannot be. No man can heartily trust him, especially in so great a matter as his salvation, whom he takes for a liar. Thou wouldst not give God the lie ? If he be not perfectly good, he is not God. No marvel then if you be liars yourselves, if you think God be one ; for no man is bound to be better than God. And therefore I will never marvel to see any man do that evil which he apprehends that God himself will do.

But what will sinners get by this unbelief ? It is but the way of their own self-delusion and undoing. He that will not believe God, I cannot expect he should believe me, or any man ; nor can he rationally expect to be believed himself. Yet I will ask him the question.

You that see what Christ saith, and yet say you will not believe it, but that unconverted men may be saved ; what say you ? Do you know any man in the world that you will believe, if he speak to you with such protestation as Christ here doth ? If you do not, it seems you measure other men by yourselves : if you do, I would wish to know of you whether you think that any man is better than God ? I had rather believe that God is true, and every man a liar, than that men are true, and God is a liar. And I would further ask you, would you have any man believe you, or take your words. If you say no ;

he is not wise that will have any thing to do with you, if he can choose : and then you openly proclaim what you are, even such liars that you would not wish men to believe you : but if you say yes, then I would further ask you whether you dare take on you to be better than God ? Why, thou frail, imperfect, mutable sinner, wouldst thou be believed thyself, and wilt thou not believe God ? Darest thou say that thou art more true and better than God, and that thy word is to be taken before his word ? If thou dare, do not blame him if he shortly stop that presumptuous mouth of thine, with his confounding indignation ; and if he make that blaspheming tongue to be speechless, when he shall say, ' take him, bind him hand and foot, and cast him into utter darkness.' And then thou wilt have ' weeping and gnashing of teeth.'

Well then, if God is not to be believed, no one is ; and if God is to be believed, then no unconverted man shall enter into the kingdom of heaven. Is it not time for you then to consider of your condition, and look about whether you be converted, or not ? I pray you be not so silly, as to take these words as mine, and so to think that it is I that make the matter so terrible. If I had not found them in the Bible, I had never preached them to you ; and we have nothing to preach, but what we here find, and to open this to you, that you may understand it. It will be nevertheless true, if neither I, nor any preacher in England should tell you of it ; or if none of us did believe it. For our unbelief makes not the word of God of none effect. I do therefore intreat you all, as you are men of reason, see that you be truly converted, because no unconverted man shall be saved ; it is God that saith it, it is the devil that denies it, and will you believe the devil before God ? This was it that brought destruction first upon the world, when God told our first parents that if they sinned they should die ; and the devil told them they should not die, and they believed the devil rather than God. And have you this warning, and will you do so too ? Is that a Christian, yea, is that a man, or worthy the name of a man, that will considerately believe the devil before God ; and believe his own flesh and carnal reason before God ? Whether is God or the devil, think you, the better, and more to be believed, and the better friend to your souls, and more to be trusted and regarded ? O horrible wickedness ! That ever men should put us on such a question, or make any comparison ! And what are you, that you should presume to set your reason against Christ ?

God saith, ' verily the unconverted shall not be saved,' and you say, for all this you hope they shall : and what are you, that you should be believed before God? What! do you know more than he? Why, where had you that knowledge? Is there any knowledge in the world that comes not from God? And doth he give you more than he hath himself? Is a dungeon more clear than the sun? Or is there any light here below, but what comes from the sun mediately or immediately? Why, a dungeon may better compare with the sun, and say, I have more light than thou ; than thou canst compare with God, and say, I have more knowledge than thou. O that ever dust and ashes should be so blind, as not to know this ; and that ever they should prefer their blindness to the infinite knowledge of him that made them ! If you do not, how dare you say, you hope that will prove false which God hath spoken? But do you think that this unbelief will make your danger the less? No, it is this that increases your danger. What if a man in the midst of evil, will wink, or put his eyes out, is he therefore safe, because he sees not his danger? Again, therefore, I beseech you, if you be men of reason, if you be not resolved to be your own enemies, and to do the worst you can against yourselves, if you do not long for damnation: O then believe God, and take time while you have it, and make out for conversion without delay. And instead of hoping to be saved against the word of God, and as it were in despite of him, and whether he will or not ; see that you presently yield to the word by which he would convert you if you do not resist it. Believe your present misery, and look out presently to Christ for the remedy, and thank God that you may, and that the day of his patience is not past. And if the devil and sin do still so harden your hearts, that you will not believe, nor take this counsel, remember that thou was told that the unconverted shall not enter into heaven. Remember that this was preached to thee from the word of God, and thou wouldst not believe it. Yea, thou shalt remember it whether thou wilt or not.

SECTION III.

THE UNCONVERTED MAN IS IN AN UNPARDONED STATE.

I beseech you consider further, that while a man is unconverted, he hath no sin pardoned ; all the sin that ever he committed is yet upon his own head, and he shall answer for it before God, and suffer for it for ever, if he thus continue. Nor I do not speak this of mine own head: I will now give you but three texts of scripture to prove it, which is as good as three hundred. When Christ speaks of those that were judicially hardened, because they had wilfully resisted grace, he addeth, ' lest at any time they should be converted, and their sin should be forgiven them.' By which you see, that till men are converted, their sin is not forgiven them. ' I send thee to open their eyes, and turn them from darkness to light, and from the power of satan unto God, that they may receive forgiveness of sins, and an inheritance.' You see then that men receive not forgiveness of sins till they are turned from the power of sin to God ; this is the order of God's saving grace. ' Whom he calleth,' that is, converteth, ' them he justifieth ; and whom he justifieth, them he glorifieth.' So that no man is justified before he be called.

Consider then what a fearful case it is to have a load of unpardoned sins upon your souls. One unpardoned sin would as surely condemn a man for ever, as one stab at the heart would kill a man. What then will so many thousands do? Poor sinner, if Christianity and humanity did not bind me to compassionate thy soul, I would not tell thee these things to trouble thee. But I cannot forbear, unless I would be cruel to thee. It seems an easy matter to a felon to think of his crime, while he is not apprehended, because he lives in hope to escape, and therefore he can laugh when he talks of the gallows : but when he comes to it, the case is altered : offenders may escape the justice of men, but no man can so escape the hand of God. It may now seem a small and easy matter to you to think and talk of unpardoned sin, but the day is coming when you would give all the world if you had it, for a pardon, as light as you do now make of it : all are sinners, but all are not unpardoned sinners : it is not all sinners that shall perish ; for then we should all perish ; but all unpardoned sinners shall perish ; and all unconverted sinners are unpardoned.

When sin is pardoned, the terror of it is gone ; then a man hath a sure refuge against the accusation : he can say at judgment, if he be accused of his sin, that he hath a pardon of all through the blood of Christ, and then there is no more to be done against him : but so cannot the unpardoned. O, heavy case for a poor trembling sinner to hear, At such a time thou didst abuse God's creature, his name, his word, and his ordinances ; at such a time thou didst neglect duty, and mis-spend thy time, even the Lord's day, and to have nothing to say against the accusation. What a sight will it be for him, to have all his sins set in order before him? All the sins of his youth, and his riper age, of ignorance, and of knowledge; and have no remedy against the justice and the wrath of God! Once there was a remedy offered them, but being finally neglected, there remains no more sacrifice for sin, ' but a certain looking for of judgment, and fiery indignation that shall devour the adversary.' Tell me, I beseech you, what do you think to do by the sins that you are guilty of? Do you believe that you shall come to judgment for them or not? If not; what do you here among Christians? If you do, will you tell me what you mean to say, or how do you think to come off, and to escape? Either you must have a pardon or not. If you have not pardon, what do you think will become of you? There is no question of it, but an unpardoned sinner must be damned, as sure as the devils themselves are damned: for Christ tells you this will be the sentence, ' Depart, ye cursed, into everlasting fire, prepared for the devil and his angels.' Wo to that man that ever he was born, that shall stand at God's bar with unpardoned sin. It will be heavier upon thy soul than a mountain upon thy body, and press thee down to everlasting misery. Unpardoned sin is the very fuel of hell. If angels and men snould all join together to save an unpardoned sinner at judgment, they could not do it. What hope have you then to escape, or to see the face of God with comfort? I beseech you, bethink you what you mean to say, or how you think to come off? Should a wise man be going to such a judgment, and never once think what to say for himself, or how to escape when he comes thither? Will you then plead that ' you hope you are pardoned by the blood of Christ?' Why, alas, that will be utterly vain; for there is no hope that God will be false to his word; and God hath assured you, that the blood of Christ and the mercy of God shall never pardon any sinner but he that repents and is converted from his sin. Will you say, ' Though I am not pardoned now, yet I hope I may beg pardon then.' And do you think to cry loud, and persuade the judge? If that would do; what a cry would there then be! How many thousand and ten thousand souls would cry, Mercy, mercy, Lord, on a poor miserable wretch! O pity a lost sinner; O do not condemn thy creature; do not deliver me up to the tormentor; do not send me away from thy presence into those flames; as ever thou hadst pity on a sinner, have pity on me. If crying and praying would then be sufficient, how would they ring in the ears of Christ!

But it is then too late, sinners; you should have done this sooner. The day of grace is now past, and there is no remedy. Now prayer might do good (with forsaking sin through the blood of Christ) and men will not use it, but then it will do no good at all.

Do not say, that I make this terrible doctrine of myself, the scripture is full of it. Christ hath told you over and over of it, that if you are then found without the oil of saving grace in your lamps, you shall in vain cry, Lord, Lord, open to us; and long enough may you knock, before you can have any hearing: but Christ will say, ' verily, I know you not.' It is not they that will cry, ' Lord, Lord, that shall enter into the kingdom of heaven; but they that do the will of our Father which is in heaven.' For many in that day will plead acquaintance with Christ, to whom he will profess, ' I never knew you, depart from me, all ye that work iniquity.' I tell you again, if all the angels in heaven should fall down before the Lord Jesus Christ, and beg for you, (which they will never do) and beseech him to pardon your sins, he will not do it. For it is in this life that pardon must be got, or never. We have no hope to be wholly free from sin, but we may procure the pardon of it through Christ, and if it be not done now, it will never be done. Now must the pardon be procured, and sued out, and then it must be brought forth that you may not be condemned.

Now, sinners, as ever you would stand with boldness in judgment, repent and be converted, that you may have the pardon of all your sins. As ever you would stand then at Christ's right hand, and not be sent into everlasting torment, look about you now for the pardon of your sins; for there was never a man that got a pardon after he was dead, who died unpardoned. I give you but the same counsel which Peter gave the Jews, ' Repent ye therefore and be converted, that your sins may be blotted out, when the times of refreshing shall come from the presence of the Lord.' I pray you mark these words; you see that no man's sins will then be blotted out, but those that now repent and are converted.

SECTION IV.

UNCONVERTED MEN ARE THE SLAVES OF SIN AND SATAN.

The next thing that I would entreat you to consider, is this: that as long as you are unconverted, you are the servants and slaves of Satan.

and under his power, and led about as his captives at his will. It may be you do not think so
much, nor believe this, but perhaps would take
it ill to be told so: but God hath told us that so
it is. There are but two sorts of men in the
world—the slaves of sin and the servants of
Christ. All the world is in two armies: Satan is the
general of one, and Christ of the other, and these
two are in continual conflicts with one another.
In his first assault of Adam, our first father,
Satan overcame him by drawing him to sin, and
thereby got him and his posterity into his power:
the Lord Jesus comes on purpose to rescue us
out of his hands, and this he doth by converting
grace, and justification thereupon. So that, till
a man be converted, he remains in the bondage
and slavery of the devil; and when he is converted, he is entered among the freemen and sons
of God.

What think you of this? Is it not a miserable state to be the devil's bond-slaves? Why,
if you will believe God, it is the case of all that
are unconverted: nay, you may feel it in yourselves. Do you not feel that your wills are to
do evil? That he leads you to worldliness, to
drunkenness, or wickedness at his will? If he
bid you rail or swear, you do it. If he bid you
neglect everlasting life, you do it, and you have
no heart to God and the life to come: why,
these are the marks of Satan's bondage. Hear
whether the scripture speaks it not plainly,
' Know ye not that to whom ye yield yourselves
servants to obey, his servants ye are whom
ye obey, whether of sin unto death, or of obedience unto righteousness.—He that committeth
sin is of the devil. In this the children of God
are manifest, and the children of the devil; whosoever doth not righteousness, is not of God.'
The meaning of both is, that he that hath the
whole bent of his heart and life for sin, that is,
for the flesh and the world, is of the devil; and
he that hath the chief bent of his heart and life
for God, that is, for righteousness, is a converted
child of God. ' For of whom a man is overcome, of the same is he brought into bondage.'
In Timothy, they are said to be in the ' snare
of the devil, taken captive of him at his will,'
and in Acts, it is expressly said that conversion
' turneth men from the power of Satan unto
God.' So that you see the case is plain in
scripture, that, ' till men are converted, they
are in the power of Satan.'

It may be you perceive not the misery of
your condition; and no marvel, for Satan's servants are all volunteers, and he usually keeps
his possession in peace till a stronger than he

shall come upon him, and cast him out. O
that the eyes of poor sinners were but opened
to see who it is that leads them captive. Poor
soul, didst thou but see that the devil is thy
ruler, that he stands by thee, and goads thee on
in all thy wickedness, it would surely make thee
desire to change thy master. You are afraid of
seeing him appear to you in any shape, and if
you should but see him, it would make your
joints tremble. O why are you not more
afraid to be ruled by him, and to follow him
to your destruction? Why are you not more
afraid lest you should dwell with him for ever?
A man that is in the favour of God, were not
much the worse if he should see all the devils in
hell, no more than a soldier to see the enemies,
when they are conquered; but a man that is unconverted, whether he see them or not, should
tremble to think that he is yet in their snares.
O that you did but know, and well consider,
that it is the devil himself within you that cavils
against the word of God, contradicts the truth,
draws you to doubt, and entices you to sin. If
you did hear the devil say to you with a voice,
Come follow me to the alehouse, it would surely
frighten you from going. Or if you heard him
speak out, and say against the gospel, It is not
true, do not believe it; how would this affect you?
Why, it is he that speaks this in you, whenever
you have these thoughts in your hearts. Your
own corrupt hearts are the mother, but he is the
father of them all. When you feel such thoughts
as these within you, that sin is a small matter,
and that God doth not hate it so much as
preachers talk of, that God will not condemn
all the unconverted, who so live and die, that
men may be saved without a holy life, and
that this is but preciseness, and more ado than
needs,—all this is as truly the very inward persuasions and motions of the devil, as if you
heard him speak it openly in a voice. It is he
that bids you go on in sin and fear not, and yet
at least take a little more of your fleshly pleasure, and if you must turn, let it not be yet. It
is he that bids you hate them that endeavour
your conversion, and make a scorn of those that
fear God. It is he that bids you lose your time,
especially on the Lord's day, and talk of filthiness or vanity, and rail, lie, backbite, or hate
your brother: the scripture tells us that this
is his work, which Christ came into the world
to destroy. We can certainly know the workman by his work. So bad a work hath no better an author.

I beseech you, therefore, in the name of God,
bethink you where you are, and what a case you

are in. Have you known all this time, that you were in the power and captivity of the devil? What, and yet be so merry or careless as you have been? What, sleep quietly, and live quietly, and yet be in such a case? How many a sigh and groan comes from him, to think where he is, and what a case he is in, in comparison of other men! And many a time he cries, O that I were free! And yet all the servants of Satan are willing in their bondage. This is it that makes you deserve the less pity, because it is your own doing, and you will not be delivered. A slave would be delivered if he could, and would give a thousand thanks to him that would deliver him: but you might be delivered, and will not. Christ hath provided a remedy in his blood, he offers it to you, and entreats you to accept it, and yet you will not. He hath commanded us to entreat you, and you will not be entreated. 'God would have all men saved, and come to the knowledge of his truth;' and many will not be saved. Christ 'would gather them as a hen gathers her chickens under her wing, and they will not.' When God, ministers, and godly friends offer you help, and earnestly would have you delivered, and you will not, what pity do you deserve, if you perish everlastingly? It is a strange thing to see how people hate the devil, and yet love his service! How they speak evil of him and yet obey him! How they even affect to fear his name, as men that abhor him, and yet will not be persuaded by any means that we can use, to come out of this captivity, when the doors are set open by Christ that bought them. Not that I suspect that any of you do really love him; for I know that God hath put an enmity in the beginning, even between the nature of Satan and of man. I know you hate him, even while you wilfully serve him. But the matter lies here, though you hate him you love the sin, because it is pleasant to flesh and blood, and you do not know, or will not consider, that it is he indeed that leads you to it; or else you durst not continue in that case. Lay this then to heart, and believe that all men are slaves to Satan, till they be converted, and if you are not willing to live and die his slaves, and to be used for ever as his slaves, delay not your conversion.

SECTION V.

THE UNCONVERTED CANNOT PLEASE GOD.

Moreover, the misery of the unconverted doth further appear in this: that while men are unconverted, nothing that they do can truly please God. There are many works, which for the matter of them are commanded, which such men may do, but yet there are so many defects and so much of the venom of their corruption mixed in them, that God hath no delight in them, but doth abhor them. I would not be misunderstood in this, as if I said or thought that therefore all that the unconverted can do is to no purpose, in order to their salvation: and that therefore it is as good for them to let all alone, and sit still and be careless till God shall convert them; or as if it were better, or as good for them not to pray, as to pray, and not to hear or read, or ask advice, as to do it, because that all is displeasing to God. But I mean, and say, that there is more in their best duties to displease God than to please him, and that they are such as he hath made them no promise of accepting, so far as to give them any special grace or reward on that account. Or if this please not any, yet this much is out of controversy, that the duties of no unconverted man are pleasing to God, so as to prove their persons pleasing to him, as his own servants are; and that God takes no such delight in their duties, as he doth in those that are performed by the righteous. And thus at least you may take it as beyond all question, that God is comparatively displeased with, and abhors even the best works that are performed by the unconverted. The works of wicked men are of four sorts. 1. Some are such as have no tendency to their conversion and recovery, nor to the good of any others; but are either plainly wicked for the substance, or but indifferent for the matter, and wicked in the ends and manner: these God abhors in the highest degree. 2. And there are some that are common civil actions, in themselves neither good nor evil, nor yet designed to any special wicked end: but yet because the common aim of such is wrong, and the manner sinful, these therefore are said to be abomination to the Lord. 3. And then there are their best works which are done by them with evil intents, to settle them in their present state, without any thoughts of turning from it, as their alms-deeds which are done to merit, or to quiet their consciences in a sinful state, or the like. These also God abhors for all the good that is in them; for these they do as wicked men, wickedly, for all the goodness that is in the action. 4. But then, there are some actions of the unconverted that are in order to their conversion, and these God accepts not, so as to accept their persons, as of one reconciled to him in Christ, nor as he accepts the works of his people, nor so as to be engaged by promise for their reward. But yet he so far accepts them that they are ordinarily the way in which he will be found; and in which he will give them greater things: they are means of his appointing for the conversion of their souls, which he hath not appointed them to use in vain. So that by this time you may see my meaning here in this particular; the three first sorts of the works of wicked men, God doth plainly abhor, even their wicked works that are both such for matter and end; and their civil and natural works that are wicked for the end; and their religious works, that are wicked for the end; but the fourth sort, which are works that are done in order to their conversion, though they please not God as the works of the regenerated do, yet he abhors them not as he doth the rest; for as they come from a common faith, though not from a special faith, so they may please God in a common manner, though not in a special: and as they have an end that is good in its place, that is, the saving of their souls by turning from their sins, though they have not the true ultimate end of the saints, that is, the glory and pleasing of God, and the enjoyment of him therein, so are they proportionably acceptable to God. So that it is the first three sorts of actions that I mean in this application. And in regard to them, I say it is a matter of great terror to the unconverted, that God abhors all that they do.*

I will first prove it to you, and then show you the terror of it. As for their wicked works there is no question, they are abominable to God, and he hates them. The very thoughts of the wicked are abominable to him. But the question is of their better works: and we find in scripture, that their very trades, and works of their callings, is sin. The 'ploughing of the wicked is sin,' or if perhaps the sense of that text may be that their preparations and contrivances are sinful, which are metaphorically called ploughing, yet of their best works the scripture is plain; the 'sacrifice of the wicked is an abomination to the Lord, but the prayer of the upright is his delight.' Note, that he saith not, the humiliation, or the repentance, or thoughts of conversion that may be in a wicked man, but his sacrifice, which is somewhat that he thinks God should accept, as a matter of worth: and therefore it was that Cain's sacrifice was abhorred, when Abel's was accepted. And that you may see that it is not only because of the wicked designs that they may have in it,

the Spirit of God speaks of both. 'The sacrifice of the wicked is an abomination,' how much more when he brings it with a wicked mind? Yea, the very 'prayer of wicked men is abominable.' Yet do not say that God is a respecter of persons, and will take that well from one which he hates from another, without any just cause. For there is just cause. If you will not do the main things that God requires, he cares not for the rest. 'He that turns away his ear from hearing the law, even his prayer shall be abomination.' The law of God commands you to take another course, and condemns your wicked life, and if you will turn away your ear from this law, that would turn away your heart from sin, God will not accept your prayer. 'If I regard iniquity in my heart, God will not hear my prayer.—He that calleth on the name of the Lord, must depart from iniquity.' Yea, the fasting and self-afflicting of the wicked is disregarded.

Little doth a poor blind sinner think when he is boasting of his praying and religious duties, that God abhors them; but if they be unconverted, they will find it so. 'Ye are they that justify yourselves before men, but God knoweth your hearts: for that which is highly esteemed among men, is abomination in the sight of God. And one reason is, because that the person himself is such as God doth hate; and therefore no wonder if he hate his work: for a fig-tree bears not thorns and thistles, nor the bramble grapes, but as the tree is, so is the fruit. 'Thou hatest all the workers of iniquity: the wicked is made for the day of evil, and every one that is proud in heart, is an abomination to the Lord.' Though men bless, yet the Lord abhors them. When he sees their wickedness, he abhors even those that profess themselves his people. Yea, and his own sanctuary, and the very place of his worship. Especially when they often deal falsely with him. And no wonder when wicked men do lothe the Lord and his service, if he do also lothe them. 'My soul lotheth them, and their soul also abhorreth me.' Sinners, the case in a word is this: God is a Spirit, and will be worshipped in spirit and in truth, and such worshippers only doth he choose; and wicked man can give him but the shadow of his service: God made all things for himself, and will accept of nothing but what is intended for himself: but wicked men are turned from God, and do all for their carnal selves, even when they pretend to do it for God. It is your hearts that God hath lost, and your hearts that he regards, and your hearts he will have again, or he will have nothing; but you may even keep all to yourselves if you will, except you will give him this. What need hath God of your prayers, or other services, or what good can you do him by all? It is yourselves that he desires, and then he will accept your service, though he need it not, and will make it good to you, though it can do no good to him. Therefore this is his first demand, 'My son, give me thine heart;' and if you deny him this, you deny him all. He cares not for your lips, nor your religious duties, without it. If you will not first give him yourselves, he will not accept of any thing that you offer him.

And indeed, when it is not in a returning way, but in an offering way, that wicked men will serve him, he plainly tells them it is in vain, and tells them he hates it, and bids them keep it with them; for he will have none of it till they leave their sins, and give up themselves to him. ' To what purpose is the multitude of your sacrifices to me, saith the Lord? I am full of your burnt-offerings, when you come to appear before me; who hath required this at your hands, to tread in my courts? Bring no more vain oblations; incense is an abomination to me; the new moons, and sabbaths, and solemn assemblies, I cannot away with it; it is iniquity, even the solemn meetings; your new moons and appointed feasts, my soul hateth, they are a trouble to me; I am weary to bear them; and when ye spread forth your hands, I will hide mine eyes from you; yea, when you make many prayers, I will not hear; your hands are full of blood. Wash ye, make you clean, put away the evil of your doings from before mine eyes; cease to do evil; learn to do well; come now, and let us reason together, saith the Lord.' If a prince have subjects, that are in rebellion, he will not take any gift at their hands, till they come in themselves: no more will God at your hands. There is no true minister of the gospel, but feels some exposition of this in his own heart. If the people would send us any tokens of their love and expressions of kindness, if it were not for exasperating them, who would not return it them with contempt, as long as they refuse to be reformed, and will not yield to the word of the gospel? To let go their goods, if it were all they have, for us, is a matter that we regard not, if they will not let go their sins; because we seek not theirs, but them: and much more is it so with Jesus Christ. If you should be as punctual in his worship as any, and give him never so much of your knees or tongues, yea, or your goods, and all you have, he will not take it as a thing that pleases him, unless withal you give him yourselves. 'If I suffer my body to be

burnt,' saith Paul, 'and have not love, it availeth nothing.' Many a poor unconverted sinner considers not this, who comes constantly to church. receives the sacrament, and uses some kind of praying every day, and thinks, that if God should not accept of such as him, there should almost nobody be saved; and therefore they make no question of his acceptance. O but one thing is necessary, and that is yet wanting. If God had your hearts first, then he would take the rest in good part; but when the world hath your hearts, and though you sit and hear with some delight, as if you were his people, yet your heart goes after your covetousness. When your fleshly pleasure and profit have your hearts, God will not regard your service, were it much more.

Now it is the work of conversion to bring the heart to God, that was never brought to him, and set upon him before: therefore till this work be done, all is but abominable. 'For without faith it is impossible to please God.' You think to live to the flesh, and then to please God by your good praying and meanings, or by being of the right religion, or by some good works; but remember what God himself hath told you, who best knows what it is that pleases him, 'they that are in the flesh, cannot please God,' and all that are unconverted, are said to be in the flesh, because 'they mind the things of the flesh,' and live according to their carnal inclinations, and for carnal ends. What a sad consideration would this be to your hearts, if you did but understand and feel your own condition! You talk against this man and that man for being of a wrong religion, and you think you are better than this party or that, whereas you are miserable, whatsoever your religion be, because you are heartily of no religion. You think God will be pleased with your service, and it doth but add to the load of your sin; you read the word, and think you do God service by it, when you do but read your own condemnation, because you have your hearts against the doctrine that you read; you think you serve God by coming to church, but if you refuse to let the word convert you, how should God be pleased with such a service as this? It is as if you should tell your servant what you have for him to do, and because he hath given you the hearing, he thinks he should have his wages, though he do nothing of that which you set him to do: were not this an unreasonable servant? Or would you give him according to his expectation? It is a strange thing that men should think that God will save them for dissembling with him: and save them for abusing his name and ordinances : every time you hear, or pray, or praise God, or receive the sacrament, while you deny God your heart, and remain unconverted, you do but despise him, and show more of your rebellion than your obedience. Would you take that man for a good tenant that at every rent-day would duly wait on you, and show you outward respect, but never bring you a penny of rent? Or would you take him for a good debtor, that brings you nothing but an empty purse, and expects you should take that for payment? For God bids you come to church, to hear the word, and so you do, and so far you do well : but withal he charges you to suffer the word to work upon your hearts, to take it home and consider of it, to obey it, cast away your former courses, and give up your hearts and lives to him, but this you will not do : yet you think that he will accept of your service. Dare you plead such services with God for a reward and say, Lord, though we shut thee out of our hearts, yet we gave thee the hearing.

I beseech you then, lay this well to heart, what will you do in a day of affliction? What will you do at an hour of death? Will you not fall a praying? Will you not call to God for mercy, when you see that nothing but his mercy can relieve you? Why, if you be unconverted, God will not hear your prayers : he abhors them, because he hath not your hearts. O sad case, for a man in misery to look about him, and see no hope in heaven or earth, but God alone, and when he begins to cry for help to him, he will lothe their prayers, turn away his ears, and will not hear! Hear his own word, 'because I have called, and ye refused, I have stretched forth my hands, and no man regarded,' &c. For my part, I foresee the day is coming, when I would not take all the world to be without a God to pray to. O then, to have a man's prayers themselves thought but iniquity, and charged on him as his sin, when he must have present help or perish! What case more sad can there be? For a man that is going into another world, and calling to God to receive his soul, to have prayers and soul cast out together, how sad a case is it! Do not mistake me, as if I took you off from prayers or other holy duties by this ; but I tell you, that if you go on in any kind of duty, and remain unconverted, you cannot expect that God should take any kind of pleasure in them or in you. If you say then 'it is as good never a whit, as never the better :' I answer ; do your great duty first, and then all the rest will be accepted : yield to the word and Spirit, resist not the grace of God any

longer ; give him your hearts, and give them no longer to this deceitful world, and then come and welcome. And for the duties that tend to conversion, as hearing the word and begging true grace of God, which may convert you, and considering of those truths that must be the instruments to do it,—these are the very beginnings of the work, and therefore it is not these that we discourage you from : it is time for you to use these, that the rest may be accepted.

SECTION VI.

THE UNCONVERTED ARE IN CONSTANT DANGER OF EVERLASTING PERDITION.

Another sad consideration, concerning the state of an unconverted man, is this : as long as they remain in that condition, they live in continual danger of damnation ; they are under the wrath of God ; and though patience have long forborne them, to try whether they will repent, yet are they not sure whether it will stay for them one day longer : they are under the curse of the law, and when it will be executed they cannot tell. I have told you already, from the word of God, that an unconverted man cannot be saved, and I need not tell you surely that he is uncertain how long he shall continue in this world : and methinks a man that is sure to go to hell if he dies and knows not whether it may not be this day, should have little comfort in his life till he were changed. Now the Lord have mercy on poor hard-hearted sinners. What do they mean then that they look no more about them? Why will not the word of the living God awaken them, which tells them how near they are to perdition? I do here make known to you, from the word of truth, that if there be any unconverted souls in this assembly, they are not certain to be out of hell an hour. God knows, I would not tell you of this if it were needless ; but alas, do you mean to continue in such a case as this? As sure as the word of God is true, every soul that goes unconverted out of the body, is shut out of all hope of mercy for ever, and enters into a remediless misery.

Remember then, man, in the name of God, every morning thou arisest, and every night thou liest down, that thou art uncertain to be out of hell till the next day. Alas, it is enough to amaze a poor Christian that is indeed converted, when he doth but find himself in doubt of it ; how much more should it awaken them that are yet in the flesh! Many a one that truly fears

God, having wanted assurance at the time of death, O, how terrible it hath made death to them! to look before them and think they must be gone, and they know not whither; to think that it is but one day or two more, and my soul will be among angels or devils, and I know not which of the two it will be! what a dreadful thought is this, even to many that are converted, for want of assurance at the time of death! but alas, this is but a small matter in comparison of the case of the unconverted: for as soon as the soul is out of the flesh, all the fears of the godly are at an end, and they shall never more have a doubting thought; but for the rest, if you should die with never so great confidence, death would dispel it all; and as soon as you were out of the body, your eyes would be opened to see that which would never let you have a thought of hope or comfort more. I speak none of this of myself. ' When a wicked man dies his expectation shall perish; and the hope of the unjust man perisheth.—For what is the hope of the wicked, though he have gained, when God takes away his soul? Will God hear his cry when trouble comes upon him?—So are the paths of all that forget God, and the hypocrite's hope shall perish; whose hope shall be cut off, and whose trust shall be a spider's web. He shall lean upon his house, but it shall not stand; he shall hold it fast, but it shall not endure.—The eyes of the wicked shall fail, and they shall not escape, and their hope shall be as the giving up of the ghost.' Take this home with you then, and let it cause you to have no rest till you are truly converted, that till then you are never certain to be one day or hour more in safety.

SECTION VII.

THE UNCONVERTED CANNOT POSSESS SOLID PEACE NOR SPIRITUAL COMFORT.

From all this you may see another sad consideration, which is, that as long as a man is unconverted, he hath no ground for one hour's true peace and comfort, but hath reason to live in continual terror, and to be the grief of all that know his misery. For should a man be merry that is in such a case as this? O no, if his eyes were opened, it would certainly affrighten him, either out of his sins, or out of his wits. Many worldly vanities and sensual delights such men may have to delight their thoughts; but this is their weakness, and not their happiness. Some malefactors, when they are to be hanged, will make themselves drunk beforehand, that death may not be terrible to them; that is but a medicine against repentance, and not against hell. So do thousands of poor sinners make themselves drunk with merry company, false conceits, worldly business, and fleshly pleasures: but though this ease their hearts a while, and keep away the feeling of their misery, it will not do so long, but only till the hope of cure be past. Brethren, the desire of my soul is to advance the consolation of the saints, and to take from you no peace or hope, but what death will take from you if it be not done before; and if I had any hopes that your merry days would last after death, and would not end in everlasting sorrow, I would not be the one that should interrupt your mirth. Truly you should hold on in your careless, drowsy course for me, if I did not see the after-reckoning: but seeing the case is such as I have proved, with all that are unconverted, I must say to all in that condition, that mirth is very unsuitable to your state, and laughter doth ill become you. And if ever a man might say of it, as Solomon, 'thou art mad,' it is when it appears in the face of such a man that stands all the while on the very brink of hell. What! be merry in the power of Satan, under the wrath of God, before you are pardoned, and before you know whether ever you will be saved, or escape the everlasting pains of hell! O doleful mirth!

What wise man would be partner with you in such pleasure? Now, I beseech you that are in this case, for your poor soul's sake, when you are next among your merry companions, let this thought come into your mind, ' O but I am not yet converted.' When you are next in your worldly cares and businesses, or careless for your souls, bethink you then, ' O but I am not yet converted.' And every day and night, wherever you are, whatever you do, think still, ' I am yet unconverted,' that so you may look about you, come to yourselves, and get into that condition wherein you may have cause indeed to be merry. Methinks every time you hear the bell toll, it should frighten you. Every time you go among the sick, or see any brought to the grave, it should frighten you: yea, every thing that you look on should be matter of terror to you, till you are out of this condition. Surely there is no believing friend that you have, that knows your case, but must needs pity you. They are bound to lament you. Only this comfort doth yet remain, that a sufficient remedy is provided in the blood of Christ, which will recover you, if you do not proceed to value it lightly.

This is all your comfort, that your case is not without a remedy, as long as you are under the calls of grace. Take heed, in the name of God take heed of going on any longer in that condition, lest you make it remediless: there is yet a possibility of your salvation, but not without your conversion; you have to do with a merciful God, and that you find by experience, or else you had not been here now. But O! go not out of the reach of mercy: never did God's mercy save one unconverted soul, any other way than by converting them. And the greater are your possibilities now, and the more freely the blood of Christ is offered you, the greater will be your sorrow if you lose all this, and by neglecting it, make your case remediless.

SECTION VIII.

NEGLECTED WARNINGS WILL AGGRAVATE THE MISERY OF THE UNCONVERTED WHO DIE IN THEIR SINS.

Consider further, the warnings that the unconverted have of their danger, are so many and so great, that if they be neglected, they will multiply their misery. To be an unconverted man among the Turks or heathens, is no wonder, no more than to be in the dark at midnight. To be unconverted among papists, is not so much wonder, no more than to miss your way by moonshine: but to be unconverted in the midst of gospel-light, this is a sin that hath no excuse, and a misery that continues by neglecting the remedy. All the preachers that have told you of your misery, and persuaded you to turn, shall be witnesses against you. Yea, all the examples of the wicked that have gone before you, that were set forth for your bettering, shall be witnesses against you. The way to hell is a beaten road, and most of the world tread it continually; and therefore you might have known and avoided it, when God had told you how to know it. God hath not left you in darkness, but you shut your eyes: the light shines round about you, and you will not see: you have bibles, and you have other good books, and you have teachers, and you have neighbours that are able and willing to help you, but you will not make use of them. Consider then, I beseech you, to get well to heaven is a business and not a play. It is a matter to be inquired after, prayed for, and learned with all diligence and care, and not to be put off with heartless shows. Hear then, O hear the call of God that sounds in thine ears, to bring thee to conversion: wilt thou run on when God is calling after thee? He calls by his word; he calls by his ministers; he calls by his judgments, and by his mercies, by conscience, and by his Spirit; and will you stop your ears and slight them all? Many a one hath come in at the first call that ever they had by the preaching of the gospel, and you have had hundreds, and yet you will not return? Believe it, the calls of God will convert you or confound you: his word will not return in vain: you cannot resist his grace after all this warning, at such easy and cheap rates as many others in the world may do. Your impenitency and wilfulness hath the more obstinacy in it, by how much the greater light you do resist. If the gospel do not convert you, you will wish you had never heard or read it. Hear what Christ himself says of those that were not converted by his word, 'Whosoever shall not receive you, nor hear your word, when you depart out of that house or city, shake off the dust of your feet; verily I say unto you, It shall be more tolerable for Sodom and Gomorrah in the day of judgment than for that city.' Christ upbraided the cities where his works were done, because they repented not: 'wo to thee, Chorazin, wo to thee, Bethsaida; for if the mighty works which have been done in thee, had been done in Tyre and Sidon, they had repented long ago, in sackcloth and ashes; but I say unto you, It shall be more tolerable for Tyre and Sidon in the day of judgment than for you. And thou Capernaum, which art exalted to heaven, shalt be brought down to hell; for if the mighty works which have been done in thee,' &c. The Lord grant that I may never hear Christ upbraiding any of this congregation with the warnings that they did neglect. It is a heavy case, that when Christ sends to men the gospel of salvation, they must be upbraided with it, because they would not be saved by it. And that Sodom and Gomorrah, those places of abomination that bore the most remarkable plagues of God, being consumed with fire and brimstone from the Lord, should yet speed better in the day of judgment, than many of our people that sit under our teaching from day to day. In a word, my hearers, remember this, all unconverted sinners that so lived and died, shall be condemned, but those that had the greatest means and warnings, shall have the greatest condemnation.

SECTION IX.

PERSEVERING IMPENITENCE RENDERS CONVERSION MORE IMPROBABLE, AND PUNISHMENTS MORE CERTAIN.

Consider further, that the longer men go on in an unconverted state, the deeper is their sin, the harder is their cure, and the greater will be their punishment. It is not a state wherein you may safely abide, no, not a day, if you were sure to have time for repentance. Is it a small thing to go on in sin, and to add to that heap which is so great already, and to increase that mountain which is so unsupportable? As long as you are unconverted, you live in the continual abuse of God and all his mercies: you abuse him most unworthily, for you prefer the unworthy creature before him, as if he and his glory were no better than this earth; nor even so good: you abuse him by denying him that which is his own: you deny him your hearts; you deny him your service—that which he hath made and redeemed; you deny him that which none can lay claim to but himself. You abuse his word by rejecting it; you abuse his sabbaths by profaning them; you abuse his image in his servants by contemning it: you abuse his name by taking it in vain: you abuse his mercy and all his creatures by beholding them in vain, and receiving them in vain: and by advancing them into the throne, and giving them that which is not their due: though you worship not sun and moon, yet you worship meat and drink, ease and money, and thus you live in the abuse of all things: besides the rest, you abuse your own souls. They were made for the high God, fitted to love him and know him, live to him here, and to see his face in glory hereafter; yet all unconverted men abuse them to the basest drudgery of the devil: they make them sinks of sin. God hath advanced you above the beasts that perish, and made you for a life with angels in his glory, if you would but believe it, and set your hearts upon it: and you debase your own souls, and make them brutish, as if they had no better a happiness than a mere animal; or as if you were worms that live in the earth. Who can marvel if a carnal man abuse God, and the godly, and all things else, when he wilfully and delightfully doth so abuse himself? It may turn the passion of those they abuse into compassion, when they consider, whatsoever they do against others, they do an hundred times more against themselves: they scorn us, and they wound themselves: they tempt others to sin, but they cast themselves into it: they wrong our names, or estates, or bodies, and they damn their own souls. Alas, poor wretches, who would have thoughts of revenge on such men that are the most cruel persecutors and destroyers of themselves! What a base indignity do they put upon a noble and immortal soul, to make it like the body, inclining unto earth, as if it had been taken hence as the body was, to take it down from living upon God, and engage it in a life of mere vanity.

Moreover consider, that all the while you continue unconverted, you grow hardened in your sin; and as you forsake God more, so doth his Spirit withdraw from you: and custom will make you still worse and worse. Your recovery will be harder the next week than this, and therefore it is not a state to be continued in: but of this we shall speak, when we shall come to the particular exhortation.

SECTION X.

THE UNCONVERTED DEPRIVE THEMSELVES OF HAPPINESS HERE, AND ETERNAL LIFE HEREAFTER.

As long as you remain in an unconverted state, you deprive yourselves of a world of happiness that God doth offer you, and you might possess. You might have God instead of the creature; and Christ instead of a carnal self; and the Spirit instead of the devil that doth deceive you: you might have holiness instead of the filth of wickedness; and justification for condemnation; and a blessing for the curse, and the state of reconciliation instead of the enmity that you are in to God: you might have peace of conscience, instead of terrors or groundless security: you might serve a better master now and in better company: and have better wages both here and hereafter. You do not know what you lose every day that you remain unconverted; more than all the pleasures of sin can afford you. Ask any of them that have escaped out of that condition that you are in, whether they are willing to return? You see not perhaps that they have got any thing by the change, and therefore you think you lose nothing by continuing as you are, but their gain is out of sight; it is most out of their own sight, and therefore it may well be out of yours. But if themselves should deny it, it is not therefore an uncertain or contemptible thing; for 'the foundation of God standeth sure; he knoweth who are his.' If it were but to be employed upon higher things, and to escape the deadly wounds of conscience, which you give yourselves, or else prepare for, it is no small gain to be a true believer; and if they found themselves in no better a case than they were before, they would be tempted to return to their former state; but that they will not do for a world. I dare say, if you did know but the danger and horrible misery of the life that you now live, you would make as much haste out of it, as a man would do out of a house that were a fire over his head; or as a man that were at sea in a leaking vessel, that if he did not bestir himself as for his life to get it to the shore, would sink and drown him. And if you knew but the case of a converted soul, even of those that walk most heavily, and most bewail their own condition, you would not be out of it one day longer, if you could possibly help it. Well, I have showed you what it is to be unconverted: if any of you dare yet go on in such a case, and unbelievingly cavil at the word of God, or carelessly trample it under your feet; if God forsake you and leave you to yourselves and if death find you in that sad state, you may thank yourselves.

CHAPTER V.

SOME OF THE SPECIAL BENEFITS OF CONVERSION.

SECTION I.

INTRODUCTION.

Having said thus much to you by way of terror, if it may be to drive you from an unconverted state, I shall not so leave you; but shall next say somewhat also by way of allurement to draw you to a better state. For as there is enough in your misery to drive a sober man from it, so is there enough in the hope that is set before you, to draw any believing heart to embrace it. The gospel is a joyful message, and brings glad tidings of salvation to all that entertain it; if you will not shut your eyes by unbelief, or inconsiderateness, you shall see that God calls you not to your hurt or loss. If there be not more to be had in his service, than in the service of the world, the flesh, or the devil, take your course, and never regard me more. If I do not give you sufficient reason to prove to you that you may make a better bargain by speedy conversion, than by continuing in your carnal, unconverted state, I am contented that you never more give me a hearing: for my part, I would not persuade you to your hurt or loss, nor make such a stir

about an uncertain gain; nor about a small matter, were it never so certain: but my principal arguments are yet behind: fear is not the principal affection of a true convert; and therefore terrifying arguments are not the principal means; yet these must be used, or else God had never put such an affection into man's heart, nor such terrifying passages into his word: and we all feel the need and usefulness of it; for in reason he that is in danger should know it: but yet it is love that must be the predominant affection, and therefore it is the discovery of the amiableness of God, and the wonderful gain that comes by godliness, that must be the principal argument that we must use with you. For we know that men will not be directly affrighted into love, though they must be affrighted from the contrary that hinders it: do not think that God hath no better argument to use with you than to take you by the throat, and say, 'love me, or I will damn thee.' Thus he will endeavour to wean you from the contrary love, and to let you know the fruit of your folly, that he may equally carry on his work upon all the affections of your souls together.

But he that principally requires your love, doth give you undeniable reason why you *should love* him: and he that calls for your hearts doth show you that which might take with your hearts, and effectually win them, if your eyes were opened to see what he shows you. He draws them as a loadstone doth the iron, by the force of his attractive love. If there be not more in God that is worth your love than in all the world, if all were yours, then hold on your present course and spare not. But why make I any comparison in such a case? It were a want of reverence in me, but that your necessity requires it: because wicked men do not only make a comparison first, but also prefer the world before God, though not in their tongues, yet in their hearts and lives: if I were but able to make you thoroughly know what that condition is to which I persuade you, I would desire no better argument to prevail with you; were it in my power but to open your eyes to make you know what conversion is, and what it doth for those that have it, I should make no doubt of your speedy conversion: for none withdraw their hearts from God, but for want of knowing him; and none are against a holy life, but those that understand not sufficiently what it is: and none prefer this world, and the pleasures and profits of it before the glorious things that God doth offer them, but only they that are cheated and bewitched by it, and know not what it is that they dote upon. If I were but able to give you such a sight as Stephen had, when he saw the heavens opened, and Christ standing at the right hand of God, I should have no need to call you from your fleshly vanities. How contemptuously would you throw away your former pleasure, and run to see and be possessors of that glory! If I could but bring you with Paul into the third heaven, to see the unutterable things that every true believer shall possess, I would give you no thanks to cast off this world, and presently to turn to God. Nay, if you had but the light about you that Paul had at his conversion, it would do much: but why talk I of these extraordinary things? If you did but know by a sound belief, such as all the converted have, what a blessed life it is that we invite you to, away you would come without delay; as the apostles when Christ called them from their trades and friends, and bade them follow him, they presently left all, though they saw nothing in the world to draw them on; so would you, if you were but well illuminated. And because all that I can do in this work, is to exhibit to your understandings the excellency of that condition to which I persuade you, I shall next fall upon that, and leave the issue to God, desiring him to open your eyes, to see what shall be propounded.

SECTION II.

THE CONVERTED ARE DELIVERED FROM THE DOMINION OF SATAN, AND THE SLAVERY OF SIN.

When a sinner is converted, he is delivered from the power of Satan, the bonds of your captivity will all be broken in your return to Christ, as Peter's chains fell off him, and the prison doors were set open, when the angel roused him up. So it will be with thy soul when God converts thee. Ignorance and wilfulness in fleshly pleasures, and the love of this world, these are the chains that Satan holds men in; and conversion will bring thee from darkness to light, even from the power of darkness into the kingdom of Christ; it will bring such a marvellous light into thy mind, as thou never hadst before, which will make thee marvel at the riches of grace and glory, and marvel at the wonderful love of God, and wonder that during thy former folly thou couldst neglect it. Thus will God bring thee out of darkness into his marvellous light. Telling you what this light is will not be sufficient to make you know it, till you see it yourselves. You shall then have other apprehensions of

things than now you have, even of the same things which you see and seem to know. You will have another knowledge of the world, of Christ, grace, duty, and all spiritual things, even of good and evil than now you have. As the first sin did open Adam's eyes to know good and evil by sad experience, as having lost the good and felt the evil, and also to know them in a separated sense, as distinct and separated in his thoughts from God: so true conversion will open your eyes to know good and evil by a blessed experience, even to see God, the chief good, as recovered to you for your felicity; and sin and hell the greatest evils from which you are delivered; and to see God in all the creatures, and the respect and tendency they all have to him. I cannot by telling you make you conceive what a marvellous change will be in your understanding; what an excellent and marvellous light you will see, when once conversion hath opened your eyes. Let me endeavour, by a familiar comparison, to acquaint you with somewhat of it in general, though I cannot give you the thing itself.

You know that a dog that lives in the house with you doth see the same things, place, and persons in the house as you do; he hath some kind of knowledge of them; he knows every room, and every person in the house: suppose now that God should turn this dog suddenly into a man; do you think there would not be a marvellous change in his apprehension? Would he not see something in every thing, place, and person to marvel at? Would he not know all these things in another manner than before he did? I do not say that the change which conversion makes is just of such a kind as this; but it is very marvellous, and we may by such a similitude help our apprehensions of it. When some of the poor naked Indians have been brought into this land, how strange did every thing seem to them? When they came into London, with what wondering would they gaze about them, as if they had been in another world. And will not a poor converted soul do so, when God hath newly opened his eyes, and made him see that which he never saw before? Then he sees that evil in sin, that ravishing love in Christ, that amiable glory in the face of God, and that truth in the promises of eternal blessedness, that make him wonder: when before he could see nothing to wonder at in any of them. If you knew but the pleasure of this marvellous light that God by conversion would let into your souls, you would never rest till you found yourselves converted. Every man hath a natural desire of knowledge, and in a natural way they are seeking after it ; and many even in the use of these means, which should be spiritual, employ themselves but in natural seeking. One man thinks that common learning can help him to this light, and therefore he reads and studies day and night; and I deny not but in its place it is good: another thinks that among this or that party it is to be found, and in the discovery of this or that opinion it doth consist; but when all is done, it is the great and common truths that are most wonderful; and converting grace that must show men the glory of them. It is not in new discoveries, nor strange principles that were never heard of till now, that this light is to be found, but it is in the substance of Christian verity. I tell you that now usually mutter over your creed for a prayer and hear the catechism without understanding it, if your eyes were opened by converting grace, you would marvel at the very doctrine of the creed and catechism. You would see that excellency, and feel that weight in common truths, that would exceedingly engage your very hearts. You now know not what it is to believe in God the Father, the Son, and Holy Ghost: but then these three words would seem to you of greater glory than the sun at noon-day; they would find you both work and wonder, and yet delight, if you had no more than these to think of.

And do you love the darkness rather than such light? Have you been so long in the dungeon, that you are fallen in love with it, and are loth to come out? Is all this light so small a matter in your eyes? Are you like an owl or bat that cannot endure the light of the sun? Or rather like a thief that hates the day-light, because he is afraid of being made known? Sinners, I beseech you come away and leave your dungeon state of darkness, and live in the light of the countenance of God. ' It is a pleasant thing for the eyes to see the sun.' Deprive not yourselves of the pleasure which is offered you.

It is not only your chains of darkness, but also your wilfulness and blind affections that converting grace will turn you from: these bonds of worldly profits and pleasure that seem so strong to others that they cannot overcome them, you will shake them off as Samson did his bonds, and they will not be able to separate you from the love of God : the same tempter that so easily prevails with others, will not be able to prevail against you; ' the God of peace will tread him under your feet.' In the work of conversion Christ lays siege to the heart of a sinner, which naturally is Satan's garrison; he batters, starves it, and forces it to yield, ' and binds that 'strong man that possesses it in peace.' So he is cast out of his possession by converting grace ; he hath not the same power there that he had before ; once he could have commanded the man to swear, or be drunk, or neglect his soul, and he would have done it; but now he hath no such power ; once he could have turned their thoughts against Christ, and their tongues to cavil against his word, but now he cannot ; they are now under another government. They have now that ' repentance to the acknowledgment of the truth,' by which they are recovered out of the snares of the devil, who formerly led them captive at his will. The very first day that you are converted, you are the freemen of Christ, who were the bond-slaves of the devil all your lives before. As ever then you would partake of this blessed privilege, resist no longer, but yield to the call of grace, that you may be converted.

SECTION III.

THEY ARE VITALLY UNITED TO THE LORD JESUS.

Another excellent privilege of a converted soul is this : as soon as ever a man is converted, he is united or joined to Jesus Christ : this is the very root of all the rest. Conversion turns men from Satan to God ; it breaks them off from their former lovers, and unites them to Christ as the husband of their souls. He is the vine, and we are the branches, and into him we must be grafted, if we will have life. He is the head, and conversion is that which makes us his members, giving us that faith by which we receive him to dwell in our hearts. So that as the sovereign and subject make one commonwealth; as the head and the body make one man, so Christ and his church are one. Whether or not the union be any more than relative, taking union in the strictest sense, yet it is wonderful and glorious, and a communication of holy qualifications follows it. We are one in relation and one in judgment, as being of the same mind; and one in affection, one in regard of the similitude of nature, and many ways one in a larger sense. Here is the root of the saints' felicity. If you were one with the prince, you would not fear the want of honour or riches ; you would not fear any thing that he could save you from.

When Jonathan loved David as his own soul, he ventured his life to save him from his father's indignation : when Lazarus, whom Christ loved, was sick, he raised him from the dead. If you be once so near to Christ as to be one with him, what will he not do for you? Will he neglect his own members? Will he hurt himself? The apostle could use this argument with husbands to love their wives, because they are as their own body, and 'whoever hated his own flesh? but nourisheth it and cherisheth it, even as Christ doth the church.' From hence doth the apostle fetch the example of conjugal love; 'husbands love your wives, even as Christ loved the church; yea, from this union: for we are members of his body, of his flesh, and of his bones.—This is a mystery,' saith the apostle, speaking of Christ and the church, and a mystery of unspeakable consolation to the saints. Therefore resist not that grace which should convert you: if you would be united to Christ, come to him, and yield to the drawings of his love, that you may be one with him who is one with the Father, according to your capacity, for that is his will, concerning all that are truly converted. Judge now whether it be not a most honourable and inconceivable felicity, that conversion doth advance the soul into. It was the greatest miracle of all God's works, that ever he revealed to the sons of men, to take the human nature into union with the divine, that Christ, who was God, should condescend to be made man; and the next is, that he will take his church into union with himself, and will magnify his love, in such a wonderful advancement of poor sinners, that without his grace they could not well believe it.

SECTION IV.

THEY ARE CONSTITUTED LIVING MEMBERS OF THE CHURCH OF CHRIST.

Another benefit that follows conversion is this: as soon as ever a man is truly converted, he is made a member of the true church of Christ, for he is at once united to the head and to the body: a man may be a member of the visible church, or rather, be visibly made a member of the church before conversion: yet that is but as a wooden leg to the body; or as Bellarmine himself acknowledges, they are not living but dead members: and as many of his friends whom he mentions, confess they are but as the hair, or the nails, which are not properly members of the body, though they are in the body; or as Austin saith, like the chaff among the corn, which is so a part of the field as to be an appendage of the

corn. So that till conversion, even the baptized and the most intelligent men, are but as the straw and chaff in God's barn, and as the tares in his field, as Christ himself compares them. But conversion doth effectually ingraft them into the body, and make them living members; and so 'by one Spirit we are all baptized into one body.' And so 'we are the body of Christ and members in particular.—All are not Israel that are of Israel,' saith the apostle to the Romans. And 'in Christ Jesus neither circumcision availeth any thing, nor uncircumcision, but a new creature; and faith that worketh by love.—For circumcision is that of the heart, in the Spirit, not in the letter.—They are the circumcision that worship God in the Spirit.' And it is not the mere baptism of water, but the baptism of the Holy Ghost, which is given in conversion, that makes you living members of the body.

SECTION V.

THEY ARE MADE THE SUBJECTS OF PARDONING LOVE.

As soon as ever a sinner is truly converted, he hath a pardon of all the sins that ever he committed, be they ever so many and ever so great: though with Paul he have been a persecutor of the church of God; though he have with Manasseh, been a very sorcerer; though he have hated godliness, and made a mock at it; though his very heart hath been against Christ all his days; yet when he is once truly converted, he is pardoned: though he have spent the flower of his youth in vanity; though he have been a drudge for this world, and forgotten his soul and the world to come; though he have hindered others from conversion and salvation; yet when he is once truly converted, he is forgiven; though he have long resisted grace, and striven against his own salvation; though he have stifled many convictions of conscience, and broken many purposes and promises, and much abused the patience of God: yet if the work of conversion be true, all this shall be pardoned and done away. For the Lord Jesus hath made satisfaction for all; and thereupon hath made a conditional promise, that all who truly repent and believe shall be pardoned: and as soon as ever they perform the condition through his grace, the promise becomes effectual to them, and their iniquities are therein forgiven them.

What news is this to a weary heavy-laden

sinner; to them that are bruised and broken under the sense of sin and wrath, that would give a world if they had it, for a pardon! Why, come to Christ, sinner, and take it freely: he hath purchased it, and he freely offers it, but only to them that take himself: for God hath made these benefits parts of his salvation; take Christ himself, and all is thine. What comfort was it to such a sinner as Mary, that lay wiping Christ's feet with the hairs of her head, and washed them with her tears, to hear him say, 'thy sins are forgiven thee.' Those sins that so terrify the conscience, and those that lie asleep till conscience be enlightened; thy secret sins, which the world knows not of, and thine open sins, that have been thy shame, at the very hour of true conversion will be pardoned: all thy sinful thoughts, words and actions: sins against knowledge, conscience, consideration: sins of ignorance and presumptuous sins, all shall be done away. 'Whom he calleth, them he justifieth.—Christ is exalted to be a prince and a Saviour, to give repentance and forgiveness of sins.' Thus doth 'he bless them, in turning them from their iniquities;' and in turning away from them the punishment of that iniquity. He who sent John Baptist first to preach 're- pentance for the remission of sins,' who hath shed his own blood for their remission, and who calls men to repent for that end, hath promised to give it to all that thus repent and believe in him, and are converted to him; and commanded his ministers to join these together, and 'that repent- ance and remission of sins be preached in his name.' May we not then say with David, and after him with Paul, that they are 'blessed whose iniquities are forgiven, whose sins are covered, and to whom the Lord will not impute sin?' Therefore receive ye converting grace, that you may be made partakers of this blessedness: take the counsel of Peter to Simon Magus, 'Repent of thy wickedness, and pray God, if perhaps the thoughts of thy heart may be forgiven thee.' Or as the same Peter to the Jews, 'Repent ye therefore and be converted, that your sins may be blotted out.' O blessed hour that frees the soul from such a load, that else would have sunk it as low as hell! A day and a mercy that must never be forgotten by us.

SECTION VI.

CONVERTS ARE RECONCILED TO GOD.

Another benefit is this: as soon as a sinner is converted, he is reconciled to God: the former enmity is done away: though this be in substance the same with the former, yet doth it show us our happiness in another consideration. A fu- ture reconciliation was purchased before by the blood of Christ, and a conditional reconciliation given out in the gospel; but the soul was never actually reconciled till the time of conversion. Hitherto a sinner either presumptuously intruded into the presence of God to his own danger, or else fled back through the terrors of his con- science. The frowns of the face of God were indeed enough to deter a guilty soul! What comfort could that man have to think of God, who lay under his continual curse and wrath? But when once they are converted, the face of God then smiles on them, and his arms are open to embrace them, as the father's were to the re- turning prodigal. God cannot show himself pleased with a graceless, carnal soul: nor can he choose but be reconciled to the soul that is once possessed of his image, and reconciled unto him: as you are, so will he be to you. He did but stay for the turning of your hearts, that you might be fit to receive that kindness from him, which you are not fit for in the bondage of your sins. This is the happiness of a converted soul, that he hath the love and favour of almighty God. Therefore doth Christ call them his friends. And what is it that he will not do for his friends, who did so much for us while we were enemies? Therefore yield ye to the calls of God. The word of conversion is a word of reconciliation: and this is it that he hath committed to us, that we might 'beseech men in his name and stead to be reconciled to God,' which is only by being converted to God. Did you know the worth of peace with God, you would quickly yield to return unto him.

SECTION VII.

THEY ARE ADOPTED INTO HIS FAMILY.

Another precious benefit to the converted is, that they are the adopted sons of God; which is a step higher than to be barely reconciled and his friends. When they are planted into Christ the natural Son, they become adopted sons; for 'God sent his own Son made of a woman, made under the law, to redeem them that were under the law, that we might receive the adoption of sons; wherefore we are no more servants only but sons.' This is a benefit not common to all. 'It is as many as are led by the Spirit of God that are his sons.—And they that are in their measure blameless and harmless, without rebuke in the midst of a crooked and perverse nation, among whom they shine as lights in the world.' Christians, know your own felicity, that you may rejoice in it, and give glory to God. You may boldly draw near him, and call him your father, and look for the love and bounty of a father, at his hands. O wretched world, to despise so great a mercy as this is! Doth it seem a small thing to them to be the sons of God? It raised the blessed apostle into an admiration, 'Behold what manner of love the Father hath bestowed upon us, that we should be called the sons of God :' and as a father compassionates a son that he delights in, so doth the Lord the poorest of his people. The world, I told you, is divided into the children of God and the children of the devil, and it is by conversion from sin to God that men are known to be the children of God. If therefore you value this wonderful privilege, yield then to the grace of God, which would convert you.

SECTION VIII.

THEY POSSESS THE SPIRIT OF CHRIST.

Another benefit of the converted is, that they have the Spirit of Christ within them : by it doth Christ possess and govern them ; by it doth he make them like to himself, and work out all that is contrary to his holiness. For it is a cleansing Spirit and a Spirit of holiness ; by this he helps them against the flesh and effectually mortifies it ; by this doth he quicken them to newness of life, for it is a quickening Spirit; by this it is that 'he helpeth their infirmities, and teacheth them to pray ;' by this he teaches them his law, and writes it in their hearts; by this he possesses them with filial affection, and causes them to 'cry to him, Abba, Father ;' by this one Spirit all his people have access to him, and by this they are made his habitation ; and in the unity of this Spirit they are one with the Lord, and among themselves. This Spirit is the earnest of their future glory; and 'where this Spirit is, there is liberty' from former slavery. So that you see how great a mercy it is to have the Spirit of Jesus Christ within us; and this is the case of all that are converted, and none but them. 'For if any man have not the Spirit of Christ, the same is none of his.' If you did but know what it is to be possessed by the Holy Ghost, when ungodly men have the spirit of uncleanness, you would not rest without this blessedness.

SECTION IX.

THEY INHERIT THE PROMISES.

Another part of the happiness of the converted is : that all the promises of grace are theirs: they are the children of the promise, and God is, as it were, obliged to them, and hath engaged his word for their security. 'All the promises are in Christ, yea, and amen.' They therefore that are in Christ must needs have part in them. How full is the book of God of free and precious promises to his people! which all belong to thee, if converted. There hast thou promises for remission ; promises for assistance against temptation ; promises for acceptance of thy person and duties, and promises for protection and deliverance from evil ; and when thou readest them, thou mayest say, 'all those are mine.' He that knows that God is true, will not take a promise as an inconsiderable mercy. If men account it such a matter to have a lease or deed of gift of land and worldly riches, how should we value that covenant and testament of our Lord? In a word, 'godliness is profitable to all things, having the promise of the life that now is, and of that which is to come.' What can any man desire more ?

Yield therefore to the voice of grace that you may be converted, and all the promises of grace will be yours: it will then be an unspeakable comfort to you, that whatsoever condition you are in, you have a promise of God that you shall be better. If you be in poverty, in sickness, or at the hour of death, yet you have a promise, which is enough to support a believing soul. As one saith, 'I had rather be at the bottom of the sea with a promise, than in paradise without it.' For there is no misery so deep, but we shall certainly be delivered from it, if we have but a promise : but without it Adam was not safe in innocency.

CHAPTER X.

THEIR SERVICES ARE ACCEPTABLE TO GOD.

Another benefit of the converted is, that all their duties are pleasing to God. I mean not their sins nor the failings of their duties; for God will never be reconciled to these, when he is reconciled to the sinner : but the failings of all their duties are forgiven them, through the blood of Christ, and the failing being forgiven, the duty is accepted, and well pleasing to God. 'By faith, Abel offered a more excellent sacrifice than Cain, by which he obtained witness that he was righteous, God testifying of his gifts.—By faith, Enoch had this testimony that he pleased God.' The sacrifice of their good works is pleasing to him; their 'prayers and alms-deeds come up before him; for in every nation he that feareth God and worketh righteousness, is accepted of him.' It is their study and work to do those things that please him and walk in all obedience, for such are accepted of him. And all this is through Christ, in whom the Father was first well pleased. How great a consolation is this to the saints! See that you be truly converted, and go to God, and fear not lest he will reject you further than is necessary to reverence and caution. When he abhors the gilded sacrifice of the hypocrite, he will accept that which seems weaker from thee. He will hear thy very groans, tears, and broken expressions: lament over thy weakness and see that thou disown them, and then thou shalt find that God will not disown thy services for them. What a comfort is this in a time of extremity, in trouble of conscience, in sickness and at death, to have God to be well pleased with all our duties, and to know that he will not abhor our prayers. The time is near, Christian, when thou wilt find this privilege more worth to thee than a thousand worlds, that God will let thee come near him with acceptance, bid thee welcome, and hear thy prayers, and the time is coming when unconverted sinners would give a world if they had it, for such a privilege, and say, O that I could go to God, and have a gracious hearing as well as they: but it will not be, because they knew not the day of their visitation.

SECTION XI.

THEY ARE THE OBJECTS OF ANGELIC CARE.

Another benefit of the converted is this: the angels of God have a special order and commission to attend them. They are all ministering spirits sent forth to minister for them who shall be heirs of salvation. Note here, that angels are servants, not to us, but to God for us; and that it is in a special manner for the heirs of salvation: and that it seems it is all the angels that are designed to this office. I say not all the glorious spirits that are before the throne of God: for I presume not to determine whether there be not other spirits besides the angels; for the word angel signifies a messenger, and there-

fore it is only these that are employed as God's messengers that are called by that name; and those that believe in Christ are said to have their own angels always beholding the face of God. These doth he send to deliver his servants in distress, as they did. For 'he giveth his angels charge over them to keep them in all their ways, they shall bear them up in their hands, lest they dash their foot against a stone.' Yea, they have their office also for the good of souls: an angel appeared to Christ himself and strengthened him in his agony. As evil spirits can hurt the souls of the wicked, so no doubt but the good can help the souls of the righteous; and therefore when Satan comes to deceive, he is said to be 'transformed into an angel of light.' Yea, when the soul goes out of the body, these angels are the conductors of it into the presence of God, where we shall be made equal to the angels themselves. If the eyes of true Christians were but opened to see their glorious attendance, they would be more sensible of this privilege, and more thankful for it, than now they are. God could do all things for us without instruments if he pleased; but as he rather chooses to work by instruments and second causes for our bodies, so also by these invisible instruments both for body and soul. When Saul had sinned against God, and was forsaken by him, the good spirit was taken from him, and an evil spirit given to him. Some common benefits even common men may have by these angels while they forfeit not their helps, but not that special benefit as the saints. The world cannot distinguish the righteous from the wicked, but the angels of God can; for they must needs know their own charge, and who it is that Christ hath especially committed to their trust.

SECTION XII.

THEY ARE FIT SUBJECTS FOR COMMUNION WITH GOD'S REDEEMED CHURCH.

Another excellent benefit of the converted is this: as they are true members of the catholic church (whatsoever any schismatics may say to the contrary, that would confine the catholic church to their own party,) so have they communion with the whole church, and many spiritual advantages by that communion. Besides that external communion in church order and ordinances, which the ungodly may have as well as they; there is a spiritual internal communion and communication, which is proper to the living converted members. All the saints have one spirit of holiness to animate them; they all intend the same end, and conspire in the same way for the accomplishment: God is their common end, as he is their common original; they have 'all one God, one Christ, one faith,' though they may differ in many smaller opinions, and to 'every one of them is given grace, according to the measure of the gift of Christ,' and so they 'are all one body and one Spirit, and must endeavour to keep the unity of the Spirit in the bond of peace; they are members of one heavenly city, 'even Jerusalem, which is above, the mother of us all;' where they shall be perfected, and of the militant church, the city of God, while they are here on earth. It is the design of God, in the fulness of time, to gather them all into one, in Christ, yea, to make them and the angels in heaven to be one body; they have here the same officers and means, even apostles, and prophets, and their holy writings, pastors and teachers, and the use of ordinances, and this for the edifying and perfection of the body, 'till they all come in the unity of the faith and of the knowledge of the Son of God, to a perfect man, to the measure of the stature of the fulness of Christ. That speaking the truth in love, they may grow up into him in all things which is the head, Christ, from whom the whole body, fitly joined together and compacted by that which every joint supplieth, according to the effectual working in the measure of every part, maketh increase of the body, to the edifying of itself in love.'

Moreover the whole church doth constantly pray for every member; not only as for those that are yet unconverted, that they may have grace, because they have no absolute promise to be heard in that, and that they shall not be heard for all men in general, they are certain, and therefore may not so ask it; but when they pray for the godly, it is as for those for whom they have a promise. As they live in the constant love of one another, which is the mark by which the world must know them, and an effect of the Spirit, which doth animate the whole body; so doth this love express itself in the breathings forth of constant desires for the prosperity of the whole, and each part. Christians, what an excellent privilege is this, that the poorest man or woman of you that is converted, hath thousands and tens of thousands of the prayers of the saints going for you to God from day to day: which ever way you are going, or whatsoever you are doing, this stock is improving for you, this work is going on. When you are about other matters and think not of it, there are thousands of holy people praying for you: when you grow cold and faint in prayer, there are thousands of fervent Christians at prayer for you. When you have backslidden, and conscience is troubled, and you dare scarcely go to God again, there are thousands of Christians that are at prayer for you, who have clearer consciences and boldness with God. Is not this a comfort when your graces are weak, when temptations are strong, and troubles, fears, and doubts, are many, to remember you have thousands of the people of God at prayer for you? Is not this a great comfort, in the greatest dangers, when you are afraid of your salvation, to remember how many thousands are at prayer for your salvation? Nay, it is even the whole church of God: and you may well think that God will not easily deny the prayer of his whole church: he that hath promised to hear two or three, yea, every single person that asks any thing in the name of Christ, according to his will, is unlikely to deny his whole church when they join together for any such thing?

This is a matter that is according to his will, that his truly converted people should persevere, and be preserved in his love, and safely brought on to his heavenly kingdom. O remember this in your doubts and troubles, that all the church of Christ is daily at prayer with God for your salvation. Is not this a great comfort to you, in time of sickness, or at the hour of death, to remember that now the whole church of God is at prayer for you? You send to this friend and that friend, whom you think have interest in God, and you are glad if you can but get them to pray for you: how glad then should you be, that all the church prays for you, who most certainly have so great an interest in him? The Spirit of prayer which teaches the people of God to pray, will not forget you, nor suffer them to forget you, but will make them pray for all the body, and every member of it, as the very tenor of the Lord's prayer shows you: then if you be wise, yield to that grace of Christ that would convert you, that you may be members of this body, and live in the spiritual communion of it: for alas, to join externally in the communion of the church, when you have not communion with them in the spirit, will but increase your condemnation at the last. You are every day among the saints of God, but you know them not, nor the Spirit by which they live, nor the spiritual part of the work which they do. Such a communion as the dead bodies have together which you tread upon (whose bones and dust lie mingled in the earth) in comparison of our communion who are here together in the presence of God among the living; even such a communion have the unconverted in the visible church in comparison of that spiritual communion of the people that are converted.

SECTION XIII.

THEY HAVE AN INTEREST IN THE CONSTANT INTERCESSION OF CHRIST.

Another excellent benefit to the converted is: that they have the constant intercession of Jesus Christ, God and man, in his heavenly priesthood, at his Father's right hand, in the heavenly glory. Their Head is not insensible of their wants, nor doth he disregard them; the wrong that is done you, he takes as done to himself. 'Saul, Saul, why persecutest thou me?' said he to one that trod upon his foot. And the good that is done or denied to you by others, he takes as done or denied to himself. Surely then he doth not forget us, though he be exalted to his glory. He is not like the poor silly creatures that cannot bear exaltation without being puffed up, and forgetting themselves : yea, their friends and their God. No ; his exaltation is spiritual and heavenly, perfecting his human nature to the greatest height that it is capable of : he lives in the face of God, who is love ; nay, into the personal union with the Godhead, which is love, hath he assumed our nature long ago ; he was never more tender of Jerusalem, when he wept over them, or of his people when he wept, bled, and died for them, than he is now of them in his glory. Though he cannot weep or grieve now as he did on earth yet he can love now as much as ever he loved : and therefore his eye is still upon our wants, his heart is set upon us for our good ; he looks down from heaven upon every particular member ; he sees that this man wants this grace, and that man wants that, and the other is in danger of this or that corruption or temptation ; and he is daily carrying on the cure. It is he that sends this minister and the other minister as his apothecaries, with his medicines, and persuades you to take them for your good ; it is he that directs this or that affliction to be a medicine for some dangerous disease, when he sees that easier means prevail not. You see not your chief physician, he stands out of your sight ; but he sees you, and it is he that doth all for you that is done : as he prepared a medicine of his own blood to cure sick souls, while he was here upon earth, so is he now continually applying it to them for their cure. Do not think that all his love was shown upon the cross, or that all that

he doth for you by his blood was then done. No : he is still pleading as it were that blood on your behalf unto his Father, and offering the sacrifice for you again in the holiest, which he once offered for you on the cross ; and is there a priest for ever after the order of Melchizedeck. 'And because he continueth ever, he hath an unchangeable priesthood ; wherefore he is able also to save them to the uttermost that come unto God by him, seeing he ever liveth to make intercession for them.—For as by his own blood he entered once into the holy place, having obtained eternal redemption : so shall this blood of Christ, who through the eternal Spirit offered himself without spot to God, purge our consciences from dead works to serve the living God.—For Christ is not entered into the holy place made with hands, which is the figure of the true, but into heaven itself, now to appear in the presence of God for us.—For after he had offered one sacrifice for sins, for ever he is set down on the right hand of God, from henceforth expecting till his, and our, enemies be made his footstool ; for by one offering he hath perfected for ever them that are sanctified.'

So that we have a perfect high priest that perfectly loves us, who is representing our case before his Father, and pleading a perfect sacrifice for us ; and through him it is that we ourselves 'have boldness to enter into the holiest, even by his blood, by the new and living way which he hath consecrated for us, through the veil, even his flesh : for, having such an high priest over the house of God, we may draw near in full assurance of faith, if we have a true heart, sprinkled from an evil conscience, as our bodies are washed with pure water.' What an unspeakable comfort is this to every truly converted soul? The Son of God is at prayer for thee, Christian. If thou think that God will not hear thine own prayers : no, nor hear the whole church's prayers : dost thou think he will hear his Son's prayers, or not? The poor man that was born blind could tell that God heareth not sinners, that is, unconverted sinners ; 'but if any man be a worshipper of God, and doth his will, him he heareth.' How then can he choose but hear him that had no sin ; and hear him that takes away the sins of the world? He that said, 'This is my beloved Son, in whom I am well pleased, hear him ;' will surely hear him himself, because he is so. He tells his Father, 'I know that thou hearest me always ;' and it is not only his common intercession for his common salvation, which he gives to the world ; for so, 'when he poured out his soul to death, and was numbered among the transgressors, and bare the sins of many, he made intercession for the transgressors.' And said, Father, forgive them, for they know not what they do.' And so he procures them a conditional pardon and salvation, with the means and mercies that have a tendency thereto. But it is the special intercession for that special grace which he communicates to none but his living members. Read that excellent prayer which he puts up to the Father for his own, and remember that these requests are for you, and that it is for all that shall believe in him through the world, that he thus intercedes. O what a comfort is it to a poor Christian, that in his greatest infirmities, and deepest sense of unworthiness, he hath the beloved of the Father to take his prayers and present them to God, and to plead his cause more effectually than he can do his own. What say you then to this, you that are yet in the flesh and unacquainted with the life of grace; would you have a Saviour to speak for you to the Father? Yea, one who hath all power in heaven and earth committed to him, and 'is able to save to the uttermost all those that come to God by him?' Yield then speedily to converting grace, and rest not till this work be wrought upon your souls: this blessed state may be yours as well as other men's, if you do not now neglect it and refuse it.

SECTION XIV.

ALL THINGS ARE THEIRS AND WORK TOGETHER FOR THEIR GOOD.

Another excellent benefit to the converted is: that God hath assured them that all things are theirs, and shall work to their good. The promise is expressed. Not that they have a propriety in other men's possessions, in civil respects; but finally, other men, and their possessions, and all the world are for their good. As the world at first was made for Adam and his offspring, so is it redeemed from ruin for the second Adam and his offspring, in a special manner; the earthly inheritors shall have it in possession, and many of them not have a thousandth part of the benefit by it, as others that possess it not: the physician hath his skill in his own possession, but the patient who is recovered by it, may have more benefit by it than he that possesses it: the whole frame of heaven and earth are in perpetual motion for the glory of the saints: are all conjoined by the over-ruling providence, and are carrying on the same design of God, when they seem at the greatest odds among themselves. When the instruments themselves are unacquainted with their own employment, and know not what it is that they are doing, yet God knows, who sees and rules them all. The business that God hath in hand is to build the heavenly Jerusalem, to gather to himself the whole number of his elect that are scattered through the world, and to make them a city for his own habitation, and a people for his everlasting praise; and the very persecutors of the church are but now hewing them and squaring them, and fitting them for the building: when God sees us sick of a fever, he often uses the sword of an enemy to let blood, which shall as certainly do the cure as the tenderest hand. The medicine knows not that it is healing a man's disease; the lance knows not that it is saving a man's life by taking away his blood, but he that uses them knows what he is doing. Herod and Pilate, and the people of the Jews thought they had been securing their own seats, and the liberty of their nation, by crucifying one that called himself King of the Jews; they little knew that they were shedding that blood which was to be a sacrifice for the sins of the world, and crucifying that flesh that was given for the life of the world. But God knew what he was doing by them: for they did nothing but what 'his council had determined should come to pass.'

Pharaoh thought he was securing his interest; but God knew he was getting himself glory, and his people a wonderful deliverance by his obstinacy. And even Satan himself is as much over-reached in his devices and enterprizes against the saints, as their earthly enemies are. He is but exercising their graces, driving them to Christ, and honouring the power of his blood and Spirit eventually, when he seeks to devour them; his temptations but make them the more watchful; or if they fall, they rise with the greater hatred of sin, love to Christ, and thankfulness for his blood and pardoning grace, and renewed resolution to walk more carefully for the time to come. O blessed state, where all the world, both good and bad, both friends and foes, both angels and devils, are all carrying on the work of our salvation; some with delight and some unwillingly, some with understanding and some not knowing what they do! What a state of comfort hath that man, that may be assured that whatsoever befalls him shall be for his good, and that all things work together for the best! I confess I have had myself so much comfort from that one promise in Rom. viii. 28. that I would not have been without it for a world. When I have had no particular discovery of the tendency of a providence under affliction, and the appearance of death, having had nothing from below to support me, that one promise hath appeared so full, that I thought if there were no more, it might abundantly supply my soul with consolation : what fear should we have of want or enemies, of sickness or death, or any thing that may be terrible to the flesh, as long as we know that all things do but conspire for our salvation ? And though none of the wheels in the chariot of providence should know which way or whither they are moving themselves, yet they all serve to convey us to our glory : it is a matter that is past the belief of the carnal world, but it is a certain sealed truth, that when the persecutor is treading down and tormenting the poor despised saints, it is the saint that is the gainer, and all that is for his good, and his ignorant enemy is scouring off his rust, and preparing him for his master's use and for his glory, and is himself the loser, and the miserable wretch, when he is highest in his honour, and deepest in his cruelty, and proudest in his triumphs. Why poor sinners, do not your hearts within you long to be partakers of this blessed state ? Is it not worth all that you can do or suffer, yea, worth ten thousand worlds, to be such a one as I have now described to you ? Why, you may be such if your own folly and neglect exclude you not, God hath not shut you out of the promise ; O do not shut out yourselves by refusing his converting grace.

SECTION XV.

THEY ARE IN A SAFE STATE TO LIVE OR TO DIE.

Another most excellent benefit to the converted is : that they are past their greatest danger, and have done the greatest business of their lives, and now are ready for death and judgment, whensoever it shall come. Not that all danger is over, or all enemies yet overcome, or all their work done, nor that they are yet perfectly ready to die : but the principal work is done, and the great conquest of the enemy is over and the chief danger is past, and upon the whole they are prepared for their change. What had we to do here but to prepare for glory, and in this short and troublesome life to get interest in a better that shall never end ? and with all that are truly converted this is done : at the very hour that God converted them, he made them his sons, he pardoned their sins, and gave them right to everlasting glory : when he gives you Christ, he gives you all things, or puts you into a condition wherein you may well think he will give you all things. O happy day, may that man or woman say, as long as they live, when God translated them out of the kingdom of darkness into the kingdom of his dear Son ! Many keep their birth days as a day of rejoicing or feasting while they live, when Solomon saith, the day of death is better than the day of birth, but they that know the day of their new-birth may well make that a day of rejoicing while they live. What a blessed change doth that one day or hour make, when God shall presently bring up the heart of a sinner to himself, and join them truly to Jesus Christ, and forgive all the sins that ever they did, and give them right to everlasting glory. You are like a man that is pursued by his enemies, and as soon as ever he can but get into such a castle or garrison, he is safe : so when you first get into Christ by a living, effectual faith, that very hour were you out of the reach of the prevailing, commanding power of hell ; then was the strong man cast out of your souls—then were you brought from under the curse of the law and the wrath of God. If death had found you one hour before that change, you had been damned wretches in hell for ever : and if death should come but one hour after that change, you will certainly be glorified saints with Christ This is true, how strange soever it may seem to you : and the reason is at hand, because that the hour before your conversion you were the members of Satan, you were in the flesh, and had no saving interest in Christ or in the promise : and the hour after true conversion, you are members of Christ, children of the promise, and have part in him who is Lord of all. I deny not but you must still 'watch and pray, that you enter not into temptation ;' and for all the 'promise that is left you of entering into rest,' you must 'fear lest you should seem to come short of it ;' you must still stand on your guard in all the spiritual armour, and work and fight out your salvation, and acquit yourselves like men to the end : but yet I may well say that the chief difficulty is over : the enemy is dispossessed of his chief hold : he that ruled you is now cast out, and though he be not quite under your feet, yet he shortly will be so. Your greatest business now is to keep him out and to stand on your defence, 'and keep what you have, that none may take your crown from you ;' to follow on the conquered enemy in the pursuit, till none remain : 'to grow in grace, and perfect your holiness in the fear of God,' and cast out the remnants of your former filthiness. Hearken therefore, poor sinners, and as ever you are friends to your own souls, neglect not that grace that would bring you into this condition. Would you not think yourselves happy, if it were thus with you?

SECTION XVI.

THEY ARE HEIRS OF GLORY—HAVE THE EARNEST, AND SHALL SOON HAVE THE FULL POSSESSION OF IT.

Another most excellent benefit of the converted is: that they are the rightful heirs of everlasting glory, and as soon as the soul is gone out of the body, they shall have possession of it: at the day of judgment they shall have a blessed resurrection, they shall themselves be justified in judgment, and also with Christ shall judge the world, and so shall be fully possessed of that glory in soul and body, and shall live in the everlasting praise of their Redeemer. Here are many particular benefits, which for brevity I join together. 1. They are now the heirs of glory; for being the sons of God, they are co-heirs with Christ, though they must follow him in sufferings before they come to the possession of their inheritance. 'The Spirit witnesseth with our spirits that we are the children of God; and if children, then heirs, heirs of God, and joint-heirs with Christ, if so be that we suffer with him, that we may also be glorified together.' Though now in our minority, we differ not from servants, yet 'being sons, we are heirs of all.' When moved with holy fear we prepare the ark, and hide ourselves in Christ by faith, and become the heirs of the righteousness of faith, even then also do we become heirs of the end of that righteousness. When we receive our interest in the promise, that promise makes us heirs. O brethren, that you could but conceive the greatness of this blessedness, which even the poorest beggar in the world may have that is rich in faith; for even 'they are heirs of that kingdom which God hath promised to them that love him.' How certainly shall these be partakers of that glory, when they 'have finished their course, and fought the good fight?' For God hath 'laid up a crown of salvation for all such as love his appearing.'

It is conversion that brings us into this blessed state, and the unconverted have no part or fellowship in it. 'But after that the kindness and love of God our Saviour toward man appeared, not by works of righteousness which we have done, but according to his mercy he saved us, by the washing of regeneration and renewing of the Holy Ghost, which is shed on us abundantly through Jesus Christ our Saviour: that being justified by his grace, we should be made heirs according to the hope of eternal life.' So that it is conversion that brings us into this happy condition: therefore bless God if you find that he hath wrought this work upon your souls. Yet be not careless for the time to come, but 'let every one of you show the same diligence to the full assurance of hope unto the end: that ye be not slothful, but followers of them who through faith and patience inherit the promises.' And then doubt not; God hath confirmed your salvation by his oath. 'For God, being willing abundantly to show to the heirs of promise the immutability of his counsel, confirmed it by an oath,' saith the apostle, 'that by two immutable things, in which it was impossible for God to lie, we might have a strong consolation, who have fled for refuge to lay hold on the hope set before us, which hope we have as an anchor of the soul both sure and steadfast, and which entereth into that which is within the veil; whither Jesus Christ the fore-runner is for us entered.'

2. Hereupon it follows that whensoever the righteous die, their souls are conveyed by angels into that glory; when they 'depart, they are with Christ;' and when they 'are absent from the body, they are present with the Lord.' Of which they may 'be confident, as walking by faith, and not by sight, and knowing that if our earthly house of this tabernacle were dissolved, we have a building of God, an house not made with hands, eternal in the heavens;' and therefore may 'groan earnestly, desiring to be clothed upon with our house which is from heaven.' When we die, we may say with Stephen, 'Lord Jesus, receive my spirit'. And were our death as ignominious as the thief's on the cross, yet that 'day should we be with Christ in paradise.' Blessed people that live in such a case, so near the door of a more blessed life! How can you endure to be out of his condition of hope and peace one day or hour? O that you did but know the blessedness that you neglect!

3. Yet this is not all, but the greatest part of the blessedness remains till the day of judgment, and then there are these four benefits to be received. First, The righteous shall have a blessed resurrection: not the resurrection of damnation, which will be the lot of all the rest, but the resurrection of life, as Christ distinguishes them. The graves shall be no longer able to detain them, but he that conquered death

by his own resurrection, will by the same divine power again overcome it by the resurrection of his people. As his natural body hath already triumphed over it, so shall his mystical body at that day: he that made heaven and earth of nothing, will by the same almighty power accomplish this. Second, Being raised and brought to judgment, the next benefit will be their final justification. They have now the justification and pardon of the gospel, and then they shall have the final justification of the judge. For he will give to every man according to right, and his promise made this their right through the blood of Christ. For, 'there is no condemnation to them that are in Christ Jesus, who walk not after the flesh, but after the Spirit.' Whatsoever sin can then be charged on them, they can answer all by showing the gospel pardon in the blood of Christ, and if their title be questioned, they can prove it by their faith and sincere obedience. So all that repent and are converted will then 'have their sins blotted out, when that time of refreshing shall come from the presence of the Lord.' It is not possible that Christ should condemn his own body and condemn those that have believed in him, and sincerely loved him: so dear a friend, so tender-hearted a Saviour, that hath bought us so dearly, sanctified us and cleansed us, and given us a right to that justification by his promise, cannot possibly condemn us after all this. As certainly as Christ himself is justified, his promise true, and his love unchangeable, so certainly shall all the converted be then absolved. Third, Not only so, but also ' with Christ they shall judge the world:' for so is the plain word of promise. Yea, they shall judge the angels themselves. And lastly, they shall take possession of their glory, and enter into the joy of their Lord. ' Then shall the righteous shine forth as the sun in the kingdom of their Father, when the wicked are cast into that furnace of fire, where shall be wailing and gnashing of teeth.—He that hath ears to hear let him hear,' saith Christ, when he had spoken these words: and he that will not hear such things as these, and regard them, will one day wish that he had never had ears, and never had a heart in his breast, or else that it had been better.

Dear friends! would that I were but able to make you know the difference between the righteous and the wicked at that day. Surely I should not need then to say any more to you to make you apprehensive of the necessity of conversion, and to make haste to entertain that grace which is offered you. If the crown of glory be worth seeking, then must converting grace be sought: if an everlasting blessedness with Christ and his holy angels be worth the having, renewing grace is certainly so. Lift up your heads then, Christians, and rejoice in the hope that is set before you. Bless the Lord that ever he brought you into the kingdom of grace, which is but the beginning of the kingdom of glory. As sure as your natural birth was your entrance into this natural world, so sure was your new birth the entrance into a better world. For your life eternal was begun when you began to have the saving knowledge of God, and his Son Jesus Christ. He that hath given you the 'earnest of his Spirit;' who ' hath sealed us with the Holy Spirit of promise, which is the earnest of our inheritance, till the redemption of the purchased possession,' will doubtless give us the inheritance itself. Fear not, Christian, the Lord that hath promised will not deceive thee; for he never yet deceived any. But as sure as the sun shines in the firmament, so surely shalt thou live in the heavenly Jerusalem, and be joined with the holy angels of God in his everlasting praises, and then thou wilt better know than now thou canst do, what God did for thee that day that he converted thee. I know it is the business of the enemy of thy salvation, if it might be, to draw thee back into thy former state of death and darkness; and when he cannot do that, to rob thee at least of the comfort of thy felicity, that thou mightest doubt, fear, and live in perplexity, as if thou wert not the heir of glory. Because as he is loth to be tormented before the time, so is he loth that thou shouldst be comforted before the time; but do not thou believe him: suffer him not to hide thy blessedness from thine eyes, remember it cannot be loved, if it be not believed; thou wilt lose thy joy and God his praise, if the tempter prevail with thee to deny thy mercy. Believe then, and give God the glory by believing.

SECTION XVII.

CONVERSION IS THE COMMENCEMENT OF ETERNAL LIFE.

Another of the blessings of a converted man is: that new life which he hath begun, is a life of health and peace, comfort, and the very beginning of his everlasting peace and life; and the more he hath of it, the more happy will his life be. It is not only our suffering that is the way to reigning, and our tribulation by which we must enter into the kingdom of God; but we have also peace the way to peace; and life the way to life, and joy the way to joy and glory. Our tribulation and sufferings are but some accidental attendants of this our militant state; but the life itself consists of other kind of matter. How blessed a life is it to live in so near relation to God as is above mentioned! And how pleasant a thing is the believing exercise of his graces! How sweet is it to live here in any lively beginnings of the love of God! How pleasant is it to know that we are beloved of him! How sweet is it to draw near him, and plead our cause with him in faith, and to call him Father in confidence through Christ! How sweet is it to live under the power of his ordinances, when by his Spirit he blesses them to our souls! What a joy is it, by believing, to think beforehand of their eternal blessedness! And what comfortable communion have the people of God together, and what good doth it do them to hear and speak of the glory that they shall possess! O poor deceived sinners, that think the way of the Lord to be so grievous, and fly from it as if it were an insufferable toil; did you but know the safety and the comfort which the life of godliness doth afford, you would be of another mind, and take another course than you do. I here profess to you all, in the name of the Lord, that you will never have a safe, nor truly peaceable and comfortable life, till you are converted and live a spiritual and heavenly life: the joy of the world is sorrow in comparison of that you might have from Christ.

The laughter of a fool doth not so much differ from the highest content of the greatest prince on earth, as your carnal mirth and peace differs from that which is brought by true faith from the face of God and the life to come. You fly from godliness for fear of sorrow and trouble, and I tell you it is joy and peace that you fly from, and sorrow and trouble that you continue in, and that you are preparing for. Believe the Lord Jesus himself, if you will not believe those that have tried, ' Come to me all you that are weary and heavy laden, and I will give you rest; take my yoke upon you, and learn of me, for I am meek and lowly in heart, and ye shall find rest to your souls: for my yoke is easy and my burden is light.—For this is the love of God, that we keep his commandments, and his commandments are not grievous.—Being justified by faith, we have peace with God, through our Lord Jesus Christ, by whom also we have access by faith into this grace, wherein we stand, and rejoice in the hope of the glory of God: and not only so, but we glory in tribulation.—Whom having not seen, ye love; though now ye see him not, yet believing, ye rejoice with joy unspeakable and full of glory, receiving the end of your faith, even the salvation of your souls.—We are the circumcision that worship God in the spirit, and rejoice in Christ Jesus, and have no confidence in the flesh.—Rejoice evermore.—Rejoice in the Lord always, and again I say, rejoice.—Rejoice in the Lord, ye righteous, for praise is comely for the upright.— Ye that love the Lord, hate evil; he preserveth the souls of his saints, he delivereth them out of the hands of the wicked: light is sown for the righteous, and gladness for the upright in heart: rejoice in the Lord, O ye righteous, and shout for joy, all ye that are upright in heart.'

What say you to all this now? Is it a life of trouble and misery that God hath prescribed for his people to live in? Is this a burdensome, grievous life? Will you not believe him, concerning his own way? I tell you again, and declare to you from the Lord, that you shall never have any true peace and comfort till you are converted and lead an holy life: and you that say you shall never have an agreeable day more, if you leave your sins, and give up yourselves to a life of holiness, I profess and proclaim to you, that you shall never have a happy life indeed till you do it: I mean, you shall never have that solid and lasting joy, which beseems a man of wisdom to regard: believe the Lord himself that hath told you it twice over, ' There is no peace, saith the Lord, to the wicked.—There is no peace, saith my God, to the wicked.—The way of peace they know not, there is no judgment in their goings; they have made them crooked paths; whosoever goeth therein shall not know peace.' I confess a carnal peace you may maintain, and for a time may have a comfortable dream, but the day is near, when you will have a terrible awakening. You may think that the godly have no such joy, because you see it not, or because you see them sad and heavy; but their joy is such as strangers meddle not with. I know the righteous have many troubles, and are oftener in tears and groans than others; but that is from the remnants of their sins, which, as it consists with prevailing grace, so doth that sorrow, with prevailing joy, or may do at least: a dead man groans not, when a sick man doth: and yet that is no disparagement to life: what is sweeter than life, and yet sickness may make it grievous; but we do not therefore prefer death before life, because some are sick. So what is sweeter than the life of grace, and yet spiritual sickness may make us walk heavily, and yet we do not therefore prefer a death in sin before it. Come and try, sinners, the pleasures that are in the ways of God, and do not for shame speak against them, till you have thoroughly tried them. The Lord himself doth testify of them, ' happy is the man that findeth wisdom, and the man that getteth understanding; for the merchandise of it is better than the merchandise of silver, and the gain thereof than fine gold : she is more precious than rubies ; all the things thou canst desire are not to be compared to her : length of days is in her right hand, and in her left hand riches and honour ; her ways are ways of pleasantness, and all her paths are peace : she is a tree of life to them that lay hold upon her, and happy is every one that retaineth her.' You see then that conversion is the beginning of consolation.

SECTION XVIII.

THE FURTHER THEY ADVANCE IN THE DIVINE LIFE THE GREATER THEIR HAPPINESS.

Another of the privileges of the converted is this : as he hath cause of continual joy, so no evil that can befal him is a sufficient reason to lay by these joys, as to the habit at least, and the prevailing degree. I know that so far as we have sin, we may, we shall, we must have sorrow ; but then, so far as we have that sin pardoned and mortified, we may, we should have greater joy : and because a converted man hath no unmortified, unpardoned sin, therefore his cause of joy is greater than his cause of sorrow. Though yet I must say, that there are seasons when sorrow must be most expressed, as in days of humiliation, in great falls, and in some afflictions ; yet habitually then our joy should be the greater, though it be not the season to express it. But my special meaning here is about the evil of affliction, which is sanctified to the godly, and hath lost its sting, and is turned by a hand of grace to their advantage. Should not that man live in continual joy that is the heir of heaven, a friend of God, a member of Christ, and doth but wait for the hour of death to be possessed of that unspeakable, endless glory ? What should trouble the heart of him that is escaped out of the power of Satan, and the greatest trouble, which is the wrath of God, and the danger of everlasting misery ? That which may torment the heart day and night, even the thoughts of hell, this is not only taken out of his way, but turned into the matter of his joy and praise ; to think but of the fearful misery that he hath escaped. What heart that hath received a pardon of all sins, and is saved thereby from the everlasting torments, can choose but to daily rejoice in that salvation ? Would not a Judas have been glad, while he was hanging himself in despair, if any one would have given him assurance, yea, or but hope of that salvation ?

Go to any despairing sinner, or any one under the terrors of the Lord, and ask them whether or not they would be glad if they could but be assured that they should escape that misery, which they fear ? You need not doubt what answer they would give you. They would be glad, and a thousand times glad, much more if you could assure them of an everlasting glory, instead of that deserved misery. Then, what a blessed state are all those in, that are truly converted ! How many times doth the mouth of Christ pronounce them blessed ! ' Blessed are the poor in spirit, for theirs is the kingdom of heaven : blessed are the pure in heart, for they shall see God : blessed are they that hunger and thirst after righteousness, for they shall be filled : blessed are they that are persecuted for righteousness' sake, for theirs is the kingdom of God.' What case soever that man be in that is the heir of heaven, he cannot choose but be a blessed man. If any thing might make him seem miserable, it would be to be persecuted and hated, and made the scorn of the world ; and yet Christ saith, that even then he is blessed : and bids them even ' then rejoice and be exceeding glad, for great is your reward in heaven ; for so persecuted they the prophets that were before you. That man who hath a reward in heaven, may be exceeding glad, whatsoever befall him here on earth. That man who hath not clothes to his back, nor a house to put his head in, nor a good word from any about him, and yet hath assurance of living in glory with God and his holy angels, as soon as ever he is gone out of the flesh, I think is a happy man in the eye of reason itself. And he that professes to have assurance of such a glory, and yet lives not comfortably in every condition, I will not believe him, whatsoever he profess. Sure I am, the great monarchs and princes of the world, when they are parting with their crowns, would be glad to have assurance of the everlasting crown, on condition they had lived as poor as the vilest beggar on the earth. There is not the stoutest gallant, and proudest sinner, but would be glad to change states with the poorest saint when he sees the end : but they must be wise in time that will be ever the better for their wisdom. Balaam could say, ' O that I may die the death of the righteous, and that my last end may be like his.' All the world would say at last as the foolish virgins, if it would do any good, ' give us of your oil, for our lamps are gone out.' Who would not be a saint, when he is past the pleasure of his sin, and cast off by the world, which deceived him in his prosperity ?

Methinks the greatest men on earth should tremble in the midst of all their glory, to remember the everlasting misery that they are near, if they be not living members of Christ, as Belshazzar did in the midst of his mirth. And methinks the poorest true believer should have his heart abound with joy, to remember the things which God hath promised him, and he must certainly ere long possess. Think not what you are, Christians, only, but what you shall be. Yet a little while, and you shall groan, weep, 'and complain no more : you shall not know what poverty, or trouble, or any other sufferings mean. You are almost past all your sorrow, as the unconverted are almost past their joy. What a difference is between their part and yours; between the good things which they have here, and the portion which you have there! Is it not better to go by the cross to the everlasting crown, than by a fading crown to everlasting torments ? They will forget their honour and delicious fare, when they want a drop of water to cool their tongues ; and you will forget your present sorrow when you are in Abraham's bosom, or in the presence of the Lamb. If one day in the courts of God on earth seemed better to David than a thousand elsewhere, what will an endless life in glory seem to a believing soul ? We want nothing but soundness of faith, spiritual life, and seriousness to make our hearts to leap within us, to make our lives a foretaste of heaven, and to make us pity poor worldlings in the height of their vain glory. What should be a terror to that man who hath overcome the prince of terrors,—who hath God on his side, who hath a promise of everlasting life, who hath evidence to show for his interest in the promise, and a lively faith to improve it and live upon it ? Methinks if the devil should appear to him in his way : if he should walk before him in the most fearful shape, he should but look upon him as a conquered foe. Methinks if he were passing by death from this world, it would be a joyful hour to him, that is presently to step into a world of glory. Now dearly beloved neighbours and friends, I beseech you, for the Lord's sake, hear these things, as men that believe the word of God. Is it not a thousand pities that God should offer you such consolations as these, and you refuse them ? Is it not consummate folly that you should neglect such a blessed state as this, when it is set before you? God hath made you for high and excellent things, even to live with angels in the heavens in glory. Yield but to the work of converting grace, and see that Christ be formed in you once, and all is yours. These things are far off you, and out of sight, and therefore seem strange to flesh and blood, and carnal hearts will not believe them ; but they are true as the living God is true.

The souls of all the converted that are dead in Christ from the beginning to this day, are now in the possession of that glory that I am speaking of. They see it, though we do not ; and we shall see it, if unbelief and neglect do not hinder us : believing is the only way to seeing and possessing. I told you before what a miserable case it is that every unconverted sinner is in, that he is not sure to be safe an hour ; and would you not be out of that state ? Would it not be a blessed state for you to be sure that you shall live with Christ an endless life ? Then you may challenge death with Paul : ' O death, where is thy sting ? O grave, where is thy victory r' Then you may challenge all the world, even earth and hell as he did : 'If God be for us, who shall be against us ? It is God that justifieth, who shall condemn ? Who shall separate us from the love of God ? Shall life or death,' &c. I here proclaim to you, in the name of the Lord, that you may have this blessedness if you will be converted, and that without conversion, it will never be had. Get once into this state, and you may have cause to joy as long as you live, and far greater cause when your present life is ended. I tell you a true converted man is never in so sad or low a case, but still he hath more matter for his joy than for his sorrow. Therefore do not set light by such a happiness, and choose not to yourselves a life of terror, when you may have better if you will.

SECTION XIX.

CONVERSION INDUCES A DESIRE TO BE USEFUL TO OTHERS.

Another great benefit of the converted is this the longer they go on, and the further they proceed, the greater will be their felicity : the case of the wicked is the longer the worse, but the case of the converted is the longer the better

When a wicked man hath had the sweetness, it may kill his heart to think what a bitter cup is kept for the last: but when the godly have had the bitterest here, it may sweeten all to think of what remains. If a wicked man should have never so much trouble in the flesh, there is another kind of trouble to be endured hereafter—the worst of their condition is still behind; but the best is still behind with the converted: you shall have what is good for you here, you shall have pardon of sin, and peace with God through Jesus Christ, and access to him in peace, when other men are shut out; help in your distress, and strength against temptation: but all this is as nothing in comparison of that which is yet to come. You know partly what you are, but you know not what you shall be, but only in general, that when Christ appears you shall be like him. Your glory is not within the sight of flesh and blood. You walk here as other men, in the same frail flesh, compassed with infirmities, and as men of sorrows; and the world knows not that you are the children of the God of heaven, and that you shall reign with him in glory: for the heir in his minority differs not to outward appearance from a servant, but yet by right he is Lord of all. No wonder if it be thus with you, for so it was with your Head, the Lord of all: he was found in form as a man, and there appeared no worldly glory or comeliness in him, for which he should be desired, but was despised, and became a man of sorrows, bearing our iniquity, and the chastisement of our peace. But he that was among men of no reputation, was worshipped by angels and dearly beloved by the Father, and for his humiliation is highly exalted, and hath a name given him above every name, and hath seen of the travail of his soul and been satisfied. So it is also in their measure with his members; for if you suffer with him, you shall also reign with him; and if you be made conformable to him in his death, so shall you also be in his resurrection and glorification. Though your way to heaven may seem uneven and troublesome, yet still the further you go, the nearer you are to it; and though sometimes you must pass through the valley of the shadow of death, where the place of your happiness may seem out of sight, yet still you are going on towards it; and the foul way as well as the fair is the way to heaven, and the waves and storms shall help you to the harbour. Though you be delivered to death for Jesus' sake, it is that the life of Jesus might be manifested in you. And though you 'always bear about in the body the dying of the Lord Jesus, it is that his life may be

manifested in your bodies.—For we know that he which raised up the Lord Jesus, will also raise us up by Jesus; for which cause we faint not; for though our outward man perish, yet our inward man is renewed day by day: for our light affliction, which is but for a moment, worketh for us a far more exceeding and eternal weight of glory; while we look not at the things that are seen, but at the things that are not seen; for the things which are seen are temporal, but the things which are not seen are eternal.' Great cause therefore have we to 'groan earnestly, desiring to be clothed with our house, which is from heaven, that immortality may be swallowed up of life.' As Christ was nearer his glory on the cross, and in the grave than before, when no man laid hands on him; so are his members in the last of their afflictions: for though the last enemy, death, must yet be encountered with, yet he also shall be overcome through the strength of him that hath conquered him for us; and who through death destroyed him that had the power of death.

If there were but this one thing to show you the difference between a converted and unconverted state, methinks it should sink down into your hearts; that the last day of the ungodly is still the worst, because that all ends in their eternal misery; and the last state of converted souls is still the best, because all will end in everlasting glory. Careless sinners seem to have some joyful days for a while; but how will they answer that question of Peter's, 'Judgment must begin at the house of God: and if it first begin at us, what shall the end be of them that obey not the gospel of God? And if the righteous scarcely be saved, where shall the ungodly and the sinner appear?' Their 'ways do now seem right in their own eyes, but the end thereof are the ways of death.—O that they were wise to consider this, and that they would remember their latter end.' The not considering of their end, is the cause that it proves so miserable. But the end of a believing, holy life is another kind of end. 'Mark the upright man, and behold the just, for the end of that man is peace. But the transgressors shall be destroyed together; the end of the wicked shall be cut off. For eye hath not seen, nor ear heard, nor hath it entered into the heart of man, what God hath prepared for them that love him.' Nor is this end far off. We have but a little while to wait, and we shall see the Lord upon the throne of his glory, and see the accomplishment of his promise to his saints. For yet a little while, and he that comes will come, and will not tarry.

It is many ages since the apostle said, 'the end of all things is at hand; seeing therefore all these things shall be dissolved, what manner of persons ought you to be in all holy conversation and godliness?' O therefore yield to that grace that would convert you. Conversion is the first gate, and an holy life the way to heaven: though this gate be strait, and this way be narrow, and few find it, yet the end will pay for all: as ever you would have this blessed end, see that you make this happy beginning.

Yet this is not all; but besides all these benefits to yourselves, conversion will make you useful to others—it will make you become a blessing to the place where you live. As a wicked man hath a curse upon him, so usually he is a curse to others: judgments many times follow him, and those about him may fare the worse for his sake. And as a true Christian hath a heart full of the blessing of God's right hand, and is himself a blessed man, so is he usually a blessing to others, and many fare the better for his sake, as you may see in the case of Joseph. While you are ignorant and ungodly, what are you but hinderers of other men's salvation, and temptations to those about you? But when God hath illuminated you, and changed your hearts, you will be forward to do good to others, and to help them to that life and hope which you have received. If they want instruction, you will be more able to instruct them: if they are ignorant or careless, you will have some words to say to them for the awakening of their souls: if they be in danger, you can tell them of it; and you can go to God, and pray for them in their distress: you have a spirit of prayer, which you had not before; and you have interest in God, which you had not before, and therefore you may speed better for others, though not so certainly as for yourselves.

I tell you, sinners, the stoutest of you all may be glad of the fellowship of a godly man, if it be but for the benefit of his prayers. Jeroboam, who stretched forth his hand against the prophet, was glad to beg his prayers for the restoring of that hand, and Simon Magus was glad to crave the prayer of Peter. A few more such as Lot was might have saved Sodom from the flames, when his ungodly neighbours were the cause of that heavy judgment. You are made fitter to do God service, when you are converted, for that is it which makes you his servants: this is it that bends your hearts and thoughts to God, and causes you to devote yourselves, and all that you have, to him, and therefore you can never do him acceptable service till this work be wrought. That is the most happy and honourable nation, which hath most of these converted people in it. Let the world think of them as basely as they please, these are the honour and safety of your country, and of your towns and parishes, and of the families where they live. If England be any better than the nations of infidels, it is by the godly. If the Lord would make this town to abound more with true converts and godliness than any other, I dare say it would be a happier town than any other. I tell you that is the best place where there is most of the fear of God; that is the best family in the town which hath most true converted persons in it; or where those that are, are the most eminent in holiness. Were there but such hearts within you, that you would all agree together to yield to the saving work of the gospel, and set yourselves in good earnest to the work of your salvation, this would make you the happiest, the most honourable place in the world. Every good man is a common good; their light shines abroad to others, and such light will not be hid: the heat of their graces help to warm others, and happy are they that live near them, and have but the opportunity of conversing with them, if they have hearts to improve such opportunities.

SECTION XX.

THE CONVERSION OF SINNERS MAKES AN ACCESSION TO THE HAPPINESS OF HEAVEN.

If all this be not enough to show you the blessedness of the truly converted; consider, in the last place, that it is not only themselves, nor only to the world about them, that the comfort doth redound, but the heavenly host of God in some sort partake of it. For the Lord Jesus tells us 'there is joy in heaven at the conversion of a sinner who repenteth.' Hearken to this all you who live a worldly, fleshly life; it would be the very joy of angels to see your true conversion; and will you rob them of their joy? They know what good this change would do you, when you do not know it; and therefore they have compassion of you in your misery, and it would rejoice them to see your recovery. O that you did believe this, and that you did consider it. Can you find in your hearts to stand out any longer, when you consider how many would be glad of your conversion? Turn then, turn to Christ, poor sinners, and make glad the very angels of God by your returning.

Yea, more than that, the Son of God himself would rejoice at your conversion. For the recovery of sinners is the fruit of his blood: and when he ' sees the travail of his soul, he will be satisfied :' he that came into the wilderness of this world to seek such lost and scattered sheep, doth bring them home with joy when he finds them ; ' he came to seek and save that which is lost.—He came not to condemn the world, but that the world through him might be saved,' though he must and will condemn them if they reject his salvation. Nothing pleases him better than the conversion and salvation of straying souls : or else he would never have done so much to accomplish it as he hath done : he would never have sent abroad the doctrine of salvation, and established a ministry in the church to that end, if a returning sinner were not his delight. O that you knew how welcome you would be to Christ, after all the wrong that you have done him, if you would but speedily and heartily return. Those arms that were nailed upon the cross, are still ready to embrace a returning soul: he that had tears to weep over his enemies in their obstinacy, hath joy for them that return from their impenitency. He that would have gathered Jerusalem as an hen gathereth her chickens under her wing, if they would have been gathered, doth show what kind and tender welcome repenting sinners should find with him : if you had but hearts to repent, you would find that Christ hath a heart to receive you. I have formerly told you how tenderly he would meet a poor sinner half way, fall upon his neck, comfort his broken heart, forget his miscarriages, and remember his sins no more ; as the father did by the returning prodigal. If you did but know the worth of Christ's endearments and tender love that he hath to show toward you, you could not find in your heart to stand out so long. You would rather be in your Saviour's arms than among the swine, where you have nothing but the husks.. Can you find in your hearts to delay your return, and to despise this love ? In the name of God, take heed what you do ; for I must tell you, if you are so barbarous, and will so abuse that grace that would save you, you will find that he hath wrath as well as grace ; and the Lamb of God is a lion to his enemies, and will slay those without mercy, that would not have him rule over them, nor accept of his mercy : abuse not mercy so much, lest it turn to unavoidable indignation. For ' our God is also a consuming fire,' and if his wrath be kindled, yea, but a little, then blessed are they that put their trust in him: then blessed are they that were converted by his grace, for only they shall be saved from his burning indignation, and be made partakers of the kingdom of his glory.'

SECTION XXI.

EXPOSTULATION WITH SINNERS.

By this time you may see, if you be not wilfully blinded, that when we persuade you to be converted, we are not drawing you into a miserable life ; and that it is no ill bargain which we offer you from the Lord. If I had nothing to plead with you but the danger of damnation, I might justly expect you should believe and tremble, and yield such obedience as fear alone can cause : but I could not expect that you should receive it with love, nor yield the delightful obedience of the saints : but now you may see that we move you, not to your loss. I dare say I have shown you enough to win the heart of any man that is not obstinately blind and wicked. If you would be rich, I have showed you the only riches ; if you would be honourable, it is only conversion that can make you so ; if you would have pleasure, I have showed you the way to pleasure, and how you may be possessed even of your Master's joy. In a word, if you would be happy, I have showed you the only way to happiness—a life of peace and safety ; a life of honour and pleasure hath been offered you, and remember that it was offered you. If you refuse it, remember you might have been happy if you would : you might have lived with the image of God upon your souls, with the Holy Ghost within you, and the everlasting kingdom a little before you ; with the eye of faith upon the promise of it in the word, and the eye of hope upon the glory that is promised : with the love of God in your hearts, now breathing after him in holy desires, which, when you have reached him, and are come to him, will turn into those endless and unconceivable enjoyments. You might have lived here in the spiritual communion of the saints, in the spiritual and fruitful use of God's ordinances—the chariots to convey your souls to life, and that glass in which you may see the Lord; you might have been much freed from the terrible qualms of conscience, which the guilty feel, or certainly shall feel ; and secured from that sin that lies at the door, and from all the everlasting misery that now waits for you. In a word, instead of a life of brutish sensuality and folly, slavery to

Satan, and preparation to eternal torment, you were offered that life which consists in 'righteousness and peace, and joy in the Holy Ghost.'

Beloved hearers, I now beseech you, in the name of the Lord, that you would not wilfully refuse to be happy; and that you would not neglect so great salvation : our office obliges us to invite you, and to be earnest with you ; and O that we were able even to compel you to come in. The nature of Christian charity obliges us to desire that you might partake of that felicity which is offered you. We know that you may live for ever in glory, if you prefer not the world and your flesh before it. Through the great mercy of God, we have tasted somewhat of this felicity ourselves, and cannot choose but wish that you might be companions of our joy. Methinks I should be of so much credit with you myself, as that you should take my word in a matter that I have tried. If you will take my word, I profess to you, before the Searcher of hearts, that the safety, peace, and comfort of a converted state is such, that I would not be without it for all the world: shall I say, I would not change it for a life of drunkenness, or filthiness, or fleshly pleasure, or for all the gains of a covetous worldling ? I am ashamed of the comparison. As bad as we know our own hearts to be, I will confidently say, through the grace of God, that if the kingdoms of the world were offered us in exchange, we should scorn them, and tread them under foot. I give you my word and experience, but to persuade you to come near and try : but alas, if you will not believe God, how can I expect my words should be believed ? O that you would but come and try, and when you have tried the way of holiness, but a quarter as much as you have done the ways of the world and the flesh, then if you like it not, take your course. If you find by experience that the way of sin is safer and better, when you have tried both, then turn back again and spare not ; I would trouble you no more, would you but come and try ; it is all that I now desire of you. But to think hardly of a state that you never tried ; to draw back from a life that you never tried,—this is not equal dealing with God, nor impartial faithful dealing for your souls. I know some that have forborne some outward sins a while, and stepped into an outward profession and into the company of the godly, have fallen back again. But if you will but try the inward nature and spiritual life of a saint ; the love, the trust, the zeal, the joy, the endeavours, and the hopes of a saint, then judge and spare not, as experience shall direct you, and forsake God if

you really find that the flesh and the world are better. Remember what I say to you: it will leave you inexcusable, and be the confusion of your faces, when you shall answer this another day, that when your everlasting joy or torment lay upon it, you would not be persuaded by all that we could say, so much as to leave your sins a while, and come and make trial of a godly life. O my fellow men! you will one day be ready to gnaw your own hearts, to think that you wilfully, impenitently and obstinately refused so fair, so necessary, so good an invitation.

CHAPTER VI.

TEN APPLICATORY QUESTIONS.

Beloved hearers, I do not address you to-day of my own head, nor in my own name, nor on my own business ; but in the name of Christ, and on the business of your salvation. I know this great assembly will be all very shortly in another world, and we shall meet ere long in a far greater assembly at the day of Christ's judgment, which will be upon us for all the seeming delay, before the careless world is aware. That you may be ready for that day, and stand with boldness before the judge, when the unconverted world stands trembling and amazed, as overwhelmed with the unexpected terrors of the Lord, —this is the business that I come hither about to-day ; no less, no lower business than this. That I have not trifled with you, and filled your ears with trifles and strange matters, I hope you will easily pardon me, when you have considered your condition and the business of our office. I hate that preaching which passes over the one thing necessary, and only tickles the ears of miserable men, when it should endeavour their relief. If the town were on fire, it were no commendable matter to be fiddling and dancing, when you should quench it. If I saw you but sinking in a broken vessel, and ready to drown, if you had not help, it would seem no part of wisdom to me to make a learned oration to you, when I should be helping you out of present danger : I must tell you therefore, that I came not hither only to talk to you, that you might go home and say, you had heard a fine or a learned sermon: but I come to help you out of the misery of an unconverted state. I see the gulf of remediless destruction is a little before you, and I come to require you, in the name of the Lord, to make a stand, and go no further in the way of wickedness; but look about you and consider your way, and presently return. Have you been ignorant, inconsiderate worldlings, forgetting the God that should have had your hearts, and forgetting the life where you must live for ever? Be awakened then, and look before you; lift up the eye of faith, and see that joy or torment is even at hand: have you lived to the flesh, as if you had nothing but it to care for, and thought it more ado than needs to provide for eternity? In a word, have your hearts been set more on this life, than that to come, and on the things below, than on God above? If this be so, flatter not yourselves in vain hopes: delay not a day longer, but presently return from that condition: believe the word of God, or your ruin will be certain. ' For if you live after the flesh, ye shall die.—For they that are far from thee shall perish; but it is good for me to draw nigh to God.— Where your treasure is, there will your heart be also.' What say you, will you return to God from the lusts of the flesh, the love of this world, and a lazy, careless, ungodly life, or will you not? Will you justify yourselves no longer in a state of death; nor excuse nor befriend the sins that have endangered you, but yield to the converting work of the Spirit, and strive not against that grace that would recover you? I pray you give me not the bare hearing, but let your hearts make answer, yes, or no? Will you return and be converted, or will you not? Dare any of you say no? I hope you dare not. But it is next to saying no, if your hearts say nothing. Tell me not of your cold wishes and purposes, and you hope you shall: a thousand such faint and heartless resolutions have left souls to perish in endless misery: it is resolution, strong resolution, and present resolution that you must have, and that God expects. What say you? Are you resolved to return, or are you not? Take heed what you say, for God is here present and sees your hearts. Do not halt between two opinions; but if Baal be God, follow him; if the flesh and the world be God, and will make you happy, follow them; but if the Lord be God, follow him, do not put me off with to-morrow, or sometime hereafter, as if it were not yet time, or you could not spare your sin as yet: no resolution is sincere, but present resolution; he that would keep his sins a day longer, would keep them a year, and seven years, and for ever if he might. He that would not yield to Christ to-day, would never do it by his good will. No man loves God, that longs not presently to be such as God would have him be. Again therefore, I ask you, are you resolved presently to return, or not?

This is the business I come hither upon, and 1 do not mean to go away thus, till I have my errand; I am resolved to leave you better, or worse, either converted, or more inexcusable than you were before, and to say that which shall be a witness against you, if it convert you not: and now, if you be not yet resolved, I shall desire that you will soberly answer me these few questions following.

1. What do you think had come of you, if God had cut you off by death all this while before you were converted? Where do you think you should have been this very hour, if death had found you in an unconverted state? Do you not know? Why, doth not my text tell you? Will not you believe Jesus Christ? I know, if you do not, you had been as sure in hell, as you are now on earth. How many a fair advantage hath God had against you? He could have killed you with one frown; with a morsel of bread, with a draught of drink, by the turning of a hand, by the slipping of a foot, by the stumbling of a horse: besides many hundred diseases that would have opened the door, or rather have broken down your dusty cottages, and let out your guilty unprepared souls into another world. You cannot now apprehend what a dreadful thing it is for an unchanged soul to appear before the holy God! Doth it not sometimes amaze the best to think what a change it is that death makes? And what it is for a man that hath lived among mortals on earth, to find himself in a moment among angels and other spirits? How much more should the thoughts of a more lamentable change amaze the unconverted? It is only or chiefly some doubts, and some strangeness to that heavenly state, that amazes the godly; which will all be dispelled in the twinkling of an eye, by that joy and glory that they shall find themselves possessed of. But it is another kind of matter, even the everlasting misery, that should amaze the wicked. Dear friends, what a case had you been in, if you had died before conversion? Your hearts are not able to conceive of the thousandth part of the misery that you would have been in. Have you lived all this while in so much danger, and will you live in it still? God forbid. Hath a wonder of mercy kept you out of hell so long, and will you loiter yet longer in the old condition? Methinks I look upon you as imitating Lot, when he was called out of Sodom. That after he had been warned by the angel to get away out of Sodom with all that he had, as he loved his life; yet sons and daughters, or one thing or other, so long detain him, that he lingers away the time, till God being merciful unto him,

the angels even carried him forth, and said, 'escape now for thy life, look not behind thee, and make no stay.' So God hath mercifully called you out of the Sodom of your sins, and you have lingered till now. O that the Lord would be so merciful to you as to lay hands as it were upon those hearts, and take them off the world and your lusts, and bring you away: this warning, however, I am bound to give you. Escape now for your lives, look not behind you, stay not any longer, lest you perish in your negligence. So much for my first question, what had become of you if you had died before conversion?

2. My next question is this: are you sure if you delay returning another day, that you shall be that day out of hell? If you refuse this offer that God makes you now, are you sure you shall ever have another? Can you say, that your bodies shall not lie in the church-yard, and your souls be past hope and help in misery, before the next meeting in this place, if you so long delay and harden your hearts? You are not sure of it: if you are, let us see your evidence of security. Hath God any where promised you another day? Why! can you live a day whether God will or not? You know you cannot: I dare say, you know it. You know that many a one as strong as you, and that feared death as little, hath been quickly cut off; and go you must, however, at the last. Well, brethren, do I need to ask you such a question now, whether it be wisdom, or madness rather, for any man wilfully or negligently to live one day or night longer in such a condition, as if you should die in it, you were undone for ever? Will you venture to live another day in such a case in which you cannot be sure that one day to be out of hell? Methinks while you are unconverted, this saying of Christ should be still ringing in your ears; 'Verily, I say unto you, except ye be converted, and become as little children, you cannot enter into the kingdom of heaven.' Methinks every night you lie down in bed, you should think with yourselves, what if I should die in an unconverted state before the next morning? Methinks the very dreams of this should awaken you with terror. Methinks when you rise in the morning, you should think with yourselves, what if I should die in an unconverted state before night? Methinks the daily thoughts of this should mar your mirth, and sour to you all the sweetness of the world! How can you forbear in such a danger to think of it, in your shops, and at your plough; at home and abroad, which way soever you go, or whatsoever you are doing? If you say, though

I am not sure to live a day, yet I am likely, for I have lived many a one already, when I had no assurance of it. I answer: but who would leave such a matter as his everlasting salvation upon such hazard? I warn thee therefore from God, in the words of God, 'Boast not thyself of to-morrow, for who knoweth what a day may bring forth?'

3. My third question to you is this: which dost thou really think is better, God or the creature, heaven or earth, a life in glory, or the present pleasure of sin? Is it indeed thy settled judgment, that it is better to be drunk than sober, and better to take the delight of thy flesh, and follow this world, than to live to God here, and with God hereafter? Is this thy settled judgment, or is it not? If it be, thou art an infidel, or an atheist, and not a Christian. Nay, worse than most infidels or heathens in the world. If it be not thy judgment, how darest thou do it? Wilt thou go against thy own knowledge? Wilt thou not do that which thou knowest is both pleasing to God, and best for thyself? Shall God show thee thy misery; and wilt thou wilfully run into it? Shall he show thee thy happiness, and wilt thou wilfully forsake it? Dost thou think that it is better to be converted, or not? If thou think it to be a better state, how darest thou neglect it, or refuse it as thou dost? Who can help thee, if thou know that thou doest evil, and yet wilt do it; if thou know that thy way is the way of death, and yet wilt go on in it? And who shall pity thee, if knowingly thou wilt damn thyself?

4. My fourth question to you is this: dost thou believe that man is made for this world only, or for a better? If heaven were never so desirable, if it be not attainable, it is in vain to seek it: but if it may be had, what hearts have they that will neglect it, or prefer any other thing before it? Do you think that man was made only to take a life of pleasure on this earth, and go no further, and there is an end of him? If you think so, you are blinder than most heathens in the world. Three sorts of creatures did God create; one sort are pure spirits without flesh, and these were placed in their happiness at the first to be nearest to God, and employed by him in his noblest works: only being not at first confirmed, some of them fell away, and are become devils: another sort of creatures have flesh without immortal souls, having no other life than what is fitted to their earthly state; I mean beasts, birds and all other unreasonable creatures: these are not capable of any higher felicity than they here enjoy:

388 A TREATISE ON CONVERSION.

they were never intended for it, and therefore their natures are not fitted to it. But man is of a middle sort, partaking somewhat of both these; he hath flesh like the beasts, because he must live on earth as they, and so must eat, drink, sleep and die, and his flesh must perish as well as theirs. But with this flesh he hath a soul that is akin to angels, and therefore is capable of an endless life, and fitted for it: so that so far as he is fleshly, so far he is earthly, and is like the beasts that perish; but as he is a living soul he is disposed to an endless life, and may there be like to the angels of God. You may see this difference between brutes and men in their very natures here. They know not that there is another life, but we do; they live not in hopes and fears of another life, but we do. Experience certainly discovers this; they fear but one death, and we fear two, in fearing a misery after death. We govern them only by present objects: but God rules us by promises and threatenings of unseen things, and by the hopes and fears of another life: it is our nature to be thus governed, and theirs to be ruled by sensual objects.

Well then, if man was made for higher things, should he not seek them, and live for them? Remember then, I beseech you, that the work of conversion is but to set your hearts on the things that you were made for: it is to make you know that you are men and not beasts, and to bring you to live the life of men. Sin doth unman us, and in a sort even brutalize us; conversion restores us, in our present measure, to the ends that we were created for, and to the image of God that we were created in, which disposes us to those ends: if you believe then that man is not a beast, but made for an everlasting life with God, away with fleshly, worldly vanities, and live as strangers here, and as those that are heirs of that everlasting life.

5. My next question to you is; have you ever soberly and considerately compared the gain and the loss that conversion will bring you? Did you ever, on the one side, consider of all the present peace and safety, and that everlasting glory, which is the portion of them that cleave to God, and of the misery of all others, as I have before discovered it to you? And on the other side, have you considered how small a matter it is that you can lose, if you yield to that grace that would prepare you for this glory? Surely if you had ever considered both of the winning and the losing, and laid one in the one end of the scales, and the other in the other, the case might have been resolved with you long before now. Sinners, when God and his ministers make such a stir with

you to persuade you to be converted, and all will not serve, but year after year you are still the same, there is somewhat surely that is the cause. If somewhat did not stick with you, you would have yielded before this time. Somewhat there is surely that you are afraid of losing by the change, or else what should be the matter that you refuse, or delay? Well, let us hear what it is that you are afraid it will deprive you of? Is it any thing that is better than God, than heaven, than the saving of your souls? This is the benefit that conversion brings, and if it would take from you any thing that is better, refuse it then, and spare not. I tell you, sinners, God hath no need of you; it is for your own good, and that honour and pleasure that he takes in doing good, that he is so earnest with you to come in. And if any of you dare charge the God of heaven with dissembling, as if he meant your hurt, while he thus pretends your good, and would take from you more than he offers you, or would give you; make good thy charge, if thou canst, or rather take heed, if thou love thyself, of such blasphemous imaginations. Poor soul, if God would do thee harm, who dost thou think will do thee good? If the chief good be not good, where wilt thou find good? Dost thou fear lest the sun should deprive thee of thy light, when thou canst have none but what it affords thee? Dost thou run away from the fire, lest it should make thee cold? What, fear lest God should do thee harm, when there is no good but what doth stream from him? Who wilt thou go to for any good, if thou flee from him? Hath any creature the least relief for thee, except they receive it from God, and he send it thee by their hands? They have nothing but what he lends them, nor can they give thee any succour, but by his consent.

What is it then that thou art afraid of losing, by being converted? Is it any thing that is worth the keeping? It is incredible that God should envy thee thy happiness; that is the work of the devil, which moved him to tempt us from it! Dare you make God like him; or father on God his nature or his works? It is incredible wrong that men do to God while they question his goodness, and dislike his holy laws and ways, and quarrel with him, as if he were their enemy: when he would draw them out of the prison of the devil, and the power of sin, they draw back, as if he would draw them into bondage. O base, unthankful creatures! Must salvation be so dearly bought, and so kindly offered you, and do you thus reject it? Foolish, self-destroying sinners, are you so far delivered from all your enemies, that your happiness is brought to your own choice, and you may freely have it if you will, and now will you not have it? Will you be the last and deadly enemy to yourselves? Why, what is it that you are so loth to leave? Is it your sins? Is it your fleshly pleasures; or your worldly profits, or your ease, or credit, or which of these? Is it not a sad case that reasonable men should come to such a pass, that they are afraid of returning to the favour of God, and of coming from the thraldom of the devil, into his service, lest they should lose their pleasure? As if there were less delight in the love of God, than in flesh-pleasing filthiness; or as if the joys of heaven were less than the mirth of an ale-house. Is it not a sad case that ever men should be afraid of being losers by God? or of missing their money, or their houses, or lands, when they come to heaven? As if there were any want there where all are glorious kings: and as if Lazarus had not changed his state! Is it not a shameful thing, that men should be ashamed to be the servants of the God of heaven, and think it a discredit to be the heirs of glory? Is it to any purpose to talk to such men as these? Will they ever hear reason that are so unreasonable? If preaching were not the ordinance of God, which he hath commanded us to use, and therefore may set in with his blessing, when he pleases, we should even throw by all, and look on such as these as madmen and think, till God shall bring them to their judgment, there is no good to be done by speaking to them. If a man will fly from God, to an ale-house, or gaming-house for pleasure, or from God to the world for profit or honour, what shall we say to such a man, but even take him in this as beside himself?

For who will think better of him that will run into a prison, or to his enemies for his liberty? Or that will tumble in the channel, or lie down in the mire, and will not come out for fear of being fouled? I would ask the drunkard, or fornicator, or worldling, or whosoever he be that hath the most that sin can do for him, Dost thou think that thou hast a more comfortable life than those that are farthest from thy sin? Dost thou think that they who abhor thy drunkenness, whoredom, or worldly courses of life, have not a more comfortable life than thou? Besides that which they shall have in heaven; when sin hath brought thee into torment (if true conversion do not prevent it) even in this life; which, think you, have the more peaceable and comfortable life? I am even ashamed to make the comparison. A wise and godly man abhors these things that are the felicity of ungodly men. Your

filthy lives which you are loth to leave, would make the heart of a sober man to rise thinking of them. What wise man would not think it a misery, if he were condemned to live your lives but a few days; a swine takes pleasure to tumble in the mire, but a man in his senses will take no pleasure to bear him company. And is this all that you are like to lose by it, if you be converted, and yet will you stand off? Well, I say no more of it now but this; if after all this you take the world to be better than God, and the pleasures of sin to be greater than the pleasures of a holy life, and the joy that God would give you with himself; if you are afraid of turning to God lest you be the losers by him, you may take your course, and stay till the end shall make you wiser, to your cost.

6. My next question to you is this: have you now any reason to give against your speedy, effectual conversion, which you will undertake to stand to, and justify at the bar of God? Do you know any harm by that state and life that God by converting grace would bring you to? You have heard much that may be said for it; what now have you to lay against it? I know that a great many senseless words are poured out by foolish sinners against the holy ways of God: but they are such as show their folly and malice, and proceed from wilfulness and not from reason. Not one of all these that you hear in a corner scorning at godliness, or reasoning against it, dare stand to these reasons when God shall deal with him. For my part, I would persuade you to nothing unreasonable and unfit: I have told you my reasons for the necessity of conversion: if you are against it now, either you have reason to be against it, or you have not; if you have no reason for it, how dare you, how can you do it? What! will you renounce your reason in the greatest matters, where you have the greatest use for it? Will you be wilfully brutes; or will you set yourselves knowingly against God and your own souls? In the name of God, consider first what you do: it must be either deluded reason or mere wilfulness that causes you now to refuse or delay to be converted. I beseech you, let me have the answer of your hearts here before the Lord. Deal truly; have you any reason why you should not be converted and turn to God before to-morrow? I pray you do not pass it over carelessly, but give me your answer. Have you any reason for it, or have you not? If you have not, your conscience is then witness that you are wilful in your neglect. You turn not to God because you will not turn: you go on in sin because you will go on. You do then in your

hearts as it were set God at defiance, and say, I confess I have no reason to sin, but yet I will do it: I have no reason to delay my return to God an hour, but yet I will do it: and I will do it though reason as well as the word of God cry out against it. Who can you blame then, if the plagues of God shall reach such a rebel, and if he deal with you as wilful sinners should be dealt with?

If you had done it ignorantly, you had some excuse, or you might have been beaten with the fewer stripes; but wilful sin hath no excuse, and on such the Lord will pour out his wrath. If your own reason tell you, you should presently return to God, and you will not, how can you expect in reason to find mercy with the Lord? O that you knew what a heinous thing it is to sin wilfully after the knowledge of the truth: it would make every joint of you to tremble, lest if you go a little further, there should be no more sacrifice for sin, ' but a certain fearful looking for of judgment, and fire which devoureth the adversary.' Well, let me again put the question to you: What say you; will you presently return to God, or will you not? Halt not between both, but resolve off, or no. Say plainly, you will or you will not: if you will not, tell me then why will you not? Have you any reason for it, or have you none? If none, how dare you be wilful? But if you have any reason, I pray you answer my next question. Is your reason such as you will undertake to stand to at the bar of God? It is an easy matter to deceive yourselves and others, and to daub over a cause that is apparently naught, and to bring fair pretences for the most foul actions. Something men will have to say, to stop the mouth of those that would convince them, be their course never so ungodly; but the question is, whether you have any reasons for your sin, and against your speedy and effectual return, which you will undertake to stand to before the Lord.

I pray you, bethink yourselves soberly of an answer, before you hold on your course any longer; lest you be at the bar before you are aware. One man's reason is, his sin is sweet, and he hopes he may safely keep it a little longer, and then he means to let it go. It seems then you had rather sin, than not, and that shows that at present thou art a graceless man. But is the sweetness of thy sin a sufficient reason for thee to refuse the sweetness of a pardon, of the reconciled face of God, and of everlasting glory? Dare you stand to such a reason as this is before God? I know you dare not. How then dare you delay your conversion upon such rea-

sons? Is sin sweet to thee, and is not holiness sweeter? Is not pardon, life, grace, Christ, and God and glory sweeter? O what kind of reasons are these for a reasonable man to venture his salvation upon! I shall not stand to try the rest of them, because they will fall under a more particular consideration hereafter: only in general I charge and require you, plead not such reasons as you dare not stand to at the bar of God.

7. My next question to you is this, have you ever well considered who they be that are for your conversion, and who they be that are against it? You may easily conjecture by this whether it be good or bad. You have heard already who they be that are for it: God, Christ, the Holy Ghost, the angels of heaven, the ministers of the gospel, and every wise and godly man is for it. God is so much for it, that he sent his Son to purchase it, and his word to command and call you to it, and to give you directions how it must be done, and his ministers to persuade you to hear and submit. He is so much for it, that he follows you with mercies and afflictions, and all to this end, to lead you to repentance: he is so much for it, that he hath sworn that he hath ' no pleasure in the death of the wicked, but rather that he return and live;' and pleads the case with you, and asks you ' why you will die. Christ is so much for it, that he hath made it his office; he took the nature of man on him to that end, that he might seek and save that which was lost; and for that end he submitted to the cursed death of the cross; for that end hath he made the promises of the gospel, and sent abroad his ministers to proclaim them: he is so much for it, that he is purposely become the Captain of our salvation: and having first given us his own example, doth lead us on in all encounters, and calls us to follow him, that we may conquer as he hath done: he is so much for it, that upon this very ground will he condemn at last the impenitent world, because they would not be converted by him. The Holy Ghost is so much for it, that he moves and importunes sinners thereunto, and effectually works it in all the elect. The angels of heaven, as you have heard, are so much for it, that it is their joy when a sinner is converted. The ministers of Christ are so much for it, that they make it their business, study, preach, pray, and suffer for it, and think nothing too much if they might but accomplish it. ' They are willing to spend and be spent for this end;' they account not their lives dear to them, so they may but finish their course with joy, and the ministry which they have received

of the Lord in preaching the gospel of the grace of God. They are content to instruct those in meekness that oppose themselves, 'if God peradventure will give them repentance to the acknowledging of the truth, that they may escape out of the snares of Satan.' All the godly are so much for it, that it is their daily prayer and earnest desire, and they would do any thing they could to accomplish it. How heartily do they pray for your conversion, that the kingdom of God may come in your hearts! How glad are they when they hear of the conversion of a sinner! Well, sinners, methinks you should consider with yourselves, for what reason do all these desire my conversion? Who is it that shall be the gainer by it? What doth God get by it? What doth Christ the redeemer get by it? What doth the Spirit that moves me get by it? What profit is it to the minister of the gospel? Might they not as easily let me alone, and please me in my sins, and tell me of no danger? What profit is it to all my godly friends, that they should so earnestly desire it, and pray for it? Is it not I that am like to have the gain? And should I set against all the friends I have that endeavour for my own good, even my everlasting good?

You see who they be that are for your conversion; will you now consider who they be that are against it? Are they better than God? Are they more true friends to you than Christ and his ministers, and those that persuade you to repent and live? Are they such as love you better than all these do? Why, who are they? First, the chief enemy to your conversion is the devil himself. It is he that dissuades you; that raises doubts and temptations in your mind, and casts so many stumbling-blocks in your way: he would not have you converted if he could hinder it: if all his subtilty, if all his power and malice, if all the instruments that he can raise up against it, can hinder it, you shall never be converted. He knows he shall lose a servant and subject of his kingdom; he shall be cast out of that possession which he hath kept in peace: if he do not rule you, he shall not torment you, which is pleasant to his malice. No one in all the world is so much against your conversion as the devil. When you say, you will never be so pure, nor so godly, nor live so holy and heavenly a life, O how you please him! You could not have said a word that he more delights to hear; for it is as much as if you had said, I will never leave my master the devil to serve Christ. Nay, it is all one as if you had said, I am resolved I will never be saved, seeing there is no salvation without conversion. When you say you will do as your forefathers have done; will take your pleasure and follow the world; and not be so precise, nor trouble your minds so much about the case of your souls, or the matters of eternal life; O how you please the devil by this! This is what he would have. You speak even as he would have you speak: for indeed it is he who tempts you to speak it. But for God's sake, and your soul's sake, sinners, will you consider whether God or the devil is your better friend? You are the cause that I am put upon such a strange question to you: whether that be more likely to be for your good, which God, Christ, and the Holy Ghost, and ministers and all godly people would have; or that which the devil himself would have? Do I need to bid you consider of this? A little consideration surely may resolve it. Can you think that all these forementioned are against you, and Satan is your friend? If you will indeed take God and Christ, and his Spirit, and people, for your enemies, and him that is your greatest enemy for your friend, after such warnings as you have received; you may reap those fruits of his friendship which you little think of.

But there are some others besides the devil against your conversion. True; but who are they? None but his agents, and those that are deceived by him themselves. Perhaps, you will hardly think so; for one may be your father, another your mother, another a husband or wife, or those that profess themselves your friends, and some perhaps may be thought wise and learned in the world. But what doth God say of them; who is most to be believed? He tells you they are foolish, wicked, and enemies to the cross of Christ: you call them friends, but God tells you they are your enemies. If you think I speak too harshly of them, in telling you that they are ignorant, blinded sinners, believe God who says the same: I hope you will not accuse him of wronging them, or any one: never man spake against conversion that knew what he said, and was converted himself. It is only those that never knew or tried the ways of God, that persuade you from them. Will you go to the blind for direction, or to the slaves of Satan for counsel whether you should return to God? If they were wise men, they would return themselves; if they be not wise, they are unfit to give you counsel. Methinks your own reason might tell you, that that man cannot be wise who would draw the hearts of others from God, and would have them venture upon the drawn sword of his vengeance: and do that which he hath threatened everlasting destruction to. Can that be a wise man who doth himself prefer this sinful world, and the sinful mirth of a sinner before all the holy joy and glory of the saints, even before the present life of grace and the future life of glory? Ask your reason whether this can be a wise man? I may boldly say then, that there is none but the devil and wicked fools that are against your conversion. Tell them how I call them and spare not; for God calls them more, and their own consciences will call them so for ever, if they do not that themselves which they would dissuade you from doing. I say it again, there is not one in the world, but the devil and wicked fools, that are against your conversion: and if these shall be your counsellors, and ye will be ruled more by them than by God, and all the true friends you have in the world, let your own consciences judge whether you have dealt well with God, or with yourselves?

8. Yet I have some more questions to ask you, and my next is this: had you rather die in a converted, or an unconverted state? And in which of these had you rather appear before the Lord? I pray you, put this question to your own hearts, and soberly answer it. I say, which of these two conditions had you rather be in at death and judgment? Had you rather die the death of the righteous, or of the wicked? Had you rather stand among the unconverted, or the converted, at the bar of God? Had you rather that death should find you with clean hands, an innocent life, and an heavenly mind, delighting in God, and hoping for Christ's appearing; or that it should find you either in your ignorance, worldliness, fornication, or drunkenness, or with the guilt of any of these upon your souls, and with an heart that is not unfeignedly turned from them unto God? I do not think there is the most stout-hearted sinners among you, no, not they that make a mock at godliness, and discourage others from it, but they had rather be among the godly, than the ungodly, at the last. Is it not a strange thing, that men should set against that course, which they would wish to be found in? And should live contrary to it, when yet at the same time they had rather die in it, than as they are? Sinners, should you not be now such as you would be found then? And should you not live in that state as you would die in? Will it be best then, and is it worst now? how can that be? Believe it, you have neither your lives, nor the grace of God at your will. If you would be found among the converted at the last, become such quickly, lest the last should come before you are aware. If life forsake you

not, you cannot tell whether the Spirit of God may forsake you. If grace must be had, or else you are undone, take it while you may have it, lest you be given over to the hardness of your hearts.

9. My next question is this; if God should send an angel from heaven to you, to plead against your sinful course, and to persuade you to be converted, would you hearken to him and obey him; or would you not? If he should appear to you in your careless and worldly course of life, or if he should come to you in the very act of your sin, and tell you how the Lord abhors your iniquity; how his vengeance hangs over your head, and will fall upon you, if you speedily repent not; and should persuade and entreat you to lament your folly, and turn to God with all your heart, without delay, what would you do? What answer would you give? Would you tell him to his face, I will not be converted; I will take my pleasure, and follow the world, and venture my soul rather than live so strict a life? Would you say thus to him? You would not; surely you durst not do it. Would you not tell him, I am sorry for my sins, and resolve to turn without delay; but if you should so tell him, if you did not do it, your promise would but prove you hypocrites, and rise up against you to your condemnation. You do not know how such a sight would amaze you, and awaken you from security. A hand that appeared writing upon a wall, made the knees of a sensual king to tremble; it loosed his very loins, changed his countenance, and troubled his thoughts. The appearance of an angel, at the resurrection of Christ, made the keepers of the grave to shake, and become as dead men. How an angel's appearance affected Cornelius; and an earthquake, with the effects, moved the jailor, may be seen in Acts x. 16. and many similar examples we might give you. What if an angel of God should but come and speak over this very text to you that I am preaching: 'Verily, except you be converted, you shall not enter into the kingdom of heaven?' Would you yield or would you not? If you would not, you are hardened with a witness. If you would, let me follow my question a little further with you. Should not the written word of Christ himself, and the voice of his messengers that speak in his name, and all the judgments and mercies that second these, I say, should not all these prevail with you as much, and more than an angel's voice? You have here the protestation, or vehement asseveration of the Lord himself, and should not that be of greatest authority with

us? Angels are but servants of Christ and ministering spirits for the good of his elect: would you hear them, and will you not hear their Master? Would you hear an unusual messenger, and will you not learn in Christ's appointed way? If it be a doctrine to be received from angels, tell me if you can, why it should not be received now from the word of God, and from his min-isters?

10. The last question that I shall now trouble you with is this: do you think that man who after all this shall refuse to turn to God, and after all this shall remain unconverted, will have any just excuse before the Lord; or will he not be left speechless and under the condemnation of his own conscience for ever? Is it any pity to cast away that man, who will without all pity cast away himself, and no saying will serve him, and no reason will satisfy him? Or when he is convinced and silenced, yet for all that will not be converted? When it is their own doing, and they were their own undoing; and when God did not spare for cost and persuasion to have done them good; and when he shall say after all, 'What could have been done more to my vineyard, that I have not done in it?' What should I have said more to this sinner, than I have said? What plea is left for such a sinner? Or what can he say why he should not be sentenced to perdition? Will you say you did it ignorantly, or you had no warning? you cannot say it. Indians may say it, and many barbarous nations of the world may say it, but England cannot say it, nor can you that hear me say it. You have warning after warning, and all said to you that we knew how to say, which was likely to move the heart of a sinner. Will you say you were not able, because it was a work above your power? Why, you cannot thus excuse your sin: for if you had been but truly willing, you might have done it? Your disability lay in your obstinate unwillingness. Are you willing this day, unfeignedly willing, to turn to God, or are you not? If you be, you will return without delay: for if you are willing, who can hinder you? But if you be not truly willing, how can you say that you would have done it if you could? Or how can you excuse yourselves by your disability? Unwillingness is a disability which excuses no men, but aggravates their sin. If you could have said that you would have returned with all your hearts, but were not able for all that you were willing, then you had some excuse; but now you have nothing to say for yourselves.

People may object and say, we know there is no pleading for ourselves, nor any excuse to be made with God, but yet we hope we may be saved for all that?

To which I answer, how can you have any hope, if you have no ground of hope to show? If you have no reason to give against the sentence of your condemnation, how can you think to escape it? God is just, and will judge in righteousness according to his word; and they that have not now a title in the word for their justification at judgment, shall never be there justified, whatsoever they may dream.

SECTION III.

OBJECTIONS STATED AND ANSWERED—EXPOSTULATION.

Beloved hearers, I have been all this while pleading with you, by the reasons of the word of God, to see if it were possible for me to persuade you to yield to the light, and be converted, that you may live. I have meant you no harm, unless salvation be your harm. The threatenings of the scripture, and the miserable death of unconverted souls were all this while before me, which moved me to use so many persuasions with you. Have I prevailed with you, or have I not? Are you resolved for conversion, fully resolved, or are you not? God hath all this while stood by and heard what I have said to you, and perceives now what answer is in your hearts and what effect these words have had. Shall all this be lost? And when we have said all that we can, must we sit down in sorrow, and say, Who hath believed our report? Is there one man or woman of you that dare go on in an unconverted state and draw back from God, loiter out your time, and still return to your former sins, after all that I have said? If you do so, do it at your peril; and when you find yourselves in hell, remember the sermons that have been preached to you on this text, and blame not me, but your wilful negligence. Think not much that I bid you remember these sermons when you find yourselves in hell, for you shall do it then whether you will, or not: there is not a soul of you that shall live or die in an unconverted state, but shall remember the warnings that I have now and formerly given you. Sermons will be remembered in hell, that are forgotten on earth: and they that were weary to hear them here, and would not be at the small labour to repeat them, or hear them repeated, or else ponder in secret of what they heard, shall there think of it, and think again to their sorrow. As Abraham said to the condemned worldling, ' Remember that thou in thy life receivedst thy good things, and Lazarus his evil things, but now he is comforted and thou art tormented. So shall you remember the time, means, and warnings that you once had. If you ask me how I know that? Why, because the word of God tells me that the consciences of wicked men will be their accusers. And that they shall mourn at the last, and say, ' how have I hated instruction, and my heart despised reproofs, and have not obeyed the voice of my teachers; nor inclined mine ear to them that instructed me!'

Many other scripture texts also assure me of the same. How much better were it now to believe the Lord, foresee this evil, and think of your way while you have opportunity to escape? How much safer were this for you; and how much more pleasing would it be to God and us? Do not cast away your souls, and displease God and all the true friends you have, only to please the devil and your flesh! Let me urge you a little further in the words of your Maker, and I charge you to regard them, as you will answer the contempt of them at your peril. Did you never observe how God doth pity the stir that poor sinners make in the world for nothing, and the unprofitable trade of sinning that they drive on, and how he invites them to himself as the true gain and felicity? 'Wherefore do you spend your money for that which is not bread; and your labour for that which satisfieth not? Hearken diligently to me, and eat ye that which is good, and let your soul delight itself in fatness: incline your ear and come unto me; hear and your souls shall live.—Wash you, make you clean; put away the evil of your doings from before mine eyes: cease to do evil, learn to do well: come now and let us reason together, saith the Lord; though your sins be as scarlet, they shall be as white as snow.—How long, ye simple ones, will ye love simplicity? and ye scorners delight in scorning, and fools hate knowledge? Turn ye at my reproof: behold I will pour out my Spirit on you. I will make known my words to you.—Turn ye even to me with all your hearts; with fasting, weeping, and mourning: rend your hearts and not your garments, and turn to the Lord your God; for he is gracious and merciful to them that turn, but not to them that go on in their iniquity.—When a wicked man turneth away from his wickedness, which he hath committed, and doth that which is lawful and right, he shall save his soul alive. Repent, and turn yourselves from all your transgressions, so iniquity shall not be your ruin. For I have

no pleasure in the death of him that dieth, wherefore turn yourselves and live ye.'

These are the calls of the God of mercy, inviting you into the way wherein his saving mercy is only to be found. How glad would many thousands be that are now past hope, if they had but the call of God to repent, as you have this day! How glad should you be that you have such an offer, and that it is not yet too late? And therefore how cheerfully should you yield to be converted? I shall in conclusion say but this: if ever a man or woman of you all shall appear before the Lord in judgment, in a carnal, unconverted state, after all the warnings you have received, I hope God will not charge it upon me, who faithfully, though weakly, endeavoured to prevent it. *

CHAPTER VII.

HINDERANCES TO CONVERSION STATED, AND OBJECTIONS OBVIATED.

By this time I hope many of you are willing to be converted, and are ready to inquire what you should do to that end; and whether there be any thing on your parts to be done that may further it? In hope that you are willing, I shall next proceed to give you my best advice herein. If it were so that you could do nothing to further it, because I am sure you may do much to hinder it, and have done all this while, or else it had been better with you than it is; therefore I shall show you what are the common hinderances of conversion, which you must carefully endeavour to remove or conquer; and with them I shall adjoin the contrary directions, which concern your necessary duty to this end. Though some of their contraries are real parts of conversion; yet the reason that I mention them here is, because the not yielding to the initial acts in the understanding, is the hinderance of the subsequent acts on the heart and life.

Hinderance 1. *The wilful neglect of God's appointed means of salvation. Objections answered.* The first hinderance of conversion that I shall warn you of is; the wilful neglect of those ordinary means which God hath appointed

---

* Our Author is not more copious in his doctrinal statements,— ample in his arguments—and happy in his illustrations—than he is varied, and urgent, and irresistible in his *appeals to the conscience.* The whole regions of *matter* and mind are ransacked for illustration and argument to urge the principles and blessings of the common salvation upon the sinner's heart. In this, a great part of the moral grandeur and utility of the writings of the non-conformist school consists.—*Editor.*

for the working of conversion. When God will give any man saving grace, ordinarily he will do it by the means of grace. He that hath appointed his ordinances to that end will so far stand to his own appointment, and honour his own ordinances, as to work by them, and not ordinarily without them. If men therefore will not use God's means, no wonder if they go without his grace. For first, such are out of the way of grace, and when they avoid the causes, they cannot in reason look for the effects. And moreover, they provoke God to withhold and deny his grace when they so disesteem it, as that they will not so much as use the means to get it. For example, one particular means of conversion is, the hearing of the word preached by the ministers of Christ in the public assembly. ' How shall they believe in him of whom they have not heard? And how shall they hear without a preacher? So then, faith cometh by hearing, and hearing by the word of God.' God sent Paul to open men's eyes and convert them. God would so far favour Cornelius, as to send an angel to him, but not to preach the gospel, but only to bid him send for a preacher, because he would keep to his standing ordinance, and make use of his ministers and appointed means. So he would stop Paul by a vision in his way, and do more for him in acquainting him extraordinarily with his name, than he doth with others; and yet he sends him to Ananias for instruction. It was by hearing Peter preach that the Jews were pricked at the heart, and converted, and three thousand added to the church at once. It was God that must open the heart of Lydia; but what did he open it for, but to ' attend the things that were spoken by Paul;' that thereby she might be converted? God would vouchsafe an earthquake to prepare the heart of the jailor for conversion, but he would not convert him without the preaching of Paul and Silas. It was those that had ears and heard not, and hearts that were hardened against the word, that were not converted, healed, or forgiven. By teaching sinners the way of God, David assured himself, ' they shall be converted to him.' The word of God is the seed of life, which is sown and takes root in the hearts of them that God will save. It is the word of God which abideth for ever, which is the incorruptible seed by which we are born again. God hath made those promises of a blessing on his word, which should draw us to attend it. ' Incline your ears, come unto me, hear and your souls shall live.' He hath severely threatened those that will not hear and obey. If a people will not hear the ministers of Christ, they must ' shake off the dust of their feet in witness against them:' Christ hath attested that it shall be more tolerable for Sodom and Gomorrah in the day of judgment than for that people. It is by his ministers that Christ doth teach his church, and ' every soul that hears not him, shall be cut off from his people.' If you will be at home when the message of God is delivered to the congregation, you cannot expect the blessing and benefit of it. If you can find something else to do when you should hear the word of God, God will find something else to do when he should give you his saving grace.

To him who objects that the minister is but a weak man, and I cannot profit by him; I answer, Doth he not deliver the profitable word of God? Doth he not preach the doctrine of faith, repentance, and justification by Christ, and show you the way of life? If you can hear the doctrine of everlasting life, and not profit by it, because the minister is not so able as others, blame your own hearts, and give more attendance and regard to what you hear: and lament that ignorance or carelessness of your own which hinders you from profiting.

And to him who murmurs, by saying, I have more temptations in the congregation than I have when I sit at home; Satan is troubling me with vain thoughts, and I cannot attend,—I say, is that a reason against duty, and so necessary a duty? Will you think to overcome the devil's temptations by yielding to them? That is what he would have. If he could drive you from God's ordinances, he hath his will. Will you make your own sin a pretence against your necessary duty? That is to make one sin a pretence for another: yea, a lesser sin a pretence for a greater: It is your sin to hear with a careless, wandering mind, but it is a greater sin not to hear at all.

To the man who thus objects, I can profit as much by staying at home, and reading the scriptures, or some good book: it is the word of God which they preach, and it is that which I read at home: the books that are written by learned men, are better than the sermons that are preached by our ministers,—I will show, 1. What foolish pretences these are against the plain command of God, and our own necessary duty. When God hath appointed you your duty, will he allow you to forsake it upon your own reason, as if you were wiser than God, and knew what will profit you better than he? If your physician give you a medicine, and bid you take it for the cure of your disease, will you be wiser than he, and say, Why may not such and such a thing serve as well, or better? If you will needs be your own physician, forsake God's direction, and cure yourselves, do it as well as you can, and see what will become of it. It is a strange thing that a sinner should think himself wiser than God, take upon him to mend his word, and find out a better way to heaven than he hath prescribed him. 2. Can you have grace, think you, without the gift of God? If you cannot, do you think God will give it you in a way of disobedience, when you run from his appointed means; or rather in a way of duty and obedience, when you wait on him in that which he hath promised to bless? Find you such promises to those that turn their back on God's public ordinances, as we can show you to them that diligently use them, if you can. 3. Is it not horrible pride in you to think that you are able to understand the word of God as well without a teacher, as with one? The Eunuch said to Philip, when he asked him whether he understood what he read, ' how can I, except some man should guide me?' Yet you think you can read the word at home as profitably without a guide: as if your children that go to school should say, ' we have the same books at home, and therefore we will not go to school, our master doth but teach us our grammar, and other books, and these we can read at home.' You are wise men meanwhile, that know no more of your own ignorance; and humble men, that think you have no need of teaching; as if God had appointed his ministers and ordinances in vain. 4. It is a certain mark that you never heard or read as you should; or else your hearing or reading would have taught you that both must go together, and not one shut out the other; and that the greatest, which is God's public work, must be preferred. It is a mark of a graceless heart and worse; even of one that hath much blinded common reason itself, when wretched sinners do know no more of their own necessity, but think they can live as well without God's public means as with it. If ever sermon or book had done you saving good, and you had the least spark of grace, and had felt the power of divine truth upon your soul, you would have been far from these conceits: you would feel the necessity of the preaching of the word, as an hungry man feels the need of his food. Your own necessity would drive you, the good which you feel by the word would draw you, and your love to it would not suffer you to forbear. If you were necessarily kept away by any business, you would take it for your loss, when it is not your sin, and would lament that you are deprived of that which you find so sweet and

profitable. To find no profit by the preaching of the word of God, nor any great need of it, is a mark of a dead and graceless soul. 5. Look through the scripture, and see whether the common way of conversion were not by the hearing the word of God preached. 6. If you may thus forbear it, then why may not all others? Then all Christian assemblies should be dissolved; then what churches should we have? Do you think that this is the will of God? All sorts of Christians in the world would have assemblies. Papists have their meetings, and Socinians have theirs; and even the separatists have theirs; and would you have none? Doth not God expressly charge you, that ' you forsake not the assembling of yourselves together, as the manner of some is;' to what end else hath he appointed ministers in his church? 7. Do you think that there should be any ministers, or not? If not; then no church, no baptism, and then no Christ and no salvation. If there should; what should they do, if not preach the gospel? Paul so far preferred it before other ordinances, that he thanks God that he baptized not any himself save some few among them, because of an inconveniency that might have followed. ' For God sent me not,' saith he, ' to baptize, but to preach the gospel.' If you would have no preaching, you should have no ministers. If you would have us preach, who should we preach to? To walls, or to men? If to men, why not to you as well as to others? Are others bound to hear any more than you? And how can we preach without hearers? Paul saith, and so must we, ' necessity is laid upon me, and wo to me if I preach not the gospel:' and may we not then say, necessity is laid on you, and wo to you if you hear not the gospel? The scripture saith, ' how beautiful are the very feet of them that bring the glad tidings of peace?' And you can profit as well without them at home. Is not your spirit then contrary to God's Spirit, which thus speaks; what spirit is it that is contrary to God's Spirit, but the devil's? 8. It was never God's end in writing the scripture; nor the end of ministers in writing good books to keep you from the public hearing of the word. Each duty must know its place. I had rather the books that I have written were all burned, than that men should by them be kept from the public and greater ordinances. Do not these very books which you say you read, command you to hear, and condemn those that do not hear? Do they not show you that your words are the words of wickedness; and say as much for hearing as now I do? What an hypocritical trick of you is this, when the Bible and other good books command you to be constant hearers, and condemn you if you will not, that you will say you can profit more by reading these books than by hearing? What! can you profit more by reading your duty, when you refuse to do it, than by obediently doing it? Can you profit most by reading your own condemnation? You read in scripture that 'he that turneth away his ear from hearing the law, even his prayer shall be abomination.' The truth is, you show by this, that you do but make reading a pretence against hearing, when indeed you never did either of them with understanding and grace in your hearts. 9. What do you, by withdrawing from the public assemblies, but excommunicate yourselves? And is it not our duty then to excommunicate or avoid you if you continue obstinate after admonition? Do you believe the communion of saints, and yet do you avoid it? If you had any grace in your hearts, you would make the assembly and public worship of God, the delight of your souls, and it would do you so much good to call on God, praise him with his people, and hear his instruction, that you could not be without it. You would do as David, when he was banished from the temple and worship of God; he crieth out, 'As the heart panteth after the water-brooks, so panteth my soul after thee, O God. My soul thirsteth for God, for the living God, when shall I come and appear before God? My tears have been my meat day and night, while they continually say to me, where is thy God? When I remember these things, I pour out my soul in me. For I had gone with the multitude; I went with them to the house of God, with the voice of joy and praise, with the multitude that kept holy-day.'

The sixth council at Constance decreed, that whosoever was absent from the congregation three Lord's-days together, without necessity, if he were a minister, should be put from the ministry, and if he were a private man, he should be cast from the communion of the church. If you cast out yourselves, blame not us if we cast you out.

But say some, when a minister preaches a month, or two, or three, or a year upon one text, how can he choose but add to the word of God, and therefore why should we hear them?

That is a foolish cavil. What! is expounding and applying the word of God, adding to it? Do we tell you that any thing is the word of God which is not? Why doth not one of these ignorant objectors come and tell us in any one particular, what it is that we have added to the word of God? I am now persuading you to hear the word of God; is this adding to it? Doth not the word do the like? Doth not God in the word bid us acquaint you with it, and make it plain to you, and press it upon you? What if a lawyer bestow a day or twenty days in pleading your cause before the judge, that he may save your estate, or your life from the malice of an adversary? Will you say, that this lawyer doth add to the law of the land by his pleading? What if the judge pass sentence according to law, and give the reason of it? Or what if he make a charge of many hours' length wherever he comes; doth he add to, or diminish from the law by so doing? I must crave pardon of the hearers that are but of common reason, that I have spent so much time in answering such senseless cavils as these. But they must consider that such people we have to deal with, and the more unreasonable they are, the greater need they have to be taught.

Another means that God hath appointed for conversion is the reading of his word, and of such good books as are written for the opening and applying of it. Though this must not thrust out hearing, yet is it an excellent means in its own time and place, or else God would not have appointed it as he hath done. Many a soul hath had happy experience of the success of reading. The word read is the word, and therefore may convert, for 'the law of the Lord is perfect, converting the soul;' it is a very great privilege to have the truths of God before our eyes, where we may view them over and over at our leisure, till they be fastened in our hearts.

Another means that God hath appointed us to use for the obtaining of his grace is, a serious inquiry of those that should and can instruct us. In common easy matters, you may go either to ministers or to private Christians, as you see fit; but in matters of great difficulty, where private men are in danger of mistaking, or are not able to do it as your case requires, there is it your duty especially to repair to your teachers; or the most able, faithful ministers that you can well get, and make known your case to them, and desire their direction for your effectual recovery. Nicodemus came to Jesus by night for counsel, because he perceived that he was a teacher sent from God: and Christ thereupon did give him advice in the matter of the new birth. Another inquires what he shall do that he may have eternal life. The Eunuch desires instruction of Philip, Paul of Ananias, and Cornelius of Peter, as was said before. The Jews that were pricked at the heart, ask Peter and the rest of the apostles what they shall do ? The jailor asks Paul and Silas what he shall do to be saved ? See further in Malachi, ' The priests' lips should keep knowledge, and they should seek the law at his mouth ; for he is the messenger of the Lord of hosts.' If poor unconverted sinners would but take his course, go to their teachers for direction for their salvation, and resolve to practise it when it is given them, conversion would not be so rare, nor so many miscarry as now do : but most are so careless that they feel no need of it, and think it were but to trouble themselves and their teachers, to no purpose ; and others are so stout that they will not stoop to it ; but if we send for them to come and speak with us, that we may afford them the best advice we can, they ask us by what authority we do it, and think it too much to come near us and speak to us : others are so sinfully bashful, that they cannot open their mouths when their salvation is concerned in the matter; and others are conceited beforehand that ministers will but slight them, and are too stout to speak to them, at least with any seriousness and tenderness of their case. And thus Satan keeps men from grace, by keeping them from the means of grace.

Another means of conversion is, the frequent company of those that fear God, and would afford us their help in the way to heaven, and conference with them about these things. Company hath a transforming power, and the speeches and examples of heavenly Christians will do much to bring others to a consideration of their ways. Commonly men are, or seem to be, such as their familiar company is.

Another means for conversion is, frequent and earnest prayers to God. When we know we want grace, and that God is the giver of it, what should we do to betake ourselves to him, and ask saving grace 'and wisdom of him, who giveth to all men liberally, and upbraideth not ?" I know some would persuade us that we may not exhort unconverted men to pray ; because their prayer is an abomination to God, and without faith they cannot please God. To whom I answer briefly. First, Nature itself teaches a man in misery to cry to him who is able to relieve him, to beg pardon of him whom he hath offended, and especially when he knows that he is of a merciful nature : may we not persuade men to that which the very light of nature doth direct them to, and the law of nature oblige them to ; or will these men go against the light and law of nature ? Second, Scripture commands these to pray, and seek God ; ' seek the Lord while he may be found, call upon him while he is near. Let the wicked forsake his ways, and the unrighteous man his thoughts,' &c. Peter exhorts Simon Magus ' to pray, if perhaps the thoughts of his heart may be forgiven him,' when he pronounces him ' in the gall of bitterness and bond of iniquity.' Third, We do not exhort men to pray, while they continue wicked, but to return with prayer in their mouths from their wickedness. Our exhortation is as those before mentioned ; ' let the wicked forsake his way :' and thus 'seek the Lord.—Repent of this thy wickedness,' and so pray for pardon, as Peter exhorts. When we bid them pray, we bid them desire, for desire is the soul of prayer, and words are but the body ; and when we exhort them to desire grace, we exhort them to the beginning of grace. Praying is a returning act, and when we exhort them to pray, we exhort them to return, and by prayer to begin the work, and so this beginning may be a means of the rest of the change that is yet behind.

Direction 1. Having showed you the first hinderance of conversion, I come to give you the first direction, which is contrary thereto : and that is, that you would presently fall upon the use of those means that God hath appointed you to use for your conversion. Are you sensible of the necessity of it ; and are you truly willing to be converted, or are you not ? If you would, let us see your willingness in the use of the means without delay. Particularly let me intreat of you these following things.

1. See that you be constant hearers of the word preached, and take delight in the public assembly of the church, and let nothing but necessity keep you at home. Live under the ablest ministry that you can ; and neglect not one such opportunity for your souls. If you be absent without necessity but from one sermon, God may justly deny you the blessing of the rest : and you know not which it is that is most suit-able to your condition, and therefore miss not any. The devil is aware what a minister is studying about all the week, and when he sees that we have provided that which is likeliest to do you good, he will do all that he can to keep you away that day. He will find one business or other to tempt you to be negligent ; because he is afraid, lest if you come, you should be converted. Miss not one sermon therefore, lest you miss that one which should have done you good. And as you hear, so take heed how you hear, and attend to it as to a message sent from God, concerning your salvation ; and ' set your hearts to all the words that you hear, for it is not a vain

thing, but it is for your life.—He that hath ears to hear, let him hear,' saith Christ often in cases of greatest moment. And he that will not hear, and diligently hear a message of free grace for the saving of his soul, is unworthy to have ears. 2. If you would be converted by the word, do not let it slip as soon as you have heard it; but call it to remembrance again, and bring it home to your hearts: ponder of what you have heard, and speak of it to those about you. And if you be not able to remember it through the weakness of your memories, go to some of your neighbours' houses that repeat it, that you may have the benefit of their assistance. Have not you as much need as they? And should not you be at as much pains as they? Make the word your own before you leave it. 3. Be much in reading the word of God, and such practical books, as will help you to apply it? And lay to heart the truths you shall read. 4. Especially do all this on the Lord's-day, which is purposely set apart for such holy works. Lose none of that precious season of grace: but when the public worship is over, betake yourselves with your families, and in secret, to the improvement of it; and take as much pains that day for your souls, as you do on the rest of the days of the week for your bodies. You cannot then pretend that you have no leisure, when it is at a time that is wholly to be employed in such things. O make the best of that day, and seek after the knowledge of God therein, if you would be partakers of his grace. 5. Will you go, in case you want direction, to those that are able to direct you? Especially to your teachers, and ask them what course you must take for conversion, and tell them your case, and the hinderances that you meet with, and resolve to obey the counsel that they shall give you? 6. Will you betake yourselves daily to God in hearty prayer, and beg of him that he would give you converting grace? Beseech him to open your eyes, and show you the greatness of your sin and misery, till you be unfeignedly humbled, and that he would show you the need of his grace in Christ, till you can thirst after him and his righteousness; and that he would show you the certainty and excellency of his glory, till your hearts be set upon it above all? O beg hard of God that he would not let you live unconverted any longer, lest death should find you in that miserable state. Beseech him to pardon all your former rebellions and resistance of his Spirit, and now at last to give you that grace that you have so undervalued; and bring you into the hatred of those ways of sinful pleasure or profit, which had your hearts before.

These are the means that God hath appointed to bring you into a state of saving grace. What say you? Are you willing? Are you resolved to use these means, or are you not? If you think that this is too much, and that your salvation is not worth it, you may take your ease and go without it. But if God have not given you up to so much unreasonableness, but that you had rather be at the sweet and comfortable pains of duty, than endure the intolerable pains of hell: if you do not set more by the ease of your flesh for a few days, than the ease and peace of soul and body for ever, then take my counsel, and set upon these means without delay. Look who doth most for God, and their salvation of all that you know, and strive to do as much as they. You have the same God, the same law, and the same, and greater necessity, than they: you are further behind hand: you have more work undone which must be done: your danger is greater, and your souls should be as precious to you, as theirs to them. O therefore take time while you have it, and set yourselves to the work.

Hinderance 2. *Indulgence in bad company.* The second hinderance of conversion which I shall mention is, bad company. It is a dangerous thing to be wilfully a companion of ignorant, careless, ungodly men. If they will say nothing directly against that which is good, yet will they do much to hinder your salvation by keeping your thoughts, conversation, and delight upon other things, and by giving you an evil example, as if these matters were not necessary. Vain talk and vain practices settle the minds of men in vanity, and in a forgetfulness and neglect of heavenly things. Besides, they will be enticing you to such kind of business and delight as strengthen the flesh, contradict the Spirit, and harden you in sin, and are the common causes of the perdition of the world. The noise of their foolish laughter and giddy discourse, will drown the voice of conscience and of the Spirit of God. It is hard keeping the heart in a sense of duty, or the evil of sin in the midst of sin. As it is certainly a vain and graceless heart that delights most in vain company, so such will make the heart more vain. When men sit over their cups, cherishing their flesh (which they once vowed to fight against as their enemy) pouring out a deal of foolish discourse, the sense of the evil of sin, of the love of Christ, and of the worth of glory, is then far from the heart: and if they do make any mention of God or holy things, it is commonly unreverently and most abusively, taking the name of God in vain, and sinning more by their scripture discourse than by any other: and it is a wonder if the devil and their fleshly reason do not lead them to plead against God, and to take part with the flesh, and perhaps to make a scorn of godliness. What a dangerous thing it is, to live among such company as will be still hindering, but never helping, in the way to heaven; especially among those that are worldly or sensual, or that are enemies to godliness, and set themselves against it to their power. In a way that is up hill, and all against the interest and inclination of our flesh, and in which we are so weak and backward ourselves, we had need of all the help that we can get; and a little hinderance may be our undoing. But when poor sinners shall live among such, where they shall hear almost no discourse, but vain, and almost no talk of religion, but in distaste and contempt of it, despising the way to heaven, which is in effect to despise heaven itself; how can it be expected that such should be brought to the knowledge of the truth, and the love of those ways that they hear so much reproached? I know God can do it, and sometimes doth, where people are unavoidably cast into such company; but if men will choose such, when they may avoid it, the case is dangerous indeed. 'He that walketh with wise men shall be yet wiser, but a companion of fools shall be destroyed.' Some of these ungodly wretches are so cunning in their discourse, that weak, silly people are not able to discern their folly: some of them also have some worldly interest in them, and therefore are the more likely to do them hurt: when those that they dwell with, those that they depend upon, and those that seem to love them are ungodly, and speak against the way of salvation, it commonly takes so much with the ignorant, that they either say as they say, and are of their minds, or at least it hinders them from thorough conversion, and setting themselves diligently to the saving of their souls. Thousands have been for ever undone by evil company.

Direction 2. The second direction therefore that I shall give you is this: do all that you can to avoid the company of those that would hinder you, and to live in the company of those that would help you, in the matters of your salvation. I do not mean that a servant who is bound should go from his master before he hath served according to their agreement; nor that a child should forsake his parents that are ungodly; nor that a woman should forsake her husband, or a man his wife on this account; for here they are not at their own choice, but are fixed to their relations.

which tie them to duty and faithfulness in their places; but I mean, that no man should willingly cast himself into evil company that can avoid it. Particularly, If a master be to take a servant, take not such as are ungodly, if you can have better: if a servant be to choose a master, come not into an ungodly family, if you can help it. If young people be intended to marry, take heed of being yoked unequally, and joining yourselves with the members of the devil, and the enemies of Christ, and those that are likely to be hinderers of your salvation, and so to prove the damnation of your souls. You will be backward enough and bad enough in the best company that you can get; what then will you be in the worst? Especially when it is so near you, and continually with you, and that of your own choice. I confess a minister, or other Christian, when he hath a call to endeavour the good of such, and to reprove their sin, may go among them as a physician among the sick; and so did Christ himself when he was on earth: but to make them our companions willingly, we may not. Grace is hardly got, and hardly kept, and more hardly increased in such company as this.

On the other side, get into the company of such as will further you. 'The tongue of the just is as choice silver; the heart of the wicked is little worth; the lips of the righteous feed many, but fools die for want of wisdom.—The lips of the righteous know what is acceptable, but the mouth of the wicked speaketh frowardness.—Go from the presence of a foolish man, when thou perceivest not in him the lips of knowledge.' If you were children of God yourselves, you would delight in those that are such: for, by this we know that we 'are translated from death to life, because we love the brethren;' and David saith, that 'the saints on the earth, and the excellent are all his delight. Get therefore, if it be possible, into the company of such; with them you shall hear that which may humble you for sin, and you shall hear that of Christ which may tend to kindle the love of him in your breasts; and you shall hear that of the goodness of God, his way, and the privilege of the saints, the precious promises of the gospel, the life of grace, and the hopes of everlasting glory, which may make your hearts to burn within you. When you live with those that by their example disgrace sin to you, and draw you from it, watch you against it, and that will be still reminding you of those truths that should sanctify your hearts. O what an advantage is this to your salvation! If you be ignorant, they will teach you; if you are unskilful in prayer, or other holy duties, they will help you by their instruction and example. Choose therefore the best company you can get, if you be free, and all little enough. Live among that company on earth that you must live with in heaven, if ever you come thither.

Hinderance 3. *Ignorance of those truths which are the means of conversion.* The next hinderance of conversion to be mentioned is : a gross ignorance of those truths which should be the instruments of their conversion : he that turns to God, must needs know God ; and he that turns from sin, must needs know the evil and danger of sin. No man will make so great a change, and not know why : no man will part with his present contents, and set upon a course that his nature is against ; nor forsake all the world, even that which is dearest to him, till he know that there is a pressing necessity of so doing, or know of something better to be had by the change. When we find that even men of knowledge are too often ungodly, and they will not leave sin even when they know the evil of it, and know that everlasting damnation is threatened against it : how then can they forsake it that know not this ? When many that can speak of the vanity of this world, the glory of the saints in the life to come, and the amiableness of God, and his all-sufficiency to make them happy, do yet cleave to this world, neglect God, and the glory which they so extol, how then can we expect that they should turn to God, and set their minds to seek his kingdom that do not know him ? All the wickedness in the world is cherished by ignorance, total or partial. Even those that say they know these things, and yet live ungodly, do not soundly know them, but hold them as an opinion, and not as a point of saving faith. If poor sinners, that set so light by the everlasting kingdom, did but thoroughly know what they slight, they would quickly change their minds and courses : if you knew heaven as well as you know your own houses and lands, and if you saw what the souls do now enjoy that depart in the faith, as you see what is done in the houses where you dwell, I would not thank the worst of you all to become far more devout and diligent than the best in the town or country is now : I would not thank the vilest worldling to become heavenly ; or the vilest drunkard to become sober ; or the scorner of godliness to be the most godly in the country. If you knew heaven as well as you know earth, it were no thanks to you if every family of you were a society of saints, but this cannot be expected : God will not have us live by sight and

sense, but by faith : but yet a knowledge of divine revelation we may and must have : no man loves sin but for want of knowing what he loves : no man dotes upon this deceitful world, but for want of knowing the worthlessness of it : no man makes light of eternal glory, but for want of knowing what he makes light of : and no man is against a holy life, but he that knows not what it is, nor what will be the end of it. O if you but knew God, your hearts would be enflamed with love to him. Some of you now stand gazing in wonder at the diligence of the godly, and some of you are secretly reproaching them, and casting forth your ignorant scorns against them ; but if you did but know what it is that they are doing, and who it is that urges them on work, and for what it is that they make all this ado, you would wonder more at your own folly, and would be as forward as they, and would presently take that course which you now reproach. Alas ! poor sinners durst not sport with sin if they knew what they did : they durst not run in crowds to damnation if they knew what they did. The kingdom of Satan is a kingdom of darkness ; his works are the works of darkness ; and himself the ruler of the darkness of this world, and under chains of darkness is he reserved to the judgment of•the great day ; and the mist and blackness of darkness is reserved to him and his servants for ever ; 'if the gospel be hid, it is hid to them that are lost ; in whom the God of this world hath blinded the minds of them which believe not, lest the glorious gospel of Christ, who is the image of God, should shine unto them. He that walketh in darkness knoweth not whither he goeth.' They that are converted can truly say, ' we were sometimes darkness, but now we are light in the Lord.' For they are translated from the power of darkness.

Direction 3. If ever you would be converted, labour for true knowledge : come into the light, that your deeds may be manifested ; and that your own hearts may be manifest to yourselves. Nothing but light will expel your darkness ; the devil haunts men during the night of ignorance, and seldom appears in the open day-light : bring in but the saving light of knowledge and he will vanish and be gone : the first part of saving grace is illumination. The opening of the eye causes the opening of the heart : if you had but a little of the heavenly light of the saints, it would show you that which would turn your hearts ; you could not be of the same mind as you are, if you had but saving light : now you think highly of the world, and meanly of the world to come; you now think nothing too much for your flesh, and all too much that is done for heaven; you could not be of this mind if you had the light of the Spirit: you labour now for that which profits not, and neglect that which would pay you for your labour: you vilify Christ, grace, and holiness, while you magnify the dreams and dust of the world; you could not do thus if you were savingly illuminated. I beseech you therefore, if ever you would be converted and saved, labour presently to know the Lord, and his will and ways; lament your former ignorance and negligence which did maintain it. It is not so great a shame for you to be ignorant how to do your work in the world; no, nor how to eat or drink, or how to dress yourselves, as it is to be ignorant of the kingdom of heaven, and the way thereto: you will never find the way to heaven if you do not know it: he that knows most knows too little; what then will they do that know almost nothing at all? O think not knowledge a needless thing, but pursue after it, and rest not till you obtain it; to which end you must use these means following :—

1. Be much in hearing and reading the word of God, as was before directed; for that is it which ‘giveth light to the simple;’ this ‘will make you wise unto salvation.’ 2. Read good books that are written for the expounding and applying of the scripture. Many have received much information by these. 3. Converse with wise and godly men: these are the means of knowledge that were before made mention of.

We, you object, are not learned, and therefore God will not require much knowledge at our hands. To which I reply, You may say, therefore God will not require learning at your hands, further than you are without it through your own neglect. But, 1. Every man that hath a reasonable soul should know God that made him; know the end for which he should live; and know the way to his eternal happiness as well as the learned: have not you souls to save or lose as well as the learned have? 2. God hath made plain his will to you in his word; he hath given you teachers and many other helps; so that you have no excuse if you are ignorant; you must know how to be Christians if you are no scholars. You may learn the way to heaven in English, though you have no skill in Hebrew or Greek: but in the darkness of ignorance you can never reach it. 3. Will not God judge you as well as the learned? Will not he require an account of the talents which you possess? He hath set you on his work as well as others, and therefore

you must know how to do his work. If you think therefore that you may be excused from knowledge, you may as well think that you may be excused from love and from all obedience; for there can be none of this without knowledge.

But I am, you say, not of so quick an apprehension as others; and therefore I cannot learn so well. And I have been brought up in ignorance, and therefore it cannot be expected from me.

Can any man, I answer, have excuse for ignorance that lives among such teaching, books, and Christian company as we now do? You may as well shut your eyes at noon-day, and say you cannot do your work for want of light. Were you but as willing to get the knowledge of God and heavenly things as you are to know how to work in your trade, you would have set yourselves to it before this day, and you would have spared no cost nor pains till you had got it. But you account seven years little enough to learn your trade, and will not bestow one day in seven in diligent learning the matters of your salvation. Is there not many an opportunity of getting knowledge, which you omit through your own neglect? You are at home or upon other business, when you might have been hearing the word of God and in the company of diligent Christians who are inquiring and learning these necessary things; and when you neglect the means, you think to be excused for your ignorance. The way that God commands you to get knowledge is, that you ‘receive the word of God and hide his commandments with you; incline your ears to wisdom, apply your hearts to understanding, and that you cry after knowledge; lift up your voice for understanding, and seek it as silver, and search for it as for hid treasures.’ If you would do thus, the Lord hath promised that ‘ you shall understand the fear of the Lord, and find the knowledge of God.’ Methinks light itself should be pleasant to you. Did Adam so desire unnecessary knowledge as to undo himself and his posterity to procure it; and will not you so desire that knowledge which is necessary to your salvation, and by which you may be recovered from that miserable estate? How many years' study will men spend to know a little of the creature, and will you not take pains to know the Maker and end of the whole creation?

But may we not hope that we may be saved without so much knowledge?

No; not without knowing the necessary, fundamental points of Christianity, and a desire to know more. Doth Christ say, 'it is life eternal to know God and Jesus Christ,' and do you think to have life eternal without it? God saith of people that have no understanding, ' that he that made them will not save them, and he that formed them will shew them no favour;' that ' Christ shall come in flaming fire, to render vengeance to them that know not God, and obey not the gospel of our Lord Jesus Christ;' and that they 'shall be punished with everlasting destruction from the presence of the Lord.'

Hinderance 4. *The power of unbelief.* The next hinderance of conversion is unbelief: when men will not be persuaded that the word of God is true, but doubt of the things which he hath revealed to them concerning the everlasting state of men. Men have but a slight opinion of the truth of the word of God, which will not serve turn to prevail against their fleshly inclination.

Three great enemies of the Christian faith we have to deal with, which if we overcome not, we lose all. 1. The one is our own unbelieving hearts, and our carnal inclinations and interests; flesh and blood cannot reveal the things of God to us, nor discern them when they are revealed. A sound belief of the life to come, and of the whole Christian faith, would certainly turn the heart to God, and turn the course of all your lives. It is this faith that purifies the heart, and without it no wonder if the word be unprofitable, as to the producing of any further work of sanctification, for it must first beget faith before it can do the rest. 2. Another enemy to the Christian faith is the devil; who believes and trembles himself, but labours to keep others unbelieving and secure. So great is his malice against Christ and our souls, that when he sees that he cannot make a poor sinner forget God, and make light of his word any longer, he flies openly in the very face of God, and disturbs the soul with blasphemous suggestions, and tempts them to doubt whether there be a God, or not ; or whether scripture be his word ; or whether it be true. It was his first way of deceiving, to make the woman doubt of the truth of God's word, which had told her, that if she sinned, she should die. And experience teaches him to follow on in this course, which he hath found to be so successful ; most of the world are destroyed by this unbelief. How sensible is many a poor Christian of the incessant malice of Satan in this point ! When he follows them from day to day with such violence, that their hearts are ready to be overwhelmed with the horror of the temptation. But the ungodly yield to them

without so much reluctance. 3. Another sort of enemies of the Christian faith are notorious ungodly men ; such as, either by the power of their own unbelieving hearts, have prevailed against the light that should have drawn them to believe, or such as have, by the reasonings of infidels, been made infidels themselves, and are desirous to make others such as they are : these are the devil's instruments to draw men to unbelief.

Direction. If ever you would be savingly converted, see that you soundly believe the word of God: believe soundly that there is an everlasting happiness, which is the reward of a holy life, and an everlasting torment, which is the punishment of ungodliness ; and you cannot choose but forsake your ungodliness and become holy. To this end observe these few things following: 1. Watch over your carnal hearts with jealousy : do not take your hearts to be clear and impartial ; and therefore commit not the matter to their trust : they are naturally enemies to the word of God, and therefore no wonder if they hardly believe it. 2. Do not think too highly of your own understandings, as if you were able to comprehend the depths of God ; or were competent judges of each passage in his word, before you have had time and means to understand them, or before you have improved your time and means by diligent study and prayer to God : search the scriptures as a learner, and not as a foolish caviller. 3. Abhor the very first temptation of Satan that tends to draw your souls to unbelief, and suffer not his malice to make too deep impressions in your fancies: cast out such horrid thoughts with detestation, and give them not the least countenance or willing entertainment. 4. Detest the company of atheistical men, or infidels that dare open their mouths to speak against the word of God. Yea, though they pretend to do it but by way of question. Hear every word against the scripture from such deceivers, as if you heard it from the devil himself, or as if you saw him behind them, prompting them what to say, and putting them on: for it is he that doth it by their mouth. As it was Satan that caused Judas to betray Christ, and filled the heart of Ananias and Saphira to lie against the Holy Ghost; so is it Satan that fills the hearts of these unbelievers to speak against Christ, and to contradict the word which the Holy Ghost hath delivered. 5. Labour to understand the sense of scripture, and the great evidence of its truth, and of the Christian faith ; and have recourse to those for your confirmation that are of better understandings herein, than yourselves, and read those books which are written to that end, to manifest the divine authority of scripture. 6. Submit to the truth, which you know, and strive not against the light, but let it have its due impress upon your souls, that you may have the experience of its power and excellency to confirm you: by these means you may do much to overcome your unbelief; and if that were once done, the rest of the work would go on apace.

Hinderance 5. *Want of consideration on spiritual subjects.* The next hinderance is, inconsiderateness: of which I spoke in the beginning, but shall add somewhat in this place. When truths are not considered of, they are but as medicines that lie in a box, and therefore are not like to work; it is the work of consideration to bring down truths from the understanding to the heart, and to hold them there till they work. We cannot get poor sinners so much as soberly to bethink them of their ways, to call to mind the things we speak to them, and consider of them for their good. Because I intend, if the Lord will, to speak hereafter more fully of this subject, I shall pass it over now thus briefly.

Direction. If ever you would be truly converted, consider frequently and seriously of those truths of God that must do the work. The word of God is pure and powerful to convert the soul, but can you imagine it should convert you, if you will not so much as soberly think upon it? How can that work upon your hearts, which is out of your minds? It is you that must join with us for your own conversion, and do the rest of the work, when you come home, and not think that a sermon can do it, when you forget it, and never mind it more. If you seek to the ablest physician for your body, he can but give you physic, it is you that must take it and keep it, and observe directions till it work. If you will presently vomit it up again, how can it do you good? We tell you of those truths that are most useful to your conversion, and if you will take them home, keep them, and ponder on them when you are alone, till they sink into your hearts, and take root, you may be happy men; but if you will cast them all up again, and will not be persuaded to bestow now and then a few of your deepest, serious thoughts for the further entertainment of them, how should they do you saving good? If I could prevail with this congregation to be but considerate, and now and then to bestow some time to get the truth to their hearts, I should have great hopes of the conversion of you all: for light is stronger than dark-

ness: if you would but open the window by consideration, and let it in, you should find the darkness presently dispelled, and it would be day with you who have sat in the shadow of death.

The Spirit of God is able to overcome the flesh, and Christ is able to conquer Satan, bind him, and cast him out of your souls. If you would but set in, and take his part, and open him the door by sober consideration, when he knocks and seeks admittance, and not discourage him by your wilful neglect, you would feel the working of his power to your salvation. There have now been many sermons preached to you on this text; have you considered of them, when you came home? Have you taken yourselves alone, and asked your own hearts whether you are converted or not? Have you bethought you of the blessedness of the converted, and the misery of the unconverted, which you have heard? Have you dwelt upon these thoughts, till they have sunk down into your hearts? If you have, I dare say this doctrine hath done you good; but if you have not, what wonder if you be unconverted still, and if you live and die so, and if you be damned among the unconverted, when you will not be persuaded so much as seriously to consider of the matter? If it be not a matter worthy the thinking of, it is not worth the hearing, and if this be not to be thought on, I know not what is. We do not go home with you from church into your houses, nor see what you think of there in secret, nor whether you fall down there before the Lord, and pray over the sermons that you hear; nor do we hear what you say of it to others, but God follows you home, and he sees and hears all; and he that is here ready with his grace to enter into your hearts, if you do not resist or slight him, is there also ready to help you to make use of what you have heard, if you do not wilfully throw it off yourselves. Did you but earnestly consider what God is, what your duty is, what you were made for, whither you are going, what sin and the world is, what grace is, what Christ is, and hath done for you, what death is, what judgment is, what heaven is, and what hell is, how is it possible you should continue unconverted,? How is it possible but you should presently run out of your present carnal, worldly state, as you should do out of a house that is all on fire over your head; and should become most zealous and diligent Christians? Certainly consideration would do very much to your conversion, 'I thought on my ways, and turned my feet to thy testimonies; I made haste, and delayed not to keep thy commandments.'

Hinderance 6. *Hardness of heart and a seared conscience are powerful obstructions to conversion.* Though every man have some of these evil principles of human nature in his original corruption, yet the resisting of light and motions of grace, doth usually bring men to a far greater measure of them ; both by the nature of the thing, and by the just judgment of an over-ruling God. When men have sinned often or long against knowledge and conscience, and receive not the truth in the love of it, that they may be saved, but suppress the light, and live not up to the convictions that are upon their consciences, it is usual for such to grow hardened and sense-less, and for the brutish part so far to prevail, that they are in a sort unreasonable men. Men are naturally dead in sin, but when they have sinned wilfully, they grow more dead ; that is, they are more insensible, and have more of the marks of death upon them. When they fall, especially from former conviction and profession, they become twice dead, and plucked up by the roots, and then the work of conversion is hard indeed : when the heart is thus hardened, no words are much regarded by them : no saying will serve ; you speak as to a post. We shoot our arrows at a wall of flint, where they will not enter : the dew of holy instructions doth fall upon a stone where no fruit can be expected. You cannot devise what to say that will touch them, because they are stupid, and will not lay it to heart : you cannot tell how to sharpen your words to make them enter. The Lord have mercy upon these poor men, for their case is lamentable. It would make a man of consideration wonder to see what piercing, weighty truths a hard heart will make light of. Speak to them as from the God that made them, and they regard you not. Speak to them of their everlasting state, and they regard you not : tell them of the heinous evil of sin, and all its aggravations, and they take it all but as words of course ; and will say, God help us, we are all sinners, and there is an end of it. Tell them of the infinite love of God ; the precious blood of Christ that was shed for them, the free pardon that is offered, the rich, abundant grace which they might have, and it will increase their presumption and security, but it will not raise their estimation of it, nor quicken their desire after it, nor make them forsake all, and follow Christ. Tell them of an everlasting state of glory which they may obtain in the presence of the Lord, they make light of it, and hear it as they do a story of the fortunate Islands, or the Elysian fields : tell them of the endless torments of the damned that despised grace in the day of their visitation, and either they feel not, or fear not what you say ; or if they fear a little, it is not so much as to move them from their courses, nor bring them to a change of heart and life. What a sad work it is to have to deal with a hardened heart ! It is to hew at a stone, and to cleave a knotty tree that will not receive the wedge ; to plough and sow on a rock, where you cannot make the plough to enter. This is the trouble of a preacher's life : this damps his hopes ; this wearies and tires him ; this makes him say, I have laboured in vain, and spent my strength for nought ; and this hath broken many of their hearts.

Alas ! to see our poor people within a few days or years of eternal fire, which they might prevent if they would look about them in time, and we cannot get them to lay it to heart ! Alas ! to hear what a feeling they must have for ever, and yet we cannot get them to feel or fear, and prevent it now. O ! thinks a poor minister, if I could but awaken him, and make him regard the case of his soul, I should have hope yet to prevent his damnation : for no man can destroy him against his will ; and the light is so clear, that methinks he should see it, if he would not wilfully shut his eyes. But alas ! we cannot get them to regard it. How sad a case is it to think of an everlasting glory, which they might have, how freely Christ hath purchased it, how freely he doth offer it to them, and they might have it if they would, and if they did not wilfully slight it and reject it ; and yet that we cannot awaken them to consideration, nor bring such matters as these to their hearts. I have formerly said it, and I will say it again, that I profess that I often marvel that the weight of everlasting matters doth not rather over-match your spirits and overwhelm them. I have wondered that it doth not even amaze and astonish you to think how great a change you are near ; and what a thing it is to be for ever in heaven or in hell : and yet we cannot get our people to feel, or lay to heart these things. O, what lamentable hearts are these ! What will they regard and feel if they will not feel everlasting matters ? What words will ever pierce their hearts if the words of the living God will not do it, and the words by which they know they shall be judged ? Do but call one of them by some disgraceful name, and he will quickly feel : threaten him with death ; promise him but an hundred pounds, and he will regard it : but let God declare his sin and misery to him, and he will not feel it : let God threaten him with hell, and promise him everlasting life, if he will return, and he will not regard it. O, what a happy life might a minister have if it were not for hard-hearted men! If we could deal with them but on such terms for their souls as we do for their bodies, how certainly should we prevail, and then how comfortable would our employments be! If a lawyer tell them their evidence, or cause is nought, they will hear and regard him: if a physician tell them they must take physic or die, they will lay it to heart: if their landlord tell them they must pay their rent, or be turned out of their houses, they can feel what he saith; but if we tell them that they must repent and be converted, or be condemned for ever, and lose salvation, we cannot be regarded. Their hearts are shut up from us by the world, pride, lust, and sin, and we cannot get into their bosom: we know not how to come at their hearts. Alas! if it were not for their own sakes this trouble were small to us; for what good else should it do to us to trouble them, and break their hearts and change them? But when we consider if we could but convert them we should save them; and if we could help them to grace, we might meet them in everlasting glory, this makes us long for better success. Gladly then would we get them to hear, regard, and feel what we say, that it might go well with them for ever: but we cannot. Alas! to the grief of our hearts we cannot. It is a tiring life to have none but hard-hearted sinners to persuade: we lose our study for them; we lose our breath upon them. Some of them can think of other things while we are speaking to them of the greatest matters in all the world; and some of them can drop asleep under it, and some of them sit as dead as stock; and some of them will look upon us as if they were affected, and yet it never goes to the quick: and some of them that seem to be somewhat sensible, do shake off all again in a few days time, and when they have been a while among their old companions, and about their old business, they show us that they are the old men, and that it is one thing to be a little affrighted for a few days, and another thing to have a changed, softened heart.

Were it not for this sin of hardness of heart, it were not possible that so many sermons should be lost; nor that so many ministers in England should see so little fruit of their labours. Why alas, sinners, what else can be the matter? We come on as reasonable an errand as any men in the world can come on; it is but that men would accept salvation that is freely purchased and offered them, and that they would be content to change a life of sin and misery for a life of grace and everlasting glory: one would think

that such a message as this should take with every man and woman in the congregation; especially when it is sent from God himself, and brought to them with such evidence of certain truth, and themselves profess to believe what we say. One would think a message so reasonable as this should prevail with every man in a whole country or kingdom where it comes: and yet it doth not. Nay, alas! how few are they with whom it doth prevail? If we come hither to offer every man in this congregation that he should live in a palace as a prince, on condition he would leave his cottage and accept it, who would make any question of the success? I should not doubt but every man and woman of you would yield: and yet when we come in the name of God to offer them grace and glory on free cost, if they will but let go sin and the world, they will not be persuaded; say what we can, though they will not tell us so, yet they will not be persuaded; and whence can this come but from an hardened heart? Did we not speak to men that have lost their sense and reason, and are past feeling, it could not be. When every man naturally desires his own happiness, and yet men will not be happy when it is offered them.

Yea, this is not all: but when the heart is thus hardened, some of them are given over to such a desperate case that they hear the word with a malicious mind; and instead of receiving it in power to their salvation, they do but cavil at it, and pick quarrels with it to their condemnation; and prate among their companions against that which they understand not, nor ever laid to heart. If a physician would heal them for nothing, and they should maliciously reproach him or quarrel with all that he doth for them, did they not deserve to be left to perish by the disease? If they had forfeited their lives and a free pardon were offered them, what would you think of him that, instead of a thankful accepting of the pardon, would pick quarrels with it, and prove it nonsense, or scorn the messenger; his is the case of many of our hearers. Poor souls, their lives declare their misery, and God sends us to them with the offers of a remedy, and one goes home and makes a jest of it; another foolishly cavils against it, and another thinks it a needless thing; and this is our success with hard-hearted men. Now the Lord have mercy upon you that hear me in this congregation, and grant that this may be none of your case; or if it be, that he would powerfully and quickly cure it: for it is one of the saddest cases in this world: and of all sorts of men there is few or none that we have so little hope of as hard-hearted men. If a man were never so much mistaken and never so far out of the way, yet if he had but any regard or feeling with him, we might hope, by the force of reason and the light of the word of God, to bring him to himself, and set him in the way : but when men are past feeling, what shall we say to them, or what can we do for them ? Nay, it is not only words but even the works of God that are lost upon such men : mercies do but harden them, and judgments themselves do but harden them, which one would think should humble and soften them, if any outward means could do it.

When the Jews had sinned, God punished them with war, and let loose plundering, robbing soldiers upon their estates, and destroyers upon their bodies, and yet they were so far from being humbled and softened by it, that they did not so much as regard the cause, nor the hand that did it. 'Who gave Jacob for a spoil, and Israel to the robbers? Did not the Lord, he against whom we have sinned? For they would not walk in his way, neither were they obedient to his law. Therefore he hath poured upon him the fury of his anger, and the strength of battle, and it hath set him on fire round about; yet he knew not, and it burned him, yet he laid it not to heart.' And hath not this been our own case in England? Who would have thought, if people had but had life, sense, and reason in them, but that so many afflictions should have humbled them for their sins, and made them willing to learn and to be reformed? Who would have thought but they would ' have searched and tried their ways, and turned to the Lord ' that did afflict them; have loved his word, have given up themselves to his will, and even in the open assemblies have voluntarily acknowledged and bewailed their iniquities? and yet we see how many are the same. As the plague found them, so it hath left them, if not worse : and if the fury of God's anger cannot be felt, no wonder if they cannot feel our preaching : and if they lay not to heart the fire that burns them up, what wonder if they lay not to heart the message we deliver? If Peter and Paul, yea, or Christ himself, had preached to one of those hardened sinners, they would have made light of it ; or gone home and ignorantly cavilled against them as they do against the ministers now, unless the powerful arm of God had inwardly concurred to the softening of their hearts: for indeed they did thus by Christ and his apostles while they were upon earth, and by all the prophets that went before them. Saith the Lord,

' Son of man, get thee to the house of Israel, and speak with my words to them. Not to many people of a strange speech and a hard language, whose words thou canst not understand. Surely had I sent thee to them, they would have hearkened to thee ; but the house of Israel will not hearken to thee, for they will not hearken to me, for all the house of Israel are impudent and hardhearted.' And Christ himself when he had wrought even miracles to confirm his doctrine, was ' grieved for the hardness of their hearts.' And when the apostles preached the gospel of salvation, ' divers were hardened and believed not, but spoke evil of the way of God before the people,' till the apostles resolved to leave them to themselves. So that hardness of heart is the great impediment of conversion.

Direction. The advice therefore that I would give you for this work of conversion is: that you especially take heed of this dangerous case, of an hardened heart : in the name of God, see that you run not into this miserable state ; or if you be in it, O that I could awaken you, that you might speedily be brought out of it. Have you yet time of repentance ; and are your souls and bodies yet together? Yet hath God's patience kept you out of hell? O harden not your hearts, lest time be gone, and death and darkness be upon you before you are aware. ' Behold now is the accepted time, behold now is the day of salvation,' saith the Holy Ghost. Doth God give you warning once again before he smites you into everlasting vengeance, and doth he once more call you to repent before he summon you to judgment ? O take the counsel of the Holy Ghost ; ' to-day, if ye will hear his voice, harden not your hearts :' I say, to-day, lest he bear not with thee till to-morrow; 'boast not of to-morrow, for thou knowest not what a day may bring forth;' and if God do call thine impenitent soul out of this world before our next meeting in this place, or at least, ere long, remember then that thou hadst time to have prevented the misery which thou must feel to all eternity.

There is not a more fearful plague on earth than a hardened heart : none is more likely to be sealed up to damnation than such a one. Dost thou hear of the greatness of thy sin, and hear of judgment and eternal life, and hear of the love and severity of the Lord, and yet dost thou not feel it ? O sad case, and sadly to be lamented by all that understand it ! For from thyself it cannot be expected. Believe it, sinner, God hath a voice that will be heard and regarded ; if the voice of mercy be made light of, the voice of judgment shall not be made light of. When we have told thee of thy danger, and of the remedy by Christ, thou canst go home and cast it out of thy mind: but when God hath said, 'go, ye cursed, to everlasting fire prepared for the devil and his angels,' then make light of that if thou canst. When he hath newly said, 'take him and bind him hand and foot, and cast him into utter darkness where shall be weeping and gnashing of teeth,' then forget this, and cast this out of thy mind if thou canst. Poor wretch, if thou hadst to do but with such a one as I, or any one of the sons of men, perhaps thou mightest think to escape well enough: but thou hast to do with the eternal Majesty, and how then wilt thou escape? Canst thou grapple with his almighty strength; or canst thou make good thy part against him? When we call on thee to repent and reform, thou wilt not; when we call on thee to a holy and heavenly life, thou wilt not; but when he shall say, Depart from me, thou cursed wretch, wilt thou then say, thou wilt not? When he shall deliver thee to the devils to be tormented by them for ever, who deceived thee in thy lifetime, and bid them take thee to everlasting flames, wilt thou then say, thou wilt not go? Alas, poor wretch! what power hast thou to resist? It is the same almighty God that made all the world of nothing, and bears it up in his hand, and disposes of it at his will, which then will command thee to remediless perdition. If he bid the sun in the firmament move, it moves; and once when he bade it stand still, it stood still, and nothing is able to resist his power; and canst thou resist it? Why, if he send but a disease upon thee thou art unable to resist it? If he bid thee die, wilt thou say, I will not die? Alas! if sinners could have resisted God, and saved themselves from the stroke of justice, the church-yard would not have been so full of graves, nor hell so full of damned souls as it is at this day. 'But who hath hardened himself against him, and hath prospered?' Name me the man and tell me where he dwells, that hardened his heart against the Lord, and sped well by it in the latter end? I tell you again, if sermons cannot make you feel, if mercies and warning, if threatening and affliction cannot make you feel, judgment and hell shall make you feel. Say not but thou wast told so, and remember this when thou seest not me. Remember that I foretold thee that God will not be always mocked or abused, and that thou canst not so lightly sneer at hell as thou didst at the warnings of God and man. If thou be turned into a rock, God hath an hammer that can batter and dash in pieces that rock.

You may aver, if God will harden my heart, how can I help it? It is he that hardened Pharaoh's heart, and so he did the Jews, and if he will do it, what remedy? To which I respond, dost thou think to have any excuse or comfort by accusing the righteous and holy God? What a foolish thing is sin, and how it bereaves poor sinners of their understanding! Thou mightest better have laid the blame upon any one in the world than upon the righteous and most Holy God. For never sin came from him, nor was caused by him. Dost thou think he will not be justified in his judging? God's hardening men is but his leaving them to themselves, to go on in that hardness that he found them in, and denying them that grace which he no way owes them. God doth not this neither till thou abusest his grace, strivest against the light, and castest away thy own mercy; is it not just then that he should take his mercy from thee? If children will play with their meat or cast it to the dogs, and tread it under feet, it is time to take it away. This is God's hardening of the hearts of sinners, he leaves them as he found them, after they have abused and refused his grace: and withal, he lets loose the tempter upon them, that seeing they will be wicked, they may be taken in their own wickedness, and destroy themselves by it: as you will lay a purse in his way to catch a thief by, when you do not make him thievish; so God will try and catch a sinner when yet he never gives him any inclination to the sin: but when he sees that they are and will be such, it is just with him to let them take their course, and smart by their folly: and as if you see a thief that is running into a pit, you are not bound to keep him out, no more is God to keep a sinner from destroying of himself, especially when he hath so often refused his assistance.

But what can I do for the softening of my own heart? you ask.—Hear the reply. O that thou wert but willing to do what thou shouldest and mightest do: if thou be willing. 1. Get alone and consider of the misery of thy condition; and of the time when thou shalt feel whether thou wilt or not. 2. Keep under the most powerful preaching of the word, which is God's ordinary means for melting of the heart. 3. Keep the company of those that will remember thee of those holy truths which have a softening nature, and will bring everlasting things into thy mind. 4. Keep out of the company of foolish and ungodly men, who by their words and practices will harden thee more. 5. Resolve that thou go not on in the practice of thy known sin; no not once more: for sinning against knowledge hardens the heart, and tempts the Lord to leave thee to thyself. If thou wilt be drunk when thou knowest it to be a sin; and wilt be worldly, and wilt be fleshly, when God and conscience speak against it; this will desperately harden thy heart. 6. Beg daily of God that he would soften thy heart: beseech him upon thy knees to pardon those sins by which thou hast hardened it, and to give thee his Spirit which must deliver thee from this misery: and follow him hard with these requests from day to day; for if thou prevail not, thou art undone and lost for ever. For, saith the Holy Ghost, 'he that covereth his sins shall not prosper; but he that confesseth and forsaketh them shall have mercy. —Happy is the man that feareth always, but he that hardeneth his heart shall fall into mischief. —He that being often reproved, hardeneth his neck, shall suddenly be destroyed, and that without remedy.'

Hinderance 7. *Idolatrous esteem of the world and the things of it, is another hinderance of conversion.* Another hinderance of conversion is: the too great esteem that men have of this world, and the great interest that it has gotten in their hearts; by this it is that God is shut out; that Christ is so neglected, that heavenly things are so much undervalued; because men have that in their hands already, or at least in their eyes, which they like better. God and Mammon cannot both be loved; these two masters cannot be both served. While the world is leaned to, Christ will be made light of. The glory to come can never be obtained but by the hearty forsaking of this present world; it is this that stole the heart from God, and it is this that possesses it, till grace recovers it to God again. And therefore it is the work of grace to cast out the world, and to set up God, to dethrone this usurper, and to give God again the possession of his own. As truly as darkness goes out of the room when light comes in, so truly doth the love of the world depart where the love of God doth enter into the soul: for if any man, predominantly, love the world, the love of the Father is not in him. Men cannot make God their end, and the world their end too. They cannot love God above all, and the world above all too. They cannot set their hearts on heaven, nor make it their treasure and their chief good, while they set their hearts on earth, and make it their treasure, 'for where their treasure is, their hearts will be.' When men are drowned in worldly cares, and taken up so much with worldly contrivances and business, there is then no room for the matters of their salvation. If

they would go to consider of their sin and misery, and think of these things that might further their conversion, their worldly matters step in, and turn away their thoughts. So that, when they are alone, and have opportunity for such considerations, yet they have no hearts to such a work. When they are considering, and begin to perceive that they must either change or perish, and that this life will not serve the turn, presently the world doth turn their minds, and tells them of other matters to be minded, and so all is forgotten again. If their hearts be a little awakened and troubled for sin, the pleasure or business of the world doth quiet them, and sometimes it makes them forget their misery; they live as if it were cured, and all their trouble vanishes away. If they are moved to set up the worship of God in their families, to read, pray, and instruct those that are under them, the world will not give them leave, they have somewhat else to mind, which it seems they think of greater necessity: and thus the world is an enemy to God, the love of it keeps out the love of God, the serving of it excludes his service, and they that are friends of it, are certainly his enemies. And this is a grievous hinderance of conversion.

Direction. Let go the world then, if ever you would be converted. You renounced it in your baptism; see that your hearts now unfeignedly renounce it, unless you will renounce your part in Christ and the world to come. Think not to keep both, and make up a felicity to yourselves between them: it is now become your enemy, and as an enemy it must be affected and used, or else as an enemy it will effectually destroy you. It is a killing, conquering enemy to those that take it not heartily for their enemy: but it is only a troubling, though a conquered enemy, to them that take it and use it as an enemy. O that poor worldlings did but know what a feather, what a shadow, what an empty, unprofitable thing they pursue. You run after it eagerly, but when you overtake it, you will befool yourselves, and say, What have I gotten? Is this all that I have cared and toiled for; is this all that I forsook God and my salvation for? For your soul's sake, sinners, forsake not God till you know for what. Neglect not heaven till you have somewhat better to regard. Renounce not your salvation till you know such reason for it as you dare own, and stand to at death and judgment. Is a small portion of wealth and worldly trifles a matter for a man to sell his soul for? You think, I know, that you do not sell your salvation for it, because you hope that you may have both: but this is merely your wilful delusion. If you will not believe God now that tells you cannot have two portions, two treasures, two ends, or two masters, you will find it true when your deceit hath undone you. Doth God tell you that you cannot love both, and that the world and he cannot both have your hearts, and will you not believe him? If the world be better than God, then take it and let him go: if it be more durable than heaven, then follow it and spare not. But alas! what a dream, what a shadow is it! How soon will it be gone! Will you always dwell in these houses? Or will your friends and riches stay with you for ever? Will you carry your lands, wealth, and fleshly provision to another world? Alas, that men should wilfully undo themselves!

There is not a worldling but will confess all this to be true that I say, yet their hearts are still the same; the world hath their love, care, and pleasure, and worldlings they will be still. What a self-condemning sinner is a worldling, and how much against his knowledge doth he sin. He knows that he mis-places his affections, and yet he will do it. He foresees that the world will deceive him at the last, and yet he will follow it, to the neglect of his salvation. Christ hath made but one thing necessary. Do that and do all: get that and get all: but they needlessly cumber themselves about many things, and make themselves more work than God hath made them: they will not see that they have lost their labour, till they find that they have lost their souls. O poor foolish sinners, that now are so busy for you know not what, and rejoicing in your possessions as if you were happy, when ' your souls shall be required of you, whose then shall these things be?' When death and judgment shall awaken you to your account, and help you better to understand your reckoning; then make your boast of the world, and boast of your gain, if you find it worth your boasting of: then tell us who was the wiser merchant, he that sold all for the pearl of grace and glory, or he that let go that treasure for the world: then tell us whether an heavenly or an earthly conversation was the wiser course; and who it was that choose the better part.

Hinderance 8. *Custom and the power of bad habits are hinderances.* Another great impediment to conversion is: when custom in sinning hath given it the mastery, and made the flesh the ruler of your reason, and made men think that they have a kind of necessity to sin. Nature, as corrupted, doth bring forth sin in too great strength; but custom doth make it stronger, and blots out the remnants of moral wisdom and honesty from the soul: when men have long taken a custom of sinning, they grow hardened and senseless, as the high way doth by being often trod upon, or as a labourer's hand grows hard by constant labour: and so sin becomes familiar to them, and they become past feeling, and are 'given up to work uncleannesss with greediness.' A custom of sinning against reason doth make men in a sort unreasonable, by giving their sensuality the rule of their reason. We see, by sad experience, when men grow old in ignorance, how hardly they are brought to knowledge, yea, or to be willing to learn: and when men are often drunk, or commit any other heinous sin, how it prostitutes their souls to the next temptation, and makes sin as familiar to them as water to the fish. It must be by a miracle, or next to a miracle, that an old, ignorant, worldly or sensual sinner must be converted: by often sinning they have lost their understandings, hardened their hearts, think the greatest good to be evil, and think they cannot live without their sin. But as a man in a fever calls for cold water, so do they for the pleasure of their flesh: they must have it, they cannot forbear it, their flesh will have no denial. ' If the Ethiopian can change his skin, or the leopard his spots, then may they that are accustomed to do evil, learn to do well.' We see, in public cases, what a power custom hath: if men be but used to any thing in God's worship, that is unmeet or contrary to the word of God, they will not hearken to scripture, but cry out custom, custom, against that plain word that must judge them and should direct them; as if the custom of their forefathers were of more authority than the word of God; no wonder then if a custom of swearing, drunkenness, worldliness, wickedness, or contempt of a religious, godly life, do prevail with thousands to harden them to perdition; and this is a grievous hinderance to their conversion.

Direction. You that are yet young, take heed of a custom in sin, and you that are hardened in it already, in the fear of God make a stand and go no further: it is sad that you have gone so far: but if you wilfully go on but one day more, you know not but God may leave you to yourselves; and if you wilfully add but one sin more to the account, it may seal you to perdition, and sink you into hell. What a folly is it then for men to delay their repentance to the last, when custom in sinning doth make the work of their conversion to be more difficult: remember, I beseech you, that your custom is the aggravation of your sin, and not any just excuse. The oftener you have sinned, the oftener you have wronged God; and the oftener you have wronged him, the more should you now bewail it, and not therefore go on to wrong him more. If you had oftentimes hurt yourselves by falls, or cut your fingers by negligence or carelessness, will you do so still to keep a custom? What greater madness can there be than to plead custom for sinning against the living God, and hastening your own souls to everlasting perdition? You shall have custom for suffering then, as you have for sinning now, and see whether you will therefore love your suffering. If you will love sin, because you are accustomed to it, you shall try whether you can love hell, because you are accustomed to it.

Hinderance 9. *Self-love, presumption, and false hope, deceive men on the subject of conversion.* Another hinderance of conversion is foolish self-love, which makes men unwilling to know the worst of themselves, and so keeps them from believing their sinfulness and misery; and causes them to presume and keep up false, deceiving hopes, that they may be saved whether they are converted or not; or that they are converted, when indeed they are not. They think it is every one's duty to hope well of themselves, and therefore they will do so; and so while they hope they are converted already, or may be saved without conversion, no wonder if they look not seriously after it: like many a sick man that I have known in the beginning of a consumption, or some grievous disease, they hope there is no danger in it; or they hope it will go away of itself, and it is but some cold; or they hope that such or such an easy medicine may cure it, till they are past hope, and then they must give up these hopes, and their lives together, whether they will or no. Just so do poor wretches by their souls: they know that all is not well with them, but they hope God is so merciful, that he will not damn them, or they hope to be converted sometime hereafter, or they hope that less ado may serve the turn, and that their good wishes and prayers may save their souls; and in these hopes they hold on, till they find themselves to be past remedy, and their hopes and they be dead together. I speak not this without the scripture, for 'when a wicked man dieth, his expectation shall perish, and the hope of the unjust man perisheth.—What is the hope of the hypocrite, though he have gained, when God taketh away his soul? Will God hear his cry, when trouble cometh upon him?—And the eyes of the wicked shall fail, and they shall not

escape; and their hope shall be as the giving up of the ghost.' There is scarcely a greater hinderance of conversion than these false deceiving hopes of sinners; that think they are converted, when they are not; or hope to be saved, when they have no ground for their hopes: were it not for this, men would look about them, and return.

Direction. I have formerly spoke and wrote to you of this point, and I have told you that it is none of my desire that any man should absolutely despair. But despair you must of ever being saved without conversion, or finding heaven in the way to hell: till that kind of despair possess your hearts, we cannot expect a saving change: for men will not let go all their pleasure, and cast themselves upon these difficulties, which flesh and blood apprehends to be in the way of God, as long as they hope to do well enough without it. No wonder if men be unholy, that hope to be saved whether they be holy or not. It is hope that keeps your hearts from breaking, which must be broken for your former sins. It is hope of doing well enough in your present case, that keeps you from seeking out for a better; if you knew that you must be converted or condemned, and had no hopes of being saved, unless you were born again, then you would look about you, and run to God by prayer for his grace, and run to the word by reading for instruction, and run to the minister with inquiry for direction, and be glad of that company, which would help you to heaven. I tell you, it is these carnal hopes that deceive the world, and hinder them from seeking Christ and life.

The thing therefore that I request of you for the sake of your own souls, is but this, that you would but try your hopes by the word of God, prove them sound before you trust them, and content not yourselves to say, I hope I shall be saved, but prove and try, whether you are such as God hath promised salvation to, or not: for there are hopes that will never deceive men, that is, those that are well grounded on the word of God; and there are hopes, as you have heard, that will die with men, and undo them; that is, those that had no ground but their own self-love; when men hope they shall be saved because they would have it so, and hope to come to heaven, when they will not go the way to heaven; is it not one of the most dreadful sights in the world, to see a man ready to leave this world, and have no hopes but what will die when he dies? O if you did but know what a terrible thing it will be for a man in his life-time to hope for salvation, and as soon as he is dead to find himself in damnation, and all his hopes to vanish like a dream, you would surely be persuaded to try your hopes. Prove once by the marks of grace in your souls, that thou art one of those that God hath promised salvation to, that is, one of the regenerated, the heavenly and the holy, and then hope for salvation and spare not, and the Lord confirm and maintain thy hopes. For these hopes are grounded on the word of God, which never yet deceived any. But if you hope well, and know not why, and you have nothing to show for your hopes of heaven, but what an ungodly man can show, or the most of the world may show that shall perish, and cannot prove that you are new creatures, and holy and heavenly, these hopes do but hinder your conversion and salvation.

Hinderance 10. *Counterfeit graces, or favourable appearances put in the room of conversion.* The next hinderance of conversion is, those counterfeit graces, or half conversion, which are like to true graces, but are not them, and so do not bring over the soul to God, but strengthen the false hopes, which we mentioned before. There is somewhat in the heart of an unconverted man, which is like in his eyes to true conversion. Some fears and accusation of conscience he may have, and some change thereupon : he may be convinced of his sin and misery, and see the necessity of another course, and hereupon may change his company, and betake himself to many duties, and break off many of his former sins, and seem to himself to be truly converted, and glory in this as long as he lives, and think verily that he is indeed a converted man : he may know the very time, the book, the sermon, the words that were the means of doing this work upon his soul, and therefore think that it is truly done : he may remember so great a change that was made on him, that he may confidently conclude that it was a saving change, and yet it may be but common preparation, or mere terrors or convictions, or some common works, which many that perish partake of : he may have hereupon somewhat that in his eye is like to every grace of the Spirit, and therefore think that these are they indeed ; and this is a fearful, deceiving state, and mightily quiets men in a miserable condition ; when these common gifts should be otherwise used.

Direction. Take heed therefore of trusting to counterfeit graces, or superficial works that do not effectually convert the soul ; labour to discern, by the light of the word of God, whether the work be savingly done or not ; how you

may discern it, I have told you before : if God be set up highest in your souls, and brought nearest to your hearts, and your hopes are set upon the life to come, and all things in this world seem vain to you in comparison of it : if sin be bitter to you, and Christ, and grace, and holiness be sweet, then you may conclude that it is a saving work, but otherwise not. And therefore rest not in common works.

Hinderance 11. *Numerous and strong temptations to sin.* Another hinderance is, when men live among strong temptations and occasions of sin ; as when they depend upon some great men, or parents, or other friends that are enemies to godliness, and would undo them if they should follow it : or when they are so engaged in a course of sin, that they cannot break it off without their worldly undoing or suffering : when their credit or their gain depends upon it ; as the oppressor lives by oppression, and the ale-seller lives by the sins of drunkards, or tippling, idle companions, and because they think this gain is sweet, therefore they will not leave the sin. Because Demetrius and the rest of the craftsmen had their wealth and living by making shrines for the idol Diana, therefore they stirred up the people against the gospel and the preachers of it, that would take down the idol that caused their pecuniary advantage ; in like manner, when men that are addicted to drunkenness will live among such company or temptations as will draw them to it : when lustful persons will live among those that do provoke or tempt them : when ignorant, unresolved persons live among those that speak ill of godliness, it is a hard thing to be converted under these temptations : especially if men wilfully cast themselves upon them.

Direction. Fly therefore the occasions and appearances of evil. If you would not be drowned, what do you so near the water-side ? If you would not be wounded, why do you thrust yourselves among your enemies ? If you would escape the hook, meddle not with the bait : walk not among the lime twigs if you would not be intangled : you may fly from temptation, and yet resist the devil, and make him fly : be not too confident of your own strength ; consider whether it be safe to die in your sin and ungodliness ? If not : why should you live in it ? And if you may not live in it, why should you commit it ? If you cannot digest it when it is down, but it must up again by repentance, or you perish ; why then should you let it down ? If you may not let it down, what reason have you to be tasting it ? And if you may not taste it, why should you once look upon it, to entice your taste? And if you may not look on it, why should you think on it, and make your own imagination to be your tempter: present and strong temptations have shaken those that seemed to be cedars; therefore take heed of them; for they may much more hinder the conversion of the impenitent, and such difficulties may easily block up the way of life to you.

Hinderance 12. *Another hinderance is the scandalous lives of professors.* When those that seem godly, or indeed are so, shall fall into division among themselves, withdraw from each other, censure one another, and cry out against one another as deceived; when the common people see so many religions, as they think, and so many several minds and ways, they think it is as good be of none, as to venture among so many, where they are not sure to hit on the right; and it makes them question all, when they see so many that they know not which to own. When they see men change their opinions, which a while ago they seemed so zealous for, this makes them think that the rest may be as uncertain as these: and thus we have seen by sad experience in these times, that many have been kept off from the approving and practice of a godly life, because of the unhappy differences that are among us: and alas! when they see one that seemed religious to be worldly, and another to fall into this or that sin, this makes them think that religon is but hypocrisy, and themselves are already in as good a condition as the godly are.

Direction. I will not excuse the sins of any: offence must come, but woe to him by whom it comes. If they be godly, their profession doth aggravate it, and therefore I do not intend to extenuate it: but yet, as I must needs say, that the malice of the ungodly doth frequently make even holiness to be a crime, virtue itself to be the greatest vice, those to be faults that are really none, those to be common that are seldom and but the case of very few, and those to be great that are not so; so, I must needs tell you, that there is no sufficient reason in the faults and divisions of those that are religious, to dissuade any from religion, or excuse them in their sin, or sinful neglect of their own salvation: for consider these things following:—

1. It is not men's lives that are any disgrace to the word of God, no more than it is a dishonour to the sun that some men are blind, or others wilfully abuse his light; will you fall a railing at the sun, because a thief may steal by the light of it; or a murderer may kill men by the light of it; or some men may miss their way? This is not owing to it, but to themselves. 2. Yea, consider that it is for want of being more religious that men are so bad, and not because they are religious: can you prove that ever religion taught men to be bad; doth the word of God teach men to be worldly, to be proud, to divide the church, and abuse one another? You know it doth not; nay, you know that it forbids and condemns all this; and that no one in the world hath said and done so much against these sins, as God hath done: and no religion is so much against them as the Christian religion: and is it not an abuse beyond all modesty then, to think ill of the word of God, or of his way, because men offend against it, and forsake it? To accuse the law, because men break it? To wrong God, because others have wronged him? 3. Consider that the sins of others will be no excuse to you: their fall should be your warning and not your hardening. Will God pardon or save without repentance and faith, because some that seemed religious have miscarried? If they are wicked while they seem religious, they and you, if you so continue, shall be damned together: but if they rise by repentance, and hate and forsake the sins which they fell into, and you stumble upon them, and will not rise with them, but quarrel with religion, because of their falls, they shall be pardoned, and you shall perish. I tell thee, if all the world should fall from God, he will not therefore change his law, nor admit one unconverted sinner into heaven. Do you think to be saved without holiness, because some men counterfeit holiness that have it not? Methinks this should cast you into greater terrors, and make you think with yourselves how much you have yet to do, that must go further, and be better than ever any hypocrite was, before you can have any durable hopes of salvation: if you will have any part in God, you must stick to him, though all men else should forsake him, and not forsake him, because you think that others do so that seemed to stick to him. 4. Consider also, that as to the divisions that offend you, it is not every difference in judgment or practice that makes a new religion. While we are here we shall know but in part, and therefore shall differ in part, but as long as we all agree in the fundamentals and live to God, we are of one religion for all our differences. 5. And can you think that it will excuse you to be of no religion, because that other men are of a wrong religion? Will you sit still and let heaven go, because some men have missed the way to it? Do you think that this is

a reasonable conclusion? Surely they that would fain know the way if they could and are diligent to seek it, are more likely to be accepted, though they fall into many errors, than those that mind it not, but prefer the things of the world before it. 6. The more bye-ways there are, the more need have you to look about you, and see that you miss not the way yourselves. Salvation is not a matter that we can spare, and therefore the difficulty must make us more diligent, and not more negligent. 7. Among all the religions and opinions in the world, God hath not left you at a loss, he hath given his word to tell you which is the right, and many means to understand it: so that, if proud or careless men will err, it follows not that therefore the humble and diligent may not be certain which way is the right. Go you to the scripture with an humble reverence, willing to know the will of God, that you may do it, and take the helps which you may have from ministers and private Christians, and show not by your neglect that you despise the word of God and your salvation, and then you shall have no cause to complain that you cannot find the right religion, and not hit the way to heaven, because there are so many opinions. 8. I pray you consider of that which I have often answered you to this objection. Will you but faithfully practise that which all or almost all these different parties are agreed in? If not, then make not their differences any more a pretence for your ungodliness: if you will, then consider whether they be not all agreed on the necessity of conversion and a holy life. Will they not all acknowledge that there is no salvation without sanctification and newness of life? Let their agreement then move you, and do not for shame neglect so great and necessary a thing, which is owned by them all who differ much in other things.

Hinderance 13. *Parental neglect, or a bad system of training up children.* The next hinderance of conversion is the bad education of children: when they are trained up in ignorance, or kept unacquainted with the truths of God till they are grown hardened in their evil way: especially when they are taught from their childhood to think hardly of godliness, and speak reproachfully of it, and hear nothing of the godly, but by way of slander or contempt. That which people receive in their youth doth usually possess them all their days: they receive it with more advantage, when they are most teachable and tractable: when they receive it from parents, and those that have the greatest interest in their affections, and the most absolute rule over them.

Therefore we see most of the world are such as they were taught in their childhood to be : and it is hard to change them from the way in which they were brought up.

Direction. You that have children, remember they are Christ's. If you are Christians, both you and yours are devoted to God: will you be so forward to devote them to God in baptism, and will you rob him afterwards of his own ; and break these covenants, and, contrary to your own promises, will you hinder them from the knowledge and fear of God? O what desperate hypocrisy and wickedness is this? Will you come here, in the face of the congregation, and consecrate and offer your children to Christ, and when you have done, will you keep them from the way of Christ, and make them believe that godliness is more ado than needs, and that holiness is but foolish preciseness? Will you here undertake to bring them up in the nurture and admonition of the Lord, and when you have done, never once instruct them in his fear, nor persuade them to a holy life, nor restrain them from sin, but rather teach them to rail, curse, swear, and be carnal? O cruel creatures, who dare thus murder your children's souls! To murder the body is a heinous sin, yea, though it were the body of an enemy; but to murder the soul, yea, and the soul of a child, and so to be guilty of their eternal damnation; what greater sin can you commit? O what a horror it will be to you to see your own children in eternal flames by your own conduct; and to hear them there cry out against you, and say you hardened them in evil; you discouraged them from good. You gave them bad examples, you used to rail, curse and swear before them: you took no pains to convince them of their natural sin and misery: and to get them to Christ that they might be healed by him. O pity your poor children, and do not hinder them from that glory that is offered them: if the devil be against their salvation, be not you so too. It is more excusable in the devil himself to seek to destroy the souls of your children, than it is in their own parents to do it : for nature and Christianity doth bind them to do otherwise. If you settle them in an ignorant, carnal course, they will remember it as long as they live; and if you possess them with hard thoughts of the holy ways of God, they will make this an argument against us whenever we should seek to reform and convert them. Do we not hear it from them daily? Our fathers, say they, taught us otherwise, and we hope they are saved, and therefore we will venture to do as they did: so that it is the false conceits that you put into their minds in their childhood, which ministers have to encounter with all their days after. The devil hath instruments enough to seek your children's damnation besides you: be not you his instruments if ever you would not lie down with them in everlasting misery; take some more pity on yourselves and them. You could not find in your hearts to dash your children against the stones, or cut their throats, and if you should, the world would ring of your wickedness, and the law of the land would deservedly put you to a painful death; and will you do them a greater mischief? Will you blind them, and keep them off from Christ and godliness; and will you embolden them in the way of sin, and help them to damnation? God forbid. But alas! they who have no more pity on their own souls but to use them thus, what wonder if they have no more pity of others.

2. The next part of my direction therefore is to you that have been brought up in ignorance and ungodliness from your youth. Look about you while you have time and means: if your parents have been false to you, be not false to God and your souls. If your parents have betrayed your souls, do not you betray your own. They kept you in ignorance because they were ignorant themselves; they bred you up in worldliness and ungodliness, because they were worldly and ungodly themselves; they spoke against holiness because they knew it not, but were themselves unholy: but you have one that hath more interest in you than your parents, who calls to you for your conversion. Hearken to him if all the world should gainsay it: do not care as little for your own souls as your parents cared for them: do not take on you, even to love your parents so well as to follow them to perdition. Their company will not make hell any easier to you. Should not the love of your heavenly Father do more to draw you to heaven, than the love of your parents to draw you to hell? Hearken then to God and to his word, though all the world should say against it.

Hinderance 14. *Striving against the Spirit.* Another hinderance of conversion is, striving against the Spirit of grace. When God would illuminate a sinner, and he is unwilling to see; when God would take off a sinner from his lusts and evil ways, and he is loth to be taken off; God shows him his sin to humble him, and he is unwilling to be humbled, but strives against the Spirit, and runs into worldly businesses, or merry company, or turns his thoughts to other things. As Christ said to the Jews, 'how oft would I have gathered you, but you would not?' So he

may say to many a sinner, how oft did I show thee a better way, and thou wouldst not walk in it? How oft did I show thee the sinfulness and misery of thy estate, and thou wouldst not come off from it? When men fight against Christ, and purposely wink because they hate the light that would reform them, and when they strive against the Spirit that would convert them, what wonder if they be unconverted?

Direction. If ever you would be converted, yield to the Spirit of God that would convert you. It is his office to sanctify all that shall be saved: be not you unwilling to be sanctified by him. If you refuse help when it is offered you, you may justly be left helpless and perish for want of that which you despise. You are baptized into the name of the Holy Ghost, by which you have professed to take him for your sanctifier, and are you now unwilling to be sanctified by him? And will you now strive against him when you are so solemnly engaged to him? You cannot be saved unless you be sanctified, and you cannot be sanctified unless it be done by the Holy Ghost, whom you now resist. How easily and prosperously doth the work go on, when the Spirit of God assists, and how impossible is it to be done without him! They that would have a prosperous voyage will take wind and tide, and not be so foolish as to set against them when they stand to their advantage: he that would have health will not abuse the physician or drive him away from him. Take heed how you use the Spirit of God if ever you would be converted!

Hinderance 15. *Want of resolution, and halting between two opinions.* Another hinderance of conversion is, unresolvedness and half-purposes; when men will hang wavering between God and the world; and though the light be never so clear to convince them, yet they will not be persuaded to resolve. ' A double-minded man,' saith James, ' is unstable in all his ways.' How many shall perish for want of resolution! They have been convinced that they must be changed or else they are undone, and yet they would not resolve: they have long been inclining to a better course, and had some thoughts of it, but the world hinders, or friends hinder, or the flesh hinders, and they will not resolve: and thus they hang loose from God, and never unfeignedly resign up themselves to him till either God in judgment leave them to themselves, or death and hell do find them unresolved.

Direction. If you would be converted and saved, do not stand wavering, but resolve, and presently turn to God. If it were a doubtful business, I would not persuade you to do it rashly, or if there were any danger to your souls in resolving, then I would say no more. But when it is a case that should be beyond all dispute with men of reason, why should you stand staggering, as if it were a doubtful case? What a horrible shame is it to be unresolved whether God or the world should have your hearts? Were it not a disgrace to that man's understanding that were unresolved whether gold or tin were better? whether a bed of thorns, or a feather bed, were the easier? whether the sun, or a clod of earth, were the more light and glorious? It is a far greater shame for a man to be unresolved, whether it be God or the world that must make him happy, and that should have his heart, and whether a life of sin or holiness be the better. What! have you read scripture, and heard sermons so long, and yet are you unresolved of this? Nay, have you common reason, and do you believe that there is a God, and a world to come, and yet are you unresolved whether you must be godly or not? I say to you, as Elias said to Israel, 'how long halt ye between two opinions? If God be God follow him, if Baal be God follow him.' If it be better to be damned than leave your sins, then keep them, and the curse of God with them: but if it be better to deny your flesh, than to suffer through eternity the wrath of God, then away with your iniquities, and meddle with them no more. If it be better to live in an ale-house a while, than in heaven for ever, then drink on and spare not; but if it be not, why do you not consider and come away. If God and holiness be not better than the world and wickedness, then take your course; but if they be, why do you stand wavering, and do not resolve to be the people of God with all your hearts? What a blind and miserable creature is a wicked man, that such matters as these should seem doubtful to him; or that he should yet be unresolved of them! What, unresolved whether it be best to go to heaven, or not; whether it be best to be damned, or not! and all this for the love of a vile, unprofitable lust! If this be wisdom, what then is folly?

Hinderance 16. *Criminal delay.* Another hinderance of conversion is, delay. When men are resolved that they must be converted or condemned, and purpose to let go sin, and to take another course, yet they delay and put off the time: they would yet have a little more of the pleasure of their sin before they part with it: yet they cannot spare it, but shortly they will do it: they are yet young, and they hope they have day-light and time enough before them: they are yet in health, and therefore they hope there is no such haste, but they may have time to think on it: because God will receive a sinner whensoever he returns, they think they may stay a little longer: and thus some grow hardened by custom in their sin, and others are cut off while they are purposing to return; and many thousand souls are lost for ever that once were purposed to have turned to God, and all because they delayed their return. As the sluggard saith, 'yet a little sleep, a little slumber;' so saith the sinner, yet I may sin a little while, till they have sinned themselves into a reprobate sense, or provoked God to leave them to themselves, and so they must perish for ever by their delay.

Direction. Consider therefore, sinners, that conversion is not a work to be delayed. Would a man lie under the wrath and curse of God one day, that knew what it is? Methinks he should not. Are you loth to come out of the bondage of the devil? Why, your delay doth show that your heart is false, and that you are not willing truly to be converted: he that is loth to leave his sin this day or hour, would never leave it if he knew how to keep it: if he did not love it, he would be willing to be rid of it without delay. He that loves God had rather return and be reconciled to him, and partake of the joy of his Spirit to-day, than to-morrow; did you but know what God is, you would not delay your conversion to him: did you but know what the glory is that he offers you, you would not delay to make sure of it any longer: did you but see the nature of sin, and know the miserable effects of it, how hastily would you endeavour to be rid of it? If you had so many serpents in your bosoms, you would not say, I will cast them out to-morrow, but how quickly would you shake them from you? If you had but felt the sting of sin, it would appear another matter to you than now it doth. It is one kind of face that sin hath in an ale-house, or in the height of your filthy lust, or in the seeming gain of your covetous practices; and it is another kind of face that it hath when God will reckon for it with the guilty soul. Should a man trifle in such a course, wherein, if he die, he is lost for ever? Why, poor wretched sinner, how long wilt thou delay, and why wilt thou delay? Wilt thou delay till death shall seize upon thee, and thou drop into hell before thou art aware? Dost thou not know that sin gets advantage by thy delay? God has not promised thee that ever his Spirit shall be offered to thee more, if thou refuse his assistance, and delay thy conversion but one day longer. Wo be to thee if he depart from thee.

When people will have none of God, nor will

hearken to his voice, he often gives them up to their own heart's lusts, to walk in their own counsels. Unworthy wretch! if thou hadst any of the ingenuity of a Christian within thy breast, thou wouldst say, I have abused Christ, and his grace so long that I am utterly ashamed of it, and will abuse him no more: have too long slighted Christ already, and too long hearkened to his enemies' voice. If thy dead heart were but well awakened to consider and feel thy own condition, thou wouldst be quickly affrighted out of thy delay, and run as hastily from thy state of sin, as thou wouldst out of a house that were all on fire over thy head, or out of a boat that were sinking under thee. What, hast thou not yet served the devil long enough? Hast thou not yet sufficiently abused Christ, nor often enough rejected the grace of God? Hast thou not yet wallowed long enough in the filth of sin? But must thou needs have more of it? Hast thou not yet done enough to the destruction of thy soul? Nor drunk in enough of that deadly poison, nor stabbed thyself sufficiently by thy wickedness, but thou must needs have more? Will sin come up easier, when it is deeper rooted? Canst thou more easily be converted, when thou hast driven away the Spirit of God that should convert thee? Wilt thou travel out of thy way till night, before thou wilt turn back again? And wilt thou drive the nail yet faster to the head, which thou knowest must be drawn out again? O be not wilfully befooled by sin. Wilt thou be converted, or wilt thou not? If not, thou art a lost man: if thou know thou must, why not to-day rather than to-morrow? What reason have you for any longer delay? Is a state of sin, or a state of grace better? If sin be better keep it, and make thy best of it: but if grace, holiness, and happiness be better, why then should you delay? If you were sick you would not care how soon you were well; and if you had a bone broken, you care not how soon it were set; and when your souls are in a state of sin and misery, are you afraid of being safe and happy too soon? Remember another day, that a day, and many a day of grace thou hadst; and if thou lose this day, thou mayst thank thyself, if thou lose thy soul, and if thou never have another day like this; 'to-day while it is called to-day, therefore hear his voice, and harden not your hearts.' When David thought of his ways, he made haste and delayed not to turn to God, and keep his precepts, as has been already mentioned.

Hinderance 17. *When gracious impressions are not followed up.* Another great hinderance

of conversion is, when good beginnings are not followed on, but suffered to die and come to nothing before they bring men over to God. Commonly preparing works of grace go before through sanctifying works; and men have many convictions and half reformations and troubles of mind, before they come to embrace Christ upon the terms that he is offered: these common preparatory works are the way to more; if men would but cherish these, and follow them on, and improve the light and motions which they have, they know not what a blessed issue they might see: but when they will forget the truth that once did move them, and lose the purposes that once they had, and turn back again to the sins they were in before; no wonder if these be left in their iniquities: is not this the case of you that hear me this day? You have been convinced that God and your souls must be regarded, whatsoever else be neglected; and did you not thereupon begin to pray, to use means, and take the helps in public and private that are necessary for your salvation? Have not some of you fallen into company that have taken you off by foolish cavils or vain objections, and evil examples, and tempting you to sin? Have not others of you grown cold, and lost your feeling, as if you were not the same men, and had never heard or felt such things; and others of you turned to this present world, and choked the word, with the cares of this life? And so the hopeful beginnings that you once had, are turned to a relapse into your old condition.

Direction. If there be any such sinners that hear me this day, as I fear there may be too many, consider whence you are fallen, and be zealous and amend; are you turned with 'the dog to his vomit, and with the sow that was washed, to wallow in the mire?' What! 'do you look back when you had put your hand to the plough of God?' Did Christ give you any cause to repent of his service, or to forsake him? Have you found indeed that the devil is the better master, and that the way of sin is the better way, and the wages of sin the better wages? What, did the thoughts of everlasting life once move you, and will they not move you now? Is heaven become as no heaven to you, God as no God, Christ as no Christ, and the promises as no promises? Are you grown abler to resist the terrors of the Lord? O poor souls, that you did but know the misery of apostates! The Lord hath professed, that 'if any draw back, his soul shall have no pleasure in him,' and they that draw back, shall find they do it to their own perdition; when they should have believed and persevered to the saving of their souls, there are none of all the damned more miserable than they that were sometimes fair for heaven, and once begin to look after godliness ; 'for the latter end of these men is worse than their beginning.' Alas! how sad will it be to see the faces of such among the wicked and condemned at the last, and to think that once we saw the faces of these men among the godly, that once they seemed to set themselves for heaven, and are they fallen off to this—is this the end of them! In the name of God, I warn and charge every one of you that ever had a thought of returning to God, and giving up yourselves to a holy life, that you presently bethink you what is gone with these thoughts and purposes, and why did you turn from these beginnings? What reason had you for it ; and what cause hath Christ given you? What! will the world now be a faster friend to you than before ; and will you now continue with it, and never die? Or can you better be without God and his grace than before? O be awakened from this desperate folly, and once again renew your former resolutions, and consider whether you are not nearer eternity than you were, and have not as much need of Christ as ever? Sleep not on till hell awaken you.

Hinderance 18. *Ignorance and error on divine subjects is another hinderance. Various instances stated.* The next hinderance of conversion to be mentioned is, a misunderstanding of scripture and erroneous thoughts of the ways of God. If error possess the mind, it will keep out grace from possessing the heart, so far as the error prevails. I shall instance in some few particulars.

1. Some men know not what true grace or conversion is, and therefore think they have it when they have none, and do not set themselves to look after it : they think that it is but to forsake some gross sins, and to use some outward service of God, and do no one any wrong, and then they think they have true conversion ; because they have turned from many sins that once they lived in : but these must know that conversion is the withdrawing of the soul from the world, from carnal-self, and the devoting of ourselves and all that we have to God. If you should be never so zealous in forms, and take up never so strict principles, and stick to the strictest party ; this is no proof of true conversion, if your souls do not cleave to God, as your portion, and to Christ as the only way to God.

2. Some there be that do not think there is any such thing as saving grace, or true conversion in the world ; because they have none themselves, they do not think that any one else hath : when they hear of a hope and heart in heaven, and of loving God above all creatures, they do not think that any one doth reach to it, but that men merely talk of such things, which they never had experience of : but these men must know, that it is an arrogant madness to contradict the scope of the word of God, and the common experience of the best men in the world, and all because they are so bad themselves. Doth God talk so much of sanctifying his people, of putting the spirit of Jesus into their hearts, ruling them, dwelling in them, crucifying the world to them, and purifying a peculiar people to himself, that are zealous of good works, —dare they now say there is no such thing? whether is God or they to be believed? What, hath Christ died to procure it, and is it the office of the Holy Ghost to work it, and is there now no such thing? Are the word, ministers and all the ordinances to that end, and is there now no such thing? God will make them know that such a thing was offered once to them, and such a thing as grace and a heavenly life was necessary to their salvation. If they will not believe the experience of the saints, or will not see the graces of God, as they shine in the conversation of his people, they shall be forced one day to see, and be ashamed.

3. Others there be that think holiness is but needless preciseness, and that to meditate on God and heaven, and make it our chief business, is more ado than needs ; that this is but to be godly overmuch, that God will accept less, and that this is the way even to drive men beside themselves.

Though I have formerly answered this objection, yet because it here again falls in my way, I shall distinctly answer it in these particulars : 1. Tell me truly, do you think that God or you are fitter to be judges of what is necessary to the salvation of a sinner? Doth God command it, and dare you say it is more ado than needs? Why, what is this but plainly to say, that God hath set us upon a needless work,— that you are wiser than he? There is no master so foolish and unmerciful, as will set his servant to pick straws, and labour to no purpose ; and will you impute such unmerciful folly to God? Dare you say, he makes you do more than is needful. 2. Then I ask, is it more than what scripture doth require? Doth not the word of God make it necessary ; which you call unnecessary? Read and judge. 'Lay not up for yourselves treasures on earth : but lay up for yourselves treasures in heaven. Seek first the kingdom of God and his righteousness.—The kingdom of heaven suffers violence, and the violent take it by force.—Strive to enter in at the strait gate; for many, I say to you, shall seek to enter in, and shall not be able.—Labour not for the food which perisheth, but for that which endureth to everlasting life.—See that ye walk circumspectly, redeeming the time.—What manner of persons ought ye to be in all holy conversation and godliness?' And a hundred more such places may be mentioned. So that if it be an error to require so much ado for our salvation, it is God himself that is the cause of it: and who is likelier to be in the right,—the Lord that made you, or such silly, ignorant worms as you? You scarce know good from bad, and will you take on you to be wiser than God, and to control his law? 3. Do you think indeed in your consciences, that a man can do too much for heaven, as long as he doth but what God bids him; and that he can be at more cost and labour for it than it is worth? Is that man worthy or meet to see the face of God in glory, that thinks it not worth his utmost diligence? Do you set so much by your labour, or do you so lightly prize God and glory, as to think the everlasting enjoyment of it to be unworthy of your pains? 4. Do you think there ever was a man that got well to heaven, that repented of coming thither at so dear a rate, or that was there of your mind, that this godliness is more ado than needs? If we could but speak with one of the glorified saints that see the face of God, and put the case to him, Whether is the wiser man, he that doth all that he can to be saved, or he that saith what needs all this ado? which side do you think he would be on? Cannot you easily conjecture? 5. Is Christ, or the apostles, or any of the servants of God of your mind? Judge by their conversations whether they thought it more ado than needs: the best of his saints never had so much grace but they longed for more; they never were so holy but they longed to be better; do you think that you are wiser than all they, and that neither prophets, apostles, nor any saints of God did know what they did? 6. What is it that you think is so painful a life as to be too much for God and heaven? Do you know what you talk of? Why, it is the only joyful life on earth: it is more a receiving from God, than a giving to him. It is an employment that is suited both to the new nature of the saints, and to their necessity and good. What is holiness but a living in the love of God, the joy of the Holy Ghost, the hope of the life to come, and a daily communion with God in the Spirit, in the use of his holy ordinances? To hear of his love and the promise of his glory, the pardon of our sins, to beg of him what we want, and thank and praise him for what we have received? And do you think this is so tedious a life? Is it a toil to you to eat and drink of the best, when your bodies require it; to rest when you are weary; or to love your dearest friend, and to be in his company? If not, why should we think it a toil to live in the love of God, and in holy communion with him in his service? 7. Is it not a certain mark of a graceless heart to think that this is such a grievous work? Surely that soul is void of the love of God, that thinks it a grievous thing to love him. A man that hates his wife, and loves harlots, will say, I cannot love her, nor abide to dwell with her; but if he loved her he would think otherwise. If you did not hate God you would not think it so grievous to live in the love of him, and to be much in his holy worship. 8. Do you desire to come to heaven, or not: if not, then remember, if you are shut out, it is by your own consent. If you would come thither, then do you not know that all your employment there must be such as this, and much more holy and perfect than this? Will you account heaven itself grievous; and the praises of God there to be more ado than needs? If not, how dare you say so of a far lower degree which we have in this life? If you are weary of this little, how weary would you be of heaven? 9. I pray you tell me, do you think indeed that any man on earth is so good as he should be? Do you not know, that he that is best, is too bad; he that doth most, comes unspeakably too short of what he should do? Dare you say then, that this is more ado than needs? Why if you had spoken to Peter or Paul, or the holiest man that ever lived, he would have rather complained that he could be no better, and cried out, O that I were more holy, and could be more taken up in the love of God; alas, I fall exceedingly short of what is my duty! And shall such sinners as we are, yea, some of the vilest sinners, say, that this is more ado than needs? Why, thou proud, insensible man, dost thou not better know thy own needs than this? Doth not thy soul need this and more than this? What, darest thou justify thyself in thy ungodliness, and judge of godliness as a needless thing? 10. Canst thou tell me how long thou wilt be of that mind? When thou liest a-dying wilt thou then think that holiness was more ado than needs? When thou seest that the world hath left thee, and that thou art presently to appear before the Lord, speak as thou thinkest; hadst thou not rather then be found in the case of the holiest and most diligent saints on earth, than in the case of the careless, proud or carnal? Will holy duty, or the neglect and deriding of it, be then more comfortable? Wouldst thou not then change state with one of those that did the most for God, and for their souls, and wouldst thou not say with Balaam, 'let me die the death of the righteous, and let my last end be as his?' 11. What is it, do you think, that is worth a man's pains and care, if God and everlasting glory be not? Is there any thing of greater worth? Man was not made for nothing, and idleness is no delight to him: something he would be doing and looking after, and something he expects to make him happy, and that which he takes for his happiness, he cannot choose but think it worth all his pains: have you found out any thing that is better than heaven? Will this world last longer; or stand you in greater stead at last? Alas, that we should be put to ask or answer such questions as these! Why either heaven or earth must have your love, care, and labour, and which, do you think, doth more deserve it? You can talk of the world from day to day, you can work and toil for the world all the year long, and yet you never say it is more ado than needs? If your servant labour harder for you in a day than God's servants do for him in a week, you will not tell him that he doth more than needs. Foolish worldlings, let me deal plainly with you, and tell you to your faces, it is you that make more ado than needs: is the world worth all this care and stir that you make about it? Is it worth your thoughts and unwearied diligence, and is it worth the venturing of your salvation to obtain it? I tell you it is not; and you partly know yourselves it is not. Why, where are your wits, to toil yourselves all your lives for these trifles; and to tell them that labour for salvation, that they make more ado than needs? Well, hearken of the end, and then you shall see whether it be labour for heaven or for earth, that will be repented of. If you know not now, you shall shortly know it. 12. One question more I shall yet put to you. Do you think the pains of duty to be greater than the pains of hell? If you do not, should not we choose the lesser to escape the greater? If you had not the love of God to make you delight in his service, methinks you should have that love of yourselves to make you fear his everlasting wrath: never flatter yourselves with other thoughts. Believe it, if you will needs take it for a pain which should be your pleasure, you must undergo the pain of an unfeignedly holy life, or the pain of hell; choose you whether.

4. Another of the errors that hinder conversion is, that their own good meanings, praying and good works will make God amends for their sins, and after all will procure their acceptance with God. And if these will not do, they think the case is bad, for there is nothing else for us to do: and so they see not the evil of their own meanings and good works, and how much sin is in them to be cast off, nor do they see the need of a Christ in all, nor the need of a thorough change of their condition, that they may be made the justified sons of God, and have new hearts and new conversations. But they think while they live to the world and the flesh, to make up all and procure acceptance by good meaning, good praying, and good works. I would not be misunderstood, as if I were speaking against that which is truly good in any, but I would desire these people well to consider: 1. That the meanings and works of unconverted men are not truly and properly good; for it is the end that denominates the work; and seeing no unconverted man doth make God his ultimate end, therefore he hath properly no good meaning nor work: for he means all ultimately for his carnal self, for the flesh, and for the world, and for these are his works. As the true Christian doth make his worldly labour to be ultimately for God, so doth the ungodly make his seeming service of God to be ultimately for his flesh. 2. You should consider that all your good works must have a pardon themselves, and therefore cannot satisfy for your sins. 3. That if your works were perfectly good, without any blemish, yet could they not satisfy for that sin which is past, but that must be expected only from the blood of Christ. It is therefore a lamentable case to hear many of the grossly ignorant people talk of all their good meanings and praying, as if their confidence were all in these, while they make no mention of the blood of a redeemer; or feel not the need of it; nor what it is that Christ hath done for them, nor how much they are beholden to him. 4. It is no patching up of your old unregenerated state that will serve for your salvation, but you must be wholly made new. He that 'is in Christ is a new creature; old things are past away, behold all things are become new.' It is not forsaking this or that sin, or falling betimes to your prayers, that will serve the purpose; but you must have new hearts, new ends, a new conversation, and the chief business and scope of your lives must be new. Those hearts that were set on the world before

must be set on God; and those desires that run to the pleasures of the flesh, must run out after the pleasing of God. I say, it is not patching up the old condition, but all must be new.

5. Another error that hinders conversion is, the misunderstanding of those scriptures that promise salvation to some particular graces or duties. As because the scripture saith ' whosoever believes in him shall not perish,' therefore they say that they truly believe, and therefore, though they have not such holiness of life, yet God hath promised them salvation: so also, where it is said, ' that whosoever shall call on the name of the Lord, shall be saved,' therefore, say they, we call on the name of the Lord, and so shall be saved, though we be not converted, nor so holy as you require. To these men I have these several things to say, for the cure of this dangerous error.

1. Poor, ignorant souls, they talk of they know not what; and suffer themselves to be deceived by words which they understand not. If they did but know well what faith is, and what calling upon God is, they would never be troubled with this objection. To believe in Christ, is to believe him to be the Saviour of his church, to save them from their sins, and heartily to consent that he shall be so to us, to *save us from our sins ;* and can you believe in him as a Saviour, and yet be unwilling to be saved by him? Sin is the mischief from which he saves you, and conversion is one half of his saving work; and can you then say you believe, and therefore need not be converted ? Why you may as well say : I take such a man for my physician, and I trust in him for a cure, and therefore I need not be cured. Is not this nonsense or a contradiction ? What! is it better to say, I believe in Christ as my Saviour, that is to save me from my sins, and therefore I may be saved though I be not saved from my sins. These are the wise reasonings that many of our self-conceited hearers make use of to delude themselves and other men. And the very nature of faith is to take Christ as Christ, as he is offered in the gospel: as our teacher to guide us in the way of holiness, and as our king to rule us, as well as a sacrifice for our sins: and how can he do this for us if we will not be converted ? 2. Moreover, faith in Jesus Christ is always annexed to a belief in God the Father. ' You believe in God, believe also in me.—This is life eternal, to know thee the only true God, and Jesus Christ whom thou hast sent.' Now to believe in God is to take him for our Maker, that hath absolute right in us, and absolute power over us, whom we must

obey before all, and our happiness and chief good, whom we must love and desire above all. And can this be done without conversion ? 3. To believe in Christ is ever accompanied with believing in the Holy Ghost, which is the receiving him to be our sanctifier; and can you do this and yet be unconverted. 4. By this much that has been said, you may perceive that conversion and faith is in a sort one and the same thing ; to be a true believer, and to be converted, is all one: for conversion is to make you true believers: and is it not then a wise kind of cavil to say, that if you believe, you may be saved without conversion? As much as to say, if I have the sun-shine, I may see without light ; or if I have a soul, I need not life or understanding: I tell you there is no such thing as true faith without conversion. 5. Moreover, where true faith is, all other saving graces do accompany it ; there is ever repentance, hope, love, humility, and an heavenly mind. So that it is no true faith which is separated from these, and which the ungodly deceive themselves with, but an opinion and a mere ungrounded presumption. 6. Another error which hinders men's conversion is, some false apprehensions of the doctrine of God's eternal decree of election or predestination: from which many desperate consequences are raised by them, to the deceiving of their own souls: by this I find abundance among us in this country deluded ; how the devil hath brought it to pass, I know not. They have many of them learned this foolish pretence; 'If God has chosen us, we shall be saved, and if he have not, we shall not, whatsoever we do. No diligence will save a man that is not elected, and 'it is not in him that willeth, nor in him that runneth, but in God that sheweth mercy.' Those that God will save, shall be saved, whatsoever they be; and those that he will damn, shall be damned ; and no man can have grace except God give it to him ; for we can do nothing of ourselves.' Upon these grounds they think they may be secure, and cast all upon God, as a matter that they have little to do with; and think that their endeavours are to little purpose; if they should make ever so much ado.

Ans. One would think common reason should teach men to answer such silly cavils as these ; but because I find so many ignorant souls stick at them, I shall give you a full answer in these particulars.

1. God elects no man to the end without means, but to the end and means together: all that he elects to salvation he elects to conversion and sanctification, and all to whom he de-

nies conversion to them he also denies salvation.
2. If therefore you care whether you are saved or
damned, it concerns you 'to make both your calling and election sure.' Make but your calling
sure, and you need not make any question of your
election. Make sure that you are converted, and
hold fast what you have, and then you may be
certain you shall be saved. You begin at the
wrong end, if you would first ask whether you
are elected, that you may know whether you
shall be saved: but you must first try whether
you are converted and saved from the power of
sin, and then you may certainly gather that you
are elected and shall be saved from hell. Will
you begin at the top of the ladder, and not at
the bottom? Did God ever damn any man that
was truly converted and sanctified, because he
was not elected? No such thing; prove any
such thing if you can: nay, we can fully prove
the contrary, for he hath promised salvation
to all that are truly converted and sanctified,
'Blessed are the pure in heart, for they shall see
God:' with many similar texts which have been
named frequently to you. And can you prove
that ever God saved any man that was not converted, because he was elected? Not at all;
for he elects all that are converted. And he
hath resolved to save none but the converted, as
is plain from many places formerly quoted. 3.
These reasonings therefore of yours, if they keep
you from conversion and an heavenly life, are a
certain mark that you are without the evidence
of your election; and if you so live and die,
that you are none of the elect. And therefore
by such reasonings you do but show your own
misery, like a man that hath the plague, who will
glory in the symptoms of it: it should make
your hearts tremble to find so sad a mark as
this upon your souls, that you have a heart that
dares hold off from conversion, and bring vain
pretences from the decree of God. 4. Consider also, that God's decrees are not the cause of
your impenitency or any sin; though his grace
be the cause of men's conversion, he is the be-
ginner of our good, but we are the cause of our
own evil: all our grace is from him, but all our
sin is from ourselves: he gives us grace before
we so much as willed it, and accordingly he decreed to give it before the foresight of our own
willing it: but he causes not our sin, but only
permits us to cause it, and accordingly he decreed not the event of sin before he did foresee
that we would be sinners, and our wills of themselves would turn from God, and so proceed till
grace recover us. You have no more ground
therefore of excusing yourselves, because of the

decree of God, than if he had made no such decree at all. What if I could foretell, from the
obstinate wickedness of such a thief, or such a
drunkard, that he will never be cured: is it owing to me because I foreknew it? What if the
prophet foretell Hazael what cruelty he shall
commit on the children of Israel, is the prophet
therefore the cause of it? 5. Consider also, that
if you knew not how to answer any objection of
this nature, yet you have the very principles of
reason and all religion to assure you that God is
most wise, good, just, and holy: therefore that
he cannot be the author of your sin, nor shall
you ever be able to produce any just excuse from
him: you might better have looked about you
any where in the world for one to bear the blame
of your miscarriages than the most wise and
holy God. For nothing is more certain than
that the infinite good cannot be the author of
evil; and whosoever it comes from, it cannot
come from him; O how easily will God stop
those mouths that excuse themselves by accusing
him in so foul a case!

6. Why do you not consider what madness
it would be to argue about your bodies as you
do about your souls: it is as true that God
hath decreed how many years and days you
shall live, as that he hath decreed whether you
shall be saved. I will refer it to your own reason, what you would think of the wit of that man
who would give over eating and drinking, and
say, 'God hath decreed how long I shall live, and
if he have decreed that I shall live any longer, I
shall, whether I eat and drink or not; and if he
have not decreed that I shall live, it is not eating
nor drinking that will keep me alive?' What
would you say to such a man but this, that God
decrees no man to live, but by the ordinary
means of living: therefore ordinarily if you will
give over eating and drinking, it is certain that
you will give over living; and that God hath
made no decree to save you alive whether you eat
and drink, or not? so if a man should have a
journey to go on life or death, what would you
think of that man who will say, 'if God have decreed that I shall come to my journey's end, I
shall do it, whether I go or not; and if he have
not decreed it, I shall never come thither, though
I travel never so hard?' This is true; but if you
hence infer, that therefore it is as good sit still as
go, you will show your own folly, and not procure an excuse for your neglect. Why, even so
it is in our present case. If you will say, if God
have elected me, I shall be saved, and if he have
not, I shall not, whatsoever I do, and therefore
I may spare my pains, it is no wiser than to give

over eating and drinking, because God hath decreed how long you shall live; or to give over travelling because God hath decreed whether you shall come to your journey's end: will you be thus mad about the matters of your trades and callings in the world? Why do you not give over ploughing and sowing, and say, If God have decreed that I shall have a crop, I shall have one, whether I plough and sow, or not; and if he have not, I shall not, whatsoever I do? If you will needs be fools, let it be about these worldly things, which you may better spare: try your own opinion a while, and give over eating, drinking and working: but do not befool yourselves about the one thing necessary: play not the madman about the flames of hell: and do not in such jest throw away your salvation. It were an hundred times a wiser course for a man to set his house on fire, and say, 'if God have decreed the saving of it, the fire shall not burn it, if he have not, it will perish whatsoever I do.' I tell you again, God hath not ordinarily decreed the end without the means: if you will neglect the means of salvation, it is a certain mark that God hath not decreed you to salvation. But you shall find that he hath left you no excuse, because he hath not thus predestinated you.

7. But you say, we cannot convert ourselves; what can man do without the grace of God? and therefore if God give us not grace we are excusable.

Still, do your consciences justify you, that you have done all that you can? Can you not go to church when you stay at home? Can you not go among the servants of God when you go to your worldly businesses, or to an ale-house? Cannot you keep out of evil company? Or cannot you so much as consider of your ways, or bethink you of the things of the life to come? I say, cannot you do these things if you will? Have you done these, or have you not? Have you avoided temptations and occasions of evil, and used the means of grace; attended God in the use of his ordinances; marked diligently what is said to you, and considered it when you came home? Have you not sinned and neglected the means of grace, both knowingly and wilfully? Conscience may tell you that you have, and God shall make you know that you have: shortly you shall be convinced, past denial, that you did not all that you could, nor forbore the evil that you might have forborne: if you will refuse and abuse the help of God, can you expect that he should follow you still with his assistance? God will make you know one day, that nobody carried you into an ale-house, nor opened your mouth, nor poured down the drink; and nobody forced you to swear, or to rail, or hate religion, or quarrel with the word that should have saved you, but it was the malicious wickedness of your naughty hearts.

For the power of conversion and believing itself, you must know that there is a two-fold power—one natural, the other moral: the natural faculty of understanding and willing every man hath: if they have the use of reason, they have no physical impediment, but they may use them; and if they hear the word they have no such absence of the necessary object, as may make the work impossible to them: the moral power is nothing but a disposition or habit of the soul to believe or repent, &c. or a freedom from contrary habits: this it is acknowledged that none have, but those that have proportionably received that grace that doth effect it; or to speak as plainly as I can to you; there is a power which lies in being able to believe and repent if we will, or to do whatsoever we will that concerns us to do; and there is a willingness itself to execute this power, and that both actual and habitual: the former every one hath, the latter none but the godly have in sincerity, and those that make so great a stir about this in the church, do seem to be agreed in it, and do not know it. For every man on both parties confesses that all men have the natural faculty of understanding and will, and that they have so much power that they can believe and love God above all, if they will; and on the other side, I hope we are all agreed that wicked unregenerated men are not truly willing to repent and believe, and that they have not the habit and disposition thereto, but have the contrary habits. Experience tells us this without any more ado.

The latter sort of power then, about which all the controversy lies, is nothing but the very willing or grace itself, actual or habitual, or the absence of the contrary: therefore it is all one to ask whether a wicked man have power to believe; and to ask whether he be a believer actually or habitually, or not an unbeliever; so that when we are all agreed that the natural power or faculty is present, and the moral, which is but the willingness, is absent, you can ground none of your excuses on the differences of the church in this point: as I have formerly said to you, if you will but reduce this last kind of power and impotency to its most proper expression, you will open the shame of your own excuses: for morally to be unable to believe, is no more than to be unwilling to believe: if you should say, 'I will not believe or repent, and therefore I am excusable:' what would your own conscience say to such an excuse? Natural impotency excuses faults: he that can say, I would believe, but cannot, is excusable: but never a one of you all shall ever be able to say this; but moral impotency aggravates faults; the more will, the more sin. All the government and justice in the world is grounded upon this principle, and therefore all rewards and punishments are founded in the will of man, and all moral virtue and vice is resolved into that: and if you can but prove that a man offended willingly, you have proved him culpable: for nature hath taught all the world to bring the fault to the will, and there to leave it, and look no further for the cause: unless as seducers may be made accessory by their persuasions, which yet is no excuse to the offender.

8. Whereas you alledge that of the apostle, ' It is not in him that willeth, or in him that runneth, but in God that showeth mercy.'

I answer, that the meaning is not, that our salvation is not in him that wills, or in him that runs: the apostle talks of no such thing: but it is about the giving of the gospel to them that had it not, and taking it from them that had forfeited it by their sin; or the giving of the first special grace to them that had it not, and the denying it to them that had forfeited it by their neglect; and the meaning is no more than this, that the reason why God gives one man or nation the preaching of the gospel when others for their sins are left in darkness, is not from any merit or willing or running of their own, but from his mere mercy. The reason why he blesses the gospel to the conversion of some, when he leaves others to despise it by their wilful obstinacy, is not from the merits of any of those unregenerated men, or from any willing or running of theirs, but from God that shows mercy. So that you must note, it is, 1. One thing to ask the cause of man's damnation in himself considered, and this is not said to be because God will damn him, but because he hath *deserved it by his sin;* and so the cause of his failure in the matter of special grace, is not barely because God will pass him by, but because he hath deserved it; for God denies the gospel, and faith by the gospel, or his grace to effect it, to no man that hath not first deserved that denial. 2. It is another thing to ask the reason of men's salvation, which is not given in scripture barely from the will of God, but from the faith and obedience of men, for it is an act of rewarding justice as well as of paternal love and mercy. 3. It is yet another thing to ask the reason why

God gives any man the first special grace to repent and believe, considering him simply in himself, and this is, because that God is gracious, and no reason can be given but his own mercy; and thus far most of us are agreed. 4. It is yet another thing to ask the reason why God gives the special grace to this man, rather than that, comparatively considered, when he might justly have denied it to them both, and neither of them could plead their desert of it? To this it is that the apostle's answer does most correspond, or at least is fitly applied; ' It is not in him that willeth or runneth, but of God that showeth mercy.' So that, though no man can give any reason besides the mere will of God, why God should give this grace to Peter rather than to Judas, yet we well know that he denies it not to Judas without his own desert; though he gives it to Peter contrary to his desert.

9. Whereas it is further objected, that whom he will, he hardeneth, and if God will harden us, how can we repent? We must consider, First, That he hardens no man without his own desert; it is not till you have forfeited his softening grace by your resisting and abuse of it. Second, That his hardening is but this leaving you to yourselves, and taking away or denying you that Spirit which you have quenched; or his carrying the just course of his providence so as he knows your corrupt natures will be hardened thereby: but *he doth not put any hardness into your hearts,* and therefore these afford you no excuse.

7. Another error that hinders conversion is: the placing of holiness in holding of certain opinions, and so turning from the life of faith and love, to speculation and vain janglings. If once men place their religion in their opinions, they may as well be hypocrites and self-deceivers in a true opinion, as in a false. This is a habit by which the devil hath caught multitudes of souls in all ages of the church, and especially of late: when he cannot keep men in open profaneness, then he will tempt them to think that such a party and such a sect are the only right and holy people; and therefore if thou get but among them, and be one of that opinion and party, then thou shalt be saved. Hence it is that we see that men who are so zealous for their parties, and glory so much in several opinions, do yet many, very many of them live so unacquainted with God and heaven, are such strangers to Christian charity, can freely reproach both common Christians and ministers, ' speak evil of the things they understand not,' take their railing accusations for their piety, walk in discord, hatred, and disunion from the church of God,

and are glad when they can bear down the reputation of their brethren whose labours are necessary for the good of souls. It is a common mark of an opinionative hypocrite, that he prefers the interest of his opinion and party, before the interest of those common truths which salvation is clearly laid upon, and all Christians are agreed in: he cares not to hinder ministers from propagating these common truths for the conversion of souls, so he might withal but hinder them from propagating that opinion which is contrary to his: and he lays out more of his zeal and diligence for these opinions than for the mortification of his lusts, the maintaining of the union and communion of the saints, and walking holily with God, and uprightly with men.

I shall now say no more to these, but that ' the kingdom of God consists not in meats and in drink, but in righteousness, peace, and joy in the Holy Ghost.—That circumcision availeth nothing, nor uncircumcision, but faith that worketh by love.—And the new creature.—For in Christ Jesus there is neither Jew nor Gentile, bond nor free, male nor female;' and why may I not say on the same ground, ' young nor old, but Christ is all, and in all.' We have many promises of life and salvation to as many as repent and believe, love God, and hope for the coming of Christ, but we have none to those that are of this or that party or opinion without these graces. We know how tender God is of the unity of his church and people, and how much he hath spoken against division, and they that know not this, when they pretend to know things that are not half so clearly revealed, may be ashamed of their ignorance. I do not know where God hath commanded men to avoid them that hold this or that tolerable different opinion, or that follow this or that tolerable different practice: but I know where he hath commanded us 'to mark them that cause division, and avoid them.'

8. Another error that hinders conversion is: when men have gotten false conceits against the lawfulness or necessity of those holy ordinances, that are used by the people of God: for the life of religion lies so much in the use of holy ordinances, that if people be brought out of conceit with these, they will not know what it is to be religious, nor what necessity there is of it. To give an instance in some particulars.

(1.) Some grow into doubt of the necessity of family duty, and ask, where hath God commanded us to pray in our families,—and that so oft? To which I answer, that it is sufficient that he hath bid us ' pray always, and in all things make our requests known to God with prayers,

supplication and thanksgiving.—All things are sanctified by the word and prayer ;' and therefore our families and callings are so. What have we common reason for, but to circumstantiate these duties that God hath commanded to us for the substance : and common reason tells us, that as we daily need God we must daily seek supply of our needs, and so not only our persons but our families, as families, need this mercy, and receive his mercy, and are related to him as the head, so our families, as families, must call on him, praise him, and love his headship. Besides the example of Daniel, who prayed three times a day in his house so openly that his enemies had matter of accusation from the matter of his prayer. But I have had occasion to write more largely of this, and therefore wilt not now stand on it.

(2.) Others are brought to question the lawfulness of joining with our solemn assemblies, in hearing, or praying, or other public worship of God : the reasons are such as I am ashamed to stand to mention and confute them, and shall be weary to go over them, they are so vain and superficial, and answered at large by many. Some of their reasons are, because we are so bad, when many of the accusers are such themselves, that they deserve to be severely censured by the church, and because the church will not deal with them, they will judge the church, and think themselves too good to have communion with it: and the church unworthy to have communion with them. In a word, they would have not one but many cast out, whom they never dealt with in Christ's way by admonition : and because it is not done out of Christ's way, to save a labour, they will turn schismatics.

Others of them withdraw on the pretence that we have no ministry : how prove they that ? You may wait long enough till you can have a word of scripture or reason for the proof, or before they can answer that sufficient proof that is brought of the contrary. If you do but put them to tell you which is the true church and ministers, and where it hath been ; you shall see what work they will make in the end.

Others withdraw on pretence that we are unbaptized, to which end they must coin a new baptism, or else they are at a loss : their arguing with us, will be much like the papists in the point of transubstantiation, which requires that men renounce their sense, and say, that they see not that which they see, and feel not, or taste not, that which indeed they feel and taste, and then they may come to be in the right: so we must believe that we see none baptized in our churches, nor hear it, nor know of any such thing, and then we may come to be a church. If these brethren had half so much humility or Christian love, and sense of the unity of the church of Christ as they should have, they would think on it, and think again, before they would either say of the universal church of Christ for one age, much more for so many ages, that it was no church, or not to be joined with. For he that dares renounce communion with the whole, doth make it hard to be discerned that he is a part : he that is not a member of the body, will not find another body of Christ, whose communion is desireable. For my part, I believe the church hath had many errors in many ages, but I know no age since the creation, in which, if I had lived, I durst have disclaimed communion with her. Much less dare I think of running out of the way to heaven, which almost all they went in that are there ; or of separating from all the church of Christ, from Adam till within this two hundred years, or thereabout : for if there were no church till then, there was no head, no Christ, and so no Christianity. Yea, if there were none but for any one time. If it were the will of God, that we could have as clear light in some other weighty points, as we have in scripture for the baptism of the children of believers ; how much would it do to quiet the understandings of many that are willing to know.

(3.) Others there be that despise the solemn praises of the congregations, because some psalms are such as all cannot truly, they think, recite. As if no recital were lawful, but that which personally owneth the words, which can never be proved. Do they not know that God himself hath prevented their objection ? That it flieth in his own face ? Who knows not that these psalms, or at least very many of them, were appointed for the solemn praise of God in the temple and congregations of the Jews in those times ? If those could lawfully use them whose hearts were generally no more fitted to them, than ours, may not we do so too ?

Do they not know that their objection doth make, not only against psalms, but all public prayer also to be unlawful ? For you cannot so speak in any such public prayers, or praises, but there will be somewhat which will not suit with the particular dispositions of many in the congregation personally to own, or else your duty will be very defective. If you express rejoicing, must all drooping spirits separate from the assembly that cannot rejoice ? But I will trouble you no more with this. If they will in this, and the aforesaid cases of baptism, separation and the rest, divide from the church, and venture on

damnation to save themselves the labour of reading that which is written to give them information, they must take what they get by it. Who can help it ?

Hinderance 19. *A proud, unteachable spirit is another hinderance to conversion.* Another hinderance of conversion, is : a proud unteachable frame of spirit—when people are so wise in their own eyes, that they think they know enough already ; and they scorn to be taught. If the wisest minister in England should live with such, they would but despise his counsel in every thing almost that crosses their conceits. As long as he will humour them, and say as they say, he shall be a good man, and well spoken of by all ; but if he will trouble them, cross them, and tell them that which is against their present opinion, they think themselves wiser in this than he, and if they do not bid him look to himself, and let them alone, at least they will give him little thanks, and show it by their small regard.

Some of them will not come near us, nor give us the hearing, when we would teach them ; and others, though they hear, do think themselves too wise to believe or obey. And thus they are fixed in a state of misery.

Direction. If ever you will be converted, humbly submit to the word of God, and the instructions of those whom he hath appointed to inform you. What unreasonable pride is it in you that are ignorant, unlearned men, to despise the counsel of the most able, godly ministers, and that in points wherein the godly through all the world are agreed ? Yea, where God himself doth lead them by his word ? Are not they likely to know more than you, that have studied it all their days ? Discourse with them, and try whether they or you have more knowledge. Consider what you do when you proudly reason against the necessity of conversion and a holy life. What ! are you wiser than your teachers, and than the ablest teachers in the land ; yea, than all the ministers in the world, and than all the godly people in the world ? Silly souls that scarcely know any of the principles of religion, are yet so proud as to despise the instruction from the wisest. But if you think yourselves wiser than all the ministers in the world, will you also think yourselves wiser than God ? I tell you, either illuminating grace, or the conviction of God's judgment, shall take down your lofty hearts ere long, and make you wish you had stooped to instruction. The day is coming that will abate your pride, and make you talk a little more submissively. Hearken therefore in time, lest that befal you that is mentioned. ' Lest thou mourn at last when thy flesh and body are consumed; and say, How have I hated instruction, and my heart despised reproof; and have not obeyed the voice of my teachers, nor inclined mine ear to them that instructed me !' If you are too wise to learn, you will prove in the end too foolish to be saved.

Hinderance 20. *Wilful obstinacy.* The last hinderance of conversion that I shall mention is, wilful obstinacy. When men have long resisted grace, they are given over oftentimes to themselves, and then they grow wilful: and when they have nothing else to say why they should not be converted, and become the people of God, they can say, they will not: they will never be so holy, nor deny their flesh, nor forsake the world, nor set themselves to a heavenly life: they will not believe that this is so necessary: nor will they ever yield to such a course: come on it what will, they are resolved against it; before they will do it they will venture their souls; and let God do with them what he will: this desperate wilfulness is the devil's last hold.

Direction. What direction should I give you against this hinderance? When the will is so corrupt and obstinate, whatsoever I give, it will be rejected. If you were but willing I should make no doubt but the work might prosper; or if you were but reasonable, teachable and persuadable, I should make no doubt, through the blessing of God, but the former means might make you yield: but if men be wilful and resolved to perish, what remedy? If men could give us any reason against conversion and a holy life, and did err through the mere mistake of their understandings, I should make no doubt, through the blessing of God, but by bare reason they might be rectified. But when their will is their reason, and they are resolved, whatsoever comes of it, to hold on, and stop their ears against advice, what can we say to these men? All that I can do, is to commend to them the former considerations, and to desire them to think of those motives before delivered, which may change their wills. But I have but little hope to prevail with them so much as soberly to think of it. And because so many of our poor people are in this state, I am forced here to end this subject with lamentation.

CHAPTER VIII.

THE AUTHOR'S CONCLUDING REMARKS UPON THIS BRANCH OF CONVERSION.

I have delivered now many discourses to you of conversion, and whether any souls be con-verted by it, the Lord knows, I know not. But the sad observation of the state of the world, and the partial impressions made by such endeavours, do justly make me fear the issue. I know that both I and this congregation shall shortly appear before our Judge, to give a strict account of our lives; and if I have not preached these sermons in sincerity, with a true desire after the saving of your souls, then how shall I stand before the Lord, if the blood of Christ, through faith and repentance, prevail not for remission? If any man or woman in this town or parish shall there appear in an unconverted state, what will they be able to say for themselves; or how will they escape the threatened damnation? I am not out of hope that I shall meet some souls there, though yet I know not of them, that will be able to say, they were converted by these sermons. But I am so much afraid lest I shall meet abundance of you in an unconverted state, that I could even find in my heart to sit down and weep over these sermons, now that I have preached them. Alas! that you should be condemned by that which was intended to further your salvation. Have I studied and preached all this to be a witness against you? I know as true as you sit in these seats, that every soul of you shall be for ever in hell, that passes out of the body in an unconverted state. I know when you have heard so much of it, and been so often warned, and now are left without excuse, you will have a double condemnation. For now it is your mere wilfulness that must keep you unconverted. If you say, you cannot convert yourselves; I ask you in a word, will you do what you can? Tell me, will you, or will you not? If you will not, what remedy? If you will, look over the directions I have given you, and set upon the faithful practice of them. Particularly, see that you presently search the scriptures, read good books, forsake your evil company, and come not near them, but get among those that fear the Lord, and take all opportunities, public and private, and inquire of your teachers and neighbours that can help you, what you shall do to be saved? And sin no more wilfully, but avoid the very temptations and appearances of evil, and be much with God in secret and open prayer: and dwell in the consideration of your own estate, of your own sin and danger, of Christ and duty, of grace and glory, and think not any pains too much for your salvation. What say you? Will you do but thus much, or will you not? If you will, you shall find no cause to repent of it, and God will not be wanting to that soul that doth not wilfully forsake him, but is willing to be conformed to the image of his Son; and to be what God would have him be. But alas! it is this wilfulness and obstinacy that undoes men: that is that which shuts up the heart of God and man from compassionating the wicked in their everlasting misery. They did it wilfully; they would take no warning; they would hear no counsel; no saying would serve them; they chose their own destruction; it was their own doing; they were told of it an hundred times; they were entreated to consider, but they would not be entreated. What could have been said more to them? What could we do more for them? O that any one of you could tell me what I should say more, or what I should do now to save the souls of ignorant, fleshly, worldly sinners from damnation; to convert the unconverted, and turn the hearts of men to God! O that you could but tell me how I might accomplish it! Would I not do it? The Lord knows, if any lawful and honest means would accomplish it, I would do it, if I know my own heart. But if Christ could not be heard, why should I wonder if many will make light of what is said by such a one as I. If they will not hear the Lord that made them, speaking in his word, why should I wonder if they will not hear him speaking by such a worm as I? Sinners, what shall I say more to you? I have told you of an everlasting glory which you might have; if you will neglect it, and prefer your worldly things before it, who can help it? I have told you of eternal misery that you are in danger of; if you will venture on it, and not believe it till you feel it, and are past remedy, who can help it? I have proved to you, from the word of God, that without conversion there is no salvation: if you dare go on in an unconverted state, keep your sin, follow your fleshly desires and delights, and your worldly vanities and wicked company, if you will not be drawn to the ways of God, what remedy? I have delivered my message, and I hope God will not require your blood at my hands. You shall all be forced to bear me witness that I told you there was no salvation without conversion: and that I manifested to you the reasonableness of the offers of God: if you be not converted, it is because you would not: what a torment it will be everlastingly to your consciences to think that you wilfully damned yourselves, and to think that you wilfully refused your salvation; and that you might have been in heaven as well as others, if you had not wilfully and obstinately rejected it: I say, what tormenting thoughts these will prove to you through eternity, you cannot possibly now conceive, but then you shall know and feel it, if true conversion do not prevent it. Which that it may do, as it hath been the end of all these discourses, so shall it now, and as long as I have life and strength, be the matter of my prayers for you.

A

CALL TO THE UNCONVERTED

TO

TURN AND LIVE,

AND ACCEPT OF MERCY WHILE MERCY MAY BE HAD, AS EVER THEY WOULD FIND
MERCY IN THE DAY OF THEIR EXTREMITY FROM THE LIVING GOD.

PREFATORY REMARKS.

THE "CALL TO THE UNCONVERTED" has been more widely circulated than any other of Baxter's publications. The preface is dated 10th December, 1657: the "Treatise of Conversion" had appeared in June of the same year. To a work so well known as the "Call to the Unconverted," little seems required in the way of prefatory remark. It is worthy, however, of historical record, that he was induced to undertake these works on Conversion by Archbishop Usher. That eminent man, no doubt, perceived what constituted the *forte* of Baxter, and therefore suggested an employment so well suited to his powers. The following passage of his preface to the "Call" contains this circumstance, and gives some account of the order in which he intended to pursue his task.

"In the short acquaintance I had with that reverend, learned servant of Christ, Bishop Usher, he was oft, from first to last, importuning me to write a Directory for the several ranks of professed Christians, which might distinctly give each one their portion; beginning with the unconverted, and then proceeding to the babes in Christ, and then to the strong; and mixing some special helps against the several sins that they are addicted to. By the suddenness of his motion at our first congress, I perceived it was in his mind before; and I told him, both that it was abundantly done by many already, and that his unacquaintedness with my weakness might make him think me fitter for it than I was. But this did not satisfy him, he still made it his request. I confess I was not moved by his reasons, nor did I apprehend any great need of doing more than is done in that way; nor that I was likely to do more. And, therefore, I parted

from him without the least purpose to answer his desire. But since his death his words often came into my mind; and the great reverence which I bore to him did the more incline me to think with some complacency of his motion. Having of late intended to write a 'Family Directory,' I began to apprehend how congruously the forementioned work should lead the way; and the several conditions of men's souls be spoken of, before we come to the several relations. Hereupon I resolved, by God's assistance, to proceed in the order following. First, to speak to the impenitent, unconverted sinners, who are not yet so much as purposing to turn; or at least are not setting about the work. With these, I thought, a wakening persuasive was a more necessary means than mere directions; for directions suppose men willing to obey them. But the persons that we have first to deal with are wilful and asleep in sin, and as men that are past feeling, having given themselves over to sin with greediness. My next work must be for those that have some purposes to turn, and are about the work, to direct them for a thorough and a true conversion, that they miscarry not in the birth. The third part must be directions for the younger and weaker sort of Christians, that they may be established, built up, and persevere. The fourth part, directions for lapsed and backsliding Christians, for their safe recovery. Beside these, there is intended some short persuasions against some special errors of the times, and against some common killing sins. As for directions to doubting troubled consciences, that is done already; and the strong I shall not write directions for, because they are so much taught of God already. And then the last part is in-

tended more especially for families, as such,
directing the several relations in their duties."

The "Call" appears to be the substance of a
sermon which he had previously preached from
Ezekiel xxxiii. 11. He prefixes to it a prefatory
address to "all unsanctified persons who shall
read the book, especially his hearers in the
parish of Kidderminster;" which is itself a
powerfully-awakening sermon, full of the most
faithful statements and expostulations. The
results in the conversion of men, arising from
this book, have been greater probably than have
arisen from any other mere human performance.
His own account of the effects produced by it,
which had come to his knowledge long before his
death, must be given in his own language. And
as it has passed through editions almost innumerable since, the good effected by it is beyond all
calculation.

"God hath blessed it with unexpected success
beyond all the rest that I have written, except
the 'Saints' Rest.' In a little more than a year,
there were about twenty thousand of them printed
by my own consent, and about ten thousand
since, besides many thousands by stolen impression, which poor men stole for lucre' sake.
Through God's mercy, I have had information of
almost whole households converted by this small
book, which I set so light by; and, as if all this
in England, Scotland, and Ireland, were not
mercy enough to me, God, since I was silenced,
hath sent it over on his message to many beyond the seas. For when Mr. Elliot had printed
all the Bible in the Indians' language, he next
translated this my 'Call to the Unconverted,' as
he wrote to us here; and though it was here
thought prudent to begin with the 'Practice of
Piety,' because of the envy and distaste of the
times against me, he had finished it before that
advice came to him. Yet God would make some
further use of it, for Mr. Stoop, the pastor of
the French church in London, being driven hence
by the displeasure of superiors, was pleased to
translate it into elegant French, and print it in
a very curious letter; and I hope it will not be
unprofitable there, nor in Germany, where it is
printed in Dutch."

Dr. Bates tells us, in his funeral sermon for
Baxter, that six brothers were at one time converted by this book. It has been translated into
Welsh and Gaelic, and most of the European languages; and Cotton Mather, in his Life, mentions
an Indian prince who was so affected with it
that he kept reading it with tears till he died.

The "Call" naturally leads us to connect with
it the tract which immediately follows it: namely,
"Now or Never," a discourse founded on Ecclesi-
astes ix. 10; and in which "the holy, serious,
diligent believer is justified, encouraged, excited,
and directed; and the opposers and neglecters
convinced by the light of Scripture and reason."
These tracts are so similar in character, style, and
design, that I know not where the preference is
due in point of excellence. They are both characterized by one strongly-marked feature—INTENSE
EARNESTNESS—the earnestness of the author's
deep convictions of the awfully perilous condition of unconverted men. This was the result
of the clear and powerful perceptions which he
had of the present guilt and wretchedness, and
the future loss and ruin of such persons. It is
not the working up of mental excitement till it
becomes passion, nor is it a laboured effort of
human eloquence, which we admire in these
treatises. Baxter was thinking of everything
rather than of the clothing of his thoughts, his
words or figures. He was thinking of the character and desert of a sinner, and intent only on
arresting him before it might be too late. His
object was to gain his attention, to convince his
understanding, and to impress his heart. For
this purpose he describes, he reasons, he expostu-
lates, he threatens, he implores. He avails himself of every topic calculated to alarm or to allure.
The character of God—the responsibility of man
—the uncertainty of time—the misery of hell—
the glory of heaven—are all brought forward and
urged with an irresistible force of language, and
in the tenderest appeals to the conscience and
the heart.

The work of Baxter I cannot help thinking
preferable to a similar production of one of his
own brethren, Joseph Alleine's "Alarm;" to
which indeed Baxter writes a long preface, where
he unites with the author in sounding the alarm
to the unconverted. Alleine's tract is written
in a style of almost unmitigated severity. There
is a forbidding sternness in it. Full of "the
terrors of the Lord," it is calculated to frighten
rather than to persuade. Some of the topics
also are not happily chosen, or discreetly urged;
yet it is a powerful appeal, and on some minds
may be fitted to prepare the way for the consideration of the "mercies of the Lord." Baxter's
"Call" is adapted for more general usefulness.
It breathes a softer and kindlier spirit, while it is
no less pointed and faithful than the production
of his friend and brother.—*Orme.*

A
CALL TO THE UNCONVERTED.

MEN AND BRETHREN,

THE eternal God that made you for life everlasting, and hath redeemed you by his only Son, when you had lost it, and yourselves; being mindful of you in your sin and misery, hath indited' the gospel, sealed it by his Spirit, and commanded his ministers to preach it to the world, that pardon being freely offered you, and heaven being set before you, he might call you off from your fleshly pleasures, and from following after this deceitful world, and acquaint you with the life you were created and redeemed for, before you are dead and past remedy. He sends you not prophets or apostles, that receive their message by immediate revelation, but yet he calls you by his ordinary ministers, who are commissioned by him to preach the same gospel which Christ and his apostles first delivered. The Lord stands over you, and sees how you forget him and your latter end, and how light you make of everlasting things, as men that understand not what they have to do or suffer: he sees how bold you are in sin, how fearless of his threatenings, how careless of your souls, and how the works of infidels are in your lives, while the belief of Christians is in your mouths. He sees the dreadful day at hand, when your sorrows will begin, and you must lament all this with fruitless cries in torment and desperation; and then the remembrance of your folly will tear your hearts, if true conversion now prevent it not. In compassion of your sinful, miserable souls, the Lord, who better knows your case than you can know it, hath made it our duty to speak to you in his name, to tell you plainly of your sin and misery, and what will be your end, and how sad a change you will shortly see, if yet you go on a little longer. Having bought you at so dear a rate as the blood of his Son Jesus Christ, and made you so free and general a promise of pardon, grace, and everlasting glory, he commands us to tender all this to you, as the gift of God, and to intreat you to consider of the necessity and worth of what he offers. He sees and pities you, while you are drowned in worldly cares and pleasures, and eagerly following childish toys, and wasting that short and precious time for a thing of nought, in which you should make ready for an everlasting life; and therefore he hath commanded us to call after you, and to tell you how you lose your labour, and are about to lose your souls, and to tell you what greater and better things you might certainly have, if you would hearken to his call.

We believe and obey the voice of God: and come to you daily on his message, who hath charged us to preach and be instant with you in season, and out of season, and to lift up our voice like a trumpet, and show you your transgressions and your sins; but woe and alas! to the grief of our souls, and your own undoing you stop your ears, you stiffen your necks, you harden your hearts, and break our hearts, and send us back to God with groans, to tell him that we had done his message, but can do no good, nor scarcely get a sober hearing. O that our eyes were as a fountain of tears, that we might lament our ignorant, careless, people, that have Christ before them, and pardon and life, and heaven before them, and have not hearts to know and value them! That might have Christ, grace, and glory, as well as others, if it were not for their wilful negligence and contempt: O that the Lord would fill our hearts with more compassion to these miserable souls, that we might cast ourselves even at their feet, and follow them to their houses, and speak to them with our bitter tears. For long have we preached to many of them as in vain: we study plainness to make them understand, and many of them will not understand us: we study serious, piercing words to make them feel, but they will not feel. If the greatest matters would work with them, we should awake them. If the sweetest things would work, we should entice them, and win their hearts. If the most dreadful things would work, we should at least affright them from their wickedness: if truth and sincerity would take with them, we should soon convince them: if the God that made them, and the Saviour that bought them, might be heard, the case would soon be altered with them: if scripture might be heard, we should soon prevail: if reason, even the best and strongest reason, might be heard, we should not doubt but we should speedily convince them: if experience might be heard, even their own experience, and the experience of all the world, the matter might be mended : yea, if the conscience within them might be heard, the case would be better with them than it is. But if nothing can be heard, what then shall we do for them ? If the dreadful God of heaven be slighted, who then shall be regarded ? If the inestimable love and blood of a Redeemer be made light of, what then shall be valued ? If heaven have no desirable glory with them, and everlasting joys be worth nothing ; if they can jest at hell, and dance about a bottomless pit, and play with the consuming fire, and that when God and man do warn them of it : what shall we do for such souls as these?

Once more, in the name of the God of heaven, I shall deliver the message to you which he hath commanded us, and leave it in these standing lines to convert you or condemn you : to change you, or rise up in judgment against you, and to be a witness to your faces that once you had a serious call to turn. Hear all you that are the drudges of the world, the servants of the flesh and Satan,—that spend your days in looking after prosperity on earth, and drown your consciences in drinking, gluttony, idleness, and foolish sports, and know your sin, and yet will sin, as if you set God at defiance, bid him do his worst, and spare not ! Hearken all you that mind not God, and have no heart to holy things, and feel no savour in the word or worship of the Lord, or in the thoughts or mention of eternal life ; that are careless of your immortal souls, and never bestow'ed one hour in inquiring what case they are in, whether sanctified or unsanctified, and whether you are ready to appear before the Lord ! Hearken all you that by sinning in the light, have sinned yourselves into atheism and infidelity, and do not believe the word of God. He that hath an ear to hear let him hear the gracious and yet dreadful call of God ! His eye is all this while upon you, your sins are registered, and you shall surely hear of them again : God keeps the book now ; and he will write it upon your consciences with his terrors ; and then you also shall keep it yourselves : O sinners, that you knew but what you are doing ! and who you are all this while offending : the sun itself is darkness before the glory of that Majesty which you daily abuse and carelessly provoke. The sinning angels were not able to stand before him, but were cast down to be tormented with devils ; and dare such silly worms as you so carelessly offend, and set yourselves against your Maker ! O that you did but a little know what a case that wretched soul is in, that hath engaged the living God against him ! The word of his mouth who made thee can unmake thee ; a frown of his face will cut thee off, and cast thee out into utter darkness. How eager are the devils to be doing with thee that have tempted thee ; they but wait for the word from God to take and use thee as their own ! And then in a moment thou wilt be in hell. If God be against thee, all things are against thee. This world is but thy prison for all that thou so lovest it : thou art but reserved in it to the day of wrath. The Judge is coming, thy soul is even going. Yea, a little while and thy friends shall say of thee, He is dead ; and thou shalt see the things that thou dost now despise, and feel what now thou wilt not believe. Death will bring such an argument as thou canst not answer : an argument that shall effectually confute thy cavils against the word and ways of God, and all thy self-conceited dreams : and then how soon will thy mind be changed ? Then be an unbeliever if thou canst ! Stand then to all thy former words which thou wast wont to utter against the scriptures, or against a holy and heavenly life ! Make good that cause then before the Lord, which thou wast wont to plead against thy teachers, and against the people that feared God. Then stand to thy old opinions, and contemptuous thoughts of the diligence of the saints.

Make ready now thy strongest reasons, and stand up then before the judge, and plead like a man, for thy fleshly, thy worldly, and ungodly life ; but know that thou must have one to plead with thee, that will not be looked out of countenance by thee, nor so easily put off as we thy fellow creatures. O poor, deceived, wretched soul, there is nothing but a slender vail of flesh betwixt thee and that amazing sight, which will quickly silence thee and turn thy tune, and make thee of another mind ! As soon as death has drawn this curtain, thou shalt see that which will quickly leave thee speechless. And how quickly will that day and hour come ? When thou hast had but a few more merry hours, and but a few more pleasant draughts and morsels, and a little more of the honours and riches of the world, thy portion will be spent, and thy pleasures ended, and all is then gone that thou settest thy heart upon, of all that thou soldest thy Saviour and salvation for ; there is nothing left but the heavy reckoning. As a thief that sits merrily spending the money in an ale-house which he hath stolen, when men are riding in post-haste to apprehend him, so it is with you ; while you are drowned in cares or fleshly pleasures, and making merry with your own shame, death is coming in post-haste to seize upon you and carry your souls to such a place and state as now you little know or think of. Suppose when you are bold and busy in your sin, that a messenger were but coming post from London to apprehend you, and take away your life, though you saw him not ; yet if you knew of his coming it would mar your mirth and you would be thinking of the haste he makes, and hearkening when he knocks at your door : O that ye could but see what haste death makes, though yet it hath not overtaken you ! No post so swift ! No messenger more sure ! As sure as the sun will be with you in the morning, though it hath many thousand and hundred thousand miles to go in the night : so sure will death be quickly with you, and then where is your sport and pleasure ? Then will you jest and brave it out ? Then will you mock at them that warned you ? Then is it better to be a believing saint, or a sensual worldling ? And then whose shall all those things be that you have gathered ? Do you not observe that days and weeks are quickly gone, and nights and mornings come apace, and speedily succeed each other ? You sleep, but your 'damnation slumbereth not ;' you linger, ' but your judgment this long time lingereth not ;' to which you are reserved for punishment. ' O that you were wise to understand this, and that you did consider your latter end !—He that hath an ear to hear, let him hear the call of God in this day of his salvation.'

O careless sinners, that you did but know the love that you unthankfully neglect, and the preciousness of the blood of Christ which you despise ! O that you did but know the riches of our Lord ! O that you did but know the riches of the gospel ! O that you did but know a little the certainty, the glory, and blessedness of that everlasting life, which now you will not set your hearts upon, nor be persuaded first and diligently to seek. Did you but know the endless life with God which you now neglect, how quickly would you cast away your sin ! How quickly would you change your mind and life, your course and company, and turn the streams of your affections, and lay out your care another way ? How resolutely would you scorn to yield to such temptations as now deceive you, and carry you away ? How zealously would you bestir yourselves for that most blessed life ? How earnest would you be with God in prayer ? How diligent in hearing, learning, and inquiring ? How serious in meditating on the laws of God ? How fearful of sinning in thought, word or deed ? And how careful to please God and grow in holiness ? O what a changed people you would be ! And why should not the certain word of God be believed, and prevail with you, which opens to you these glorious and eternal things ? Yea, let me tell you, that even here upon earth, you little know the difference between the life you refuse and the life you choose. The sanctified are conversing with God, when you scarce dare think of him, and when you are conversing but with earth and flesh, their conversation is in heaven, when you are utter strangers to it, and your belly is your God, and you are minding earthly things. They are seeking after the face of God, when you seek for nothing higher than this world. They are busily laying out for an endless life, where they shall be equal with the angels, when you are taken up with a shadow, and a transitory thing of nought. How low and base is your earthly, fleshly, sinful life, in comparison of the noble, spiritual life of true believers ? Many a time have I looked on such men with grief and pity to see them trudge about the world, and spend their lives, care and labour for nothing but a little food and raiment, or a little fading treasure, or fleshly pleasures, or empty honours, as if they had no higher thing to mind.

What difference is there between the lives of these men, and of the beasts that perish, who spend their time in working, eating, and living, merely that they may live ? They taste not of the inward heavenly pleasures which believers taste and live upon. I had rather have a little of their comfort, which the fore-thoughts of their heavenly inheritance doth afford them, though I had all their scorn and sufferings with it, than to have all your pleasures and treacherous prosperities : I would not have one of your secret misgivings of conscience, dark and dreadful thoughts of death and life to come, for all that ever the world hath done for you, or all that you should reasonably hope that it should do. If I were in your unconverted, carnal state, and knew but what I know, believed but what I now believe, methinks my life would be a foretaste of hell: how oft should I be thinking of the terrors of the Lord, and of the dismal day that is hastening on ? Surely death and hell would be still before me. I should think of them by day, and dream of them by night ; I should lie down in fear, rise in fear, and live in fear, least death should come before I were converted : I should have small felicity in any thing that I possessed, and little pleasure in any company, and little joy in any thing in the world, as long as I knew myself to be under the curse and wrath of God : I should still be afraid of hearing that voice, ' Thou fool, this night shall thy soul be required of thee.' And that fearful sentence would be written upon my conscience, ' There is no peace, saith my God, to the wicked.' O poor sinner ! it is a more joyful life than this that you might live, if you were but willing, but truly willing to hearken to Christ, and to come home to God. You might then draw near to God with boldness, and call him your Father, and comfortably trust him with your souls and bodies. If you look upon promises, you may say, They are all mine ; if upon the curse, you may say, From this I am delivered! When you read the law, you may see what you are saved from : when you read the gospel, you may see him that redeemed you, and see the course of his love, holy life, and sufferings, and trace him in his temptations, tears and blood, in the work of your salvation. You may see death conquered, heaven opened, and your resurrection and glorification provided for, in the resurrection and glorification of your Lord. If you look on the saints, you may say, They are my brethren and companions. If on the unsanctified, you may rejoice to think that you are saved from that state : if you look upon the heavens, the sun, the moon, and stars innumerable, you may think and say, My Father's face is infinitely more glorious ; it is higher matters that he hath prepared for his saints. Yonder is but the outward court of heaven. The blessedness that he hath promised me is so much higher, that flesh and blood cannot behold it. If you think of the grave you may remember that the glorified Spirit, a living Head, and a loving Father, have all so near relation to your dust, that it cannot be forgotten or neglected, but will more certainly revive than the plants and flowers in the spring : because the soul is still alive, that is the root of the body, and Christ is alive, who is the root of both. Even death, which is the king of fears, may be remembered and entertained with joy, as being the day of your deliverance from the remains of sin and sorrow, and the day which you believed, hoped, and waited for, when you shall see the blessed things which you have heard of, and shall find, by present joyful experience, what it was to choose the better part, and be a sincere believing saint. What say you, sirs ? Is not this a more delightful life, to be assured of salvation, and prepared to die, than to live as the ungodly, that have their hearts ' overcharged with surfeiting and drunkenness, and the cares of this life, and so that day comes upon them unawares.' Might you not live a comfortable life, if once you were made the heirs of heaven, and sure to be saved when you leave the world ? O look about you then, and think what you do, and cast not away such hopes as these for very nothing. The flesh and world can give you no such hopes or comforts.

And besides all the misery that you bring upon yourselves, you are the troublers of others as long as you are unconverted. You trouble magistrates to rule you by their laws. You trouble ministers by resisting the light and guidance which they offer you : your sin and misery is the greatest grief and trouble to them in the world. You trouble the commonwealth, and draw the judgments of God upon us: it is you that most disturb the holy peace and order of the churches, and hinder our union and reformation, and are the shame and trouble of the churches where you intrude, and of all the places where you are. Ah Lord ! how heavy and sad a case is this, that even in Britain, where the gospel doth abound above any other nation in the world; where teaching is so plain and common, and all the helps we can desire, are at hand, when the sword hath been hewing us, and judgment hath run as a fire through the land ; when deliverance has relieved us, and so many admirable mercies have engaged us to God, to the gospel, to an holy life: that yet after all this, our cities, towns, and countries, abound with multitudes of unsanctified men, and swarm with so much sensuality, as every where to our grief we see ! One would have thought, that after all this light, and all this experience, all these judgments and mercies of God, the people of this nation should have joined together, as one man, to turn to the Lord; and should have come to their godly teachers, lamented all their former sins, and desired them to join with them in public humiliation to confess them openly, and beg pardon of them from the Lord, and should have craved their instruction for the time to come, and be glad to be ruled by the Spirit within, and the ministers of Christ without, according to the word of God. One would think, that after such reason and scripture evidence as they hear; and after all these means and mercies, there should not be an ungodly person left among us, nor a worldling, a drunkard, a hater of reformation, or an enemy to holiness, be found in all our towns, or countries.

If we be not all agreed about some ceremonies or forms of government, one would think that, before this, we should have been all agreed to live a holy and heavenly life, in obedience to God, his word and ministers, and in love and peace with one another. But alas! how far are our people from this course? Most of them, in most places, do set their hearts on earthly things, and seek not first the kingdom of God, and the righteousness thereof, but look at holiness as a needless thing; their families are prayerless, or else a few heartless, lifeless words, must serve instead of hearty, fervent, daily prayer; their children are not taught the knowledge of Christ, and the covenant of grace, nor brought up in the nurture of the Lord, though they falsely promised this in their baptism. They instruct not their servants in the matters of salvation; but so their work be done, they care not. There are more oaths, curses, and railing speeches in their families, than gracious words that tend to edification. How few are the families that fear the Lord, and inquire after his word and ministers, how they should live, and what they should do; and are willing to be taught and ruled, and that heartily look after everlasting life! And those few that God hath made so happy, are commonly the bye-word of their neighbours: when we see some live in drunkenness, and some in pride and worldliness, and most of them have little care of their salvation, though the cause be gross, and past all controversy, yet will they hardly be convinced of their misery, and more hardly recovered and reformed; but when we have done all that we are able to save them from their sins, we leave them, most of them, as we find them. And if, according to the law of God, we cast them out of the communion of

the church, when they have obstinately rejected all our admonitions, they rage at us as if we were their enemies, and their hearts are filled with malice against us, and they will sooner set themselves against the Lord, his laws, church, and ministers, than against their deadly sins.

This is the doleful case of Britain; we have magistrates that countenance the ways of godliness, and a happy opportunity for unity and reformation is before us; and faithful ministers long to see the right ordering of the church and of the ordinances of God: but the power of sin in our people doth frustrate almost all. No where almost can a faithful minister set up the unquestionable discipline of Christ, or put back the most scandalous impenitent sinners from the communion of the church, and participation of the sacrament, but the most of the people rail at them and revile them: as if these ignorant careless souls were wiser than their teachers, or than God himself; and fitter to rule the church than they. Thus in the day of our visitation when God calls upon us to reform his church, though magistrates seem willing, and faithful ministers are willing, yet are the multitude of the people still unwilling; and sin hath so blinded them, and hardened their hearts, that even in these days of light and grace, they are the obstinate enemies of light and grace, and will not be brought by the calls of God, to see their folly, and know what is for their good. O that the people of England 'knew, at least in this their day, the things that belong unto their peace, before they are hid from their eyes.' O foolish and miserable souls! Who hath bewitched your minds into such madness, and your hearts into such deadness, that you should be such mortal enemies to yourselves, and go on so obstinately towards damnation, that neither the word of God, nor the persuasions of men, can change your minds, or hold your hands, or stop you till you are past remedy! Well, sinner! This life will not last always; this patience will not wait upon you still. Do not think that you shall abuse your maker and redeemer, serve his enemies, debase your souls, trouble the world, wrong the church, reproach the godly, grieve your teachers, hinder reformation, and all this upon free cost. You know not yet what this must cost you, but you must shortly know, when the righteous God shall take you in hand, who will handle you in another manner than the sharpest magistrates, or the plainest dealing pastors did, unless you prevent the everlasting torments by a sound conversion, and a speedy obeying the call of God. 'He that hath an ear to hear, let him hear,' while mercy hath a voice to call.

One common objection, which I have after touched, but with too much brevity, I find adheres close to the hearts of many ungodly men. They think that God doth not so much care what men think, or say or do, as we persuade them; and therefore they care so little themselves. For the convincing of such atheistical men as these, I shall propound the following questions:—

1. Dost thou think God cares whether thou be a man or not? If not, who made thee, and preserved thee? If he do, then surely he cares whether thou behave thyself as a man. No man is so foolish as to make any instrument, build an house, or a ship, and not care, when he hath done, whether it be good for the use he made it. Do not, for shame then, impute such folly to the God of wisdom, as if he made so noble a creature as man, and endowed him with such noble faculties, all for nothing, caring not what becomes of him when he hath done. Why should God give thee a mind that can know him, and a heart that can love him, when he cares not whether thou know him, love him, or not? Do you not see, that in the course of nature every thing is fitted to its use? The beasts know not God, nor are capable of loving him, because they were made for no such use; but thy capacity shows that thou wast made for God, and for a life to come.

2. Dost thou think that God is every where present, infinite, and all-sufficient? If not, thou dost not believe that he is God, and it is unreasonable to imagine that God hath made a world that is greater, and more extensive or comprehensive than himself! For none can communicate more than he hath. But if thou art forced to confess that God is every where, and as sufficient for every single man, as if he had never another creature to regard, thou must needs confess then that he is not careless of the hearts and ways of the sons of men: for they are things that are still before his eyes. Base and blasphemous thoughts of God, as if he were limited, absent or insufficient, are what make men think him so regardless of their hearts and ways.

3. Dost thou think that God cares what becomes of thy body,—whether thou be sick or well; whether thou live or die? If not, then how camest thou by thy life, health, and mercies? If they came from any other fountain, tell us from whence: is it not to God that thou prayest for thy life and health? Darest thou say to him I will not depend upon thee? I

will not be beholding to thee for the life and mercies of another day? If so, then thou art a blind atheist. But if thou thinkest he cares for thy body, canst thou think he cares not more for thy soul? If he must regard to furnish thee with mercies, he will surely have a regard whether thou love and live to him that gave them.

4. Dost thou believe that God is the governor of the world, or not? If not, then there can be no rightful government; for as no magistrate can have a power, but from the sovereign, so no sovereign can have power but from God, nor be a lawful governor, but under him: and then all the world would be turned into confusion. But if thou must needs confess that God is the governor of the world, what an unwise, unrighteous governor wouldst thou make him, if thou thinkest that he regards not the hearts and ways of those whom he doth govern? This still is but to deny him to be God.

5. If God do not care so much what is in our hearts, or what we do, why then should he make a law for our hearts, words, and ways? Would he command us that which he doth not care for? Would he so strictly forbid sin, if he were indifferent whither we sin or not? Would he promise eternal life to the holy and obedient, if he cared not whether we be holy and obedient, or not? Would he threaten hell to all that are ungodly, if he cared not whether we are godly or not? Darest thou say, that the almighty, holy God designs to rule the world by a lie, and to deceive men into obedience? Yea, the very law of nature itself doth contain not only precepts of our duty, but the hopes and fears of the life to come, without which the world could not be governed; and certainly they are no deceits by which an infinite wisdom, power, and goodness, governs the world.

6. If God did not much regard our hearts and lives, why doth he make all the world to be our servants? Doth he give us the sun, the moon, the stars, the earth, and all the creatures, to attend us and serve us with their lives and virtues, and yet doth he not care for our hearts or service? this is as foolish as to say, that he hath made all the world in vain, and cares not for it, now he hath made it.

7. If he cared not for the frame of our hearts and lives, he would not have sent his Son to redeem us, and to cleanse us from iniquity, and sanctify us a 'peculiar people to himself.' Surely the price that was paid for sinners, and the wonderful design of God in our redemption, shows that he makes not light of sin, and that he is wonderfully in love with holiness.

8. If God doth not regard our hearts and lives, he would not have made it the office of his ministers to call us daily to repentance and an holy life; nor commanded them to make such a stir with sinners to win them unto God; he would not have appointed all his ordinances, public and private, also to this end. Doth God command all this ado for a thing he regards not?

9. Nor would he punish the world with hell hereafter, or so many dreadful judgments here, as thousands feel, if he cared not what they think or do. Methinks, men that are so often groaning under his rod, should feel that he looks after their hearts and ways.

10. And how can the Holy Ghost be our sanctifier, if God be so indifferent, whether we be clean or unclean? Dare you think that the Holy Ghost doth take upon him a needless work?

11. Methinks you might perceive, even in the malice of the tempter, that God is holy, and hateth iniquity; and his word is true, that tells us of the eternal punishment of sin. The scripture tells us of the angels' fall, and that many of them are become devils by their sin, and are malicious enemies of man's salvation. And do you not easily perceive it to be true? How came they else to be such importunate tempters of men, which we feel, alas, by too much experience? Or if this evidence be not palpable enough to convince the infidel, how come they to make so many bargains with deceivers, to draw them from God and salvation, as they have done?

12. Lastly, if yet you think that God, the sovereign ruler of the world, who is every where present, and preserves all, cares so little what men are, or what they do, whether they are holy or unholy, obedient or disobedient to his laws, then methinks that you yourselves, and all the rest of your fellow-creatures, should little care.

Two other questions therefore I must propound to you.

First, do not you care what men say of you, or do to you? Are you contented that men slander you, or abuse you, or set your houses or towns on fire, or destroy your cattle, or wives, or children, and imprison, wound, or kill yourselves? If you will make a great matter what men say or do against you, can you be so mad, (for it is no better) as to think that the omnipotent, holy God, should little regard what is said, or done against himself, and against his servants, and that by such silly worms as men, who are his workmanship? Did not selfishness make you blind

and partial, you would know that one sin against God deserves more punishment than ten thousand thousand times as much against such silly things as you. Do you make no matter of difference between a bad servant and a good one: an obedient and a disobedient child; a son that will lay down his life for you, and a son that longs for your death, that he may have your land; between a faithful friend, and a deadly enemy? If you do not, you are not men, but something else in human shape. If you do, then you are somewhat worse than men, if yet you would have the blessed God to make no great difference between those that love him above all the world, and those that regard him not; between the holy and unholy soul.

Second, I would ask you, whether you would have the rulers of the world to take care what men say or do, or would you not? If not, then you would have all the world turned loose, and you would have every man that is poorer than you, have leave to rob you: and every man that hates you, have leave to beat, or kill you; and every man that likes your house, or lands, or goods, or cattle, to have leave to take them from you; and every man defile your wives or daughters, that hath a mind to it? And so we should see whither it is that infidelity leads men. But if you like not this, then you are most unreasonable, if you would have magistrates to be regardful of men's actions, and not God. If magistrates must hang men for wronging you, and the eternal majesty must not punish them for wronging him, and breaking his laws, which is infinitely a great matter. As if you would have a constable punish men, and the king or judge to have no regard of it. For kings are under God, as constables are under kings, and a thousand-fold lower.

The truth is, wicked men are fallen so far from God to themselves, that they are as gods to themselves in their own esteem, and besides themselves they know no God; and therefore any wrong that is done against them, or any good that is done for them, they would have regarded: but the wrong and disobedience that is against God they would have nothing made of it. And they have such narrow, blasphemous thoughts of God, as if he were a finite creature like themselves, that can be but in one place at once, that makes them so blaspheme his providence, and think he minds no good or evil, and will not regard the godly, or punish the ungodly, but were like the idols of the heathen, that have eyes and see not, ears and hear not, and hands without an executive power. But when the memorial book of God is opened, which is written for them that fear the Lord, and think upon his name ; and when the Lord shall say of them, ' These are mine,' as he is making up his jewels, and spares them, as a man spares his son that serves him, then shall these infidels return to their senses and the righteous shall return from their fears and sufferings, and shall discern between the righteous and the wicked, between those that serve God, and those that serve him not.

Another objection I find most common in the mouths of the ungodly, especially of late years: they say, We can do nothing without God ; we cannot have grace, if God will not give it us ; and if he will, we shall quickly turn ; if he have not predestinated us, and will not turn us, how can we turn ourselves, or be saved. It is not in him that wills, or in him that runs : and thus they think they are excused.

I have answered this formerly, and in this book ; but now let me now say this much. 1. Though you cannot cure yourselves, you can hurt and poison yourselves ; it is God that must sanctify your hearts ; but who corrupted them? Will you wilfully take poison, because you cannot cure yourselves ? Methinks you should the more forbear it : you should the more take heed of sinning, if you cannot mend what sin doth mar. 2. Though you cannot be converted without the special grace of God, yet you must know that God gives his grace in the use of his holy means which he hath appointed to that end ; and common grace may enable you to forbear your gross sinning, as to the outward act, and to use those means. Can you truly say, that you do as much as you are able to do ? Are you not able to go by an ale-house door, or to shut your mouths and keep out the drink? Or to forbear the company that hardens you to sin? Are you not able to go to hear the word, and think of what you heard when you come home? And to consider with yourselves of your own condition, and of everlasting things? Are you not able to read good books from day to day, at least on the Lord's day, and to converse with those that fear the Lord ? You cannot say that you have done what you are able. 3. Therefore you must know that you can forfeit the grace and help of God, by your wilful sinning or negligence, though you cannot, without grace, turn to God. If you will not do what you can, it is just with God to deny you that grace by which you might do more. 4. And for God's decrees, you must know that they separate not the end and means, but bind them together. God never

decreed to save any but the sanctified, nor to damn any but the unsanctified. God doth as truly decree from everlasting, whether your land this year shall be barren, or fruitful, and just how long you shall live in the world, as he hath decreed whether you shall be saved or not. And yet you would think that man but a fool, that would forbear ploughing and sowing and say, If God have decreed that my ground shall bear corn, it will bear whether I plough and sow or not. If God have decreed that I shall live, I shall live whether I eat or not; but if he have not, it is not eating will keep me alive. Do you know how to answer such a man, or do you not? If you do, then you know how to answer yourselves : for the case is alike : God's decree is as peremptory about your bodies as your souls ; if you do not then try first these conclusions upon your bodies, before you venture to try them on your souls : see first whether God will keep you alive without food or raiment, and whether he will give you corn without tillage and labour, and whether he will bring you to your journey's end without your travel or carriage : and if you speed well in this, then try whether he will bring you to heaven without your diligent use of means and sit down and say, We cannot sanctify ourselves.

And for the point of free will, which you harp so long upon ; divines are not so much disagreed about it as you imagine. Augustin as well as Pelagius, Calvin as well as Arminius, the Dominicans as well as the Jesuits, all generally maintain, that man hath free-will ; the Orthodox say, that free-will is corrupted and disposed to evil. Epiphanius condemned Origen for saying, that man had lost the image of God, and makes it a point of heresy. And yet one may truly say, that man hath lost God's image ; and another may truly say, that he hath not lost it. For there is a two-fold image of God on man : the one is natural, and that is our reason and free-will, and this is not lost, the other is qualitative and ethical, and this is our holiness, and this is lost, and by grace restored. No man of judgment denies that a man hath a will that is naturally free ; it is free from violence, and it is a self-determining principle ; but it is not free from evil dispositions. It is habitually averse to God and holiness, and inclined to earthly, fleshly things. It is enslaved by a sinful bias. This no man, methinks, that is a Christian, should deny ; and of the aged, I see not how an infidel can deny it. Alas, we easily confess to you, that you have not the spiritual, moral free-will, which is but your right inclinations. I had no need to write such books as these, to persuade you to be willing in a case on which your own salvation lies. To the grief of our souls, we perceive after all our preachings and persuasions, that the ungodly have not this spiritual free-will. But this is nothing but your willingness itself, and inclination to be willing; and therefore the want of it is so far from excusing you, that the more you want it, that is, the more you are wilful in sin, the worse you are, and the sorer will be your punishment. Our preachings and persuasions, your hearing and considering, are the appointed means to get this moral power of freedom, that is, to make you truly willing.

I have but three requests to you, and I have done. First, That you will seriously read over this small treatise; and if you have such that need it in your families, that you read it over and over to them: if those that fear God, would go now and then to their ignorant neighbours, and read this or some other book to them of this subject, they might be a means of winning souls. If we cannot entreat so small a labour of men for their own salvation, as to read such short instructions as these, they greatly abuse themselves, and will most justly perish. Secondly, When you have read over this book, I would entreat you to go alone, and ponder a little what you have read, and bethink you, as in the sight of God, whether it be not true, and do not nearly touch your souls, and whether it be not time for you to consider your ways: and also intreat that you will fall upon your knees and beseech the Lord that he will open your eyes to understand the truth, and turn your hearts to the love of God, and beg of him all that saving grace, that you have so long neglected, and follow it on from day to day, till your hearts be changed. And withal, that you will go to your pastors that are set over you, to take care of the health and safety of your souls, as physicians do for the health of your bodies, and desire them to direct you what course to take, and acquaint them with your spiritual estate, that you may have the benefit of their advice and ministerial help. Or if you have not a faithful pastor at home, make use of some other in so great a need. Thirdly, When by reading, consideration, prayer and ministerial advice, you are once acquainted with your sin and misery, with your duty and remedy, delay not, but presently forsake your sinful company and courses, turn unto God, obeying his call, and as you love your souls, take heed that you go not on against so loud a call of God, and against your own knowledge and conscience, lest it go worse with you in the day of judgment than with Sodom and Gomorrah.

Inquire of God, as a man that is willing to know the truth, and not be a wilful deceiver of your own soul. Search the holy scriptures daily, and see whether these things be so or not: try impartially whether it be safer to trust heaven or earth; and whether it be better to follow God or man, the Spirit or the flesh; and better to live in holiness or sin. Whether an unsanctified state be safe for you to abide in one day longer; and when you have found out which is best, resolve accordingly, and make your choice without any more ado. If you will be true to your own souls, and do not love everlasting torments, I beseech you, as from the Lord, that you will but take this reasonable advice. O what happy towns and countries, and what a happy nation might we have, if we could but persuade our neighbours to agree to such a necessary motion! What joyful men would all faithful ministers be, if they could but see their people truly heavenly and holy! This would be the unity, the peace, the safety, the glory of our churches, the happiness of our neighbours, and the comfort of our souls. Then how comfortably should we preach pardon and peace to you, and deliver the sacraments, which are the seals of peace, to you! With what love and joy might we live among you! At your death bed, how boldly might we comfort and encourage your departing souls! At your burial, how comfortably might we leave you in the grave, in expectation to meet your souls in heaven, and to see your bodies raised to that glory.

But if still the most of you will go on in a careless, ignorant, fleshly, worldly, or unholy life; and all our desires and labours cannot so far prevail, as to keep you from the wilful damning of yourselves, we must then imitate our Lord, who delights himself in those few that are his jewels, and the little flock that shall receive the kingdom, when the most shall reap the misery which they sowed. In nature excellent things are few. The world hath not many suns nor moons; it is but a little of the earth that is gold or silver; princes and nobles are but a small part of the sons of men. And it is no great number that are learned, judicious or wise, in this world. And therefore if the gate being strait, and the way narrow, there be but few that find salvation; yet God will have his glory and pleasure in those few. And when Christ ' shall come with his mighty angels in flaming fire, taking vengeance on them that know not God, and obey not the gospel of our Lord Jesus Christ, his coming will be glorified in his saints, and admired in all true believers.'

For the rest, as God the Father vouchsafed to create them, and God the Son disdained not to bear the penalty of their sins upon the cross: and did not judge such sufferings vain, though he knew that by refusing the sanctification of the Holy Ghost, they would finally destroy themselves, so we that are his ministers, though these be not gathered, judge not our labour wholly lost.

Reader, I have done with thee, (when thou hast perused this book;) but sin hath not yet done with thee, even those that thou thoughtest had been forgotten long ago; and Satan hath not yet done with thee though now he be out of sight; and God hath not yet done with thee, because thou wilt not be persuaded to have done with deadly reigning sin. I have written thee this persuasive discourse, as one that is going into another world, where the things are seen that I here speak of, and as one that knows thou must shortly be there thyself. As ever thou wouldest meet me with comfort before the Lord that made us: as ever thou wilt escape the everlasting plagues prepared for the final neglecters of salvation, and for all that are not sanctified by the Holy Ghost, and love not the communion of the saints, as members of the holy catholic church; and as ever thou hopest to see the face of Christ the judge, and of the majesty of the Father, with peace and comfort, to be received into glory, when thou art turned naked out of this world: I beseech thee, I charge thee to hear, and obey the call of God, and resolutely to turn, that thou mayest live. But if thou wilt not, even when thou hast no true reason for it, but because thou wilt not; I summon thee, answer for it before the Lord, and require thee there to bear me witness I gave thee warning, and that thou wert not condemned for want of a ' call to turn and live,' but because thou wouldst not believe it, and obey it; which also must be the testimony of thy serious monitor,

RICHARD BAXTER.

" *Say unto them, As I live, saith the Lord God, I have no pleasure in the death of the wicked, but that the wicked turn from his way, and live: turn ye, turn ye, from your evil ways; for why will ye die, O house of Israel."*— EZEK. xxxiii. 11.

It hath been the astonishing wonder of many a man, as well as me, to read in the holy scriptures how few will be saved, and that the greatest part even of those that are called, will be for ever shut out of the kingdom of heaven, and tormented with the devils in eternal fire. Infidels believe not this when they read it, and therefore must feel it. Those that do believe it, are forced to cry out with Paul, ' O the depth of the riches both of the wisdom and knowledge of God! How unsearchable are his judgments, and his ways past finding out! But nature itself doth teach us all, to lay the blame of evil works upon the doers, and therefore when we see any heinous thing done, a principle of justice doth provoke us to inquire after him that did it, that the evil of the work may return the evil of shame upon the author. If we saw a man killed and cut in pieces by the way, we should presently ask, O! who did this cruel deed? If the town were wilfully set on fire, you would ask, What wicked wretch did this? So when we read that the most will be firebrands of hell for ever, we must needs think with ourselves, How comes this to pass, and to whom is it owing; who is it that is so cruel as to be the cause of such a thing as this? And we can meet with few that will own the guilt. It is indeed confessed by all, that Satan is the cause, but that doth not resolve the doubt, because he is not the principal cause. He doth not force men to sin, but tempt them to it, and leaves it to their own wills, whether they will do it or not. He doth not carry men to an ale-house, and force open their mouths, and pour in the drink; nor doth he hold them that they cannot go to God's service, nor doth he force their hearts from holy thoughts. It lies therefore between God himself and the sinner, one of them must needs be the principal cause of all this misery, which ever it is; for there is no other to cast it upon. God disclaims it: he will not take it upon him. The wicked disclaim it usually, and they will not take it upon them, and this is the controversy that is here managed in the text.

The Lord complains of the people, and the people think the fault is with God. They plainly say, ' that the way of the Lord is not equal.' And God saith, ' it is their ways that are not equal.' So here they say, ' if our transgressions and our sins be upon us, and we pine away in them, how shall we then live?' As if they should say, if we must die and be miserable, how can we help it? As if it were not owing to them, but to God. But God, in my text, doth clear himself of it, and tells them how they may help it if they will, and persuades them to use the means; and if they will not be persuaded, he lets them know that it is of themselves; and if this will not satisfy them he will not therefore forbear to punish them. It is he that will be the judge, and he will judge them according to their ways, they are no judges of him, or of themselves, as wanting authority, wisdom and impartiality ; nor is it their caviling and quarreling with God, that shall serve their turn, or save them from the execution of justice against which they murmur.

The words of this verse contain, 1. God's purgation of clearing himself from the blame of their destruction. This he doth, *not* by disowning his *law*, that the wicked shall die, nor by disowning his *judgments* and execution according to that law, or giving them any hope that the law shall not be executed ; but by profession, that it is not their death that he takes pleasure in, but their returning rather, that they may live : and this he confirms to them by his oath. 2. An express exhortation to the wicked to return ; wherein God doth not only command, but persuade and condescend also to reason the case with them, Why will they die ? The direct end of this exhortation is, That they may turn and live. The secondary, or reserved ends, upon supposition that this is not attained, are these two : First, To convince them by the means which he used, that it is not the will of God, if they be miserable. Secondly, To convince them, from their manifest wilfulness, in rejecting all his commands and persuasions, that it is of themselves ; and they die even because they will die.

The substance of the text doth lie in these observations following :

DOCT. I. It is the unchangeable law of God, that wicked men must turn, or die.

DOCT. II. It is the promise of God, that the wicked shall live, if they will but turn.

DOCT. III. God takes pleasure in men's conversion and salvation, but not in their death or damnation : he had rather they would return and live, than go on and die.

DOCT. IV. This is a most certain truth, which because God would not have men to question, he hath confirmed it to them solemnly by his oath.

DOCT. V. The Lord redoubles his commands and persuasions to the wicked to turn.

DOCT. VI. The Lord condescends to reason the case with them, and asks the wicked why they will die.

DOCT. VII. If after all this, the wicked will not return, it is not the will of God that they perish, but of themselves : their own wilfulness is the cause of their damnation ; they therefore die because they will die. Having laid the text open before you, in these plain propositions,

I shall next speak somewhat of each of them in order, though very briefly.

DOCT. I. It is the unchangeable law of God, that wicked men must turn or die.

If you will believe God, believe this ; there is but one of these two ways for every wicked man, either *conversion* or *damnation*. I know the wicked will hardly be persuaded either of the truth or equity of this. No wonder if the guilty quarrel with the law. Few men are apt to believe that which they would not have to be true ; and fewer would have that to be true, which they apprehend to be against them. But it is not quarreling with the law, or with the judge, that will save the malefactor : believing and regarding the law might have prevented his death ; but denying and accusing it, will but hasten it. If it were not so, an hundred would bring their reasons against the law, for one that would bring his reason to the law : and men would rather choose to give their reasons why they should not be punished, than to hear the commands and reasons of their governors, which require them to obey. The law was not made for you to judge, but that you might be ruled and judged by it. But if there be any so blind, as to venture to question either the truth or justice of the law of God, I shall briefly give you that evidence of both, which, methinks, would satisfy a reasonable man. And first, if you doubt whether this be the word of God or not, besides a hundred other texts, you may be satisfied by these few. 'Verily I say unto you, Except ye be converted, and become as little children, ye cannot enter into the kingdom of heaven.— Verily, verily, I say unto thee, except a man be born again, he cannot see the kingdom of God. —If a man be in Christ, he is a new creature : old things are passed away, behold all things are become new.—Ye have put off the old man with his deeds, and have put on the new man, which is renewed in knowledge, after the image of him that created him.—Without holiness none shall see God.—So then, they that are in the flesh cannot please God. Now if any man have not the Spirit of Christ, he is none of his.—For in Christ Jesus neither circumcision availeth any thing, nor uncircumcision, but a new creature. —According to his abundant grace, he hath begotten us again to a lively hope.—Being born again, not of corruptible seed, but of incorruptible, by the word of God, which liveth and abideth for ever.—Wherefore, laying aside all malice and all guile, and hypocrisies, and envies, and evil-speakings, as new-born babes, desire the sincere milk of the word, that ye may grow thereby.—

The wicked shall be turned into hell; and all the nations that forget God.—And the Lord loveth the righteous, but the wicked his soul hateth.'

As I need not stay to open these texts which are so plain, so I think I need not add any more of that multitude which speak the like: if thou be a man that dost believe the word of God, here is already enough to satisfy thee that the wicked must be converted or condemned. You are already brought so far, that you must either confess that this is true, or say plainly, you will not believe the word of God. If once you are come to that pass, there is but small hopes of you: look to yourselves as well as you can; for it is likely you will not be long out of hell. You would be ready to fly in the face of him that should give you the lie: and yet dare you give the lie to God? But if you tell God plainly you will not believe him, blame him not if he never warn you more, or if he forsake you, and give you up as hopeless: for, to what purpose should he warn you, if you would not believe him, should he send an angel from heaven to you; it seems you would not believe, for an angel can speak but the word of God, but if an angel should bring you any other gospel, you are not to receive it, but to hold him accursed; surely there is no angel to be believed before the Son of God, who came from the Father to bring us this doctrine. If he is not to be believed, then all the angels in heaven are not to be believed. If you stand on these terms with God, I shall leave you till he deal with you in a more convincing way. God hath a voice that will make you hear; though he intreat you to hear the voice of his gospel, he will make you hear the voice of his condemning sentence, without intreaty. We cannot make you believe against your wills, but God will make you feel against your wills. But let us hear what reason you have, why you will not believe this word of God, which tells us that the wicked must be converted or condemned. I know your reason; it is because that you judge it unlikely that God should be so unmerciful; you think it cruelty to damn men everlastingly for so small a thing as a sinful life. And this leads us to the second thing, which is to justify the equity of God in his laws and judgment.

First, I think you will not deny, but that it is most suitable to an immortal soul to be ruled by laws that promise an immortal reward, and threaten an endless punishment. Otherwise, the law should not be suited to the nature of the subject; who will not be fully ruled by any lower means than the hopes or fears of everlasting things: as it is in case of temporal punishment. If a law were now made that the most heinous crimes should be punished with a hundred years' captivity, this might be of some efficacy, as being equal to our lives. But if there had been no other penalties before the flood, when men lived eight or nine hundred years, it would not have been sufficient, because men would know that they might have so many hundred years' impunity afterwards. So it is in our present case.

Second, I suppose you will confess, that the promise of an endless and unconceivable glory is not unsuitable to the wisdom of God, or the case of man: and why then should you not think so of the threatening of an endless and unspeakable misery?

Third, When you find it in the word of God that so it is, and so it will be, do you think yourselves fit to contradict this word? Will you call your Maker to the bar, and examine his word upon the accusation of falsehood? Will you sit upon him and judge him by the law of your conceits? Are you wiser and better, and more righteous than he? Must the God of heaven come to school to you to learn wisdom; must infinite wisdom learn of folly; and infinite goodness be corrected by an erring sinner, that cannot keep himself an hour clean? Must the Almighty stand at the bar of a worm? O horrid arrogancy of senseless dust! Where were you, when the Almighty made the laws, that he did not call you to his council? Surely he made them before you were born, without desiring your advice, and you came into the world too late to reverse them: if you could have done so great a work, you should have stepped out of your nothingness, and have contradicted Christ when he was on earth, or Moses before him, or have saved Adam and his sinful progeny from the threatening death; that so there might have been no need of Christ. And what if God withdraw his patience and preservation, and let you drop into hell while you are quarreling with his words, will you then believe that there is an hell?

Fourth, If sin be such an evil that it required the death of Christ for its expiation, no wonder if it deserve our everlasting misery.

Fifth, If the sins of the devils deserved an endless torment, why not also the sins of man?

Sixth, You should perceive that it is not possible for the best of men, much less for the wicked, to be competent judges of the desert of sin. Alas, we are both blind and partial. You can never know fully the desert of sin till you fully know the evil of sin: and you can never fully know the evil of sin, till you fully know, 1. The excellency of the soul which it deforms. 2. And the excellency of holiness, which it obliterates. 3. The reason and the excellency of the law which it violates. 4. The excellency of the glory which it despises. 5. The excellency and office of reason which it treads down. 6. No, nor till you know the infinite excellency, almightiness, and holiness of that God, against whom it is committed. When you fully know all these, you shall fully know the desert of sin. Besides, you know that the offender is too partial to judge the law, or the proceedings of this judge. We judge by feeling, which blinds our reason. We see in common worldly things, that most men think the cause is right which is their own: and that all is wrong that is done against them: and let the most wise, or just, impartial friends, persuade them to the contrary, and it is all in vain. There are few children but think the father unmerciful, or deals hardly with them, if he whip them. There is scarcely the vilest transgressor, but thinks the church doth wrong him, if they excommunicate him; or scarcely a thief or murderer that is hanged, but would accuse the law, and judge it cruelty, if that would serve his turn.

Seventh, Can you think that an unholy soul is fit for heaven? Alas, they cannot love God here, nor do him any service which he can accept. They are contrary to God; they lothe that which he most loves; and love that which he abhors: they are incapable of that imperfect communion with him which his saints here partake of. How then can they live in that perfect love of him, and full delights and communion with him, which is the blessedness of heaven? You do not accuse yourselves of unmercifulness, if you make not your enemy your bosom counsellor; or if you take not an animal to bed and board with you: no, nor if you take away his life, though he never sinned: and yet will you blame the absolute Lord, the most wise and gracious sovereign of the world, if he condemn the unconverted man to perpetual misery.

Use, I beseech you now, all that love your souls, that instead of quarreling with God, and with his word, you will presently stoop to it, and use it for your good. All you that are yet unconverted in this assembly, take this as the undoubted truth of God, you must ere long be converted or condemned, there is no other way but turn or die. When God, that cannot lie, hath told you this, when you hear from the maker and judge of the world, it is time for him that hath ears to hear; by this time you may see what you have to trust to. You are but dead and damned men, except you will be converted. Should I tell you otherwise I should deceive you with a lie. Should I hide this from you I should undo you, and be guilty of your blood, as the verses before my text assure me, 'When I say to the wicked man, O wicked man, thou shalt surely die; if thou dost not speak to warn the wicked from his way, that wicked man shall die in his iniquity, but his blood will I require at thine hand.' You see then, though this be a rough, unwelcome doctrine, it is such as we must preach, and you must hear. It is easier to hear of hell than feel it. If your necessities did not require it, we should not grate your tender ears with truths that seem so harsh and grievous. Hell would not be so full, if people were but willing to know their case, and to hear and think of it. The reason why so few escape it, is, because they strive not to enter in at the strait gate of conversion, and to go the narrow way of holiness while they have time, and they strive not, because they are not awakened to a lively feeling of the danger they are in: and they are not awakened, because they are loth to hear or think of it; and that is partly, through foolish tenderness and carnal self-love; and partly, because they do not well believe the word that threatens it. If you will not thoroughly believe this truth, methinks the weight of it should force you to remember it, and it should follow you and give you no rest till you are converted. If you had but once heard this word, by the voice of an angel, Thou must be converted or condemned: turn or die! would it not sink into your mind, and haunt you night and day? So that in your sinning you would remember it, as if the voice were still in your ears, Turn or die! O happy were your souls, if it might thus work with you, and never be forgotten, or let you alone till it hath driven home your hearts to God. But if you will cast it out by forgetfulness, or unbelief, how can it work to your conversion and salvation? But take this with you, to your sorrow, though you may put this out of your minds, you cannot put it out of the bible; but there it will stand as a sealed truth, which you shall experimentally know for ever, that there is no other way but turn or die.

O what is the matter then that the hearts of sinners are not pierced with such a weighty truth! A man would think now that every unconverted soul that hears these words should be pricked to the heart, and think with themselves, This is my own case, and never be quiet till they found themselves converted. Believe it, this drowsy careless temper will not last long. Conversion and condemnation, are both of them awakening things: and one of them will make you feel ere long, I can foretell it as truly, as if I saw it with my eyes, that either grace or hell, will shortly bring these matters to the quick, and make you say, ' What have I done; what foolish wicked courses have I taken?' The scornful and the stupid state of sinners will last but a little while. As soon as they either turn or die, the presumptuous dream will be at an end, and then their wits and feeling will return.

But I foresee there are two things that are like to harden the unconverted, and make me lose all my labour, except they can be taken out of the way: and that is, the misunderstanding of those two words *the wicked* and *turn.* Some will think with themselves, It is true, the wicked must turn or die: but what is that to me? I am not wicked, though I am a sinner, as all men are. Others will think, It is true that we must turn from our evil ways; but I am turned long ago, I hope this is not now to do. Thus, while wicked men think they are not wicked, but are already converted, we lose all our labour in persuading them to turn. I shall therefore, before I go any further, tell you here who are meant by the wicked, and who they are that must turn or die, and also what is meant by turning; and who they are that are truly converted; this I have purposely reserved for this place, preferring the method that fits my end.

And here you may observe, that in the sense of the text, a wicked man and a converted man are contraries. No man is a wicked man that is converted, and no man is a converted man that is wicked: so that to be a *wicked man* and to be *an unconverted man*, is *all one.* And therefore in opening one, we shall open both.

Before I can tell you what either wickedness or conversion is, I must go to the bottom, and fetch up the matter from the beginning.

It pleased the great Creator of the world, to make three sorts of living creatures; angels he made pure spirits, without flesh, and therefore he made them only for heaven and not to dwell on earth. Beasts were made flesh, without immortal souls; and therefore they were made only for earth, and not for heaven. Man is of a middle nature, between both, as partaking of both flesh and spirit: therefore he was made both for heaven and earth. But as his flesh is made to be but a servant to his spirit, so is he made for earth; but as his passage, or way to heaven, and not that this should be his home or happiness. The blessed state that man was made for, was to behold the glorious majesty of the Lord, and to praise him among his holy angels, to love him, and be filled with his love for ever. As this was the end that man was made for, so God did give him means that were fitted to the attaining of it. These means were principally two. First, The right inclination and disposition of the mind of man. Secondly, The right ordering of his life and practice. For the first, God suited the disposition of man unto his end; giving him such knowledge of God, as was fit for his present state, and an heart disposed and inclined to God in holy love. But yet he did not fix or confirm him in this condition; but having made him a free agent, he left him in the hands of his own free will. For the second, God did that which belonged to him; that is, he gave man a perfect law requiring him to continue in the love of God, and perfectly to obey him. By the wilful breach of this law, man did not only forfeit his hopes of everlasting life, but also turned his heart from God, and fixed it on these lower fleshly things, and hereby did blot out the spiritual image of God from his soul. So that man did both fall short of the glory of God, which was his end, and put himself out of the way, by which he should have attained it; and this, both as to the frame of his heart, and of his life. The holy inclination and love of his soul to God, he lost; and instead of it, he contracted an inclination and love to the pleasing of his flesh, or carnal self, by earthly things! Growing strange to God, and acquainted with the creature: the course of his life was suited to the bent and inclination of his heart; he lived to his carnal self, and not to God: he sought the creature for the pleasing of his flesh, instead of seeking to please the Lord. With this nature or corrupt inclination, we are all now born into the world; for ' who can bring a clean thing out of an unclean?' As a lion hath a fierce and cruel nature before he doth devour, and as an adder hath a venomous nature before it stings, so in our very infancy we have those sinful natures or inclinations, before we think, or speak, or do amiss. Hence springs all the sin of our lives. Not only so, but when God hath of his mercy provided us a remedy, even the Lord Jesus Christ, to be the Saviour of our souls, and bring us back to God again, we naturally love our present state, and are loth to be brought out of it, and therefore are set against the means of our recovery: though custom hath taught us to thank Christ for his good will, yet carnal self persuades us to refuse his remedies, and to desire to be excused when we are commanded to take the medicines which he offers, and are called to forsake all, and follow him to God and glory.

I pray you, read over this leaf again, and mark it; for in these few words you have a true description of our natural state; and consequently of a wicked man. For every man that is in this state of corrupted nature, is a wicked man, and in a state of death.

By this also you are prepared to understand what it is to be converted, to which end you must further know, that the mercy of God, not willing that man should perish in his sin, provided a remedy, by causing his Son to take our nature, and being in one person God and man, to become a Mediator between God and man; and by dying for our sins on the cross, to ransom us from the curse of God and the power of the devil: he having thus redeemed us, the Father hath delivered us into his hands, as his own. Hereupon the Father and Mediator do make a new law and covenant for man. Not like the first, which gave life to none but the perfectly obedient, and condemned man for every sin: but Christ hath made a law of grace, * or a promise of pardon and everlasting life to all, that by true repentance, and by faith in Christ, are converted unto God. Like an act of oblivion, which is made by a prince, to a company of rebels, on condition they will lay down their arms, come in, and be loyal subjects for the time to come.

But because the Lord knows that the heart of man is grown so wicked that, for all this, men will not accept of the remedy if they be left to themselves; therefore the Holy Ghost hath undertaken it as his office, to inspire the apostles, and seal up the scripture by miracles and wonders, and to illuminate and convert the souls of the elect.

So that by this much you see, that as there are three persons in the Trinity, the Father, the Son, and the Holy Ghost; so each of these persons have their several works, which are eminently ascribed to them.

The Father's works were, to create us, to rule us as his rational creatures, by the law of nature, and judge us thereby: in mercy to provide us a Redeemer when we were lost; and to send his Son, and accept his ransom.

The works of the Son for us were these: to ransom and redeem us by his sufferings and righteousness, to give out the promise or law of grace, and rule and judge the world as their Redeemer, on terms of grace, and to make intercession for us, that the benefits of his death may be communicated, and to send the Holy Ghost, which the Father also doth by the Son.

The works of the Holy Ghost for us are these: to indite the holy scriptures, by inspiring and guiding the prophets and apostles; sealing the word, by his miraculous gifts and works: illuminating and exciting the ordinary ministers of the gospel; so enabling them, and helping them to publish that word, and by the same word illuminating and converting the souls of men. So that as you could not have been reasonable creatures, if the Father had not created you; not have had any access to God, if the Son had not redeemed you; so neither can you have a part in Christ, or be saved, except the Holy Ghost do sanctify you.

So that by this time you may see the several causes of this work. The Father sends the Son; the Son redeems us, and makes the promise of grace; the Holy Ghost indites and seals this gospel: the apostles are the secretaries of the Spirit, to write it: the preachers of the gospel to proclaim it, and persuade men to obey it; and the Holy Ghost doth make their preaching effectual, by opening the hearts of men to intertain it. All this is to repair the image of God upon the soul, and to set the heart upon God again, and take it off the creature, and carnal self, to which it is revolted, and so turn the current of this life into an heavenly course, which before was earthly; and all this by the entertainment of Christ by faith, who is the physician of the soul.

By this which I have said, you may see what it is to be wicked, and what it is to be unconverted. Which I think, will be yet plainer to you, if I describe them, as consisting of their several parts: thus a wicked man may be known by these three things:

First, He is one that places his chief happiness on earth; loves the creature more than God, and his fleshly prosperity above the heavenly felicity: he savours the things of the flesh, but neither discerns nor savours the things of the Spirit: though he will say, that heaven is better than earth, yet doth he not really so esteem it himself. If he might be sure of earth, he would let go heaven; and had rather stay here, than be removed thither. A life of perfect holiness, in the sight of God, and in his love, and praises for ever in heaven, doth not find such liking with his heart as a life of health, wealth, and honour here upon earth. Though he falsely profess that he loves God above all, yet indeed

---

* Our Author here does not mean what some call 'a remedial law, in which God accepts what they call 'man's sincerity in perfect obedience. Baxter 'had not so learned Christ.

he never felt the power of divine love within him, but his mind is more set on the world, or fleshly pleasures, than on God. In a word, whoever loves earth above heaven, and fleshly prosperity more than God, is a wicked, unconverted man.

On the other side, a converted man is illuminated to discern the loveliness of God ; and so far believes the glory that is to be had with God, that his heart is taken up to it, and set more upon it than on any thing in this world. He had rather see the face of God, and live in his everlasting love and praises, than have all the wealth or pleasure of the world. He sees that all things else are vanity, and nothing but God can fill the soul : and therefore let the world go which way it will, he lays up his treasures and hopes in heaven ; and for that he is resolved to let go all. As the fire doth mount upward, and the needle that is touched with the load-stone, still turns to the north, so the converted soul is inclined unto God. Nothing else can satisfy him : nor can he find any content and rest but in his love. In a word, all that are converted esteem and love God better than all the world, and the heavenly felicity is dearer to them than their fleshly prosperity. The proof of what I have said, you may find in many places of scripture.

Secondly. A wicked man is one that makes it the principal business of his life to prosper in the world, and attain his fleshly ends. And though he may read and hear, do much in the outward duties of religion, and forbear disgraceful sins ; yet this is all but mere form, and he never makes it the principal business of his life to please God, and attain everlasting glory, but puts off God with the dregs of the world, and gives him no more service than the flesh can spare ; for he will not part with all for heaven.

On the contrary, a converted man is one that makes it the principal care and business of his life to please God, and to be saved; takes all the blessings of this life but as accommodations in his journey towards another life, and uses the creature in subordination unto God ; he loves an holy life, and longs to be more holy; he hath no sin but what he hates, longs, prays, and strives to be rid of. The bent of his life is for God : and if he sin, it is contrary to the very bent of his heart and life, and therefore he rises again, and laments it, and dare not wilfully live in any known sin. There is nothing in this world so dear to him but he can give it up to God, and forsake it for him and the hopes of glory.

Thirdly, The soul of a wicked man did never truly discern and relish the mystery of redemption, nor thankfully entertain an offered Saviour, nor is he taken up with the love of the Redeemer, nor willing to be ruled by him as the physician of his soul, that he may be saved from the guilt and power of his sins, and recovered unto God ; but his heart is insensible of this unspeakable benefit, and is quite against the healing means by which he should be recovered. Though he may be willing to be carnally religious, yet he never resigned up his soul to Christ, and to the motions and conduct of his word and Spirit.

On the contrary, the converted soul having felt himself undone by sin ; perceiving that he hath lost his peace with God, hopes of heaven, and is in danger of everlasting misery, doth thankfully entertain the tidings of redemption, and believing in the Lord Jesus as his only Saviour, resigns up himself to him for wisdom, righteousness, sanctification, and redemption. He takes Christ as the life of his soul, lives by him, and uses him as a salve for every sore, admiring the wisdom and love of God in his wonderful work of man's redemption. In a word, Christ doth even dwell in his heart by the faith, and the life that he 'now liveth is by faith of the Son of God, that hath loved him, and gave himself for him.' Yea, it is not so much he that lives, as Christ in him.

You see now, in plain terms, from the word of God, who are the wicked and who are the converted. Ignorant people think, that if a man be no swearer, curser, railer, drunkard, fornicator, extortioner, nor wrong any body in their dealings, and if they come to church, and say their prayers, these cannot be wicked men. Or if a man that hath been guilty of drunkenness, swearing, gaming, or the like vices, do but forbear them for the time to come, they think that this is a converted man. Others think, if a man that hath been an enemy, and a scorner of godliness, do but approve it, join himself with those that are godly, and be hated for it by the wicked, as the godly are, that this needs must be a converted man. Some are so foolish as to think they are converted, by taking up some new and false opinion. Some think, if they have but been affrighted by the fears of hell, and had convictions of conscience, and thereupon have purposed, promised amendment, taken up a life of civil behaviour, and outward religion, that this must needs be true conversion. These are the poor deluded souls that are like to lose the benefit of all our persuasions. When they hear that the wicked must turn or die, they think that this is not spoken of them; for they are not wicked, but are turned already. Therefore it is, that Christ told some of the rulers of the Jews, who were more grave and civil than the common people, that 'publicans and harlots do go into the kingdom of God before them.' Not that an harlot or gross sinner can be saved without conversion, but because it was easier to make those gross sinners perceive their sin and misery, and the necessity of a change, when the more civil sort do delude themselves by thinking that they are converted already when they be not.

Conversion is another kind of work than most are aware of. It is not a small matter to bring an earthly mind to heaven, and to show man the amiable excellencies of God, till he be taken up in such love to him, that can never be quenched, to break the heart for sin, and make him fly for refuge unto Christ, and thankfully embrace him as the life of his soul; to have the very drift and bent of the heart and life to be changed; so that a man renounces that which he took for his felicity, places his felicity where he never did before, lives not to the same end, and drives not on the same design in the world as formerly he did: in a word, he that is in Christ, is 'a new creature: old things are passed away, behold all things are become new.' He hath a new understanding, a new will and resolution, new sorrows, desires, love and delight; new thoughts, new speeches, new company, if possible, and a new conversation. Sin, that before was a jesting matter with him, is now so odious and terrible to him, that he flies from it as from death. The world that was so lovely in his eyes, doth now appear but as vanity and vexation; God, that was before neglected, is now the only happiness of his soul; before he was forgotten and every lust preferred before him, but now he is set next the heart, and all things must give place to him; the heart is taken up in the attendance and observance of him, is grieved when he hides his face, and never thinks itself well without him. Christ himself, that was wont to be slightly thought of, is now his only hope and refuge, he lives upon him, as on his daily bread, he cannot pray without him, nor rejoice without him, nor think, nor speak, nor live without him. Heaven itself, that before was looked upon but as a tolerable reserve, which he hoped might serve better than hell, when he could not stay any longer in the world, is now taken for his home, the place of his only hope and rest, where he shall see, love, and praise that God which hath his heart already. Hell, that did seem before but as a bugbear to frighten men from sin, doth now appear to be a real misery, that is not to be ventured on or jested with. The works of holiness, which before he was weary of, and seemed to be more ado than needs, are now both his recreation, his business, and the trade he lives upon.

The Bible, which was before to him but almost as a common book, is now as the law of God, as a letter written to him from heaven, and subscribed with the name of the eternal majesty; it is the rule of his thoughts, words, and deeds; the commands are binding, the threats are dreadful, and the promises of it speak life to the soul. The godly, that seemed to him but like other men, are now the most excellent and happiest on earth. The wicked, that were his play-fellows, are now his grief; and he that could laugh at their sins is readier now to weep for their sin and misery. In short, he hath a new end in his thoughts, and a new way in his endeavours, and therefore his heart and life are new. Before, his carnal self was his end? His pleasure and worldly profits and credits were his way: now God and everlasting glory is his end; Christ, the Spirit, word, and ordinances, holiness to God righteousness and mercy to men, these are his way. Before, self was the chief ruler, to which the matters of God and conscience must stoop and give place; and now God, in Christ, by the Spirit, word and ministry, is the chief ruler, to whom both self, and all the matters of self, must give place: so that this is not a change in one, or two, or twenty points: but in the whole soul; and the very end, and bent of the conversation. A man may step out of one path into another, and yet have his face still the same way, and be still going towards the same place, but it is another matter to turn quite back again, and take his journey the contrary way to a contrary place. So is it here; a man may turn from drunkenness to soberness, and forsake his good fellowship, and other gross, disgraceful sins, and set upon some duties of religion, and yet be going still to the same end as before, intending his carnal self above all, and giving it still the government of his soul. But when he is converted, this self is denied, taken down, God is set up, and his face is turned the contrary way, and he that before was addicted to himself, and lived to himself, is now, by sanctification, devoted to God and lives unto God: before he asked himself what he should do with his time, his parts, and his estate, and for himself he used them; but now he asks God what he shall do with them and uses them for him; before he would please God so far as might stand with the pleasure of his flesh, and carnal self, but not to any great displeasure of them; but now he will please God, let flesh and self be never so much displeased. This is the great change that God will make upon all that shall be saved.

You can say that the Holy Ghost is our sanctifier; but do you know what sanctification is? Why, this is it that I have now opened to you: and every man and woman in the world must have this, or be condemned to everlasting misery. They must turn or die.

Do you believe all this, or do you not? Surely you dare not say you do not: for it is past all doubt or denial; these are not controversies, where one learned, pious man is of one mind, and another of another; where one party saith this, and the other saith that; every sect among us, that deserves to be called Christians, are all agreed in this that I have said, and if you will not believe the God of truth, and that in a case where every sect and party doth believe him, you are utterly inexcusable.

But if you do believe this, how comes it to pass that you are so quiet in an unconverted state? Do you think you are converted; and can you find this wonderful change upon your souls? Have you been thus born again, and made anew; are not these strange matters to many of you, and such as you never felt upon yourselves? If you cannot tell the day or week of your change, or the very sermon that converted you, yet do you find that the work is done, and such a change indeed there is, and that you have such hearts as are before described? Alas, the most follow their worldly business, and little trouble their minds with such thoughts. If they be but restrained from scandalous sins, and can say, I am no whoremonger, nor thief, nor curser, nor swearer, nor tippler, nor extortioner, I go to the church and say my prayers; they think that this is true conversion, and they shall be saved as well as any. Alas, this is foolish deceiving of yourselves; this is too much contempt of an endless glory, and too gross neglect of your immortal souls. Can you make so light of heaven and hell; your corpse will shortly be in the dust, and angels or devils will presently seize upon your souls. Every man or woman of you all will shortly be among other company, and in another case than now you are: you will dwell in these houses but a little longer; you will work in your shops and fields but a little longer, you will sit in these seats, and dwell on this earth but a little longer; you will see with those eyes, hear with those ears, and speak with those tongues, but a little longer, till the resurrection day; and can you make shift to forget this? What a place will you be shortly in of joy or torment! What a sight will you shortly see in heaven or hell! What thoughts will shortly fill your hearts with unspeakable delight or horror! What work will you be employed in? To praise the Lord with saints and angels, or to cry out in fire unquenchable with devils: and should all this be forgotten? And all this is to be endless, and sealed up by an unchangeable degree. Eternity, eternity will be the measure of your joys or sorrows, and can this be forgotten? And all this is true, most certainly true: when you have gone up and down a little longer, and slept and awaked but a few times more, you will be dead and gone, and find all true that now I tell you; and yet can you now so much forget it? You shall then remember you heard this sermon, and that this day, in this place, you were remembered of these things, and perceive them matters a thousand times greater than either you or I could here conceive, and yet shall they be now so much forgotten.

Beloved friends, if the Lord had not awakened me to believe and lay to heart these things myself, I should have remained in the dark and selfish state, and have perished for ever: but if he have truly made me sensible of them, it will constrain me to compassionate you, as well as myself. If your eyes were so far open as to see hell, and you saw your neighbours that were unconverted, dragged thither with hideous cries; though they were such as you accounted honest people on earth, and feared no such matter by themselves, such a sight would make you go home and think of it, and think again, and make you warn all about you as Dives would have had his brethren warned, lest they come to that place of torment. Why, faith is a kind of sight, it is the eye of the soul, the evidence of things not seen: if I believe God, it is next to seeing: therefore I beseech you to excuse me, if I be half as earnest with you about these matters, as if I had seen them. If I must die to-morrow, and it were in my power to come again from another world, and tell you what I had seen, would you not be willing to hear me; would you not believe, and regard what I should tell you? If I might preach one sermon to you after I am dead, and have seen what is done in the world to come, would you not have me plainly speak the truth; would you not crowd to hear me; would you not lay it to heart? But this must not be: God hath his appointed way of teaching you by scripture and ministers ; and he will not humour unbelievers so far, as to send men from the dead to them, and alter his established way ; if any man quarrel with the sun, God will not humour him so far as to set up a clearer light. Friends, I beseech you regard me now, as you would do if I should come from the dead to you : for I can give you the full assurance of the truth of what I say to you, as if I had been there and seen it with my eyes ; for it is possible for one from the dead to deceive you : but Jesus Christ can never deceive you ; the word of God, delivered in scripture, and sealed up by the miracles and holy workings of the Spirit, can never deceive you. Believe this, or believe nothing. Believe, and obey this, or you are undone. Now, as ever you believe the word of God, and as ever you care for the salvation of your souls, let me beg of you this reasonable request, and I beseech you deny me not, that you would without any more delay when you are gone from hence, remember what you heard, and enter into an earnest search of your hearts, and say unto yourselves,

' Is it so indeed ; must I turn or die ; must I be converted or condemned? It is time for me then to look about me, before it be too late. O why did not I look after this till now ; why did I venturously put off or skim over so great a business ; was I awake, or in my senses ? O blessed God, what a mercy is it that thou didst not cut off my life all this while, before I had any certain hope of eternal life. Well, God forbid that I should neglect this work any longer. What state is my soul in ; am I converted, or am I not ? Was ever such a change or work done upon my soul ; have I been illuminated by the word and Spirit of the Lord, to see the odiousness of sin, the need of a Saviour, the love of Christ, and the excellencies of God and glory ; is my heart broken, or humbled within me for my former life ; have I thankfully entertained my Saviour and Lord, that offered himself with pardon and life to my soul ; do I hate my former sinful life, and the remnant of every sin that is in me ; do I fly from them as my deadly enemies ; do I give up myself to a life of holiness, and obedience to God ? Do I love it, and delight in it ? Can I truly say that I am dead to the world and carnal self ; that I live for God, and the glory which he hath promised. Hath heaven more of estimation and resolution than earth ; is God the dearest and highest in my soul ? Once, I am sure, I lived principally to the world and flesh, and God had nothing but some heartless services which the world could spare, and which were the refuse of flesh. Is my heart now turned another way ; have I a new design, a new end, and a new train of holy affections ; have I set my hope and heart in heaven ; is it the scope, design, and bent of my heart and life, to get well to heaven, to see the glorious face of God, and live in his everlasting love and praise ; when I sin, is it against the habitual bent and design of my heart ; do I conquer all gross sins, and am I weary and willing to be rid of my infirmities ? This is the state of a converted soul. Thus must it be with me, or I must perish. Is it thus with me indeed, or is it not ? It is time to get this doubt resolved, before the dreadful Judge resolve it. I am not such a stranger to my own heart and life, but I may somewhat perceive whether I am thus converted or not : if I be not, it will do me no good to flatter my soul with false conceits and hopes. I am resolved no more to deceive myself, but endeavour to know truly, off or on, whether I be converted, yea or no ; that if I be, I may rejoice in it, and glorify my gracious Lord, and comfortably go on till I reach the crown : and if I am not, I may set myself to beg and seek after the grace that should convert me and may turn without any more delay : for, if I find in time that I am out of the way, by the help of Christ I may turn and be received ; but if I stay till either my heart be forsaken of God in blindness and hardness, or till I be snatched away by death, it is then too late. There is no place for repentance and conversion then ; I know it must be now or never '

This is my request of you, that you will but take your hearts to task, and thus examine them, till you see, if it may be, whether you are converted or not ; and if you cannot find it out by your own endeavours, go to your ministers, if they be faithful and experienced men, and desire their assistance. The matter is great, let not bashfulness nor carelessness hinder you. They are set over you, to advise you for the saving of your souls, as physicians advise you for the curing of your bodies. It undoes many thousands, that they think they are in the way to salvation when they are not ; and think that they are converted, when it is no such thing. When we call to them daily to turn, they go away as they came, and think that this concerns not them ; for they are turned already, and hope they shall do well enough in the way that they are in, at least if they pick the fairest path, and avoid some of the foulest steps ; when alas, all this while they live but to the world, the flesh, are strangers to God, and eternal life, and are quite out of the way to heaven. All this is much, because we cannot persuade them to a few serious thoughts of their condition, and to spend a few hours in the examining of their states. Is there not many a self-conceited sinner that hears me this day, that never bestowed one hour, or a quarter of an hour in all their lives, to examine their souls, and try whether they are truly converted or not? O merciful God, that will care for such sinners that care no more for themselves; that will do so much to save them from hell, and help them to heaven, who will do so little for it themselves! If all that are in the way to hell, and in the state of condemnation, did but know it, they durst not continue in it. The greatest hope that the devil hath of bringing you to damnation without a rescue, is by keeping you blindfold, ignorant of your state, and making you believe that you may do well enough in the way that you are in. If you knew that you were out of the way to heaven, and were lost for ever, if you should die as you are, durst you sleep another night in the state that you are in? Durst you live another day in it? Could you heartily laugh, or be merry in such a state? What, and not know but you may be snatched away to hell in an hour! Surely it would constrain you to forsake your former company and courses, and to betake yourselves to the ways of holiness, and the communion of the saints. Surely it would drive you to cry to God for a new heart, and to seek help of those that are fit to counsel you. There is none of you surely that cares not for being damned. Well then, I beseech you presently make inquiry into your hearts, and give them no rest, till you find out your condition; that if it be good, you may rejoice in it and go on: if it be bad, you may presently look about you for recovery, as men that believe they must turn or die. What say you, will you resolve and promise to be at thus much labour for your souls? Will you fall upon this self-examination when you come home? Is my request unreasonable? Your consciences know it is not; resolve on it, then, before you stir; knowing how much it concerns your souls. I beseech you, for the sake of that God that commands you, at whose bar you will shortly appear, that you will not deny me this reasonable request. For the sake of those souls that must turn or die, I beseech you deny me not; even but to make it your business to understand your own conditions, and build upon sure ground, and know whether you are converted or not and venture not your souls on negligent security.

But perhaps you will say, What if we should find ourselves yet unconverted, what shall we do then? This question leads me to my second doctrine; which will do much to the answering of it, to which I shall now proceed.

DOCT. II. It is the promise of God, that the wicked shall live if they will but turn; unfeignedly and thoroughly turn.

The Lord here professes, that this is it he takes pleasure in, that the wicked turn and live. Heaven is made as sure to the converted, as hell is to the unconverted. Turn and live, is as certain a truth as turn or die. God was not bound to provide us a Saviour, nor open to us the door of hope, nor call to us to repent and turn, when once we had cast ourselves away by sin. But he hath freely done it to magnify his mercy. Sinners, there are none of you shall have cause to go home, and say I preach desperation to you. Do we use to shut up the door of mercy against you? O that you would not shut it up against yourselves! Do we use to tell you that God will have no mercy on you, though you turn and be sanctified? When did you ever hear a preacher say such a word? You that bark at the preachers of the gospel, for desiring to keep you out of hell, and say that they preach desperation; tell me, if you can, when did you ever hear any sober man say that there is no hope for you, though ye repent and be converted? No, it is quite the contrary that we daily proclaim from the Lord, that whosoever is born again, and by faith and repentance doth become a new creature, shall certainly be saved; and so far we are from persuading you to despair of this, that we persuade you not to make any doubt of it. It is life, and not death, that is the first part of our message to you; our commission is to offer salvation—certain salvation, a speedy, glorious, everlasting salvation, to every one of you: to the poorest beggar as well as to the greatest lord: to the worst of you, even to the drunkards, swearers, worldlings, thieves, yea, to the despisers and reproachers of the holy way of salvation.

We are commanded, by our Lord and Master, to offer you a pardon for all that is past, if you will but now at last return and live; we are commanded to beseech and intreat you to accept the offer and return; to tell you what preparation is made by Christ, what mercy stays for you, what patience waits on you, what thoughts of kindness God hath towards you; and how happy, how certainly and unspeakably happy you may be if you will. We have indeed, also, a message of wrath and death: yea, of a twofold wrath and death: but neither of them is our principal message: we must tell you of the wrath that is on you already, and the death that you are born under, for the breach of the law of works: but this is only to show you the need of mercy, and provoke you to esteem the grace of the Redeemer. And we tell you nothing but the truth, which you must know: for who will seek for physic, that knows not that he is sick? For telling you of your misery, is not what makes you miserable, but drives you to seek for mercy; it is you that have brought this death upon yourselves. We tell you also of another death, even remediless, and much greater torment which will fall on those that will not be converted. But as this is true, and must be told you, so it is but the last, and saddest part of our message; we are first to offer you mercy, if you will turn: and it is only those that will not turn nor hear the voice of mercy, that we must foretel damnation to. Will you but cast away your transgressions, delay no longer, but come away at the call of Christ; be converted, and become new creatures, and we have not a word of damning wrath or death to speak against you. I do here, in the name of the Lord of life, proclaim to you all that hear me this day, to the worst of you, to the greatest, to the oldest sinner, that you may have mercy and salvation if you will but turn. There is mercy in God, there is sufficiency in the satisfaction of Christ; the promise is free, full, and universal: you may have life if you will but turn. But then, as you love your souls, remember what turning it is the scripture speaks of; it is not to mend the old house, but to pull down all, and build a new on Christ the rock and sure foundation; it is not to mend somewhat in a carnal course of life, but to mortify the flesh, and live after the Spirit; it is not to serve the flesh and the world in a more reformed way, without any scandalous, disgraceful sins, and with a certain kind of self-devised religion; but it is to change your master, your works, and end, set your face contrary ways, do all for the life that you never saw, and dedicate yourselves and all you have to God. This is the change that must be made, if you will live.

Yourselves are witness now, that it is salvation and not damnation, that is the great doctrine I preach to you; and the first part of my message to you. Accept of this and we shall go no farther with you; for we would not so much as affright or trouble you with the name of damnation, without necessity. But if you will not be saved, there is no remedy, but damnation must take place: for there is no middle place between the two: you must have either life or death. And we are not only to offer you life but to show you the grounds on which we do it, and call you to believe, that God doth mean indeed as he speaks: that the promise is true, and extends conditionally to you as well as others, and that heaven is no fancy, but a true felicity.

If you ask, where is our commission for this offer? Among an hundred texts of scripture, I will show it unto you in these few:

First, You see it here in my text, and the following verses, as plain as can possibly be spoken. And in 2 Cor. v. 17—21. you have the very sum of our commission. 'If any man be in Christ, he is a new creature: old things are past away, behold all things are become new: and all things are of God, who hath reconciled us to himself by Jesus Christ, who hath given to us the ministry of reconciliation: to wit, that God was in Christ reconciling the world unto himself; not imputing their trespasses to them, and hath committed unto us the word of reconciliation: now then we are ambassadors for Christ, as though God did beseech you by us, we pray you in Christ's stead, be ye reconciled unto God; for he hath made him to be sin for us who knew no sin, that we might be made the righteousness of God in him.—Go ye into all the world, and preach the gospel to every creature.—He that believeth (that is, with such a converting faith as is expressed) and is baptized, shall be saved; and he that believeth not, shall be damned.—Thus it behoved Christ to suffer, and to rise from the dead the third day, and that repentance (which is conversion) and remission of sins, should be preached in his name among all nations.—The God of our fathers raised up Jesus, whom ye slew and hanged on a tree; him hath God exalted with his right hand to be a prince and a Saviour, to give repentance to Israel, and forgiveness of sins.—Be it known unto you, therefore, men and brethren, that through this man is preached unto you the forgiveness of sins; and by him all that believe are justified from all things, from which ye could not be justified by the law of Moses.' Do not think this offer is restrained to the Jews, 'for in Christ Jesus neither circumcision availeth any thing, nor uncircumcision, but a new creature. —Come, for all things are now ready.'

You see by this time, that we are commanded to offer life to you all, and to tell you from God, that if you will turn you may live.

Here you may safely trust your souls; for the love of God is the fountain of this offer, and the blood of the Son of God hath purchased it; the faithfulness and truth of God is engaged to make the promise good; miracles oft sealed up the truth of it ; preachers are sent through the world to proclaim it ; the sacraments are instituted and used for the solemn delivery of the mercy offered, to them that will accept it ; and the Spirit doth open the heart to entertain it, and is itself the earnest of the full possession. So that the truth of it is past controversy, that the worst of you all, and every one of you, if you will but be converted, may be saved.

Indeed, if you will needs believe you shall be saved without conversion, then you believe a falsehood ; and if I should preach that to you, I should preach a lie ; this were not to believe God, but the devil and your own deceitful hearts. God hath his promise of life, and the devil hath his promise of life. God's promise is, ' Return and live ;' the devil's is, ' Thou shalt live whether thou turn or not.' The words of God are, as I have showed you, ' Except ye be converted, and become as little children, ye cannot enter into the kingdom of heaven.—Except a man be born again, he cannot enter into the kingdom of God.—Without holiness none shall see God.' The devil's word is, You may be saved without being born again and converted, you may go to heaven well enough, without being holy ; God doth but frighten you, he is more merciful than to do as he saith, he will be better to you than his word. Alas, the greatest part of the world believe this word of the devil before the word of God, just as our first sin and misery came into the world. God saith to our first parents, If ye eat ye shall die ; the devil contradicts him, and saith, Ye shall not die ; and the woman believed the devil before God. So now the Lord saith, Turn or die ; and the devil saith, You shall not die if you do but cry mercy at last, and give over the acts of sin, when you can practise it no longer. And this is the word that the world believes. O heinous wickedness, to believe the devil before God!

Yet that is not the worst, but blasphemously they call this a believing and trusting in God, when they put him in the shape of Satan, who was a liar from the beginning ; and when they believe that the word of God is a lie, they call this a trusting God, and say they believe in him, and trust on him for salvation : where did ever God say that the unregenerated, unconverted, unsanctified, shall be saved? Show such a word in scripture ; I challenge you if you can. Why, this is the devil's word, and to believe it is to believe the devil, and is the sin that is commonly called presumption : and do you call this a believing and trusting God : there is enough in the word of God to comfort and strengthen the

hearts of the sanctified : but not a word to strengthen the hands of wickedness, nor to give men the least hope of being saved, though they be never sanctified.

But if you will turn, and come into the way of mercy, the mercy of the Lord is ready to entertain you. Then trust God for salvation, boldly and confidently ; for he is engaged by his word to save you.

He will be a Father to none but his children, and he will save none but those that forsake the world, the devil, and the flesh, and come into his family, to be members of his Son, and have communion with the saints. But if they will not come in, it is wrong of themselves ; his doors are open, he keeps none back ; he never sent such a message as this to any of you, ' it is not too late, I will not receive thee, though thou be converted.' He might have done so and done you no wrong, but he did not, he doth not to this day, he is still ready to receive you, if you were but ready unfeignedly, and with all your hearts to turn. The fulness of this truth will yet more appear in the two following doctrines, which I shall therefore next proceed to, before I make a farther application of this.

Doct. III. God takes pleasure in men's conversion and salvation, but not in their death and damnation : he had rather they would return and live, than go on and die.

I shall first teach you how to understand this ; and then clear up the truth of it to you.

And for the first ; you must observe these following things : 1. A simple willingness and complacency is the first act of the will, following the simple apprehension of the understanding ; before it proceeds to compare things together. But the choosing act of the will is a following act, and supposes the comparing practical act of the understanding ; and these two acts may often be carried to contrary objects, without any fault at all in the person. 2. An unfeigned willingness may have several degrees. Some things I am so far willing of, as that I will do all that lies in my power to accomplish them : and some things I am truly willing another should do, when yet I will not do all that ever I am able to procure it, having many reasons to dissuade me therefrom ; though yet I will do all that belongs to me to do. 3. The will of a ruler, as such, is manifest in making and executing laws ; but the will of a man in his simple natural capacity, or as absolute lord of his own, is manifested in desiring, or resolving of events. 4. A ruler's will, as lawgiver, is first and principally that his law be obeyed, and not at all that the penalty be executed on any, but only on supposition that they will not obey his laws. But a ruler's will, as judge, supposes the law already either kept or broken : therefore he resolves on reward or punishment accordingly.

Having given you these necessary distinctions, I shall next apply them to the case in hand, in these following propositions :

1. It is in the glass of the word that as creatures in this life we must know God : and so according to the nature of man, we ascribe to him understanding and will, removing all the imperfections that we can, because we are capable of no higher positive conceptions of him. 2. On the same grounds we do, with the scriptures, distinguish between the acts of God's will, as diversified from the respects, or the objects, though as to God's essence they are all one. 3. And the bolder, because that when we speak of Christ, we have the more ground for it from his human nature. 4. Thus we say, that the simple complacency, will, or love of God, is to all that is naturally or morally good, according to the nature and degree of its goodness. And so he hath pleasure in the conversion and salvation of all, which yet will never come to pass. 5. And God, as Ruler and Lawgiver of the world, had so far a practical will for their salvation, as to make them a free exhibition and offer of Christ and life, and an act of oblivion for all their sins, so be it they will not unthankfully reject it ; and to command his messengers to offer this gift to all the world, and persuade them to accept it. And so he doth all, that as lawgiver or promiser, belongs to him to do for their salvation. 6. But yet he resolves, as lawgiver, that they that will not turn, shall die : and as judge when their day of grace is past, he will execute that decree. 7. So that he thus unfeignedly wills the conversion of those that never will be converted, but not as absolute Lord, with the fullest efficacious resolution, nor as a thing which he resolves shall undoubtedly come to pass, or would engage all his power to accomplish : it is in the power of a prince to set a guard upon a murderer, to see that he shall not murder and be hanged. But if upon good reason he forbear this, and send to his subjects, and warn and intreat them not to be murderers, I hope he may well say, that he would not have them murder and be hanged ; he takes no pleasure in it, but rather that they forbear, and live. If he do more for some, upon some special reason, he is not bound to do so by all. The king may well say to all the murderers and felons in the land, I have no pleasure in your death, but rather that you would obey my laws and live ; but if you will not, I am resolved for all this, that you shall die. The judge may truly say to a thief, or a murderer, Alas, man, I have no delight in thy death, I had rather thou hadst kept the law, and saved thy life, but seeing thou hast not, I must condemn thee, or else I should be unjust. So, though God have no pleasure in your damnation, and therefore calls upon you to return and live, yet he hath pleasure in the demonstration of his own justice, and the executing his laws, and therefore he is for all this fully resolved, that if you will not be converted, you shall be condemned. If God were so much against the death of the wicked, as that he were resolved to do all that he can to hinder it, then no man should be condemned, whereas Christ tells you, that few will be saved. But so far God is against your damnation, as that he will teach you, warn you, set before you life and death, offer you your choice, and command his ministers to intreat you not to damn yourselves, but accept his mercy, and so to leave you without excuse ; but if this will not do, if still you be unconverted, he professes to you he is resolved of your damnation, and hath commanded us to say to you in his name, O wicked man, thou shalt surely die ! Christ hath little less than sworn it over and over, with a ' Verily, verily, except ye be converted and born again, ye cannot enter into the kingdom of heaven.' Mark that he saith, You cannot. It is in vain to hope for it, and in vain to dream that God is willing of it ; for it is a thing that cannot be.

In a word, you see then the meaning of the text, that God, the great lawgiver of the world, takes no pleasure in the death of the wicked, but rather that they turn and live ; though yet he be resolved that none shall live but those that turn ; and as a judge even delights in justice, and manifests his hatred of sin, though not in their misery which they have brought upon themselves, in itself considered.

2. And for the proofs of this point, I shall be very brief in them, because I suppose you easily believe it already.

First, The very gracious nature of God proclaimed, Exod. xxxiv. 6. and xx. 5. and frequently elsewhere, may assure you of this, that he hath no pleasure in your death.

Second, If God had more pleasure in thy death than in thy conversion and life, he would not have so frequently commanded thee in his word to turn ; he would not have made thee such promises of life, if thou wilt but turn ; he would not have persuaded thee to it by so many reasons. The tenor of his Gospel proves the point.

Third, His commission that he hath given to the ministers of the gospel, doth fully prove it. If God had taken more pleasure in thy damnation, than in thy conversion and salvation, he would never have charged us to offer you mercy, and to teach you the way of life, both publicly and privately; to intreat and beseech you to turn and live; to acquaint you of your sins, and foretell you of your danger; to do all that possibly we can for your conversion, and to continue patiently so doing, though you should hate or abuse us for our pains. Would God have done this and appointed his ordinances for your good, if he had taken pleasure in your death.

Fourth, It is proved also by the course of his providence. If God had rather you were damned than converted and saved, he would not second his word with his works, and invite you by his daily kindness to himself, and give you all the mercies of this life, which are his means to lead you to repentance, and bring you so often under his rod, to force you into your wits: he would not set so many examples before your eyes, no, nor wait on you so patiently as he doth from day to day, and year to year. These are not signs of one that takes pleasure in your death; if this had been his delight, how easily could he have had thee long ago in hell! How oft before this, could he have snatched thee away in the midst of thy sins, with a curse, or oath, or lie in thy mouth, in thy ignorance and pride, and sensuality; when thou wert last in thy drunkenness, or last deriding the ways of God! How easily could he have stopped thy breath, and tamed thee with his plagues, and made thee sober in another world! Alas, how small a matter it is for the Almighty to rule the tongue of the most profane railer, and tie the hands of the most malicious persecutor; or calm the fury of the bitterest of his enemies, and make them know they are but worms: if he should but frown upon thee, thou wouldest drop into thy grave; if he gave commission to one of his angels to go and destroy ten thousand sinners, how quickly would it be done! How easily can he lay thee upon the bed of languishing, and make thee lie roaring there in pain, and eating the words of reproach which thou hast spoken against his servants, his word, his worship, and his holy ways; and make thee send to beg their prayers, whom thou didst despise in thy presumption! How easily can he lay that flesh under pains and groans, and make it too weak to hold their soul, and make it more lothsome than the mire of the earth! That flesh which now must have what it loves, must not be displeased, and must be humoured with meat, drink, and clothes, whatsoever God says to the contrary, how quickly would the frowns of God consume it! When thou wast passionately defending thy sin, and quarrelling with them that would have drawn thee from it, and showing thy spleen against the reprovers, and pleading for the *works of darkness;* how easily could God snatch thee away in a moment, and set thee before his dreadful majesty, where thou mayest see ten thousand times ten thousand of glorious angels waiting on his throne; and call thee there to plead thy cause, and ask thee, what hast thou now to say against thy Creator, his truth, his servants, or his holy ways; now plead thy cause, and make the best of it thou canst. Now what canst thou say in excuse of thy sins? Now give account of thy worldliness and fleshly life, of thy time, of all thy mercies thou hast had. O how thy stubborn heart would have melted, thy proud looks been taken down, thy countenance appalled, and thy stout words turned into speechless silence, or dreadful cries; if God had but set thee thus at his bar, and pleaded his own cause with thee, which thou hast here so maliciously pleaded against. How easily can he, at any time, say to thy guilty soul, 'come away, and live in that flesh no longer, till the resurrection,' and it cannot resist? A word of his mouth would take off the noise of thy present life, and then all thy parts and powers would stand still; and if he say unto thee, 'live no longer; or live in hell,' thou couldst not disobey.

But God hath yet done none of this; but hath patiently forborn thee, and mercifully upheld thee: hath given thee that breath which thou didst breath out against him, hath given those mercies which thou didst sacrifice to the flesh, and afforded thee that provision which thou spentest to satisfy thy greedy appetite; he gave thee every minute of that time which thou didst waste in idleness, or drunkenness, or worldliness; and doth not all his patience and mercy show that he desired not thy damnation; can the candle burn without thy oil? Can your houses stand without the earth to bear them? As well you can live one hour without the support of God. Why did he so long support thy life, but to see when thou wouldest bethink thee of the folly of thy ways, and return and live: will any man purposely put arms into his enemies' hands to resist him? Or hold a candle to a murderer that is killing his children? Or to an idle servant that plays, and sleeps the while? Surely it is to see whether thou wilt at last return and live, that God hath so long waited on thee.

Fifth, It is further proved by the sufferings of his Son, that God takes no pleasure in the death of the wicked. Would he have ransomed them from death at so dear a rate? Would he have astonished angels and men by his condescension; would God have dwelt in flesh, and have come in the form of a servant, and have assumed humanity into one person with the Godhead? Would Christ have lived a life of suffering, and died a cursed death for sinners, if he had rather taken pleasure in their death? Suppose you saw him but so busy in preaching and healing of them, or so long in fasting, or all night in prayer, or praying with the drops of blood trickling from him instead of sweat, or suffering a cursed death upon the cross, and pouring out his soul as a sacrifice for our sins,—would you have thought these the signs of one that delights in the death of the wicked?

Think not to extenuate it by saying, that it was only for his elect. For it was thy sin, and the sin of all the world, that lay upon our redeemer; and his sacrifice and satisfaction is sufficient for all, and the fruits of it are offered to one as well as to another; but it is true, that it was never the intent of his mind, to pardon and save any that would not by faith and repentance be converted. If you had seen and heard him weeping and bemoaning the state of disobedience in impenitent people, or complaining of their stubbornness, 'O Jerusalem, Jerusalem, how oft would I have gathered thy children together, even as a hen gathereth her chickens under her wings, and ye would not!' Or if you had seen and heard him on the cross, praying for his persecutors, 'Father, forgive them, for they know not what they do;' would you have suspected that he had delighted in the death of the wicked, even of those that perish by their wilful unbelief? 'When God hath so loved (not only loved, but so loved) the world as to give his only begotten Son, that whosoever believeth in him, (by an effectual faith) should not perish, but have everlasting life,' I think he hath hereby proved, against the malice of men and devils, that he takes no pleasure in the death of the wicked, but had rather that they would turn and live.

Lastly, If all this will not yet satisfy you, take his own word, that knows best his own mind, or at least believe his oath: but this leads me to the fourth doctrine.

Doct. IV. The Lord hath confirmed it to us by his oath, that he hath no pleasure in the death of the wicked, but rather that he turn and live; that he may leave man no pretence to question the truth of it.

If you dare question his word, I hope you dare not question his oath. As Christ hath solemnly protested, that the unregenerated and unconverted cannot enter into the kingdom of heaven, so God hath sworn that his pleasure is not in their death, but in their conversion and life: and as the apostle saith, 'because he can swear by no greater than himself, he saith, As I live,' &c.; 'for men verily swear by the greater, and an oath for confirmation is to them an end of strife, wherein God willing more abundantly to show unto the heirs of promise the immutability of his council, confirmed it by an oath, that by two immutable things, in which it was impossible for God to lie, we might have a strong consolation, who had fled for refuge to lay hold on the hope set before us, which we have as an anchor of the soul, both sure and stedfast.' If there be any man that cannot reconcile this truth with the doctrine of predestination, or the actual damnation of the wicked, that is his own ignorance; he hath no pretence left to deny or question therefore the truth of the point in hand; for this is confirmed by the oath of God, and therefore must not be distorted, to reduce it to other points, but doubtful points must rather be reduced to it, and certain truths must be believed to agree with it, though our shallow understandings do hardly discern the agreement.

I earnestly intreat thee, if thou be an unconverted sinner that hearest these words, that thou wouldest ponder a little upon the forementioned doctrines, and bethink thyself a while, who it is that takes no pleasure in thy sin and damnation. Certainly, it is not God: he hath sworn for his part, that he takes no pleasure in it. I know it is not the pleasing of him that you intend in it. You dare not say that you drink and swear, and neglect holy duties, and quench the motions of the Spirit, to please God. That were as if you should reproach the prince, break his laws, seek his death, and say, you did all this to please him.

Who is it then that takes pleasure in your sin and death? Not any that bear the image of God, for they must be like minded to him. God knows it is small pleasure to your faithful teachers, to see you serve your deadly enemy, and madly venture your eternal state, and wilfully run into the flames of hell. It is small pleasure to them, to see upon your souls (in the sad effects,) such blindness, hard-heartedness, carelessness, and presumption; such wilfulness in evil, such uncharitableness, and stiffness, against the ways of life and peace; they know these are marks of death, and of the wrath of God, and they know from the word of God what is like to be the end of them; and therefore it is no more pleasure to them, than to a tender physician to see the plague marks break out upon his patient. Alas, to foresee your everlasting torments, and know not how to prevent them! To see how near you are to hell, and we cannot make you believe it, and consider it! To see how easily, how certainly you might escape, if we knew but how to make you willing! How fair you are for everlasting salvation, if you would but turn, and make it the care and business of your lives to obey the gospel! But you will not do it; if our lives lay on it, we cannot persuade you to do it. We study day and night what to say to you, that may convince you and persuade you, and yet it is undone: we lay before you the word of God, and show you the very chapter and verse where it is written, that you cannot be saved except you be converted; and yet we leave the most of you as we find you: we hope ye will believe the word of God, though you believe not us, and that you will regard it when we show you plain scripture for it: but we hope in vain, and labour in vain, as to any saving change upon your hearts. Do you think that this is a pleasant thing to us? Many a time in secret prayers we are constrained to complain to God with sad hearts,

'Alas, Lord, we have spoken it to them, in thy name, but they little regard us? We have told them what thou bidst us tell them, concerning the danger of an unconverted state, but they do not believe us; we have told them that thou hast protested that there is no peace to the wicked; but the worst of them all will scarcely believe that they are wicked. We have showed them the word, where thou hast said, that if they live after the flesh they shall die; but they say, they will believe in thee, when they will not believe thee; and that they will trust in thee, when they give no credit to thy word, and when they hope that the threatenings of thy word are false, they will yet call this a hoping in God, and though we show them where thou hast said, that when a wicked man dies all his hopes perish, yet cannot we persuade them from their deceitful hopes. We tell them what a base unprofitable thing sin is, but they love it, and therefore will not leave it. We tell them how dear they buy their pleasure, and what they must pay for it in everlasting torment, and they bless themselves and will not believe it, but will do as the most do; and because God is merciful, they will not be-

lieve him, but will venture their souls, come on it what will. We tell them how ready the Lord is to receive them; and this does but make them delay their repentance, and be bolder in their sin. Some of them say they purpose to repent, but they are still the same; and some say they repent already, while yet they are not converted from their sins. We exhort them, we intreat them, we offer them our help, but we cannot prevail with them; but they that were drunkards are drunkards still, and they that were voluptuous flesh-pleasing sinners are such still, and they that were worldlings are worldlings still; and they that were ignorant, proud, and self-conceited, are so still. Few of them will see and confess their sins, and fewer will forsake them, but comfort themselves that all men are sinners. as if there were no difference between a converted sinner and an unconverted. Some of them will not come near us when we are willing to instruct them, but think they know enough already, and need not our instruction: and some of them will give us the hearing, and do what they list; and most of them are like dead men that cannot feel; so that when we tell them of the matters of everlasting consequence, we cannot get a word of it to their hearts. If we do not obey them, and humour them in baptizing children of the most obstinately wicked, and giving them the Lord's Supper, and doing all that they would have us, though never so much against the word of God, they will hate us, and rail at us; but if we beseech them to confess and forsake their sins, and save their souls, they will not do it. We tell them if they will but turn, we will deny them none of the ordinances of God, neither baptism to their children, nor the Lord's Supper to themselves; but they will not hear us: they would have us to disobey God, damn our souls to please them, and yet they will not turn, and save their own souls to please God. They are wiser in their own eyes than all their teachers; they rage, and are confident in their own way; and if we would never so willingly, we cannot change them. Lord, this is the case of our miserable neighbours, and we cannot help it; we see them ready to drop into hell, and we cannot help it: we know if they would unfeignedly turn, they might be saved; but we cannot persuade them: If we would beg it of them on our knees, we cannot persuade them to it; if we would beg it of them with tears, we cannot persuade them: and what more can we do?'

These are the secret complaints that many a poor minister pours out before God, and do you think that he hath any pleasure in this? Is it a pleasure to him to see you go on in sin, and cannot stop you? To see you so miserable, and cannot so much as make you sensible of it? To see you merry, when you are not sure to be an hour out of hell? To think what you must for ever suffer because you will not turn? And to think what an everlasting life of glory you wilfully despise and cast away? What sadder things can you bring to their hearts, and how can you devise to grieve them more?

Who is it then that you please by your sin and death? It is none of your sensible, godly friends. Alas, it is the grief of their souls to see your misery, and they lament you many a time, when you give them little thanks for it, and when you have not hearts to lament yourselves.

Who is it then that takes pleasure in your sin? It is none but the three great enemies of God, whom you renounced in your baptism, and now are turned falsely to serve.

1. The devil indeed takes pleasure in your sin and death; for this is the very end of all his temptations: for this he watches night and day: you cannot devise to please him better, than to go on in sin: how glad is he when he sees thee going to the alehouse, or other sin; when he hears thee curse or swear, or rail? How glad is he when he hears thee revile the minister that would draw thee from thy sin, and help to save thee? These are his delight.

2. The wicked are also delighted in it, for it is agreeable to their nature.

3. But I know, for all this, that it is not the pleasure of the devil that you intend, even when you please him; but it is your own flesh, the greatest and most dangerous enemy, that you intend to please. It is the flesh that would be pampered, that would be pleased in meat and drink, and clothing, that would be pleased in your company, pleased in applause and credit with the world, pleased in sports and lusts, and idleness; this is the gulph that devours all. This is the very God that you serve, for the scripture saith of such, ' that their bellies are their God.'

But I beseech you stay a little and consider the business.

1. Should your flesh be pleased before your Maker? Will you displease the Lord, displease your teacher, and your godly friends, and all to please your sensual desires? Is not God worthy to be a ruler of your flesh; if he shall not rule it, he will not save it: you cannot in reason expect that he should.

2. Your flesh is pleased with your sin; but is your conscience pleased? Doth not it grudge

within you, tell you sometimes that all is not well, and that your case is not so safe as you think it to be? Should not your souls and consciences be pleased before that corruptible flesh?

3. But is not your flesh preparing for its own displeasure also? It loves the bait, but doth it love the hook? It loves the strong drink and sweet morsels; it loves its ease, sport and merriment; it loves to be rich, well spoken of by men, and to be somebody in the world, but doth it love the curse of God? Doth it love to stand trembling before his bar, and to be judged to everlasting fire? Doth it love to be tormented with the devils for ever? Take all together; for there is no separating sin and hell, but only by faith and true conversion; if you will keep one, you must have the other. If death and hell be pleasant to thee, no wonder then if thou go on in sin; but if they be not (as I am sure they are not) then what if sin be ever so pleasant, is it worth the loss of life eternal? Is a little drink, meat, ease, the good word of sinners, or the riches of this world, to be valued above the joys of heaven? Or are they worth the sufferings of eternal fire? These questions should be considered before you go any farther by every any man that hath reason to consider, and that believes he hath a soul to save or lose.

Well, the Lord here swears that he hath no pleasure in your death, but rather that you would turn and live: if yet you will go on and die, rather than turn, remember it was not to please God that you did it; it was to please the world, and to please yourself. If men will damn themselves to please themselves, run into endless torments for delight, and have not the heart, the grace, to hearken to God or man that would reclaim them, what remedy? But they must take what they get by it, and repent in another manner, when it is too late. Before I proceed any farther in the application, I shall come to the next doctrine; which gives a fuller ground for it.

DOCT. V. So earnest is God for the conversion of sinners, that he doubles his commands and exhortations with vehemency; ' Turn ye, turn ye, why will ye die?'

This doctrine is the application of the former, as by a use of exhortation, and accordingly I shall handle it. Is there an unconverted sinner, that hears these vehement words of God; is there a man or woman in this assembly, that is yet a stranger to the renewing, sanctifying works of the Holy Ghost? It is a happy assembly if it be not so with the most: hearken then to the voice of your Maker, and turn to him by

Christ without delay. Would you know the will of God? Why this is his will, that you presently turn. Shall the living God send so earnest a message to his creatures, and should they not obey? Hearken then all you that live after the flesh, the Lord that gave thee thy breath and being, hath sent a message to thee from heaven, and this is his message, ' Turn ye, turn ye, why will you die?' He that hath ears to hear let him hear. Shall the voice of the eternal Majesty be neglected? If he but terribly thunder, thou art afraid. O but this voice doth more nearly concern thee; if he but tell thee that thou shalt die to-morrow, thou wouldst not make light of it, but this word concerns thy life or death everlasting. It is both a command and an exhortation. As if he had said to thee, I charge thee, upon the allegiance thou owest to me thy Creator and Redeemer, that thou renounce the flesh, the world and the devil, and turn to me, that thou mayest live. I condescend to intreat thee, as thou lovest or fearest him that made thee; as thou lovest thine own life, even thine everlasting life, turn and live; as ever thou wouldst escape eternal misery, turn, turn, for why wilt thou die? And is there a heart in man, in a reasonable creature, that can once refuse such a message, such a command, such an exhortation as this? O what a thing then is the heart of man!

Hearken then, all that love yourselves, and all that regard your own salvation. Here is the most joyful message that ever was sent to the ears of man, ' Turn ye, turn ye, why will you die?' You are not yet shut up under desperation. Here is mercy offered you, turn and you shall have it. O sirs, with what glad and joyful hearts should you receive these tidings! I know that this is not the first time that you have heard it; but how have you regarded it, or how do you regard it now? Hear, all you ignorant, careless sinners, the word of the Lord. Hear, all you worldlings, you sensual flesh-pleasers, you gluttons, drunkards, whoremongers, and swearers; you railers, backbiters, slanderers, and liars; ' turn ye, turn ye, why will ye die?'

Hear, all you cold and formal professors, and all that are strangers to the life of Christ, who never knew the power of his cross and resurrection, who never felt your hearts warmed with his love, and live not on him as the strength of your souls; ' turn ye, turn ye, why will ye die?'

Hear, all that are void of the love of God, whose hearts are not toward him, nor taken up with the hopes of glory, but set more by your earthly prosperity and delights, than by the joys of heaven; you that are religious but a little, and give God no more than your flesh can spare; that have not denied your carnal selves, and forsaken all that you have for Christ, in the estimation and grounded resolution of your souls, but have some one thing in the world so dear to you, that you cannot spare it for Christ, if he requires it, but will rather even venture on his displeasure, than forsake it; ' turn ye, turn ye, why will you die?

If you never heard it, or observed it before; remember that ye were told it from the word of God this day, that if you will but turn, you may live; and if you will not turn ' you shall surely die.'

What now will you do : what is your resolution; will you turn or will you not? Halt not any longer between two opinions : if the Lord be God, follow him : if your flesh be God, then serve it still. If heaven be better than earth and fleshly pleasures, come away then and seek a better country, and lay up your treasure where rust and moths do not corrupt, and thieves cannot break through and steal, and be awakened at last with all your might to seek the kingdom that cannot be moved. Employ your lives on a higher design, and turn the stream of your cares and labours another way than formerly you have done : but if earth be better than heaven, or will do more for you, or last you longer, then keep it and make your best of it, and follow it still. Are you resolved what to do ? If you be not, I will set a few more moving considerations before you, to see if reason will make you resolve.

1. Consider what preparations mercy hath made for your salvation : and what pity it is that any man should be damned after all this. The time was when the flaming sword was in the way, and the curse of God's law would have kept thee back, if thou hadst been ever so willing to turn to God : the time was when thyself, and all the friends that thou hadst in the world, could never have procured thee the pardon of thy sins past, though thou hadst never so much lamented, and reformed them. But Christ hath removed this impediment, by the ransom of his blood. The time was, that God was wholly unreconciled, as being not satisfied for the violation of his law : but now he is so far satisfied and reconciled, as that he hath made thee a free act of oblivion, and a free deed of the gift of Christ and life, and offers it to thee, and intreats thee to accept it, and it may be thine if thou wilt. For, ' he was in Christ reconciling the world to himself, and hath committed to us the word of actual recon-

ciliation.' Sinners, we are commanded to do this message to you all, as from the Lord. ' Come, for all things are ready.' Are 'all things ready,' and are you unready? God is ready to entertain you and pardon all that you have done against him, if you will but come. As long as you have sinned, as wilfully as you have sinned, as heinously as you have sinned, he is ready to cast all behind his back, if you will but come. Though you have been prodigals, and run away from God, and have staid so long, he is ready even to meet you, and embrace you in his arms, and rejoice in your conversion, if you will but turn. Even the earthly worldling and debauched drunkard may find God ready to bid him welcome, if they will but come. Doth not this turn thy heart within thee? O sinner, if thou hast a heart of flesh, and not of stone in thee, methinks this should melt it; shall the dreadful infinite Majesty of heaven, even wait for thy returning, and be ready to receive thee who hast abused him, and forgotten him so long? Shall he delight in thy conversion, that might at any time glorify his justice in thy damnation; and doth it not yet melt thy heart within thee, and art thou not yet ready to come in? Hast thou not as much reason to be ready to come, as God hath to invite thee and bid thee welcome?

But that is not all; Christ hath done his part on the cross, and made such a way for thee to the Father that on his account thou mayest be welcome, if thou wilt come. And yet art thou not ready?

A pardon is already expressly granted, and offered thee in the gospel. And yet art thou not ready?

The ministers of the gospel are ready to assist thee, to instruct thee, and pronounce the absolving words of peace to thy soul; they are ready to pray for thee, and to seal up thy pardon by the administration of the holy sacrament; and yet art thou not ready?

All that fear God about thee, are ready to rejoice in thy conversion, and to receive thee into the communion of saints, and to give thee the right hand of fellowship, yea, though thou hadst been one that had been cast out of their society: they dare not but forgive, where God forgives, when it is manifest to them by thy confession and amendment: they dare not so much as reproach thee with thy former sins, because they know that God will not upbraid thee with them. If thou hadst been never so scandalous, if thou wouldst but heartily be converted and come in, they would not refuse thee, let the world say what they would against it. Are all these ready to receive thee, and yet art thou not ready to come in?

Yea, heaven itself is ready: the Lord will receive thee into the glory of the saints, vile as thou hast been; if thou wilt but be cleansed thou mayest have a place before his throne: his angels will be ready to guard thy soul to the place of joy, if thou but unfeignedly come in. And is God ready, the sacrifice of Christ ready, the promise ready, and pardon ready? Are ministers ready, the people of God ready, heaven itself ready, and angels ready, and all these but waiting for thy conversion; and yet art thou not ready? What! not ready to live, when thou hast been dead so long? Not ready to come to thy right understanding; as the prodigal is said to come to himself, when thou hast been beside thyself so long? Not ready to be saved, when thou art even ready to be condemned? Art thou not ready to lay hold on Christ that would deliver thee, when thou art even ready to drown, and sink into damnation? Art thou not ready to be saved from hell, when thou art even ready to be cast remediless into it; alas, man! dost thou know what thou dost? If thou die unconverted, there is no doubt to be made of thy damnation: thou art not sure to live an hour: and yet art thou not ready to turn, and to come in? O miserable wretch! hast thou not served the flesh and the devil long enough! Yet hast thou not enough of sin. Is it so good to thee, or so profitable for thee? Dost thou know what it is, that thou wouldest yet have more of it? Hast thou had so many calls, so many mercies, so many blows and so many examples? Hast thou seen so many laid in the grave, and yet art thou not ready to let go thy sins, and come to Christ? What! after so many convictions and misgivings of conscience, after so many purposes and promises, art thou not yet ready to turn and live? O that thy eyes, thy heart were opened, to know how fair an offer is now made to thee! What a joyful message it is that we are sent on, to bid thee come, for all things are ready.

2. Consider also what calls thou hast to turn and live. How many, how loud, how earnest, how dreadful, and yet what encouraging, joyful calls.

For the principal invitor it is God himself. He that commands heaven and earth, commands thee to turn: and presently, without delay, to turn; he commands the sun to run its course, and to rise upon thee every morning; though it be so glorious a creature, and many times bigger than all the earth, yet it obeys him, and fails not one minute of its appointed time. He commands all the planets, and orbs of heaven, and they obey: he commands the sea to ebb and flow, and the whole creation to keep its course, and they all obey him: the angels of heaven obey his will, when he sends them to minister to such silly worms as we on earth. And yet if he command but a sinner to turn, he will not obey him: he only thinks himself wiser than God, he cavils and pleads the cause of sin, and will not obey. If the Lord Almighty says the word, the heavens and all therein obey him; but if he call a drunkard out of an ale-house he will not obey; or if he call a worldly, fleshly sinner to deny himself, mortify the flesh, and set his heart on a better inheritance, he will not obey.

If thou hadst any love in thee, thou wouldst know the voice, and say, O this is my Father's call! How can I find in my heart to disobey? For the sheep of Christ 'know and hear his voice, and they follow him, and he giveth them eternal life.' If thou hast any spiritual life and sense in thee, at least thou wouldst say, This call is the dreadful voice of God, and who dare disobey? For saith the prophet, 'The lion hath roared, who will not fear?' God is not a man, that thou shouldst trifle and play with him. Remember what he said to Paul at his conversion, 'it is hard for thee to kick against the pricks.' Wilt thou yet go on and despise his word, resist his Spirit, and stop thine ears against his call? Who is it that will have the worst of this? Dost thou know whom thou disobeyest and contendest with, and what thou art doing? It were a far wiser and easier task for thee, to contend with the thorns, and spurn them with thy bare feet, and beat them with thy bare hands, or put thy head into the burning fire. 'Be not deceived, God will not be mocked.' Whosoever else be mocked God will not; you had better play with the fire among gunpowder than with the fire of his burning wrath. 'For our God is a consuming fire.' O how unmeet a match art thou for God; 'it is a fearful thing to fall into his hands.' Therefore it is a fearful thing to contend with him, or resist him. As you love your own souls, take heed what you do. What will you say, if he begin in wrath to plead with you? What will you do if he take you once in hand? Will you then strive against his judgment, as now you do against his grace? Saith the Lord, 'Fury is not in me,' that is, I delight not to destroy: I do it as it were unwillingly; but yet, 'who would set the briars and thorns against me in battle? I would go through them, I would burn them together. Or let him take hold of my strength, that he may make peace

with me, and he shall make peace with me.' It is an unequal combat for the briars and stubble to make war with the fire.

Thus you see who it is that calls you, that should move you to hear this call, and turn: so consider also, by what instruments, how often, and how earnestly he doth it.

Every leaf of the blessed book of God hath, as it were, a voice, and calls out unto thee, Turn and live, turn or thou wilt die. How canst thou open it, and read a leaf, or hear a chapter, and not perceive God bids thee turn?

It is the voice of every sermon thou hearest; for what else is the scope of all, but to call, persuade, and intreat thee to turn.

It is the voice of many a motion of the Spirit, that secretly speaks over these words again, and urges thee to turn.

It is likely sometimes, it is the voice of thy own conscience. Art thou not sometimes convinced, that all is not well with thee; doth not thy conscience tell thee, that thou must be a new man, take a new course, and often call upon thee to return?

It is the voice of the gracious examples of the godly. When thou seest them live an heavenly life, and fly from the sin which is thy delight, this really calls upon thee to turn.

It is the voice of all the works of God. For they also are God's books that teach thee this lesson, by showing thee his greatness, wisdom, and goodness, and calling thee to observe them, and admire the Creator. 'The heavens declare the glory of God, and the firmament showeth his handy work; day unto day uttereth speech, night unto night showeth knowledge:' every time the sun rises upon thee, it really calls thee to turn, as if it should say, 'What do I travel and compass the world for, but to declare to men the glory of their Maker, and to light them to do his work? And do I still find thee doing the work of sin and sleeping out thy life in negligence? Awake thou that sleepest, and arise from the dead, and Christ shall give thee light. The night is spent, the day is at hand. It is now high time to awake out of sleep, let us therefore cast off the works of darkness, and let us put on the armour of light. Let us walk honestly as in the day, not in rioting and drunkenness, not in chambering and wantonness, not in strife and envying; but put ye on the Lord Jesus Christ, and make no provision for the flesh, to fulfil the lusts thereof.' This text was the means of Augustine's conversion.

It is the voice of every mercy thou dost possess. If thou couldst but hear, and understand them, they all cry out unto thee, Turn: why doth the earth bear thee, but to seek and serve the Lord? Why doth it afford thee fruit, but to serve him? Why doth the air afford thee breath, to serve him? Why do all the creatures serve thee with their labours, and their lives, but that thou mightest serve the Lord of them and thee? Why doth he give thee time, health, and strength, but to serve him? Why hast thou meat, drink and clothes, but for his service? Hast thou any thing which thou hast not received? If thou didst receive them, it is reason thou shouldest bethink thee from whom, and to what end and use thou didst receive them. Didst thou never cry to him for help in thy distress? And didst thou not then understand that it was thy part to turn and serve him, if he would deliver thee? He hath done his part, and spared thee yet longer, and tried thee another and another year, yet thou dost not turn. You know the parable of the unfruitful fig-tree; when the Lord had said, 'Cut it down, why cumbereth it the ground?' he was intreated to try it one year longer, and then if it proved not fruitful, to cut it down. Christ himself there makes the application twice over, 'Except ye repent, ye shall all likewise perish.' How many years hath God looked for the fruits of love and holiness from thee, and hath found none? And yet hath spared thee. How many times by thy wilful ignorance, carelessness, and disobedience, hast thou provoked justice to say, Cut him down, why cumbereth he the ground? Yet mercy hath prevailed, and patience hath forborne the killing, damning blow to this day. If thou hadst the understanding of a man within thee, thou wouldst know that all this calls thee to turn. 'Dost thou think thou shalt still escape the judgment of God? Or despisest thou the riches of his goodness, forbearance, and long suffering, not knowing that the goodness of God leadeth thee to repentance? But after thy hardness and impenitent heart treasurest up unto thyself wrath against the day of wrath, and revelation of the righteous God, who will render to every one according to his deeds.'

Moreover, it is the voice of every *affliction*, to call thee to make haste and turn. Sickness and pain cry turn: poverty, the loss of friends, and every twig of the chastising rod cry turn; yet wilt thou not hearken to the call? These have come near thee, and made thee feel: they have made thee groan, and can they not make thee turn.

The very frame of thy nature and being itself bespeaks thy return. Why hast thou reason, but to rule thy flesh, and serve thy Lord? Why hast thou an *understanding soul*, but to learn and know his will, and do it? Why hast thou an heart within thee that can love, fear and desire, but that thou shouldest fear him, love him, and desire after him?

Yea, thine own engagements by promise to the Lord, call upon thee to turn and serve him. Thou hast bound thyself to him by a baptismal covenant, and renounced the world, the flesh, and the devil; this thou hast confirmed by the profession of Christianity, and renewed it at sacraments, and in times of affliction: wilt thou promise and vow, but never perform, and turn to God?

Lay all these together now, and see what should be the issue. The *holy scriptures* call upon thee to turn: the ministers of Christ call upon thee to turn: the Spirit, thy conscience, and the godly, by persuasions and examples, cry turn: the whole world and all the creatures therein that are presented to thy consideration, cry turn: the patient forbearance of God, all the mercies which thou receivest, the rod of God's chastisement cry turn: thy reason, and the frame of thy nature bespeaks thy turning: and so do all thy promises to God, and yet *art thou not resolved to* turn?

3. Moreover, poor hard-hearted sinner, didst thou ever consider upon what terms thou standest all this while with him that calleth on thee to turn? Thou art his own, and owest him thyself, and all thou hast; and may he not command his own? Thou art his absolute servant, and shouldest serve no other master, thou standest at his mercy, and thy life is in his hand; and he is resolved to save thee upon no other terms: thou hast many malicious spiritual enemies, that would be glad if God would but forsake thee; and let them alone with thee, and leave thee to their will; how quickly would they deal with thee in another manner? Thou canst not be delivered from them, but by turning unto God. Thou art fallen under his wrath by thy sin already; and thou knowest not how long his patience will yet wait. Perhaps this is the last year; perhaps the last day: his sword is even at thy heart, while the word is in thine ear; if thou turn not, thou art a dead and undone man. Were thy eyes but open to see where thou standest, even upon the brink of hell, and to see how many thousands are there already that did not turn, thou wouldst see that it is time to look about thee.

Look inwards now, and tell me, how are your hearts affected with these offers of the Lord: you hear what is his mind; he delights not in your death : he calls to you, Turn, turn; it is a fearful sign if all this move thee not, or if it but half move thee, and much more if it make thee more careless in thy misery, because thou hearest of the mercy of God. The working of the medicine will partly tell us, whether there be any hope of the cure. O what glad tidings would it be to those that are now in hell, if they had but such a message from God ! What a joyful word would it be to hear this, Turn and live ! Yea, what a welcome word would it be to thyself, when thou hast felt that wrath of God but an hour: or, if after a thousand, and ten thousand years' torment, thou couldst but hear such a word from God, Turn and live ; and yet wilt thou neglect it, and suffer us to return without our errand?

Behold, sinners, we are set here as the messengers of the Lord, to set before you life and death ; what say you, which of them will you choose ? Christ stands as it were by thee, with heaven in one hand, and hell in the other, and offers thee thy choice, which wilt thou choose ? ' The voice of the Lord makes the rocks to tremble.' And is it nothing to hear him threaten thee, if thou wilt not turn ? Dost thou not understand and feel this voice, ' turn ye, turn ye, why will ye die ?' Why, it is the voice of love, of infinite love, of thy best and kindest friend, as thou mightest easily perceive by the motion, and yet canst thou neglect it ? It is the voice of pity and compassion. The Lord sees whither thou art going, better than thou dost, which makes him call after thee, Turn, turn: he sees what will become of thee, if thou turn not: he thinks with himself, Ah this poor sinner will cast himself into endless torment, if he do not turn : I must in justice deal with him according to my righteous law ; and therefore he calls after thee, Turn, turn. O sinner ! If thou didst but know the thousandth part as well as God doth, the danger that is near you, and the misery that you are running into, we should have no more need to call after you to turn.

Moreover, this voice that calls to thee, is the same that hath prevailed with thousands already, and called all to heaven that are now there : they would not now for a thousand worlds that they had neglected it, and not turned to God. Now what are they possessing that turned at God's call? Now they perceive indeed that it was the voice of love, that meant them no more harm than their salvation. And if thou wilt obey the same call thou shalt come to the same happiness. There are millions that must . for ever lament that they turned not, but there is not a soul in heaven that is sorry that they were converted.

Are you yet resolved, or are you not ; do I need to say no more to you; what will you do ; will you turn or not ? Speak in thy heart to God, though thou speak not out to me : speak, lest he take thy silence for a denial ; speak quickly, lest he never make thee like offer more. Speak resolvedly, and not waveringly ; for he will have no indifferent persons to be his followers. Say in thy heart now, without any more delay, even before thou stir hence, ' By the grace of God, I am resolved presently to turn. Because I know mine own insufficiency, I am resolved to wait on God for his grace, follow him in his ways, forsake my former courses and companions, and give up myself to the guidance of the Lord.'

You are not shut up in the darkness of heathenism, nor in the desperation of the damned. Life is before you, and you may have it on reasonable terms if you will ; yea, on free cost, if you will accept it. The way of God lies plain before you, the church is open to you, and you may have Christ, pardon and holiness, if you will. What say you; will you or will you not ? If you say nay, or say nothing, and still go on, God is witness, this congregation is witness, he who now announces to you these awful truths is witness, and your own consciences are witness, how fair an offer you had this day. Remember you might have had Christ, and you would not; remember, when you have lost it, that you might have had eternal life, as well as others, and would not : and all this because you would not turn!

But let us come to the next doctrine, and hear your reasons.

DOCT. VI. The Lord condescends to reason the case with unconverted sinners, and to ask them why they will die.

A strange disputation it is, both as to the controversy, and as to the disputants.

The controversy or question propounded to dispute of is, why wicked men will damn themselves? Or, whether they will rather die than turn ? Whether they have any sufficient reason for so doing?

The disputants are God and man : the most holy God, and wicked unconverted sinners.

Is it not a strange thing which God doth seem here to suppose, that any man should be willing to die, and be damned; yea, that this should be the case of all the wicked ; that is, of the greatest part of the world ? But you will say, this cannot be ; for nature desires the preservation and felicity of itself, and the wicked are more selfish than others, not less; and therefore how can any man be willing to be damned?

To which I answer, First, It is a certain truth, that no man can be willing of any evil, as evil, but only as it hath some appearance of good; much less can any man be willing to be eternally tormented. Misery, as such, is desired by none. Second, But yet for all that, it is most true, which God here teaches us, that the cause why the wicked die and are damned, is, because they will die and be damned. This is true in several respects.

1. Because they will go the way that leads to hell, though they are told by God and man whether it goes, and where it ends. Though God hath so often professed in his word, that if they hold on in that way they shall be condemned; that they shall not be saved unless they turn. ' There is no peace, saith the Lord, unto the wicked.—The way of peace they know not; there is no judgment in their going; they have made them crooked paths, whosoever goeth therein shall not know peace.' They have the word and the oath of the living God for it, that if they will not turn, they shall not enter into his rest. Yet wicked they are, and wicked they will be, let God and man say what they will: fleshly they are, and fleshly they will be; worldlings they are, and worldlings they will be; though God hath told them that 'the love of the world is enmity to God; and that if any man love the world (in that measure) the love of the Father is not in him.' So that consequently these men are willing to be damned, though not directly: they are willing of the way to hell, and love the certain cause of their torment, though they be not willing of hell itself, and do not love the pain which they must endure.

Is not this the truth of your case? You would not burn in hell, but you will kindle the fire by your sins, and cast yourselves into it; you would not be tormented with devils in hell, but you will do that which will certainly procure it in despite of all that can be said against it. It is just as if you would say, ' I will drink poison, but yet I will not die. I will cast myself headlong from the top of a steeple, but yet I will not kill myself. I will thrust my knife into my heart, but yet I will not take away my life. I will put this fire into my bosom, but yet I will not be burned by it.' Just so it is with wicked men; they will be wicked, and live after the flesh and the world, yet they would not be damned. But do you not know, that the means

lead unto the end; and that God hath, by his righteous law, concluded, that ye must repent or perish? He that will take poison may as well say, I will kill myself, for it will prove no better in the end: though perhaps he loved it for the sweetness of the sugar that was mixed with it, and would not be persuaded it was poison, but that he might take it and do well enough? But it is not his conceits and confidence that will save his life: so if you will be drunkards, fornicators, worldlings, or live after the flesh, you may as well say plainly, we will be damned; for so you shall be unless you turn. Would you not rebuke the folly of a thief or murderer that would say, I will steal or kill, but I will not be hanged; when he knows, that if he do the one, the judge in justice will see that the other be done: if he says, I will steal and murder, he may as well say plainly, I will be hanged; so if you will go on in a carnal life, you may as well say plainly, we will go to hell.

2. Moreover, the wicked will not use those means without which there is no hope of their salvation: he that will not eat, may as well say plainly he will not live, unless he can tell how to live without meat. He that will not go his journey, may as well say plainly, he will not come to the end. He that falls into the water, and will not come out, nor suffer another to help him out, may as well say plainly, he will be drowned. So if you be carnal and ungodly, and will not be converted, nor use the means by which you should be converted, but think it more ado than needs, you may as well say plainly, you will be damned. For if you have found out a way to be saved without conversion, you have done that which was never done before.

3. Yea this is not all, but the wicked are unwilling, even of salvation itself. Though they may desire somewhat which they call by the name of heaven, yet heaven itself, considered in the true nature of the felicity, they desire not: yea, their hearts are quite against it. Heaven is a state of perfect holiness, and of continual love and praise to God, and the wicked have no heart to this. The imperfect love, praise, and holiness which is here to be obtained, they have no mind of; much less of that which is so much greater; the joys of heaven are of so pure and spiritual a nature, that the heart of the wicked cannot truly desire them.

So that by this time you may see on what ground it is that God supposes that the wicked are willing of their own destruction: they will not turn, though they must turn or die: they will rather venture on certain misery, than be converted ; and then to quiet themselves in their sins, they will make themselves believe, that they shall nevertheless escape.

As the controversy is matter of wonder, that ever men should be such enemies to themselves, as wilfully to cast away their souls, so are the disputants too. That God should stoop so low, as thus to plead the case with man ; and that man should be so strangely blind and obstinate as to need all this in so plain a case, yea, and to resist all this, when their own salvation lies upon the issue.

No wonder, if they will not hear us that are men, when they will not hear the Lord himself : as God saith, when he sent the prophet to the Israelites, ' the house of Israel will not hearken unto thee : for they will not hearken unto me : for all the house of Israel are impudent, and hardhearted.' No wonder, if they can plead against a minister, or a godly neighbour, when they will plead against the Lord himself, even against the plainest passages of his word, and think they have reason on their side : when they 'weary the Lord with their words ;' they say, ' wherein have we wearied him ?' The priests that despised his name, durst ask, ' wherein have we despised thy name.' And when they 'polluted his altar, and made the tables of the Lord contemptible,' they durst say, ' wherein have we polluted thee ;' but ' woe unto him,' saith the Lord, ' that striveth with his Maker ! Let the potsherd strive with the potsherds of the earth ; shall the clay say to him that fashioneth it, what makest thou ?'

But why is it that God will reason the case with man ?

Because that man, being a reasonable creature, is accordingly to be dealt with ; and by reason to be persuaded and overcome. God hath therefore endowed them with reason, that they might use it for him. One would think a reasonable creature should not go against the clearest and greatest reason in the world, when it is set before him.

At least men shall see that God did require nothing of them that was unreasonable, but that whatever he commands them, and whatever he forbids them, he hath all the right reason in the world on his side, and they have good reason to obey him, but none to disobey. And thus even the damned shall be forced to justify God, and confess that it was but reason that they should have turned to him, and they shall be forced to condemn themselves, and confess that they have little reason to cast away themselves by the neglecting of his grace in the day of their visitation.

Look up your best and strongest reason, sinners, if you will make good your way : you see now with whom you have to deal. What sayest thou, O unconverted, sensual sinner ? Darest thou venture upon a dispute with God : art thou able to confute him ? Art thou ready to enter the list ? God asks thee, why wilt thou die ? Art thou furnished with a sufficient answer ? Wilt thou undertake to prove that God is mistaken, and that thou art in the right ? O what an undertaking is that ! Why, either he or you is mistaken, when he is for your conversion, and you are against it : he calls upon you to turn, and you will not : he bids you do it presently, even to-day, while it is called to-day, but you delay, and think it time enough hereafter. He saith it must be a total change, that you must be holy and new creatures, and born again ; but you think that less may serve the turn, and that it is enough to patch up the old man, without becoming new. Who is in the right now, God or you ; God calls on you to turn and to live an holy life, and you will not ; by your disobedient lives, it appears you will not. If you will, why do you not ? Why have you not done it all this while ? And why do you not fall upon it yet ? Your wills have the command of your lives, we may certainly conclude, that you are unwilling to turn, when you do not turn. Why will you not ? Can you give any reason for it, that is worthy to be called a reason ?

I that am but a worm, your fellow creature, of a shallow capacity, dare challenge the wisest of you all to reason the case with me, while I plead my Maker's cause, and I need not be discouraged, when I know I plead but the cause that God pleads, and contend for him that will have the best at last. Had I but these two general grounds against you, I am sure that you have no good reason on your side.

1. I am sure it can be no good reason which is against the God of truth and reason ; it cannot be light, that is contrary to the sun. There is no knowledge in any creature, but what it had from God, and therefore none can be wiser than God ; it were reckless presumption for the highest angel to compare with his Creator. It is one of the fullest discoveries of the horrible wickedness of carnal men, and the madness of such who sin, that so silly a worm dare contradict his Maker, and call in question the word of God : yea, that those people in your parishes, that are so beastly ignorant, that they cannot give us a reasonable answer concerning the very principles of religion, and yet so wise in their own conceit, that they dare question the

plainest truths of God, yea, contradict them, and cavil against them, when they can scarcely speak sense, and will believe them no farther than agrees with their foolish wisdom.

2. As I know that God must needs be in the right, so I know the case is so palpable and gross which he pleads against, that no man can have reason for it. Is it possible that a man can have any good reason to break his master's laws, reason to dishonour the Lord of glory, and reason to abuse the Lord that bought him? Is it possible that a man can have any good reason to damn his own immortal soul? Mark the Lord's question, ' Turn ye, turn ye, why will ye die?' Is eternal death a thing to be desired; are you in love with hell; what reason have you wilfully to perish? If you think you have some reason to sin, should you not remember that death is the wages of sin, and think whether you have any reason to undo yourselves body and soul for ever? You should not only ask whether you love the adder, but whether you love the sting. It is such a thing for a man to cast away his everlasting happiness, and to sin against God, that no good reason can be given for it; but the more any one pleads for it, the more mad he shows himself to be. Had you a lordship or a kingdom offered to you, for every sin that you commit, it were not reason but madness to except it. Could you by every sin obtain the highest thing on earth that flesh desires, it were of no considerable value to persuade you in reason to commit it. If it were to please your greatest and dearest friends, or obey the greatest prince on earth, or save your lives, or escape the greatest earthly misery, all these are of no consideration to draw a man in reason to the committing of one sin. If it were a right hand or a right eye that would hinder your salvation, it would be your bounden duty to cast it away, rather than go to hell to save it. For there is no saving a part, when you lose the whole. So exceeding great are the matters of eternity, that nothing in this world deserves once to be named in comparison with them, nor can any earthly thing, though it were life, or crowns and kingdoms, be a reasonable excuse for matters of so high and everlasting consequence. A man can have no reason to cross his ultimate end. Heaven is such a thing, that if you lose it, nothing can supply the want, or make up the loss; and hell is such a thing, that if you suffer it, nothing can remove your misery, or give you ease and comfort. Therefore nothing can be a valuable consideration to excuse you for neglecting your own salvation. For saith

our Saviour, ' What shall it profit a man to gain all the world and lose his own soul?'

O did you but know what matters they are we are now speaking to you of! The saints in heaven have other kind of thoughts of these things. If the devil could come to them that live in the sight and love of God, and should offer them all the luxuries of life to entice them away from God and glory; I pray you tell me, how do you think they would entertain the motion. Nay, if he should offer them to be kings on the earth, do you think this would entice them down from heaven? O with what hatred, and holy scorn would they disdain and reject the motion, and why should not you do so that have heaven opened to your faith, if you had but faith to see it? There is never a soul in hell, but knows by this time, that it was a mad exchange to let go heaven for fleshly pleasure: and that it is not a little mirth, a pleasure, or worldly riches or honour, or the good will, or the word of men, that will quench hell fire, or make him amends that loses his soul. O if you had heard, what I believe, if you had seen what I believe, and that on the credit of the word of God, you would say, there can be no reason to warrant a man to damn his soul; you durst not sleep quietly another night, before you had resolved to turn and live.

If you see a man put his hand in the fire till it burn off, you marvel at it; but this is a thing that a man may have reason for, as bishop Cranmer had when he burnt off his hand for subscribing to popery. If you see a man cut off a leg, or an arm, it is a sad sight; but this is a thing a man may have good reason for; as many a man doth to save his life. If you see a man give his body to be burned to ashes, and to be tormented with stripes and racks, and refuse deliverance when it is offered; this is a hard case to flesh and blood. But this a man may have good reason for; and as many a hundred martyrs have done. But for a man to forsake the Lord that made him, and for a man to run into the fire of hell, when he is told of it, and intreated to turn, that he may be saved; this is a thing that can have no reason in the world, that is reason indeed, to justify or excuse it. For heaven will pay for the loss of any thing that we can lose to get it, or for any labour which we bestow for it. But nothing can pay for the loss of heaven.

I beseech you now, let his word come nearer to your hearts. As you are convinced you have no reason to destroy yourselves, so tell me what reason you have to refuse to turn, and live to God; what reason hath the worldling or drunkard, or ignorant careless sinner of you all, why you should not be as holy as any you know, and be as careful for your souls as any other? Will not hell be as hot to you as to others? Should not your own souls be as dear to you as theirs to them? Hath not God as much authority over you? Why then will ye not become a sanctified people, as well as they?

When God brings down the matter to the very principles of nature, and shows you that you have no more reason to be ungodly, than you have to damn your own souls: if yet you will not understand and turn, it seems a desperate case that you are in.

Now either you have reason for what you do, or you have not. If not, will you go on against reason itself? Will you do that which you have no reason for? But if you think you have, produce them, and make the best of your matter, reason the case a little while with your fellow creature, which is far easier than to reason the case with God. Tell me here, before the Lord, as if thou wert to die this hour, why shouldest thou not resolve to turn this day, before thou stir from the place thou standest in? What reason hast thou to deny, or to delay? Hast thou any reason that satisfies thine own conscience for it? Or any that thou darest own and plead at the bar of God? If thou hast, let us hear them, bring them forth, and make them good. But alas, what false arguments, what excuses, instead of sacred reasons, do we daily hear from ungodly men? But for their necessity, I should be ashamed to name them.

1. One saith, if none shall be saved but such converted and sanctified ones as you talk of, heaven would be but empty; then, God help a great many.

Ans. What! it seems you think God doth not know, or else that he is not to be believed: measure not all by yourselves; God hath thousands and millions of his sanctified ones; but yet they are few in comparison of the world, as Christ himself hath told us. It better beseems you to make that use of this truth which Christ teaches you; 'Strive to enter in at the strait gate; for strait is the gate, and narrow is the way that leadeth unto life, and few there be that find it; but wide is the gate, and broad is the way that leadeth to destruction, and many there be that go in thereat.—And fear not little flock, saith Christ to his sanctified ones, for it is your Father's good pleasure to give you the kingdom.'

Object. 2. I am sure if such as I go to hell, we shall have store of company.

Ans. Will that be any ease or comfort to you?

Or, do you think you may not have company enough in heaven? Will you be undone for company? Or, will you not believe that God will execute his threatenings, because there are so many that are guilty? All these are silly, unreasonable conceits.

Object. 3. But all men are sinners, even the best of you all.

Ans. But all are not *unconverted* sinners. The godly live not in gross sins; and their very infirmities are their grief and burden, which they daily long, pray, and strive to be rid of. Sin hath not dominion over them.

Object. 4. I do not see that professors are any better than other men: they will over-reach and oppress, and are as covetous as any.

Ans. Whatever hypocrites are, it is not so with those that are sanctified. God hath thousands and ten thousands that are otherwise. Though the malicious world doth accuse them of what they can never prove, and of that which never entered into their hearts. And commonly they charge them with heart-sins, which none can see but God; because they can charge them with no such wickedness in their lives, as they are guilty of themselves.

Object. 5. But I am no whoremonger, drunkard, nor oppressor; and therefore why should you call upon me to be converted?

Ans. As if you were not born after the flesh, and had not lived after the flesh; as well as others. Is it not as great a sin, as any of these, for a man to have an earthly mind, to love the world above God, and to have a faithless unhumbled heart? Nay, let me tell you more, that many persons who avoid disgraceful sins, are fast glued to the world, as much slaves to the flesh, as strange to God, and averse to heaven in their more civil course, as others are in their more shameful notorious sins.

Object. 6. But I mean nobody any harm, or do no harm; and why then should God condemn me?

Ans. Is it no harm to neglect the Lord that made thee, the work for which thou camest into the world, and prefer the creature before the Creator; and neglect grace that is daily offered thee? It is the depth of thy sinfulness to be insensible of it. The dead feel not that they are dead. If once thou were made alive, thou wouldst see more amiss in thyself, and marvel at thyself, for making so light of it.

Object. 7. I think you will make men mad under a pretence of converting them: it is enough to rack the brains of simple people, to muse so much on matters too high for them.

Answ. 1. Can you be more foolish than you are already? Or at least, can there be a more dangerous madness, than to neglect your everlasting welfare and wilfully undo yourselves.

2. A man is never well in his senses till he be converted; he neither knows God, nor sin, nor Christ, nor the world, nor himself, nor what his business is on the earth, so as to set himself about it till he be converted. The scripture saith that the wicked are 'unreasonable men,' and 'that the wisdom of the world is foolishness with God;' it is said of the prodigal, that when he came to himself, he resolved to return. It is a wise world when men will disobey God and run to hell for fear of being out of their wits.

3. What is there in the work that Christ calls you to, that should drive a man out of his senses? Is it the loving of God, and calling upon him, and comfortable thinking of the glory to come, and the forsaking of our sins, and the loving of one another, and delighting ourselves in the service of God? Are these such things as should make men mad?

4. And whereas you say, that these matters are too high for us, you accuse God himself for making this our work, giving us his word, and commanding all that will be blessed, to meditate in it day and night. Are the matters which we are made for, and which we live for, too high for us to study? This is plainly to unman us, and to make beasts of us, as if we were like to them that must attend to no higher matters than what belongs to flesh and earth; if heaven be too high for you to think on, and to provide for, it will be too high for you ever to possess.

5. If God should sometimes suffer any weakheaded person to be distracted by thinking of eternal things; this is because they misunderstand them, and run without a guide. Of the two, I had rather be in the case of such a one, than of the mad unconverted world, that take their distraction to be their wisdom.

Object. 8. I do not think that God doth care so much what men think, or speak, or do, as to make so great a matter of it.

Answ. It seems then you take the word of God to be false, and then what will you believe? But your own reason might teach you better, if you believe not the scriptures: for you see God doth not disneglect us, but that he vouchsafed to make us, still preserves us, daily upholds us, and provides for us; and will any wise man make a curious frame for nothing? Will you make or buy a clock, or a watch, and daily look to it, and not care whether it go truly or falsely? Surely if you believe not a particular eye of providence observing your hearts and lives, you cannot believe or expect any particular providence to observe your wants and troubles, to relieve you. And if God had so little cared for you, as you imagine, you would never have lived till now: an hundred diseases would have striven which should first destroy you. Yea, the devil would have haunted you, and brought you away alive, as the great fishes devour the less; and as ravenous beasts and birds devour others. You cannot think that God made man for no end, or use: if he made him for any, it was surely for himself. Can you think he cares not whether his end be accomplished, and whether we do the work that we are made for?

Yea, by this atheistical objection, you make God to have made and upheld all the world in vain. For, what are all other lower creatures for, but for man? What doth the earth but bear us, and nourish us? The beasts serve us with their labours and lives: and so of the rest. Hath God made so glorious an habitation, and set man to dwell in it, and made all his servants: now doth he look for nothing at his hands; nor care how he thinks, or speaks, or lives? This is most unreasonable.

Object. 9. It was a better world when men did not make so much ado about religion.

Answ. 1. It hath ever been the custom to praise the time past. That world that you speak of, was wont to say, It was a better world in our forefathers' days, and so did they of their forefathers. This is but an old custom, because we all feel the evil of our own times, but we see not that which was before us.

2. Perhaps you speak as you think: worldlings think the world is best when it is agreeable to their minds; and when they have most mirth and worldly pleasure. I doubt not but the devil, as well as you, would say, that then it was a better world; for then he had more service and less disturbance; but the world is best, when God is most loved, regarded and obeyed. How else will you know when the world is good or bad, but by this?

Object. 10. There are so many ways and religions, that we know not which to be of; and therefore we will be even as we are.

Answ. Because there are many, will you be in that way that you may be sure is wrong? None are farther out of the way, than worldly, fleshly, unconverted sinners. For they do not err in this or that opinion, as many sects do; but in the very scope of their lives. If you were going a journey that your life lay on, would you stop or turn again, because you meet some cross ways, or because you saw some travellers go the main-way, some the foot-way, and some perhaps break over the hedge, yea, and some miss the way? Or would you not rather be the more careful to inquire the way? If you have some servants that know not how to do your work right, and some that are unfaithful, would you take it well at any of the rest, that would therefore be idle and do you no service, because they see the rest so bad?

Object. 11. I do not see that it goes any better with those that are so godly, than with other men. They are as poor, and in as much trouble as others.

Answ. Perhaps in much more, when God sees it meet. They take not an earthly prosperity for their wages. They have laid up their treasure and hopes in another world, or else they are not Christians indeed. The less they have, the more is behind: and they are content to wait till then.

Object. 12. When you have said all that you can, I am resolved to hope well, and trust in God, and do as well as I can, and not make so much ado.

Answ. 1. Is that doing as well as you can, when you will not turn to God, but your heart is against his holy and diligent service? It is as well as you will indeed; but that is your misery.

2. My desire is that you should hope and trust in God. But for what is it that you will hope; is it to be saved, if you turn and be sanctified? For this you have God's promise; and therefore hope for it, and spare not; but if you hope to be saved without conversion and a holy life, this is not to hope in God but in Satan, or yourselves: for God hath given you no such promise, but told you the contrary; but it is Satan and self-love that made you such promises, and raised you to such hopes.

Well, if these, and such as these, be all you have to say against conversion, and a holy life, your all is nothing, and worse than nothing; and if these and such as these seem reasons sufficient to persuade you to forsake God, and cast yourselves into hell, the Lord deliver you from such reasons, from such blind understandings, and from such senseless hardened hearts. Dare you stand to every one of these reasons at the bar of God? Do you think it will then serve your turn to say, 'Lord, I did not turn, because I had so much to do in the world, or because I did not like the lives of some professors, or because I saw men of so many minds?' How

easily will the light of that day confound and shame such reasons as these? Had you the world to look after? Let the world which you served, now pay you your wages, and save you if it can! Had you not a better world to look after first? And were ye not commanded to 'seek first God's kingdom and righteousness,' and promised, that 'other things shall be added to you?' And were you not told, 'that godliness was profitable to all things, having the promise of this life, and of that which is to come?' Did the sins of professors hinder you? You should rather have been the more watchful, and learned by their falls to beware; and have been the more careful, and not to be more careless; it was the scripture and not their lives, that was your rule. Did the many opinions of the world hinder you? Why, the scripture, that was your rule, did teach you but one way and that was the right way: if you had followed that, even in so much as was plain and easy, you would never have miscarried. Will not such answers as these confound and silence you? If these will not, God hath those that will. When he asks the man, 'Friend, how camest thou in hither, not having on a wedding garment?' That is, what dost thou in my church amongst professed Christians, without a holy heart and life; what answer did he make? Why, the text saith, 'he was speechless,' he had nothing to say. The clearness of the case, and the majesty of God, will then easily stop the mouths of the most confident of you, though you will not be put down by any thing that we can say to you now, but will make good your cause, be it ever so bad. I know already, that not a reason that now you can give me, will do you any good at last, when your case must be opened before the Lord and all the world.

Nay, I scarcely think that your own consciences are well satisfied with your reasons. For if they are, it seems then you have not so much as a purpose to repent: but if you do but purpose to repent, it seems you do not put much confidence in your reasons which you bring against it.

What say you, unconverted sinners; have you any good reason to give, why you should not turn, and presently turn with all your heart; or will you go to hell regardless of reason itself? Bethink you what you do in time, for it will shortly be too late to bethink you. Can you find any fault with God, or his work, or wages; is he a bad master; is the devil, whom ye serve, a better; or is the flesh a better? Is there any harm in a holy life? Is a life of worldliness and ungodliness better? Do you think, in your conscience, that it would do you any harm to be converted, and live an holy life? What harm can it do you? Is it harm to you to have the Spirit of Christ within you, and to have a purified heart? If it be bad to be holy, why doth God say, 'be ye holy, for I am holy?' Is it evil to be like God? Is it not said, that 'God made man in his own image?' Why, this holiness is his image: this Adam lost, and this, Christ, by his word and Spirit, would restore you, as he doth to all that he will save. Why were you baptized into the Holy Ghost; and why do you baptize your children into the Holy Ghost, as your sanctifier, if ye will not be sanctified by him, but think it an hurt to be sanctified? Tell me truly, as before the Lord; though you are loth to live an holy life, had you not rather die in the case of those that do so, than of others? If you were to die this day, had you not rather die in the case of a converted man, than of the unconverted—of an holy and heavenly man, than of a carnal, earthly man? Would you not say as Balaam, 'Let me die the death of the righteous, and let my last end be like his:' and why will you not now be of the mind that you will be of then? First or last, you must come to this: either to be converted, or to wish you had been, when it is too late.

But what is it that you are afraid of losing, if you turn? Is it your friends? You will but change them: God will be your friend, Christ and the Spirit will be your friend, and every Christian will be your friend. You will get one friend that will stand in more stead than all the friends in the world could have done. The friends you lose would have but enticed you to hell, but could not have delivered you; but the friend you get will save you from hell, and bring you to his own eternal rest.

Is it your pleasures that you are afraid of losing; you think you shall never have a happy day again, if once you be converted: alas, that you should think it a greater pleasure to live in foolish sports and merriments, and please your flesh, than live in the believing thoughts of glory, in the love of God, in righteousness and peace, and joy in the Holy Ghost, in which the state of grace consists. If it be a greater pleasure to you to think of your lands, and inheritance, if you were lord of all the country, than it is to a child to play with toys, why should it not be a greater joy to you to think of the kingdom of heaven being yours, than all the riches or pleasures of the world? As it is but foolish child-

ishness, that makes children so delight in trifles, that they would not leave them for all your lands; so it is but foolish worldliness, fleshliness, and wickedness, that makes you so much delight in your houses, lands, meat, drink, ease, and honour, as that you would not part with them for heavenly delights. But what will you do for pleasure when these are gone? Do you not think of that? When your pleasures end in horror, and go out with a foul flavour, the pleasures of the saints are then at the best; I have had myself but a little taste of the heavenly pleasures in the fore-thoughts of the blessed approaching day, and in the present persuasions of the love of God in Christ; but I have taken too deep a draught of earthly pleasures, so that you may see, if I be partial, it is on your side, yet I must profess, from that little experience, that there is no comparison: there is more joy to be had in a day, if the sun of life shine clear upon us, in the state of holiness, than in a whole life of sinful pleasure. 'I had rather be a doorkeeper in the house of God, than to dwell in the tents of wickedness; a day in his courts are better than a thousand any where else.'

The mirth of the wicked is like the laughter of a madman, that knows not his own misery: therefore Solomon saith of such laughter, 'it is mad; and of mirth, what doth it?—It is better to go to the house of mourning, than to go to the house of feasting; for that is the end of all men, and the living will lay it to his heart: sorrow is better than laughter; for by the sadness of the countenance, the heart is made better. The heart of the wise is in the house of mourning, but the heart of fools is in the house of mirth. It is better to hear the rebuke of the wise, than to hear the song of fools; for as the crackling of thorns under a pot, so is the laughter of a fool.' All the pleasure of fleshly things is but like passing vapour. Your loudest laughter is but like that of a man that is tickled, he laughs when he hath no cause of joy. It is a wiser thing for a man to give all his estate, and his life, to be tickled to make him laugh, than for you to part with the love of God, the comforts of holiness, the hopes of heaven, and to cast yourselves into damnation, that you may have your flesh gratified with the pleasure of sin for a little while. Judge as you are men, whether this be a wise man's part. It is your carnal unsanctified nature, that makes an holy life seem grievous to you, and a course of sensuality seem more delightful. If you will but turn, the Holy Ghost will give you another nature and inclination, and then it will be more pleasant to you to be rid of your sin, than now it is to keep it; and you will then say, that you knew not what a comfortable life was till now, and that it was never well with you till God and holiness were your delight:

Quest. But how comes it to pass, that men should be so unreasonable in the matters of salvation? They have wisdom enough in other matters; what makes them so loth to be converted, that there should need so many words in so plain a case, and all will not do, but the most will live and die unconverted?

Ans. To name them only in few words, the causes are these:

1. Men are naturally in love with earth and flesh, they are born sinners, and their nature hath an enmity to God and godliness, as the nature of a serpent hath to a man: and when all that we can say, goes against the habitual inclinations of their natures, no marvel if it little prevail.

2. They are in darkness, and know not the very things that they hear. Like a man that was born blind, and hears a high commendation of the light; but what will hearing do, unless he sees it? They know not what God is, nor what is the power of the cross of Christ, nor what the spirit of holiness is, nor what it is to live in love by faith: they know not the certainty, suitableness, and excellency of the heavenly inheritance. They know not what conversion, and a holy mind and conversation is, even when they hear of it. They are in a mist of ignorance, they are lost and bewildered in sin, like a man that hath lost himself in the night, and knows not where he is, nor how to come to himself again, till the day light recover him.

3. They are wilfully confident, that they need no conversion, but some partial amendment; that they are in the way to heaven already, and are converted, when they are not. If you meet a man that is quite out of his way, you may long enough call on him to turn back again, if he will not believe you that he is out of the way.

4. They are become slaves to their flesh, and drowned in the world to make provision for it. Their lusts, passions, and appetites, have distracted them, and got such an hand over them, that they cannot tell how to deny them, or how to mind any thing else: so that the drunkard saith, I love a cup of good drink and cannot forbear it; the glutton saith, I love good cheer and I cannot forbear; the fornicator saith, I love to have my lusts fulfilled, and I cannot forbear; and the gamester loves to have his sports, and he cannot forbear. So that they are even become captivated slaves to their flesh, and their

very wilfulness is become an impotency, and what they would not do, they say they cannot. The worldling is so taken up with earthly things that he hath neither heart, nor mind, nor time, for heavenly; but as in Pharoah's dream the lean kine did eat up the fat ones, so this lean and barren earth eats up all the thoughts of heaven.

5. Some are so carried away by the stream of evil company, that they are possessed with hard thoughts of a godly life, by hearing them speak against it: or at least they think they may venture to do as they see most do, and so they hold on in their sinful ways; and when one is cut off and cast into hell, and another snatched away from among them, to the same condemnation, it doth not much daunt them, because they see not whither they are gone. Poor sinners! They hold on in their ungodliness for all this; for they little know that their companions are now lamenting it in torments. In Luke xvi. the rich man in hell would willingly have had one to warn his five brethren, lest they should come to that place of torment. He knew their minds and lives, and knew that they were hastening thither, and little dreamed that he was there, yea, and little would have believed one that should have told him so. I remember a passage a gentleman told me he saw upon a bridge over Severn. A man was driving a flock of fat lambs, and something meeting them and hindering their passage, one of the lambs leaped upon the wall of the bridge, and his legs slipping from under him, he fell into the stream, and the rest seeing him, did one after another leap over the bridge into the stream, and were all, or almost all, drowned. Those that were behind, did little know what was become of them that were gone before, but thought that they might venture to follow their companions; but as soon as ever they were over the wall, and falling headlong, the case was altered. Even so it is with unconverted carnal men. One dies by them, and drops into hell, and another follows the same way; and yet they will go after them, because they think not whither they are going. Oh, but when death has once opened their eyes, and they see what is on the other side of the wall, even in another world, then what would they give to be where they were!

6. Moreover, they have a subtile, malicious enemy that is unseen of them, and plays his game in the dark; and it is his principal business to hinder their conversion; and therefore to keep them where they are, by persuading them not to believe the scriptures, or not to trouble their minds with these matters, or by persuading them to think ill of a godly life; or to think

that it is more ado than needs, and that they may be saved without conversion, and without all this stir ; and that God is so merciful, that he will not damn any such as they, or at least, that they may stay a little longer, and take their pleasure, follow the world yet a little longer, then let it go, and repent hereafter, and by such juggling, deluding cheats as these the devil keeps most in his captivity, and leads them to misery.

These, and such like impediments as these, do keep so many thousands unconverted, when God hath done so much, Christ hath suffered so much, and ministers have said so much for their conversion ; when their reasons are silenced, and they are not able to answer the Lord that calls after them, ' Turn ye, turn ye, why will ye die ?' Yet all comes to nothing with the greatest part of them ; and they leave us no more to do after all, but to sit down and lament their wilful misery.

I have now showed you the reasonableness of God's commands, and the unreasonableness of wicked men's disobedience. If nothing will serve but men will yet refuse to turn, we are next to consider who is to blame if they be damned. And this brings me to the last doctrine ; which is,

DOCT. VII. That if after all this, men will not turn, it is not owing to God that they are condemned, but of themselves, even their own wilfulness. They die because they will die, that is, because they will not turn.

If you will go to hell, what remedy ? God here acquits himself of your blood ; it shall not lie on him if you be lost. A negligent minister may draw it upon him ; and those that encourage you, or hinder you not in sin, may draw it upon them ; but be sure of it, it shall not lie upon God. Saith the Lord concerning his unprofitable vineyard, ' Judge, I pray you, between me and my vineyard ; what could have been done more to my vineyard, that I have not done to it ?' When he had ' planted it in a fruitful soil, and fenced it, and gathered out the stones, and planted it with the choicest vines,' what should he have done more to it ? He hath made you men, and endued you with reason ; he hath furnished you with external necessaries, all creatures are at your service : he hath given you a righteous perfect law ; when you had broken it, and undone yourselves, he had pity on you, and sent his Son, by a miracle of condescending mercy, to die for you, and be a sacrifice for your sins, and he 'was in Christ reconciling the world to himself.' The Lord Jesus hath made you a free offer of himself, and eternal life with him, on the

condition you will but accept it, and return. He hath on this reasonable condition offered you the free pardon of all your sins: he hath written this in his word, and sealed it by his Spirit, and sent it to you by his ministers ; they have made the offer to you a hundred, and a hundred times, and called you to accept it, and turn to God. They have in his name intreated you, reasoned the case with you, and answered all your frivolous objections. He hath long waited on you, staid your leisure, and suffered you to abuse him to his face. He hath mercifully sustained you in the midst of your sins : he hath compassed you about with all sorts of mercies. He hath also intermixed afflictions, to mind you of your folly, and call you to reflection: his Spirit hath been often striving with your hearts, and saying there, ' Turn, sinner, turn to him that calleth thee : whither art thou going ; what art thou doing ; dost thou know what will be the end ; how long wilt thou hate thy friends, and love thine enemies ; when wilt thou let go all, and turn, and deliver up thyself to God, and give thy Redeemer the possession of thy soul ; when shall it once be ?'

These pleadings have been used with thee ; when thou hast delayed, thou hast been urged to make haste, and God hath called to thee. ' To-day, while it is called to-day, harden not thy heart ; why not now without any more delay ?' Life hath been set before you ; the joys of heaven have been opened to you in the gospel: the certainty of them have been manifested ; the certainty of the everlasting torments of the damned have been declared to you ; unless you would have had a sight of heaven and hell, what could you desire more ? Christ hath been, as it were, set forth crucified before your eyes. You have been a hundred times told, that you are but lost men, till you come unto him ; as oft as you have been told of the evil of sin, of the vanity of sin, the world, and all the pleasures and wealth it can afford ; of the shortness and uncertainty of your lives, and the endless duration of the joy or torment of the life to come. All this, and more than this, have you been told, and told again ; even till you were weary of hearing it, till you could make the lighter of it, because you had so often heard it; like the smith's dog, that is brought by custom to sleep under the noise of the hammers, when the sparks do fly about his ears ; and though all this have not converted you, yet you are alive, and might have mercy, to this day, if you had but hearts to entertain it. Now let reason itself be judge, whether it be owing to God or you, if after all this you will be unconverted, and be damned? If you die now it is because you will die. What should be said more to you? Or what course should be taken, that is more likely to prevail? Are you able to say and make it good, 'we would willingly have been converted and become new creatures, but we could not; we would have changed our company, our thoughts, and our discourse, but we could not.' Why could you not if you would? What hindered you but the wickedness of your hearts? Who forced you to sin; or who did hold you back from duty? Had you not the same teaching, and time and liberty to be godly as your godly neighbours had? Why then could you not have been godly as well as they? Were the church doors shut against you, or did you not keep away yourselves, or sit and sleep, or hear as if you did not hear? Did God put in any exceptions against you in his word, when he invited sinners to return, and when he promised mercy to those that do return? Did he say, 'I will pardon all that repent except thee?' Did he shut you out from the liberty of his holy worship, or did he forbid you to pray to him any more than others? You know he did not. God did not drive you away from him, but you forsook him, and ran away yourselves. When he called you to him, you would not come. If God had excepted you out of the general promise and offer of mercy, or had said to you, 'Stand off, I will have nothing to do with such as you; pray not to me, for I will not hear you. If you repent never so much, and cry for mercy never so much, I will not regard you.' If God had left you nothing to trust to but desperation, then you had had a fair excuse. You might have said, 'To what end should I repent and turn, when it will do no good?' But this was not your case. You might have had Christ to be your Lord and Saviour, your head and husband, as well as others, and you would not; because ye felt not yourselves sick enough for the physician; and because you could not spare your disease; in your hearts ye said as those rebels, 'We will not have this man to reign over us.' Christ 'would have gathered you under the wings of his salvation, and you would not.'

What desires of your welfare did the Lord express in his holy word? With what compassion did he stand over you and say, 'O that my people had hearkened unto me, and that they had walked in my way.—O that there were such a heart in this people, that they would fear me, and keep all my commandments always, that it might be well with them, and with their children

for ever!—O that they were wise, that they understood this; and that they would consider their latter end.' He would have been your God, and done all for you that your souls could well desire; but you loved the world and your flesh above him; and therefore you would not hearken to him; though you complimented with him, and gave him high titles, yet when he came to the closing, you would have none of him. No marvel then if 'he give you up to your own heart's lusts, and you walked in your own counsels.' He condescends to reason, and pleads the case with you, and asks you 'what is there in me, or my service, that you should be so much against me? What harm have I done thee, sinner? Have I deserved this unkind dealing at thy hands? Many mercies have I showed thee; for which of them dost thou despise me? Is it I, or is it Satan, that is thy enemy? Is it I, or is it thy carnal self, that would undo thee? Is it a holy life, or a life of sin, that thou hast cause to fly from? If thou be undone, thou procurest this to thyself, by forsaking me the Lord that would have saved thee.—Doth not thine own wickedness correct thee, and thy sin reprove thee; thou mayest see that it is an evil and bitter thing, that thou hast forsaken me.— What iniquity have ye found in me, that ye have followed after vanity, and forsaken me.' He calls out, as it were, to the brutes to hear the controversy he hath against you. 'Hear, O ye mountains, the Lord's controversy, and ye strong foundations of the earth: for the Lord hath a controversy with his people, and he will plead with Israel. O my people, what have I done to thee, and wherein have I wearied thee; testify against me, for I brought thee out of Egypt, and redeemed thee, &c. Hear, O heavens, and give ear, O earth, for the Lord hath spoken. I have nourished and brought up children, and they have rebelled against me. The ox knoweth his owner, and the ass his master's crib, but Israel doth not know, my people doth not consider: ah, sinful nation, a people laden with iniquity, a seed of evildoers! &c.—Do you thus requite the Lord, O foolish people and unwise? Is not he thy Father that bought thee, made thee, and established thee?' When he saw that you forsook him even for nothing, and turned away from your Lord and life, to hunt after the chaff of the world, he told you of your folly, and called you to a more profitable employment, 'wherefore do you spend your money for that which is not bread, and your labour for that which satisfieth not? Hearken diligently unto me, and eat ye that which is good, and let your soul delight itself in fatness.

—Incline your ear and come unto me ; hear and your soul shall live, and I will make an everlasting covenant with you, even the sure mercies of David.—Seek ye the Lord while he may be found, call ye upon him, while he is near.—Let the wicked forsake his way, and the unrighteous man his thoughts, and let him return unto the Lord, and he will have mercy upon him, and to our God, for he will abundantly pardon.'

And when you would not hear, what complaints have you put him to, charging it on you, as your wilfulness and stubbornness! ' Be astonished, O heavens, at this, and be horribly afraid : for my people have committed two evils ; they have forsaken me, the fountain of living waters ; and hewed them out cisterns, broken cisterns, that can hold no water.' Many a time hath Christ proclaimed that free invitation to you, ' let him that is athirst come : and whosoever will, let him take the water of life freely.' But you put him to complain after all his offers ; ' they will not come to me that they may have life. He hath invited you to feast with him in the kingdom of his grace ; and you have had excuses from your grounds, your cattle, your worldly business, and when you would not come, you have said you could not, and provoked him to resolve that you should never ' taste of his supper,' and who is to blame but yourselves ? And what can you say is the chief cause of your damnation, but your own wills ? You would be damned. The whole case is laid open by Jesus Christ himself in Prov. i. 20—23. ' Wisdom crieth without, she uttereth her voice in the streets, she crieth in the chief place of the concourse, How long, ye simple ones, will ye love simplicity, and ye scorners delight in their scorning, and fools hate knowledge ? Turn ye at my reproof ; behold I will pour out my Spirit upon you ; I will make known my words unto you. Because I have called and ye refused, I have stretched out my hands, and no man regarded, but ye have set at nought all my counsel, and would have none of my reproofs : I also will laugh at your calamity, I will mock when your fear cometh ; when your fear cometh as desolation, and your destruction cometh as a whirlwind ; when distress and anguish cometh upon you, then shall they call upon me, but I will not answer ; they shall seek me early, but they shall not find me. For that they hated knowledge, and did not choose the fear of the Lord. They would none of my counsels, they despised all my reproof ; therefore shall they eat of the fruit of their own way, and be filled with their own devices. For the turning away of the simple shall

slay them, and the prosperity of fools shall destroy them : but whoso hearkeneth to me, shall dwell safely, and shall be quiet from the fear of evil.' I thought best to recite the whole text at large to you, because it doth show the cause and destruction of the wicked. It is not because God would not teach them, but because they would not learn. It is not because God would not call them, but because they would not turn at his reproof. Their wilfulness is their ruin.

From what hath been said, you may farther learn these following things :

1. From hence you may see, not only what blasphemy and impiety it is, to lay the blame of men's destruction upon God ; but also how unfit these wicked men are to bring in such a charge against their Maker. They cry out upon God, and say he gives them no grace, and his threatenings are severe, and God forbid that all should be damned that be not converted and sanctified, and they think it hard measure, that a short sin should have an endless suffering ; and if they be damned, they say they cannot help it. When in the mean time they are busy about their own destruction, even working the overthrow of their own souls, and will not be persuaded to hold their hand. They think God were cruel if he should damn them, and yet they are cruel to themselves, and they will run into the fire of hell, when God hath told them it is a little before them, and neither intreaties nor threatenings, nor any thing that can be said, will stop them. We see them almost undone ; their careless, worldly, fleshly lives do tell us, that they are in the power of the devil ; we know, if they die before they are converted, all the world cannot save them ; and knowing the uncertainty of their lives, we are afraid every day lest they drop into the fire. And therefore we intreat them to pity their own souls, and not to undo themselves when mercy is at hand, and they will not hear us. We intreat them to cast away their sin, and come to Christ without delay, and to have some mercy on themselves : but they will have none. And yet they think that God must be cruel if he condemn them. O wilful wretched sinners ! It is not God that is so cruel to you ; it is you that are cruel to yourselves. You are told you must turn or burn, and yet you turn not. You are told, that if you will needs keep your sins, you shall keep the curse of God with them ; and yet you will keep them. You are told, that there is no way to happiness but by holiness, and yet you will not be holy. What would you have God say more to you ; what would you have him do

with his mercy; he offered it to you, and you will not have it. You are in the toils of sin and misery, and he would give you his hand to help you out, and you refuse his help; he would cleanse you of your sins, and you had rather keep them. You love your lusts, and love your gluttony, and sports, and drunkenness, and will not let them go; and would you have him bring you to heaven whether you will or not? Or would you have him to bring you and your sins to heaven together? Why, that is an impossibility; you may as well expect he should turn the sun into darkness. What! an unsanctified, fleshly heart be in heaven! It cannot be. 'There entereth nothing that is unclean.—For what communication hath light with darkness, or Christ with Belial?—All the day long hath he stretched out his hands to a disobedient and gainsaying people.'

What will ye do now? Will you cry to God for mercy? Why, God calleth upon you to have mercy upon yourselves, and you will not; ministers see the poisoned cup in the drunkard's hand, and tell him there is poison in it, and desire him to have mercy on his soul, and forbear, and he will not hear us; drink it he must and will, he loves it, and therefore though hell comes next, he saith he cannot help it. What should one say to such men as these? We tell the ungodly, careless worldlings, 'it is not such a life that will serve the turn, or ever bring you to heaven. If a bear were at your back, you would mend your pace; and when the curse of God is at your back, and Satan and hell are at your back, you will not stir, but ask, what needs all this ado? Is an immortal soul of no more worth? O have mercy upon yourselves!' But they will have no mercy on themselves, nor once regard us. We tell them the end will be bitter. Who can dwell with the everlasting fire? Yet they will have no mercy upon themselves. Yet will these shameful transgressors say, that God is more merciful than to condemn them, when it is themselves that cruelly and unmercifully run upon condemnation? And if we should go to them and intreat them, we cannot stop them; if we should fall down on our knees to them, we cannot stop them; but to hell they will, and yet will not believe that they are going thither. If we beg of them for the sake of God that made them, and preserves them; for the sake of Christ that died for them; for the sake of their own poor soul, to pity themselves, and go no farther in the way to hell, but come to Christ while his arms are open, and enter into the state of life, while the door stands open, and now take mercy while mercy may be had,

they will not be persuaded. If we should die for it, we cannot get them so much as now and then to consider with themselves of the matter and to turn. And yet they can say, 'I hope God will be merciful.' Did you never consider what he saith, 'it is a people of no understanding, therefore he that made them will not have mercy on them; and he that formed them will show them no favour.' If another man will not clothe you when you are naked, and feed you when you are hungry, you will say he is unmerciful; if he should cast you into prison, or beat or torment you, you would say he is unmerciful. And yet you would do a thousand times more against yourselves, even cast away both soul and body for ever, and never complain of your own unmercifulness. Yea, and God that waited upon you all the while with his mercy, must be taken to be unmerciful, if he punish you after all this. Unless the holy God of heaven will give these hardened men leave to trample upon his Son's blood, and with the Jews, as it were again to spit in his face, do despite to the Spirit of grace, make a jest of sin, a mock at holiness, and more disesteem saving mercy than the filth of their fleshly pleasure; and unless, after all this, he will save them by the mercy which they cast away, and would have none of, God himself must be called unmerciful by them; but he will be justified when he judgeth; and he will not stand or fall at the bar of a sinful worm.

I know there are many particular cavils that are brought by them against the Lord, but I shall not here stay to answer them particularly, having done it already in my Treatise of Judgment, to which I shall refer them. Had the disputing part of the world been as careful to avoid sin and destruction, as they have been busy in searching after the cause of them, and forward indirectly to impute it to God, they might have exercised their judgment more profitably, and have less wronged God, and sped better themselves. When so vile a monster as sin is within us, and so heavy a thing as punishment is on us, and so dreadful a thing as hell is before us, one would think it should be an easy question who is in the fault, and whether God or man be the principal or culpable cause? Some men are such favourable judges of themselves, that they are more prone to accuse infinite perfection and goodness itself, than their own hearts; and imitate their first parents who said, 'the serpent tempted me, and the woman that thou gavest me, gave unto me, and I did eat,' secretly implying that God was the cause. So, say they, 'the understanding that thou gavest me, was unable to discern ; the will that thou gavest me, was unable to make a better choice; the objects which thou didst set before me, did entice me; the temptation which thou didst permit to assault me, prevailed against me.' And some are so loth to think that God can make a self-determining creature, that they dare not deny him that which they take to be his prerogative, to be the determiner of the will in every sin, as the first efficient immediate physical cause. And many could be content to acquit God from so much causing of evil, if they could but reconcile it with his being the chief cause of good: as if truths would be no longer truths, than we are able to see them in their perfect order and coherence. Because our shallow understandings cannot set them right together, nor assign each truth its proper place, we presume to conclude, that some must be cast away. This is the fruit of proud self-conceit, when men receive not God's truth as a child his lesson, in a holy submission to the holy omniscience of our teacher, but as censurers that are too wise to learn.

Object. But we cannot convert ourselves till God convert us ; we can do nothing without his grace. It is not in him that willeth, nor in him that runneth, but in God that showeth mercy.

Ans. 1. God hath two degrees of mercy to show: the mercy of conversion first ; and the mercy of salvation last: the latter he will give to none but those that will and run, and hath promised it to them only. The former is to make them willing that were unwilling ; and though your own willingness and endeavours deserve not his grace, yet your wilful refusal deserves that it should be denied unto you. Your *disability is your very unwillingness itself,* which excuses not your sin, but makes it the greater. You could turn, if you were but truly willing, and if your wills themselves are so corrupted, that nothing but effectual grace will move them, you have the more cause to seek for that grace, and yield to it, and do what you can in the use of the means, and not neglect it, nor set against it. Do what you are able first, and then complain of God for denying you grace, if you have cause.

Object. But you seem to intimate all this while that man hath free-will.

Ans. The dispute about free-will is beyond your capacity, I shall therefore now trouble you with no more but this about it. Your will is naturally a free, that is, a self-determining faculty, but it is viciously inclined, and backward to do good; and therefore we see by sad experience

that it hath not a virtuous moral freedom. But that it is the wickedness of it which deserves the punishment. I pray you let us not befool ourselves with opinions. Let the case be your own. If you had an enemy so malicious, that he falls upon you and beats you every time he meets you, and takes away the lives of your children, will you excuse him, because he saith, I have not free-will, it is my nature, I cannot choose, unless God give me grace ? If you have a servant that robs you, will you take such an answer from him ? Might not every thief and murderer that is hanged at the assizes give such an answer, I have not free-will, I cannot change my own heart: what can I do without God's grace ? Shall they therefore be acquitted ? If not, why then should you think to be acquitted for a course of sin against the Lord ?

2. From hence also you may observe these three things together. First, What a subtle tempter Satan is. Second What a deceitful thing sin is. Third, What a foolish creature corrupted man is. A subtle tempter indeed, that can persuade the greatest part of the world to go wilfully into everlasting fire, when they have so many warnings and dissuasives as they have! A deceitful thing is sin indeed, that can bewitch so many thousands to part with everlasting life, for a thing so base and utterly unworthy: a foolish creature is man indeed, that will be so cheated of his salvation for nothing, yea, for a known nothing ; and that by an enemy, a known enemy! You would think it impossible that any man in his senses should be persuaded, for a trifle, to cast himself into the fire or water, into a coal-pit, to the destruction of his life? And yet men will be enticed to cast themselves into hell. If your natural lives were in your own hands, that you should not die till you would kill yourselves, how long would most of you live? Yet when your everlasting life is so far in your own hands, under God, that you cannot be undone till you undo yourselves, how few of you will forbear your own undoing! Ah, what a silly thing is man ; and what a bewitching and befooling thing is sin !

3. From hence also you may learn, that it is no great wonder if wicked men be hinderers of others in the way to heaven, and would have as many unconverted as they can, and would draw them into sin, and keep them in it. Can you expect that they should have mercy on others, that have none upon themselves; and that they should much stick at the destruction of others, that stick not to destroy themselves ? They do no worse by others, than they do by themselves.

4. Lastly, You may hence learn that the greatest enemy to man is himself, and the greatest judgment in this life that can befall him is to be left to himself; that the greatest work that grace hath to do is to save us from ourselves, and the greatest accusations and complaints of men should be against themselves; that the greatest work we have to do ourselves, is to resist ourselves, and that the greatest enemy we should daily pray and strive against, is our carnal hearts and wills; and the greatest part of your work, if you would do good to others, and help them to heaven, is to save them from themselves, even from their own blind understandings, corrupted wills, perverse affections, violent passions, and unruly senses. I only name all these for brevity sake, and leave them to your farther consideration.

Now we have found out the great delinquent and murderer of souls, even men's selves, their own wills; what remains, but that you judge according to the evidence, and confess this great iniquity before the Lord, be humbled for it, and do so no more? To these three ends distinctly, I shall add a few words more. First, Farther to convince you. Second, To humble you. And Third, To reform you, if there be yet any hopes.

1. We know so much of the exceedingly gracious nature of God, who is willing to do good, and delights to show mercy, that we have no reason to suspect him of being the culpable cause of our death, or call him cruel: he made all good, and he preserves and maintains all: 'the eyes of all things do wait upon him, and he giveth them their meat in due season; he openeth his hand, and satisfieth the desires of the living.' He is not only 'righteous in all his ways,' and therefore will deal justly, and holily in all his works (and therefore not the author of sin) but 'he is also good to all, and his tender mercies are over all his works.'

But as for man, we know his mind is dark, his will perverse, and his affections carry him headlong, so that he is fitted by folly and corruption, to such a work, as the destroying of himself. If you saw a lamb lie killed in the way, would you sooner suspect the sheep or the dog, or wolf to be the author of it, if they both stand by; or if you see an house broken, and the people murdered, would you sooner suspect the prince, or judge, that is wise and just, and had no need; or a 'known thief, or murderer?' I say, therefore, 'Let no man say when he is tempted, that he is tempted of God; for God cannot be tempted with evil, neither tempteth he any man (to draw him to sin) but every man is tempted, when he is drawn away of his own lust, and enticed. Then when lust hath conceived it bringeth forth sin; and sin, when it is finished, bringeth forth death.'

You see here that sin is the offspring of your own depraved desires, and not to be fathered on God; that death is the offspring of your own sin, and the fruit which it will yield you as soon as it is ripe. You have a treasure of evil in yourselves, as a spider hath of poison, from whence you are bringing forth hurt to yourselves; and spinning such webs as intangle your own souls. Your nature shows that you are the cause.

2. It is evident you are your own destroyers, in that you are so ready to entertain any temptation almost that is offered you. Satan is scarcely readier to move you to any evil, than you are ready to hear, and to do as he would have you. If he would tempt your understanding to error and prejudice, you yield. If he hinder you from good resolutions, it is soon done: if he would cool any good desires or affections, it is soon done: if he would kindle any lust, or vile affections and desires in you, it is soon done: if he would put you on to evil thoughts, words, or deeds, you are so free that he needs no rod or spur: if he would keep you from holy thoughts, words, and ways, a little doth it; you need no curb. You examine not his suggestions, nor resist them with any resolution, nor cast them out as he casts them in, nor quench the sparks which he endeavours to kindle. But you set in with him, meet him half-way, embrace his motions, and tempt him to tempt you. It is easy to catch such greedy fish that are ranging for a bait, and will take the bare hook.

3. Your destruction is evidently procured by yourselves, in that you resist all that would help to save you, and would do you good, or hinder you from undoing yourselves. God would help and save you by his word, and you resist it, it is too strict for you. He would sanctify you by his Spirit, and you resist and quench it. If any man reprove you for your sin, you fly in his face with evil words; and if he would draw you to a holy life, and tell you of your present danger, you give him little thanks, but either bid him look to himself, he shall not answer for you; or else at best you put him off with heartless thanks, and will not turn when you are persuaded. If ministers would privately instruct and help you, you will not come to them, your unhumbled souls feel but little need of their help. If they would catechise you, you are too old to be catechised, though you are not too

old to be ignorant and unholy. Whatever they can say to you for your good, you are so self-conceited and wise in your own eyes, even in the depth of ignorance, that you will regard nothing that agrees not with your present conceits, but contradict your teachers, as if you were wiser than they; you resist all that they can say to you, by your ignorance and wilfulness, foolish cavils, shifting evasions, and unthankful rejections; so that no good that is offered, can find any welcome acceptance or entertainment with you.

4. Moreover, it is apparent that you are self-destroyers, in that you draw the matter of your sin and destruction even from the blessed God himself; you like not the contrivance of his wisdom: you like not his justice, but take it for cruelty: you like not his holiness, but are ready to think he is such a one as yourselves, and makes as light of sin as you: you like not his truth, but would have his threatenings, even his peremptory threatenings, prove false. His goodness, which you seem most highly to approve, you partly abuse to the strengthening of your sin, as if you might the more freely sin because God is merciful, and because his grace doth so much abound.

5. Yea, you draw destruction from your blessed Redeemer, and death from the Lord of life himself, and nothing more emboldens you in sin, than that Christ hath died for you; as if now the danger of death were over, and you might boldly venture: as if Christ were become a servant to Satan, and your sins, and must wait upon you while you are abusing him; because he is become the physician of souls, and is able to save to the utmost, all that come to God by him, you think he must suffer you to refuse his help, and throw away his medicines, and must save you, whether you will come to God by him or not; so that a great part of your sins are occasioned by your bold presumption upon the death of Christ, and from not considering that he came to redeem his people from their sins, to sanctify them a peculiar people to himself, and to conform them in holiness to the image of their heavenly Father, and to their head.

6. You also procure your own destruction from all the providences and works of God. When you think of his eternal fore-knowledge and decrees, it is to harden you in your sin, or possess your minds with quarrelling thoughts, as if his decrees might spare you the labour of repentance, and an holy life, or else were the cause of your sin and death. If he afflict you, you

repine; if he prosper you, you the more forget him, and are the more backward to the thoughts of the life to come: if the wicked prosper, you forget the end that will set all reckonings straight; and are ready to think it is as good to be wicked as godly. And thus you draw your death from all.

7. The like you do from all the creatures and mercies of God to you; he gives them to you as the tokens of his love, and furniture for his service, and you turn them against him to the pleasing of your flesh. You eat and drink to please your appetite, not for the glory of God, and to enable you for his work; your clothes you abuse to pride; your riches draw your hearts from heaven; your honours and applause puff you up; if you have health and strength, it makes you more secure, and forget your end. Yea, other men's mercies are abused by you to your hurt: if you see their honours and dignity, you are provoked to envy them; if you see their riches, you are ready to covet them; if you look upon beauty, you are stirred up to lust; and it is well if godliness be not an eye-sore to you.

8. The very gifts that God bestows on you, and the ordinances of grace which he hath instituted for his church, you turn into your sin. If you have better parts than others, you grow proud and self-conceited: if you have but common gifts, you take them for special grace. You take the bare hearing of your duty for so good a work, as if it would excuse you for not obeying it. Your prayers are turned into sin, because you 'regard iniquity in your hearts,—and depart not from iniquity when you call on the name of the Lord.—Your prayers are abominable, because you turn away your ear from hearing the law,' and are more ready to 'offer the sacrifice of fools,' thinking you do God some special service, than to hear his word and obey it. You examine not yourselves before you receive the supper of the Lord, but not discerning the Lord's body, eat and drink judgment to yourselves.

9. Yea, the persons you converse with, and all their actions, you make the occasions of your sin and destruction. If they live in the fear of God, you hate them; if they live ungodly, you imitate them; if the wicked are many, you think you may the more boldly follow them; if the godly be few, you are the more emboldened to despise them: if they walk exactly, you think they are too precise: if one of them fall into a particular temptation, you stumble upon them, and turn away from holiness, because others are imperfectly holy; as if you were warranted to break your necks be-

cause some others have, by their heedlessness, sprained a sinew or disjointed a bone. If a hypocrite discover himself, you say, they are all alike, and think yourselves as honest as the best. A professor can scarcely slip into any miscarriage, but because he cuts his finger, you think you may boldly cut your throats. If ministers deal plainly with you, you say they rail; if they speak gently or coldly, you either sleep under them, or are little more affected than the seats you sit upon. If any errors creep into the church, some greedily entertain them, and others reproach the Christian doctrine for them, which is most against them. And if we would draw you from any ancient rooted error, which can but plead two, or three, or six, or seven hundred years' custom, you are as much offended with a motion for reformation, as if you were to lose your life by it, and hold fast old errors while you cry out against new ones. Scarce a difference can arise among the ministers of the gospel, but you will fetch your own death from it. And you will not hear, or at least, not obey the unquestionable doctrine of any of those that agree not with your conceits: one will not hear a minister, because he reads his sermons, and another will not hear him, because he doth not read them: one will not hear him, because he saith the Lord's prayer; and another will not hear him, because he doth not use it: one will not hear them that are for episcopacy, and another will not hear them that are against it. And thus I might show you in many other cases, how you turn all that comes near you to your own destruction; so clear is it, that the ungodly are self-destroyers, and that their perdition is of themselves. Methinks now, upon the consideration of what is said, and the review of your own ways, you should bethink you what you have done, be ashamed, and deeply humbled, to remember it. If you be not, I pray you consider these following truths.

1. To be your own destroyers, is to sin against the deepest principle in your natures, even the principle of self-preservation; every thing naturally desires or inclines to its own felicity, welfare, or perfection? And will you set yourselves to your own destruction? When you are commanded to love your neighbours as yourselves, it is supposed that you naturally love yourselves; but if you love your neighbours no better than yourselves, it seems you would have all the world to be damned.

2. How extremely do you cross your own intentions! I know you intend not your own damnation, even when you are procuring it; you think you are but doing good to yourselves by gratifying the desires of your flesh. But alas, it is but as a draught of cold water in a burning fever. If indeed you would have pleasure, profit, or honour, seek them where they are to be found, and do not hunt after them in the way to hell.

3. What pity is it, that you should do that against yourselves, which none else in earth or hell can do! If all the world were combined against you, or all the devils in hell were combined against you, they could not destroy you without yourselves, nor make you sin, but by your own consent. Will you do that against yourselves which none else can do; you have hateful thoughts of the devil, because he is your enemy, and endeavours your destruction; and will you be worse than devils to yourselves? Why thus it is with you, if you had hearts to understand it; when you run into sin, and run from godliness, and refuse to turn at the call of God, you do more against your own souls than men or devils could do besides. If you should set yourselves and bend your minds to do yourselves the greatest mischief, you could not devise to do a greater.

4. You are false to the trust that God hath reposed in you. He hath much intrusted you with your own salvation; and will you betray your trust? He hath set you with all diligence to keep your hearts; and is this the keeping of them.

5. You do even forbid all others to pity you, when you will have no pity on yourselves: if you cry to God, for mercy, in the day of your calamity, what can you expect but that he should thrust you away, and say, nay, thou wouldst not have mercy on thyself; who brought this upon thee but thy own wilfulness? And if your brethren see you for ever in misery, how should they pity you, that were your own destroyers, and would not be persuaded.

6. It will for ever make you your own tormentors in hell, to think on it, that you brought yourselves wilfully to that misery. Oh, what an agonizing thought it will be for ever, to think with yourselves that this was your own doing; that you were warned of this day, and warned again, but it would not do; that you wilfully sinned and turned from God; that you had time as well as others, but you abused it. You had teachers as well as others, but you refused their instruction; you had holy examples, but you did not imitate them; you were offered Christ, grace, and glory as well as others, but you had more mind to fleshly pleasures; you had a prize in your hands, but had not a heart to lay it out. Can it choose but torment you, to

think of this your present folly? Oh, that your eyes were opened to see what you have done in the wilful wronging of your own souls! And that you better understood those words of God, 'hear instruction, and be wise, and refuse it not: blessed is the man that heareth me, watching daily at my gates, waiting at the posts of my doors; for whoso findeth me, findeth life, and shall obtain favour of the Lord; but he that sinneth against me, wrongeth his own soul; and they that hate me, love death.'

Now I am come to the conclusion of this work, my heart is troubled to think how I shall leave you, lest after this the flesh should deceive you, and the world and the devil should keep you asleep, and I should leave you as I found you, till you awake in hell. Though in care of your poor souls, I am afraid of this, as knowing the obstinacy of a carnal heart; yet I can say with the prophet Jeremiah, 'I have not desired the woful day, the Lord knoweth.' I have not with James and John, desired that fire might come down from heaven, to consume them that refused Jesus Christ. But it is the preventing of the eternal fire that I have been all this while endeavouring: and O, that it had been a needless work! That God and conscience might have been as willing to spare me this labour, as some of you could have been. But dear friends, I am so loth you should lie in everlasting fire, and be shut out of heaven, if it be possible to prevent it, that I shall once more ask you, what do you now resolve? Will you turn, or die? I look upon you as a physician on his patient, in a dangerous disease, that saith unto him, though you are so far gone, take but this medicine, forbear but these few things that are so hurtful to you, and I dare warrant your life; but if you will not do this, you are a dead man. What would you think of such a man, if the physician and all the friends he hath, cannot persuade him to take one medicine to save his life, or to forbear one or two poisonous things that would kill him? This is your case. As far as you are gone in sin, do but now turn and come to Christ, take his remedies, and your souls shall live. Cast up your deadly sins by repentance, and return not to your poisonous vomit any more, and you shall do well. But yet if it were your bodies, that we had to deal with, we might partly know what to do for you. Though you would not consent, you might be held or bound, while the medicine was poured down your throats, and hurtful things might be kept from you. But about your souls it cannot be so; we cannot convert you against your wills.

There is no carrying madmen to heaven in fetters. You may be condemned against your wills, because you sinned with your wills; but you cannot be saved against your wills. The wisdom of God hath thought meet to lay man's salvation or destruction very much upon the choice of their own wills: that no man shall come to heaven that chose not the way to heaven; and no man shall come to hell, but shall be forced to say, I have the thing I chose, my own will did bring me hither. Now if I could but get you to be willing, to be thoroughly, resolvedly, and habitually willing, the work were more than half done. Alas, must we lose our friends, and must they lose their God, their happiness, their souls, for want of this? O God forbid! It is a strange thing to me, that men are so inhuman and stupid in the greatest matters, that in lesser things are very civil and courteous, and good neighbours. For ought I know, I have the love of all, or almost all, my neighbours, so far, that if I should send to every man in the town, parish, or country, and request a reasonable courtesy of them, they will grant it me; and yet when I come to request of them the greatest matter in the world, for themselves, and not for me, I can have nothing of many of them, but a patient hearing. I know not whether people think a man in the pulpit is in good earnest or not, and means as he speaks. For I think I have few neighbours, but if I were sitting familiarly with them, and telling them of what I have seen or done, or known in the world, they would believe me, and regard what I say; but when I tell them from the infallible word of God, what they themselves shall see and know in the world to come, they show by their lives that they do either not believe it, or not much regard it. If I meet any one of them on the way, and told them, yonder is a coal pit, or there is a quick-sand, or there are thieves lay in wait for you, I could persuade them to turn by. But when I tell them that Satan lies in wait for them, and that sin is poison to them, and that hell is not a matter to be jested with, they go on as if they did not hear me. Truly neighbours, I am in as good earnest with you in the pulpit, as I am in any familiar discourse, and if ever you will regard me, I beseech you let it be here. I think there is not a man of you all, but if my own soul lay at your wills, you would be willing to save it; though I cannot promise that you would leave your sins for it.

Tell me, thou drunkard, art thou so cruel to me that speaks to thee, that thou wouldst not forbear a few cups of drink, if thou knewest it would save my soul from hell? Hadst thou rather I did burn there for ever, than thou shouldst live soberly as other men do? If so, may I not say, thou art an unmerciful monster, and not a man? If I came hungry or naked to one of your doors, would you not part with more than a cup of drink to relieve me? I am confident you would: if it were to save my life, I know you would, some of you, hazard your own. And yet will not be intreated to part with your sensual pleasures for your own salvation? Wouldst thou forbear an hundred cups of drink, to save my life, if it were in thy power, and wilt thou not do it to save thy own soul? I profess to you, I am as hearty a beggar with you this day, for the saving of your souls, as I would be for my own supply, if I were forced to come a begging to your doors. Therefore if you would hear me then, hear me now. If you would pity me then, be entreated now to pity yourselves. I do again beseech you, as if it were on my bended knees, that you would hearken to your Redeemer, and turn, that you may live. All you that have lived in ignorance and carelessness, and presumption, to this day; all you that have been drowned in the cares of the world, and have no mind of God and eternal glory: all you that are enslaved to your fleshly desires of meats and drinks, sports and lust: and all you that know not the necessity of holiness, and never were acquainted with the sanctifying work of the Holy Ghost upon your souls; that never embraced your blessed Redeemer by a lively faith, with admiring and thankful apprehensions of his love, that never felt an higher estimation of God and heaven, and a heartier love to them, than to your fleshly prosperity, and the things below: I earnestly beseech you, not only for my sake, but for the Lord's sake, and for your soul's sake, that you go not on one day longer in your former condition, but look about you and cry to God for converting grace, that you may be made new creatures, and may escape the plagues that are a little before you. If ever you will do any thing for me, grant me this request, to turn from your evil ways and live: deny me any thing that ever I shall ask you for myself, if you will, but grant me this. If you deny me this, I care not for any thing else that you would grant me. Nay, as ever you will do any thing at the request of the Lord that made you, and redeemed you, deny him not this: for if you deny him this, he cares for nothing that you shall grant him. As ever you would have him hear your prayers, and grant your requests, and do for you at the hour of death and day of judgment, or in any of

your extremities, deny not his request now in the day of your prosperity. Believe it, death and judgment, heaven and hell, are other matters when you come near them, than they seem to carnal eyes afar off. Then you will hear such a message as I bring you, with more awakened regardful hearts.

Well, though I cannot hope so well of all, I will hope that some of you are by this time purposing to turn and live; and that you are ready to ask me, as the Jews did Peter when they were pricked to their hearts, and said, 'Men and brethren, what shall we do? How might we come to be truly converted? We are willing, if we did but know our duty. God forbid, that we should choose destruction, by refusing conversion, as hitherto we have done.'

If these be the thoughts and purposes of your hearts I say of you, as God did of a promising people, 'They have well said all that they have spoken; O that there was such an heart in them, that they would fear me, and keep all my commandments always.' Your purposes are good; O that there were but hearts in you to perform these purposes! In hope thereof, I shall gladly give you directions what to do; and that but briefly, that you may the more easily remember them for your practice.

Direction I. If you would be converted and saved, labour to understand the necessity and true nature of conversion; for what, from what, to what, and by what it is, that you must turn.

Consider what a lamentable condition you are in till the hour of your conversion, that you may see it is not a state to be rested in. You are under the guilt of all the sins that ever you committed; under the wrath of God, and the curse of his law; you are bond-slaves to the devil, and daily employed in his work against the Lord, yourselves and others. You are spiritually dead and deformed, as being void of the holy life, nature, and image of the Lord. You are unfit for any holy work, and do nothing that is truly pleasing unto God. You are without any promise or assurance of his protection; and live in continual danger of his justice, not knowing what hour you may be sent to hell, and most certain to be damned if you die in that condition. Nothing short of conversion, can prevent it. Whatever civilities, amendments, or virtues are short of true conversion, will never procure the saving of your souls. Keep the true sense of this natural misery, and so of the necessity of conversion on your hearts.

Then you must understand what it is to

be converted ; it is to have a new heart or disposition and a new conversation.

Quest. For what must we turn?

Answ. For these ends following, which you may attain. First, You shall immediately be made living members of Christ, have an interest in him, be renewed after the image of God, be adorned with all his graces, quickened with a new and heavenly life, saved from the tyranny of Satan and the dominion of sin, be justified from the curse of the law, have the pardon of all the sins of your whole lives, be accepted of God, made his sons, have liberty with boldness to call him Father, and go to him by prayer, in all your needs, with a promise of acceptance ; you shall have the Holy Ghost to dwell in you, to sanctify and guide you. You shall have part in the brotherhood, communion and prayers of the saints. You shall be fitted for God's service; be freed from the dominion of sin, be useful and a blessing to the place where you live, and shall have the promise of this life and that which is to come. You shall want nothing that is truly good for you, and your necessary afflictions you will be enabled to bear; you may have some taste of the communion of God in the spirit; especially in all holy ordinances, where God prepares a feast for your souls; you shall be heirs of heaven while you live on earth, and may foresee, by faith, the everlasting glory, and so may live and die in peace : you shall never be so low, but your peace and happiness will be incomparably greater than your misery.

How precious is every one of these blessings, which I do but briefly name, and which in this life you may receive !

Then, Second, At death your souls shall go to Christ and at the day of judgment both soul and body shall be justified and glorified, and enter into your Master's joy : where your happiness will consist in these particulars :—

1. You shall be perfected yourselves: your mortal bodies shall be made immortal, and the corruptible shall put on incorruption ; you shall no more be hungry, thirsty, weary, or sick : nor shall you need to fear either shame, sorrow, death, or hell. Your souls shall be perfectly freed from sin, perfectly fitted for the knowledge, love, and praises of the Lord.

2. Your employment shall be to behold your glorified Redeemer, with all your holy fellow-citizens of heaven : to see the glory of the most blessed God, to love him perfectly, be loved by him, and to praise him everlastingly.

3. Your glory will contribute to the glory of the new Jerusalem, the city of the living God,

which is more than to have a private felicity to yourselves.

4. Your glory will contribute to the glorifying of your Redeemer, who will for ever be magnified and pleased in you that are the travail of his soul : and this is more than the glorifying of yourselves.

5. The eternal Majesty, the living God, will be glorified in your glory: both as he is magnified by your praises, as he communicates of his glory and goodness to you, as he is pleased in you, and in the accomplishment of his glorious works, in the glory of the new Jerusalem, and of his Son.

All this, the poorest beggar of you that is converted shall certainly and endlessly enjoy.

You see for what you must turn: next you must understand from what you must turn : and that is, in a word, from your carnal self, which is the end of all the unconverted ; from the flesh, that would be pleased before God, and would still be enticing you thereto; from the world that is the bait ; and from the devil, that is the angler for souls, and the deceiver ; and so from all known and wilful sins.

Next you must know to what you must turn, and that is, to God as your end ; to Christ as the way to the Father ; to holiness as the way appointed you by Christ ; and so to the use of all the helps and means of grace offered you by the Lord.

Lastly, You must know by what you must turn. That is, by Christ as the only Redeemer, intercessor, and by the Holy Ghost as the Sanctifier : by the word as his instrument or means : and by faith and repentance, as the means and duties on your part to be performed. All this is of necessity.

Direction II. If you would be converted and saved, be much in secret, serious consideration. Inconsiderateness undoes the world. Withdraw yourselves off into retired secrecy, and there bethink you of the end why you were made, of the life you have lived, the time you have lost, the sins you have committed ; of the love, sufferings, and fulness of Christ ; of the danger you are in ; of the nearness of death and judgment ; of the certainty and excellency of the joys of heaven ; of the certainty and terror of the torments of hell, and eternity of both ; of the necessity of conversion, and a holy life ; bathe your hearts in such considerations as these.

Direction III. If you will be converted and saved, attend upon the word of God, which is the ordinary means. Read the scripture, or hear it read, and other holy writings that do apply it;

constantly attend upon the public preaching of the word. As God will lighten the world by the sun, and not by himself alone without it; so will he convert and save men by his ministers, who are the lights of the world. When he hath miraculously humbled Paul, he sends him to Ananias. And when he hath sent an angel to Cornelius, it is but to bid him send for Peter, who must tell him what he is to believe and do.

Direction IV. Betake yourselves to God, in a course of earnest, constant prayer. Confess and lament your former lives, and beg his grace to illuminate and convert you. Beseech him to pardon what is past and give you his Spirit, change your hearts and lives, lead you in his ways, and save you from temptation. Ply this work daily, and be not weary of it.

Direction V. Presently give over your known and wilful sins, make a stand, and go that way no farther: be drunk no more, but avoid the places and occasion of it; cast away your lusts and sinful pleasures with detestation; curse, swear, and rail no more; and if you have wronged any, restore, as Zaccheus did. If you will commit again your old sins, what blessing can you expect on the means for conversion?

Direction VI. Presently, if possible, change your company, if it hath hitherto been bad. Not by forsaking your necessary relations, but your unnecessary sinful companions, and join yourselves with those that fear the Lord, and inquire of them the way to heaven.

Direction VII. Deliver up yourselves to the Lord Jesus, as the physician of your souls, that he may pardon you by his blood, and sanctify you by his Spirit, by his word and ministers, the instruments of his Spirit. 'He is the way, the truth, and the life; there is no coming to the Father but by him.—Nor is there any other name under heaven, by which you can be saved.' Study therefore his person, his nature, what he hath done and suffered for you, and what he is to you; what he will be, and how he is fitted to the full supply of all your necessities.

Direction VIII. If you mean indeed to turn and live, do it speedily, without delay. If you be not willing to turn to-day, you will not be willing to do it at all. Remember you are all this while in your blood; under the guilt of many thousand sins, and under God's wrath, and you stand at the very brink of hell; there is but a step between you and death. This is not a case for a man that is well in his judgment to be quiet in. Up therefore presently and fly as for your lives: as you would be gone out of your house if it were all on fire over your heads. O if you

did but know what continual danger you live in, what daily unspeakable loss you sustain, and what a safer and sweeter life you might live, you would not stand trifling, but presently turn. Multitudes miscarry that wilfully delay when they are convinced that it must be done. Your lives are short and uncertain; and what a case are you in, if you die before you thoroughly turn! You have staid too long already; and wronged God too long; sin gets strength, and rooting; while you delay, your conversion will grow more hard and doubtful. You have much to do, and therefore put not all off to the last, lest God forsake you, and give you up to yourselves, and then you are undone for ever.

Direction IX. If you will turn and live, do it unreservedly, absolutely and universally. Think not to capitulate with Christ, and divide your heart between him and the world, to part with some sins, and keep the rest: and to let go that which your flesh can spare. This is but self-deluding: you must in heart and resolution forsake all that you have, or else you cannot be his disciples. If you will not take God and heaven for your portion, and lay all below at the feet of Christ, but you must needs also have your good things here, have an earthly portion, and God and glory is not enough for you; it is in vain to dream of salvation on these terms: for it will not be. If you seem ever so religious, if yet it be but a carnal righteousness, and the flesh's prosperity, or pleasure, or safety, be still excepted in your devotedness to God; this is as certain a way to death, as open profaneness, though it be more plausible.

Direction X. If you will turn and live, do it resolvedly, and stand not still deliberating, as if it were a doubtful case. Stand not wavering as if you were yet· uncertain whether God or the flesh be the better master; whether heaven or hell be the better end; or whether sin or holiness be the better way: but away with your former lusts, and presently, habitually fixedly resolve: be not one day of one mind, and the next of another; but be at a point with all the world, and resolvedly give up yourselves and all you have to God. Now while you are reading or hearing this, resolve. Before you sleep another night, resolve. Before you stir from the place, resolve. Before Satan hath time to take you off, resolve. You will never turn indeed till you resolve: and that with a firm unchangeable resolution. So much for the direction.

Now I have done my part in this work, that you may turn at the call of God and live. What will become of it, I cannot tell. I have cast the seed at God's command; but it is not in my power to give the increase. I can go no farther with my message, I cannot bring it to your hearts, nor make it work; I cannot do your parts for you to entertain it, and consider of it; nor I cannot do God's part, by opening your heart to cause you to entertain it; nor can I show you heaven or hell to your eye-sight, nor give you new and tender hearts. If I knew what more to do for your conversion, I hope I should do it.

But O thou that art the gracious Father of spirits, that hast sworn thou delightest not in the death of the wicked, but rather that they turn and live; deny not thy blessing to these persuasions and directions, and suffer not thine enemies to triumph in thy sight, and the great deceiver of souls to prevail over thy Son, thy Spirit, and thy word. O pity poor unconverted sinners; that have no hearts to pity or help themselves: command the blind to see, the deaf to hear, and the dead to live, and let not sin and death be able to resist thee. Awaken the secure; resolve the unresolved; confirm the wavering; let the eyes of sinners, who read these lines, be next employed in weeping over their sins; and bring them to themselves and to thy Son, before their sins have brought them to perdition. If thou say but the word, these poor endeavours shall prosper, to the winning of many a soul to their everlasting joy, and thine everlasting glory. Amen.

NOW OR NEVER;

OR.

THE BELIEVER JUSTIFIED AND DIRECTED,

AND THE

OPPOSERS AND NEGLECTERS OF THE GOSPEL CONVINCED.

PREFACE.

It is a question more boldly than accurately debated by many, whether a man may not be saved in any religion, who is faithful to the principles of it by serious, diligent practice? The true solution is this: religion is that which men hold and do to serve and please God. 1. If men make themselves a religion of serving idols or devils instead of God. 2. Or if they place their service to God himself in things that are evil (as what evil is there that some men have not brought into their religion, and fathered upon God?) the more diligent such men are in their religion, the more they sin. 3. Or if they make themselves a religion of irrational, ludicrous ceremonies, their greatest diligence in this will not save them. 4. Or if they hold all the essentials of the true religion, except some one, it cannot save them while one thing is wanting which is essential to that religion, and so necessary to salvation, which is the case of real heretics: for they are not indeed of that religion, if they want that which is essential to it. 5. Or if they hold all that is essential to the true religion only notionally, and hold any thing with it practically which is contradictory and inconsistent with it, the soundness of the notional belief will not save them from the mortal poison of their practical heresy or error.

But, 1. Whosoever holds all that is necessary to salvation, and is serious and diligent in living according thereunto, shall be saved, whatever error he holds with it. For if he be serious and diligent in the practice of all things necessary to salvation, he hath all that is necessary to salvation, viz. in belief and practice: and it must needs follow, that his errors are either not contradictory to the things necessary which he holds and practises, or that he holds not those errors practically but notionally, as an opinion, or ineffectual cogitation in a dream, which provokes not to action; and in such a case the error keeps no man from salvation.

What is necessary to be believed by them that never hear the gospel, it so little concerns us to know, that God hath not thought meet to make it so plain to us, as things that more concern ourselves. But as it is certain, that without the atonement, satisfaction, and reconciliation made by Christ, and without new terms of grace to be judged by, and without his grace for the performance of their part, no man can be saved that hath the use of reason, so there is so much knowledge necessary to salvation, as is necessary to engage the heart to love God above all, and sincerely to obey his revealed will, and to prefer the life to come before the transitory pleasures of this life. Now if any man can prove to me, that those that never heard the gospel, can thus love God, and the life to come, and obey sincerely, without the knowledge of the person, life, death, resurrection of Jesus Christ, and the declaration of the attractive love and goodness of God in him, and in the work of our redemption, then I should believe that such negative infidels may be saved; for God cannot damn a sanctified soul that sincerely loves him. But if the discovery of the love of God in our redemption be so necessary a moral means to engage the heart, now corrupted by sin and creature-love to the true love of God, that this love cannot be wrought without it; or if Christ give not his Spirit to produce the love of God in any but those that hear the gospel, and believe in him, then no such persons can be saved by their religion. For Christ is the way to the Father, and no man comes to the Father but by him ; and the love of God is absolutely and of itself necessary to salvation ; and faith in Christ is so far necessary to salvation, as it is necessary to bring men to the love of God, as pardoning sin and reconciled to them.

But if any should ever so confidently conclude, that some that hear not of Christ may be saved, yet he must needs confess that the want of this clear and great discovery of the love and goodness of God in his pardoning grace, and of the glorious life which he hath prepared for us, must needs make the love of God a very rare and difficult thing, and consequently their salvation rare and difficult, in comparison of ours.

The Christian faith is the believing an everlasting life of happiness to be offered by God, with the pardon of all sin, as procured by the sufferings and merits of Jesus Christ, to all that are sanctified by the Holy Ghost, persevere in love to God, and to each other, and in a holy and heavenly conversation. This is saving faith and Christianity, if we consent as well as assent. All that was necessary to salvation to be believed, was. formerly thought to be contained in the creed, and that was the test or symbol of the Christian faith; and the Christian religion is the same, hath the same rule, test, and symbol in all ages. But since faction and tyranny, pride and covetousness, became the matters of the religion of too many, vice and selfish interest hath commanded them to change the rule of faith by their additions, and to make so much necessary to salvation, as is necessary to their affected universal dominion, and to their carnal ends. And since faction entered, and hath torn the church into many sects (the Greek, Roman, Armenian, Jacobites, Abassine, and many more) it seems meet to the more tyrannical sect to call these several religions, and to say that every man that differs from them in any of their opinions or additions, which they please to call articles of faith, is of another religion.

If the word religion be taken in this sense, and if all that agree in one Christian religion, are said to be of as many religions, as different opinions, in points that some call necessary, then I answer the question thus : He is the true catholic Christian that hath but one, even the Christian religion : and this is the case of the Protestants, who, casting off the additions of popery, adhere to the primitive simplicity and unity : if Papists, or any others, corrupt this re

ligion with human additions and innovations, the great danger of these corruptions is, lest they draw them from the sound belief and serious practice of that ancient Christianity which we are all agreed in : among Papists, or any other sect, where their corruptions do not thus corrupt their faith and practice in the true essentials, it is certain that those corruptions shall not damn them. For he that truly believes all things that are essential to Christianity, and lives accordingly with serious diligence, hath the promise of salvation: and it is certain, that whatever error that man holds, it is either not inconsistent with true Christianity, or not practically, but notionally held, and so not inconsistent as held by him : for how can that be inconsistent which actually doth consist with it ?

If a Papist or any other sectarian seriously love God, and his brother, and set his heart upon the life to come, give up himself to the merits and grace of Jesus Christ, and the sanctification of the Holy Spirit, to be fitted for that glory, lives by faith above the world, mortifies the desires of the flesh, and lives wilfully in no known sin, but presses after further degrees of holiness, I doubt not of the salvation of that person; no more than of the life of him that hath taken poison but into his mouth and spit it out again, or let down so little as nature and antidotes do expel : but I will not therefore plead for poison, nor take it, because men may live that thus take it.

Having answered this great question, reader, I am now come up to the subject of my following discourse, and to tell thee that though it be a great question whether serious diligence in a corrupt religion will save a man, it is past all question, and agreed on by all sides, that no religion will save a man who is not serious, sincere, and diligent in it. If thou be of the truest religion in the world, and are not true thyself to that religion, the religion is good, but it is none of thine. Objectively thou art of a true and good religion, the things in themselves are true and good, but subjectively thou art sincerely of no religion at all ; for if thou art not serious, hearty and diligent in it, it is certain that thou dost not truly entertain it, and make it thine ; but it is thy books that have the true religion, or thy tongue, or fantasy, or brain, but not thy heart : and the best meat on thy table, or that goes no further than thy mouth, will never feed thee, or preserve thy life. So certain is the salvation of every holy mortified Christian, and so certain the damnation of every ungodly, worldly, fleshly sensualist, that I had a thousand-fold rather have my soul in the case of any sectarian, that lives a truly heavenly life, in the love of God and man, and in a serious, diligent obedience to God, according to his knowledge, than in the case of a Protestant, or whomsoever you can imagine to be right in his opinions, that is worldly, sensual, and a stranger, if not an enemy, to the power and serious practice of his own professed religion, and void of a holy and heavenly heart and life. If ever such a man be saved, the principles of all religion* deceive us.

Certainly such men's hypocrisy doth aggravate their sin, and will increase their misery. So many as there are in the world that profess themselves Christians, and yet are not serious and diligent in their religion, but are ungodly neglecters or enemies of a holy life, so many hypocrites are in the world. I wonder that their consciences call them not hypocrites when they stand up at the creed, or profess themselves believers; though the congregation sees not 'hypocrite' written in their foreheads, God sees it written on their hearts, and those that converse with them may see it written in their lives. Yet these men are the most forward to cry out against hypocrites. The devil hath taught it them to stop the suspicion of conscience, as he hath taught the greatest schismatics, or church-dividers, the papists, to cry out most against schism and division, and pretend to unity. But these shifts blind none but fools and forsaken consciences; and the cheat that is now detected by the wise, will quickly by God be detected before all the world. Till then let them make merry in their deceits: who would envy the drunkard the pleasure of an hour's sickly delight? This is their portion, and this is their time. As we have chosen and covenanted for another portion, we are content to stay the time assigned, till God shall tell them and all the world who was sincere, and who the hypocrite. For our parts, we believe that he is most or least sincere, that is most or least serious in the practice of his own professed religion.

For my part, I must profess that, by the mercy of God, I have made it the work of many a year, to look about me, and think wherein the felicity of man doth indeed consist: I have long been past doubt, as much as I am that I am a man, that it is not in transitory, sensual delights, and that these are such lean, dry commodities, and pitiful pleasures, leaving men so speedily in a forlorn state, that I am contented that my greatest enemy have my part of them. I have renounced them

to God, as any part of my felicity, and I renounce them to men. Let them do with me about these things as God will give them leave. I will have a portion after death, or I will have none.

The case is so palpable, that it seems wonderful to me that the contrary deceit is consistent with the nature and reason of a man; that so many gentlemen, scholars, and persons of an ingenuous education, can no better distinguish, and can possibly conquer their reason so easily with the presence of sensual delights, and so easily make nothing of that which will be to-morrow and for ever, merely because it is not to-day. Well, I must say, the wisdom and justice of God is abundantly seen in the government of the world with the liberty of the will, and determining that all men should speed as they choose.

TREATISE.

" Whatsoever thy hand findeth to do, do it with thy might : for there is no work, nor device, nor knowledge, nor wisdom in the grave, whither thou goest."—Eccles. ix. 10.

The mortality of man being the principal subject of Solomon in this chapter, and observing that wisdom and piety exempt not men from death, he first hence infers, that God's love or hatred to one man above another, is not to be gathered by his dealing with them here, where all things in the common course of providence come alike to all. The common sin hath introduced death as a common punishment, which levels all, and ends all the contrivances, businesses, and enjoyments of this life, to good and bad ; and the discriminating justice is not ordinarily manifested here : an epicure or infidel would think Solomon were here pleading their unmanly, impious cause : but it is not the cessation of the life, or operations, or enjoyments of the soul that he is speaking of, as if there were no life to come, or the soul of man were not immortal ; but it is the cessation of all the actions, honours, and pleasures of this life, which to good or bad shall be no more. Here they have no more reward, the memory of them will be here forgotten. ' They have no more a portion for ever in any thing that is done under the sun.' From hence he further infers, that the comforts

---

* By "religion" here the author seems to mean *profession* or denomination. There may be a plurality of systems of superstition ;— but there is but *one* religion that God himself has given, contained in the inspired volume.—*Ed.*

of life are but short and transitory, and therefore that what the creature can afford, must be presently taken : and as the wicked shall have no more but present pleasures, so the faithful may take their lawful comforts in the present moderate use of creatures ; for if their delightful goodness be of right and use to any, it is to them : and therefore though they may not use them to their hurt, to the pampering of their flesh, strengthening their lusts, and hindering spiritual duties, benefits, and salvation, yet must they ' serve the Lord with joyfulness, and with gladness of heart, for the abundance of all things which he gives them.'

Next he infers, from the brevity of man's life, the necessity of speed and diligence in his duty. This is in the words of my text: where you have, First, The duty commanded. Second, The reason or motive to enforce it.

The duty is in the first part, ' whatsoever thy hand findeth to do,' that is, whatever work is assigned thee by God to do in this thy transitory life, ' do it with thy might,' that is, First, Speedily, without delay. Second, Diligently ; and as well as thou art able, and not with slothfulness, or by halves.

The motive is in the latter part ; ' for there is no work nor device, nor knowledge, nor wisdom in the grave, whither thou goest,' that is, it must be now or never : the grave, where thy work cannot be done, will quickly end thy opportunities. The Chaldee paraphrase appropriates the sense too narrowly to works of charity, or alms ; ' whatsoever good and alms-giving thou findest to do.' And the moving reason they read accordingly ' for nothing but thy works of righteousness and mercy follow thee.' But the words are more general, and the sense is obvious, contained in these two propositions.

DOCT. I. The work of this life cannot be done, when this life is ended. Or, there is no working in the grave, to which we are all making haste.

DOCT. II. Therefore while we have time, we must do our best : or do the work of this present life with vigour and diligence.

It is from an unquestionable and commonly acknowledged truth, that Solomon here urges us to diligence in duty ; and therefore to prove it would be but loss of time. As there are two worlds for man to live in, and so two lives for man to live, so each of these lives hath its peculiar employment. This is the life of preparation: the next is the life of our reward or punishment : we are now but in the womb of eternity, and must live hereafter in the open world.

We are now but set to school to learn the work that we must do for ever. This is the time of our apprenticeship ; we are learning the trade that we must live upon in heaven. We run now, that we may then receive the crown ; we fight now, that we may then triumph in victory. The grave hath no work, but heaven hath work and hell hath suffering: there is no 'repentance unto life' hereafter : but there is repentance unto torment, and to desperation. There is no believing of a happiness unseen in order to the obtaining of it ; or of a misery unseen in order to the escaping of it ; nor believing in a Saviour in order to these ends: but there is the fruition of the happiness which was here believed ; and feeling of the misery that men would not believe ; and suffering from him as a righteous judge, whom they rejected as a merciful Saviour. So that it is not all work that ceases at our death: but only the work of this present life.

Indeed no reason can show us the least probability of doing our work when our time is done, that was given us to do it in. If it can be done, it must be, First, By the recalling of our time. Second, By the return of life. Third, Or by opportunity in another life: but there is no hope of any of these.

1. Who knows not that time cannot be recalled ? That which once was, will be no more. Yesterday will never come again. To-day is passing, and will not return. You may work while it is day ; but when you have lost that day, it will not return for you to work in. While your candle burns, you may make use of its light, but when it is done, it is too late to use it. No force of medicine, no orator's elegant persuasions, no worldling's wealth, no prince's power, can call back one day or hour of time. If they could, what endeavours would there be used, when extremity hath taught them to value what they now despise ; what murmurings would there be at last, if time could be purchased for any thing that man can give ! Then misery would bring out their wealth and say, All this will I give for one day's time of repentance more : lords and knights would lay down their honours, and say, Take all, and let us be the basest beggars, if we may but have one year of the time that we misspent ! Then kings would lay down their crowns and say, Let us be equal with the lowest subjects, so we may but have the time again that we wasted in the cares and pleasures of the world. Kingdoms would then seem a contemptible price for the recovery of time. The time that is now idled and talked away ; the time that is now

feasted and complimented away, that is unnecessarily sported and slept away; that is wickedly and presumptuously sinned away; how precious will it one day seem to all! How happy a bargain would they think that they had made, if at the dearest rates they could redeem it! The most profane mariner falls a praying, when he fears his time is at an end. If importunity would then prevail, how earnestly would they pray for the recovery of time, that formerly derided praying, or minded it not, or mocked God with lip-service, and customary forms, and feigned words instead of praying? What a lesson would death teach the trifling time-despising sinners; the idle, busy, dreaming, active, ambitious, covetous lovers of this world, if time could be intreated to return! How passionately then would they roar out their requests, 'O that we might once see the days of hope, means, and mercy, which once we saw, and would not see! O that we had those days to spend in penitential tears, prayers, and holy preparations for an endless life, which we spent at cards, in needless recreations, in idle talk, in humouring others, on the pleasing of our flesh, or in the inordinate cares and businesses of the world! O that our youthful vigour might return; that our years might be renewed; that the days we spent in vanity might be recalled! That ministers might again be sent to us publicly and privately, with the message of grace, which we once made light of! That the sun would once more shine upon us; that patience and mercy would once more reassume their work!' If cries or tears, or price or pains, would bring back lost-abused time, how happy were the now-distracted, dreaming, dead-hearted, and impenitent world! If it would then serve their turn to say to the vigilant believers, 'Give us of your oil, for our lamps are gone out,' or to cry, 'Lord, Lord, open to us,' when the door is shut, the foolish would be saved as well as the wise; but 'this is the day of salvation; this is the accepted time.' While it is called to-day, hearken, and harden not your hearts. Awake thou that sleepest, stand up from thy slothful, wilful death, and use the light that is afforded thee by Christ, or else the everlasting utter darkness will shortly end thy time and hope.

2. As time can never be recalled, so life shall never be here restored. 'If a man die, shall he live (here) again?' All the days of our appointed time we must therefore wait, in faith and diligence, till our change shall come. One life is appointed us on earth to dispatch the work that our everlasting life depends on: we shall have but one; lose that, and all is lost for ever: yet you may hear, read, learn, and pray; but when this life is ended, it shall be so no more. You shall rise from the dead indeed to judgment, and to the life that now you are preparing for; but never to such a life as this on earth: your life is as the fighting of a battle, that must be won or lost at once. There is no coming hither again to mend what is done amiss. Over-sights must be presently corrected by repentance, or else they are for ever past remedy. Now if you be not truly converted, you may be; if you find that you are carnal and miserable, you may be healed; if you are unpardoned, you may be pardoned; if you are enemies, you may be reconciled to God; but when once the thread of life is cut, your opportunities are at an end. Now you may inquire of your friends and teachers what a poor soul must do that he may be saved, and you may receive particular instructions and exhortations, and God may bless them to the illuminating, renewing, and saving of your souls; but when life is past, it will be so no more. O then, if desperate souls might but return, and once more be tried with the means of life, what joyful tidings would it be! How welcome would the messenger be that brings it! Had hell but such an offer as this, and would any cries procure it from their righteous judge, O what a change would be among them! How importunately would they cry to God, 'O send us once again unto the earth! Once more let us see the face of mercy, and hear the tenders of Christ and of salvation! Once more let the ministers offer us their helps, and teach in season and out of season, in public and in private, and we will refuse their help and exhortations no more: we will hate them and drive them away from our houses and towns no more: once more let us have thy word, and ordinances, and try whether we will not believe them, and use them better than we did: once more let us have the help and company of thy saints, and we will scorn them, abuse them, and persecute them no more. O for the great invaluable mercy of such a life as once we had! O try us once more with such a life, and see whether we will not contemn the world, close with Christ, live as strictly, and pray as earnestly, as those that we hated and abused for so doing! O that we might once more be admitted into the holy assemblies, and have the Lord's day to spend in the business of our salvation! We would plead no more against the power and purity of the ordinances; we would no more call that day a burden; nor hate them that spent it in works of holiness, nor plead for the liberty of the flesh therein.'

It makes my heart even shake within me to think with what cries those damned souls would strive with God, and how they would roar out, ' O try us once again,' if they had but the least encouragement of hope! But it will not be, it must not be. They had their day, and would not know it: they cannot lose their time and have it. They had faithful guides, and would not follow them: teachers they had, but would not learn. The dust of their feet must witness against them, because their entertained obeyed message cannot witness for them. Long did Christ wait with the patient tenders of his blood and Spirit: his grace was long and earnestly offered them, but could not be regarded and received: they cannot finally refuse a Christ, and yet have a Christ; or refuse his mercy, and yet be saved by it. He that would have Lazarus sent from the dead to warn his unbelieving brethren on earth, no doubt would have strongly purposed himself on a reformation, if he might once more have been tried: how earnestly would he have begged for such a trial, that begged so hard for a drop of water! But alas! Such mouths must be stopped for ever with a ' Remember that thou in thy life time receivedst thy good things.'

So that it is appointed for all men once to die, and after that the judgment. But there is no return to earth again: the places of your abode, employment and delight shall know you no more. You must see these faces of your friends, and converse in flesh with men no more! This world, these houses, that wealth and honour, as to any fruition, must be to you as if you had never known them. You must assemble here but a little while; yet a little longer, and we must preach, and you must hear it no more for ever. That therefore which you will do, must presently be done, or it will be too late. If ever you will repent and believe, it must be now. If ever you will be converted and sanctified, it must be now. If ever you will be pardoned and reconciled to God, it must be now. If ever you will reign, it is now that you must fight and conquer. O that you were wise, that you understood this, and that you would consider your latter end; that you would let those words sink down into your hearts, which came from the heart of the Redeemer, as was witnessed by his tears. ' If thou hadst known, even thou, at least in this thy day, the things which belong unto thy peace. But now they are hidden from thine eyes;' and that these warnings may not be the less regarded, because you have so often heard them, when often hearing increases your obligation, and diminishes not the truth, or your danger.

3. As there is no return to earth, so is there no doing this work hereafter. Heaven and hell are for other work. If the infant be dead born, the open world will not revive him; that which is generated, and born an animal or serpent, will not, by all the influences of the heavens, or all the powers of sun or earth, become a man. The second and third operation presuppose the first; the harvest doth presuppose the seed time and the labour of the husbandman. It is now that you must sow, and hereafter that you must reap. It is now that you must work, and then that you must receive your wages. Is this believed and considered by the sleepy world? Alas, do you live as men that must live here no more? Do you work as men that must work no more, and pray as men that must pray no more, when, once the time of work is ended? What thinkest thou, poor unhappy sinner! will God command the sun to stand still while thou rebellest or forgettest thy work and him? Dost thou think he should pervert the course of nature, and continue the spring and seed-time till thou hast a mind to sow; or that he will return the dead-born infant into the womb, that it may be better formed or quickened? Will he renew thy age and make thee young again, and call back the hours that thou prodigally wastedst on thy lusts and idleness? Canst thou look for this at the hand of God, when nature and scripture assure thee of the contrary? If not, why hast thou not yet done with thy beloved sins; why hast thou not yet begun to live? Why sittest thou still while thy soul is unrenewed, and all thy preparation for death and judgment is yet to make? How fondly would Satan find thee thus at death; how anxiously would he have leave to blow out thy candle, before thou hast entered into the way of life? Dost thou look to have preachers sent after thee, to bring thee the mercy which thy contempt here left behind? Wilt thou hear and be converted in the grave and hell; or wilt thou be saved without holiness; that is, in spite of God, that hath resolved it shall not be. O ye sons of sleep, of death, of darkness, awake, live, and hear the Lord, before the grave and hell have shut their mouths upon you! Hear now, lest hearing be too late; hear now if you will ever hear; hear now if you have ears to hear. And O ye sons of light, that see what sleeping sinners see not, call to them, and ring them such a peal of lamentations, tears and compassionate intreaties, as is suited to such a dead and doleful state; who knows but God may bless it to awake them?

If any of you be so far awakened, as to ask

me what I am calling you to do, my text tells you in general, up and be doing: look about you, and see what you have to do, and do it with your might.

1. ' Whatsoever thy hand finds to do,' that is, whatsoever is a duty imposed by the Lord, whatsoever is a means conducing to thy own or others' welfare; whatsoever necessity calls thee to do, and opportunity allows thee to do.

' Thy hand findeth,' that is, thy executive power, by the conduct of thy understanding, is now to do.

' Do it with thy might:' do thy best in it. Trifle not, but do it presently, without unnecessary delay. Do it resolutely. Remain not doubtful, unresolved, in suspense, as if it were yet a question with thee whether thou shouldst do it, or not.

Do it with thy most awakened affections, and serious intention of the powers of thy soul. Sleepiness and insensibility are most unsuitable to such works. It is a peculiar people, zealous of good works, that Christ hath purchased to himself.

Do it with all necessary forethought and contrivance: not with a distracting, hindering care; but with such a care as may show that you despise not your master, and are not regardless of his work: and with such a care as is suited to the difficulties and nature of the thing, and is necessary to the due accomplishment of it.

Do it not slothfully, but vigorously, and with diligence. Stick not at thy labour: lest thou hear, ' thou wicked and slothful servant.—Hide not thy hand in thy bosom with the slothful, and say not there is a lion in the way.' The negligent and the vicious, the waster and the slothful, differ but as one brother from another, as the self-murder of the wilfully ungodly, so also the desire of the slothful kills him, because his hands refuse to labour, the soul of the sluggard desireth and hath nothing; but the soul of the diligent shall be made fat; ' be not slothful in business, but be fervent in spirit, serving the Lord.'

Do it with constancy, and not with destructive pauses and intermissions, or with weariness and turning back. ' The righteous shall hold on his way, and he that is of clean hands shall be stronger and stronger.—Be stedfast, unmoveable, always abounding in the work of the Lord; forasmuch as you know that your labour is not in vain in the Lord.—Be not weary of well doing: for in due season we shall reap if we faint not.' These six particulars are necessary, if you will observe the precept in my text.

But that misunderstanding may not hinder the performance, I shall acquaint you further with the sense, by these few explicatory cautions.

The energy and diligence here required, excludes not the necessity of deliberation and prudent conduct. Otherwise, the faster you go, the further you may go out of the way; and misguided zeal may spoil all the work, and make it but an injury to others or yourselves. A little imprudence in the season, order, and manner of a duty, sometimes may spoil it, and hinder the success, and make it do more hurt than good. How many a sermon, or prayer, or reproof, is made the matter of derision and contempt, for some imprudent passages or deportment! God sends not his servants to be triflers of the world, or to play the madman, as David in his fears: we must be wise and innocent, as well as resolute and valiant: though fleshly and worldly wisdom be not desirable, as being but foolishness with God; yet the wisdom which is from above, and is first pure, and then peaceable, and is acquainted with the high and hidden mysteries, and is justified of her children, must be the guide of all our holy actions. Holiness is not blind: illumination is the first part of sanctification. Believers are ' children of the light.' Nothing requires so much wisdom as the matters of God, and of our salvation. Folly is most unsuitable to such excellent employments, and most unbeseeming the sons of the Most High. It is a spirit of wisdom that animates all the saints; it is the treasures of wisdom that dwell in Christ, and are communicated to his members. We must ' walk in wisdom toward them that are without,' and our ' work must be shown out of a good conversation, with meekness of wisdom;' yet I must needs say, that it is more in great things than in small, in the substance than the circumstances; in a sound judgment and estimate of things, and suitable choice and prosecution, than in fine expressions or deportment answering proud men's expectations.

Though you must work with all your energy, yet with a diversity agreeable to the quality of your several works. Some works must be preferred before others: all cannot be done at once. That is a sin out of season, which in season is a duty. The greatest, and the most urgent work, must be preferred. And some works must be done with double fervour and resolution, and some with less. Buying, selling, marrying, possessing, and using the world, must be done with a fear of overdoing, and in a sort as if we did them not, though they also must have a necessary diligence. God's kingdom and its rightcousness must be first sought, and our labour for the meat that perishes must be comparatively as none.

Lastly, It is not an irregular, nor a self-disturbing, vexatious violence that is required of us: but a sweet, well-settled resolution, and a delightful expeditious diligence, that makes the wheels go smoothly on, and the more easily get over those difficulties, that clog and stop a slothful soul.

Now will you lend me the assistance of your consciences, for the transcribing of this command of God upon your hearts, and taking out a copy of this order, for the regulating of your lives? *Whatsoever* is not a word so comprehensive as to include any vanity or sin; but so comprehensive as to include all your duty.

1. To begin with the lowest: the very works of your bodily callings must have diligence. 'In the sweat of your brows you must eat your bread.—Six days shalt thou labour, and do all that thou hast to do.—He that will not work, let him not eat.—Disorderly walkers, busy bodies, that will not work with quietness, and eat their own bread, are to be avoided and shamed by the church.' Lazy servants are unfaithful to men, and disobedient to God, who commands them to obey their masters according to the flesh (unbelieving, ungodly masters) in all things that concern their service, and that not with eye service, as men pleasers, but in singleness of heart, and in the fear of God, doing whatsoever they do as to the Lord, and not unto men; knowing that of the Lord, even for this, they shall receive the reward of the inheritance. But he that doth wrong by slothfulness, or unfaithfulness, shall receive for the wrong which he hath done.

Success is God's ordinary temporal reward of diligence; and diseases, poverty, shame, disappointment, or self-tormenting melancholy, are his usual punishments of sloth. Hard labour redeems time: you will have the more to lay out on greater works: the slothful is still behind, and therefore must leave much of his work undone.

2. Are you parents or governors of families; you have work to do for God, and for your children's and servants' souls: do it with your might: deal wisely, but seriously and frequently with them about their sins, their duty, and their hopes of heaven; tell them whither they are going, and which way they must go: make them understand that they have a higher Father and Master that must be first served, and greater work than yours. Waken them from their na-

tural insensibility and sloth: turn not all your family duties into lifeless customary forms: speak about God, heaven, hell, and holiness, with that seriousness as beseems men that believe what they say, and would have those they speak to, to believe it. Talk not either drowsily, or lightly, of such dreadful, or joyful, inexpressible things. Remember, that your families and you are going to the grave, and to the world where there is no more room for your exhortations. There is no catechising, examining, or serious instructing them in the grave, whither they and you are going. It must be now or never: therefore do it with your might. The words of God must be in your hearts, and you 'must diligently teach them to your children, talking of them when you sit in your houses, when you walk by the way, when you lie down, and when you rise up.'

3. Have you ignorant or ungodly neighbours, whose misery calls for your compassion and relief? Speak to them and help them with prudent diligence. Lose not your opportunities: stay not till death hath stopped your mouths, or stopped their ears. Stay not till they are out of hearing, and taken from your converse. Stay not till they are in hell, before you warn them of it, or till heaven be lost, before you have seriously called to them to remember it. Go to their houses: take all opportunities: stoop to their infirmities: bear with unthankful frowardness: it is for men's salvation: remember there is no place for your instructions or exhortations in the grave or hell. Your dust cannot speak, and their dust cannot hear: up therefore and be doing with all your might.

4. Hath God intrusted you with the riches of the world; with many talents or with few, by which he expects you should relieve the needy, and especially should promote those works of piety which are the greatest charity? Give prudently, but willingly and liberally, while you have to give. It is your gain: the time of market for your souls; of laying up a treasure in heaven, and setting your money to the most gainful usury; and of 'making you friends of the mammon of unrighteousness;' and furthering your salvation by that which hinders other men's, and occasions their perdition. 'As you have opportunity, do good to all men, but especially to them of the household of faith.—Cast thy bread upon the waters; for thou shalt find it after many days. Give a portion to seven and to eight; for thou knowest not what evil may be upon the earth.—In the morning sow thy seed, and in the evening withhold not thy hand: for thou knowest not whether shall pros-

per, this or that, or whether they both shall be alike good.—Withhold not good from them to whom it is due, when it is in the power of thy hand to do it : say not to thy neighbour, go, and come again, and to-morrow I will give, when thou hast it by thee.—Lay up a foundation for the time to come. Do good before thy heart be hardened, thy riches blasted and consumed, thy opportunities taken away ; part with it before it part with thee.' Remember it must be now or never: there is no working in the grave.

5. Hath God intrusted you with power or interest, by which you may promote his honour in the world, relieve the oppressed, and restrain the rage of impious malice ! Hath he made you governors, and put the sword of justice into your hands ? up then and be doing with your might. Defend the innocent, protect the servants of the Lord, cherish them that do well, be a terror to the wicked, encourage the strictest obedience to the universal Governor, discountenance the breakers of his laws : look not to be reverenced or obeyed before him, or more carefully than he: openly maintain his truth and worship without fear or shame : deal gently and tenderly with his lambs and little ones : search after vice that you may successfully frown upon it. Hate those temptations that would draw you to man-pleasing, temporizing, remissness, or countenancing sin ; but especially those that would ensnare you in a controversy with heaven, and in quarrels against the ways of holiness, or in that self-confounding sin of abusing and opposing the people that are most careful to please the Lord. Your trust is great, and so is your advantage to do good; how great will be your account, and how dreadful, if you be unfaithful! As you signify more than hundreds or thousands of the meaner sort, and your actions do most good or hurt ; so you must expect to be accordingly dealt with, when you come to the impartial, final judgment. Befriend the gospel as the charter of your everlasting privileges ; own those that Christ hath told you he will own. Use them as men that are ready to hear 'insomuch as you did it to one of the least of these my brethren, you did it unto me.—Know not a wicked person : but let your eyes be on the faithful of the land, that they may dwell therein, and lead a quiet and peaceable life, in all godliness and honesty. —Let those that work the work of the Lord, be with you without fear.' Remember that it is the character of a pharisee and hypocrite, to see the mote of the non-observance of a ceremony, or tradition, or smaller matter of difference in religion in their brother's eye, and not to see the

beam of hypocrisy, injustice and malicious cruel opposition of Christ and his disciples in their own eyes : that it is the brand of them that please not God, that are filling up their sins, on whom God's wrath is coming to the utmost, to persecute the servants of the Lord, ' forbidding them to preach to the people that they might be saved.

Learn well the second and the hundred and first psalm : and write these sentences on your walls and doors, as an antidote against that self-undoing sin : ' whosoever shall offend one of these little ones which believe in me, it were better for him that a mill-stone were hanged about his neck, and that he were drowned in the depth of the sea.—He that toucheth you toucheth the apple of his eye.—Him that is weak in the faith receive you ; but not to doubtful disputations. For God hath received him.—He that receiveth you, receiveth me; and he that receiveth me, receiveth him that sent me. He that receiveth a righteous man in the name of a righteous man, shall receive a righteous man's reward : and whoso shall give to drink to one of these little ones, a cup of cold water only, in the name of a disciple, verily I say unto you, he shall in no wise lose his reward.' If you love not the godly, love yourselves, so far as such self-love is possible ; wound not your own hearts, to injure them. Damn not your souls, and that by the surest, nearest way, that you may hurt their bodies. Provoke not God to thrust you from his presence, and deny your suits, by your dealing so with them : stop not your own mouths, when your misery will bespeak your loudest cries for mercy, by your stopping the mouths of the servants of the Lord, and refusing to hear their requests for justice. If you have the serpent's enmity against the woman's seed, you must expect the serpent's doom : ' your heads will be bruised,' when you have ' bruised their heels.—Kick not against the pricks.' Let not ' briars and thorns set themselves in battle against the Lord, lest he go therefore through them, and burn them together.'

I speak not any of this by way of accusation or dishonourable reflection on the magistrate. Blessed be God that hath given us the comfort of your defence. But knowing what the tempter aims at, where it is that your danger lies, and by what means the rulers of the earth have been undone, faithfulness commands me to tell you of the snare, and to set before you good and evil, as ever I would escape the guilt of betraying you by flattery, or cruel and cowardly silence.

Especially when your magistracy is but annual,

or for a short time, it concerns you to be doing with your might. It is but this year, or short space of time that you have to do this special service in; lose this and lose all. By what men on earth should God be eminently served and honoured, if not by magistrates, whom he hath eminently advanced, impowered and intrusted? With considerate foresight, seriously ask yourselves the question, are you willing to hear, at the day of your accounts, that you had but one year, or a few, to do God special service in, and that you knew this, and yet would not do it? Can your hearts bear it then, to hear and think that you lost, and wilfully lost, such an opportunity? Look about you then, and see what is to be done. Are there not alehouses to be suppressed, drunkards and riotous persons to be restrained; preaching and piety to be promoted? Do it with your might: for it must be now or never.

6. To come yet a little nearer you, and speak of the work that is yet to be done in your own souls; are any of you yet in the state of unrenewed nature, born only of the flesh, and not of the Spirit, ' minding the things of the flesh and not the things of the Spirit;' and consequently yet in the 'power of Satan, taken captive by him at his will;' up and be doing, if thou love thy soul. If thou care whether thou be in joy or misery for ever, bewail thy sin and spiritual distress: make out to Christ, cry mightily to him for his renewing and reconciling, pardoning grace; plead his satisfaction, his merits and his promises; away with thy rebellion, and thy beloved sin; deliver up thy soul entirely to Christ, to be sanctified, governed and saved by him. Make no more delays about it; it is not a matter to be questioned, or trifled in. Let the earth be acquainted with thy bended knees, the air with thy complaints and cries, and men with thy confessions and inquiries after the way of life; and heaven with thy sorrows, desires and resolutions, till thy soul be acquainted with the Spirit of Christ, and with the new, the holy and heavenly nature; and thy heart have received the transcript of God's law, the impress of the gospel, and so the image of thy creator and redeemer. Ply this work with all thy might; for there is no conversion, renovation, or repentance unto life, in the grave whither thou goest. It must be now or never, and never saved, if never sanctified.

7. Hast thou any prevailing sin to mortify, that either reigns in thee, or wounds thee and keeps thy soul in darkness and unacquaintedness with God? Assault it resolutely: reject it speedily: abhor the motions of it: turn away from the persons or things that would entice thee. Hate the doors of the harlot, and of the alehouse, or the gaming house: and go not as the ox to the slaughter, as a bird to the fowler's snare, and as a fool to the correction of the stocks, as if thou knewest not that it is for thy life. Why, thou befooled soul, wilt thou be tasting of the poisoned cup? Wilt thou be sporting thee with the bait? Hast thou no where to walk or play thee, but at the brink of hell? Must not the flesh be crucified with its affections and lusts? Must it not be tamed, and mortified, or thy soul condemned? ' Run not therefore as at uncertainty: fight not as one that beats the air.' Seeing this must be done, or thou art undone, delay with sin no longer: let this be the day; resolve, and resist it with thy might: it must be now or never: when death comes, it is too late. It will be then no reward to leave thy sin, which thou canst keep no longer: no part of holiness or happiness that thou art not drunk, or proud, or lustful in the grave or hell. As thou art wise, therefore, know and take thy time.

8. Art thou in a declined, lapsed state; decayed in grace; hast thou lost thy first desires and love; do thy first works, and do them with thy might. Delay not, but remember from whence thou art fallen, and what thou hast lost by it, and into how sad a case thy folly and negligence hath brought thee: say, ' I will go and return to my first husband; for then was it better with me than now.' Cry out with Job, ' O that I were as in months past! as in the days when God preserved me! when his candle shined upon my head and when by his light I walked through darkness. As I was in the days of my youth, when the secret of God was on my tabernacle, when the Almighty was yet with me.' Return while thou hast day, lest the night surprise thee: loiter and delay no more: thou hast lost by it already: thou art far behind; bestir thee therefore with all thy might.

9. Art thou in the darkness of uncertainty concerning thy conversion and thy everlasting state? Dost thou not know whether thou be in a state of life or death; and what should become of thee, if this were the day or hour of thy change? If thou art careful about it, and inquirest, and usest the means that God hath appointed thee for assurance, I have then no more to say to thee now, but wait on God, and thou shalt not be disappointed or ashamed. Thou shalt have assurance in due time, or be saved before thou wouldst believe thou shouldst be saved. Be patient and obedient, and the light of Christ will

shine upon thee, and yet thou shalt see the days of peace. But if thou art careless in thy uncertainty, and mindest not so great a business, be awakened and call thy soul to its account; search and examine thy heart and life: read, consider, and take advice of faithful guides. Canst thou carelessly sleep, laugh, sport, and follow thy lesser business, as if thy salvation were made sure, when thou knowest not where thou must dwell for ever? 'Examine yourselves whether you be in the faith? prove yourselves; know ye not your own selves that Christ is in you except you are reprobates?—Give all diligence in time to make your calling and election sure.' In the grave and hell there is no making sure of heaven: you are then past inquiries and self-examinations, in order to any recovery or hope. Another kind of trial will finally resolve you. Up therefore and diligently ply the work: it must be now or never.

10. In all the duties of thy profession of piety, justice, or charity, to God, thyself, or others, up and be doing with thy might. Art thou seeking to inflame thy soul with love to God? plunge thyself in the ocean of his love; admire his mercies; gaze upon the representations of his transcendent goodness; ' O taste and see that the Lord is gracious!' Remember that he must be 'loved with all thy heart and soul and might.' Canst thou pour out thy love upon a creature, and give but a few barren drops to God?

When thou art fearing him, let his fear command thy soul, and conquer all the fear of man.

When thou art trusting him, do it without distrust, and cast all thy care and thyself upon him: trust him as a creature should trust his God, and the members of Christ should trust their head and dear Redeemer.

When thou art making mention of his great and dreadful name, O do it with reverence, awe, and admiration: and take not the name of God in vain.

When thou art reading his word, let the majesty of the author, the greatness of the matter, and gravity of the style, possess thee with an obedient fear. Love it, and let it be sweeter to thee than the honeycomb, and more precious than thousands of gold and silver. Resolve to do what there thou findest to be the will of God. When thou art praying in secret, or in thy family, do it with thy might: cry mightily to God as a soul under sin, wants, and danger, that is stepping into an endless life, should do. Let the reverence and the fervour of thy prayers show that it is God himself thou art speaking to; that it is heaven itself that thou art praying for;

hell itself that thou art praying to be saved from. Wilt thou be dull and senseless on such an errand to the living God? Remember what lies upon thy failing or prevailing, and that it must be now or never.

Art thou a preacher of the gospel, and takest charge of the souls of men? ' Take heed to thyself and to the whole flock, over which the Holy Ghost hath made thee an overseer, to feed the church of God, which he hath purchased with his own blood.' Let not the blood of souls, and the blood that purchased them, be required at thy hands; thou 'art charged before God, and the Lord Jesus Christ, who shall judge the quick and the dead at his appearing, and his kingdom, that thou preach the word; be instant in season and out of season; reprove, rebuke, and exhort with all long-suffering and doctrine.—Teach every man, and exhort every man.—Even night and day with tears.—Save men with fear, pulling them out of the fire.—Cry aloud; lift up thy voice like a trumpet; tell them of their transgressions.' Yet thou art alive, and they alive; yet thou hast a tongue, and they have ears: the final sentence hath not yet cut off their hopes. Preach therefore, and preach with all thy might. Exhort them privately and personally with all the seriousness thou canst. Quickly, or it will be too late. Prudently, or Satan will over-reach thee: fervently, or thy words are like to be disregarded. Remember when thou lookest them in the face, when thou beholdest the assemblies, that they must be converted or condemned, sanctified on earth or tormented in hell; and that this is the day: it must be now or never.

In a word: apply this quickening precept to all the duties of the Christian course. Be religious, just, and charitable in good earnest, if you would be taken for such when you look for the reward. ' Work out your salvation with fear and trembling.—Strive to enter in at the strait gate; for many shall seek to enter and shall not be able.—Many run, but few receive the prize: so run that you may obtain.—If the righteous scarcely be saved, where shall the ungodly and the sinner appear?' Let the doating world deride your diligence, and set themselves to hinder and afflict you: it will be but a little while before experience change their minds, and make them see it in a true light. Follow Christ fully: ply your work, and lose no time. The judge is coming. Let not words nor any thing that man can do, prevail with you to sit down, or stop you in a journey of such importance. Please God, though flesh, friends, and all the world should be displeased. Whatever come of your reputation, or estates, liberties or lives, be sure you look to life eternal; and cast not that on any hazard, for a withering flower, or a pleasant dream, or a picture of pleasure, or any vanity that the deceiver can present. ' For what shall it profit you to win the whole world and lose your soul;' or to have been honoured and obeyed on earth, when you are under the wrath of God in hell; or that your flesh was once provided with variety of delights, when it is turned to rottenness, and must be raised to torments? Hold on therefore in faith, holiness, and hope, though earth and hell should rage against you; though all the world, by force or flattery, should do the worst they can to hinder you. This is your trial; your warfare is the resisting of deceit, and of all that would tempt you to consent to the means of your own destruction: consent not and you conquer: conquer, and you are crowned. The combat is all about your wills; yield, and you have lost the day. If the prating of ungodly fools, or the contemptuous sneers of hardened sinners, or the frowns of unsanctified superiors, could prevail against the Spirit of Christ, and the workings of an enlightened mind, then what man would be saved? You deserve damnation, if you will run into it to avoid a mock, or the loss of any thing that man can take from you. You are unfit for heaven, if you can part with it to save your purses. ' Fear not them that can kill the body, and after that have no more that they can do: but fear him that can destroy both soul and body in hell.' Obey God, though all the world forbid you. No power can save you from his justice: and none of them can deprive you of his reward. Though you lose your heads, you shall save your crowns: you no way save your lives so certainly, as by such losing them, one thing is necessary: do that with speed, care, and diligence, which must be done, or you are lost for ever. They that are now against your much and earnest praying, will shortly cry as loud themselves in vain. When it is too late, how fervently will they beg for mercy, that now deride you for valuing and seeking it in time! ' But then they shall call upon God, but he will not answer; they shall seek him early, but shall not find him: for that they hated knowledge, and did not choose the fear of the Lord: they would none of his counsel, but despised all his reproof.'

Up therefore and work with all thy might. Let unbelievers trifle, who know not that the righteous God stands over them, who know not that they are now to work for eternity, and know not that heaven or hell is at the end. Let them delay, laugh, play, and dream away their time, that are drunk with prosperity, and mad with fleshly lusts and pleasures, and have lost their reason in the cares, delusions, and vain-glory of the world. But shall it be so with thee whose eyes are opened, who seest the God, the heaven, and the hell, which they but hear of as unlikely things? Wilt thou live awake, as they that are asleep? Wilt thou do in the day-light, as they do in the dark? Shall freemen live as Satan's slaves; shall the living lie as still and useless as the dead? Work then while it is day; for the night is coming when none can work.

It is not the works of the Mosaical law, nor works that are conceived for their proper value, to deserve any thing at the hands of God, that I am all this while persuading you to: but it is the works prescribed you by Christ in the gospel, according to which you shall be shortly judged to joy or misery, by Christ himself, that will call you to account. These must be done with all your might.

Object. But you will say perhaps, Alas! what might have we? we have no sufficiency of ourselves; without Christ we can do nothing; and this we find when it comes to the trial.

Ans. 1. It is not a might that is originally thine own, that I am to call thee to exercise: but that which thou hast already received from God, and that which he is ready to bestow. Use well but all the might thou hast, and thou shalt find thy labour is not in vain. Even the strength of nature, and of common grace, are talents which thou must improve.

2. Art thou willing to use the might thou hast, and to have more, and use it if thou hadst it? If thou art, thou hast then the strength of Christ: thou standest not and workest not by thy own strength; his promise is engaged to thee, and his strength is sufficient for thee. But if thou art not willing, thou art without excuse; when thou hadst heaven and hell set open in the word of God to make thee willing, God will distinguish thy wilfulness from unwilling weakness.

3. There is more power in all of you than you use, or than you are well aware of. It wants but awakening to bring it into act. Do you not find in your repentings, that the change is more in your will than in your power; and in the awaking of your will and reason into act, than in the addition of mere abilities; and that therefore you befool yourselves for your sins and your neglects, and wonder that you had no more use of your understandings? Let but a storm at sea, or violent sickness, or approaching death, rouse up and awaken the powers which you have,

and you will find there was much more asleep in you than you used.

I shall therefore next endeavour to awaken your abilities, or tell you how you should awaken them.

When your souls are drowsy, and you are forgetting your God, and your latter end, and matters of eternity have little force and savour with you; when you grow lazy and superficial, or religion seems a lifeless thing and you do your duty as if it were in vain, or against your wills; when you can lose your time, and delay repentance, and friends, profit, reputation, and pleasure can be heard against the word of God, and take you off; when you do all by halves, and languish in your Christian course, as near to death ; stir up your souls with the urgency of such questions as these.

Quest. 1. Can I do no more than this for God; who gave me all ; who deserves all ; who sees me in my duties and my sins ; when he puts me purposely on the trial, what I can do for his sake and service, can I do no more ; can I love him no more ; obey, watch, and work no more ?

2. Can I do no more than this for Christ ; for him that did so much for me; that lived so exactly ; obeyed so perfectly ; walked so inoffensively and meekly ; despising all the baits, honours, and riches of the world ? That loved me to the death, and offers me freely all his benefits, and would bring me to eternal glory ; are these careless, cold and dull endeavours my best return for all this mercy ?

3. Can I do no more when my salvation is the prize; when heaven or hell depend much on it ? When I know this beforehand, and may see in the glass of the holy scriptures what is prepared for the diligent and the negligent, and what work there is and will be for ever in heaven and hell on these accounts; could I not do more, if my house were on fire, or my estate or life, or friend in danger, than I do for my salvation?

4. Can I do no more for the souls of men ; when they are undone for ever, if they be not speedily delivered; is this my love and compassion to my neighbour, my servant, friend or child ?

5. Can I do no more for the church of God ; for the public good ; for the peace and welfare of the nation and our posterity ; in suppressing sin; in praying for deliverance ; or in promoting works of public benefit ?

6. Can I do no more, that have loitered so long ; and go no faster, that have slept till the evening of my days, when diligence must be the discovery of my repentance ?

7. Can I do no more, that know not now but I am doing my last ; that see how fast my time makes haste, and know I must be quickly gone ; that know it must be now or never ; and that this is all the time I shall have, on which an endless life depends ?

8. Can I do no better, when I know beforehand, what different aspects diligence and negligence will have, to the awakened soul in the review, and what a comfort it will be at death and judgment, to be able to say, I did my best, or loitered not away the time I had ? And what a vexatious and heart-disquieting thing it will then be to look back on time as irrecoverably lost, and on a life of trial, as cast away upon impertinencies, while the work that we lived for lay undone?   Shall I now, by trifling, prepare such tormenting thoughts for my awakened conscience ?

9. Can I do no more, when I am sure I cannot do too much, and am sure there is nothing else to be preferred ?   And that it is this I live for: and that life is for action ; and disposes thereunto ; and holy life for holy action, and that it is better not live, than not attain the ends of living ; when I have so many and unwearied enemies ; when sloth is my danger, and the advantage of my enemy, when I know that resolution and vigorous diligence is so necessary, that all is lost without it. Will temptations be resisted and self-denied, concupiscence mortified, and fleshly desires tamed and subdued, sin cast out, and a holy communion with heaven maintained with idleness and sloth ; will families be well ordered, and church, or city, or country well governed; will the careless sinners that I am bound to help, be converted and saved, with sitting still, and with some heartless cold endeavours ?

10. Can I do no more that have so much help ; that have mercies of all sorts encouraging me, and creatures attending me ; that have health to enable me, or affliction to remember and excite me, that have such a master, such a work, such a reward, as better cannot be desired ; who is less excusable for neglect than I ?

11. Could I do no more, if I were sure that my salvation lay on this one duty ; that according to this prayer, it should go with me for ever ; or if the soul of my child, or servant, or neighbour must speed for ever, as my endeavours speed with them now for their conversion ; for ought I know it may be thus.

12. Would I have God to come with the spur and rod ; how do I complain when affliction is upon me ; and will I neither endure it, nor be

4

quickened without it; is it not better to mend my pace and work on easier terms?

I would not have distressed souls use these considerations merely to disquiet themselves for their infirmities, and so live in heaviness and self-vexation, because they cannot be as good as they desire, or do as much and as well as they should do: It is not despair that will mend the matter, but make it worse. But I would wish the lazy slothful soul to plead these questions with itself, and try whether they have no quickening power, if closely urged, and seriously considered.

Believe it, it is the deceitfulness of prosperity that keeps up the reputation of a slothful life, and makes holy diligence seem unnecessary. When affliction comes, awakened reason is ashamed of this, and sees it as an odious thing.

By this time you may see what difference there is between the judgment of God, and of the world, and what to think of the understandings of those men, be they high or low, learned or unlearned, that hate or oppose this holy diligence. God bids us love, seek, and serve him, with all our heart, soul, and might: and these men call them zealots, enthusiasts, and puritans, that endeavour it; though alas, they fall exceedingly short, when they have done their best. It is one of the most wonderful monstrosities and deformities that ever befell the nature of man, that men, that learned men, that men that in other things are wise, should seriously think that the utmost diligence to obey the Lord and save our souls, is needless, that ever they should take it for a crime, and make it a matter of reproach: that the serious, diligent obeying of God's laws, should be the matter of the common disdain and hatred of the world; that no men are more generally abhorred, and tossed up and down by impatient men; that great and small, the rulers and vulgar rabble, in most places of the earth cannot endure them. To think how the first man that ever was born into the world, did hate his own brother till he had proceeded to murder him, because he served God better than himself, 'because his own works were evil, and his brother's righteous;' and how constantly this horrid unnatural madness hath succeeded and raged in the world from Cain until this day. It is not in vain that the Holy Ghost adds in the next words, 'Marvel not, my brethren, if the world hate you.' Implying that we are apt to marvel at it, as I confess I have often and greatly done. Methinks, it is so wonderful a plague and stain in nature, that it doth very much to confirm me of the truth of scripture; of the doctrine of man's fall and original sin, and the necessity of a Redeemer, and of renewing grace.

Distracted, miserable souls! Is it not enough for you to refuse your own salvation, but you must be angry with all that will not imitate you! Is it not mad enough, and bad enough to choose damnation, but you must be offended with all that are not of your mind. If you will not believe God, that without regeneration, conversion, holiness, and a heavenly, spiritual life, there is no salvation to be hoped for, must we all be unbelievers with you? If you will laugh at hell till you are in it, must we do so too? If God and glory seem less worth to you than your fleshly pleasures for a time, must we renounce our Christianity and our reason for fear of differing from you? If you dare differ from your Maker, the Redeemer, and the Holy Ghost, from all the prophets, apostles, and evangelists, and all that ever came to heaven, might not we be bold to differ from you? If you will needs be ungodly, and choose your everlasting woe, be patient with them that have more understanding, and dare not be so hardy as to leap after you into the unquenchable fire: Mock not at holiness if you have no mind of it. Hinder not them that strive to enter in at the strait gate, if you refrain yourselves. Be not so desirous of company in hell. It will prove no comfort to you, or abatement of your pain.

But because you have the faces to contradict the God of truth, and to reproach that work which he commands, and to say, What needs so much ado? when he bids us do it with all our might; I will briefly tell you what you are doing, and show you the deformed face of the scorner, and the filthy hearts of the enemies of holiness, that if it may be, you may lothe yourselves.

1. These enemies of holy diligence deny God with their works and lives, and are practical atheists; and it seems are so near of kin to 'that wicked one,' that they would have all others to do so too. And then how soon would earth be turned into hell! The case is plain: if God deserve not to be loved and served with all thy heart, soul and might, he is not God. And if thy wealth, or honour, or flesh, or friend deserve more of thy love, care, and diligence than God, then that is thy God that deserves best. See now what these deriders of purity and obedience think of God, and of the world.

2. These Cainites blaspheme the Governor of the world: when he hath given laws to the creatures that he made of nothing, these sinners deride and hate men for obeying them. If God have not commanded that which you oppose,

contradict it, and spare not: I would you were much more against that pretended religion which he commands not. But if he have commanded it, and yet you dare revile them as too pure and precise that would obey it, what do you but charge the King of saints with making laws that are not to be obeyed; which must needs imply that they are foolish, or bad, though made by the most wise and good.

3. These enemies of holiness oppose the practice of the very first principles of all religion. For 'he that cometh to God, must believe that God is, and that he is the rewarder of them that diligently seek him.' It is diligent seeking him that they hate and set themselves against.

4. Do not they judge heaven to be less worth than earth; when they will do less for it, and would have others to do so too?

5. They would have us all unchristian and unman ourselves, as if there were no life to come; as if our reason and all our faculties were given us in vain. For if they are not given us for greater matters than all the honours and pleasures of the world, they are in vain, or worse; and the life of man is but a dream and misery. Were not an irrational animal less miserable, if this were all?'

6. How base a price do these Cainites set on the immortal soul of man, that think it not worth so much ado, as the careful obedience of the laws of Christ; nor worth so much as they do themselves for their filthy sins and perishing flesh? But would have us so mad as to sell heaven and our souls for a little sinful sloth and ease.

7. These enemies of holiness would have men take their mercies for their hurt, and their greatest blessings for a burden or a plague, and to run into hell to be delivered from them. Why man, dost thou know what holiness is; and what it is to have access to God? I tell thee it is the foretaste of heaven on earth. It is the highest glory, sweetest delight, and chief enjoyment of the soul. Art thou afraid of having too much of this? What, thou that hast none, which should make thee tremble, art thou afraid of having too much? Thou that never fearest too much money, nor too much honour, nor too much health, art thou afraid of too much spiritual health and holiness? What shall be thy desire, if thou lothe and fly from thy felicity?

8. You that are loyal subjects, take heed of these ungodly scorners: for by consequence they would tempt you to despise your king, and make a mock at the obeying of his commands and laws. For if a man persuade you to despise a judge, he implies that you may despise a constable. No king is so great in comparison of God, as the meanest insect to that king. He therefore that would relax the laws of God, and make it seem a needless thing to obey him diligently and exactly, implies that obedience to any of the sons of men is much more needless.

And you that are children or servants, take heed of the doctrine of these men: masters, admit it not into your families. If he be worthy to be scorned as a puritan, who is careful to please and obey the Lord, what scorn do your children and servants deserve, if they will be obedient and pleasing to such as you?

9. All you that are poor tradesmen, take heed of the consequences of the Cainites' scorns, lest it make you give over the labours of your calling, and turn yourselves and families into beggary. For if heaven be not worth your greatest labour, your bodies are not worth the least.

10. These Cainites speak against the awakened consciences, and the confessions of all the world. Whatsoever they may say in the dream of their blind presumption and security, at last, when death hath opened their eyes, they all cry, O that we had been saints! O that we might die the death of the righteous, and that our last end might be as his! O that we had spent that time, care, and labour for our souls, which we spent on that which now is gall to our remembrance! And yet these men will take no warning, but now oppose and deride that course that all the world do wish at last they had been as zealous for as any.

11. The enemy himself hath a conscience within him, that either grudges against his malicious impiety, and witnesses that he abuses them that are far better than himself, or at least will shortly call him to a reckoning, and tell him better what he did, make him change his views, and wish himself in the case of those that he did oppose.

12. To conclude, the Cainite is of that wicked one, of his father the devil, and is his walking, speaking instrument on earth, saying what he himself would say: he is the open enemy of God. For who are his enemies, but the enemies of holiness, of his laws, of our obedience, of his image, and of his saints? How will Christ deal at last with his enemies? O that they knew, that, foreseeing, they might escape! This is the true picture of a Cainite, or enemy of a holy life, that reproaches serious diligence as a precise and needless thing, when God commands us, and death, the grave, and eternity admonish us to do his work with all our might. 'Now con

sider this ye that forget God, lest he tear you in pieces, and there be none to deliver you.'

But of all the opposers of serious holiness in the world, there are none more inexcusable and deplorably miserable, than those that profess themselves ministers of Christ. Would one believe that had not known them, that there are such men in the world? Alas, there are too many. Though education, and the laws of the land engage them to preach true doctrine, yet are they false teachers in the application. For they never well learned the holy and heavenly doctrine which they preach, nor digested it, nor received the power and impress of it upon their hearts; and therefore retaining their natural corruptions, impiety and enmity to the life, power, and practice of that doctrine, they indirectly destroy what directly they would seem to build; and preach both for God, and against him, for Christ, and the Holy Spirit, and against them; for godliness, and against it, both in the same sermon. In general, they must needs speak for the word of God, and a holy life; but when they come to the particulars, they secretly reproach it, and condemn the parts, while they commend the whole. In general they speak well of religious, godly, holy people; but when they meet with them, they hate them, and make them enthusiasts, a sect that is every where spoken against, pestilent fellows, and movers of sedition, as the apostles were accused, and any thing that malice can invent to make them odious. And what they cannot prove, they will closely intimate, in the false application of their doctrines, describing them so as may induce the hearers to believe that they are a company of self-conceited hypocrites, factious, proud, disobedient, turbulent, peevish, affecting singularity, desiring to ingross the reputation of godliness to themselves, but secretly as bad as others. And when they have thus represented them to the ignorant sort of people, they have made the way of godliness odious, and sufficiently furnished miserable souls with prejudice and dislike; so that because the persons are thus made hateful to them, all serious diligence for heaven, all tenderness of conscience, and fear of sinning, all heavenly discourse, and serious preaching, reading, or praying, are also made odious for their sakes: for hearing so ill of the persons, and seeing that these are the things wherein they differ from others, they reduce their judgment of their practices to their foresettled judgment of the persons.

When their diligence in their families, in prayer and instructions, in reading, and fruitful improvement of the Lord's day, or any other actions of strictness and holy industry are mentioned, these ungodly ministers are ready to blame them with some open calumnies, or secret reproaches, or words of suspicion, to vindicate their own unholy lives, and make people believe that serious piety is faction and hypocrisy. The black tincture of their minds, and the design and drift of their preaching may be perceived in the sneers and slanderous intimations against the most diligent servants of the Lord. The controverted truths that such maintain, they represent as errors: their unavoidable errors they represent as heresy: their duties they represent as faults; and their human frailties as enormous crimes: they feign them to be guilty of the things that never entered into their thoughts, and if some that have professed godliness be guilty of greater crimes, they would make men believe that the rest are such, and that the family of Christ is to be judged of by a Judas, and the scope is to intimate that either their profession is culpable, or needless, and less commendable. Regeneration they would make to be but the entrance into the church by baptism, and any further conversion, than the leaving off some gross sins, and taking up some heartless forms of duty, to be but a fancy or unnecessary thing: and they would draw poor people to believe, that if they be born again sacramentally of water, they may be saved, though they be not born again by the renewing of the Holy Spirit. Being strangers themselves to the mystery of regeneration, and to the life of faith and a heavenly conversation, and to the loving and serving of God with all their soul and might: they first endeavour to quiet themselves with a belief that these are but fancies or unnecessary, and then to deceive the people with that by which they have first deceived themselves.

And it is worthy of your observation, what it is in religion that these formal hypocrites are against. There are scarcely any words so sound or holy, but they can bear them, if they be but deprived of their life: nor scarcely any duty, if it be but mortified, but they can endure. But it is the spirit and life of all religion which they cannot bear. As a body differs from a carcass, not by the parts, but by the life; so there is a certain life in preaching, prayer, and all other acts of worship, which is perceived by several sorts of hearers. The godly perceive it to their edification and delight. For here it is that they are quickened and encouraged. Life begets life, as fire kindles fire. The ungodly often perceive it to their vexation, if not to their conviction and conversion : this life in preaching, praying, discipline, reproof, and conference, is that which galls, goads, and disquiets their consciences. This they kick and rail against : this is the thing that will not let them sleep quietly in their sin and misery ; but is calling and inciting them to awake, and will not let them sin in peace, but will either convert them, or torment them before the time. It is the life of religion that the hypocrite wants ; and the life that he is most against. A painted fire burns not ; a dead lion bites not. The lifeless body of an enemy is not formidable. Let the words of that sermon that most offends them, be separated from the life, and put into a homily, and said or read in a formal, drowsy, or a school-boy tone, and they can bear it and commend it. Let the same words of prayer which now they like not, be said over as a lifeless, customary form, and they can like it well. I speak not against the use of forms, but the abuse of them : not against the body but the shadow. Let forms themselves be used by a spiritual serious man, in a spiritual serious manner, with the interposition of any quickening exhortations, or occasional passages, that tend to keep them awake and attentive, make them feel what you mean and are about, and you shall see they love not such animated forms. It is the living, Christian, lively worship, and serious, spiritual religion, which they hate : kill it and they can bear it. Let the picture of my enemy be nearer and comelier than his person was, and I can endure it in my bed chamber, better than himself in the meanest dress.

It is the living Christians that in all parts of the world are chiefly persecuted. Let them be once dead, and dead-hearted hypocrites themselves will honour them, especially at a sufficient distance : they will destroy the living saints, and keep holidays for the dead ones. ' Woe to you, scribes and pharisees, hypocrites, because ye build the tombs of the prophets, and garnish the sepulchres of the righteous, and say, if we had been in the days of our fathers, we would not have been partakers with them in the blood of the prophets ; wherefore ye be witnesses unto yourselves, that ye are the children of them which kill the prophets : fill ye up the measure of your fathers: ye serpents, ye generation of vipers, how can ye escape the damnation of hell !' The dog that will not meddle with the dead creature, will pursue the living ; and when he sees it stir no more, will leave it. Christianity without seriousness is not Christianity, and therefore not liable to the hatred of its enemies as such. Say any thing, and do any thing how strict soever, if you will but act it as a player on the stage, or do it coldly, slightly, and as if you were but in jest, you may have their approbation. But it is this life, seriousness, and worshipping God in spirit and truth, that convinces them that they themselves are lifeless, consequently troubles their deceitful peace, and therefore must not have their friendship. If it were the mere bulk of duty that they are weary of, how comes it to pass that a Papist at his psalter, beads, and mass-books, can spend more hours without much weariness or opposition, than we can do in serious worship ? Turn all but into words, beads, canonical hours and days, shows, and ceremony, and you may be as religious as you will, and be righteous overmuch, and few will hate, or reproach, or persecute you among them, as too precise or strict. But living Christians and worship, come among them like fire, that burns them, and makes them smart, with a ' word that is quick and powerful, sharper than any two-edged sword, piercing even to the dividing of soul and spirit, joints and marrow, and is a discerner of the thoughts and intents of the heart.'

The enmity of the Cainites may teach the Christian what he should be, and wherein his excellency lies. It is life and seriousness that your enemies hate : and therefore it is life and seriousness that you must above all maintain ; though dead-hearted hypocrites never so much oppose and contradict you.

They are no trifles, but the greatest things that God hath set before you in his word, and called you out to prosecute and possess : your time of seeking them is short, and therefore you have no time for trifles, nor any to lose in idleness and sloth. And of all men, preachers should be most sensible of this. If they were not against serious holiness in others, it is double wickedness for such as they, to be against it in themselves. It is great things that they have to study and to speak of : such as call for the greatest seriousness, reverence and gravity in the speaker, and condemn all trifling in matter or in manner. A man that is sent of Christ to run for an immortal crown, or to direct others in such a race, to save his own, or other men's souls, from endless misery, should be ashamed to fill up his time with trifles, or to be slight and cold about such great and weighty things. All the heart, soul, and might, is little enough for matters of such unspeakable importance. When I hear preachers or people spend their time in little impertinent fruitless things, that do but divert them from the great business of their lives, or to trifle with the greatest matters rather than to use them and treat of them with a seriousness suitable to their importance; I oft think of the words of Seneca, the serious moralist, as shaming the hypocrisy of such trifling preachers and professors of the Christian faith : ' You compose copious words, and tie hard knots by curious questions; and you say, O these are acute things ! What is more acute than the peal of corn ? and yet what is it good for ? Subtilty itself makes some things unprofitable and ineffectual.' Again, ' Leave these toys or fooleries to poets, whose business is to delight the ear, and to compose a pleasant fable. But they that mean to heal men's understandings, and retain credibility among men, and to bring into men's minds the remembrance of their duties, must speak seriously, and do their business with all their might.'

Did a Seneca see, by the light of nature, so much of the necessity of seriousness and diligence about the matters of the soul ; and so much of the madness of spending words and time and trifles ? And yet shall there be found a man among professed Christians, and among the preachers of faith and holiness, that pleads for trifling, scorns at seriousness, and accounts them moderate and wise that a heathen brands as toyish and distracted ?

What is it that clouds the glory of Christianity, and keeps so great a part of the world in heathenism and infidelity, but this, that among Christians there are so few that are Christians indeed ? And those few are so obscured by the multitude of formal trifling hypocrites, that Christianity is measured and judged of by the lives of those that are not Christians ? Religion is a thing to be demonstrated, honoured, and commended by practice : words alone are ineffectual to represent its excellency to so blind a world, that must know by feeling, having lost their sight. In our professed faith we mount unto the heavens, and leave poor unbelievers wallowing in the mire. O what a transcendant, inconceivable glory, do we profess to expect with God unto eternity, and what manner of persons should they be, in all holy conversation and godliness, that look for such a life as this ! How basely should they esteem those transitory things, that are the food and felicity of the sensual world ! How patiently should they undergo contempt and scorn, and whatsoever man can inflict upon them ! How studiously should they devote and refer all their time, strength, wealth, and interest, to this their glorious, blessed end ! How seriously should they speak of, and how industriously should they seek sure, near, and endless joys ! Did professed Christians more exactly conform their hearts and lives to their profession and holy rule, their lives would confute the reproaches of their enemies, and command a reverend and awful estimation from the observers, and do more to convince the unbelieving world of the truth and dignity of the Christian faith, than all the words of the most subtle disputants. Christianity being an affecting practical science, must practically and affectionately be declared, according to its nature : arguments do but paint it out : and pictures do no more make known its excellency, than the picture of meat and drink makes known its sweetness. When a doctrine so holy, is visibly exemplified, and lives, walks, and works in serious Christians before the world : either this or nothing will convince them, and constrain them, to glorify our Lord, and say that ' God is among us, or in us of a truth,' but it is unchristian lives that darkens the glory of the Christian faith. When men that profess such glorious hopes, shall be as sordidly earthly, sensual, ambitious, impotent, and impatient as other men, they seem but dissemblers.

Yet shall there be found such a perfidious wretch under the heavens of God, as a professed minister of Christ, that shall subtilly or openly labour to make an exact, holy, and heavenly conversation a matter of reproach and scorn ; and that, under pretence of reproving the sins of hypocrites and schismatics, shall make the exactest conformity to the Christian rule, and faithfullest obedience to the almighty sovereign, to seem to be but hypocrisy or self-conceitedness, or needless trouble, if not the way of sedition, and public trouble, and turning all things upside down ? That cannot reprove sin, without malicious, insinuating slanders or suspicions against the holy law, and holy life, that are most contrary to sin, as life to death, as health to sickness, and as light to darkness ?

For any man, especially any professed Christian, any where to oppose or scorn at godliness, is a dreadful sign, as well as a heinous sin : but for a preacher of godliness to oppose and scorn at godliness, and that in the pulpit, while he pretends to promote it, and plead for it in the name of Christ, is a sin that should strike the heart of man with horror to conceive of.

Though I look upon this sort of the enemies of holiness as those that are as unlikely to be recovered and saved, as almost any people in the world, except apostates and malicious blasphemers of the Holy Ghost, yet in compassion to the people and themselves, I shall plead the cause of God with their consciences, and try what light can do with their understandings, and the terrors of the Lord with their hardened hearts.

1. A preacher of the gospel should much excel the people in understanding: and therefore this sin is greater in them than other men: what means, what light do they sin against? Either thou knowest the necessity of striving for salvation with the greatest diligence, or thou dost not. If not, what a sin and shame is it to undertake the sacred office of the ministry, while thou knowest not the things that are necessary to salvation, and that which every infant in the faith doth know? But if thou dost know it, how dost thou make shift maliciously to oppose it, without feeling the beginnings of hell upon thy conscience? When it is thy work to read the Scriptures, and meditate on them, dost thou not read thy doom, and meditate terror? How canst thou choose but perceive that the scope of the word of God is contrary to the bent of thy affections and suggestions? Yea, what is more evident by the light of nature, than that God and our salvation cannot be regarded with too much holy seriousness, exactness and industry? Should not the best things be best loved; and the greatest matters have our greatest care? Is there any thing to be compared with God and our eternal state? O what overwhelming subjects are these to a sober and considerate mind! what toys are all things in comparison of them: yet dost thou make light of them, and also teach men so to do? As if there were something else that better deserved men's greatest care and diligence than they. What! a preacher, and not a believer; or a believer, and yet not see enough in the matters of eternity to engage all our powers of soul and body against all the world that should stand in competition?

2. Is it not sinful and terrible enough, to be thyself in a carnal, unrenewed state: and to be without the Spirit and life of Christ, but thou must be so cruel as to make others miserable also? 'But to the wicked, saith God, What hast thou to do to declare my statutes; or that thou shouldest take my covenant in thy mouth, seeing thou hatest instruction and castest my words behind thee?—Whosoever shall break one of these least commandments, and shall teach men so, he shall be called the least in the kingdom of heaven: but whosoever shall do and teach the same, shall be called great in the kingdom of heaven.'

3. What an aggravation is it of thy impiety and soul-murder, that thou art bound by office to teach men that life of holiness which thou opposest: and to persuade them to that with all thy might, which thou endeavourest closely and cunningly to disgrace! And wilt thou be a traitor to Christ in the name of a messenger and preacher of the gospel? Wilt thou engage thyself to promote his interest, and to use all thy skill and power to build men up in holiness and obedience; and when thou hast done this, wilt thou disgrace and hinder it? Dost thou take on thee to go on the message of Christ, and then speak against him? We do not find that Judas dealt thus with him: when he sent him as he did other preachers, we read not that he preached against him. O let not my soul be numbered with such men in the day of the Lord! It will be easier for Sodom and Gomorrah, than for the refusers of the word and grace of Christ. What then will be the doom of the opposers? And above all of those treacherous opposers, that pretend themselves to propagate and promote them?

If the wit and malice of Satan's instruments were sharpened against the ways and servants of the Lord, it belongs to you to plead Christ's cause, shame these absurd unreasonable gainsayers, and stop the mouth of impious contradiction. Will you join with gainsayers, and secretly or openly say as they? Who should confound the deriders of a holy life but you? Who should lay open the excellencies of Christ, the glory of heaven, the terrors of the Lord, and all other obligations to the most serious, but you that have undertaken it as your calling and employment? If any man in the parish were so atheistical and brutish, as to think God unworthy of our dearest love, our most exact obedience, and most laborious service, who should display this atheist's folly, but you that are doubly, as Christians and ministers, obliged to defend the honour of your Lord? If any of the people should fall into such a dream or dotage, as to question the necessity of our utmost diligence in our preparations for eternal life, who should awake them by lifting up their voices as a trumpet, and help to recover their understandings, but you that are the watchmen, and know their blood will be required at your hands, if you give them not loud and timely warning? If any subtle, malicious servant of the devil should plead against the necessity of holiness, and dissuade the people from serving God with all their might, who should be ready to confirm the weak, and strengthen and encourage them that are thus assaulted, and help to keep up their zeal and forwardness, but you that are leaders in the army of the Lord? Is it not a holy God that you are engaged to serve; and a holy church in which you have your station; and a communion of saints in which you have undertaken to administer the holy things of God? Have you not read what was done to Nadab and Abihu, when Moses told Aaron, 'This is it that the Lord spake, saying, I will be sanctified in them that come nigh me, and before the people I will be glorified.' Is it not a holy law and gospel which you publish? You have undertaken to warn the slothful, the sensual, the worldly, and the profane, 'that they strive to enter in at the strait gate, and seek first the kingdom of God and his righteousness.—To give diligence to make sure their calling and election.—To give all diligence in adding virtue to their faith. —With all diligence to keep their hearts.' And are you the men that would quench their zeal, and destroy the holy diligence which you should preach? The Lord touch your hearts, and recover you in time, or how woeful will it be with such hardened hypocrites, that in the light, in his family and livery, and under his standard and colours, dare prove traitors and enemies to the Lord.

4. And what an addition is it to your guilt, that you speak against God in his own name? By office, you are to deliver his message, and speak to the people in his name and in his stead. Dare you, before the sun, and under the heavens of God, and in his hearing, persuade men that the most holy God is against holiness; and the King of saints is an adversary to sanctity; and that he that made his holy law, is against the most exact obeying of it? Dare you prefix a ' Thus saith the Lord,' to so impious a speech as 'It is in vain to serve the Lord?' What needs there so much ado for your salvation? Dare you go to men as from the Lord, and say, ' You are too careful and diligent in his service; less ado may serve the turn; what need of this fervour and redeeming of time; this is but puritanism or preciseness! It is better to do as the most, and venture your souls without so much ado.' Who could at last hold up his face, or stand before the dreadful tribunal, that should be found in the guilt of such a crime? What, to put God into the similitude of Satan, and describe the most holy as the enemy of holiness! To make him plead against himself, disgrace his own image, and dissuade men from that which he himself hath made of necessity to their salvation! What viler blasphemy can be uttered?

5. It aggravates your sin, that your relation obliges you to the most tender affections to your people: and yet that you should seduce them to condemnation. For the nurse to poison them: for the parents to cut the children's throats, is worse than for an enemy to do it. If the devil, our professed enemy, should himself appear to us and say, Prepare not so seriously for death : be not so strict, so diligent, and holy ; it were not, in many respects, so bad as for you to do it, that should help to save us from his snares. You that profess yourselves their fathers ; that should travail in birth till Christ be formed in your people's hearts; that should love your people as your own bowels, foster the weak, pity the wicked, and stick at no labour, suffering, or cost, that might advance their holiness, and further their salvation; for you to tempt men into a careless life, and turn them out of the holy way, is an aggravated cruelty. It is worse for the shepherd to destroy us than the wolf.

6. Are you not ashamed thus to contradict yourselves; what can you find to preach from the word of God, that tends not to this holy diligence which you are against; how can you make shift to preach an hour, and not acquaint men with the duty and necessity of seeking God with all their might? Do you not tell them, that 'Except they be converted and be born again, they shall not enter into the kingdom of God.' And 'that without holiness none shall see the Lord.—That if they live after the flesh, they shall die.—That except their righteousness exceed the righteousness of the scribes and pharisees, they shall in no case enter into the kingdom of heaven.' And will you, in your application or private discourses, unsay all this again and give God and yourselves the lie ; letting people see that the pulpit is to you but as a stage, and that you believe not what you speak?

7. Consider, that your place and calling make you the most successful servants of the devil, and so the most bloody murderers of souls, while you give your judgment against a strict and heavenly life. For a drunkard in an alehouse to mock the minister, and rail at serious religion, is less regarded by sober men, and of small injury to his master's cause ; nay, the wickedness of his life is so great a shame to his judgment, that it inclines many to think well of those that he speaks against. But when a man that pretends to learning and understanding, to be himself a pastor of the church, and preacher of the mysteries of Christ, shall make them odious that are most careful of their souls, most exact in pleasing God, and shall make all serious diligence for heaven to seem but intemperate zeal and self-conceitedness : and shall describe a saint as if the formal, lifeless hypocrite, that gives God but

the leavings of the world, and never sets his heart on heaven, were indeed the man: what a snare is here for the perdition of the ignorant! They that are naturally averse from holiness, and are easily persuaded to think that to be unnecessary or bad, which seems so much above them and against them, will be much confirmed in their mistakes and misery, when they hear their teachers speak without them, the same that Satan by his suggestions doth within them. This turns a trembling sinner into a hardened scorner: he that before went under the daily correction of his conscience, for neglecting God, and omitting holy duties, and living to the flesh, grows bold and fearless when he hears the preacher disgrace the stricter, purer way. By that time he hath heard a while the fear of God derided as preciseness, and tender conscience reproached as a scrupulous foolish thing, his conscience grows more pliable to his lusts, and hath little more to say against them. When God's own professed ministers, who should be wiser and better than the people, are against this zeal and industry for heaven, the people will soon think, that at least it is tolerable in them: and they will sooner learn to deride a saint from a sermon or discourse of a preacher or a learned man, than from the scorns or talk of hundreds of the ignorant. Wilt thou teach them to hate godliness, who hast undertaken, before the righteous God, to teach them to practise it? He that despises it, though under the names, and represents it as odious, though masked with the title of some odious vice, doth indeed endeavour to make men hate it. And what a terrible account wilt thou have to make, when the seduction and transgression of all these sinners shall be charged upon thee; when Christ shall say to the haters, deriders, and opposers of his holy ways and servants, 'in as much as you did it to one of the least of these my brethren, you did it unto me? How durst you scorn the image of your Maker; nate the saints whose communion you professed to believe; and deride, or oppose that serious holiness, without which you had no hope of being saved? If then the sinners become your accusers, and say, 'Lord, we thought it had been but unnecessary preciseness, and that serious Christians had been but self-conceited, factious hypocrites, and that lip-service with a common worldly life, might have served the turn; we heard our preachers represent such strict and zealous men as turbulent, seditious, and refractory, as odious and not as imitable : their application was against them: their discourse derided them: of them we learnt it: we thought they were wiser and better than we : of whom should we learn but of our teachers ?' Wo to the teachers that ever they were born, that must be then found guilty of this crime.

If Adam's excuse was Eve's accusation; 'the woman which thou gavest to be with me, she gave me of the tree, and I did eat,' and the woman's excuse did charge the serpent, 'the serpent beguiled me and I did eat,' though it freed not the excusers, how will it load you, when your people shall say, 'the teachers that we thought thou gavest us, did teach us and go before us in setting against this holy diligence, and we did but learn of them, and follow them !'

8. Are not the people backward enough to the serving of God with all their might, unless you hinder them? Is not the corrupted heart of lapsed man averse enough to the matters of salvation, but you must make them worse? If you had to do with the best and holiest person in the world that walks with God in the most heavenly conversation, he would tell you that his dull and backward heart hath no need of clogs, and discouragements, but of all the help that can be afforded him, to quicken him up to greater diligence. The most zealous lament that they are so cold: the most heavenly lament that they are so earthly and so strange to heaven: the most laborious lament that they are so slothful, and the most fruitful believers, that they are so unprofitable ; those that are most watchful of their words and deeds, that they are so careless ; those that most diligently redeem their time, lament it, that they lose so much ; and those that walk most accurately and exactly, that they are so loose, and keep no closer to the rule. Yet darest thou increase the backwardness of the ungodly ! will not their carnal interest and lusts serve to keep them from a holy life ? Is not Satan strong enough of himself ? Will not the common distaste of godliness in the world, sufficiently prejudice and avert them without thy help? Do you see your people so forward to do too much for heaven, that you must pull them back ? Cannot souls be condemned without your furtherance ; or is it a desirable work ; and will it pay for your cost and labour ? The way is up-hill; the best of us are weak, and frequently ready to sit down. A thousand impediments are cast before us by Satan and the world, to make us linger till the time be past ; and many a charm of pleasure and diversion, to make us sleep till the door be shut. Ministers are sent to keep us walking, and take us by the hand, to lead us on, and remove impediments : and shall they set in with the enemy, and be our chief

hinderers? O treacherous guides! O miserable helps! Are not our dark understandings, our earthly, dull and backward hearts, our passions and troubled affections, our appetites and sensual inclinations, our natural strangeness and averseness to God, heaven and holiness, enough to hinder us without you? Are not all the temptations of the devil, the allurements of the flesh and world, the impediments of poverty and riches, of flattery and of frowns, of friends and foes, in our callings, are not all these enough to cool us and keep us from serving God too much, and being too careful and diligent for our souls, but preachers themselves must be our impediments and snares? Now the Lord deliver our souls from such impediments, and his church from such unhappy guides!

9. Consider whom thou imitatest in this. Is it Christ, or Satan? Christ calls men to 'strive,' to 'labour,' to 'seek first,' to 'watch,' to 'pray always,' and 'not wax faint.' The apostles call men to be 'fervent in spirit, serving the Lord; to be a peculiar people, zealous of good works, to pray continually, to be a chosen generation, a royal priesthood, a holy nation, a peculiar people, to show forth the praises of him that hath called us, and offer up spiritual sacrifices acceptable to God by Jesus Christ.—To fight the good fight of faith, and lay hold upon eternal life.—To serve God acceptably (being as a consuming fire) with reverence and godly fear.—To be stedfast, unmoveable, always abounding in the work of the Lord, forasmuch as we know that our labour is not in vain in the Lord.' And dare you gainsay the Lord and his apostles, concur with Satan, and the Pharisees and enemies of Christ?

10. You do your worst to make the sacred office of the ministry become contemptible, as Eli's sons did: poor people that cannot sufficiently distinguish the doctrine from the application, the office from the person, the use from the abuse, will be tempted to run from the ordinances of God, and think the worse of others for your sakes, and suspect all their food, because you mix such poison in it. The more holy and necessary the office and work is, the greater is your sin in corrupting it, or making it suspected or abhorred.

Consider soberly of these things, and then go on and speak against a life of holy diligence, if you dare.

I know you say it is not godliness, but singularity, or humour, or disobedience, or hypocrisy, or faction, that you oppose; and perhaps you instance in some that are guilty of some of these, or seem so at the least.

But, 1. I here solemnly profess that I hate these crimes as well as you; and that it is not any part of my intention to plead for intemperance, disobedience in lawful things, for schism, or faction, or any irregularity: this I here put in against those that are disposed to misunderstand and misrepresent us, and leave it, as on record, to prove them slanderers, that shall accuse me of defending any such thing. I protest against those on the other side, that will seek encouragement for any transgression from my necessary plea for the holy industry and vigilance of believers. And moreover, I profess that it is only the opposers of holiness that I mean in this defence, and have not the least intent to intimate that any others are guilty of that crime who are not. But having premised this protestation, to prevent mistakes and false reports, I answer now to the guilty.

2. If it be crimes only that you are against, deliver yourself so, as you may not lay reproach or suspicion on godliness, which is most opposite to all crimes. Cannot you preach against divisions, disobedience, or any other sin, without any scornful intimations or reflections against men's diligent serving of the Lord.

3. Why do not you commend those that are not liable to your accusations, encourage them in holiness, and draw others to imitate them? And why do you not commend the good, while you discommend the evil that is mingled with it?

4. Shall health and life be made a scorn, because there are few but have some distemper or disease? Shall Christianity and holiness be secretly reproached, because all Christians have some fault to be accused of? If men be faulty you should persuade them to be more strict and diligent, and not less; it is for want of watchfulness and strictness that they sin. Nothing is more contrary to their faults than holiness. There is no other way for their full reformation. And therefore all true humbled Christians are ready to confess their faultiness themselves; but so far are they from thinking the worse of piety for it, that it is one great reason that moves them to go on, to read, hear, pray, meditate, and do so much, that they may get more strength against their faults. Must they think ill of food, physic, and exercise, because they are infirm? All faithful ministers tell their people plainly of their sins, so far as they are acquainted with them, as well as you: but they do it not in a way reproachful to their holy diligence: they do not therefore call them off from godliness, nor tempt them to be less in the use of means, but more, by how much their need is greater. A holy

heart, and a malignant heart, will show their difference in the reproving of the same fault. The one lays all the odium on the vice, and honours the holy obedience of the saints. The other fastens his sting upon the godly, and under pretence of dishonouring their faults, doth seek to fasten the dishonour on their holiness. Those that are so minded, will never want occasion or pretence, for the worst that Satan would have them say. The church will never be without some hypocrites, and scandals, nor the best without some faults and passions; nor the holiest action without some mixture of human frailty and infirmity; nor will the very goodness and holiness of the action, be free from plausible calumnies and scorns, while there is the wit and venom of the serpent in the heads and hearts of wicked men.

How easy is it to put a name of ignominy upon every person and every duty; to charge any man with hypocrisy, or pride; to take the wisest man for self-conceited, because he is not of the accuser's mind; to call our obedience to God, by the name of disobedience unto man, when man forbids it, as they used the three witnesses, and Daniel himself, for praying in his house, though they confessed they had nothing else against him; to call God's truth by the name of heresy, and heresy by the name of truth; to charge all with schism that dare not subject their souls to the usurpation and arrogant impositions of the sons of pride, that have neither authority nor ability to govern us, as the Papists deal with the greatest part of the Christian world; to lay snares for men's consciences, and then accuse them for falling into those snares; to make new articles of faith, till they have transcended the capacity of divine and rational belief, and then condemn us for not believing them; to make laws for the church, unnecessary in their own opinion, and sinful in other men's; command things which they know that others think the Lord forbids, and then load them with the sufferings and reproaches of the disobedient, turbulent, heretical, schismatical, or seditious; to call men factious, if they will not be of their faction, and sectarians, if they will not unreasonably subject their souls to them, and join with an imperious sect against the catholic unity and simplicity, all which the Romanists practise upon the church of Christ. How easy, but how unreasonable, and yet how irresistible is all this; how easy is it to call a meeting of sober Christians, for prayer and mutual edification, such as that was, by the name of a factious, schismatical conventicle; and a meeting of drunkards, or

gamesters, by a more gentle, less disgraceful name; to say a man becomes a preacher, when he modestly reproves another for his sins, or charitably exhorts him in order to his salvation, or gives any necessary plain instruction to his family, for whom he must give account? Believe it, it will be a poor excuse to any man, that becomes an enemy to the diligence of a saint, that he could thus cloak his malice, and clothe a saint with the vizor of a hypocrite, and the rags of any odious sect.

If the pharisees were to be believed, it was not they, but Christ that was the hypocrite; nor was it the Son of God, but an enemy to Cæsar, and a blasphemer, that they put to death. But will not Christ know his sheep though he find them torn in a wolf's skin? You say it is turbulent precisians that you strike; but what if Christ find but one of the least of his brethren bleeding by it? It is but hypocrites or schismatics that you reproach; but if Christ find an humble, serious Christian suffering by your abuse, and you to answer it, I would not be in your place for all the greatness and honour that you shall have before your everlasting shame. If Tertullus accuse a ' pestilent fellow, and a mover of sedition,' and Christ find a holy, laborious apostle in bonds and suffering by it, it is not his names that will excuse him, and make an apostle, or persecution to be another thing.

To return to the endangered flocks: look upwards, my hearers, and think whether heaven be worth your labour. Look downwards, and think whether earth be more worthy of it. Lay up your treasures where you must dwell for ever. If that be here, then gather, flatter, and get all that you can: but if it be not here, but in another life, then hearken to your Lord, lay up for yourselves a treasure in heaven, and there let your very hearts be set. And upon the peril of everlasting misery, hearken not to any man that will tempt you from a diligent holy life. It is a serious business, deal seriously in it; and be not laughed or mocked out of heaven, by the sneers of a distracted sensual atheist. If any of them will pretend sobriety and wisdom, and undertake to prove that God should not be loved and served, and your salvation sought with all your might, with greater care and diligence than any earthly thing, procure me a sober conference with that man, and try whether I prove him to be a befooled servant of the devil, a mischievous enemy of your salvation and his own. O that we might have but sober debates, instead of jeers and scorns and railing, with this sort of men! How quickly should we show you that they must renounce the scripture, and renounce Christianity; and, if that be nothing with them, that they must renounce God, renounce right reason, unman themselves, if they will renounce a holy heavenly life, and blame them that make it their principal business in the world to prepare for the world to come.

But if they will not be intreated to such a sober conference, will you that hear them, if you care what becomes of you, but come to us, and hear what we can say for a holy life, before you hearken to them; let your souls have fair play, and show that you have so much love to yourselves, as not to cast away salvation at the derision of a fool, before you have heard the other side.

If I make not good the strictest law of God Almighty, against the most subtle cavils of any of the instruments of Satan, then tell me that infidels or epicures are in the right. Compare their words with words of God. Consider well but that one text, and tell me whether it suit with their opinions, ' Seeing all these things must be dissolved, what manner of persons ought we to be in all manner of holy conversation and godliness; looking for and hastening to the coming of the day of God!' Did these words but sink into your hearts, the next time you heard any man reproach a holy, heavenly life, it would perhaps make you think of the words of Paul to such another, ' O full of all subtilty and all mischief, thou child of the devil; thou enemy of all righteousness, wilt thou not cease to pervert the right ways of the Lord?'

If holiness be evil spoken of by them that never tried it, what wonder! Christ hath foretold us that it must be so. ' Blessed are ye when men shall revile you and persecute you, and say all manner of evil against you falsely, for my sake. Rejoice and be exceeding glad, for great is your reward in heaven; for so persecuted they the prophets which were before you. —If ye were of the world, the world would love his own; but because ye are not of the world, but I have chosen you out of the world, therefore the world hateth you.—They think it strange that you run not with them to the same excess of riot, speaking evil of you, who shall give account to him that is ready to judge the quick and dead.—If ye be reproached for the name of Christ, happy are ye; for the Spirit of glory, and of God, resteth upon you. On their part he is evil spoken of, but on your part he is glorified.' Seneca himself often tells us, that among the heathens virtue was a derision, so far is the nature of man degenerated. The question is

not what you are called or taken to be, but what you are. Says he, 'Inwardly consider of thyself and judge not what thou art by the words of others: for the most part good men are called fools and dotards: let me be so derided. The reproaches of the ignorant or unskilful, must be patiently heard, and this contempt of one that follows virtue, must be contemned.' Yea, it is the highest honour to be content to be accounted bad, that we may not be so; and the greatest trial whether we be indeed sincere, to put to it, to be either accounted hypocrites, or to be such. Methinks I can scarcely too often recite that excellent saying of Seneca, ' No man seems to set a higher price on virtue; no man seems to be more devoted to it, than he that hath lost the reputation of being a good man, lest he should lose his conscience.

But perhaps you will ask, may not a man be righteous overmuch?

I answer, it is making a man's self overwise or righteous, that is there reproved. And no doubt but, 1. Many take on them or make themselves more wise and righteous than they are; that is, are hypocrites. 2. As righteousness is taken materially and in common estimation, so a man may be too righteous. He may be too rigorous, which is called justice; too much in grief or fear, or trouble; and too much in any outward act that goes under the name of duty. But it is not then truly and formally duty and righteousness, but sin. As, to fast to the disabling the body for God's service: to pray when we should hear: to hear when we should be about some greater work of mercy or necessity: to neglect our outward labour and calling on pretence of religion: to set up sacrifice against or before mercy: to sorrow when we should rejoice: to meditate, fear, and grieve, beyond what the mind can bear, till it distract us: this is called, being righteous overmuch— as also to make us a religion of our own invention, to overdo with will-worship and the traditions of men, as the pharisees and papists. But indeed this is not righteousness but sin: to be formally overmuch righteous, is a contradiction, and impossible. For to go beyond the rule is unrighteousness: and to do too much is to go beyond the rule. Unless you dare imagine, that God hath erred, that the rule itself is overstrict, and the law is unrighteous: but then 'how shall God judge the world?' saith the apostle. ' Shall not the Judge of all the world do righteously?' Nay, how then should he be God?

And is there any thing now left but ignorance or wickedness to stand up against thy speedy diligence? Away then with thy delays and slothfulness. If thou wilt serve God with all thy might, let it be seen; if thou wilt be a Christian indeed, let deeds declare it. Christianity is not a dead opinion. If really thou live in hope of heaven, such hopes will make thee stir for the attainment. Why standest thou idle, when thou art born for work, and all thy faculties are given thee for work, and thou art redeemed for work; for evangelical work. If thou be sanctified, thou hast the Spirit of Christ, a quickening, working principle within thee; which way canst thou look, that thou mayest see that which would shame a slothful soul, and fire a cold and frozen heart, and call thee up to a speedy industry? What quickening words shalt thou find in scripture, if thou wilt but bring thy heart thither, as one that is willing to be quickened? What powerful commands, what promises, what threatenings, what holy examples of exceeding diligence of Christ and his apostles? See how the godly about thee are at work, though the world oppose them and deride them! How earnestly they pray! how carefully they walk! how sadly they complain that they are no better! Hast thou not an immortal soul to save or lose as well as they? See what a stir the proud ambitious person makes for less than nothing; what a stir the covetous and the voluptuous make for a sweetened draught of mortal poison! And shall we be idle that are engaged for heaven? Is it reason that we should do less for God and our salvation, than they do for sinful pleasure to damnation? You cannot mock them out of their pride or covetousness: and shall they mock thee out of thy religion, and thy hopes of heaven? All the commands, promises, and threatenings of God, the most powerful preaching, that, as it were, sets open heaven and hell to them, doth not prevail with fleshly men to leave the most unmanly sin: and shall the words or frowns of dust prevail with thee against the work for which thou livest in the world, when thou hast still at hand unanswerable arguments from God, from thyself, from heaven and hell, to put thee on? Were it but for thy life, or the life of thy children, friend, yea, or enemy, or for the quenching of a fire in thy house, or in the town, wouldst thou not stir and do thy best? And wilt thou be idle when eternal life lies on it? Let Satan frown against thee by his instruments. Let senseless sinners talk a while of they know not what, till God hath made them change their note, let what will be the consequence to thy flesh.

These are not matters for a man much to observe, that is engaged for an endless life. O

what are these to the things that thou art called to prosecute! Hold on then, Christians, in the work that you have begun. Do it prudently, and do it universally. Take it together, both works of piety, justice, and charity: but do it now without delay, and do it seriously with your might. I know not what cloud of darkness hath seized on those men's minds that speak against this, or what deadly damp hath seized on their hearts, that hath so benumbed and unmanned them. For my own part, though I have long lived in a sense of the preciousness of time, and have not been wholly idle in the world; yet when I have the deepest thoughts of the great everlasting consequences of my work, and of the uncertainty and shortness of my time, I am even amazed to think that my heart can be so slow and senseless, as to do no more in such a case. The Lord knows, and my accusing, wounded conscience knows, that my slothfulness is so much my shame and admiration, that I am astonished to think that my resolutions are no stronger, my affections no livelier, and my labour and diligence no greater, when God is the commander, his love the encourager, his wrath the spur, and heaven or hell must be the issue. O what lives should all of us live, that have things of such unspeakable consequence on our hands, if our hearts were not almost dead within us! Let who will speak against such a lie, it shall be my daily grief and regret that I am so dull, and do so little. I know that our works do not profit the Almighty, nor bear any proportion with his reward; nor can they stand in his sight, but as accepted in the Lord our righteousness, and perfumed by the odour of his merits. But I know they are necessary, and they are sweet. Without the holy employment of our faculties, this life will be but a burden or a dream, and the next an inexpressible misery. O therefore that I had more of the love of God, that my soul could get but nearer to him, and more swiftly move upward by faith and love! O that I had more of that holy life, and active diligence, which the serpentine, Cainish nature doth abhor, though I had with it the scorns of all about me, and though they made me as they once did better men, as the filth of the world, and the off-scouring of all things! O that I had more of this derided diligence, and holy converse with the Lord, though my name were cast out as an evil doer, and I were spit at and buffeted by those that do now but secretly reproach! Might I nearly follow Christ in holiness, why should I grudge to bear his cross, and to be used as he was used? Knowing that 'if we suffer with him, we shall also reign with him ; and the sufferings of this present time are not worthy to be compared with the glory which shall be revealed in us.'

If when we have done all, we are but unprofitable servants, and must say, we have done but our duty, have we not all more need of monitors to humble us for doing so much less than our duty, than to be reprehended for being too diligent and exact ?

I again protest, that it is not any works of super-errogation, or human invention, superstition, or self-appointment, that I am defending, but only the accurate obeying of the laws of God, and the utmost diligence in such obedience, for the obtaining of everlasting life. Either God hath commanded these works of holiness, justice, and charity, or not. If he have not, then I have done, and yield the cause : it is only what he hath commanded that I plead for. O that before you either speak against any holy duty, or yourselves neglect it, you would but come to us, and soberly join in ' searching the holy scriptures,' to see whether it be required there or not ; and resolve but to obey it, if we prove it thence : and if it be not a matter of human imposition, we leave you to yourselves, and should desire that you may be much left to yourselves in such things ; that you place not too much of your religion therein. But if indeed it be commanded in the word of God, I beseech you, as you are Christians, and as you are men, remember that whenever you blame or scorn a holy duty, it is God himself that you blame or scorn. If it be naught, it belongs to him that did command it : the subject must obey : should not such worms as we obey the infinite God that made us ? If it be a fault to obey, it is a duty to rebel, or disobey ; that must be because that God hath no authority to command, and that must be because he is not God. See whether you bring your opposition to an holy life : and dare you stand to this ? Dare you as openly mock God for making these strict and holy laws, as you do men for obeying them ? None but a professed atheist dare.

Alas, it is nothing but intoxicating prosperity, sensual delights, and worldly diversions, that turn your brains, and leave you not the sober use of reason, that makes you think well of ungodly slothfulness, and makes you think so contemptuously of a heavenly life. I tell you, and remember another day that you were told of it, that there is not the boldest infidel in the world, nor the bitterest enemy to holiness in this assembly, but shortly would wish they had rather been saints in rags, with all the scorn and cruelty that malice can inflict on such, than to have braved it out in pride and gallantry, with the neglect of the great salvation. I tell you again, there is not an ungodly person that hears me, but ere long would give a world if he were owner of a holy heart and life, that he had spent his days in holy watchful preparations for his change, which he spent for that which will deceive him and forsake him.

Methinks I even see how you will passionately rage against yourselves, and tear your hearts with self-revenge, if grace prevent it not by a more safe repentance, when you think too late how you lived on earth, what golden times of grace you lost, and vilified all that would not lose them as foolishly as you. If repentance unto life made Paul so call himself 'foolish, disobedient, deceived, and exceeding mad,' you may imagine how tormenting repentance will make you call yourselves too late.

You cannot now conceive, while you sit here in health, ease and honour, what different thoughts will then possess you of a holy and unholy life ! How mad you will think them that had but one life's time of preparation for eternal life, and desperately neglected it : how sensible you will then be of the wisdom of believers, that knew their time, and used it while they had it. ' Now wisdom is justified of all her children :' but then how sensibly will it be justified of all its enemies ! With what pangs will undone souls look back on a life of mercy and opportunities, thus basely undervalued, slept away in dreaming idleness, and fooled away for things of nought.

The language of that condemned rich man, in Luke xvi. may help you in your predictions. O how will you wonder at yourselves that ever you could be so blind and senseless, as to be no more affected with the warnings of the Lord, and with the forethoughts of everlasting joy or misery ! To have but one small part of time to do all that ever must be done by you for eternity, and say all that ever you must say for your own or others' souls, and that this was spent in worse than nothing ; to have but one uncertain life, in which you must run the race that wins or loses heaven for ever ; that you should be tempted by a thing of nought, to lose that one irrecoverable opportunity, and to sit still or run another way, when you should have been making haste with all your might ; the thoughts of this will be other kind of thoughts another day, than now you feel them ; you cannot now think how the thoughts of this will then affect you ! That you had a time in which you might have prayed, with promise of acceptance, and had no hearts to take that time; that Christ was offered you as well as he was offered them that entertained him; that you were called on and warned as well as they, but obstinately despised and neglected all; that life and death were set before you, and the everlasting joys were offered to your choice, against the charms of sinful pleasures; you might have freely had them if you would, and were told that holiness was the only way, that it must be now or never, and yet you chose your own destruction! These thoughts will be part of hell to the ungodly. They will wonder that reason could be so unreasonable; and they that had the common wit of man in other matters, should be so far beside themselves in that which is the only thing that it is commendable to be wise for; that such sottish reasonings should prevail with them against the clearest light, that nothing should be preferred before all things, and arguments brought from chaff and dust, should conquer those that were sent from heaven! What heart-rending thoughts will these be, when eternity shall afford them leisure for an impartial review; yea, that they should deceive others also with such a gross deceit, and scorn at all that would not be as mad as they; that being drunken with the world's delusion, they should abuse all that were truly sober; that the one thing needful, should seem to them a needless thing; that their tongues should plead for these delusions of their wicked hearts; that they should be enemies to those that would not be enemies to God and to themselves, and cast away their time and souls as they did! They will wonder, with self-indignation, what could bewitch them into so great unreasonableness, below a man, against the light of nature, as well as of supernatural revelation.

Honourable and beloved hearers, I beseech you do not take it ill, that I speak so much of these matters that are so unpleasant and unwelcome to unbelieving, careless, carnal hearts: it is that I may prevent all this in time, by the awakenings of true repentance. O that this might be the success felt—that I might hear, by your penitent confessions, and see by your universal speedy reformations, that God hath so great mercy for you, that these persuasions might be the means of so much happiness to you, and comfort unto me! However this assembly shall be witnesses that you were warned; conscience shall be witness, that if you waste the rest of your days in the pleasures and vanities of this deceitful world, it was not because you could have no better, and were not called to higher things. That if you yet stand idle, it is not because you could not be hired. For in the name

of Christ I have called you into his vineyard, told you of your work and wages, and shamed your excuses and objections this day. Come away then speedily from the snares of sinners, the company of deceived, hardened men, and cast away the works of darkness! Heaven is before you; death is at hand; the eternal God hath sent to call you; mercy doth yet stretch forth its arms; you have stayed too long, and abused patience too much already: stay no longer! O now please God, and comfort us, and save yourselves by resolving that this shall be the day; faithfully performing of this your resolution. Up and be doing: believe, repent, desire, obey, and do all this with all your might. Love him that you must love for ever, and love him with all your soul and might; seek that which is truly worth the seeking, and will pay for all your cost and pains: and seek it first with all your might; remembering still it must be now or never.

Before I conclude, I have two messages yet to deliver to the servants of the Lord: the one is of encouragement; the other of direction.

I know that many of you have a threefold trouble, which requires a threefold comfort and encouragement.

One is, that you have done so little of your work; but lost so much of your time already: another is, that you are so opposed and hindered. The greatest of all is, that you are yet so dull and slow: the cure of which must be the matter of my directions.

1. For the first: that you have lost your time, must be the matter of your humiliation: but that all is not lost, before you see your sin and duty; but yet the patience and mercy of the Lord are attending you, and continuing your hope; this is the matter of your comfort and encouragement. Repent therefore that you came no sooner home: but rejoice that you are come home at last; and now be more diligent in redeeming your time, in remembrance of the time already lost: though it must be your grief that your Master hath been deprived of so much of his service, and others of so much good which you should have done them, and that time is lost which cannot be recalled; yet it is your comfort, that your own reward may be equal with them that have borne the burden and heat of the day: for many that are last, in the time of their coming in, shall be first in receiving the reward. This is the meaning of that parable in Mat. xx. which was spoken to encourage them that had stood out too long, and to rebuke the envy and high expectations of them that came in sooner:

and it is no whit contradictory to those passages in Mat. xxv. which intimate a different degree of glory to be given to them that have different degrees of grace upon their industrious improvement. The former parable shows that men shall not be rewarded differently for their longer or shorter continuance in the work, but that those that come in late, and yet are found with equal holiness, shall be rewarded equally with the first: and more, if their holiness be more, which the latter parable expresses, declaring God's purpose to give them the greatest glory, that have improved their holiness to the greatest measure. O therefore that the sense of your former unkindness might provoke you the more resolvedly to give up yourselves in fervent love and full obedience! and then you will find that your time is redeemed, though it cannot be recalled; and that mercy hath secured your full reward. What an unspeakable mercy is this! that if yet you will devote yourselves entirely to Christ, and serve him with your might, the little time that yet remains, he will take it as if you had come in at the first hour of the day!

2. As for the opposition and hinderances in your way, they are no other than what your Lord foretold. He hath gone before you, and conquered much more than ever you will encounter from without, though he had not a body of sin to conquer; and in that respect the conquest of his Spirit in his members, hath the pre-eminence of his personal conquest. He hath bid you be of good cheer, because he hath overcome the world. If you will not take up your cross and follow him, you cannot be his disciples. would you be soldiers on condition you may not fight, or fight and yet have no opposition? Follow the Captain of your salvation. If mocking, or buffeting, or spitting in his face, or hanging him upon a cross, or piercing his side, would have made him give up the work of your redemption, you had been left to utter desperation. The opposition that is conquerable, should serve but to excite your courage and resolution in a case of such necessity, where you must prevail, or perish. Have you God himself on your side, and Christ your captain, and the Spirit of Christ to give you courage, and the promise to invite you, and heaven before you, hell behind you, and the examples of such an army of conquering believers: and shall the scorns or threats of a worm prevail against all these for your discouragement? You are not afraid lest any man should pull down the sun, or dry up the sea, or overturn the earth: and are you afraid that man should conquer God: or take you out of the

hands of Christ? Mark how they used David; 'every day they wrest my words: all their thoughts are against me for evil: they gather themselves together: they hide themselves: they mark my steps when they wait for my soul.' But did he therefore fear, or fly from God? No, 'what time I am afraid, I will trust in thee; in God will I praise his word; in God have I put my trust; I will not fear what flesh can do unto me.—Hearken to me ye that know righteousness, the people in whose heart is my law; fear ye not the reproach of men, neither be ye afraid of their revilings; for the moth shall eat them up like a garment, and the worm shall eat them like wool: but my righteousness shall be for ever, and my salvation from generation to generation.' You deserve to be shut out of heaven, if you will not bear the breath of a fool's derision for it.

3. But saith the self-accusing soul, I am convinced that I ought to be laborious for my salvation, and that all this is too little that I can do; but I am dull, cold, and negligent in all: I am far from doing it with my might: I hear, read, and pray as if I did it not, and as if I were half asleep, or my heart were away upon somewhat else. I fear I am but a lazy hypocrite.

Answ. I shall first speak to thy doubt, and then proceed to direct thee against thy sin.

First. You must be resolved whether your sloth be such as is predominant, or mortified; such as proves that you are dead in sin; or only such as proves you but diseased and infirm.

To know this you must distinguish, 1. Between the dullness and coldness of the affections, and the unresolvedness and disobedience of the soul. 2. Between a slothfulness that keeps men from a godly life in a life of wickedness; and that which only keeps them from some particular act of duty, or abates the degree of their sincere affection and obedience. 3. Between that sloth which is the vicious habit of the will, and that which is the effect of age, or sickness, or melancholy, or other distemper of the body.

So the case lies plain before you. 1. If it be not only your affections that are dull, but your will through sloth is unresolved; and this not only in a temptation to the abatement of some degrees, and the neglect of some particular duty, but against a holy life, and against the forsaking of your reigning sin; and this be not only through some bodily distemper, disabling your reason, but from the vicious habit of your wills; then is your sloth a mortal sign, and proves you in a graceless state: but if the sloth which you complain of be only dullness of your affections, and the backwardness of your wills to some high degrees, or particular duties, and the effect of some bodily distemper, or the weakness of your spiritual life, while your wills are habitually resolved for God and a holy life, against a worldly, fleshly life : this is your infirmity, and a sin to be lamented, but not a mark of death and gracelessness.

You will have a backward, slothful heart to strive with while you live : but bless God that you are offended with it, and would fain be delivered from it.   This was Paul's evidence.   You will have flesh, and flesh will plead for its interest, and will be striving against the Spirit ; but bless God that you have also the Spirit to strive against the flesh.   Be thankful that you have life to feel your sickness, though you languish under it, and cannot work as healthful men ; and that you are in the way to heaven, though you go not so fast as you should and would.

2. But yet though you have life, it is so grievous to be diseased and languish under such an infirmity as sloth, that I advise you to stir up yourselves to the utmost, and give not way to a lazy temper : and that you may serve the Lord with all your might, I recommend these few directions to your observation.

Direction 1. When you would be quickened up to seriousness and diligence, have ready at hand such quickening considerations as are here before propounded to you ; set them before you, and labour to work them upon your hearts.   Powerful truths would have some power upon your souls, if you will but soberly apply your reason to them, and plead them with yourselves, as you would do with another in any of your reproofs or exhortations.

Direction 2. Take heed lest any worldly design or interest, or any lusts or sensual delight, divert your minds from God and duty.   For all the powers of your soul will languish, when you should set them on work on spiritual things, and your hearts will be abroad, when you should be wholly taken up with God, if once they be entangled with worldly things.   Watch therefore over them in your callings, lest the creature steal too deep into your affections : for if you be alive to the world, you will be in that measure dead to God.

Direction 3. If it be possible, live under a lively ministry, that when your hearts go cold and dull unto the assemblies, they may come warm and quickened home.   Life cherishes life as fire kindles fire.   The word and ordinances of God are quick, powerful, and sharper than any two-edged sword, piercing even to the dividing asunder of soul and spirit, and it is a discerner of the thoughts and intents of the heart.   Therefore it may do much to make you feel.   Many a thousand hath it pricked at the heart, and sent them home alive, that before were dead.   Much more may you expect, that it should excite the principle which you have already.

Direction 4. If it may be, converse with lively, active, stirring Christians : but especially have one such for a bosom friend, that will warm you when you are cold, help to awake you when you drop asleep, and will not comply with you in a declining, lazy and unprofitable course. ' Two are better than one, because they have a good reward for their labour : for if they fall, the one will lift up his fellow ; but woe to him that is alone when he falleth ; for he hath not another to help him up.   Again, if two lie together, then they have heat ; but how can one alone be warm?   And if one prevail against him, two shall withstand him ; and a threefold cord is not quickly broken.'

Direction 5. Put not away from you the day of death.   Look not for long life.   It is the life to come that must be the life of all your duties here, and distant things lose their force.   Set death, judgment, and eternal life continually as near at hand : live in a watchful expectation of your change : do all as dying men, and as passing to receive the recompence of endless joy or woe, and this will quicken you.   To this end, go often to the house of mourning, and be not unseasonably or immoderately in the house of mirth.   When you observe what is the end of all men, the heart will be made better by it.   But excess of carnal mirth doth infatuate men, destroy their wisdom, seriousness, and sobriety.   Keep always a sense of the brevity of life, and of the preciousness of time, and remember that it is posting on whether you work or play : methinks, if you forget any of the rest, this one consideration that we have in hand, should make you bestir with your might, that it must be now or never.

I shall only add two needful cautions, lest while we cure one disease, we cause another, as knowing that corrupted nature is used to run from one extreme into another.

1. Desire and labour more for an high estimation of things spiritual and eternal, and a fixed resolution, and an even and diligent endeavour, than for passionate feelings and affections.   For these latter are more unconstant in the best, and depend much on the temper of the body, and are not of so great necessity as the former.

though excellent in a just degree and season. For it is possible that passion even about good things may be too much; when estimation, resolution, and regular endeavours cannot.

2. Be suspicious when you have the warmest and liveliest affections, lest your judgment should be perverted by following, when they should lead. It is very common for zeal and strong affections, even to that which is good, to occasion the mistakes of the understanding, and make men look all on one side, and think they can never go far enough from some particular sins, till ignorantly they are carried into some perhaps as great on the other hand. Be warned, by the sad experience of these times, to suspect your judgments in the fervour of your affections.

Observing these cautions, let nothing abate your zeal and diligence; but whatever duty is set before you, do it with your might; for it must be now or never.

Though I know that the enmity to a holy, heavenly life is so deeply seated in corrupted nature, that all that I have said is necessary and too little; yet some, I know, will think it strange that I should intimate that any who preach the gospel are guilty of any measure of this sin, and will think that I intend by it to reflect upon some parties above the rest. But again I profess, that it is no party but the devil's party, and the ungodly party, that I mean. It is hard if you will not believe me concerning my own sense. Nor is it my desire that any of the odiousness of schism, sedition, rebellion, or disobedience to authority, should be so much as diminished by any man's profession of godliness. No, I beseech you, by how much the more godly you are, by so much the more you will detest all these; godliness tends to shame and condemn these odious sins, and not to be a cloak for them or any extenuation; Nay, what can more aggravate them, than that they should be found in the professors of godliness? I again profess that I have no design but to plead for serious diligence in the religion which we are all agreed in, and to stop the mouth of those that wickedly speak against it.

But alas! it is too evident that I have too many to speak to, that are not innocent; why else doth scripture tell us that such there will be still to the end of the world; and that there are some that preach Christ of strife and envy, to add affliction to the bonds of the afflicted? Can we already forget what abundance of antinomian teachers were among us, that turned out the very doctrine of practical diligence, cried it down as a setting up ourselves and our own works, as injurious to free grace, and under pretence of exalting Christ, did set up a heartless, lifeless doctrine, that tended to turn out the life of Christianity, and take men off their necessary diligence, as a legal, dangerous thing?

What ordinance of God hath not been cast out by preachers themselves upon religious pretences; as family duties, catechising, singing of psalms, baptism, the Lord's Supper, and what not? If all these were down, wherein should the practice of religion consist? And what abundance of pamphlets had we, that laboured to make the orthodox, faithful ministry a very scorn, and derided them for their faithful service of God, and their faithfulness to their superiors in opposition to their unrighteous ways?

Let no Papist, or any enemy of our church, reproach us because such enemies to holiness are found among us. Can it be expected that our church should be better than the family of Adam, that had a Cain; or of Noah, that had a Ham; or of Christ, that had a Judas? And are there not far more enemies to serious godliness among the Papists themselves, than among us? There is no place, no rank of men in the world, where some of the enemies of a holy life are not to be found, even among those that profess the same religion in doctrinals, with those whom they oppose. Christ and the devil have their several armies; if once the devil disband his soldiers, and have none to oppose a holy life, then tell me that it is a needless thing to defend it and to confute them. But I am listed under Christ, and will never give over pleading for him, till his adversaries give over pleading against him, and his cause, as long as he continues my liberty and duty. Blessed be the Lord, that if a hypocritical preacher be found among us, who secretly or openly disgraces a diligent, holy life, there are more able, holy, faithful ones to confute him, both by doctrine and by their lives, than are to be found in any other kingdom in the world proportionably, that ever I could hear of. And that the faithful disciples are so many, and the Judases so few, how great a blessing is it to this land, how great an honour to his Majesty's government, and to the church in his dominions. The Lord teach this sinful nation to be thankful, pardon their ingratitude, and never deprive them of this forfeited mercy. The Lord teach them to hearken to the friends, not to the enemies of holiness, and never to receive a wound at the heart of their religion, however they hear their smaller differences about things circumstantial.

Now when I should conclude, I am loth to end, for fear lest I have not yet prevailed with you. What are you now resolved to do, from this day forward? It is work that we have been speaking of, necessary work of endless consequence, which must be done, quickly done, and thoroughly done. Are you not convinced that it is so? That ploughing and sowing are not more necessary to your harvest, than the work of holiness in this day of grace is necessary to your salvation? You are blind if you see not this; you are dead if you feel it not; what then will you do? For God's sake, and for your own sake, stand not demurring till time be gone. It is all that the devil desires, if he can but find you one thing or other to be thinking, talking, and doing about, to keep you from this till time be gone; and then he that kept you from seeing and feeling, will help you to see and feel to your calamity: then the devil will make you feel that which preachers could not make you feel; and he will make you think of that, and lay it close enough to your hearts, which we could not get you to lay to heart. Now we study and preach to you in hope; but then alas, it breaks our hearts to think of it, we have done with you for ever, because all hope is gone. Then the devil may challenge a minister, Now do thy worst to bring this sinner to repentance: now call him to consider, believe, and come to Christ: now offer him mercy, and intreat him to accept it: now cry to him to take heed of sin and of temptations, that he come not to this place of torments: now tell him of the beauty or necessity of holiness, and call upon him to turn and live: now do thy worst to rescue him from my power, and save his soul. Alas, poor sinners! will you stop your ears, go on in sin, and damn yourselves, and break our hearts to foresee that day? Must we see the devil go away with such a prey, and shall we not rescue your captivated souls, because you will not hear, you will not stir, you will not consent? Hear the God of heaven, if you will not hear us, who calls to you, return and live! Hear him that shed his blood for souls, and offers you now salvation by his blood! O hear, without any more delay, before all is gone, and you are gone, and he that now deceives you, torments you!

Yet hold on a little longer in a carnal, earthly, unsanctified state, and it is too late to hope, or pray, or strive for your salvation: yet a little longer, and mercy will have done with you for ever; Christ will never invite you more, nor never offer to cleanse you by his blood, or sanctify by his Spirit. Yet a little longer, and you shall never hear a sermon more, and never more be troubled with those preachers that were in good earnest with you, and longed once for your conversion and salvation. O sleepy, dead-hearted sinners, what should I do to show you how near you stand to eternity, and what is now doing in the world that you are going to, and how these things are thought on there? What should I do to make you know how time is valued, how sin and holiness are esteemed in the world where you must live for ever? What should I do to make you know those things to-day, which I will not thank you to know when you are gone hence? O that the Lord would open your eyes in time! Could I but make you know these things as believers should know them, I say not as those that see them, nor yet as dreamers that do not regard them, but as those that believe that they must shortly see them, what a joyful hour's work should I esteem this; how happy would it be to you and me, if every word were accompanied with tears! If I followed you home and begged your consideration on my bare knees, or as a beggar begs an alms at your doors: if this sermon cost me as many censures or slanders as ever sermon did, I should not think it too dear, if I could but help you to such a sight of the things we speak of, as that you might truly understand them as they are; that you had but a truly awakened apprehension of the shortness of your day, of the nearness of eternity, and of the endless consequence of your present work, and what holy labour and sinful loitering will be thought of in the world to come for ever! But when we see you sin, trifle, and no more regard your endless life, and see also what haste your time is making, and yet cannot make you understand these things; when we know ourselves, as sure as we speak to you, that you will shortly be astonished at the review of your present sloth and folly, and when we know that these matters are not thought of in another world, as they are among the sleepy or the infatuated sinners here, and yet know not how to make you know it, whom it doth so exceedingly much concern, this amazes us, and almost breaks our hearts! Yea, when we tell you of things that are past doubt, and can be no further matter of controversy then, men have sold their understandings, and betrayed their reason to their sordid lusts, and yet we cannot get reasonable men to know that which they cannot choose but know; to know that seriously and practically which always hath a witness in their breasts, and which none but the profligate dare deny.

I tell you, sinners, this, even this, is worse than a prison to us: it is you that are our persecutors; it is you that are the daily sorrow of our hearts; it is you that disappoint us of our hopes, and make us lose so much of the labour of our lives! And if all others did as some do by us, alas, how sad an employment should we have! and how little would it trouble us to be silenced and laid aside! If we were sick of the ambitious, or covetous thirst, we should then say, that it is they that deny us wealth and honour that disappoint us. But if we are Christians, this is not our case, but it is the thirst after your conversion and salvation which affects us : therefore it is you, even you that linger in your sins and delay repentance, forget your home, and neglect your souls; it is you that disappoint, and you that occasion our affliction ; and as much as you think you befriend us when you plead our cause against men of violence and rage, it is you that shall answer for the loss of our time, labour, and hope, and for the grieving of your teachers' hearts.

Sinners, whatever the devil and raging passion may say against a holy life, God and your own consciences shall be our witnesses, that we desired nothing unreasonable or unnecessary at your hands. I know it is the master-piece of the devil's craft, when he cannot keep all religion in contempt, to raise up a dust of controversy in the world about names, forms, and circumstances in religion, that he may keep men busily striving about these, while religion itself is neglected or unknown; and that he may make men believe that they have some religion, because they are for one side or other in these controversies ; especially that he may entice men to number the substantials of religion itself among these lesser doubtful points, and make sinners believe that it is but the precise opinion of one party that they reject, while they reject the serious practice of all true religion. So the devil gets more by these petty quarrels and controversies, occasioned by contentious empty men, than he could have done by the open opposition of infidels, heathens, or the profane: so that neither I nor any man, that opinionative men have a mind to quarrel with, can tell how to exhort you to the very practice of Christianity itself, but you are presently casting your thoughts upon some points wherein we are reported to differ from you, or remembering some clamours of malicious men, that prejudice against the person of the speaker, may keep your souls from profiting salvation by the doctrine which even yourselves profess.

If this be the case of any one of you, I do not mean your consciences shall so escape the power or evidence of the truth. Dost thou talk of our differences about forms and ceremonies?

Alas! what is that to the message which we come about to thee; what is that to the business that we are preaching of ? The question I am putting to you, is not whether you will be for this form of church-government, or for that, for a ceremony or against it ; but it is, whether you will hearken in time to God and conscience, and be as busy to provide for heaven, as ever you have been to provide for earth ; whether you will set yourselves to do the work that you are created and redeemed for ? This is the business that I am sent to call you to; what say you ; will you do it, and do it seriously without delay; you shall not be able to say that I called you to a party, a faction, or some opinion of my own, or laid your salvation upon some doubtful controversy. No, sinner, thy conscience shall have no such shift for its deceit: it is godliness, serious and practical godliness that thou art called to. It is nothing but what all Christians in the world, both papists, Greeks, protestants, and all the parties among those that are true Christians, are agreed in the profession of. That I may not leave thee in any darkness which I can deliver thee from, I will tell thee distinctly, though succinctly, what it is that thou art thus importuned to ; and tell me then, whether it be that which any Christian can make doubt of.

1. That which I intreat of thee, is but to live as one that verily believes there is a God, and that this God is the Creator, the Lord, and Ruler of the world : that it is incomparably more of our business to understand and obey his laws, and as faithful subjects to be conformed to them, than to observe or be conformed to the laws of man : to live as men that believe, that this God is almighty, and that the greatest of men are less than worms to him ; that he is infinitely wise, and the wisdom of man is foolishness to him ; that he is infinitely good and amiable ; that the best of creatures is dung in comparison of him ; that his love is the only felicity of man ; that none are happy but those that do enjoy it ; that none that enjoy it can be miserable; and that riches, honour, and fleshly delights are brutish vanities in comparison of the eternal love of God. Live but as men that heartily believe all this, and I have that I come for. Is any of this matter of controversy or doubt ? Not among Christians, I am sure ; not among wise men. It is no doubt to those in heaven, nor to those in hell, nor to those that have not lost their understandings upon earth. Live then according to these truths.

2. Live as men that verily believe that mankind is fallen into sin and misery ; and that all

men are corrupted, and under the condemnation of the law of God, till they are delivered, pardoned, reconciled to God, and made new creatures by a renewing, restoring, sanctifying change. Live but as men that believe that this cure must be wrought, and this great restoring change must be made upon ourselves, if it be not done already. Live as men that have so great a work to look after. Is this a matter of any doubt or controversy? Surely it is not to a Christian: and methinks it should not be to any man else that knows himself, any more than to a man in a dropsy, whether he be diseased, when he feels the thirst, and sees the swelling. Did you but know what cures and changes are necessarily to be made upon your diseased, miserable souls, if you care what becomes of them, you would soon see cause to look about you.

3. Live but as men that verily believe that you are redeemed by the Son of God, who hath suffered for your sins, and brought you the tidings of pardon and salvation, which you may have if you will give up yourselves to him who is the physician of souls, to be healed by him: live as men that believe that the infinite love of God, revealed to lost mankind in the Redeemer, doth bind us to love him with all our hearts, serve him with all our restored faculties, and to work as those that have the greatest thankfulness to show, as well as the greatest mercies to receive, and misery to escape; and as those that believe that if sinners that without Christ had no hope, shall now love their sins and refuse to leave them, to repent, or be converted, and unthankfully reject the mercy of salvation so dearly bought, and so freely offered them, their damnation will be doubled as their sin is doubled. Live but as men that have such redemption to admire, such mercy to entertain, and such a salvation to attain, and that are sure they can never escape if they continue to neglect so great salvation; and is there any controversy among Christians in any of this? There is not, certainly.

4. Live but as men that believe that the Holy Ghost is given by Jesus Christ to convert, to quicken, to sanctify all that he will save; that except you be born again of the Spirit, you shall not enter into the kingdom of heaven; that 'if any man have not the Spirit of Christ, the same is none of his,' and that without this no patching or mending of your lives by any common principles, will serve the purpose for your salvation, or make you acceptable to God. Live as men that believe that this Spirit is given by

the hearing of the word of God, and must be prayed for, obeyed, and not resisted, quenched and grieved. Is there any controversy among Christians in any of this? Ask those that make a mock at holiness, sanctification and the Spirit, whether they be not baptized into the name of the Holy Ghost, and profess to believe in him as their sanctifier, as well as in the Son their Redeemer? And then ask them whether it be not a thing that should make even a devil to tremble, to come so near the blasphemy against the Holy Ghost, as to mock at his office and sanctifying work, and at the holiness without which no man shall see the Lord; and this after they are baptized and profess to believe in the Holy Ghost, as their sanctifier.

5. Live but as men that believe that sin is the greatest evil, the thing which the Holy God abhors. And then you will never make a mock of it, as Solomon saith the foolish do, nor say, what harm is in it.

6. Live but as men that believe no sin is pardoned without repentance: and that repentance is the lothing and forsaking of sin; and that if it be true, it will not suffer you to live wilfully in any gross sin, nor to desire to keep the least infirmity, nor to be loth to know your unknown sins.

7. Live as those that believe that you are to be members of the holy catholic church, and therein to hold the communion of saints. Then you will know that it is not as a member of any sect or party, but as a holy member of this holy church, that you must be saved; and that it is the name of a Christian which is more honourable than the name of any division or subdivision among Christians, whether Greek, or Papists, or Protestant, or Prelates, or Presbyterian, or Independent, or Baptist. It is easy to be of any one of these parties; but to be a Christian, which all pretend to, is not so easy. It is easy to have a burning zeal for any divided party or cause; but the zeal for the Christian religion is not so easy to be kindled or kept alive; but requires as much diligence to maintain it, as dividing zeal requires to quench it. It is easy to love a party as a party: but to keep up catholic charity to all Christians, and to live in that holy love and converse which is requisite to a communion of saints, is not so easy. Satan and corrupted nature befriend the love and zeal of faction, which is confined to a party on a controverted cause; but they are enemies to the love of saints, to the zeal for holiness, and to the catholic charity which is from the spirit of Christ. You see I call you not to division,

nor to side with sects; but to live as members of a holy catholic church, which consists of all that are holy in the world; and to live as those that believe the communion of saints.

8. Live as those that believe that there is a life everlasting, where the sanctified shall live in endless joy, and the unsanctified in endless punishment and woe: live but as men that verily believe a heaven, a hell, and a day of judgment, in which all the actions of this life must be revised, and all men judged to their endless state. Believe these things heartily, and then think a holy diligence needless if you can: then be of the mind of the deriders and enemies of godliness if you can! If one sight of heaven or hell would serve, without any more ado, instead of other arguments, to confute all the cavils of the distracted world, and to justify the most diligent saints in the judgment of those that now abhor them, why should not a sound belief of the same thing in its measure do the same?

9. Live but as those that believe this life is given us as the only time to make preparation for eternal life, and that all ever shall be done for your salvation must be *now, just now,* before your time is ended. Live as those that know, and need not faith to tell them, that this time is short and almost at an end already, and stays for no man, but as a post doth haste away. It will not stay while you are trimming you, or sporting you: it will not stay while you are taking up the stage-plays, in compliments, in idle visits, or any impertinent, needless things: it will not tarry while you spend yet the other year, or month, or day, in your worldliness, or ambition, or in your lusts and sensual delights, and put off your repentance to another time. For the Lord's sake, do but live as men that must shortly be buried in the grave, and their souls appear before the Lord, and as men that have but this little time to do all for their everlasting life, that ever must be done. Live as men that are sure to die, and are not sure to live till morrow: and let not the noise of pleasure or worldly business, or the chat or scorns of miserable fools, bear down your reason, and make you live as if you knew not what you know, or as if there were any doubt about these things. Who is the man, and what is his name, that dares contradict them, and can make it good? Do not sin against your knowledge: do not stand still and see your glass running, and time making such haste, yet make no more haste yourselves, than if you were not concerned in it: do not, O do not slumber, when time and judgment never slumber, nor sit still when you have so much to do, and know all that is now

left undone must be undone for ever! Alas, how many questions of exceeding weight have you yet to be resolved in; whether you are truly sanctified; whether your sins be pardoned; whether you shall be saved when you die; whether you are ready to leave this world, and enter upon another? I tell you, the answering of these, and many more such questions, is a matter of no small difficulty or concern. And all these must be done in this little and uncertain time. It must be now or never. Live but as men that believe and consider these certain, unquestionable things.

10. Lastly, Will you but live as men that believe that the world and the flesh are the deadly enemies of your salvation: that believe 'that if any man love the world, the love of the Father is not in him.' As men that believe, that 'if ye live after the flesh, ye shall die; but if, by the Spirit, ye mortify the deeds of the body, ye shall live;' that those who are in Christ Jesus, and are freed from condemnation, are such as 'walk not after the flesh, but after the Spirit.' That we must make no provision for the flesh to satisfy the will or lusts thereof; we must not walk in gluttony and drunkenness, in chambering and wantonness, in strife and envying, but must have hearts where our treasure is, and our converse in heaven, that being risen with Christ, we must seek the things that are above, set our affections on them, and not on the things that are on the earth.

Will you say that any of this is our singular opinion, or matter of controversy and doubt; are not all Christians agreed in it; do you not, your own selves profess that you believe it? Live then but as those that believe it, and condemn not yourselves in the things that you confess?

I tell thee, if now thou wilt refuse to live according to these common acknowledged truths, thou shalt never be able to say before the Lord, that men's controversy about a ceremony, or church government, or the manner of worship, were the things that hindered thee. But all sorts and sects shall be witnesses against thee, and condemn thee; for they are all agreed in these things; even the bloodiest sects, that imprison, torment, and kill others for their differences in smaller matters, are yet agreed, with those that they persecute and murder, about these things: papists are agreed in them, and protestants are agreed in them: all the sects that are now quarreling among us, and in the world, are agreed in them, who are but meet for the name of Christians. All these will be ready to bear witness against the profane, the sensual, the slothful neglecter of God and his salvation, and to say, we all confessed, notwithstanding our other differences, that all these things were certain truths, and that men's lives should be ordered according unto these.

But if yet you pretend controversy to cover your malignity or ungodliness, I will go a little further, and tell you that in the matter, as well as in the principles, it is things that we are all agreed in, which I call you to, and which the ungodly do refuse: I will briefly name them.

1. One part of your work which we urge you to do with all your might, is seriously and soberly to consider often of all these truths before mentioned, which you say you believe: is it any controversy with reasonable men whether they should use their reason; or with believers, whether they should consider and lay to heart the weight and use of the things which they believe?

2. Another part of your work, is to love God with all your soul and might; to make him your delight, to seek first his kingdom, and the righteousness thereof; to set your affections on the things above, and to live on earth as the heirs of heaven: is there any controversy among protestants, papists, or any, about this?

3. Another part of your work is, to see the honouring of God in the world, the promoting of his kingdom and government in yourselves and others, the doing of his will, and the obeying of his laws: is there any controversy in this?

4. Another part of your work is, to mortify the flesh, reject its conceits, desires, and lusts, which resist the aforesaid obedience to God; and to cast out the inordinate love and care of worldly things: to refuse the counsels, the commands, the will, the enticements and persuasions of men, which contradict the commands and will of God; to forsake all that you have in the world rather than forsake your dear Redeemer, and hazard your salvation by any wilful sin: to take up your cross and follow Christ through a life of suffering to glory. I know there is difficulty enough in all this, and that flesh will repine against it and abhor it: but is there any controversy about it among any true believers? Is not all this the express command of God, and necessary to salvation?

5. Another part of your work is to avoid temptations, and fly from the occasions and appearances of evil; not only to avoid that which is directly evil itself, but that also which would draw you into evil, as far as you can, to keep as far as may be from the brink of hell and danger, and to have no fellowship with the unfruitful works of darkness, nor be companions with them, but reprove them, and mourn for the unclean and wicked conversation of the world. This is it that we intreat of you; is there any matter of controversy in all this?

6. Another part of the work which we call you to, is, to redeem this little time that is allotted you: to make the best of it, and improve it to the greatest furtherance of your salvation: to lose none of it upon unprofitable things: to spend it in those works which will comfort you most when time is gone. If it will be more comfortable to you in the day of judgment, that you have spent your time in plays, sports, idleness, worldly cares, and pleasures, than in serving God, and preparing for another life, then hold on, and do so to the end: but if it will not, then do what you would hear of, seeing you must hear of it: spend none of your time in idleness and unfruitful things, till you have no better and more necessary things to spend it in, and till you have time to spare from more important work. This is our request to you, that you would not lose one hour of your precious time, but spend it as those that have lost too much, and have but a little more to spend in preparation for eternity. Is this any schismatical or factious notion? Is there any thing controvertible, or which any Christian can speak against, in any of this?

7. Another part of your work is, to search the scriptures, as that which contains your directions for eternal life. To love the word of God more than thousands of gold and silver, and prefer it before your necessary food, to meditate on it day and night, as that which is your pleasure and delight; and as that which is able to make you wise unto salvation, to build you up, and give you an inheritance among the sanctified. That you lay up the word of God in your hearts, teach them diligently to your children, talk of them when you sit in your houses, when you walk by the way, when you lie down and when you rise up, that so you and your households may serve the Lord. This is the work that we call you to: is there any thing that a Christian can make a controversy of in all this? Is there any thing here that protestants are not agreed in?

8. Another part of your work is, that you guard your tongues, take not the name of God in vain, and speak no reproaches or slanders against your brethren; 'that no corrupt communication proceed out of your mouths, but that which is good to the use of edifying, and that it may minister grace unto the hearers;—that fornication, uncleanness, and covetousness be not once named among you, as becometh saints; neither filthi-

ness nor foolish talking, nor jesting, which are not convenient, but rather giving of thanks.' Is there any thing of doubt or controversy in this?

9. Another part of the work which we persuade you to, is to pray continually, and not to wax faint, to be fervent and importunate with God, as those that know the greatness of their necessity, that you pray with all prayer and supplication in the Spirit, and 'in every thing, by prayer and supplication, to make known your requests unto God; that you pray for kings and all in authority, that we may lead a quiet and peaceable life in all godliness and honesty.' Is there any thing in all this that any Christian can deny?

10. Lastly, the work we call you to is, 'to love your neighbour as yourselves, and to do to others, as you would have them do to you.' To scorn, deride, molest, imprison, slander, or hurt no man, till you would be so used yourselves on the like occasion; to rejoice in other men's profit and reputation as your own; to envy none, to hate no man, to wrong none in their persons, estates, or names; to preserve the chastity, honour, and estate of your neighbour as your own; to love your enemies, forgive them that wrong, pray for them that hate, hurt, and persecute you. This is your work: and is there any thing of faction, schism, or controversy in this? No, you shall shortly be convinced, that the differences and controversies of believers, and the many opinions about religion, were a wretched hypocritical pretence for your neglect and contempt of the substance of religion, about which there was no difference, but all parties were agreed in the confession of the truth, however hypocrites would not live according to their own professions.

But perhaps you will say, that there is such difference in the manner yet among them that agree in the principles and the matter, that you know not which way God is to be worshipped.

I answer, first, do you practise as aforesaid, according to the principles and matter agreed on, or not? If you do not, it is but gross hypocrisy to pretend disagreements in the manner, as an excuse for your contempt or omission of the matter, which all agree in. Forsooth, your families shall be prayerless, and you will make a jest of serious prayer, because some pray on a book, and some without, and some that are wisest, think that either way is lawful. Will God be deceived by such silly reasonings as these? Second, But this shall not hide the nakedness of your impiety. Will you also, in the manner of your obedience, but go so far as all Christians are agreed in? I will briefly then give you some particular instances.

1. The work of God must be done with reverence, in his fear; not like the common works of men, with a common, careless frame of mind, ' God will be sanctified of all that draw near him,' he will be served as God, and not as man: he will not be prayed to with a regardless mind, as those do that can divide their tongues from their hearts, and say over some customary words while they think of something else. It is a dreadful thing for dust to speak to God Almighty: and a dangerous thing to speak to him as slightly and regardlessly, as if we were talking to one of our companions. It beseems a believer to have more of the fear of God upon his heart, in his ordinary converse in the world, than hypocrites and formalists have in their most solemn prayers. Knowest thou the difference between God and man? Put then such a difference between God and man in thy addresses, as his majesty requires. And see also that thy family compose themselves to a reverent behaviour, when they join with thee in the worshipping of God. What have you to say now against this reverent manner of behaviour? Is there any think controvertible in this?

2. It is also requisite that you be serious and sober in all the service you perform to God. Do it not ludicrously, and with half a heart. Be as much more fervent and serious in seeking God and your salvation, than you are in seeking worldly things, as God and your salvation is better than any thing in the world: or if that be beyond your reach, though else there is reason for it, at least let the greatest things have the greatest power upon your hearts. You cannot pray more fervently for heaven than heaven deserves. O let but the excellency and greatness of your work appear in the serious manner of your performance. I hope you cannot say that this is any point of controversy, unless it be a controversy whether a man should be an hypocrite, or be serious in the religion which he professes.

3. It is requisite that your service of God be performed understandingly. God delights not in the blind devotion of men that know not what they do. Prayers not understood are indeed no prayers: for no man's desire goes further than his knowledge. And he expresses not his desires that knows not what he expresses himself. Nor can he expect the concurrence of another man's desires, that speaks what another

understands not. The word that is not understood cannot sink into the heart and sanctify it; or if it be not well and soundly understood, it is easily stolen away by the tempter. If understanding be necessary in our common conversations, much more in our holy addresses to the Almighty. ' A man of understanding is of an excellent spirit;' but God hath ' no pleasure in fools' or in their 'sacrifices,' nor is pleased with a parrot-like lip-service, which is not understood. He saith, in detestation of the hypocrites, ' This people draweth near unto me with their mouth, and honoureth me with their lips, but their heart is far from me.' I hope then when we call you to serve God in judgment, and with understanding, we call you to nothing that a Christian should make question of.

4. ' God is a Spirit,' and they that serve him must 'serve him in spirit and in truth.—The Father seeketh such to worship him.' He calls for the heart; he looks for the inward desires of the soul: he converses with minds that are abstracted from vanity, are seriously taken up in attending him, and are intent upon the work they do: the words of a prayer, separated from the life of it, is abhorred before the holy God. As he will be loved, so will he be ' served. with all the heart, and soul, and might.' Do we call you then to any thing that is doubtful, when we call you to the spiritual worshipping of God ?

5. Yet we maintain that the body hath its part in the service of God as well as the soul, and the body must express the inward reverence and devotion of the soul; though not in a way of hypocritical ostentation, yet in a way of serious adoration. The bowing of the knee, the uncovering of the head, reverent deportment, and whatsoever nature, or common use, and holy institution hath made an expression of holy affections, and a decent and grave behaviour of ourselves, should be carefully observed in the presence of the Most High ; and the holy things of God more reverently to be respected than the presence of any mortal man. And they rather, because that a grave, reverent, and holy manner of deportment in God's worship, reflects upon the heart, and helps us in our inward and spiritual devotion; it helps the beholders, and awakens them to reverent thoughts of God, and holy things, which a regardless and common manner of deportment would extinguish. It is no dishonour to reverent behaviour, that it is the use of hypocrites, but rather an honour to it; for it is something that is good that the hypocrite uses for the cloak of his secret emptiness or evil: if there were nothing good in reverent behaviour before God, it would not serve the hypocrite's

turn. As it is a commendation to long prayer, that the pharisees made it their pretence for the devouring of widows' houses: and those that call them hypocrites that are much in holy exercises and speeches, should consider that if holy exercises and speeches were not good, they were not fit for the hypocrite's design; evil will not be a fit cloak for evil ; that which the hypocrite thinks necessary to the covering of his sin, we must think more necessary to the cure of our sin and the saving of our souls; the way to avoid hypocrisy, is not by running into impiety and profaneness ; we must do more than the hypocrite, and not less, else he will rise up in judgment against you and condemn you, if he would do more to seem good, than you would do to be good, and to please your Maker ; if a pharisee will pray longer to colour his oppression, than you will do to attain salvation. The mischief of hypocrisy is, that the soul of religion is wanting, while the body is present: will you cast away both soul and body, both inside and outside, in opposition to hypocrisy ? If others seem to love God when they do not, will you therefore not so much as seem to do it? So here about reverence in the service of God: the hypocrite should not exceed the sincere in any thing that is truly good. This is the manner of God's service that I persuade you to, and to no other : is there any thing of controversy in this? Prefer but the spiritual part, and know but what that means, ' I will have mercy and not sacrifice,' that so you 'may not condemn the innocent;' and you shall never say that we will be more backward than you to decency, and reverent behaviour in God's service.

6. God will be served in purity and holiness, with clean hearts and hands, and not with such as remain defiled with guilt of any sinful sin. He abhors the sacrifice of the wicked and disobedient. ' He that turneth away his ear from hearing the law, his prayers are abominable.—To what purpose is the multitude of your sacrifices unto me ? saith the Lord (to oppressing wicked men).—When you come to appear before me, who hath required this at your hand, to tread my courts? Bring no more vain oblations: incense is an abomination to me; the new moons and sabbaths, the calling of assemblies, I cannot away with : it is iniquity even the solemn meeting, &c.—And when you spread forth your hands I will hide mine eyes from you ; yea, when you make many prayers, I will not hear: your hands are full of blood. Wash you, make ye clean, put away the evil of your doings from before mine eyes; cease to do evil, learn to do well, seek judgment, relieve the oppressed, judge the fatherless, plead

for the widow; come now and let us reason together, saith the Lord.'

To play the glutton, or drunkard, or filthy fornicator, in the day time, and then to come to God at night, as if it were to make him amends by a hypocritical prayer; to blaspheme God's name and oppose his rule, yea, oppose his kingdom and government in yourselves and others, to do your own will, to hate and scorn them that do his will, and study his will that they may do it, and then to 'pray that God's name may be hallowed, his kingdom come, and his will be done,' is an abusing God, and not serving or pleasing him. Live according to your prayers, and let your lives show, as well as your words, what it is that you desire. This is the service of God that we call you to: and can you say that there is any thing controvertible in all this; are there any men of any party among Christians, or sober infidels, that dare contradict it?

7. God will be served entirely and universally, in all his commands, and with all your faculties; in works of piety, justice, and charity, which must never be separated. You must not hold up your charity against duties of piety; for God is to be preferred in your estimation, love, and service; and all that is done for man must be done for his sake. You must not set up duties of piety against duties of justice, charity, and sobriety: it is not true piety that will not bring forth these. God must be loved above all, and our neighbour as ourselves; and these two sorts of love are inseparable. Do all the good you can to all while 'you have opportunity; especially to them of the household of faith.' What good you would hear of in the day of your accounts, that do now, speedily, diligently, and sincerely, according to your power. Say not, I may come to want myself, but 'cast thy bread upon the waters, for thou shalt find it after many days; give a portion to seven, and also to eight, for thou knowest not what evil shall be upon the earth,' and whether all may not quickly be taken from thee; and then thou wilt wish thou hadst done good with it while thou hadst it, lent it to the Lord, and trusted him with thy remainder, who intrusted thee with his blessings; and hadst 'made thee friends of the mammon of unrighteousness, that when all fail they might receive thee into the everlasting habitations.' Drop not now and then a scanty and grudging alms, as if thou wert a loser by it, and God must be beholden to thee; but believe, that the greatest gain is to thyself, and look after such bargain, and do good as readily, gladly, and liberally, as one that verily expects a full reward

in heaven. This is part of the service of God that we exhort you to, even to visit, relieve, and love Christ in his members and brethren. Is there any thing of doubt or controversy in all this?

8. Moreover, God will be served with love, willingness, and delight: it is the most gainful, honourable, blessed, and pleasant work in the world, which he hath appointed you, and not a toilsome task or slavery; and therefore it is not a melancholy, pining, troublesome course of life that we persuade you to, under the name of godliness; but it is to rejoice in the Lord, and to live in the joyful expectations of eternal life, and in the sense and assurance of the love of God. If you could show us any probability of a more pleasant and joyful life on earth, than that which serious holiness doth afford, I should be glad with all my heart to hearken to you. I am ready to tell you what is the ground of our comforts, which faith reveals: if you will come, and soberly debate the case, and show us the matter and ground of your comforts, which you have or hope for in any other way; if yours prove greater, better, and surer than the joys of faith, we will hearken to you, and be of your mind and side.

The matter of the joys of a believer is, that all his sins are pardoned; that God is reconciled to him in Christ; that he hath the promise of God, that all things, even the greatest sufferings, shall work together for his good; that he is always in the love, care, and hands of God; that he hath leave to draw near him by holy prayer, and open his heart to him in all his straits and wants; that he may solace himself in his praise and thanksgiving, and in other parts of holy worship; that he may read and hear his holy word, the sure discovery of the will of God, and revelation of the things unseen, and the charter of his inheritance; that he may exercise his soul in the serious believing thoughts of the love of God revealed in the wonderful work of our redemption, of the person, offices, and grace of Jesus Christ our Redeemer; and that he may love that God who hath so wonderfully loved him; that he hath the Spirit of God to quicken and actuate his soul, to supply his spiritual defects, kill his sins, and help him to believe, to love, to rejoice, to pray: that this Spirit is God's seal upon him, and the earnest of everlasting life; that death shall not kill his hopes, nor end his happiness, but that his felicity and fullest joy begins, when that of worldlings hath an end, and their endless misery begins; that he is delivered from everlasting torment by the redemption of Christ, and the sanctification of the Spirit; that angels will attend his departing soul into the presence of his Father; that he shall be with his glorified Redeemer and behold his glory; that his body shall be raised to everlasting life; that he shall be justified by Christ from all the accusations of the devil, and all the slanders of the malicious world; that he shall live with God in endless glory, and see and enjoy the glory of his Creator, and shall never more be troubled with enemies, with sin or sorrow, but among his holy ones shall perfectly and most joyfully love and praise the Lord for ever.

These are the matter of a believer's joy: these, purchased by Christ, revealed in his word, sealed by his miracles, his blood, his ordinances, and his Spirit, are our comfort. This is the religion, the labour that we invite you to: it is not to despair, nor to some dry, unprofitable toil, nor to self-troubling, grieving, miserable melancholy, nor to costly sacrifices, or idle ceremonies, or irrational service, such as the heathens offered to their idols; it is not to cast away all mirth and comfort, to turn unsociable, morose, and sour; but it is to the greatest joys that the world allows, and nature is here capable of, and reason can discern and own: it is to begin a truly sociable life: it is to fly from fear and sorrow, in flying from sin and hell, and from the consuming wrath of God: it is to the foretastes of everlasting joys, and to the beginnings of eternal life. This is the labour, the religion which we would have you to follow with all your might.

If you have better things to seek, follow, and find, let us see them, that we may be as wise as you. If you have not, for your soul's sake, make not choice of vanity, which will deceive you in the day of your necessity.

But you must not think to make us believe that a great house, or a horse, or a licentious course, or a feast, or a flatterer, or fine clothes, or any childish toys, or brutish filthiness, are more comfortable things than Christ, and everlasting life; or that it is sweeter and better to love a harlot, or lands, or money, than to love God, grace, and glory; nor that any thing that will go no further than the grave with you, is as good as that which will endure to eternity; nor that any pleasure which an animal hath, is equal to the delights of the angels of heaven: if you would have us of your mind, you must not be of this mind, nor persuade us to such horrible things as these. But we profess to you and all the world, that we are not so in love with sorrows or sourness, nor so fallen out with joy and plea-

sure, as to choose a life of miserable sadness, or refuse a life of true delight. If we could hear from any man, or find, by the most diligent inquiry, that there is a more full, sweet, rational, satisfactory, and durable delight to be had in any other way than that of serious faith and holiness, which Christ in scripture hath revealed to us, we are like enough to hearken after it.

But can the distracted, sensual world believe that it is sweeter and happier to brave it out in fleshly gallantry and sport, and to rage against the godly for a while till the vengeance of God lay hold upon them, and give them their reward, than to live in the love of God, and wait in patience for the performance of God's promise of everlasting joy? O what a thing is fleshly passion, raging sensuality, and blind unbelief! The Lord have mercy upon deluded sinners; the devil's business is to turn the world into a bedlam; and alas, how strangely hath he prevailed; that so many men can take their greatest misery for their happiness, and the only happiness for an intolerable life! Yea, and be so angry with all that are not of their mind, and will not set as much by filth and foolery, and as little by God and glory as they! Like the nobleman that was lunatic, or mad by fits, and whenever he was mad, he would swear all were mad, that said not as he said, and would make all his servants be sent to bedlam that would not imitate him, and there they must lie as madmen till their lord was recovered from his madness. So are God's servants used and talked of in the world, as if they were beside themselves, as long as the world is not cured of its madness. As the man is, so is his judgment, and such is his relish, desire, and delight. When I was a child, I had far more desire to fill my pin-box, than now I have to fill my purse, and accounted it a greater treasure, and had much more delight and contentment in it. And alas, we may remember since we were strangers to the relish of heavenly things, that we found more pleasure in that of which we are now ashamed, than we did in the most high and excellent things. Let us therefore pity and pray for those that are distempered with the same disease.

I have been longer on this than I thought to have been, because men think that we call them from all mirth, joy, and pleasure, to a heavy, melancholy life, when we call them to a serious diligence for their salvation. As if levity and folly were the only friends to pleasure, and it were only to be found in childish, worthless, transitory things. And as if the greatest everlasting happiness were no matter of true delight, nor seriousness; nor diligence, a friend to joy.

9. Moreover, as to the manner; God will be served with absolute self-resignation, without exceptions, limitations or reserves: not with the dregs of the flesh, nor with a proviso that you may not suffer by your religion, or be poor, or despised, or abused by the world: but with self-denial you must lay down all the interests of the flesh at his feet; you must take up your cross, and follow a suffering Christ to glory. You must serve him as those that are wholly his, and not your own; have nothing but what is his, and therefore nothing to be excepted, reserved, or saved from him; but must be content that you and all your interests be in his hands, and saved by him, if saved at all. I know these terms seem hard to flesh and blood; but should heaven be the crown and reward to them that have undergone no trial for it? But here is nothing but what is past all controversy, and what all Christians confess is the word of Christ.

10. Lastly, God will be served resolvedly and constantly: if you will reign, you must conquer and endure to the end. Opposition you must expect; and overcome it if you would not be overcome. It is not good beginnings that will serve the purpose, unless you also persevere, and fight out the good fight of faith, finish your course, and patiently wait to the last breath, for 'the crown of righteousness, which the righteous judge will give' the conquerors, when the unbelieving world shall say of all their delight and hope, 'It is past and gone, we shall never see or taste it more, but must now taste of that endless wrath of God which we were treasuring up, when we should have worked out our salvation.'

I have all this while been describing to you, both as to the principles, the matter and the manner, what that religion and service of God is, in which you must labour with all your might; that you may see that it is no factious or private opinions or practices that we call you to do; and that your consciences may no longer be deluded with the pretences of men's different opinions in religion; that the names of prelatical, presbyterian, puritan, papist, nor any other sounding in your ears, may not so distract you, as to make you forget the name of Christian, which you have all undertaken, nor what the Christian religion is. You see now that it is nothing, no not a syllable or tittle, which all sober Christians are not agreed in, that we persuade you to do as the work of your religion: therefore I tell you again here, before that God that shall be your judge, and that conscience that

shall be as a thousand witnesses, that if you will go on in ungodly, worldly lives, and refuse the serious diligence of Christians in this religion which yourselves profess, it shall be so far from being any excuse or ease to you, that there were hypocrites, or heretics, or schismatics, or different opinions in religion in the world; that this very thing shall aggravate your sin and condemnation; that all these hypocrites, schismatics, or different parties in the church, did agree in the confession of all these things, and yet for all that you would not practise them; no, nor practise what yourselves confessed: all these parties or sects shall rise up against the sensual and profane ungodly sinner, and say, 'Though we are ignorant or doubtful of many other things, yet we are all agreed in these; we gave our concurrent testimony of them; we tempted no man to doubt of these, or to deny them.' If you will err more than a hypocrite or a schismatic, and be far worse than those that are such, or you account such, and think to excuse it, because they erred in lesser things, it is as if the devil should excuse his sin by saying, Lord, thy saints did none of them love thee as they should, hypocrites did but seem to love thee, and therefore I thought I might hate thee and set against thy ways.

But, saith the ungodly sensualist, I will never believe that God delights in long and earnest prayers; or that he is moved by the passions or the words of men; and therefore I take this but for babbling, which you call the serious diligence of believers, in their serving God.

To this impious objection, I return these several answers.

1. Suppose this were true as you imagine, what is this to you that serve God no way at all with any serious diligence; that live in sensuality, and wilful disobedience to his laws, do more for your bodies than for your souls, and for temporal things than for eternal?

2. Who, do you think, is likeliest to understand God's mind, and what is pleasing to him,—himself or you? Is any thing more plainly commanded in God's word, than praying with frequency, fervency, and importunity. And will you tell God that he hath but dissembled with you, and told you that he is pleased with that which is not pleasing to him?

3. What is the reason of your unbelief? forsooth, because God is not moved with human words or passions! I grant he is not. But what of that; hath prayer no other use to move God? It is enough, First, That it moves and fits us to receive his mercies. Second, That God hath made it necessary to the effect, and a means or condi-

tion without which he will not give the blessing. Do you think, if you judge but by natural reason, that a person is as fit for a mercy that knows not the want or worth of it, and would not be thankful for it if he had it, as one that values it, and is disposed to thankfulness and improvement? Do not you know that holy prayer is nothing but the actuating of holy desires, and the exercise of all those graces which are suited to the due estimation and improvement of the mercy? If God be not moved and drawn to us, it is enough that we are moved and drawn to God: and withal that God may give us his own blessings, to whom and upon what terms he please, and that he hath assured us he will give them only to those that value, desire, and seek them, and that with faith, fervency, and importunity.

And yet I may add, that God is so far above us, as that his incomprehensible essence and blessed nature is very little known to us; and therefore though we know and confess that he hath no human passions nor imperfections, yet if he assume to himself the title of such a thing as love, desire, joy, or wrath, we must in reason believe, that though these are not in God as they are in man, with any imperfection, yet there is something in God that cannot be represented to man, nor be understood by man, than by the images of such expressions as God himself is pleased to use.

3. But I beseech you hearken to nature itself. Doth it not teach all rational creatures, in necessity, to pray to God? A storm will teach the profane seaman to pray, and that with continuance and fervency. The mariners could say to Jonah in their danger, 'what meanest thou, O sleeper! arise, call upon thy God; if so be that God will think upon us, that we perish not.' And they themselves cried every man unto his god. When thou comest to die, and seest there is no more delay, nor any more hope from the pleasures of sin, or from any of thy old companions or old deceits, then tell me whether nature teach thee not to cry, and cry mightily for pardon, mercy, and help to God? Then we shall hear thee crying, O mercy, mercy, Lord, upon a miserable sinner, though now thou wilt not believe that prayer doth any good.

I will say no more to thee of this: if nature be not conquered, and grace have not forsaken thee, thou wilt be taught at home to answer this objection. Surely thou canst not easily so far conquer reason, as to believe that there is no God. If thou believe that there is a God, thou canst not believe that he is not to be worshipped,

and that with the greatest seriousness and diligence; nor that he is not the giver of all that thou dost want; or that the governor of the world regards not the dispositions and actions of his subjects, but will equally reward the good and bad, give to all alike, and have no respect to men's preparations for his reward. What heathen that believes that there is a God, doth not believe that prayer to him is a necessary part of his worship?

Obj. But is not your strict observation of the Lord's day a controverted thing?

Answ. In this also I will strip thee of this excuse. Spend the Lord's day but according to the common principles of Christianity and reason, and it shall suffice: spend it but as one that loves God better than any thing in the world, and that takes more pleasure in his service than in sin and vanity: spend it but as the necessities of thy own soul and thy families require; as one that is glad of so honourable, gainful, and delightful an employment, as the public and private worshipping of God, and the serious contemplation of the life to come: as one that knows the need and benefit of having stated times for the service of God; and what would come of all religion, if the time were left to each one's will? Spend it as men that put a just difference between the common business of this world, and the things that concern your endless state; and that have considered the proportion of one day in seven, in reference to this different consequence of the work: spend it as men that have lost as much time as you have done, and have need to make the best of the little that is left; and that are behind-hand so far in the matters of your salvation, and have need to work with all your might, and should be more glad of the helps of such a day, than of thousands of gold and silver: spend it as those that believe that we owe God as much service as the Jews did: spend it as the ancient Christians spent it, that were wont to stay together almost from morning till night in public worship and communion: spend it as the King's declaration requires, which saith, 'our purpose and resolution is, and shall be, to take care that the Lord's day be applied to holy exercise, without unnecessary divertisements.'

I have done my part to open to you the necessity of serious diligence, and to call up the sluggish souls of sinners to mind the work of their salvation, and to do it speedily and with all their might; I must now leave the success to God and you. What use you will make of it, and what you will be and do for the time to come, is a matter that more concerns yourselves than me. If long speaking, or multitude of words, were the way to prevail with you, I should willingly speak here while my strength would endure, and lengthen out my exhortations yet seven-fold. But that is not the way: a little wearies you: you love long feasts, long visits, plays, and sports, much better than long sermons, or books, or prayers. But it is no small grief to us, to leave you in a case of such importance, without some considerable hopes of your deliverance.

The matter is now laid before you, and much in your own hands; it will not be so long. What will you now do? Have I convinced you now, that God and your salvation are to be sought with all your might? If I have not, it is not for want of evidence in what is said, but for want of willingness in yourselves to know the truth: I have proved to you, that it is a matter out of controversy, unless your lusts, passions, and carnal interest will make a controversy of it. I beseech you tell me, if you be of any religion at all, why are you not strict, serious, diligent, mortified, and heavenly in that religion which you are of? Surely you will not so far shame your own religion, whatever it be, as to say that your religion is not for mortification, holiness, heavenliness, self-denial, or that your religion allows you to be sensual, ambitious, covetous, gluttonous, drunken, to curse, swear, and rail and oppress the innocent: it is not religion, but diabolical serpentine malignity that is for any of this.

It is wonderful to think, that learned men, gentlemen, and men that pretend to reason and ingenuity, can quietly betray their souls to the devil upon such silly grounds, do the evil that they have no more to say for, and neglect that duty which they have no more to say against, when they know they must do it now or never! That while they confess that there is a God, and a life to come, a heaven and a hell, and that this life is purposely given us for preparation of eternity; while they confess that God is most wise, holy, good, and just, that sin is the greatest evil, and that the word of God is true, they can yet make shift to quiet themselves in an unholy, sensual, careless life: that while they honour the apostles and martyrs, and saints that are dead and gone, they hate their successors and imitators, the lives that they lived, and are inclined to make more martyrs by their malicious cruelty.

Alas, all this comes from the want of a sound belief of the things which they never saw; and the distance of those things, the power of passion, and sensual objects and inclinations, that hurry them away after present vanities, conquer reason, and rob them of their humanity; by the noise of the company of sensual sinners, that harden and deaden one another, and by the just judgment of God forsaking those that would not know him, leaving them to the blindness and hardness of their hearts. But is there no remedy? O thou, the fountain of mercy and relief, vouchsafe these miserable sinners a remedy! O thou, the Saviour of lost mankind, have mercy upon these sinners in the depth of their security, presumption and misery! O thou, the illuminator and sanctifier of souls, apply the remedy so dearly purchased! We are constrained often to fear lest it be on account of us, that should more seriously apply the awakening truths of God unto men's hearts. Verily our consciences cannot but accuse us, that when we are most lively and serious, alas, we seem but almost to trifle, considering on what a message we come, and of what transcendent things we speak. But Satan hath got his advantage upon our hearts that should be instrumental to kindle theirs, as well as on theirs that should receive the truth. O that we could thirst more after their salvation! O that we could pray harder for it; and intreat them more earnestly; as those that were loth to take a denial from God or man. I must confess to you all, with shame and sorrow, that I am even amazed to think of the hardness of my own heart, that melts not more in compassion for the miserable, and is not more earnest and importunate with sinners when I am upon such a subject as this; and am telling them that it must be now or never; when the messenger of death within, and the fame of men's displeasure from without, doth tell me how likely it is that my time shall be but short, and that if I will say any thing that may reach the hearts of sinners, for ought I know, it must be now or never. What an obstinate, what a lamentable disease is this insensibility, and hardness of heart! If I were sure this were the last sermon that ever I should preach, I find now my heart would show its sluggishness, and rob poor souls of the serious fervour which is suitable to the subject and their case, and needful to the desired success.

But yet, poor sleepy sinners, hear us: though we speak not to you as men would do, that had seen heaven and hell, and were themselves in a perfectly awakened frame, yet hear us while we speak to you the words of truth, with some seriousness and compassionate desire of your salvation. O look up to your God! Look out unto eternity: look inwardly upon your souls: look wisely upon your short and hasty time; then bethink you how the little remnant of your time should be employed; and what it is that most concerns you to dispatch and secure before you die. Now you have sermons, books, and warnings: it will not be so long: preachers must have done: God threatens them, death threatens them, men threaten them, and it is you, it is you that are most severely threatened, and that are called on by God's warnings, ' If any man have an ear to hear, let him hear.' Now you have abundance of private helps, you have abundance of understanding, gracious companions; you have the Lord's days to spend in holy exercises, for the edification and solace of your souls; you have choice of sound and serious books; and blessed be God, you have the protection of a Christian and a protestant king and magistracy: O what invaluable mercies are all these! O know your time, and use these with industry; and improve this harvest for your souls! For it will not be thus always: it must be now or never.

You have yet time and leave to pray and cry to God in hope: yet if you have hearts and tongues, he hath an hearing ear; the Spirit of grace is ready to assist you: it will not be thus always: the time is coming when the loudest cries will do no good: O pray, pray, pray, poor, needy, miserable sinners: for it must be now or never.

You have yet health, strength, and bodies fit to serve your souls: it will not be so always: languishing, pains, and death are coming. O use your health and strength for God; for it must be now or never.

Yet there *are* some stirrings of conviction in your consciences: you find that all is not well with you: and you have some thoughts or purposes to repent and be new creatures: there is some hope in this, that yet God hath not quite forsaken you. O trifle not and stifle not the convictions of your consciences, but hearken to the witness of God within you: it must be now or never.

Would you not be loth to be left to the despairing case of many poor distressed souls, that cry out, ' O it is now too late! I fear my day of grace is past; God will not hear me now if I should call upon him: he hath forsaken me, and given me over to myself. It is too late to repent, too late to pray, too late to think of a new life; all is too late.' This case is sad: but yet many of these are in a safer and better case than they imagine, are but frightened by the tempter, and it is not too late; while they cry out, It is too late. But if you are left to cry in hell, It is too late, alas! how long and how doleful a cry and lamentation will it be!

Consider, poor sinner, that God knows the time and season of thy mercies: he gives the spring and harvest in their season, and all his mercies in their season, and wilt thou not know thy time and season, for love, duty, and thanks to him?

Consider, that God who hath commanded thee thy work, hath also appointed thee thy time. And this is his appointed time. To-day therefore hearken to his voice, and see that thou harden not thy heart: he that bids thee ' Repent and work out thy salvation with fear and trembling,' doth also bid thee do it now: obey him in the time, if thou wilt be indeed obedient; he best understands the fittest time. One would think, to men that have lost so much already, loitered so long, are so lamentably behind-hand, and stand so near the bar of God and their everlasting state, there should be no need to say any more, to persuade them to be up and doing. I shall add but this: you are never like to have a better time. Take this or the work will grow more difficult, more doubtful, if through the just judgment of God, it become not desperate. If all this will not serve, but still you will loiter till time be gone, what can your poor friends do but lament your misery! The Lord knows, if we knew what words, what pains, what cost would tend to your awakening, conversion and salvation, we should be glad to submit to it; and we hope we should not think our labours, or liberties, or our lives too dear to promote so blessed and so necessary a work. But if when all is done that we can do, you will leave us nothing but our tears and groans for self-destroyers, the *sin is yours* and the *suffering shall be yours:* if I can do no more, I shall leave this upon record, that we took our time to tell you most pointedly, that serious diligence is necessary to your salvation; and that God is the rewarder of them that diligently seek him, and that this was your day, your only day: it must be now or never.

DIRECTIONS AND PERSUASIONS

TO A

SOUND CONVERSION,

FOR PREVENTION OF THAT DECEIT AND DAMNATION OF SOULS, AND OF THOSE
SCANDALS, HERESIES, AND DESPERATE APOSTASIES THAT ARE THE
CONSEQUENTS OF A COUNTERFEIT OR SUPERFICIAL CHANGE.

PREFATORY REMARKS.

LITTLE more than five months after the publication of the "Call to the Unconverted," Baxter sent from the press his "DIRECTIONS AND PERSUASIONS TO A SOUND CONVERSION," the preface to which is dated 29th May, 1658. This, according to his own arrangement, was the next in order of his books on Conversion. "Having," he says, "in my 'Call to the Unconverted,' endeavoured to awaken careless souls, and persuade the obstinate to turn and live, I have here spoken to them that seem to be about the work, and given them some directions and persuasions to prevent their perishing in the birth, and so to prevent that hypocrisy, which else they are like to be formed into; and the deceit of their hearts, the error of their lives, and the misery at their death, which are likely to follow. That they live not as those that flatter God with their mouths, and 'lie unto him with their tongues, because their heart is not right with him, neither are they steadfast in his covenant.' Lest, denying deep entertainment and rooting to the seed of life, or choking it by the radicated, predominant love and cares of the world, they wither when the heat of persecutions shall break forth: and lest, building on the sands, they fall when the winds and storms arise, and their fall be great: and so 'they go out from us, that they may be made manifest that they were not of us; for if they had been of us they would no doubt have continued with us.'"

This work is well calculated to undeceive those who take it for granted that they have been the subjects of a divine change, when no such change has been effected. While great alarm is experienced, it is not so well fitted to be useful, as after the alarm has subsided, and the conscience begins to be satisfied, though the great change has not taken place. Baxter's directions for conversion are frequently so expressed, as if men could accomplish the change themselves; or as if they would do certain things with a view to their being converted. For instance, he says, "If you would be truly converted, be sure that you make an absolute resignation of yourselves, and all that you have, to God." Now, it is as plain as possible that only a converted person will make such a surrender as this. The same remark will apply to many other of his directions. No man, however, had a stronger conviction than he, that conversion is peculiarly the work of God. His views of its nature and consequences, as well as his general sentiments, afford the most satisfactory evidence

that this must have been the case. But he did not always sufficiently discriminate what belongs to God, from what falls within the province of man in the affairs of religion. He did not distinguish between *our* using all suitable means to convert men, and calling upon men to do certain things to convert themselves. Almost everything he said, considered as an appeal to the understandings and the consciences of sinners, is strictly correct as means which God has appointed his servants to employ for the conversion of the world: but when put in the form of requesting sinners to perform certain acts with a view to God's converting them, the nature and tendency of the address are considerably altered. This gives to some of Baxter's preaching the aspect of a self-righteous system, in which the work of salvation is divided between God and man. But nothing could be further from his design. He meant, in fact, nothing more than is intended by those solemn appeals in which the prophets and apostles call upon men to repent, to turn, to be converted, to make to them new hearts and right spirits, that they may live and not die. This language is the voice of God to the sinner, sleeping in security, and dead in his sins; it is the moral means suited to the understanding, and appointed to induce consideration and repentance, which the divine Spirit brings to bear on the heart, while the heart receives the impression from which salvation and eternal life arise.

This is one of the numerous books, many of them considerable quarto volumes, which Baxter wrote and published during the time of his ministry in Kidderminster, a period of which was so fully occupied in writing that he tells us the labours of the pulpit and the congregation were but his recreation. The account of these labours, their successes, and those advantages by which under God they were procured forms one of the most interesting portions of his "Life and Times." He says, "Before the wars, I preached twice each Lord's-day; but after the war, but once, and once every Thursday, beside occasional sermons. Every Thursday evening, my neighbours who were most desirous, and had opportunity, met at my house and there one of them repeated the sermon; afterwards they proposed what doubts any of them had about the sermon, or any other case of conscience; and I resolved their doubts. Last of all I caused sometimes one and sometimes another of them to pray, to exercise them; and sometimes I prayed with them myself : which beside singing a psalm was all they did. Once a week, also, some of the younger sort, who were not fit to pray in so great an assembly, met among a few more privately, where they spent three hours in prayer together. Every Saturday night they met at some of their houses, to repeat the sermon of the former Lord's-day, and to pray and prepare themselves for the following day. Once in a few weeks, we had a day of humiliation on one occasion or other. Every religious woman that was safely delivered, instead of the old feastings and gossipings, if she was able, did keep a day of thanksgiving with some of her neighbours, with them praising God, and singing psalms, and soberly feasting together. Two days every week, my assistant and myself took fourteen families between us, for private catechizing and conference; he going through the parish, and the town coming to me. I first heard them recite the words of the catechism, and then examined them about the sense ; and lastly, urged them, with all possible engaging reason and vehemency, to answerable affection and practice. If any of them were stalled through ignorance or bashfulness, I forbore to press them any further to answers, but made them hearers, and either examined others, or turned all into instruction and exhortation. I spent about an hour with each family, and admitted no others to be present ; lest bashfulness should make it burthensome, or any should talk of the weaknesses of others : so that all the afternoons on Mondays and Tuesdays I spent in this way, after I had begun it (for it was many years before I did attempt it); and my assistant spent the morning of the same day in the same employment. Before that, I only catechized them in the church, and conferred occasionally with an individual.

"Beside all this, I was forced, five or six years, by the people's necessity, to practise physic. A common pleurisy happening one year, and no physician being near, I was forced to advise them to save their lives; and I could not afterwards avoid the importunity of the town and country round about. Because I never once took a penny of any one, I was crowded with patients ; so that almost twenty would be at my door at once: and though God, by more success than I expected, so long encouraged me, yet at last I could endure it no longer; partly because it hindered my other studies, and partly because the very fear of miscuring and doing any one harm, did make it an intolerable burden to me. So that, after some years' practice, I procured a godly diligent physician to come and live in the town, and bound myself, by promise, to practise no more, unless in consultation with him, in case of any seeming necessity; and so with that answer I turned them all off, and never meddled with it again.

"But all these my labours (except my private conference with the families), even preaching and preparing for it, were but my recreation, and, as it were, the work of my spare hours ; for my writings were my chief daily labour; which yet went the more slowly on, that I never one hour had an amanuensis to dictate to, and especially because my weakness took up so much of my time. All the pains that my infirmities ever brought upon me were never half so grievous an affliction as the unavoidable loss of time which they occasioned. I could not bear, through the weakness of my stomach, to rise before seven o'clock in the morning, and afterwards not till much later; and some infirmities I laboured under made it above an hour before I could be dressed. An hour I must of necessity have

to walk before dinner, and another before supper ; and after supper I could seldom study : all which, beside times of family duties and prayer, and eating, &c., left me but little time to study: which hath been the greatest external personal affliction of all my life.

"Every first Wednesday in the month was our monthly meeting for parish discipline ; and every first Thursday of the month was the ministers' meeting for discipline and disputation. In those disputations it fell to my lot to be almost constant moderator; and for every such day, I usually prepared a written determination; all which I mention as my mercies and delights, and not as my burdens. Every Thursday, besides, I had the company of divers godly ministers at my house, after the lecture, with whom I spent that afternoon in the truest recreation, till my neighbours came to meet for their exercise of repetition and prayer.

"For ever blessed be the God of my mercies, who brought me from the grave, and gave me, after wars and sickness, fourteen years' liberty in such sweet employment! How strange that, in times of usurpation I had all this mercy and happy freedom ; when under our rightful king and governor, I, and many hundreds more, are silenced and laid by as broken vessels, and suspected and vilified as scarce to be tolerated to live privately and quietly in the land!

"I have mentioned my secret and acceptable employment; let me, to the praise of my gracious Lord, acquaint you with some of my success ; and I will not suppress it, though I foreknow that the malignant will impute the mention of it to pride and ostentation. For it is the sacrifice of thanksgiving which I owe to my most gracious God, which I will not deny him, for fear of being censured as proud ; lest I prove myself proud indeed, while I cannot undergo the imputation of pride in the performance of my thanks for such undeserved mercies.

"My public preaching met with an attentive, diligent auditory. Having broke over the brunt of the opposition of the rabble before the wars, I found them afterwards tractable and unprejudiced. Before I entered into the ministry, God blessed my private conference to the conversion of some, who remain firm and eminent in holiness to this day : but then, and in the beginning of my ministry, I was wont to number them as jewels; but since then I could not keep any number of them. The congregation was usually full, so that we were fain to build five galleries after my coming thither ; the church itself being very capacious, and the most commodious and convenient that ever I was in. Our private meetings, also, were full. On the Lord's-days there was no disorder to be seen in the streets; but you might hear a hundred families singing psalms and repeating sermons as you passed through them. In a word, when I came thither first, there was about one family in a street that worshipped God and called on his name, and when I came away, there were some streets where there was not one poor family in the side that did not so ; and that did not, by professing serious godliness, give us hopes of their sincerity. And in those families which were the worst, being inns and alehouses, usually some persons in each house did seem to be religious."

The causes conducive to this great success he thus enumerates :—"One advantage was that I came to a people that never had any awakening ministry before, but a few cold formal sermons of the curate; for if they had been hardened under a powerful ministry, and been sermon-proof, I should have expected less.

"Another advantage was, that at first I was in the vigour of my spirits, and had naturally a familiar, moving voice, which is a great matter with the common hearers; and doing all in bodily weakness, as a dying man, my soul was the more easily brought to seriousness, and to preach as a dying man to dying men. For drowsy formality and customariness do but stupify the hearers, and rock them asleep. It must be serious preaching which must make men serious in hearing and obeying it.

"Another advantage was, that most of the bitter enemies of godliness in the town, that rose in tumults against me before, in their very hatred of Puritans, had gone out into the wars, into the king's armies, and were quickly killed, and few of them ever returned; and so there were few to make any great opposition to godliness.

"Another, and the greatest advantage was, the change that was made in public affairs by the success of the wars. . . . . I bless God, who gave me, under an usurper [Cromwell] whom I opposed, such liberty and advantage to preach the gospel with success, which I cannot have under a king to whom I have sworn and performed true subjection and obedience. Sure I am that when it became a matter of reputation and honour to be godly, it abundantly furthered the successes of the ministry.

"The holy, humble, blameless lives of the religious sort were a great advantage to me. The malicious people cared not to say, You professors here are as proud and covetous as any; but the blameless lives of godly people did shame opposers, and put to silence the ignorance of foolish men, and many were won by their good conversation.

"Our unity and concord were a great advantage, and our freedom from those sects and heresies which many other places were infected with. We had not pastor against pastor, nor church against church, nor sect against sect, nor Christian against Christian; but we were all of one mind, and mouth, and way.

"Another furtherance of my work was the writings which I wrote and gave among them. Some small books I gave each family, one of which came to about eight hundred, and of the bigger I gave fewer. Every family that was poor, and had not a Bible, I gave a Bible to. And I had found myself the benefit of reading to be so great, that I could not but think it would be profitable to others.

"And it was a great advantage to me that my neighbours were of such a trade as allowed them to read or talk of holy things. For the town liveth upon the weaving of Kidderminster stuffs; and as they stand in their loom, they can set a book before them, or edify one another; whereas ploughmen and many others are so wearied, or continually employed, either in the labours or the cares of their callings, that it is a great impediment to their salvation. Freeholders and tradesmen are the strength of religion and civility in the land; and gentlemen, and beggars, and servile tenants, are the strength of iniquity. Their constant converse and traffic with London doth much promote civility and piety amongst tradesmen.

"And it was a great advantage to me that at last there were few that were bad but some of their relations were converted. Many children did God work upon at fourteen, or fifteen, or sixteen years

of age; and thus did marvellously reconcile the minds of the parents and elder sort to godliness. They that would not hear me, would hear their own children. Many that would not be brought to it themselves, were proud that they had understanding, religious children. And we had some old persons of near eighty years of age, who are, I hope, in heaven, and the conversion of their own children was the chief means to overcome their prejudice, and old customs, and conceits.

"Another great help to my success was the fore-described work of personal conference with every family apart, and catechizing and instructing them. That which was spoken to them personally, and put them sometimes upon answers, awakened their attention, and was more easily applied than public preaching, and seemed to do much more upon them."

In this retrospect Baxter says little about his preaching, which assuredly was more conducive to his singular usefulness as a minister than all other helps united. With his tall and slender figure, his melting voice, his beaming eye—with a saintly smile shining through his ascetic and pain-worn features —with an aspect which spoke more of another world than of this one, and with that veneration which in good men's minds encircled his person—his very appearance in the pulpit awakened a profound impression, which never failed to be deepened as, taking up some topic of weightiest import, he set it before his auditory, in language, plain, vivid, and unmistakeable; and as he proceeded to descant on the claims and perfections of that God who was evidently his dearest friend and chiefest joy, and on the vast concerns of that eternity from which he looked like a returning sojourner; and, as with an accumulation of argument, remonstrance, persuasion, which seemed as if it could never cease, he kept urging their immortal interests and their immediate duty on men who envied the blessed speaker, and who felt that there was only One other who had shown greater compassion for their souls, he often left the excited throng dissolved in a passion of universal tenderness, and reluctant to leave the spot which had brought them so near the gate of heaven. Of popularity, in its best and safest form, he enjoyed an abundant share. Even at Dudley, the first sphere of his labours, the rough and almost savage miners were attracted to his ministry in such multitudes that the church could not hold them. They hung like bees around the doors and windows, and climbed on the very leads; and even one short year sufficed to work a notable reformation among these drunken and brawling pitmen. The unprecedented work which he was allowed to accomplish in Kidderminster has been already noticed; and even a hundred years after—in the days of Joseph Williams, and Benjamin Fawcett, and Job Orton—the result was still perceptible. And in London, wherever he was expected—whether it were the morning lecture in Cripplegate, or preaching before "the Parliament men" in St. Margaret's, Westminster, or before the lord-mayor in St. Paul's—no building could contain the thronging multitude; and of those who came within range of the preacher's voice, few could ever utterly forget the emotions which, for once at least in their lives, had been awakened by his sacred oratory.—*Baxter's Life and Writings, by Orme; and Our Christian Classics, by Dr. Hamilton.*

DIRECTIONS

TO

A SOUND CONVERSION.

PREFACE.

IT is a weight so unconceivable that depends on the soundness of conversion and sanctification, that our care and diligence cannot be too great to make it sure. As the professed atheist. heathens and infidels without, so the self-deceiving hypocrites within the church, do wilfully cast away themselves for ever, by neglecting such a business of everlasting consequence, when they have time, warnings, and assistance to dispatch it. Multitudes live like brutes or atheists, forgetting that they are born in sin and misery, settled in it by wilful custom, and must be converted or condemned. These know not, many of them, what need they have of a conversion, nor what conversion or sanctification is. And some that have been preachers of the gospel, have been so lamentably ignorant in so great a matter, that they have persuaded the poor deluded people that it is only the gross and heinous sinners that need conversion ; branding them with the name of puritans, that will not take a dead profession, joined with civility, for true sanctification ; and promise salvation to those, that Christ hath with many asseverations professed shall not enter into the kingdom of God. Others that confess that a thorough sanctification is a necessary thing, delude their souls with something that is like it. Hence is the misery and dishonour of the church. Holiness itself is disgraced by the sins of them that are unholy, because they pretend to that which they have not. Hence it is, that we have thousands, who call themselves Christians, that live a worldly, fleshly life, and some of them hating the way of godliness, and yet think they are converted, because they are sorry when they have sinned, wish, when it is past, that they had not done it, implore God's mercy for it, and confess that they are sinners ; and this they take for true repentance : when sin was never mortified in their souls, nor their hearts ever brought to hate it, and forsake it : but when they have had the profit and pleasure of sin, they are sorry for the danger, but are never regenerated and made new creatures by the Spirit of Christ. Hence also it is, that we have such abundance of mere opinionists, that take themselves for religious people, because they have changed their opinions, and their parties, and can prate contentiously against those that are not of their mind, and join themselves with those that seem to be the strictest, they take themselves to be truly sanctified : and this makes such gadding from one opinion to another, and such censuring, reviling, and divisions, upon that account : because their religion is most in their opinions, and hath not mortified their carnal, selfish inclinations and passions, nor brought them to a holy, heavenly mind. Hence also it is that we have so many sensual, scandalous professors, that ' seem to be religious, but bridle not their tongues,' their appetites, or their lusts, but are railers, or backbiters, or tipplers, or gluttons, or filthy and lascivious, or some way scandalous to their holy profession, because they are strangers to a thorough conversion, but take up with the counterfeit of a superficial change. Hence also we have so many worldlings, that think themselves religious men ; that make Christ but a servant to their worldly interest, and seek heaven but for a reserve, when earth forsakes them, and have something in this world that is so dear to them that they cannot forsake it for the hopes of glory : but give up themselves to Christ, with secret exceptions and reserves, for their prosperity in the world: and all, because they never knew a sound conversion, which should have rooted out of their hearts this worldly interest, and delivered them up entirely and absolutely to Christ. Hence also it is that we have so few professors that can lay by their pride, bear disesteem or injury, love their enemies, and bless them that curse them, yea, or love their godly friends that cross them, or dishonour them; and so few that can deny themselves in their honour, or any considerable thing, for the sake of Christ, in obedience, and conformity to his will. And all because they never had that saving change, which takes down self, and sets up Christ as sovereign in the soul. Hence also it is that we have in this age so many dreadful instances of apostasy. So many reproaching the scripture, that once they thought had converted them, and the way of holiness, that once they did profess; and denying the Lórd himself that bought them; and all because they formerly took up with a superficial counterfeit conversion. O how commonly, and how lamentably doth this misery appear among professors in their unsavoury discourse, their strife and envy, on religious pretences, their dead formality and their passionate divisions, or their selfish, proud, and earthly minds! A thorough conversion would have cured all this, at least as to the dominion of it.

Having therefore in my Call to the Unconverted endeavoured to awaken careless souls, and persuade the obstinate to turn and live, I have here spoken to them that seem to be about the work, and given them some directions and persuasions, to prevent their perishing in the birth, and so to prevent that hypocrisy which else they are like to be formed into, the deceit of their hearts, the error of their lives, and the misery at their death, which is likely to follow. That they live not as those that 'flatter God with their mouths, and lie unto him with their tongues, because their heart is not right with him, neither are they stedfast in his covenant.' Lest denying deep entertainment, and rooting to the seed of life, or choking it by the eradicated predominant love and cares of the world, they wither, when the heat of persecution shall break forth. Lest building on the sands, they fall when the winds and storms arise, and their fall be great, and so 'they go out from us, that they may be made manifest that they were not of us: for if they had been of us, they would no doubt have continued with us.' Look therefore to this great, important business, and 'give all diligence to make your calling and election sure,' and trust not your hearts too

easily, or too confidently: 'but turn to the Lord with all your hearts.' Cleave to him resolvedly, or with purpose of heart, and see that you sell all, buy the pearl, and stick not at the price, but absolutely resign yourselves to Christ, and turn to him, as Zaccheus and other primitive converts did, surrendering all that you have unto his will. Leave not any root of bitterness behind; make no exceptions, or reserves; but deny yourselves; forsake all, and follow him that hath led you this self-denying way; and trust to his blood, merits, and promise, for a treasure in heaven, and then you are his disciples, and true Christians indeed. Reader, if thou heartily make this resolution and keep it, thou shalt find that Christ will not deceive thee, when the world deceives them that choose it, in their greatest extremity: but if thou draw back, and think these terms too hard, remember that everlasting life was offered thee, and remember why and for what thou didst reject it. If in this life-time thou wilt have thy good things, expect to be tormented, when the believing, self-denying souls are comforted.

RICHARD BAXTER.

DIRECTIONS TO SINNERS THAT HAVE PURPOSED TO TURN, AND ARE UNDER THE WORK OF CONVERSION—THAT IT MISCARRY NOT.

The first and greatest matter in the seeking after the salvation of our souls, is to be sure that we lay the foundation well, and that the work of conversion be thoroughly wrought. To this end I have already used many persuasions with the unconverted to return, as thinking all further directions vain, till we have persuaded men to a consent and willingness to practise them. And in the end of that discourse, I added a few directions for the use of such as are willing to be converted. But because I know that this is a matter of great consequence, I dare not thus leave it, before I have added some further directions, to prevent the miscarrying of this work where it is begun. And lest I should lose my labour, through the unpreparedness of the reader; I shall first give you some preparing considerations, which may awaken you to the practice of the directions which I shall give you.

INTRODUCTORY CONSIDERATIONS.

Consider, 1. That half conversions are the undoing of many thousand souls. If you are but like Aggrippa, almost persuaded to be Christians, you will be but almost saved. Many thousands that are now past help, have had the word come near them, and cast them into a fear, and make some stir and trouble in their souls, awakening their consciences, and forcing them to some good purposes and promises ; yea, and bringing them to the performance of a half-reformation ; but this is not what will serve your turn. Many have been so much changed, as not to be ' far from the kingdom of God,' who yet came short of it. There is no promise in scripture that you shall be pardoned if you almost repent and believe ; or be saved, if you be almost sanctified and obedient : but on the contrary, the Lord hath plainly resolved, that you must turn or die, though you almost turn ; repent, or perish, though you almost repent : and that you shall not enter into the kingdom of heaven, without conversion and a new birth, though you came ever so near it. God hath resolved upon the terms of your salvation ; and it is in vain to hope for salvation upon any other terms. God will not change nor come down to your terms ; it is you that must change and come quite over to *his terms*, or you are lost for ever. If you come ever so near them, you are but lost men if you come not up to them. The Lord well knew what he did, when he made his covenant and law, and he imposed nothing on the sons of men but what his infinite wisdom told him it was fit for him to impose ; he will not now compound with sinners, and take less than he requires ; that is, less than the pre-eminency in their hearts ; nor will he ever come down to any lower terms with you, than those which he proposes to you in his gospel. Therefore, poor sinners, as you love your souls, do not stand halting and wavering with God ; but give up yourselves entirely to him ; do not stop at the beginnings of a conversion, but go through with it, till you are become new creatures indeed, or you are undone when you have done all. A half, unsound convert will as certainly perish as a drunkard or a whoremonger ; though his torment may not be so great.

2. Consider also, that if you do not go through with the work when you are upon it, you may perhaps make it more difficult than it was before ever you meddled with it, and make it a very doubtful case whether ever it will be done. As it is with a wound or other sore ; if you tamper with it with salves that are not agreeable to it, or are disorderly applied ; or if you skin it over before it be searched to the bottom, it must be opened again, and will cost you double pain before it be cured. Or as I have seen it with some that have had a bone broken, or out of joint, and it hath been set amiss at first, O what torments were the poor creatures made to undergo, in having it broken, or stretched and set again ; which might have been spared, if it had been thoroughly done at first. So, if you will be shrinking, drawing back, favouring your flesh, and will not go to the quick, you will make your conversion much more difficult ; you must be brought to it again, and your groans will be yet deeper than before : and weep over all your former tears : your doubts will be multiplied ; your fears and sorrows will be increased ; and all will go sorer with you than at first. O what a case will you be in, when your sores must be lanced a second time, and your bones as it were broken again ! Then you will wish you had gone through with it at the first.

Yea, perhaps you may put God to it to fetch you in by some sharp affliction, and send out so boisterous and churlish a messenger to call you home, as may make you wish you had hearkened to a more gentle call : when the sheep will stray, the dog must be sent to affright them home. Many a foolish sinner makes light of the gentle invitations of grace, and they stand hovering between their sins and Christ ; sometimes they have a mind to turn, but the next temptation they are off again, and then they come on again coldly and with half a heart ; thus they stand trifling with the God of heaven, till he is induced to take another course with them, and resolves to use some sharper means : when he lays them under his rod, they can neither fly from, nor resist him, but see that their lives and souls are at his mercy, then they begin to look about them, see their folly, and change their minds. You can tarry, and delay, with the dreadful God, in the time of your prosperity, and we may ask you over and over whether you will turn before we can have a hearty answer ; but what will you do when God shall begin to frown, when he takes you in hand by his irresistible power, and lets loose upon you the terrors of his wrath ? Will you then make as light of his mercy as you do now ; have you not read, Dan. v. 6. how small an apparition of his anger did make a carousing king look pale, and his joints to tremble in the midst of his mirth ? A Manasseh will bethink himself and come in when he is laid in irons, though he could forget his God before. If Jonah will run away from God, he can send a boisterous messenger to arrest him, cast him as it were into the belly of hell, and make him cry for mercy to him that he disobeyed. So if you will stand trifling with God, and will not, by fair means, be persuaded to yield and come away, you may shortly look to hear from him in another manner ; for he hath a voice that will make the proudest face look pale, and the most stubborn heart to tremble. If an idle, stubborn child will not learn nor be ruled, the master or parent will teach him with the rod, give him a lash, and ask him, Will you yet learn ? another lash, and ask him, What say you now, will you yet obey? So will God do by you, if he love you, and mean to save you : when he hath taken away your wealth, your friends and your children, will you then hearken to him, or will you not? When you lie groaning on your couch, and all your parts are overwhelmed with pains, death begins to lay hands upon you, and bids you now come and answer for your rebellions and delays before the living God, what will you do then ? Will you turn or not? O the lamentable folly of sinners, that put themselves to so much sorrow, and great calamity for themselves. When sickness comes and death draws near, you beg and cry, and groan and promise : when you feel the rod, what Christians will you then be ? And why not without so much ado? You then think God deals somewhat hardly with you: why will you not turn then by gentler means ? You might spare yourselves much of this misery if you would ; and you will not. Is it a seemly thing for a man to be driven to heaven by scourges ? Is God so bad a Master, and heaven so bad a place, that you will not turn to them, mind them, and seek them, till there be no remedy, and you are as it were driven to it against your will ? Is the world such an inheritance, sin so good a thing, and the flesh or devil so good a master, that you will not leave them till you are whipped away ? What a shameful, unreasonable course is this!

The case is plain before you. Turn you must at one time or other, or be the firebrands of hell. Seeing it is a thing that must be done, were it not best for you to take the easiest and the surest way to do it ? Why, this is the easiest and the surest way ; even to strike while the iron is hot, before it cool again ; and to go through with it when God doth move you and persuade you ; if you love your flesh itself, do not put him to take up the rod, and fetch you home by stripes and terrors.

But that is not the worst; for it will sorely hazard the work itself, and consequently your salvation, if you do not go through with it at the first attempt. I know there is many a one that hath been converted and saved, after many purposes, promises, and half conversions. But yet I must tell you, that this is a very dangerous course. For you do not know when you grieve the Spirit of grace, and basely refuse mercy when it is offered you, whether that Spirit may not utterly forsake you, leave you to your own ungodly wills, and let you take your lusts and pleasures, and say, Let this wretch be filthy still : let him keep his drunkenness, his companions, his worldliness, and the curse of God with them, till he have tried what it is that they will do for him : let him follow his own conceits, and the pride and obstinacy of his own heart, till he find whither they will bring him : let him serve the flesh and the world, till he understand whether God or they be the better master. Seeing he will not be wise on earth, let him learn in hell, and let torments teach him, seeing mercy might not teach him. O poor soul ! what a case art thou in, if this should once be the resolution of God?

Moreover, you may easily know that the longer you stay, the more leisure you give the devil to assault you, to try one way when he cannot prevail by another, and to strengthen his temptations: like a foolish soldier, that will stand still to be shot at, rather than assault the enemy.

The longer you delay, the more your sin gets strength and root. If you cannot bend a twig, how will you be able to bend it when it is a tree ? If you cannot pluck up a tender plant, are you likely to pluck up a sturdy oak ? Custom gives strength and root to vices. 'A black may as well change his skin, or a leopard his spots, as those that are accustomed to do evil, can learn to do well.'

If you stick at conversion as a difficult matter to-day, it will be more difficult to-morrow, or the next month, and the next year, than it is now.

Yea, the very resistance of the Spirit doth harden the heart, and the delays and triflings of the soul do bring it to an insensibility and boldness in sin, and drive away the fear of God from the heart. Now it may be you are somewhat awakened, and begin to see that you must turn or die ; but if you trifle and delay, this light may be gone, and leave you in greater darkness than before ; and the voice that now awakens you, may be silent and leave you to fall asleep again.

Moreover, you know that you are uncertain of the continuance of the gospel. You know not whether you shall have such lively, serious preachers as you now have, nor you know not whether you shall have such godly neighbours and company to encourage you and help you in the work. God will remove them one after another to himself, then you will have fewer prayers for you, fewer warnings, and good examples, and perhaps be left wholly to the company of deceived, ungodly fools, that will do nothing but hinder and discourage you from conversion. And you are not sure that religion will continue in that reputation as now it is in. The times may turn, before you turn; godliness may become a scorn again, it may be a matter of suffering, and may cost you your lives to live as the servants of Christ must do. Therefore if you stop at it now as a difficult thing, when you have all the helps and encouragements that you can expect, and the way to heaven is made so fair; when magistrates, ministers, and neighbours are ready to encourage and help you; what will you do in times of persecution and discouragement? If you cannot turn when you have all these helps and means, what will you do when they are taken from you? If you cannot row with the stream, how will you row against it? If you dare not set to sea, when you have wind, tide, and sunshine; what will you do in storms and tempests, when all is against you? O what would some of your forefathers have given to have seen the days that you see! How glad would many thousands in other countries of the world be, to have the helps to heaven that you have! Never look to have the way fairer and easier while you live. If you think heaven is offered you at too dear a rate now, you may even let it go, and try whether hell be better; for the next offer is likely to be upon harder terms rather than easier. If you cannot now find in your hearts to turn and live an holy life, what would you have done in the days of the apostles, or ancient Christians; and what would you have done in Spain or Italy, where it would cost you your lives? He that will not be converted now, but thinks the terms of grace too hard, is so impious a despiser of Christ and heaven, that it is no wonder if God resolve that he shall never taste of the salvation that was offered him.

Moreover, you know upon what uncertainties you hold your lives; you have no assurance of them for an hour, but you are sure that they are passing away whilst you delay; and will you trifle then in a work that must be done; what a case are you in, if death find you unconverted? The heart of man is not able now to conceive the misery of your case. How dare you venture to live another day in an unconverted state, lest death should find you so? Are you not afraid when you lie down at night, and afraid when you go out of your doors in the morning, lest death surprise you before you are converted? If you be not, it is owing to your deadness and presumption.

I would fain hear what it is that should thus stop you. What are you afraid of; is God an enemy, that you are loth to come to him; is the devil a friend, that you are so loth to leave him? Is sin a paradise; is holiness a misery; is it a pleasanter life to love your money, or your lands, or your meat, drink, and lusts, than to love the most blessed God the Creator of the world, the life of our souls, and our eternal felicity; is it better to pamper a body that must shortly be reduced to dust, than to provide for a living, immortal soul; whether do you think that earth or heaven will be the more glorious and durable felicity?

What is it that you stick at that you make so many delays before you will turn? Is there any difficulty in the point? Do you think it a hard question whether you should turn or not? Why, how can you be so blind? Do you stand pausing upon the business, as if it were a doubt, whether God or the world were better, and whether sin or holiness, Christ or death, heaven or hell, were to be preferred? I pray you consider; can you reasonably think that conversion will do you any harm; can it bring you into a worse condition than you are in? Surely you cannot fear such a thing: you are in your blood; you are dead in sin; you are children of wrath, while you are unconverted; you are under the curse of the law of God; you are the slaves of the devil, you are the heirs of hell, and under the guilt of all your sins; your life is a continued rebellion against God; you are employed every day in the destroying of yourselves, in kindling the flames that must for ever torment you, and laying in fuel for the perpetuating of your misery; fighting against your friends, that would deliver you, unthankfully abusing Christ, grace, ministers, and friends that would save your souls. This is the condition that every one of you are in, till you are converted. And can you fear lest conversion would bring you into a worse condition than this? These truths are sure and plain; and if yet you stick at them, your error is so palpably gross, that unless you are madmen, I may be bold to say, it is a *wilful* error. If you love to be deceived, and wilfully choose a lie, you must take what you get by it.

3. Consider further, that half conversions often prove an occasion of deluding men's souls, making them quiet in a miserable state, and so of keeping them from being converted to the last. If you had never done any thing in it, you would more easily be persuaded that your case is bad, and that there is still a necessity of your change. But when you have had some

convictions and troubles of mind, fears, and sorrows, and so have fallen into an outside, partial reformation, and now are persuaded that you are truly converted, when it is no such matter, what a dangerous impediment to your conversion may this prove? And all because you slight the work, cut it off before it reaches to sincerity, strive against the workings of the Spirit, break away from your physician before he hath done the cure, and would not follow it on to the end. I know that a half-conversion, if it be known to be no more, is much better than none; and doth often prepare men for a saving work. But when this half-conversion is taken to be a true and saving change, as too commonly it is, it proves one of the greatest impediments of salvation. Whenever Christ shall afterwards knock at your door, you will not know him, as thinking that he dwells with you already. If you read any books that call on you to be converted, or hear any preachers that call on you to turn, you have this at hand to deceive yourselves with, and frustrate all. You will think, this is not spoken to me; for I am converted already. O how quietly do such poor deluded sinners daily read and hear their own doom and misery, and never once dream that they are the men that are meant, and therefore are never dismayed at the matter! This forms you into a state of hypocrisy, and makes the course of your duties and your lives to be hypocritical. If another man, that knows himself to be still unconverted, but read the threatenings of the word against such, or hear of the terrors of the Lord from a minister; he may be brought to confess that this is his own case, and so to perceive the misery of his condition. But when such as you read and hear these things, they never trouble you, for you think that they do not refer to you: you are scripture-proof and sermon-proof; and all by the delusion of your half-conversion. O how zealously will such a man cry out against the sins of others; and tell them of their misery, persuade them to turn, and show them the danger that is near them if they do not; and in the mean time little thinks that this is his own case, and that he speaks all this against his own soul! How will such men applaud a sermon that drives at the conversion of a sinner, and that tells them their misery while they are unconverted! O, thinks he, this touched such and such; I am glad that such a man and such a man heard it: and he little thinks that it as nearly touched himself.

How smoothly will he go on in any discourse against wicked, unregenerated men, as David heard the parable of Nathan, and it never once enters into their thoughts, that they speak all this against themselves; till the judge shall tell them when it is too late, thou art the man? It will turn not only the stream of your thoughts into hypocrisy and self-deceit, but also the stream of your speeches to others; yea, and the current of your prayers, and all the rest of your religious performances. When in confession you should acknowledge and lament an unregenerated, carnal state, you will only confess that you have the infirmities of the saints, and that you have this or that sin, which yet you think is mortified. When you should importunately beg for renewing grace, you will beg only for strengthening grace, or assurance; when you should be labouring to break your hearts, you will be studying to heal them; and will be hearkening after present comforts, when you have more need of godly sorrow. It will fill your mouths in prayer with pharisaical thanksgivings for the mercies of regeneration, justification, adoption, sanctification, which you never received. Little doth many a soul know what sanctification, and the several graces of the Spirit are, that use to give God thanks for them: there is many and many a one that must for ever be in hell, that were used in their prayers to give God thanks for their hopes of glory: and the common cause of all this deceit and misery is, that men do run from under the hands of their physician before he ever went to the bottom of their sore, and go away with a half-conversion, and so spend all the rest of their lives, in a mere delusion, as verily thinking they are converted, when they are not. How confidently will such receive the Lord's supper, and thrust themselves into the communion of the saints, as if they had as good right as others to be there, till the Lord of the feast shall take them to task, and say, 'friend, how camest thou in hither, not having on a wedding garment? and then they will be speechless.' How many false, deceiving comforts, and perhaps even seeming raptures, and assurance, may these have in themselves, as verily thinking their case is good, when alas, they never yet laid the foundation? Yea, and it is to be observed, that Satan is a friend to the comforts of this kind of men, and therefore will do all that he can to promote them. For he would willingly keep his garrison in peace, and therefore he may possibly be a comforting spirit to them himself, and imitate the Holy Ghost, the comforter of the saints: and it may be give them such raptures as seem higher than those which the spirit of holiness doth give. He envies the saints their peace and comfort, because he foresees how durable they will prove : but he can be content that deluded hypocrites may have joy, because their comforts do not weaken his kingdom within them, and he knows they are like to endure but for a while.

And thus you may perceive, how hard it is to convert one of these half-converted men, that have strangled the new creature as it were in the birth, and that are fortified against all the means of grace, by a false conceit that they are sanctified already. See therefore that you make sure work, take not up in the middle, with halves, but take your present time, and give up your souls to a total change.

4. Consider, if you take up short of a thorough conversion, you lose all your labour, sufferings, and hopes, as to the matter of your salvation.

What pity is it that so much should be lost. Alas, to see many of our hearers touched at a sermon, come to a minister and bewail their sin, seem to be humbled, promise to be new men, and yet all this to be lost: how sad a case is this to think of ? To see them leave their company and former course of life, come among the professors of holiness, and all men take them for real converts ; yet all this to be lost, and their souls lost after all : how sad a case is this ! If you grow up to the greatest parts for outward duty, and be able to discourse, or pray, or preach, even to the admiration of the hearers ; yet if you do not ground this on a thorough conversion, all is but lost, as to your own salvation. If you keep up the highest strain of profession, and get the highest esteem in the church, so that others depend upon you as oracles ; yea, if the pope with all his infallibility should canonize you for saints ; it were all but loss. If you should keep up the most confident persuasion of your salvation, and hope to go to heaven, to the last hour of your lives ; it were all but lost if you build not all on a thorough conversion. Yea, if you should be taken by persecutors for one of the party to which you join, and should suffer for the cause of religion among them ; all were but lost without a sound conversion.

It is a pitiful case to see some poor unsanctified souls how they wander and change from one opinion to another, and from party to party, to find out that which they want within. They turn to this party first, and that party next, then to another, and then think they are sure in the way to heaven, when they never thoroughly turned to God by Jesus Christ ; and therefore are certainly out of the way, whatever party it be that they join with. Some go to the giddy sects that make the highest pretences to strictness: some go to Rome, because they think that there they shall have more company, and hear the deluding sound of unity, universality, antiquity, succession, miracles, and such like : and then they think they have found the way. Alas, poor souls ! if God were but nearest and dearest to your hearts, Christ and his righteousness exalted within you, and your souls unfeignedly turned from your sins, you would be in the certain way to heaven, in what country or company, or church soever you were ; supposing that you believe and do nothing there, which is inconsistent with this life of grace. Though yet every Christian should choose that particular society, if he can, where he may not only be saved, but most certainly saved, and find the *greatest helps* and *least hinderances*, or else where he may *do God the greatest service.* But choose what company you will in all the world, the strictest, the most reformed, the most splendid in outward pomp and glory, or of whatever excellency else you can imagine, you will never be saved in it yourselves, as long as your hearts are unconverted. I know the papists have found out many devices, by sacraments, ceremonies, and the merits of the saints, to patch up the defect of a thorough conversion ; but all are mere delusions that pretend to such a thing.

O then think of this, poor sinner : hast thou gone so far, done so much, and shall all be lost because thou wilt not follow it to the end ? Hast thou groaned, wept, confessed, and bemoaned thine own condition ? Hast thou prayed, read, heard, fasted, changed thy company, and much of thy course of life : and shall all this be lost, for want of going to the bottom, and making a thorough work of it ? What a loss will this be !

5. Consider also, what an admirable help and advantage it will be to you through the whole course of your lives, if the work of conversion be once thoroughly wrought. I will show you this in some particulars.

First, It will be an excellent help to your understandings, against the grosser errors of the world, and will establish you in the truth much more than mere arguments can do ; for you will be able to speak for the truth from feeling and experience : he that hath the law written both in his Bible and in his heart, is likely to hold it faster than he that hath it in his Bible alone.

Secondly, If you be but thoroughly converted, you have that within you which will be a continual help against temptations : you have not only experience of the mischief of sinning, and the folly of those reasons that are brought for its defence; but you have also a new nature, which is against the temptation, as life is against poison: and as it is a great disadvantage to the law of Christ, that it speaks against the nature of the ungodly; so is it a disadvantage to the temptations of the devil, that they would draw a Christian against his new nature. You have that within you that will plead more effectually against sensuality, uncharitableness, pride, or worldliness, or any the like sin, than learning or reason alone can do, as in the fore-cited book I have further manifested.

Thirdly, If conversion be thoroughly wrought, you will have within you a continual helper of your graces, a remembrancer to put you in mind of duty, a spur to put you on to the performance, and a furtherer of your souls in the performance itself: it is out of this spark and principle within you that the Holy Ghost doth raise the acts of grace. This is it that the word, prayer, conference, sacraments, and all the means of grace must work upon. If we see you do amiss, we have hopes that you will hear us; if we plainly reprove you, we may look you should take it in good part: for you have that within you that saith as we say, and is at deadly enmity with the sin, which we reprove. If we provoke you to love and to good works, we dare almost promise ourselves that you will obey; for you have that within you that disposes you to the duty, and preaches out sermons to you over again. O what an advantage it is to our teaching, when you are all taught of God within, as well as by his messengers without! But when we speak to the unconverted, we have little to work upon: we give physic to the dead; we speak all against the bent of their souls; every reproof and exhortation to holiness goes against their very natures; and therefore what wonder if we have the smaller hopes to prevail?

Fourthly, If the work be thoroughly done at first, it will help to resolve many doubts that may be afterwards cast into your minds: you need not be still at a loss and looking behind you, and questioning your foundation, but may go cheerfully and boldly on. O what an excellent encouragement is this! to know that you have hitherto made good your ground, left all safe and sure behind you, and have nothing to do but to look before you, and press on towards the mark, till you lay hold upon the prize: whereas if you be in any great doubt of your conversion, it will be stopping you and discouraging you in all your work; you will be still looking behind you, and saying, What if I should yet be unconverted?

When you should cheerfully address yourselves to prayer or sacraments, how sadly will you go, as being utterly uncertain whether you have a saving right to them; or whether God will accept a sacrifice at your hand? When you should grow and go forward, you will have little heart to it, because you know not whether you are yet in the way; and this will damp your life and comfort in every duty, when you must say, ' I know not whether yet I be thoroughly converted.' O therefore stop not the work at first.

Fifthly, If the work be thoroughly done at first, you will persevere, when others fall away. You will have root in yourselves, entertaining the seed as into depth of earth; you will have the Holy Ghost within you, and more than so engaged for your preservation, and the perfecting of your salvation; when they that received the word as seed upon a rock, and never give it deep entertainment, will wither and fall away in the time of trial; and from them that have not saving grace, shall be taken away, even that which they seemed to have.

6. And lastly, Consider, If you fall short of a true conversion at the first, the devil will take occasion by it, to tempt you at last to utter despair. When you have made many essays and trials, and been about the work again and again, he will persuade you that there is no possibility of accomplishing it. If we convince an openly profane person who is unconverted, he may more easily say that yet there are hopes of it, but if a man have been half converted, lived long in a formal, self-deceiving profession of religion, and been taken by himself and others for a godly man, as it is very hard to convince this man that he is unconverted, so when he is convinced of it, he will easily fall into desperation. For Satan will suggest to him, ' If thou be yet unconverted after so many confessions and prayers, and after so long a course of religion, what hope canst thou have that yet it should be done? Thou wilt never have better opportunities than thou hast had. If such sermons as thou hast heard could not do it, what hope is there of it? If such books, such company, such mercies, and such afflictions have not done it, what hope canst thou have; canst thou hear any livelier teaching than thou hast heard; or speak any holier words than thou hast spoken? If yet the work be quite undone, it is not forsaking another sin, nor going a step further, that will do it; and therefore never think of it; for there is no hope: dost thou not know how oft thou hast tried in vain, and what canst thou do more?' And thus you give advantage to the tempter by your first de-

lays, and taking up in mere preparatories. And therefore I beseech you, as you love your souls, take heed of resisting the Spirit of grace, and breaking off the work before it is thoroughly done, but go to the bottom, and follow it on, till it be accomplished in sincerity. And now hoping that upon these considerations you are resolved to do your best, I shall come to the thing which I principally intended; which is to give you certain directions, which if you will obey, you may be CONVERTS AND SAINTS INDEED.

DIRECTION I.

Lest the work of conversion should miscarry where it seems to be begun, or in a hopeful way, I first advise you, to 'labour after a right understanding of the true nature of Christianity, and the meaning of the gospel which is sent to convert you.' You are naturally slaves to the prince of darkness; you live in a state of darkness, do the works of darkness, and are hasting apace to utter darkness. And it is the light of saving knowledge that must recover you, or there is no recovery. God is 'the Father of light, and dwelleth in light:' Christ is 'the light of the world;' his ministers are also the 'lights of the world,' as under him; and are sent to 'turn men from darkness to light, by the gospel which is the light to our feet; and this is to make us children of light, that we may no more do the works of darkness, but may be partakers of the inheritance of the saints in light.' Believe it, darkness is not the way to the celestial glory. Ignorance is your disease, and knowledge must be your cure. I know the ignorant have many excuses, and are apt to think that the case is not so bad with them as we make it to be; and that there is no such need of knowledge, but a man may be saved without it. But this is because they want that knowledge that should show them the misery of their ignorance, and the worth of knowledge. Has not the scripture plainly told you, that 'if the gospel be hid, it is hid to them that are lost, whose minds the god of this world hath blinded, lest the light of the glorious gospel of Christ, who is the image of God, should shine unto them?' I know that many that have much knowledge are ungodly. But what of that? Can any man therefore be godly or be saved, without knowledge? You may have a bad servant, that yet is skilful enough in his work, but yet you will not mend the matter, by taking one that hath no skill at all. You may send a man on your errand that knows the way, and yet will not go it, but loiter and deceive you:

but what of that, will you therefore think to mend the matter by sending one that knows not a step of the way, nor will not learn it? Though a man of knowledge may be the servant of the devil, yet no man without knowledge, that hath the use of his reason, can be the servant of God. A man may go to hell with knowledge; but he certainly shall go to hell without it. I do not say that you must all be men of learning, and skilled in the arts, sciences, and languages: but you must have the knowledge of a Christian, though not of a scholar. Can you love or serve a God that you know not? Can you let go friends, goods, and life, for a glory which you have no knowledge of? Can you make it the principal business of your lives to seek for a heaven whose excellencies you know not of? Can you lament your sin and misery, when you are unacquainted with it? Or will you strive against sin as the greatest evil, when you know not the evil of it? Will you believe in a Christ, whom you do not know, and trust your souls and all upon him? Will you rest upon a promise, or fear a threatening, or be ruled by a law, which you do not understand? It is not possible to be Christians without knowing the substance of Christianity: nor is it possible for you to be saved without knowing the way of salvation.

Labour therefore to be well acquainted with the grounds, reasons, and nature of your religion. The clearer your light is, the warmer and livelier your hearts will be. Illumination is the first part of sanctification. The head is the passage to the heart. O if you did but thoroughly know what sin is, and what a life it is to serve the flesh, and what the end of this will prove, with what detestation would you cast it away? If you did thoroughly know what a life of holiness is, how speedily would you choose it? If you did truly know what God is, how infinitely powerful, wise, and good; how holy, just, and true, and what title he hath to you, authority over you, and what an eternal portion he would be to you, how is it possible that you could prefer the dust of the world before him, or delay any longer to return unto him? If you did but truly know what Christ is, and what he hath done and suffered for you: and what that pardon, grace, and glory are which he hath purchased for you, and offers to you, and how sure his promise is by which it is offered; it is not possible that you should refuse to entertain him, or delay to give up your souls unto him. Do you think a man that truly knows what heaven is, and what hell is, can still be in doubt whether he should turn or not? If God would but open your eyes, to see where you are, and what you are doing, you would run as for your lives, and quickly change your minds and ways. You would no more stay in your carnal state, than you would stay in a house that were falling down on your heads, or in a ship that you perceived sinking under you, or on the sands when you see the tide coming towards you. If you did but see your chamber full of devils this night, you would not stand to ask whether you should be gone: surely then, if you knew how the devils are about you, how they deceive you, rule you, and wait to drag you away to hell, you would never stay a night longer willingly in such a state.

While men understand not what the gospel means, nor what a minister saith to them, no wonder if they regard them not, but continue in their sin. If you see a bear or a mad dog making towards a man, tell him of it, and call to him to be gone, if he be a man of another language and do not understand you, he will make never the more haste; but if he understand and believe you, he will away. If people think that ministers are in jest with them, or that they are uncertain of what they say, no marvel if they hear us in jest, or as men that believe not what they hear: but if you knew that your lives lay on it, yea, your everlasting life, would you not regard it and look about you? Now you stand deliberating and questioning the business whether you should turn, and let go sin, or not: but if you knew that you must certainly have hell with it if you keep it, methinks your doubt should quickly be resolved, and you should be loth to give another night's lodging to so chargeable and dangerous a guest. Now when we persuade you to holiness of life, you will demur on it, as if there were some doubtfulness in the matter: but if you knew the nature and end of holiness, you would soon be out of doubt; and if you knew but how much happier you might be with God, you would never stick at the parting with your most delightful sins. As the Jews rejected Christ, preferred a murderer before him, and cried out, Crucify him, and all because they did not know him; so you let Christ knock and call, and offer you salvation; you stand questioning whether you should obey his call, and whether you should not prefer your lusts before him; all because you know him not, nor the grace and glory which he tenders to you. When men understand not the reasons of God, that should prevail with them, no wonder if they part not with that which is as dear to them as their lives. But when once they know the reasons of Christianity, those moving, weighty, un-

deniable reasons that are brought from God, heaven, and hell, they will then stand questioning the matter no longer; but they will resign up all, even life itself. All this I speak of a spiritual, powerful, and a practical knowledge, and not of every swimming opinion and conceit.

Study therefore what God is, what he is to you, and what he would be to you. Study what sin is, and what the damnation is which it deserves. Study what Christ is, hath done and suffered for you, and what he is willing to do, if you neglect him not. Study what the world is, and what is the utmost that sin will do for you. Study what the everlasting glory is which you may have with God, if you lose it not by your folly. Study what faith is, what repentance is, what love and joy, and a holy and heavenly life are, and how little reason you have to be afraid of them. If this understanding have but deeply possessed you, it will bias your hearts, and make you resolved, settled converts.

Whereas if you seem to turn and scarce know why, and seem to take up a Christian life, before you are thoroughly possessed with the nature, grounds, and reasons of it, no marvel if you are quickly lost again in the dark, and if every caviller that you meet with can nonplus you, and make you stagger, call in question all that you have done, and perplex all your work; or if you do but run from one party to another, follow every one that tells you a fair tale, and never know what to fix upon, nor when you are in the way and when you are out.

The apprehensions of the mind move the whole man: wisdom is the guide and stay of the soul. Sinning is doing foolishly, and sinners are fools. Their mirth is but the mirth of fools, and their song, the song of fools. Yea, the best of their services, while they refuse to hear and obey, is but the sacrifice of fools. Such are not fit for the house of God; 'for God hath no pleasure in fools.' He hath need to have his wits about him, and know what he doth, that will be the servant of the God of heaven, escape the deceits of a subtle devil, and get to heaven through so many difculties as are before him. Above all getting, therefore, 'GET WISDOM.'

DIRECTION II.

If you would not have the work of your conversion miscarry, when you understand what is offered you, then 'search the scriptures daily to see whether those things be so or not.'

So did the Bereans, and the text saith, that 'therefore they believed.' We come not to deceive you ; and therefore we desire not that you should take any thing from us, but what we can prove to you from the word of God to be certainly true. We desire not to lead you in the dark, but by the light to lead you out of darkness ; and therefore we refuse not to submit all our doctrine to an equal trial. Though we would not have you wrong your souls by an unjust distrust of us, yet would we not desire you to take these great and weighty things merely upon our words ; for then your faith will be in man ; then no marvel if it be weak, ineffectual, and quickly shaken : if you trust a man to-day, you may distrust him to-morrow ; and if one man be of greatest credit with you this year, perhaps another of a contrary mind may be of more credit with you the next year. Therefore we desire no further to be believed by you, than is necessary to lead you up to God, and to help you to understand that word which you must believe : our desire therefore is that you search the scripture, and try whether the things that we tell you be the truth. The word will never work on you to purpose till you see and hear God in it, and perceive that it is he, and not man only, that speaks to you. When you hear none speaking to you but the minister, no marvel if you dare despise him ; for he is a frail and mortal man like yourselves ; when you think that the doctrine which we preach to you is merely of our own devising, and the conjecture of our own brain, no marvel if you do not value it, and will not let go all that you have, at the persuasion of a preacher. But when you have searched the scriptures, and find that it is the word of the God of heaven, dare you despise it then ? When you there find that we said no more than we were commanded, and God that hath spoken this word will stand to it ; then surely it will go nearer you, you will consider of it, and make light of it no more. If we offered you bad wares, we should desire a dark shop ; and if our gold were light or bad, we would not call for the balance and the touchstone. But when we are sure the things that we speak are true, we desire nothing more than trial. Beauty and comeliness have no advantage of lothsome deformity, when they are both together in the dark, but the light will show the difference. Error may be a loser by the light, and therefore shuns it. But truth is a gainer by it, and therefore seeks it. Let papists hide the scripture from the people, forbid the reading of them in a tongue which they understand, and teach them to speak to God they know not what ; we dare not do so, nor do we desire it ; our doctrine will not go off well

in the dark ; and therefore we call you ' to the law and to the testimony, desire you to take our words into the light, and see whether they be according to the word of the Lord. Nothing troubles us more than that we cannot persuade our hearers to this trial. Some of them are so hardened in their sin and misery, that they will not be at so much labour as to open their bibles, and try whether we say true or not ; some of them will not trouble their minds with the thoughts of it ; ' God is not in all their thoughts.' Some are already too wise to learn ; and they will not so long abate their confidence of their former opinions ; though poor souls, their ignorance doth threaten their damnation. And some are so engaged in a sinful party, that their companions will not give them leave to make so much question of the way that they are in ; and some will scarce take the scripture for the rule by which they must try and be tried, but look more to custom, and the will of those in power over them. Most are unwilling to try, because they are unwilling to know the truth, and cannot endure to find themselves miserable, nor see the sin which they would not leave, nor see the duty which they love not to practise. And thus we cannot get them to try whether the things that we teach them be so.

For want of this it is that men deceive themselves, and think their case to be safe when it is miserable, because they will not try it by the word. This makes them rage and be confident in their folly, laugh and sing at the brink of hell, and swim as merrily down the stream to the devouring gulf as if no evil were near them. This makes them in the depth of misery to have no pity on themselves, and to do so little to escape it ; though they have time, means, and helps at hand, yet there are not hearts in them to make use of them ; yea, they run themselves daily further on the score ; all because we cannot get them to search the scripture, try whether sin be so small a matter, and whether this will not be bitterness in the end. Hence it is that they are so easily drawn by a temptation ; that they dislike an holy life, have base thoughts of them that are most diligent for salvation, and are most precious in the eyes of God ; and that they can even deride the way that they should walk in, because they will not search the scripture, to see what it saith to these matters. The word is a light would aid much to open their eyes, and win them over to God, if they would but come to it with a desire to know the truth. You think that the ungodly that are rich and great, are in a better condition than a godly man, that is poor and despised.

And why is this, but because you will not go into the sanctuary, and see in what a slippery place they stand, and what will be the end of these men? In a word, this is the undoing of millions of souls. They are all their lifetime out of the way to heaven ; and yet will not be persuaded to ask the way ; but they run on, shut their eyes, and put it to the venture. Many thousands are gone out of world, before they ever spent the quantity of one day in trying by the scripture whether their state were good, and their way were right. Nay, let their teachers tell them that they must be sanctified and take another course, they will differ from their teachers though they be never so wise or learned ; and they will contradict them, and not believe or regard them. And yet we cannot get them to come to us, and put the case to the trial, and let the scripture be the judge. Would they but do this, they could never have such hard thoughts of their teachers, and be offended at their plainest, closest dealing. You would then say, ' I see now the minister says not this of himself, he speaks but that which God commands him ; and if he would not deliver the message of the Lord, he were unworthy and unfit to be his ambassador : he were cruel to me if he would not pull me out of the fire, by the plainest, closest means. He hated me if he would not rebuke me, but suffer sin upon me. If he would please men, he should not be the servant of Christ. I know it is no pleasure to him to trouble me, or to provoke me ; but it would be his own destruction if he tell me not of my danger. And I have no reason to wish him to damn his own soul, and suffer me to do the like by mine ; and all for fear of displeasing me in my sin.' These would be your thoughts if you would but try our words by the scripture, and see whether we speak not the mind of God.

Surely it would. go somewhat deeper in your hearts, and it would stick by you, and be more before your eyes, when you once understood that it is the word of God.

This then is my request to you, that the work of your conversion may not miscarry, that you would carry all that you hear to the scripture, search there, and see whether it be so or not, that you may be put out of doubt, and may be at a certainty, and not stand wavering ; and that your faith may be resolved into the authority of God ; and so the work may be divine, and consequently powerful and prevailing, when the ground and motive is divine. If you be not satisfied in the doctrine which the minister delivers to you, first search the scripture yourselves ; and if that will not do, go to him, and desire him to show you his grounds for it in the word of God, and join with you in prayer for a right understanding of it. Do you question whether there be so severe a judgment, a heaven, and a hell, as ministers tell you? Search the scripture in Mat. xxv. and 2 Thess. i. 8, 9, 10 ; John v. 29 ; Mat. xiii. Do you question whether a man may not be saved without conversion, regeneration, and holiness? Open your bibles, and see what God saith, John iii. 3, 6 ; Mat. xviii. 3 ; 2 Cor. v. 17 ; Rom. viii. 9 ; Heb. xii. 14. Do you think a man may be saved without knowledge? Let scripture judge ; 2 Cor. iv. 3, 4 ; John xvii. 3 ; Hos. iv. 6. Do you think a man may be saved that doth as the most do, and goeth in the common way of the world? Search the scripture and see, Mat. vii. 13, 20 ; xvi. 22, 14 ; Luke xii. 32. Do you think an unhumbled soul may be saved, that never was contrite and broken hearted for sin? Try by Isa. lvii. 15, 66 ; Psalm li. 17 ; Luke iv. 18 ; Mat. xi. 28. Do you think a man can be the servant of God, that lives a fleshly life, and will keep his sin? Try by Rom. viii. 13 ; Gal. vi. 8 ; Ephes. v. 5, 6 ; 1 John iii. 9, 10. Do you doubt whether it be necessary to make so much ado to be saved, and to be so strict, and make religion our chief business? Try by Psalm i. 1, 2, 3 ; 1 Pet. iv. 18 ; Heb. xii. 14 ; Luke x. 42 ; Luke xiii. 24 ; Eph. v. 15, 16. Do you think a man can be saved that is a worldling, whose heart is more on earth than heaven? Try by 1 John ii. 15 ; Phil. iii. 19 ; Col. iii. 1 ; Luke xiv. 26, 33. Do you doubt whether you should serve God with your families, and instruct them and pray with them? Try by Jos. xxiv. 15 ; Deut. vi. 6, 7 ; Dan. vi. 10, 11 ; Exod. xx. 10.

Thus if you will in all these weighty matters but go to the scriptures, and see whether it say as your teachers say, you might soon be resolved, and that by the surest authority in the world. If you think that your ministers may be deceived, I hope you will confess that God cannot be deceived. If you think that your ministers are passionate, or self-conceited, or speak out of ill will to you, I hope you dare not say so by the Lord ; he owes you no ill will, nor speaks a word but what is most sure. If you think us partial, sure God is impartial. What better judge can you have now. than he that is infallible, and must judge you all at the last? If any papist put it into your head to ask, ' Who shall be judge of the sense of scripture?' I answer, who shall be judge of the Judge of all the world? The law is made to judge you, and not to be judged by you. None can be the proper judges of the sense of a law but the maker of it; though others must judge their cases by the law. Your work is to discern, understand and obey it; and our work is to help you to understand it; but it is neither our work nor yours to be the proper, or absolute judges of it. At least where it speaks plain it needs no judge. Come then to the word in meekness and humility, with a teachable frame of spirit, a willingness to know the truth, a resolution to stand to it, and yield to what shall be revealed to you; beg of God to show you his will, to lead you into the truth, and you will find that he will be found of them that seek him.

DIRECTION III.

If you would not have the work of your conversion miscarry, my next advice is this:—

' See that you be much in the SERIOUS CONSIDERATION of the truths which you understand betwixt God and you in secret.'

I have often spoken of this heretofore; but although I apprehend it to be a point of very great moment, I shall be no longer on it again, than on the rest.

The greatest matters in the world will not work much upon him that will not think of them. Consideration opens the ear that was stopped, and the heart that was shut up; it sets the powers of the soul to work, and awakens it from the sleep of indifference and security. The thoughts are the first actings of the soul, that set to work the rest. Thinking on the matters that must make us wise, and do the work of God on the heart, is that which lies on us to do, in order to our conversion. By consideration a sinner makes use of the truth, which before lay by, and therefore could do nothing. By consideration he takes in the medicine to his soul, which before stood by, and could not work. By consideration a man makes use of his reason, which before was laid asleep, and therefore could not do its work. When the master is from home the scholars will be at play. When the coachman is asleep, the horses may miss the way, and possibly break his neck and their own. If the plough-man go his way the oxen will stand still, or make but bad work. So when reason is laid asleep, and out of the way, what may not the appetite do; what may not the passions do; and what may not temptations do with the soul? A wise man, when he is asleep, hath as little use of his wisdom as a fool. A learned man, when he is asleep, can hardly dispute with an unlearned man that is awake. A strong man that is ever so skilful at his weapons, is scarcely able in his sleep to deal with the weakest child that is awake. Why all the powers of your soul are as it were asleep till consideration awake them, and set them on work: and what the better are you for being men and having reason, if you have not the use of your reason when you need it? As men are inconsiderate because they are wicked, so they are the more wicked because they are inconsiderate. The keenest sword, the greatest cannon, will do no execution against an enemy, while they lie by and are not used. There is a mighty power in the word of God, and the example of Christ, to pull down strong holds, and conquer the strongest lusts and corruptions. But they will not do this while they are forgotten and neglected. Will heaven entice the man that thinks not of it; will hell deter the man that thinks not of it? Why is it that all the reasoning in the world, will do no more good on a man that is deaf, than if you said nothing? Just because the passage to his thoughts and understanding is stopped up. If you have eyes and see not, ears and hear not, and wilfully cast it out of your thought, what good can any thing do to you that is spoken? It is not holding your meat in your mouth that will nourish you, if you will not let it down; not taking it unto your stomach, if you will not keep it, but presently cast it up again; but it must be kept till it be digested and distributed. So it is not the most excellent truths in the world that will change your hearts, if you let them not down to your hearts, and keep them not there by meditation till they are digested and turned into spiritual life. The plaster must be laid upon the sore, if you would be cured. The wound and sickness is at your heart; and if you will not take in the word to your heart, where the sickness is, I know not how you should expect a cure. The soul will not be charmed into holiness by the bare hearing or saying over a few good words, as wizards use to cure diseases, or seem to cure them. It must be truth at the heart that must change the heart. And if you will not think on it, and think on it again, how can you expect it should come at your hearts?

You say you would gladly have Christ and grace, and are ready to lay the blame on God, because he doth not give it you, and say, We cannot convert ourselves: but would you have the Spirit come in, while you hold the door against him? He knocks and desires you to open and let him in, and you wish him to come in; but you bar the door, and no intreaty will procure you to open it. It is consideration of the saving doctrine of the gospel that opens the heart, and gives it entertainment. Set yourselves therefore on purpose to this work, open the doors of your heart which are now shut, and let the king of glory come in. Who will believe that you love the light, when you shut the windows, and draw the curtains? If you will set yourselves to consider of the truth, the windows of your soul will be set open, and then the light will certainly come in. Now you read over whole chapters, and hear sermon after sermon, either they never stir you, or at least, it is but a little for a fit, like a man that hath a little warmed himself at the fire in the winter, and when he goes from it is colder than before: but if you would but set yourselves to consider of what you hear or read, one line of a chapter, or one sentence of a sermon, would lay you in tears, or make you groan, or at least do more than now is done. Satan hath garrisoned the heart of every carnal man: and consideration is the principal means to cast him out. If by considering of the terrible threatenings of the word, you would discharge these cannons of God against them, what a battery would it make in the corruptions of your souls! Our God is a consuming fire, and the fire of hell is threatened in his law, as the wages of sin: by serious consideration you may, as it were, bring fire from God and from his word, set fire to the very gates of Satan's garrison, and fire him out of many of his holds.

But because this is so needful a point, I shall be so large upon it as, First, To tell you some of those things that you should consider of. Second, To tell you in what manner you should do it. And, Third, to give you some motives to put you on.

SECT. I. *Some of the things to be considered.* The first thing that I would have you often to think on, is, the nature of that God with whom ye have to do. Consider that if he be the most wise, it is all the reason in the world that he should rule you. If he be good, and infinitely good, there is all the reason in the world that you should love him; and there is no show of reason that you should love the world or sin before him. If he be faithful and true, his threatenings must be feared, and his promises must not be distrusted; and there is no reason that you should make any question of his word. If he be holy, then holiness must needs be most excellent, and those that are the holiest must needs be the best, because they are like to God; then he must be an enemy to sin, and to all that are unholy, because they are contrary to his nature. Consider that he is almighty, and there is no re-

sisting him, or standing out against him; in the twinkling of an eye can he snatch thy guilty soul from thy body, and cast it where sin is better known. A word of his mouth can set all the world against thee, and set thine own conscience against thee too; a frown of his face can turn thee into hell; and if he be thine enemy, it is no matter who is thy friend, for all the world cannot save thee, if he condemn thee. They are blessed whom he blesses, and they are cursed indeed whom he curses. He was from eternity, and thou art but as it were of yesterday: thy being is from him; thy life is always in his hands, thou canst not live an hour without him, thou canst not draw a breath without him, nor think a thought, nor speak a word, nor stir a foot or hand without him; thou mayest better live without bread or drink, fire, air, earth, or water, than without him. All the world is before him but as the drop of a bucket or a little sand of dust that should be laid in balance with all the earth. Hadst thou but compassed about this lower world, and seen all the nations of it, its wonderful furniture, the great deeps of the mighty ocean, and the abundance of creatures that be in all, O what thoughts then wouldest thou have of God! But if thou hadst been above the stars, seen the sun in all its glory, seen the frame and course of those orbs, seen the blessed, glorious angels, and all the inhabitants of the higher world, O then what thoughts of God wouldst thou entertain! O but if it were possible that thou hadst seen his glory, or seen but his backparts, as Moses did, or seen him in Christ, the now glorified Redeemer, what apprehensions wouldst thou have of him then? Then how wouldst thou abhor the name of sin, and how weary wouldst thou be of the pleasantest life that sensuality could afford thee? Then thou wouldst quickly know that no love can be great enough, no praises can be high enough, and no service can be holy and good enough for such a God: then you would soon know, that this is not a God to be neglected, or trifled with; nor a God to be resisted, or provoked by the wilful breaking of his laws. It is eternal life to know this God, and for want of knowing him, it is that sin abounds in the world. This makes holiness so scarce and lean: men worship they care not how, because they worship they know not whom. O therefore dwell on the meditations of the Almighty. So far as he doth possess thy mind there will be no place for sin and vanity. One would think if I should set you no further task, and tell you of no other matters for meditation, this one should be enough; for this one is in a manner all. What will not the due know-ledge of God do upon the soul? That is the best Christian, and the most happy man, who knows most of him; that is the most vile and miserable wretch who is furthest from him, and strangest to him: it is the character of the fool of fools, to have a heart whose disposition and practice saith, 'there is no God,' that is, to be so affected and employed in their hearts, as if there were no God, and when 'God is not in all his thoughts.' It was better with man when he had less knowledge for himself, and fewer thoughts for himself, and more of God. And there is no way to restore us to sound un-derstanding, and to perfect our knowledge, but to turn our eye upon God again; for in know-ing him, we know all that is worth the knowing. Take hold then of the blessed God in thy medi-tations, and fill thy thoughts with him, and dwell upon those thoughts. Remember he is always with thee, and wherever thou art, or whatever thou art doing, most certainly he sees thee. As sure as thou art there, the Lord is there. He knows thy thoughts, he hears thy words, he sees all thy ways. And is such a God as this to be provoked or despised! Were it not better to provoke and despise all the world? Is his fa-vour to be slighted? Were it not better to lose the favour of all the world? Consider of this.

2. Another thing that I would have you oft think of, is, what end you were made for, and what business it is that you came for into the world. You may well think that God made you not in vain; and that he made you for no lower end, than for himself: and that he would never have made you, nor so long preserved you, if he had not cared what you do. He would never have endued you with a reasonable and immortal soul, but for some high, noble, and immortal end. Surely it was that you might be happy in knowing him, that he made you capable of know-ing him; for he made nothing in vain. It is useful for a horse to know his pasture, provender, work, and perhaps his master; but he needs not know whether there be a God; and accordingly he is qualified. But it is surely man's chief con-cern to know that there is a God, and what he is, how to serve him, what he is, and will be to us; or else we should never have been capable of such things. He would never have made you capable of loving him, but that you should be exercised and made happy in that love. The frame, faculties, capacity of your souls, and the scope of scripture, all declare, that you were sent into this world to seek after God, to love him, obey him, rejoice in him in your measure; and to prepare for a life of nearer communion, where you may enjoy him and praise him in the highest perfection. Consider with yourselves, whether a life of sin be that which you were made for; or whether God sent you hither to break his laws, and follow your own lusts; and whe-ther the satisfying of your flesh, and the gather-ing a little worldly wealth, and the feathering of a nest which you must so quickly leave, be like to be the business that you were sent about into the world.

3. The next thing that I would have you con-sider of, is, how you have answered the ends of your creation, and how you have done the busi-ness that you came into the world to do. Look back upon the drift of your hearts and lives; read over the most ancient records of your con-sciences, and see what you have been, and what you have been doing in the world till now. Have you spent your days in seeking after God, and your estates and strength in faithfully serving him? Have you lived all this time in the ad-miration of his excellencies, in the fervent love, the delightful remembrance, and the zealous worship of him? If you have done this, you had not need of a conversion. But consider; have you not forgotten what business you had in the world, and little minded the world that you should have prepared for, and lived as it you knew not him that made you, or why he made you? Was sport and merriment the end that you were created for? Was ease and idle-ness, or eating, or drinking, or vain discourses, or recreation, the business that you came into the world about? Was living to the flesh, and scraping up riches, or gaping after the esteem of men, the work that God sent you hither to do? Was this it that he preserved you for, and daily gave you in provision for? What was it to for-get him, slight him, turn him out of your hearts, and rob him of his service and honour; to set up your flesh in his stead, and give that to it that was due to him? Bethink you what you have done, and whether you have done the work that you were sent to do, or not.

4. The next thing you should use to consider of, is, how grievously you have sinned, and what a case it is that your sin hath brought you into. If you take but an impartial view of your lives, you may see how far you have looked below your mark, and how far you have been from what you should have been; and how little you have done of that which was your business. O what abundance of aggravations have your sins! which I shall pass over now, because I must men-tion them under another head. It is not only some actual out breakings against the bent of your

heart and life: but your very heart was false and gone from God, and set in you to do evil.

O the time that you have lost; the means and helps that you have neglected; the motions that you have resisted; the swarms of evil thoughts that have filled your imaginations; the streams of vain and idle words that have flowed from your mouth; the works of darkness, in public and in secret, that God hath seen you in! And all this while, how empty were you in inward holiness, and how barren of good works, to God or men? What have you done with all your talents; and how little or nothing hath God had of all?

Now consider what a case you are in, while you remain unconverted. You have made yourselves the sinks of sin, the slaves of Satan, and the flesh, and are skilful in nothing but doing evil; if you be called to prayer or holy meditation, your hearts are against it, and you are not used to it, therefore you know not how to do it to any purpose: but to think the thoughts of lust or covetousness, or hatred, or malice, or revenge, this you can do without any toil: to speak of the world, or of your sports and pleasures, or against those that you bear ill will to, this you can do without any study. You are such as are spoken of, ' My people is foolish, they have not known me: they are sottish children, and they have no understanding: they are wise to do evil, but to do good they have no knowledge.' You are grown strangers to the God that made you, in whose love and service you should live and find your chief delights. Your hearts are hardened, and you are dead in your sins: the guilt of the sins of your lives are still upon you; you can neither look into your hearts or lives, no, not on one day of your lives, or the best hour that you have spent, but you must see the deformed face of sin, which deserves condemnation. You have made God your enemy, who should have been your only felicity. Yet you are always at his mercy, and in his hands. Little do you know how long his patience will yet endure to you; or what hour he will call away your souls: if death come, alas, what a case will it find you in; how lamentably unready are you to meet him; how unready to appear before the dreadful God whom you have offended; and what a terrible appearance do you think that will be to you? Most certainly, if you die before you are converted, you will not be from among the devils and lost souls an hour. The law hath cursed you already, and the execution will be answerable, if you die in your sins. Thus you may see the gain of sin, and what it is that you have been doing all this while for your own souls; what a case it is that you have brought yourselves into: and what need you have speedily to look about you!

5. The next step of your consideration should be this: Bethink yourselves what a blessed condition you might be in, if by conversion you were but recovered from this misery, and brought home to God. This moved the heart of the prodigal son to return, ' When he came to himself, he said, how many hired servants of my father's have bread enough, and to spare, and I perish with hunger?' He that had not husks to feed on with the swine, considered the plenty that he had forsaken at home. The poorest member of the household of Christ, is in a better condition than the greatest king on earth who is unconverted. You might have lived another kind of life, than you have done, for safety, benefit, and true content, if you would have turned your mind and life to God. Were you but converted, you would be the living members of Christ, and his precious benefits would be yours; his blood would cleanse you from all your sins, and they would be all freely forgiven you; God would be reconciled to you, and become your friend, yea, your Father and your God, and will take you for his household servants, and adopted children: the Holy Ghost would dwell in you, guide your understandings, show you that which flesh and blood cannot reveal, and bring you into acquaintance with the mysteries of God: he will be a Spirit of light and life within you, work your hearts yet more to God, and give you yet stronger inclinations and affections to the things above. He will help you when you are weak, and quicken you when you are dull, and be your remembrancer when you are forgetful of necessary things.. He will help you in prayer, both for matter and for manner, help you in meditation, conference, and other duties: he will warn you of your danger, strengthen you against temptations, and cause you to overcome; and if you fall, he will cause you to rise again: he will be an in-dwelling comforter to you, and so effectually speak peace to you in the midst of your disquietness, that by speaking it, he will create it in you: and in the multitude of your thoughts within you, his comforts will delight your souls. O what a life might you live, if Christ, by his Spirit, live in you!

You may easily conjecture how tender Christ would be of his own members, how dearly he would love them, how constantly he would watch over them, how plentifully he would provide for them, and how safely he would preserve them.

If you should come into a rougher way, he would lead you out: afflictions should never be laid on you but for your good, nor continue longer than your condition rendered them necessary, and be taken off at last, to your satisfaction and contentment. Indeed your life would be a life of mercies; and that which is but a common mercy to common men, would be a special mercy to you, as coming from your Father's love, furthering your salvation, and pointing out to you your everlasting mercies. You could not open your eyes, but you would see that which may encourage and comfort you; all the works of God, which you behold, would show you his majesty, his love and power, and lead you to himself. You could not open your bible, but you would find in it the blessed lines of love: O what good it would do you, to read there the blessed attributes of your God; to look upon his name; to peruse the description of his most perfect nature! What good would it do you to read of the nature and incarnation, the life, death, resurrection, ascension, intercession, and return, of your blessed Redeemer; what good would it do you to find those holy rules which your new nature is agreeable to, and to read over the law that is written in your hearts, and read the curse from which you are delivered! What life and joy would your souls receive from the many, full, and free promises of grace! Were you once but truly sanctified and made new, your condition would be often comfortable, but always safe; and when you were in the greatest fears and perplexities, you would still be fast in the arms of Christ: what a life would that be, to have daily access to God in prayer; to have leave, in all your wants and danger, to seek to him with a promise of hearing and success; that you may be sure of much more from him, than a child can from the tenderest father, or a wife from the most loving husband upon the earth What a life would it be, when you may always think on God as your felicity, and fetch your highest delights from him, from whom the ungodly have their greatest terrors? And it is no contemptible part of your benefits, that you may live among his people, and in their special love, and have a special communion with them, and interest in their prayers, and may possess among them the privileges of the saints and the ordinances of God: that instead of idle talk, and the unprofitable fellowship of the children and works of darkness, you may join with the church of God in his praises, and feed with them at his table on the body and blood of Christ, and then have conveyances of renewed grace, and a re-

newed pardon sealed to your souls: but how long should I stay, if I should tell you but one half of the blessings of a sanctified and spiritual state? In a word, God would be yours, Christ would be yours, the Holy Ghost would be yours, all things would be yours; the whole world would have some relation to your welfare; devils would be subdued to you, and cast out of your souls; sin would be both pardoned and overcome; angels would be ministering spirits unto you for your good: the promises of scripture would be yours, and everlasting glory would at last be yours; and while you staid on earth, you might comfort yourselves as oft as you would, with the believing foresight of that inconceivable, unspeakable, endless felicity.

What a treasure have I here expressed in a few words; what hearts would you have if you were but possessed, lively and sensible of all that is contained in this leaf or two! you would not envy the greatest prince on earth his glory, nor change states with any man that were a stranger to these things. Did you but use to consider of the state of the saints; how could you keep off, or stay with sin, and make so many delays in turning unto God! Surely this consideration might turn the scales.

6. The next part of your meditation should be, of the gracious and wonderful work of our redemption, and the means and remedies which are provided for your souls, and the terms on which salvation may be obtained.

For all the sins that you have committed, you are not given over to despair; the Lord hath not left you without a remedy. Your conversion and salvation is not a thing impossible. Nay, so much is done by Christ already, that it is brought upon reasonable terms even to your hands. A new and living way is consecrated for us by Christ, through the vail of his flesh, and by his blood we may have boldness to enter into the holiest; he hath borne your burden, and offers you, instead of it, his burden, which is light; he hath removed the impossibility, and nailed to his cross the hand-writing that was against you, and instead of it offers you his easy yoke; he hath spoiled the principalities and powers that had captivated you, and also triumphed over them on the cross. You are not left under the care of making satisfaction to God for your own sins; but only of accepting the Redeemer that hath satisfied. This much I dare confidently say to you all, without extending his benefits too far. It would be from want of faith in you, and not from want of satisfaction by the Redeemer, if any of you perish. O how free are his offers; how full are his promises! And the condition which is imposed on you is not some meritorious or mercenary work, but the accepting of the benefit freely given, according to its nature, use and ends. This is the faith by which you must be justified; these are the terms on which you may be saved. And what is more, the Lord hath provided means, even excellent, plentiful, and powerful means, for the furthering of your souls in the performance of this condition, helping you to believe, and repent, that you may live: if the Spirit make not these means effectual, and adjoin not his special grace, and after this you remain unconverted, it will not be owing to him, but of yourselves. So that you may perceive how hopeful a case you are yet in, by the blood of your Redeemer. If you destroy not your own hopes, and make not your case desperate by wilful impenitency, and refusal of free grace, how fair are you yet for heaven; and what happy advantages have you for salvation! It is brought even to your doors; it is thrust as it were into your hands; the Redeemer hath done so much for you all, as to bring your salvation to the choice of your own wills; and if you be his chosen ones, he will also make you willing. You have precepts to believe; you are threatened if you will not believe; you have promise upon promise, and Christ himself offers you pardon, and life, and salvation with him, if you are but truly and heartily willing. You have God himself condescending to beseech you to accept them; and ambassadors intreating you in his name and stead. You have ordinances fitted to your necessities; both reading and preaching, sacraments, and prayer. You have store of plain and powerful books; you have the godly about you, most desirous to assist you, who would be glad to see or hear of your conversion; you have the sight of the wicked, who are wallowing in their own impurity, and that of the world, to make you hate such wicked ways. You have reason and conscience within you to consider of these matters, set them home, and apply them to yourselves; you have time and strength to do all this, if you will not abuse them, and provoke God to take them from you for your negligence. You have mercies of many sorts, outward and inward, to win upon you, and encourage you in the work; and sometimes afflictions to remember you, awaken you, and spur you on. The devil and all your enemies are so far disabled, that they cannot destroy you against your wills, nor keep you from Christ, but by your own consents. The angels in heaven are ready to help you, and would even rejoice at your conversion.

This is your case, these are your helps and encouragements; you are not shut up under desperation. God never told you, it is in vain to think of conversion; it is too late; if any have told you so, it was the devil, and not God; one would think that such considerations as these should drive the nail to the head, and be effectual to move you to resolve and turn.

7. The last thing that I would set before you to be considered, is, what is like to be the end of it, if after all this you should die unconverted.

Your hearts are not able now to conceive of it, nor the tongue of any mortal man to utter it. But so much of it we can certainly utter, as one would think should make your hearts to tremble. You have seen, it may be, a dying man, in what pangs and agonies he parts with his soul: and you have seen it is like the corpse that was left there behind; and seen it laid in the common earth. But you see not what became of the soul, nor what an appearance it made in another world, nor what company did attend it, nor what place or state it passed into. When the hour is at hand that this must be your own case, it will awaken you to other kind of affections than you have or can have at the reading of these words. It is wonderful that a little distance should make us so insensible of that change which we are all certain will come to pass; and yet through the folly and deadness of our hearts it is so; but they are other kind of thoughts of these weighty matters, which we shall have the next hour after death, than the liveliest affections beforehand can afford us.

The misery was great that the Redeemer found you in, and which you deserved by your sin against the law of your Creator. But if you be found unconverted at last, your punishment will be much sorer, and your case far worse than it was before. The Redeemer's law or gospel hath its peculiar threatening, which differs from the law of the mere Creator in several respects; 1. In the nature of the punishment, which will be torments of conscience for the neglect of a Redeemer, and recovering grace, which you should never have felt if you had never been offered redemption. 2. In the degree of the punishment, which will be far sorer. And, 3, in the remedilessness of it, the sentence being irreversible and peremptory. The first law indeed provided no remedy, but did not exclude remedy, nor make it impossible; but the law of Christ doth positively and expressly exclude all remedy, and leave the soul that goes unconverted out of the body, to utter desperation and misery, without help or hope. But I shall not stand now to describe to you the terrors of judgment or of hell, because I have done it already in other books, which I desire you to compare with the rest of this meditation; that is, my Treatise of Judgment, and the beginning of the third part of my Book of Rest.

SECT. II. *In what manner they are to be considered.* Having told you what should be the matter of your consideration, I shall next tell you, but briefly, in what manner you should perform it. Here I shall not stand to prescribe to you any long or exact method for meditation, both because it agrees not with my present resolved brevity, and because the persons that I now deal with are not capable of observing such rules; and if any desire such helps, they may transfer the directions which are given on another subject in my Book of Rest, to the subject now in hand.

1. Do not stay till such thoughts will come of themselves into your minds, but set yourselves purposely to consider of these matters. Take some time to call your souls to an account concerning their present state, and their preparations for eternity. If a heathen Seneca could call himself every night to an account for the evil committed, and the good omitted in the day past, as he professes that he ordinarily did; why may not even an unconverted man, that hath the helps which are now among us, bethink himself of the state of his soul? But I know that a carnal heart is exceedingly backward to serious consideration, and is loth to be troubled with such thoughts as these; and the devil will do what he can to hinder it, by himself and others: but yet if men would but do what they may do, it might be better with them than it is. Will you but now and then purposely withdraw yourselves from company into some secret place, and there set the Lord before your eyes, and call your souls to a strict account about the matters that I have mentioned even now, and make it your business to exercise your reason upon them; and as you purposely go to church to hear, so purposely set yourselves to this duty of consideration as a necessary thing?

2. When you are upon it, labour to awaken your souls, and to be very serious in all your thoughts; and do not think of the matters of salvation, as you would do of an ordinary trivial business, which you do not much regard or care how it goes. But remember that your life lies on it, even your everlasting life: and therefore call up the most earnest of your thoughts, and rouse up all the powers of your souls, and suffer them not to draw back, but command them to the work; and then set the several points that I mentioned even now before you; and as you think of them, labour to be affected with them, in some measure, according to their exceeding weight. As Moses said to Israel, 'set your hearts to all the words which I testify among you this day; which you shall command your children to do,' &c. 'For it is not a vain thing for you; because it is your life.' And as Christ said, 'let these sayings sink into your ears,' so I say to you, let the matters which you think of go to your hearts, and sink down to the quick of your affections.

And if your hearts would slip away from the work, and other thoughts would creep into your mind, and you are weary of these considerations before they have done their work, see that you give not way to this laziness, or unwillingness, but remember it is a work that must be done, and therefore hold your thoughts upon it, till your hearts are stirred, and warmed within you.

And if, after all, you cannot awake them to seriousness and sensibility, put two or three such awakening questions as these to yourselves.

(1.) Quest. What if it were but the case of my body, or state, or name, should I not earnestly consider of it? If one but wrong me, how easily can I think of it, and how tenderly do I feel it; and can scarcely forget it? If my good name be blemished, and I be but disgraced, I can think of it night and day: if I lose but a beast, or have any cross in the world, or decay in my estate, I can think of it with sensibility: if I lose a child or a friend, I can feel it as well as think on it. If my health be decayed, and my life in danger, I am in good earnest in thinking of this. And should I not be as serious in the matters of everlasting life? Should I not think of it, and soberly and earnestly think on it, when body and soul lie at stake, and when it concerns my everlasting joy or torment?

(2.) Quest. What if I had but heard the Son of God himself calling on me to repent, and be converted, and seconding his commands with that earnest expression, 'he that hath an ear to hear, let him hear,' would it not have brought me to some serious thoughts of my state? Why this he hath done in his word, and doth it by his ambassadors, and why then should I not consider it?

(3.) Quest. If I did but know that death were at my back, and ready to arrest me, and that I should be in another world before this day sevennight, I should then begin to bethink me in good earnest: and why do I not so now, when I have no hold of my life an hour, and when I am sure that shortly that time will come?

(4.) If my eyes were but open to see that which I pretend to believe, and which is certainly true; even to see a glimpse of the majesty of the Lord, to see the saints in joy and glory, to see the lost souls in misery, and if I heard their lamentations, would not this even force my heart to consideration? O then how earnestly should I think of these things; and why should I not do so now, when they are as sure as if I saw them, and when I must see them ere it be long.

Many more such awakening questions are at hand, but I give you but these brief touches on the things that are most common and obvious, that the most ignorant may be able to make some use of them. With such thoughts as these, you must bring on your backward hearts, shake them out of their insensibility, and awaken them to the work.

Sect. III. *Some motives to move to consideration.* When you have brought your hearts to be serious, be sure that you drive on your considerations to a resolution. Break not off in the middle, or before you bring the matter to an issue; but let all be done in order to practice. When you have been thinking of the excellencies of God and the world to come, and comparing them with all the delights on earth; put the question then to your hearts, and say, ' What sayest thou now, O my soul; which of these is the better for thee? which is the more desirable; and which of them shouldst thou prefer? Resolve then, and make thy choice according to the light and convictions which thou hast received.' When you are thinking of the reasons that should move you to be converted, ask yourselves, ' whether these reasons be not clear, and what you have to say against them? And whether any thing that can be said to the contrary can prove it better for you to be as you are, and to remain unconverted?' Ask yourselves, ' Is my judgment resolved, or is it not? And if it be, as sure it must be, if you be not beside yourselves, then write it down under your hands, or at least in your hearts. I here confess before the Lord, that his commands are just, his motions are reasonable, his offers are exceeding merciful: I am satisfied that it is best for me to turn to him speedily, and with all my heart: I confess before him that I have no reason to the contrary that deserves to be owned, and called reason: this is my own judgment; of this I am convinced: if I turn not after this, the light that is in me, and the judgment that now I possess, must needs be a witness against my soul.' If you would but thus drive on the case to a resolution of your judgments, you would have a great ad-

vantage for the resolving of your wills, which is the next thing that you must proceed to: and therefore next ask yourselves, ' Why should I not now resolve, and fixedly resolve to turn without any more delay? Is not the case plain before me; what reason have I to stand questioning the matter any longer, and to be unwilling to be happy; shall I provoke God by dallying with him, and hazard my soul by lingering out my time in such a miserable state? No; by the grace of God I will return; even this hour, without any more delay.' Thus drive on all your consideration to resolution. But of this, I have more to say afterwards.

By this time you may see of what necessity this duty of consideration is, and how it must be performed, that it may further your conversion: but because it is a matter of so great necessity, I am loth to leave it thus, till I have done what I can to persuade you to the practice of it. To which end I intreat you to think of these following motives:—

1. Consideration is a duty that you may perform if you will. You cannot say that it is wholly out of your power; so that you are left inexcusable, if you will not be persuaded to it. You say you cannot convert yourselves: but can you not set yourselves to ' consider of your ways,' and bethink you of those truths that must be the instruments of your conversion? Your thoughts are partly at the command of your will: you can turn them up and down from one thing to another. Even an unsanctified minister, that hath no saving relish of spiritual things, can think of them, and spend most of his time in thinking of them, that he may preach them to others: and why cannot you then turn your thoughts to them for yourselves? You can think of house, land, friends, trading, and of any thing that ails you, or any thing that you want, or any thing that you love or think would do you good: and why cannot you think of your sin and danger of God, of his word and works, of the state of your souls, and of everlasting life? Are you not able to go sometimes by yourselves, and consider of these matters? Are you not able when you are alone in your beds, or as you travel in the way, or at your labour, to bethink how things stand with your souls; why are you not able; what is it that could hinder you, if you were but willing?

2. Yea, further consideration is so cheap a remedy, that if you will not use this, you despise your souls: yea, and you despise the Lord himself, and the everlasting things which you are called to consider of. A man who is in dan-

ger of losing his estate, or health, or life, and will not do so much as bethink him of a remedy, doth certainly despise them, and lose them by his contempt. A man that had but his house on fire, and would not so much as think how to quench it, doth deserve that it should be burned. If your parents, or children, or friends, were in distress, if you would not so much as think of them, it were a sign you did not much value them. Why, are not your souls worth the thinking on? Is not God, is not your Redeemer, worth the thinking on? And yet you will hypocritically pretend that you love God above all, when you will not so much as seriously think of him; how can you show greater contempt of any thing, than to cast it out of your minds as unworthy to be thought on? And how can you more plainly show that you despise God, and heaven; than by such a course as this? If it be not worth the thinking on, it is worth nothing.

3. Consider that God doth not set so little value on your salvation. He thought it worth a great deal more: must Christ think it worth his bloody sufferings and with such a life of labour and sorrow, and will not you judge it worth your serious considerations; if he had not thought on it, and thought again, how miserable should we have remained? Ministers also must think on it, and study how to save your souls. And should you not study how to save your own? Must another man make it the business of his life to think how to do you good, that you may be saved; and are you not as much bound to do good to yourselves? Yea, all that fear God about you are bound to study to do you good; and should you not bethink you then of the things that concern your own good?

4. Moreover, what have you your reason for, but to consider? And wherein do you differ from the beasts, so much as in your reason? If you have reason and will not use it, you brutify yourselves; you live like madmen: for what is madness, but a loss of the use of reason? And do you think it a small thing to deface so noble a creature as man, and to turn yourselves into beasts and madmen? Do you think that God will not call you to account for your reason, how you have used it? Doubtless he gave it you for an higher employment, than to enable you to plough, sow, follow your trades, and provide for your flesh. If this were all that a man did exceed a beast in, what a silly wretched creature were man? Yea, so much more miserable than beasts, as his knowledge begets more care, sorrow, and fear, than theirs. What matter is it for having reason at all, if it be not that we may use it for the matters of God, and eternal life?

5. Moreover, your soul is an active principle, which will be working one way or other; your thoughts will be going on one thing or other; and therefore the bare consideration is no great labour to you. And if you must lay out your thoughts on something, is it not better to lay them out on these things, than on any other? Have you any better matters to think on than these; have you any greater matters, or matters of greater necessity to think of? You cannot imagine it; at least you will not say so for shame. This makes your inconsiderateness an inexcusable sin. If thinking were a toil to you, it were another matter. But when you must think of something, why not of God, your eternal state, and the way to heaven, as well as of other matters? Will you rather throw away your thoughts than God shall have them? If a man command his servant who is lame, to go on his business, the servant hath a good excuse: I cannot go, or not without a great pain and danger; but if he have a son or a servant who is so wanton that he cannot stand on his legs, but spends his time in running up and down, dancing, and leaping, this person hath no excuse, if he will refuse to go on his master's or his father's errand, but will gad about on his pleasure all day, and will not go a few steps when he is desired: especially if it were for his own life or welfare. So when you have thoughts that will not be kept idle, but will be gadding abroad through the world, and yet you will not think of God, and the matters of your peace, what wilfulness is this? If you should ask one that hath it not, for meat, or drink, or money, they might well deny you. But if you ask these of one that hath abundance, and knows not what to do with them, but would throw them down the channel, rather than you should have them, what would you think of such a one; especially if it were your servant or your child that owed you much more? Thus do you by God, and your own souls. You have thoughts enough and to spare, you know not what to do with them; and yet rather than you will spend one hour in a day or a week in serious thoughts of the state of your souls and the life to come, you will cast them away upon news, tales, and other folk's business, that do not concern you; yea, you will cast them down the sink of covetousness, malice, lust, wantonness, and make them servants to the devil and the flesh. If you have a brook running by your land, you will endeavour to turn it over your ground, that seeing it must run, it may as well run that way where it may do good,

as run in vain : so when your thoughts must run, is it not better that you turn them to your own hearts and states, to prepare for the world that you are ready to step into, than to let them run in vain ? If you see a man go into a wine-cellar, though it be his own, and pull out all the spigots, and let all the wine run about the cellar, and suffer nobody to catch it, or be the better for it, what would you conceive of the wisdom and charity of that man ? Your thoughts are a thing more precious than wine, and such a thing as should not be spilt; and yet is not this your daily practice ? You are before him who knows your thoughts : deny it if you can. What hour of the day can a man come to you and find your thoughts altogether idle ; what minute of an hour can a man come and ask you, What are you now thinking on ? and you can truly say, nothing ! I know as long as you are awake you are always thinking of somewhat, and perhaps when you are asleep, and what is it on ? This body shall have a thought, and that body a thought ; every word you hear, every wrong that is done you, and almost every thing you look upon, shall have a thought ; and God and your own salvation shall have none ; that is, you will lose them, and let them run in waste ; but you will do no good with them, nor take in any profit by them to yourselves.

6. Have you any thing that better deserves your consideration, than God and your salvation ? Certainly God hath more right to your thoughts than any thing else that you can place them on. Your flesh, your friends, your worldly business, are neither so honourable, so necessary, or so profitable subjects, as God and heaven are. As there is more profit to be got by the tillage of fruitful land, than barren heath ; or by digging in a mine of gold, than in a clay-pit ; so is there more pleasure and profit to be gotten in one hour's serious thoughts of your salvation, than in thinking all your life time of the world.

7. At least methinks you should consider, how disproportionably and unequally you lay out your thoughts. Cannot you deny God the tenth ; no nor the hundredth part of them ? Look back upon your lives, trace your thoughts from day to day, and tell me how many hours in a week, in a month, in a year, you have spent in serious thoughts of the state of your souls, and of the life to come ; is it one hour of a hundred, of a thousand, of ten thousand, with some of you that is thus spent ? Nay, I have very great cause to fear that there are some, yea, that there are many, yea, that there is far the greatest number, that never spent one hour since they were born, in

withdrawing themselves purposely from all other business, soberly, and in good earnest bethinking themselves what case they are in, what evidence they have of their salvation, or how they must be justified at the bar of God ; no, nor what business they have in the world, to what end they were made, and how they have done the work that they were made for. Doth conscience justify you in this ; or rather, will it not torment you one day to remember it ? What ! did thy land, livings, and worldly matters deserve all thy thoughts, and did not the saving of thy soul deserve some of them ? Did thy lusts, sports, and wantonness deserve all ; and did not God deserve some of them? Was it not worth now and then an hour's time, no, nor one hour's study, in all thy life, to bethink thee in good earnest how to make sure of a life of endless joy and glory, and how to escape the flames of hell? This is not an equal distribution of thy thoughts, as thou wilt confess at last in the horror of thy soul.

8. It is the end of your present time and warnings, that you may consider, and prepare for your everlasting state. What have you to do on earth but to consider how to get well to heaven ? O that you did but know what a mercy it is, before you enter upon an endless life, to have but time to bethink you of it, and to make your election sure ! If you were to be called away suddenly this night, and the angel of the Lord should say to any of you, Prepare ; for within this hour thou must die, and appear before the living God. Then would you not cry out, O not so suddenly, Lord ! Let me have a little more time to consider of my condition : let me have one month longer, to bethink me of the case of my soul, and make sure that I am justified from the guilt of my sins. Let me have one day more at least to prepare for my everlasting state ; for alas, I am yet unready. Would not these be your cries, if God should call you presently away ? And yet now you have time, you will not consider of these matters and prepare.

9. Moreover, is it not time for you to consider your ways, when God doth consider them? If he would forget them, or did not regard them, you might regard them the less yourselves : but be sure of it, he doth observe them, whether you do or not ; and he remembers them though you forget them. Dost thou not know that all the sins of thy life are still on record before the Lord ? Job saith, ' Thou numberest my steps ; dost thou not watch over my sin ? My transgression is sealed up in a bag, and thou sowest

up mine iniquity.' Do you think that God forgets your sins, as you forget them? Saith the Lord by the prophet Hosea, ' They consider not in their hearts, that I remember all their wickedness ; now their doings have beset them about, they are before my face. But you will say, What if God do consider our ways? why surely then it is not for nothing, but evil is near if not prevented. As the Lord saith, ' Is not this laid up in store with me, and sealed up among my treasures? To me belongs vengeance, and recompence ; their foot shall slide in due time. For the day of their calamity is at hand, and the things that shall come upon them make haste.' If God be registering up thy sins, thou hast cause to tremble, to think what that portends : for in this ' hardness and impenitency of thy heart, thou art treasuring up wrath against the day of wrath, and revelation of the righteous judgments of God.' As grace is the seed of glory, so sin is the seed of shame, trouble, and everlasting torment ; though it may seem long before the harvest, you will taste the bitter fruit at last ; and whatsoever you have sowed, that shall you reap.

10. Moreover, if any thing ailed you, you look that God should presently consider you : or if you want any thing, you think he should consider your wants : yet will you not consider of him, and of your own wants? When you are in trouble, you cry to God, ' Have mercy upon me, O Lord, consider my trouble.—Consider and hear me, O God.' When you lie in pain and sickness, you will then cry to God, ' Consider mine affliction, and deliver me.' If you be oppressed or abused, you will groan as the Israelites under their taskmasters, and perhaps cry to God, as the captive people, ' See, O Lord, and consider ; for I am become vile : remember, O Lord, what is come upon us ; consider and behold our reproach.' And must God consider of you, that will not consider of him, or your own souls? Or may you not rather expect that dreadful answer, which he gives to such regardless sinners ; and hear your cries, as you hear his counsel, and think of you, as you thought of him.

Nay, more ; even while you forget him, the Lord doth daily consider you, supply your wants, and save you from dangers ; and should you then cast him out of your thoughts? If he did not think on you, you would quickly feel it to your cost and sorrow.

11. Moreover, the nature of the matter is such as, one would think, should force a reasonable creature to consider of it, and often and earnestly to consider. When all these things concur in the matter, he must be a fool or a madman that will not consider,—When they are the most excellent, or the greatest things in all the world. —When they are our own matters, or much concern us.—When they are the most necessary, profitable, and delightful things.—When there is much difficulty in getting them, and danger of losing them ; and all these go together in the matter of your salvation.

(1.) If you will not think of God, and your souls, of heaven, and hell, what then will you think of? All other things in the world are but toys and jesting matters to these. Crowns, kingdoms, lands, and lordships are but chaff, and bawbles, to these everlasting things. The acts of renowned kings and conquerors, are but as puppet-plays in comparison of the working out of your salvation. Yet will you not be drawn to the consideration of such astonishing things as these? One would think that the exceeding greatness of the matter should force you to consider it whether you will or not : when smaller objects affect not the senses, yet greater will even force their way. He that hath so hard a skin that he cannot feel a feather, methinks should feel the weight of a mill-stone ; and if he feel not the prick of a pin, methinks he should feel a dagger. He that cannot hear one whisper, methinks should hear a cannon, or a clap of thunder, if he have any such thing as hearing left him. He hath bad eyes that cannot see the sun. One would think so glorious an object as God, should so entice the eyes of men, that they should not look off him. One would think that such matters as heaven and hell should follow thy thoughts which way soever thou goest, so that thou shouldst not be able to look besides them, or to think almost of any thing else, unless with great neglect and disesteem. O what a thing is a stony heart, that can forget not only the God that he lives by, but also the place where he must live for ever! Yea, that will not be persuaded to the sober consideration of it for an hour.

(2.) As these are the greatest matters, so they are your own matters, and therefore one would think you should not need so much ado to bring you to consider them. If it were only other men's matters, I should not wonder at it ; but self-love should make you regard your own. In outward matters, all seek their own things. And have they not more reason to seek their own salvation? It is your own souls, your own danger, your own sin, your own duty, that I persuade you to consider of. It is that God, that Christ, that would be your own : it is that heaven, that blessedness that may be your own, if you lose it not by neglect: it is that hell, and torment, that will certainly be your own, if you prevent it not. Should not this be thought on? You will think of your own goods, lands, or riches; of your own families, your own business, your own lives, and why not also of your own salvation?

(3.) Especially, when it is not only your own, but it is the one thing needful. It is that which your life, or death, your everlasting joy or torment, lies on; and therefore must be considered of, or you are utterly undone for ever. Necessity lies upon you; and woe be to you, if you consider not of these things. It is not so necessary that you eat, or drink, or sleep, or live, as it is necessary that you make sure your everlasting life; and the profit also doth answer the necessity. Buy but this one pearl, and you will be infinite gainers, though you sell all that you have in the world to buy it. Get God, and get all; make sure of heaven, and then fear no loss, nor want, nor sorrow. If you count not all the world as dust for the winning of Christ, that you may be found in him, possessed of his righteousness, it is because you know neither the world nor Christ. Yea, the delight will also answer the commodity: ' For in the presence of God is fulness of joy, and at his right hand are pleasures for evermore.' And the fore-thoughts of them may well make ' glad our hearts, and cause our glory to rejoice.—For goodness and mercy shall follow us all the days of our lives, and we shall dwell in the house of the Lord for ever.—He shall guide with his counsel, and afterward receive us into glory.' And lest yet you should suspect any lack of comfort, he tells you, you shall ' enter into the joy of your Lord.—And that you shall be with him where he is, to behold his glory.'

(4.) And yet if all this might be had with a wet finger; if heaven were the portion of worldlings, and sluggards, that trouble not their thoughts much about it, then you might have some excuse for your inconsiderateness. But it is not so; there are difficulties in your way; and they are many and great. What a dark understanding have you to inform; what a dull and backward nature to spur on; what an unreasonable appetite; what raging passions; what violent rebellious senses to contend with, to master and to rule! Abundance of adversaries on every hand: a subtle devil, as malicious as subtle, and as furious and able to do you a mischief, if God restrain him not. A world of wicked men about you; each one more stiff in error than you in

the truth; and more fast to the devil than you are to God, if his grace do not hold you faster than you will hold yourselves; and therefore they are abler to deceive you, than you are to undeceive them: many of them are crafty and can puzzle such ignorant beginners as you, and can put a face of reverence and truth upon damnable errors and pernicious ways; while those that have not wisdom, have foolish violence, scorn and passion, and can drive you towards hell, if they cannot draw you. All these enemies you must conquer or you are lost. Is it not time for a man in so much danger to consider of them, that he may know how to escape; and for one that is compassed about with such difficulties, to consider how he may well get through them? What abundance of things have you to consider of! Of all your life past; of the relations you have borne, and how you have performed the duties of those relations; of the time you have had, and how you have spent it; of the means you have had, and what you have received by them; of the present state of your souls, your sins, your miseries, your hopes, and the duties that are incumbent on you, in order to your recovery; of the temptations to be encountered with; and the graces that are daily to be exercised and confirmed! Would not a man bethink himself with all possible care, and consider, an hundred times consider, that hath all this to do, or be undone for ever? You have much to know that will not easily be known, and yet must be known; much to do, receive and suffer, that hath difficulty adjoined with necessity: were it necessary and not hard, the facility might draw you to make light of it. And were it hard and not necessary, the difficulty might more discourage you than the matter would excite you: but when it must be done, or you must be shut out of heaven, and lie in hell for it world without end, yet there are so many difficulties in the way, I think it is time to look about you, and seriously consider.

12. To conclude; consideration would prevent a world of misery, which else would make you consider when it is too late. It must be a principal means of your salvation if ever you be saved. If God have so much mercy for you, he will make you consider; set your sins in order before you, set hell fire before your face, and hold your thoughts on it that you cannot look off. He will set before you a crucified Christ, and tell you that this your sins have done, and make you think of the reason of his sufferings; what there is in sin that could require it; and what it is to rebel against the Lord, and run

yourselves into the consuming fire. Now your thoughts are gadding abroad the world, and running after every trifle, and going away from God; but if ever God will save you, he will overtake your hearts, bring them home, and show them that they have somewhat else to think on. If commands will not serve, he will send out his threatenings, terrors shall come upon you, and pursue your soul as the wind; he will bring you out of the alehouse and the gaming house, and take you off the trifling humour, and lay that upon your heart that you shall not easily shake off. If you are taken up with the cares of the world, he will show you that you have somewhat else to care for; and drown those cares in greater cares. If you have such giddy, unsettled, vagrant minds, that you cannot call in your thoughts of God, nor hold them with him, he will lay those clogs and bolts upon them at first, that shall restrain them from their idle vagaries; and then he will set upon them such a bias, as shall better order them, and fix them for the time to come. Men do not go to heaven, and never think of it: and to escape hell fire, the plague of sin, the curse of the law, the wrath of God, the rage of Satan, and never think on it; nor do they use to mind other matters, and find themselves in heaven, before they ever dreamed of it, or before their hearts were set upon it. No; if ever God will save you, he will make you consider, and again consider, and perhaps with many a sigh and groan: and bring these things so near your hearts, that you shall not only think on them, but feel them; they shall be as written before your eyes; you shall think of them when you lie down, and when you rise up, as if they were written upon the tester of your beds; you shall think of them when you sit at home, when you go abroad, as carrying them still with you, which way soever you go. As before, God was not in all your thoughts, so now he will be the sum and end of them all.

If by your resistance you escape these considerations, believe it, God will bring you to consideration by a severer and more dreadful way. If he but give your conscience a commission, it will follow you, and bring you to such a consideration as Judas was brought to. If he lay you under his judgments, and speak to you by his rod, and give you a lash with every word, and ask you whether yet you will consider of it, it may bring such things to your thoughts, as you were little troubled with before. If he say but the word, how soon will your soul be required of you! And when you lie in hell and feel the smart, you will then consider of it. Now we

cannot beg of you to bestow one hour in sober consideration; but then you shall do it without intreaty; then you will be as a man that hath the stone, or gout, or toothache, that cannot forget it, if he would never so willingly. Forget your folly, your obstinacy, and unthankfulness then, if you can; forget God's wrath, and the torment which you then feel, if you can. Now you were so busy that you could not have time to think of the matters of the world to come; but then God will give you leisure; you shall have little else to do: you shall have time enough: when you have thought of these things ten thousand years, you shall still have time enough before you to think of them again. You will not consider now, but when 'God hath performed the intents of his heart, in the latter days, you shall perfectly consider it.—O that you were wise, that you understood this; that you would consider your latter end!'

What brings so many thousand souls to hell, but because they would not consider in time? If you could speak with any of those hopeless souls, and ask them, how came you to this place of torment; they would tell you, 'because we did not consider of our case in time; we little thought of this day, though we were told of it; we had a load of sin upon us, and did not consider how we might be relieved: we had Christ and mercy set before us, but we did not consider the worth of them, nor how to be made partakers of them: we had time, but we considered not how to make the best of it: we had the work of our salvation lying upon our hands, but we did not consider how we might accomplish it: O had we but considered what now we feel, we might have escaped all this, and have lived with God!' These would be the answers of those miserable souls, if you could but ask them the cause of their misery. There is scarcely a thief or a murderer hanged at the gallows, but will cry out, O if I had but had the wit and grace to have considered this in time, I need not have come to this! There is scarcely a spendthrift that falls into beggary, no, nor a man that comes into any mischance, but will say, If I had considered it beforehand, I might have prevented it. Most of the calamities of the world might have been prevented, by timely and sober considerations. God himself doth place men's wickedness much in their inconsiderateness, and lays the cause of their destruction upon it. Whence is it that Israel was rebellious to astonishment? 'Why, Israel doth not know, my people doth not consider.—He shall break in pieces mighty men without number, and set others in their stead:

therefore he knoweth their works, he overturneth them in the night, so that they are destroyed. —He striketh them as wicked men in the open sight of others, because they turned back from him, and would not consider any of his ways.' Why do men live so wilfully in sin, but because 'they consider not that they do evil ; how many such hath the world that God pronounces a woe to, who drink, play, and give themselves to their merriments, 'but they regard not the work of the Lord ; neither consider the operation of his hands. They consider not in their hearts the folly of their ways.' When they see God's judgments, they consider not the meaning of them, and therefore lay them not to heart.

When God calls men to conversion, or reformation, he calls them to consideration as the way to it ; ' Thus saith the Lord of hosts, consider your ways.' The son that shall escape the misery of his father, is he that, 'considereth, and turneth away from his transgressions, considereth, and doth not his forefathers' work.' When he sends the prophet to them, it is but with this encouragement ; ' Though they are a rebellious house, it may be they will consider.' David professes, that consideration was the beginning of his conversion, 'I thought on my ways, and turned my feet unto thy testimonies. I made haste, and delayed not to keep thy statutes.'

I know that it is the Lord that must renew and revive a sinful soul ; but yet, under God, consideration must do much. O could we but persuade our people to consider, it is not certainly possible that they could be as they are, or act as they do. Would so many thousands live in ease, and quietness under the guilt of so many sins, and the wrath of God, if they did but well consider of it. Durst they live so peaceably in a state of death and in the slavery of the devil, if they did but well consider of it? Would they do no more to prepare for their speedy appearing before God, and for the escaping of hell fire, if they did but consider of it ? Would they swallow down their cups so greedily, and give up themselves to the world so eagerly, if they did but well consider what they do ? Methinks they should not. The cause of sin, and the devil, is so bad, that I should hope to shame it with the most of the ungodly, if I could but bring them to a serious consideration of it. O how the kingdom of Satan would fall, if we could but tell how to make them considerate ! How fast the devil would lose his servants ! What abundance Christ would gain ! How many would be saved, if we could but tell how to make men considerate ! One would think

that this should be easily done, seeing man is a self-loving and reasonable creature: but yet to our grief, and great sorrow, we cannot bring them to it. I should not doubt, but one sermon, or one sentence of a sermon, might do more good than a hundred do now ; if I were but able to persuade the hearers when they come home, to follow it by serious consideration. But we cannot bring them to it : if our lives lay on it, we could not bring them to it ; though we know that their own lives and salvation lies on it, yet can we not bring them to it. They think, and talk of other matters almost as soon as the sermon is done ; and they turn loose their thoughts ; or if they do read, hear, or repeat a little, yet cannot we get them to one half-hour's secret and sober consideration of their case. This is the reason why it is so rare a thing to see men thoroughly turn to God. This is much of the use of all God's teachings, and afflictions too, but to bring men to sober consideration. God knows that sin hath unmanned us, and lost us the use of our reason, where we have most use for it ; therefore the means and works of God, are to recover us to our reason, and to make us men again : the very graces of his Spirit are to make us to be more reasonable.

Now, before I dismiss this direction, I have a question, and a request, to make to thee, whoever thou art, that readest these lines. My question is this, hast thou ever soberly considered of thy ways and laid these greatest matters to heart, or hast thou not ? Dost thou ever use to retire into thyself, and spend any time in this needful work ? If thou dost not, my request to thee is, that now at last thou wouldst do it without delay. Shall I beg this of thee ; shall the Lord that made thee, that bought thee, that preserves thee, request this of thee ; that thou wouldst sometimes betake thyself into some secret place and set thyself purposely to this work of consideration, follow it earnestly, and close with thy heart till thou hast made something of it, and brought it to a resolution ? Wilt thou then spend a little time in reasoning the case with thyself, calling thy heart to a strict account, and ask thyself, ' What is it that I was made for ; and what business was I sent into the world about ; how have I despatched it ; how have I spent my time, my thoughts, my words ; and how shall I answer for them ? Am I ready to die, if it were this hour ; am I sure of my salvation ; is my soul converted, and truly sanctified by the Holy Ghost ? If not, what reason have I to delay ? Why do I not set about it, and speedily resolve ? Shall I linger till death come and find me unconverted? O then what a sad appearance shall I make before the Lord! And thus follow on the discourse with your hearts. What say you? Will you here promise me to bestow but some few hours, if it be but on the Lord's day, or when you are private on the way, or in your beds, or in your shops, in these considerations? I beseech you, as ever you will do any thing at my request, deny me not this request. It is nothing that is unreasonable. If I desired one of you to spend an hour in talking with me, you would grant it; yea, or if it were to ride, or go for me: and will you not be intreated to spend now and then a little time in thinking of the matters of your own salvation? Deny not this much to yourselves, deny it not to God, if you will deny it me. Should you not bethink you a few hours, of the place and state that you must live in for ever? Men will build strong where they think to live long; but a tent or a hut will serve a soldier for a few nights. O, eternity is a long day. In the name of God, let not conscience have such a charge as this against you hereafter; thou art come to thy long home, to thy endless state, before ever thou spentest the space of an hour, in deep, sad, and serious considerations of it, or in trying thy title to it. O what a confounding charge would this be! I am confident I have the witness of your consciences going along with me, telling you it is but reasonable, yea, and needful, which I say. If yet you will not do it, and I cannot beg one hour's sober discourse in secret, between you and your hearts, about these things, then what remedy, but even to leave you to your misery. But I shall tell you, in the conclusion, that I have no hope of that soul that will not be persuaded to this duty of consideration: but if I could persuade you to this reasonable, this cheap, this necessary work, and to follow it close, I should have exceeding great hopes of the salvation of you all. I have told you the truth, 'consider what I say, and the Lord give you understanding.' Or if you put me to conclude in harsher terms, they shall be still the oracles of God; 'Now consider this, ye that forget God, lest I tear you in pieces, and there be none to deliver you.'

So much for the third direction, about consideration; on which I have staid somewhat long, because I apprehend it of exceeding necessity.

DIRECTION IV.

The fourth direction which I shall give you, that the work of your conversion may not mis-

carry, is this: 'See that the work of humiliation be thoroughly done, and break not away from the Spirit of contrition before he have done with you; yet see that you mistake not the nature, the ends of the work, and that you drive it not on further than God requires you.'

Here I shall, 1. Show you the true nature of humiliation: 2. The use and ends of it; 3. The mistakes about it, that you must avoid; and, 4. I shall improve the substance of the direction, and show you the necessity of it.

SECT. I. There is a preparatory humiliation that goes before a saving change, which is not to be despised, because it is a drawing nearer unto God, though it be not a full submission to him. This preparatory humiliation, which many have that perish, doth chiefly consist in these things following. It lies most in the fear of being damned: as it is most in the passions, so most in this of fear. It consists also in some apprehensions of the greatness of our sins, the wrath of God that hangs over our heads, and the danger that we are in of being damned for ever. It consists also in some apprehensions of the folly that we are guilty of in sinning, and of some repentings that ever we did it, and some remorse of conscience for it. Hereto may be joined some passions of sorrow, and this expressed by groans and tears. All this may be accompanied with confessions of sin to God and man; lamentations for our misery, and in some it proceeds to desperation itself. And lastly, it may proceed to an indignation against ourselves, and to the taking of a severe revenge on ourselves, yea, more than God would have men take; as Judas did by self-destroying. This desperation and self-execution are no parts of the preparatory humiliation; but the excess, the error of it, and the entrance upon hell.

But there is also a humiliation that is proper to the converted, which accompanies salvation, and this contains in it all that is in the former, and much more: even as the rational soul contains the sensitive, vegetative, and much more. And this saving humiliation consists in these following particulars.

It begins in the understanding; it is rooted in the will. It works in the affections; and when there is opportunity it shows itself in outward expressions and actions.

1. Humiliation in the understanding consists in a low esteem of ourselves, and in a self-abasing, self-condemning judgment on ourselves; and that in these particulars.

It consists in a deep and solid apprehension of the odiousness of our own sins, habitual and actual, and of ourselves for our sins ; that because they are contrary to the blessed nature and law of God, and so contrary to our own perfection and chief good. It consists also in a solid and fixed apprehension of our own ill-deserving, because of these sins ; so that our judgments subscribe to the equity of the condemning sentence of the law ; and we judge ourselves unworthy of the smallest mercy, and worthy of everlasting punishment. It consists in an apprehension of our undone and miserable condition in ourselves: not only as we are the heirs of torment, but as we are void of the image and Spirit of God, have lost his favour, are under his displeasure and enmity by our sin, have forfeited our part in everlasting glory, and how unable we are to help ourselves.

This is in such a measure, that we truly judge our sin, and ourselves for sin, to be more odious than any thing else could have made us, and our misery by sin in the foresaid particulars, to be greater than any outward calamity in the flesh, and than any worldly loss could have procured us. This we apprehend by a practical judgment, and not only by a bare, ineffectual speculation. The spring of this is some knowledge of God himself, whose Majesty is so glorious, and whose wisdom is so infinite ; who is so good in himself, and unto us, whose holy nature is contrary to sin, who hath an absolute propriety in us, and sovereignty over us. It also proceeds from a knowledge of the true state of man's felicity, which by sin he hath cast away ; that it consists in the pleasing, glorifying, and enjoying of God, in loving and delighting in him ; and praising him for ever, and having a nature perfectly holy, and fitted hereunto. To see that sin is contrary to this felicity, and hath deprived us of it, is one of the springs of true humiliation. It proceeds also from a believing knowledge of Christ cruci-fied, whom our sins did put to death, who hath declared in the most lively manner to the world by his cross, and sufferings, what sin is, what it hath done, and what a case we had brought our-selves into. Thus much of saving humiliation consisting in the understanding.

The principal seat of this humiliation is in the will, and there it consists in these following acts. As we think basely of ourselves, so the will has a fixed displeasure against ourselves for our sins, and a kind of lothing of ourselves for all our abominations. A humble sinner is fallen out with himself, and as he is evil, his heart is against himself.

There is also in the will a deep repenting that ever we sinned, wronged God, abused grace, and have brought ourselves to this as we have done ; so that the humbled soul could wish that he had spent his days in prison, in beggary, or in bodily misery, so that he had not spent them in sin ; and if it were to do again, he would rather choose such a life of shame and calamity in the world, than a life of sin, and would be glad of the exchange.

An humbled soul is truly willing to grieve for the sins which he hath committed, and to be as deeply sensible of them, and afflicted for them, as God would have him. Even when he cannot shed a tear, yet his will is to shed them. When he cannot feel any deep afflicting of his soul for sin, his hearty desire is, that he might feel it. He doth an hundred times weep in desire, when he doth it not in act.

An humble soul is truly willing to humble the flesh itself, by the use of those appointed means by which God would have him bring it in subjection, as by fasting, or abstinence, or mean attire, hard labour, and denying it unnecessary delights. It is a doubt worth the considering, whether any such humbling act must be used, purposely in revenge on ourselves for sin. To which I answer, that we may do nothing in such revenge that God doth not allow, or that makes our body less fit for his service; for that were to be revenged of God, and our souls; but those humbling means which are needful to tame the body, may well be used with this double intention : first and chiefly, as a means for our safety and duty for the time to come; that the flesh may not prevail, and then collaterally we should be the more content that the flesh is put to so much suffering, because it hath been and still is so great an enemy to God and us, and the cause of all our sin and misery ; this is the revenge that is warrantable in the penitent, and some think is meant.

As the humbled soul hath base thoughts of himself, so he is willing that others should es-teem and think of him accordingly, even as a vile unworthy sinner, so far as his disgrace may be no wrong to the gospel, or to others, or dis-honour to God. His pride is so far taken down, that he cannot endure to be vilified with some consent ; not approving of the sin of any man that doth it maliciously, but consenting to the judgment and rebukes of those that do it truly, and to the judgment of God, even by them that do it maliciously. The humbled soul does not stand defending and unjustly extenuating his sin, excusing himself, and swelling against the re-prover ; whatever he may do in a temptation, if this tempter were predominant, his pride, and not humility must be predominant. But he judges himself as much as others can justly judge him, and humbly consents to be base in men's eyes, till God shall think it meet to raise him and recover his esteem.

The root of all this in the will is, a love to God, whom we have offended ; a hatred of sin that hath offended him, and that hath made us vile ; a believing sense of the love and sufferings of Christ, that in his flesh hath condemned sin. Thus you see what humiliation is in the will, which is the very life and soul of true humiliation.

3. Humiliation also consists in the affections ; in an unfeigned sorrow for the sin which we have committed ; the corruption that is in sin ; a shame for these sins ; a holy fear of God whom we have offended, and of his judgments which we have deserved ; and the hatred of our sins by which we have deserved them. But, as I must further show you, it is not the measure, but the sincerity of these passions, by which you must make a judgment of your state ; and that will be hardly discerned by the passions themselves, but only by so much of the will as is in them, and therefore the will is the safest to judge by.

4. Humiliation also consists expressively in the outward action, when opportunity is offered ; and it is not true in the heart, if it refuse to appear without, when God requires it in your ordinary course. The outward acts of humiliation are these : a voluntary confession of sin to God, and to men, when God requires it, and that is, when it is necessary to his honour, to the healing of them that we have endangered, and satisfying the offended ; at least in the hearing of men, in such cases as these to confess them openly to God : an unhumbled soul will refuse this for the shame ; but the humble will freely take shame to themselves, and warn their brethren, and justify God, and give him the glory, ' if we confess our sins, he is faithful and just to forgive us.— Confess your faults one to another, and pray one for another that ye may be healed.—He that hideth his sins shall not prosper : but he who confesseth and forsaketh them, shall have mercy.' Not that any man is to confess his secret sins to others, except in case that he cannot otherwise find relief ; nor that a man is to publish those offences of his own, by which he may further dishonour God, and hinder the gospel : but when the sin is open already, and especially when the offence of others, the hardening of the wicked, the satisfaction of the church, concerning our repentance, require our confession, and open lamentation, the humble soul both must and will

submit to it ; but the rotten-hearted, unhumbled hypocrite will confess but in these cases ; when the secrecy of the confession, or the smallness of the fault, or the custom of such confession, makes it to be a matter of no great disgrace. Or when it is so open, that it is in vain to attempt to hide it, and his confession will do nothing to increase the disgrace. Or when conscience is awakened, or they see they must die, or are forced by some terrible judgment of God ; in all these cases the wicked may confess. So Judas will confess, ' I have sinned in betraying the innocent blood ;' Pharaoh will confess ' I and my people have sinned.' A thief on the gallows will confess ; and the vilest wretches on their death-bed will confess : but we have more death-bed confessions than voluntary confessions before the church. Nay, so far hath pride and hypocrisy prevailed, and the ancient discipline of the church been neglected, that I think in most places in England there are many more that make confessions on the gallows, than personally in the congregation.

Humiliation must be also expressed by all those external means and signs which God, by scripture or nature, calls us to. As by tears and groans, so far as we can seasonably procure them ; by fasting, and laying by our worldly pomp and folly, and using mean, although decent attire ; by condescending to men of the lower sort, and stooping to the meanest : by humble language and carriage ; and by forgiving others, on this account, that we are sensible of the greatness of our debts to God. Thus I have briefly showed you the true nature of humiliation, that you may know what it is that I am persuading you to, and which you must submit your hearts unto.

SECT. II. When I have told you the use and ends of humiliation, you will see more of the reason of its necessity to yourselves. And first, it is one use of humiliation, to help on the mortification of the flesh, or carnal self, and to annihilate it as it is the idol of the soul. The nature of man's sinful and miserable estate, is, that he is fallen from God to himself ; and lives now to himself, studying, loving, and pleasing himself, his natural self above God. A sinner will let go many outward sins, and be driven from the out-works before he will let go carnal-self and be driven from the castle and strength of sin. There is no part of mortification so necessary and so hard, as self-denial : indeed this doth virtually comprehend all the rest, and if this be done, all is done. If it were but his friends, his superfluities, his house, his lands, perhaps a carnal heart might part with it. But to part with his life, his all, his self, this is a hard saying to him, and enough to make him go away sorrowful; therefore here appears the necessity of humiliation: this lays all the load on self, and breaks the heart of the old man, and makes a man lothe himself, that formerly doted on himself. It lays this tower of Babel in the dust, and makes us abhor ourselves in dust and ashes: it sets the house on fire about our ears, which we both trusted and delighted in; and makes us not only see, but feel, that it is time for us to be gone. Pride is the master vice in the unsanctified, and it is the part of humiliation to cast it down. Self-seeking is the business of their lives, till humiliation help to turn the stream: and then if you did but see their thoughts, you should see them think most vilely of themselves: and if you do but overhear their prayers or complaints, you shall hear them still cry out upon themselves, as their greatest enemies.

Second, The next use of humiliation, and implied in this, is, to mortify those sins which carnal-self doth live upon, and is maintained by; and to stop all the avenues or passages of its provision. Sin is sweet and dear to all that are unsanctified; but humiliation makes it bitter and base. As children are persuaded from playing with a bee-hive, when they are once or twice stung by them, or from playing with snappish dogs, when they are bitten by them: so God will teach his children to know what it is to play with sin when they are smitten by it. They will know a nettle from a harmless herb, when they feel the sting; we are so apt to live by sense, that God sees it needful that our faith have something of sense to help it. When the conscience doth accuse, the heart is smarting, and groaning in pain, and we feel that no shifting or striving will deliver us, then we begin to be wiser than before, and to know what sin is, and what it will do for us. When that which was our delight, is become our burden, and a burden too heavy for us to bear, it cures our delighting in it. When David was watering his couch with his tears, and made them his drink, his sin was not the same thing to him as it was in the committing. Humiliation washes away the painting of this harlot, and shows her in her deformity. It unmasks sin, which had got the vizard of virtue, or of a small matter, or harmless thing. It unmasks Satan, who was transformed into a friend, or an angel of light, and shows him, as we say, with his cloven feet. How hard is it to cure a worldling of the love of money? But when God hath laid such a load of it on his conscience,

that makes him groan, and cry for help, he hath then enough of it. When he begins to weep and howl for the miseries that are coming on him, and he sees the effect of his corrupted riches, and the canker of his gold and silver begin to eat his flesh as fire, and his idol is but a witness against him, then he is better able to judge of it, than he was before. The wanton thinks he hath a happy life, when the harlot's lips drop as the honey-comb: but when he perceives her end is bitter as wormwood, and sharp as a two-edged sword, and that her feet go down to death, and her steps take hold on hell, and he lies in sorrow, complaining of his folly, he is then of a more rectified judgment than he was. Manasseh humbled in irons, is not the same as he was upon the throne: though grace did more to it than his fetters, yet were they some way serviceable to that end. Humiliation opens the door of the heart, and tells you what sin is to the quick; and lets in the word of life, which passed no further than the ear or brain.

It is a tiring work to talk to dead men, that have lost their feeling; especially when it is an effective and practical doctrine, which we must deliver to them, which is lost if it be not felt and practised: till humiliation comes, we speak to dead men, or at least to men that are fast asleep. How many sermons have I heard that, one would think, should have turned men's hearts within them, and made them cry out against their sins, with sorrow and shame in the face of the congregation, and never meddle with them more! When yet the hearers have scarcely been moved by them, but gone away as they came, as if they knew not what the preacher said, because their hearts were all the while asleep within them. But a humbled soul, is an awakened soul: it will regard what is said to it; especially when they perceive that it comes from the Lord, and concerns their salvation. It is a great encouragement to us to speak to a man that hath ears, life, and feeling; that will meet the word with an appetite, take it with some relish, and let down the food that is put into their mouth. The will is the chief fort of sin. If we can there get in upon it, we may do something: but if it keep the heart, and we can get no nearer it than the ear or brain, there will no good be done. Now humiliation opens us a passage to the heart, that we may assault sin in its strength. When I tell you of the abominable nature of sin, that caused the death of Christ, and causes hell, and tell you that it is better to run into the fire, than to commit the least sin wilfully, though it be such as the world makes nothing of: another man may hear all this, and superficially believe it, and say it is true, but it is the humbled soul that feels what I say. What a stir have we with a drunkard, or worldling, or any other sensual sinner, in persuading him to cast away his sins with detestation; and all to little purpose! Sometimes he will, and sometimes he must needs be tasting them again; and thus he stands dallying, because the word hath not mastered his heart. But when God comes in upon the soul as with a tempest, throws open the doors, and as it were thunders and lightens in the conscience; lays hold upon the sinner, and shakes him all in pieces by his terrors, and asks him, Is sinning good for thee? Is a fleshly, careless life so good? Thou wretched worm! Thou foolish piece of clay! Darest thou thus abuse me to my face? Dost thou not know that I look on? Is this the work that I made thee for, that I feed and preserve thee, and continue thee alive for? Away with thy sin, without any more ado, or I will take thy soul away, and deliver thee to the tormentors. This awakens him out of his dalliance and delays; makes him see that God is in good earnest with him, and therefore he must be so with God.

If a physician have a patient that is addicted to his appetite, who hath the gout or stone, or other disease, and he forbid him wine, strong drink, or such meats as he desires; as long as he feels himself at ease, he will be venturing on them, and will not be curbed by the words of the physician; but when the fit is on him, and he feels the torment, then he will be ruled. Pain will teach him more effectually than words could do. When he feels what is hurtful to him, and feels that it always makes him sick, it will restrain him more than hearing of it could do. So when humiliation doth break your hearts, make you feel that you are sick of sin, and fills your soul with smart and sorrow, then you will be the more willing that God should destroy it in you. When it lies so heavy on you, that you are unable to look up, and makes you go to God with groans and tears, and cry, O Lord, be merciful to me, a sinner! When you are glad to go to ministers for ease to your consciences, fill their ears with accusations of yourselves, and open even your odious, shameful sins, then you will be content to let them go. Now there is no talking to you of mortification, and the resolute rejecting of your sins; the precepts of the gospel are too strict for you to submit to. But a broken heart would change your minds. The healthful ploughman saith, Give me that which I love: these physicians would bring us all to their rules, that they may get money by us; I never mean to follow their directions: but when sickness is upon him, and he hath tried all his own skill in vain, and pain gives him no rest, then send for the physician, then he will do any thing, take any thing whatever he will give him, so that he may but be eased and recovered. So when your hearts are whole and unhumbled, these preachers and scriptures are too strict for you; you must have that which you love: self-conceited, precise ministers must have leave to talk; but you will never believe that God is of their mind, or will damn men for taking that which they have a mind of. But when these sins are as swords in your hearts, and you begin to feel what ministers told you of, then you will be of another mind: away then with this sin; there is nothing so odious, so hurtful, so intolerable. O that you could be rid of it, whatever it cost you! Then he will be your best friend that can tell you how to kill it, and be free from it; and he who would draw you out, would be as Satan himself to you. Humiliation digs so deep, that it undermines sin, and the fortress of the devil: and when the foundation is rooted up, it will soon be overthrown. When the murderers of Christ were pricked to the heart, they then cried out for counsel to the apostles. When a murderer of the saints is stricken blindfold to the earth, and the Spirit withal doth humble his soul, he will then cry out, Lord what wouldst thou have me to do? When a cruel jailor that scourged the servants of Christ, is by an earthquake brought to a heart-quake, he will then cry out, 'What shall I do to be saved?'

Here comes in the usefulness of afflictions; even because they are so great advantages to humiliation. Men will be brought to some reason by extremities. When they lie a dying, a man may talk to them, and they will not so proudly fly in his face, or make a scorn at the word of the Lord, as in their prosperity they did. God will be more regarded when he pleads with them with the rod in his hand: stripes are the best logic and rhetoric for a fool. When sin hath captivated their reason to their flesh, the arguments to convince them may be such as the flesh is capable of perceiving. Sensuality doth brutify men in too great a measure: and so far as they are brutish, it is not the clearest reasons that will prevail; and if God did not maintain in corrupted man some remnants of free reason, we might preach to beasts as hopefully as to men. But afflictions tend to weaken the enemy that doth captivate them; as prosperity by accident tends to strengthen him. The flesh understands the language of the rod, better than the language of reason or of the word of God.

As the sensible part of our humiliation promotes mortification; so the rational and voluntary humiliation, which is proper to the sanctified, is a principal part of mortification itself. And thus you may see that it is necessary that we be thoroughly humbled, that sin may be thoroughly killed in us.

Third, Another use of humiliation is to fit the soul for a meet entertainment of further grace, and that both for the honour of Christ and grace, and for our own welfare.

(1.) In respect of Christ, it is equal that he should dwell in such souls only as are fit to entertain him. Neither his person, nor his business are such as can suit with the unhumbled heart. Till humiliation make a sinner feel his sin and misery, it is not possible that Christ, as Christ, should be heartily welcome to him, or received in that sort as his honour doth expect. Who cares for the physician that feels no sickness, and fears not death? He may pass by the doors of such a man, and he will not call him in; but when pain and fears of death are on him, he will send, seek, and bid him welcome. Will any man fly to Christ for succour, that feels not his wants and danger? Will they hold on him, as the only refuge of their souls, and cleave to him as their only hope, that feel no great need of him; will they lie at his feet, and beg for mercy, that feel themselves well enough without him? When men but hear of sin and misery, and superficially believe it, they may coldly look after Christ and grace; and feel the worth of the latter, in such a manner as they feel the weight of the former. But never is Christ valued and sought after as Christ, till sorrow have taught us how to value him; nor is he entertained in the necessary honour of a Redeemer, till humiliation throw open all the doors; no man can seek him with his whole heart, that seeks him not with a broken heart.

It is also certain that Christ will come on no lower terms into the soul. Though he come to do us good, yet he will have the honour of doing it; though he come to heal us, and not for any need he hath of us, yet he will have the welcome that is due to a physician. He came to save us, but he will be honoured in our salvation. He invites all to the marriage supper, and even compels them to come in; but he expects that they bring * a wedding garment, and come not in a garb that will dishonour his house.

Though his grace be free, yet he will not expose it to contempt, but will have the fulness and freeness of it glorified. Though he came not to redeem himself but us, yet he came to be glorified in the work of our redemption. He hath no grace so free, as to save them that will not esteem it, and give him thanks for it. Therefore though faith is enough to accept the gift, yet must it be a thankful faith, that will magnify the giver, and an humble faith that will feel the worth of it, and an obedient faith that will answer the ends of it. Therefore that faith which is the condition of our justification, is fitted as well to the honour of the giver, as the necessity of the receiver. And as reason tells us that it should be so, so Christian ingenuity consents that it be so. The soul that is truly united to Christ, and partakes of his nature, doth think its own receiving greatest, where the honour of Christ is greatest; and it cannot take pleasure in the thoughts of such a kind of grace as should dishonour the Lord of grace himself. As Christ is solicitous for the saving of the soul, so he makes the soul solicitous of the right entertainment of him that saves it. Therefore through his blood, and not his teaching or his government, was the ransom of our souls; yet he is resolved to justify none by his blood, but on the condition of that faith, which is a hearty consent to his teaching and dominion. It is not in the application, or bestowing of Christ's benefits, as it was in the purchasing of them. When he came to ransom us, he consented to be a sufferer, gave his cheeks to the smiter, and submitted to reproach; he endured the cross, despising the shame, and being reviled, he reviled not, but prayed for his persecutors: but when he comes by his saving grace into the soul, he will not there be entertained with contempt: for in the flesh he came on purpose to be humbled: but in the Spirit he comes to be exalted: in the flesh he came to condemn the sin that reigned in our flesh, and so was made sin for us, that is, a sacrifice for sin. But in the Spirit he comes to conquer our flesh, and by the law of his quickening Spirit, to free us from the law of sin and death; both that the righteousness of the law might be fulfilled in us, and also that there might be no condemnation to us, who walk not after the flesh, but after the Spirit.

The kingdom of Christ was not worldly; for if it had been worldly, he would have sought to establish it by strength of arms, and fighting, which are worldly means. But his kingdom is *within* us: it is a spiritual kingdom; and therefore though in the world he was used with con-

---

* It is customary among the orientals, that he who provides the feast, also furnishes the proper apparel for the occasion.—*Ed.*

tempt, as a fool, as a sinner, and a man of sorrows; yet within us he will be used with honour, and reverence, as a king and absolute Lord. It was the hour of the executioner and the power of darkness, when he was in his suffering; but it is the hour of his triumph, and marriage, and the prevailing power of the heavenly light, when he comes by saving grace into the soul. On the cross he was as a sinner, and stood in our place, and bore what was our due, and not his own. But in the soul he is the conqueror of sin, and comes to take possession of his own, and doth the work that belongs to him in his dignity; and therefore he will there be acknowledged and honoured. On the cross he was pulling down the kingdom of Satan, and setting up his own, but in the preparatory purchase: but in the soul he doth both by immediate execution. On the cross, sin and Satan had their full blow at him; but when he enters the soul, he hath his blow at them, and ceases not till he have destroyed them. In purchasing he expended his own: but in converting he takes possession of that which he purchased. In a word, he came into the world in flesh for his undertaking humiliation; but he comes into the soul, by his Spirit, for his deserved exaltation: therefore though he endured to be spit upon in the flesh, he will not endure to be slighted in the soul: as in the world he was scorned with the title of a king, and crowned with thorns, and clothed in such kingly robes, as might make him the fitter object for their reproach: so when his Spirit enters into the soul, he will be there enthroned in our most reverent, subjective, and deepest esteem, crowned with our highest love, and thankfulness, and bowed to with the tenders of obedience and our praise. The cross shall there be the portion of his enemies, and the crown and sceptre shall be his; and as all were preferred before him on earth, even Barabbas himself, so all things shall be put under him in the sanctified soul, and he shall be preferred before all.

This is the end of humiliation, to make ready the heart for a fuller entertainment of the Lord that bought it; and to prepare the way before him, and fit the soul to be the temple of his Spirit. An humbled soul would never have put him off with excuses from oxen, farms, and wives; but the unhumbled will care little for him.

(2.) As Christ himself will be honourably received, or not at all, so must the mercies, and graces, which he offers. He will not apply his blood and righteousness to them that care not for them: he will not pardon such a mass of iniquities, and remove such mountains as lie upon the soul, for them that feel not the necessity of such a mercy. He will not take men from the power of the devil, the drudgery of sin, the suburbs of hell, and make them his members and the sons of God, and the heirs of heaven, that have not learned the value of these benefits, but set more by their very sin and misery and the trifles of the world. Christ doth not despise his blood, his Spirit, his covenant, his pardon, nor his heavenly inheritance, and therefore he will give them to none that despise them, till he teaches them better to know their worth. Do you think it would stand with the wisdom of Christ, to give such unspeakable blessings as these to men that have not hearts to value them? Why, it is more to give a man justification, and adoption, than to give him all this visible world; the sun, the moon, the firmament, and the earth. And should these be given to one that cares not for them? Why, by this means God should miss of his ends: he should not have the love, the honour, or the thanks that he intended by his gift. It is necessary therefore that the soul be thoroughly humbled, that pardon may be received as pardon, and grace as grace, and not unduly neglected.

(3.) As this is necessary for the honour both of Christ and grace, so also it is necessary for our own benefit and consolation. The mercy cannot indeed be ours, if humiliation do not make us capable of it. These cordials must be taken into an empty stomach, and not be drowned in vanity and impiety. A man on the gallows will be glad of a pardon; but a stander by that thinks he is innocent, would not regard it, but take it for an accusation. There is no great sweetness in the name of a Redeemer, to an unhumbled soul. It values not the Spirit; the gospel is no gospel to it; the tidings of salvation are not so glad to such a one, as the tidings of riches or worldly delights would be. As it is the preparation of the stomach that makes our meat sweet to us; and the coarsest fare is more pleasant to the sound, than sweetmeats to the sick; so if we were not emptied of ourselves, vile, and lost in our own apprehensions, and if contrition did not quicken our appetites, the Lord himself, and all the miracles of saving grace, would be but as a thing of nought in our eyes; and we should be but weary to hear or think of them. But O what an unestimable treasure is Christ to the humbled soul! What life is in his promises! What sweetness in every passage of his grace, and what a feast in his immeasureable love!

(4.) The use of humiliation, implied in the former, is, that it is necessary to bring men to yield to the terms of the covenant of grace: nature holds fast its fleshly pleasures, and lives by feeling and upon present things, and knows not how to live upon invisibles, by a life of faith. This is the new life that all must live that will live in Christ: and therefore he calls them to the forsaking of all; the crucifying the world and flesh, the denying of themselves, if they will be his disciples: but O how loth is nature to part with all, and make a full resignation unto Christ! But anxiously it would make sure of present things, for fear lest the promises of heaven should but deceive them, and then they would have heaven at last as a reserve. On these terms it is that hypocrites are religious, and thus it is that they deceive their souls. But when the heart is truly broken; it will then stand no longer on such terms with Christ, but yield up all: it will then no longer propose conditions with him, but stand to his conditions, and thankfully accept them. Any thing will then serve with Christ, grace, and the hopes of glory.

(5.) Another use of humiliation is, to fit us for the retaining and improving of grace, when we have received it. The proverb is, 'lightly come, lightly go.' If God should give the pardon of sin to the unhumbled, how soon would it be cast away! How easily would such be hearkening to temptation, and returning to their vomit! 'The burned child,' we say, 'dreads the fire.' When sin hath killed you once, and broken your hearts, you will think the worse of it while you live. When a temptation comes, you will think of your former smart: 'Is not this it that cost me so many groans, laid me in the dust, and had almost damned me; and shall I go to it again? Was I so hardly recovered, by a miracle of mercy; and shall I run again into the misery that I was saved from? Had I not sorrow, fear, and care enough, but I must go back again for more, and renew my trouble? Thus the remembrance of your sorrows will be a continual preservative to you. A contrite spirit that is emptied of itself, and is taught the worth of Christ and mercy, will not only hold them fast, but will know how to use them, in thankfulness to God and benefit to himself.

(6.) Another use of humiliation is, to fit the soul for its approach to God himself, from whom it had revolted. As it beseems not any creature to approach the God of heaven, but in reverential humility, so it beseems not any sinner to approach him, but in contrite humility: who can come out of such wickedness and misery, and not bring along the sense of it on his heart? It

beseems not a prodigal to meet his father as confidently and boldly, as if he had never departed from him; but to say, 'Father, I have sinned against heaven, and before thee, and am no more worthy to be called thy son.' It is not ingenuous for a guilty soul, or one that is snatched as a brand out of the fire, to look towards God with a brazen face, but with shame and sorrow to hang down the head, and smite upon the breast, and say, 'O Lord, be merciful to me a sinner.—For God resisteth the proud, but giveth grace to the humble.—Though the Lord be high, yet he hath regard unto the lowly: but the proud he knoweth afar off.—For thus saith the high and holy One, that inhabiteth eternity; whose name is Holy; and I dwell in the high and holy place: with him also that is of a contrite and humble spirit, to revive the spirit of the humble, and to revive the hearts of the contrite ones.—To this man will I look, even to him that is poor, and of a contrite spirit, and that trembles at my word.—The Lord is nigh to them that are of a broken heart, and saveth such as be of a contrite spirit.—The sacrifices of God are a broken spirit: a broken and contrite heart, O God, thou wilt not despise.' There is no turning to God, unless we 'lothe ourselves for all our abominations.'

The nearer we approach him, the more we must abhor ourselves in dust and ashes. He will not embrace a sinner in his sins; but will first wash and cleanse him. Conversion must make us humble, as little children, that are teachable, and look not after great matters in the world, or else there is no entering the kingdom of God. And thus you see the uses and necessity of humiliation.

SECT. III. By what hath been already said, you may perceive what mistakes are carefully to be avoided, about your humiliation, and with what caution it must be sought.

1. One error that you must take heed of, is that you take not humiliation for an indifferent thing, or for such an appendage of faith as may be spared: think not an unhumbled soul, while such, can be sanctified. Some carnal hearts conceive, that it is only more heinous sinners that must be contrite and broken-hearted; and that this is not necessary to them that have been brought up civilly or religiously from their youth. But it is as possible to be saved without faith, as without repentance, and that special humiliation, which I described to you before, it is part of your sanctification.

2. Another mistake to be carefully avoided, is, the placing of your humiliation, either only, or principally in the passionate part, or in the

DIRECTIONS TO A SOUND CONVERSION.

outward expression of those passions. I mean, either in pinching grief, and sorrow of heart, or else in tears. But you must remember that the life of it is, as was said before, in the judgment and the will. It is not the measure of passionate sorrow and anguish, that will best show the measure of your sincere humiliation; much less is it your tears or outward expressions. But it is your low esteem of yourselves, and contentedness to be vile in the eyes of others; your displeasure with yourselves, and willingness to mourn and weep for sin as much as God would have you, with the rest of the judgment and will before described.

Two great dangers are here before you to be avoided. Some there be that have terrible pangs of sorrow, and are ready to tear their own hair, yea, to make away with themselves, as Judas, in the horror of their consciences; and these may seem to have true humiliation, and yet have none. And some can weep abundantly at a sermon, or in a prayer, or in mentioning their sin to others; therefore think that they are truly humbled; and yet it may be nothing. For if, at the same time, their hearts are in love with sin, or had rather keep it than let it go, or have not an habitual hatred to it, and a predominant superlative love to God, their humiliation is no saving work. That which is in the passions and tears, may be even forced against your wills; and it signifies scarcely so much as a common grace, where you are not willing of it. Many a one can weep through a passionate, womanish tender-nature, and yet not only remain unhumbled, but be proud in a very high degree. How many such do we ordinarily see! especially women, that can weep more at a duty or conference, than some that are truly broken-hearted could do in all their lives; and yet be so far from being vile in their own eyes, and willing to be so in the eyes of others, that they will hate, reproach, and rail at those that charge them with the faults which they seemed to lament; or at least that charge them with disgraceful sins; they will excuse and mince their sins, make a small matter of them, and love none so well as those that have the highest thoughts of them. So that pride does ordinarily reign in their hearts, break out in their words and lives, make them hate the most faithful reprovers, and live in contention with any that dishonour them, for all the tears that come from their eyes. Judge not therefore by passions, or tears alone, but by the judgment and the will, as is aforesaid. Another sort there are much better and happier than the former, that yet to their great trouble are mistaken in this point; and that is, they who think they have no true humiliation because they find not such pangs of sorrow, and freedom of tears, as others have, when as their hearts are contrite, even when they cannot weep a tear. Tell me but this; are you vile in your own eyes, because you are guilty of sin, and that against the Lord, whom you chiefly love? Do you lothe your sins, because of your abominations, and could you heartily wish that you had been suffering when you were sinning? And if it were to do again, would you choose to *suffer* rather than to *sin*; have you a desire to grieve, when you cannot passionately grieve, and a desire to weep when you cannot weep? Can you quietly bear it, when you are vilified by others, because you know yourselves to be so vile? And are you thankful to a plain reprover, though he tell you of the most disgraceful sin? Do you think meanly of your own sayings and doings, and think better of others, where there is any ground, than of yourselves? Do you justify God's afflictions and men's true rebukes, and think yourselves unworthy of the communion of the saints, or to see their faces, and unworthy to live on the face of the earth? Yea, would you justify if he should condemn you? This is the state of an humbled soul. Find but this, and you need not doubt of God's acceptance, though you were unable to shed a tear. There is more humiliation in a base esteem of ourselves, than in a thousand tears; and more in a will, or desire to weep for sin, than in tears, that come through force of terror, or moisture of the brain, or passionate tenderness of nature. If the will be right, you need not fear. It is he that most hates sin, and is most hard drawn to it, that is humbled for it. He that will lament it to-day, and commit it to-morrow, is far less humbled and penitent, than he that would not be drawn to it with the hopes of all the pleasures of the world, nor commit it, if it were to save his life.

3. To avoid this, some run into the contrary mistake, and think that sorrow and tears are unnecessary, and that they may repent as well without them as with them; they lay all in some dull, ineffectual wishes; and so they think the heart is changed. But certainly God made not the affections in vain. It cannot be that any man can have a sanctified will, but his affections will hold some correspondence with it, and be commanded by it. Though we cannot mourn in that measure as we desire, yet some sorrow there will be wherever the heart is truly changed, and apparently this sorrow will be the greatest. No man can heartily believe that sin is the greatest

evil to his soul, and not to be grieved for it; indeed our liveliest affections should be exercised about these weightiest things. It is a shame to see a man mourn for a friend, and repine under a cross, that touches but the flesh, yet be so insensible of the plague of sin, the anger of the Lord, and to laugh and jest with such mountains on his soul. Though grief and tears be not the heart, or principal part of our humiliation, yet are they to be looked after as our duty; yea, sorrow in some measure is of absolute necessity; and the want of tears is no good sign in them, that have tears for other things. Indeed the sense of our folly and unkindness should be so great, that it should even turn our hearts into sorrow, melt them in our breasts, and draw forth streams of tears from our eyes; if we cannot bring ourselves to this, we must yet lament the hardness of our hearts, and not excuse it.

4. In the next place you are hence informed, now to answer that question, whether it be possible for a man to be humbled, and repent too much. That part of humiliation which consists in the acts of the understanding and the will, cannot be too much as to the intention of the act; if it be too much as to the objective extent, then as it is misguided, so it changes its nature, and ceases to be the thing that it was before. A man may think worse of himself than he is, by thinking falsely of himself, as that he is guilty of the sin, which he is not guilty of; but this is not the same thing with true humiliation. But to have too clear an apprehension of the evil of his sin and his own vileness, this he need not fear. In the will it is more clear: no man can be too willing to be rid of sin, in God's time and way; nor be too much averse from it, as it is against the Lord. But then the other part of humiliation, which consists in the depth of sorrow, or in tears, may possibly be too much; though I know very few that are guilty of it, or need to fear it; because the common case of the world is to be stupid and hard-hearted; and most of the godly are lamentably insensible. But yet some few there are, that have need of this advice, that they strive not for too great a measure of grief. Let your hearts be against sin as much as is possible; but yet let there be some limits in your grief and tears. This counsel is necessary to these sorts of people. (1.) To melancholy people, who are in danger of being distracted, and made unreasonable and useless, by overmuch sorrow. Their thoughts will be fixing, musing, sad, dark and full of fears, and either make things worse than they are, or else be more deeply affected with them than their

heads can bear. (2.) This is the case of some weak-spirited women, that are not melancholy; but yet, by natural weakness of their brains and strength of their passions, are unable to endure those serious, deep, affecting apprehensions which others may desire; but the depth of their sensibility, and greatness of their passion, doth presently endanger the injuring of their judgment, and quickly cast them into melancholy, or worse.

This is a very heavy affliction, where it comes, both to the persons themselves, and those about them. To be deprived of the use of reason, is one of the greatest corporal calamities in this life. It is matter of offence, and dishonour to the gospel in the eyes of the ungodly, who understand not the case. When they see any languish in unmeasureable sorrow, or fall into distraction, it is a grievous temptation to them to fly from religion, avoid godly sorrow, and all serious thoughts of heavenly things, and it occasions the foolish scorners to say, that religion makes men mad; and that this humiliation and conversion which we call them to, is the way to bring them out of their senses. So that by reason of the grief of the godly, and the hardening of the ungodly, the case is so bad, that it requires our greatest care to avoid it.

Quest. But if it be so dangerous to sorrow, either too little or too much, what shall a poor sinner do in such a strait; and how shall he know when to restrain his sorrow?

Ans. There are but very few in the world that have cause to fear excess of this kind of sorrow. The common case of men is to be insensible; worldly sorrow doth cast more into melancholy and distraction than godly sorrow: but for those few who are in danger of excess, I shall first tell you how to discern it, and then how to remedy it.

When your sorrow is greater than your judgment can bear, without apparent danger of distraction, or a melancholy disturbance and diminution of your understanding, then it is certainly too much, and to be restrained. For if you overthrow your reason, you will be a reproach to religion, and you will be fit for nothing that is truly good, either to your own edification, or the service of God.

If you be in any grievous disease, which sorrow would increase to the hazard of your life, you have reason to restrain it: though you may not forbear repenting, or carefulness of your salvation, yet the passion of grief you must moderate and abate.

When sorrow is so great as to discompose your mind, or enfeeble your body, so as to unfit you for the service of God, and make you more unable to do good, or receive good, you have reason then to moderate and restrain it.

When the greatness of your sorrow doth overmatch the necessary measure of your love, or joy, or thanks, and keep out these, and takes up more of your spirit than its part, having no room for greater duties, then it is excessive and to be restrained. There are some that will strive and struggle with their hearts, to wring out a few tears, and increase their sorrow, that yet make little conscience of other affections, and will not strive half so much to increase their faith, love, and joy.

When your sorrow, by the greatness of it, doth draw you into temptation, either to despair, or think hardly of God and his service, or to undervalue his grace and the satisfaction of Christ, as if it were too scanty and insufficient for you, you have then cause to moderate and restrain it.

When your sorrow is unseasonable, and will needs thrust in at those times when you are called to thankfulness and joy, you have then cause to moderate and restrain it at that season. Not that we should wholly lay by sorrow in any day of joy and thanksgiving, unless we could lay by all our sin in the duties of that day. Nor should we wholly lay by spiritual comfort and delight, in days of greatest humiliation. For as our state is here mixed, of grace and sin, so must all our duties be mixed of joy and sorrow. It is only in heaven where we must have unmixed joys, and only in hell that there are unmixed sorrows; or at least, not in any state of grace. But yet for all that there are seasons now, when one of these must be more eminently exercised, and the other in a lower measure. As in times of calamity, and after a fall, we are called out so much to humiliation, that comfort should but moderate our sorrows, and the exercise of it be vailed for that time: so in times of special mercies from the Lord, we may be called out to exercise our thanks, praise, and joy so eminently, that sorrow should keep us humble, and be, as it were, serviceable to our joys. When grace and mercy is most eminent, then joy and praise should be predominant, which is through the most of a Christian's life, who walks uprightly and carefully with God: and when sin and judgments are most eminent, sorrow must be then predominant, as being a necessary means to solid joy. And therefore ordinarily a sinner that is but in the work of conversion, and newly coming to God from a rebellious state, must entertain more sorrow, and give himself more to groans and tears

than afterward, when he is brought to reconciliation with God, and walks in integrity.

Quest. But when is it that my sorrow is too short, and I should labour to increase it?

Answ. 1. When there is no apparent danger of the last-mentioned evils, that is, of destroying your bodies, distracting your minds, discomposing your faculties, and drowning other graces, duties, and the rest; then you have little cause to be afraid of an excess.

2. When you have not sorrow enough to cause you to value the love of Christ, to highly prize his blood, and the effects of it, to hunger and thirst after him and his righteousness, and earnestly beg for the pardon of your sin; you have cause to desire then more sorrow: if you feel no great need of Christ, but pass by him as lightly as the full stomach by the food, as if you could do well enough without him; you may be sure then you have need to be broken more. If you set not so much by the love of God, that you would part with any thing in the world to enjoy it, and would think no terms too dear for heaven; you have need to lie under the sense of your sin and misery a little longer, and to beseech the Lord to save you from that heart of stone, When you can hear of the love and suffering of your Redeemer without any warmth of love to him again, and can read or hear the promise of grace, offers of Christ, and eternal life, without any considerable joy, or thankfulness, it is time for you then to beg of God a tender heart.

3. When you make many pauses in the work of your conversion, and are sometimes in a good mind, and then again at a stand, as if you were yet unresolved whether to turn or not: when you stick at Christ's terms of denying yourselves, crucifying the flesh, and forsaking all, for the hopes of glory; and think these sayings somewhat hard, and are considering of the matter, whether you should yield to them or not; or are secretly reserving somewhat to yourselves; this certainly shows that you are not yet sufficiently humbled, or else you would never stand trifling thus with God. He must yet set your sins in order before you, and hold you a while over the fire of hell, and sound in your consciences such a peal as shall make you yield and resolve your doubts, and teach you not to dally with your Maker. If Pharoah himself be off and on with God, and sometime he will let Israel go, and then again he will not; God will follow him with plague after plague, till he make him yield, and be glad to drive, or hasten them away. Even where he deals in ways of grace, he makes so much use of sorrows, as to make men yield

the sooner to his terms, and glad to have mercy on such terms, if they were harder.

4. When you are heartless and dull under the ordinances of God, and scripture hath little life or sweetness to you, and you are almost indifferent whether you call upon God in secret or not; whether you go to the congregation, hear the word, join in God's praises and the communion of the saints; and you have no great relish in holy conference, or any ordinance, but do them almost merely for custom, or to please your consciences, and not for any great need you feel of them, or good you find by them; this shows for certain you want some more of the rod and spur; your hearts are not awakened and broken sufficiently, but God must take you in hand again.

5. When you are unmindful of God, and of the life to come, and forget both your sins and Saviour's blood, and set out your thoughts almost continually upon worldly vanities or common things, as if you were over-grown the need of Christ; this shows that the stone is yet in your hearts, that God must keep you to harder fare to mend your appetites, and make you feel your sin and misery, till it call off your thoughts from things that less concern you, and teach you to mind your everlasting state. If you begin to forget yourselves and him, it is time for you to have a remembrancer.

6. When you begin to taste more sweetness in the creature, to be more tickled with applause and honour, pleased more with a full estate, and more impatient with poverty, or wants, or wrongs from men, and crosses in the world; when you are set upon a thriving course, and are eager to grow rich, and fall in love with money; when you drown yourselves in worldly cares and business, and are cumbered about many things, through your own choice; this shows indeed that you are dangerously unhumbled; if God have mercy for you, he will bring you low and make your riches gall and wormwood to you, abate your appetite, and teach you to know that one thing is needful; to be more eager after the food that perishes not, and hereafter to choose the better part.

7. When you can return to play with the occasions of sin, or look upon it with a reconcilable mind, as if you had yet some mind on it, and could almost find in your heart to be doing with it again; when you begin to have a mind for your old company and courses, or begin to draw as near it as you dare, are gazing upon the bait, tasting of the forbidden thing, and can scarce tell how to deny your fancies, your appetites, your senses, your desires; this shows that you want some awakening work: God must yet read you another lecture in the black-book, and set you to spell those lines of blood which it seems you have forgotten; and kindle a little of that fire in your consciences, which else you would run into, till you feel and understand whether it be good playing with sin, the wrath of God, and everlasting fire.

8. When you begin to be indifferent as to your communion with God, think not much whether he accept you, and manifest his love to you or not, but can huddle up your prayers, and look no more after them, or what becomes of them, use ordinances, and seldom inquire of the success: when you can spare the spiritual consolations of the saints, and derive little of your comforts from Christ, or heaven; but from your friends, health, prosperity, and accommodations; and perhaps can be as merry in carnal company, when you say and do as they, as if you were considering of the love of Christ, this shows that the threatenings went not deep enough. Sorrow hath yet another part to play: you must be taught better to know your home, to take more pleasure in your father, your husband, your brethren, and your inheritance, than in strangers, or enemies to God and you.

9. When you begin to grow wanton with ordinances or other mercies, and instead of thankfully receiving them, and feeding on them, you pick quarrels with them, and nothing will please you; either the minister is too weak, or he is too curious, or too formal; you must have it this way or that way; either you must have more of a form, or no form; in this gesture, or that order, and something or other is still amiss: this shows that you want humbling, and that you are fitter for the rod, than for meat. If God but open you a door into your hearts and show you the evils and emptiness that are there, you will see, that the fault lay somewhere else than in the minister, or the ordinances: if it were in them, it was more in you. The cause of your lothing, and quarreling with the world, was the fulness of your own stomach; and God must give you a searching medicine, that shall make your hearts ache before it hath done working, and then your appetites will be mended, and your wantonness will cease; and that will be sweet to you which before you slighted.

10. When you begin to be leavened with pride, think highly of yourselves, have good conceits of your own parts and performances, would be noted and taken for somebody among the godly, and cannot endure to be overlooked or past by: when you think meanly of other men's parts

and duties in comparison of yours, think yourselves as wise as your teachers, begin to hear them as judges with a magisterial spirit, and think you could do as well as this yourselves; when you are finding fault with that which should nourish you, and in every sermon you are most noting the defects, and think that this you could have mended; when you itch to be teachers yourselves, and think yourselves fitter to preach than to learn, to rule than to be ruled, to answer than to ask for resolution; when you think so well of yourselves, that the church is not pure or good enough for your company, though Christ disowns it not, and they force you not to sin; when you grow censorious, and aggravate the faults of others, extenuate their graces, and can see a mote in another's eye, but will discern none of their graces, if they be not as high as mountains; and none can pass for godly with you, but those of the most eminent magnitude; when you are itching after novelties in religion, and setting your wisdom against the present or ancient church; and affecting singularity, because you will be of no common way; when you cannot hear this minister, nor that minister, though the ministers of Christ; and you are harping upon that, ' Come out from among them, and be ye separate;' as if Christ had called you to come out of the church, when he called you to come out of the company of infidels: all this cries aloud for farther humiliation; you have a swelling that must be opened, to let out the wind that puffs you up: if you be not for perdition, to be forsaken, and given over to yourselves, you must be brought over again and humbled with a witness. When God hath turned you inside outward and showed you that you are poor, miserable, blind and naked, and that you are empty nothings, who thought so well of yourselves; he will then make you stoop to those that you despised, and think yourselves unworthy of the communion of those that before you thought unworthy of yours. He will make you think you are unworthy to hear those ministers that you turned your back upon; he will take down your teaching, vain-talking, and make you glad again to be learners: in a word, he will by conversion make you as little children, or you shall never enter into the kingdom of heaven.

This spiritual pride is a most lamentable disease, and the issue usually is exceedingly sad. For with many, it is the forerunner of damnable apostasy; God gives them over to their own conceits, and the wisdom which they so esteem, till it have led them to perdition. And those that are cured, are many of them cured by the saddest way of any men in the world. For it is usual with God to let them alone, till they have run themselves into some abominable error, or fallen into some shameful scandalous sin, till they are made an hissing and by-word among men; that shame and confusion may bring them to their senses, that they may learn to know what it was that they were proud of, and see that they were but silly worms.

Thus I have showed you, when you must seek after deeper humiliation, and may conclude that you are not humbled enough. Yea, and when a greater measure is of some necessity to your souls.

Quest. Well, but yet you have not told us what course a poor sinner should take in such a strait, when he knows not whether his humiliation, as to the affectionate part, be too little or too much.

Answ. 1. You may partly discern yourselves by what is said, whether you have need of more or less humiliation, if you can but try your hearts by these signs. 2. But yet I would advise, and earnestly persuade you, in cases of difficulty, to betake yourselves to some able, faithful minister for resolution. If you feel sorrow seize so deep upon your spirits, that it distempers you, or threatens your understanding, or your health, especially if you are either passionate women, or melancholy persons: stay not then any longer, lest delay do that which easily cannot be undone, but go and open your case, and crave advice. This is a principal use of pastors, that you should have them at hand, to advise with in the diseases and dangers of your souls, as you do with physicians, in the diseases and dangers of the body. Lay by all sinful bashfulness, and trust not yourselves any longer with your own skill, but go to them that God hath set in office over you for such uses as these, and tell them your case: this is God's way, and he will bless his own ordinance: melancholy and passionate distempered persons are not fit judges of their own condition. In this case you must distrust your own understanding, and be not self-conceited, nor stick obstinately to every fancy that comes into your heads, but in the sense of your weakness rely upon the guidance of your faithful overseers; till your distempers are overcome, and you are made more capable of discerning for yourselves.

5. You are further here to be informed, that it is not for itself that sorrow and tears are so desirable; but as they are expressions of a gracious temper of the will, and as they help on the ends that humiliation is appointed to. Therefore you may hence learn in what way you must seek after it. (1.) You must not place the

chief part of your religion in it, as if it were a life of mere sorrow, that we are called to by the gospel. But you must make it a servant to your faith, love, and joy in the Holy Ghost, and other graces. As the use of the needle is but to make way for the thread, and then it is the thread, and not the needle that makes the seam; so much of our sorrow is but to prepare for faith and love, and these are they that unite the soul to Christ. It is therefore a sore mistake of some, that are very apprehensive of their want of sorrow, but little of their want of faith, or love; and that pray and strive to break their hearts, or weep for sin, but not much for those higher graces, which it tends to. One must be done, and not the other left undone.

(2.) As tears are the expression of the heart, so those are the most kindly and sincere which voluntarily flow from the inward feeling of the evil that we lament; if you could weep ever so much, merely because you think that tears are in themselves necessary, and had not within the hatred of sin, and sense of its vile and killing nature; this were not true humiliation at all. If the heart be humbled before the Lord, it is not the want of tears that will cause him to despise it. Some are so backward to weep by nature, that they cannot weep for any outward thing, no, not for the loss of the dearest friend, when yet they would have done ten times more to redeem his life, than some that have tears at will. Groans are as sure expressions of sorrow as tears, with such as these; and the hearty rejecting and detestation of sin, is yet a better evidence than either. But where men have naturally a weeping disposition, which they can manifest about crosses in the world, and yet cannot shed a tear for sin, there the case is the more suspicious.

(3.) The principal cause why you must strive for deeper sorrow, is, that you may obtain the ends of that sorrow; that sin may be more odious to you, and more effectually mortified; that self may be taken down, that Christ may be valued, desired, and exalted, and that you may be fitted for a holy communion with God for the time to come, saved from pride, and kept in watchfulness.

6. From this that was last said, you have a rule by which you may certainly discern, what measure of humiliation it is that must be had. It must go so deep as to undermine our pride; so far the heart must needs be broken, as is necessary to break the heart of sin and carnal self. If this be not done, there is nothing done, though you weep out your eyes. You must be brought so low, that the blood of Christ, and the favour

of God, may be more precious in your eyes than all the world, and in your very hearts preferred before it: and then you may be sure that your humiliation is sincere, whether you have tears or none.

7. From hence also you may see, that you must take heed of ascribing to your own humiliation any part of the office and honour of Christ: think not that you can satisfy the justice of the law, or merit any thing of God by the worth of your sorrows, though you should weep even tears of blood. It is not true humiliation if it consist not in the sense and acknowledgment of your unworthiness and desert of condemnation, and if it do not lead you to look out for pardon and life from Christ, as being lost and wholly insufficient for yourselves. Therefore it would be a plain contradiction, if true humiliation should be taken as satisfaction or merit, or trusted on instead of Christ.

SECT. IV. Having thus far opened the nature and reasons of true humiliation, I conclude with that advice which I principally here intended; refuse not to be thoroughly and deeply humbled. Be not weary of the humbling workings of the Spirit. Grief is an unwelcome guest to nature; but grace can see reason to bid it welcome. Grace is ingenuous, and cannot look back on so great unkindness, with unwillingness to mourn over it. There is somewhat of God in godly sorrow, therefore the soul consents to it, seeks for it, and calls it in: yea, and is grieved that it can grieve no more. Not that sorrow, as sorrow, is desirable, but as a necessary consequence of our grievous sinning, and a necessary antecedent of our further recovery: as we may submit to death itself, with a cheerful willingness, because it is sanctified to be the passage into glory, how dreadful soever it be to nature in itself; so much more may we submit to humiliation and brokenness of heart with a holy willingness, because it is sanctified to be the entrance into the state of grace. Consider for your satisfaction of these following things.

The main part of your sorrows will be but in the beginning: and when once you are settled in a holy course, you will find more peace and comfort than ever you could have had in any other way. I know if you will be meddling with sin again, it will in its measure breed sorrow again: but a godly life is a life of uprightness, conversion is a departing from sin, and consequently a departing from the cause of sorrows. Can you not bear such a sorrow for a little while?

2. Consider but whence you are coming: is

it not out of a state of wrath? Where have you have been all this while; was it not in the power of Satan? What have you been doing all your lives; hath it not been the drudgery of sin, the offending of your Lord, the destroying of yourselves? Is it meet, is it reasonable, is it ingenuous, to come out of such a case, without lamentation that you staid in it so long?

Consider also, that it is necessary to your own recovery and salvation. Do you think to take so dangerous a surfeit, and then to be cured without a suitable application? You will endure, for the health of your bodies, the bitterest pills and most lothsome potions, the shortest diet, and the letting out of your blood; for you know that your life lies on it, and there is no remedy. And should you not endure, for the saving of your souls, the bitterest sorrows, the keenest rebukes, the freest confessions, and the most plentiful tears? Sin will not be put down at easier rates: self will not be conquered else: the heart of it will not be broken, till your hearts be broken. We know your sorrows merit nothing, and make not God amends for your sins, nor is it for want of sufficiency in the blood of Christ that we require them. But it is part of the fruit of his blood upon your souls. If his blood do not melt and break your hearts, you have no part in him. It becomes you to mourn over him whom you have pierced; and this fruit of his blood is a preparative to more. You may as well think of being saved without faith, as without repentance and humiliation. Consider so much as is bitter in it, is of your own preparation; you may thank yourselves for it. Who was it that brought you to this necessity of sorrow? Have you been all your life-time surfeiting on the creature and causing your own disease, and now will you grudge at the trouble of a cure? Whom have you to blame and find fault with, but yourselves; was it not you that sinned; was it not you that laid in the fuel of sorrows, sowed the seeds of this bitter fruit, and cherished the cause of trouble in yourselves? God did not do this; it was you yourselves. He doth but undo that which you have been doing. Grudge not therefore at your physician, if you must be purged, bled, and dieted strictly, but thank yourselves for it that have made it so necessary.

Consider also, that you have a wise and tender physician, that hath known what sorrow and grief is himself, for he was made for you a man of sorrows, and therefore can pity those that be in sorrow; he delights not in your trouble and grief, but in your cure and after-consolations. Therefore you may be sure that he will deal gently and moderately with you, and lay no more on you than is necessary for your good; nor give you any bitterer cup, than your disease doth require. When he shows his greatest liking of the contrite, it is that he may revive their hearts; and he professes withal, that 'he will not contend for ever, nor be always wroth, lest the spirit should fail before him, and the souls which he hath made.' He calls to him 'the weary and heavy-laden, that he may give them ease. —He was sent to heal the broken-hearted; to preach deliverance to the captives, and recovering of sight to the blind, and to set at liberty them that are bruised.' When he hath broken your hearts, he will 'as tenderly bind them up and as safely heal them,' as you can reasonably desire. Even his ministers, who labour to break your hearts, and bring you low, even to the dust, have no worse meaning in it than to bring you to Christ, life, and comfort; though they are glad to see the weeping eyes of their hearers, and to hear their free confessions and lamentations, yet this is not because they take pleasure in your trouble, but because they foresee the saving fruits of it, and know it to be necessary to your everlasting peace. You may read what their thoughts are in the words of Paul, 'Now I rejoice, not that you were made sorry, but that ye sorrowed to repentance; for ye were made sorry after a godly manner, that ye might receive no damage by us in nothing. For godly sorrow worketh repentance to salvation, not to be repented of; but the sorrow of the world worketh death. For behold this self-same thing that ye sorrowed for after a godly sort, what carefulness it wrought in you: yea, what clearing of yourselves, yea, what indignation, yea, what fear, yea, what vehement desire, yea, what zeal, yea, what revenge.' Indeed neither Christ nor his ministers have that fond foolish love to you, and pity of you, as you have to yourselves. they are not so tender of you, as to save you from the sorrow which is needful to the saving of you from hell. But they would not put you to any more than is needful; nor have you taste a drop of the vinegar and gall, or shed one tear but what shall tend to your comfort and salvation.

Consider what sorrows they are that these sorrows prevent, and what those suffer in hell, that avoid this godly sorrow on earth. Your repenting sorrows are joys to those; yours have hope, but theirs are quickened with desperation; yours are small and but a drop to their ocean; yours are curing, but theirs are tormenting; yours are a father's rod, but theirs are the rack and gallows; yours are mixed with love, but theirs are unmixed, overwhelming them with confusion;

yours are short, but theirs are endless. Had you rather sorrow as they do, than as the godly do? Had you rather howl with devils and rebels, than weep with saints and children? Had you rather be broken in hell by torments, than on earth by grace? Is it not an unreasonable thing of you, to make such a stir at the sorrow that must save you, when you remember what it would save you from, and what all must suffer that are not humbled here by grace! O it is another kind of sorrow that others are now enduring. Grudge not at the opening of a vein, when so many thousands are for ever bleeding at the heart.

Consider, the more you are rightly humbled, the sweeter will Christ and all his mercies be to you ever after while you live. One taste of the healing love of Christ, will make you bless those sorrows that prepared for it. The same Christ is not equally esteemed even by all that he will save: had you not rather be emptied yet more of yourselves, that you may be fuller of Christ hereafter? When you do but feel his arms embracing you, and perceive him in that posture as the prodigal's father was, you will thank that sorrow which fitted you for his arms.

If you be thoroughly humbled, you will walk the more safely all your days, if other things correspond. It will make you hate the sin you smarted by, and fly the occasions of that which cost you so dear.

The sin of pride is one of the most mortal damning sins in the world; and that which thousands of professors miscarry by. Humiliation is most directly contrary to this; and therefore must needs be an amiable and necessary thing. It is worth all the sorrow that a hundred men endure here, to be saved from this dangerous sin of pride.

A thorough humiliation is usually a sign of the greater exaltation to come after. 'For those that humble themselves shall be exalted, and those that exalt themselves shall be brought low.— Humble yourselves therefore under the mighty hand of God, and he shall lift you up;' the higher you mean to build, the deeper you will dig to lay the foundation. Your consolations are like to be greater, as your sorrows have been greater: you may be free from those doubts that follow others all their days, lest they were never truly humbled. You need not be still questioning, or pulling up your foundations, as if you were to begin again. It is a sign that you are intended to greater employments, if other things concur. Paul must be laid exceedingly low in his conversion, that he might be the fitter as a 'chosen vessel, to bear Christ's name among the Gentiles.

Lay all this now together, and consider what cause you have to cherish the humbling works of grace and not to quench them. When your hearts begin to be afflicted for sin, go not among foolish and merry companions to drink or laugh it away: drive it not out of your minds, as unkindly, as if it came to do you hurt: but get alone, and consider of the matter, and on your knees in secret, beseech the Lord to follow it home, and break your hearts, and make you meet for his healing consolations; and not to leave you in this red sea, but to bring you through and put the songs of praise into your mouths.

DIRECTION V.

Having thus directed you about your humiliation, the next direction which I would offer you, that you may not miscarry in the work of conversion, is this: see that you submit to the Lord Jesus Christ, intelligibly, heartily, and entirely, as he is revealed and offered to you in the gospel. In this your Christianity consists, upon this your justification and salvation lie. This is the sum of your conversion, and the very heart of the new creature. The rest is all but the preparatives to this, or the fruits of it. Christ is the end and the fulfilling of the law; the substance of the gospel, the way to the Father, the life, the help, and the hope of the believer; if you know not him, you know nothing: if you possess not him, you have nothing, and if you are out of him, you can do nothing that hath a promise of salvation. Therefore I shall distinctly, though briefly, tell you what it is to obey Christ with the understanding, heartily, and with the whole soul, as he is offered in the gospel.

SECT. I. That you may obey Christ with the understanding, you must look to these things: that you understand who Christ is, as in his person and his offices; that you understand the reason of his undertaking; that you understand what it is that he hath done and suffered for us; that you understand the nature and worth of his benefits, and what he will do for you; that you understand the terms on which he conveys these benefits to men, and what is the nature, extent, and condition of his promise; and that you understand the certain truth of all this.

For the first, you must understand that Jesus Christ hath two natures in one person; that he is both God and man: as he is God of the same substance with his Father, and one in essence with him, the second person in the blessed Trinity; the word of God, the only begotten Son of the Father, eternal, incomprehensible, and infinite: as man he hath a true human soul and body as men have; so that his Godhead, his human soul, and his body, are really distinct. This human nature was conceived by the Holy Ghost in the Virgin Mary, without man, born of her, and is so truly united to the divine nature, as that they are one person: not that the Godhead is turned into the manhood, nor the manhood into the Godhead; but the Godhead hath taken the manhood into personal unity with itself. This was not from eternity, but when man had sinned, had lost himself, and needed a Redeemer. By reason of his miraculous conception, he was free from all original sin, being holy, harmless, and undefiled. His person and natures were fit for his office; which was to be Mediator between God and man, to make reconciliation, and recover us to God. Had he not been God, but mere man, his dignity would not have been sufficient for such an interposition, nor his obedience or sufferings of any such value, as to be the price of our redemption: nor could he have borne our burden, or conquered death, risen again, and overcome the prince of death, the devil; nor have ruled his church, and preserved, and sanctified them, and prospered his cause, and subdued his enemies, nor effectually interceded with the Father, nor judged the world, or raised the dead, and done the work of a perfect Saviour. Nor was the angelic nature sufficient for this office. Had he not been man, he had not been near enough to us to have suffered in our stead, taught us by his doctrine, and given us his example, nor could he have suffered, or died for us: for God cannot die or suffer. As he is God he is one in nature with the Father; and as he is man, he is one in nature with us; therefore is fit to mediate for us; and in him we are brought thus nigh to God. To this office of the Mediator there are many acts belonging, from whence it hath several denominations, of which more anon. So much of Christ's person.

The next thing that you must understand, is, the reasons and ends of his undertaking; which though we are not able fully to comprehend, nor the reason of any of the works of God, yet must we observe so much as is revealed. These following ends or reasons of this work, show themselves clearly in the scripture, and in the event.

(1.) One is, the demonstration of God's justice, as he is governor of the world, according to the law of nature. He made man a rational and voluntary agent, capable of good or evil, with desires and hopes of the good, fears of the evil, and so to be ruled according to his nature. He made for him a law that revealed good and evil, with promises to move him by desire and hope, and with threatenings to drive him by necessary fear. By these means God resolved to govern mankind. This law was the rule of man's duty, and of his receiving, or of God's judgment: according to this law, the world was to be governed by God. His governing justice consists in giving all their due according to his law: at least so far as that the end of the law may be attained, that is, the honour of the lawgiver preserved, transgression made odious by the terror of penalty, and obedience made honourable by its fruits and reward: otherwise the law would not have deterred effectually from evil, nor encouraged to good, especially to so much as creatures must go through for the crown of life: so the law would have been no fit instrument for the government of the world; that is, the law would have been no law. But this the wise and righteous God would not be guilty of, by making a law that was no law; that was unmeet for the ends to which he made it; which were essential to it as a law. There was no way to avoid this intolerable consequence when man had sinned, but strict execution of the law, or by sufficient satisfaction instead of such an execution. The execution would have destroyed the common-wealth, even the whole inferior world, at least the reasonable creature who was the subject. The wisdom and love, and mercy of God would not give way to this, that the world should be destroyed so soon after it was made, and man left remediless in everlasting misery: satisfaction therefore must be the remedy; this must be such as might be as fit to procure the ends of the law, as if the law itself had been executed; that is, as if the offenders had all died the death that it did threaten. It must therefore be a public demonstration of justice, and of the odiousness of sin, to the terror and warning of sinners for the future: and this was done by Jesus Christ, when none else in heaven, or earth could do it: for it did as fully demonstrate the justice of God, preserved his honour, and the usefulness of his law and government, that a person so high and glorious, and so dear to him, should suffer so much for sin, as if all the world had suffered for themselves. Thus God made him to be sin for us, who knew no sin. And thus Christ hath redeemed us from the curse of the law, being made a curse for us.

(2.) Hereby also God demonstrated the holiness of his nature ; how much he hates sin ; and how unreconcilable he is to it ; as light to darkness : as the law and judgments of God proceed from his perfect nature and will, so they bear the image of that perfection, and demonstrate it to the world. This therefore is the nobler end and work of Christ in our redemption, to declare the holiness and perfection of God in his nature and will ; though the former, the declaring of his governing justice, be the nearer end. If the death of Aaron's two sons were such a declaration, 'that he will be sanctified in all that draw near him ;' if his laws and present judgments declare him to be a holy and jealous God, that will not forgive sin, without a valuable consideration, or satisfaction, how much more evidently is this declaration in the death of Christ ? If the Bethshemites cry out, 'Who is able to stand before this holy Lord God ?' upon the death of five thousand and seventy men ; how much more may the guilty soul say so, when he thinks on the crucified Son of God ? As it is the end of God's execution on transgressors that ' the Lord may be exalted in judgment, and that God, who is holy, may be sanctified in righteousness ;' so was it his end in the sacrifice of his Son.

(3.) Another end of our redemption by Christ is, the demonstration of the infinite wisdom of God. His wisdom in the preventing the ruin of the created world ; that it might not be said that sin and Satan had frustrated him of the glory of his creation, and destroyed it almost as soon as he had made it : yea, in getting an advantage, by the malice of his enemies, for the more admirable attainment of the ends of his law, and the glorifying of all his governing attributes : he would not have made man a free agent, left him in the hand of his own will, and suffered him to sin, if his wisdom had not known how to secure his own interest and honour to the full. So also in the economy and admirable frame of his gracious and wise government by Christ, the manifold wisdom of God doth shine. As the wonderful structure of heaven and earth, and every part of this natural frame, doth gloriously reveal the wisdom of the Creator ; so the wonderful contrivance of our redemption by Christ, the restoration of the world by him, and the moral frame of this evangelical dispensation, doth wonderfully demonstrate the wisdom of the Redeemer. As the observation of our natures may give us cause to say with David, ' I will praise thee, for I am fearfully and wonderfully made ;' so the observation of our natures and condition may well cause us to say, ' I will praise thee :

for I am graciously and wonderfully redeemed ; marvellous are thy works, and that my soul knoweth right well.' As nature may teach us to admire the frame of nature ; so grace will teach us to admire the frame of grace ; to see the beauty of its several parts ; and much more of the whole, where all the parts are orderly composed.

(4.) Yea, the very power of God is demonstrated in Christ. Therefore he is called, ' the power of God, and the wisdom of God :' not only formally, because Christ himself is the wise and powerful God ; nor only efficiently, because God exercises his power and wisdom, by his Son in creation, redemption, and government ; but also effectually and objectively, as Christ is the great and most admirable demonstration of the power and wisdom of God in the world.

What work transcends the incomprehensible miracle of the incarnation ; that God should assume the nature of man into personal union ? The creation of the sun is no greater a work of power, than the incarnation and sending of the Son of God, the intellectual sun, the light of the world, ' that living light, that lighteneth every one that cometh into the world : though yet the darkness comprehendeth not his light.' What was he but the living visible power of God, when he healed all diseases, cast out devils, raised the dead, rose from the dead himself, ascended into glory, and sent down the Holy Spirit on his church, enduing them with power from on high. When he was on earth he was ' anointed with the Holy Ghost, and with power, and went about doing good, and healing all that were oppressed of the devil.' Being dead, ' he was declared to be the Son of God with power, by the resurrection from the dead.—When he ascended up on high, he led captivity captive.' Yea, he filled his servants with power. Even such as was admired and desired by the ungodly. He being 'the brightness of God's glory, and the express image of his person, and upholding all things by the word of his power, when he had by himself purged our sins, sat down on the right hand of the Majesty on high, being made so much better than the angels, as he hath by inheritance obtained a more excellent name than they.' As Christ therefore in his glorified humanity united to the godhead, is far more excellent than the angels of God, and more glorious than the sun, so is the power of God more abundantly demonstrated in him, than in the sun, or the angels, or any other creature. The illuminated know this, ' and what is the exceeding greatness of his power, to us-ward who believe, according to the working of his mighty power, which he wrought in Christ when he raised him from the dead and set him at his own right hand in the celestials, far above all principality, power, might, dominion, and every name that is named, not only in this world, but also in that which is to come ; and hath put all things under his feet, and given him to be head over all things to the church, which is his body, the fulness of him that filleth all in all.'

Besides this, even in the works of Christ for his church, his calling, sanctifying, ruling, and preserving them, his subduing their enemies, and raising them from the dead, and glorifying them with himself, how glorious is the very power of God by his Son ; and therefore his gospel may well be called ' the power of God to salvation,' which hath been the instrument of his power in doing such wonderful works in the world.

(5.) But the most sweet and conspicuous end of our redemption, was the demonstration of God's love and mercy to mankind, and that he might make known the riches of his glory on the vessels of mercy prepared unto glory. Of all God's attributes, there is none shines more illustriously in the work of our redemption than love and mercy. ' Hereby perceive we the love of God, because he laid down his life for us.' By the creation and sustaining of us we perceive the love of God, but more abundantly by our redemption. ' In this was manifested the love of God towards us, because that God sent his only begotten Son into the world, that we might live through him.' O wonderful love, which condescends to such rebels, and embraces such unworthy and polluted sinners, and pities them even in their blood ! Even after we had sold ourselves to Satan, cast away the mercies of our creation, had all come short of the glory of God, and were sentenced to death and ready for the execution, then did this wonderful love step in, and rescue and recover us. Not staying till we repented and cried for mercy, and cast ourselves at his feet ; but seeking us in the wilderness, and finding us before we felt that we were lost, and being found of us before we sought him, and beginning to us in the depth of our misery. ' Herein is love, not that we loved God, but that he loved us, and sent his Son to be the propitiation for our sins.' Though God love us not in our sin and misery before our conversion, so far as in that state to justify us, adopt us, and take pleasure in us, or have communion with us in the Spirit, yet doth he so far love us in that state, as to redeem us by the blood of Christ and tender us his salvation, and to bring in his chosen

effectually to entertain his offer. ' And thus the love of God is shed abroad in our hearts by the Holy Ghost which is given to us ; for when we were yet without strength, in due time Christ died for the ungodly, and commended his love towards us, in that while we were yet sinners, Christ died for us.—Greater love hath no man than this, that a man lay down his life for his friend.'

What was the Son of God, but love incarnate ? Love born of a virgin ; love coming down from heaven to earth, and walking in flesh among the miserable, seeking and saving that which was lost : was it not love that spoke those words of life, those comfortable promises, those necessary precepts, those gracious encouragements which the gospel doth abound with? Was it not love itself that went preaching salvation to the sons of death, and deliverance to the captives, and offered to bind up broken hearts ? Was it not love that invited ' the weary and heavy laden,' and that sent even to ' the highways, and the hedges to compel men to come in, that his house may be filled ?' Was it not love itself that went up and down healing diseases and doing good ; that suffered them for whom he suffered, to scorn him, spit upon him, buffet him, and condemn him; that being reviled, reviled not again ; that gave his life an offering for sin, died, and prayed for them that murdered him ? No wonder if the gospel be it that teaches us to call God by the name of love itself, for it is the gospel that hath most fully revealed him to be so. No wonder if the gospel do so frequently and importunately require us to love one another, and even to lay down our lives for Christ, and for one another, when it hath given us such a ground, motive, and precedent for our love. He that sees the true face of redemption, and understands and savours the gospel and the grace of Christ, must needs see most cogent reasons for such duties ; ' Beloved, let us love one another, for love is of God ; and every one that loveth is born of God, and knoweth God ; he that loveth not knoweth not God, for God is love.—If God so loved us, we ought also to love one another.—If we love one another, God dwelleth in us.' No wonder if by this love we know that we are translated from death to life ; and if by it the children of God be known from the children of the devil, for love is the very nature and image of our Father. No wonder if this be the ' new commandment,' which had newly such a powerful motive and example : and no wonder if it be the great distinguishing character, by which all men shall know that we are the disciples of Christ. When he had set us such a copy, and taught us this lesson by such effectual means, writing it out for us in lines of blood, even of his own most precious blood; and shedding it abroad in our hearts by the Holy Ghost.

But if we should come down to the particular benefits of Christ's death, and see what love is manifested in them. even in our calling, our justification, our adoption or sanctification, our preservation, and our everlasting glorification, we should find ourselves in an ocean that hath neither banks nor bottom; and when we have fathomed as far as we can, we must be contented to stand and admire it, and to say with the beloved apostle, 'Behold what manner of love the Father hath bestowed upon us, that we should be called the sons of God!'

This is the blessed employment of the saints, which they are called to by the gospel, to live in the participation, consideration and admiration of this wondrous love, 'that Christ may dwell in their hearts by faith, and so being rooted and grounded in love, they may be able to comprehend with all saints what is the breadth, and length, and depth, and height, and to know the love of Christ, which passeth knowledge, and be filled with all the fulness of God.—And withal, to be followers of God as dear children, and walk in love as Christ hath loved us, and given himself for us, an offering, and a sacrifice to God, for a sweet smelling savour.—And to love without dissimulation.—Even from a pure heart fervently.—That we love as brethren, being compassionate, pitiful and courteous; not rendering evil for evil, but contrariwise blessing; knowing that we are thereunto called, that we should inherit a blessing.—And that we keep ourselves in the love of God, that nothing may be able to separate us from it.' And if we thus imitate our heavenly pattern, 'the God of love and peace will be with us.' Thus I have showed you the principal ends of the undertaking of Christ in the work of our redemption, especially as they are attained directly by his cross, and resurrection.

Another end also is apparent in the scripture; which is the glorifying of God's rewarding justice, together with his mercy in the salvation of his elect. This end he partly attains here; God hath his ends continually: in this life his servants have much of his mercy; and the beginnings of their reward in the beginning of their salvation; but the fulness is hereafter in their glorification. All his promises he performs in their seasons. Even in the present pardon of our sins he honours his faithfulness and justice;

his faithfulness in making good his promise, his justice in rewarding the performers of the condition, and giving what his promise had made their due; that so men may even here, in part, 'discern between the righteous and the wicked, between him that serveth God and him that serveth him not;' while they see God's esteem of his people 'as his jewels, and spare them as a man spareth his son that serveth him.—The King of Zion is just, having salvation.—The righteousness of God is manifested in our justification.—Even the righteousness of God, which is by faith of Jesus Christ, unto all, and upon all them that believe; for there is no difference: for all have sinned and come short of the glory of God; being justified freely by his grace, through the redemption that is in Jesus Christ, whom God hath set forth to be a propitiation, through faith in his blood, to declare his righteousness for the remission of sins that are past, through the forbearance of God: to declare, I say, at this time his righteousness, that he might be just, and the justifier of him that believeth in Jesus.'

But it is most eminently at judgment, and in the world to come, that this remunerative justice with mercy will be glorified: when Christ shall come purposely, 'to be glorified in his saints, and to be admired in all them that believe,' not only in himself, but in them: and that because they were believers. When 'we have fought the good fight, and finished our course, and kept the faith, we shall find that there is laid up for us a crown of righteousness, which the Lord the righteous Judge shall give us, and all that love his appearing at that day.' He will justify and applaud them before all the world, yea, and adjudge them to everlasting life, with a 'well done, good and faithful servant, enter thou into the joy of thy Lord. I will make thee ruler over many things; even because they had been faithful in a little.' Because they showed their love to him and his members, he will say to them, 'Come, ye blessed of my Father, inherit the kingdom prepared for you from the foundation of the world.' He that now commands us to 'say to the righteous, it shall be well with him, will in righteousness cause it then to be well with him.—Then shall the righteous shine forth as the sun in the kingdom of their Father.' And the righteousness and mercy of their Father shall as conspicuously and gloriously shine in them. For it is a day appointed for the 'revelation of the righteous judgment of God, who will render to every man according to his deeds.—The present faith and patience of the saints in all the persecutions and tribulations which they endure, is a manifest token of the righteous judgment of God, that they may be accounted worthy of the kingdom of God, for which they suffer : it being a righteous thing with God to recompence tribulation to them that trouble us, and to us that are troubled, rest with the saints.—For the righteous Lord loveth righteousness.—And in righteousness will he judge the world.' And therefore ' in the keeping of his word there is a great reward.—Yea, a cup of water given in love to him, shall not be unrewarded.—To him that soweth righteousness shall be a sure reward.' If in this life men are forced to say, ' Verily, there is a reward for the righteous ; verily, there is a God that judgeth in the earth ;' much more when we receive the reward of the inheritance. This causes the saints to forsake the pleasures of sin, because ' they have respect to the recompence of reward.' This is what makes them rejoice and be exceeding glad in their persecutions, because that great is their reward in heaven: and therefore it is that they cast not away their confidence, because it hath great recompence of reward. If we let no man beguile us of our reward, and if we look to ourselves that we lose not those things that we have wrought, we shall receive a full reward. For the Lord hath said, ' Behold, I come quickly, and my reward is with me, to give every man according as his work shall be.'

7. Another end of Christ's undertaking in this blessed work is, the complacency and glory of God in the love, praise, and service of his redeemed ones ; in some measure here, but in perfection when they are perfected. Sin had made us unserviceable to God : Christ brings us back into a fitness for his service : he disposes us God-ward by faith and love : he hath redeemed us from our iniquity, and purifieth to himself a peculiar people, zealous of good works. To which he creates us, that we should walk in them. ' And with such sacrifice God is well-pleased.' The blood of the covenant was therefore shed, ' to make us perfect in every good work to do his will, who worketh in us that which is wellpleasing in his sight. This must be our care, ' to walk worthy of the Lord in all well-pleasing, being fruitful in every good work.—Then whatsoever we ask, we shall receive of him, because we keep his commandments and do those things that are pleasing in his sight.'

But principally when we are glorified, and fitted by our perfection for the perfect love and praises of God, then will God perfectly take pleasure in us, and in our love and praise. The glory of the new Jerusalem and the harmony of everlasting praise and thanksgiving will be his delight. He will rejoice over us with joy, he will rest in his love ; he will joy over us with singing.

Another end of Christ's undertaking this blessed work is, the everlasting glory of God which shall shine forth in the glorified manhood of the Redeemer, and the everlasting complacency that God will have in him, for his own perfection, and the work that he hath wrought.

Though Christ had no need to suffer for any sin or want of his own ; yet was it his personal dignity, dominion, and everlasting glory, as well as our salvation, that was intended by him and by the Father in this work, and which he was to receive as the reward of his performances. Nay, if we may make comparisons, this seems the highest part of God's end, in the sending of his Son. As there is no part of all the works of God to be compared to the person of the Redeemer, so consequently there is none in which the glory of God will shine forth so admirably and illustriously as in Christ. If on earth the heavenly voice bear witness that it was in him that the Father was well pleased, which was uttered both at his baptism, and transfiguration, when his disciples saw a glimpse of his glory, and he was the chosen servant of God in whom his soul delighted ; much more is it apparent, that in his heavenly glory he will be the Father's everlasting pleasure and delight: both in him, and by him, and for the work that he hath wrought, the redeemed in glory will honour him for ever. ' He is the head of the body, the church, the beginning, the first-born from the dead, that in all things he might have the pre-eminence : for it pleased the Father that in him should all fulness dwell. Therefore in him the glory of God will shine in fulness, and he shall have the pre-eminence in the Father's everlasting love. When Christ prayed, 'Father, glorify thy name,' he was answered by a voice from heaven, ' I have glorified it, and will glorify it again ;' even in the Son that thus desired it. He hath done it on earth, and he will do it again more perfectly in heaven. ' He hath glorified the Son, that the Son also may glorify him.' As he glorified his Father on earth, and finished the work which he gave him to do, so the Father hath now glorified him with himself, that in his glory he may be yet more glorified.

In his transfiguration his face did shine as the sun, and in his appearance to Paul, his shining light did cast him blindfold and trembling on the earth. It was Stephen's encouragement to the suffering of his martyrdom to see the glory of

God, and Jesus standing on God's right hand. When John saw him on the Lord's day in the spirit, he beheld his eyes as a flame of fire, his feet like burning brass in the furnace, and his voice was as the sound of many waters, in his right hand were the stars, out of his mouth went a sharp two-edged sword, and his countenance was the sun that shineth in his strength, his voice also did proclaim his glory, 'I am the first and the last. I am he that liveth and was dead; and behold I am alive for ever more, Amen, and have the keys of hell and of death.' It was the Lord of glory that was crucified; 'God was manifest in the flesh, justified in the Spirit, seen of angels, preached to the Gentiles, believed on in the world, received up into glory,' where he is glorified with the Father in the praises of the saints. The glory in the holy mount was great at the giving of the law; but it was no glory compared with that of the gospel administration, much more to that of the glorified Redeemer, who hath overcome, and is set down with the Father in his throne, yea, the glory that will be given to God for ever, will be through Jesus Christ.

Indeed it is a very great question whether we shall immediately see the essence of God in heaven, or only see him in the glorified Redeemer; and whether Christ will not then be the mediator of our fruition, as he was here the mediator of acquisition. But certain we are, that God will be for ever pleased and glorified in the person of the Redeemer, as well as in the church, which is his body.

It may be said to be God's end in this blessed work, that he may more fully demonstrate his vindictive justice, according to the gospel, or law of the Redeemer, upon them that finally reject his grace, than it would have been manifested on the terms of the law of the creation on Adam and his offspring. Though Christ came not into the world, primarily, 'to condemn the world, but that the world through him might be saved;' yet was it his purpose that unbelievers, who love darkness rather than light, should fall under the special condemnation, and that 'they should not see life, but that the wrath of God should abide upon them.' God would not so much as permit them to reject his salvation, but that he knows how he may be no loser by them: 'he suffers with much patience the vessels of wrath, to make his wrath and power known;' the mouth of the condemned will be utterly stopped, and they will be left speechless, when they are judged on terms of grace, much more than they would have been if they had been judged

only by the first law: when they see Christ and heaven that was offered them, and remember their wilful and obstinate contempt of them, their own consciences and tongues shall justify God, and confess that he is righteous in the most dreadful of his judgments. 'If the word spoken by angels was stedfast, and every transgression and disobedience received a just recompense of reward, how shall they escape that neglect so great salvation, which at first began to be spoken by the Lord, and then was confirmed by them that heard him, God also bearing them witness with signs, wonders, and with divers miracles and gifts of the Holy Ghost.—And if they escaped not, that refused him that spake on earth, much more shall not they escape that turn away from him that speaks from heaven: for our God is a consuming fire.' So much of the ends of Christ's undertaking in our redemption.

In which you may see that there are several things which demonstrate the glory of the forementioned attributes of God, in this gospel dispensation. 1. It shines forth in the person of the Redeemer as he was on earth, in his nature and wonderful conception, and in his perfections. 2. It also shines forth in the actions of his life, overcoming the world and the devil, and perfectly fulfilling the law of God: so that the image of his Father did shine forth in his conversation. 3. In his death and sufferings was the Father glorified, as I showed before. 4. In the most wise and holy frame of those laws by which the grace of the mediator is conveyed, and the church governed. 5. By the image of God, by the impress of those laws on the souls of his saints, and by the holiness of their lives, the glory of God is also demonstrated. 6. By the justifying sentence of the judge, and the glorious reward bestowed on the faithful. 7. By the condemning sentence and execution on the ungodly, in whom vindictive justice will be honoured. 8. In the perfection of the individual saints, and their perfect love and praise. 9. In the saints as imbodied in the heavenly Jerusalem, the glory of which will be the glory of God. 10. And principally in the blessed person and work of the Redeemer. In all these will God's glory shine forth for ever.

Quest. But to whom is it that God doth thus demonstrate his glory?

Ans. 1. To the saints in this life, in that degree as is suited to a state of grace, and the condition of a traveller that lives by faith. We are apt to look upward, long after fuller revelations of the heavenly kingdom and mystery, and marvel that God will not show himself more fully to his saints on earth. Gladly we would know more of God, Christ, and the life to come; and it is often matter of some temptation to us, that God doth not satisfy these desires, but leaves them in so much darkness, that they are willing of his light. But this is because we do not consider how much of glory consists in the light; and that grace is more in the desires of it than in the possession: and if we should have as much of it as we desire,* it were but to bring down heaven to earth. Means must be suited to their ends. God will discover to us so much of his glory as may quicken our desires, and keep alive our hope, patience and endeavours; but not so much as shall satisfy us, and answer our expectations. For heaven is not here. We must not carry our home about with us, but travel towards it, that we may reach it at the last.

2. God doth even now demonstrate the glory of his forementioned attributes, in the work of redemption, not only to his saints, but to the angels of heaven. The consideration of this hath often satisfied me, when I have been tempted to wonder at the work of redemption, that God should so far condescend as to be incarnate, and make such glorious discoveries of himself, yet that so few in the world should take notice of it, and he should have from men so little of the honour that he seems by his preparations to expect. But the most part of the world did never once see the glory that shines to them in the Redeemer. But God hath another world besides this, and other creatures besides man, in all likelihood incomparably more numerous, perhaps thousands for one, and certainly more excellent. Though Christ did not assume the nature of angels, and came not to redeem them that needed no Redeemer, yet may the lustre of this work of redemption appear to the angels more clearly than to man; and God may have a thousand-fold more glory from them that are but the spectators and admirers, than from us in our present darkness, that are yet possessors. As we that are here on earth, look upon and admire the glory of the sun, which is as it were in another world, and out of our reach; so the angels much more may gaze upon the glory of the Son of God, and admire the Lord in the work of our redemption though they were not the redeemed ones. So that unto them doth God shine forth by it in his excellencies.

Perhaps you will say, that cannot be: because this is but seeing him in a glass; when the angels see him face to face, and immediately behold his blessed essence: or else how can the saints expect that beatific vision? To which I answer; first, that I am uncertain whether seeing face to face be an immediate intuition of the essence of God, or only such a sight of his glory in those emanations, that are as appropriated to the place or state of bliss. God's essence is every where: but that glory is not every where: so I know not whether our present knowledge be not called enigmatical, and as in a glass, comparatively to that glory prepared for the saints: but, secondly, I answer that certainly I think that God is demonstrated to his angels in the Redeemer, yea, in the church itself, which is the subject of his grace, that they are both affected, and employed about us accordingly. He that 'spoiled principalities, and powers, and openly triumphed over them, and by death overcame him that had the power of death,' and had so much to do against the evil angels as enemies, no doubt is joyfully observed by the good angels. He that is set so 'far above principalities, and powers, and might, and dominion, and every name that is named in this world, or that which is to come,' and 'is gone into heaven, and is on the right hand of God, angels, and authorities, and powers being made subject to him,' no doubt is honoured and admired by angels. Indeed it is expressly said, 'Let all the angels of God worship him.' And what are 'they all but ministering spirits, sent forth to minister for them who shall be heirs of salvation?' therefore sent forth by Jesus Christ, the Lord of saints; which makes some think that the title of angels was never given to any of these spirits, till the Mediator's undertaking, and that it was only as they were his deputed messengers, or servants, for the ends of that undertaking. Sure we are, they attended his birth with their acclamations, his life and sufferings as far as was meet, with their service, and that they are deputed to bear his servants in their hands, that they dash not their foot against a stone; that they are ascending and descending, are present with the churches in their holy worship, and that they rejoice at the conversion of one sinner; and that the least of Christ's servants have their angels beholding the face of God; that the law was given by their disposition or ordination, and they attend the departing souls of believers; and that they contend against evil spirits for our good, and are encamped about us, and that they shall attend the Lord at his coming to judgment, and be his glorious retinue, and instruments in the work; and that they are numbered with us, as members of the same heavenly Jerusalem, and

---

* It is proper here to guard the reader against a common assertion and popular error—'That the desire of grace is grace. This is a fallacious and delusive mistake in the loose way in which it is often uttered, and understood.—*Editor*.

that we shall be like or equal to them. Yea, men must be either confessed or denied, owned, or disowned, before the angels, but if all this seem not sufficient to persuade you that the angels are so far interested in the affairs of God about the redeemed as to behold and admire him in this blessed work, to take notice of the express affirmations of the scriptures, 'which things the angels desire to look into.' And why, but to see and admire the wisdom, power, goodness, mercy, and justice of God, shining forth in the Redeemer? If this be not plain enough, mark well those words, ' to the intent that now unto the principalities and powers in heavenly places, might be known by the church, the manifold wisdom of God.' You see here, that the church of the redeemed is that admirable looking-glass which God hath set up to this very intent, that his angels may in it, or by it, behold the manifold wisdom of God; yea, and that upon the full revelation of Christ by the gospel, they saw that which did more fully inform, and illuminate them. No doubt but the very work of the creation, yea, of this inferior world, that are made for the habitation and use of man, are far better known to angels than to man: for we know but little of what we daily see and use: consequently it is by angels more than men that God is beheld, admired, and glorified in them. If it be so in these works of creation, we may well say, it is so in the works of redemption.

3. But when we are perfected in glory, then we ourselves shall clearly see the glory of this mystery, and of Go l therein. As it is not till we come to heaven that we shall have the fullest benefits of redemption, so is it not till then, that we shall have the fullest understanding of it, and God have his fullest praises for it. As we are here but sowing the seed of our own glory, which we must reap in the everlasting fruition of God; so God is here but sowing those seeds of his praise, and glory, which he will eternally reap by this blessed work. Do not therefore judge of the ends, and fruits of Christ's undertakings, by what you see him attain on earth, but by what he shall attain in heaven, when he hath fully seen the travail of his soul, to his satisfaction, and hath presented the whole church without spot unto God, and when the glorious marriage of the Lamb with the heavenly Jerusalem is solemnized, and the kingdom delivered up to the Father, it will be another manner of conceiving which we shall have in heaven of this blessed work; when we see the face of our glorified Lord, and fully possess the fruits of his redemption, then this is that we have now by our weak believing. We shall then have another manner of sight of the wisdom, power, love, and justice that appear to man, in the face of Christ, than now we have.

Yea, the tormenting discoveries of the glory of redemption to the condemned rejectors of it, shall also contribute to the glory of God.

You see then that this work hath most glorious ends; which I have mentioned the more largely, both to remove their temptations who are apt to think that it was an unnecessary thing, and the less to be regarded, and to teach men the true value of it, by showing them the true ends.

For the former, I say, there was no necessity that God should make the world, and reveal his power, wisdom, and goodness, in this excellent frame, but what did suppose the free will of God the original cause. Will you therefore say, that the creation is vain; and undervalue God's admirable works, in which he thus reveals himself to the intellectual creatures? So here; we confess that there could be no necessity of redemption, but what was originally derived from the will of God, though a final necessity there was for the constitution of things, upon supposition of what went before the undertaking. But yet shall we undervalue so glorious a work, in which the divine perfections do so fully reveal themselves to the world?

I say the more of this, because I observe that it is the not apprehending the high and excellent ends of redemption, that makes it so much slighted, and consequently tempts many to infidelity. For the ends and uses do set the value on the means. That is of little worth, that is to little purpose, and doth but little good. If men understood more the ends of redemption, and how much God doth shine forth in the world, in the person, life, and laws, and works of the Son of God, they would then live in the admiration of it, and be always searching and prying into it, and desire to know nothing but God in Christ crucified, and account all things else but as loss and dung for this excellent knowledge: but alas, the most scarcely discern any higher ends of Christ, or other use of him, than to save themselves from hell, for want of faith, and through humiliation, they have but little sense of that; therefore no wonder if the Redeemer be neglected, and God denied the honour of the work.

So much of this second point, the reasons and ends of Christ's undertaking. I shall purposely be shorter on the rest.

The third point to be understood concerning our Redeemer is, what he hath done and suffered for mankind, and wherein his redeeming work consisted both as to the general and special part. Should I stand on these at large, I must needs be voluminous; and therefore I shall but briefly recite them for your remembrance.

The first thing that Christ did for the saving of the world, was his interposing between offending man and the wrath of God; and so preserving the world from that destruction which the execution of the violated law would have procured: undertaking then to become the seed of the woman, and so to break the serpent's head; and revealing this grace by slow degrees, till the time of his coming.

Then when the fulness of time was come, he was made man, being conceived by the Holy Ghost, and born of the virgin Mary, and so 'the Word was made flesh, and dwelt among men, who beheld his glory, as the glory of the only begotten of the Father, full of grace and truth.' Thus God was manifested to men in the flesh.

As he was perfectly holy in his nature, without any stain or guilt of original sin; so was he perfectly holy in his life, and never broke the least command of God in thought, word or deed. Never could any convince him of sin. He fulfilled the law of nature, which all the world was under; the Mosaical law which the Jews were under, and the special law that was given to himself as mediator, and was common to no other creature in the world.

And thus he performed these excellent works. 1. By the fulfilling of all righteousness he pleased the Father, always accomplishing his will; and so did much of the work of a Saviour, in meriting for us. 'For such an high-priest became us, who is holy, harmless, undefiled, separate from sinners.'

2. He hath conquered the tempter, who conquered us. Therefore did he purposely yield himself to such sore temptations, that his victory might be glorious, and the second Adam might overcome him that had overcome the first. Thus he hath done much to the rescue of the captivated.

3. Hereby also he hath overcome the world, which overcame the first Adam and his posterity; he trampled upon its seeming glory; he neglected and despised its baits and allurements; he went through all its cruel persecutions and oppositions, so that the world now, as well as the devil, are conquered things; by which he hath made way for the victory of his followers, and given them ground of great encouragement. 'Be of good cheer, I have overcome the world.' Yea, I may say, in a sort, he hath overcome the flesh also. For though Christ had no corrupted flesh as we

have to contend with, yet had he a natural and sensitive appetite, which the command of God did forbid him to fulfil. And therefore when innocent nature desired that the cup might pass from him, and abhor death by a simple averseness; yet perfect holiness permitted not this to proceed to a refusal by the comparing intellect, and choosing, or refusing will; but saith, 'Not my will, but thine be done.' And when Christ was hungry and weary, the desire of food and rest by the sensitive appetite was no sin; but when the work of God forbade the fulfilling of such desires, he still denied them.

4. Hereby also he hath set us a perfect pattern of obedience, and is become our example, whom we must endeavour to imitate. For he knew that it is the most effectual teaching, to do it by words and deeds together. It is a great help to us, when we do not only hear his voice, but see also which way he hath gone before us. When he saith, 'Learn of me,' he directs us not only to his words, but to himself, who was meek and lowly.

5. Moreover Christ received of the Father fulness of the Spirit, and power, for the benefit of the redeemed: that he might be meet to be the head and the treasury of the church, and to shower down the streams of grace upon his members, and when all power was given him in heaven and earth, he might be fitted to the following application of his benefits, to rule, support, and defend his people.

6. Moreover he was pleased himself to become a preacher of the gospel of salvation, not to all the world, but principally as a minister of the circumcision, that is, the Jews. He that purchases salvation, condescended also to proclaim it. The preaching of the gospel is a work that Christ thought not himself too good for; sometimes to many, sometimes to one or two, as he had opportunity, often with tears, and always with earnestness and compassion, did he go about doing good, seeking the lost, healing the diseased, calling men to faith and repentance, and offering them the grace and life which he purchased.

7. He was pleased also to seal up his doctrine by his works, casting out devils, healing all diseases, raising the dead, and working divers other miracles, to assure them that he came from God and did his work, and revealed his will, that so the world might have no excuse for their unbelief; but that they that would not believe upon any other account, might yet believe him for the sake of his works.

8. Besides all this, he gave up himself to a life of suffering, being despised by his creatures

whom he came to redeem, destitute voluntarily of fleshly pleasures, and of that riches and worldly provision that might procure it: he was a man of sorrows, afflicted from his youth, persecuted from the cradle; he gave his cheeks to the smiters, and his person to be made the scorn of fools; he was crowned with thorns, spit upon and buffeted, and having sweat water and blood, in his agony in the garden, he was hanged on a cross, where thieves were both his companions and revilers, where they gave him gall and vinegar to drink, pierced his blessed body with a spear, and put him to a shameful, cursed death. But he endured the cross, despising the shame, gave up himself thus a sacrifice for sin, and bore our transgressions, that we might be healed by his stripes; and having ransomed us by his blood, he was buried as an offender, continuing for a time in the power of the grave. All this he consented to undergo, though he consented not to the sin of them that did inflict it, for he laid down his life, it was not taken from him against his will.

9. Having thus paid the price of our reconciliation to God, the third day he rose again from the dead; though soldiers watch his grave, because he had foretold them that he would rise the third day, yet were they soon daunted by the glory of an angel, that came and rolled away the stone. So Christ made known his divine power and victory, and the finishing of his work: and as by death, he overcame him that had the power of death, that is, the devil; so by his resurrection he triumphed over death itself. For how should the grave detain the innocent, and death overcome the Lord of life? This was the glorious day of triumph; in remembrance of this, he appointed the Lord's day to be observed by the church. The resurrection of Christ, was the confusion of all the powers of darkness; the great argument to confirm the truth of his doctrine, and prove his Godhead to the unbelieving world.

10. Being risen, he more fully revealed his gospel, and sent forth his apostles and disciples, to proclaim the offers of life to the world, and settle the churches in an holy order, when they had gathered them, and to ordain such ministers to succeed them, as might carry on his work to the end of the world. Thus he is the faithful Lawgiver to the church.

11. When he had abode thus forty days on earth, he ascended up into heaven while his disciples stood by, and gazed after him; and there hath taken possession in our nature, advancing it to the Father's right hand in glory, which was by sin depressed so low in misery. So he is gone 'to prepare a place for us,' leaving us a certain word of promise that he 'will come again, and take us to himself, that where he is, there we may be also.' And 'as our life now is hid there with Christ in God, so when he shall appear, we shall appear with him in glory.'

12. Being ascended, he manifested his power and his truth in sending down the Holy Ghost upon his disciples, enabling them to do such works as he had done, such as were necessary to convince the unbelieving world, and to conquer the opposing wisdom and power of the flesh: enabling them to speak in variety of languages, which they had never before learned: as also to understand, and powerfully preach the mysteries of the gospel, to confirm their doctrine by miracles, healing the lame, the blind, the sick, casting out devils, raising the dead, and conquering the resistance of principalities and powers, in seeming weakness, and in a contemptible garb. Not to speak now of the sanctifying work of the same Spirit on them and on the rest of the church.

13. Lastly, In this glory Christ intercedes for us, and is our High-priest in the heavens with God, living for ever, procuring and conveying to us the mercies which we need upon the account of his sacrifice: ruling his church, and preserving them; succeeding his cause and servants; restraining and subduing his enemies and ours: and will perfect his work at the day of his coming to judgment. So much of the works of Christ.

The fourth point to be understood concerning our redemption, is, the nature and worth of the benefits that are procured for us. Which though you may gather much from what is said, and the full handling of them would be a larger work than is suitable to my present ends, yet such a brief recital I shall here give you, as my ends require.

In general, we have all from Jesus the mediator that is worth the having; even all the blessings of this present life, and of the life to come. As we lost our right to all by sin, so we have our restored right by Christ alone, who came to destroy sin, and its effects. Had not he interposed, we might have had materially life, and natural faculties, and other things which now are mercies; but not as mercies, but as the requisites to our deserved punishment: even as the devils have their being, and natural perfections to sustain them in their sufferings. Nature itself, so far as good, and all natural blessings, are now of grace: and that not only of such grace as they were to Adam, which was mercy without proper merit, but of gospel grace procured by Christ; which is mercy contrary to merit. It is no sounder doctrine to say, that God doth without the merit of his Son bestow our common forfeited mercies, either on the elect, or others, than that he gives us his saving grace without it. As all things are delivered into the hands of Christ, so none can receive any good but from his hands. To give mercies to men that forfeit them, and deserve misery, is so far to pardon their sin; for to remit the sin, is to remit the punishment: but the scripture is not acquainted with any pardon of sin, but what is on the account of the merits of Christ. They that deny this mercy of God, in giving even to the ungodly such a measure of forgiveness, do speak against the daily and hourly experience of all the world; and therefore need no other confutation.

More particularly, (1.) Christ having taken the human nature into union with the divine, our nature is thereby unconceivably advanced, and brought nigh to God.

(2.) Having fulfilled the law and offered himself a sacrifice for sin, God's justice, wisdom, holiness, and goodness, are admirably demonstrated: and this sacrifice is both satisfactory and meritorious, on our behalf.

(3.) The world, the devil, death, and the grave, are conquered by him, in preparation to our conquest.

(4.) The Lord Jesus himself being risen, and justified, hath received all power in heaven and earth, and is enabled to do all things that are necessary for his further ends. As the Redeemer he is become Lord of ourselves, and of all we have: and he is made the sovereign ruler of all, having full power to relax the law that cursed, and to deal with the world on terms of grace.

(5.) Accordingly he hath kept off the stroke of the justice of God, and hindered the strict execution of the law of works, and gives still abundance of forfeited mercies to the sinful world, keeping them from deserved torments, while he is treating them on terms of life.

(6.) He hath made an universal deed of gift, of Christ, and life to all the world, on condition that they will but accept the offer. In this testament, or promise, or act of oblivion, the sins of all the world are conditionally justified, and reconciled to God.*

(7.) He hath given apostles, evangelists, pas-

tors, and teachers to proclaim this act of grace to the world, commanding them to go into all the world, and preach this gospel to every creature, and promise salvation to all that by faith will become his true disciples, so that their promulgation is universal.

(8.) Though his servants have most lamentably neglected their duty, and have not gone abroad in the world, to divulge the gospel according to his will; imagining that this work had been proper to the apostles; and though the nations have sinfully neglected a due inquiry after this blessed light, yet hath he not left himself among them without witness, but hath given them some dawning of the day, or some moonlight in the reflections of evangelical truth, who have not seen the sun itself: much mercy they have had notwithstanding their transgressions; and while they served devils, they have been provided for by God, 'in whom they live, move, and be: doing them good, and giving them rain from heaven, and fruitful seasons, filling their hearts with food and gladness; and this to teach them, that they should seek the Lord, if happily they might feel after him, and find him, though he be not far from every one of them. And that which may be known of God, is manifest among them, for God hath showed it to them; for the invisible things of him from the creation of the world are clearly seen, being understood by the things that are made, even his eternal power and godhead: so that they are without excuse.' By experience they may find, that God deals not now in rigour of justice, but on terms of grace, and that sin is not now unpardonable: and they should know that the 'goodness of God leadeth them to repentance.'

(9.) As the gospel conditionally pardons all their sins, and offers them everlasting life, so it contains the clearest reasons, and most effectual motives, to persuade them to accept the offer. It affords them most excellent precepts, instructions, exhortations, and other helps to bring them to a willingness, that salvation may be theirs.

(10.) To which also is added abundance of outward providential helps, to further the working of the gospel; as seasonable afflictions and mercies of various sorts.

(11.) And with these are usually concurrent some inward motions, and assistance of the Holy Ghost; as knocking at the door, where he is not yet let in, and entertained.

(12.) And by their presence in the visible church, even the ungodly have many benefits in the ordinances, instructions, and examples of the

---

* I submit if this paragraph be not *exceptionable*, it seems to border on, or merge in, the modern controversy of universal pardon. To preach the gospel to every creature, and proclaim pardon through Christ to the chief of sinners, is a different thing from a universal *deed of gift* of life to all the world.—*Ed.*

saints. All these, besides a resurrection, are common effects of general redemption, and not appropriated to the elect.

Besides which there are others that the elect only receive. As, 1. God is pleased, by effectual grace, to draw them to his Son, and make the gospel successful to their conversion, insuperably teaching and changing them by his Spirit, causing them to repent, believe in Christ, and to perform the conditions of his fore-mentioned promises. That love which brought the Lord on earth, that clothed him with flesh, that lifted him up upon the cross, doth stream forth in his season into the hearts of his elect, touches them with a changing power, wins them to his Father, and himself, and drops into them those heavenly principles which will grow up in them to everlasting life.

2. Hereupon the soul believing in Christ is united to him, as a member of his body, even of his true catholic church; and Christ is become the Head, the Husband, the Lord, the Saviour of that soul in a special sort. Christ himself is first given to us in these relations; and from him, as our head, his following benefits are conveyed. 'He that hath the Son hath life, and he that hath not the Son hath not life; for this life is in the Son.' He is the 'vine, and we are the branches, and out of him we can do nothing.' As it was not we that purchased our own salvation, so it is not we, but Christ, that must have the keeping and dispensing of the purchased benefits. 'For it pleased the Father, that in him should all fulness dwell, and that he should be the head over all things to his church,' that it might by communication become his fulness. He is our treasury, and from him we must have our continual supplies: for 'with him the Father will give us all things.' And thus 'Christ will dwell in our hearts by faith;' and set up the kingdom of God within us.

3. Hereupon we have the pardon of all our sins; not only as to the temporal punishment, nor only as to the bestowing of temporal mercies, or common helps of creatures, and providences; for this is but a 'winking at the days of our ignorance,' in comparison of the pardon which afterward we receive. Nor is it only a conditional, or offered pardon; but it is an actual remission of the eternal, and of all the destructive punishment. And thus we are justified from all that might be charged on us from the law, and accepted, and used as just by God. There is a kind of forgiveness that was promised to the sacrificers. But as that was upon Christ's account, so it extended not to the pardon of the

eternal punishment to any but true believers. He that was once crucified, 'is exalted by God's right hand a prince and a Saviour, to give repentance to Israel, and forgiveness of sins.— Through this man is preached the forgiveness of sins; and by him all that believe are justified from all things, from which they could not be justified by the law of Moses.' When our eyes are opened, and we are turned from darkness to light, and from the power of Satan unto God, we then receive remission of our sins.' When we are 'delivered from the power of darkness, and translated into the kingdom of Christ; in him we have then redemption through his blood, even the forgiveness of sins.' And 'blessed are they whose iniquities are forgiven, and whose sins are covered, to whom the Lord imputeth not sin.' Now 'who shall condemn us? It is God that justifieth us: for there is no condemnation to them that are in Christ Jesus, that walk not after the flesh, but after the Spirit.'

4. With this benefit concurs our reconciliation to God, and our adoption; by which we are made his sons, and God is pleased to own us as our Father. For being one with Christ, the Son of God, we are sons by him; 'to as many as received him, to them gave he power to become the sons of God, even to them that believe in his name.' This is the wonderful love that the Father hath bestowed on those that were his enemies; that they should not only be reconciled to him by the death of his Son, but also be called the sons of God. For he hath 'chosen us in him, before the foundation of the world, that we should be holy, and without blame before him in love; having predestinated us to the adoption of children, by Jesus Christ, to himself, according to the good pleasure of his will, to the praise of the glory of his grace, wherein he hath made us accepted in the Beloved.' O what an unspeakable mercy is it to have the blessed God, whom we had so oft offended, to become our reconciled Father in Christ! For it is not an empty title that he assumes; but he hath more abundant love to us, and tenderness of our welfare, than any title can make us understand.

5. Hereupon it doth immediately follow, that we have a right to the blessed inheritance of his sons, and are certain heirs of his heavenly kingdom. For 'if sons, then heirs, heirs of God, and joint heirs with Christ.—Being saved by the washing of regeneration, and renewing of the Holy Ghost, and justified by grace through Christ, we are made heirs, according to the hope of eternal life.—Being begotten again to a lively hope, by the resurrection of Jesus

Christ from the dead, to an inheritance incorruptible, and undefiled, and that fadeth not away, reserved in heaven for us.'

6. Withal the Holy Ghost is given to us, not only to close us at first with Christ, but to take up his abode in us as his temples, and to be the agent, and life of Christ within us, to do his work, maintain his interest, cleanse us of all filthiness of flesh and spirit, sanctify us throughout, to strive against the flesh and conquer it, and to keep us by divine power through faith unto salvation, 'for because we are sons, God sendeth forth the Spirit of his Son into our hearts, whereby we cry, Abba, Father.' This 'Spirit of adoption,' which we receive, ' doth bear witness with our spirits that we are the sons of God.— For if any man have not the Spirit of Christ, the same is none of his.' By this Spirit is the spirit of the world cast out of us ; the spirit of pride, and of blindness, of delusion, hard-heartedness, of sensuality, malice, and hypocrisy, are cast out. By this is God's image imprinted on our souls ; we are conformed to his blessed will ; 'we are made partakers of the divine nature, being holy, as God is holy.' Hereby also we are fitted for the service of God, to which before we were undisposed and unfit. O what an ease is it to the soul, to be free from so much of the burden of sin ? What an honour is it to have the Spirit of God within us, and to have a nature so truly heavenly and divine ? How can it go ill with him that hath ' God dwelling in him, and that dwells in God ?'

7. Another of our precious benefits by Christ, is, that we shall be actually employed in the special and nearest service of God, that on earth is to be performed. Let diseased souls desire idleness, and sensual sinners take pleasure in the mire ; but the saints will ever rejoice in God, and take it for the most blessed life on earth, when they can do him the greatest service. Let his enemies that hate his service, be weary of it, as if it were a toil or drudgery ; but his children will desire no sweeter work: they never think themselves so well as when they are most serviceable to their blessed Lord, though at the greatest cost and labour to the flesh So sweet is God's service, that the more of it we can do, the more is our pleasure, honour, and content. Other work spends strength ; but this increases it : other work must have recreation intermixed, but this is itself the most delightful recreation : other service is undertaken for the *love* of the *wages*, but this is undertaken for the *love* of the *Master* and the work, and is wages itself to them that go through with it. For other service is but a

means, and that to some inferior end ; but this is a means to the everlasting perfection and blessedness of the soul ; and such a means, as contains, or presently procures, somewhat of the end. All the saints are even here 'a chosen generation, a royal priesthood, a holy nation, a peculiar people, that they should show forth the praises of him that hath called them out of darkness, into his marvellous light : they are a holy priesthood, to offer up a spiritual sacrifice, acceptable to God by Jesus Christ.' Their very bodies 'are a living sacrifice, holy and acceptable to God, which is their reasonable service.' What a sweet work is it to live in the daily love of God ; in his praises, in the hopes, and sweet fore-thoughts of everlasting joys ! The world affords not such a Master, nor such a work.

8. Another of the precious benefits by Christ is, the liberty of access in all our wants to God by prayer, with a promise to be heard. The flaming sword did keep the way to the tree of life, till Christ had taken it down, and consecrated for us a new and living way, through the vail, which is his flesh : and now 'we have boldness to enter into the holiest, by the blood of Jesus ; and therefore may draw near with a true heart, in full assurance of faith.' When worldlings cry to their Baal in vain, the 'righteous cry, and the Lord heareth them, and delivereth them out of all their (hurtful) troubles.' O what a mercy is it in our falls, in our distresses, in our dangers, in our wants, to have a God, a faithful, merciful Father to go to, and make our complaint for relief ? What a mercy is it, when our flesh and our hearts fail us, when friends and worldly things all fail us, to have God for the rock of our hearts, of our portion ? When sickness begins to break these bodies, and earthly delights all forsake us, and death calls us to come to our endless state, then to have a reconciled Father to go to, and crave his aid, upon the encouragement of a promise, recommend our souls into his hand as to a faithful Creator, and our surest, dearest friend ; this is a mercy that no man can well value, till he come to use it. To know every day, that as often as ever we come to God, we are always welcome ; that our persons and prayers are pleasing to him, through his Son ; what a mercy is it ! One would think we should live joyfully, if we had but one such promise as this for faith to live upon: 'Call upon me in the day of trouble, and I will deliver thee, and thou shalt glorify me.—Whatsoever ye shall ask in my name, that will I do, that the Father may be glorified in the Son.' No wonder if they be rich, that have so free access to such a treasure ;

and if they be safe, that have access to so sure a help; for 'God is a very present help in trouble.'

9. Another precious benefit is, that we have peace of conscience, or ground for it at the least, in our peace with God ; and so may come to assurance of salvation, and may partake of the joy in the Holy Ghost: for in this peace and joy the kingdom of God doth much consist. When the chief cause of all our fear and sorrow is done away, what then is left to break our peace? When we have no cause to fear the flames of hell, nor the sting of death, or the appearance of our judge, any further than to move us to make ready, what then should greatly trouble the soul? If God and heaven be not matter of comfort, I know not what is. If we saw a man that had got many kingdoms, to be still sad and peevish because he had no more : we would say, he was very ambitious, or covetous ; and yet he might have reason for it: but if you have the love of God, and a title by promise to the heavenly inheritance, and yet you are discontented, and God and glory is not enough for you, this is most unreasonable.

10. Another of our precious benefits by Christ is, our spiritual communion with his church, and holy members. We do not only join with them in outward communion, but we unite our desires, and there is an harmony of affections. We are in the main of one mind, will, and way, and we jointly constitute the body of our Lord : ' we are come unto mount Zion, and unto the city of the living God, the heavenly Jerusalem, and to an innumerable company of angels, to the general assembly, and church of the first born, which are written in heaven, and to God the judge of all, and to the spirits of just men made perfect, and to Jesus the mediator of the new covenant.' We are joined to that body, and have communion with it, which consists both of militant and triumphant saints, and of the angels also. ' We are no more strangers and foreigners, but fellow citizen with the saints, and of the household of God, and are built on the foundation of the apostles and prophets, Jesus Christ himself being the chief corner stone, in whom all the building, fitly framed together, groweth unto an holy temple in the Lord ; in whom we also are builded together, for an habitation of God, through the Spirit.' And as in holy concord we serve the Lord, having ' one God, one Christ, one Spirit, one faith, one baptism,' one rule, the word of God, one mind, one heart, one work of holiness and righteousness in the main, one hope, and one heaven, the place of our expectations: so have we the fruit of the prayers of each other,

and of all the church, and have the honour, the safety, and other benefits of being members of so blessed a society.

Yea, we have, in this communion, the whole church obliged and disposed, according to their capacity, to endeavour the good of every member. So that ministers and magistrates, yea, though they were apostles, or prophets, Paul, or Apollos, all are ours ; kings have their power for us, and for us they must use them. If we suffer, every member must be as forward to assist us, and if we want, to relieve us, according to their power, as if they suffered with us.

Yea, the angels are our brethren and fellow-servants, yea, ' ministering spirits, sent forth to minister for them that shall be heirs of salvation,' to encamp about them, and to bear them in their arms, rejoicing to behold their graces, and prosperity, as was showed before.

11. Another of our precious benefits by Christ, is, that 'all things shall work together for our good ;' when we are sanctified to God, all things are sanctified to us, to serve us for God, and help us to him. Every creature that we have to do with, is as it were another thing to the saints, than to other men. They are all wheels in that universal engine of grace, to carry us to salvation. The same things that are *common* mercies to others, are *special* to us, as proceeding from a special love, and being designed to a *special use*. As flesh-pleasing is the ultimate end of the ungodly, and all things are thereby debased, to be but means to that ignoble end : so the pleasing and fruition of God is the end of all the saints, and thereby all things that they have to do with, are advanced to the honour of being sanctified means to this most high and noble end, and as they are engaged to use them to this end, and consequently to their own greatest advantage ; so God hath engaged himself to bless them in that holy use, and to cause them all by his gracious providence to co-operate to their good. The greatest afflictions, the most cruel persecutions from the most violent enemies, our wants, our weaknesses, and death itself, all must concur to carry on this work. What then should a Christian fear, but sin ? How honourable, and how happy a life may he live, that hath all these assured for his service ; and what causeless fears are they that use to afflict the servants of God, concerning their outward troubles and necessities ? What do we fear, groan under, and complain of, but our Father's physic, and the means of our salvation? If this one truth were but believed, received and used according to its worth, O what a life would Christians live !

The last and greatest of our benefits by Christ is, resurrection, and our justification at the bar of God, and our reception into glory. This is the end of all, and therefore contains all. For this Christ died; for this we are Christians; for this we believe, hope, and labour; for this we suffer, and deny ourselves and renounce this world. Our bodies shall then be spiritual and glorious, no more troubled with infirmities, diseases or necessities. Our souls shall be both naturally and graciously perfected; both in their faculties and qualities. We shall be brought nigh to God: we shall be numbered with the inhabitants of the heavenly Jerusalem, be members and companions of that blessed society, and equal with the angels of God: we shall for ever behold our glorified Redeemer, and see our own nature united to the Godhead; and we shall have the greatest and nearest intuition and fruition of God, the fullest love to him and the sweetest rest, content, and delight in him, that our created natures are capable of: we shall everlastingly be employed in this love, and delight, and in his praises, with all the heavenly host: the glory of God will shine forth in our glory, and the abundance of his goodness will be communicated to us; he will be well pleased with us, with our praises, with all that blessed society, and with our Head: and this will endure to all eternity.

Christians, I have now named, in a few words, those benefits by Christ which the heart of man is not able to value, in any proportion to their inexpressible worth: I have named that in an hour, which you will enjoy for ever. So much of our benefits by Christ.

The fifth point to be understood in the right knowledge of Christ is, the terms on which he conveys his benefits to men, and how we must be made partakers of them.

These mercies are of two sorts. First, Common. Second, Proper to them who are heirs of salvation. The common are those discoveries of grace that are made even to heathens in the creatures, and the merciful providences of God. These are absolutely and freely bestowed in some measure upon all, but in a greater measure upon some, as pleases the Giver.—The supernatural, or instituted means of revealing Christ, and life to the world, and drawing them to a saving consent of faith,—these are the gospel written and preached, with other corresponding helps. The commission Christ hath given to his ambassadors is to preach this gospel to all the world, even to every reasonable creature, without exception or restriction. And it is absolutely and freely given, where it is given; but as to the providential disposal of the event, God causes it not to be sent to all, but to whom he sees meet.

The proper or special mercies are of two sorts. First, Some are physical inherent qualities, or performed acts. Second, Some are adherent rights, or relations.

Of the former inherent sort, there are these three degrees; namely, there is the first special work of vocation, conversion, or regeneration, causing the sinner to repent and believe, and giving him the principle of spiritual life. There is the bestowing of the indwelling Spirit of God, and progressive sanctification of heart and life, and perseverance with victory. There is the perfecting of all this, in our glorious perfection in the life to come.

For the first of these, God hath not promised it conditionally or absolutely to any individual person that hath it not. He hath bound all to repent and believe, but hath not promised to make them do it: only he hath revealed that there are certain persons so given to Christ, as that they shall be infallibly drawn to believe. But he hath appointed certain means for the ungodly, which they are bound to use in order to their conversion; and if they will not use them, they are without excuse. If they will, they have very much encouragement from God, both, 1. In the nature of the means, which are fitted to their ends, and are mighty to bring down all opposition. 2. In the commands and institution of God; whose wisdom and goodness may easily resolve us, that he will not appoint us means in vain, nor set his creatures on fruitless labour; and, 3. From the issue; for no man can stand forth, and say, such an one did his best in the use of means, and yet could not attain the end, but fell short of the grace and glory of God.

The diseases of men's souls are wilfulness and blindness; the means of cure are the persuasions, with the revelation of the gospel. Men have two natural powers of understanding and will: but they want that right disposition which we call the habit, or moral power, which is no more than to say they are habitually blind and wilful. It is so far from being unreasonable to teach and persuade men that are under such an impotency as this, that there is nothing in the world that doth more bespeak our teaching and persuasions: for this is the natural and instituted way to cure them, and give them power. What means of overcoming ignorance like teaching; and what means of overcoming habituated wilfulness, like persuasion, added to informing truths? We do not use to reason men out of a natural impotency, nor to persuade them to do that for which they have no faculties or object; but it is the very means of overcoming a moral impotency, and making men willing of the good which they rejected. With this means doth God set in and infallibly cause it to be effectual with his chosen. Thus no man comes to the Son except the Father draw him; and then for the two following degrees of holiness in our sanctification and glorious perfection, God hath promised them to those that have this first degree. For the Spirit of holiness is promised to all that truly repent and believe, and salvation to all that are sanctified and persevere. So that the right to the inheritance being a relation, is conveyed as other rights and relations, of which we are next to speak.

As the Spirit, by the operation of the word upon the heart, conveys the foresaid inherent benefits, or qualities and acts, so the promise of grace, indited by Christ and the Spirit, doth as a deed of gift, or testament or act of oblivion, bestow on us our rights and spiritual relations; and from these they result, as the immediate instrumental cause. Thus doth he give power or right to as many as receive him, to become the sons of God. Thus doth he give us pardon, justification, adoption, and our right to further grace and glory. These promises are conditional; and our repenting and believing in Christ, is the condition.* And therefore till conversion bring us to repent and believe, we have no right to any of these benefits of the promise. Therefore though our repentance and faith be none of the proper cause of our justification, or right; yet the main work, in order to the procurement of these benefits that is now to be done, is to persuade the sinner to *repent* and *believe;* to turn that he may live; for God's act of grace is past already, the conditional pardon is granted long ago, and will effectually pardon us as soon as we perform the condition, and not till then we hinder the efficacy of the deed of gift; for unbelief and impenitency are true causes of men's condemnation, though faith and repentance are no proper causes of their salvation.

These promises being conditional, we cannot be assured of our part in the benefits, but by being assured that we perform the condition. By this you may see the nature of presumption; when men say they believe that which never was promised; or believe that they have right to the blessings that are promised to others, and thus they believe that they shall have the benefits promised, when they perform not the conditions;

all this is presuming, and not true believing. If men believe that God is reconciled to them, will pardon them, justify them, and save them, when they are unconverted, impenitent, unregenerated men; this is not indeed a believing of God, that hath never made them any such promise, nor ever told them any such matter, but the contrary; but it is a believing the false delusions of the devil and their own hearts. He that will claim any title to Christ, pardon, and salvation, must have something more to show for it than you, and more than the most of the world have to show; for the most shall be shut out. Every man therefore that regards his salvation, must seriously ask his soul this question, What have I to show for my title to salvation more than the most of the world can show? It is not saying, I hope to be saved, that will serve the turn, except I can give a reason of my hopes. Thousands that lay claim to salvation shall miss of it, because they have no title to it. That which you must have to show is this, a promise, or deed of gift on God's part, and the fulfilling of the condition on your part. God saith to all men, Whosoever repents, believes, or is converted, shall be saved. When you have found that you repent of all your sins, truly believe, and are converted to God, *then,* and *not till then,* you may conclude that you shall be saved.

The sixth point to be understood and believed, concerning these benefits of Christ, is the infallible certainty of them. While men look on the promised glory to come as on an uncertain thing, they will hardly be drawn to venture, to let go the profits and pleasures of the world to attain it; much less to part with life itself. The life of all our Christian motion is the unfeigned belief of the truth of God's word, and especially of the unseen things of the world to come. Such as men's belief of heaven and hell is, such will be the bent of their hearts, the course of their lives, and such they will be in their yielding to sin, or in resisting it, and in all the service they do for God. As all men would take another course, if they did but see heaven and hell with their eyes; so all men would presently throw away their worldly, fleshly pleasures, turn to God, and an holy life, if they did but as thoroughly believe the joys and torments to come, as if they saw them. Flesh and blood can hardly judge of things, without the help of sense; and fleshly men take all things to be phantasms or nothings, that are not within the judgment of their senses. They must see it, feel it, taste it, or hear it; and believing is a way that hardly satisfies them; though it be God himself that they are to believe. Believing is trusting the credit of another; and we are naturally loth to trust to any, but our eyes or other senses. We are so false ourselves, that we are ready to measure God by ourselves; and to think that he is a deceiver, because that we are such. Hence it is that the world is so ungodly that they venture on sin, and will not be at the cost and labour of a heavenly life; because they take the matters of the life to come to be but uncertainties, and have not so true a belief of them as might possess them with a deep apprehension of their reality. How should the word profit them that mix it not with faith, unless by begetting faith itself? O what a change would a sound belief of the scriptures make in the world! But having spoken so oft of this in other writings, I shall say no more of it now. So much of the knowledge of Christ.

SECT. II. I have showed you the first part of this direction, how Christ must be received with the understanding; I now come to the second, which is, that he must be received heartily. As God must be beloved, so Christ must be believed in, with all the heart, and soul, and strength. If not with all in a perfect degree—for that will not be till we come to heaven—yet with all in a predominant prevalent degree. There are many convictions, good meanings, wishes, and purposes, which may proceed from common grace,* and be found in those that never shall be saved: these may be called, analogically, faith, love, and desire, as those are that are found in the truly regenerated; and yet the persons in whom they are found, may not fitly be called believers or lovers of God; because a man is to be denominated from that in him which is predominant, and hath the chief power on his heart. The soul of man is not so simple as to move but one way: its state in this life is to stand between two differing competitors, God and the world, spirit and flesh; and there is no man that is totally given up to either of them. No man is so good and spiritual, who hath not something in him that is bad and carnal: and no man is so fully addicted to God, but the creature hath too much interest in his heart. Nor is there any man so given up to the creature, in whom God hath no manner of interest at all, in his estimation and affections; if he indeed believe that there is a God. At least it is not so with all that are unconverted. Otherwise, 1. What is it that common grace doth, if it do not dispose them towards God? Certainly it would not else be grace. 2. And if this were not so, then we must say, that no unregenerated man hath any

good in him, that is truly moral: for if there be no interest of God in his mind or will, there can be no good in him. But this is contrary to scripture and experience. It was undoubtedly some moral good † which Christ loved the man for, in Mark x. 21. who was not far from the kingdom of God. 3. Otherwise all men must be equally departed from God, which is contrary to experience. 4. Yea, all men must be as bad on earth, privately, as in hell; which certainly is false. I may well say, that on earth there is some good in the worst; much more in those that are almost persuaded to be converted Christians. Many a thought of the goodness of God, of the necessity of a Saviour, and of the love of Christ, and of the joys of heaven, may be stirring and working in the minds of the unsanctified; but if they take not up the heart for Christ, the person is not a true believer. As the gospel must be believed to be true, so Christ, who is offered to us in the gospel as good, must be heartily, and thankfully accepted accordingly: and the glory, the justification, reconciliation with God, and other benefits procured by him, and offered with him, must be valued, and desired above all earthly fleshly things. If you are convinced that sin is evil, as contrary to God, and hurtful to you, and hereupon have some mind to let it go, some wishes that Christ would save you from it, yet still have a love to it that is greater than your dislike; the bent of your hearts being more for it, than against it, and your habitual desires rather to keep than to leave it: this is not sanctification, nor a saving consent to be saved by Christ. If you have some convictions that holiness is good, as being the image of God, as pleasing to him, and necessary to your salvation, and so should have some mind of holiness on these grounds; yet if you have on the other side a greater averseness to it, because it would deprive you of the pleasures of your sin, and the habitual inclination of your will is more against it than for it; certainly this will not stand with true sanctification, or faith in Christ, to save you from the power of sin by his Spirit.

Thousands deceive themselves by misunderstanding some common passages, that are spoken to comfort afflicted consciences; viz. That the least true desires after grace, prove the soul to be gracious. This is true, if you speak of the least desires, which are predominant in the soul; when our desire is more habitual than our unwillingness, and we thus prefer Christ before all the world, the least of this is an evidence

---

* Or rather from natural conviction, a Christian education and example, and the influence of habit. – Ed.

† It was the love of *benevolence* and *commiseration*, NOT *complacency.—Ed.*

of saving grace. But such desires as are sub-dued by the contrary desires; and such a will as is accompanied with a greater unwillingness, habitually; and such a faith, as is drowned in greater unbelief; these are not evidences of a saving change, nor can you justly gather any special comfort from them. He that hath more unbelief than belief, is not to be called a believer, but an unbeliever; and he that hath more hatred, or dislike of God and holiness than love to them, is not to be called godly, but ungodly, nor a lover of God, but a hater of him. I am easily persuaded, that many of you that are ungodly could be contented that God be glorified, if his glory do not cross your carnal interest; and so you desire God's glory even for itself, as that which is absolutely good in itself. But if your fleshly interest be so dear to you, that you will sacrifice God's glory to it, and had rather God were dishonoured, than your fleshly interest contradicted, it is your flesh then that is made your god, and your chief end. It is not every wish, or minding of Christ, no, not to save you from sin as sin, that will prove you true believers: nor is it every minding of God, or love to him, no, nor as one apprehending by you to be the chief good, and desirable for himself, as your end, that will prove indeed that you savingly love him; as long as the contrary mind and will is habitually predominant in you. Such as the very habit and bent of a man's heart is, such indeed is the man. It is possible for a man, even a good man, to have two contrary ends and intentions, yea, ultimate ends; as that which is desired for itself, and referred to nothing else, is called ultimate; but it is not possible for him to have two principal predominant ends. So far as we are carnal still, we make the pleasing of our flesh our ultimate end: for doubtless we do not sin only by pleasing the flesh, as a means to God's glory, nor only in the mischoosing of other means: but yet this is none of our principal ends, so far as men are truly sanctified. Because that is called a man's mind, or will, which is the chief and highest in his mind and will; therefore we use to denominate men from that only which bears rule in them. Thus we may say with Paul, 'It is not I, but sin that dwelleth in me.' For a disowned act that proceeds from us against the bent and habit of our wills and the course of our lives, and from the remnants of a carnal misguided will, is not that which must denominate the person, nor is so fully ours as the contrary act. Therefore though indeed we sinfully participate of it; yet when the question is, whether believing or unbelief, sinning or obeying, be my

work; it is not comparatively to be called mine, which I am much more against than for. So on the other side, if the unsanctified have some transient, superficial, ineffectual acts of desire or faith, or love to God, which are contrary to the bent and habit of their hearts, this is not theirs, nor imputable to them, so far as hence to give them their denomination. It is not they that do it, but the common workings of the Spirit upon them.

If ever then you would be assured that you are Christians, look to the habitual bent of your hearts, and see that you do not only talk of scripture, and slightly believe it, and speak well of Christ, with some good wishes, meanings, and purposes; but as you love your souls, see that Christ be received as your dearest Saviour, with thankfulness, and greatest love, and as your sovereign Lord, with true subjection; and that he have your superlative estimation and affections, and all things in the world be put under him in your souls. This must be so, if you will have the portion of believers. No faith that is short of this, will prove you Christ's disciples indeed, or heirs of the promises made to believers. The voice of Christ that calls to you in the gospel, is, 'My son give me thy heart.' Do what thou wilt in ways of duty, and think as highly as thou wilt of thyself, thou art no true believer in Christ's account till thou hast given him thy heart. If he have thy tongue, if he have thy good opinion—nay, if thy body were burnt in his cause, if he had not thy love, thy heart, it were as nothing. For thy works and sufferings are so far acceptable, through Christ, as they are testimonies of this, that Christ hath thy heart. If he have not thy heart, he takes it as if he had nothing: and if he have this, he takes it as if he had all. For this is not only preferred by him before all; but also he knows that this commands all. If Christ have thy heart, the devil will not have thy tongue and life; the alehouse, or a brothel, will not have thy body; nor the world will not have the principal part of thy life. If Christ have thy heart, it will be heard much in thy conference; it will be seen in thy labours. For that which hath a man's heart will hardly be hid, unless he purposely hide it, which a Christian neither can nor ought to do. It would make a man wonder to hear some foolish people, who will run from God as fast as they can, and yet assert that God hath their hearts: who have no mind, so much as to meditate, or talk of Christ or his precious blood, or mysterious redemption, or the glorious kingdom purchased by him; that will be at neither cost nor labour in his service, and yet profess that Christ hath their hearts : that will refuse a holy, heavenly life, perhaps make a scorn of it, and maliciously prate against the sanctified, and yet will stand to it that the Holy Ghost, the sanctifier of the elect, hath their hearts. No wonder if those hearts are ill-managed, and in a miserable deceived state, that are so unacquainted with themselves.

Faith enters at the understanding ; but it hath not all its essential parts, and is not the gospel faith indeed, till it hath possessed the will. The heart of faith is wanting, till faith hath taken possession of the heart. For by faith Christ dwells in the heart ; if he dwell not in the heart, he dwells not in the man, in a saving manner. He had some interest in Judas, Simon Magus, Ananias, and Sapphira, as to the head, and perhaps somewhat more in a superficial sort. But Satan entered into the heart of one, and filled the heart of another of them with a lie, and the heart of the third was not right in the sight of God, and therefore he had no part or lot in Christ, but was still in the gall of bitterness and bond of iniquity : and all because Christ was not heartily entertained. It is in the heart that the word must have its rooting, or else it will wither in time of trial. It is 'seeking with the whole heart' that is the evidence of the blessed, and it is a feigned turning when men turn not to God with the whole heart. This is God's promise concerning his elect ; 'I will give them a heart to know me that I am the Lord, and they shall be my people, and I will be their God : for they shall return unto me with their whole heart.' See then that the heart be unfeignedly delivered up to Christ : for if Christ have it not, the flesh, the world, and the devil, will have it. Your hearts must be a dwelling for one of these masters ; choose you whether.

It is the damnation of the most professed Christians, that they have nothing for Christ but a good opinion, or a few good words, or outside services, or some slight professions, when the flesh and the world go away with their hearts, and yet they will not know it, nor confess it. Christ will not be an underling or servant to your flesh. Your hearts he hath bought, and your hearts he will have ; or you are none of his. If he shall have nothing from you but a name, you shall have nothing but the name of his purchased salvation.

SECT. III. The last part of the direction yet remains, viz. that you must submit to Christ entirely, as well with the understanding as with the heart. It is whole Christ that must be received with the whole heart.

For the understanding of this, it must be known, both how and why Christ is offered to us.

As he came into the world ' to destroy the works of the devil, and to seek and save that which was lost,' and by his mediation to reconcile us to God, and bring us up to glory ; so two things were to be done for the accomplishment of this. First, he was himself to merit our salvation, and pay the price of our redemption on the cross, and in his own person to conquer the world, the devil, death, and the grave : and then he was, by his intercession in the heavens, to make application of this, and bestow the benefits thus purchased by him. Because it was he, and not we, that made the purchase, it therefore pleased the Father that the purchased treasure should be put into his hands, and not immediately put into ours. He is become our treasury, and authorised to be our head : all power is given him in heaven and earth. We have so foully miscarried already, that he will no more trust his honour in our hands, as at first he did. We shall have nothing of pardon, or grace, or glory, but what we have *in* and *from* the *Son.* ' God hath given us eternal life, and this life is in his Son : he that hath the Son hath life ; and he that hath not the Son, hath not life.' It is not only the nature and person of Christ that is to be believed in ; but it is the person as empowered to certain ends, and clothed with his office, that we must now entertain. Now the office of Christ being for our salvation, and the glory of God, is suited to these happy ends.

Our necessities are principally in these three points. 1. We have the guilt of sin upon us to be pardoned, and the wrath of God, the curse of the law, and the punishment of sin to be removed. 2. We have the corruption of our nature to be healed ; the power of sin to be destroyed ; the image of God repaired on us, and our hearts and lives to be actuated and ordered according to the will of God ; and to these ends, temptations to be conquered ; and our souls directed, strengthened, and preserved to the end. 3. We must be raised from the grave at the last day : we must be justified in judgment, and possessed of that glory which is the end of our faith To this, justification, sanctification, and glorification may the rest be reduced.

Now the office of Christ is suited to these necessities of ours ; and as we cannot possibly be saved, unless all these necessities be supplied, and these works done for us : so we cannot possibly have these things done but by accepting of Christ, as authorised, and impowered by his office and perfections, to do them.

The glory that God will have by this work, I have before expressed to you at large. He will have his justice, wisdom, power, holiness, and mercy, to be demonstrated and honoured by Christ. And therefore Christ hath resolved to give out none of his benefits, but in such manner and ways as may best attain these highest ends.

These several points therefore I must intreat you here to note distinctly. 1. That you must be brought into a special relation to the person of Christ, as clothed with his office, before you can lay claim to his saving benefits; he is the head, and you must become his spouse; and so of the rest. This is called our uniting to Christ, which must go before our further communion with him. It is the will of God, that you shall never receive his benefits before you receive his Son: except only those benefits which go before your union with Christ himself, in order to the accomplishing it; as the gospel, the gift of faith to the elect, &c. You shall never have actual pardon, justification, adoption, sanctification, or glory, till you have first saving interest in Christ himself. He is the vine, and we are the branches: we must be planted into him, and live in him, or else we can have nothing further from God, nor do nothing acceptable to God. Therefore the first and great work of faith is to receive and rely on the person of Christ, as clothed with his office.

2. Understand and note, that as you shall not have his great benefits before, or without his person; so God hath resolved, that you shall not have his special benefits, unless you will take them all together. I speak of men at age, that are capable of all. You shall not have pardon and justification, or glory, without sanctification; nor the comforts of Christ without the guidance and government of Christ. You must have all or none.

3. From hence it follows, that therefore you must receive and close with Christ entirely, in his whole office, as he is to accomplish all these works, or else you cannot be united to him. He will not be divided: you shall not have Christ as a justifier of you, if you will not have him as a guide, ruler, and sanctifier of you. He will not be a partial Saviour: if you will not consent that he shall save you from your sins, he will not consent to save you from hell.

4. Understand and note that Christ will look to his Father's interest and honour, and his own, as well as to your salvation; yea, and before it. Therefore you must not hope for any mercy from him, in any way that is dishonourable to him, or that is inconsistent with his own blessed ends and interest. Therefore do not look for any such grace from him as shall discharge you from your duty, or give you liberty to dishonour or disobey him; nor do not think that you shall have him related to you only for your own ends, but on terms of highest honour to God and your Redeemer. Do not think that your grace is ever the less free, because God's honour is thus preferred: for if you are Christians indeed, you will take God's interest, as your own highest interest, and will confess, that you could not have your own ends and welfare any other way.

5. Understand and note also, that as all your mercies are in the hand of Christ, so Christ hath appointed, in his gospel, a certain way and course of means in which he will bestow it: and you cannot expect it from him in any other way but his own. As God hath made Christ the way, and no man comes to the Father but by him, so Christ hath ordained a standing course of means, which are his way for the making over of his benefits; and here you must have them, or go without them.

6. Understand and note, that there are some of Christ's ends and benefits, that the very natural man desires, and some that corrupted nature is against. Now it is therefore the established way of Christ to promise us those which we can desire, on condition that we will also accept of and submit to those that we are against. Not but that his grace doth dispose men to the performance of such conditions: but his grace works by means: and a conditional promise is his established means, to draw men's hearts to the performance of the condition, which, well considered, is a sufficient answer to the arguments that are commonly urged against the condition of the promise. As the Spirit doth powerfully work within; so he uses that word from without, as his instrument, which works wisely and powerfully to the same work. If a physician have two medicines to give his patient, as necessary for his cure, the one very sweet, and the other bitter; the one which he loves, and the other which he lothes, he will promise him the sweeter, if he will take the bitter one; that by the love of one, he may prevail against the lothing of the other, and may entice it down. He will not promise the bitter one which is lothed, and make the taking of the sweet one the condition: he will not say, I will give thee this aloes, on condition thou wilt take this sugar; but contrary, I will give thee the sweeter, if thou wilt take the bitter.

In Christ's ends, and works, First, We naturally are more willing of that which makes for ourselves directly, than of that which makes directly for the honour of God and the Redeemer. We prefer our own ends before God's glory: therefore Christ hath so ordered the condition of his promises, that unless we will take him in his relations of dignity as King and Lord, and will make the glory and pleasing of God our principal end, we shall have none of him, or his saving benefits. For he came not to fulfil our selfish desires, but to bring us off from ourselves, and recover us to God, that he might have his own. If we will not have our all in God, we shall have nothing. Second, Naturally we are willing, as to our own benefits, to be pardoned, freed from the curse of the law, the flames of hell, natural death, and punishment: therefore we are thus far naturally willing of free justification; but we are unwilling to let go the seeming profit, credit, and pleasure of sin, and to deny the flesh, and forsake the world; we are averse to the spiritual felicity of the saints, to the holiness of heart and life, that is the way to it. Therefore Christ hath most wisely so ordered it, in the tenor of his promises, that our repentance and faith shall be the condition of our justification and deliverance from death and hell: this faith is the believing in him, and accepting him entirely in his whole office, to sanctify us, and rule us, as well as to justify us: thus we must take him wholly, or we shall have none of him. The accepting him as our teacher, sanctifier, and king, is as much at least the condition of our justification, pardon, and deliverance from hell, as is the accepting of him as a justifier of us. He that had the power in his own hands, and that made the free promise, hath put in such conditions, as his own wisdom saw best; and they are such as suit most congruously to all his ends; even the glory of God, in all his attributes, the Redeemer's glory, our own, and most full and free salvation: on his conditions must we have his benefits, or we shall never have them.

7. Lastly, Understand and note, that the means which Christ hath resolved on for teaching and ruling us, ordinarily are his word, his ministers, and his Spirit; all must be submitted to together, where they may be had, and none of them laid by, by separation. His word is the grammar, or book as it were, that we must learn: his ministers must teach us this book: and his Spirit, who in the apostles and prophets indited and sealed it, must inwardly teach us, by powerful illumination. The word is God's laws:

the ministers are his ambassadors, or heralds to proclaim them, and command obedience in his name; and his Spirit must open men's hearts to entertain them. The word is God's seed; the ministers are the husbandmen, or servants that sow it; the Spirit must give the increase, without which our planting and watering will do nothing. He therefore that takes Christ for his Master and King, must resolve to be taught and ruled by his established means, even by his word, ministers, and Spirit: for he that refuses and despises these, doth refuse and despise Christ; and consequently the Father that sent him. For it was never the meaning of Christ, when he became the teacher and king of the church, to stay on earth, and personally and visibly to teach them himself; but these three are his means, which all must submit to, that will be his subjects and disciples. And he that despises the word, shall be destroyed. He that will not have the word, ministry, and Spirit teach him, will not have Christ teach him: and he that refuses to be ruled by these three, shall be destroyed as a rebel against Christ himself. Still it is supposed that ministers must teach and rule according to this word.

The society in which Christ will teach and govern us, is his church; as members therefore of the universal church and in communion with his particular church where we live and have opportunity, we must wait on Christ for his teaching and benefits. For this is his school, where his disciples must diligently attend and learn.

Lay all this together, and this is the sum. the object of justifying, saving faith, is one only undivided Christ, one in person, but of two natures, God and man; in office the Mediator between God and man, who hath already done the work of satisfaction and merit, and is authorized further to bestow the benefits: by the gospel grant he hath given himself as Head, Husband, Teacher, King, and Saviour, to all that will entirely and heartily accept him; and with himself he gives justification by the promise; sanctification by the word, ministry, and Spirit; final forgiveness, and everlasting life. If ever then you will have Christ and life, you must accept him in all these essentials of his person and offices, and that to the ends which his redemption was intended for: you must be willing to be sanctified by him, as well as to be justified: you must at once unfeignedly become his disciples, his subjects, his members, if you would become his saved ones. You must consent, that as your Teacher and your Lord, he shall teach and rule your heart and life, by his word, ministers, and

Spirit in communion with his church. No bar of exception must be put in, nor reservation made against any one of these parts of his office. If you yield not to these parts of his saving work that tend but to the complete growth, you sin, and deprive yourselves of the benefit: but if you yield not to those that must make you truly sanctified and justified men, you cannot be saved. The essentials of Christ's person and office, constitute him the Christ, and if he be not received in all those essential points, he is not received as Christ.

Thus I have given you the sum of the gospel, and the description of faith and true Christianity, in this direction for a right closing with the Lord Jesus Christ. And experience of most that I discourse with, persuades me to think this direction of great importance, and to intreat you thoroughly to peruse and consider it. I find abundance of ignorant people, that talk much of Christ, but know very little of him; that can scarce tell us whether he be God or man, or which person in the trinity he is, nor to what end he became incarnate and died, nor what relation he stands in to us, or what use he is of, or what he now is, or what he is engaged to do for us. But if we ask them about their hopes of salvation, they almost overlook the redemption by Christ, and tell us of nothing but God's mercies, and their own good meanings and endeavours. I am afraid too many professors of piety look almost all at the natural part of religion, and the mending of their own hearts and lives (and I would this were better done) while they forget the supernatural part, and are little affected with the infinite love of God in Christ. I desire such to consider these things: First, You overlook the sum of your religion, which is Christ crucified, besides whom Paul desired to know nothing. Second, You overlook the fountain of your own life, and the author of your supplies; and you strive in vain for sanctification or justification, if you seek them not from a crucified Christ. Third, You leave undone the principal part of your work, and live like moral heathens, while you have the name of Christians. Your daily work is to study God in the face of his Son; and to labour with 'all saints to comprehend the height, breadth, length, and depth, and to know the love of Christ, which passeth knowledge.' All your graces should be daily quickened, and set to work by the life of faith, in the contemplation of the Redeemer and his blessed work. This is the weight that must set all the wheels agoing. You do God no service, that he can accept, if you serve him not in this gospel work, of loving, trusting, admiring, and praising him in the Redeemer, and for his redemption. Fourth, And so you rob God of the principal part of his glory which you are to give him; which is for his most glorious work of our redemption. I pray you read over again the ends of this work, which I laid down in the beginning of this direction. Fifth, Moreover you rob yourselves of your principal comfort, which must all come in, by living upon Christ. Sixth, You harden the Antinomians and Libertines, and tempt men to their extremes, that run from us as legalists and as men that savour not the doctrine of free grace, and are not of a gospel spirit and conversation. I would our great neglect of Christ had not been a snare to these mistaken souls, and a stumbling block in their way.

If a thought of your hearts, if a word of your mouths, have not some relation to Christ, suspect it, yea, reject it. Call it not a sermon or a prayer, or a duty, that hath nothing of Christ in it. Though the pure godhead be your principal end, yet there is no way to this end but by Christ; and though love, which is exercised on that end, must animate all your graces and duties, as they are means to that end; yet faith hath love in it, or else it is not the Christian faith; and Christ is the object of your faith and love; and your perfect everlasting love will be animated by Christ: for your love and praise will be to him that was slain, and redeemed us to God by his blood, out of every kindred, tongue, and nation, and made us kings and priests to God. So much for the fifth direction.

DIRECTION VI.

The next direction which I would give you for a thorough conversion, is this: see that the flesh be thoroughly mortified, and your hearts be thoroughly taken off the world, and all its pleasures, profits, and honours, and that the root of your fleshly interest prevail not at the heart, and that you think not of reconciling God and the world, as if you might secure your interest in both.

This is a very common cause of the deceit and destruction of such as verily think they are converted. It is the very nature and business of true conversion, to turn men's hearts from the flesh, from the world to God, and from an earthly and seeming happiness, to a heavenly, real, everlasting happiness. When men are affrighted into some kind of religiousness, yet never learn to deny themselves, and never mortify their fleshly mind, but the love of this world is still the chief principle at their hearts; and so go on in a profession of godliness, with a secret reserve that they will look as well as they can to their outward prosperity, whatever become of their religion, and they will have no more to do with the matters of another world, than may stand with their bodily safety in this world; these are the miserable, deluded hypocrites, whose hopes will prove as the giving up of the ghost; whom Christ will disown in their greatest extremities, after all their seeming religion. Look to this, my reader, as ever you would be happy. It is an easy, it is a common, it is a most dangerous thing, to set upon a course of outward piety, yet keep the world next your hearts, take it still as a great part of your felicity, and secretly to love your former lusts, while you seem to be converted. The heart is so deceitful that you have great cause to watch it narrowly in this point: it will closely cherish the love of the world, and your fleshly pleasures, when it seems to renounce them, and when your tongue can speak contemptuously of them. It was not for nothing Christ would have the first-fruits of his gospel-church, who were to be the example of their successors, to sell all, and lay it down at the feet of his apostles: and it is his standing rule, that 'whoever he be, that forsaketh not all that he hath, he cannot be his disciple.' In estimation, affection, and resolution, it must be forsaken by all that will be saved; and also in practice, whenever God calls us to it. You can have but one happiness; if you will needs have it in this world, in the contenting of your flesh, there is no hope of having it also in another world, in the fruition of God. If you think not God and heaven enough for you, and cannot let go the prosperity of the flesh for them, you must let go all your hopes of them. God will not halve it with the world in your hearts, nor part stakes with the flesh; much less will he be below them, and take the dregs: heaven will not be theirs, that set not by it more than earth. God will not call that love to him sincere, which is not a superlative love, and able to make you even to hate all those things that would draw away your affections and obedience from him. There is no possibility of serving God and mammon, and compounding you a happiness of earth and heaven. Do therefore as Christ bids you in Luke xiv. 21, 29, 30.

Sit down and count what it must cost you, if you will be saved, and on what rates it is that you must follow Christ. Can you voluntarily, for the love of him, and the hope of glory, take up your cross, and follow him in poverty, in losses, in reproaches, through scorns, scourgings, and prisons and death? Do you value his loving-kindness better than life? Can you deny your eyes and your appetites their desire? Can you consent to be vile in the eyes of men, to tame your own flesh, keep it in subjection, and live a fleshly, displeasing life, that having suffered with Christ, you may also be glorified with him? If you cannot consent to these terms, you cannot be Christians, nor can you be saved. If you must needs be rich, or must be honourable, yea, if you must needs save your estates, or liberties, or lives, it is past all question you must needs let go Christ and glory: if you must needs have the world, you must needs lose your souls. If you must have your good things here, you must not have them hereafter too, but be tormented, when Christ's sufferers are comforted. These hopes of purveying for the flesh, as long as they can, and then of being saved, when they can stay here no longer, is it that hath deceived many thousands to their destruction. It is a strange thing to see how the world doth blind very knowing men, and how unacquainted these hypocrites are with their own hearts. What a confident profession of down-right godliness many of them will make; yea, of some extraordinary height in religion, when nothing is so dear to them as their present prosperity, and God hath not near so much interest in them as the flesh? What contrivances some of them make for riches, or rising in the world! How tender others are of their honour with men; and how tenacious they are of their mammon of unrighteousness; how much money, and great men, can do with them. If the times but change and countenance any error, how small an argument will make their judgments bend with the times: if truth or duty must cost them dear, O how they will shift, stretch, and wriggle, to prove truth to be no truth, and duty to be no duty; and no argument is strong enough to satisfy them, when the flesh doth but say, It is bitter, it is dangerous, it may be my undoing.

It is none of my meaning, that any should needlessly run into suffering, or cross their governors and themselves, through a spirit of pride, singularity, and contradiction: but that men should think themselves truly religious, that keep such reserves for their fleshly interest, and show, by the very drift of their lives, that they are worldlings, and never felt what it was to be crucified to the world, and deny themselves, but are religious on this supposition only, that it may stand with worldly ends, or at least not undo them in the world; this is a lamentable hypocritical self-deceit. When God hath so plainly said, 'Love not the world, nor the things that are in the world: if any man love the world, the love of the Father is not in him.' Nay, that the neighbourhood, and all the country that know them, should ring of the worldliness of some, who think themselves good Christians; and yet they will not see themselves. What a cheating, blinding thing is the world!

If you will be Christians, count what it must cost you: and if you will be heirs of heaven, away with the world: cast it out of your hearts: and if your hands must yet trade in it, yet trade not for it: use it for God, but enjoy it not for itself. Take yourselves as strangers here; and look on the world as a desolate wilderness; through which, in the communion of the militant saints, you may safely travel on to heaven; but do not make it your home, nor take it for the smallest part of your felicity. To be sanctified without mortification, is a palpable contradiction. Be at a point with all things below, if you will groundedly hope for the heavenly inheritance. But I shall purposely forbear to enlarge this any further, because I have preached and written a treatise on this subject, which I desire you to peruse.

DIRECTION VII.

My next direction is this: If you would be truly converted, be sure that you make an absolute resignation of yourselves, and all that you have, to God.

This is the very form and life of sanctification. To be sanctified, is to be separated in heart, life, and profession, from all other masters and ends, to God. When the heart that was set upon the word and flesh, is separated from them, and inclined to God by the power of love, and devoted to him, to serve and please him; this is indeed a sanctified heart: and when the life that before was spent in the service of Satan, the world, and the flesh, is now taken off them, and spent, as to the drift, and course of it, in the service of God, for the pleasing and glorifying of him, from the impulse of love, this is indeed a holy life. Herein consists the very nature of our sanctity. When a man does but profess to renounce the devil, the world and the flesh, and to give up his heart and life to God, this is a profession of holiness. God is both on the title of creation, preservation, and redemption, our absolute Lord or Owner, and we are not our own, but his; therefore we must give to God

the things that are God's, and glorify him in our souls and bodies which are his. As we are his own, so he will have his own, and be served by his own: do not imagine that you have any title to yourselves, or propriety in yourselves: but without any more ado, make a full, unreserved, absolute resignation of yourselves, of your understandings, and of your wills, of your bodies, and of your names, and of every penny-worth of your estates to God, from whom, and for whom you have them. Think not that you have power to dispose of yourselves, or of any thing that you have. Ask not flesh and blood, what life you shall lead, or what mind or will, you shall be of. But ask God, to whom you belong. Ask not your carnal selves, what you shall do with any of your estates, but ask God, and then ask conscience, which is the way that God would have me use it in, that is, which way may I use it to be most serviceable to God? and that resolve upon. No service that you do to God will prove you sanctified, unless you have heartily and absolutely given up, and devoted yourselves to him; and he that gives up himself, must needs give up all that he hath with himself. For he cannot keep it for himself, ultimately, when even himself is given up to God. Though you be not bound to give all that you have to the poor, nor all to the church, nor to deny your own bodies, or families their due supplies; yet must it all be given up to God, even that which you make use of for yourselves and families: for as you are given up to God yourselves, so you must feed yourselves as his, and clothe yourselves, and your families as his, to fit yourselves and them for his service, and not as your own, for the satisfying of your flesh.

Thus it is that all comes to be pure to the pure, sanctified to them that are themselves first sanctified; because when you feed yourself you but feed a servant of God, that is consecrated to him, and separated from things common and unclean. And even as the tithes and offerings, that were given for the food and maintenance of the priests and Levites, were called the Lord's portion, and holy to the Lord, because they were their portion that were separated to his altar; even so that which is necessary to fit you for God's service, while you use it to that very end, is sanctified in your sanctification, and is holy to God; for all his saints are a 'holy nation, a royal priesthood, to offer up acceptable sacrifice to him.' And thus, 'whether you eat, or drink, or whatever you do, you must do all to the glory of God.—For of him, and through him, and to him, are all things, and therefore to him must be the glory for ever.' God, who is the end of your hearts and lives, must be the end of every action of them, unless you will step out of the way of order, safety, and holiness. For every action that is not from God, and by God, and for God, is contrary to the nature of true sanctification. If then you would be Christians indeed, be heartily willing that God should have his own. Understand what an excellent honour, privilege, and happiness it is to you to be his. If his right to you will not move you, let your own necessity and benefit at least move you to give up yourselves and all you have to God. Bring your hearts to the bar, and plead the cause of God with them, and convince them of God's title to them, and how sinfully they have robbed him of his own all this while. Have your days and hours, your wealth and interest, been used purposely for God as his own? O what abundance is there, that in word, and confident profession, give up themselves, and all to God, and yet the use of themselves and all plainly shows that it is no such matter; but they dissembled with God, and yet never knew so much by themselves. How little they use for God, when they have with seeming devotion resigned all to him! One would think, by their lives, that they look to be saved by robbing God, and confessing the robbery, by saying that all is God's, while they allow him next to nothing.

The devoted, resigned, sanctified soul hath the true principle of all obedience, and that which will do much to repel all temptations and carry him through the greatest straits and trials. If I am not my own, I need not be over solicitous for myself, but may expect that he that owns me should care for me: nor do I need to use any sinful shifts for my own preservation. If I have nothing of my own, what need I to sin for the saving of any thing; what need I to venture upon unwarrantable means, to preserve either credit or goods, or life? It is self that is the root of all sin, the heart of the old man, and seed of hell: nothing else is pleaded against God, and our salvation. If the flesh would have you abuse God's creatures, you must remember they are not your own. If the devil would entice you to sin against God, either for the getting, or keeping of any creature, it would easily repel the temptation, were you but rightly sensible, that nothing is your own: for God hath no need that you should sin, to get riches, or honours, for him. If you are called to let go your houses, or lands, or friends, or lives, or to deliver up your bodies to the flames, did you but rightly take them as none of your own, how easy would it be! You

can be content that another man give his goods, or life itself to God, whenever God requires it; but your own, you cannot be content to part with; and that because it is your own. But if you had rightly resigned all to God, and took not yourselves, or any thing for your own, but looked upon yourselves, and all as God's, the greatest works of obedience, or suffering, would be much more easy to you; and you would have little difficulty, or hinderance in your way. Self-denial is but sanctification itself, denominated from the wrong end and principle, which we forsake. Where self is denied and dead, what is there left to draw us from God, or stand up against him, in any part of our lives? So much interest as self hath in you, so much the world and the devil hath in you. And nothing is more proper to a miserable hypocrite, than deep reserves of life, or worldly things, to themselves, while they seem to give up all to God.

O happy soul, that is wrought to this sincerity by the Spirit of grace; to say unfeignedly, O Lord, I devote and resign myself wholly unto thee! I am not my own, nor desire any further to be, than to be thine: I have nothing that is my own, nor desire to have any thing that shall not be thine. Happy and truly wise is that man, that keeps as constant and faithful a reckoning, how he lays out himself, and all that he hath for God, as a faithful steward doth, of his receiving, and laying out for his master's use. Every penny that is reserved from God, is the fuel of sin and a sacrifice to the devil, and the flesh; and if it be pardoned to the truly penitent, by the sacrifice of Christ, that is no thanks to us, that would else have made it the fuel of hell. God is not so careless of us, or his mercies, but that he keeps an exact account of all that we have from him, and will require an account of our improvement of all: not only requiring his own again, but his own with advantage. Why else did he give us such leisure and ability to approve it? I can never forget what a sinful thought was once in my mind, which I will venture to confess, because it may possibly be the case of others, that so they may beware: Hearing of some that used to lay by the tenth part of their yearly comings in, for charitable uses, I purposed to do so too, and thought it a fair proportion: but since I have perceived what a vile and wicked thought that was, to offer to cut out a scantling for God, or give him a limited share of his own, or say that so much he shall have, and no more. Though we cannot say that God must have all in any one kind of service only; either only for the church, or only for the

poor, or only for public uses ; yet must we resolve, that in one way or other he must have all ;
and the particular portions to the poor, or church,
or other uses, must be assigned by truly sanc-
tificd prudence, considering which way it may
be most serviceable to God. I must relieve my
own family, or kindred, if they want, but not
because they are my own, but because God hath
commanded me, and so hath made it a part of
my obedience. But if I see where I may do
more service to God by relieving a stranger, and
that God doth more require it, I must yet prefer them before all the kindred that I have in the
world.

When the Christian pattern was set up by the
primitive church, they sold all, and laid down
the whole price at the apostles' feet, which was
not distributed to their natural kindred only, but
to all the poor Christians that had no other relation to them, even as every one had need. And
as it is the loving of our spiritual brethren in
Christ, that is made the sign of our translation
from death to life, so is it the relieving of Christ
in these his members, that is, the relieving them
because they are his members, that is made the
very matter of our cause in the last judgment,
and the ground of the sentence of life, or death.
I must provide for my own body, and you must
provide for your children, but that is, as I said
before, not as I am my own, nor as your children
are your own ; but as I am a servant of Christ,
that must be supported in his service, or as
yourselves, and yours are put under your care
and duty by God. So that I may give it to
myself, or others, when I can truly say, I do
but use it principally for God, and think that
the principal service I can do him by it, but I may
neither take to myself, nor give to any that are
nearest to me, any more than God commands, or
his service doth require. When you and yours have
your daily bread, which also must be used for him,
you must not go to flesh and blood, but to God, to
ask which way you will dispose of the remainder. This is a strange doctrine to the unsanctified world, but that is because they are unsanctified. And it is a doctrine that a worldly hypocrite is loth to believe and understand ; but
that is because of carnality and hypocrisy, that
always deal with God, like Ananias and Sapphira,
lying to the Holy Ghost, and giving God but
half, and few so much as half, when they daily
confess that all is from him, and should be his,
and pretend to be wholly devoted to him. There
are but few men so bad, but will spare God
something rather than go to hell: but indeed
this is not to devote it to God, but to use it for

themselves, thinking by their sacrifices to stop
the mouth of justice, and to please God by a
part, when they have displeased him in the rest.
I much fear, and not without apparent cause,
that abundance among us, who think themselves
Christians, worship and serve God as some
Indians are said to offer sacrifice to the devil,
not for any love they have to him, or his service,
but for fear he should hurt them. There are
few hypocrites but will pretend it is from very
love.

It is a greater matter to resign and give up
yourselves and all you have to God, and heartily to
quit all claim to yourselves and all things, than
many a thousand self-deluded professors imagine. Many look at this but as some high extraordinary strain of piety ; and the papists
almost appropriate it to a few that live in mo-
nastic orders, when indeed the sincerity of this
resignation, and dedication, is the very sincerity
of sanctification itself.

Let me tell you, that the unfeigned convert
who attains to this, hath not only plucked up the
root of sin, though all of us have too many strings
of it left, not only stopped up the spring of
temptation, and got the surest evidence of his
uprightness, but also is got himself into the
safest and most comfortable state. For when
he hath absolutely resigned himself, and all to
God, how confidently may he expect that God
should accept him, and use him as his own ; and
how comfortably may he commit himself and his
cause, and all good affairs to God, as knowing
that God cannot be negligent and careless of
his own ? It is an argument that may make us
confident of success, when we can say as David,
' I am thine ; save me.' Even Christ himself
commends his elect to the Father on this account ; ' Thine they were, and thou gavest them
to me : I pray for them : I pray not for the
world, but for them which thou hast given me :
for they are thine ; and all mine are thine, and
thine are mine, and I am glorified in them.'
And indeed, by resigning all to God, it is the
more our own ; that is, we have unspeakably
more of the benefit of it, and so there is no way
to make it our own, but by quitting it absolutely
up to God : this is the mystery that the world
will not learn, but God will teach it all that
shall be saved by the Spirit, and by faith.
' Then Jesus said to his disciples, if any man
will come after me, let him deny himself, take
up his cross, and follow me : for whosoever will
save his life shall lose it ; and whosoever will
lose his life for my sake shall find it.' Methinks a man who hath time, strength, and mo-

ney, should long to be disbursing all for God, that he might put it in the surest hands, and it may be out of danger; yea, that it may be set to the most honest and profitable usury. For when God hath it from the dedication of an upright heart, it is sure; but till God have it, it is in hazard; and all that he hath not, is lost, and worse than lost. When it is in our hands, thieves may steal it, bad servants, or unadvised children may consume it, and our own thievish flesh may steal it, which is worst of all, and consume it in our lusts; or if our children consume it not, their children may: or if they save it, they may lose it most of all, by feeding their pride and fleshly minds by it: but if once it be in God's hands, it is safe. You can make no comfortable account of one penny, nor of one hour's time, unless you can tell God that he had it himself; that you used it for him; or that you live to him in the main, and that the rest is pardoned. O that those parents understood this doctrine, who had rather strengthen the fetters and temptations of their children with it, and help them in that state which few are saved in, than to devote and use their estates for God! Though Christ hath told them how hardly the rich are saved, and how few of such come to heaven, yet what care is taken to leave their children rich, and how little to further the work of God, or their own accounts, that they may hear the 'Well done, good and faithful servant, thou hast been faithful over a few things: I will make thee ruler over many things: enter thou into the joys of thy Lord.'

If you would be good husbands, and provident indeed for your souls, see that your hearts prove not false to you in this, and make no secret reserves for yourselves, but that God have yourselves first, and all things with yourselves; as Christ first gives himself to you and all things with himself. Never think your hearts right, but when they can readily say, 'We are not our own.' Think not that you come aright to God in any duty, if you do not heartily devote yourselves to him, and intreat him to accept you, as wholly his, who neither are, nor desire to be your own; and intreat him accordingly to use you for himself. Say not that any thing is your own that you possess. In respect to God, and a communion of charity, though it be your own, as a talent that God doth intrust you with, in respect of men, by a legal propriety.

Then trust God boldly, for you are his own: serve him cheerfully, and draw near him in faith, for you are his own. In poverty, sickness, temptations, and the approach of death, rejoice in him confidently, for you are his own. Into his hands commend your departing spirits, for they are his own. What reason of distrustful fears can you now have? Do you fear lest God will yet hate you; why remember that 'no man ever yet hated his own flesh?' Nay for shame, think not the blessed God to be worse than the wicked world; for Christ saith of the world, 'If ye were of the world, the world would love his own.' Will not God then love his own, do you think? If you are willing to be his own, Christ is certainly willing that you should be his own, and will own all that own not themselves, but him. 'He calleth his own sheep by name, and leadeth them out: and when he putteth forth his own sheep he goeth before them, and the sheep follow him: for they know his voice.— Having loved his own which are in the world, to the end he loved them.'

If you are but truly willing to be his own people, he is certainly willing to be your own Saviour and your own God. Not that you can have such a propriety in him, as he hath in you. But in these relations he will be your own; glory, help, and salvation shall be yours. You may well conclude that 'God, even our own God, shall bless us.' Much comfort may be brought from that in Luke xv. 31. though parables must not be stretched too far: 'Son, thou art ever with me, and all that I have is thine.'

Upon this ground it is that we have the greater encouragement, to believe that God accepts of. our very infants themselves; because it is his will that they should be devoted, engaged, and dedicated to him: and that which he would have us dedicate and offer to him, he will surely accept in that relation to which he would have it offered.

I beseech you therefore remember what it is to be truly converted: it is to be called from things common and unclean, and separated to God; it is to be brought nigh to him, as the children of his household, that are themselves and all that they have, in his hands: it is to be taken off yourselves and your own, and to lose yourselves and all you have in God, by the most gainful loss; lest indeed you lose yourselves, and all, while you persuade yourselves you save, or gain. It is a taking God in Christ for your all, and so being content to have nothing but him, and for him. It is a changing of your old master, self, for God, a better master: your old work, which was self-seeking and pleasing, to self-denial, and to the seeking and pleasing of God. See now that this be done, and that your treacherous hearts hide nothing for themselves, as Rachel, under pretence of necessity, hid her idols, but say, ' Here I am, to be thine, O Lord, and to do thy will.'

DIRECTION VIII.

My next advice, that the work of conversion may not miscarry, is this ; take heed, lest you mistake a mere change of your opinions, outward profession, and behaviour, for a true saving change.

Wicked opinions must be changed, and so must evil professions and outward practices ; but if no more be changed you are wicked still. I have great cause to fear that this is the most common condemning deceit, that befals professors of godliness, and that it is the case of most hypocrites in the church. A man may be brought to hold any truth in scripture as an opinion ; and so far be sound, and orthodox ; yet never be indeed a sound believer, nor have his heart possessed with the life and power of those sacred truths. It is one thing to have a man's *opinion changed*, and another thing to have his heart *renewed*, by the change of his practical estimation, resolutions, and dispositions. It is one thing to turn from loose profane opinions, to strict opinions ; and think the godly are indeed in the right, that their case and way is safest and best ; and it is another thing to be made one of them in newness, spirituality of heart, and life. A lively faith differs much from opinion, and that which is in unsanctified men, which we call faith ; which is a kind of faith indeed, but a mere opinionative faith : I call it an opinionative faith, because it differs from saving faith, much like as opinion doth from knowledge. Merely speculative it is not ; for some intention of practice there is : but the practical intention of such persons differs from the predominant intentions of the sanctified ; even as their opinionative faith differs from the saving faith.

It is no wonder if there be abundance of these opinionative believers in the world : for the truths of God have very great evidence ; especially some of them ; and men are yet men, and consequently reasonable creatures ; and therefore have some aptitude to discern the evidence of truth : some truths will compel assent even from the unwilling : many a thousand ungodly men believe that to be true which they would not have to be true, if they could help it ; because they do not heartily take it to be good in respect to themselves. Truth as truth, is the natural object of the understanding : though the same truth, as seeming evil to them, may be hated by them that are forced to assent to it. I know

that sin hath much blinded men's understanding, and that ' the natural man receiveth not the things of the Spirit, because they are foolishness to him, and must be spiritually discerned,' but though he cannot savingly receive them without the special illumination of the Spirit, nor opinionatively receive them without a common illumination of the Spirit, yet he may have this opinionative conviction and an answerable reformation, by the common grace of the Spirit, without the special grace. An unsanctified man may have something more than nature in him : and every unregenerated man is not merely, or only natural. Many are far convinced, that are far from being savingly converted. I can make you know that you shall die ; that you must part with all your wealth, and fleshly pleasures, and divers such truths, whether you will or not. And one of these truths, doth let in many more, that depend upon them. So that as dark as the minds of natural men are, they yet lie open to many wholesome truths.

As the understanding is thus far open to conviction, so the will itself, which is the heart of the old man, will far sooner yield to the changing of your opinions than to the saving change of heart and life. It is not the bare opinion, that your fleshly interest doth fight against, but it is the power and practice of godliness ; and opinions as they lead to these. It is one thing to be of opinion that conversion is necessary, that sin must be forsaken, and God preferred before all the world ; and it is another thing to be indeed converted, to forsake sin, and to prefer God before the world. It is a far more easy matter to convince a worldling that he should not love the world, than to cure him of his worldly love ; and to convince a drunkard that he should leave his drunkenness, and the whoremonger, that he should abhor his lusts, than to bring them to do these things which they are convinced of. It will cost them dear, as the flesh accounts it, to deny themselves, and cast away the sin ; but it costs not so dear to take up the opinion that these things should be done. It will cost them dear to be upright with God, and practically religious ; but they can take up an opinion that godliness is the best and necessary course, at a cheaper rate. Strict practices mortify the flesh, but strict opinions may stand with its liberty. O what abundance of our poor neighbours would go to heaven, who are now in the way to hell, if an opinion that godliness is the wisest course, would serve the turn. If instead of conversion, God would take up with an opinion that they ought to turn ; and if instead of a holy, heavenly life, God would accept of an opinion, that such are the happiest men that live such a life; and if instead of temperance, meekness, self-denial, and forgiving wrongs, God would accept of an opinion and confession, that they should be temperate, meek, and self-denying, and should forbear others, and forgive them; then O what abundance would be saved, that are now in little hope of salvation! If instead of a diligent life of holiness, and good works, it would serve turn to lie still, and be of a good opinion, that men should strive, and labour for salvation, and lay out all they have for God, how happy then were our towns and countries, in comparison of what they are!

I am afraid this deceit will be the ruin of many, that they take a change of their opinions for a true conversion. Have not some of you been formerly of the mind, that the best way is to eat, drink, be merry, venture your souls, follow your worldly business, and never trouble yourselves with any deep and searching thoughts about your spiritual state, or your salvation? Have you not thought that this diligent godliness is but a needless strictness and preciseness; and have you not since been convinced of your error, and perceived that this is the wisest course, which you before thought to be needless, and thereupon have betaken you to the company of the godly, and set upon a course of outward duties; and now you think that you are made new creatures and that this is regeneration, and the work is done. I fear lest this be all the conversion that many forward professors are acquainted with! but woe to them that have no more.

Because the face of our present times doth plainly show the commonness and prevalency of this disease, and because it is a matter of so great concern to you, I shall here give you, as briefly as I well can, some signs by which a true conversion may be known from this mere opinionative change.

1. The true convert is brought to an unfeigned hatred of the whole body of sin; and especially of those secret, or beloved sins, that did most powerfully captivate him before. But the opinionative convert is still carnal, unmortified, and inwardly at the heart the interest of the flesh is habitually predominant. He is not brought to an irreconcilable hatred to the great master sins that ruled him, and lay deepest; but only hath cropt off some of the branches of the tree of death. The thorns of worldly desires and cares, are still rooted in his heart; and therefore no wonder if they choke the seed of wholesome truth, and there be a greater harvest for the devil than for God.

2. Another sign that follows upon this is, that the sound convert doth carry on the course of his obedience, in a way of self-denial, as living in a continual conflict with his own flesh, and expecting his comfort and salvation to come in upon the conquest: and therefore he can suffer for Christ, as well as be found in cheaper obedience, and he dare not ordinarily refuse the most costly service. For the spoils of his fleshly desires are his prey, and crown of glorifying in the Lord.

But the opinionative convert still lives to his carnal self: and therefore, secretly at least, seeks himself: and lays hold on present things, as the true convert lays hold on eternal life. The truths of God being received but into his opinion, do not go deep enough to conquer self, and to take down his great idol, nor make him go through fire and water, and to serve God with the best, and honour him with his substance much less with his sufferings and death: he hath something that he cannot spare for God.

3. The sound convert has taken God for his portion, and heaven for that sure and full felicity, which he is resolved to venture upon: that is it upon which he has set his heart and hopes, and thither tends the scope of his life.

But he that is changed only in his opinions, had never such sure apprehensions of the life to come; nor so full a confidence in the promises of God, as to set his heart unfeignedly upon God, and make him truly heavenly-minded. He may have a heavenly tongue, but he hath an earthly heart. A bare opinion, be it ever so true, will not raise men's hearts so high, as to make their affections, and the very design and business of their lives, to be heavenly.

4. The sound convert hath seen the vileness of himself, in the sinfulness of his heart and life, and the misery thereby deserved; and so is a sincerely humbled, self-accusing man.

But the opinionist is commonly unhumbled, and conceited of himself, and a self-justifying pharisee; unless it be that self-accusing will cost him no disgrace, and he take it up as a custom, or that which may bring him into the repute of being humbled and sincere. For his opinion will not search, and pierce his heart, nor batter down his self-exalting thoughts, nor root up the master sin of pride. These are too great works for an opinionist to perform. And therefore you shall hear him more in the excusing of his sin, the magnifying of himself, or stiffly maintaining of his own conceits, than in unfeigned self-abasing.

5. The sound convert is so acquainted with the

defects, sins, and necessities of his own soul, that he is much taken up at home, in his studies, cares, censures, and his daily work : the acting and strengthening of grace, the subduing of corruption, and his daily walk with God, are much of his employment : above all keeping, he keeps his heart, as knowing that thence are the issues of life. He cannot have leisure to spy out the faults of others, and meddle with their affairs, where duty binds him not, as others can do ; because he hath so much to do at home.

But the opinionist is most employed abroad, and about mere notions and opinions ; but he is little employed in such heart-searching or heart-observing work. His light doth not pierce so deep as to show him his heart, and the work that is there to be necessarily done. As the change is little upon his heart, so his employment is little there. He is little in bewailing his secret defects and corruptions, and little in keeping his soul's accounts ; and little in secret striving with his heart to work it into communion with God, and into a spiritual, lively, fruitful frame. He is forward to aggravate others, and oft-times severe enough in censuring them. But he is a very gentle censurer of himself, and a patient man with his own corruptions, and puts the best construction upon all that is his own. He hath much labour perhaps in shaping his opinions, but little for the humbling and sanctifying of his heart, by the power of the truth.

6. As the difference lies thus constantly in the heart, so it is usually manifested by the tongue. The sound convert is most desirous to discourse of those great and saving truths, which his very heart hath taken in, which he hath found to be the seed of God for his regeneration, and the instruments of that holy and happy change that is made upon him : he feels most savour and life in these great and most necessary points, which formed the image of God upon him : and upon these he daily feeds and lives.

But the opinionist is most forward to discourse of mere opinions ; to feed upon the air of notions, and controversies of lesser moment. For one hour's holy, heavenly, experimental, heart-searching discourse, that you shall have from him, you shall have many and many hours discourse of his opinions. I mean it indifferently of all his opinions. I mean it, I say, of all his opinions, whether true or false. For though falsehoods cannot be fit food for the soul, yet truths themselves may also be made of little service to them. A man may be a mere opinionist that hath true opinions, as well as he that hath false. Almost all the free and zealous discourse

of these men, on matters of religion, is about their several sides, parties, and opinions : if they be set upon a point, especially wherein they seem to themselves to be wiser than others, they have a fire of zeal for it in their breasts, that makes them desirous to be propagating it to others. About the orders and ceremonies of the church ; about the forms of prayer, and the accidents of worship ; about infant baptism, or other such controversies in religion, is the freest of their discourse.

Yea, you may perceive much of the difference, even in the very manner of their conference. A serious Christian, even when he is necessitated to speak of lower controverted points, yet doth it in a spiritual manner, as one that more savours higher truths, and makes a holy and heavenly life his end, even in these lower matters ; and deals about such controversies in a practical manner, in order to the growth of holiness.

But the opinionists, even when they speak of the most weighty truths, do speak of them but as opinions ; and when they discourse of God, of Christ, of grace, of heaven, it is but as they discourse of a point in philosophy, or little better. They go not through the shell to the kernel ; they look after the truth, but they have but little relish of the goodness.

The like may be said of their reading and hearing of sermons. The sound convert *feels life* and *spirit*, in that which is little savoury to the opinionist. It is one thing in a sermon or text, that is pleasant to a true Christian, and another thing usually that is most pleasant to the opinionist. The true Christian delights in and feeds on the inward life of spiritual doctrine, and the good which they offer him ; that is, indeed it is upon God, and Christ himself, he is feasting his soul in reading and hearing : for this is the soul of all, without which letters and words are but a carcass. But the superficial opinionist is much more taken up, either with the history, or the elegance of speech, or with the rational light of the discourse, still sticking in the bark, and savouring not Christ and the Father, in all. As a man that reads the deeds, or lease of his own lands, delights in one thing ; and a clerk that reads the same, or the like, in a book of precedents, for his learning, delights in another thing, so is it in this case.

7. Hence it follows, that there are several sorts of duties and exercises, usually, that these several sorts of persons are most addicted to. The sound convert is most addicted to those spiritual means that tend most to the strengthening of his faith, warming his heart with the

love of God, promoting holiness, and destroying sin; but tend to furnish him with speculative knowledge and discourse, and to satisfy his fancy, or curious mind. The sound convert is much addicted to prayer, even in secret, and to heavenly meditations and gracious discourse. But the opinionist is much more addicted to reading histories, controversies, dogmatical divinity, or civil and political matters. The sound convert savours best those preachers and books that speak the most weighty spiritual truths, in the most weighty spiritual manner, in power and demonstration of the Spirit : but the opinionist relishes those preachers and books most, that either speak curiously to please the ear, or exactly and learnedly to please the natural intellect, or that speak for the opinions or party that he is addicted to: but others, he cares little about.

8. Moreover the sound Christian lays out most of his zeal, affections, and endeavours, about the great essentials of religion, and that, as I said, in a practical manner. But the opinionist lays out his zeal upon opinions : right or wrong it is but as opinions : of these he makes his religion ; for these he contends. He loves those best that are of his own opinion, though there be nothing of the special image of God upon his soul ; or if he love a true Christian, it is not so much for his holiness and spirituality, as because he is of his mind in those matters of opinion. Hence it is that he is usually a bitter censurer of those that are not of his opinion, how upright soever they may be ; his very esteem of men and love to them is partial and factious to those that are of his mind and sect ; a papist will esteem and love men of the popish sect; yea, a protestant, if he be an opinionist, doth esteem of men and love them as a sect : whereas the true Christian, as he is truly catholic, and of the catholic church, which is not confined to papists, no, nor protestants, so he hath truly catholic affections, and loves a Christian as a Christian, a godly man, as godly ; yea, if he saw more serious godliness in one that is not of his opinion in lesser things, yet would he love him more than one that is in such matters of his opinion, that is ungodly, or of more doubtful piety. For as it is God in Christ that he principally loves, so it is Christ that he admires in his members ; and so much of Christ as he sees in many, so much are his special affections towards them.

9. Ordinarily the mere opinionist will sacrifice the very ends of the gospel, and the honour and success of the great fundamental truths of God, to the interest of those opinions, which he hath in a singular manner made his own. He will rather hinder the propagation of the common truths, and the conversion of the ignorant, than he will silence his opinions, or suffer them to lose any advantages with the world. Hence it is, that we cannot prevail with the papists to silence a while the differences between us and them, till we have taught their ignorant in Ireland, and other barbarous parts, the knowledge of those truths that all are agreed in, Nor can we get many anabaptists, or any such sect, that is engaged in a division, to forbear their opinions, till we have endeavoured to lay the necessary grounds, on which all must build, that will be saved. But though it be apparent to the world, that their disputes and contentions exceedingly harden the ignorant and ungodly against all religion, and hinder their conversion and salvation ; yet will they go on in the unseasonable, intemperate declaration of their conceits, and will not be persuaded to agree on those terms, for the managing of differences, as most tend to secure the interest of Christ and his gospel in the world. If an opinionist be for the truth, he is usually without much zeal for it, because that nature doth not befriend the great spiritual truths of the gospel, so much as it doth errors and private conceits. But if he be of erroneous opinions, he is usually very zealous for them : for corrupted nature, self, Satan, and the world ofttimes, do more befriend these, furnish him with a zeal for them, and blow the coal. The counterfeit angel of light is very ordinarily also a spirit of heat, and great activity ; not a reviving fire, nor a refining fire, but a consuming fire, devouring Christian love, meekness, and patience, and therewith the church and truth of God so far as it can prevail. For lesser matters, that minister questions, such men can lay by that which tends to godly edifying in faith. Yea, that 'charity, which is the very end of the commandment, out of a pure heart, a good conscience, and faith unfeigned.—From these they swerve, and turn aside to vain jangling ; ofttimes desiring to be teachers of such things in which they understand not what they say, nor whereof they speak.—Consenting not to the wholesome words of Christ, and the doctrine which is according to godliness, they teach otherwise, being proud, knowing nothing, but doating about questions, and strife of words, whereof cometh envy, strife, railings, evil surmisings, perverse disputing of men of corrupt minds, and destitute of the truth.' Yea, they sometimes take their opinions, or their worldly gain that they often aim at, to be instead of godliness : and think, that to be godly, is to be of their mind and way. They 'use to

strive about words to no profit, but to the subverting of the hearers, and their vain babblings increase to more ungodliness.'

But the true convert looks principally to internal principles: he loves every known truth of God, but in their order, and according to their worth and weight: he will not, for his own opinions, wilfully do that which will hazard the chief matter, or hinder the gospel, and the saving of men's souls. Though he will not be false to any truth, yet he will 'avoid foolish and unlearned questions, knowing that they gender strife; and the servant of the Lord must not strive, but be gentle to all men, and meekly instruct opposers: following righteousness, faith, charity, peace with them that call on the Lord out of a pure heart.'

10. Lastly, true converts are stedfast, but opinionists are usually mutable and unconstant. The sound convert receives the greatest truths, and receives the goodness as well as the truth; and takes it not only into the head, but into the heart, and gives it deep root. He yields himself to God as his only felicity, and to Christ as his only refuge, and Redeemer, and with heaven as the sure everlasting glory, to which the world is but a mole-hill, or a dungeon. No wonder then if this man be 'stedfast, and unmoveable, always abounding in the work of the Lord, that knows his labour is not in vain in the Lord.'

But the opinionist either fastens on smaller matters, or else holds these great matters but as bare opinions, and therefore they have no such interest in his heart, as to establish him against shaking trials and temptations. For two sorts there are of these opinionists, the one sort have no zeal for their own opinions, because they are but opinions: and these are time servers, and will change, as the king, or their landlords change, and fit their opinions to their worldly end. The other sort have a burning zeal for their opinions; and these use to wander from one opinion to another, not able to resist the subtilty of seducers, but are taken with fair and plausible reasonings, not able to see into the heart of the cause. These are as ' children tossed to and fro, and carried about with every wind of doctrine, by the slight and cunning craftiness of men, whereby they lie in wait to deceive.' When with great confidence they have held one sort of opinions a while, and railed against those that were not of their mind; ere long they will themselves forsake them, and take up another way, and be as confident in that, and take no warning by the experience of their former deceit. And thus they go oft from one opinion

to another, till at last finding themselves deceived so oft, some of them cast off all religion, and think there is no certainty to be found in any: suspecting religion, when they should have suspected their false hearts: all this comes to pass because they never received the truth of the love of it, that they might be sanctified and saved by it, nor ever gave it deep entertainment in their hearts, that it might thoroughly convert them; but as a bare opinion into the brain, to polish their tongues, and outsides, and deceive themselves as much as others.

Thus I have showed you the difference between a sound convert, and an opinionist, or one that hath but superficial change, that you may see which of these is your own condition.

To return now to my advice and exhortation. I entreat every person that reads, or hears these words, to see that they stick not in an opinionative conversion. To which end I further desire you, 1. To consider that it is a higher matter that Christ came into the world for, than to change men's bare opinions; and it is a higher matter that the gospel is intended for and that ministers are sent to you for. For it is more than a corruption of men's opinions, that sin hath brought upon you; and therefore it is a deeper disease that must be cured. The work of Christ, by his gospel, is no less, than to draw you off from that which flesh and blood accounts your happiness, and to unite you to himself, and make you holy, as God is holy, and to give you a new nature, and make you as the dwellers or citizens of heaven, while you walk on earth, and these are greater matters than the changing of a party or opinion. The Holy Ghost himself must dwell in you, work in you, and employ your soul and life for God, that you may study him and love him, live to him here, and live with him for ever. Do but think well of the ends and meaning of the gospel, and how much greater matters it proposes, and then you will see that there is no taking up with an opinionative profession.

2. Keep company, if it be possible, with the most sober, spiritual, and heavenly professors, that will be drawing you to the observation of your own heart and life, and opening to you the riches of the love of Christ, and winning up your affections to God and heaven: and be not the companions of inexperienced wranglers, that have no other religion but a zeal for their opinions, and will endeavour rather to make you like satan, than like God, by possessing your minds with malice, and bitter thoughts of your brethren, employing your tongues in reproaches and vain strivings, and making you fire-

brands in the places where you live : neither be companions of them that hold the truth no deeper than opinion; for though some such may be useful to you in their places, yet if you have not more edifying associates, your danger will be very great, lest you should let go the life of religion, and take up with mere notions and formalities as they.

3. When you have considered, tnat every truth of God is a message to your hearts, as well as to your heads, and hath a work of God to do upon them, look after that work ; and when you have heard, or read a truth, go down into your hearts, and see what it hath done there : and if you find not in your will, resolutions, and affections, the image and fruits of the truth you have heard, bring it up again, and ruminate upon it, and do not think you have received it, or done with it, till this be done: yea, take it but as lost, and sinfully rejected, if it have not done you some good at the very heart.

4. Also be sure that you practise all practical truths, upon the first opportunity, as soon as you have heard them.   Imprison them not in unrighteousness: cast them not out in forgetfulness ; use not a lecture of divinity as if it were a lesson of music, or a mere philosophical or historical discourse. Read not the doctrine of salvation, the promise of heaven, and the forewarnings of everlasting misery, as you read a common story, or a groundless conjecture in an almanac : but as a message from God, which tells you where you must dwell for ever, and as a direction sent from heaven, to teach you the way thither. Fall to work then, and practise what you know, if you would be Christians indeed. ' Be ye doers of the word, and not hearers only, deceiving your own selves.' For the opinionative hearer sees but a slight appearance of the truth, as a man that looks on his face in a glass, which he quickly forgets : but he that is a sound believer and practiser, and not only an opinionative forgetful hearer, is the man that shall be blessed in his deed. Opinion without practice, is building on the sand ; but hearing, sound believing, and doing, is building upon the rock, where the building will stand after all assaults. An opinionist doth but seem to be religious, while he keeps his reigning sins, and therefore his ' religion is in vain:' but the practical religion is the pure and 'undefiled religion.' Hearty obedience will not only show that your religion is deeper than mere opinion, but it will also advance it to a greater purity, and root it more deeply than it was before. A man that hath studied the art of navigation in his closet, may talk of it almost as well as he that hath been at sea ; but when he comes to practise it, he will find that he has much yet to learn : but let this man go to sea, join practice and experience to his theory, and then he may have a knowledge of the right kind. So, if a man that hath only read over military books, would be a true soldier ; or a man that hath only studied physic, would be a true physician, what better way is there, than to fall to practice ? So you must, if you would have a religion that shall save your souls ; and not only a religion that will furnish you with good opinions and expressions.

5. Moreover, if you would get above opinion, be still searching more and more after the evidences of the ancient fundamental truths that you have received ; and lay open your hearts to the power of them.   Think it not enough that you take the Christian religion for true, but labour after a clearer sight of its truth : for you may possibly, upon some conjecture, take it for a truth, by bare opinion, when as the sight of fuller evidences, and a full sight of those evidences, might raise you from opinion to a working, saving faith.

6. Lastly, Take heed lest any thing be suffered to keep possession of your hearts, and so to confine the truth to your memory. When the world is kept up in life and power, and is nearest the heart, there is no room for the word there, but it must float upon the top, and swim in your opinion, because it can go no deeper, your lusts and profits having possession before it. The word can never go to the heart with unmortified men, but by casting your idols out of your hearts ; nor will it take rooting in you, but by rooting out the world.

If you knew the misery of a mere opinionist, you would surely be persuaded now to practise these directions, that may raise you higher.   An opinionist is a deceiver of himself, and often of others : a troubler of the church, if he have any zeal for opinions, and hit, as usually he doth, on the wrong ; and when his religion is right, he is wrong himself, being out of the way, even when he is in the right way, because he is not right in that right way ; for he doth but sit down in it, when he should travel it. A runner shall not win the prize by being in the right way only, unless he make haste. The knowledge of the opinionist doth but serve to aggravate his sin, and cause him to be beaten with many stripes ; but is not of force to sanctify his heart and life, and to save him. Stick not therefore in an opinionative profession of religion.

DIRECTION IX.

My next direction that your conversion may prove sound, is this, Acquaint your souls, by faith, with the glory of the everlasting kingdom, and see that you make it your portion, your end, and from thence let the rest of your endeavours be animated.

No man can be a sound Christian, that knows not the ends and portion of a Christian. There is a great deal of difference between the desires of heaven in a sanctified man, and in an unsanctified. The believer prizes it above earth, and had rather be with God, than here, though death, that stands in the way, may possibly have harder thoughts from him, but to the ungodly there is nothing seems more desirable than this world; therefore he only chooses heaven before hell, but not before earth; and therefore shall not have it upon such a choice. We hear of gold and silver mines in the Indies: if you offer a golden mountain there to an Englishman that hath an estate and family here, that are dear unto him, perhaps he will say, ' I am uncertain whether their golden mountains be not mere fictions to deceive men; and if it be true, that there are such things, yet it is a great way thither, and the seas are perilous; and I am well enough already where I am, and therefore let who will go thither for me, I will stay at home as long as I can.' But if this man must needs be banished out of England, and had his choice whether he would go to the golden islands, or to dig in a coal-pit, or live in a wilderness, he would rather choose the better than the worse. So it is with an ungodly man's desires, in respect to this world and that to come. If he could stay here, in fleshly pleasure for ever, he would; because he looks at heaven as uncertain, and a great way off, and the passage seems to him more troublesome and dangerous than it is; and he is where he would be already: but when he sees that there is no staying here for ever, but death will have him away; he had rather go to heaven than to hell, and therefore will be religious, as far as the flesh and the world will give him leave, lest he should be cast into hell, when he is taken from the earth.

But take an Englishman that is in poverty and reproach, and hath neither house nor land, nor friend to comfort him, and let him have the offer of a golden island, and a person of unquestionable skilfulness and fidelity, who will promise in short time to bring him safe thither; if he believe this person, and can put his trust in him, doubtless he will depart and follow him over sea and land; and though the passage may somewhat daunt him, yet the promised possession will carry him through all. So is it with the true Christian; he is dead to this world, and sees nothing here in which he can be happy; he is burdened and wearied with sin and suffering; he is firmly persuaded of the truth of the gospel; and sees by faith the world that is to flesh invisible, and believes in Jesus Christ who hath promised to convey him safely thither, and therefore he would away; and though he love not death, the stormy passage, yet he will submit to it, having so sure a pilot, because he loves the life which through death he must pass into, and had rather be there than here.

Such as a man's principal end is, such is the man, and such is the course of his life. He that takes this world for his portion, and makes the felicity of it his end, is a carnal, worldly, unsanctified man, whatever good and godly actions may come in upon his mind. It is he, and only he, that is a sanctified believer, who looks on heaven as his only portion, and his sailing through the troublesome seas of this world, on purpose to come to that desired harbour; not loving these seas better than the land of rest, which he is sailing to; but patiently and painfully passing through them, because there is no other way to glory. As it is the desire of the land to which he is sailing, that moves the mariner or passenger to do all that he doth in his voyage; the desire of his home or journey's end, that moves the traveller all the way; and the desire of seeing a perfect building that moves the builder in every stroke of his work; so it must be the love of God, and the desire of everlasting blessedness, that must be the very engine to move the rest of the affections and endeavours of the saints, and must make men resolve on the necessary labour and patience of believers. Take off this weight, and all the motions of Christianity will cease. No man will be at labour and sufferings for nothing, if he can avoid them. It is a life of labour, though sweet to the spirit, yet tedious to the flesh, which Christianity doth engage us in; there is much suffering to be undergone; even to the very last, and to the denial of ourselves; and if God require it, to the loss of all the comforts of the world; for no less than forsaking all that we have will serve to make us Christ's disciples. And will any man do this for he knows not what; will any man forsake all that he has, unless it be for something better, which may be as sure to him as that he has, and may make him more happy? Look to it therefore, that you have right and believing thoughts of heaven, that unfeignedly you take it for your home and happiness, and look not for any other portion. Till you see so much of the certainty and excellency of everlasting glory, as shall prevail with you to lay out your faithful labour for it, and to be at a point with all this world, as having laid up your treasure and hopes in the world to come, you have no ground to conclude that you are true Christian converts.

Seeing therefore that it is heaven that is the very reason, the end, the life of all your religion, it follows that you must necessarily understand somewhat of its excellency, believe its certainty, accordingly set your hearts upon it, and make the attainment of it your daily work and business in the world: this is to be a convert indeed.

Remember therefore first what I told you before, wherein the nature of this blessedness consists. I will only name the essentials of it, that your comprehension may be right, and forbear to say much as being done already.

1. The first thing considerable in our everlasting blessedness, will be our personal perfection of the whole man; this is in order to the perfection of our everlasting operations and enjoyments. Our bodies shall be no more flesh and blood, nor corruptible, or mortal, or subject to hunger, pain, or weariness, nor to passions that rebel against the reasonable soul; but they shall be spiritual bodies, immortal, incorruptible, and undefiled. Our souls will be perfected in their natural perfections, and in their moral. They shall be of more advanced understanding and comprehensive wisdom than now. Our wills shall attain to perfect rectitude in a perfect conformity to the will of God, and every affection shall be brought to its perfect order and elevation: all sin shall be done away, whether it were in the understanding, will, affections, or the actions. The executive power will be answerable to the rest of the perfections, and to the blessed work which it hath to do: and thus we shall be like the angels of God.

2. The next thing to be noticed in our blessedness is, our approximation or approach to God: we shall be admitted into the holiest, and brought as near him as our natures are capable of, and we are fit for.

3. Moreover, we shall be members of the new Jerusalem, and receive our glory in communion with that blessed society, and so as members contribute to her glory.

4. We shall behold the glorified person of our Redeemer, and he will be glorified in us as the fruits of his victory.

5. We shall behold the face of the blessed God, and see his wisdom, power, and glory, and know as we are known. Though we cannot now fully know the manner, yet in that sense as our angels are said to 'behold the face of God,' we also shall behold it.

6. We shall also enjoy him in the nearest relation, and by the most raised vigorous affections of our soul: we shall be filled with his love as full as we can hold, and we shall abound with perfect love to him again: and the joy that is in his presence, which this intuition and everlasting love will afford us, is such as no heart is here able to conceive.

7. Being thus furnished, we shall be employed in his perfect practices, in singing and rejoicing to him with the heavenly host, and magnifying his great and holy name.

8. In all this will the glory of God shine forth, and he will be admired in his saints; in us it shall appear how abundant he is in power, wisdom, goodness, holiness, faithfulness, and righteousness.

9. God himself will be well pleased with us, and with the new Jerusalem, and glorified Son, and will take complacency in this manifestation and communication of his glory and of himself unto his creatures. And this is his ultimate end, and should be the highest point of ours. The change hath now brought all to that centre, which is both the alpha and omega, the beginning and the end. His will is the fountain or efficiency of all; and it is the ultimate end and perfection of all.

There is no more to add, as to the matter, but that as to the duration, first we may take it as that which leaves no room for any addition, that all this will be everlasting, leaving not any doubts or fears of a cessation. Abundance of glorious adjuncts of this felicity might be mentioned; but I pass them all by, and but name these few which are the essential constitutive parts of our happiness, because I have touched them before, and spoken of them in the Saints' Rest. Thus much I thought meet to mention here, that you may have somewhat of that in your eye that I am persuading you to intend and seek; and the rather, because I perceive that many of the godly have not such distinct apprehensions of the constitutive parts of the felicity, as they should have; but much wrong their souls, God himself, and the glory of their profession, by looking but at some of the parts.

Believe God that this is the life that you shall live, if you will take it for your portion, and set your hearts upon it, and follow the conduct of Christ for the obtaining of it. Can you be content with heaven alone? Is it enough for you, though you be despised and persecuted in the world; do you account this for certainty and excellency to be worth all; yea, that all is dross to this? This must you do if you will be true converts. For all such are heavenly in their minds and hearts, and in the drift of all their lives and conversations.

DIRECTION X.

My next advice that you may prove sound converts, is this, Rest not and count not yourselves truly converted, till God and his holy ways have your very love, desire, and delight; and take not that for a saving change, when you had rather live a worldly, ungodly life, if it were not for the fear of punishment.

I shall speak but little of this, because I touched upon it before, when I told you that Christ must have your hearts, and because it is but a consequence of the last, or contained in it. But yet I think it best to present it here distinctly to your consideration, because a slavish kind of religion deceives so many, and because the life of grace is here expressed. I deny not but holy fear is exceedingly useful to us; even a fear of the threatenings and judgments of God. But yet I must tell you, that in fear there is much more that is common to the unsanctified, than there is in love, desire and delight. Though the fear of God be the beginning of wisdom, it is love that is the perfection; that fear is not filial, and of the right stamp, if love be not its companion. Fear of punishment shows that you love your natural selves; but it shows that you love God, and are true-hearted to him. The devils fear and tremble, but they do not love. It is love and not fear that is the bias, the inclination, and, as I may say, the nature of the will of man. By his love it is that you must know what the man is. The philosopher saith, 'Such as a man is, such is his end,' which is all one as to say, 'Such as a man is, such is his love.' You may fear a thing at the same time when you hate it; and it is too common to have some hatred mixed with fear. You may be as much against God and his holy ways, when fear only drives you to some kind of outward form, as others are that scarce meddle with religion at all. The first thing that God looks at, is what you would do; and the next is, what you do. If you do it, but had rather leave it undone, you lose your reward, and God will take it as if you had not done it: for it was not you that did it, if you did it not from love; but it was fear that

dwells in you. God takes men's hearty desires and will, instead of the deed, where they have not power to fulfil it; but he never took the bare deed instead of the will. An external form of worship, consisting in outward actions, without the heart, is fit to be given to a graven image; but the true and living God abhors it. He is a Spirit, and will be worshipped in spirit and in truth; such worshippers he seeks, and such he will accept. A beggar will be glad of your alms, though you leave it with an ill will, because he needs it; but God hath no need of you, or of your service, therefore think not that he will accept you on such terms. That people worship God in vain, 'who draw near him with their mouth, and honour him with their lips, when their heart is far from him.' A man's heart is where his love is, rather than where his fear is. If you should lie still upon your knees, or in the holy assembly; if you should be the strictest observer of the ordinances on the Lord's days, and yet had such hearts in you, as had rather let all these alone, if it were not for fear of punishment; it will all be disregarded, and reckoned to you according to your wills, as if it had never been done by you at all. It is love that must beget love, or make you fit for love to entertain. If you give your goods to the poor, or your bodies to be burned in a cause that in itself is good, and yet have not love, it avails nothing.

You will not think your wife hath conjugal affection that loves another man better than you, and had rather be gone from you, if she could live without you. He is an unnatural son that loves not his father, but had rather be from him than with him. If God called you to a drudgery or slavery, he would then look but for your work, and not care much whether you be willing or unwilling. If your ox draw your plough, and your horse carry his burden, you care not much whether it be willingly or unwillingly. Or if it be an enemy that you have to deal with, you will look for no more than a forced submission, or that he be disabled from doing you hurt. But this is not your case: it is a state of *friendship* that the gospel calls you to, you must be nigh to God, his children, and the members of his Son, espoused to him in the dearest, strongest bonds: and do you think that it is possible that this should be done without your wills and affections? If you can be content with the portion of a slave and an enemy, then do your task, and deny God your affections: but if you look for the entertainment and portion of a friend, a child, a spouse; you must bring the heart of a friend, of a child, and of a spouse. Fear may do good by driving you to the use of means, and taking out of your hands the things by which you would do yourselves a mischief: it may prepare you for saving grace, and when you are sanctified, it will prove a necessary servant of love, to keep you in awe, and save you from temptations. But love is the ruling affection in the sanctified, fear is therefore necessary, because of the present imperfection of love, and because of the variety of temptations that here beset us: think not therefore that you are savingly renewed, till God have your very hearts. When you do but believe and tremble, it is better than to be unbelieving, stupid, and secure; but *you are not true Christians till you believe and love.* We fly from the thing which we fear, and therefore apprehend it to be evil to us. We avoid the presence and company of those that we are afraid of, but we draw nigh them that we love, and delight in their company. We fear an enemy, we love a friend: we fear the devil naturally, but we do not love him. Love is that affection of the soul which entertains God as God, even as good; though that love must be accompanied with a filial fear, even a dread and reverence of his majesty, his greatness, and a fear of displeasing him. If you should toil out yourselves in religious duties, with a heart that had rather forbear them, if you durst, you have not the hearts of God's children in your breasts.

The magistrate can frighten men to the congregation and outward worship: you may lock a man in the church, who had rather be away: and will any man think that this makes him acceptable to God? You may keep a thief from stealing by prison and irons, but this makes him not accepted with God as a true man: you may cure a man of cursing, swearing, railing, idleness, and ribaldry, even in a minute of an hour, by cutting off his tongue; but will God accept him ever the more, so long as he hath a heart that would do it if he could? There is abundance of people at this day who are kept from abusing the Lord's day, and from swearing, and stealing, yea, and from laying hands on all about them that are godly, and this by the law of man, and the fear of present punishment. Do you think that these are therefore innocent or acceptable with God? By this account you may make the devil a saint, when he is chained up from doing mischief: you may as well say, that a lion is become a lamb, when he is shut up in his den: or that a mastiff-dog is become harmless and gentle, when he is muzzled. Believe it, you are never Christians, till you see what it is in God that wins your hearts to him, so that

you would not change your master for any in the world; and till you see that in the hopes of everlasting glory, that you would not change it for any thing else that can be imagined by the heart of man; and till you see that goodness in a heavenly life, that you had rather live it, than any life in the world: you are not converted to God indeed, till you had rather live in holiness, than in sin, if you had your freest choice; and till you would gladly be the strictest, holiest person that you know in the world; and long after more and more of it, and anxiously reach perfection itself; for though we cannot be perfect here, yet no man is upright that desires not to be perfect. For he that loves holiness, as holiness, must needs love the greatest measure of holiness with the greatest love. This is it that makes sound converts to be so faithful and constant with God. A man is forward and ready to a work that he loves; when he draws back from it, as if it were a mischief, he hath no mind to do it. A man is hardly kept from the persons, places, and employments that he loves; but a little will withdraw him from that which he loves not. Why is it that we have so much ado to take off a drunkard from his companions and his lusts, but because he loves them better than temperance and gracious company? Why can we so hardly draw the lustful wretch from his filthy lusts, or the glutton, or the idle sensual person from his needless or excessive recreations, but because they love them? Why is it that you cannot draw the worldling from his covetousness, but he parts with his money almost as hardly as with his blood, but because he loves it? Therefore what wonder if temptations be resisted, and the fairest baits of the world despised by him, that is truly in love with God?

No wonder if nothing can turn back that man from the way to heaven, who is in love both with heaven and with the way. No wonder if that man stick close to Christ, and never forsake a holy life, who tastes the sweetness of it, and feels it to do him good, and had rather go that way than any in the world. There is no true Christian but can say with David, ' that a day in God's courts is better than a thousand, and he had rather be a door-keeper in the house of God, than dwell in the tents, yea, or the palaces of wickedness.' Do but mark those professors that prove apostates, and forsake the way of godliness which they seemed to embrace, and see whether they be not such as either took up some bare opinions and outward duties upon a flash of superficial illumination, or else such as were frightened into a course of religion, and so went on from duty to duty, for fear of being damned, when all the while their hearts were more another way, and they had rather have been excused. These hypocrites are they that are disputing so oft the obligations to their duty, and asking, how do you prove that it is a duty to pray in my family, or a duty to observe the Lord's day, or to come constantly to the congregation, or to use the communion of the godly in private meetings, or to repeat sermons, or sing psalms, and the like? Intimating, that they are as birds in a cage, or hens in a pen, that are boring to get out, and had rather be at liberty: if it were not for the fear of the law of God that is upon them, they had rather let all these duties alone, or take them up but now and then at an idle time, when Satan and the flesh will give them leave. If a feast be prepared and spread before them, a good stomach will not stand to ask, How can you prove it my duty to eat? but perhaps the sick that loth it, may do so. If the cup be before the drunkard, he doth not stand on those terms, How do you prove it my duty now to drink this cup, and the other cup. No, if he might have but leave, he would drink on, without any questioning whether it be a duty: if the gamester, or the whoremonger, might but be sure that he should escape the punishment, he would never stick at the want of a precept, and ask, Is it my duty? If there were but a gift of twenty pounds a man to be given to all the poor of the town, yea, and to all the people in general, I do not think I should meet with many people in the town that would draw back and say, What word of God commands me to take it; or how can you prove that it is my duty? Why is all this, but because they have an inward love to the thing; and love will carry a man to that which seems good for him, without any command or threatening? If these ungodly wretches had one spark of spiritual life within them, and any taste and feeling of the matters that concern their own salvation, instead of asking, How can you prove that I must pray with my family, or that I must keep the Lord's day, or that I must converse with the godly, and live a holy life? they would be readier to say, How can you prove that I may not pray with my family; and that I may not sanctify the Lord's day; and that I may not have communion with the saints in holiness? Seeing so great a mercy is offered to the world, why may not I partake of it as well as others? I can perceive in many that I converse with, the great difference between a heart that loves God and holiness, and a heart that seems religious and

honest without such a love: the true convert perceives so much sweetness in holy duties, and so much spiritual advantage by them to his soul, that he is loth to be kept back; he cannot spare these ordinances and mercies, no more than he can spare the bread from his mouth, or the clothes from his back; yea, or the skin from his flesh, no, not so much. He loves them, he cannot live without them: at the worst that ever he may be, he had rather be holy than unholy, and live a godly than a fleshly, worldly life. Therefore if he had but a bare leave from God, without a command, to sanctify the Lord's day, and to live in the holy communion of the saints, he would joyfully take it with many thanks: for he need not be driven to his rest when he is weary, nor to his spiritual food when he is hungry, nor to Christ, the refuge of his soul, when the curse and accuser are pursuing him. But the unsanctified hypocrite who never loved God or godliness in his heart, stands questioning and inquiring for some proof of a necessity of these courses. If he can but bring himself to hope that God will save him without so much ado, which by the help of the devil he may easily be brought to hope, away then goes the duty: if you could not show him that there is a necessity of family prayer, a necessity of sanctifying the Lord's day, a necessity of forsaking his tippling and voluptuousness, and a necessity of living a heavenly life, he would quickly resolve on another course: for he had rather do otherwise if he durst. He never was religious from a true predominant love to God and a holy life, but for fear of hell, and for other inferior objects.

Remember this when you have precious opportunities before you, of doing or receiving good, and when you see that you have leave to take these opportunities, and yet you draw back, and are questioning, How we can prove it to be your duty; or that you cannot be saved without it? Do not these questions plainly show that you love not the work and delight not in a holy life; and that you had rather let it alone? Are you not blind if you see not this is in yourselves? Yea, it is plain that you have such an averseness or hatred to God and a holy course of life, that if you did but know what shift to make to escape damnation, you would fly away from God and holiness, and have as little to do with them as you can. Your questions and cavils plainly declare this wicked enmity and backwardness of your hearts; and consequently show how far you are from true conversion.

Not that I am of their mind who think there is any good which the law of Christ obliges us not to accept, and which we can refuse without sin and danger to ourselves : for God doth both draw us, and drive us at once. But when the threatening and punishment only can prevail with men, and men love not God and godliness for themselves, but had rather have liberty to live as the ungodly, I shall never take one of these for a sanctified man, nor have any hope of the saving of such a soul how far soever his fears may carry him from his outward sins, or to outward duties ; till God shall give him a better conversion than this ; I say, I have not the smallest hope of this man's salvation. Then you are God's children, when the honour, the work, the family, the name of your Father are lovely and delightful to you: and when you grieve that there are any remnants of sin in your souls, and when your sins are to you as lameness to the lame, that pains them every step they go; and as sickness to the sick, that makes them groan, and groan again, and long to be rid of it: and when you think those the happiest men on earth that are the most holy, and wish from your hearts that you were such as they, though you had not a house to put your head in : when you look toward God with longing thoughts, and are grieved that your understandings can reach no nearer him, and know no more of him, and that your hearts cannot embrace him with a more burning love : when you admire the beauty of a meek, a patient, a mortified, spiritual, heavenly mind, and long to have more of this yourself, yea, to be perfect in all holiness and obedience : when your hearts are thus brought over to God, that you had rather have him than any other, and rather live in his family any where, and rather walk in his ways than in any ; then are you indeed converted, and never till then, whatever other dispositions you may have.

Now if that were my business, what abundance of reason might I show you, to make you willing to come over unto God, with love and with delight ? Whom else can you love, if he that is love itself seem not lovely to you. All loveliness is in him and from him, the creature hath none of it itself, nor for itself: to love a life of sin, is to love the image and service of the devil, and to love that which feeds the flames of hell ; what is it then to love this sin so well, as for the love of it to fly from God and godliness? Methinks men at the worst should love that which will do them good, and not prefer that before it which will hurt them. Do sinners indeed believe that God and holiness will do them hurt, and that sin will do them greater good ? Is there a man so mad, that he dare speak

this and stand to it? If indeed you think it best to live in sin, and therefore had rather keep it than leave it, your understandings are befooled ; I had almost used Paul's phrase, and said, bewitched. Will it do you any hurt to leave your sensual lives, and to 'live soberly, righteously, and godly, in the world, denying ungodliness, and worldly lusts, and looking for the blessed hope, and the glorious appearing of the great God, and our Saviour Jesus Christ ?' This is the doctrine of saving grace. Would it do you any harm to be assured of salvation, and ready to die, and to know that angels shall conduct your departing souls to Christ, and that you shall live in joy with him for ever ; or to be employed in those holy works that must prepare you for this day, and help you to this assurance ? If God be undervalued by you, if holiness, righteousness, and temperance be nothing to you, then you may as well say, heaven is nothing to you; and therefore you must resolve for sin and hell, and see whether that be good for you. I shall say no more of this point, because I have written of it already, in the conclusion of the Saints' Rest, which I desire you to peruse.

DIRECTION XI.

The next part of my advice is, if you would not have this saving work miscarry, turn then this present day and hour, without any more delay.

Somewhat I have spoke of this already, and therefore shall say the less. But yet I shall back this direction with such reasons as will certainly convince you, if you be not unreasonable, of the folly of delay, and show you that it concerns you presently to return. Though my reasons will be numerous, it is not the number, but the strength of them, that I shall urge you principally to consider ; and because of the number, I will go over them with the greater brevity.

1. Consider to whom it is that you are commanded to turn: and then tell me whether there can be any reason for delay. It is not to an empty, deceitful creature, but to the faithful, all-sufficient God : to him that is the cause of all things ; the strength of the creation ; the joy of angels ; the felicity of the saints ; the sun and shield of all the righteous, and refuge of the distressed ; and the glory of the whole world. Of such power, that his word can take down the sun from the firmament, and turn the earth and all things into nothing ; for he doth more in giving them their being and continuance. Of such wisdom, that was never guilty of mistake, and

therefore will not mislead you, nor draw you to any thing that is not for the best. Of such goodness as that, evil cannot stand in his sight, and nothing but your evil could make him displeased with you ; and it is from nothing but evil that he calls you to turn. It is not to a malicious enemy, that would do you a mischief, but it is to a gracious God, who is love itself : not to an implacable judge, but to a reconciled Father : not to revenging indignation, but to the embrace of those arms, and the mercy of that compassionate Lord, that is enough to melt the hardest heart, when you find yourself as the poor returning prodigal, in his bosom, when you deserved to have been under his feet. Will the great and blessed God invite thee to his favour, and wilt thou delay and demur upon the return ? The greatest of the angels of heaven are glad of his favour, and value no happiness but the light of his countenance ; heaven and earth are supported by him, and nothing can stand without him ; how glad would those very devils be of his favour, that tempt thee to neglect his favour : and wilt thou delay to turn to such a God ? Why, thou art every minute at his mercy ; if thou turn not, he can throw thee into hell when he will, more easily than I can throw this book to the ground ; and yet dost thou delay ? There are all things imaginable in him to draw thee : there is nothing that is good for thee, but it is perfectly in him ; where thou mayest have it certain and perpetuated. There is nothing in him to give the least discouragement : let all the devils in hell, and all the enemies of God on earth, say the worst they can against his majesty, and they are not to find the smallest blemish in his absolute holiness, wisdom, and goodness : yet wilt thou delay to turn ?

2. Consider also, as to whom, so to what it is that thou must turn. Not to uncleanness, but unto holiness : not to the sensual life of a beast, but to the noble rational life of a man, and the more noble heavenly life of a believer : not to an unprofitable worldly toil, but to the most gainful employment that ever the sons of men were acquainted with : not to the deceitful drudgery of sin, but to that 'godliness which is profitable to all things, having the promise of the life that now is, and of that which is to come.' Do you know what a life of holiness is ? You do not know it, if you turn away from it : I am sure if you knew it, you would never fly from it, no, nor endure to live without it : why, a life of holiness is nothing but a living unto God ; to be conversant with him, as the wicked are with the world ; and to be devoted to his

service, as sensualists are to the flesh. It is to live in the love of God and our Redeemer ; in the foretastes of his everlasting glory, and of his love : in the sweet forethoughts of that blessed life that shall never end, and in the honest self-denying course that leads to that blessedness. A godly life is nothing else but a sowing the seed of heaven on earth ; and a learning, in the school of Christ, the songs of praise which we must use before the throne of God ; and by suffering, a learning how to triumph and reign with Christ. Is there any thing in this life which you have cause to be afraid of ? The sins and weaknesses of the godly are contrary to godliness ; and therefore godliness is no more dishonoured by them, than health and life is dishonoured by your sicknesses. As health is never the worse to be liked, but the better, because of the painful grievousness of sickness, so godliness is to be liked the better, because the very failings of the saints are so grievous. If a true believer step out of the way of God, he is wounded, he is out of joint, he is undone till he come in again ; though it was but in one particular. Can you endure to continue strangers to it altogether so long ? I know you may find faults in the godly till they are perfect ; but let the most malicious enemy of Christ on earth find any fault in godliness itself, if he can.

Can you delay to come into your Father's family ; into the ' vineyard of the Lord ;' into the ' kingdom of God on earth ;' to be ' fellow-citizens of the saints ;' and ' of the household of God ;' to have ' the pardon of all your sins,' and ' the sealed promise of everlasting glory ?' When you are called on to turn, you are called to the porch of heaven, into the beginning of salvation ; and will you delay to accept ' everlasting life ?'

3. Consider also, from what you are called to turn ; and then judge whether there be any reason of delay. It is from the devil, your enemy ; from the love of a deceitful world : from the seduction of corrupted brutish flesh ; it is from sin, the greatest evil : what is there in sin that you should delay to part with it ; is there any good in it ; or what hath it ever done for you that you should love it ; did it ever do you good ; or did it ever do any man good ? It is the deadly enemy of Christ and you : that caused his death, and will cause yours, and is working for your damnation, if converting and pardoning grace prevent it not : and are you loth to leave it ? It is the cause of all the miseries of the world, of all the sorrows that ever did befal you, and the cause of the damnation of them that perish : and do you delay to part with it ?

4. Your delaying shows that you love not God, that you prefer your sin before him, and that you would never part with it if you might have your will. For if you loved God, you would long to be restored to his favour, to be near him, employed in his service, and his family. Love is quick and diligent, and will not draw back : and it is a sign also that you are in love with sin ; for else, why should you be so loth to leave it ? He that would not leave his sin, and turn to God, till the next week, or next month, or year, would never turn if he might have his desire ; for that which makes you desirous to stay a day or week longer, doth indeed make you loth to turn at all. And therefore it is but hypocrisy to think that you are willing to turn hereafter, if you be not willing to do it *now* without delay.

5. Consider, what a case you are in while you thus delay. Do you think you stand on firm ground, or in a safe condition ? If you knew where you are, you would sit as upon thorns, as long as you are unconverted ; you would be as a man that stood up to the knees in the sea, and saw the tide coming towards him : who certainly would think that there is no standing still in such a place. Read what I have said of the state of the unconverted, and in my first Treatise of Conversion. In a word, you are the drudges of sin, the slaves of the devil, the enemies of God, the abusers of his grace and Spirit, the despisers of Christ, the heirs of hell. And is this a state to stay in an hour ? You have all your sin unpardoned ; you are under the curse of the law : the wrath of God is upon you ; and the fulness of it hangs over your heads ; judgment is coming to pass upon you the dreadful doom ; the Lord is at hand ; death is at the door, and waits but for the word from the mouth of God, that it may arrest you, and bring you to everlasting misery : and is this a state for a man to stay in ?

6. Moreover, your delaying gives great advantage to the tempter. If you would presently turn and forsake your sins, and enter into a faithful covenant with God, the devil would be almost out of hope, and the very heart of his temptations would be broken : he would see that now it is too late : there is no getting you out of the arms of Christ. But as long as you delay, you keep him still in heart and hope : he hath time to strengthen his prison and fetters, and to renew his snares : and if one temptation serve not, he hath time to try another, and another ; as if you would stand as a mark for Satan to shoot at, as long as he pleases. What likelihood is there, that ever so foolish a sinner should be recovered and saved from his sin ?

7. Moreover, your delaying is a vile abuse of Christ and the Holy Ghost, and may so far provoke him, as to leave you to yourself, and then you are past help. If you delight so to trample on your crucified Lord, and will so long put him off by refusing his grace, and grieving his Spirit ; what can you expect but that he should turn away in wrath, and utterly forsake you, and say, Let him keep his sin, seeing he had rather have it than my grace ; let him continue ungodly, seeing he is so loth to be sanctified ; let him take his own course, die in his sin, and repent in hell, seeing he would not repent on earth ? You provoke Christ thus to give you up.

8. Consider also, I beseech you, if you ever mean to turn, what is it that you stay for. Do you think to bring down Christ and heaven to lower terms, and to be saved hereafter with less attention ? Surely you cannot be so foolish ; for God will be still the same, and Christ the same, and his promise hath still the same condition, which he will never change ; and godliness will be the same, and as much against your carnal interest hereafter as it is now. When you have looked about you ever so long, you will never find a fairer or nearer way ; but this same way you must go, or perish. If you cannot leave sin now, how should you leave it then ? It will be still as sweet to your flesh as now : or if one sin grow stale by the decay of nature, another that is worse will spring up in its stead, and though the acts abate, they will all live still at the root ; for sin was never mortified by age. So that if ever you will turn, you may best turn now.

9. Yea, more than that, the longer you stay, the harder it will be. If it be hard to-day, it is like to be harder to-morrow. For as the Spirit of Christ is like to forsake you for your wilful delays, so custom will strengthen sin ; and custom in sinning will harden your hearts, and make you as past feeling, to work all uncleanness with greediness. Cannot you crush this serpent when it is but in the spawn, and can you encounter it in its serpentine strength ? Cannot you pluck up a tender plant, and can you pluck up an oak or cedar ? O sinners ! What do you do, to make your recovery so difficult by delay ? You are never like to be fairer for heaven, and to find conversion an easier work, than now you may do. Will you stay till the work be ten times harder, and yet do you think it so hard already ?

10. Consider also, that sin gets daily victories by your delay. We lay our batteries against it, and preach, exhort, and pray against it, and it gets a kind a kind of victory over all,

as long as we prevail not with you to turn. It conquers our persuasions and advice: it conquers all the stirrings of your consciences: it conquers all your heartless purposes, and deceitful promises. These frequent conquests strengthen your sin, weaken your resistance, and leave the matter almost hopeless. Before a physician hath used remedies, he hath more hope of a cure, than when he hath tried all means and finds that the best medicines do no good, but the man is still as bad or worse. So when all means have been tried with you, and yet you are unconverted, the case draws towards desperation itself: the very means are disabled more than before, that is, your hearts are more unapt to be wrought upon by them: when you have long been under sermons and reading, and among good examples, and yet you are unconverted, these ordinances lose much of their force with you: custom will make you slight them, and be dead-hearted under them. It is these very same means and truths that you have frustrated that do the work, or it will never be done: the same medicine must heal you, that you have abandoned so often. What a sad case is this, that there is no hope left but in the very same medicine which you have taken so often in vain!

11. Moreover, age itself hath many inconveniences, and youth hath many great advantages, and therefore it is folly to delay. In age the understanding and memory grow dull, people grow incapable, and almost unchangeable. We see, by our daily experience, that men think they should not change when they are old; that opinion or practice that they have been brought up in, they think that they should not then forsake it: to *learn* when they are old, and to *turn* when they are old, you see how much they are against it. Besides, how unfit is age to be at that pains, that you can undergo. How unfit to begin the holy warfare against the flesh, the world, and the devil! God's way is, to enlist his soldiers as soon as may be, even in their infancy; which they must own as soon as ever they come to age: the devil would not have it done at all, and therefore he would have it put off as long as may be. In infancy he will tell the parents, with the anabaptists, it is too soon to be dedicated to God, and entered into covenant: when they come to their childhood, and youthful state, he will then persuade them that it is yet too soon; and when he can no longer persuade them that it is yet too soon, he will then persuade them that it is too late. O what a happy thing it is to come unto God betimes, and with the first! What advantage hath youth! They have the vigour of wit and of body: they are not rooted and hardened in sin; not

filled with prejudice and obstinacy against godliness, as others are; besides, the capacity of serving God, of which more immediately.

12. You have such times of advantage and encouragement, as few ages of the world have ever seen, and few nations on earth enjoy at this day. What plain and plentiful teaching have you; what abundance of good examples, and the society of the godly! Private and public helps are common. Godliness is under as little suffering as ever you can expect to see it; yea, it is grown into reputation among us, so that it is an honour to serve God, and a dishonour to neglect it, as well it may. Our rulers countenance the practices of godliness, they proclaim themselves the forward professors and patrons of it, and take this as their glory. This is not ordinary in the world. Seldom has the church seen such days on earth. Yet is not the way to heaven fair enough for you; yet are you not ready to turn to God; when should men make hay, but when the sun shines; will you delay till this harvest time be over, and the winter of persecution come again; can you better turn to God, when a godly life is the common scorn of the country, as it was a while ago; and when every one will be deriding and railing at you; or when it may possibly cost you your lives; have you sun, wind, and tide, to serve you, and will you stay to set out in storms and darkness?

13. Moreover, your delay doth cast your conversion and salvation upon hazard, yea, upon many and grievous hazards. Is your everlasting happiness a matter to be wilfully hazarded, by causeless and unreasonable delays? If you delay to-day, you are utterly uncertain of living till to-morrow. If you put by this one motion, you know not whether ever you shall have another. Alas! that ever the heart of man should be so senseless, as to delay, when they know not but it may prove their damnation, and when heaven or hell must certainly follow; that they dare put off a day or hour, when they know not whether ever they shall see another. As your life is uncertain, so are the means uncertain by which God uses to do the work. He may remove your teachers, and other helps; and then you will be further off than before. And if both should continue, yet grace itself is uncertain. You know not whether ever the Spirit of God will put another thought of turning into your hearts: or at least whether he will give you hearts to turn.

14. Moreover, the delay of conversion continues your sin, and so you will daily increase the number, and increase your guilt, and make your

souls more abundantly miserable. Are you not deep enough in debt to God already, and have you not sins enough to answer for upon your souls; would you have one year's sin more, or one day's sin more to be charged upon you? O, if you did but know what sin is, it would amaze you to think what a mountain lies already upon your consciences. One sin unpardoned will sink the stoutest sinner into hell: and you have many a thousand upon your souls already, and would you yet have more? Methinks you should rather look about you, and bethink you how you may get a pardon for all that is past.

15. And as this sin increased daily by delay, so consequently the wrath of God increases; you will run further into his displeasure; possibly you may cut down the bough that you stand upon, and hasten even bodily destruction to yourselves. When you live daily upon God, and are kept out of hell, by a miracle of his mercy, methinks you should not desire yet longer to provoke him, lest he withdraw his mercy, and let you fall into misery.

16. Do but consider, what will become of you, if you be found in these delays. You are then lost, body and soul, for ever. Now if you had but hearts to know what is good for you, the worst of you might be converted and saved; for God doth freely offer you his grace. But if you die in your delays, in the twinkling of an eye, you will find yourselves utterly undone for ever. Now there is hope of a change, but when delays have brought you to hell, there is no more change, nor no more hope.

17. Consider, that your very time which you lose by these delays, is an inconceivable loss. When time is gone, what would you then give for one of those years, or days or hours, which now you foolishly trifle away? O wretched sinners! are there so many thousand souls in hell, that would give a world if they had it, for one of your days, and yet can you afford to throw them away, in worldliness, sensuality, and loitering delays? I tell you, time is better worth, than all the wealth and honours of the world. The day is coming when you will set by time: when it is gone, you will know what a blessing you made light of. But then all the world cannot call back one day or hour of this precious time, which you can sacrifice now to the service of your flesh, and cast away on unprofitable sinning.

18. Consider also, that God hath given you no time to spare. He hath not lent you one day or hour, more than is needful for the work that you have to do, and therefore you have no reason to lose any by your delays. Do you imagine that God would give a man an hour's time for nothing; much less, for abusing him, and serving his enemy. No, let me tell you, that if you make your best of every hour, if you should never lose a minute of your lives, you would find all little enough for the work you have to do. I know not how others think of time, but for my part, I am forced daily to say, How swift, how short is time; how great is our work; and when we have done our best, how slowly goes it on! O precious time! What hearts have they, what lives do those men lead, that think time long; that have time to spare and pass it in idleness!

19. To convince you more, consider, I beseech you, the exceeding greatness of the work you have to do; and tell me then, whether it be time for you to delay? Especially you that are yet unconverted, and strangers to the heavenly nature of the saints, you have far more to do than other men. You have a multitude of headstrong passions to subdue, and abundance of deadly sins to kill, and rooted vices to root up: you have many a false opinion of God and his ways, to be plucked up, and the customs of many years standing to be broken: you have blinded minds that must be enlightened with heavenly knowledge; and abundance of spiritual truths, that are above the reach of flesh and blood, that you must needs learn and understand: you have much to know, that is hard to be known: you have a dead soul to be made alive, a hard heart to be melted, a seared conscience to be softened and made tender, and the guilt of many thousand sins to be pardoned: you have a new heart to get, a new end to aim at, and seek after, and a new life to live; abundance of enemies you have to fight with and overcome, abundance of temptations to resist and conquer. Many graces to get, preserve, exercise, and increase, and abundance of holy works to do for the service of God, and the good of yourselves and others. O what a deal of work doth every one of these words contain; and yet what abundance more might I name! Have you all this to do, and yet will you delay? They are not indifferent matters that are before you; it is no less than the saving of your souls, and the obtaining the blessed glory of the saints. Necessity is upon you; these are things that must be done, or else woe to you that ever you were born: and yet have you another day to lose! Why, if you had a hundred miles to go, in a day or two, upon pain of death, would you delay? O think of the work that you have to do, and then judge whether it be not time to stir.

20. And methinks it should exceedingly terrify you to consider, What numbers perish by such delays; and how few that wilfully delay are ever converted and saved. Many a soul that once had purposes hereafter to repent, is now in the misery, where there is no repentance that will do them any good. For my part, though I have known some very few converted when they are old; yet I must needs say, both that they were very few indeed, and that I had reason to believe, that they were such that had sinned before in ignorance, and did not wilfully put off repentance, when they were convinced that they must turn. Though I doubt not but God may convert even these if he please, yet I cannot say that I have ever known many, if any such, to be converted. Sure I am that God's usual time is in childhood, or youth, before they have long abused grace, and wilfully delayed to turn when they were convinced. Some considerable time, I confess, many have before their first convictions and purposes be brought to any great ripeness of performance: but O how dangerous is it to delay!

21. Consider also, either conversion is good or bad for you: either it is needful, or unnecessary. If it be bad, and a needless thing, then let it alone altogether. But if you are convinced that it is good, and necessary, is it not better now, than to stay any longer? Is it not the sooner the better? Are you afraid of being safe, or happy, too soon? If you are sick, you care not how soon you are well: if you have a bone out of joint, you care not how soon it is set; if you fall into water, you care not how soon you get out: if your house be on fire, you care not how soon it be quenched: if you are but in fears by any doubts, or evil tidings, you care not how soon your fears are over. And yet are you afraid of being too soon out of the power of the devil, and the danger of hell; and of being too soon the sons of God, and the holy, justified heirs of heaven?

22. Consider also, either you can turn now, or not. If you can, and yet will not, you are utterly without excuse. If you cannot to-day, how much less will you be able hereafter, when strength is less, difficulties greater, and burdens more. Is it not time therefore to make out to Christ for strength; and should not the very sense of your inability dissuade you from delay?

23. Consider how long you have staid already, and put God's patience to trial by your folly: hath not the devil, the world and the flesh, had many years' time of your life already? Have you not long enough been swallowing the poison of sin; and long enough been abusing the Lord that made you, and the blood of the Son of God, that was shed for you, and the Spirit of grace, that hath moved and persuaded with you? Are you not yet gone far enough from God; and have you not yet done enough to the condemning of yourselves, and casting away everlasting life? O wretched sinners! It is rather time for you to fall down on your faces before the Lord, and with tears and groans, to lament it day and night, that ever you have gone so far in sin, and delayed so long to turn to him as you have done. Surely, if after so many years' rebellion, you are yet so far from lamenting it, that you had rather have more of it, and had rather hold on a little longer, no wonder if God forsake you, and let you alone.

24. Have you any hopes of God's acceptance, and your salvation, or not? If you have such hopes, that when you turn, God will pardon all your sins, and give you everlasting life; is it, think you, an ingenuous thing to desire to offend him yet a little longer, from whom you expect such exceeding mercy and glory as you do? Have you the face to speak what is in your hearts and practice, and to go to God with such words as these? ' Lord, I know I cannot have the pardon of one sin, without the blood of Christ, and the riches of thy mercy: nor can I be saved from hell without it; but yet I hope for all this from thy grace; I beseech thee let me live a little longer in my sins, a little longer let me trample on the blood of Christ, and despise thy commands, and abuse thy mercies; a little longer let me contemn thy goodness, and prefer the flesh and the world before thee, and then pardon me all that ever I did, and take me into glory.' Could you for shame put up such a request to God as this? If you could, you are past shame: if not, then do not practise and desire that which you cannot for shame speak out and request.

25. Moreover, it is an exceeding advantage to you, to come unto God betimes, and an exceeding loss, that you will suffer by delay. If you were sure to be converted at the last, if you speedily come in, you may have time to learn, and get more understanding in the matters of God, than else can be expected: for knowledge will not be had but by time and study. You may also have time to get strength of grace, when young beginners can expect no more than an infant's strength: you may grow to be men of parts and abilities, to be useful in the church, and profitable to those about you, when others cannot go or stand, unless they lean on the

stronger for support. If you come in betime, you may do God a great deal of service; which in the evening of the day, you will neither have strength, nor time to do. You may have time to get assurance of salvation, and to be ready with comfort when death shall call; when a babe is like to be perplexed with doubts, and fears, and death is like to be terrible, because of their unreadiness.

26. Did you ever consider, who and how many do stay for you while you delay? Do you know who it is that you make to wait your leisure? God himself stands over you with the offers of his mercy, as if he thought it long till you return, saying, ' O that there were such a heart in them; and when will it once be?—How long, ye simple, will ye love simplicity, and scorners delight in scorning, and fools hate knowledge; turn ye at my reproof.' Do you think it wise, or safe, or mannerly, for you to make the God of heaven to wait on you, while you are serving his enemy? Can you offer God a baser indignity, than to expect that he should support your lives, feed you, preserve you, and patiently forbear you, while you abuse him to his face, and drudge for the flesh, the world, and the devil? Should a worm thus use the Lord that made him? You will not yourselves hold a candle in your hands, while it burns your own fingers; nor will you hold a nettle, or a wasp, in your hand, to sting you; nor will you keep a dog in your house, that is good for nothing but to snarl at you, and bite your children, or worry your sheep: and yet God hath long held up your lives, while instead of light, you have yielded nothing but a stinking snuff; and instead of grapes, you have brought forth nothing but thorns and thistles; and while you have snarled at his children, and his flock, and done the worst you could against him. Would you indeed put God to wait on you thus, while you serve the devil yet one day more? Must God as it were hold the drunkard the candle while he reels and staggers? Must he draw the curtain, while the filthy wretch doth once more please his fleshly lusts? Marvel not, if he withdraw his supporting mercy, and let such transgressors drop into hell.

It is not God only, but his servants, creatures, and ordinances, that all are waiting on you. The angels stay for the joy that is due to them upon your conversion. Ministers are studying, preaching, and praying for you. Godly neighbours are praying, and longing for your change. The springs and rivers are flowing for you: the winds blow for you: the sun shines for you: the clouds rain for you: the earth bears fruit for

you: the beasts must labour, suffer, and die for you: all things are doing, and would you stand still, or else do worse? What haste makes the sun about the world, to return in its time to give you light? What haste make other creatures in your services? And yet must you delay? Must God stay, and Christ, and the Spirit stay? Must angels stay; must ministers stay; must the godly stay; and the ordinances stay; and all the creatures stay your leisure, while you are abusing God, your souls, and others, while you delay, as if it were too soon to turn.

27. Consider, that when you were lost, the Son of God did not delay the work of your redemption. He presently undertook it, and turned by the stroke of condemning justice. In the fulness of time he came and performed what he undertook; he failed not one day of his appointed time. And will you now delay to accept the benefit, and turn to him? Must he make such haste to save you at so dear a rate? And now will you delay to be saved?

28. Moreover, God doth not delay to do you good: you have the day and night in their proper seasons; the sun doth not fail to rise upon you at the appointed time; you have the spring and harvest, in their meetest seasons, the former and latter rain in season. When you are in want, you have seasonable supplies, and when you are in danger, you have seasonable deliverance: and is it meet or equal that you should refuse to bring forth seasonable fruit, but still be putting off God with your delays?

29. Moreover, when you are in trouble and necessity, you are then in haste for deliverance and relief. Then you think every day a week, till your danger or suffering be past. If you be under the pain of a disease, or in danger of death, or under poverty, or oppression, or disgrace, you would have God relieve you without delay; and yet you will not turn to him without delay. Then you are ready to cry out, How long, Lord, how long till deliverance come? But you will not hear God, when he cries to you in your sins, how long will it be ere you turn from your transgressions; when shall it once be? When you are to receive any outward deliverance, you care not how soon; the sooner the better: but when you are to turn to God, receive his grace, and title to glory, then you care not how late, as if you had no mind of it. Can you for shame beg of God to hasten your deliverances, when you remember your delays, and still continue to trifle with him and draw back?

30. Your present prosperity and worldly delights are posting away without delay; and should

you delay to make sure of better in their stead? Time is going, and health is going, youth is going, yea, life is going, your riches are taking wing, your fleshly pleasures perish in the very using; your meat and drink is sweet to you little longer than it is in your mouth. Shortly you must part with house and lands, with goods and friends, and all your mirth and earthly business will be done. All this you know, and yet will you delay to lay up a durable treasure which you may trust upon, and to provide you a better tenement before you be turned out of this? What will you do for an habitation, for pleasures and contents, when all that you have is spent and gone, and earth will afford you nothing but a grave? If you could but keep that you have, I should not much wonder, that knowing so little of God, and another world, you look not much after it; but when you perceive death knocking at your doors, and see that all your worldly comforts are packing up, and hasting away: methinks, if you have your senses about you, you should presently turn, and make sure of heaven, without any more delay.

31. Consider also whether it be equal, that you should delay your conversion, when you can seasonably dispatch your worldly business, and when your flesh would be provided for, you can hearken to it without delay. You have wisdom enough to sow your seed in season, and will not delay it to the time of harvest: you will reap your corn when it is ripe, and gather your fruit when it is ripe, without delay. You observe the seasons in the course of your labours, day by day, and year by year: you will not lie in bed when ye should be at your work, nor delay all night to go to your rest; nor suffer your servants to delay your business: you will know your dinner time and supper time, day by day: if you be sick, you will seek help without delay, lest your disease should grow to be incurable. And yet will you delay your conversion, and the making sure of heaven? Why, shall these trifles be done without delay; and shall your salvation be put off? In the name of God, what do you think of? Do you imagine that you can better suffer hell-fire, than hunger, or nakedness; or that you can better bear the loss of everlasting joys, than the loss of your earthly comforts and provisions in the world? Surely, if you believe the life to come, you cannot think so. And can you have time for every thing, except that one thing, which all the rest are merely to promote, and in comparison of which they are all but dreams? Can you have leisure to work, to plough, sow, and reap, and cannot you have time to prepare for eternal life? Why, if you cannot find time yet to search your hearts and prepare for death; turn to God and give over eating, drinking, and sleeping, and say, I cannot have time for these. You may as wisely say so for these smaller matters, as for the greater.

32. Moreover, If men offer you courtesies, and commodities for your bodies, you will not stand delaying, and need so many persuasions to accept them. If your landlord would for nothing renew your lease, if any man would give you houses, or lands, would you delay so long before you would accept of them? A beggar at your door will not only thankfully take your alms, without your intreaty, and importunity, but will beg for it, and be importunate with you to give it. And yet will you delay to accept the blessed offers of grace, which is a greater thing?

33. Yet consider, that it is God that is the giver, and you that are the miserable beggars, and receivers: and therefore it is fitter that you should wait on God, and call on him for his grace, when he seems to delay, and not that he should wait on you. He can live without your receiving, but you cannot live without his giving. The beggar must be glad of alms at any time, and the condemned person of a pardon at any time; but the giver may well expect that his gift be received without delay, or else he may let them go without it.

34. Methinks you should not deal worse with God, when he comes to you as a physician to save your own souls, than you would do with a neglecter, or a friend, when it is not for your own good but for theirs. If your neighbour lay a dying, you would go and visit him without delay; if he fell down in a swoon, you would catch him up without delay: if he fell into the fire, or water, you would pluck him out without delay: yea, you would do thus much for a very beast. And yet will you delay when it is not another, but yourselves, that are sinking and drowning, and within a step of death and desperation? If a woman be but in travail, her neighbours will come to her without delay; yet when their souls are in bondage to sin and Satan, and a state of death, they will let them lie there, year after year, and when we desire them to be converted, there is nothing but delays.

35. If yet you perceive not how unreasonable you deal with God, and your souls, I beseech you consider whether you do not deal worse with him, than you do with the devil himself. If Satan or his servants persuade you to sin, you delay not so long but you are presently at it.

You are ready to follow every tippling companion, or gamester, that entices you. You are ready to go, as they invite you: the very sight of the cup doth presently prevail with the drunkard, and the sight of his paramour prevails with the fornicator; and sin can be presently entertained without delay. But when God comes, when Christ calls, when the Spirit moves, when the minister persuades, when conscience is convinced, we can have nothing after all, but wishes, purposes, and promises with delays. Thus deal ungodly wretches between their poisonous sins, and the saving means and grace of Christ.

Nay, more than this, so eager are they on their sin, that we are not able to intreat them to delay it. When the passionate man is but provoked, we cannot persuade him to delay his railing language, so long as to consider first of the issue. We cannot intreat the drunkard to put off his drunkenness but for one twelvemonth, while he tries another course: all the ministers in the country cannot persuade the worldling to forbear his worldliness, and the proud persons their pride, and the ungodly person his ungodliness, for the space of one month, or week, or day. And yet when God hath a command, and a request to them, to turn to him, and be saved, here they can delay without our intreaty.

36. Consider also, that it is not possible for you to turn too soon; nor will you ever have cause to repent of your speediness. Delay may undo you, but speedy turning can do you no harm. I wonder what hurt you think it can do you, to be quickly reconciled to God! And why then should there be any delay, where it is not possible to be too hasty? Do you think that there is ever a saint in heaven, yea, or on earth either, that is sorry that he staid not longer unconverted? No, you shall never hear of such a repentance from the mouth of any that is indeed converted.

37. But I must tell you on the contrary, that if ever you be so happy as to be converted, you will repent it, and an hundred times repent it, that you delayed so long before you yielded. O how it will grieve you when your hearts are melted with the love of God, and are overcome with the infinite kindness of his pardoning, saving grace; that ever you had the hearts to abuse such a God, deal so unkindly with him, and stand out so long against that compassion that was seeking your salvation! O how it will grieve your hearts to consider, that you have spent so much of your lives in sin, for the devil, the flesh, and the deceitful world! O you would think with yourselves; was not God more worthy of my youthful days; had I not been better to have spent it in his service and the work of my salvation? Alas, that I should waste such precious days, and now be so far behind hand as I am! Now I want that faith, that hope, that love, that peace, that assurance, that joy in the Holy Ghost, which I might have had, if I had spent those years for God, which I spent in the service of the world and the flesh. Then I might have had the comfort of a well spent life, and with joy have now looked back upon those days, and seen the good I had done to others, and the honour I had brought to God; whereas I must now look back upon all those years with sorrow, shame, and anguish of mind. You will think to yourselves then a hundred times, O that I had but that time again to spend for God, which I spent for sin, and to use for my soul, which I wasted for my mortal body! Believe it, if ever you be converted, you must look for these repenting sorrows for all your delays, and that is the best that can come of it. And who would now wilfully make work for sorrow?

38. I pray consider, whether it belongs of right to God or you, to determine of the day and hour of your coming in? It is he that must give you the pardon of your sins; and doth it not then belong to him to appoint the time of your receiving it? You cannot have Christ and life without him: it is he that must give you the kingdom of heaven; and is he not worthy then to appoint the time of your conversion, that you may be made partakers of it? But if he say, To-day, dare you say, I will stay till to-morrow?

39. Nay, consider whether God or you be most likely to know the meetest time? Dare you say that you know better when to turn, than God doth? I suppose you dare not: and if you dare not say so, for shame let not your practice say so. God saith, ' To-day, while it is called to-day, hear my voice, and harden not your hearts.' And dare you say, It is better to stay one month longer, or one day longer? God saith, ' Behold this is the accepted time! Behold, this is the day of salvation.' And will you say, it is time enough to-morrow? Do you know better than God? If your physician but tell you in a pleurisy, or a fever, you must have blood drawn this day, you will have so much reason as to submit to his understanding, and think that he knows better than you: and cannot you allow as much to the God of wisdom?

40. Consider also, that the speediness of your conversion when God first calls you, doth make you the more welcome, and is a thing exceed-

ingly pleasing to God. Our proverb is, A speedy gift is a double gift. If you ask any thing of a friend, and he give it you presently and cheerfully at the first asking, you will think you have it with a good will; but if he stand delaying first, and demurring upon it, you will think you have it with a grudge, and that you owe him the smaller thanks. If a very beggar at your door must stay long for alms, he will think he is the less beholden to you. How much more may God be displeased, when he must stay so long for his own, and that for your benefit? God loves a cheerful giver, and consequently a cheerful obedience of his call: and if it be hearty and cheerful, it is the more likely to be speedy, without such delays.

41. I would desire you but to do with God as you would be done by. Would you take it well of your children if they should tear all their clothes, and cast their meat to the dogs, and tread it in the dust, and when you intreat them to give over, they will not regard you? Would you stand month after month entreating and waiting on them, as God doth on you, in a foolish course; or rather would you not either soundly whip them, or take their meat from them till hunger teach them to use it better? If your servant will spend the whole day and year in drinking and playing when he should do your work, will you wait on him all the year with entreaties, and pay him at last, as if he had served you? Can you expect then that God should deal so by you?

42. Consider, I pray you, that your delay is a denial, and so may God interpret it. For the time of your turning is part of the command. He that saith turn, saith now, even to-day, without delay. He gives you no longer day: if time be lengthened, and the offer made again and again, that is more than he promised you, or you could have promised yourselves. His command is, Now return, and live. If you refuse the time, the present time, you refuse the offer, and forfeit the benefit. And if you knew but what it is to give God a denial in such a case as this, and what a case you were in if he should turn away in wrath, and never come near you more, you would then be afraid of jesting with his hot displeasure, or trifling with the Lord.

43. Methinks you should remember, that God doth not stay thus on all as he doth on you. Thousands are under burning and despair, and past all remedy, while patience is waiting yet upon you. Can you forget that others are in hell at this very hour, for as small sins as those that you are yet intangled, and linger in? Good

Lord, what a thing is a senseless heart! That at the same time when millions are in misery for delaying or refusing to be converted, their successors should fiercely venture in their steps. Surely if faith had but opened your ears to hear the cries of those damned souls, you durst not imitate them by your delays.

44. And I must tell you, that God will not always thus wait on you, and attend you by his patience, as hitherto he hath done. Patience hath his appointed time. And if you outstay that time, you are miserable creatures. I can assure you, the glass is turned upon you, and when it is run out, you shall never have an hour of patience more: then God will no more intreat you to be converted. He will not always stand over you with salvation, and say, O that this sinner would repent and live! O that he would take the mercies that I have provided for him! Do not expect that God should do thus always with you; for it will not be.

45. Your delays weary the servants of Christ that are employed for your recovery. Ministers will grow weary of preaching to you, and persuading you: when we come to men that were never warned before, we come in hopes that they will hear and obey: and this hope puts life and earnestness into our persuasions: but when we have persuaded men but a few times in vain, and leave them as we found them, our spirits begin to droop and flag: much more when we have preached and persuaded you many years, and still you are the same, and are but where you were: this damps a minister's spirit, and makes him preach heavily and coldly, when he is almost out of heart and hope. I do not justify ministers in this, and say, they should do thus; I know they should not; and if they were perfect they would not: but they are but men, and imperfect themselves; and what man is able to be lively and fervent in his work, when people stir not, and he sees no good done on the miserable hearers, as if he had the encouragement of success? O when we do but see the hearts of hardened, stubborn sinners relent, break, and melt before the power of the word, and when we hear them cry out for Christ and mercy, and cry out against themselves for their former folly, and confess their sins, and ask us what they shall do to be saved, and are but willing to be ruled by Christ the physician of their souls: this would put life into a preacher who was cold and dull; this would even make a stone to speak. But when we tell men of God's threatenings till they are past believing them, and tell them of God's anger till they seem to be past fearing it, and tell

them of the plague of sin, till they are past feeling; when instead of preaching men to faith and repentance, fear, and tenderness of heart, we preach them into greater unbelief and carelessness, and dead stupidity: this is enough to depress or break the heart of almost any preacher in the world. What man is able to follow so fruitless a work with liveliness? And then it is you that will have the loss and danger of it; when you have dried the breasts, the child may famish: if your preachers could not awake, and change you, with all their convincing arguments and fervency, how quietly may you sleep on when you have flattened them by discouragements? If Satan can either dismount, or make useless these cannons that were wont to batter his garrison, he may then possess your souls in peace. You talk against persecutors that silenced ministers: but it is you that are our greatest persecutors, that refuse and delay to yield to the calls of Christ, by our ministry, and make us labour so much in vain: though it be not vain as to our own souls, yet you make it in vain as to yours: when we studied till we had worn out our minds, preached till we have quite broke our strength, and we are consumed, and worn away with the labour and bodily pains that it procures, then you come after, and make us requital by breaking our hearts by your delays, and refusing to turn and live. Truly, I must tell you, for my own part, that if it had not been for those that gave me better encouragement by their obedience, I should never have held out with you a quarter of this time: if all had profited as little as some, and all had stuck as fast in an unconverted state as some; if the humble, penitent, obedient ones among you had not been my comfort and encouragement under Christ, I had been gone from you many a year ago, I could never have held out till now: either my corruption would have made me run away with Jonas, or my judgment would have commanded me to shake off the dust of my feet, as a witness against you, and depart.

But to what end do I speak all this to you? To what end? Why, to let you see how you abuse both God and man by your delays and disobedience. You cannot possibly do us, who are your teachers, a greater injury or mischief than by thus delaying your own happiness. Are our studies and our labours worth nothing, think you? Are our watchings and waiting worth nothing; are our prayers, tears, and groans to be despised? God will not despise them if you do: believe it, he will set them all on your score, and you will one day have a heavy reckoning of

them, and pay full dear for them. Is it equal dealing with us, that when we are watching for your souls, as men that know we must give an account, you should rob us of our comfort, and make us do it with sighs and sorrow; yea, that you should undo all that we are doing, and make us lose our labour and hopes: yet do you not think to pay for this? I tell you again, unconverted sinners, we are wearied with your delays: many years we have been persuading you to turn and live, yet you have not turned; you have been convinced long, and thinking on it, wishing long, and talking of it, promising long, yet it is undone, and here is nothing but delays. We see, while you delay, death takes away one this week, another the next week, and you are passing into another world apace; yet those who are left behind will take no warning, but still delay. We see that Satan delays not while you delay: he is day and night at work against you: if he seem to make a truce with you, it is that he may be doing secretly while you suspect him not. We see that sin delays not while you delay: it is working like poison or infection in your bodies, and seizing upon your vital powers; it is daily blinding you more and more; it is hardening your hearts more, and searing up your consciences, to bring you past all feeling and hope. Must we stand by and see this miserable work with our people's souls, and all be frustrated and rejected by themselves, that we do for their deliverance? How long must we stand by with the light in our hands, while you are serving the flesh, and neglecting that which we are sent to call you to? It is not our business to hold you the candle to play by, or to sleep by, or to sin by; these are works that better agree with the dark: but God sent us to you on another message,—even to light you out of your sins to him, that you might be saved. Truly, beloved hearers, I must needs say, that the time seems long, and very long to me, that I have been preaching so many years to you for your conversion, and for an holy, heavenly life, even since I first knew you, and that yet so many of you are drowned in sin and ignorance, and are unconverted, when I think your very consciences tell you that it is a thing that must be done: I tell you, all these years seem to me a long time to wait on you in vain. Blessed be the Lord, that it hath not been in vain with some, or else I would scarcely preach any more than one other sermon to you, even to bid you farewell. I pray you deal but fairly with us, and tell us whether ever you will turn or not; if you will not, but are resolved for sin and hell, say so, that we may know the worst;

speak out your minds, that we may know what to trust to; for if we once knew you would not turn, we would soon have done with you, and leave you to the justice of God. But if still you say, you will turn, when will you do it? You will do it, and you hope you shall; but when? How long would you have us wait yet; have you not abused us enough? Nay, I must tell you, that you even weary God himself; it is his own expression, 'Thou hast wearied me with thine iniquities.' And I must say to you, as the prophet, 'Is it a small thing for you to weary men, but you must weary my God also?' Consider what it is that you do.

46. Consider also, that you are at a constant unspeakable loss every day and hour that you delay your conversion. O little do you know what you deprive yourselves of every day! If a slave in the galleys or prison, might live at court as a favourite of the prince, in honour, delight, and ease, would he delay either years or hours? Or would he not rather think with himself, is it not better to be at ease, and in honour, than to be here? As the prodigal said, 'how many hired servants of my father's have bread enough, and to spare, and I perish with hunger!' All this while I might be in plenty, and delight. All the while that you live in sin, you might be in the favour of God, in the high and heavenly employments of the saints; you might have the comforts of daily communion with Christ, and with the saints; you might be laying up for another world, and might look death in the face with faith and confidence, as one that cannot be conquered by it; you might live as the heirs of heaven on earth: all this, and more than this, you lose by your delays: all the mercies of God are lost upon you: your food and raiment, your health and wealth, which you set so much by, all is but lost and worse than lost, for they turn to your greater hurt: all our pains with you, and all the ordinances of God, which you possess; and all your time, is lost and worse. Do you think it indeed a wise man's part, to live any longer at such a loss as this, and that wilfully and for nothing? If you knew your loss, you would not think so.

47. Nay more, you are all this while doing that which must be undone again, or you will be undone for ever. You are running from God, but you must come back again, or perish when all is done. You are learning an hundred carnal lessons and false conceits, that must be all unlearned again; you are shutting up your eyes in wilful ignorance, which must be opened again; you must learn the doctrine of Christ, the great teacher of the church. if you stay ever so long, or else you shall be cut off from his people; when you have been long accustoming yourselves to sin, you must unlearn, and break all those customs again; you are hardening your hearts daily, and they must again be softened. I must tell you, though a little time and labour may serve to do mischief, yet it is not quickly undone again. You may sooner set your house on fire, than quench it when you have done: you may sooner cut and wound your bodies, than heal them again; and sooner catch a cold, or a disease, than cure it; you may quickly do that which must be longer in undoing. Besides, the cure is accompanied with pain; you must take many a bitter draught, in groans or tears of godly sorrow, for these delays? The wounds that you are now giving your souls, must smart, and smart again, before they are searched and healed to the bottom. And what man of wisdom would make himself such work and sorrow? Who would travel on an hour longer, that knows he is out of his way, and must come back again? Would you not think him a madman that would say, I will go on a little further, and then I will turn back?

I know Mr Bilney, the martyr, was offended with this comparison, because he thought it was against free grace. But comparisons extend not to every respect: there are two things in your sins to be undone, the one is the guilt, and the other is the habit and power of sin; the first indeed is done away when you are converted, but at the cost of Christ, which should not be made light of. Yet some scars may be left behind, and such twigs of God's rod may fall upon you, as shall make you wish you had come sooner in. And for the habit of sin, though conversion break the heart of it, yet will it live and trouble you while you live: those sins that now you are strengthening by your delays, will be thorns in your sides, and rebels in your country, and find you work as long as you live. Thus I may well say that you are doing that while you delay, that must be long in undoing, and will not be undone so easily as it is done; and you are going on that way that must be all trod backward.

48. If it were but this, it should terrify you from your delays, that it is likely to make your conversion more grievous, if you should have so great mercy from God, as after all to be converted. There are very few who escape, that are so exceeding long in travail; but if you come to the birth, it is likely to be with double pain. For God must send either some grievous affliction to fire and frighten you out of your sins, or

else some terrible pangs of conscience that shall make you groan, and groan again, in the feeling of your folly. The throes of conscience, in the work of conversion, are far more grievous in some than in others. Some are even on the rack, and almost brought beside themselves, and the next step to desperation, with horror of soul and the sense of the wrath of God; so that they lie in doubts and complaints many a year together, and think that they are even forsaken of God. To delay your conversion, is the way to draw on either this, or worse.

49. Consider also, that delays are contrary to the very nature of the work, and the nature of your souls themselves. If indeed you ever mean to turn, it is a work of haste, violence, and diligence, that you must needs set upon: you must ' strive to enter in, for the gate is strait, and the way is narrow that leads to life, and few there be that find it. Many shall seek to enter, and shall not be able.—When once the master of the house is risen up, and hath shut the door, and ye begin to stand without, and knock at the door, saying, Lord, Lord, open to us, he shall answer, I know you not whence you are; depart from me, all you workers of iniquity.' It is a race that you are to run, and heaven is the prize. ' And you know that they which run in a race, run all, but one receiveth the prize; and therefore you must so run, as that you may win and obtain.' What is more contrary to this than delay? You are soldiers in fight, and your salvation lies on the victory; will you trifle in such a case, when death or life is even at hand? You are travellers to another world, and will you stay till the day is almost past before you will begin your journey? Christianity is a work of that infinite consequence, and requires such speedy and vigorous dispatch, that delay is more unreasonable in this than any thing in all the world.

Besides, your souls are spirits, of an excellent active nature, that will not be kept idle: therefore delay is unsuitable to their excellency. The best and noblest creatures are most active: the basest are most dull and unfit for action: the earth will stand still: you may easily keep clods and stones from moving; but fire and winds, that are purer things, the sun, and such nobler, sublimer creatures, you are not able to keep idle for an hour. Who can cause the sun to delay its course; or who can stay the ascending flames? Therefore to your more excellent, immortal souls, and that in a work that must needs be done, how exceeding unsuitable are delays?

50. If all this will not serve the purpose, let me tell you, that while you are delaying, your judgment doth not delay; and that when it comes, these delays will multiply your misery, and the remembrance of them will be your everlasting torment. Whatever you are thinking of, or whatever you are doing, your dreadful doom is drawing on apace, and misery will overtake you before you are aware. When you are in the ale-house, little thinking of damnation, even then is your damnation coming in haste; when you are drowned in the pleasures, or cares of the world, your judgment is still hastening. You may delay, but it will not delay. It is the saying of the Holy Ghost, ' Whose judgment now of a long time lingereth not, and their damnation slumbereth not.' You may slumber, and that so carelessly, that we cannot awake you, but your damnation slumbers not, nor hath not done of a long time, while you thought it slumbered; and when it comes, it will awaken you. As a man who is in a coach on the road, or a boat on the water, whatever he is speaking, or thinking, or doing, he is still going on, and hastening to his journey's end, or going down the stream: so whatever you think, or speak, or do, whether you believe it, or mock at it, whether you sleep or wake, whether you remember it, or forget it, you are hastening to damnation, and you are every day a day nearer to it than before; and it is but a little while till you shall feel it. ' Behold, the Judge standeth before the door!' The Holy Ghost hath told you, ' The Lord is at hand.—The day is at hand, the time is at hand, the end of all things is at hand.—Behold, saith the Lord, I come quickly, and my reward is with me, to give to every man according as his work shall be.' Do you, as it were, see the judge approaching, and damnation hastening on, yet will you delay?

Consider withal, that when it comes, it will be most sore to such as you; and then what thoughts, do you think, shall you have of these delays? You are unable to conceive how it will torment your consciences, when you see that all your hopes are gone, to think what you have brought yourselves to, by your trifling; to feel yourselves in remediless misery, and remember how long the remedy was offered you, and you delayed to use it, till it was too late,—to see that you are shut out of heaven, and remember that you might have had it as well as others, but you lost it by delay. O then it will come with horror in your mind, ' How oft was I persuaded, and told of this; how often had I inward motions to return; how often was I purposed to be holy, and to give up my heart and life unto God! I was even ready to have yielded; but I still delayed, and now it is too late.' Then you shall pay for all your warnings, and all the sermons and motions which you lost.

Now having laid you down no less than fifty moving considerations, if it be possible to save you from these delays, I conclude with this request to you, whoever you be that read these words ; that you would but consider of all these reasons, and then entertain them as they deserve. There is not one of them that you are able to gainsay ; much less all of them. If after the reading of all these, you can yet believe that you have reason to delay, your understandings are forsaken of God ; but if you are forced to confess that you should not delay, what will you do then? Will you obey God, and your own consciences, or will you not ? Will you turn this hour without delay ? Take heed of denying it, lest you have never such a motion more : you know not, but God, who calls you to it, may be resolved, that it should be now or never. I beseech you, yea, as his messenger I charge you in his name, that you delay not an hour longer, but presently be resolved, and make an unchangeable covenant with God ; and as ever you would have favour in that day of your distress, delay not now to accept his favour, in the day of your visitation. O what a blessed family were that, which upon the reading of this, would presently say, We have done exceeding foolishly in delaying so great a matter so long : let us agree together to give up ourselves to God, without any more delay. This shall be the day ; we will stay no longer. The flesh, the world, and the devil, have had too much already : it is a wonder of patience that hath borne with us so long : we will abuse the patience of God no longer, but begin to be absolutely his this day. If this may be the effect of these exhortations, you shall have the everlasting blessing : but if still you delay, I hope I am free from the guilt of your blood.

DIRECTION XII.

The last directions that I shall give you, for preventing your miscarriage in the work of conversion, is this, Stop not in weak, wavering purposes, and faint attempts : but see that you be well grounded, unreservedly, and habitually resolved.

There are many good thoughts and meanings in the soul before resolution ; but you are not truly converted till you are resolved, and thus resolved as is here expressed. Here I shall show you, 1. What this resolution is. 2. Why it is so necessary. 3. I shall urge you to resolve ; and, 4. I shall direct you in it.

1. Resolution is the firm or prevalent determination of the will upon deliberation.

In opening this definition, I shall first show you how we are led up to resolution by deliberation ; and then what is this determination of the will.

There are several steps by which the will doth rise up to resolution, which I shall set before you. And first it is presupposed, that in the state of corrupted nature, the soul is unresolved for God, if not, in many that are exceedingly wicked, resolved against him. At first the sinner doth either resolve to be as he is, or else he hath no resolution to return. But God breaks many a wicked resolution, or else woe to the ungodly ; for there were no hope. Many wicked persons have not only neglected their souls, but also resolved that they would never lead a holy life, nor ever join themselves to the communion of saints, nor ever leave their drunken company, or be so precise, and make so great a matter of sin, as the godly do. When we urge them with the plainest words of God, and the most unquestionable reasons, so that they have not a word of sense to speak against it : when we have told them of the command of God, and told them of the certain danger of their souls, they will plainly tell us that they are resolved never to be so precise : when they have nothing else to say, but nonsense, they will put us off with this, that they are resolved to venture their souls without so much ado. But as resolute as they are, God will break and change their resolution, and make them as much resolved of the contrary, if ever he will save them. For woe to them that ever they were born, if he should take them at their word, and resolve as they resolve.

Now in this case there are many degrees that men go through, before they come to be resolved for God.

1. The first thing usually that befalls such a soul, is some further light, which shows him that which before he understood not. 2. This light causes him to begin to doubt, whether all be so well with him as he thought it had been, and whether he were so wise in his former resolutions, as he thought himself. 3. When light hath bred these doubts in his mind, these doubts breed some fears with him, and he begins to be a little awakened ; lest evil be nearer him than he was aware of, and lest the threatenings of God and his ministers should prove true. 4. These fears drive him to consider of the matter, and to deliberate what he is best to do : to consider whether these things be so or not, and

what course he must take if they should prove true. 5. Though sometimes God may bless the very first considerations to be the present means of true conversion, yet that is no usual thing; but ordinarily the first considerations help the mind to some slight convictions, so that the man begins to see a great deal more than he did before; and so much as puts him now past doubt that he was before mistaken, and out of the way. 6. Finding himself in this case, his fears increase, and his grief comes on for his former folly, and he finds himself in a miserable case, and at a loss for a remedy. 7. By thus much he is quickened to a purpose or resolution, to hearken to those that can instruct him, and inquire of them that he thinks are in the right, and to use such means as he is acquainted with, to find out what he must do to be saved. Accordingly he goes among good company, begins to hear more diligently and sensibly, and to mark and regard what he hears and reads, and also to cry to God, in prayer for mercy and relief. But all this is but from the natural fear of misery, awakened in him by common preparing grace. 8. In the use of these means of grace, he begins better to understand and relish the doctrine of redemption by Jesus Christ, and the nature and necessity of true sanctification by the Holy Ghost. Though sometimes these evangelical illuminations may be special saving works at the very first, yet it is more usual, especially with us that are bred up under the gospel, to have a more superficial common illumination, before the saving light come in. By this common light, men have at first but a general, glimmering, confused knowledge of a Saviour, of redemption, and of mercy to be had by him. Sometimes they have a distinct knowledge of some parts only of the Christian faith, and sometimes a distinct knowledge and belief of every article; but only superficial, and not savingly effectual. 9. By this general, or superficial, knowledge of Christ and mercy, a kind of hope arises in the heart, that yet there is a possibility of escape, and a kind of comfort answerable to this hope. 10. These hopes are accompanied with some desires to understand yet more of the mystery of the gospel; and to be made partakers of the saving mercy of which he hath had a confused light. 11. Hereupon there is further kindled in the will a purpose, or resolution, to go further on in learning, inquiring into the will of God, and using his means: and, 12. This purpose is performed, and means are further used. Thus far the soul is but in preparation, and under the common works of grace, and pos-

sibly may fall off and perish. The first degree may be so stifled, that it shall not reach unto the second; or the second so stifled that it shall not reach unto the third: but the most common stop is at the third degree. When men are a little frightened, they will not follow it on to consideration: they that follow consideration diligently, usually speed well, and get through all the rest.

But when the soul is brought thus far, if God will save it, he next proceeds to this much more. He gives a clearer light into the soul, which gives a more distinct, or at least a more piercing, convincing, deep and savoury apprehension of the essentials of Christianity, than he ever had before.

Where note, of this special heavenly light, 1. That being usually the consequent of a more common knowledge, therefore most ordinarily the sum of Christian doctrine is in some manner known before. 2. That it doth not reveal only some one point of faith alone, and then another, and so on; as if we savingly knew one essential point of faith, when we have no saving knowledge of the rest; for that is a contradiction. But finding all these truths received in the mind before by a common knowledge, the special light comes in upon them all at once; and shows us the anatomy of Christianity, or the part of God's image in one frame, as to the essentials. 3. For the understanding of which you must further know, that there is such an inseparable connexion of these truths, and such a dependence of one upon another, that it is not possible to know one of them truly, and not know all. For example, believing in Jesus Christ is an act so inseparable from the rest, that if the essentials of Christianity be not essential to it, certainly you cannot do this without them. For to believe in Christ, is essentially to believe in him as God and man, two natures in one person, by office the Mediator, our Redeemer and Saviour, to save us from guilt and sin, from punishment and pollution, and to give us, by the Holy Ghost, a holy nature and life, to give us the forgiveness of sin, and everlasting life, and so to restore us to the mutual love of God here, and fruition of him hereafter; and all this as merited and procured by his death, obedience, resurrection, ascension, and intercession for his church. Whether here be all that is essential to Christianity, and absolutely necessary to salvation to be believed, I leave to consideration; but sure I am, that all this is essential to saving, justifying faith. Christ is not taken as Christ, if he be not thus taken: for the ends thus enter the definition of his relation as the Redeemer, Saviour and Lord.

So that the love of God as our felicity and

end, and the belief in Christ as the way, are both together in the same minute of time, which soever of them be first in order of nature : which is a question that I dare not here so unseasonably handle.

Upon this special illumination of the soul, and the special consideration with which it doth concur, the deliberating soul is presently resolved. In these two acts, which always go together, consists the special sanctifying work : even in the illumination and estimation of the understanding, and in the true resolution of the will.

The determination of the will, is its own free act, performed by its natural self-determining power, procured by the special grace of God ; I mean in this special case, it follows deliberation. While we are unresolved, we deliberate what to resolve upon ; that is, we are considering which is best and most eligible, and which not: and as we practically judge, we use to determine, and to choose. When this choice after deliberation is peremptory and full, it is called resolution.

So that my meaning is to let you understand, that when the matter of our faith is set open to the soul, it is not a wavering, fickle purpose, that is a saving closure with it, but it must be a firm resolution. Much less will it ever bring a man to heaven, to be thinking and deliberating what to do, as long as he is unresolved. Now I shall prove the necessity of this.

SECT. II. Till you are resolved, you are not converted, and that appears by these evidences. 1. If you are not firmly resolved, it is certain that you do not firmly believe. For such as your belief is, such will be the effects of it upon the will. An unsound opinionative belief, will produce but tottering, languishing purposes ; but a firm belief will cause a firm resolution of the will. If your belief be unsound, you must confess you are unconverted.

2. Moreover, if you do not esteem God above all creatures, heaven above earth, and Christ and grace above sin, you are certainly unconverted. But if you have such a true estimation, you will certainly have a firm resolution. For you will resolve for that which you highly esteem.

3. If God have not your firm resolution, he hath not indeed your heart and will : for to give God your hearts and wills, is principally by firm resolving for him. If God have not your hearts, you are surely unconverted.

4. Moreover, if you are not firmly resolved, your affections will not be sincere and stedfast. For all the affections are such as to their sincerity, as the will is, which doth excite or command them. Nothing is more mutable than the affec-

tions in themselves considered ; they will be hot to-day, and cold to-morrow, if they be not rooted in the firm resolution of the will, which is the life of them.

5. Lastly, without a firm resolution, there can be no faithful obedience and execution of the will of God. For if men be not resolved, they will heavily go on, and lazily proceed, and easily come off: for their hands go to work without their hearts. It is the greatest work in all the world, that God calls you to ; and none but the resolved are able to go through with it. Of which we shall give you a fuller account immediately.

SECT. III. In the next place, let me intreat you, in the fear of God, to look after this great and necessary part of your conversion. There are many degrees of good motions in the mind ; but all that falls short of resolution is unsound. Many are brought to doubt whether all be well with them, and to have some fears thereupon, that yet will not be brought so far as to consider soberly of the matter, and deliberate what is best to be done, and to advise with their ministers for the furthering of their salvation. Many that are persuaded so far as to consider, deliberate, and take advice, yet go no further than some cold wishes, or purposes, which are all overcome by the love of the world, and the power of their sins. Many that proceed to some kind of practice, do only take a taste or an essay of religion, to try how they can like it ; and begin some kind of outward reformation, without any firm resolution to go through with it : or if their purposes seem strong, it is but occasioned by something without, and not from a settled habit within. All these are short of a state of special saving grace, and must be numbered with the unconverted.

It is a common and very dangerous mistake, that many are undone by, to think that every good desire is a certain sign of saving grace : whereas you may have more than bare desires, even purposes, promises, and some performances, and yet perish for want of resolution and regeneration. Do you think that Judas himself had not some good desires, who followed Christ so long, and preached the gospel? Do you think that Herod had not some good desires, who heard John so gladly, and did many things accordingly ? Agrippa had some good desires, when he was almost persuaded to be a Christian. They that for a time believe, have surely some good desires ; and so had the young man that went away sorrowful from Christ, when he could not be his disciple, unless he would part with all that he had. And doubtless those had more than good desires, 'that had known the way of righteous- ness, and had escaped the pollutions of the world, through the knowledge of the Lord and Saviour Jesus Christ.' So had those that had received the knowledge of the truth, and were sanctified by the blood of the covenant,' and those 'that were once enlightened, and tasted of the heavenly gift, and were made par- takers of the Holy Ghost, and tasted the good word of God, and the powers of the world to come.' Surely Ananias and Sapphira had more than some good desires, when they 'sold all, and brought half the price to the apostles.'

Believe it, there are none of your desires or endeavours that will serve a profitable purpose, to prove you in a state of grace, unless they be accompanied with firm resolution. Be it known to you, that you are unconverted, if you are not habitually resolved. Therefore I must here in- treat you all, to put the question close to your hearts: are you resolved, firmly resolved, to give up yourselves and all to Christ, to be wholly his, and follow his conduct; or are you not? The question is not, what good meanings, or wishes, or purposes you may have; but whether you are resolved, and firmly resolved? Take heed, what you venture your souls upon: God will not be trifled with, nor be deceived; he will have no unresolved, false-hearted servants.

Before I proceed to urge you further, I shall here tell you what kind of resolution it must be, that will prove a man converted; and then I shall give you such motives as should persuade you to it.

It is not all kinds of resolution that will serve you; but it is only that which hath these follow- ing properties, that will evidence a state of grace.

1. As to the matter, it must be the whole es- sence of Christianity that must be resolved on. It must be no less than embracing God as your chief happiness, to be loved above all, and as your chief Lord, to be obeyed before all; and a submitting Jesus Christ as your only Saviour, your Teacher, and your Lord; to bring your hearts again to God, and reconcile you to him; and a closing with the Holy Ghost as your sanc- tifier, to make you a holy people, cleanse you from all your sin of heart and life, and guide you by the ministry, word, and ordinances, to everlast- ing life. Thus must you resolve to deliver up yourselves to God the Father, Son, and Holy Ghost, to be made a peculiar people, zealous of good works. Should you be ever so reso- lute in some point of religion, and as Ananias, to give God half, and to become half religious, half holy, and half heavenly, this is but to be half

Christians, and will not bring you half way to heaven: it is entire Christianity that must be re- solved on.

2. You must also be resolved for present obe- dience, and to turn without any more delay; and not only resolve to turn to-morrow, or sometime hereafter. No resolution is sincere in this case, if it be but for the future: if you had rather stay but one day or hour longer in the state of sin, and service of the flesh, you are no true disciples of Christ, though you should be resolved to turn to-morrow.

3. Your resolution must be absolute and pe- remptory, not only without any secret reserves, but positively against any such reserves. Here it is that hypocrites commonly fall short. They see they must mend, they are convinced that a holy life is necessary, and they resolve hereupon to change their course, and turn religious; but either it is with this secret reserve, provided al- ways that I look to my credit, or estate, or life, whatever I do; and provided that I go no fur- ther in religion than will stand with these; pro- vided that godliness be not my undoing in the world. Or else, if he have not actually such thoughts, he hath them always virtually, and ha- bitually: he is not resolved against such re- serves; he hath not considered that Christ will have no disciples that cannot and will not part with all; and that if he hope for heaven, he must not look for a treasure on earth, but only pass through the world as a traveller, or labour in it as the harvest of the Lord, in expectation of a reward and rest hereafter; and so resolved to take Christ on these self-denying terms. But he that will be saved, must be thus resolved, even to sell all, to buy the invaluable pearl. To make sure of heaven, though he lose all on earth by it; to lay up his hopes in the life to come, and venture, and let go all rather than those hopes; to take Christ absolutely upon his own terms, 'for better and worse,' as being certain that there is no other way to life, and that there is no danger of losing by him. The hypocrite is like a man that when he delivers up the pos- session of his house, will make his bargain that he will keep this room or that room to himself, for his own use. Or like a servant that will not be hired, but on condition that his master shall not set him to such and such work that he loves not: but Christ will have no such servants; you must deliver up all to him, or he will ac- cept of none: you must give him leave to make his conditions for you, and tell you on what terms you must serve him, and wholly refer the matter to him, even for life itself, and not offer to put

conditions upon him, and think to bring him to any terms of yours. It is not true resolution unless it be absolute and unreserved, and against all reserves ; yea, and that also as to perseverance ; that you resolve to give up yourselves finally as well as totally, not only without any reserve of a revocation, but against any such revocation : it must not be a coming to Christ upon essay, or mere trial, that if he like it, he will stand to it, but he must make an unchangeable, everlasting covenant : it must be part of your covenant, that you will never revoke it.

4. Moreover, your resolution must be well grounded ; you must know what the essentials are of that religion which you resolve on, and you must be moved to it by right and weighty considerations ; and go upon reasons that will hold up your resolution. For should you resolve on the most necessary work, as this is, upon mistakes, or wrong, or insufficient, as the will of man, the custom of the country, the reputation of Christianity, or only such like ; there is no likelihood that your resolution should endure, and it is not sincere while it doth endure.

5. Your resolution must be accompanied with a sense of your own insufficiency, to stand to it immutably, and execute it faithfully by your own strength ; as knowing the corruption and deceitfulness of your own heart : and it must be strengthened and supported by a confidence or dependence on the sufficiency of Christ, on whose grace and Spirit you must rely, both for the continuing and the performing of your resolutions ; as knowing, that without him you can do nothing, but that you can do all necessary things, through Christ strengthening you.

Lastly, Your resolution is not savingly sincere, unless it be habitual. It is a very hard question, how far some moving exhortation, or the approach of death in sickness, may prevail with the unsanctified, for an actual resolution ; undoubtedly very far : but that is man's mind and will which is habitually his mind and will ; when the very inclination and bent of your will is right, then only is your heart right. A stone will move upwards against its nature, while it is followed by the strength of the hand that cast it ; but when the strength is spent, it will quickly fall again. It is not an extraordinary act, that you can try yourselves by, but such a free course and tenour of your lives, as will prove that you have a new nature, or a heart inclined and habituated to God. The main business therefore, is to prove that you are habitually resolved. Set all these together now, and you may see what resolution it is that must prove you to be converted. 1. It must be

a resolution for all the essence of Christianity, and not only some part. 2. It must be a resolution for present obedience, and not only for some distant time to come. 3. It must be an absolute, peremptory resolution, without and against reserves for the flesh, both total and final, without and against any revocation. 4. It must be soundly grounded, and moved by right principles. 5. It must be joined with an humble sense of your insufficiency, and a dependence on Christ, for continuing and performing it. And, 6. It must be habitual, and such as sets right the bent and drift of heart and life. All this is of necessity.

You see now what you must do ; the next question then is, What you will do. A great many motions God hath made to you, to let go your worldliness and wickedness, become new creatures, and live to God ; and never could you be got to resolve and obey them. Many thoughts you have had of it, I suppose, and long you have been purposing that. Turn you would, but all have come to little or nothing, because you were never fully resolved. I am once more sent to you on this message from God, to see whether you will resolve: whether, after all your trifling delays, and after all your wilful sinning, and abuse of God's patience, against your own knowledge and consciences, you will yet resolve. What say you ? Shall God be your master indeed, and shall Christ be your Saviour and Lord ; shall heaven be your happiness, and have your hearts indeed ? Shall holiness be your business indeed, and shall sin be your hatred, and the flesh and the world be your enemies indeed ; and used accordingly from this day forward, without any more ado ? I beseech you resolve, and fully resolve.

Because I know if we prevail not with you in this, you are undone for ever ; and therefore I am loth to let you go before we have brought you, if it may be, to resolve : I will give you here some considerations to turn the scales, and if you will but read them, and soberly consider of them, I shall have great hope to prevail with you, yet after all. One would think that the fifty considerations under the last direction, might suffice : but lest all should be too little, I will add these following.

1. Consider, I beseech you, what leisure you have had to think of the matter. You have lived many years in the world already, and you have had nothing to do in it, but to seek after true happiness : even your worldly labours ought to have been all but in order to this ; and yet are you unresolved ? Alas, have you lived some twenty,

some thirty years and more in the world, and yet are you not resolved what you came hither for, or what have you to do here? It is twenty, or thirty, or forty years since you set out, and should by this time have been far on your journey, and are you yet unresolved whither to go, or which way to go; as if you were newly entering the world, or if you had never heard of your business? I think so many years are a fair time of consideration, and it is time to be resolved, if you will resolve at all.

2. I pray you consider, what helps you have had to have resolved you before this: if you did not know what you had to look after, and which way to take, you should have inquired; you had the word of God to advise with; and many experienced Christians to advise with: you wanted not for the wisest, and most faithful counsellors; if you had been but willing and diligent, certainly you might have been resolved long ago.

3. Consider, I beseech you, what a case it is that you are unresolved in. Is it so hard a question, that all this time, and all these helps, cannot resolve you? What! whether God or the flesh should be first obeyed and loved; whether heaven or earth, eternal glory, or the transitory pleasures of sin should be preferred? Whether you should care and labour more to be saved from sin and hell, or from poverty and worldly crosses and reproaches? These, and such like, are the questions to be resolved; and are these so hard, that all your wit, and all the advice you can have from scripture and ministers, would not suffice to help you to a resolution, no, not in twenty or thirty years' time? O wonderful; that ever the devil should be able so to befool men: that reasonable creatures should be so stupified, that they cannot be resolved whether it be better to be saved, or be condemned? Or whether sin, with hell after it, be better than holiness with heaven after? The Lord have mercy upon the poor distracted world, and bring some more of them to their wits! We have wise men, if themselves may be judges, very wise in their own conceit, who know many great matters in the world, and yet do not practically know whether God or the devil be the better master; whether sin or holiness be the better work, and whether heaven or hell be the better wages? If they say they know these things, judge by their lives whether they know them practically or not. Resolve they will not for God, holiness, and heaven, nor against the flesh, the world and sin, whatever they may be brought to confess to their self-condemnation. Is it not a pitiful case, that such points as these,

should seem so hard to reasonable men, as to be so long in resolving of them?

4. I pray you consider, how horribly by this you disgrace your understandings. You that cannot abide to be derided as fools in the world, do yet abuse yourselves thus grossly, as if there were never greater fools upon the earth. We have proud men that are so high in their own eyes, that they can hardly endure contempt from others, and love almost none that think meanly or dishonourably of them; yet what a horrible contempt and dishonour do they cast upon themselves? If one of these our wise neighbours should study seven years to know whether the sea be fire or water; whether a mountain be heavy, whether the fire be hot or cold; and could not be resolved after so many years' consideration; what would you think and say of these wise men? It is far grosser folly, I tell you again, it is far grosser folly to be unresolved whether you should be holy or unholy; which is, in plain English, whether it be better to go to heaven or to hell? For faith and holiness is the way to heaven; and an unholy life is the way to hell: if you will needs forsake the way to heaven, you may hope to come thither as long as you will; but you may as well hope to touch the moon with your finger, or run up and down with a mountain on your backs. If you will hold on in the way to hell, that is, in an unsanctified state, you may say you hope for all that to escape hell, even as wisely as to leap into the sea, and say I hope to escape drowning me, as well as you. I beseech you do not abuse God, and abuse Christ, and the Spirit, and scripture, and withal abuse your immortal souls, for I know not what; for a momentary gratification: for a thing of nought: your souls are noble creatures, and your understandings are noble faculties: why will you expose them to be the scorn of Satan, and make them so base and sottish as you do? You can see the folly of a poor drunkard, that will make a beast of himself, and go reeling and talking nonsense about the street for the boys to mock at him, and make himself the laughing-stock of the town: I pray you, why do you not understand, that till you are resolved for a holy heavenly life, you are all drunk, while you think yourselves to be sober? You are as miserable as the other, and more in this, that yours is in your natures, and theirs is but an accident; yours is continued, and theirs in that particular, but by fits. In the name of God bethink you, whether you can possibly more disgrace your wits, than to be unresolved of a case as plain as the high-way, and which your everlasting salvation or damnation lies on? If one of

you could not in twenty years be resolved whether the sun be light or dark, or the day or the night be fitter for rest; or whether it be better to plough and sow, or let all alone, and hope God will give you a crop without labour; would you take this for a wise man?

Again I tell you, your folly is more gross, that cannot all this while be resolved, whether you should cast away your wilful sins, and give up yourselves to Christ, and a holy life, to obtain the glory, and escape the misery that is hard at hand. If you stood up to the neck in water, or stood but in a storm of rain, you would not be so long in deliberating whether it were better for you to stay there longer or come out. If your finger were but in the fire, you need not so long a deliberation, whether you should take it out. Yet these wise men are, under many thousand unpardoned sins, under the curse of the law of God, within a step of everlasting fire, and have no way possible to escape, but by conversion, faith and holiness; this God hath told them, as plain as the tongue of man can speak, and yet they are considering of it, whether it be best to come out of it; yet they cannot be resolved. Did I say they are considering? Nay, the Lord be merciful to them, they are so dead-hearted and besotted, that they do not so much as seriously consider of it, but even run on without consideration. Ah, poor wretches! They are ready to go to another world, and may look every day when the bell tolls for them, and when death will bring them to their endless life, and yet they have not wit enough to resolve whether they should make ready; no, nor wit enough in their most careless, worldly state, to know that they are unready. Death is coming, judgment is coming, and the burning wrath of God is coming, and are even at the door: and yet these wise men are unresolved of that only way which is of absolute necessity to their safety; they must have more time yet to consider of the matter, whether it be best for them to turn or not? They stand at the very brink of hell; and yet they must further consider of it, whether it be better to turn back or to go on? Nay, they will go on without consideration! Yet these men would take it heinously, if one should lay hands on them, and carry them to bedlam; or but tell them of the hundredth part of the sottishness that they are guilty of.

A man that is well in his senses, would think that these matters should be more out of doubt than the former, and the more speedily resolved on? One would think it should be an easier question, whether you should turn to God and a holy life, for the saving of your immortal souls, than whether you should eat or drink, or sleep, for the preservation of your bodies? For I can in many cases bring some reason that should persuade you to forbear eating or drinking, or sleeping, for a considerable time; but no man breathing can speak a word of reason, except men's folly should be called reason, that should persuade you to forbear your conversion for a minute. If you mistake about these bodily matters, the loss may be repaired, at least in the world to come: but if you die before you are resolved, and firmly resolved to give up your soul and body to Christ, and live a holy, heavenly life, you are undone, body and soul, for ever, and all the world can never save you.

What a strange and horrible thing is it, that a man that hath the wit to manage his affairs as plausibly as any of his neighbours; who can overwit others in the matters of the world; who can govern towns and countries; who is learned in his profession, in law, in physic, in merchandize, in navigation, or the like: I say, that a man of so deep a research, so plodding, and active a wit as this, should yet be unresolved, yea, at thirty or forty years old be unresolved, whether to be sanctified or unsanctified; whether to be holy and be saved, or to be unholy, though God hath professed expressly, 'That such shall not see the face of God.' These are our wise men, these are too many, besides the ignorant countrymen, of our gentlemen, our worshipful, and honourable men, our great scholars, and men of noble or reverend esteem; that yet are unresolved, whether to be saved, or to be damned. Though God hath written the bible, and a thousand books are written, preachers are studying and preaching to resolve them; and a thousand mercies are cast into the scales, that one would think should help to turn them; some sharp afflictions are helping to resolve them, and twenty or forty years' certain experience of the vanity of this world, the deceitfulness of riches, honour, and pleasure, and the unprofitableness of sin, one would think should resolve them; yet after all this they are unresolved, whether they should presently let go their sin, and whether God or the flesh should be pleased or displeased? If this be the wisdom of these men, the Lord bless me and all his chosen from such wisdom!

6. Nay, consider further of your unreasonable wickedness: are not many of your judgments resolved, when yet your hearts and wills are not resolved? I am confident, nay, I am certain it is so: you are at once both resolved and unresolved. What a confusion and war do you thus

make in your own souls? The judgment is for one thing, and the will and affections are for another thing. What! are you not led by reason; will you let out your affections, and lead your lives, quite contrary to your knowledge; would not most of you give it me as your judgments under your hands, that it is a thousand times better to cast away your drunkenness, your filthiness, your worldliness, and your known sins, than to keep them any longer? , What say you? Are you not convinced that it were your wisest course to part with them this very day and hour? Undoubtedly many of you are. Yet for all this, will you not resolve to do it? Are you not persuaded in your consciences, that it is better to die in a holy and heavenly state, than in a loose, careless, and worldly state; and that it were your safest and wisest course to become new men, and lead a holy, heavenly life without delay? Dare you deny this; is it not your judgment; yet will you not do it; are you resolved that it should be done, and must be done, and yet will you not resolve to do it? Why, what is this but to be condemners of yourselves; to carry a judge about with you in your own breasts, who is still passing sentence against you? 'Happy is he,' saith the Spirit of God, 'that condemneth not himself in that which he alloweth.' If your judgments be resolved, let your wills resolve, or else you are wilful adversaries of the light, fight against reason, unman yourselves, and sinning wilfully against your knowledge, 'shall be beaten with many stripes.'

7. Methinks also it should somewhat quicken you to resolve, when you consider what a case you had now been in, if death had found you unresolved. For if you are unresolved, you are unsanctified; if not sanctified, you are not pardoned, or justified; and therefore undoubtedly you had been past all help, in endless misery, if you had died all this while, before you were firmly resolved for God. O what a dangerous condition have you stood in all this while! What wise man would live an hour in such a case for all the world, for fear lest that hour should be his last; yet would you stay longer in it; still are you unresolved?

8. Believe it, Christ will not own you as his servants, nor trust you whatever promises you may make him, as long as you are unresolved. Who will take a servant that is not resolved to do any service; who will take an unresolved person if he knows it, as a wife, or a friend, into his intimate love? Indeed you are not truly Christians till you are resolved to take Christ for your Saviour and portion. Whatever

state is short of this, is also short of true sanctification, and will fall short of heaven. Christ is resolved to stand by his servants, and he will have no servants that are not resolved to stand by him.

9. Indeed if you be unresolved, as you are false-hearted at the first setting out, so it is certain that you will never go well on, nor endure to the end in case of trial, nor can you do the business of a Christian's life, without resolution. If you will be Christ's disciples, you must reckon upon persecutions: 'you must take up your cross and follow him: you must be hated of all men for his sake and the gospel's:' you must prepare for prison, fire, and sword: there is no hope of being saved, while you purpose to save your pleasures, riches, liberties, or lives. Will a man that is unresolved forsake his friends, estate, and life, for the sake of Christ and the hopes of glory? He cannot do it. I know that a carnal, ungrounded resolution, may deceive a man in the day of trial, when the self-suspecting, fearful Christian may hold out: but yet without an humble self-denying resolution, joined with an adherence to Christ for strength, there is no man will hold out. If thou be a wavering-minded man, thou wilt be unstedfast in all thy ways. If thou be not resolved, the words of a man's mouth will turn thee out of the way: the very mockery and scorn of a drunkard, or a fool that hath no understanding in the matters of salvation, will make thee shrink and hide thy profession, and be ashamed of Christ, in whom alone thou hast cause to glory. If thou be not a resolved man, what better can be expected, but that thou turn as the weather-cock with every wind, fit thy religion to thy worldly ends, and as another Judas, sell thy Lord for a little money. If thou fall not away, it will be but for want of a trial to procure it; therefore in God's account thou art gone already; because thy resolution was never with it.

When you turn to God, there will remain within you the remnants of your corruption, a body of death, a rebelling flesh; this will be still tempting you, and drawing you from God. O how strong do these temptations seem to the soul that is unresolved! Yea, without a firm resolution, it is impossible to overcome them. Your whole way to heaven is a continual warfare: you have enemies that will dispute every foot of the way with you. There is no going a step forward but as the ship doth in the sea,, by cutting its way through the waves and billows; and as the plough doth in the earth, by cutting through the resisting soil: there is self, which is your principal enemy, and there is Satan, and the world, and almost all that you meet with in it, will prove hinderances: you must make your way by valour and holy violence through all: and will an unresolved man do this? You will scarce ever bow your knee to God in secret prayer, or set yourselves upon serious meditations, but the flesh and the devil will be drawing you off: you will never attempt a faithful reproof, a liberal work of charity, a hazardous confession of Christ, or any dangerous or costly duty, but the flesh and the devil will plead against it, and put you to it. In these and in many such cases of your lives, you will never break through, nor do any good on it, without resolution. Do I need to tell you, how hard the way of salvation is, that fly from it on mistake, because you think it harder than it is? Do I need to tell you how false you will prove to Christ, if you have not resolution; that you know it by your ordinary, miserable experience, that a poor temptation will make you sin against your knowledge? How many good wishes and purposes have you had already, in sickness, or at a lively sermon, that are all come to nothing, for want of a firm resolution? What abundance of time-servers, and of light professors are lately fallen off, to the way of rising and riches in the world, or to the pride and levity of dividers, that oppose the truth of God and their teachers, and trouble the church, and all because they were never well rooted by a sound resolution! They that take Christ but upon liking, do usually dislike him, when he calls them to self-denial. For they had never that natural principle that should effectually dispose their souls to like him; nor had they ever the inward experiences of power and sweetness, which are proper to the sincere, and should increase their love to him. Either resolve therefore, or stand by and perish.

10. I beseech you consider also, what abundance of clear, undeniable reasons doth God give in to thee, to turn the scales, and cause thee to resolve. He brings reasons from his own dominion and sovereignty. Should not a creature obey the Lord that made him? He reasons with you from his daily preservations. Do you live upon him, and should you not obey him? He reasons with you from his almightiness; you are all at his mercy, and wholly in his hands; and yet dare you disobey him? He reasons with you from his love and goodness: never did evil come from him; nor did he ever do any wrong: never was there man or angel that was a loser by him; it is not possible to have so good a master, and yet will you not obey him? He exhibits rea-

sons from all his mercies; every morsel of bread is from him, and should be an argument with thee to obey him: every day's health, strength, and comforts, every night's rest and ease; thy mercies at home, thy mercies abroad, in private, and in public; all should be so many arguments with thee to resolve. You cannot look upon a plant, or a flower under your feet, upon the sun or a star that is over your heads, or upon any creature, but you may see so many reasons, that should move you to resolve. If all these will not serve, he gives yet stronger reasons from the incarnation, example, and blood of the Son of God. Canst thou look on God incarnate for sin, combating with Satan, and conquering for thee, and dying, bleeding, and buried for thy sin; yet be unresolved to leave that sin, and turn to him who hath bought thee by his blood? If all this will not serve, he reasons with thee from thy own benefit. If thou care not for God, dost thou care for thyself? Dost thou regard thy own soul? If thou do, it is high time to resolve. He reasons with thee from everlasting glory. Is a certain kingdom and an everlasting, glorious kingdom, nothing to thee? Art thou content to be thrust out of that eternal inheritance? Are the filthy pleasures of the flesh for a few hours, better than the endless joys of the saints? He pleads also with thee from the danger that thou art near. Poor soul! thou little seest what others see, that are dead before thee. Thou little knowest what they feel, that died before they were resolved for God. He brings his reasons from the certain and everlasting flames of hell; and is there not force enough in these for to resolve thee? O Lord, what a thing is a senseless sinner! Dost thou believe in heaven and hell as thou takest on thee to do? If thou believe in them, is it possible for thee believingly to think of heaven and its eternal glory, and yet be unresolved whether to turn or not; or canst thou think of the endless miseries of the damned, and yet be unresolved whether to turn or not? Can any heart be so senseless or deluded?

Moreover, he pleads with thee from the equity and sweetness of his service. It is but to love him, to seek his kingdom, and forbear those things that hurt thy soul. His commands are not unreasonable nor grievous. Darest thou speak out and say, that sin is better; and that Satan hath provided thee a better work than God hath done? He reasons with thee also from his wisdom and his justice. He tells thee, that as Satan hath nothing to do with thee, and as he is none of thy friends, and means thee not so well as God doth; so he is not able to prescribe thee a more just and perfect law than God hath done. Follow God, and thou art sure thou shalt never be deceived or misled: for he wants not wisdom, or power, or goodness to be a meet law-giver and guide: but if thou follow the devil, the world, or the flesh, thou followest a blind and a deceitful guide. And yet after all these reasons, art thou not resolved?

He reasons with thee also from thy own ex-perience. What good hath sin done thee, and what hurt would holiness do thee? Yea, he rea-sons with thee from the experience of all the world. Who was ever the better for sinning, and who was ever the worse for holiness? How long will thy fleshly delights endure; what will this do for thee in thy extremity; was ever man made happy by it? Thou knowest well enough thou must shortly leave it, and that it will for-sake thee in thy greatest need: but so would not God, if thou hadst resolvedly given up thy-self to him. All men who refuse a heavenly life, sooner or later wish that they had chosen it.

Abundance of such reasonings God uses with thee in his word, and by his ministers; and dost thou think indeed that there is not weight enough in these to give thee cause immediately to re-solve? How little canst thou say against them? Canst thou bring any reason, that is reason in-deed, against these or any of these reasons of the Lord; darest thou say, that one of them is false, or insufficient; and what are the reasons which you have on the contrary to hinder you from resolving? Forsooth, because your sins are sweet, you would anxiously have the plea-sure of them a little longer yet. O wretched souls! that find more pleasure in the abusing of your Maker and Redeemer, than in loving, hon-ouring and pleasing him: that delight more in serving the flesh and the devil, than in serving God, and seeking after his favour and your own salvation. You are a hundred times worse than a man that lies in the mire, and will not rise out of it to receive a kingdom, because it is so soft and so sweet that he is loth yet to leave it; you are more foolish than Nebuchadnezzar had been, if he had been loth to return again to his king-dom, because he would wish to stay longer among the beasts of the field, among whom, in his distraction, he had betaken himself. And what other reasons have you against resolving? Forsooth, you shall be mocked or jested at by others; by whom, I pray you? Not a man but a miserable fool will do it. Yea, but you are told you must forsake all, and be ready to die

for Christ, if he call you to it. Very true! and can you keep that which he calls you to forsake? How long will you keep it? Silly souls! do you not know that you forsake it by not forsaking it, and lose all, by saving any thing; and that you have no way to save it, but by losing and for-saking it? Suppose you were by enemies ba-nished out of England, and upon pain of death you must be gone within a twelvemonth: and a king that loves you, invites you to his coun-try, and tells you, for the poor livings that you have lost, he will make you lords and princes, so you will bring with you the little goods you have, and leave nothing behind you: hereupon one man takes the next wind, and ships over all his riches, that he may have it when he comes there: another saith, I am loth to leave my goods, I have a while longer to stay here, and what shall I do without them? I am loth to see the habitation of my ancestors impoverished; and so when his time is expired, he is desirous to leave them all behind him, and hath none that will receive him in the country where he must abide; which of these, think you, is the wiser man? Which of them was it that lost his goods, and which did save them? I speak to you but such another parable as Christ used to you himself, where you are advised to send your riches be-fore you; and to make you 'friends of the mammon of unrighteousness, that when you die, you may be received into the everlasting habita-tions.'

I know there are other vain delusions that hinder you from resolving: I will not call them reasons; for they are unreasonable. I shall only say this to you, that if there be a man of you that hears his words, that dare be such a blasphemer, as to reproach the laws and image of his Maker, and say, that he hath made you too strict a law, and laid too heavy a task upon you, and a heavenly life is troublesome and unneces-sary: if there be a man of you that is so devil-ish, as that you dare plead the devil's cause, justify his work before the Lord's, and say, that it is better to please the flesh; let that man prepare himself to make good these words before the Lord and his holy angels; and be sure that he shall be there put to it in another manner than he is here by me: and if you have such reasons as you will stand to before the bar of God, to prove the devil the better master, and an unholy life to be better than a heavenly; see then that you lock them up, and there make your best of them; and expect to live with the master that you served, to reap as you sowed, and eat the fruit of your fleshly ways which you took to be the best. But if you have no such reasons, but your consciences are convinced that God should be served, that sin should be speedily forsaken, and heaven should be provided for above all; resolve then to do it before you stir: or else say plainly, I have no reason to be wicked, but because I will be wicked; I will forsake God, and damn my own soul without any reason, because I will do it. If you are at this pass, you may take your course.

11. Another thing that I would intreat you to consider of, is this, it is a most base and treacherous abuse of God to make any question of this which you are so long unresolved of. I confess, when a blind mind hath raised such a question, it is lawful for a reasonable man to answer it. But in him that makes a doubt of such a thing, as it is a shame to himself so it is a heinous indignity to God. If you set a rebel before your prince, and make a question which of them hath the better title to the crown, what entertainment might you expect? I tell you it is ten thousand thousand times a baser affront and wrong to God, to set the pleasure of sin before him, and make a question which of them is the better, and to set your riches, sports, drunkenness, gluttony, whoredom, and revenge, in competition with your Redeemer and everlasting glory, and to make a question which of them is to be preferred? To make once a question, whether God or the flesh should be pleased; whether Christ or the world should be loved and followed; whether the Holy Ghost, or the devil, should dwell in us, and guide us; whether the saints of God, or the servants of the devil, should be our chosen company; whether the word and ministers of Christ, or the examples and words of wicked men, should more prevail with us; whether heaven or earth should be more carefully sought after; whether a holy, or a careless wicked life be more to be desired; or whether it be better to turn to God, or not? I say, to make such a question as this, or one of these, is little better than to put a scorn upon the God of heaven; and savours of such malice as is more like a devil, than a reasonable man; or else of such folly as is below the devil, and as none of you would be guilty of in the matters of this world. There is but one infinite, inconceivable, perfect God, and shall he be abased by such a question? There is but one thing that is contrary to God in all the world, which is worse than the devil himself, and that is sin: shall this be put in question or comparison with God? There is but one that hath loved us to the death, but with a matchless, inconceivable, saving love,

and that is Jesus Christ: there is but one thing that is a deadly enemy to us and him, and that would condemn us, when he is endeavouring to save us; and that is sin. Must there be a question or comparison between these? There is one sanctifying Spirit, that would cleanse, heal, and save us: there is a malicious spirit that would deceive us, defile us, and destroy us: must there be any question or comparison made between these? There is but one eternal happiness, and one holy way to it; and there is but one everlasting misery, and fleshly, filthy, sinful way to it: must there be made any question which of these should be preferred? Consider, I beseech you, what you do; if it be so vile a thing to make any question of it, what is it then to be still unresolved? Yea, and to choose the worst part and cleave to it in your heart and life?

12. Consider also, that present resolution would put an end to a great many fruitless, troublesome deliberations and delays. If a man had but a weighty business of the world upon his hand, that his estate or life lies on, it is a perplexity to him as long as he is unresolved what course he should take: it will be troubling him when he should rest, and break his sleep: it will fill him with musings, and disturb and distract his mind, and even make him melancholy; how can it choose but be a troublesome, distracting thing to your mind, to be unresolved what course to take for your everlasting state? I know some hearts are so desperately hardened and past feeling, and some men's consciences so seared as with an hot iron, that they can throw away all thoughts of resolution, and never be much troubled: but I hope that many are not so desperate: it is not thus with all that are unconverted. How long have some of your minds been troubled whether to turn or not? Resolve, if thou love thy soul, and put an end to such troubles.

13. Consider also, that resolving will put an end to a great many of those troublesome temptations that assault you, and will break the heart of Satan's hopes. As long as you are unresolved, he hath still possession of you, and is still in hopes to keep possession. As long as he hath any hope, he will never give over, but will be repairing his garrison, and making up all the breaches that the ordinances of God had made. When one temptation takes not, he will be offering you another, and will be following and disquieting you day and night: but if once he see you firmly resolved, his hopes will fail him, and you may be much freer from his temptations than you were before. I do not say he will give over: for even when you are broken

away from him, he will make after you again. But it is a greater advantage to you to fight against him in the open field, under such a captain as Jesus Christ, who will assure you of the victory, than to be in his own prison with his fetters on your heels. You know the way to be troubled with an unwelcome suitor, is to delay your answer, and take time to consider of it; and the way to be eased of him, is to give him a peremptory resolute answer. When he sees you resolved, he will cease.

14. Moreover, till you are resolved on your conversion, you cannot rationally resolve on any one word or action of your lives; nay, till then they are all misemployed to their hurt. For no man can resolve of the means till he is resolved of the end. You must resolve whither to go, before you can resolve which way to go. Before conversion, men's end is wrong; their intention and business is to please the flesh, and all their thoughts, words, and actions, that have such an end, are wicked, and pernicious. Till you are resolved by conversion to be for God, you have never a right end, in a prevailing sense: and therefore you cannot order one thought, or word, or deed aright. I tell you, every thought you think, and every word you speak, and every deed you do, while you are unconverted, are so many steps towards hell, except only those that tend towards conversion, and some way further it; resolve therefore of this, or you can resolve of nothing.

15. Moreover, if you would presently and firmly resolve, you would ease your friends and the ministers of Christ of much of their sorrows, fears, and cares for you; and of much of the most troublesome part of their work. As long as you are unconverted, they can look on you but as the heirs of hell, that will be quickly in those torments, if conversion prevent it not; and therefore their hearts are full of sorrow for you, when you sorrow not for yourselves; and their care is, how they might prevent your condemnation, which they know, without conversion, can never be done. Many a groan doth your misery cost them, and many a thought have they of your danger, which you are not aware of. O what a grief is it to believing ministers, to see so many of their people in the power of Satan, and in the highway to hell, after all their care and labour for their recovery! We cannot say that the unconverted shall certainly perish, because we have yet hopes that they may be converted, though they be not: but we know that if they die in the case that they are in, there is no hope of them at all, and we know they are uncertain to live an hour: and

therefore, as long as they are in this condition, how can we choose but be filled with fear, grief, and care for them? All the troubles that befal a faithful minister, in his worldly affairs, by crosses and persecutions, are nothing to the trouble that your sin and misery brings to their minds. O what a comfortable life were it for a minister to live with bread and water, among a people that would obey the gospel; and give us hopes that we should live with them in heaven! O how cheerfully may we study for them, and preach to them, when we see that it is not lost upon them! How willingly should we prepare them the bread of life, when we see they feed and live upon it! How joyfully may we pray and praise God with them, when we think how they must join with us in the celestial praises! I beseech you, grudge not your ministers this comfort: do not destroy yourselves to grieve and trouble them. O put them once out of their fears and grief for you, by your resolving and speedy return to God: that they that have many a time thought in their hearts, I am afraid this poor sinner will never be recovered; I am afraid he will be a firebrand in hell; may now rejoice with you when they see you coming home, and may meet you as the father himself doth meet his prodigal children, and weep over you for joy, as they were wont to do in sorrow. You would ease our hearts of abundance of sad thoughts, if we could but perceive you once resolved, and see you come home. Now you think our preaching harsh to you, because we tell you so much of sin and damnation; and you think our discipline more harsh, when we refuse to have communion with you. But if you would once resolve and turn, how gladly should we open our doors and our hearts to you; and how gladly should we turn the stream of our preaching, and tell you of nothing but Christ, heaven, peace, and comfort, further than your own necessities should require it? What say you to this reasonable request? Will you resolve without any more ado, and ease us of our grief and fears, and give us leave to preach more comfortable doctrine to you?

16. Moreover consider, that you have much work to do when you are resolved and converted, and a great way to go when you have begun your journey towards heaven. Till you are resolved, none can be done. You can go no further, till conversion have set you in the right way. Till then, the farther you go, the farther you are out of the way. Will you be unresolved till the night come on? Shall all the rest of your work be undone? Will you begin your race when

you should be at the end? Alas! if you should not be able to say, as Paul, ' I have fought a good fight, I have finished my course; henceforth there is laid up for me a crown of righteousness;' when as you cannot yet say, I have begun my course: I am set in the right way.

17. Consider also, that resolution makes work easy and successful. The resolute army is seldom conquered. A resolute traveller will go through with his journey, and it is easier to himself: his spirits are excited; and doing it with vivacity, he finds less trouble in it. A slow and lazy pace doth sometimes soonest weary us: a slow motion is most easily stopped; when a swift one bears down that which would resist it. A man that resolvedly sets himself to the work of God, and is past any further deliberating of the matter, and is at a point with all the world, will make a pleasure of that which will stop an unresolved professor. Resolve therefore for your own success and ease.

I tell you, by resolving it is that you must conquer, and by conquering, you must obtain the crown. The unresolved are wavering at every assault, like cowardly soldiers, even ready to run before they fight. They will not be at the cost or labour; they are soon weary; they cannot say nay to an old companion, or a tempting bait. But the resolved breaks through all, and treads that under his feet as dust, which another sells his soul for. If he meet with reproaches and scorn from men, he remembers that Christ foretold him this, and suffered much more of the like before him. If his friends turn enemies for the gospel's sake, he saith, I was told of this before, even that I must be hated of all men for Christ. If he be enticed by lewd and wanton company, he saith as David, ' Depart from me, ye evil doers, for I will keep the commandments of my God.' If he be tempted with rewards and honours in the world, he will not stand wavering and longing after it, as Balaam; but he will say the same which Balaam was forced to do : ' If you will give me a house full of gold and silver, I cannot go beyond the word of the Lord.' Let their money perish with them, that think all the gold in the world worth the peace of a good conscience, and the favour of God. If he be threatened by men to move him to forsake his duty, he saith, ' Whether it be better to obey God or man, judge ye?' If he hear seducers, he is rooted in the Spirit, and the infallible word, and is not shaken by every wind. If he see ever so many fall off by backsliding, he saith, it was not only for their company that I chose the holy way : God is still the same; heaven is the same, and scripture

is the same; and therefore I am resolved to be the same. If God afflict him by poverty, sickness, or other trials, he saith, I did not become a Christian to escape affliction, but to escape condemnation. ' If he kill me, yet will I trust in him : shall I receive good at the hands of God, and not evil? Naked came I out of my mother's womb, and naked must I return to dust. The Lord giveth, the Lord taketh away; blessed be his name.' If oppressing enemies insult over him, he can say, ' Rejoice not against me, O mine enemy; when I fall, I shall arise; when I sit in darkness, the Lord will be a light to me: I will bear the indignation of the Lord, because I have sinned against him, until he plead my cause, and execute judgment for me: he will bring me forth to the light, and I shall behold his righteousness.' If the wicked cast in his teeth his profession, and the name of his God, ' he rejoiceth that he is counted worthy to suffer for that name;' and yet ' he will hope to see the goodness of the Lord in the land of the living.' If he must go to heaven through poverty and a mean estate, he hath ' learned to want, as well as to abound; and in what estate soever he be, therewith to be contented.' And so in the work of conversion itself, for want of resolution, many are hanging so long between heaven and hell, that it is a wonder of mercy that God doth not cut them off, and let them perish. But the well resolved soul doth deal more faithfully with the light that is revealed to him, and doth not stand struggling so long against it, nor hold Christ and his Spirit so long in hand; but is glad to make sure work in so great a business, and take so good a match while it is offered : and being engaged once, he is firm as mount Zion, that cannot be moved. Resolve therefore that your work may be the more easy and successful, and conquer by resolving.

18. I suppose you dare not resolve against conversion and a heavenly life; and why then will you not resolve for it? What purpose you to do for the time to come? Is it your resolution to live and die as you are? Have you not purposes in your mind to repent hereafter? Dare you say, I am resolved never to be converted? Some may be so desperate; yet I think it is but few even of the ungodly. Why this shows that there is a secret conviction in your consciences; O do not stifle it : neutrality never saved a soul : Seeing you dare not resolve against it, resolve for it.

19. Consider, I beseech you, how much it doth concern yourselves, to have this question well and speedily resolved. God asked you, whether you will be converted and sanctified, or not?

Resolve this question, and you resolve yourselves of a great many more that depend upon it.

The answer to this must be the answer to the rest. If the question were, Whether you will be pardoned or not; whether you will live in heaven or hell for ever; whether you will dwell with God and angels, or with devils: you would not be long in answering this; you would resolve without an hour's delay. Why this is the question: but the answer to it must be the answer to the first question: for without sanctification, there is no salvation: if you will not be converted, you shall be condemned whether you will or not; for God hath resolved of this already, and there is no resisting the resolution of God. The true state of the question is, whether you will turn or burn? Choose you whether, for it must be one: O therefore, if you will but resolve for Christ and us this one question, that you will be converted, Christ will resolve you the principal questions that concern you in the world, even whether you shall be pardoned or saved; and where, and with whom, you must live for ever.

20. Lastly, consider, that if you receive the sentence of death, it is two to one but that will force you to resolve: but a forced resolution will not serve the purpose: and then it will be very hard for you to discern whether it be any better than merely from your fears: you put off all till sickness come, and you see that you must die, there is no remedy; and then you will cry, O if the Lord would but recover me, and try me once again with life, I would delay no longer, but I would become a new man, and live a holy and heavenly life; I am resolved of it, by the grace of God. Yea, but who knows whether these last resolutions be sincere. We hear very many speak this in their sickness, that never turn when they come to health, but forget all, and live in a manner as they did before. Is it not most likely to be only the fear of death that makes you take up these resolutions? If it be so, they will never save you if you die, nor hold you to your promise if you live: for it is not bare fear that is true conversion, but it is a changed heart, that is fallen in love with God and holiness, and into a settled hatred of former sins. No late repentance and resolutions but these, will be any thing worth as to the saving of your souls: and therefore if you will have true resolutions at the last, which is too rare, you cannot choose but be much in doubt of them, when you find so much of fear upon your spirit, and consider that you would never resolve till then. Therefore if you would have a comfortable change, resolve now in your prosperity, before the face of death affright you to it, and those fears, and the lateness, make you question the truth and soundness of it, and so deprive you of the comfort which you have so much need of at a dying hour.

Thus I have given you twenty considerations to persuade you, if it may be, presently to resolve. I am sure there is truth, reason, and weight in them; but what good they will do you, I am not sure, because I know not how you will receive them.

IV. Now I come to the last part of my task, which is to direct you how to perform the work that I have persuaded you to. But because it is merely the determination of the will, it is persuasion that must do more to the work than direction: and therefore I shall only desire you to look back upon the qualifications of sound resolution, which I before laid down to you, and then take heed of the hinderances in your way, and to set yourselves to do your duty.

Remember that I before told you, that it is not a holy, saving resolution, unless it be, First, Entire for the matter of it, comprehending all that is essential to Christianity. Second, Unless you resolve upon present obedience without delay. Third, Also unless it be absolute and peremptory, taking Christ for your 'all in all,' without any reserve. Fourth, Unless it be well grounded. Fifth, Unless it be built on the strength of Christ, and not only a carnal confidence of your own. Sixth, Unless it be habitual and firm, and become your ordinary frame and bias, and as it were the new nature and inclination of your souls. By this much you see already what manner of resolution it is that you must have.

The next thing is, to advise you of the hinderances that you may avoid them. 1. The principal hinderance of resolution is secret unbelief; when everlasting life is taken but as an uncertainty, or men have no more but a slight opinion of it. The cure of this disease, I have often, and a little before, delivered to you. 2. Another thing that hinders resolution is inconsiderateness, of which also I have spoken purposely before. 3. Another hinderance is a sleepy insensibility, when the heart is hardened, and men are past feeling. We cannot tell how to awaken these men to be sensible of the things that should move them to resolve. Of this also I have spoken by itself. 4. Another great hinderance is, the natural strangeness and averseness of the mind of corrupted men to these high and spiritual things. So that we drive men, by all our arguments, against the bias of their sinful habits: and those habits plead against us more forcibly without a word of reason, than all the reason in the world could do. See therefore that you keep under changing means till your hearts be changed ; and the perusing of such weighty arguments as we offer you may be of use to the changing of your hearts. For God useth to work on the will by the understanding ; and therefore light hath an aptitude to change the will itself. 5. Moreover, the rooted interest of this world doth much hinder men from resolving to turn : it is always drawing them another way, or putting objections and cavils into their minds ; and if they will needs resolve, it is this that secretly entices them to reserves, and to resign themselves to God but with conditions and exceptions ; thus making them hypocrites, when they think themselves converts ; and cheats them with a half-deceitful resolution, instead of one that is absolute and firm. Against this impediment also I have spoken before. 6. Another hinderance is, the nearness of fleshly, enticing objects. When the covetous man sees his houses and lands, his goods and money, the very sight of them breaks the heart of all his better resolutions : the drunkard seems to be resolved till he sees the cup, and then his resolution is broken. The whoremonger seems to be resolved, till the bait is brought near him, and then he goes as an ox to the slaughter, and as a fool to the correction of the stocks. Certainly, if these resolutions were sound, they would either cause men to fly from the bait, and not come near it, or else to refuse it when it is presented them. In the course of their lives, their resolution would govern them if they were sincere. 7. Satan himself will do all that he can to hinder you when he sees you ready to resolve. He knows that he must bestir him now or never. You never put him to it indeed till you are resolving to forsake him. One stumbling-block or other he will be sure then to cast in your way : either he tells you it is but folly and melancholy to trouble yourself with these matters, or that you may be saved without all this ado, or that God is more merciful than to cast away all that be not sanctified, or that godliness doth but trouble and distract people, and that the professors of it are secretly no better than others, that it is but hypocrisy for them to make such a stir with their religion, and that we must be moderate in our godliness, and take heed of being godly over much. A hundred such foolish suggestions as these the devil hath at hand to cast in your way, when he sees you ready to resolve.

If these will not serve, he will set some of his wicked disciples on railing or deriding you ; and perhaps some cunning fool a cavilling with you, to see if they can over-match you, and draw you back.

If that will not do, perhaps he will open the falls of professors to you, and labour to persuade you that all are such : or he will show you what divisions and differences are among them : or he will take advantage of some difficulties in religion, or some controversies in which he sees you already engaged to a party, or he will tell you of some false doctrine that some forward professors may be tainted with, to make them, and consequently godliness itself, more odious, or at least suspected by you. If all this will not do, he will endeavour to set your very parents, or natural kindred, against you ; that those that should most promote your salvation, and on whom your livelihood much depends, shall become your enemies, and hate you for offering to give up yourselves to Christ. If that will not do, he will endeavour to entice you with the baits of fleshly pleasure, or of preferments, or much business, or light company, or some great matters that you may hope for in the world. Usually this snare is the strongest of all : or else he will tell you, that if you will resolve, it is time enough hereafter : you may yet take more of your worldly pleasure before you leave it ; you may yet suck the breast of the world a little drier, and then turn to God and cast it off. If all this will not prevail with you, he will tell you it is now too late, you have sinned so long, or done such aggravated sins, that God will not have mercy on you ; he will make you believe that God hath utterly forsaken you, and there is no remedy ; and you may as well spare your thoughts of turning now, for Christ will not receive or welcome you ; and therefore it is even as good to go on, and take up the rest that the world can afford you, for there is no hope of better.

But the most desperate temptation of all the rest, is, to put some blasphemous, unbelieving thoughts into your mind ; especially if you fall into company with infidels, that will draw you to question the word of God, and the immortality of the soul, and the truth of Christianity, or the life to come, whether there be any such things or not : where these once take, and are received with approbation, the soul is in a miserable case : though I know many tempted, melancholy Christians, are haunted with such temptations, who yet abhor them, and do well at last, for all this. Sometimes also, when he cannot take you off from resolving, he will lead you among some disputing opinionists, and they shall entice you to take up with their opinionative speculations instead of true sanctification, of which I have spoken in the eighth direction. By these and many such wiles as these, doth the old serpent do all that possibly he can, to hinder you from sound resolution and conversion. Therefore you must be armed against his temptations, and meet them with abhorrence ; and if you feel them too hard for you, go daily to Christ by faith and prayer for renewed strength, and call to your faithful friends and ministers for help. Open your case to some one that is able, experienced, and faithful; that he may help you with arguments to resist those temptations which you know not how yourselves to deal with. God hath appointed pastors in his church to be spiritual fathers in the Lord, and when they have sowed in you the seed of eternal life, they watch over it till they see the blade and fruit: they 'travail as in birth for you, till Christ be formed in you.' It is their office to help you, and God gives to them that are faithful, abilities and affections agreeable to their office. Therefore lean upon the hand of your faithful guides, and think not to break through temptations alone, and get to heaven without the means that God hath appointed you.

Having told you the hinderances, and what to do against them, I shall add but these two words more of direction.

Direct. 1. When you are resolving, give up yourselves to God with a holy covenant or vow. I mean not any rash vow, nor any unnecessary vow ; but the same that you made in baptism, which your age itself doth call you to renew, but your sins against it do call you more.

Perhaps you will say, that you are not able to perform it by your own strength, and you are uncertain of God's assistance, and therefore how can you promise or vow ?

To this I answer, 1. You may be sure that this objection is frivolous, because it makes against the frequent, express commands of God, the practice of his church in all ages, and the nature of Christianity itself. God hath in all ages been pleased to receive men into his service and church in a covenant way, and baptism itself is our solemn covenanting with him, and the Lord's supper is appointed for a solemn renewing of it. Indeed it is implicitly and virtually renewed by a true Christian every day of his life. In every duty he gives up himself to God: and if he should cease this heart covenant, he would cease to be a Christian ; for the very essence of his Christianity consists in it ; it is his faith itself. 2. When you covenant for the time to come you do not take on you to foretell infallibly your own perseverance, but

you profess your present consent to be Christ's, and to continue his, and you engage yourselves thereto. And should you not choose the strictest engagements ? 1. Where there is the greatest need of them, because of the looseness of the heart, and the strength of temptations, that would draw us away. 2. Where there is the most absolute necessity, because if we miscarry we are undone. 3. Where you are already obliged by God's commands whether you vow or not. 4. Where God hath made your consent to the obligation of necessity to salvation. He that intends to keep covenant, and knows that he must keep it, or be condemned, hath little reason to be loth to make it. 5. For God's assistance, you have much more cause to expect it in the way of covenanting, which himself hath appointed you, than in the neglect of his appointed means.

But you will say perhaps, I am afraid of breaking my vows again, and it is better to forbear them, than not to perform them.

To which I answer, 1. This reason makes as much against the inward vow and resolution of the heart, so that by this rule you would never be Christians, for fear of falling away, and being worse. 2. There is an absolute necessity of your resolving and covenanting, and of keeping your resolution and covenants : and when it must be kept, or you are utterly undone. It is but a madness to refuse to make a covenant for fear of breaking it : for this is but the make choice of an easier place in hell, for fear of having a worse, if you should resolve for heaven ; when as heaven is set open before you, and you thus wilfully cast away your hopes. Nay, your place in hell is not likely to be the easier, when you thus deliberately and wilfully refuse the covenant. 3. Your resolutions and holy vows, are means of God's appointment to keep you from breaking his imposed covenant. Is not a resolved, engaged, devoted Christian more likely to be accepted, and to persevere, than a waverer that saith, I dare not vow, for fear lest I perform not ?

In unnecessary matters, I had rather you were too backward to vow. Some will vow poverty, and some a single life, and some will vow that they will never drink wine or strong drink more , such vows as these may be good for some, in cases of special necessity, as the last remedies of a dangerous disease ; but they are not for all, nor rashly to be made. But the resolution and vow of cleaving unto God in faith and holy obedience and of renouncing the flesh, the world, and the devil; this is for all, and must be made and kept by all that will be saved.

Direct. 2. As I would have you second your resolution by a covenant with God, so I would advise you ordinarily to go further, and openly profess the resolution and covenant that you have made. 'For as with the heart men believe unto righteousness, so with the mouth confession is made unto salvation.' Christ will confess those that confess him, and disown, and be ashamed of those that are ashamed of him. When you have escaped the greatest misery in the world, and obtained the greatest mercy in the world, the greatness of it calls you to acknowledge and give glory unto God. Go to your old companions in sin, and tell them what God hath revealed to you, and done for you. Tell them, 'I see now that which I never saw before ; I wonder how I could venture so madly upon sin; and how I could make light of God, of Christ, of death, of judgment, and everlasting life. I have been hitherto your companion in sin, but I would not take the same course again for all the world. I see now there is a better portion hereafter to be obtained, which I was unmindful of. I see now we were all this while making merry at the brink of hell, and there was but a step between us and death : now I see that the course that we have taken is wicked and deceitful, and will not secure my salvation: if I serve the flesh, it will reward me but with rottenness : I will therefore hereafter serve that God, who will certainly reward me with everlasting life. I beseech you, come away with me, and see and try what I have seen and tried : I have lived with you in sin, O now let us join together in repentance, and a holy life! I shall be glad of your company to heaven ; but if you will not do it, take your course : for my part I am resolved, by the grace of God, I am fully resolved, to be from this day forward a new man, and never to join with you more in a fleshly and ungodly life. Never tempt me or persuade me to it, for I am resolved.'

Thus if you will declare your resolutions to others, and seek to win them, you may possibly do them good; but however, you will be the more deeply engaged to God yourselves.

Yea, though I would have no ostentation of conversion, nothing done rashly in public, nor without the advice of a faithful minister beforehand ; yet with these cautions, I must say, that it is a shame that we hear no more in public of the conversion of sinners. As baptism is to be in public, that the congregation may witness your engagement, pray for you, and rejoice at the receiving of a member: so the solemn renewing of the same covenant by repentance after a wicked life, should ordinarily be in public, to give warning to others to avoid the sin, to give God the honour, to have the prayers of the church, and to satisfy them of our repentance, that they may have communion with us. The papists do more offend, of the two, in so much confining confession and penitence to the priest's ear in secret, and not bringing it before the church, than they do in making a sacrament of it. I wonder that people should every day thrust into our hands their requests to pray for them when they are sick, and that it is so rare a matter to have any desire of our prayers for the pardon of all the sins of their natural, unconverted state.

I would here seriously advise all those that it concerns, that when God hath showed them so great a mercy as to convert them, and make them new creatures, they would go to their faithful minister, and by his advice, put up such a request as this, 'Such a man of this parish, having long lived in blindness, deadness, and ungodliness, and name the particular sins if they were publicly known, and being by the great mercy of God convinced of his sin and misery ; and sustained with some hopes of mercy by the blood and merits of Jesus Christ, and being now resolved, by the grace of God, to forsake this fleshly, worldly life, and to give up himself to Christ and holiness, doth earnestly intreat the church to pray for him, that his many and aggravated sins, may be all forgiven, that God would again receive him into mercy, and that he may hold on in faith and holiness to the last, and never turn again to the course of his iniquity.

If the minister think it meet, refuse not to make yourselves an open confession of your former life of sin and misery, and to profess openly your resolution to walk with God for the time to come.

This course should be more frequently with us ; and if conversion itself were not so rare, or else so defective, that it doth too little to quicken men to a sense of duty, and sin and mercy ; or so doubtful, and by slow degrees, and that it is scarcely discerned by many that have it ; were it not for some of these, more often would it be to the great rejoicing and benefit of the church.

THE CONCLUSION.—Now I have given you directions in the most great and necessary business in the world : they are such as I have received of God, and if faithfully practised, will put your salvation past all hazard. But what they have done, or what they will do, I cannot tell, but must leave the issue to God and you. It is a pity eternal glory should be lost for want of yielding to so holy, sweet, and reasonable a course. It is lamentable to observe, what ignorant, base, unworthy thoughts the most have of the very office of the Holy Ghost, who is the Sanctifier of all that God will save. The very name of regeneration and sanctification is not understood by some, and is but matter of derision to others : the most think that it is another kind of matter than indeed it is. To be baptized and come to church, and to say some cold and heartless prayers, and to forbear some gross, disgraceful sins, is all the sanctification that most are acquainted with ; and all have not this : thus they debase the work of the Holy Ghost. If a prince have built a sumptuous palace, and you will show men a ruinous hovel, and say, ' This is the palace that the prince hath been so long a building,' were not this to abuse him by contempt ? If he built a navy, and you show a man two or three troughs, and say, ' These are the king's ships,' would he not take it for a scorn ? Take heed of such dealing with the Holy Ghost. Remember what it is to believe in the name of the Father, Son and Holy Ghost ; and remember that you were baptized into the name of the Father, Son, and Holy Ghost. Do you not yet know why; nor know the meaning of your baptismal covenant ? It is not only to believe that there are three persons in the trinity, but to consent to the relations and duty to them, in respect to their several relations and works. If the Father had not created you, how could you have been men ? The Lord of nature must be acknowledged as the end and governor of nature, and accordingly obeyed. This is to believe and be baptized into the name of God the Father. If the Son had not redeemed you, you had been as the devils were, forsaken and given over to despair. The purchaser, procurer, and author of grace, of pardon, and salvation, must be acknowledged to be such, and himself, and his salvation accordingly accepted, and his terms submitted to. This is to believe in the name of the Son ; and in baptism we make profession hereof. Certainly the work of the Holy Ghost is as necessary to your salvation.

Without the sanctifying work of the Spirit, you could never be delivered from sin and Satan, nor restored to God's image ; and consequently could never be the members of Christ, nor have any saving benefit by his sufferings. Would you not think him unworthy to live, that would reproach the Father's work of nature, and say, that the whole creation is but some poor contemptible work ; and would you not think

him unworthy the name of a Christian, that had contemptible thoughts of the Son's redemption, as if we could be saved as well without a Saviour ; or as if it were some poor and trivial commodity that Christ had purchased for us ? I know you would confess the misery of that man, who believes no better in the Father and the Son : how comes it to pass that you think not of your own misery, that believe no better in the Holy Ghost ? Do not you debase the sanctifying office of the Holy Spirit, when you show us your knowledge and parts, and outward duties and civility, and tell us that these are the works of sanctification ? What ! is sanctification but such a thing as this? Why, holiness is a new life and spirit in us ; and these that you talk of, are but a few flowers that are stuck upon a corpse to keep it a while from corrupting among men, till death convey it to a burial in hell. Sanctification is another kind of matter than the forsaking of some of our fouler vices, and speaking well of a godly life : it is not the patching up of the old man, but the creating of a new man. I give you warning therefore from God, that you think not basely of the work of the Holy Ghost ; and that you think no more to be saved without the sanctifying work of the Spirit than without the redeeming work of the Son ; or creation, government, or love of the Father. Sanctification must turn the very bent and stream of heart and life to God, to Christ, to heaven ; it must mortify carnal self and the world to you ; it must make you a people devoted, consecrated, and resigned up to God, with all that you have : it must make all sin odious to you, and make God the love and desire of your souls ; so that it must give you a new heart, a new end, a new master, a new law, and a new conversation. This is that noble, heavenly work which the Holy Ghost hath vouchsafed to make the business of his office : to slight and despise this, is to slight and despise the Holy Ghost : to refuse this, is to refuse the Holy Ghost, and not to believe in him. To be without this work is to be without the Holy Ghost : and if any man have not the Spirit of Christ, the same is none of his. The holy catholic church is composed of all through the world that have this work upon them, and therefore it is called holy : the communion of saints is the blessed vital fellowship of these sanctified ones ; for these only is the resurrection unto blessedness, and the life everlasting with the Lord of life : for all others is the resurrection of condemnation, and the everlasting punishment.

But if the other two articles of our faith have been so denied by the blind, it is less wonder if this be so. Some heretics denied God to be the Creator of the world, and because they saw so much evil in the world, they said that it was made by devils or evil angels, who indeed made the sin, but not the world. So dealt the Jews by the Son, and the second article of our faith: the sacrifice of bulls and goats, and such beasts, was all the sacrifice for sin that they believed in. And thus deal the multitude of the ungodly by the Spirit. Indeed they know not themselves sufficiently to know the need and worth of sanctification. They are too whole to value the skill and care of Christ or the Holy Ghost. The insensibility of spiritual death and misery, and thinking too lightly of original corruption, and too well of our depraved nature, is both the cause of many of the heresies of the learned, and of the common contempt of Christ, of the Spirit, and recovering grace, in all the unregenerated. For it is not possible that men should have any deeper sense of the need or worth of the remedy, than they have of the greatness of their sin and misery.

Did we not come upon this great disadvantage to you, that we speak to dead men, who have indeed a natural life, which doth but take pleasure in their spiritual death; how confidently should we expect to prevail with you all! But while you think lightly of your disease, we can expect no better, but that you think as lightly of Christ and holiness, and all the means that tend to your recovery; and think of the new man, as the poets fabled of the Promethean race, that it grows out of the earth, of your own poor, sorry purposes and performances, like ordinary plants.

Truly, I have led you even as far as I can; and what more to say to you, or what more to do for you, to procure your conversion, I do not know. If it had been in my power to have showed you heaven and hell itself, that you might better have known the matters that we speak of, I think I should have done it. But God will not have men live by sense in this life, but by faith. If I could but help you all to such a knowledge and apprehension of these invisible things, as the worst of you shall have as soon as you are dead, then I should make but little doubt of your conversion and salvation. Surely if you had but such a sight, the force of it would so work upon you, that before I went out of the congregation, you would all cry out that you are resolved to be new creatures. But though this be beyond my power, and though I cannot show you your great and wonderful things that every eye here must shortly see; yet I come not to you without a glass of God's own making, and in that glass

you may see them. There, if you have but an eye of faith, you may see that God that you have so long offended, and that now so earnestly invites you to return: there you may see that crucified Christ that hath opened you a way for repentance by his blood, and pleads that blood with you for the melting of your impenitent, obstinate hearts. There you may see the odious face of sin, and the amiable face of holiness, which is the image of God. There you may see both heaven and hell, for all that they are invisible: and may know what will be, and that to all eternity as well as what is.

Will not such a sight, in the glass of God's word, serve to move thee presently to give up the trade of sinning, and to resolve before thou stir, for God? I am now come to the end of this part of my work; if the reading of it have brought thee to the end of thy ungodly, careless life, it will be happy for thee, and I shall so far attain the end of my labour. I have purposely put this direction of the necessity of resolution in the last place, that I might leave upon thy spirit the reasons for resolution, that here I have laid down. Now I beseech thee, reader, whoever thou art, with all the earnestness that I am able to use with thee, as ever thou wouldst escape the fruits of all thy sin, as ever thou wouldst see the face of God with comfort, and have him thy reconciled Father in Christ; as ever thou wouldst have a saving part in Christ, and have him stand thy friend in thy extremities; as ever thou wouldst have hope in thy death, and stand on the right hand, and be justified at judgment; as ever thou wouldst escape the day of vengeance prepared for the unconverted, and the endless misery that will fall upon all unsanctified souls, as sure as the heaven is over thy head: see that thou resolve and turn to God, and trifle with him no more. Away with thy old transgressions, away with thy careless, worldly life, away with thy ungodly company, and set thyself presently to seek after thy salvation with all thy heart, mind, and might. I tell thee once more, that heaven and hell are not matters to be jested with, nor to be carelessly thought of, or spoken, or regarded. The God of heaven stands over thee now while thou art reading all these words, and he sees thy heart, whether thou art resolved to turn or not. Shall he see thee read such urgent reason, and yet wilt not resolve? Shall he read these earnest requests, and yet not resolve? What! not to come home to thy God, to thy Father, to thy Saviour, to thyself, after so long and wilful sinning? What! not to accept of mercy, now it is even thrust into thy hands, when thou hast neglected and abused mercy so long? O let not the just and jealous God stand over thee, and see thee guilty of such wickedness. If thou be a Christian, show thyself a Christian, use thy belief, and come to God. If thou be a man, show thyself a man, use thy reason, and come away to God. I beseech thee read over and over again the reasons that I have here offered thee, and judge whether a reasonable man should resist them, and delay an hour to come unto God. I that am now writing these lines of exhortation to thee, must shortly meet thee at the bar of Christ. I now adjure thee, and charge thee, in the name of the living God, that thou do not thyself and me that wrong, as to make me lose this labour with thee, and that thou put me not to come in as a witness against thee, to thy confusion and condemnation. Resolve therefore presently in the strength of Christ, and strike an unchangeable covenant with him; get thee to thy knees, and bewail with tears thy former life, and deliver up thyself wholly now to Christ, and never break this covenant more.

If thou lay by the book, and go away the same, and no persuasion will do any good upon thee, but unholy thou wilt still be, and sensual, and worldly still thou wilt be; I call thy conscience to witness, that thou wast warned of the evil that is near thee; and conscience shall obey this call, and bear me witness whether thou wilt or not: and this book which thou hast read, which I intended for thy conversion and salvation, shall be a witness against thee: though age or fire consume the leaves and lines of it, yet God and conscience shall bring it to thy memory, and thou shalt then be the more confounded to think what reasons, and earnest persuasions thou didst reject in so plain, so great and necessary a case.

But if the Holy Ghost will now become thy tutor, and at once both put this book into thy hand, and his heavenly light into thy understanding, and his life into thy heart, and effectually persuade thee to resolve and turn, how happy wilt thou be to all eternity? Make no more words on it; but answer my request, as thou wouldst do if thou wert in a burning fire, and I entreated thee to come out. Thou hast long enough grieved Christ and his Spirit, and long enough grieved thy friends and teachers: resolve this hour, and rejoice them that thou hast grieved; and now grieve the devil, that thou hast hitherto rejoiced; and hereafter grieve the wicked, and thy own deceitful flesh, whose sinful desires thou hast hitherto followed: and if thou also grieve thyself a little while, by that moderate sorrow that thy sin hath made necessary for thee, it will be but a preparative to thy endless joys, and the day is promised, and coming speedily, when Satan, that thou *turnest* from, shall trouble thee no more, and GOD, that thou *turnest to*, shall wipe away all tears from thy eyes. And if the reading of this book may be but a means of so blessed an end, as God shall have the glory, so when Christ comes to be glorified in his saints, and admired of all them that believe, both thou and I shall then partake of the communication of his glory; if so be that I be sincere in writing, and thou and I sincere in obeying the doctrine of this book. Amen.

DIRECTIONS

FOR

WEAK DISTEMPERED CHRISTIANS,

TO GROW UP IN A CONFIRMED STATE OF GRACE:
WITH MOTIVES OPENING THE EFFECTS OF THEIR WEAKNESS AND DISTEMPERS.

PREFATORY REMARKS.

THIS treatise is the next in order of those on Conversion, though following after a considerable interval. It was preached in a lecture at Kidderminster in 1658, but was not published by Baxter till 1668. The dedication is an affecting address to his "Dearly beloved, the Church at Kidderminster." In this letter he expresses great respect for them, and unabated confidence and affection. "The things which I especially loved in you," he says, "I will freely praise, which were a special measure of humility; a plain simplicity in religion; a freedom from common errors; a readiness to receive the truth; a catholic temper, without addictedness to any sect; a freedom from schism and separating ways, and a unity and unanimity in religion; a hatred and disowning of the usurpations, perturbations, and rebellions against the civil government; and an open bearing of your testimony in all these cases; together with seriousness in religion, and sober, righteous, charitable, and godly conversation. But yet, with all this, which is truly amiable, I know you have your frailties and imperfections. The weaker sort of Christians, either in knowledge or in holiness, to say nothing of the unsound, are the greater number in the best congregation that I ever yet knew. And what may be your case these eight years, since I have been separated from your presence, I cannot tell, though, through the mercy of God, I hear not of your declining. It is our sin which hath parted us asunder; let us lay the blame upon ourselves. I have now done expecting my ancient comforts in labouring among you any

more. For these six years' time, in which I thought my great experience had made me more capable of serving my Master better than before, his wisdom and justice have caused me to spend in grievous silence. And now my decays and disability of body are so much increased, that if I had leave, I have not strength, nor can ever reasonably expect it; therefore, once more I am glad to speak to you as I may, and shall be thankful, if authority will permit these instructions to come to your view, that the weak may have some more counsel and assistance. And if any shall miscarry, and disgrace religion, there may remain on record one more testimony, what doctrine it was that you were taught. The Lord be your teacher and your strength, and save you from yourselves, and from this present evil world, and preserve you to his heavenly kingdom through Jesus Christ."

He assigns another reason for its publication, beside that of its being the third part of his intended plan.

"The last sermon which I preached publicly, was at Blackfriars, on this text, Col. ii. 6, 7; and presently after there came forth a book called 'Farewell Sermons,' among which, this of mine was one. Who did it, or to what end, I know not, nor doth it concern me to inquire. But I took it as an injury, both as it was done without my knowledge, and against my will, and to the offence of my superiors; and because it was taken by the notary so imperfectly, that much of it was nonsense: especially when some foreigners that lived in Poland, Hungary, and Helvetia, were earnest to buy this with the rest of my writings, I perceived how far the injury was likely to go, both against me and many others of my brethren. Therefore, finding since among the relics of my scattered papers, this imperfect piece, which I had before written on that text, I was desirous to publish it, as for the benefit of weak Christians, so to right myself, and to cashier that farewell sermon."

The second part of this treatise came out the following year, under the title of " The Character of a sound, confirmed Christian; as also of a weak Christian, and of a seeming Christian." The preface to this is addressed to his friend, Henry Ashurst, Esq., and is dated from " his lodgings in New Prison, June 14, 1669." In reference to this work, he says, in his Life:—

" The great weaknesses, passions, and injudiciousness of many religious persons, and their ill effects; and especially perceiving that the temptations of the times, yea, the very reproofs of the conformists did but increase these things among the separating party, caused me to offer a book to be licensed, called, ' Directions to weak Christians how to grow in Grace,' with a second part, being ' Sixty Characters of a sound Christian, with as many of the weak Christian and the Hypocrite;' which I the rather writ to imprint on men's minds a right apprehension of Christianity, and to be as a confession of our judgment in this malignant age, when some conformists would make the world believe that it is some monstrous thing, composed of folly and sedition, which the nonconformists mean by a Christian and a godly man. This book came forth when I was in prison, having been long before refused by Mr. Grigg."

Of the reasons of this refusal by the bishop's chaplain, he gives the following account in another place:—" This short treatise I offered to Mr. Thomas Grigg, the Bishop of London's chaplain, to be licensed for the press; a man who had but lately conformed, and who possessed special respect to me; but he utterly refused it, pretending that it savoured of discontent, and would be interpreted as against the bishops and the times. The matter was, that in several passages I spoke of the prosperity of the wicked and the adversity of the godly; described hypocrites by their enmity to the godly, and their forsaking the truth for fear of suffering; and described the godly by

their undergoing the enmity of the wicked world, and being steadfast, whatever it shall cost them. All this was interpreted as against the church or prelatists. I asked them whether they would not license that of mine, which they would do of another man's, against whom they had no displeasure; and he told me no; because the words would receive their interpretation with the mind of the author. He asked me whether I did not myself think that nonconformists would interpret it as against the times. I answered him, yes; I thought they would: and so they do all those passages of Scripture which speak of persecution and the sufferings of the godly; but I hoped Bibles should be licensed for all that. I asked him whether that was the rule which they went by, that they would license nothing of mine which they thought any readers would interpret as against the bishops or their party. And when he told me plainly that it was their rule or resolution, I took it for my final answer, and purposed never to offer him more: for I despaired of writing that which men would not interpret according to their own condition and opinion; especially against those whose crimes are notorious before the world. This made me think what a troublesome thing is guilt, which, as Seneca saith, is like a sore, which is pained not only with a little touch, but sometimes upon a conceit that it is touched. It maketh a man think that every brier is a sergeant to arrest him; or, with Cain, that every one who seeth him will kill him. A Cainite's heart and life have usually the attendance of a Cainite's conscience. I did but try the licenser with this small, inconsiderable script, that I might know what to expect for my more valued writings; I then told him that I had troubled the world with so much already, and said enough for one man's part, that I could not think it very necessary to say any more to them; and therefore I should accept of his discharge. But fain they would have had my controversial writings about universal redemption, predetermination, &c., in which my judgment is more pleasing to them; but I was unwilling to publish them alone, while the practical writings are refused. I give God thanks that I once saw times of greater liberty, though under an usurper; or else, as far as I can discern, scarce any of my books had ever seen the light."—*Orme's Life of Baxter.*

DIRECTIONS TO WEAK CHRISTIANS,

ESTABLISHMENT, GROWTH, AND PERSEVERANCE.

PREFACE.

If the reader will but peruse these directions impartially, and read them as he doth the prescriptions of his physicians, which are not written merely to be read, but must be daily practised, whatever it cost him, as he loves his life; then I make no doubt, notwithstanding the weakness of the composition, but it may further the cure of his spiritual weaknesses and distempers, and of the consequent troubles and losses of others and himself. I hope I shall not meet with many, besides malignant hypocrites, who will be so impenitent and peevish, as to fly in the face of the reprover and director, and say that I open the nakedness of many servants of Christ, to the reproach and dishonour of religion. I have told you from the word of God, that it is God's way, and must be ours, to lay the just dishonour upon the sinner, that it may not fall upon religion and on God: and that the defending or excusing of odious sins, in tenderness of the persons who committed them, is the surest and worst way to bring dishonour, first or last, both upon religion and on them. A Noah, a Lot, a David, a Solomon, a Peter, &c., shall be dishonoured by God in the divine record to all ages, that God may not be more dishonoured by them! The truly penitent are willing that it should be so; and account their honour a very cheap sacrifice, to offer up to the honour of religion which they have wronged. Till you come to this, you come short of true repentance. He that defends his open sin, unless he could deny the fact, doth as much as say, God likes it; Christ bids me do it; the scripture is for it, or not against it: religion taught it me, or doth not forbid it me; the godly allow it, and will do the like. And what can be said more blasphemously against God, or more injuriously against religion, the scriptures, and the saints? But he that confesses his sin, doth as good as say, Lay all the blame on me, for I deserve it; and not on God, on Christ, on scripture, on religion, or on the servants of God; for I learned it not from any of them, nor was encouraged to it by them; none are greater enemies to it than they; if I had hearkened to them, I had done otherwise. It is one of the chief reasons why repentance is so necessary, because it justifies God and holiness.

Alas! it is too late to talk of concealing those weaknesses and crimes of Christians, which are so visible before all the world; which have had such public effects upon churches, kingdoms, and states; which have kept almost all the Christian churches in a torn and bleeding woeful state, for so many hundred years, to this present day; which have separated the churches of the east and west, and defiled both: and have drawn so much blood in Christian countries, and keep us yet like distracted persons, gazing strangely at our nearest friends, and running away by peevish separation, from our brethren, with whom we must live in heaven; and mistakingly using those as enemies, with whom, if we are Christians, as we profess, we are united in the same Head, and by the same Spirit, which is a Spirit of love. In a word, when our faults are so conspicuous as to harden infidels, heathens and the ungodly, and to hinder the conversion of the world; and when they sound so loud in the mouths of our common reproaching enemies; and when they have contracted so much malignity as to refuse a cure by such wars, divisions, church desolations, plagues and flames, as has been seen; it is then too late to say to the preachers of repentance, 'Be silent, lest you open the nakedness of Christians, and disgrace religion and the church.' We must not be silent, lest we disgrace religion and the church, to save the credit of sinners.

Whoever reads the holy scriptures, and ever understood the Christian faith, must needs know that nothing in all the world is so much against every one of our errors and evil deeds. It is only for want of more religion, that any professors of religion miscarry: nothing but the doctrine of Christianity and godliness did at first destroy the reign of their sin; and nothing else can subdue the rest, and finish the cure. It is no disgrace to life that so many men's lives are burdensome with sickness, which the dead are not troubled with; nor is it any disgrace to learning, that scholars for want of more learning, have troubled the world with their contentious disputes; nor is it any disgrace to reason, that men's different reasons, for want of more reason, doth set the world together by the ears. We can never magnify you enough as you are Christians and godly, unless we should ascribe more to you than your bounteous Lord hath given you, who hath made you little lower than angels, and crowned you with glory and honour. But your sins are so much the more odious, as they are brought so near the holy presence; and as they are aggravated by greater mercies and professions: and God is so far from being reconciled, or reconcileable to any one of them, and though he see not such iniquity in Jacob, as is in heathens and the ungodly, because it is not in them to be seen, yet he sees more aggravated iniquity in such sins as you commit, in many respects, than in the heathens. That which is our common trouble is, that you hurt not yourselves alone by your iniquities; families are hurt by them; neighbours are hurt by them; churches are distracted by them; kingdoms are afflicted by them; and thousands of blind sinners are hardened and everlastingly undone by them. The ignorant husband saith, I will never follow sermons nor scriptures, nor be so religious, while I see my wife, who makes so much ado with religion, to be as peevish and discontented, foul-tongued and unkind, contemptuous and disobedient, as those that have no religion. The master who is profane saith, I like not your religion, when that servant which most professes religion in my house, is as lazy, as negligent, as surly, as ready to dishonour me, and answer again, and as proud of his little knowledge, as those that have no religion at all. The like I might say of all other relations. All the dishonour that this casts upon grace is, that you have too little of it; and it is so weak in you, that its victory over your flesh and passions is lamentably imperfect A servant hearing a high commendation of a gentleman, that he was of extraordinary wisdom, godliness, bounty, patience, affability, and what not, did think with himself, how happy a man were I, if I could but dwell in this man's house: which at last he procured, but ere long went away. His friend meeting him, asked him how he came so quickly to forsake his happiness? Did not his master prove as was reported? He answered, Yes, and better than report could make him, or I could ever have believed: but though my master was so good, my mistress was so unreasonable, clamorous and cruel, that she would beat us, and there was no living with her. So faith, I hope, is the master in your hearts: and that is as good as can be well believed. But the flesh is mistress, which should be but a servant: and that makes such troublesome work with some of you, that some quiet-natured infidels are less vexatious companions than you. Nay, and I wonder if you can be very confident of your own sincerity, as long as such fleshly vices, and headstrong passions, keep up the power of a mistress in you.

I wonder if you do not fear, lest, as a woman said, I will call my husband Lord, with Sarah, if I may have my will fulfilled, so grace and faith should have no more than the regent titles, while your flesh hath so much of its will fulfilled. I know too many cheat themselves into comfort, with the false opinion, that because they have a party in them that strives against their sins, it is a certain sign that they have the Spirit, and are sanctified, though the flesh even in the main doth get the victory: and I know that many have sincerity indeed, who yet have many a foil by boisterous passions, and fleshly inclinations: but I am sure till you know which party is predominant, and truly bears the governing sway, you can never know whether you are sincere. As once a servant, when his master and mistress were fighting, answered one at the door, who desired to speak with the master of the house, You must stay till I see who gets the better, before I can tell you who is master of the house. So truly I fear the conflict is so hard with many Christians, between the spirit and the flesh, and holds them so long in a doubtful state, and sense, passion, unbelief and pride, worldliness, and selfishness prevail so much, that they may stay themselves a great while before they can be well resolved which is master. For—to prosecute my similitude—in innocent men, spiritual reason was absolutely master, and fleshly sense was an obsequious servant, though yet it had an appetite which needed government and restraint. In wicked men the fleshly sense and appetite is master, and reason is a servant, though reason and the motions of the Spirit may make some resistance. In strong Christians, spiritual reason is master, and the fleshly sense and appetite is a servant, but a boisterous and rebellious servant, tamed according to the degrees of grace and spiritual victory: like a horse that is broken and well ridden, but oft needs the spur, and oft the reins. So that Paul may cry out, 'O wretched man,' &c. In a weak Christian the Spirit is master, but the flesh is mistress, and is not kept in the servitude which it was made for, as it ought. Therefore his life is blemished with scandals, and his soul with many foul corruptions; he is a trouble to himself and others: the good which he doth, is done with much reluctance and weakness; and the evil which he forbears, is oftentimes very hardly forborn: his flesh hath so much power left, that he is usually uncertain of his own sincerity; and yet too patient both with his sin and his uncertainty: and he is many times a greater troubler of the church, than any moderate unbelievers. The hypocrite or almost Christian, hath the flesh for his master, as other wicked men, but reason and the common grace of the Spirit, may be as mistress with him, and may have so much power and respect, above a state of utter servitude, as may delude him into a confident conceit that grace hath the victory, and that he is truly spiritual: when yet the supremacy is exercised by the flesh. 'He that hath an ear to hear, let him hear: to him that overcometh will I give to eat of the tree of life.—He shall not be hurt of the second death.—He shall eat of the hidden manna.—He shall have power over the nations.—I will give him the morning star.—I will confess him before my Father and the angels.—He shall be a pillar in the temple of God, and go out no more. I will grant him to sit with me in my throne.'

PART I.

EXPOSITION OF THE TEXT, AND EXHORTATIONS
GROUNDED ON IT.

" *As ye have therefore received Christ Jesus the Lord, so walk ye in him, rooted and built up in him, and stablished in the faith, as ye have been taught, abounding therein with thanksgiving.*"—COL. ii. 6, 7.

As ministers are called in God's word the fathers of those that are converted by their min-

istry, so are they likened thus far to mothers, that they travail. as in birth, of their people's souls till Christ be formed in them. As Christ saith, ' A woman when she is in travail hath sorrow, because her hour is come; but as soon as she is delivered of the child, she remembers no more the anguish, for joy that a man is born into the world.' So while we are seeking and hoping for your conversion, and are as in travail of you till you are born again; not only our labour, but much more our fears of you, and cares for you, and compassion of you in your danger and misery, doth make the time seem very long to us; and O what happy men would we think ourselves, if all or the most of our people were converted ! When we see but now and then one come home, we remember no more the anguish of our fears and sorrows, nor think all our labour ill bestowed, for joy that a Christian is new born unto Christ. But yet for all the mother's joy, her work, care, and sorrow, is not at an end as soon as she is delivered: many a foul hand, many a troublesome hour, and many a waking night, she must have with the child, whose birth she so rejoiced in ; and after that, many a year of care and labour to bring it up, and provide for it in the world; and in her old age, when she expects from her children the love, honour, and thanks, and comfort that was due to her as a mother, and for all her labour, care and pains, perhaps one child will prove kind, and of another she must take it well that he is not very unkind, and a third perhaps may break her heart: and yet she must still be a mother to them all. So it befalls us; when we have greatly rejoiced at the real or seeming conversion of now and then one of our hearers, our work with them is not at an end, nor may we lay aside our care and labour for them. We have, for some years, usually the nurse's work to do ; and many a troublesome day and night, the weakness, the uncleanness, the peevish, childish exceptions, the querulous and quarrelsome dispositions of our beloved converts, will trouble us: and after all that, when they begin to go on their own legs, and think themselves sufficient for themselves without our help, many a fall and hurt they may catch, and many fallings out may they have with one another, to the great trouble of themselves and us. And when they are grown up to strength of parts and gifts, some that seemed sincere may turn prodigals or apostates; some fall a quarreling about the inheritance, and make most woful divisions in Christ's family; and some perhaps despise us that have thus spent our days and strength in studies, prayers, fears, cares and labours for their salvation; yea, perhaps be ready to treat us with contempt and reproach our persons, yea, and our very office and calling itself, as the experience of these times of ours, seconding the experience of all ages of the church before us, doth, alas, too evidently and openly testify.

Yet some will be faithful and constant, and thankful to Christ and us. And that all might be so, for Christ's sake, and for their own, must still be our care, desires, and endeavours. In these several cases we find blessed Paul with his children, in his epistles, sometimes rejoicing with them in their stedfastness; sometimes defending himself and his ministry against their unkind and childish wranglings; as with the Corinthians you may find him; sometimes he is put, but seldom, to a severe correction of the obstinate, delivering them up to Satan, for a warning to the rest; sometimes he is anxious to watch with them, as in their sickness, when they are infected with some dangerous error, or other disease; and is brought even to make great question of their lives, lest he hath laboured for them in vain, and themselves have run in vain, and lest they be fallen from grace, and Christ should profit them nothing; receiving himself no better requital of all his labours from them that once would have pulled out their eyes for him, than to be taken for their enemy, because he tells them the truth; and the more he loves them, the less to be loved of them. But with the most we find him as one that is yet between hope and fear of them, directing and exhorting them to spiritual stedfastness, growth, and perseverance to the end; and this is the work which we here find him upon with the Colossians in this text; which contains, 1. A supposition of a work (the great work) already done, viz. that, 'they have received Christ Jesus the Lord.' 2. An inference of further duty, and exhortation thereto, which is their confirmation and progress. The parts of this duty are expressed in several metaphors. The first is taken from a tree or other plant, and is called our 'rooting in Christ.' After the 'receiving of Christ,' there is a further rootedness in him to be sought. The second is taken from a building, and is called, a 'being built up in him,' as a house is upon the foundation. All the work is not done when the chief corner stone and foundation is laid. The third part is taken from those pillars and stronger parts of the building, which are firm upon the foundation, and it is called a being 'stablished or confirmed in faith.'

Having made mention of faith, lest they should

hearken to innovations and the conceits of men under pretence of faith, he adds, 'as ye have been taught,' to show them what faith or religion it is that they must be established in; even that which by the apostles they had been taught. And, lastly, he expresses the measure that they should aim at, and one special way in which their faith should be exercised, 'abounding therein with thanksgiving.' The matter is not great, whether we take the relative to refer to Christ, and read it with the vulgar Latin, 'abounding in him with thanksgiving;' or as the Æthiopian, 'abound with thanksgiving to him;' or whether we take it as relating to thanksgiving itself, as the Arabic translator, and some Greek copies have it, 'abounding in thanksgiving;' or, 'abounding in such thanksgiving:' or as the ordinary Greek copies, and the Syriac translator, referring it to faith, 'abounding in it,' that is, in that faith with thanksgiving. For in the end it comes to the same, 'to abound in Christ,' and 'to abound in faith in Christ,' and 'to abound in a believing thanksgiving to Christ.' All this is generally comprehended in 'walking in Christ;' the whole life of a Christian being divided into these two parts, 'receiving Christ, and walking in him.'

Here are these several terms therefore briefly to be opened. 1. What is meant by receiving Christ Jesus the Lord. 2. What is meant by walking in him. 3. What by being rooted in him. 4. What by being built up in him. 5. What by being confirmed or stablished in the faith. 6. What by this directive limitation, 'as ye have been taught.' 7. What by abounding therein with thanksgiving.

For the first, you must observe the act and the object. The act is 'receiving:' the object is 'Christ Jesus the Lord.'

To receive Christ is not only, as some annotators mistake it, to receive his doctrine, though it is certain that his doctrine must be received, and that the rest is implied in this. But when the understanding receives the gospel by assent, the will also accepts or receives Christ as he is offered, by consent; and both these together are the receiving of Christ; that is, the true justifying faith of God's elect. It is not therefore a physical passive reception, as wood receives the fire, and as our souls receive the graces of the spirit; but it is a moral reception, which is active and metaphorical. This will be better understood when the object is considered, which is 'Christ Jesus the Lord.' To receive Christ as Christ, or the anointed Messias, and as the Saviour and our Lord, is to believe that he is such, and to consent that he be such to us, and to trust in him, and resign ourselves to him as such. The relation we indeed receive by a proper passive reception; I mean our relation of being the redeemed members, subjects, and disciples of this Christ. But the person of Christ we only receive by such an active, moral reception, as a servant by consent receives a master; a patient by consent receives a physician; a wife by consent receives a husband; and a scholar or pupil by consent receives a teacher or tutor; or the subject by consent receives a sovereign. So that it is the same thing that is called 'receiving Jesus the Lord,' and believing in him as it is expounded. There are three great observable acts of faith essential to it; the first is, assent to the truth of the gospel: the second is, consent or acceptance of Christ and life, as the offered good: the third is, affiance in Christ for the accomplishing of the ends of his office. Now the word *faith* doth most properly express the first act and the last; and the word *receiving*, doth most properly express the middle one. But which ever term is used, when it is justifying faith that is spoken of, all three are intended or included. By what hath been said, you may discern whether you have received Christ or not: for faith may be known by these acts, which are its parts. 1. If you sincerely believe the gospel to be true; which must be with a belief so strong at least, as that you are resolved to venture your happiness upon this belief, and let go all for the hope that is set before you. 2. If an offered Christ, in his relation as a full and perfect Saviour, be heartily welcome to you. If you consent to the gospel offer, and are but truly willing to be his, and that he be yours in that relation. Faith is not only called a receiving of Christ, but is often expressed by this term of willing him. Therefore the promise is to whosoever will, and the wicked are denied a part in Christ, because they will not have him reign over them, or will not come to him that they may have life, even because they would have none of him, which is because they are not true believers or disciples of Christ. 3. If you thus by consent take Christ for your Saviour, teacher, and Lord, it must needs follow that you stedfastly rely upon him, or trust him to accomplish the ends of his relations; that you trust to him for deliverance from the guilt, power, and punishment of sin, and for quickening, strengthening, and preserving grace, and for everlasting life; that you resign yourselves up to him as his disciple, to learn of him, with a confidence or trust, that he will infallibly

teach you the way to happiness; that you also give up yourselves to him as his subjects, with a trust that he will govern you in truth and righteousness, in order to your salvation, and will defend you from destroying enemies. This much is of the very being of faith, or the receiving Christ Jesus the Lord. And these parts are inseparable; he that hath one in truth, hath all. Whenever we find in scripture the promise of justification or salvation made to us, if we believe, it is this believing, and none but this, that is intended. It is not only believing in Christ as a sacrifice or priest, that is the faith which justifies, and believing in him as a teacher or Lord that sanctifies: the effects are not thus parcelled out to several essential parts of this same faith; but it is this one entire faith in all these essential parts, that is the undivided condition of all these benefits; and in that way of a condition of the free promise it doth procure them. So much for the meaning of the first words, 'receiving Christ Jesus the Lord.' I will be more brief about the next. The second is 'walking in him,' which is no more but the living as Christians, when once we are become Christians, and using that Christ to the ends which we received him for, when once we have received him. Two things are necessary to such as we that have lost our way: the first is, to get into the right way, and that is to get into Christ, who is the way: the other is to travel on, when we are in it: for it is not enough to bring us to our journey's end, that we have found out the right way. The next word to be explained is 'rooted,' which doth not intimate that any are really planted into Christ, without any rooting in him at all: but by 'rooted' is meant 'deeply rooted.' For the roots increase under ground, as well as the tree above ground. Rooting hath two ends, and both are here implied. The first is for the fibres of the tree, that fierce winds may not overturn it. The second is for nutriment, that it may receive that nourishment from the earth which may cause its preservation, growth, and fruitfulness. This is the rootedness of Christians in Christ, that they may be confirmed in him against all assaults, and may draw from him that nutriment that is necessary to their growth and fruit. The next term is 'built up in him.' No house consists of a bare foundation. Five things are expressly contained in our being 'built up in him.' The first is, that we are united or conjoined to him, as the building is on the foundation. The second is, that we rest wholly on him, as our support, as the building doth on the foundation. The third is, that we are also conjoined one unto another, and are become one spiritual building in the Lord. The fourth is, that the fabric doth increase in size, as the house doth by being built up ; so that it importeth our increase in grace, and increase of the church by us. The fifth is, the fitness of the building to its intended ends and use : till it be built up, it is not fit for habitation. And till Christians are built up, God hath not that use of them to which he doth intend them. The next term is, 'stablished or confirmed in the faith,' which signifies, that strengthening and fixing of us that may prevent our fall or shaking ; and it comprises these two things. First, that we be found bottomed on Christ, who is our foundation. And, secondly, that we be cemented and firmly joined to each other. This comprehends their stability in the doctrine of faith : therefore he adds, 'as ye have been taught,' to fortify them against heresies, which indeed are all but novelties ; that so they may know how to try the doctrines that afterwards should be offered them, and stick fast to that which the apostles taught. He next requires them, to 'abound therein,' to let them know, that as it is no small matters that they expect by Christ, so they should not rest in small degrees of grace or duty ; but especially the duty of 'thanksgiving,' which is an evangelical and celestial duty, and so admirably beseems a people who have partaken of such admirable salvation, and is so suitable to our mercies, and our condition, and God's just expectation. As it is love and grace whose eternal praise is designed by the gospel, and are magnified in the church by the Redeemer's great and blessed work : so it is returns of love, praise, and joy, that should be the most abounding or overflowing part of all our Christian affections and performances. After this explication, you may see that the sense of the text lies plain in this proposition :

Doct. Those that have savingly received Christ Jesus the Lord, must be so far from resting here, as if all were done, that they must spend the rest of their days in walking in him, being rooted and built up in him, stablished in the faith as the apostles taught it, and abounding in it, especially with joyful praises to our Redeemer.

Because that my design is only to direct young Christians how they may come to be established and confirmed in Christ, I shall therefore pass over all other things that the full handling of this text requires ; and shall only give you, I. A short intimation here, what this confirmation and stability is, which shall be more fully opened to you in the directions. II. Show you the need of seeking it. III. How you may attain it.

I. This confirmation is the habitual strength of grace, distinct from present actual confirmation by the influence of grace from God ; for though God may in an instant confirm a weak person against some particular temptation, by his free assistance, yet that is not it which we have here to speak of, but habitual confirmation in a state of grace. And ordinarily we may expect, that God's co-operating, assisting grace, should bear some proportion with our habitual grace ; even as in nature he concurs with the strongest men, to do greater works than he causes the weak to do ; and with the wisest men to understand more than the foolish do ; I say but that ordinarily it is thus.

A confirmed Christian, as contrary to a weak one, 1. Is not to be judged of by his freedom from all scruples, doubts, or fears. 2. Nor by his eminency in men's esteem or observation. 3. Nor by his strength of memory. 4. Or freedom of utterance in praying, preaching, or discourse. 5. Or by his seemly deportment and courtesy towards others. 6. Nor by his sedate, calm, and lovely temper, and freedom from some haste and heats which other tempers are more prone to. 7. Nor by a man-pleasing or dissembling faculty to bridle the tongue, when it would open the corruption of the mind, and to suppress all words which would make others know how bad the heart is. There are many endowments laudable and desirable, which will not show so much as sincerity in grace ; and much less a state of confirmation and stability.

But confirmation lies in the *great degree of all those graces which constitute a Christian,* and the great degree appears in the operations of them. As, 1. When holiness is as a new nature in us, gives us a promptitude to holy actions, makes us free and ready to them, and makes them easy and familiar to us : whereas the weak go heavily, and can scarcely drive on and force their minds. 2. When there is a constancy or frequency of holy actions ; which shows the strength and stability of holy inclinations. 3. When they are powerful to bear down oppositions and temptations, can get over the greatest impediments in the way, make an advantage of all resistance, and despise the most splendid baits of sin. 4. When it is still getting ground, and drawing the soul upward, and nearer to God, its rest and end ; when the heart grows more heavenly and divine, and a stranger to earth and earthly things. 5. And when holy and heavenly things are more sweet and pleasant to the soul, and are sought and used with more love and pleasure. All these show that the operations of grace are vigorous and strong, and consequently that the habits are so also.

This confirmation should be found, 1. In the understanding. 2. In the will. 3. In the affections. 4. In the life.

1. When the mind of a man hath a larger comprehension of the truths of God, and the order, method, and usefulness of every truth, with a deeper apprehension of the certainty of them, and of the goodness of the matter expressed in them; when knowledge and faith come nearest unto sight or intention, and we have a full, true, firm, and most certain apprehension of things revealed and unseen; when the nature, the reasons, the ends and benefits of the Christian religion are all most clearly, orderly, decently, constantly, and powerfully printed on the mind, then is that mind in a confirmed state.

2. When the will is guided by such a confirmed understanding, and is not foolishly resolved, he knows not for what, or why; when light hath fixed it in such resolutions as are past all notable doubtings, deliberations, waverings, or unwilling backwardness, and a man is in seeking God and his salvation, and avoiding known sin, as a natural man is about the questions, whether he should preserve his life and make provision for it, and whether he should poison, or famish, or torment himself; when the inclination of the will to God, heaven and holiness, are likest to its natural·inclination to good as good, and to its own felicity, and its action is so free as to have least indetermination, and to be likest to natural necessary acts, as those are of blessed spirits in heaven; when the least intimation from God prevails, and the will doth answer him with readiness and delight; and when it takes pleasure to trample upon all opposition, and when all that can be offered to corrupt the heart, and draw it to sin, and loosen it from God, prevails but as so much dust and dross would do, —this is a confirmed state of will.

3. When the affections proceed from such a will, and are ready to assist, excite, and serve it, and to carry us on in necessary duties; when the lower affections of fear and sorrow cleanse, restrain, and prepare the way, and the higher affections of love and delight adhere to God, and desire and hope make out after him, and set the soul on just endeavours; when fear and grief have less to do, and are delivering up the heart still more and more to the possession of holy delight and love, and when those affections, which are rather profound than very sensible immediately towards God himself, are sensible towards his word, his servants, his graces, and his ways, and against all sin; then are the affections, and so the man, in a confirmed state.

4. When ourselves, our time, and all that we have, are taken to be God's, and not our own, and are entirely, and unreservedly resigned to him and used for him; when we study our duty, and trust him for our reward; when we live as those that have much more to do for heaven than for earth, and with God than with man or any creature; when our consciences are absolutely subjected to the authority and laws of God, and bow not to competitors; when we are habitually disposed, as his servants, to be constantly employed in his works, and make it our calling and business in the world, as judging that we have nothing to do on earth, but with God, or for God; when we keep not up any secret desires and hopes of a worldly felicity, nor pursue the pleasure of the flesh, under the cloak of faith and piety, but subdue the flesh as our most dangerous enemy, and can easily deny its appetite and concupiscence; when we guard all our senses, and keep our passions, thoughts, and tongues, in obedience to the holy law; when we do not inordinately set up ourselves in our esteem or desire above or against our neighbour and his welfare; but love him as ourselves, seek his good, and resist his hurt as heartily as our own; and love the godly with a love of complacence, and the ungodly with a love of benevolence, though they be our enemies; when we are faithful in all our relations, and have judgment to discern our duty, that we run not into extremes; and skill, and readiness, and pleasure in performing it, and patience under all our suffering; this is the life of a confirmed Christian, in various degrees, as their strength is various.

I shall now proceed to persuade such to value and seek this confirmation, lest with dull, unprepared minds my following directions should be lost; and then I shall give you the directions themselves, which are the part that is principally intended. First for the motives.

I. Consider that your first entrance into Christianity is an engagement to proceed; your receiving Christ obliges you to walk and grow up in him. A fourfold obligation, your very Christianity lays upon you, to grow stronger, and to persevere. 1. The first is, from the very nature of it; even from the office of Christ, and the use and ends to which we receive him. You receive Christ as a physician of your diseased souls; and doth not this engage you to go on to use his medicines till you are cured? What do men choose a physician for, but to heal them? It were but a foolish patient that would say, Though my disease be deadly, yet now I have chosen the best physicians, I have no more to do; I doubt not of recovery. You took Christ for a saviour, which engages you to use his saving means, and submit to his saving works. You took him for your teacher and master; and gave up yourselves to be his disciples, and what sense was in all this if you did not mean to proceed in learning of him. It is a silly conceit for any man to think that he is a good scholar, merely because he hath chosen a good master, or tutor, without any further learning of him. When Christ sent out his apostles, it was for these two works: first to disciple nations, and baptize them; and then to go on in teaching them to observe all things whatsoever he commandeth them. Christ is the way to the Father; but to what purpose did you come into this way, if you meant not to travel on in it?

2. Moreover, when you became Christians, you entered a solemn covenant with Christ; and bound yourselves by a vow, to be faithful to him to the death: and this vow is upon you: 'it is better not to vow, than to vow and not perform.' In taking him to be the captain of your salvation, and lifting yourselves under him, and taking this oath of fidelity to him, you did engage yourselves to fight as faithful soldiers, under his conduct and command to your life's end. And as it is a foolish soldier who thinks that he hath no more to do, but list himself and take colours, and need not fight; so it is a foolish and ungodly professor who thinks he hath nothing to do but to promise, and may be excused from performance, because that promising was enough; when the promise was purposely to bind him to perform.

3. Moreover, when you became Christians, you put yourselves under the laws of Christ; and these laws require you to go further till you are confirmed; so that you must go on, or renounce your obedience to Christ.

4. Lastly, when you became Christians, you received such exceeding mercies, as oblige you to go much higher in your affections, and much further in your obedience to God. A man who is newly snatched, as from the jaws of hell, and hath received the free forgiveness of his sins, and is put into such a state of blessedness as we are, must needs feel abundance of obligations upon him to proceed to stronger resolutions and affections, and not to stop in those low beginnings. So that if you lay these four things together, you will perceive that the very purpose

of your receiving Christ was that you might walk in him, and be confirmed and built up.

II. Consider also, that conversion is not sound if you are not heartily desirous to increase. Grace is not true, if there be not a desire after more; yea, if you desire no perfection itself. An infant is not born to continue an infant, for that were to be a monster; but to grow up unto manhood. As the kingdom of Christ in the word is likened by him to a little leaven, and to a grain of mustard seed, in the beginning, which afterward makes a wonderful increase; so his kingdom in the soul is of the same nature too. If you are contented with that measure of holiness that you have, you have none at all, but a shadow and conceit of it. Let those men think of this that stint themselves in holiness, and plead for a moderation in it, as if it were intemperance or fury to love God or fear him, or seek him or obey him, any more than they do; or as if we were in danger of excess in these: if ever these men had feelingly, and by experience known what holiness is, they would never have been possessed with such conceits as these.

III. Consider what abundance of labour hath been lost, and what hopes have been frustrated, for want of proceeding to a rooted confirmation. I say not that such were truly sanctified; but I say, they were in a very hopeful way, and went far, and by going further might have attained to salvation. The heart of many a minister hath been glad to see their hearers humbled, bewailing sin, changing their minds and lives, and becoming forward professors of godliness; when a few years' time hath turned all this joy into sorrow; and one of our hopeful seeming converts doth grow cold, and lose his former forwardness; another falls to desperate sensuality, and turns drunkard, or fornicator, or gamester; another turns worldling, and drowns all his seeming zeal in the love of riches, and the cares of this life; and another, if not many to one, is deluded by some deceiver, and infected with some deadly errors, casts of duty, and sets himself, like a hired instrument of Satan, to divide the church, oppose the gospel, reproach, slander, and rail at the ministers and professors of it, to weaken the hands of the builders, strengthen the ungodly, and serve the secret enemies of the truth. Those that once comforted our hearts in the hopes of their conversion, break our hearts by their apostacy and subversion, and become greater hinderances to the work of Christ, and greater plagues to the church of God, than those that never professed to be religious. Those that were wont to join with us in holy worship, and went up with us to the house of God as our companions, do afterwards despise both worshippers and worship. Whereas if these men had been rooted and confirmed, you should never have seen them fall into this misery. O how many prayers, confessions, and duties do these men lose! How many years have some of them seemed to be religious, and after all have proved apostates; and the world, the flesh, and pride and error swallow up all. See then what need you have to be rooted, confirmed, and built up in Christ.

IV. Consider also, how much of the work of your salvation is yet to do, when you are converted. You have happily begun; but you have not finished. You have hit on the right way, but you have your journey to go; you have chosen the best commander and fellow soldiers; but you have many a battle yet to fight. If you are Christians indeed, you know yourselves that you have many a corruption to resist and conquer, many a temptation yet to overcome, and many a necessary work to do; and there is a necessity for these after-works as well as of the first. For these are the use and end of your conversion, that you may 'live soberly, righteously and godly in this present world, denying ungodliness and worldly lusts.—For we are his workmanship, created in Christ Jesus for good works, which God hath ordained that we should walk in them.' How can infants go through all these works? Which of you would desire an infant or cripple to be your servant; but though God be in this more merciful than man, yet he may well expect that you should not be always infants. What work are you like to make him, in this decrepit and weak condition? O pitiful blindness! that any man who knows that he hath a soul to be saved, should think an infant's strength proportionable to those works and difficulties that stand between him and everlasting life! In the matters of this life, you feel the need and worth of strength; you will not think an infant fit to plough or sow, reap or mow, or travel, or act the soldier, and yet will you rest satisfied with an infant's strength, to do those great and matchless works which your salvation lies on.

V. Moreover, the weak, unconfirmed souls are usually full of trouble, and live without that assurance of God's love, and that spiritual peace and comfort, which others possess. One would think no other argument should be necessary to make men weary of their spiritual weaknesses and diseases, than the pain and trouble that always attend them. It is more pain to a sick man to travel a mile, than to a sound man

to go ten. To the lame or feeble, every step hath pain, and all that they do is grievous to them; when far more would be a recreation to one that is in health. O therefore, delight not in your own languishings; choose not to live in pain and sorrow; but strive after confirmation and growth in grace, that overgrowing your infirmities you may overcome your sad complaints and groans, and may be acquainted with the comfortable life of the confirmed. O how roundly and cheerfully would you go through your work; how easy, sweet and profitable would it prove to you, if once you were strong confirmed Christians! Alas, the souls of those that are not confirmed, lie open to every temptation of the malicious enemy of their peace; how small a matter will disquiet and unsettle them; every passage in scripture which they understand not, and which seems to make against them, will disturb them. A minister cannot preach so plainly or so cautiously, but somewhat which they understand not will be the matter of disquiet. Providences will trouble them, because they understand them not: afflictions will be bitter to the mind as well as the body, and will immoderately perplex them, because they understand them not, or have not strength to bear them and improve them. The sweeter mercies of prosperity will much lose their sweetness, for want of holy wisdom and strength to digest them. What man would choose such a weak and languishing state as this, before a confirmed, healthful state? Will you run up and down for physic when you are sick; will you no more regard the health and stability, and spiritual peace and vigour of your souls.

VI. Moreover it is the strong, confirmed Christian that hath the true use and benefit of all God's ordinances: meat is digested by the healthful stomach, and it is seen upon them; we use to say, it is not lost: it is sweet to them, and doth them good; and they are strengthened more by it. So is the confirmed Christian by God's ordinances. But to the weak, unconfirmed soul, how much of the means of grace is even as lost! How little sweetness do they find in means; and how little good can they say they get by them! I deny not but some good they get, and that they must use them still; for though the sick have little relish of his meat, yet he cannot long live without it; and though it breed not strength or health, yet it maintains that languishing life; but this is all, or almost all. What a sad thing is this to yourselves, and unto us, when ministers that are as the nurses of the church, or stewards of the household, must see that all that ever they can do for you, will do no more than keep you alive? Yea, how often are you quarreling with your food; and you do not like it? Or you cannot get it down, something still ails it for matter or manner: or else if the minister displease you, your feeble stomachs lothe the food, because you like not the cook that dresses it, or because his hands are not so clean as you desire. 'The full soul lothed an honey-comb, but to the hungry every bitter thing is sweet.' Or if you get it down, you can hardly keep it, but are ready to cast it up to our faces. Thus a great deal of our labour is lost with you, holy doctrine lost, and sacraments and other ordinances lost, because you have not strength to digest them. Labour therefore to be established and built up.

VII. I beseech you look upon the face of the world, and see whether it have not need of the strongest help. Whereas the weak and sick are burthensome to others, rather than fit to help the distressed. There are a multitude among us and abroad in the world, that are ignorant and ungodly, and in the depth of misery. And if there be but a few to help them, those few should not be babes. Abundance of this multitude are obstinate in their sin, blind and wilful, captivated by the devil, and have sold themselves to do evil; and shall such miserable souls as these have none but children or sick folks to help them? I tell you, their diseases prove too hard for the most skilful physicians: it will put the wisest man in England to it, to persuade one obstinate enemy of godliness to the hearty love of a holy life; or to cause one old superstitious person of his self-conceitedness; or one covetous person of his love of the world; or one old drunkard or glutton of his sensuality. How then will silly, ignorant Christians be able to persuade them? I know it is not the ability of the instrument, but the will of God, that is the principal cause; but yet God uses to work by instruments according to their fitness for the work. What a case is that hospital in where all are sick, and no healthful persons among them to help them! Poor weak Christians; you are not able much to help one another; how much less to help the dead ungodly world. Woe to the world if it had no better helpers! and woe to yourselves, if you had not the help of stronger than yourselves, seeing it is God's way to work by means. Alas, a child or sick person is so unfit to labour for the family, and to work for others, that they are the burdens of the family, and must be provided for by others. They are so unmeet to help others in their weakness, that they must be carried, or attended and waited on themselves. What a life is this

to be the burdens of the church, when you might be the pillars of it? To be so blind and lame, when you might be eyes to the blind, and feet to the lame.

I speak not this to extenuate God's mercies to you; nor to undervalue the great felicity of the saints, even the poorest and weakest of them. I know that Christ is tender of the weakest that are sincere, and will not forsake them. But though you are so far above the dead world, even in the bed of your groaning and languishing, yet O how far are you below the confirmed, healthful Christian! You are happy in being alive, but you are unhappy in being so diseased and weak. You are happy in being of the family, and fellow citizens with the saints; but you are unhappy in being so useless, unprofitable and burdensome: for indeed you live but as the poor of the parish; not only on the alms of Christ, for so we do all, but on the alms of your brethren's assistance and support: I know that in worldly matters you will 'rather labour with your hands, that you may have to give to them that need,' than be troublesome to others, and live upon charity. I know that the time is not yet come that there shall not be a beggar in Israel; I mean, one that needs not our continual relief: 'the poor we shall have always with us;' even the poor in grace to exercise our charity; I know that 'the strong must bear with their infirmities,' and exercise compassion on them. But yet you should remember the words of Christ, 'It is more honourable to give than to receive.' Therefore be persuaded to bestir yourselves for spiritual health, strength and riches, that the multitudes of needy, miserable souls may have some help from you; that when they come to your doors, you may not turn them away with so cold an answer, Alas, we have nothing for ourselves. Were you but strong, confirmed Christians, what blessings might you be to all about you; what a stay to the places where you live; your lips would feed many as the tree of life. The ear that heard you would bless you, and the eye that saw you would bear you witness. You would be to poor souls, as bountiful rich men are to their bodies; the support and relief of many that are needy. You would not eat your morsels alone, nor would you see any perish for lack of clothing, but the poor would bless you. O pity the poor world that needs more than children's help, and grow up unto confirmation. O pity the poor church that abounds with weaklings, that is pestered with childish, self-conceited quarrellers, and needs more than children's help; and grow up to a confirmation. O pity yourselves, and live not still in so childish, sickly, and beggarly a condition, when the way of riches and health is before you ; but up and be doing till you have attained confirmation.

VIII. Yea, this is not all; you not only deny the church your assistance, but most of the troubles and divisions of the church, are from such unsettled weaklings as you. In all ages almost, these have made the church more work than the heathen persecutors did with fire and sword. These novices, as Paul calls them ; that is, young beginners in religion, are they that most commonly are puffed up with pride, and fall into the condemnation of the devil ; these are they that are most easily deceived by seducers, as being not able to make good the truth, nor to confute the plausible reasonings of the adversaries ; and withal, they have not that rooted love to the truth and ways of God, which should hold them fast ; and they quickly yield like cowardly soldiers, that are able to make but small resistance. As Paul speaks, they are ‘ like children tossed to and fro, and carried about with every wind of doctrine, by the sleight of men, and cunning craftiness, whereby they lie in wait to deceive.’ If you will still continue children, what better can we expect of you, but thus to be tossed and carried about. Thus you gratify Satan and seducers, when you little think on it : and thus you harden the ungodly in their way ; and thus you grieve the hearts of the godly, and especially of the faithful guides of the flocks. Alas, that so many of the children of the church, should become the scourges and troublers of the church ; and should set their teeth so deep in the breasts that were drawn out for their nourishment ! If you were never drawn to do any thing to the reproach of the church, yet what a grief must it be to us, to see so many of yourselves miscarry ? Ah, thinks a poor minister, what hopes had I once of these professors ; and are they come to this ? O mark the apostle’s warning, ‘ be not carried about with divers and strange doctrines.’ His way of prevention is, that the heart be established with grace.

IX. Consider also, that it is a dishonour to Christ, that so many of his family should be such weaklings ; so mutable, unsettled, and unprofitable as you are ! I do not mean that it is any real dishonour to him ; for if all the world should forsake him, they would dishonour themselves, and not him, with any competent judge : as it would dishonour the beholders more than the sun, if all the world should say that it is darkness. But you are guilty of dishonouring him

in the eyes of the misguided world. O what a reproach it is to godliness, that so many professors should be so ignorant and imprudent ; so many so giddy and unconstant ; and so many that manifest so little of the glory of their holy profession ; all the enemies of Christ without the church, are not capable of dishonouring him so much as you, that bear his name, and wear his livery ; while your graces are weak, your corruptions will be strong : and all those corruptions will be the dishonour of your profession ! Will it not break your hearts to hear the ungodly pointing at you as you pass by, to say, yonder goes a covetous professor; or yonder goes a proud, or a tippling, or a contentious, professor? If you have any love to God, and sense of his dishonour, methinks such sayings should touch you at the heart ! While you are weak and unconfirmed, you will, like children, stumble at every stone, catch many a fall, and yield to temptations, which the stronger easily resist : and then being scandalous, all your faults by foolish men will be charged on your religion. If do but speak an ill word of another, or rail, or deceive, or over-reach in bargaining, or fall into any scandalous opinions or practice, your religion must bear all the blame with the world. Ever since I can remember, it hath been one of the principal hinderances of men’s conversion, and strengtheners of the wicked in their way, that the godly were accounted a sort of peevish, unpeaceable, covetous, proud, self-seeking persons ; which was a slander as to many, but too much occasioned by the scandalousness of some. Methinks you should be afraid of that woe from Christ, ‘ woe be to him by whom offence cometh.’ If you be children, you may have the woe of sharp castigations ; and if you be hypocrites, you shall have the woe of everlasting sufferings. The world can judge no farther than they see : and when they see professors of holiness to be so like to common men, and in some things worse than many of them, what can you expect but that they despise religion, and judge of it by the professors of it, and say, If this be their religion, let them keep it to themselves, we are as well without it as they are with it. Thus will the holy ways of God be vilified through you. If you will not excel others in the beauty of your conversations, that in this glass the world may see the beauty of your religion, you must expect that they should take it but for a common thing, which brings forth but common fruits, to their discerning. You should be such that God may boast of, and the church may boast of, to the face of the accuser ; then would you be an honour to the church, when God may say of you as he did of Job, 'hast thou considered my servant Job, that there is none like him on the earth, a perfect and an upright man, one that feareth God and escheweth evil.' If we could say so of you to the malignant enemies, See what men the godly are, there is none such among you; men of holiness, wisdom, uprightness, sobriety, meekness, patience, peaceable, and harmless, living wholly to God, as strangers on earth, and citizens of heaven, then you would be ornaments to your holy profession. Were you such Christians as the old Christians were, we might boast of you then to the reproaching adversaries.

X. Moreover, till you are confirmed and built up, you may too easily be made the instruments of Satan, to further his designs. The weakness of your understandings, and the strength of your passions, and especially the interest that carnal-self hath remaining in you, may lay you open to temptations, and engage you in many a cause of Satan, to take his part against the truth. How sad a case is this, to any that have felt the love of Christ! Have you been warmed with his wondrous love, washed with his blood, and saved by his matchless mercy? And may it not even break your hearts to think, that after all this, you should be drawn by Satan to wound your Lord, to abuse his honour, to resist his cause, to hurt his church, to confirm his enemies, and gratify the devil! I tell you, with shame and grief of heart, that the abundance of weak, unsettled professors, that we hope have upright hearts in the main, have been more powerful instruments for Satan to do his work by, for the hindering of the gospel, the vilifying of the ministry, the dividing of the church, and the hindering of reformation, than most of the notoriously profane have been! What excellent hopes had we once in England, of the flourishing of piety and happy union among the churches and servants of Christ? And who hath not only frustrated these hopes, but almost broke them all to pieces? Have any had more to do in it than weak, unstable professors of religion? What sad confusions are in most parts of England at this day, by reason of the breaking of churches into sects, and the contentions and reproaches of Christians against Christians, and the odious abuse of holy truth and ordinances! Who is it that doth all this, so much as unstable professors of piety? What greater reproach almost could have befallen us, than for the adversary to stand by, and see men pulling out each other's eyes; hating, persecuting, and reproaching one another; and that our own hands should pull down the house of God,

and tear in pieces the miserable churches, while men are striving who shall be the master of the reformation? O what a sport is this to the devil, when he can set his professed enemies by the ears, and make them fall upon one another! When if he have any notable work to do against the church and cause of Christ, he can call out unstable Christians to do it! If he would have godliness to be scandalized, who hath he to do it but professors of godliness? Some of them to give the scandal, and others to aggravate and divulge it.

Would he have a church divided; how quickly doth he find a bone of contention? And who should do it but the unstable members of it? Would he have the truth opposed, and error and darkness to be promoted; who must do it but professors of the truth? Persuade some of them that truth is error, and error is truth, and the work will be done: they will furiously march out against their master, and think they do him service while they are fighting against him, scorning, and shaming, if not killing his servants. Would he have public divisions maintained among all the churches of the world? It is but possessing the weaker unstable pastors and people, with a perverse zeal for mere words and notions, as if the life of the church did therein consist; and they will be the devil's instruments at a call, and carry it perhaps by the major vote; and all that will not word it as they, shall be called heretics, and the church shall have new articles added to their faith, under pretence of preserving and expounding the old ones. Thus when Satan hath a work to do, if heathens and infidels cannot do it, it is no more but call out Christians to do it: if drunkards and malignant enemies cannot do it, it is but calling out some unstable professors of godliness to do it, and possessing the more injudicious part of the pastors with some carnal ends, or blind, consuming zeal.

O Christians! in the name of God, as you would avoid these devilish employments, labour for confirming, strengthening grace, and rest not in your childish weakness and instability. If you are delivered from Satan, and have truly renounced him, and tasted the great salvation of Christ, methinks you should even tremble to consider what a thing it would be, if, after all this, you should prove, through your weakness, so serviceable to the devil, and so injurious to your dearest Lord! What! must those abuse him whom he hath redeemed from condemnation? Must those hands be employed to demolish his kingdom, that were washed by him, and should have built it up? As if you were like Judas, that even now hath his hand with his master in the dish, and presently lifts it up against him.

XI. Moreover, while you are weaklings and unconfirmed, you will exceedingly encourage the ungodly in their false hopes, by being so like them as you are. When they see that you excel them so little, and in many things are as bad or worse than they, it strongly persuades them that their state is as good as yours, and that they may be saved as well as others, seeing the difference seems to be so small. They know that heaven and hell are much unlike, and vastly distant; and therefore they will hardly believe that they must be thrust into hell, when men who seem so little to differ from them must go to heaven. You would not believe how it hardens them in their sin, when they see professors do as bad; and how it settles them in presumption and impenitency to perceive your faults! When a minister hath laboured to make the sins of the ungodly odious to him, and to break his heart with the terrors of the Lord. O how it quiets him, and heals all again, to see the like sins, or others as bad, in the professors of religion! If these, saith he, may be saved, for all such and such sins, what cause have I to fear? O wretched, unprofitable, scandalous professors; when we have studied and preached for men's conversion many a year, you go and undo all that we have done, by the scandal, or levity, or imprudence of an hour! When we have almost persuaded men to be Christians, you persuade them, and turn them back again, and do more harm by the weakness and scandal of your lives, than many of us can do good by life and doctrine: when we have brought sinners even to the door of life, you prove their enemies, take them out of our hands again, and bring them back to their old captivity. Doth it not pierce your very hearts to think on it, that ever one soul, much more so many, should be shut out of glory, and burn in everlasting misery, and you should have a hand in it! Consider of this, and methinks you should desire confirming grace.

XII. And methinks it should be very grievous to you, to be so like to the ungodly yourselves, and that Satan should still have so much interest in you. Holiness is God's image; and doth it not grieve you that you are so little like him! By his graces he keeps possession of you; and doth it not grieve you that God hath no more possession of you; but that Satan and sin should so defraud him of his own? Will he condescend to dwell in so low a worm, so oft defiled with the impurity of his iniquities; and doth it not wound you to think, that even there he should be so straitened, and thrust into corners by an implacable enemy, as if that simple habitation were too much for him, and that impure dwelling were too good for him; and as if you grudged him so much of the dregs of Satan, that had taken up the beginning of your days in sin.

Your corruption is the very image of the devil, and doth it not affright you to think that you should be so like him? You are charged not to be 'conformed to this world, but to be transformed by the renewing of your mind, that ye may prove what is that good, that acceptable, and perfect will of God,' and yet will you stop in a state so like to those that perish? He that hath the least measure of saving grace, is likest to the children of the devil of any man in the world, that is not one of them. Seek therefore to increase.

XIII. I beseech you consider, that your excellency, and the glory and lustre of your graces, is one of God's appointed means for the honour of his Son, his gospel, and church, and for the conviction and conversion of the unbelieving world: therefore if you use not this means, you rob God and the church of that which is their due, and deprive sinners of one of the means of their salvation. You are commanded to 'let your light so shine before men, that they may see your good works, and glorify your Father which is in heaven.' Christians, be awakened to consider what you have to do with your graces! You have the living God to please and honour by them! As the excellency of the work doth honour the workman, so must your graces and lives honour God. You have the souls of the weak to confirm by your lives, and the souls of the ungodly to win by your lives. You should all be preachers, and even preach as you go up and down in the world, as a candle lighteth which way ever it goes. As we are sent to save sinners, as ambassadors of Christ, by public proclamation of his will; so are you sent to save them as his servants and our helpers, and must preach by your lives and familiar exhortations, as we must do by authoritative instruction. A good life is a good sermon; yea, those may be won by your sermons, that will not come to ours; or will not obey the doctrine which they hear. Even to women that must keep silence in the church, doth Peter command this way of preaching, 'that if any of them have husbands that obey not the word, they may without the word be won by the conversation of the wives.' Thousands can understand the meaning of a good life, that cannot understand the meaning of a good sermon. By this way you may preach to men of all languages, though your tongues had never learned but one : for a holy, harmless, humble life, doth speak in all the languages of the world, to men that have eyes to read it. This is the universal character and language, in which all sorts may perceive you speak the wondrous works of the Holy Ghost. I charge you therefore, Christians, deprive not God of the honour you owe him, nor the church, or souls of wicked men, of this excellent, powerful help which you owe them, by continuing in your weakness and unsettled minds, and spotted lives; but grow up to that measure that may be fit for such a work. As you durst not silence the preachers of the gospel, so do not dare to silence yourselves from preaching by your holy, exemplary lives. Alas, do you think that feeble, giddy, scandalous professors, are like to do any great matters by their lives! Would you wish the poor world to write after such a crooked and blotted copy? Will it win men's hearts to a love of holiness, to talk with a Christian that can scarcely speak a word of sense for his religion; or to see a professor as greedy for a little gain as the veriest worldling that hath no other hope ; or to hear them rail, lie or slander; or to see them turn up and down like a weathercock, according as the wind of temptation fits; and to follow every new opinion that is but put off with a plausible fervency? Do you think that men are likely to be won by such lives these?

XIV. Do you consider of what great things you must make account to suffer for Christ? You must forsake all that you have. You must not save your lives, if he bid you lose them. You must suffer with him, if you will be glorified with him. You may be called to confess Christ before the kings or judges of the earth; then if you deny him he will deny you, and if you be ashamed of him he will be ashamed of you, unless you be brought to a better state. You may be called to the fiery trial, 'and to suffer also the spoiling of your goods,' and in a word, the loss of all. Do you think that you shall not find use for the strongest graces then? Have you not need to be confirmed, rooted Christians, that must expect such storms? Are infants meet for such encounters? Have you not seen how many that seemed strong, have been overthrown in a time of trial, and yet will you stop in a weak estate? Perhaps you will say, we cannot stand by our own strength, and therefore Christ may uphold the weakest, when the strongest may fall. To which I answer, it is true : but it is God's

common way to work by means, and to imitate nature in his works of grace ; and therefore he roots and strengthens those that he will have to stand and conquer; yea, and arms them as well as strengthens them, and then teaches them to use their arms. ' Finally, my brethren, be strong in the Lord, and in the power of his might : put on the whole armour of God, that ye may be able to stand against the wiles of the devil. For we wrestle not against flesh and blood, but against principalities, against powers, against the rulers of the darkness of this world, and against spiritual wickedness in high places: wherefore take unto you the whole armour of God, that you may be able to withstand in the evil day, and having done all, to stand.' You must look when 'you are illuminated, to endure a great fight of afflictions, to be made a gazing-stock both by reproaches and afflictions, and to be companions of them that are so used ; therefore you have need of patience, that after you have done the will of God, you may receive the promise.' If you will endure, in the time of persecution, the word must take deep root in your hearts. You must be founded on a rock, if you look to stand in time of storms.

In the mean time, it is a fearful thing to see in what a wavering condition you seem to stand, like a tree that shakes as if it were even falling, or like a cowardly army, that are ready to run before they fight ; like cowardly soldiers, you are still looking behind you, and a small matter troubles, perplexes and staggers you, as if you were ready to repent of your repentings. Must God have such servants as these, that upon every rumour, word or trouble, are wavering and looking back, and ready to forsake him.

XV. Consider also, that the same reasons that moved you at first to be Christians, should now move you to be confirmed, thriving Christians : for they are of force as well for this as for that You would not have lost your part in Christ for all the world, if indeed you have the least degree of grace. If the beginning be good and necessary, the increase is neither bad nor needless. If a little grace be desirable, surely more is desirable. If it was then but a reasonable thing, that you should forsake all for Christ and follow him, it is surely as reasonable that you should follow him to the end, till you reach that blessedness which was the end for which at first you followed him. What, Christian! hast thou found God a hard master, a barren wilderness to thee; or his service an unprofitable thing? Say so, and I dare say thou art a bastard, to use the apostle's phrase, and not a Christian. Some trial thou hast made of him, what evil hast thou found in him; or what wrong hath he ever done thee; that thou shouldst now begin to make a stand, as if thou wert in doubt, whether it be best to go further? If ever Christ were needful, he is needful still? If ever heaven and holiness were good, they are good still; therefore go on till thou hast obtained more, and forget not the reasons that first persuaded thee.

XVI. Nay, more than so, you have the addition of much experience, which should be an exceeding help to quicken your affections. When you first repented and came into Christ, you had never had any experience in yourselves of his saving special grace before; but you came in upon the bare hearing and believing of it: but now you have tasted that the Lord is gracious; you have received at his hands the pardon of sin, the spirit of adoption, the hope of glory, which before you had not; you have had many a prayer answered, many a deliverance granted; and will you make a stand when all these experiences call you forward? Should not new motives and helps thus added to the old, be the means of adding to your zeal and holiness? Surely more wages and encouragement, doth bespeak more work and diligence. Therefore see that you increase.

XVII. Most, or many of you, have cause to consider how long you have been already in the family and school of Christ. If you are but newly entered, I may well exhort you to increase, but I cannot reprove you for not increasing. Alas, what a multitude of dwarfs hath Christ, that are like infants at twenty, or forty, or threescore years of age. What! be so many years in his school, and yet be in the lowest form. 'For when for the time ye ought to be teachers, you have need that one teach you again which be the first principles of the oracles of God, and are become such as have need of milk, and not of strong meat: for every one that uses milk is unskilful in the word of righteousness; for he is a babe: but strong meat belongs to them that are of full age, that by reason of use have their senses exercised to discern both good and evil.' O poor, weak, diseased Christian! hast thou been so many years beholding the face of God by faith; yet art thou no more in love with him than at the first? Hast thou been so long making trial of his goodness, and dost thou see it and savour it no more than in the beginning? Hast thou been so long under his cure; and art thou no more healed than the first year or day? Hast thou been hearing and talking of heaven so long, yet art thou no more heavenly nor ready for heaven? Hast thou heard and talked so much against the world and the flesh, yet is the world as high in thee as at first, the flesh as strong as in the beginning of thy profession? O what a sin and shame is this—what a wrong to God and thee!

Yea, consider here also what means thou hast had, as well as what time. O who hath gone beyond thee for power, plenty, and purity of ordinances; or at least how few. Surely few parts of all the earth are like to England, for the showers of heaven, and the riches of the precious ordinances of God. You have sermons till you can scarcely desire more; and that so plain, that men can scarcely tell how to speak plainer; so earnest, as if the servants of Christ would take no denial; even almost as if they must perish if you perished. You have as frequent, plain, and powerful books. You have the warnings and examples of the godly about you. What yet would you have more? Should a people thus fed be dwarfs continually? Is ignorance, dullness, earthliness, and selfishness, excusable after all these means? Surely, it is but just that God should expect you all to be giants,—even heavenly, grown, confirmed Christians: whatever others do, it should be so with you.

XVIII. Methinks it should somewhat move you to consider, how others have advanced in less time, by smaller means by far than you have had, and how some of your neighbours can yet thrive by the same means that you so little thrive by: Job, who was so magnified by God himself, had not such means as you: Abraham, Isaac, Jacob, Joseph, had none of them all such means as you! 'Many prophets and righteous men have desired to see those things that you see, and have not seen them; to hear those things which ye hear, and have not heard them.' Though John the Baptist was greater than any of the prophets, yet the least of you who are in the gospel kingdom, are greater than he, in respect of means. As the times of the gospel have far clearer light, and give out greater measures of grace; so the true genuine children of the gospel should, taking them one with another, be far more confirmed, strong and heavenly, than those that were under the darker and scantier administration of the promise.

Do you not see and hear how far you are outstripped by many of your poor neighbours, who are as low in natural parts, and as low in the world, and the esteem of men as you? How many, in this place I dare bodily speak it, shine before you in knowledge, meekness, and patience, and a blameless, upright life; in fervent prayers, and a heavenly conversation! Men that have had as much need to look after the world as you, and no longer time to get these qualifications ; and no other means but what you have had, or might have had as well as they. Now they shine as stars in the church on earth, while you are like sparks, if not like clods. I know that God is the free disposer of his graces ; but yet he so seldom fails any, even in degrees, that are not wanting to themselves, that I may well ask you, why you might not have reached to some more eminency, as well as these about you, if you had but been as careful and industrious as they.

XIX. Consider also, that your holiness is your personal perfection, and that of the same kind you must have in glory, though not in the same degree. Therefore if you be not desirous of its increase, it seems you are out of love with your souls, and with heaven itself : when you cease to grow in holiness, you cease to go on any further to salvation. If you would indeed yourselves be perfect and blessed, you must be perfected in this holiness, which must make you capable of the perfect fruition of the most holy God, and capable of his perfect love and praise. There is no heaven without a perfection in holiness. If therefore you let fall your desires of this, it seems you let fall your desires of salvation. Up then and be doing, and grow as men that are growing up to glory ; and if you believe that you are in your progress to heaven, being nearer your salvation than when you first believed, see then that you make progress in heavenly-mindedness, and that you be riper for salvation than when you first believed. How ill doth it become men to make any stand in the way to heaven, especially when they have been in the way so long, that we might have expected before this they should have been as it were almost within sight of it ?

XX. Consider also, that with little grace, is little glory ; and the greater measure of holiness, the greater measure will you have of happiness. I know that the glory of the lowest saint in heaven will be exceeding great ; but doubtless the greatest measure is unspeakably most desirable. And as it will not stand with the truth of grace for a man to be satisfied with a low degree of grace, though he plead the happiness of the lowest Christian, and his own unworthiness of the least degree : so at least it ill becomes an heir of glory to desire but the lowest degree of glory, though he plead the happiness of the lowest saint in heaven, and his own unworthiness of the lowest place. For he that will be so content with the smallest degree of glory, as not to have hearty desires of more, is accordingly content to have in himself the smallest measure of the knowledge and love of God, to be loved in the smallest measure by

him ; to have the least enjoyment of him ; and to bear the smallest part in his praises, and in pleasing and glorifying him for ever : for all these things are our happiness itself. How well this agrees with a gracious frame of mind, I need not any further tell you.

But because some make question of it, whether the degree of glory will be answerable to the degree of holiness, I shall prove it in a few words.

1. It is the very drift of the parable of the talents in Matth. xxv. He that had got most by improvement, was made ruler proportionably over most cities. Not he that had been at the greatest bodily labour in religion, nor every one that had passed the greatest sufferings : but he that had got most holiness to himself, and honour to God, by the improvement of his talents, and so had doubled them.

2. The degrees of holiness hereafter will be divers, as are the degrees of holiness here : for as men sow they will reap ; and there is no promise in scripture, that men that die with the smallest holiness shall be made equal to them that died with the greatest holiness. That the greatest holiness hereafter must have the greatest happiness, is past denial. For holiness in heaven is an essential part of the felicity itself. It is the perfection of the soul. The use of it is for perfect fruition, and perfect exercise of love and praise ; which are the other parts of glory. God will not give men powers, capacities, and dispositions in heaven which shall be in vain ; as he gives hungering, thirsting, and love, so will he give proportionable satisfaction, and not tantalize his servants in their blessedness, and leave a part of hell in heaven. Holiness is pleasing to God in its own nature ; therefore the greatest holiness will most please him ; he that most pleases God, hath the greatest glory. These things are plain.

3. Moreover, we have great reason to conceive of the state of the glorified, in some conformity with the rest of the workmanship of God. But in all the rest there is a difference, therefore we have reason to think it is so here. On earth there are princes and subjects in the commonwealth ; and pastors and people in the churches, and several degrees among the people as to gifts and comforts : among the devils there are degrees ; and among angels themselves there are principalities and powers, thrones and dominions. Why then should we imagine that the heavenly Jerusalem shall not be so too ?

4. Christ plainly intimates that there is a place, on his right hand and his left, to give, in that kingdom, though as the Son of man he had not

the principal disposal of it. And then the kingdom must be delivered to the Father, and God be all in all; therefore the Mediator, as such, has somewhat less to do, than now. When Christ tells us of Lazarus in Abraham's bosom, and of many from the east and west sitting down with Abraham, Isaac, and Jacob, he intimates to us, that every place in heaven is not so high as Abraham's bosom, nor a sitting with Abranam, Isaac, and Jacob. So that I take it as a plain revealed truth, that divers degrees of holiness will have divers degrees of glory hereafter.

The chief argument to the contrary is brought from the parable of the labourers, who coming in at several hours, received every one a penny. But this is misunderstood: for there is not a word in it contrary to our assertion. The parable only saith that glory shall not be proportioned to the time; but they that come later shall have never the less for that. Which is nothing to our question about the degrees of holiness. For many that are first in time may be least and last in holiness; many that are last in time, may in that little time come to be best and greatest in holiness, and consequently in glory. The parable in Matth. xxv. shows that God will give different degrees of glory according to the difference in improvement of our talents: the other parable shows that he will not give out his glory according to men's time and standing in the church, seeing a weaker Christian may be of longer standing, and a stronger of a later coming in. What show of discord is there between these? Yet it is doubtful, in the judgment of good expositors, whether the parable of the penny speak of heaven at all or not; or whether it speak not only of the calling of the Gentiles, and taking them into the gospel church in equality with the believing Jews; though the Jews, being God's ancient people, had been longer in the vineyard, and the Gentiles were called but at the eleventh hour, yet God will make the Gentiles equal in the grace of calling, because in this he hath not engaged himself, but may do with his own as he will: which ever of these two is the thing intended in the text, or possibly both, it is certain that this general is the sum of the parable, 'that the first may be last, and the last first,' that is, that God will not give men the greatest reward that were first called: but he never said that he would not reward them most that had done him the truest service, and were highest in holiness.

Object. But the reason is, may I not do as I will with my own. True, but you must remember what it is a reason of; even of the cause in question, and may not by you be extended to other causes without a warrant. You never read that he equally pardons the believer and the unbeliever, or saves the regenerated and unregenerated, and then gives this reason of it, 'may I not do as I will with my own.' For this can be no reason for any thing which he hath revealed that he will not do: prove first that he will do it, and then bring your reasons why; but not before. So that it extends not to the case of different glory upon different degrees of holiness; for this he hath revealed that he will do.

So much to satisfy the doubtful: now I desire to return to the dull and languishing Christian, and beseech him to remember what a difference there will be between one saint and another in glory! O who would not aspire after the highest measure of holiness, in hope of a high degree of glory? Christian, hadst thou not infinitely rather love God with the greatest love than with a less, and be beloved again with the greatest of his love? I mean, by partaking of the greatest effects of it, and the fullest sense of his everlasting favour? Remember this, and surely it will persuade thee to gird up thy loins, and run as for the incorruptible crown, and press on to the mark for the prize of the high calling, and not to sit down with weak beginnings, especially when the way is so sweet as well as the end; the greatest holiness hath here also the greatest spiritual reward; and is attended with the greatest peace and joy, in the ordinary course of God's dispensations. When all the knocks, falls, and cries of Christians in this life, proceed from the childish weakness of their spirits: almost all the woes and calamities that attend us, our shames, our pains, our contentions and divisions, and the lamentable difficulty, that seems an impossibility, of healing them, or preventing more, all is from the corruptions that are the companions of our weakness: could we but grow up to a manhood of understanding, humility, meekness, self-denial, and the love of God in Christ, and of one another, we might then have some hope of the cure of all. Alas! that men who are so sensible of the difference between a weak body and a strong, a sick and a sound, a child and a man, an idiot and a man of wisdom, though all of them have human nature, should yet be so little sensible of the great difference between a weak Christian and a strong, a sick and a sound, a childish and manly, wise, confirmed Christian! Did you well know the difference, you would show us that you make a greater matter of it.

Now, Christian reader, I entreat thee soberly to consider of these twenty motives, whether they do not show thee reason enough to move thee to look after higher things, and not to stay in an infancy of holiness. It is a blessed mercy I confess that God hath given thee a true conversion, and the smallest measure of the heavenly life; I do not move thee to undervalue it; nay, I am blaming thee for undervaluing it: for if thou didst not undervalue it, thou wouldst earnestly desire more. Thou hast cause to bless God to all eternity, and to all eternity thou shalt bless him, for making thee a new creature, even a living member of his Son: and I know that thy condition is unspeakably better than the greatest prince's or emperor's upon earth, that is void of holiness. I know that thou hast still ground of exceeding consolation: I am not taking thy comforts from thee: I know God despises not the day of small things: and that Christ will not quench the smoking flax, nor break the bruised reed, nor cast off the poorest infants of his family, or lose any one of the lambs of his flock. But yet for all this I must tell thee, that there is a great deal of difference in excellency, strength, comfort, and happiness, between one sanctified person and another: and if thou be so apt to be over-covetous of worldly riches, where God forbids it, and limits thy desires, and where there is no such necessity or excellency to entice thee, why shouldst thou not cherish that holy covetousness which God expressly commands thee? ' Covet earnestly the best gifts.' And which he hath promised a blessing to, ' blessed are they which do hunger and thirst after righteousness, for they shall be filled.' This is not spoken of them that have no righteousness, but of them that have it, and would have more. For there is no such promise made to any that are short of saving faith. It is not any common grace that God makes this promise to, but a special grace. It is evident that no man can thus hunger and thirst after righteousness without righteousness; for even this hungering and thirsting is a degree of true sanctification. You would not take up with a cottage or smoky cabin if you could have a palace; nor with dry bread if you could lawfully have plenty; nor with a torn or threadbare coat, if you can have better; nor with a poor, laborious, toilsome life, in disgrace and the reproach of men, if you could have honour, ease, and abundance. And yet will you take up with so poor a stock of holiness, so dark a mind, so small a measure of heavenly light, so cold a love to God and glory, and so barren and common a kind of life? God hath commanded you, ' that having food and raiment, you should there-

with be content;' but he never commanded you that being once converted and made an infant in grace, you should therewith be content: so content you must be as not to murmur; but not so content as not to desire more.

You can see the difference, I doubt not, in others, between a little grace and more: O that you would but see this for yourselves! If you have a froward wife, or husband, or child, who hath a harsh and passionate nature, and hath so much grace only as to lament this when they are calmed, and to strive against it, but not to forbear the frequent exercise of it; though such a nature may be pardoned to the penitent, yet it may prove such a thorn in your own side, and such a smoke or continual dropping in your house, as will make you weary of it. I have often known men that had wives of so much folly, passion, and unruliness of tongue, that yet they hoped had some saving grace, that made them even aweary of their lives, and wish that they had met with a gentle nature. And methinks you should know that corruption in yourselves is much more dangerous and hurtful to you than any that can be in wife or husband; and should be much more offensive, wearisome, and grievous to you. It is a desperate sign of a bad heart, that can bear with corruption in themselves, and cannot bear with it in wife or husband, or those that do them wrong by their corruptions. If weakness of grace leave your nearest friends thus liable to wrong and abuse you, and this trouble you; consider that your own weakness leaves you liable to far greater and more frequent offences against God: and this should trouble you much more.

Let me give you another instance: if you have a pastor who is truly godly, and yet is so weak that he can scarcely speak with any understanding or life, the message that he should deliver, and withal is indiscreet, and as scandalous as will stand with grace; what good is this man like to do for all his godliness? At least you will soon see a lamentable difference between such a one and a judicious, convincing, holy, heavenly, powerful, and unspotted man! O what a blessing is the one to the place, and the other may be a grievous judgment; and you would be ready to run away from his ministry. Why, if there be so great a difference between pastor and pastor, where both have grace; methinks you should see what a difference there is also between people and people, even where all have grace. For truly poor ministers find this to their sorrow in their people, as well as you can find it in them. Some ministers have a stayed, confirmed, judicious, humble, meek, self-denying, teachable, peaceable, and experienced people: these walk comfortably, guide them peaceably, and labour with them cheerfully; O what beauty and glory is upon such assemblies, and what order, growth, and comfort is among them? Alas, how many ministers have a flock, even of those that we hope are godly, that grieve them by their levity, or weary them by their unteachable ignorance or self-conceit, or hinder their labours by errors, quarrels, and perverse opposition to the truths which they do not understand. So that there is a great difference between people and people that are godly.

Brethren, it is far from the desire of my heart, to cast any unjust dishonour upon saints; much less to dishonour the graces of God in them. No, I take it rather for an honour to that immortal spark, that it can live among its enemies and not be conquered, and in the waters of corruption, and not be quenched. But yet I must take up a just complaint, that few of us answer the cost of our redemption and the provisions of God; or are near such a people as our receivings or professions require we should be. It is one of the most grievous thoughts that ever came to my heart, to observe how the lives of the greatest part of professors tend to dishonour the power and worth of grace in the eyes of the world, and that the ungodly should see that grace doth make no greater a difference, and do no more upon us than it doth. Yea, it is a sore temptation oftentimes to believers, to see that grace doth no more in the most; but that so many are still a shame to their profession.

I must confess that I once thought more highly of professors as to the measure of their grace, than experience now will suffer me to think. Little did I think that they had been so unstable, so light, so ignorant, so giddy, as to follow almost any that do but nod for them. What a dreadful sight it is to see, how quickly the most odious heresies infect and destroy even multitudes of them, and that in a moment, as soon as they appear? The grossest mists of the bottomless pit are presently admired as the light of God.

If a church divider but arise, how quickly doth he get disciples.

If a papist have but opportunity, he will lightly catch some as oft as he doth cast his net. If he cannot prevail barefaced, it is but putting on the visor of some other sect.

Even the odious heresies of the Quakers themselves, and their railings, which an honest pagan would abhor, presently find entertainment with professors; let the matter or manner be ever so senseless, yet it is accepted, if it be but zealously put off. O who would have thought that our people that seemed godly, should be so greedy of the devil's baits, as to catch at any thing, yea, and to devour the bare hooks! O who would have thought that so many that seemed lovers of God, would so readily believe every deceiver that speaks against him, if he can but do it with a pious pretence.

Yea, if infidels themselves but cast in their objections, how many of our people are presently at a loss, and their faith is muddied, and they have to seek for a ministry, to seek for a church, to seek for ordinances, and to seek for a scripture, even for the gospel itself; therefore it is like they have to seek for a Christ, or to seek for a religion, if not to seek for God, and for heaven.

O sad day! that ever these things should come to pass, and that we are forced to utter them, having no possibility of concealing them from the world. Were these men confirmed and stablished in the faith? Were these men rooted and built up in Christ? Alas, if any deceivers come among us, how few of our people are able to withstand them, and defend the truth of God against them? But they are caught up by the devil's hunter, as the poor chickens by the kite, except those that fly under the wings of a judicious minister.

If an anabaptist assault some with their baptism, how few of them can defend it. Silly souls, when they find themselves nonplussed, they suspect not their own unfurnished understandings, or inexperienced, unsettled hearts, but suspect the truth of God, and suspect their teachers, be they ever so far beyond them in knowledge and holiness; as if their teachers had misled them, whenever these unprofitable infants are thus stalled.

If a papist be to plead his cause with them, how few have we that can answer him.

If an infidel should oppose the scripture, or Christ himself, how few among us are able to defend them, and solidly give proof either of the truth of scripture, or of the faith that they profess.

This is not all, though it is a heart-breaking case, but even in their practice, alas, what remissness and what corruptions appear! How few in secret keep any constant watch upon their hearts, and fear and abhor the approach of an evil thought? Nay, how few are they that do not leave their fancy almost common, and ordinarily even feed on covetous, proud, malicious, or lustful thoughts, and make no great matter of it, but live in it from day to day! How few keep up life and constancy in secret prayer or meditation! How few are the families where the cause, worship and government of Christ is kept up in life and honour, and where all is not dissolved into a little weary, disordered, heartless, performance.

Look into our congregations, and judge but by their very looks, carriage, and gestures, how many, even of those that we think the best, so much as seem to be earnest in prayer and praise, when the church is upon that work! Though it be the highest and noblest part of worship, and should be done with all the heart and might, and with a participation of a kind of angelical reverence, devotion, and spirituality; if it were so, we should see it by some of the signs of reverence and affection: yet, alas, when we think the best of them should be striving with God, or wrapt up in his praises, they but hear us pray as they hear us preach, and think they have done fair to give us the hearing. They sit on their seats in prayer, or use some crooked, leaning gesture, perhaps looking up and down about them, perhaps half asleep; but few of them with eyes, hands and hearts lifted up to heaven, behave themselves as if they believed that they had so nearly to do with God. I know reverent gestures may easily be counterfeited; but that shows that they are good, when hypocrites think them a fit cover for hypocrisy, for they use not to borrow credit from evil, but from some good to be a cover to the evil: it leaves the neglects of the godly more inexcusable, when they will not go so far herein as hypocrites themselves, nor by their behaviour in a public ordinance, so much as seem to be seriously employed with God.

If we try the graces or obedience of professors, alas, how small shall we find them in the most! How little are most acquainted with the life of faith! How little they admire the Redeemer and his blessed work! How unacquainted are they with the daily use and high improvement of a Saviour, for access to God, support, and corroboration of the soul, for conveyance of daily supplies of grace, and help against our spiritual enemies! How few are they that can rejoice in tribulation, persecution, and bodily distresses, because of the hopes laid up in heaven; that can live upon a promise, and comfortably wait on God for the accomplishment! How few live as men that are content with God alone, and can cheerfully leave their flesh, credit, and worldly estate, to his disposal, and be content to want or suffer when he sees it good for them! What repinings and troubles possess our minds if the flesh be not provided for, and if

God but cross us in these worldly things; as if we had made our bargain with him for the flesh, and for this world. and had not taken him alone for our portion! How few can use prosperity in riches, health, and reputation, with a mortified, weaned, heavenly mind! Nay, how few are there that do not live much to the pleasure of the flesh, and pamper it as indulgently under the appearance of temperance and religion, as others do in grosser ways! Do but try the godly themselves by plain and faithful reproof of their corruptions, and see how many of them you will find, that will not excuse them and take part with the enemy, and be offended with you for your close reproof. If any of them be overtaken with a scandalous fault, and the pastors of the church shall call them to open confession, and expression of repentance, though you would little think a penitent man should once stick at this, and refuse to do any thing that he can do, to repair the honour of God and his profession, and to save the souls of others whom he hath endangered, yet how many will you find that will add a wilful obstinacy to their scandal, and will deliberately refuse so great, clear and necessary a duty: so great is the interest of self and flesh in them, and consequently so little the interest of Christ, that they will live in impenitency in the eye of the church, and venture on the high displeasure of God, come of it what will, and resist the advice of their best, wisest and most impartial friends, rather than they will so far deny themselves as to make such a free and faithful confession. They are many of them so much for holy discipline, that they are ready to fall out with the church and ministers, and to be gone to a purer society, because it is not exercised. But on whom? On others only, and not upon them. When they need discipline themselves, how impatient are they of it, and how do they abhor it; what a stir they make before they will submit; even more sometimes than a drunkard or a swearer, so small is their repentance and detestation of their sin; whereby they show that their zeal for discipline and reformation is much out of pride, that others may be brought to stoop, or be cast out from them; and not out of a sincere desire to have the refining and humbling benefit of it themselves.

If any among them be either faulty or reported so to be, who is forwarder than many professors of godliness, to backbite them, and speak of their faults when they cannot hear, nor answer for themselves, nor receive any benefit by it? and if another that hates backbiting but reprove them, they will slander him also for a defender of men's sin! But when they should go in Christ's way, tell men of their faults, and draw them to repentance, and if they hear not, take two or three, and speak to them again, how hardly can you draw them to the performance of this duty; what shifts and frivolous excuses have they then. Nay, they will reproach the church or minister for not casting such out, or not keeping them from communion, before they have done or will be persuaded to do these duties that must go before.

Alas, how little hearty love is there to Christ in his members, even in them that are confident they love the brethren. How few will do or suffer much for them, or relieve them in their want as suffering with them. How small a matter, a word, a seeming wrong or disrespect, will turn their love in estrangement, or bitterness; if they be tried by an ill word, or a wrong, how touchy, froward, and impatient do they appear. And it is well if they prove not down-right malicious, or return not reviling for reviling.

Alas, how much pride prevails with many that seem to go far in the way of piety; how wise are they in their own conceits; how able to judge of controversies, and how much wiser than their teachers, before they can give a good account of the catechism, or fundamental truths; how well do they think of themselves and their own parts and performances; how ill do they bear dis-esteem or undervaluing; and they must needs be noted for some body in the world!

How worldly, close-handed, and eager of gain, are many that say they despise the world, and take it for their enemy. If any duty be cross to their profit or credit with men, how obstinate are they against it; and such interest hath the flesh in them, that they will hardly believe that it is their duty.

How censorious are they of others, especially that differ from them in lesser things; and how unapt to judge themselves. O how few are the Christians that are eminent in humility, meekness and self-denial, that are content to be accounted nothing, so that Christ may be all, and his honour may be secured; that live as men devoted to God, honour him with their substance, and freely expend, yea, study for advantages, to improve all their riches and interest to his service! How few are they that live as in heaven upon earth, with the world under their feet, and their hearts above with God their happiness; that feel themselves to live in the workings and warmth of love to God, and make him their delight, and are content with his approbation whoever disapproveth them: that are still

groaning or reaching and seeking after him, long to be with him, to be rid of sin, see his blessed face, and live in his perfect love and praises; that love and long for the appearance of Jesus Christ, and can heartily say, Come, Lord Jesus, come quickly. How few are they that stand in a day of trial! If they are tried but with a foul word, if tried but with any thing that touches their case: if tried but with the emptiest reasonings of deceivers, much more if they be tried with the honours and greatness of the world, how few of them stand in trial, and do not fall and forget themselves, as if they were not the men that they seemed to be before! What then would they prove if they were tried by the flames?

Mistake me not in all this sad complaint; as I intend not the dishonour of godliness by this, but of ungodliness, for it is not because men are godly that they have these faults, but because they are not more godly. So here is no encouragement to the unsanctified to think themselves as good as the more religious, because they are charged with so many faults: nor do I affirm all these things to be consistent with true grace that I have here expressed: but only this, that professors that seem godly to others, are thus too many of them guilty: and those that have true grace may have any of these faults in a mortified degree, though not in a reigning, predominant measure.

But, methinks you should by this time be convinced and sensible, how much we dishonour God by our infirmities. What a lamentable case it is, that the church should consist of so many infants; and so many should be sò little serviceable to God or the common good, but rather be troublers of all about them. Alas, that we should reach no higher, that yet no greater things should be attained. O what an honour would you be to your profession, and what a blessing to the church, if you did but answer the cost and pains of God and man, and answer the high things that you have been acquainted with and profess. That we could but boast of you as God did of Job, and could say to Satan or any of his instruments, Here are Christians rooted and stablished in the faith; try whether you can shake them or make them stagger, and do your worst. Here is a man eminent in meekness, humility, patience, and self-denial; discompose and disturb his mind if you can; draw him to pride or immoderate passion, or censoriousness or uncharitableness if you can: here are a people that are in unity, and knit together in faith and love; of one heart, one soul, and one lip: do your worst to divide them or break them into parties, or draw them into several minds and ways, or exasperate them against each other. Here are a people established in mortification, and that have crucified the flesh with its affections and lusts. Do your worst to draw them to intemperance in eating or drinking or recreations, or any of the delights of the flesh ; or to puff them up by greatness and prosperity, and make them forget themselves or God. Try them with riches, or beauty, or vain-glory, or other sensual delights, and see whether they will turn aside, and be ever the less in communion with God, and enticed to forget the joy that is set before them, or will not rather despise your baits, and run away from alluring objects as their greatest dangers ; daunt them if you can by threatenings ! Try them by persecution, by fire and sword, and see whether they are not past your shaking, even rooted, confirmed, and built up in Christ.

O what a glory would you be to your profession, if you could attain to this degree. Could we but truly thus boast of you, we might say our people are Christians of the right strain. But when we must come about you like men in a swoon, and can hardly perceive whether you are alive or dead, and can scarcely discern whether you have any grace or none, what a grief is this to our hearts ; what a perplexity to us in our administrations, not knowing whether comfort or terror be your due ; and what a languishing, uncomfortable life is this to yourselves, in comparison of what you might attain to.

Rouse up yourselves, Christians, and look after higher and greater things, and think it not enough that you are barely alive. It is an exceeding righteousness that you must have if you will be saved, even exceeding all that the unsanctified attain : for 'except your righteousness exceed even the righteousness of scribes and pharisees, you shall in no case enter into the kingdom of heaven.' But it is yet a more exceeding righteousness that you must have if you will be confirmed, built up, and abound, would honour your profession, and cheerfully, successfully, and constantly go on in the journey, the race, the warfare that you have begun : you must then exceed yourselves, and exceed all the feeble, unstable, wavering, infant Christians, that are about you. To persuade you yet further to look after this, I shall here annex a few motives more.

1. Consider, Christian, that it is a God of exceeding infinite greatness and goodness that thou hast to do with, and therefore it is not small and low matters that are suitable to his service. O if thou hadst but a glimpse of his glory, thou wouldst say that it is not common things that are meet for such a dreadful majesty : hadst thou but a fuller taste of his goodness, thy heart would say, this pittance of love and service is unworthy of him. You will not offer the basest things to a king, much less to the highest King of kings. ' If ye offer the blind for sacrifice, is it not evil ? and if ye offer the lame and sick, is it not evil ? offer it now to thy governor : will he be pleased with thee, or accept thy person, saith the Lord of hosts.—But ye have profaned it, (his great name,) in that ye say, The table of the Lord is polluted, and the fruits thereof, even his meat is contemptible : ye have said also, What a weariness is it, and ye have snuffed at it, saith the Lord of hosts, and ye bought that which was torn, and the lame and the sick : thus ye brought an offering. Should I accept this of your hand, saith the Lord ; but cursed be the deceiver, which hath in his flock a male, and voweth and sacrificeth to the Lord a corrupt thing : for I am a great king, saith the Lord of hosts, and my name is dreadful among the heathen.' If you better knew the majesty of God, you would know that the best is too little for him, and trifling is not tolerable in his service. When Nadab and Abihu ventured with false fire to his altar, and he smote them dead, he silenced Aaron with this reason of his judgment, ' I will be sanctified in them that come nigh me, and before all the people will I be glorified,' that is, I will have nothing common offered to me, but be served with my own holy, peculiar service. When five thousand of the Bethshemites were smitten dead, they found that God would not be trifled with, and cried out, 'who is able to stand before this holy Lord God ?'

2. Consider also, it was an exceeding great price that was paid for your redemption : for ' you were not redeemed with corruptible things, as silver and gold, from your vain conversation, received by tradition from your fathers, but by the precious blood of Jesus Christ.' It was an exceeding great love that was manifested by God the Father and by Christ in this work of redemption ; such as even perplexes angels and men to study and comprehend it. Should all this be answered but with trifling from you ? Should such a matchless miracle of love be answered with no greater love ; especially when you were purposely ' redeemed from all iniquity, that you might be sanctified to Christ a peculiar people, zealous of good works.' It being therefore so great a price that you are bought with, remember that you are ' none of your own, but

must glorify him that bought you, in body and spirit.'

3. Consider also, that it is not a small, but an exceeding glory that is promised you in the gospel, and which you live in hope to possess for ever: therefore it should be an exceeding love that you should have to it, and an exceeding care that you should have of it. To make light of heaven is to make light of all. Truly, it is an unsuitable, unreasonable thing, to have one low thought, or one careless word, or one cold prayer, or other performance, about such a matter as eternal glory. Shall such a thing as heaven be coldly or carelessly minded and sought after? Shall the endless fruition of God in glory be looked at with sleepy, heartless wishes. I tell you, if you will have such high hopes, you must have high and strong endeavours. A slow pace becomes not him that travels to such a home as this. If you are resolved for heaven, behave yourselves accordingly. A gracious, reverent, godly frame of spirit, producing an acceptable service of God, is fit for them that look to 'receive the kingdom that cannot be moved.' The believing thoughts of the end of all our labours, must needs convince us that we should be 'stedfast and unmoveable, always abounding in the work of the Lord. O hearken, thou sleepy, slothful Christian! Doth not God call, and conscience call? Awake, up and be doing; for it is for heaven. Hearken, thou negligent Christian; do not God and conscience call out to thee, O man, make haste and mend thy pace, it is for heaven. Hearken, thou cowardly, faint-hearted Christian; do not God and conscience call out to thee, Arm, man, and see that thou stand thy ground; do not give back, nor look behind thee; but fall on, and fight in the strength of Christ; for it is for the crown of endless glory. O what a heart hath that man, that will not be stimulated with such calls as these? Methinks the very name of God and heaven should awaken you, and make you stir, if there be any stirring power within you! Remissness in worldly matters hath an excuse, for they are but trifles: but slackness in the matters of salvation, is made inexcusable by the greatness of those matters. O let the noble greatness of your hopes appear in the resolution, exactness and diligence of your lives.

4. Consider, also, that it is not only low and smaller mercies that you receive from God; but mercies innumerable, inestimable, and exceeding great. Therefore it is not cold affections and dull endeavours, that you should return to God for all these mercies. Mercy brought you into the world; mercy hath nourished you and bred you up; and mercy hath defended and maintained you, and plentifully provided for you. Your bodies live upon it: your souls were recovered by it; it gave you your being: it rescued you from misery: it saves you from sin, Satan, and yourselves: all that you have at present, you must hold by it: all that you can hope for, for the future, must be from it. It is most sweet in quality: what sweeter to miserable souls than mercy? It is exceeding great in quantity; 'the mercy of the Lord is in the heavens, and his faithfulness reaches to the clouds. His righteousness is like the great mountains; his judgments are a great deep.—O how great is his goodness which he hath laid up for them that fear him; which he hath for them that trust in him before the sons of men.—His mercy is great unto the heavens, and his truth unto the clouds.' And O what an insensible heart hath he that doth not understand the voice of all this wondrous mercy! Doubtless it speaks the plainest language in the world: commanding great returns from us of love, praise, and obedience to the bountiful bestower of them. With David we must say, 'blessed be the Lord, for he hath showed me marvellous kindness in a strong city; O love the Lord, all ye his saints, for the Lord preserveth all the faithful.—Teach me thy way, O Lord, I will walk in thy truth: unite my heart to fear thy name.—I will praise thee, O Lord my God, with all my heart: and I will glorify thy name for evermore, for great is thy mercy towards me; and thou hast delivered my soul from the lowest hell.' Unspeakable mercies must needs be felt in deep impressions, and be so savoury with the gracious soul, that methinks it should work us to the highest resolutions: unthankfulness is a crime that heathens detested: and it is exceeding great unthankfulness, if we have not exceeding great love and obedience, under such exceeding great and many mercies as we possess.

5. Consider, that they are exceeding great helps and means, that you possess, to further your holiness and obedience to God: and therefore your holiness and obedience should also be exceeding great. You have all the book of nature to instruct you. Every creature may teach you God, and calls loud upon you to persuade your hearts yet nearer to him. Every work of disposing providence is an instructor and persuader of you. Every leaf and line of scripture is a guide or spur to you. You have ministers able and willing to help you: you have the help of the communion of saints: the help of the examples of the good, and the warning of the judg-

ments of God upon the wicked : the helps of sermons, the helps of sacraments ; the helps of prayer, and holy meditation and conference ; mercies to encourage you ; afflictions to excite you. What more would you have ? Yet will you be infants, and do no more with all your helps ? But this I touched upon before.

6. It is an exceeding great necessity that is upon you : and therefore your resolutions should be exceeding high, and your diligence exceeding great. For all you are converted, your salvation lies yet upon your stability and perseverance. ' Christ hath reconciled you in the body of his flesh through death, to present you holy, unblameable, and unreproveable, in his sight ; if ye continue in the faith, grounded and settled, and be not moved away from the hope of the gospel which you have heard.' God will not be an accepter of persons. You must stick to his terms, if you will partake of his salvation. He will not make two words with you. He hath told you what he expects of you ; and that he will have. Death will not be bribed, nor put by. Judgment is coming on. There is no shifting out of the hands of God. Under such pressing necessities as these, what Christians should we be ; how stable, and abundant in faith and righteousness !

7. It is a great account that you have to make, and therefore a great preparation that should be made. When you shall be brought before the living God, and all your times, thoughts, and ways, must be called over, and you see what follows, and are waiting for the final doom, then there will be no dull thoughts in your hearts, all will be then lively, and quite above this careless frame. Then even the wicked will have strong desires, O that we had taken another course ! that we had but prevented this dreadful doom, whatever it had cost us ! Should not believers now, be awakened to great and careful preparations, for such a day as this.

8. For trifles here are great endeavours used. To climb up into honour or riches in the world ; to satisfy the flesh ; to lay up a treasure on earth, and labour for the meat that perisheth. O what endeavours then should be used for the heavenly, everlasting treasure.

9. Consider also, how forward and diligent should those men be, that are sure they can never go too high, nor be too diligent, when they have done their best ; nay, that are certain, that the best do come so abundantly short, that they must after sit down and lament that they were no better. O there is not the holiest saint on earth, but will confess, with lamentation, how little his love to God is in comparison of what it should be ; how short all falls below our duty, below the glorious majesty of God ; below the precious love of Christ ; below the worth of precious souls ; below the weight of endless glory ; below the mercies that should warm our hearts ; below the great necessity that is on us ; and consequently, below their own desires. Look therefore after greater things, while you may attain them.

Lastly, Consider what abundance of great engagements are on you, who are sincere believers, more than upon others.

(1.) You are more nearly related to Christ than any others are. Therefore you should be more tender of offending him, and more eminent in love and service to him. You are his household servants ; and will you not labour for him and stick to him ? You are his friends ; and should a friend abuse him ; should not a friend be faithful ? You are his dear adopted children, and his spouse : and should not you be faithful to him to the death ? Should not all the love and service that you have be his.

(2.) You have bound yourselves to him by more serious frequent vows and covenants than other men have done. How many persons, places, and necessities of yours, can witness against you, if you be not firm and forward for the Lord. As Joshua said to Israel, ' Behold this stone, it shall be a witness unto you, lest you deny your God ;' so I may say, the places where you have kneeled, prayed, and promised, will be witnesses against you, if you be not firm to God : the churches that you have assembled in, the places you have walked in, in your solitary meditations ; the persons that have heard your promises and professions ; the world about you that hath seen your forwardness, will all witness against you if you be not firm.

(3.) It is you that have the life and kernel of mercies ; others have but the crumbs that fall from your tables : others have common mercies, but you have the great and special mercies that accompany salvation : ' all things are yours,' and should not you be Christ's. Of you it is that God is so exceeding tender, that he charges your enemies not to touch you, and tells them that touch you, that they ' touch the apple of his eye.' Should not you abound in love and holiness ; should you not be as tender of his favour and his law, and honour, as of the apple of your eye ? Should not he that touches the name, law, and honour of God, by profaning them by sin, be as one that touches the apple of your eye.

(4.) You have a spirit and heavenly life within you, which the rest of the world are unacquainted with. Can you think it is something extraordinary, that God must needs expect from you? Will you not walk in the spirit which is given you, and mortify the flesh by it. Is there not more expected from the living than the dead? Surely he that hath made you new creatures, and made you partakers of the divine nature, doth expect somewhat divine in your affections and devotions, and that you be somewhat more than men.

(5.) Moreover, it is you above others, for whom the word and messengers of God are sent. We must speak to all: but it is you that God's special eye is upon; it is your salvation that he intends to accomplish by us. There were many widows in the days of Elias, and many lepers in the days of Elisha: but it was but to one of them that the prophet was sent. We make the ungodly multitude even rage against us, and ministers are hated for magnifying the grace of God to you, and declaring his special love to you above others. When Christ himself had spoken the forecited words, it is said in the next verses, that 'all they in the synagogue, when they heard these things, were filled with wrath, and rose up and thrust him out of the city, and led him to the brow of the hill whereon their city was built, that they might cast him down headlong.' This was the entertainment of Christ himself, when he did but declare how few it is that God will save, and for whose sakes he specially sends his messengers. Must we incur all this for magnifying you; and will you dishonour yourselves? Is all our study and labour for you, and our lives for you, and all things for you; and will not you be wholly, and to the utmost of your strength, for God? Are you chosen out of all the world, for salvation, and will you not answer this admirable, distinguishing grace, by an admirable difference from those that must perish, and by an admirable excellency in meekness, humility, self-denial, and heavenliness, above other men.

(6.) Moreover, you know more, and have a greater experience to assist you than others have; therefore you should excel them accordingly. Others have but heard of the odiousness of sin, but you have seen and felt it. Others have heard of God's displeasure, but you have tasted it to the breaking or bruising of your hearts. You have been warned at the very quick, as if Christ had spoken to your very flesh and bones, 'go thy way, sin no more, lest a worse thing come unto thee.' As Ezra said, 'After all that is come upon us, should we again break thy commandments; wouldst thou not be angry with us till thou hast consumed us?' So, if after all

your spiritual experiences, after so many tastes of the bitterness of sin, groans, prayers, and cries against it, you shall yet live as like to the wicked as you dare, and be familiar with that which hath cost you so dear, how do you think that God must take this at your hands? You have tasted of the sweetness of the love of Christ, and wondered at the unspeakable riches of his grace? You have tasted the sweetness of the hopes of glory, and of the powers of the world to come. You have perceived the necessity and excellency of holiness, by inward experience; and if after all this you will grovel in the earth, and live below your own experiences, contenting yourselves with an infancy of love, life, and fruitfulness, how much do you then transgress against the rules of reason, and of equity.

(7.) Moreover, all the world expects much more from you, than from any others. God expects more from you; for he hath given you more, and means to do more for you. Must you be in the eternal joys of heaven, when all your unsanctified neighbours are in torments, and yet will you not more endeavour to excel them? Is it not unreasonable to expect to be set eternally at so vast a distance from the ungodly world, even as far as heaven is from hell, and yet to be content to differ here but a little from them in holiness? The Lord knows that poor, forsaken, impenitent sinners will do no better, but rage and be confident till they are past remedy; he looks for no better from them than to neglect him, and slight his Son, word, and ways; and to go on in worldliness and fleshly living; to be filthy still, careless, presumptuous, and self-conceited still. But it is higher matters that he expects from you; and good reason, he hath done more for you, and prepared you for better things. The ministers of Christ look for little better from many of their poor, ignorant, ungodly neighbours, but even to live out their days in security and self-deceit, and to be barren after all their labours, if not to hate us for seeking to have saved them. But it is you that their eyes are most upon, and you that their hearts are most upon. Their comfort, and the fruit of their lives, lie much in your hands. Saith Paul, 'Brethren, we were comforted over you, in all our affliction and distress, by your faith: for now we live, if you stand fast in the Lord. For what thanks can we render to God again for you, for all the joy wherewith we joy for your sakes before our God: night and day praying exceedingly, that we might see your face, and might perfect that which is lacking in your faith.' You see here, that your pastors' lives are in your hands: if you stand fast, they live : for the end of life is more than life ; and your salvation is the end of our lives. If the impenitent world reproach us, and abuse, and persecute us, we suffer it joyfully, as long as our work goes on with you : but when you are at a stand ; when you are barren, scandalous, and passionate, dishonour your profession, and put us in fears, lest we have bestowed all our labour on you in vain: this breaks our hearts above any worldly crosses whatsoever. O when the people that we should rejoice and glory in shall prove unruly, self-conceited, peevish, proud, every one running his own way, falling into divisions, contentions, or scandals, this is the killing of the comforts of your ministers : when the ungodly shall hit us in the teeth with your scandals or divisions, and say, ' these are the godly people that you boasted of, see now what is become of them,' this is the smoke to our eyes, and the gall and vinegar that is given us by the adversary : though still we know that our reward is with the Lord, yet can we not choose but be wounded for your sakes, and for the sake of the cause and name of God.

Yea, the world itself expects more from you than others. When men talk of great matters, and profess as every Christian doth, to look for the greatest matters of eternity, and to live for no lower things than everlasting fellowship with God and angels, no wonder then if the world look for extraordinary matters from you. If you tell them of reaching heaven, they will look to see you winged like angels, and not to creep on earth like worms. If you say that you are more than men, they look you should show it, by doing more than men can do ; even by denying yourselves, forgiving injuries, loving your enemies, blessing those that curse you, contemning this world, and having your conversation in heaven. Believe it, it is not small or common things that will satisfy the expectations of God or men, of ministers, or of the world themselves, concerning you.

8. Yea, moreover, God himself doth make his boast of you, and all out of the world to observe your excellency; he sets you up as the light of the world, to be beheld by others. He calls you in his word, his ' peculiar treasure above all people, a peculiar people, purified, and zealous of good works ;' he called you a chosen generation, a royal priesthood, an holy nation, a peculiar people, that ye should shew forth the praises of him that hath called you out of darkness into his marvellous light : ye are as lively stones, built up a spiritual house, an holy priesthood; to offer up spiritual sacrifice, acceptable to God, by Jesus Christ.' You are ' born again, not of corruptible seed, but of incorruptible, and are made meet to be partakers of the inheritance of the saints in light.—God hath delivered you from the power of darkness, and translated you into the kingdom of his dear Son, in whom you have redemption through his blood, the remission of sins.— The Spirit itself beareth witness with our spirit, that we are the children of God ; and if children, then heirs ; heirs of God, and joint heirs with Christ.—All things shall work together for your good : he that spared not his own Son, but gave him up for us all, how shall he not with him also freely give us all things.' Nothing but the illuminated soul can discern the riches of the glory of God's inheritance in the saints, and what is the exceeding greatness of his power to usward who believe, according to the work of his mighty power.—When we were dead in sins, he hath quickened us together, with Christ, and hath raised us up together, and made us sit together in heavenly places in Christ Jesus : that in the ages to come he might show the exceeding riches of his grace, in his kindness towards us through Jesus Christ.' He hath ' brought us nigh that were afar off, so that by one Spirit we have access to the Father by Christ ; and are now no more strangers and foreigners, but fellow-citizens of the saints, and of the household of God.—We are members of the body of Christ, we are come to mount Zion, and unto the city of the living God, the heavenly Jerusalem, and an innumerable company of angels, to the general assembly and church of the first-born, which are written in heaven, and to God the judge of all, and to the spirits of just men made perfect, and to Jesus the mediator of the new covenant.'

Brethren, shall the Lord speak all this, and more than this, in the scripture, of your glory, and will you not prove yourselves glorious, and study to make good this precious word ? Doth he say, ' the righteous is more excellent than his neighbour,' and will you not study to show yourselves more excellent indeed? Shall all these high things be spoken of you, and will you live so far below them all ? What a heinous wrong is this to God ? He sticks not in boasting of you, to call you his jewels, and tells the world he will make them one day discern the ' difference between the righteous and the wicked, between him that serveth God, and him that serveth him not.' He tells the world, that his coming in judgment will be ' to be glorified in his saints, and to be admired in them that believe.' It is openly professed by the apostle John, ' we know that we are of God, and the whole world lieth in wickedness.' He challenges any 'to condemn you, or lay any thing to your charge, professing that it is he that justifieth you;' casting the saints into admiration by his love. 'What shall we say to these things; if God be for us, who can be against us?' He challenges 'tribulation, distress, persecution, famine, or nakedness, peril, or sword, to separate you, if they can, from the love of God.' He challenges 'death and life, angels, principalities and powers, things present, and things to come, height and depth, or any other creature, to separate you, if they are able, from the love of God in Christ Jesus our Lord.' Shall the Lord of heaven thus make his boast of you to all the world, and will you not make good his boasting? Yea, I must tell you, he will see that it be made good to a word! If you be not careful of it yourselves, and it be not made good in you, then you are not the people that God thus boasts of. He tells the greatest persecutors to their faces, that the meek, the humble, little ones of his flock, 'have their angels beholding the face of God in heaven,' and that at the great and dreadful day of judgment, they shall be set at his right hand as his sheep, with a 'come, ye blessed, inherit the kingdom,' when others are set at his left hand as goats, with a 'go, ye cursed, into everlasting fire.' He tells the world, that he that receiveth a converted man, that is become as a little child, receiveth Christ himself; and that whoever shall offend one of these little ones, that believe in him, it were better for him that a millstone were hanged about his neck, and he were drowned in the depth of the sea.'

Must God be thus wonderfully tender of you, and will you not now be very tender of his interest and your duty? Shall he thus distinguish you from all the rest of the world, and will you not study to declare the difference? The ungodly even gnash the teeth at ministers, and scriptures, and Christ himself, for making such a difference between them and you; and will you not let them see that it is not without cause? I entreat you, I require you, in the name of God, see that you answer these high commendations, and show us that God hath not boasted of you beyond your worth.

9. Consider this as the highest motive of all; God doth not only magnify you and boast of you, but also he hath made you the living images of his blessed self, his Son Jesus Christ, his Spirit and his holy word; and so he hath exposed himself, his Son, his Spirit, and his word, to be censured by the world, according to your lives.

The express image of the Father's person is the Son. The Son is declared to the world by the Holy Ghost: the Holy Ghost hath indited the holy scriptures, which therefore bear the image of Father, Son, and Holy Ghost. This holy word, both law and promise, is written in your hearts, and put into your inner parts, by the same Spirit. So that as God hath imprinted his holy nature in the scripture, so hath he made this world the seal, to imprint again his image on your hearts. And you know that common eyes can better discern the image in the wax, than on the seal: though I know that the hardness of the wax, or something lying between, or the imperfect application, may cause an imperfection in the image on the wax, when yet the image on the seal is perfect: therefore the world hath no just cause to censure God, or Christ, or the Spirit, or the word, to be imperfect, because that you are so; but yet they will do it, and their temptation is great. O how would your prince take it of you, or how would your poorest friend take it of you, if you should hang forth a deformed picture of them, to the view of all that shall pass by; and should represent them as blind, or leprous, or lame, wanting a leg, or an arm, or an eye? Would they not say that you unworthily exposed them to scorn? So if you will take on you to be the living images of God, of Christ, of the Spirit, and the word; and yet will be blind, worldly, passionate, proud, unruly, obstinate, or lazy, and negligent, and little differing from those that bear the image of the devil; what do you but proclaim that the image of God, of Satan, and of the world, do little differ; and that God is thus unrighteous and unholy as you are.

10. Lastly, consider, that the faithful servants of Christ are few; and therefore if those few dishonour him, and prove not fast to him; what do you but provoke him to forsake all the world, and make an end of all the sons of men. It is but a little flock to whom he will give the kingdom. It is but a few from whom God expects any great matter; and shall those few prove deceitful to him? It must be you or none that must honour the gospel! You or none that must be exemplary to the world; and shall it be none at all? Shall all the workmanship of God abuse him? Shall he have no honour from any inferior creature? How can you then expect that he should preserve the world? For will he be at so much care to keep up a world to dishonour and abuse him? If the turning of men's hearts prevent it not, he would come and 'smite the earth with a curse,' for the land that 'beareth thorns

and briars is rejected, and is nigh unto cursing, whose end is to be burned;' if therefore Israel play the harlot yet let not Judah sin. If the vessels of wrath, prepared to destruction, will be blind, sensual, and filthy still, yet let pollution be far from the sanctified. 'Such were some of you, but ye are washed, ye are sanctified, ye are justified.' O let the Lord be magnified in his saints: blot not out his image: receive not his impressions defectively and by halves. Let the name of the most holy one be written in your very foreheads. O that you would be so tender of the honour of the Lord, and shine forth so brightly in holiness and righteousness, that he that runs might read whose servants you are, and know the image and superscription of God upon the face of your conversations! That as clearly as light is seen in and from the sun, and the power, wisdom, and goodness of God, is seen in the frame of the creation, and of scripture; so might the same shine forth in you, that you might 'be holy as God is holy,' and 'perfect as your heavenly Father is perfect.' That they that would know God, may see him in his saints, where his image is, or should be, so lively and discernible; that they who cannot read and understand the scripture, or the works of creation, or disposing providence, may read and understand the holy and heavenly representations of your lives.

Men are apt to look after images of the Godhead, because they are carnal and far from God: O you who are appointed to bear his image, see that you so represent him to the eyes of the world, as may be to his glory, and not to his dishonour, and take not the name of God in vain.

It is so desirable for God, and for the church, and for your own peace and happiness, that Christians should grow up to a ripeness in grace, and be rooted, built up, confirmed, and abound, according to my text, that it hath drawn out from me all these words of exhortation thereunto: though one would think, that to men of such holy principles and experience, it should be more than needs: but if all will but serve to awaken the weak to a diligent progress, I shall be glad, and have my end. The great matter that I intended, when I began this discourse, is yet behind; that is, the giving you such directions as may tend to your confirmation and perseverance; which I shall now proceed to: but I entreat every reader who hath any spark of grace in his soul, that he will resolve to put these directions in practice, and turn them not off with a bare perusal, or approbation. Let me reap but this much fruit of all my foregoing exhortations, and I shall not think my labour lost.

PART II.

Direct. 1. *Be sure that the foundation be well laid, both in your heads and hearts; or else you can never attain to confirmation nor be savingly built up.*

To this end you must know what the foundation is, and how it must be soundly laid. The foundation hath two parts or respects, according to the faculties of the soul where it must be laid. The first is the truth of the doctrine and matter, and the second is the goodness of it. As true, the foundation is laid in our understandings; as good, it is laid in the will. Concerning both these, we must therefore first consider of the matter of the foundation, and then of the manner how that must be received or laid. The foundation is that matter or object of our faith, hope, and love, which is essential to a Christian; that is, to the Christian saving faith, hope, and love. This hath been always contained in our baptism, because baptizing us is making us visible Christians, or the solemn entrance into the state of Christianity. As therefore we are baptized into the name of the Father, Son, and Holy Ghost, renouncing the flesh, the world, and the devil; so the doing of this unfeignedly, without equivocation, according to the scripture sense of the words, is the essence of Christianity, or the right laying of the foundation. So that the foundation-principle, or fundamental matter is, God the Father, Son, and Holy Ghost: the secondary foundation, or fundamental doctrine, is those scripture propositions that express our faith in God the Father, Son, and Holy Ghost. When we name the three persons as the object of the Christian faith, we express the names of relation, which contains both the persons, nature, and offices, or undertaken works; without either of which, God were not God, and Christ were not Christ, and the Holy Ghost were not, in the sense of our articles of faith, the Holy Ghost. As we must therefore believe that there is one only God: so we must believe that God the Father is the first in the holy trinity of persons; that the whole Godhead is perfect and infinite in being, power, wisdom, and goodness, in which all his attributes are comprehended; but yet a distinct understanding of them all is not of absolute necessity to salvation; that this God is the creator, preserver, and disposer of all things, and the owner and ruler of mankind, most just and merciful : that as he is the beginning of all, so he is the ultimate end, and the chief good of man, which before all things else, must be loved and sought. This is to be believed concerning the Godhead, and the Father in person. Concerning the Son, we must moreover believe, that he is the same God with the Father, the second person in trinity, incarnate, and so become man, by a personal union of the Godhead and manhood : that he was without original or actual sin, having a sinless nature, and a sinless life ; that he fulfilled all righteousness, and was put to death as a sacrifice for our sins, and gave himself a ransom for us ; and being buried, he rose again from the dead, and afterwards ascended into heaven, where he is Lord of all, and intercedes for believers ; that he will come again and raise the dead, and judge the world, the righteous to everlasting life, and the wicked to everlasting punishment : that this is the only redeemer, the way, the truth, and the life ; neither is their access to the Father but by him, nor salvation in any other. Concerning the Holy Ghost, we must believe that he is the same one God, the third person in trinity, sent by the Father and the Son, to inspire the prophets and apostles ; that the doctrine inspired and miraculously attested by him is true : that he is the sanctifier of those who shall be saved, renewing them after the image of God, in holiness and righteousness, giving them true repentance, faith, hope, love, and sincere obedience ; causing them to overcome the flesh, the world, and the devil ; thus gathering a holy church on earth to Christ, who have by his blood the pardon of all their sins, and shall have everlasting blessedness with God.

This is the essence of the Christian faith, as to the matter of it. As to the manner of receiving it by the understanding, 1. It must be received as certain truth of God's revelation, upon the credit of his word, by a lively, effectual belief ; piercing so deep as is necessary for its prevalency with the will. 2. It must be entirely received, and not only a part of it : though all men have not so exactly formed distinct apprehensions of every member of this belief, as some have, yet all true Christians have a true apprehension of them. We feel by daily experience, that with the wisest some matters are truly understood by us, which yet are not so distinctly and clearly understood, as to be ready for an expression. I have often, in matters that I am but studying, a light that gives me a general, imperfect, but true conception, which I cannot yet express ; but when

another hath helped me to form my conception, I can quickly and truly say, that was it of which I had an unformed apprehension before, and what I meant but could not utter ; not so much for want of words, as for want of a full and distinct conception.

The matter of our Christianity to be received by the will, is as follows : As we must consent to all the forementioned truths, by the belief of the understanding, so the pure Godhead must be received as the fountain, and our end : the Father as our owner, ruler, and benefactor, on the title of creation and redemption ; as our everlasting happiness. The Son as our only Saviour by redemption, bringing us pardon, reconciliation, holiness and glory, and delivering us from sin and Satan, the wrath and curse of God, and from hell. The Holy Ghost as our guide and sanctifier. All which contains our renouncing the flesh, the world, and the devil, and carnal self, that is the point of their unity and heart of the old man. This is the good that must be embraced, or accepted by the will.

As to the manner of receiving it, it must be done unfeignedly, resolvedly, unreservedly, or absolutely, and habitually, by an inward devoting of the heart, as I have formerly explained it. This is the essence of Christianity ; this is true believing in God the Father, Son, and Holy Ghost : this is the foundation, and this is the right laying of it.

And now the thing that I am persuading you to is, to see that this foundation be surely laid, in head and heart.

That it may be surely laid in the head. you must labour, 1. To understand these articles. 2. To see the evidence of their truth, that you may thoroughly believe them. 3. To consider of the worth and necessity of the matter revealed in them, that your judgments may most highly esteem it. This is the sure laying of the foundation in the head.

To these ends you should first learn some catechism, and be well acquainted with the principles of religion ; and also be much in reading or hearing the holy scripture, and inquiring of your teachers, and others that can help you ; see that you take your work before you, and step not higher till this be done. Then all other following truths, duties, and promised benefits, must all be so learned, as to be built upon this foundation, and joined to it, as receiving their life and strength from hence, and never looked upon as separated from this ; nor as more excellent and necessary.

For want of learning well, and believing

soundly these principles, essentials, or fundamentals of Christianity, some of our people can
go no further, but stand all their days in their
ignorance, at a non-plus : some of them go on in
a blind profession, deceiving themselves by building upon the sand, and hold true doctrine by a
false, unsound belief of it : and when the floods and
storms do beat upon their building, it falls, and
great is the fall thereof. With some of them it
falls upon the first assault of any seducer, who
hath interest in them, or advantage on them ;
and abundance swallow up errors, because they
never well understood, or firmly believed, fundamental truths. With others of them, the building falls not until death, because they lived not
under any shaking temptations. But it being
but a perseverance in an unsound profession,
will nevertheless be ineffectual to salvation.

When you have thus laid the foundation in
your understanding, be sure, above all, that it be
firmly laid in your *heart* or *will*. Take heed
lest you should prove false and unstedfast in the
holy covenant ; and lest you should take in the
word but into the furnace of the soul, and not
give it depth of earth and rooting ; and lest you
should come to Christ but as a servant upon trial,
and make an absolute resignation of yourselves
to him : of which I warned you in the former
directions.

O this is it that makes our people fall so fast in
a day of trial ; some shrink in adversity ; and
some are enticed away by prosperity : greatness
and honour deceive one, riches run away with
another, fleshly pleasure poisons a third, and his
conscience, religion, salvation and all, he sacrifices to his belly, and swallows it down ; and
all the love and goodness of God, the blood of
Christ, the workings of his Spirit, the precepts
and promises, and threatenings of the word, and
the joy and torments which once they seemed to
believe, all are forgotten, or have lost their force:
and all because the foundation was not laid well
at the first. But because this was the very
business of the former directions, I will dismiss
it now.

Direct. II. *Think not that all is done when
once you are converted ; but remember that the
work of your Christianity then comes in, and
must be as long as the time of your lives.*

Of this also I shall say but little, because it is
the drift of all the preceding considerations. I
doubt it is the undoing of many to imagine, that
if once they are sanctified, they are so sure in
the hands of Christ, that they have no more care
to take, nor no more danger to be afraid of, and
at last think that they have no more to do, as of

necessity to salvation ; and thus prove that indeed they were never sanctified. I confess when
a man is truly converted, the principal part of
his danger is over ; he is safe in the love and
care of Christ, and none can take him out of his
hands. But this is but part of the truth ; the
other must be taken with it, or we deceive ourselves. There is still a great deal of work before
us ; and holiness is still the way to happiness ;
and much care and diligence is required at our
hands : and it is no more certain that we shall
be saved by Christ, than it is that we shall be
kept in faith, love, and holy obedience by him.
It is as true that none can separate us from the
love of God, and from a care to please him, and
from a holy diligence in the work of our salvation, as that none can take us out of his hands,
and bring us into a state of condemnation. He
that is resolved to bring us to glory, is as much
resolved to bring us to it by perseverance in
holiness and diligent obedience ; for he never decrees one without the other ; and he will never
save us by any other way.

Indeed, when we are converted we have escaped many and grievous dangers ; but yet there
are many more before us, which we must by
care and diligence escape. We are translated
from death to life, but not from earth to heaven.
We have the life of grace, but yet we are short
of the life of glory. And why have we the life
of grace but to use it, and to live by it ? Why
came we into the vineyard, but to work ; and
why came we into the army of Christ but to
fight ; why came we into the race but to run for
the prize ; or why turned we into the right way,
but to travel in it : we never did God faithful
service till the day of our conversion, and then
it is that we begin : and shall we be so sottish
as to think we have done, when we have but begun ? Now you begin to live, who before were
dead : now you begin to awake that before were
asleep : therefore now you should begin to work
that before did nothing, or rather a thousand-fold
worse than nothing. Work is the effect of life ;
it is the dead that lie still in darkness, and do
nothing : if you had rather be alive than dead,
you should rather delight in action than in idleness. It is now that you set to sea, and begin
your voyage for the blessed land ; many a
storm, and wave, and tempest, must you yet expect. Many a combat with temptations must
you undergo ; many a hearty prayer have you
yet to pour forth. Many and many a duty to
perform, to God and man. Think not to have
done your care and work, till you have done
your lives. Whether you come in at the first

hour or the last, you must work till night if you will receive your wages. And think not this a grievous doctrine. It is your privilege, it is your joy, your earthly happiness, that you may be so employed; that you that till now have lived an animal life, may now take wing and fly to God, and walk in heaven, and talk with saints and be guarded by angels; is this a life to be accounted grievous.

Now you begin to come to yourselves; to understand what you have to do in the world; to live like men, that you may live like angels! Therefore now you should begin accordingly to bestir you. I would not have you retain the same measure of fears of God's displeasure, nor the same apprehensions of your misery, nor the doubts and perplexities of mind which you were under at your first conversion; for these were occasioned by the passage in your change, and the weakness of your grace in that beginning, and your former folly made them necessary for a time: but I would have you retain your fear of sinning, and be much more in the love of God, and in his service, than you were at first. Temptations will haunt you to the last hour of your lives: if therefore you would not fall by these temptations, you must watch and pray to the last. Give not over watching till Satan give over tempting and watching advantages against you. The promise is still but on condition that you persevere and abide in Christ, and continue rooted and stedfast in the faith, and overcome and be faithful to the death, as you may see in John xv. throughout. 'Work out therefore your salvation with fear and trembling.' If you have begun resolvedly, proceed resolvedly. It is the undoing of men's souls to think that all the danger is over, and lose their apprehensions of it, when they are yet but in the way; when their care and holy fears abate, their watch goes down; the soul is laid open as a common wilderness, and made a prey to every lust. Therefore still know, your work is not done till your life be done.

Direct. III. *Be sure that you understand wherein your establishment and growth consists, that you may not miscarry by seeking somewhat else instead of it; nor think you have it when you have it not, or that you want it, when you have it, and so be needlessly disquieted about it.*

For your assistance in this, I shall further show you wherein your confirmation and growth consists in its several parts, both as it is subjected or exercised in your *understandings*, your *wills* and *affections*, and your *conversations*.

I. As holiness is in the understanding, it is commonly in scripture called light and knowledge, as comprehending the several parts. The confirmation and growth of this must consist in these seven following parts.

1. It is ordinary with new converted Christians to see the great essential truths of the Christian profession with a great imperfection as to the evidences that discover them. Either they see but some of the solid evidence, over-looking much more than they see; or more usually they receive the truth itself upon some low, insufficient evidence at first, and then proceed to a kind of mixture; taking it upon some evidences that are valid and sufficient, and joining some that are invalid with them. But you must grow beyond this infancy of understanding; when you see greater and sounder evidences for the truth than you did before: and when you see more of these solid evidences, and leave not out so many as you did; and when you lay smaller stress upon the smaller evidences, and none upon those that are invalid and indeed no evidences, then are your understandings more confirmed in the truth, and this is a principal part of their growth. So we find the Samaritans of Sychar; 'many of them believed on him for the saying of the woman, which testified, he told me all that ever I did. This was the first faith upon a weaker evidence, 'and many more believed, because of his own words, and said unto the woman, Now we believe, not because of thy saying, for we have heard him ourselves, and know that this is indeed the Christ, the Saviour of the world.' Here is a notable confirmation and growth, by believing and knowing the same thing which they believed before; it was before believed on weaker evidence, and now upon stronger. Thus Nathaniel, by Philip's persuasion, was drawn to Christ, but when he perceived his omniscience, that he knew the heart and things that were distant, and out of the reach of common knowledge, he is confirmed, and saith, 'Rabbi, thou art the Son of God, thou art the King of Israel.' Yet Christ tells him, that there were far greater evidences yet to be revealed, which might beget a more confirmed, stronger faith; 'because I said unto thee, I saw thee under the fig tree, believest thou, thou shalt see greater things than these; verily, verily, I say unto you, hereafter ye shall see heaven open, and the angels of God ascending and descending upon the Son of man.'

There is not one Christian of many thousands, that at first hath a full sight of the solid evidences of the Christian doctrine; but must grow more and more in discerning those reasons for the truth which he believes, which in the beginning he did not well discern. It is not the most confident belief that is always the strongest confirmed belief; but there must be sound grounds and evidence to support that confidence, or else the confidence may soon be shaken; and is not sound even while it seems unshaken. Here young beginners must be forewarned of a most dangerous snare of the deceiver, because at first the truth itself is commonly received upon feeble and defective grounds or evidence. It is the custom of the devil and his deceiving instruments, to show the young Christian the weakness of those grounds, and thence to conclude that his cause is naught: for it is too easy to persuade such that the cause has no better grounds than they have seen, for having not seen any better, they can have no particular knowledge of them. They are too apt to think over highly of their knowledge, as if there were no more reasons for the truth than they themselves have reached to, and other men did see no more than they. Thus poor souls forsake the truth, which they should be built up and confirmed in; and take that for a reason against the truth, which is but a proof of their own infirmity. I meet with very few that turn to any heresy or sect, but this is the cause: they were at first of the right mind, but not upon sound and well-laid grounds; but held the truth upon insufficient reasons: then comes some deceiver, and beats them out of their former grounds, and so having no better, they let go the truth, and conclude that they were all this while mistaken. Just as if in my infancy I should know my father only by his clothes; and when I grow a little bigger, one should tell me that I was deceived, this is not my father, and to convince me would put his clothes upon another, or tell me that another may have such clothes, and hereupon I should be so foolish as to yield that I was mistaken, and that this is not my father. As if the thing were false, because my reasons were insufficient. Or as if you should ask the right way in your travel, and one should tell you, that by such and such marks you may know your way; and think you have found those marks a mile or two short of the place where they are; but when you understand that those are not the marks that you were told of, you turn back again before you come at them, and conclude that you have lost the way. So is it with these poor deluded souls, that think all discoveries of their own imperfections, and every confutation of their own silly arguments, to be a confutation of the truths of God, which they did hold; when, alas, a strong, well-grounded Christian would make nothing of defending the cause which they give up against more strong and subtle enemies; or at least, would hold it fast themselves. This is the first part of your growth in knowledge, when you can see more or better evidences, for the great truth of Christianity, than you saw before.

2. Moreover, you must grow to a clearer apprehension of the very same reasons and evidences of the truth, which you saw before. For when a weak Christian hath the best arguments and grounds in the world, yet he hath so dim a sight of them, that makes them find the slighter entertainment in his affections. The best reason in the world can work but little on him that hath but a little understanding of it. There are various degrees of knowledge, not only of one and the same truth, because of the diversity of evidence, but of one and the same evidence and reason of that truth. I can well remember myself, that I have many a year had a common argument for some weighty truth, and I have made use of it, and thought it good, but yet had but little apprehension of the force of it; and many years after, a sudden light hath given me in my studies, so clear an apprehension of the force of that same argument which I knew so long, as that it hath exceedingly confirmed and satisfied me, more than ever I was before. I beseech you, Christians, consider of this weighty truth; it is not the knowledge of the truth that will serve you without a true and solid knowledge of that truth; nor is it the hearing or understanding of the best grounds and reasons or proofs, in the world, that will serve the purpose, unless you have a deep and solid apprehension of those proofs and reasons. A man that hath the best arguments may forsake the truth, because he hath not a good understanding of those arguments. As a man that hath the best weapons in the world may be killed, for want of strength and skill to use them. I tell you, if you knew every truth in the bible, you may grow much in knowledge of the very same truths which you know.

3. Moreover, a young, ungrounded Christian, when he sees all the fundamental truths, and sees good evidence and reasons of them, perhaps may be yet ignorant of the right order and place of every truth. It is a rare thing to have young professors to understand the necessary truths methodically: and this is a very great defect. For a great part of the usefulness and excellency of particular truths consists in the respect they have to one another. This therefore will be a considerable part of your confirmation and growth

in your understandings, to see the body of Christian doctrine as it were at one view, as the several parts of it are united in one perfect frame; to know what aspect one point hath upon another, and which is their due places. There is a great difference between the sight of the several parts of a clock or watch, as they are disjointed and scattered about, and the seeing of them conjoined and in use and motion. To see here a pin, and there a wheel, and not know how to set them all together, nor ever see them in their due places, will give but little satisfaction. It is the frame and design of holy doctrine that must be known, and every part should be discerned as it hath its particular use to that design, and as it is connected with the other parts. By this means only can the true nature of theology, together with the harmony and perfection of truth, be clearly understood. Every single truth also, will be much better perceived by him that sees its place and order, than by any other. For one truth exceedingly illustrates and leads in another into our understanding. Nay, more than so, your own hearts and lives will not be well ordered, if the method or order of the truths received should be mistaken. For the truths of God are the very instruments of your sanctification, which is nothing but their effect upon your understandings and wills, as they are set home by the Holy Ghost. Truths are the seal, and your souls are the wax, and holiness is the impression made. If you receive but some truths, you will have but some part of the due impression: nay, indeed, they are so coherent, and make up the sense by their necessary conjunction, that you cannot receive any one of them sincerely, without receiving every one that is of the essence of the Christian belief. If you receive them disorderly, the image of them on your souls will be as disorderly; as if your bodily members were monstrously displaced. Study therefore to grow in the more methodical knowledge of the same truths which you have received. Though you are not yet ripe enough to discern the whole body of theology in due method, yet see so much as you have attained to know, in the right order and placing of every part. As in anatomy, it is hard for the wisest physician to discern the course of every branch of veins and arteries, but yet they may easily discern the place and order of the principal parts and greater vessels: so it is in divinity, where no man hath a perfect view of the whole, till he come to the state of perfection with God; but every true Christian hath the knowledge of all the essentials, and may know the order and place of them all.

4. Another part of your confirmation and growth in understanding, is, in discerning the same truths more practically than you did before, and perceiving the usefulness of every truth, for the doing of its work on your hearts and lives. It was never the will of God that bare speculation should be the end of his revelations, or of our belief. Divinity is an effective practical science, therefore must truths be known and believed, that the good may be received, and a holy change may be made by them on the heart and life. Even the doctrine of the trinity itself is practical, and the fountain of that which is more easily discerned to be practical. There is not one article of our faith, but has a special work to do upon our hearts and lives; and therefore a special fitness for that work. Now the understandings of young Christians discern many truths, when they see but little of the work to be done by them, and the special usefulness of those truths to those works. This therefore must be your daily inquiry, and in this you must grow. As if you come into a workman's shop, and see a hundred tools about you, it is a small matter to discern the shape and fashion of them, and what metal they are made of: but you will further ask, what is this tool to do, and what is that to do: if ever you will learn the trade, you must know the use of every tool. So must you, if you will be skilful Christians, be acquainted with the truths which you have received; and know that this truth is to do this work, and that truth to do that work, upon the soul and life. A husbandman may know as many herbs, flowers, and fruits, as a physician, and be able to tell them all by name, and say this is such an herb, and that is such a one; and to perceive the shape and beauty of them. But he knows little or nothing that they are good for, unless to feed his cattle: whereas the physician can tell you, that this herb is good for this disease, and that herb for another disease, and can make use of those same herbs to save men's lives, which other men tread under foot as useless. A countryman may see the names that are written on the apothecary's boxes, but it is the physician that knows the medicinal use of the drugs. So, many men that are unsanctified, may know the outside of holy doctrine, that little know what use is to be made of it: the weak Christian knows less of this than the grown, confirmed Christian doth. Learn therefore every day more and more, to know what every truth is good for, that this is for the exercise and strengthening of such a grace, and this is good against such or such a disease of the soul. Every leaf in the bible hath a

healing virtue in it: they are the leaves of the tree of life. Every sentence is good for something. ' All scripture is given by inspiration of God, and is profitable for doctrine, for reproof, for correction, for instruction, in righteousness, that the man of God may be perfect, thoroughly furnished unto all good works.' Not a word is without its usefulness.

5. Moreover, you must grow, not only in knowing the usefulness of truths, but also in knowing how to use them, that you may have the benefit of that worth which is in them. Many a man knows what use a workman's tools are for, that yet knows not how to use them. Many a one knows the use and virtue of herbs and drugs, that knows not how to make a medicine of them, and compound and apply them. There is much skill to be used in knowing the seasons of applications, and the measure, and what is fit for one, and what for another, that we may make that necessary variation which diversity of conditions require. As it is a work of skill in the pastors of the caurch, to ' divide the word of God aright, and speak a word in season to the weary, and give the children their meat in due season;' so is it also a work of skill to do this for yourselves, to know what scripture it is that doth concern you ; and when and in what measure to apply it, and in what order, and with what advantages or correctives, to use it, as may be most for your own good. You may grow in this skill as long as you live ; even in understanding how to use the same truths which you have long known. O what excellent Christians should we be, if we had but this holy skill, and hearts to use it. We have the whole armour of God to put on and use ; but all the matter is how to use it. The same sword of the Spirit in the hand of a strong and skilful Christian, may do very much, which in the hand of a young, unskilful Christian, will do very little and next to nothing. A young physician may know the same medicines as an able, experienced physician doth ; but the great difference lies in the skill to use them. This is it that must make you rich in grace, when you increase in the skilful use of truths.

6. Moreover, your understandings may be much advanced, by knowing the same truths more experimentally than you did before : I mean such truths as are capable of experimental knowledge. Experience gives us a far more satisfactory manner of knowledge, than others have that have no such experience. To know by hearsay, is like the knowing of a country in a map ; and to know by experience, is like the knowing of the same country by sight. An experienced navigator, or soldier, or physician, or governor, hath another manner of knowledge than the most learned can have without experience ; even a knowledge that confirms a man, and makes him confident. Thus may you daily increase in knowledge, about the same points that you knew long ago. When you have ' tasted and seen that the Lord is gracious,' you will know him more experimentally than you did before : when you have tasted the sweetness of the promise, and of pardon of sin, and peace with God, and the hopes of glory, you will have a more experimental knowledge of the riches of grace than you had before : and when you have lived a while in communion with Christ and the saints, walked a while with God in a heavenly conversation, maintained your integrity, and kept yourselves unspotted of the world, you will then know the nature and worth of holiness by a knowledge more experimental and satisfactory than before. This is confirmation and growth in knowledge.

7. Moreover, you must labour to grow in higher estimation of the same truths which you knew before. This will be a consequence of the forementioned acts. A child that finds a jewel may prize it, for its shining beauty ; when yet he may value it many thousand pounds below its worth. You see so much wisdom and goodness in God, the first hour of your new life, as causes you to prefer him before the world ; and you see so much necessity of a Saviour, so much love and mercy in Jesus Christ, as draws up your hearts to him ; and you see so much certainty and glorious excellency of the life to come, that makes you value it even more than your lives. But yet there is in all these such an unsearchable treasure, that you can never value them near their worth ; for all that you have seen of God, of Christ, and glory, there is a thousand times more excellency in them yet to be discerned. For all the beauty thou hast seen in holiness, it is a thousand fold more beautiful than ever thou didst apprehend it : for all the evil thou hast seen in sin, it is a thousand fold worse than ever thou didst perceive it to be. So that if you should live a thousand years, you might still be growing in your estimation of those things which you knew the first day of your true conversion. For the deeper you dig into this precious mine, the greater riches will still appear to you. There is an ocean of excellency in one article of your belief, and you will never find the banks or bottom, till you come to heaven, and then you will find that it had neither banks nor bottom.

Thus I have showed you what confirmation and growth is needful for your understandings, even about the very same truths, which at first you knew. And now I shall add, that you must also labour to understand many more truths than at the first you understood, and to reach to as much of the revealed will of God, as you can, and not to stop in the mere essentials. For all divine revelations are precious, and of great use; and none must be neglected. The knowledge of many other truths is of some necessity to our clear understanding of the essentials; and also to our holding them fast, and practising them. ' Secret things belong to God, but things revealed, to us and to our children.'

But here I must give you this further advice. 1. That you proceed in due order, from the fundamental points to those that lie next them; and do not overpass the points of next necessity and weight, and go to higher and less needful matters, before you are ready for them. 2. Also see that you receive all following truths which are taught you, as flowing from the foundation, and conjoined with it. Disorderly proceedings have unspeakably wronged the souls of many thousands, when they are presently upon controversies and smaller matters, before they understand abundance of more necessary things that must be first understood. This course doth make them lose their labour, and worse; it deceives the understanding instead of informing it: and thereupon it perverts the will itself, and turns men to an heretical, proud, or perverse frame of spirit; and then it must needs mislead their practices, and cause them, like deluded men, to be zealous in doing mischief, while they think they are doing good. In common matters you can see, that you must learn and do things in their due order, or else you will but make fools of yourselves. Will you go to the top of the stairs or ladder, without beginning at the lower steps? Will you sow your ground before you manure or plough it; or can you reap before you sow it; will you ride your colt before you break him; will you rear an house before you frame it; or will you teach your children Hebrew, Greek, and Latin, before they learn English; or to read the hardest books before they learn the easiest; or can they read before they learn to spell, or know their letters? No more can you learn the difficult controversies in divinity, as about the exposition of obscure prophecies, or doctrinal doubts, till you have taken up before you those many, great and necessary truths that lie between. It would make a wise man pity them and be ashamed to hear them, when

young, self-conceited professors, will fall into confident expositions of Daniel, the Revelations, or the Canticles, or such like, or into disputes about free-will, or predestination, or about the many controversies of the times, when, alas, they are ignorant of a hundred truths about the covenants, justification, and the like, which must be known before they can reach the rest!

By this much that I have said already, you may understand, that, though we should reach as far as we can in knowing all necessary revealed truths; yet the principal part of your growth in knowledge, when once you are converted, consists not in knowing more than you knew before, as to the number of truths, but in knowing better the very same fundamental truths, which you knew at first. This is the principal thing that I would here teach you. Many are deluded, by not understanding this; you see here you have seven several things in which you must daily grow in knowledge about the same truths which you first received. 1. You must see better and sounder reasons and evidences for the fundamental truths than you saw at first: or more such evidences than you did then perceive. 2. You must grow to a clearer sight or apprehension of those same evidences. 3. You must see truths more methodically, all as it were at one view, and all in their due proportion and place, as the members of a well composed body; and how they grow together, and what strength one truth affords to another. 4. You must see every truth more practically than before, and know what use it is of, for your hearts and lives, and what you must do with it. 5. You must learn more skill in the using of these truths, when you know what they are good for; and must be better able to manage them on yourselves and others. 6. You must know more experimentally than you did at first. 7. You must grow into a higher esteem of truths. All this you have to do, besides your growing in the number of truths. I must likewise tell you, that as these essentials of Christianity were the instrumental causes of your first conversion, and were more needful and useful to you then, than ten thousand others; so it is the very same points that you must always live upon, and the confirmation and growth of your souls in these, will be more useful to you than the adding of ten thousand more truths, which yet you know not: therefore take this advice, as you love your peace and growth; neglect not to know more, but bestow many and many hours in labouring to know better, the great truths which you have received, for one hour that you bestow in seeking to know more truths which you know not, believe it, this is the safe and sure way. You know already that God is all-sufficient, infinitely wise, good, and powerful. And you know not perhaps the nature of free will, or of God's decrees of election, or a hundred the like points. True knowledge of any of the revealed things of God, is very desirable: but yet, I must tell you that you are forty times more defective here in your knowledge of that of God which you know, than of the other which you know not; that is, the want of more degrees of this necessary knowledge, is more dangerous to your souls than the total want of the less necessary knowledge. The addition of more degrees to the more needful parts of knowledge, will strengthen and enrich you more than the knowing of less necessary things, which you knew not before at all.

You know Christ crucified already, but perhaps you know not certain controversies about church-government, or the definitions and distinctions of many matters in divinity. It will be a greater growth now to your knowledge, to know a little more of Christ crucified, whom you know already, than to know these lesser matters, which you know not yet at all. If you had already a hundred pounds in gold, and not a penny of silver, it will more enrich you to have another purse full of gold, than a purse full of silver. Trading in the richest commodities, is likelier to raise men to greater estates, than trading for matters of a smaller rate. They that go to the Indies for gold and pearl, may be rich if they get but little in quantity; when he may be poor that brings home ships laden with the greatest store of poor commodity. That man who hath a double measure of the knowledge of God in Christ, and the clearest, deepest, and most effectual apprehensions of the riches of grace and glory to come, and yet never heard of most of the questions in Scotus, or Ockam, or Aquinas's sums, is far richer in knowledge, and a much wiser man, than he that hath those controversies at his finger ends, and yet hath but half his clearness and solidity of the knowledge of God, of Christ, of grace and glory. There is enough in some one of the articles of your faith, in one of God's attributes, in one of Christ's benefits, in one of the Spirit's graces, to hold you studying all your lives, and afford you still an increase of knowledge. To know God the Father, Son, and Spirit, and their relations to you, and operations for you, and your duties to them, and the way of communion with them, is that knowledge in which you must still be growing, till it be perfected by the celestial beatific vision. Those are not the wisest men that can answer most questions; but those that have the fullest intellectual reception of the infinite wisdom. You will confess that he is a wiser man, that hath wisdom to get and rule a kingdom, than he that hath wisdom enough to talk of a hundred trivial matters, which the other is ignorant of. He is the wisest physician that can do most to save men's lives; not he that can best read a lecture of anatomy, or is readiest in the terms of his art. Knowledge is to be esteemed according to the use of it, and the dignity of its objects, and not according to the number and subtilty of notions. Therefore I beseech you all, that are young and weak in the faith, take much more pains to grow in the fuller acquaintance with that same faith which you have received, than to be acquainted with smaller controversial truths which you never knew. Men use to call these higher points, because they are more difficult; but certainly the articles of your faith are much higher in point of excellency, though they are lower in the due order of learning them, as the foundation is the lowest part of the building, and is first laid, but is that which must bear up all the rest.

Here you must observe, how gracelessly and unlike to Christians those men speak, that say, they care not for reading such a book, or hearing such or such a minister, because he tells them no more than they know already. And on that account some of them stay from church, because they hear nothing but what they know already. It is a certain sign that they do not know already the blessed nature of God, and the riches of Christ, which they say they know: for if they did, they could not hear or think too much of them: they would long to know more, and therefore to hear more of the same things. It is a sign the minister takes the course that tends to your edification and enriching in knowledge, when he is most upon the great and most necessary truths. All saints make it their study to 'comprehend the height, and breadth, and length, and depth, and know the love of God in Christ.' But when they have done, they confess that it 'passeth knowledge.' It is a graceless, wicked soul, in a state of damnation, that thinks he knows so much of God and Jesus Christ, and the essentials of Christianity, that he cares not for hearing these things any more, but had rather have novelties, and let these alone; and feels not need of knowing much more and more of the same truths; of using and living upon these vital principles which he knows. You have eaten bread, and drank water an hundred times; but perhaps you never did eat of sturgeon, or many strange and dangerous fruits, in all your life. And yet I hope you will not seek after these, because they are novelties, and give over eating bread because you have eaten of it already? Nor will you churlishly refuse to go to a feast, because there is no meat but what you have eaten of before. We have not a new God to preach to you, nor a new Christ, nor a new Spirit, nor a new gospel, nor a new church, nor a new faith, nor a new baptismal covenant, nor a new heaven, or hope, or happiness, to propound. Your growth in methods, definitions, and distinctions, and in additional points of knowledge, is principally to be valued as it clears your understandings in the foresaid great essential points, and brings you up to God himself. Some think they quickly learned past the essential articles of the faith, and ere long they are past the higher points; and shortly they are past the scripture itself, and throw it by, as a scholar that hath learned one book, and must be entered into another. They understand not, that the ministry and Spirit are but to teach them the word of the gospel; but they think they must outgrow the word and ministry, and the Spirit must teach them some other doctrine, or gospel, which the written word doth not contain. I pray mark the apostle's warning, 'Be not carried about with divers and strange doctrines; for it is a good thing that the heart be established with grace;' and, 'that we henceforth be no more children, tossed to and fro, and carried about with every wind of doctrine, by the sleight of men, and cunning craftiness.'

II. Having showed you wherein your growth consists in the understanding, I shall be short in the rest, and next I must tell you wherein it consists in the will.

And that is, 1. When upon good understanding and deep consideration, you are most fixedly, habitually, absolutely and practically resolved for God and glory than before. So that you are grown more beyond all doubtfulness or wavering of mind, and beyond all unevenness, mutability and unconstancy. When a man is thus satisfied, that none but God hath title to him, or can make him happy, and that none but Christ can reconcile him to God, and that it were a madness to make any other choice, and thereupon is settled and firm as mount Zion, and says, 'whom have I in heaven but thee, and there is none on earth that I desire besides thee.' When you are firmly resolved, that let God do with you what he will, and come of it what will, you will never choose another master, or saviour, or rule, or happiness, or way, or body, than you are in; and will never forsake the path of holiness: this is the fixed sta-

bility of the will, and the more of this, the more you grow.

2. And when you have the lowest esteem of the creatures, and the greatest and most resolved averseness to all that would draw you from God, and can meet the greatest worldly or fleshly allurements with a holy contempt; this shows a settled, confirmed will.

3. Also when you are speedy in holy resolutions, and see nothing in a temptation, how great soever, that can make you demur upon it, or make a stop in a Christian course; but go on to duty, as if the tempter had said nothing to you, and the flesh and the world had no interest in you; you do not so much as stand to think on it, whether you should yield to sin or not, as abhorring to call such a matter into question. This shows a confirmed fixed will; and the more of this, the more of holiness.

III. The strength and growth of holy affections, consists principally in these particulars; 1. When the affections are lively, and not dull; so that we thirst after God and heaven with vigour and alacrity. 2. When they are ready at hand, and not to seek, and need not a great deal ado to quicken them, or call them in. 3. When they are most pure and unmixed, having least of the creature and most of God in them. 4. But principally (and the surest point to try them by) when they contain in them, or accompany the foresaid confirmation and resolvedness of the will; for it is more the willingness that is in, or with our affections, than the heat of them that we must judge them by. 5. And lastly, when they follow the best guidance of the understanding, when they are hottest about the greatest matters, and not about the smaller or more doubtful things; when they are obedient and yielding to faith and holy reason, and not too ready to harken to sense, and be moved about fleshly, sensible things. In these things lies the growth of your affections.

IV. Then lastly, for your conversations, your stability and growth consisteth, 1. In the readiness of your obedience. 2. In the fulness and universal exactness of it. 3. In the resolved conquest of all temptations that would pervert you. 4. In the diligent use of all those means that may farther confirm and strengthen you. 5. In the evenness of it, that it be constant and not mixed with scandals and stops in the way, or stepping out into by-paths. 6. In your fruitfulness and profitableness to others, according to the proportion of your talents; that you study to do good, and do it with all the care, wisdom and diligence you can. 7. In the spirituality of it, that God be the principal and the end of all, and that all be animated from the believing consideration of his attributes, and the views of everlasting blessedness. So that you have such lively, fixed intentions of God, that you can perceive that you do all, even common things, of purpose for his pleasure, will, and glory; and that the love of God doth carry you about from duty to duty, and constrain you to it. 8. Lastly, in the measure of your present attainments of the end and fruits of your obedience. For a taste of these ends are here to be attained. When your inward graces are more confirmed and increased, and your talents are doubled, and when you bring God a great deal of honour in the world, so that by his graces shining in your works, your Father is glorified; and when yourselves are readier to go to God, and meet your Redeemer, and long more for his appearing: in all these consists the stability, growth, and excellency of your conversations.

Now by all that I have said you may see wherein your stability, strength, and growth doth not consist. 1. It doth not most, or much consist in speculations, or less useful truths. 2. It doth not consist in the mere heat of affections; for zeal may be misguided, and do hurt, and may prove sometimes but a mere natural or distempered, sinful passion. 3. It consists not in mere fears, or purposes, that you are frightened into against your wills. 4. Nor doth it consist in the common gifts of grace or nature. 5. Nor yet in running into groundless singularities, and unusual strains. But in a word, it consists in holy love, kindled by effectual faith. When a firmly believing soul is fullest of love to God, Christ, and holiness, this is the most confirmed state of the soul; and in this your chief growth confirmeth.

Direct. IV. *Grow downwards in humility; be low and small in your own eyes; affect not to be high or great in the eyes of others; and still keep a deep apprehension of the greatness and danger of the sin of pride; but especially of that called spiritual pride.*

The tree that hath the shallowest, weakest root, is the most shaken, and is soonest overthrown: the deeper roots, the higher growth, for the most part. The building that hath not a deep foundation, is soonest shaken and overthrown. Christ is our foundation; and humiliation digs deep and lets him into the heart. Pride is commonly thought to be the devil's first or chief sin. Sure I am, it is the proud that fall into his condemnation. The pride of our first parents, affecting to be as gods in knowledge, was the in-

let of all our sin and misery; and the tempter still follows the way that he hath found to be so successful. It is pride, that like a storm or tempest, doth set all the world in the rage, contention, differences, and confusion, that we see them in. It is pride that hath filled the church with divisions; and it is pride that causes the apostacy of most that fall away. The more men have of it, the less do they usually discern it in themselves. I am sure the less do they hate it and lament it. Though one would think, that young beginners, and weak Christians that have little to be proud of, should be out of the danger of this temptation, yet experience tells us, that it is they that fall by it, more than the wiser and stronger Christians that have more to glory in: for the more men increase in wisdom, the more do they know their own unworthiness, their emptiness, and ignorance, and manifold sins: the more do they know of the holiness and jealousy of God: the more do they know of the evil of sin, and see what abundance of knowledge and grace they yet want: so that the more holy wisdom and experience, the less pride. But folly is the parent and nurse of pride. Children will be proud of toys and things of no value. There are two or three things that make young Christians in greater danger of spiritual pride than others. 1. Because they come so lately out of darkness, and so great a change is made upon their souls, that it makes them the more sensible of it; and therefore the more ready to have high thoughts of themselves. Though one would think that the remembrance of former folly, and late dejection, should keep them low, yet with too many that is quickly gone, and they know not how to receive a comforting message, but they make it an occasion of lifting up. 2. The ignorance of these novices or young Christians is such, that they little know what abundance of things they are yet ignorant of. Little do they know what knowledge they yet want: they think there is little more to be reached to than is in their sight, and therefore suppose themselves somebody in the school of Christ, because they have learned the first lesson. 3. By reason of this ignorance, they know not how to value the higher attainments and understandings of others, but look on the wisest as little wiser than themselves, because they are unacquainted with the matter of their wisdom, and therefore overlook it as if it were none, and consequently think too highly of themselves. 4. And withal, they have not that experience of their own hearts, that should make them jealous of them, as ancient Christians have.

The humble soul is still in an empty craving temper; he hungers and thirsts after righteousness, and therefore shall be satisfied. No man sets so high a price on Christ and grace, and all the means of grace. Even the crumbs are welcome to him, which the proud despise. ' The full soul lothes the honey-comb; but to the hungry every bitter thing is sweet.' Therefore such beggars are welcome to God : he hath respect to the humble, contrite soul, ' The hungry he filleth with good, but the rich he sendeth empty away. —He giveth more grace to the humble,' when the proud are abhorred by him. The church of Laodicea, that said, ' I am rich, and increased with goods, and have need of nothing, was miserable, and poor, and blind, and naked.' As many that are proud of their honour and birth, run out of all, by living above their estates, when meaner persons grow rich, because they are still gathering, and make much of every little: so proud professors of religion are in a consumption of the grace they have, while the humble increase, by making much of every little help, which is slighted and neglected by the proud, and by shunning all those spending courses which the proud are plunged in. Be sure to keep mean thoughts of yourselves, of your knowledge, parts, grace, and duties, and be content to be mean in the esteem of others, if you would not be worse than mean in the esteem of God.

Direct. V. *Exercise yourselves daily in a life of faith upon Jesus Christ, as your Saviour, your Teacher, your Mediator, and your King; as your example, your wisdom, your righteousness, and your hope.*

All other studies and knowledge must be merely subservient to the study and knowledge of Christ. That vain kind of philosophy which St Paul so much cautions Christians against, is so far yet from being accounted vain, that by many called Christians it is preferred before Christianity itself; and to show that it is vain while they overvalue it, they can show no solid worth or virtue, which they have got by it; but only an elated mind, and an idle tongue, like a tinkling cymbal. We are ' complete in Christ, in whom dwelleth all the fulness of the Godhead bodily.' No study in the world will so much lead you up to God, and acquaint you with him, especially in his love and goodness, as the study of Christ, his person, his office, his doctrine, his example, his kingdom, and his benefits. As the deity is your ultimate end, to which all things else are but helps and means; so Christ is that great and principal means, by whom all other means are animated. Remember that you are in continual need of him, for direction, intercession, pardon, sanctification, for support and comfort, and for peace with God. Let no thoughts therefore be so sweet and frequent in your hearts, nor any discourse so ready in your mouths (next to the excellencies of the eternal Godhead) as this of the design of man's redemption. Let Christ be to your souls as the air, the earth, the sun, and your food are in your bodies, without which your life would presently fail. As you had never come home to the Father but by him, so without him you cannot a moment continue in the Father's love, nor be accepted in one duty, nor be protected from one danger, nor be supplied in any want: for it pleased the Father, that in him should all fulness dwell, ' and by him it is, that being justified by faith, we have peace with God, and have access by faith unto this grace wherein we stand, and rejoice in hope of the glory of God.' And it is in him the head, that we must 'grow up in all things, from whom the whole body doth receive its increase.' You grow no more in grace, than you grow in the true knowledge and daily use of Jesus Christ. But of this I will say no more, because I have said so much in my Directions for a Sound Conversion.

Direct. VI. *Let the knowledge and love of God, and your obedience to him, be the works of your religion; and the everlasting fruition of him in heaven be the continual end and ruling motive of your hearts and lives, that your very conversation may be with God in heaven.*

You are so far holy as you are divine and heavenly. A Christian indeed in casting up his accounts, being certain that this world doth make no man happy, hath been led up by Christ to seek a happiness with God above. If you live not for this everlasting happiness, if you trade not for this, if this be not your treasure, your hope and home, the chief matter of your desires, love and joy, and if all things be not pressed to serve it, and despised when they stand against it, you live not indeed a Christian life. God and heaven, or God in heaven, is the life and soul, the beginning and the end, the sum, the all, of true religion. Therefore it is that we are directed to lift up our heads and hearts, and begin our prayers with ' our Father which art in heaven,' and end them with ascribing to ' him the kingdom, the power, and the glory for ever.' It is not the creatures, but God, the creator, that is the Father, the guide, and the felicity of souls, and therefore the ultimate end and object of all religious actions and affections. Dwell still upon God, and dwell in heaven, if you would understand the nature and design of

Christianity. Take God for all; that is, for God; study after the knowledge of him in all his works; study him in his word; study him in Christ; and never study him barely to know him, but to know him that you may love him: take yourselves as dead, when you live not in the love of God: keep still upon your hearts a lively sense of the infinite difference between him and the creature: look on all the world as a shadow, and on God as the substance: take the very worst that man can do, to be in comparison of the punishments of God, but as a slight wound to the sorest death: and take all the dreaming pleasures of the world, to be less in comparison with the joys of heaven than one mouthful of honey is to a thousand years' possession of all the felicities on earth. Think not all the pleasures, honours, or riches of the world, to be worthy to be named in comparison of heaven; nor the greatest of men to be worthy to be once thought on, in comparison of God. As one straw or feather won or lost, would neither much rejoice or trouble you, if all the city or land were yours. So live as men whose eyes are open, and who discern a greater disproportion between the portion of a worldling and a saint. Let God be your king, your father, your master, your friend, your wealth, your joy, your all. Let not a day go over your heads, in which your hearts have no converse with God in heaven. When any trouble overtakes you on earth, look up to heaven, and remember, that it is there that rest and joy are prepared for believers. When you are under any want, or cross, or sorrow, draw not your comfort from any hopes of deliverance here on earth, but from the place of your final full deliverance. If you feel any strangeness and backwardness on your minds to heavenly contemplations, do not make light of them, but presently by faith get up to Christ, who must make your thoughts of heaven familiar, and seek remedy before your estrangedness increase. The soul is in a sad condition, when it cannot draw comfort and encouragement from heaven; for then it must have none, or worse than none. When the thoughts of heaven will not sweeten all your crosses, and relieve your minds against all the encumbrances of earth, your souls are not in a healthful state; it is time then to search out the cause, and seek a cure, before it come to worse.

There are three great causes of this dark and dangerous state of soul, which make the thoughts of heaven ineffectual and uncomfortable to us, which therefore must be overcome with the daily care and diligence of your whole lives. First, Un-belief, which makes you look towards the life to come with doubting and uncertainty: this is the most common, radical, powerful, and pernicious impediment to a heavenly life. The second is, the love of present things, which being the vanity of a poor, low, fleshly mind, the reviving of reason may do much to overcome it; but it is the sound belief of the life to come that must indeed prevail. The third is the inordinate fear of death, which hath so great advantage in the constitution of our nature, that it is commonly the last enemy which we overcome, (as death itself is the last enemy which Christ overcomes for us.) Bend all your strength, and spend your days in striving against these three great impediments of a heavenly conversation; and remember, that so far as you suffer your hearts to retire from heaven, so far they retire from a life of Christianity and peace.

Direct. VII. *In the work of mortification, let self-denial be the first and last of all your study, care, and diligence.*

Understand how much of the fallen, depraved state of man consists in the sin of selfishness: how he is sunk into himself, in his fall from the love of God, and of his neighbour; of the public or private good of others: and how this inordinate self-love is now the grand enemy of all true love to God or man; and the root and heart of covetousness, pride, voluptuousness, and all iniquity. Let it be your work therefore all your days, to mortify it, and watch against it. When you feel yourselves partial in your own cause, and apt to be drawing from others to yourselves, in point of reputation, precedency, or gain, and apt to make too great a matter of every word that is spoken against you, or every little wrong that is done you, observe then the pernicious root of selfishness, from whence all this mischief doth proceed. Read more of this in my Treatise of Self-denial.

Direct. VIII. *Take your corrupted fleshly desires for the greatest enemy of your souls, and let it be every day your constant work to mortify the flesh, and to keep a watch upon your lusts and appetites, and every sense.*

Remember that our senses were not made to govern themselves, but to be governed by right reason; and that God made them at the first to be the ordinary passage of his love and mercy to our hearts, by the means of the creatures which represent or manifest him unto us: but now in the depraved state of man, the senses have cast off the government of reason, and are become the ruling power, and so man is become like the beasts that perish. Remember then, that to be sensual is to be brutish: and though grace doth not destroy the appetite and sense, yet it subjects it to God and reason. Therefore let your appetite be pleased in nothing, but by the allowance of right reason; and think not that you have reason to take any meat, or drink, or sport, merely because your flesh desires it; but consider whether it will do you good or hurt, and how it conduces to your ultimate end. It is a base and sinful state to be in servitude to your appetite and sense; when by using to please it, you have so increased its desires, that now you know not how to deny it and to displease it. When you have taught it to be like a hungry dog or swine, that will never be quiet till his hunger be satisfied; whereas a well governed appetite and sense is easily quieted with a rational denial.

Direct. IX. *Take heed lest you fall in love with the world or any thing therein, and lest your thoughts of any place or condition which you either possess or hope for, grow too sweet and pleasing to you.*

For there is no one perishes, but for loving some creatures more than God: and complacency is the formal act of love. 'Love not the world, nor the things that are in the world, for if any man love the world, the love of the Father is not in him.' Value all earthly things as they conduce to your Master's service, or to your salvation; and not as they tend to the pleasing of your flesh: it is the commonest and most dangerous folly in the world, to be eager to have our houses, lands, provisions, and every thing about us, in the most pleasing and amiable state; when as this is the acknowledged way to hell, and the only poison of the soul. Are you not in more danger of overloving a pleasing and prosperous condition, than a bitter and vexatious state; and of overloving riches, honour, and sensual fulness and delights, rather than poverty, reproach, and mortification? And do you not know that if ever you be damned, it will be for loving the world too much, and God too little? Is it for nothing that Christ describes a saint to you as a Lazarus in poverty and sores, and a condemned sinner as one that was 'clothed in purple and silk, and fared sumptuously every day.' Did not Christ know what he did when he put the rich man upon this trial, to part with all his worldly riches, and follow Christ for a treasure in heaven? All things must be esteemed as loss and dung for the knowledge of Christ, and the hopes of heaven, if ever you will be saved. You must so live by faith, and not by sight, as not to look at the temporal things that are seen, but at the things eternal which are unseen. One that is running in a race for his life, would not so much as turn his head to look back on any one that called to him to stay; or to look aside to any one that would stay with him in his way. Thus must we forget the things that are behind, as counting them not worthy a thought, or remembrance, or a look. If you feel this poison seize upon your hearts, and your condition in the world, or at least your hopes, begin to grow too sweet and pleasing to you, presently make haste to Christ your physician, and take his antidote, and cast up the poison as you love your souls. You must know no other pleasure in your outward mercies, but as God appears in and by them, and as they tend to profit you, and further you in God's service, or to promote your own or others' good; but not as they are provision for the flesh.

Direct. X. *Cast not yourselves wilfully upon temptations, but avoid them as far as lawfully you can: and if you are cast upon them unwillingly, resist them resolutely, as knowing that they come to entice you into sin and hell, from God and your everlasting happiness; and therefore be well acquainted with the particular temptations of every company, calling, relation, business, time, place, and condition of life; and go always furnished with particular antidotes against them all.*

Strong grace will do no more against strong temptations, than weak grace against weak ones. Temptation is the way to sin, and sin is the way to hell. If you saw the danger of your station, when you cast yourself upon temptations, you would tremble and fly as for your lives. I take that man as almost gone already, who chooses temptations, or avoids them not when he may. Especially be acquainted with the diseases and greatest dangers of your soul; and there keep up a constant watch. Are you liable to a gluttonous pleasing of your appetite? Avoid the temptation; set not that before you which may be your snare: let a little, and that of the least tempting kind of food, be your ordinary provision. Sit not at the glutton's table, who fares deliciously every day, if you would escape the glutton's sin and misery. Or if the provision be of other men's choice, at least rise quickly and be gone. Are you inclined to please your appetite in drinking? Avoid such strong drink as may tempt your appetite; and avoid the place and company that draws you to it. Are you inclined to fleshly lust? Avoid the presence of such of the other sex as are a temptation to you: look not on them, nor talk of them; but above all take heed of nearness and familiarity, and privacy with them; and of all opportunity of sin. When the devil hath brought the bait to your hand, and tells you, now you may sin without any molestation or discovery, you are then in a very dangerous case. Some that think they would not be guilty of the sin, will yet tempt themselves, and delight to have it in their power, and to have the opportunity of sinning, and to come as near it as they dare; these are gone before they well perceive their danger. So if you are inclined to pride and ambition, avoid the society of those that tempt you to it: come not among vain men, or such as kindle your ambition. A retired life, in company of mean and humble persons, is fittest for one that hath your disease. 'Mind not high things, but condescend to men of low estate.'

But if you cannot avoid the temptation, be sure yet to avoid the sin; take it as if you saw and heard the devil himself persuading you to sin, and ruin your souls. Abhor the motion, and give not the devil a patient hearing, when you know what he comes about: resolution escapes many a danger, which those are ruined by, who stand disputing and dallying with the tempter. Especially look about you, when the tempter employs great men, or learned men, or godly men, or nearest friends, to be his instruments. If their subtilty puzzle you, go to the stronger and more experienced Christians for advice and help. 'Watch and pray that you enter not into temptation.' It is a dreadful thing to think what persons temptations have overthrown. How wise, learned, and excellent men have been over-witted by Satan, and sinned like fools, when they have let go their watch: if we be as resolved as Peter, temptations may quickly change our resolutions, if God leave us to ourselves, and we grow presumptuous or secure: then our very reason will lose its power; and false representations will make things appear to us quite contrary to what indeed they are; those reasonings will seem probable to us, which at another time we could easily see through as mere deceit. Temptation as it prevails, doth damp and lay asleep our graces, and charm and bewitch all the faculties of the soul.

Direct. XI. *If it be possible, make choice of such a pastor for the help and guidance of your souls, as is judicious, experienced, humble, holy, heavenly, faithful, diligent, lively, and peaceable, who lives not in separation from the generality of sober, godly ministers and Christians where he lives.*

1. Think not of being sufficient for yourselves, without the help of those whom Christ hath appointed to be watchmen for your souls. As you cannot live without the teaching and the grace of Christ; so Christ doth vouchsafe you his teaching, and his grace, by the ministry of his own officers, whom he hath appointed to that end and use. It is marvellous to observe, how Christ chose rather to convert men by the preaching and miracles of his apostles than by his own: and how he would not fully convert Paul without the ministry of Ananias, though he spoke to him from heaven himself, and reasoned the case with him against his persecution. How he would not fully convert Cornelius and his household, without the ministry of Peter, though he sent an angel to direct him to a teacher: nor would he convert the Ethiopian eunuch without the ministry of Philip, nor the jailor without the ministry of Paul and Silas, though he wrought a miracle to prepare for his conversion. Paul must plant, and Apollos must water, before God will give the increase. Though all true Christians are taught of God, and must call no man on earth the master of their faith but Christ, yet have they their teachers, fathers, and instructors under Christ, who are helpers of their joy, though they have not dominion over their faith, and are overseers, though not lords and owners of the flock, and are ministers of Christ by whom he teaches, and stewards of the mysteries of God, and ambassadors by whom he beseeches sinners to be reconciled to God, having committed to them the word of reconciliation. These are 'labourers together with God' upon his 'husbandry and building;' some being master builders, and others under labourers. Christ knew the necessity that the infants of his family had of such nurses, and he knew what numbers of such weak ones there would be in comparison of the strong; or else he had never appointed the strong to such an office: having appointed it, he will keep up the honour of his officers, and will send you his alms, your food, your physic, your pardon, your privileges, by their hands. If you be drawn by seducers to forsake or neglect the ministry of Christ's officers, you forsake or neglect your helps and mercies, you refuse his grace, you are like infants that scorn their nurses' help; and like subjects who reject all the officers of the king, and like the chickens that forsake the hen; you forsake the school and church of Christ, and may expect to be quickly catched up by the devil, as stragglers that have no defence or guide.

2. Yet is there great difference between one minister or pastor and another, as much as be-

'tween physicians, lawyers, or men of any other function. There being no case in the world that you are so much concerned to be careful in, as the instructing, conduct, and safety of your souls, you have exceeding great reason to take heed whom you choose to commit the care and conduct of your souls to. It is not enough to say, that he is a true ordained minister, and that his administrations are not nullities, no more than to say of an ignorant physician, or cowardly captain, that he hath a valid licence or commission; when for all that, if you trust him, it may cost you your lives. Nor is it a wise man's answer to say that God gives his grace by the worst as soon as by the best, and by the weakest as soon as by the strongest, and therefore I need not be so careful in my choice. For though God hath not confined the working of his Spirit to the most excellent means, yet ordinarily he works according to the means he uses: and this both scripture, reason and daily experience fully prove. God works rationally on man as man; that is, as a rational free agent, by moral operation, and not by a mere physical injection of his grace. When we see the man that is made wise unto salvation by mere infusion of wisdom, without a teacher or the study of the word of God, or when we see God work by his word as by a charm, that a few words shall convert a man, though the speaker or hearer understood them not, then we may hearken to this conceit: and then we may think that a heretic may as well teach you the truth as the orthodox, or a schismatic teach you unity and peace as well as a catholic, peaceable pastor; or a man that is ignorant of the mysteries of regeneration and holy communion with God, may best teach you that which he knows not himself, and an enemy to piety and charity, may teach you to be pious and charitable as well as any other. But I need not say much more of this, for all parties would never so strive to have such ministers as they like, and to put out such as they dislike, if they thought not that the difference between ministers and ministers was very great.

See therefore that the guide whom you choose for your souls be, 1. Judicious, for an injudicious man may pervert the scripture, and lead you into error, heresy, and sin, before you are aware: as an unskilful coachman may soon overturn you, or an unskilful waterman may drown you; yea, though he be a zealous, fervent preacher, yet if he be injudicious, he may ignorantly give you poison in your food, as the experience of this age hath lamentably proved.

2. See if possible that he be an experienced man, who knows by experience on himself not only what it is to be regenerated and sanctified, and made a new creature, but also how all the combat between the Spirit and the flesh is to be managed, and what are the methods and stratagems of the tempter, and what are the chief helps and safeguards of the soul, and how they are all to be used: for it is not harder to be a judicious physician, or lawyer, or soldier, without experience, than a judicious pastor. Therefore the Holy Ghost commands that he be not a novice, or raw, inexperienced Christian.

3. See that he be humble, for if he be puffed up with pride, he falls into the condemnation of the devil. Then he will either scorn the labour of the ministry as a drudgery (to preach in season and out of season, to beseech and exhort, and stoop to the poorest of the flock;) or else he will 'speak perverse things to draw away disciples after him,' or he will, as 'Diotrephes, reject the brethren' as loving himself, to 'have the pre-eminence,' and will oversee the church 'by constraint, for filthy lucre, as being a lord over God's heritage.'

4. See that he be holy in his life. The unholy are inexperienced, yea, and have a secret enmity in their hearts against that holiness which they should daily preach; and will usually be showing it in their close, disgracing, discouraging speeches, against that serious piety which they should promote: they will neglect most of the personal care of their flock; and will undo, by their lives, the good which they preach by their tongues, hardening and emboldening the people in their sins, and making them believe that they believe not what they preach themselves. Choose not an enemy of holiness to lead you in the way of holiness (a way that he never went himself,) nor an enemy of Christ to conduct you in the Christian warfare, when he is a servant of the devil, the world, the flesh, against whom you fight.

5. See that he be of a heavenly mind, or else his doctrine will be unsavoury and dry, and he will be preaching some speculations or barren controversies, instead of heavenly, edifying truth.

6. See that he be faithful and diligent in his ministry, as one that knows the worth of souls, and will not sell them or betray them to the devil for filthy lucre, or his fleshly ends; or make merchandise of them, as desiring rather theirs than them, and preferring their fleece before the safety of the flock. But one that imitates the pattern, and 'in meekness instructeth those that are opposers.'

7. See that he be a lively, serious preacher; for all will be little enough to keep up a lively

seriousness in such dull and frozen hearts as ours : a cold preacher, with a cold heart, is like to make cold work. He that speaks senselessly and sleepily about such matters as heaven and hell, doth by the manner of his speech contradict the matter. When hard-heartedness, security, deadness, and lethargic drowsiness, is the common and dangerous disease of souls, let him that loves his soul, and would not perish by his disease, make use of a physician and remedy that is suited to the cure, and not of one to lull him asleep, or give him an opiate to increase his malady.

8. See also that he be one who is of a truly catholic spirit, not addicted to a sect, nor to divisions in the church, nor one that lives in a separation or distance from the generality of godly, sober ministers. For if you take him not for your guide, as separated from the catholic church, but as united to it, and a member of it ; as valuing the judgment of all the church above the judgment of any one pastor, and knowing that you are yourselves to be kept in the unity of the church, and not seduced into a sect ; and that the pastors are to be the bonds and ligaments of the body, that by their help it may grow up in love and unity, and not the dividers of the body. As captains and inferior officers in an army, that are to conduct each soldier in unity with the army, and not to separate, and make every troop or regiment an army by itself, that they may be the petty generals. In a word, read some good visitation sermons, which tell you what a minister must be, and choose, if possible, to live under such a minister ; I say, if possible ; for I know to many it is not possible. Wives, children and servants, while they abound, cannot leave their husbands, parents, or masters ; and strong Christians who are called to do good to others, must prefer that before such advantages to themselves, and many other impediments may deny men such a blessing. But yet I say, undervalue not so great a mercy, and neglect it not where lawfully it may be had, and prefer nothing before it, as a just impediment, which is not really more worth. And remember that divines commonly resolve the case of the infidel nations of the world, that they are inexcusable in their infidelity, because when they hear that other nations profess to know the way to heaven, they do not in so great a case go over sea and land to inquire after the doctrine which we profess. And if the Tartars, Indians, and other nations are bound to send to Christian nations for preachers of the gospel, I only leave you proportionably to measure your

case by theirs, allowing for the disproportion : and to consider how far you should deny your worldly profit in removing your habitations, for such helps as your own necessities require.

Direct. XII. *Make choice of such Christians for your familiar friends, and the companions of your lives, as are holy, humble, heavenly, serious, mortified, charitable, peaceable, judicious, experienced and fixed in the ways of God ; and not of ungodly persons, or proud, self-conceited, censorious, dividing, injudicious, inexperienced, sensual, worldly, opinionative, superficial, lukewarm or unsettled professors.*

The reasons of this direction you may perceive in what I said under the last. Your company is a matter of exceeding great concern to you, as one of the greatest helps or hinderances, comforts or discomforts of all your lives, especially those that you dwell with, and those that you choose for your familiars and bosom friends. And therefore, so far as God's providence doth not forbid you, and make it impossible, choose such as are here described ; or at least one such for your bosom friend, if you can have acquaintance with no more. It is of unspeakable importance to your salvation, with whom you are associated for most familiar converse. A good companion will teach you what you know not, or remember you of that which you forget, or stir you up when you are dull, or warm you when you are cold, and watch over you and warn you of your danger, and save you from the poison of ill companions. O what a help and delight it is to have a holy, judicious, faithful friend to open your heart to, and to walk with, in the ways of life ! And how exceeding hard it is to escape sin and hell, and get well to heaven, in company and familiarity of the servants of the devil, who are posting unto hell ? Let not your companions be worse than yourselves, lest they make you worse ; but as much wiser and better as you can procure.

Direct. XIII. *Subdue your passions, and abhor all uncharitable principles and practices, and live in love ; maintaining peace in your families and with your neighbours, but especially in the church of God.*

Love as you would be loved ; yea, love if you would be loved ; for there is no surer way to purchase love ; and love because you are so freely loved by that God whose wrath you have so oft deserved ; let the thankful feeling of his love in Christ, even turn you wholly into love to God and man : abhor every thought, word, and deed, which is contrary to love, and tends to the hurt of others ; and hate the backbitings and bitter words of any, which tend to make another odious, and to destroy your love to any one that God commands you to love. Allow that moderate passion which is the fruit of love, and tends only to do good; but resist that which inclines you to hatred or to do evil. The more men wrong you, remember that you are the more watchfully to maintain your love, knowing that these temptations are sent by the devil on purpose to destroy and quench it and fill your heart with uncharitableness and wrath. Give place to the wrath of others, and stand not resisting it by words or deeds. 'Recompence to no man evil for evil,' in word or action. Especially be most tender of the union of true Christians, and of the church's peace: when you hear the men of several sects representing one another as odious, understand that it is the language of the devil to draw you from love, into hatred and divisions: and when you must speak odiously of men's sin, speak charitably of their persons, and be as ready to speak of the good that is in them, as of the evil. Believe not that dividing, ungrounded doctrine, which tells you that you cannot sufficiently disown the errors of any party in doctrine, worship, and discipline, without a separation or withdrawing from their communion; which tells you that you are guilty of the ministerial faults of every pastor that you join with, or of the faults of all that worship which you are present at, which would first separate you from every worshipping society and person upon earth, and then lead you to give over the worshipping of God yourselves. You must love Christians as Christians, though they have errors and faults repugnant to their Christianity. You must join in worship with Christians as Christians, though their worship hath errors and faults repugnant to the right order and manner of worship: so be it you join not in that worship which is substantially evil, and such as God doth utterly disown; or that you commit no actual sin yourselves, or that you approve not of the errors and faults of the worshippers, and justify not their smallest evil; or that you prefer not defective, faulty worship before that which is more pure and agreeable to the will of God. For while all the worshippers are faulty and imperfect, all their worship will be so too: and if your actual sin, when you pray or preach effectively yourselves, doth not signify that you approve your faultiness; much less will your presence prove that you allow of the faultiness of others. The business that you come upon is to join with a Christian congregation in the use of those ordinances which God hath appointed, supposing that the ministers and worshippers will all be sinfully defective, in method, order, words, or circumstances: and to bear with that which God doth bear with, and not to refuse that which is God's for the adherent faults of men, no more than you will refuse every dish of meat which is unhandsomely cooked, as long as there is no poison in it, and you prefer it not before better.

Direct. XIV. *Keep up a constant government over your thoughts and tongues, especially against those particular sins which you are most tempted to, and which you see other Christians most overtaken with.*

Keep your thoughts employed upon something that is good and profitable; either about some useful truths, or about some duty to God or man, of your general or particular calling; yea, about all these in their several seasons: learn how to watch your thoughts, and stop them at their first excursions, and how to quicken them and make them serviceable to every grace, and every duty. You can never improve your solitary hours, if you have not the government of your thoughts.

As the thoughts must be governed, because they are the first and intimate actings of good or evil; so the tongue must be governed as the first expositor of the mind, and the first instrument of good or hurt to others. Especially take heed of these sins which the faultiness of most professors of religion doth warn you to avoid. 1. An ordinary course of vain jesting, and unprofitable talk. 2. Provoking, passionate, inconsiderate words, that tend to kindle wrath in others. 3. Backbiting, censuring, and speaking evil of others, without any just call, when it is either upon uncertain reports, or uncharitable suspicion, or tends more to hurt than good. 4. A forward venting of our own conceits, and a confident pleading for our uncertain unproved opinions in religion, and a contentious wrangling for them, as if the kingdom of God lay in them; and a forwardness in all company to be the speakers rather than the hearers, and to talk in a magisterial teaching way, as if we took ourselves to be the wisest, and others to have need to learn of us. But especially take heed of speaking evil of those that have wronged you, or of those that differ from you in some tolerable opinions in religion: and hate that uncharitable vice which makes men ready to believe any thing, or say any thing, be it ever so false, of those that are against their sect; yea, of whole parties of men who differ from them, when there is not one of a thousand of all the party that ever they were acquainted with, or ever could prove the thing by, of which they are accused. By the means of these bold, uncharitable reports, the devil hath unspeakably gained against Christ; and the kingdom of malice hath won upon the kingdom of love : and most Christians are more easily known to be factious, by hating or slandering one another, than they can be known to be Christ's disciples by loving one another. While every sect, without remorse, doth speak reproachfully and hatefully of the rest, they learn hereby to hate one another, and harden the infidel and ungodly world, in hating and speaking evil of them all : so that a Turk or heathen need no other witness of the odiousness of all Christians, than the venomous words which they speak against each other. And as foul words in quarrels prepare for blows, so these malicious invectives, upon differences in religion, prepare for the most cruel persecutions.

From my own observation, which, with a grievous soul, I have made in this generation, I hereby give warning to this and all succeeding ages, that if they have any regard to truth or charity, they take heed how they believe any factious, partial historian or divine, in any evil that he saith of the party which he is against : for, though there be good and credible persons of most parties, yet you shall find that passion and partiality prevail against conscience, truth and charity in most that are sick of this disease. And that the envious zeal which is described in James iii. doth make them think they do God service; first, in believing false reports, and then in venting them against those that their zeal or faction doth call the enemies of truth; so that there is little credit to be given to their reproaches, farther than some better evidence is brought to prove the thing. Nay, it would astonish a man to read the impudent lies which I have often read, obtruded upon the world with such confidence, that the reader will be tempted to think, surely all this cannot be false. Yea, about public words or actions, where you would think that the multitude of witnesses would deter them from speaking it, if it were not true ; and yet all as false as tongue can speak. Therefore believe not pride, or faction, or malice in any evil that it saith, unless you have better evidence of the truth.

Most Christian is that advice of Dr H. More, that ' all parties of Christians would mark all the good which is in other parties, and be more forward to speak of that, than of the evil :' and this would promote the work of charity in the church, and the interest of Christianity in the world : whereas the overlooking of all that is good, and aggravating all the evil, and falsely feigning more

than is true, is the work of greatest service to the devil, and of greatest enmity to Christianity and love, that I know commonly practised in the world. Keep your tongues from all such hellish work as this.

Direct. XV. *Let every state of life and relation that you are in, be sanctified unto God, and conscionably used : and to that end understand the advantages and duties of every condition and relation, and the sins, hinderances, and dangers to which you are most liable.*

The duties of our relations are a great part of the work of a Christian's life : as magistrates and subjects, pastors and flocks, parents and children, husband and wife, masters and servants ; as superiors in gifts or places, or inferiors or equals ; as neighbours or companions : in our teaching and learning, ruling and obeying, buying and selling. Be upright in all these which are your own relations, if you will live as Christians, and be acceptable unto God. An ungodly or oppressing magistrate, a murmuring, rebellious subject, an ungodly, negligent, or factious pastor, an unteachable, refractory, ungodly flock, a husband, parent, or master, without religion, love, or justice ; a wife, child, or servant, without love, dutiful obedience, and faithful diligence ; a proud, contemptuous superior, a malicious, censorious inferior, an unjust, uncharitable neighbour ; a deceitful buyer or seller, borrower or lender, and a self-seeking friend, and seducing, unprofitable companion, are all as far from pleasing God by the rest of their works or profession of religion, as they are from being obedient to his will : they provoke him to abhor their prayers and profession, and to tell them that he will rather have obedience than sacrifice. If you are false to men, you are not true to God. It is he that ' feareth God, and worketh righteousness, that is accepted of him :' and the unrighteous shall not inherit the kingdom of God.

Direct. XVI. *Live as those that have all their powers, receivings, and opportunities to do good with in the world ; and must be answerable how they have improved all : and as those that believe that the more good they do, the more they receive, and the greater is the honour, the profit, and the pleasure of their lives.*

To do no harm, is an honour which is common to a stone or a clod of clay, with the most innocent man. If this were all the excellency that you aim at, it were better that you had never been born; for then you would certainly have done no harm : remember that to do good is the highest imitation of God, supposing that it proceeded from holy love, and be done to the pleasing and glorifying of God, that the principle and the end be suitable to the work. Remember who hath told you, that 'it is more blessed to give than to receive,' and hath promised, that 'he that receives a prophet, in the name of a prophet, shall receive a prophet's reward; and he that receives a righteous man, in the name of a righteous man, shall receive a righteous man's reward. And whosoever shall give to drink unto one of these little ones, a cup of cold water only, in the name of a disciple, verily, I say unto you, he shall in no wise lose his reward,' supposing that he have no better to give. 'Give to every man that asketh of thee,' according to thy ability, 'give, and it shall be given to you.' Take that day or hour as lost, in which you do no good, directly or preparatorily: and take that part of your estate as lost, with which directly or remotely, you do no good. Remember how the judgment must pass on you at last, according to the improvement of your several talents. When your time is past, and your estates are gone, or your understandings or your strength decayed, and your power and greatness is levelled with the poorest, it will be an unspeakable comfort to you, if you are able to say, we laid them out sincerely to our master's use; and an unspeakable terror for you to say, they were lost and cast away on the service of the flesh. If therefore you are rulers, and are entrusted with power, study how to do all the good within your power that possibly you can: if you are ministers of Christ, lay out your time, strength, and parts, in doing good to the souls of all about you; study how you may be most serviceable to the church and cause of Christ. If you are rich men, study how to do all the good with your riches that possibly you can do, not violating the order appointed you by God: in your neighbourhood, and in all your families and relations, study to do the greatest good you can. Take it thankfully as a great mercy to yourselves, when opportunity to do good is offered you. And content not yourselves to do a little, while you are able to do more. 'Be not deceived, God is not mocked; for whatsoever a man soweth, that shall he also reap; for he that soweth to his flesh, shall of the flesh reap corruption; but he that soweth to the spirit, shall of the spirit reap everlasting life. And let us not be weary in well-doing, for in due season we shall reap if we faint not. As we have therefore opportunity, let us do good to all men, especially unto them who are of the household of faith.—He that soweth sparingly shall reap sparingly, and he that soweth bountifully shall reap bountifully: every

man according as he purposeth in his heart, so let him give, not grudgingly, or of necessity; for God loves a cheerful giver.—To do good, and to communicate, forget not, for with such sacrifice God is well pleased.' For we are his workmanship, created in Christ Jesus to good works, which God hath ordained, that we should walk in them.' Let doing good be the business and employment of your lives; preferring still the public good, before the private good of any; and the good of men's souls before that of the body. But yet neglecting none, but doing the lesser, in order to the greater.

Object. But I am a poor, obscure person, that have neither abilities of mind, or body, or estate; and what good can I do?

Answ. There is not one rational person that is not entrusted with one talent at the least; and that is not in a capacity of doing good in the world, if they have but hearts and be but willing. If you had neither money to give, nor tongues to speak, for God, and to provoke others to do good, yet a holy, humble, heavenly, patient, blameless life, is a powerful means of doing good, by showing the excellency of grace, convincing the ungodly, stopping the mouths of the enemies of piety, and honouring the ways of God in the world: such a holy, harmless, exemplary life, is a continual, and a powerful sermon: and for giving, 'if there be first a willing mind, it is accepted according to that a man hath, and not according to that he hath not.' If you are unfeignedly willing to give, if you had it, God takes it as done: what you would have given, is set down on your account as given indeed. The widow's two mites were praised by Christ as a bountiful gift, and a cup of cold water is not unrewarded to the willing soul. No one therefore is excusable that lives unprofitably in the world. But yet men of power, parts, and wealth, have the greatest reckoning to make: their ten talents must have a proportionable improvement: it is a great deal of good that they must do: 'for to whomsoever much is given, of him shall be much required; and to whom men have committed much, of him they will ask the more.'

Direct. XVII. *Redeem your time, and highly value every minute; and spare for no labour in the work of your salvation: dream not of an easy, idle, sluggish life, as sufficient to your high and glorious ends; nor rest in a customary and outside way of duty, without regard to the life and the success.*

If any thing in all the world require all our power and time, it is that for which all our powers and time are given us; and which we are sure will a thousand fold recompence us for all. O what a sottish kind of stupidity is it, for a man to trifle in the way to eternity, that hath an endless life of joy or sorrow depending on the preparations of so short a life. How little doth he know the worth of his soul, the joys of heaven, the terrors of hell, the malicious diligence of Satan, òr the difficulty of salvation, that can idle and play away whole hours of time; pray as if he prayed not, and seem to be religious when he is not in good earnest! Who bestirs not himself so much to escape hell fire, and to obtain everlasting joys with Christ, as he would do to escape a temporal death or misery, or to obtain some dignity or riches in the world. O therefore, as ever you care what becomes of your souls, and as ever you will have comfort in the review of your present life, make not a jest of heaven and hell: trifle not in your race and warfare; dally not with God and conscience; play not and dream not away your time. Know the worth of an hour's time, for the sake of your work, and of your souls, as it is commonly known by dying men. But of this I have spoken already in my Now or Never, in the Carnal and Spiritual Man Compared and Contrasted, and in the Saints' Rest.

Direct. XVIII. *Sit down and count what it may cost you to be Christians indeed, and to be saved: reckon not on prosperity, or a cheap religion, but resolve to take up the cross and follow Christ in suffering, and to be crucified to the world, and by many tribulations, to enter into the kingdom of heaven.*

All who will live godly in Christ shall suffer persecution. It is not all that are baptized and called Christians, but ' all that will live godly in Christ Jesus:' it is godliness, and not the bare name of Christianity, which the serpent's seed have so great an enmity to. I have elsewhere cited an excellent saying of Dr Thos. Jackson's, to prove that this is to be expected under Christian, as well as heathen governments, and that it is not through the goodness of the great ones of the world, but the cowardliness of our hearts, that the ministers of Christ are not ordinarily martyrs. Though God may possibly exempt you from any notable suffering for his cause, yet it is not wise or safe to expect such an exemption: for that will hinder your preparation for suffering: a mind prepared to suffer, is essential to true Christianity: and no man that is not a martyr in resolution and disposition can be saved. If the fiery trial come upon you, let it not seem a strange, unexpected thing. When persecution arises because of the word, the unrooted, un-

sound, unsettled Christian, is presently offended, and falls away. Then they will fall to distinguishing and carnal reasoning, and prove any thing lawful which is necessary to their peace. ' As many as desire to make a fair show in the flesh, they constrain you to be circumcised, only lest they should suffer persecution for the cross of Christ.' Shrink not for sufferings; ' fear not them that can but kill the body.' Never doth the Spirit of God and glory so much rest upon believers, as in their greatest sufferings for righteousness' sake, and never have they cause of more exceeding joy. Prosperity doth not so well agree with a life of faith, as sufferings and adversity. ' Our light affliction, which is but for a moment, works for us a far more exceeding and eternal weight of glory; while we look not at the (temporal) things which are seen, but at the things (eternal) which are not seen.'

Direct. XIX. *If you fall into any sin, rise speedily by a thorough repentance; and take heed both of delay, and of a palliating cure.*

Take heed of trusting to a general repentance, or a converted state, instead of a particular repentance and conversion from any known sin, especially which is more than the ordinary unavoidable infirmities of a saint; for it is not general repentance indeed which reaches not to every known particular. If temptation have cast you down, take heed of lying there, but presently get up again: what the apostle saith of wrath, the same I may say of other falls, let not the sun go down upon them: but go out with Peter and weep with him, if you have sinned with him. If your bones be out of joint, or broken, get them set presently, before they settle in their dislocation: and let the cure be thorough, and spare not for a little pain at first; let as open confession as the case requires, and as full restitution, signify the sincerity of your repentance: for a gentle handling of yourselves may undo you; and palliation is the hypocrite's cure. O take heed, lest you presume to sleep one night in your unrepented sin; and take heed, lest delay encourage the tempter to offer you the bait again and again, and to say, why not once more; why may you not be as well pardoned for twice as for once; and for thrice as for twice, &c. It is dangerous playing or sleeping at the brink of hell. Away from the temptation and occasion of your sin; stand not disputing, but resolve and be gone; and ' sin no more, lest a worse thing come unto you.' Stick not at the shame or loss or suffering, which confession, restitution or reformation may bring; but remember that you can never escape damnation at too dear a rate.

This is Christ's meaning, when he speaks of 'cutting off a right hand, or plucking out a right eye, if it offend;' that is, ensnare and tempt you unto sin. Not that you should do so indeed, for you have an easier way to avoid the sin; but that, this is far the lesser of the two evils, to lose a hand or eye, than to lose the soul, and therefore to be chosen if there were no other remedy. If the thief had no other way to forbear stealing than to cut off his hand; or the fornicator to cure his lust, than to put out his eyes, it were a cheap remedy. A cheap and easy, superficial repentance, may skin over the sore and deceive an hypocrite; but he that would be sure of pardon, and free from fear, must go to the bottom.

Direct. XX. *Live as with death continually in your eye, and spend every day in serious preparation for it, that when it comes, you may find your work dispatched; and may not then cry out in vain to God to try you once again.*

Promise not yourselves long life : think not of death as at many years' distance, but as at hand. Think what will then be needful to your peace and comfort, and order all your life accordingly, and prepare that now, which will be needful then : live now while you have time, as you will resolve and promise God to live, when on your death bed you are praying for a little time of trial more. It is a great work to die in a joyful assurance and hope of everlasting life, and with a longing desire to depart and be with Christ as best of all. O then what a burden and terror it will be, to have an unbelieving, or a worldly heart, or a guilty conscience. Now therefore use all possible diligence to strengthen faith, to increase love, to be acquitted from guilt, to be above the world, to have the mind set free from the captivity of the flesh, to walk with God, and to obtain the deepest, most delectable apprehensions of his love in Christ, and of the heavenly blessedness which you expect. Do you feel any doubts of the state of immortality, or staggering at the promise of God through unbelief ? Presently do all you can to conquer them, and get a clear resolution to your souls, and leave it not all to do at the time of sickness. Are the thoughts of God and heaven unpleasant or terrible to you ? Presently search out the cause of all, and labour in the cure of it as for your lives. Is there any former or present sin, which is a burden or terror to your consciences ? Presently seek out to Christ for a cure by faith and true repentance ; and do that to disburden your consciences now, which you would do on a sick bed; and leave not so great and necessary a work to so uncertain, short and unfit

a time. Is there any thing in this world that is sweeter to your thoughts than God and heaven, and which you cannot willingly let go ? Mortify it without delay, considering of its vanity ; compare it with heaven ; crucify it by the cross of Christ ; cease not till you account it loss and dross, for the excellent knowledge of Christ and life eternal. Let not death surprise you as a thing that you never seriously expected : can you do no more in preparation for it than you do ? If not, why do you wish at death to be tried once again ; and why are you troubled that you lived no better ; but if you can, when think you should it be done ; is the time of uncertain, painful sickness better than this ? O how doth sensuality besot the world ; and inconsiderateness deprive them of the benefit of their reason ; if you know indeed that you must shortly die, live then as dying men should live ; choose your condition in the world, and manage it as men that must shortly die : use your power, command, and honour ; use all your neighbours, and especially use the cause and servants of Christ, as men should do that must shortly die. Build and plant, buy and sell, and use your riches as those that must die, remembering that the fashion of all these things is passing away. Yea, pray and read, hear and meditate, as those that must die. Seeing you are as sure of it as if it were this hour, delay not your preparations. It is a terrible thing for an immortal soul to pass out of the body in a carnal, unregenerated, unprepared state ; and to leave a world which they loved and were familiar with, and go to a world which they neither know nor love, and where they have neither heart nor treasure.

The measure of faith which may help you to bear an easy cross, is not sufficient to fortify and encourage your souls, to enter upon so great a change. So also bear all your wants and crosses as men that must shortly die : fear the cruelties of men, but as beseems those that are ready to die : he that can die well, can do any thing, or suffer any thing : and he that is unready to die, is unfit for a fruitful and comfortable life. What can rationally rejoice that man, who is sure to die, and is unready to die, and is yet unfurnished of dying comforts ? Let nothing be now sweet to you, which will be bitter to your dying thoughts. Let nothing be much desired now, which will be unprofitable and uncomfortable then. Let nothing seem very heavy or grievous now, which will be light and easy then : let nothing now seem honourable, which will then seem despicable and vile. Consider of every thing as it will look at death ; that when the day shall come which ends all the joys of the ungodly, you may look up with joy, and say, Welcome heaven, this is the day which I so long expected, which all my days were spent in preparation for, which shall end my fears, begin my felicity, and put me into possession of all that I desired, prayed, and laboured for; when my soul shall see its glorified Lord: for he hath said, 'if any man serve me, let him follow me; and where I am, there shall also my servant be: if any man serve me, him will my Father honour: even so, Lord Jesus, remember me, now thou art in thy kingdom, and let me be with thee in paradise.' O thou that spakest those words, so full of inexpressible comfort, to a sinful woman, in the first speech after thy blessed resurrection, 'Go to my brethren, and say unto them, I ascend unto my Father and your Father, and to my God and your God,' take up now this soul that is thine own, that it may see the glory given thee with the Father, and instead of this life of temptation, trouble, darkness, distance, and sinful imperfection, I may delightfully behold, love, and praise thy Father and my Father, thy God and my God. 'Lord, now lettest thou thy servant depart in peace; Lord Jesus, receive my spirit.'

Now I have given you all these directions, I shall only request you in the close, that you will set your very hearts to the daily serious practice of them; for there is no other way for a ripe, confirmed state of grace; and as ever you regard the glory of God, the honour of your religion, the welfare of the church, and those about you, and the living and dying comforts of yourselves, O do not sluggishly rest in an infant state of grace! Did you but know how a weak and strong faith differ, and how a weak and a sound confirmed Christian differ as to the honour of God, the good of others, and especially to themselves, both in life and death, it would quickly awaken you to a cheerful diligence, for so high and excellent an end. Did you but well understand the wrong that Christ and the gospel have sustained in the world, yea, in England, by weak, diseased, distempered Christians, your hearts would bleed, and with shame and grief, it would be your secret and open lamentation. Stir up then the grace that is given you, use Christ's means, and do your best, and you will find that Christ is not an insufficient physician, nor an ineffectual Saviour, or an empty fountain; but that he is filled with all the fulness of God, hath spirit and life to communicate to his members, and that there is no want which he cannot supply, and no corruption or temptation, which his grace is not sufficient to overcome.

THE CHARACTER

OF

A SOUND CONFIRMED CHRISTIAN;

AS ALSO

OF A WEAK AND SEEMING CHRISTIAN.

ADDRESS TO THE READER.

IT is a matter of a greater moment than I can express, what idea or image of the nature of godliness and Christianity is imprinted upon men's minds: the description which is expressed in the sacred scriptures, is true and full: the thing described is rational, pure, perfect, unblameable and amiable. That which is expressed in the lives of the most, is not so; but it is purblind, defiled, maimed, imperfect, culpable, and mixed with so much of the contrary quality, that to them that cannot distinguish the chaff from the wheat, the sickness from the life, it seems an unreasonable, fanciful, lothesome and vexatious thing, and so far from being worthy to be preferred before all the riches, honours and pleasures of the world, that it seems worthy to be kept under as a troubler of kingdoms, societies, and souls. And doubtless this monstrous expression of it in men's lives, is because the perfect expression of it in God's word, hath not made a true impression upon the mind, and consequently upon the heart. For as it is sound doctrine which must make sound Christians; so doctrine works on the will and affections, not as it is in itself, and as delivered, but as it is understood, believed, remembered, considered; even as it is imprinted on the mind, and used by it. And as interposed matter, or defective application, may cause the image on the wax to be imperfect, though made by the most perfect seal: so is it in this case, when one man doth defectively understand the scripture description of a godly man or Christian, and another by misunderstanding mixes false conceptions of his own; and another by a corrupt, depraved will hinders the understanding from believing, or remembering, or considering and using what it partly apprehends; what wonder if the godliness and Christianity in their hearts be unlike the godliness and Christianity in the scriptures: when the law of God, in nature and scripture, is pure and uncorrupt, and the law of God written imperfectly on the heart, is there mixed with the carnal law in their members, no marvel if it be expressed accordingly in their lives.

I have therefore much endeavoured in all my writings, and especially in this, to draw out the full portraiture of a Christian or godly man indeed, and to describe God's image on the soul of man, in such a manner as tends to the just information of the reader's mind, and the filling up of the wants, and rectifying the errors which may be found in his former conceptions of it. And I purposely inculcate the same things oft, in several writings, as when I preached I did in all my sermons, that the reader may find that I bring him not undigested, needless novelties, and that the frequent repetition of them may help to make the deeper and fuller impression: for my work is to subserve the Holy Ghost, in putting God's law into men's hearts, and writing it out truly, clearly, and fully upon their inward parts; that they may be made such themselves, by understanding thoroughly what they must be, and what a solid Christian is: and that thus they may be born again by the incorruptible, immortal seed, the word of God, which will live and abide for ever; and may purify their souls in obeying the truth, through the Spirit. He is the best lawyer, physician, soldier, &c. who hath his doctrine in his soul, and not only in his books, and hath digested his reading into an intellectual system and habit of knowledge. If ministers had an hundred times over repeated the integral portraiture or character of a sound Christian, till it had been as familiar to the minds and memories of their hearers, as is the description of a magistrate, a physician, a schoolmaster, a husbandman, a shepherd, and such things as they are well acquainted with, it would have been a powerful means to make sound Christians. But when men's minds conceive of a Christian, as a man that differs from heathens and infidels in nothing but holding the Christian opinions, and using different words and ceremonies of worship, and such like, no wonder if such be but opinionative, lifeless Christians: and if their religion make them no better than a Seneca or a Plutarch, I shall never believe that they are any surer to be saved than they. And such a sort of men there are, that suppose Christianity to consist but of these three parts: 1. The Christian doctrine acknowledged, which they call faith. 2. The orders and ordinances of the Christian church and worship, submitted to, and decently used, which they call godliness. And, 3. The heart and life of a Cato, Cicero, or Socrates adjoined. But all that goes beyond this, which is the life of Christianity and godliness, a lively faith, hope, and love ; a heavenly and holy mind and life, from the renewing indwelling Spirit of God, which is described in this treatise, they are strangers to it, and take it to be but fancy and hypocrisy. These non-Christians do much to reduce the church to infidelity ; that there may be indeed no Christians in the world. For my part I must confess. if there were no better Christians in the world than these, I think I should be no Christian myself ; and if Christ made men no better than the religion of Socrates, Cato, or Seneca, and did no more to the reparation and perfecting of men's hearts and lives, I should think no better of the Christian religion than of theirs ; for the means is to be estimated by the end and use : and he is the best physician who hath the remedies which are fittest to work the cure. If God had not acquainted me with a sort of men that have really more holiness, mortification, spirituality, love to God, and to one another, and even to enemies, and more heavenly desires, expectations and delights, than these men before described have, it would have been a very great hinderance to my faith.

The same may I say of those that place godliness and Christianity only in holding strict opinions, and in affected, needless singularities, and in the fluent oratory and length of prayer, and

avoiding other men's forms and modes of worship, and in any thing short of a renewed, holy, heavenly heart and life.

Undoubtedly, if a true full character of godliness had been imprinted in their minds, we should never have seen the professors of it so blotted with sensuality, selfishness, pride, ambition, worldliness, distrust of God, self-conceitedness, heresy, schism, rebellions, unquietness, impatiency, unmercifulness, and cruelty to men's souls and bodies, as we have seen them in this age ; and all this justified as consistent with religion.

I fear, that because this treatise will speak to few that are not some way guilty, every face which hath a spot or blemish will be offended with the glass : that the faulty will say, that I particularly intended to disgrace them. But I must here tell the reader, to prevent his misunderstanding, that if he shall imagine that I have my eyes upon particular parties, and as a discontented person, intend to blame those that differ from myself, or to grieve inferiors, or dishonour and asperse superiors, they will mistake me, and wrong themselves, and me, who professedly intend but the true description of sound Christians, diseased Christians, and seeming Christians.

For the manner of this writing, I am conscious it hath but little to commend it. The matter is that for which it is published. The Lord Verulam, in his essays, truly saith, that much reading makes one full ; much discourse doth make one ready, and much writing doth make a man exact. Though I have had my part of all these means, yet being parted five years from my books, and three years from my preaching, the effects may decay : and you must expect neither quotations or testimonies, or ornament of style : but having not yet wholly ceased from writing, I may own so much of the exactness, as will allow me to intreat the reader, not to use me as many have done ; who by overlooking some one word, have made the sense another thing, and have made it a crime to be exact in writing, because they cannot, or will not, be exact in reading, or charitable or humane in interpreting.

PRELIMINARY REMARKS.

In the explication of the text, which I made the ground of ' Directions to Weak Christians,' I have showed you that there is a degree of grace to be expected and sought after by all true Christians, which puts the soul into a sound, confirmed, established state. in comparison of that weak, diseased, tottering condition, which most Christians now continue in. And I have showed you how desirable a state that is, and what calamities follow the languishing, unhealthful state, even of such as may be saved. Indeed did we but rightly understand, how deeply the errors and sins of many well-meaning Christians have wounded the interest of religion in this age; and how heinously they have dishonoured God, and caused the enemies of holiness to blaspheme, and hardened thousands in popery and ungodliness, in probability to their perdition. Had we well observed when God's judgments have begun, and understood what sins have caused our wars, plagues, flames, and worse than all these, our great heart divisions, and church-distractions and convulsions; we should ere this have given over the flattering of ourselves and one another, in such a heaven-provoking state; and the ostentation of that little goodness, which hath been eclipsed by such lamentable evils. Instead of these, we should have betaken ourselves to the exercise of such a serious, deep repentance as the quality of our sins, and the greatness of God's chastisements, require. It is a doleful case, to see how light many make of all the rest of their distempers, when once they think that they have so much grace and mortification, as is absolutely necessary to save their souls: and expect that preachers should say little to weak Christians, but words of comfort, setting forth their happiness: yet if one of them, when he hath the gout, or stone, or cholic, or dropsy, doth send for a physician, he would think himself derided or abused, if his physician, instead of curing his disease, should only comfort him, by telling him, that he is not dead. What excellent disputations have Cicero and Seneca, the Platonists and Stoicks, to prove, that virtue is of itself sufficient to make man happy? Yet many Christians live as if holiness were but the way and means to their felicity, or at best but a small part of their felicity itself; or as if felicity itself grew burdensome, or were not desirable in this life; or a small degree of it were as good as a greater.

Too many mistake the will of God, and the nature of sanctification, and place their religion in the hot prosecution of those mistakes: they make a composition of error and passion, and an unyielding stiffness in them, and siding with the church or party which maintains them, and uncharitable censuring of those that are against them, and an unpeaceable contending for them: and this composition they mistake for godliness, especially if there be but a few drams of godliness and truth in the com-

position, though corrupted and overpowered by the rest.

For these miscarriages of many well-meaning, zealous persons, the land mourns, the churches groan; kingdoms are disturbed by them; families are disquieted by them; godliness is hindered, and much dishonoured by them; the wicked are hardened by them, and encouraged to hate, blaspheme, and oppose religion; the glory of the Christian faith is obscured by them; and the infidel, Mahometan, and heathen world, are kept from faith in Jesus Christ, and many millions of souls destroyed by them. I mean by the miscarriages of the weaker sort of Christians, and by the wicked lives of those carnal hypocrites, who for custom or worldly interest, profess that Christianity, which was never received by their hearts.

All this is much promoted by their indiscretion, who are so intent upon the consolatory opening of the safety and happiness of believers, that they omit the due explication of their description, their dangers, and their duties.

One part of this too much neglected work I have endeavoured to perform in the foregoing treatise; another I shall attempt in this second part: there are five degrees or ranks of true Christians observable. 1. The weakest Christians, who have only the essentials of Christianity, or very little more: as infants that are alive, but of little strength or use to others. 2. Those who are lapsed into some wounding sin, though not into a state of condemnation, like men in old age, who have lost the use of some one member for the present, though they are strong in other parts. 3. Those who having the integral parts of Christianity in a considerable measure, are in a sound and healthful state, though neither perfect, nor of the highest form or rank of Christians in this life, nor without such infirmities, as are the matter of their daily watchfulness and humiliation. 4. Those who are so strong as to attain extraordinary degrees of grace, who are therefore comparatively called perfect. 5. Those that have an absolute perfection, without sin, that is, the heavenly inhabitants.

I meddle not now with the lapsed Christian as such, nor with those giants in holiness of extraordinary strength, nor with the perfect blessed souls in heaven: but it is the Christian who hath attained that confirmation in grace, and composed, quiet, fruitful state, which we might ordinarily expect, if we were industrious, whose image or character I shall now present you with: I call him oft-times a Christian indeed, in allusion to Christ's description of Nathaniel, and as we commonly use that word, for one that answers his own profession without any notable dishonour or defect : as we say such a man is a scholar indeed ; and not as signifying his mere sincerity. I mean one whose heart and life is so conformable to the principles, the rule, and the hopes of Christianity, that to the honour of Christ, the true nature of our religion is discernible in his conversation,—in whom an impartial infidel might perceive the true nature of the Christian faith and godliness. If the world were fuller of such living images of Christ, who, like true regenerated children, represent their heavenly Father, Christianity would not have met with so much prejudice, nor had so many enemies in the world, nor would so many millions have been kept in the darkness of heathenism and infidelity, by flying from Christians, as a sort of people that are common and unclean.

Among Christians, there are babes, who must be fed with milk, and not with strong meat, that are ' unskilful in the word of righteousness,' and novices, who are unsettled, and in danger of an overthrow. In these the nature and excellency of Christianity, is little more apparent than reason in a little child. And there are strong, confirmed Christians, ' who by reason of use have their senses exercised to discern both good and evil,' and ' who show forth the glory of him that hath called them out of darkness into his marvellous light ;' of whom God himself may say to Satan and their malicious enemies, as once of Job, ' hast thou not seen my servant Job,' &c. This Christian indeed I shall now describe to you, both to confute the infidel's slanders of Christianity, and to show men those false descriptions which have caused the presumption of the profane, and the irregularities of erroneous sectaries ; and to tell you what manner of persons they are that God is honoured by ; and what you must be if you will understand your own religion. Be Christians indeed, and you will have the comforts indeed of Christianity ; and will find that its fruits and joys are not dreams, shadows, and imaginations, if you content not yourselves with an imagination, dream and shadow of Christianity, or with some spark or buried seed.

THREE DIFFERENT CLASSES OF CHARACTERS
COMPARED.

I. A Christian indeed—by which I still mean, a sound, confirmed Christian—is one that contents not himself to have a seed or habit of faith, but he lives by faith, as the sensualist by sight

or sense : not putting out the eye of sense, nor living as if he had no body, or lived not in a world of sensible objects ; but as he is a reasonable creature, which exalts him above the sensitive nature, so faith is the true information of his reason, about those high and excellent things, which must take him up above things sensible. He hath so firm a belief of the life to come, as procured by Christ, and promised in the gospel, as that it serves him for the government of his soul, as his bodily sight doth for the conduct of his body. I say not, that he is assaulted with no temptations, nor that his faith is perfect in degree, nor that believing moves him as passionately as sight or sense would do : but it doth effectually move him through the course and tenor of his life, to do those things for the life to come, which he would do if he saw the glory of heaven ; and to shun those things for the avoiding of damnation, which he would shun, if he saw the flames of hell. Whether he do these things so fervently or not, his belief is 'powerful, effectual, and victorious. Let sight and sense invite him to their objects, and entice him to sin, and forsake his God, the objects of faith shall prevail against them, in the bent of an even, a constant and resolved life. It is things unseen which he takes for his treasure, and which have his heart, hope, and chief labours. All things else, which he hath to do are but subservient to his faith and heavenly interest, as his sensitive faculties are ruled by his reason. His faith is not only his opinion, which teaches him to choose what church or party he will be of ; but it is his intellectual light ; by which he lives, and in the confidence and comfort of which he dies, ' for we walk by faith, not by sight.—We groan to be clothed upon with our heavenly house.—Wherefore we labour that, whether present or absent, we may be accepted of him.—Now the just shall live by faith.—Now faith is the substance of things hoped for, the evidence of things not seen.' Most of the examples in Heb. xi. show you this truth, that true Christians live and govern their actions by the firm belief of the promise of God, and of another life when this is ended. ' By faith Noah being warned of God of things not seen as yet, moved with fear, prepared an ark, to the saving of his house ; by which he condemned the world, and became heir of the righteousness which is by faith.— Abraham looked for a city which had foundations, whose builder and maker is God.—Moses feared not the wrath of the king ; for he endured, as seeing him who is invisible.' So the three witnesses, Dan. iii. and Daniel himself, and all believers, have lived this life, as Abraham the father of the faithful did ; who, as it is said of him, 'staggered not at the promise of God through unbelief, but was strong in faith, giving glory to God.' The faith of a Christian is truly divine ; and he knows that God's truth is as certain as sight itself can be, however sight be apt to move the passions : therefore, if you can judge but what a rational man would be, if he saw heaven and hell, and all that God hath appointed us to believe, then you may conjecture what a confirmed Christian is ; though sense cause more sensible apprehensions.

2. The weak Christian also hath a faith that is divine, as caused by God, and resting on his word and truth. He so far lives by this faith, as that it commands and guides the scope and drift of his heart and life: but he believes with a great deal of staggering and unbelief: therefore his hopes are interrupted by his troublesome doubts and fears ; and the dimness and languor of his faith is seen in the faintness of his desires, and the many blemishes of his heart and life : and sight and sensual objects are so much the more powerful with him, by how much the light and life of faith is dark and weak.

3. The hypocrite or best of the unregenerated, believes but either with a human faith, which rests but on the word of man, or else with a dead, opinionative faith, which is overpowered by infidelity, or is like the dreaming thoughts of a man asleep, which stir him not to action : he lives by sight and not by faith : for he hath not a faith that will overpower sense and sensual objects.

II. 1. A Christian indeed not only knows why he is a Christian, but sees those reasons for his religion, which disgrace all that the atheist or infidel can say against it; and so far satisfy, confirm and establish him, that difficulties, temptations and objections, do not at all stagger him, or raise any deliberate doubts in him of the truth of the word of God: he sees first the natural evidence of those foundation-truths which nature itself makes known ; as that there is a God of infinite being, power, wisdom and goodness, the Creator, the owner, the ruler, and the Father, felicity and end of man ; that we owe him all our love and service ; that none of our fidelity shall be in vain or unrewarded, and none shall be finally a loser by his duty; that man, who is naturally governed by the hopes and fears of another life, is made and lives for that other life, where his soul shall be sentenced by God, his judge, to happiness or misery, &c. Then he discerns the attestation of God to those supernatural, superadded revelations of the gospel, containing the doctrine of man's redemption : and he sees how wonderfully these are built upon the former, and how excellently the Creator's and Redeemer's doctrine and laws agree ; and how much countenance supernatural truths receive from the presupposed naturals ; so that he doth not adhere to Christ and religion by the mere engagement of education, friends, or worldly advantages ; nor by a blind resolution, which wants nothing but a strong temptation from a deceiver or a worldly interest, to shake or overthrow it : but he is built upon the rock, which will stand in the assault of Satan's storms, and the gates of hell shall not prevail against it.

2. But a weak Christian hath but a dim and general kind of knowledge of the reasons of his religion; or at least but a weak apprehension of them, though he have the best and most unanswerable reasons: and either he is confident in the dark upon grounds which he cannot make good, and which want but a strong assault to shake them ; or else he is troubled and ready to stagger at every difficulty which occurs : every hard saying in the scripture offends him ; every seeming contradiction shakes him : and the depth of mysteries, which pass his understanding, make him say as Nicodemus of regeneration, how can these things be? And if he meet with the objections of a cunning infidel, he is unable so to defend the truth, and clear his way through them, as to come off unwounded and unshaken, and to be the more confirmed in the truth of his belief, by discerning the vanity of all that is said against it.

3. The seeming Christian either hath no solid reasons at all for his religion, or else if he have the best, he hath no sound apprehension of them ; but though he be ever so learned and orthodox, and can preach and defend the faith, it is not so rooted in him as to endure the trial; but if a strong temptation from subtilty or carnal interest assault him, you shall see that he was built upon the sand, and that there was in him a secret root of bitterness, and an evil heart of unbelief, which causes him to depart from the living God.

III. 1. A Christian indeed, is not only confirmed in the essentials of Christianity, but he hath a clear, delightful sight of those useful truths, which are the integral parts of Christianity, and are built upon the fundamentals, and are the branches of the master-points of faith. Though he see not all the lesser truths, which are branched out at last into innumerable particles, yet he sees the main body of sacred verities, delivered by Christ for man's sanctification ; and sees them methodically in their proper places ; sees how one supports another, and in how beautiful an order and contexture they are placed : and as he sticks not in the bare principles, so he receives all these additions of knowledge, not notionally only, but practically, as the food on which his soul must live.

2. A weak Christian in knowledge, besides the principles or essentials of religion, doth know but a few disordered, scattered truths; which are also but *half known ;* because while he hath some knowledge of those points, he is ignorant of many others, which are needful to the supporting, and clearing, and improving of them : and because he knows them not in their places, order, relation, and aspect upon other truths. Therefore if temptations be strong, and come with advantage, the weak Christian in such points is easily drawn into many errors; thence into great confidence and conceitedness in those errors ; and thence into sinful, dangerous courses in the prosecution and practice of them : such are like 'children tossed up and down, and carried to and fro by every wind of doctrine, through the cunning sleight and subtilty of men, whereby they lie in wait to deceive.'

3. The seeming Christian having no saving practical knowledge of the essentials of Christianity themselves, doth therefore either neglect to know the rest, or knows them but notionally, as common sciences, and subjects them all to his worldly interest : and therefore is still of that side or party in religion, which upon the account of safety, honour or preferment, his flesh commands him to follow. Either he is still on the greater, rising side, and of the ruler's religion, be it what it will ; or if he dissent, it is in pursuit of another game, which pride or fleshly ends have started.

IV. 1. The Christian indeed, hath not only reason for his religion, but also hath an inward continual principle, even the Spirit of Christ, which is as a new nature, inclining and enlivening him to a holy life ; whereby he minds and savours the things of the Spirit : not that his nature doth work blindly, as nature doth in the irrational creatures ; but at least it much intimates nature as it is found in rational creatures, where the inclination is necessary, but the operations free, and subject to reason : it is a spiritual appetite in the rational appetite, even the will, and a spiritual visive disposition in the understanding : not a faculty in a faculty ; but the right disposition of the faculties to their highest objects, to which they are by corruption made unsuitable. So that it is neither a proper power in the natural sense, nor a mere act : but nearest to the nature of a seminal disposition or habit. It is the health and rectitude of the faculties of the soul. Even as nature hath made the understanding disposed to truth in general, and the will disposed or inclined to good in general, and to self-preservation and felicity in particular ; so the Spirit of Christ doth dispose the understanding to spiritual truth, to know God and the matters of salvation, and doth incline the will to God and holiness ; not blindly, as they are unknown, but to love and serve a known God. So that whether this be properly or only analogically called a nature, or rather should be called a habit, I determine not ; but certainly it is a fixed disposition and inclination, which scripture calls the divine nature, and 'the seed of God abiding in us,' but most usually it is called 'the Spirit of God, or of Christ in us.—If any man have not the Spirit of Christ the same is none of his.—By one spirit we are all baptized into one body.' Therefore we are said to be in 'the spirit, and walk after the spirit, and by the spirit, to mortify the deeds of the body.' And it is called 'the spirit of the Son, and the spirit of adoption, whereby we cry, Abba, Father,' or are inclined to God, as children to their father ; and the spirit of grace and supplication. From this Spirit and the fruits of it, we are called new creatures, quickened and made alive to God. It is a great controversy whether this holy disposition and inclination, was unnatural to Adam or not, and consequently, whether it be a restored nature in us, or not ? It was as natural to him, as health is natural to the body; but not so natural as to be a necessitating principle.

2. This same spirit and holy inclination is in the weakest Christian also, but in a small degree, and remissly operating, so as that the fleshly inclination oft seems to be the stronger, when he judges by its passionate strugglings within him : though indeed the Spirit of life doth not only strive, but conquer in the main, even in the weakest Christians.

3. The seeming Christian hath only the ineffectual motions of the spirit to a holy life, and effectual motions, and inward dispositions to some common duties of religion : and from these, with the natural principles of self love and common honesty, with the outward persuasions of company and advantages, his religion is maintained, without the regeneration of the spirit.

V. From hence it follows, 1. That a Christian indeed doth not serve God for fear only, but for love ; even for love both of himself, and of his holy work and service ; yea, the strong Christian's love to God and holiness, is not only greater than his love to creatures ; but greater than his fear of wrath and punishment. The love of God constrains him to duty ; love is the fulfilling of the law, therefore the gospel cannot be obeyed without it. He saith not, O that this were no duty, and O that this forbidden thing were lawful, though his flesh say so, the spirit, which is the predominant part, doth not. But he saith, ' O how I love thy law ! O that my ways were so directed that I might keep thy statutes !' For the spirit is willing even when the flesh is weak : he serves not God against his will : but his will is to serve him more and better than he doth : he longs to be perfect, and perfectly to do the will of God, and takes the remnant of his sinful infirmities to be a kind of bondage to him, which he groans to be delivered from : to will even perfection is present with him, though not perfectly ; and though he do not all that he wills : and this is the true meaning of Paul's complaints. Because the flesh wars against the spirit, he cannot do the good that he would ; that is, he cannot be perfect, for so he would be. His love and will excel his practice.

2. The weak Christian also hath more love to God and holiness than to the world and fleshly pleasure : but yet his fear of punishment is greater than his love to God and holiness. To have no love to God, is inconsistent with a state of grace, and so it is to have less love to God than to the world, and less love to holiness than to sin : but to have more fear than love is consistent with sincerity of grace : yea, the weak Christian's love to God and holiness is joined with so much backwardness and averseness, and interrupted with weariness, and with the carnal allurements and diversions of the creature, that he cannot certainly perceive whether his love and willingness be sincere or not. He goes on in a course of duty, but so heavily, that he scarcely knows whether his love or lothing of it be the greater. He goes to it as a sick man to his meat, or labour : all that he doth is with so much pain or indisposedness, that to his feeling his averseness seems greater than his willingness, were it not that necessity makes him willing. For the habitual love and complacency which he hath towards God and duty is so oppressed by fear, and by averseness, that it is not so much felt in act as they.

3. A seeming Christian hath no true love of God and holiness at all, but some ineffectual liking and wishes which are overborn by a greater backwardness, and by a greater love to earthly things ; so that fear alone, without any true ef-

fectual love, is the spring and principle of his religion and obedience. God hath not his heart, when he draws near him with his lips ; he doth more than he would do, if he were not forced by necessity and fear ; and had rather be excused, and lead another kind of life. Though necessity and fear are very helpful to the most sincere yet fear alone, without love or willingness, is a graceless state.

VI. 1. A Christian indeed doth love God in these three gradations : he loves him much for his mercy to himself, and for that goodness which consists in benignity to himself ; but he loves him more for his mercy to the church, and for that goodness which consists in his benignity to the church. But he loves him most of all for his infinite perfections and essential excellencies ; his infinite power, wisdom, and goodness, simply in himself considered. For he knows that love to himself obliges him to returns of love ; especially saving grace : and he knows that the souls of millions are of more worth incomparably than his own, and that God may be much more honoured by them, than by him alone ; and therefore he knows that the mercy to many is greater mercy, and a greater demonstration of the goodness of God, therefore doth render him more amiable to man. Yet he knows that essential perfection and goodness of God, as simply in himself and for himself, is much more amiable than his benignity to the creature ; and that he that is the first efficient, must needs be the ultimate final cause of all things ; and that God is not finally for the creature, but the creature for God, (for all that he needs it not) for of him, and through him, and to him, are all things. As he is infinitely better than ourselves, so he is to be better loved than ourselves. As I love a wise and virtuous person, though he be one I never expect to receive any thing from, and therefore love him for his own sake, and not for his benignity or usefulness to me : so must I love God most for his essential perfections, though his benignity also doth represent him amiable. As he is blindly selfish that would not rather himself be annihilated or perish, than whole kingdoms should all perish, or the sun be taken out of the world ; because that which is best must be loved as best, and therefore be best loved : so is he more blind, who in his estimation prefers not infinite, eternal goodness, before such an imperfect silly creature as himself, or all the world : we are commanded to love our neighbour as ourselves, when God is to be loved with all the heart, and soul, and might, which therefore signifies more than to love him as ourselves ; (or else he were to be loved no more than our neighbour,) so that the strong Christian loves God so much above himself, as that he accounts himself, and all his interests, as nothing in comparison of God, yea, and loves himself more for God than for himself : though his own salvation be loved and desired by him, and God must be loved for his mercy and benignity ; yet that salvation itself which he desires, is nothing else but the love of God : wherein his love is the final felicitating act, and God is the final felicitating object, and the felicity of loving is not first desired ; but the attractive object doth draw out our love, and thereby make us consequentially happy in the enjoying exercise thereof.   Thus God is all and in all to the soul.

2. A weak Christian also loves God as one that is infinitely better than himself and all things ; or else he did not love him at all as God.   But in the exercise he is so much in the minding of himself, and so seldom and weak in the contemplation of God's perfections, that he feels more of his love to himself, than unto God; and feels more of his love to God, as for the benefits which he receives in and by himself, then as for his own perfections ; yea, and often feels the love of himself to work more strongly than his love to the church, and all else in the world.   The care of his own salvation is the highest principle which he ordinarily perceives in any great strength in him ; and he is very little and weakly carried out to the love of the whole church, and to the love of God above himself.

3. A seeming Christian hath a common love of God as he is good, both in himself, unto the world, and unto him.   But this is not for his holiness ; and it is but a general, ineffectual approbation and praise of God, which follows a dead, ineffectual unbelief : but his chief predominant love is always to his carnal self, and the love both of his soul, and of God, is subjected to his fleshly self-love : his chief love to God is for prospering him in the world, and such as is subservient to his sensuality, pride, covetousness, presumption, and false hopes.

VII. 1. A Christian indeed doth practically take this love of God, and the holy expressions of it, to be the very life of his religion, and the very life, beauty, and pleasure of his soul : he makes it his work in the world, and loves himself, but so far as he finds in himself the love of God ; and so far as he finds himself without it, he lothes himself as an unlovely subject : and so far as his prayers and obedience are without it, he looks on them but as unacceptable, lothesome things : therefore he is taken up in the study of

redemption, because he can no where so clearly see the love and loveliness of God, as in the face of a Redeemer, even in the wonders of love revealed in Christ.   And he studies them, that love may kindle love : therefore he delights in the contemplating of God's attributes and infinite perfections ; in the beholding of him in the frame of the creation, and reading his name in the book of his works, that his soul may by such steps, be raised in love and admiration of his Maker.   And as it is a pleasant thing for the eyes to behold the sun or light, so is it to the mind of the Christian indeed, to be frequently and seriously contemplating the nature and glory of God : and the exercise of love in such contemplations, is most of his daily walk with God. Therefore it is also, that he is more taken up in the exercises of thanksgiving, and the praises of the Almighty, than in the lower parts of godliness ; so that though he neglect not confession of sin and humiliation, yet doth he use them but in subserviency to the love and praise of God.   He places not the chief part of his religion in any outward duties, nor in any lower preparatory acts ; nor doth he rest in any of these, however he neglect them not.   But he uses them all to advance his soul in the love of God ; and uses them the more diligently, because the love of God, to which they conduce, as to their proper end, is so high and excellent a work. Therefore in David's psalms you find a heart delighting itself in the praises of God, and in love with his word and works, in order to his praises.

2. The weak Christian is taken up but very little with the lively exercises of love and praise, nor with any studies higher than his own distempered heart : the care of his poor soul, and the complaining of his manifold infirmities, and corruptions, is the most of his religion : and if he set himself to the praising of God, or to thanksgiving, he is as dull and short in it as if it were not his proper work.

3. The seeming Christian lives to the flesh ; and carnal self-love is the active principle of his life ; and he is neither exercised in humiliation nor in praise sincerely, being unacquainted both with holy joy and sorrow : but knowing that he is in the hands of God, to prosper or destroy him, he will humble himself to him to escape his judgments, and praise him with some gladness for the sunshine of prosperity ; and he will seem to be piously thanking God, when he is but rejoicing in the accommodations of his flesh, or strengthening his presumption and false hopes of heaven.

VIII. 1. A Christian indeed is one that is so apprehensive of his lost condition, unworthiness, and utter insufficiency for himself, and of the office, perfection, and sufficiency of Christ, that he hath absolutely put his soul and all his hopes into the hands of Christ, and now lives in him and upon him; as having no life but what he hath from Christ, nor any other way of access to God, or acceptance of his person, or his service, but by him. In him he beholds and delightfully admires the love and goodness of the Father: in him he hath access with boldness unto God: through him the most terrible avenging judge is become a reconciled God, and he that we could not remember but with trembling, is become the most desirable object of our thoughts. He is delightfully employed in prying into the unsearchable mystery: and Christ doth even dwell in his heart by faith; and being rooted and grounded in love, he apprehends with all saints, what is the breadth, and length, and depth, and height, and knoweth the love of Christ, which passeth knowledge. He perceives that he is daily beholden to Christ that he is not in hell, that sin doth not make him like to devils, and that he is not utterly forsaken of God: he feels that he is beholden to Christ for every hour's time, and every mercy to his soul and body, and for all his hope of mercy in this life, or in the life to come. He perceives that he is dead in himself, and that his life is hid with Christ in God. And therefore he is as buried and risen again with Christ; even dead to sin, but alive to God through Jesus Christ. He saith with Paul, ' I am crucified with Christ: nevertheless I live: yet not I, but Christ liveth in me: and the life which I now live in the flesh, I live by the faith of the Son of God, who loved me and gave himself for me.' Thus doth he live as truly and constantly by the second Adam, who is a quickening spirit, as he doth by the first Adam, who was a living soul. This is a confirmed Christian's life.

2. But the weak Christian, though he be also united unto Christ, and live by faith, yet how languid are the operations of that faith! How dark and dull are his thoughts of Christ! How little is his sense of the wonders of God's love revealed to the world, in the mystery of redemption! How little use doth he make of Christ; and how little life receives he from him! How little comfort finds he in believing, in comparison of that which the confirmed find! He is to Christ as a sick person to his food: he only picks here and there a little of the crumbs of the bread of life, to keep him from dying; but is wofully unacquainted with the most powerful works of faith. He is such a believer as is next to an unbeliever, and such a member of Christ, as is next to a mere stranger.

3. And for the seeming Christian, he may understand the letter of the gospel, and number himself with Christ's disciples, and be baptized with water, and have such a faith as is a dead opinion: but he hath not an effectual living faith, nor is baptized with the Holy Ghost; nor is his soul engaged absolutely and entirely in the covenant of Christianity to his Redeemer: he may have a handsome well made image of Christianity, but it is the flesh and sense, and not Christ and faith, by which his life is actuated and ordered.

IX. 1. A Christian indeed doth firmly believe that Christ is a teacher sent from God, that he came from heaven to reveal his Father's will, and to bring life and immortality more fully to light by his gospel; and that if an angel had been sent to tell us of the life to come, and the way thereto, he had not been so credible and venerable a messenger as the Son of God: therefore he takes him alone for his chief teacher, and knows no master on earth but him, and such as he appoints under him: his study in the world is to know a crucified and glorified Christ, and God by him, and he regards no other knowledge, nor uses any other studies but this, and such as are subservient to this. Even when he studies the works of nature, it is as by the conduct of the restorer of nature, and as one help appointed him by Christ, to lead him up to the knowledge of God. Therefore he perceives that Christ is made of God unto us, wisdom as well as righteousness: that Christianity is the true philosophy; and that the wisdom of the world, which is only about worldly things, from worldly principles, to a worldly end, is foolishness with God: he takes nothing for wisdom which tends not to acquaint him more with God, or lead him up to everlasting happiness. Christ is his teacher, either by natural or supernatural revelation, and God is his ultimate end in all his studies, and all that he desires to know in the world. He values knowledge according to its usefulness: and he knows that its chief use is to lead us to the love of God.

2. Though the weak Christian hath the same master, yet alas, how little doth he learn! How oft is he hearkening to the teaching of the flesh, and how carnal and common is much of his knowledge! How little doth he depend on Christ, in his inquiries after the things of nature! How apt is he to think almost as highly of the teaching of Aristotle, Plato, Seneca, or at least of some excellent preacher, as of Christ's! And

to forget that these are but his messengers and instruments, to convey unto us several parcels of that truth, which is his, and not theirs, and which, naturally or supernaturally, they received from him ; and all these candles were lighted by him, who is the sun ! How little doth this weak Christian refer his common knowledge to God, or use it for him or to the furtherance of his own and others' happiness !

3. And the seeming Christian, though materially he may be eminent for knowledge, yet is so far from resigning himself to the teaching of Christ, that he makes even his knowledge of Christian verities to be to him but a common carnal thing, while he knows it but in a common manner, and uses it to the service of the flesh, and never yet learned so much as to be a new creature, nor to love God as God, above the world.

X. 1. A Christian indeed is one whose repentance hath been deep, serious, universal, and unchangeable : it hath gone to the very root of sin, and to the bottom of the sore, and hath not left behind it any reigning unmortified sin, nor any prevalent love to fleshly pleasures : his repentance did not only disgrace his sin, and cast some reproachful words against it, and use confessions to excuse him from mortification, to save its life, and hide it from the mortal blow. Nor doth he only repent of his open sins, and those that are most censured by the beholders of his life ; but he especially perceives the dangerous poison of pride, unbelief, and worldliness, and the want of the love of God, and all his outward and smaller sins, serve to show him the greater malignity of these, and these are the matter of his greatest lamentations. He takes not up a profession of religion, with strong corruptions secretly covered in his heart ; but his religion consists in the death of his corruptions, and the purifying of his heart ; he doth not secretly cherish any sin as too sweet or too profitable to be utterly forsaken, nor overlook it as a small inconsiderable matter. But he feels sin to be his enemy and his disease, and as he desires not one enemy, one sickness, one wound, one broken bone, one serpent in his bed, so he desires not any one sin to be spared in his soul. But saith with David, 'search me, O God, and know my heart ; try me and know my thoughts, and see if there be any wicked way in me ; and lead me in the way everlasting.' He lives in no gross or scandalous sin : and his infirmities are comparatively few and small ; so that if he were not a sharper accuser of himself, than the most observant spectators are (that are just,) there would

little be known by him that is culpable and matter of reproof. He 'walketh in all the commandments and ordinances of God blameless,' as to any notable miscarriage ; 'he is blameless and harmless, as the Son of God, without rebuke, in the midst of a crooked and perverse generation ; among whom he shineth as a light in the world.' The fear, love, and obedience of God, is the work and tenor of his life.

2. But the weak Christian, though he hath no sin but what he hates, and wishes to be delivered from, yet alas, how imperfect is his deliverance ! And how weak is the hatred of his sin, and mixed with so much proneness to it, that his life is much blemished with the spots of his offences. Though his unbelief and pride, and worldliness, are not predominant in him, yet are they, or some of them, still so strong, and fight so much against his faith, humility, and heavenliness, that he can scarcely tell which hath the upper hand ; nor can others that see the failings of his life, discern whether the good or the evil be most prevalent. Though it be heaven which he most seeks, yet earth is so much regarded by him, that his heavenly-mindedness is greatly damped and suppressed by it. Though it be the way of godliness and obedience which he walks in, yet is it with so many stumblings and falls, if not deviations also, that makes him oft a burthen to himself, a shame to his profession, and a snare or trouble to those about him. His heart is like an ill swept house, that hath many a foul corner in it, and his life is like a moth-eaten garment, which hath many a hole, which you may see if you bring it into the light.

3. And for the seeming Christian, his repentance doth but crop the branches, it goes not to the root and heart of his sin : it leaves his fleshly mind and interest in the dominion : it polishes his life, but makes him not a new creature. It casts away those sins which the flesh can spare, and which bring more shame, or loss, or trouble, with them, than worldly honour, gain or pleasure : but still he is a worldling at heart ; and the sins which his fleshly pleasures and felicity consist in, he will hide by confessions and seeming oppositions, but never mortify and forsake. As Judas, that while he followed Christ was yet a thief and a covetous hypocrite.

XI. 1. Hence it follows that a Christian indeed doth heartily love the searching light, that it may fully acquaint him with his sins : he is truly desirous to know the worst of himself : therefore uses the word of God, as a candle to show him what is in his heart ; and brings himself willingly into the light ; he loves the most searching books and preachers; not only because they disclose the faults of other men, but his own: he is not one that loves his pleasant and profitable sins, as to fly the light, lest he should be forced to know them, and so to forsake them: but because he hates them, and is resolved to forsake them, therefore he would know them; therefore he is not only patient under reproofs but loves them, and is thankful to a charitable reprover; and makes a good use even of malicious and passionate reproofs. He saith 'that which I see not, teach thou me.—If I have done iniquity, I will do no more.' His hatred of the sin, and desire to be reformed, suffer not his heart by pride to rise up against the remedy, and reject reproof. Though he will not falsely confess his duty to be his sin, nor take the judgment of every selfish, passionate, or ignorant reprover, to be infallible, nor to be his rule; yet if a judicious, impartial person but suspect him of a fault, he is ready to suspect himself of it, unless he be certain that he is clear. He loves him better that would save him from his sin, than him that would entice him to it; and takes him for his best friend who deals freely with him, and is the greatest enemy to his faults: and a flatterer he takes but for the most dangerous insinuating kind of foe.

2. But the weak Christian, though he hate his sin, and love reformation, and loves the most searching books and preachers, and loves a gentle kind of reproof, yet hath so much pride and selfishness remaining, that any reproof that seems disgraceful to him, goes very hardly down with him; like a bitter medicine to a disordered stomach: if you reprove him before others, or if your reproof be not very carefully expressed; so that it rather extenuate than aggravate his fault, he will be ready to cast it up into your face, and with retortions to tell you of some faults of your own, or some way show you how little he loves it, and how little thanks he gives you for it. If you will not let him alone with his infirmities, he will dislike you, if not fall out with you, and let you know by his smart and impatience, that you have touched him in the sore and galled place. He must be a man of very great skill in managing a reproof, that shall not somewhat provoke him to distaste.

3. For the seeming Christian, this 'is his condemnation, that light is come into the world, and he loveth darkness rather than light, because his deeds are evil.' He comes not to the light, lest his deeds should be discovered and reproved. He likes a searching preacher for others, and loves to hear their sins laid open, if it no way reflect upon himself. But for himself he likes best a general or a smoothing preacher; and he flies from a quick and searching ministry, lest he should be proved and convinced to be in a state of sin and misery. Guilt makes him fear or hate a lively, searching preacher, even as the guilty prisoner hates the judge. He loves no company so well as that which thinks highly of him, and applauds and commends him, and neither by their reproofs nor stricter lives, will trouble his conscience with the remembrance of his sin, or the knowledge of his misery. He will take you for his enemy for telling him the truth, if you go about to convince him of his undone condition, and tell him of his beloved sin: sin is taken to be as himself; it is he that doth evil, and not only sin that dwells in him: therefore all that you say against his sin, he takes it as spoken against himself, and he will defend his sins as he would defend himself: he will hear you till you come to touch himself, as the Jews did by Stephen. When they heard him call them stiffnecked resisters of God, and persecutors, then they were cut to the heart, and grind their teeth at him. And as they did by Paul, 'they gave audience to this word, and then lift up their voices and said, Away with such a fellow from the earth, for it is not fit that he should live.' The priests and pharisees would have laid hands on Christ, when 'they perceived that he spake of them.' And Ahab hated Michaiah, 'because he did not prophesy good of him, but evil.' Deservedly do they perish in their sin and misery, who hate him that would deliver them, and refuse the remedy. 'Whoso loveth instruction loveth knowledge, but he that hateth reproof is brutish.—He that being often reproved, hardeneth his neck, shall suddenly be destroyed, and that without remedy.'

XII. 1. A Christian indeed, is one that unfeignedly desires to attain to the highest degree of holiness, and to be perfectly freed from every thing that is sin. He desires perfection, though not with a perfect desire. He sits not down contentedly in any low degree of grace. He looks on the holiest, how poor soever, with much more reverence and esteem than on the most rich and honourable in the world. And he had far rather be one of the most holy, than one of the most prosperous and great: he had rather be a Paul or Timothy, than a Cæsar or an Alexander. He complains of nothing with so much sorrow, as that he can know and love his God no more. How happy an exchange would he count it, if he had more of the knowledge and love of God though he lost all his wealth and honour in the world. His smallest sins are a greater burden to him, than his greatest corporal wants and sufferings. As Paul, who because he could not perfectly fulfil God's law, and be as good as he would, he cries out as in bondage, ' O wretched man that I am ! who shall deliver me from this body of death?'

2. Though the weak Christian is habitually and resolvedly of the same mind, yet, alas, his desires after perfection are much more languid in him: and he hath too much patience and partiality to some of his sins, and sometimes takes them to be sweet : so that his enmity to his pride, or covetousness, or passion, is much abated, and suffers his sin to waste his grace and wound his conscience, and hinder much of his communion with God. He sees not the odiousness of sin, nor the beauty of holiness, with so clear a sight as the confirmed Christian doth. He hates sin more for the ill effects of it, than for its malignant, hateful nature. He sees not clearly the intrinsic evil that is in sin, which makes it deserve the pains of hell. Nor doth he discern the difference between a holy and unholy soul so clearly as the stronger Christian doth.

3. As for the seeming Christian, though he may approve of perfect holiness in another, and may wish for it himself, when he thinks of it but in the general, and not as it is exclusive and destructive of his beloved sin ; yet when it comes to particulars, he cannot away with it : he is so far from desiring it, that he will not endure it. The name of holiness he likes ; and that preservation from hell which is the consequence of it : but when he understands what it is, he hath no mind of it. That holiness which should cure his ambition and pride, and make him contented with a low condition, he doth not like: he loves not that holiness, which would deprive him of his covetousness, his intemperance in pleasant meats and drinks, his fleshly lusts, and inordinate pleasures ! Nor doth he desire that holiness should employ his soul in the love of God, and in daily prayer and meditating on his word, and raise him to a heavenly life on earth.

XIII. 1. A Christian indeed is one that makes God and heaven the end, reward and motive of his life : he lives not in the world for any thing in the world, but for that endless happiness which the next world only can afford. The reasons which actuate his thoughts, and choice, and all his life, are drawn from heaven. The interest of God and his soul as to eternity, is the ruling interest in him. As a traveller goes all the way, and bears all the difficulties of it, for the sake of the end or place that he is going to : however he may talk of many other matters by the way, so is it with a Christian ; he knows nothing worthy of his life and labours, but that which he hopes for hereafter. This world is too sinful, and too vile and short, to be his felicity. His very trade and work in the world is to lay up a treasure in heaven, 'and to lay up a good foundation against the time to come, and to lay hold on eternal life.' Therefore his very heart is there, and he is employed in seeking and 'setting his affections on the things above, and his conversation and traffic is in heaven. 'He looks not at the things which are seen, which are temporal, but at the things which are not seen, which are eternal.' He is a stranger upon earth, and heaven is to him as his home.

2. The weak Christian also hath the same end, hope, and motive ; and prefers his hopes of the life to come before all the wealth and pleasures of this life : but yet his thoughts of heaven are much more strange and dull : he hath so much doubting and fear yet mixed with his faith and hope, that he looks before him to his everlasting state with backwardness and trouble, and with small desire and delight. He hath so much hope of heaven, as to abate his fears of hell, and make him think of eternity with more quietness, than he could do if he found himself unregenerated : but not so much as to make his thoughts of heaven so free, sweet, and frequent, nor his desires after it so strong, as the confirmed Christian's are. Therefore his duties and his speech of heaven, and his endeavours to obtain it, are all more languid and inconstant : he is much more prone to fall in love with earth, and to entertain the motions of reconciliation to the world, and to have his heart too much set upon some place, or person or thing below, and to be either delighted too much in the possession of it, or afflicted and troubled too much with the loss of it. Earthly things are too much the motives of his life, and the reasons of his joys and griefs : though he hath the true belief of a life to come, and it prevails in the main against the world, yet it is but little that he uses to the commanding, raising, and comforting his soul, in comparison of what a strong believer doth.

3. But the seeming Christian would serve God and mammon, and places his chief and most certain happiness practically upon earth : though speculatively he know and say that heaven is better, yet doth he not practically judge it to be so to him : therefore he loves the world above it, and he doth most carefully ' lay up a treasure on earth,' and is resolved first to seek and secure his portion here below ; and yet he takes heaven for a reserve, as knowing that the world will cast

him off at last, and die he must, there is no remedy ; therefore he takes heaven as next unto the best ; as his second hope, as better than hell, and will go in religion as far as he can, without the loss of his prosperity here ; so that earth and flesh govern and command the design and tenor of his life ; but heaven and his soul shall have all that they can spare ; which may be enough to make him pass with men for eminently religious.

XIV. 1. A Christian indeed is one that having taken heaven for his felicity, accounts no labour or cost too great for the obtaining of it : he hath nothing so dear to him in this world, which he cannot spare and part with for God and the world to come. He doth not only notionally know that nothing should seem too dear or hard for the securing of our salvation ; but he knows this practically, and is resolved accordingly. Though difficulties may hinder him in particular acts, and his executions come not up to the height of his desires, yet he is resolved that he will never break on terms with Christ : there is no duty so hard which he is not willing and resolved to perform ; and no sin so sweet or gainful which he is not willing to forsake : he knows how unprofitable a bargain he makes, who wins the world, and loses his own soul ; and that no gain can ransom his soul, or recompence him for the loss of his salvation. He knows that it is impossible to be a loser by God ; or to purchase heaven at too dear a rate ; he knows that whatsoever it cost him, heaven will fully pay for all : and that it is the worldling's labour, and not the saint's, that is repented of at last. He marvels more at distracted sinners, for making such a stir for wealth, honours, and command, than they marvel at him for making so much ado for heaven. He knows that this world may be too dear bought, but so cannot his salvation ; yea, he knows that even our duty itself, is not our smallest privilege and mercy : and that the more we do for God, the more we receive, and the greater is our gain and honour ; and that the sufferings of believers for righteousness' sake, do not only prognosticate their joys in heaven, but occasion here the greatest joys, that any short of heaven partake of. He is not one that desires the end without the means, and would be saved so it may be on cheap and easy terms : but he absolutely yields to the terms of Christ, and says with Austin, ' Cause me to do what thou commandest, and command what thou wilt.' Though Pelagius contradicted the first sentence, and the flesh the second, yet Augustine owned both ; and so doth every true believer. He greatly complains of his backwardness to obey, but never complains of the strict-

ness of the command. He loves the holiness justness and goodness of the laws, when he bewails the unholiness and badness of his heart : he desires not God to command him less, but desires grace and ability to do more. He is so far from the mind of the ungodly world, who cry out against too much holiness, and making so much ado for heaven, that he desires even to reach to the degree of angels, and would gladly have ' God's will to be done on earth, as it is done in heaven ;' therefore the more desires to be in heaven, that he may do it better.

2. The weak Christian hath the same estimation and resolution : but when it comes to practice, as his will is less confirmed and more corrupted and divided, so little impediments and difficulties are great temptations to him, and stop him more in the way of his obedience. All his duty is much more tedious to him, and all his sufferings are much more burthensome to him, than to confirmed Christians : therefore he is more easily tempted into omissions and impatience, and walks not so evenly, or comfortably, with God. When the spirit is willing, it yields often to the weakness of the flesh, because it is willing in too remiss a degree.

3. But the seeming Christian, though notionally and generally he may approve of strictness, yet secretly at the heart hath always this reserve, that he will not serve God at too dear a rate. His worldly felicity he cannot part with, for all the hopes of the life to come : and yet he will not, he dare not renounce and give up those hopes : therefore he makes himself a religion of the easiest and cheapest parts of Christianity, among which sometimes the strictest opinions may fall out to be one part, so be it they be separated from the strictest practice ; and this easy, cheap religion he will needs believe to be true Christianity and godliness ; and so will hope to be saved upon these terms : though he cannot but know that it is the certain character of a hypocrite, to have any thing nearer and dearer to his heart than God, yet he hopes that it is not so with him, because his convinced judgment can say that God is best and the world is vanity, while yet his heart and affections so much contradict his opinion, as almost to say, there is no God : for his heart knows and loves no God as God, that is, above his worldly happiness. He is resolved to do so much in religion as he finds necessary to delude his conscience, and make himself believe that he is godly and shall be saved ; but when he comes to forsake all and take up the cross, and practise the costliest parts of duty, then you shall see

that mammon was better loved than God, and he will go away sorrowful, and hope to be saved upon easier terms, for he was never resigned absolutely to God.

XV. 1. A confirmed Christian is one that takes self-denial for the one half of his religion : therefore hath bestowed one half of his endeavours to attain and exercise it. He knows that the fall of man was a turning to himself from God ; and that selfishness and want of love to God, are the sum of all corruption and ungodliness : that the love of God and self-denial are the sum of all religion, and that conversion is nothing but the turning of the heart from carnal self to God by Christ : therefore on this hath his care and labour been so successfully laid out, that he hath truly and practically found out something that is much better than himself, and to be loved and preferred before himself; and which is to be his chief ultimate end. He makes not a God of himself any more, but uses himself for God, to fulfil his will, as a creature of his own, that hath no other end and use. He no more prefers himself above all the world, but esteems himself a poor and despicable part of the world ; and more highly values the honour of God, the welfare of the church, and the good of many, than any interest of his own. Though God in nature hath taught him to regard his own felicity and to love himself, and not to seek the glory of God, and the good of many souls, in opposition to his own, yet he hath taught him to prefer them (though in conjunction) much before his own : for reason tells him that man is nothing in comparison of God, and that we are made by him and for him ; and that the welfare of the church or public societies is better, in order to the highest ends, than the welfare of some one. Selfishness in the unregenerated, is like an inflammation which draws the humours from other parts of the body to itself: the interest of God and man are all swallowed up in the regard that men have to self-interest : and the love of God and our neighbour are turned into self-love. But self is as annihilated in the confirmed Christian, so that it rules not his judgment, his affections, or his choice : and he that lived in and to himself, as if God and all the world were but for him, doth now live to God, as one that is good for nothing else, and finds himself in seeking him that is infinitely above himself.

2. The weak Christian hath attained to so much self-denial, that self is not predominant in him against the love of God and his neighbour ; but yet above all other sins, too great a measure of selfishness still remains in him : these words *own*, *mine*, and *self*, are too insignificant with him ; every thing of his own is regarded inordinately, with partiality, and too much selfishness. A word against himself, or an injury to himself, is more to him, than worse against his brother : he is too little mindful of the glory of God, of the public good, and the souls of others ; and even when he is mindful of his own soul, he is too regardless of the souls of many, that by prayer, or exhortation, or other means, he ought to help : as a small candle lights but a little way, and a small fire heats not far off, so is his love so much confined, that it reaches not far from him : he values his friends too much upon their respect to please himself, and loves men too much, as they are partial for him ; and too little upon the pure account of grace, and their love to Christ and service to the church : he easily overvalues his own abilities, and is too confident of his own understanding, and apt to have too high conceits of any opinions that are his own ; he is too apt to be tempted unto uncharitableness, against those that cross him in his interest or way : he is apt to be too negligent in the work of God, when any self-interest doth stand against it ; and too much to seek himself, his own esteem, when he should devote himself to the good of souls, and give up himself to the work of God : though he is not like the hypocrite, that prefers himself before the will of God and the common good, yet selfishness greatly stops, interrupts, and hinders him in God's work ; and any great danger, or loss, or shame, or other concern of his own, doth seem a greater matter to him, and oftener turns him out of the way, than it will with a confirmed Christian. They were not all hypocrites that Paul speaks of in that sad complaint, 'for I have no man like minded to Timothy, who will naturally care for your state ; for all seek their own, not the things which are Jesus Christ's,' that is, they too much seek their own, and not entirely enough the things that are Christ's: which Timothy did naturally, as if he had been born to it ; grace had made the love of Christ, the souls of men, and the good of others, as natural to him, as the love of himself. Alas, how loudly do their own distempers, soul miscarriages, and the divisions and calamities of the church, proclaim, that the weaker sort of Christians have yet too much selfishness, and that self-denial is lamentably imperfect in them.

3. But in the seeming Christian, selfishness is still the predominant principle ; he loves God but for himself ; and he never had any higher end than self: all his religion, his opinions, his

practice is animated by self-love, and governed by it, even by the love of carnal-self: self-esteem, self-conceit, self-love, self-will, self-seeking and self-saving, are the constitution of his heart and life. He will be of that opinion, way and party in religion, which selfishness directs him to choose: he will go no further in religion than self-interest and safety will allow him to go. He can change his friend, turn his love into hatred, and his praises into reproach, whenever self-interest shall require it. He can make himself believe, and labour to make others believe, that the wisest and holiest servants of God are erroneous, hypocrites, and unsufferable, if they but stand cross to his opinions and interest. For he judges of them, and loves or hates them, principally as they conform to his will and interest, or as they are against it: as the godly measure all persons and things by the will and interest of God, so do all ungodly men esteem them as they stand in reference to themselves. When their factious interest required it, the Jews, and especially the pharisees, could make themselves and others believe, that the Son of God himself was a breaker of the law, an enemy to Cæsar, a blasphemer, and unworthy to live on the earth; that Paul was a pestilent fellow, a mover of sedition among the people, a ringleader of a sect, and a profaner of the temple; and which of the prophets and apostles did they not persecute? Because Christ's doctrine crosses the interest of selfish men, therefore the world doth so generally rise up against it with indignation, even as a country will rise against an invading enemy: for he comes to take away that which is dearest to them. Selfishness is so general and deeply rooted, that, except with a few self-denying saints, self-love and self-interest rules the world. If you would know how to please a graceless man, serve but his carnal interest, and you have done it: be of his opinion, or take on you to be so, applaud him, admire him, flatter him, obey him, promote his preferment, honour and wealth, be against his enemies; in a word, make him your God, and sell your soul to gain his favour, and so it is possible you may gain it.

XVI. A Christian indeed hath so far mortified the flesh, and brought all his senses and appetites into subjection to sanctified reason, as that there is no great rebellion or perturbation in his mind but a little matter, a holy thought, or a word from God, presently rebukes and quiets his inordinate desires: the flesh is as a well broken horse, that goes on his journey obediently and quietly, and not with striving and chasing, and

vexatious resisting: though still flesh will be flesh, and will be weak, and will fight against the spirit, so that we cannot do all the good we would; yet in the confirmed Christian, it is so far tamed and subdued, that its rebellion is much less, and its resistance weaker, and more easily overcome: it causes not any notable unevenness in his obedience, or blemishes in his life; it is no other than consists with a readiness to obey the will of God. 'They that are Christ's have crucified the flesh, with the affections and lusts thereof: they run not as uncertainly; they fight not as one that beats the air; but they keep under their bodies, and bring them into subjection, lest by any means they should be castaways: they put on the Lord Jesus Christ, and make no provision for the flesh to fulfil the lusts thereof.' As we see to a temperate man how sweet and easy temperance is, when to a glutton or drunkard, or riotous liver, it is exceeding hard; so it is in all other points with a confirmed Christian. He hath so far crucified the flesh, that it is as dead to its former lusts; and so far mastered it, that it easily and quickly yields. This makes the life of such a Christian not only pure, but very easy to him, in comparison of other men's. Nay, more than this, he can use his sense, as he can use the world, the objects of sense, in subserviency to faith and his salvation. His eye but opens a window to his mind, to hold and admire the Creator in his work. His taste of the sweetness of the creatures is but a means, by which the sweeter love of God doth pass directly to his heart. His sense of pleasure is but the passage of spiritual, holy pleasure to his mind. His sense of bitterness and pain is but the messenger to tell his heart of the bitterness and vexatiousness of sin. As God in the creation of us, made our senses but as the inlet and passage for himself into our minds, even as he made all the creatures to represent him to us by this passage; so grace restores our very senses, with the creature, to this their holy original use; that the goodness of God, through the goodness of the creature, may pass to our hearts, and be the effect and end of all.

2. But, for the weak Christian, though he have mortified the deeds of the body by the spirit, and live not after the flesh, but be freed from its captivity or reign, yet hath he such remnants of concupiscence and sensuality, as make it a far harder matter to him to live in temperance, deny his appetite, govern his senses, and restrain them from rebellion and excess: he is like a weak man upon an ill ridden headstrong horse, who hath much ado to keep his saddle and keep

his way. He is more strongly inclined to fleshly lusts, or excess in meat, or drink, or sleep, or sports, or some fleshly pleasure, than the mortified temperate person is, and therefore is more frequently guilty of some excess ; so that this life is a very tiresome conflict, and very uneasy to himself, because the less the flesh is mortified, the more able it is to raise perturbations, and to put faith and reason to a continual fight. Most of the scandals and blemishes of his life arise from hence, even the successes of the flesh against the Spirit ; so that, though he live not in any gross or wilful sins, yet in lesser measures of excess he is too frequently overtaken. How few be there that in meat and sleep do not usually exceed their measure ! They are easily tempted to libertine opinions, which indulge the flesh, having a weaker preservative against them than stronger Christians have.

3. But the seeming Christian is really carnal. The flesh is the predominant part with him ; and the interest of the flesh is the ruling interest. He washes away the outward filth, and, in hope of salvation, will be as religious as the flesh will give him leave ; he will deny it in some smaller matters, and will serve it in a religious way, and not in so gross and impudent a manner as the atheists and openly profane. But for all that he never conquered the flesh indeed ; but seeks its prosperity more than the pleasing of God and his salvation : and among prayers and sermons, holy conference, and books, yea, and formal fastings too, he is serving the flesh, with so much the more dangerous impenitency, by how much the more his cloak of formality hinders him from the discerning of his sin ; many a one that is of unblemished reputation in religion, doth constantly serve his appetite in meat and drink, though without any notable excess, and his fleshly mind in the pleasure of his dwelling, wealth and accommodations, as much as some profane ones do, if not much more. Whenever it comes to a parting trial, they will show that the flesh was the ruling part, and will venture their souls to secure its interest.

XVII. 1. Hence it follows that a Christian indeed prefers the means of his spiritual benefit and salvation incomparably before all corporal ease and pleasures. He had rather dwell under the teaching and guidance of an able experienced pastor, though it be cross to his prosperity and worldly gain, than to live under an ignorant or dead-hearted preacher, when it furthers his trading or more accommodates his flesh : though yet he must not remove when God lays any restraint upon him, by his duty to his family, or others :

he had rather, if he be a servant, dwell in a family where he may do or receive most spiritual good, than in a carnal family, where he may have more ease, better fare, and greater wages. If he be to marry, he had rather have one that hath wisdom and piety without wealth, than one that hath riches without wisdom and piety. He is more glad of an opportunity, in public or private, for the profit of his soul, than of a feast, or a good bargain, or an opportunity for some gain in worldly things.

2. The weak Christian is of the same mind in the main. He values mercies and helps for his soul, above those for his body : but it is with less zeal and more indifference : and therefore is more easily and frequently drawn to the omitting of spiritual duties, and neglect of spiritual helps and mercies ; and goes to them with more averseness, and as driven by necessity, and is much less sensible of his loss when he misses of any such spiritual helps.

3. But the seeming Christian, being a real worldling, doth serve God and mammon ; and mammon with the first and best : he had rather miss a sermon than a good bargain ; he had rather dwell where he may thrive best, or have most ease and pleasure, than where he may find the greatest helps for heaven ; he will be religious, but it must be with an easy, a pleasant, and merry religion ; which may not be too niggardly with his flesh, nor use it too strictly ; unless when one day's austerity may procure him an indulgence for his liberty all the week following. He will make his bargain with Christ so as to be sure that he may not lose by him : and he will not believe that God is pleased with that which is much displeasing to his flesh.

XVIII. 1. The Christian indeed is one that is crucified to the world, and the world is as a crucified thing to him. He hath overcome the world by faith, and follows Christ in the pursuit of it, to a perfect conquest. He hath seen through all its glossing vanity, and foreseen what it will prove at last. He hath found that it cannot quiet conscience, nor reconcile the guilty soul to God, nor save it from his consuming wrath ; nor serve instead of God or heaven, of Christ or grace ; but will cast off its servants in their last extremity, naked and desolate, into remediless despair : therefore he is resolvedly at a point with all things under the sun : let them take the world for their portion and felicity that will : for his part he accounts all things in it dung and dross in comparison of Christ and things eternal. All the preferments, honours, command, wealth, and greatness of the world, do not seem to him a bait considerable, to make a wise man once question whether he should persevere in faithfulness to God, or to tempt him to commit one wilful sin: he would not speak, or own a lie, or approve the sin of another, for all that worldlings enjoy in their greatest prosperity while they live. He accounts his peace with God and conscience, and his communion with Christ in the greatest poverty, to be incomparably better than all the pleasures and profits of sin; yea, the very reproach of Christ is better to him than all the treasures of court or country. Grace hath mortified and annihilated the world to him: and that which is dead and nothing, can do nothing with him against God and his soul. He looks on it as a dead animal, which dogs may love and fight for, but is unfit to be the food of man: he is going to the land of promise, and therefore will not contend for an inheritance in this howling wilderness. Whether he be high or low, rich or poor, are so small a part of his concerns, that he is almost indifferent to them, farther than as the interest of God and souls may accidentally be concerned in them. The world set against God, heaven, and holiness, weighs no more in his estimation, than a feather that is put in the balance against a mountain, or all the world. He feels no great force in such temptations, as would draw him to win the world and lose his soul. His eye and heart are where his God and treasure is, above; and worldly wealth and greatness are below him, even under his feet: he thinks not things temporal worth the looking at, in comparison of things eternal. He thinks that their money and riches deservedly perish with them, who think all the money in the world to be a thing comparable with grace.

2. The weak Christian is of the same judgment and resolution in the main; but yet the world retains a greater interest in his heart; it grieves him more to lose it; it is a stronger temptation to him: to deny all the preferments, and honours, and riches of it, seems a great matter to him; and he does it with more striving and less ease; and sometimes the respect of worldly things prevails with him in lesser matters, to wound his conscience, and makes work for repentance; and such are so entangled in worldly cares, and prosperity tastes so sweet with them, that grace even languishes and falls into a consumption, and almost into a swoon. So much do some such let out our hearts to the world, which they renounced, and scrape for it with so much care and eagerness, and contend with others about their rights, that they seem to

the standers-by to be as worldly as worldlings themselves are; and become a shame to their profession, making ungodly persons say, your godly professors are as covetous as any.

3. But the seeming Christians are the servants of the world; when they have learned to speak hardest of it, it hath their hearts: heaven, as I said before, is valued but as a reserve, when they know they can keep the world no longer: they have more sweet and pleasing thoughts and speeches of the world, than they have of God and the world to come: it hath most of their hearts when God is most preferred by their tongues: there it is that they are daily laying up their treasure, and there they must leave it at the parting hour, when they go naked out as they came in: the love of deceitful riches chokes the word of God, and it withers in them, and becomes unfruitful. They go away sorrowful because of their beloved riches, when they should part with all for the hopes of heaven, yea, though they are beggars, that never have a day's prosperity in the world; for all that, they love it better than heaven, and desire that which they cannot get; because they have not an eye of faith, to see that better world which they neglect, therefore take it for an uncertain thing: nor are their carnal natures suitable to it, therefore they mind it not. When an hypocrite is at the best, he is but a religious worldling; the world is nearer to his heart than God is, but pure religion keeps a man unspotted with the world.

XIX. 1. A confirmed Christian is one that still sees the end in all that he doth, and that is before him in his way; and looks not at things as at the present they seem or relish to the flesh, or to short-sighted men; but as they will appear and be judged of at last. The first letter makes not the word, nor the first word the sentence, without the last. Present time is quickly past, therefore he less regards what things seem at present, than what they will prove to all eternity, when temptations offer him a bait to sin, with the present profit, or pleasure, or honour, he sees at once the final shame; he sees all worldly things as they are seen by a dying man, and as after the general conflagration they will be. He sees the godly in his adversity and patience, as entering into his master's joys; he sees the derided, vilified saint, as ready to stand justified by Christ at his right hand; and the lies of the malicious world as ready to cover themselves with shame: he sees the wicked in the height of their prosperity, as ready to be cut down and withered, and their pampered flesh to turn to dust; and their filthy and malicious souls to stand condemned by Christ at his left hand; and to near, 'go, ye cursed, into everlasting fire, prepared for the devil and his angels.' Therefore it is that he values grace, because he knows what it will be ; therefore it is that he flies from sin, because he knows the terrors of the Lord, and what it will prove to the sinner in the end ; and how sinners themselves will curse the day that ever they did commit it ; and wish, when it is too late, that they had chosen the holiness and patience of the saints : therefore it is that he pities rather than envies the prosperous enemies of the church, because he foresees what the ' end will be of them that obey not the gospel of Christ. And if the righteous be scarcely saved, where shall the ungodly and sinner appear ?' If the wicked unbelievers saw the ending of all things as he doth, they would be all then of his mind and way. This puts so much life into his prayers, his obedience, and patience, because he sees the end in all.

2. The weak Christian doth the same in the main, so far as to turn his heart from things temporal to things eternal; and to resolve him in his principal choice, and to conduct the course of his life towards heaven. But yet in particular actions he is often stopped in present things, and forgetfully loses sight of the end, and so is deluded and enticed into sin, for want of seeing that which should have preserved him. He is like one that travels over hills and valleys, who when he is upon the hills doth see the place that he is going to ; but when he comes into the valleys it is out of his sight. Too often the weak Christian thinks of things as they appear at the present, with little sense of the change that is near : when he sees the baits of sin, whether riches or beauty, meat or drink, or any thing that is pleasing to the senses ; the remembrance of the end doth not so quickly and powerfully work, to prevent his deceived imaginations, as it ought. And when poverty, or shame, or sufferings, or sickness, are presented to him, the foresight of the end is not so speedy and powerful in clearing his judgment, settling his resolution, and preventing his misapprehension and trouble, as it ought. Hence comes his frequent mistakes and falls ; and herein consists much of that foolishness which he confesses when repentance brings him to himself.

3. But the seeming Christian hath so dim and doubtful a foresight of the end, and it is so frequently out of his mind, that things present carry away his heart, and have the greatest power and interest with him ; and are most regarded and sought after in this life. For he is purblind, not seeing afar off, as it is said; he wants that faith which is the substance of things hoped for, and the evidence of things unseen ; things promised in another world seem to him too uncertain, or too far off, to be preferred before all the happiness of this world ; he is resolved to make his best of that which he hath in hand, and to prefer possession before such hopes. Little doth his heart perceive what a change is near, and how the face of all things will be altered! How sin will look, and how the minds of sinners will be changed, and what all the riches, pleasures, and honours of the world, will appear at the latter end! He foresees not the day when the slothful, the worldly, the fleshly, the proud, and the enemies of godliness, shall all wish in vain ; 'O that we had laid up our treasure in heaven, and laboured for the food that perishes not, and had set less by all the vanities of the world ; and had imitated the holiest and most mortified believers! Though the hypocrite can himself foretell all this, and talk of it to others, yet his belief of it is so dead, and his sensuality so strong, that he lives by sense, and not by that belief: and present things are practically preferred by him, and bear the sway, so that he needs those warnings of God, as well as the profane, 'O that they were wise, that they understood this, and that they would consider their latter end. He is one of the foolish ones, who are seeking oil for their lamps when it is too late, and are crying out, 'Lord, Lord, open to us,' when the door is shut; and will not know the time of their visitation, nor know effectually in this their day the things which belong to their everlasting peace.

XX. 1. The Christian indeed is one that lives upon God alone ; his faith is divine ; his love, obedience, and confidence, are divine ; his chief converse is divine ; his hopes and comforts are divine. As it is God that he depends on, trusts to, and studies to please above all the world, so it is God's approbation that he takes up with for his justification and reward. He took him for his absolute governor and judge, and full felicity, in the day when he took him for his God. He can live in peace without man's approbation. If men are never acquainted with his sincerity, or virtues, or good deeds, it doth not discourage him nor hinder him from his holy course ; he is therefore the same in secret as in public, because no place is secret from God. If men turn his greatest virtues or duties to his reproach, and slander him, and make him odious to men, and represent him as they did Paul, 'a pestilent fellow, a mover of sedition, and the ring-leader of a sect,' and make him as the filth of the world, and the off-scouring of all things, this changes him not, for it changes not his felicity, nor doth he miss of his reward. Read the words in the text: though he hath so much suspicion of his own understanding, and reverence for wiser men's, that he will be glad to learn, and will hear reason from any one: yet praise and dispraise are matters of very small regard with him; and as to himself, he accounts it but a small thing to be judged of men, whether they justify or condemn him; because they are fallible, and have not the power of determining any thing to his great interest or detriment; nor is it their judgment by which he stands or falls, he hath a more dreadful or comfortable judgment to prepare for: man is of small account with him in comparison of God.

2. Though with the weakest true Christian it is so also as to the predominancy of God's esteem and interest in him, yet is his weakness daily visible in the culpable effects. Though God have the chief place in his esteem, yet man hath much more than his due. The thoughts and words of men seem to such of far greater importance than they should. Praise and dispraise, favours and injuries, are things which affect their hearts too much; they bear not the contempts and wrongs of men with so quiet and satisfied a mind, as beseems those that live upon God. They have so small experience of the comforts of God in Christ, that they are tasting the deeper of other delights, and spare them not so easily as they ought to do: God, without friends, or house, or land, or maintenance, or esteem in the world, doth not fully quiet them; but there is a deal of peevish impatience left in their minds, though it doth not drive them away from God.

3. But the seeming Christian can better take up with the world alone than with God alone; God is not so much missed by him as the world; he always breaks with Christ when it comes to forsaking all; he is godly notionally and professedly, and therefore may easily say that God is his portion, and enough for those that put their trust in him; but his heart never consented truly to reduce these words to practice. When it comes to the trial, the praise or dispraise of man, and the prosperity or matters of the world, signify more with him than the favour or displeasure of God; and can do more with him. Christ, riches, and esteem, he could be content with; but he cannot away with a naked Christ alone. Therefore he is indeed a practical atheist, even when he seems most religious: for if he

had ever taken God for his God indeed, he had certainly taken him as his portion, felicity, and all; and therefore as enough for him without the creature.

XXI. 1. For all this it follows that a Christian indeed hath with himself devoted all that he hath to God, and so all that he hath is sanctified: he is only in doubt ofttimes in particular cases, what God would have him do with himself and his estate; but never in doubt whether they are to be wholly employed for God, in obedience to his will, so far as he can know it; and therefore doth estimate every creature and condition, purely as it relates unto God and life eternal. 'Holiness to the Lord' is written upon all that he hath and doth; he takes it as sent from God, and uses it as his master's goods and talents, not chiefly for himself, but for his master's ends and will: God appears to him in the creature, and is the life, sweetness, and glory of the creature to him: his first question in every business he undertakes, or every place or condition that he chooses, is, how it conduces to the pleasing of God, and to his spiritual ends; 'whether he eateth or drinketh, or whatever he doth, he doth all to the glory of God.' The image engraven on his heart is the name of God, with 'of him, and through him, and to him are all things, to him be glory for ever. Amen.' He lives as a steward that uses not his own, though yet he have a sufficient reward for his fidelity; and he keeps accounts both of his receiving and laying out, and reckons all to be worse than lost, which he finds not expended on his Lord's account. For himself he asks not that which is sweetest to the flesh, but that which is fittest to his end and work; and therefore desires not riches for himself, but his daily bread, and food convenient for him; and having food and raiment is therewith content,' having taken godliness for his gain. He asks not for superfluity, nor for any thing to consume on his lusts, nor to become provision for his flesh, to satisfy the desires thereof. But as a runner in his race desires not any provisions which may hinder him; and 'therefore forgetting the things which are behind (the world which he hath turned his back upon) he reacheth forth to the things which are before (the crown of glory), and presseth toward the mark, for the prize of the high calling of God in Christ Jesus:' not turning an eye to any thing that would stop him in his course. Thus while he is employed about things below, his mind and conversation is heavenly and divine, while all things are estimated and used purely for God and heaven.

2. But the weak Christian, though he have all

this in desire, and be thus affected and resolved in the main, and lives to God in the scope and course of his life, yet is too often looking aside, and valuing the creature carnally for itself; and oft-times uses it for the pleasing of the flesh, and almost like a common man; his house, land, friends, and pleasures, are relished too carnally, as his own accommodations; and though he walk not after the flesh, but after the Spirit, yet he hath too much of the fleshly taste, and is greatly out in his accounts with God; and turns many a thing from his master's use to the service of the flesh; and though he be not as the slothful wicked servant, yet is it but little improvement that he makes of his talent.

3. But the seeming Christian being carnal and selfish, while his notions and professions are spiritual and divine, and his selfish and fleshly interest being predominant, it must needs follow that he estimates all things principally as they respect his fleshly interest, and uses them principally for his carnal self, even when in the manner he seems to use them most religiously, as I have said before, and so to the defiled nothing is pure.

XXII. 1. A Christian indeed hath a promptitude to obey, and a ready compliance of his will to the will of God. He hath not any great averseness and withdrawing, and doth not the good which he doth with much backwardness and striving against it; but as in a well ordered watch or clock, the spring or balance easily sets all the wheels a going, and the first wheel easily moves the rest: so is the will of a confirmed Christian presently moved, as soon as he knows the will of God. He stays not for other moving reasons; God's will is his reason. This is the habit of subjection and obedience, which makes him say, 'Speak, Lord, for thy servant heareth;' and 'Lord, what wouldst thou have me do?' And 'teach me to do thy will, O God. I delight to do thy will, O God; yea, thy law is within my heart.' The law written in our heart is nothing else but the knowledge of God's laws, with this habit or promptitude to obey them, the special fruit of the Spirit of grace.

2. But a weak Christian, though he love God's will and way, and be sincerely obedient to him; yet in many particulars, where his corruption contradicts, hath a great deal of backwardness and striving of the flesh against the spirit; and there needs many words and many considerations, and vehement persuasions; yea, and sharp afflictions sometimes to bring him to obey: and he is anxious to drive on his backward heart, and hath frequent use for the rod and spur, and therefore is more slow and uneven in his obedience.

3. The seeming Christian is forward in those easy, cheaper parts of duty, which serve to delude his carnal heart, and quiet him in a worldly life; but he is so backward to thorough, sincere obedience in the most flesh-displeasing parts of duty, that he is never brought to it at all; but either he will fit his opinions in religion to his will, and will not believe them to be duties, or else he will do something like them in a superficial, formal way; but the thing itself he will not do. For he is more obedient to his carnal mind and lusts, than he is to God, and much more forward to sacrifice than obedience.

XXIII. 1. A Christian indeed daily delights himself in God, and finds more solid content and pleasure in his commands and promises, than in all this world; his duties are sweet to him, and his hopes are sweeter. Religion is not a tiresome task to him, the yoke of Christ is easy to him, his burden light, and his commandments are not grievous. That which others take as physic, for mere necessity, against their wills, he goes to as a feast, with appetite and delight; he prays because he loves to pray; and he thinks and speaks of holy things, because he loves to do it. Hence it is that he is so much in holy duty, and so unwearied, because he loves it, and takes pleasure in it. As voluptuous persons are oft and long at their sports, or merry company, because they love them, and take pleasure in them: so are such Christians oft and long in holy exercises, because their hearts are set upon them as their recreation, and the way and means of their felicity. If it be a delight to a studious man to read those books which most clearly open the most abstruse mysteries of the sciences, or to converse with the most wise and learned men: and if it be a delight to men to converse with their dearest friends, or to hear from them and read their letters, no marvel if it be a delight to a Christian indeed, to read the gospel mysteries of love, and to find there the promises of everlasting happiness, and to see in the face of Jesus Christ the clearest image of the eternal deity; and foresee the joys which he shall have for ever. He sticks not in superficial formality, but breaking the shell, doth feed upon the kernel. It is not bare external duty which he is taken up with, nor any mere creature that is his content; but it is God in creatures and ordinances that he seeks and lives upon; and therefore it is that religion is so pleasant to him. He would not change his heavenly delights, which he finds in the exercise of faith, hope, and love to God, for all the carnal pleasures of this world; he had rather be a door-keeper in the house of God, than dwell in the tents or palaces of wickedness. A day in God's court is better to him than a thousand in the court of the greatest prince on earth. He is not a stranger to the joy in the Holy Ghost, in which the kingdom of God in part consists. 'In the multitude of his thoughts within him, the comforts of God delight his soul.—His meditation of God is sweet, and he is glad in the Lord.' The freest and sweetest of his thoughts and words run out upon God and the matters of salvation. The word of God is sweeter to him than honey, and better than thousands of gold and silver. And because his delight is in the law of the Lord, therefore he meditates in it day and night, he sees great reason for all those commands, 'rejoice evermore, let the righteous be glad, let them rejoice before God, yea, let them exceedingly rejoice. Be glad in the Lord and rejoice, ye righteous: and shout for joy all that are upright in heart.' He is sorry for the poor unhappy world, that have no better things than meat, drink, clothes, house, land, money, lust, play, and domineering over others, to rejoice in; and heartily he wishes that they had but a taste of the saint's delights, that it might make them abandon their luscious, unclean, unwholesome pleasures. One look to Christ, one promise of the gospel, one serious thought of the life which he must live with God for ever, doth afford his soul more solid comfort than all the kingdoms on earth can afford. Though he live not continually in these high delights, yet peace with God, peace of conscience, and some delight in God, and godliness, is the ordinary temperature of his soul, and higher degrees are given him in season for his cordials and his feasts.

2. But the weak Christian hath little of these spiritual delights; his ordinary temper is to apprehend that God and his ways are indeed most delectable; his very heart acknowledges that they are worthiest and fittest to be the matter of his delights: and if he could attain assurance of his special interest in the love of God and his part in Christ and life eternal, he would then rejoice in them indeed, and would be more glad than if he were the lord of all the world: but in the mean time, either his fears and doubts are damping his delights; or else, (which is much worse), his appetite is dull, and God and holiness relish not with him half so sweetly as they do with the confirmed Christian; and he is too busy in tasting of fleshly and forbidden pleasures, which yet more deprave his appetite, and dull his de-

sires to the things of God; so that though in his estimation, choice, resolution and endeavour, he much prefers God before the world; yet as to any delightful sweetness in him, it is but little that he tastes. He loves God with a desiring love, and with a seeking love, but with very little of a delighting love. The remnant of corrupt and alien affections weaken his affections to the things above; and his infant measure of spiritual life, joined with many troublesome diseases, allow him very little of the joy of the Holy Ghost. Nay, perhaps he hath more grief, fear, doubts, trouble, and perplexity of mind, than ever he had before he turned unto God, and perhaps he hath yet less pleasure in God than he had before in sin and sensuality. Because he had his sin in a state of fruition, but he hath God only in a seeking, hoping state; he had the best of sin, and all that ever it will afford him; but he hath yet none of the full felicity which he expects in God: the fruition of him is yet but in the prospect of hope. His sensual, sinful life was in its maturity, and the object present in its most alluring state; but his spiritual life of faith and love is but yet in its weak beginnings, and the object absent from our sight: he is so busy at first in blowing up his little spark, not knowing whether the fire will kindle or go out, that he hath little of the use or pleasure either of its light or warmth. Infants come crying into the world, and afterwards oftener cry than laugh: their senses and reason are not yet perfected or exercised to partake of the pleasures of life. And when they come to know what laughter is, they will laugh and cry almost in a breath: and those weak Christians that come to taste of joy and pleasure in their religious state, it is commonly but as a flash of lightning, which leaves them as dark as they were before.

Sometimes in the beginning, upon their first apprehensions of the love of God in Christ, and of the pardon of their sins, and the privileges of their new condition, and the hopes of everlasting joy, their hearts are transported with unspeakable delight; which is partly from the newness of the thing and partly because God will let them have some encouraging taste to draw them further, and to convince them of the difference between the pleasures of sin and the comforts of believing: but these first rejoicings soon abate, and turn into a life of doubts, fears, griefs, and care, till they are grown to greater understanding, experience, and settledness in the things of God; the root must grow greater and deeper, before it will bear a greater top. Those Christians that in the weakness of grace have frequent joys, are usually persons whose weak and passionate nature doth occasion it (some women especially), that have strong fancies and passions, are always passionately affected with whatsoever they apprehend. These are like a ship that is tossed in a tempest; that is one time lifted up as to the clouds, and presently cast down as into an infernal gulf: they are one day in great joy, and quickly after in as great perplexity and sorrow, because their comforts or sorrows follow their present feeling, or mutable apprehensions. But when they come to be confirmed Christians, they will keep a more constant judgment of themselves, and their own condition, and constantly see their grounds of comfort; and when they cannot raise their souls to any high and passionate joys, they yet walk in a settled peace of soul, and in such competent comforts, as make their lives to be easy and delightful; being well pleased and contented with the happy condition that Christ hath brought them to, and thankful that he left them not in those foolish, vain, pernicious pleasures, which were the way to endless sorrows.

3. But the seeming Christian seeks and takes up his chief contentment in some carnal thing: if he be so poor and miserable as to have nothing in possession that can much delight him, he will hope for better days hereafter, and that hope shall be his chief delight; or if he have no such hope, he will be without delight, and show his love to the world and flesh, by mourning for that which he cannot have, as others do in rejoicing in what they possess; and he will, in such a desperate case of misery, be such to the world as the weak Christian is to God, who hath a mourning and desiring love, when he cannot reach to an enjoying and delighting love. His carnal mind most savours the things of the flesh, and therefore in them he finds or seeks his chief delights. Though yet he may have also a delight in his superficial kind of religion, his hearing, reading, and praying, and in his ill-grounded hopes of life eternal: but all this is but subordinate to his chief earthly pleasure: 'yet they seek me daily, and delight to know my ways, as a nation that did righteousness, and forsook not the ordinances of their God; they ask of me the ordinances of justice; they take delight in approaching unto God.' And yet all this was subjected to a covetous oppressing mind: 'he that received the seed into stony places, the same is he that heareth the word, and anon with joy receiveth it, yet hath he not root in himself, but dureth for a while, for when tribulation or persecution ariseth because of the word, by and by

he is offended.' Whereby it appears that his love to the word, was subjected to his love to the world.

Object. But there are two sorts of people that seem to have no fleshly delights at all, and yet are not in the way to salvation, viz. the Quakers and Behmenists, who live in great austerity, and some of the religious orders of the Papists, who afflict their flesh.

Answ. Some of them undergo their fastings and penance for a day, that they may sin the more quietly all the week after; and some of them proudly comfort themselves with the fancies and conceit of being and appearing more excellent in austerity than others; and all these take up with a carnal sort of pleasure. As proud persons are pleased with their own, or others' conceits, of their beauty, or wit, or worldly greatness; so prouder persons are pleased with their own and others' conceits of their holiness. And verily they have their reward. But those of them that place their chief happiness in the love of God, and the eternal fruition of him in heaven, and seek this sincerely according to their helps and power, though they are misled into some superstitious errors, I hope I may number with those that are sincere; notwithstanding their errors and the ill effect of them.

XXIV. 1. A confirmed Christian ordinarily discerns the sincerity of his own heart, and consequently hath some well grounded assurance of the pardon of his sins, and of the favour of God, and of his everlasting happiness; and therefore no wonder if he live a peaceable and joyful life. For his grace is not so small as to be undiscernable, nor is it as a sleepy buried seed or principle; but it is almost a continual act: and they that have a great degree of grace, and also keep it in lively exercise, seldom doubt of it. Besides, that they blot not their evidence by so many infirmities and falls. They are more in the light, and have more acquaintance with themselves, and more sense of the abundant love of God, and of his exceeding mercies, than weak Christians have; and therefore must needs have more assurance. They have boldness of access to the throne of grace, without irreverent contempt. They have more of the spirit of adoption, and therefore more childlike confidence in God, and can call him Father with greater freedom and comfort than any others can; 'and we know that we are of God, and that the whole world lieth in wickedness.'

2. But the weak Christian hath so small a degree of grace, and so much corruption, and his grace is so little in act, and his sin so

much, that he seldom, if ever, attains to any well-grounded assurance, till he attain to a greater measure of grace. He differs so little from the seeming Christian, that neither himself nor others certainly discern the difference. When he searches after the truth of his faith, love, and heavenly-mindedness, he finds so much unbelief and averseness from God, and earthly-mindedness, that he cannot be certain which of them is predominant; and whether the interest of this world or that to come, bear the sway. So that he is often in perplexities and fears, and more often in a dull uncertainty. And if he seem at any time to have assurance, it is usually but an ill grounded persuasion of the truth; though it be true which he apprehends, when he takes himself to be the child of God, yet it is upon unsound reasons that he judges so, or else upon sound reasons weakly and uncertainly discerned; so that there is commonly much of security, presumption, fancy, or mistake, in his greatest comforts. He is not in a condition fit for full assurance, till his love and obedience be more full.

2. But the seeming Christian cannot possibly in that estate, have either certainty, or good probability that he is a child of God, because it is not true: his seeming certainty is merely self-deceit, and his greatest confidence is but presumption, because the Spirit of Christ is not within him, and therefore he is certainly none of his.

XXV. 1. The assurance of a confirmed Christian increases his alacrity and diligence in duty, and is always seen in his more obedient, holy, fruitful life. The sense of the love and mercy of God, is as the rain upon the tender grass. He is never so fruitful, so thankful, so heavenly, as when he hath the greatest certainty that he shall be saved. The love of God is then shed abroad upon his heart by the Holy Ghost, which makes him abound in love to God. He is the more stedfast, unmoveable, and always abounding in the work of the Lord, when he is most certain that his labour shall not be in vain in the Lord.

2. But the weak Christian is unfit yet to manage assurance well, and therefore it is that it is not given him; graces must grow proportionably together. If he be but confidently persuaded that he is justified and shall be saved, he is very apt to gather some consequence from it, that tends to security and to the remitting of his watchfulness and care: he is ready to be the bolder with sin, and stretch his conscience, and omit some duties, and take more fleshly liberty and ease, and think, Now I am a child of God, I am out of danger, I am sure I cannot totally fall away. And though his judgment conclude

not, 'therefore I may venture further upon worldly, fleshly pleasures, and need not be so strict and diligent as I was,' yet his heart and practice thus conclude. And he is most obedient when he is most in fear of hell, and he is worst in his heart and life, when he is most confident that all his danger is past.

3. But the seeming Christian, though he have no assurance, is hardening in his carnal state by his presumption. Had he but assurance to be saved without a holy life, he would cast off that very image of godliness which he yet retains. The conceit of his own sincerity and salvation, is that which deludes and undoes him. What sin would not gain, or pleasure draw him to commit, if he were but sure to be forgiven? It is fear of hell that causes that seeming religion which he hath: therefore if that fear be gone, all is gone; and all his piety, and diligence, and righteousness, is come to nought.

XXVI. 1. For all his assurance, a confirmed Christian is so well acquainted with his manifold imperfections, and daily failings, and great unworthiness, that he is very low and vile in his own eyes; and therefore can easily endure to be low and vile in the eyes of others: he hath a constant sense of the burthen of his remaining sin; especially he doth even abhor himself, when he finds the averseness of his heart to God, and how little he knows of him, and how little he loves him, in comparison of what he ought, and how little of heaven is upon his heart, and how strange and backward his thoughts are to the life to come. These are as fetters upon his soul; he daily groans under them as a captive, that he should be yet so carnal, and unable to shake off the remnant of his infirmities, as if he were sold under sin, that is, in bondage to it; he hates himself more for the imperfections of his love and obedience to God, than hypocrites do for their reigning sin. And O how he longs for the day of his deliverance. He thinks it no great injury for another to judge of him as he judges of himself, even to be less than the least of all God's mercies: he is more troubled for being overpraised and overvalued, than for being dispraised and vilified; as thinking those that praise him are more mistaken, and lay the more dangerous snare for his soul. For he hath a special antipathy to pride; and wonders that any rational man can be so blind as not to see enough to humble him: for his own part, in the midst of all God's graces, he sees in himself so much darkness, imperfection, corruption, and want of further grace, that he is lothesome and burdensome continually to himself: if you see him sad or troubled, and ask him the cause, it is ten to one but it is himself that he complains of. The most froward wife, the most undutiful child, the most disobedient servant, the most injurious neighbour, the most malicious enemy, is not half so great a trouble to him as he is to himself. He prays abundantly more against his own corruption, than against any of these. O could he but know and love God more, be more in heaven, more willing to die, and more free from his own distempers, how easily could he bear all crosses, or injuries from others! He came to Christ's school as a little child, and still he is little in his own esteem: therefore disesteem and contempt from others, is no great matter with him. He thinks it can be no great matter with him. He thinks it can be no great wrong that is done against so poor a worm, and so unworthy a sinner as himself, except as God or the souls of men may be interested in the cause. He heartily approves of the justice of God, in abhorring the proud; and hath learned that duty 'in honour preferring one another,' and ' let us not be desirous of vain glory, provoking one another, envying one another.'

2. But the remnant of pride is usually the most notable sin of the weak Christian; though it reigns not, it foully blemishes him. He would wish to be taken for some body in the church; he is ready to step up into a higher room, and to think himself wiser and better than he is. If he can but speak confidently of the principles of religion, and some few controversies which he hath made himself sick with, he is ready to think himself fit to be a preacher. He looks through a magnifying glass upon all his own performances and gifts, he loves to be valued and praised; he can hardly bear to be slighted and dispraised, but is ready to think hardly of those that do it, if not to hate them in some degree. He loves not to be found fault with, though it be necessary to his amendment. And though all this vice of pride be not so predominant in him, as to conquer his humility, yet doth it much obscure and interrupt it: and though he hate this his pride and strive against it, and lament it before God, yet still it is the sorest ulcer in his soul. And should it prevail and overcome him, he would be abhorred of God, and it would be his ruin.

3. But in the hypocrite, pride is the reigning sin. The praise of men is the air which he lives in. He was never well acquainted with himself; and never felt aright the burden of his sins and wants; and therefore cannot bear contempt from others. Indeed if his corrupt disposition turn most to the way of covetousness, tyranny, or lust, he can more easily bear contempt from others, as long as he hath his will at home; and he can spare their love, if he can be but feared and domineer. But still his pride is predominant; and when it affects not much the reputation of goodness, it affects the name of being rich or great. Sin may make him sordid, but grace doth not make him humble. Pride is the vital spirit of the corrupted state of man.

XXVII. 1. A confirmed Christian is acquainted with the deceitfulness of man's heart, and the particular corrupt inclinations that are in it; and especially with his own; he is acquainted with the wiles and methods of the tempter, what are the materials which he makes his baits of, and what is the manner in which he spreads his nets. He sees always some snares before him. And what company soever he is in, or what business soever he is about, he walks as among snares, which are visible to his sight: and it is part of his business continually to avoid them. He lives in a continual watch and warfare. He can resist much stronger and subtle temptations than the weak can do. He is always armed, and knows what are the special remedies against each particular snare and sin. And he carries always his antidotes about him, as one that lives in an infectious world, and in the midst of a froward and perverse generation, from which he is charged to save himself.

2. The weak Christian is a soldier in the army of Christ, and is engaged in striving against sin, and really takes the flesh and world, as well as the devil, to be his enemies, and doth not only strive, but conquer in the main; but yet, alas, how poorly is he armed! How unskilfully doth he manage his Christian armour! How often is he foiled and wounded; how many a temptation is he much acquainted with; how many a snare lies before him which he never did observe! And oft he is overcome in particular temptations, when he never perceives it, but thinks that he hath conquered.

3. But the hypocrite is fast ensnared when he glories most of his integrity, and is deceived by his own heart, thinking he is something, when he is nothing. When he is thanking God that he is not as other men, he is rejoicing in his dreams, and sacrificing for the victory which he never obtained; he is led by Satan captive at his will, when he is boasting of his uprightness, and hath a beam of covetousness, or pride, or cruelty in his own eye, while he is reviling, or censuring another for the mote of some difference about a cere-

mony, or tolerable opinion. And usually such grow worse and worse, deceiving and being deceived.

XXVIII. 1. A Christian indeed, is one that hath deliberately counted, what it may cost him to follow Christ and to save his soul ; and knowing that suffering with Christ is the way to our reigning with him, he hath fully consented to the terms of Christ : he finds that bearing the cross and forsaking all, is necessary to those that will be Christ's disciples : and accordingly in resolution he hath forsaken all ; and looks not for a smooth and easy way to heaven : he considers that ' all that who will live godly in Christ Jesus must suffer persecution,' and that ' through many tribulations we must enter into heaven :' therefore he takes it not for a strange or unexpected thing, if the fiery trial come upon him. He doth not wonder at the unrighteousness of the world, as if he expected reason, or honesty, justice or truth, or mercy, in the enemies of Christ, and the instruments of Satan : he will not bring his action against the devil, for unjustly afflicting him. He will rather turn the other cheek to him that smites him, than he will hinder the good of any soul by seeking right ; much less will he exercise unjust revenge. Though where government is exercised for truth and righteousness, he will not refuse to make use of the justice of it to punish iniquity, and discourage evil doers, yet this is for God and the common good, and for the suppression of sin, much more than for himself. Suffering doth not surprise him as a thing unlooked for : he hath been long preparing for it, and it finds him garrisoned in the love of Christ ; yea, though his flesh will be as the flesh of others, sensible of the smart, and his mind is not senseless of the sufferings of his body ; yet it is some pleasure and satisfaction to his soul, to find himself in the common way to heaven, and to see the predictions of Christ fulfilled, and to feel himself so far conformed to Jesus Christ his head, and to trace the footsteps of a humbled Redeemer in the way before: 'as Christ hath suffered for us in the flesh, so doth the Christian arm himself with the same mind.—He rejoiceth that he is made partaker of the sufferings of Christ, that when his glory shall be revealed, he may also be partaker of the exceeding joy ;' yea, he takes the reproach of Christ for a treasure, yea, a greater treasure than riches or men's favours can afford. For he knows if he be reproached for the name or sake of Christ, he is happy : for thereby he glorifies that God whom the enemy blasphemes, and so the spirit of God and of glory rests on him.

He lives and suffers as one that from his heart believes, that ' they are blessed that are persecuted for righteousness' sake, for great is their reward in heaven. They are blessed when men shall revile them, and persecute them, and say all manner of evil against them falsely for Christ's sake : in this they rejoice and are exceeding glad, as knowing that herein they are ' followers of them who through faith and patience inherit the promise.' If he be offered upon the sacrifice and service of the faith of God's elect, he can rejoice in it as having greater good than evil. He can ' suffer the loss of all things, and account them dung that he may win Christ, and be found in him, and know him, and the power of his resurrection, and the fellowship of his sufferings, being made conformable to his death.' Not out of sullenness and pride does he rejoice in sufferings ; as some do, that they may carry the reputation of holy, undaunted men ; and seem to be far better and more constant than others. When pride makes men suffer, they are partly the devil's martyrs, though the cause be ever so good : though it is much more ordinary for pride to make men suffer gladly in a bad cause than in a good one ; the devil having more power on his own ground than on Christ's. But it is the love of Christ, the belief of the reward, the humble neglect of the mortified flesh, and the contempt of the conquered world, that makes the Christian suffer with so much joy. For he sees that the judge is at the door : and what torments the wicked are preparing for themselves : that as certainly as there is a God that governs the world, and that in righteousness, so certainly are his eyes upon the righteous, and his face is set against them that do evil ; and ' though sinners do evil an hundred times,' and escape unpunished till their days be prolonged, yet vengeance will overtake them in due time, and it shall be well with them that fear the Lord ; and that he keeps all the tears of his servants till the reckoning day. And if ' judgment begin at the house of God,' and the righteous be saved through so much suffering and labour, what then ' shall be their end that obey not the gospel ? and where shall the ungodly and sinner appear ?'

2. The weak Christian is one that will forsake all for the sake of Christ, and suffer with him that he may be glorified with him ; and will take his treasure in heaven for all. But he does it not with that easiness, alacrity, and joy, as the confirmed Christian doth. He hearkens more to the flesh, which says, Favour thyself. Suffering is much more grievous to him : and sometimes he is wavering before he can bring himself fully to resolve, and let go all.

3 But the seeming Christian looks not for much suffering : he reads of it in the gospel, but he saw no probability of it, and never believed that he should be called to it in any notable degree : he thought it probable that he might well escape it, and therefore, though he agreed verbally to take Christ for his portion, and to follow him through sufferings, he thought he would never put him to it. And indeed his heart is secretly resolved, that he will never be undone in the world for Christ : some reparable loss he may undergo, but he will not let go life and all. He will still be religious and hope for heaven : but he will make himself believe, and others if he can, that the truth lies on the safer side, and not on the suffering side ; and that it is but for their own conceits and scrupulosity, that other men suffer, who go beyond him ; and that many good men are of his opinion, and therefore he may be good also in the same opinion, though he would never have been of that opinion, if it had not been necessary to his escaping of sufferings, what flourish soever he makes for a time, when persecution arises he is offended and withers. Unless he be so deeply engaged among the suffering party, that he cannot come off without perpetual reproach ; and then perhaps pride will make him suffer more than the belief of heaven, or the love of Christ could do : and all this is because his very belief is unrooted and unsound, and he hath secretly at the heart a fear, that if he should suffer death for Christ, he should be a loser by him, and he would not reward him according to his promise, with everlasting life.

XXIX. 1. A Christian indeed is one that follows not Christ for company, nor holds his belief in trust upon the credit of any in the world, and therefore he would stick to Christ, if all that he knows or converses with should forsake him. If the rulers of the earth should change their religion, and turn against Christ, he would not forsake him : if the multitude of the people turn against him ; nay, if the professors of godliness should fall off, yet would he stand his ground and be still the same : if the most learned men, and the pastors of the church, should turn from Christ, he would not forsake him : yea, if his nearest relations and friends, or even that minister who was the means of his conversion, should change their minds, forsake the truth, and turn from Christ or a holy life, he would yet be constant, and be still the same. What Peter resolved on, he would truly practise, 'though all men should be offended because of thee, yet would not I be offended : though I should die with thee, yet will I not deny thee.' If he thought him-

self, as Elias did, that he was left alone, yet would he not bow the knee to Baal. If he hear that this eminent minister falls off one day, and the other another day, till all be gone, yet still ' the foundation of God stands sure ;' he falls not because he is built upon the rock, his heart saith, Alas, whither shall I go, if I go from Christ ? Is there any other that hath the word and spirit of eternal life ; can I be a gainer if I lose my soul ? He uses his teachers to bring him that light and evidence of truth, which dwells in him when they are gone : and therefore though they fall away, he falls not with them.

2. The weakest Christian believes with a divine faith of his own, and depends more on God than man : but yet if he should be put to so great a trial, as to see all the pastors and Christians that he knows change their minds, I know not what he would do : for though God will uphold all his own, whom he will save, yet he doth it by means and outward helps, together with his internal grace ; and keeps them from temptations, when he will deliver them from the evil ; and therefore it is a doubt, whether there be not degrees of grace so weak, as would fail, in case the strongest temptations were permitted to assault them. A strong man can stand and go of himself, but an infant must be carried ; and the lame and sick must have others to support them. The weak Christian falls, if his teacher or most esteemed company fall. If they run into an error, sect, or schism, he keeps them company. He grows cold, if he have not warming company : he forgets himself, and lets loose his sense and passion, if he have not some to watch over him, and warn him. No man should refuse the help of others, that can have it ; and the best have need of all God's means : but the weak Christian needs them much more than the strong, and is much less able to stand without them.

3. But the seeming Christian is built upon the sand, and therefore cannot stand a storm ; he is a Christian more for company, or the credit of man, or the interest that others have in him, or the encouragement of the times, than from a firm belief and love of Christ, and therefore falls when his props are gone.

XXX. 1. A strong Christian can digest the hardest truths, and the hardest works of providence : he sees more of the reasons and evidence of truths than others ; and he hath usually a more comprehensive knowledge, and can reconcile those truths which short-sighted persons suspect to be inconsistent and contradictory ; and when he cannot reconcile them, he knows they are reconcileable: for he hath laid his foundation well, and then he reduces other truths to that, and builds them on it. And so he doth by the hardest providences. Whoever is high or low, whosoever prospers or is afflicted, however human affairs are carried, and all things seem to go against the church and cause of Christ, he knows yet that ' God is good to Israel,' and that he is ' the righteous judge of all the earth;' and that the ' righteous shall have dominion in the morning,' and it ' shall go well with them that fear the Lord.' For he goes into the sanctuary, and foresees the end.

2. But the weak Christian is very hard put to it, when he meets with difficult passages of scripture, and when he sees it go with the righteous according to the work of the wicked, and with the wicked according to the work of the righteous. Though he is not overturned by such difficulties, yet his foot is ready to slip, and he digests them with much perplexity and trouble.

3. But the seeming unsettled Christian is often overcome by them, and turns away from Christ, and saith, These are hard sayings, or hard providences, who can bear them. Thus unbelief thence gathers matter for its increase.

XXXI. 1. A Christian indeed is one that can exercise all God's graces in conjunction, and in their proper places and proportion, without setting one against another, on neglecting one while he is exercising another. He can be humbled without hindering his thankfulness and joy; and he can be thankful and joyful without hindering his due humility. His knowledge doth not destroy, but quicken his zeal: his wisdom hinders not, but furthers his innocency: his faith is a help to his repentance, and his repentance to his faith. His love to himself doth not hinder, but help his love to others: and his love to God is the end of both. He can mourn for the sins of the times, and the calamities of the church, yea, for his own sins and imperfections, and yet rejoice for the mercies which he hath in possession or in hope. He finds that piety and charity are necessarily united; and every grace and duty is a help to all the rest. Yea, he can exercise his graces methodically, which is the comeliness and beauty of his heart and life.

2. But the weak Christian, though he have every grace, and his obedience is universal, yet can he hardly set himself to any duty, but it hinders him from some other duty, through the narrowness and weakness of his mind. When he is humbling himself in confession of sin, he can scarcely be lively in thankfulness for mercy: when he rejoices, it hinders his humiliation; he can hardly do one duty without omitting or hindering another. He is either all for joy, or all for sorrow; all for love, or all for fear; and cannot well do many things at once, but is apt to separate the truths and duties which God hath inseparably conjoined.

3. For the seeming Christian, he exercises no grace in sincerity, nor is he universal in his obedience to God; though he may have the image of every grace and duty.

XXXII. 1. A Christian indeed is more in getting and using his graces, than in inquiring whether he have them: he is very desirous to be assured that he is sincere, but he is more desirous to be so. He knows that even assurance is got more by the exercise and increase of grace, than by bare inquiry, whether we have it already: not that he is a neglecter of self-examination: but he oftener asks, ' what shall I do to be saved?' than, how shall I know that I shall be saved?

2. But the weak Christian hath more of self, and less of God in his solicitude. Though he be willing to obey the whole law of Christ, yet he is much more solicitous to know that he is out of danger, and shall be saved, than to be fully pleasing unto God. Therefore proportionably, he is more in inquiring by what marks he may know that he shall be saved, than by what means he may attain more holiness, and what diligence is necessary to his salvation.

3. But the seeming Christian is most careful how to prosper in the world, or please his flesh: and next, how he may be sure to escape damnation, when he hath done; and least of all, how he may be made like to Christ in holiness.

XXXIII. 1. A Christian indeed, studies duty more than events; and is more careful what he shall be towards God, than what he shall have from God in this life. He looks to his own part more than unto God's; as knowing that it is he that is like to fail: but God will never fail of his part. He is much more suspicious of himself than of God. When any thing goes amiss he blames himself, and not God's providence: he knows that the hairs of his head are numbered, and that his Father knows what he needs; and that God is infinitely wiser and fitter to dispose of him, than he is to choose for himself; and that God loves him better than he can love himself: therefore he thankfully accepts that easy, indulgent command, ' cast all your care on him, for he careth for you. Take no thought what you shall eat or drink, or wherewith you shall be clothed.'

2. But alas, how guilty is the weak Christian of meddling with God's part of the work. How

sinfully careful what will become of him, and of his family, affairs, and of the church, as if he were afraid lest God would prove forgetful, unfaithful, or insufficient for his work: so imperfect is his trust in God.

3. And the seeming Christian really trusts him not at all, for any thing that he can trust himself or the creature for; he will have two strings to his bow if he can: but it is in man that he places his greatest trust for any thing that man can do. Indeed to save his soul he knows none but God is to be trusted, and therefore his life is still preferred before his soul: and consequently man whom he trusted most with his life and prosperity, is really trusted before God; however God may have the name.

XXXIV. 1. A Christian indeed is much more studious of his own duty towards others, than of theirs to him; he is much more fearful of doing wrong, than of receiving wrong: he is more troubled if he say ill of others, than if others speak ill of him: he had far rather be slandered himself, than slander others; or be censured himself than censure others; or be unjustly hurt himself, than unjustly hurt another: or to be put out of his own possessions or right, than to put another out of his. He is oftener and sharper in judging and reproving himself than others: ne falls out with himself more frequently than with others; and is more troubled with himself than with all the world besides: he takes himself for his greatest enemy, and knows that his danger is most at home; and that if he can escape but from himself, no one in earth or hell can undo him. He is more careful of his duty to his prince, his parents, his pastor, or his master, than of theirs to him: he is much more unwilling 'to be disobedient to them in any lawful thing, or to dishonour them, than to be oppressed, or unjustly afflicted, or abused by them. And all this is, because he knows that sin is worse than present suffering; and that he is not to answer for other men's sins but for his own: nor shall he be condemned for the sins of any but himself: and that many millions are condemned for wronging others, but no one for being wronged by others.

2. The weak Christian is of the same mind in general; but with so much imperfection, that he is much more frequent in censuring others, complaining of their wrongs, finding fault with them, and aggravating all that is said or done against himself, which he is hardly made so sensible of as great miscarriages in himself, as having much more uncharitableness, partiality, and selfishness, than a confirmed Christian hath. There

are few things which weakness of grace doth more ordinarily appear in, than this partiality and selfishness, in judging of the faults or duties of others, and of his own. How apt are not only hypocrites, but weak Christians, to aggravate all that is done against them; and to extenuate or justify all that they do against another? O what a noise they make of it, if they think that any one hath wronged them, defamed them, disparaged them, or encroached on their right? If God himself be blasphemed or abused, they can more patiently bear it, and make not so great a matter of it. Who hears of such angry complaints on God's behalf, as on men's own? Of such passionate invectives, such sharp prosecutions, against those that wrong both God and men's souls, as against those that wrong a selfish person; and usually every man seems to wrong him, who keeps from him any thing which he would have, or saith any thing of him which is displeasing to him. Go to the assizes and courts of justice; look into the prisons, and inquire whether it be zeal for God, or for men's selves, which is the plaintiff and prosecutor; and whether it be for wronging God or them, that all the stir is made. Men are ready to say, God is sufficient to right himself: as if he were not the original and the end of laws and government, and as if magistrates were not his officers, to promote obedience to him in the world.

At this time how universal is men's complaint against their governors! How common are the cries of the poor and sufferers, of the greatness of their burdens, miseries, and wants. But how few lament the sins against government, which this land hath been sadly guilty of. The pastors complain of the people's contempt: the people complain of the pastor's insufficiency and lives. The master complains how hard it is to get good servants, that will mind their business and profit, as if it were their own: servants complaining of their masters for over-labouring them, or using them too hardly. Landlords say that their tenants cheat them: and tenants say that their landlords oppress and grind them. But if you were Christians indeed, the commonest and saddest complaints would be against yourselves. I am not so good a ruler, so peaceable a subject, so good a landlord, so good a tenant, so good a master, so good a servant, as I ought to be. Your rulers', subjects', landlords', tenants', masters', servants' sin, shall not be charged upon you in judgment, nor condemn you, but your own sin. How much more therefore should you fear, feel, and complain of your own, than of theirs.

3. As for the seeming Christian, I have told you already, that selfishness is his nature and predominant constitution ; and according to self-interest he judges of almost all things ; of the faults and duties of others and himself : and therefore no man seems honest or innocent to him who displeases him, and is against his worldly interest. Cross him about mine and thine, and he will deceive the most honest man alive, and call his ancient friend his enemy. But of his dealings with them, he is not so scrupulous nor so censorious of himself.

XXXV. 1. A Christian indeed is much taken up in the government of his thoughts, and hath them so much ordinarily in obedience, that God and his service, and the matters of his salvation, have that precedency in them, and his eye is fixed on his end and duty ; and his thoughts refuse not to serve him for any work of God to which he calls them. He suffers them not to be the inlets or agents for pride, or lust, or envy, or voluptuousness, or to contrive iniquity : but if any such sparks from hell are cast into his thoughts, he presently labours to extinguish them : if they intrude, he lets them not lodge or dwell there. Though he cannot keep out all disorder or vanity, or inordinate delights, yet it is his endeavour, and he leaves not his heart in any thing to itself.

2. The weak Christian also makes conscience of his thoughts, and allows them not to be the inlets or servants of any reigning sin : but alas, how imperfectly he governs them ! What a deal of vanity and confusion is in them ! How carelessly doth he watch them ! How remissly doth he rebuke, excite, and command them ! How often are they defiled with impurity and uncharitableness ! How little doth he repent of this, or endeavour to reform it ; and little serviceable are his thoughts, to any high and heavenly work, in comparison of the confirmed Christian.

3. The seeming Christian is very little employed about his thoughts, but leaves them to be the servants of his pride, worldliness, or sensuality, or some reigning sin.

XXXVI. 1. A Christian indeed is much employed in the government of his passions ; and hath so far mastered them, as that they prevail not to pervert his judgment, nor to discompose his heart so far as to interrupt much his communion with God, or to ensnare his heart to any creature, or to breed any fixed uncharitableness or malice in him, nor to cause his tongue to speak things injurious to God or man, to curse, swear, rail, or lie ; nor yet to cause him to hurt and injure any in his heart. But when passion would be inordinate, either in delights or desires, or anger, or grief, or fear, or hope, he flies to his help to suppress and govern them. Though fear is more out of man's power than the rest, and therefore ordinarily hath less of sin ; he knows that Christ hath blessed the meek, and bids us learn of him to be meek and lowly, and that a meek and quiet spirit is in the sight of God of great price. It is therefore his care and course to give place to wrath, when others are angry, and ' if it be possible, as much as in him lieth, to live peaceably with all men,' yea, to follow peace when it flies from him, and not when ' he is reviled to revile again,' nor to threaten or revenge himself on them that injure him. Reason and charity hold the reins, and passion is kept under ; yea, it is used wholly for God. Slow to anger he is in his own cause, and watchful over his anger even in God's cause.

2. But the weak Christian greatly shows his weakness, in his unruly passions, (if he have a temper of body disposed to passion ;) they are often rising, and not easily kept under ; yea, and too often prevail for such unseemly words, as make him become a dishonour to his profession. Oft he resolves, promises, and prays for help, and yet the next provocation shows how little grace he hath to hold the reins. His passionate desires, delights, love, and sorrows, are often as unruly as his anger, to the further weakening of his soul. They are like ague fits, which leave the health impaired.

3. The seeming Christian hath much less power over those passions, which must subserve his carnal mind. For anger depends much upon the temperature of the body ; and if that incline him not strongly to it, his credit or common discretion may suppress it : unless you touch his chief carnal interest, and then he will not only be angry, but cruel, malicious, and revengeful : but his carnal love, desire, and delight, which are placed upon that pleasure, or profit, or honour, which is his idol, are indeed the reigning passions in him : and his grief, and fear, and anger are but the servants unto these.

XXXVII. 1. A Christian indeed is one that keeps a constant government of his tongue ; he knows how much duty or sin it will be the instrument of : according to his ability and opportunity he uses it to the service and honour of his Creator : in speaking of his excellencies, his works and word ; inquiring after the knowledge of him and his will ; instructing others, and pleading for the truth and ways of God, and rebuking the impiety and iniquities of the world, as his place and calling doth allow him. He bridles his tongue from uttering vanity, filthiness, ribaldry, and foolish and uncomely talk and jests ; from rash and irreverent talk of God, and taking of his name in vain ; from the venting of undigested and uncertain doctrines which may prove erroneous and perilous to men's souls ; from speaking imprudently, unhandsomely, or unseasonably about holy things, so as to expose them to contempt and scorn ; from lying, censuring others without a warrantable ground and call ; from backbiting, slandering, false-accusing, railing, and reviling, malicious, envious, injurious speech, which tends to extinguish the love of the hearers to those he speaks of ; from proud and boasting speeches of himself, much more from swearing, cursing, and blasphemous speech, and opposition to the truths and holy ways of God, or opprobrious speeches, or derision of his servants. And in the government of his tongue, he always begins with his heart, that he may understand and love the good which he speaks of, and may hate the evil which his tongue forbears ; and does not hypocritically force his tongue against or without his heart. His tongue doth not run before his heart, but is ruled by it.

2. But the weak Christian, though his tongue be sincerely subject to the laws of God yet frequently miscarries and blemishes his soul by the words of his lips, being much oftener than the confirmed Christian overtaken with words of vanity, meddling, folly, imprudence, uncharitableness, wrath, boasting, venting uncertain or erroneous opinions, &c. so that the unruliness of his tongue is the trouble of his heart, if not also of the family, and all about him.

3. The seeming Christian uses his tongue in the service of his carnal ends, and therefore allows it so much injustice, uncharitableness, falsehood, and other sins, as his carnal interest and designs require ; but the rest perhaps he may suppress, especially if natural sobriety, good education and prudence assist him ; and his tongue is always better than his heart.

XXXVIII. 1. The religious discourse of a confirmed Christian is most about the greatest and most necessary matters : heart-work and heaven-work are the usual employment of his tongue and thoughts : unprofitable controversies and hurtful wranglings he abhors : and profitable controversies he manages sparingly, seasonably, charitably, peaceably, and with caution and sobriety, as knowing that ' the servant of the Lord must not strive,' and that strife of words perverts the hearers, and hinders edifying. His ordinary discourse is about the glorious excellencies, attributes, relations, and works of God ; and the mystery of redemption, the person, office, covenant and grace of Christ ; the renewing, illuminating, sanctifying works of the Holy Ghost ; the mercies of this life, and that to come ; the duty of man to God as his Creator, Redeemer, and Regenerator ; the corruption and deceitfulness of the heart ; the methods of the tempter ; the danger of particular temptations ; and the means of our escape, and of our growth in grace ; and how to be profitable to others, and especially to the church. And if he be called to open any truth which others understand not, he doth it not proudly, to set up himself as the master of a sect, or to draw disciples after him, nor make divisions about it in the church ; but soberly, to the edification of the weak. Though he be ready to defend the truth against perverse gainsayers in due season, yet doth he not turn his ordinary edifying discourse into disputes, or talk of controversies ; nor hath such a proud, pugnacious soul, as to assault every one that he thinks erroneous, as a man that takes himself for the great champion of the truth.

2. But the weak Christian hath a more unfruitful wandering tongue ; and his religious discourse is most about his opinions or party, or some external thing : as which is the best preacher, or person, or book. Or if he talk of any text of scripture, or doctrine of religion, it is much of the outside of it ; and his discourse is less feeling, lively, and experimental : yea, many a time he hinders the more edifying savoury discourse of others, by such religious discourse as is imprudent, impertinent, or turns them away from the heart and life of the matter in hand. But especially his opinions, and distinct manner of worship, are the chief of his discourse.

3. For the seeming Christian, though he can affectedly force his tongue to talk of any subject in religion, especially that which he thinks will most honour him in the esteem of the hearers ; yet when he speaks according to the inclination of his heart, his discourse is first about his fleshly interest and concerns, and next to that of the mere externals of religion, as controversies, parties, and the several modes of worship.

XXXIX. 1. A Christian indeed is one that so lives upon the great substantial matters of religion, as yet not willingly to commit the smallest sin, nor to own the smallest falsehood, nor to renounce or betray the smallest holy truth or duty, for any price that man can offer him. The works of repentance, faith, and love, are his daily busi-

CHARACTER OF A CONFIRMED CHRISTIAN.

ness, which take up his greatest care and diligence. Whatever opinions or controversies are a-foot, his work is still the same; whatever changes come, his religion changes not; he places not 'the kingdom of God in meats, and drinks,' and circumstances, and ceremonies, either being for them or against them; but 'in righteousness, peace, and joy in the Holy Ghost.—And he that in these things serveth Christ, as he is acceptable to God, so is he approved' by such a Christian as this, however factious persons may revile him. The strong Christian can bear the infirmities of the weak, and not take the course that most pleases himself, but that which pleases his neighbour for his good to edification. The essentials of religion—faith, love, and obedience, are as bread and drink, the substance of his food. These he meditates on, and these he practises, and according to these he esteems of others.

But yet no price can seem sufficient to him, to buy his innocency; nor will he wilfully sin, and say, it is a little one, nor do evil that good may come by it: nor offer to God the sacrifice of disobedient fools, and then say, I knew not that I did evil: for he knows that God will rather have obedience than sacrifice, and that 'disobedience is as the sin of witchcraft.' And 'he that breaketh one of the least commands, and teacheth men so, shall be called least in the kingdom of God.' He that teaches men to sin by the example of his own practice, can little expect to turn them from sin, by his better instructions and exhortations. He that will deliberately sin in a small matter, sets but a small price on the favour of God and his salvation. Wilful disobedience is odious to God, how small soever the matter be about which it is committed. Who can expect that he should refrain from any sin, when his temptation is great, who will considerately commit the least; especially if he will approve and justify it. Therefore the sound Christian will rather forsake his riches, his liberty, his reputation, his friends, and his country, than his conscience; and rather lay down liberty, and life itself, than choose to sin against his God, as knowing that never man gained by his sin.

The sin that Saul was rejected for, seemed but a little thing; or the sin that Uzzah was slain for; and the service of God, even his sacrifice and his ark were the pretence for both. The sin of the Bethshemites, of Achan, of Gehezi, of Ananias and Saphira, which had grievous punishments, would seem but little things to us. It is a great aggravation of our sin to be chosen, deliberate, justified, and fathered upon God: and to pretend that we do it for his service, for the worshipping of him, or the doing good to others; as if God would own and bless sinful means, or needed a lie to his service or glory, when he hates all the workers of iniquity, and requires only the sacrifices of righteousness. He abhors sacrifice from polluted hands; they are to him as the offering a dog; and he will ask who hath required this at your hand. 'The sacrifice of the wicked is abomination to the Lord.—It is not pleasing to him; all that eat thereof shall be polluted.' The preaching, the praying, the sacraments of wilful sinners, especially when they choose sin as necessary to his service, are a scorn and mockery put upon the most holy one: as if your servant should set poison and impunity before you on your table for your food; such offer Christ vinegar and gall to drink.

2. In all this the weakest Christian that is sincere, is of the same mind, saving that in his ordinary course, he places too much of his religion in controversies, parties, modes, and ceremonies, whether being for them or against them, and allows too great a proportion in his thoughts, speech, zeal, and practice; and hinders the growth of his grace, by living upon less edifying things, and turning too much from the more substantial nutriment.

3. The seeming Christians are here of different ways. One sort of them place almost all their religion in pharisaical observations of little, external, ceremonial matters; as their washings, fastings, tithings, formalities, and the traditions of the elders: or in their several opinions, ways, and parties, which they call being of the true church: as if their sect were all the church. But living to God in faith and love, and in a heavenly conversation, and worshipping him in spirit and truth, they are utterly unacquainted with. The other sort are truly void of these essential parts of Christianity, in the life and power, as well as the former. But yet being secretly resolved to take up no more of Christianity than will consist with their worldly prosperity and ends, when any sin seems necessary to their preferment or safety in the world, their way is to pretend their high esteem of greater matters, for the swallowing of such a sin as an inconsiderable thing: and then they extol those larger souls that live not upon circumstantials but upon the great and common truths and duties, and pity those men of narrow principles and spirits, who by unnecessary scrupulosity make sin of that which is no sin, and expose themselves to needless trouble. They would make themselves and others believe that it is their excellency and wisdom to be above such trifling scruples. And all is because they

never took God and heaven for their all, and therefore are resolved never to lose all for the hopes of heaven; and therefore to do that, whatever it be, which their worldly interest shall require, and not to be of any religion that will undo them.

Three great pretences are effectual means in this their deceit. One is, because indeed there are a sort of persons that tithe mint and cummin, while they pass by the greatest matters of the law, and that are causelessly scrupulous, and make that to be sin, which indeed is no sin; and when such a scrupulous people are noted by their weaknes, and under dishonour among wiser men, the hypocrite hath a very plausible pretence for his hypocrisy, in seeming only to avoid this ignorant scrupulosity, and taking all for such who judge not his sin to be a thing indifferent.

Another great shelter to the credit and conscience of this hypocrite, is the charity of the best Christians, who always judge rigidly of themselves, and gently of others. They would rather die than wilfully choose to commit the smallest sin themselves; but if they see another commit it, they judge as favourably of it as the case will bear, and hope that he did it not knowingly, or wilfully: for they are bound to hope the best till the worse be evident. This being the upright Christian's case, the hypocrite knows that he shall still have a place in the esteem and love of those charitable Christians, whose integrity and moderation makes their judgments most valuable: and then for the judgment of God, he will venture on it; and for the censures of weaker persons, who themselves are censured by the best for their censoriousness, he can easily bear them.

Another covert for the hypocrite in this case, is the different judgments of learned and religious men, who make a controversy of the matter: and what duty or sin is there that is not become a controversy? Yea, and among men otherwise well esteemed of, except in the essentials of religion. And if once it be a controversy, whether it be a sin or not, the hypocrite can say, I am of the judgment of such and such good learned men; they are very judicious, excellent persons; and we must not judge one another in controverted cases; though we differ in judgment, we must not differ in affection: and thus because he hath a shelter for his reputation from the censures of men, by the countenance of such as accompany him in his sin, he is as quiet as if he were secured from the censures of the Almighty.

XL. 1. A Christian indeed is one that highly values time: he abhors idleness, and all diversions which would rob him of his time, and hinder him from his work: he knows how much work he hath to do, and of what unspeakable consequence to his soul, if not also to others, he knows that he hath a soul to save or lose; a heaven to win; a hell to escape; a death and judgment to prepare for; many a sin to mortify, many graces to get, exercise, and increase; many enemies and temptations to overcome; and that he shall never have more time of trial; but what is now undone, must be undone for ever: he knows how short and hasty time is, and also how uncertain; and how short many hundred years is to prepare for an everlasting state, if all were spent in greatest diligence: therefore he wonders at those miserable souls, that have time to spare, and waste in those fooleries which they call pastimes, even in stage-plays, cards and dice, and long and tedious feastings, delights, complements, idleness, and overlong or needless visits, or recreations. He marvels at the distraction or sottishness of those persons, that can play, prate, loiter, and feast away precious hours, as if their poor unprepared souls had nothing to do, while they stand at the very brink of a dreadful eternity; and are so fearfully unready as they are. He takes that person who would cheat him of his time, by any of these forenamed baits, to be worse to him than a thief that would take his purse from him by the highway. O precious time! how highly doth he value it, when he thinks of his everlasting state, and thinks what haste his death is making, and what reckoning he must make for every moment; what abundance of work hath he for every hour, which he is grieved that he cannot do? He hath a calling to follow, and he hath a heart to search, watch, and study; a God to seek and faithfully serve, and many to do good to; and abundance of particular duties to perform, in order to every one of these; but, alas, time doth make such haste away, that many things are left undone, and he is afraid lest death will find him very much behind hand: therefore he is up and doing, as one that hath use for every minute; and works while it is day, because he knows that the night is coming, when none can work. Redeeming time is much of his wisdom and his work. He had rather labour in the house of correction, than live the life of idle and voluptuous gentlemen, or beggars, that live to no higher end than to live, or to please their flesh; or to live as worldlings, that lose all their lives in the service of a perishing world. He knows how precious time will be ere long, in the eyes of those that now make light of it, and trifle it away as a contemned thing as if they had too much.

2. The weak Christian is of the same mind in the main : but when it comes to particular practice, he is like a weak or weary traveller, that goes but slowly, and makes many a stop : though his face is still heaven-wards, he goes but a little way in a day : he is too easily tempted to idle, or talk, or feast, or play away an hour unlawfully, so it be not his ordinary course, and he do it but seldom : he takes not the loss of an hour for so great a loss as the confirmed Christian doth : he could sooner be persuaded to live, though not an idle and unprofitable, yet an easier, less profitable life. The world and the flesh have far more of his hours, than they ought to have. Though his weakness tell him, that he hath most need of diligence.

3. But the time of a seeming Christian is most at the service of his fleshly interest ; and for that it is principally employed : and for that he can redeem it, and grudge if it be lost. But as he lives not to God, so he cannot redeem his time for God. He loses it even when he seems to employ it best ; when he is praying, or otherwise worshipping God, and doing that good which feeds his false hopes, he is not redeeming his time in all this. While he is sleeping in security, and deluding his soul with a few formal words, and an image of religion, his time passes on, he is hurried away to the dreadful day, and his damnation slumbers not.

XLI. 1. A Christian indeed is one whose very heart is set upon doing good : as one that is made to be profitable to others, according to his ability and place ; even as the sun is made to shine upon the world; he could not be content to live idly, or to labour unprofitably, or to get ever so much to himself, and live in ever so much plenty himself, unless he some way contribute to the good of others: not that he grudges at the smallness of his talents, and lowness or obscurity of his place, for he knows that God may dispose his creatures and talents as he pleases ; and that where much is given, much is required. But what his Lord hath entrusted him with, he is loth to hide, and willing to improve to his Master's use. He is so far from thinking that God is beholden to him for his good works, that he takes it for one of his greatest mercies in the world, that God will use him in doing any good. He would take it for a very great suffering to be deprived of such opportunities, or turned out of service, or called

to less of that kind of duty. If he were a physician and denied liberty to practise, or a minister and denied liberty to preach, it would far more trouble him that he is hindered from doing good, than that he is deprived of any profits, or honours, to himself. He doth not only comfort himself with the foresight of the reward, but in the very doing of good he finds so much pleasure, as makes him think it the most delightful life in the world : and he looks for most of his receivings from God, in a way of duty.

2. But the weak Christian, though he have the same disposition, is far less profitable in the world : he is more for himself, and less able to do good to others ; he wants either parts or prudence, or zeal, or strength : yea, he is often like the infants and sick persons of a family, that are not helpful, but troublesome to the rest. They find work for the stronger Christians, to bear their infirmities, to watch them, and support and help them. Indeed as an infant is a comfort to the mother, through the power of her own love, even when she endures the trouble of its crying and uncleanness ; so weak Christians are a comfort to charitable ministers and people ; we are glad that they are alive, but saddened often by their distempers.

3. The seeming Christian lives to himself, and all his good works are done but for himself, to keep up his credit, or quiet his guilty conscience, and deceive himself with the false hopes of a reward, for that which his false-heartedness makes to be his sin : if he be a man of learning and good parts, he may be very serviceable to the church : but the thanks of that is due to God, and little to him, who seeks himself more than God, or the good of others, in all that he doth.

XLII. 1. A Christian indeed doth truly love his neighbour as himself : he is not all for his own accommodation : his neighbour's profit or good name is as his own. He feels himself hurt when his neighbour is hurt : and if his neighbour prosper, he rejoices as if he prospered himself. Though his neighbour be not united to him, in the nearest bonds of Christianity or piety, yet he is not disregardful of the common unity of humanity. Love is the very soul of life.

2. But the love that is in weaker Christians, though it be sincere, is weak as they are ; and mixed with too much selfishness ; and with too much sourness and wrath : little matters cause differences and fallings out : when it comes to mine and thine, and their neighbours cross their interest or ease, or stand in their way when they are seeking any preferment or profit to them-

selves ; you shall see too easily by their sourness and contention, how weak their love is.

3. But in the seeming Christian, selfishness is so predominant, that he loves none but for himself with any considerable love : all his kindness is from self-love, because men love him, or highly value him, or praise him, or have done him some good turn, or may do him good hereafter, or the like. If he hath any love to any for his own worth, yet self-love can turn all that to hatred, if they seem against him or cross him in his way: for no man that is a lover of the world and flesh, and carnal-self, can even be a true friend to any other. For he loves them but for his own ends; and any cross interests will show the falsehood of his love.

XLIII. 1. A Christian indeed hath a special love to all the godly ; such as endears his heart unto them ; and such as will enable him to visit them, and relieve them in their wants, to his own loss and hazard, according to his ability and opportunity. For the image of God is beautiful and honourable in his eyes : he loves not them so much as God in them ; Christ in them ; and the Holy Spirit in them. He foresees the day when he shall meet them in heaven, and there rejoice in God with them to eternity. He loves their company and converse ; and delights in their gracious words and lives: and the converse of ungodly and empty men is a weariness to him, unless in a way of duty, or when he can do them good. 'In his eyes a vile person is contemned, but he honoureth them that fear the Lord.' Other men grieve his soul with their iniquities, while he is delighted with the appearances of God in his holy ones, even the excellent ones on earth. Yea, the infirmities of believers destroy not his love ; for he hath learned of God himself to distinguish between their abhorred frailties and their predominant grace ; and to love the very infants in the family of Christ. Yea, though they wrong him, or quarrel with him, or censure him in their weakness, he can honour their sincerity, and love them still : if some of them prove scandalous, and some seeming Christians fall away, or fall into the most odious crimes, he loves religion nevertheless ; but continues as high an esteem of piety, and of all that are upright, as he had before.

2. The weak Christian sincerely loves all that bear his Father's image : but it is with a love so weak, even when it is most passionate, as will sooner be abated or interrupted by any tempting differences : he is usually quarrelsome and froward with his brethren, and apter to confine his love to those that are of his own opinion or par-

ty : and because God hath taught him to love all that are sincere, the devil tempts him to censure them as not sincere, that so he may justify himself in the abatement of his love. Weak Christians are usually the most censorious, because they have the smallest degree of love, which covers faults, and thinks no evil, and is not suspicious, but ever apt to judge the best, till the worst be evident. 'It beareth all things, believeth all things,' (that are credible) ' hopeth all things, endureth all things.' But it is no wonder to see children fall out, even about their childish toys and trifles, and what the dissensions of the children of the church have done against themselves in these kingdoms, I need not, I delight not, to record. 'And I, brethren, could not speak unto you, as unto spiritual, but as unto carnal, even as unto babes in Christ. I have fed you with milk, and not with meat ; for hitherto ye were not able to bear it, neither yet now are ye able : for ye are yet carnal: for whereas there is among you envying, and strife, and divisions, are you not carnal, and walk as men ?'

3. The seeming Christian may have some love to real Christians, even for their goodness' sake: but it is a love subservient to his carnal self love : therefore it shall not cost him much : as he hath some love to Christ, so he may have some love to Christians ; but he hath more to the world and fleshly pleasures : therefore all his love to Christ or Christians, will not make him leave his worldly happiness for them. Therefore Christ, at the day of judgment, will not inquire after empty, barren love, but after that love which visited and relieved suffering saints. An hypocrite can allow both Christ and Christians such a cheap, superficial kind of love, as will cost him little : he will bid them lovingly 'depart in peace, be you warmed and filled.' But still the world is most beloved.

XLIV. 1. A Christian indeed doth love his enemies, and forgive those that injure him, and this out of a thankful sense of that grace which forgave him a far greater debt: not that he thinks it unlawful to make use of the justice of the government which he is under, for his necessary protection, or for the restraint of men's abuse and violence : nor is he bound to love the malice or injury, though he must love the man : nor can he forgive a crime as it is against God or the common good, or against another, though he can forgive an injury or debt that is his own. Nor is he bound to forgive every debt, though he is bound so far to forgive every wrong, as heartily to desire the good of him that did it. Even God's enemies he so far loves, as to desire

God to convert and pardon them, while he hates their sin, and hates them as God's enemies, and desires their restraint. But those that hate, and curse, and persecute himself, he can unfeignedly love, and bless, and pray for. For he knows that else he cannot be a child of God, and that to love those that love him is not much praiseworthy, being no more than heathens and wicked men can do. He is so deeply sensible of that wondrous love which so dearly redeemed him, and saved him from hell, and forgave him a thousand-fold worse than the worst that ever was done against himself, that thankfulness and imitation, or conformity to Christ in his great compassions, overcomes his desires of revenge, and makes him willing to do good to his most cruel enemies, and pray for them as Christ and Stephen did at their deaths. He knows that he is so inconsiderable a worm, that a wrong done to him as such, is the less considerable; and he knows that he daily wrongs God more than any man can wrong him, and that he can hope for pardon, but on condition that he himself forgive; and that he is far more hurtful to himself, than any other can be to him.

2. The weakest Christian can truly love an enemy, and forgive a wrong; but he doth it not so easily and so fully as the other. But it is with much striving, and some unwillingness and averseness; and there remains some grudge or strangeness upon the mind. He doth not sufficiently forget the wrong which he forgives. Indeed his forgiving is very imperfect, like himself, not with that freeness and readiness required. 'With all lowliness and meekness, with longsuffering, forbearing one another in love. Put on therefore, as the elect of God, holy and beloved, bowels of mercies, kindness, humbleness of mind, meekness, long-suffering, forbearing one another, and forgiving one another; even as Christ forgave you, so also do ye. Avenge not yourselves,' &c.

3. As for the seeming Christian, he can seem to forgive wrongs for the sake of Christ, but if he do it indeed, it is for his own sake: as because it is for his honour, or because the person hath humbled himself to him, or his pleasure requires it, or he can make use of his love and service for his advantage, or some one hath interposed for reconciliation who must not be denied, or the like. But to love an enemy indeed, and to love that man, be he ever so good, who stands in the way of his preferment, honour or ease in the world, he ever doth it from his heart, whatever he may seem to do. The love of Christ doth not constrain him.

XLV. 1. A Christian indeed is as precise in the justice of his dealings with men, as in acts of piety to God. For he knows that God requires this as strictly at his hands, 'that no man go beyond, or defraud his brother in any matter; for the Lord is the avenger of all such, as we also have forewarned and testified.' He is one that 'walketh uprightly, and worketh righteousness, and speaketh the truth in his heart, that backbiteth not with his tongue, nor doth evil to his neighbour, nor taketh up a reproach against his neighbour. If he swear to his own hurt, he changeth not: he puts not out his money to (unjust or unmerciful) usury; nor taketh reward against the innocent.' He obeys that, 'thou shalt not defraud thy neighbour, neither rob him; the wages of him that is hired shall not abide with thee all night until the morning. He can say as Samuel, 'whose ox or ass have I taken? Or whom have I defrauded? Whom have I oppressed? Or of whose hand have I received any bribe, to blind mine eyes therewith, and I will restore it? And they said, thou hast not defrauded us, nor oppressed us, neither hast thou taken ought of any man's hand.' If heretofore he was ever guilty of defrauding any, he is willing to his power to make restitution, and saith as Zaccheus, if I have taken any thing from any man by false accusation, I restore him four fold. Though flesh and blood persuade him to the contrary, and though it leave him in want, he will pay his debts, and make restitution of that which is ill gotten, as being none of his own. He will not sell for as much as he can get, but for as much as it is truly worth: he will not take advantage of the weakness, or ignorance, or necessity of his neighbour: he knows that 'a false balance is abomination to the Lord, but a just weight is his delight.' He is afraid of believing ill reports, and rebukes the backbiter. He is apt to take part with any man behind his back, who is not notoriously inexcusable; not to justify any evil, but to show his charity, and his hatred of evil speaking, especially where it can do no good. He will not believe evil of another till the evidence compel him to believe it. If he have wronged any by incautious words, he readily confesses his fault to him, asks him forgiveness, and is ready to make any just satisfaction for any wrong that he hath done. He borrows not when he sees not a great probability that he is likely to pay it. Nor will remain in debt by retaining that which is another man's against his will, without an absolute necessity. 'Owe no man any thing, but love one another.' For to borrow when he cannot pay is but to steal

92

Begging is better than borrowing for such. ' The wicked borroweth and payeth not.'

2. The weak Christian makes conscience of justice as well as acts of piety, as knowing that God hath no need of our sacrifices, but loves to see us do that which is good for human society, and which we have need of from each other. But yet he hath more selfishness and partiality than the confirmed Christian hath, and therefore is often overcome by temptations to unrighteous things : as to stretch his conscience for his convenience, in buying or selling, and concealing the faults of what he sells, and sometimes overreaching others : especially he is ordinarily too censorious of others, and apt to be credulous of evil reports, and to be overbold and forward in speaking ill of men behind their backs, and without a call ; especially against persons that differ from him in matters of religion, where he is usually most unjust and apt to go beyond his bounds.

3. The seeming Christian may have a seeming justice. But really he hath none but what must give place to his fleshly interest : and if his honour, comfort, and safety require it, he will not stick to be unjust. And that justice which wants but a strong temptation to overturn it, is almost as bad as none. If he will not seize on Naboth's vineyard, nor make himself odious by oppression or deceit ; yet if he can raise or enrich himself by secret flattery, and get so fair a pretence for his injustice, as shall cloak the matter from the sight of men, he seldom hesitates at it. It is an easy matter to make an Achan think that he doth no harm, or a Gehazi think that he wrongs no man, in taking that which was offered and due. Covetousness will not confess its name ; but will find some reasonings to make good all the injustice which it doth.

XLVI. 1. A Christian indeed is faithful and laborious in his particular calling, and that not out of a covetous mind ; but in obedience to God, and that he may maintain his family, and be able to do good to others. For God hath said, ' in the sweat of thy face thou shalt eat thy bread.' And six days shalt thou labour. And with quietness men must work, and eat their own bread ; and if any will not work, neither should he eat. Abraham and Noah, and Adam, laboured in a constant course of employment. He knows that a sanctified calling and labour is a help, and not a hinderance to devotion; and that the body must have work as well as the soul, and that religion must not be pretended for slothful idleness, nor against obedience to our master's will.

2. The weak Christian is here more easily deceived, and made believe that religion will excuse a man from bodily labour ; and under the colour of devotion to live idly. ' They learn to be idle, wandering about from house to house, and not only idle, but tatlers also and busybodies, speaking things which they ought not.' Slothfulness is a sin much condemned in the scriptures.

3. The seeming Christian in his labour is ruled chiefly by his flesh : if he be rich, and it incline him most to sloth, he makes small conscience of living in idleness, under the pretence of his gentility or wealth : but if the flesh incline him more to covetousness, he will be laborious enough ; but it shall not be to please God by obedience, but to increase his estate, and enrich himself and his posterity, whatever better reason he pretend.

XLVII. 1. A Christian indeed is exactly conscientious in the duties of his relation to others in the family and place of his abode : if he be a husband, he is loving and patient, and faithful to his wife ; if he be a father, he is careful of the holy education of his children : if he be a master, he is just and merciful to his servants, and careful for the saving of their souls. If he be a child or servant, he is obedient, trusty, diligent and careful, as well behind his parents' or his master's back, as before his face. He dare not lie, or steal, or deceive, or neglect his duty, or speak dishonourably of his superiors, though he were sure he could conceal it all. For he knows that the fifth commandment is enforced with a special promise. And that a bad child, or a bad servant, a bad husband or wife, a bad parent or master, cannot be a good Christian.

2. But weak Christians, though sincere, are ordinarily weak in this part of their duty ; and apt to yield to temptations, and carry themselves proudly, stubbornly, idly, disobediently, as eye servants that are good in sight ; or to be unmerciful to inferiors and neglect their souls : and to excuse all this from the faults of those that they have to do with, and lay all upon others ; as if the fault of husband, wife, parent, master or servant, would justify them in theirs ; and passion and partiality would serve for innocency.

3. The hypocrite ordinarily shows his hypocrisies, by being false in his relations to man, while he pretends to be pious and obedient unto God. He is a bad master, and a bad servant, when his filthy interest requires it, and yet thinks himself a good Christian for all that. For all men being faulty, it is easy to find a pretence from all men that he doth abuse, to cover the injury of his abuse. Cain, Ham, Eli, Absalom, Judas, &c. are sad examples of this.

XLVIII. 1. A Christian indeed is the best subject, whether his prince be good or bad: though by infidel and ungodly rulers he be often mistaken for the worst. He obeys not his rulers only for his own ends, but in obedience to God; and not only for fear of punishment, but for conscience sake: he looks on them in their relations as the officers of God, and armed with his authority, and therefore obeys God in them. He permits not dishonourable thoughts of them in his heart; much less dare he speak dishonourably of them. He knows that 'every soul must be subject to the higher powers, and not resist;' and that 'there is no power but of God: whosoever therefore resisteth the power, resisteth the ordinance of God; and he that resisteth shall receive to himself damnation.' Therefore in all things lawful he obeys them: and though he must not, or will not obey them against God, yet will he suffer patiently when he is wronged by them; and not only forbear resistance by arms or violence, but also all reproachful words, as knowing that the righting of himself is not so necessary to the public order and good, as the honour of his rulers is. Usurpers may probably charge him to be a traitor, seditious, and rebellious, because he dare not approve of their usurpations; and when several are contending for the government, and in a litigious title the lawyers mislead him, when the controversy is only among them, and belongs to their profession, it is possible he may mistake as well as the lawyers, and take him to have the better title that hath the worse: but in divinity he knows there is no controversy whether every soul must be subject to the highest power, so far as he can know it; that prayers and patience are the subject's arms; that religion is so far from being a warrant to resist, that it plainly forbids disobedience and resistance; that none are more obliged to submission and quietness than Christians are: the spirit of Christianity is not of this world: its kingdom and its hopes are not of this world: and therefore they contend not for dignities and rule; much less by resisting or rebelling against their lawful governors. But they are resolved to obey God, and secure their everlasting portion, and bear all the injuries which they meet with in the way, especially from those whom God hath set over them. There is no doctrine that ever was received in the world, so far from befriending seditions and rebellion as the doctrine of Christ; nor any people in the world so loyal as Christians, while Christianity retained its genuine simplicity; till proud, domineering, worldly men, for carnal ends, pre-

tended themselves to be Christians, and perverted the doctrine of Christ, to make it warp to their ambitious ends; suffering seems not so great a matter to a holy, mortified, heavenly mind, as to tempt him to hazard his salvation to resist it. No man is so likely to be true to kings, as he that believes that his salvation lies on it, by the ordinance of God. And princes that are wise and just do always discern that the best Christians are their best subjects: though those that are unbelieving and ungodly themselves, have ever hated them as the greatest troublers of the earth.

It hath ever been the practice of the enemies of Christ and godliness, to do all they can to engage the rulers of the earth against them; and to persuade them that the most godly Christians are persons of disloyal and unquiet minds; and by vexing and persecuting them, they do their worst to make them such as they falsely called them: even Christ himself was crucified as an enemy to Cæsar, and Pilate driven to it by the noise of them that cried out, that if he let him go, he was not Cæsar's friend. They first tempted him with the question, whether it were lawful to give tribute unto Cæsar, and though they could in this way take no hold of him, yet this was the first article of his accusation, 'we have found this fellow perverting the nation, and forbidding to give tribute to Cæsar.' And how loyal would those rebellious Jews seem, when they thought it the only way to engage the Roman power against Christ! Then they cry out 'we have no king but Cæsar.' This was the common accusation against the Christians, both by Jews and Gentiles: the language of the Jews you may hear from Tertullus, 'we have found this man a pestilent fellow, and a mover of sedition among all the Jews throughout the world, and a ring-leader of the sect of the Nazarenes.' And at Thessalonica, the charge against them was, that 'they turned the world upside down, and did all contrary to the decrees of Cæsar.' Thus the best Christians have by such been slandered from age to age; because the devil and his instruments know not how sufficiently to molest them, except they engage the rulers against them. But yet all this doth not conquer the patience and loyalty of confirmed Christians. They are wiser than that wise man that Solomon saith 'oppression maketh mad.' If usurpers or malicious liars shall a thousand times call them rebellious and seditious, it shall not drive them from their due subjection: they can patiently follow their Lord and the ancient Christians, in the enduring of such slanders, and suffering as enemies to Cæsar, so they but escape the sin, and be not such as malice calls them. They had rather die as reputed enemies to government, than be such indeed. They prefer subjection before the reputation of it; for they look not for their reward from princes, but from God. If they can preserve their innocency, they can bear the defamation of their names, being satisfied in the hopes of the joyful day of the judgment of Christ, which will fully justify them, and set all straight. Indeed they know that a state of subjection is easier and safer than places of command; and that it is more easy to obey than govern. And so far are they from envying men's greatness, and from desiring dominions, that they pity the tempted, dangerous, and troublesome state of those in power, and are thankful to God for their quieter and safer station. They heartily pray for kings, and all that are in authority; not that by their favour they may rise to places of wealth and honour, but 'that under them they may live a quiet and peaceable life, in all godliness and honesty.' Yea, though infidel princes hate and persecute them, they continue to pray for them, and to honour their authority, and will not thereby be driven from their duty.

If God cast their lot under infidel, ungodly and malicious governors, they do not run to arms to save themselves, or save the gospel; as if God had called them to reform the world, or keep it from the oppression of the highest powers. Nor do they think it a strange intolerable matter for the best man to be lowest, and to be on the suffering side, and so fall to fighting that Christ and the saints may have the rule. For they know that Christ's 'kingdom is not of this world,' that is, not a visible monarchy, as his usurping vicar doth pretend; and that Christ doth most eminently rule unseen, and disposes of all the kingdoms of the world, even where he is hated and resisted; that the reign of saints is in their state of glory; and that all God's graces do fit them more for a suffering life than for worldly power: their humility, meekness, patience, self-denial, contempt of the world, and heavenly-mindedness, are better exercised and promoted in a suffering, than a prosperous reigning state. When they think of the holy blood which hath been shed by heathen Rome, from Christ and Stephen till the days of Constantine; and the far greater streams which have been shed by the bloody papal Rome, wherever they had power, in Piedmont, Germany, Poland, Hungary, in Belgia, England, and in other lands; the 30,000, or 40,000 murdered in a few days at the Bartholomew massacre in France; the two hundred thousand murdered in a few weeks in Ireland, they are not so unlike their suffering brethren, as to think that striving for honours and command is their way to heaven. When Christ hath foretold them that self-denial under the cross, tribulation, and persecution, is the common way. So far are they from fighting against the injuries and cruelties of their governors, that they account the reproach of Christ to be greater riches than all their treasures, and think they are blessed when they are persecuted, and say with Paul, ' God forbid that I should glory, save in the cross of our Lord Jesus Christ, by whom the world is crucified to me, and I unto the world.—Therefore I take pleasure in infirmities, in reproaches, in necessities, in persecutions, in distresses for Christ's sake; for when I am weak, then I am strong.—Nay, in all these things (when persecuted and killed all the day long, and counted as sheep to the slaughter) they are more than conquerors through Christ.' They obtain a nobler conquest than that which is obtained by the sword.

2. But the weak Christian having less patience, and more selfishness and passion, is more easily tempted to break his bounds, and with Peter, run to his unauthorised sword, when he should submit to suffering. His interest and sufferings cause his passion to have too great a power on his judgment, so that he is more easily tempted to believe that to be lawful which he thinks to be necessary to his own preservation; and to think that the gospel and the church are falling, when the power of men is turned against them; and therefore he must, with Uzzah, put forth his hand to save the ark of God from falling. He is more troubled at men's injustice and cruelty, and makes a wonder of it, to find the enemies of Christ and godliness to be unreasonably impudent and bloody; as if he expected reason and righteousness in the malicious world. His sufferings fill him more with discontent, and desires of revenge from God, and his prosperity too much lifts him up, and in the litigious titles of pretenders to supremacy, he is often too hasty to interest himself in their contentions, as if he understood not, that whoever is the conqueror will count these rebels that were on the other side; and that the enemies of Christ will cast all the odium upon Christianity and piety, when the controversy is only among the statesmen and lawyers, and belongs not to religion at all.

3. The seeming Christian will seem to excel all others in loyalty and obedience, when it makes for his carnal ends: he will flatter rulers for

honours and preferment, and always be on the rising side, unless when his pride engages him in murmurings and rebellions. He hath a great advantage above true Christians and honest men, to seem the most obedient subject; because he hath a stretching conscience, that can do any thing for his safety or his worldly end. If he be among papists, he can be a papist; if among protestants, he is a protestant; and if he were among Turks, it is likely he would rather turn a Mahometan than be undone. No prince or power can command him any thing which he cannot yield to, if his worldly interest require it. If there be a law for worshipping the golden image, it is the conscientious servants of God, and not the time-servers, that refuse to obey it. If there be a law against praying, it is Daniel, and not the ungodly multitude, that disobey it. If there be a command against preaching, it is the holy apostles and best Christians that plead the command of God against it, and refuse obedience to it. The self-seeking temporizing hypocrite can do any thing: and yet he obeys not while he seems to obey. For it is not for the authority of the commander that he doth it, but for his own ends: he never truly honours his superiors; for he doth not respect them as the officers of God, nor obey them for his sake with a conscientious obedience: he fears the higher powers as bears or tigers, that are able to hurt him; or uses their favour as he uses his horse, to do him service. Were it not for himself, he would little regard them. The true Christian honours the basest creature more than the hypocrite and worldling honours his king: For he sees God in all, and uses the smallest things unto his glory; whereas the worldling debases the highest, by the baseness of his esteem, use and end; for he knows not how to esteem or use the greatest prince, but for himself or for some worldly ends.

XLIX. 1. A Christian indeed, is a man of courage and fortitude in every cause of God; for he trusts God, and firmly believes that he will bear him out: he knows his superiors, and hath a charitable respect to all men: but as for any selfish or timorous respect, he hath the least regard to man. For he knows that the greatest are but worms, whose breath is in their nostrils, that pass away as shadows, and return to dust; that the most potent are impotent when they contend with God, and are unequal matches to strive against their Maker; that it will prove hard for them to kick against the pricks; and that whoever seems now to have the day, it is God that will be conqueror at last. ' Put not your trust in princes, nor in the son of man, in whom there is no help; his breath goeth forth; he returneth to his earth: in that very day his thoughts perish. Happy is he that hath the God of Jacob for his help; whose hope is in the Lord his God. Woe to him that striveth with his Maker.' He knows that it is more irrational to fear man against God, than to fear a fly against the greatest man. The infinite disproportion between the creature that is against him, and the Creator that is for him, doth resolve him to obey the command of Christ. ' Be not afraid of them that kill the body, and after that have no more that they can do: but I will forewarn you whom you shall fear: fear him, which after he hath killed, hath power to cast into hell: yea, I say unto you, fear him.—Hearken unto me, ye that know righteousness, the people in whose 'heart is my law: fear ye not the reproof of man, neither be afraid of their revilings: for the moth shall eat them up like a garment, and the worm shall eat them like wool; but my righteousness shall be for ever, and my salvation from generation to generation.—I gave my back to the smiters, and my cheeks to them that plucked off the hair: I hid not my face from shame and spitting. For the Lord God will help me: therefore shall I not be confounded: therefore have I set my face like a flint; and I know that I shall not be ashamed. He is near that justifieth me; who will contend with me? Let us stand together; who is mine adversary? Let him come near to me. Behold, the Lord God will help me: who is he that shall condemn me? Lo, they all shall wax old as a garment; the moth shall eat them up.—Cease ye from man, whose breath is in his nostrils; for wherein is he to be accounted of.—Cursed is the man that trusteth in man.—Blessed is the man that trusteth in the Lord.' Alas, how terrible is the wrath of God, in comparison of the wrath of man! And how easy an enemy is the most cruel persecutor, in comparison of a holy sin-revenging God. Therefore the confirmed Christian saith as the three witnesses, ' We are not careful to answer thee in this matter: the God whom we serve is able to deliver us. But if not, be it known unto thee, O king, that we will not serve thy gods, nor worship the golden image which thou hast set up.' When Daniel knew that the decree was past, he prayed openly in his house, as heretofore. ' Moses feared not the wrath of the king, for he endured as seeing him that is invisible.' ' The righteous is bold as a lion.—When they saw the boldness of Peter and John they marvelled.' Paul's bonds made others bold. ' Perfect love casteth out fear.—If ye suffer for righteousness' sake, happy are ye ; and be not afraid of their terror, neither be troubled.—So that we may boldly say, the Lord is my helper, and I will not fear what man shall do unto me.

2. But the weak Christian, though he also trust in God, is much more fearful, and easily daunted and discouraged; and ready with Peter to be afraid, if he perceive himself in danger. He is not valiant for the truth. Though he can forsake all, even life itself, for Christ, yet is it with a deal of fear and trouble. Man is a more significant thing to him than to the stronger Christian.

3. But the seeming Christian fears men more than God, and will venture upon the displeasure of God, to avoid the displeasure of men that can do him hurt ; because he doth not soundly believe the threatenings of the word of God.

L. 1. A Christian indeed is made up of judgment and zeal united. His judgment is not a patron of lukewarmness, nor his zeal an enemy to knowledge : his judgment doth not destroy, but increase his zeal ; and his zeal is not blind nor self-conceited, nor runs before, or without judgment. If he be of the most excellent sort of Christians, he hath so large a knowledge of the mysteries of godliness, that he sees the body of sacred truth with its parts, or joints, as it were at once. It is all written deeply and methodically in his understanding ; he hath by long use his senses exercised, to discern both good and evil. He presently discerns where mistaken men go out of the way, and lose the truth by false suppositions, or by false definitions, or by confounding things that differ. Therefore he pities the contentious sects and disputers, who raise a dust to blind themselves and others, and make a stir to the trouble of the church, about things which they never understood : and in the sight of that truth which others obscure or contradict, he enjoys much content or pleasure in his own mind, though incapable persons zealously reject it. Therefore he is stedfast, as knowing on what ground he sets his foot. Though he be the greatest lover of truth, and would with greatest joy receive any addition to his knowledge, yet ordinarily by erroneous zealots he is censured as too stiff, self-conceited, and tenacious of his own opinions ; because he will not entertain their errors, and obey them in their self-conceitedness. For he that knows that it is truth which he holds, is neither able nor willing to hold the contrary, unless he imprison the truth in unrighteousness. But if he be one that hath not attained to such a clear comprehensive judgment, yet

with that measure of judgment which he hath, he doth guide and regulate his zeal, and makes it follow after, while understanding goes before. He treads on sure ground, and knows it to be duty indeed which he is zealous for, and sin indeed which he is zealous against ; and is not put to excuse all his favour and forwardness after with a *non putarem*, or 'I had thought it had been otherwise.'

2. But the weak Christian either hearkens too much to carnal wisdom, which suppresses his zeal, and makes him too heavy, dull, and indifferent in many of his duties, and the concerns of his soul, permitting the world to take up too much of the vigour of his spirit ; or else he is confident in his mistakes, and verily thinks that he understands better than many wiser men, these things which he never understood at all. He chooses his party by the zeal that he finds in them, without any judicious trial of the truth of what they hold and teach : he is very earnest for many a supposed truth and duty, which proves at last to be no truth or duty at all ; and he censures many a wiser Christian than himself, for many a supposed sin which is no sin, but perhaps a duty. For he is always injudicious, and his heat is greater than his light, or else his light is too flashy without heat : peremptorily he sets down some among the number of the most wise and excellent men, for keeping him company in his mistakes. He boldly numbers the best and wisest of his teachers with the transgressors, for being of a more sound understanding than himself, and doing those duties which he calls sins. Hence it is that he is a person apt to be misled by appearances of zeal ; and the passions of his teachers prevail more with him than the evidence of truth. He that prays and preaches most fervently is the man that carries him away, though none of his arguments be truly cogent. If he hear any hard name against any opinion, or manner of worship, he receives that prejudice which turns him more against it than reason could have done ; so the bugbear name of heresy, Lutheranism, and Calvinism, frightens many a well-meaning Papist both from the truth, and almost from his wits. And the names of Popery, Arminianism, Prelacy, Presbyterianism, Independency, &c. turn away the hearts of many, from things which they never tried or understood. If a zealous preacher but call any opinion or practice antichristian or idolatrous, it is a more effectual terror than the clearest proof. Big and terrible words move the passions, while the understanding is abused, or a stranger to the cause. And passion is much

of their religion   Hence, alas, is much of the calamity of the church.

3. But the seeming Christian is only zealous finally for himself, or zealous about the smaller matters of religion, as the pharisees were for their ceremonies and traditions, or for his own inventions, or some opinions or ways, in which his honour seems to be interested, and pride inflames his zeal. But as for a holy zeal about the substance and practice of religion, and that for God as the final cause, he is a stranger to it. He may have a zeal of God, and of, and for the law and worship of God as the material cause, but not a true zeal for God, as the chief final cause.

LI. 1. A Christian indeed can bear the infirmities of the weak: though he love not their weakness, yet he pities it, because he truly loves their persons. Christ hath taught him not ' to break the bruised reed, and to gather the lambs in his arms, and carry them in his bosom, and gently lead them that are with young.' If they have diseases and distempers, he seeks in tenderness to cure them, and not in wrath to hurt and vex them. He turns not the infants or sick persons from the family, because they cry, or are unquiet, unclean, infirm, and troublesome; but he exercises his love and pity upon their weaknesses. If they mistake their way, or are ignorant, peevish, and froward in their mistakes, he seeks not to undo them, but gently to reduce them. If they censure him, and call him erroneous, heretical, antichristian, idolatrous, because he concurs not with them in their mistakes, he bears it with love and patience, as he would do the peevish chidings of a child, or the frowardness of the sick. He doth not lose his charity, and set his wit against a child, or aggravate the crimes, and being reviled revile again; and say, you are schismatics, hypocrites, obstinate, and fit to be severely dealt with: but he overcomes them with love and patience, which is the conquest of a saint, and the happiest victory both for himself and them. ' It is a small matter to him to be judged of man. He is more troubled for the weakness and disease of the censorious, than for his own being wronged by their censures.

2. But the weak Christian is more ready to censure others, than patiently to bear a censure himself. Either he storms against the censurers, as if they did him some insufferable wrong, through the over-great esteem of himself and his reputation; or else to escape the fangs of censure, and keep up his repute with them, he complies with the censorious, and over-runs his

judgment and conscience to be well spoken of and counted a sincere and stedfast man.

3. But the seeming Christian is so proud and selfish, and wants charity and tenderness to the weak, that he is impatient of their provocations; and would cure the diseases of the servants of Christ by cutting their throats, or ridding the country of them. If a child but wrangle with him, he cries, Away with him, he is a troubler of the world. He takes more notice of one of their infirmities, than of all their graces; yea, he can see nothing but obstinacy and hypocrisy in them, if they but cross him in his opinions, or reputation, or worldly ends. Selfishness can turn his hypocrisy into malignity and cruelty, if once he take them to be against his interest. Indeed his interest can make him patient: he can bear with them that he looks to gain by, but not with them that seem to be against him. The radical enmity against sincerity, that was not mortified, but covered in his heart, will easily be again uncovered.

LII. 1. A Christian indeed is one who greatly esteems the unity of the church, and is greatly averse to all divisions among believers. As there is in the natural body an abhorring of dismembering or separating any part from the whole; so there is in the mystical body of Christ. The members that have life, cannot but feel the smart of any distempering attempt: for abscission is destruction. The members die that are separated from the body. And if there be but any obstruction or hinderance of communion, they will be painful or useless: he feels in himself the reason of all those strict commands, and earnest exhortations. ' Now I beseech you, brethren, by the name of our Lord Jesus Christ, that ye all speak the same thing, and that there be no divisions among you, but that ye be perfectly joined together in the same mind, and in the same judgment.—If there be any consolation in Christ, if any comfort of love, if any fellowship of the Spirit, if any bowels and mercies; fulfil ye my joy, that ye be like minded, having the same love, being of one accord, of one mind. —Let nothing be done through strife or vainglory; but in lowliness of mind, let each esteem other better than themselves.—Look not every man on his own things, but every man also on the things of others.—I therefore, the prisoner of the Lord, beseech you, that ye walk worthy of the vocation wherewith ye are called, with all lowliness and meekness, with long-suffering, forbearing one another in love; endeavouring to keep the unity of the spirit in the bond of peace. There is one body and one Spirit, even as ye are called in one hope of your calling ; one Lord, one faith, one baptism, one God and Father of all, who is above all, and through all, and in you all. But unto every one of us is given grace, according to the measure of the gift of Christ.' He looks at uncharitableness and divisions, with more abhorrence than weak Christians do at drunkenness or whoredom, or such other heinous sins. He fears such dreadful warnings as Acts xx. 29, 30. 'For I know this, that after my departing shall grievous wolves enter in among you, not sparing the flock. Also, of your ownselves shall men arise, speaking perverse things, to draw away disciples after them ;' and he cannot slight such a vehement exhortation as Rom. xvi. 17, 18. 'Now I beseech you, brethren, mark them which cause divisions and offences, contrary to the doctrine which ye have learned, and avoid them. For they that are such serve not our Lord Jesus Christ, but their own belly, and by good words and fair speeches deceive the hearts of the simple.' Therefore he is so far from being a divider himself, that when he sees any one making divisions among Christians, he looks on him as on one that is mangling the body of his dearest friend, or as one that is setting fire to his house, and therefore doth all that he can to quench it ; as knowing the confusion and calamity to which it tends. He is a Christian, and therefore of a truly catholic spirit ; that is, he makes not himself a member of a divided party, or a sect ; he regards the interest and welfare of the body, the universal church, above the interest or prosperity of any party whatsoever ; and he will do nothing for a party which is injurious to the whole, or to the Christian cause. The very names of sects and parties are displeasing to him ; and he could wish that there were no name but that of Christians among us, save only the necessary names of the criminal, such as that of the Nicolaitans, by which those that are to be avoided by Christians must be known.

Christianity is confined to so narrow a compass in the world, that he is unwilling to contract it yet into a narrower. The greatest party of divided Christians, whether it be the Greeks or Papists, is too small a body for him to take for the catholic (or universal) church. He grieves at the blindness and cruelty of faction, that can make men damn all the rest of the church for the interest of their proper sect ; and take all those as non-Christians that are better Christians than themselves : especially the papists, who unchurch all the church of Christ, except their sect, and make it as necessary to salvation to be a subject of the pope, as to be a Christian : and when by

their great corruption and abuses of Christianity, they have more need of charitable censures themselves than almost any sort of Christians, yet are they the boldest condemners of all others. The confirmed Christian can distinguish between the strong and weak, the sound and unsound members of the church, without dismembering any, and without unwarrantable separations from any. He will worship God in the purest manner he can, and locally join with those assemblies, where, all things considered, he may most honour God, and receive most edification ; and will not sin for communion with any. He will sufficiently distinguish between a holy, orderly assembly, and a corrupt, disordered one ; and between an able, faithful pastor, and an ignorant or worldly hireling. He desires that the pastors of the church may make that due separation by the holy discipline of Christ, which may prevent the people's disorderly separation. But for all this, he will not deny his presence upon just occasion, to any Christian congregation that worships God in truth, though with many modal imperfections, so be it they impose no sin upon him as necessary to his communion with them. Nor will he deny the spiritual communion of faith and love to those that he holds not local communion with : he knows that all our worship of God is sinfully imperfect, and that it is a dividing principle to hold, that we may join with none that worship God in a faulty manner ; for then we must join with none on earth. He knows that his presence in the worship of God, is no sign of his approbation of all the failings of pastors or people, in their personal or modal imperfections, as long as he joins not in a worship so corrupt as to be itself unacceptable to God.

While men who are all imperfect and corrupt, are the worshippers, the manner of their worship will be such as they, in some degree, imperfect and corrupt. The solid Christian hath an eye upon all the churches in the world, in the determining of such questions ; he considers what worship is offered to God in the churches of the several parties of Christians, the Greeks, Armenians, Abassines, Lutherans, &c. as well as what is done in the country where he lives ; and he considers whether God disown and reject the worship of almost all the churches in the world, or not ; for he dares no further reject them than God rejects them. Nor will he voluntarily separate from those assemblies where the presence of Christ, in his spirit and acceptance yet remains. His fuller acquaintance with the gracious nature, office, and tenderness of Christ, together with greater love to his brethren, causes him in this to judge more gently than young censorious Christians do. And his humble acquaintance with his own infirmities, makes him the more compassionate to others. If he should think that God would reject all that order not, and word not their prayers aright, he would be afraid of being rejected himself, who is still conscious of greater faultiness in his own prayers, than a mere defect in words and order; even of a great defectiveness in that faith, desire, love, zeal, and reverence which should be manifested in prayer. Though he be more apprehensive than others, of the excellency and necessity of the holiness and spirituality of the soul in worship; yet withal he is more judicious and charitable than the peevish and passionate infant Christians, who think that God doth judge as they do, and sees no grace where they see none; and takes all to be superstitious or fanatical, that differ from their opinions or manner of worship; or that he is as ready to call every error in the method or the words of prayer, idolatry or will-worship, as those are that speak not what they know, but what they have heard some teachers, whom they reverence, say before them. ' He that dwelleth in love, dwells in God, and God in him :' and he that dwells with God, is likelier to be best acquainted with his mind, concerning his children and his worship, than he that dwells in wrath, pride, and partiality.

2. But the weak Christian, though so far as he hath grace, he is of the same mind, and abhors discord and division among the flock of Christ; yet being more dark, selfish, and distempered, he is much more prone to unwarrantable separations and divisions than the stronger Christian is. He is narrower sighted, and looks little further than his own acquaintance, and the country where he lives; and minds not sufficiently the general state of the churches through the world, nor understands well the interest of Christ and Christianity in the earth. His knowledge and experience being small, his charity also is but small; and a little thing tempts him to condemn another, aggravate his faults, and think him unworthy of the communion of the saints. He is much more sensible of the judgment, affections, and concerns of those few with whom he converses, and that are of his opinion, than of the judgment, and practice, and concerns of the universal church. He knows not how to prefer the judgments and holiness of some that he thinks more excellent than the rest, without much undervaluing and censuring of all others that are not of their opinion: he cannot choose the actual local communion of the best society,

without some unjust contempt of others, or separation from them. He hath not so much knowledge as may sufficiently acquaint him with his ignorance; therefore he is apt to be unreasonably confident of his present apprehensions, and to think verily that all his own conceptions are the certain truth; and to think them ignorant or ungodly, or very weak at least, that differ from him. For he hath not thoroughly and impartially studied all that may be said on the other side. The authority of his chosen teacher and sect is greater with him, if he fall into that way, than the authority of all the most wise and holy persons in the world besides. What the scripture speaks of the unbelieving world, he is apt to apply to all those of the church of Christ who are not of his mind and party : when Christ commands us to come out of the world, he is prone to understand it of coming out from the church into some stricter and more narrow society; and is apt, with the papists, to appropriate the name and privileges of the church to his party alone, and to condemn all others : especially if the church-governors be carnal and self-seeking, or otherwise very culpable : and if discipline be neglected, and if profaneness be not sufficiently discountenanced, and godliness promoted, he thinks that such a church is no church, but a profane society : God hath taught him by repentance to see the mischief of ungodliness, but he yet wants that experience which is needful to make him know the mischief of church-divisions. He had too much experience himself of the evil of profaneness before his conversion; but he hath not tried the evil of schism; and without some sad experience of its fruits, in himself or others, he will hardly know it as it should be known; because it is the custom of some malignant enemies of godliness to call the godly heretics, schismatics, factious sectarians, &c. therefore the very names come into credit with him; and he thinks there are no such persons in the world, or that there is no danger of any such crimes, till he be taught, by sad experience, that the professors of sincerity are in as much danger on that side as on the other; and that the church, as well as Christ, doth suffer between two thieves, the profane and the dividers.

Paul was unjustly called the ringleader of a sect, and Christianity called a heresy and a sect every where spoken against. But for all that, heresy is a fruit of the flesh, and some of them are called damnable; they are the trial of the church, to distinguish the approved members from the chaff. An obstinate heretic is to be avoided by true believers. Dividers and divisions are justly branded in scripture, as aforesaid. There must be no schism in the body of Christ, the following of selected teachers, in a way of division from the rest, or opposition to them, shows that men are carnal in too great a measure, though it be not in predominancy, as in the profane. ' And I, brethren, could not speak unto you as unto spiritual, but as unto carnal, as unto babes in Christ: I have fed you with milk, and not with meat; for hitherto ye were not able to bear it, neither yet now are ye able. For ye are yet carnal: for whereas there is among you envying, strife, and divisions, are ye not carnal, and walk as men ? For while one saith, I am of Paul, and another, I am of Apollos, are ye not carnal?' How much more when he that is for Paul censures and rails at Cephas and Apollos ? He that hath seen the course of men professing godliness in England in this age, may easily and sadly know how prone weak Christians are to unjust separations and divisions, and what are the effects: he that had heard many zealous in prayer, and other duties, and the next year see them turning Quakers, and railing in the open congregations at the ablest, holiest, self-denying ministers of Christ, and at their flocks, with a ' come down, thou deceiver, thou hireling, thou wolf; ye are all greedy dogs,' &c. and shall see how yet poor souls run into that reviling and irrational sect, to say nothing of all other sects among us, will no longer doubt whether the weak be inclinable to schism, but will rather lament the danger of their station ; and know that all is not done when a sinner is converted from an ungodly state. Study the reason of those three texts : ' For the edifying the body of Christ, till we all come in the unity of the faith, and of the knowledge of the Son of God, unto a perfect man : unto the measure of the stature of the fulness of Christ ; that we henceforth be no more children tossed to and fro, and carried about with every wind of doctrine, by the sleight of men, and cunning craftiness whereby they lie in wait to deceive ; but speaking the truth in love, may grow up unto him in all things, which is the head, even Christ; from whom the whole body fitly joined together and compacted, by that which every joint supplies, according to the effectual working in the measure of every part, maketh increase of the body, to the edifying of itself in love.' Here you see the children are apt to be carried into dividing parties. And that they are most apt to be proud, and in that way to miscarry. ' Not a novice (or raw young Christian) lest being lifted up with pride, he fall into the condemnation of the devil ;' and then follows the effect, ' also of your own selves shall men arise, speaking perverse things, to draw away disciples after them.' I would not have you groundlessly accuse any Christian with a charge of pride : but I must tell you, that the childish pride of apparel, is a petty business in comparison of that pride which many in sordid attire have manifested, who in their ignorance rage and foam out words of falsehood and reproach against Christ's ministers and servants, as if they were all fools or impious in comparison of them, speaking evil of that which they never understood : the lifting up the heart above the people of the Lord, in the pride of supposed holiness, is incomparably worse than pride of learning, honour, greatness, wit or wealth. Nay, it hath often been to me a matter of wonder to observe how little all those plain and urgent texts of scripture, which cry down division, work upon many of the younger Christians, who yet are as quickly touched as any with a text that speaks against profaneness and lukewarmness. In a word, they are often of the temper of James and John, when they would have had Christ revenge himself on his opposers by fire from heaven, ' they know not what manner of spirit they are of.' They think verily that it is a holy zeal for God, when it is the boiling of passion, pride and selfishness: they feel not the sense of such words as Christ's, ' I pray also for them who shall believe on me, through their word, that they all may be one, as thou Father art in me, and I in thee, that they also may be one in us, that the world may believe that thou hast sent me,' &c.

3. As for the seeming Christian, in this they are of several sorts. When their carnal interest lies in compliance with the major part and stronger side, then no men more cry up unity and obedience. What a noise do many thousand Papists, prelates, Jesuits, and friars, make with these two words throughout the world ? Unity and obedience unto them, upon their terms, signify principally their worldly greatness, wealth and power. But if the hypocrite be engaged in point of honour, or other carnal interest on the suffering side, or be out of hope of any advantage in the common road ; then no man is so much for separation and singularity as he. For he must needs be noted for some body in the world, and this is the chief way that he finds to accomplish it. And so being ' lifted up with pride, he falleth into the condemnation of the devil,' and becomes a fire-brand in the church.

LIII. 1. A Christian indeed is not only zealous for the unity and concord of believers, but he seeks it on the right terms, and in the way that is fittest to attain it. Unity, peace and concord, are like piety and honesty, things so unquestionably good, that there are scarcely any men of reason and common sobriety, that ever were heard to oppose them directly and for themselves: therefore all that are enemies to them, are yet pretenders to them and oppose them. 1. In their causes only. 2. Or covertly and under some other name. Every man would have unity, concord and peace in his own way, and upon his own terms: but if the right terms had been understood and consented to as sufficient, the Christian world had not been so many hundred years in the sin, shame, and ruins as it hath lain. The cause of all is, that Christians indeed, that have clear confirmed judgments and strength of grace, are very few; and for number and strength unable to persuade or over-rule the weak, the passionate and the false-hearted worldly hypocritical multitude, who bear down all the counsels and endeavours of the wise.

The judicious, faithful Christian knows, that there are three degrees or sorts of Christian communion, which have their several terms. 1. The universal church communion, which all Christians, as such, must hold among themselves. 2. Particular church communion, which those that are united for personal communion in worship, hold under the same pastors and among themselves. 3. The extraordinary intimate communion that some Christians hold together, who are bosom friends, or are specially able and fit to be helpful and comfortable to each other.

The last concerns not our present business; we must hold church communion with many that are unfit to be our bosom friends, and that have no eminency of parts or piety, or any strong persuading evidence of sincerity. But the terms of catholic communion, he knows, are such as these: 1. They must be such as were the terms of church communion in the days of the apostles. 2. They must be such as are plainly and certainly expressed in the holy scriptures. 3. And such as the universal church has in some ages since been actually agreed in. 4. And those points are likeliest to be such, which all the differing parties of Christians are agreed in as necessary to communion to this day (so we call not those Christians that deny the essentials of Christianity.) 5. Every man in the former ages of the church was admitted to this catholic church communion, who in the baptismal vow or covenant gave up himself to God, the Father, Son and Holy Ghost, as his Creator, Redeemer and Sanctifier, his Owner, Governor and Father,

renouncing the flesh, the world and the devil. More particularly, as man hath an understanding, a will and an executive power, which must all be sanctified to God, so the creed was the particular rule for the *credenda* or things to be believed, and the Lord's prayer for the *pretenda* or things to be willed, loved and desired, and the ten commandments for the *agenda* or things to be done; so that to consent to these rules particularly, and to all the holy scriptures implicitly and generally, was the thing then required to catholic communion. The belief of the doctrine being necessary for the sanctifying of the heart and life, the belief of so much is of necessity, without which the heart cannot be sanctified, or devoted in covenant to God our Creator, Redeemer and Regenerator; and without which we cannot love God, as reconciled to us in Christ, above all, and our neighbours as ourselves. So that, in a word, he that can tell what the baptismal vow or covenant is, can tell what is necessary to that catholic church communion, which belongs to Christians as Christians, at how great a distance soever they dwell from one another.

Then for particular church communion, which is local and personal, it is moreover necessary, 1. That each member agree to acknowledge and submit to the same pastors. 2. That they be guided by them in the convenient circumstances and adjuncts of worship: for if some persons will not consent or submit to the same pastors that the body of the church consents and submits to, they cannot have communion particularly and locally with that church, nor are they members of it; no more than they can be members of the same kingdom that have not the same king: and there being no solemn worship performed but by the ministry of those pastors, they cannot join in the worship that join not with the minister. And if some members will not consent and submit to the necessary determination of the adjuncts or external modes of worship, they cannot join in local, particular church communion where that worship is performed: as if the pastor and the body of the church will meet in such a place, at such a day and hour, and some members will not meet with them at that place, day, and hour, they cannot possibly then have their local personal communion. Or if the pastor will use such a translation of the scriptures, or such a version of the psalms, or such a method in preaching and prayer, or such notes or books, and other like helps; if any members will not submit, nor hold communion with the rest, unless that translation, or version, or method of preaching, or praying, or notes or books be laid aside, he cannot have communion while he refuses it. If the pastor and all the rest will not yield to him, he must join with some other church that he can agree with. As long as the catholic church communion is maintained, which consists in unity of the Christian covenant, or of Christianity, or of faith, love, and obedience, the difference of modes and circumstances between particular churches must be allowed without any breach of charity, or without disowning one another: and he that cannot be a member of one particular church, may quietly join himself to another, without condemning that which he dissents from, so far as to hinder his catholic communion with it, even as among the papists, men may be of what order or religious persons they best like, as long as they submit to their general government. Here the strong, judicious Christian, for his part, will never be guilty of church divisions : for, 1. He will make nothing necessary to church communion which any sober, pious, peaceable minds shall have any just reason to except against, or which may not well be manifested to be for the edification of the church. 2. He will bear with the weak dissenters so far as will stand with the peace and welfare of the church. 3. He will particularly give leave to such weak ones as cannot yet hold communion with him, being peaceable, and not promoting heresy, ungodliness or sedition, to join another church where they can hold communion, with peace to their own consciences ; as long as they continue their aforesaid catholic communion. For the strong know that they must not only 'bear with, but bear the infirmities of the weak, and not to please themselves, but every one of them to please his neighbour for good to edification. For even Christ pleased not himself.' And so they will ' receive one another, as Christ also received us to the glory of God, not despising the weak, nor rejecting them that God receiveth.' Thus you may see how easy a matter it were to unite and reconcile all the Christian world, if the principles of the judicious, confirmed Christian might be received and prevail ; and that it is not he that is the cause of the abundance of sin and calamity which divisions have caused, and continued in the church. But that which now seems an impossible thing, may quickly and easily be accomplished, if all were such as he : and that the difficulty of reconciling and uniting Christians, lies not first in finding out the terms, but in making men fit to receive and practise the terms from the beginning received by the churches.

2. But the weak Christian is too easily tempted to be the divider of the church, by expecting that it be united upon his impossible or unrighteous terms. Sometimes he will be orthodox overmuch, or rather wise in his own conceit, and then none are judged for his communion that are not of his opinion, in controverted doctrinals; e. g. predestination, the manner of the work of grace, free-will, perseverance, and abundance such. Sometimes he will be righteous overmuch, or, to speak more properly, superstitious : and then none are fit for his communion, that worship not God in that method and manner for circumstantials, which he esteems best : and his charity is so weak that it frees him not from thinking evil, and so narrow that it covers not either many or great infirmities. The more need he hath of the forbearance and charity of others, the less can he bear or forbear others himself. The strong Christian must bear the infirmities of the weak ; but the weak Christian can scarcely bear with the weak or strong : nay, he is often too impatient with some of their virtues and duties, as well as with their infirmities. He is of too private a spirit, and too insensible of the public interest of the church of Christ. Therefore he must have all the world come over to him, and be conformed to his opinion and party, and unite upon his mistaken narrow terms, if they will have communion with him : I mean, it is thus with him, when the temptation on that side prevails. Sometimes he is overcome with the temptation of domination, to make his judgment the rule to others ; then he quite overvalues his own understanding, and will needs be judge of all the controversies in the church, and takes it as unsufferable if wiser and better men do not take him as infallible, and in every thing observe his will. When his brethren give him the reason of their dissent, as his judgment is not clear enough to understand them, so his passion and partiality are too strong to suffer his judgment to do its part. Thus oftentimes he is a greater hinderance to the church's unity, than the enemies of the church themselves : for he hath not judgment enough to guide him the right way, and yet he hath so much zeal as will not suffer him to keep his errors to himself.

3. All these distempers that are but in a lower degree in the weak Christian, are predominant in the hypocrite. The church shall have no concord or peace if he can hinder it, but what is consistent with his carnal interest, his honour, or wealth, or dignity in the world. The pride and covetousness which rule himself, he would have to make the terms of concord, and to rule all others

It is hypocrites in the church that are the greatest cause of discord and divisions, having selfish spirits, principles and ends, and having always a work of their own to do, which suits not well with the work of Christ; and yet Christ's work must be subjected to it, and ordered and over-ruled by it. While they pretend to go to the scriptures, or to councils, or fathers for their reasons, indeed they go first for them to their worldly interest; and then would hire or press the scripture, church or fathers to serve their turn, and come in as witnesses on their side. Thus the church, as well as Christ, is betrayed by the covetous Judases of his own family: and the servants of the world, the flesh and the devil, that take up the livery of Christ, and usurp the name and honour of Christians, more effectually hinder the concord and prosperity of the church, than any open enemies do. Those that are indeed non-Christians cause Christianity to be reproached; even as spies and traitors that are hired by the enemy to take up arms in the army which they fight against, that they may betray it by their fraud, and do more harm to it, by raising mutinies, and by false conduct, than a multitude of professed enemies could have done. It is proud, and worldly carnal hypocrites, that hinder most the concord of believers.

LIV. 1. A confirmed Christian is of a peaceable spirit. He is not masterly, domineering, turbulent, hurtful, cruel, seditious, factious, or contentious. He is like ripened fruits that are mellow and sweet, when the younger, greener fruits are sour and harsh. He is not wise in his own conceit, and therefore not over urgent in obtruding his conceits on others, not quarrelsome with all that cannot entertain them, nor will he easily lay men's salvation or damnation, no, nor the church's peace upon them. He is 'kindly affectioned to others with brotherly love, yea, loveth his neighbour as himself.' Therefore he doth to others as he would they should do to him; and uses them as he would be used by them: then how far they are like to suffer by him, you may easily judge. For 'love worketh no ill to his neighbour.' He is above the portion of the worldling, and a contemner of that vanity which carnal men account their felicity; and therefore he prefers love and quietness before it, and can lose his right when the interest of love and peace requires it. He is become as a little child in his conversion; and is low and little in his own eyes, and therefore contends not for superiority or pre-eminence, either in place or power, or reputation of his learning, wisdom, or piety; but in honour preferreth others before

himself. 'He mindeth not high things, but condescendeth to men of low estate,' and therefore will not contend for estimation or precedency, nor scramble to be highest, though he rise by the ruins of men's bodies and souls. 'If it be possible, as much as lieth in him, he will live peaceably with all men.' For he is not one that by word or deed will avenge himself; but when the wrath of others is up like a blustering storm, he gives place to it, he bows before it, or goes out of the way. 'If his enemy hunger, he feedeth him, if he thirst, he giveth him drink,' when oppressors would deprive not only an enemy, but the righteous of their meat and drink; and thus he melts his hardened enemies, by heaping kindnesses upon them when they are wrathful, proud, contentious, and do him wrong, or use provoking words against him; he is not overcome of their evil to imitate them, but he overcomes their evil with his good. If God have given him more knowledge and abilities than others, he doth not presently set up himself to be admired for it, nor speak disdainfully and contemptuously of those that are not of his mind: but he shows the eminence of his wisdom, 'with meekness, by the works of a good conversation,' and by doing better than the unwiser do. He is endued with 'the wisdom from above, which is first pure, then peaceable, gentle, easy to be entreated, full of mercy and good fruits, without partiality,' (or wavering in persecution, as Dr Hammond renders it,) 'and without hypocrisy.' And thus 'the fruit of righteousness is sown in peace of them that make peace.' As he is taught of God to love his brother, so that same teaching with experience of the effects, assures him, that they that pretend to be wiser and better than others, when 'they have bitter, envious zeal and strife in their hearts, they vainly glory and lie against the truth. This wisdom descendeth not from above, but is earthly, sensual, and devilish. For where envying and strife is, there is confusion and every evil work.' Read but the story of the Jewish zealots in Josephus, and heretical zealots in all the ages of the church, and you will perceive the truth of this, when such quarrelsome spirits are filling the church with contentions or vexations about their meats, drinks, days, &c. The Christian indeed understands that the kingdom of God consists not of such things as these, but in righteousness and peace, and joy in the Holy Ghost; 'and he that in these things serveth Christ, is acceptable to God, and approveth of (wise and sober) men. Therefore he follows after things which make for peace and things wherewith one may edify another; and will not for meats, &c. destroy the work of God.' He stays not till peace be offered him, or brought home to him, but ' he followeth peace with all men, as well as holiness.' If it fly from him, he pursues it; if it be denied him, he seeks it, and will not refuse to stoop to the poorest for it, and to beg it of his inferiors, if it were upon his knees, rather than be denied it, and live an unpeaceable, disquiet life, for he believes that 'blessed are the peace-makers, for they shall be called the children of God.'

2. And the weak Christian hath the same spirit, and therefore the love of peace is most predominant in him: but alas, he is too easily tempted into religious passions, discontents, contentious disputations, quarrelsome and opprobrious words; and his judgment lamentably darkened and perverted whenever contentious zeal prevails, and passions perturb the quiet and orderly operations of his soul. He wants both the knowledge and the experience, and the mellowness of spirit, which riper Christians have attained: he hath a less degree of charity, and is less acquainted with the mischiefs of contention: therefore it is the common course of young professors to be easily tempted into unpeaceable ways; and when they have long tried them, if they prove not hypocrites, to come off at last upon experience of the evils of them; and so the young Christians united with some hypocrites, make up the rigorous, fierce, contentious and vexatious party, and the aged riper Christians make up the holy, moderate, healing party, that groan and pray for the church's peace, and mourn in secret both for the ungodliness and violence which they cannot heal. Yea, the difference is much apparent in the books and sermons which each of them is best pleased with. The ripe experienced Christian loves those sermons that kindle love, and tend to peace; and love such healing books as narrow differences and tend to peace; and love such healing books as narrow differences, and tend to reconcile and heal; but the younger, sour, uncharitable Christians are better pleased with such books and sermons as call them aloud to be very zealous for this or that controverted point of doctrine, or for or against some circumstance of worship or church discipline, or about some fashions, or customs, or indifferent things, as if the kingdom of God were in them.

3. But the seeming Christian is either a mere temporizer that will be of that religion, whatever it be, which is most in fashion, or which the higher powers are of, or which will cost him least: or else he will run into the other extreme, and lift up himself by affected singularities, and by making a bustle and stir in the world about some small and controverted point, and cares not to sacrifice the peace and safety of the church to the honour of his own opinions. And as small as the Christian church is, he must be of a smaller society than it, that he may be sure to be amongst the best: while indeed he hath no sincerity at all, but places his hopes in being of the right church or party, or opinion: and for his party or church, he burns with a feverish kind of zeal, and is ready to call for fire from heaven, and to deceive him, the devil sends him some from hell, to consume those that are not of his mind: yet doth he bring it as an angel of light to defend the truth and church of Christ: and indeed, when the devil will be the defender of truth, or of the church, or of peace, or order, or piety, he doth it with the most burning zeal: you may know him by the means he uses. He defends the church by forbidding the people to read the scriptures in a known tongue, and by imprisoning and burning the soundest and holiest members of it, and abusing the most learned faithful pastors, and defends the flock by casting out the shepherds, and such like means; as the murders of the Waldenses, and the massacres of France and Ireland, the Spanish inquisition, Queen Mary's bonfires, and the powder-plot; yea, and the Munster, the English rage and phrensies, may give you fuller notice of: he that hath no holiness, or charity to be zealous for, will be zealous for his church, or sect, or customs, or opinions. And then this zeal must be the evidence of his piety; and so the inquisitors have thought they have religiously served God, by murdering his servants; and it is the badge of their honour to be the devil's hangmen, to execute his malice on the members of Christ; and all this is done in zeal for religion by irreligious hypocrites. There is no standing before the malicious zeal of a graceless pharisee, when it rises up for his carnal interest, or the honour, traditions, and customs of his sect; ' and they were filled with madness, and communed with one another what they might do to Jesus.' The zeal of a true Christian consumes himself with grief to see the madness of the wicked: but the zeal of the hypocrite consumes others, that by the light of the fire his religion may be seen; you may see the Christian's fervent love to God, by the fervent flames which he can suffer for his sake: and you may see the fervent love of the hypocrite, by the flames which he kindles for others; by these he cries with Jehu, ' come and see my zeal for the Lord.'

LV. 1. A Christian indeed is one that most

highly esteems and regards the interest of God and men's salvation in the world; and takes all things else to be inconsiderable in comparison of these. The interest of great men, nobles, and commanders, yea, and his own in corporal respects, as riches, honour, health, and life, he takes to be things unworthy to be named in competition with the interest of Christ and souls. The thing that his heart is most set upon in the world, is that God be glorified, that the world acknowledge him their king, that his laws be obeyed, and that darkness, infidelity, and ungodliness, may be cast out: and that pride, worldliness, and fleshly lusts, may not hurry the miserable world unto perdition. It is one of the saddest and most amazing thoughts that ever enters into his heart, to consider how much of the world is overwhelmed in ignorance and wickedness, and how great the kingdom of the devil is in comparison of the kingdom of Christ: that God should forsake so much of his creation; that Christianity should not be owned in above the sixth part of the world; and popish pride and ignorance, with the corruptions of many other sects, and the worldly, carnal minds of hypocrites, should rob Christ of so much of this little part, and leave him so small a flock of holy ones, that must possess the kingdom. His soul consents to the method of the Lord's prayer, as prescribing us the order of our desires. And in his prayers he seeks first, in order of estimation and intention, the 'hallowing of God's name, and the coming of his kingdom, and the doing of his will on earth as it is done in heaven,' before his daily bread, or the pardon of his sins, or the deliverance of his own soul from temptations and the evil one. Mark him in his prayers, and you shall find that he is above other men, taken up in earnest petitions for the conversion of the heathen and infidel world, and the undeceiving of Mahometans, Jews, and heretics, and the clearing of the church from those papal tyrannies, fopperies, and corruptions, which make Christianity hateful or contemptible in the eyes of the heathen and Mahometan world, and hinder their conversion. No man so much laments the pride, covetousness, laziness, and unfaithfulness of the pastors of the church, because of the doleful consequents to the gospel, and the souls of men; and yet with all possible honour to the sacred office which they thus profane. No man so heartily laments the contentions and divisions among Christians, and the doleful destruction of charity thereby. It grieves him to see how much selfishness, pride, and malice, prevails with them that should shine as lights in a benighted world,

and how obstinate and incurable they seem to be, against the plainest means, and humblest motions, for the church's edification and peace. He envies not kings and great men their dominions, wealth, or pleasure; nor is he at all ambitious to participate in their exaltation: but the thing that his heart is set upon is, that 'the kingdoms of the world may all become the kingdoms of the Lord,' and that the gospel may every where have free course and be glorified, and the preachers of it be encouraged, or at least delivered from unreasonable wicked men. Little cares he who is uppermost or conquers in the world, or who goes away with the preferments or riches of the earth (supposing that he fail not of his duty to his rulers), so that if it may go well with the affairs of the gospel, and souls be but helped in the way to heaven. Let God be honoured, and souls converted and edified, and he is satisfied. This is it that makes the times good in his account: he thinks not as the proud and carnal church of Rome, that the times are best when the clergy are richest and greatest in the world, overtop princes, claim the secular power, and live in worldly pomp and pleasures, but when holiness most abounds, when the members of Christ are most like to their Head, when multitudes of sincere believers are daily added to the church, and when the mercy and holiness of God shine forth in the numbers and purity of his saints. It is no riches or honour that can be heaped upon himself, or any others, that make the times seem good to him, if knowledge and godliness are discountenanced and hindered, and the way to heaven is made more difficult; if atheism, infidelity, ungodliness, pride, and malignity prevail; and truth and sincerity are driven into the dark, and when 'he that departeth from evil maketh himself a prey,' when 'the godly man ceaseth, and the faithful fail from among the children of men, when every man speaketh vanity to his neighbour, and the poor are oppressed, the needy sigh, and the wicked walk on every side, when the vilest men are exalted.' The times are good when the men are good; and evil when the men are evil, be they ever so great or prosperous. As Nehemiah, when he was cup-bearer to the king himself, yet wept and mourned for the desolations of Jerusalem. Whoever prospers, the times are ill when there is a 'famine of the word of the Lord, and when the chief of the priests and people transgress, mock God's messengers, despise his words, and misuse his prophets;' when the apostles are 'charged to speak no more in the name of Christ.' It is a text enough to make one tremble, to think into what a desperate condition the Jews were carried by a partial, selfish zeal, 'who both killed the Lord Jesus, and their own prophets, and have persecuted us, and they please not God, and are contrary to all men; forbidding us to speak to the Gentiles that they might be saved; to fill up their sin alway: for the wrath is come upon them to the uttermost.' When the interest of themselves and their own nation, and priesthood, did so far blind and pervert them, that they durst persecute the preachers of the gospel, 'and forbid them to speak to the people that they may be saved, it was a sign that wrath was come upon them to the uttermost.' A Christian indeed had rather be without Jeroboam's kingdom, than make Israel to sin, and make the basest of the people priests, and stretch out his hand against the prophet of the Lord. He had rather labour with his hands, as Paul, and live in poverty and rags, so that the gospel may be powerfully and plentifully preached, and holiness abound, than to live in all the prosperity of the world, with the hinderance of men's salvation. He had rather be a door-keeper in the house of God, than be a lord in the kingdom of Satan: he cannot rise by the ruins of the church, nor feed upon those morsels that are the price of the blood of souls.

2. The weakest Christian is in all this of the same mind, saving that private and selfish interest is not so fully overcome, nor so easily and resolutely denied.

3. But here the hypocrite shows the falseness of his heart: his own interest is it that chooses his religion; and that he may not torment himself by being wicked in the open light, he makes himself believe that whatsoever is most for his own interest, is most pleasing unto God, and most for the good of souls, and the interest of the gospel; so that the carnal Romish clergy can persuade their consciences, that all the darkness and superstitions of their kingdom, and all their opposition to the light of the gospel of Christ, make for the honour of God and the good of souls, because they uphold their tyranny, wealth, pomp, and pleasure. Or if they cannot persuade their consciences to believe so gross a lie, let church and souls speed how they will, they will favour nothing that favours not their interest and ends. The interest of the flesh and spirit, of the world and Christ, are so repugnant, that commonly such worldlings take the serious practice of godliness for the most hateful thing, and the serious practisers of it for the most unsufferable persons. The enmity of interests, with the enmity of nature, between the woman's and the serpent's seed, will maintain that warfare to the end of the world, in which the prince of the powers of darkness shall seem to prevail, as he did against our crucified Lord: but he shall be overcome by his own successes, and the just shall conquer by patience when they seem most conquered. The name, form, and image of religion, the carnal hypocrite not only bears, but favours, and himself accepts: but the life and serious practice he abhors, as inconsistent with his worldly interest and ends. For these he can find in his heart, with Ahab, to hate and imprison Micaiah, and prefer his four hundred flattering prophets. If Luther will touch the pope's crown, and the friars' bellies, they will not scruple to oppose and ruin both him and all such preachers in the world, if they were able.

LVI. 1. A Christian indeed is one whose holiness usually makes him an eye-sore to the ungodly world; and his charity, peaceableness, and moderation, make him to be censured as not strict enough, by the superstitious and dividing sects of Christians. For seeing the church hath suffered between these two sorts of opposers, ever since the suffering of Christ himself, it cannot be but the solid Christian offends them both, because he hath that which both dislike. All the ungodly hate him for his holiness, which is cross to their interest and way; and all the dividers will censure him for that universal charity and moderation, which is against their factious and destroying zeal. Even Christ himself was not strict enough, in superstitious observances, for the ceremonious, zealous pharisees. He transgressed, with his disciples, the tradition of the elders, in neglecting their observances, who transgressed the commandment of God by their tradition. He was not strict enough in their uncharitable observation of the sabbath-day. John, who was eminent for fasting, they said had a devil. 'The son of man came eating and drinking; and they say, behold a man gluttonous, and a wine bibber, a friend of publicans and sinners. But wisdom is justified of her children.' And the weak Christians censured those that durst eat those meats and do those things which they conceived to be unlawful. They that err themselves, and make God a service which he never appointed, will censure all as lukewarm, or temporizers, or wide conscienced men, that err not with them, and place not their religion in such superstitious observances, as 'touch not, taste not, handle not,' &c. The raw censorious Christians are offended with the charitable Christian, because he condemns not as many and as readily as they, and shuts not others out of the number of believers, and judges not rigorously enough of their ways. In a word, he is taken by one sort to be too strict, and by the other to be too pliant or indifferent in religion, because he places not the kingdom of God in meats and days, and such like circumstances, but in ‘ righteousness, peace, and joy in the Holy Ghost.’ And as Paul withstood Peter to his face, for drawing men to make scruple or conscience of things lawful, so is the sound Christian withstood by the superstitious, for not making scruple of lawful things.

2. The weak Christian is in the same case, so long as he follows prudent, pious, charitable guides : but if he be taken in the snares of superstition, he pleases the superstitious party, though he displease the world.

3. Whereas the solid Christian will not stir an inch from truth and duty, to escape either the hatred of the wicked, or the bitterest censures of the sectary or the weak ; the hypocrite must needs have one party on his side : for if both condemn him, and neither applaud him, he loses his peculiar reward.

LVII. 1. The confirmed Christian understands the necessity of a faithful ministry, for the safety of the weak, as well as the conversion of the wicked, and for the preservation of the interest of religion upon earth. Therefore no personal unworthiness of ministers, nor any calumnies of enemies, can make him think or speak dishonourably of that sacred office : but he reverences it as instituted by Christ ; and though he lothes the sottishness and wickedness of those that run before they are sent, and are utterly insufficient or ungodly, and take it up for a living or trade only, as they would a common work ; and are sons of Belial, that know not the Lord, and ‘ cause the offering of the Lord to be abhorred.’ Yet no such temptation shall overthrow his reverence to the office, which is the ordinance of Christ ; much less will he be unthankful to those who are able and faithful in their office, and labour instantly for the good of souls, as willing to spend and be spent for their salvation. When the world abuses, derides, and injures them, he is one that honours them both for their work and Master's sake, and the experience which he hath had of the blessing of God on their labours to himself. For he knows that the smiting of the shepherds is but the devil's ancient way for the scattering of the flock : though he knows that ‘ if the salt have lost its savour, it is good for nothing, neither fit for the land, nor yet for the dung-hill, but men cast it out, and it is trodden under foot : he

that hath ears to hear, let him hear.’ Yet he also knows, that ‘ he that receiveth a prophet in the name of a prophet, shall receive a prophet's reward.’ And that ‘ he that receiveth them, receiveth Christ, and he that despiseth them that are sent by him, despiseth him.’ He therefore readily obeys those commands. ‘ Obey them that have the rule over you, and submit yourselves ; for they watch for your souls as those that must give account. We beseech you brethren, to know them which labour among you, and are over you in the Lord, and admonish you ; and to esteem them very highly in love for their works' sake, and be at peace among yourselves. Let the elders that rule well, be counted worthy of double honour ; especially they who labour in the word and doctrine.’

2. But though the weak Christian be of the same mind so far as he is sanctified, yet is he much more easily tempted into a wrangling censoriousness against his teachers, though they be ever so able and holy men ; and by seducers may be drawn to oppose them, or speak contemptuously of them, as the Galatians did of Paul, and some of the Corinthians ; accounting him as their enemy for telling them the truth, when lately they would have plucked out their eyes to do him good.

3. But the hypocrite is most easily engaged against them, either when they grate upon the guilt of his bosom sin, or open his hypocrisy, or plainly cross him in his carnal interest, or else when his pride hath conquered his sobriety, and engaged him in some sect or erroneous way, which his teachers are against, and would reduce him from.

LVIII. 1. A Christian indeed is one that hath stored up such manifold experience of the fulfilling of God's promises, of the hearing of prayers, and of the goodness of his holy ways, as will greatly fortify him against all temptations to infidelity, apostacy, or distrust. No one hath stronger temptations usually than he, and no one is so well furnished with weapons to resist them. The arguments of most others are drawn out of their books only ; but he hath moreover a life of experience to confirm his faith, and so hath the witness in himself. He hath tried and found that in God, in holiness, in faith, in prayer, which will never suffer him to forsake them. Yea, it is like that he hath upon record some such wonders in the answer of prayers, as might do much to silence an infidel himself. I am sure many Christians have had such strange appearances of the extraordinary hand of God, that hath done much to destroy the remnants of their own unbelief.

2. But the experiences of the younger, weaker Christians are much shorter, and less serviceable to their faith; and they have not judgment enough to understand and make use of the dealings of God; but are ready to plead his providences unto evil ends and consequences, and to take their own passionate imaginations for the workings of the Spirit. It is ordinary with them to say, this or that was set upon my heart, or spoken to me, as if it had been some divine inspiration, when it was nothing but the troubled workings of a weak, distempered brain: and it is their own fancy and heart that saith that to them, which they think the Spirit of God within them said.

3. The hypocrite wants those establishing experiments of the power of the gospel, and the hearing of prayers, and fulfilling of promises, and communion with Christ in the Spirit: therefore he is the more open to the power of temptations, and a subtle disputer will more easily corrupt him, and carry him away to apostacy: for he wants the root and witness in himself.

LIX. 1. A Christian indeed is one that highly values sanctified affections and passions, that all he doth may be done as lively as possibly he can: and also holy abilities for expression. But he much more values the three great essential constant parts of the new creature within him; that is, 1. A high estimation of God, Christ, and heaven, and holiness in his understanding, above all that can be set in any competition. 2. A resolved choice and adhesion of the will, by which he prefers God, Christ, heaven, and holiness, above all that can be set against them, and is fixedly resolved here to place his happiness and his hopes. 3. The drift and endeavours of his life, in which he seeks first the kingdom of God and his righteousness. In these three, his highest estimation, his resolved choice and complacencies, and his chief endeavours, he takes his standing constant evidences of his sincerity to consist: and by these he tries himself as to his state, and not by the passionate feelings or affections of his heart, nor by his memory, or gifts, or orderly thinking or expression. It is these rational operations of his soul, in which he knows that holiness principally consists; and therefore he chiefly labours to be strong in these. 1. To ground his judgment well. 2. To resolve to fix his will. 3. And to order his conversation aright, yet highly valuing sensible affections and gifts of utterance, but in subserviency to those which are the vital acts.

2. But the weak Christian usually places most of his religion in the more affectionate and expressive part: he strives more with his heart for passionate apprehensions, than for complacency and fixed resolution. He is often in doubt of his sincerity, when he wants the feeling, affectionate workings which he desires, &c. thinks he hath no more grace than that he hath sensibility of expressive gifts. And so as he builds his comfort upon these unconstant signs, his comforts are accordingly unconstant. Sometimes he thinks he hath grace, when his body, or other advantages do help the excitation of his lively affections: and when the dulness of his body, or other impediments hinder this, he questions his grace again, because he understands not aright the nature and chief acts of grace.

3. The hypocrite hath neither the rational, nor the passionate part in sincerity: but he may go much further in the latter than in the former: a quick and passionate nature, though unsanctified, may be brought to shed more tears, and express more fervour than many a holy person can; especially upon the excitement of some quickening sermon, or some sharp affliction, or great conviction, or at the approach of death. Few of the most holy persons can constantly retain so lively, fervent, passionate repentings, desires, and resolutions to amend, as some carnal persons have in sickness. The power of fear alone makes them more earnest, than love makes many a gracious soul: but when the fear is over, they are the same again. How often have I heard a sick man most vehemently profess his resolutions for a holy life, which all have come to nothing afterwards? How often have I heard a common drunkard, with tears, cry out against himself for his sin, and yet go on in it? And how many gracious persons have I known, whose judgments and wills have been resolved for God and holiness, and their lives have been holy, fruitful, and obedient, who yet could not shed a tear for sin, nor feel any very great sorrows or joys? If you judge of a man by his earnestness in some good moods, and not by the constant tenor of his life, you will think many an hypocrite to be better than most saints. Who would have thought that had seen him only in that fit, but that Saul had been a penitent man, when ' he lifted up his voice and wept, and said to David, Thou art more righteous than I; for thou hast rewarded me good, whereas I have rewarded thee evil.' A smaller matter will raise some sudden passions that will renew the soul, and give the pre-eminence to God, holiness, and heaven, in the judgment, will, and conversation.

LX. 1. A Christian indeed, confirmed in grace, is one that makes it the business of his life to prepare for death; and delays not his serious thoughts of it, and preparations for it till it surprise him; and therefore when it comes it finds him prepared, and he gladly entertains it as the messenger of his Father, to call him to his everlasting home. It is not a strange unexpected thing to him, to hear he must die: he dieth daily in his daily sufferings, and mortified contempt of worldly things, and in his daily expectation of his change. He wonders to see men at a dying time, surprised with astonishment and terror, who gaily or carelessly neglected it before, as if they had never known till then that they must die; or as if a few years' time were reason enough for so great a difference. For that which he certainly knows will be, he looks at as if it were even at hand; and his preparation for it is more serious in his health than other men's is on their death bed. He more carefully bethinks himself what graces he shall need at a dying time, and in what case he shall then wish his soul to be; and accordingly he labours in his provisions now, even as if it were to be to-morrow. He verily believes that it is incomparably better for him to be with Christ, than to abide on earth, and therefore, though death of itself be an enemy, and terrible to nature, yet being the only passage into happiness, he gladly entertains it. Though he have not himself any clear and satisfactory apprehensions of the place and state of the happiness of departed souls, yet it quiets him to know that they shall be with Christ, and that Christ knows all, and prepares and secures for him that promised rest. Though he is not free from all the natural fears of death, yet his belief and hope of endless happiness abates those fears, by the joyful expectation of the gain which follows.

But especially he loves and longs for the coming of Christ to judgment, as knowing that then the marriage-day of the Lamb is come, and then the desires and hopes of all believers shall be satisfied; ' then shall the righteous shine as stars in the kingdom of their Father;' and the hand of violence shall not reach them. Every enemy then is overcome, and all the Redeemer's work is consummated, and the kingdom delivered up unto the Father: then shall the ungodly and the unmerciful be confounded, and the righteous filled with everlasting joy, when their Lord shall thoroughly plead their cause, and justify them against the accusations of Satan, and all the lies of his malicious instruments. O blessed, glorious, joyful day, when Christ shall come with thousands of his angels, to execute vengeance on the ungodly world, and to be glorified in his saints, and admired in all them that now believe. When the patient followers of the Lamb shall behold him in glory, whom they have believed in, and shall see that they did not pray, or hope, or wait in vain! When Christ himself and his sacred truth, shall be justified and glorified in the presence of the world, and his enemies' mouths for ever stopped. ' When he shall convince all that are ungodly of all their ungodly deeds, which they have impiously committed, and of all their hard speeches, which ungodly sinners have spoken against him.' Where then is the mouth that pleads the cause of infidelity and impiety, reproached the serious holiness of believers, and made a jest of the judgments of the Lord? Then what terrors, confusion, and shame, what fruitless repentings will seize upon that man, that set himself against the holy ones of the Lord, and knew not the day of his visitation, and embraced the image and form of godliness, while he abhorred the power. The joys which will then possess the hearts of the justified, will be such as now no heart can comprehend. When love shall come to be glorified in the highest expression, to those that lately were so low; when all their doubts, fears, and sorrows, shall be turned into full contenting sight, and all tears shall be wiped away, and all reproaches turned into glory, and every enemy overcome, sin destroyed, and holiness perfected, and our ' vile bodies changed, and made like the glorious body of Christ,' then will the love and work of our redemption be fully understood: and then a saint will be a saint indeed, when with Christ they shall judge the angels and the world, and shall hear from Christ, ' come ye blessed of my Father, inherit the kingdom prepared for you from the foundation of the world, enter ye into the joy of your Lord;' then ' every knee shall bow to Christ, and every tongue shall confess that he is Lord, to the glory of God the Father.' Then sin will fully appear in its malignity, and holiness in its lustre unto all: the proud will then be abased, and the mouths of all the wicked stopped, when they shall see to their confusion, the glory of that Christ whom they despised, and of those holy ones whom they made their scorn. In vain will they then ' knock when the door is shut and cry, Lord, Lord, open unto us,' and in vain will they then say, O that we had known the day of our visitation, that we might have ' died the death of the righteous, and our latter end might have been as his.'

The day of death is to true believers a day of happiness and joy: but it is much easier for them to think with joy on the coming of Christ and the day of judgment, because it is a day of fuller joy, and soul and body shall be joined in the blessedness; and there is nothing in it to be so great a stop to our desires, as death is, which naturally is an enemy. God hath put a love of life, and fear of death, into the nature of every sensible creature, as necessary for the preservation of themselves and others, and the orderly government of the world: but what is there in the blessed day of judgment, which a justified child of God should be averse to? O if he were but sure that this would be the day, or week, or year of the coming of his Lord, how glad would the confirmed Christian be! And with what longings would he be looking up, to see that most desired sight.

2. The weak Christian is so far of the same mind, that he had rather come to God by death and judgment, than not all; except when temptations make him fear that he shall be condemned. He hath fixedly made choice of that felicity, which till then he cannot attain. He would not take all the pleasures of this world for his hopes of the happiness of that day: but yet he thinks not of it with so strong a faith and great consolation, nor with such boldness and desire, as the confirmed Christian doth; but either with much more dull security, or more perplexity and fear. His thoughts of God and of the world to come, are much more dark and doubtful, and his fears of that day, are usually so great as make his desires and joys scarcely felt: only he thinks not of it with that contempt or stupidity as the infidel or hardened sinner, nor with the terrors of those that have no God, no Christ, no hope: except when temptation brings him near to the borders of despair. His death indeed is unspeakably safer than the death of the ungodly, and the joys which he is entering into will quickly end the terror; but yet he hath no great comfort at the present, but only so much trust in Christ, as keeps his heart from sinking into despair.

3. But to the hypocrite or seeming Christian, death and judgment are the most unwelcome days, and the thoughts of them the most unwelcome thoughts: he would take any tolerable life on earth, at any time, for all his hopes of heaven; and that not only through the doubts of his own sincerity (which may sometimes be the case of a tempted Christian) but through the unsoundness of his belief of the life to come, or the utter unsuitableness of his soul to such a blessedness; which makes him look at it as less desirable to him, than a life of fleshly pleasures here. All that he doth for heaven is upon mere necessity, because he knows that die he must, and he had

rather be in heaven than in hell, though he had rather be in prosperity on earth than either. As he takes heaven but as a reserve or second good, so he seeks it with reserves, and in the second place. Having no better preparations for death and judgment, no marvel if they be his greatest terror. He may possibly, by his self-deceit, have some abatement of his fears, and he may by pride and wit seem very valiant and comfortable at his death, to hide his fear and pusillanimity from the world. But the cause of all his misery is, that he ' sought not first the kingdom of God and his righteousness, and laid not up a treasure in heaven, but upon earth, and loved this world above God, and above the world to come, and so his heart is not set on heaven, nor his affections on the things above; therefore he hath not that love to God, to Christ, to saints, to perfect holiness, which should make that world most desirable in his eyes, and make him think unfeignedly that it is best for him to depart and live with Christ forever. Having not the divine nature, nor having lived the divine life in walking with God, his complacency and desires are carnal, according to the nature which he hath. This is the true cause, and not alone his doubts of his own sincerity, of his unwillingness to die, or to see the day of Christ's appearance.

Thus I have showed you from the word of God, and the nature of Christianity, the true characters of the confirmed Christian, of the weak Christian, and of the seeming Christian.

The uses for which I have drawn up these characters, and which the reader is to make of them, are these.

I. Here the weak Christian and the hypocrite may see what manner of persons they ought to be: not only how unsafe it is to remain in a state of hypocrisy, but also how uncomfortable, and unserviceable, and troublesome it is, to remain in a state of weakness and disease; what a folly, and indeed a sign of hypocrisy is it to think, If I had but grace enough to save me, I would desire no more, or I would be well content. Are you content if you have but life here to distinguish you from the dead? If you were continually infants that must be fed, carried, and made clean by others; or if you had a continual gout, or stone, or leprosy, and lived in continual want and misery, you would think that life alone is not enough; and that life is uncomfortable when we have nothing but life, and all the delights of life are gone. He that lies in continual pain and want is weary of his life, if he cannot separate it from those calamities. He that knows how necessary strength is, as well as life, to do any considerable service for God, and how many pains attend the diseases and infirmities of the weak, and what great dishonour comes to Christ and religion, by the faults and childishness of many that shall be pardoned and saved, would certainly bestir him with all possible care to get out of this sick or infant state.

II. By this you may see who are the strong Christians, and who are the weak: it is not always the man of learning and free expressions, that can speak longest and most wisely of holy things, who is the strong confirmed Christian; but he who most excels in the love of God and man, and in a heavenly mind and holy life. Nor is it he that is unlearned, or of a weak memory, or slow expression, who is the weakest Christian; but he who hath least love to God and man, and the most love to his carnal self and to the world, and the strongest corruptions, and the weakest grace. Many a poor day-labourer or woman, that can scarcely speak sense, is a stronger Christian, as being stronger in faith, love, patience, humility, mortification, and self-denial, than many great preachers and doctors of the church.

III. You see here what kind of men they be that we call the godly; and what that godliness is which we plead for, against the malicious serpentine generation. The liars would make men believe that by godliness we mean a few affected strains, or hypocritical shows, or heartless lip-service, or singular opinions, or needless scrupulosity, or ignorant zeal; yea, a schism, or faction, or sedition, or rebellion, or what the devil pleases to say. If these sixty characters describe any such thing, then I will not deny, that in the way that such men call heresy, faction, schism, singularity, so worship we the God of our fathers; but if not, the Lord rebuke thee satan, and hasten the day when the 'lying lips shall be put to silence.'

IV. By this also you may see how inexcusable the enemies of Christianity and godliness are, and for what it is that they hate and injure it. Is there any thing in all this character of a Christian, that deserves the suspicion or hatred of the world, what harm is there in it; or what will it do against them? I may say to them of his servants as Christ did of himself, 'many good works have I showed you from my Father, for which of these works do ye stone me?' Many heavenly graces are in the sanctified believer: for which of these do you hate and injure him? I know that goodness is so far in credit with human nature, that you will answer as the Jews did, 'for a good work we stone thee not, but for blasphemy.' We hate them not for godliness, but for hypocrisy and sin. But if it be so indeed, 1. Speak not against godliness itself, nor against the strictest performance of our duty. 2. Yea, plead for godliness, and countenance and promote it, while you speak against hypocrisy and sin. 3. Choose out the hypocrite whose character is here truly set before you; and let him be the object of your enmity and distaste: let it fall on those that are worldlings and time-servers, and will stretch their consciences to their carnal interest, and can do any thing to save their skin; and being false to Christ, can hardly be true to any of their superiors, but only in subordination to themselves. As it is said of Constantius, that he commanded that all his servants should be turned out of their places who would not renounce Christianity: and when he had thereby tried them, he turned out all the apostates, and kept in the sincere, and told them they could not be true to him, that were not true to their God and Saviour. 4. See that you be not hypocrites yourselves. You profess yourselves Christians; and what is it to be a Christian indeed, you may here perceive. If any that fall under the character of hypocrites or worse, shall vilify or hate the sincere Christians as hypocrites, what a horrid aggravation of their hypocrisy will it be.

Indeed they are the best and strongest Christians who have most of the hatred both of the unbelieving and the hypocritical world. For my own part I must confess, that the very observation of the universal implacable enmity which is undeniably seen throughout the world, between the woman's and the serpent's seed, being such as is not found among any other sorts of men on other occasions, doth not a little confirm my belief of the holy scriptures, and seems to be an argument not well to be answered by any enemy of the Christian cause. That it should begin between the two first brothers that ever were born in the world, and stop in nothing lower than shedding the righteous blood of Abel, for no other cause, but because the works of Cain were evil, and his brother's righteous, and that it should go down to the prophets, and Christ, the apostles, and primitive saints, and continue to this day throughout the earth; and that the profession of the same religion doth not alter it, but rather enrage the enmity of hypocrites against all that are serious and sincere in the religion which they themselves profess: these are things that no good account can be given of, save only from the predictions and verities of the word of God.

V. Also you may hence perceive how exceedingly injurious hypocrites and scandalous Christians are, to the name of Christ, and cause of Christianity and godliness in the world. The blind malicious enemies of faith and godliness instead of judging of them by the sacred rule, look only to the professors, and think of religion as they think of them. If they see the professors of Christianity to be covetous, proud, usurpers, time-servers, self-exalters, cruel, schismatical, rebellious, they presently charge all this upon their religion; and godliness must bear the blame, when all comes but from want of godliness and religion. All the world hath not done so much against these and all other sins, as Christ hath done. What if Christ's disciples strive who shall be the greatest, is it a small matter of him who girds himself to wash and wipe their feet; and tells them, that 'except they be converted, and become as little children, they shall not enter into the kingdom of God;' and tells them, that though 'the kings of the Gentiles do exercise lordship over them, and they that exercise authority upon them are called benefactors, yet ye shall not be so?' Is it nothing of him that hath said to the elders, 'feed the flock of God which is among you, taking the oversight thereof, not by constraint, but willingly, not for filthy lucre, but of a ready mind; neither as being lords over God's heritage, but being examples to the flock?' Who hath set the elders such a lesson as you find in Acts xx. and 2 Tim. iv. 1, 2, 3. and 1 Tim. v. 17. If any called Christians should be truly schismatical, factious or turbulent, is it nothing of him that hath prayed the Father that they may all be one: and hath so vehemently intreated them that 'they speak the same thing, and that there be no divisions among them, and that they be perfectly joined together in the same mind, and in the same judgment;' and hath charged them to 'mark them that cause divisions and offences contrary to the doctrine which they had learned, and to avoid them?'

If any called Christians shall be seditious, or rebellious, or as the papists believe, that the clergy are from under the jurisdiction of kings, and that the pope hath power to excommunicate princes, and absolve their subjects from their allegiance, and give their dominions to others, as it is decreed in the general council at the Lateran under Innocent the Third. Is all this as nothing of Christ, who paid tribute to Cæsar, and hath commanded that every soul be subject to the highest powers, and not resist, and this for conscience sake; and hath bid his disciples rather to turn the other cheek, than to seek revenge;

and hath told them that they that use the sword of rebellion, or revenge, or cruelty, shall perish by the sword. If any Christians will, under pretence of religion, set up a cruel inquisition, or kill men to convert them, or become self-lovers, covetous, boasters, proud, blasphemers, disobedient to parents, unthankful, unholy, without natural affection, truce-breakers, false-accusers, incontinent, fierce, despisers of those that are good, &c. is it nothing of him that hath forbid all this? If for their own domination, lust or covetousness, men called Christians, will be worse than heathens and wolves to one another, is this nothing of him that hath made it his sheep mark, by which we must be known to all men to be his disciples, that we love one another; and hath told them, that if they bite and devour one another, they shall be devoured one of another; and hath blessed the merciful, as those that shall find mercy, and hath told men that what they do to his little ones, shall be taken as if it were done to himself, and hath commanded the 'strong to bear with the infirmities of the weak, and not to please themselves,' and 'to receive one another as Christ received us,' and hath told those that offend but one of his little ones, that it were good for that man that a millstone were hanged about his neck, and he were drowned in the depth of the sea, and hath told him that 'smiteth his fellow servants, that his Lord will come in a day when he looketh not for him, and shall cut him asunder, and appoint him his portion with the hypocrites, where shall be weeping and gnashing of teeth.' I wonder what men would have Christ do, to free himself and the Christian religion from the imputation of the sins of the hypocrites, and the weak distempered Christians. Would they have him yet make stricter laws, when they hate these for being so strict already; or would they have him condemn sinners to more grievous punishment, when they are already offended at the severity of his threatenings? O what an unrighteous generation are his enemies that blame the law, because men break it, and blame religion because many are not religious enough: as if the sun must be hated, because that shadows and dungeons want light; or life and health must be hated, because many are sick and pained by their diseases! But Christ will shortly stop all the mouths of these unreasonable men. O how easily will he justify himself, his laws, and all his holy ways, when all iniquity shall be for ever silent. And though 'it must needs be that offences come, yet woe to the world because of offences, and woe to the man by whom they come.'

The wrong that Christ receives from hypocrites and scandalous Christians, of all ranks and places, is not to be estimated. These are the causes that Christianity and godliness are so contemptible in the eyes of the world; that Jews, heathens, and Mahometans, are still unconverted and deriders of the faith; because they see such scandalous tyranny and worship among the papists, and such scandalous lives among the greatest part of professed Christians in the world; whereas if the papal tyranny were turned into the Christian ministry, and their irrational fopperies, and historical hypocritical worship were changed into a reverent, rational and spiritual worship; and the cruel, carnal, worldly lives of men called Christians, were changed into self-denial, love and holiness; in a word, if Christians were Christians indeed, and such as I have here described from their rule; what a powerful means would it be of the conversion of all the unbelieving world! Christianity would then be in the eye of the world, as the sun in its brightness, and the glory of it would dazzle the eyes of beholders, and draw in millions to inquire after Christ, who are now driven from him by the sins of hypocrites and scandalous believers.

This doth not contradict what I said before of the enmity of the world to holiness, and that the best are most abused by the ungodly: for even this enmity must be rationally cured, as by the error of reason it is fed. God by the power of intellectual light, brings all those out of darkness whom he saves, and so brings them from the power of Satan to himself. Men hate not holiness as good, but as misconceived to be evil. Evil I say to them, because it is opposite to the sensual pleasures, which they take to be their chief good. The way of curing their enmity, is by showing them their error: and that is by showing them the excellency and necessity of that which they unreasonably distaste.

VI. Lastly. In these characters you have some help in the work of self-examination, for the trial both of the truth and strength of grace. I suppose it will be objected, that in other treatises I have reduced all the infallible marks of grace to a smaller number. To which I answer, I still say, that the predominancy or prevalency of the interest of God as our God, and Christ as our Saviour, and the Spirit as our Sanctifier, in the estimation of the understanding, the resolved choice of the will, and the government of the life, against all the worldly interest of the flesh, is the only infallible sign of a justified regenerated soul. But this whole hath many parts, and it is abundance of particulars materially in which

this sincerity is to be found: even all the sixty characters which I have here named are animated by that one, and contained in it. I think to the most, the full description of a Christian in his essential and integral parts, yet showing which are indeed essential, is the best way to acquaint them with the nature of Christianity, and to help them in the trial of themselves. As it were an abuse of human nature, for a painter to draw the picture of a man, without arms, legs, nose, or eyes, because he may be a man without them; so would it have been in me to draw only a maimed picture of a Christian, because a maimed Christian is a Christian. Yet, because there are so many maimed Christians in the world, I have also showed you their lamentable defects; not in a manner which tends to encourage them in their sins and wants, under pretence of comforting them, but in that manner which may best excite them to their duty, in order to their recovery, without destroying their necessary supporting comforts.

O happy church, and state, and family, which are composed of such confirmed Christians! Where the predominate temperature is such as I have here described; yea, happy is the place where magistrates and ministers are such; who are the vital parts of state and church, and the instruments appointed to communicate these perfections to the rest. But how much more happy is the new Jerusalem, the city of the living God, where the perfected spirits of the just in perfect life, light, and love, are perfectly beholding, admiring, praising, and pleasing the eternal God, their creator, redeemer, and sanctifier for ever; where the least and meanest is greater and more perfect than the confirmed Christian here described. Where hypocrisy is utterly excluded, and imperfection ceases, with scandal, censures, uncharitableness, division, and all its other sad effects: where the souls that thirsted after righteousness shall be fully satisfied, and love God more than they can now desire, and never grieve themselves or others with their wants or weaknesses, or evil deeds any more. O blessed day, when our most blessed head shall be revealed from heaven with his mighty angels, and shall come to be glorified in his saints, and admired in all them that now believe; whose weakness here occasioned his dishonour, and their own contempt! When the seed of grace is grown up into glory, and all the world, whether they will or not, shall discern between the righteous and the wicked, between him that serves God, and him that serves him not; between the clean and the unclean, and between him that swears, and him that fears an oath : though now our life is hid with Christ in God, and it yet 'appeareth not (to the sight of ourselves or others) what we shall be ; yet then when Christ, who is our life, shall appear, we also shall appear with him in glory.'

Away then, my soul, from this dark, deceitful and vexatious world ! Love not thy diseases, thy fetters and calamities: groan daily to thy Lord, and earnestly groan to be clothed upon with thy house which is from heaven, that mortality may be swallowed up of life. Join in the harmonious desires of the creatures, who groan to be delivered from the bondage of corruption, into the glorious liberty of the sons of God. 'Abide in him, and walk in righteousness, that when he shall appear, thou mayest have confidence, and not be ashamed before him at his coming.' Join not with the evil servants, who say in their hearts, Our Lord delays his coming, and begin to smite their fellow servants, and to eat and drink with the drunken ; whose lord shall come in a day when they look not for him, and in an hour that they are not aware of, and shall cut them asunder, and appoint them their portion with the hypocrites, where shall be weeping and gnashing of teeth. O watch and pray that thou enter not into temptation ! And be patient, for the judge is at the door ; lift up thy head with earnest expectation, O my soul, for thy redemption draws near ! Rejoice in hope before thy Lord, for he comes ; he comes to judge the world in righteousness and truth. Behold he comes quickly, though faith be failing, and iniquity abound, and love wax cold, and scoffers say, Where is the promise of his coming? Make haste, O thou whom my soul desires, and come in glory as thou first camest in humility, and conform them to thyself in glory, whom thou madest conformable to thy sufferings and humility.

Let the holy city, new Jerusalem, be prepared as a bride adorned for her husband ; and let God's tabernacle be with men, that he may dwell with them and be their God, and wipe away their tears, and death, and sorrow, and crying ; and pain may be no more, but former things may pass away. Keep up our faith, our hope, our love, and daily vouchsafe us some beams of thy directing consolatory light in this our darkness : be not as a stranger to thy scattered flock, in this desolate wilderness ; but let them hear thy voice, and find thy presence, and have such conversation with thee in heaven, in the exercise of faith, hope, and love, which is agreeable to their low and distant state : testify to their souls that thou art their Saviour and Head, and that they abide in thee by the Spirit which thou hast given them, abiding, and overcoming in them, and as thy agent preparing them for eternal life. O let not our darkness, nor thy strangeness feed our odious unbelief ! O show thyself more clearly to thy redeemed ones. Come and dwell in our hearts by faith ; and by holy love let us dwell in God, and God in us, that we grope not after him, as those that worship an unknown God. O save us from temptation ! If the messenger of Satan be sent to buffet us, let thy strength be manifest in our weakness, and thy grace appear sufficient for us. Give us the patience which thou tellest us we need, that having done thy will, we may inherit the promise : and bring us to the sight and fruition of our Creator, of whom, and through whom, and to whom, are all things; to whom be glory for ever. Amen.

THE

MISCHIEFS OF SELF-IGNORANCE,

AND THE

BENEFITS OF SELF-ACQUAINTANCE,

OPENED IN DIVERS SERMONS AT ST. DUNSTAN'S-WEST, AND PUBLISHED IN ANSWER TO
THE ACCUSATIONS OF SOME AND THE DESIRES OF OTHERS.

PREFATORY REMARKS.

THIS treatise was published in 1662. It is preceded by a long dedicatory epistle to Anne, Countess of Balcarras, in course of which Baxter gives a series of directions to acquiring self-acquaintance. The chief part of this dedication, including the whole of these directions, will be found printed as the introduction in this edition. This dedication bears date 25th August, 1661, and a postscript is added, 1st November, 1661. Then follows an address to the people of Kidderminster, giving the reasons why he was not allowed to preach in the diocese of Worcester, and which led to a controversy between him and Bishop Morley. This address bears date 11th November, 1662.

The subject of which he discourses is one of great importance, and lies at the foundation of all proper knowledge and experience of the power of religion. It is founded on 1 Cor. xiii. 5, "Know ye not your own selves?" This treatise is probably less known to the reading public, than many of the practical works of Baxter, not because it is less valuable, but because it has not been regularly supplied in separate and successive editions. Its excellence consists not in doctrinally unfolding the economy of grace, or in directly pressing upon the reader the necessity of repentance towards God, or faith towards our Lord Jesus Christ, but in tracing out the involutions of that most intricate economy of thought and feeling, judgment and action, moral liking and moral antipathy, which exists entire, and works apart in the bosom of every individual: and in this way it is powerfully subservient to repentance and faith, by disturbing the apathy, and combating the ignorant indifference, which so fatally shut them out from men's consciences and hearts. Its general scheme of thought is instructively arranged; and although its topics are numerous, they are not diffusely treated; while under each of them, there is a rich variety of illustrative matter, judiciously selected, and very aptly introduced. It is idle to say more of the manner of the writing, than that it is the manner of Richard Baxter; showing the writer in every page, but clear concise, and simple, beyond several of his other pieces; while it is second to none of them in persuasive eloquence and impressive fervour, clothing thoughts which are not familiar, in very conspicuous language, and adapting itself, with uncommon felicity, to the inexperienced and the undisciplined. The whole style and spirit of the work are exactly suited to the nature of the subject; and we think it well entitled to a place among the few books which the parent selects for his child, or the pastor for the young of his flock, or the guardian for his pupil, as a means of awakening religious inquiry, and forming habits of early reflection.

Of the Countess of Balcarras, to whom this work is dedicated, and her husband, of whose piety the author speaks in terms of warm commendation, the following account will interest the reader:

"She was daughter to the late Earl of Seaforth in Scotland, towards the Highlands, and was married to the Earl of Balcarras, a Covenanter, but an enemy to Cromwell's perfidiousness, and true to the person and authority of the king.

With the Earl of Glencarne, he kept up the last war for the king against Cromwell; and his lady, through dearness of affection, marched with him and lay out of doors with him on the mountains. At last Cromwell drove them out of Scotland, and they went together beyond sea to the king, whom they long followed. He was taken for the head of the Presbyterians with the king; but, by evil instruments, he fell out with the lord-chancellor, who, prevailing against him upon some advantage, he was for a time forbidden the court; the grief whereof, added to the distempers he had contracted by his warfare on the cold and hungry mountains, cast him into a consumption, of which he died. He was a lord of excellent learning, judgment, and honesty; none being praised equally with him for learning and understanding in all Scotland.

"When the Earl of Lauderdale (his near kinsman and great friend) was prisoner in Portsmouth and Windsor Castle, he fell into acquaintance with my books, and so valued them, that he read them all, and took notes of them, and earnestly commended them to the Earl of Balcarras, then with the king. The earl met, at the first sight, with some passages where he thought I spake too favourably of the Papists, and differed from many other Protestants; so he cast them by, and sent the reason of his distaste to the Earl of Lauderdale, who pressed him but to read one of the books over; which he did, and then read them all (as I have seen many of them marked with his hand), and was drawn to over-value them more than the Earl of Lauderdale. Hereupon his lady reading them also, and being a woman of very strong love and friendship, with extraordinary entireness swallowed up in her husband's love, she, for the books' sake, and her husband's sake, became a most affectionate friend to me before she ever saw me. While she was in France, being zealous for the king's restoration (in whose cause her husband had pawned and ruined his estate), by the Earl of Lauderdale's direction, she, with Sir Robert Murray, got divers letters from the pastors and others there to bear witness of the king's sincerity in the Protestant religion; among which there was one to me from Mr. Gaches. Her great wisdom, modesty, piety, and sincerity, made her accounted the saint at court. When she came over with the king, her extraordinary respect obliged me to be so often with her, as gave me acquaintance with her eminency in all the foresaid virtues. She was of solid understanding for her sex; of prudence, much more than ordinary; of great integrity and constancy in her religion; a great hater of hypocrisy; and faithful to Christ in an unfaithful world. She was somewhat over affectionate to her friends, which hath cost her a great deal of sorrow in the loss of her husband, and since of other special friends; and may cost her more, when the rest forsake her, as many in prosperity do to those that will not forsake their fidelity to Christ. Her eldest son, the young Earl of Balcarras, a very hopeful youth, died of a strange disease; two stones being found in his heart, of which one was very great. Being my constant auditor, and over-respectful friend, I had occasion for the just praises and acknowledgments which I have given her; which the occasioning of these books hath caused me to mention."

Lord Balcarras died at Breda on the 30th August, 1659, at the early age of forty-one; his body was brought over to Scotland and buried in the church at Balcarras. His eldest son, referred to above, died in 1662. The countess, after remaining in a state of widowhood for upwards of ten years, was secondly married, on the 28th January, 1670, to Archibald Mull, Earl of Argyle, who suffered martyrdom in 1685, and whom she survived for above twenty years.—See Introductory Essay by Rev. David Young, Bath, in *Collins' Select Christian Authors—Baxter's Life* —and *Anderson's Ladies of the Covenant*, in which there is a full and interesting life of the countess.

MISCHIEFS OF SELF-IGNORANCE,

BENEFITS OF SELF-ACQUAINTANCE.

"For if a man think himself to be something when he is nothing, he deceiveth himself; but let every man prove his own work, and then shall he have rejoicing in himself alone, and not in another. For every man shall bear his own burden."—GAL. VI. 3—5.

INTRODUCTION.

PRELIMINARY DIRECTIONS IN ACQUIRING SELF-KNOWLEDGE.

He that is a stranger to himself, his sin, his misery, his necessity, &c., is a stranger to God, and to all that might denominate him wise or happy. To have taken the true measure of our capacities, abilities, infirmities and necessities, and thereupon to perceive what is really best for us, and most agreeable to our case, is the first part of true practical saving knowledge. Did the distracted mindless world consider, what work they have at home for their most serious thoughts, and care and diligence, and of what unspeakable importance and necessity it is, that men carry within them the matter of their final doom, and the beginning of endless joy or sorrow, they would be called home from their busy-idleness, their laborious-loss of precious time, and unprofitable vagaries, and would be studying their hearts, while they are doting about a multitude of impertinencies, and would be pleasing God while they are purveying for the flesh; and they would see that it more concerneth them to know the day of their salvation, and now to lay up a treasure in heaven, that they may die in faith, and live in everlasting joy and glory, than in the crowd and noise of the ambitious, covetous, voluptuous sensualists, to run after a feather, till time is past, and mercy gone, and endless woe hath unexpectedly surprised them. Yet do these dead men think they live, because they laugh, and talk, and ride, and go, and dwell among gnats and flies in the sun-shine, and not with worms and dust in darkness: they think they are awake, because they dream that they are busy; and that they are doing the works of men, because they make a noise for finer clothes, and larger room, and sweeter morsels, than their poorer undeceived neighbours have: they think they are sailing to felicity, because they are tossed up and down: and if they can play the pike among the fishes, or the wolves or foxes in the flocks of Christ; or if they can attain to the honour of a pestilence, to be able to do a great deal of hurt, they are proud of it, and look as high as if they saw neither the grave nor hell, nor knew how quickly they must be taken down, and laid so low, that 'the righteous shall see it and fear, and laugh at them, saying, Lo, this is the man that made not God his strength, but trusted in the abundance of his riches, and strengthened himself in his wickedness.' 'Behold, these are the ungodly that prosper in the world, and increase in riches; surely they are set in slippery places, and cast down to destruction, and brought to desolation as in a moment; and utterly consumed with terrors: as a dream when one awaketh, so, O Lord, when thou awakest, thou shalt despise their image.' 'Though while they lived they blessed themselves, and were praised by men; yet when they die they carry nothing away; their glory shall not descend after them; like sheep they are laid in the grave : death shall feed on them, and the upright shall have dominion over them in the morning ; man in honour abideth not; he is like the beasts that perish; this their way is their folly ; yet their posterity approve their sayings.' As the proverb is, 'at last the wolf's skin is brought to the market, and the fox's to the furrier.' They shall find that God is not afraid to lay the hand of justice on the stoutest of them, and will be as bold with silken shining gallants, as with the poorest worms; and will contemn that man's glory, who durst despise the glory of his Redeemer ; and will trample upon the interest which is set up against the interest of Christ. The jovial world do now think that self-study is too melancholy a thing ; and they choose to be distracted for fear of being melancholy; and will be mad in Solomon's sense, that they may be wise and happy in their own. ' The heart of fools is in the house of mirth, and the heart of the wise in the house of mourning.' And yet there is most joy in the hearts of the wise, and least solid peace in the hearts of fools : they know that conscience hath so much against them, that they dare not hear its accusations and its sentence: they dare not look into the hideous dungeon of their hearts, nor peruse the accounts of their bankrupt souls, nor read the history of their impious unprofitable lives, lest they should be tormented before the time : they dare not live like serious men, lest they should lose thereby the delights of brutes. O sinful men ! against what light both natural and supernatural, do they offend! They see how all things haste away : the names of their predecessors are left as a warning to them ; every corpse that is carried to the grave, being dead, yet speaketh : and every bone that is thence cast up, doth rise as a witness against their luxury and lust; and yet they will have their will and pleasure while they may, whatever it cost them : and they will set their house on fire that they might have one merry blaze, and warm them once before they die. I shall give a few directions to those that would be well acquainted with themselves, and would comfortably converse at home.

Direct. 1. Let him not overvalue or mind the deceitful world, that would have fruitful converse with God and with himself: trust not such a deceiver, as hath robbed so many thousands before us, especially when God and common experience do call out to us to take heed: the study of riches, and rising, and reputation, and pleasures, agreeth not with this study of God, and of our hearts : and though the world will not take acquaintance with us, if we come not in their fashion, nor see us, if we stand not on the higher ground: yet it is much better to be unknown to others, than to ourselves. A retirement therefore must be made, from the inordinate pursuit of worldly things, and the charms of honours, riches, and delights: and if some present loss do seem to follow, it is indeed no loss, which tendeth unto gain. Methinks they that sincerely pray 'lead us not into temptation,' should not desire to have bolts and bars between God and them, and to dwell where salvation is hardest to be attained ! Desire not to be planted in any such place, though it seem a paradise, where God is most unknown, and used as a stranger, and where saints are wonders, and examples of serious piety are most rare, and where a heavenly conversation is known but by reports, and reported of according to the malice of the serpent, and represented but as fancy, hypocrisy or faction; where sin most prospereth, and is in least disgrace ; and where it is a greater shame to be a saint than to be a fool; a serious Christian, than a seared stupified sensualist: bless you from that place where the weeds of vice are so rank, as that no good plant can prosper near them : where gain is godliness; and impiety is necessary to acceptable observance, and a tender conscience, and the fear of God, are characters of one too surly and unpliable to be countenanced by men: where the tongue that nature formed to be the index of the mind, is made the chiefest instrument to hide it ; and men are so conscious of their own incredibility, that no one doth believe or trust another ; where no words are heart-deep, but those that are spoken against Christ's cause and interest, or for their own ; where a vile person is honoured, and those contemned that fear the Lord; bless you from the place where truth is intolerable, and untruth cloaked with its name ; where holiness is looked at as an owl or enemy, and yet hypocrisy must steal its honour from it : where he is a saint that is less wicked than infamous transgressors; and where Dives' life is blameless temperance ; and where pride, idleness, fulness of bread, and filthy fornication and lasciviousness, are the infirmities of pious and excellent persons : where great sins are small ones, and small ones are none ; and where the greatest must have no reproof, and the physician is taken for the greatest enemy, where chaff is valued at the price of wheat, and yet the famine is of choice : where persons and things are measured by interest ; and duty to God derided as folly, whenever it crosseth the wisdom of the world, and hated as some hurtful thing when it crosseth fleshly men in their desires: and where Dives' brethren are unwarned; and none are more secure and frolicsome, than those that to-morrow may be in hell. Old travellers are usually most addicted to end their days in solitude: learn to contemn the world at cheaper rates than they: neither hope, nor wish to live an Alexander, and die a Socrates; a crowd or concourse, though of the greatest, where is the greatest tumult of affairs, and confluence of temptations, is not the safest place to die in: and I have most mind to live where I would die. Where men are Christians in name, and infidels in conversation, the sweetness of their Christian names will not preserve them or you from the danger of their unchristian lives: it was not the whole of Lot's deliverance to be saved from the flames of Sodom, but it was much of it to be freed from their malicious rage, and filthy grievous conversation: the best medicine against the plague, is to keep far enough from the place that hath it. Desire not that condition, where all seem friends, but none are friends indeed; but they that seem to be your servants, are by flattery serving themselves by you: where few persons or things are truly represented; but men are judged of by the descriptions of their enemies, and the lambs have the skins and names of wolves; and the best are odious when bold calumniators load them with odious accusations. In a word, desire not the place where the more men seek, the less they find, and the more they find, the less they have, and the more they have, the less they do enjoy: where the more are their provisions, the less are their supplies; the more their wealth, the more their want; the more their pleasure, the less their peace; the greater their mirth, the less their joy; the greater their confidence, the less their safety: where the great mistake about their happiness, their best, their end, doth make their lives a constant error, and death a doleful disappointment.

Direct. 2. Keep all clean and sound within, that there may be little of loathsomeness to disaffect you, or terror to frighten you from yourselves. It is a frightful thing to be much conversing with a guilty soul, and hearing the accusations of a conscience not cleansed by the blood of Christ; and it is an unpleasant thing to be searching in our wounds, and reading the history of a life of folly, especially of wilful sin, and of ungrateful neglect of offered grace. Make not such work for yourself, if you love it not. We make our beds ill, and then we are weary of them, because they are so hard: our comforts are more in our own hands than in any others: the best

friend or pastor cannot do so much to promote them, nor the greatest enemy so much to destroy them, as ourselves. If we will surfeit, and make ourselves sick, we must endure it. If wasps and vipers be our guests, no wonder if we dwell not quietly at home; and if we sit not at ease, when we carry thorns about us. Folly and concupiscence breed our misery: it is the smoke of our own corruptions that troubleth our eyes, and the scent and smart of our ulcerated minds that most annoyeth us. We cannot waste our peace, and have it. Turk and pope, and all the terrible names on earth, are not so terrible deservedly to a sinner as his own: the nearest evil is the most hurtful evil. If a scolding wife be such a continual dropping, and troublesome companion, as Solomon tells us, what then is a distempered, troubled mind, and a chiding conscience? It is a pity that man should be his own afflicter, but so it is: and, as the proverb is, he hath great need of a fool, that will play the fool himself, so I may say, he hath great need of a tormentor, that will be a tormentor to himself. Folly, and lust, and rashness and passion are sorry keepers of our peace: darkness and filth do make a dungeon, and not a delightful habitation of our hearts: God would take pleasure in them, if we kept them clean, and would walk with us in those gardens, if we kept them dressed; but if we will defile his temple, and make it unpleasing unto him, he will make it unpleasing unto us. Terror and trouble are the shadow of sin, that follow it, though the sun shine never so brightly. If we carry fire in our clothes, we shall smell it at the least. Keep close to God; obey his will; make sure of your reconciliation and adoption; keep clear your evidences, and grieve not the Holy Spirit which sealeth you, and must comfort you. And then it will do you good to look into your heart, and there you shall find the most delightful company; and the spirit that you have there entertained, will there entertain you with these joys.

But if disorder have prevailed and made your hearts a place of trouble, yet fly not from it, and refuse not to converse with it: for though it be not at the present a work of pleasure, it is a work of necessity, and may tend to pleasure in the end. Conversing wisely and faithfully with a disordered troubled heart, is the way to make it a well ordered and quiet heart.

Direct. 3. In judging of your present state and actions, let one eye be always on the end: this will both quicken you to be serious in the duty, and direct you in all particular cases to judge aright. As the approach of death doth convince

almost all men of the necessity of studying themselves, and calleth them to it from all other
studies; so the considerate foresight of it, would
do the like in better time. And it is the end
that communicateth the good or evil to all things
in the way: and therefore as they have relation
to the end, they must be judged of. When you
peruse your actions, consider them as done by
one that is entering into eternity, and as those
that must all be opened in a clearer light. If we
separate our actions in our considerations from
their ends, they are not of the same signification,
but taken to be other things than indeed they
are. If the oaths, the lies, the slanders, the sensuality and filthiness of impure sinners, had not
relation to the loss of heaven, and to the pains
of hell, they were not matters of that exceeding
moment as now they are. And if the holiness,
obedience and watchfulness of believers, had no
relation to the escaping of hell fire, and the attainment of eternal life, they would be of lower
value than they are. The more clearly men discern that God is present, that judgment is at
hand, that they are near to heaven or hell, where
millions have already received their reward, the
more seriously will they study, and the better
will they know themselves.

Direct. 4. Though you must endeavour to
judge yourself truly as you are, yet rather incline to think meanly, than highly of yourself,
and be rather too suspicious than too presumptuous. My reasons for this direction are, because man's nature is generally disposed to self-
exalting; and pride and self-love are sins so
common and so strong, as that it is a thing of
wondrous difficulty to overcome them, so far as
to judge ourselves impartially, and to err as little
in our own cause, as if it were another's: and
because self-exalting hath far more dangerous
effects than self-abasing, supposing them to exceed their bounds. Prudent humility is a quieting grace, and avoideth many storms and tempests, which trouble and shake the peace of
others. It maketh men thankful for that little as
undeserved, which others repine at as short of
their expectations: it telleth the sufferer that
God doth afflict him much less than he deser-
veth, and causeth him to say, 'I will bear the
indignation of the Lord, because I have sinned
against him.' It teacheth us a cautious suspicion
of our own understandings, and a just submission to those that are wiser than ourselves; when
pride keepeth out wisdom, by keeping out the
knowledge of our ignorance. And as Pliny
tells us of some nations, where they are grey
headed in their infancy, and black-headed when

they are old: so pride maketh many wise so
soon, that they never come to be truly wise:
they think in youth that they have more than
the wisdom of age, and therefore in age they
have less than what beseemed them in youth.
Every hard report or usage is ready to break a
proud man's heart; when contempt doth little
disquiet the humble, because they judge so
meanly of themselves. The proud are frequently
disturbed, because they climb into the seats of
others; when humility sits quietly, and no one
bids it rise, because it knoweth and keepeth its
own place. Therefore it is, that true contrition
having once told us of our folly to the heart,
doth make us walk more circumspectly while we
live; and that no man is better resolved than he
that was once in doubt, and that no man standeth
faster than he that hath had a fall: and no man
is more safe, than he that hath had most assaults.
If you love your safety, desire not either to be, or
to seem too high. Be little in your own eyes,
and be content to be so in the eyes of others.
As for worldly greatness, affect neither the thing
nor the reputation of it. Look up, if you please,
to the tops of steeples, masts and mountains;
but stand below if you would be safe. And for
spiritual endowments, desire them, and improve
them; but desire not inordinately the reputation
of them. It seldom increaseth a man's humility
to be reputed humble: and though humility help
you to bear applause, yet the remnants of pride
are ready to take fire, and other sins to get advantage by it.

Direct. 5. Improve your self-acquaintance to a
due apprehension of what is most suitable, most
profitable, and necessary for you, and what is
most hurtful, unsuitable and unnecessary. He
that hath taken a just measure of himself, is the
better able to judge of all things else. How
suitable will Christ and grace appear, and how
unsuitable will worldly pomp appear to one that
truly knows himself? How suitable will serious
fervent worship appear, and how unsuitable the
ludicrous shows of hypocrites? And one pair
of eyes will be valued above many pairs of spectacles, and one pair of legs before two pairs
of crutches, by one that is not a stranger to
himself. If a man knew aright the capacity
and tendency of the reasonable nature, and
the evil of sin, and the necessity and distress
of an unrenewed soul, what sweet, what longing thoughts would he have of God, and all
that tendeth to the pleasing and enjoying of
him? How little would he think himself concerned in the trivial matters of honour or dishonour, riches or poverty, favour or displeasure

further than as they help or hinder him in the things that are of more regard? Know yourself, and you will know what to love and what to hate; what to choose and what to refuse; what to hold and what to lose; what to esteem and what to slight; what to fear, and when to be courageous and secure: the curing the dotage thus, would cure the night-walks of the dreaming vagrant world. And they that find that music cureth not the stone or gout, would know that mirth and gallantry, and vain-glory, are no preservatives from hell, nor sufficient cure for a guilty soul: and that if an aching head must have a better remedy than a golden crown, and a diseased body a more suitable cure than a silken suit, a diseased soul doth call for more.

Direct. 6. Value not yourself by mutable accidents, but by the essence and substance of Christianity. 'A man's life consisteth not in the abundance which he possesseth.' Paul knew better what he said, when he accounted all but loss and dung for the knowledge and fruition of Jesus Christ, than they that dote on wealth as their felicity. And is a man to be valued, applauded, and magnified for his wealth, or for his personal endowments? Judge not of the person by his apparel, when the foolishest and the worst may wear the same. The master and inhabitants honour the house more than the house doth the master and inhabitants. All the wit and learning in the world, with all the riches, honour and applause, yea, and all the civility and winning deportment, will not make a Christian of an infidel or atheist, nor a happy of a miserable man. As nothing will make a man honourable indeed, that hath not the use of reason, which distinguishes men from brutes; so nothing will make or prove him holy or happy, or safe, that hath not the holy image of God, which must mark his children from his enemies. If he be unsanctified, and be not a new creature, and have not the spirit of Christ within him, he is an atheist, or infidel, or an ungodly wretch, let him be never so rich, or great, or honourable. And as a harlot is never beautiful in the eyes of the wise and chaste, so a wicked man is never happy in the eyes of any but his own favourite society.

Direct. 7. Think not that a few occasional hasty thoughts will bring and keep you in acquaintance with yourself. It must be diligent observation, and serious consideration that must accomplish this. Many a man walketh where he doth not dwell. A transient salute is not a sign of intimate familiarity. It is enough sometimes to step into your neighbour's house for a charitable visit; but you must dwell in your own: be more busy and censorious at home than the proud and malicious are abroad; and be as seldom and tender in censuring others, as such hypocrites are in censuring themselves. Put on your spectacles at home, when you are reading over the register of your consciences; but wear them not as you walk the streets; but take up with so much knowledge of ordinary passengers as you can have without them. Think not that you are unconcerned in the danger or safety of your neighbour, but remember that you are more concerned in your own. It is here most reasonable to say, that charity begins at home, when self-neglect will disable you to help another. And if sometimes your falls or frailty do find you matter for searching, troublesome thoughts, and interrupt your sweeter, comfortable meditations, refuse not the trouble when you have made it necessary. It is many a sad and serious thought that the ministers of Christ have for the cure and safety of their flocks, and should not the people have as serious thoughts for themselves. Your reason, your wisdom, care and diligence, are more your own than any one's else; and therefore should be more used for yourself, than for any. And if after much thoughtfulness and labour, you find your heart to be no whit better, yet labour and believe. It is not the last blow of the axe alone that cuts down the tree, though it fall not till the last. The growth of grace, as of plants and fruits, and flowers, is not perceived by immediate inspection. There is much good obtained when we discern it not: and nothing is more certain, than that honest diligence is never lost in the things of God and our salvation. It is worth all our labour, if we grow no better, to keep our spark from going out, and to see that we grow no worse. And the preventing of evil is here an excellent good. Many a thousand eat and drink, that never hope to grow any fatter or stronger than they are. It is something to be sustained for our daily work, and to have our oil renewed daily as it wasteth. The mill gets by going, saith the proverb, though it stir not from the place. O 'keep the heart with all diligence, for out of it are the issues of life:' actions receive their specification and quality from the heart. 'Death and life are in the power of the tongue, but the tongue' is in the power of the heart.

Direct. 8. Let not your self-knowledge be merely speculative, but also practical. Be not contented that you know what you are, and what you have done, nor that your heart is much affected with it: but let all tend to action to mend what is amiss, and to maintain, improve, and increase what is good: and let the next question be, what am I now to do? Or, what must I be for time to come? It is a lamentable mistake of many that tire themselves with striving, to make deep affecting impressions on their hearts; and when they have got much sorrow, or much joy, they think they have done the greatest matter, and there they stop. But affections are the spring that move to action; and if you proceed not to your duty, affection is much lost: and if with smaller affection or passion you can stedfastly and resolutely cleave to God, and do your duty, you have the principal thing, and are accepted: not that outward actions are accepted without the heart; but that there is most of the heart, where there is most of the estimation and will, though less of passion; and there is most of will, where there is most endeavour: and inward action is the first part of obedience; and without these no speculations will avail. However you find your heart, be up and doing in the use of means, to make it better, and wait on God for further grace.

Direct. 9. Manage your self-acquaintance prudently, cautiously, and with the help of your skilful friend or pastor. Think not that it is a work that you need no helper in: if you mistake in your accounts, and put down a wrong sum, and call yourself confidently what you are not, or deny God's graces, whenever through melancholy or distemper you cannot find them, and pass false conclusions against God's mercies and yourself, this were to turn a duty into a sin and snare.

And you must do it seasonably: melancholy persons are most incapable of it, who do nothing but pore upon themselves to little purpose; such must do more of other duty, but lay by much of this till they are more capable, and make much use of the judgment of their guides. And weaker heads must take but a due proportion of time for self-searching meditations, lest they contract that troublesome disease: duties must be used with profitable variety, and all done under good advice. But young persons, and those that are yet unconverted, have need to fall upon it without delay; and to follow it till they have made sure their calling and election. O what a dreadful thing it is, for a man to come newly to the study of his soul, as a thing that he is unacquainted with, when sickness is upon him, and death at hand, and he is ready to pass into another world! To be then newly to ask, what am I? and what have I done? and whither am I going? and what will become of me for ever? is a most fearful state of folly.

Direct. 10. Terminate not your knowledge ultimately in yourself; but pass up unto God in Christ, and to the blessed privileges of the saints and the joyful state of endless glory, and there let your meditations be most frequent and most sweet.

CHAPTER I.

SELF-KNOWLEDGE DEFINED—ITS PROPER PROVINCE.

Know ye not your ownselves?—2 Cor. xiii. 5.

The Corinthians being much abused by false teachers, to the corrupting of their faith and manners, and the questioning of the apostle's ministry, he acquainteth them in my text with an obvious remedy for both these maladies; and lets them know, that their miscarriages call them to question themselves, rather than to question his authority or gifts, and that if they find Christ in themselves, they must acknowledge him in his ministry.

He therefore first most importunately urgeth them to the immediate duty of self-examination: 'Examine yourselves, whether you be in the faith: prove your ownselves:' self-examination is but the means of self-knowledge. This therefore he next urgeth, and that first in general; by way of interrogation, 'Know ye not your ownselves?' and then more particularly he tells them, what it is of themselves, that it most concerneth them to know, 'How that Jesus Christ is in you, except ye be reprobates.' As if he should say, Alas, poor souls, you have more cause to question yourselves than me: go to therefore, examine and prove yourselves. It is a shame for a man to be ignorant of himself. Know ye not your ownselves? Either Christ is in you, by faith, and by his Spirit, or he is not: if he be not, you are yet but reprobates, that is, disapproved of God, and at present in a forsaken, or condemned state yourselves; which is a conclusion that you will be loath to admit, but more concerneth you: if Christ be in you, it was by the means of my ministry; and therefore that ministry hath been powerful and effectual to you, and you are my witnesses; the seal of my ministry is upon your own souls; Christ within you bears me witness, and therefore of all men, you have least cause to question or quarrel with my ministry.

This paraphrase opening all that may seem difficult in the text, I shall immediately offer you a double observation, which the words afford us; first, as considered in themselves, and then as respecting the inference for which they are premised by the apostle.

The first is, that all men should know themselves: or, it is a shame for a man to be unacquainted with himself.

The second is, that not knowing ourselves, is the cause of other errors; or, the knowledge of ourselves would much conduce to the cure of many other errors.

In handling this, I shall show you,

I. *What it is to know ourselves.*

II. *How far it is, or is it not a shame to be ignorant of ourselves.*

III. *What evils follow this ignorance of ourselves, and what benefits self-knowledge would procure.*

IV. *How we should improve this doctrine by application and practice.*

I. Self-knowledge is thus distinguished according to the object. 1. There is a physical self-knowledge; when a man knows what he is as a man; what his soul is, and what his body, and what the compound called man. The doctrine of man's nature, or this part of physics, is so necessary to all, that it is first laid down even in the holy scriptures, in Genesis, chap. 1, 2, 3. before his duty is expressed. And it is pre-supposed in all the moral passages of the word, and in all the preaching of the gospel. The subject is pre-supposed to the adjuncts. The subjects of God's kingdom belong to the constitution; and therefore to be known before the legislation and judgment, which are the parts of the administration. Morality always pre-supposeth nature. The species is in order before the separable accidents. Most ridiculously therefore doth ignorance plead for itself against knowledge, in them that cry down this part of physics, as human learning, unnecessary to the disciples of Christ. What excellent holy meditations of human nature do you find often in Job and in David's Psalms, concluding in the praise of the incomprehensible Creator; ' I will praise thee, for I am fearfully and wonderfully made: marvellous are thy works, and that my soul knoweth right well.'

2. There is a moral self-knowledge very necessary. And this is, the knowing of ourselves in relation to God's law, or to his judgment. The former is the knowledge of ourselves, in respect of our duty: the second, in respect of the reward or punishment. And both of them have respect to the law of nature and works, or to the remedying law of grace.

The ethical knowledge of ourselves, or that which respecteth the precept and our duty, is twofold. The first is, as we have performed that duty: the second, as we have violated the law by non-performance or transgression. The first is, the knowledge of ourselves as good; the second as evil. And both are either the knowledge of our habits (good or evil) or of our acts; how we are morally inclined, disposed, or habituated; or what, and how we have done: we must know the good estate of our nature that we were created in; the bad estate of sinful nature that we are fallen into; the actual sin committed against the law of nature, and what sin we have committed against the law of grace; and whether we have obeyed the call of the gospel of salvation or not. So that as man's state, considered ethically, is threefold—the state of upright nature; the state of sin, original and actual; and the state of grace; we must know what we are in respect to every one of these.

And as to the judicial knowledge of ourselves, that is, as we stand related to the promises and threatenings, the judgment, the reward and punishment, we must know first, what is due to us according to the law of nature, and then what is due to us according to the tenor of the law of grace. By the law of nature or of works, death is the due of fallen mankind; but no man by it can lay claim to heaven. All men are under its curse or condemnation, till pardoned by Christ; but no man can be justified by it. By the promise of the gospel, all true believers renewed and sanctified by the Spirit of Christ, are justified and made the sons of God, and heirs of everlasting glory. To know whether we are yet delivered from the condemnation of the law, and whether our sins are pardoned or not, and whether we are the children of God, and have any part in the heavenly glory, is much of the self-knowledge that is here in the text, and that which most nearly concerneth the solid comfort of our souls.

II. But is all self-ignorance a shame, or dangerous? Answ. 1. It is no other shame than what is common to human frailty, to be ignorant of much of the mystery of our natural generation, constitution, integral parts, and temperament. There is not a nerve, or artery, or vein, nor the breadth of a hand from head to foot, but hath something unknown to the most excellent philosopher on earth. This little world called man, is a compound of wonders. Both soul and body have afforded matter of endless controversy, and voluminous disputations to the most learned men; which will not admit of a full decision, till we are past this state of darkness and mortality.

2. There are many controversies about the nature, derivation, and punishment of original sin, which an humble and diligent Christian may possibly be ignorant of.

3. The degrees of habitual sin, considered simply, or proportionably and respectively to each other, may be much unknown to many that are willing and diligent to know; and so may divers actual sins, such as we know not to be sin, through our imperfect understanding of the law; and such as through frailty, in a crowd of actions, escape our particular observation. And the sinfulness or aggravations of every sin, are but imperfectly known and observed by the best.

4. The nature and beauty of the image of God, as first planted on created man, and since restored to man redeemed; the manner of the Spirit's access, operation, testimony and inhabitation, are all but imperfectly known by the wisest of believers.

The frame or admirable composure or contexture of the new man in each of the renewed faculties; the connexion, order, beauty and special use of each particular grace, are observed but imperfectly by the best.

5. The very uprightness and sincerity of our own hearts, in faith, hope, love, repentance and obedience, is usually unknown to young beginners in religion; and to the weaker sort of Christians, how old soever in profession, and to melancholy persons, who can have no thoughts of themselves but sad and fearful, tending to despair; and to lapsed and declining Christians, and also to many an upright soul, from whom in some cases of special trial, God seems to hide his pleased face. And though these infirmities are their shame, yet are they not the characters or prognostics of their misery and everlasting shame.

6. The same persons must needs be unacquainted with their justification, reconciliation, adoption and title to everlasting blessedness, as long as they are uncertain of their sincerity. Yea, though they uprightly examine themselves, and desire help of their guides, and watch and pore continually upon their hearts and ways, and daily beg of God to acquaint them with their spiritual condition, they may yet be so far unacquainted with it, as to pass an unrighteous judgment on themselves, and condemn themselves when God hath justified them.

But, 1. To be totally ignorant of the excellency and capacity of your immortal souls. 2. To be void of an effectual knowledge of your sin and misery, and need of the remedy. 3. To think you have saving grace, when you have none; that you are regenerate by the Spirit, when you are only sacramentally dedicated by baptism; that you are the members of Christ, when it is no such matter; that you are justified,

adopted, and the heirs of heaven, when it is not so; all this is doleful and damnable ignorance of yourselves.

To be unacquainted with a state of life, when you are in such a state, is sad and troublesome, and casts you upon many and great inconveniencies. But to be unacquainted with a state of death, when you are in it, doth fasten your chains, and hinder your recovery. To be willing and diligent to know your state, and yet be unable to attain an assurance and satisfaction, is ordinary with many true believers: but to be ignorant of it, because you have no grace to find, and because you mind not the matters of your souls, or think it not worth your diligent consideration or inquiry; this is the case of the miserable despisers of salvation.

CHAPTER II.

THE MISCHIEFS OF SELF-IGNORANCE.

1. Atheism is cherished by self-ignorance. The knowledge of ourselves, as men, doth notably conduce to our knowledge of God. Here God is known but darkly, and as in a glass, and by his image; and not as face to face. And, except his incarnate and his written word, what glass revealeth him so clearly as the soul of man? We bear a double image of our Maker: his natural image in the nature of our faculties; and his moral image in their holy qualifications, in the nature of grace, and frame of the new man. By knowing ourselves, it is easy to know that there is a God; and it much assisteth us to know what he is, not only in his attributes and relations, but even in the trinity itself. He may easily know that there is a primitive being and life, that knoweth he hath himself a derived being and life. He must know that there is a creator, that knoweth he is a creature. He that findeth a capacious intellect, a will, and power in the creature, and that is conscious of any wisdom and goodness in himself, may well know that all these are infinite in the first cause that must thus have in itself whatsoever it doth communicate. He that knoweth that he made not, and preserveth not himself, may well know that he is not his own, but his that made him and preserveth him, who must needs be his absolute proprietor and Lord. He that knoweth that he is an intellectual free agent, and therefore to act morally, and therefore to be moved by moral means, and that he is a sociable creature, a member of the universe, living among men, may well be sure, that

he is made to be a subject, and governed by laws, and by moral means to be directed and moved to his end; and therefore, that none but his absolute Lord, the infinite wisdom, goodness, and power, can be his absolute and highest sovereign. He that is convinced that he is, he lives, he hopeth and enjoyeth all that is good, from a superior bounty, may be sure that God is his principal benefactor. And to be the first and infinite being, intellect, will, and power, wisdom, goodness, and cause of all things; the absolute owner, the most righteous governor, and the most bounteous benefactor, this is to be God.

This being the description of him that is so called: such a description as is fetched from his created image man, and expressed in the terms that himself hath chosen, and used in his word, as knowing that if he will be understood by man, he must use the notions and expressions of man. And though these are spoken but analogically of God, yet are there no fitter conceptions of him that the soul of man, in flesh, is capable of. So that the atheist carrieth about him that impress and evidence of the deity, which may convince him, or condemn him for his foolishness and impiety. He is a fool indeed, that saith in his heart, there is no God, since that heart itself in its being, and life, and motion, is his witness; and soul and body, with all their faculties, are nothing but the effects of this Almighty cause: and since they prove that there is a God, even by questioning or denying it, being unable, without him so much as to deny him; that is, to think, or speak, or be. As if a fool should write a volume, to prove that there is no ink or paper in the world, when it is ink and paper by which he writes.

And whether there be no representation of the trinity in unity in the nature of man, let them judge that have well considered, how in one body there are the natural, vital and animal parts and spirits: and in one life or soul, there are the vegetative, sensitive and rational faculties; and in one rational soul as such, there are an intellect, will, and executive power, morally perfected by wisdom, goodness and promptitude to well-doing: as in one sun there is light and heat, and moving force. So that man is both the beholder and the glass; the reader and the book: he is the index of the godhead to himself: yea, partly of the trinity in unity. We need not say, who shall go up into heaven? God is nigh us, with us, within us; a holy spirit resideth within us, the observer of our evil and good, and our preserver: he useth us as he is used by us: no good man is without God. Augustine saith, ' God is

in himself as the Alpha and Omega : in the world, as its governor and author: in angels, as their sweetness and comeliness : in the church, as the master of the family in his house : in the soul, as the bridegroom in his bed-chamber : in the righteous, as their helper and protector, &c. And as all declareth him, so all should praise him. Let the mind be exercised in loving him, the tongue in singing him, the hand in writing him ; let these holy studies be the believer's work.'

2. He that knoweth himself, may certainly know that there is another life of happiness or misery for man to live when this is ended. For he must needs know that his soul is capable of a spiritual and glorious felicity with God, and of immaterial objects, and that time is as nothing to it, and transitory creatures afford it no satisfaction or rest: and that the hopes and fears of the life to come, are the divine engines by which the moral government of the world is carried on ; and that the very nature of man is such, as that without such apprehensions, hopes and fears, he could not in a connatural way be governed, and brought unto the end, to which his nature is inclined and adapted ; but the world would be as a wilderness, and men as brutes. And he may well know that God made not such faculties in vain, nor suited them to an end which cannot be attained, nor to a work which would prove but their trouble and deceit : he may be sure that a mere probability or possibility of an everlasting life, should engage a reasonable creature in all possible diligence in piety and righteousness, and charity to attain it ; and so religious and holy endeavours become the duty of man as man ; there being few such infidels or atheists to be found on earth, as dare say they are sure there is no other life for man. And doubtless whatsoever is by nature and reason made man's duty, is not delusory and vain: nor is it reasonable to think that falsehood, frustration and deceit, are the ordinary way by which mankind is governed by the most wise and holy God. So that the end of man may be clearly gathered from his nature : forasmuch as God doth certainly suit his works unto their proper use and ends. It is therefore the ignorance of ourselves, that makes men question the immortality of souls: and I may add, it is the ignorance of the nature of conscience, and of all morality, and of the reason of justice among men, that makes men doubt of the discriminating justice of the Lord, which is hereafter to be manifested.

3. Did men know themselves, they would better know the evil and odiousness of sin. As poverty and sickness are better known by feeling

than by hearsay; so also is sin. To hear a discourse, or read a book of the nature, prognostics and cure of the plague, consumption, or dropsy, doth little affect us, while we seem to be sound and safe ourselves: but when we find the malady in our flesh, and perceive the danger, we have then another manner of knowledge of it. Did you but see and feel sin as it is in your hearts and lives, as oft as you read and hear of it in the law of God, I dare say sin would not seem a jesting matter, nor would those be censured as too precise, that are careful to avoid it, any more than they that are careful to avoid infectious diseases, or crimes against the laws of man, that hazard their temporal felicity or lives.

4. It is want of self-acquaintance that keeps the soul from kindly humiliation: that men are insensible of their spiritual calamities, and lie under a load of unpardoned sin and God's displeasure, and never feel it, nor loath themselves for all the abominations of their hearts and lives, nor make complaint to God or man with any seriousness and sense. How many hearts would be filled with wholesome grief and care, that now are careless and almost past feeling; and how many eyes would stream forth tears that now are dry, if men were but truly acquainted with themselves? It is self-knowledge that causeth the solid peace and joy of a believer, as conscious of that grace that warranteth his peace and joy: but it is self-deceit and ignorance that quieteth the presumptuous, that walk as carelessly, and sleep as quietly, and bless themselves from hell as confidently, when it is ready to devour them, as if the bitterness of death were past, and hypocrisy would never be discovered.

5. It is unacquaintedness with themselves that makes Christ so undervalued by the unhumbled world: that his name is reverenced, but his office and saving grace are disregarded. Men could not set so light by the physician, that felt their sickness, and understood their danger. Were you sensible that you are under the wrath of God, and shall shortly and certainly be in hell, if Christ, received by a hearty, working, purifying faith, do not deliver you, you would have more serious savoury thoughts of Christ, more yearnings after him, more fervent prayers for his healing grace, and sweet remembrance of his love and merits, example, doctrine and inestimable benefits, than lifeless hypocrites ever were acquainted with.

Imagine with what desires and expectations the diseased, blind and lame cried after him for healing to their bodies, when he was on earth.

And would you not more highly value him, more importunately solicit him for your souls, if you knew yourselves?

6. It is unacquaintedness with themselves that makes men think so unworthily of a holy, heavenly conversation; and that possesseth them with foolish prejudice against the holy care and diligence of believers. Did men but value their immortal souls as reason itself requireth them to do, is it possible they should venture them so easily upon everlasting misery, and account it unnecessary strictness in them that dare not be as desperately venturous as they, but fly from sin, and fear the threatenings of the Lord? Did men but considerately understand the worth and concern of their souls, is it possible they should hazard them for a thing of nought, and set them at sale for the favour of superiors, or the transitory pleasures and honours of the world? Could they think the greatest care and labour of so short a life to be too much for the securing of their salvation? Could they think so many studious careful days, and so much toil, to be but meet and necessary for their bodies; and yet think all too much that is done for their immortal souls? Did men but practically know that they are the subjects of the God of heaven, they durst not think the diligent obeying him to be a needless thing, when they like that child or servant best, that is most willing and diligent in their service. Alas! were men but acquainted with their weakness, and sinful failings, when they have done their best, and how much short the holiest persons do come of what they are obliged to by the laws and mercies of the Lord, they durst not make a scorn of diligence, nor hate or blame men for endeavouring to be better, that are sure at best they shall be too bad. When the worst of men, that are themselves the greatest neglecters of God and their salvation, shall cry out against a holy life, and making so much ado for heaven, (as if a man that lieth in bed should cry out against working too much or going too fast) this shows men's strangeness to themselves. Did the careless world but know themselves, and see where they stand, and what is before them, and how much lieth on this inch of time; did they but know the nature and employment of a soul, and why their Creator did place them for a little while in flesh, and whether they must go when time is ended, you should then see them in that serious frame themselves which formerly they disliked in others: and they would then confess, that if any thing in the world deserved seriousness and diligence, it is the pleasing of God, and the saving of our souls.

7. It is for want of acquaintance with themselves, that men are so deceived by the vanities of the world: that they are drowned in the love of pleasures and sensual delights: that they are so greedy for riches, and so desirous to be higher than those about them, and to waste their days in the pursuit of that which will not help them in the hour of their extremity. Did the voluptuous sensualist know aright that he is a man, he would not take up with the pleasures and felicity of a brute; nor enslave his reason to the violence of his appetite. He would know that there are higher pleasures which beseem a man; even those that consist in the well being and integrity of the soul, in peace of conscience, in the favour of God, and communion with him in the Spirit, and in a holy life, and in the fore-thoughts and hopes of endless glory.

Did the covetous worldling know himself, he would know that it must be another kind of riches that must satisfy his soul, and that he hath wants of another nature to be supplied; and that it more concerneth him to lay up a treasure in heaven, and think where he must dwell for ever, than to accommodate his perishing flesh, and make provision with so much ado, for a life that posteth away while he is providing for it: he would rather make him friends with the mammon of unrighteousness, and lay up a foundation for the time to come, and labour for the food that never perisheth, than to make such a stir for that which will serve him for so short a time; that so he might hear, 'Well done, thou good and faithful servant,' &c. rather than, 'Thou fool, this night thy soul shall be required of thee; then whose shall those things be which thou hast provided?'

Self-knowledge would teach ambitious men to prefer the calmest safest station before the highest; and to seek first the kingdom of God and its righteousness, and to please him most carefully that hath the keys of heaven and hell, and to be content with food and raiment in the way, while they are ambitious of a higher glory. It would tell them, that so dark and frail a creature should be more solicitous to obey than to have dominion; and that large possessions are not the most desirable passage to a narrow grave; and that it is the highest dignity to be an heir of heaven. Would men but spend some hours' time in the study of themselves, and seriously consider what it is to be a man, a sinner, a passenger to an endless life, an expectant of so great a change, and withal to be a professed believer, what a turn would it make in the cares, and the desires, and conversations of the most!

'What strive you for, O worldlings? What is here but a brittle glass full of dangers? And by how many dangers must you come to greater dangers? Away with these vanities and toys, and let us set ourselves to seek the things that have no end;' saith Augustine.

8. It is for want of self-acquaintance that any man is proud. Did men considerately know what they are, how quickly would it bring them low? Would corruptible flesh, that must shortly turn to loathsome rottenness, be stout and lordly, and look so high, and set forth itself in gaudy ornaments, if men did not forget themselves? Did rulers behave themselves as those that are subjects to the Lord of all, and have the greatest need to fear his judgment, and prepare for their account: did great ones live as men that know that rich and poor are equal with the Lord, who respects not persons; and that they must speedily be levelled with the lowest, and their dust be mixed with the common earth, what an alteration would it make in their deportment and affairs? And what a mercy would it prove to their inferiors and themselves? If men that swell with pride of parts, and overvalue their knowledge, wit, or elocution, did know how little indeed they know, and how much they are ignorant of, it would much abate their pride and confidence. The more men know indeed, the more they know to humble them. It is the novices, that being lifted up with pride, do fall into the condemnation of the devil; they would loathe themselves if they knew themselves.

9. It is self-ignorance that makes men rush upon temptations, and choose them, when they customarily pray against them. Did you know what tinder or gunpowder lodgeth in your natures, you would guard your eyes and ears, and appetites, and be afraid of the least spark; you would not be indifferent as to your company, nor choose a life of danger to your souls, for the pleasing of your flesh; to live among the snares of honour or beauty, and bravery, or sensual delights; you would not wilfully draw so near the brink of hell, nor be tampering with the bait, nor looking on the forbidden fruit, nor dallying with allurements, nor hearkening to the deceiver, or to his messengers. It is ignorance of the weakness and badness of your hearts, that maketh you so confident of yourselves, as to think that you can hear any thing, and see any thing, and approach the snare, and treat with a deceiver without any danger. Self-acquaintance would cause more fear and self-suspicion.

If you should escape well a while in your self-chosen dangers, you may catch that at last that may prove your woe.

Temptation puts you on a combat with the powers of the earth, and flesh, and hell! And are toil and danger your delight? Danger is never overcome without danger, saith Seneca; it is necessary valour to charge through all, which you are in; but it is temerity to seek for danger, and invite such enemies when we are so weak. Goliah's saying, 'give me a man to fight with,' is a prognostic of no good success. Rather foresee all your dangers to avoid them; understand where each temptation lieth that you may go another way if possible. Chastity is endangered in delights; humility in riches; piety in businesses; truth in too much talk; and charity in this world, saith Bernard. Alas, did we but think what temptations did with a Noah, a Lot, a David, a Solomon, a Peter, we would be afraid of the enemy and weapon that such worthies have been so wounded by, and of the quicksands where they have so dangerously fallen. When Satan durst assault the Lord himself, what hope will he have of such as we? When we consider the millions that are blinded, and hardened, and damned by temptations, are we in our wits if we will cast ourselves into them?

10. Self-acquaintance would confute temptations, and easily resolve the case when you are tempted. Did you considerately know the preciousness of your souls, and your own concerns, and where your true felicity lieth, you would abhor allurements, and encounter them with that argument of Christ, 'what shall it profit a man, if he gain the world and lose his soul? or what shall a man give in exchange for his soul?' The fear of man would be conquered, by a greater fear; as the Lord commandeth, 'and I say unto you, my friends, be not afraid of them that kill the body, and after that have no more that they can do: but I will fore-warn you whom you shall fear: fear him which after he hath killed, hath power to cast into hell: yea, I say unto you, fear him.'

11. It is unacquaintedness with themselves, that make men quarrel with the word of God, rejecting it when it suits not with their deceived reason, and to be offended with his faithful ministers when they cross them in their opinions or ways, or deal with them with that serious plainness which the weight of the case and their necessity doth require. Alas, sirs, if you were acquainted with yourselves you would know that the holy rule is straight, and the crookedness is in your conceits and misapprehensions; and that your frail understandings should rather be suspected than the word of God, and that your work is to learn and obey the law, and not to censure it;

and that quarreling with the holy word, which you should obey, will not excuse but aggravate your sin, nor save you from the condemnation, but fasten it and make it greater. You would know that it is more wisdom to stoop than to contend with God: and that it is not your physicians nor the medicine that you should fall out with, nor desire to be delivered from, but the disease.

12. Self-acquaintance would teach men to be charitable to others, and cure the common censoriousness, and envy, and malice of the world. Hath thy neighbour some mistakes about the disputable points of doctrine, or doubtful modes of discipline or worship? Is he for the opinion, or form, or policy, or ceremony, which thou dislikest? Or is he against them when thou approvest them? Or afraid to use them, when thou thinkest them laudable? If thou know thyself, thou darest not break charity or peace for this. Thou darest not censure or despise him: but wilt remember the frailty of thine own understanding, which is not infallible in matters of this kind; and in many things is certainly mistaken, and needs forbearance as well as he. Thou wouldst be afraid of inviting God or man to condemn thyself, by thy condemning others; and wouldst think with thyself; 'if every error of no more importance in persons that hold the essentials of religion, and conscientiously practise what they know, must go for heresy or make men sectaries, or cut them off from the favour of God, or the communion of the church, or the protection of the magistrate, and subject them to damnation, to misery, to censures and reproach: alas, what then must become of so frail a wretch as I—of so dark a mind, of so blameable a heart and life—that am like to be mistaken in matters as great, where I least suspect it?' It is ignorance of themselves that makes men so easily think ill of their brethren, and entertain all misreports of them, and look at them so strangely, or speak of them so contemptuously and bitterly, and use them so uncompassionately, because they are not in all things of their opinion and way. They consider not their own infirmities, and that they teach men how to use themselves. The fall of brethren would not be over-aggravated, nor be the matter of insulting or contempt, but of compassion, if men knew themselves. This is implied in the charge of the Holy Ghost, 'Brethren, if a man be overtaken in a fault, ye which are spiritual, restore such a one, in the spirit of meekness, considering thyself lest thou also be tempted: bear ye one another's burdens, and so fulfil the law of Christ.

The pharisee that seeth not the beam of mortal formality and hypocrisy in his own eye, is most censorious against the motes of tolerable particular errors in his brother's eye. None are more uncharitable against the real or supposed errors or slips of serious believers, than hypocrites that have no saving serious faith and knowledge, but place their religion in opinion and out-side shows, and wholly err from the path of life.

13. It is ignorance of themselves that makes men divide the church of Christ, and pertinaciously keep open its bleeding wounds, and hinder concord, and disturb its peace. How far would self-acquaintance go to the cure of all our discords and divisions? Is it possible that the pope should take upon him the government of the antipodes, even of all the world, (and that as to spiritual government, which requireth more personal attendance than secular,) if he knew himself, and consequently his natural incapacity, and the terror of his account for such an usurped charge? Self-acquaintance would depose their inquisitions, and quench their flames; and make them know what spirit they are of, that inclineth not to save men's lives, but to destroy them. Did they know themselves, the papists durst not multiply new articles of faith and ceremonies, and depart from the ancient simplicity of the gospel, and turn the creed or scripture into all the volumes of their councils, and say, All these decrees or determinations of the church are necessary to salvation; and so make the way of life more difficult, if not impossible, (had they indeed the keys) by multiplying their supposed necessaries. Did they but know themselves aright, it were impossible they should dare to pass the sentence of damnation on the far greatest part of the Christian world, because they are not subject to their pretended vicar of Christ. Durst one of the most leprous corrupted sort of Christians in the world unchurch all the rest that will not be as bad as they, and condemn all other Christians as heretics or schismatics, either for their adhering to the truth, or for errors and faults, far smaller than their own? Did they know themselves and their own corruptions, they durst not thus condemn themselves, by so presumptuous and blind a condemnation of the best and greatest part of the church of Christ, which is dearest to him, as purchased by his blood. If either the Protestants or the Greeks, or the Armenians, Georgians, Syrians, Egyptians, or Ethiopian churches, be in as bad and dangerous a case as these usurping censurers tell the world they are, what then will become of the tyrannous, superstitious, polluted, blood-thirsty church of Rome?

What is it but self-ignorance that perverteth the unsettled among us, and sends them over to the Roman tents? No man could rationally become a papist, if he knew himself. Let me prove this to you in these four instances.

1. If he had but the knowledge of his natural senses, he could not take them to be all deceived (and the senses of all others as well as his,) about their proper object; and believe the priests that bread is no bread, or wine no wine, when all men's senses testify the contrary.

2. Some of them turn papists because they see some differences among other Christians, and hear them call one another by names of contumely and reproach; and therefore they think that such can be no true churches of Christ: but if they knew themselves, they would be acquainted with more culpable errors in themselves, than those for which many others are reproached; and see how irrational a thing it is to change their religion upon the scolding words or slanders of another; or which is worse, upon their own uncharitable censures.

3. Some turn to the papists, as apprehending their ceremonious kind of religion to be an easier way to heaven than ours: but if they knew themselves they would know that it is a more solid and spiritual sort of food that their nature doth require, and a more searching physic that must cure their diseases; and that chaff will not feed, but choke and starve their souls.

4. All that turn papists must believe, that they were unjustified and out of the catholic church before, and consequently void of the love of God and special grace: for they receive it as one of the Romish articles, that out of their church there is no salvation. But if these persons were indeed before ungodly, if they knew themselves, they would find that there is a greater matter necessary, than believing in the pope, and turning to that faction; even to turn to God by faith in Christ, without which no opinions or profession can save them. But if they had the love of God before, then they were justified and in the church before; and therefore protestants are of the true church, and it is not confined to the Roman subjects: so that if they knew this, they could not turn papists without a palpable contradiction.

The papists' fugitives tell us, we are no true ministers, nor our ministry effectual and blessed of God. What need we more than imitate Paul, when his ministry was accused, and call them to the knowledge of themselves—'examine yourselves, whether ye be in the faith? Prove yourselves: know ye not your ownselves, how that Jesus

Christ is in you, except ye be reprobates.' If they were ungodly, and void of the love of God, while they were under our ministry, no wonder if they turn papists. For it is just with God, that those that ' receive not the love of the truth that they may be saved, be given over to strong delusions to believe a lie.' But if they received the love of God while in our churches by our ministry, they shall be our witnesses against themselves.

And others as well as papists would be kept from church divisions, if they did but know themselves. Church governors would be afraid of laying things unnecessary, as stumbling-blocks before the weak, and of laying the unity and peace of the church upon them ; and casting out of the vineyard of the Lord, and out of their communion, all such as are not in such unnecessary or little things, of their opinion or way. The words of the great apostle of the Gentiles so plainly and fully deciding this matter, would not have stood so long in the bible, as utterly insignificant, in the eyes of so many rulers of the churches, if they had known themselves, as having need of their brethren's charity and forbearance : ' Him that is weak in the faith receive ye, but not to doubtful disputations : for one believeth that he may eat all things, another that is weak eateth herbs. Let not him that eateth despise him that eateth not,' (much less destroy him or excommunicate him) 'and let not him which eateth not, judge him that eateth : for God hath received him. Who art thou that judgest another man's servant? To his own master he standeth or falleth ; yea, he shall be holden up, for God is able to make him stand. One man esteemeth one day above another; another esteemeth every day alike : let every man be fully persuaded in his own mind.—Let us not therefore judge one another any more ; but judge this rather, that no man put a stumbling-block, or an occasion to fall in his brother's way.'—' For the kingdom of God is not meat and drink, but righteousness, and peace, and joy in the Holy Ghost. —For he that in these things serveth Christ, is acceptable to God, and approved of men.'—' We then that are strong, ought to bear with the infirmities of the weak, and not to please ourselves.' —' Wherefore receive ye one another, as Christ also received us, to the glory of God.' Self-acquaintance would help men to understand these precepts ; and be patient with the weak, when we ourselves have so much weakness, and not to vex or reject our brethren for little or unnecessary things, lest Christ reject or grieve us that have greater faults.

Self-acquaintance also would do much to heal the dividing humour of the people ; and instead of separating from all that are not of their mind, they would think themselves more unworthy of the communion of the church, than the church of theirs.

Self-acquaintance makes men tender and compassionate, and cureth a censorious contemptuous mind. It also silenceth passionate contentious disputes, and makes men suspicious of their own understandings, and therefore forbiddeth them intemperately to condemn dissenters. It also teacheth men to submit to the faithful directions and conduct of their pastors ; and not to vilify, forsake, and disobey them, as if they were above them in understanding, and fitter to be guides themselves ; so that in all these respects, it is ignorance of themselves that makes men troublers of the church, and the knowledge of themselves would much remedy it.

14. And it is ignorance of themselves also, that makes men troublers of the state. A man that doth not know himself is unfit for all society ; if he be a ruler he will forget the common-good, and instead of clemency and justice, will violently exercise an imperious will. If he be a subject, he will be censuring the actions of his rulers, when distance and unacquaintance makes him an incompetent judge. He will think himself fitter to rule than they, and whatever they do, he imagineth that he could do it better. And hence come suspicions and murmurings against them, and Korah's censures, ' ye take too much upon you : are not all the people holy ?' Were men acquainted with themselves, their weaknesses, their concerns, and their duties, they would rather inquire whether they obey well, than whether their superiors rule well ; and would think the lowest place to be most suitable to them ; and would quiet themselves in the discharge of their own duty, making ' supplications, prayers, intercessions, and thanksgivings for all men ; for kings, and for all that are in authority, that we may lead a quiet and peaceable life, in all godliness and honesty ; for this is good and acceptable in the sight of God our Saviour. It would quiet all the seditions and tumults of the world, if men were well acquainted with themselves.

15. Self-acquaintance would end abundance of controversies, and very much help men to discern the truth. In the controversy of free-will or human power ; to know ourselves as we are men, would be to know that we have the natural power and freedom consisting in the self-determining faculty and principle. To know ourselves as sinful, would certify us how much we

want of the moral power which consisteth in right inclinations, and the moral liberty from vicious dispositions and habits. Would time permit, I might show it in the instances of original corruption, of the nature of grace, of merit, of the cause of sin, and many other controversies, how much error is promoted by the ignorance of ourselves.

16. Self-acquaintance maketh men both just and merciful. One cannot be so much as a good neighbour without it, nor yet a faithful friend. It will teach you to put up with injuries and to forgive; as remembering that you are likely to be injurious to others, and certainly are daily so to God; and that it is no great fault that is done against such poor unworthy persons as ourselves, if it had no higher a respect than to us. It is such only that 'with all lowliness, and meekness, and long-suffering, forbear one another in love,' —'and recompense to no man evil for evil,'— and 'be not overcome of evil, but overcome evil with good.' He that is drawn to passion and revenge, is overcome, when he seems to overcome by that revenge. It teacheth us to forgive, to know that much is forgiven us by Christ, or at least, what need we have of such forgiveness. 'Let all bitterness, and wrath, and anger, and clamour, and evil-speaking, be put away from you, with all malice: and be ye kind one to another, tender hearted, forgiving one another, even as God for Christ's sake hath forgiven you.' O that this lesson were well learned!

17. Self-acquaintance will teach us the right estimate of all our mercies: when we know how unworthy we are of the least, and what it is we principally need, it will teach us thankfulness for all; and teach us which of our mercies to prefer. Men know not themselves and their own necessities, and therefore they slight their chief mercies, accounting them burdens, and are unthankful for the rest.

18. Self-acquaintance is necessary to the solid peace and comfort of the soul. Security and stupidity may quiet the ungodly for a while, and self-flattery may deceive the hypocrite into a dream of heaven; but he that will have a durable joy, must find some matter of joy within him, as the effects and evidence of the love of God, and the prognostics of his endless love. To know what Christ hath suffered, and done, and merited, and promised, is to know the general and principal ground of our rejoicing: but something is wanting to make it peace and joy to us, till we find the fruits of his Spirit within us, without which no man can be his. 'If a man think himself to be something, when he is nothing,

he deceiveth himself. But let every man prove his own work, and then shall he have rejoicing in himself alone, and not in another.' The seal and witness, and beginnings of life, must be within you, if you will know that you are the heirs of life.

19. Self-ignorance causeth men to mis-interpret and repine at the providence of God, and to be froward under his most righteous judgments, because men know not what they have deserved, and what is good for them; they know not the reason and intent of providence; and therefore they quarrel with their Maker, and murmur as if he did them wrong, when self-acquaintance would teach them to justify God in all his dealings, and resolve the blame of all into themselves. The nature of man doth teach all the world, when any hurt is done to societies or persons, to inquire by whose will as well as by whose hands it was perpetrated; and to resolve all the crimes that are committed in the world into the will of man, and there to leave the guilt and blame, and not to excuse the malefactors upon any pretence of the predetermination of the first or any superior cause: and to justify the judge and executioner that takes away men's lives, or their estates, as long as themselves are proved to deserve it. And surely the knowledge of the nature and depravity of man should teach us to deal as equally with God, and finally resolve all guilt and blame into the free and vitiated will of man. Humbling self-knowledge maketh us say with Job, 'Behold, I am vile, what shall I answer thee? I will lay my hand upon my mouth:' And when God is glorifying himself on our relations, or ourselves by his judgments, it teacheth us with Aaron to hold our peace, and to say with Eli, 'It is the Lord, let him do what seemeth him good.' And with David, 'If I shall find favour in the eyes of the Lord he will bring me again, and show me it, and his habitation: but if he thus say, I have no delight in thee; behold here am I, let him do to me as seemeth good to him.' And as the afflicted church, 'I will bear the indignation of the Lord, because I have sinned against him.' Even a Pharaoh, when affliction hath taught him a little to know himself, will say, 'The Lord is righteous, and I and my people are wicked.' When Rehoboam and his princes are humbled, they say, 'The Lord is righteous.'

20. Lastly, it is for want of the knowledge of ourselves, that precious time is so much lost, and hastening death no more prepared for. Did we carry still about us the sensible knowledge of our mortality, and the inconceivable change that

is made by death, we should then live as men that are continually waiting for the coming of their Lord, and as if we still beheld our graves. For we carry about us that sin and frailty, such corruptible flesh, as may tell us of death as plainly as a grave or a skeleton. So great, so unspeakably necessary a work as the serious, diligent preparation for our end, could not be so sottishly neglected by the ungodly, did they thoroughly and feelingly know what it is to be a mortal man, and what to have an immortal soul; what it is to be a sinner, and what to pass into an endless life of joy or misery.

CHAPTER III.

SELF-IGNORANCE EXPOSED, AND CORRECTED.

And now I may suppose that the best of you all, the most honourable, the most learned, the most religious, of them I dare affirm it, will acknowledge, that I want not sufficient reason to urge you, with the question in my text, ' know ye not your own selves?' Judge by the forementioned effects, whether self-acquaintance, even in the most weighty and necessary respects, be common among professed Christians. Doth he duly know himself as a man, that doubteth of a Deity whose image is his very essence, though not the moral image that must be produced by renewing grace? Or he that doubteth of a particular providence, of which he hath daily and hourly experience? Or he that doubteth of the immortality of his soul, or of the life to come, which is the end of his creation and endowments, and is legibly engraven on the nature and faculties of his soul? Do they morally know themselves that make a jest of sin, and make it their delight? That bear it as the lightest burden, and are not so much humbled by all the distempers and miseries of their souls, as they would be by a leprosy, an imprisonment, or disgrace? That have as cold unthankful thoughts of Christ, and of his grace and benefits, as a sick stomach of a feast? That compliment him at the door, but will not be persuaded to let him in, unless he will come upon their terms, and will dwell with their unmortified sin, and be a servant to their flesh, and leave them their worldly prosperity and delights, and save them for these compliments and fruits of the flesh, when sin and the world shall cast them off?

Do those men truly know themselves, that think they need not the spirit of Christ for regeneration, conversion, and sanctification, nor need a diligent holy life, nor to be half so careful and serious for their salvation, as they are for a shadow of happiness in the world? That would without entreaty bestir themselves, if their houses were on fire, or they were drowning in the water, or were assaulted by a thief or enemy; and yet think he is too troublesome and precise that intreateth them to bestir themselves for heaven, and to quit themselves like men for their salvation, and to look about them, and spare no pains for the escaping everlasting misery; when this is the time, the only time, when all this must be done, or they are utterly undone for ever?

Do they know themselves, and what they want, and what indeed would do them good, that itch after sensual delights, and please their appetites and lusts, and waste their time in needless sports, and long for honour and greatness in the world, and study for preferment more than for salvation, and think they can never stand too high nor have too much: as if it were so desirable to fall from the highest pinnacle, or to die forsaken by that for which they forsook the Lord.

Do our feathered, gaudy gallants, or our frizzled, wanton dames, understand what it is that they are so proud of, or do so carefully trim up and adorn? Do they know what flesh is, as they would do, if they saw the comeliest of their companions, when he hath lain a month or twelve months in the grave? Do they know what sin is, as a sight of hell would make them know, or the true belief of such a state? If they did, they would think that another garb doth better beseem such miserable sinners; and that persons in their case have something else to mind and do, than toyishly to spruce up themselves, like handsome pictures for men to look upon, and something else to spend their hours in than dalliance and compliments, and unnecessary ornaments; and that the amiable and honourable beauty, and comeliness, and worth consist in the holy image of God, the wisdom and heavenly endowments of the soul, and in a heavenly, charitable, righteous conversation, and good works; and not in a curious dress or gaudy attire, which a fool may wear as well as a wise man, and a Dives that must lie in hell, when a Lazarus may lie in sores and rags.

Do they know themselves that fear no snares, but choose the life of the greatest temptations and danger to their souls, because it is highest, or hath most provision for the flesh? and that think they can keep in their candle in the greatest storms, and in any company maintain their innocency? And yet cannot understand so much of the will of God, nor of their own interest and danger, as to resist a temptation when it comes, though it offer them but the most inconsiderable trifle, or the most sordid and unmanly lust.

Do they know themselves, that are prying into unrevealed things, and will be wise, in matters of theology, above what is written? That dare set their shallow brains, and dark, unfurnished understandings, against the infallible word of God; and question the truth of it, because it suiteth not with their lame and carnal apprehensions; or because they cannot reconcile what seemeth to them to be contradiction; nor answer the objections of every bold and ignorant infidel? In a word, when God must not be God unless he please them; nor his word be true, unless it be all within the reach of them, that never employed the time and study to understand it, as they do to understand the books that teach them languages, arts, and sciences, and treat of lower things: and when scripture truth must be called in question, as oft as an ignorant eye shall read it, or an unlearned graceless person misunderstand it? When offenders that should bewail, and reform their own transgressions of the law, shall turn their accusations against the law, and call it too precise or strict, and believe and practise no more than stands with their obedience to the law of sin, and will quarrel with God, when they should humbly learn, and carefully obey him; and despise a life of holy obedience, instead of practising it; and in effect, behave themselves as if they were fitter to rule themselves and the world, than God is; and as if it were not God, but they, that should give the law, and be the judge; and God were the subject, and man were God? Do you think, that sinful worms, that stand so near the grave and hell, do know themselves, when they think, or speak, or live at such rates, and according to such unreasonable arrogancy? Do they know themselves, that reproach their brethren for human frailties, and difference of opinion in modes and circumstances, and errors smaller than their own? And that by calling all men heretics, sectaries or schismatics, that differ from them, do tempt men to turn infidels or papists, and to take us all for such as we account each other? And that instead of receiving the weak in faith, whom God receiveth, will rather cast out the most faithful labourers, and cut off Christ's living members from his church, than forbear the imposing of unnecessary things? I dare say, were it not for unacquaintedness with our brethren and ourselves, we should put those in our bosoms as the beloved

of the Lord, that now we load with censures and titles of reproach: and the restoring of our charity would be the restoring of our unity. If blind men would make laws for the banishment of all that cannot read the smallest characters, you would say they had forgot themselves. Nay, when men turn papists or separatists and fly from our churches, to shun those that perhaps are better than themselves, and to get far enough from the smaller faults of others, while they carry with them far greater of their own; when people are more apt to accuse the church than themselves, and say the church is unworthy of their communion, rather than that they are unworthy of the communion of the church, and think no room in the house of God is clean and good enough for them, while they overlook their own uncleanness; when men endure an hundred calumnies to be spoken of their brethren, better than a plain reprehension to themselves; as if their persons only would render their actions justifiable, and the reprover culpable; judge whether these men are well acquainted with themselves.

Why should we go farther in the search; when in all ages and countries of the world the unmercifulness of the rich, the murmuring of the poor, the hard usage by superiors, the disobedience of inferiors, the commotions of the state, the wars and rebellions that disquiet the world, the cruelty covered with pretences of religion, the unthankfulness for mercies, the murmuring under afflictions, too openly declare that most men have little knowledge of themselves. To conclude, when we see that none are more self-accusing and complaining than the most sincere, and none more self-justifying and confident than ungodly careless souls; that none walk more heavily than many of the heirs of life, and none are merrier than many that must lie in hell for ever: that all that a minister can say, will not convince many upright ones of their integrity, nor any skill or industry suffice to convince most wicked men that they are wicked; nor if our lives lay on it, can we make them see the necessity of conversion, nor know their misery till feeling tell them it is now too late: when so many walk sadly and lamentingly to heaven; and so many go fearlessly and presumptuously to hell, and will not believe it till they are there; by all this judge what work self-ignorance maketh in the world.

'Know thyself' is many a man's motto, that is a stranger to himself; as the house may be dark within that hath the sign of the sun hanging at the door. It is easy to say, men should know themselves, and, out of the book or brain, to speak of the matters of the heart: but indeed to know ourselves as men, as sinners, as Christians, is a work of greater difficulty, and such as few are well acquainted with. Shall I go a little further in the discovery of it?

1. Whence is it that most are so unhumbled; so great and good in their own esteem; so strange to true contrition and self-abhorrence, but that they are voluntary strangers to themselves? To loathe themselves for sin, to be little in their own eyes, to come to Christ as little children, is the case of all that know themselves aright. And Christ 'made himself of no reputation, but took upon him the form of a servant,' and set us a pattern of the most wonderful humiliation that ever was performed, to convince us of the necessity of it, that have sin to humble us, when he had none; 'Learn of me, for I am meek and lowly.' And one would think it were a lesson easily learned by such as we, that carry about us, within and without, so much sensible matter of humiliation. 'Had Christ,' saith Augustine 'bid us learn of him to make a world, to raise the dead, and work miracles, the lesson had been strange: but to be meek and lowly is so suitable to our low condition, that if we knew ourselves we could not be otherwise.'

To be holy without humility, is to be a man without the essentials of nature, or to build without a foundation. It is the contrite heart that is the habitation and delight of God on earth; the acceptable sacrifice; 'he that humbleth himself shall be exalted, and he that exalteth himself shall be brought low.' We must not overvalue ourselves, if we would have God esteem us; we must be vile and loathed either in his eyes or our own. It is special to the elect to think more meanly of themselves than they are. But I urge you not to err in your humility. It were low enough, if we were as low in our own esteem as we are indeed: which self-acquaintance must procure. 'He is least displeased with himself, that least knoweth himself; and he that hath the greatest light of grace, perceiveth most in himself to be reprehended,' saith Gregory. Illumination is the first part of conversion and of the new creature: and self-discovery is not the least part of illumination. There can be no salvation without it, because no humiliation.

But how rare this is, let experience determine. To have a poor habitation, a poor attire, and perhaps of choice (though that is not usual) is much more common than a humble soul. It is the most ill-favoured pride that stealeth some rags of humility to hide its shame. It is easier to change our clothing than our mind, and to put off a gaudy habit than our self-flattering hearts. Many a one can live quietly without gold rings and jewels, or sumptuous houses and attendance, that cannot live quietly without the esteem and applause of men, nor endure to be accounted as indeed he is.

O therefore, as you would escape divine contempt, and the most desperate precipitation, know yourselves. For that which cast angels out of heaven, will keep you out, if it prevail. As Hugo acutely saith, 'Pride was bred in heaven (no other wise than as death, in life) but can never hit the way thither again, from whence it fell.' Open the windows of our breast to the gospel light, to the law's conviction, to the light of reason, and then be unhumbled if you can.

2. The abounding of hypocrisy showeth how little men are acquainted with themselves. I speak not here of that gross hypocrisy, which is always known to him that hath it, but of that close hypocrisy which is a professing to be what we are not, or to believe what we believe not, or to have what we have not, or to do what we do not. What article of the faith do not most among us confidently profess? What petition of the Lord's prayer will they not put up? Which of the commandments will they not profess their obedience to? While the stream of their conversation testifieth, that in their hearts there is none of the belief, the desire, or the obedience in sincerity, which they profess. Did they know themselves they would be ashamed of the vanity of their profession, and of the miserable want of the things professed; and that God who is so nigh their mouths is so far from their hearts. If you heard an illiterate man profess that he understandeth all the languages and sciences, or a beggar boasting of his wealth, would you take any of these to be the words of one that knows himself? Sure they are in the dark that spend their days in dreaming visions: but they have their eyes so much on the beholders, that they have no leisure to peruse themselves: they are so careful to be esteemed good, that they are careless of being what they seem.

Especially if they practise not the vicious inclinations of their hearts, they think they have not the vice they practise not, and that the root is dead because it is winter: when it is the absence of temptations and occasions, and not of vitious habits, or inclinations, that smooths their lives with seeming innocency, and keeps their sins from breaking forth to their own or others' observation. The feeble vices of many lie hid:

there are wanting instruments of drawing forth their wickedness. So a poisonous serpent may be safely handled, while he is stiff with cold, and yet it is not because he hath no venom, but because he is stupified: so is it with the cruelty, luxury and ambition of many.'—Seneca. The knowledge of yourselves is the bringing in of light into your souls, which will awaken you from the hypocrite's dream, and make such apparitions vanish. Come near this fire, and the paint of hypocrisy will melt away.

3. The common impatience of plain reproof, and the love of flattery, shows us how much self-ignorance doth abound. Most men love those that have the highest estimation of them, be it true or false. They are seldom offended with any for over-valuing them. They desire not much to be accounted well when they are sick, or rich when they are poor, but to be ac· counted wise though they are foolish, and godly when they are ungodly, and honest and faithful when they are deceitful and corrupt; this is a courtesy that you must not deny them—they take it for their due. They will never call you heretics for such errors as these. And why is it, but because they themselves err about themselves, and therefore would have others do so too.

A wise man loveth himself so well, that he would not be flattered into hell, nor die as Sisera or Samson, by good words, as the harbingers of his woe. He loveth ingenuous penitence so well, that he cannot love the flatterer's voice that contradicteth it. Faithful reprovers are the messengers of Christ, that call us to repentance, that is, to life. Unfaithful flatterers are the messengers of the devil, to keep us from repentance, and harden us in impenitency unto death. If we know ourselves, we shall know that when we are over-loved and over-praised as being more learned, wise, or holy than we are, it is not we that are loved and praised; for we are not such as that love or praise supposeth us to be. Vices, like worms, are bred and crawl in the inward parts, unseen, unfelt of him, that carrieth them about him: and therefore by the sweetmeats of flattery and sensuality they are ignorantly fed: but it is bitter medicines that must kill them, which those only will endure, that know they have them, and what they are. 'You speak bitterly,' saith the impatient sinner to the plain reprover, 'but such are sweet and excellent men that meddle not with the sore.' But it is bitter things that are wholesome to your souls; that befriend your virtues, and kill the worms of your corruption, which sweet things cherish. Sermons not ·pier-

cing, but pleasing, are not wise. But, alas, men follow the appetite of their vices, not only in choosing their meat, and drink, and company, and recreations, but also in the choice of the church that they will hold communion with, and the preachers that they will hear: and they will have the sweet, and that which their corruption loveth, come of it what will. Nay, pride hath got so great dominion, that flattery goeth for due civility; and he is accounted cynical or morose that useth it not. To call men as they are (even when we have a call to do it), or to tell them of their faults with necessary freedom, though with the greatest love and caution and deprecation of offence, is a thing that most, especially great ones, cannot digest. A man is supposed to rail, that speaketh without flattery; and to reproach them, that would save them from their sins. Jerome saith, ' The vice of flattery now so reigneth, and which is worst, goeth under the name of humility and good will, that he that knoweth not how to flatter, is reputed envious or proud.' Indeed some men have the wit to hate a feigned hypocritical flatterer, and also modestly to take on them to disown the excessive commendations of a friend; but these mistaken friendly flatterers seldom displease men at the heart. Jerome saith, ' We can say we are unworthy, and modestly blush; but within, the heart is glad at its own commendation.' Seneca saith, ' We soon please ourselves to meet with those that call us good men, wise and holy; and we are not content with a little praise: whatever flattery heapeth on us without shame, we lay hold on it as due; we assent to them that say we are the best and most holy, when we ofttimes know ourselves that they lie!' All this is for want of the true knowledge of themselves. When God hath acquainted a sinner effectually with himself, he quickly calleth himself by other names than flatterers do: with Paul he saith, ' we ourselves were sometime foolish, disobedient, serving divers lusts and pleasures:' that he was mad against the saints in persecuting them. He then speaks so much against himself, that if tender ministers and experienced friends, did not think better of him than he of himself, and persuade him to more comfortable thoughts, he would be ready to despair, and think himself unworthy to live upon the earth.

4. Judge also how well men know themselves, when you have observed, what different apprehensions they have of their own faults and of other men's; and of those that are suitable to their dispositions or interests, and those that are against them. They seem to judge of the

actions by the persons, and not the persons by the actions. Though he be himself a sensualist, a worldling, drowned in ambition and pride, whose heart is turned away from God, and utterly strange to the mystery of regeneration and a heavenly life, yet all this is scarce discerned by him, and is little troublesome, and less odious than the failings of another, whose heart and life are devoted unto God. The different opinions, or modes and circumstances of worship, in another that truly feareth God, are matter of severer censures and reproach with them than their own omissions, and averseness and enmity to holiness, and the dominion of their deadly sins. It seems to them more intolerable for another to pray without a book, than for themselves to pray without any serious belief, or love, or holy desire, without any feeling of their sins, or misery or wants; that is, to pray with the lips without a heart; to pray to God without God, even without the knowledge or love of God, and to pray without prayers. It seemed to the hypocritical Pharisees a greater crime in Christ and his disciples, to violate their traditions in not washing before they eat, to break the ceremonious rest of their sabbath by healing the diseased, or plucking ears of corn, than in themselves to hate and persecute the true believers and worshippers of God, and to kill the Lord of life himself. They censured the Samaritans for not worshipping at Jerusalem: but censured not themselves for not worshipping God that is a Spirit, in spirit and in truth. Which makes me remember the course of their successors, the ceremonious papists, that condemn others for heretics, and burn them in the flames, for not believing that bread is no bread, and wine is no wine, and that bread is to be adored as God, and that the souls of dead men know the hearts of all that pray to them in the world at once; and that the pope is the vice-Christ and sovereign of all the Christians in the world; and for reading the scriptures and praying in a known tongue, when they forbid it, and for not observing a world of ceremonies; when all this enmity to reason, piety, charity, humanity, all their religious tyranny, hypocrisy, and cruelty, do seem but holy zeal and laudable in themselves. To lie, dissemble, forswear, depose and murder princes, is a smaller matter to them when the pope dispenseth with it, and when it tends to the advantage of their faction, which they call the church, than to eat flesh on Friday or in Lent, to neglect the mass, or images, or crossing, &c.

And it makes me remember bishop's Hall's description of an hypocrite: 'He turneth all gnats into camels, and cares not to undo the world for a circumstance. Flesh on Friday is more abominable to him than his neighbour's bed: he abhors more not to uncover at the name of Jesus, than to swear by the name of God.' It seems that prelates were guilty of this in Bernard's days, who saith, ' Our prelates strain at a gnat, and swallow a camel; while permitting greater matters, they discuss (or sift) the less: excellent estimators of things indeed, that in the smallest matters employ great diligence, but in the greatest little or none at all.' And the cause of all this partiality is, that men are unacquainted with themselves. They love and cherish the same corruptions in themselves, which they should hate and reprehend in others. And saith Jerome, ' How can a prelate of the church reform the evil that is in it, that rusheth into the like offence? Or with what freedom can he rebuke a sinner, when his conscience secretly tells him, that he hath himself committed the same faults which he reproveth?'

Would men but first be acquainted with themselves, and pass an impartial judgment on the affections and actions that are nearest them, and that most concern them, they would be more competent and more compassionate judges of their brethren, that are now so hardly used by them. It is excellent advice that Austin gives us, ' When necessity constraineth us to reprove any one, let us think whether it be such a vice as we never had ourselves; and then let us think that we are men, and might have had it: or if we once had such, but have it not now, then let the remembrance of common frailty touch us, that compassion and not hatred may lead the way to our reproof: but if we find that we have the same vice ourselves, let us not chide, but groan, and move (or desire) that we may both equally lay it by.'

5. It shows how little men know themselves, when they must needs be the rule to all other men, as far as they are able to command it: and that in the matters that men's salvation dependeth on; and also in the smallest, most tender and disputable points; and even in those things where themselves are most unfit to judge. In every controverted point of doctrine, (though such as others have much better studied than himself) he that hath strength to suppress all those that differ from him, must ordinarily be the umpire: so is it even in the modes and circumstances of worship. Perhaps Christ may have the honour to be called the king of the church, and the scriptures have the honour to be called his laws. But indeed such men would be the lords themselves; and it is their wills and words that must

be the laws; and this under pretence of serving Christ, and interpreting his laws; when they have talked the utmost for councils, fathers, church, tradition, it is themselves that indeed must be all these; for nothing but their own conceits and wills must go for the sense of decrees, or canons, fathers, or tradition. Even they that hate the power and serious practice of religion, would fain be the rule of religion to all others: and they that never knew what it was to worship God in spirit and truth, with delight and love, and suitableness of soul, would needs be the rule of worship to all others, even in the smallest circumstances and ceremonies. And they would be the governors of the church, or the determiners of its mode of government, that never would be brought under the government of Christ themselves. If it please them better to spend the Lord's day in plays or sports, or compliment or idleness, than in learning the will of God in his word, or worshipping him, and begging his mercy and salvation, and seriously preparing for an endless life, they would have all others to do the like.

'If their full souls loathe the honey-comb,' and they are weary of being instructed above an hour, or twice a day, they would have all others forced to their measure, that they may seem as diligent as others, when others are compelled to be as negligent as they. Alas, did men but know themselves, the weakness of their understandings, the sinful bias that personal interest and carnal inclinations have set upon their wills, they would be less arrogant and more compassionate, and not think, by making themselves as gods, to reduce the unavoidable diversities that will be found among mankind, to a unity in conformity to their minds and wills, and that in the matters of God and of salvation; while every man's conscience that is wise and faithful, will be tenacious of a double interest of God and of his soul which he cannot sacrifice to the will of any. But be so just as not to mistake and misrepresent me in all this, as if I pleaded for libertinism or disorder, or spoke against government, civil or ecclesiastical; when it is only private ambition, uncharitableness, and cruelty, and papal usurpations over the church and consciences of men, that I am speaking of; which men, I am sure, will have other thoughts of, when God hath made them know themselves, than they have while passion hindereth them from knowing what spirit they are of: they will then see, that the weak in faith should have been received, and that catholic unity is only to be founded in the universal head, and end, and rule.

6. The dreadful change that is made upon men's minds, when misery or approaching death awakes them, doth show how little they knew themselves before. If they have taken the true estimate of themselves in their prosperity, how come they to be so much changed in adversity? Why do they begin then to cry out of their sins, and of the folly of their worldliness and sensuality, and of the vanity of the honours and pleasures of this life? Why do they then begin to wish, with gripes of conscience, that they had better have spent their precious time, and minded more the matters of eternity, and taken the course as those did whom they once derided, as making more ado than needs? Why do they then tremble under the apprehensions of their unreadiness to die, and to appear before the dreadful God, when formerly such thoughts did little trouble them? Now there is no such sense of their sin or danger upon their hearts. Who is it now that ever hears such lamentations and self-accusations from them, as then it is likely will be heard? The same man that then will wish with Balaam, that he might 'die the death of the righteous and that his latter end might be as his,' will now despise and grieve the righteous. The same man that then will passionately wish that he had spent his days in holy preparation for his change, and lived as strictly as the best about him, is now so much of another mind that he perceives no need of all this diligence; but thinks it is timorous superstition, or at least that he may do well enough without it. The same man that will then cry, 'Mercy, mercy, O mercy, Lord, to a departing soul, that is loaden with sin, and trembleth under the fear of thy judgment,' is now perhaps an enemy to serious earnest prayer, and hates the families and persons that most use it; or at least is prayerless, or cold and dull himself in his desires, and can shut up all with a few careless customary words, and feel no pinching necessity to awaken him importunately to cry and strive with God. Doth not all this show, that men are befooled by prosperity, and unacquainted with themselves, till danger or calamity call them to the bar, and force them better to know themselves?

Your mutability proveth your ignorance and mistakes. If indeed your case be now as good as your present confidence or security do import, lament it not in your adversity; fear it not when death is calling you to the bar of the impartial judge! Cry not out then of your ungodliness and sensuality; of your trifling hypocrisy, your slight contemptuous thoughts of God, and of your casting away your hopes of heaven, by wilful negligence and delays! If you are sure that you are now in the right, and diligent, serious believers in the wrong, then stand to it before the Lord : set a good face on your cause if it be good—be not cast down when it is tried; God will do you no wrong: if your cause be good, he will surely justify you, and will not mar it. Wish not to die the death of the righteous : say not to them, 'give us of your oil, for our lamps are gone out.' If all their care, and love, and labour, in seeking first the kingdom of God and its righteousness, be a needless thing, wish not for it in your extremity, but call it needless then. If fervent prayer may be spared now, while prayer may be heard, and a few lifeless words that you have learned by rote may serve the turn, then call not on God when answering is past, seek him not when he will not be found, 'when your fear cometh as desolation, and your destruction as a whirlwind; when distress and anguish come upon you.' Cry not 'Lord, Lord, open unto us,' when the door is shut. Call them not foolish then that slept, but them that watch, if Christ was mistaken, and you are in the right.

O sirs, stand but at the bed side of one of these ungodly, careless men, and hear what he saith of his former life, of his approaching change, of a holy or a carnal course, whether a heavenly or worldly life is better, unless God have left him to that deplorable stupidity which an hour's time will put an end to; hearken then whether he thinks that God or the world, heaven or earth, soul or body, be more worthy of man's chief care and diligence, and then judge whether such men did know themselves in their health and pride, when all this talk would have been derided by them as too precise, and such a life accounted over-strict and needless, as then they are approving and wishing they had lived. When that minister or friend should have once been taken for censorious, abusive, self-conceited, and unsufferable, that would have talked of them in such language as, when death approacheth, they talk of themselves; or would have spoken as plainly and hardly of them, as they will then do of themselves. Doth not this mutability show, how few men now have a true knowledge of themselves?

What is the repentance of the living, and the desperation of the damned, but a declaration that the persons repenting and despairing were unacquainted with themselves before? Indeed the erroneous despair of men, while grace is offered them, comes from ignorance of the mercy of God and willingness of Christ to receive all that are willing to return. But yet the sense of sin and misery, that occasioneth this erroneous despair, doth show that men were before erroneous in their presumption and self-esteem. Bernard saith, 'Both the knowledge of God and of thyself is necessary to salvation; because as from the knowledge of thyself, the fear of God cometh into thee, and love from the knowledge of God : so on the contrary, from the ignorance of thyself cometh pride, and from the ignorance of God cometh desperation.'

Poor men that must confess their sin and misery at last, would show a more seasonable acquaintance with themselves, if they would do it now, and say with the prodigal, 'I will arise and go to my Father, and say to him, Father I have sinned against heaven and before thee, and am no more worthy to be called thy son.' In time this knowledge and confession may be saving Even a Seneca could say, without the scripture, 'The knowledge of sin is the beginning of recovery, or health : for he that knows not that he sinneth, will not be corrected. Reprehend thyself therefore as much as thou canst. Inquire into thyself : first play the part of an accuser, then of a judge, and lastly, of one that asketh pardon.'

It is not because men are innocent or safe, that we now hear so little confession or complaint; but because they are sinful and miserable in so great a measure, as not to know or feel it. Seneca says, 'Why doth no man confess his vices? Because he is yet in them. To tell his dreams is the part of a man that is awake : and to confess his faults is a sign of health.' If you call a poor man rich, or a deformed person beautiful, or a vile, ungodly person virtuous, or an ignorant barbarian learned, will not the hearers think you do not know them? And how should they think better of your knowledge of yourselves, if any of you that are yet in the flesh will say you are spiritual; and those that hate the holiness, and justice, and government of God, will say they love him; or those that are in a state of enmity to God, and are as near to hell as the execution is to the sentence of the law, will persuade themselves and others, that they are the members of Christ, the children of God, and the heirs of heaven; and take it ill of any that would question it, though only to persuade them to make it sure, and to take heed what they trust to, when endless joy or misery must be the issue?

7. Doth it not manifest how little men know themselves, when in every suffering that befalls them, they overlook the cause of all within them, and fall upon others or quarrel with every thing

that standeth in their way? Their contempt of God doth cast them into some affliction, and they quarrel with the instruments, and meddle not with the mortal cause at home. Their sin finds them out, and testifieth against them; and they are angry with the rod, and repine at providence, as though God himself were more to be suspected of the cause than they: yea, it is become with many a serious doubt, whether God doth not necessitate them to sin, and whether they omit not duty merely because he will not give them power to perform it; and, whether their sin be any other than a relation unavoidably resulting from a foundation laid by the hand of God himself. Do those men know themselves, that will sooner suspect and blame the most righteous, holy God, than their own unrighteous, carnal hearts? Man drinketh up iniquity like water, but there is no unrighteousness with God. And is not such a frail and sinful weight more likely to be the cause of sin than God, and to be culpable in all the ill that doth befall us?

It shows that men little know themselves, when all their complaints are poured out more fluently on others than themselves: like sick stomachs, that find fault with every dish, when the fault is within themselves; or like pained, weak, or froward children, that quarrel with every thing that toucheth them, when the cause is in themselves. If they want peace, content, or rest, they lay the blame on this place or that, this or that person, or estate: they think if they had their mind in this or that, they should be well; and therefore they are still contriving for somewhat which they want, and studying changes, or longing after this or that, which they imagine would work the cure: when alas, poor souls, the sin, the sickness, the want are in themselves. It is a wiser mind, a better, more holy, heavenly will, that are wanting to them; without which nothing in the world will solidly content and comfort them.

Did you know yourselves in all your griefs, it is there that you would suspect and find your malady, and there that you would most solicitously seek the cure.

By this time, if you are willing, you may see where lie the disease and misery of the world, and also what must be the cure. Man hath lost himself, by seeking himself, he hath lost himself in the loss of God: he departed from God, that he might enjoy himself, and so is estranged from God and himself. He left the sun, and retired into darkness, that he might behold himself, and not the light; and now beholdeth neither himself nor the light: for he cannot behold himself but by the light. As if the body should forsake the soul, and say, I will no longer serve another, but will be my own. What would such a selfish separation procure, but the converting of a body into a loathsome carcass and a senseless clod? Thus hath the soul dejected itself, by turning to itself, and separating from God; without whom it hath neither life, nor light, nor joy. By desiring a selfish kind of knowledge of good and evil, withdrawing from its just dependence upon God, it hath involved itself in care and misery, and lost the quieting, delighting knowledge which it had in God. And now poor man! he is lost in error; he has strayed so far from home that he knoweth not where he is, nor which way to return, till Christ in mercy seek and save him.

Yet could we but get men to know that they do not know themselves, there were the greater hope of their recovery. But this is contrary to the nature of their distemper. An eye that is blinded by a suffusion or cataract, seeth not the thing that blindeth it: it is the same light that must show them themselves and their ignorance of themselves. Their self-ignorance is part of the self-evil which they have to know. Those troubled souls that complain that they know not themselves, do show that they begin at least to know themselves. But a pharisee will say, 'are we blind also?' They are too blind to know that they are blind. The gospel shall be rejected, the apostles persecuted, Christ himself abused and put to death, the nation ruined, themselves and their posterity undone, by the blindness of these hypocrites, before they will perceive that they are blind, and that they know not God or themselves. Alas, the long calamities of the church, the distempers and confusions in the state, the lamentable divisions and dissensions among believers, have told the world how little most men know themselves, and yet they themselves will not perceive it. They tell it aloud to all about them, by their self-conceit and cruelty, uncharitable censures, reproaches and impositions, that they know not themselves, and yet you cannot make them know it. Their afflicted brethren feel it to their smart; the suffering grieved churches feel it; thousands groan under it, that never wronged them; and yet you cannot make them feel it.

Did they well know themselves to be men, so many would not use themselves like beasts, and care so little for their most noble part. Did they know themselves aright to be but men, so many would not set up themselves as gods; they would not arrogate a divine authority in the matters of God, and the consciences of others, as the Roman prelates do: nor would they desire so much that the observation, reverence, admiration, love, and applause of all should be turned upon them; nor be so impatient when they seem to be neglected; nor make so great a matter of their wrongs, as if it were some deity that were injured.

O what a change it would make in the world, if men were brought to the knowledge of themselves? How many would weep, that now laugh, and live in mirth and pleasure? How many would lament their sin and misery, that are now pharisaically confident of their integrity? How many would seek to faithful ministers for advice, and inquire what they should do to be saved, that now deride them, and scorn their counsel, and cannot bear their plain reproof or come not near them? How many would ask directions for the cure of their unbelief, and pride and sensuality, that now take little notice of any such sins within them? How many would cry day and night for mercy, and beg importunately for the life of their immortal souls, that now take up with a few words of course, instead of serious fervent prayer? Do but once know yourselves aright, know what you are, and what you have done, and what you want, and what is your danger; and then be prayerless and careless if you can: then sit still and trifle out your time, and make a jest of holy diligence, and put God off with lifeless words and compliments if you can. Men could not think so lightly and contemptuously of Christ, so unworthily and falsely of a holy life, so delightfully of sin, so carelessly of duty, so fearlessly of hell, so senselessly and atheistically of God, and so disregardfully of heaven, as now they do, if they did but thoroughly know themselves.

And now, sirs, methinks your consciences should begin to stir, and your thoughts should be turned inwards upon yourselves, and you should seriously consider, what measure of acquaintance you have at home, and what you have done to procure and maintain such acquaintance. Hath conscience no use to make of this doctrine, and of all that hath been said upon it? Doth it not reprove you for your self-neglect, and your wanderings of mind, and your alien, unnecessary fruitless cogitations? Had you been but as strange to your familiar friend, and as regardless of his acquaintance, correspondence, and affairs, as too many of you have been of your own, you may imagine how he would have taken it, and what use he would have made of it: some such use it beseemeth you to make of estrangedness to yourselves. Would not he ask, what is the matter that my friend so seldom looketh at me, and no more mindeth me or my affairs? What have I done to him? How have I deserved this? What more beloved company or employment hath he got? You have this and much more to plead against your great neglect and ignorance of yourselves.

CHAPTER IV.

REASONS AND MOTIVES TO CULTIVATE SELF-ACQUAINTANCE.

In order to your conviction and reformation, I shall first show you some of those reasons that should move you to know yourselves, and consequently should humble you for neglecting it: and then I shall show you what are the hinderances that keep men from self-acquaintance, and give you some directions necessary to attain it.

In general, consider it is by the light of knowledge that all the affairs of your souls must be directed: and therefore while you know not yourselves, you are in the dark, and unfit to manage your own affairs. Your principal error about yourselves will have influence upon all the transactions of your lives, you will neglect the greatest duties, and abuse and corrupt those which you think you do perform. While you know not yourselves, you know not what you do, nor what you have to do, and therefore can do nothing well. For instance,

1. When you should repent of sin, you know it not as in yourselves, and therefore cannot savingly repent of it. If you know in general that you are sinners, or know your gross and crying sins, which conscience cannot overlook, yet the sins which you know not, because you will not know them, may condemn you. How can you repent of your pride, hypocrisy, self-love, self-seeking, your want of love and fear, and trust in God, or any such sins which you never did observe? Or if you perceive some sins, yet if you perceive not that they reign and are predominant, and that you are in a state of sin, how can you repent of that state which you perceive not? Or if you have but a slight and superficial sight of your sinful state and your particular sins, you can have but a superficial false repentance.

2. If you know not yourselves, you cannot be duly sensible of your misery. Could it be expected that the pharisees should lament that they were of their father the devil, as long as they boasted that they were the children of God. Will they lament that they are under the wrath of God, the curse of the law, and the bondage of

the devil, that know not of any such misery that they are in, but hope they are the heirs of heaven? What think you is the reason that when scripture telleth us that few shall be saved, and none at all but those that are new creatures, and have the Spirit of Christ, that yet there is not one of many that is sensible that the case is theirs? though scripture peremptorily concludeth, ' that they that are in the flesh cannot please God,' and that ' to be carnally minded is death,' and that ' without holiness none shall see God,' and that all 'they shall be damned that believe not the truth, but have pleasure in unrighteousness,' and that ' Christ will come in flaming fire, taking vengeance on them that know not God, and that obey not the gospel of our Lord Jesus Christ; who shall be punished with everlasting destruction from the presence of the Lord and the glory of his power, when he shall come to be glorified in his saints, and admired in all them that believe.' And would not a man think that such words as these should awake the guilty soul that doth believe them, and make us all to look about us? I confess it is no wonder, if a complete atheist or infidel should slight them and deride them. But is it not a wonder if they stir not those that profess to believe the word of God, and are the men of whom these scriptures speak? And yet among a thousand that are thus condemned already—I say, by the word, that is the rule of judgment, even condemned already, for so God saith—how few shall you see that with penitent tears lament their misery? How few shall you hear with true remorse complain of their spiritual distress, and cry out as those that were pricked at the heart, ' men and brethren, what shall we do?' How few hearts are affected with so miserable a case?

Do you see by the tears, or hear by the complaints of those about you, that they know what it is to be unpardoned sinners, under the wrath of the most holy God? And what is the matter that there is no more such lamentation? Is it because there are few or none so miserable? Alas! no. The scripture, and their worldly, fleshly, and ungodly lives, assure us of the contrary. But it is because men are strangers to themselves. They little think that it is themselves, that all the terrible threatenings of God do mean. Most of them little believe or consider what scripture saith; but fewer consider what conscience hath to say within, when once it is awakened, and the curtain is drawn back, and the light appeareth. The first proposition inferreth not the conclusion; and the assumption they overlook. Did all that read and hear the

scriptures know themselves, I will tell you how they would hear and read it. When the scripture saith, ' to be carnally minded is death : and if ye live after the flesh ye shall die:' the guilty hearer would say, 'I am carnally minded, and I live after the flesh; therefore I must turn or die.' When the scripture saith, ' where your treasure is, there will your hearts be also:' the guilty conscience would assume, ' My heart is not in heaven, therefore my treasure is not there.' When scripture saith, ' except ye be converted and become as little children, ye shall not enter into the kingdom of heaven;' and 'except a man be regenerated and born again, he cannot enter into the kingdom of God;' and 'if any man be in Christ, he is a new creature, old things are passed away, behold all things are become new;' and 'if any man have not the Spirit of Christ, he is none of his:' the guilty hearer would assume, 'I was never thus converted, regenerated, born again, and made a new creature; I have not the Spirit of Christ; therefore I am none of his, and cannot enter into the kingdom of heaven, till this change be wrought upon me.' When the scripture saith, 'whoremongers and adulterers God will judge,' the guilty hearer would say, ' how then shall I be able to stand before him?'

Yea, did hearers but know themselves, they would perceive their danger from remoter principles, that mention the dealing of God with others. When they hear of the judgments of God upon the ungodly and the enemies of the church, they would say, ' except I repent, I shall likewise perish.' When they hear that 'judgment must begin at the house of God,' they would infer ' what then shall be the end of them that obey not the gospel of God?' And when they hear that 'the righteous are scarcely saved,' they would think ' where then shall the ungodly and the sinner appear?'

3. If you know not yourselves, you cannot be Christians : and cannot have a practical belief in Christ: for he is offered to you in the gospel, as the remedy for your misery; as the ransom for your enthralled souls; as the propitiation for your sin, and your peace-maker with the Father; without whose merit, satisfaction, righteousness, and intercession, your guilty souls can have no hope. And can you savingly value him in these respects, if you know not that sin and misery, that guilt and thraldom, in which your need of Christ consisteth? Christ is esteemed by you according to the judgment you pass upon yourselves.

They that say they are sinners, from a general head knowledge, will accordingly say Christ is their Saviour and their hope, with a superficial belief, and will honour him with their lips with all the titles belonging to the Redeemer of the world: but they that feel that they are deadly sick of sin at the very heart, and are lost for ever if he do not save them, will feel what the name of a Saviour signifieth, and will look to him as the Israelites to the brazen serpent, and cast themselves at his feet for the crums of grace, and yield up themselves to be saved by him in his own way. An ineffectual knowledge of yourselves may make you believe in a Redeemer, as all the city do of a learned, able physician, that will speak well of his skill, and resolve to use him when necessity constraineth them, but at present they find no such necessity. But an effectual sight and sense of your condition will bring you to Christ, as a man in a dropsy or consumption comes to the physician, that feels he must have help or die. Saith Bernard, ' You will not take the Son of God for a Saviour if you be not affrighted by his threatenings.' And if you perceive not that you are lost you will not heartily thank him that came to seek and save you. Can you seek to Christ to take you up, till you find that you have fallen and hurt yourselves? Will you seek to him to bring you from the gates of hell, that find not that you are there?

But to the self-condemning soul that knoweth itself, how welcome would a Saviour be? How ready is such a soul for Christ? Thou judgest that thyself art the person that must come to Christ to be justified. Now thou art ready to be healed by him, when thou findest that thou art sick and dead. Hast thou received the sentence of death in thyself? come to him now and thou shalt have life. Art thou weary and heavy laden; come to him for rest: come and fear not, for he bids thee come. Dost thou know that thou hast sinned against heaven and before God, and art not worthy to be called a son? do but cast thyself then at his feet, and tell him so, and ask forgiveness, and try whether he will not welcome and embrace thee, pardon and entertain thee, clothe thee and feast thee, and rejoice over thee as one that was lost, and is found, was dead, and is alive? for he came to seek and to save that which was lost. While thou saidst, I am rich and increased in goods, and have need of nothing, and knewest not that thou wert wretched, and miserable, and poor, and blind, and naked; thou wouldst not buy the tried gold that thou mightest be rich, nor his white raiment that thou mightest be clothed, that the shame of thy nakedness might not appear; nor Christ's eye salve that

thou mightest see; but now thou art poor in spirit, and findest that thou art nothing, and hast nothing, and of thyself canst do nothing that is acceptably good, and that of thyself thou art insufficient to think any thing that is good; now thou art readier for the help of Christ, and a patient fit for the tender, healing hand of the physician. Whilst thou saidst, ' God, I thank thee that I am not as other men are, extortioners, unjust, adulterers, nor as this publican,' thou wast further from Christ and justification, than now that thou standest afar off, and darest scarcely look up to heaven, but smitest on thy breast and saith, ' Lord be merciful to me a sinner.' Not that extortioners, unjust, adulterers, or any that are ungodly, are justified or can be saved, while they are such; nor that smiting on the breast, or saying, ' Lord, be merciful to me a sinner,' will serve their turn while they continue in their wicked lives: but when thou art brought to accuse and condemn thyself, thou art prepared for his grace that must renew and justify thee. None sped better with Christ than the woman that confessed herself a dog, and begged but for the children's crums: and the centurion that sent friends to Christ to mediate for him, as being unworthy to come himself, and unworthy that Christ should enter under his roof: for of the first Christ said, ' O woman, great is thy faith: be it unto thee even as thou wilt;' and of the second he saith with admiration, ' I have not found so great faith, no, not in Israel.' Though thou art ready to deny the title of a child, and to number thyself with the dogs, yet go to him and beg his crums of mercy. Though thou think that Christ will not come to such a one as thou, and though thou beg prayers of others, as thinking he will not hear thy own, thou little thinkest how this self-abasement and self-denial prepare thee for his tenderest mercies and his esteem. When thou art contrite and poor, and tremblest at the word, then will he look at thee with compassion and respect. ' For thus saith the high and lofty One that inhabiteth eternity, whose name is holy; I dwell in the high and holy place: with him also that is of a contrite and humble spirit, to revive the spirit of the humble, and to revive the heart of the contrite ones: for I will not contend for ever, neither will I be always wroth; for the spirit should fail before me, and the souls which I have made.' When thou art using the self-condemning words of Paul, ' I am carnal, sold under sin; what I would, that do I not, and what I hate, that do I; for I know that in me, that is, in my flesh, dwelleth no good thing; I find a law, that when I would do good, evil is present with me; a law in my members warring against the law of my mind, and bringing me into captivity to the law of sin;' when thou criest out with him, 'O wretched man that I am, who shall deliver me from the body of this death:' thou art then fitter to look to thy Redeemer, and use the following words, 'I thank God, through Jesus Christ our Lord.' When thou didst exalt thyself, thou wast obnoxious to the storms of justice, which were engaged to bring thee low: but now that thou humblest thyself, thou liest in the way of mercy, which is engaged to exalt thee; mercy looketh downward, and can quickly espy a sinner in the dust, but cannot leave him there, nor deny him compassion and relief. Art thou cast out as helpless, wounded by thy sin, and neglected by all others that pass by? thou art the fittest object for the skill and mercy of him that washeth sinners in his blood, and tenderly bindeth up their wounds, and undertakes the perfecting of the cure; though yet thou must bear the surgeon's hand, till his time of perfect cure be come. Now that thou perceivest the greatness of thy sin and misery, thou art fit to study the greatness of his mercy, and with all saints to strive to comprehend what is the breadth, and length, and depth, and height, and to know the love of Christ which passeth knowledge.

Now that thou hast smitten upon the thigh, and said, 'What have I done?' thou art fitter to look unto him that was wounded and smitten for thy transgressions, and to consider what he hath done and suffered: how he 'hath borne thy grief and carried thy sorrows, and was bruised for thy iniquities; the chastisement of our peace was laid upon him, and we are healed by his stripes: all we like sheep have gone astray, we have turned every one to his own way, and the Lord hath laid on him the iniquity of us all.' Art thou in doubt whether there be any forgiveness for thy sins, and whether there be any place for repentance? Remember that Christ is 'exalted by God's right hand to be a prince and a saviour, to give repentance unto Israel, and forgiveness of sins.' And that he himself hath spoken it, that 'all manner of sin and blasphemy shall be forgiven unto men, except the blasphemy against the Spirit.' And this forgiveness of sins thou art bound to believe as an article of thy creed: that it is purchased by Christ, and freely offered in the gospel. Mercy did but wait all this while, till thou wast brought to understand the want and worth of it, that it might be thine. When a Peter that denieth Christ with oaths and cursing, goeth out and weepeth, he speedily finds mercy from him without, whom he but now denied within.

When so bloody a persecutor as Paul findeth mercy, upon his prostration and confession, and when so great an offender as Manasseh is forgiven upon his penitence, in bonds; when all his witchcraft, idolatry and cruelties are pardoned, upon a repentance that might seem to have been forced by a grievous scourge; what sinner that perceives his sin and misery, can question his entertainment if he come to Christ. Come to him, sinner, with thy load and burden; come to him, with all thy acknowledged unworthiness: and try whether he will refuse thee. He hath professed that 'him that cometh to him, he will in no wise cast out.' He refused not his very murderers, when they were pricked at the heart and inquired after a remedy, and will he refuse thee? Hath our physician poured out his blood to make a medicine for distracted sinners, and now is he unwilling to work the cure? O sinner! now that thou art brought to know thyself, know Christ also, and the cure is done. Let thy thoughts of the remedy be deeper and larger, and longer, than all thy thoughts of thy misery: it is thy sin and shame if it be not so. Why wilt thou have twenty thoughts of sin and misery, for one that thou hast of Christ and mercy? when mercy is so large, and great, and wonderful as to triumph over misery, and grace aboundeth much more where sin hath abounded. 'Behold the wounds of Christ as he is hanging; the blood of him dying, the price of him redeeming, the scars of him rising. His head is bowed to kiss thee, his heart open to love thee, his arms open to embrace thee, his whole body exposed to redeem thee.'—'The Maker of man was made man, that he who rules the stars might be a suckling, that bread might hunger, the fountain might thirst, the light might sleep, the way might be weary in his journey, the truth might be hidden by false-witnesses, the judge of quick and dead might be judged by a mortal judge, justice might be condemned by the unjust, discipline might be scourged, the cluster of grapes might be crowned with thorns, the foundation might be hanged on a tree, strength might be weakened, health might be wounded, and life itself might die.'—Augustine. This is the wonderful mystery of love, which will entertain the soul that comes to Christ, and which thou must study to know when thou knowest thyself. But till then all these will be riddles to thee, or little relished: and Christ will seem to thy neglecting heart to have died and done all this in vain.

And hence it is, that as proud, ungodly, sensual men, were never sound believers, so they oft-times fall from that opinionative, common faith which they had, and of all men do most easily turn apostates: it being just with God that they should be so far forsaken as to vilify the remedy, who would not know their sin and misery, but love it, and pertinaciously hold it as their felicity.

4. If you know not yourselves, you will not know what to do with yourselves, nor to what end, and for what work you are to live. This makes the holy work neglected, and most men live to little purpose, wasting their days in matters that themselves will call impertinent when they come to die; as if they were good for nothing else: whereas if they knew themselves, they would know that they are made and fitted for more noble works. O man, if thou wert acquainted well with thy faculties and frame, thou wouldst perceive the name of God thy Maker to be so deeply engraven in thy nature, even in all thy parts and powers, as should convince thee that thou wast made for him; that all thou art and all thou hast, are nothing worth, but for his service: as all the parts and motions of a clock or watch are but to tell the hour of the day. Thou wouldst know then the meaning of sanctification and holiness; that it signifieth but the giving God his own, and is the first part of justice, without which no rendering men their due can prove thee just. Thou wouldst then know the unreasonableness and injustice of ungodliness and all sin: and that to serve thy fleshly lusts and pleasures with those noble faculties that were purposely formed to love and serve the eternal God, is absurd and villanous. O man! didst thou but know thyself, and for what employment thy faculties are made, thou wouldst lift up thy head, and seriously think who holds the reins,—who keeps the breath yet in thy nostrils, and continueth thee in life; and where it is that thou must shortly fix thy unchangeable abode; and what is now to be done in preparation for such a day. Thou wouldest know that thy higher faculties were not made to serve the lower: thy reason to serve thy sensual delight. O man! hadst thou not lost the knowledge of thyself, thou wouldst be so far from wondering at a holy life, that thou wouldst look upon an unholy person as a monster.

I confess my soul is too apt to lose its lively sense of all these things: but whenever it is awake, I am forced to say, in meditations such as these, 'If I had not a God to know and think on, to love and honour, to seek and serve, what had I to do with my understanding, will, and all my powers? What should I do with life and time? What use should I make of God's provisions? What could I find to do in the world, that is worthy of a man? Were it not as good to lie still, and sleep out my days, and professedly do nothing, as to go dreaming with a seeming seriousness, and wander about the world as in my sleep, and do nothing with such a troublesome stir, as sensual worldly persons do? Could not I have lived as a beast without a reasonable, free-working soul?' Let them turn from God, and neglect the conduct of the Redeemer, and disregard the holy approaches, and breathings, and workings of the soul towards its beloved centre and felicity, that know not what an immortal soul is, or know how else to employ their faculties with satisfaction or content unto themselves. I profess here, as in his presence, who is the Father of spirits, and before angels and men, I do not; I know not what else to do with my soul that is worth the doing, but what is subservient to its proper object, its end and everlasting rest. If the holy service of God, and the preparation for heaven, and seeking after Christ and happiness, be forbidden me, I have no more to do in the world that will satisfy my reason, or satisfy my affections, or that as a man or a Christian I can own. And it is as good not to live, as to be deprived of the uses and ends of life. Though my love and desires are infinitely below the eternal goodness, and glory, which they should prosecute and embrace, yet do my little tastes, and dull desires, and cold affections consent unfeignedly to say, ' Let me have God or nothing : let me know him and his will, and what will please him, and how I may enjoy him: or, O that I had never had an understanding to know any thing ! Let me remember him; or, O that I had never had a memory! Let me love him and be beloved of him; or, O that I had never had such a thing as love within me! Let me hear his teachings, or have no ears: let me serve him with my riches, or let me have none ; and with any interest or honour, or let me be despised.' It is nothing that he gives not being to: and it is useless that is not for his glory and his will. If God have nothing to do with me, I have nothing to do with myself, nor have the world anything to do with me.

Let dark and dreaming sinners declare their shame, and speak evil of what they never knew, and neglect the good they never saw; let them that know not themselves or God, refuse to give up themselves to God, and think a life of sensuality more suitable to them : but ' Lord, lift thou up the light of thy countenance on me,' and let me no longer be a man, nor have reason, or any of thy talents in my trust, if I shall not be thine.

and live to thee. I say as Bernard—'Worthy is that man, O Christ, to die, that refuseth to live to thee: and he that is not wise to thee, is but a fool; and he that careth to be, unless it be for thee, is good for nothing, and is nothing. For thyself, O God, hast thou made all things; and he that would be to himself and not to thee, among all things beginneth to be nothing.'

5. If you know not yourselves, you know not how to apply the word of God, which you read or hear; you know not how to use either promises or threatenings to the benefit of your souls: nay, you will misapply them to your hurt. If you are unregenerate, and know it not. you will reject all the calls of God that invite you to come in and be converted, and think that they belong to grosser sinners but not to you. All the descriptions of the unsanctified and their misery will little affect you, and all God's threatenings to such will little move you; for you will think they are not meant for you; you will be pharisaically blessing yourselves, when you should be pricked at the heart, and laid in contrition at the feet of Christ: you will be thanking God that you are not such as indeed you are; you will be making application of the threatenings to others, and pitying them when you should lament yourselves; you will be thundering when you should be trembling; and speaking that evil of others that is your own; and convincing others of that which you had need to be convinced of; and wakening others by talking in your sleep; and calling other men hypocrites, proud, self-conceited, ignorant, and other such names that are indeed your own; you will read or hear your own condemnation, and not be moved at it, as not knowing your own description when you hear it, but thinking that this thunderbolt is levelled at another sort of men. All the words of peace and comfort, you will think are meant of such as you. When you read of pardon, reconciliation, adoption, and right to everlasting life, you will imagine that all these are yours. And thus you will be dreaming that you are rich and safe, when you are poor and miserable, and in the greatest peril. And is it not a pity that the celestial, undeceiving light should be abused to so dangerous self-deceit,—and that truth itself should be made the furtherance of so great an error,—and that the eye-salve should only put out your eyes? Is it not sad to consider that you should now be emboldened to presumption, by that very word which (unless you be converted) will judge you to damnation; and that self-deceit should be increased by the glass of verity that should undeceive you?

6. If you know not yourselves, you know not how to confess or pray. This makes men confess their sins so seldom, and with so little remorse to God and man; you hide them because they are hidden from yourselves; and therefore God will open them to your shame: whereas if they were opened to you, they would be opened by you, and covered by God. Saith Augustine, 'I did not cover, but open, that thou mayest cover: I concealed not, that thou mightest hide, for when man discloseth, God covereth; when man hideth, God maketh bare; when man confesseth, God forgiveth.' For want of self-acquaintance it is that men hypocritically confess to God, in a way of custom, the sins which they will deny or excuse to man; and will tell God formally of much, which they cannot endure to be told of seriously by a reprover: or, if they confess it generally with a seeming humility to others, they cannot bear that another should faithfully charge it upon them, in order to their true humiliation and amendment. Saith Bernard, 'It is the sign of true confession, if, as every one saith he is a sinner, he contradicts not another that saith it of him. For he desireth not to seem a sinner, but righteous, when one confesseth himself a sinner when none reproveth him. It is the vice of pride, for a man to disdain to have that spoken to him of others, which he stuck not to confess of his own accord concerning himself.'

And for prayer, it is men's ignorance of themselves that makes prayer so little in request: hunger best teacheth men to beg. You would be oftener on your knees, if you were oftener in your hearts. Prayer would not seem needless, if you knew your needs. Know yourselves, and be prayerless if you can. When the prodigal was convinced, he presently purposeth to confess and pray; when Paul was converted, Ananias hath this evidence of it from God, 'behold he prayeth.' Indeed the inward part of prayer is the motion of a returning soul to God. Saith Hugo, 'Prayer is the turning of a pious, humble soul to God, leaning upon faith, hope and love. It is the relief of the petitioner, the sacrifice of God, the scourge of devils.'

Self-knowledge would teach men how to pray. Your own hearts would be the best prayer-books to you, if you were skilful in reading them. Did you see what sin is, and in what relation you stand to God, to heaven and hell, it would drive you above your beads and lifeless words of course, and make you know, that to pray to God for pardon and salvation, is not a work for a sleepy soul. Saith Gregory, 'He offereth the truest prayer to God that knoweth himself, that humbly seeth he is but dust, and ascribeth not virtue to himself.' Nothing quencheth prayer more than to be mistaken or forgetful of ourselves. When we go from home this fire goes out; but when we return, and search our hearts, and see the sins, the wants, the weaknesses that are there, and perceive the danger that is before us, and withal the glorious hopes that are offered us, here are fuel and bellows to inflame the soul, and cure it of its drowsiness and numbness. Help any sinner to a clearer light, to see into his heart and life, and to a livelier sense of his own condition, and I warrant you he will be more disposed to fervent prayer, and will better understand the meaning of those words, 'that men ought always to pray and not to faint,' and 'pray without ceasing.' You may hear some impious persons now disputing against frequent and fervent prayer, and saying, What need of all this ado? But if you were able to open these men's eyes, and show them what is within them and before them, you would quickly answer all their arguments, and convince them better than words can do, and put an end to the dispute. You would set all the prayerless families in town and country, gentlemen's and poor men's, on fervent calling upon God, if you could but help them to such a sight of their sin and danger, as shortly the stoutest of them must have. Why do they pray, and call for prayers, when they come to die, but that they begin a little better to know themselves? They see then that youth, and health, and honour, are not the things, and make them not so happy, as befooling prosperity once persuaded them. Did they believe and consider what God saith of them, and not what flattery and self-love say, it would open the mouths of them that are most speechless. But those that are born deaf are always dumb. How can they speak that language with desire to God, which they never learned by faith from God or by knowledge of themselves?

Self-knowledge would also teach men what to ask. They would feel most need of spiritual mercies and beg hardest for them; and instead of outward things, they would ask but for their daily bread, and not be foolishly importunate with God for that which they know not to be suitable or good for them. It is a mercy to be sometimes denied when we pray for outward things: our physician, and not we, must choose our physic, and prescribe our diet.

If men knew themselves, it would teach them on what terms to expect the hearing of their prayers: neither to be accepted for their merits, nor yet to be accepted without that faith repentance and desire, that seriousness, humility, and sincerity of heart, which the very nature of prayer to God doth contain or presuppose. 'He that nameth the name of Christ, must depart from iniquity,' and must 'wash himself and make him clean, and put away the evil of his doings from before the eyes of God, and cease to do evil, and learn to do well:' as knowing that though a Simon Magus must repent and pray; and the wicked in forsaking his way, and thoughts, and returning to the Lord, must 'seek him while he may be found, and call upon him while he is near;' and the prayers of an humbled publican are heard, when he sets his prayer against his sins: yet if he would cherish his sin by prayer, and flatter himself into a presumption and security in a wicked life, because he useth to ask God forgiveness; if he thus regard iniquity in his heart, God will not hear his prayers. And ' we know that such impenitent sinners God heareth not.' And thus the prayers of the wicked, as wicked, (which are not a withdrawing from his wickedness, but a bolster of his security, and as a craving of protection and leave to sin) are but an abomination to the Lord: the bullet, the thorn must be first got out, efore any medicine can heal their wounds. Did men know themselves, and who they have to do with in their prayers, they would not go from cards, and dice, and gluttony, and fornication, and railing, lying, or reviling at the servants of the Lord, to a few hypocritical words of prayer, to salve all till the next time, as if one sin had procured the forgiveness of another. Nor would they conclude a day of worldliness, ambition, sensuality, or profaneness, with a few heartless words of confession and supplication; or with the words of penitence, while their hearts are impenitent; as if when they have abused God by sin, they would make him amends, or reconcile him, by their mockery. Nor would they think to be accepted by praying for that which they would not have; for holiness, when they hate it, and for deliverance from the sins which they would not be delivered from, and would not have their prayers granted.

7. If you know not yourselves, it will unfit you for thanksgiving: your greatest mercies will be least esteemed; and the lesser will be most esteemed. And while you are unthankful for what you have, you will be absurdly thanking God for that which indeed you have not.

What inestimable mercies are daily trodden under feet by sinners, that know not their worth, because they know not their own necessities! They have time to repent, and make preparation for an endless life: but they know not the worth of it, but unthankfully neglect it, and cast it away on the basest vanities; as if worldly cares, or wicked company, or fleshly lusts, or cards, or dice, or revellings, or idleness, were exercises in which they might better improve it, than the works of holiness, justice, and mercy, which God hath made the business of their lives: or as if the profits and pleasures, and vain glory of this world, did better deserve it than their Creator, and their own souls, and the heavenly inheritance. But if their eyes were opened to see where they stand, and what they are, and what are their dangers and necessities, how thankful would they be for one year, one month, one day, one hour, to repent and cry to God for mercy! And how sensibly would they perceive that a hundred years is not too long to spend in serious preparation for eternity?

They have now the faithful ministers of Christ, inviting them in his name to come to him and receive the riches of his grace, and 'beseeching them in his stead to be reconciled unto God.' But they stop their ears, and harden their hearts, and stiffen their necks, and love not to be disturbed in their sins, but are angry with those that are solicitous for their salvation, and revile those as too precise and strict that tell them of the one thing needful, and persuade them to choose the better part, and tell them where their sin will leave them. They take them for their friends that will encourage them in the way that God condemneth, and be merry with them in the way to endless sorrow, and flatter them into security and impenitence till the time of grace be past; but they hate them as their enemies that faithfully reprove them, and tell them of their folly, and call them to a safer, better way. Alas, sirs, there would not be so many nations, congregations, and souls now left in darkness and misery by their own doing, having driven away the mercy of the gospel, and thrust their faithful teachers from them, if they knew themselves. Men would not triumph in their own calamity, when they have expelled their faithful teachers, the dust of whose feet, the sweat of whose brows, the tears of whose eyes, and the fervent prayers and groans of whose hearts, must witness against them, if they knew themselves. They would not be like a madman that glorieth that he hath beaten away his physician and his friends, and is left to himself, if they knew themselves. When they have the earnest calls of the word without, and convictions and urgings of the Spirit of God and their consciences within, they would not wilfully go on, and

cast these mercies at their heels, if they knew themselves.

They have leave to join in the communion of saints, and to enjoy the benefit of holy society in prayer, and conference, and mutual love and spiritual assistance, and in the public worship of God: but they pass these by, as having more of trouble and burden than of mercy, because they little know themselves.

And their inferior mercies of health, and wealth, and food, and raiment, and friends, and accommodations they misesteem and misuse: and value them but as provision for the flesh, and the satisfaction of their sensual and inordinate desires, and not as necessary provision for their duty in the way to heaven! And therefore they are most thankful for their greatest snares: for that honour and abundance which are stronger temptations than they can overcome; for those fleshly contentments and delights which are the enemies of grace, and the prison of their noblest faculties, and the undoing of their souls. If they could for shame speak out, they would thank God more for a successful game, or the favour of their earthly gods, or for preferment, or profit, lands or houses, than ever they did for all the offers of Christ and grace, and all the invitations to a holy life; for there is much more joy and pleasure in their hearts for the former than the latter.

And self-ignorance will also corrupt your thanksgiving, and turn it into sin and folly. Is it not a shame and pity to hear an unpardoned enemy of God and of holiness thank God that he is justified and reconciled to God, and adopted to be his child, and made a member of Jesus Christ; and to hear a carnal, unregenerated person give thanks for his regeneration and sanctification by the Holy Ghost; as it is to hear a leper give thanks for perfect health, or a fool or madman thank God for making him wiser than his neighbours. Is it not a pity to hear a miserable soul thank God for the grace which he never had; and one that is near eternal misery thanking God for making him an heir of glory? O how many have thanked God pharisaically for the pardon of their sins, that must for ever suffer for those sins! How many have thanked him for giving them the assured hopes of glory, that must be thrust out into endless misery! I have known many, that by their friends and by themselves have been flattered into confident hopes of life, when they were ready to die, have thanked God that they were pretty well, and the worst was past; which, in the eyes of judicious standers-by, was not the least aggravation of their sad and deplorable state. Methinks it is one of the saddest spectacles in the world to hear a man thanking God for the assurance of salvation, that is in a state of condemnation, and like to be in hell for ever! These absurdities could not corrupt your highest duties, and turn them into sin, if you knew yourselves.

A man that knoweth his own necessities and unworthiness, is thankful for a little, to God and man. Mercy is as no mercy, where there is no sense of need or misery. Therefore God useth to humble them so low in the work of conversion, whom he meaneth ever after to employ in the magnifying of his grace. And then that which is folly and hypocrisy from a pharisee, will be an acceptable sacrifice from a humble, grateful soul; and he that by grace is made to differ from other men, may (modestly) thank God that he is not as other men. For had he nothing more to thank God for, than the ungodly world, he would be rejected and perish with the world : and if he have more than the world, and yet be no more thankful than the world, he would be guilty of greater unthankfulness than the world. 'This,' saith Augustine, ' is not the pride of one lifted up, but the acknowledgment of one that is not unthankful: know that thou hast, and know that thou hast nothing of thyself, that thou mayst neither be proud, nor yet unthankful. Say to thy God, I am holy, for thou hast sanctified me: for I have received what I had not; and thou hast given me what I deserved not.' The thanksgiving of a faithful soul is so far from being displeasing to God as a pharisaical ostentation, that it is a great and excellent duty, and a most sweet and acceptable sacrifice. ' Offer unto God thanksgiving,—he that offereth praise, glorifieth me.'

8. And as to the Lord's supper, what work they are there like to make, that are unacquainted with themselves, you may conjecture from the nature of the work, and the command of self-examination and self-judging. Though some may be welcomed by Christ that have faith and love, though they doubt of their sincerity, and know not themselves to be children of God ; yet none can be welcome that know not themselves to be sinners condemned by the law, and needing a Saviour to reconcile and justify them. Who will be there humbled and thankful for a Redeemer, and hunger and thirst for sacramental benefits, that knoweth not his own unworthiness and necessities? O what inestimable mercy would appear in a sacrament to us, in the offers of Christ and saving grace, and communion with God and with his saints, if our appetites were but quickened by the knowledge of ourselves?

9. I beseech you consider, whether all your studies, and learning and employments, be not irrational, preposterous and impertinent, while you study not first to know yourselves ? You are nearest to yourselves, and therefore should be best acquainted with yourselves. What should you more observe than the case of your own souls ; and what should you know better than what is within you, and that which, methinks, you should always feel ? even the bent of your own estimations and affections; the sickness of your souls ; your guilt, your wants, and greatest necessities. All your learning is but the concomitant of your dotage, till you know yourselves. Your wisest studies are but the workings of a distracted mind, while you study not yourselves, and the things of everlasting consequence. To study whether it be the sun or earth that moveth, and not consider what motion is predominant in thy soul and life, is a pitiful preposterous study : to think more what stars are in the firmament, than what grace is in thy heart ; and what planet reigneth, than what disposition reigneth in thyself, and whether the spirit or flesh have the dominion, is but to be learnedly besides thyself.

Is it not a laborious madness to travel into far countries, and compass sea and land, to satisfy curiosity ; and to be at so much cost and pains to know the situation, government, and manners, of the cities and countries of the world, and in the mean time to be utterly strange at home, and never bestow one day or hour in a serious survey of heart and life ; to carry about a dark, unknown, neglected soul, while they are travelling to know remote things that less concern them ? Methinks it is a pitiful thing to hear men ingeniously discoursing of the quality, laws and customs of other nations, and of the affairs of princes, and commonwealths, and of the riches and commodities of sea and land, and to be mute when they should express their acquaintance with themselves, either in confession and prayer to God, or in any humble, experimental conference with men ; to trade abroad, and utterly neglect the trade of godliness at home; to keep correspondence with persons of all degrees, and to have no correspondence with themselves ; to keep their shop-books and accounts with diligence, and never regard the book of conscience, nor keep account of that for which they must ere long be accountable to God. It is a pitiful thing to see men turn over voluminous histories, to know what hath been done from the beginning of the world, and regard no more the history of their own lives, nor once look back with penitent remorse upon their ungodly careless conversations, nor say, what have we done? to see men have well-furnished libraries, and read over a multitude of books, and never read the state and records of their souls?

It maketh you but objects of wonder and compassion, to read laws and records, and understand all cases, and never endeavour to understand the case of your immortal souls; to counsel others for their temporal estates, and never understand your spiritual state; to study the mysteries of nature, and search into all the works of God, except yourselves, and that on which your happiness or misery doth depend; to study the nature, and causes and signs of bodily diseases, and their several remedies, and never study the diseases of your own souls, nor the precious remedy which mercy hath provided you; to cure the sicknesses of other men's bodies, and never feel a stony, proud or sensual heart; to know the matters of all arts and sciences, to be able to discourse of them all to the admiration of the hearers, is but an aggravation of thy lamentable folly, if thou be all this while a stranger to thyself, and that because thou art forgetful of thy soul's condition. It is more necessary to know yourselves, your sin, your duty, your hopes, your dangers, than to know how to eat, or drink, or clothe yourselves. Alas, it is a pitiful kind of knowledge that will not keep you out of hell; and a foolish wisdom that teaches you not to save your souls. Till you know yourselves, the rest of your knowledge is but a confused dream. Self-knowledge will direct you in all your studies, and still employ you on that which is necessary, and will do you good, when others are studying but unprofitable, impertinent things; and indeed they are but proud, knowing nothing, when they seem to excel in knowledge, 'but doting about questions and strifes of words, whereof cometh envy, strife, railings, evil surmisings, perverse disputings of men of corrupt minds and destitute of the truth, that take gain for godliness.' Self-knowledge will help you in all your studies. 'You will know in what order, with what study, and to what end every thing should be known: in what order; that that may go first which most promoteth our salvation: with what study or desire; that we may know that most ardently, which most vehemently provoketh love: to what end; that it be not for vain glory and ostentation, but for your own and other men's salvation.'—Bernard.

And as it is ourselves and our own affairs that are nearest to us, and therefore first in order to be known; so it is ourselves that we have a

special charge of, and that we are most obliged to study and to know; and it is our own condition and the affairs of our souls that most concern us. Though sun, and moon, and earth, be not little things in themselves; yet the knowledge of them is a small inconsiderable matter to thee in comparison of the knowledge of thyself.

When our nearer, greater works are done, then those that are more distant will be seasonable, and useful, and excellent in their proper places. When men understand the state and affairs of their souls, and have made sure of their everlasting happiness, they may then seasonably and wisely manage political and economical affairs, and prudently order and prosecute their temporal concerns: when they 'first seek the kingdom of God and his righteousness,' subordinate things may be seasonably considered. But for a man to be taken up about matters of law, or trade, or pleasure, when he mindeth not the matters of his salvation; and to study languages, arts and sciences, when he studieth not how to escape damnation, is not to be learned, but to dote; nor to be honourably or prudently employed, but to walk as a man in a dream, and live contrary to the reason of man, as well as below the faith of a Christian. These seemingly wise and honourable worldlings, that labour not to know what state and relation they stand in towards God, and his judgment, do live in a more pernicious distraction than he that is disputing in mood and figure while his house is burning over his head.

Even works of charity seem but absurd, preposterous acts, in those that are not charitable to themselves. To be careful to feed or clothe the bodies of the poor, and to be senseless of the nakedness and misery of your own souls, is an irrational, distracted course of mercy; as if a man should be busy to pull a thorn out of another's finger, and senseless of a stab that is given himself in the bowels or at the heart. To love yourself and not your neighbour, is selfish, unsociable, and uncharitable; to love neither your neighbour nor yourself, is inhuman; to love your neighbour and not yourself is preposterous, irrational, and scarcely possible. But to love first yourself (next to God), and then to love your neighbour as yourself, is regular, orderly, Christian charity.

10. Consider also, that the ignorance of yourselves doth much unfit you to be useful unto others. If you are magistrates, you will never be soundly faithful against the sin of others, till you have felt how hurtful it is to yourselves. If you are ministers, you will scarcely ever be good at heart-searching work, till you have searched

your own: nor will you know the deceitfulness of sin, and the turnings and windings of the crooked serpent, till you have observed them in yourselves: nor will you have due compassion on the ignorant, impenitent, ungodly, unconverted, or on tempted, weak, disconsolate souls, till you have learned rightly to be affected with sin and misery in yourselves. If men see a magistrate punish offenders, or hear a minister reprove them, who is as bad or worse himself, they will but deride the justice of the one, and reproofs of the other, as the acts or words of blind partiality or hypocrisy; and accost them with 'Physician heal thyself.' The eye of the soul is not like the eye of the body, that can see other things, but not itself. There are two evils that Christ noteth in the reproofs of such as are unacquainted with themselves—hypocrisy and unfitness to reprove. 'Why beholdest thou the mote that is in thy brother's eye, but considerest not the beam that is in thine own eye? Or how wilt thou say to thy brother, let me pull out the mote out of thine eye, and behold a beam is in thine own eye? thou hypocrite, first cast the beam out of thine own eye, and then thou shalt see clearly to cast out the mote out of thy brother's eye.' Thine own vices do corrupt thy judgment, and cause thee to excuse the like in others, and to accuse the virtue that in others is the condemner of thy vice, and to represent all as odious that is done by those that by their piety and reproofs are become odious to thy guilty and malicious soul. Dost thou hate a holy, heavenly life, and art thou void of the love of God, and of his servants; hast thou a carnal, dead, unconverted heart; art thou a presumptuous, careless, worldly wretch; hast thou these beams in thine own eye; and art thou fit to quarrel with others that are better than thyself, about a ceremony, or a holiday, or a circumstance of church-government or worship, or a doubtful, controverted opinion; and to be pulling these motes out of thy brother's eye? Yea, wouldest thou rather pull out his eyes, to get out the mote? first get an illuminated mind and a renewed, sanctified heart; be acquainted with the love of God and of his image; and cast out the beam of infidelity, ungodliness, worldliness, sensuality, malice and hypocrisy, from thine own eye; and then come and play the oculist with thy brother, and help to cure him of his lesser involuntary errors and infirmities. Till then the beam of thy sensuality and impiety will make thee a very incompetent judge, of the mote of a different opinion in thy brother. Every word that thou speakest in condemnation of thy brother, for his opinion or infirmity, is a double condemnation of thyself for thine ungodly, fleshly life. If thou wilt needs have judgment to begin at the house of God, for the failings of his sincere and faithful servants, it may remind thee, to thy terror, what 'the end of them shall be that obey not the gospel of God.' And if you will condemn the righteous for their lamented weaknesses, where, think you, 'shall the ungodly and the sinner appear?'

11. If you begin not at yourselves, you can make no progress to a just and edifying knowledge of extrinsic things. Man's self is the alphabet or primer of his learning. Hugo says, 'In vain doth he lift up his heart to see God, that is yet unfit to see himself. For thou must first know the invisible things of thy own spirit, before thou canst be fit to know the invisible things of God. And if thou canst not know thyself, presume not to know the things that are above thyself.' You cannot see the face which it representeth, if you will not look upon the glass which representeth it. God is not visible, but appeareth to us in his creatures; and especially in ourselves. And if we know not ourselves, we cannot know God in ourselves. The principal glass for the beholding of God, is the reasonable soul beholding itself.

You will make but an unhappy progress in your study of the works of God, if you begin not with yourselves. You can know but little of the works of nature, till you know your own nature: and you can know as little of the works of grace, till self-acquaintance help you to know the nature and danger of those diseases that grace must cure. The unhappy error of presumptuous students, about their own hearts, misleadeth and perverteth them in the whole course of their studies. It is a lamentable sight to see a man turning over fathers and councils, and diligently studying words and notions, who is himself in the gall of bitterness and bond of iniquity, and never knew it, nor studieth the cure. It is a pitiful thing to see such in a pulpit, teaching the people to know the mysteries of salvation, that know not, nor ever laboured to know what sins are predominant in their own hearts and lives; or whether they stand before God in a justified or a condemned state; to hear a poor, unsanctified man boldly treating of the mysteries of sanctification, as if he had felt them in himself; and a man that is condemned already, and stayeth but a while for death,—for final execution,—treat as calmly of judgment and damnation, as if he were out of danger, and exhort others to escape the misery which he is in himself, and never dreameth of it! This showeth how sad a thing it is for men to be ignorant of themselves. To see men running into damnable and dangerous errors on each hand, some into the proud self-conceitedness of the fanatics, enthusiasts and libertines, and some into contempt and scorn of holiness, and every one confident even to rage in his own distractions; this doth but show us whither men will go, that are unacquainted with themselves. This also maketh us so troubled with our auditors, who, when they should learn the truth that should convert and save them, are carping and quarreling with us, and hear us as the pharisees and Herodians heard Christ—to catch us in our words; and they must tell us themselves what medicine must be given them, what doctrine and what administrations they must have.

They that will not be directed or healed by us, will blame us if others be not healed, and hit the minister in the teeth with the errors and faults of his unteachable hearers. Though we do our best in season and out of season, and they cannot tell us what we have neglected on our part, that was likely to effect the cure (though I confess we are too often negligent:) and though we succeed in the conversion of many others, yet must we be reproached with the disobedience of the impenitent! As if it were not grief enough to us, to have our labour frustrated, and see them obstinate in their sin and misery, but we must also be blamed or derided for our calamity! As if they knew not the power of the disease; and what a wonder of mercy it is that any and so many are recovered.

12. Lastly, consider how many great and necessary things concerning yourselves, you have to know, and it will show you how needful it is to make this the first of your studies. To know what you are as men, with what faculties you are endowed, and to what use, for what end you live, in what relation you stand to God and to your fellow creatures, what duties you owe, what sin is in your hearts, and what hath been by commission and omission in your lives, what humiliation, contrition, and repentance you have for your sin, whether you have truly entertained an offered Christ, and are renewed and sanctified by his Spirit, and unreservedly devoted to God, and resolved to be entirely his: whether you love him above all, and your neighbours as yourselves: whether you are justified and have forgiveness of all your sins: whether you can bear afflictions from the hand, or for the sake of Christ, even to the forsaking of all the world, for the hopes of the heavenly, everlasting treasure: how you perform the daily works of your relations and callings; whether you are ready to die, and are safe from the danger of damnation. O did you but know how it concerneth you to get all these questions well resolved, you would find more matter for your studies in yourselves than in many volumes; you would then perceive that the matters of your own hearts and lives are not so lightly and carelessly to be passed over, as they ordinarily are by drowsy sinners.

If you have but many and weighty businesses to think on in the world, you are so taken up with care, that you cannot turn away your thoughts. And yet do you find no work at home, where you have such a world of things to think on, and such as of all the matters in the world, do most nearly concern you?

CHAPTER V.

THE DUTY OF CULTIVATING SELF-ACQUAINTANCE.

Having showed you so much reason for this duty, let me now take leave to invite you all to the serious study of yourselves. It is a duty past all controversy, agreed on by heathens as well as Christians, and urged by them in the general, though many of the particulars necessary to be known are beyond their light. It brutifieth man to be ignorant of himself. Man that is in honour and understandeth not (himself especially) is as the beasts that perish. 'It is worse than beastly to be ignorant of ourselves, it being a vice in us, which is nature in them,' saith Boethius.

Come home, you wandering, self-neglecting souls; lose not yourselves in a wilderness or tumult of impertinent, vain distracting things; your work is near you, the country that you should first survey and travel is within you. From it you must pass to that above you; while by losing yourselves in that which is without you, you will find yourselves, before you are aware, in that which is below you. And then (as Gregory speaks) 'he that was a fool in sinning, will be wise in suffering!' You shall then have time enough to review your lives, and such constraining help to know yourselves, as you cannot resist. O that you did now know but a little of that, which then you must else know in that overwhelming evidence which will everlastingly confound you; and that you would now think of that for a timely cure, which else must be thought of endlessly in despair! Come home, then, and see what work is there: let the eyes of fools be in the corners of the earth ! Leave it to men beside themselves, to live as without themselves, and to be still from home, and waste that time in other business that was given them to prepare for life eternal. The soul is more laudable that knows its own infirmity, than he that, without discerning this, doth search after the compass of the world, the courses of the stars, the foundations of the earth, and the heights of the heavens;' says Augustine. Dost thou delight in the mysteries of nature? Consider well the mysteries of thy own. ' Some men admire the heights of mountains, the huge waves of the sea, the great falls of the rivers, the compass of the ocean, and the circuit of the stars, and they pass by themselves without admiration.'—Augustine. The compendium of all that thou studiest without thee, is near thee, even within thee, thyself being the epitome of the world. If either necessity or duty, nature or grace, reason or faith, internal inducements, external repulses, or eternal attractions and motives, might determine the subject of your studies and contemplations, you would call home your lost, distracted thoughts, and employ them more on yourselves and God.

But before I urge this duty further, I must prevent the misapplication of some troubled souls. I must confess it is a grievous thing for a guilty soul to judge itself, and see its own deformity and danger: and I observe many troubled, humbled souls, especially where melancholy much prevails, are exceedingly prone to abuse this duty, by excess and misdoing it. Though wandering minds must be called home, we must not run into the other extreme, and shut up ourselves, and wholly dwell on the motions of our own distempered hearts. Though straggling thoughts must be turned inward, and our hearts must be watched, yet must we not be always poring on ourselves, and neglect the rest of our intellectual converse ; to look too long on the running of a stream, will make our eyes misjudge of what we afterwards look on, as if all things had the same kind of motion ; to look too long on the turning of a wheel, will make us dizzy, as if all turned round ; and to pore too long on the disordered motions, the confused thoughts, the wants, the passions of our diseased minds, will but molest us, and cast us into greater disquiet and confusion. The words of Anselme notably express the straits that Christians are here put to ; ' O grievous strait ! if I look into myself, I cannot endure myself ; if I look not into myself, I cannot know myself. If I consider myself, my own face affrighteth me ; if I consider not myself, my damnation deceiveth me; if I see myself, the horror is intolerable ; if I see not myself, death is unavoidable.' In this strait we must be careful to avoid both extremes ; and neither neglect the study of ourselves, nor yet exceed in poring on ourselves. To be carelessly ignorant of ourselves, is to undo ourselves for ever: to be too much about ourselves, is to disquiet rather than to edify ourselves, and to turn a great and necessary duty into a great and unnecessary trouble.

Consider, 1. That we have many other matters of great importance to study and know, even when we know ourselves. We must chiefly study God himself, and all the books of scripture, nature, and governing providence, which make him known. What abundance of great and excellent truths have we in all these to study ; what time, what industry is necessary to understand them ; and should we lay out all this time about our own hearts and actions, which is but one part of our study, what sinful omissions should we be guilty of in the neglecting of all these! It is indeed but the burying of our talent of understanding, to confine it to so narrow a compass as ourselves, and to omit the study of God, and his word and works, which are all with delight and diligence to be studied. We have also Christ, and his gospel mysteries and benefits, to study ; we have the church's ease, its dangers, sufferings, and deliverances to study ; we have the state of our neighbours and brethren to consider of; the mercies, and dangers, and sufferings both of their souls and bodies ; we have our enemies to think of with due compassion; and our duty to all these.

2. As it is negligence and omission to be all at home, and pass by so great a part of duty, so is it a double frustration of our labour, and will make even this study of ourselves to be in vain. (1.) We cannot come by all our study to the true knowledge of ourselves, unless we also study other things besides ourselves: for we are related to God, as his creatures, his subjects, his dependent children, his redeemed, and his sanctified ones. And if we know not God as creator, redeemer, and sanctifier ; as our owner, ruler and benefactor ; and know not what his creation, redemption, sanctification, his title, government, and benefits mean, it is not possible that we should know ourselves. Mutual relations must be known together, or neither can be known. (2.) And if we could know ourselves, and know no more, it were but to know nothing, and lose that knowledge; for this is but the entrance into wisdom, and the means and way to higher knowledge. This learning of our alpha-

bet or primer is lost, if we learn no further: you are therefore to study and know yourselves, that you may advance to the knowledge of Christ and his grace, and be acquainted with the remedy of all that you find amiss at home; and that by Christ you may be brought unto the Father, and know God as your happiness and rest; you are not your own ultimate ends, and therefore must go further in your studies than yourselves. (3.) We shall never attain to rectitude, or solid comfort and content, unless our studies go further than ourselves: for we are not the rule to ourselves, but crooked lines, and cannot know what is right and wrong, if we study not the rule as well as ourselves. And alas! we are diseased, miserable sinners. To be always looking on so sad a spectacle, can bring no peace or comfort to the mind; to be still looking on the sore, and hearing only the cry of conscience, will be but a foretaste of hell. When we would be humbled and have matter of lamentation, we must look homeward, where the troubling thorns and nettles of corruption grow; but if we would be comforted and lifted up, we must look higher—to Christ and his promises, and to everlasting life: our garden beareth no flowers or fruits that are so cordial.

Two sorts of persons have great need of this caution, that they dwell not too much on themselves. One is poor, melancholy people, that can think of almost nothing else: their distemper disposeth them to be always poring on themselves, and fixing their thoughts on their sin and misery, and searching into all their own miscarriages and making them worse than indeed they are: you cannot call off their thoughts from continual self-condemning, and musing on their own misdoings and unhappiness. They have a God, a Christ, a heaven, a treasure of precious promises to meditate on: yet they cannot turn their thoughts to these, unless as they aggravate their sin and sorrows, but live as if they had nothing to think on but themselves, and were made to be their own tormentors: day and night, even when they should labour, and when they should sleep, they are busy in a fruitless vexation of themselves. These poor, afflicted souls have need to be called from the excessive study of themselves.

Another sort is, those Christians that wholly taken up in inquiring whether they have saving grace or not; while they neglect that exercise of their grace in doing all the good they can to others, and following on the way of faithful duty, which might do more to their assurance than solitary trials.

The former sort, by overdoing in this one part of their work, disable themselves for all the rest: they tire and distract their minds, and raise such fears as hinder their understandings, and cast their thoughts into such confusion, that they quite lose the command of them, and cannot gather them up for any holy work: yea, while they study nothing but themselves, they lose even the knowledge of themselves: they gaze so long upon their faults and wants, that they can see nothing else, and know no apprehensions but those which are dark and sad; they wilfully unlearn the language of thanksgiving and praise; therefore the burden of all their thoughts and speeches is, miserable and undone; as if there were for them no mercy, no help, no hope, but they are utterly forsaken and cast off by God.

The other sort do so exceed in the measure of that self-love, which in itself is good, that they neglect the study of the love of God; and are still thinking what they are and have been, when they should consider what they must be. They spend so much time in trying their foundation, that they can make but little progress in the building: they are putting on their armour, and preparing their weapons, when they should be fighting; and inquiring which is the way, while they should be travelling. When they should instruct the ignorant, exhort the obstinate, confirm the weak, or comfort the afflicted, they are complaining of their own ignorance, obstinacy, weakness, or affliction, and help not others, because they feel such need of help themselves; as if they were like beggars, that had nothing to give, but must live by asking and receiving. They understand not that it is one of the mysteries of godliness, that teaching others doth inform themselves, and the light which they bring in for others, will serve themselves to work by; and that reproving others doth correct themselves; that exhorting others doth prevail with themselves; that persuading the obstinate wills of others, doth tend to bend and resolve their own; and that comforting others doth tend to revive and raise themselves: their own spirits may be a little revived, by the very smell of the cordials they prepare for others. In this case, giving is both begging and receiving. Doing good is not the least effectual kind of prayer; and that we may be so employed is not the smallest mercy. Many a one hath thus grown rich by giving: many a one hath convinced himself, by confuting his own objections from another: and many a one hath raised and comforted himself, by offering comfort to others that have the same infirmities, and have banished their own excessive doubts and fears, by frequent compassionate answering the same in others, whose sincerity they have less suspected than their own.

None thrive more than they that grow in the sunshine of God's blessing: for God blesseth those most that are most faithful in his work: and the work of love, is the work of God. To do good, is to be most like him, and they that are most like him, do best please him: in subordination to Christ, in whom we are accepted, we must, by his Spirit, be made thus acceptable in ourselves: we must be amiable if we will be loved. Those that God loveth best, and is most pleased with, are like to receive most plenteously from his love. It is necessary therefore to our own safety, and holiness, and consolation, that we look much abroad at the necessities of others, and study our brethren, and the church of God, as well as ourselves: 'that we look not every man on his own things, but every man also on the things of others.'

There may be somewhat of inordinate selfishness even about our souls, and sinful selfishness is always a losing course. As he that will be a self-saver, in point of estate, or honour, or life, taketh the ready way to lose them; so he that for the saving of his soul will confine all his care and charity to his own soul, taketh not the way indeed to save it. We keep not ourselves; we quicken not, we comfort not, we save not ourselves; but only as agents under Christ, manuring the land, and sowing the seed, to which he alone can give the blessing: it is not therefore our inordinate self-studying that will do it: with all our care, without his blessing, we cannot add one cubit to the stature of our graces: therefore it must needs be our safest course to be as careful and faithful, as we can, in duty, and lay out most of our study to please him; and then if we come not to assurance of his love, or discern not his image and grace upon us, yet we must trust him with our souls, and leave the rest to his care and goodness, who hath undertaken that none shall be losers by him, nor be ashamed or have their hopes frustrated that wait upon and obey him: let us 'commit the keeping of our souls to him in well doing, as unto a faithful Creator.' 'As the eyes of servants look to the hand of their masters,' so our eyes (in a way of duty) must 'wait upon the Lord our God, till he have mercy upon us.' Though we 'grow weary of crying, and our throat be dried, and our eyes fail while we wait for God,' yet our hope is only in him, and therefore we must continue to wait upon him, for 'they that wait for him shall not be ashamed.'

It is not the pretended necessity of one work that will excuse him that hath many as necessary to do; especially when they are conjunct in nature and necessity, and must go together, to attain their end. Concerning God, as we may well say that we must love and serve him only, and none but him, because we must love nothing but for his sake, and as a means to him, the end of all; and so while it is God in all things that we love, we are more properly said to love God than the creature by that act, because he is the ultimate, first intended end, and principal object of that love; and as the means (as a means) hath its essence in its relation to the end, so the love of the means (as such) is accordingly specified: and we may say of our study and knowledge of God, that nothing but God is to be studied or known, because it is God in the creature that must be studied: it is a defective similitude (as all are) to say, 'it is for the face that we behold the glass,' for God is more in the creature than the face in the glass. But though all the means be united in the end, yet are they various among themselves. And therefore though we must study, know, and love nothing but God, yet must we study, know, and love many things besides ourselves: the means that are many, must all be thought on. More strings must be touched than one, how near soever, if we will have any music. More letters must be learned than one or we shall never learn to read.

All men will confess, that to confine our charity to ourselves, and to do no good to others, is unlike a Christian. To refuse to feed and clothe our brother in his need, is to deny it unto Christ: and it will be no excuse, if we were able, to say, 'I laid it out upon myself.' The objects of our charity must be the objects of our thoughts and care: and it will not suffice for our excuse to say, 'I was taken up at home, I had a miserable soul of my own to think on.'

If these self-studying souls, that confine almost all their thoughts unto themselves, would but seek after God in themselves, and see his grace and benefits, it were the better: but poor souls, in the darkness of temptation, they overlook their God, and most of their study of themselves, is to see Satan and his workings in themselves: to find as much of his image as they can, in the deformities or infirmities of their souls; but the image of God they overlook, and hardly will acknowledge. As noble objects raise the soul, and amiable objects kindle love, and comfortable objects fill it with delight, and God, who is all in each perfection, doth elevate and perfect it, and make it happy; so inferior objects do express it, and ugly objects fill it with distaste and loathing, and sad and mournful objects turn it into grief: and therefore to be still looking on our miseries and deformities, must needs turn calamity and woe into the temperament and complexion of the soul.

This much I thought needful to be spoken here, to prevent misunderstanding and misapplication; that while I am pressing you to study and know yourselves I may not encourage any in extremes, nor tempt them to make an ill use of so great and necessary a doctrine. And indeed the observation of the sad calamity of many poor, drooping, afflicted souls, that are still poring excessively on their own hearts commanded me not to overlook this caution; yet when I have done it, I am afraid lest those in the contrary extreme will take encouragement to neglect themselves, by my reprehensions of those that are so unlike them.

And therefore I must add, to save them from deceit; 1. that is but very few that are faulty in over studying themselves, in comparison of the many thousands that err on the other hand, in the careless neglecting of themselves. 2. That it is symptomatically and effectively far more dangerous to study yourselves too little than too much. Though it be a fault here to exceed, yet it is for the most part a sign of an honest heart to be much at home, and a sign of a hypocrite to be much abroad. Sincerity maketh men censurers of themselves. For it maketh them more impartial, and willing to know the truth of their condition: it cureth them of that folly, which before made them think that presumption shall deliver them, and that they shall be justified by believing promises of their own, though contrary to the word of God; yea, by believing the promises of the devil, and calling this a faith in Christ: they are awakened from that sleep in which they dreamed, that winking would save them from the stroke of justice, and that a strong conceit that they shall not be damned, will deliver them from damnation; and that they are safe from hell if they can but believe that there is no hell, or can but forget it, or escape the fears of it. These are the pernicious conclusions of the ungodly, discernable in their lives, and intimated in their presumptuous reasonings, though too gross to be openly and expressly owned; and therefore they are indisposed to any impartial acquaintance with themselves.

But grace recovereth men from this distraction, and makes them know that the judgment of God will not follow the conceits of men; that the knowledge of their disease is necessary to their cure, and the knowledge of their danger is necessary to its prevention; that it is the greatest madness to go on to hell, for fear of knowing that we are in the way to it; and to refuse to know it, for fear of being troubled at the news.

An upright soul is so far fallen out with sin, that he taketh it seriously for his enemy, and therefore is willing to discover it, in order to its destruction, and willing to search after it in order to a discovery.

He hath in him some measure of the heavenly illumination, which maketh him a child of light, and disposeth him to love the light, and therefore cometh to it, 'that his deeds may be made manifest.' Hypocrites are quick sighted in discovering the infirmities of others; but at home they shut the windows, and draw the curtains, that they may not be disturbed or frightened in their sin: darkness suits the works of darkness. It is a good sign when a man dare see his own face in the glass of God's word, and when he dare hear his conscience speak. I have ever observed it in the most sincere-hearted Christians, that their eye is more upon their own hearts and lives than upon others: and I have still observed the most unsound professors to be least censorious and regardful of themselves, and hardly drawn to converse at home and to pass an impartial judgment on themselves.

Hence therefore you may be informed of the reason of many other differences between sincere believers and the ungodly; why it is that the sincere are so ready to discourse about matters of the heart; that they so much relish such discourse; and that they have so much to say when you come to such a subject. It is because they know themselves in some good measure. They have studied, and are acquainted with the heart, and therefore can talk the more sensibly of what is contained in a book which they have so often read, and are so conversant with. Talk with them about the matters of the world, and perhaps you may find them more simple and ignorant than many of their neighbours: but when you talk about the corruptions of the heart, and its secret workings; the matter, order, and government of the thoughts, affections and passions; the wants and weaknesses of believers; the nature and workings of inward temptations; the ways of grace, and of the exercise of each grace; the motions and operations of the Spirit upon the heart; the breathings of love and desire after God; the addresses of the soul to Christ by faith, and dependence on him, and receivings from him; about these secret matters of the heart, he is usually more able in discourse than many learned men that are unsanctified.

Hence it is that upright, self-observing souls are so full in prayer, and able to pour out their hearts so enlargedly before the Lord, in confessing their sins, petitioning for grace, opening their necessities, and thanking God for his spiritual mercies! Some that are themselves acquainted with themselves, and the workings of grace, despise all this, and say, It is but an ability to speak of the things which they are most used to. I doubt not but mere acquired abilities and custom may advance some hypocrites, to pray in the language of experienced Christians. I also doubt not but natural impediments, and want of use, and of right education, may cause many to want convenient expressions, that have true desires. But the question is, from whence it comes to pass, that so great a number of those that are most careful and diligent for their souls, are so full in holy conference and prayer, when very few others that excel them in learning and natural parts, have any such ability? Doubtless the chief reason is, that the care and study of these Christians hath been most about their spiritual state; and that which they set their hearts upon, they use their tongues upon: generally it cannot be imagined, why they should use themselves to those studies and exercises which procure those abilities, but that they more highly esteem and more seriously regard the matters that concern their salvation, which are the subject. I doubt not but God bestoweth his gifts upon men in the use of means, and that it is partly use that maketh men able and ready in these services of God. But what reason can be given, why one part of men use themselves to such employments, and another part are unable through disuse, but that some do set their hearts upon it, and make it their business to know themselves, their sins and wants, and seek relief, when by the others all this is neglected. Some hypocrites may be moved by lower ends, both in this and in other duties of religion; but that is no rule for our judging of the intentions of the generality, or of any that are sincere. As a man that hath lived in the East or West Indies, is able to discourse of the places and people which he hath seen; and perhaps another by a map or history may say somewhat of the same subject, though less distinctly and sensibly; while others can say nothing of it: so a man of holy experience in the mysteries of sanctification, who is much conversant at home, and acquainted with his own heart, is able, if other helps concur, to speak what he feels, to God and man, and from his particular observation and experience, to frame his prayers and spiritual conference; and a hypocrite, from reading and common observation, may do something affectedly that is like it: but careless, self-neglecting worldlings, are usually dumb about such matters, and hear you as they do men of another country, that talk in a language which they do not understand, or at least cannot make them any answer in.

But if any of you will needs think more basely and maliciously of the cause of holy prayer and conference in believers, let us leave them for the present to the justification of him that gave them the spirit of supplication, which you reproach, and let us only inquire what is the reason that men who can discourse as distinctly as others, about worldly matters, have nothing to say beyond a few cold, affected words, which they have learned by rote, either to God or man, about the matters of the soul, the methods of the Spirit, the workings of a truly penitent heart, or the elevations of faith, and the pantings of desire after God. Why are you dumb when you should speak this language, and frequently and delightfully speak it? Is it because your reason is lower than those men's that do speak it, whom you despise? No, you are wise enough to do evil: you can talk of your trades, your honours, or employments, your acquaintances and correspondence all the day long; you are more wordy about these little things, than the preachers themselves, whom you count most tedious, are about the greatest; you are much longer in discoursing of your delusory toys, than the lovers of God, whose souls long after him, are in those prayers which trouble you with their length. Many a time have I been forced to hear your dreaming, incoherent dotage; how copious you are in words that signify no greater matters than flesh-pleasing, or fanciful honours and accommodations—I had almost said, than chaff or straw. As the ridiculous orator, 'you strain and gape an hour or a day together to say nothing.' Set all the words of a day together, and peruse them at night, and see what they are worth. There is little higher than visible materials, than meat and drink, than play and compliment, than houses, or lands, or domineering affections or actions, in many hour's or day's discourse. I think of you sometimes when I see how ingeniously and busily children make up their babies of patches, how seriously they talk about them, how every pin and patch is matter of employment and discourse, how highly they value them, and how many days they can unweariedly spend about them. Pardon my comparison : if you repent not of your discourses and employments more than they, and do not one day call yourselves far worse fools than them, then let me be stigmatized with the most contumelious brand of folly.

It is not then your want of natural faculties and parts that makes you mute in the matters of God and your salvation, when men of meaner natural parts than you do speak of those things with the greatest freedom and delight ; and surely it is not for want of an ingenious education. As you would take it ill to be thought below them in natural endowments, so much more in those acquisitions and furniture of the mind, which come by due culture of your faculties. You would disdain in these to be compared with many poor rustics and mechanics, that are almost as fluent in speaking of the great things of immortality, as you are in talking of your transient occurrences, your sublunary felicities, and the provisions of your appetites. What then can be the cause of this dumb disease, but that you are unacquainted with yourselves ? As you have not a new-birth, and a divine nature, and the Spirit of Christ, to be either the spring and principle, or the matter of your discourse ; so you have not the due knowledge of your sin and misery, which should teach you the language of serious penitents, before you have the language of justified believers.

If you say again, It is because we have not been used to this kind of speech ; I answer, And whence is it that you have not been used to it ? If you had known the greatness and goodness of the Lord, as sensibly as they, would not you have used to pray to him and speak of him as well as they? If you had known and considered your sin, and wants, and miseries, or dangers, as well as they, would you not have been used to beg mercy, pardon and relief, and to complain of your distress as much as they? If you did as highly value matters of eternal consequence as they do, and laid them to heart as seriously as they, would not your minds and hearts have appeared in your speeches, and made you apply yourselves to prayer and holy conference as well as others ?

If you say, That many have that within them which they are not able to express, or which they think not meet to open unto others, I answer,

1. As to ability, it is true of those that have excessive bashfulness, melancholy, or the like ; and of those that are so lately converted, that they have not had time to learn, and use themselves to, a holy language ; but what is this to those that are of as good natural parts and elocution as other men, and suppose themselves to have long been true Christians?

2. As to the point of prudence which is pleaded for this silence, it is so much against nature, and so much against the word of God, that there is no room at all for this pretence, unless it be for inferiors, or such as want an opportunity to speak to their superiors or to strangers ; or unless it be only for some particular omissions, when the thing would be unseasonable.

Nature hath made the tongue the index of the mind ; especially to express the matters of most urgency and concern. Do you keep silent ordinarily on the matters which you most highly esteem, which you oftenest think of, which you take your life and happiness to consist in, and which you are most deeply affected with, and prefer before all other matters of the world ? What a shameful pretence is it, for those that are dumb as to prayer and holy conference, for want of any due sense of their condition, or love to God, which should open their lips, to talk on them ? Is it because their prudence directeth them to silence, when they hold not their tongues about those matters which they must confess are ten thousand fold less useful ? They can discourse unweariedly about their wealth, their sport their friend, their honour, because they love them : and if a man should here tell them, that the heart is not to be opened or exercised by the tongue, they would think he knew not the natural use of heart or tongue. Yet while they pretend to love God above all, they have neither skill nor will to make expression of it ; you strike them dumb when you turn the stream of conference that way ; and you may almost as well bid them speak in a strange language, as pray to God from the sense of their necessities, and yet they say their hearts are good.

Let the word of God be judge whether a holy experienced heart should hide itself, and not appear in prayer and holy conference by the tongue. 'Pray continually.—Christ spake a parable to this end, that men ought always to pray and not wax faint.—Be careful for nothing : but in every thing, by prayer and supplication, with thanksgiving, let your requests be made known unto God.'

How they must pray, you may gather from 2 Chron. vi. 29. In case of dearth, pestilence, blasting, mildews, locusts, caterpillars, enemies, sicknesses or sores, ' Then what prayer or supplication soever shall be made of any man, or of all the people, when every one shall know his own sore, and his own grief, and shall spread forth his hands in this house, then hear thou from heaven.' I am not speaking of the prescribed prayers of the church, nor denying the lawfulness of such in private: but if you have no words but what you say by rote, and pray not from the knowledge of your own particular sore and grief, it is because you are too much unacquainted with yourselves, and strangers to those hearts, where the greatest of your sores and griefs are lodged.

Whether good hearts should be opened in holy conference, as well as prayer, you may easily determine from the command of God. ' As every man hath received the gift, so minister the same one to another, as good stewards of the manifold grace of God;' 'if any man speak, let him speak as the oracles of God;' 'let no corrupt communication proceed out of your mouth, but that which is good to the use of edifying, that it may minister grace unto the hearers;' 'exhort one another daily while it is called to-day, lest any of you be hardened through the deceitfulness of sin;' 'the mouth of the righteous speaketh wisdom, and his tongue talketh of judgment: the law of his God is in his heart;' ' let my mouth be filled with thy praise and with thy honour all the day;' ' the mouth of a righteous man is a well of life;' ' the lips of the righteous feed many.' Christ himself decideth it expressly, ' out of the abundance of the heart the mouth speaketh: a good man out of the good treasure of his heart bringeth forth good things.

For a man that hath no heart to prayer or holy conference, but loathes them, and is weary of them, and had rather talk of fleshly pleasures, to pretend that yet his heart is good, and that God will excuse him for not expressing it ; and that it is his prudence, and his freedom from hypocrisy that maketh his tongue to be so much unacquainted with the goodness of his heart, this is but to play the hypocrite to prove that he is no hypocrite, and to cover his ignorance in the matters of his salvation, with the expression of his ignorance of the very nature and use of the heart and tongue, and to cast by the laws of God, and his own duty, and cover this impiety with the name of prudence. If heart and tongue be not used for God, what do you either with a heart or tongue?

The case is plain, to men that can see, that it is your ignorance of yourselves that is the cause that you have little to say against yourselves, when you should confess your sins to God ; and so little to say for yourselves, when you should beg his grace ; and so little to say of yourselves, when you should open your hearts to those that can advise you. But that you see not that this is the cause of your dumbness, who see so little of your own corruptions, is no wonder while you are so strange at home. Had you but as much knowledge of yourselves as to see that it is the ignorance of yourselves that maketh you so prayerless and mute ; and as much sense as to complain of your darkness, and be willing to come into the light, it were a sign that light is coming into you, and that you are in a hopeful way of cure. But when you neither know yourselves, nor know that you do not know yourselves, your ignorance and pride are likely to cherish your presumption and impiety, till the light of grace or the fire of hell, have taught you better to know yourselves.

2. And here you may understand the reason why people fearing God are so apt to accuse and condemn themselves and to be too much cast down ; and why they that have cause of greatest joy, do sometimes walk more heavily than others. It is because they know more of their sinfulness, and take more notice of their inward corruptions and outward failings, than presumptuous sinners do of theirs : because they know their faults and wants, they are cast down ; but when they come farther to see their interest in Christ and grace, they will be raised up again. Before they are converted they usually presume, as being ignorant of their sin and misery. In the infancy of grace they know these, but yet languish for want of more knowledge of Christ and mercy. But he that knoweth fully both himself and Christ, both misery and mercy, is humbled and comforted, cast down and exalted. As a man that never saw the sea is not afraid of it ; he that seeth it but afar off, and thinks he shall never come near it, is not much afraid of it ; he that is drowned in it is worse than afraid ; he that is tossed by the waves, and doubteth of ever coming safe to harbour, is the fearful person ; he that is tossed, but hath good hopes of a safe arrival, hath fears that are abated or overcome with hope; but he that is safe-landed is past his fears. The first is like him that never saw the misery of the ungodly ; the second is like him that seeth it in general, but thinks it doth not belong to him; the third is like the damned that are past remedy ; the fourth is like the humbled, doubting Christian, that seeth the danger, but doth too much question or forget his helps; the fifth is like the Christian of a stronger faith, that sees

the danger, but withal seeth his help and safety; the sixth is like the glorified saints, that are past the danger.

Though the doubting Christian knoweth not his sincerity, and therefore knoweth not himself so well as the strong believer doth, yet in that he knoweth his sinfulness and unworthiness he knoweth himself better than the presumptuous world.

CHAPTER VI.

EXHORTATIONS TO THE UNGODLY ON THE DANGERS OF SELF-IGNORANCE.

All persons to whom I can address this exhortation are either godly or ungodly; in the state of sin, or in the state of grace. And both of them have need to study themselves.

I. And to begin with the unrenewed, carnal sort, it is they that have the greatest need to be better acquainted with themselves. O that I knew how to make them sensible of it; if any thing will do it, methinks it should be done by acquainting them how much their endless state is concerned in it. In order hereunto, let me yet add, to all that has been said already, these few considerations:

1. If you know not yourselves, you know not whether you are the children of God or not; nor whether you must be for ever in heaven or hell; no, nor whether you may not within this hour behold the angry face of God, which will frown you into damnation. Is this a matter for a man of reason to be quietly and contentedly ignorant of? It is a business of such unspeakable concern to know whether you must be everlastingly in heaven or hell, that no man can spare his cost or pains about it, without betraying and disgracing his understanding. You are sure you shall be here but a little while. Your bodies, you all know, will hold your souls but a little longer; and I think there is not the proudest of you but would be humbled, nor the most sluggish or dead-hearted but would be awakened, if you knew that you must go to endless misery, and that your dying hour would be your entrance into hell. And if you know not yourselves, you know not but it may be so. To know nothing to the contrary, would be terrible to you if you well considered it, especially when you have so much cause to fear it. O sirs, for a man to live here senselessly that knows not but he may burn in hell for ever, and knows it not because he is blind and careless; how unsuitable

is it to the principle of self-love and self-preservation? And how very unbeseeming the rational nature to have no sense or care, when you look before you to the unquenchable fire and the utter darkness.

If any of you think that all these matters are to be put to the adventure, and cannot now be known, you are dangerously mistaken. As you may certainly know by scripture that there is a future life of joy to the godly, and of misery to the wicked, so may you know, by a faithful trial of yourselves, to which of these at present you belong, and whether you are under the promise or the threatening. Know yourselves, and you may know whether you are justified or condemned already, and whether you are the heirs of heaven or hell. Surely he that comforteth his servants with the promise of glory to all that believe, and are new creatures, and are sanctified by his Spirit, did suppose that we may know whether we believe, and are renewed and sanctified, or not: or else what comfort can it be to us? If blinded infidels have no means to quiet themselves but their unbelief, and a conceit that there is no such life of misery, they have the most pitiful opiate to ease them in the world; and may as well think to become immortal by a confident conceit that they shall never die. If they befool themselves with the ordinary questions, Where is hell, and what kind of fire is it? &c. I answer them, with Augustine, 'It is better to be in doubt about things that are hidden from us, than to quarrel about things that are uncertain to us. I do not doubt that we must understand that the rich man was in the heat of pain, and the poor man in a refreshing place of joys; but how to understand that flame in hell, that bosom of Abraham, that tongue of the rich man, that finger of the poor man, that thirst of torment, that drop for cooling or refreshment, perhaps will hardly be found by the most humble inquirers, but never by contentious strivers.'

Therefore I conclude that the greatness and dreadfulness of the case, should make every person that hath an eye to see, an ear to hear, and a heart to understand, to read, inquire and consider, and never rest till they know themselves, and understand where it is that they are going to take up their everlasting abode.

2. Consider that all men must shortly know themselves. Presumption will be but of short continuance. Though so confident of being saved without holiness, you will speedily be undeceived. If the Spirit's illumination do not convince and undeceive you, death will undoubtedly do it at the furthest. Thousands and mil-

lions know their sin and misery now when it is too late, that would not know it when the remedy was at hand. Sinners, your souls are now in darkness: your bodies are your dungeon: but when death brings you out into the open light, you will see what we could never make you see. O how glad would a faithful minister of Christ be, if by any information he could now give you half the light that you shall then have, and now make you know at the heart, with the feeling of repentance, that which you must else quickly know, even at the heart, with the feeling of despair. Sirs, I hope you think not that I speak mere fancies to you, or any thing that is questionable and uncertain ; you cannot say so without denying yourselves to be Christians, no, nor without contradicting the light of nature, and debasing your souls below the heathen, who believe an immortality of souls in a state of joy or misery in the life to come; and if you are once below heathens, what are you better than brute beasts ? ye are better in your natural faculties and powers, as being not made brutes by your Creator; but worse as to the use of them, and the consequences to yourselves, because you are voluntary self-abusing brutes. To believe you shall die as a beast, will not prevent the miserable life of an impenitent sinner. It will not make your souls to be mortal, to believe they are mortal, no more than it will make a beast to be immortal, if he could but think so. Faith and reason can both assure you that your souls lie not down with your bodies in the dust, nor are annihilated by the falling of your earthly tabernacle ; no more than the spirits, when the glass is broken that held them; nor than the angels that appeared to the apostles or others, were annihilated when they disappeared : or, if I must speak more suitably to the ungodly, no more than the devil who sometimes appeareth in a bodily shape, is annihilated when that appearance vanisheth. As I suppose there is not a person in all this populous city that was here but sevenscore years ago, so I suppose there is none of you that expect to be here so long a time. The former inhabitants are gone before you into a world where there is no presumption or security : and you are going after them apace and are almost there. O sirs, that world is a world of light. To the damned souls it is called outer darkness, because they have none of the light of glory or of comfort: but they shall have the light of a self-accusing, self-tormenting conscience, that is gone out of the darkness of self-ignorance and self-deceit, and is fully cured of its slumber and insensibility.

Do you now take a civilized person for a saint? You will not do so long. Doth the baptism of water only, go with you now for the regeneration of the Spirit ? It will not be so long ; you will shortly be undeceived. Doth a ceremonious pharisee thank God for the sincerity and holiness which he never had ? He will shortly be taught better to know the nature of holiness and sincerity, and that God justifieth not all that justify themselves. Doth a little formal, heartless, hypocritical devotion, now cover a sensual, worldly mind ? The cover will be shortly taken off, and the nakedness and deformity of the pharisee will appear. Doth the name of a Christian, and the heartless use of outward ordinances, and the good esteem of others, now go for godliness and saving grace ? The autumn is at hand, when these leaves will all lie in the dust, and will go for fruit no longer. Do you take it now for true religion, to be hot for lust, and pride, and gain, and cold for God and your salvation ; and to obey God so far as will stand with your outward prosperity, and as the flesh or your other masters will give leave ? This is an opinion that never accompanied any man beyond the grave. Do you think to be saved by that devotion which gives God but the leavings of the flesh and the world, and by a religion that gives him but the outer rooms (when pleasure and gain are next your hearts) and that makes him but an underling to your covetousness and ambition ? Think so if you can, when you are gone hence. Cannot the preacher now make the ungodly to know that they are ungodly, the unsanctified to know they are but carnal, and the pharisee to know that his religion is vain ? Death can convince the awakened soul of all this in a moment.

You can choose whether you will believe us ; but death will so speak as to be believed. You must be voluntary in knowing your misery now ; but then you shall know it against your wills. You must open your eyes if you would see yourselves by the light which we bring to you; but death irresistibly throws open all. To say in pride and obstinacy, ' I will not believe it,' will now serve to quiet your consciences, and make you seem as safe as any; but when God saith, ' You shall feel it,' your unbelief is ineffectual : it can then torment you, but it can no longer ease you. There is then no room for ' I will not believe it.' God can, without a word, persuade you of that which you were resolved you would never be persuaded of. While you are in the body, you are every one affected according as you apprehend your state to be, whether it be indeed as you apprehend it; or not, but when death hath opened to you the door into eternity, you will be all affected with your conditions as they are indeed. To-day you are quiet, because you think your souls are safe; some are troubled that think they are in a state of misery; and it is likely that some on both sides are mistaken. The quiet of one, and the disquiet of another, may arise from the want of knowledge of yourselves; but death will rectify both these errors: and then, if you are unsanctified, no false opinions, no unbelief, no confident conceits of your integrity, will abate your desperation, or give any ease to your tormented minds. Nor will there be any doubts, or fears, or despairing self-afflicting thoughts, to disquiet those that Christ hath justified, or abate their joys.

O how many thousands will then think much otherwise of themselves than they now do! Death turns you out of the company of flatterers, and calls you out of the world of error, where men laugh and cry in their sleep, and brings you among awakened souls, where all things are called by their proper names, and all men are taken by themselves to be as they are indeed. Serious religion is not there a derision; and loving, and seeking, and serving God with all the heart, and soul and might, is not there taken for unnecessary preciseness. God judgeth not as man, by outward appearances, but with righteous judgment. That which is highly esteemed among men, is an abomination in the sight of God, and he will make you then to judge of yourselves as he hath judged you. Though wisdom now be justified only by her children, it shall then be justified by all, not by a sanctifying, but constrained, involuntary, tormenting light. And though now men can believe as well of themselves, as self-love and the quieting of their consciences doth require, yet then they will have lost this mastery over their own conceits.

O therefore, seeing you are all going into an irresistibly convincing light, and are almost in that world where all must fully know themselves; seeing nothing is covered that shall not be revealed, nor hid that shall not be made known, and no unsanctified hypocrite doth flatter himself into such high presumption but that a dying hour will humble him, and turn it all into endless desperation, if true conversion prevent it not; I beseech you be more conversant with conscience than you have been: be ashamed that you who know nothing better than flesh to adorn and to be careful of, should bestow more hours in looking into the glass, than you bestow to look into God's word and your own hearts, yea, more

in a year than you have thus bestowed in all your lives.

O that you knew what a profitable companion conscience is for you to converse with! You would not then think yourselves so solitary as to be destitute of company and employment, while you have so much to do at home, and one in your bosom that you have so much business with. It is a necessary and inseparable companion. If conscience should chide you when you had rather be flattered, yet there is no running from it for more pleasant company; home is homely; it is there that you must dwell; conscience is married to you, please it on safe terms as well as you can, but do not think to over-run it, for it will follow you, or you must return to it home again, when you have gone your furthest and done your worst. You have taken conscience for better and for worse. There is expectation of a divorce not even by death: it will follow you to eternity; and therefore, O be not strange to conscience, that will be your comforter or tormentor at the hour of death; that can do so much to make sickness and all suffering light or grievous; and to make death welcome or terrible to you. Fly not from conscience that must dwell with you for ever.

O foolish sinners! Do you want company and business to pass away your time? Are you fain to go to cards or dice to waste this treasure, which is more precious than your money? Do you go to an ale-house, or a play-house, to seek for company and pastime? Do you forget what company and business you have at home? As you love your peace and happiness, instead of conversing with vain, lascivious, or ungodly persons, O spend that time in converse with your consciences. You may there have a thousand times more profitable discourse. Be not offended to give conscience a sober, faithful answer: if it ask you what you have done with all your time; how you have lived in the world; how you have obeyed the calls of grace; how you have entertained Christ in your hearts; whether you have obeyed him or his enemy; whether you have been led by the Spirit or the flesh; what forwardness the work of your salvation is in, for which you came into the world; what assurance you have of your justification and salvation; and what readiness to die? think it not presumption in conscience thus to examine you. Though you have perhaps unthankfully disdained to be thus examined by your pastors, your external guides, whose office it is to help you, and watch for your souls, yet do not disdain to be accountable to yourselves. Accountable you must be ere long to God; and that friend that would help you to make ready such accounts, on which so great a weight dependeth, methinks should be welcomed with a thousand thanks. Ministers and conscience should be acceptable to you, that come on so necessary a work.

The chidings of conscience are more friendly language than the flattery of your ignorant or proud associates, and should be more pleasant to you than the laughter of fools, which is like the crackling of thorns in the fire. Thy own home, though it be a house of mourning, is better for thee than such a sinful house of mirth. Hear but what conscience hath to say to you. No one will speak with you, that hath words to speak which more nearly concern you. I beseech you, sirs, be more frequent and familiar with conscience than most men are. Think not the time lost, when you walk and talk with it alone. Confer with it about your endless state, and where you are likely to be for ever, and what way you are in, and what thoughts you will have of your sins and duties, of the world and God, of yielding or overcoming, at the last. Is there no sense in this discourse? Thou art dead and senseless if thou think so. Is idle talk and prating better? I hope you are not so distracted as to say so. If you have not blinded, deceived or bribed it, I tell you conscience hath other kind of discourse for you; more excellent and necessary things to talk of, than wantons or worldlings have. It is better to be giving conscience an account, what business thou hast had so often in such company, and how thou wouldst have looked if death had found thee there, than without leave from God or conscience to go thither again.

The thriving way is neither to be always at home, nor always abroad; but to be at home when home work is to be done, and to be abroad only for doing and for getting good, in a way of diligent Christian trading; and to bring that home that is got abroad, but never to go abroad upon loitering, vain, expensive occasions. When you have done with conscience, converse with others that your business lieth with, and go abroad when it is for your master's work, but go not upon idle errands: converse not with prodigal wasters of your time, and enemies to your souls. One time or other conscience will speak, and have a hearing: the sooner the better, put it not off to a time so unseasonable as death: I say not unseasonable for conscience to speak in, but unseasonable for it to begin to speak in; and unseasonable for those terrible words that need a calmer time for answer; and unseasonable

for so many things and so great, as self-betrayers use to put off until then, which need a longer time for due consideration and dispatch.

3. And I beseech you consider, with what amazing horror it must needs surprise you, to find on a sudden and unexpectedly, when you die, that all is worse with you than you imagined or would believe? After a whole life of confident presumption, to be suddenly convinced by so dreadful an experience of your so long and wilful mistake! To find in a moment that you have flattered your souls, into so desperate a state of woe! To see and feel all the selfish cavils and reasonings confuted, in one hour, which the wisest and holiest men on earth could never beat you from before! O sirs, you know not now what a day, what a conviction, that will be! You know not what it is for a guilty soul to pass out of the body, and find itself in the plague of an unsanctified state, and hated of the holy God, that never would know it till it was too late. You know not what it is to be turned, by death, into the world of spirits, where all self-deceit is detected by experience, and all must undergo a righteous judgment; where blindness and self-love can no more persuade the miserable that they are happy, the unholy that they are sanctified, the fleshly-minded men that they are spiritual, the lovers of the world that they are the lovers of God. Men cannot there believe what they list, nor take that for a truth which makes for their security, be it never so false: men cannot there believe that they are accepted of God, while they are in the bonds of their iniquity; or that their hearts are as good as the best, while their tongues and lives are opposite to goodness; or that they shall be saved as soon as the godly, though they be ungodly.

It is easy for a man to hear of waves, and gulfs and shipwrecks, that never saw the sea; and without any fear to hear of battles, that never saw the face of an enemy; and without any trouble, to hear of sickness and tormenting pains, and burning, and cutting off of limbs, that never felt or saw such things. It is easy for you here, in these seats, in the midst of health, and peace, and quietness, to hear of a departing soul, and where it shall appear, and what it shall there see, and how great a discovery death will make. But, O sirs, when this must be your case, as you know it must be, alas, how speedily! these matters will then seem considerable: they will be new and strange to those that have heard of them an hundred times, because they never heard of them sensibly till now. One of those souls that have been here before you, and have past into eternity, have other thoughts of these things than what you have! O how do they think now, of the fearless slumber and stupidity of those that they have left behind? What think they now of those that wilfully fly the light, and flatter themselves in guilt and misery, and make light of all the joys and torments of the other world. Even as Dives thought of his poor brethren that remained in prosperity and presumption upon earth, and little thought what company he was in, what a sight he saw, and what he did endure!

Poor careless souls, you know not now what it is, for the ungodly to see that they are ungodly, by the irresistible light of another world; and for the unholy to feel in hell that they are unholy, and to be taught by flames and the wrath of the Almighty, what is the difference between the sanctified and the carnal; between an obedient and a rebellious life. While here, you little know these things: you see them not: you feel them not: and the Lord grant you may never so know them by woful experience. That you may escape such a knowledge, is the end of all that I am saying to you; but that will not be, but by another kind of knowledge, even the knowledge of belief and serious consideration.

For your soul's sake therefore come into the light, and try yourselves, and huddle not over a work of such unspeakable consequence as the searching of your hearts and judging of your spiritual state? O be glad to know what you are indeed! Put home the question, Am I sanctified or not? Am I in the Spirit or in the flesh? Be glad of any help for the sure resolution of such doubts. Take not up with slight and venturous presumptions. It is your own case; your nearest and your greatest case; all lies upon it: who should be so willing of the plainest dealing, the speediest and the closest search as you? O be not surprised by an unexpected sight of an unrenewed, miserable soul at death. If it be so, see it now, while seeing it may do good: if it be not so, a faithful search can do you no harm, but comfort you by the discovery of your sincerity. Say not too late, I thought I had been born again of the Spirit, and had been in a state of grace: I thought I had been a child of God, and reconciled to him, and justified by faith! O what a heart-tearing word would it be to you, when time is past, to say, I thought it had been better with me!

4. Consider also, that it is one of Satan's principal designs for your damnation, to keep you ignorant of yourselves. He knows if he can but make you believe, that you are regenerate when

you are not, you will never seek to be regenerate: and that if he can make you think that you are godly, when you are ungodly, and have the Spirit of Christ, while you are servants to the flesh, he may defeat all the labours of your teachers, and let them call on you to be converted till their hearts ache, to no purpose, but leave you as you are: he knows how lightly you will value the physician, if he can but make you believe that you are well! And how little care you will take for a pardon, if you think that you need it not, or have one already. In vain may we call on you to turn and become new creatures, and give up yourselves to Christ, if you think that you are good Christians, and are in the way to heaven already.

And when you know before hand, that there lieth the principal game of the deceiver, and that it will be his chief contrivance to keep you unacquainted with your sin and danger, till you are past recovery, one would think there should be no need to bid you be diligent to know yourselves.

5. I beseech you consider also, that without this design there is no likelihood that Satan could undo you: if he keep you not ignorant of yourselves, he is never like to keep you in his power: you come out of his kingdom when you come out of darkness. He knoweth that if once you did but see how near you stand to the brink of hell, you would think it time to change your standing.

There is a double principle in nature, that would do something towards your repentance and recovery, if your eyes were opened to see where you are.

(1.) There is, since the seduction and ruin of man, by Satan's temptations, an enmity put into the whole nature of man against the whole satanical serpentine nature: so that this natural enmity would so much conduce to your deliverance, as that you would not be contented with your relation, if you knew that you are the slaves of the devil; nor would you be charmed into sin so easily, if you knew that it is he indeed that doth invite you; no language would be so taking with you as that which you knew was uttered by his voice. It would do much to affright you from his service, if you knew that it is he indeed that setteth you on work, and is gratified by it. He keepeth men in his bondage, by making them believe that they are free: he persuadeth men to obey him, by persuading them that it is God that they obey: and he draweth them to hell, by making them believe that they are following Christ to heaven; or at least, that they are following the inclination of their nature in a pardonable infirmity.

(2.) The natural principle of self-love would, in order to self-preparation, do much to drive you from your sinful state, if you did but know what a state it is. There is no man so far hateth himself, as to be willing to be damned. You cannot choose a habitation in hell; such a place can never be desired. Sure he that cannot choose but fly from an enemy that pursues him, or fly from fire, or water, or pestilence, when he perceives his danger, would fly from hell if he perceived his danger.

I beseech you all, that are secure in an unsanctified state, do but look inwards, and help me in preaching this doctrine to your hearts, and tell yourselves whether you do not think that your state is good, and that you are the children of God as well as others; and that though you are sinners, yet your sins are pardoned by the blood of Christ, and that you shall be saved if you die in the state that you are in? Are not these thoughts the reason why you venture to continue in your present state, and look not after so great a change as scripture speaketh of as necessary?

I pray you, deal plainly with your hearts, and tell me, you careless sinners, young or old, that live here as quietly as if all were well with you: if you did but know that you are at this hour unregenerate, and that without regeneration there is no salvation; if you did but know that you are yet carnal and unholy, and that without holiness none shall see God; if you did but know that you are yet in a state of enmity to God, while you call him Father, and of enmity to Christ, while you call him your Saviour, and of enmity to the Holy Spirit, while you call him your Sanctifier; if you did but know that your sins are unpardoned, and your souls unjustified, and that you are condemned already, and shall certainly be damned if you die as you are, could you live quietly in such a state? Could you sleep, and eat, and drink quietly, and follow your trades, and let time run on, without repenting and returning unto God, if you knew that you are past hope, if death surprise you in this condition? For the Lord's sake, sirs, rouse up yourselves a little, and be serious in a business that concerneth you more than ten thousand natural lives, and tell me, or rather tell yourselves, if you did but know that while you live here, you are unrenewed, and therefore under the curse of God, and in the bondage of the devil, and are hastening towards perdition, and are gone for ever, if you be not sanctified and made

new creatures before you die, could you forbear going alone, and there bethink yourselves, 'O what a sinful, dreadful condition are we in! What will become of us, if we be not regenerated before we die? Had we no understandings, no hearts, no life or sense, that we have lingered so long, and lived so carelessly in such a state? O where had we been now, if we died unregenerate! How often have we been near to death? How many sicknesses might have put an end to life and hope? Had we died before this day, we had now been in hell without remedy.' Could any of you that knew this to be your case, forbear to betake yourselves to God, and cry to him in the bitterness of your souls, 'O Lord, what rebels, what wretches have we been? We have sinned against heaven and before thee, and are no more worthy to be called thy children! O how sin hath captivated our understandings, and conquered our very sense, and made us live like men that were dead, as to the love and service of God, and the work of our salvation, which we were created and redeemed for! O Lord, have mercy upon these blind and senseless, miserable souls; have mercy upon these despisers and abusers of thy mercy! O save us, or we perish; save us from our sins, from Satan, from thy curse and wrath; save us or we are undone and lost for ever; save us from the unquenchable fire, from the worm that never dieth; from the bottomless pit, the outer darkness, the horrid gulf of endless misery! O let the bowels of thy compassion yearn over us; O save us for thy mercy sake; shut not out the cries of miserable sinners. Regenerate, renew and sanctify our hearts; O make us new creatures! O plant thine image on our souls, and incline them towards thee, that they may be wholly thine: O make us such as thou commandest us to be: away with our sins, and sinful pleasures, and sinful company! We have had too much, too much of them already! Let us now be thine, associated with them that love and fear thee; employed in the works of holiness and obedience all our days! Lord, we are willing to let go our sins, and to be thy servants: or if we be not, make us willing.

What say you, sirs, if you knew that you were this hour in a state of condemnation, could you forbear making haste with such confessions, complaints, and earnest supplications to God? Could you forbear going presently to some faithful minister, or godly friend, and telling him your case and danger, and begging his advice, and prayers, and asking him what a poor sinner must do to be recovered, pardoned, and saved.

that is so deep in sin and misery, and hath despised Christ and grace so long? Could you tell how to sleep quietly many nights more, before you had earnestly sought for help, and made this change? How could you choose but presently betake yourselves to the company, and converse, and examples of the godly that are within your reach! (For whenever a man is truly changed, his friendship and company is changed, if he have opportunity.) And how could you choose but go and take your leave of your old companions, and with tears and sorrow tell them how foolishly and sinfully you have done, and what wrong you have done each other's souls, and intreat them to repent and do so no more, or else you will renounce them, and fly from their company as from a pesthouse?

Can a man forbear thus to fly from hell, if he saw that he is as near it as a condemned traitor to the gallows? He that will beg for bread if he be hungry, would beg for grace if he saw and felt how much he needeth it. And as seeing it is the way to feel it, he that will seek for medicines when he is sick, and would do almost any thing to escape a temporal death, would he not seek to Christ, the remedy of his soul, if he knew and felt that otherwise there is no recovery? And would he not do much against eternal death? 'Skin for skin, and all that a man hath, he will give for his life', was a truth that the devil knew and maketh use of in his temptations. And will a man then be regardless of his soul, that knows he hath an immortal soul; and of life eternal, that knows his danger of eternal death?

O, Sirs, it is not possible but that the true knowledge of your state of sin and danger, would do very much to save you from it, for it is a wilful, chosen state. All the devils in hell cannot bring you to it, and continue you in it against your will. You are willing of the sin, though unwilling of the punishment. And if you truly knew the punishment, and your danger of it, you would be the more unwilling of the sin; for God hath affixed punishment to sin, for this end, that they that else would love the serpent, may hate it for the sting. Foreseeing is to a man, what seeing is to a beast : if a beast see a coalpit or a gulf before his eyes, he will not easily be driven into it; he will draw back and strive, if you go about to kill him. And is he a man, or some monster that wants a name, that will go on to hell, when he seeth it as it were before him ; and that will continue in a state of sin, when he knows he must be damned in hell for ever, if he so continue to the end? Indeed sin is the deformity of the soul. He is a mons-

ter of blindness that seeth not the folly and peril of such a state, and that a state of holiness is better. He is a monster of stupidity that finds himself in such a state, and doth not feel it, but maketh light of it. And he is a monster of slothfulness that will not stir when he finds himself in such a case, and seek for mercy, and value the remedy, and use the means, and forsake his sinful course and company, till further mercy take him up and bring him home, and make him welcome, as one that was lost but now is found, was dead but is now alive.

I do not doubt for all these expostulations, but some men may be such monsters as thus to see that they are in a state of wrath and misery, and yet continue in it.

As, 1. Such as have but a glimmering, insufficient sight of it, and a half belief, while a greater belief and hope of the contrary, that is, presumption, is predominant at the heart. These are rather to be called men ignorant of their misery, than men that know it ; and men that believe it not, than men that do believe it, as long as ignorance and presumption is the prevailing part.

2. Such as by the rage of appetite and passion are hurried into deadly sin, and so continue, whenever the tempter offereth them the bait against their conscience, and some apprehension of their misery. But these have commonly a prevalent self-flattery secretly within, encouraging and upholding them in their sin, and telling them, that the reluctancies of their consciences are the Spirit's strivings against the flesh, and their fits of remorse are true repentance ; and though they are sinners, they hope they are pardoned, and shall be saved, so that these do not know themselves indeed.

3. Such as by their deep engagements to the world, and love of its prosperity, and a custom in sinning, are so hardened, and cast into a slumber, that though they have a secret knowledge or suspicion that their case is miserable, yet they are now awakened to the due consideration and feeling of it ; and therefore they go on as if they knew it not ; but these have not their knowledge in exercise. It is but a candle in a dark lantern, that now and then gives them a convincing flash, when the right side happens to be towards them ; or like lightning, that rather frightens and amazes them, than directeth them. As I said of the former, their self-ignorance is the predominant part, and therefore they cannot be said indeed to know themselves.

4. Such as being in youth or health, do promise themselves long life, or any others that foolishly put away the day of death, and think

they have yet time enough before them; and therefore though they are convinced of their misery, and know they must be converted or condemned, do yet delay, and quiet themselves with purposes to repent hereafter, when death draws near, and there is no other remedy but they must leave their sins, or give up all their hopes of heaven. Though these know somewhat of their present misery, it is but an ineffectual knowledge, and they know little of the wickedness of their hearts, while they confess them wicked. Otherwise they could not imagine that repentance is so easy a work to such as they, as that they can perform it when their hearts are further hardened, and that so easily and certainly, as that their salvation may be ventured on it by delays. Did they know themselves, they would know the backwardness of their hearts, and manifold difficulties should make them see the madness of delays, and of longer resisting and abusing the grace of the Spirit that must convert them, if ever they be saved.

5. Such as have light to show them their misery, but live where they hear not the discovery of the remedy, and are left without any knowledge of a Saviour. I deny not but such may go on in a state of misery, though they know it, when they know no way out of it.

6. Such as believe not the remedy, though they hear of it, but think that Christ is not to be believed in, as the Saviour of the world.

7. Such as believe that Christ is the Redeemer, but believe not that he will have mercy upon them, as supposing their hearts are not qualified for his salvation, nor ever will be, because the day of grace is past, and that they are under a sentence of reprobation. Therefore thinking that there is no hope, and that their endeavours would be all in vain, they cast off all endeavours, and give up themselves to the pleasures of the flesh, and say, It is as good to be damned for something, or for a greater matter, as for a less.

So that there are three sorts of despair that are not equally dangerous. 1. A despair of pardon and salvation, arising from infidelity, as if the gospel were not true, nor Christ a Saviour to be trusted with our souls, if predominant, is damnable. 2. A despair of pardon and salvation, arising from a misunderstanding of the promise, as if it pardoned not such sins as ours, and denied mercy to those that have sinned so long as we; this is not damnable necessarily of itself, because it implieth faith in Christ, and not infidelity, but misunderstanding hindereth the applying, comforting act. Therefore, this actual personal despair is accompanied with a general

actual hope, and with a particular personal, virtual hope. 3. A despair of pardon and salvation, upon the misunderstanding of ourselves as thinking both that we are graceless, and always shall be so, because of the blindness and hardness of our hearts. Of this despair, I say as of the former, it is joined with faith, and with general and virtual hope; and therefore is not the despair that of itself condemneth. Many may be saved that are too much guilty of it.

But if either of these two latter sorts shall so far prevail, as to turn men off from a holy, to a fleshly, worldly interest and life, and make them say, ' we will take our pleasure while we may, and will have something for our souls before we lose them,' and do accordingly; this kind of desperation is damnable by the effects, because it takes men off the means of life, and giveth them up to damning sins.

Thus I have showed you seven sorts of persons that may know themselves, their sin and danger, with such an ineffectual partial knowledge as I have described, and yet continue in that; in and misery.

In two cases even sound believers may possibly go on to sin, when they see the sin; and not only see the danger of it, but despairingly think it greater than it is. As, 1. In the case of common unavoidable failings, infirmities, and low degrees of grace. We are all imperfect, and yet we all know that it is our duty to be perfect, as perfection is opposed to sinful, and not to innocent imperfection, and yet this knowledge maketh us not perfect. We know we should be more humbled, and more believing, and more watchful, and love God more, and fear and trust him more, and be more fruitful and diligent, and obedient and zealous; and yet we are not what we know we should be in any of these. In these we all live in sin against knowledge; else we should be all as good as we know we ought to be, which no man is. And if through temptation any of us should be ready to despair, because of any of such infirmities, as that we cannot repent, or love God, watch, or pray, or obey more perfectly, or as we should, yet grace ceaseth not to be grace, though in the least degree, because we are ready to despair for want of more. Nor will the sincerity of this spark, or grain of mustard-seed, be unsuccessful, as to our salvation, because we think so, and take ourselves to be insincere, and our sanctification to be none: nor yet because we cannot be as obedient and good as we know we should be. For the gospel saith not,' he that knoweth he hath faith or sincerity shall be saved; and he that knoweth it not, shall be damned:' or ' he that is less holy or obedient than his conscience tells him he should be, shall be damned:' but 'he that believeth and repenteth, shall be saved,' whether he know it to be done in sincerity or not: and ' he that doth not, shall be damned,' though he never so confidently think he doth. So that in the degrees of holiness and obedience, all Christians ordinarily sin against knowledge.

2. Besides what is ordinary, some extraordinarily, in the time of powerful temptation, go further than ordinarily they do. And some under melancholy, or violent diseases or distempers of body, or under a diseased violent appetite, may transgress more against their knowledge than otherwise they would do. When the spirits are excited, the thoughts confused, the reason weakened, the passions strengthened, and the executive faculties indisposed, so that their actions are but imperfectly human or moral, imperfectly capable of virtue or vice, good or evil, it is no wonder if poor souls then not only perceive their sin, but think it and the danger to be tenfold greater than they are ; and still go on against their knowledge, and yet have true grace.

This much I have said, both to prevent you from misunderstanding what I said before, concerning the power of conviction to conversion, and also to help you to the fuller understanding of the matter itself of which I treat. But exceptions strengthen and do not weaken any rule or proposition, in the points not excepted. Still I say, that out of these cases the true knowledge of a sinful, miserable state, is so great a help to bring us out of it, that it is hardly imaginable how rational men can wilfully continue in a state of such exceeding danger, if they be but well acquainted that they are in it. I know a hardened heart hath an unreasonable obstinate opposition against the means of its own recovery: but yet men have some use of reason and self-preserving love and care, or they are not men. Though little transient lightnings often come to nothing, but leave some men in greater darkness; yet could we but set up a standing light in all your consciences, could we fully convince the unregenerated that they cannot be saved in the carnal state they are in, but must be sanctified or never saved, what hopes should we have, that all the subtilties and snares of Satan, and all the pleasures and gain of sin, and all the allurements of ungodly company, could no longer hinder you, from falling down at the feet of mercy, and begging forgiveness, through the blood of Christ, and giving up yourselves in covenant to the

Lord, and speedily and resolutely betaking yourselves to an holy life! Could I but make you thoroughly known unto yourselves, I should hope that all the unsanctified that hear me would date their conversion from this very day ; and that you would not delay till the next morning, to bewail your sin and misery, and fly to Christ, lest you should die and be past hope this night.

Doth so much of our work, and of your recovery, lie upon this point, and yet shall we not be able to accomplish it? Might you not be brought into the way to heaven, if we could but persuade you that you are yet out of the way; and will you be undone, because you will not suffer so small and reasonable a part of the cure as this is ? O God forbid! O that we knew how to illuminate your minds so far, as to make you find that you are lost ? How ready would Christ be then to find you, and to receive and welcome you, upon your return? Here is the first difficulty, which if we could but overcome, we should hope to conquer all the rest. O that any of you that know the nature of self-deceit and know the fallacious reasonings of the heart, could tell us but how we might undeceive them! O that any of you that know the nature of the human understanding, with its several maladies, and their cure, and know the power of saving truth, could tell us what key will open this lock,—what medicine will cure this disease of wilful, obstinate, self-deceiving ? Think but on the case of our poor people, and of ours, and sure you cannot but pity both them and us. We are all professors of the Christian faith, and all say we believe the word of God. This word assureth us, that all men are fallen in Adam, and are by nature children of wrath, and increase in sin and misery, till supernatural grace recover them. It tells us, that the Redeemer is become, by office, the physician or Saviour of souls, washing away their guilt by his blood, and renewing and cleansing their corrupted natures by his Spirit. It tells us, that he will freely work the cure, for all that will take him for their physician, and will forgive and save them that penitently fly to him, and value, and accept, and trust in his grace : and that except they be thus made new creatures, all the world cannot save them from everlasting wrath. This is the doctrine that we all believe, or say we believe. Thus doth it open the case of sinners. We come now according to our office, and the trust reposed in us, and we tell our hearers what the scripture saith of man, and what it commandeth us to tell them. We tell them of their fall, their sin and misery; of the Redeemer, and the sure and free salvation which they may have if they will but come to him. But, alas, we cannot make them believe that they are so sick, as to have so much need of the physician: and that they are dead, and have need of a new creation, as to the inclinations of their hearts, and the end, and bent, and business of their lives. We are sent to tender them the mercy of Christ, but we cannot make them believe that they are miserable. We are sent to offer them the riches, and eye-salve, and white raiment of the gospel; but we cannot make them know that they are poor, and blind, and naked. We are sent to call them to repent and turn, that they may be saved; and we cannot make them know that they need a change of heart and life. Here they sit before us, and we look on them with pity, and know not how to help them. We look on them, and think, alas, poor souls, you little see what death will quickly make you see. You will then see that there is no salvation, by all the blood and merits of Christ, for any but the sanctified; O that we could now but make you understand it! We look on them with compassion; and think, alas, poor souls, as easily and quietly as you sit here, a change is near. It will be thus with you but a little while, and where will you be next? We know, as sure as the word of God is true, that they must be converted and sanctified, or be lost for ever; and we cannot make them believe, but that the work is done already. The Lord knoweth, and our consciences witness to our shame, that we are not half so sensible of their misery, nor so compassionate towards them as we ought to be. Yet sometimes our hearts melt over them, and fain we would save them from the wrath to come; and we should have great hopes of success, if we could but make them know their danger. It melts our hearts to look on them, and think that they are so near damnation, and never likely to escape it, till they know it, and till they know that their corruption is so great that nothing but the quickening Spirit can recover them, and nothing less than to become new creatures will serve the turn. O that we knew how to get within them, and to open the windows, that the light of Christ might show them their condition! But when we have done all, we find it past our power. We know they will be past help in hell, if they die before they are regenerated. And could we but get themselves to know it, we could not but hope that they would look about them and be saved. But we are not able. It is more than we can do. We cannot get the grossest worldling, the basest sensualist, the proudest child of the spirit of pride, to know that he is in a state of condemnation, and must be sanctified or be damned. Much less can we procure the formal pharisee, thus to know himself. We can easily get them to confess that they are sinners, and deserve damnation, and cannot be saved without Christ; but this will not serve: the best saint on earth must say as much as this. There are converted and unconverted sinners; sanctified and unsanctified sinners; pardoned and unpardoned sinners; sinners that are members of Christ, and the children of God, and heirs of heaven, and sinners that are not so, but the contrary. They must know not only that they are sinners, but that they are yet unconverted, unsanctified, unpardoned sinners; not only that they cannot be saved without Christ, but that yet they have no special interest in Christ. They will not so value and seek for conversion, and remission, and adoption, as to obtain them, while they think they have them already. They will not come to Christ that they may have life, while they think they have part in Christ already. Paul after his conversion was a sinner, and had need of Christ, but Paul before his conversion was an unsanctified, unjustified sinner, and had no part in Christ. This is the state of sin and misery that you must come out of, or you are lost, and how can you be brought out of it, till you know that you are in it?

O therefore that we knew how to make you know it! How should we make poor sinners see that they are within a few steps of everlasting fire, that we might induce them to run away from it, and be saved? We cry so often, and lose our labour, and leave so many in their security and self-deceits, that we are discouraged, and remit our desires, and lose our compassion, and alas, grow dull and too insensible of their case, and preach too often as coldly as if we could be content to let them perish. We are too apt to grow weary of holding the light to men asleep, or that shut their eyes and will not see by it. When all that we have said is not regarded, and we know not what more to say, this damps our spirits; this makes so many of us preach almost as carelessly as we are heard. Regardless, sleepy hearers make regardless, sleepy preachers; frequent frustration abateth hope; and the fervour and diligence of prosecution ceaseth as hope abateth. This is our fault. Your insensibility is no good excuse for ours, but it is a fault not easily avoided.

When we are stopped at the first door, and cannot conquer Satan's out-works, what hopes have we of going further? If all that we can say will not convince you that you are yet unsanctified and unjustified, how shall we get you to the duties that belong to such, in order to the attainment of this desirable state?

And here I think it not unseasonable to inform you why the most able, faithful ministers of Christ do search so deep, and speak so hardly of the case of unrenewed souls, as much displeaseth many of their hearers, and makes them say they are too severe and terrible preachers: the zealous Antinomian saith they are legalists; and the profane Antinomian saith they rail, and preach not mercy, but judgment only, and would drive men to despair, but will they tell God he is a legalist for making the law, even the gospel law as well as the law of nature, and commanding us to preach it to the world? Shall they escape the sentence by reproaching the lawmaker? Will not God judge the world, and judge them by a law? And will he not be just and beyond the reach of their reproach? O sinner, this is not the smallest part of thy terror, that it is the gospel that speaks this terror to thee, and excludes thee from salvation, unless thou be made new: it is mercy itself that thus condemneth thee, and judgeth thee to endless misery. You are mistaken, sirs, when you say we preach not mercy, and say we preach not the gospel, but the law: it is the gospel that saith, ' except a man be born again, he cannot enter into the kingdom of heaven;' and that ' if any man have not the Spirit of Christ, the same is none of his.' The same gospel that saith, ' he that believeth shall be saved,' saith also, ' that he that believeth not shall be damned.' Will you tell Christ, the Saviour of the world, that he is not merciful, because he talks to you of damnation? Mercy itself, when it tells you that ' there is no condemnation,' doth limit this pardon to them ' that are in Christ Jesus, who walk not after the flesh, but after the Spirit.' It is sanctifying mercy that must save you, if ever you be saved, as well as justifying mercy. Will you refuse this mercy, and by no entreaty yield to have it, and yet think to be saved by it? What, saved by that mercy which you will not have? And will you say, we preach not mercy, because we tell you, that mercy will not save you, if you continue to reject it? To be saved by mercy without sanctification, is to be saved and not saved: to be saved by mercy without mercy: your words have no better sense than this: and are those afraid, lest preachers should make them mad by showing them their need of mercy, that are no wiser than to cast away their souls upon such senseless, self-contradicting conceits as these?

I beseech you tell us whose words are they that say, ' without holiness none shall see God?' and that, ' he that is in Christ, is a new creature,' and such like passages which offend you; are they ours, or are they God's? Did we indite the holy scriptures, or did the Holy Ghost? Is it severe of us if there be any words there that cross your flesh, and that you call bitter! Can we help it, if God will save none but sanctified believers? If you have any thing to say against it, you must say it to him: we are sure that this is in his word: and we are sure he cannot lie; and therefore we are sure it is true: we are sure that he may do with his own as he will, and that he oweth you nothing, and that he may give his pardon and salvation to whom, and upon what terms he pleaseth: and therefore we are sure he doth you no wrong. But if you think otherwise, reproach not us that are but messengers: but prepare your charge, and make it good against your Maker, if you dare and can: you shall shortly come before him, and be put to it to justify yourselves: if you can do it by recrimination, and can prevent your condemnation, by condemning the law and the judge, try your strength and do your worst.

Ah poor worms! Dare you lift up the head and move a tongue against the Lord? Did infinite wisdom itself want wisdom, to make a law to rule the world? And did infinite goodness want goodness to deal mercifully, and as was best, with man! And shall justice itself be judged to be unjust? And that by you! By such silly, ignorant, unrighteous ones as you! As if you had the wisdom and goodness, which you think God wanted when he made his laws!

And whereas you tell us of preaching terribly to you, we cannot help it, if the true and righteous threatenings of God be terrible to the guilty. It is because we know the terrors of the Lord, that we preach them, to warn you to prevent them. And so did the apostles before us; either it is true that the unquenchable fire will be the portion of impenitent, unbelieving, fleshly, worldly, unsanctified men, or it is not true: if it were not true, the word of God were not true: and then what should you do with any preaching at all, or any religion? But if you confess it to be true, do you think in reason it should be silenced? Or can we tell men of so terrible a thing as hell, and tell them that it will certainly be their lot, unless they be new creatures, and not speak terribly to them? O, sirs, it is the wonder of my soul that it seemeth no more terrible to all the ungodly who think they do believe it. Yea, and I would it did seem more terrible, that it might affright you from your sin to God, and you might be saved. If you were running ignorantly into a pit, would you revile him that told you of it, and bid you stop if you love your life? Would you tell him that he speaks bitterly or terribly to you? It is not the preacher that is the cause of your danger: he doth but tell you of it, that you may escape. If you are saved, you may thank him: but if you are lost, you may thank yourselves. It is you that deal bitterly and terribly with yourselves. Telling you of hell, doth not make hell: warning you of it, is not causing it: nor is it God that is unmerciful, but you who are foolishly cruel and unmerciful to yourselves. Do not think to despise the patience and mercy of the Lord, and then think to escape by accusing him of being unmerciful, and by saying it is terrible doctrine that we preach to you impenitent sinners! I confess to thee it is terrible, and more terrible than thy senseless heart imagineth: one day, if grace prevent it not, thou shalt find it ten thousand times more terrible than thou canst apprehend it now. When thou seest thy judge with millions of his angels coming to condemn thee, thou wilt then say his laws are terrible indeed. Thou hast to do with a holy, jealous God who is a consuming fire, and can such a God be despised, and not be terrible to thee? He is called, ' the great, the mighty, and the terrible God.—With God is terrible majesty.—He is terrible out of his holy place.—He is terrible to the greatest, even to the kings of the earth.' It is time for you therefore to tremble and submit, and think how unable you are to contend with him: and not revile his word or works, because they are terrible, but fear him for them, and study them on purpose that you may fear and glorify him. And as David, say unto God, ' how terrible art thou in thy works! Through the greatness of thy power shall thy enemies submit themselves unto thee.—Come and see the works of the Lord! He is terrible in his doings towards the children of men.—Let them praise thy great and terrible name, for it is holy.' And will you reproach God or his word or works, or ministers, with that which is the matter of his praise? If it be terrible to hear of the wrath of God, how terrible will it be to feel it? Choose not a state of terror to yourselves, and preaching will be less terrible to you. Yield to the sanctifying work of Christ, and receive his Spirit, and then that which is terrible to others will be comfortable to you. What terror is it to the regenerated, that knoweth himself to be such, to hear that none but the regenerated shall be saved? What terror is it to them that mind the things of the Spirit, to hear of the misery of a fleshly mind, and that they who live after the flesh shall die? The word of God is full of terror to the ungodly: but return with all your hearts to God, and then what word of God speaks terror to you? Truly, sirs, it is more in your power than ours, to make our preaching easy and less terrible to you! We cannot change our doctrine, but you may change your state and lives: we cannot preach another gospel: but you may obey the gospel which we preach. Obey it, and it will be the most comfortable word to you in the world. We cannot make void the word of God: but you may avoid the stroke by penitent submission. Do you think it is fitter for us to change our master's word, and falsify the laws of God Almighty; or for you to change your crooked courses, which are condemned by his word, and to let go the sin which the law forbiddeth? It is you that must change, and not the law. It is you that must be conformed to it, and not the rule that must be bent to conform to you.

Say not as Ahab of Micaiah, of the minister: ' I hate him, for he prophesieth not good of me, but evil,' for a Balaam could profess that if ' the king would give him his house full of silver and gold, he could not go beyond the word of the Lord his God, to do less or more ; to do either good or bad of his own mind.' What good would it do you for a preacher to tell you a lie, and say that you may be pardoned and saved in an impenitent, unsanctified state? Do you think our saying so would make it so? Will God falsify his word to make good ours? Or would he not deal with us as perfidious messengers who had betrayed our trust, and belied him, and deceived your souls? And would it save an unregenerated man to have Christ condemn the minister for deceiving him, and telling him that he may be saved in such a state? Do but let go the odious sin that the word of God doth speak so ill of, and then it will speak no ill of you.

Alas, sirs, what would you have a poor minister do, when God's command doth cross your pleasure, and when he is sure to offend either God or you? Which should he venture to offend? If he help not the ungodly to know their misery, he offendeth God: if he do it, he offendeth them. If he tell you, that ' all they shall be damned that believe not the truth, but have pleasure in unrighteousness,' your hearts rise against him for talking of damnation to you: and yet it is but the words of the Holy Ghost which we are bound to preach! If he tell you that, ' if ye live after the flesh, ye shall die,' you will be angry, and if he do not tell you so, God will be angry, for it is his express determination; and whose anger, think you, should a wise man choose, or whose should he most resolutely avoid; the anger of the dreadful God of heaven, or yours? Your anger we can bear, but his anger is intolerable. When you have railed and slandered us and our doctrine, we can live yet; or if you kill the body, you can do no more, you do but send us before, to be witnesses against you, when you come to judgment. But who can live, when God will pour out wrath upon him? We may keep your slanders and indignation from our hearts: but it is the heart that the heart-searching God contendeth with: and who can heal the heart which he will break? You may reach the flesh; but he that is a Spirit can afflict and wound the spirit: 'and a wounded spirit (and wounded by him) who can bear?'

Would you not yourselves say he were worse than mad, who would rather abuse the eternal God, than cross the misguided desires of such worms as you; who would displease God to please you, and sell his love to purchase yours? Will you be instead of God to us when we have lost his favour? Will you save us from him, when he sendeth for our souls by death, or sentenceth us to hell by judgment? Silly souls! How happy were you could you save yourselves! Will you be our gods if we forsake our God? We have one God, and but one, and he must be obeyed, whether you like or dislike it: 'There is one law-giver that is able to save and to destroy,' and he must be pleased, whether it please your carnal minds or not: if your wisdom now will take the chair, and judge the preaching of the gospel to be foolishness, or the searching application of it to be too much harshness and severity, I am sure you shall come down ere long, and hear his sentence that will convince you, that the 'wisdom of the world is foolishness with God, and the foolishness of God (as blasphemy dare call it) is wiser than men,' and God will be the final judge, and his word shall stand when you have done your worst. The worst that the serpent can do, is but to hiss a while and put forth the sting, and bruise our heel: but God's day will be the bruising of his head, and Satan shall be bruised under feet.

The sun will shine, and the light thereof discover your deformities, whether you will or not. And if adulterers or thieves, that love the works of darkness, will do their worst by force or flattery, they cannot make it cease its shining, though they may shut their eyes, or hide themselves in darkness from its light: faithful teachers are the lights of the world; they are not lighted by the Holy Ghost, to be 'put under a bushel, but on a candlestick, that they may give light to all that are in the house; what would you do with teachers but to teach you, and what should they make known to you, if not yourselves?

Verily, sirs, a sinner under the curse of the law, unsanctified and unpardoned, is not in a state to be jested and dallied with, unless you can play in the flames of hell: it is plain dealing that he needs. A quibbling, flashy sermon, is not the proper medicine for a lethargic, miserable soul, nor fit to break a stony heart, nor to bind up a heart that is kindly broken. Heaven and hell should not be talked of in a canting or pedantic strain. A Seneca can tell you that it is a physician that is skilful, and not one that is eloquent, whom we need. It is a cure that we need; and the means are best, be they ever so sharp, that will accomplish it. Serious, reverend gravity suiteth best with matters of such incomprehensible concern. But as dropping of beads is too ludicrous for one that is praying to be saved from the flames of hell; so a sleepy, or a histrionical speech is too light and unlikely a means to call back a sinner that is posting to perdition, and must be humbled and renewed by the Spirit, or be for ever damned. This is your case, sirs: and do you think the playing of a part upon a stage doth fit your case? O, no! So great a business requireth all the serious earnestness in the speaker that he can use. I am sure you will think so ere long yourselves; and you will then think well of the preachers that faithfully acquainted you with your case: and you will curse those that smoothed you up in your presumption, and hid your danger, by false doctrine, or misapplication, if they succeed to your perdition. God can make use of clay and spittle to open the eyes of men born blind; and of rams' horns to bring down the walls of Jericho: but usually he fitteth the means unto the end, and works on man agreeably to his nature: and therefore if a blind understanding must be enlightened, you cannot expect that it should be done by squibs and glow-worms, but by bringing into your souls the powerful celestial truth, which shall show you the hidden corners of your hearts, and the hidden mysteries of the gospel, and the unseen things of the other world. If a hardened heart be to be broken, it is not stroking, but striking that must do it. It is not the sounding brass, the tinkling cymbal, the carnal mind puffed up with superficial knowledge, that is the instrument fitted to the renewing of men's souls: but it is he that can acquaint you with what he himself hath been savingly acquainted: the heart is not melted into godly sorrow, nor raised to the life of faith and love, by a game at words, or useless notions, but by the illuminating beams of sacred truth, and the attraction of divine displayed goodness, communicated from a mind that by faith hath seen the glory of God, and by experience found that he is good, and that liveth in the love of God: such a one is fitted to assist you first in the knowledge of yourselves, and then in the knowledge of God in Christ.

Did you consider what is the office of the ministry, you would soon know what ministers do most faithfully perform their office, and what kind of teaching and oversight you should desire: and then you would be reconciled to the light, and would choose the teacher, could you have your choice, that would do most to help you to know yourselves and know the Lord.

I beseech you judge of our work by our commission, and judge of it by your own necessities. Have you more need to be acquainted with your sin and danger; or to be pleased with a set of words, which, when they are said, do leave you as they found you; and leave no light and life, and heavenly love, upon your hearts; that have no substance that you can feed upon in the review?

And what our commission is, you may find in many places of the scripture, 'When I say unto the wicked, thou shalt surely die; and thou givest him not warning, nor speakest to warn the wicked from his wicked way, to save his life; the same wicked man shall die in his iniquity, but his blood will I require at thy hand: yet if thou warn the wicked, and he turn not from his wickedness, nor from his wicked way, he shall die in his iniquity, but thou hast delivered thy soul:' and 'if thou warn the righteous man, that the righteous sin not, and he doth not sin, he shall surely live, because he is warned, also thou hast delivered thy soul.'

And what if they distaste our doctrine, must we forbear? 'Tell them, thus saith the Lord God, whether they will hear, or whether they will forbear.' You know what became of Jonah for refusing to deliver God's threatenings against Nineveh.

Christ's stewards must give to each his portion. He himself threateneth damnation to the impenitent, the hypocrites, and unbelievers. Paul saith of himself 'if I yet pleased men, I should not be the servant of Christ,' patience and meekness is commanded to the ministers of Christ, even in the instructing of opposers, but to what end? 'that they may escape out of the snare of the devil, who are taken captive by him at his will.' So that with all our meekness we must be so plain with you, as to make you know that you are Satan's captives, taken alive by him in his snares, till God by giving you repentance shall recover you.

The very office of the preachers sent by Christ was 'to open men's eyes, and turn them from darkness to light, and from the power of Satan unto God, that they may receive remission of sins, and inheritance with the sanctified by faith in Christ,' which telleth you, that we must let men understand, that till they are converted and sanctified, they are blind, and in the power of Satan—far from God—unpardoned, and having no part in the inheritance of saints.

Christ tells the pharisees, that they were of their father the devil, when they boasted that God was their father, and how plainly he tells them of their hypocrisy, and asketh them how they can escape the damnation of hell, you may see in Matt. xxiii.

Paul thought it his duty to tell Elymas that he 'was full of all subtilty and mischief, the child of the devil, and the enemy of all righteousness, a perverter of the right ways of the Lord.' And Peter thought meet to tell Simon Magus, that he had neither part nor lot in that matter; that his heart was not right in the sight of God; that he was in the gall of bitterness and bond of iniquity.

The charge of Paul to Timothy is plain and urgent, 'I charge thee before God, and the Lord Jesus Christ, who shall judge the quick and the dead at his appearing and his kingdom, preach the word, be instant in season and out of season, reprove, rebuke, exhort.' And to Titus, 'rebuke them sharply, that they may be sound in the faith.'

Judge now whether ministers must deal plainly or deceitfully with you, and whether it be the searching, healing truth that they must bring you, or a smooth tale that hath no salt or savour in it: and would you have us break these laws of God, for nothing but to deceive you, and tell you a lie, and make the ungodly believe that he is godly, or to hide the truth that is necessary to your salvation? Is the knowledge of yourselves so intolerable a thing to you?

Beloved, either it is true that you are yet unsanctified or it is not: If it be not, it is none of our desire you should think so: but if it be true, tell me, why would you not know it? I hope it is not because you would not be tormented before the time. I hope you think not that we delight to vex men's consciences with fear, or to see men live in grief and trouble, rather than in well grounded peace and joy. And if indeed you are yet unregenerated, that is not the fault of us that tell you of it, but of yourselves that wilfully continue it. Do we make you ungodly, by telling you of your ungodliness? Is it we that hinder the forgiveness of your sins, by letting you know that they are not forgiven? O no! we strive for your conversion, to this end, that your sins may be forgiven you; and you hinder the forgiveness of them, by refusing to be converted. When God forsaketh stubborn souls for resisting his grace, note how he expresseth his severity against them; 'that seeing they may see and not perceive, and hearing they may hear and not understand, lest at any time they should be converted, and their sins should be forgiven them.' You see here, that till they are converted, men's sins are not forgiven them. And that whoever procureth the forgiveness of their sins, must do it by procuring their conversion; and that the hindering of their conversion is the hindering of their forgiveness. And that blindness of mind is the great hinderance of conversion; and therefore undoubtedly the teacher that brings you a light into your minds, and first sheweth you yourselves, and your unconverted and your unpardoned state, is he that takes the way to your conversion and forgiveness: as the fore-cited text showeth you, 'I send thee to open their eyes, and to turn them from darkness to light,' that they may first know themselves, and then know God in Jesus Christ, 'and from the power of Satan,' who ruled them as their prince and captivated them as their jailor, 'unto God', whom they had forsaken as a guide and governor, and were deprived of as their protector, portion, and felicity; 'that they may receive forgiveness of sins', which none receive but the converted, 'and an inheritance among them that are sanctified,' for glory is the inheritance of the saints alone, and all this 'through faith that is in me,' by believing in me, and giving up themselves unto me, that by my satisfaction, merits, teaching, Spirit, intercession, and judgment, it may be accomplished.

Truly, sirs, if we knew how to procure your conversion and forgiveness, without making you know that you are unconverted and unpardoned, we would do it, and not trouble you needlessly with so sad a discovery. Let him be accounted unworthy to be a preacher of the gospel, that envieth you your peace and comfort. We would not have you think one jot worse of your condi-

tion than it is. Know but the very truth, what case you are in, and we desire no more.

And so far are we by this from driving you to desperation, that it is your desperation that we would prevent by it; which can no other way be prevented. When you are past remedy, desperation cannot be avoided; and this is necessary to your remedy. There is a conditional despair, and an absolute despair. The former is necessary to prevent the latter, and to bring you to a state of hope. A man that hath the tooth-ache, may perhaps despair of being eased without drawing the tooth: or a man that hath a gangrened foot may despair of life, unless it be cut off; that so by the cure he may not be left to an absolute despair of life. So you must despair of being pardoned or saved without conversion, that you may be converted, and so have hope of your salvation, and be saved from final, absolute despair. I hope you will not be offended with him that would persuade you to despair of living, unless you will eat and drink. You have no more reason to be offended with him that would have you despair of being pardoned or saved without Christ, or without his sanctifying Spirit.

Having said so much of the necessity of ministers endeavouring to make unregenerated sinners know themselves, I shall next try what I can do towards it, with those that hear, by proposing these few questions to your consideration.

Quest. 1. Do you think that you were ever unsanctified, and in a state of wrath and condemnation or not? If not, then you are not the offspring of Adam; you are not then of the human race; for the scripture telleth you that 'we are conceived in sin,' and 'that by one man sin entered into the world, and death by sin, and so death passed upon all men, for that all have sinned;—that by the offence of one, judgment came upon all men to condemnation,' and that 'all have sinned, and come short of the glory of God;' 'if we say we have no sin, we deceive ourselves, and the truth is not in us;—and the wages of sin is death.'

I hope you will confess that you cannot be pardoned and saved without a saviour; and therefore that as you need a saviour, so you must have a special interest in him. It is as certain that Christ saveth not all, as that he saveth any: for the same word assureth us of the one and of the other.

Quest. 2. But if you confess that once you were children of wrath, my next question is, whether you know how, and when you were delivered from so sad a state? or at least, whether it be done, or not? Perhaps you will say it was done in your baptism, which washeth away original sin. But granting you, that all have a promise of pardon before, have that promise sealed, and that pardon delivered them by baptism, I ask you,

Quest. 3. Do you think that baptism by water alone will save, unless you be also baptized by the Spirit? Christ telleth you the contrary, with a vehement asseveration, 'verily, verily, I say unto thee, except a man be born of water and of the Spirit, he cannot enter into the kingdom of God.' And Peter tells you that it is 'not the putting away the filth of the flesh, but the answer of a good conscience towards God;' 'if therefore you have not the Spirit of Christ,' for all your baptism, 'you are none of his,' for that which is born of the flesh is flesh, and you must be born of the Spirit if you will be spiritual.

I shall further grant you, that many receive the Spirit of Christ even in their infancy, and may be savingly as well as sacramentally then regenerated. And if this be your case, you have a very great cause to be thankful for it. But I next inquire of you,

Quest. 4. Have you not lived an unholy, carnal life, since you came to the use of reason? Have you not since then declared, that you did not live the life of faith, nor walk after the Spirit but after the flesh? If so, then it is certain that you have need of a conversion from that ungodly state, whatever baptism did for you; and therefore you are still to inquire, whether you have been converted since you came to age.

And I must needs remind you, that your infant covenant made in baptism, being upon your parents' faith and consent, and not your own, will serve your turn no longer than your infancy, unless when you come to the use of reason, you renew and own that covenant yourselves, and have a personal faith and repentance of your own. And whatever you received in baptism, this must be our next inquiry.

Quest. 5. Did you ever since you came to age, upon sound repentance, and renunciation of the flesh, the world, and the devil, give up yourselves unfeignedly by faith, to God the Father, Son, and Holy Ghost; and show by the performance of this holy covenant that you were sincere in the making of it?

I confess it is a matter so hard to most, to assign the time and manner of their conversion, that I think it no safe way of trial. And therefore I will issue all in this one question:

Quest. 6. Have you the necessary parts of the new creature now; though perhaps you know

not just when, or how it was formed in you? The question is, Whether you are now in a state of sanctification; and not, Whether you can tell just when you did receive it? It beginneth so early with some, and so obscurely with others and in others the preparations are so long or notable, that it is hard to say when special grace came in. But you may well discern, whether it be there or not. And that is the question which must be resolved, if you would know yourselves.

And though I have been long in these exhortations, to incline your wills, I shall be short in giving you those evidences of the holy life, which must be before your eyes, while you are upon the trial.

In fine, if your very hearts do now unfeignedly consent to the covenant which you made in baptism, and your lives express it to be a true consent, I dare say you are regenerated, though you know not just when you first consented. Come on then, and let us inquire what you say to the several parts of your baptismal covenant.

1. If you are sincere in the covenant you have made with Christ you do resolvedly consent, that God shall be your only God, as reconciled to you by Jesus Christ. Which is, (1.) That you will take him for your owner or your absolute Lord, and give up yourselves to him as his own. (2.) That you will take him for your supreme governor, and consent to be subject to his government and laws, taking his wisdom for your guide, and his will for the rule of your wills and lives. (3.) That you will take him for your chief benefactor, from whom you receive and expect all your happiness, and to whom you owe yourselves and all, by way of thankfulness. And that you take his love and favour for your happiness itself, and prefer the everlasting enjoyment of his glorious sight and love in heaven, before all the sensual pleasures of the world.

I would prove the necessity of all these by scripture as we go, but that it is evident in itself; these three relations being essential to God, as our God in covenant. He is not our God, if not our owner, ruler, and benefactor. You profess all this, when you profess but to love God, or take him for your God.

2. In the covenant of baptism you do profess to believe in Christ, and take him for your only Saviour. If you do this in sincerity, (1.) You do unfeignedly believe the doctrine of his gospel, and the articles of the Christian faith, concerning his person, his offices, his sufferings and works. (2.) You do take him unfeignedly for the only Redeemer and Saviour of mankind, and give up yourselves to be saved by his

merits, righteousness, intercession, &c. as he hath promised in his word. (3.) You trust upon him and his promises, for the attainment of your reconciliation and peace with God, your justification, adoption, sanctification, and the glory of the life to come. (4.) You take him for your Lord and king, your owner and ruler by the right of redemption ; and your grand benefactor, that hath obliged you to love and gratitude by saving you from the wrath to come, and purchasing eternal glory for you, by his most wonderful condescension, life and sufferings.

3. In the baptismal covenant, you are engaged to the Holy Ghost. If you are sincere in this branch of your covenant, (1.) You discern your sins as odious and dangerous, as the corruption of your souls, and that which displeaseth the most holy God. (2.) You see an excellency in holiness of heart and life, as the image of God, the rectitude of man, and that which fits him for eternal blessedness, and maketh him amiable in the eyes of God. (3.) You unfeignedly desire to be rid of your sin, how dear soever it hath been to you ; and to be perfectly sanctified by the Holy Spirit, by his degrees, in the use of the means which he hath appointed : and you consent that the Holy Ghost, as your sanctifier, do purify you and kindle the love of God in you, and bring it to perfection.

4. In baptism, you profess to renounce the world, the flesh, and the devil ; that is, as they stand for your hearts against the will and love of God, and against the happiness of the unseen world; and against your faith in Christ your Saviour ; and against the sanctifying work of the Holy Ghost. If therefore you are sincere in this part of your covenant, you do upon deliberation perceive all the pleasures, profits, and honours of this world to be so vain and worthless, that you are habitually resolved to prefer the love and favour of God, and your salvation, before them ; and to be ruled by Jesus Christ, and his Spirit and word, rather than by the desires of the flesh, or the world's allurements, or the will of man, or the suggestions of the devil ; and to forsake all rather than forsake the Father, the Saviour, the Sanctifier, to whom you are devoted, and the everlasting life, which upon his promise you have taken for your hope and portion. This is the sense of baptism, and all this in profession being essential to your baptism, must be essential to your Christianity. Your parents' profession of it was necessary to your infant title to the outward privileges of the church. Your own personal profession is necessary to the continuance of those privileges, and your visible Chris-

tianity and communion with the adult. And the truth of what you profess, is necessary to your real Christianity before God, and to your title to salvation : and this is what is to be now inquired after. You cannot hope to be admitted into heaven, upon lower terms than the sincerity of that profession which entereth you into the church : while we tell you of no higher matters necessary to your salvation, than the sincerity of that which is necessary to baptism and Christianity, I hope you will not say we deal too strictly with you. Inquire now by a diligent trial of your hearts, whether you truly consent to all these articles of your baptismal vow or covenant. If you do, you are regenerated by the Spirit : if you do not, you have but the sacrament of regeneration ; which aggravateth your guilt, as a violated profession and covenant must needs do. And I do not think that any man worthy to be discoursed with, will have the face to tell you, that any man, at the use of reason, is by his baptism, or any thing else, in a state of justification and salvation, whose heart doth not sincerely consent to the covenant of baptism, and whose life expresseth not that consent.

Hence therefore you may perceive that it is a thing unquestionable, that all these persons are yet unregenerated, and in the bond of their iniquity.

1. All those that have not unfeignedly devoted themselves to God, as being not their own, but his. His by the title of creation; ' know ye that the Lord he is God ; it is he that hath made us, and not we ourselves, we are his people, and the sheep of his pasture.' And his by the title of redemption ; for ' we are bought with a price,' and he that unfeignedly taketh God for his owner, and absolute Lord, will heartily give up himself unto him, as Paul saith of the Corinthians, ' they first gave up their own selves to the Lord, and to us by the will of God.

He that entirely giveth up himself to God, doth with himself surrender all that he hath in desire and resolution. As Christ with himself doth give us all things, and addeth other things to them that seek first his kingdom and its righteousness, so Christians with themselves do give up all they have to Christ.

He that giveth up himself to God, will live to God ; and he that taketh not himself to be his own, will take nothing for his own, but will study the interest of his Lord, and think he is best disposed of, when he honoureth him most, and serveth him best ; ' ye are not your own, for ye are bought with a price ; therefore glorify God in your body, and in your spirit, which are God's.'

If any of you devote not yourselves unfeignedly to God, and make it not your first inquiry, what God would have you be and do, but live to yourselves, and yet think yourselves in a state of grace, you are mistaken, and do not know yourselves. How many might easily see their miserable condition in this discovery, who say in effect ' our lips are our own, who is Lord over us ?' and rather hate and oppose the interest of God and holiness in the world, than devote themselves to the promoting of it! ' Do ye thus requite the Lord, ye foolish people and unwise ? Is not he thy father that hath bought thee ? Hath he not made thee, and established thee ?'

2. All those are unregenerated and in a state of death, that are not sincerely subjected to the governing will of God, but are ruled by their carnal interest and desires ; and the word of a man that can gratify or hurt them, can do more with them than the word of God : to show them the command of a man that they think can undo them if they disobey, doth more prevail with them, than to show them the command of God, that can condemn them unto endless misery. They more fear men that can kill the body, than God that can destroy both soul and body in hell fire. When the lust of the flesh and the will of man, do bear more sway than the will of God, it is certain that such a soul is unregenerated ; 'know ye not that so many of us as were baptized into Jesus Christ, were baptized into his death? Therefore we are buried with him by baptism into death, that like as Christ was raised from the dead, by the glory of the Father, even so we also should walk in newness of life.—Knowing this, that our old man is crucified with him, that the body of sin might be destroyed ; that henceforth we should not serve sin.—Know ye not to whom ye yield yourselves servants to obey, his servants ye are to whom ye obey, whether of sin unto death, or of obedience unto righteousness.—Forasmuch then as Christ hath suffered for us in the flesh, arm yourselves likewise with the same mind ; for he that hath suffered in the flesh, hath ceased from sin : that he no longer should live the rest of his time in the flesh, to the lusts of men, but to the will of God.'

3. All those are unregenerated that depend not upon God as their chief benefactor ; and do not most carefully apply themselves to him, as knowing that in his favour is life, and that ' his loving kindness is better than life,' and that to his judgment we must finally stand or fall: but do ambitiously seek the favour of men, and call them their benefactors, whatever become of the favour of God. He is no child of God that preferreth not the love of God before the love of all the world. He is no heir of heaven that preferreth not the fruition of God in heaven, before all worldly glory and felicity. 'If ye be risen with Christ, seek the things that are above, where Christ sitteth on the right hand of God : set your affections on things above, not on things on the earth.' The love of God is the sum of holiness—the heart of the new creature ; the perfecting of it is the perfection and felicity of man.

4. They are certainly unregenerated that believe not the gospel, and take not Christ for their only Saviour, and his promises of grace and glory, as purchased by his sacrifice and merits, for the foundation of their hopes, on which they resolve to trust their souls for pardon and for peace with God, and endless happiness ; 'neither is there salvation in any other: for there is none other name under heaven given among men, whereby we must be saved.—This is the record, that God hath given us eternal life, and this life is in his Son : he that hath the Son, hath life ; and he that hath not the Son, hath not life.'

When our happiness was in Adam's hands, he lost it : it is now put into safer hands, and Jesus Christ, the second Adam, is become our treasury. He is the head of the body, from whom each member hath quickening influence ; the life of saints is in him, as the life of the tree is in the root, unseen ; holiness is a living unto God in Christ ; though we are dead with Christ, to the law, the world, and the flesh, we are alive to God. So Paul describeth our case in his own : ' I through the law am dead to the law, that I might live unto God : I am crucified with Christ, nevertheless I live : yet not I, but Christ liveth in me : and the life which I now live in the flesh, I live by the faith of the Son of God, who loved me, and gave himself for me.—Likewise reckon ye also yourselves to be dead indeed unto sin, but alive unto God through Jesus Christ our Lord.—Christ is the vine, and we are the branches ; without him we can do nothing : if you abide not in him, and his words in you, you are cast forth as a branch, and withered, which men gather and cast into the fire, and they are burned.' In baptism you are married unto Christ, as to the external solemnization ; and in spiritual regeneration your hearts do inwardly close with him, entertain him and resign themselves unto him by faith and love, and by a resolved covenant become his own.

5. That person is certainly unregenerated that never was convinced of a necessity of sanctification, or never perceived an excellency and amiableness in holiness of heart and life, and loved

it in others, and desired it himself; and never gave up himself to the Holy Ghost, to be further sanctified in the use of his appointed means; desiring to be perfect, and willing to press forward towards the mark, and to abound in grace. Much less is that person renewed by the Holy Ghost, that hateth holiness, and had rather be without it, and would not walk in the fear and obedience of the Lord.

The Spirit of holiness is that life by which Christ quickeneth all that are his members. He is no member of Christ that is without it: 'according to his mercy, he saveth us by the washing of regeneration, and renewing of the Holy Ghost.'

6. That person is unregenerated, that is under the dominion of his fleshly desires, and 'mindeth the things of the flesh above the things of the Spirit;' and hath not mortified it so far as not to live according to it. A carnal mind and a carnal life, are opposite to holiness, as sickness is to health, and darkness unto light. 'There is no condemnation to them that are in Christ Jesus, that walk not after the flesh, but after the Spirit. —For they that are after the flesh do mind the things of the flesh; but they that are after the Spirit, the things of the Spirit. For to be carnally minded is death, but to be spiritually minded is life and peace; because the carnal mind is enmity against God; for it is not subject to the law of God, neither indeed can be: so then they that are in the flesh, cannot please God. —For if ye live after the flesh, ye shall die: but if, by the Spirit, ye mortify the deeds of the body, ye shall live.—Now the works of the flesh are manifest, which are adultery, fornication, uncleanness, lasciviousness, idolatry, witchcraft, hatred, variance, emulations, wrath, strife, seditions, heresies, envyings, murders, drunkenness, revellings, and such like; of which I tell you before, as I have also told you in time past, that they which do such things shall not inherit the kingdom of God. But the fruit of the Spirit is love, joy, peace, long-suffering, gentleness, goodness, faith, meekness, temperance: against such there is no law. And they that are Christ's have crucified the flesh, with the affections and lusts.'

7. Lastly, that person is certainly unregenerated that so far valueth and loveth this world, or any of the carnal accommodations therein, as practically to prefer them before the love of God, and the hopes of everlasting glory: seeking it first, with highest estimation, and holding it fastest; so as that he will rather venture his soul upon the threatened wrath of God than his body upon the wrath of man; and will be religious no further than may consist with his prosperity or safety in the world, and hath something that he cannot part with for Christ and heaven, because it is dearer to him than these: let this man go never so far in religion, as long as he goeth farther for the world, and sets it nearest to his heart, and holds it fastest, and will do most for it, and consequently loves it better than Christ, he is no true Christian, nor in a state of grace.

The scriptures put this also out of doubt. 'He that loveth father or mother more than me, is not worthy of me. Whosoever doth not bear his cross and come after me, cannot be my disciple. Whosoever he be of you that forsaketh not all that he hath, he cannot be my disciple.— Know ye not that the friendship of the world, is enmity with God? Whosoever therefore will be a friend of the world, is the enemy of God;' no wonder then if the world must be renounced in our baptism. 'Love not the world, neither the things that are in the world: if any man love the world, the love of the Father is not in him.'

You see, by this time, what it is to be regenerated and to be a Christian indeed, by what is contained even in our baptism: consequently how you may know yourselves, whether you are sanctified, and the heirs of heaven, or not.

Again therefore I summon you to appear before your consciences: and if indeed these evidences of regeneration are not in you, wait not for the sentence, but confess your sinful, miserable state, and condemn yourselves, and say no longer I hope yet that my present condition may serve the turn, and that God will forgive me, though I should die without any further change. Those hopes that you may be saved without regeneration, or that you are regenerated when you are not, are the pillars of Satan's fortress in your hearts, and keep you from the saving hopes of the regenerated, that will never make you ashamed. Uphold not that which Christ is engaged against: down it must, either by grace or judgment; and therefore abuse not your souls by under-propping such an ill-grounded, false, deceitful hope. You have now time to take it down so orderly and safely, that it shall not fall on your heads, and overwhelm you for ever; but if you stay till death will undermine it, the fall will be great, and your ruin irreparable. If you are wise, therefore, know yourselves in time.

———

CHAPTER VII.

EXHORTATIONS TO THE GODLY, TO KNOW THEIR SINS, AND THEIR SPIRITUAL NECESSITIES.

I have now done with that part of my special exhortations which concerned the unregenerated: I am next to speak to those of you that by grace are brought into a better state, and to tell you, that it very much concerneth you also, even the best of you, to labour to be well acquainted with yourselves; and that both in respect of, 1. Your sins and wants, and, 2. Your graces and your duties.

1. Be acquainted with the root of your sins ; with your particular inclinations and corrupt affections ; with their quality, their degree and strength ; with the weaknesses of every grace; with your inability to duty ; and with the omissions or sinful practices of your lives. Search diligently and deeply; frequently and accurately peruse your hearts and ways, till you certainly and thoroughly know yourselves.

I beseech you let it not suffice you that you know your states, and have found yourselves in the love of God, in the faith of Christ, and possessed by his Spirit. Though this be a mercy worth many worlds, yet this is not all concerning yourselves that you have to know. ' If yet you say that you have no sin, you deceive yourselves.' If yet you think you are past all danger, your danger is the greater for this mistake. As much as you have been humbled for sin, as much as you have loathed it because of it, as oft as you have confessed it, lamented it, and complained and prayed against it, yet it is alive; though it be mortified, it is alive. It is said to be mortified as to its prevalency and reign, but the relics of it yet survive : were it perfectly dead, you were perfectly delivered from it, and might say you have no sin ; but it is not yet so happy with you. It will find work for the blood and Spirit of Christ, and for yourselves, as long as you are in the flesh. And, alas, too many that know themselves to be upright in the main, are yet so much unacquainted with their hearts and lives, as to the degrees of grace and sin, that it much impedes them in their Christian progress. Go along with me in the careful observation of the following evils, that may befal even the regenerated by the remains of self-ignorance.

1. The work of mortification is very much hindered, because you know yourselves no better, as may appear in all the following discoveries.

(1.) You confess not sin to God or man so penitently and sensibly as you ought, because you know yourselves no better. Did you see your hearts more fully, how heavily would you charge yourselves? Repentance would be more intense and more effectual ; and when you were more contrite, you would be more meet for the sense of pardon, and for delight in God. It would fill you more with godly shame and self-abhorrence, if you better knew yourselves. It would make you more feelingly say with Paul, ' I see another law in my members warring against the law of my mind, and bringing me into captivity to the law of sin, which is in my members. O wretched man that I am, who shall deliver me from the body of this death !' And with David, ' I will declare my iniquity, I will be sorry for my sin; they are more than the hairs of my head. I acknowledged my sin unto thee, and mine iniquity have I not hid : I said I will confess my transgressions to the Lord, and thou forgavest the iniquity of my sin.' Repentance is the death of sin: and the knowledge of ourselves, and the sight of our sins, are the life of repentance.

(2.) You pray not against sin, and for grace and pardon, so earnestly as you should, because you know yourselves no better. O that God would but open these too close hearts, and show us all the recesses of our self-deceit, and the filth of worldliness and of carnal inclinations that lurk within us, and read us a lecture upon every part, what prayers would it teach us to indite.' That you be not proud of your holiness, let me tell you, Christians, that a full display of the corruptions which the best of-you have in you, would not only put down self-exalting thoughts, but would teach you to pray with fervour and importunity, and waken you out of your sleepy indifference, and make you cry, ' O wretched man that I am, who shall deliver me ?' If the sight of a person, lame or in rags, move you to compassion, though they use no words ; surely the sight of your own deformities, wants and dangers, would affect you, if you saw them as they are. How many sins do you forget in your confessions that should have a particular repentance ; how many wants do you overlook in prayer, that should have particular petitions for a merciful supply ; and how many are slightly referred to with words of course, that would be earnestly insisted on, if you did but better know yourselves ! O that God would persuade you better to study your hearts, and pray accordingly whenever you draw nigh him, that you might not be like the hypocrites, who ' draw near to him with their lips, when their hearts are far from him.' To my shame I must confess, that my soul is too dry and barren in holy supplications to God, and too little affected with my confessed sins and wants: but I am forced to lay all in a very great measure upon the imperfect acquaintance that I have with myself. I cannot think I should want matter to pour out before the Lord in confession and petition, nor so much want of fervour and earnestness with God, if my heart and life lay open to my view, while I am upon my knees.

3. It is for want of a fuller knowledge of your-selves that you are so negligent in your Christian, watchfulness; that you do no better guard your senses; that you make no stricter a covenant with your eyes, your appetites, your tongues: that you do not more examine what you think, feel and say; that you call not yourselves more fre-quently to account, while days run on, and duties are carelessly performed as matters of course, and no daily or weekly reckoning is made to conscience. The knowledge of your weaknesses, and readiness to yield, and of your treacherous corruptions, that comply with the enemy, would make you more suspicious of yourselves, and to walk more circumspectly, 'not as fools, but as wise,' and to look under your feet, and consider your ways before you were too bold and ventu-rous. The consciousness of their own infirmity should have moved the disciples to watch and pray. 'Watch and pray that ye enter not into temptation; the Spirit indeed is willing, but the flesh is weak.' And all have the same charge, because all have the same infirmity and danger; 'what I say to you, I say unto all, watch.' Did we better know how many advantages our own corruptions give the tempter, that charge of the Holy Ghost would awaken us all to stand to our arms and look about us: 'watch ye, stand fast in the faith, quit you like men, be strong.—Put on the whole armour of God, that ye may be able to stand against the wiles of the devil: for we wrestle not against flesh and blood, but against principalities and powers, against the rulers of the darkness of this world, against spiritual wickedness in high places.' The know-ledge of ourselves doth show us all the ad-vantages of the tempter,—what he hath to work upon, and what in us to take his part, and conse-quently where he is likeliest to assault us: and thus it puts us into so prepared a posture for defence, as very much hinders his success. But so far as we do not know ourselves, we are like blind men in fencing, whom the adversary may hit in what part he pleases. What sin may not Satan tempt a man into, that is not acquainted with the corruptions and frailties of his own heart?

4. It is for want of self-acquaintance that we seek not, for help against our sin, to ministers or other friends that could assist us, and that we use the confirming ordinances with no more care and diligence. All the ability and willingness of others, and all the helps of God's appointment, will be neglected, when we should employ them against our sins, so far as self-ignorance doth keep us from discerning the necessity of them.

5. It is for want of a fuller self-knowledge that many lie long in sins unobserved by them-selves; and that many are on the declining hand, and take no notice of it. How little resistance or mortifying endeavours we are likely to bestow upon unknown or unobserved sins, it is easy to conceive. How many may we observe to have notorious blemishes of pride, ostentation, desire of pre-eminence and esteem, envy, malice, self-conceit, self-seeking, censoriousness, uncharita-bleness, and such like, that see no more of it in themselves than is in more mortified men? How ordinarily do we hear the pastors that watch over them, and their friends that are best acquainted with them, lamenting the miscarriages, and the careless walking and declining of many that seem religious, when they lament it not themselves, nor will be convinced that they are sick of any such disease, any more than all other Christians are? Hence it is that we have all need to la-ment in general our unknown sins, and say with David, 'Who can understand his errors? cleanse thou me from secret faults.'

There are few of us, that observe our hearts at all, but find, both upon any special illumina-tion, and in the hour of searching trials, that there are many distempers in our hearts, and many miscarriages in our lives, that we never took notice of before. The heart hath such secret corners of uncleanness, such mysteries of iniquity, and depths of deceitfulness, that many fearers of God are strangely unacquainted with themselves, as to the particular motions and degrees of sin, till some notable providence or gracious light assist them in the discovery. I think it not un-profitable here, to give you some instances of sin undiscerned by the servants of the Lord themselves that have it, till the light come in that makes them wonder at their former dark-ness. In general, first observe these two. (1.) The secret habits of sin, being discernible only by some acts, are many times unknown to us, because we are under no strong temptation to commit such sins. And it is a wonderful hard thing for a man, that hath little or no tempta-tion, to know himself, and what he would do if he had the temptations of other men. And O what sad discoveries are made in the hour of temptation! What swarms of vices break out in some, like vermin that lay hid in the cold of winter, and crawl about when they feel the summer's heat! What horrid corruptions which we never observed in ourselves before, do show themselves in the hour of temptation! Who would have thought that righteous Noah had in the ark such a heart, as would by carelessness fall into the sin of drunkenness; that righteous Lot had carried from Sodom the seed of drunkenness and incest in him; or that David, a man so eminent in holiness, and a man after God's own heart, had a heart that had in it the seeds of adultery and murder? Little thought Peter, when he professed Christ, that there had been in him such carnality and unbelief, as would have so soon provoked Christ to say, 'get thee behind me, Satan, thou art an offence unto me, for thou savourest not the things that be of God, but those that be of men.' And little did he think when he so vehemently professed his resolution rather to die with Christ than deny him, that there had been then in his heart the seed that would bring forth this bitter fruit. Who knows what is virtually in a seed, that never saw the tree, or tasted of the fruit?

Especially when we have not only a freedom from temptations, but also the most powerful means to repress vicious habits, it is hard to know how far they are mortified at the root. When men are among those that countenance the contrary virtue where the vice is in disgrace, and where examples of piety and temperance are still before their eyes; if they dwell in places and company, where authority, friendship and reason do all take part with good, and cry down the evil; no wonder if the evil that is unmortified in men's hearts, do not much break out to their own or other's observation through all this opposition. The instance of king Joash is famous for this, who did that which was right in the sight of the Lord, all the days of Jehoiadah the priest that instructed him; but after his death, when the princes of Judah flattered him with their obeisance, he left the house of God and served idols, till wrath came upon the land; and he was so hardened in sin as to murder Zechariah the prophet of God, and son of that Jehoiadah who had brought him out of obscurity, and set him upon the throne, even because he spake in the name of the Lord against his sin. Who would have thought that it had been in the heart of Solomon, a man so wise, so holy, and so solemnly engaged to God, by his public professions and works, to have committed the abominations recorded of him?

If you say, that all this proveth not that there was any seed or root of such a sin in the heart before, but only that the temptation did prevail to cause the acts first, and then such habits as those acts did tend to; I answer, 1. I grant that temptations do not only discover what is in the heart, but also make it worse when they prevail; and that this is no full proof that a man had a proper habit of sin before, because by temptation he commits the act: for Adam sinned by temptation without an antecedent habit. 2. But we know the nature of man to be now corrupted; and that this corruption is virtually or seminally sin of every kind, and disposing us to all sin; and that this disposition is strong enough to be called a general habit. When grace in the sanctified is called a nature, there is the same reason to call the sinful inclination also a nature; which can signify nothing else than a strong and rooted inclination. Knowing therefore that the heart is so corrupted, we may well say, when the evil fruit appears, that the seed of it was there before. The easy and frequent yielding to the temptation, shows there was a friend to sin within. 3. But if it were not so, yet that our hearts should be so frail, mutable, and easily drawn to sin, is a part of self-knowledge necessary to our preservation, and not to be disregarded. 4. I am sure Christ himself tells us, that out of the heart proceed the sins of the life, and that the evil things of evil men come out of the evil treasure of their hearts, and when God permitted the fall of good king Hezekiah, the text saith, 'God left him to try him, that he might know all that was in his heart,' that is, that he might show all that was in his heart; so that the weakness and the remaining corruption of Hezekiah's heart was shown in the sin which he committed.

2. As the sinful inclinations are with difficulty discerned, and long lie hid till some temptation draw them out; so the act itself is scarcely discerned in any of its malignity, till it be done and past, and the soul is brought to a deliberate review. For while a man is in the act of sin, either his understanding is so far deluded, as to think it no sin, or at least none to him that then committeth it; or that it is better to venture on it than not, for attaining some seeming good, or avoiding some evil: or else the restraining activity of the understanding is suspended, and it discerneth not practically the pernicious evil of the sin, and forbiddeth not the committing of it, or forbids it with so low a voice, as is drowned by the clamour of contradicting passion: and thus the prohibition is not heard. How can it be expected that, when a man has not wisdom enough to see his sin so far as to forbear it, he

should even then see it so far as rightly to judge of himself and it; and that when reason is low, and sensuality prevaileth, we should then have the right use of reason for self-discerning? When a storm of passion hath blown out the light, and error hath extinguished it, we are unlikely then to know ourselves. When the sensual part is pleasing itself with its forbidden objects the pleasantness of this so corrupts the judgment that men will easily believe that it is lawful, or not very bad : thus sin is usually least known and felt, when it is greatest and most active, and when one would think it should be most perceptible ; like a phrenzy or madness, or other delirium, which is least known when it is greatest and most in action, because its nature is destructive to the reason that should know it. And thus you see, that through self-ignorance it comes to pass that both secret habits and the most open acts of sin are oft-times little known. A man that is drunk is in an unfit state to know what drunkenness is, and so is a man that is in a passion: you will hardly bring him to repentance till it be allayed. And so is a man in the brutifying heat of lust ; and therefore abundance of unknown sin, may remain in a soul that laboureth not to be well acquainted with itself. And as I have showed you this in general, both of habits and acts of sin, let us consider of some instances in particular, which will yet more discover the necessity of studying ourselves.

1. Little do we think what odious and dangerous errors may befall a person that now is orthodox; what a slippery mutability the mind of man is liable to ; what a variety of representations causeth a variety of apprehensions : like some pictures that seem one thing when you look on them on one side, and another thing when on another side; yet if you change your place or your light, they seem to change. Indeed God's word hath nothing in it thus fitted to deceive; but our weakness hath that which disposeth us to mistakes. The person that now is a zealous lover of the truth, when it hath procured entertainment by the happy advantage of friends, acquaintance, ministers, magistrates, or by common consent, may possibly turn a zealous adversary to it, when it loseth these advantages. When a minister shall change his mind, how many of the flock may be misled ? When you marry or contract any intimate friendship with a person of unsound and dangerous principles, how easily are they received ? When the stream of the times and authority shall change, and put the name of truth on falsehood, how many may be carried down the stream? How zealous have

many been for faithful ministers that have turned their persecutors, or made it a great part of their religion to revile them, when once they have turned to some sect that is possessed by a malicious spirit.

O! that we could stop here, and not remind you how faithfully and honestly some have seemed to love and obey the word of God, and to delight in the communion of saints, that by seducers have been brought to deny the divine authority of the scriptures, and to turn their backs on all God's public ordinances of worship, and excommunicate themselves from the society of the saints, and vilify or deny the works of the Spirit in them ! Little did these men once think how far they should fall under the conceit of rising higher : little would they have believed him that had told them what a change they would make. Had these men known themselves in time, and known what tinder was in their hearts, they would have walked more warily, and likely would have escaped the snare. But they fell into it, because they feared it not; and they feared it not, because they knew not, or observed not, how prone they were to be infected.

2. Little do many think in their adversity, or low estate, what seeds are in their hearts, which prosperity would turn into very odious, scandalous sins, unless their vigilancy, and a special preservation, should prevent it. Many a man that in his shop, or at his plough, is censuring the great miscarriages of his superiors, doth little think how bad he might prove, if he were in the place of those whom he censures. Many a poor man that freely talks against the luxury, pride, and cruelty of the rich, doth little think how like them he should be, if he had their temptations and estates. How many persons that lived in good repute for humility, temperance, and piety, have we seen become proud, and sensual, and ungodly, when they have been exalted ! I must say that this age hath given us such lamentable instances, as should make all our hearts to ache and fear, when we consider the crimes and their effects. Would the persons that once walked with us in the ways of peace, and concord, and obedience, have believed that man who should have foretold them twenty years ago, that very many should be puffed up and deluded by success, and by the ebullition of pride make themselves believe that victories authorized them to deny subjection to the higher powers, by right or wrong take down all that stood in their way, take the government into their own hands, and depose their rightful governors ; never once condescending to ask themselves the question that

Christ asked, ' man, who made me a judge, or a divider over you ?' as if authority had been nothing but strength, and he had the best right to govern that could use the greatest force to compel obedience. Little were the seeds of all this evil discerned in the heart, till prosperity and success cherished them, and brought them to that which, with grief, we have long observed. If one had told them before, that God has charged every soul to be subject on pain of condemnation ; that they have vowed fidelity, but yet would break all these commands and vows ; and all because they were able to do it : they would have said, as Hazael, ' am I a dog that I should do this ?' When the ministers of the gospel, and their dearest friends, bore witness against the sin, the heart could not, by all this, be brought to perceive its guilt, or that it was any sin to overturn, overturn, overturn, till they had overturned all, and left not themselves a bough to stand upon. Their unrighteous conduct toward magistracy and ministry, and the licentious indulgence of the open enemies and revilers of both, and of all the ordinances and churches of the Lord, do proclaim aloud to all that fear God, 'the depths and deceits of the heart are wonderful, and you little think what an hour of temptation may discover in you, or bring you to.'—O therefore know yourselves, and fear, and watch !

3. A man that in adversity is touched with penitent and mortifying considerations, and strongly resolves that he will live hereafter holily and diligently ; if he be recovered or delivered from his suffering, doth oft-times little think what a treacherous heart he hath, and how little he may retain of all this sense of sin or duty, when he is delivered, and that he may be so much worse than he seemed or promised, as that he may have cause to wish he had been afflicted still. O how many sick-bed promises are as pious as we can desire, that wither away and come to almost nothing, when health hath scattered the fears that caused them ! How many with a celebrated imprisoned lord do, as it were, write the story of Christ upon their prison walls, and forget him when they are set at liberty ! How many have tender consciences in a low estate, who, when they are exalted, and converse with great ones, think that they may waste their time in idleness and scandalous recreations, be silent witnesses of the most odious sins from day to day, pray God to be merciful to them when they go to the house of Rimmon, and dare scarcely own the honest servant, or hated and reproached cause of God ! O what a preservative would it be to us in prosperity, to know the corruption

of our hearts, and foresee in adversity what we are in danger of ! We should then be less ambitious to place our dwellings on the highest ground, and more fearful of the storms that must be expected there. How few are there that grow better by worldly greatness and prosperity? Yea, how few that hold their own, and grow not worse ? And yet how fewer still are there that refuse or that desire not this perilous station, rather than to stand safer on the lower ground ! Verily, the lamentable fruits of prosperity, and the mutability of men that make great professions and promises in adversity, should make the best of us jealous of our hearts, and convince us that there is greater corruption in them that are never put to such a trial, than most are acquainted with. The height of prosperity shows what the man is indeed, as much as the depth of adversity.

Would one have thought that had read of Hezekiah's earnest prayer in his sickness, the miracle wrought to signify his deliverance, and his recorded song of praise, that yet his heart should so deceive him as to prove unthankful? You may see by his expressions, how high his resolutions were to spend his life in the praise of God, ' the living, the living he shall praise thee, as I do this day : the fathers to the children shall make known thy truth. The Lord was ready to save me : therefore we will sing our songs to the stringed instruments all the days of our life in the house of the Lord !' Would you think that a holy man, thus wrapt up in God's praise should yet miscarry, and be charged with ingratitude? And yet it is said of him, ' Hezekiah rendered not again according to the benefit done unto him ; for his heart was lifted up : therefore there was wrath upon him and upon Judah and Jerusalem.' God was fain to bring him to a review, and humble him for being thus lifted up, as the next words show, ' Hezekiah humbled himself for the pride of his heart.' O sirs, what Christian that ever was in deep affliction, and hath been recovered by the tender hand of mercy, hath not found how false a thing the heart is, and how little to be trusted in its best resolutions, and most confident promises ! Hezekiah still remained a holy faithful man ; but yet thus failed in particulars and degrees. Which of us can say, who have had the most affecting deliverances, that ever our hearts did fully answer the resolutions and promises of our afflicted state : and that we had as constant, sensible thanksgivings after, as our complaints and prayers were before ! Not I ; with grief I must say, not I, though God hath tried me many a time. Alas !

we are too like the deceitful Israelites, 'when he slew them, then they sought him; and they returned and inquired early after God: and they remembered that God was their rock, and the high God their redeemer. Nevertheless they did flatter him with their mouths, and they lied unto him with their tongues ; for their heart was not right with him, neither were they stedfast in his covenant.' Prosperity often shows more of the hypocrisy of the unsound, and the infirmity of the upright, than appeared in adversity. When we feel the strong resolutions of our hearts to cast off our sin, to walk more thankfully, fruitfully, and circumspectly with God than we have done, we can hardly believe that ever those hearts should lose so much of these affections and resolutions as in a little time we find they do. Alas how quickly and insensibly do we slide into our former insensibility, and into our dull and heavy fruitless course, when once the pain and fear are gone! And then when the next affliction comes, we are confounded and covered with shame, and have not such confidence with God in our prayers and cries as we had before, because we are conscious of our covenant-breaking and backsliding; and at last we grow so distrustful of our hearts, that we know not how to believe any promises which they make, nor how to be confident of any evidence of grace that is in them ; and so we lose the comfort of our sincerity, and are cast into a state of too much heaviness, and unthankful denial of our dearest mercies? And all this comes from the foul unexpected relapses of the heart that comes not up to the promises we made to God in our distress.

But if exaltation be added to deliverance, how often doth it make the reason drunk, so that the man seems not the same! If you see them drowned in ambition, or worldly cares, or pleasures ; if you see how boldly they can play with a sin that once they would have trembled at; how powerful fleshly arguments are with them ; how strangely they now look at plain-hearted, zealous, heavenly Christians, whose case they once desired to be in; and how much they are ashamed or afraid, to appear openly for an opposed cause of Christ, or openly to justify the persons that he justifieth, as if they had forgot that a day is coming when they will be loth that Christ should be ashamed of them, and refuse to justify them, when the grand accuser is pleading for their condemnation ; I say, if you see these men in their prosperity, would you not ask with wonder, are these the men that lately in distress did seem so humble, penitent, and sincere ; that seemed so much above these vani-

ties ; that could speak with so much contempt of all the glory and pleasures of the world, and with so much pity of those giddy men that they now admire?

O what pillars have been shaken by prosperity; what promises broken; what sad eruptions of pride and worldliness ? What openings and sad discoveries of heart, doth this alluring trial make! And why is it that men know not themselves when they are exalted, but because they did not sufficiently know themselves when they were brought low, nor suspected enough the purposes and promises of their hearts in the day of their distress?

4. We would little think, when the heart is warmed and raised even to heaven, in holy ordinances, how cold it will grow again, and how low it will fall down? And when we have attained the clearest sight of our sincerity, we little think how quickly all such apprehensions may be lost; and how the soul, that reckons upon nothing but what it sees, or feels at present, may be at as great a loss, as if it had never perceived any fruits of the Spirit, or lineaments of the image of God upon itself. How confident, upon good grounds, is many an honest heart of its sincerity ; how certain that it desireth to be perfectly holy? (1.) That it would be rid of the nearest and dearest sin. (2.) That it loves the saints. (3.) That it loves the light of the most searching ministry. (4.) That it loves the most practical, sanctifying truths. (5.) And that it loves the ministry and means that have the greatest and most powerful tendency to make themselves more holy—all which are certain evidences of sincerity :—how clearly may the heart perceive all these, and write them down ; and yet ere long have lost the sight and sense of them all, and find itself in darkness and confusion, and perhaps be persuaded that all is contrary with them ! And when they read in their diary, or book of heart accounts, that, at such a day in examination, they found such or such an evidence, and such a one at another, and many at a third ; yet now they may be questioning whether all this were not deceit, because it seems contrary to their present sight and feeling! It is by present light that the mind discerneth, and not by that which is past and gone, and of which we cannot so easily judge by looking back. They find in their accounts, at such a time I had my soul enlarged in prayer ; at such a time I was full of joy ; at another time I had strong assurance, and boldness with God, and confidence of his love in Christ, and doubted not of the pardon of all my sins, or the justification or acceptance

of my person: but now, no joy, no assurance, no boldness, or confidence, or sense of love and pardon appear; but the soul seemeth dead, and carnal, and unrenewed: as the same trees that in summer are beautified with pleasant fruits and flowers, in winter are deprived of their natural ornaments, and seem as dead, when the life is retired to the root. The soul that once would have defied the accuser, if he had told him that he did not love the brethren, nor love the sanctifying word and means, nor desire to be holy, and to be free from sin, is now as ready to believe the accusation, and will sooner believe the tempter than the minister that watcheth for them, as one that must give account. Yea, now it will turn its own accuser, and say as Satan says, and falsely charge itself with that which Christ will acquit it of. The same work that a well composed believer hath in confuting the calumnies of Satan, the same hath a minister to do in confuting the false accusations of disturbed souls against themselves. And how subtile, how obstinate and pertinacious are they! as if they had learned some of the accuser's art—such as the uncharitable and malicious are against their neighbour.

There is not a soul so high in joy and sweet assurance, but is liable to fall as low as this. It makes our case to be much more grievous than otherwise it would be, because we know not ourselves in the hour of our consolations, and think not how apt we are to lose all our joy, and what seeds of doubts, fears, and griefs, are still within us and what cause we have to expect a change. And therefore when so sad a change befalleth us, so contrary to our expectations, it surpriseth us with terror, and casteth the poor soul almost into despair. Then crieth the distressed sinner, 'Did I ever think to see this day! Are my hopes and comforts come to this! Did I think so long that I was a child of God, and must I now perceive that he disowneth me! Did I draw near to him as my Father, and place my hope in his relief! and now must my mouth be stopped with unbelief, and must I look at him afar off, and pass by the doors of mercy with despair! Is all my sweet familiarity with the godly, and all my comfortable hours under the precious means of grace, now come to this?' O how the poor soul exclaims, 'O vile, apostate, miserable sinner! O that I had never lived to see this gloomy day! It had been better for me never to have known the way of righteousness, than thus to have relapsed; and have all the prayers that I have put up, and all the sermons I have heard, and the books that I have read, to aggravate my sin and misery. O how many a poor Christian in

this dark, mistaking case, is ready with Job to curse the day that he was born, and to say of it, 'let it be darkness, let not God regard it from above, neither let the light shine upon it: let it not be joined to the days of the year: let it not come into the number of the months, because it shut not up the doors of the womb, and hid not sorrow from mine eyes. Why died I not from the womb? Why did I not give up the ghost when I came out of the belly? Why did the knees prevent me, or why the breasts that I should suck? For now should I have lain still and been quiet. Wherefore is light given to him that is in misery, and life unto the bitter in soul; which long for death, and it cometh not; which rejoice exceedingly, and are glad when they can find the grave? Why is light given to a man whose way is hid and whom God hath hedged in?' Such are the lamentations of distressed souls, that lately were as in the arms of Christ. Their lives are a burden to them; their food is bitter to them; their health is a sickness to them; their liberty is as a prison to them; their dearest relations are become as strangers; and all their comforts are turned into sorrows, and the world seems to them as a howling wilderness, and themselves as desolate, forsaken souls. They are still as upon the cross, and will own no titles, but vile, unworthy, lost, undone, forlorn, and desolate; as if they had learned no words from Christ but 'my God, my God, why hast thou forsaken me!'

Much of this comes from the ignorance of ourselves in the time of peace and consolation. We are as David, that saith, 'in my prosperity I said, I shall never be moved: Lord, by thy favour thou hast made my mountain to stand strong: but thou didst hide thy face and I was troubled.' One frown of God, or withdrawing the light of his countenance from us, would quickly turn our day into night, cover us with sackcloth, and lay us in the dust.

Take warning therefore, dear Christians, you that are yet in the sunshine of mercy, and were never at so sad a loss, nor put to grope in the darkness of mistake and terror. No man is so well in health, but must reckon on it that he may be sick. When you feel nothing but peace and quietness of mind, expect a stormy night of fears, that may disquiet you; when you are feasting upon the sweet entertainments of your Father's love, consider that feasting is not likely to be your ordinary diet, but harder fare must be expected. Look on poor Christians in spiritual distress, with compassion; join in hearty prayer for them; and remember that this may prove your case. If you say, to what purpose should you know beforehand, how subject your are to this falling sickness.? I answer, not to anticipate, or bring on your sorrows; but if it may be, to prevent them; or if that may not be, at least to prevent the extremity and terror, and to be provided for such a storm. When you are now in health of body, and not disabled by melancholy, or other corruptions of your imagination or passion, or overwhelmed with the troubles of your mind, you have leisure calmly to understand the case of such mis-judging and distressed souls; accordingly you may avoid the things that cause it; you may be furnished with right principles, and with promises, and experiences, and recorded evidences of grace; and when comfort is withdrawn, you may by such provision understand that God changeth not, nor breaks his covenant, nor abates his love, when your apprehensions change; and that this is no sign of a forsaken soul; and that the ceasing of our feast, and withdrawing of the table, is not a turning us out of the family.

What I have said of the loss of comfort, may be said also of the diminished and interrupted operations of all grace. We little think, in the vigour of our holy progress, what falls and languishings we may find. When you have access with boldness in prayer unto God, and lively affections and words at will, and comfortable returns, remember that you may be in a sadder case; and that many a true Christian hath such withdrawings of the Spirit of prayer, as makes them think they are possessed with a dumb devil, and question whether ever they prayed acceptably at all, and cannot so much as observe the groanings of the Spirit in them.

When you are warm and vigorous in the work of God, and find delight in all the ordinances, remember that you are subject to such sicknesses as may take away your appetite, and make you say, I have no mind to hear, or read, or pray: methinks I feel no sweetness in them! I was wont to go up with comfort to the house of God; I was glad when the Lord's day was come or nigh; it did me good to see the faces of the saints: O the meltings, the strivings, the lively workings of soul that I have had in their sweet communion, when they have preached and prayed as full of the Holy Ghost, and of faith: but now I do but force myself to duty; I go to prayer as against my will; I feel small relish in the word of life. O how many Christians that little thought of such a day, cry out that spiritual death is upon them; that they are dead to prayer, and dead to meditation, and dead to holy confer-

ence; and that once they thought they were dead to the world and now they find they are dead to God. Understand beforehand that you are liable to this, and you may do much to prevent it; and if you should fall into a sickness and loss of appetite, you may be able to distinguish it from death.

When you are sweetly refreshed at the table of the Lord, and have there received a sealed pardon, as from heaven, into your bosoms, and have found delightful entertainment with the Lord, remember that the day may come, when dulness, and unbelief, and fears, may so prevail, as to make that an ordinance of greatest terror to you; that you may sit there in trembling, lest you should eat and drink your own damnation; that you may go home in fears lest Satan have there taken possession of you, or lest it have sealed you up to wrath; or you may fly from that feast which is your due, and Christ invites you to, through fears, lest it belong not to you, and should but harden you more in sin. For, alas, this sad and sinful case is too often that of true believers, who little feared it in their spiritual prosperity. This the very high expectations of such workings of soul, which they cannot often or ordinarily reach, and the frustrating of those expectations, do so often turn the table of the Lord into the bitterness of wormwood, into distracting fears and troubles, that I cannot tell whether any other part of worship occasions so much distress to many that are upright at the heart as this doth, which is appointed for their special consolation.

So when you are clear and vigorous in the life of faith, and can abhor all temptations to unbelief, and the beams of sacred truth in the scriptures have showed you that it is the undoubted word of God, and you have quietly established your soul on Christ, and built your hopes upon his promises, and can with a cheerful contempt let go the world for the accomplishment of your hopes; remember yet that there is a secret root of unbelief remaining in you, and that this odious sin is but imperfectly mortified in the best: and that it is more than possible that you may see the day when the tempter will assault you with questionings of the word of God, and trouble you with the injections of blasphemous thoughts and doubts, whether it be true or not; and that you who have thought of God, of Christ, of heaven, of the immortal state of souls, with joy, and satisfied confidence, may be in the dark about them, affrighted with wicked suggestions of the enemy, and may think of them all with troublesome, distracting doubts, and be forced to cry with the disciples, 'Lord, increase our faith.—Lord, I believe, help thou my unbelief.' Yea, worse than this; some upright souls have been so amazed and distracted by the tempter, and their distempered hearts, as to think they do not believe at all, nor yet are able sincerely to say, ' Lord, help thou my unbelief;' when yet at that time their fears and their abstaining from iniquity show that they believe the threatenings, and therefore indeed believe the word. Now if we did but thoroughly know ourselves, when faith is in its exercise and strength, and consider whether the secret seeds of remaining unbelief may bring us, being forewarned we should be fore-armed, and should fortify our faith the better, and be provided against these sad assaults. And if the malignant spirit be suffered to storm this fortress of the soul, we should more manfully resist: we should not be overwhelmed with horror, as soon as any hideous and blasphemous temptations do assault us; since Christ himself was not exempted from the most blasphemous temptation, even the worshipping of the devil instead of God ; though in him there was no sinful disposition to entertain it.

O watch and pray, Christians, in your most prosperous and comfortable state! Watch and pray, lest ye enter into temptation : for you little think what is yet within you, and what advantage the deceiver hath ; how much of your own to take his part, and how low he may bring you, both in point of grace and peace, though he cannot damn you. I am troubled that I must tell you of so sad a case, that even the children of God may fall into, lest by troubling you with the opening of your danger, I should do any thing to bring you into it. But because self-ignorance, and not being beforehand acquainted with it, may do much more, I have timely showed you the danger with the remedy.

5. Another instance of the darkness even of a heart that in part is sanctified, is in the successes of the temptations of adversity. When we want nothing, we think we value not the world, and we could bear the loss of all, but when poverty or danger comes, what trouble and unseemly murmuring is there, as if it were by a worldling that is deprived of his idol, and all the portion that ever he must have. And by the shameful complaint and stir that we make for what we want, we show more sinful overvaluing of it, and love to it, than before we observed or would believe. O how confidently and piously have I heard some inveigh against the love of the world, as if there had been no such thing in them; who yet have been so basely dejected when they have been unexpectedly stripped of their estates, as if they had been quite undone!

How patiently do we think we could bear affliction till we feel it! And how easily and piously can we exhort others unto patience, when we have no sense of what they suffer ! But when our turn is come, alas, we seem to be other men. Suffering is now another thing, and patience harder than we imagined. And how inclinable are we to hearken to temptations, to use sinful means to come out of our sufferings! Who would have thought that faithful Abraham should have been so unbelieving, as to equivocate in such a danger, and expose the chastity of his wife to hazard, as we read in Gen. xii. and that he should fall into the same sin again, on the same occasion, Gen. xx. to Abimelech, as before he had done with Pharaoh! And that Isaac should, after him, fall into the same sin, in the same place ! The life of faith doth set us so much above the fear of man, and show us the weakness and nothingness of mortal worms, and the faithfulness and all-sufficiency of God, that one would think the frowns and threatenings of a man should signify nothing to us, when God stands by, and giveth us such ample promises and security for our confirmation and encouragement ; and yet what base dejection and sinful compliances are many brought to, through the fear of man, that before the hour of temptation, could talk as courageously as any ! This was the case of Peter, and of many that have a wounded conscience, and have wronged their profession by too cowardly a disposition. If this were foreknown, we might do more for our confirmation, and betake ourselves in time to Christ, in the use of means for strength. Few turn their backs on Christ, or a good cause, in time of trial, that are jealous of themselves beforehand, and are afraid lest they should forsake him. Few fall that are afraid of falling; but the self-ignorant and self-confident are careless of their way, and it is they that fall.

. 6. Another instance that I may give you, is, in the unexpected appearances of pride in those that yet are truly humble. Humility speaks in their confessions, aggravating their sin, and searching heart and life for matter of self-accusation : they call themselves less than the least of all God's mercies. They are ready, with the woman of Canaan, even to own the name of dogs, and to confess themselves unworthy of the children's crumbs, and unworthy to tread upon the common earth, or to breathe the air, or to live upon the patience and provisions of God. They will spend whole hours and days of humiliation, in confessing their sin, and bewailing their weaknesses and want of grace, and lamenting their desert of misery. They are oft cast down so much too low, that they dare not own the title of God's children, nor any of his special grace, but take themselves for mere unsanctified hardened sinners; and all that can be said will not convince them that they have any saving interest in Christ, nor hinder them from pouring out unjust accusations against themselves. All this is done by them in the uprightness of their hearts, and not in dissimulation. And yet would you think, that with all this humility, there should be any pride; and that the same persons should lift up themselves and resist their helps to further humiliation? Do they think in their dejections, that it is in their hearts so much to exalt themselves? I confess many of them are sensible of their pride, even to the increase of their humility; and as it is said of Hezekiah, do humble themselves for the pride of their hearts, so that God's wrath doth not come upon them. But yet too few are so well acquainted with the power and rootedness of this sin at the heart, and the workings of it in the hour of temptation, as they should be. Observe it but at such times as these, and you will see that break forth which before appeared not. (1.) When we are undervalued or slighted, and meaner persons preferred before us; when our words and judgments are made light of, and our parts thought to be poor and low; when any blot or dishonour is cast upon us, deserved or undeserved; when we are slandered or reproached, and used with despite: what a matter do we make of it, and how much then doth our pride appear in our distaste, and offence, and impatience! Thus the same person that can pour out words of blame and shame against himself, cannot bear half as much from others, without displeasure and disquietness of mind. It would help us much to know this by ourselves, in the time of our humility, that we may be engaged to more watchfulness and resistance of our pride. (2.) When we are reproved for any disgraceful sin, how hardly goes it down, and how many excuses have we? How seldom are we brought to downright penitent confessions? What secret distaste is apt to be rising in our hearts against the reprover; and how seldom hath he that hearty thanks, which so great a benefit deserves! Yet would any think in our humiliations and large confessions unto God, that we were so proud? To know this of ourselves, would make us more suspicious and ashamed to be guilty of it. (3.) When any preferment or honour is to be given, or any work

to be done that is a mark of dignity, how apt are we to think ourselves as fit for it as any, and to be displeased if the honour or employment do pass by us! (4.) When we are admired, applauded, or excessively esteemed and loved, how apt are we to be too much pleased with it! This shows a proud desire to stand high in the world; and that there is much of this venom at the bottom in our hearts, even when we lay ourselves in the dust, and walk in sackcloth, and pass the heaviest judgment on ourselves.

7. Another instance of our unacquaintedness with our hearts, and the latent, undiscerned corruption of them, is our little discerning or bewailing those secret master-sins, which lie at the root of all the rest, and are the life of the old man, and the cause of all the miscarriages of our lives. As, (1.) Unbelief of the truth of the holy scriptures, of the immortality of the soul, and the life of joy or misery hereafter, and the other articles of the Christian faith. What abundance of Christians are sensible of their unbelief, as to the applying acts of faith that tend to their assurance of their own salvation, that are little sensible of any defect in the assenting act, or of any secret root of unbelief about the truth of the gospel revelations? And yet, alas, it is this that weakeneth all our graces; it is this that feedeth all our woe! O happy men were we free from this; what prayers should we put up; what lives should we lead; how watchfully should we walk; with what contempt should we look on the allurements of the world; with what disdain should we think on fleshly lusts; with what indignation should we meet the tempter, and scorn his base unreasonable motions, if we did but perfectly believe the very truth of the gospel and world to come! How careful and earnest should we be to make our calling and election sure; how great a matter should we make of sin, and of helps and hinderances in the way to heaven; how much should we prefer that state of life that furthereth our salvation, before that which strengtheneth our snares by furthering our prosperity and pleasure in the world, if we were not weak or wanting in our belief of the certain verity of these things? Did we better know the badness of our hearts herein, it would engage us more in fortifying the vitals, and looking better to our foundation, and winding up this spring of faith, which must give life to all right motions of the soul. (2.) How insensible are too many of the great imperfection of their love to God! What passionate complaints have we of their want of sorrow for their sin, and want of memory, and of ability to pray, &c. when their complaints for

want of love to God, and more affecting knowledge of him, are so cold and customary, as shows us they little observe the greatness of this sinful want! This is the very heart and poison of all the sins of our soul and life. So much as a man loves God, so much he is holy; so much he hath of the Spirit and image of Jesus Christ; so much he hath of all saving graces; so much he will abhor iniquity; and so much he will love the commands of God. As love is the sum of the law and prophets, so should it be the sum of our care and study through all our lives to exercise and strengthen it. (3.) How little are most Christians troubled for want of love to men—to brethren, neighbours and enemies: how cold are their complaints for their defects in this, in comparison of other of their complaints! But is there not cause of as deep humiliation for this sin, as almost any other? It seems to me that want of love is one of the most prevalent diseases among us, when I hear it so little seriously lamented. I often hear people say, O that we could hear more attentively and affectionately, pray more fervently, and weep for sin more plenteously: but how seldom do I hear them say, O that we did love our brethren more ardently, and our neighbours and enemies more heartily than we do, and set ourselves to do them good! There is so little pains taken to bring the heart to the love of others, and so few and cold requests put up for it, when yet the heart is backward to it, that makes me conclude that charity is weaker in most of us than we observe. And indeed it appeareth so when it comes to trial, to that trial which Christ will judge it by at last; when love must be showed by any self-denial, or costly demonstration, by parting with our food and raiment to supply the wants of others, and by hazarding ourselves for them in their distress, then see how much we love indeed! Good words cost little: so cheap an exercise of charity as, 'depart in peace, be warmed, and filled,' is an insufficient evidence of the life of grace, and will do as little for the soul of the giver, as for the body of the receiver. And how little hazardous or costly love is found among us, either to enemies, neighbours, or saints! Did we better know our hearts, there would be more care and diligence used to bring them to effectual, fervent love, than to those duties which are of less importance; and we should learn what this meaneth, 'I will have mercy and not sacrifice,' which Christ sets the pharisees twice to learn.

8. Another instance of unobserved corruption of the heart, is, the frequent and secret insinuations of selfishness in all that we do toward God or man; when we think we are serving God alone, and have cleansed our hearts from deceit, before we are aware self-interest, self-esteem, self-conceit, self-love, self-will, or self-seeking, do secretly creep in and mar the work. We think we are studying and preaching, and writing purely for God, and the common good or the benefit of souls; and perhaps little observe how subtilly selfishness insinuates, and makes a party, and sways us from holy ends, and the simplicity and sincerity which we thought we had carefully maintained: so that we are studying and preaching, and writing for ourselves, when we take no notice of it. When we enter upon any office, or desire preferment, or riches, or honour in the world, we think we do it purely for God, to furnish us for his service, and little think how much of selfishness is in our desires. When we are doing justice, or showing mercy, in giving alms, or exhorting the ungodly to repent, or doing any other work of piety or charity, we little think how much of selfishness is secretly latent in the bent and intention of the heart. When we think we are defending the truth and cause of God, by disputing, writing, or by the sword; or when we think we are faithfully maintaining on one side order and obedience against confusion and turbulent, disquiet spirits, or the unity of the church against division; or on the other hand, that we are sincerely opposing pharisaical corruptions and hypocrisy, and tyranny, and persecution, and defending the purity of divine worship, and the power and spirituality of religion; in all these cases we little know how much of carnal self may be unobserved in the work.

But above all others, Christ himself, and the Holy Ghost, that searcheth the hidden things of the heart, hath warned one sort to be suspicious of their hearts; and that is, those that cannot bear the dissent and infirmities of their brethren in tolerable things, and those that are calling for fire from heaven, and are wholly for force and cruelty in religion; for vexing, imprisoning, banishing, burning, hanging, or otherwise doing as they would not be done by, in their own case. Christ tells his two disciples, in such a case, 'ye know not what manner of spirit ye are of,' as if he should say, 'you think you purely seek my honour in the punishment of this contempt and opposition of unbelievers, and you think it will much redound to the propagation of the faith; and therefore you think that all this zeal is purely from my Spirit: but you little know how much of a proud, a carnal, selfish spirit is in these desires! You would fain have me, and your-selves with me, to be openly vindicated by fire from heaven, and be so owned by God that all men may admire you, and you may exercise a dominion in the world; and you stick not at the sufferings and ruin of these sinners, that you may attain your end: but I tell you this selfish, cruel spirit, is unlike my Spirit, which inclineth to patience, forbearance and compassion.' 'Him that is weak in the faith, receive ye; who art thou that judgest another man's servant? Why dost thou judge thy brother, and why dost thou set at nought thy brother? We shall all stand before the judgment seat of Christ.—Every one of us shall give account of himself to God.—We then that are strong, ought to bear the infirmities of the weak, and not to please ourselves. Let every one of us please his neighbour for his good to edification. Brethren, if a man be overtaken in a fault, ye which are spiritual restore such a one in the Spirit of meekness, considering thy-self, lest thou also be tempted. Bear ye one another's burden, and so fulfil the law of Christ.'

So also men are frequently mistaken, when they are zealously contending against their faith-ful pastors and their brethren, and vilifying others, and quenching love, and troubling the church, upon pretence of greater knowledge or integrity in themselves, which is notably dis-covered, and vehemently pressed by the apostle, James iii. 1., &c. where you may see how greatly the judgment of the Spirit of God, concerning our hearts, doth differ from men's judgment of themselves. They that had a domineering, con-tentious, envious zeal, did think they were of the wiser sort of Christians, and of the highest form in the school of Christ; when yet the Holy Ghost telleth them that their wisdom descended not from above, but was earthly, sensual and devilish, and that their envy and strife bring confusion and every evil work; and that the wisdom from above is neither unholy nor contentious, 'but first pure, and then peaceable, gentle and easy to be entreated.'

You see then how oft and dangerously we are deceived by ignorance of ourselves; and how selfish, carnal principles, ends and motives, are often mixed in the actions which we think are the most excellent for wisdom, zeal and piety, that ever we did perform. O therefore what cause have we to study, and search, and watch such hearts, and not too boldly or carelessly to trust them! And it is not only hypocrites that are subject to these deceitful sins, who have them in dominion, but true believers, that have a remnant of this carnal, selfish principle contin-

ually offering to insinuate itself and corrupt their most excellent works, and even all that they do.

9. The strong eruption of those passions that seemed to be quite mortified, doth show that there is more evil lurking in the heart than ordin-arily doth appear. How calmly do we converse together, how mildly do we speak, till some provoking word or wrong blows the coals, and then the dove appeareth to partake of a fierce nature, and we can perceive that in the flame which we perceive not in the spark? When a provocation can bring forth censorious, reviling, scornful words, it shows what before was latent in the heart.

10. We are very apt to think those affections to be purely spiritual, which in the issue appear to be mixed with carnality. Our very love to the assemblies and ordinances of worship, to min-isters and other servants of the Lord; to books and knowledge, are ordinarily mixed; and good and bad are strangely twisted together in the same affections and works. And the love that begin-neth in the Spirit, is apt to degenerate into carnal love, and to have too much respect to riches, or honour, or personage, or birth, or particular con-cerns of our own; and thus it is corrupted, as wine that turns into vinegar, before we are aware. And though still there be uprightness of heart, yet too much hypocrisy is joined with it, when it is little perceived or suspected.

Thus in ten instances I have showed you how much the servants of Christ themselves may be mistaken or unacquainted with their hearts; and how the work of mortification is hindered by this covering of so many secret, unob-served sins. But I must here desire you to take heed of running into the extreme of those, who hereupon conclude that their hearts being so dark and so deceitful, are not at all to be under-stood; and who therefore are still so suspicious of the worst, that they will not be persuaded of the grace that plainly worketh in them, and will condemn themselves for that which they are not guilty of, upon suspicion that they may be guilty and not know it, and think that all the sin that they forbear is but for want of a temptation: and that if they had the same temptations, they should be as bad as any others.

I would intreat these persons to consider of these truths, for their better information:

1. Temptations do not only show the evil that is in the heart, but breed much more, and turn a spark into a flame. Adam was made a sin-ner by temptation.

2. There is no Christian so mortified, but hath such remnants of corruption as would quickly

bring forth heinous sins, if temptations beyond strength were let loose upon him. What need you more proof than the sad instances of Noah, Lot, David, Solomon, and Peter? It did not prove that any of these were graceless hypocrites before, because they fell so foully by temptations; yet these objectors think they are graceless, because some strong temptations might make them fall.

3. Is it not God's way of saving men, to give them so much inward grace as no temptation can overcome, but to preserve and bring them safe to heaven, by moral conduct, together with an internal change of their hearts. And therefore he keepeth men from sin, by keeping them from temptations that are too strong for them. All human strength is limited: and there are none on earth have such a measure of grace, but a temptation may be imagined so strong as to overcome them. If God should let Satan do his worst, there must be extraordinary assistances to preserve us, or we should fall. Bless God if he lead you not into temptation, but deliver you from the evil, by keeping you far enough from the snare. This is the way of preservation that we are taught to pray and hope for.

4. It is our own duty to keep as far from temptations as we can; and if we have grace to avoid the sin by avoiding the temptation, we have such grace as God useth for the saving of his own: not that he hath saving grace that would live wickedly, if he were but tempted to it by those ordinary trials that human nature may expect: but the soul that preferreth God and glory before the pleasures of sin for a season, if it so continue, shall be saved, though possibly there might have been a temptation so strong as would have conquered the measure of grace that he had, if he had not been fortified with new supplies. It is therefore mere dotage in those that could find in their hearts to put themselves in the way of some temptation, to try whether they are sincere by the success. Avoid temptation, that you may avoid the sin and punishment. Make not yourselves worse on pretence of discovering how bad you are. All men are liable to fall, and capable of every sin, and must be saved from it by that grace which worketh on nature according to that nature, and prevaileth with reason by means agreeable to reason. If we think we are wicked, because we find that we have hearts that could be wicked, were they let alone, and because we are not removed so far from sin as to be incapable of it, we may as well say Adam was wicked in his innocency, much more David, Solomon, and Peter, before their falls.

It is not he that can sin that shall be punished; but he that doth sin, or would sin if he could, and had rather have the sin for its pleasantness to the flesh, than be free from it, and be holy, in order to salvation, and the favour, and pleasing, and enjoying of God in endless glory.

5. Lastly, let such persons try themselves by their conquest over the temptations which they have, and not by imaginary conflicts with all that they think may possibly at any time assault them. You have still the same flesh to deal with, and the same world and devil, that will not let you go to heaven without temptation: if the temptations which you have already, keep you not from preferring the love and fruition of God before the pleasure of the flesh, and a life of faith and holiness, before a life of infidelity, and impiety, and sensuality, so that you had rather live the former than the latter, I am sure your temptations have not kept you from a state of grace. And you may be assured that for the time to come, if you watch and pray, you may escape the danger of temptation; and that God will increase your strength if he increase your trials; be not secure, be you ever so holy. Think not that you have a nature that cannot sin, or cannot be tempted to a love of sin: but 'let him that thinketh he standeth, take heed lest he fall. There hath no temptation taken you, but such as is moderate, or common to man: but God is faithful, who will not suffer you to be tempted above that you are able; but will with the temptation also make a way to escape, that ye may be able to bear it.' Thus I have showed you how self-ignorance hindereth the conquest and mortifying of sin even in the godly, and now shall add some further motives.

1. Not knowing ourselves, and the secret corruptions of our hearts, doth make sin surprise us the more dangerously, and break forth the more shamefully, and wound our consciences the more terribly. The unsuspected sin hath least opposition, and when it breaks out doth, like an unobserved fire, go far before we are awakened to quench it. And it confoundeth us with shame, to find ourselves so much worse than we imagined. It overwhelmeth the soul with despairing thoughts to find itself so bad, when it thought it had been better. We are still ready to think whatever we discern that is good within us, that we may as well be mistaken now as we were before. And thus our present self-ignorance, when discovered, may hinder all the comforts of our lives.

2. Lastly, not knowing ourselves, and our particular sins, and wants, and weaknesses, doth

keep us from a particular application of the promises, and from seeking those particular remedies from Christ, which our case requireth: and so our mercies lie by neglected, while we need them and do not understand our need.

CHAPTER VIII.

EXHORTATIONS TO PIOUS PERSONS, TO KNOW AND CULTIVATE THEIR GRACES AND DUTIES.

I am next to persuade believers to know their graces and their happiness. Good is the object of voluntary knowledge, but evil of forced involuntary knowledge, unless as the knowledge of evil tendeth to some good. Therefore you should be readiest to this part of the study of yourselves: and yet, alas, the presumptuous are not more unwilling to know their sin and misery, than some perplexed Christians are backward to acknowledge their grace and happiness. How hard is it to convince them of the tender love of God towards them, and of the sincerity of their love to him; and to make them believe that they are dear to God when they loathe themselves! How hard is it to persuade them that the riches of Christ, the promises of the gospel, and the inheritance of the saints, belong to them! And the reasons, among others, are principally these,

1. The remnant of sins are so great, and so active and troublesome, as that the feeling of these contrary dispositions doth hinder them from observing the operations of grace. It is not easy to discern the sincerity of faith among so much unbelief, or the sincerity of love where there is so much averseness: or of humility where there is so much pride: or of repentance and mortification, where there is so much inclination to sin: especially when grace by its enmity to sin doth make the soul so suspicious and sensible of it, as that the observation of it turns their mind from the observation of the contrary good that is in them. Health is not observed in other parts, when the feeling of the stone, or but a tooth-ache, takes us up. The thoughts are called all to the part affected; and sickness and wounds are felt more sensibly than health. The fears of misery by sin are more easily excited, and are more passionate than love and hope, and all the affections that are employed in the prosecution of good. And in the midst of fear it is hard to feel the matter of our joys: fear is a tyrant if it exceed, and will not permit us to believe or observe the cause of hope. 'What we too much fear, we too easily believe, and hardly believe

that it is gone,' and the danger past. These fears are useful to our preservation, but they too often pervert our judgments, and hinder our due consolation. Saith Seneca, 'he that feareth snares, doth not fall into them: nor doth he quickly perish by ruin that feareth ruin: a wise man escapeth evil by always fearing it.' And the Holy Ghost saith, 'happy is the man that feareth always; but he that hardeneth his heart shall fall into mischief.'

Moderate fears, then, are given to believers for their necessary preservation, that walking among enemies and snares, they may take heed and escape them. But when this passion doth exceed, it abuseth us, and drowns the voice of reason: it maketh us believe that every temptation is a sin, and every sin is such as cannot stand with grace, and will hardly ever be pardoned by Christ. Every sin against knowledge and conscience doth seem almost unpardonable: and if it were deliberated after profession of religion, it seems to be the sin against the Holy Ghost. As children and other frightful persons that fear the devil by way of apparitions, do think in the dark he is ready to lay hold on them, so the fearful Christian is ever thinking that thing he feareth is upon him, or coming upon him. The fear of an unregenerated, unpardoned state, doth make him think he is in it; and the fear of the wrath of God doth make him think that he is under it. It is wonderfully hard, in a frighted state, or indeed in any passion that is strong, to have the free use of judgment for the knowing of ourselves, and to discern any grace, or evidence, or mercy, which is contrary to our fears, especially when the feeling of much corruption doth turn our eyes from the observation of the good, and we are still taken up with the matter of our disease.

2. Another cause that we hardly know our graces, is, because they are weak and small; and therefore in the midst of so much corruption are oftentimes hardly discerned from none. A little faith, even as a grain of mustard seed, may save us: a little love to God that is sincere will be accepted, and weak desires may be fulfilled: but they are frequently undiscerned, or their sincerity questioned by those that have them, and therefore bring but little comfort. Peter's little faith did keep him from drowning, but not from doubting and fearing he should be drowned, nor from beginning to sink; 'he walked on the water to go to Jesus; but when he saw the wind boisterous he was afraid, and beginning to sink, he cried, saying, Lord, save me. And immediately Jesus stretched forth his hand and caught him, and

said unto him, O thou of little faith, wherefore didst thou doubt?' So the little faith of the disciples kept them from perishing, but not from their fear of perishing, ' when a great tempest arose, so that the ship was covered with waves, they cry, Lord, save us, we perish: and he saith to them, Why are ye afraid, O ye of little faith?' The little faith of the same disciples entitled them to the fatherly protection and provision of God: but it kept them not from sinful cares and fears, ' about what they should eat or drink, or wherewith they should be clothed.—Take no thought for your life, what you shall eat, or drink, or for your body, what you shall put on.—Why take ye thought for raiment?—If God so clothe the grass of the field, which to day is, and to-morrow is cast into the oven, shall he not much more clothe you, O ye of little faith?' The seed that Christ likeneth his kingdom to, hath life while it is buried in the earth, and is visible while a little seed; but is not so observed as when it cometh to be as a tree. Though God despise not the day of little things, and though he will not break the bruised reed, or quench the smoking flax, yet ourselves or others cannot discern and value these obscure beginnings as God doth. But because we cannot easily find a little faith, and a little love, when we are looking for it, we take the non-appearance for a non-existence, and call it none.

3. Sanctification is often unknown to those that have it, because they do not try and judge themselves by sure infallible marks—the essentials of the new man; but by uncertain qualifications, that are mutable, and belong but to the beauty and activity of the soul.

The essence of holiness, as denominated from the object, is the consent to the three articles of the covenant of grace. (1.) That we give up ourselves to God, as our God and reconciled Father in Jesus Christ. (2.) That we give up ourselves to Jesus Christ, as our Redeemer and Saviour, to recover us, reconcile us, and bring us unto God. (3.) That we give up ourselves to the Holy Ghost as our sanctifier, to guide and illuminate us, and perfect the image of God upon us, and prepare us for glory. The essence of sanctification, as denominated from its opposite objects, is nothing but our renunciation and rejection of the flesh, the world, and the devil; of pleasures, profits, and honours, as they would be preferred before God, and draw us to forsake him. The essence of sanctification, as denominated from our faculties, which are the subject of it, is nothing but this preferring of God, and grace, and glory, above the said pleasures, profits, and honours. (1.) By the estimation of our understandings. (2.) By the resolved, habituated choice of our wills. (3.) And in the bent and drift of our endeavours in our conver ations. In these three acts, as upon the first three objects, and against the other three objects, lieth all that is essential to sanctification, and that we should judge of our sincerity and title to salvation by, as I before showed. But beside these, there are many desirable qualities and gifts, which we may seek for, and be thankful for; but are not essential to our sanctification. Such are (1.) The knowledge of other truths, besides the essentials of faith and duty, and the soundness of judgment, and freedom from error in these lesser points. (2.) A strong memory to carry away the things that we read and hear. (3.) A right order of our thoughts, when we can keep them from confusion, roving, and distraction. (4.) Freedom from too strong affections about the creatures, and from disturbing passions. (5.) Lively affections and feeling operations of the soul towards God, in holy duty; and tender meltings of the heart for sin; which are very desirable, but depend so much on temperature of the body, and outward accidents, and are but the vigour, and not the life and being of the new creature, that we must not judge of our sincerity by them. Some Christians scarcely know what any such lively feelings are; and some have them very seldom, and, I think, no one constantly: and therefore if our peace, or judgment of ourselves, be laid on these, we shall be still wavering and unsettled, and tossed up and down as the waves of the sea: sometimes seeming to be almost in heaven, and presently near the gates of hell: when our state doth not change at all, as these feelings and affectionate motions of the soul do: but we are still in our safe relation to God while our first essential graces do continue, though our failings, dulness, weaknesses and wants, must be matter of moderate filial humiliation to us.

6. The same must be said of all common gifts of utterance, in conference, or prayer, and of quickness of understanding, and such like.

7. Lastly, the same must be said also of all that rectitude of life, and those degrees of obedience that are above mere sincerity; in which one true Christian doth exceed another, and in which we should all desire to abound; but must not judge ourselves to be unsanctified, merely because we are imperfect; or to be unjustified sinners, merely because we are sinners.

In our judging of ourselves by our lives and practices, two extremes must be carefully avoided: on the left hand that of the profane, and of the Antinomians. The former cannot distinguish between sinners and sinners, sanctified and unsanctified, justified and unjustified sinners; and when they have once taken the conceit that they are in the favour of God, whatever they do, they say, we are but sinners, and so are the best. The latter teach men, that when once they are justified, they are not for any sins to doubt again of their justified state, lest they should seem to make God changeable. On the other hand must be avoided this extreme of perplexed doubting Christians, that make all their sins, or too many of them, to be matter of doubting, which should be but matter of humiliation. I know it is a very great difficulty that hath long perplexed the doctors of the church, to define what sins are consistent, and what inconsistent with a state of holiness and salvation, which if any distinguish by the names of mortal and venial, taking the words in no other sense, I shall not quarrel with them. At the present I shall say but this, for the resolving of this great and weighty question,

1. It is not the bare act of sin in itself considered, that must determine the case; but the act compared with the life of grace, and with true repentance. Whoever hath the love of God and life of grace is in a state of salvation; and therefore whatever sin consisteth with the forementioned essentials of sanctification, viz. The habitual devotion of the soul to God, the Father, Son, and Holy Ghost, and the habitual renunciation of the flesh, the world, and devil, consisteth with a state of life. True repentance proveth the pardon of all sin: and therefore whatever sin consisteth with habitual repentance, which is the hatred of sin, as sin, and hath actual repentance when it is observed, and there is time for deliberation, consisteth with a state of grace. Now in habitual conversion or repentance, the habitual willingness to leave our sins, must be more than our sinful habitual willingness to keep it. Now you may by this much discern, as to particular acts, whether they are consistent with habitual hatred of sin. For some sins are so much in the power of the will, that he that hath an habitual hatred of them, cannot frequently commit them. And some sins are also of so heinous a nature or degree, that he that habitually hateth sin, cannot frequently commit them; nor at all, while his hatred to them is in act. And he that truly repenteth of them, cannot frequently return to them; because that showeth that repentance was indeed either but superficial or not habitual. But some sins are not so great and heinous, and therefore do not so much deter

the soul, and some are not so fully in the power, of a sanctified will, as passions, thoughts, &c., and therefore may oftener be committed in consistency with habitual repentance or hatred of sin. To examine particulars would be tedious.

2. I must further answer, that our safety, and consequently our peace and comfort, lieth in flying as far from sin as we can: and therefore he that will sin as much as will consist with any sparks of grace, will bury those sparks by his sin, and shall not know that he hath any grace, nor have the comfort of it; as being in a condition unfit for actual assurance and comfort, till he be brought to actual repentance and amendment.

Thus I have shown you, by what you must try your sanctification, if you will know it; which I before proved to you from scripture.

4. Another cause that many Christians are ignorant of their state of grace, is their looking so much at what they should be, and what others are that have a high degree of grace, and what is commanded as our duty, that they observe not what they have already, because it is short of what they ought to have. We are thus too much about outward mercies. We mourn more for our friend that is dead, than we rejoice in many that are alive. We are more troubled for one mercy taken from us, than comforted in many that are left with us. We observe our diseases and our sores more sensibly than our health. David for one Absalom is so afflicted, that he wished he had died for him, though a rebel! when his comfort in Solomon, and his other children is laid aside. As all the humours flew to the pained place, so do our thoughts, as was aforesaid, and so we overlook the matter of our comfort.

5. It very much hindereth the knowledge of our graces, that we search upon so great disadvantages as hinder a true discovery. Among many others, I will instance but in two or three. (1.) We surprise our souls with sudden questions, and look for a full and satisfactory answer, before we can well recollect ourselves, and call up our evidences; and we expect to know the sum or product, before our consciences have had leisure deliberately to cast up their accounts. Yea, when we have set to it, and by diligent search with the best assistances, have discovered our sincerity, and recorded the judgment, if conscience cannot presently recall its proofs, and make it out upon every surprise, we unjustly question all is past, and will never rest in any judgment, but are still calling over all again, as if the cause

nad never been tried. And then the judgment passeth according to our present temper and disposition, when many of the circumstances are forgotten, and many of the witnesses are out of the way, that last assisted us. (2.) Perhaps we judge, as I said before, in a fit of passion, of fear, or grief, which imperiously over-ruleth or disturbeth reason : and then no wonder, if in our haste we say, that all men that would comfort us are liars. And if with David, ' In the day of our trouble, our souls do even refuse to be comforted;' and if we 'remember God, and are troubled more,' and if our ' spirit be overwhelmed in us : when he holdeth our eyes waking, and we are so troubled that we cannot speak.' And if we question whether ' the Lord will cast off for ever, and will be favourable no more :' whether ' his mercy be clean gone for ever, and his promise fail for evermore: whether he hath forgotten to be gracious, and hath shut up his tender mercies in displeasure:' till a calm deliver us from the mistake, and make us say, ' this is our infirmity,' we think that God doth cast off our souls, and ' hideth his face from us, when our soul is full of troubles, and our life draweth nigh unto the grave: when we are afflicted and ready to die from our youth up, and are distracted, while we suffer the terrors of the Lord;' as he complaineth, passion judgeth according to its nature, and not according to truth. (3.) Or perhaps we judge, when our friends, our memory, and other helps are out of the way, and we are destitute of due assistance. (4.) Or when our bodies are weak or distempered with melancholy, which representeth all this in black and terrible colours to the soul, and will hear no language but ' forsaken, miserable, and undone.' You may as well take the judgment of a man half drunk, or half asleep, about the greatest matters of your lives, as take the judgment of conscience in such a state of disadvantage, about the condition of your souls. (5.) Another hinderance to us, is, that we cannot take comfort from the former sight of grace that we have had, unless we have a continued present sight. And so all our labour in trying, and all our experiences, and all God's former manifestations of himself to the soul are lost, as to our present comfort, when our grace is out of sight: like foolish travellers, that think they are out of the way, and are ready to turn back, whenever any hill doth interpose, and hinder them from seeing the place they go to. As if it were no matter of comfort to us, to say, I did find the evidences of grace ; I once recorded a judgment of my sincerity : but the former is still questioned rather than the latter. When

with David, we should ' consider the days of old, the years of ancient times, and call to remembrance our songs in the night, and commune with our hearts in such a diligent search,' and remembrance of the mercies formerly received. (6.) Lastly, The operations of man's soul are naturally so various, and from corruption are so confused and so dark, that we are oft-times in a maze and at a loss, when we are most desirous to judge aright ; and scarcely know where, in so great disorder, to find any thing that we seek; and know it not when we find it : so that our hearts are almost as strange to themselves as to one another ; and sometimes more confident of other men's sincerity than our own, where there is no more matter for our confidence.

CHAPTER IX.

MOTIVES TO ASCERTAIN THE EVIDENCE OF OUR SANCTIFICATION.

Having thus showed you the causes of our ignorance of our sanctification, I shall briefly state some reasons that should move you to seek to be acquainted with it, where it is.

1. The knowledge of God is the most excellent knowledge ; and therefore the best sort of creature-knowledge is, that which hath the most of God in it. And undoubtedly there is more of God in holiness, which is his image, than in common things. Sins and wants have nothing of God in them; they must be fathered on the devil and yourselves. And therefore the knowledge of them is good but by accident, because the knowledge even of evil hath a tendency to good; and therefore it is commanded and made our duty, for the good which it tendeth to. It is the divine nature and image within you, which hath the most of God ; and therefore to know this is the high and noble knowledge. To know Christ within us, is our happiness on earth, in order to the knowledge of him in glory, face to face, which is the happiness of heaven. To know God, though darkly through a glass, and but in part, is far above all creature-knowledge. The knowledge of him raiseth, quickeneth, sanctifieth, enlargeth, and advanceth all our faculties. It is life eternal to know God in Christ, therefore where God appeareth most, there should our understandings be most diligently exercised in study and observation.

2. It is a most delightful, felicitating knowledge, to know that Christ is in you. If it be delightful to the rich to see their wealth, their

houses, and lands, and goods, and money: and if it be delightful to the honourable to see their attendance and hear their own commendations and applause; how delightful must it be to a true believer to find Christ within him, and to know his title to eternal life? If the knowledge of full barns, and much goods laid up for many years, can make a sensual worldling say, 'Soul, take thy ease, eat, drink, and be merry,' the knowledge of our interest in Christ and heaven, should make us say, 'Thou hast put gladness in my heart, more than in the time that their corn and wine increased; return unto thy rest, O my soul, for the Lord hath dealt bountifully with thee. If we say with David, 'blessed are they that dwell in thy house; they will be still praising thee,' much more may we say, 'blessed are they in whom Christ dwelleth, and the Holy Ghost hath made his temple'; they should be still praising thee; blessed is the man whom thou choosest, and causest to approach unto thee, that he may dwell in thy courts: we shall be satisfied with the goodness of thy house, even of thy holy temple.'

If you ask, how it is that Christ dwelleth in us; I answer, 1. Objectively, as he is apprehended by our faith and love: as the things or persons that we think of, and love and delight in, are said to dwell in our minds or hearts. 2. By the Holy Ghost, who as a principle of new and heavenly life, is given by Christ the head, unto his members; and as the agent of Christ doth illuminate, sanctify, and guide the soul. 'He that keepeth his commandments, dwelleth in him, and he in him: and hereby we know that he abideth in us, by the Spirit which he hath given us.' That of Ephes. iii. 17. may be taken in either, or both senses comprehensively, 'that Christ may dwell in your hearts by faith.'

3. Did you know that Christ is in you by his Spirit, it might make every place and condition comfortable to you! If you are alone, it may rejoice you to think what company dwelleth continually with you in your hearts. If you are wearied with evil company without, it may comfort you to think that you have better within: when you have communion with the saints, it is your joy to think that you have nearer communion with the Lord of saints. You may well say with David, 'when I awake I am still with thee; I have set the Lord always before me; because he is at my right hand, I shall not be moved.'

4. Did you know Christ within you, it would much help you in believing what is written of him in the gospel. Though to the ungodly the mysteries of the kingdom of God do seem incredible, yet when you have experience of the power of it on your souls, and find the image of it on your hearts, and the same Christ within you, conforming you to what he commandeth in his word, this will work such a suitableness to the gospel in your hearts, as will make the work of faith more easy. Saith the apostle, 'we have seen, and do testify, that the Father sent the Son to be the Saviour of the world'—there is their outward experience,—'and we have known and believed the love that God hath to us: God is love, and he that dwelleth in love dwelleth in God, and God in him:' there is their faith confirmed by their inward evidence. No wonder if they that have God dwelling in them by holy love, do believe the love that God hath to them. This is the great advantage that the sanctified have in the work of faith, above those that much excel them in disputing, and are furnished with more arguments for the Christian verity; Christ hath his witness abiding in them. The fruits of the Spirit bear witness to the 'incorruptible seed, the word of God that liveth and abideth for ever;' the impress on the heart bears witness to the seal that caused it. Labour to know the truth of your sanctification, that you may be confirmed by it in the truth of the word that sanctifieth you, and may rejoice in him 'that hath chosen you to salvation, through sanctification of the Spirit, and belief of the truth.'

5. If you can come to the knowledge of Christ within you, it will be much easier to trust upon him, and fly to him in all your particular necessities, and to make use of his mediatorship with holy confidence. When others fly from Christ with trembling, and know not whether he will speak for them, or help them, but look at him with strange and doubtful thoughts, it will be otherwise with you that have assurance of his continual love and presence. When you find Christ so near you, as to dwell within you, and so particular and abundant in his love to you, as to have given you his Spirit, and all his graces, it will produce a sweet delightful boldness, and make you run to him as your help and refuge, in all your necessities. When you find the great promise fulfilled to yourselves, 'I will put my law in their hearts, and in their minds will I write them, and their sins and iniquities will I remember no more,' you will 'have boldness to enter into the holiest by the blood of Jesus; by the new and living way which he hath consecrated for us, through the veil, that is to say, his flesh. And having an high priest over the house of God, you may draw near with a true

heart, in full assurance of faith, having your hearts sprinkled from an evil conscience, (or the conscience of evil) as your bodies are washed (in baptism) with pure water. In Christ we may have boldness and access with confidence, by the faith of him.' This intimate acquaintance with our great high priest, who is passed into the heavens, and yet abideth and reigneth in our hearts, will encourage us to 'hold fast our profession, and to come boldly to the throne of grace, that we may obtain mercy, and find grace to help in time of need,' when by unfeigned love, we 'know that we are of the truth, and may assure our hearts before him, and our heart condemneth us not, then we have confidence towards God; and whatever we ask we receive of him, because we keep his commandments, and do those things that are pleasing in his sight.'

6. When once you know that you have Christ within you, you may cheerfully proceed in the way of life ; when doubting Christians, that know not whether they are in the way or not, are still looking behind them, and spend their time in perplexed fears, lest they be out of the way, and go on with heaviness and trouble, as uncertain whether they may not lose their labour ; and are still questioning their ground work, when the building should go on. It is an unspeakable mercy, when a believing soul is freed from these distracting, hindering doubts, and may boldly and cheerfully hold on his way, and be walking or working, when other men are fearing and inquiring the way; and may with patience and comfort wait for the reward, the crown of life, when others are still questioning whether they were ever regenerated, and whether their hopes have any ground. We may be 'stedfast, unmoveable, always abounding in the work of the Lord, when we know that our labour is not in vain in the Lord;' we may then 'gird up the loins of the mind, and in sobriety hope unto the end, for the grace that is to be brought us at the revelation of Jesus Christ.'

7. When you are assured that you have Christ within you, it may preserve you from those terrors of soul that affright them that have no such assurance. He that knoweth what it is to think of the intolerable wrath of God, and says, I fear I am the object of this wrath, and must bear this intolerable load everlastingly, may know what a mercy it is to be assured of our escape. He that knows what it is to think of hell, and say, I know not but those endless flames may be my portion, will know what a mercy it is to be assured of a deliverance, and to be able to say, I know I am saved from the wrath to come ; and that 'we are not of them that draw back to perdition, but of them that believe, to the saving of the soul ;' and that 'God hath not appointed us to wrath, but to obtain salvation by our Lord Jesus Christ, who died for us, that whether we wake or sleep, we should live together with him :' we may comfort ourselves together, and edify one another,' when we have this assurance.

They who have felt the burden of a wounded spirit, and know what it is to feel the terrors of the Lord, to see hell fire as it were before their eyes, to be kept waking by the dreadful apprehensions of their danger, and to be pursued daily by an accusing conscience, setting their sins in order before them, and bringing the threatenings of God to their remembrance ; these persons will understand, that to be assured of a Christ within us, and consequently of a Christ that is preparing a place of glory for us, is a mercy that the mind of man is now unable to value, according to the ten thousandth part of its worth.

8. Were you assured that Christ himself is in you, it would sweeten all the mercies of your lives. It would assure you that they are all the pledges of his love ; and love in all, would be the substance and the life of all your friends, your health, your wealth, your deliverances, would be steeped in the dearest love of Christ, and have a spiritual sweetness in them, when to the worldling they have but a carnal, unwholesome, luscious sweetness : and to the doubting Christians they will be turned into troubles ; while they are questioning the love, and meaning of the giver; and whether they are sent for good to them, or to aggravate their condemnation ; and the company of the giver will advance your estimation of the gift. Lowly things with the company of our dearest friends, are sweeter than abundance in their absence. Your money, your goods, your books and your friends in near and sweet society, are all advanced to a higher value, when you know that you have also Christ in your hearts ; and that all these are but the attendants of your Lord, and the fruits that drop from the tree of life, and the tokens of his love, importing greater things to follow. Whereas in the crowd of all those mercies, the soul would be uncomfortable, or worse, if it missed the presence of its dearest friend : and in the midst of all, would live but as in a wilderness, and go seeking after Christ with tears, as Mary at his sepulchre, because they had taken away her Lord, and she knew not where they had laid him, all mercies would be bitter to us, if the presence of

Christ did not put into them that special sweetness which is above the estimate of sense.

9. This assurance would do much to preserve you from the temptation of sensual delights. While you had within you matter of more excellent contentment, and when you find that these inferior pleasures are enemies to those which are your happiness and life, you will not be easily taken with the bait. The poorest brutish pleasures are made much of by them that never were acquainted with any better. But after the sweetness of assurance of the love of God, how little relish is there to be found in the pleasures that are so valued by sensual unbelievers! Let them take them for me, saith the believing soul; may I but still have the comforts of the presence of my Lord, how little shall I miss them? How easily can I spare them? Silver will be cast by, if it be set in competition with gold. The company of common acquaintance may be acceptable, till better and greater come; and then they must give place. Men that are taken up with the pleasing entertainment of Christ within them, can scarcely afford any more than a transient salutation or observance to those earthly things that are the felicity of the carnal mind, and take up its desires, endeavours and delight; when the soul is tempted to turn from Christ, to those deceiving vanities that promise him more content and pleasure, the comfortable thoughts of the love of Christ, and his abode within us, and our abode with him, do sensibly scatter and confound such temptations. The presence of Christ, the great reconciler, doth reconcile us to ourselves, and make us willing to be more at home. He that is out of love with the company that he hath at home, is easily drawn to go abroad. But who can endure to be much abroad, that knoweth of such a guest as Christ at home? We shall say as Peter, 'Lord, to whom shall we go? Thou hast the words of eternal life; and we believe, and are sure, that thou art that Christ, the Son of the living God.' And as when he saw him in a little of his glory, 'Master, it is good for us to be here.' And if the riches of the world were offered to draw a soul from Christ, that hath the knowledge of his special love and presence, the tempter would have no better entertainment than Simon Magus had with Peter, their money perish with them that think Christ and his graces to be no better than money.

10. How easy and sweet would all God's service be to you, if you were assured that Christ abideth in you? What delightful access might you have in prayer, when you know that Christ himself speaks for you! Not as if the Father himself were unwilling to do us good, but that he will do it in the name, and for the sake and merits of his Son: which is the meaning of Christ in those words, which seem to deny his intercession: 'At that day ye shall ask in my name; and I say not unto you, that I will pray the Father for you: for the Father himself loveth you, because ye have loved me,' &c. I appeal to your own hearts, Christians, whether you would not be much more willing and ready to pray? And whether prayer would not be a sweeter employment to you, if you were sure of Christ's abode within you, and intercession for you, and consequently that all your prayers are graciously accepted of the Lord! You would not then desire the vain society of empty persons; nor seek for recreation in their insipid, insignificant discourse. The opening of your heart to your heavenly Father, and pleading the merits of his Son in your believing petitions for his saving benefits, would be a more satisfactory kind of pleasure to you.

How sweet would meditation be to you, if you could still think on Christ, and all the riches of his kingdom, as your own? Could you look up to heaven, and say with grounded confidence, it is mine, and there I must abide and reign for ever! Could you think of the heavenly host, as those that must be your own companions, and of their holy employments as that which must be your own for ever, it would make the assent of your minds to be more frequent, and meditation to be a more pleasant work. Were you but assured of your special interest in God, and that all his attributes are by his love and covenant engaged for your happiness, experience would make you say, ' in the multitude of my thoughts within me, thy comforts do delight my soul.—I will sing unto the Lord as long as I live: I will sing praise to my God while I have my being: my meditation of him shall be sweet; I will be glad in the Lord.' Could you say with full assurance, that you are the children of the promises, and that they are all your own, how sweet would the reading and meditation on the holy scriptures be to you! How dearly would you love the word! What a treasure would you judge it! 'your delight would be then in the law of the Lord, and you would meditate in it day and night.' To find such grounds of faith, and hope, and riches of consolation in every page, and assuredly to say, 'all this is mine,' would make you better understand why David did indite all the 119th Psalm, in high commendations of the word of God, and would make you join in his affectionate expressions, ' O how I love thy law! It is my meditation all the day. Thou through thy commandments hast made me wiser than mine enemies; for it is ever with me.'

Sermons also would be much sweeter to you, when you could confidently take home the consolatory part, and use our ministry as a help to your faith, and hope, and joy; whereas your doubts and fears, lest you are still unregenerated, will turn all that you hear, or read, or meditate on, into food and fuel for themselves to work upon; and you will gather up all that tends to your disquietude, and say, it is your part; and cast away all that tendeth to your consolation, and say, it belongeth not to you. The most comforting passages of the word will be turned into your discomfort: the promises will seem to you as none, while you imagine that they are none of yours: and the loss of your peace and comfort will not be the worst. But this will increase your backwardness to duty; and when your delight in the worship of God is gone, your inclination to it will abate, and it will seem a burden to you, as meat to the stomachs of the sick.

The same I may say of the sacrament of the Lord's supper. How sweet will it be to you, if you are assured that the same Christ that is there represented as broken and bleeding for your sins, doth dwell within you by his Spirit. What welcome entertainment would you expect to find, if you knew that you brought the feast, and the master of the feast with you in your hearts; and had there entirely entertained him, with whom you expect communion in the sacrament! How boldly and comfortably would your hungry souls then feed upon him! With what refreshing acts of faith would you there take the sealed promise and pardon of your sins! Whereas when you come in fears and doubting, and must take the body and blood of Christ in their representations, with your hand and mouth, while you know not whether you receive him with the heart, and whether you have any special interest in him, O what a damp it casteth on the soul! How it stifleth its hopes and joys, and turneth the sacrament, which is appointed for their comfort, into their greater trouble! It hath many a time grieved me to observe that no ordinance doth cast many upright souls into greater perplexities, and discouragements, and distresses, than the Lord's supper, because they come to it with double reverence, and by the doubtings of their title, the questioning of their preparedness, and by their fears of eating and drinking unworthily, their souls are utterly discomposed with perplexing passions, and turned from the pleasant exercise of faith, and the delightful intercourse

that they should have with God; are distempered and put out of relish to all the sweetness of the gospel: and frightened from the sacrament by such sad experiences that they dare come thither no more, for fear of eating judgment to themselves. Therefore should not Christians labour to remove the cause of such miserable distracting fears, that so much wrong both Christ and them, and try to recover their well-grounded peace and comfort?

Your love to God, which is the heart and life of the new creature, doth so much depend upon your knowledge of his love to you, as should make you much more desirous of such a knowledge. Love is the end of faith; and faith the way to love. So much of love as is in every duty, so much holiness is in it, and no more. Love is the sum of the commandments. It is the fulfilling of the law; though God loved us first, as purposing our good, before we loved him. And we therefore love him, because he first loved us, yet doth he love us by complacency and acceptance, because we love the Father and the Son: 'for the Father himself loveth you, because ye have loved me, and have believed that I came out from God.' And what will more effectually kindle in you the fervent love of Christ, than to know that he loveth you, and dwelleth in you? All this is expressed by Christ himself; 'at that day ye shall know that I am in my Father, and you in me, and I in you: he that hath my commandments and keepeth them, he it is that loveth me; and he that loveth me, shall be loved of my Father, and I will love him, and will manifest myself to him.—If a man love me, he will keep my words, and my Father will love him, and we will come unto him, and make our abode with him.—If any man love God the same is known of him,' with a knowledge of special love and approbation. This is no disparagement to faith, whose nature and use is to work by love; what a man loveth, such he is. The love is the man. Our love is judged by our life, as the cause by the effect: but the life is judged by the love, as the fruits by the tree, the effects by the cause. 'Our manners are not used to be judged of,' saith Augustine, 'according to that which every man knoweth, but according to that which he loveth: it is only good or evil love, that maketh good or evil manners.' If Plato could say, 'to be a philosopher is to love God;' much more should we say, this is the doctrine and the work of a Christian, even the love of God. Indeed it is the work of the redeemer, to recover the heart of man to God, and to bring us to love him by representing him to us as the most amiable, suitable object of our love: and the perfection of love is heaven itself. 'The yoke of holy love, O how sweetly dost thou surprise? How gloriously dost thou enthral? How pleasantly dost thou press? How delightfully dost thou load? How strongly dost thou bind? How prudently dost thou instruct.' Again, 'O happy love, from which ariseth the strength of manners, the purity of affections, the subtilty of intellects, the sanctity of desires, the excellency of works, the fruitfulness of virtues, the dignity of deserts, the sublimity of the reward!' I appeal to your own consciences, Christians, would you not think it a fore-taste of heaven upon earth, if you could but love God as much as you desire? Would any kind of life that you can imagine, be so desirable and delightful to you? Would any thing be more acceptable unto God? And on the contrary, a soul without the love of God, is worse than a corpse without a soul. 'If any man love not the Lord Jesus Christ, let him be anathema, maranatha.'

And do I need to tell you what a powerful incentive it is to love, to know that you are beloved? It will make Christ much more dear to you, to know how dear you are to him. What is said of affective love in us, may partly be said of attractive love in Christ; 'many waters cannot quench love, neither can the floods drown it:' no riches can purchase what it can attract. When you find that he hath set you as a seal upon his arm and heart, and that you are dear to him as the apple of his eye, what holy flames will this kindle in your breast! If it be almost impossible with your equals upon earth not to love them that love you (which Christ telleth you that even publicans will do,) how much more should the love of Christ constrain us abundantly to love him, when being infinitely above us, his love descendeth that ours may ascend! His love puts forth the hand from heaven to draw us up.

O Christians, you little know how Satan wrongeth you, by drawing you to deny, or doubt of the special love of God. How can you love him that you apprehend to be your enemy, and to intend your ruin? Doubtless not so easily as if you know him to be your friend. In reason is there any more likely way to draw you to hate God, than to draw you to believe that he hateth you? Can your thoughts be pleasant of him? Or your speeches of him sweet? Or can you attend him, or draw near to him with delight, while you think he hateth you, and hath decreed your damnation? You may fear him, as he is a terrible avenger; and you may confess his judg-

ments to be just: but can you amicably embrace the consuming fire, and love to dwell with the everlasting burnings!

O therefore, as ever you would have the love of God to animate, and sanctify, and delight your souls, study the greatness of his love to you, and labour with all possible speed and diligence, to find that Christ by his Spirit is within you. It is the whole work of sanctification that Satan would destroy or weaken by your doubts: and it is the whole work of sanctification that by love would be promoted, if you knew your interest in the love of Christ.

12. It is the knowledge of Christ dwelling in you, and so of the special love of God, that must acquaint you with a life of holy thankfulness and praise. These highest and most acceptable duties, will be out of your reach if Satan can hide from you that mercy which must be the chief matter of your thanksgiving. Will that soul be in tune for the high praises of the Lord, that thinks he meaneth to treat him as an enemy? Can you look for any cheerful thanksgiving from him that looks to lie in hell? Will he not rather cry with David, 'in death there is no remembrance of thee: in the grave who shall give thee thanks? What profit is there in my blood, when I go down to the pit? Shall the dust praise thee? Shall it declare thy truth?' Shall the damned praise thee, or shall they give thee thanks that must be scorched with the flames of thine indignation? Can you expect that joy should be in their hearts, or cheerfulness in their countenances, or praises in their mouths, that think they are reprobated? Undoubtedly Satan is not ignorant, that this is the way to deprive God of the service which is most acceptable to him, and you of the pleasures of so sweet a life. And therefore he that envieth both, will do his worst to damp your spirits, and breed uncomfortable doubts and fears, and wrongful suspicions in your minds. Whereas the knowledge of your interest in Christ, would be a continual store-house of thanksgiving and praise, and teach your hearts as well as your tongues, to say with David, 'blessed is the man whose transgression is forgiven, whose sin is covered; blessed is the man unto whom the Lord imputeth not iniquity, and in whose spirit there is no guile.—Be glad in the Lord, and rejoice ye righteous, and shout for joy all ye that are upright in heart.—Bless the Lord, O my soul, and all that is within me bless his holy name: bless the Lord, O my soul, and forget not all his benefits: who forgiveth all thine iniquities: who healeth all thy diseases: who redeemeth thy life from destruction, and crowneth thee with loving kindness and tender

mercies. O Lord, my God, I cried unto thee, and thou hast healed me: O Lord, thou hast brought up my soul from the grave; thou hast kept me alive that I should not go down to the pit; sing unto the Lord, O ye saints of his, and give thanks at the remembrance of his holiness: for his anger endureth but for a moment: in his favour is life.' Thanksgiving would be the very pulse and breath of your assurance of Christ dwelling in you. You would say with Paul, 'blessed be the God and Father of our Lord Jesus Christ, who hath blessed us with all spiritual blessings in celestials in Christ: according as he hath chosen us in him before the foundation of the world, that we should be holy and blameless before him in love: having predestinated us to the adoption of children by Jesus Christ to himself, according to the good pleasure of his will, to the praise of the glory of his grace, wherein he hath made us accepted in the Beloved, in whom we have redemption through his blood, the remission of sins, according to the riches of his grace, wherein he hath abounded toward us,' &c. Thus faith and assurance, as they have an unspeakable store to work upon, so it is natural to them to expatiate in the praise of our redeemer, and to delight in amplifications and commemorations of the ways of grace. Just so doth Peter begin his first epistle; 'blessed be the God and Father of our Lord Jesus Christ, which according to his abundant mercy hath begotten us again unto a lively hope, by the resurrection of Jesus Christ from the dead, to an inheritance incorruptible, undefiled, and that fadeth not away, reserved in heaven for you who are kept by the power of God, through faith unto salvation, ready to be revealed in the last time, wherein ye greatly rejoice.'

No wonder if the heirs of heaven be inclined to the language and the work of heaven. I think there are few of you that would not rejoice, and by your speech and countenance express your joy, if you had assurance but of the dignities and dominions of this world. And can he choose but to express his joy and thankfulness that hath assurance of the crown of life? What fragrant thoughts should possess the mind that knoweth itself to be possessed by the Spirit of the living God! How thankful will he be who knows he hath Christ and heaven to be thankful for! What sweet delights should fill up the hours of that man's life, who knows the Son of God liveth in him, and that he shall live in joy with Christ for ever! How gladly will he be exercised in the praises of his creator, redeemer and sanctifier, who knows it must be his work for ever!

No wonder if this joy be a stranger to their hearts, that are strangers to Christ, or strangers to their interest in his love: no wonder if they have no hearts for these celestial works, that have no part in the celestial inheritance, or that know not that they have any part therein. How can they joyfully give thanks for that which they know not that they have or ever shall have, or have any probability to attain?

But to that man who is assured of Christ within him, heaven and earth, and all their store, do offer themselves as the matter of his thanks, and do furnish him with provisions to feed his praises. What a shame is it that an assured heir of heaven should be barren in comfort to himself, or in thanks and praise to Jesus Christ, when he hath so much love and mercy to bring his motives from, and hath two worlds to furnish him with the materials; and hath no less than infinite goodness, even God himself, to be the subject of his praise! 'O give thanks unto the Lord, for he is good, because his mercy endureth for ever; let Israel say, let the house of Aaron say, let them that fear the Lord say, that his mercy endureth for ever.' The knowledge of our interest fitteth us for his praise. 'Thou art my God, and I will praise thee: thou art my God, and I will exalt thee. O Lord, truly I am thy servant, I am thy servant, and the son of thine handmaid: thou hast loosed my bonds; I will offer to thee the sacrifice of thanksgiving, and will call upon the name of the Lord.' His praise is for the congregation of his saints, 'let Israel rejoice in him that made him; let the children of Zion be joyful in their king.—Let them praise the name of the Lord; for his name alone is excellent, his glory is above the earth and heaven. He also exalteth the horn of his people; the praise of all his saints, even of the children of Israel, a people near unto him. I will also clothe his priests with salvation, and his saints shall shout aloud for joy.' Praise is a work so proper for the saints, and thanksgiving must be so fed with the knowledge of your mercies, that Satan well knoweth what he shall get by it, and what you will lose, if he can but hide your mercies from you. The height of his malice is against the Lord, and the next is against you. And how can he show it more than by drawing you to rob God of his thanks and praise, when he hath blessed and enriched you with the chiefest of his mercies? Labour therefore, Christians, to know that you have that grace that may be the matter and cause of so sweet and acceptable an employment as the praises of your Lord.

13. Moreover, you should consider that with-

out the knowledge of your interest in Christ, you cannot live to the honour of your redeemer, in such a measure as the gospel doth require. The excellency of gospel-mercies will be veiled and obscured by you, and will not be revealed and honoured by your lives. Your low and poor dejected spirits will be a dishonour to the faith and hope of the saints, and to the glorious inheritance, of which you have so full a prospect in the promises. The heirs of heaven, that know not themselves to be such, may live like the heirs of heaven, as to uprightness and humility, but not in the triumphant joy, nor in the courageous boldness, which becometh a believer. What an injury and dishonour is it to our redeemer, that when he hath done and suffered so much to make us happy, we should walk as heavily as if he had done nothing for us at all! And when he hath so fully secured us of everlasting happiness, and told us of it so expressly that our joy may be full, we should live as if the gospel were not the gospel, and such things had never been promised or revealed! When heaven is the object, and the promise of God is the ground work of our faith, we should live above all earthly things, as having the honours and pleasures of the world under our feet, accounting all as loss and dung for the excellency of the knowledge of Jesus Christ, whom we should love, though, ' we have not seen him ; in whom though now we see him not, yet believing, we should rejoice with joy unspeakable and full of glory, as those that must receive the end of their faith, the salvation of our souls.' And how can we do this, if we are still questioning the love of Christ, or our interest in it!

Believers should with undaunted resolution charge through the armies of temptation, and conquer difficulties, and suffer for the name of Christ with joy ; accounting it a blessed thing to be persecuted for righteousness' sake, because theirs is the kingdom of heaven. Because of the greatness of the reward, they should rejoice and be exceeding glad; and how can they do this, that believe not that the reward and kingdom will be theirs? The joys of faith and confidence on the promise and strength of Christ, should overcome all inordinate fears of man ; ' for he hath said, I will never fail thee nor forsake thee : so that we may boldly say, the Lord is my helper, and I will not fear what man shall do unto me,' and how can we do this, while we are questioning our part in Christ and the promise that we should thus boldly trust upon?

14. Lastly consider, that the knowledge of your part in Christ may make all sufferings easy to you. You will be so much satisfied in God your portion, as will abate the desires and drown the joys and sorrows of the world. You will judge the sufferings of this present time unworthy to be compared to the glory that shall be revealed in us ; you will choose 'rather to suffer affliction with the people of God, than to enjoy the pleasures of sin for a season, esteeming the reproach of Christ greater riches than the treasures of the world, as having respect to the recompence of reward.' All this must be done, and will be done by true believers, that have an assurance of their own sincerity ; they must and will forsake all, and take up the cross and follow Christ, in hope of a reward in heaven, as it is offered them in the gospel, when they know their special interest in it. For these are Christ's terms which he imposeth on all that will be his disciples. But you may certainly perceive that it will be much more easy to part with all, and undergo and do all this, when we have the great encouragement of our assured interest, than when we have no more but the common offer. To instance in some particulars.

1. Do you live where serious godliness is derided, and you cannot obey the word of God, and seek first the kingdom of God, and its righteousness, without being made the common scorn, and the daily jest and by-word of the company ? Let it be so : if you know that you have Christ within you, and are secured of everlasting joys, will you feel, will you regard such things as these ? Shall the jest of a distracted, miserable fool, abate the joy of your assured happiness ? Princes and noblemen will not forsake their dominions or lordships, nor cast away the esteem and comfort of all they have, because the poor do ordinarily reproach them as proud and unmerciful oppressors. They think they may bear the words of the miserable, while they have the pleasure of prosperity. And shall not we give losers leave to talk ? We will not be mocked out of the comfort of our health or wealth, our habitations or our friends; and shall we be mocked out of the comfort of Christ, and out of the presence of the comforter himself! If they that go naked deride you for having clothes, and they that are out of doors in the cold and rain deride you that are warm and dry within ; or they that are sick deride you for being well, this will but make you more sensible of your felicity, and pity them that have added such folly to their wants : so will it increase the sense of your felicity to find that you are possessed of so unspeakable a mercy, which others have not so far tasted of as to know its worth.

2. If you have the contradictions and opposition of the ignorant or malicious, speaking evil of things they know not, and persuading you from the ways of righteousness, how easily may all this be borne while you have Christ within you to strengthen and encourage you! Had you but his example before you, who is 'the author and finisher of your faith, who for the joy that was set before him endured the cross, despising the shame, and endured the contradiction of sinners against himself,' it should keep you from being weary and fainting in your minds. But when you have his presence, his Spirit, and his help, how much should it corroborate and confirm you?

3. How easily may you bear the slanders of your own or the gospel's enemies, as long as you are sure of your interest in Christ? How easily may you suffer them to call you by their own names, 'pestilent fellows, movers of sedition among the people, ring-leaders of a sect, profaners of the temple,' as Paul was called, so long as you have Christ within you, who was called Beelzebub for your sakes. Your judge that must finally decide the case, is your dearest friend, and dwelleth in you: it is he that will justify you; who is he that condemneth you? His approbation is your life and comfort. How inconsiderable is it as to your own felicity, what mortal worms shall say or think of you? What if they call you all that is naught, and stain your names, and obscure your innocency, and make others believe the falsest accusations that Satan can use their tongues to utter of you? You have enough against all this within you. What if you go for hypocrites, or factious or whatever malignity can call you, until the day of judgment? As long as you have so good security of being then fully cleared of all, and your righteousness vindicated by your judge, how easily may you now bear the slanders of men, that prove themselves wicked, by falsely affirming it of you? And you may well endure to be called proud, while you are humble; and factious, while you are the lovers of unity and peace; or hypocrites, while you are sincere. How boldly may you say with the prophet, 'the Lord God will help me, therefore shall I not be confounded; therefore have I set my face like a flint, and I know that I shall not be ashamed. He is near that justifieth me: who will contend with me? let us stand together: who is mine adversary? let him come near to me: behold the Lord God will help me; who is he that shall condemn me? Lo, they shall all wax old as a garment; the moth shall eat them up.'

Had you but Paul's assurance and experience of Christ dwelling in you, you might imitate him in a holy contempt of all the slanders and revilings of the world. 'I think that God hath set forth us the apostles last, as it were men appointed to death; for we are made a spectacle to the world, and to angels, and to men; we are fools for Christ's sake, but ye are wise in Christ; we are weak, but ye are strong; ye are honourable, but we are despised: even unto this present hour we both hunger, and thirst, and are naked, and are buffeted, and have no certain dwelling place; and labour, working with our own hands. Being reviled, we bless; being persecuted, we suffer it; being defamed, we intreat: we are made as the filth of the world, and are the off-scouring of all things unto this day.' Thus may we do and suffer all things through Christ that strengtheneth us. What matter is it what men call us, if God call us his children and friends, and Christ be not ashamed to call us brethren? With us it will be a very small thing to be judged of man, while we know the Lord that must judge us is on our side. It lieth not on our hands to justify ourselves: it is Christ that hath undertaken to answer for us, and made it the work of his office to justify us: to him we may boldly and comfortably leave it, and let all the accusers prepare their charge, and deal with him, and do their worst.

4. How easily may you bear imprisonment, banishment, or other persecution, as long as you are assured of the love of Christ? Can you fear to dwell where Christ dwells with you? If he will go with you through fire and water, what need you fear? God's owning, appropriating words, may make us venture upon the greatest perils. 'Fear not, for I have redeemed thee; I have called thee by thy name, thou art mine: when thou passest through the waters, I will be with thee, and through the rivers, they shall not overflow thee; when thou walkest through the fire, thou shalt not be burnt.—For I am the Lord thy God, the holy One of Israel, thy Saviour.' Who would not with Peter cast himself into the sea, or walk with confidence upon the waters, if Christ be there and call us to him?

The eleventh chapter to the Hebrews doth recapitulate the victories of faith, and show us what the hope of unseen things can cause believers patiently to undergo. How cheerfully will he endure the foulest way, who is assured to come safe to such a home? What will a man stick at, that knows he is following Christ to heaven, and knoweth that he shall reign with him, when he hath suffered with him? He is unworthy of

Christ, and of salvation, that thinks any thing in the world too good to lose for them. What matter is it whether death finds us in honour or dishonour, in our own country or in another, at liberty or in prison, so we are sure it finds us not in a state of death? Who would not rather pass to glory by as strait a way as John the Baptist, Stephen, or other martyrs did, than, with their persecutors, to prosper in the way to misery? Who can for shame repine at the loss of temporal commodities, that is secured of the eternal joys? If assurance of the love of God, will not embolden you to patient suffering, and to lay down life and all for Christ, what do you think will ever do it? But when you are afraid lest death will turn you into hell, what wonder if you timorously draw back? When you know not whether ever you shall have any better, no wonder if you are loathe to part with the seeming happiness which you have. Those doubts and fears enfeeble the soul, and spoil you of that valour that becomes a soldier of Christ.

5. All personal crosses in your estates, your families, your friends, your health, will be easily borne, if you are once assured of your salvation. To a man that is passing to heaven, all these are almost inconsiderable things. What is Lazarus the worse now for his sores or rags; or what is the rich man the better for his sumptuous attire and fare? Whether you be poor or rich, sick or sound; whether you are used kindly or unkindly in this world, are questions of so small importance that you are not much concerned in the answer of them: but whether you have Christ within you, or be reprobates—whether you are the heirs of the promise, or are under the curse, are questions of everlasting consequence.

6. Lastly, you may comfortably receive the sentence of death, when once you are assured of the life of grace, and that you have escaped everlasting death. Though nature will be still averse to a dissolution, yet faith will make you cheerfully submit, desiring to depart and be with Christ, as the best condition for you. When you ' know that if the earthly house of this tabernacle were dissolved, you have a building of God, a house not made with hands, eternal in the heavens; you will then groan earnestly, desiring to be clothed upon with your house, which is from heaven:' not to be unclothed, (for the union of soul and body is the constitution of the man, which nature cannot but desire) but to be clothed upon, that mortality might be swallowed up of life.' This ' God doth work you for,' who 'giveth you the earnest of the Spirit: therefore as men that know while you are at home in the body,

you are absent from the Lord ; and that walk by faith, and not by sight, you would be always confident, and willing rather to be absent from the body, and present with the Lord.'

Though it be troublesome to remove your dwelling, yet you would not hesitate about the trouble, if you were sure to change a cottage for a palace ; nor would you refuse to cross the seas, to change a prison for a kingdom. The holy desires of believers do prepare them for a safe death; but it is the assurance of their future happiness, or the believing expectation of it, that must prepare them for a death that is safe and comfortable. The death of the presumptuous may be quiet, but not safe: the death of doubting, troubled believers may be safe, but not quiet: the death of the ungodly, that have awakened, undeceived consciences, is neither safe nor quiet : but the death of strong believers, that have attained assurance, is both. And he that findeth Christ within him, may know, that when he dieth, he shall be with Christ : his dwelling in us by faith, by love, and by his Spirit, is a pledge that we shall dwell with him. Christ within, will certainly carry us to Christ above. Let Socinians question the happiness of such departed souls, or doubt whether they be in heaven before the resurrection, I am sure that they are with Christ, as the following places show, 2 Cor. v. 7, 8. and Phil. i. 23. and many others. We are following him, who when he had conquered death, and went before us, did send that message to his doubting, troubled disciples, which is to me so full of sweetness, that methinks I can scarcely too oft recite it, ' go to my brethren, and say unto them, I ascend unto my Father and your Father, and to my God and to your God.' O piercing, melting words, which write themselves upon my heart, whenever I read them with attention and consideration! Know once that you are his brethren, and that his Father is your Father, and his God is your God, and that he is ascended and glorified in your nature ; and then how can you be unwilling to be dismissed from the bondage of this flesh, and be with Christ! For in his ' Father's house are many mansions ; and he is gone before to prepare a place for us ; and will come again and receive us unto himself, that where he is, there we may be also ;' and that this is his will for all his servants, he hath declared in that comfortable promise, which also I have found so full of sweetness, that I value it above all the riches of the world, ' If any man serve me, let him follow me ; and where I am, there shall also my servant be :—if any man will serve me, him will my Father honour.' The Spirit of Christ within us, is the earnest of all this. Be assured of your faith, and hope, and love, and you may be assured of possessing the good believed, and hoped for, and loved. The incorruptible seed, which liveth and abideth for ever, of which you are new born, doth tend to the incorruptible crown, even the ' crown of righteousness, which the righteous judge will give to all that love his appearing—and so shall we ever be with the Lord,' as the apostle comfortably says, seasonably annexing the use of such a cordial, ' wherefore comfort one another with these words.'

Whether we are to die by the decay of nature, by the storm of any violent disease, by the hand of persecutors, or by any other instrument of Satan, the difference is small: they are but several ways of landing at the shore of happiness, which we are making toward, through all the duties and difficulties of life. So as we by any death are sent to Christ, let those domineer a while that stay behind, and are conquerors and happy in their dream: we shall neither miss nor desire their felicity. So as I die assured of the love of God, how little to be regarded is it, whether I be poor or rich till then, or in what manner death shall do its execution? And how little cause have blessed souls to envy them that are left on earth, in a quiet and prosperous passage to damnation?

And what an ease and pleasure is this to a man's mind through all this life, to be able, with well-grounded comfort, to think of death? What cares can vex him that hath secured his everlasting state; what losses should afflict him that is sure he shall not lose his soul, and is sure to gain eternal life? What fears should disquiet him that is sure to escape the wrath of God; what wants should trouble him that knoweth he is an heir of heaven? Why should the indignation or threatenings of man, be any temptation to turn him out of the way of duty, or dismay his mind, who knoweth that they can but kill the body, and dismiss the soul into his blessed presence, whom it loveth, and laboureth, and longs to see? What should inordinately grieve that man who is certain of eternal joy? What else should he thirst for, that hath in him the well of living waters springing up to everlasting life? And what should deprive that man of comfort, who knoweth he hath the comforter within him, and shall be for ever comforted with his Master's joy? And what should break the peace and patience of him that is assured of everlasting rest? If the assurance of a happy death cannot make it welcome, and cannot make affliction

easy, and fill our lives with the joys of hope, I know not what can do it.

But, alas, for those poor souls that know not whither death will send them, or at least have not good grounds of hope; what wonder if, ' through the fear of death, they be all their lifetime subject unto bondage !' Methinks in the midst of their wealth and pleasure, they should not be so stupid as to forget the millions that are gone before them, that lately were as jovial and secure as they; and how short their dreaming feast will be. Methinks all the beauty of their fleshly idols should be blasted with those nipping frosts and storms, that in their serious fore-thoughts come in upon them, from the black and dreadful regions of death ! Methinks at any time it should damp their mirth, and allay the ebullition of their frenetick blood, to remember ' for all this I must die,' and it may be ' this night,' ' that the fool must deliver up his soul ; and then, whose shall those things be which he hath provided !' Then who shall be the lord, and who the knight or gentleman? Methinks, Solomon's memento should bring them to themselves, ' rejoice, O young man, in thy youth, and let thy heart cheer thee in the days of thy youth, and walk in the ways of thine heart, and in the sight of thine eyes; but know thou, that for all these things God will bring thee into judgment. And as the sound of these words, ' I must shortly die,' methinks should be always in your ears; so in reason, the question, ' whither must I then go?' should be always as it were before your eyes, till your souls have received a satisfactory answer to it. O what an amazing, dreadful thing it is, when an unsanctified, unprepared soul must say, ' I must depart from earth, but I know not whither ! I know not whether into heaven or hell ; here I am now, but where must I be for ever?' When men believe that their next habitation must be everlasting, methinks the question ' whither must I go?' should be day and night upon their minds, till they can say upon good grounds, I shall go to the blessed presence of the Lord: O had you but the hearts of men within you, methinks the sense of this one question, ' whither must I go when I leave the flesh' should so possess you, that it should give your souls no rest, till you were able to say, we shall be with Christ, because he dwelleth in us here, and hath sealed us and given us the earnest of his Spirit ; or at least, till you have good hopes of this, and have done your best to make it sure.

And thus I have told you of how great importance it is to believers, to attain assurance of the love of God, and to know that Christ abideth in them. And now I think you will confess I have proved the necessity of self-knowledge, both to the unregenerated and the regenerated, though in several degrees: and having opened the disease, and showed you the need of a remedy, I am next to direct you in the application for the cure.

CHAPTER X.

THE EXTERNAL HINDERANCES TO SELF-ACQUAINTANCE.

I doubt not but there are many of the hearers, who by this time are desirous to be instructed, how this self-knowledge may be attained: for whose satisfaction, and for the reducing of all that hath been spoken into practice, I shall next acquaint you with the hinderances of self-knowledge (the removing of them being not the least point in the cure) and with the positive directions to be practised for the attainment of it. And because the hinderances and helps are contrary, I shall open both together as we go on.

The hinderances of self-knowledge are some of them without us, and some within us; and so must be the helps.

I. The external hinderances are these.

1. The failing of ministers in their part of the work, through unskilfulness or unfaithfulness, is a great cause that so many are ignorant of themselves. They are the lights of the world; and if they are eclipsed, or put under a bushel; if they are darkened by the influences of their own corruptions; or if they feed not their light by the oil of diligent studies, and other endeavours; or if they will not go along with men into the dark and unknown corners of the heart, what wonder if men's hearts remain in darkness, when those that by office are appointed to afford them light, do fail them? It is not a general dull discourse, or critical observations upon words, or the subtle decision of some nice and curious questions of the schools, though these may be useful to their proper ends, nor is it a neat and well composed speech, about some other distant matters, that is likely to acquaint a sinner with himself. How many sermons may we hear, that to other ends are not unprofitable, but are levelled at some mark or other, that is very far from the hearers' hearts, and therefore are never like to convince them, or prick them, or open and convert them? And if our congregations were in such a case, as that they needed no closer quickening work, such preaching might be borne with and commended; but when so many usually sit

before us that must shortly die, and are unprepared, and are condemned by the law of God, and must be pardoned or finally condemned; that must be saved from their sins, that they may be saved from everlasting misery; I think it is time for us to talk to them of such things as most concern them; and that in such a manner as may most effectually convince, awaken, and change them. When we come to them on their sick-beds, we talk not then to them of distant or impertinent things; but of the state of their souls, and their appearing before the Lord, and how they may be ready, that death may be both safe and comfortable to them: though a superstitious, miserable fellow, that knoweth no better things himself, may talk to the sick of beads, and relics, and of being on this side or that, for this ceremony or the other, and may think to conjure the unholy spirit out of him, by some affected words of devotions, uttered from a graceless, senseless heart, or to command him out by papal authority, as if they would charm his soul to heaven, by saying over some lifeless forms, and using the gospel as a spell: yet ministers indeed, that know themselves what faith and what repentance are, and what it is to be regenerated, and to be prepared to die, do know that they have other work to do.

The gospel offereth men their choice, whether they will have holiness or sin; and to be ruled by Christ or by their fleshly lusts; and so whether they will have spiritual, carnal, eternal, or transitory joys. And our work is to persuade them to make that choice which will be their happiness, if we can prevail, and which eternal joy depends upon; whether we come to them in sickness or in health, this is our business with them. A man that is ready to be drowned, is not at leisure for a song or dance: and a man that is ready to be damned, methinks should not find himself at leisure to hear a man show his wit and reading only, if not his folly and malice against a life of holiness: nor should you think that suitable to such men's case, that doth not evidently tend to save them. But, alas, how often have we heard such sermons, as tend more to diversion than direction, to fill their minds with other matters, and find men something else to think on, lest they should study themselves, and know their misery! A preacher that seems to speak religiously, by a sapless, dry discourse that is called a sermon, may more plausibly and easily divert him: and his conscience will more quietly suffer him to be taken off the necessary care of his salvation, by something that is like it, and pretends to do the work as well, than by the grosser avocations, or the scorn of fools: and he will more tamely be turned from religion by something tnat is called religion, and which he hopes may serve the turn, than by open wickedness, or impious defiance of God and reason. But how often do we hear applauded sermons, which force us, in compassion to men's souls, to think, O what is all this to the opening a sinner's heart unto himself, and showing him his unregenerated state? What is this to the conviction a self-deluding soul, that is passing unto hell with the confident expectation of heaven; to the opening of men's eyes, and turning them from darkness unto light, and from the power of Satan unto God? What is this to show men their undone condition, and the absolute necessity of Christ, and of renewing grace? What is in this to lead men up from earth to heaven, and to acquaint them with the unseen world, and to help them to the life of faith and love, and to the mortifying and the pardon of their sins? How little skill have many miserable preachers in the searching of the heart, and helping men to know themselves, whether Christ be in them, or whether they be reprobates? And how little care and diligence are used by them to call men to the trial, and help them in the examining and judging of themselves, as if it were a work of no necessity! 'They have healed also the hurt of the daughter of my people slightly, saying, Peace, peace, when there is no peace, saith the Lord.—Because, even because they have seduced my people, saying, peace, and there was no peace; and one built up a wall, and lo, others daubed it with untempered mortar: say unto them that daub it with untempered mortar, that it shall fall: there shall be an overflowing shower, and ye, O great hailstones, shall fall, and a stormy wind shall rend it. Lo, when the wall is fallen, shall it not be said unto you, where is the daubing wherewith ye have daubed it?'

It is a plain and terrible passage, 'He that saith to the wicked, thou art righteous, him shall the people curse; nations shall abhor him.' Such injustice in a judge, or witnesses, is odious, that determine but in order to temporal rewards or punishments: but in a messenger that professeth to speak to men in the name of God, and in the stead of Jesus Christ, when the determination hath respect to the consciences of men, and to their endless joy or torment, how odious and horrid a crime must it be reckoned to persuade the wicked that he is righteous: or to speak that which tendeth to persuade him of it, though not in open, plain expressions! What perfidious dealing is this against the holy God! What an

abuse of our redeemer, that his pretended messengers shall make him seem to judge contrary to his holiness, and to his law, and to the judgment which indeed he passeth, and will pass on all that live and die unsanctified! What vile deceit and cruelty against the souls of men are such preachers guilty of, that would make them believe that all is well with them, or that their state is safe or tolerable, till they must find it otherwise to their woe! When diseased souls have but a short and limited time allowed them for their cure, that a man shall come to them, as in the name of their physician, and tell them that they are pretty well, and need not make so much ado about the business, and thus keep them from their only help till it be too late! What shame, what punishment can be too great for such a wretch, when the neglect and making light of Christ and his salvation, is the common road to hell? And most men perish, because they value not, and use not the necessary means of their recovery; for a man in the name of a minister of the gospel, to cheat them into such undervaluings and neglects, as are likely to prove their condemnation: what is this but to play the minister of Satan, and to do his work, in the name and garb of a minister of Christ? It is damnable treachery against Christ, and against the people's souls, to hide their misery, when it is your office to reveal it; and to let people deceive themselves in the matters of salvation, and not to labour diligently to undeceive them; and to see them live upon presumption and ungrounded hopes, and not to labour with faithful plainness to acquaint them with their need of better hopes.

But some go farther, and more openly act the part of Satan, by reproaching the most faithful servants of the Lord, and labouring to bring the people into a conceit, that seriousness and carefulness in the matters of God and our salvation, are but hypocrisy and unnecessary strictness: and in their company and converse they give so much countenance to the ungodly, and cast so much secret or open scorn upon those that would live according to the scriptures, as hardeneth multitudes in their impenitency. O dreadful reckoning to these unfaithful shepherds, when they must answer for the ruin of their miserable flocks! How great will their damnation be, which must be aggravated by the damnation of so many others! When the question is, how came so many souls to perish? the answer must be, because they set light by Christ and holiness, which should have saved them. But what made them set light by Christ and holiness? It was their deceitful confidence, that they had so much part in Christ and holiness, as would suffice to save them, though indeed they were unsanctified strangers to both. They were not practically acquainted with their necessities. But how came they to continue thus ignorant of themselves till it was too late? Because they had teachers that kept them strangers to the nature of true holiness, and did not labour publicly and privately to convince them of their undone condition, and drive them to Christ, that by him they might have life. Woe to such teachers that ever they were born, that must then be found under the guilt of such perfidiousness and cruelty! Had they ever felt themselves, what it is to be pursued by the law of conscience, and with broken hearts to cast themselves on Christ as their only hope and refuge, and what it is to be pardoned, and saved by him from the wrath of God; and what it is to be sanctified, and to be sensible of all his love, they would take another course with sinners, and talk of sin, and Christ, and holiness at other rates, and not deceive their people with themselves.

Direct. 1. My first direction therefore to you is, in order to the knowledge of yourselves, that if it be possible, you will live under a faithful, soul-searching, skilful pastor, and that you will make use of his public and personal help, to bring you, and keep you in continual acquaintance with yourselves.

As there is a double use of physicians; one general, to teach men the common principles of physic, and the other particular, to apply those common precepts to each individual person as they need: so is there a double use of ministers of the gospel; one to deliver publicly the common doctrines of Christianity, concerning man's sin and misery, and the remedy, &c., and the other to help people in the personal application of all this to themselves. And they that take up only with the former, deprive themselves of half the benefit of the ministry.

1. In public how skilful and diligent should we be, in opening the hearts of sinners to themselves! The pulpit is but our candlestick from which we should diffuse the holy light into all the assembly: not speaking the same things of all that are before us, as if it were our work only to trouble men, or only to comfort them. But as the same light will show every man the things which he beholdeth in their varieties and differences; so the same word of truth which we deliver, must be so discovering and discriminating, as to manifest the ungodly to be ungodly, and the carnal to be carnal, the worldling to be a worldling; the hypocrite to be a hypocrite,

and the enemies of holiness to be as they are and the sincere to be sincere, and the renewed soul to be indeed renewed. The same light must show the excellency of sanctification and the filthiness of sin: the glory of the image of Christ, and the deformity of that spiritual death which is its privation. It must show the righteous to be ' more excellent than his neighbour,' and help men to ' discern between the righteous and the wicked; between him that serveth God, and him that serveth him not.' We must not be like the miserable ungodly preachers, that cannot describe the state of grace with clearness and feelingly, because they never knew it: or that dare not discover the unsanctified, lest they detect themselves, nor judge them according to their office, lest they condemn themselves; and that preach to the ungodly as if all were well with them; and they dare not awaken the consciences of others, lest they should awaken and affright their own, and therefore are ready to scorn all distinguishing preachers, and to take the discovery of regeneration to be but the boasting of hypocrisy, as if he that would differ from the most, or did pretend to the special privileges of the saints, did but as the pharisee, ' thank God that he is not like other men;' or say, ' stand by, I am more holy than thou.' If these preachers could prove that all men should be saved that will but say that they are Christians, they might then have hope of being saved themselves, without that serious piety which they so distaste. No wonder therefore if they preach in the language of Korah; ' ye take too much upon you, seeing all the congregation are holy, every one of them, and the Lord is among them: wherefore then lift you up yourselves above the congregation of the Lord.' But the Lord saith, ' if you take forth the precious from the vile, thou shalt be as my mouth: let them return unto thee, but return not thou unto them.'

If you love not discriminating preaching, make no difference from the true members of Christ by your hypocrisy or ungodly living; be such as they, and we shall not difference you from them. Read but the first Psalm, the fifteenth Psalm, the third of John, the eighth to the Romans, and the first epistle of John, and then tell me whether the scripture be not a discriminating word, condemning some and justifying others, and showing the true state of the difference betwixt them. What! is there no difference between the heirs of heaven and hell? Or is the difference no more than that one hath the name of a Christian, and not the other? Or that one had the distinguishing lot to be born where the gospel was received, and Christianity was the religion of the country, and the other the unhappiness to be born where it was not known? O no, when the differencing day is come, men shall find that there was another kind of difference between the way of life and of death when many shall say, ' Lord, Lord, have we not prophesied in thy name, and in thy name have cast out devils, and in thy name done many wonderful works!' to whom Christ will profess, ' I never knew you: depart from me, ye that work iniquity.' When ' many shall come from the east and west, and shall sit down with Abraham, Isaac and Jacob, in the kingdom of heaven; but the children of the kingdom shall be cast out into utter darkness: there shall be weeping and gnashing of teeth.' What a difference will appear between those that now converse together, between whom the world that judgeth by the outside, discerns but little or no difference? When those things shall be executed that are written in Matt. xxv. and 2 Thess. i. O what a difference will then appear! When of those that were in the same church, the same house, the same shop, the same bed, one shall be taken, and the other left: and the felicity that was hid in the seed of grace, shall shine forth to the astonishment of the world, in the fulness of eternal glory!

I know preachers are ordinarily hated that thus distinguish between the godly and ungodly; the very names of differences are matter of scorn to guilty souls, because they imply the matter of their terror! I have oft noted this with admiration, in the success of Christ's own doctrine upon the Jews, when he had so preached the gospel, as that he had the testimony of the multitude that ' wondered at the gracious words that proceeded out of his mouth,' yet some were cavilling and believed not; and he saith ' I tell you of a truth, many widows were in Israel in the days of Elias, when the heaven was shut up three years, but unto none of them was Elias sent, save unto Sarepta, a city of Sidon, to a woman that was a widow. And many lepers were in Israel in the time of Eliseus the prophet: and none of them was cleansed, saving Naaman the Syrian.' But how was this distinguishing doctrine of Christ entertained by the Jews? It is said, ' all they in the synagogue when they heard these things, were filled with wrath, and rose up and thrust him out of the city, and led him to the brow of the hill, whereon their city was built, that they might cast him down headlong.' Read it, and consider what moved these men to so much rage against Christ himself for preaching this doctrine, which restrained the fruit of the gospel to a few;

and then you will not wonder if those preachers that imitate Christ in this, be used no better than their master.

But let ministers know that this is their duty, to show every man himself, his deeds, and state, as indeed they are: and let Christians choose and love such ministers. Choose not the glass that makes you fairest, but that which is truest, and representeth you to yourselves as God accounteth you, whether he do it with more eloquence or less, with smoother or with rougher language; hear him, if you may, that will best acquaint you with the truth of your condition, and choose not those that speak not to the heart.

2. And when you have heard the best, the clearest, the most searching preacher, do not think that now you can do all the rest of the work yourselves, and that you have no further need of help, but make use of their more particular personal advice in these following cases: (1.) In case that after your most diligent self-examination, you are yet at uncertainty and doubt whether you are truly sanctified or not, the settling of your state for eternity, and the well-grounding of your hopes and comforts, is a matter of such unspeakable moment, as that you should not remain in careless, negligent uncertainty, while God hath provided you any further means that may be used for assurance. Yea, if you were not troubled with doubting, yet if you have opportunity of opening your evidences to a judicious, faithful minister or friend, I think it may be worth your labour, for the confirmation of the peace and comforts which you have. You cannot make too sure of everlasting happiness. (2.) Not only in the first settling of your peace, but also when any notable assault or dangerous temptation shall afterward shake it, which you cannot overcome without assistance, it is seasonable to betake yourselves to a physician. (3.) Also in case of any dangerous lapse of declining that hath brought you into a state of darkness. The sick and wounded must have help, for they are not sufficient for themselves. (4.) Also in case of any particular corruption or temptation, your particular sinful inclinations may be opened to a faithful guide, that by his prudent and lively counsel you may be strengthened.

If you say, ' to what end do ministers preach to me, and why do I hear them opening the nature of grace and of hypocrisy, if I cannot judge of myself by the doctrine which they preach? I answer, (1.) You may and must judge yourselves by the public common helps, as far as you are able: but a personal applying help, added unto this, is a further advantage. And humility should teach you, not to think better of your understandings than there is cause; nor to think you are so wise as to need but one help, when God hath provided you two, or that you need but the lesser, when he hath provided you a greater. And doth not your own experience convince you? Do you not find, that after the best public preaching, you are yet in doubt, and at a loss about your spiritual state, and therefore that you have need of further help? (2.) I further answer you: there is so great a diversity of particular circumstances in the cases of particular persons, that a great deal of help is necessary to most, to pass a right judgment, when they do understand both the law and the fact. Will you think it enough that you have the statutes of the land, and the law-books, to judge of all your own cases by? Or will you not think that you have also need of the counsel of the wisest lawyer, in your weightiest cases, to help you to judge of your cause by the particular application of the law to it? So in physic, who is so foolish, as to think that by the help of the most learned book, or approved prescriptions, he is able to be his own physician, without any more particular advice? You must be long in studying law or physic before you can understand them so well as those that have made them the study and business of their lives. It is not reading a book only, or hearing a lecture of them, that can make you as understanding as the masters of the profession; and also to have all passages at hand that must be observed in the judging of your case. So is it in matters of the soul. When you have heard much, and understand much, you cannot in modesty think that all the sense of scripture, about those points is known as exactly to you as to your most judicious teachers; and that you are as able at once to see all the passages of the word, and of the fact, as may enable you to pass so clear a judgment on it. Perhaps you will say, that you know your own hearts and actions better than they do. I answer, you do so, or should do so, and it is you that they must know it from: yet when you have done, you may not be able to judge of your state by those acts which you say you know: you must show the lawyer all your evidences: he cannot see them till you show them him: and yet when he seeth them, he can judge of them whether they are good or bad, and of your title by them, better than you can that have the keeping of them, because he better understands the law.

But perhaps you will say, that when you have gone to ministers, and opened your case to them, they cannot resolve you, but you are still in doubt; I answer, (1.) Perhaps when they have resolved them, yet you would not be resolved. Have they not told you the truth and you would not believe it? or directed you to remedies which you would not use? They cannot, when they have told you the truth, compel you to believe it; and when they have told you what will do the cure, they cannot make you use it if you refuse. (2.) And what if the nature of the disease be obstinate, and will not be cured easily and at once, but with time, and diligence, and patience? Will you therefore think the means are vain? Must you at once, or in a short time, be resolved, and delivered from all your doubts about your title to eternal life, or else will you cast off all advice? Should your children learn thus of their teachers, they were like to make unhappy scholars. As you will not have done with Christ if he cure you not at once, nor give over praying if you have not all your desires at once (if you love yourselves,) so you must not have done with the counsel of your guides, if they satisfy not your doubts at once. As you cease not hearing them in public, though you have still your doubtings; so why should you cease advising with them personally upon that account? Use God's means, and be thankful, if by degrees they cure, and prevail at last.

Object. But I find it is God only that can speak peace; and therefore it is vain to hang on men.

I answer, God speaketh by his word and Spirit: his word is to be delivered, expounded, and applied to you by his ministers: if therefore you will have it from God, you must not refuse his own appointed ordinary means. The Spirit comforteth by the promise: as in conversion God useth not to do it by the Spirit, without, but in and by, the ministry of the word, so also in all our directions, and satisfaction and comfort afterwards. As he that will run from the ministry of the word, because it is God that must convert, doth indeed run from God, and is not likely to be converted, so is it in point of assurance and consolation. The teachers of the church are ' to be accounted of as the ministers of Christ, and stewards of the mysteries of God;—by whom the people have believed, not having dominion over their faith, but being helpers of their joy;' who ' are comforted in all their tribulations, that they might be able to comfort them that are in any trouble, by the comfort wherewith they themselves are comforted of God.' They are to be ' faithful and wise stewards, whom the Lord maketh rulers over his household, to give them their portion of meat in due season.' Thus Christ hath given ' authority to his servants, and appointed to every man his work,' and 'given pastors and teachers to his church, for the perfecting of the saints, for the work of the ministry, for the edifying of the body of Christ, till we all come in the unity of the faith, and of the knowledge of the Son of God to a perfect man. These therefore being Christ's officers, and this their appointed work, we must receive so much of God's mercies by their hands, as belongeth to their office to administer.   ' If there be a messenger with him, an interpreter, one among a thousand, to show unto man his uprightness, then God is gracious unto him, and saith, Deliver him from going down to the pit; I have found a ransom.' So that you see it is God's way to show to man his uprightness, and to speak peace to souls by his messengers and interpreters, that are fitted and authorized thereto.

Object. It is but few that are able thus to discuss the case of unsettled doubting souls, and to give them clear and safe directions, that may save them both from presumption and despair : in many places the ministers are senseless of these things, and unacquainted with the concerns and works of conscience, and have nothing to say to us, unless to deride us as scrupulous and precise, and bid us not trouble our heads about such matters, seeing God is merciful, and Christ died for sinners : they will discourse with us long enough about news, or worldly businesses or opinions, or controversies ; but when we open to them the state of our souls, and desire their advice for the making of our calling and election sure, they have no sense or savour of such discourse : and many ministers that are truly conscientious are yet so unskilful and so weak, that we have no encouragement to acquaint them with our state.

To this I answer : it cannot be denied but all this is too true ; and it is matter of lamentation, and must send us to God with the old petition which Christ himself hath put into our mouths, ' the harvest truly is plenteous, but the labourers are few : pray ye therefore the Lord of the harvest that he will send forth labourers into his harvest.'

But consider that this is no unusual thing : for all this, there is no nation under heaven that hath more able, faithful ministers of Christ than are in these nations. Alas, how much of the church is guided by mere ignorant readers ! And how much by superstitious deceivers ! Did you know the case of the poor Christians in the Ethiopian, the Greek, and the Roman churches, you would bless God that it is so well with us. Even when the church was in a narrower room,

yet God complained, ' many pastors have destroyed my vineyard : they have trodden my portion under foot ; they have made my pleasant portion a desolate wilderness ; they have made it desolate : and being desolate, it mourneth unto me. Woe be to the pastors that destroy and scatter the sheep of my pasture, saith the Lord ; therefore thus saith the Lord God of Israel against the pastors that feed my people : ye have scattered my flock and driven them away, and have not visited them ; behold I will visit on you the evil of your doings, saith the Lord. And I will set up shepherds over them who shall feed them, and they shall fear no more, nor be dismayed.' Then was the church fain to take up this lamentation, ' woe is me, my hurt ; for my wound is grievous : but I said, truly this is a grief, and I must bear it : my tabernacle is spoiled, and all my cords are broken ; my children are gone forth of me, and they are not ; there is none to stretch forth my tent any more, and to set up my curtains : for the pastors are become brutish, and have not sought the Lord : therefore they shall not prosper, and all their flocks shall be scattered.' But the voice of healing mercy saith ' only acknowledge thine iniquity, &c.   Turn, O back-sliding children, &c. and I will give you pastors according to my heart, which shall feed you with knowledge and understanding.'

You see in all other professions that require not supernatural illumination, that there are but few that attain to excellency ; it is but in few that nature layeth the foundation or giveth that capacity to be excellent, which grace doth elevate and improve. I will not persuade you to go always to the minister of your parish, to open the case of your souls, be he fit or unfit, but to the fittest that you can have access to.   The papists themselves will give men leave to choose others for their confessors. Where there is most of the heavenly illumination, and holy skill in the matters of the soul ; where there is the soundest and most exact judgment, joined with experience and tender compassion, and faithful plainness, and cautious secrecy, there open your hearts if you have opportunity, and take the help of such faithful counsellors to acquaint you with yourselves.

Object. But such ministers being few, and having more of greater work than they can turn them to, are not to be spoken with as oft as my necessity requireth help. Answ. Use then the best that are at leisure ; and it is not only ministers that you must use, but any other Christian friend that hath such abilities and qualifications as fit them to assist you ; whosoever hath the light, refuse not to come to it ; God's gifts and graces may be helpful to you in a parent, a husband, a neighbour, and not only in a minister.

Quest. But how far may a dark and doubting person take up and rest in the judgment of a minister, or of others, about the state of his soul, when he is not satisfied himself? Answ. This question is of very great use, and therefore the more carefully to be resolved ; I shall answer it therefore, 1. Negatively, and, 2. Affirmatively.

1. Negatively. (1.) No man's judgment of your state is to be taken as absolutely infallible or divine : nor is man to be believed as God is, with a divine belief. When they tell you, that, if you are regenerated, you are justified, then they do but tell you what God hath told you, and therefore this is to be taken as of infallible certainty, not as it is their word, but as it is God's : so also when they tell you, that if you are unconverted you are not forgiven. But when they tell you, that you are converted or unconverted, pardoned or unpardoned, this judgment is not to be taken as infallible or divine. (2.) For the bare matter of fact whether you repent or not ; whether you had rather be holy or unholy, &c. there is no minister that can know your heart so well as you yourselves may know it, except in case when melancholy or passion, or a weakness of understanding on one side, or a wilfulness of presumption on the other side, doth make men judge of their own condition quite contrary to the evidence that appeareth in their lives to others. (3.) It is not safe to rest on the judgment of one that is either an enemy or stranger to the workings of a careful, troubled soul ; or of one that is fond of any private opinion of his own, and layeth out his zeal to form people into his opinion, as if the life of religion lay in that ; nor yet of a weak, unskilful man. (4.) It is not safe for you to rest much on the judgment of one that knows you not, and is not acquainted with the bent and manner of your lives, but must judge only by the present expressions of your own mouths. (5.) It is not safe for you to rest on the judgment of any one single person, when the judgment of most of your judicious acquaintance is contrary to it.

2. Affirmatively. I answer (1.) By a divine faith you are bound to believe all the promises of scripture that your pastor or any other shall acquaint you with. (2.) As a disciple of Christ, you are bound to learn the meaning of these promises and other passages of the scripture from your teachers duly authorized to instruct you: and with such a human belief, as a scholar oweth to his teacher in arts or sciences, you are bound to

believe your teachers concerning the meaning of the promises, in cases wherein you are unable yourselves to understand the word by its proper light and evidence, as well as they ; and in case you see no evidence of falsehood in their exposition, nor have any special reason to distrust them. He that will believe nothing that his teacher telleth him, in order to his own understanding, shall never understand by teaching. If you know as much as he already, you need no teacher ; if you do not, you must believe him, or else you can never learn of him. But this is not to take him for omniscient, or infallible in himself, but to credit him as a man. (3.) You are bound, when he judgeth of your particular case, upon your opening to him the matter of fact, to allow him so much credit as is due to the proportion of his understanding. You tell him how you feel your hearts affected, and what the actions of your lives have been ; when you have told it him, he judgeth by God's word, whether this be a state of saving grace which you describe, or not; if upon much stronger parts, or longer study, and more experience, he know more of the meaning of the word, and of the nature of grace, and so be abler to judge than you, modesty requireth that you do in that measure submit your understanding unto his, and believe him according to the measure of his skill, upon supposition that you deceive him not in your information. Even as you will believe a lawyer about your title to your lands, when you have showed him your evidence ; or a physician about your disease, when you have told him what you feel. (4.) You are bound to add also, all that credit that his honesty and fidelity requireth, if he be a godly man, unwilling to deceive you. (5.) And you are bound to add so much belief, as in the case is due to a stander by that is not blinded by self-love, or partiality, or passions, or any selfish bias, as most men are to themselves. (6.) If you are darkened by melancholy, or any other weakening distemper, that maketh you incapable of judging for yourselves, you are bound to allow another so much credit, as the advantage of his sounder understanding, and more composed judgment require. If every child, or sick person, will believe no body that doth not say as they, their self-conceit and their distrust of others will be their wrong. (7.) In the manner of reception, you are bound to do all this with such a submission as belongeth to an officer of Christ : not that you are to believe any falsehood that he bringeth you, and fathereth upon Christ ; nor to put out your own eyes, and see with his, but to learn of him to understand your-

107

selves, and receive what he bringeth you, according to his office. (8.) You may yet more boldly and confidently give credit to the judgment of such a minister of Christ when he is not singular, but speaks according to the concurrent judgment of the generality of able, experienced men ; modesty will forbid you to think yourselves wiser than all the able ministers about you. (9.) You have the less reason to suspect his judgment, when you may be sure that he is not perverted by any self-interest or self-respect, and frustrateth not the truth for fear of displeasing you, or bringing any discredit or suffering on himself. (10.) Lastly, when all these things concur, you may with the greater confidence rest upon his judgment. And though still he is but an imperfect man, and no absolute certainty of your state can be had from his bare judgment, though from his doctrine, and the effects and signs there may ; yet such a judgment should weigh very much with you, to the raising of fear, and care in the ungodly, and for the quieting of a troubled soul.

Let us now apply this direction to both parties. Beloved, if any of you can look before you to eternity, and do not with awakened thoughts conclude that all probable means should be used in time, to make sure of your final justification at the dreadful day of God, that man wants either the faith of a Christian, or the feeling of a considerate man. Are you all desirous to be sure before hand, what sentence shall pass upon you then, or are you not ? If you are, come on, and let me make a motion that you cannot reasonably refuse. The business is of unspeakable consequence. To be deceived, may be to be undone for ever. Will you advise with those that God hath appointed to give you advice in so great a case ? Well then ! will you go and faithfully open your state, to some able faithful minister of Christ ? Not to an ignorant, or a carnal, inexperienced man, but unto one that is skilled in spiritual affairs, and that will be faithful to you, and deal with that serious gravity and reverence as bescems him that is helping to prepare a soul for the bar of Christ. Will you tell him, whether ever you were convinced of your sin and misery ; whether ever you saw the need of Christ ; whether you have loathed yourselves for your iniquities, and fled to Christ as your only refuge from the wrath of God, and have turned away with resolution from your former ungodly, careless life, and have changed your company, your business, and your delights ; whether you make it your chief business to please God, and to save your souls, and resolve to take

up with the hopes of heaven as your only portion, and not to hazard it for any worldly interest, or fleshly pleasure whatsoever ; whether in ' your eyes a vile person be contemned, but you love and honour them that fear the Lord ?' Tell these and other such particulars of your state to your faithful pastors. Answer to these, and such like questions, and then take their judgment, with the cautions before expressed, of your spiritual state. Hear what they will tell you of it. Might not this course convince thee of thy miserable state, that never hadst any such evidences as these to show ; and might it not awaken thee in time, to bethink thee of a safer course ?

Go to any faithful minister in the world, and tell him the plain truth, that yet thou art a secret fornicator, or a drunkard, or flesh-pleaser in some sensual way ; or if thou sinnest not so grossly, that yet thou art a formal hypocrite, and hast a secret enmity to those that are most seriously religious, and live the most heavenly lives, and that thou art thyself a stranger to sanctification : and I dare assure thee that he will tell thee, if thou art thus indeed, thou art in the gall of bitterness, and the bond of iniquity, and must be speedily renewed, and sanctified, and justified, or thou art undone for ever. I tell thee, there is not a man that is worthy the name of a minister in all the world, but will pass this judgment on the condition of thy soul. And yet wilt thou bear it out with a senseless heart, a seared conscience, and a brazen face, and still live as carelessly as if all were well with thee ? What ! is thy soul of no more worth ? Is it so small a matter with thee, what becometh of thee ? Or is the judgment of able, faithful ministers, in the way of their own office, of no more regard with thee ? They show thee the plain word of God against thee ; and that his threatening contains the virtual sentence of thy condemnation. They are by office the interpreters of the law of God to you ; it hath been the study of their lives. Do they pronounce you miserable, as being strangers to the Spirit of Christ ? So they did by themselves, when they saw their sin ; and therefore they are impartial : they have had before them multitudes, alas too many, in your case ; and you will regard the judgment of a physician that hath had many hundreds in hand, that had the same disease as you. They are men that are not willing to deceive you ; they deny themselves in telling you of your danger ; they know that smoother words would please you better ; and they have natures that desire men's love and favour, rather than displeasure. They are more impartial than you are, and have not your self-interest and passion to blind them. They are not abused in their judgment by the temptations of evil company, or of worldly fleshly things, as you are; for these temptations more hinder us from judging ourselves than other men. They are the messengers of Christ, appointed to give to each their portion; and should not their judgment be regarded in the business committed to their trust? And it is not one man or two, or a hundred only, that are of this mind. Open thy case to all the judicious, faithful ministers in the land, and open it truly, and they will all tell thee, that if thou die without converting, sanctifying grace, thou art lost for ever; and that all the world cannot save thee from the everlasting wrath of God. Try as many of them as you will, and see if all of them tell you not the same thing. And is all this nothing to thee, presumptuous sinner, that in the judgment of all the most able, faithful ministers of Christ, thy soul should be in a state of death? If all the physicians in the country should tell thee, that thou hast a disease that will certainly be thy death, unless thou take some one effectual medicine in time, I think thou wouldst not slight their judgment, and say they are too censorious, and that thou knowest thy condition better than they? I think it would affright thee to seek after the remedy. And why should not the judgment of faithful ministers, about the state of thy soul, be so far regarded, as to awaken thee to a more careful inquiry, and stir up a preventing and remedying fear? If the judgment of Christ's officers be not regarded, then there is no matter of terror in excommunication; nor no matter of comfort in ministerial assistance.

O the madness of a hardened sinner! that when he showeth by the fruits of an ungodly life, that he is a stranger to sanctification, and liveth in the sins which the scripture threateneth damnation to, and hath no evidence of true conversion to show, will yet be confident of pardon and salvation, let God and his ministers say what they will against it; and will rather be offended with his spiritual physicians for telling him of the danger of his state, and rail at them as if they did him wrong, than he will see his danger and prevent his misery! Let such a one hear the word of God, if he have ears to hear. ' Lest there should be among you a root that beareth gall and wormwood, and it come to pass when he heareth the words of this curse, that he bless himself in his heart, saying, I shall have peace, though I walk in the imagination of mine heart, to add drunkenness to thirst: the Lord will not spare him, but then the anger of the Lord and his jealousy shall smoke against that man, and all the curses that are written in this book shall lie upon him, and the Lord shall blot out his name from under heaven. And the Lord shall separate him unto evil.'

And on the other hand, is there any soul among you, that in doubts and trouble, hath opened his case to the faithful ministers of Christ, and their judgment is, that your state is safe? Is this the judgment, not only of the weakest, but the wisest; not only of strangers, but of those that know you best; not only of one or two, but of all, or most, of the judicious ministers that ever you opened your case to; even of the most honest and impartial, that would not flatter you nor deceive you? Yea, and perhaps, when desertions, or melancholy, or passion, or ignorance, do make you unmeet to judge of yourselves. And doth all this seem nothing to you; or a small matter? It is not small. I confess it is no ground of certainty: they are but men: it is a human testimony: but yet it is a testimony that may weigh down many of your own surmises, and take off much of your distressing fears, and may give much ease to troubled souls, while they are seeking after surer knowledge. It is a ground of comfort, not to be despised or made light of. Till you can come to see your evidences yourselves, and to be acquainted with the indwelling Spirit as your witness, you may much quiet your minds, and take much comfort, in this judgment and witness of the servants of the Lord, that have a spirit of discerning, and have that grace which acquainteth them with the nature of grace in others, and that have been long exercised in the discerning of men's states. It is possible an hypocrite, especially one that wilfully giveth them a false relation of himself, may deceive them: but it is probable that it is not one of many they are deceived in, when they know or have a good description of the person. If in a fever, all the ablest physicians tell you the danger is past, it is possible yet that they may be all deceived, but yet I think you would take some comfort in such a testimony; so should you here. Though the judgment of ministers be not infallible, it may be much better than your own, though about yourselves; and it may be set against the jealousies and fears of a disquieted soul, and against abundance of the molesting suggestions of the accuser.

I do not by all this draw you to lay too much on man; I advance them not too high, and make them not lords of your faith, but helpers of your joy. I draw you not to any deceitful course, nor into any way of danger to your souls. I bid you not fully and finally rest in the judgment of man ; I bid you not neglect any means to come to fuller knowledge and certainty of your own sincerity. I bid you not forbear any means that tend to the getting of true grace. If you have it, and know it not, the same means for the most part may increase it, which you use to get it : and if you have it not, when it is thought you have it, the means may work it, that are intended to increase it. Do all that you can to repent, believe, and love God, and live to him, whether you ever did these before or not. But yet let the judgment of your faithful pastors, the officers and experienced servants of the Lord, keep off despondency and despair, that would disable you from the use of means, and would weaken your hands, and make you sit down in unprofitable complaints, and give up all as hopeless. Let their judgment quiet you in the way of duty ; lean on them in the dark, till you come into the light. Yea, be glad that you have so much encouragement and hope, from those that are by Christ appointed to subserve the Spirit, in the comforting as well as the sanctifying work, and to 'show to man his uprightness,' and to say to the righteous, it shall be well with him.' I tell you, all the wealth of the world is not worth even this much ground of comfort: live upon this much till by diligent attendance, and waiting on the Spirit of grace and comfort, you can get higher.

The second extrinsic hinderance of self-knowledge is prosperity, and the flattery that usually attendeth it. The one disposeth men to be deceived, and the other putteth the vail over their eyes, and tells them the falsehoods which deceive them.

When men prosper in the world, their minds are lifted up with their estates ; and they can hardly believe that they are indeed so ill, while they feel themselves so well ; and that so much misery is joined with so much content and pleasure. They cannot taste the bitterness of their sin, and God's displeasure, while the sweetness of worldly delights and honours is in their mouths. The rich man in Luke xvi. would have given a man but an unwelcome entertainment, that had come to tell him that within a few days and years he should lie in hell, and not be able to get a drop of water to cool his tongue! What need we doubt of that, when his five brethren, that he left on earth behind him, would not be persuaded to know their danger of those flames, and to use the necessary means to escape

them though one had come to them from the dead ! You plead against their feeling, when you tell them of their misery, when they feel prosperity. Their fleshly appetite and sense, which is in them the reigning faculty, doth tell them they are well and happy : and that which must confute this, and tell them they are miserable, must be an inward sense of the sin and diseases of their souls, and a foreseeing faith that must look before them unto eternity, and bring its proofs from the word of God, and its motives from another world: and alas, they have no such inward sense, nor no such faith, as can prevail against their sensual feeling. And therefore it is a matter of lamentable difficulty, to make a prospering sinner well acquainted with his misery. He is drunken with fleshly pleasures and content: and when the drink is in a man's head, you can hardly make him sensible of his misery. The devil is therefore willing to reach his servants as full a cup of prosperity as he can, that their drunkenness may keep them from the true use of their reason : for if they once come to themselves, they will come home to God. When misery brought the prodigal to himself, he resolved presently on going to his father ; the bustle of his worldly business, and the vain discourse that is in his ears, and the mirth and sport that takes him up, will not allow him so much of reason, as seriously to consider of his soul's condition. Alas ! when poor men, that must labour all day for food and raiment, can find some time for serious converse with God and with their consciences, the great ones of the world have no such leisure. How many are going apace towards hell, and say they cannot have time to bethink themselves what way they are in, or whither it is that they are going! That which they have all their time for, they have no time for, because they have no hearts for it. Prosperity doth so please their flesh, that they can give no heed to conscience or to reason : it doth so charm their minds, and enslave their wills to sense and appetite, that they cannot endure to be so melancholy as to prepare for death and judgment, or to consider seriously how this will relish with them at the end ; nor scarcely to remember that they are men, that should rule their senses, and be ruled by God, and that have another life to live.

As prosperity in itself is so great a hinderance to the knowledge of yourselves, so flatterers, that are the flies of summer, are always ready to blow upon the prosperous, and increase the danger. What miserable men are extolled as wise and virtuous, and religious, if they be but rich and great! Their vices are masked or extenuated, and made but little human frailties: though they were gluttons or drunkards, or filthy fornicators, or mere flesh-pleasing, sensual persons, that waste most of their lives in ease and sports, and eating and drinking, and such delights; yet with their flatterers all these shall go for prudent, pious, worthy persons, if they can but seek when they have done, to mock God and their consciences with some lip service and lifeless carcass of religion. O happy men, if God would judge of them as their flatterers do; and would make as small a matter of their wickedness, and as great a matter of their outside, hypocritical, heartless worship! But they must be greater than men or angels, and higher than either earth or heaven, before God will flatter them. When they can make him afraid of their high looks or threatenings, or when they can put him in hope of rising by their preferment, then they may look that he should comply with their parasites, and compliment with his enemies, and justify the ungodly; but not till then. O did they consider how little flattery doth secure them, and how little the Judge of all the world regards their worldly pomp and splendour; yea, how greatly their greatness doth aggravate their sin and misery, they would frown their flatterers out of doors, and call for plain and faithful dealers. Of all the miseries of worldly greatness, this is not the least, that usually such want the necessary blessing of a glass that will truly show them their faces; of a friend at hand that will deal plainly and justly with their souls; who tells them plainly of the odiousness, and bitter fruits of sin, and of the wrath of God and endless misery? How few such true and faithful friends have they? And what wonder, when it is a carnal inducement that draweth men to follow them: it is their wealth and honour, and their power, to do men good or hurt in outward things, that makes their friends. They are attended by these flies and wasps, because they carry the honey-pot which they love. God saith to his followers, 'love not the world, nor the things that are in the world: if any man love the world, the love of the Father is not in him;' and it is for love of worldly things—even the lust of the flesh, the lust of the eye, and pride of life, which are not of the Father, but of the world—it is for these that great men have their friends and followers for the most part: and therefore it is plain that the worst sort of men are ordinarily their friends: for those are the worst men that have not the love of the Father in them, but are the friends of the world and therefore the enemies

of God; and the best, though fit to be their truest friends, are seldom their followers, as knowing that the attraction of the sensual world is a shadow unfit to deceive those that are acquainted with its vanity, and a snare unfit to take those that have observed how Satan lays and baits the trap, and how they have fared that have been taken in it. A despised Christ that hath the words of eternal life, is much more followed by men that have the heavenly relish. Such gracious souls, whose appetites are not corrupted by the creatures and their sickness, have more mind to flock after a spiritual and powerful messenger of Christ, who talks to them of his kingdom, and the righteousness thereof, which they first seek, than to gape after the preferment and vain-glory of prosperity. Christ, who despised the offer of all the kingdoms and glory of the world, doth teach his followers to despise them.

Seeing then the ordinary attendants of the prosperous are the worst of men, that seek themselves, and are purveying for the flesh, what wonder if they be flatterers, that have neither skill nor will to speak that unpleasing language of reproof, that should make the prosperous know themselves! O how seldom or never do they hear, what the poor can hear from every mouth! If a man of low degree be wicked, or offend, his enemy dares tell him of it, and his friend dares tell him of it, and his angry neighbour or companion will be sure to tell him of it; and they dare tell him frequently till he amend, and tell him plainly. But if great ones be as bad and need more help, as having more temptation, yet alas! they may sin, and sin again, and perish, for any body that will deal faithfully with their souls, except some faithful minister of Christ, whose plainness is taken but for a thing of course. And usually even ministers themselves are some of them so unfaithful, and some so fearful, and some so prudently cautious that such persons have no such help from them to know themselves, as the poorer sort of people have. If we deal freely with them, it will be well taken; or if it offend, yet offence may easily be borne, as bringing no ill consequences to our ministry: but if we deal so with the great ones of the world, what outcries would it raise, and by what names should we and our preaching be called! If it were not for fear lest some malicious hearers would misunderstand me, and misapply my words, as spoken of those that we are bound to honour, and as tending to diminish the reputation of any of our superiors, which I detest, I should have showed you all this in scripture instances. When Haman could not bear the omission of one man's obeisance, what wonder if such cannot bear to be spoken to, as indeed they are! Not only an Ahab hateth one faithful plain Micaiah, because he prophesieth not good of him, but evil, but Asa, that destroyed idolatry, can imprison the prophet that reproveth him for his sin. I will not tell you of the words that were spoken to Amos by the priest of Bethel, or to the prophet, lest malice mis-interpret and mis-report me: for it is none of my intent to fix on any particular persons, but to tell you in general the lamentable disadvantage that the great and prosperous have, as to the knowledge of themselves; how little plain-dealing they have, and how hardly most of them can bear it; though yet I doubt not but it is borne and loved by those that have true grace: and that if David sin, he can endure to hear from Nathan, ' thou art the man;' and an Eli can bear the prophecy of Samuel, and say, 'it is the Lord, let him do what seemeth him good;' and an Hezekiah can say, ' good is the word of the Lord which thou hast spoken;' and Josiah can bear the threatenings of Huldah; and it is a double honour in persons that have so great temptations to love the plain discoveries of their sin: but a Joash will slay even Zechariah, the son of Jehoiadah, that set him up; and a Herod, that hath so much religion as to fear John, ' as knowing that he was a just man, and an holy; and to observe him, when he heard of him doing many things, and hear him gladly,' had yet so much love to his fleshly lust, and so little power to resist a flatterer, as that he could sell both the head of John and his own soul for so pitiful a price as this. So true is that of Christ himself, 'for every one that doeth evil hateth the light, neither cometh to the light, lest his deeds should be reproved : but he that doeth truth, cometh to the light, that his deeds may be made manifest that they are wrought in God.'

And indeed there is none that more opposeth Micaiah than Zedekiah, as being concerned for the honour of his flattering prophecy to bring plain-dealing into disgrace. It is he that smiteth him, and saith, 'which way went the Spirit of the Lord from me, to speak unto thee ?' But saith Solomon, ' he that rebuketh a man, afterward shall find more favour than he that flattereth with the tongue.' And ' faithful are the wounds of a friend; but the kisses of an enemy are deceitful.' When prosperity is vanished, the flatterer and the faithful dealer will be better known. Deceitful prosperity, and deceitful men, will at once forsake you. None of them will admire or applaud you when you are low, and the tide is gone, and hath left you in contempt :

these kind of men will be as ready as any to reproach you ; as Shimei that honoured David in his prosperity, but curseth him, and revileth him as a rebel against Saul, and casteth stones at him, when he saw him flying in distress.

But whom can the prosperous blame so much as themselves, if they are undone by the deceit of flatterers? It is their own choice ; they love to have it so; they will not endure faithful dealing. When they contract those diseases which will not be cured without bitter medicines, they hate the physician that offereth them : their appetites and sensual lust, and not their believing reason, doth choose their work, their pleasures and their company, and prescribe what language must be spoken to them. And he that resolves to cast away the remedy, and will please his appetite and fancy, come of it what will, must take what he gets by it, and bear the endless wrath of God, that could not bear the necessary warnings and self-knowledge that should have prevented it. Did these men hate sin, and the messengers of Satan, they would not hate the justice and messengers of God : but while they love fleshly pleasures, they cannot savingly love the word that chargeth them to let go those pleasures, nor the persons that cross them in the things they love. And thus poor worldlings are ruined by their own desires: it seemeth so sweet to them to live in sin, that they cannot endure to know the bitter fruits of misery, which it will at last bring forth. They are conquered by their fleshly lusts, and therefore they hate the messengers of that Spirit which would fight against them. Satan doth perfect his former victories in them, by dispelling or dispersing the auxiliaries of Christ, that were sent for their rescue and relief. They live as if they were purposely made great, that they may be able to drive away the messengers of salvation, and to keep the voice of mercy far enough from their ears ; and to command that which the Gadarenes did intreat, that Christ would go out of their coasts, because they would not be troubled with him. They so much love the way to hell, that they cannot abide to be told whither it leadeth them ; therefore they come thither before they are aware, and must know themselves by the unquenchable fire, because they would not know themselves by the discovering, recovering light. Thus by prosperity and flattery, Satan pursues and wins his game.

Direct. 2. In opposition to this hinderance, two things are to be done.

(1.) Desire not so perilous a station as worldly prosperity and greatness is. Love not, and seek not a condition so hazardous to your souls

Leave that to them that take it for their portion, as not believing what they must lose and suffer by it; or what God hath revealed of the life to come.

Or if you be in such prosperity, not by your desire, but by the will and providence of God, let your fear and watchfulness be doubled, as your dangers are: be not like those sensualists that 'feed themselves without fear.' Use not prosperity to the pleasing of the flesh, and the prospering of your lusts, but deny yourselves in the midst of your abundance; and turn it into an adversity to your sensual inclinations, by taming the body, and bringing it into subjection, and suspecting yourselves, and walking humbly with God and man.

And when adversity is upon you, improve the opportunity for the knowledge of yourselves. Then take a just survey of your former course of life. Then try your ways, when the drunkenness and deceits of prosperity are past, and the hand of God hath brought you into a sober and considerate state. O how many souls do know that in one day, when adversity hath made them wise and sensible, which before they knew and would not know; they saw it, but did not understand and feel it! Then on a sudden they are able to pass a right judgment upon their yielding to temptations, and the value of the things that tempted them, and upon their worldly designs and fleshly wisdom, and their neglects of God and heaven, and duty, than before they could do, though they had ever so much instruction, and though they could speak the same words of sin as now. Affliction taketh away the deceiving advantages of fleshly objects, and unmasketh the glory and profit of the world, and awakeneth the rational faculties to perform their office, and therefore is an excellent opportunity for self-acquaintance. The prodigal came to himself, when he was denied to fill his belly with the food of swine; nature teacheth men to understand that it is the principal lesson that affliction readeth to us, to know ourselves and our ways, as they are related to God and to his judgment.

(2.) If you are in prosperity, be the more suspicious of flatterers, and drive them away with the greater detestation: be more careful to keep them from you, than to keep your bodies clean from defilement. And be the more solicitous to procure such faithful overseers and physicians for your souls, as will do their best to save you, though they displease you. O that you knew what an advantage it is to have a faithful pastor, and a faithful friend, that seek not yours but you, and make no advantage to themselves by flatter-

ing you, but choose the means that tend most to your salvation! And O that you knew the great disadvantage of those that want such a pastor, and such a friend! You would then be sure to give it as your strictest charge to both to deal plainly with you, and never to hide or extenuate your sin or danger. You would thus charge your teachers, 'whatever you do, deal faithfully with my soul! If you see me in any dangerous course, I beseech you tell me of it: if I should be hardened against your warnings and reproofs, I beseech you deal not lightly with me, but labour to awaken me, and set it home, and pull me out of the fire, and save me as with fear, O suffer me not to be quiet in my sins.' The like charge also you would give to your friends that are about you, and converse with you; choose such pastors, and such friends as are fittest thus to prove your friends indeed: and charge them and intreat them, as they love your souls, and as they will answer it before God, that they suffer you not to sin for fear of displeasing you by plain reproofs; and resolve to submit and take it well. A stander by hath the great advantage of impartiality, and therefore may see that in you which you observe not in yourselves; self-love doth not hinder us so much in judging of other men's cases as our own. Friendly and faithful dealing in the matters of eternal consequence, is the principal use and benefit of friendship. This distinguishes the communion of saints from Beelzebub's swarm of flies and caterpillars. Thus 'two are better than one: for if they fall, the one will lift up his fellow: but woe to him that is alone when he falleth, for he hath not another to help him up;' much more woe to him that hath a multitude to cast and to keep him down.

Hind. 3. The third extrinsic impediment to self-knowledge, is conversing only with such as are as bad as ourselves; and not with such whose lives display the spiritual endowment and excellencies which we want. Though Christians that know better the common disease, do know that there must be a common humiliation and remedy; yet these indeed are the thoughts of most: they know not that it is a matter of dishonour and lamentation, to be no better than the most, and to lie in the common corruptions of the world, and to have no better hearts than they had by nature. To hear preachers talk of holiness, and a divine nature, and a new birth, and of being made new creatures, and of living in the love of God, and in the joyful hopes of endless glory, doth seem to them but as the talk of a world in the sun, or the description of an angel, which humbleth not them at all, for not being such, nor exciteth in them any great desires to be such : as long as they see not the persons that are such, they think these are but devout imaginations, or the pious dreams of melancholy men ; and that indeed there are no such persons in the world: they judge of all the world, or almost all, by those about them; and they think that God should be unmerciful if he should condemn so great a number as they see are like themselves ; and should save none but those few transcendent souls that they hear described, but are unacquainted with.

It sometimes melteth my heart in pity of many great ones of the world, to think how hard a matter it is for them to know indeed what holiness is ; when they seldom hear so much as one heavenly prayer or discourse, or any serious talk of the matters of sanctification, and communion with Christ: when profaneness and inhuman wickedness dwell about them, and make such as are but civil and temperate, and good-natured persons, to seem saints : when they see but few that fear the Lord, and love him unfeignedly, and live by faith : and those few are perhaps of the more cold, and timorous, and temporizing strain, that show forth but little of the heavenly nature, and the virtues of their holy faith: that dare scarce open their mouths to speak against the wickedness which they see or hear ; that dare not discourse like the saints of the most High, and the heirs of heaven, for fear of being made the scorn and by-word of the rest, or of falling under the frowns and dislike of their superiors ; so that they live among others almost like common men, save only that they run not with them to their excess of riot ; and think it enough that by such forbearance of gross sin they are in some measure evil spoken of : when they that should ' let their light so shine before men, that they might see their good works, and glorify their heavenly Father,' do hide their religion, and put their light as under a bushel, and not in a candlestick, that it might give light unto all that are in the house ; and so when religion never appeareth in its proper splendour and power, and heavenly tendency, to those great ones that have no better company, what wonder if they never know themselves, nor truly understand the nature, necessity or excellency of religion ? When they know it, for the most part, but by hearsay, yea, and when they hear it more reproached than applauded, it must be a miracle of mercy that must make such men to be sincerely and heartily religious. When they see so many about them worse than themselves, and so few

better, and those few that are better do hide it, and live almost as if they were no better; and when the godly, whom they see not, are described to them by the serpent's seed, as if they were but a company of whining, melancholy, brain-sick hypocrites, who can expect that ever such men should savingly know themselves or Christ, unless a wonder of mercy rescue them, and bring them from this darkness and delusion into the light ? O how oft have I wished, in compassion to many of the great ones of the world, that they had but the company which we that are their inferiors have ; that they did but hear the humble, holy, heavenly language, that we have heard ; and hear the faithful, fervent prayers that many poor Christians pour out before the Lord ; and saw but the humble, harmless, exemplary and heavenly lives of many poor Christians, that are represented to them as the filth and the off-scouring of the world, and perhaps no more regarded than Lazarus was at the rich man's gate! Did they but see and hear, and know such holy and heavenly believers, and were as well acquainted with them as we are, how many of them would better know themselves, and see what they want, and what they must be, and better discern between the righteous and the wicked, between those that fear God and those that fear him not!

Direct. 3. It will therefore be a great help to the knowledge of yourselves, if you will converse with those that bear the holy image of their Creator, and whose lives will tell you what it is to live by faith, and what it is to walk in the Spirit, to mortify the flesh, and to live above all the alluring vanities of the world. We can more sensibly perceive the nature of holiness, when we see it in action before our eyes, than when we only read a description of it. Who could have known what life is, or what reason is, by bare reading or hearing their descriptions, if he knew them not in himself and others, by another kind of demonstration? Many thousands can honour the name of a saint, and the scripture descriptions of a saint, that hate the life of holiness, when it appeareth to them in practice, and cannot endure a saint indeed. It will most convincingly tell you what you want, when you see what others have. To see how naturally they breathe after heaven, will most convincingly show you the dulness and earthliness of your minds: to see how easily they can love an enemy and forgive a wrong, will acquaint you most sensibly with the evils of your passionate, revengeful minds. Do but lay by your prejudice and partiality, and see whether there be not in serious Christians another spirit than in the world: and whether they live not upon the things above, which your belief and love did never reach: look upon believers, and consider why they pray, and watch and study to please God, and then bethink yourselves whether you have not as much need to do so as they: and so you may perceive your negligence by their diligence, your senselessness by their tenderness of heart and conscience; your fleshliness by their spirituality, and the rest of your sins by the lustre of their graces. As Gregory saith, 'He that would fully understand what he is, must look on such as are better than himself, that in the comeliness of the good, he may take the measure of his own deformity.' 'Men know not themselves by themselves alone.'—Isidore.

Hence therefore the servants of God may see how exactly they should live, and of what consequence it is that they be eminently holy, when it is they that, by their heavenly excellency, must convince the world of their sinfulness and misery. O Christians, do you live such exemplary and convincing lives? Is there indeed that excellency of holiness appearing in you, which may show men, to the glory of your Redeemer, how the heirs of heaven do differ from the world? Alas, our common, careless living doth wrong to multitudes as well as to ourselves; and is a cruelty to the souls whose salvation we are bound by our examples to promote. What then do those men, that by their vicious, scandalous conversation harden the ungodly, and cause them to think contemptuously, and to speak scornfully of the holy way! O woe to them, if they repent not, by whom such offence cometh!

Especially ministers should see that their lives be a continual lecture; as Hierome saith, 'The house and conversation of a bishop is set as in a glass (or to be beheld) as the teacher of public discipline: all think they should do whatever he doth.' And therefore Chrysostom concludeth, 'that a priest that is bad, doth acquire by his priesthood, not dignity but disgrace: for,' saith he, 'thou sittest in judgment on thyself: if thou live well and preach well, thou instructest the people: if thou preach well and live ill, thou condemnest thyself. For by living well and preaching well, thou instructest the people how to live: but by preaching well and living ill, thou instructest God, as it were, how to condemn thee.'

Hence it is also that the servants of God should have a care of their fame, as well as of their conversation, because the reputation of re-

ligion dependeth much on the reputation of the religious: and reputation doth much to the encouraging or discouraging of the ungodly that are strangers to the things themselves. Augustin saith, ' Conscience is necessary for thyself: and thy good name is necessary for thy neighbour. He that hunteth after fame, and neglecteth conscience, is an hypocrite: and he that so trusteth to a good conscience as to neglect his good name, is cruel to others.' When we mind our fame for the good of others, and the service of God, and not to please a proud, vain-glorious mind; and when we do it without immoderate care, seeking it only by righteous means, and referring the issue to the will of God, as being prepared for evil report as well as good, this is but to improve our talent to our master's use.

CHAPTER XI.

THE INTERNAL HINDERANCES TO SELF-ACQUAINTANCE.

II. I come next to the internal impediments to self-acquaintance, especially in the worse sort of men.

1. The first that I shall acquaint you with is, that natural deep-rooted sin of pride, which strongly inclineth men to think well of themselves, and to desire that all others do so too. So that where pride is not discovered and subdued by grace, men will scarcely endure to be closely questioned by ministers or other friends about their sin, and the condition of their souls: what! question them whether they are ungodly, unsanctified, the servants of sin and Satan; in a state of death and condemnation? Their hearts will rise with indignation against him that will put such questions to them. What! question them whether they have any saving grace; whether they are regenerated, pardoned, and have any well-grounded hopes of heaven! They love not the searching word of God; they love not the distinguishing passages of scripture; they love not a faithful, searching minister, because they would dishonour and trouble them with such doubts as these. A proud man judgeth not of himself as he is, but as his distempered fancy representeth him to himself to be: to think himself something when he is nothing, and so to be wilfully his own deceiver, is his disease; and as pride is one of the deepest-rooted sins in man, and of greatest strength, and hardest to be extirpated and overcome, so true self-acquaintance must be accordingly difficult, it being carried on but by such degrees

as we get ground and victory against our pride. As melancholy men that are wise in all other things, may be far from the right use of reason in some one point where the imagination is crazed and the distemper lieth; so a proud man, how wise soever in any other matter, as to the right knowledge of himself, is like one that hath not indeed the use of reason: pride was his first tutor, and taught him what to believe of himself: so that Christ, who comes after with a humbling doctrine, cannot be believed, nor scarcely with any patience heard. O what a disease is to be cured before a proud person will well know himself! what labour do we lose in all our sermons! yea, how often doth the medicine irritate the disease! so that a poor wretch that is under the wrath of God, and knoweth not when he is gone out of the assembly, whether the justice of heaven will not take vengeance on him before he come hither again, yet cannot abide to hear of this, but, with Ahab, hateth the preacher that prophesieth evil of him, be it ever so true. It is pride that leadeth up that army of corruptions, that here strive against the light of truth, that is sent to convince and convert the guilty. And is a man like to be saved by the word, while he hateth it, and bends his thoughts and passions all against it?

Direct. 1. He therefore that will ever know himself, must first let in so much of the light as may take down his arrogancy, and bring him as a little child to the school of Christ. First know what thou art as a man; and then know what thou art as a sinner, and sentenced by God, that so thou mayest come to know what thou art as one that is under the hopes and duties of the redeemed. When thy proud heart rebelleth against conviction, remember with whom thou hast to do. Will God speak submissively to thee for fear of offending thee? Will he bribe thee with mercy, for handling thee so roughly as to tell thee thou art yet the child of wrath? Is he afraid to talk to thee of death or of damnation? Will he recall his threatenings, and repent him of the severity of his laws, because such worms are angry with them, or will not believe them? Perhaps thou mayst make a false-hearted, fearful, man-pleasing minister, to change his strain of plain-dealing, and become thy flatterer, or be silent: but will God be silenced? Will he stoop to thee, and bend or stretch his word to humour thee? O no; he will one day tell thee what thou art with another voice than this of a mortal and despised man, and in another manner than preachers tell it thee. If thou canst frown the preacher out of the pulpit, or out of his fidelity

to God and thee, yet thou canst not frown God out of heaven. He will speak to thee more terribly than the most terrible preacher that ever thou heardst; and if thy pride shall rise up, and tell him that he doth thee wrong, how quickly will thy mouth be stopped, and thou be forced to confess thy guilt! O stoop, man, to the humbling word of grace, or God will make thee stoop to the words and strokes of wrath. Fear him that will make the proudest fear, before he hath done with them. Judged thou must be; by thyself, to self-abasing and conversion, or by God to desolation and confusion: and canst thou easier bear God's judgment than thy own? Stoop, foolish, self-deluding dust! Stoop, sinful man, and know thy misery! If thou stand it out a little longer, an undiscerned blow will bring thee down, and thou shalt not see the hand that strikes thee, till thou art humbled to the grave and hell. O how absurd, yet pitiful a sight is it, to see poor sinners brave it out against the humbling message of the Lord, as if they could make good their cause against him; and scorn to know that they are going to hell, till they are there! And then will pride preserve them from the knowledge of it? It is shameful folly to be proud and obstinate, where a man knoweth before-hand that he must submit at last, and is not able to stand it out.

2. The second internal impediment to self-acquaintance is an unreasonable tenderness of ourselves; when an inordinate love of ease and quietness of mind doth prevail with us to hold fast all that thus quieteth us at the present, without regard of due provision for the time to come; in this there is a mixture of unreasonableness and self-love: it is indeed the very brutish disposition. A beast will not willingly be dieted for his future health: let him have at present what he loveth and you please him, though you feed him for the slaughter. For he hath not reason to foresee what followeth. Fleshly-minded men have thus brutified themselves, so that they judge of things by present feeling, and have not reason and faith to look before them, and judge of things by what they tend to, even by the good or hurt that will follow in the end. It is a very terrible, troublesome thing for a man that is unregenerated, unjustified, and unreconciled to God, to know it: for a man that hath any feeling left, to find himself in a state of condemnation: this is to stir up all the terrors of his soul, and cast him into perplexing fears and disquietude of mind; so that he cannot eat or drink, or sleep in quietness, but the troublesome thoughts of sin and everlasting wrath torment him: and the in-

considerate man that judgeth of things by present feeling, will not endure this. As most men hate those that speak against them, be the matter ever so true, so they cannot endure those thoughts that accuse them, nor to have a reprover so near them, even in their own breasts: a conscience within them, to preach to them night and day; not one hour in a week, but wherever they go, and whatever they are doing. To be so near, so constant, so precise, and so severe and terrible a preacher, as usually a newly enlightened and awakened conscience is, this seemeth intolerable to themselves; and whatever come of it, this preacher must be silenced, as turbulent and vexatious, and one that would make them melancholy or mad. And this is the condemnation of these miserable souls, that light is come into the world, and they loved darkness rather than light, because their deeds were evil: for every one that doeth evil, hateth the light, neither cometh to the light, lest his deeds should be reproved; and thus while men are so tender of themselves, that they will do nothing that troubleth or hurteth them at the present, they venture upon all the miseries that they are forewarned of.

Direct. 2. Be not unreasonably tender of a little disturbance at the present, nor unbelievingly careless of the misery to come. Cannot you endure to know your sin and misery, and yet can you endure to bear it? Will you go to hell for fear of knowing that you are in the way? Must you not know it with everlasting woe and vengeance when you come thither, if by knowing your danger you prevent not your coming thither? Is it easier to bear God's wrath for ever, than to find at present that you have offended him? Sirs, the question is whether you are under the condemnation of the law, or not,—whether you are regenerated and justified, or yet in your sin? If you are justified, far be it from me to persuade you to think that you are under condemnation: I leave that to Satan and the malicious world, who are the condemners of those that Christ doth justify. But if you are unregenerated and unjustified, what will you do at death and judgment? Can you stand before God, or be saved upon any other terms? You cannot; if God is to be believed, you cannot; and if you know the scriptures, you know you cannot. And if you cannot be saved in an unrenewed, unjustified state, is it not needful that you know it? Will you cry for help before you find yourselves in danger? Or strive to get out of sin and misery, before you believe that you are in it? If you think that you have no other sin than the pardoned infirmities of the godly, you will never

so value Jesus Christ, and pray and strive for such grace as is necessary to them that have the unpardoned reigning sins of the ungodly. If it be necessary that you be saved, it is necessary that you value and seek salvation; and if so, it is necessary that you know your need of it, and what you must be and do if you will obtain it. It is a childish thing, below a man of reason, to stick at a little present trouble, when death cannot otherwise be prevented: if you can prove that ever any was converted and saved by any other way than by coming to the knowledge of their sin and misery, then you have some excuse for your presumption: but if scripture tell us of no other way, yea, that there is no other way, and you know of none that ever was saved by any other, I think it is time to fall to work, and search and try your hearts and lives, since damnation is as it were at your backs. You should rather think with yourselves, if we can so hardly bear the fore-thoughts of hell, how shall we be able everlastingly to bear the torments?

And consider, that Christ hath made the discovery of your sin and misery to be now comparatively an easy burden, in that he hath made them pardonable and curable: if you had not had a Saviour to fly to, but must have looked on your misery as a remediless case, it had then been terrible indeed; and it had been no great mistake to have thought it the best way to take a little ease at present, rather than to disquiet yourselves in vain. But through the great mercy of God, this is not your case; you need not despair of pardon and salvation, if you will but hear while it is called to-day. The task that you are called to, is not to torment yourselves as the damned do, with the thought of unpardonable sin, and of a misery that hath no help or hope; but it is only to find out your disease, and come and open it to the physician, and submit to his advice, and use his means, and he will freely and infallibly work the cure. It is but to find out the folly that you have been guilty of, and the danger that you have brought yourselves into; to come to Christ, and with hearty sorrow and resolution to give up yourselves unto his grace, to cast away your iniquities, and enter into his safe and comfortable service. And will you lie in hell, and say, we are suffering here, that we might escape the trouble of foreseeing our danger of it, or of endeavouring in time to have prevented it,—we died for fear of knowing that we were sick,—we suffered our house to burn to ashes for fear of knowing that it was on fire! O sirs, be warned in time, and own not and practise not such egregious folly, in a business of everlasting consequence. Believe it, if you sin, you must know that you have sinned: and if you are in the power of Satan it cannot long be hid. Did you but know the difference between discovering it now while there is hope, and hereafter when there is none, I should have no need to persuade you to be presently willing to know the truth, whatever it should cost you.

Hind. 3. Another great impediment of the knowledge of ourselves, is, that self-love so blindeth men that they can see no great evil in themselves or any thing that is their own: it makes them believe that all things are as they would have them be ; yea, and better than they would have them: for he that would not indeed be holy, is willing by himself and others to be thought so : did not the lamentable experience of all the world confirm it, it were incredible that self-love could so exceedingly blind men. If charity think no evil of another, and we are very hardly brought to believe any great harm by those we love ; much more will self-love cause men to see no evil in themselves. No arguments so cogent, no light so clear, no oratory so persuading, as can make a self-lover think himself as bad as indeed he is, till God, by grace or terror, shall convince him. When you are preaching the most searching sermons to convince him, self-love confuteth or misapplieth them ; when the marks of trial are most plainly opened, and most closely urged, self-love doth frustrate the preacher's greatest skill and diligence: when nothing of sense can be said to prove the piety of the impious, and the sincerity of the formal hypocrite, yet self-love is that wonderful alchemist, that can make gold not only of the basest metal, but of dross itself. No cause so bad which it cannot justify ; and no person so miserable but it will pronounce him happy, till God by grace or wrath confute it. Self-love is the grand deceiver of the world.

Direct. 3. Subdue this inordinate self-love, and bring your minds to a just impartiality in judging. Remember that self-love is only powerful at your private bar ; and it is not there that your cause must be finally decided ; it can do nothing at the bar of God ; it cannot there justify, where it is condemned itself ; God will not so much as hear it, though you will hear none that speak against it. Self-love is but the vicegerent of the grand usurper, that shall be deposed, and have no show of power, at Christ's appearing, when he will judge his enemies.

Here it will be a helpful course to see your own sin and misery in others ; and put the case as if it were theirs, and then see how you can dis-

cern the evil of it. O how easy is it with the most to see and aggravate the faults of others? How safe were we, if we were as impartial to ourselves! And also it will be very useful to desire often the help of more impartial judgments than your own : others can quickly spy our faults, as we can quickly find out theirs : therefore as poets and painters do expose their works before they finish them, to the common view, that so what is blamed by many may be considered and amended ; so should we, in order to the judging of ourselves, observe both what our friends and enemies say of us, and the more suspiciously try what others blame. But especially have some near judicious friends, that will prudently and faithfully assist you. ' A true friend is an excellent looking-glass,' saith Seneca. Deliberate well, first in the choosing of a friend, and then with him deliberate on all things.

And if you would have the benefits of friendship, discourage not plain-dealing. I know a reprover should be wise, and love must be predominant if he will expect success : but we must take heed of judging that we are hated, because we are reproved ; that is, that a friend is not a friend, because he doth the office of a friend. Of the two, it is fitter to say of a reproving enemy, he dealeth with me like a friend, than of a reproving friend, he dealeth with me like an enemy. It is a happy enmity that helpeth to deliver you from sin and hell; and a cruel friendship that will let you undo your soul for ever, for fear of displeasing you by hindering it.

There are two sorts that deprive themselves of the saving benefit of necessary reproof, and the most desirable fruits of friendship. The one is the hypocrite, that so cunningly hideth his greatest faults, that his friend and enemy never tell him of them. He hath the happiness of keeping his physician unacquainted with his disease, and consequently of keeping the disease. The other is the proud, that can better endure to be ungodly than to be told of it, and to live in many sins, than to be freely admonished of one. Consider therefore that it will prove self-hatred in the effect, which is now called self-love; and that it would seem but a strange kind of love from another to suffer you to fall into a coal-pit, for fear of telling you that you are near it; if you love another no better than thus, you have no reason to call yourself his friend ; and shall this be your wisest loving of yourselves? If it be love to damn your souls for fear of knowing your danger of damnation, the devil loveth you. If it be friendship to keep you out of heaven, for fear of disquieting you with the light that should have saved you, then you have no enemies in hell. The devil himself can be content to grant you a temporal quietness and ease, in order to your everlasting woe. Let go your hopes of heaven, and he can let you be merry a while on earth; while the strong armed man keepeth his house, the things that he possesseth are in peace. If it be not friendship, but enmity, to trouble you with the sight of sin and danger, in order to your deliverance, then you have none but enemies in heaven; for God himself doth take this course with the dearest of his chosen. No star doth give such light as the sun doth. No minister doth so much to make a sinner know himself, as God doth. Love yourselves therefore in the way that God loveth you. Be impartially willing that God and man should help you to be thoroughly acquainted with your state. Love not to be flattered by others, or yourselves. Vice is never the more lovely, because it is yours: and you know that pain is never the more easy or desirable to you, because it is yours. Your own diseases, losses, injuries, and miseries, seem the worst and most grievous to you; and why should not your own sins also be most grievous? You love not poverty, or pain, because it is your own; O love not sin, because it is your own.

Hind. 4. Another impediment to self-acquaintance, is, that men observe not their hearts in a time of trial, but take them always at the best, when no great temptation puts them to it. A man that never had any opportunity to rise in the world, perhaps doth think he is not ambitious, and desireth not much to be higher than he is, because the coal was never blown. When a little affront doth ferment their pride into disquietude, and desires of revenge; or applause doth ferment it into self-exaltation, they observe not then the distemper when it is most observable, because the nature of sin is to please and blind, and cheat the mind into a consent. And when the sin seems past, and they find themselves in a seeming humility and meekness, they judge of themselves as then they find themselves, as thinking the distemper is past and cured, and they are not to judge of themselves by what they were, but what they are. And by that rule every drunkard or whoremonger should judge themselves temperate, and chaste, as soon as they forbear the act of sin. And what if poverty, age, or sickness, hinder them from ever committing either of them again? For all this the person is a drunkard or fornicator still; because the act is not pardoned, the heart sanctified, nor the habit or corrupt inclination mortified. And thus passionate persons do judge of themselves by their milder temper, when no temptation kindleth the flame. But little doth many a one know what corruption is latent in his heart, till trial shall disclose it, and draw it into sight. ' If these persons be not always sinning, they will not take themselves for sinners: but he that hath once sinned knowingly, in God's account continueth in the sin, till his heart be changed by true repentance.'—Augustine. Yet on the other side, I would not wrong any upright soul, by persuading them to judge of themselves as they are at the worst, in the hour of temptation; for so they will be mistaken as certainly, though not as dangerously as the other.

You may ask then, what is to be done in such a difficult case? If we must neither judge of ourselves as we are at the best out of temptation, nor yet as we are at the worst in the hour of temptation, when, and how then shall we judge of ourselves? I answer, it is one thing to know our particular sins, and their degrees, and another thing to know our state in general, whether we are justified and sanctified or not. To discern what particular sin is in us, and how apt it is to break forth into act, we must watch all the stirrings and appearings of it, in the time of the temptation: but to discern whether it be unmortified and have dominion, we must observe these rules. (1.) There is no man on earth that is perfectly free from sin; and therefore it is no good consequence that sin reigneth unto death, because it is not perfectly extinguished, or because it is sometimes committed, unless in the cases after expressed. (2.) No sin that is truly mortified and repented of, shall condemn the sinner; for pardon is promised to the truly penitent. (3.) Whatever sin the will, according to its habitual inclination, had rather leave than keep, is truly repented of and mortified. For the will is the principal seat of sin: and there is no more sinfulness than there is wilfulness. (4.) There are some sins which cannot be frequently committed in consistency with true grace, or sincere repentance; and some which may be frequently committed in consistency with these. As where sins are known and great, or such as are easily subject to the power of a sanctified will, so that he that will reject them, may. As one such sin must have actual repentance, if actually known; so the frequent committing of such will not consist with habitual repentance. Whereas those sins that are so small as upright persons, perhaps, may not be sufficiently excited to resistance; or such as upon the sincere use of means are still unknown, or such as a truly sanctified will may not subdue, are all of them consistent with repentance, and a justified state: and in this sense we reject not that distinction betwixt mortal and venial sin ; that is, between sin inconsistent with a state of spiritual life, and sin consistent with it, and consequently pardoned. He that had rather leave the former sort (the mortal sins) will leave them ; and he that truly repents of them, will forsake them. But for the other consistent with life we must say, that a man may retain them, that yet had rather leave them, and doth truly repent of them. (5.) A sin of carnal interest, esteemed good, in order to something which the flesh desireth ; and so loved and deliberately kept, hath more of the will, and is more inconsistent with repentance, than a sin of mere passion or surprise, which is not so valued upon the account of such an interest. (6.) They that have grace enough to avoid temptations to mortal or reigning sin, and consequently in that way to avoid the sin, shall not be condemned for it, whatever a stronger temptation might have done. (7.) Where bodily diseases necessitate to an act, or the omission of an act, the will is not to be charged with that which it cannot overcome, notwithstanding an unfeigned willingness. As if a man in a frenzy or distraction should swear or curse, or blaspheme ; or one in a lethargy, or potent melancholy, cannot read, or pray, or meditate, &c. (8.) As frequent commissions of venial sins, or such as are consistent with true grace, will not prove the soul unsanctified ; so the once committing of a gross sin by surprise, which is afterward truly repented of, will not prove the absence of habitual repentance, or spiritual life, as the frequent committing of such sins will.

Thus I conclude, in order to the detection of the sin itself, we must all take notice of ourselves as at the worst, and see what it is that temptation can do ; but in order to the discovery of our state, and whether our sins are pardoned or not, we must especially observe whether their eruptions are such as will consist with true habitual repentance, and note what temptations do with us.

Direct. 4. Observe then the workings and discoveries of the heart, and judge of its abundance, or habits, by your words and deeds. Note what you were when you had opportunity to sin, when the full cup of pleasure was held out to you, when preferment was before you, when injury or provoking words did blow the coal: if then sin appeared, judge not that you are free, and that none of the roots are latent in your hearts: or if you are sure that such dispositions are hated, repented of and mortified, yet you may hence observe what diseases of soul you should chiefly

strive against, to keep them under, and prevent a new surprise or increase. It is so usual for such licentiousness, such self-seeking, such pride and passion, to break forth upon some special temptations, which for many years together did never appear to the person that is guilty, or to any other, that it should keep the best in fear and self-suspicion, and cause them to live in constant watchfulness, and to observe the bent and motions of their souls ; and to make use afterward of such discoveries as they have made to their cost in time of trial.

It much concerneth all true Christians to keep in remembrance the exercise and discoveries of grace, which formerly upon trial did undoubtedly appear, and convinced them of the sincerity which afterward they are apt again to question. Will you not believe that there is a sun in the firmament, unless it always shine upon you? It is weakness and injurious rashness in those Christians, that upon every damp that seizeth on their spirits, will venture to deny God's former mercies, and say that they had never special grace, because they feel it not at present ; that they never prayed in sincerity, because some distemper at present discomposeth or overwhelmeth them ; that their former zeal and life was counterfeit, because they are grown more cold and dull ; that former comforts were all but hypocritical delusions, because they are turned now to sorrows : as much as to say, because I am now sick, I was never well. O were it not for the tender compassions of our Father, and the sure performance of our Lord and Comforter, and that our peace is more in his hand than our own, it could never be that a poor, distempered, imperfect soul, should here have any constancy of peace, considering the power of self-love and partiality on one side, and of grief and fear, and other passions on the other ; and how little a thing doth shake so moveable and weak a thing, and trouble a mind so easily disturbed ; and how hard it is, again to quiet and compose a mind so troubled, and bring a grieved soul to reason, and make passion understand the truth, and to cause a weak, afflicted soul to judge quite contrary to what they feel. All this considered, no wonder if the peace and comfort of many Christians be yet but little, and interrupted and uneven.

To show us the sun at midnight, and convince us of love while we feel the rod ; and to give us the comfortable sense of grace, while we have the uncomfortable sense of the greatness of our sin ; to give us the joyful hopes of glory, in a troubled, melancholy, dejected state ; all this is a work that requireth the special help of the

Almighty, and exceeds the strength of feeble worms. Let God give us never so full discoveries of his tenderest love and our own sincerity, as if a voice from heaven had witnessed it unto us, we are questioning all if once we seem to feel the contrary, and are perplexed in the tumult of our thoughts and passions, and bewildered and lost in the errors of our own disturbed minds. Though we have walked with God, we are questioning whether indeed we ever knew him, as soon as he seemeth to hide his face. Though we have felt another life and spirit possess and actuate us than heretofore, and found that we love the things and persons which once we loved not, and that we were quite fallen out with that which was our former pleasure, and that our souls broke off from their old delights, and hopes, and ways, and resolvedly did engage themselves to God, and unfeignedly delivered themselves unto him, yet all is forgotten, or the convincing evidence of all forgotten, if the lively influence of heaven be but once so far withdrawn, as that our present state is clouded and afflicted, and our former vigour and assurance is abated. And thus unthankfully we deny God the praise and acknowledgment of his mercies, longer than we are tasting them, or they are still before us. All that he hath done for us is as nothing; and all the love which he hath manifested to us, is called hatred; and all the witnesses that have put their hands to his acts of grace, are questioned, and his very seals denied, and his earnest misinterpreted, as long as our darkened, distempered souls are in a condition unfit for the apprehension of mercy, and usually when a diseased or afflicted body doth draw the mind into too great a participation of the affliction. And thus, as we are disposed ourselves so we judge ourselves and all our receivings, and all God's dealings with us. When we feel ourselves well, all goes well with us, and we put a good interpretation upon all things: but when we are out of order, we complain of every thing and take pleasure in nothing. And thus, while the discoveries, both of sin and grace, are at present overlooked or afterwards forgotten, and almost all men judge of themselves by present feeling, no wonder if few are well acquainted with themselves.

But as the word and the works of God must be taken together, if they be understood, and not a sentence, part or parcel taken separated from the rest, which must make up the sense ; so also the workings of God upon your souls must be taken all together, and you must read them over from the first till now and set altogether, and not forget the letters, the part that went before, or else you will make no sense of that which followeth. I beseech all weak and troubled Christians to remember also, that they are but children and scholars in the school of Christ; and therefore when they cannot set the several parts together, let them not overvalue their inexperienced understandings, but by the help of their skilful, faithful teachers, do that which of themselves they cannot do. Inquire what your former mercies signify. Open them to your guides, and tell them how God hath dealt with you from the beginning, and how it is with you now. Desire them to help you to perceive how one conduceth to the right understanding of the other. Be not of froward, but of tractable, submissive minds ; and thus your self-acquaintance may be maintained, at least to safety, and to some degree of peace, if not to the joys which you desire, which God reserves for their proper season.

I should have added more on this necessary subject, but that I have said so much of it in other writings, especially in the Saints' Rest, Part 3. Chap. 7. and in my Treatise of Self-denial, and in The Right Method for Peace of Conscience.

I must confess I have written on this subject as I did of Self-denial, viz. with expectation that all men should confess the truth of what I say; and yet so few are cured by it of their self-ignorance, as that still we must stand by and see the world distracted by it, the church divided, the love of brethren interrupted, and the work of Satan carried on by error, violence, and pride ; and the hearts of men so strangely stupified, as to go on incorrigibly in all this mischief, while the cause and cure are open before them, and all in vain, while they confess the truth ! so that they will leave us nothing to do, but exercise our compassion, by lamenting the delirium of madmen, while we are unable to save the church, their brethren, or their own souls, from the lacerations and calamitous effects of their furious self-ignorance. But Christ that hath sent us with the light which may be resisted, and abused, and in part blown out, will teach the proud, the scornful, the unmerciful, the self-conceited, the malicious, and the violent, so effectually to know themselves, as that no more exhortations shall be necessary for the reception of his convictions; nor will he or his servants any more beseech men to consider and know their sin and misery, nor be beholden to them to believe and confess it. Yet is there no remedy for a stupified inconsiderate soul ? Is there no prevention of so terrible a self-knowledge, as the light of judgment, and the fire of hell will else procure? Yes, the remedy is certain, easy, and at hand: even to know themselves, till they are driven to study, and seek and know the Father, and his Son Jesus Christ. And yet is the salvation of most as hopeless almost as if there were no remedy, because no persuasion can prevail with them to use it. Lord, what hath thus locked up the minds and hearts of sinners against thy truth and thee? What hath made reasonable man so unreasonable, and a self-loving nature so mortally to hate itself? O thou that openest, and no man shutteth, use the key that openeth hearts; come in with thy wisdom, and thy love, and all this blindness and obstinacy will be gone. At least commit not the safety of thy flock to such as will not know themselves: but ' gather thy remnant, and bring them to their folds, and let them be fruitful and increase; and set up shepherds over them, which shall feed them, and let them fear no more, nor be dismayed, nor be lacking.—Ordain a place for them, plant them, and let them dwell therein unmoved; and let not the children of wickedness waste them any more.—As a shepherd seeketh out his flock in the day, that he is among his sheep that are scattered, so seek out thy sheep, and deliver them out of all places where they have been scattered in the cloudy and dark day. Save thy people and bless thine inheritance: feed them also, and lift them up for ever.

MR. BAXTER'S
DYING THOUGHTS,

UPON PHILIPPIANS I. 23.

WRITTEN FOR HIS OWN USE IN THE LATTER TIMES OF HIS CORPORAL PAINS AND WEAKNESS.

PREFATORY REMARKS.

This work was first published in 1683, and is preceded by the following "Preface to the Reader:"—

Reader,—I have no other use for a preface to this book, but to give you a true excuse for its publication. I wrote it for myself, unresolved whether any one should ever see it, but at last inclined to leave that to the will of my executors, to publish or suppress it when I am dead, as they saw cause. But my person being seized on, and my library and all my goods distrained on by constables, and sold, and I constrained to relinquish my house (for preaching and being in London), I knew not what to do with multitudes of manuscripts that had long lain by me; having no house to go to, but a narrow hired lodging with strangers: wherefore I cast away whole volumes, which I could not carry away, both controversies and letters practical, and cases of conscience, but having newly lain divers weeks, night and day, in waking torments, nephritic and colic, after other long pains and languor, I took this book with me in my removal, for my own use in my further sickness. Three weeks after, falling into another extreme fit, and expecting death, where I had no friend with me to commit my papers to, merely lest it should be lost, I thought best to give it to the printer. I think it is so much of the work of all men's lives to prepare to die with safety and comfort, that the same thoughts may be needful for others that are so for me. If any mislike the title, as if it imported that the author is dead, let him know that I die daily, and that which quickly will be, almost is: it is suited to my own use: they that it is unsuitable to may pass it by. If those men's lives were spent in serious, preparing thoughts of death, who are now studying to destroy each other, and tear in pieces a distressed land, they would prevent much dolorous repentance.

RICHARD BAXTER.

These "Dying Thoughts" abound in admirable sentiments, expressed in appropriate and beautiful language, worthy of a believer in the near prospect of eternity. They were written for his own use, and originally intended to be left to his executors for publication, but were finally brought out by himself. Calamy puts them under the date of 1685, and represents them as having furnished great consolation to Lord William Russell before his execution. But, as he speaks of himself as in the seventy-sixth year of his age, and the fifty-third of his ministry, which was the year of his death, he must have altered and improved the work shortly before he died.

In these Thoughts, as there are few raptures, so there are no depressions or despondencies. They discover throughout a solemn, calm, undisturbed serenity; the steady contemplation of dissolution and all its consequences, without alarm or terror. He knew in whom he had believed; to him, therefore, death had no sting. Its poison had been extracted, and the grim tyrant deprived of his power to injure. In Christ, his soul had found rest; his life was made sure by the covenant of redemption: so that he could lay down his head and die in the sure and certain hope of a resurrection to glory. Unenviable must be the state of that man's feelings, who can read these reflections as the honest and sincere expressions of a soul ready to take its flight into eternity, without exclaiming, "Let me die the death of this righteous man, and let my latter end be like his."

The last few years of his life Baxter resided in Charterhouse Square, in London, and preached every Lord's-day in the meeting-house of his friend, Mr. Sylvester. His last effort in preaching so exhausted the small remainder of vitality, that he nearly expired in the pulpit; and doubtless, as Dr. Bates remarks, "it would have been his joy to be transfigured in the mount." But he was able to creep home; and until he took to his bed, he kept his door open to receive all who came to his family worship, and the feeble but earnest exhortations which he there delivered. At last he felt the approaches of death, and could rise no more. Of such a man, in such circumstances, every utterance is memorable; and not the least memorable are those which, in the vestibule of eternity, identify with the lowliest of penitents and the latest of converts, the mighty theologian and the saint of sixty years' standing. " 'God be merciful to me a sinner.' I bless God that this is left on record in the gospel as an effectual prayer." " God may justly condemn me for the best duty I ever did; all my hopes are from his free mercy in Christ." When waking from a slumber, he said, " I shall rest from my labours;" a minister added, "And your works will follow you;" but he answered, " No works! I will leave out works, if God will grant me the other." And when a friend recalled the great good which had been done by his writings, he replied, " I was but a pen in God's hand; and what praise is due to a pen?" " Almost well," was the answer to inquiries how he did; and at last, on Tuesday, the 8th of December, 1691, he entered into the rest which remains for the people of God. His funeral was attended by a concourse of distinguished persons of various ranks, including many of the ministers of the Church of England; and a spectator tells how the train of mourning coaches extended from Merchant Taylor's Hall, whence the procession set out, to the gate of Christ Church, where his body lies buried.

The threescore years and fifteen of this good man's pilgrimage included the most eventful period of our national history, and joined the old Elizabethan England to the England that now is; for although James was on the throne when Baxter was in the cradle, it was practically the England of the Tudors on which his eyes first opened. But he lived to see great changes. He lived to see the practical despotism of both Tudors and Stuarts replaced by a constitutional monarchy. He lived to see the despised and persecuted Puritanism within the Church of England expand into a dominant Presbyterianism, and after another interval of suppression, emerge in the shape of modern Nonconformity. And he lived to see the principle of religious toleration—in his younger days the heresy of an insignificant handful—practically, though grudgingly, recognized by the laws of England. And it is curious to think who all were Baxter's contemporaries; but sure and certain he lived alongside of Pope and Addison, as well as Shakspeare; of Isaac Watts, as well as Giles Fletcher and George Herbert; of Sir Robert Walpole, as well as Sir Walter Raleigh. When he was a boy the model preacher was Bishop Andrews; in his old age, the lights of the pulpit were Bates, and South, and Francis Atterbury. His own ministry commenced under the primacy of Laud; and when he closed it, Tillotson had ascended the throne of Canterbury.

But Baxter was the citizen of a kingdom which cannot be moved, and the times which passed over him wrought little change on his theology, his temperament, or even his mode of expression. Retain-ing many of his "Baxterian" opinions to the last, during all these long years he withal maintained his intense and affectionate grasp of that truth supreme which alone is saving; and as long as breath and being lasted, he continued to urge it with unabating fervour on the minds of men; and amidst all the changes in public taste, he continued to write the same copious, manly, unfettered English which made his earliest works precocious, and which, even now, prevents them from being obsolete. His practical writings fill four great folios, and have been reprinted in twenty-two octavos; and were his controversial treatises collected, they would occupy a space at least twice as large; good work, surely, for a constant invalid, and one who was, during his best days, a busy pastor; but of all his hundred and sixty-eight separate publications, there is not one which, in a life of leisure, we should deem it a hardship to read through, and scarcely one through which the reader might not hope to be made wiser and better.

"Deposit one of those gray folios on a resting-place equal to that venerable burden," says the eloquent professor of modern history at Cambridge, " then call up the patient and serious thoughts which its very aspect should inspire, and confess that among the writings of uninspired men, there are none better fitted to awaken, to invigorate, to enlarge, or to console the mind which can raise itself to such celestial colloquy. True, they abound in undistinguishable distinctions; the current of emotion, when flowing most freely, is but too often obstructed by metaphysical rocks and shallows, or diverted from its course into some dialectic winding; one while the argument is obscured by fervent expostulation; at another, the passion is dried up by the analysis of the ten thousand springs of which it is compounded; here is a maze of subtleties to be unravelled, and there a crowd of the obscurely learned to be refuted. The unbroken solemnity may now and then shed some gloom on the traveller's path, and the length of the way may occasionally entice him to slumber; but where else can be found an exhibition, at once so vivid and so chaste, of the diseases of the human heart—a detection so fearfully exact of the sophistries of which we are first the voluntary, and then the unconscious victims—a light thrown with such intensity on the madness and the woe of every departure from the rules of virtue—a development of those rules at once so comprehensive and so elevated—counsels more shrewd or more persuasive—or a proclamation more consolatory of the resources provided by Christianity for escaping the dangers by which we are surrounded, of the eternal rewards she promises, or of the temporal blessings she imparts, as an earnest and a foretaste of them?"[1]

---

[1] Orme's *Life of Baxter*, Hamilton's *Christian Classics*, and Sir J. Stephen's *Essays in Ecclesiastical Biography*.

DYING THOUGHTS

On Phil. i. 23.

PRELIMINARY OBSERVATIONS.

The exercise of three sorts of love—to God, to others, and to myself—affords me a threefold satisfaction to be willing to depart.

I. I am sure my departure will be the fulfilling of that will which is love itself, which I am bound above all things to love and please, and which is the beginning, rule, and end of all. Antonine could hence fetch good thoughts of death.

II. The world dies not with me when I die: nor the church, nor the praise and glory of God, which he will have in, and from this world unto the end: and if I love others as myself, their lives and comforts will now be to my thoughts, as if I were to live myself in them. God will be praised and honoured by posterity when I am dead and gone. Were I to be annihilated this would comfort me now, if I lived and died in perfect love.

III. But a better and glorious world is before me, into which I hope by death to be translated, whither all these three sorts of love should wrap up the desires of my ascending soul; even the love of myself, that I may be fully happy; the love of the triumphant church, Christ, angels, and glorified men, and the glory of all the universe which I shall see; and above all, the love of the most glorious God, infinite life, and light, and love, the ultimate amiable object of man's love: in whom to be perfectly pleased and delighted, and to whom to be perfectly pleasing for ever, is the chief and ultimate end of me, and of the highest, wisest, and best of creatures. Amen.

THE INTRODUCTION.

I write for myself, and therefore supposing the sense of the text, shall only observe what is useful to my heart and practice.

It was a happy state into which grace had brought this apostle, who saw so much not only tolerable, but greatly desirable, both in living and dying. To live to him was Christ, that is, Christ's interest or work: to die would be gain, that is, his own interest and reward. His strait was not whether it would be good to live or good to depart: both were good, but which was more desirable was the doubt.

I. Quest. But was there any doubt to be made between Christ's interest and his own? Answer., No, if it had been a full and fixed competition: But by Christ, or Christ's interest, he means his work for his church's interest in this world: but he knew that Christ also had an interest in his saints above; and that he could raise up more to serve him here: yet because he was to judge by what appeared, and he saw a defect of such on earth, this did turn the scales in his choice; and for the work of Christ and his church's good, he more inclined to the delay of his reward, by self-denial: yet knowing that the delay would tend to its increase. It is useful to me here to note:—That even in this world, short of death, there is some good so much to be regarded, as may justly prevail with believers to prefer it before the present hastening of their reward.

I the rather note this, that no temptation carry me into that extreme, of taking nothing but heaven to be worthy of our minding or regard; and so to cast off the world in a sinful sort, on pretence of mortification, and a heavenly mind and life.

I. As to the sense, the meaning is not that anything on earth is better than heaven, or simply, and in itself, to be preferred before it:

the end is better than the means as such: and perfection better than imperfection.

But the present use of the means may be preferred sometimes before the present possession of the end; and the use of means for a higher end may be preferred before the present possession of a lower end: and everything hath its season. Planting, sowing, and building are not so good as reaping, and fruit-gathering, and dwelling: but in their season they must be first done.

II. Quest. But what is there so desirable in this life?

Answer. 1. While it continues it is the fulfilling of the will of God, who will have us here: and that is best which God wills.

2. The life to come depends upon this: as the life of man in the world upon his generation in the womb; or as the reward upon the work; or as the runner's or soldier's prize upon his race or fighting; or as the merchant's gain upon his voyage. Heaven is won or lost on earth; the possession is there, but the preparation is here: Christ will judge all men according to their works on earth: 'Well done, good and faithful servant,' must go before 'Enter thou into the joy of thy Lord:' 'I have fought a good fight, I have finished my course' goes before, 'the crown of righteousness which God the righteous judge will give:' all that ever must be done for salvation by us, must here be done. It was on earth that Christ himself wrought the work of our redemption, fulfilled all righteousness, became our ransom, and paid the price of our salvation: and it is here that our part is to be done.

The bestowing of the reward is God's work, who we are sure will never fail: there is no place for the least suspicion or fear of his misdoing or failing in any of his undertaken work. But the danger and fear is of our own miscarrying: lest we be not found capable of receiving what God will certainly give to all that are disposed receivers. To distrust God is heinous sin and folly: but to distrust ourselves we have great cause. So that if we will make sure of heaven, it must be by giving all diligence to make firm our title, our calling, and our election here on earth. If we fear hell, we must fear what leads to it.

It is great and difficult work that must be here done: it is here that we must be cured of all damning sin; that we must be regenerated and new born; that we must be pardoned and justified by faith. It is here that we must be united to Christ, made wise to salvation, renewed by his Spirit, and conformed to his likeness: it is here that we must overcome all the temptations of the devil, the world, and the flesh, and perform all the duties towards God and man, that must be rewarded: it is here that Christ must be believed in with the heart to righteousness, and with the mouth confessed to salvation. It is here that we must suffer with him that we may reign with him, and be faithful to the death that we may receive the crown of life: here we must so run that we may obtain.

3. Yea, we have greater work here to do than merely securing our own salvation. We are members of the world and church, and we must labour to do good to many; we are trusted with our Master's talents for his service: in our places to do our best to propagate his truth, and grace, and church; and to bring home souls, honour his cause, edify his flock, and further the salvation of as many as we can. All this is to be done on earth, if we will secure the end of all in heaven.

Use 1. It is then an error, though it is but few I think that are guilty of it, to think that all religion lies in minding only the life to come, and disregarding all things in this present life: all true Christians must seriously mind both the end, and the means or way: if they mind not believingly the end, they will never be faithful in the use of means: if they mind not and use not diligently the means, they will never obtain the end. None can use earth well that prefer not heaven; and none come to heaven, that are not prepared by well using earth. Heaven must have the deepest esteem, and habituated love, desire, and joy: but earth must have more of our daily thoughts for present practice. A man that travels to the most desirable home, hath a habit of desire to it all the way, but his present business is his travel: and horse, company, inns, ways, weariness, &c. may take up more of his sensible thoughts, and of his talk and action, than his home.

Use 2. I have often marvelled to find David in the psalms, and other saints before Christ's coming, to have expressed so great a sense of the things of this present life, and to have said so little of another. To have made so great a matter of prosperity, dominions, and victories on one hand, and of enemies, success, and persecution on the other. But I consider that it was not for mere personal, carnal interest, but for the church of God, and for his honour, word, and worship: and they knew that if things go well with us on earth they will be sure to go well in heaven: if the militant church prosper in holiness, there is no doubt but it will triumph in glory: God will be sure to do his part in receiving souls, if they be here prepared for his kingdom. Satan doth much of his damning work by men: if we escape their temptations we escape much of our danger. If idolators prospered, Israel was tempted to idolatry: the Greek church is almost swallowed up by Turkish prosperity and dominion. Most follow the powerful and prosperous side. Therefore for God's cause, and for heavenly, everlasting interest, our own state, but much more the church's, must be greatly regarded here on earth.

Indeed if earth be desired only for earth, and prosperity loved but for the present welfare of the flesh, it is the certain mark of an earthly mind. But to desire peace, and prosperity, and power to be in the hands of wise and faithful men, for the sake of souls, and the increase of the church, and the honour of God, that his name may be hallowed, his kingdom come, and his will done on earth, as it is in heaven: this is to be the chief of our prayers to God.

Use 3. Be not unthankful then, O my soul, for the mercies of this present life, for those to thy body, to thy friends, to the land of thy nativity, and specially to the church of God.

This body is so nearly united to thee, that it must needs be a great help or hinderance: had it been more afflicted, it might have been a discouraging clog; like a tired horse in a journey, or an ill tool to a workman, or an untuned instrument in music: a sick or bad servant in a house is a great trouble: a bad wife much more. But thy body is nearer thee than either, and will be more of thy concern.

Yet if it had been more strong and healthful, sense and appetite would have been strong; and lust would have been strong; and therefore danger would have been greater, and victory and salvation much more difficult. Even weak senses and temptations have too often prevailed. How knowest thou then what stronger ones might have done: when I see a thirsty man in a fever or dropsy; and specially when I see strong and healthful youths, bred up in fulness, and among temptations, how mad they are in sin, and how violently they are carried to it, bearing down God's rebukes, conscience, parents, and friends, and all regard to their salvation, it tells me how great a mercy I had even in a body not liable to their case.

Many a bodily deliverance hath been of great use to my soul, renewing my time, opportunity, and strength for service, and bringing frequent and fresh reports of the love of God.

If bodily mercies were not of great use to the soul, Christ would not so much have showed his saving love, by healing all manner of diseases as he did. Nor would God promise us a resurrection of the body, if a congruous body did not further the welfare of the soul.

I am obliged to great thankfulness to God for the mercies of this life which he hath showed to my friends; that which furthers their joy should increase mine: I ought to rejoice with them that rejoice: nature and grace teach us to be glad when our friends are well and prosper: though all in order to better things than bodily warfare.

Such mercies of this life to the land of our habitation, must not be undervalued. The want of them are parts of God's threatened curse; and godliness hath the promise of this life, and of that which is to come; and so is profitable to all things. When God sends on a land the plagues of famine, pestilence, war, persecution, especially a famine of the word of God, it is a great sin to be insensible of it: if any shall say, While heaven is sure we have no cause to accuse God, or to cast away comfort, hope, or duty, they say well: but if they say, Because heaven is all, we must make light of all that befalls us on earth, they say amiss.

Good princes, magistrates, and public-spirited men that promote the safety, peace, and true prosperity of the commonwealth, do thereby very much befriend religion, and men's salvation; and are greatly to be loved and honoured by all. If the civil state, called the commonwealth, miscarry, or fall into ruins and calamity, the church will fare the worse for it, as the soul doth by the ruins of the body. The Turkish, Muscovite, and such other empires, tell us, how the church consumes and dwindles away into contempt; or withered ceremony and formality, where tyranny brings slavery, beggary, or long persecution on the subjects. Doubtless divers passages in the Revelations contain the church's glorifying of God for their power and prosperity on earth, when emperors became Christians: What else can be meant well by Rev. ix. 10. 'Hath made us kings and priests to God, and we shall reign on the earth;' but that Christians shall be brought from under heathen persecution, and have rule and sacred honour in the world, some of them being princes, some honoured church guides, and all a peculiar honoured people. Had not Satan found out that cursed way of getting wicked men that hate true godliness and peace, into the sacred places of princes and pastors, to do his work against Christ, as in

Christ's name, surely no good Christians would have grudged at the power of rulers of state or church : sure I am that many called fifth monarchy men seem to make this their great hope, that rule shall be in the hands of righteous men : and I think most religious parties would rejoice if those had very great power whom they take to be the best and trustiest men : which shows that it is not the greatness of power in most princes, or sound bishops, that they dislike, but the badness, real or supposed, of those whose power they dislike. Who will blame power to do good ?

Surely the three first and great petitions of the Lord's prayer include some temporal welfare of the world and church, without which the spiritual rarely prospers extensively, (though intensively in a few it may) since miracles ceased.

4. Be thankful therefore for all the church's mercies here on earth : for all the protection of magistracy, the plenty of preachers, the preservation from enemies, the restraint of persecution, the concord of Christians, and increase of godliness, which in this land it hath had in our ages, notwithstanding all Satan's malignant rage, and all the bloody wars that have interrupted our tranquillity. How many psalms of joyful thanksgiving be there for Israel's deliverances, and the preservation of Zion, and God's worship in his sanctuary : 'pray for the peace of Jerusalem : they shall prosper that love it :' especially, that the gospel is continued, while so many rage against it, is a mercy not to be made light of.

Use IV. Be specially thankful, O my soul, that God hath made any use of thee for the service of his church on earth. My God, my soul for this doth magnify thee, and my spirit rejoices in the review of thy great undeserved mercy ! O what am I whom thou tookest up from the dunghill, or low obscurity, that I should live myself in the constant relish of thy sweet and sacred truth, and with such encouraging success communicate it to others ? That I must say now my public work seems ended, that these forty-three or forty-four years I have no reason to think that ever I laboured in vain ! O with what gratitude must I look upon all places where I lived and laboured, but above all, that place that had my strength. I bless thee for the great numbers gone to heaven, and for the continuance of piety, humility, concord and peace among them.

For all that by my writings have received any saving light and grace. O my God, let not my own heart be barren while I labour in thy husbandry, to bring others unto holy fruit. Let me not be a stranger to the life and power of that saving truth which I have done so much to communicate to others. O let not my own words and writings condemn me as void of that divine and heavenly nature and life, which I have said so much for to the world.

Use V. Stir up then, O my soul, thy sincere desires and all thy faculties, to do the remnant of the work of Christ appointed thee on earth, and then joyfully wait for the heavenly perfection in God's own time.

Thou canst truly say, ' to live, to me is Christ : it is his work for which thou livest : thou hast no other business in the world : but thou dost his work with the mixture of many oversights and imperfections, and too much troublest thy thoughts distrustfully about God's part, who never fails if thy work be done. Be thankful for what is past, and that thou art come so near the port of rest : if God will add any more to thy days, serve him with double alacrity, now thou art so near the end : the prize is almost within sight ; time is swift and short : thou hast told others that there is no working in the grave, and that it must be ' now or never :' though the conceit of meriting of commutative justice be no better than madness, dream not that God will save the wicked ; no, nor equally reward the slothful and the diligent, because Christ's righteousness was perfect. Paternal justice makes difference according to that worthiness which is so denominated by the law of grace : and as sin is its own punishment, holiness and obedience is much of its own reward ; whatever God appoints thee to do, see that thou do it sincerely, and with all thy might : if sin dispose men to be angry because it is detected, disgraced and resisted, if God be pleased, their wrath should be patiently borne, who will shortly be far more angry with themselves. If slander and obloquy survive, so will the better effects on those that are converted : and there is no comparison between these. I shall not be hurt, when I am with Christ, by the calumnies of men on earth : but the saving benefit will, by converted sinners, be enjoyed for ever. Words and actions are transient things, and being once past are nothing : but the effect of them on an immortal soul may be endless. All the sermons that I have preached are nothing now ; but the grace of God on sanctified souls is the beginning of eternal life. It is unspeakable mercy to be sincerely thus employed with success, therefore I had reason all this while to be in Paul's strait, and make no haste in my desires to depart. The crown will come in its due time : eternity is long enough to enjoy it, how long soever it be delayed : but if I will do that which must obtain it for myself and others, it must be quickly done before my declining sun be set.

O that I had no worse causes of my unwillingness yet to die, than my desire to do the work of life for my own and other men's salvation, and to ' finish my course with joy, and the ministry committed to me by the Lord.'

Use VI. As it is on earth that I must do good to others, so it must be in a manner suited to their state on earth. Souls are here closely united to bodies, by which they must receive much good or hurt : do good to men's bodies, if thou wouldst do good to their souls : say not, things corporeal are worthless trifles, for which the receivers will be never the better : they are things that nature is easily sensible of, and sense is the passage to the mind and will. Dost not thou find what a help it is to thyself, to have at any time any ease and alacrity of body : what a burden and hinderance, pains and cares are ? Labour then to free others from such burdens and temptations, and be not regardless of them. If thou must rejoice with them that rejoice, and mourn with them that mourn, further thy own joy in furthering theirs ; and avoid thy own sorrows, in avoiding or curing theirs.

But, alas ! What power hath selfishness in most ? How easily do we bear our brethren's pains, reproaches, wants and afflictions, in comparison of our own : how few thoughts, and how little cost or labour, do we use for their supply, in comparison of what we do for ourselves. Nature indeed teaches us to be most sensible of our own case : but grace tells us that we should not make so great a difference as we do, but should love our neighbours as ourselves.

Use VII. Now, O my soul, consider how mercifully God hath dealt with thee, that thy strait should be between two conditions so desirable ? I shall either die speedily, or stay yet longer upon earth : which ever it be, it will be a merciful and comfortable state. That it is desirable to depart and be with Christ, I must not doubt, and shall afterwards more copiously consider, And if my abode on earth yet longer be so great a mercy as to be put in the balance against my present possession of heaven, surely it must be a state which obliges me to great thankfulness to God, and comfortable acknowledgment. Surely it is not my pain, or sickness, or my suffering from malicious men, that should make this life on earth unacceptable, while God will continue it. Paul had his ' thorn in the flesh, the messenger of Satan, to buffet him,' and suffered more from men (though less in his health,) than

I have done : yet he gloried in such infirmities, and rejoiced in his tribulations, and was in a strait between living and dying, yea, rather chose to live yet longer.

Alas, it is another kind of strait that most of the world are in : the strait of most is between the desire of life for fleshly interest, and the fear of death as ending their felicity : the strait of many is between a tiring world and body which makes them weary of living, and the dreadful prospect of future danger which makes them afraid of dying : if they live, it is in misery ; if they must die, they are afraid of greater misery : which way ever they look, behind or before them, to this world or the next, fear and trouble is their lot ; yea, many an upright Christian, through the weakness of their trust in God, doth live in this perplexed strait ; weary of living, and afraid of dying ; between grief and fear, they are pressed continually : but Paul's strait was between two joys, which of them he should desire most : if that be my case, what should much interrupt my peace or pleasure. If I live, it is for Christ ; for his work, and for his church, for preparation, for my own and others' everlasting felicity. Should any suffering which makes me not unserviceable, make me impatient with such a work, and such a life ? If I die presently, it is my gain : God, who appointeth me my work, doth limit my time, and surely his glorious reward can never be unseasonable, or come too soon, if it be the time that he appoints. When I first engaged myself to preach the gospel, I reckoned, as probable, but upon one or two years : God hath continued me yet above forty-four, with such interruptions as others in these times have had. What reason have I now to be unwilling either to live or die ? God's service hath been so sweet to me, that it hath overcome the trouble of constant pains or weakness of the flesh, and all that men have said or done against me.

But the following crown exceeds this pleasure, more than I am here capable to conceive. There is some trouble in all this pleasant work, from which the soul and flesh would rest : ' blessed are the dead that die in the Lord : even so saith the Spirit ; for they rest from their labours, and their works follow them.'

But, O my soul, what needest thou be troubled in this kind of strait ? It is not left to thee to choose whether or when thou wilt live or die. It is God that will determine it, who is infinitely fitter to choose than thou : leave therefore his own work to himself, and mind that which is thine ; whilst thou livest, live to Christ, and when thou diest, thou shalt die to

Christ, even into his blessed hands ; so live, that thou mayest say,' It is Christ liveth in me, and the life that I live in the flesh, I live by the faith of the Son of God, who loved me, and gave himself for me : and then as thou hast lived in the comfort of hope, thou shalt die unto the comfort of vision and fruition : and when thou canst say, he is the ' God whose I am, and whom I serve,' thou mayst boldly add, and whom I trust, and to whom I commend my departing soul : and I know whom I have trusted.

CHAP. I.

EXPOSITION OF THE TEXT, AND BASIS OF THE TREATISE.

" *For I am in a strait betwixt two, having a desire to depart, and to be with Christ, which is far better ;*" or, *for this is much rather to be preferred, or better.*—PHIL. I. 23.

'MAN that is born of a woman, is of few days, and full of trouble: he cometh forth like a flower, and is cut down : he fleeth also as a shadow, and continueth not ; and dost thou open thine eyes upon such a one, and bringest me into judgment with thee ?' saith Job. As a watch when it is wound up, or as a candle newly lighted ; so man newly conceived or born, begins a motion which incessantly hastens to its appointed period. An action, and its time, that is past, is nothing : so vain a thing would man be, and so vain his life, were it not for the hopes of a more durable life, which this refers to. But those hopes, and the means, do not only distinguish a believer from an infidel, but a man from a beast. When Solomon describes the difference in respect to the time and things of this life only, he truly tells us that one end here befalling both shows that both are here but vanity, but man's vexation is greater than the beasts'. And Paul truly saith of Christians, that, ' if our hope were only in this life,' that is, in the time and things of this life and world, ' we were of all men most miserable.' Though even in this life, as related to a better, and as we are exercised about things of a higher nature than the concerns of temporal life, we are far happier than any worldlings.

Being to speak of myself, I shall pass by all the rest of the matter of this text, and suppose its due explication, and spread before my soul only the doctrine and uses of these two parts contained in it.

Part I. That the souls of believers, wnen departed hence, shall be with Christ.

Part II. That so to be with Christ is far better for them than to be here in the body.

Concerning the first, my thoughts shall keep this order :

1st. I shall consider the necessity of believing it. 2d. Whether it be best believing it, without consideration of the proofs or difficulties. 3d. The certainty of it manifested for the exercise of faith.

Whether the words signify that we shall be in the same place with Christ, which Grotius groundlessly denies, or only in his hand, care, and love, I will not stay to dispute : many other texts concurring do assure us that ' we shall be with him where he is.' At least, ' with him' can mean no less than a state of communion, and a participation of felicity. To believe such a state of happiness for departed souls, is of manifold necessity or use.

If this be not soundly believed, a man must live without or below the end of life : he must have a false end, or be uncertain what should be his end.

I know it may be objected, that if I make it my end to please God, by obeying him, and doing all the good I can, and trust him with my soul and future estate, as one that is utterly uncertain what he will do with me, I have an end intended, which will make me godly, charitable, just, and happy, so far as I am made for happiness : for the pleasing of God is the right end of all.

Must I desire to please him no better than I do in this imperfect state, in which I have, and do, so much which is displeasing to him ? He that must desire to please him, must desire to please him perfectly : and the desire of our ultimate end must have no bounds or check. Am I capable of pleasing God no better, than by such a sinful life as this ? God hath made the desire of our own felicity so necessary to the soul of man, that it cannot be expected that our desire to please him, should be separated from this. Therefore both in respect of God as the end, and of our felicity as our second end, we must believe that he is the ' rewarder of them that diligently seek him.'

If we make such an ill description of God, as that he will turn our pleasing him to our loss, or will not turn it to our gain and welfare, or that we know not whether he will do so or not, it will hinder our love, trust, and joy in him, by which we must please him, and consequently hinder the alacrity, soundness, and constancy of our obedience.

It will much dismiss that self-love which

must excite us, and it will take off part of our necessary end: and I think the objectors will confess, that if they have no certainty what God will do with them, they must have some probability and hope, before they can be sincerely devoted here to please him.

If a man be but uncertain what he should make the end of his life, or what he should live for, how can he pitch upon an uncertain end? And if he waver so as to have no end, he can use no means: and if end and means be all laid by, the man lives not as a man, but as a brute. What a torment must it be to a considerate mind to be uncertain what to intend and do in all the tenor and actions of his life? Like a man going out at his door, not knowing whither, or what to do, or which way to go; either he will stand still, or move as brutes do by present sense, or a windmill or weather-cock, as he is moved.

But if he pitch upon a wrong end, it may yet be worse than none; for he will but do hurt, or make work for repentance: and all the actions of his life must be formally wrong, how good soever materially, if the end of them be wrong.

If I fetch them not from this end, and believe not in God as a rewarder of his servants, in a better life, what motives shall I have, which in our present difficulties, will be sufficient to cause me to live a holy, yea, or a truly honest life? All piety and honesty indeed is good, and goodness is desirable for itself: but the goodness of a means, is its aptitude for the end; and we have here abundance of impediments, competitors, diversions and temptations, and difficulties of many sorts; and all these must be overcome by him that will live in piety or honesty. Our natures, we find, are diseased, and greatly indisposed to unquestionable duties; and will they ever discharge them, and conquer all these difficulties and temptations, if the necessary motive be not believed? Duty to God and man is accidentally hard and costly to the flesh, though amiable in itself: it may cost us our estates, our liberties and lives. The world is not so happy as commonly to know good men from bad, or to encourage piety and virtue, or to forbear opposing them. Who will let go his present welfare, without some hope of better as a reward? Men use not to serve God for nought; nor that think it will be their loss to serve him.

A life of sin will not be avoided upon lower ends and motives: nay, those lower ends, when alone, will be a constant sin themselves: a preferring vanity to glory, the creature to God, and a setting our heart on that which will never

make us happy: and when lust and appetite incline men strongly and constantly to their several objects, what shall sufficiently restrain them, except the greater and more durable delights or motives drawn from divine things? Lust and appetite distinguish not between lawful and unlawful. We may see in the brutish politics of Benedictus Spinosa, * whither the principles of infidelity tend. If sin so overspreads the earth, that the whole world is as drowned in wickedness, notwithstanding all the hopes and fears of a life to come, what would it do were there no such hopes and fears?

No mercy can be truly known and estimated, nor rightly used and improved by him that sees not its tendency to the end, and perceives not that it leads to a better life, and uses it not thereunto God deals more bountifully with us than worldlings understand: he gives us all the mercies of this life, as helps to an immortal state of glory, and as earnests of it. Sensualists know not what a soul is, nor what soul-mercies are; and therefore not what the soul of all bodily mercies are: but take up only with the shadow. If the king would give me a lordship, and send me a horse or coach to carry me to it, and I should only ride about the fields for my pleasure, and make no other use of it, should I not undervalue and lose the principal benefit of my horse or coach? No wonder if unbelievers be unthankful, when they know not at all that part of God's mercies which is the life and real excellency of them.

Alas! How should I bear with comfort the sufferings of this wretched life, without the hopes of a life with Christ? What should support and comfort me under my bodily languishings and pains, my weary hours, and my daily experience of the vanity and vexation of all things under the sun, had I not a prospect of a comfortable end of all? I that have lived in the midst of great and precious mercies, have all my life had something to do, to overcome the temptation of wishing that I had never been born, and had never overcome it, but by the belief of a blessed life hereafter. Solomon's sense of vanity and vexation, has long made all the business, wealth, honour, and pleasure of this world, as such, appear such a dream and shadow to me, that were it not for the end, I could not have much distinguished men's sleeping and their waking thoughts, nor have much more valued the waking than the sleeping part of life, but should have thought it a kind of happiness to have slept from the birth unto the death. Children cry when they come into the world : and I am often sorry when I am awakened out of a quiet sleep, especially to the business of an unquiet day. We should be strongly tempted in our considering state, to murmur at our Creator, as dealing much harder by us than by the brutes : if we must have had all those cares, griefs, and fears, by the knowledge of what we want, and the prospect of death, and future evils, which they are exempted from, and had not withal had the hopes of a future felicity to support us. Seneca and his stoics had no better argument to silence such murmurers, who believed not a better life, than to tell them, that if this life had more evil than good, and they thought God did them wrong, they might remedy themselves by ending it when they would : but that would not cure the repinings of a nature, which found itself necessarily weary of the miseries of life, and yet afraid of dying. It is no great wonder that many thought that pre-existent souls were put into these bodies as a punishment of something done in a former life, while they foresaw not the hoped end of all our fears and sorrows. ' O how contemptible a thing is man !' saith the same Seneca, ' unless he lift up himself above human things.' Therefore, saith Solomon, when he had glutted himself with all temporal pleasures, ' I hated life, because the work that is wrought under the sun, is grievous to me : for all is vanity and vexation of spirit.'

I have often thought whether an implicit belief of a future happiness, without any search into its nature, and thinking of any thing that can be said against it, or the searching, trying way, be better. On the one side, I have known many godly women that never disputed the matter, but served God comfortably to a very old age, (between 80 and 100) to have lived many years in a cheerful readiness and desire of death, and such as few learned, studious men do ever attain to in that degree ; who, no doubt, had this as a divine reward of their long and faithful service of God, and trusting in him. On the other side, a studious man can hardly keep off all objections, or secure his mind against the suggestions of difficulties and doubts ; and if they come in, they must be answered ; seeing we give them half a victory, if we cast them off before we can answer them. A faith that is not upheld by such evidence of truth, as reason can discern and justify, is often joined with much secret doubting, which men dare not open, but do not therefore overcome : its weakness may have a weakening deficiency, as to all the graces and duties which should be strengthened by it. Who

knows how soon a temptation from satan, or infidels, or our own dark hearts, may assault us, which will not, without such evidence and resolving light, be overcome ? Yet many that try reason, and dispute most, have not the strongest, or most powerful faith.

My thoughts of this have had this issue. There is a great difference between that light which shows us the thing itself, and that artificial skill by which we have right notions, names, definitions, and formed arguments, and answers to objections. This artificial, logical, organical, kind of knowledge is good and useful in its kind, if right ; like speech itself : but he that hath much of this, may have little of the former : unlearned persons that have little of this, may have more of the former, and may have those inward perceptions of the vanity of the promises and rewards of God, which they cannot bring forth into artificial reasonings to themselves or others ; who are taught of God by the effective sort of teaching, which reaches the heart or will, as well as the understanding, and is a giving of what is taught, and a making us such as we are told we must be. Who finds not need to pray hard for this effective teaching of God, when he hath got all organical knowledge, words and arguments in themselves most apt, at his finger ends, as we say ? When I can prove the truth of the word of God, and the life to come, with the most convincing, undeniable reasons, I feel need to cry and pray daily to God to increase my faith, and to give me that light which may satisfy the soul, and reach the end.

Yet man being a rational creature, is not taught by mere instinct and inspiration : therefore this effective teaching of God doth ordinarily suppose a rational, objective, organical teaching and knowledge. The foresaid unlearned Christians are convinced by good evidence, that God's word is true, and his rewards are sure, though they have but a confused conception of this evidence, and cannot word it, nor reduce it to fit notions. To drive these that have fundamental evidence, unseasonably and hastily to dispute their faith, and so to puzzle them by words and artificial objections, is but to hurt them, by setting the artificial, organical, lower part, (which is the body of knowledge) against the real light and perception of the thing (which is as the soul), even as carnal men set the creatures against God, that should lead us to God ; so do they by logical, artificial knowledge.

But they that are prepared for such disputes, and furnished with all artificial helps, may make good use of them for defending and clearing up the truth to themselves and others; so be it they use them as a means to the due end, and in a right manner, and set them not up against, or instead of the real and effective light.

But the revealed and necessary part must here be distinguished from the unrevealed and unnecessary. To study till we as clearly as may be understand the certainty of a future happiness, and wherein it consists, in the sight of God's glory, and in perfect, holy, mutual love, in union with Christ, and all the blessed, this is of great use to our holiness and peace. But when we will know more than God would have us, it doth but tend, as gazing on the sun, to make us blind, and to doubt of certainties, because we cannot be resolved of uncertainties. To trouble our heads too much in thinking how souls out of the body subsist and act, sensitively or not, by organs, or without; how far they are one, and how far still individuate, in what place they still remain, and where is their paradise or heaven; how they shall be again united to the body; whether by their own emission, as the sun-beams touch their objects here; and whether the body shall be restored, as the consumed flesh of restored sick men, or only from the old materials: a hundred of these questions are better left to the knowledge of Christ, lest we but foolishly make snares for ourselves. Had all these been needful to us, they had been revealed. In respect to all such curiosities and needless knowledge, it is a believer's wisdom implicitly to trust his soul to Christ, and to be satisfied that he knows what we know not, and to fear that vain, vexatious knowledge, or inquisitiveness into good and evil, which is selfish, and savours of a distrust of God, and is that sin, and fruit of sin, which the learned world too little fears.

That God is the rewarder of them that diligently seek him, and that holy souls shall be in blessedness with Christ, these following evidences conjoined do evince; on which my soul raises its hopes.

The soul, which is an immortal spirit, must be immortally in a good or bad condition: but man's soul is an immortal spirit, and the good are not in a bad condition. Its immortality is proved thus: A spiritual, or most pure, invisible substance, naturally endowed with the power, virtue, or faculty of vital action and volition, which is not annihilated, nor destroyed by separation of parts, nor ceases or loses either its power, species, individuality or action, is an immortal spirit. But such is the soul of man, as shall be manifested by what follows.

The soul is a substance: for that which is nothing, can do nothing; but it doth move, understand and will. No man will deny that this is done by something in us, and by some substance; and that substance is it which we call the soul: it is not nothing, and it is within us.

As to them that say, It is the temperament of several parts united, I have elsewhere fully confuted them, and proved that it is some one part that is the agent on the rest, which all they confess that think it to be the material spirits, or fiery part: it is not bones and flesh that understand, but a purer substance, as all acknowledge. What part soever it be, it can do no more than it is able to do: a conjunction of many parts, of which no one hath the power of vitality, or volition, formally or eminently can never by contemperation do those acts: for there can be no more in the effect than is in the cause, otherwise it were no effect.

The vanity of their objections, that tell us, a lute, a watch, a book, perform that by co-operation, which no one part can do, I have elsewhere manifested. Many strings indeed have many motions, and so have many effects on the ear, and imagination, which in us are sound and harmony: but all is but a percussion of the air by the strings, and were not that motion received by a sensitive soul, it would be no music or melody; so that there is nothing done but what each part had power to do. But intellect and volition are not the united motions of all parts of the body, receiving their form in a nobler, intellectual nature, as the sound of the strings makes melody in man: if it were so, that receptive nature still would be as excellent as the effect imports. The watch or clock doth but move according to the action of the spring or poise; but that it moves in such an order as becomes to man a sign and measure of time, this is from man who orders it to that use. But there is nothing in the motion but what the parts have their power to cause: that it signifies the hour of the day to us, is no action, but an object used by a rational soul as it can use the shadow of a tree or house, that yet doth nothing. So a book doth nothing at all, but is merely an objective ordination of passive signs, by which man's active intellect can understand what the writer did intend; so that here is nothing done beyond the power of the agent, nor any thing in the effect which was not in the cause, either formally or eminently. But for a company of atoms, of which no one hath sense or reason, to become sensitive and rational by mere united motion, is an effect beyond the power of the supposed cause.

But as some think so lowly of our noblest acts, as to think that contempered, agitated atoms can perform them, that have no natural intellect or sensitive virtue or power in themselves, so others think so highly of them, as to take them to be the acts only of God, or some universal soul, in the body of man; and so that there is no life, sense, or reason in the world, but God himself or such an universal soul; and so that either every man is God, as to his soul, or that it is the body only that is to be called man, as distinct from God. But this is the self-ensnaring and self-perplexing temerity of busy, bold and arrogant heads, that know not their own capacity and measure. On the like reasons they must at last come, with others, to say, that all passive matter also is God, and that God is the universe, consisting of an active soul and passive body. As if God were no cause, and could make nothing, or nothing with life, or sense, or reason.

But why depart we from things certain, by such presumptions as these? Is it not certain that there are lower creatures in the world than men or angels? Is it not certain that one man is not another? Is it not certain that some men are in torment of body and mind? And will it be a comfort to a man in such torment to tell him that he is God, or that he is part of a universal soul? Would not a man on the rack, or in the stone, or other misery, say, 'call me by what name you please, that eases not my pain: if I be a part of God, or a universal soul, I am sure I am a tormented, miserable part! And if you could make me believe that God hath some parts which are not serpents, devils, or wicked or tormented men, you must give me other senses, and perceptive powers, before it will comfort me, to hear that I am not such a part. If God had wicked and tormented parts on earth, why may he not have such, and I be one of them, hereafter? and if I be a holy and happy part of God, or of a universal soul on earth, why may not I hope to be such hereafter?'

We deny not but that God is the continued first cause of all being whatsoever; and that the branches and fruit depend not as effects so much on the causality of the stock and roots, as the creature doth on God; and that it is an impious conceit to think that the world, or any part of it, is a Being independent, and separated totally from God, or subsisting without his continued causation. But cannot God cause as a creator, by making that which is not himself? This yields the self-deceiver no other honour or happiness but what equally belongs to a devil, to a fly or to a worm!

As man's soul is a substance, so is it a substance distinguished formally from all inferior substances, by an innate, power, virtue, or faculty, of vital action, intellect, and free-will: for we find all these acts performed by it, as motion, light, and heat are by the fire or sun. If any should think that these actions are like those of a musician, compounded of the agents, the several principal and organical parts; could he prove it, no more would follow but that the lower powers, the sensitive or spirits, are to the higher as a passive organ, receiving its operations; and that the intellectual soul hath the power of causing intellection and volition by its action on the inferior parts, as a man can cause such motions of his lute, as shall be melody, not to it, but to himself; and consequently, that as music is but a lower operation of man, whose proper acts of intellection and volition are above it, so intellection and volition in the body are not the noblest acts of the soul, but are performed by an eminent power, which can do greater things. If this could be proved, what would it tend to the unbeliever's ends, or to the disadvantage of our hopes and comforts.

That man's soul at death is not annihilated, even the Atomists and Epicureans will grant, who think that no atom in the universe is annihilated: and we that see not only the sun and heavens continued, but every grain of matter, and that compounds are changed by dissolution of parts, and rarefaction, or migration, &c. and not by annihilation,—have no reason to dream that God will annihilate one soul (though he can do it if he please, yea, and annihilate all the world:) it is a thing beyond a rational expectation.

A destruction by the dissolution of the parts of the soul, we need not fear. For, either an intellectual spirit is divisible, or not; if not, we need not fear it: if it be, either it is a thing that nature tends to, or not: but that nature doth not tend to it, is evident. There is naturally so strange and strong an inclination to unity, and averseness to separation in all things, that even earth and stones, that have no other natural motion, have yet an aggregative motion in their gravitation: but if you will separate the parts from the rest, it must be by force. Water is yet more averse to partition without force, and more inclined to union than earth, and air than water, and fire than air, so he that will cut a sun-beam into pieces, and make many of one, must be an extraordinary agent. Surely spirits, even intellectual spirits, will be no less averse to partition, and inclined to keep their unity, than fire or a sun-beam is ; so that naturally it is not a thing to be feared, that it should fall into pieces.

He that will say, that the God of nature will change and overcome the nature that he hath made, must give us good proofs of it, or it is not to be feared. If he should do it as a punishment, we must find such a punishment somewhat threatened, either in his natural or supernatural law, which we do not, and therefore need not fear it.

But if it were to be feared, that souls were partible, and would be broken into parts, this would be no destruction of them, either as to their substance, powers, form or actions, but only a breaking of one soul into many : for being not compounded of heterogeneous parts, but as simple elements of homogeneous only, as every atom of earth is earth, and every drop of water in the sea is water, and every particle of air and fire is air and fire, and have all the properties of earth, water, air and fire ; so would it be with every particle of an intellectual spirit. But who can see cause to dream of such a partition never threatened by God.

That souls lose not their formal powers or virtues, we have great reason to conceive ; because they are their natural essence, not as mixed, but simple substances : though some imagine that the passive elements may by attenuation be transmuted one into another, yet we see that earth is still earth, water is water, and air is air ; and their conceit hath no proof : were it proved, it would but prove that none of these are a first or proper element. But what should an intellectual spirit be changed into ; how should it lose its formal power ? Not by nature ; for its nature hath nothing that tends to deterioration, or decay, or self-destruction? The sun doth not decay by its wonderful motion, light and heat: why should spirits ? Not by God's destroying them, or changing their nature ; for, though all things are in constant motion or revolution, he continues the natures of the simple beings, and shows us, that he delights in a constancy of operations, insomuch that hence Aristotle thought the world eternal. God hath made no law that threatens to do it as a penalty. Therefore to dream that intellectual spirits shall be turned into other things, and lose their essential, formal powers, which specify them, is without and against all sober reason. Let them first but prove that the sun loses motion, light and heat, and is turned into air, or water, or earth. Such changes are beyond a rational fear.

But some men dream that souls shall sleep, and cease their acts, though they lose not their powers. But this is more unreasonable than the former. For it must be remembered that it is not a mere obedient, passive power that we speak of ; but an active power consisting in as great an inclination to act, as passive natures have to forbear actions. So that if such a nature act not, it must be because its natural inclination is hindered by a stronger : who shall hinder it ?

God would not continue an active power, force and inclination in nature, and forcibly hinder the operation of that nature which he himself continues, unless penalty for some special cause, which he never gave us any notice of by any threatening, but the contrary.

Objects will not be wanting, for all the world will be still at hand, and God above all. It is therefore an unreasonable conceit to think that God will continue an active, vital, intellectual nature, form, power, force, inclination, in a noble substance, which shall use none of these for many hundred or thousand years, and so continue them in vain.

It is rather to be thought that some action is their constant state, without which the cessation of their very form would be inferred.

But all that can be said with reason is, that separated souls, and souls hereafter in spiritual bodies, will have actions of another mode, and very different from these that we now perceive in flesh. Be it so. They will yet be radically of the same kind, and they will be formally or eminently such as we now call vitality, intellect and volition ; and they will be no lower or less excellent, if not far more ; and then what the difference will be, Christ knows whom I trust, and in season I shall know. But to talk of a dead life, and an inactive activity, or a sleeping soul, is fitter for a sleeping than a waking man.

It is true that diseases or hurts do now hinder the soul's intellectual perceptions in the body, and in infancy and sleep they are imperfect. Which proves indeed that the acts commonly called intellectual and volition, have now something in them also of sensation, and that sensitive operations are diversified by the organs of the several senses. And that bare intellect and volition without any sensation is now scarcely to be observed in us, though the soul may have such acts intrinsically, and in its profundity. For it is now so united to this body, that it acts on it, as our form ; and indeed the acts observed by us cannot be denied to be such as are specified or modified at least by the agents, and the recipients, and sub-agents' parts united. But as the sun would certainly do the same thing, if it sent forth its beams only into empty space; though this were no illumination or calefaction, because there were no recipient to be illuminated and heated by it; and it would lose nothing by the want of objects; so the soul, had it no body to act on, would have its profound immanent acts of self living, self-perceiving, self-loving, and all its external acts on other objects, which need not organs of sense for their approximation. Its sensitive faculty is itself, or such as it is not separated from, though the particular sorts of sensation may be altered with their uses: therefore it may still act on or with the sense: and if one way of sensation be hindered, it hath another. How far this lantern of flesh doth help or hinder its operations, we know not yet, but shall know hereafter. Sondius, though a heretical writer, hath said much to prove that the body is a hinderance, and not a help to the soul's intuition: and if ratiocination be a compound act, yet intuition may be done for ever by the soul alone. But as we are not to judge what powers the soul hath when the acts are hindered, but when they are done; nor what souls were made by God for, by their state in the womb or infancy, or diseases, but by our ordinary mature state of life; so we have little reason to think that the same God who made them for life, intellect, and volitions here, will not continue the same powers to the same, or as noble uses hereafter, whether with organs, or without, as pleases him. If in this flesh our spirits were not inactive and useless, we have no reason to think that they will be so hereafter, and that for ever.

This greatest and hardest of all objections, doth make us confess, with Contarenus, that 'though by the light of nature we may know the immortality of souls, and that they lose not their powers or activity; yet, without supernatural light we know not what manner of action they will have in their separated state, or in another world, because here they act according to objective termination, and the receptivity of the sense, and in the womb we perceive not that it acts intellectually at all.'

But we know that, if even then it differed not in its formal power from the souls of brutes, it would not so much afterward differ in act: and it would never be raised to that which was not virtually in its nature at the first. We find, that even very little children have quick and strong knowledge of such objects as are brought within their reach: that their ignorance is not for want of an intellectual power, but for want of objects, or images of things, which time and use, and

conversation among objects must furnish their imaginations and memories with. So a soul in the womb, or in an apoplexy, hath not objects of intellect within its reach to act upon; but is as the sun to a room that hath no windows to let in its light. What if its profound vitality, self-perception, and self-love be by a kind of sensation and intuition, rather than by discursive reason? I doubt not but some late philosophers make snares to themselves and others, by too much vilifying sense and sensitive souls, as if sense were but some loseable accident of contempered atoms: but sensation, though diversified by organs and uses, and so far mutable, is the act of a noble, spiritual form and virtue. As Chambre and some others make brutes a lower rank of rationals, and man another higher species, as having his nobler reason for higher ends: so for man to be the noblest order, here, of sensitives, and to have an intellect to order, and govern sensations, and connect them and improve them, were a noble work, if we had no higher. If intellect and volition were but a higher species of internal sensation than imagination, and memory are, it might yet be a height that should set man specifically above brutes. I am daily more and more persuaded, that intellectual souls are essentially sensitive and more, and that their sensation never ceases. Still I say, that it is to nature itself a thing unlikely, that the God of nature will long continue a soul that hath formally or naturally an intellectual power, in a state in which it shall have no use of it. Let others that will inquire whether it shall have a vehicle or none to act in, and whether aereal, or igneous, and ethereal, and whether it be really an intellectual sort of fire, as material as the solar fire, which is an igneous substance, and formal virtue of life, sense, and intellect, with other such puzzling doubts; it satisfies me, that God will not continue its noblest powers in vain; and how they shall be exercised, is known to him: and that God's word tells us more than nature. Withal, life, intuition and love, or volition, are acts so natural to the soul, as motion, light and heat to fire, that I cannot conceive how its separation should hinder them, but rather that its incorporation hinders the two latter by hiding objects, whatever be said of abstract knowledge and memory.

But the greatest difficulty to natural knowledge is, whether souls shall continue their individuality, or rather fall into one common soul, or return so to God that gave them, as to be no more divers, or many individuals, as now; as extinguished candles are united to the illuminated air, or to the sun beams. But of this I have elsewhere said much for others; and for myself I find I need but this: that as I said before, either souls are partible substances, or not: if not partible, how are they unible? If many may be made one by conjunction of substances, then that one may, by God, be made many again by partition. Either all, or many, souls are now but one, individuated only by matter, as many gulfs in the sea, or many candles lighted by the sun, or not: if they are not one now in several bodies, what reason have we to think that they will be one hereafter, any more than now? Augustine was put on the questions, whether souls are one, and not many: and that he utterly denies. Whether they are many, and not one; and that it seems he could not digest. Whether they were at once both one and many: which he thought would seem to some ridiculous, but he seems most to incline to: as God is the God of nature, so nature, even of the devils themselves, depends on him, as I said, more than the leaves or fruit do on the tree: we are all his offspring, and live, move, and are in him. But we are certain for all this, that we are not God; that we are yet many individuals, and not all one soul or man. If our union should be as near as the leaves and fruit on the same tree, yet those leaves and fruit are numerous, and individual leaves and fruits, though parts of the tree. Were this proved of our present, or future state, it would not alter our hopes or fears: for as now, though we all live, move, and be in God, and as some dream, are parts of a common soul, yet it is certain that some are better and happier than others; some wise and good, and some foolish and evil; some in pain and misery, and some at ease and in pleasure; and, as I said, it is now no ease to the miserable to be told, that radically all souls are one; no more will it be hereafter, nor can men reasonably hope for, or fear such an union, as shall make their state the same. We see in nature, as I have elsewhere said, that if you graff many sorts of scions, some sweet, some bitter, some crabs, on the same stock, they will be one tree, and yet have diversity of fruit. If souls be not unible, nor partible substances, there is no place for this doubt: if they be, they will be still what they are, notwithstanding any such union with a common soul. As a drop of water in the sea is a separable part, and still itself; and as a crab upon the foresaid stock, or tree. The good or bad quality ceases not by any union with others.

Sure we are, that all creatures are in God, by close dependence, and yet that the good are good, and the bad are bad, and that God is good, and hath no evil; and that when man is tormented or miserable, God suffers nothing by it, as the whole man doth, when but a tooth doth ache. For he would not hurt himself were he passive. Therefore to dream of any such cessation of our individuality, by any union with a creature, as shall make the good less good or happy, or the bad less bad or miserable, is a groundless folly.

Yet it is very probable that there will be a nearer union of holy souls with God and Christ, and one another, than we can here conceive of: but this is so far from being to be feared, that it is the highest of our hopes. God himself, though equally everywhere in his essence, doth operate very variously on his creatures. On the wicked he operates as the first cause of nature, as his sun shines on them: on some he operates by common grace: to some he gives faith to prepare them for the in-dwelling of his Spirit: in believers he dwells by love, and they in him: if we may use such a comparison as Satan acts on some only by suggestions, but on others so despotically as that it is called his possessing them; so God's Spirit works on holy souls so powerfully and constantly as is called his possessing them. Yet on the human nature of Christ, the divine nature of the second person hath such a further extraordinary operation, as is justly called a personal union: which is not by a more essential presence (for that is everywhere), but by a peculiar operation and relation: so holy souls being under a more felicitating operation of God, may well be said to have a nearer union with him than now they have.

I observe, that, as is foresaid, all things have naturally a strong inclination to union and communion with their like: every clod and stone inclines to the earth: water would go to water, air to air, fire to fire; birds and beasts associate with their like. The noblest natures are most strongly thus inclined: therefore I have natural reason to think that it will be so with holy souls.

I find that the inordinate contraction of man to himself, and to the interest of this individual person, with the defect of love to all about us, according to every creature's goodness, and especially to God the infinite good, whom we should love above ourselves, is the very sum of all the pravity of man. All the injustice and injury to others, and all the neglect of good works in the world, and all our daily terrors, and self-distracting, self-tormenting cares, griefs, and fears, proceed from this inordinate love and adhesion to ourselves: therefore I have reason to think that in our better state, we shall perfectly love others as ourselves, and the selfish love will turn into a common and a divine love, which must be by our preferring the common and the divine good and interest.

I am so sensible of the power and plague of selfishness, and how it now corrupts, tempts, and disquiets me, that when I feel any fears, lest individuality cease, and my soul fall into one common soul, as the Stoics thought all souls did at death, I find great cause to suspect that this arises from the power of this corrupting selfishness: for reason sees no cause at all to fear it, were it so. For I find also that the nature of love is to desire as near a union as is possible ; and the strongest love doth strongly desire it. Fervent lovers think they can scarcely be too much one. Love is our perfection, and therefore so is union. I find that when Christians had the first and full pourings out of the Spirit they had the ferventest love, the nearest union, and the least desire of propriety and distance. I find that Christ's prayer for the felicity of his disciples is a prayer for their unity, and in this he places much of their perfection. I find also that man is of a sociable nature, and that all men find by experience, that conjunction in societies is needful for their safety, strength, and pleasure. I find that my soul would fain be nearer God, and that darkness and distance is my misery, and near communion is it that would answer all the tendencies of my soul : why then should I fear too near a union. I think it utterly improbable, that my soul should become more nearly united to any creature than to God : though it be of the same kind with other souls, and infinitely below God ; for God is as near me as I am to myself: I still depend on him as the effect upon its total, constant cause ; and that not as the fruit upon the tree, which borrows all from the earth, water, air, and fire, which it communicates to its fruit: but as a creature on its Creator, who hath no being but what it receives totally from God, by constant communication. Hence Antonine, Seneca, and the rest of the Stoics, thought that all the world was God, or one great animal consisting of divine spirit and matter, as man of soul and body ; sometimes calling the supposed soul of the world, God ; and sometimes calling the whole world, God ; but still meaning, that the universe was but one spirit and body united, and that we are all parts of God, or of the body of God, or accidents at least.*

* This Stoical philosophy is still prevalent over a great part of India ; and is usually taught and held, so as to exonerate man of all responsibility to his Maker. It renders him a kind of machine ; and is in fact atheism in a heathen garb.—*Ed.*

Even the popish mystical divines, in their pretensions to the highest perfection, say the same in sense : such as Benedict. Anglus, in his Rule of Perfection, approved of by many doctors, who places much of his supereminent life in our believing verily that there is nothing but God, and living accordingly ; maintaining that all creatures are nothing distinct from God, but are to God, as the beams are to the sun, and as the heat is to the fire, which really is itself: and so teaching us to rest in all things as good, as being nothing but God's essential will, which is himself, resolving even our sins and imperfections accordingly into God, so that they are God's or none.

All these men have as fair a pretence for the conceits of such a union with God now, as for such a union after death : for their reason is that God being infinite, there can be no more beings than his own. But God and the smallest distinct being, would be more entity than God alone: but infinity can have no addition : but God only is good. If we are, notwithstanding all this, distinct beings from God now, we shall be so then. For we shall not be annihilated, and we shall not be so advanced as to be deified, and of creatures or distinct beings, turned into a Being infinitely above us. If we be not parts of God now, we shall not be so then.

But if they could prove that we are so now, we should quickly prove to them that then God hath material, divisible parts, as the Stoics thought. And that we are no such parts as are not distinct from one another ; but some are tormented, and some happy. That, as is said, it will be no abatement of the misery of the tormented, nor of the felicity of the blessed, to tell them that they are all parts of God : for though the manner of our union with him, and dependence on him, be past our comprehension, yet that we are distinct and distant from each other, and have each one a joy or misery of his own, is past all doubt. Therefore there is no union with God to be feared by holy souls, but the utmost possible to be most desired.

If our union with God shall not cease our individuality, or resolve us into a principle to be feared, we may say so also of our union with any common soul, or many : if we be unible, we are partible, and so have a distinct though not a divided substance, which will have its proper accidents. All plants are parts of the earth, really united to it, and radicated in it, and live, and are nourished by it : and yet a vine is a vine, and an apple is an apple, and a rose is a rose, and a nettle is a nettle. Few men would be toiled horses, if it were proved that they are animated by a common soul.

But God lets us see, that though the world be one, yet he delights in a wonderful diversity and multiplicity of individuals. How various and numerous are they in the sea, and on the land, and in the air? Are there none in the other world? How come the stars therein to be so numerous, which are of the same element? Though perhaps Saturn, or some other planets, or many stars, may send forth their radiant effluvia or parts into the same air, which the sunbeams seem totally to fill and illuminate, yet the rays of the sun, and of other stars, are not the same, how near soever in the same air.

Were there now no more contraction by egotism or propriety among men, nor mine and thine did signify no more, nor the distance were greater than that of the several drops of water in the sea, or particles of light in the illuminated air, but I had all my part in such a perfect unity and communion with all others, and knew that all were as happy as I, so that there were no divisions by cross interests or minds, but all were one, certainly it would make my own comforts greater by far than they are now? Are not an hundred candles set together and united, as splendid a flame as if they were all set asunder? So one soul, one love, one joy would be.

Object. But it is only the fomes that individuates lights; as when the same sun by a burning glass lights a thousand candles, they are individuate only by the matter contracting, being still all united parts of the same sun-beams. When they are extinct, they are nothing, or all one again.

Ans. They were before they were extinct, both one and many; none but fools think that extinction annihilates them, or any part of them. They are after as much substance, and as much solar fire, though diffused, and as much and no more one than before, but not indeed many as before, but parts of one. Nature hath made the equal diffused sun-beams to be to the air and surface of the earth, as the blood equally moving in the body: our candles and fires seem to be like the same blood contracted in a bile or inflammation, which indeed is more felt than the equally diffused blood, but it is as the pain of a disease. So when our fires go out they are but like a healed scattered inflammation, and the same substance is more naturally and equally diffused. If the individuation of souls were only by corporeal matter, and the union thus as great at their departure, it would not diminish, if it did not too much increase their perfection and feli-

city: for there would be no diminution of any substance, or power, or activity, or perfection whatsoever.

This would confute their fond opinion, who think that separated souls sleep for want of an organized body to operate in: for no doubt but if all holy souls were one, this world, either in heaven or earth, hath a common body, enough for such a soul to operate in. Even those stoics that think departed souls are one, do think that one soul hath a nobler operation than ours, in our narrow bodies, and that when our souls cease animating this body, they have the nobler and sweeter work in part, of animating the whole world: those that thought several orbs had their several souls, of which the particular person participated, said the like of separated souls, as animating the bodies of their globes or orbs. Though all these men trouble their heads with their own vain imaginations, yet this much the nature of the matter tells us, which is considerable, that whereas the utmost fear of the infidel is that souls departed lose their individuality or activity, and are resolved into one common soul, or continue in a sleep for want of a body to operate in, they do but contradict themselves, seeing it is a notorious truth that if all holy souls were one, no one would be a loser by the union, but it would be a greater gain than we must hope for: for a part of one is as much, as noble, and as active a substance, as if it were a separated person: annihilation, or loss of specific powers, is not to be rationally feared. That one soul is now either self-subsisting without a body, or animates a suitable body, as some ancients thought the angels stars. If that one soul can act without a body, so may ours, whether as parts of it, or not; if that one soul animate a suitable body, ours, were they united parts of it, would have part of that employment; so that hereby they confute themselves.

Object. But this would equalize the good and bad, or at least those that were good in several degrees; where then were the reward and punishment?

Answ. It would not equal them at all, any more than distinct personality would do: for the souls of all holy persons may be so united, as that the souls of the wicked shall have no part in that union. Whether the souls of the wicked shall be united in one sinful miserable soul, or rather but in one sinful society, or be separated, disunited, contrary to each other, and militant, as part of their sin and misery, is nothing to this case. Yet natural and moral union must be different. God is the root of nature to the worst, and however in one sense it is said, that there is nothing in God but God, yet it is true that in him all live, and move, and have their being. But yet the wicked's in-being in God affords them no sanctifying, or beatifying communion with him, as experience shows us, in this life; which yet holy souls have, as being made capable recipients of it. As I said, different plants, briars, and cedars, the stinking and the sweet, are implanted parts, or accidents, of the same world or earth. The godly themselves may have as different a share of happiness in one common soul, as they have now of holiness, and so as different rewards, even as roses and rosemary, and other herbs, differ in the same garden, and several fruits in the same orchard, or on the same tree. For if souls are unible, and so partible, substances, they have neither more nor less of substance or holiness for their union; and so will each have his proper measure. As a tun of water cast into the sea will there still be the same, and more than a spoonful cast into it.

Obj. But spirits are not as bodies, extensive and quantitative, and so not partible or divisible, and therefore your supposition is vain.

My supposition is but the objectors'; for if they confess that spirits are substances, as cannot with reason be denied; for they that specify their operations by motion only, yet suppose a pure, proper substance to be the subject or thing moved, then when they talk of many souls becoming one, it must be by conjunction and increase of the substance of that one. Or when they say that they were always one, they will confess withal that they now differ in number, as in the body: and who will say that millions of millions are no more than one of all those millions. Number is a sort of quantity: and all souls in the world are more than Cain's or Abel's only. One feels not what another feels: one knows not what another knows: and indeed, though souls have not such corporeal extension, as passive, gross, bodily matter hath, yet, as they are more noble, they have a more noble sort of extension, quantity or degrees; according to which all mankind conceive of all the spiritual substance of the universe, yea, all the angels, or all the souls on earth, as being more, and having more substance than one man's soul alone. The fathers for the most part, especially the Greeks, yea, and the second council of Nice, thought that spirits created had a purer sort of material being, which Tertullian called a body: and doubtless all created spirits have somewhat of passiveness; for they do undergo emotions from the divine influx: only God is wholly impassive. We

are moved when we move, and acted when we act; and it is hard to conceive that, when matter is commonly called passive, that which is passive should have no sort of matter in a large sense taken: and if it have any parts distinguishable, they are by God divisible. But if the contrary be supposed, that all souls are no more than one, and so that there is no place for uniting or partition, there is no place then for the objection of all souls becoming one, and of losing individuation, unless they mean by annihilation.

But that God who,—as is said, delights both in the union, and yet in the wonderful multiplicity of creatures, and will not make all stars to be only one, though fire have a most uniting or aggregative inclination,—hath further given experimental notice that there is individuation in the other world as well as here, even innumerable angels and devils, and not one only: as the revelations of scripture history and many other evidences prove, of which more anon. So that all things considered, there is no reason to fear that the souls shall lose their individuality or activity, though they change their manner of action, any more than their being or formal power: and so it is naturally certain that they are immortal.

If holy souls are so far immortal, I need not prove that they will be immortally happy: for their holiness will infer it; and few will ever dream that it shall there go ill with them that are good, and that the most just and holy God will not use those well whom he makes holy.

That holy souls shall be hereafter happy, seems to be one of the common notices of nature planted in the consciences of mankind; and it is therefore acknowledged by the generality of the world that freely use their understandings. Most, yea, almost all the heathen nations at this day believe it, besides the Mahometans; and it is the most barbarous cannibals and heathens that do not, whose understandings have had the least improvement, and who have rather an inconsiderate ignorance of it, than a denying opposition. Though some philosophers denied it, they were a small and contemned party: and though many of the rest were somewhat dubious, it was only a certainty which they professed to want, and not a probability or opinion that it was true. Both the vulgar and the deep studied men believed it, and those that questioned it were the half-studied philosophers, who not resting in the natural notice, nor yet reaching full intellectual evidence of it by discourse, had found out matter of difficulty to puzzle them, and came not to that degree of wisdom as would have resolved them.

Even among apostates from Christianity most, or many, still acknowledge the soul's immortality, and the felicity and reward of holy souls, to be of the common notices, known by nature to mankind. Julian was so much persuaded of it, that on that account he exhorts his priests and subjects to great strictness and holiness of life, and to see that the Christians did not exceed them. Among us, many that seem not to believe our supernatural revelations of Christianity, do fully acknowledge it. As also those philosophers who most opposed Christianity, as Porphyrius, Maximus Tyrius, and such others.

We find that this notice hath so deep a root in nature, that few of those that study and labour themselves into sensuality or sadducism, are able to silence the fears of future misery, but conscience overcomes or troubles them much at least, when they have done the worst they can against it. Whence should all this be in man and not in beasts, if man had no further reason of hopes and fears, than they? Are a few sadducees wiser by their forced or crude conceits, than all the world that are taught by nature itself.

If the God of nature have made it every man's certain duty to make it his chief care and work in this life, to seek for happiness hereafter, then such a happiness there is for them that truly seek it. But the antecedent is certain, as I have elsewhere proved.

As to the antecedent, the world is made up of three sorts of men, as to the belief of future retribution. Such as take it for a certain truth—Christians, Mahometans, and most heathens; such as take it for uncertain, but most probable or most likely to be true; such as take it for uncertain, but rather think it untrue. For as none can be certain that it is false, which indeed is true, so I never yet met with one that would say he was certain it was false. So that I need not trouble you with the mention of any other party or opinion. But if any should say so, it is easy to prove that he speaks falsely of himself.

That it is the duty of all these, but especially of the two former sorts, to make it their chief care and work to seek their happiness in the life to come, is easily proved thus: Natural reason requires every man to seek that which is best for himself, with the greatest diligence; but natural reason saith that a probability or possibility of the future, everlasting happiness is better and more worthy to be sought, than any thing attainable in this present life, which doth not suppose it.

The major is past doubt. Good and felicity being necessarily desired by the will of man, that which is best and known so to be, must be most desired.

The minor should be as far past doubt to men that use not their sense against their reason. In this life there is nothing certain to be continued one hour. It is certain that all will quickly end: and that the longest life is short. It is certain that time and pleasure past are nothing, properly nothing; and so no better to us than if they had never been. It is certain that while we possess them, they are poor unsatisfactory things, the pleasure of the flesh being no sweeter to a man than to a beast; and the trouble that accompanies it much more. Beasts have not the cares, fears, and sorrows upon foresight which man hath: they fear not death upon the fore-knowledge of it, nor fear any misery after death, nor are put upon any labour, sufferings or trials, to obtain a future happiness, or avoid a future misery: all which considered, he speaks not by reason, who saith this vain, vexatious life is better than the possibility or probability of the everlasting glory.

Now as to the consequence, or major, of the first argument, it is evident of itself, from God's perfection, and the nature of his works. God makes it not man's natural duty to lay out his chief care and labour of all his life on that which is not, or to seek that which man was never made to attain: for then all his duty should result from mere deceit and falsehood, and God should govern all the world by a lie, which cannot be his part who wants neither power, wisdom, nor love, to rule them by truth and righteousness; and who hath printed his image both on his laws and on his servants; in which laws lying is condemned: and the better any man is, the more he hates it; and liars are lothed by all mankind. Then the better any man is, and the more he doth his duty, the more deluded, erroneous and miserable should he be. For he should spend that care and labour of his life upon deceit, for that which he shall never have, and so should lose his time and labour. He should deny his flesh those temporal pleasures which bad men take and suffer persecutions and injuries from the wicked, and all for nothing, and on mistake: the more wicked or more unbelieving any man is, the wiser and happier should he be, as being in the right when he denies the life to come, and all duty and labour in seeking it, or in avoiding future punishment; and while he takes his utmost pleasure here, he hath all that man was made for. But all this is utterly unsuitable to God's perfection, and to his other works: for he makes nothing in vain, nor can he lie; much less will he make holiness itself, and all that duty and work of life which reason itself obliges all men to, to be not only vain, but hurtful to them. But of this argument I have enlarged elsewhere.

Man differs so much from brutes in the knowledge of God, and of his future possibilities, that it proves that he differs as much in his capacity and certain hopes. As to the antecedent, man knows that there is a God by his works: he knows that this God is our absolute Lord, our ruler, and our end: he knows that naturally we owe him all our love and obedience: he knows that good men use not to let their most faithful servants be losers by their fidelity, nor do they use to set them to labour in vain; he knows that man's soul is immortal, or at least that it is far more probable that it is so; and therefore that it must accordingly be well or ill for ever; and that this should be most cared for. Why should God give him all this knowledge more than to the brutes, if he were made for no more enjoyment than the brutes, of what he knows: every wise man makes his work fit for the use that he intends it to, and will not God? So that the consequence also is proved from the divine perfection; and if God were not perfect, he were not God: the denial of a God therefore, is the result of the denial of man's future hopes.

Indeed, though it be but an analogical reason that brutes have, those men seem to be in the right, who place the difference between man and brutes, more in the objects, tendency, and work of our reason, than in our reason itself as such, and so make *animal religiosum* to be more of his description than *animal rationale*. About their own low concerns, a fox, a dog, yea, an ass and a goose, have such actions as we know not well how to ascribe to any thing below some kind of reasoning, or a perception of the same importance. But they think not of God, and his goverment and laws, nor of obeying, trusting or loving him, nor of the hopes or fears of another life, or of the joyful prospect of it: these are that work that man was made for, which is the chief difference from the brutes. Shall we unman ourselves?

The justice of God, as governor of the world, infers different rewards hereafter, as I have largely elsewhere proved. God is not only a mover of all that moves, but a moral ruler of man by laws, judgment, and executions. Else there were no proper law of nature, which few are so unnatural as to deny: and man should

have no proper duty, but only motion, as he is moved; and then how comes a government by laws to be set up under God by men? Then there were no sin or fault in any; for if there were no law and duty, but only necessitated motion, all would be moved as the mover pleased, and there could be no sin; and then there would be no moral good, but forced or necessary motion: but all this is most absurd: and experience tells us that God doth indeed morally govern the world; and his right is unquestionable.

If God were not the ruler of the world, by law and judgment, the world would have no universal laws; for there is no man that is the universal ruler. Then kings, and other supreme powers, would be utterly lawless and ungoverned, as having none above them to give them laws, and so they would be capable of no sin or fault. and of no punishment; which yet neither their subjects' interest, nor their own consciences, will grant or allow them thoroughly to believe.

If God be a ruler, he is just; or else he were not perfect, nor so good, as he requires princes and judges on earth to be. An unjust ruler or judge is abominable to all mankind. Righteousness is the great attribute of the universal king.

But how were he a righteous ruler, if he drew all men to obey him by deceit? If he obliged them to seek and expect a felicity or reward which he will never give them? If he make man's duty his misery; if he require him to labour in vain; if he suffer the wicked to prosecute his servants to the death, and make duty costly, and give no after recompence; or if he let the most wicked on the earth pass unpunished, or to escape as well hereafter as the best, and to live in greater pleasure here? The objections brought from the intrinsical good of duty, I have elsewhere answered.

But God hath not left us to the light of mere nature, as being too dark for men so blind as we: the gospel revelation is the clear foundation of our faith and hopes. Christ hath brought life and immortality to light: one from heaven that is greater than an angel was sent to tell us what is there, and which is the way to secure our hopes. He hath risen and conquered death, and entered before us as our captain and fore-runner into the everlasting habitations. He hath all power in heaven and earth, and all judgment is committed to him, that he might give eternal life to his elect: he hath frequently and expressly promised it them, that they shall live because he lives, and shall not perish, but have everlasting life. How fully he hath proved and sealed the truth of his word and office to us, I have so largely opened in my Reasons of the Christian Religion, and Unreasonableness of Infidelity, and in my Life of Faith, &c. and since in my Household Catechising, that I will not here repeat it.

As all his word is full of promises of our future glory at the resurrection, so we are not without assurance that at death the departing soul doth enter upon a state of joy and blessedness. He expressly promised the penitent crucified thief, 'this day shalt thou be with me in paradise.' He gave us the narrative or parable of the condemned sensualist, and of Lazarus, to instruct us, and not to deceive us. He tells the sadducees that God is not the God of the dead, as his subjects and beneficiaries, but of the living. Enoch and Elias were taken up to heaven, and Moses, who died, appeared with Elias on the mount. He tells us, that they that kill the body, are not able to kill the soul.* Christ's own soul was commended into his Father's hands, and was in paradise, when his body was in the grave, to show us what shall become of ours. He hath promised, that ' where he is, there shall his servant be also.' That the life here begun in us is eternal life, and that he that believes in him shall not die, but shall live by him, as he lives by the Father; for he dwells in God, and God in him, and in Christ, and Christ in him. Accordingly Stephen that saw heaven opened, prayed the Lord Jesus to receive his spirit. We are come to mount Sion, &c. to an innumerable company of angels, and to the spirits of the just made perfect. Paul desired to depart and be with Christ as far better : ' to be absent from the body, and be present with the Lord.' ' The dead that die in the Lord are blessed, from henceforth, that they may rest from their labours, and their works follow them.' If the disobedient spirits be in prison, and the cities of Sodom and Gomorrah suffer the vengeance of eternal fire, then the just have eternal life. If the Jews had not thought the soul immortal, Saul had not desired the witch to call up Samuel to speak with him : the rest I now pass by. We have many great and precious promises on which a departed soul may trust.— Christ expressly says, that when we fail, that is, must leave this world, we shall be received into the everlasting habitations.

It is not nothing to encourage us to hope in him that hath made all these promises, when we find how he hears prayers in this life, and

thereby assures his servants that he is their true and faithful Saviour. We are apt in our distress to cry aloud for mercy and deliverances ; and when human help fails, to promise God, that if he now will save us, we will thankfully acknowledge it his work ; and yet when we are delivered, to return not only to security, but to ingratitude : and think that our deliverance came but in the course of common providence, and not indeed as an answer to our prayers. Therefore God in mercy renews both our distresses, and our deliverances, that what once or twice will not convince us of, many and great deliverances may. This is my own case. O ! how often have I cried to him when men and means were nothing, and when no help in second causes did appear, and how often, suddenly, and mercifully hath he delivered me ? What sudden ease, what removal of long afflictions have I had ; such extraordinary changes, and beyond my own and others' expectations, when many plain-hearted, upright Christians have by fasting and prayer sought God on my behalf, as have over and over convinced me of special providence, and that God is indeed a hearer of prayer. Wonders I have seen done for others also, upon such prayers, more than for myself: yea, and wonders for the church and public societies. Though I and others are too like those Israelites who cried to God in their troubles, and he often delivered them out of their distress, but they quickly forgot his mercies, and their convictions, purposes, and promises, when they should have praised the Lord for his goodness, and declared his works with thanksgiving to the sons of men.

What were all these answers and mercies but the fruits of Christ's power, fidelity, and love, the fulfilling of his promises, and the earnest of the greater blessings of immortality, which the same promises give me title to.

I know that no promise of hearing prayer sets up our wills in absoluteness, or above God's, as if every will of ours must be fulfilled if we do but put it into a fervent or confident prayer : but if we ask any thing through Christ, according to his will, expressed in his promise, he will hear us. If a sinful love of this present life, or of ease, wealth, or honour, should cause me to pray to God against death, or against all sickness, want, reproach, or other trials, as if I must live here in prosperity for ever if I ask it ; this sinful desire and expectation is not the work of faith, but of presumption : What if God will not abate me my last, or daily pains ? What if he will continue my life no longer, whoever pray for it, and how earnestly soever ? Shall I there-

---

* Indeed if the soul were not immortal, the resurrection were impossible : it might be a new creation of another soul, but not a resurrection of the same, if the same be annihilated. It is certain that the Jews believed the immortality of the soul, in that they believed the resurrection and future life of the same man.

fore forget how often he hath heard prayers for me; and how wonderfully he hath helped both me and others? My faith hath often been helped by such experiences, and shall I forget them, or question them, without cause at last?

It is a subordinate help to my belief of immortality with Christ, to find so much evidence that angels have friendly communion with us here, and therefore we shall have communion with them hereafter. They have charge of us, and pitch their tents about us; they bear us up; they rejoice at our repentance, they are the regardful witnesses of our behaviour: they are ministering spirits for our good; they are our angels, beholding the face of our heavenly Father. They will come with Christ in glorious attendance at the great and joyful day: and as his executioners, they will separate the just from the unjust.

It is not only the testimony of scripture, by which we know their communion with us, but also some degree of experience: not only of old did they appear to the faithful as messengers, from God, but of late times there have been testimonies of their ministration for us: of which see Zanchy, On Angels, and Mr J. Ambrose, On our Communion with Angels. Many a mercy doth God give us by their ministry: and they that are now so friendly to us, and suitable to our communion and help, and make up one society with us, do hereby greatly encourage us to hope that we are made for the same religion, work and company, with these our blessed, loving friends. They were once in a life of trial, as we are now, though not on earth. They that overcame and are confirmed, rejoice in our victory and confirmation. It is not an uninhabited world which is above us; nor such as is beyond our capacity and hope: we are come to an innumerable company of angels, and to the spirits of the perfected just.

But the great and sure prognostics of our immortal happiness, is from the renewing operations of the Spirit of holiness on the soul. That such a renewing work there is, all true believers in some measure feel; and that it is the earnest of heaven is proved thus.

If it be a change of greatest benefit to man; if heaven be the very sum and end of it; if it overcome all fleshly, worldly opposition; if it can be wrought by none but God; if it was before promised by Jesus Christ to all sound believers, and is universally wrought in them all, either only, or eminently above all others; and was promised them as a pledge and earnest of glory; then it can be no less than such a pledge and earnest. But the former are all true, &c.

That the change is of grand importance unto man, appears in that it is the renovation of his mind, will, and life: it repairs his depraved faculties: it causes man to live as man, who is degenerated to a life too like to brutes: by God's permitting many to live in blindness, wickedness, and confusion, and to be tormentors of themselves and one another, by temptations, injuries, wars, and cruelty, we the more fully see what it is that grace doth save men from, and what a difference it makes in the world. Those that have lived unholily in their youth, easily find the difference in themselves when they are renewed: but to them that have been piously inclined from their childhood, it is harder to discern the difference, unless they mark the case of others. If man be worth any thing, it is for the use that his faculties were made: and if he be not good for the knowledge, love, and service of his Creator, what is he good for? Certainly the generality of ungodly worldlings are indisposed to all such works as this, till the Spirit of Christ effectually change them. Men are slaves to sin till Christ thus make them free. But 'where the Spirit of the Lord is, there is liberty.' If the divine nature and image, and 'the love of God shed abroad on the heart, be not our excellency, health, and beauty, what is? And that which 'is born of the flesh, is flesh; but that which is born of the Spirit, is spirit.' Without Christ and his Spirit, we can do nothing: our dead notions and reason, when we see the truth, have not power to overcome temptations, nor to raise up man's soul to its original and end, nor to possess us with the love and joyful hopes of future blessedness. It were better for us to have no souls, than that those souls should be void of the Spirit of God.

That heaven is the sum and end of all the Spirit's operations, appears in all that are truly conscious of them in themselves; and to them and others by all God's precepts, which the Spirit causes us to obey, and the doctrine which it causes us to believe, and by the description of all God's graces which he works in us. What is our knowledge and faith, but our knowledge and belief of heaven, as consisting in the glory and love of God there manifested, and as purchased by Christ, and given by his covenant? What is our hope, but the hope of glory? 'And through the Spirit we wait for all this hope.' What is our love but a desire of communion with the blessed God here, and perfectly hereafter? As the sum of Christ's gospel was 'take up the cross, forsake all here, and follow me, and thou shalt have a reward in heaven' The consolation of his gospel is, 'rejoice, and be exceeding glad, for great is your reward in heaven.' So the same is the sum of his Spirit's operations : for what he teaches and commands that he works, for he works by that word ; and the impress must be like the signet, what arm soever set it on. He sends not his Spirit to make men more crafty than others for this world ; but to make them wiser for salvation : and to make them more heavenly and holy : for the children of this world are wiser in their generation than the children of light.' Heavenliness is the Spirit's special work.

In working this it conquers the inward averseness of a fleshly, worldly mind and will, and the customs of a carnal life ; and the outward temptations of Satan, and all the allurements of the world. Christ first overcame the world, and teaches and causes us to overcome it ; even its flatteries and its frowns : our faith is our victory : whether this victory be easy, and any honour to the Spirit of Christ, let our experience of the wickedness of the ungodly world, and of our own weakness, and of our falls, when the Spirit of God forsakes us, be our informer.

That none but God can do this work on the soul of man, both the knowledge of causes and experience prove. The most learned, wise, and noly teachers cannot, as they confess and show ; the wisest and most loving parents cannot ; and therefore must pray to him that can : the greatest princes cannot : evil angels neither can nor will. What good angels can do on the heart we know not ; but we know that they do nothing, but as the obedient ministers of God. Though we have some power on ourselves, yet that we ourselves cannot do it ; that we cannot quicken, illuminate, or sanctify ourselves, and that we have nothing but what we have received, conscience and experience fully tell us.

That Christ promised this Spirit in a special measure, to all true believers, that it should be in them his advocate, agent, seal, and mark, is yet visible in the gospel ; yea, and in the former prophets. Indeed the Spirit here, and heaven hereafter, are the chief of all the promises of Christ.

That this Spirit is given, not to hypocrites that abuse Christ, and do not seriously believe him, nor to mere pretending nominal Christians, but to all that sincerely believe the gospel, is evident not only to themselves in certainty, if they are in a condition to know themselves, but to others in part, by the effects : they have other ends, other affections, other lives, than the rest of mankind have ; though their heavenly nature and design be the less discerned and honoured in the world, because their chief difference is out of the sight of man, in the heart, and in their secret actions, and because their imperfections blemish them, and because the malignant world is by strangeness and enmity an incompetent judge, yet it is discernable to others, that they live upon the hopes of a better life, and that their heavenly interest overrules all the adverse interests of this world, and that in order thereunto they live under the conduct of divine authority, and that God's will is highest and most prevalent with them, and that to obey and please him as far as they know it, is the greatest business of their lives, though ignorance and adverse flesh make their holiness and obedience imperfect. The universal noise and opposition of the world against them, show that men discern a very great difference, which error, and cross interests, and carnal inclinations, render displeasing to those who find them condemned by their heavenly designs and conversations.

But whether others discern it, or deny it, or detest it, the true believer is conscious of it in himself : even when he groans to be better, to believe, trust, and love God more, and to have more of the heavenly life and comforts, those very desires signify another appetite and mind, than worldlings have ; and even when his frailties and weaknesses make him doubt of his own sincerity, he would not change his governor, rule, or hopes, for all that the world can offer him. He hath the witness in himself, that there is in believers a sanctifying Spirit, calling up their minds to God and glory, and warring victoriously against the flesh ; so that to will is present with them ; and they love and delight in a holy conformity to their rule, and it is never so well and pleasant with them, as when they can trust and love God most ; and in their worst and weakest condition, they would wish to be perfect. This spirit, and its renewing work, so greatly different from the temper and desires of worldly men, is given by Christ to all sound believers.

It is true, that some that know not of an incarnate Saviour, have much in them that is very laudable. Whether it be real saving holiness, and whether Abraham were erroneous in thinking that even the Sodoms of the world were likely to have had fifty righteous persons in them, I am not now to inquire : but it is sure that the world had really a Saviour, about four thousand years before Christ's incarnation, even the God of pardoning mercy, who promised and undertook what after was performed, and shall be to the end. The Spirit of this Saviour did sanctify God's elect from the beginning; and gave them the same holy and heavenly dispositions, in some degree, before Christ's incarnation, as is given since: yea, it is called 'the Spirit of Christ,' which was before given: and this Spirit was then given to more than the Jews. Christ hath put that part of the world that hear not of his incarnation, into no worse a condition than he found them in: that as the Jews' covenant of peculiarity was no repeal of the universal law of grace, made by God with fallen mankind in Adam and Noah; so the covenant of grace of the second edition, made with Christ's peculiar people, is no repeal of the foresaid law in the first edition, to them that hear not of the second. All that wisdom and goodness, that is in any without the Christian church, is the work of the Spirit of the Redeemer; as the light which goes before sun-rising, and after sun-setting, and in a cloudy day, is of the same sun which others see, even to them that see not the sun itself. The more any without the church are like to the sanctified believers, the better they are, and the more unlike the worst; so that all these things being undeniable, it appears, that it is the same Spirit of Christ which now gives all men what real goodness is any where to be found. But it is notorious that no part of the world is, in heavenliness and virtue, comparable to true and serious Christians.

Let it be added, that Christ, who promised the greatest measures of the Spirit, which he accordingly hath given, did expressly promise this, as a means and pledge, first-fruits and earnest of the heavenly glory: therefore it is a certain proof that such a glory we shall have. He that can and doth give us a spiritual change or renovation, which in its nature and tendency is heavenly, and sets our hopes and hearts on heaven, and turns the endeavours of our lives to the seeking of a future blessedness, and told us before-hand that he would give us this preparatory grace, as the earnest of that felicity, may well be trusted to perform his word in our actual glorification.

Now, O weak and fearful soul! why shouldst thou draw back, as if the case were yet left doubtful? is not thy foundation firm? Is not the way of life through the valley of death, made safe by him that conquers death? Art thou not yet delivered from the bondage of thy fears, when the jailor and executioner who had the power of death, hath by Christ been put out of his power, as to thee? Is not all this evidence true and sure? Hast thou not the witness in thyself? Hast thou not found the motions, the effectual operations, the renewing changes of this Spirit in thee, long ago; and is he not still the agent and witness of Christ, residing and operating in thee? Whence else are thy groanings after God; thy desires to be nearer to his glory: to know him better, to love him more? Whence came all the pleasures thou hast had in his sacred truth, ways, and service? Who else overcame thy folly, pride, and vain desires, so far as they are overcome? Who made it thy choice to sit at the feet of Christ, and hear his word, as the better part, and to despise the honours and preferments of the world, and to account them all as dung and dross? Who breathed in thee all those requests that thou hast sent up to God? Overvalue not corrupted nature; it brings not forth such fruits as these: if thou doubt of that, remember what thou wast in the hour of temptation; even of poor and weak temptations: and how small a matter hath drawn thee to sin, when God did but leave thee to thyself: forget not the days of youthful vanity: overlook not the case of the miserable world; even of thy sinful neighbours, who in the midst of light still live in darkness, and hear not the loudest calls of God. Look about on thousands, that in the same land, and under the same teaching, and after the greatest judgments and deliverance, run on to all excess of riot, and, as past feeling, are greedily vicious and unclean. Is it no work of Christ's Spirit that hath made thee to differ? Thou hast nothing to boast of, and much to be humbled for: but thou hast also much to be thankful for.

Thy holy desires are, alas! too weak; but they are holy: thy love hath been too cold; but it is holiness, and the most holy God, that thou hast loved. Thy hopes in God have been too low; but it is God thou hast hoped in, and his love and glory that thou hast hoped for. Thy prayers have been too dull and interrupted; but it is holiness and heaven that thou hast most prayed for: thy labours and endeavours have been too slothful; but it is God and glory, and the good of mankind, that thou hast laboured for. Though thy motion were too weak and slow, it hath been Godward; and therefore it was from God. O bless the Lord, that hath not only given thee a word that bears the image of God, and is sealed by uncontrolled miracles to be the matter of thy belief, but hath also fulfilled his promises so often and notably to thee, in the answer of prayers, and in great and convincing deliverances of thyself and many others! And hath by wonders often assisted thy faith. Bless that God of light and love, who, besides the universal attestation of his word, long ago given to all the church, hath given thee the internal seal, the nearer indwelling attestation, the effects of power, light, and love, imprinted on thy nature, mind, and will, the witness in thyself that the word of God is not a human dream, or lifeless thing; that by regeneration hath been here preparing thee for the light of glory, as by generation he prepared thee to see this light, and converse with men. And wilt thou yet doubt and fear against all this evidence, experience, and foretaste?

I think it not needless labour to confirm my soul in the full persuasion of the truth of its own immortal nature, and of a future life of joy or misery to mankind, and of the certain truth of the Christian faith. The being of God, and his perfection, hath so great evidence, that I find no great temptation to doubt of it, any more than whether there be an earth or a sun; and the atheist seems to me to be in that no better than mad: the Christian verity is known only by supernatural revelation; but by such revelation it is so attested externally to the world, and internally to holy souls, as makes faith the ruling, victorious, consolatory principle, by which we must live, and not by sight: but the soul's immortality and reward hereafter is of a middle nature, viz. of natural revelation, but incomparably less clear than the being of a God; and therefore by the addition of evangelical, supernatural revelation, is made to us much more clear and sure. I find among the infidels of this age, that most who deny the Christian verity, do almost as much deny or question the retribution of a future life: they that are fully satisfied of this, find Christianity so excellently congruous to it, as greatly facilitates the work of faith. Therefore I think that there is scarcely any verity more needful to be thoroughly digested into a full assurance, than this of the soul's immortality, and hope of future happiness.

When I consider the great unlikeness of men's hearts and lives to such a belief, as we all profess, I cannot but fear that not only the ungodly, but most that truly hope for glory, have a far weaker belief, in habit and act, of the soul's immortality, and the truth of the gospel, than they seem to take notice of in themselves. Can I be certain or fully persuaded, in habit and act, of the future rewards and punishments of souls, and that we shall be all shortly judged as we have lived here, and yet not despise all the vanities of this world, and set my heart with resolution and diligence to the preparation which must be made by a holy, heavenly, fruitful life, as one whose soul is taken up with the hopes and fears of things of such unspeakable importance? Who could stand dallying as most men do, at the door of eternity, that did verily believe his immortal soul must be shortly there? Though such a one had no certainty of his own particular title to salvation, the certainty of such a grand concern, that joy or misery is at hand, would surely awaken him to try, cry, or search; to beg, to strive, to watch, to spare no care, or cost, or labour, to make all sure in a matter of such weight: it could not be but he would do it with speed, and do it with a full resolved soul, and do it with earnest zeal and diligence. What man that once saw the things which we hear of, even heaven and hell, would not afterwards, at least in deep regard and seriousness, exceed the most resolved believer that you know: one would think in reason it should be so thought: I confess a wicked heart is very senseless.

I confess that there is much weakness of the belief of things unseen, where yet there is sincerity: but surely there will be some proportion between our belief and its effects. Where there is little regard, or fear, or hope, or sorrow, or joy, or resolved diligence, for the world to come, I must think that there is, in act at least, but little belief of it, and that such persons little know themselves how much they secretly doubt whether it be true. I know that most complain almost altogether of the uncertainty of their title to salvation, and little of their uncertainty of a heaven and a hell: but were they more certain of this, and truly persuaded of it at the heart, it would do more to bring them to that serious, resolved faithfulness in religion, which would help them more easily to be sure of their sincerity, than long examinations, and many marks talked of, without this, will do.

I confess that the great wisdom of God hath not thought meet that in the body we should have as clear, sensible, and lively apprehensions of heaven and hell, as sight would cause. For that would be to have too much of heaven or hell on earth; for the participation would follow the perception, and so full a sense would be some sort of a possession, which we are not fit for in this world. Therefore it must be a darker revelation than sight would be, that it may be a lower perception, lest this world and the next should be confounded; and faith and reason should be put out of office, and not duly tried, exercised, and fitted for reward. But yet faith is faith, and knowledge is knowledge; and he that verily believes such great transcendent things, and though he see them not, will have some proportionable affections and endeavours.

I confess also that man's soul in flesh is not fit to bear so deep a sense of heaven and hell, as sight would cause ; because it here operates on and with the body, and according to its capacity, which cannot bear so deep a sense without distraction, by straining up the organs too much, till they break, and so over-doing would undo all : but yet there is an over-ruling seriousness, which a certain belief of future things must needs bring the soul to, that truly hath it. He that is careful and serious for this world, and looks after a better, but with a slight, unwilling, half-regard, as if in the second place ; must give me leave to think, that he believes but as he lives, and that his doubting or unbelief of the reality of a heaven and hell, is greater than his belief.

O then ! for what should my soul more pray, than for a clearer and a stronger faith. ' I believe, Lord, help my unbelief :' I have many a thousand times groaned to thee under the burden of this remnant of darkness and unbelief : I have many a thousand times thought of the evidences of the Christian verity, and of the great necessity of a lively, powerful, active faith. I have begged it : I have cried to thee night and day, Lord, increase my faith : I have written and spoken that to others, which might be most useful to myself, to raise the apprehensions of faith yet higher, and make them more like those of sense : but yet, yet, Lord, how dark is this world ? what a dungeon is this flesh ? How little clearer is my sight, and little quicker are my perceptions, of unseen things, than long ago ? Am I at the highest that man on earth can reach ; and that when I am so dark and low ? Is there no growth of these apprehensions more to be expected ? Does the soul cease its increase in vigorous perception, when the body ceases its increase or vigour of sensation ? Must I sit down in so low a measure, while I am drawing nearer to the things believed ; and am almost there where belief must pass into sight and love ? Or must I take up with the passive silence and inactivity, which some friars persuade us is nearer to perfection ? and under pretence of annihilation and receptivity, let my sluggish heart alone, and say, that in this neglect I wait for thy operation ? O let not a soul that is driven from this world, and weary of vanity, and can think of little else but immortality ; that seeks and cries both night and day, for the heavenly light, and fain would have some foretaste of glory, and some more of the first-fruits of the promised joys : let not such a

soul either long, or cry, or strive in vain. Punish not my former grieving of thy Spirit, by deserting a soul that cries for thy grace, so near its great and inconceivable change : let me not languish in vain desires, at the door of hope ; nor pass with doubtful thoughts and fears from this vale of misery : which should be the season of triumphant faith, hope, and joy, if not when I am entering on the world of joy ? O thou that hast left us so many consolatory words of promise, that our joy may be full, send, O send, the promised Comforter, without whose approaches and heavenly beams, when all is said, and a thousand thoughts and strivings have been assayed, it will still be night and winter with the soul.

But have I not expected more particular and more sensitive conceptions of heaven, and the state of blessed souls, than I should have done, and remained less satisfied, because I expected such distinct perceptions to my satisfaction, which God doth not ordinarily give to souls in flesh ? I fear it hath been too much so : a distrust of God, and a distrustful desire to know much good and evil, for ourselves, as necessary to our quiet and satisfaction, was that sin which has deeply corrupted man's nature, and is more of our common depravity than is commonly observed : I find that this distrust of God, and of my Redeemer, hath had too great a hand in my desires of a more distinct and more sensible knowledge : I know that I should implicitly, and absolutely, and quietly trust my soul into my Redeemer's hands ; of which I must speak more afterwards. It is not only for the body, but also for the soul, that a distrustful care is our great sin and misery. But yet we must desire that our knowledge and belief may be as distinct and particular as God's revelations are ; and we can love no further than we know ; and the more we know of God and glory, the more we shall love, desire, and trust him : it is a known, and not merely an unknown, God and happiness that the soul doth joyfully desire. If I may not be ambitious of too sensible and distinct perceptions here of the things unseen ; yet must I desire and beg the most fervent and sensible love to them that I am capable of. I am willing in part, to take up with that unavoidable ignorance, and that low degree of such knowledge, which God confines us to in the flesh, so be it he will give me but such consolatory foretastes in love and joy, which such a general imperfect knowledge may consist with, that my soul may not pass with distrust and terror, but with suitable triumphant hopes to the everlasting pleasures.

O Father of lights, who givest wisdom to them that ask it of thee, shut not up this sinful soul in darkness! Leave me not to grope in unsatisfied doubts at the door of the celestial light! Or if my knowledge must be general, let it be clear and powerful; and deny me not now the lively exercise of faith, hope, and love, which are the stirrings of the new creature, and the dawnings of the everlasting light, and the earnest of the promised inheritance.

But we are often ready to say with Cicero, when he had been reading such as Plato, that while the book is in our hands, we seem confident of our immortality, and when we lay it by, our doubts return; so our arguments seem clear and cogent, and yet when we think not of them with the best advantage, we are often surprised with fear, lest we should be mistaken, and our hopes be vain; and hereupon, and from the common fear of death, that even good men too often manifest, the infidels gather that we do but force ourselves into such a hope as we desire to be true, against the tendency of man's nature, and that we were not made for a better world.

.But this fallacy arises from men's not distinguishing sensitive fears from rational uncertainty, or doubts; and the mind that is in the darkness of unbelief, from that which hath the light of faith.

When I look into eternity, I find in myself too much of fear, interrupting and weakening my desires and joy. But I find that it is very much an irrational, sensitive fear, which the darkness of man's mind, the greatness of the change, the dreadful majesty of God, and man's natural aversion to die, do in some degree necessitate, even when reason is fully satisfied that such fears are consistent with certain safety. If I were bound with the strongest chains, or stood on the surest battlement, on the top of a castle or steeple, I could not possibly look down without fear, and such as would go near to overcome me; and yet I should be rationally sure that I am there fast and safe, and cannot fall. So is it with our prospect into the life to come: fear is often a necessitated passion: when a man is certain of his safe foundation, it will violently rob him of the comfort of that certainty: yea, it is a passion that irrationally doth much to corrupt our reason itself, and would make us doubt because we fear that we know not why: a fearful man doth hardly trust his own apprehensions of his safety, but among other fears is still ready to fear lest he be deceived: like timorous, melancholy persons about their bodies, who are ready still to think that every little distemper is a mortal symptom,

and that worse is still nearer them than they feel, and they hardly believe any words of hope.

Satan knowing the power of these passions, and having easier access to the sensitive than to the intellectual faculties, doth labour to get in at this back-door, and to frighten poor souls into doubt and unbelief: in timorous natures he doth it with too great success, as to the consolatory acts of faith. Though yet God's mercy is wonderfully seen in preserving many honest, tender souls from the damning part of unbelief, and by their fears preserves them from being bold with sin: when many bold and impudent sinners turn infidels or atheists, by forfeiting the helps of grace.

Indeed irrational fears have so much power to raise doubts, that they are seldom separated; insomuch that many scarcely know or observe the difference between doubts and fears: many say they not only fear but doubt, when they can scarcely tell why, as if it were no intellectual act which they meant, but an irrational passion.

If therefore my soul see undeniable evidence of immortality; and if it be able by irrefragable argument, to prove the future blessedness expected, and if it be convinced that God's promises are true, and sufficiently sealed and attested by him, to warrant the most confident belief, and if I trust my soul and all my hopes upon this word, and evidences of truth, it is not then our aversion to die, nor the sensible fears of a soul that looks into eternity, that invalidate any of the reasons of my hope, or prove the unsoundness of my faith.

But yet these fears prove its weakness, and were they prevalent against the choice, obedience, resolutions, and endeavours of faith, they would be prevalent against the truth of faith, or prove its nullity; for faith is trust; and trust is a securing, quieting thing: 'why are ye fearful, O ye of little faith,' was a just reproof of Christ to his disciples, when sensible dangers raised up their fears. For the established will hath a political or imperfect, though not a despotical and absolute power over our passions. Therefore our fears show our unbelief, and stronger faith is the best means of conquering even irrational fears. 'Why art thou cast down, O my soul, and why art thou so disquieted in me! trust in God,' &c. is a needful way of chiding a timorous heart.

And though many say that faith hath not evidence, and think that it is an assent of the mind, merely commanded by the empire of the will, without a knowledge of the verity of the testimony; yet certainly the same assent is ordinarily in the scriptures called indifferently, knowing and believing: and as a bare command will not cause love, unless we perceive an amiableness in the object; so a bare command of the law or of the will, cannot alone cause belief, unless we perceive a truth in the testimony believed: for it is a contradiction, or an act without its object. Truth is perceived only so far as it is some way evident: for evidence is nothing but the objective perceptibility of truth; or that which is metaphorically called light. So that we must say that faith hath not sensible evidence of the invisible things believed; but faith is nothing else but the willing perception of the evidence of truth in the word of the assertor, and a trust therein. We have and must have evidence that scripture is God's word, and that his word is true, before, by any command of the word or will, we can believe it.

I do therefore neither despise evidence as unnecessary, nor trust to it alone as the sufficient, total cause of my belief: for if God's grace do not open mine eyes, and come down in power upon my will, and insinuate into it a sweet acquaintance with the things unseen, and a taste of their goodness to delight my soul, no reasons will serve to establish and comfort me, how undeniable soever: reason is desirous first to make use of notions, words, or signs; and to know terms, propositions, and arguments, which are but means to the knowledge of things, is its first employment, and that, alas! which multitudes of learned men take up with: but it is the illumination of God that must give us an effectual acquaintance with the things spiritual and invisible which these notions signify, and to which our organical knowledge is but a means.

To sum up all, that our hopes of heaven have a certain ground appears from Nature, from Grace, from other works of gracious Providence. I. From the Nature of man,—made capable of it,—obliged even by the law of nature to seek it before all;—naturally desiring perfection, habitual, active, and objective. From the nature of God,—as good and communicative,—as holy and righteous,—as wise: making none of his works in vain.

II. From Grace,—purchasing it,—declaring it by a messenger from heaven, both by word, and by Christ's own and others' resurrection.—Promising it,—sealing that promise by miracles there;—and by the work of sanctification to the end of the world.

III. By subordinate Providence,—God's actual governing the world by the hopes and fears of another life,—the many helps which he gives us for a heavenly life, and for attaining it, which are not vain,—especially the ministration of angels, and their love to us, and communion with us;—and, by accident, devils themselves convince us by the nature of their temptations,—by possessions: which though it be but a satanical operation on the body, yet is so extraordinary an operation, that it differs from the more usual, as if I may so compare them, God's Spirit's operations on the saints, that are called his dwelling in them, or possessing them, are different from his lower operations on others.

Chap. II.

the hope, the certainty, and bliss of being with christ.

Having proved that faith and hope have a certain future happiness to expect, the text directs me next to consider why it is described by 'being with Christ;' viz. What is included in our 'being with Christ,' that we shall be with him: why we shall be with him.

To be with Christ, includes presence, union, communion, or participation of felicity with him.

Is it Christ's Godhead, or his human soul, or his human body, that we shall be present with, and united to, or is it all? It is all, but variously.

We shall be present with the divine nature of Christ. But are we not always so? And are not all creatures always so? Yes, as his essence comprehends all place and beings: but not, as it is operative and manifested in and by his glory. Christ directs our hearts and tongues to pray, ' our Father which art in heaven:' and yet he knew that all place is in and with God: because it is in heaven that he gloriously operates and shines forth to holy souls: even as man's soul is eminently said to be in the head, because it understands and reasons in the head, and not in the foot or hand, though it be also there. As we look a man in the face when we talk to him, so we look up to heaven when we pray to God. God who is, and operates as the root of nature in all the works of creation, ' for in him we live, and move, and are,' and by the way of grace in all the gracious, doth operate, and is by the works and splendour of his glory, eminently in heaven: by which glory therefore we must mean some created glory: for his essence hath no inequality.

We shall be present with the human nature of Christ both soul and body: but here our present narrow thoughts must not too boldly presume to resolve the difficulties, which to a distinct understanding of this, should be overcome ; for we must not here expect any more than a dark and general knowledge of them. What is the formal difference between Christ's glorified body, and his flesh on earth ; where Christ's glorified body is, and how far it extends ; and wherein the soul and the glorified body differ, seeing it is called a spiritual body : these things are beyond our present reach.

For what conceptions can we have of a spiritual body, save that it is pure, incorruptible, invisible to mortal eyes, and fitted to the most perfect state of the soul ? How near the nature of it is to a spirit, and so to the soul, and how far they agree or differ in substance, extensiveness, divisibility, or activity ; little do we know.

Nor do we know where and how far Christ's body is present by extent. The sun is commonly taken for a body, and its motion, light, and heat are, by the most probable philosophy, taken to be a real emanant part of its substance, and so that it is essentially as extensive as those beams ; that is, it at once fills all our air, and touches the surface of the earth ; and how much farther it extends we cannot tell : what difference there is between Christ's glorified body, and the sun, in purity, splendour, extent, or excellency of nature, little do poor mortals know. And so of the rest.

Let no man therefore cavil and say, How can a whole world of glorified bodies be all present with the one body of Christ, when each must possess its proper room ? for as the body of the solar beams, and the extensive air, are so compresent, as that none can discern the difference of the places which they possess, and a world of bodies are present with them both, so may all our bodies be with Christ's body, and that without any real confusion.

Besides presence with Christ, there will be such an union as we cannot now distinctly know. A political relative union is past doubt, such as subjects have in one kingdom with their king : but little know we how much more. We see that there is a wonderful corporeal continuity or contact among the material works of God : the more spiritual, pure, and noble, the more inclination each nature hath to union. Every plant on earth hath a union with the whole earth in which it lives ; they are real parts of it. What natural conjunction our bodies shall have to Christ's, and what influence from it, is past our knowledge : though his similitudes in John xv. and John vi. Eph. v. and 1 Cor. xii. seem to extend far, yet

being but similitudes, we cannot fully know how far.

The same we may say of our union with Christ's human soul. Seeing souls are more inclinable to union than bodies, when we see all vegetables to be united parts of one earth, and yet to have each one its proper individuating form and matter, we cannot, though animals seem to walk more disunited, imagine that there is no kind of union or conjunction of invisible souls ; though they retain their severable substances and forms. Nor yet that our bodies shall have a nearer union with Christ's body, than our souls with his soul : but the nature, manner, and measure of it, we know not.

Far be it from us to think that Christ's glorified spiritual body, is such in forms, parts, and dimensions, as his earthly body was : that it hath hands, feet, brains, heart, stomach, liver, intestines, as on earth : or that it is such a compound of earth, water, and air, as here it was, and of such confined extent : for then as his disciples and a few Jews only were present with him, and all the world besides were absent, and had none of his company, so it would be in heaven. But it is such as not only Paul, but all true believers in the world, from the creation to the end, shall ' be with Christ, and see his glory.' Though inequality of fitness, or degrees of holiness, will make an inequality of glory, no man can prove an inequality by local distance from Christ ; or if such there be, for it is beyond our reach, yet none in heaven are at such a distance from him as not to enjoy the felicity of his presence.

Therefore when we dispute against them that hold transubstantiation, and the ubiquity of Christ's body, we assuredly conclude that sense is judge, whether there be real bread and wine present, or not : but it is no judge, whether Christ's spiritual body be present or not, no more than whether an angel be present : we conclude that Christ's body is not infinite or immense as is his godhead ; but what are its dimensions, limits, or extent, and where it is absent, far be it from us to determine, when we cannot tell how far the sun extends its secondary substance, or emanant beams ; nor well what locality is as to Christ's soul or any spirit, if to a spiritual body.

Their fear is vain and carnal, who are afraid lest their union with Christ or one another will be too near ; even lest thereby they lose their individuality, as rivers that fall into the sea, or extinguished candles, whose fire is after but a sun-beam, or part of the common element of fire in the air ; or as the vegetative spirits, which in autumn retire from the leaves into the branches and trunk of the tree : I have proved before, that our individuality, or numerical existence, ceases not : and that no union is to be feared, were it ever so sure, which destroys not the being, or formal powers or action of the soul ; and that it is the great radical disease of selfishness, and want of holy love to God and our Saviour, and one another, which causes these unreasonable fears ; even that selfishness which now makes men so partially desirous of their own wills and pleasure in comparison of God's, and their own felicity in comparison of others, and which makes them so easily bear God's injuries, and the sufferings of a thousand others, in comparison of their own. But he that put a great desire of the body's preservation into the soul while it is its form, will abate that desire when the time of separation is come, because there is then no use for it till the resurrection : else it would be a torment to the soul.

As we shall have union, so also communion with the divine and human nature of Christ, respectively. Both as they will be the objects of our soul's most noble and constant acts, and as they will be the fountain or communicative cause of our receptions.

We find now that our various faculties have various objects suitable to their natures. The objects of sense are things sensible ; and the objects of imagination, things imaginable, and the objects of intellect, things intelligible, and the objects of the will, things amiable : the eye, that is a nobler sense than some others, hath light for its object, which to other senses is none : and so of the rest. Therefore we have cause to suppose, that as far as our glorified souls, and our spiritual glorified bodies will differ, so far Christ's glorified soul and body will respectively be their several objects : and beholding the glory of both, will be part of our glory.

Yet is it not hence to be gathered, that the separated soul before the resurrection shall not have Christ's glorified body for its object : for the objects of the body are also the objects of the soul, or to speak more properly, the objects of sense are also the objects of intellect and will, though all the objects of the intellect and will are not objects of sense. The separated soul can know Christ's glorified body, though our present bodies cannot see a soul. But how much our spiritual bodies will excel in capacity and activity these passive bodies, that have so much earth and water, we cannot tell.

Though now our souls are as a candle in a lantern, and must have extrinsic objects admitted by the senses before they can be understood, yet it follows not, that therefore a separated soul cannot know such objects : because it now knows them abstractly, because its act of ratiocination is compound as to the cause, soul and body. But it will then know such things intuitively, as now it can do itself, when the lantern is cast by. Whatever many of late that have given themselves the title of ingenious, have said to the contrary, we have little reason to think that the sensitive faculty is not an essential, inseparable power of the same soul that is intellectual, and that sensation ceases to separated souls, however the modes of it may cease with their several uses and organs. To feel intellectually, or to understand, and will feelingly, we have cause to think will be the action of separated souls ; and if so, why may they not have communion with Christ's body and soul as their objects in their separated state ? Besides that we are uncertain whether the separated soul have no vehicle or body at all. Things unknown to us must not be supposed true or false : some think that the sensitive soul is material, and as a body to the intellectual, never separated : I am not of their opinion that make them two substances, but I cannot say, I am certain that they err : some think that the soul is material, of a purer substance than things visible, and that the common notion of its substantiality means nothing else but a pure, as they call it, spiritual, materiality : thus thought not only Tertullian, but almost all the old Greek doctors of the church that write of it, and most of the Latin, or very many, as I have elsewhere showed ; and as Faustus recites them in the treatise answered by Mammertus : some think that the soul, as vegetative, is an igneous body, such as we call æther or solar fire, or rather of a higher, purer kind, and that sensation and intellect are those formal faculties which specifically distinguish it from inferior mere fire or æther. There were few of the old doctors that thought it not some of these ways material ; and consequently extensive and divisible by divine power, though not naturally, or of its own inclination, because most strongly inclined to unity. If any of all these uncertain opinions should prove true, the objections in hand will find no place. To say nothing of their conceit, who say, that as the spirit that retires from the falling leaves in autumn, continues to animate the tree, so man's soul may do when departed, with that to which it is united, to animate some more noble universal body : but as all these are the too bold cogitations of men that had better let unknown things alone, so yet they may be mentioned to refute that more perilous boldness which denies the soul's action which is certain, upon, at best, uncertain reasons.

I may boldly conclude, notwithstanding such objections, that Christ's divine and human nature, soul and body, shall be the felicitating objects of intuition and holy love to the separated soul before the resurrection ; and that to be with Christ is to have such communion with him, and not only to be present where he is.

The chief part of this communion will be that in which we are receptive , even Christ's communications to the soul. As the infinite incomprehensible deity is the root or first cause of all communication, natural, gracious, and glorious, to being, motion, life, rule, reason, holiness, and happiness; and the whole creation is more dependent on God, than the fruit on the tree, or the plants on the earth, or the members on the body, though yet they are not parts of the deity, nor deified, because the communication is creative ; so God uses second causes in his communication to inferior natures. It is more than probable, that the human soul of Christ primarily, and his body secondarily, are the chief second cause of influence and communication both of grace and glory, both to man in the body, and to the separated soul. As the sun is first an efficient communicative second cause of seeing to the eye, and then also is the object of our sight : so Christ is to the soul.* For as God, so the Lamb is the light and glory of the heavenly Jerusalem : in his light we shall have light. Though he give up the kingdom to the Father, so far as that God shall be all in all, and his creature be fully restored to his favour, and there shall be need of a healing government no more, for the recovering of lapsed souls to God ; yet surely he will not cease to be our Mediator, and to be the church's head, and to be the conveying cause of everlasting life, light, and love, to all his members : as now we live because he lives, even as the branches in the vine, and the Spirit that quickens, enlightens, and sanctifies us, is first the Spirit of Christ before it is ours, and is communicated from God, by him, to us ; so will it be in the state of glory ; for we shall have our union and communion with him perfected and not destroyed or diminished. Unless I could be so proud as to think that I am or shall be the most excellent of all the creatures of God, and therefore nearest him, and above all others, how could I think that I am under the influence of no

* This one truth will give great light into the controversies about God's gracious operations on the soul: for when he uses second causes, we see he operates according to their limited aptitude : and Christ's human nature, and all other second causes are limited, and operate variously and resistibly, according to the recipient's capacity.

second cause, but have either grace or glory from God alone.

So far am I from such arrogancy, as to think that I shall be so near to God, as to be above the need and use of Christ and his communications, as that I dare not say that I shall be above the need and help of other subordinate causes : as I am now lower than angels, and need their help, and as I am under the government of my superiors, and, as a poor weak member, am little worth in comparison of the whole body, the church of Christ, and receive continual help from the whole : so how far it will be thus in glory, I know not ; but that God will still use second causes for our joy, I doubt not ; and also that there will not be an equality ; that it will be consistent with God's all-sufficiency to us, and our felicity in him, that we shall for ever have use for one another, and that to ' sit down with Abraham, Isaac, and Jacob in the kingdom of God, and to be in Abraham's bosom, and sit at Christ's right and left hand in his kingdom, and to be ruler over ten cities, and to join with the heavenly host or choir in the joyful love and praise of God, and of the Lamb, and many such like, are not false nor useless notes and notions of our celestial glory.

Certainly if I be with Christ, I shall be with all that are with Christ ; even with all the heavenly society. Though these bodies of gross passive matter must have so much room, that the earth is little enough for all its inhabitants ; and those at the antipodes are almost as strange to us as if they were in another world ; and those of another kingdom, another province or country, and often another parish, yea, another house, are strangers to us, so narrow is our capacity of communion here ; yet we have great cause to think, by many scripture expressions, that our heavenly union and communion will be nearer, and more extensive ; and that all the glorified shall know each other, or at least be far less distant, and less strange, than now we are. As I said before, when I see how far the sun-beams extend, how they penetrate our closest glass, and puzzle them that say that all bodies are impenetrable ; when I see how little they hinder the placing or presence of other creatures, and how intimately they mix themselves with all ; and seem to possess the whole region of the air, when yet the air seems itself to fill it, &c. I dare not think that glorified spirits, no, nor spiritual bodies, will be such strangers to one another as we are here on earth.

I must needs say, that it is a pleasant thought to me, and greatly helps my willingness to die, to think that I shall go to all the holy ones, both Christ, and angels, and departed blessed souls. God hath convinced me, that they are better than I, each singly, and therefore more amiable than myself; and that many are better than one, and the whole than a poor sinful part, and the new Jerusalem is the glory of the creation. God nath given me a love to all his holy ones as such; a love to the work of love and praise, which they continually and perfectly perform to God; and a love to the celestial Jerusalem as it is complete, and to his glory shining in them. My old acquaintance with many a holy person gone to Christ, doth make my thoughts of heaven the more familiar to me. O how many of them could I name! It is no small encouragement to one that is to enter upon an unseen world, to think that he goes not an untrodden path, nor enters into a solitary or singular state; but follows all from the creation, to this day, that have passed by death to endless life. Is it not an emboldening consideration, to think, that I am to go no other way, nor to no other place or state, than all the believers and saints have gone to before me, from the beginning to this time? Of this more afterwards.

Chap. III.

to be with christ, it is needful to depart.

But I must be loosed or depart before I can thus be with Christ: and I must here consider from what I must depart. How, or in what manner; and I must not refuse to know the worst.

I know that I must depart from this body itself, and the life which consists in the animating of it. These eyes must here see no more; this hand must move no more; these feet must walk no more; this tongue must speak no more: as much as I have loved and over-loved this body, I must leave it to the grave. There must it lie and dissolve in darkness, as a neglected thing.

This is the fruit of sin, and nature would not have it so: I mean the nature of this compound man: but what though it be so? It is but my shell or tabernacle, and the clothing of my soul, and not itself. It is but an elementary composition dissolved; and earth going to earth, and water to water, and air to air, and fire to fire, into that union which the elementary nature doth incline to.

It is but an instrument laid by when all its work is done, and a servant dismissed when his service is at an end. What should I do with a horse when I shall need to ride or travel no more, or with a pen when I must write no more? It is but the laying by the passive receiver of my soul's operations, when the soul hath no more to do upon it: as I cast by my lute, or other instrument, when I have better employment than music to take up my time!

Or at most, it is but as flowers die in the fall and plants in winter, when the retiring spirits have done their work, and are indisposed to dwell in so cold and unmeet a habitation, as the season makes their former matter then to be. Its retirement is not its annihilation, but its taking up a fitter place.

It is but a separation from a troublesome companion, and putting off a shoe that pinched me. Many a sad and painful hour I have had in this frail and faultering flesh; many a weary night and day: what cares, what fears, what griefs, and what groans, hath this body cost me? Alas! how many hours of my precious time have been spent to maintain it, please it, or repair it? How considerable a part of all my life hath been spent in necessary sleep and rest? How much in eating, drinking, dressing, physic: and how much in labouring, or using means to procure these and other necessaries? Many a hundred times I have thought, that it costs me so dear to live, yea, to live a painful, weary life, that were it not for the work and higher ends of life, I had little reason to be much in love with it, or to be loth to leave it. Had not God put into our nature itself a necessary, unavoidable, sensitive love of the body, and of life, as he puts into the mother, and into every brute, a love of their young ones, how unclean, impotent, and troublesome soever, for the propagation and continuance of man on earth,—had God but left it to mere reason, without this necessary pre-engagement of our natures, it would have been a matter of more doubt and difficulty than it is, whether this life should be loved and desired, and no small number would daily wish that they had never been born; a wish that I have had much ado to forbear, even when I have known that it is sinful, and when the work and pleasure of my life have been such to overcome the evils of it, as few have had.

Yea, to depart from such a body, is but to be removed from a very foul, uncleanly and sordid habitation. I know that the body of man and brutes is the curious, wonderful work of God, and not to be despised, nor injuriously dishonoured, but admired and well used: but yet it is a wonder to our reason, that so noble a spirit should be so meanly housed : we may call it ' our vile body,' as the apostle doth. It is made up of the airy, watery and earthly parts of our daily food, influenced and actuated by the fiery part, as the instrument of the soul. The greater part of the same food, which, with great cost, pomp, and pleasure, is first upon our tables, and then in our mouths to-day, is to-morrow a lothesome excrement, and cast out into the draught, that the sight and smell of that annoy us not, which yesterday was the sumptuous fruit of our abundance, and the glory of that which is called great house-keeping,-and the pleasure of our eyes and taste.

Yet more : to depart from such a body, is but to be loosed from the bondage of corruption, and from a clog and prison of the soul. I say not that God put a pre-existent soul into this prison penally, for former faults : I must say no more than I can prove, or than I know : but that body which was an apt serpent to innocent man's soul. is become as a prison to him now : what alteration sin made upon the nature of the body, as whether it be more terrene and gross than else it would have been, I have no reason to assert : of earth or dust it was at first, and to dust it is sentenced to return. But no doubt but it hath its part in that dispositive deprivation which is the fruit of sin. We find that the soul, as sensitive, is so imprisoned or shut up in flesh, that sometimes it is more than one door that must be opened before the object and the faculty can meet : in the eye indeed, the soul seems to have a window to look out at, and to be almost itself visible to others : yet there are many interposing tunicles, and a suffusion or winking can make the clearest sight to be as useless for the time as if it were none : if sense be thus shut up from its object, no wonder if reason also be under difficulties from corporeal impediments ; and if the soul that is yoked with such a body can go no faster than its heavy pace.

Yet further : to depart from such a body, is but to be separated from an accidental enemy, and one of our greatest and most hurtful enemies : though still we say, that it is not by any default in the work of our Creator, but by the effects of sin, that it is such : what could Satan, or any other enemy of our souls, have done against us without our flesh ? What is it but the interest of this body, that stands in competition against the interest of our souls and God ? What else do the profane sell their heavenly inheritance for, as Esau his birthright ? No man loves evil, as evil, but as some way a real or seeming good ? What good is it but that which seems good for the body ? What else is the bait of ambition, covetousness, and sensuality, but the interest and pleasure of this flesh ? What takes up the thoughts and care which we would lay out upon things spiritual and heavenly, but this body and its life ? What pleasures be they that steal away men's hearts from the heavenly pleasures of faith, hope, and love, but the pleasures of this flesh ? This draws us to sin : this hinders us from and in our duty. This body hath its interest which must be minded, and its ordinate appetite which must be pleased ; or else what murmurings and disquiet must we expect ? Were it not for bodily interest, and its temptations, how much more innocently and holily might I live ? I should have nothing to care for, but to please God, and to be pleased in him, were it not for the care of this bodily life. What employment should my will and love have, but to delight in God, and love him and his interest, were it not for the love of the body, and its concerns ? By this the mind is darkened, and the thoughts diverted : by this our wills are perverted and corrupted, and by loving things corporeal, contract a strangeness and aversion from things spiritual : by this, heart and time are alienated from God ; our guilt is increased, and our heavenly desire and hopes destroyed ; life made unholy and uncomfortable, and death made terrible, God and our souls separated, and life eternal set by, and in danger of being utterly lost. I know that it is the sinful soul that is in all this the chief cause and agent : but what is it but bodily interest that is its temptation, bait, and end ? What but the body, its life, and pleasure, is the chief, objective, alluring cause of all this sin and misery ? Shall I take such a body to be better than heaven, or be loth to be loosed from so troublesome a yoke-fellow, or to be separated from so burdensome and dangerous a companion ?

Object. But I know this habitation, but the next I know not ; I have long been acquainted with this body, and this world, but the next I am unacquainted with.

Answ. If you know it, you know all that of it which I have mentioned before ; you know it to be a burden and snare : I am sure I know by long experience, that this flesh hath been a painful lodging to my soul, and this world as a tumultuous ocean, or like the uncertain and stormy region of the air. Well he deserves bondage, pain, and enmity, who will love them because he is acquainted with them and is loth to leave them because he hath had them long, and is afraid of being well because he hath been long sick.

Do you not know the next and better habitation? Is faith no knowledge? If you believe God's promise, you know that such a state there is: and you know in general that it is better than this world; and you know that we shall be in holiness and glorious happiness with Christ: and is this no knowledge? What we know not, Christ, that prepares and promises it, doth know: and is that nothing to us, if we really trust our souls to him? He that knows not more good by heaven than by earth, is yet so earthly and unbelieving, that it is no wonder if he be afraid and unwilling to depart.

In departing from this body and life, I must depart from all its ancient pleasures: I must taste no more sweetness in meat, drink, rest, sport, or any such thing that now delights me: house, lands, goods and wealth, must all be left; and the place where I live must know me no more. All my possessions must be no more to me, nor all that I laboured for or took delight in, than if they had never been at all.

What though it must be so? Consider, O my soul, thy ancient pleasures are all past already. Thou losest none of them by death, for they are all lost before, if immortal grace have not by sanctifying them, made the benefits of them to become immortal. All the sweet draughts, morsels, sports, and laughter; all the sweet thoughts of thy worldly possessions, or thy hopes, that ever thou hadst till this present hour, are past by, dead, and gone already. All that death doth to such as these, is to prevent such, that on earth thou shalt have no more.

Is not that the case of every brute, that hath no comfort from the prospect of another life, to repair his loss: and yet as our dominion diminishes their pleasure while they live, by our keeping them under fear and labour, so at our will their lives must end. To please a gentleman's appetite for half an hour or less, birds, beasts, and fishes, must lose life itself, and all the pleasure which light might have afforded them for many years; yea, perhaps many of these, birds and fishes at least, must die to become but one feast to a rich man, if not one ordinary meal.

Is not their sensual pleasure of the same nature as ours? Meat is as sweet to them, and ease as welcome, and desire as strong in season; and the pleasure that death deprives our flesh of, is such as is common to man with brutes: why then should it seem hard to us to lose that in the course of nature, which our wills deprive them of at our pleasure? When, if we are believers, we can say that we but exchange these delights of life, for the greater delights of a life with

Christ, which is a comfort that our fellow-creatures, the brutes, have not!

Indeed the pleasures of life are usually imbittered with so much pain, that to a great part of the world doth seem to exceed them: the vanity and vexation is so great and grievous, as the pleasure seldom countervails. It is true, that nature desires life, even under sufferings that are but tolerable, rather than to die: but that is not so much from the sensible pleasure of life, as from mere natural inclination; which God hath laid so deep, that free-will hath not full power against it. As before I said, that the body of man is such a thing, that could we see through the skin, as men may look through a glass-hive upon the bees, and see all the parts and motion, the filth that are in it, the soul would hardly be willing to actuate, love, and cherish such a mass of unclean matter, and to dwell in such a lothesome place, unless God had necessitated it by nature, deeper than reason or sense, to such a love, and such a labour, by the spring of inclination: even as the cow would not else lick the unclean calf, nor women themselves be at so much labour and trouble with their children, while there is little of them to be pleasing; but uncleanness, and crying, and helpless impatiency, to make wearisome, had not necessitating inclination done more hereto than any other sense or reason; even so I now say of the pleasure of living, that the sorrows are so much greater to multitudes than the sensible delight, that life would not be so commonly chosen and endured under so much trouble, were not men determined thereto by natural, necessitating inclination; or deterred from death by the fears of misery to the separated soul; and yet all this kept not some who are counted the best and wisest of the heathens, from taking it for the valour and wisdom of a man to take away his life in times of extremity, and from making this the great answer to them that grudge at God for making their lives so miserable, 'If the misery be greater than the good of life, why dost thou not end it? Thou mayst do that when thou wilt.'

Our meat and drink is pleasant to the healthful; but it costs poor men so much toil, labour, care, and trouble, to procure a poor diet for themselves and their families, that, I think, could they live without eating and drinking, they would thankfully exchange the pleasure of it all, to be eased of their care and toil in getting it: and when sickness comes, even the pleasantest food is lothesome.

Do we not willingly interrupt and lay by these pleasures every night, when we betake ourselves to sleep? It is possible, indeed, that a man may then have pleasant dreams: but I think few go to sleep for the pleasure of dreaming: either no dreams, or vain, or troublesome dreams, are much more common. To say that rest and ease is my pleasure, is but to say that my daily labour and cares are so much greater than my waking pleasure, that I am glad to lay by both together: for what is ease but deliverance from weariness and pain? For in deep and dreamless sleep there is little positive sense of the pleasure of rest itself. But indeed it is more from nature's necessitated inclination to this self-easing and repairing means, than from the positive pleasure of it, that we desire sleep. If we can thus be contented every night to die, as it were, to all our waking pleasures, why should we be unwilling to die to them at once.

If it be the inordinate pleasures forbidden of God, which you are loth to leave, those must be left before you die, or else it had been better for you never to have been born: yea, every wise and godly man doth cast them off with detestation: you must be against holiness on that account as well as against death: indeed, the same cause which makes men unwilling to live a holy life, hath a great hand in making them unwilling to die; even because they are loth to leave the pleasure of sin: if the wicked be converted, he must be gluttonous and drunken no more; he must live in pride, vain glory, worldliness, and sensual pleasures, no more: therefore he draws back from a holy life, as if it were from death itself. So he is the more loth to die, because he must have no more of the pleasures of his riches, pomp, and honours, his sports and lust, and pleased appetite; no more for ever: but what is this to them that have mortified the flesh with the affections and lusts thereof?

Yea, it is these forbidden pleasures which are great impediments both of our holiness and our true pleasures: one of the reasons why God forbids them, is, because they hinder us from better. If for our own good we must forsake them when we turn to God, it must be supposed that they should be no reason against our willingness to die, but rather that to be free from the danger of them, we should be the more willing.

But the great satisfying answer of this objection is, that death will pass us to far greater pleasures, with which all these are not worthy to be compared. But of this more in due place. But,

When I die, I must depart not only from sensual delights, but from the more manly pleasures of my studies, knowledge, and converse with many wise and godly men, and from all my pleasure in reading, hearing, public and private exercises of religion, &c.; I must leave my library, and turn over those pleasant books no more: I must no more come among the living, nor see the faces of my faithful friends, nor be seen of man: houses and cities, fields and countries, gardens and walks, will be nothing as to me. I shall no more hear of the affairs of the world, of man, or wars, or other news, nor see what becomes of that beloved interest of wisdom, piety, and peace, which I desire may prosper, &c.

Though these delights are far above those of sensual sinners, yet, alas, how low and little are they? How small is our knowledge in comparison of our ignorance? How little doth the knowledge of learned doctors differ from the thoughts of a silly child? For from our childhood we take it in by drops; and as trifles are the matter of childish knowledge, so words, and notions, and artificial forms, do make up more of the learning of the world, than is commonly understood; and many such learned men know little more of any great and excellent things themselves, than rustics that are contemned by them for their ignorance. God and the life to come, are little better known by them, if not much less, than by many of the unlearned. What is it but a child's game, that many logicians, rhetoricians, grammarians, yea, metaphysicians, and other philosophers, in their most eager studies and disputes, are exercised in? Of how little use is it to know what is contained in many hundreds of the volumes that fill our libraries? Yea, or to know many of the most glorious speculations in physics, mathematics, &c. which have given some the title of *virtuosi* and *ingeniosi* in these times, who have little the more wit or virtue to live to God, or overcome temptations from the flesh and world, and to secure their everlasting hopes: what pleasure or quiet doth it give to a dying man to know almost any of their trifles.

Yea, it were well if much of our reading and learning did us no harm, nay, more than good: I fear lest books are to some but a more honourable kind of temptation than cards or dice; lest many a precious hour be lost in them, that should be employed on much higher matters, and lest many make such knowledge but an unholy, natural, yea, carnal pleasure, as worldlings do the thoughts of their lands and honours; and lest they be the more dangerous by how much the less suspected: but the best is, it is a pleasure so fenced from the slothful with thorny labour of hard and long studies, that laziness saves more from it than grace and holy wisdom doth. But doubtless, fancy and the natural intellect may, with as little sanctity, live in the pleasure of reading, knowing, disputing, and writing, as others spend their time at a game of chess, or other ingenious sport.

For my own part, I know that the knowledge of natural things is valuable, and may be sanctified; much more theological knowledge; when it is so, it is of good use; and I have little knowledge which I find not some way useful to my highest ends. If wishing or money could procure more, I would wish and empty my purse for it; but yet if many score or hundred books which I have read, had been all unread, and I had that time now to lay out upon higher things, I should think myself much richer than now I am. I must earnestly pray, the Lord forgive me the hours that I have spent in reading things less profitable, for the pleasing of a mind that would wish to know all, which I should have spent for the increase of holiness in myself and others: yet I must thankfully acknowledge to God, that from my youth he taught me to begin with things of greatest weight, and to refer most of my other studies thereto, and to spend my days under the motives of necessity and profit to myself, and those with whom I had to do. I now think better of the course of Paul, who determined to know nothing but a crucified Christ, among the Corinthians, that is, so to converse with them as to use, and glorying as if he knew, nothing else: so of the rest of the apostles and primitive ages: though I still love and honour the fullest knowledge, yet I less censure even that Carthage council which forbade the reading of the heathen books of learning and arts, than formerly I have done. I would have men favour most that learning in their health, which they will, or should, favour most in sickness, and near to death.

Alas, how dear a vanity is this knowledge! That which is but theoretic and notional is but a tickling of the fancy or mind, little differing from a pleasant dream: but how many hours, what gazing of the wearied eye, what stretching thoughts of the impatient brain, must it cost us, if we will attain to any excellency? Well saith Solomon, 'much reading is a weariness to the flesh, and he that increaseth knowledge increaseth sorrow.' How many hundred studious days and weeks, and how many hard and tearing thoughts, hath my little, very little, knowledge cost me? How much infirmity and painfulness to my flesh, increase of painful diseases, and loss of bodily ease and health? How much pleasure to myself of other kinds, and how much acceptance with

men, have I lost by it, which I might easily have had in a more conversant and plausible way of life? When all is done, if I reach to know any more than others of my place and order, I must differ so much, usually, from them: if I manifest not that difference, but keep all that knowledge to myself, I sin against conscience and nature itself: the love of man, and the love of truth oblige me to be soberly communicative: were I so indifferent to truth and knowledge, as easily to forbear their propagation, I must also be so indifferent to them, as not to think them worth so dear a price as they have cost me, though they are the free gifts of God: as nature is universally inclined to the propagation of the kind by generation, so is the intellectual nature to the communication of knowledge, which yet hath its lust and inordinancy in proud, ignorant, hasty teachers and disputers.

But if I obey nature and conscience in communicating that knowledge which contains my difference aforesaid, the dissenters too often think themselves disparaged by it, how peaceably soever I manage it: as bad men take the piety of the godly to be an accusation of their impiety, so many teachers take themselves to be accused of ignorance, by such as condemn their errors by the light of truth? If you meddle not with any person, yet take they their opinions to be so much their interest, as that all that is said against them, they take as said against themselves. Then, alas, what envyings, what whispering disparagements, and what backbitings, if not malicious slanders and underminings, do we meet with from the carnal clergy. O that it were all from them alone, and that among the zealous and suffering party of faithful preachers, there were not much of such iniquity, and that none of them preached Christ in strife and envy; it is sad that error should find so much shelter under the selfishness and pride of pious men; and that the friends of truth should be tempted to reject and abuse so much of it in their ignorance as they do: but the matter of fact is too evident to be hid.

But especially if we meet with a clergy that are high, and have a great deal of worldly interest at the stake: or if they be in councils and synods, and have got the major vote, they too easily believe that either their grandeur, reverence, names, or numbers, must give them the reputation of being orthodox, and in the right, and will warrant them to account and defame him as erroneous, heretical, schismatical, singular, factious, or proud, that presumes to contradict them, and to know more than they:

of which not only the case of Nazianzen, Martin, Chrysostom, are sad proofs, but also the proceedings of too many general and provincial councils. So our hard studies and darling truth must make us as owls, or reproached persons, among those reverend brethren, who are ignorant at easier rates, and who find it a far softer kind of life to think and say as the most or best esteemed do, than to purchase reproach and obloquy so dearly.

The religious people of the several parts will say as they hear their teachers do, and be the militant followers of their too militant leaders: and it will be their house talk, their shop talk, their street talk, if not their church talk, that such a one is an erroneous, dangerous man, because he is not as ignorant and erroneous as they, especially if they be the followers of a teacher much exasperated by confutation, and engaged in the controversy; and also if it should be suffering confessors that are contracted, or men most highly esteemed for extraordinary degrees of piety: then what cruel censures must he expect, who ever so tenderly would suppress their errors?

O what sad instances of this are the case of the confessors in Cyprian's days, who, as many of his epistles show, became the great disturbers of that church; and of the Egyptian monks at Alexandria, in the days of Theophilus, who turned Anthropomorphites, and raised abominable tumults, with woeful scandal, and odious bloodshed. O that this age had not yet greater instances to prove the matter than any of these! Now should a man be loth to die, for fear of leaving such troublesome, costly learning and knowledge, as the wisest men can here attain?

But the chief answer is yet behind. No knowledge is lost, but perfected, and changed for much nobler, sweeter, greater knowledge: let men be ever so uncertain in particular de modo, whether acquired habits of intellect and memory die with us, as being dependent on the body: yet, by what manner soever, that a far clearer knowledge we shall have, than is here attainable, is not to be doubted of. The cessation of our present mode of knowing, is but the cessation of our ignorance and imperfection: as our wakening ends a dreaming knowledge, and our maturity ends the trifling knowledge of a child: for so saith the Holy Ghost, 'Love never faileth,' and we can love no more than we know: but whether there be prophesies they shall fail: that is, cease: whether there be tongues they shall cease: whether there be knowledge, notional and abstractive, such as we have now, it shall vanish away: 'when I was a child I spoke as a child, understood as a child, I thought as a child; but when I became a man, I put away childish things:' for now we see through a glass darkly, as men understand a thing by a metaphor, parable or riddle, but then face to face, even creatures intuitively as in themselves naked and open to our sight: now I know in part, but then shall I know, even as I am known: not as God knows us: for our knowledge and his must not be so comparatively likened: but as holy spirits know us both now and for ever, we shall both know and be known by immediate intuition.

If a physician be to describe the parts of man, and the latent diseases of his patient, he is anxious to search hard, and bestow many thoughts of it, besides his long reading and converse to make him capable of knowing: and when all is done, he goes much upon conjectures, and his knowledge is mixed with many uncertainties, yea, and mistakes; but when he opens the corpse, he sees all, and his knowledge is more full, more true, and more certain, besides that it is easily and quickly attained, even by a present look: a countryman knows the town, the fields, and rivers where he dwells, yea, and the plants and animals, with ease and certain clearness; when he that must know the same things by the study of geographical writings and tables, must know them, but with a general, an unsatisfactory, and often a much mistaken kind of knowledge: alas, when our present knowledge hath cost a man the study of forty, or fifty, or sixty years, how lean and poor, how doubtful and unsatisfactory is it after all? But when God will show us himself, and all things; and when heaven is known as the sun by its own light, this will be the clear, sure, and satisfactory knowledge; 'blessed are the pure in heart, for they shall see God.' 'And without holiness none can see him.' This sight will be worthy the name of wisdom, when our present glimpse is but philosophy, a love and desire of wisdom; so far should we be from fearing death through the fear of losing our knowledge, or any of the means of knowledge, that it should make us rather long for the world of glorious light, that we might get out of this darkness, and know all that with an easy look, to our joy and satisfaction, which here we know with troublesome doubtings, or not at all. Shall we be afraid of darkness in the heavenly light, or of ignorance, when we see the Lord of glory.

As for the loss of sermons, books, and other means, surely it is no loss to cease the means when we have attained the end: cannot we spare our winter clothes, as troublesome in the heat of summer, and sit by the hot fire without our gloves? Cannot we sit at home without a horse or coach? or set them by at our journey's end? Cannot we lie in bed without boots and spurs? Is it grievous to us to cease our physic when we are well: even here, he is happier that hath least of the creature, and needs least, than he that hath much and needs much: because all creature comforts and helps have also their inconveniences: the very applying and using so many remedies of our want, is tedious of itself. As God only needeth nothing but is self-sufficient, and therefore only perfectly and essentially happy, so those are likest God that need least from without, and have the greatest plenitude of internal goodness. What need we to preach, hear, read, pray, to bring us to heaven when we are there?

As for our friends, and our converse with them, as relations, or as wise, religious, and faithful to us, he that believes not that there are far more, and far better, in heaven than are on earth, doth not believe, as he ought, that there is a heaven: our friends here are wise, but they are unwise also: they are faithful, but partly unfaithful; they are holy, but also, alas, too sinful: they have the image of God, but blotted and dishonoured by their faults: they do God and his church much service; but they also do too much against him, and too much for Satan, even when they intend the honour of God: they promote the gospel; but they also hinder it: their weakness, ignorance, error, selfishness, pride, passion, division, contention, scandals, and remissness, do often so much hurt, that it is hard to discern whether it be not greater than their good to the church or to their neighbours. Our friends are our helpers and comforters; but how often also are they our hinderers, troubles, and grief? But in heaven they are altogether wise, holy, faithful, and concordant, and have nothing in them, nor there done by them, but what is amiable to God and man.

With our faithful friends, we have here a mixture, partly of useless and burdensome persons, and partly of unfaithful hypocrites, and partly of self-conceited, factious wranglers, and partly of malicious, envious underminers, and partly of implacable enemies: how many of all these set together is there for one worthy, faithful friend? How great a number is there to trouble you, for one that will indeed comfort you? But in heaven there are none but the wise and holy: no hypocrites, no burdensome neighbours, no treacherous, or oppressing, or persecuting enemies are there: is not all good and amiable better than

a little good with so troublesome a mixture of noisome evil?

Christ loved his disciples, his kindred, yea, and all mankind, and took pleasure in doing good to all; and so did his apostles: but how poor a requital had he or they from any but from God? Christ's own brethren believed not in him, but wrangled with him; almost like those that said to him on the cross, 'If thou be the Son of God, come down, and we will believe.' Peter himself was once a Satan to him, and after, with cursing and swearing, denied him: all his disciples forsook him and fled: what then from others could be expected?

No friends have a perfect suitableness to each other; and roughness and inequalities that are nearest us are most troublesome. The wonderful variety and contrariety of apprehensions, interest, educations, temperaments, occasions, temptations, &c. are such, that whilst we are scandalized at the discord and confusions of the world, we must recall ourselves, and admire that all-ruling providence which keeps up so much order and concord as there is: we are, indeed, like people in crowded streets, who, going several ways, molest each other with their jostling oppositions; or, like boys at foot-ball, striving to overthrow each other for the ball: but it is a wonder of divine power and wisdom, that all the world is not continually in moral war.

If I do men no harm, yet if I do but cross their wills, it goes for a provoking injury: When there are as many wills as persons, who is it than can please them all? Who hath money enough to please all the poor that need it, or the covetous that desire it? Or, who can live with displeased men, and not feel some of the fruits of their displeasure? What day goes over my head in which very many desire not, or expect not impossibilities from me? How great is the number of them that expect unrighteous things? By nothing do I displease so many, as by not displeasing God and my conscience: for nothing am I so deeply accused of sin, as for not sinning; the world will not think well of any thing that crosses their opinion and carnal interest, be it ever so conformable to God's commands; I must confess, that while I suffer from all sides, few men have more common and open praises from their persecutors than I: but while they praise me in general, and for other particulars, they aggravate my nonconformity to their opinions and wills, and take me to be so much the more hurtful to them. The greatest crimes that have been charged on me have been for the things which I thought to be my greatest duties; and for those parts of my obedience to my conscience and God, which cost me dearest : and where I pleased my flesh least, I pleased the world least. At how cheap a rate to my flesh could I have got the applause of factious men, if that had been my end and business ? Would I have conformed to their wills, and taken a bishopric, and the honours and riches of the world, how good a man had I been called by the diocesan party ! O what praise I should have with the Papists, could I turn Papist ! And all the backbitings and bitter censures of the Antinomians, Anabaptists, and Separatists, had been turned into praise, could I have said as they, or not contradicted them. But otherwise there is no escaping their accusations. And is this tumultuous, militant, yea, malignant world, a place that I should be loth to leave ?

Alas, our darkness, and weakness, and passions, are such, that it is hard for a family or a few faithful friends, to live so evenly in the exercise of love, as not to have often unpleasant jars ! What then is to be expected from strangers and from enemies ? Ten thousand persons will judge of abundance of my words and actions, who never knew the reasons of them : every one's conceptions are as the report and conveyance of the matter to them is : and while they have a various light, and false reports, and defectiveness will make them false, what can be expected but false, injurious censures ?

Though no outward thing on earth is more precious than the holy word, worship, and ordinances of God, yet even here I see that which points me up higher, and tells me it is much better to be with Christ. Shall I love the name of heaven, better than heaven itself ? The holy scriptures are precious, because I have there the promise of glory ; but is not the possession better than the promise ? If a light and guide thither through this wilderness be good, surely the end must needs be better : and it hath pleased God that all things on earth, and therefore even the sacred scriptures, should bear the marks of our state of imperfection : imperfect persons were the penmen ; and imperfect human language is the conveying, signal, organical part of the matter. The method and phrase, though true and blameless, are far short of the heavenly perfection. Else so many commentators had not found so hard a task of it to expound innumerable difficulties, and reconcile so many seeming contradictions ; nor would infidels find matter of so strong temptation, and so much cavil as they do ; nor would Peter have told us of the difficulties of Paul's epistles, and such occasions of

men's wresting them to their own destruction. Heaven will not be made, to perfect spirits, the occasion of so many errors, controversies, and quarrels, as the scriptures are to us imperfect men on earth : yea, heaven is the more desirable, because there I shall better understand the scriptures than here I can ever hope to do. All the hard passages now misunderstood, will be there made plain, and all the seeming contradictions reconciled ; and, which is much more, that God, that Christ, that new Jerusalem, that glory, and that felicity of souls, which are now known but darkly and enigmatically in the glass, will then be known intuitively as we see the face itself, whose image only the glass first showed us. To leave my bible, and go to the God and the heaven that is revealed, will be no otherwise a loss to me, than to lay by my crutches or spectacles when I need them not, or to leave his image for the presence of my friend.

Much less do I need to fear the loss of all other books, sermons, or other verbal information. Much reading hath often been a weariness to my flesh ; and the pleasure of my mind is much abated by the great imperfection of the means. Many books must be partly read, that I may know that they are scarcely worth the reading : and many must be read to enable us to satisfy other men's expectations, and to confute those who abuse the authority of the authors against the truth : and many good books must be read, that have little to add to what we have read in many others before ; and many that are blotted with ensnaring errors : which, if we detect not, we leave snares for such as see them not : and if we detect them, ever so tenderly, if truly, we are taken to be injurious to the honour of the learned, godly authors, and proudly to overvalue our own conceits. So lamentable is the case of all mankind, by the imperfections of human language, that those words which are invented for the communication of conceptions, are so little fitted to their use, as rather to occasion misunderstanding and contentions : there being scarcely a word that hath not many significations, and that needs not many more words to bring us to the true notice of the speaker's mind. Every word is a *sign*, that hath three relations,—to the matter spoken of;—to the mind of the speaker, as signifying his conceptions of that matter ;—and to the mind of the hearer or reader which is to be informed by it. Hence it is so hard to find and use words that are fitted indeed to all these uses, and to have store of such, and mix no other, that few, if any, in the world were ever so happy as to attain it. If words be not fitted to the matter or things, they are false as to their first and proper use : and yet the penury of apt words, and the redundancy of others, and the authority of the masters of sciences imposing arbitrary terms and notions on their disciples, and the custom of the vulgar, who have the empire as to the sense of words, have all conspired to make words of very uncertain signification. So that when students have learned words by long and hard studies, they are often little the nearer the true knowledge of the things ; and too often, by their ineptitude, misled to false conceptions. So their saying is too often true, that a great book is a great evil, while it contains so great a number of uncertain words, which become the matter of great contentions.

When the mind of the speaker or writer is no better informed by such notions, but his conceptions of things are some false, some confused and undigested, what wonder if his words do not otherwise express his mind to others, when even men of clearest understanding find it difficult to have words still ready to communicate their conceptions with truth and clearness. To form true sentiments of things into apt significant words, is a matter of mere art, and requires an apt teacher, a serious learner, and long use : too many take their art of speaking in prayer, conference, or preaching, to have more in it of wisdom and piety, than it hath ; and some too much condemn the unaccustomed that want it.

If we could fit our words well to the matter, and to our minds, with that double verity, yet still it is hard to fit them to the reader or hearer : for want of which they are lost as to him : his information being our end, they are therefore so far lost to us. That which is spoken most congruously to the matter, is seldom fitted to the capacity of the receiver. Some readers or hearers, yea, almost all, are so used to unapt words and notions, obtruded on mankind by the master of words, that they cannot understand us if we change their terms and offer them fitter, and yet least understand those which they think that they best understand : all men must have long time to learn the art of words, before they can understand them, as well as before they can readily use them. The duller any man is, and of less understanding, the more words are necessary to make him understand : yet his memory is the less capable of retaining many. This is our difficulty, not only in catechising, but in all our writings and teaching, a short catechism, or a short style, the ignorant understand not ; and a long one they remember not. He that will accommodate one judicious reader or hearer, with profound matter, or an accurate style, must incommodate multitudes that are incapable of it. Therefore such must be content with few approvers, and leave the applause of the multitude to the more popular, unless he be one that can seasonably suit himself to both.

A man that resolves not to be deceived by ambiguous words, and makes it his first work in all his readings and disputings to distinguish between words, sense, and things, and strictly to examine each disputed term, till the speaker's meaning be distinctly known, will see the lamentable case of the church, and all mankind, and what shadows of knowledge deceive the world, and in what useless dreams the greatest part of men, yea, of learned men, do spend their days : much of that which some men unweariedly study, and take to be the honour of their understandings, and their lives, and much of that, in which multitudes place their piety and hopes of salvation, being a mere game at words, and useless notions, and as truly to be called vanity and vexation as is the rest of the vain-show that most men walk in. My sad and bitter thoughts of the heathen, infidel, mahometan world, and of the common corruptions of rulers and teachers, cities and countries, senates and councils, I will not here open to others, lest they offend ; nor cry out as Seneca, 'We all are bad,' or, ' Fools exist everywhere,' nor describe the furious spirits of the clergy, and their ignorance, and unrighteous calumnies and schisms, as Gregory Nazianzen and others do, nor voluminously lament the seeming hopeless case of earth, by the boldness, blindness, and fury of men that make use of such sad considerations, to loosen my love from such a world, and make me willing to be with Christ.

If other men's word and writings are blemished with so much imperfection, why should I think that my own are blameless ? I must for ever be thankful for the holy instructions and writings of others, notwithstanding human frailty, and contentious men's abuse of words : and so I must be thankful that God hath made any use of my own, for the good of souls, and his church's edification. But with how many drawbacks are such comforts here mixed : we are not the teachers of a well ruled school, where learners are ranked into several forms, that every one may have the teaching which is agreeable to his capacity : but we must set open the door to all that will crowd in, and publish our writings to all sorts of readers : and there being as various degrees of capacity as there are men and women, and consequently great variety and contrariety of apprehensions, it is easy to anticipate what various reception we must expect : we cast out our doctrine almost as a foot-ball is turned out among boys in the street, in some congregations ; few understand it, but every one censures it. Few come as learners, or teachable disciples, but most come to sit as judges on their teacher's words ; and yet have not either the skill, or the patience, or the diligence, which is necessary in a just trial, to a righteous judgment. But as our words agree or disagree with the former conceptions of every hearer, so are they judged to be wise or foolish, sound or unsound, true or false, fit or unfit.

Few sermons that I preach, but one extols them, and wishes they were printed, and another accuses them of some heinous fault : some men are pleased with clearness and accurateness of doctrine ; and others account it too high, and say we shoot over the hearers' heads, and like nothing but the fervent application of what they knew before : most hearers are displeased with that which they most need : if they err, they reproach that doctrine as erroneous that would cure them : if they are guilty of any prevailing distemper and sin, they take that application to be injurious to them, which would convince them, and save them from that guilt. Most are much pleased with plain and zealous reproof of sin ; but it must be other men's sins, and not their own. The poor love to hear of the evil of oppression and unmercifulness, of pride, fulness and idleness, and all the sins of the rich : subjects love to hear of their rulers' faults, and say, O this man is no flatterer ; he dares tell the greatest of their sins : but if they hear of their own, they take it for an injury. Rulers like a sermon for submission and obedience, but how few love to hear of the evil of injustice and oppression, or pride and sensuality, or to hear of the necessity of holiness, justice, temperance, of death, judgment, and the life to come ? Every sectarian and dogmatist delights to have his own opinion cried up, and his party praised as the chief saints : but all that tends to the praise of those that he dissents from, and accounts adversaries to the truth, is distasteful to him, as a complying with iniquity, and a strengthening of the enemies of Christ : and all that uncharitableness which he expects from us against others, is as much expected by others against him, and such as he.

This day, while I am writing these words, my pockets are full of letters sent me, on one side importunately charging it on me as my duty to conform to the oaths, declarations, covenants, and practices, now imposed, or else to give over preaching, which would please them ; and on the other side vehemently censuring me as guilty of grievous sin, for declaring my judgment for so much of conformity as I have done ; and charging me by predictions as guilty of the sufferings of all that are otherwise minded, for communicating in the sacrament, and the common prayers of the church ; and others in the mid-way, persuading me equally to bear my testimony against unjust separation and persecution, and to endeavour still, if possible, to save a self-destroying people, from the tearing fury of these two extremes : and how should I answer these contrary expectations, or escape the censures of such expectations ?

It hath pleased God, who thirty years and more hath tried me by human applause, of late, in this city, where multitudes of persons of contrary minds are, like passengers in crowded streets still jostling and offending one another, to exercise me with men's daily backbitings and cavils : and so many have chosen me for the subject of their discourse, that I may say as Paul, 'We are made a spectacle (or theatre) to the world, and to angels, and to men : we are fools for Christ's sake, but ye are wise in Christ,' &c. Did I not live out of the noise in retirement, taken up with pain, and expectations of my change, what an annoyance to me would it be to hear religious persons, that have a God, a Christ, a heaven to talk of, to abuse their time and tongues in so much talking of one so inconsiderable, and that hath so little to do with them, or they with him ; while with some overvaluing me, and others still quarrelling, I am the matter of their idle, sinful talk. The persecutors for divers years after first silencing, if not still, and the separatists for two or three years past, have been possessed with so strange a jealousy and quarrelsome a disposition against me, that they seem to take it for their interest to promote my defamation, and for much of their work to search what may afford them any matter of accusation in every sermon that I preach, and every book that I write. Though the fury of the persecutors be such as makes them incapable of such converse and sober consideration as is needful to their true information and satisfaction : yet most of the more religious cavillers are satisfied as soon as I have spoken with them : for want of accurateness and patience, they judge rashly before they understand, and when they understand confess their error ; and yet many go on and take no warning after many times conviction of their mistake.

Even in books that are still before their eyes,

as well as in transient words and sermons, they heedlessly leave out, or put in, or alter, and misreport plain words, and with confidence affirm those things to have been said that never were said, but perhaps the contrary. When all people will judge of the good or evil of our words, as they think we have reason to use them or forbear them, how can we satisfy men that are out of our hearing, and to whom we cannot tell our reasons? Most men are of private, narrow observation, and judge of the good or hurt that our words do, by those that they themselves converse with: and when I convince them that my decisions of many questions, which they are offended at, are true; they say, It is an unseasonable and a hurtful truth: and when I have called them to look further abroad in the world, and told them my reasons; they say, Had these been all set down, men would have been satisfied. On how hard terms do we instruct such persons, whose narrow understandings cannot know obvious reasons of what we say till they are particularly told them? So to tell men the reasons of all that such can quarrel with, will make every book to swell with commentaries to such a size as they can neither buy nor read: and they come not to us to know our reasons; nor have we leisure to open them to every single person: and thus suspicious men, when their understandings want the humbling acquaintance with their ignorance, and their consciences, that tenderness which should restrain them from rash judging, go on to accuse such needful truths of which they know not the use and reason. What man living hath the leisure and opportunity to acquaint all the ignorant persons in city and country, with all the reasons of all that he shall say, write, or do? Or who, that writes not a page instead of a sentence, can so write, that every unprepared reader shall understand him? What hopes hath that tutor or schoolmaster of preserving his reputation, who shall be accounted erroneous, and accused of unsound or injurious doctrine, by every scholar that understands not his words, and all the reasons of them?

But God in great mercy to me hath made this my lot, not causing, but permitting, the sins of the contentious, that I might before death be better weaned from all below: had my temptations from inordinate applause had no alloy, they might have been more dangerously strong. Even yet while church-dividers, on both extremes, do make me the object of their daily obloquy, the continued respects of the sober and peaceable, are so great, as to be a temptation strong enough, to so weak a person, to give a check to my desires to leave the world. It is long since riches and worldly honour appeared to me as they are, as not rendering the world either lovely or desirable. But the love and concord of religious persons hath a more amiable aspect: there is so much holiness in these, that I was loth to call them vanity and vexation: but yet as flesh and blood would refer them to selfish ends, and any way value them as a carnal interest, I must so call them, and number them with the things that are loss and dung. Selfishness can serve itself upon things good and holy: and if good men, and good books, and good sermons, would make the world seem overlovely to us, it will be a mercy of God to abate the temptation: and if my soul, looking toward the heavenly Jerusalem, be hindered as Paul was, in his journey to Jerusalem, by the love of ancient friends and hearers, I must say, ' What mean you to weep and break my heart!' I am ready to leave the dearest friends on earth, and life, and all the pleasures of life, for the presence of far better friends with Christ, and the sweeter pleasures of a better life. That little amiableness which is in things below, is in godly men as life in the heart, which dies last: when that is all gone, when we are dead to the love of the godly themselves, and to learning, books, and mediate ordinances, so far as they serve a selfish interest, and tempt down our hearts from heavenly aspirings, the world is then crucified to us indeed, and we to it. I rejoice to tread in the footsteps of my Lord, who had some indeed weeping about his cross, but was forsaken by all his disciples, while in the hour of temptation they all fled! But my desertion is far less, for it is less that I am fit to bear. If God will justify, who shall condemn? If he be for me, who shall be against me? O may I not be put to that dreadful ease, to cry out, 'My God, my God, why hast thou forsaken me?' And may nothing separate me from his love! Then were I forsaken of the sober and peaceable, as I am, in part, of some quarrelsome dividers, how tolerable a trial would it be? Man is as dust in the balance, that adds little to it, and signifies nothing when God is in the other end. But I suspect still that I make too much account of man, when this case hath taken up too much of my observation.

Of all things, surely a departing soul hath least cause to fear the losing of its notice of the affairs of the world; of peace, wars, church, or kingdoms. If the sun can send forth its material beams, and operate by motion, light, and heat, at such a distance as this earth, why should I think that blessed spirits are such local, confined and impotent substances, as not to have notice of the things of earth? Had I but bodily eyes, I could see more from the top of a tower or hill, than any one that is below can do. Shall I know less of earth from heaven than I do now? It is unlike that my capacity will be so little: if it were, it is unlike that Christ and all the angels will be so strange to me, as to give me no notice of things that so much concern my God and my Redeemer, to whom I am united, and the holy society of which I am a part, and myself as a member of Christ and that society! I do not think that the communion of the celestial inhabitants is so narrow and slow, as it is of walking clods of earth, and of souls that are confined to such dark lanthorns as this body is? Stars can shine one to another. We on earth can see them so far off in their heaven. Surely then, if they have a seeing faculty, each of them can see many of us; even the kingdoms of the world. Spirits are most active, and of powerful and quick communication. They need not send letters, or write books to one another, nor lift up a voice to make each other hear: nor is there any unkindness, division, or unsociable selfishness among them, which may cause them to conceal their notices or their joys: but as activity, so unity, is greatest, where there is most perfection: they will so be many, as yet to be one; and their knowledge will be one knowledge, their love one love, and their joy one joy: not by so perfect a unity as in God himself, who is one and but one; but such as is suitable to created imperfection, which participates of the perfection of the Creator, as the effect doth of the virtue of the cause, and therefore hath some participation of his unity. O foolish soul! If I shall fear this unity with God, Christ, and all the holy spirits, lest I should lose my present separate individuality, when perfection and unity are so near a-kin. In a word, I have no cause to think that my celestial advancement will be a diminution of any desirable knowledge, even of things on earth; but contrarily, that it will be inconceivably increased.

But if indeed I shall know less of things below, it will be because that the knowledge of them is a part of vanity and vexation, which hath no place in heaven. So much knowledge of good and evil in lower matters, as came to us by sin, is unworthy of our fond tenaciousness, and fear of losing it? Surely the sad tidings which we have weekly in our news books, our lamentable notices of heathen and infidel kingdoms, of the over-spreading prevalency of barbarism, idolatry, ignorance, and infidelity; of the rage and success of cruel tyrants; of the bloody wars of proud, unquiet, worldly men, of the misery of the oppressed, desolate countries, the dissipated churches, the persecuted, innocent Christians, are no such pleasing things as that we should be afraid to hear of such no more. To know or hear of the poor in famine, the rich in folly, the church distracted, the kingdom discontented, the godly scandalous by the effects of their errors, imperfections, and divisions, the wicked outrageous and waxing worse, the falseness or miscarriages, or sufferings of friends, the fury or success of enemies, is this an intelligence which I cannot spare? What is the daily tidings that I hear, but of bloody wars, the undone countries, the persecuted churches, the silenced, banished, or imprisoned preachers, of the best removed in judgment from an unworthy world by death, and worse succeeding in their rooms, of the renewed designs and endeavours of the church's enemies; the implacable rage of the worldly and unquiet clergy, and the new divisions of self-conceited sectaries, and the obloquy and backbitings of each party against the other? How often hear I the sad tidings of this friend's sickness or death, and that friend's discontent, and of another's fall, and of many, very many's sufferings? My ears are daily filled with the cries of the poor whom I cannot relieve, with the endless complaints of fearful, melancholy, despairing persons: with the wranglings of the ignorant and proud professors, and contentious divines, who censure most boldly where they are most erroneous or dark; or with the troublesome discontents of those that I converse with: should I be afraid of the ending of so sad a tragedy, or of awaking out of such an unpleasant dream? Have I not many times thought of the privilege of the deaf, that hear not these troublesome and provoking things; and of the blind, that see not the vanities and temptations of this world; it is one part of the benefit of solitude, or a private life and habitation, to free me from many of these unpleasing objects; and a great part of the benefit of sleep, that with my clothes I may lay by these troublesome thoughts.

But other men tell me, the church cannot yet spare you: there is yet this and that necessary work to be done: there is this and that need, &c.

But is it we or God that must choose his servants, and cut out their work? Whose work am I doing? Is it my own, or his? If his, is it not he that must tell me what, and when, and how long? And will not his will and choice be best? If I believe not this, how do I take him for my

God? Doth God or I know better what he hath yet to do? And who is fittest to do it? The church's service and benefits must be measured out by our master and benefactor, and not by ourselves.

What am I to those more excellent persons whom, in all ages, he hath taken out of the world? And would men's thoughts of the church's needs detain them? The poor heathen, infidel, mahometan nations have no preachers of the gospel? And if their need prove not that God will send them such, no country's need will prove that God will continue them such. Many more useful servants of Christ have died in their youth: John Janeway preached but one sermon: Joseph Allen, and many other excellent men, died young in the midst of their vigorous, successful labours: both of them far more fit for God's work, and likely to win souls, and glorify God, than I am or ever was, however their greater light was partly kindled from my lesser. Yet did both these, under painful, consuming languishings of the flesh, die as they had long lived, in the lively triumphant praises of their Redeemer, and joyful desires and hopes of glory? Shall I at seventy-six years of age, after such a life of unspeakable mercies, and almost fifty-three years of comfortable help in the service of my Lord, be now afraid of my reward, and shrink at the sentence of death, and still be desiring to stay here, upon pretence of further service: we know not what is best for the church as God doth: the church and the world are not ours, but his; not our desires, but his will, must measure out its mercies: we are not so merciful as he is: it is not unmeet for us to desire many things which God will not give, nor sees it meet to grant the particulars of such desires. Nothing ever lay so heavy on my heart as the sin and misery of mankind, and to think how much of the world lies in folly and wickedness. For what can I pray so heartily as for the world's recovery: and it is his will that I should show a holy and universal love by praying,—'Let thy name be hallowed. Thy kingdom come, Thy will be done on earth as it is done in heaven:' yet alas, how unlike is earth to heaven, and what ignorance, sin, confusions, and cruelties, here reign and prosper? Unless there is a wonderful change to be expected, even as by a general miracle, how little hope appears that ever these prayers should be granted in the things? It makes us better to desire that others may be better: but God is the free disposer of his own gifts: and it seems to be his will, that the permitted ignorance and confusion of this world should help us the more

to value and desire that world of light, love, and order, which he calls us to prefer and hope for.

If I am any way useful to the world, it is undeserved mercy that hath made me so; for which I must be thankful: but how long I shall be so, is not my business to determine, but my Lord's. My many sweet and beautiful flowers arise and appear in their beauty and sweetness, but for one summer's time, and they murmur not that they flourish for so short a space. The beasts, birds, and fishes, which I feed on, live till I will have them die: and as God will be served and pleased by wonderful variety at once, of animals and vegetables, &c. so will he by many successive generations: if one flower fall or die, it suffices that others shall summer after summer arise from the same root: and if my pears, apples, plums, &c. fall or serve me when they are ripe, it suffices that, not they, but others, the next year shall do the same; God will have other generations to succeed us: let us thank him that we have had our time: and could we overcome the grand crime of selfishness, and could we love others as ourselves, and God, as God, above all the world, it would comfort us at death, that others shall survive us, and the world shall continue, and God will be still God, and be glorified in his works: and love will say, I shall live in my successors, and I shall more than live in the life of the world; and yet most of all in the eternal life and glory of God.

God, who made us not gods, but poor creatures, as it pleased him, knows best our measures: and he will not try us with too long a life of temptations, lest we should grow too familiar where we should be strangers, and utterly strangers to our home: no wonder if that world was ready for a deluge, by a deluge of sin, in which men lived to six, seven, eight, and nine hundred years of age: had our great sensualists any hope of so long a life, they would be more like incarnate devils, and there would be no dwelling near them for the holy seed: if angels were among them, they would, like the sodomites, seek furiously to abuse them.

Nor will God tire us out with too long a life of earthly sufferings: we think short cares, fears, and sorrows, persecutions, sickness, and crosses, to be long: and shall we grudge at the wisdom and love which shortens them. Yea, though holy duty itself be excellent and sweet, yet the weakness of the flesh makes us liable to weariness, and abates the willingness of the spirit: and our wise and merciful God will not make our warfare, or our race, too long, lest we be wearied and faint, and fall short of the prize. By our weariness, complaints, fears and groans, one would think that we thought this life too long, and yet when we should yield to the call of God, we draw back as if we would have it everlasting.

Willingly submit then, O my soul: it is not thou, but this flesh, that must be dissolved; this troublesome, vile, and corruptible flesh: it is but the other half of thy meat and drink, which thy presence kept longer uncorrupted. Thou diest not when man dieth, by thy departure; as thou livest not to thyself, thou diest not to thyself; whether I live or die, I am the Lord's: he that set up the candle, knows how long he hath use for the light of it. Study thy duty, and work while it is day, and let God choose thy time, and willingly stand to his disposal. The gospel dies not when I die: the church dies not: the praises of God die not: the world dies not: perhaps it shall grow better, and those prayers shall be answered which seemed lost: yea, and it may be some of the seed that I have sown, shall spring up to some benefit of the dark and unpeaceable world when I am dead. Is not this much of the end of life? Is not that life good which attains its end? If my end was to do good and glorify God, if good be done, and God glorified, when I am dead, yea though I were annihilated, is not my end attained? Feign not thyself to be God, whose interest—that is, the pleasing of his will—is the end of all things; and whose will is the measure of all created good: feign not thyself to be all the world: God hath not lost his work; the world is not dissolved when I am dissolved. O how strong and unreasonable a disease is this inordinate selfishness! Is not God's will infinitely better than mine, and fitter to be fulfilled? Choose the fulfilling of his will, and thou shalt always have thy choice: if a man be well that can always have his will, let this always be thy will, that God's will may be done, and thou shalt always have it.

Lord, let thy servant depart in peace; even in thy peace, which passes understanding, and which Christ, the Prince of peace, doth give, and nothing in the world can take away. O give me that peace which is suited to a soul which is so near the harbour, even the world of endless peace and love; where perfect union, such as I am capable of, will free me from all the sins and troubles which are caused by the convulsions and confusions of this divided, selfish world. Call home this soul by the encouraging voice of love, that it may joyfully hear, and say, It is my Father's voice: invite it to thee by the heavenly messenger: attract it by the tokens and the foretastes of love: the messengers that invited me to the feast of grace, compelled me to come in without constraint: thy effectual call did make me willing: is not glory better than preparing grace? Shall I not come more willingly to the celestial feast? What was thy grace for, but to make me willing of glory, and the way to it? Why didst thou dart down thy beams o. love, but to make me love thee, and to call me up to the everlasting centre? Was not the feast of grace as a sacrament of the feast of glory: Did I not take it in remembrance of my Lord until he come? Did not he that told me all things are ready, tell me also that he is gone to prepare a place for us, and it is his will that we shall be with him, and see his glory. They that are given him, and drawn to him by the Father on earth, do come to Christ: give now and draw my departing soul to my glorified Head: as I have glorified thee on earth, in the measure that thy grace hath prevailed in me, pardon the sins by which I have offended thee, and glorify me in the beholding and participation of the glory of my Redeemer; come, Lord Jesus, come quickly, with fuller life, light, and love, into this too dead, dark, and disaffected soul, that it may come with joyful willingness unto thee.

Willingly depart, O lingering soul! It is from a Sodom, though in it there be righteous Lots, who yet are not without their woeful blemishes! Hast thou so often groaned for the general blindness and wickedness of the world, and art thou loth to leave it for a better? How often wouldst thou have rejoiced to have seen but the dawning of a day of universal peace and reformation? Wouldst thou not see it where it shines forth in its fullest glory? Would a light at midnight have pleased thee so well? Hast thou prayed and laboured for it so hard? Wouldst thou not see the sun? Will the things of heaven please thee no where but on earth, where they come in the least and weakest influences, and are terminated in gross, terrene, obscure, and unkind recipients? Away, away, the vindictive flames are ready to consume this sinful world! Sinners that blindly rage in sin, must quickly rage in the effects of sin, and of God's justice: the pangs of lust prepared for these pangs! They are treasuring up wrath against this day: look not then behind thee: away from this unhappy world! Press on unto the mark, 'looking towards, and hastening to the coming of the day of God.'

As this world hath used thee, it would use thee still, and it will use others: if thou hast sped well in it, no thanks to it, but unto God: if thou hast had manifold deliverances, and marvellous preservatıons, and hast been fed with angels' food, love not this wilderness for it, but God and his angel which was thy guide, protector, and deliverer.

Hath this troublesome flesh been so comfortable a companion to thee, that thou shouldest be so loth to leave it ? Have thy pains, thy weariness, thy languishings, thy labours, thy cares and fears about this body, been pleasing to thee ? Art thou loth that they should have an end ? Didst thou not find a need of patience to undergo them ; and of greater patience than mere nature gave thee ? And canst thou hope now for better when nature fails, and that an aged, consumed, more diseased body, should be a more pleasant habitation to thee than it was heretofore ? If from thy youth up it hath been both a tempting and a troublesome thing to thee, surely though it be less tempting, it will not be less troubling when it is falling to the dust, and above ground savours of the grave ! Had things sensible been ever so pleasant in thy youth, and hadst thou glutted thyself in health with that sort of delight, in age thou art to say, by nature : 'I have no pleasure in them.' Doth God in great mercy make pain and feebleness the harbingers of death, and wilt thou not understand their business ? Doth he mercifully beforehand, take away the pleasures of all fleshly things, and worldly vanities, that there may be nothing to relieve a departing soul, as the shell breaks when the bird is hatched, and the womb relaxes when the infant must be born ; and yet shall we stay when nothing holds us, and still be loth to come away ? Wouldst thou dwell with thy beloved body in the grave, where corruption reigns ? If not, why should it now, in its painful languor, seem to thee a more pleasant habitation than the glorious presence of thy Lord ? In the grave it will be at rest, and not tormented as now it is, nor wish at night, O that it were morning ! nor say at morning, When will it be night ? And is this a dwelling fit for thy delight ? Patience in it, while God will so try thee, is thy duty : but is such patience a better and sweeter life than rest and joy ?

But, alas, how deaf is flesh to reason ? Faith hath the reason which easily may shame all contrary reasoning ; but sense is unreasonable, and especially this inordinate, tenacious love of present life. I have reason enough to be willing to depart, even much more willing than I am : O that I could be as willing as I am convinced, that I have reason to be ! Could I love God as much as I know that I should love him, then I should desire to depart, and to be with Christ

as much as I know that I should desire it : but God in nature hath there laid upon me some necessity of aversion, though the inordinateness came from sin : else Christ had not so feared, and deprecated the cup : death must be a penalty, even where it is a gain ; and therefore it must meet with some unwillingness : because we willingly sinned, we must unwillingly suffer : the gain is not the pain or dissolution in itself, but the happy consequences of it. All the faith and reason in the world, will not make death to be no penalty, and therefore will not take away all unwillingness. No man ever yet reasoned or believed himself into a love of pain and death, as such : but seeing that the gain is unspeakably greater than the pain and loss, faith and holy reason may make our willingness to be greater than our unwillingness, and our hope and joy than our fear and sorrow : and it is the deep and effectual notice of goodness, which is God's way, in nature and grace, to change and draw the will of man. Come then, my soul, and think believingly, what is best for thee, and wilt thou not love and desire most that which is certainly the best ?

CHAP. IV.

THE INCONCEIVABLE ADVANTAGES OF BEING WITH CHRIST—IT IS FAR BETTER.

To say and hear that it is far better to be with Christ, is not enough to make us willing ; words and notions are such instruments as God uses to work on souls, but the convincing, satisfying, powerful light, and the inclining love, are other things. The soul now operates on and with the corporeal spirits and organs ; and it perceives now its own perceptions ; but it is a stranger to the mode of its future action, when separated from the body, and can have no formal conception of such conceptions as yet it never had. Therefore its thoughts of its future state, must be analogical and general, and partly strange. But general notices, when certain, may be very powerful, and satisfy us in so much as ıs needful to our consent, and to such a measure of joy as is suitable to this earthly state. Such notices we have from the nature of the soul, with the nature of God, the course of providence, and government of mankind, the internal and external conflicts which we perceive about men's souls, the testimony and promises of the word of God, the testimony of conscience, with the witness of the sanctifying Spirit of Christ, and in it the earnest and the foretaste of glory, and the beginnings of life eternal here; all which I have before considered.

The Socinians, who would interpret this of the state of resurrection only, against plain evidence violate the text: seeing Paul expressly speaks of his gain by death, which will be his abode with Christ, and this upon his departure hence: which he calls his being 'absent from the body, and present with the Lord:' which Christ, to the penitent thief, calls his being 'with him in paradise;' in the parable of the steward, Christ intimates to us, that wise stewards, when they go hence, are received into the everlasting habitations; as he there further tells us Lazarus was in Abraham's bosom.

Goodness is primary or secondary: the first is God's perfect essence and will: the second is either proper and simple good, or analogical. The former is the creature's conformity to the will of God, or its pleasingness to his will: the latter is the greater, which is the welfare or perfection of the universe. The lesser, which is the perfection of the several parts of the universe, either in the nobler respect, as they are parts contributing to the perfection of the whole; or in the lower respect, as they are perfect or happy in themselves; or, in the lowest respect of all, as they are good to their fellow-creatures which are below themselves.

Accordingly, it is far better to be with Christ, properly and simply, as it is the fulfilling of God's will; analogically, as it tends to the perfection of the universe and the church; as it will be our own good or felicity; and as it will be good to our inferior fellow-creatures; though this last be most questionable, and seems not included in the meaning of this text.

It is an odious effect of idolatrous selfishness, to acknowledge no goodness above our own felicity, and accordingly to make the goodness of God to be but formally his usefulness, benevolence, and beneficence to his creatures, which is by making the creature the ultimate end, and God but the means; to make the creature to be God, and deny God indeed, while we honour his name: as also it is, to acknowledge no higher goodness formally in the creature, than in its own felicity as such, as if neither the pleasing of God's will, nor the perfection of the church and world, were better than we are. We are not of ourselves, and therefore we are not chiefly for ourselves, and therefore we have a higher good to love.

That is simply best which God wills. Therefore to live here is best whilst I do live here; and to depart is best when the time of my de-

parture comes: that is best which is, for it is the work of God. The world cannot be better at this instant than it is, nor any thing better, which is of God, because it is as he wills it to be: but when God hath changed them, it will then be best that they are changed. Were there no other good in my departure hence but this simple good, the fulfilling of God's will, my reason tells me that I should be fully satisfied in it: but there is also a subordinate sort of good.

For my change will tend to the perfection of the universe, even that material good or perfection which is its aptitude for the use to which God hath created and doth preserve it: as all the parts, the modes, the situation, the motions of a clock, a watch, or other engine, do to the ends of the artificer. Though God hath not told me particularly, why every thing, mode, and motion is as it is, I know it is all done in perfect wisdom, and suited to its proper use and end. If the hen or bird knows how to make her nest, to lay her eggs secretly together, when and how to sit on them till they are hatched, and how to feed them and preserve them, and when to forsake them, as sufficient for themselves without her help, &c; if the bee knows when, whence, and how, to gather her honey and wax, and how to form the repository combs, and how to lay it up, and all the rest of her marvellous economy, shall I think that God doth he knows not what, or what is not absolutely the best? Doth he want either skill, will, or power.

Should the stone grudge to be hewed, the brick to be burnt, the trees to be cut down, and sawed and framed, the lead and iron to be melted, &c. when it is but to form an useful edifice, and to adapt and compose every part to the perfecting of the whole?

Shall the waters grudge that they must glide away, and the plants that they must die, and half die every winter, and the fruits and flowers that they must fall, or the moon that it must have its changing motions, or the sun that it must rise and set so often, &c. when all is but the action and order which makes up that harmony and perfection which was designed by the Creator, and is pleasing to his will?

But lawful self-love is yet futher herein gratified: the goodness expressed in the text is that analogical subordinate good which is my own felicity, and that which tends thereunto: it is most reasonable to love God best, and that next which is likest him. Why should it not be the easiest and the sweetest? But experience finds it so easy to love ourselves, that certainly, if I firmly believe that it is best for me, I shall desire to depart and to be with Christ, have I not reason to believe it?

The reasons of it I will consider in this order: 1st. The general reasons from the efficients and the means. 2d. The final reasons. 3d. The constitutive reasons from the state of my intellect, and its action and fruition there. 4th. The constitutive reasons from the state of my will. 5th. The constitutive reasons from my practice there, leaving out those which the resurrection will give me, because I am speaking but of my present departure unto Christ.

SECTION I.—GENERAL REASONS FOR DEPARTURE.

That is best for me, which love itself, my heavenly Father designs, and chooses for my good. I hope I shall never dare to think, or say, that he is mistaken, or that he wanted skill or love, or that I could have chosen better for myself than he doth, if he had left all to my choice. Many a time the wise and gracious will of God hath crossed my foolish rebellious will on earth: and afterward I have still perceived that it was best; usually for myself, but always for a higher good than mine. It is not an enemy, nor a tyrant that made me, that hath preserved me, and that calls me hence. He hath not used me as an enemy: the more I have tried him, the better I have found him. Had I better obeyed his ruling will, how happy had I been; and is not his disposing and rewarding will as good? Man's work is like man, and evil corrupts it; but God's work is like God, and uncorrupted. If I should not die till my dearest friend would have it, much more till I myself would choose it, not constrained by misery, I should rejoice, and think my life were safe! O foolish, sinful soul, if I take it not to be far better to be at God's choice, than at my own, or any man's; and if I had not rather that he choose the time than I!

Be of good cheer then, O my soul, it is thy Father's voice that calls thee hence. His voice that called thee into the world, and bade thee live, that called thee out of a state of sin and death, and bade thee live hereafter unto him; that called thee so often from the grave, and forgiving thy sins, renewed thy strength, restored thee to the comforts of his house and service; and hath so graciously led thee through this howling wilderness, and brought thee almost to the sight of the promised land. Wilt thou not willingly go, when infinite fatherly love calls thee? Art thou not desirous of his presence? Art thou afraid to go to him who is the only

cure of thy fears? What was it but this glory to which he did finally elect thee? Where dost thou read that he elected thee to the riches and honours of this world, or to the pleasures of the flesh? But he elected us in Christ to the heavenly inheritance. Indeed he elected thee also to bear the cross, and to manifold sufferings here; but is it that which thou preferrest before the crown? That was but as a mean unto the kingdom, that thou mightest be conformed to Christ, and reign with him when thou hast suffered with him. If God choose thee to blessedness, refuse it not thyself, nor behave thyself like one who does so.

Surely that state is my best which my Saviour purchased and promised me as best: as he bought me not with silver and gold, so neither to silver and gold. Did he live and die to make me rich or advanced in the world? Surely his incarnation, merits, sacrifice, and intercession, had a low design if that were all; and who hath more of these than they that have least of Christ? But he purchased us to an incorruptible crown; to an inheritance undefiled, that fades not away, reserved in heaven for us, that are kept by God's power, through faith, unto salvation. Is it heaven that cost so dear a price for me, and is the end of so wonderful a design of grace, and shall I be unwilling now to receive the gift?

That sure is best for me for which God's Holy Spirit is preparing me; that for which he is given to believers; and that which is the end of all his holy operations on my soul. But it is not to love this world that he is persuading me from day to day, but to come off from such love, and to set my heart on the things above. Is it to love this life and fleshly interest, this vanity and vexation, or rather to love the invisible perfection, that this blessed Spirit hath done so much to work my heart? Would I now undo all, or cross and frustrate all his operations? Hath grace been so long preparing me for glory, and shall I be loth to take possession of it? If I am not willing, I am not yet sufficiently prepared?

If heaven be not better for me than earth, God's word and ordinances have been all in vain? Surely that is my best which is the gift of the better covenant, and which is secured to me by so many sealed promises, and which I am directed to, by so many sacred precepts, doctrines, and examples; and for which I have been called to hear, read, meditate, pray, and watch so long. Was it the interest of the flesh on earth, or a longer life of worldly prosperity, which the gospel covenant secured to me; which the sacraments and Spirit sealed to me; which the Bible was written to direct me to; which ministers preached to me; which my books were written for; which I prayed for; and for which I served God? Or was it not for his grace on earth, and glory in heaven? Is it not better for me to have the end of all these means, than lose them all, and lose my hopes? Why have I used them, if I would not attain their end?

That is my best state which all the course of God's fatherly providence tends to. All his sweeter mercies, and all his sharper corrections, are to make me partaker of his holiness, and to lead me to glory in the way that my Saviour and all his saints have gone before me: all things work together for the best to me, by preparing me for that which is best indeed. Both calms and storms are to bring me to this harbour: if I take them but for themselves, and this present life, I mistake them, and understand them not, but unthankfully vilify them, and lose their end, life, and sweetness. Every word and work of God; every day's mercies, changes, and usages, look at heaven, and intend eternity; God leads me no other way. If I follow him not, I forsake my hope in forsaking him: if I follow him, shall I be unwilling to be at home, and come to the end of all this way?

Surely that is best for me, which God hath required me principally to value, love, and seek, and that as the business of all my life, referring all things else thereto; that this is my duty, I am fully certain, as is proved elsewhere. Is my business in the world only for the things of this world? How vain a creature then were man; and how little were the difference between waking and sleeping, life and death. No wonder if he that believes that there is no life but this to seek or hope for, lives in uncomfortable despair, and only seeks to palliate his misery with the brutish pleasures of a wicked life, and if he stick at no villany which his fleshly lusts incline him to: especially tyrants and multitudes who have none but God to fear. It is my certain duty to seek heaven with all the fervour of my soul, and diligence of my life, and is it not best to find it?

That must needs be best for me which all other things must be forsaken for. It is folly to forsake the better for the worse; but scripture, reason, and conscience, tell me, that all this world, when it stands in competition, or opposition, should be forsaken for heaven; yea, for the least hopes of it. A possible everlasting glory should be preferred before a certainly perishing vanity. I am sure this life will shortly be nothing to me; and therefore it is next to nothing now. Must I forsake all for my everlasting hopes, and yet be unwilling to pass unto the possession of them.

That is like to be our best which is our maturest state. Nature carries all things towards their perfection: our apples, pears, grapes, and every fruit, is best when it is ripe, though they then hasten to corruption, that is, through the incapacity of the corporeal materials any longer to retain the vegetative spirit, which is not annihilated at its separation; and being not made for its own felicity, but for man's, its ripeness is the state in which man uses it, before it doth corrupt of itself, that its corruption may be for his nutriment; and the spirits and best matter of his said food doth become his very substance. Doth God cause saints to grow up unto ripeness, only to perish and drop down into useless rottenness? It is not credible. Though our bodies fall into corruption, our souls return to God that gave them; though he need them not, he uses them in their separated state; and that to such heavenly uses as the heavenly maturity and mellowness hath disposed them to. Seeing then love hath ripened me for itself, shall I not willingly drop into its hand.

That is like to be the best which the wisest and holiest in all ages of the world have preferred before all, and have most desired; which also almost all mankind do acknowledge to be best at last. It is not likely that all the best men in the world should be most deceived, and be put upon fruitless labours and sufferings by this deceit, and be undone by their duty; and that God should by such deceits rule all, or almost all mankind: also that the common notices of human nature, and conscience's last and deepest impressions, should be all in vain. But it is past all doubt, that no men usually are worse than those that have no belief or hopes of any life but this; that none are so holy, just, and sober, so charitable to others, and so useful to mankind, as those that most firmly believe and hope for the state of immortality. Shall I fear that state which all that were wise and holy, in all ages, have preferred and desired?

It is not unlikely that my best state is that which my greatest enemies are most against. How much Satan doth to keep me and other men from heaven, and how much worldly honour, pleasure, and wealth he could afford us to accomplish it, I need not here again be copious in reciting, having said so much of it elsewhere. Shall I be towards myself, so much of Satan's mind: he would not have me come to heaven: and shall I also be unwilling? All these things tell me, that it is best to be with Christ.

SECTION II.—ULTERIOR REASONS.

Is it not far better to dwell with God in glory, than with sinful men, in such a world as this? Though he be every where, his glory, which we must behold to our felicity, and the perfecting operations and communications of his love, are in the glorious world, and not on earth. As the eye is made to see the light, and then to see other things by the light, so is man's mind made to see God, and to love him; and other things, as in, by, and for him. He that is our beginning is our end: and our end is the first motive of all moral action, and for it, it is that all means are used. The end attained is the rest of souls. How often hath my soul groaned under the sense of distance, darkness, and estrangement from God? How often hath it looked up, and aspired after him, and said, O when shall I be nearer and better acquainted with my God? 'As the hart panteth after the water brooks, so panteth my soul after thee, O God: my soul thirsteth for God, for the living God: when shall I come and appear before God?' Would I not have my prayers heard, and my desires granted? What else is the sum of lawful prayers, but God himself? If I desire any thing more than God, what sinfulness is in those desires, and how sad is their signification? How often have I said, 'Whom have I in heaven but thee, and there is none on earth that I desire besides thee? It is good for me to draw near to God.' Woe to me, if I did dissemble; if not, why should my soul draw back: is it because that death stands in the way? Do not my fellow-creatures die for my daily food? And is not my passage secured by the love of my Father, and the resurrection and intercession of my Lord? Can I see the light of heavenly glory in this darksome shell and womb of flesh?

All creatures are more or less excellent and glorious, as God is more or less operative and refulgent in them, and by that operation communicates most of himself unto them: though he be immense and indivisible, his operations and communications are not equal; and that is said to be nearest to him, which hath most of those operations on it, and that without the intervening causality of any second created cause; and so all those are in their order near unto him, as they have noblest natures, and fewest intervening causes. Far am I from presuming to think that I am, or shall be, the best and noblest of God's creatures, and so that I shall be so near him, as to be under the influx of no second or created causes; of which more in the sequel. But to be as near as my nature was ordained to approach, is but to attain the end and perfection of my nature.

As I must not look to be the nearest to him, as he is the first efficient, no more must I as he is the governing cause: as now I am under the government of his officers on earth, I look for ever to be under sub-governors in heaven: my glorified Saviour must be my Lord and Ruler; and who else under him I know not. If angels are not equal in perfection, nor, as is commonly supposed, equal in power, nor without some regimental order among themselves, I must not conclude that no created angel or spirit shall have any government over me: but it will be so pure and divine, as that the blessed effects of God's own government will be sweetly powerful therein. If the law was given by angels, and the angel of God was in the burning bush, and the angel conducted the people through the wilderness, and yet all these things are ascribed to God, much more near and glorious will the divine rule there be, whoever are the administrators.

As I must expect to be under some created efficient causes there, so must I expect to have some subordinate ends: else there would not be a proportion and harmony in causalities; whatever nobler creatures are above me, and have their causalities upon me, I must look to be finally for those nobler creatures. When I look up and think what a world of glorious beings are now over me, I dare not presume to think that I shall finally, any more than receptively, be the nearest unto God, and that I am made for none but him. I find here that I am made, ruled, and sanctified, for the public or common good of many as above my own, of which I am past doubt. I am sure that I must be finally for my glorified Redeemer; and for what other spiritual beings or intelligences that are above me, little do I know: and God hath so ordered all his creatures, as that they are mutually ends and means for and to one another, though not in an equality nor in the same respects. But whatever nearer ends there will be, I am sure that he who is the first efficient, will be the ultimate final cause. I shall be, in this respect, as near him as is due to the rank and order of my nature. I shall be useful to the ends which are answerable to my perfection.

If it be the honour of a servant to have an honourable master, and to be appointed to the most honourable work: if it be some honour to a horse above a swine, or a worm, or fly, that he serves more nearly for the use of man, yea, for a prince, will it not be also my advancement to be ultimately for God, and subordinately for the highest created natures; and this in such services as are suitable to my spiritual and heavenly state?

For I am far from thinking that I shall be above service, and have none to do, for activity will be my perfection and my rest; all such activity must be regular in harmony and order of causes, and for its proper use. What though I know not now fully what service it is that I must do? I know it will be good, and suitable to the blessed state which I shall be in: it is enough that God and my Redeemer know it, and that I shall know it in due time, when I come to practice it; of which more afterward.

The inordinate love of this body and present composition, seduces souls to think that all their use and work is for its maintenance and prosperity, and when the soul hath done that, and is separated from flesh, it hath nothing to do, but must lie idle, or be as nothing, or have no considerable work or pleasure: as if there were nothing in the whole world, but this little fluid mass of matter for a soul to work upon, or as if itself, and all the creatures, and God, were nothing, or no fit objects for a soul: why not hereafter as well as now? Or, as if that which in our compounded state, operates on and by its organs, had no other way of operation without them. As if the musician lost all his power, or were dead, when his instrument is out of tune, or broken, and could do nothing else but play on that: as if the fiery part of the candle were annihilated or transmutated, as some philosophers imagine, when the candle goes out, and were not fire, and in action still: or as if that sunbeam which I shut out, or which passes from our horizon, were annihilated, or did nothing, when it shines not with us? Had it no other individual to illuminate, or to terminate its beams or action, were it nothing to illuminate the common air? Though I shall not always have a body to operate in and upon, I shall always have God, a Saviour, and a world of fellow-creatures; and when I shine not in this lantern, and see not by these spectacles, nor imaginarily in a glass, I shall yet see things suitable intuitively, and as face to face. That which is essentially life, as a living principle, will live: that which is essentially an active, intellectual principle, force, and virtue, will still be such while it is itself, and is not annihilated, or changed into another thing; which is not to be feared: that

which is such can never want an object till all things be annihilated.

Reason assures me, that were my will now what it should be, and fully obsequious herein to my understanding, to fulfil God's will would be the fulfilling my own will, for my will should perfectly comply with his, and to please him perfectly would be my perfect pleasure. It is the unreasonable adhesion to this body, and sinful selfishness, which makes any one think otherwise now. I am sure that my soul shall live, for it is life itself, and I am sure that I shall live to God, and that I shall fulfil and please his blessed will; and this is as incomparably better than my felicity. Yet so far as I am pleased in so doing, it will be my felicity.

I begin now to think, that the strange love which the soul hath to this body, so far as it is not inordinate, is put into us of God, partly to signify to us the great love which Christ hath to his mystical body, and to every member of it, even the least. He will gather all his elect out of the world, and none that come to him shall be shut out, and none that are given him shall be lost. As his flesh is to them meat indeed, and his blood is to them drink indeed, and he nourishes them for life eternal;—his spirit in them, turning the sacrament, the word, and Christ himself, as believed in, into spirit and life to us, as the soul and our natural spirits turn our food into flesh, blood, and spirits, which, in a dead body, or any lifeless repository, it would never be;—so as we delights in the ease and prosperity of our body, and each member, and have pleasure in the pleasant food that nourishes it, and other pleasant objects which accommodate it; Christ also delights in the welfare of his church, and of all the faithful, and is pleased when they are fed with good and pleasant food, and when hereby they prosper: Christ loves the church, not only as a man must love his wife, but as we love our bodies: no man ever hated his own flesh. Herein I must allow my Saviour the pre-eminence, to out-go me in powerful, faithful love: he will save me better from pain and death, than I can save my body; and will more inseparably hold me to himself. If it please my soul to dwell in such a house of clay, and to operate on so mean a thing as flesh, how greatly will it please my glorified Lord to dwell with his glorified body, the triumphant church, and to cherish and bless each member of it? It would be a kind of death to Christ to be separated from his body, and to have it die. Whether Augustine and the rest of the fathers were in the right or not, who thought, that as our bodies do not only shed their hairs, but by sicknesses and waste lose much of their very flesh, so Christ's militant body doth not only lose hypocrites, but also some who seem to be living, justified members ; yet certain it is, that confirmed members, and more certain that glorified members, shall not be lost : heaven is not a place for Christ or us to suffer such loss in. Will Christ love me better than I love my body ? Will he be more loth to lose me than I am to lose a member, or to die ? Will he not take incomparably greater pleasure in animating and actuating me for ever, than my soul doth in animating and actuating this body ? O then let me long to be with him ! And though I am naturally loth to be absent from the body, let me be by his Spirit more unwilling to be absent from the Lord ; and though I would not be unclothed had not sin made it necessary, let me groan to be clothed upon with my heavenly habitation, and to become the delight of my Redeemer, and to be perfectly loved by Love itself.

Even this blessed susceptibility of my soul, in terminating the love and delight of my glorified Head, must needs be a felicity to me ! The insensible creatures are but beautified by the sun's communication of its light and heat ; but sensitives have also the pleasure of it. Shall my soul be senseless ? Will it be a clod or stone ? Shall that which is now the form of man, be then more lifeless, senseless, or incapable than the form of brutes is now ? Doubtless it will be a living, perceiving, sensible recipient of the felicitating love of God and my Redeemer. I shall be loved as a living Spirit, and not as a dead and senseless thing, that doth not comfortably perceive it.

If I must rejoice with my fellow servants that rejoice, shall I not be glad to think that my blessed Lord will rejoice in me, and in all his glorified ones ? Union will make his pleasure to be much mine : and it will be aptly said by him to the faithful soul, ' Enter thou into the joy of thy Lord.' His own active joy will objectively be ours, as ours will be efficiently his, or from him. Can that be an ill condition to me, in which my Lord will most rejoice ? It is best to him, and therefore best to me.

The heavenly society will joyfully welcome a holy soul. If there be now ' joy in heaven among the angels for one sinner that repenteth,' who hath yet so little holiness and so much sin, what joy will there be over a perfected, glorified soul ! Surely if our angels there behold our Father's face, they will be glad, in season of our company. The angels that carried Lazarus to Abraham's bosom, no doubt rejoiced in their work and their success. Is the joy of angels and the heavenly host as nothing to me ? Will not love and union make their joy to be my own ; if love here must make all my friends and neighbours' comforts to become my own ? As their joy, according to their perfection, is greater than any that I am now capable of, so the participation of so great a joy of theirs, will be far better than to have my little separated apartment. Surely that will be my best condition which angels and blessed spirits will be best pleased in, and I shall rejoice most in that which they most rejoice in.

SECTION III.—SPECIAL REASONS ARISING OUT OF THE INTELLECTUAL CHARACTER OF THE MIND.

Though the tempter would persuade men because of the case of infants in the womb, &c. that the understanding will be but an inactive power when separated from these corporeal organs, I have seen before sufficient reasons to repel this temptation. I will suppose that it will not have such a mode of conception as it hath now by these organs : but, 1. The soul will be still essentially a vital, intellectual substance, disposed to act naturally ; and that is to those acts which it is formally inclined to, as fire to illuminate and warm. As it cannot die while it is what it is in essence, because it is life itself, that is, the vital substance ; so it cannot but be intellectual as to an inclined power, because it is such essentially, though God can change or annihilate any thing if he would. 2. It will be among a world of objects. 3. It will still have its dependence on the first cause, and receive his continual actuating influx. 4. No man can give the least show of true reason to prove that it shall cease sensation, whether the sensitive faculties be in the same substance which is intellect, which is most probable, or in one as some imagine, though the species and modes of sensation cease which are denominated from the various organs. 5. Yea, no man can prove that the departing soul doth not carry with it its igneous spirits, which in the body it did immediately actuate: if it were ever so certain that those Greek fathers were mistaken, as well as Hippocrates, who took the soul itself to be a sublime intellectual fire.

As to the objection, some hold that the soul pre-existed before it was in the body ; others, and most, that it then received its first being. If the first were true, it would be true that the soul had its intellectual activity before, though the soul itself incorporate, remembers it not, because it operates but in human form, and its oblivion they take to be part of its penalty: they that think it a ray of the soul or system of the world, must think that then it did intellectually animate this world or a part of the world: to do so again, is the worst they can conjecture of it. As the rays of the sun which heat a burning glass, and by it set a candle on fire, are the same rays still diffused in the air, and illuminating, heating, and moving it, and terminated on some other body, and not annihilated or debilitated when their contracted operation ceases by breaking the glass or putting out the candle: as the spirit of a tree still animates the tree, when it retires from the leaves and lets them fall. But this being an unproved imagination of men's own brains, we have no further use of it than to confute themselves. But if the soul existed not till its incorporation, what wonder if it operate but as a form, when it is united to the body for that use? What wonder if its initial operations, like a spark of fire in tinder, or the first lighting of a candle be weak, and scarcely by us perceptible? What wonder if it operate but to the uses that the creation did appoint it; and first, as vegetative, fabricate its own body, as the maker's Instrument, and then feel, and then understand? What wonder if it operate no further than objects are admitted? Therefore what wonder if in apoplexies, &c. such operations are intercepted? But the departing soul is, 1. In its maturity. 2. No more united to this body, and so not confined to sense and imagination in its operations, and the admission of its objects. 3. It is *sub ratione meriti*, and as a governed subject is ordinate to its reward; which it was not capable of receiving in the womb or in an apoplexy, as we have the reasons before alleged to hold that it shall not be annihilated, nor dissolved, nor lose its essential faculties or powers, nor those essential powers be continued useless by the wise and merciful Creator, though by natural revelation we know not in what manner they shall act; whether on any other body, and by what conjunction, and how far; so by supernatural revelation we are assured, that there is a reward for the righteous, and that holy souls are still members of Christ, and live, because he lives, and that in the day of their departure they shall be with him in paradise, and being absent from the body, shall be present with the Lord; and that Christ therefore died, rose, and revived, that he might be Lord both of the dead and of the living, that is, of those that being dead, hence do live with him, and of those that yet live in the body: for he that said, God is not the God of the dead, but of the living, that is, stands not related to them as his people, as a king to his subjects, is not himself the Lord of the absolute dead but of the living.

Therefore the immortality of the soul is provable by the light of nature, but the manner of its future operation must be known by faith. Blessed be the Father of spirits, and our Redeemer, who hath sent and set up this excellent light, by which we see further than infidels can do.

But I deny not but even the scripture itself doth tell us but little of the manner of our intellectual constitution, when we are out of the body; and it is not improbable that there is more imperfection in this mode of abstract knowledge which the soul exercises in the body, than most consider of: that as the eye hath the visual faculty in sleep, and when we wink, and an internal action of the visual spirits, no doubt, and yet sees not any thing without, till the eye-lids are opened, and was not made to see its own sight; so the soul in the body is as a winking eye to all things that are not by the sense and imagination intromitted or brought within its reach: but I am very suspicious that the body is more a lantern to the soul than some will admit; and that this abstract knowledge of things by organical images, names, and notions, is occasioned by the union of the soul with the body as forms, and is that childish knowledge which the apostle saith shall be done away. How much of man's fall might consist in such a knowing of good and evil I cannnot tell, or in the over-valuing such a knowledge. I think that when vain philosophy at Athens had called the thoughts and desires of mankind from great realities to the logical and philological game at words and notions, it was Socrates's wisdom to call them to more substantial studies, and Paul's greater wisdom to warn men to take heed of such vain philosophy, and to labour to know God and Jesus Christ, and the things of the Spirit, and not to overvalue this ludicrous, dreaming, worldly wisdom. If I have none of this kind of notional, childish knowledge when I am absent from the body, the glass and spectacles may then be spared, when I come to see with open face, or as face to face. Our future knowledge is usually in scripture called seeing: 'Blessed are the pure in heart, for they shall see God.'—'We shall see face to face.'—'We shall see him as he is.'—'Father, I will that those which thou hast given me, be with me where I am, that they may behold my glory which thou hast given me,' &c. An intuitive knowledge of all things, as in themselves immediately, is a more excellent sort of knowledge than this by similitudes, names, and notions, which our learning now consists in, and is but an art acquired by many acts and use.

If the sun were, as the heathens thought it, an intellectual animal, and its emitted rays were vitally visive, and when one of those rays were received by prepared seminal matter, as in insects, it became the soul of an inferior animal; in this case the said ray would operate in that insect or animal but according to the capacity of the recipient matter; whereas the sun itself, by all its emitted rays, would see all things intellectually, and with delight; and when that insect were dead, that ray would be what it was, an intellectual, intuitive emanation. Though the soul in flesh do not know itself, how it shall be united to Christ, and to all other holy souls, and to God himself, nor how near, or just of what sort that union will be, yet united it will be; and therefore will participate accordingly of the universal light of understanding to which it is united. The soul now as it is, or operates in the foot or hand, doth not understand, but only as it is, and operates in the head: and yet the same soul which is in the hand, understands in the head; and the soul operates not so selfishly or dividedly in the hand, as to repine there because it understands not there; but it is quiet in that it understands in the head, and performs its due operation in the hand. But this diversity of operations seems to be from the organs and body's use or need: but souls dismissed from the body seem to be as all eye, or intuitive light. Therefore though it might content us to say that our head sees all things, and we are united to him, yet we may say further, that we ourselves shall see God, and all things that are meet for us to see.

Seeing it is most certain that the superior glorious regions are full of blessed spirits, who see God and one another, having much more perfect operations than we have, whose effects we mortals find here below, why should I that find an intellectual nature in myself, make any doubt of my more perfect operations when I am dismissed hence, being satisfied that a soul will not lose its simple essence. Either those superior spirits have ethereal bodies to act in, or are such themselves, or not: if they are or have such, why should I doubt of the like, and think that my substance or vehicle will not be according to the region of my abode? If not, why should I think that my departed soul may not know or see without an ethereal body or vehicle, as well as all those worlds of spirits.

These things reviewed, being partly mentioned before, assuring me that I shall have actual intellect in my separated state, the region, with the objects, but above all the holy scriptures, will tell me as much as it is meet that I should here know what it is that I shall intuitively understand. The apostle doth distinguish our knowing in part and knowing perfectly, knowing as a child, and as a man, knowing darkly and enigmatically as in a glass, and knowing face to face as we are known. The great question is, when this time of perfection is? Whether he mean at death, or at the resurrection. If Dr. Hammond's observation hold that ἀνάστασις in scripture, when, the flesh or body, is not joined with it, signifies that life which the soul enters upon immediately after our death, and so that the soul hath that, after living, which is signified by the very word which we translate resurrection, then it will lead men to think that there is less difference between man's state, at his first departure, and at his last resurrection, than most think, even than Calvin himself thought. But the difference between our first and last state of after-life, or resurrection, cannot be now distinctly known. What difference there is now between Enoch, Elias, and those who rose at Christ's resurrection, and the rest of the saints, even the spirits of the perfected just, and whether the first have as much greater glory than the rest, as it is conceived that we shall have at the resurrection above that which immediately follows death, what mortal man can tell? I am past doubt that, 'Flesh and blood,' formally so called, and not only as sinful, 'shall not inherit the kingdom of God,' but that our natural bodies shall be made spiritual bodies: and how a spiritual body differs from a spirit or soul, I pretend not well to understand, but must stay till God, by experience or fuller light, inform me. But surely the difference is not like to be so great, as that a soul in flesh shall know in part, and a soul in a spiritual body shall know perfectly, and a soul between both shall not know at all. If it be perfection which we shall have in our spiritual body, it is likely that we are nearer to that perfection, in knowledge and felicity, while we are between both, than when we are in the flesh.

Surely a soul that, even Solomon saith goes upward, and to God that gave it, is more likely to know God, than that which is terminated in flesh, and operates according to its capacity and state: and a soul that is with Christ, is more likely to know Christ, and the Father in him, than that which is present with the body, and absent from the Lord. What less can the promise of being with him signify?

As to the kind of knowledge, how excellent and more satisfactory a way will that of intuition or intellectual sense be than is our present way of abstraction, similitudes, and signs: what abundance of time, thoughts, and labour doth it cost us now to learn our grammar, our rhetoric, and our logic; to learn our wordy rules and axioms, in metaphysics, physics, &c. When we have learned them all, if all can be learned, how little the nearer are many to the knowing of the signified realities! We often get but a set of words to play with, to take up our time, and divert us from the matter: even as carnal men use the creatures which signify God, and are made to lead them up to him, to intangle them, and be the greatest and most pernicious diversion of their souls from God; so do too many learned men do by their knowledge. They use it as men do cards, romances, and plays, to delight their fancies; but they know less of the things that are worth their knowing, than many unlearned persons do, as I said before. Had not much of the Athenian learning been then a mere game, for men to play away their precious time at, and to grow proud of, while they were ignorant of saving realities, Christ and his apostles had not so much neglected it as they did, nor Paul so much warned men to take heed of being deceived by that vain kind of philosophy; in which he seems to me to have greater respect to the universal esteemed Athenian arts, than, as Dr Hammond thought, to the mere Gnostic pretensions.

This poor, dreaming, signal artificial knowledge is costly, uncertain, contentious, and unsatisfactory, in comparison of intuitive knowledge.

It is costly, as to the hard labour and precious time, which must be laid out for it, as aforesaid; we grow old in getting us horses, boots, and spurs, for our journey, and it is well if we begin it at the last: like a man that would study the new found planets, and the shape of Saturn and Jupiter's satellites, and the milky way, &c. and he spends his whole life in getting him the best tubes or telescopes, and never uses them to his ends: or like one that instead of learning to write spends his life in getting the best ink, paper, and pens: or rather like one that learns to write and print exactly, and not to understand what any of his words signify. Men take their spectacles instead of eyes.

When this learning is got, how uncertain are we whether the words have no ambiguity? Whether they give us the true notice of the speaker's mind, and of the matter spoken of. As I said before, what penury, and yet redundancy of words, have we? Of how various and uncertain signification? Changed by custom, or arbitrary design: sometimes by the vulgar use, and sometimes by learned men, that being conscious of the defectiveness of the speaking art, are still tampering, and attempting to amend it. Some men speak obscurely on purpose, to raise in their readers a conceit of their subtle and sublime conceptions. He that understands things most clearly, and speaks them most plainly, which are the parts of true learning, shall have much ado to get the matter out of dark and bewildering uncertainties, and to make others understand both it and him.

Hence come the greatest part of the contentions of the world, which are hottest among men that most pretend to wordy knowledge: as in traffic and converse, the more men and business we have to do with, usually the more quarrels and differences we have; so the more of this wordy learning, instead of realities, men pretend to, the more disputes and controversies they make; and the instruments of knowledge prove the instruments of error and contention. Alas, how many applauded volumes are the snares and troublers of the world! How great a part of our libraries are vain janglings, and strife of words, and traps for the more ingenuous sort, that will not be taken with cards and dice, robbing us of our time, destroying our love, depressing our minds, that should ascend to God, and diverting them from the great and holy things which should be the matter of our thoughts and joys; and filling the church with sects and strife, while every one strives for the pre-eminence of his wit and notions, and few strive for holy love, unity, and good works.

All this while, alas, too many learned men do but lick the outside of the glass, and leave the wine within untasted. To know God, Christ, heaven, and holiness, gives the soul a nourishing and strengthening kind of pleasure, like that of the appetite in its food: but this game at words is but a knowing of images, signs, and shadows, and so is but an image and shadow of true knowledge: it is not that grace which Austin's definition saith, 'no one makes ill use of,' but it is that which the sanctified use well, and the unsanctified are puffed up by, and use to the opposition of truth, the ostentation of a foolish wit, and the deceit of their own souls. If it be sanctified knowledge, it is but mediate in order to our knowledge of things thus signified: it is the real good which contents and beatifies, though the notions may be a subordinate recreation. Intuition feasts on these realities.

As to the objects of this intuition, their excellency will be the excellency of our knowledge. I. I shall know God better. II. I shall know the universe better. III. I shall know Christ better. IV. I shall know the church, his body, better with the holy angels. V. I shall better know the methods and perfection of the scripture, and all God's word and will. VI. I shall know the methods and sense of disposing providence better. VII. I shall know the divine benefits, which are the fruits of love, better. VIII. I shall know myself better. IX. I shall better know every fellow-creature which I am concerned to know. X. And I shall better know all that evil, sin, Satan, and misery, from which I am delivered.

I. Aquinas, and many others, took it for the chief natural proof of the soul's immortality, that man, by nature, desires not only to know effects and second causes, but to rise up to the knowledge of the first cause ; and therefore was made for such knowledge in the state of his perfection: but grace hath much more of this desire than nature. Not that we must not be content to be without a great deal of knowledge, which would be unmeet for us, useless, troublesome, or dangerous to us ; nor must we aspire to that which is above our capacity ; and to know the unsearchable things of God : but not to know God is to know nothing, and to have an understanding worse than none. I presume not to pry into the secret of the Almighty, nor to pretend to know more of God than indeed I do ; but O that I might know more of his glorious perfections, of his will, love, and ways, with that knowledge which is eternal life ? Blessed be that love that sent the Son of God from heaven to reveal him to us in the gospel as he hath done : but all that hear the same words, and believe them, have not the same degree of light or faith. If an angel from heaven came down on earth to tell us all of God that we would know, and might lawfully desire and ask him, who would not turn his back on libraries, universities, and learned men, to go and discourse with such a messenger ? What travel should I think too far ? What cost too great for one hour's talk with such a messenger? But we must have here but such intimations as will exercise faith, and excite desire, and try us under the temptations of the world and flesh : the glorious light is the reward of the victory obtained by the conduct of the light of grace. God in great mercy even here begins the reward: they that are true to the initial light, and faithfully follow on to know the Lord, do find usually such increase of light, not of vain notions, but of quickening and comforting knowledge of God as greatly encourages them, and draws them still on to seek for more. It is very pleasant here to increase in holy knowledge, though it usually bring an increase of malignant opposition, and so of sorrows to the flesh.

The pleasure that the mind hath in common knowledge, brings men through a great deal of labour to attain it : how many years travel over land and sea do some men take, to see and know more of this lower world ? Though it is little that they bring home, but more acquaintance with sin, vanity, and vexation. How many more years do thousands spend in the reading multitudes of tedious volumes, that they may know what others knew before them. Printers and booksellers live by our desire of knowledge. What soul then on earth can possibly conceive how great a pleasure it will be for a glorified soul to see the Lord ? Though I cannot now conceive what that intuition of God himself will be, and whether it will not be a glorious kind of concluding or abstract knowledge ; whether the glory which we shall see be only a created appearance of God, or be his very essence, it satisfies me that it will be as perfect a knowledge as is fit for me to desire ; and I shall then desire no more than is fit : and what it is I shall then know by itself, for it is not otherwise to be clearly known. All the pleasure that I shall have in heaven in knowing any of the works of God, will be in my beholding God himself, his being, his vital power and action, his wisdom, and his love and goodness in those works : for he is the life and glory of them all. ' Blessed are the pure in heart, for they shall see God.'

II. Doubtless it will be no small part of my delight, to see and know God's perfect works, I mean, the universe itself ; I cannot say that I shall have so large a capacity as to comprehend all the world, or know it perfectly, and with an adequate knowledge : but I shall know it in such perfection as is suitable to my capacity. It is exceedingly pleasant to know the least particles of the works of God : with what diligence and delight have men endeavoured to anatomize a body, yea, a small part of one, and to know and describe poor worms and insects, plants and minerals ? No man ever yet perfectly knew the least of them all ; no herbalist or physician ever yet knew the nature and uses of any one herb with an adequate knowledge : with what delight and diligence are physical researches carried on in the world, though still we are all but groping in the dark, and ignorant of many things for one that we know, and therefore know no one perfectly, because we are ignorant of the rest. But if indeed we were above our dreaming, erroneous hypotheses, and saw the nature of every creature, even in sea and land, this little spot of God's creation, and the appendages of all, O, what a delightful spectacle would it be! How much more to see the whole creation, yea, or one system of the globes, and to know their union and communion, and to behold their beauteous symmetry, and to hear them in concord and melodious harmony praising the glory of their great, wise, amiable Creator; this were a delectable sight indeed! I shall have as much of this as I shall be capable of: the wonders and glories of the works of God, shall wrap up my soul, in admiring, joyful praise for ever. Though here it be but little of God's works that we know, I have great reason to think that it will be far otherwise there. 1. Because the state of perfection must far excel our dark and infant state of imperfection: we have now desires after such a knowledge: 'his works are great, sought out of them that have pleasure therein.' These desires being of God, shall not be frustrated. 2. Because there will be proportionable parts of our perfection; and therefore as our love to God and his works will be there perfected, so will be our knowledge. 3. Because we shall know God himself as much as we are capable, and therefore we shall know his works in him, or by a subordinate knowledge, the less being in the greater. 4. Because God hath made his works to be known to his glory: but it is little that is here known of them by mortals; therefore they are known by them in heaven, who are fitted to improve that knowledge to his praise.

If Christ, who is the wisdom of God, will teach me the true philosophy, how to love God, and live here in all well-pleasing unto him, I shall quickly in heaven be a perfect philosopher; and experience will tell me, that the surest way to be truly learned, and know the wonderful works of God, was to know, love, and serve the great Creator, and in him we shall have all, and without him we know nothing, and have nothing at all.

Satan tempted Christ by showing him the kingdoms and glory of the world, and promising them all to him if he would have worshipped him: but God will show me more than Satan could show, and give me more of that which is best, than Satan could give.

III. That in heaven I shall better know Jesus Christ, and all the mystery of our redemption by him, will not be the least of my felicity, for in him are hid all the treasures of wisdom. To know the mystery of his eternal Godhead, in the second person, and his created nature, and the union of these, and to see God's wonderful design and work of grace in him laid open to our clearest view, O what beatifying knowledge would this be! All dark texts concerning his person, his office, and his works, will then be expounded and fully understood: all those strange and difficult things which were the great exercise and honour of faith, will then be plain: difficulties will no more be Satan's advantage to tempt us to unbelief or doubting. The sight of the glory of my Lord will be my glory. If Paul had not then attained to perfection in the knowledge of Christ, and the power of his resurrection, but was pressing forward to reach that crown in the life to come, which he calls 'the resurrection of the dead,' such as I must not expect here to attain it; but when that which is perfect is come, this imperfect knowledge of faith will be done away, as childish knowledge is in manly: the glass and riddle shall be laid aside, when we 'shall see face to face, and shall know as we are known,' as to our sight and knowledge of Christ and his triumphant body: for I dare not apply that phrase to the sight and knowledge of the divine essence; nor yet deny it.

If now though we see not Christ, yet believing we love him, and rejoice in him with unspeakable glorying joy: what love and joy will the everlasting sight of our blessed Head excite there in the souls of all the glorified.

IV. I shall better, O much better, know the heavenly Jerusalem, the triumphant church, the blessed angels and glorified saints: as my love to them, so my knowledge of them, will not be the least part of my heavenly delight. As strangely as I now look upward to that world, because I cannot see it with these eyes, it shall be my well known everlasting habitation. O what a sight, what a joyful sight, will death show me by drawing aside the vail! Or rather the Lord of life by turning death to my advantage! When I am there at home, I shall no more think with confusion, fear, or doubting, of that blessed place or state. My fears, which now come from the smallness of my faith, will end when faith is turned into vision. As I now know the several rooms in my house, and houses in the street, and streets in the city, so shall I then know the many mansions which Christ hath said are in his Father's house. Words now give me so poor, imperfect a conception of the world and things which I never saw, as that sometimes I can scarcely tell whether the joy of my faith, or the trouble of my dark apprehensions, be the greater: but when I shall see the place and persons, the glory which I heard of, that will be the delightful, satisfying, and possessing kind of knowledge. If Nehemiah and the godly Jews made so great a matter of seeing the walls of Jerusalem repaired, and others of the imperfect rebuilding of the temple, O what a joyful sight to me will the heavenly Jerusalem then be! The most glorious sight will be at the great marriage-day of the Lamb, when ' Christ shall come to be glorified in his saints, and admired in all them that now believe.' But the next to that will be the day of my particular deliverance, when I shall come to Christ, and see the saints admiring him in glory.

If I were of the opinion of those Greek fathers, who thought that stars were angels, or had intellectual souls, (matters unknown to us,) I should love them as my guardians, and take it to be yet more of my concern to be advanced to the fuller knowledge of them. But seeing I know that angels love us, and by office attend and keep us, and rejoice at our good, and at our repentance, and, which is far more, are more holy and excellent creatures than we are; it is therefore my comfort to think that I shall better know them, and live in near and perpetual acquaintance and communion with them, a more sensible and sweet communion than we can have with them here. Devils are aerial, and near to this dark and sinful world, and more often appear to men than angels: but the angels affect not such descending appearances, till love and obedience to their Lord make it pleasing to them. Therefore we have but little knowledge, even of those that know, love, and keep us: but when we come home to their nearest society and converse, to know them will be sweet and joyful knowledge. For they are more excellent creatures than the most glorious that are here below the intellectual nature: they are full of light, and full of love to God and man. Had God bid me pray to them, I would not have refused it, but taken it for my honour: but seeing he hath not, I will do that which he hath bid me, even love them, and rejoice in my relation to the innumerable company of them, in the city of the living God, the heavenly Jerusalem, and long to know and love them more; expecting ere long to bear my part in the praises of God and of the Lamb, in the same choir where they are the precentors.

That I shall know the spirits of the perfected just, and be of their communion, will be no small addition to my joy. How sweet hath one wise and holy, though weak and blemished, companion been to me here on earth! And how lovely have God's graces in such, though sullied, appeared to me! O then what a sight will it be when we shall see the millions of souls that shine in perfect wisdom and holiness with Christ! To see a garden that hath some beautiful flowers in it, is something: but if you saw whole fields and countries shining with them, it would be a glory, though fading, to the earth. A well-built city is a more pleasant sight than a single house; and a navy than a ship; and an army than one man. If this poor, low world did all consist of wise, just, and holy persons, O what an orderly, lovely world would it be! If one kingdom consisted, (prince, magistrates, pastors, and people,) all of such, what a blessed kingdom would that be! The plague of wicked men's deceits, falsehoods, oppressions, and iniquities, may help to make us sensible of this. It would be a great temptation to us to be loth to die, and leave such a country, were it not that the more the beauty of goodness appears, the more the state of perfection is desired. It is pleasant to me to pray in hope as Christ hath commanded me, that earth may be made liker unto heaven, which now is become so like to hell: but when I shall see the society perfected, in number, in holiness, in glory, in heavenly employment, the joyful praises of Jehovah, the glory of God and the Lamb shining on them, and God rejoicing over them as his delight, and myself partaking of the same, that will be the truly blessed day! And why doth my soul, imprisoned in flesh, no more desire it?

V. I shall better understand all the word of God: the matter, and the method of it; though I shall not have that use for it as I have now in this life of faith, yet I shall see more of God's wisdom and his goodness, his love, mercy, and justice appearing in it, than ever man on earth could do! As the creatures, so the scriptures, are perfectly known only by perfect spirits. I shall then know now to solve all doubts, and reconcile all seeming contradictions, and to expound the hardest prophecies: that light will show me the admirable methods of those sacred words, where dark minds now suspect confusion! How evident and clear then will every thing appear to me! Like a small print when the light comes in, which I could not read in the glimmering twilight. How easily shall I then confute the cavils of all our present unbelievers! How joyfully shall I praise that God and Saviour, that gave his church so clear a light to guide them through this darksome world, and so sure a promise to support them till they came to life eternal! How joyfully shall I bless him that by that immortal seed regenerated me to the hopes of glory, and that ruled me by so holy and just a law!

VI. In that world of light I shall better understand God's present and past works of providence, by which he orders the matters of this world: the wisdom and goodness of them is little understood in little parcels; it is the union and harmony of all the parts which shows the beauty of them, when the single parcels seem deformed, or are not understood. No one can see the whole together but God, and they that see it in the light of his celestial glory: it is a prospect of that end, by which we have here any true understanding of such parcels as we see. Then I shall know clearly why, or to what use, God prospered the wicked, and tried the righteous by so many afflictions: I shall know why he set up the ungodly, and put the humble under their feet; why he permitted so much ignorance, ungodliness, pride, lust, oppression, persecution, falsehood, deceit, and other sins in the world. I shall know why the faithful are so few; and why so many kingdoms of the world are left in heathenism, Mahometanism and infidelity. The strange permissions which now so puzzle me, and are the matter of my astonishment, shall all be then as clear as day, I shall know why God disposed of me as he did through all my life; and why I suffered what I did, and how many great deliverances I had, which I understood not here; and how they were accomplished. All our mis-interpretations of God's works and permissions, will be then rectified: all our controversies about them, which Satan hath made so great advantage of, by a pretended zeal for some truths of God, will then be reconciled, and at an end: all the works of divine providence from the beginning of the world, will then appear a most delectable, beauteous frame.

VII. Among all these works, I shall specially know more, the nature and excellency of God's mercies, and gifts of love, which here we too unthankfully undervalued and made light of: the special works of love should be the matter of our most constant, sweet, and serious thoughts, and the fuel of our constant love and gratitude: the lively sense of love and mercy, makes lively Christians, abounding in love to God, and mercy to others: but the enemy of God and man most labours to obscure, diminish, and disgrace God's love and mercies to us, or to make us disrelish them, that they may be unfruitful as to their excellent ends and uses. Little do most Chris-

tians know how much they wrong God and themselves, and how much they lose by the diminutive, poor thoughts which they have of God's mercies. Ingratitude is a grievous misery to the sinner, as gratitude is a very pleasant work. Many a thousand mercies we now receive, which we greatly undervalue. But when I come to the state and work of perfect gratitude, I shall have a more perfect knowledge of all the mercies which ever I received in my life, and which my neighbours, friends, God's church and the world, did ever receive: for though the thing be past, the use of it is not past. Mercies remembered must be the matter of our everlasting thanks: we cannot be perfectly thankful for them, without a perfect knowledge of them. The worth of a Christ, and all his grace, the work of the gospel, the worth of our church privileges, and all God's ordinances, the worth of our books, friends, helps of our life and health, and all conveniences, will be better understood in heaven than the most holy and thankful Christian here understands them.

VIII. It will be some addition to my future happiness, that I shall then be much better acquainted with myself; both with my nature, and with my sin and grace. I shall then better know the nature of a soul, and its faculties, three in one. I shall know the nature and way of its operations, and how far its acts are simple, or compound. I shall know how far memory, fancy, and sense internal and external belong to the rational soul, and whether the sensitive and rational are two or one; and what senses will perish, and what not. I shall know how the soul doth act upon itself, and what acts it hath that are not felt in sleep, in apoplexies, and in the womb. I shall know whether the vegetative nature be any thing else than fire; and whether it be of the same essence with the soul, sensitive or rational. I shall know how far the soul is receptive, and what the final cause doth to it; and what each object is to the constitution or production of the act; yea, and what an act is, and what a habit; and how a soul acting or habited differs from itself not acting or habited; and how its acts are many and yet but one; or its faculties at least. Many other such difficulties will all be solved, which now philosophers contend about in the dark, and pass but under doubtful conjectures; or at least are known to very few.

I shall know how God's Spirit operates on souls; and how it is sent from Christ's human nature to work on man; and whether grace be properly, or only metaphorically, called a nature (a new nature, a divine nature) in us. I shall know what freewill is, and how man's will can be the first determiner of any act of its own in a moral view, good or evil, without being such a first cause, as none but God can be: and so how far free acts are necessitated or not. I shall know what power the intellect hath on the will, and the will on the intellect; and what power the sense and fancy hath on either; and what any agent of intellect doth: whether it be to our intellect as the sun is to our sight. I shall know what is meant by the degrees of acts and habits in the soul; and whether there be divers degrees of substantiality, or of the virtue or former power of several souls. I shall know better the difference of habits called acquired and infused; and what common grace is, and what it doth; and what nature can do of itself or by common grace, without that which is proper to the justified; and how far any degrees of grace are lost.

I shall know what measure of grace I had myself; and how far I was mistaken in myself; and what acts were sincere; and how much that was not found was mixed; and what was of myself and sin.

I shall know much more of my sin than here I ever knew, the number and the greatness of them; that so I may know with greatest thankfulness and love, how much I am beholden to pardoning and healing grace.

Yea, I shall know more of my body, as it was the habitation of my soul, or the organical matter on which unitedly it worked. I shall know how far it helped or hindered me; and what were all those obscure diseases that puzzled all the physicians, and myself; and how marvellously God sustained, preserved, and often delivered me; and what of my actions was to be imputed to the body, and what of them to the soul.

IX. Every fellow-creature, which I am concerned to know, I shall know far better than now I do, both things and persons: the good and bad, the sincere and the hypocrites, will be there discerned: and many an action that here went for honourable, covered or coloured with wit or worldly advantages, or false pretences, will then be found to be odious and unjust: and wickedness will be flattered or extenuated no more: and many a good and holy work which false men, through wickedness and worldly interest, reproached as some odious crime, will there be justified, honoured, and rewarded: all sciences are there perfect, without our ambiguous terms or imperfect axioms and rules of art.

X. Lastly, I shall better know from what ene-mies, what sins, what dangers, I was here delivered: what contrivances and malicious endeavours of Satan and his instruments God defeated: how many snares I escaped: and I shall better know how great my deliverance is by Christ from the wrath to come. Though we shall not know hell by painful sense, we shall know it so far as is necessary to fill us with gratitude to our Redeemer: yea, we shall know much of it far better than the damned spirits that feel it. For we shall know by sweet and full fruition what the joy and blessedness is which they have lost; when they have no such kind of knowledge of it.

All this knowledge will be thus advanced to my glorified soul beyond what I can here conceive in flesh: and is it not then far better to be with Christ?

SECTION IV.—REASONS FROM THE CONSTITUTION OF THE WILL,—THAT IT IS FAR BETTER TO BE WITH CHRIST.

But it is the will that is to the soul, what the heart is to the body: as it is the prime seat of morality, so is it the chief seat of felicity. My greatest evil is there; and my greatest subjective good will be there. Satan did most against it, and God will do most for it. Will it not be better to be with Christ than here?

It will not there be tied to a body of cross interests and inclinations, which is now the greatest snare and enemy to my soul: which is still drawing my love, care, fears, and sorrows, to and for itself, and turning them from my highest interest. How great a deliverance will it be to be freed from the temptations, and the inordinate love, cares, and fears for this corruptible flesh?

My will shall not there be tempted by a world of inferior good, which is the bait and provision for the flesh, where meat, sleep, and possessions, house, lands, and friends, are all become my snares and danger: God's mercies will not be made there the tempter's instruments. I shall not there have the flatteries or frowns, promises or threatenings of the tyrants of the world, to tempt me: bad company will not infect me, nor divert me: the errors of good men will not seduce me, nor reputation or reverence of the wise, learned, or religious, draw me to imitate them in any sin.

I shall there have none of Satan's solicitations, to pervert my will: he will not have that advantage by my sense and fancy, nor that access unto me, as now he hath. But of this I spake before.

My will shall there be better than here. There will be nothing in it that is displeasing to God: no sinful inclination, habit or act: nothing to strive against God's Spirit; nor grudge at any word or work of God: no principles of enmity or rebellion left. There will be nothing that is against the good of others; no inclinations to injury, or any thing that is against my neighbours, or the common good. There will be nothing in it that is cross to itself; no more war striving in me; not a law in my mind, and a law in my members, that are contrary to each other: no contrariety between sense and reason, nor between the sensitive appetite and the rational: all will be at unity and peace within.

Christ will have finished his cure on my will: the work of sanctification will be perfect: my will shall there, by union and communion, be made conformable to the will of Christ, and so unto the Father's will. This must needs be meant, whatever more, in the prayer of Christ, where he prays, ' that they may be one, as thou Father art in me, and I in thee, that they may be one in us, that they may be one, even as we are one.' The will of Christ, and of the Father, will be my will, that is, I shall love and will the same that God loves and wills (in the measure of a creature, infinitely below him:) and how can the will of man have greater honour, than to be the same with the will of God? Assimilation to a king among us poor mortals, goes for honour: assimilation to angels, is much more: that we shall be like or equal to angels, is a high part of the blessed's praise: but how much more is it to be thus far like to God? Indeed God's image, and the divine in us here, can be no less than this similitude to God's will in the degree that we have it: but alas, that degree is so very low, as that we can hardly tell whether our similitude or our dissimilitude be the more; I mean, whether our wills are for more that God wills, or against more. O how many thousand wishes and desires have we had, which are against the will of God! But there we shall have the full impression of God's will upon our wills, as face answers face in a glass, or as the wax answers the seal: as the finger on the outside answers to the motion of the clock within, so, in all things which belong to our duty and perfection, we shall answer the will of God. As the echo answers the voice, defectively, but truly without contradiction or discord, so will our wills be as the echo of God's will. Then I am sure there will be nothing in my will but good; for God wills no evil. This will be virtually all obedience; for all sin is voluntary, and all moral good is primarily in the will. Then there can be no matter of disquiet in me, but all will be in perfect peace; for all that is like God will be pleasing both to God and me: no opposition will remain.

How easy and sweet then will all my obedience be, when I shall perfectly will it, without any reluctancy or averseness? All will be my very pleasure that I do.

Seeing my will shall be the same with the will of God, it follows that it shall never be frustrated, but I shall have all whatsoever I would have, and shall be and do whatsoever I would be and do, for I shall desire nothing but what God wills; and God's will shall certainly be done. I shall have as much love and joy as I would have. I shall be as happy as I would be, and desire nothing for others but it shall be done. Indeed if God's will were there unknown to me, I might ignorantly go against it, as I do here: but there before I will or desire any thing, I shall know whether it be God's will or not, so that I shall never wish any thing which shall not be accomplished. As it is God's perfection to have his will alway done, though all his laws be not obeyed, so my perfection shall consist in this likeness unto God, that my will shall be still fulfilled. Then Christ's promises will be perfectly performed, ' whatsoever ye ask the Father in my name, he will give it you.'—' Ye shall ask what you will, and it shall be done unto you.' While their will was the same with the will of Christ: but he saith not that it shall all be given us here. We ask for perfection, and we shall have it, but not here.

Yea, my will itself shall be my fruition, for it shall not be the will of one in need—a desire of what I want, for I shall want nothing: therefore it is said that we shall thirst no more. But it will be a complacency in what I possess, and in this also my perfection will be the image of God's perfection. Not but that all creatures still receive from God, and in that sense may be said to need, in that they have nothing of themselves, but all by gift and communication from him. But being still and full possessors, they cannot properly be said to want. Complacency in that which we possess, is love and pleasure in one act; and indeed, pleasure and love are the same thing: to love any thing, is to have that thing to be pleasing to my mind. Even when it is wanted, it is thought on as a pleasing thing, and therefore desired; so that the desiring act of the will is but a second act occasioned by want, and following the first act, which is complacency or simple love. I desire it because I love it. Rightly therefore is the will itself called love; for in the first act, love, will, and rational appetite, are all words of the same signification. My will therefore must needs be perpetually full of perfect joy, when enjoying love and pleasure will be my will itself. Thus shall I have in me the spring of living waters, and the Comforter will then perfectly do his work, when my constant will itself shall be comfort. Well therefore is glory said to be the perfection of sanctifying grace, when this grace is the beginning of that love and joy which glory is the perfection of; and perfection is the Spirit's work.

It will be much of my felicity that my will shall be confirmed and fixed in this conformity to the will of God, and holy love will be its nature. Now, both understanding and will are so lamentably mutable, that further than God promises to uphold us, we know not one day what we shall think, judge, or will, the next. But when love is as a fixed nature in us, we shall be still the same, adhering to amiable goodness. without intermission or cessation. It will be as easy to us to love God and holiness, as it is to the hungry and thirsty to love meat and drink, or to the proud, to love praise or domination; yea, or to any man to love his life. We shall be no more weary of loving, than the sun is of shining, or than the hungry is of feasting, or a friend of friendly love and converse. Nay, the comparison is quite too low; for all creatures here have a fading vanity which wearies the satiated or failing appetite; but tnere is no such thing in heaven. As from the nature of that act, so much more from the nature of the object, my love will appear to be my happiness.

God himself will be the full and everlasting object of my love. He that could but understand as well as those in heaven do, what this word signifies, to love God, and be beloved of him, would say, that there needs no other description of perfect happiness. Perfect joyful complacency in God is the heaven which I desire and hope for. This is my felicity, and much more. As I am the agent of love to God, and the object of God's love to me, it is my felicity: as God is the ultimate object of my love, and the agent of his love to me (that is, of the effects of it,) so it is unspeakably more high and excellent than to be my felicity. Love is the concurrence of the will of God and man, and as it is God's part or interest, efficiently or objectively, it is infinitely more excellent than as it is my part and interest.

In God there is all that love can desire for its full, everlasting feast. He is infinitely good in himself, that is, most amiable, and the nature of man's will is to love good as good. Could we love God with a love that is adequate to the object, we should be God ourselves, which is impossible: none but God can adequately know God or love him. In God's love to himself, both the act and object are infinite, and indeed are both one, there being not that formally which we know by the name of act and object; but act and object are our analogical, inadequate conceptions of that act of God which is his essence. But in our love to God the act is finite, and infinitely below the object: yea, the object, which in reality is itself infinite, yet proximately, as the known existence is the object of our love, is finite there. It is the conception or idea of God in the intellect, which is the proper and nearest object of the will, and this is as in a glass, a shadow; even the finite little shadow of an infinite Being. The same infinite good is a felicity to divers persons in divers degrees, according as they diversely love him, and are receptive of his love.

God, who is infinitely good in himself, will be that most suitable good to me, and meetest for the dearest embracements of my will. He hath all in himself that I need or can desire: there is no room, nothing above him, or beyond him, or without him, for love to cleave to: though below him the creature, though not being without him, is loved without him, by the deception of the mind.

He is willing to be loved by me; he disdains not my love. He might have refused to be embraced by such affections, as have so often and sinfully polluted themselves by embracing vanity and iniquity. As persons of state, and stately cleanliness, will not be touched by filthy hands, much less let dogs leap on them, which come from wallowing in the mire, so God might have driven me away from the happiness of loving him, and have denied me the leave for so high a work. But he commands my love, and makes it my greatest duty; he invites and intreats me, as if he were a gainer by my happiness; he seeks to me to seek to him, and as he is the first, so is he the most earnest suitor. He is far readier to receive my love, than I am to give it him. All the compassionate invitations which I have had from him here, by his word and mercies, assure me, that he will there receive me readily. He that so valued my poor cold imperfect love to him on earth, will not reject my perfect love in heaven. He that made it the great work of his Spirit to effect it, will not refuse it when it is made perfect by himself.

He is near to me, and not a distant God out of my reach, and so unsuitable to my love. Blind unbelievers may dream that he is far off, but he is as near us, even now, as we are to ourselves. He is not far from any of us, for in him we live, and move, and have our being. The light of the sun is not so near my eyes, as God will be for ever to my mind. When he would sanctify us to love him, he brings us nigh to him in Christ. As we love ourselves easily as being, as they say, the nearest to ourselves; so we shall as easily love God as ourselves, when we see that he is as near us as we are to ourselves, as well as that he is infinitely more amiable in himself.

Because of the natural inequality between the creature and the Creator, he hath provided such means to demonstrate to us his nearness, as are necessary to the exercise of our love. We shall see his glory, and taste his love, in our glorified Mediator, and in the glory of the church and world. God will condescend to show himself to us according to our capacities of beholding him. Here we see him in his works and word, and there we shall see him in the glory of all his perfect works.

Under God as I shall see, so I shall delightfully love the glorious perfection of the universe; even the image of God in all the world; as my love will be my delight, so I shall love best, that which is best, and most delight in it. The whole is better than any part; and there is a peculiar beauty and excellency in the whole world, as perfectly harmonious, which is not to be found in any part, no, not in Christ himself, as man, nor in his church.

The marvellous inclination that all things have to union, even the inanimates might persuade me, if I felt it not certainly in myself, that it is most credible that man also shall have the like inclination, and such as is agreeable to the nature of his faculties: therefore our love and delight in all things, is that uniting inclination in man.

I shall have a special love to the holy society, the triumphant universal church, consisting of Christ, angels, and saints, as they are specially amiable in the image and glory of God. God himself loves them more than his inferior works; that is, his essence, which is love, and hath no degrees or change, doth send for fuller streams of good upon them, or makes them better and happier than the rest; and my love will imitate the love of God, in my capacity. If societies on earth, more holy and wise than others, though imperfectly, are very amiable, what then will the heavenly society be? Of this I spake before, viz. of knowing them.

Think here, O my soul, how sweet a state unto thee it will be to love the Lord Jesus thy glorified Head, with perfect love! When the glory of God which shines in him, will feast thy love with full and everlasting pleasure, the highest created perfection of power, wisdom, and goodness, refulgent in him, will not give leave to thy love to cease, or intermit, or abate its fervour. When thou shalt see in the glorified church the precious fruits of Christ's redemption, grace, and love, this also will feed thy love to him, from whom this heavenly glory comes; and when thou shalt feel thyself possessed of perfect happiness, by his love to thee, will not this also do its part? Yea, the remembrance of all his former love; what he did for thee, and what he did in thee here on earth: how he called thee with an holy calling; how he washed thee in his blood from all thy sins; how he kindled in thee those desires which tended to that perfect glory; how he renewed thy nature; how he instructed, guided, and preserved thee from thy childhood; and how many and how great sins, enemies, dangers, and sufferings, he saved thee from; all this will constrain thee for ever to love him. Thus, though he give the kingdom to the Father, as ceasing his mediatory, healing, saving work of acquisition, he will be to thee the mediator of fruition. God in him will be accessible, and condescend to a suitable communion with us. As Christ is thy life, radically and efficiently, as he is the giver of grace and spirit of love, so he will be objectively thy life as he is lovely, and it will be formally thy life to love him, and God in him, for ever.

Think also, O my soul, how delectable it will be to love, as well as to know, those angels that most fervently love the Lord! They will be lovely to thee as they have loved thee, and more as they have been lovers and benefactors to the church and to mankind; but far more as they are so many refulgent stars, which continually move, shine, and burn in purest love to their Creator. O blessed difference between that amiable society of holy spirits, and this dark, mad, distracted, wicked world! Here devils tempt me within, and devils incarnate persecute me without: blaspheming of God, reviling godliness, deriding the sacred scriptures, and sacred exercises, malignant slandering of the servants of God, hating, persecuting, silencing, and saying all manner of evil falsely of them, for their righteousness' sake, while such crimes are pretended, as they once falsely charged on Christ

himself. This is the conversation of those that
I have long dwelt with in this world : atheism,
infidelity, papal church tyranny, bloody wars,
destroying the righteous, oppressing the poor,
adultery and fornication, stigmatising, perjury,
ambition, violence, covetousness, deceit, sottish
ignorance, wilfulness in sin, hatred of reproof,
revengeful malice. These, and such like, are
the fruits of the soil where I have long so-
journed, though, through the grace of Christ,
among the faithful, there have been better fruits:
and is not the company of holy angels better
than this? With them God is all ; who are even
made up of shining wisdom, and holy love, and
beneficent activity ; who are the blessed choir
that melodiously sing forth the high praises of
their Maker ; among whom God dwells as in his
presence-chamber or his temple, and in whom
he takes great delight : with these I shall see or
hear no evil : no mixture of fools or wicked ones
pollute or trouble their society. There will be
no false doctrine, no evil example, no favouring
wickedness, no accusing goodness, no hurtful
violence, but holy, powerful, operative love, will
be all and do all, as their very nature, life, and
work. Is it not better to be a door-keeper there,
than to dwell in the palaces of wickedness ? And
is not a day with them better than a thousand
here ?

With the holy angels I shall love holy souls
that are made like unto them, and joined with
them in the same society, and it is likely, with
them judge, that is, rule the world. All their
infirmities are there put off with the flesh ; they
also are spirits made up of holy life, light, and
love. There is none of their former ignorance,
error, imprudence, selfishness, contentiousness,
impatience, or any other troubling, hurtful thing.
When I think with what fervent love to God, to
Jesus Christ, and to one another, they will be
perfectly united there ; alas ! how sad and how
shameful is it, that they should here be prone
to disaffections and divisions, and hardly agree
to call each other the servants of God, or to
worship God in the same assemblies : but the
remnants of dividing principles, viz. pride, error,
and uncharitableness, will be all left behind.
Society with imperfect saints is sweet: the imperfect image of God upon them is amiable ; but
their frailties here are so vexatious, that it is hard
to live with some of them in peace. But perfect
love will make them one, and O how delightful
will that communion of saints be ! I can never
forget how sweet God hath made the course of
my pilgrimage, by the fragrance and usefulness
of his servants' graces : how sweet have my

bosom-friends been. though mutable. How
sweet hath the neighbourhood of the godly been !
How sweet hath the holy assemblies been ! And
how many hours of comfort have I there had!
How profitable have their writings, their conference, and their prayers been ! What then will
it be to live in the union of perfect love with
perfect saints in heaven for ever, and with them
concordantly to love the God of love ?

As the act and the object of love will constitute my felicity, so will my reception from the
love of God, and his creatures, be sweeter to me
than my own activity can be : for it is mutual
love that makes it up. I shall not be the fountain of my own delights; nor can I act till I am
acted, nor offer any thing to God, but what I
have first received from him. Receive I shall
abundantly and continually, and from thence
shall overflow to God, and receiving and returning, are, now, and will be, the circular endless
motion, and our true perpetual life and happiness.

All my receivings shall be from God. His
love is not a mere passive will, nor a wish which
touches not the object : but it is what heat is in
or from the sun or fire. It is an efflux of goodness : it is the most powerful, sweet, communicating principle or work. All love is communicative, but none in comparison of God's : as there
is none primitively and simply good but God.
How much doth love in the affairs of men ? All
that is pleasant in the world is it, or its effects.
Were it not for sensual love, there would be no
generation of man or brutes : God hath made it
a generating principle. Hatred causes not congress, but fighting with, or flying from, one
another. Were it not for natural love, mothers
would never endure the pain, trouble, and care,
which is necessary to human birth and education.
Were it not for love, parents would never labour
all their lives to leave their children well instructed, and well provided for, when they are
gone. My food would not please me did I not
love it, and I should neglect it to the neglect of
my life. Did I not love my books, and learning
itself, I should never have bestowed so much of
seventy years in poring on them, and searching
for knowledge, as I have done. Did I not love
my house, my conveniences, and necessaries, I
should neglect them, and they would be to me
of small use. Did I not love my friends, I should
be less profitable to them, and they to me. Did
I not love my life, I should neglect it, and never
have endured the labour and cost about it as I
have done. If a man love not his country, posterity, and the common good, he will be as a

burdensome drone in the hive, or as pernicious vermin. What is done in the world that is good, but by love?

If created love be so necessary, so active, so communicative, how much more will the infinite love of the Creator be? His love is now the life of the world: his love is the life of nature in the living; the life of holiness in saints; and the life of glory in the blessed. In this infinite love it is that I, and all the saints, shall dwell for evermore. If I dwell in love and love in me, surely I shall have its sweet and plenteous communication, and shall ever drink of the rivers of pleasure. It is pleasant to nature to be beloved of others, especially of the great, wise, and good; much more to have all the communications of love, in converse and gifts, in plenty and continuance, which may be still expressing it to our greatest benefit. Had I a friend now that did for me but the hundredth part of what God doth, how dearly should I love him? Think then, think believingly, seriously, constantly, O my soul, what a life thou shalt live for ever in the presence, the face, the bosom of infinite, eternal love. He now shines on me by the sun, and on my soul by the Sun of righteousness, but it is as through a lantern, or the crevices of my darksome habitation: but then he will shine on me and in me openly, and with the fullest streams and beams of love.

God is the same God in heaven and earth, but I shall not be the same man. Here I receive comparatively little, but live in darkness, doubtful and frequent sorrows, because my powers of reception are so small. The windows of my soul are not open to his light, sin hath raised clouds, and consequently storms, against my comforts: the entrances to my soul by the straits of flesh and sense are narrow, and they are made narrower by sin than they were by nature. Alas, how often would love have spoken comfortably to me, and I was not at home to be spoken with, but was abroad among a world of vanities; or was not at leisure, or was asleep, and not willing to be awaked! How often would love have come in and dwelt with me, and I have unkindly shut my doors against him! How often would he have been with me in secret, where he freely would embrace me, but I had some pleasing company or business which I was loth to leave! How often would he have feasted me, and had made all ready, but I was taken up and could not come! Nay, when his table hath been spread before me, Christ, grace, and glory have been offered to me, my appetite hath been gone, or dull, and all hath been almost neglected by me,

and hath scarcely seemed pleasant enough to be accepted, or to call off my mind from luscious poison! How often would he have shone upon me, and I have shut my windows or mine eyes: he was jealous indeed, and liked not a partner! He would have been all to me, if I would have been all for him, but I divided my heart, my thoughts, my love, my desires, and my kindnesses; and alas, how much did go besides him, yea, against him, to his enemies, even when I knew that all was lost, and worse than lost, which was not his? What wonder then if so foolish and unkind a sinner had little pleasure in his love; and if so great ingratitude and neglect of sovereign goodness were punished with such strangeness, fears, and faintings, as I have long with groans lamented?

But in heaven I shall have none of these obstructions. All old unkindness and ingratitude will be forgiven: the great reconciler in whom I am beloved, will then have perfected his work. I shall then be wholly separated from the vanity which here deceived me: my open soul will be prepared to receive the heavenly influx: with open face I shall behold the open face of glorifying love. I shall joyfully attend his voice, and delightfully relish the celestial provisions! No disease will corrupt my appetite: no sluggishness will make me guilty again of my old neglects. The love of the Father, by the grace of the Son, and the communion of the Holy Spirit, will have got the victory over all my deadness, folly, and disaffection, and my God-displeasing and self-undoing averseness and enmity will be gone for ever. The perfect love which God doth first effect in me, will be my everlasting spring of the fullest love of God. Benevolent love will make me good, that is, a holy lover of God; and then pleased love will make me his delight, and benevolence will still maintain me in my capacity.

Study this heavenly work of love, O my soul, these are not dead or barren studies: these are not sad, unpleasant studies; it is only love that can relish love and understand it. The will here hath its taste, so like to an understanding, as make some philosophers say, that 'the will perceives' is a proper phrase. What can poor carnal, worldlings know of glorious love, who study it without love? What sounding brass, and tinkling cymbals, a lifeless voice, as they that preach of God, Christ, and heavenly glory, without love? But gazing upon the face of love in Christ, and tasting of its gifts, and looking up to its glorious reign, is the way to kindle the sacred fire in thee. Look upwards if thou wouldst see the light that must lead thee upwards. It is not for nothing that Christ hath taught us to begin our prayers with ' Our Father which art in heaven :' it is fatherly love that must win our hearts, and that must comfort them : it is ' in heaven' where this is gloriously manifested. As I said before, as the soul is in all the body, but yet understands not in the hand as it doth in the head, or rejoices not in the foot as it doth in the heart ; so God, who is every where, doth not every where glorify his love as he doth it in heaven : thither therefore the mind and eye are even by nature taught to look up as to God, as we look a man in the face when we speak to him, rather than to his feet, though his soul be also there.

My sinful heart hath needed sorrow : my careless, rash, presumptuous soul hath needed fears, and I have had some part of these : mercy saw it good for me, as necessary to prevent my dangerous deceits and lapses. O that in the hour of sensual temptations I had feared more, and departed from evil. But it is holy love that must be my life, or else I am dead notwithstanding fear.

O come then and study the life of love : it is more of a holy nature than of art ; but yet study must do much to prepare thee to receive it. This is the great use of a heavenly conversation ! It is the contemplation, belief, and hope of the glorious state of love hereafter, that must make us like it, and kindle it in us here: the burning glass must be turned directly to the sun, if you will have it set any thing on fire. There is a carnal or common love to God, which is kindled in men by carnal pleasures ; but a holy love, like that in heaven, must be studiously drawn from heaven, and kindled by the foresight of what is there, and what we shall be there for ever: faith must ascend, and look within the vail ; thou must not live as a stranger to thy home, to thy God, and Saviour, and thy hopes. The fire that must warm thee is in heaven, and thou must come near it, or open thyself to its influence, if thou wilt feel its powerful efficacy. It is night and winter with carnal minds, when it is day and summer with those that set their faces heaven-ward.

But though all my receivings will be from God, they will not be from him alone : we must live in perfect union also with one another, and with all the heavenly society ; and therefore as we must love them all, so shall we be beloved by them all. This will be a subordinate part of our blessedness: God there will make use of second causes, even in communicating his love and glory.

The Lord Jesus Christ will not only be the object of our delightful love, but will also love us with an effectual operative love for ever. His love will be as the vital heat and motion of the heart to all the members, the root of our life and joy. The love of our Redeemer will flow out into us all as the vital spirits, and his face of glory will be the sun of the heavenly Jerusalem, and will shine upon us, and show us God : in his light we shall have light. Did his tears for a dead Lazarus make men say, ' behold how he loved him ?' O then what will the reviving beams of heavenly life make us say of that love which fills us with the pleasures of his presence, and turns our souls into joy itself ! He comforts us now by the teaching of his word ; but surely the fruition of salvation will be more gladdening than the tidings of it. When he that told us of glory in his gospel shall give it us, we shall not only believe, but feel that he loves us.

Believe, O my soul, thy Saviour's love, that thou mayest foretaste it, and be fit to feel it. We were incapable in sinful flesh of seeing him otherwise than as clothed with flesh ; and his consolations were administered by a word of promise suitable to his appearance : but when he withdrew his bodily presence, the Comforter was sent with a fuller consolation ; but all that was but the earnest and the first fruits of what he will be to us for ever. Be not seldom, nor unbelievingly, nor slight, in the thoughts of thy Saviour's love, for it is he that is the way to the infinite love. Let thy believing be so much of thy daily work, that thou mayest say, that he ' dwells in thy heart by faith,' and that, while thou livest here it is ' Christ that liveth in thee ; and that thy life in the flesh is not a fleshly life, but by the faith of the Son of God that hath loved thee, and given himself for thee.' That though thou see him not, yet believing, thou lovest him also with unspeakable joy, as believing the unspeakable, perfect joy which his love will communicate to thee for ever.

Look upon the sun, and think thus with thyself, How wonderful is the emanation of this sun : its motion, light, and heat communicated to so many millions of creatures all over the earth, and in the seas; what if all these beams of light and heat were proportionable beams of perfect knowledge, love, and joy, and that all creatures that are under the sun had from its influx as much wisdom, love and joy, as they have light, heat, and motion: would not then this earth be as a world of angels and a heaven ? O what a blessed world would it be ! What a benefactor would the sun be to the world ! Why, even such will Jesus Christ be to the celestial world: he is the Sun of glory; his influence will send forth life, and light, and joyful love upon all the blessed from the face of God, as the sun sends forth from God, its motion, light, and heat upon this world. Now therefore begin and live upon him: live upon the influence of his grace, his teaching, love-kindling, and quickening grace, that thou mayest have his name and mark, that he may find in thee something of himself or of his own, when thou comest to his righteous trial. His grace is not in my power, nor at my command. It is not meet it should be so, but he hath not bid me seek and beg in vain. If he had never told me that he will give it me, it is equal to a promise if he but bid me seek and ask. But I have more! · He teaches me to pray; he makes my prayers; he writes me out a prayer-book on my heart; he gives me desires, and he loves to be importuned by them. His Spirit is first a spirit of supplication, and after of consolation, and in both, a spirit of adoption. So far is he from being loth to be troubled with my importunity, that he seeks to me to seek his grace, and is displeased with me that I will ask and have no more.

All this is true. But how then comes my soul to be yet so low, so dark, so fond of this wretched flesh and world, and so backward to go home and dwell with Christ? Alas! a taste of heaven on earth is a mercy too precious to be cast away upon such as have long grieved and quenched the Spirit, and are not by diligent and patient seeking, prepared to receive it. He that proclaims a general peace, will give peace only to the sons of peace. If after such unkind neglects, such wilful sins as I have been guilty of, I should expect to be suddenly in my Saviour's arms, and to be feasted presently with the first-fruits of heaven, I should look that the Most Holy should too little manifest his hatred of my sin. My conscience remembers the follies of my youth, and many a later odious sin; and tells me that if heaven were quite hid from my sight, and I should never have a glimpse of the face of glorious eternal love, it were but just. I look upward from day to day; I groan to see his pleased face, and better to know my God and my home. I cry to him daily, 'My God, this little is better than all the pleasures of sin; my hopes are better than all the possessions of this world; thy gracious looks have often revived me, and thy mercies have been unmeasurable to my soul and body. But O how far short am I of what even fifty years ago I hoped sooner to have attained! Where is the peace that passeth understanding,

that should keep my heart and mind in Christ? O where is the seeing, the longing, the rejoicing, and triumphing faith? Where is that pleasant familiarity above, that should make a thought of Christ and heaven to be sweeter to me than the thoughts of friends, or health, or all the prosperity and pleasure of this world? Do those that dwell in God, and God in them, and have their hearts and conversations in heaven, attain to no more clear and satisfying perceptions of that blessed state, than I have yet attained? Is there no more acquaintance above to be here expected? No more lively sense of future joys, nor sweeter foretaste? No fuller silencing of doubts and fears? I am not so loth to go to a friend, nor to the bed where I often spend the night in restless pains and rolling, as I have too often been to come to thee! Alas, how many of thy servants are less afraid to go to a prison than to their God; and had rather be banished to a land of strangers, than sent to heaven! Lord, must I, that am called thy child, and an heir of heaven, and a co-heir with Christ, have no more acquaintance with my glorified Lord, and no more love to thee that art my portion, before I go hence, and come before thee? Shall I have no more of the heavenly life, light, and love? Alas, I have scarcely enough in my meditations, to denominate them truly heavenly meditations. I have scarcely enough in a prayer to make it indeed a heavenly prayer; or in a sermon to make it a heavenly sermon; and shall I have no more when I come to die? Must I go hence so like a stranger to my home? Wilt thou take strangers into heaven, and know them as thine that do not better know thee here? O my God, vouchsafe a sinner yet more of his Spirit that came down on earth to call up earthly minds to God; and to open heaven to all believers? O what do I beg for so frequently, so earnestly, for the sake of my Redeemer, as the Spirit of life and consolation, which may show me the pleased face of God, and unite all my affections to my glorified Head, and draw up this dark and drowsy soul to love and long to be with thee.'

But, alas, though these are my daily groans, how little yet do I ascend! I dare not blame the God of love; he is full and willing. I dare not blame my blessed Saviour; he hath showed that he is not backward to do good. I dare not accuse the Holy Spirit, it is his work to sanctify and comfort souls. If I knew no reason of this my low and dark estate, I must needs conclude that it is somewhat in myself. But, alas, my conscience wants not matter to satisfy me of the cause. Sinful resistance of the Spirit, and unthankful neglects of grace and glory, are undoubtedly the cause. But are they not a cause that mercy can forgive? That grace can overcome? May I not yet hope for such a victory before I die?

'Lord, I will lie at thy doors and groan: I will pour out my moans before thee: I will beg, and whatever thou wilt, do thou with me; thou describest the kindness of the dogs to a Lazarus that lay at a rich man's doors in sores: thou commendest the neighbourly pity of a Samaritan, that took care of a wounded man: thou condemnest those that will not show mercy to the poor and needy: thou biddest us "be merciful as our heavenly Father is merciful." If we see our brother have need of, and shut up the bowels of our compassion from him, it is because thy love dwells not in us. Shall I then wait at thy doors in vain, and go empty away from such a God, when I beg but for that which thou hast commanded me to ask, and without which I cannot serve thee or come to thee, live or die in a habit beseeming a member of Christ, a child of God, and an heir of heaven? O give me the wedding garment without which I shall but dishonour thy bounteous feast: let me wear a livery which becomes thy family, even a child of God. How often hast thou commanded me to rejoice; yea, to rejoice with exceeding and unspeakable joy! How ardently would I in this obey thee! O that I had more faithfully obeyed thee in other preparatory duties, in ruling my senses, my fancy, my tongue, and in diligent using all thy talents! Then I might more easily have obeyed thee in this. Thou knowest, Lord, that love and joy are duties that must have more than a command. O bid me do them with an effecting word. How can I rejoice in death and darkness? When the bridegroom is absent I must fast and mourn: while I look towards heaven but through the crevices of this dungeon flesh, my love and joy will be but answerable to my light: how long is it since I hoped that I had been translated from the kingdom of darkness, and delivered from the power of the prince of darkness, and brought into that light which is the entrance of the inheritance of the saints; yet alas, darkness, darkness, is still my misery! There is light round about me, in thy word and works, but darkness is within me. If my eye be dark, the sun will be no sun to me. Alas, my Lord, it is not all the learning in the world, no, not of theology, that consists in the knowledge of words and methods, which I can take for the satisfactory, heavenly light! To know what thou hast written in the sacred book, is not enough to make me know my glorified Saviour, my Father and my home. It must be a light from heaven that must show me heaven, and a light accompanied with vital heat, that must turn to love and joy within me. O let me not have only dreaming knowledge, of words and signs, but quickening light, to show the things which these words signify, to my mind and heart. Surely the faith by which we must live, must be a living faith, and must reach further than to words, how true soever. Can faith live in the dark? What is it but an effect of thine illumination? What is my unbelief but the darkness of my soul? Lord Jesus, scatter all these mists: make thy way, O thou Sun of righteousness, into this benighted mind. O send thine advocate to silence every temptation that is against thy truth and thee, and thine agent to prosecute thy cause against thine enemies and mine, and to be the resident witness of thy verity, and my sonship and salvation. Hearing of thee is not satisfactory to me: it must be the presence and operation of thy light and love, shed abroad by thy Spirit on my heart, that must quiet and content my soul. I confess with shame, that I have sinned against heaven and before thee, and am unworthy to have any glimpse or taste of heaven: but so did many that are now entertained and feasted by thy love in glory.

'My Lord, I know that heaven is not far from me: it is not, I believe, one day's or hour's journey to a separated soul: how quick is the communion of my eyes with the sun, that seems far off! Couldst thou not show it me in a moment? Is not faith a seeing grace? It can see the invisible God, the unseen world, the new Jerusalem, the innumerable angels, and the spirits of the perfected just, if it be animated by thine influx; without which it can do nothing, and is nothing; thou that often healedst the blind here in the flesh, didst tell us, that it is much more thy work to illuminate souls: it is but forgiving all my sins, and removing this film that sin hath gathered, and my illuminated soul will see thy glory. I know that the vail of flesh must be also rent before I shall see thee with open face, and know my fellow-citizens above as I am known. It is not heaven on earth that I am begging for, but that I may see it from mount Nebo, and have the bunch of grapes; the pledge, and the first-fruits; that faith and hope which may kindle love and desire, and make me run my race with patience, and live and die in the joy which beseems an heir of heaven.

'But, if my part on earth must be no greater than yet it is, let it make me the wearier of this dungeon, and groan more fervently to be with thee, and long for the day when all my longing shall be satisfied, and my soul be filled with thy light and love.'

Doubtless, as I shall love the angels and saints in heaven, so I shall some way, in subordination to Christ, be a receiver from them : our love will be mutual ; and which way soever I owe duty, I shall expect some answerable return of benefit. The sun shines upon the stars as well as on the earth, and the stars on one another. If angels are greatly useful to me here, it is likely they will be much more there, where I shall be a more capable receiver. It will be no diminution to Christ's honour, that he there makes use of my fellow-creatures to my joy, no more than it is here. The whole creation will be still one compacted frame ; and the heavenly society will for ever retain their relation to each other, and their aptitude and disposition to the duties and benefits of those relations. As we shall be far fitter for them than here we are, so shall we have far more comfort in them. How gloriously will God shine in the glory of the blessed ! How delightful will it be to see their perfection in wisdom, holiness, love, and concord ! What voices they use, or what communication instead of voices, we shall shortly know : but surely there is a blessed harmony of minds, wills, and practice. All are not equal, but all accord to love and praise their glorious God, and readily to obey him, and perfectly to love each other. There is no jarring or discordant spirit that is out of tune ; no separation or opposition to each other. As God's love in Christ is our full and final happiness ; so nature, which hath made us sociable, teaches us to desire to be loved of each other, but especially by wise and worthy persons. Saints and angels in heaven will love incomparably better than our dearest friends on earth can do ; and better than they did themselves when we were on earth ; for they will love that best which is best, and where there is most of God appearing ; else it were not intellectual love : therefore they will love us as much better when we come to heaven, as we shall be better. If we go from loving friends on earth, we shall go to them that love us far more. The love of these here doth but pity us in our pains, and go weeping with our bodies to the grave : but the love of those above will joyfully convoy or welcome our souls to their triumphing society. All the holy friends that we thought we had lost, that went before us, we shall find rejoicing there with Christ.

O what a glorious state will be that common uniting and united love ! If two or three candles joined together make a greater flame and light, what would ten thousand stars united do ? When all the love of angels and saints in full perfection, shall be so united as to make one love, to God that is one, and to one another, who are there all one in Christ, O what a glorious love will that be ! That love and joy will be the same thing : and that one universal love will be one universal joy.

Little know we how great a mercy it is to be here commanded to love our neighbours as ourselves ; and much more to be effectually taught of God so to love one another. Did we all here live in such unfeigned love, we should be like to heaven, as bearing the image of the God of love. But, alas, our societies here are small ; our goodness, which is our amiableness, wofully imperfect, and mixed with lothesome sin and discord. But there a whole heaven full of blessed spirits will flame for ever in perfect love to God, to Christ, and one another.

Go then, go willingly, O my soul ! Love joins with light to draw up thy desires ! Nature inclines all things unto union ; even the lifeless elements have an aggregative motion, by which the parts, when violently separated, hastily return to their natural adhesion. Art thou a lover of wisdom, and wouldst thou not be united to the wise ? Art thou a lover of holiness, and of love itself, and wouldst thou not be united to the holy, who are made of love ? Art thou a hater of enmity, discord, and divisions, and a lover of unity here on earth, and wouldest thou not be where all the just are one ? It is not an unnatural union to thy loss : nothing shall be taken from thee by it. Thou shalt receive by it more than thou canst contribute : it shall not be forced against thy will. It is but a union of minds and wills, a perfect union of loves. Let not natural or sinful selfishness cause thee to think suspiciously or hardly of it ; for it is thy happiness and end. What got the angels that fell to selfishness from unity ? And what got Adam that followed them herein ? The further any man goes from unity by selfishness, the deeper he falls into sin and misery from God : and what doth grace but call us back from sin and selfishness to God's unity again ? Dote not then on this dark divided world : is not thy body, while the parts by a uniting soul are kept together, and make one, in a better state than when it is crumbled into lifeless dust ? Doth not death creep on thee by a gradual dissolution ? Away then from this sandy, incoherent state : the further from the centre the further from unity : a unity indeed there is of all things ; but it is one heavenly life, light, and love which is the true felicitating union.

We dispute here whether the aggregative motion of separated parts be from a motive principle in the part, or by the attraction of the whole, or by an external impulse. It is likely that there is somewhat of all these : but surely the greatest cause is likely to do most to the effect. The body of the earth hath more power to attract a clod or stone, than the intrinsic principle to move it downwards : but intrinsic gravity is also necessary. The superior attractive love and loveliness must do more to draw up this mind to God, than my intrinsic holiness to move it upward : but without this holiness the soul would not be capable of feeling that attractive influx. Every grace comes from God to fit and lead up my soul to God ; faith therefore believes the heavenly state, and love doth with some delight desire it, and hope aspires after it, that I may at last attain it.

They that have pleaded against propriety, and would have all things common in this world, have forgotten that there is a propriety in our natural constitution, which renders some accidental propriety necessary to us. Every man hath his own bodily parts, and inherent accidents ; and every man must have his own food, his own place, clothing, and acquisitions ; his own children, and therefore his own wife, &c. But that the greatest perfection is most for community as far as nature is capable of it, God would show us, in making the first receivers of the extraordinary pourings out of his Spirit, to sell all, and voluntarily make all common, none saying, this or that is my own ; which was not done by any constraining law, but by the law or power of uniting love : they were first all as of one heart and soul.

Take not then thy inordinate desire of propriety for thy health, but for thy sickness : cherish it not, and be not afraid to lose it, and measure not the heavenly felicity by it. Spirits are penetrable : they claim not so much a propriety of place, as bodies do : it is thy weakness and state of imperfection now, which makes it so desirable to thee that thy house should be thine, and no one's but thine ; thy land be thine, and no one's but thine ; thy clothes, thy books, yea, thy knowledge and grace, be thine, and no one's but thine. How much more excellent a state were it, if we were here capable of it, if we could say, that all these are as the common light of the sun, which is mine, and every one's as well as mine ? Why are we so desirous to speak all

languages, but that we might understand all men, and be understood of all, and so might make our sentiments as common as is possible ? Whence is it that men are so addicted to talkativeness, but that nature would make all our thoughts and passions as common as it can ? Why else are learned men so desirous to propagate their learning, and godly men so desirous to make all others wise and godly ? It seems one of the greatest calamities of this life, that when a man hath with the longest and hardest study attained to much knowledge, he cannot bequeathe it, or any part of it, to his heir, or any person, when he dies, but every man must acquire it for himself. When God hath sanctified the parents, they cannot communicate their holiness to their children, though God promise to bless them on their account. Much less can any man make his grace or knowledge common. Nature and grace incline us to desire it ; but we cannot do it. For this end we talk, preach, and write ; for this end we study to be as plain, convincing, and moving as we can, that we may make our knowledge and affections as common to our hearers and readers as we can. O what a blessed work should we take preaching and writing for, if we could make them all know but what we know, and love what we are persuading them to love ! There would then be no need of schools and universities : a few hours would do more than they do in an age. But alas, how rare is it for a father of excellent learning and piety, to have one son like himself, after all his industry !

Is not the heavenly communion then desirable, where every man shall have his own, and yet his own be common to all others ? My knowledge shall be mine own, and other men's as well as mine : my goodness shall be my own and theirs : my glory and felicity shall be mine and theirs : theirs also shall be mine as well as theirs ; the knowledge, the goodness, the glory of all the heavenly society, shall be mine, according to my capacity. Grace is the seed of such a state, which makes us all one in Christ, neither barbarian nor Scythian, circumcision, nor uncircumcision, bond nor free ; by giving us to love our neighbour as ourselves, and to love both our neighbour as ourselves for Christ, and Christ in all : well might Paul say, 'all things are yours.' But it is here but as in the seed ; the perfect union and communion is hereafter. Earth and heaven must be distinguished : we must not extend our hopes or pretensions here beyond the capacity of our natures ; as perfect holiness and knowledge, so perfect unity and concord is proper to heaven, and is not here to be expected : the papal pretensions of an impossible union in one governor of all the earth, is the means to hinder that union which is possible. But the state of perfection is the state of perfect union and communion. Hasten then upwards, O my soul, with the most fervent desires, and breathe after that state with the strongest hopes ; where thou shalt not be rich, and see thy neighbours poor about thee, nor be poor while they are rich ; nor be well while they are sick, or sick while they are well. But their riches, their health, their joy, will be all thine, and thine will be all theirs, as the common light ; and none will have the less for the participation of the rest : yea, communion will be part of every one's felicity : it constitutes the very being of the city of God. This celestial communion of saints in one holy church, above what is here to be attained, is now an article of our belief: but believing will soon end in see-ing and enjoying.

SECTION V.—THE CONSTITUTIVE REASONS FROM THE HEAVENLY LIFE OR PRACTICE.

Seeing and loving will be the heavenly life. But yet it seems that, besides these, there will be executive powers, and therefore some answer-able practice. There are good works in heaven, and far more and better than on earth. For, 1. There will be more vital activity, and therefore more exercise for it : for the power is for action. 2. There will be more love to God and one another ; and love is active. 3. There will be more likeness to God and our Redeemer, who is communicative, and doth good as he is good. 4. Our union with Christ, who will be for ever beneficent as well as benevolent, will make us in our places also beneficent. 5. Our communion in the city of God will prove that we shall all bear our part as the members of the body, in contributing to the welfare of the whole, and in the common returns to God.

But what are the heavenly works, we must perfectly know when we come thither. In gen-eral we know, that they will be the works of love to God and to his creatures ; that is, such as love inclines us to exercise. They will be works of obedience to God ; that is, such as we shall do to please his will, and because he wills them to be our duty. They will be useful works to others. They will be pleasant to ourselves, and part of our felicity. They will carry all to God our end.

Somewhat of them is particularly described in the holy scriptures : as, ' We shall in concord with the whole society, or choir, give thanks and praise to God and our Redeemer.' Whether there be any voice, or only such spiritual activ-ity and exultation, as to man in flesh is not to be clearly understood, is not fit for us here to presume to determine. It will be somewhat more high and excellent than our vocal praise and singing is ; and of which this bears some analogical resemblance or signification. As all passions earnestly desire vent and exercise, so specially do our holy affections of love, joy, and admiration of God Almighty ! There is in us a desire of communion with many in such affec-tions and expressions. Methinks when we are singing or speaking God's praise in the great assemblies, with joyful and fervent souls, I have the liveliest foretaste of heaven on earth ; and I could almost wish that our voices were loud enough to reach through all the world, and unto heaven itself. Nor could I ever be offended, as many are, at the organs, and other convenient music, soberly and seasonably used, which ex-cite and help to tune my soul in so holy a work, in which no true assistance is to be despised. No work more comforts me in my greatest suf-ferings, none seems more congruous and pleasant to me while I wait for death, than psalms, and words of praise to God ; nor is there any exer-cise in which I had rather end my life ; and should I not then willingly go to the heavenly choir, where God is praised with perfect love, joy, and harmony ? Had I more of a praising frame of soul, it would make me long more for that life of praise. For I never find myself more willing to be there, than when I most joyfully speak or sing God's praise. Though the dead praise not God in the grave, and dust doth not give him thanks ; yet living souls in heaven do it joyfully, while their fleshly clothing turns to dust.

' Lord, tune my soul to thy praises now, that sweet experience may make me long to be where I shall do it better ! I see where any excellent music is, nature makes men flock to it ; and they that are but hearers, yet join by a concurrent fancy and delight. Surely, if I had once heard the heavenly choir, I should echo to their holy songs, though I could not imitate them ; and I should think it the truest blessedness to be there and bear my part. My God, the voice of thy comforting Spirit, speaking thy love effectually to my soul, would make such holy music in me, that would incline me to the celestial comfort ; and without it all these thoughts and words will be in vain. It is the inward melody of thy Spirit and my conscience, that must tune me to desire the heavenly melody. O speak thy love first to my heart, and then I shall joyfully speak it to my brethren, and shall ambitiously seek that communion of them that praise thee better than sinful, groaning mortals can : though my sins here make discord in my songs, I hope my groans for those sins, and their effects, will make no discord. Sighs and tears have had the honour to be accepted by thee, who despisest not a contrite soul ; but if thy Spirit will sing and speak within me, and help me against the discordant murmurs of my unbelieving heart, and pained flesh, I shall offer thee that which is more suitable to thy love and grace. ' I confess, Lord, that daily tears and sighs are not unsuitable to the eyes and voice of so great a sinner, who is under thy correcting rod ! What better could I expect when I grieved thy Spirit, than that it should prove my grief ? Yea, this is far better than the genuine effects of sin. But this is not it that is meet to be offered to the God of love : ' he that offereth praise doth glorify thee.' Is not this the ' spiritual sacrifice acceptable through Christ,' for which we were made priests to God ? I refuse not, Lord, to lie in tears and groans when thou requirest it, and do not thou refuse those tears and groans ; but O give me better, that I may have better of thine own to offer thee. By this prepare me for the far better which I shall find with Christ : that which is best to us thy creatures, will be accepted as best by thee, who art glorified and pleased in the perfection of thy works.

It is at least very probable that God makes glorified spirits his agents and ministers of much of his beneficence to the creatures that are below them. For, we see that where he endues any creature with the noblest endowments, he makes most use of that creature to the benefit of others. We shall in heaven be most furnished to do good, and that furniture will not be unused. Christ tells us that we shall be like or equal to the angels : which though it mean not, simply, and in all things, yet it means more than to be above carnal generation ; for it speaks of a similitude of nature and state as the reason of the other. That the angels are God's ministers for the good of his chosen in this world, and administrators of much of the affairs on earth, is past all doubt. The apostle tells us that the saints shall judge the world and angels : judging in scripture is often put for ruling ; it is therefore probable at least, that the devils and the damned shall be put under the saints, and that, with the angels, they shall be employed in some ministerial oversight of the inhabitants and affairs of the promised new earth. When even the

more noble superior bodies, even the stars, are of so great use and influx to inferior bodies, it is likely that accordingly superior spirits will be of use to the inhabitants of the world below them.

But I think it not meet to venture here upon uncertain conjectures beyond the revelation of God's word, and therefore shall add no more, but conclude, that God knows what use to make of us hereafter as well as here, and that if there were no more for us to do in heaven, but with perfect knowledge, love, and joy, to hold communion with God and all the heavenly society, it were enough to attract a sensible and considerate soul to fervent desires to be at home with God.

Here I must not over-pass my rejection of the injurious opinion of too many philosophers and divines, who exclude all sense and affection from heaven, and acknowledge nothing there but intellect and will. This is because they find sense and affection in the brutes ; and they think that the souls of brutes are but some quality, or perishing temperament of matter ; and therefore that sense and affection is in us no better.

But, what felicity can we conceive of without any affection of delight or joy ? Certainly bare volition now without these doth seem to be no felicity to us, nor knowledge either, if there were no delight in knowing.

Yea, I leave it to men's experience to judge, whether there be now any such thing in us as proper willing, which is not also some internal sense of, and affection to, the good which we will. If it be complacency or the pleasedness of the will, this signifies some pleasure ; and love, in the first act, is nothing else but such an appetite : if it be desire, it hath in it a pleasedness in the thing desired, as it is thought on by us ; and what love is without all sense and affection ?

Why doth the scripture ascribe love and joy to God and angels if there were not some reason for it ? Doubtless there is great difference between the heavenly love and joy, and ours here in the body : so there is also between their knowledge and ours, and their will and ours : but it is not that theirs is less or lower than ours, but somewhat more excellent, which ours gives us some analogical, or imperfect, formal notion of.

What though brutes have sense and affection, doth it therefore follow that we have none now, or that we shall have none hereafter ? Brutes have life, and must we therefore have no life hereafter, because it is a thing that is common to brutes ? Rather as now, we have all that the brutes have, and no more, so shall we then have life, sense, and affection of a nobler sort than brutes, and more. Is not God the living God? Shall we say that he lives not because brutes live? Or rather, that they live a sensitive life, and man a sensitive and intellectual, because God is essential, transcendent, infinite life, that makes them live.

But if they say that there is no sensation or affection but by bodily organs, I answered before to that: the body feels nothing at all, but the soul in the body. The soul unites itself most nearly to the parts, called the spirits; and in them it feels, sees, tastes, smells, &c. That soul that feels and sees, doth also inwardly love, desire, and rejoice; and that soul which doth this in the body, hath the same power and faculty out of the body. If they judge by the cessation of sensation, when the organs are indisposed, or dead, so they might as well conclude against our future intellect and will, whose operation in an apoplexy we no more perceive than that of sense. But I have before showed that the soul will not want exercise for its essential faculties, for want of objects or bodily organs; and that men conclude basely of the souls of brutes, as if they were not an enduring substance, without any proof or probability. Tell us idle dreams, that they are but vanishing temperaments, &c. which are founded on another dream, that fire is no substance either; and so our unnatural somatists know none of the most excellent substances, which actuate all the rest, but only the more base and gross which are actuated by them: and they think they have well acquitted themselves, by telling us of subtle acted matter and motion, without understanding what any living, active, motive faculty, or virtue is. Because no man knows what God doth with the souls of brutes, whether they are only one common sensitive soul of a more common body, or whether individuate still, and transmigrant from body to body, or what else. Therefore they make ignorance a plea for error, and feign them to be no substances, or to be annihilated.

I doubt not but sensation, as is aforesaid, is an excellent operation of the essential faculties of real substances called spirits; and that the highest and noblest creatures have it in the highest excellency. Though God fits every thing to its use, hath given, e. g. a dog, more perfect sense of smelling than a man; yet man's internal sense is far more excellent than the brutes', and thereby is an advantage to our intellect, volition and joy here in the flesh. That in heaven we shall have not less, but more, even more excellent sense and affections of love and joy, as well as more excellent intellect and volition; but such as we cannot now clearly conceive of.

Therefore there is great reason for all those analogical collections which I have mentioned in my book called the Saints' Rest, from the present operations and pleasures of the soul in flesh, to help our conceptions of its future pleasures. Though we cannot conclude that they will not inconceivably differ in their manner from what we now feel, I doubt not but feel and rejoice we shall, as certainly as live, and that the soul is essential life, and that our life, and feeling, and joy, will be inconceivably better.

THE APPLICATION OF THE GENERAL SUBJECT.

I am convinced that it is far better to depart and be with Christ, than to be here: but there is much more than such conviction necessary to bring up my soul to such desires. Still there resists, I. The natural aversion to death, which God hath put into every animal, and which is become inordinate and too strong by sin. II. The remnants of unbelief, taking advantage of our darkness here in the flesh, and our too much familiarity with this visible world. III. The want of more lively foretastes in a heavenly mind and love, through weakness of grace, and the fear of guilt. These stand up against all that is said, and words will not overcome them: what then must be done? Is there no remedy?

There is a special sort of the teaching of God, by which we must learn 'so to number our days as to apply our hearts to wisdom,' without which we shall never effectually, practically, and savingly learn either this, or any the most common, obvious, and easy lesson. When we have read, heard, spoken, and written, the soundest truth, and most certain arguments, we know yet as if we knew not, and believe as if we believed not, with a slight and dreaming kind of apprehension, till God by a special illumination bring the same things clearly to our minds, and awaken the soul by a special excitement to feel what we know, and suit the soul to the truth revealed, by an influx of his love, which gives us a pleasing sense of the amiableness and congruity of the things proposed. Since we separated ourselves from God, there is a hedge of separation between our senses and our understandings, and between our understandings and our wills, and affections, so that the communion between them is violated, and we are divided in ourselves, by this schism in our faculties. All men still see the demonstrations of divine perfections in the world, and every part thereof; and yet how little is God known? All men may easily know that there is a God, who is almighty, omniscient, goodness itself, eternal, omnipresent, the maker, preserver, and governor of all, who should have our whole trust, love, and obedience; and yet how little of this knowledge is to be perceived in men's hearts to themselves, or in their lives to others? All men know that the world is vanity, that men must die, that riches then profit not, that time is precious, and that we have only this little time to prepare for that which we must receive hereafter; and yet how little do men seem to know, indeed, of all such things as no man doubts of? When God doth come in with his powerful awakening light and love, then all these things have another appearance of affecting reality, than they had before; as if but now we began to know them: words, doctrines, persons, things, seem as newly known to us.

All my best reasons for our immortality and future life, are but as the new-formed body of Adam before God breathed into him the breath of life: it is he that must make them living reasons. To the Father of lights therefore I must still look up, and for his light and love I must still wait; as for his blessing on the food which I have eaten, which must concoct it into my living substance. Arguments will be but undigested food, till God's effectual influx do digest them. I must learn both as a student and a beggar. When I have thought and thought a thousand times, I must beg thy blessing, Lord, upon my thoughts, or they will all be but dulness or self-distraction. If there be no motion, light, and life here without the influx of the sun, what can souls do, or receive, or feel, without thy influx? This world will be to us, without thy grace, as a grave or dungeon, where we shall lie in death and darkness. The eye of my understanding, and all its thoughts, will be useless or vexatious to me, without thine illuminating beams. O shine the soul of thy servant into a clearer knowledge of thyself and kingdom, and love him into more divine and heavenly love, and then he will willingly come to thee!

I. Why should I strive by the fears of death, against the common course of nature, and against my only hopes of happiness? Is it not appointed for all men once to die? Would I have God to alter this determinate course, and make sinful man immortal upon earth? When we are sinless we shall be immortal. The love of life was given to teach me to preserve it carefully, and use it well, and not to torment me with the continual troubling foresight of death. Shall I make myself

more miserable than the vegetatives and brutes? Neither they nor I do grieve that my flowers must fade and die, and that my sweet and pleasant fruits must fall, and the trees be unclothed of their beauteous leaves, until the spring. Birds, beasts, fishes, and worms, have all a self-preserving fear of death, which urges them to fly from danger. But few, if any, of them, have a tormenting fear arising from the fore-thoughts that they must die. To the body, death is less troublesome than sleep; for in sleep I may have disquieting pains or dreams; and yet I fear not going to my bed. But of this before.

If it be the misery after death that is feared, O what have I now to do, but to receive the free reconciling grace that is offered me from heaven, to save me from such misery, and to devote myself totally to him, who hath promised, that those who come to him he will in no wise cast out.

But this comes by my selfishness. Had I studied my duty, and then remembered that I am not mine own, and that it is God's part, and not mine, to determine of the duration of my life, I had been quiet from these fruitless fears. But when I fell to myself from God, I am fallen to care for myself, as if it were my work to measure out my days, and now I trust not God, as I should do with his own. Had my resignation and devotedness to him been more absolute, my trust in him would have been more easy. But, Lord, thou knowest that I would fain be thine, and wholly thine; and it is to thee that I desire to live. Therefore let me quietly die to thee, and wholly trust thee with my soul.

II. Why should my want of formal conceptions of the future state of separated souls, and my strangeness to the manner of their subsistence and operations, induce me to doubt of those generals, which are evident, and beyond all rational doubting? That souls are substances, and not annihilated, and essentially the same when they forsake the body as before, I doubt not. Otherwise neither the Christians' resurrection, nor the Pythagoreans' transmigration, were a possible thing. For if the soul cease to be, it cannot pass into another body, nor can it re-enter into this. If God raise this body, then it must be by another soul: for the same soul to be annihilated, and yet to begin again to be, is a contradiction. For the second beginning would be by creation, which makes a new soul, and not the same that was before. It is the invisible things that are excellent, active, operative, and permanent: the visible, excepting light which makes all things else visible, are of themselves but lifeless dross. It is the unseen part of plants and flowers which causes all their growth and beauty, their fruit and sweetness. Passive matter is but moved up and down by the invisible active powers, as chess-men are moved from place to place by the gamester's hands. What a lothesome corpse were the world without the invisible spirits and natures that animate, actuate, or move it? To doubt of the being or continuation of the most excellent spiritual parts of the creation, when we live in a world that is actuated by them, and where every thing demonstrates them, as their effects, is more foolish than to doubt of the being of these gross materials which we see.

How often have I been convinced that there are good spirits with whom our souls have as certain communion; though not so sensible, as our life hath with the sun, and as we have with one another? That there are evil and envious spirits that fight against our holiness and peace, the authority of the scriptures, and too sad experience of temptations, do surely evince. The marvellous diversity of creatures on earth, for kind and number; yea, the diversity of stars in heaven, as well as the diversities of angels and devils, partly tell me, that though all be of one, and through one, and to one, yet absolute unity is the divine prerogative, and we must not presume to expect such perfection as to lose our specific or numerical diversity, by any union which shall befall our souls. Nor can I reasonably doubt that so noble and active a nature as souls, dwelling above in the lucid regions, in communion with their like, and with their betters, shall be without the activity, the pleasure and felicity which is suitable to their nature, their region, and their company. My Saviour hath entered into the holiest, and hath assured me that there are many mansions in his Father's house, and that when we are absent from the body, we shall be present with the Lord.

Organical sight is given me for my use here in the body; a serpent or hawk hath as much or more of this than I have. Mental knowledge reaches further than sight, and is the act of a nobler faculty, and for a higher use. Though it be the soul itself embodied in the spirits that sees, yet it is by a higher and more useful faculty that it understands. Faith is not an understanding act: it knows things unseen because they are revealed. Who can think that all believing, holy souls, that have passed hence from the beginning of the world, have been deceived in their faith and hope? That all the wicked worldly infidels, whose hope was only in this life, have been the wisest men, and have been in the right? If virtue and piety are faults or follies, and brutish sensuality be best, then why are not laws made to command sensuality, and forbid piety and virtue? To say this, is to deny humanity, and the wisdom of our Creator, and to feign the world to be governed by a lie, and to take the perfection of our nature for its disease, and our greatest disease for our perfection. But if piety and virtue be better than impiety and vice, the principles and necessary motives of them are certainly true, and the exercise of them is not in vain. What abominable folly and wickedness were it to say that the wicked only attain their ends, and that they all lose their labour, and live and die in miserable deceit, who seek to please God in hope of a better life to come, believing that God is the rewarder of them that diligently seek him? Would not this justify the foolish Manichees that thought a bad God made this world; yea, and would infer that he not only made us for a mischief, but rules us to our deceit and hurt, and gives us both natural and supernatural laws, in ill will to us, to mislead us to our misery, and to fill our lives with needless troubles? Shall I not abhor every suggestion that contains such inhuman absurdities as these? Wonderful! that Satan can keep up so much unbelief in the world, while he must make men such fools, that he may make them unbelievers and ungodly.

That my soul is no more heavenly, and my foretaste of future blessedness is so small, is partly the fruit of those many wilful sins by which I have quenched the Spirit that should be my comforter. It is partly from our common state of darkness and strangeness, while the soul is in flesh, and operates as the body forms, according to its interest and capacity. Affections are more easily stirred up to things seen, than to things that are both unseen, and known only very defectively, by general, and not by clear, distinct apprehensions. And yet this, O this is the misery and burden of my soul! Though I can say that I love God's truth and graces, his work, and his servants, and whatever of God I see in the world, and that this is a love of God in his creatures, word, and works; yet that I have no more desiring and delightful love of heaven, where his loveliness will be more fully opened to my soul, and that the thoughts of my speedy appearing there are no more joyful to me than they are, is my sin, and my calamity, and my shame: and if I did not see that it is so with other of the servants of Christ, as well as with me, I should doubt whether affections so disproportionable to my profession, did not signify unsoundness in my belief. It is strange and shameful, that one that expects quickly to see the glorious world, and to enter the holy, celestial society, should be no more joyfully affected with these hopes; and that I should make any great matter of the pain, languishing, and perishing of the flesh, when it is the common way to such an end. O hateful sin! that hath so darkened and corrupted souls, as to estrange and indispose them to the only state of their hoped happiness. Alas, what did man when he forsook the love and obedience of his God? How just it is that this flesh and world should become our prison, which we would make our home, and would not use as our Lord appointed us, as our servant and way to our better state. Though our way must not be our home, our Father would not have been so strange to us in the way if we had not unthankfully turned away from his grace and love.

It is to us that know not the mysteries of infinite wisdom, the saddest thought that ever possessed our minds, to consider that there is no more grace and holiness, knowledge of God, and communion with him in this world. That so few are saints, and those few so lamentably defective and imperfect. That when the sun shines on all the earth, the Sun of righteousness shines on so small a part of it, and so few live in the love of God, and the joyful hopes of future blessedness; and those few have so low a measure of it, and are corrupted and troubled with so many contrary affections. Infinite goodness is not indisposed to do good: he that made us capable of holy and heavenly affections, gave us not that capacity in vain. Yet, alas, how little of God and glory takes up the hearts of men!

But man hath no cause to grudge at God: the devils before their fall were not made indefectible. Divine wisdom is delighted in the diversity of his works, and makes them not all of equal excellency. Free-will was to act its part: hell is not to be as good as heaven; and sin hath made earth to be next to hell: so much sin, so much hell. What is sin but a wilful forsaking of God? Can we forsake him, and yet love him and enjoy his love: God's kingdom is not to be judged of by his jail or gibbets. We wilfully forsook the light, and made the world a dungeon to ourselves; and when recovering light doth shine unto us, how unthankfully do we usually entertain it? We cannot have the conduct and comfort of it while we shut our eyes and turn away. What though God give not all men an overcoming measure, nor to the best so much as they desire? The earth is but a spot or print of God's creation; not so much as an ant hillock to a kingdom, or perhaps to all the earth; and who is scandalized because the world hath an heap of ants in it, yea, or a nest of snakes that are not men? The vast unmeasurable worlds of light which are above us, are possessed by inhabitants suitable to their glory. A casement or crevice of light, or a candle, in this darksome world, is an unspeakable mercy; yea, that we may hear of a better world, and may seek it in hope. We must not grudge that in our prison we have not that presence of our king, and pleasures of the kingdom, as innocent and free subjects have. Hope of pardon, and a speedy deliverance, are great mercies to malefactors.

If my want of the knowledge and love of God, and joyful communion with the heavenly society, be my prison, and as the suburbs of hell, should it not make me long for the day of my redemption, and the glorious liberty of the sons of God? My true desires of deliverance, and of holiness and perfection, are my evidences that I shall obtain them. As the will is the sinner, so it is the obstinate continuance of a will to sin which is the bondage, and the cause of continued sin; and a continued hell is continued sin, as to the first part at least. Therefore they that continue in hell, continue in a sinning will, and so continue in a love and willingness of so much of hell. So far as God makes us willing to be delivered from sin, so far we are delivered; and our initial imperfect deliverance is the way to more. If pains then make me groan for ease, and sickness make me wish for health, why should not my remnants of ignorance, unbelief, and strangeness to God, occasion me to long for the day of my salvation? This is the greatest of all my troubles: and should it not then be the greatest burden from which I should earnestly desire to be eased? As grace never doth hurt efficiently, and yet may be ill used, and do hurt objectively, (as to them that are proud of it) so sin never doth good efficiently, and of itself, and yet objectively may do good: for sin may be the object of grace, and so to use it is not sin. My unbelief, darkness, disaffection, and inordinate love of this life, do of themselves most hinder my desires of deliverance, and of a better life; but objectively what more fit to make me weary of such a grievous state? Were my unbelief, and earthly mind, predominant, they would chain my affections to this world; or if I were constrainedly weary of a miserable life, I should have no comfortable hopes of a better. But as it is the nature of my sin to draw down my heart from God and glory, it is the nature of my faith, hope, and love to carry it upward, and to desire the heavenly perfection : not to love death, but to love that which is beyond it. Have I been so many years in the school of Christ, learning both how to live and die, begging and studying for this grace, and exercising it against this sinful flesh, and shall I now, after all, find flesh more powerful to draw me downward, than faith, hope, and love, to carry my desires up to God ?

'O God, forbid! O thou that freely gavest me thy grace, maintain it to the last against its enemies, and make it finally victorious! It came from thee ; it hath been preserved by thee ; it is on thy side, and wholly for thee ? O let it not now fail, and be conquered by blind and base carnality, or by the temptations of a hellish conquered enemy ; without it I had lived as a beast, and without it I should die more miserably than a beast : it is thine image which thou lovest ; it is a divine nature, and heavenly beam ; what will a soul be without it, but a dungeon of darkness, a devil for malignity, and dead to holiness and heaven ? Without it, who shall plead thy cause against the devil, world, and flesh ? Without thy glory, earth is but earth : without thy natural efficacy it would be nothing : without thy wise and potent ordination it would be but a chaos : without thy grace it would be a hell. O rather deny me the light of the sun, than the light of thy countenance ! Less miserable had I been without life or being, than without thy grace. Without thee, and my Saviour's help, I can do nothing ; I did not live without thee ; I could not pray or learn without thee ; I never could conquer a temptation without thee. Can I die, or be prepared to die, without thee ? Alas ! I shall but say as Philip of Christ, I know not whither my soul is going, and how then shall I know the way ? My Lord, having "loved his own in the world, did love them to the end." Thou lovest fidelity and perseverance in thy servants, even those that in his sufferings forsook him and fled, yet are commended and rewarded by Christ, for continuing with him in his temptations. Wilt thou forsake a sinner in his extremity, who consents to thy covenant, and would not forsake thee ? My God, I have often sinned against thee, but yet thou knowest I would desire to be thine. I have not served thee with the resolution, fidelity, and delight, as such a master should have been served, but yet I would not forsake thy service, nor change my master or my work ; I can say with thy servant Paul, that thou art the God "whose I am, and whom I serve;" and O that I could serve thee better !

For to serve thee, is but to receive thy grace, and to use it for my own, and others' good, and so to glorify thee, and please thy will, which being love itself, is best pleased when we receive and do most good.

'I have not loved thee as infinite goodness, love itself, and fatherly bounty, should have been loved ; but yet I would not forsake thy family : nothing in this world is more my grief, than that I love thee no more ; forsake not then a sinner that would not forsake thee, that looks every hour towards thee, that feels it as a piece of hell to be so dark and strange unto thee, that gropes, groans, and presses after thee ; feeling, to his greatest sorrow, though thou art every where, that while he is present in the body, he is absent from the Lord. My Lord, I have nothing to do in this world, but to seek and serve thee ; I have nothing to do with a heart and its affections, but to breathe after thee ; I have nothing to do with my tongue and pen, but to speak to thee, and for thee, and to publish thy glory and thy will : what have I to do with all my reputation, and interest in my friends, but to increase thy church, and propagate thy holy truth and service ? What have I to do with my remaining time, even these last and languishing hours, but to look up unto thee, and wait for thy grace, and thy salvation ? O pardon all my carnal thoughts, and all my unthankful neglects of thy precious grace, and love, and all my wilful sin against thy truth and thee ? Let the fuller communications of thy forfeited grace, now tell me by experience that thou dost forgive me : even under the terrible law thou didst tell man thy very nature, by proclaiming thy name, "The Lord, the Lord God, merciful and gracious, long-suffering, and abundant in goodness and truth, keeping mercy for thousands, forgiving iniquity, transgression, and sin." Is not the grace of our Lord Jesus Christ revealed in the gospel for our more abundant faith and consolation ? My God, I know, as I cannot love thee according to thy loveliness, so I cannot trust thee according to thy faithfulness. I can never be sufficiently confident of thy all-sufficient power, thy wisdom, and thy goodness. When I have said, "Will the Lord cast off for ever ? Will he be favourable no more ? Is his mercy clean gone for ever ? Doth his promise fail to generations ? Hath God forgotten to be gracious ? Hath he in anger shut up his tender mercies ?" conscience hath replied, that this is my infirmity : I never wanted comfort because thou wantedst mercy, but because I wanted faith and fitness to receive it and perceive it. But hast thou not mercy also to give me, even that fitness, and that faith? My God, all is of thee, and through thee, and all is to thee, and when I have the felicity, the glory of all for ever will be thine. None that trusts in thee, according to thy nature and promise, shall be ashamed. If I can live and die in trusting in thee, surely I shall not be confounded.'*

Why then should it seem a difficult question, how I may willingly leave this world, and my soul depart to Christ in peace? The same grace which regenerated me, must bring me to my desired end, as the same principle of vegetation which causes the end, must bring the fruit to sweet maturity. I. Believe and trust thy Father, thy Saviour, and thy Comforter. II. Hope for the joyful entertainments of his love, and for the blessed state which he hath promised. III. And long by love 'for nearer union and communion with him: and thus, O my soul, thou mayest depart in peace.

I. How sure is the promise of God! How suitable to his love, and to the nature of our souls, and to the operations of every grace! It is initially performed here, whilst our desires are turned towards him, and the heavenly seed and spark is here ingenerated in a soul that was dead, and dark, and disaffected. Is it any strange thing for fire to ascend? Yea, or the fiery principle of vegetation in a tree, to carry up the earthy matter to a great height? Is it strange that rivers should hasten to the sea? Whither should spirits go but to the region or world of spirits? And whither should Christ's members, and holy spirits go, but to himself, and the heavenly society? Is not that a more holy and glorious place and state, than this below? Earth is between heaven and hell; a place of gross and passive matter, where spirits may indeed operate upon that which needs them, and where they may be detained a while in such operation, or as incorporated forms, if not incarcerated delinquents; but it is not their centre, end, or home. Even sight and reason might persuade me, that all the noble invisible powers that operate on this lower world, principally belong unto a higher; and what can earth add to their essence, dignity, or perfection?

But why, O my soul, art thou so vainly solicitous to have formal, clear, distinct conceptions of the celestial world, and the individuality, and operations of separated souls, any more than of the angels? While thou art the formal principle of an animated body, thy conceptions must be

suitable to their present state and use. When thou art possessed of a better state, thou shalt know it as a possessor ought to do. For such a knowledge as thou lookest after, is part of the possession; and to long, to know, and love in clearness and perfection, is to long to possess. It is thy Saviour, and his glorified ones, that are comprehensors and possessors: and it is his knowledge which must now be most of thy satisfaction. To seek his prerogative to thyself, is vain, usurping arrogance; wouldst thou be a God and Saviour to thyself? O consider how much of the fall is in this selfish care and desire to be as God, in knowing that of good and evil which belongs not to thee, but to God, to know. Thou knowest, past doubt, that there is a God of infinite perfection, who is the rewarder of them that diligently seek him. Labour more to know thy duty to this God, and absolutely trust him as to the particularities of thy felicity and reward. Thou didst trust thy parents to provide thee food and raiment, when thou didst but dutifully obey them: though they could have forsaken thee or killed thee every hour, thou didst never fear it. Thou hast trusted physicians to give thee even ungrateful medicines, without inquiring after every ingredient, or fearing lest they should wilfully give thee poison. I trust a barber with my throat. I trust a boat-man or ship-master with my life: yea, my horse that might cast me: because I have no reason to distrust them, (saving their insufficiency and uncertainty as creatures.) If a pilot undertake to bring thee to the Indies, thou canst trust his conduct, though thou know thyself neither the ship, nor how to govern it, neither the way, nor the place to which thou art conveyed. Must not thy God and Saviour be trusted to bring thee safe to heaven, unless he will satisfy all thy inquiries of the individuality and operation of spirits? Leave unsearchable and useless questions to him that can easily resolve them, and to those to whom the knowledge of them doth belong.

Thou dost but entangle thyself in sin and self-vexation, while thou wouldst take God's work upon thee, and wouldst know that for thyself, which he must know for thee. Thy knowledge and care for it did not precede nor prepare for thy generation, nor for the motion of one pulse or breath, or for the concoction of one bit of all thy food, or the continuance of thy life one hour; supposing but thy care to use the means which God appointed thee, and to avoid things hurtful, and to beg his blessing. The command of being careful for nothing, and casting all thy care on God, who cares for us,

---

* There is a noble pathos, eloquence, and majesty, in the above apostrophe. There is a vast deal of soul thrown into it.—*Ed.*

obliges us in all things that are God's part; and for our souls as well as for our bodies: yea, to trust him with the greatest of our concerns, is our greatest duty; supposing we be careful about our own part, viz. to use the means and obey his precepts. To dispose of a departing soul, is God's part, and not ours. O how much evil is in this distrustful, self-providing care! If I did but know what I would know about my soul and myself; and if I might but choose what condition it should be in, and be the final disposer of it myself, O what satisfaction and joy would it afford me! Is not this to be partly a God to myself? Is he not fitter to know, choose, and dispose of me, than I am? I could trust myself easily, even my wit and will, in such a choice, if I had but power. Cannot I trust God and my Redeemer without all this care, fear, and trouble, and all these particular inquiries? If you are convoying your child in a boat, or coach, by water, or by land, and he at every turn be crying out, ' O father, whither do we go? Or, what shall I do? Or, I shall be drowned or fall,' is it not rather his trust in you than the particular satisfaction of his ignorant doubts, that must quiet and silence him? Be not then foolishly distrustful and inquisitive: make not thyself my own tormentor, by an inordinate care of thy own security. Be not cast down, O departing soul, nor by unbelief disquieted within me: trust in God, for thou shalt quickly, by experience, be taught to give him thanks and praise, who is the health of my countenance, and my God.

O what clear reason; what great experience do command me to trust him, absolutely and implicitly to trust him, and to distrust myself!

He is essential infinite perfection, power, wisdom and love: there is in him all that should invite and encourage rational trust, and nothing that should discourage it.

There is nothing in any creature to be trusted, but God in that creature, or God working in and by it. Distrust him, and there is nothing to be trusted. Not the earth to bear me, nor the air to breathe in, much less any mutable friend.

I am altogether his own, his own by right, and his own by devotion and consent: shall I not trust him with his own.

He is the great benefactor of all the world, that gives all good to every creature, not by constraint, nor by commutation, but as freely as the sun gives forth its light: shall we not trust the sun to shine?

He is my Father and special benefactor; and hath taken me into his family as his child: and shall I not trust my heavenly Father?

He hath given me his Son as the great pledge of his love: what then will he think too dear for me? Will he not with him give me all things?

His Son came purposely to reveal the Father's unspeakable love and purpose to save us. Shall I not trust him that hath proclaimed his love and reconciliation by such a messenger from heaven?

He hath given me the Spirit of his Son, even the spirit of adoption, which is the surest character of his child, the witness, pledge, and earnest of heaven, the name and mark of God upon me, ' holiness to the Lord:' yet shall I not believe his love, and trust him?

He hath made me a member of his Son, and so far already united me to him: will he not take care of the members of his Son? Will he lose those that are given him? Is not Christ to be trusted with his members?

I am his interest, and the interest of his Son: freely beloved; dearly bought! For whom so much is suffered and done, that he is pleased to call us his peculiar treasure. May I not trust him with his dear bought treasure?

He hath stated me in a relation to angels, who rejoiced at my repentance, and to the heavenly society, which shall not miss the smallest part: angels shall not lose their joy nor ministration.

He is in covenant with me; even the Father, Son, and Holy Ghost: he hath given me many great and precious promises: shall I fear lest he will break his word or covenant?

My Saviour is the fore-runner, entered into the holiest, and there appearing and interceding for me: this after he had conquered death, and risen again to assure me of a future life, and ascended into heaven, to show us whither we must ascend; and that after these comfortable words, ' Say to my brethren, I ascend to my Father, and your Father, to my God and your God.' Shall I not follow him through death, and trust such a guide and captain of my salvation?

He is there to prepare a place for me, and will take me to himself: and may I not confidently expect it.

He told a malefactor on the cross that he should be that day with him in paradise, to tell believing sinners what they may expect.

The church, by the article of his descent into the separate state, hath signified their common belief that his separated soul had its subsistence and operation, and did not sleep or perish, to tell us the immortality of separated souls.

His apostles and other servants have on earth served him with all these expectations.

The spirits of the perfected just are now in possession of what I hope for. I am a follower of them, who by faith and patience have attained the promised felicity. May I not trust him to save me, who hath already saved millions in this way, when I could trust a ferry-man to pass me over a river, that had safely passed over thousands before me, or I could trust a physician who cures all that he undertakes of the same disease ?

I must be at his disposal whether I will or not. I shall live while he will, and die when he will, and go whither he will. I may sin and vex my soul with fears, cares, and sorrows, but I shall never prevail against his will.

Therefore there is no rest for souls but in the will of God : that will created us, and that will did govern us, and that will shall be fulfilled on us. It was our efficient and our governing cause, and it shall be our end. Where else is it that we should rest ? In the will of men, or angels, or in our own wills ? All creatures are but creatures : our own wills have undone us : they have misgoverned us, and they are our greatest enemies, our disease, our prison, and our death, till they are brought over to the will of God. Till then they are like a foot out of joint ; like a child or subject in rebellion. There is no rectitude, or health, no order, no peace or true felicity, but in the conformity of our wills to the will of God. Shall I die in distrustful striving against his will, and desiring to keep up my own before it ?

What abundant experience have I had of God's fidelity and love ? After all this shall I not trust him ? His undeserved mercy gave me being ; it chose my parents ; it gave them a tender love to me, and desire of my good ; it taught them to instruct me early in his word, and to educate me in his fear ; it chose me suitable company and habitation ; it gave me betimes a teachable disposition, it chose my schoolmasters ; it brought to my hands many excellent and suitable books ; it gave me some probable public teachers ; it placed me in the best of lands on earth, and I think in the best of ages which that land had seen ; it did early destroy all great expectations and desires of the world, teaching me to bear the yoke from my youth, and causing me rather to groan under my infirmities, than to fight with strong and potent lusts ; it chastened me betimes, but did not destroy me. Great mercy hath trained me up all my days, since I was nineteen years of age, in the school of affliction, to keep my sluggish soul awake in the constant expectations of my change, and to kill my pride and over-valuing of this world, and to lead all my studies to the most necessary things, and as a spur to excite my soul to seriousness, and especially to save me from the supine neglect and loss of time. O what unspeakable mercy hath a life of constant but gentle chastisement proved to me ? It urged me against all dull delays, to make my calling and election sure, and to make ready my accounts, as one that must quickly give them up to God. The face of death and nearness of eternity, did much convince me what books to read, what studies to prefer and prosecute, what company and conversation to choose ; it drove me early into the vineyard of the Lord, and taught me to preach as a dying man to dying men. It was divine love and mercy which made sacred truth so pleasant to me, that my life hath been, under all my infirmities, almost a constant recreation and delight, in its discoveries, contemplation, and practical use. How happy a teacher have I had ! What excellent help, and sweet illumination ! How far beyond my expectation hath divine mercy encouraged me in this sacred work ! How congruously did he choose every place of my ministration and habitation to this day, without my own forecast or seeking ! When, and where, since he first sent me forth, did I labour in vain ? How many are gone to heaven, and how many are in the way, to whom he hath blessed the word, which, in weakness, I did, by his grace and providence, deliver ! Many good Christians are glad of now and then an hour's time to meditate on God's word, and recreate themselves in his holy worship ; but God hath allowed and called me to make it the constant business of my life. My library hath afforded me both profitable and pleasant company and help, at all times, whenever I would use them. I have dwelt among the shining lights, which the learned, wise, and holy men of all ages have set up, and left to illuminate the world. How many comfortable hours have I had in the society of living saints, and in the love of faithful friends ! How many joyful days have I had in the solemn assemblies, where God had been worshipped in seriousness and alacrity, by concordant, though imperfect saints. Where the Spirit of Christ had manifested his presence, by helping myself and my brethren in speaking, and the people in ready, delightful hearing, and all of us in loving and gladly receiving his doctrine, covenant, and laws. How unworthy was such a sinful worm as I who never had any academical helps, nor much from the mouth of any teacher, that books should become so great a blessing to me ; and that, quite beyond my own intentions, God should induce or constrain me to provide any such like helps for others? How unworthy was I to be kept from the multiplied snares of sects and errors which reigned in this age, and to be used as a means for other men's preservation and reduction: and to be kept in a love of unity and peace. How unworthy was I that God should make known to me so much of his reconciling truth, while extremes did round about prevail, and were commended to the churches by the advantages of piety, on one side, and of worldly prosperity and power on the other? That God should use me above forty years in so comfortable a work as to plead and write for love, peace, and concord, and to vouchsafe me so much success therein as he hath done, notwithstanding the general prevalency of the contentious military tribe. Mercy I have had in peace, and liberty in times of violence; and mercy I have had in wars, living two years in safety in a city of defence, in the very midst of the land, (Coventry) and seeing no enemy while the kingdom was in wars and flames; and only hearing of the common calamities round about. When I went abroad and saw the effects of human folly and fury, and of God's displeasure, he mercifully kept me from hurting any one, and being hurt by any. How many a time hath he preserved me by day and night, in difficulties and dangers from the malice of Satan, and from the wrath of man, and from accidents which threatened sudden death. While I beheld the ruins of towns and countries, and the fields covered with the bodies of the slain, I was preserved, and returned home in peace. O how great was the mercy which he showed me, in a teachable. tractable, peaceable, humble, unanimous people! So many in number, and so exemplary in quality; who to this day keep their integrity and concord, when violence hath separated me from them above thirty years. Yea, the like mercy of acceptance and success beyond my expectation, he hath showed me every where. I have had opportunity of free ministration; even where there were many adversaries I have had an open door; in the midst of human wrath and rage he hath preserved my liberty beyond expectation, and continued my acceptance and success. When I might not speak by voice to any single congregation, he enabled me to speak by writing to many; and for the success of my plainest and popular writings, which cost me least, I can never be sufficiently thankful. Some of which he sent to preach abroad, in other languages, in foreign lands.

When my mouth, with eighteen hundred or two thousand more, had been many years stopped, he hath since opened them in some degree; and the sufferings intended us by men have been partly put by, and partly much alleviated, by his providence; and the hardness of our terms hath not so much hindered the success of faithful labours as we feared, and as others hoped it would have done. I have had the comfort of seeing some peace and concord, and prosperity of truth and piety, kept up under the utmost opposition of diabolical and human power, policy, and wrath. When I have been sent to the common jail for my service and obedience to him, he hath there kept me in peace, and soon delivered me. He hath made the mouths of my greatest enemies, who have studied my defamation and my ruin, to become my witnesses, and to cross their own designs. How wonderful is it that I should so long dwell in so much peace, in the midst of those that seemed to want neither power nor skill, and much less will, to tread me down into contempt and misery! And O how many a danger, fear, and pain hath he delivered this frail and languishing body from! How often hath he succoured me, when flesh, heart, and art have failed! He hath cured my consuming coughs, and many a time stayed my flowing blood; he hath eased my pained limbs, and supported a weary, macerated skeleton. He hath brought me up from the jaws of death, and reversed the sentence which men have passed on me. How many thousand weary days have been sweetened with his pleasant work! How many thousand painful weary nights have had a comfortable morning! How many thousand strong and healthful persons have been taken away by death, whilst I have been upheld under all this weakness! Many a time have I cried to the Lord in my trouble, and he hath delivered me out of my distress. I have had fifty years added to my days since I would have been full glad of Hezekiah's promise of fifteen. Since the day that I first preached his gospel, I expected not, of a long time, to live above a year; and I have lived since then fifty years. When my own prayers were cold and unbelieving, how many hundreds have prayed for me! And what strange deliverances, encouraging fasting and prayer, have I often had, upon their importunate requests!

My friends have been faithful, and the few that proved unfaithful have profitably taught me to place no confidence in man, and not to be inordinately affected to any thing on earth; for I was forsaken by none of them, but those few that I excessively valued and over-loved. My relations have been comfortable to me, contrary to my deserts, and much beyond my expectations. My servants have been faithful; my neighbours have been kind; my enemies have been impotent, harmless, or profitable. My superiors have honoured me by their respectful words; and while they have afflicted me, as supposing me an abstraction to their designs, they have not destroyed but protected me. To my inferiors God hath made me, in my low capacity, somewhat helpful. I have been protected in ordinary health and safety, when the raging pestilence came near my habitation, and consumed an hundred thousand citizens. My dwelling hath been safe when I have seen the glory of the land in flames, and after beheld the dismal ruins. When violence separated me from my too much beloved library, and drove me into a poor and smoky house, I never had more help of God, nor did more difficult work than there. What pleasant retirements and quietness in the country, have been the fruits of persecuting wrath! And I must not forget, when I had more public liberty, how he saved me and all my hearers, even by a wonder, from being buried in the ruins of the fabric where we were; and others from the calamities, scandal, and lamentations which would else have followed. It is not a mercy to be extenuated, that when the tongues and pens of all sects among us, and of proud self-exalters, and of some worthy, pious, differing brethren, have been long and vehemently bent against me, when my infamy hath been endeavoured by abundance of volumes, by the backbiting of angry dividers of all sorts, and by the calumniating accusations of some that were too high to be gainsayed, and would not endure me to answer them, and vindicate my innocency; yet, all these together were never able to fasten their accusations, and procure any common belief, nor to bring me under the designed contempt, much less to break my comforts, encouragements or labours.

These, all these, and very many more than these, are my experiences of that wondrous mercy which hath measured my pilgrimage, and filled up my days. Never did God break his promise with me: never did he fail me nor forsake me. Had I not provoked him by rash and wilful sinning, how little interruption of my peace and comforts had I ever been likely to have had? And shall I now distrust him at the last? Shall I not trust, and quietly trust, that infinite wisdom, love, and power, whom I have so long trusted, and found so good?

Nature teaches man to love best those animals that are tame and tractable, that trust us and love us, that will come to our hands, and love our company, that will be familiar with us, and follow us; be it horse or dog, beasts or birds. But those that are wild and live in woods, and fly from the face of man, are taken to be the game and prey of any one that can catch and kill them. Shall my foolish soul thus wildly fly from the face of God? Shall his children be like the fearful hare? Or like a guilty Cain? Or like an unbelieving sadducee, that either believes not, or hopes not for the forgiveness of sin, and the life everlasting? Doth not the Spirit of adoption incline us to love our Father's presence, and to be loth to be long from home? To distrust all creatures, even thyself, is not unreasonable; but to distrust God, hath no just excuse. Fly from sin, from satan, from temptations, from the world, from sinful flesh and idol-self. But fly not from him that is goodness, love, and joy itself: fear thine enemy, but trust thy Father. If thy heart be reconciled to him, and his service, by the Spirit, he is certainly reconciled to thee through Christ; and if he be for thee, and justify and love thee, who shall be against thee, or who condemn thee, or separate thee from his love? If thy unreconciled will make thee doubt of his reconciliation, it is time to abhor and lay by thy enmity; consent, and be sure that he consents. Be willing to be his, and in holiness to serve him, and to be united in joyful glory to him, and then be sure that he is willing to accept thee, and receive thee to that glory. O dark and sinful soul! how little dost thou know thy friend, thyself, or God, if thou canst more easily and quietly trust thy life, thy soul, and hopes to the will of thy friend, or of thyself, if thou hadst power, than to the will of God? Every dog would be at home, and with his master; much more every ingenuous child with his father; and though enemies distrust us, wife and children will not do so, while they believe us just. Hath God ever showed himself either unfaithful or unmerciful to me?

'To thee, O Lord, as to a "faithful Creator, I commit my soul."—"I know that thou art the faithful God, who keepest covenant and mercy with them that love thee, and keep thy commandments."—"Thou art faithful who hast called me to the communion of thy Son Jesus Christ our Lord." Thy faithfulness hath saved me in and from temptations: it hath stablished me, and kept me from prevailing evil. It will keep my spirit, soul, and body to the coming of Christ. It is in faithfulness that thou hast afflicted me, and shall not I trust thee then to save me? It is thy faithful word, that all thine elect shall obtain the salvation which is in Christ Jesus with eternal glory; "and if we be dead with him we shall live with him, and if we suffer we shall also reign with him."

'To thee, O my Saviour, I commit my soul; it is thine own by redemption; it is thine own by covenant; it is marked and sealed by thy Spirit as thine own; and thou hast promised not to lose it. Thou wast made like thy brethren, that thou mightest "be a merciful and faithful high-priest in things pertaining to God, to make reconciliation for our sins." By thy blood we have boldness to enter into the holiest, even by the new and living consecrated way. Cause me to draw near with a sincere heart, in full assurance of faith, by thee that art the high-priest over the house of God: for he is faithful that has promised life through thee. Thy name is faithful and true, and faithful and true are all thy promises. Thou hast promised rest to weary souls that come to thee. I am weary of suffering, and weary of sin; weary of my flesh, and weary of my darkness, dullness, and distance, and of this wicked, blind, unrighteous and disordered world. Whither should I look for rest but home to my heavenly Father and to thee? I am but a bruised reed, but thou wilt not break me: I am but a smoking flax, but thou wilt not quench what thy grace hath kindled; but thou, in whose name the nations trust, wilt bring forth judgment unto victory. The Lord redeems the souls of his servants, and none of them that trust in thee shall be desolate, therefore will I wait on thy name, for it is good, and will trust in the mercy of God for ever. The Lord is good, a stronghold in the day of trouble, and he knows them that trust in him. Sinful fear is a snare; but he that puts his trust in the Lord shall be set on high. Blessed is the man that makes the Lord his trust, and respects not the proud, and such as turn aside to lies. Thou art my hope, O Lord God, thou art my trust from my youth: by thee have I been holden up from the womb, and my praise shall be continually of thee. Cast me not off now in the time of age; forsake me not when my strength fails. O God, thou hast taught me from my youth, and hitherto have I declared thy wondrous works: now also, when I am old and gray, O God, forsake me not. Leave not my soul destitute; for mine eyes are toward thee, and my trust is in thee. I had fainted unless I had believed to see the goodness of the Lord in the land of the living: even where they that live shall die no more. The sun may cease to shine on man, and the earth to bear us; but God will never cease to be love, nor to be faithful in his promises. Blessed be the Lord, who hath commanded me so safe and quieting a duty, as to trust him, and cast all my cares on him, as on one that hath promised to care for me!'

Blessed be God, who hath made it my duty to hope for his salvation. Hope is the ease, yea, the life of our hearts, that else would break, yea, die within us. Despair is no small part of hell. God cherishes hope as he is the lover of souls. Satan, our enemy, cherishes despair, when his way of blind presumption fails. As fear is a foretaste of evil, before it is felt; so hope doth anticipate and foretaste salvation before it is possessed. It is then worldly hypocrites' hope that perishes, for all that hope for true or durable happiness on earth, in the pleasures of this perishing flesh, must needs be deceived. 'But happy is he who hath the God of Jacob for his help, whose hope is in the Lord his God, which made heaven and earth; which keeps truth for ever.' Woe to me, were my hope only in the time and matters of this fleshly life. But the righteous hath hope in his death, and hope makes not ashamed; 'blessed is the man that trusts in the Lord, whose hope the Lord is.' Lay hold then, O my soul, upon the hope which is set before thee; it is thy firm and stedfast anchor; without it thou wilt be as a shipwrecked vessel. Thy foundation is sure; it is God himself: our faith and hope are both in God. It is Jesus our Lord who is risen from the dead, and reigns in glory Lord of all. Yea, it is the Christ who by faith doth dwell within us, who is our hope of glory. In this hope, which is better than the law that Moses gave, it is that we draw nigh to God. It is the Holy Ghost that is both our evidence and the efficient of our hope. By him we hope for that which we see not, and therefore wait in patience for it. By hope we are saved: it is an encouraging grace which will make us stir, whereas despair kills endeavours: it cures sloth, and makes us diligent and constant to the end, and by this helps us to full assurance.

It is a desiring grace, and would fain obtain the glory hoped for. It is a quieting and comforting grace. The God of hope fills us with joy and peace in believing, that we may abound in hope through the power of the Holy Ghost. Shake off despondency, O my soul, and rejoice in hope of the glory of God. Believe in hope, though dying flesh would tell thee that it is against hope. God, that cannot lie, hath confirmed his covenant by his immutable oath, that we might have strong consolation who are fled for refuge to the hope which is set before us. What blessed preparations are made for our hope? Shall we now let the tempter shake it or discourage it? The abundant mercy of God the Father hath begotten us again to a lively hope, by the resurrection of Christ, to an inheritance incorruptible and undefiled, and that fadeth not away, reserved in heaven for us. Grace teacheth us to deny ungodliness and worldly lusts, and to live soberly, righteously, and godly in this world, as looking for that blessed hope, and the glorious appearing of the great God and our Saviour. We are renewed by the Holy Ghost, and justified by grace, that we should be made heirs according to the hope of eternal life. We are illuminated, that we may know the hope of Christ's calling, and what is the riches of the glory of his inheritance in the saints. The hope that is laid up for us in heaven is the chief doctrine of the gospel, which bringeth life and immortality into clearer light. It is for this hope that we keep a conscience void of offence, and that God is served in the world, wherefore gird up the loins of thy mind; put on this helmet, the hope of salvation; and let not death seem to thee as it doth to them that have no hope.

The love of our Father, and our Saviour, have given us everlasting consolation, and good hope through grace, to comfort our hearts, and stablish them in every good word and work. Keep therefore the rejoicing of hope firm to the end. Continue grounded and settled in the faith, and be not moved away from the hope of the gospel. Now, Lord, what wait I for? my hope is in thee; uphold me according to thy word, that I may live; and let me not be ashamed of my hope. Though mine iniquities testify against me, yet, O thou that art the hope of Israel, the Saviour thereof in the time of trouble, be not as a stranger to my soul. Thy name is called upon by me, O forsake me not. Why have our eyes beheld thy wonders, and why have we had thy covenant and thy mercies, but that we might set our hope in God. Remember the word to thy servant upon which thou hast caused me to hope. If thou, Lord, shouldst mark iniquity, O Lord, who shall stand? But there is forgiveness with thee, that thou mayest be feared. I wait for the Lord; my soul doth wait, and in his word do I hope. I will hope in the Lord, for with him there is mercy and plenteous redemption. For he takes pleasure in them that fear him, in those that hope in his mercy. Though flesh and heart fail, the Lord is the rock of my heart; he is my portion, saith my soul, therefore will I hope in him. The Lord is good to them that wait for him; to the soul that seeks him. It is good that

I should both hope, and quietly wait for the salvation of the Lord. It is good for me that I have borne the yoke in my youth, and that I keep silence, and put my mouth in the dust, if so be there may be hope.

God need not flatter such worms as we, nor promise us that which he never means to perform. He hath laid the rudiments of our hope in a nature capable of desiring, seeking, and thinking of another life. He hath called me, by grace, to actual desires and endeavours; and some foretaste he hath vouchsafed. I look for no heaven, but the perfection of divine life, light, and love, in endless glory with Christ and his holy ones; and this he hath begun in me already. Shall I not boldly hope when I have the capacity, the promise, the earnest, and foretaste? Is it not God himself that hath caused me to hope? Was not nature, promise, and grace from him? And can a soul miscarry, and be deceived, that departs hence in a hope of God's own causing and encouraging? Lord, I have lived in hope, I have prayed in hope, I have laboured, suffered, and waited in hope; and, by thy grace, I will die in hope. Is not this according to thy word and will? And wilt thou cast away a soul that hopes in thee, by thine own command and operation? Had wealth and honour, or continuance on earth, or the favour of man, been my reward and hope, my hope and I had died together: were this our best, how vain were man! But the Lord lives, and my Redeemer is glorified, and intercedes for me; and the same Spirit is in heaven who is in my heart; as the same sun is in the firmament which is in my house, The promise is sure to all Christ's seed; and millions are now in heaven that once did live and die in hope; they were sinners once as now I am; they had no other Saviour, no other Sanctifier, no other promise, than I now have, confessing that they were strangers here; they looked for a better country, and for a city that had foundations, even a heavenly, where now they are; and shall I not follow them in hope that have sped so well? Hope then, O my soul, unto the end. From henceforth, and for ever, hope in the Lord. I will hope continually, and will yet praise thee more and more; my mouth shall show forth thy righteousness and salvation. The Lord is at my right hand; I shall not be moved. My heart therefore is glad, and my glory rejoices; my flesh also shall dwell confidently, and rest in hope; for God hath showed me the path of life: in his presence is fulness of joy, and at his right-hand are pleasures for evermore.

III. What then remains, O my soul, but that in trust and hope thou love thy God, thy Saviour, thy Comforter, the glorious society, thy own perfection in glorious, endless, heavenly life, light, and love, and the joyful praises of Jehovah, better than this burden of painful and corruptible flesh, and this howling wilderness, the habitation of serpents and untamed brutes, where unbelief and murmuring, lust and folly, injustice and uncharitableness, tyranny and divisions, pride and contention, have long provoked God, and wearied thee ; where the vintage and harvest is thorns and thistles, sins and sorrows, cares and crosses, manured by manifold temptations ? How odious is that darkness and unbelief, that unholiness and disaffection, that deadness and stupidity, which makes such a work as this, so reasonable, necessary, and pleasant a work, to seem unsuitable or hard ? Is it unsuitable or hard to the eye to see the sun and light ? Or by it to see the beautified world ? Or for a man to love his life or health, his father or his friend ? What should be easier to a nature that hath rational love, than to love him that is essential love itself : he that loves all, and gives to all the loving faculty, should be loved by all : he that hath specially loved me, should be specially loved by me.

Love is the perfection of all thy preparations. It desires to please God ; and therefore to be in the most pleasing state, and freed from all that is displeasing to him, which is not to be hoped for on earth. It desires all suitable nearness, acquaintance, union and communion : it is weary of distance, estrangement, and alien society and affairs. It takes advantage of every notice, intimation, or mention of God, to renew and exercise these desires. Every message and mercy from him is fuel for love, and while we are short of perfection, stir up our desires after more. When love tastes of the grapes, it would have the vine : when it tastes of the fruits, it would dwell where they grow, and possess the land : its thoughts of proximity and fruition are sweet, no other person or thing can satisfy it. The soul is where it loves : if our friend dwell in our hearts by love ; and if fleshly pleasure, riches, and honour, dwell in the heart of the voluptuous, the covetous, and the proud, surely God and our Redeemer, the heavenly society, holiness, and glory, dwell in the heart which loves them with a fervent love. If heaven dwell in my heart, shall I not desire to dwell in heaven ? Light and light, fire and fire, are not more inclined to union than love and love ; gracious love, and glorious love. Would divine, original,

universal love communicate and pour out itself more plentifully upon my heart, how easy would it be to leave this flesh and world, and to hear the sentence of my departure to my God ! Death and the grave would be but a triumph for victorious love : it would be easier to die in peace and joy, than to rest at night, or to come home from my travel to my beloved friends, or to go, when I am hungry, to a feast : a little love hath made me study willingly, preach willingly, and write willingly, yea, and suffer somewhat willingly ; and would not more make me go more willingly to God ? Shall the imagination of house, gardens, walks, libraries, prospects, meadows, orchards, hills and rivers, allure the desires of deceived minds ? Shall not the thoughts of the heavenly mansions, society, and delights, much more allure and draw up my desires ?

The reading of a known fiction of a city of the sun, an Utopia, an Atlantis, &c. hath pleased many. But if I did believingly hear of such a country in the world, where men did never die, nor were sick, or weak, or sad, where the prince was perfectly just and pious, wise and peaceable, devoted to God and the public good ; and the teachers were all wise, judicious men, of universal certain knowledge, perfectly acquainted with the matter and method of natural and theological truths, and all their duty, and all of one mind, and of one heart, tongue and practice ; loving each other, and the people as themselves, and leading the flocks heaven-ward through all temptations, with triumphant hopes and joy ; where all the people perfectly obeyed God, their commanders and their teachers, and lived in perfect love, unity, and peace, and were daily employed in the joyful praises of God, and hopes of glory, and in doing all possible good to one another, contending with none through ignorance, uncharitableness or pride, nor ever reproaching, injuring, or hurting one another, &c. I say, if I knew or heard of such a country, should I not love it before I ever see it, and earnestly desire to be there ? Nay, do I not over-love this distracted world, where tyranny sheds streams of blood, and lays desolate cities and countries, and exposes the miserable inhabitants to lamentable distress and famine ; where the same tyranny sets up the wicked, reproaches and oppresses the just and innocent, keeps out the gospel, and keeps up idolatry, infidelity, and wickedness, in the far greatest part of all the earth ; where Satan chooses pastors too often for the churches of Christ, even such as by ignorance. pride, sensuality, worldliness, and malignity, become thorns and thistles; yea, devouring wolves, to those whom they should feed and comfort; where no two persons are in all things of a mind; where evil is commended, and truth and goodness accused and oppressed, because men's minds are unacquainted with them, or unsuitable to them. Those that are tne greatest pretenders to truth, do most eagerly contend against it, and oppose it; and almost all the world are scolding or scuffling in the dark; and where there appears but little hopes of a remedy. I say, can I love such a world as this? And shall I not think more delightfully of the inheritance of the saints in light, and the uniting love and joyful praises of the church triumphant, and the heavenly choir?

Should I not love a lovely and a ,oving world much better than a world where there is, comparatively, so little loveliness or love? All that is of God is good and lovely; but it is not here that his glory shines in felicitating splendour. I am taught to look upward when I pray, and to say, ' Our Father which art in heaven.' God's works are amiable even in hell; and yet though I would know them, I would not be there; and, alas, how much of the works of man are mixed here with the works of God. Here is God's wisdom manifest; but here is man's obstinate folly. Here is God's government; but here is man's tyranny and unruliness. Here is God's love and mercies; but here are men's malice, wrath, and cruelty; by which they are worse to one another than wolves or tigers, depopulating countries, and filling the world with bloodshed, famine, misery, and lamentations; proud tyrants being worse than raging plagues; which made David choose the pestilence before his enemies' pursuit. Here is much of God's beauteous order and harmony; but here is also much of man's madness, deformity, and confusion. Here is much historical truth, and some civil and ecclesiastical justice; but, alas, with how much odious falsehood and injustice is it mixed? Here is much precious theological verity; but how dark is much of it to such blind, negligent, and corrupted minds, as every where abound? Here are wise, judicious teachers and companions to be found: but, alas, how few in comparison of the most, and how hardly known by those that need them! Here are sound and orthodox ministers of Christ, but how few that most need them know which are they, and how to value them or use them? How many thousands of seduced or sensual sinners are made believe that they are but deceivers, or, as they called Paul, pestilent fellows, and movers of sedition among the people. In how many parts of the world

are they as the prophets that Obadiah hid in caves, or as Micaiah, or Elias among the lying prophets, or the Baalites? Though such as of whom the world is not worthy. Is that world then, more worthy of our love than heaven? There are worthy and religious families which honour God, and are honoured by him: but, alas, how few! and usually by the temptations of wealth, and worldly interest, how full even of the sins of Sodom, pride, fulness of bread, and abundance of idleness, if not also unmercifulness to the poor! How are they tempted to plead for their sins and snares, and account it rustic ignorance which contradicts them? How few pious families are there of the greater sort that do not quickly degenerate, and their posterity, by false religion, error, or sensuality, grow most contrary to the minds of their pious progenitors?

There are many that educate their children wisely in the fear of God, and have accordingly comfort in them; but how many are there that, having devoted them in baptism to God, train them up in the service of the flesh, the world, and the devil, which they renounced; and never understood, or at least intended for themselves or children, what they did profess? How many parents think, that when they offer their children to God in baptism, without a sober and due con-sideration of the nature and meaning of that great covenant with God, that God must accept, and certainly regenerate and save them! Yea, too many religious parents forget that they themselves are sponsors in that covenant, and undertake to use the means on their part to make their children fit for the grace of the Son and the communion of the Spirit, as they grow up, and think that God should absolutely sanctify, keep, and save them at age, because they are theirs, and were baptized, though they keep them not from great and unnecessary tempta-tions, nor teach them plainly and seriously the meaning of the covenant which was made for them with God, as to the nature, benefits or con-ditions of it. How many send them to others to be taught in grammar, logic, philosophy, or arts, yea, and divinity, before their own parents ever taught them what they did with God in baptism, what they received, and what they promised and vowed to do? They send them to trades, or secular callings, or to travel in fo-reign lands, among a multitude of snares, among tempting company, and tempting baits, before ever at home they were instructed, armed, and settled against those temptations which they must needs encounter, and which, if they do not overcome, they are undone. How ordinarily, when they have first neglected this great duty of their own for their fortification, do they plead a necessity of thrusting them out on these temptations, though utterly unarmed, from some punctilio of honour or conformity to the world, to avoid the contempt of worldly men, or to adorn their yet naked souls with some of the plumes or painted trifles, ceremonies, or complements, which will never serve instead of heavenly wisdom, mortification, and the love of God and man: as if they were like to learn that fear of God in a crowd of diverting and tempting company, baits, and business, which they never learned under the teaching, nurture, and daily oversight of their religious parents, in a safer station: or, as if for some little reason they might send them as to sea without pilot or anchor, and think that God must save them from the waves: or, as if it were better to enter them into satan's school or army, and venture them upon the notorious danger of damnation, than to miss of preferment and wealth, or of the fashions and favour of the times. Then when they hear that they have forsaken God and true religion, and given up themselves to lust and sensuality, and perhaps as enemies to God and good men, destroy what their parents laboured to build up, these parents wonder at God's judgments, and with broken hearts lament their infelicity, when it were better to lament their own misdoing, and it had been best of all to have lamented it.

Thus families, churches, and kingdoms, run on to blindness, ungodliness, and confusion. Self-undoing, and serving the malice of Satan for fleshly lust, is the too common employment of mankind. All is wise, good, and sweet, which is prescribed us by God, in true nature, or supernatural revelation. But folly, sin, and misery, mistaking themselves to be wit, honesty, and prosperity, and raging against that which nominally they pretend to and profess, are the ordinary case and course of the most of men. When we would plead them out of their deceit and misery, it is well if we are not tempted to imitate them, or be not partly infected with their disease, or at least reproached and oppressed as their enemies. Such a bedlam is most of the world become, where madness goes for the only wisdom, and he is the bravest man that can sin and be damned with reputation and renown, and successfully drive or draw the greatest numbers with him unto hell: to which the world hath no small likeness, forsaking God, and being very much forsaken by him.

This is the world which stands in competition for my love, with the spiritual, blessed world: much of God's mercies and comforts I have here had, but their sweetness was their taste of divine love, and their tendency to heavenly perfection. What was the end and use of all the good that ever I saw, or that ever God did for my soul or body, but to teach me to love him, and long for more? How many weaning experiences; how many thousand better or contemning thoughts have I had of all the glory and pleasures of this world; how many thousand love-tokens from God have called me to believe and taste his goodness! Wherever I go, and which way soever I look, I see vanity and vexation written upon all things in this world, so far as they stand in competition with God, and would be the end and portion of a fleshly mind. I see holiness to the Lord written upon every thing, so far as it declares God, and leads me to him, as my ultimate end. God hath not for nothing engaged me in a war against this world, and commanded me to take and use it as mine enemy: the emptiness, danger, and bitterness of the world, and the all-sufficiency, trustiness, and goodness of God, have been the sum of all the experiences of my life? Shall a worldly, backward heart overcome the teachings of nature, scripture, the Spirit of grace, and all experience? Far be it from me!

But, O my God, love is thy great and special gift: all good is from thee: but love is the godlike nature, life, and image. It is given us from the love of the Father, the grace of the Son, and the quickening, illuminating, and sanctifying operation of the Holy Spirit: what can the earth return unto the sun, but its own reflected beams? If those. As how far soever man is a medium in generation, nature and that appetite which is the moving weight in the child, is thy work; so whatever is man's part in the mediate work of believing and repenting, which yet is not done without thy Spirit and grace, certainly it is the blessed regenerator which must make us new creatures, by giving us this divine nature, holy love, which is the holy appetite and weight of the soul. Come down, Lord, into this heart, for it cannot come up to thee. Can the plants for life, or the eye for light, go up unto the sun? Dwell in me by the spirit of love, and I shall dwell by love in thee. Reason is weak, and thoughts are various, and man will be a slippery, uncertain creature, if love be not his fixing principle, and do not incline his soul to thee: surely through thy grace, I easily feel that I love thy word. I love thy image, I love thy work, and O how heartily do I love to love thee, and long to know and love thee more! If all things be of thee, and through thee, and to thee, surely this love to the beams of thy glory here on earth, is eminently so! It is thee, Lord, that it means: to thee it looks: it is thee it serves: for thee it mourns, seeks, and groans. In thee it trusts; and the hope, peace, and comfort, which support me, are in thee. When I was a returning prodigal in rags, thou sawest me afar off, and met me with thy embracing, feasting love. Shall I doubt whether he that hath better clothed me, and dwelt within me, will entertain me with a feast of greater love in the heavenly mansions, the world of love?

The suitableness of things below to my fleshly nature, hath detained my affections too much on earth; and shall not the suitableness of things above to my spiritual nature much more draw up my love to heaven? There is the God whom I have sought and served. He is also here, but vailed, and but little known; but there he shines to heavenly spirits in heavenly glory. There is the Saviour in whom I have believed. He hath also dwelt in flesh on earth; but clothed in such meanness, and humbled to such a life and death, as was to the Jews a stumbling-block, and to the Gentiles matter of reproach; but he shines and reigns now in glory, above the malice and contempt of sinners. I shall there live because he lives; and in his light I shall have light. He loved me here with a redeeming, regenerating, and preserving love: but there he will love me with a perfecting, glorifying, joyful love. I had here some rays of heavenly light; but interpositions caused eclipses and nights, yea, some long and winter nights. But there I shall dwell in the city of the sun, the city of God, the heavenly Jerusalem, where there is no night, eclipse, or darkness. There are the heavenly hosts, whose holy love and joyful praises I would wish to be a partaker of! I have here had some of their loving assistance, but to me unseen, being above our fleshly way of converse; but there I shall be with them, of the like nature in the same orb, and of the same triumphant church and choir! There are perfected souls gathered home to Christ: not as here, striving like Esau and Jacob in the womb: nor yet as John when he leaped in the womb, because of his mother's joy; nor as wrangling children, that are hardly kept in the same house in peace. Not like the servants of Abraham and Lot, like Paul and Barnabas, like Epiphanius and Chrysostom, like Luther and Carolostadius, like Ridley and Hooper, or the many striving parties now among us; nor like the disciples striving who should be the greatest.

Not like Noah's family in a wicked world, or Lot in a wicked city, or Abraham in an idolatrous land, nor like Elijah left alone, nor like those that wandered in sheep-skins and goat-skins, destitute, afflicted, and tormented, hid in dens and caves of the earth; not like Job on the dung-hill, nor like Lazarus at the rich man's door. Not like the African bishops, whose tongues were cut out; nor like the preachers silenced by popish imposers in Germany, by the Interim, or elsewhere; nor like such as Tzegedine, Peucer, and many other worthy men, whose maturest age was spent in prisons. Not as we poor, bewildered sinners, seeing evil, and fearing more, confounded in folly and mad contention, some hating the only way of peace, and others groping for it in the dark, wandering and lost in the clearest light, where the illuminated can but pity the blind, but cannot make them willing to be delivered.

What is heaven to me, but God? God who is life, light, and love, communicating himself to blessed spirits, perfecting them in the reception, possession, and exercise of life, light, and love for ever. These are not the accidents, but the essence of that God who is in heaven and all to me. Should I fear that death which passes me to infinite, essential life? Should I fear a darksome passage into a world of perfect light? Should I fear to go to love itself? Think, O my soul, what the sun's quickening light and heat is to this lower corporeal world! Much more is God, even infinite life, light, and love to the blessed world above. Doth it not draw out thy desires to think of going into a world of love? When love will be our region, our company, our life. More to us than the air is for our breath, than the light is for our sight, than our food is for our life, than our friends are for our solace; and more to us than we are to ourselves, and we more for it, as our ultimate end, than for ourselves. O excellent grace of faith which foresees, and blessed word of faith that foreshows this world of love! Shall I fear to enter where there is no wrath, no fear, no strangeness, nor suspicion, nor selfish separation, but love will make every holy spirit as dear and lovely to me as myself, and me to them as lovely as themselves, and God to us all more amiable than ourselves and all. Where love will have no defects or distances, no damps or discouragements, no discontinuance or mixed disaffection; but as life will be without death, and light without darkness, a perfect everlasting day of glory, so will love be without any hatred, unkindness, or allay. As many coals make one fire, and many candles conjoined make one light, so will many living spirits make one life, and many illuminated glorious spirits, one light and glory, and many spirits naturalized into love, will make one perfect love of God, and be loved as one by God for ever: for all the body of Christ is one; even here it is one initial union of the Spirit, and relation to one God, head, and life, throughout, and shall be presented as beloved and spotless to God, when the great marriage-day of the Lamb shall come.

Hadst thou not given me, O Lord, the life of nature, I should have had no conceptions of a glorious, everlasting life: but if thou give me not the life of grace, I shall have no sufficient, delightful inclination and desire after it. Hadst thou not given me sight and reason, the light of nature, I should not have thought how desirable it is to live in the glorious light and vision; but if thou give me not the spiritual illumination of a seeing faith, I shall not yet long for the glorious light, and beatific vision. Hadst thou not given me a will and love, which is part of my very nature itself, I could not have tasted how desirable it is, to live in a world of universal, perfect, endless love: but unless thou also shed abroad thy love upon my heart, by the Spirit of Jesus, the great medium of love, and turn my very nature or inclination into divine and holy love, I shall not long for the world of love. Appetite follows nature: O give me not only the image and the art of godliness—the approaches towards it, nor only some forced or unconstant acts; but give me the divine nature, which is holy love, and then my soul will hasten towards thee, and cry, How long, O Lord, how long! O come, come quickly, make no delay. Surely the fear of dying intimates some contrary love that inclines the soul another way; and some shameful unbelief and great unapprehensiveness of the attractive glory of the world of love: otherwise no frozen person so longs for the fire, none in a dungeon so desires light, as we should long for the heavenly light and love.

God's infinite, essential self-love, in which he is eternally delighted in himself, is the most amiable object, and heaven itself to saints and angels: next to that, his love to all his works, to the world, and to the church in heaven, speaks much more of his loveliness than his love to me. But yet due self-love in me is his work, and part of his natural image; and when this by sin is grown up to excess, through the withdrawing of a contracted narrow soul, from the union and due love to my fellow-creatures, and to God, I must also, I cannot but inquire after God's love

to me. By this my desires must be moved; for I am not so capable of ascending above self-interest and self-love, as in the state of glorious union I shall be. I am glad to perceive that others do love God; and I love those most that I find most love him: but it is not other men's love to God that will be accepted by him instead of mine, nor is it God's love to others which yet rejoices me, that will satisfy me, without his love to me. But when all these are still before me, God's essential self-love and delight, his love to his creatures, especially to the glorified, and his love to me also, even to me, a vile, unworthy sinner; what then should stay my ascending love, or discourage my desires to be with God?

Dost thou doubt, canst thou doubt, O my soul, whether thou art going to a God that loves thee? If the Jews discerned the great love of Christ to Lazarus by his tears, canst thou not discern his love to thee in his blood? It is never the less, but the more obliging and amiable, that it was not shed for thee alone, but for many. May I not say as Paul, ' I live by the faith of the Son of God, that hath loved me, and given himself for me.' Yea, it is not so much I that live, as Christ that lives in me: will he forsake the habitation which his love hath chosen; and which he hath so dearly bought? O read often that triumphing chapter, Rom. viii., and conclude, ' What shall separate us from the love of God?' If life have not done it, death shall not do it. If leaning on his breast at meat was a token of Christ's special love to John, is not his dwelling in me by my faith, and his living in me by his Spirit, a sure token of his love to me. If a dark saying, ' if he tarry till I come, what is that to thee?' raised a report that the beloved disciple should not die, why should not plain promises assure me that I shall live with him that loves me for ever? Be not so unthankful, O my soul, as to question, doubtingly, whether thy heavenly Father, and thy Lord, doth love thee? Canst thou forget the sealed testimonies of it? Did I not even now repeat so many as should shame my doubts? A multitude of thy friends hath loved thee so entirely, that thou canst not doubt of it. Did any of them signify their love with the convincing evidence that God hath done? Have they done for thee what he hath done? Are they love itself? Is their love so full, so firm, and so unchangeable as his? My thoughts of heaven are the sweeter, because abundance of my ancient, lovely, and loving holy friends are there. I am the more willing by death to follow them. Should I not think of it more joyfully because my God and Father, my Saviour, and my Comforter, is there? And not alone, but with all the society of love.

Was not Lazarus in the bosom of God himself? Yet it is said that he was in Abraham's bosom; as the promise runs, that we shall sit down with Abraham, Isaac, and Jacob in the kingdom of God. What makes the society of the saints so sweet as holy love? It is comfortable to read, that, 'To love the Lord our God with all our heart, and soul, and might, is the first and great commandment; and the second is like to it, To love our neighbour as ourselves.' For God's commands proceed from that will which is his nature or essence, and they tend to the same as their objective end. Therefore he that hath made love the great command, tells us that love is the great conception of his own essence, the spring of that command; and that this commanded, imperfect love tends to perfect heavenly love, even to our communion with essential infinite love. It were strange that the love and goodness which is equal to the power that made the world, and the wisdom that orders it, should be scanty and backward to do good, and to be suspected more than the love of friends! The remembrance of the holiness, humility, love, and faithfulness of my dearest friends, of every rank with whom I have conversed on earth, in every place where I have lived, is so sweet to me, that I am often ready to recreate myself with the naming of such as are now with Christ. But in heaven they will love me better than they did on earth; and my love to them will be more pleasant. But all these sparks are little to the sun.

Every place that I have lived in was a place of divine love, which there set up its obliging monuments. Every year and hour of my life hath been a time of love. Every friend, and every neighbour, yea, every enemy, have been the messengers and instruments of love. Every state and change of my life, notwithstanding my sin, hath opened to me treasures and mysteries of love. After such a life of love, shall I doubt whether the same God do love me? Is he the God of the mountains, and not of the valleys? Did he love me in my youth and health; and doth he not love me in my age, pain, and sickness? Did he love all the faithful better in their life than at their death? If our hope be not chiefly in this life, neither is our state of love, which is principally the heavenly, endless grace. My groans grieve my friends, but abate not their love. Did he love me for my strength, my weakness might be my fear. As they that love for beauty lothe them that are deformed; and they that love for riches despise the poor. But God loved me when I was his enemy, to make me a friend, and when I was bad to make me better: whatever he takes pleasure in, is his own gift. Who made me to differ; and what have I that I have not received? God will finish the work, the building, the warfare that is his own. O the multitude of mercies to my soul and body, in peace and war, in youth and age, to myself and friends, the many great and gracious deliverances which have testified to me the love of God! Have I lived in the experience of it, and shall I die in the doubts of it? Had it been love only to my body, it would have died with me, and not have accompanied my departing soul. I am not much in doubt of the truth of my love to him. Though I have not seen him, save as in a glass, as in a glass seen I love him. I love my brethren whom I have seen, and those most that are most in love with him. I love his word, works, and ways, and fain I would be nearer to him, and love him more; and I lothe myself for loving him no better. Shall Peter say more confidently, 'Thou knowest that I love thee' than 'I know that thou lovest me?' Yes, he may; because though God's love is greater and stedfaster than ours, yet our knowledge of his great love is less than his knowledge of our little love; and as we are defective in our own love, so are we in our certainty of its sincerity.

Without the knowledge of our love to God, we can never be sure of his special love to us. But yet I am not utterly a stranger to myself. I know for what I have lived and laboured in the world, and who is it that I have desired to please. The God, 'whose I am, and whom I serve,' hath loved me in my youth, and he will love me in my aged weakness. My flesh and my heart fail; my pains seem grievous to the flesh: but it is love that chooses them, that uses them for my good, that moderates them, and will shortly end them. Why then should I doubt of my Father's love? Shall pain or dying make me doubt? Did God love none from the beginning of the world but Enoch and Elias? What am I better than my forefathers? What is in me that I should expect exemption from the common lot of mankind? Is not a competent time of great mercy on earth, in order to the unseen felicity, all that the best of men can hope for? O for a clearer, stronger faith, to show me the world that more excels this, than this excels the womb where I was conceived! Then should I not fear my third birth-day, what pangs soever go before it; nor be unwilling of my change. The grave indeed is a bed that nature doth abhor; yet there the weary be at rest; but souls new born have a double nature that is immortal, and go to the place that is agreeable to their nature; even to the region of spirits, and the region of holy love: even passive matter that hath no other natural motion, hath a natural inclination to uniting, aggregative motion. God makes all natures suitable to their proper ends and use. How can it be that a spirit should not incline to be with spirits, and souls that have the divine nature in holy love, desire to be with the God of love? Arts, sciences, and tongues, become not a nature to us; else they would not cease at death: but holy love is our new nature, and therefore ceases not with this bodily life. Shall accidental love make me desire the company of a frail and mutable friend? Shall not this ingrafted, inseparable love make me long to be with Christ? Though the love of God to all his creatures will not prove that they are all immortal, nor oblige them to expect another life, that never had capacity or faculties to expect it; yet his love to such as in nature and grace are made capable of it, doth warrant and oblige them to believe and hope for the full perfection of the work of love.

Some comfort themselves in the love of St Peter, as having the keys of heaven. How many could I name that are now with Christ, who loved me so faithfully on earth, that were I sure they had the keys and power of heaven, and were not changed in their love, I could put my departing soul into their hands, and die with joy. Is it not better in the hand of my Redeemer, and the God of love, and Father of spirits? Is any love comparable to his, or any friend so boldly to be trusted? I should take it for ungrateful kindness in my friend to doubt of my love and constancy, if I had given him all that he hath, and maintained him constantly by my kindness: but O how odious a thing is sin; which, by destroying our love to God, doth make us unmeet to believe and sweetly perceive his love: and by making us doubt of the love of God, and lose the pleasant relish of it, doth more increase our difficulty of loving him. The title that the angel gave to Daniel, 'a man greatly beloved of God,' methinks should be enough to make one joyfully love and trust God, both in life and death. Will almighty love ever hurt me or forsake me? Have not all saints that title in their degrees? What else signifies their mark and name, 'holiness to the Lord?' What is it but our separation to God as his peculiar, beloved people? How are they separated but by mutual love, and our forsaking all that alienates, or is contrary? Let scorners deride us as self-flatterers, that believe they are God's darlings—and woe to the hypocrites that believe it on their false presumption—without such belief or grounded hopes, I see not how any man can die in true peace. He that is no otherwise beloved than hypocrites and unbelievers, must have his portion with them: he that is no otherwise beloved than as the ungodly, unholy, and unregenerated, shall not stand in judgment, nor see God, nor enter into his kingdom. Most upright souls are to blame for groundless doubting of God's love; but not for acknowledging it, rejoicing in it, and in their doubts being most solicitous to make it sure. Love brought me into the world, and furnished me with a thousand mercies! Love hath provided for me, delivered me, and preserved me, till now: and will it not entertain my separated soul? Is God like false or insufficient friends, that forsake us in adversity?

I confess that I have wronged love by sin; by many and great inexcusable sins; but all, save Christ himself, were sinners, which love did purify, and receive to glory. God, who is rich in mercy, for the great love wherewith he loved us, even when we were dead in sins, hath quickened us together with Christ, (by grace we are saved), and hath raised us up together in heavenly places in Christ Jesus. O that I could love much that have so much forgiven! The glorified praise him who loved us, and washed us from our sins, in his own blood, and made us kings and priests to God. Our Father that hath loved us, gives us consolation and good hope through grace. I know no sin which I repent not of with self-lothing: I earnestly beg and labour that none of my sins may be to me unknown. I dare not justify even what is in any way uncertain; though I dare not call all that my sin, which siding men, of different judgments, on each side, passionately call so: while both sides do it on contrary accounts, and not to go contrary ways is a crime. O that God would bless my accusations to my illumination, that I may not be unknown to myself! Though some think me much better than I am, and others much worse, it most concerns me to know the truth myself; flattery would be more dangerous to me, than false accusations; I may more safely be ignorant of other men's sins than of my own. Who can understand his errors? Cleanse me, Lord, from secret sins, and let not ignorance or error keep me in impenitence; and keep thou me back from presumptuous sins. I have an advocate with the Father, and thy promise, that he that confesseth and forsaketh his sins shall have mercy. Those are, by some men, taken for my greatest sins, which my most serious thoughts did judge to be the greatest of my outward duties, and which I performed through the greatest difficulties, and which cost me dearest to the flesh, and the greatest self-denial and patience in my reluctant mind: wherever I have erred, Lord, make it known to me, that my confession may prevent the sin of others; and where I have not erred, confirm and accept me in the right.

Seeing an unworthy worm hath had so many testimonies of thy tender love, let me not be like to them, that when thou saidst, I have loved you, unthankfully asked, 'Wherein hast thou loved us?' Heaven is not more spangled with stars, than thy word and works with the refulgent signatures of love. Thy well beloved Son, the Son of thy love, undertaking the office, message and work of the greatest love, was full of that spirit which is love, which he sheds abroad in the hearts of thine elect, that the love of the Father, the grace of the Son, and the communion of the Spirit, may be their hope and life. His works, his sufferings, his gifts, as well as his comfortable word, did say to his disciples, 'as the Father loved me, so have I loved you: continue ye in my love.' And how, Lord, shall we continue in it, but by the thankful belief of thy love and loveliness, desiring still to love thee more and in all things to know and please thy will; which, thou knowest, is my soul's desire.

Behold then, O my soul, with what love the Father, Son, and Holy Spirit have loved thee, that thou shouldst be made and called a son of God, redeemed, regenerated, adopted into that covenant state of grace in which thou standest: rejoice therefore in hope of the glory of God. Being justified by faith, having peace with God, and access by faith and hope that makes not ashamed; that being reconciled, when an enemy, by the death of Christ, I shall be saved by his life. Having loved his own, to the end he loves them, and without end: his gifts and calling are without repentance: when Satan, and thy flesh, would hide God's love, look to Christ, and read the golden words of love in the sacred gospel, and peruse thy many recorded experiences, and remember the convictions which secret and open mercies have many a time afforded thee: but especially draw nearer to the Lord of love, and

be not seldom and slight in thy contemplations of his love and loveliness: dwell in the sunshine, and thou wilt know that it is light, warm, and comfortable. Distance and strangeness cherish thy doubts: acquaint thyself with him, and be at peace.

Yet look up, and often and earnestly look up, after thy ascended, glorified Head, who said, 'tell my brethren, I ascend to my Father and your Father, to my God and your God.' Think where and what he is, and what he is now doing for all his own; and how humbled, abased, suffering love is now triumphant, regnant, glorified love; and therefore no less than in all its tender expressions upon earth. As love is no where perfectly believed but in heaven, so I can no where so fully discern it, as by looking up by faith to my Father and Saviour which is in heaven, and conversing more believingly with the heavenly society. Had I done this more and better, and as I have persuaded others to do it, I had lived in more convincing delights of God's love, which would have turned the fears of death into more joyful hopes, and more earnest desires to be with Christ, in the arms, in the world, in the life of love, as far better than to be here, in a dark, a doubting, fearing world.

But, O my Father, infinite LOVE, though my arguments be many and strong, my heart is bad, and my strength is weakness, and I am insufficient to plead the cause of thy love and loveliness to myself or others. O plead thy own cause, and what heart can resist? Let it not be my word only, but thine, that thou lovest me, even me, a sinner. Speak it, as Christ said to Lazarus, Arise. If not, as thou tellest me that the sun is warm, yet as thou hast told me, that my parents and my dearest friends did love me, and much more powerfully than so. Tell it me, as thou tellest me that thou hast given me life, by the consciousness and works of life: that while I can say, 'Thou that knowest all things, knowest that I love thee;' it may include, Therefore I know that I am beloved of thee, and therefore come to thee in the confidence of thy love, and long to be nearer in the clearer sight, the fuller sense, and more joyful exercise of love for ever. 'Father, into thy hand I commend my spirit; Lord Jesus, receive my spirit.' Amen.

* The preceding treatise, especially the latter part of it, is one of great power and pathos. The venerable author expresses himself like a man upon the borders of heaven—like Jacob blessing his sons upon his death-bed—or Moses blessing the tribes of Israel when about to lay down the clay tabernacle. His whole soul seems melted into the element of divine love.—*Ed.*